Chilton's BASIC AUTO MAINTENANCE

Chilton's BASIC AUTO MAINTENANCE

Compiled and Edited by the Chilton Automotive Editorial Department

CHILTON BOOK COMPANY *Radnor, Pennsylvania*

Published by Chilton Book Company, Radnor, Pa.
and simultaneously by Thomas Nelson & Sons, Ltd., Ontario, Canada.

First Printing, October 1976
1234567890 432109876

Manufactured in the United States of America

Library of Congress Cataloging in Publication Data

Chilton Book Company. Automotive Editorial Dept.
Chilton's basic auto maintenance.

1. Automobiles—Maintenance and repair. I. Title.
II. Title: Basic auto maintenance.
TL152.C5226 1976 629.28'7'22 76-40098
ISBN 0-8019-8000-3

"Driving for Economy" starting on Page 604 was originally published as Chapter 4 of "Chilton's More Miles-Per-Gallon", *Ronald M. Weiers, Chilton Book Co., Radnor, Pa., 1974*

Although information in this book is based on industry sources and is as complete as possible at the time of publication, the possibility exists that the manufacturer made later changes which could not be included here. While striving for total accuracy, Chilton Book Company cannot assume responsibility for any errors, changes, or omissions that may occur in the compilation of this date.

Cover photo by Martin W. Kane

TABLE OF CONTENTS

American Cars

Imported Cars

General Information—Troubleshooting

General Information—How It Works

HOW TO USE THIS BOOK

This manual is indexed in two ways:

The Table of Contents, which follows the title page of the book, lists the beginning of each Car and General Information Section in the book. The Car Sections are separated into an American car group and an Import car group. Car sections are arranged alphabetically within each group.

Each Car Section has its own index at the beginning of that section. The major headings and sub-headings are listed in order of appearance.

To read about a procedure you want to perform on your car you need only find your car in the Table of Contents, turn to the beginning page of the Car Section, find the procedure in the index, turn to that page, and then do it.

Car Section

The Car Sections provide specific procedures and information that show you how to do simple maintenance chores on your car(s). Each section covers eight essential maintenance areas: Lubrication and Oil Change, Cooling System, Suspension and Tires, Ignition System, Fuel System, Safety Systems, Electrical System, and Air Conditioning. Each section ends with all necessary specifications for the maintenance procedures.

Each Car Section explains how to do the following: check fluid levels in the engine, brake master cylinder, manual or automatic transmission, and rear axle; change the engine oil and filter; replace the thermostat; adjust the fan belt; replace radiator hoses; check the shock absorbers; check the ignition system; replace spark plugs; replace ignition points and condenser; adjust point gap; set the ignition timing; replace spark plug wires; replace air filter and crankcase ventilation filter; install a new PCV valve; replace burned out bulbs and headlights; install new windshield wiper blades; check battery level; clean battery terminals; replace battery cables; replace fuses and turn signal/flasher relays.

General Information Section

There are two General Information sections. The first is a programmed section on *Troubleshooting*, which will help you determine why your car won't start or is running poorly. You may be able to fix it yourself. If you have to have it repaired, however, you can accurately describe your problem and possibly avoid having unnecessary work and expense.

For example: If your engine is misfiring, you look under General Diagnosis for the symptoms. Across from the symptoms are the numbers of diagnostic section that pertain to your problem. Following the steps outlined in the diagnostic section, you narrow your problem down to one faulty spark plug. Turn to the Car Section and follow the procedure given for spark plug replacement and your car will be running fine again.

Diagnostic charts for transmissions, brakes, air conditioning, cooling systems, and front suspensions are also featured in the Troubleshooting Section.

The second General Information section is the *How It Works* section. Each major system is fully explained in the simplest of terms. In addition, the "Towing a Trailer" section tells you how to equip your car for towing a trailer and how to tow it safely when you're ready to go.

A section on the "Metric System" consists of two parts: an introduction to explain the new units and general conversion charts to help in converting any specification.

A special section on "Driving for Economy" tells you how to save gas and money by driving smarter.

Chevelle / Monte Carlo

Lubrication and Oil Change

BRAKE FLUID LEVEL CHECK

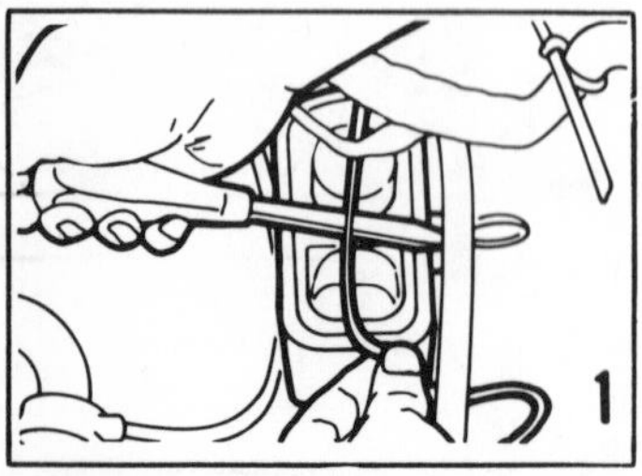
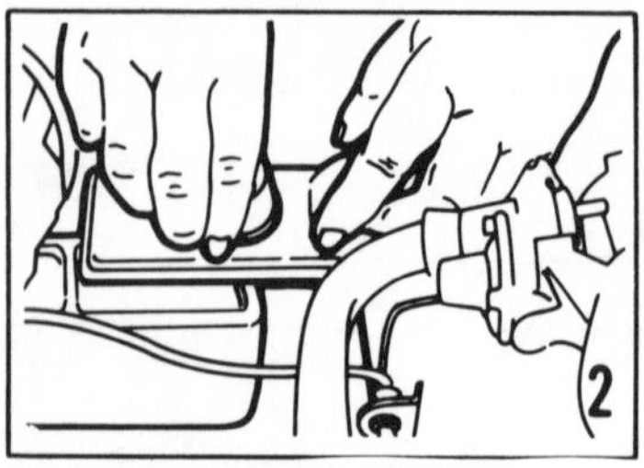
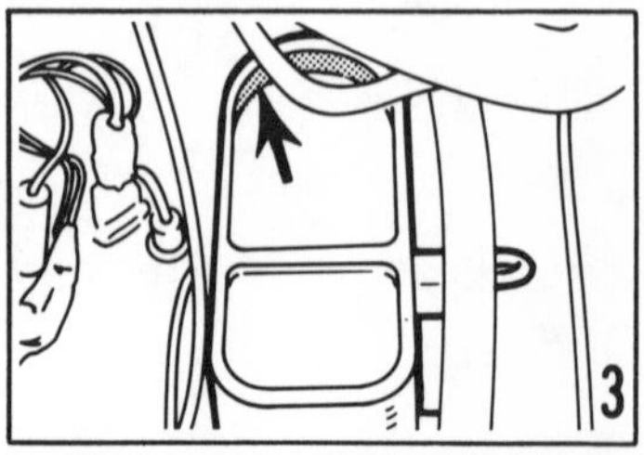

Check brake fluid level in master cylinder at least every three months . . . sooner if braking feels inadequate. Add when low.
Recommended grade: D.O.T. #3.

1. Pry wire retaining clip off cap top with screwdriver.
2. Remove cap and gasket by lifting up.
3. Fluid level should be within ¼ inch of top rim. If lower than this, add fresh fluid to appropriate level.

DO NOT OVERFILL

4. Replace cap and gasket; secure retaining clip over cap. If fluid level was low, check again in a few days.
5. If fluid repeatedly checks low, there is a leak somewhere in the system. See SAFETY SYSTEMS—WHEEL CYLINDER CHECK. Have mechanic check further. Neglect can be dangerous.

MANUAL TRANSMISSION FLUID LEVEL CHECK

Check the manual transmission fluid level every 4 months or 6000 miles (1970-74) or every 6 months or 7500 miles (1975-77). The fluid should be at operating temperature. Use SAE 80 or 90 GL-5 in all manual transmissions.

TOOLS . . . adjustable hand wrench; fluid level check device (made from coat hanger wire; bend at 90° angle 2″ from end); bulb syringe.

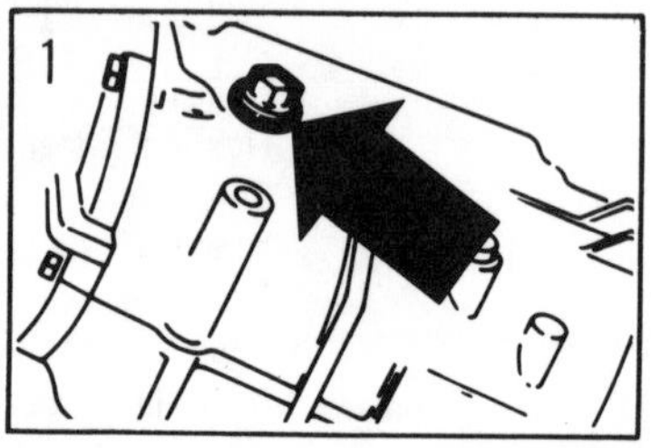

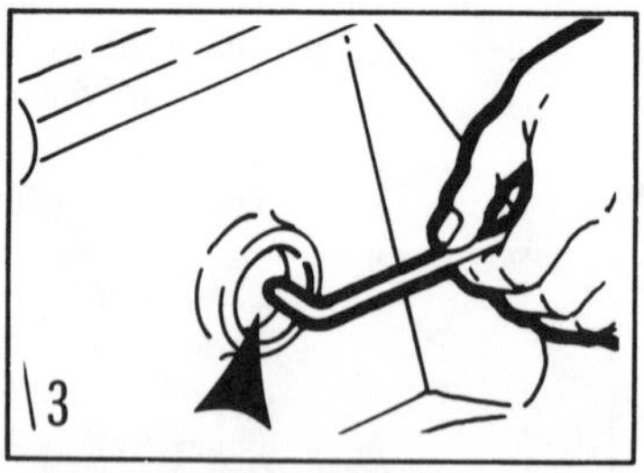
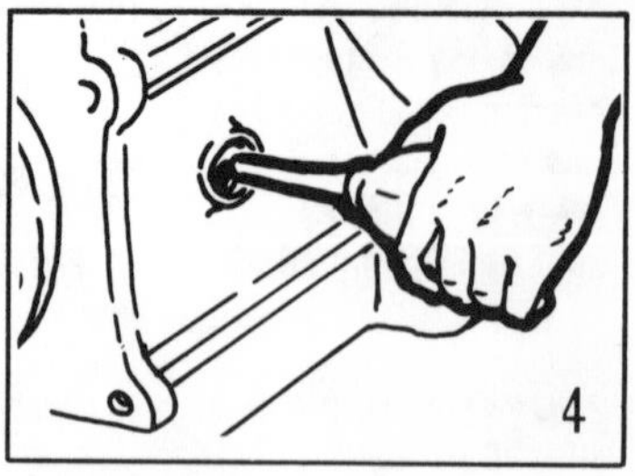

1. Locate transmission fluid filler plug on right side of transmission housing from underneath car.
2. Wipe road dirt from filler plug area before loosening. Remove plug with adjustable wrench.
3. Insert fluid level check device. Fluid level should be right up to bottom edge of filler hole.
4. Add fluid as needed with hand bulb syringe.
5. Replace filler plug; tighten.

AUTOMATIC TRANSMISSION FLUID LEVEL CHECK

GM SAYS . . . check automatic transmission fluid (ATF) level at every oil change. Recommended grade: DEXRON II®.
TOOLS . . . long neck filler funnel.
1. Engine must be warmed up and running. Place shift lever in PARK position.
2. Pull out dipstick. Wipe clean.

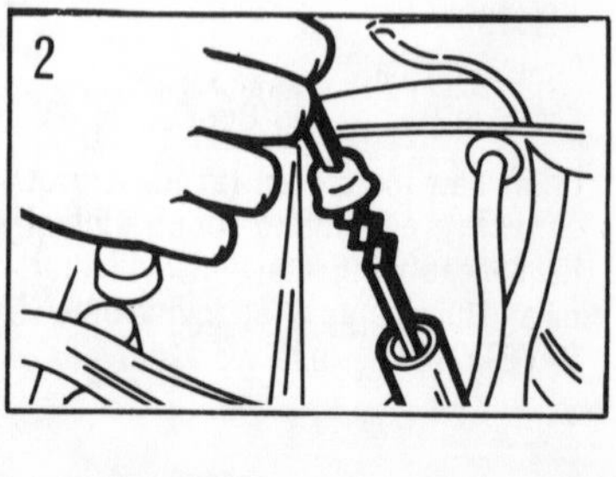

Push dipstick all the way back in; remove it again.

3. If fluid is below ADD mark, add ATF to bring level up.

DO NOT OVERFILL.

4. Add ATF thru transmission dipstick hole by means of long-neck filler funnel.

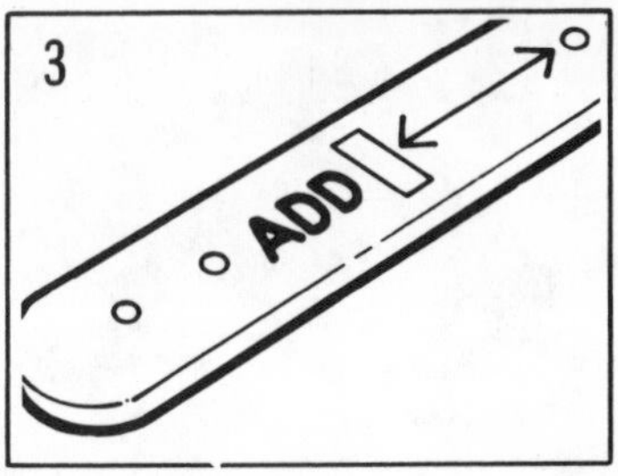

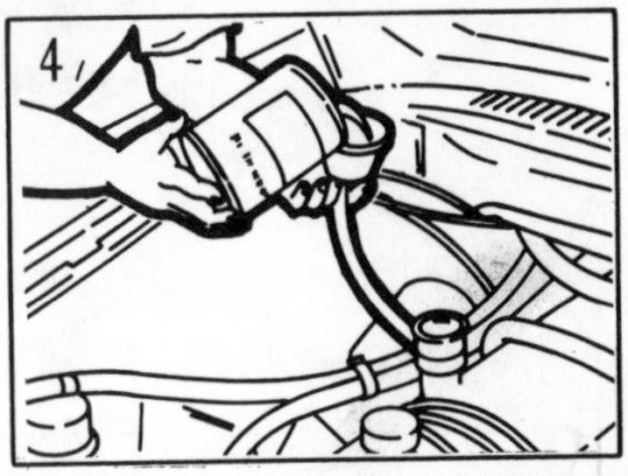

REAR AXLE LUBRICANT CHECK

Check the level of the rear axle lubricant every 4 months or 6000 miles (1970-74) or every 6 months or 7500 miles (1975-77). Use only SAE 90 hypoid gear lube for non-Positraction axles. Positraction axles require special Positraction fluid available from Chevrolet. A Positraction additive is also available to increase the quality of lubrication in Positraction axles.

TOOLS . . . adjustable hand wrench; fluid level check device (made from coat hanger wire; bend at 90° angle 2″ from end); bulb syringe.

1. Locate filler plug on forward side of rear axle housing.

2. Wipe plug area clean; remove plug with wrench.

3. Insert wire level check device; remove. Fluid level should be maintained to the bottom edge of the filler hole, but adequate fluid level will show on the last ¼ in. of the check device.

4. If fluid level is low, add as needed, with a hand bulb syringe, until level shows on last ¼-inch of wire.

5. Replace filler plug; tighten.

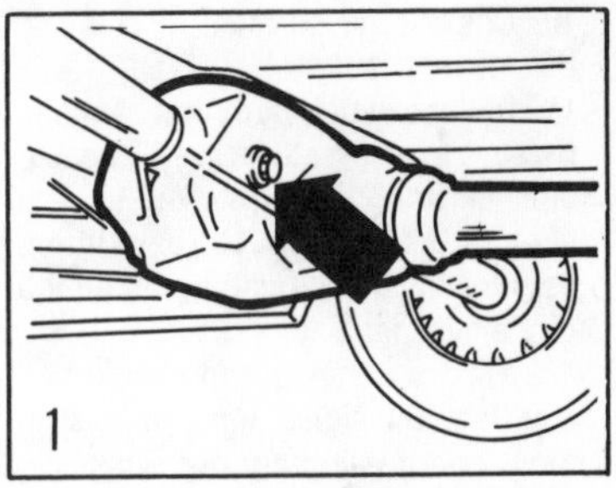

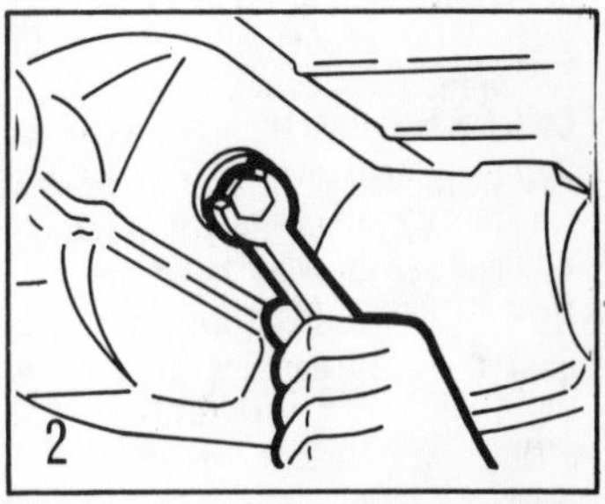

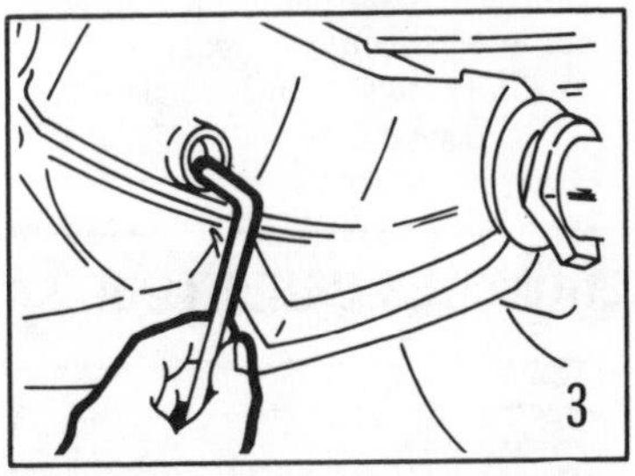

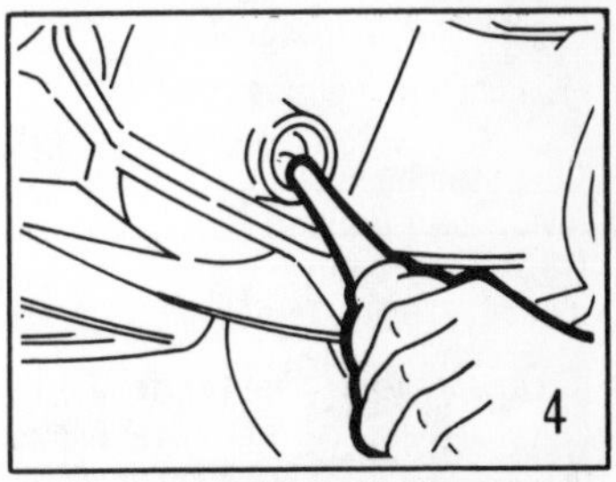

OIL AND FILTER CHANGE

Change the engine oil every 6000 miles or 4 months (1970-74) or every 7500 miles or 6 months (1975-77). Change the oil filter at least at every other oil change, preferrably at each oil change.

Cars that are used in severe service (constant trailer towing, extensive idling or driving in extreme dust conditions) should cut the oil change interval in half.

TOOLS & MATERIALS . . . adjustable wrench; medium size screwdriver; oil filter removal wrench; drain pan for old oil (at least 5 qt. capacity); oil pouring spout; 4 qt. oil (5 qt. if changing filter); new oil filter; oil and lubricants as specified below.

SAFETY TIP . . . use work gloves.

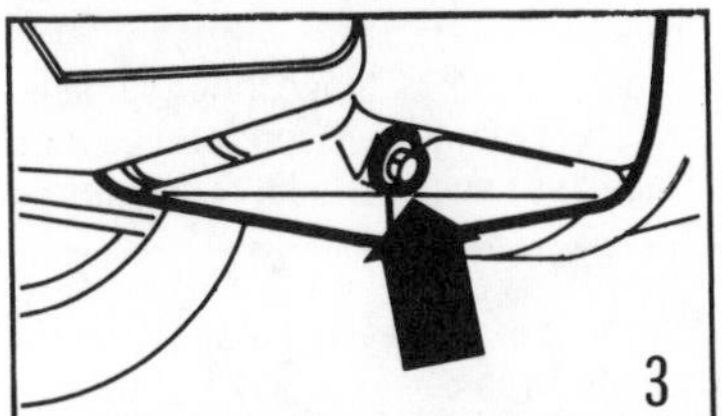

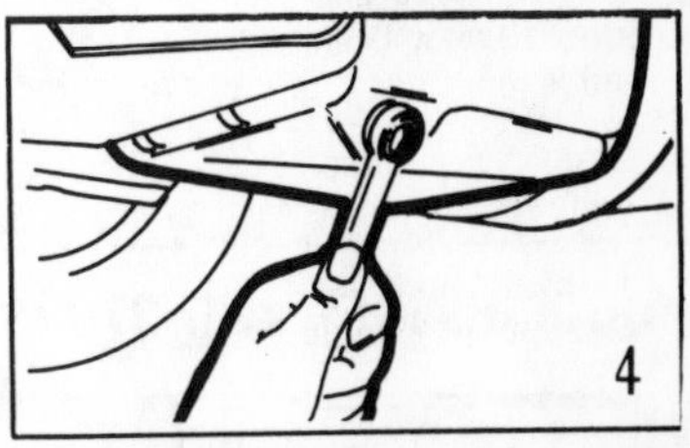

1. If engine is cold, start up and idle it until it reaches operating temperature.

2. Park car on level ground. Turn engine off.

3. Locate oil drain plug on underside of engine. Place drain pan under plug.

4. Remove drain plug with wrench. Let ALL dirty oil drain out.

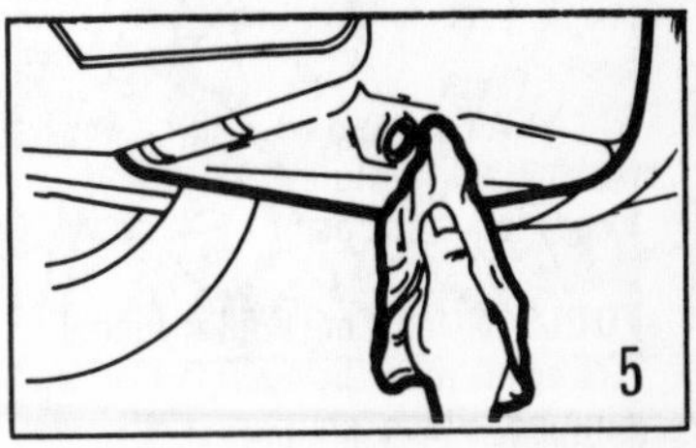

5. Wipe plug and area around drain

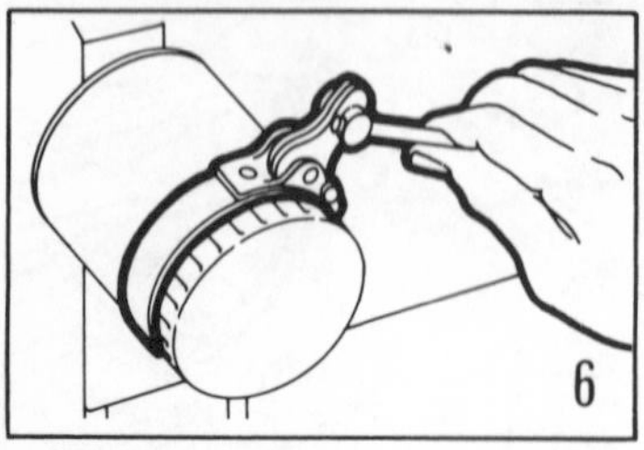

hole clean. Replace drain plug; tighten it.

6. Locate oil filter. Move drain pan under filter. Loosen filter with oil filter wrench. Unscrew; remove filter by hand.

7. Smear fresh oil over surface of rubber gasket (washer) of new filter. Install new filter by hand only. Do NOT use wrench. Turn filter until gasket makes contact. Tighten an additional half turn only . . . NO MORE.

8. Locate oil filter tube on top of engine. Remove cap.

9. Punch oil pouring spout into top

of oil can. Pour all cans of new oil into filler tube. Wipe filter cap clean and replace it.

10. Check new oil level at dipstick. Pull out dipstick, wipe clean.

11. Push dipstick back into engine. Be sure to insert all the way. Remove dipstick and check new oil level. It should be above "FULL" line. If not, be sure to check if you put in all the oil called for.

12. Start up engine and idle for 3-5 minutes. Oil signal light on instrument panel will glow red when engine is first started. Light should go out in 15 seconds or less.

13. Stop engine and check for oil

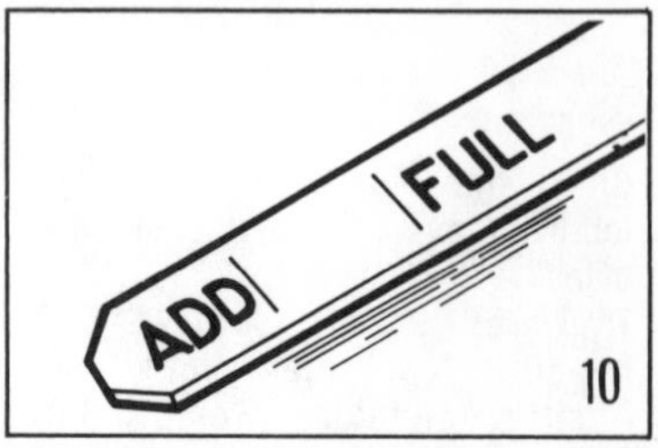

leaks at drain plug and filter. If you find any, check tightness of plug and/or filter, also for condition of filter gasket to see that it has not become pinched or damaged when installing. Recheck oil level, which should now be at "FULL".

SPEEDOMETER CABLE LUBRICATION

If speedometer pointer tends to quiver or jump, or if unit makes a low, rasping sound, lubrication may be needed.

1. Locate cable shaft attachment directly behind speedometer dial.
2. Remove retaining clip. Unscrew cable from speedometer.
3. Pull inner cable completely out of outer casing. Note carefully which end is top. Check for wear or frayed strands. If damaged, replace inner cable with new one.

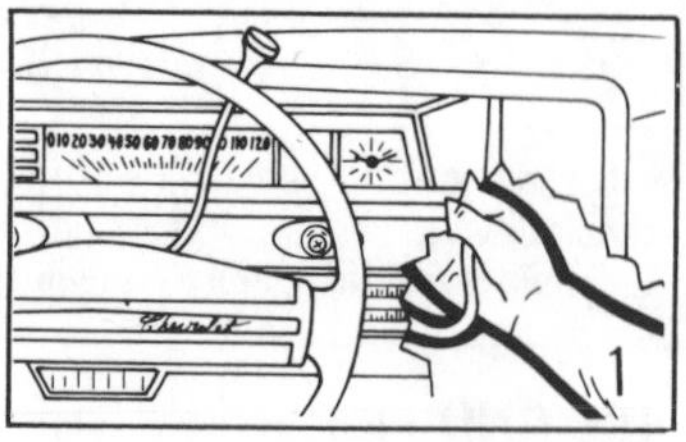

4. Apply generous amount of speedometer cable lubricant into cable casing. Replace inner cable in shaft, noting that top end is not inserted accidentally. Turn inner

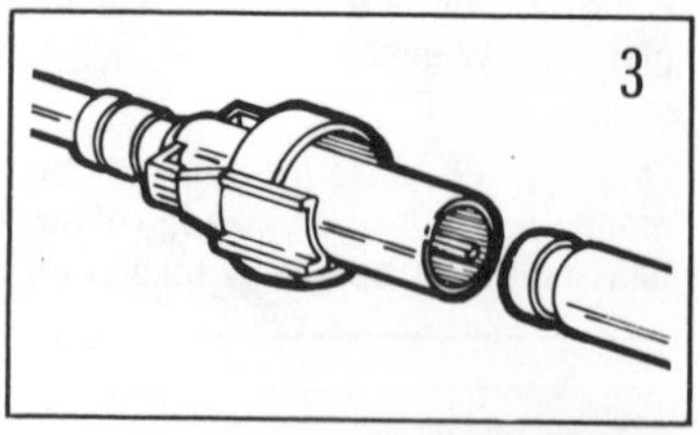

cable as it is being re-inserted. Twist cable when all the way in, to lock into position at lower end.
5. Reconnect cable to speedometer head under instrument panel.

DOOR HINGES AND STOPS

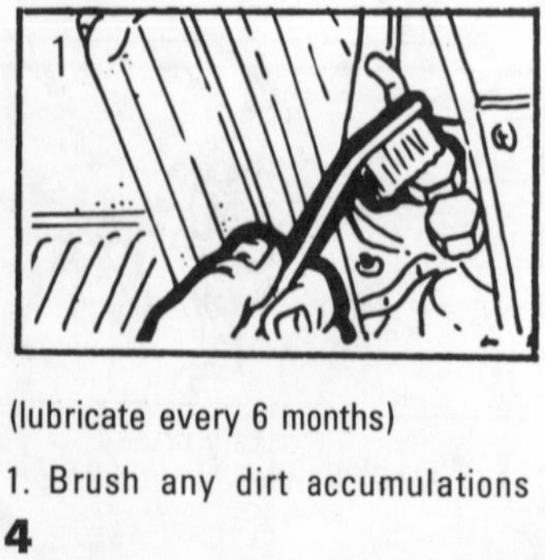

(lubricate every 6 months)

1. Brush any dirt accumulations from door hinges and stops. Use old tooth brush or rag.

2. Apply dab of white polyethylene grease to door hinges, trunk hinges, hood hinges, door stops.

DOOR LOCKS

(lubricate every 6 months)

1. Insert door key half way into lock.

2. Spray aerosol lock lubricant into lock.

3. Push key rest of way into lock; turn back and forth several times.

Cooling System

The radiator coolant should be checked at least once or twice a month, more often if you do a lot of hard driving. Check the coolant level when the engine is cold. On models with expansion tanks, do not remove the radiator cap to check the level. The level should be at the FULL COLD mark on the expansion tank if the engine is cold, or at the FULL HOT mark with the engine at operating temperature. On models without expansion tanks, the level should be at the bottom of the filler neck.

When replacing the radiator cap on models with an expansion tank, be sure the arrows on the radiator cap align with the hose to the expansion tank.

Keep coolant up to recommended level in radiator. If coolant checks frequently low, look for leaks. Tighten all hose clamps occasionally. For best results, keep a 50/50 water/antifreeze mixture year round. Change complete coolant mixture every 24 months.

CAUTION: If you must check coolant in a hot engine, cover radiator cap with thick rag before releasing. Remove cap slowly.

Cover the cap with a thick rag. Press down and turn the cap to the first stop. Wait until the hissing stops,

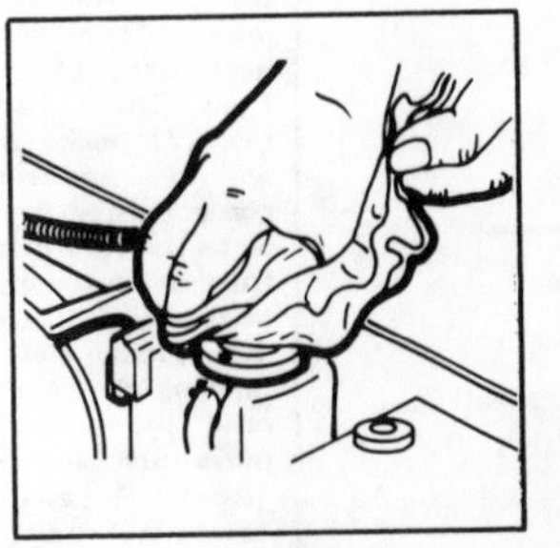

indicating that the pressure has released. Turn the cap the rest of the way and carefully remove it.

REPLACING THE THERMOSTAT

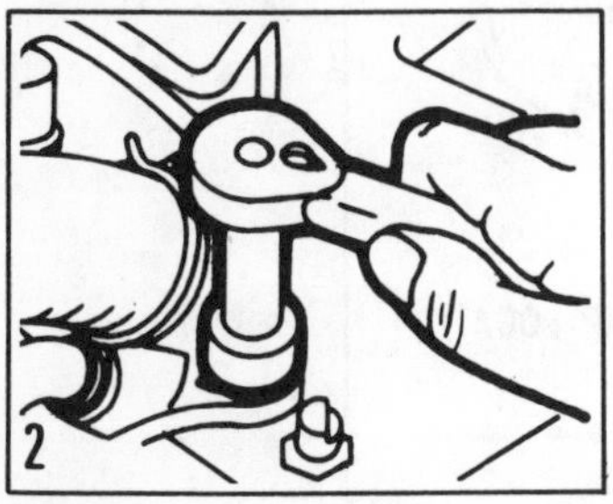

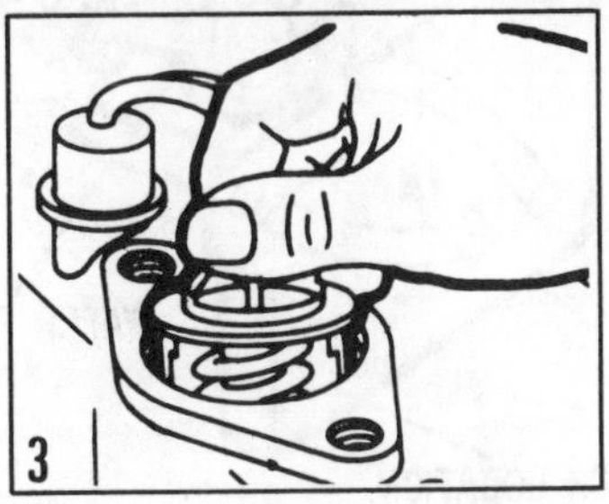

A faulty thermostat will usually cause engine overheating. The thermostat is located inside the housing where the top radiator hose connects to the engine.

TOOLS AND MATERIALS . . .
New thermostat
Gasket
Adjustable wrench

1. Drain radiator of about half its coolant. (See How To Replace Hoses).
2. Loosen and remove both retaining bolts and lift thermostat housing off the engine.

NOTE: If you're careful it won't be necessary to remove radiator hose.

3. Remove old thermostat.
4. Scrape thermostat housing flange and engine block surface to remove old gasket debris.
5. Drop new thermostat into place—spring down.
6. Install new gasket with sealer applied to both sides.
7. Replace thermostat housing and tighten both retaining bolts.

TROUBLESHOOT ENGINE OVERHEATING

1. Inspect all hoses. If any are weak, soft in spots or show cracks, replace at once.
2. Check all hose connections for tightness. Tighten loose hose clamps; they tend to loosen due to engine vibration.
3. If radiator steams or hisses when engine is switched off, check for leaks. Look for signs of coolant drips on radiator or around header tank joint.

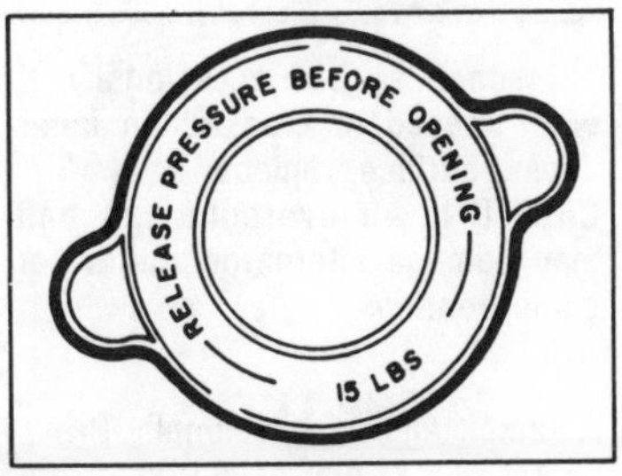

Leaks are possible at:
Upper or lower radiator hoses

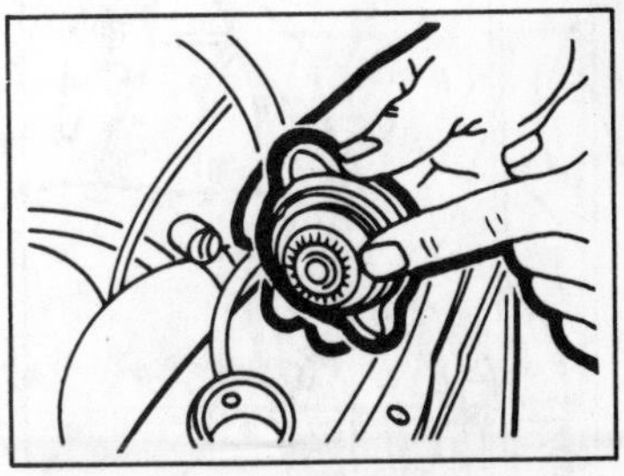

Water pump (gaskets or seal)
Heater core or connecting hoses

Automatic transmission cooler lines (at bottom of radiator)
Faulty radiator pressure cap
Faulty cylinder head gasket
Cracked cylinder head or block

Check radiator cap occasionally for worn or cracked gasket. If cap doesn't seal properly, fluid will be lost and engine will overheat. Replace worn cap with new cap rated 15 lbs. pressure.

Due to the number of joints, cooling systems have many places to leak from. Check clamp tightness. If leaks persist an anti-leak additive in the coolant may help. Noisy water pumps may benefit from a lubricating additive in the coolant. Use a cooling system cleaner when flushing during a drain and refill job. It will help remove rust and scale. Remember — additives will not cure chronic problems. But they will effect a short-term remedy in many cases.

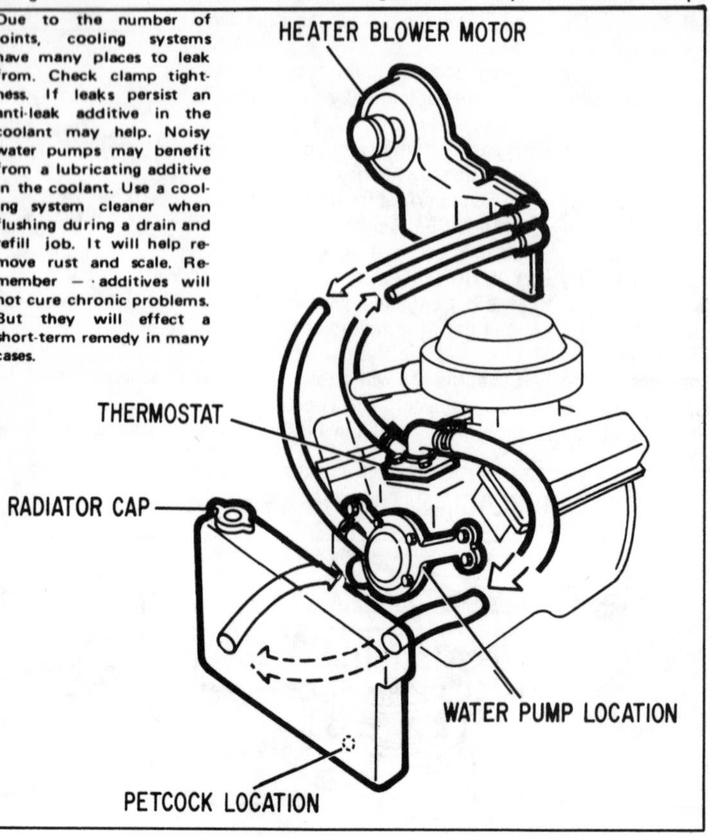

FAN BELT ADJUSTMENT

The fan belt not only drives the radiator fan, it turns the water pump and drives the alternator. It's easy to see that the condition and proper tension of the belt are vital, since almost all engine cooling and electrical power is dependent on it. The belt deserves an occasional look and tension check.

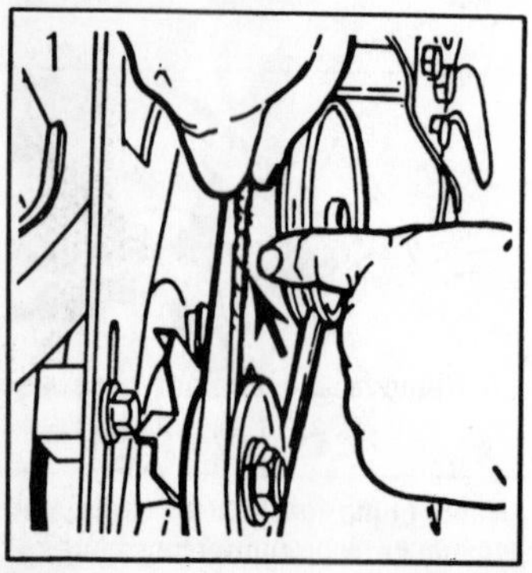

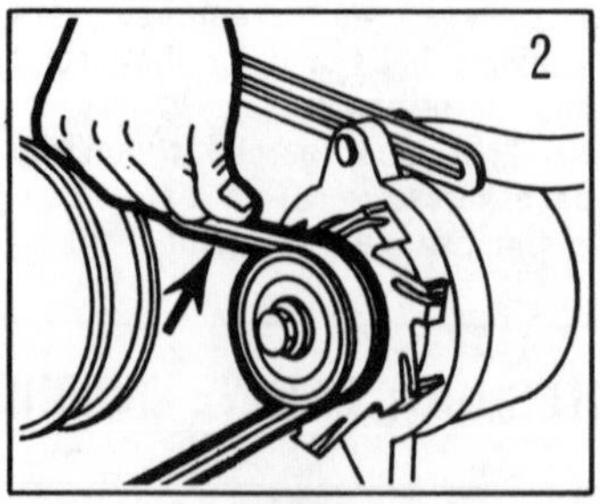

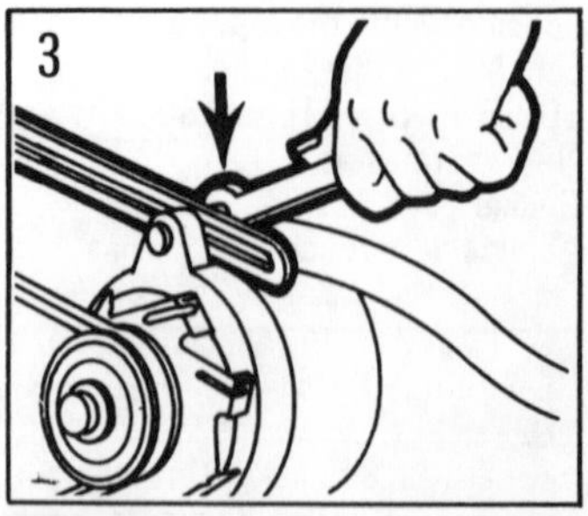

1. Inspect fan belt occasionally. If worn, frayed or cracked on inner driving surface, replace.
CAUTION: An overtightened belt may damage alternator and water pump bearings.

2. Check tension occasionally. Press thumb at midpoint of belt span between pulleys. If belt depresses more than ½ inch, tightening is needed. A too-loose belt will not drive alternator and water pump effectively.

3. To adjust loosen alternator mounting bolts, pivot the alternator over until the belt is properly tensioned (¼ in. deflection) and then tighten bolts.

HOSE REPLACEMENT

Coolant drain and refill work may be done alone; when changing hoses, coolant must also be drained as part of job. Discard all hoses with cracks or soft spots. Check hose clamps for tightness and good condition.

1. Remove radiator cap. Open radiator petcock (See 2). Drain coolant into catch basin. If near 24 months old, discard old coolant.
2. Petcock or drain plug is located at the bottom left of the radiator. Open petcock or remove plug to drain. A few models may not be equipped with a radiator drain petcock. These models are drained by removing the lower radiator hose.
3. Loosen clamps at each end of hose(s). Work loose; pull off. If old hose clamps are rusted or damaged, replace with new units.
4. Wipe all hose connections clean. Use emery cloth to get rid of residue. Check all hoses for weak spots, as well as cracks inside and out.
5. Slip clamps over each hose end. Slip hose ends all the way onto cleaned up hose connections.
6. Place hose clamp ¼ inch from hose end. Tighten. Close petcock. Refill with 50/50 coolant/water mix.
7. Start engine; allow to warm up. Check for coolant leaks.
8. Road test car; watch for temperature warning light.

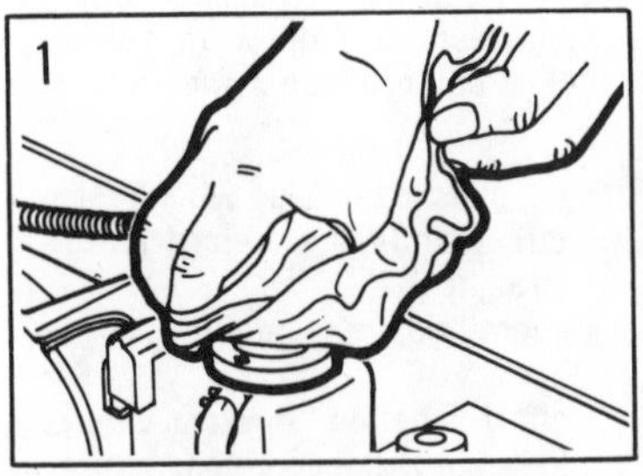

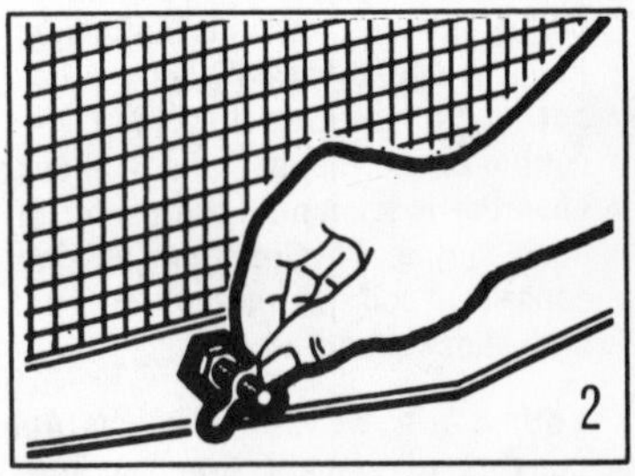

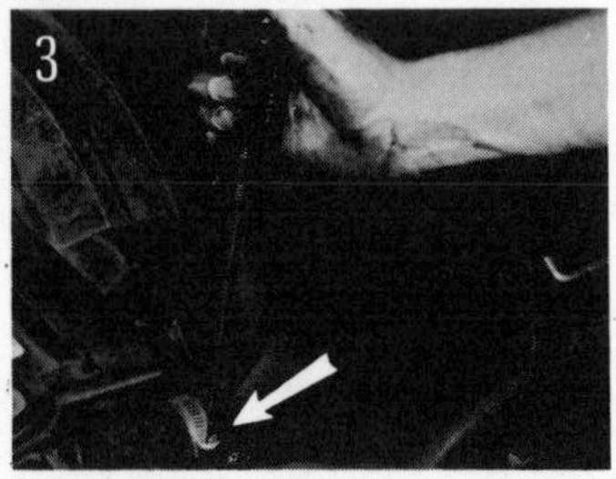

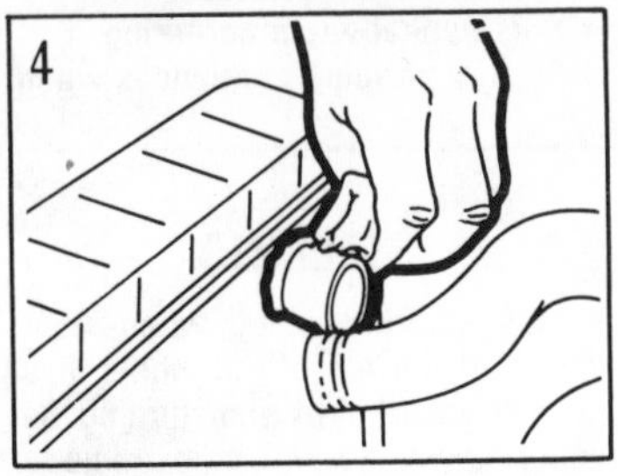

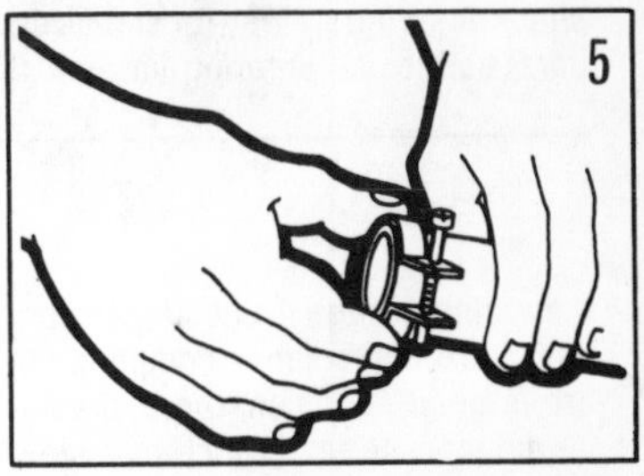

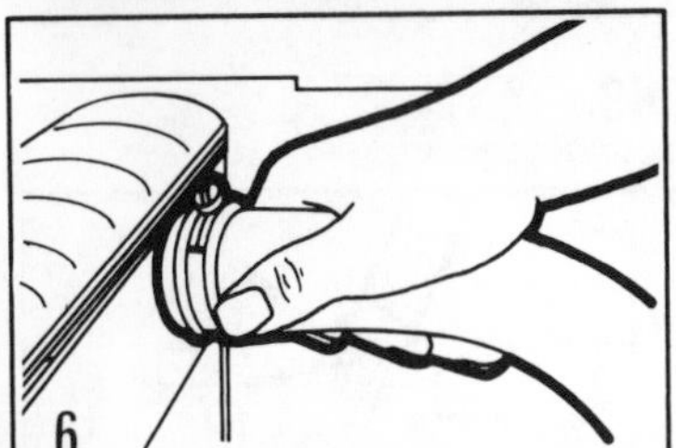

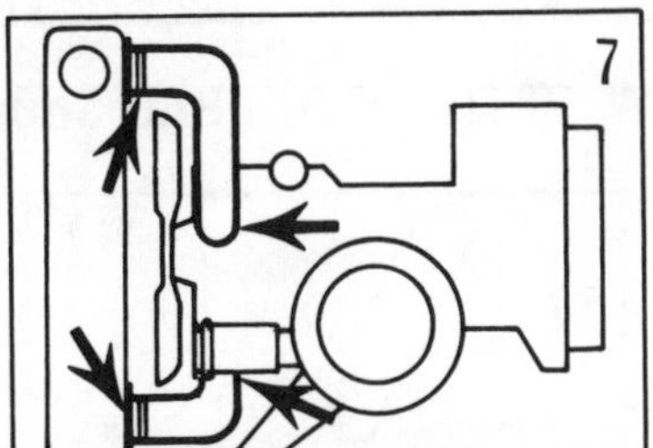

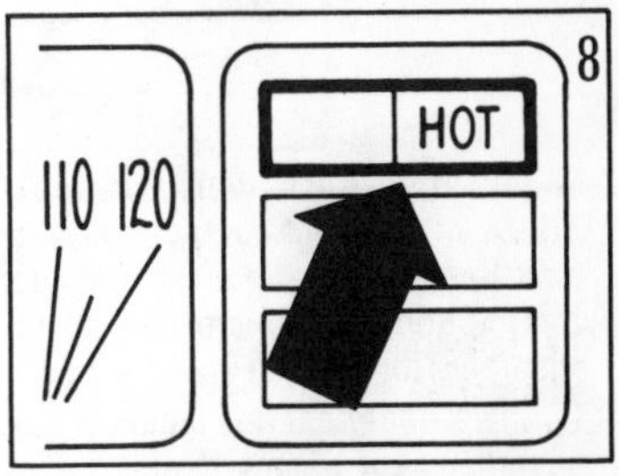

CHANGING THE ANTI-FREEZE

The cooling system anti-freeze should be drained every 2 years or 30,000 miles. Drain out the old anti-freeze, flush the system and replace with fresh coolant. The anti-freeze should be a 50/50 solution of ethylene glycol coolant and water.

1. Remove the radiator cap when the engine is cool. Slowly rotate the cap to the first detent and wait until the pressure releases (indicated by the hissing decreasing). Press down on the cap and rotate it the rest of the way.
2. With the cap removed, run the engine until the upper radiator hose is hot, indicating the thermostat is open.
3. Stop the engine and drain the coolant. Open the radiator drain petcock, or remove the lower hose from the radiator.
4. Close the valve (or replace the lower hose) and add enough water to fill the system.
5. Repeat steps 2, 3 and 4 enough times until the drained liquid is nearly colorless.
6. Allow the system to drain completely and close the radiator petcock tightly (or replace the lower hose).

7. Remove the coolant recovery tank and wash it thoroughly with detergent. Reinstall the tank.
8. Add a 50/50 mix of water and ethylene glycol coolant (or enough to

provide protection to −34° F). Fill the radiator to the base of the coolant neck or the recovery tank to the FULL HOT mark.

9. Run the engine until the upper radiator hose is hot.

10. With the engine idling, add enough coolant to fill the system to the specified level. Reinstall the radiator cap. Be sure the arrows align with the overflow tube.

Suspension and Tires

SUSPENSION SYSTEM

The front wheels mount and rotate on the spindles, which are attached to upper and lower ball joints. A coil spring is mounted between the control arms on both sides. A shock absorber is located in the center of each spring. The rear suspension consists of coil springs, control arms, and shock absorbers.

Your car's suspension system consists of wheels, tires, springs, shock absorbers, sway (or stabilizer) bars, ball joints, steering linkage. If any of these items is out of adjustment or badly worn, you may notice any of these symptoms:

- car pulls to one side when braking
- car wanders when driving a straight line
- overall ride may be either hard or bouncy
- effort is needed to steer vehicle
- tires show uneven wear
- tires squeal when cornering
- front of car dips or bounces when braking
- car rocks side-to-side when going over rough road
- wheels bounce to make slapping sound on road
- steering wheel vibrates in hands
- front of car vibrates at highway speeds

Any of above symptoms indicate corrective action is needed. Delay can: ruin tires; cause damage/failure to other suspension parts; create safety hazard.

STEERING

If steering linkage, front suspension and sterering column components are in good condition, there should be not more than 1½ inch free play in the steering wheel when measured at the rim of the wheel. If a loud knock is heard when turning the steering wheel from one extreme to the other, have mechanic check pinion bearing preload.

HOW TO CHECK FOR BAD SHOCKS

Shock absorbers work to keep wheels in constant contact with the road. Result is safe handling and ride control; longer tire life. So shock absorbers (or shocks) are important.

1. Check under car and locate shock absorber near each wheel.
2. Heavy oil streaks on outer shock housing indicate need for replacement.
3. Stand at front of car and apply body weight in a pumping action to front bumper or fender. Release pressure and allow car to stop rocking. Car should not bounce more than one more time after releasing pressure. Repeat at rear. If bouncing continues more than once, replacement is needed. Replace shocks in pairs (front pair or rear pair).

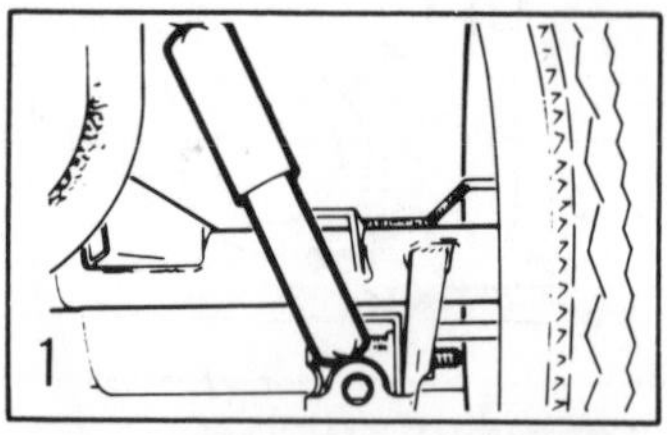

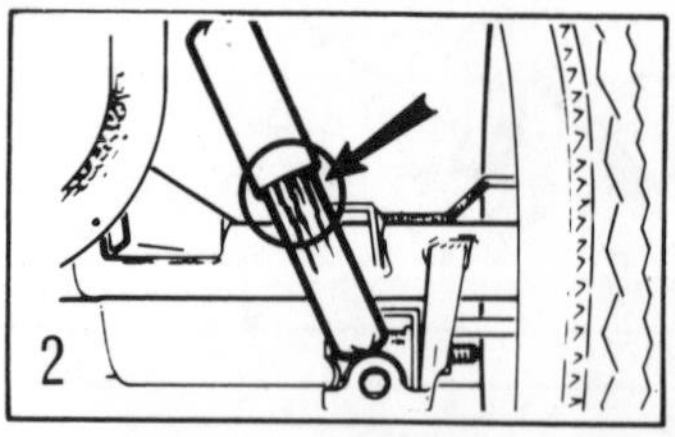

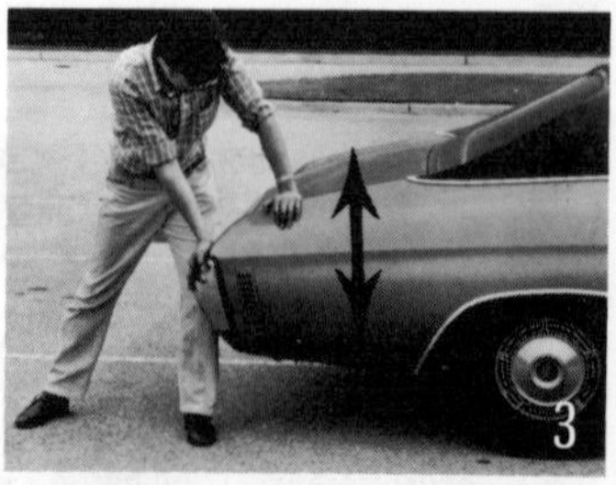

TOW HITCH INFORMATION

If your car is used for trailer towing you should check:

A. Cooling System; be sure radiator is at proper level in radiator. See Cooling System Section for checks to perform.

B. Check Transmission Fluid; keep topped up to proper level.

C. Check Rear Shock Absorbers; you

may benefit from installation of new rear shocks or air shocks.
D. Check Tire Pressures; best traction and handling can be ensured if tire pressures are properly maintained.
For safer and more trouble-free trailer towing, consider:
A. Automatic Transmission Cooler; helps remove excess heat from automatic transmission fluid built up during towing mileage. Also helps avoid radiator overheating. Some units can be self-installed.
B. Radiator Over-Flow Tank Kit; addition of a reservoir to catch radiator coolant overflow preventing coolant loss. Easy to install, these units help a tow car run cooler, avoid overheating due to coolant loss.
C. Heavy-Duty Shock Absorbers or Air Shocks; important to have on rear wheels if you intend to do a lot of towing or load carrying within the car itself. Don't forget to consider replacing factory shocks, when they are worn out, with heavy-duty units at the front as well.
D. Variable Load Flasher; this unit will accommodate the added load of trailer turn signal lamps on trailer when these are hooked into your car's electrical system.

FRONT END ALIGNMENT

When steering, handling and/or tire wear indicate front end alignment may be needed, this work can only be done at an automotive service shop. DO NOT PUT OFF NEEDED FRONT END ALIGNMENT. At the same time, have ball joints and steering linkage checked.

Ignition System

TUNE-UP SERVICES

The ignition system consists of spark plugs, plug wires, distributor, rotor, condenser and coil. These units work together to create a hot spark inside the engine (ignition) at exactly the right moment (timing). If the ignition is weak or the timing not right, the engine will be hard to start, run poorly or waste gas.
TOOLS AND MATERIALS: Parts: set of points, condenser, spark plugs. Tools: feeler gauge, 13/16 in. spark plug wrench (1970) or ⅝ in. spark plug wrench (1970-77); timing equipment, ⅛ in. allen wrench.

CHECK THE POINTS AND ROTOR

1. To open the V8 distributor, depress the screw in the cap and rotate the screw 180°. There are 2 such screws. Remove the coil wire and lift off the cap. On the 6-cylinder, unscrew the 2 screws, disconnect the coil wire and remove the cap.

2. Remove the 2 screws from the V8 rotor and lift it off. Pull the 6-cylinder rotor from the shaft. If the metal tip is badly burned or worn, replace the rotor with a new one.

3. Check the metal contacts inside the cap. If they are burned or worn, replace the cap with a new one.
4. Pry the points apart with a screwdriver, if worn or burned, replace them. If OK, check the gap.

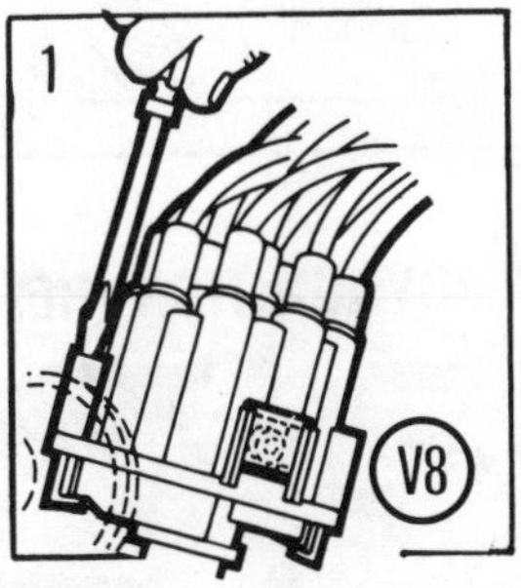

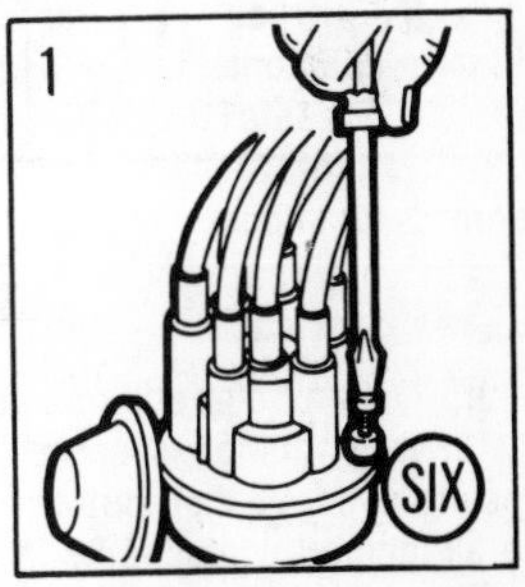

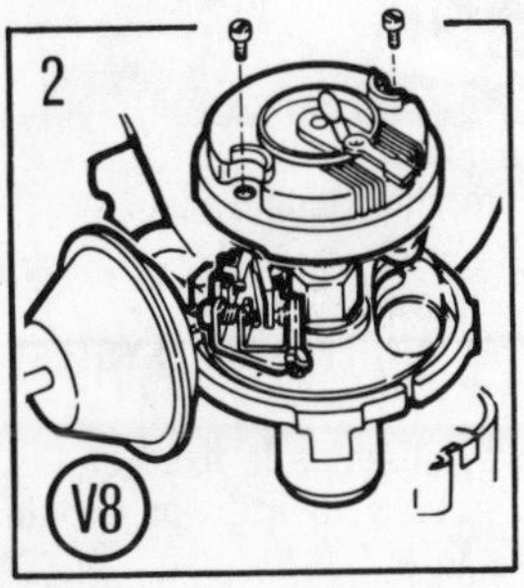

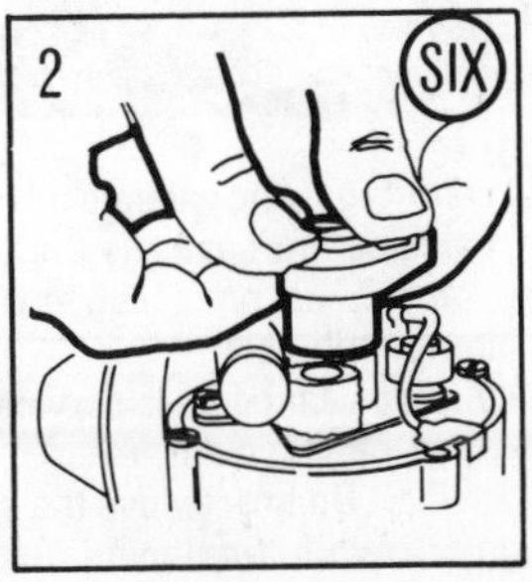

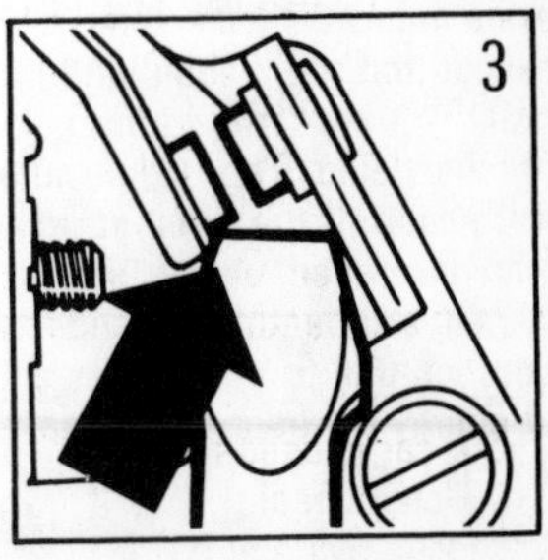

OTHER IGNITION CHECK POINTS

Inspect the spark plug wires. If cracked or brittle, entire set should be replaced. Also, check the coil wire. Inspect the distributor cap. If there are cracks or the contacts are burned, replace the cap with a new one.

SPARK PLUG REPLACEMENT

Use the firing order illustration to guide you when replacing your ignition wires and/or distributor cap.

1. Remove spark plug wire by grasping rubber boot. Do not jerk wire off. If stuck, turn boot, pulling gently.
2. Loosen spark plug using socket wrench.
3. Wipe or brush loose dirt from around plug before removing. Do not let dirt drop into engine through plug hole. Unscrew plug.
4. Check plug electrode gap on new spark plug. Adjust to 0.035 in. Plug gap is correct when the gauge drags slightly as it is pulled between plug electrodes.
5. Thread new plug into plug hole by hand. Hand tighten. Do not force or cross thread. Use socket wrench to tighten firmly but do not force. Replace plug wire. Press boot firmly.

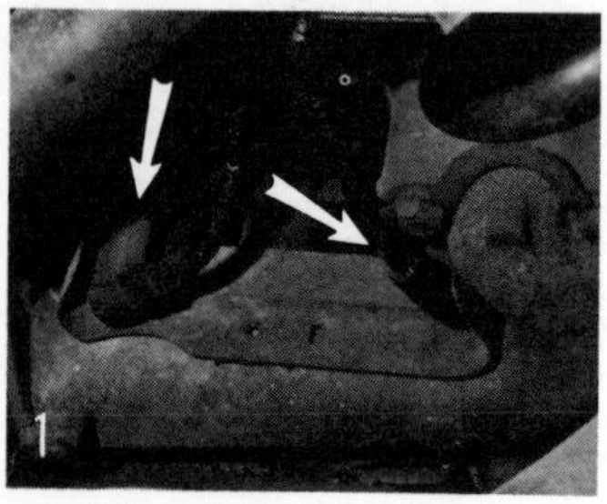

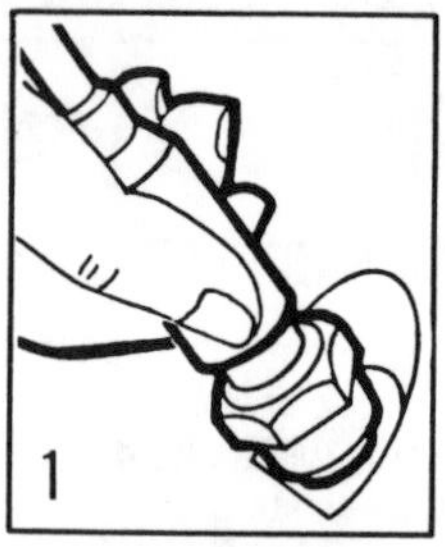

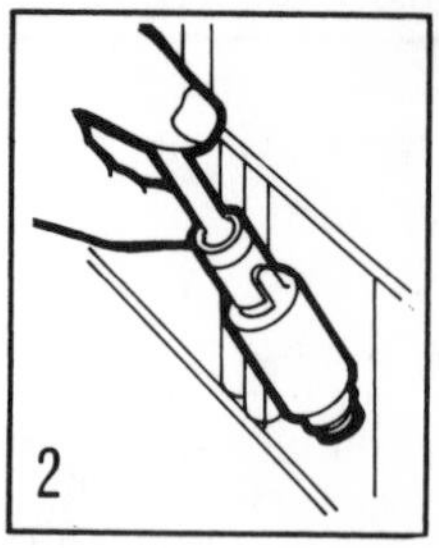

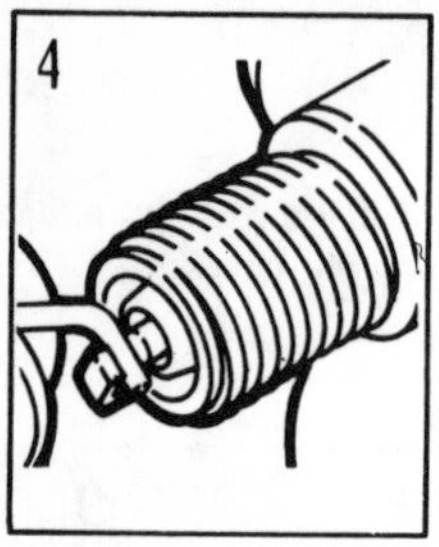

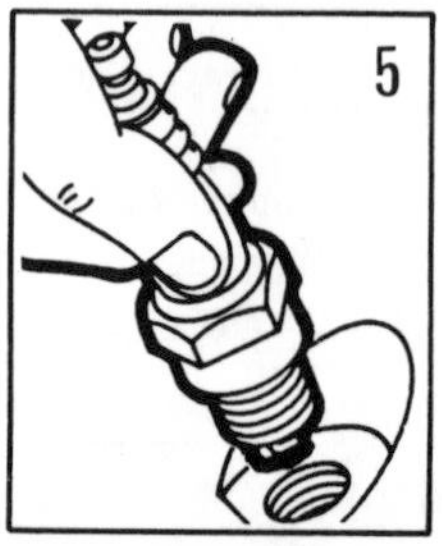

HIGH ENERGY IGNITION (HEI) SYSTEM

All 1975-77 Chevrolet engines use a High Energy Ignition system. Two types are used. V8 distributors combine all ignition components in one unit. The coil is in the distributor cap and connects directly to the rotor. The 6 cylinder distributor has an externally mounted coil. Both units operate in basically the same manner, except that the module and pick-up coil replace the conventional breaker points. The module automatically controls the dwell, stretching it with increased engine speed. The system also features a longer spark duration due to the greater amount of energy stored in the primary coil. This is necessary to fire leaner mixtures.

The centrifugal and vacuum advance mechanisms are basically the same type of unit as on a conventional ignition distributor.
The electronic module is serviced by complete replacement.
WARNING: Do not remove the spark plug wires with the engine running. Severe shock could result.

DWELL ANGLE—H.E.I. SYSTEM

The dwell angle is fixed and is not adjustable. No attempt should be made to adjust the unit.

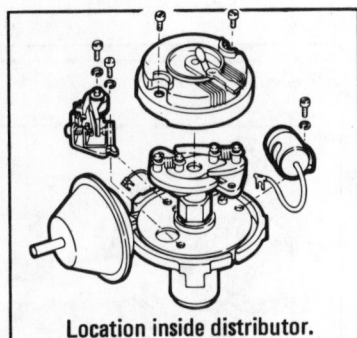

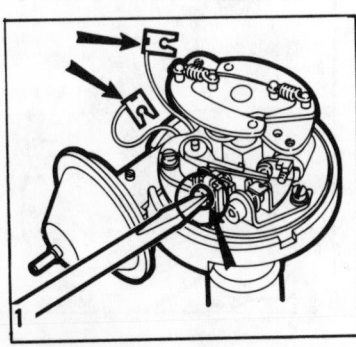

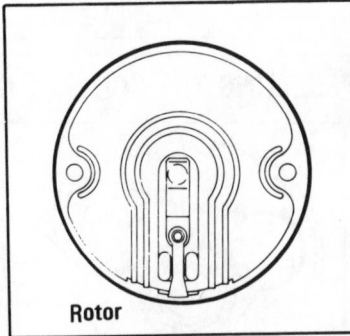

TIMING LIGHT CONNECTIONS—
H.E.I. SYSTEM

Timing light connections should be made in parallel using an adapter at the distributor No. 1 terminal.

TACHOMETER CONNECTIONS—
H.E.I. SYSTEM

There is a "tach" terminal on the distributor cap. Connect the tachometer to this terminal and ground. Follow the tachometer manufacturer's instructions.

CAUTION: Grounding the tach terminal could damage the H.E.I. ignition module.

POINTS AND CONDENSER—V8 (1970-74)

Points and condenser work together. Always replace condenser also when installing new points.

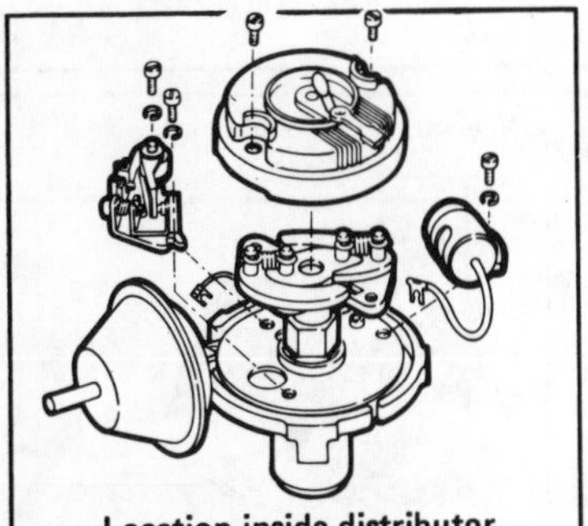

Location inside distributor.

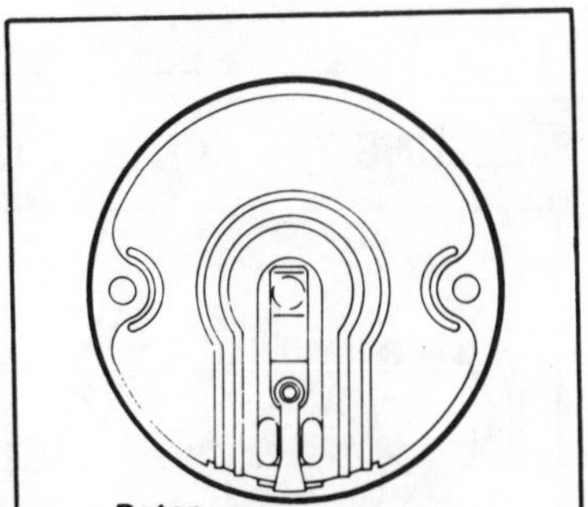

Rotor

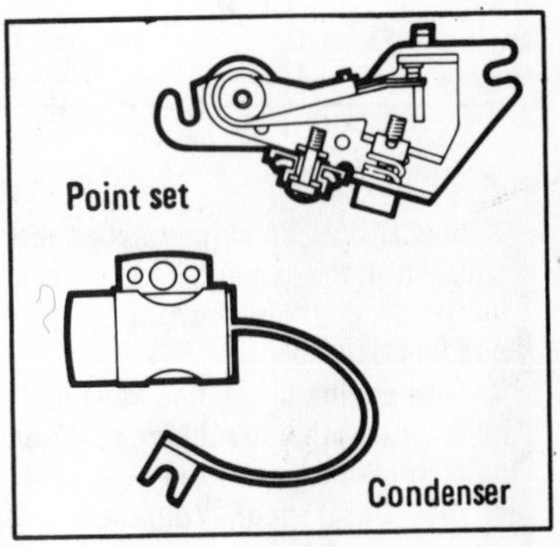

REMOVING POINTS

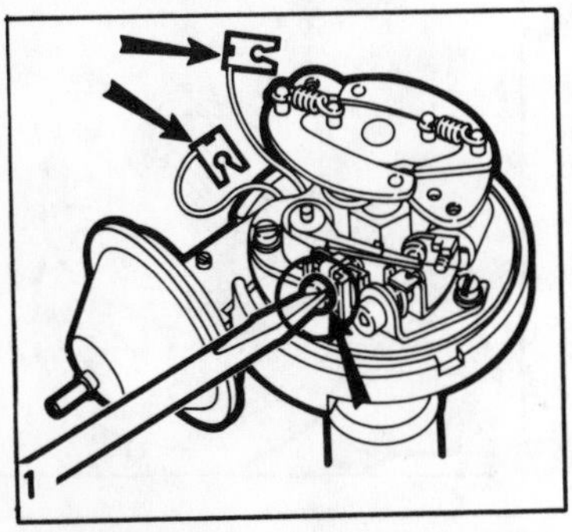

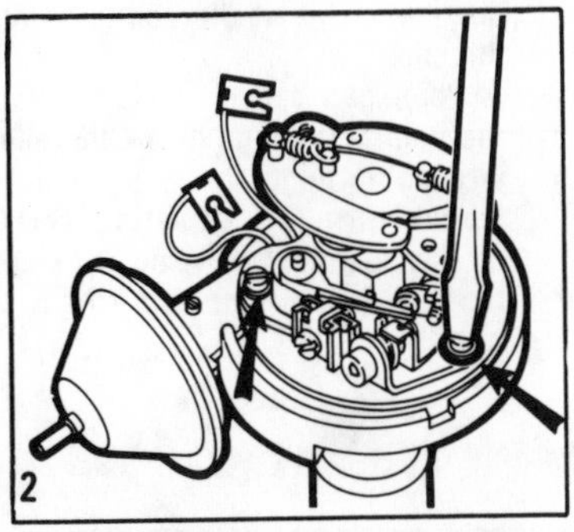

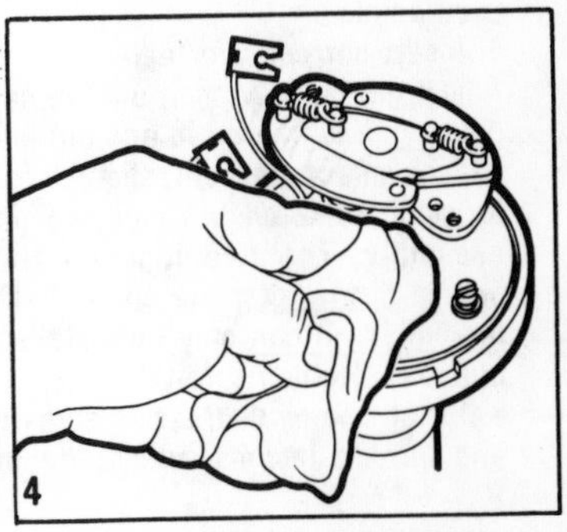

1. Disconnect the two wire terminals connected to the points set. Notice that the condenser connector is on the outside.
2. Loosen, but do not remove the two points attaching screws. Slide the points off the screws to remove.
3. Remove screw which holds condenser. DO NOT DROP SCREW. these points in early cars.
4. Wipe all dirt from distributor plate and cam with clean, lint-free rag.

NOTE: Later models use a combined points and condenser. When you remove points you also remove condenser.

CAUTION: When removing screws from distributor, be sure to avoid any screws accidentally falling through distributor opening into engine. Use magnetic screwdriver.

INSTALLING POINTS AND CONDENSER—V8 (1970-74)

1. Attach new condenser with screw.
2. Rotate or replace cam lubricator. Fiber cam lubricator must be turned 180° every 12,000 mi., replaced every 24,000. When replacing, simply pull it up and off stud; push new lubricator down over stud. DO NOT attempt to add oil or grease to fiber lubricator.
3. Position new points set in distributor by sliding onto screws. Tighten screws.

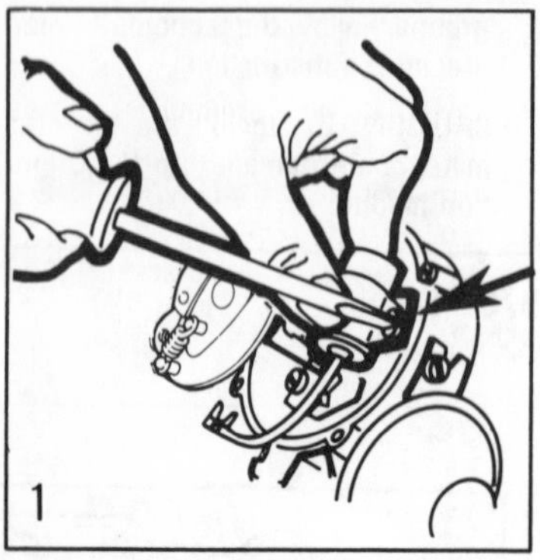

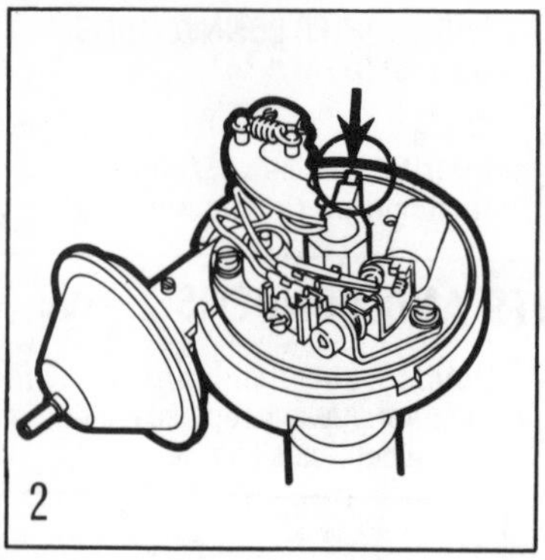

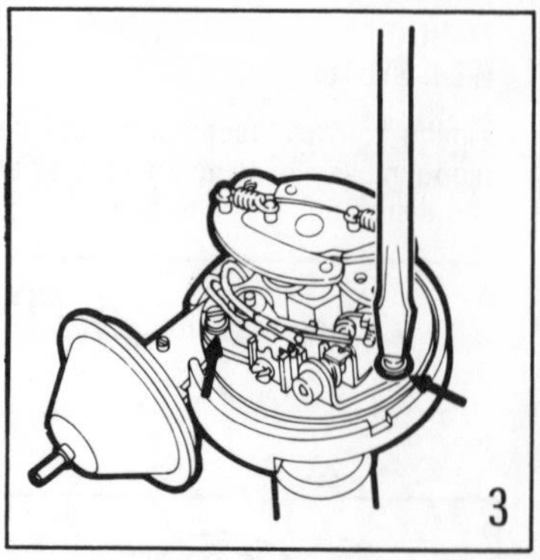

RESETTING THE CONTACT GAP

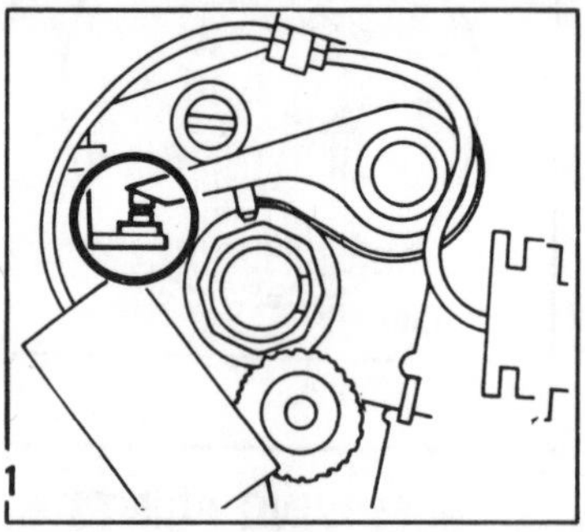

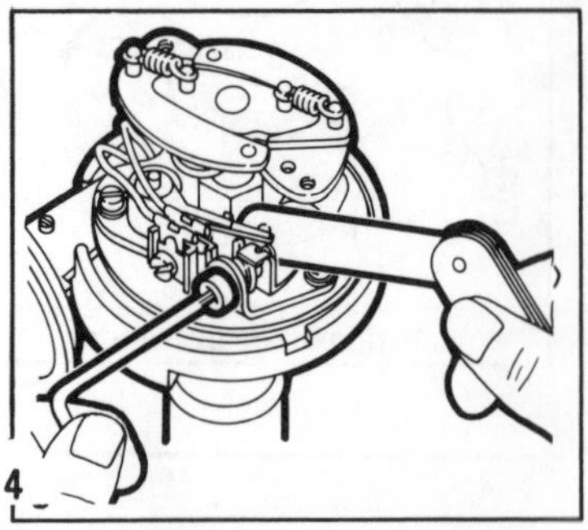

1. Check that point contacts meet squarely. If they do not, bend bracket supporting fixed contact using needle-nosed pliers.
2. Turn engine by ignition key (you'll need a helper) until rubbing block on point set is on one of the high spots of distributor cam. You may use wrench on lower engine pulley to do this.
3. Insert a ⅛ in. allen wrench into points adjusting screw. Correct gap is .019 in. for new points; .016 in. for used points.
4. Insert correct size feeler gauge. Adjust gap with wrench until feeler gauge can be moved in and out between contacts with only slight drag.
5. Install rotor on advance weight assembly. The two lugs on the bottom of the rotor are shaped differently, so it can only be installed one way. Tighten screws.
6. Install cap by depressing screws and turning latches onto body of distributor. Insert the coil wire into the cap.
7. Point gap can be adjusted with the engine running. Insert the allen wrench through the cap window, slowly turn the adjusting screw clockwise until the engine just starts to misfire, and then turn it back ½ turn.

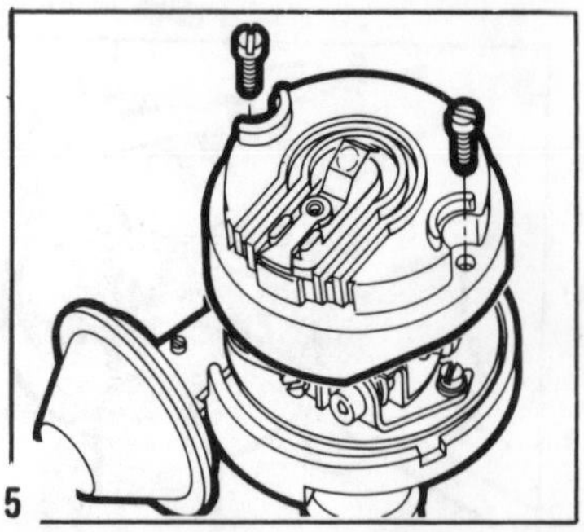

POINTS AND CONDENSER—Six Cylinder (1970-74)

Points and condenser work together. Always replace condenser also when installing new points.

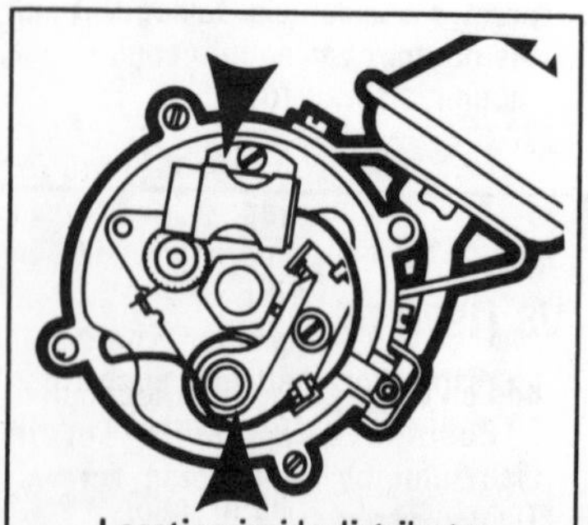
Location inside distributor.

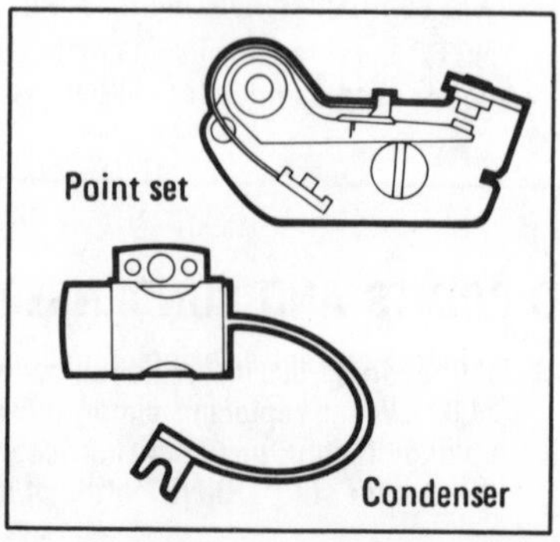

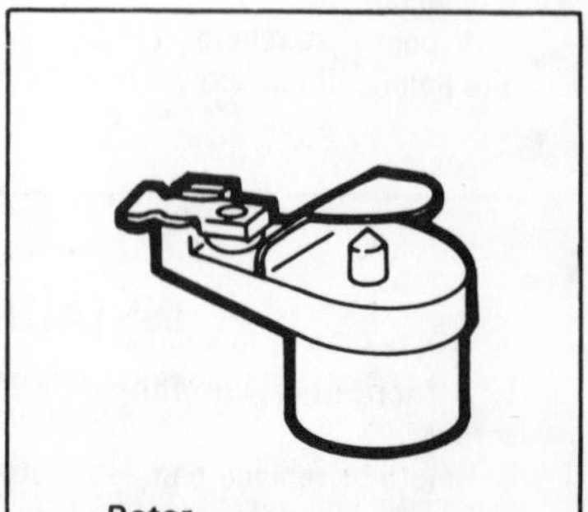
Rotor

REMOVING POINTS

1. Disconnect the two wire terminals connected to the points set. Notice that the condenser connector is on the outside.

2. Remove points attaching screw being very careful not to drop screw inside distributor.

3. Remove screw which holds condenser. DO NOT DROP SCREW.

4. Wipe all dirt from distributor plate and cam with clean, lint-free rag.

CAUTION: When removing screws from distributor, be sure to avoid any screws accidentally falling through distributor opening into engine. Use magnetic screwdriver.

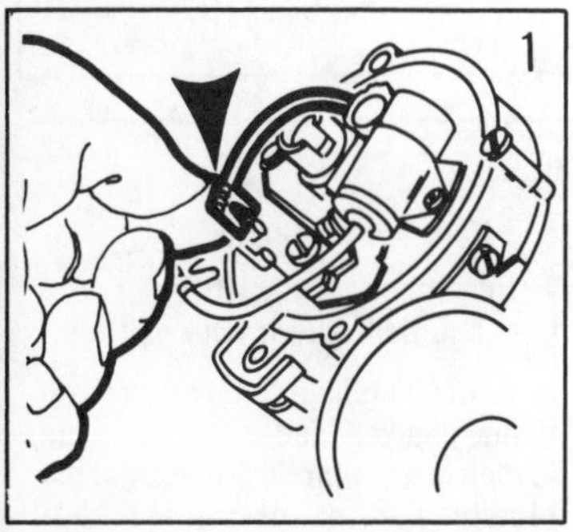

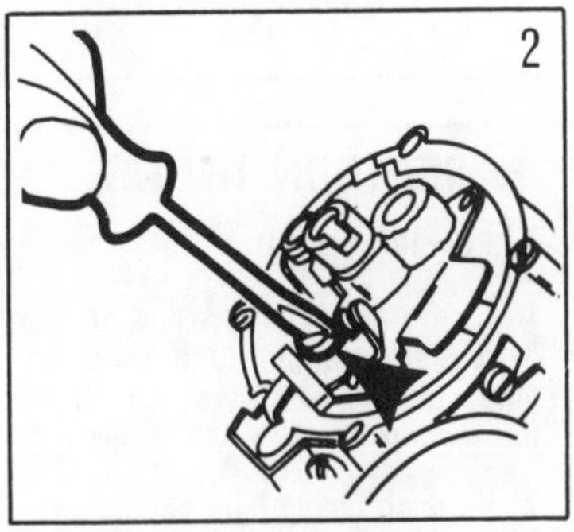

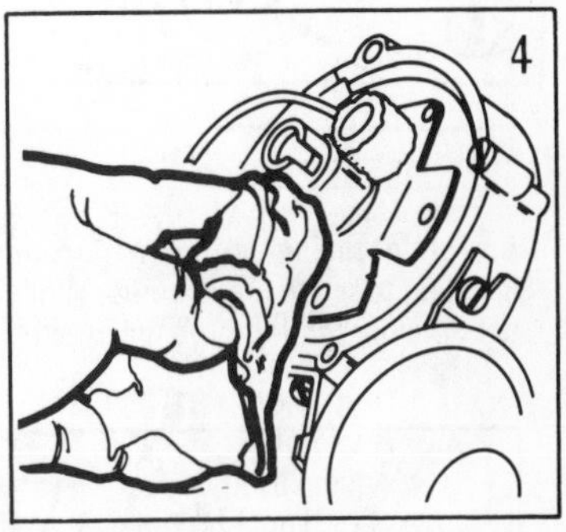

INSTALLING POINTS AND CONDENSER—Six Cylinder (1970-74)

1. Attach new condenser with screw.
2. Rotate or replace cam lubricator. Fiber cam lubricator must be turned 180° every 12,000 mi., replaced every 24,000. When replacing, simply pull it up and off stud; push new lubricator down over stud. DO NOT attempt to add oil or grease to fiber lubricator.
3. Position new points set in distributor. Attach retaining screw lightly. Replace both wire terminals. The condenser wire goes on the outside of the two.

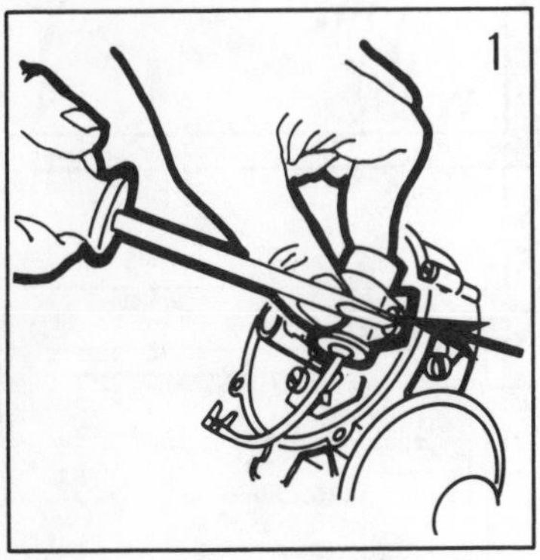

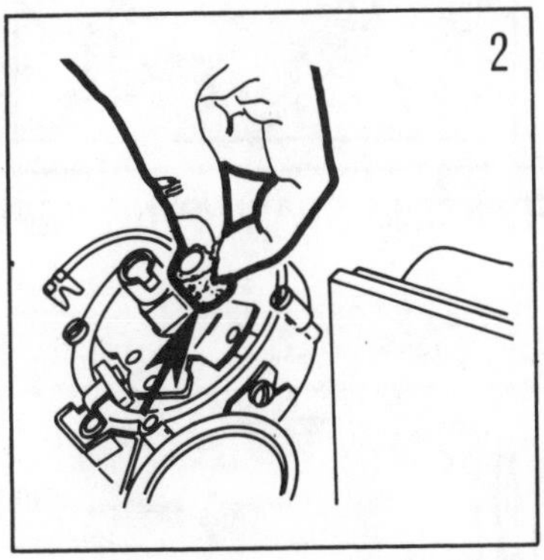

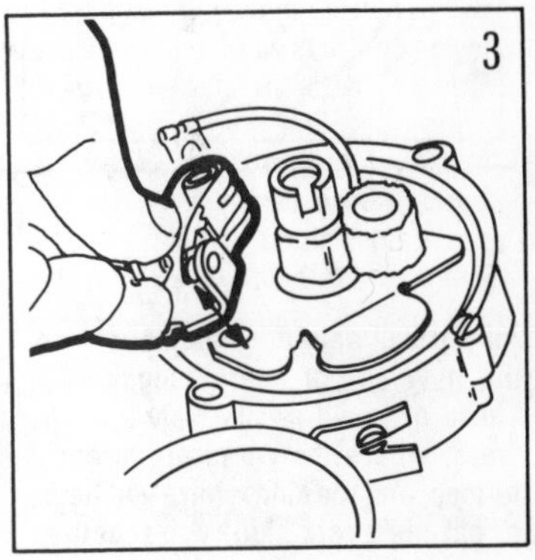

RESETTING THE CONTACT GAP

1. Check that point contacts meet squarely. If they do not, bend bracket supporting fixed contact using needle-nosed pliers.
2. Turn engine by ignition key (you'll need a helper) until rubbing block on point set is on one of the high spots of distributor cam. You may use wrench on lower engine pulley to do this.
3. Insert screwdriver in slot near point contacts; twist to open or close gap.
4. Correct gap is .019 in. for new points; .016 in. for used points.
5. Insert correct size feeler gauge. Adjust gap with screwdriver until feeler gauge can be moved in and out between contacts with only slight drag.
6. Tighten point set holddown screw. Recheck gap; it might have changed from tightening holddown screw. Re-adjust if needed.
7. Align tab inside rotor with notch on distributor shaft and push rotor onto shaft. Rotor must be fully seated on shaft.
8. Replace distributor cap; install screws.

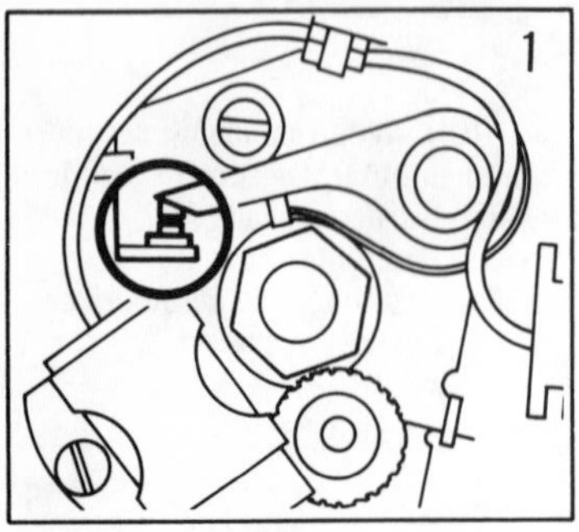

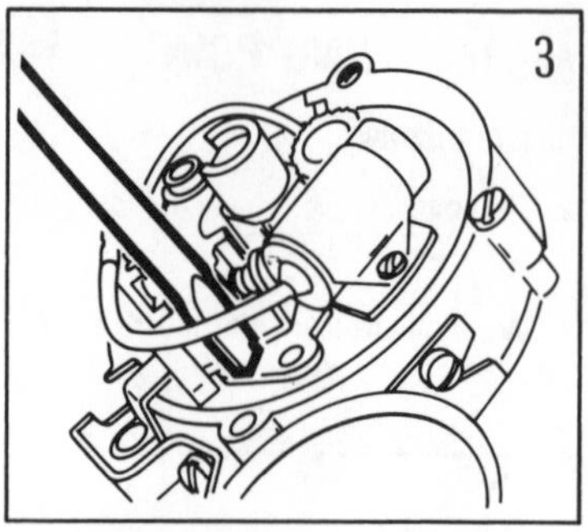

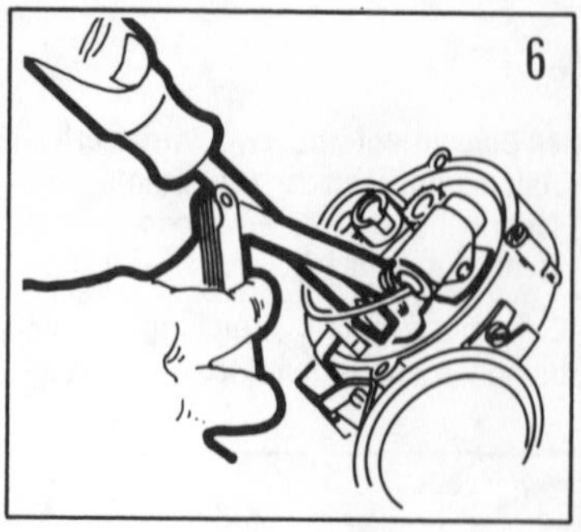

IGNITION TIMING

Adjusting timing is the important finishing touch to any tune-up. While not difficult, job requires timing light

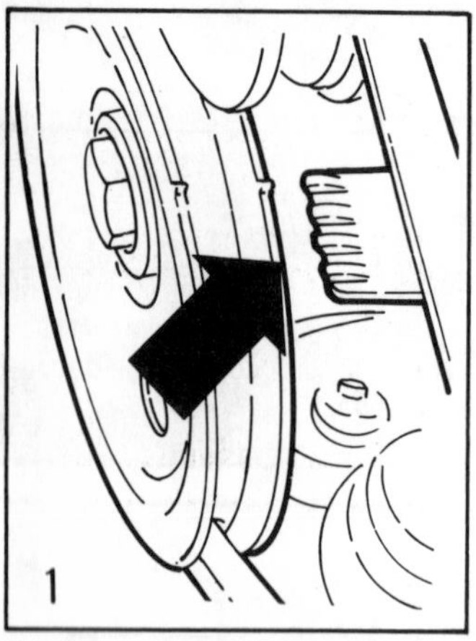

and dwell meter.

1. Locate timing marks and pointer (notches) on engine and lower engine pulley. Clean away dirt. Mark the pointer notches with chalk.

2. Hook up timing light according to instructions supplied with it.

3. Disconnect and plug the vacuum line from the distributor.

4. Disconnect the distributor vacuum line and plug it with golf tee.

5. Aim timing light at pulley mark(s). If the chalked marks do not align, loosen distributor hold-down nut and slowly rotate distributor until chalked marks align.

6. Tighten hold-down nut.

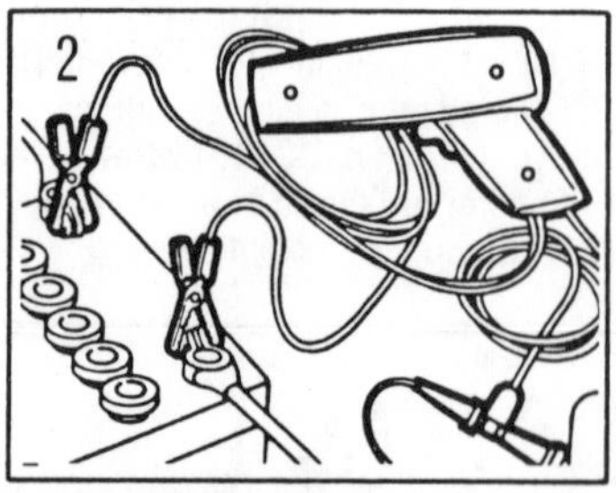

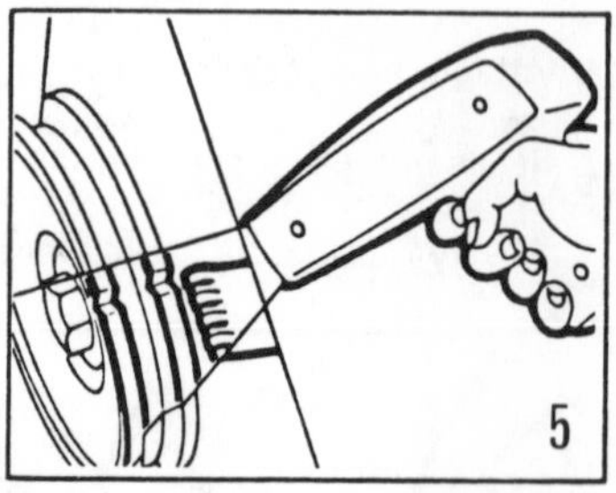

REPLACING SPARK PLUG WIRES

All you will need for this job will be the new set of spark plug wires. These are sold in kits of two basic typss; where the wires are already formed, and the kind where you have to put the spark plug wire together yourself. The preformed kits are by far the easiest to install, but with the other kit you can tailor the wire to fit your need exactly with as little surplus wire as possible. Either way, when working on spark plug wires, you only work on one at a time.

1. Lay the new wires out before you so you can match up an old wire with its replacement to ensure a correct fit.

2. Starting from the rear, twist the boot on the last plug and remove it, then remove the wire from the harness.

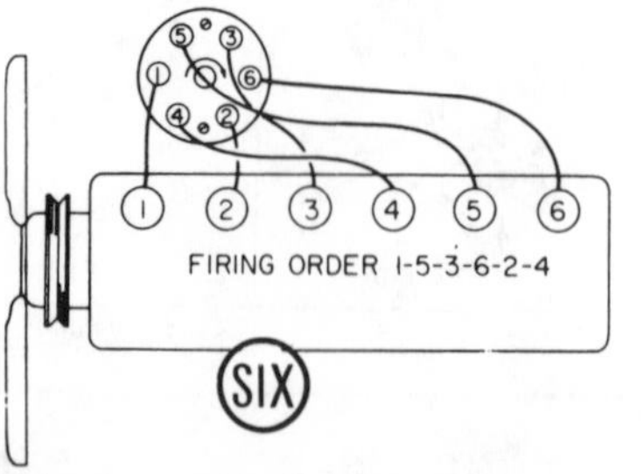

NOTE: Some wires may be routed through the engine mounts.

3. Twist off the boot on the top of the distributor cap and remove the spark plug wire.

4. Compare it with the new wires and choose the one which most nearly matches it in length. If you are using the kit where you make the wire, do not forget to add about an inch on each end for the amount of wire inside the boot.

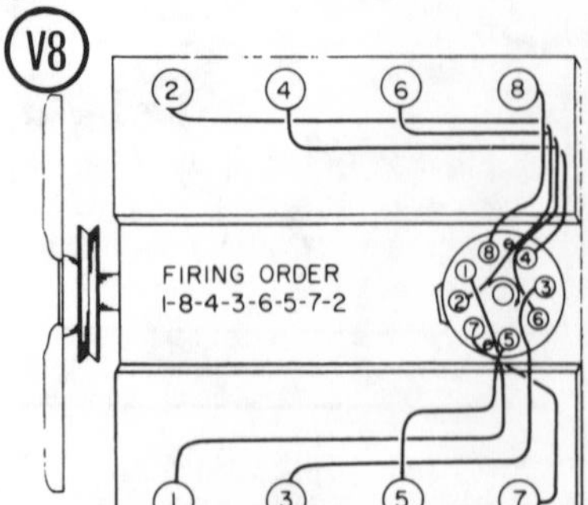

5. Insert the wire boot on the plug and make sure it is on snug. Push the wire on the harness and insert the other boot on the distributor cap, twisting it down if necessury to make sure it is snug.

6. All you have to do is follow these steps for the other plugs and your wiring job will be complete.

Fuel Systems

When gasoline is brought from the carburetor. This gas/air mixture enters engine thru the intake manifold, passes thru the intake valves and is burned in the combustion chamber. The burned exhaust gas is then passed thru the exhaust valves to the exhaust system and to the outside air. In order to keep your car's engine running cleanly with minimal pollution, and avoid dangerous carbon monoxide fumes inside the vehicle, certain items should be checked from time to time.

KEEP THE AIR INTAKE CLEAN

The large round can that sits on top of the engine is the air cleaner. The filter element is located inside and should be replaced as follows: 1970-71, all engines—every 12,000 miles; 1972-74, 6-cylinder—every 12,000 miles; 1972-74, V8—every 24,000 miles; 1975-77, 6-cylinder—every 15,000 miles; 1975-77, V8—every 30,000 miles.

1. Unscrew the wing nut and remove the air cleaner cover.
2. Remove and discard the old dirty filter.
3. Check the small crankcase breather filter. If dirty, lift out and replace it.
4. Using a clean rag, wipe out the inside of air cleaner. Install new filter and replace top cover.

1

2

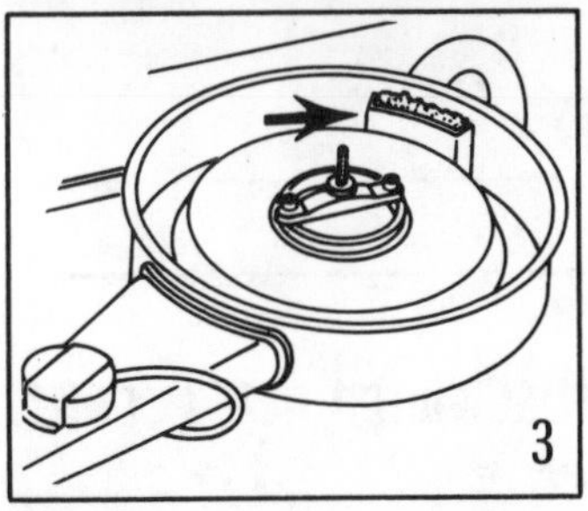
3

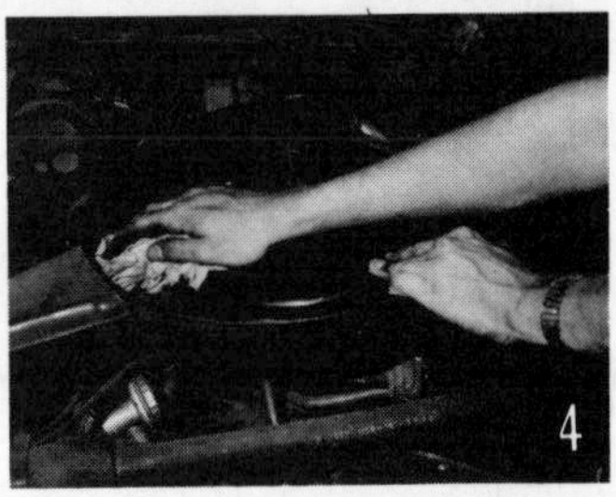
4

PCV VALVE REPLACEMENT

An important part of a car's emission control system is the Positive Crankcase Ventilation (PCV) valve and its connecting hose. The PCV valve should be replaced once every 24,000 miles (1970-74) or every 12 months or 15,000 miles (1975-77). This device keeps dirt and sludge from forming inside the engine. Make sure all PCV connections are tight. Check that the connecting hoses are clear and not clogged. Replace any brittle or broken hoses.

1. Pull valve from its location in the valve cover.
2. Squeeze the hose clamp with a pair of pliers. Remove the valve.
3. Note where the other end of the hose connects. Remove the hose and flush it with cleaning solvent.
4. Reconnect the hose. Pinch the clamp and insert the PCV valve into the hose.
5. Insert the valve into the valve cover.

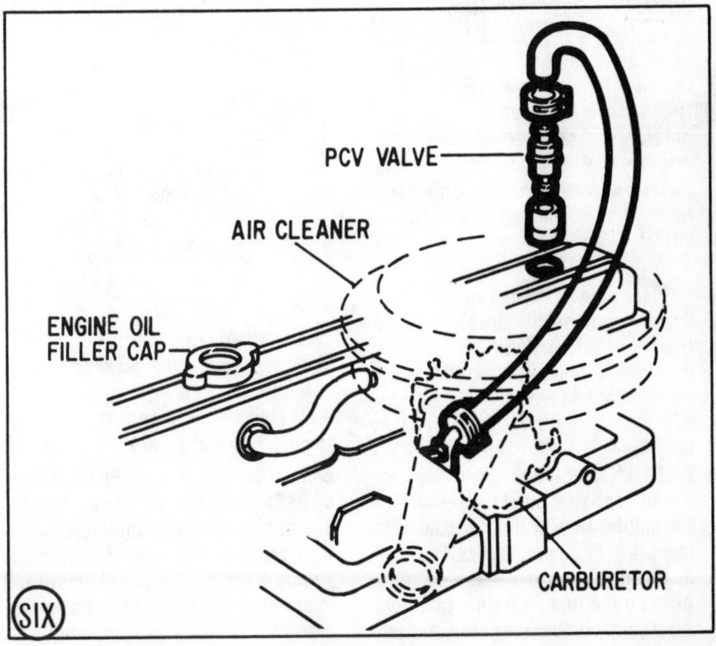

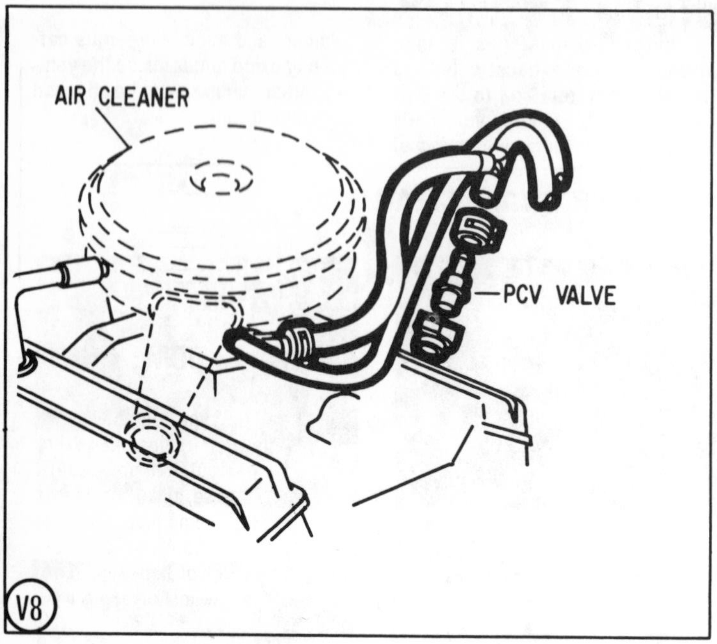

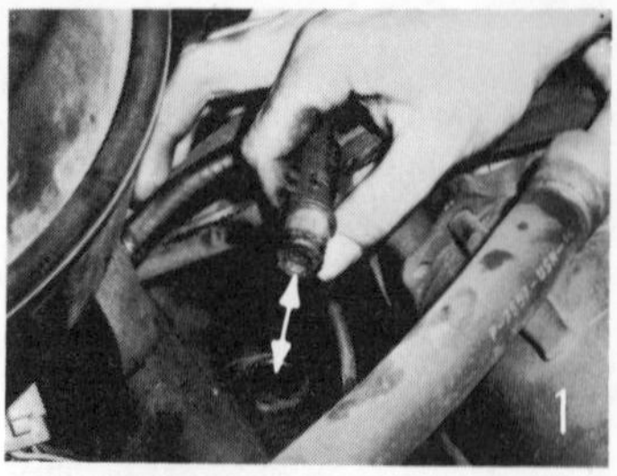

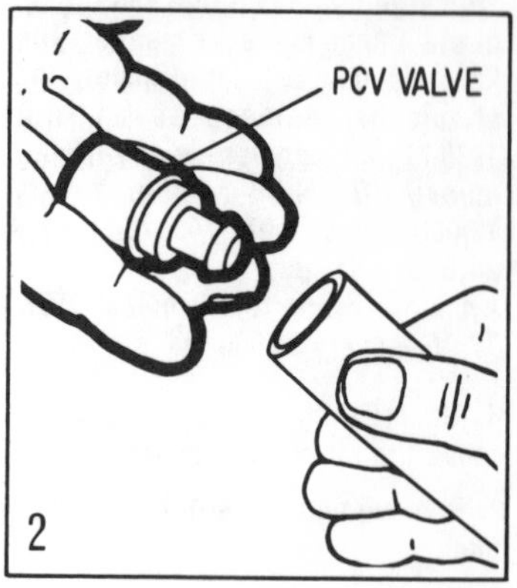

FUEL FILTER REPLACEMENT

The fuel filter is located behind the large fuel line inlet nut on the carburetor. Replace the filter every year or 12,000 miles (1970-74) or 15,000 miles (1975-77). The fuel filter prevents dirt, rust, and scale from both the gas station's tank and your own fuel tank from reaching the carburetor. A dirty filter will starve the engine and cause poor running. Some models may have an inline fuel filter which should be replaced every 30,000 miles.

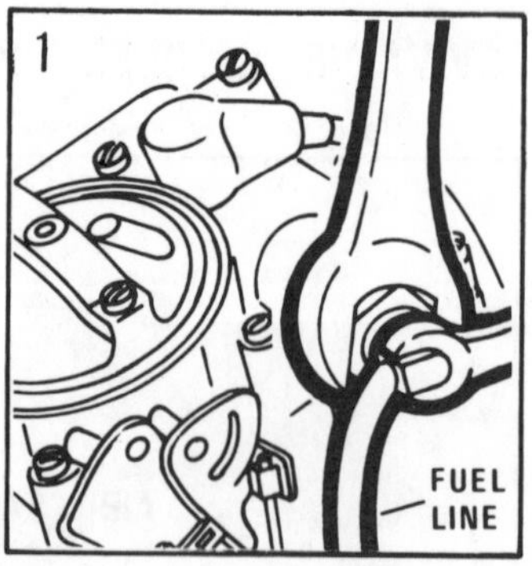

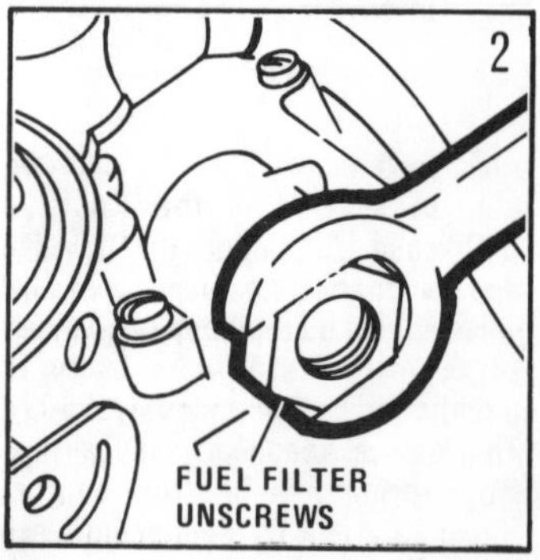

1. Place an absorbent rag under fuel line connection to absorb gas spills. Unscrew fuel line connection with ½ in. wrench while holding the larger nut with a 1 in. wrench. Be careful, fuel line fitting threads are easily stripped.
2. Remove the large filter retaining nut from the carburetor. The spring behind the filter will push it out. Remove the filter and the spring.
3. Install the spring and new filter element. Some carburetors are equipped with a paper element, others with a bronze unit. The bronze filter must have the small cone section facing out and a gasket between the filter and the retaining nut.
4. Install the new gasket on the retaining nut and screw it into place.
CAUTION: DO NOT OVERTIGHTEN
5. Reconnect the fuel line. Discard the gas soaked rag safely.
6. Start the engine and check for leaks. Addition of a can of carburetor cleaner to the fuel tank occasionally will aid in keeping the entire fuel system clean.

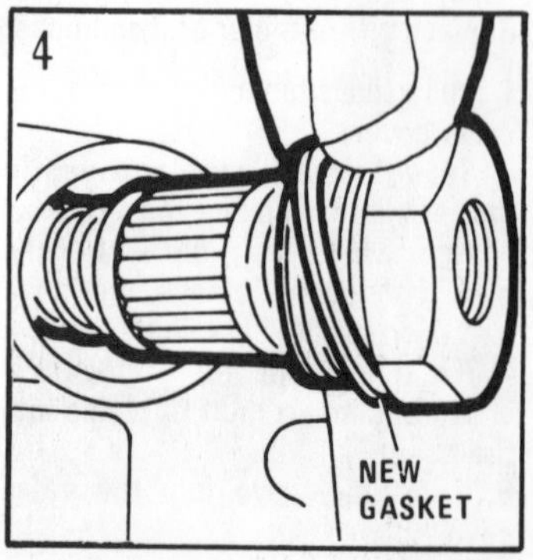

Safety Systems

LIGHTING SYSTEM

Headlights, turn signals, stop lights, and parking lights are an important part of your car's safety system. They permit you to see and be seen. Keep all lenses clean and make frequent checks to be sure that all of your lights are functioning properly. Replace any cracked lenses as soon as possible. When replacing a bulb, make a note of the number which is usually printed on the base. If you don't have a number, take the old bulb with you so that you match it for the correct replacement.

BULB REPLACEMENT

To replace a turn signal, stop light, or back-up light bulb, remove the lens, push down on bulb while turning it counterclockwise to remove it from the socket. Install the new bulb in reverse order. Be sure to match the knobs on the bulb base with the slots in the socket.

LICENSE PLATE LIGHT

Remove the screws that retain the lens to the bumpers. Push in on bulb, turning counterclockwise to remove.

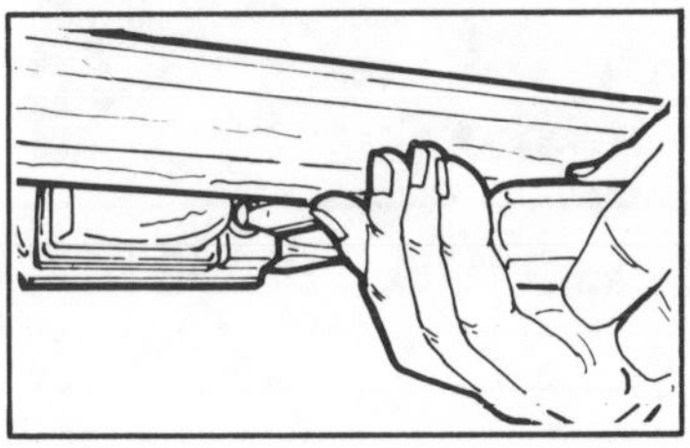

SIDE MARKER LIGHT

Reach up inside fender and turn bulb socket counterclockwise to remove from housing. Pull bulb straight out.

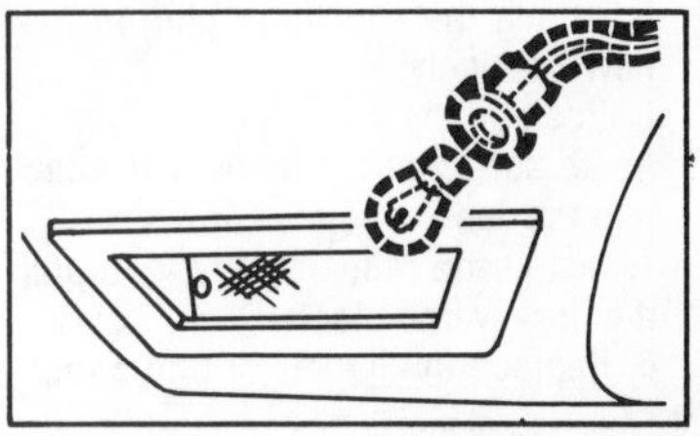

INTERIOR DOME LIGHT

This is cartridge type bulb; be sure to purchase correct replacement. Pry dome light lens out from housing. To avoid blowing fuse, make sure doors are closed and dome light switch is in OFF position. Carefully lever the bulb straight out of housing. Insert new bulb and re-install dome light lens.

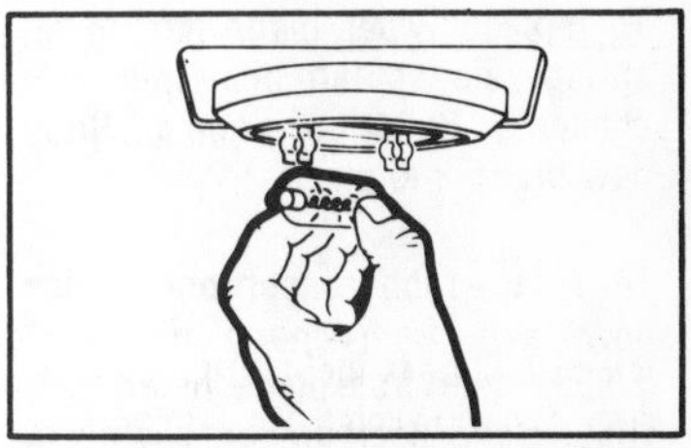

HEADLIGHT REPLACEMENT

NOTE: Some models may be equipped with "square" sealed beams. The replacement procedure is typical.

1. Remove the headlight trim retaining screws and remove the trim.
2. Unhook the spring from the headlight retaining ring.
3. Remove the two retaining ring screws. Do not disturb the long aiming screws located at 9 and 12 o'clock.

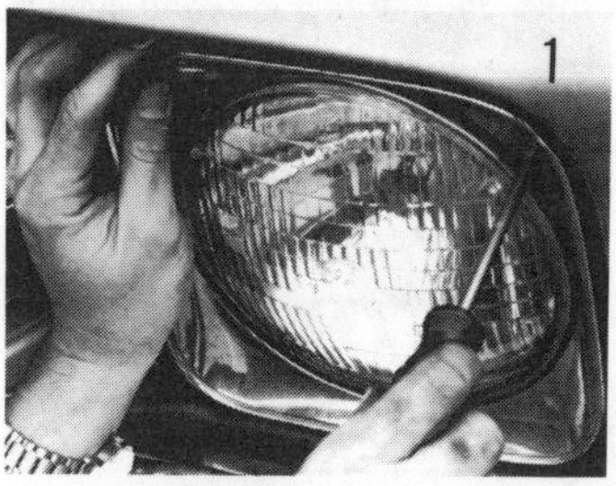

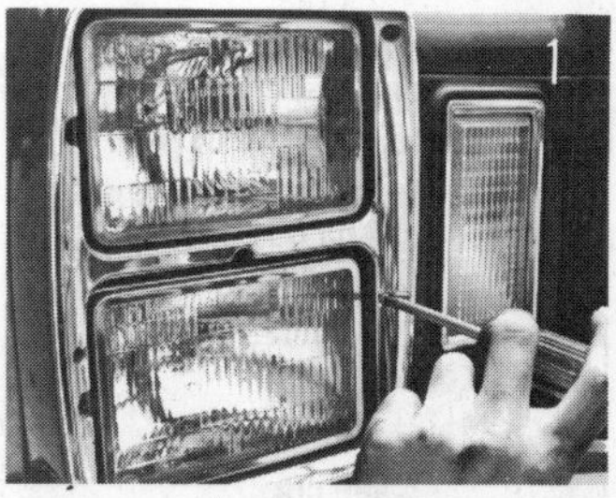

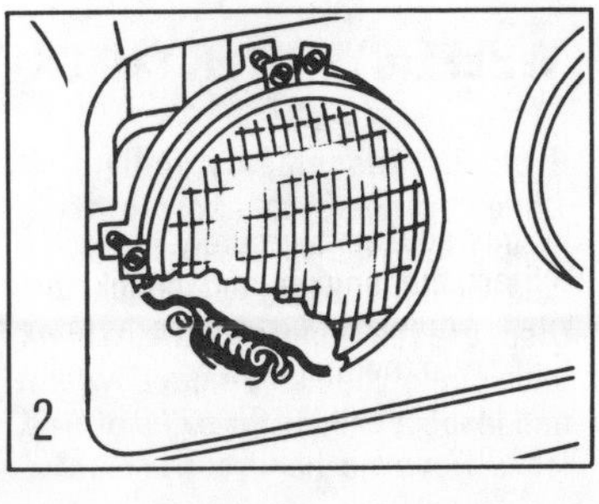

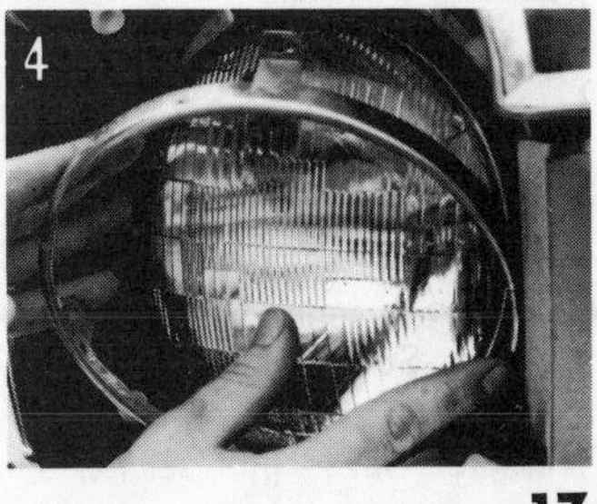

4. Remove the retaining ring. Disconnect the wiring plug and remove the bulb.
5. Attach the connector plug to the new headlight.
6. Position the new bulb in housing. Make sure that the number molded into the lens is at the top.
7. Install the retaining ring and pull the spring into place.
8. Replace the headlight trim panel.

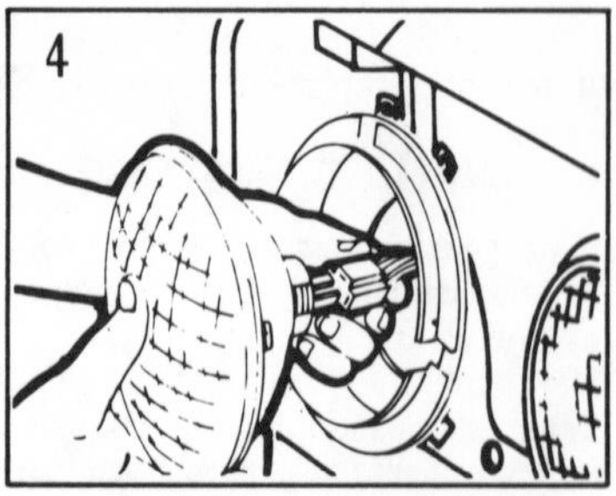

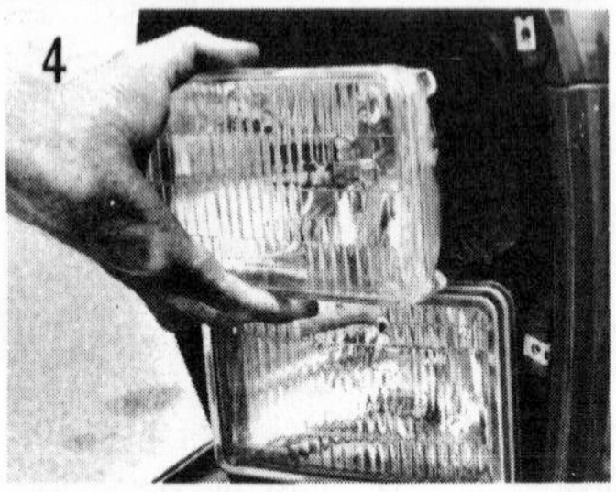

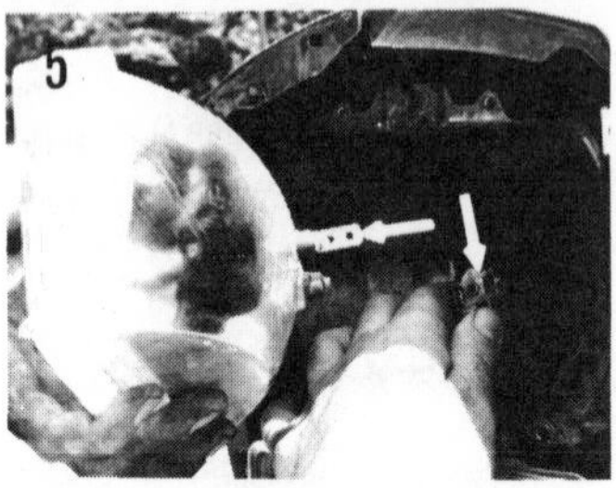

WINDSHIELD WIPER BLADE REPLACEMENT

To replace wiper blade, lift up on spring release tab on wiper arm connector. Pull wiper blade off. Snap new blade into place.

To replace rubber insert only, press down, away from wiper blade to free it. Slide insert from blade. Insert new wiper. Bend insert upward slightly to engage retaining clips.

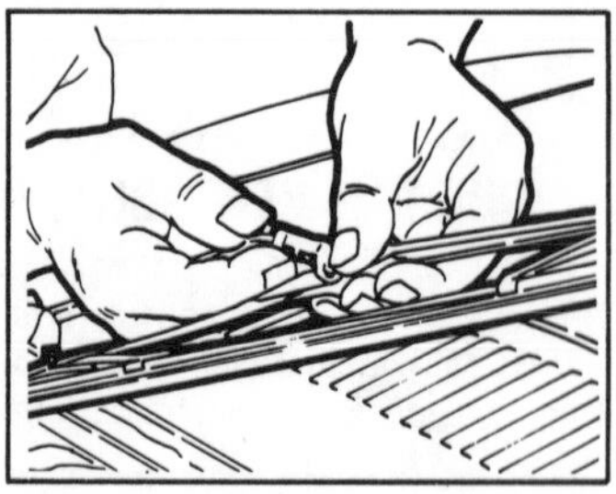

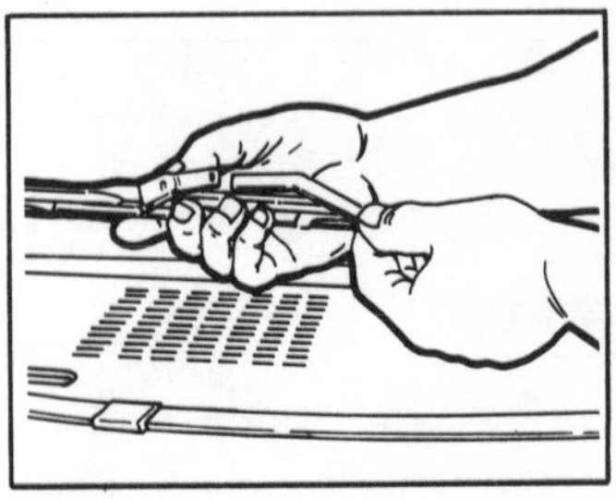

HORN PROBLEMS

If horn sounds and does not stop, this is due to short circuit in wiring. Disconnect wiring connector under hood and have professional service shop check horn wiring circuit.

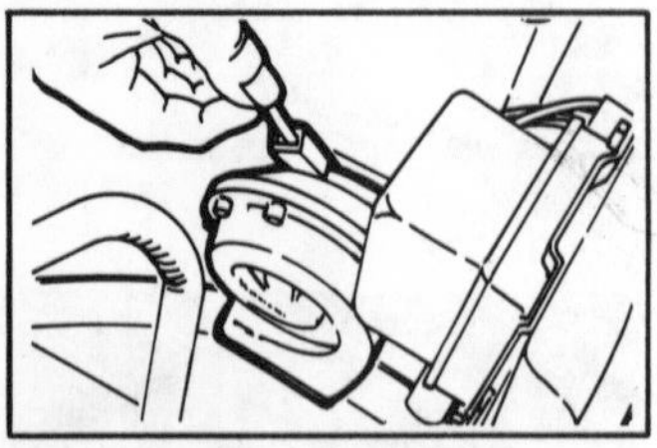

STEERING PROBLEMS

See steering system check in Suspension Section. Check tire pressures. Have a professional service shop check all components in the front end and steering system.

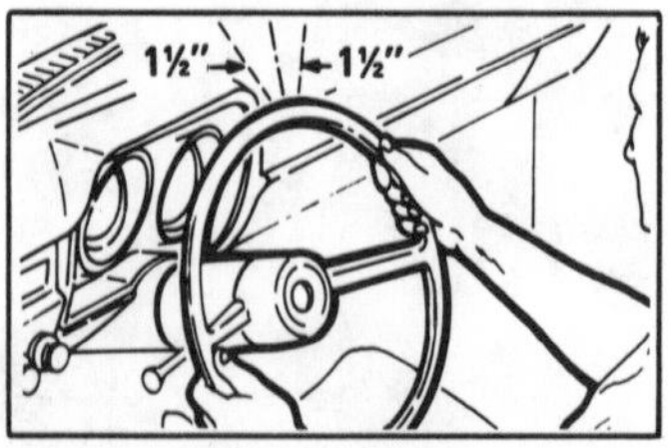

WHEEL CYLINDER CHECK

Drum brakes employ individual wheel cylinders to apply braking pressure to shoes. Check for brake fluid leaks on inside of wheel.
Disc brakes employ calipers on individual wheels. Remove wheel and inspect caliper for signs of fluid leaks. Have mechanic correct leaks.

WASHER SYSTEM

If washer fails to squirt properly, raise hood and check system hose connections. Be sure washer fluid container has fluid. Check spout openings for clogging.
Keep container filled with fluid mixture of washer solvent and water. If road spray buildup on windshield is a chronic problem, add

1 tablespoon dishwasher detergent to solvent/water mixture when refilling container.

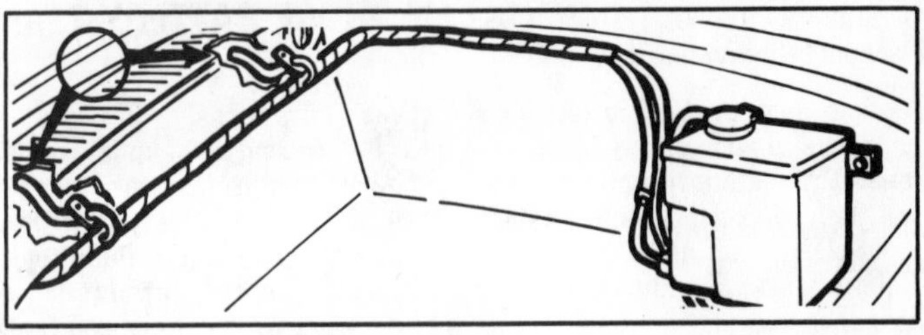

Electrical System

CHECK POINTS AND SERVICES

To ensure starting ability at all times check your battery condition periodically. You'll need to check battery electrolyte (fluid) level in each of the six cells. Check battery cable connections for tightness and inspect for accumulated corrosion. SAFETY NOTE: Wear gloves when working on battery.

CHECK BATTERY FLUID—1970-75

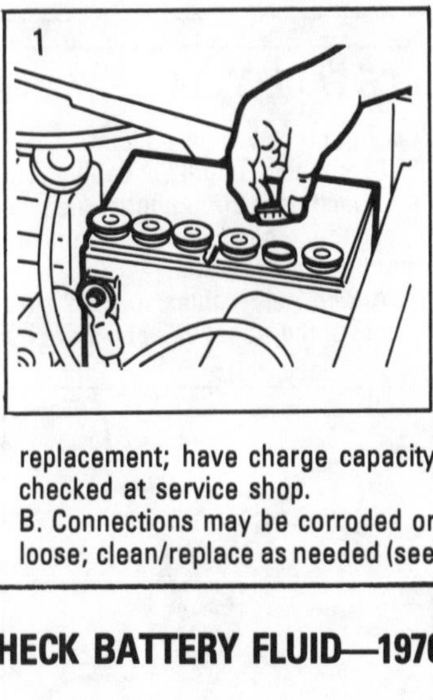

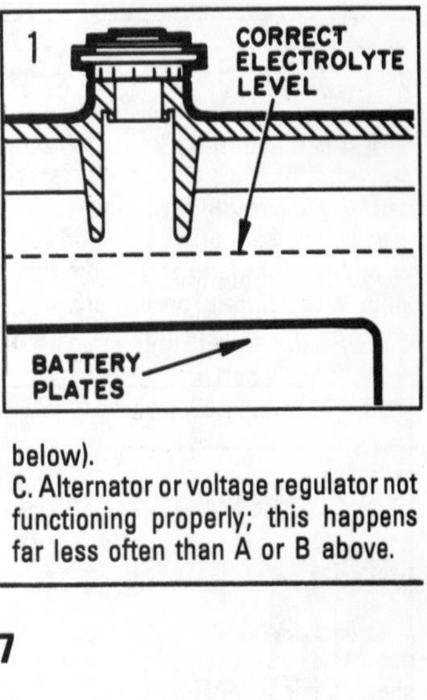

1. Remove plastic filler caps on top of battery. Fluid should be up to lower end of filler hole and covering the plates. If fluid is low add clean, cold tap water. If your area has hard water, use only distilled water available at auto supply, food or drug stores.
2. Replace any lost caps immediately.

CAUTION: NEVER LIGHT A MATCH OR SMOKE near the top of a battery. Batteries give off explosive hydrogen gas.

NOTE: Battery that often checks low on fluid could mean:

A. Battery is getting old, due for replacement; have charge capacity checked at service shop.

B. Connections may be corroded or loose; clean/replace as needed (see below).

C. Alternator or voltage regulator not functioning properly; this happens far less often than A or B above.

CHECK BATTERY FLUID—1976-77

The battery in a 1976-77 Chevelle or Monte Carlo could be a "Freedom" battery. These batteries are sealed for life and never require the checking or addition of water. There is, however, a small indicator on top of the battery to indicate battery condition. Refer to the illustration to determine the condition of your battery.

There is no maintenance with this battery, other than to keep the terminals clean and tight, as you would with any other battery. See "Cleaning Those Battery Terminals."

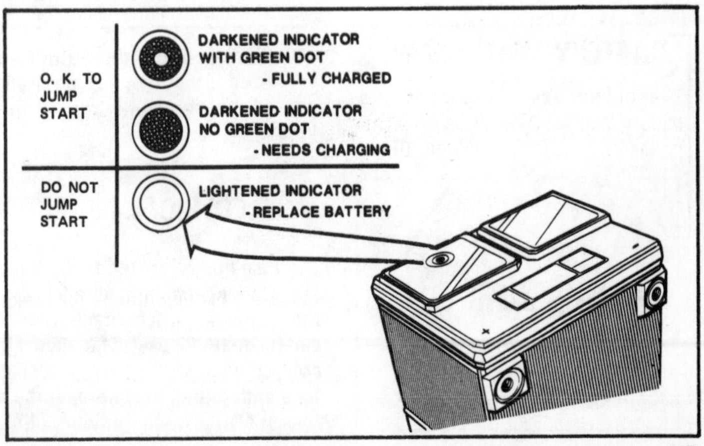

CLEAN THOSE BATTERY TERMINALS

As time goes by, battery terminals build up a dry powdery, whitish material. This material is corrosive and will gradually eat thru battery cables if not cleaned off periodically.

1. Loosen and remove battery connections.
2. Brush off all loose corrosion; use stiff bristle brush. Do not get this material into eyes or on open cuts. Wash off at once.
3. If corrosion build-up is extremely heavy and brushing does not remove all of it, mix 2 tablespoons baking soda to 1 cup water. Pour solution directly onto terminals and connectors. Allow to soak a few minutes and rinse off. Continue brushing to remove all traces of corrosion build-up. Do not allow cleaning solution to enter battery.
4. Replace connectors on battery terminal posts and tighten.
5. Liberally smear battery terminal posts and cable connectors with petroleum jelly.

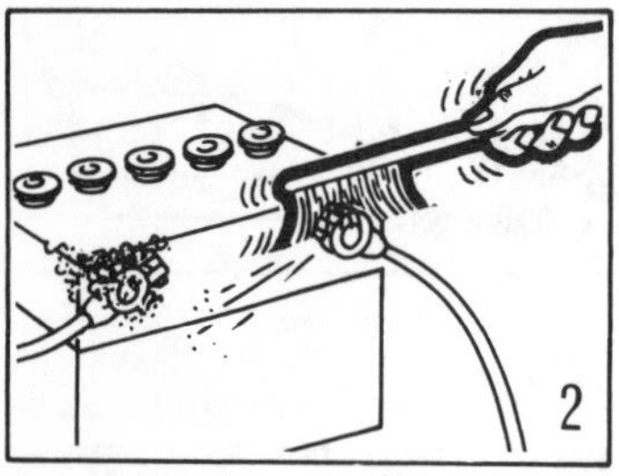

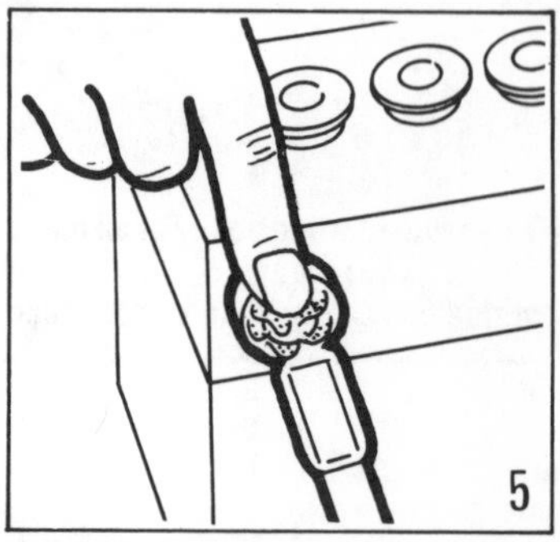

REPLACE FAULTY BATTERY CABLES

If battery cable strands become frayed, broken or corroded, replace cable immediately. Delay in correcting this condition could lead to sudden failure to start the engine and can also weaken battery.

1. Loosen and remove battery. Clean any corrosion buildup.
2. Disconnect negative cable from its attachment to engine or chassis. Disconnect positive cable from its attachment to starter relay.
3. Attach new cables making sure positive and negative cables are on proper terminals. They are not identical.
4. Replace connectors on battery terminal posts and tighten.
5. Liberally smear battery terminal posts and cable connectors with petroleum jelly.

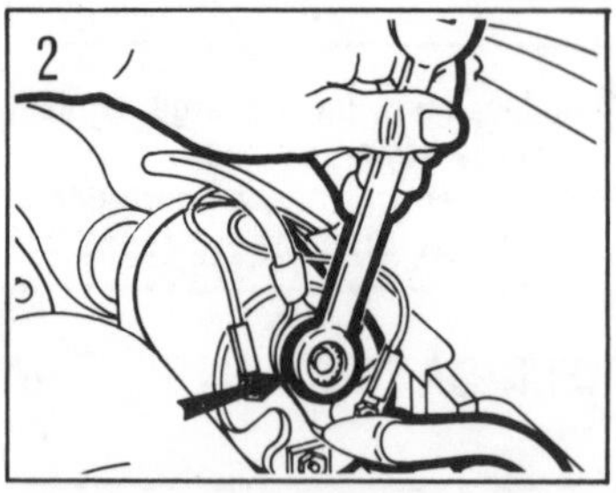

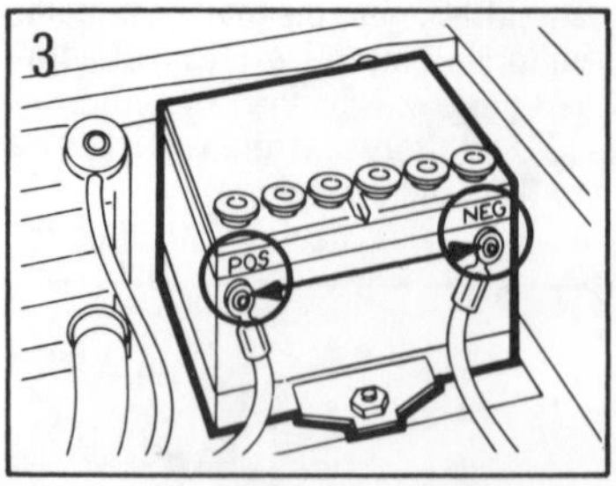

BATTERY HOLDDOWN

The clamp device which holds battery in place should be checked periodically. If loose, tighten. Clean off corrosion buildup. Severely corroded holddown components should be replaced before they break.

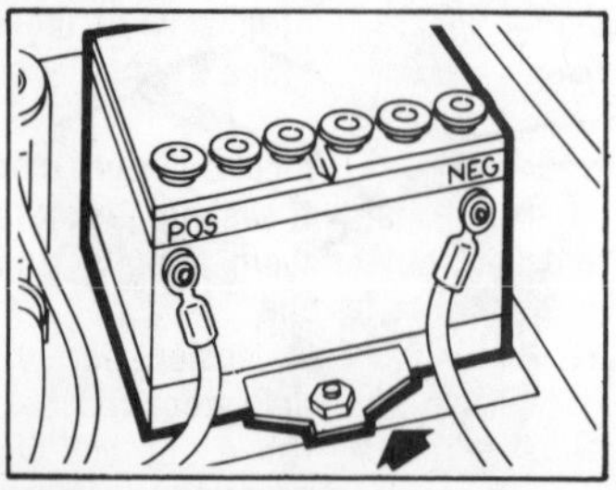

ELECTRICAL FUSES

The fuse box is located to the left of the steering column, directly over the dimmer switch. Each fuse is clearly marked as to function and correct amperage. Always replace fuse with one of same amperage. If fuses are always blowing, have checked by professional mechanic.

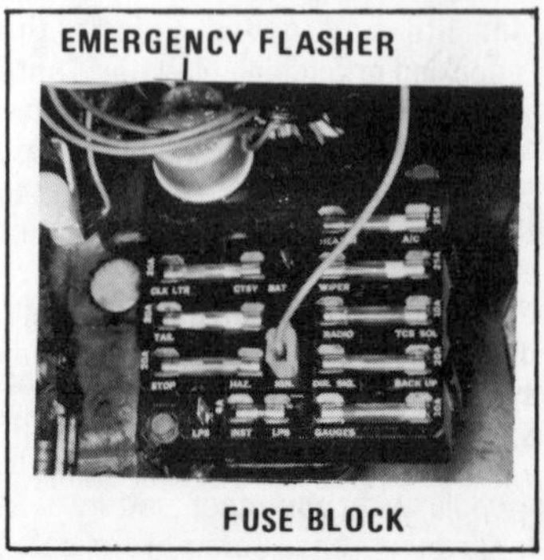

TURN SIGNAL AND 4-WAY FLASHER

Turn signals and 4-way emergency flashers will operate only if: A. All light bulbs are OK. B. Flasher units are not burned out. The car has two flasher units that work independently of each other. TURN SIGNAL FLASHER: located behind left side of instrument panel. Pull flasher from spring clip mounting. Unplug from connector. Plug in new flasher. Replace in spring clip mounting. EMERGENCY FLASHER: located in fuse block. Simply unplug and insert new flasher. REPLACE ONLY WITH SAME TYPE FLASHER.

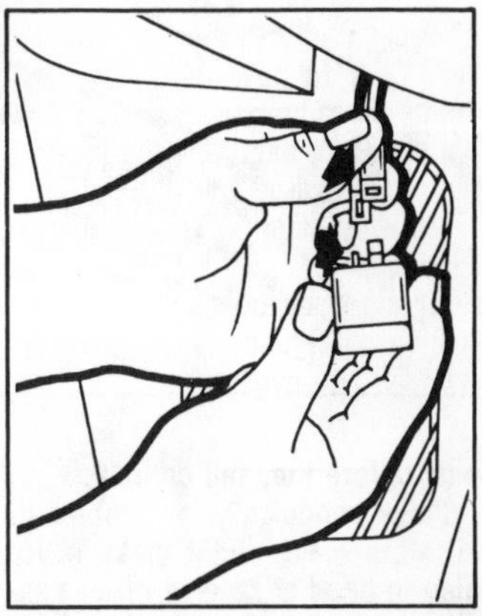

ALTERNATOR

If Alt. warning light glows red at operating speed, alternator isn't charging battery properly. Common causes are:
A. Fan belts are loose and slipping on alternator pulley. Tighten or replace belts.
B. Battery terminals, cables are loose or corroded. Clean; tighten; replace bad cables.
If A or B do not correct problem, alternator or voltage regulator may be faulty. This happens far less often, and can only be checked by mechanic with proper electrical testing equipment.

Alternator Caution: Alternator can be permanently damaged by short-circuiting terminal connections. When working around or moving alternator, always keep metal tools or engine parts from terminals.

REAR WINDOW DEFOGGER SYSTEM

Do not clean inside of rear window fitted with defogger system with any abrasive material. This could destroy carbon-copper wires. Use only soft rag and mild detergent/water mixture. Dry carefully.

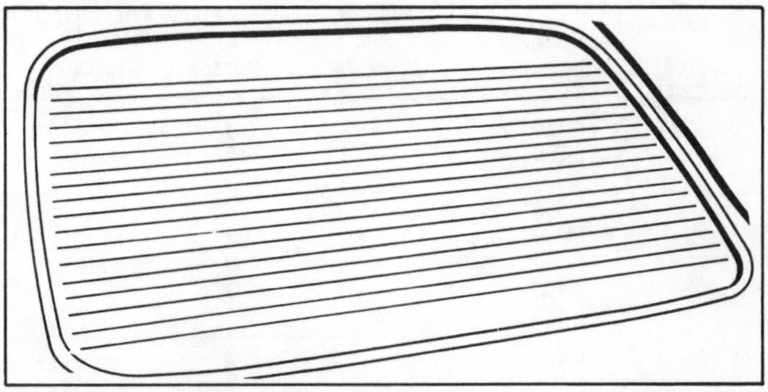

Air Conditioner

WARNING!—Never attempt to tighten fittings, disassemble or do any work on your car's A/C system. Consult a professional mechanic about A/C system problems and their correction. Your auto air conditioner (A/C) is a delicate, closed system. If air, dirt or water get into it, or if refrigerant escapes, the A/C unit will not cool a car interior. Among things you can do are:

1. Keep condenser grille clean. Check for dirt and debris; periodically remove dead insects, leaves, etc., with stiff bristle brush. Straighten any bent fins—carefully.
2. Keep radiator filled to correct level. (See Cooling System section). If fluid needs to be added, add antifreeze rather than water.
3. Keep radiator coolant at a 50/50 water/antifreeze mixture.
4. Flush cooling system and replace with fresh coolant mixture at least every 24 months. (See Cooling System section).
5. Radiator cap should be tight and sealed properly. If sealing gasket is cracked, cut or worn, replace cap with new 15 lb. unit.
6. Check fan belt tension periodically. (See Cooling System section). Replace glazed, frayed or cut fan

belts, before they fail entirely.

7. Check periodically for bubbles in A/C sight glass. Sight glass is located in head of receiver/drier vessel. Or in metal tubing leading from top of receiver/drier. Sight glass is no larger than head of large nail. It may be dirty. Wipe clean for best visibility.

PROCEED AS FOLLOWS:

a) With engine and A/C system running, look for passage of refrigerant in sight glass. You'll be looking for a stream of milky white bubbles as they pass through sight glass. It is best to watch sight glass and have someone else start the car and turn on the A/C system. Allow to run for a few minutes.

b) If you observe no bubbles, and air flow from A/C unit in the car is passing cold air, everything is OK.

c) If no bubbles appear in sight glass, and air flow from the A/C unit in the car is not delivering cold air, the system may be low on refrigerant and could need a re-charge.

d) If bubbles appear, system is low on refrigerant.

e) If you suspect refrigerant loss based on tests performed above, have system checked by a professional A/C service shop. They can confirm refrigerant loss, recharge the system and check for system leakage.

NOTE: Once a week or so, even in winter, run A/C system for about 5 minutes as you drive. This keeps system internally lubricated, prevents hoses hardening.

CAPACITIES

YEAR	ENGINE No. Cyl. Displacement (cu. in.)	ENGINE OIL Add 1 qt. with New Filter	TRANSMISSION Pts. to Refill after Draining MANUAL 3-speed	MANUAL 4-speed	AUTOMATIC	DRIVE AXLE (pts.)	COOLING SYSTEM with Heater (qts.)	COOLING SYSTEM with Air Cond. (qts.)
1970	6-230	4	3	—	6④	3.75①	12	13
	6-250	4	3	—	6④	3.75①	12	13
	8-307	4	3	—	6④	3.75①	15	16
	8-350	4	3	3	6.5②④	3.75①	16	16
	8-400	4	3	3	8	3.75①	16	16
	8-396	4	3	3	8	3.75①	23	24
	8-402	4	3	3	8	3.75①	23	24
	8-454	4	3	3	8	3.75①	22	23
1971	6-250	4	3	—	6	3.75	12	—
	8-307	4	3	—	6④	3.75	15	16
	8-350	4	3	3	6.5 ④	3.75	16	16
	8-402	4	3	3	8	3.75	23	23
	8-454	4	—	3	8	3.75	22	23
1972	6-250	4	3	—	6④	4.25	12	—
	8-307	4	3	—	6④	4.25	15	16
	8-350	4	3	3	6.5 ④	4.25	16	16
	8-402	4	—	3	8	4.25③	24	24
	8-454	4	—	3	8	4.25③	23	24
1973	6-250	4	3	—	6④	4.25	12.5	—
	8-307	4	3	—	5	425	16	17
	8-350	4	3	3	5	425	16	17
	8-454	4	3	—	8	4.25③	23	24
1974	6-250	4	3	—	8	4.25	12.5	—
	8-350	4	3	3	8	425	16	17
	8-400	4	—	—	8	4.25③	16	17
	8-454	4	—	3	9	4.9	23	24

CAPACITIES

YEAR	ENGINE No. Cyl. Displacement (cu. in.)	ENGINE OIL Add 1 qt. with New Filter	TRANSMISSION Pts. to Refill after Draining MANUAL 3-speed	MANUAL 4-speed	AUTOMATIC	DRIVE AXLE (pts.)	COOLING SYSTEM with Heater (qts.)	with Air Cond. (qts.)
1975	6-250	4	3	—	8	4.25	12.5	—
	8-350	4	—	3	8	4.25	16	17
	8-400	4	—	—	8	4.25③	16	17
	8-454	4	—	3	9	4.9	23	24
1976	6-250	4	3	—	5⑤	4.25	15	17
	V8-305	4	—	—	5⑤	4.25	17½	18½
	V8-350	4	—	—	5⑤	4.25	17½	18½
	V8-400	4	—	—	5⑤	4.25③	17½	18½
1977	6-250	4	3	—	5⑤	4.25	15	17
	V8-305	4	—	—	5⑤	4.25	17½	18½
	V8-350	4	—	—	5⑤	4.25	17½	18½

— Not Applicable.
① 4.25 pts. with 8.875 in. ring gear.
② 8 pts. with 360 Hp Engine.
③ 4.9 pts. with 8.875 in. ring gear.
④ 5 pts. with Turbo Hydra-Matic 350.
⑤ 7.5 pts. with Turbo Hydra-Matic 400.

TUNE-UP SPECIFICATIONS

YEAR	ENGINE No. Cyl. Displacement (cu. in.)	SPARK PLUGS Type	Gap (in.)	DISTRIBUTOR Point Dwell (deg.)	Point Gap (in.)	IGNITION TIMING Man. Trans.● (deg.)■	Auto Trans.● (deg.)■	IDLE SPEED Man. Trans.● (rpm)▲	Auto Trans. (rpm)▲
1970	6-250 (155 hp)	R-46T	0.035	31-34	0.019	TDC	4B	750	600/400①
	8-307 (200 hp)	R-43	0.035	28-32	0.019	2B	8B	700	600/450①
	8-350 (250 hp)	R-44	0.035	28-32	0.019	TDC	4B	750	600/450①
	8-350 (300 hp)	R-44	0.035	28-32	0.019	TDC	4B	700	600
	8-396 (350 hp)	R-44T	0.035	28-32	0.019	TDC	4B	700	600
	8-396 (375 hp)	R-43T	0.035	28-32	0.019	4B	4B	750	700
	8-400 (265 hp)	R-44	0.035	28-32	0.019	4B	8B	700	600/450①
	8-402 (330 hp)	R-44T	0.035	28-32	0.019	4B	4B	700	600
	8-454 (360 hp)	R-43T	0.035	28-32	0.019	6B	6B	700	600
1971	6-250 (145 hp)	R-46TS	0.035	31-34	0.019	4B	4B	550	500
	8-307 (200 hp)	R-45TS	0.035	29-31	0.019	4B	8B	600	550
	8-350 (245 hp)	R-45TS	0.035	29-31	0.019	2B	6B	600	550
	8-350 (270 hp)	R-44TS	0.035	29-31	0.019	4B	8B	600	550
	8-400 (255 hp)	R-44TS	0.035	29-31	0.019	4B	8B	600	550
	8-402 (300 hp)	R-44TS	0.035	29-31	0.019	8B	8B	600	600
	8-454 (365 hp)	R-42TS	0.035	29-31	0.019	8B	8B	600	600
	8-454 (425 hp)	R-42TS	0.035	29-31	0.019	8B	12B	700	700
1972	6-250 (110 hp)	R-46TS	0.035	31-34	0.019	4B	4B	700	600
	8-307 (130 hp)	R-44T	0.035	29-31	0.019	4B	8B	900	600
	8-350 (165 hp)	R-44T	0.035	29-31	0.019	6B	6B	900	600
	8-350 (175 hp)	R-44T	0.035	29-31	0.019	4B	8B	800	600
	8-402 (240 hp)	R-44T	0.035	29-31	0.019	8B	8B	750	600
	8-454 (270 hp)	R-44T	0.035	29-31	0.019	8B	8B	750	600
1973	6-250 (100 hp)	R-46T	0.035	31-34	0.019	6B	6B	700/450①	600/450
	8-307 (115 hp)	R-44T	0.035	29-31	0.019	4B	8B	900/450①	600/450
	8-350 (145 hp)	R-44T	0.035	29-31	0.019	8B	8B	900/450①	600/450
	8-350 (175 hp)	R-44T	0.035	29-31	0.019	8B	12B	900/450①	600/450
	8-454 (245 hp)	R-44T	0.035	29-31	0.019	10B	10B	900/450①	600/450

TUNE-UP SPECIFICATIONS

YEAR	ENGINE No. Cyl. Displacement (cu. in.)	SPARK PLUGS Type	SPARK PLUGS Gap (in.)	DISTRIBUTOR Point Dwell (deg.)	DISTRIBUTOR Point Gap (in.)	IGNITION TIMING Man. Trans.● (deg.)■	IGNITION TIMING Auto Trans.● (deg.)■	IDLE SPEED Man. Trans.● (rpm)▲	IDLE SPEED Auto Trans. (rpm)▲
1974	6-250 (100 hp)	R-46T	0.035	31-34	0.019	6B	6B	800/450①	600/450
	8-350 (145 hp)	R-44T	0.035	29-31	0.019	4B	8B	900/450①	600/450
	8-350 (160 hp)	R-44T	0.035	29-31	0.019	4B	8B	900/450①	600/450
	8-400 (150 hp)	R-44T	0.035	29-31	0.019	—	8B		600/450
	8-400 (180 hp)	R-44T	0.035	29-31	0.019	—	8B		600/450
	8-454 (235 hp)	R-44T	0.035	20-31	0.019	10B	10B	800/450①	600/450
1975	6-250 (105 hp)	R-46TX	0.060	②	②	10B③	10B③	800/450①	600/450①
	8-350 (145 hp) 2-bbl	R-44TX	0.060	②	②	6B	6B	900/450①	600/450①
	8-350 (155 hp) 4-bbl	R-44TX	0.060	②	②	6B④	8B⑤	600/450①	600/450①
	8-400 (175 hp)	R-44TX	0.060	②	②	—	8B	—	600/450①
	8-454 (215 hp)	R-44TX	0.060	②	②	—	16B	—	600/450①
1976	6-250 (105 hp)	R46TS	0.035	②	②	6B	6B	850/425	550/425⑥
	8-305 (125 hp)	R45TS	0.035	②	②	—	8B⑦	—	600
	8-350 (145 hp)	R45TS	0.035	②	②	—	6B⑧	—	600
	8-400 (175 hp)	R45TS	0.035	②	②	—	8B	—	600
1977	6-250	See Underhood Specifications Sticker							
	8-305	See Underhood Specifications Sticker							
	8-305	See Underhood Specifications Sticker							

▲ Adjust automatic transmissions in Drive (AMC/Ford/GM) or Neutral (Chrysler), all manual transmissions are adjusted in Neutral.
■ All figures are Before Top Dead Center.
● Figure in parentheses indicate California engine.
— Not Applicable.
① Lower figure with soleniod disconnected.
② Electronic ignition.
③ Federal without Early Fuel Evaporation—8B.
④ California—4B.
⑤ California—6B.
⑥ California—600 rpm.
⑦ California—TDC.
⑧ 350 4-bbl—California 6B.
Federal 8B.

NOTE: The underhood specifications sticker often reflects tune-up specification changes made in production. Sticker figures must be used if they disagree with those in this chart.

Chevette

Lubrication and Oil Change

BRAKE FLUID LEVEL CHECK

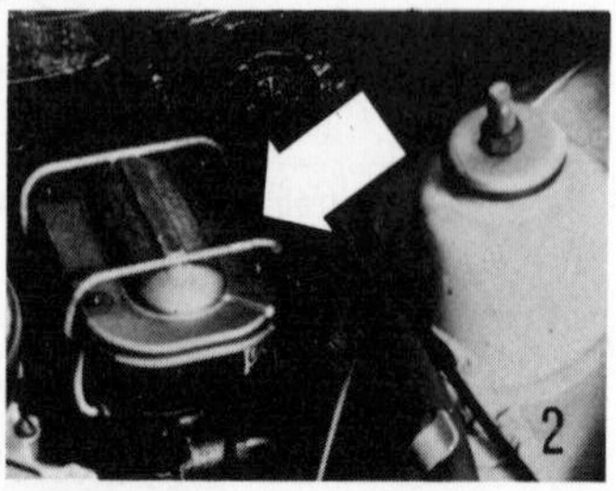

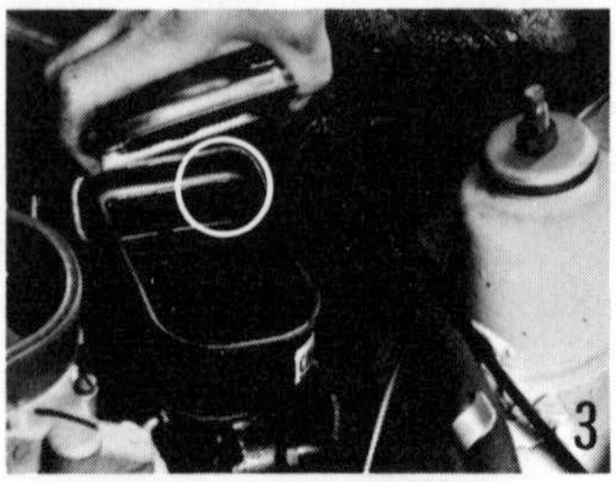

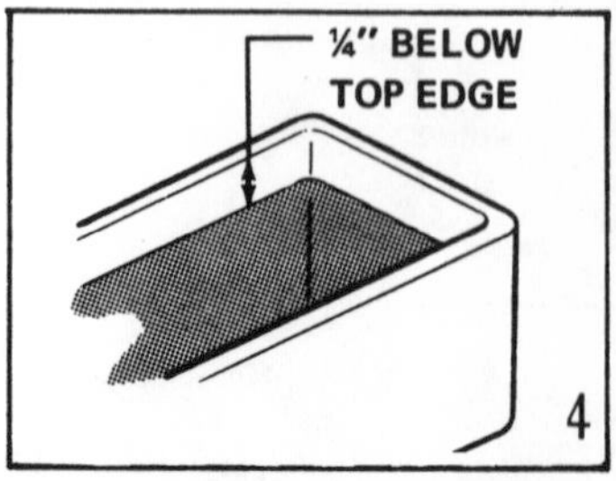

The brake master cylinder is located in the engine compartment on the left side of the firewall. Check the level of the brake fluid in the master cylinder each time you change the engine oil.
If necessary, replenish with Extra Heavy Duty (DOT 3) brake fluid.

1. Clean the dirt away from the cover.
2. Pry the wire retaining clip off the cap with a screwdriver.
3. Remove the cover.
4. The fluid level should be within ¼ in. of the top rim. If necessary, add fluid.
5. Replace the cover and snap the retaining clip into place. If the fluid level was low, recheck it in a few days. If the fluid level is repeatedly low, there is a leak in the brake system. See SAFETY SYSTEMS, WHEEL CYLINDER CHECK, and have a mechanic check further.

MANUAL TRANSMISSION FLUID LEVEL CHECK

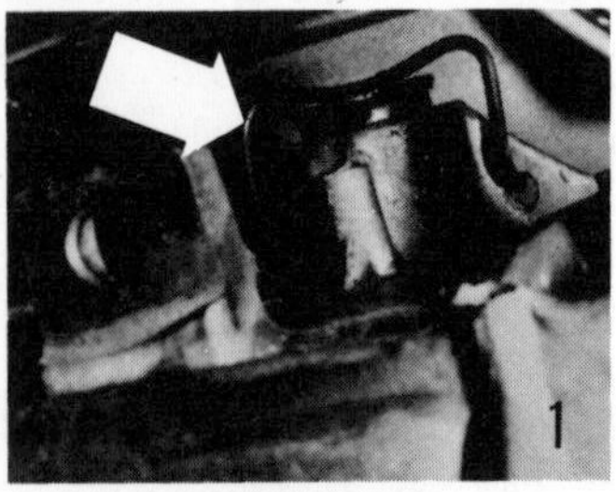

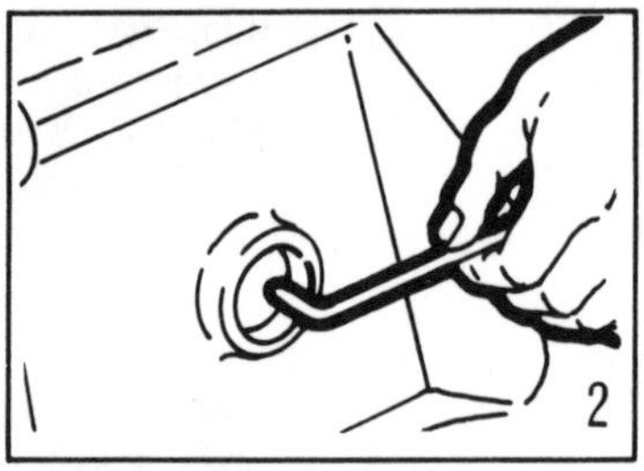

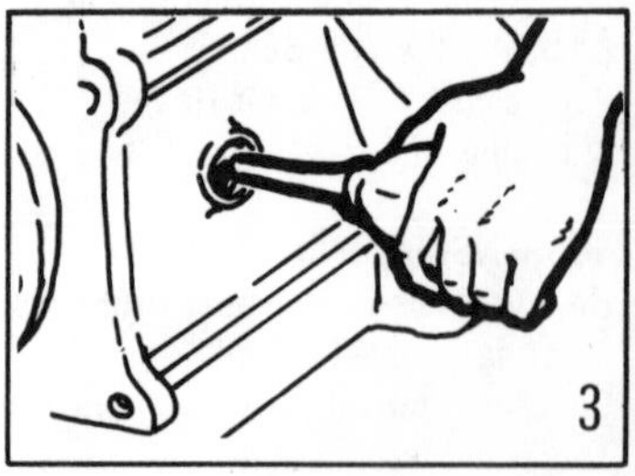

The lubricant in the manual transmission should be checked every 6 months or 7500 miles. The car should be on level ground. If necessary, refill with SAE 80W or SAE 80-90W transmission fluid.
TOOLS NEEDED: fluid level check device made from wire bent a 90° angle 2 in. from end; adjustable wrench; bulb syringe

1. Locate the transmission fluid plug on the left side of the transmission, underneath the car.
2. Clean and remove the filler plug.
3. Insert the fluid level check device. The fluid level (hot) should be even with the bottom edge of the filler plug opening, or, (cold), ½ in. below the level of the hole.
4. Add fluid as needed with a bulb syringe.

AUTOMATIC TRANSMISSION FLUID LEVEL CHECK

Check the automatic transmission fluid (ATF) level at each oil change. Use transmission fluid DEXRON® II or Type A.
TOOLS NEEDED: Long necked filler funnel

1. The car should be level, the engine running, and the gearshift lever in PARK.
2. Remove the dipstick and wipe it

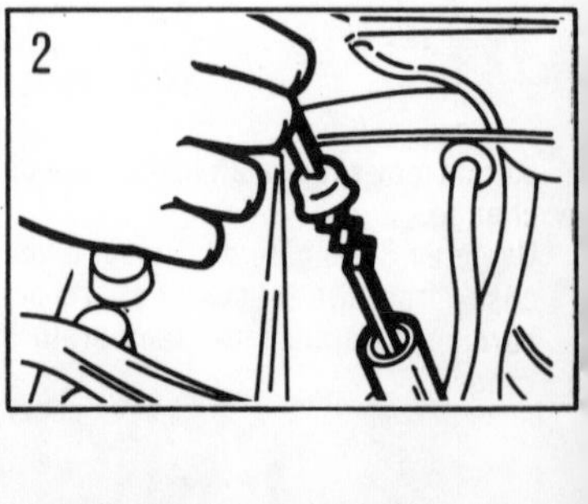

clean. Fully insert the dipstick and remove it again.

3. If the fluid is cool (room temperature), the level should be ⅛-⅜ in. below the ADD mark. If the fluid is warm, the level will show slightly above or below the ADD mark. Hot fluid (cannot be touched comfortably) will show the level between ADD and FULL.

4. Add ATF through the transmission

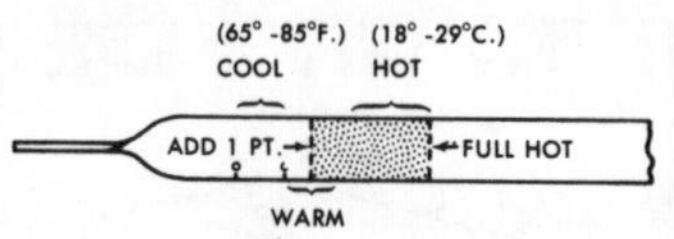

NOTE: DO NOT OVERFILL. It takes only one pint to raise level from ADD to FULL with a hot transmission.

dipstick tube with a long necked funnel. DO NOT OVERFILL. It only re-

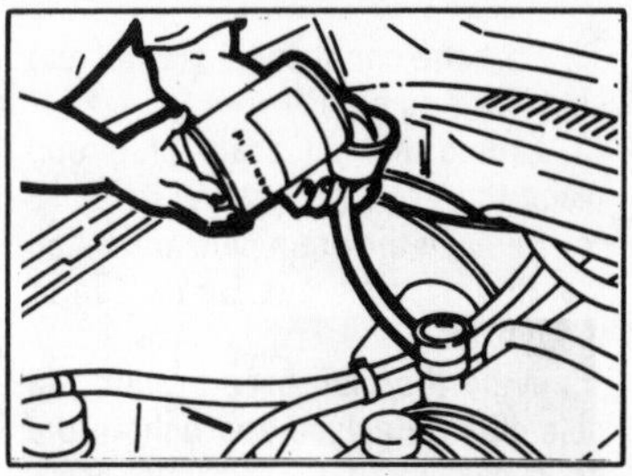

quires 1 pint to raise the level from ADD to FULL.

CHECKING REAR AXLE FLUID LEVEL

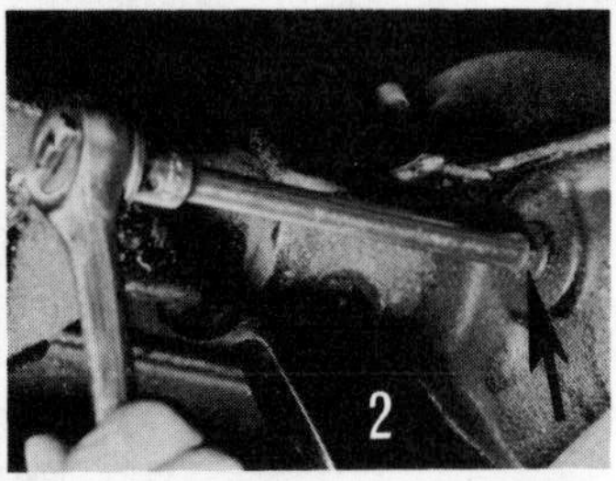

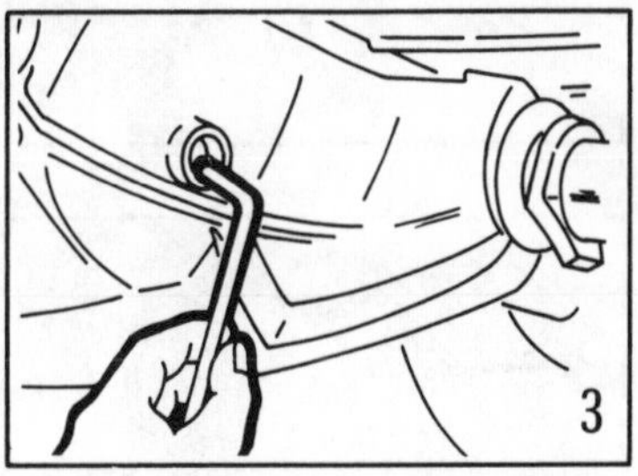

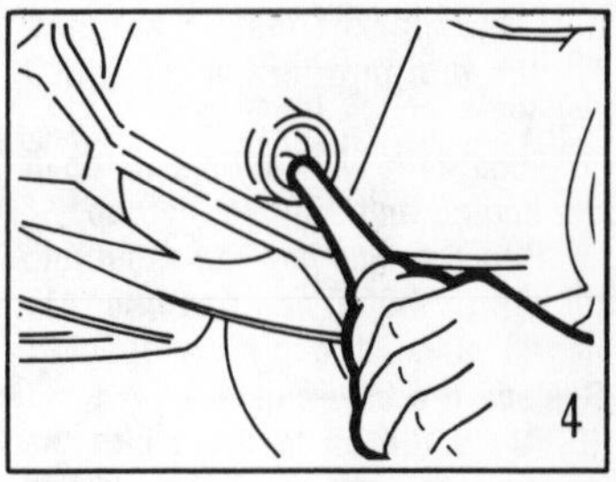

Check the rear axle lubricant level every 6 months or 7500 miles. Use SAE 80W or SAE 80-90W hypoid gear lubricant. Positraction axles require special positraction fluid.

TOOLS NEEDED: Adjustable wrench; fluid level check device made from wire bent at 90° angle 2 in. from the end; bulb syringe.

1. Locate the filler plug on the right side of the axle housing.

2. Wipe the plug area clean. Remove the plug with a wrench.

3. Insert the wire level check device and remove it. The fluid level should be even with the bottom of the filler plug hole.

4. If the level is low, add fluid with a bulb syringe until the level is as specified.

5. Reinstall and tighten the filler plug.

OIL AND FILTER CHANGE

Change the engine oil every 6 months or 7500 miles, whichever comes first, except under the following conditions.

- driving in dusty conditions
- trailer pulling
- extensive idling
- short-trip operation at freezing temperatures (engine not fully warmed)

Under any of the above conditions, change the oil every 3 months or 3000 miles. Operation in severe dust storms may require an immediate oil change.

Use only SE engine oil. Select a viscosity from the following chart, according the anticipated temperature range.

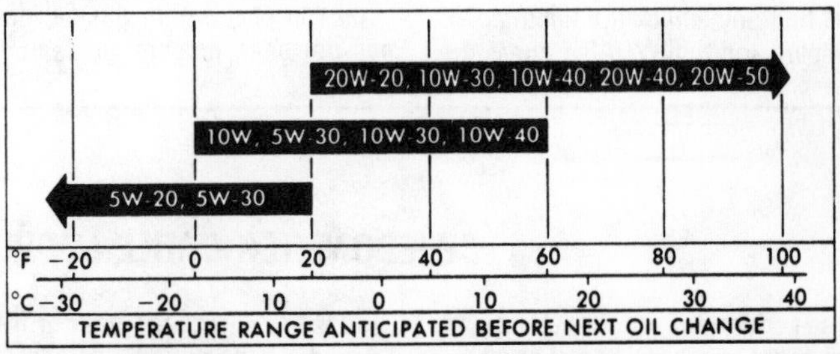

NOTE: SAE 5W-30 oils are recommended for all seasons in vehicles normally operated in Canada. SAE 5W-20 oils are not recommended for sustained high-speed driving. SAE 30 oils may be used at temperatures above 40°F. (4°C.)

TOOLS AND MATERIALS: Adjustable wrench; drain pan; oil filter wrench; oil pouring spout; 5 quarts oil; new oil filter

1. If the engine is cold, warm it to normal operating temperature.

2. Park the car on level ground and shut the engine off.
3. Locate the oil drain plug and place the drain pan below it.
4. Remove the drain plug and let all the dirty oil drain out. Be careful of the hot oil.
5. Wipe the plug area around the hole clean. Replace and tighten the drain plug.
6. Locate the oil filter and move the drain pan under the filter. Loosen the filter with a filter wrench and remove the filter by hand.
7. Smear fresh oil on the surface of the rubber gasket and install the new filter by hand. Turn the filter until the gasket makes contact. Tighten one turn further BY HAND ONLY.
8. Locate the oil filler hole on top of the engine and remove the cap.
9. Punch the oil pouring spout into the top of the oil can and pour 4½ quarts of oil through the opening. Replace the filler cap.
10. Allow the oil to drain into the engine sump and check the level on the dipstick.
11. Pull out the dipstick, next to the filler cap, and wipe it clean. Push it back into the engine. Remove it again and check the oil level. It should be at the FULL line. If not, check that you added all the oil specified.
12. Start the engine and idle it for about 3 minutes. The oil light on the instrument panel will glow when the engine is first started. It should go out in a few seconds.
13. Stop the engine and check for oil leaks at the drain plug and filter. If you find any, check the tightness of the plug and/or filter. Also, check the condition of the filter gasket, that it has not been pinched or damaged.

Recheck the oil level which should be at the FULL mark.

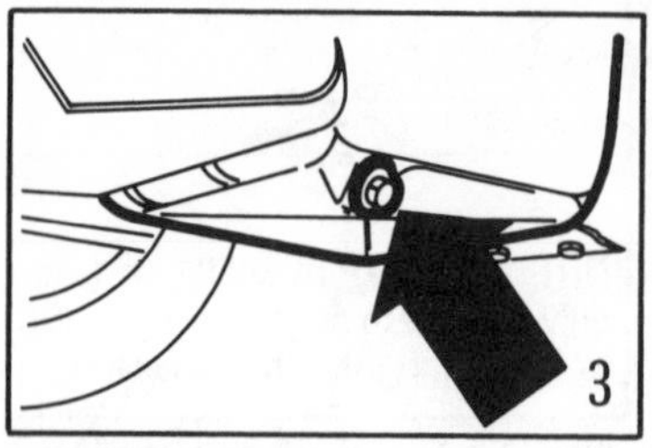
3

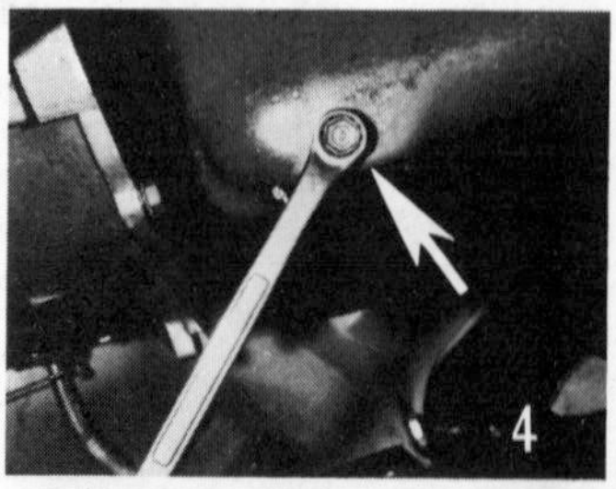
4

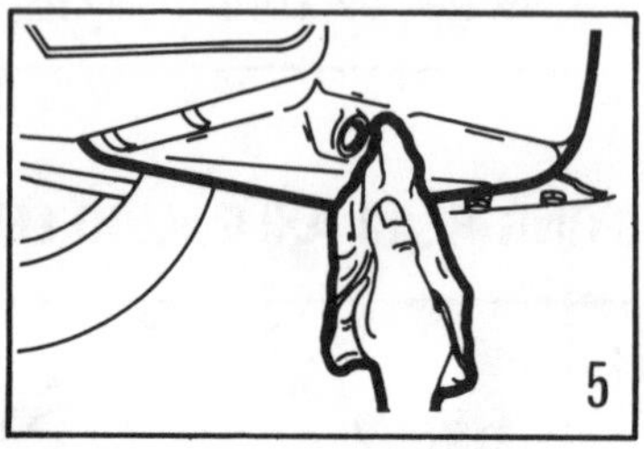
5

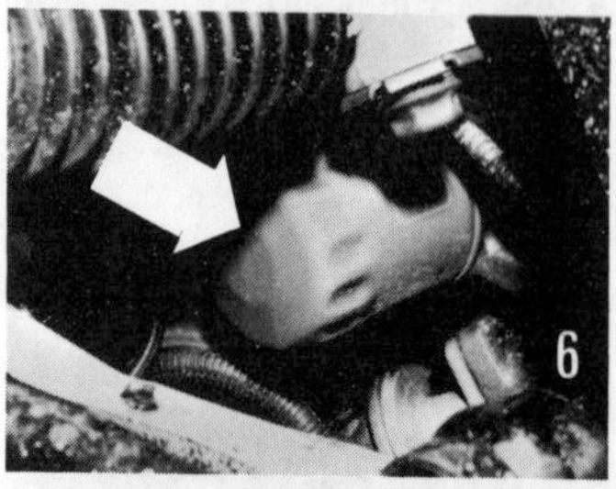
6

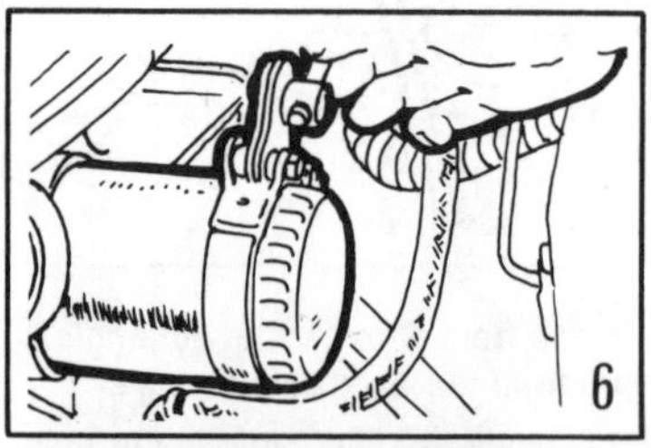
6

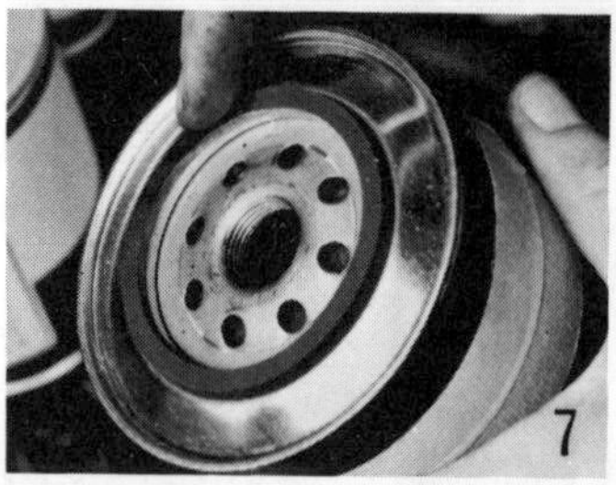
7

9

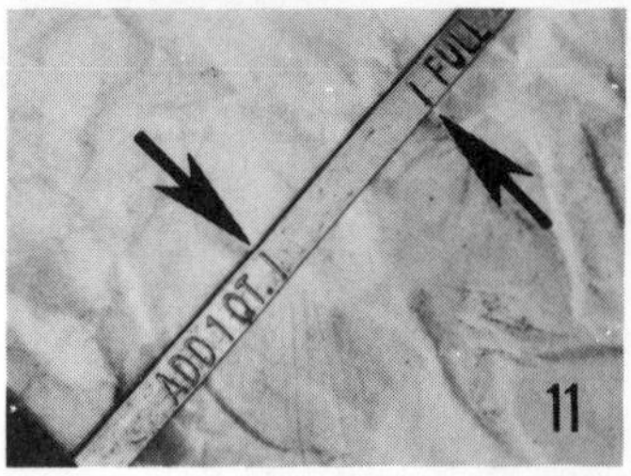

11

SPEEDOMETER CABLE LUBRICATION

If speedometer pointer tends to quiver or jump, or if unit makes a low, rasping sound, lubrication may be needed.
1. Locate cable shaft attachment directly behind speedometer dial.
2. Remove retaining clip. Unscrew cable from speedometer.
3. Pull inner cable completely out of outer casing. Note carefully which end is top. Check for wear or frayed strands. If damaged, replace inner cable with new one.
4. Apply generous amount of speedometer cable lubricant into cable casing. Replace inner cable in shaft, noting that top end is not inserted accidentally. Turn inner cable as it is being re-inserted. Twist cable when all the way in, to lock into position at lower end.
5. Re-connect cable to speedometer head under instrument panel.

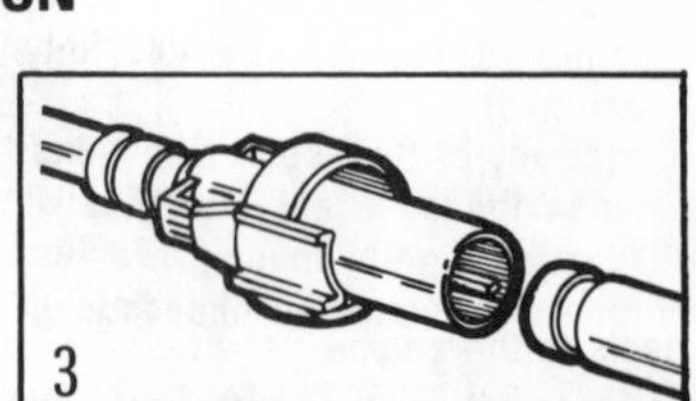
3

DOOR HINGES AND STOPS

(lubricate every 6 months)
1. Brush any dirt accumulations from door hinges and stops. Use old tooth brush or rag.
2. Apply dab of white polyethylene grease to door hinges, trunk hinges, hood hinges, door stops.

DOOR LOCKS

(lubricate every 6 months)
1. Insert door key half way into lock.
2. Spray aerosol lock lubricant into lock.
3. Push key rest of way into lock; turn back and forth several times.

Cooling System

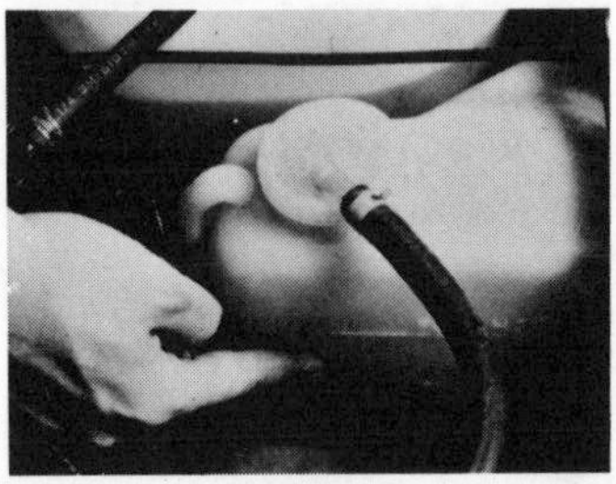

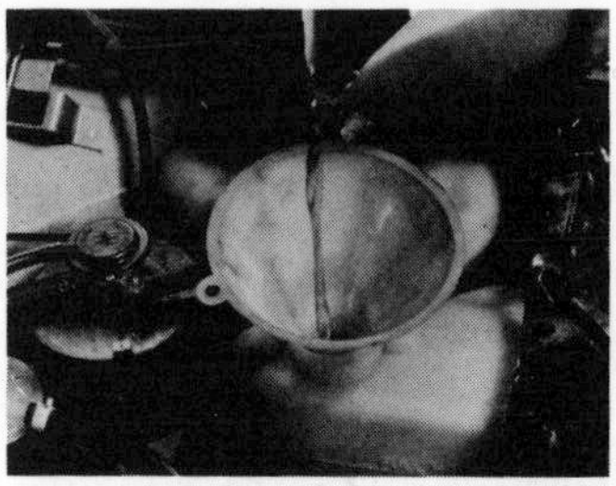

It is recommended that the radiator coolant (antifreeze) level be checked once or twice a month, more often in severe service. Check the level when the engine is COLD.
Check the coolant level without removing the cap on models with expansion tanks. On other models, remove the radiator cap cautiously, especially if the engine is hot. Slowly, rotate the cap counterclockwise to the first detent. Wait until the pressure releases (stops hissing). Cover the cap with a heavy rag, push down on the cap and turn it the rest of the way.
Coolant level should be maintained at the bottom of the radiator filler neck (models with no expansion tank) or at the appropriate mark on the expansion tank if so equipped.
Coolant concentration should be maintained to at least −20°F. for corrosion protection. If coolant must be added, add a 50/50 mix of ethylene glycol, through the radiator filler neck or through the expansion tank if equipped with a coolant recovery system.
If equipped with a coolant recovery system, make sure that the arrows on the cap align with the overflow tube.

REPLACING THE THERMOSTAT

A faulty thermostat will usually cause the engine to overheat. The thermostat is located in the housing where the top radiator hose connects to the engine.
TOOLS AND MATERIALS: New thermostat, new gasket, wrench
1. Drain the radiator about ½ way down, by opening the drain valve at

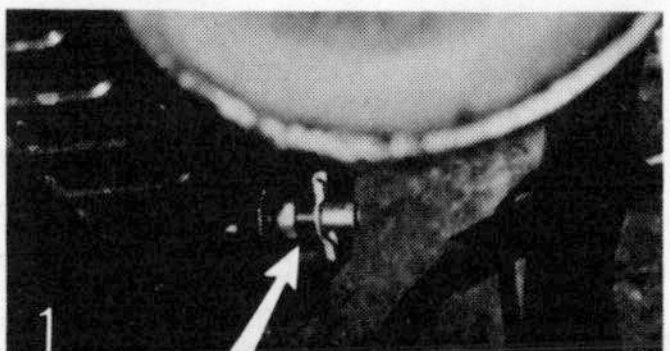

the bottom corner, driver's side of the radiator. Save the coolant.

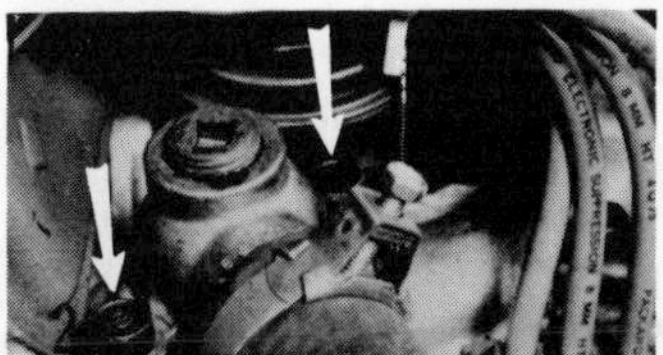

2. Loosen and remove the retaining bolts and lift the thermostat housing

off the engine. It usually isn't necessary to remove the hose.

3. Remove the thermostat.

4. Scrape away the old gasket on the engine block.

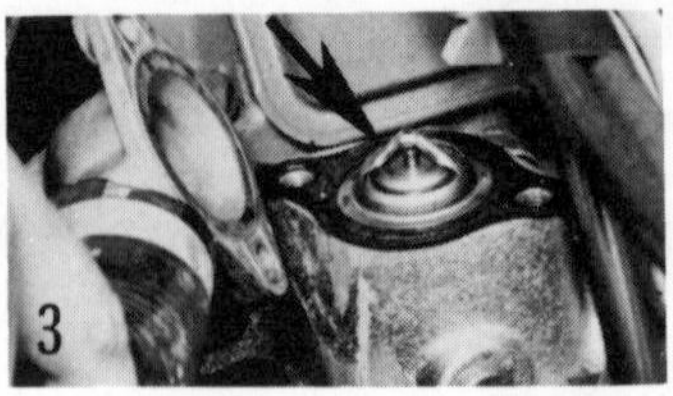

5. Drop a new thermostat into place—spring down.

6. Install a new gasket on the engine. Replace the thermostat housing and tighten the retaining bolts.

7. Refill the cooling system.

TROUBLESHOOT ENGINE OVERHEATING

1. Inspect all hoses. If any are weak, soft in spots or show cracks, replace at once.

2. Check all hose connections for tightness. Tighten loose hose clamps; they tend to loosen due to engine vibration.

3. If radiator steams or hisses when engine is switched off, check for leaks. Look for signs of coolant drips on radiator or around header tank joint.

Leaks are possible at:
Upper or lower radiator hoses
Water pump (gaskets or seal)
Heater core or connecting hoses
Automatic transmission cooler lines (at bottom of radiator)
Faulty radiator pressure cap
Faulty cylinder head gasket
Choke hoses
Cracked cylinder head or block

Check radiator cap occasionally for worn or cracked gasket. If cap doesn't seal properly, fluid will be lost and engine will overheat. Replace worn cap with new cap rated 13 to 15 lbs. pressure.

ADJUSTING THE FAN BELT

The fan belt not only drives the fan, but turns the water pump and drives the alternator and other accessories. The condition and proper tension of the drive belts are vital since almost all cooling and electrical power are dependent on them.

1. Inspect the condition of the belts occasionally (at least 12 months or 15,000 miles). If the belts are frayed, worn or cracked on the inner driving surface, replace them.

2. Check the belt tension occasionally, also. Apply moderate thumb pressure at the midpoint of the belt span. A 7-10 inch span should deflect about ¼ in.; a 13-16 inch span, about ½ in.

3. Adjust to the proper tension. A too loose belt will not drive effectively, while a too tight belt can damage water pump or alternator bearings.

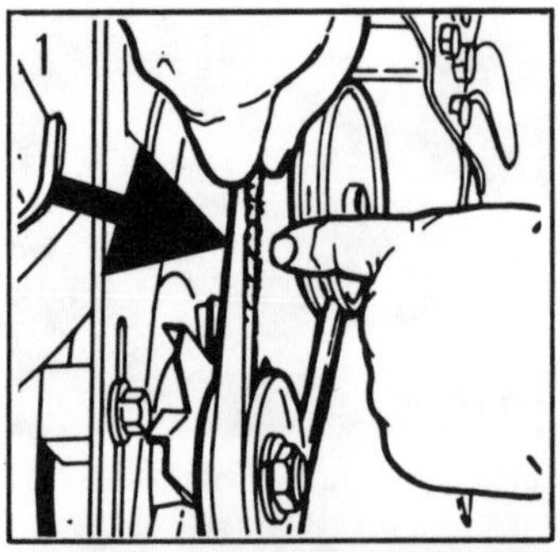

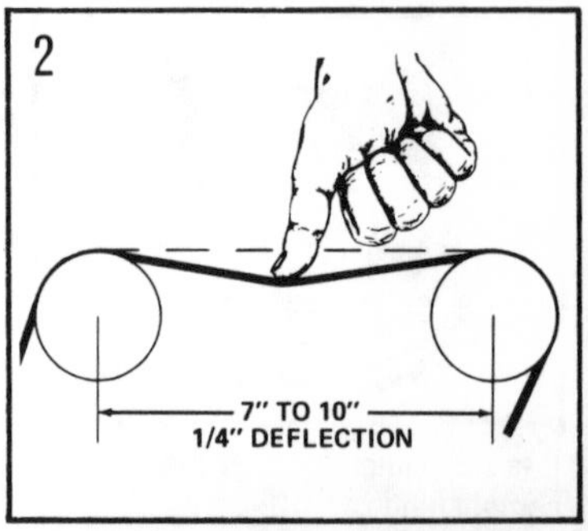

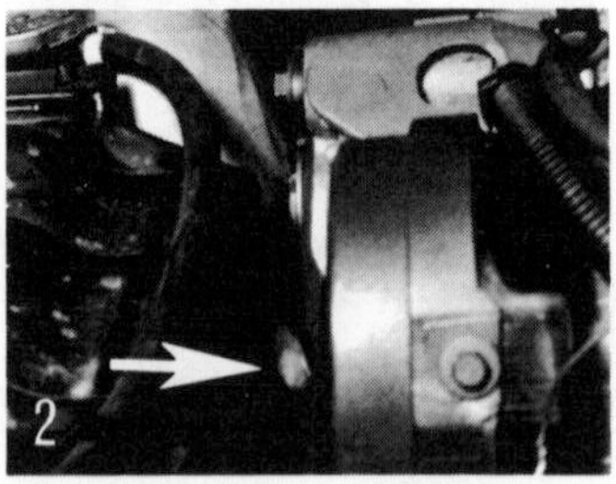

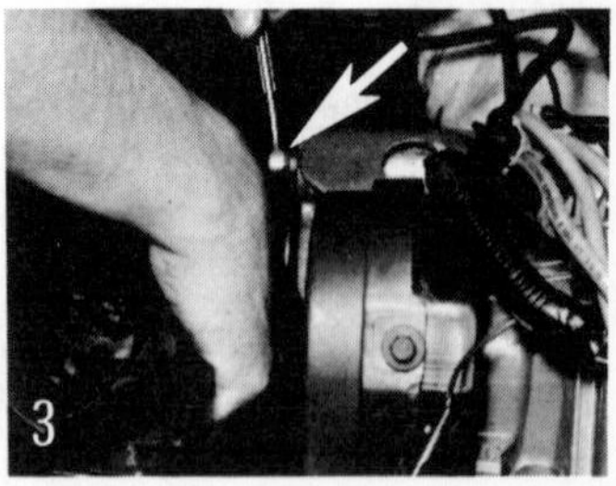

REPLACING RADIATOR HOSES

Coolant drain and refill work can be done alone. When changing hoses, coolant must be drained as part of the job. Discard all hoses with cracks or soft spots, and check the hose clamps for tightness and good condition.

1. Remove the radiator cap. Open the radiator drain cock and drain the coolant into a catch basin. If the coolant is approaching 24 months old, replace it with fresh.

2. The petcock is located on the

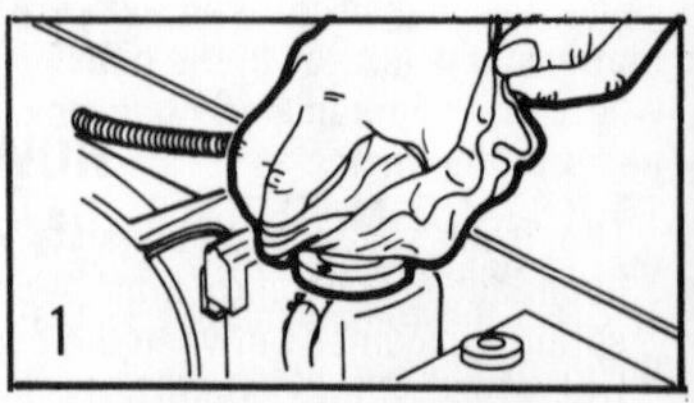

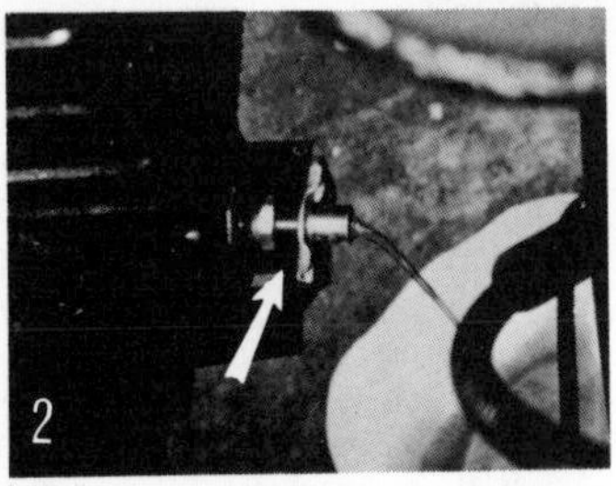

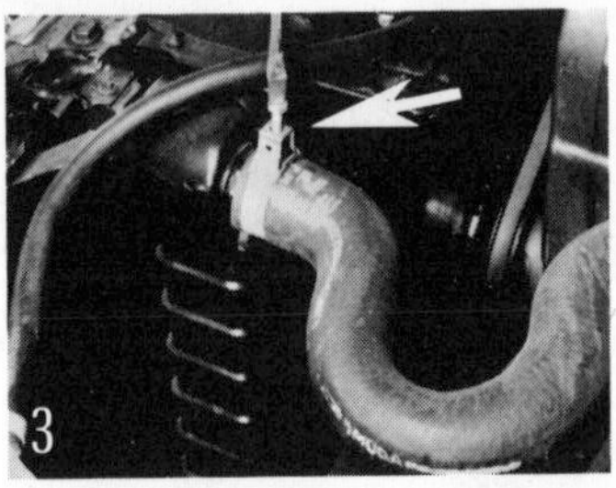

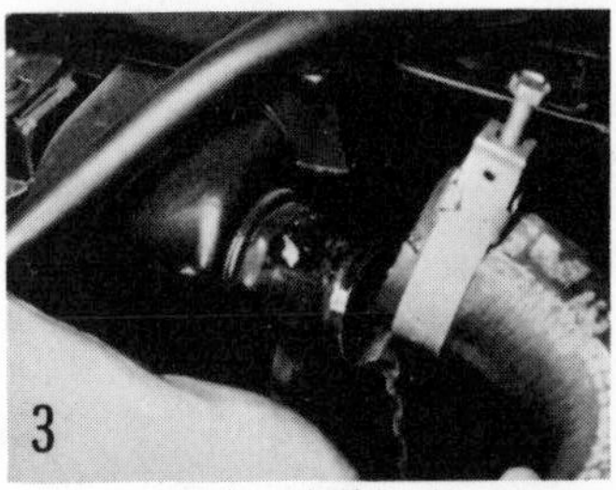

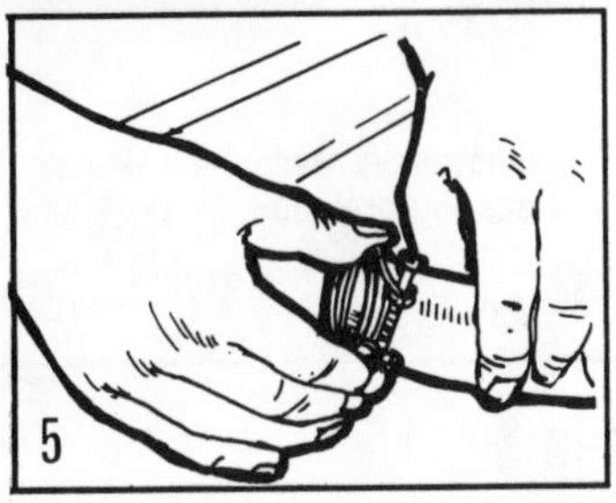

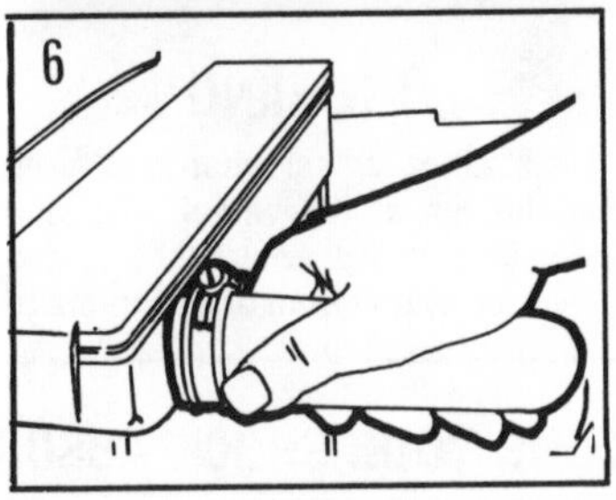

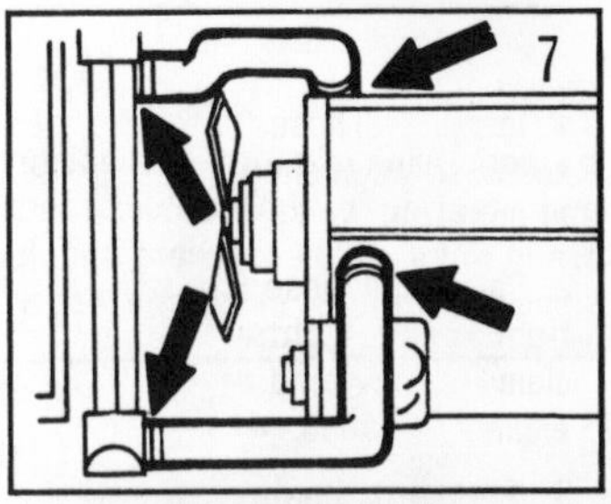

driver's side of the radiator at the bottom.

3. Loosen the clamps at each end of the hose(s). Work the hose loose and remove it. If the old hose clamps are deteriorated, replace them.

4. Wipe all hose connections clean. Use emery cloth to clean away residue.

5. Slide the clamps over each hose end. Work the hose(s) over the cleaned connections.

6. Tighten the clamps ¼ in. from the end of the hose. Close the petcock and refill the cooling system with a 50/50 solution of ethylene glycol.

7. Start the engine and allow it to warm up. Check for coolant leaks. Check the coolant level.

8. Road test the car. Watch for the temperature warning light on the dashboard.

CHANGING ANTIFREEZE

Every 2 years or 30,000 miles, whichever comes first, the cooling system should be flushed and refilled with antifreeze to provide protection to at least −20°F.

1. Remove the radiator cap when the engine is COLD. Rotate the cap to the first detent and wait until all pressure releases (hissing stops), then remove the cap.
2. Run the engine with the radiator cap removed until the upper radiator hose is hot, indicating that the thermostat is open.
3. Stop the engine. Open the radiator petcock at the bottom of the radiator and drain the coolant.
4. Close the petcock and fill the system with water.
5. Repeat steps 1,2,3, and 4 until the drained liquid is clear.
6. Allow the system to drain completely and close the petcock tightly.
7. Clean the inside of the coolant recovery tank, leaving the hoses attached.
8. Fill the cooling system with a 50/50 mix of ethylene glycol. Fill the radiator to the base of the filler neck or the mark, if equipped with a coolant recovery system.

9. Idle the engine (cap removed) until the upper hose is hot. Add coolant to the base of the neck or to the FULL HOT mark if equipped with an expansion tank.

Install the cap, making sure that the arrows align with the overflow tube.

Suspension and Tires

HOW TO PINPOINT HANDLING PROBLEMS

The front suspension consists of upper and lower control arms. A coil spring is mounted between the control arms. Shock absorbers are mounted between the upper control arms and the body attaching point. The front wheels rotate on spindles which are attached to the steering knuckles.

The rear suspension consists of coil springs, control arms and shock absorbers with a solid rear axle.

Your car's suspension system consists of wheels, tires, springs, shock absorbers, sway (or stabilizer) bars, ball joints, steering linkage. If any of these items is out of adjustment or badly worn, you may notice any of these symptoms:

- car pulls to one side when braking
- car wanders when driving a straight line
- overall ride may be either hard or bouncy
- effort is needed to steer vehicle
- tires show uneven wear
- tires squeal when cornering
- front of car dips or bounces when braking
- car rocks side-to-side when going over rough road
- wheels bounce or make slapping sound on road
- steering wheel vibrates in hands
- front of car vibrates at highway speeds

Any of above symptoms indicates corrective action is needed. Delay can: ruin tires; cause damage/failure to other suspension parts; create safety hazard.

STEERING

If steering linkage, front suspension and steering column components are in good condition, there should be no more than 1½ inch free play in the steering wheel when measured at the rim of the wheel. If a loud knock is heard when turning the steering wheel from one extreme to the other, have mechanic check pinion bearing preload.

CHECKING YOUR SHOCK ABSORBERS

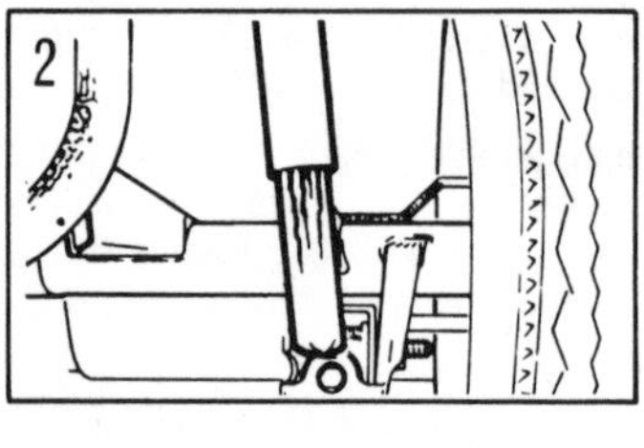

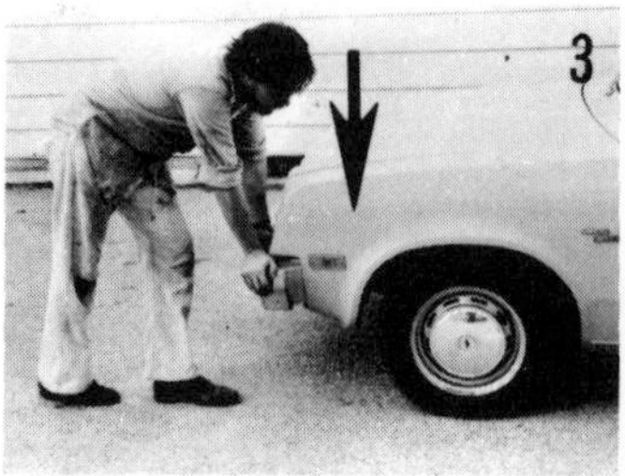

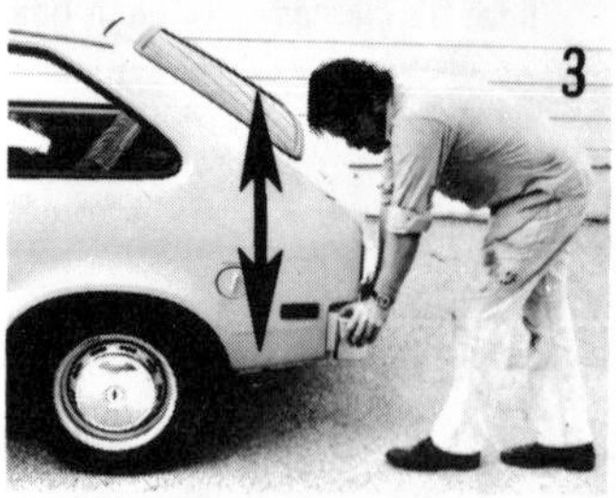

Shock absorbers work to keep the wheels in contact with the road, resulting in safe handling, comfortable ride and longer tire life.

1. Locate the shock absorber, under the car near each wheel.
2. Look for heavy oil streaks on the outside of the shock absorber. A little weeping normal, but heavy, wet streaks are cause for replacement.
3. Stand at the front of the car and apply body weight in a pumping action to the front bumper or fender. Release the pressure and allow the car to stop bouncing. The car should not bounce more than once, or twice at the most, after releasing the pressure. Repeat at the rear. If the bouncing continues more than once, or, at the utmost, twice, replacement is needed. Replace shocks in pairs (front or rear).

TOW HITCH INFORMATION

The maximum weight your Chevette can pull depends on its special equipment, but Chevrolet does not recommend pulling any trailer more than 1000 lbs. gross weight with this car.

If your car is used for trailer towing you should check:

A. Cooling System; be sure coolant is at proper level in radiator. See Cooling System Section for checks to perform.

B. Check Transmission Fluid; keep topped up to proper level.

C. Check Rear Shock Absorbers; you may benefit from installation of new rear shocks.

D. Tire Pressures: when towing trailers, inflate the tires to the highest inflation pressures shown on the decal attached to the left front door.

For safer and more trouble-free trailer towing, consider:

A. Automatic Transmission Cooler; helps remove excess heat from automatic transmission fluid built up during towing mileage. Also helps avoid radiator overheating. Some units can be self-installed.

B. Radiator Over-Flow Tank Kit; addition of a reservoir to catch radiator coolant overflow preventing coolant loss. Easy to install, these units help a tow car run cooler, avoid overheating due to coolant loss.

C. Heavy-Duty Shock Absorbers or Air Shocks; important to have on rear wheels if you intend to do a lot of towing or load carrying within the car itself. Don't forget to consider replacing factory shocks, when they are worn out, with heavy-duty units at the front as well.

D. Variable Load Flasher; this unit will accommodate the added load of trailer turn signal lamps on trailer when these are hooked into your car's electrical system.

FRONT END ALIGNMENT

When steering, handling and/or tire wear indicate front end alignment may be needed, this work can only be done at an automotive service shop. DO NOT PUT OFF NEEDED FRONT END ALIGNMENT. At the same time, have ball joints and steering linkage checked.

Ignition System

TUNE-UP SERVICES

The ignition system consists of spark plugs, plug wires, HEI (high energy ignition) distributor and ignition coil. These units provide the spark (ignition) at the proper moment (timing). If the spark is weak or if the timing is off, your engine may be hard to start, run poorly, waste gas, lose power or not run at all.

GM recommends that the spark plugs be replaced every 22,500 miles and that the spark plug wires be checked every 18 months or 22,500 miles whichever comes first.

TOOLS AND MATERIALS: Parts: 4 spark plugs. Tools: gap gauge, ⅝ in. spark plug wrench, wrenches, ratchet handle and extension, golf tee, chalk, timing light (see Ignition Timing).

SAFETY TIP: Change only one spark plug at a time to avoid crosswiring and possible engine damage.

SPARK PLUG REPLACEMENT

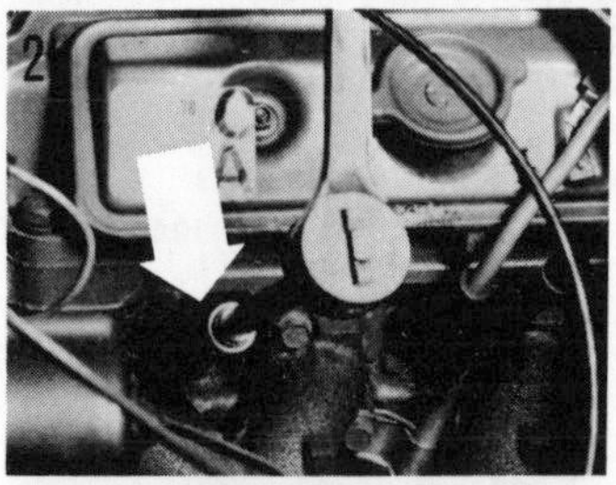

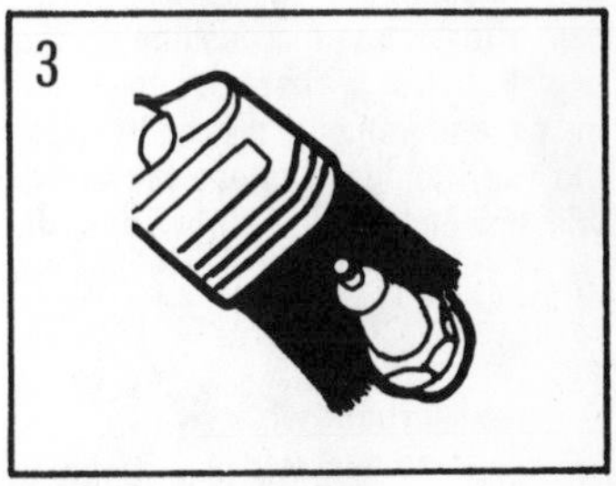

1. Grasp the spark plug wire at the boot and twist it a ½ turn to loosen it. Remove the wire by pulling on the boot, not the wire.

2. Loosen the spark plug with a spark plug socket wrench.

3. Wipe or brush the loose dirt from around the spark plug before removing. Do not let dirt drop into the engine. Unscrew the plug.

4. Check the gap on the new spark plug and adjust it to specifications if necessary. The plug gap is correct when the gauge drags slightly when passed between the center and side (outer) electrodes.

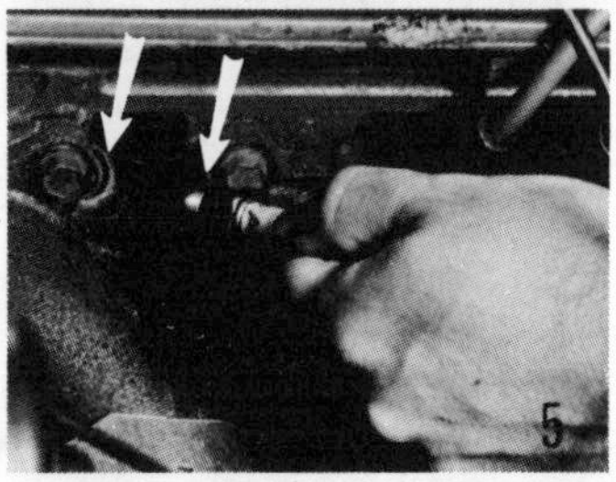

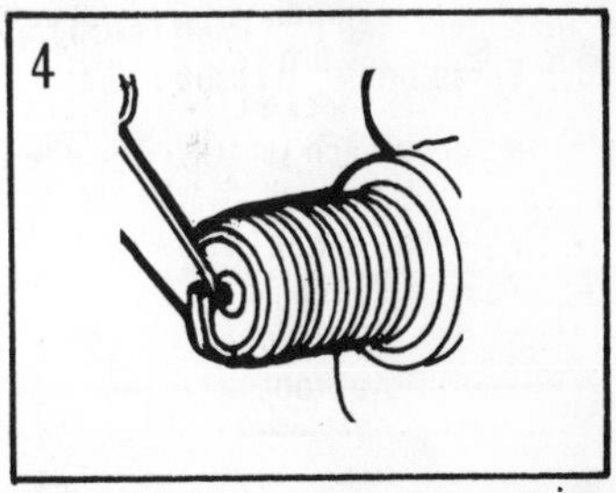

5. Thread the new plug into the hole by hand and tighten finger-tight. Tighten it firmly with a socket wrench, but do not force it. Replace the plug wire on the plug.

HEI IGNITION SYSTEM

The high energy ignition system is triggered by an electronic pulse. It is transistor controlled and uses an externally mounted ignition coil with no traditional points or condenser to be replaced. In their place is a magnetic pick-up assembly located inside the distributor, performing the same function.

The HEI system automatically controls the dwell angle (a function of contact point gap in a conventional ignition system), varying it in response to engine speed.

The HEI system is designed to be maintenance free except for the plug wires.

TACHOMETER CONNECTIONS—
H.E.I. SYSTEM

There is a "tach" terminal on the distributor cap. Connect the tachometer to this terminal and ground. Follow the tachometer manufacturer's instructions.

CAUTION: Grounding the tach terminal could damage the H.E.I. ignition module.

TIMING LIGHT CONNECTIONS—
H.E.I. SYSTEM

Timing light connections should be made in parallel using an adapter at the distributor No. 1 terminal.

CHECKING THE IGNITION SYSTEM

Wipe the ignition wires clean with a cloth. Carefully bend the wires in a tight loop, looking for brittle, cracked or loose insulation. If any wires are defective, they should be replaced immediately.
WARNING: Do not remove any spark plug wires with the engine running. The high voltage generated by the HEI is capable of rendering a healthy shock.

REPLACING SPARK PLUG WIRES

Some Chevettes may be equipped with a set of wires molded into a plate on the top of the distributor cap. In this case, merely unsnap the wire assembly from the distributor cap, after noting the position on the cap. Pull the wires from the wire looms and remove the boots from the spark plugs. Replace the entire wire assembly with a new one. To replace individual wires (if so equipped):

1. Lay out all the new wires so you can match the length of the old ones.
2. Work on one wire at a time. Twist the boot slightly to remove it from the spark plug and remove the wire from the wire loom. Remove it from the distributor.
3. Choose a new wire that nearly matches the old wire in length. If you are using wires that you have to assemble to the boots, add enough length to accommodate the boots.
4. Push the wire boot firmly onto the plug.
5. Insert the other end on the distributor. Clip the wires into the wire looms.
6. Repeat the process for all other wires, including the center coil wire.

Use the firing order illustration to guide you when replacing your ignition wires and/or distributor cap.

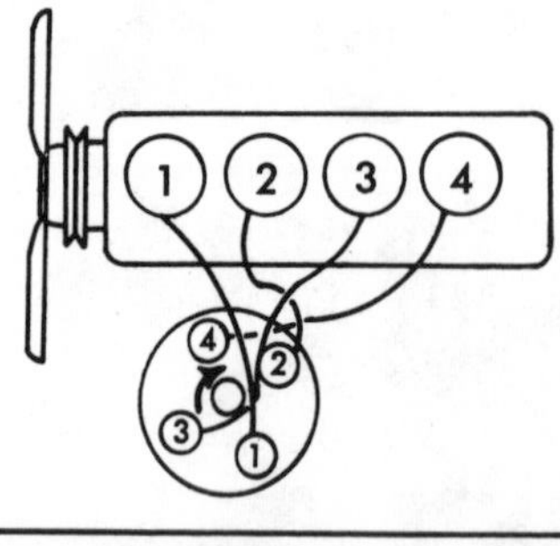

ADJUSTING IGNITION TIMING

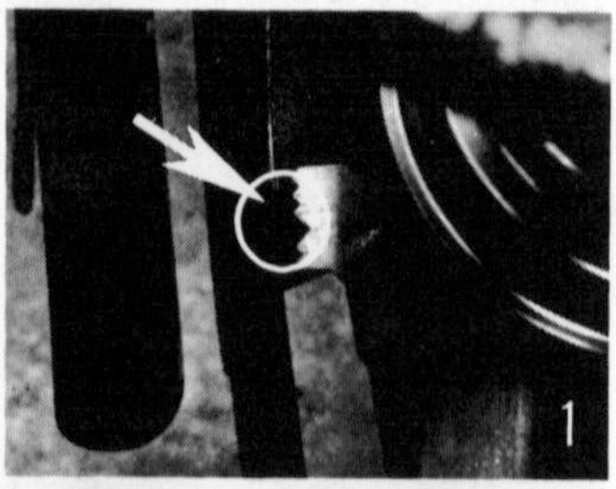

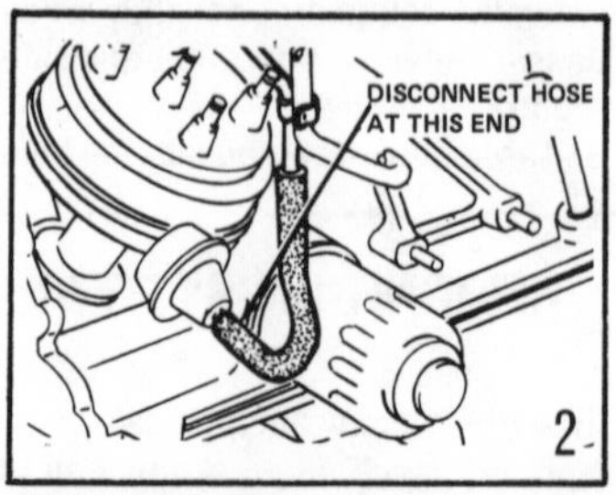

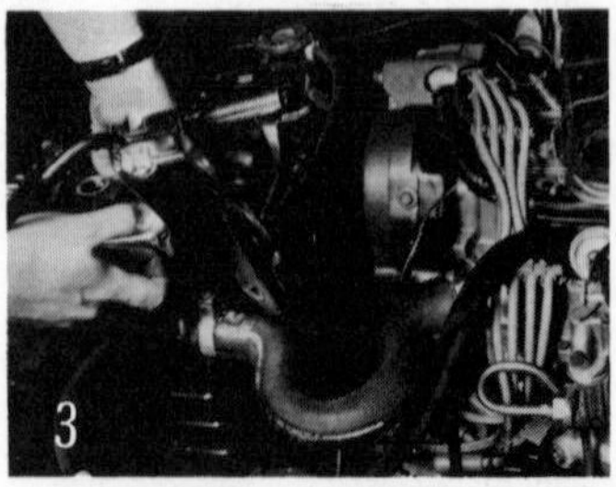

TOOLS: golf tee, wrenches, timing light, chalk
CAUTION: High voltages are generated by the secondary ignition system, including the distributor, spark plug wires and coil. Be careful working on or around these parts when the engine is running. Never run the engine in an enclosed area; keep yourself and all tune-up equipment away from the fan belts and pulleys.

1. Locate the timing mark and pointer and clean the dirt away. Mark the pointer notches with chalk.
2. Disconnect the distributor vacuum hose at the distributor and plug the line with a golf tee.
3. Connect a timing light according to the manufacturer's instructions supplied with the light.

4. Start the engine. Shine the light at the timing tab on the engine. Each peak on the tab represents 4°.
5. If the ignition timing is not as specified, shut the engine off. Loosen the distributor locknut slightly and rotate the distributor until the timing is correct, as indicated by the timing marks.
6. Tighten the distributor locknut and recheck the timing. Repeat until the timing is correct.
7. Reconnect the distributor vacuum line and disconnect the timing light.

Fuel System

The Chevette is designed to operate on unleaded gasoline. Unleaded gas is essential for proper operation of the emission control system and will help reduce spark plug fouling. In compliance with Federal regulations, pumps dispensing such fuel are labeled UNLEADED and are equipped with nozzles to fit the filler neck of your car's fuel tank.
When gasoline is brought from the fuel tank, it mixes with air in the carburetor. This gas/air mixture enters engine thru the intake manifold, passes thru the intake valves and is burned in the combustion chamber. The burned exhaust gas is then passed thru the exhaust valves to the exhaust system and to the outside air. In order to keep your car's engine running cleanly with minimal pollution, and avoid dangerous carbon monoxide fumes inside the vehicle, certain items should be checked from time to time.

General Motors recommends:

- Change fuel filter every 12 months or 15,000 miles
- Replace the PCV valve every 12 months or 15,000 miles
- Replace the air cleaner every 50,000 miles.

REPLACING THE AIR FILTER

The large round, flat can on top of the engine is the air cleaner. It is a closed, non-serviceable unit, discarded and replaced every 50,000 miles.
1. Remove the wing nut from the mounting stud.
2. Disconnect the wire clip from the air cleaner snorkel.
3. Disconnect the hose on the bottom of the air cleaner and remove the air cleaner assembly.
4. Place a new air cleaner in position, attach the hose on the bottom, reconnect the snorkel clip and attach the air cleaner to the mounting stud with the wing nut.

REPLACING THE PCV VALVE

An important part of a car's emission control system is the Positive Crankcase Ventilation (PCV) valve and its connecting hose. The PCV valve should be replaced once every 12,000 miles. This device keeps dirt and sludge from forming inside the engine. Make sure all PCV connections are tight. Check that the connecting hoses are clear and not clogged. Replace any brittle or broken hoses.

1. Pull valve from its location in the front part of the valve cover under the air cleaner.

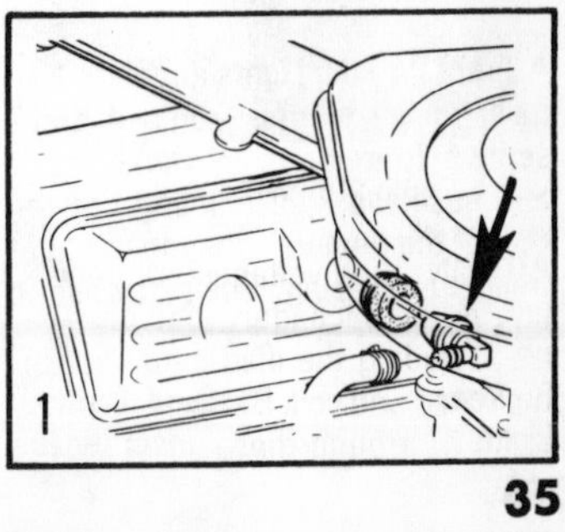

2. Squeeze the hose clamp with a pair of pliers. Remove the valve.
3. Note where the other end of the hose connects. Remove the hose and flush it with cleaning solvent.
4. Reconnect the hose. Pinch the clamp and insert the PCV valve into the hose.
5. Insert the valve into the valve cover.

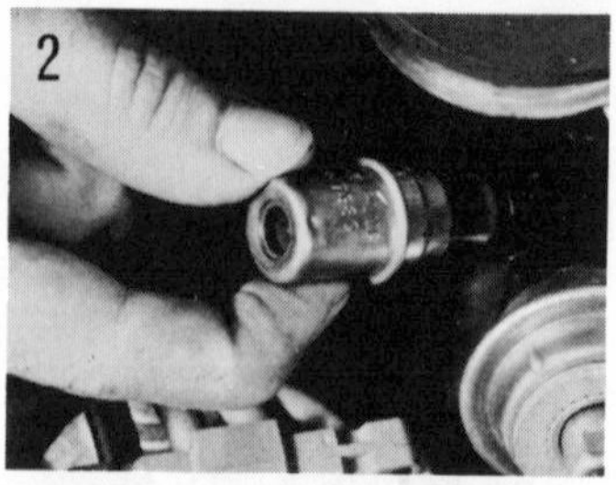

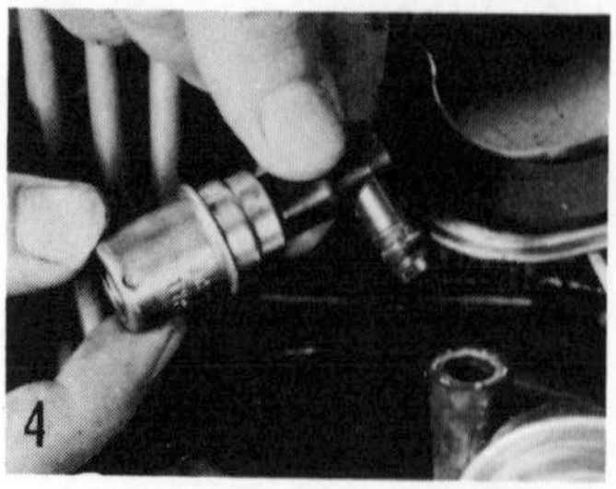

FUEL FILTER REPLACEMENT

The fuel filter is located behind the large fuel line inlet nut on the carburetor. Replace the filter every year or 15,000 miles. The fuel filter prevents dirt, rust, and scale from both the gas station's tank and your own fuel tank from reaching the carburetor. A dirty filter will starve the engine and cause poor running.

1. Place an absorbent rag under fuel line connection to absorb gas spills. Unscrew fuel line connection with wrench while holding the larger nut. Be careful, fuel line fitting threads are easily stripped.

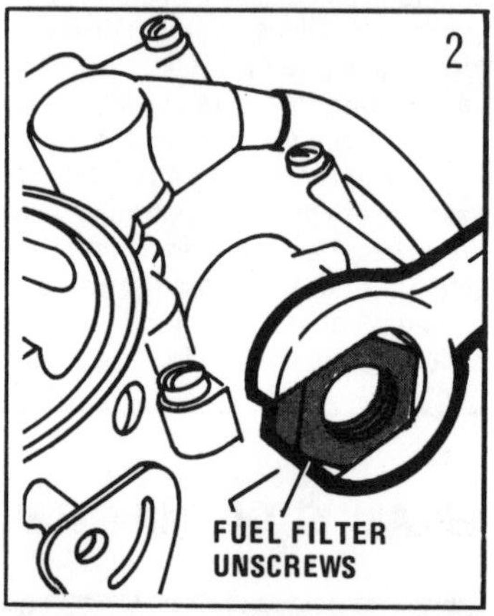

2. Remove the large filter retaining nut from the carburetor. The spring behind the filter will push it out. Remove the filter and the spring.
3. Install the spring and new filter element. Some carburetors are equipped with a paper element, others with a bronze unit. The bronze filter must have the small cone section facing out and a gasket between the filter and the retaining nut.

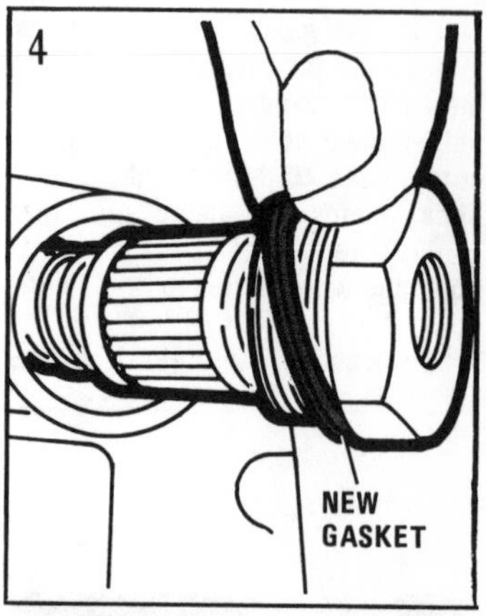

4. Install the new gasket on the retaining nut and screw it into place. CAUTION: DO NOT OVERTIGHTEN
5. Reconnect the fuel line. Discard the gas soaked rag safely.
6. Start the engine and check for leaks.

Safety Systems

LIGHTING SYSTEM

Parking lights, turn signals and stop lights function as dual element bulbs. To replace bulbs:

A. Front Parking Lights and Turn Signals: on all models, remove the 2 screws from beneath the bumper and push the light housing out the rear of the bumper. Unsnap the light from the housing. Push down and turn the bulb to remove it.

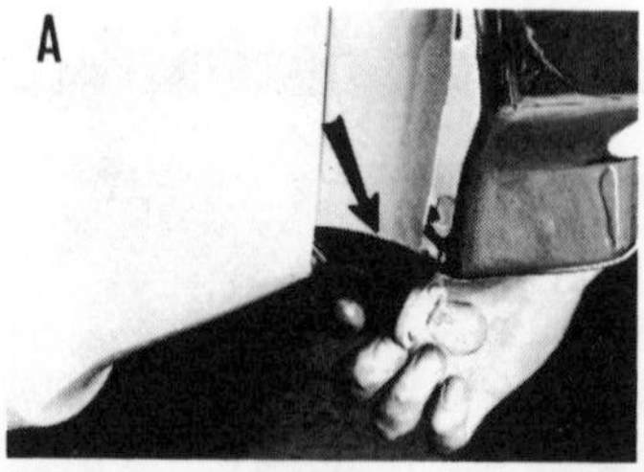

B. Rear Turn Signals and Parking Lights: on all models, unscrew the housing from the fender panel. Unsnap the bulb socket from the housing.

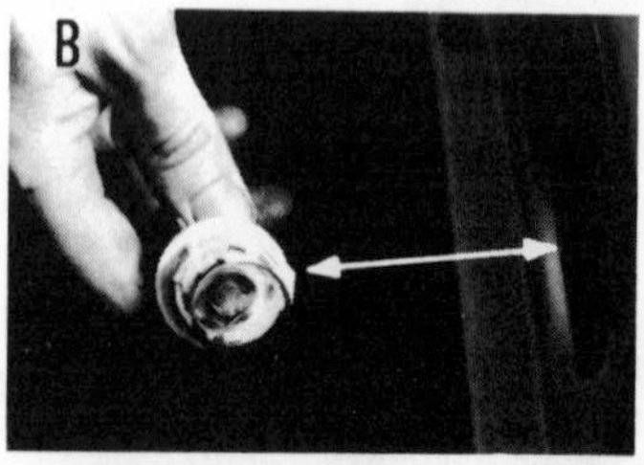

NOTE: When replacing dual element bulbs, note the lugs on the base of the bulb are in different locations on the base of the bulb. Match the lugs to the socket for proper fit.

BACK-UP LIGHTS

Unscrew the rear light housing from the fender panel above the rear bumper. Unsnap the light socket from the housing. Push down and turn the bulb to remove it.

SIDE MARKER LIGHTS

Unscrew the lens/housing from the fender. Pull the housing away from the fender and unsnap the light socket from the housing. Push the bulb down and turn it to remove.

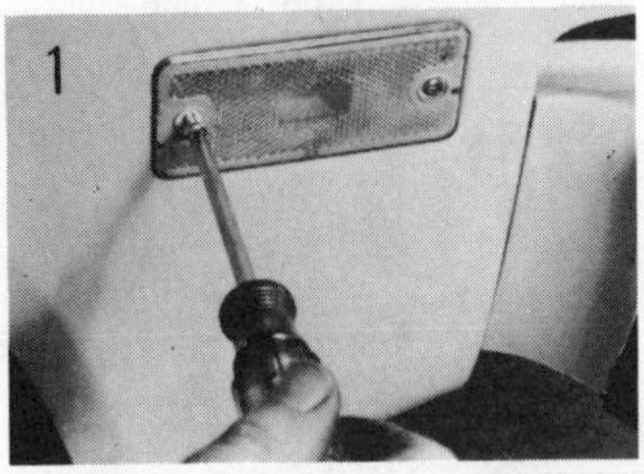

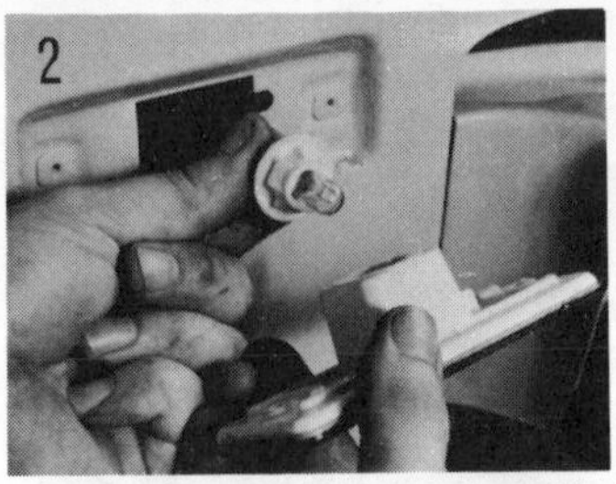

LICENSE PLATE LIGHT

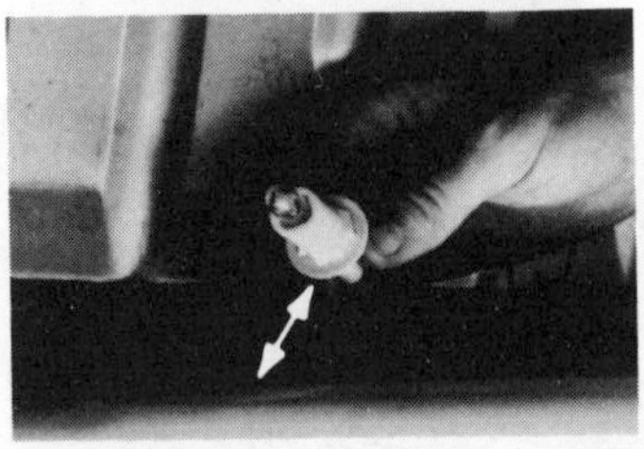

Open the trunk. Reach behind the license plate and pull the bulb socket from the housing. Push in on the bulb and turn it to remove the bulb.

INTERIOR DOME LIGHT

This is a cartridge type bulb; be sure to purchase correct replacement. Pry dome light lens out from housing. To avoid blowing fuse, make sure doors are closed and domelight switch is in OFF position. Carefully lever the bulb straight out of housing. Insert new bulb and re-install dome light lens.

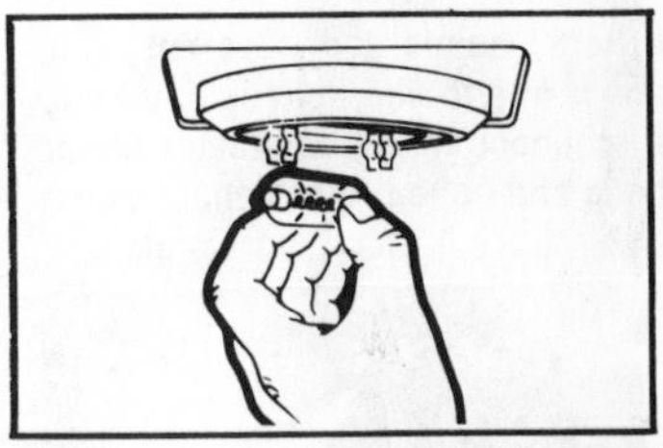

HEADLIGHT REPLACEMENT

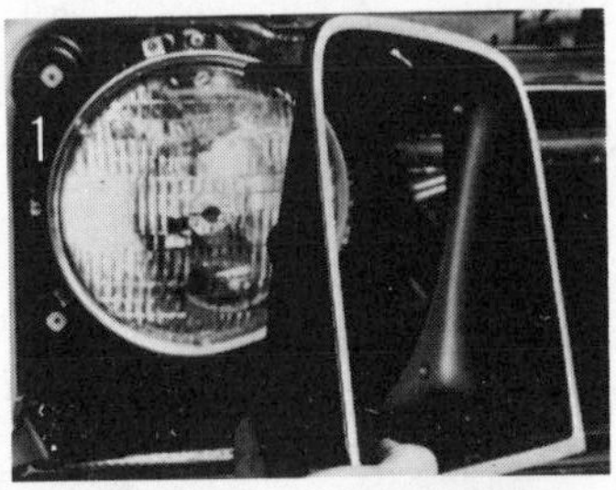

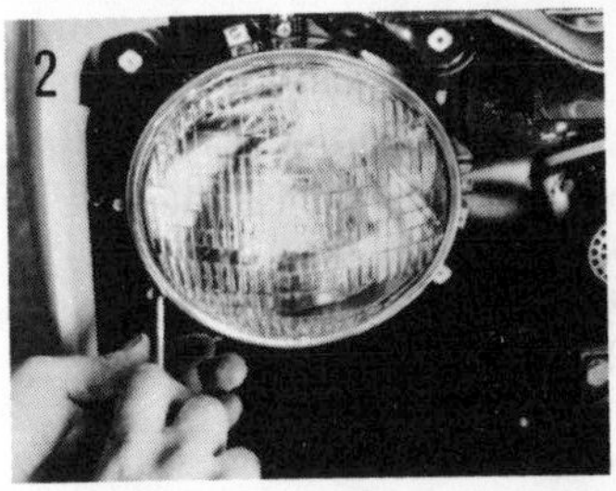

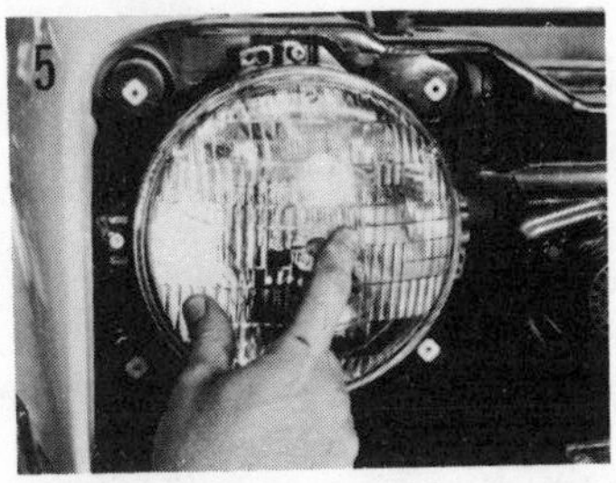

TOOLS AND MATERIALS: Tools: Phillips head screwdriver Materials; Sealed beam headlamp

1. Remove the headlamp bezel by removing the 4 Phillips head screws.
2. Remove the headlamp retaining ring by removing the 3 attaching screws. Do not disturb the headlight adjusting screws.
3. Pull the headlight sealed beam out and remove the electrical connector.
4. Connect a new headlight to the electrical connector.
5. Push the headlight in and install the retaining screws.
6. Install the headlight bezel with the 4 Phillips head screws.

REPLACING WINDSHIELD WIPER BLADES

To replace wiper blade, lift up on spring release tab on wiper arm connector. Pull wiper blade off. Snap new blade into place.

To replace rubber insert only, press down, away from wiper blade to free it. Slide insert from blade. Insert new wiper. Bend insert upward slightly to engage retaining clips.

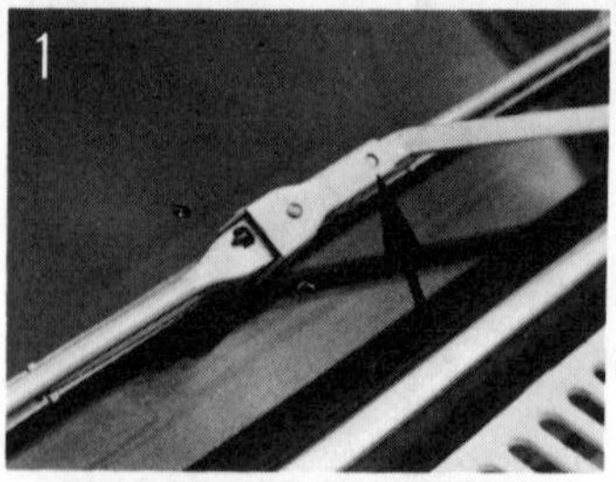

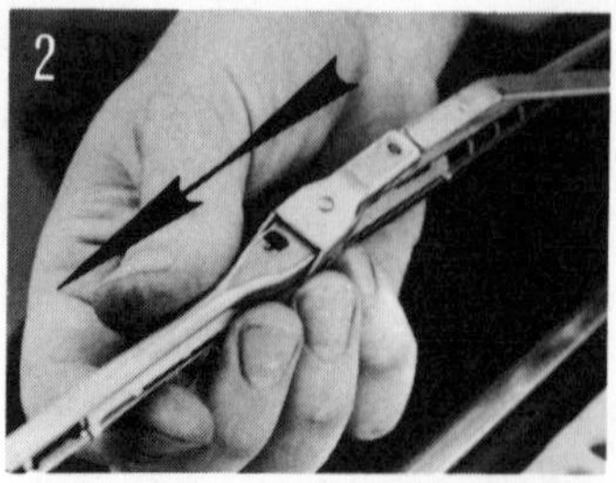

HORN PROBLEMS

If horn sounds and does not stop, this is due to short circuit in wiring. Disconnect wiring connector under hood and have professional service shop check horn wiring circuit.

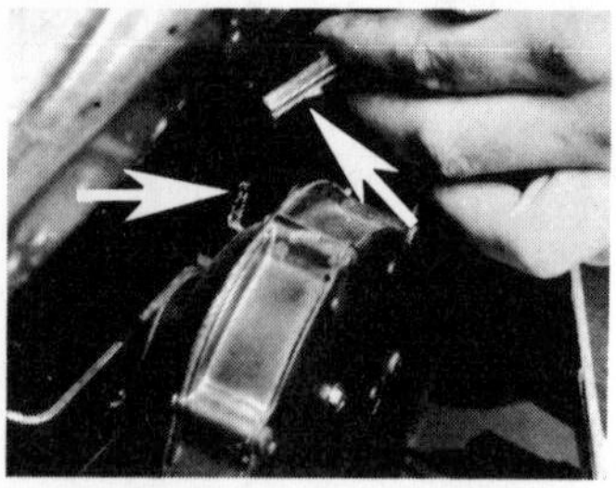

STEERING PROBLEMS

See steering system check in Suspension Section. Check tire pressures. Have a professional service shop check all compmnsnts in the front end and steering system.

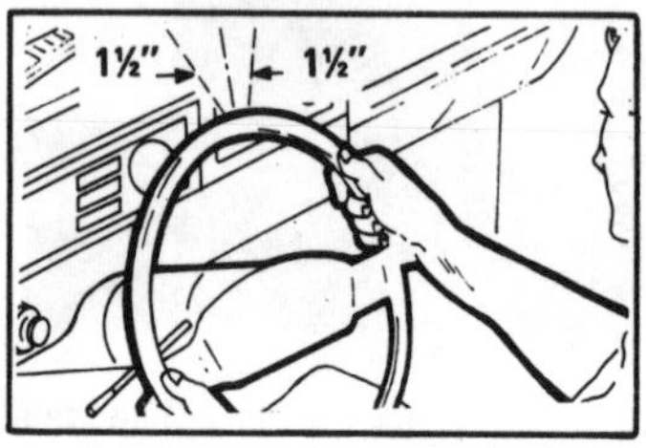

WINDSHIELD WASHER SYSTEM

If washer fails to squirt properly, raise hood and check system hose connections. Be sure washer fluid container has fluid. Check spout openings for clogging.
Keep container filled with fluid mixture of washer solvent and water. If road spray buildup on windshield is a chronic problem, add 1 tablespoon dishwasher detergent to solvent/water mixture when re-filling container.

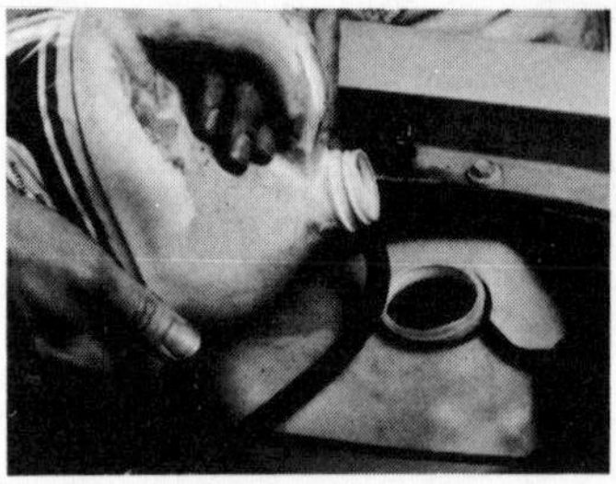

CHECKING WHEEL CYLINDERS

Drum brakes employ individual wheel cylinders to apply braking pressure to shoes. Check for brake fluid leaks on inside of wheel. Disc brakes employ calipers on individual wheels. Remove wheel and inspect caliper for signs of fluid leaks. Have mechanic correct leaks.

Electrical System

CHECK POINTS AND SERVICES

To ensure the starting ability of your battery at all times, check the battery condition periodically. Check the battery cable connections at the battery for tightness and accumulated corrosion. Also, check the condition of the battery cables periodically.
SAFETY NOTE: Wear gloves when working on the battery.

CHECKING BATTERY ELECTROLYTE LEVEL

The battery in your Chevette is a "Freedom battery", and is sealed, never requiring the addition of electrolyte. There is a "charge indicator" on top of the battery. To determine the state of charge of the battery, look at the indicator and compare it to the illustration.

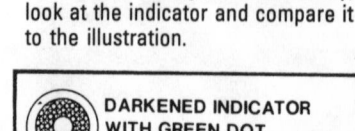

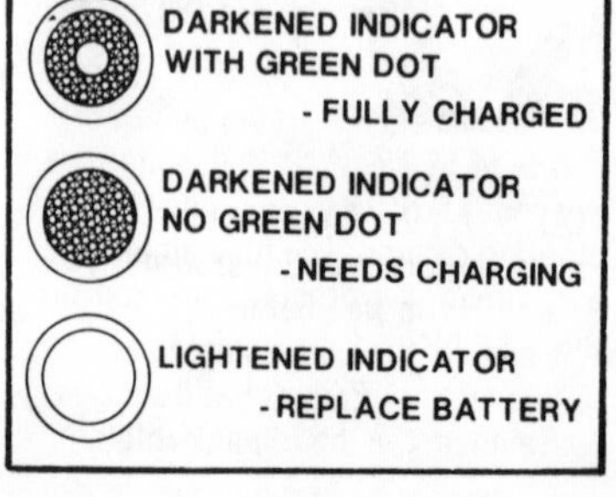

CLEANING BATTERY TERMINALS

As times goes by, battery terminals build up a dry, powdery, whitish material. This material is corrosive and will gradually eat thru battery cables if not cleaned off periodically.

1. Loosen and remove battery connections.
2. Brush off all loose corrosion; use stiff bristle brush. Do not get this material into eyes or on open cuts. Wash off at once.
3. If corrosion build-up is extremely heavy and brushing does not remove all of it, mix 2 tablespoons baking soda to 1 cup water. Pour solution directly onto terminals and connectors. Allow to soak a few minutes and rinse off. Continue brushing to remove all traces of corrosion build-up. Do not allow cleaning solution to enter battery.
4. Replace connectors on battery terminal posts and tighten.
5. Liberally smear battery terminal posts and cable connectors with petroleum jelly.

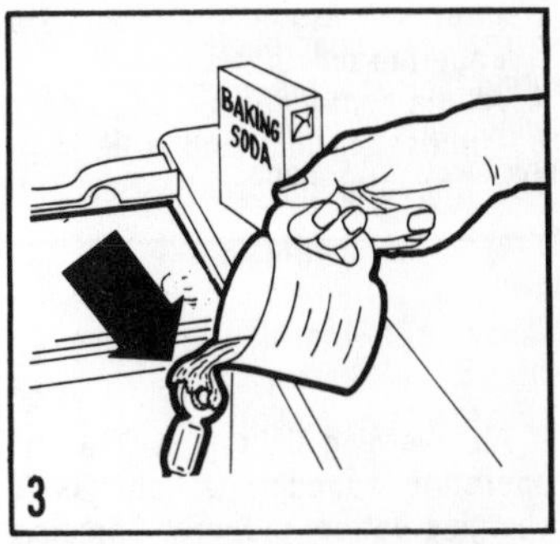

REPLACING BATTERY CABLES

If battery cable strands become frayed, broken or corroded, replace cable immediately. Delay in correcting this condition could lead to sudden failure to start the engine. Can also weaken battery.

1. Loosen and remove battery connections. Clean OFF any corrosion.

2. Disconnect negative cable from its attachment to engine or chassis. Disconnect positive cable from its attachment to starter relay.

3. Attach new cables making sure positive and negative cables are on proper terminals. They are not identical.

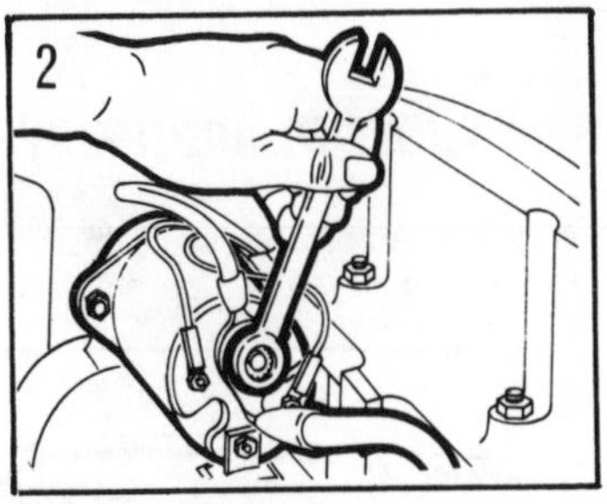

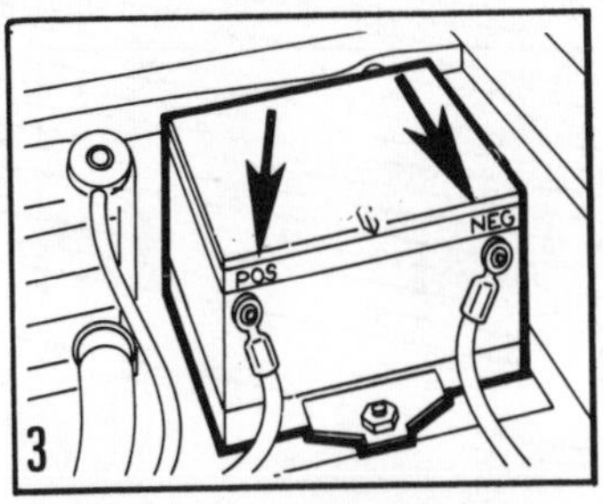

4. Replace connectors on battery terminal posts and tighten.
5. Liberally smear battery terminal posts and cable connectors with petroleum jelly.

BATTERY HOLD-DOWN

The clamp device which holds battery in place should be checked periodically. If loose, tighten. Clean off corrosion buildup. Severely corroded holddown components should be replaced before they break.

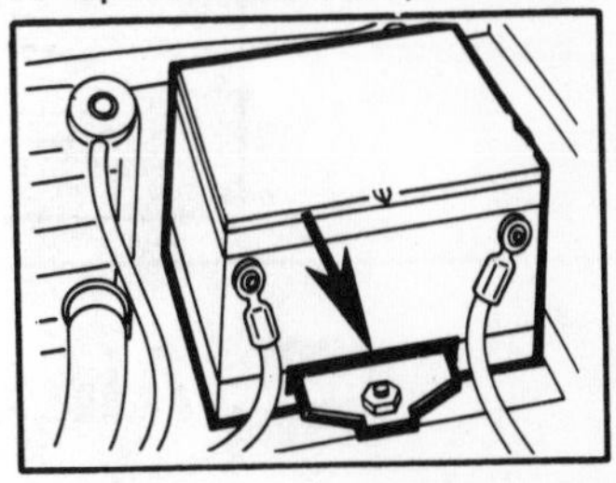

FUSE BOX LOCATION

The fuse block is located under the dashboard on the left side of the steering column. The fuse amperage and circuit it protects is marked on the fuse block.

Always replace a fuse with one of the same amperage. If fuses are constantly blowing out, have the electrical system professionally checked.

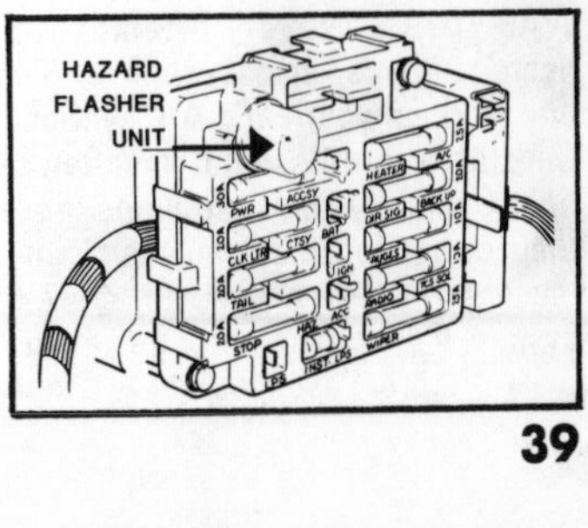

TURN SIGNAL AND 4-WAY FLASHER

The turn signals and 4-way flashers will operate only if:
A. All the light bulbs are OK, and,
B. The flasher unit itself is OK.
The Chevette hazard flasher and turn signal flasher is combined in the one unit that plugs into the upper left corner of the fuse block.
Pull the flasher from the fuse block and plug in a new flasher. It only goes in one way. If you tow a trailer, you may want to use a heavy duty flasher.

ALTERNATOR CHECKS

If Alt. warning light glows red at operating speed, alternator isn't charging battery properly. Common causes are:

A. Fan belts are loose and slipping on alternator pulley. Tighten or replace belts.

B. Battery terminals, cables are loose or corroded. Clean; tighten; replace bad cables.

If A or B do not correct problem, alternator or voltage regulator may be faulty. This happens far less often, and can only be checked by mechanic with proper electrical testing equipment.
Alternator Caution: Alternator can be permanently damaged by shortcircuiting terminal connections. When working around or moving alternator, always keep metal tools or engine parts from terminals.

REAR WINDOW DEFOGGER SYSTEM

Do not clean inside of rear window fitted with defogger system with any abrasive material. This could destroy carbon-copper wires. Use only soft rag and mild detergent/water mixture. Dry carefully.

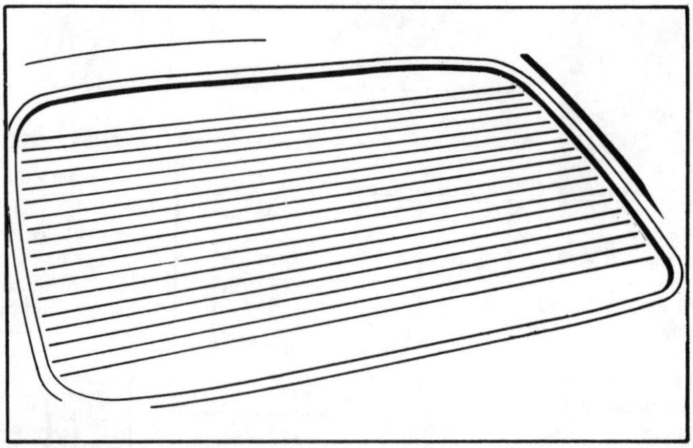

Air Conditioning System

CHECKPOINTS AND SERVICES

WARNING!—Never attempt to tighten fittings, disassemble or do any work on your car's A/C system. Consult a professional mechanic about A/C system problems and their correction. Your auto air conditioner (A/C) is a delicate, closed system. If air, dirt or water get into it, or if refrigerant escapes, the A/C unit will not cool a car interior. Among things you can do are:
1. Keep condenser grille clean. Check for dirt and debris; periodically remove dead insects, leaves, etc., with stiff bristle brush. Straighten any bent fins—carefully.
2. Keep radiator filled to correct level. (See Cooling System section). If

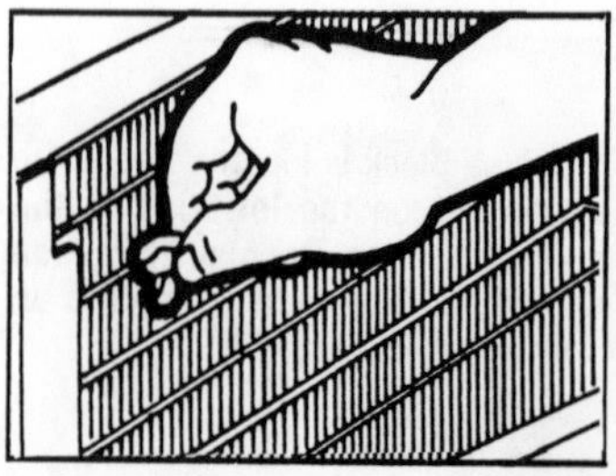

fluid needs to be added, add antifreeze rather than water.
3. Keep radiator coolant at a 50/50 water/antifreeze mixture.
4. Flush cooling system and replace with fresh coolant mixture at least every 12,000 miles. (See Cooling System section).
5. Radiator cap should be tight and sealed properly. If sealing gasket is cracked, cut or worn, replace cap with new 15 lb. unit.
6. Check fan belt tension periodically. (See Cooling System section). Replace glazed, frayed or cut fan belts, before they fail entirely.
7. Check periodically for bubbles in the A/C sight glass. Sight glass is located in the head of the receiver/drier vessel. Sight glass is no larger than the head of a large nail. It may be dirty. Wipe clean for best visibility.

TUNE-UP SPECIFICATIONS

YEAR	ENGINE No. Cyl. Displacement (cu. in.)	SPARK PLUGS Type	SPARK PLUGS Gap (in.)	DISTRIBUTOR Point Dwell (deg.)	DISTRIBUTOR Point Gap (in.)	IGNITION TIMING Man. Trans.● (deg.)■	IGNITION TIMING Auto Trans.● (deg.)■	IDLE SPEED Man. Trans.● (rpm) ▲	IDLE SPEED Auto Trans. (rpm) ▲
1976	4-85	R43TS	0.035	Electronic		10B	10B	800(1000)	800(850)
	4-97.6	R43TS	0.035	Electronic		8B	10B	800(1000)	800(850)
1977	4-85			See Underhood Specifications decal					
	4-97.6			See Underhood Specifications decal					

▲ Adjust automatic transmissions in Drive (AMC/Ford/GM) or Neutral (Chrysler), all manual transmissions are adjusted in Neutral.
■ All figures are Before Top Dead Center.
● Figure in parentheses indicate California engine.
NOTE: The underhood specifications sticker often reflects tune-up specification changes made in production. Sticker figures must be used if they disagree with those in this chart.

CAPACITIES

YEAR	ENGINE No. Cyl. Displacement (cu. in.)	ENGINE OIL Add 1 qt. with New Filter	TRANSMISSION Pts. to Refill after Draining MANUAL 3-speed	MANUAL 4-speed	AUTOMATIC	DRIVE AXLE (pts.)	COOLING SYSTEM with Heater (qts.)	COOLING SYSTEM with Air Cond. (qts.)
1976-77	4-85	4	——	3	7	2.8	8.5	9
	4-97.6	4	——	3	7	2.8	9	9

—— Not Applicable.

Service Record

Date/Mileage	Service	Next Due

Chevrolet

Lubrication and Oil Change

BRAKE FLUID LEVEL CHECK

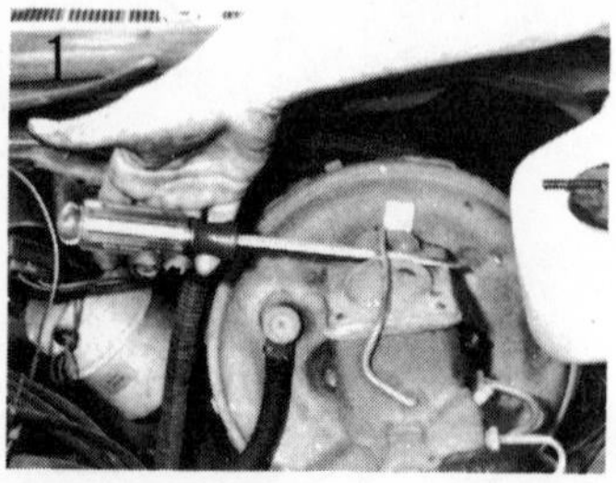

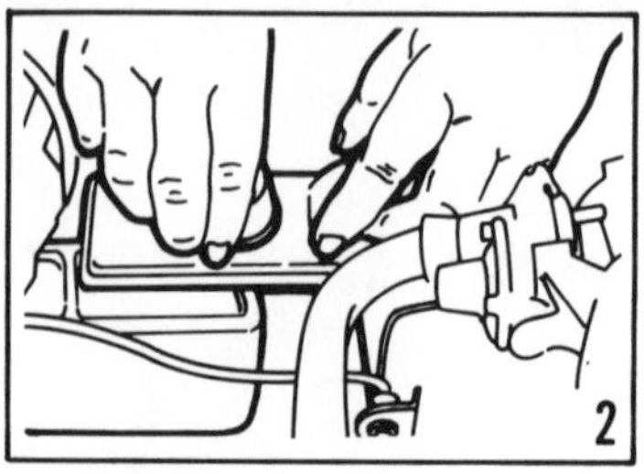

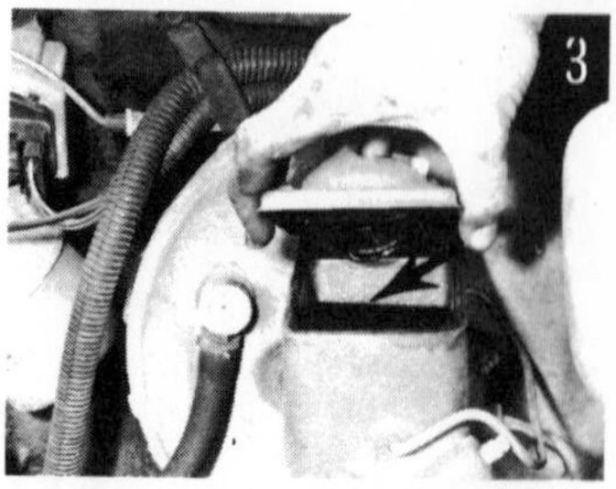

Check brake fluid level in master cylinder every three months . . . sooner if braking feels inadequate. Add when low.

Recommended grade: DOT 3.

1. Pry wire retaining clip off cap top with screwdriver.

2. Remove cap and gasket by lifting up.

3. Fluid level should be within ¼ inch of top rim. If lower than this, add fresh fluid to appropriate level. DO NOT OVERFILL

4. Replace cap and gasket; secure retaining clip over cap. If fluid level was low, check again in a few days.

5. If fluid repeatedly checks low, there is a leak somewhere in the system. See SAFETY SYSTEMS—WHEEL CYLINDER CHECK. Have mechanic check further. Neglect can be dangerous.

MANUAL TRANSMISSION FLUID LEVEL CHECK

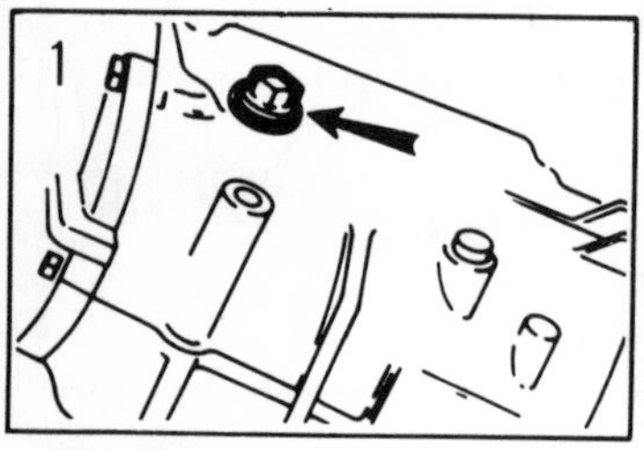

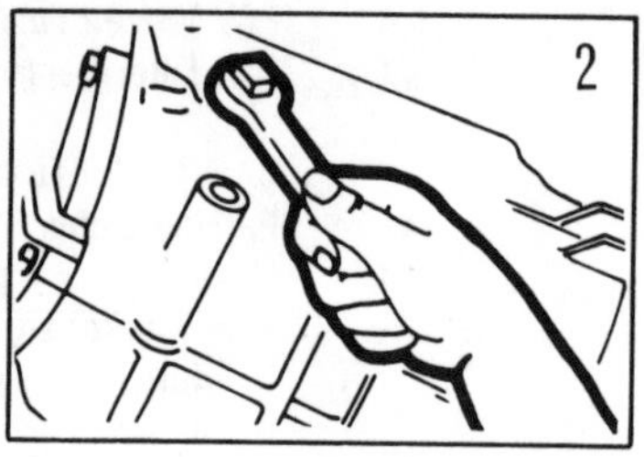

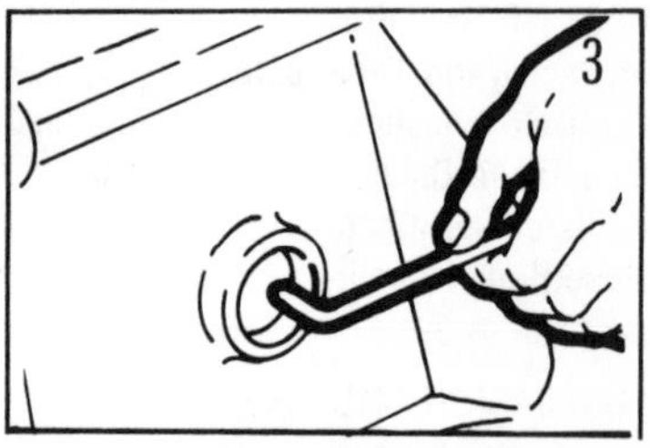

GM SAYS . . . Check transmission fluid level every four months
. . . SAE 80W or 80W-90 GL-5 gear lubricant, five speed transmission requires DEXRON® II
Tools and Materials . . . Adjustable wrench, screwdriver, suction gun, fluid as needed
Recommended grade of lubricant

1. Locate transmission fluid filler plug on right side of transmission housing from underneath car.

2. Wipe road dirt from filler plug area before loosening. Remove plug with adjustable wrench.

3. Insert fluid level check device. Fluid level should be right up to bottom edge of filler hole.

4. Add fluid as needed with hand bulb syringe.

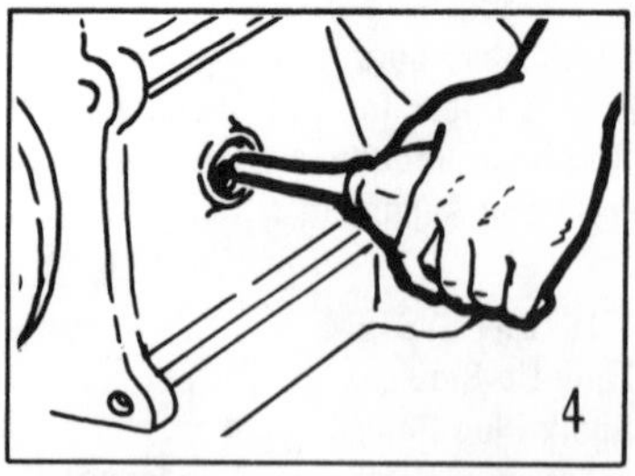

5. Replace filler plug; tighten.

AUTOMATIC TRANSMISSION FLUID LEVEL CHECK

GM SAYS . . . check automatic transmission fluid (ATF) level every 6000 miles (1970-74 models) or 7500 miles (1975-77 models). Recommended grade: DEXRON® or Type A.
TOOLS . . . Long neck filler funnel.

1. Engine must be warmed up and running. Place shift lever in PARK position.
2. Pull out dipstick. Wipe clean.

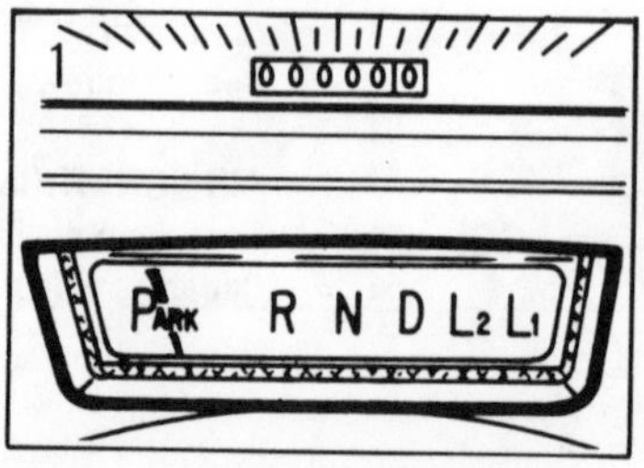

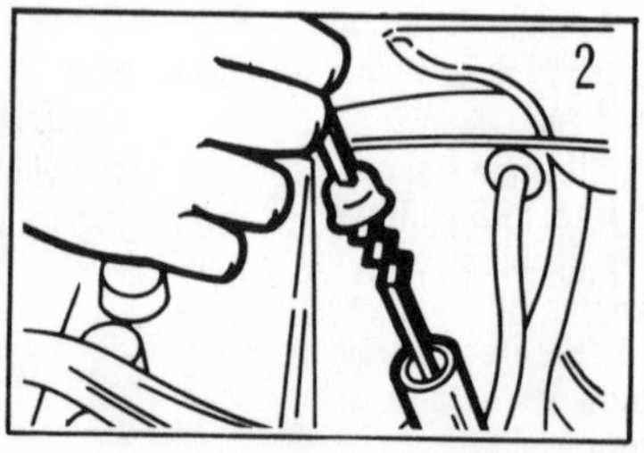

Push dipstick all the way back in; remove it again.

3. If fluid is below ADD mark, add ATF to bring level up. DO NOT OVERFILL.

4. Add ATF thru transmission dipstick hole by means of long-neck filler funnel.

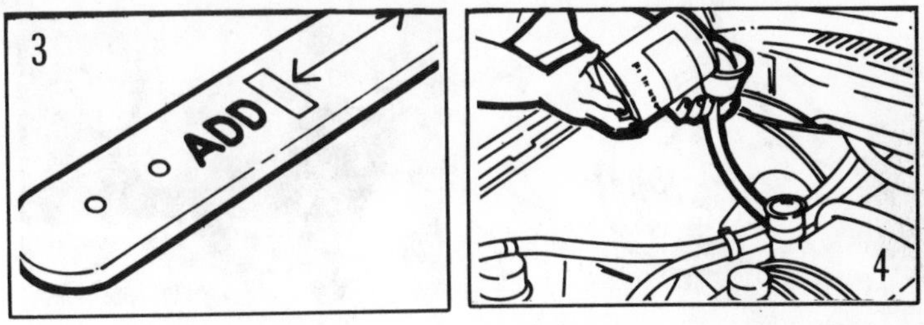

REAR AXLE LUBRICANT

GM SAYS . . . check rear axle lube level every 6000 miles (1970-74 models) or 7500 miles (1975-77 models). Recommended grade: Hypoid gear lube (SAE 90). Positraction axles require special positraction lubricant.
TOOLS . . . adjustable hand wrench; fluid level check device (made from coat hanger wire; bend at 90° angle 2″ from end); bulb syringe.
1. Locate filler plug on forward side of rear axle housing.
2. Wipe plug area clean; remove plug with wrench.
3. Insert wire level check device; remove. Adequate fluid level should show lubricant on last ¼-inch of wire.
4. If fluid level is low, add as needed, with a hand bulb syringe, until level shows on last ¼-inch of wire.
5. Replace filler plug; tighten.

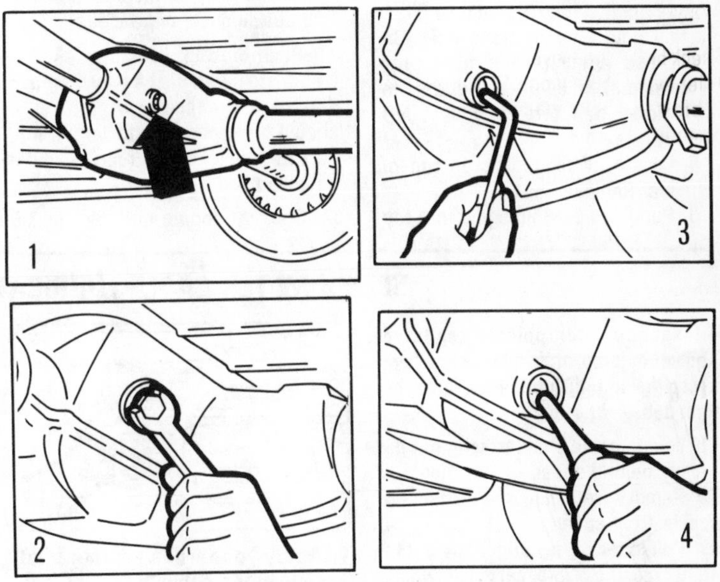

OIL AND FILTER CHANGE

GM SAYS . . . Change oil every 6000 miles (1970-74 models), 7500 miles (1975-77 models); change filter every 12,000 miles (1970-74 models) or 15,000 miles (1975-77 models). Recommended grade: SE. Check oil level at least once a week.
TOOLS & MATERIALS . . . adjustable wrench; medium size screwdriver; oil filter removal wrench; drain pan for old oil (at least 5 qt. capacity); oil pouring spout; 4 qt. oil (5 qt. if changing filter); new oil filter; oil and lubricants as specified below.
SAFETY TIP . . . use work gloves.

1. If engine is cold, start up and idle for about 5 minutes.
2. Park car on level ground. Turn engine off.
3. Locate oil drain plug on underside of engine. Place drain pan under plug.

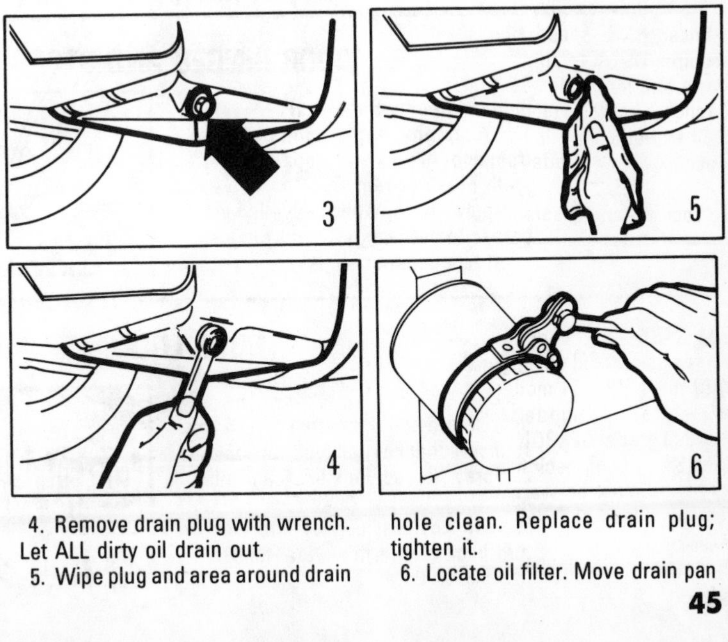

4. Remove drain plug with wrench. Let ALL dirty oil drain out.
5. Wipe plug and area around drain hole clean. Replace drain plug; tighten it.
6. Locate oil filter. Move drain pan

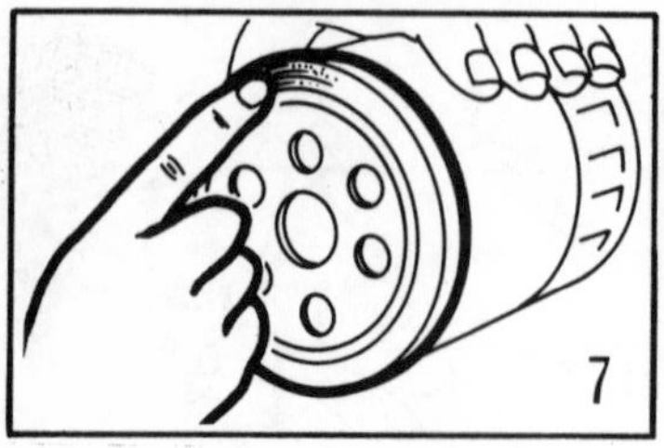

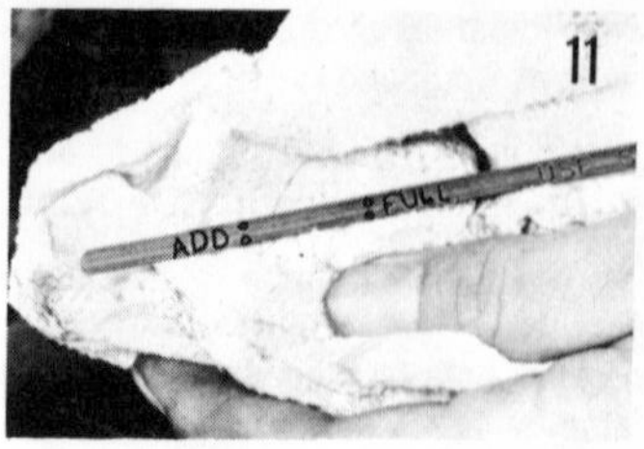

under filter. Loosen filter with oil filter wrench. Unscrew; remove filter by hand.

7. Smear fresh oil over surface of rubber gasket (washer) of new filter. Install new filter by hand only. Do NOT use wrench. Turn filter until gasket makes contact. Tighten an additional half turn only . . . NO MORE.

8. Locate oil filler tube on top of engine. Remove cap.

9. Punch oil pouring spout into top of oil can. Pour all cans of new oil into filler tube. Wipe filler cap clean and replace it.

10. Check new oil level at dipstick. Pull out dipstick, wipe clean.

11. Push dipstick back into engine. Be sure to insert all the way. Remove dipstick and check new oil level. It should be above "FULL" line. If not, be sure to check if you put in all the oil called for.

12. Start up engine and idle for 3-5 minutes. Oil signal light on instrument panel will glow red when engine is first started. Light should go out in 30 seconds or less.

13. Stop engine and check for oil leaks at drain plug and filter. If you find any, check tightness of plug and/or filter, also for condition of filter gasket to see that it has not become pinched or damaged when installing. Recheck oil level, which should now be at "FULL".

SPEEDOMETER CABLE LUBRICATION

If speedometer pointer tends to quiver or jump, or if unit makes a low, rasping sound, lubrication may be needed.

1. Locate cable shaft attachment directly behind speedometer dial.
2. Remove retaining clip. Unscrew cable from speedometer.
3. Pull inner cable completely out of outer casing. Note carefully which end is top. Check for wear or frayed strands. If damaged, replace inner cable with new one.

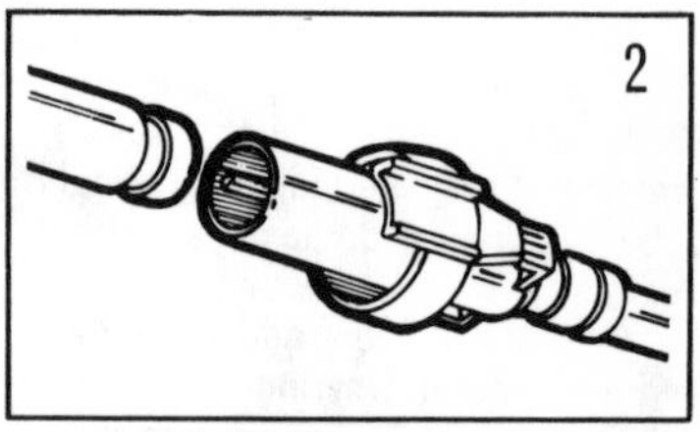

4. Apply generous amount of speedometer cable lubricant into cable casing. Replace inner cable in shaft, noting that top end is not inserted accidentally. Turn inner cable as it is being re-inserted. Twist cable when all the way in, to lock into position at lower end.
5. Reconnect cable to speedometer head under instrument panel.

DOOR HINGES AND STOPS

(lubricate every 6 months)
1. Brush any dirt accumulations from door hinges and stops. Use old tooth brush or rag.
2. Apply dab of white polyethylene grease to door hinges, trunk hinges, hood hinges, door stops.

DOOR LOCKS

(lubricate every 6 months)
1. Insert door key half way into lock.
2. Spray aerosol lock lubricant into lock.
3. Push key rest of way into lock; turn back and forth several times.

Cooling System

IT IS RECOMMENDED . . . that radiator coolant (water/antifreeze mixture) level be checked once or twice a month. Do this when engine is cold. Check more often if you do a lot of hard driving. Coolant is checked visually on models with expansion tanks.

Keep coolant up to recommended level in radiator. If coolant checks frequently low, look for leaks. Tighten all hose clamps occasionally. For best results, keep a 50/50

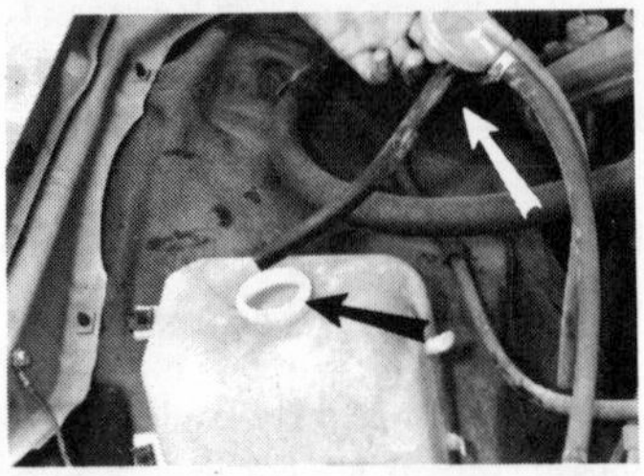

water/antifreeze mixture year round. Change complete coolant mixture every 24 months.
CAUTION: If you must check coolant

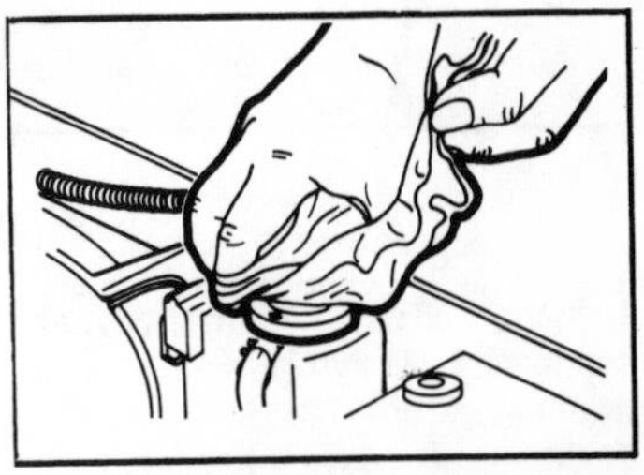

in a hot engine, cover radiator cap with thick rag before releasing. Remove cap slowly . . . press down and turn.

REPLACING THE THERMOSTAT

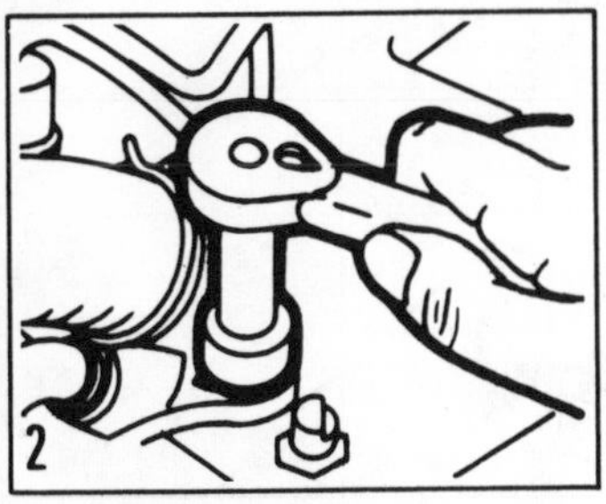

A faulty thermostat will usually cause engine overheating. The thermostat is located inside the housing where the top radiator hose connects to the engine.
TOOLS AND MATERIALS . . .
New thermostat
Gasket
Adjustable wrench

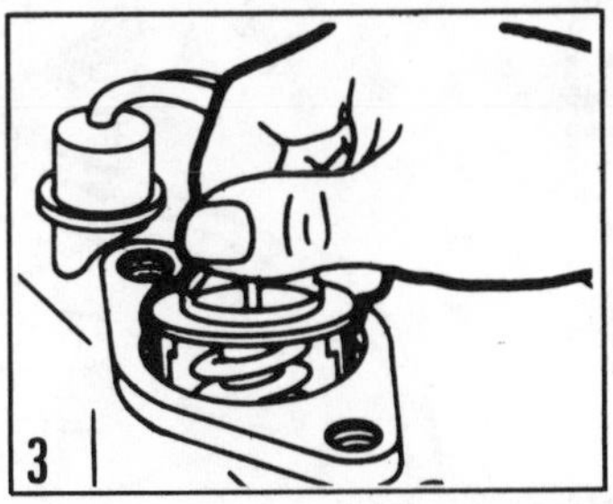

1. Drain radiator of about half its coolant. (See How To Replace Hoses).
2. Loosen and remove both retaining bolts and lift thermostat housing off the engine.
NOTE: If you're careful it won't be necessary to remove radiator hose.
3. Remove old thermostat.

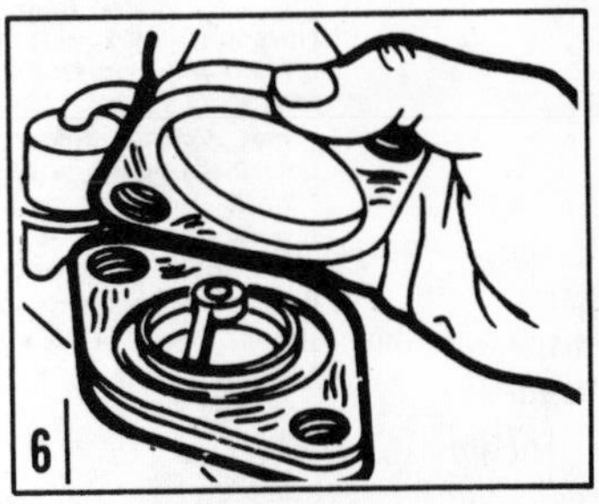

4. Scrape thermostat housing flange and engine block surface to remove old gasket debris.
5. Drop new thermostat into place—spring down.
6. Install new gasket with sealer applied to both sides.
7. Replace thermostat housing and tighten both retaining bolts.

FAN BELT ADJUSTMENT

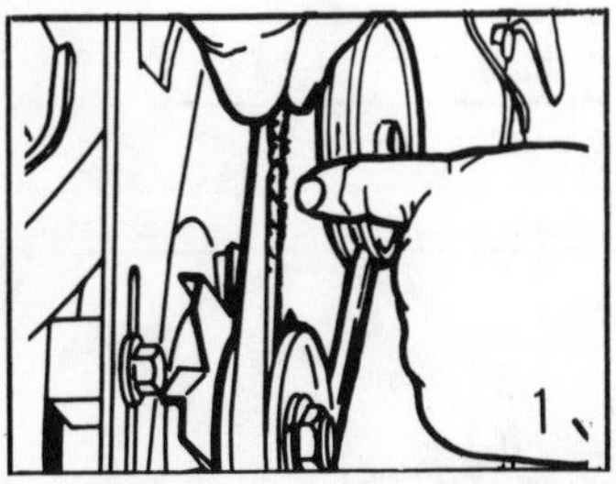

The fan belt not only drives the radiator fan, it turns the water pump and drives the alternator. It's easy to see that the condition and proper

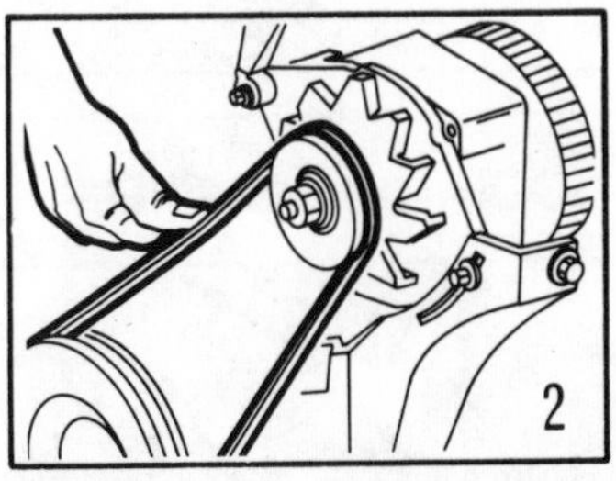

tension of the belt are vital, since almost all engine cooling and electrical power is dependent on it. The belt deserves an occasional look and

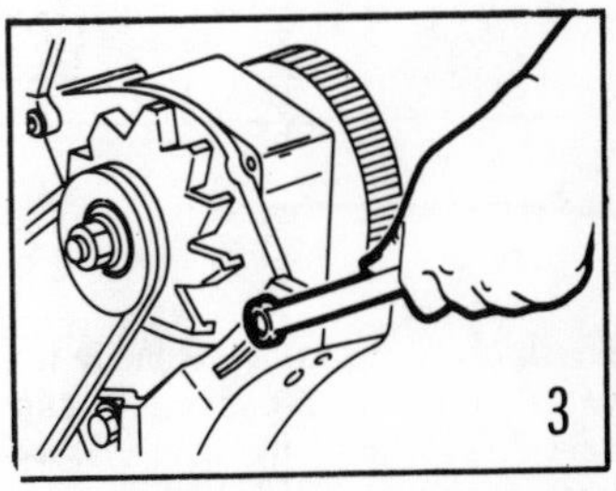

tension check.
1. Inspect fan belt occasionally. If worn, frayed or cracked on inner driving surface, replace.

CAUTION: An overtightened belt may damage alternator and water pump bearings.

2. Check tension occasionally. Press thumb at midpoint of belt span between pulleys. If belt depresses more than ½ inch, tightening is needed. A too-loose belt will not drive alternator and water pump effectively.

3. To adjust loosen alternator mounting bolts, pivot the alternator over until the belt is properly tensioned (¼ in. deflection) and then tighten bolts.

FIND THOSE COOLING SYSTEM LEAKS

1. Inspect all hoses. If any are weak, soft in spots or show cracks, replace at once.
2. Check all hose connections for tightness. Tighten loose hose clamps; they tend to loosen due to engine vibration.
3. If radiator steams or hisses when engine is switched off, check for leaks. Look for signs of coolant drips on radiator or around header tank joint.

Leaks are possible at:

Upper or lower radiator hoses
Water pump (gaskets or seal)
Heater core or connecting hoses
Automatic transmission cooler lines (at bottom of radiator)
Faulty radiator pressure cap
Faulty cylinder head gasket
Cracked cylinder head or block

Due to the number of joints, cooling systems have many places to leak from. Check clamp tightness. If leaks persist an anti-leak additive in the coolant may help. Noisy water pumps may benefit from a lubricating additive in the coolant. Use a cooling system cleaner when flushing during a drain and refill job. It will help remove rust and scale. Remember — additives will not cure chronic problems. But they will effect a short-term remedy in many cases.

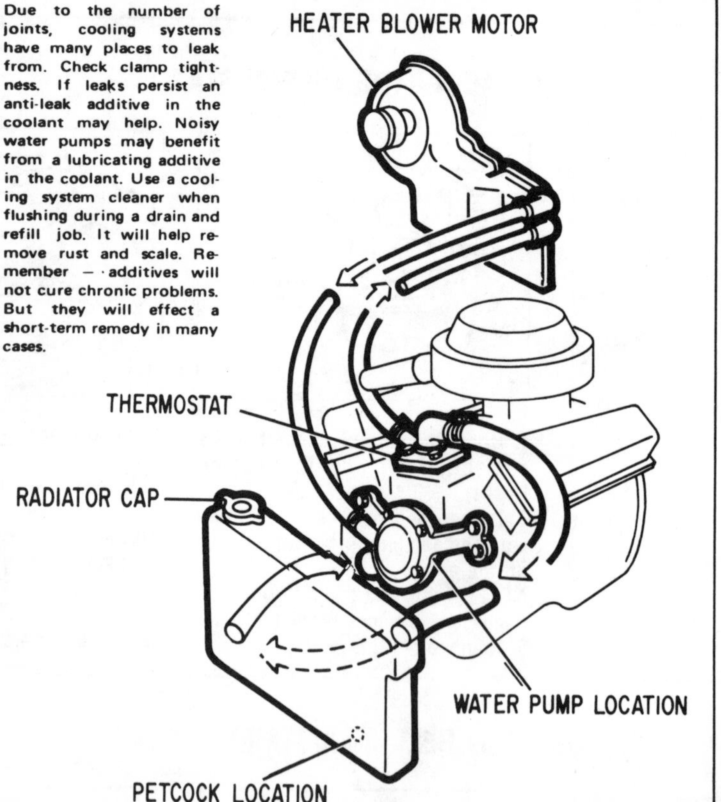

RADIATOR CAP CHECK

Check radiator cap occasionally for worn or cracked gasket. If cap doesn't seal properly, fluid will be lost and engine will overheat. Replace worn cap with new cap rated 15 lbs. pressure.

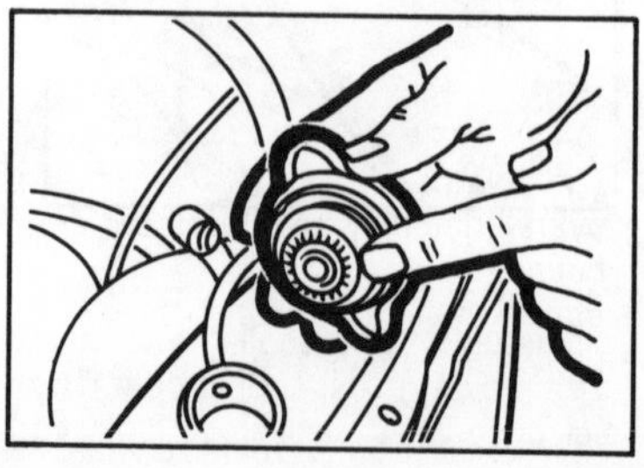

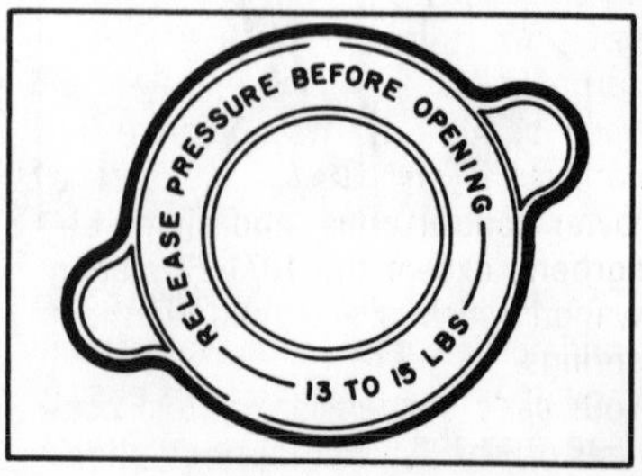

HOSE REPLACEMENT

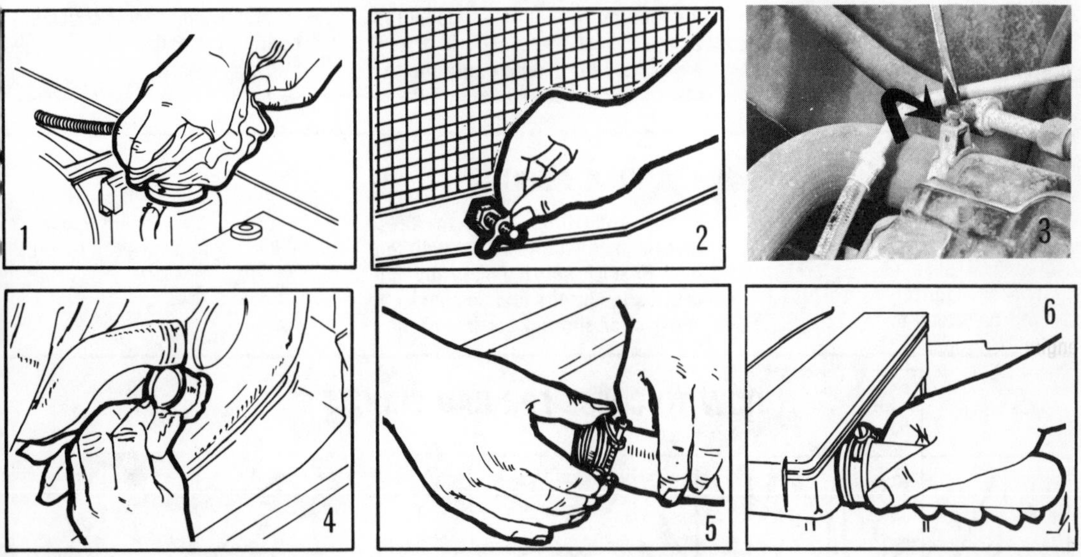

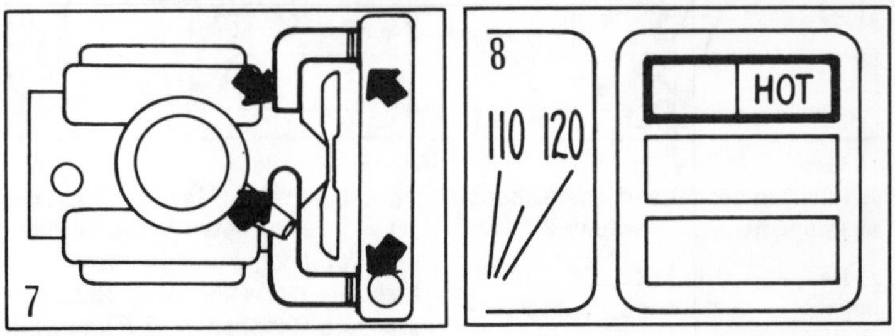

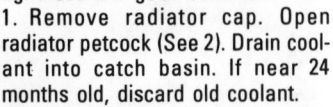

Coolant drain and refill work may be done alone; when changing hoses, coolant must also be drained as part of job. Discard all hoses with cracks or soft spots. Check hose clamps for tightness and good condition.

1. Remove radiator cap. Open radiator petcock (See 2). Drain coolant into catch basin. If near 24 months old, discard old coolant.
2. Petcock or drain plug is located at the bottom left of the radiator. Open petcock or remove plug to drain.
3. Loosen clamps at each end of hose(s). Work loose; pull off. If old hose clamps are rusted or damaged, replace with new units.
4. Wipe all hose connections clean. Use emery cloth to get rid of residue. Check all hoses for weak spots, as well as cracks inside and out.
5. Slip clamps over each hose end. Slip hose ends all the way onto cleaned up hose connections.
6. Place hose clamp ¼ inch from hose end. Tighten. Close petcock. Refill with 50/50 coolant/water mix.
7. Start engine; allow to warm up. Check for coolant leaks.
8. Road test car; watch for temperature warning light.

Suspension and Tires

The front wheels mount and rotate on the spindles, which are attached to upper and lower ball joints. A coil spring is mounted between the control arms on both sides. A shock absorber is located in the center of each spring. The rear suspension consists of coil springs, upper and lower control arms, and shock absorbers, except the 1971-77 station wagon which is equipped with leaf springs.

Your car's suspension system consists of wheels, tires, springs, shock absorbers, sway (or stabilizer) bars, ball joints, steering linkage. If any of these items is out of adjustment or badly worn, you may notice any of these symptoms:

- car pulls to one side when braking
- car wanders when driving a straight line
- overall ride may be either hard or bouncy
- effort is needed to steer vehicle
- tires show uneven wear
- tires squeal when cornering
- front of car dips or bounces when braking
- car rocks side-to-side when going over rough road
- wheels bounce to make slapping sound on road
- steering wheel vibrates in hands
- front of car vibrates at highway speeds

Any of above symptoms indicates corrective action is needed. Delay can: ruin tires; cause damage/failure to other suspension parts; create safety hazard.

STEERING

If steering linkage, front suspension and steering column components are in good condition, there should be not more than 1½ inch free play in the steering wheel when measured at the rim of the wheel. If a loud knock is heard when turning the steering wheel from one extreme to the other, have mechanic check pinion bearing preload.

SHOCK ABSORBERS

Shock absorbers work to keep wheels in constant contact with the road. Result is safe handling and ride control; longer tire life. So shock absorbers (or shocks) are important.

HOW TO CHECK FOR BAD SHOCKS

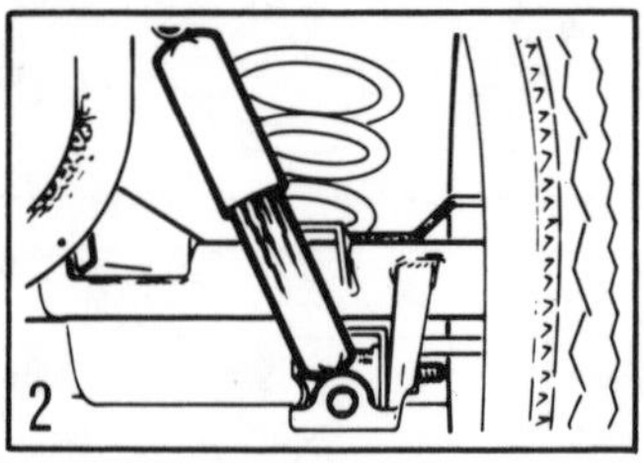

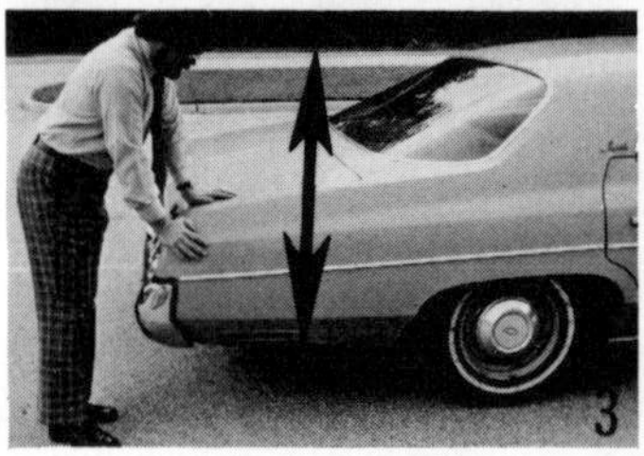

1. Check under car and locate shock absorber near each wheel.

2. Heavy oil streaks on outer shock housing indicate need for replacement.

3. Stand at front of car and apply body weight in a pumping action to front bumper or fender. Release pressure and allow car to stop rocking. Car should not bounce more than one more time after releasing pressure. Repeat at rear. If bouncing continues more than once, replacement is needed. Replace shocks in pairs (front pair or rear pair).

TOW HITCH INFORMATION

If your car is used for trailer towing you should check:
A. Cooling System; be sure radiator is at proper level in radiator. See Cooling System Section for checks to perform.
B. Check Transmission Fluid; keep topped up to proper level.
C. Check Rear Shock Absorbers; you may benefit from installation of new rear shocks.
D. Check Tire Pressures; best traction and handling can be ensured if tire pressures are properly maintained.
For safer and more trouble-free trailer towing, consider:
A. Automatic Transmission Cooler; helps remove excess heat from automatic transmission fluid built up during towing mileage. Also helps avoid radiator overheating. Some units can be self-installed.
B. Radiator Over-Flow Tank Kit; addition of a reservoir to catch radiator coolant overflow preventing coolant loss. Easy to install, these units help a tow car run cooler, avoid overheating due to coolant loss.
C. Heavy-Duty Shock Absorbers or Air Shocks; important to have on rear wheels if you intend to do a lot of towing or load carrying within the car itself. Don't forget to consider replacing factory shocks, when they are worn out, with heavy-duty units at the front as well.
D. Variable Load Flasher; this unit will accommodate the added load of trailer turn signal lamps on trailer when these are hooked into your car's electrical system.

FRONT END ALIGNMENT

When steering, handling and/or tire wear indicate front end alignment may be needed, this work can only be done at an automotive service shop. DO NOT PUT OFF NEEDED FRONT END ALIGNMENT. At the same time, have ball joints and steering linkage checked.

Ignition System

TUNE-UP SERVICES (Conventional and High Energy Ignition)

The conventional ignition system consists of spark plugs; plug wires; distributor; rotor; points; condenser; coil. These units work to create a good hot spark inside the engine (ignition) at exactly the right moment (timing). If ignition is weak or timing is off, engine may be hard to start, run poorly, waste gas, lose power, backfire or not run at all.

TOOLS & MATERIALS . . . Parts: set of points; condenser; 6 or 8 spark plugs. Tools: feeler gauge; 13/16 in. (1970) or 5/8 in. (1971-77) spark plug socket; open end box or combination wrenches; timing equipment.
SAFETY TIP . . . Change only one spark plug at a time to avoid cross-wiring and possible engine damage.
Inspect spark plug wires. If cracked or brittle, entire set should be replaced. Also, center high tension wire. Inspect distributor cap. Wipe inside clean occasionally with dry, lint-free rag. If cap is cracked or rotor contacts are excessively burned, replace cap.
Conventional Ignition–Every 6,000 miles
HEI System—Every 22,500 miles

SPARK PLUG REPLACEMENT

1. Remove spark plug wire by grasping rubber boot. Do not jerk wire off. If stuck, turn boot, pulling gently.

2. Loosen spark plug using socket wrench.

3. Wipe or brush loose dirt from around plug before removing. Do not let dirt drop into engine through plug hole. Unscrew plug.

4. Check plug electrode gap on new spark plug. Adjust to specifications. Plug gap is correct when the gauge drags slightly as it is pulled between plug electrodes.

5. Thread new plug into plug hole by hand. Hand tighten. Do not force or cross thread. Use socket wrench to tighten firmly but do not force. Replace plug wire. Press boot firmly.

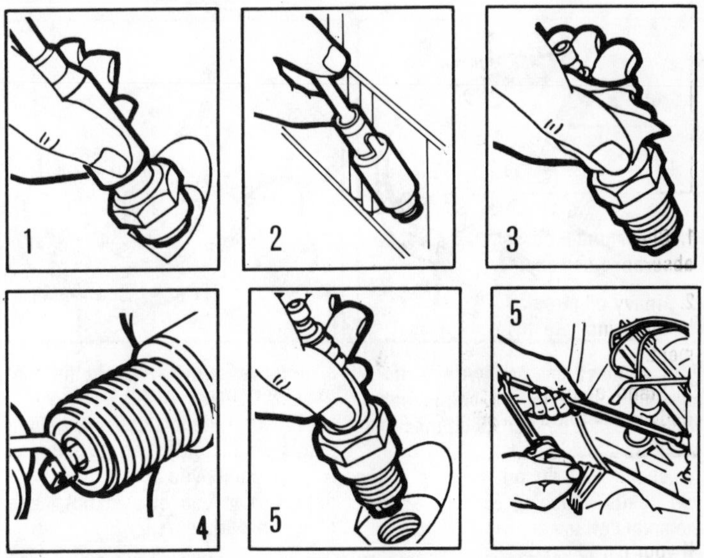

LOCATION OF POINTS AND CONDENSER—1970-74 V8

Points and condenser are located under the distributor cap. Always replace condenser also when installing new points.

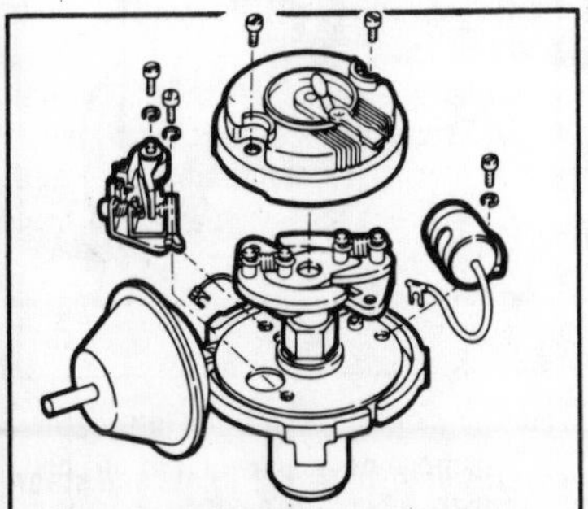

Location inside distributor.

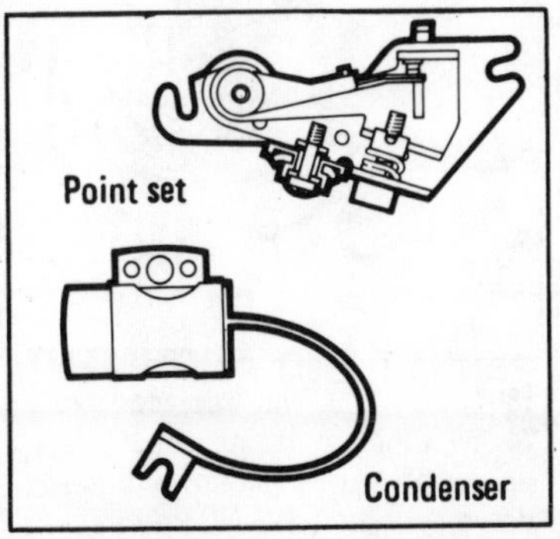

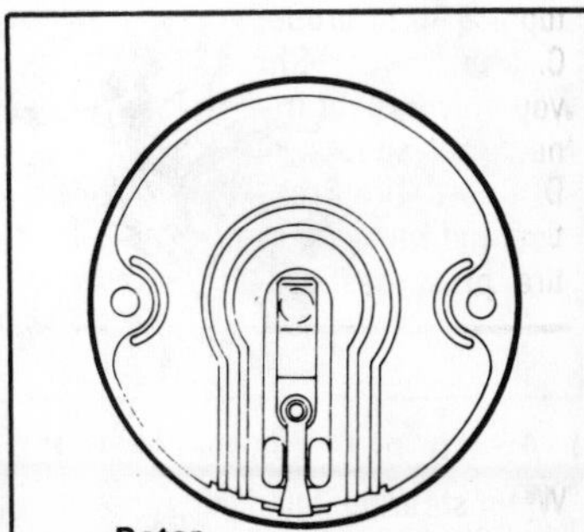

Rotor

CHECKING POINTS, AND ROTOR-V8

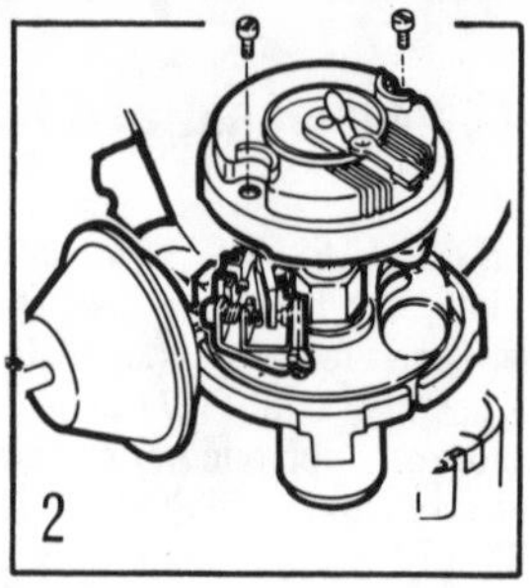

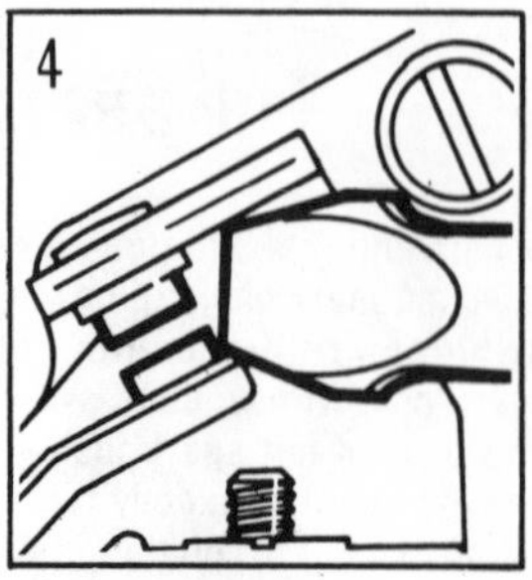

1. To open the distributor, depress the screw in the cap and rotate the latch off the distributor (there are two latches). Remove the coil wire and lift off the cap. Keep the other wires attached.
2. Remove the two screws and lift off the rotor. If it is cracked or metallic tip is badly burned, replace it.
3. Check the metal contacts inside the cap. Replace the cap if they are corroded or there are any cracks.
4. Pry the points apart with a screwdriver. If worn or burned, replace. If OK, check the gap.

REMOVING POINTS—1970-74 V8

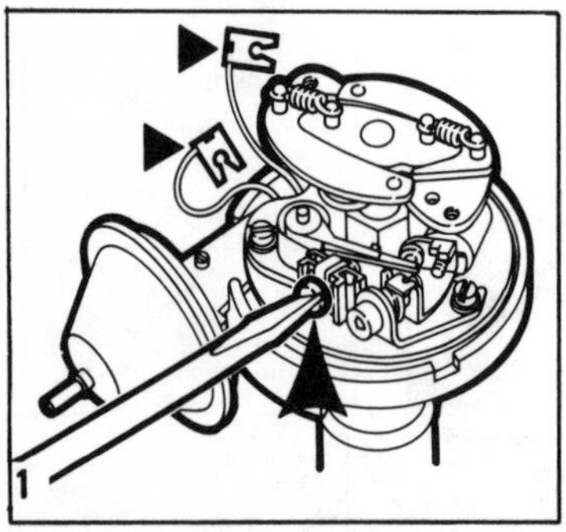

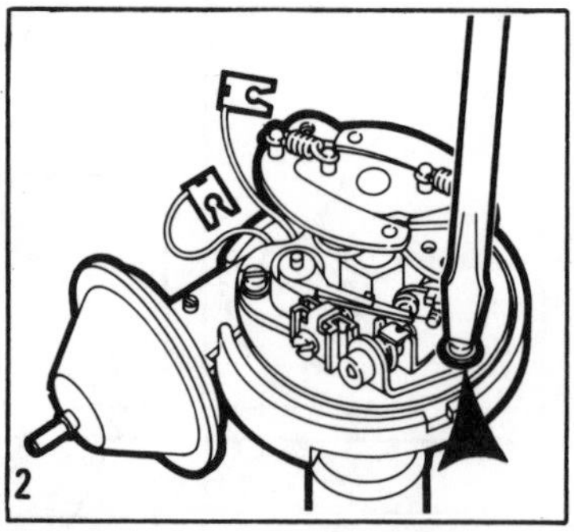

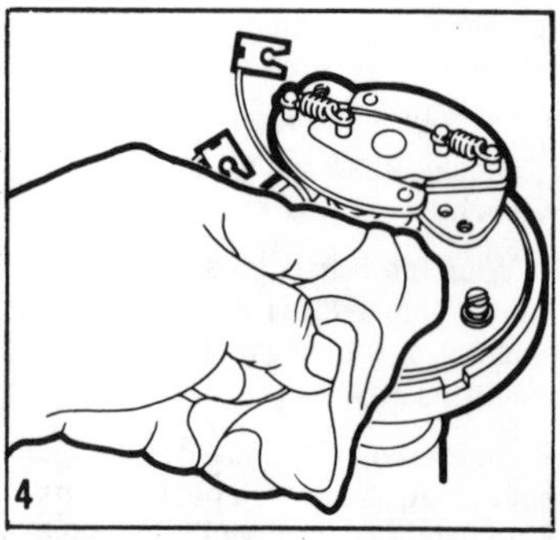

1. Disconnect the two wire terminals connected to the points set. Notice that the condenser connector is on the outside.
2. Loosen, but do not remove the two points attaching screws. Slide the points off the screws to remove.
3. Remove screw which holds condenser. DO NOT DROP SCREW.
NOTE: Later models use a combined points and condenser. When you remove points you also remove condenser. You can also install these points in early cars.
4. Wipe all dirt from distributor plate and cam with clean, lint-free rag.
CAUTION: When removing screws from distributor, be sure to avoid any screws accidentally falling through distributor opening into engine. Use magnetic screwdriver.

INSTALLING POINTS AND CONDENSER—1970-74 V8

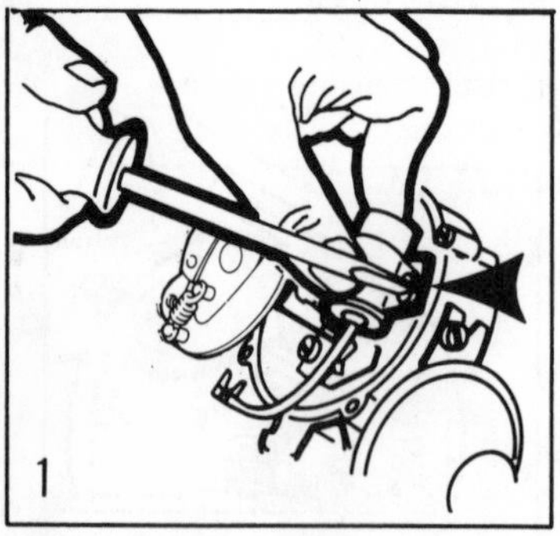

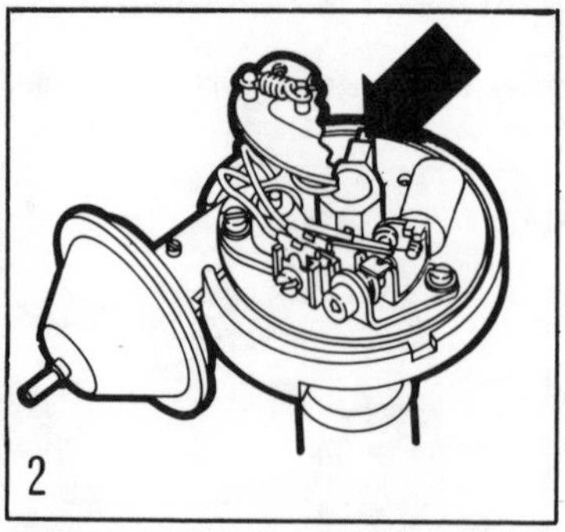

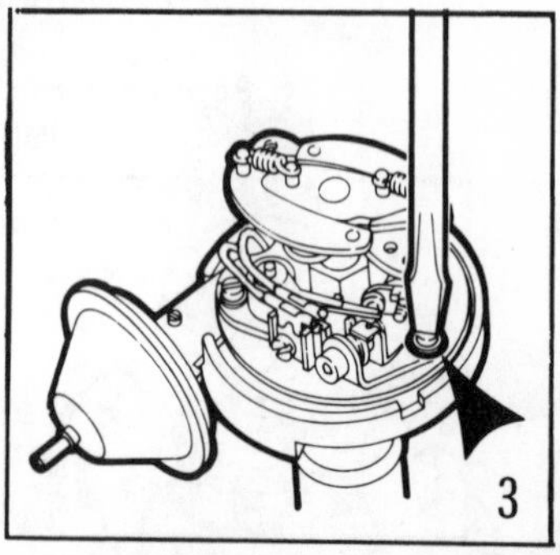

1. Attach new condenser with screw.
2. Rotate or replace cam lubricator. Fiber cam lubricator must be turned 180° every 12,000 mi., replaced every 24,000. When replacing, simply pull it up and off stud; push new lubricator down over stud. DO NOT attempt to add oil or grease to fiber lubricator.
3. Position new points set in distributor by sliding onto screws. Tighten screws.

RESETTING THE CONTACT GAP—1970-74 V8

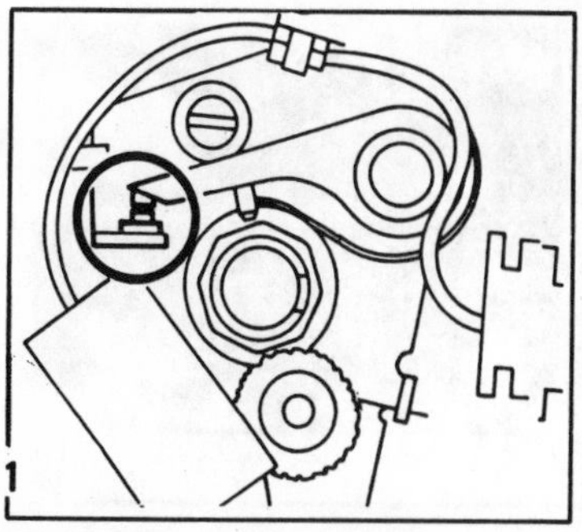

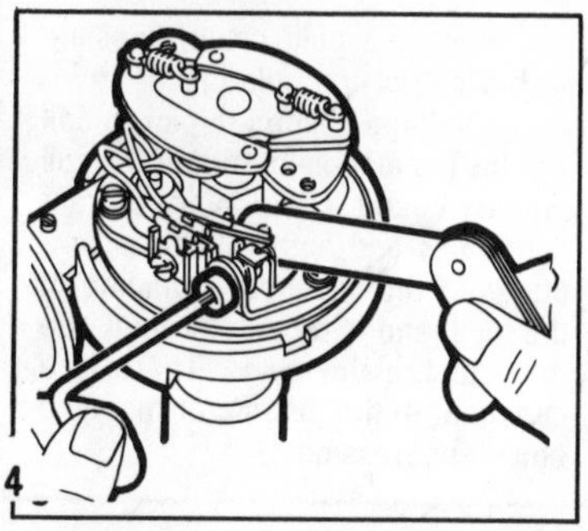

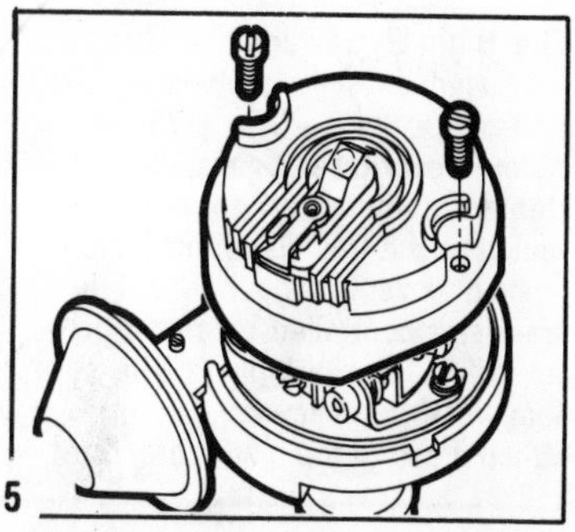

1. Check that point contacts meet squarely. If they do not, bend bracket supporting fixed contact using needle-nosed pliers.

2. Turn engine by ignition key (you'll need a helper) until rubbing block on point set is on one of the high spots of distributor cam. You may use wrench on lower engine pulley to do this.

3. Insert a 1/8 in. allen wrench into points adjusting screw. Correct gap is .019 in. for new points; .016 in. for used points.

4. Insert correct size feeler gauge. Adjust gap with wrench until feeler gauge can be moved in and out between contacts with only slight drag.

5. Install rotor on advance weight assembly. The two lugs on the bottom of the rotor are shaped differently, so it can only be installed one way. Tighten screws.

6. Install cap by depressing screws and turning latches onto body of distributor. Insert the coil wire into the cap.

7. On V8 models, point gap can be adjusted with the engine running. Insert the allen wrench through the cap window, slowly turn the adjusting screw clockwise until the engine just starts to misfire, and then turn it back 1/2 turn.

LOCATION OF POINTS AND CONDENSER—Six Cylinder

Points and condenser work together. Always replace condenser also when installing new points.

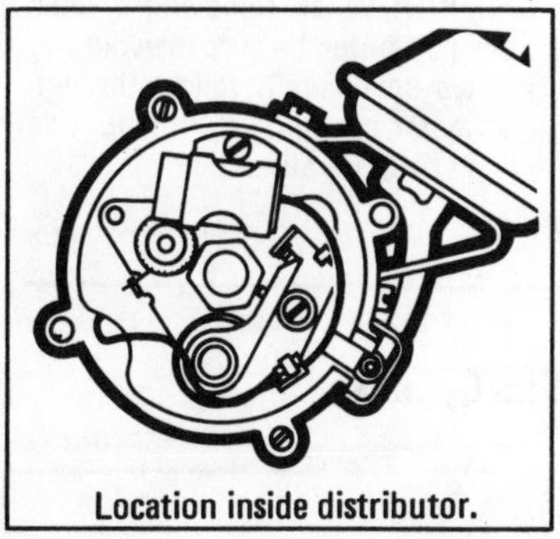
Location inside distributor.

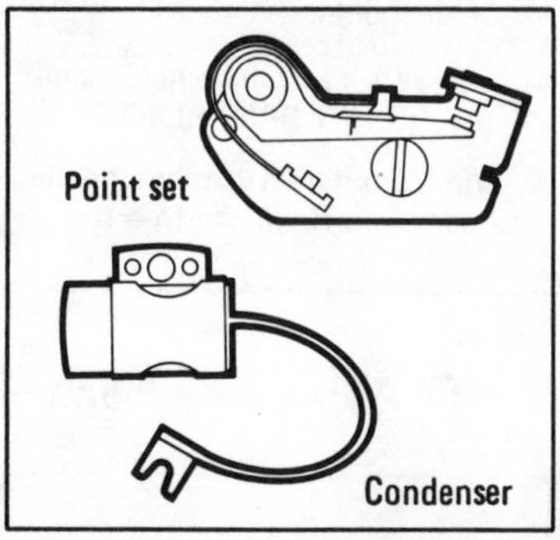

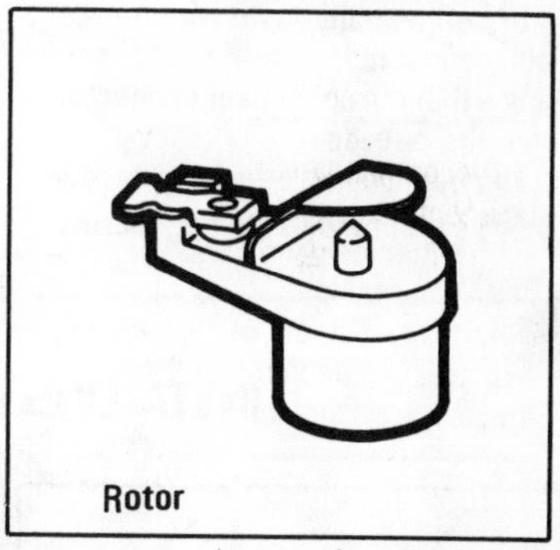

CHECKING POINTS, AND ROTOR—Six Cylinder

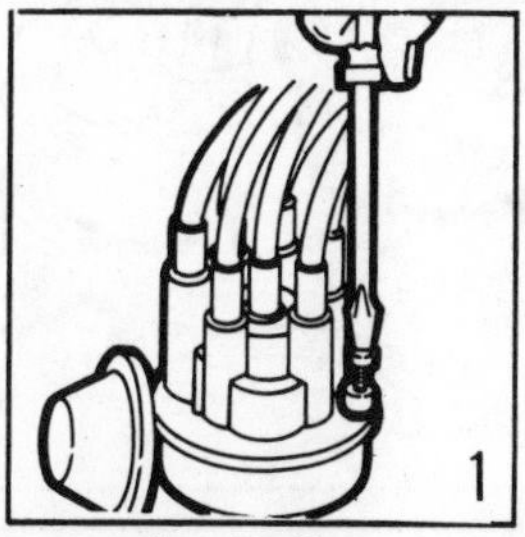

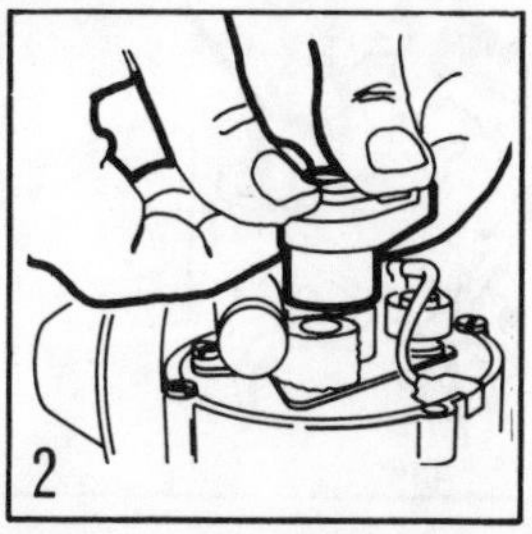

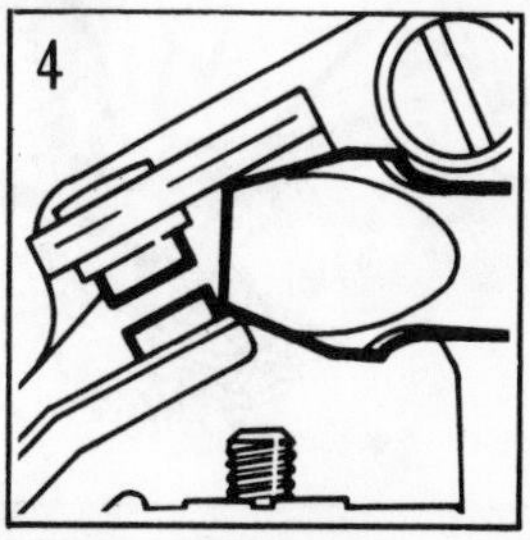

1. To open the distributor, remove the two screws retaining the cap. Remove the coil wire and lift the cap off, but keep the other wires attached.

2. Pull the rotor off (straight up). If it is cracked or metallic tip is badly burned, replace it.

3. Check the metal contacts inside the cap. Replace the cap if they are corroded or there are any cracks.

4. Pry the points apart with a screwdriver. If worn or burned, replace. If OK, check the gap.

HIGH ENERGY IGNITION (HEI) SYSTEM

The High Energy Ignition System, first used on some models in 1974 and made standard in 1975, eliminates the breaker points and condenser completely. Instead this maintenance-free electronic ignition system uses a trigger wheel and transistor controlled magnetic pick-up to fire the spark plugs. The system works as follows:
When a cog of the timer core, rotating inside the pole piece, lines up with a cog of the pole piece, an induced voltage inside the pickup coil signals the module to trigger the coil primary circuit. The primary current decreases and high voltage is produced in the secondary winding of the coil and directed through the rotor to fire the plugs. There is a capacitor in the distributor for radio noise suppression.

REMOVING POINTS—Six Cylinder

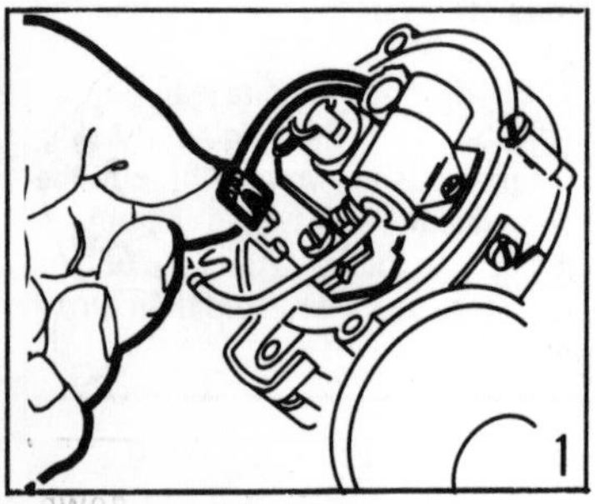

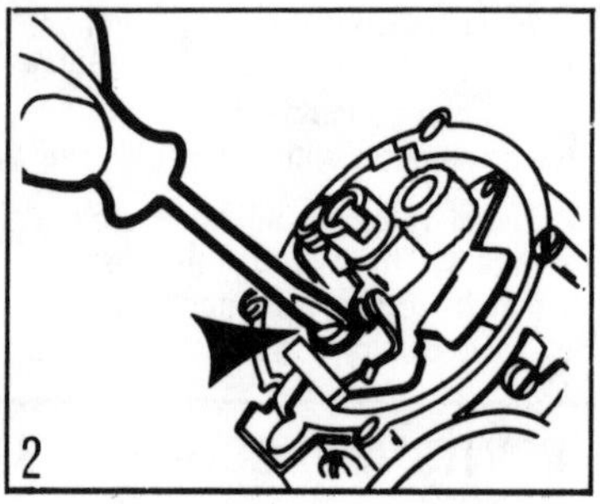

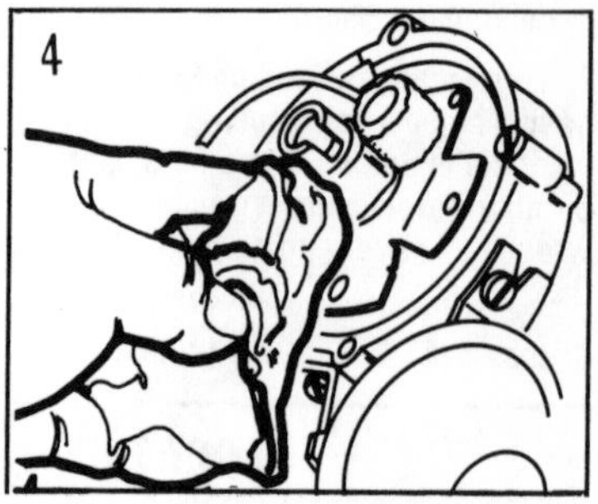

1. Disconnect the two wire terminals connected to the points set. Notice that the condenser connector is on the outside.
2. Remove points attaching screw being very careful not to drop screw inside distributor.
3. Remove screw which holds condenser. DO NOT DROP SCREW.
4. Wipe all dirt from distributor plate and cam with clean, lint-free rag.

CAUTION: When removing screws from distributor, be sure to avoid any screws accidentally falling through distributor opening into engine. Use magnetic screwdriver.

INSTALLING POINTS AND CONDENSER—Six Cylinder

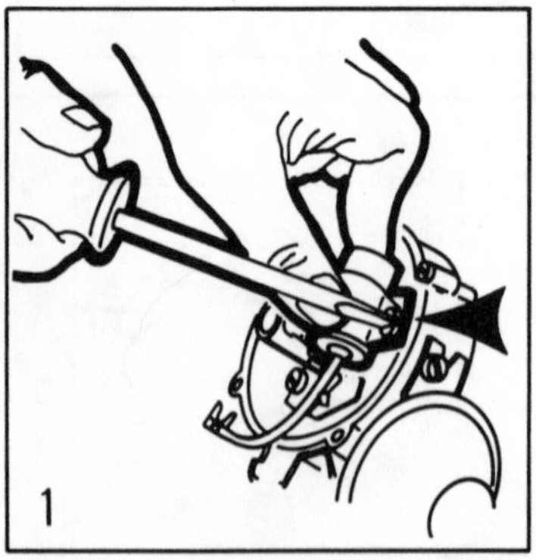

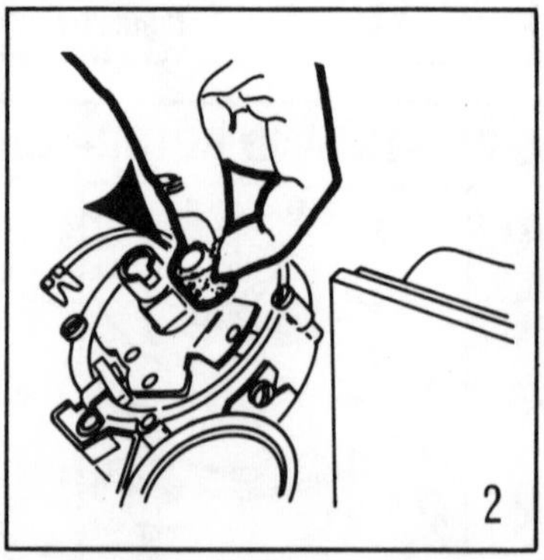

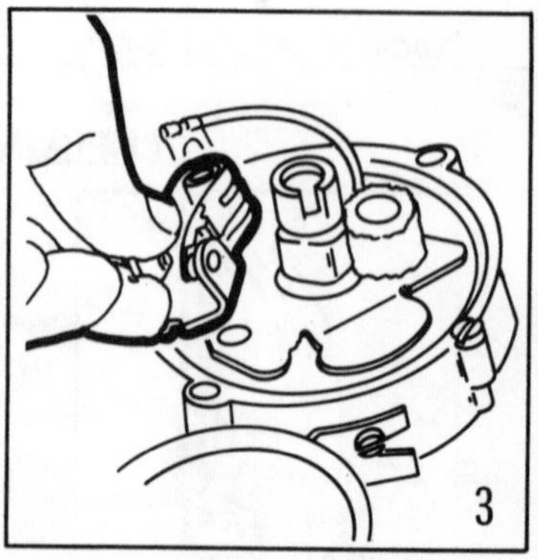

1. Attach new condenser with screw.
2. Rotate or replace cam lubricator. Fiber cam lubricator must be turned 180° every 12,000 mi., replaced every 24,000. When replacing, simply pull it up and off stud; push new lubricator down over stud. DO NOT attempt to add oil or grease to fiber lubricator.
3. Position new points set in distributor. Attach retaining screw lightly. Replace both wire terminals. The condenser wire goes on the outside of the two.

CONNECTING A TACHOMETER TO THE HEI SYSTEM

This system may not be compatible with all tachometers, so check the instruction sheet for the tachometer before attempting to hook it up to a car with electronic ignition. There is a terminal on the distributor which is marked TACH; connect a tachometer from this terminal to a suitable ground. Some tachometers may connect from this terminal to the battery positive terminal.

CAUTION: Never ground the TACH terminal; serious system damage will result. If there is any doubt as to the correct tachometer hookup, check with the tachometer manufacturer.

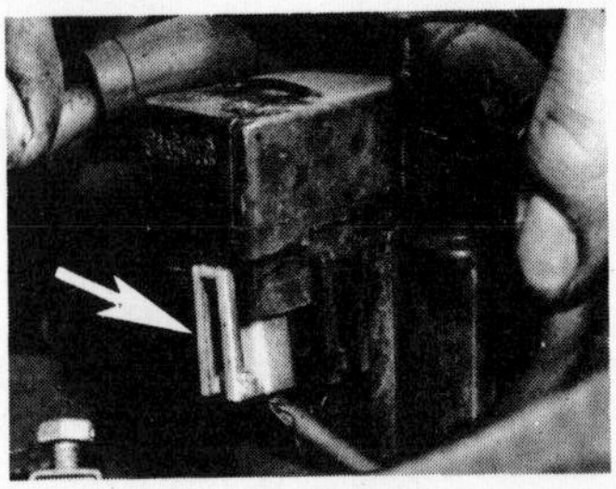

RESETTING THE CONTACT GAP—Six Cylinder

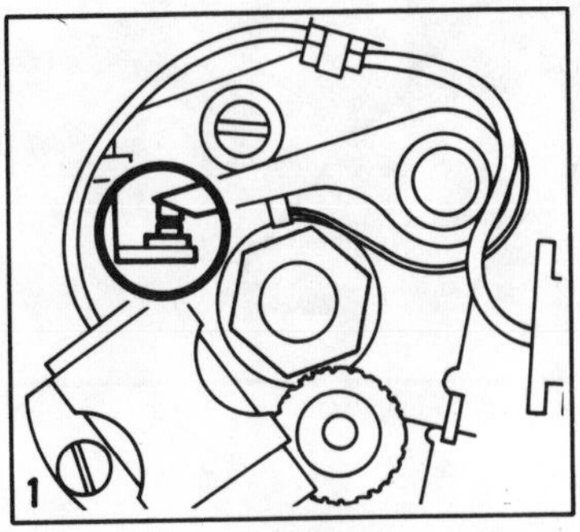

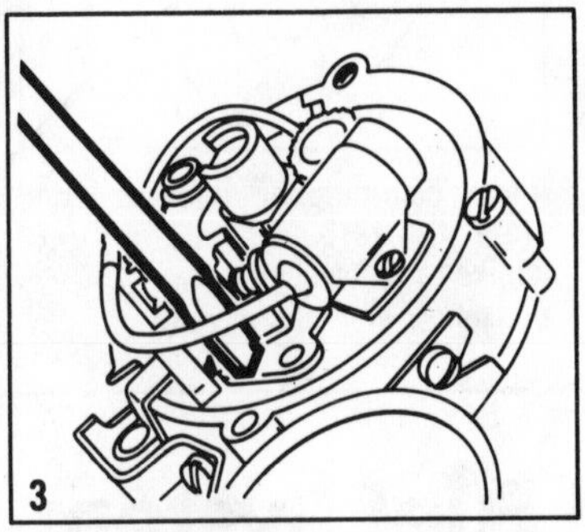

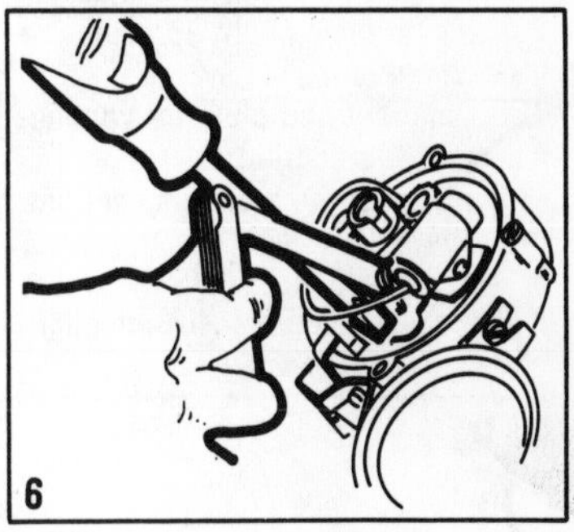

1. Check that point contacts meet squarely. If they do not, bend bracket supporting fixed contact using needle-nosed pliers.
2. Turn engine by ignition key (you'll need a helper) until rubbing block on point set is on one of the six high spots of distributor cam. You may use wrench on lower engine pulley to do this.
3. Insert screwdriver in slot near point contacts; twist to open or close gap.
4. Correct gap is .019 in. for new points; .016 in. for used points.
5. Insert correct size feeler gauge. Adjust gap with screwdriver until feeler gauge can be moved in and out between contacts with only slight drag.
6. Tighten point set hold-down screw. Recheck gap; it might have changed from tightening hold-down screw. Re-adjust if needed.
7. Align tab inside rotor with notch on distributor shaft and push rotor onto shaft. Rotor must be fully seated on shaft.
8. Replace distributor cap; install screws.

REPLACING SPARK PLUG WIRES

Use the firing order illustration to guide you when replacing your ignition wires and/or distributor cap.

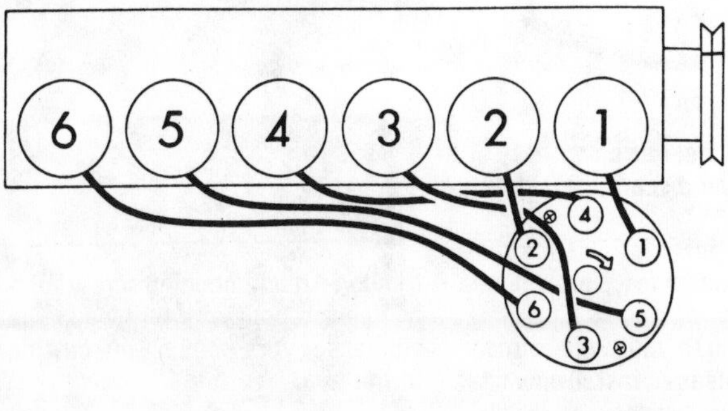

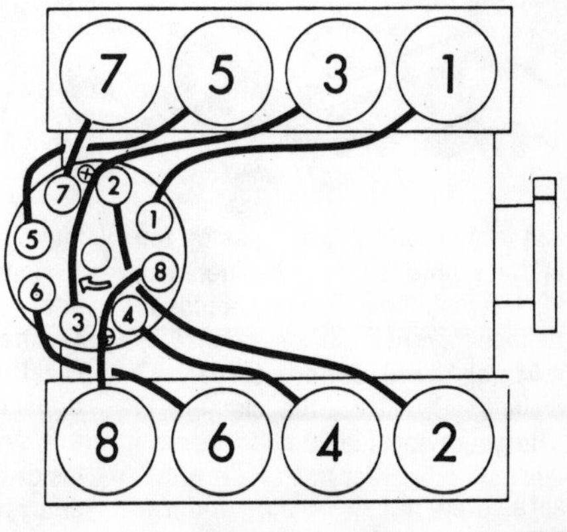

IGNITION TIMING

NOTE: Periodic adjustment of ignition timing not necessary on cars equipped with High Energy Ignition (HEI)

Adjusting timing is the important finishing touch to any tune-up. While not difficult, job requires timing light and dwell meter. Timing is listed on tune-up decal.

1. Locate timing marks and pointer (notches) on engine and lower engine pulley. Clean away dirt. Mark the pointer notches with chalk.
2. Hook up timing light according to instructions supplied with it.
3. Disconnect and plug the vacuum line from the distributor.
4. Disconnect the fuel tank vent line from the evaporative canister.
5. Aim timing light at pulley mark(s). If the chalked marks do not align, loosen distributor hold-down nut and slowly rotate distributor until chalked marks align.
6. Tighten hold-down nut.

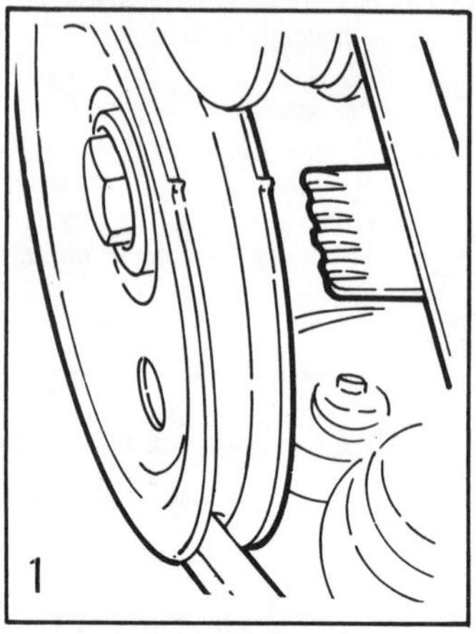

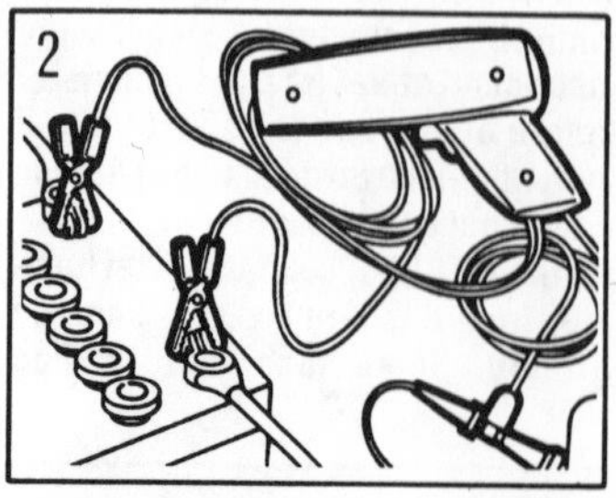

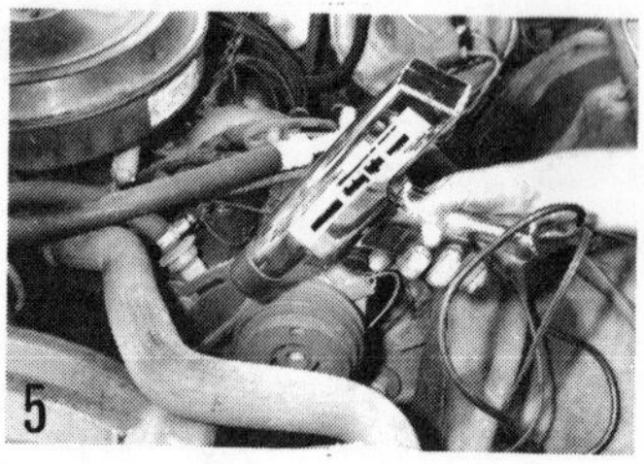

Fuel System

When gasoline is brought from the fuel tank, it mixes with air in the carburetor. This gas/air mixture then enters engine thru the intake manifold, passes thru the intake valves and is burned in the combustion chamber. The burned exhaust gas is then passed thru the exhaust valves to the exhaust system and to the outside air. In order to keep your car's engine running cleanly with minimal pollution, and avoid dangerous carbon monoxide fumes inside the vehicle, certain items should be checked from time to time.

KEEP THE AIR INTAKE CLEAN

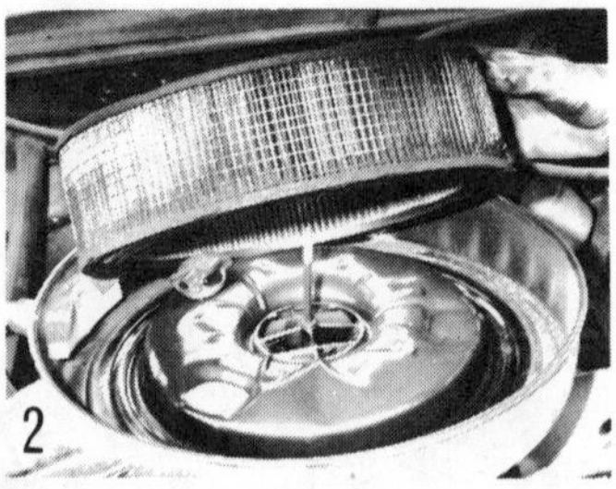

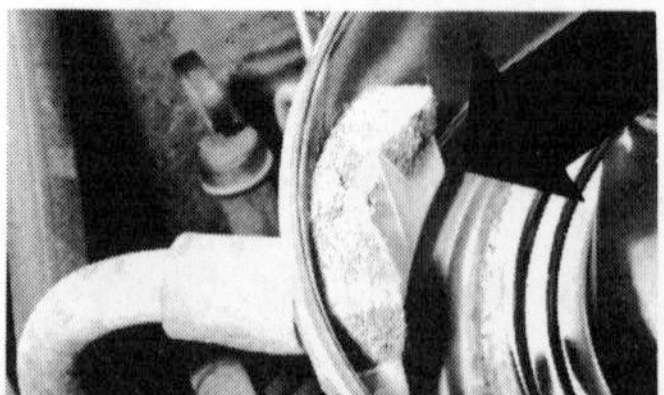

The large round can that sits on top of the engine is the air cleaner. The V8 filter element inside should be replaced every 24,000 miles (1970-74 models) or 30,000 miles (1975-77 models). On Sixes, the element is changed every 12,000 miles.

1. Unscrew the wing nut and remove the air cleaner cover.
2. Remove and discard the old dirty filter.
3. Check the small crankcase breather filter. If dirty, lift out and replace it.
4. Using a clean rag, wipe out the inside of air cleaner. Install new filter and replace top cover.

EMISSION CONTROLS SYSTEMS

An important part of a car's emission control system is the Positive Crankcase Ventilation (PCV) valve and its connecting hose. The PCV valve should be replaced once every 24,000 miles (1970-74 models) or 30,000 miles (1975-77 models). This device keeps dirt and sludge from forming inside the engine. Make sure all PCV connections are tight. Check that the connecting hoses are clear and not clogged. Replace any brittle or broken hoses.

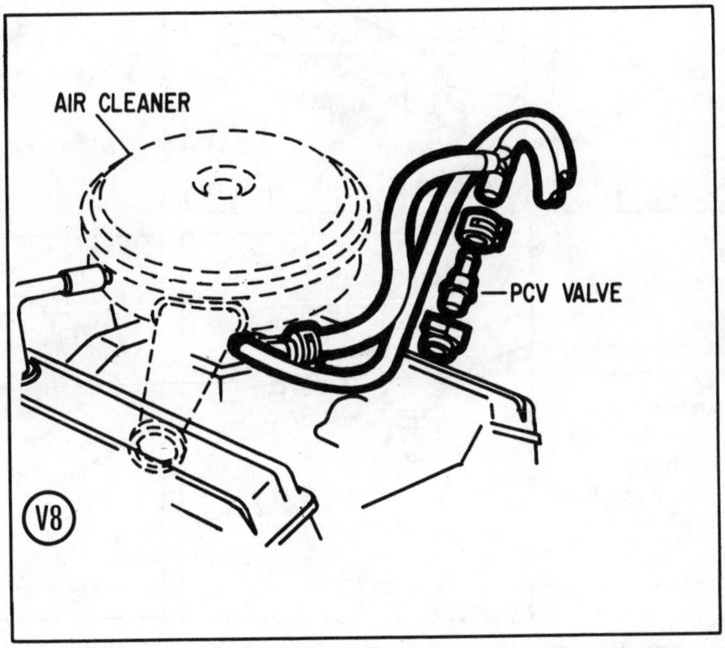

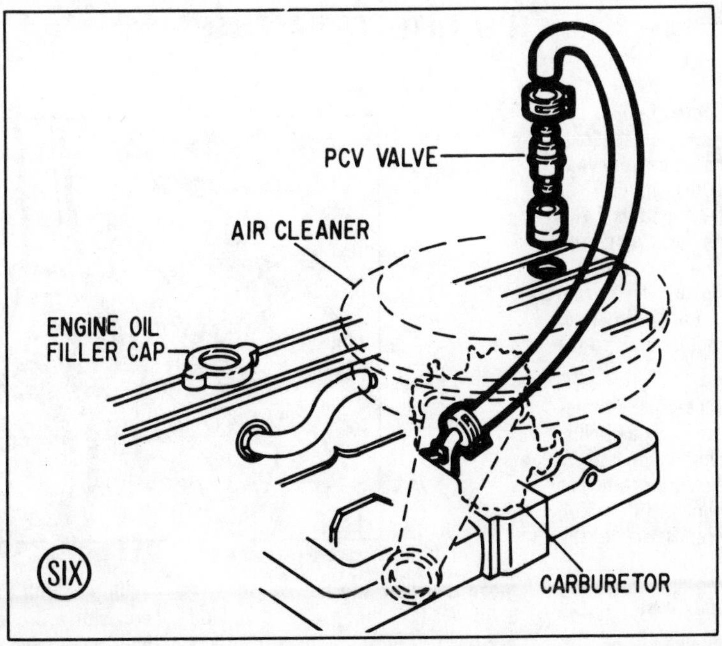

PCV VALVE REPLACEMENT

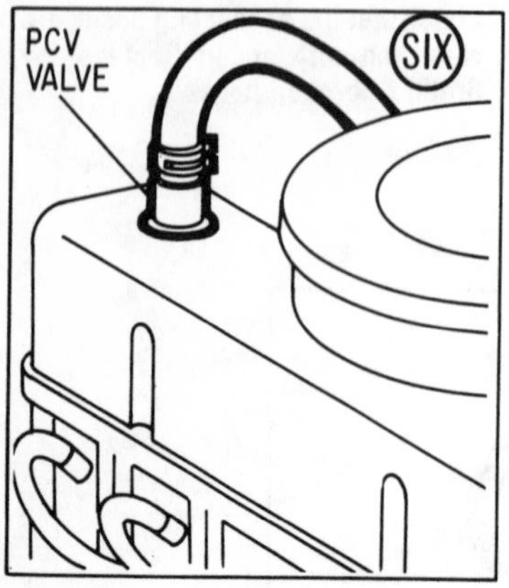

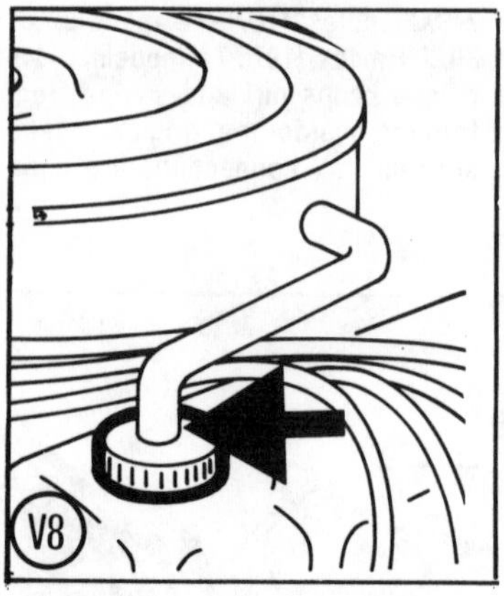

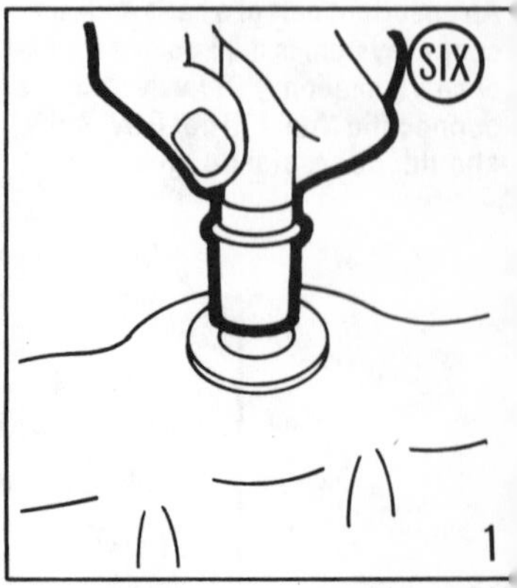

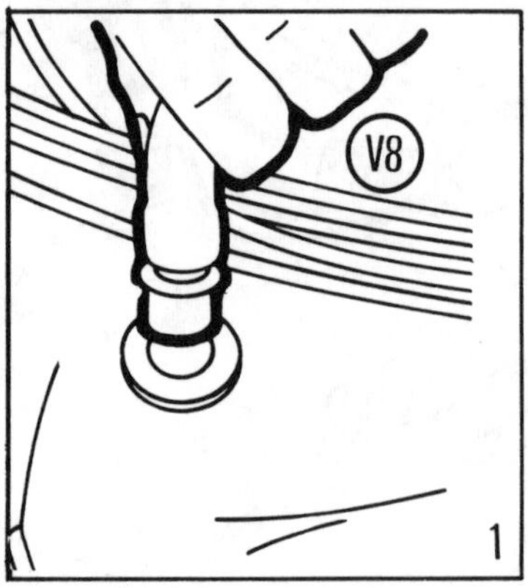

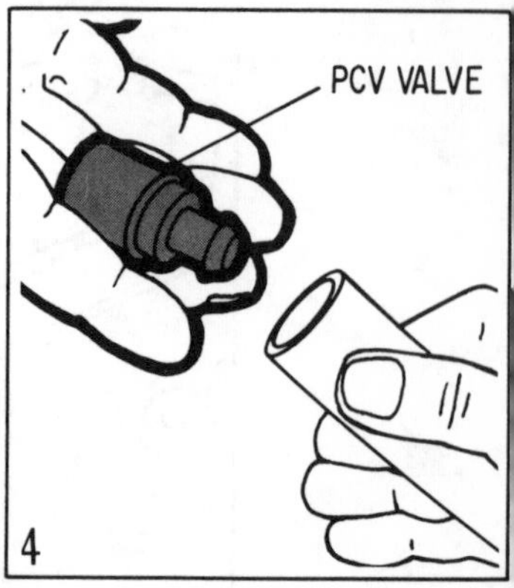

1. Pull valve from its location in left front of valve cover.
2. Squeeze the hose clamp with a pair of pliers. Remove the valve.
3. Note where the other end of the hose connects. Remove the hose and flush it with cleaning solvent.
4. Reconnect the hose. Pinch the clamp and insert the PCV valve into the hose.
5. Insert the valve into the valve cover.

FUEL FILTER REPLACEMENT

The fuel filter is located behind the large fuel line inlet nut on the carburetor. Replace the filter every year or 12,000 miles (1970-74 models) or 15,000 miles (1975-77 models). The fuel filter prevents dirt, rust, and scale from both the gas station's tank and your own fuel tank from reaching the carburetor. A dirty filter will starve the engine and cause poor running.

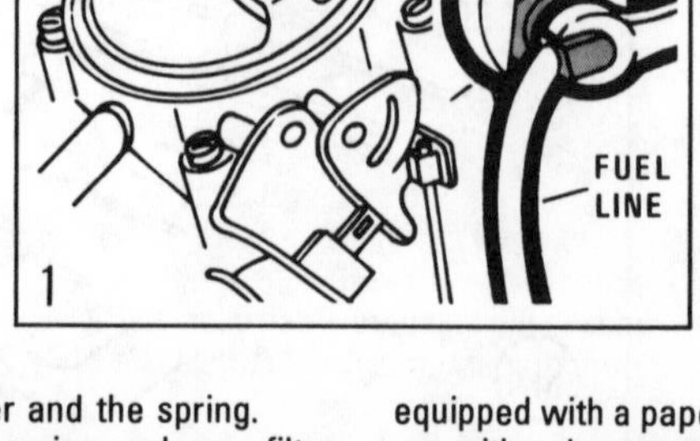

1. Place an absorbent rag under fuel line connection to absorb gas spills. Unscrew fuel line connection with ½ in. wrench while holding the larger nut with a 1 in. wrench. Be careful, fuel line fitting threads are easily stripped.
2. Remove the large filter retaining nut from the carburetor. The spring behind the filter will push it out. Remove the filter and the spring.
3. Install the spring and new filter element. Some carburetors are equipped with a paper element, others with a bronze unit. The bronze filter must have the small cone sec-

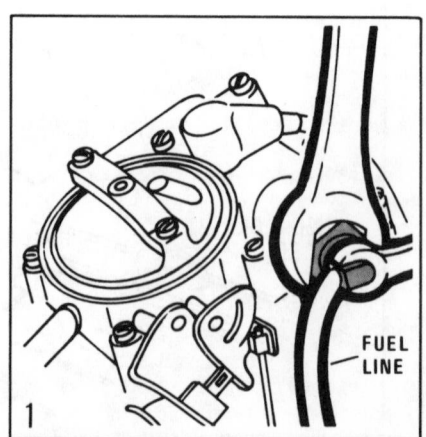

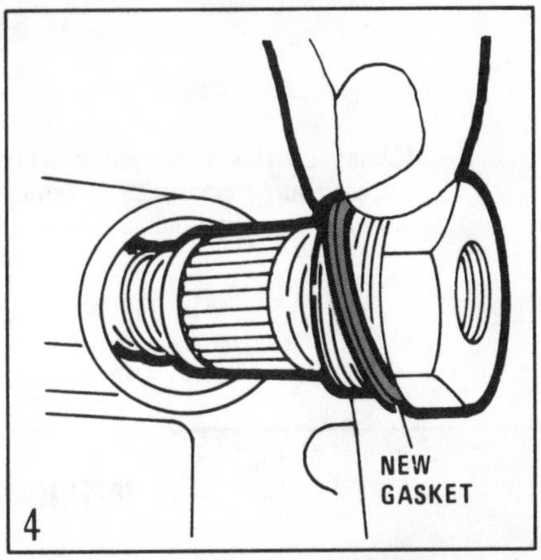

tion facing out and a gasket between the filter and the retaining nut.
4. Install the new gasket on the retaining nut and screw it into place.

CAUTION: DO NOT OVERTIGHTEN
5. Reconnect the fuel line. Discard the gas soaked rag safely.
6. Start the engine and check for leaks. Addition of a can of carburetor cleaner to the fuel tank occasionally will aid in keeping the entire fuel system clean.

Safety Systems

PARKING LIGHTS, TURN SIGNALS AND STOP LIGHTS

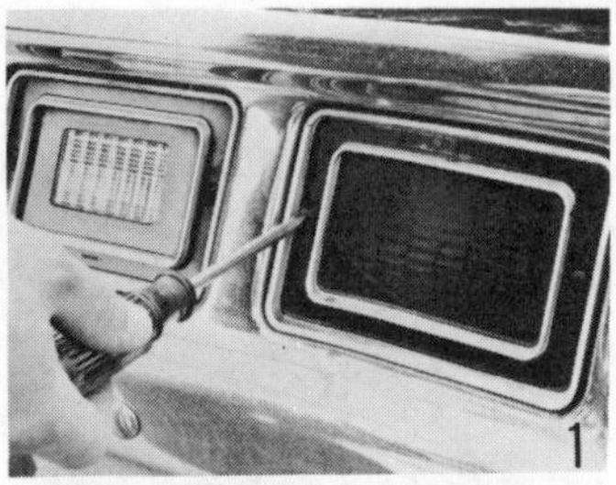

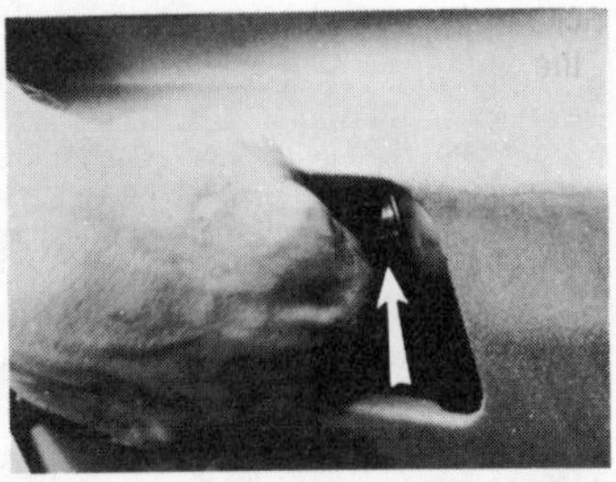

Headlights, turn signals, stop lights, and parking lights are an important part of your car's safety system. They permit you to see and be seen. Keep all lenses clean and make frequent checks to be sure that all of your lights are functioning properly. Replace any cracked lenses as soon as possible. When replacing a bulb, make a note of the number which is usually printed on the base. If you don't have a number, take the old bulb with you so that you match it for the correct replacement.
To replace a turn signal, stop light, or back-up light bulb, remove the lens, push down on bulb while turning it counterclockwise to remove it from the socket. Install the new bulb in reverse order. Be sure to match the knobs on the bulb base with the slots in the socket.

LICENSE PLATE LIGHTS

Remove the screws that retain the lens to the bumpers. Push in on bulb, turning counterclockwise to remove.

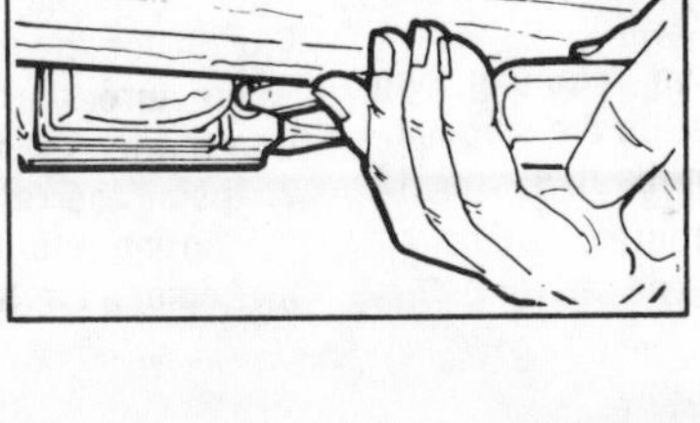

SIDE MARKER LIGHT

Reach up inside fender and turn bulb socket counterclockwise to remove from housing. Pull bulb straight out.

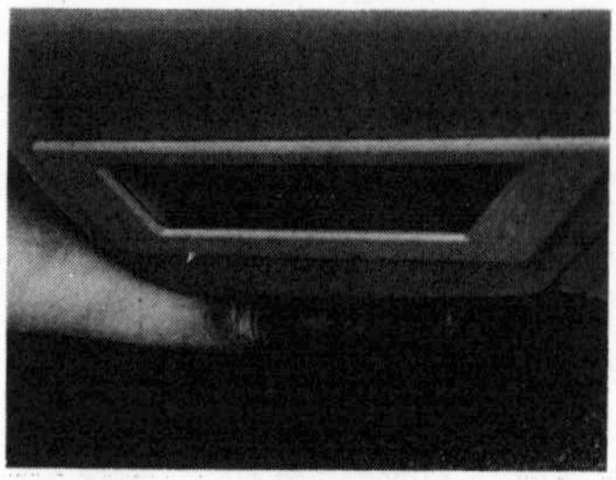

INTERIOR DOME LIGHT

This is cartridge type bulb; be sure to purchase correct replacement. Pry dome light lens out from housing. To avoid blowing fuse, make sure doors are closed and domelight switch is in OFF position. Carefully lever the bulb straight out of housing. Insert new bulb and re-install dome light lens.

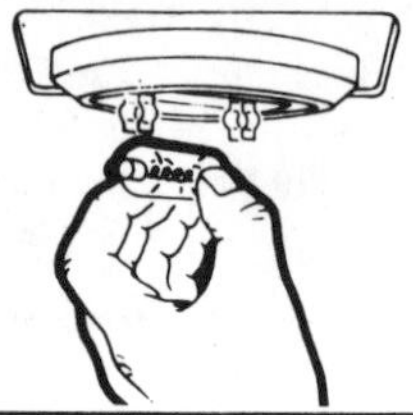

HEADLIGHT REPLACEMENT

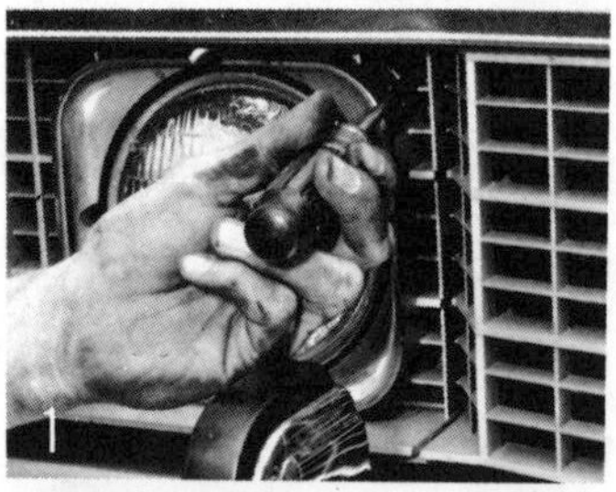

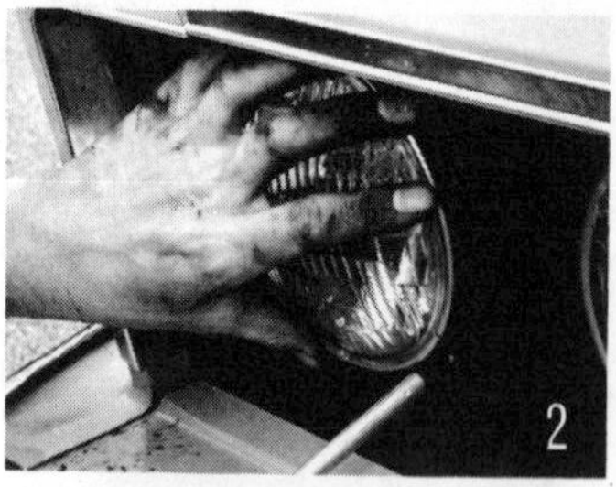

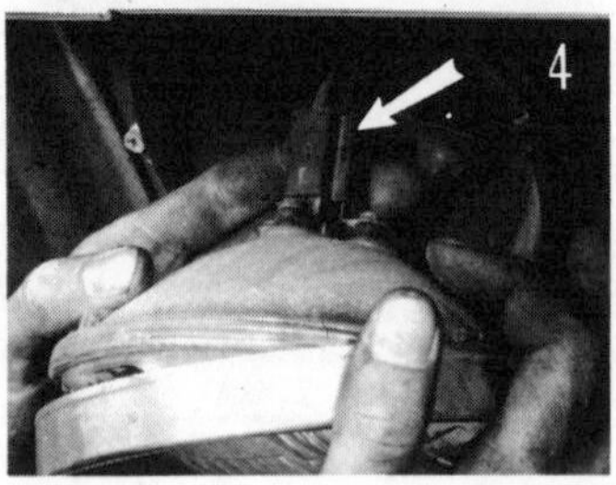

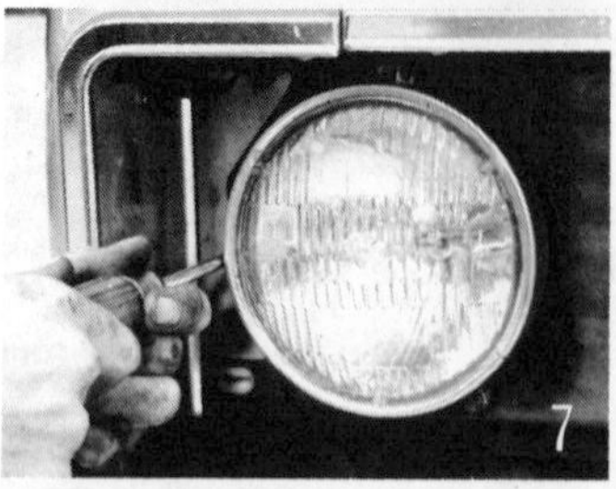

1. Remove the headlight trim retaining screws and remove the trim.

2. Unhook the spring from the headlight retaining ring.

3. Remove the two retaining ring screws. Do not disturb the long aiming screws located at 9 and 12 o'clock.

4. Remove the retaining ring. Disconnect the wiring plug and remove the bulb.

5. Attach the connector plug to the new headlight.

6. Position the new bulb in housing. Make sure that the number molded into the lens is at the top.

7. Install the retaining ring and pull the spring into place.

8. Replace the headlight trim panel.

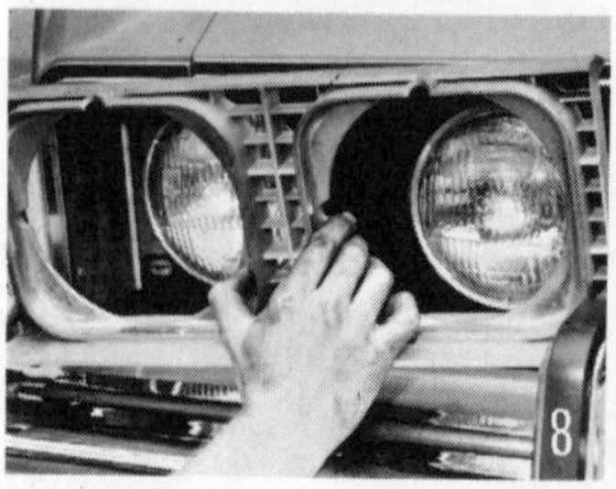

HEADLIGHT REPLACEMENT—RECTANGULAR LIGHTS

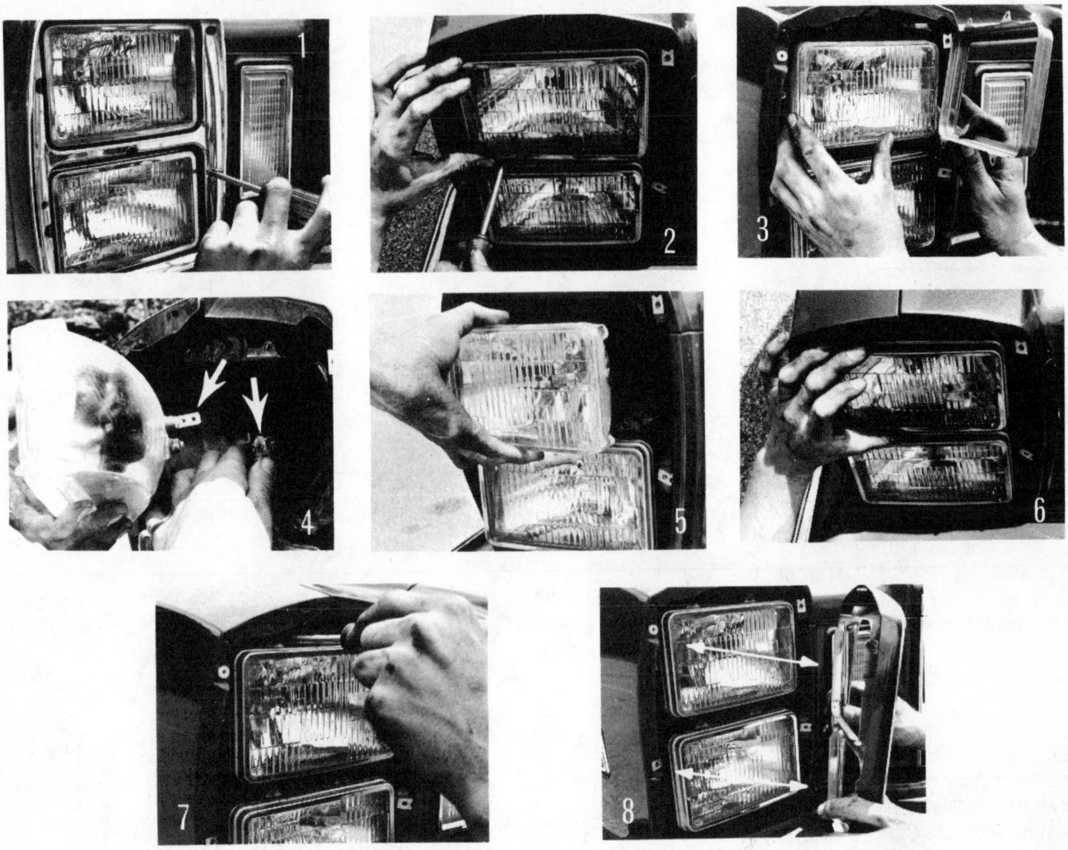

WINDSHIELD WIPER BLADE REPLACEMENT

To replace wiper blade, lift up on spring release tab on wiper arm connector. Pull wiper blade off. Snap new blade into place.
To replace rubber insert only, press down, away from wiper blade to free it. Slide insert from blade. Insert new wiper. Bend insert upward slightly to engage retaining clips.

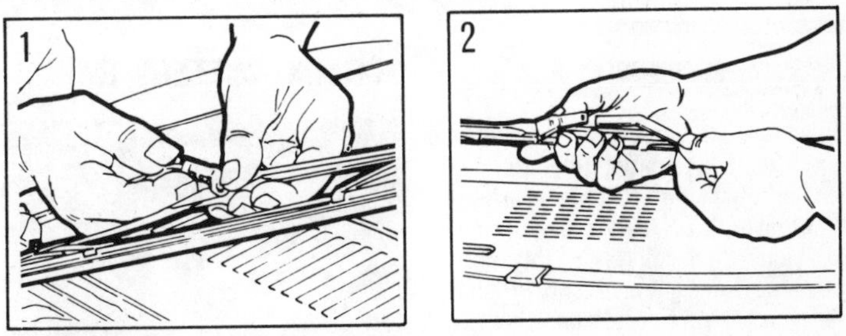

HORN PROBLEMS

If horn sounds and does not stop, this is due to short circuit in wiring. Disconnect wiring connector under hood and have professional service shop check horn wiring circuit.

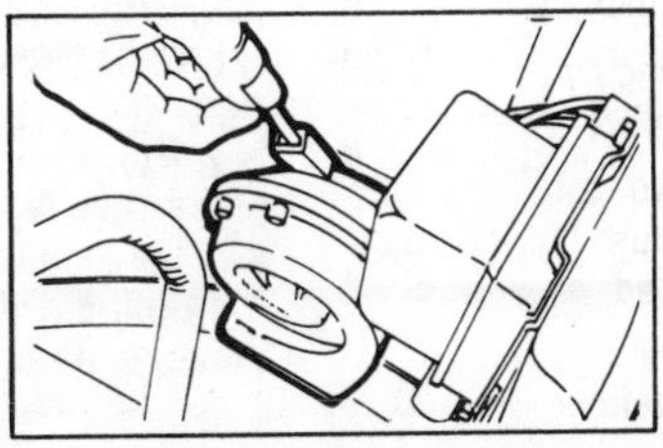

STEERING PROBLEMS

See steering system check in Suspension Section. Check tire pressures. Have a professional service shop check all components in the front end and steering system.

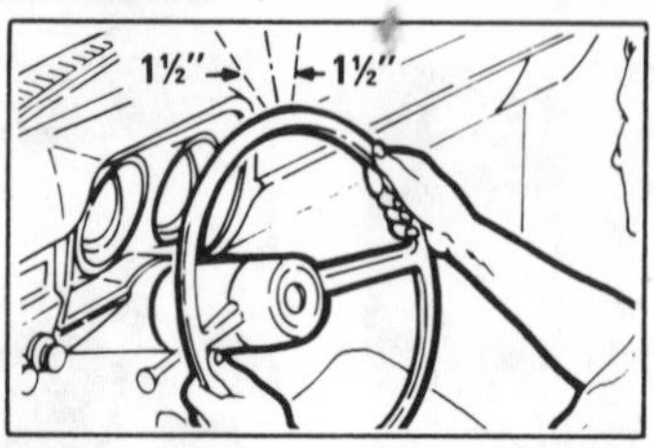

WHEEL CYLINDER CHECK

Drum brakes employ individual wheel cylinders to apply braking pressure to shoes. Check for brake fluid leaks on inside of wheel.
Disc brakes employ calipers on individual wheels. Remove wheel and inspect caliper for signs of fluid leaks. Have mechanic correct leaks.

WASHER SYSTEM

If washer fails to squirt properly, raise hood and check system hose connections. Be sure washer fluid container has fluid. Check spout openings for clogging.
Keep container filled with fluid mixture of washer solvent and water. If road spray buildup on windshield is a chronic problem, add 1 tablespoon dishwasher detergent to solvent/water mixture when re-filling container.

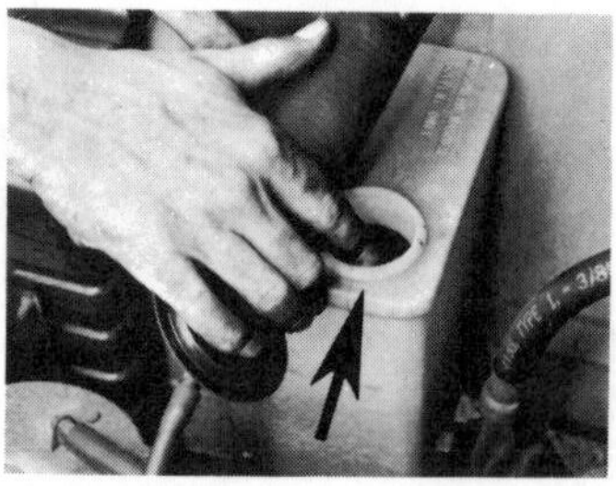

Electrical System

CHECK BATTERY FLUID

To ensure starting ability at all times check your battery condition periodically. You'll need to check battery electrolyte (fluid) level in each of the six cells. Check battery cable connections for tightness and inspect for accumulated corrosion.
SAFETY NOTE: Wear gloves when working on battery.

1. Remove plastic filler caps on top of battery. Fluid should be up to lower end of filler hole and covering the plates. If fluid is low add clean, cold tap water. If your area has hard water, use only distilled water available at auto supply, food or drug stores.
2. Replace any lost caps immediately.

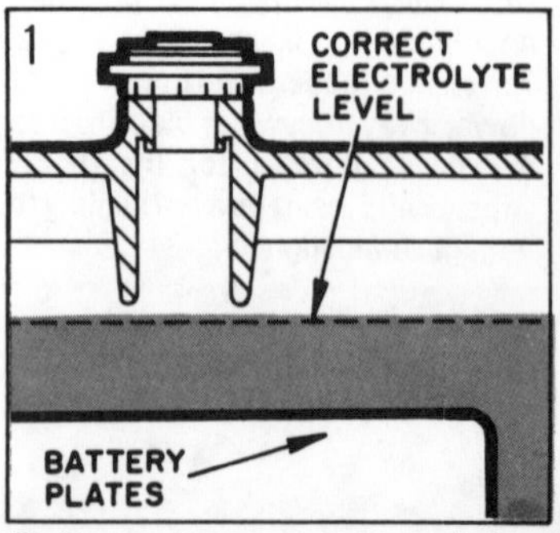

CAUTION: NEVER LIGHT A MATCH OR SMOKE near the top of a battery. Batteries give off explosive hydrogen gas.
NOTE: Battery that often checks low on fluid could mean:
A. Battery is getting old, due for replacement; have charge capacity checked at service shop.
B. Connections may be corroded or loose; clean/replace as needed (see below).
C. Alternator or voltage regulator not functioning properly; this happens far less often than A or B above.

CLEAN THOSE BATTERY TERMINALS

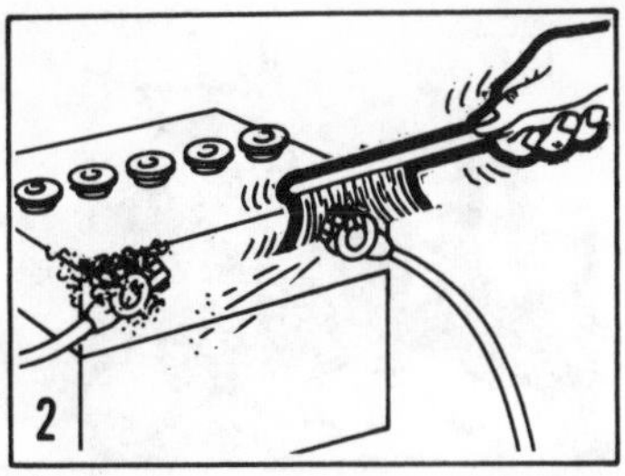

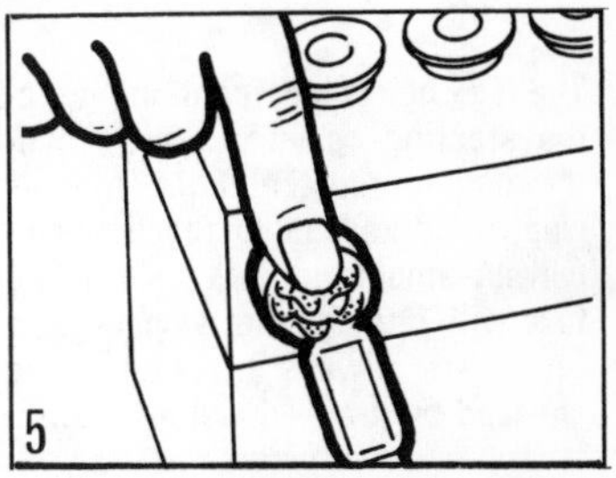

As time goes by, battery terminals build up a dry powdery, whitish material. This material is corrosive and will gradually eat thru battery cables if not cleaned off periodically.

1. Loosen and remove battery connections.

2. Brush off all loose corrosion; use stiff bristle brush. Do not get this material into eyes or on open cuts. Wash off at once.
3. If corrosion build-up is extremely heavy and brushing does not remove all of it, mix 2 tablespoons baking soda to 1 cup water. Pour solution directly onto terminals and connectors. Allow to soak a few minutes and rinse off. Continue brushing to remove all traces of corrosion build-up. Do not allow cleaning solution to enter battery.
4. Replace connectors on battery terminal posts and tighten.
5. Liberally smear battery terminal posts and cable connectors with petroleum jelly.

REPLACE FAULTY BATTERY CABLES

If battery cable strands become frayed, broken or corroded, replace cable immediately. Delay in correcting this condition could lead to sudden failure to start the engine. Can also weaken battery.

1. Loosen and remove battery connections. Clean OFF any corrosion.
2. Disconnect negative cable from its attachment to engine or chassis. Disconnect positive cable from its attachment to starter relay.
3. Attach new cables making sure positive and negative cables are on proper terminals. They are not identical.
4. Replace connectors on battery terminal posts and tighten.
5. Liberally smear battery terminal posts and cable connectors with petroleum jelly.

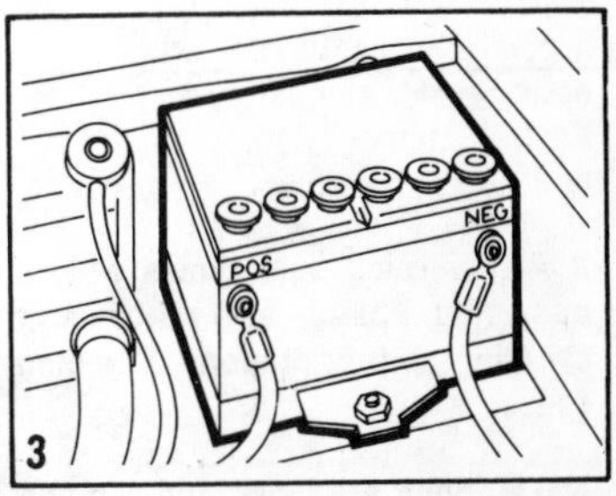

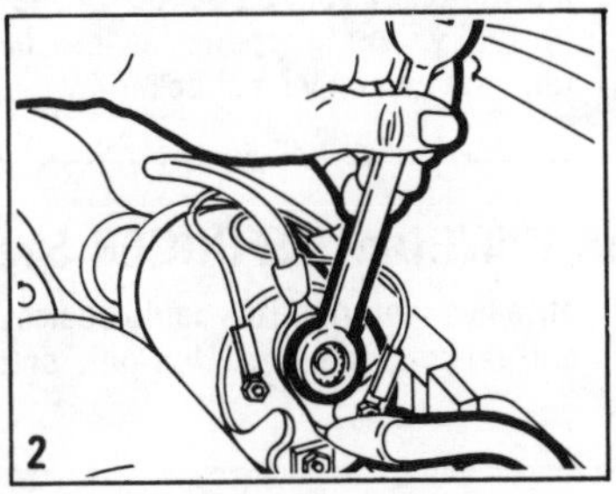

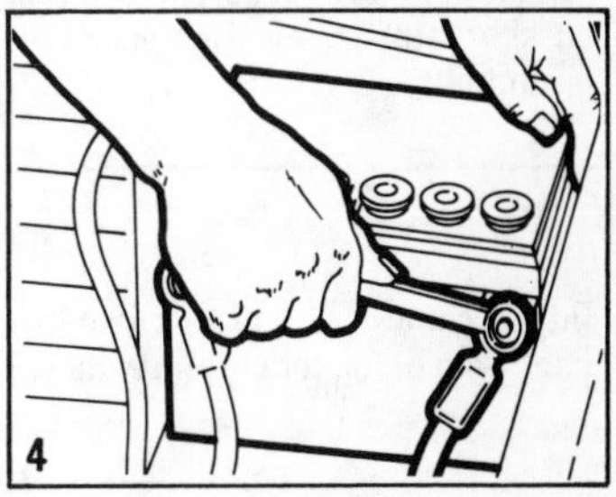

BATTERY HOLDDOWN

The clamp device which holds battery in place should be checked periodically. If loose, tighten. Clean off corrosion buildup. Severely corroded holddown components should be replaced before they break.

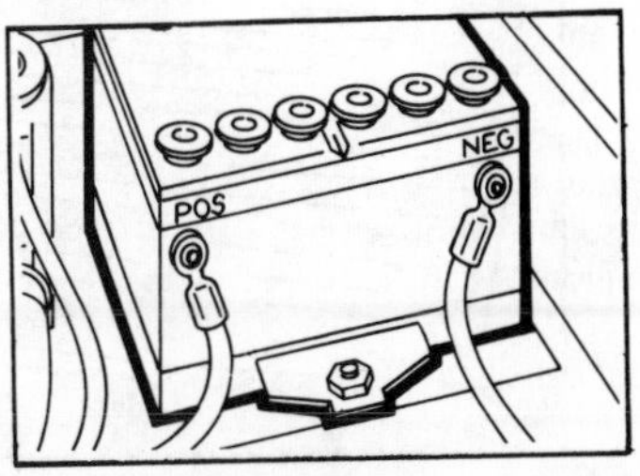

ELECTRICAL FUSES

The fuse box is located to the left of the steering column, directly over the dimmer switch. Each fuse is clearly marked as to function and correct amperage. Always replace fuse with one of same amperage. If fuses are always blowing, have checked by professional mechanic.

TURN SIGNAL AND 4-WAY FLASHER

Turn signals and 4-way emergency flashers will operate only if: A. All light bulbs are OK. B. Flasher units are not burned out. The car has two flasher units that work independently of each other. TURN SIGNAL FLASHER: located behind left side of instument panel. Pull flasher from spring clip mounting. Unplug from connector. Plug in new flasher. Replace in spring clip mounting. EMERGENCY FLASHER: located in fuse block. Simply unplug and insert new flasher. REPLACE ONLY WITH SAME TYPE FLASHER.

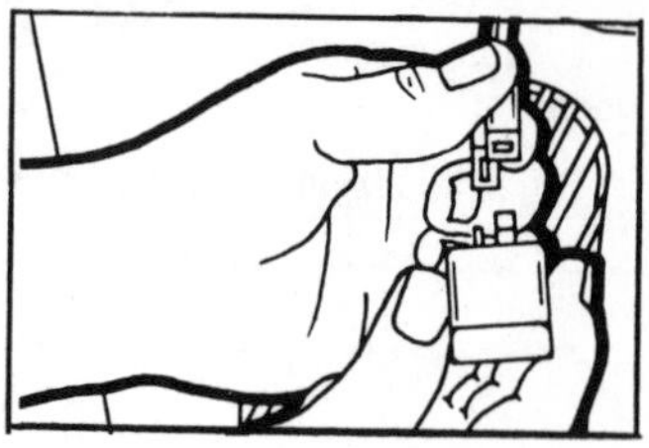

ALTERNATOR

If Alt. warning light glows red at operating speed, alternator isn't charging battery properly. Common causes are:

A. Fan belts are loose and slipping on alternator pulley. Tighten or replace belts.

B. Battery terminals, cables are loose or corroded. Clean; tighten; replace bad cables.

If A or B do not correct problem, alternator or voltage regulator may be faulty. This happens far less often, and can only be checked by mechanic with proper electrical testing equipment.

Alternator Caution: Alternator can be permanently damaged by shortcircuiting terminal connections. When working around or moving alternator, always keep metal tools or engine parts from terminals.

REAR WINDOW DEFOGGER SYSTEM

Do not clean inside of rear window fitted with defogger system with any abrasive material. This could destroy carbon-copper wires. Use only soft rag and mild detergent/water mixture. Dry carefully.

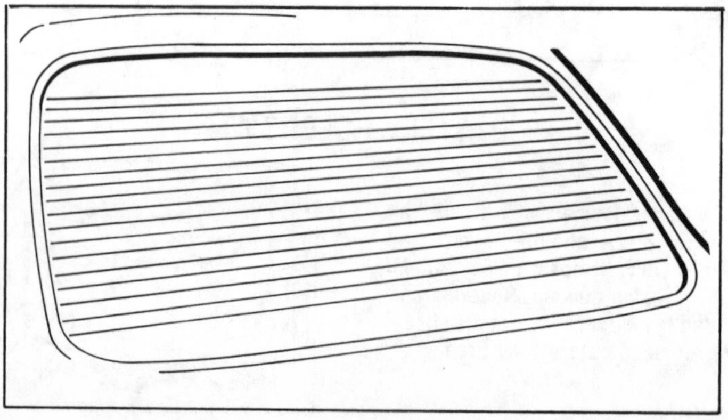

Air Conditioner

WARNING!—Never attempt to tighten fittings, disassembly or do any work on your car's A/C system. Consult a professional mechanic about A/C system problems and their correction. Your auto air conditioner (A/C) is a delicate, closed system. If air, dirt or water get into it, or if refrigerant escapes, the A/C unit will not cool a car interior. Among things you can do are:

1. Keep condenser grille clean. Check for dirt and debris; periodically remove dead insects, leaves, etc., with stiff bristle brush. Straighten any bent fins—carefully.
2. Keep radiator filled to correct level. (See Cooling System section). If fluid needs to be added, add antifreeze rather than water.
3. Keep radiator coolant at a 50/50 water/antifreeze mixture.
4. Flush cooling system and replace with fresh coolant mixture at least every 24 months. (See Cooling System section).
5. Radiator cap should be tight and sealed properly. If sealing gasket is cracked, cut or worn, replace cap with new 15 lb. unit.
6. Check fan belt tension periodically. (See Cooling System section). Replace glazed, frayed or cut fan belts, before they fail entirely.
7. Check periodically for bubbles in A/C sight glass. Sight glass is located in head of receiver/drier vessel. Or in metal tubing leading from top of receiver/drier. Sight glass is no larger than head of large nail. It may be dirty. Wipe clean for best visibility.

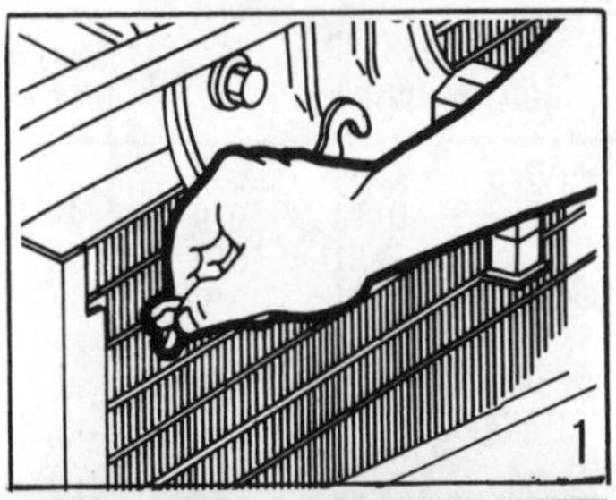

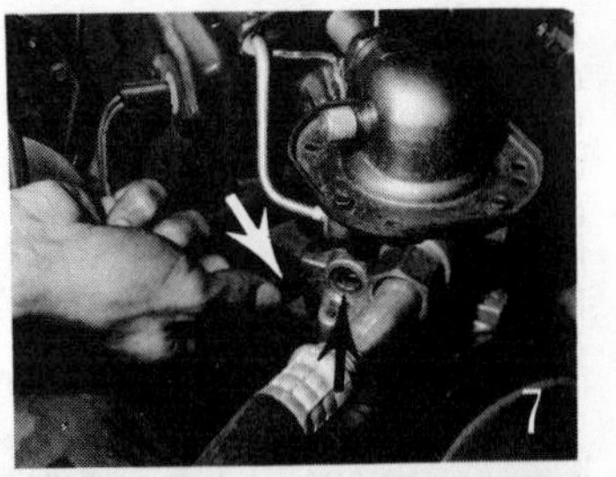

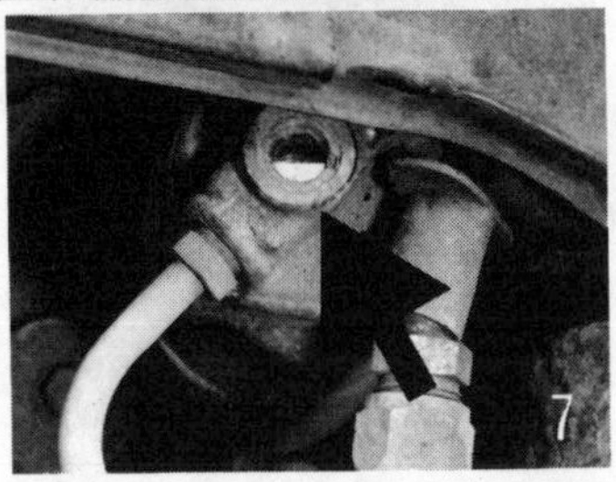

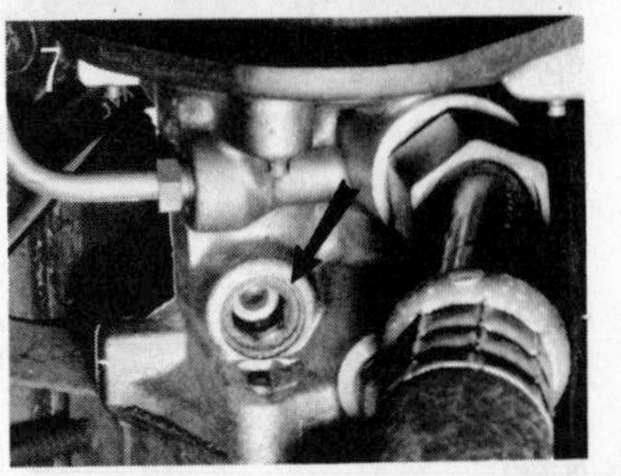

PROCEED AS FOLLOWS:

a) With engine and A/C system running, look for passage of refrigerant in sight glass. You'll be looking for a stream of milky white bubbles as they pass through sight glass. It is best to watch sight glass and have someone else start the car and turn on the A/C system. Allow to run for a few minutes.

b) If you observe no bubbles, and air flow from A/C unit in the car is passing cold air, everything is OK.

c) If no bubbles appear in sight glass, and air flow from the A/C unit in the car is not delivering cold air, the system may be low on refrigerant and could need a re-charge.

d) If bubbles appear, system is low on refrigerant.

e) If you suspect refrigerant loss based on tests performed above, have system checked by a professional A/C service shop. They can confirm refrigerant loss, recharge the system and check for system leakage.

NOTE: Once a week or so, even in winter, run A/C system for about 5 minutes as you drive. This keeps system internally lubricated, prevents hoses hardening.

TUNE-UP SPECIFICATIONS

YEAR	ENGINE No. Cyl. Displacement (cu. in.)	SPARK PLUGS Type	SPARK PLUGS Gap (in.)	DISTRIBUTOR Point Dwell (deg.)	DISTRIBUTOR Point Gap (in.)	IGNITION TIMING Man. Trans.● (deg.)■	IGNITION TIMING Auto Trans.● (deg.)■	IDLE SPEED Man. Trans.● (rpm)▲	IDLE SPEED Auto Trans. (rpm)▲
1970	6-250 (155 hp)	R46T	.035	31-34	.019	TDC	4B	750/400③	600/400②
	8-350 (250 hp)	R44	.035	29-31	.019	TDC	4B	700/450③	600/450③
	8-350 (300 hp)	R44	.035	29-31	.019	TDC	4B	700	600
	8-400 (265 hp)	R44	.035	29-31	.019	4B	8B	700	600/450②
	8-454 (345 hp)	R44T	.035	28-30	.019	6B	6B	700	600
	8-454 (390 hp)	R43T	.035	28-30	.019	6B	6B	700	600

TUNE-UP SPECIFICATIONS

YEAR	ENGINE No. Cyl. Displacement (cu. in.)	SPARK PLUGS Type	SPARK PLUGS Gap (in.)	DISTRIBUTOR Point Dwell (deg.)	DISTRIBUTOR Point Gap (in.)	IGNITION TIMING Man. Trans.● (deg.)■	IGNITION TIMING Auto Trans.● (deg.)■	IDLE SPEED Man. Trans.● (rpm) ▲	IDLE SPEED Auto Trans. (rpm) ▲
1971	6-250 (145 hp)	R46TS	.035	31-34	.019	4B	4B	550	500②
	8-350 (245 hp)	R44TS	.035	29-31	.019	2B	6B	600	550②
	8-350 (270 hp)	R44TS	.035	29-31	.019	4B	8B	600	550②
	8-400 (255 hp)	R44TS	.035	29-31	.019	4B	8B	600	550②
	8-402 (300 hp)	R44TS	.035	29-31	.019	8B	8B	600	600②
	8-454 (365 hp)	R43TS	.035	28-30	.019	8B	8B	600	600
1972	6-250 (110 hp)	R46T	.035	31-34	.019	4B	4B	700	600
	8-350 (165 hp)	R44T	.035	29-31	.019	6B	6B	900	600
	8-400 (170 hp)	R44T	.035	29-31	.019	2B	6B	900	600
	8-402 (210 hp)	R44T	.035	29-31	.019	8B	8B	750	600
	8-454 (270 hp)	R44T	.035	29-31	.019	8B	8B	750	600
1973	6-250 (100 hp)	R46T	.035	31-34	.019	6B	—	700/450③	—
	8-350 (145 hp)	R44T	.035	29-31	.019	—	8B	—	600/450③
	8-350 (175 hp)	R44T	.035	29-31	.019	—	12B	—	600/450③
	8-400 (140 hp)	R44T	.035	29-31	.019	—	8B	—	600/450③
	8-454 (245 hp⑤)	R44T	.035	29-31	.019	—	10B	—	600/450③
1974	8-350 (145 hp)	R44T	.035	29-31	.019	—	8B	—	600
	8-350 (160 hp)	R44T	.035	29-31	.019	—	12B(8B)	—	600
	8-400 (150 hp)	R44T	.035	29-31	.019	—	8B	—	600
	8-400 (180 hp)	R44T	.035	29-31	.019	—	8B	—	600
	8-454 (235 hp)	R44T	.035	29-31	.019	—	10B	—	600
1975	8-350 (145 hp)	R-44TX	.060	Electronic		—	6B	—	600
	8-350 (155 hp)	R-44TX	.060	Electronic		—	6B	—	600
	8-400 (175 hp)	R-44TX	.060	Electronic		—	8B	—	600
	8-454 (215 hp)	R-44TX	.060	Electronic		—	16B	—	650
1976	8-350 (145 hp)	R-45TS	.045	Electronic		—	6B	—	600
	8-350 (155 hp)	R-45TS	.045	Electronic		—	6B	—	600
	8-400 (175 hp)	R-45TS	.045	Electronic		—	8B	—	600
	8-454 (215 hp)	R-45TSX	.060	Electronic		—	—	—	550
1977	6-250 8-305 8-350	See Underhood Specifications Sticker							

▲ Adjust automatic transmissions in Drive (AMC/Ford/GM) or Neutral (Chrysler), all manual transmissions are adjusted in Neutral.
■ A After Top Dead Center B Before Top Dead Center TDC Top Dead Center

NOTE: The underhood specifications sticker often reflects tune-up specification changes made in production. Sticker figures must be used if they disagree with those in this chart.

● Figure in parentheses indicate California engine.
① Not used
② A/C on
③ Lower figure with Idle Solenoid disconnected
— Not applicable
④ Not used
⑤ 215 in wagons

CAPACITIES

YEAR	ENGINE No. Cyl. Displacement (cu. in.)	ENGINE OIL Add 1 qt. with New Filter	TRANSMISSION Pts. to Refill after Draining MANUAL 3-speed	4-speed	AUTOMATIC	DRIVE AXLE (pts.)	COOLING SYSTEM with Heater (qts.)	with Air Cond. (qts.)
1970	6-250	4	3	—	6	3.5③	12	12
	8-350	4	3	—	6.5⑤	3.5③	16	16①
	8-400	4	—	—	5④	3.5③	16	17
	8-454	4	—	—	8	3.5③	22	22
1971	6-250	4	3	—	6	3.5③	12	—
	8-350	4	3	—	6.5⑤	3.5③	16	17
	8-400	4	3	—	5④	3.5③	16	17
	8-402	4	—	—	8	3.5③	23	24
	8-454	4	—	—	8	3.5③	22	23
1972	6-250	4	3	—	6	4.25②	12	—
	8-350	4	—	—	5	4.25②	16	17
	8-400	4	—	—	5	4.25②	16	17
	8-402	4	—	—	8	4.25②	23	24
	8-454	4	—	—	8	4.25②	22	23
1973	6-250	4	3	—	5	4.25②	12	12
	8-350	4	—	—	5	4.25②	16	17
	8-400	4	—	—	5	4.25②	16.5	17.5
	8-454	4	—	—	8	4.25②	23	24
1974	8-350	4	—	—	8	4.25②	16	16
	8-400	4	—	—	8⑥	4.25②	16	16
	8-454	4	—	—	9	4.25②	22	23
1975-76	8-350	4	—	—	8	4.25②	16	16
	8-400	4	—	—	9	4.25②	16	16
	8-454	4	—	—	9	4.25②	22	23
1977	6-250							
	8-305							
	8-350							

① 17 qts. with 300 hp
② 4.9 pts. with 8.875 diameter ring gear
③ 4 pts. with 8.875 diameter ring gear
④ 8 pts. with Turbo Hydramatic 400
⑤ 5 pts. with Turbo Hydramatic 350
⑥ 9 with 400—4 bbl.

Service Record

DATE/MILEAGE	SERVICE	NEXT DUE

Cutlass

Lubrication and Oil Change

GM SAYS . . . Change oil every 6000 miles; change filter every 12,000 miles. Recommended grade: SE. Check oil level at least once a week.

TOOLS & MATERIALS . . . adjustable wrench; medium size screwdriver; oil filter removal wrench; drain pan for old oil (at least 5 qt. capacity); oil pouring spout; 4 qt. oil (5 qt. if changing filter); new oil filter; oil and lubricants as specified below.
SAFETY TIP . . . use work gloves.

BRAKE FLUID LEVEL CHECK

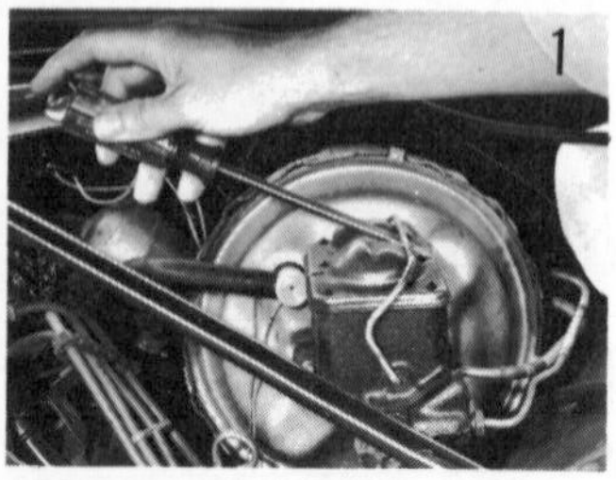

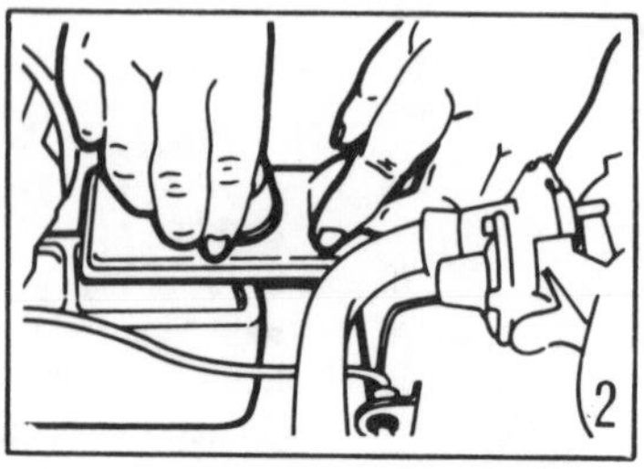

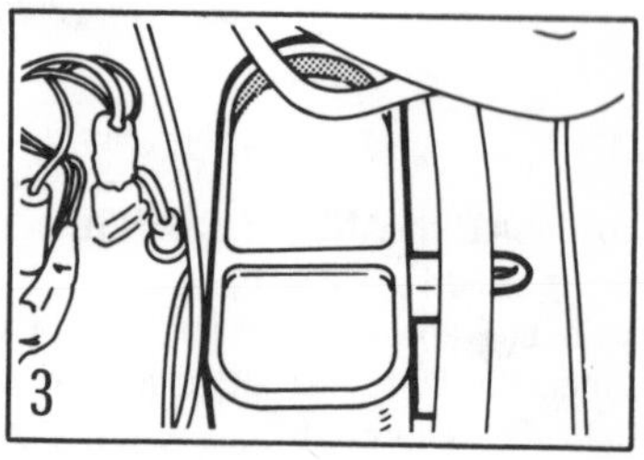

Check brake fluid level in master cylinder every three months
. . . sooner if braking feels inadequate. Add when low.
Recommended grade: DOT 3.

1. Pry wire retaining clip off cap top with screwdriver.

2. Remove cap and gasket by lifting up.

3. Fluid level should be within ¼ inch of top rim. If lower than this, add fresh fluid to appropriate level. DO NOT OVERFILL

4. Replace cap and gasket; secure retaining clip over cap. If fluid level was low, check again in a few days.

5. If fluid repeatedly checks low, there is a leak somewhere in the system. See SAFETY SYSTEMS—WHEEL CYLINDER CHECK. Have mechanic check further. Neglect can be dangerous.

MANUAL TRANSMISSION FLUID LEVEL CHECK

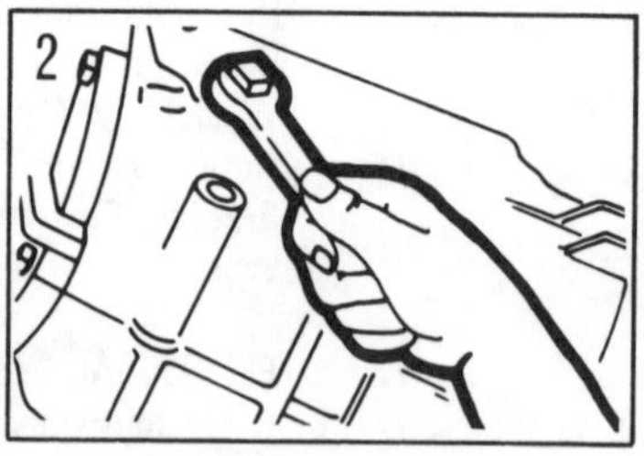

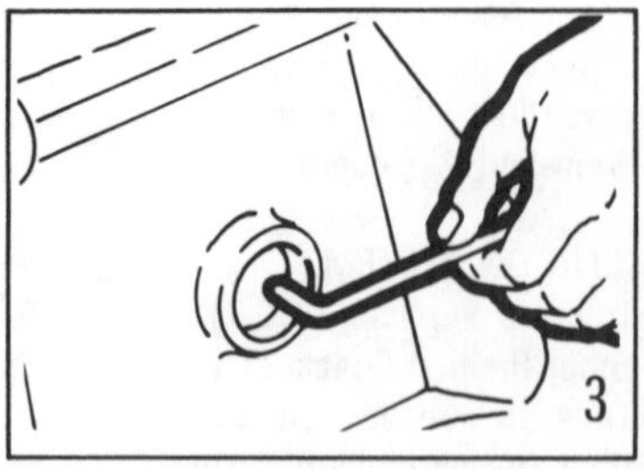

GM SAYS . . . Check the manual transmission lubricant every 6 months or 7,500 miles. Recommended grade: SAE 80W-90 GL-5 gear lube.

TOOLS . . . adjustable hand wrench; fluid level check device (made from coat hanger wire; bend at 90° angle 2″ from end); bulb syringe.

1. Locate transmission fluid filler plug on right side of transmission housing from underneath car.

2. Wipe road dirt from filler plug area before loosening. Remove plug with adjustable wrench.

3. Insert fluid level check device. Fluid level should be right up to bottom edge of filler hole.

4. Add fluid as needed with hand bulb syringe.

5. Replace filler plug; tighten.

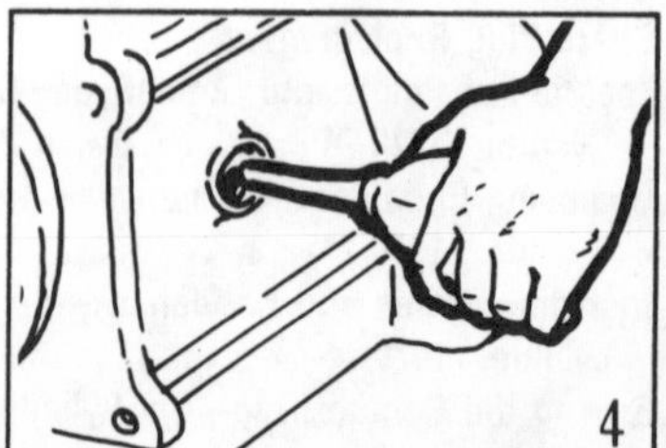

AUTOMATIC TRANSMISSION FLUID LEVEL CHECK

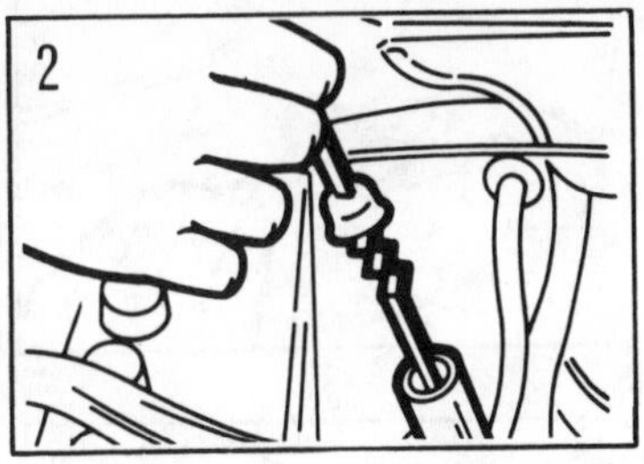

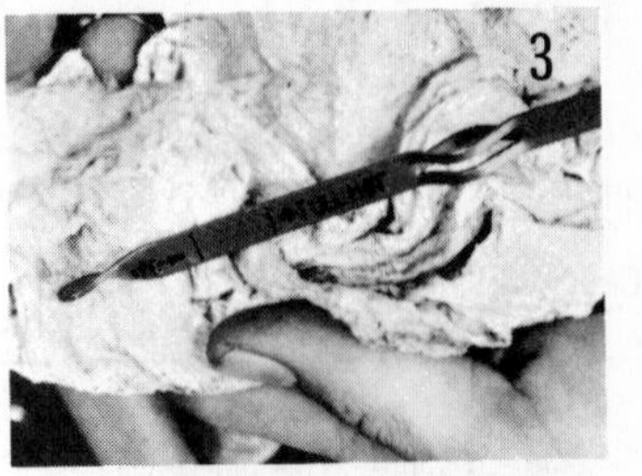

GM SAYS . . . check automatic transmission fluid (ATF) level every 6000 miles. Recommended grade: DEXRON® or Type A.
TOOLS . . . Long neck filler funnel.

1. Engine must be warmed up and running. Place shift lever in PARK position.

2. Pull out dipstick. Wipe clean. Push dipstick all the way back in; remove it again.
3. If fluid is below ADD mark, add ATF to bring level up. DO NOT OVERFILL.
4. Add ATF thru transmission dipstick hole by means of long-neck filler funnel.

REAR AXLE LUBRICANT

GM SAYS . . . check rear axle lube level every 6000 miles. Recommended grade: Hypoid gear lube (SAE 90). Positraction axles require special positraction lubricant.
TOOLS . . . adjustable hand wrench; fluid level check device (made from coat hanger wire; bend at 90° angle 2″ from end); bulb syringe.
1. Locate filler plug on forward side of rear axle housing.
2. Wipe plug area clean; remove plug with wrench.
3. Insert wire level check device; remove. Adequate fluid level should show lubricant on last ¼-inch of wire.
4. If fluid level is low, add as needed, with a hand bulb syringe, until level shows on last ¼-inch of wire.
5. Replace filler plug; tighten.

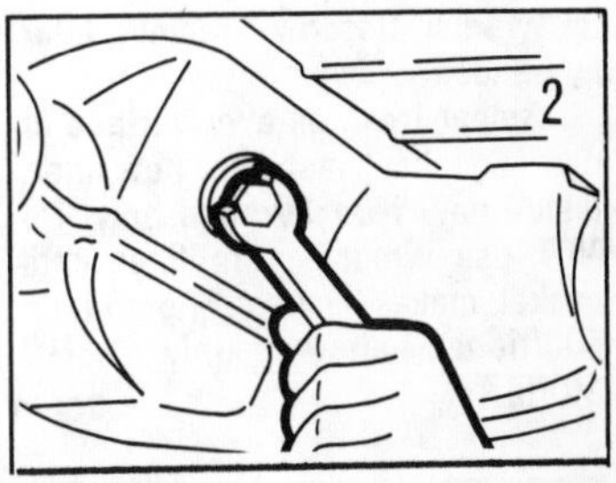

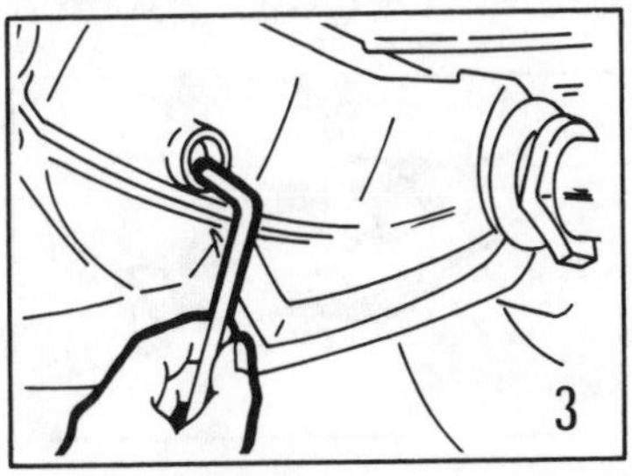

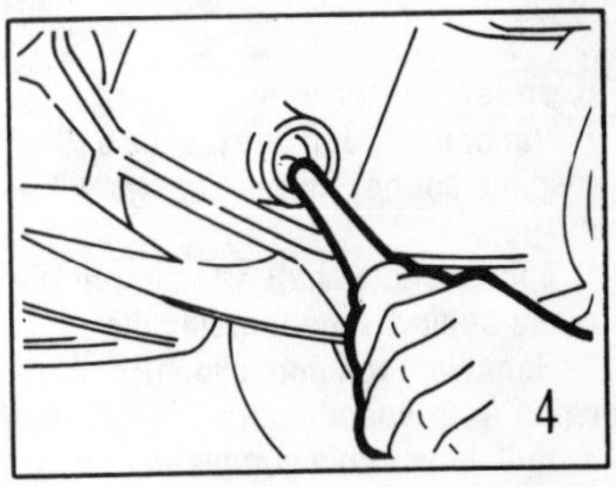

OIL AND FILTER CHANGE

1. If engine is cold, start up and idle for about 5 minutes.
2. Park car on level ground. Turn engine off.
3. Locate oil drain plug on underside of engine. Place drain pan under plug.
4. Remove drain plug with wrench. Let ALL dirty oil drain out.

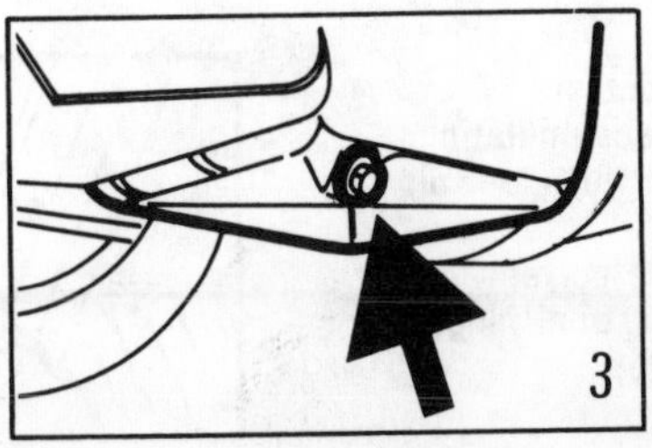

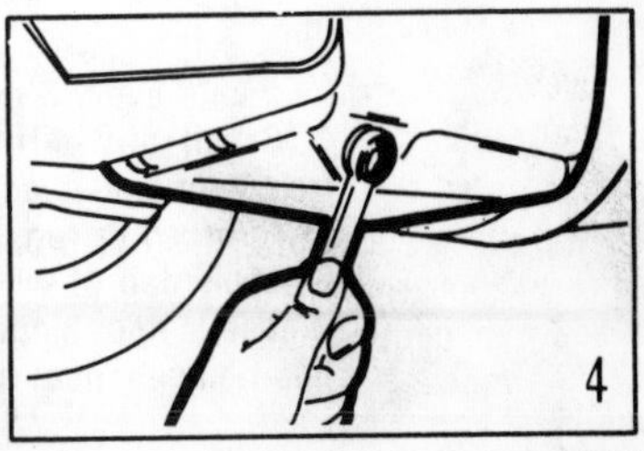

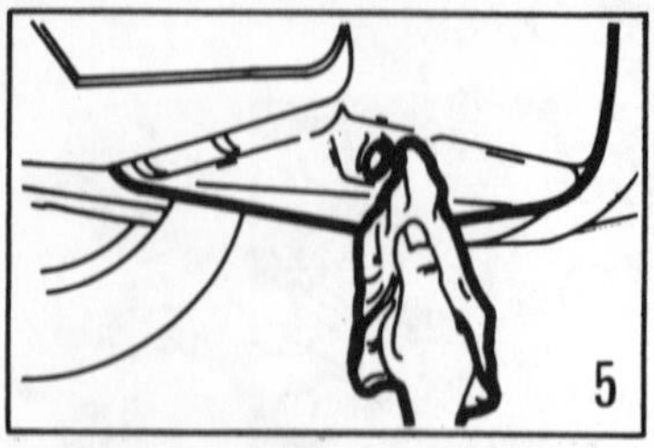

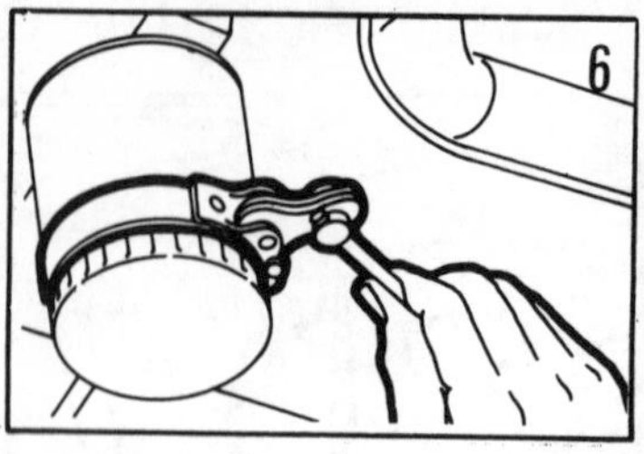

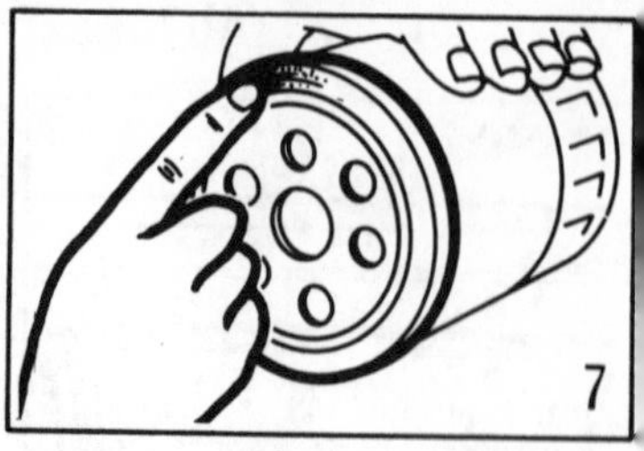

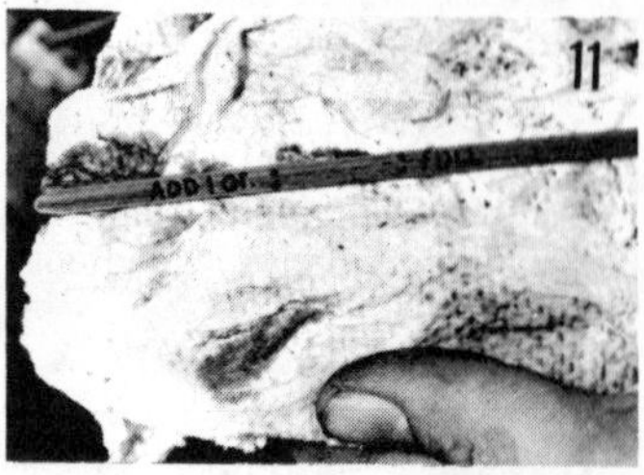

5. Wipe plug and area around drain hole clean. Replace drain plug; tighten it.
6. Locate oil filter. Move drain pan under filter. Loosen filter with oil filter wrench. Unscrew; remove filter by hand.
7. Smear fresh oil over surface of rubber gasket (washer) of new filter. Install new filter by hand only. Do NOT use wrench. Turn filter until gasket makes contact. Tighten an additional half turn only . . . NO MORE.

8. Locate oil filler tube on top of engine. Remove cap.
9. Punch oil pouring spout into top of oil can. Pour all cans of new oil into filler tube. Wipe filler cap clean and replace it.
10. Check new oil level at dipstick. Pull out dipstick, wipe clean.
11. Push dipstick back into engine. Be sure to insert all the way. Remove dipstick and check new oil level. It should be above "FULL" line. If not, be sure to check if you put in all the oil called for.

12. Start up engine and idle for 3-5 minutes. Oil signal light on instrument panel will glow red when engine is first started. Light should go out in 30 seconds or less.
13. Stop engine and check for oil leaks at drain plug and filter. If you find any, check tightness of plug and/or filter, also for condition of filter gasket to see that it has not become pinched or damaged when installing. Recheck oil level, which should now be at "FULL".

SPEEDOMETER CABLE LUBRICATION

If speedometer pointer tends to quiver or jump, or if unit makes a low, rasping sound, lubrication may be needed.
1. Locate cable shaft attachment directly behind speedometer dial.
2. Remove retaining clip. Unscrew cable from speedometer.
3. Pull inner cable completely out of outer casing. Note carefully which end is top. Check for wear or frayed strands. If damaged, replace inner cable with new one.

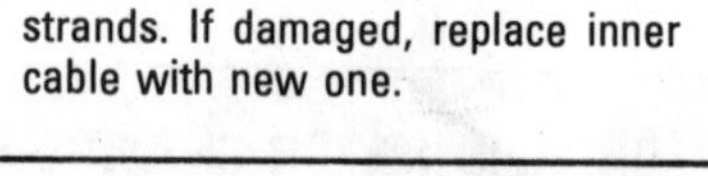

4. Apply generous amount of speedometer cable lubricant into cable casing. Replace inner cable in shaft, noting that top end is not inserted accidentally. Turn inner cable as it is being re-inserted. Twist cable when all the way in, to lock into position at lower end.
5. Reconnect cable to speedometer head under instrument panel.

DOOR HINGES AND STOPS

(lubricate every 6 months)
1. Brush any dirt accumulations from door hinges and stops. Use old tooth brush or rag.
2. Apply dab of white polyethylene grease to door hinges, trunk hinges, hood hinges, door stops.

DOOR LOCKS

(lubricate every 6 months)
1. Insert door key half way into lock.
2. Spray aerosol lock lubricant into lock.
3. Push key rest of way into lock; turn back and forth several times.

Cooling System

IT IS RECOMMENDED . . . that radiator coolant (water/antifreeze mixture) level be checked once or twice a month. Do this when engine is cold. Check more often if you do a lot of hard driving. Coolant is checked visually on models with expansion tanks.
Keep coolant up to recommended level in radiator. If coolant checks frequently low, look for leaks. Tighten all hose clamps occasionally. For best results, keep a 50/50 water/antifreeze mixture year round. Change complete coolant mixture every 24 months.
CAUTION: If you must check coolant in a hot engine, cover radiator cap with thick rag before releasing. Remove cap slowly . . . press down and turn.

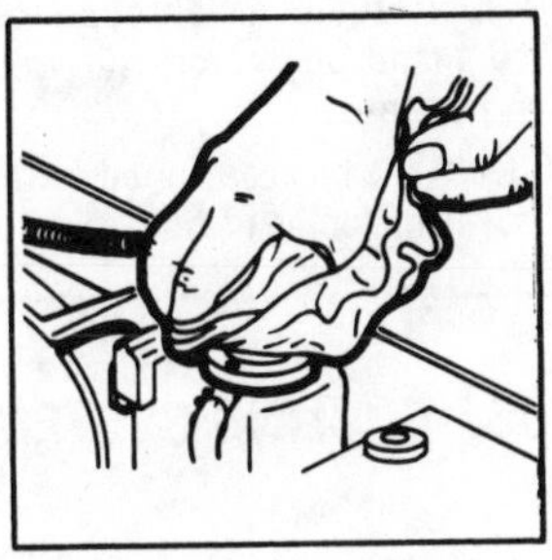

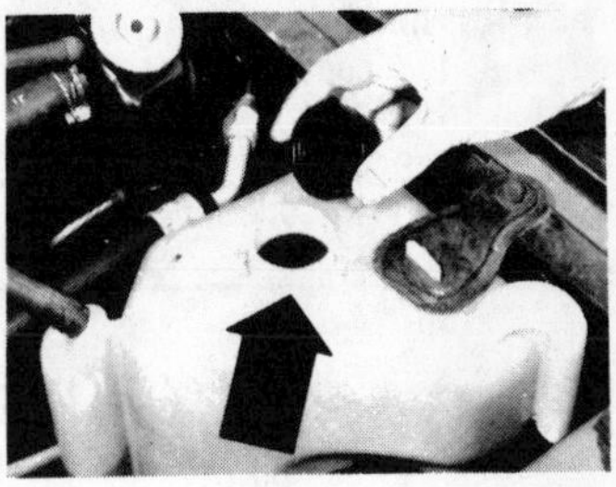

REPLACING THE THERMOSTAT

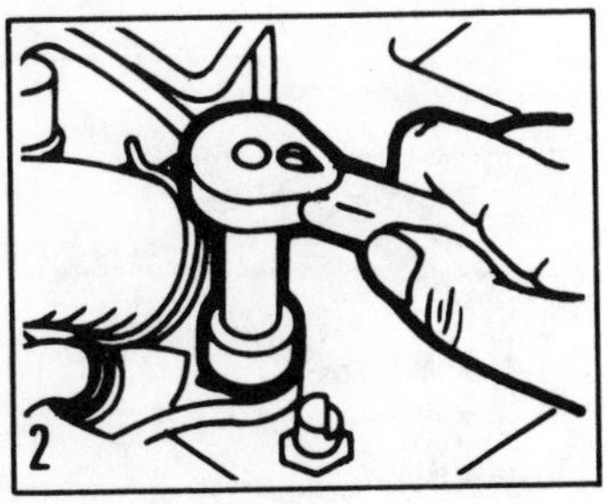

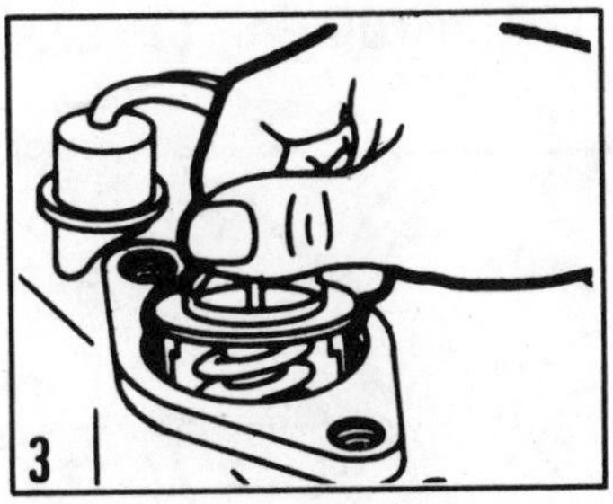

A faulty thermostat will usually cause engine overheating. The thermostat is located inside the housing where the top radiator hose connects to the engine.
TOOLS AND MATERIALS . . .
New thermostat
Gasket
Adjustable wrench

1. Drain radiator of about half its coolant. (See How To Replace Hoses).
2. Loosen and remove both retaining bolts and lift thermostat housing off the engine.
NOTE: If you're careful it won't be necessary to remove radiator hose.
3. Remove old thermostat.
4. Scrape thermostat housing flange and engine block surface to remove old gasket debris.
5. Drop new thermostat into place—spring down.
6. Install new gasket with sealer applied to both sides.
7. Replace thermostat housing and tighten both retaining bolts.

FAN BELT ADJUSTMENT

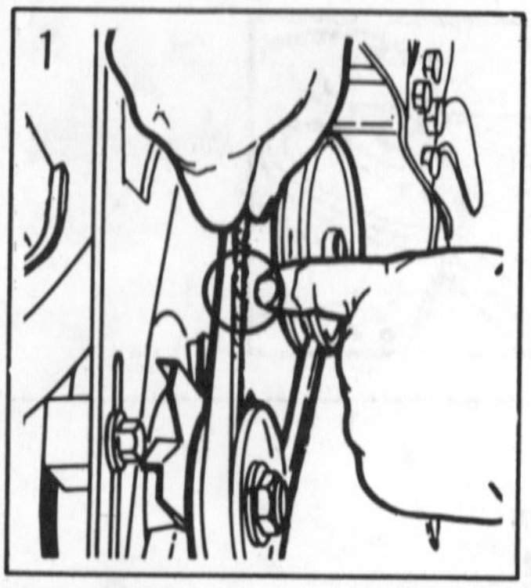

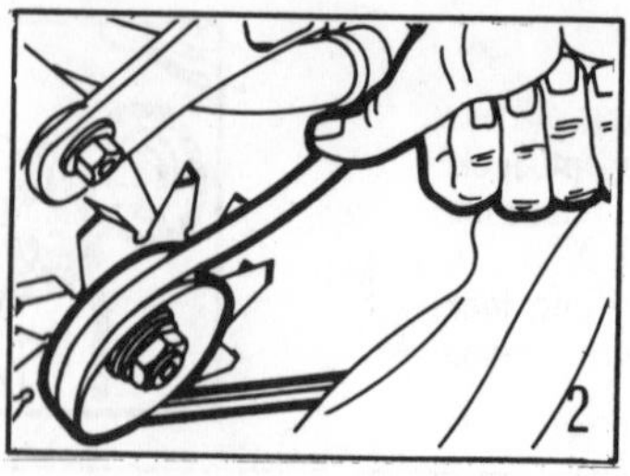

The fan belt not only drives the radiator fan, it turns the water pump and drives the alternator. It's easy to see that the condition and proper tension of the belt are vital, since almost all engine cooling and electrical power is dependent on it. The belt deserves an occasional look and tension check.

1. Inspect fan belt occasionally. If worn, frayed or cracked on inner driving surface, replace.

CAUTION: An overtightened belt may damage alternator and water pump bearings.

2. Check tension occasionally. Press thumb at midpoint of belt span between pulleys. If belt depresses more than ½ inch, tightening is needed. A too-loose belt will not drive alternator and water pump effectively.

3. To adjust loosen alternator mounting bolts, pivot the alternator over until the belt is properly tensioned (¼ in. deflection) and then tighten bolts.

FIND THOSE COOLING SYSTEM LEAKS

1. Inspect all hoses. If any are weak, soft in spots or show cracks, replace at once.
2. Check all hose connections for tightness. Tighten loose hose clamps; they tend to loosen due to engine vibration.
3. If radiator steams or hisses when engine is switched off, check for leaks. Look for signs of coolant drips on radiator or around header tank joint.

Leaks are possible at:
Upper or lower radiator hoses
Water pump (gaskets or seal)
Heater core or connecting hoses
Automatic transmission cooler lines (at bottom of radiator)
Faulty radiator pressure cap
Faulty cylinder head gasket
Cracked cylinder head or block

RADIATOR CAP CHECK

Check radiator cap occasionally for worn or cracked gasket. If cap doesn't seal properly, fluid will be lost and engine will overheat.
Replace worn cap with new cap rated 15 lbs. pressure.

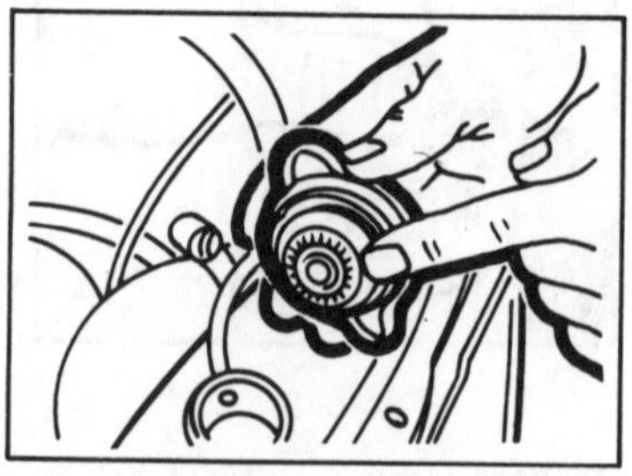

HOSE REPLACEMENT

Coolant drain and refill work may be done alone; when changing hoses, coolant must also be drained as part of job. Discard all hoses with cracks or soft spots. Check hose clamps for tightness and good condition.

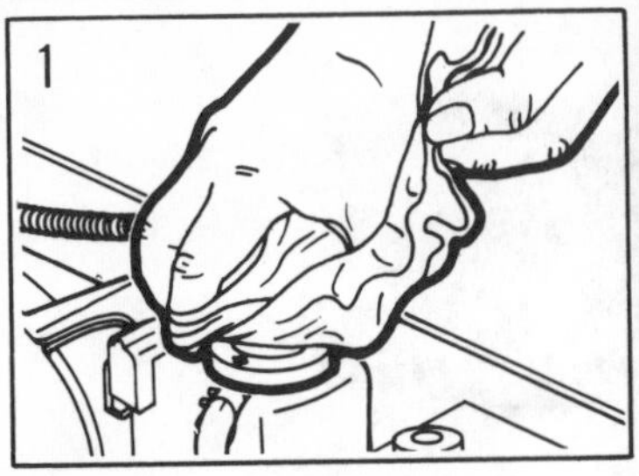

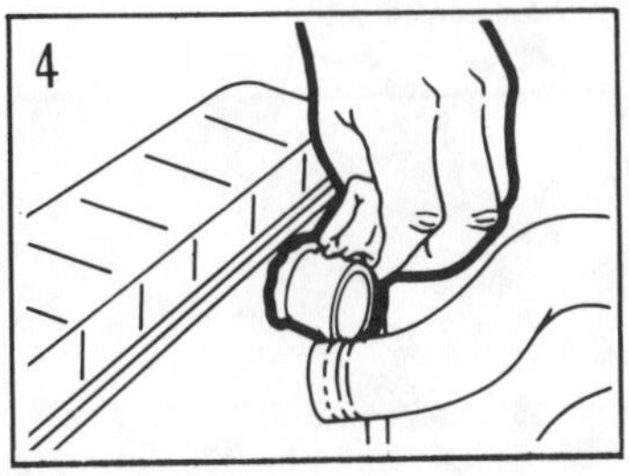

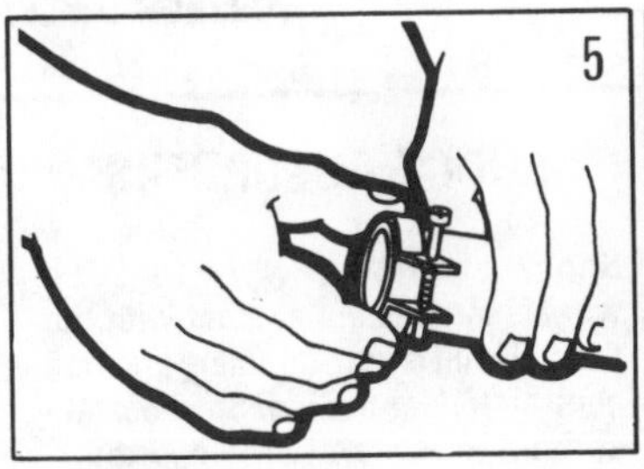

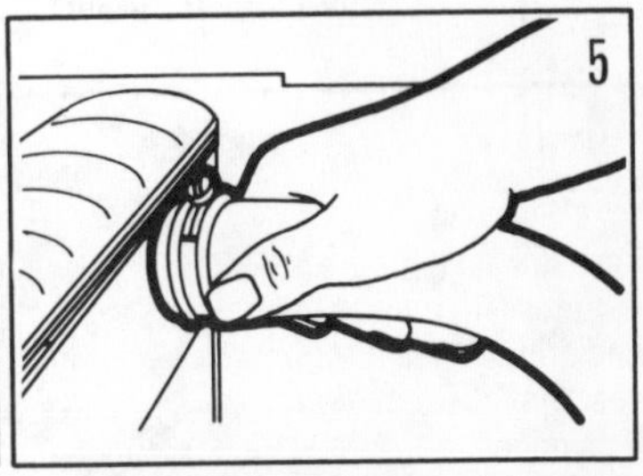

1. Remove radiator cap. Open radiator petcock (See 2). Drain coolant into catch basin. If near 24 months old, discard old coolant.

2. Petcock or drain plug is located at the bottom left of the radiator. Open petcock or remove plug to drain.

3. Loosen clamps at each end of hose(s). Work loose; pull off. If old hose clamps are rusted or damaged, replace with new units.

4. Wipe all hose connections clean. Use emery cloth to get rid of residue. Check all hoses for weak spots, as well as cracks inside and out.

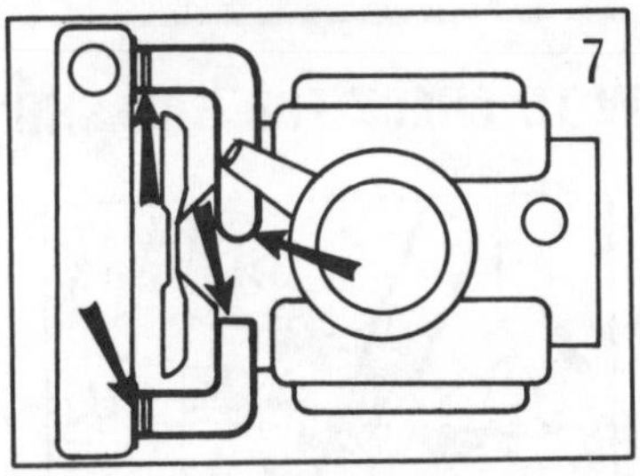

5. Slip clamps over each hose end. Slip hose ends all the way onto cleaned up hose connections.
6. Place hose clamp ¼ inch from hose end. Tighten. Close petcock.

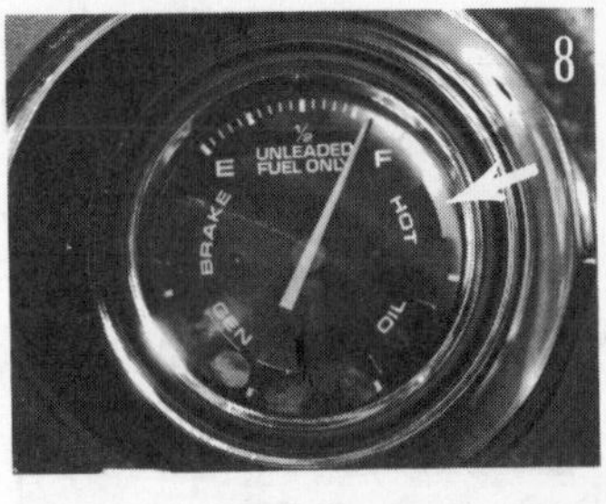

Refill with 50/50 coolant/water mix.
7. Start engine; allow to warm up. Check for coolant leaks.
8. Road test car; watch for temperature warning light.

Suspension and Tires

HANDLING TROUBLESHOOTING

The front wheels mount and rotate on the spindles, which are attached to upper and lower ball joints. A coil spring is mounted between the control arms on both sides. A shock absorber is located in the center of each spring. The rear suspension consists of coil springs, upper and lower control arms, and shock absorbers.

Your car's suspension system consists of wheels, tires, springs, shock absorbers, sway (or stabilizer) bars, ball joints, steering linkage. If any of these items is out of adjustment or badly worn, you may notice any of these symptoms:

- car pulls to one side when braking
- car wanders when driving a straight line
- overall ride may be either hard or bouncy
- effort is needed to steer vehicle
- tires show uneven wear
- tires squeal when cornering
- front of car dips or bounces when braking
- car rocks side-to-side when going over rough road
- wheels bounce to make slapping sound on road
- steering wheel vibrates in hands
- front of car vibrates at highway speeds

Any of above symptoms indicates corrective action is needed. Delay can: ruin tires; cause damage/failure to other suspension parts; create safety hazard.

STEERING

If steering linkage, front suspension and steering column components are in good condition, there should be not more than 1½ inch free play in the steering wheel when measured at the rim of the wheel. If a loud knock is heard when turning the steering wheel from one extreme to the other, have mechanic check pinion bearing preload.

SHOCK ABSORBERS

Shock absorbers work to keep wheels in constant contact with the road. Result is safe handling and ride control; longer tire life. So shock absorbers (or shocks) are important.

HOW TO CHECK FOR BAD SHOCKS

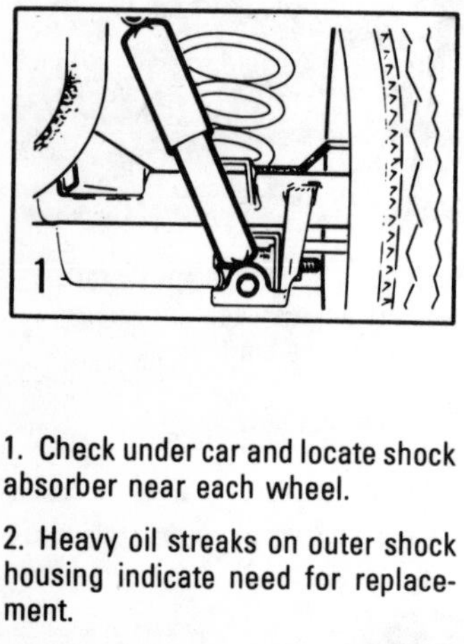

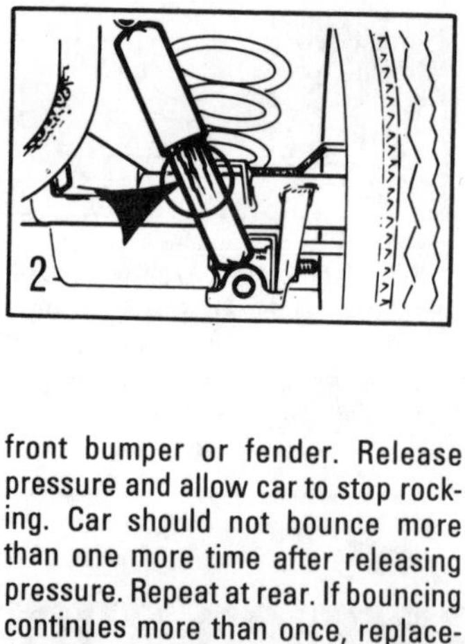

1. Check under car and locate shock absorber near each wheel.

2. Heavy oil streaks on outer shock housing indicate need for replacement.

3. Stand at front of car and apply body weight in a pumping action to front bumper or fender. Release pressure and allow car to stop rocking. Car should not bounce more than one more time after releasing pressure. Repeat at rear. If bouncing continues more than once, replacement is needed. Replace shocks in pairs (front pair or rear pair).

TOW HITCH INFORMATION

If your car is used for trailer towing you should check:
A. Cooling System; be sure radiator is at proper level in radiator. See Cooling System Section for checks to perform.
B. Check Transmission Fluid; keep topped up to proper level.
C. Check Rear Shock Absorbers; you may benefit from installation of new rear shocks.
D. Check Tire Pressures; best traction and handling can be ensured if tire pressures are properly maintained.
For safer and more trouble-free trailer towing, consider:
A. Automatic Transmission Cooler; helps remove excess heat from automatic transmission fluid built up during towing mileage. Also helps avoid radiator overheating. Some units can be self-installed.
B. Radiator Over-Flow Tank Kit; addition of a reservoir to catch radiator coolant overflow preventing coolant loss. Easy to install, these units help a tow car run cooler, avoid overheating due to coolant loss.
C. Heavy-Duty Shock Absorbers or Air Shocks; important to have on rear wheels if you intend to do a lot of towing or load carrying within the

car itself. Don't forget to consider replacing factory shocks, when they are worn out, with heavy-duty units at the front as well.
D. Variable Load Flasher; this unit will accommodate the added load of trailer turn signal lamps on trailer when these are hooked into your car's electrical system.

FRONT END ALIGNMENT

When steering, handling and/or tire wear indicate front end alignment may be needed, this work can only be done at an automotive service shop. DO NOT PUT OFF NEEDED FRONT END ALIGNMENT. At the same time, have ball joints and steering linkage checked.

Ignition System

TUNE-UP SERVICES (1970-74)

The ignition system consists of spark plugs; plug wires; distributor; rotor; points; condenser; coil. These units work to create a good hot spark inside the engine (ignition) at exactly the right moment (timing). If ignition is weak or timing is off, engine may be hard to start, run poorly, waste gas, lose power, backfire or not run at all.
TOOLS & MATERIALS . . . Parts: set of points; condenser; 6 spark plugs. Tools: feeler gauge; 13/16 in. (1970) or 5/8 in. (1971-77) spark plug socket; open end box or combination wrenches; timing equipment.
SAFETY TIP . . . Change only one spark plug at a time to avoid cross-wiring and possible engine damage.

OTHER IGNITION CHECK POINTS

Inspect spark plug wires. If cracked or brittle, entire set should be replaced. Also, center high tension wire. Inspect distributor cap. Wipe inside clean occasionally with dry, lint-free rag. If cap is cracked or rotor contacts are excessively burned, replace cap.

TUNE-UP SERVICES ELECTRONIC IGNITION (1974-77)

Cars equipped with electronic ignition systems require very little care. Spark plugs, ignition wires and timing can be checked periodically as outlined above. Major service to the electronic ignition system should be handled by your mechanic.

HIGH ENERGY IGNITION SYSTEM TACHOMETER HOOKUP

Some 1974, and all 1975 and later cars are equipped with the High Energy Ignition System which uses a different tachometer hookup than was used in previous years.

1. On the V8 engines, connect the tachometer to the TACH terminal on the distributor and to a suitable ground.

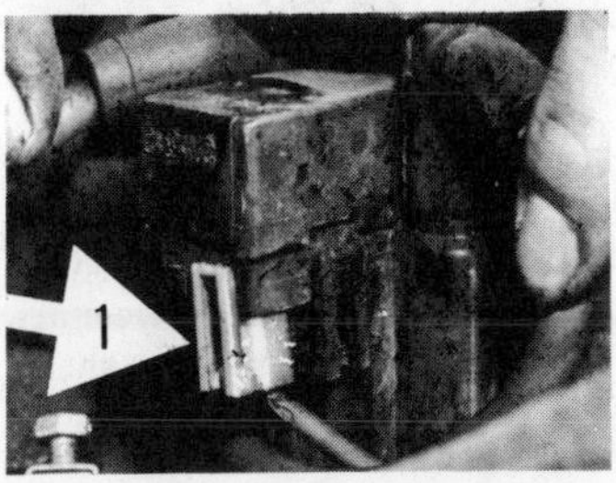

NOTE: Some tachometers must connect to the TACH terminal on the distributor and to the positive terminal on the battery. If there is any doubt check the tachometer manufacturer's instructions.

2. On the inline six cylinder, connect the tachometer to the TACH terminal on the coil, opposite the BAT terminal, and to a ground.

CHECKING POINTS AND ROTOR—Six Cylinder (1970-74)

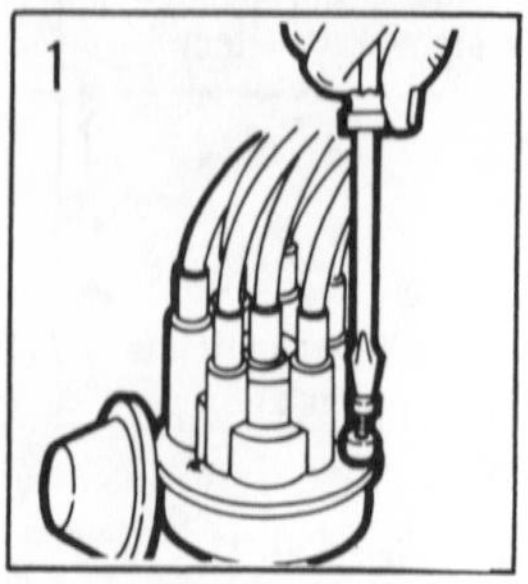

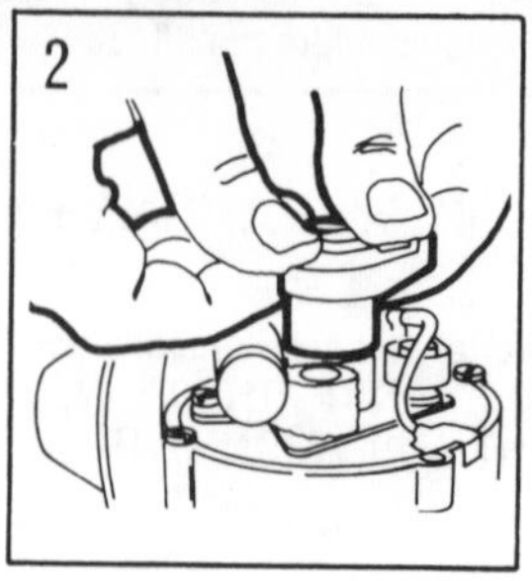

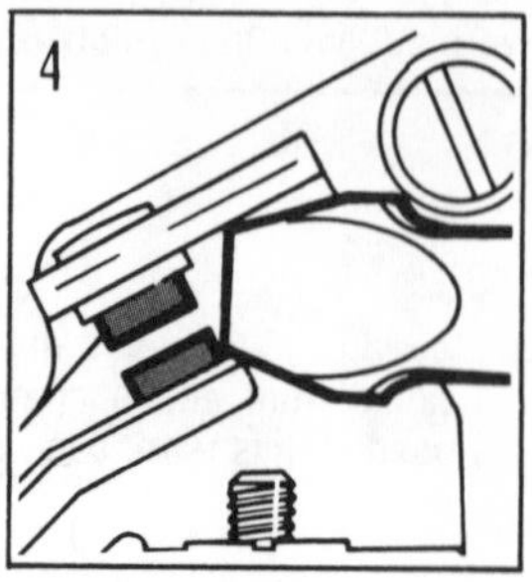

The distributor holds the points, rotor and condenser.

1. To open the distributor, remove the two screws retaining the cap. Remove the coil wire and lift the cap off, but keep the other wires attached.
2. Pull the rotor off (straight up). If it is cracked or metallic tip is badly burned, replace it.
3. Check the metal contacts inside the cap. Replace the cap if they are corroded or there are any cracks.
4. Pry the points apart with a screwdriver. If worn or burned, replace. If OK, check the gap.

CHECKING POINTS AND ROTOR—V8 (1970-74)

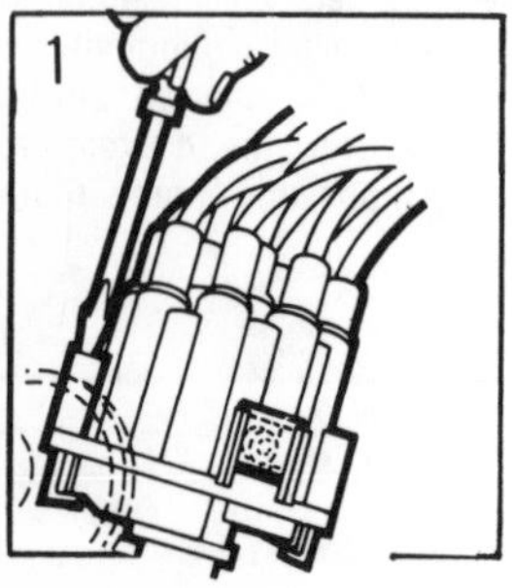

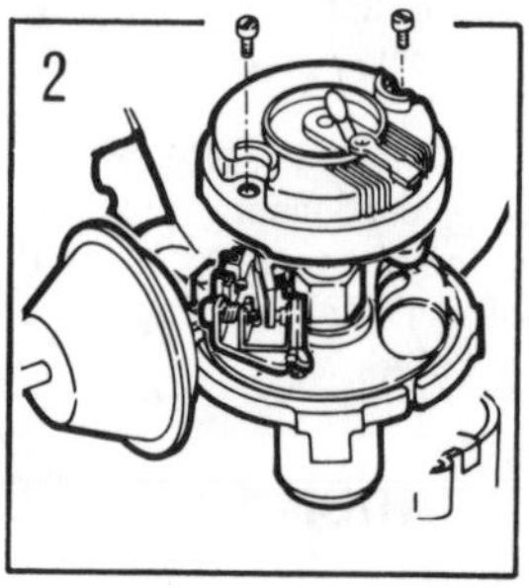

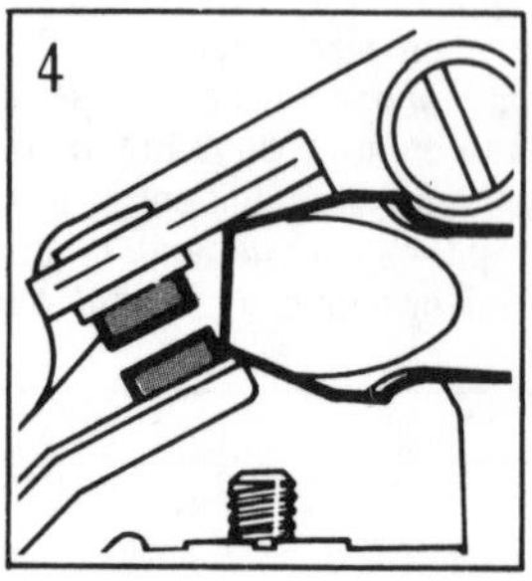

1. To open the distributor, depress the screw in the cap and rotate the latch off the distributor (there are two latches). Remove the coil wire and lift off the cap. Keep the other wires attached.
2. Remove the two screws and lift off the rotor. If it is cracked or metallic tip is badly burned, replace it.
3. Check the metal contacts inside the cap. Replace the cap if they are corroded or there are any cracks.
4. Pry the points apart with a screwdriver. If worn or burned, replace. If OK, check the gap.

SPARK PLUG REPLACEMENT

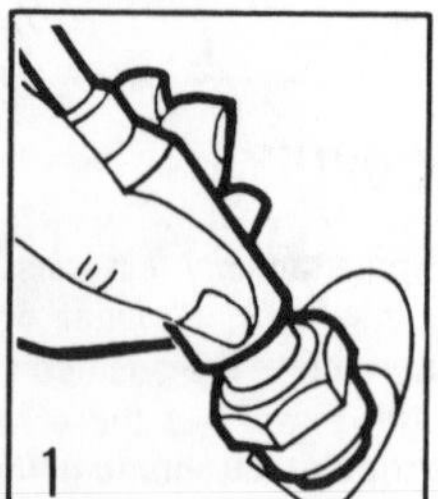

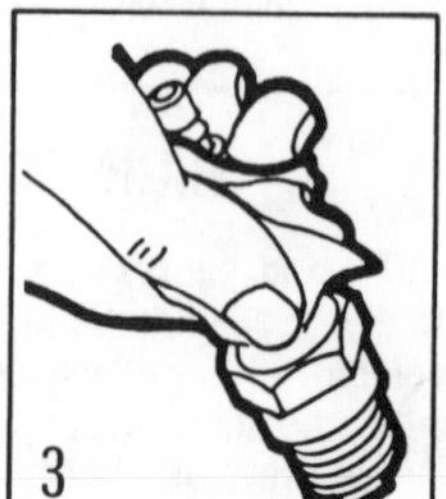

1. Remove spark plug wire by grasping rubber boot. Do not jerk wire off. If stuck, turn boot, pulling gently.
2. Loosen spark plug using socket wrench.
3. Wipe or brush loose dirt from around plug before removing. Do not let dirt drop into engine through plug hole. Unscrew plug.

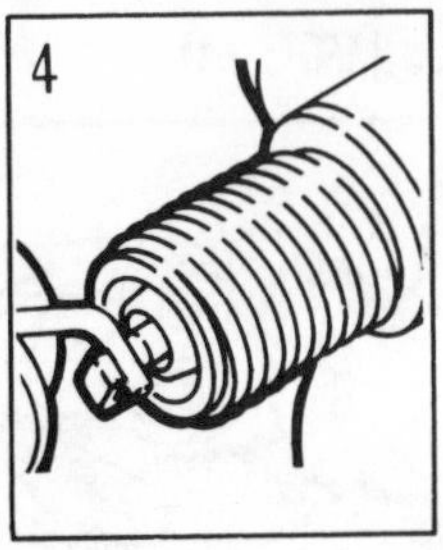

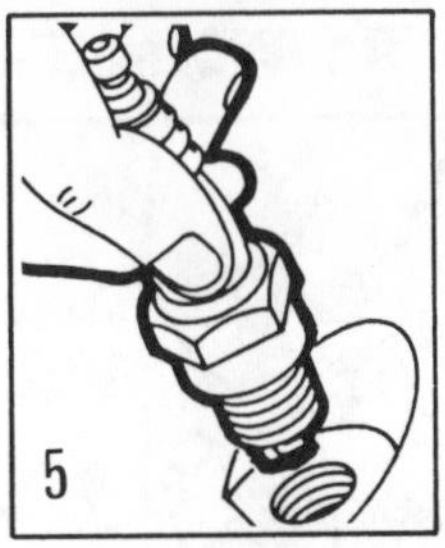

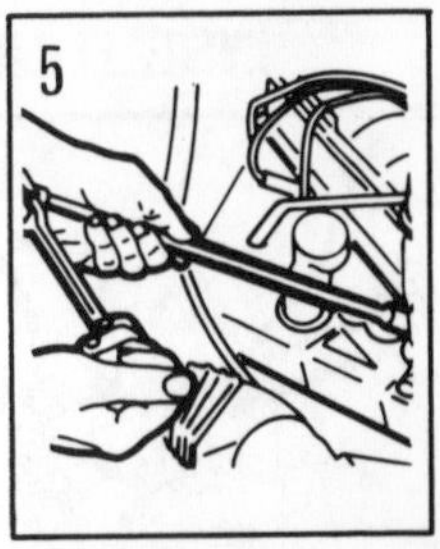

4. Check plug electrode gap on new spark plug. Adjust to **Specifications** Plug gap is correct when the gauge drags slightly as it is pulled between plug electrodes.
5. Thread new plug into plug hole by hand. Hand tighten. Do not force or cross thread. Use socket wrench to tighten firmly but do not force. Replace plug wire. Press boot firmly.

LOCATION OF POINTS AND CONDENSER—Six Cylinder (1970-74)

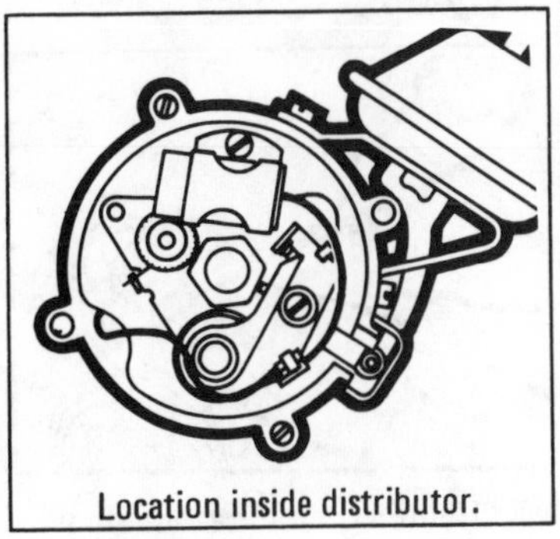
Location inside distributor.

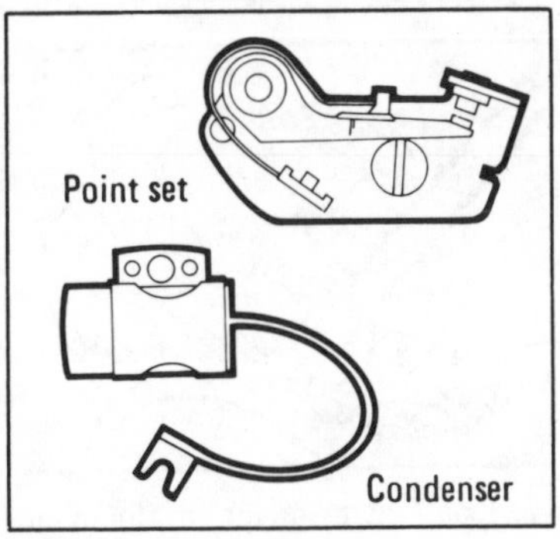

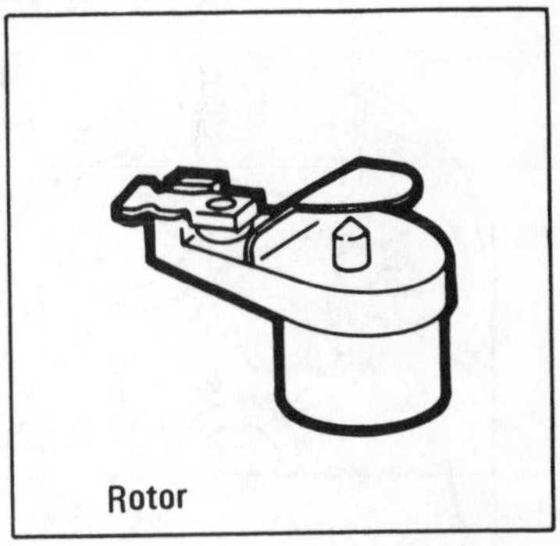
Rotor

Points and condenser work together. Always replace condenser also when installing new points.

REMOVING POINTS AND CONDENSER—Six Cylinder (1970-74)

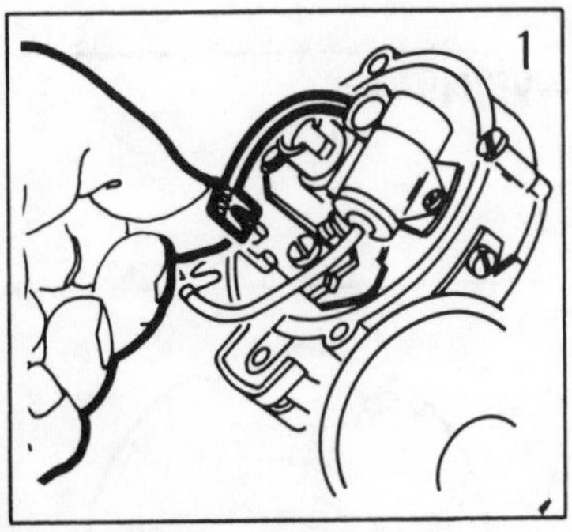

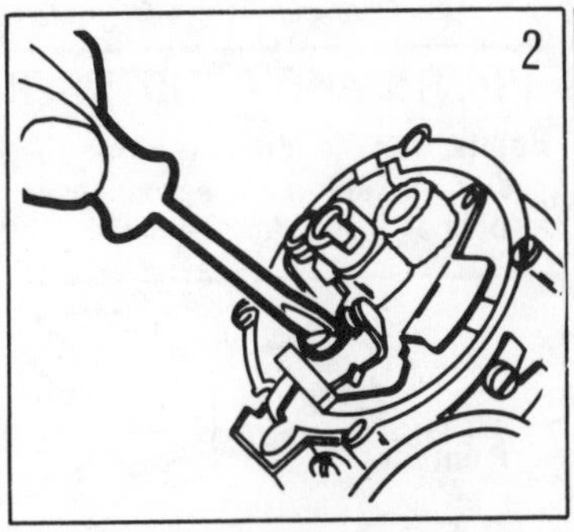

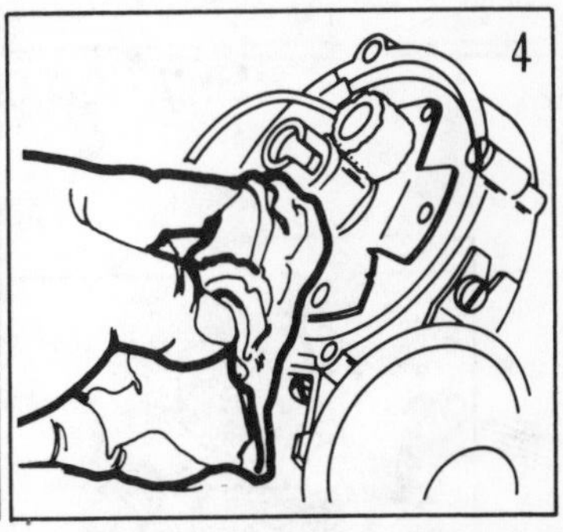

1. Disconnect the two wire terminals connected to the points set. Notice that the condenser connector is on the outside.
2. Remove points attaching screw being very careful not to drop screw inside distributor.
3. Remove screw which holds condenser. DO NOT DROP SCREW.
4. Wipe all dirt from distributor plate and cam with clean, lint-free rag.
CAUTION: When removing screws from distributor, be sure to avoid any screws accidentally falling through distributor opening into engine. Use magnetic screwdriver.

INSTALLING POINTS AND CONDENSER—Six Cylinder (1970-74)

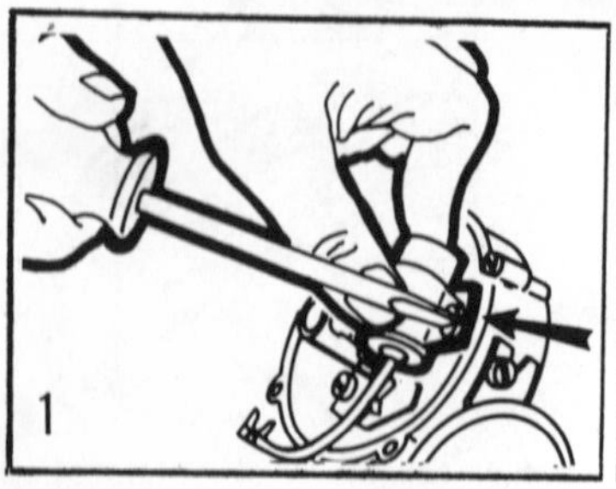

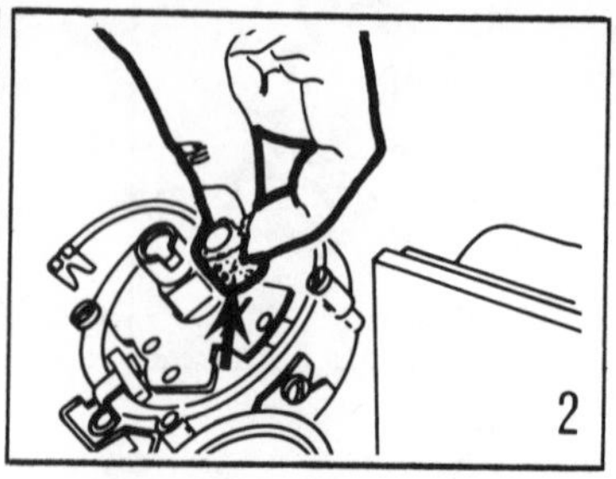

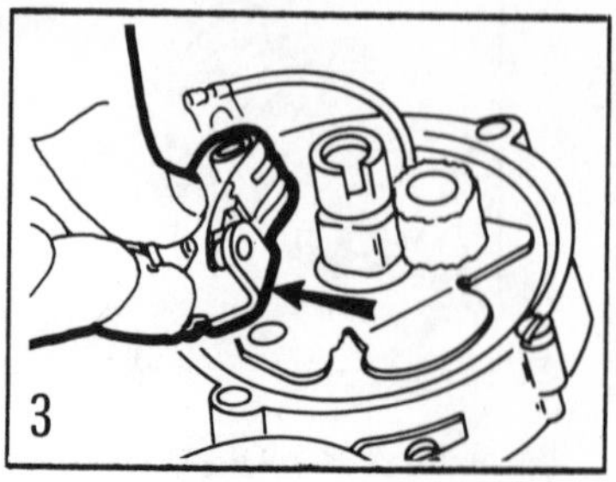

1. Attach new condenser with screw.
2. Rotate or replace cam lubricator. Fiber cam lubricator must be turned 180° every 12,000 mi., replaced every 24,000. When replacing, simply pull it up and off stud; push new lubricator down over stud. DO NOT attempt to add oil or grease to fiber lubricator.
3. Position new points set in distributor. Attach retaining screw lightly. Replace both wire terminals. The condenser wire goes on the outside of the two.

SETTING THE CONTACT GAP—Six Cylinder (1970-74)

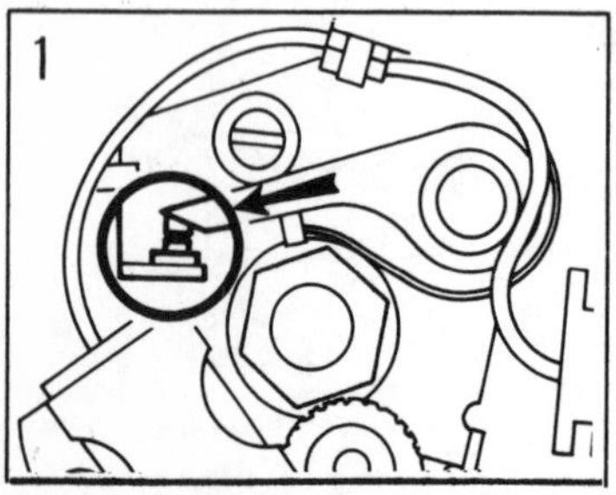

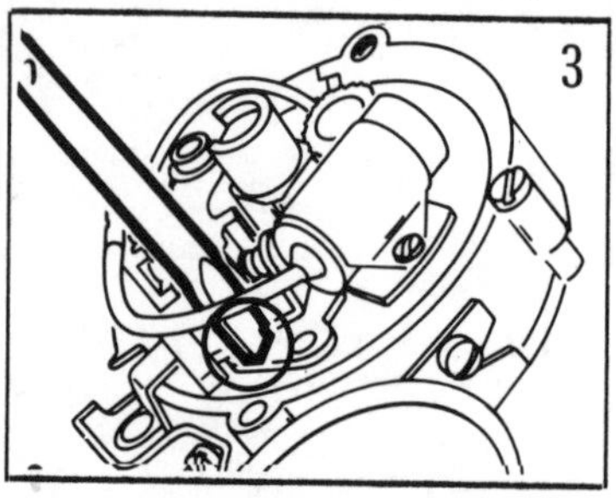

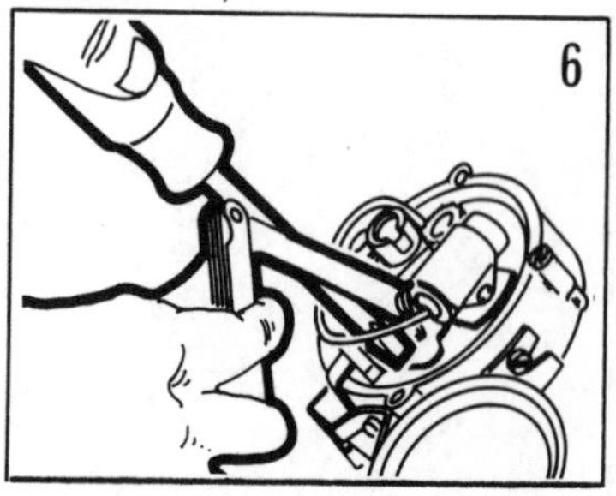

1. Check that point contacts meet squarely. If they do not, bend bracket supporting fixed contact using needle-nosed pliers.
2. Turn engine by ignition key (you'll need a helper) until rubbing block on point set is on one of the **six** high spots of distributor cam. You may use wrench on lower engine pulley to do this.
3. Insert screwdriver in slot near point contacts; twist to open or close gap.
4. Correct gap is .019 in. for new points; .016 in. for used points.
5. Insert correct size feeler gauge. Adjust gap with screwdriver until feeler gauge can be moved in and out between contacts with only slight drag.
6. Tighten point set holddown screw. Recheck gap; it might have changed from tightening holddown screw. Re-adjust if needed.
7. Align tab inside rotor with notch on distributor shaft and push rotor onto shaft. Rotor must be fully seated on shaft.
8. Replace distributor cap; install screws.

LOCATION OF POINTS AND CONDENSER—V8 (1970-74)

Points and condenser work together. Always replace condenser also when installing new points.

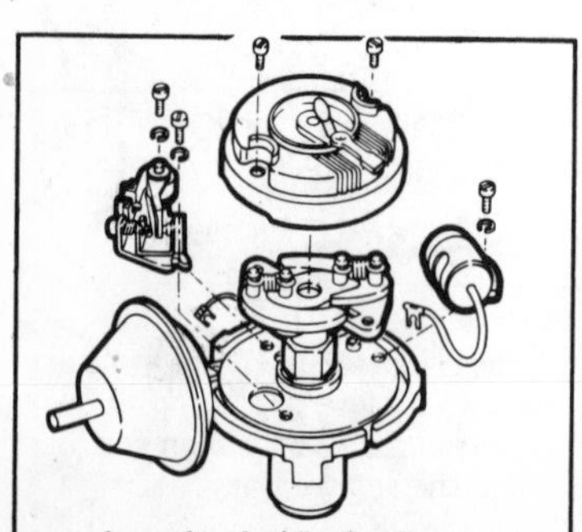

Location inside distributor.

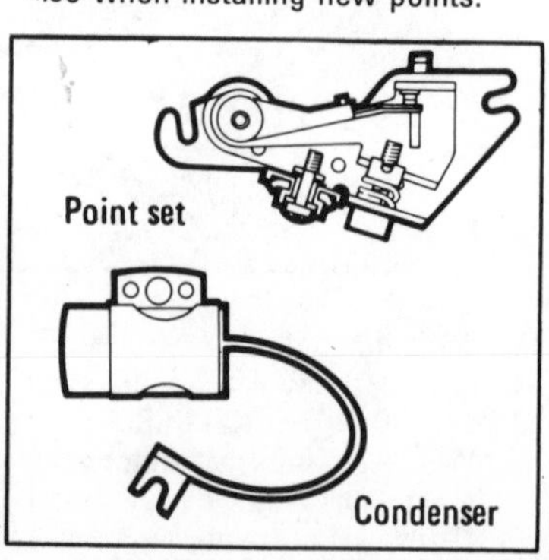

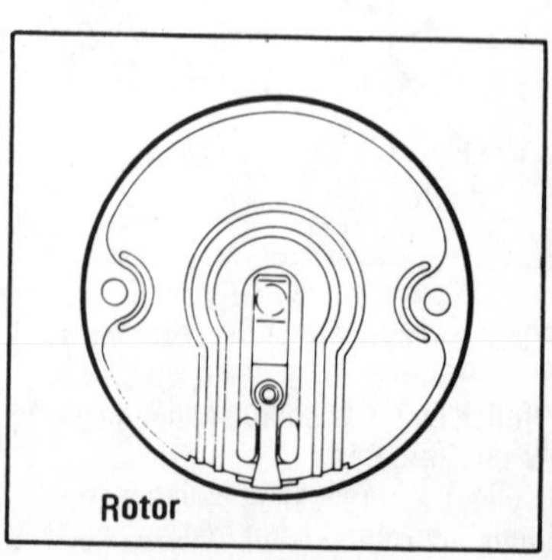

REMOVING POINTS AND CONDENSER—V8 (1970-74)

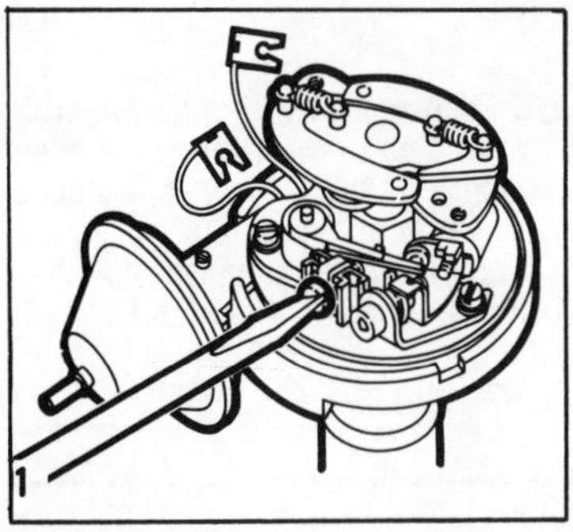

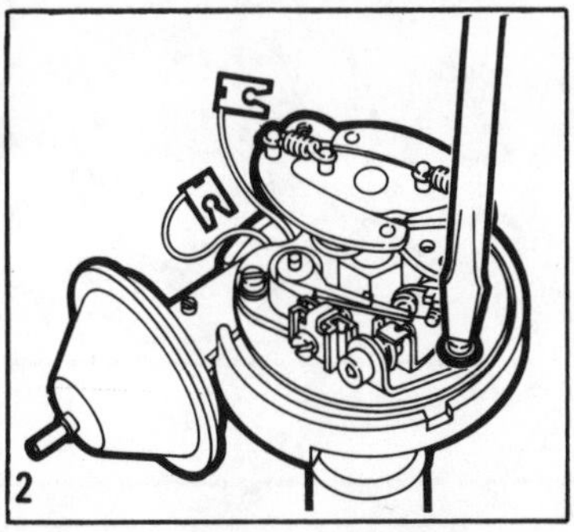

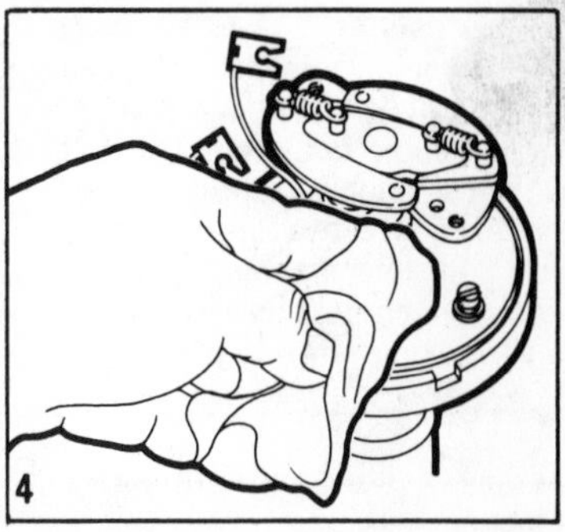

1. Disconnect the two wire terminals connected to the points set. Notice that the condenser connector is on the outside.
2. Loosen, but do not remove the two points attaching screws. Slide the points off the screws to remove.
3. Remove screw which holds condenser. DO NOT DROP SCREW. NOTE: Later models use a combined points and condenser. When you remove points you also remove condenser. You can also install these points in early cars.
4. Wipe all dirt from distributor plate and cam with clean, lint-free rag. CAUTION: When removing screws from distributor, be sure to avoid any screws accidentally falling through distributor opening into engine. Use magnetic screwdriver.

INSTALLING POINTS AND CONDENSER—V8 (1970-74)

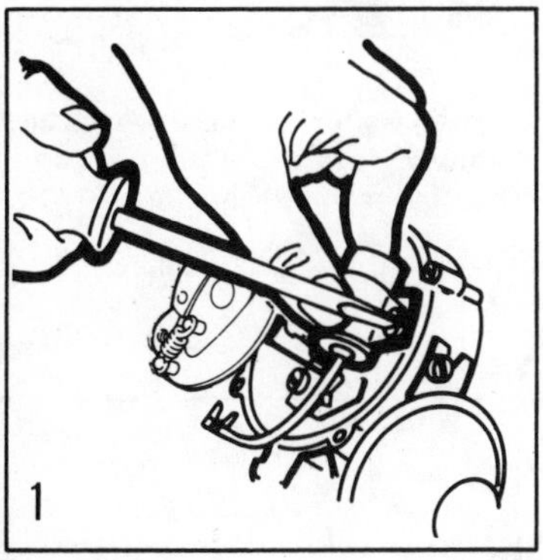

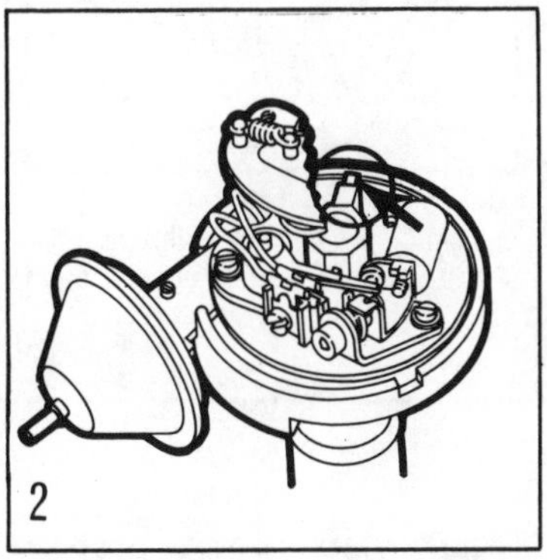

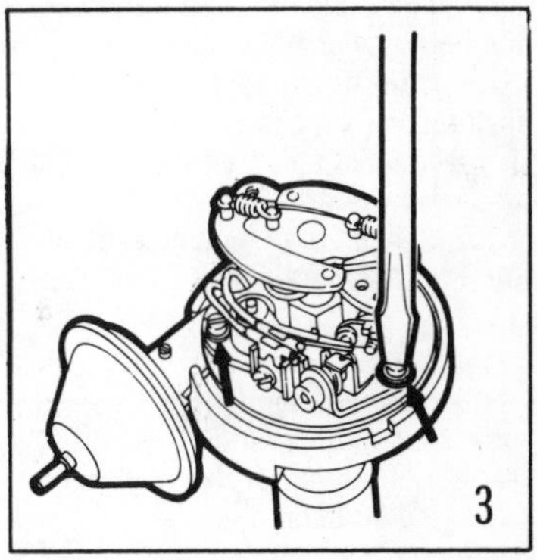

1. Attach new condenser with screw.
2. Rotate or replace cam lubricator. Fiber cam lubricator must be turned 180° every 12,000 mi., replaced every 24,000. When replacing, simply pull it up and off stud; push new lubricator down over stud. DO NOT attempt to add oil or grease to fiber lubricator.
3. Position new points set in distributor by sliding onto screws. Tighten screws.

SETTING THE CONTACT GAP—V8 (1970-74)

1. Check that point contacts meet squarely. If they do not, bend bracket supporting fixed contact using needle-nosed pliers.

2. Turn engine by ignition key (you'll need a helper) until rubbing block on point set is on one of the high spots of distributor cam. You may use wrench on lower engine pulley to do this.

3. Insert a 1/8 in. allen wrench into points adjusting screw. Correct gap

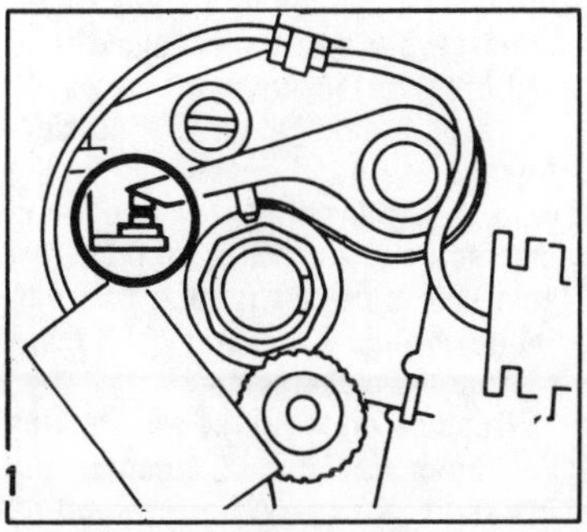

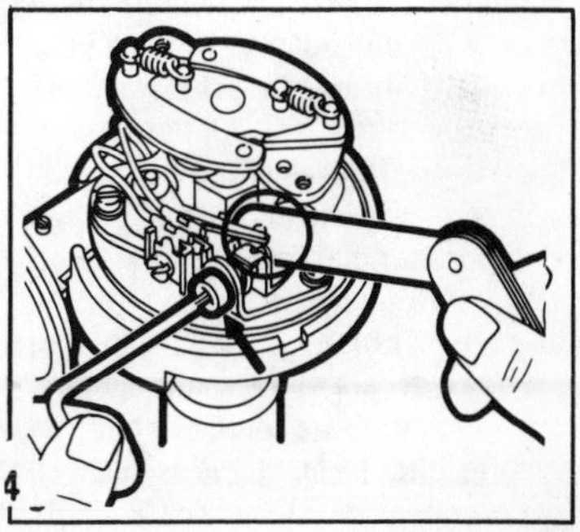

is .019 in. for new points; .016 in. for used points.
4. Insert correct size feeler gauge. Adjust gap with wrench until feeler gauge can be moved in and out between contacts with only slight drag.
5. Install rotor on advance weight assembly. The two lugs on the bottom of the rotor are shaped differently, so it can only be installed one way. Tighten screws.

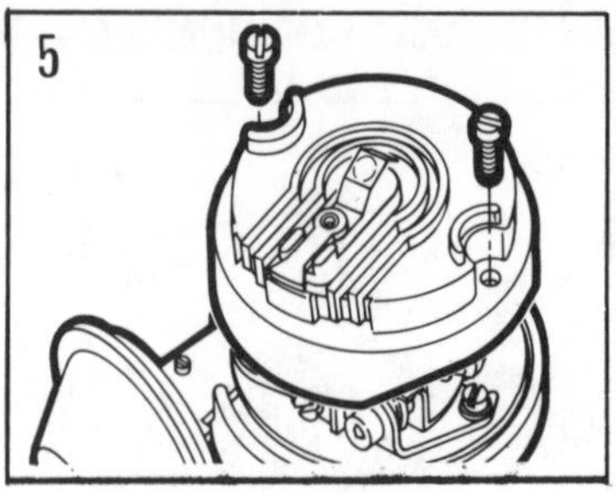

6. Install cap by depressing screws and turning latches onto body of distributor. Insert the coil wire into the cap.
7. Point gap can be adjusted with the engine running. Insert the allen wrench through the cap window, slowly turn the adjusting screw clockwise until the engine just starts to misfire, and then turn it back 1/2 turn.

IGNITION TIMING

Adjusting timing is the important finishing touch to any tune-up. While not difficult, job requires timing light and dwell meter. Timing is listed on tune-up decal.

1. Locate timing marks and pointer (notches) on engine and lower engine pulley. Clean away dirt. Mark the pointer notches with chalk.
2. Hook up timing light according to instructions supplied with it.
3. Disconnect and plug the vacuum line from the distributor.
4. Disconnect the fuel tank vent line from the evaporative canister.

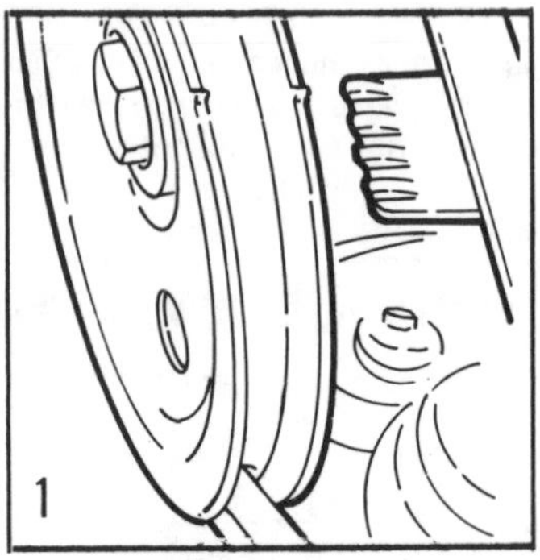

5. Aim timing light at pulley mark(s). If the chalked marks do not align,

loosen distributor holddown nut and slowly rotate distributor until chalked marks align.

6. Tighten hold-down nut.

REPLACING THE SPARK PLUG WIRES

One of the most often overlooked items in a tune-up is the spark plug wires. Your car can be in perfect tune, but if the plug wires are not carrying the spark to the plugs, your engine will run poorly. The original equipment wires that came with your car are usually good for a year or two before needing replacement. On newer cars, the higher underhood temperatures created by emission controls breaks down the wires ability to conduct electricity sooner. The spark plug boot ends of the wires will crack with age allowing the spark to arc towards the engine, not reaching the plugs. The distributor cap ends of the wires will often collect moisture, and corrode right there in your distributor cap. Sometimes a wire will contact a hot part of the engine, such as the exhaust manifold and burn through the insulation. Other times, a wire will become oil soaked and gummy, breaking down the insulation. Often, when carbon core wires get old, they will break off inside, with no visible signs of breakage on the outside. Always use good quality spark plug wire. A carbon core or cut-rate brand may seem attractive at first, but will cost you more in the long run with reduced engine efficiency and more frequent replacement.
1. Replace one wire at a time. This will keep you out of trouble with crossed wires. When removing wires, twist back and forth as you pull up. This will help free up stuck wires.
2. Take the old wire and match it up with the new one for length. If you are cutting your own, make sure there is good metal to metal contact between the end of the wire and the pinch-on connectors.
3. Make sure each wire seats all the way down in the distributor cap. First push down the wire, then the boot. The wire should click in place.
4. After you are all done, make sure all wires are clear of choke or throttle linkage, or hot exhaust manifolds.
Use the firing order illustration to guide you when replacing your ignition wires and/or distributor cap.

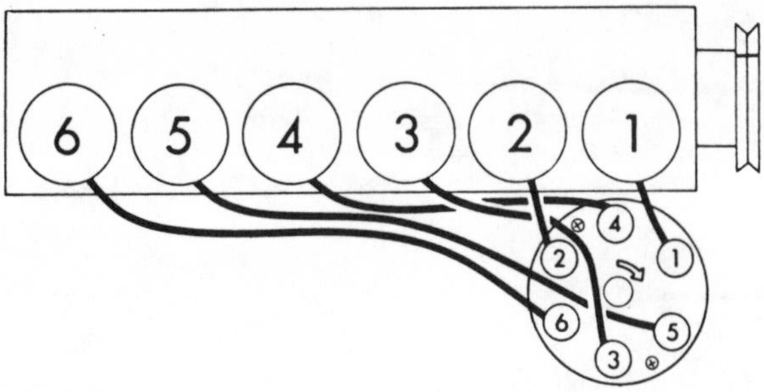

6-cyl. engine, 250 CID (1970-74)
Engine firing order: 1-5-3-6-2-4
Distributor rotation: clockwise

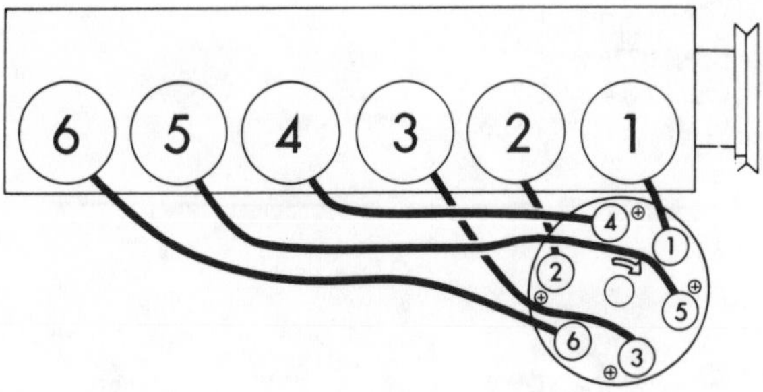

6 cyl. engine, 250 CID (1975-77)
Engine firing order: 1-5-3-6-2-4
Distributor rotation: clockwise

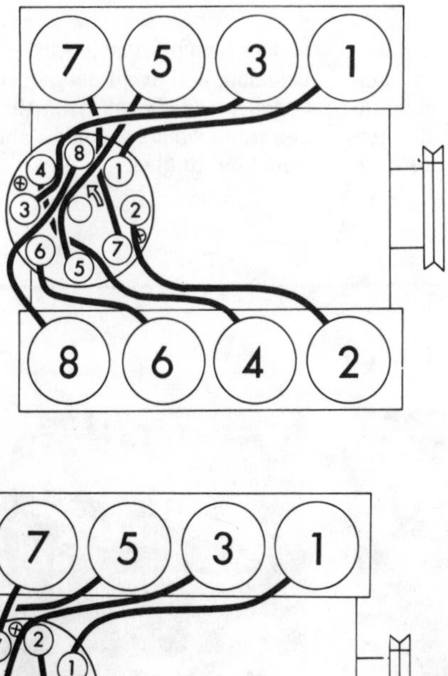

V8 engine, 350, 455 CID (1970-74)
Engine firing order: 1-8-4-3-6-5-7-2
Distributor rotation: counterclockwise

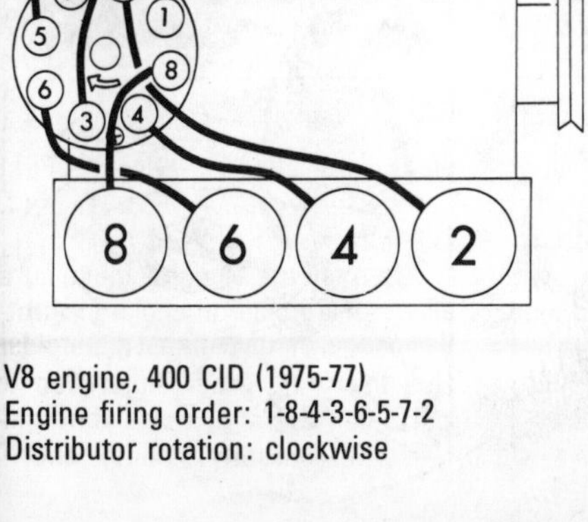

V8 engine, 400 CID (1975-77)
Engine firing order: 1-8-4-3-6-5-7-2
Distributor rotation: clockwise

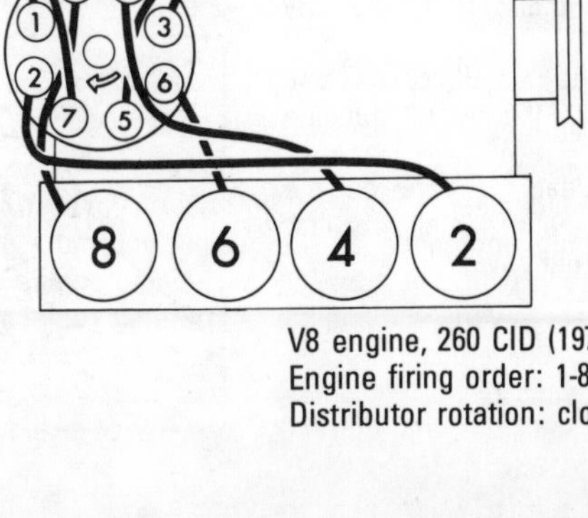

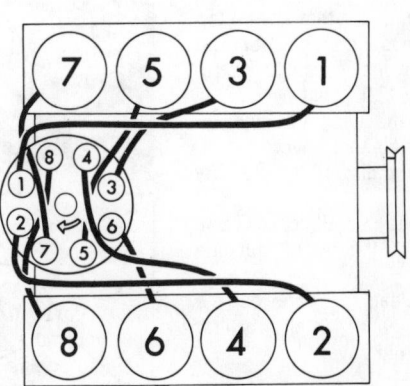

V8 engine, 260 CID (1975-77)
Engine firing order: 1-8-4-3-6-5-7-2
Distributor rotation: clockwise

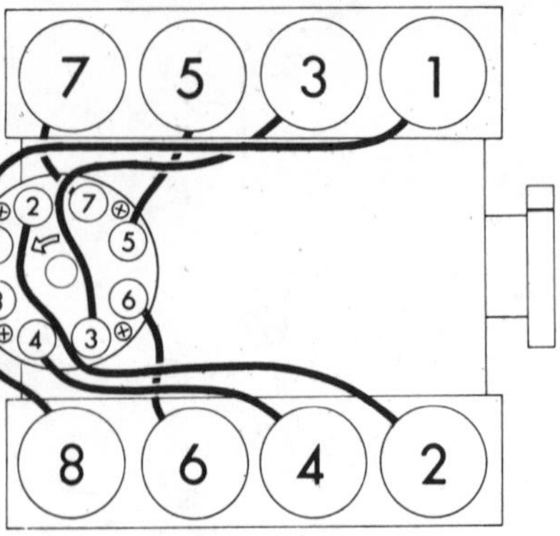

V8 engine, 350, 455 CID with full-voltage ignition (1974-77)
Engine firing order: 1-8-4-3-6-5-7-2
Distributor rotation: counterclockwise

Fuel System

When gasoline is brought from the fuel tank, it mixes with air in the carburetor. This gas/air mixture enters engine thru the intake manifold, passes thru the intake valves and is burned in the combustion chamber. The burned exhaust gas is then passed thru the exhaust valves to the exhaust system and to the outside air. In order to keep your car's engine running cleanly with minimal pollution, and avoid dangerous carbon monoxide fumes inside the vehicle, certain items should be checked from time to time.

REPLACING THE AIR FILTER

The large round can that sits on top of the engine is the air cleaner. The filter element inside should be replaced every 12,000 miles.

1. Unscrew the wing nut and remove the air cleaner cover.
2. Remove and discard the old dirty filter.
3. Check the small crankcase breather filter. If dirty, lift out and replace it.
4. Using a clean rag, wipe out the inside of air cleaner. Install new filter and replace top cover.

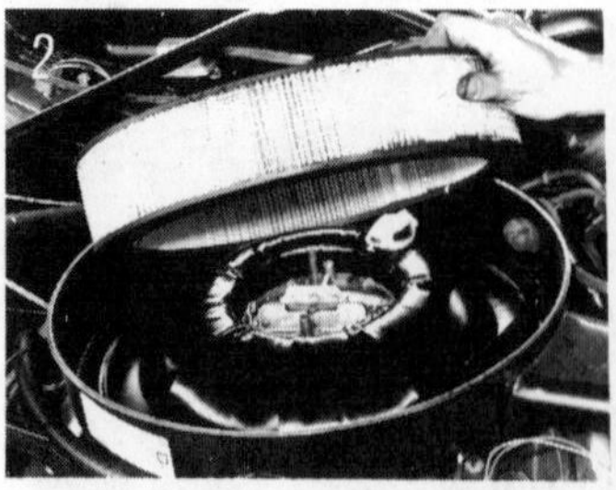

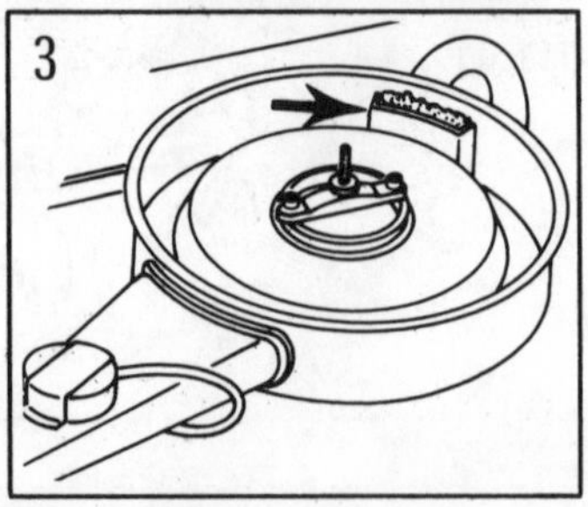

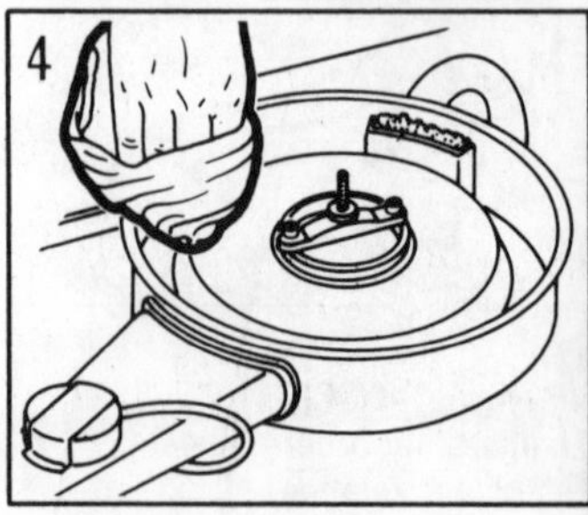

FUEL FILTER REPLACEMENT

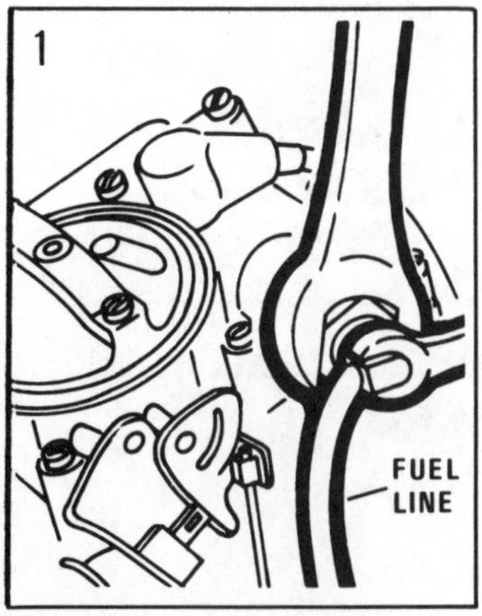

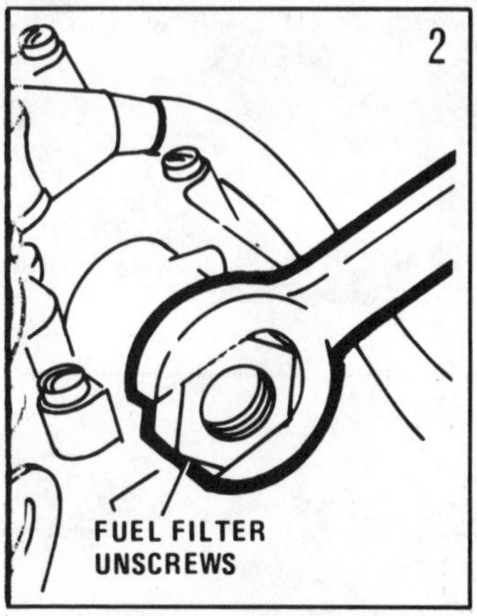

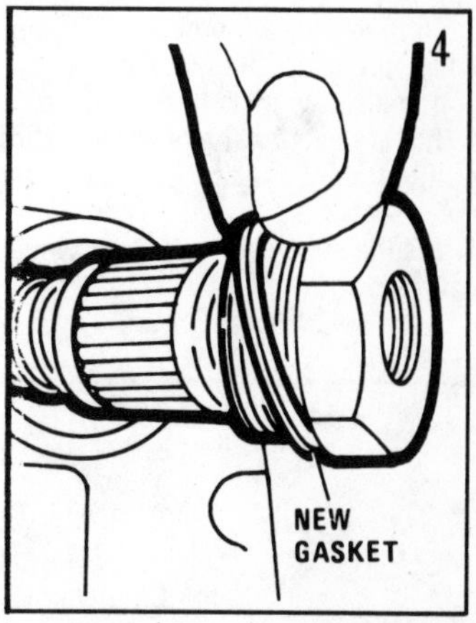

The fuel filter is located behind the large fuel line inlet nut on the carburetor. Replace the filter every year or 12,000 miles. The fuel filter prevents dirt, rust, and scale from both the gas station's tank and your own fuel tank from reaching the carburetor. A dirty filter will starve the engine and cause poor running.

1. Place an absorbent rag under fuel line connection to absorb gas spills. Unscrew fuel line connection with ½ in. wrench while holding the larger nut with a 1 in. wrench. Be careful, fuel line fitting threads are easily stripped.
2. Remove the large filter retaining nut from the carburetor. The spring behind the filter will push it out. Remove the filter and the spring.
3. Install the spring and new filter element. Some carburetors are equipped with a paper element, others with a bronze unit. The bronze filter must have the small cone section facing out and a gasket between the filter and the retaining nut.
4. Install the new gasket on the retaining nut and screw it into place. CAUTION: DO NOT OVERTIGHTEN
5. Reconnect the fuel line. Discard the gas soaked rag safely.
6. Start the engine and check for leaks. Addition of a can of carburetor cleaner to the fuel tank occasionally will aid in keeping the entire fuel system clean.

PCV VALVE REPLACEMENT

An important part of a car's emission control system is the Positive Crankcase Ventilation (PCV) valve and its connecting hose. The PCV valve should be replaced once every 24,000 miles. This device keeps dirt and sludge from forming inside the engine. Make sure all PCV connections are tight. Check that the connecting hoses are clear and not clogged. Replace any brittle or broken hoses.

1. Pull valve from its location in rear part of valve cover.

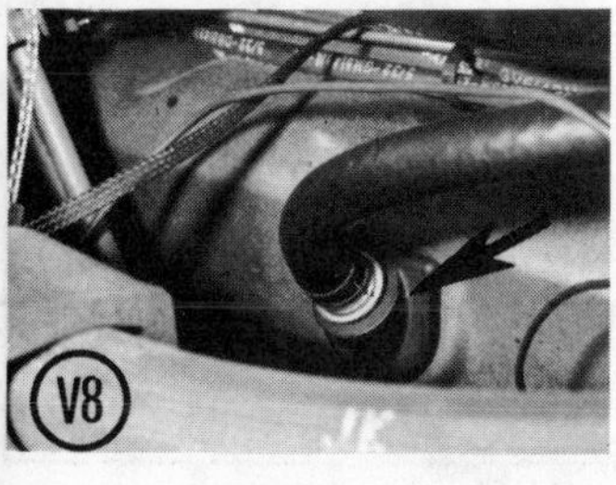

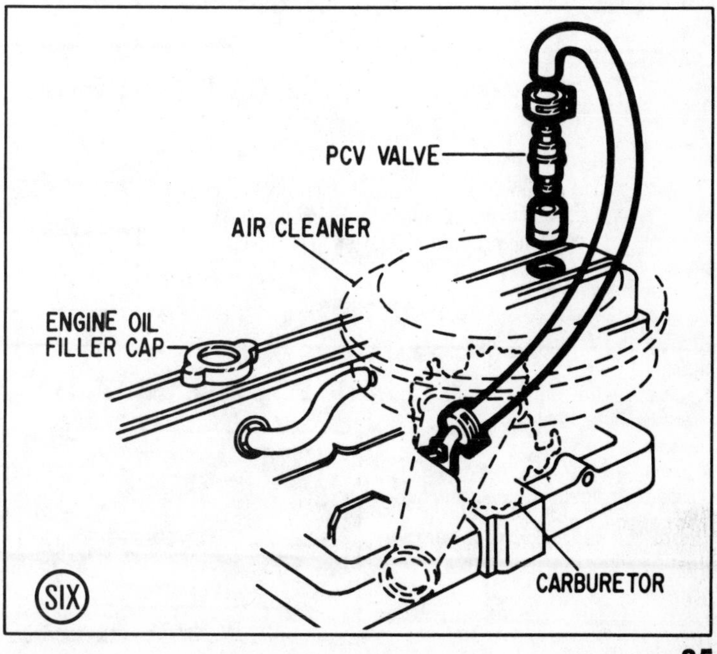

2. Squeeze the hose clamp with a pair of pliers. Remove the valve.
3. Note where the other end of the hose connects. Remove the hose and flush it with cleaning solvent.
4. Reconnect the hose. Pinch the clamp and insert the PCV valve into the hose.
5. Insert the valve into the valve cover.

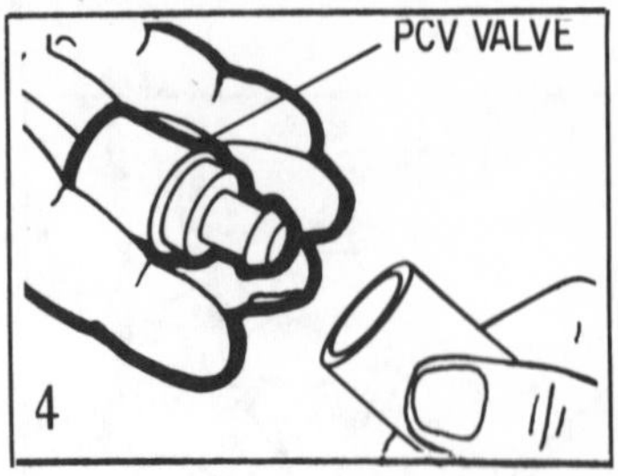

Safety Systems

LIGHTING SYSTEM

Headlights, turn signals, stop lights, and parking lights are an important part of your car's safety system. They permit you to see and be seen. Keep all lenses clean and make frequent checks to be sure that all of your lights are functioning properly. Replace any cracked lenses as soon as possible. When replacing a bulb, make a note of the number which is usually printed on the base. If you don't have a number, take the old bulb with you so that you match it for the correct replacement.

PARKING LIGHTS, TURN SIGNALS AND STOP LIGHTS

To replace a turn signal, stop light, or parking light bulb, remove the lens, push down on bulb while turning it counterclockwise to remove it from the socket. Install the new bulb in reverse order. Install the new bulb in reverse order. Be sure to match the knobs on the bulb base with the slots in the socket.

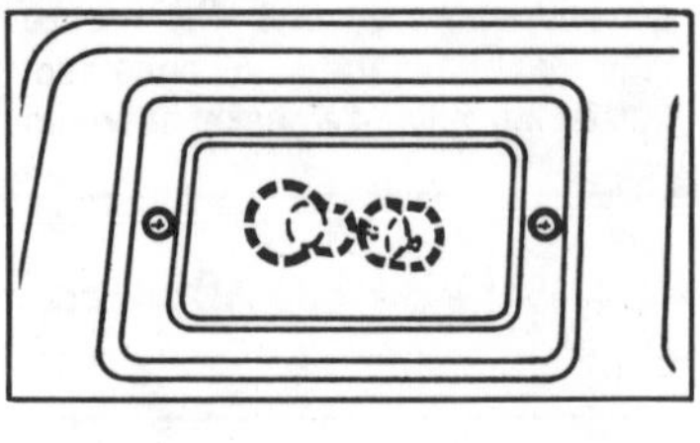

LICENSE PLATE LIGHTS

Remove the screws that retain the lens to the bumpers. Push in on bulb, turning counterclockwise to remove.

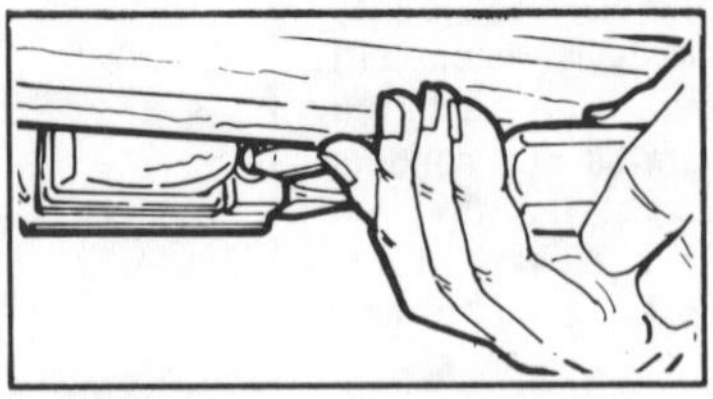

SIDE MARKER LIGHT

Reach up inside fender and turn bulb socket counterclockwise to remove from housing. Pull bulb straight out.

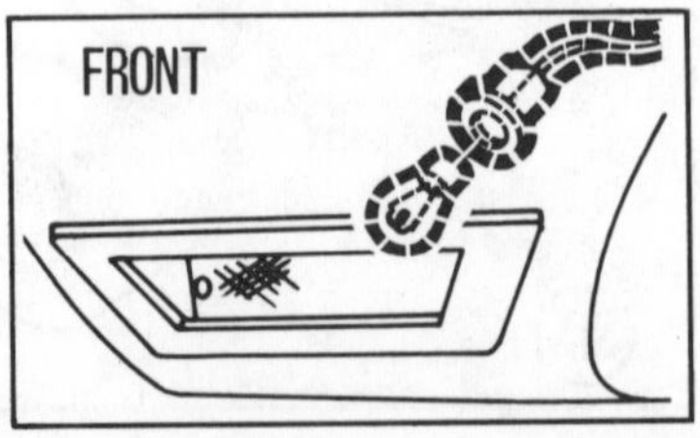

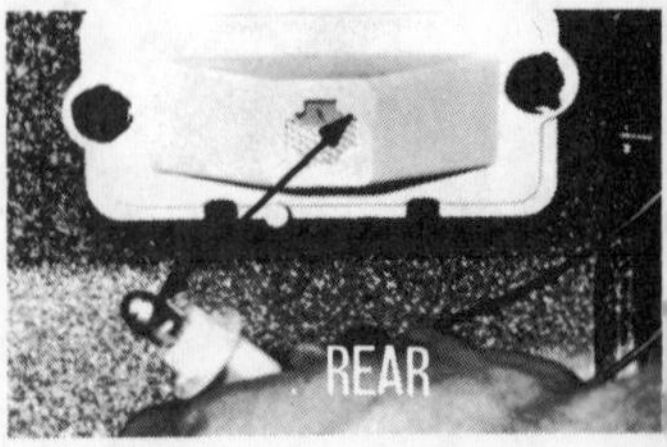

INTERIOR DOME LIGHT

This is cartridge type bulb; be sure to purchase correct replacement. Pry dome light lens out from housing. To avoid blowing fuse, make sure doors are closed and domelight switch is in OFF position. Carefully lever the bulb straight out of housing. Insert new bulb and re-install dome light lens.

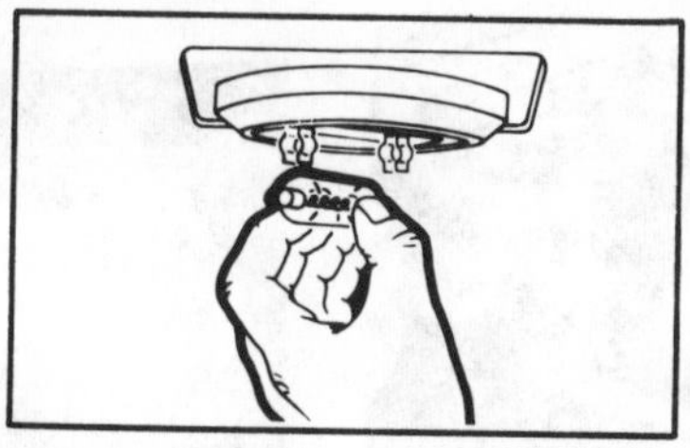

HEADLIGHT REPLACEMENT—Four Light System

1. Remove the headlight trim retaining screws and remove the trim.
2. Unhook the spring from the headlight retaining ring.
3. Remove the two retaining ring screws. Do not disturb the long aiming screws located at 9 and 12 o'clock.
4. Remove the retaining ring. Disconnect the wiring plug and remove the bulb.
5. Attach the connector plug to the new headlight.
6. Position the new bulb in housing. Make sure that the number molded into the lens is at the top.
7. Install the retaining ring and pull the spring into place.
8. Replace the headlight trim panel.

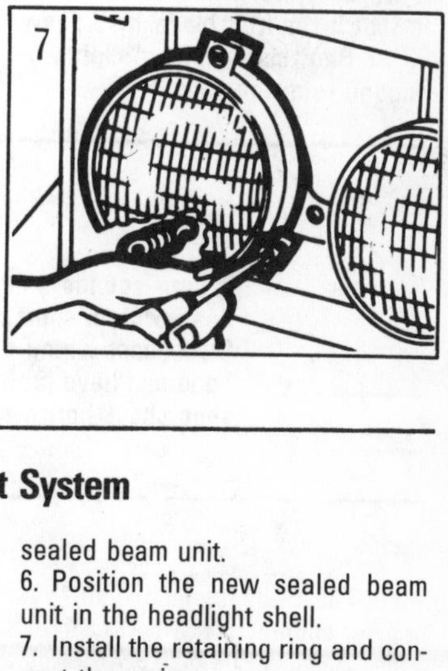

HEADLIGHT REPLACEMENT—Two Light System

1. Remove headlight cover retaining screws and cover.
2. Unhook the spring from the headlight retaining ring.
3. Unscrew the retaining ring and remove it.
NOTE: Do not mistake the headlight adjustment screws for the retaining ring screws.
4. Pull lamp (sealed beam) out of headlight shell toward front of car; disconnect wiring connector from sealed beam unit.
5. Connect wire connector to new sealed beam unit.
6. Position the new sealed beam unit in the headlight shell.
7. Install the retaining ring and connect the spring.
8. Position headlight cover; install attaching screws.

HEADLIGHT REPLACEMENT—Rectangular Lights

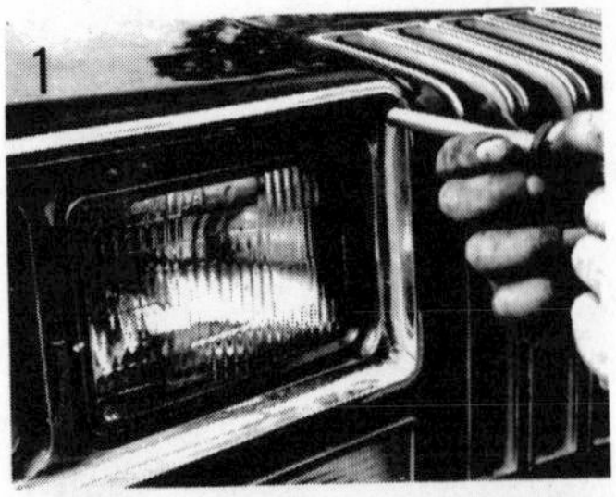

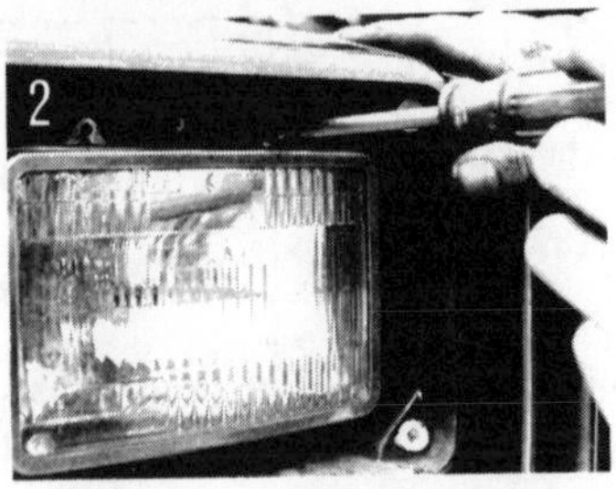

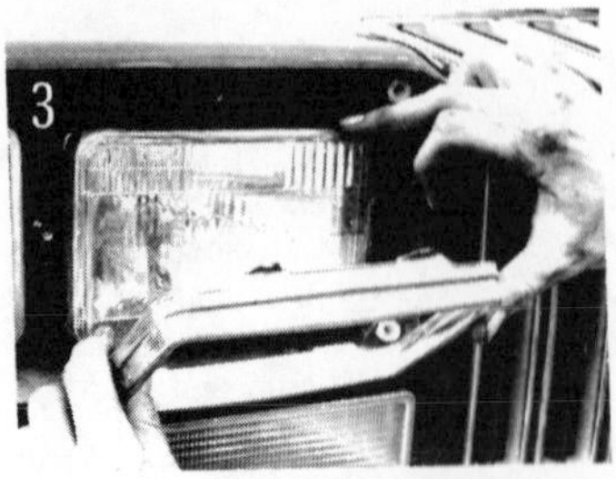

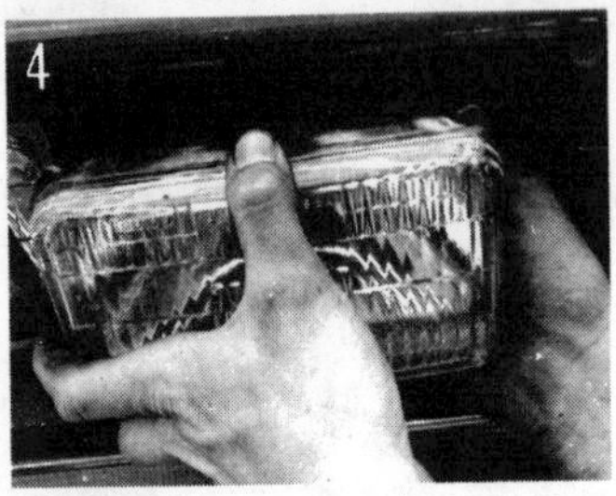

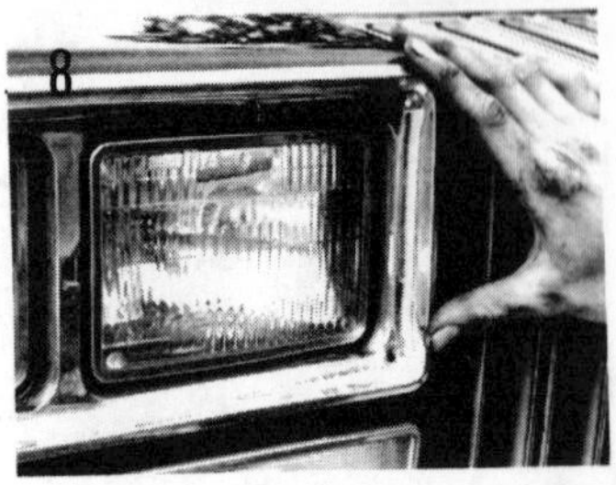

1. Remove the headlight cover retaining screws and cover.
2. Remove the headlight retainer screws.
3. Remove the headlight retainer.
4. Pull the lamp (sealed beam) out of the headlight shell toward the front of the car. Disconnect the wiring connector from the sealed beam unit.
5. Attach the wiring connector to the rear of the sealed beam unit.
6. Position the new sealed beam unit in the headlight shell.
7. Install the headlight retainer.
8. Position the headlight cover and install the attaching screws.

WINDSHIELD WIPER BLADE REPLACEMENT

To replace wiper blade, lift up on spring release tab on wiper arm connector. Pull wiper blade off. Snap new blade into place.
To replace rubber insert only, press down, away from wiper blade to free it. Slide insert from blade. Insert new wiper. Bend insert upward slightly to engage retaining clips.

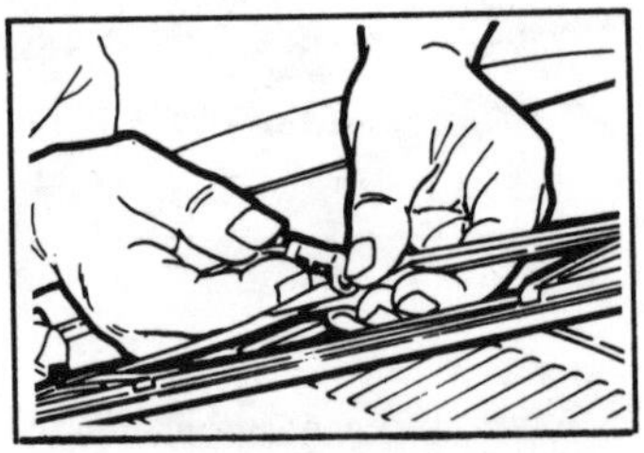

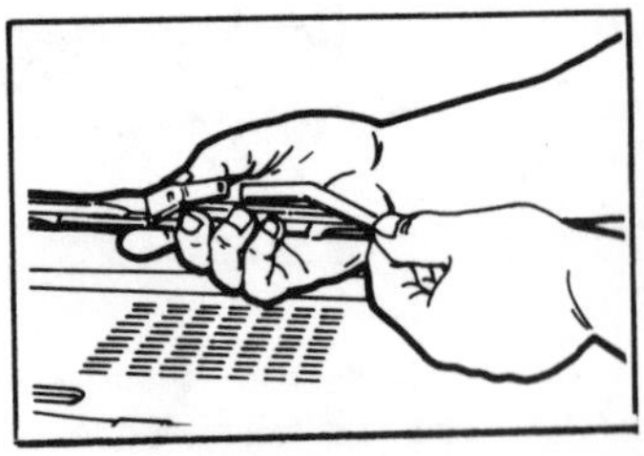

HORN PROBLEMS

If horn sounds and does not stop, this is due to short circuit in wiring. Disconnect wiring connector under hood and have professional service shop check horn wiring circuit.

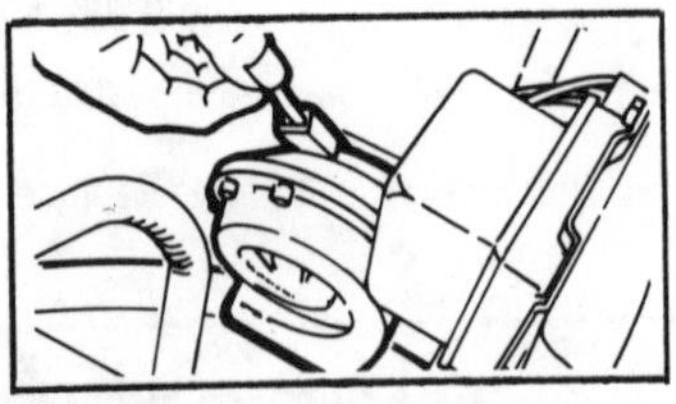

STEERING PROBLEMS

See steering system check in Suspension Section. Check tire pressures. Have a professional service shop check all components in the front end and steering system.

WASHER SYSTEM

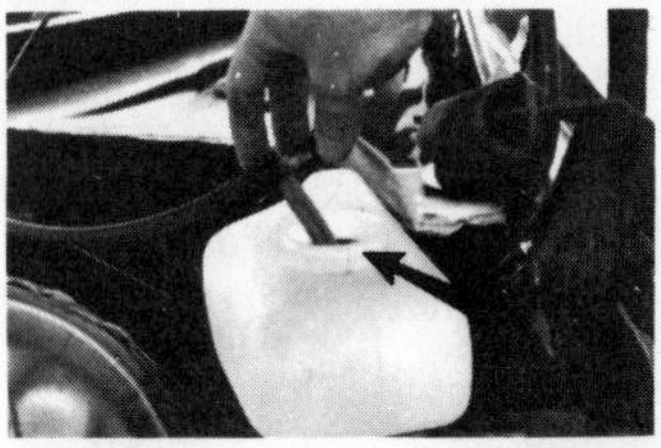

If washer fails to squirt properly, raise hood and check system hose connections. Be sure washer fluid container has fluid. Check spout openings for clogging.
Keep container filled with fluid mixture of washer solvent and water. If road spray buildup on windshield is a chronic problem, add 1 tablespoon dishwasher detergent to solvent/water mixture when re-filling container.

Electrical System

CHECKPOINTS AND SERVICES

To ensure starting ability at all times check your battery condition periodically. You'll need to check battery electrolyte (fluid) level in each of the six cells. Check battery cable connections for tightness and inspect for accumulated corrosion.
SAFETY NOTE: Wear gloves when working on battery.

CHECK BATTERY FLUID

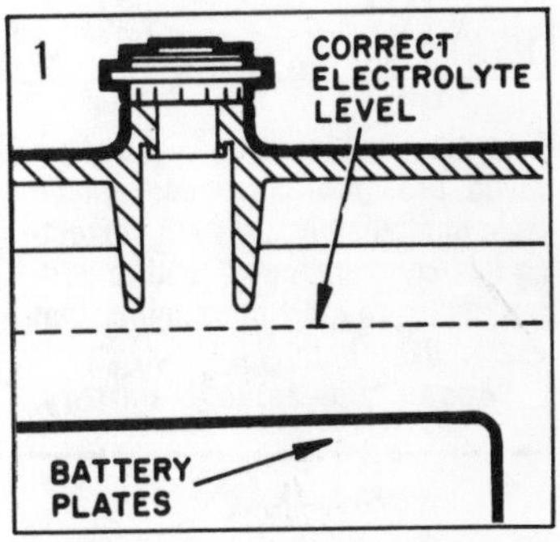

Some 1976 and all 1977 GM products are equipped with a new type of no maintenance battery. This battery requires no maintenance other than occasionally checking its state of charge by looking at the indicator on the top. If the indicator is dark with a green dot showing in the center, the battery is fully charged. If the indicator is dark but there is no green dot showing, the battery should be charged. If the indicator is light, the battery should be replaced.

1. Remove plastic filler caps on top of battery. Fluid should be up to lower end of filler hole and covering the plates. If fluid is low add clean, cold tap water. If your area has hard water, use only distilled water available at auto supply, food or drug stores.
2. Replace any lost caps immediately.

CAUTION: NEVER LIGHT A MATCH OR SMOKE near the top of a battery. Batteries give off explosive hydrogen gas.

NOTE: Battery that often checks low on fluid could mean:
A. Battery is getting old, due for replacement; have charge capacity checked at service shop.
B. Connections may be corroded or loose; clean/replace as needed (see below).
C. Alternator or voltage regulator not functioning properly; this happens far less often than A or B above.

CLEANING BATTERY TERMINALS

As time goes by battery terminals build up a dry powdery, whitish material. This material is corrosive and will gradually eat thru battery cables if not cleaned off periodically.

1. Loosen and remove battery connections.
2. Brush off all loose corrosion; use

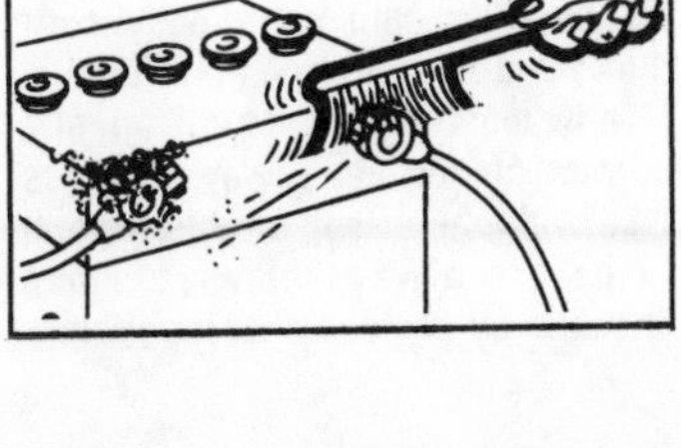

stiff bristle brush. Do not get this material into eyes or on open cuts. Wash off at once.

3. If corrosion build-up is extremely heavy and brushing does not remove all of it, mix 2 tablespoons baking soda to 1 cup water. Pour solution directly onto terminals and connectors. Allow to soak a few minutes and rinse off. Continue brushing to remove all traces of corrosion build-up. Do not allow cleaning solution to enter battery.

4. Replace connectors on battery

terminal posts and tighten.

5. Liberally smear battery terminal

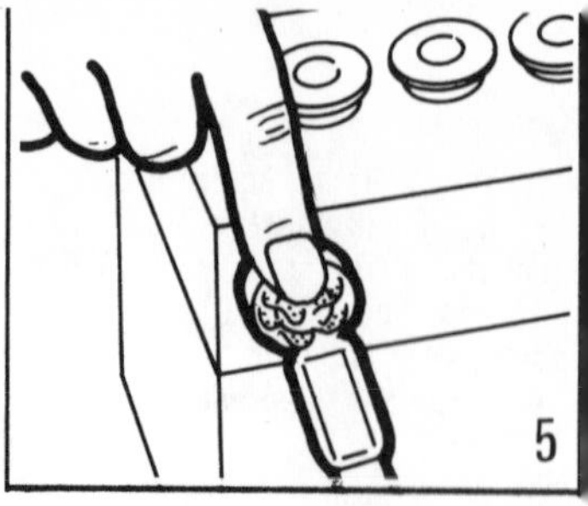

posts and cable connectors with petroleum jelly.

REPLACE FAULTY BATTERY CABLES

If battery cable strands become frayed, broken or corroded, replace cable immediately. Delay in correcting this condition could lead to sudden failure to start the engine. Can also weaken battery.

1. Loosen and remove battery.

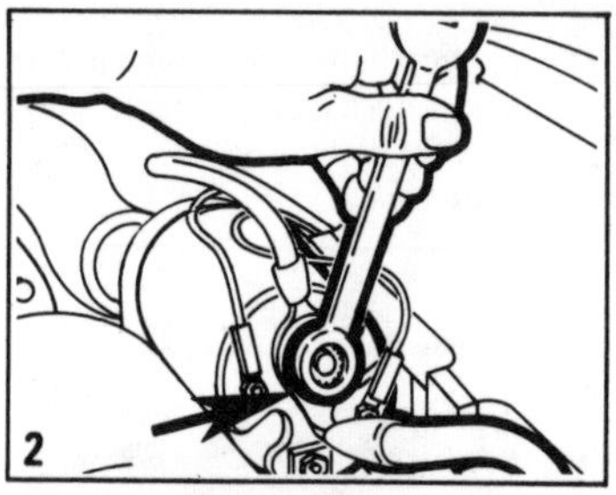

Clean any corrosion buildup

2. Disconnect negative cable from its attachment to engine or chassis. Disconnect positive cable from its attachment to starter relay.

3. Attach new cables making sure positive and negative cables are on

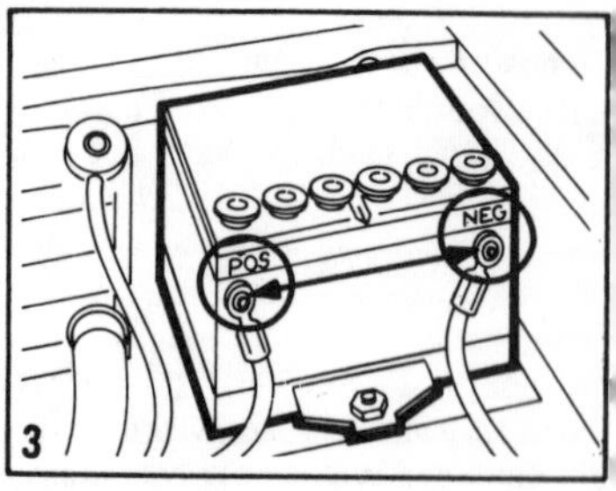

proper terminals. They are not identical.

4. Replace connectors on battery terminal posts and tighten.

5. Liberally smear battery terminal posts and cable connectors with petroleum jelly.

BATTERY HOLDDOWN

The clamp device which holds battery in place should be checked periodically. If loose, tighten. Clean off corrosion buildup. Severely corroded holddown components should be replaced before they break.

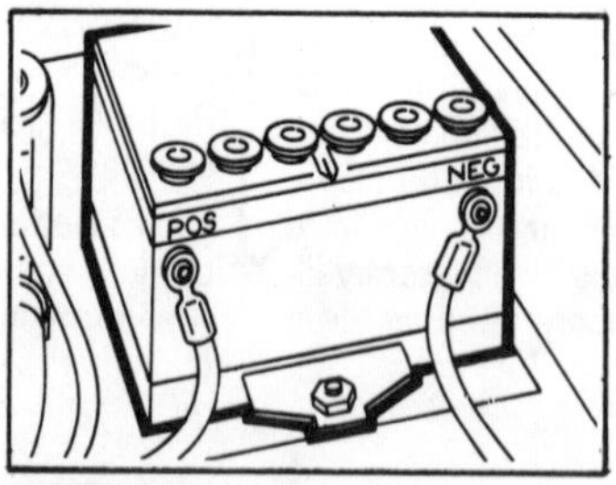

ELECTRICAL FUSES

The fuse box is located to the left of the steering column, directly over the dimmer switch. Each fuse is clearly marked as to function and correct amperage. Always replace fuse with one of same amperage. If fuses are always blowing, have checked by professional mechanic.

TURN SIGNAL AND 4-WAY FLASHER

Turn signals and 4-way emergency flashers will operate only if: A. All light bulbs are OK. B. Flasher units are not burned out. The car has two flasher units that work independently of each other. TURN SIGNAL FLASHER: located behind left side of instrument panel. Pull flasher from spring clip mounting. Unplug from connector. Plug in new flasher. Replace in spring clip mounting. EMERGENCY FLASHER: located in fuse block. Simply unplug and insert new flasher. REPLACE ONLY WITH SAME TYPE FLASHER.

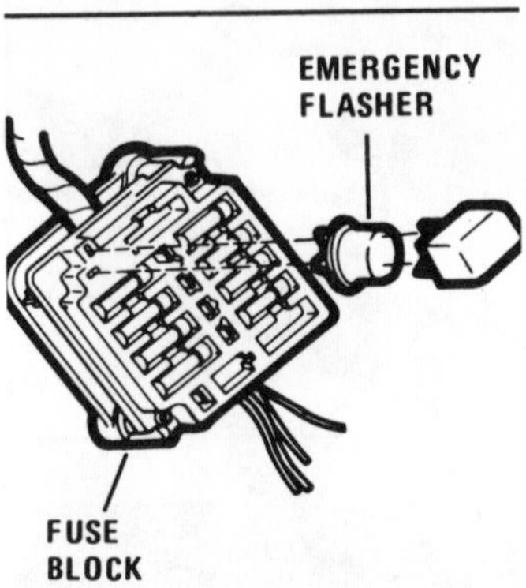

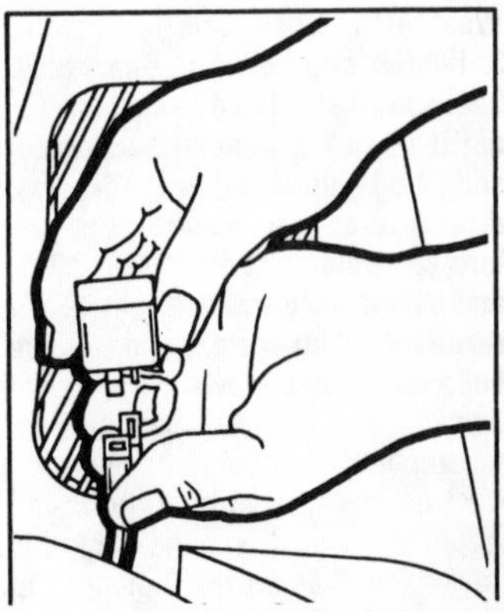

ALTERNATOR

If Alt. warning light glows red at operating speed, alternator isn't charging battery properly. Common causes are:
A. Fan belts are loose and slipping on alternator pulley. Tighten or replace belts.
B. Battery terminals, cables are loose or corroded. Clean; tighten; replace bad cables.
If A or B do not correct problem, alternator or voltage regulator may be faulty. This happens far less often, and can only be checked by mechanic with proper electrical testing equipment.

Alternator Caution: Alternator can be permanently damaged by shortcircuiting terminal connections. When working around or moving alternator, always keep metal tools or engine parts from terminals.

REAR WINDOW DEFOGGER SYSTEM

Do not clean inside of rear window fitted with defogger system with any abrasive material. This could destroy carbon-copper wires. Use only soft rag and mild detergent/water mixture. Dry carefully.

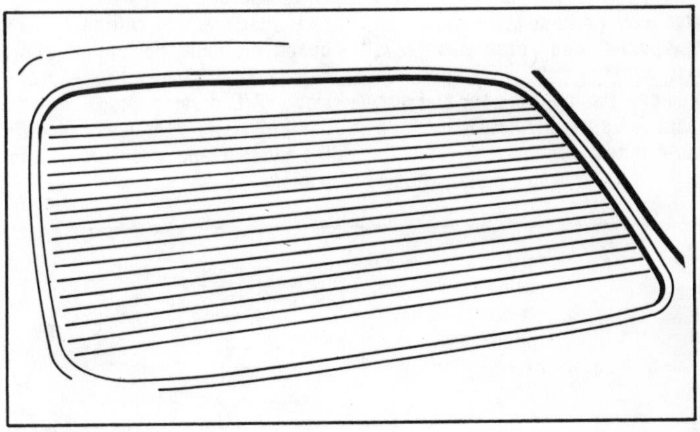

Air Conditioning System

CHECKPOINTS AND SERVICES

WARNING!—Never attempt to tighten fittings, disassemble or do any work on your car's A/C system. Consult a professional mechanic about A/C system problems and their correction. Your auto air conditioner (A/C) is a delicate, closed system. If air, dirt or water get into it, or if refrigerant escapes, the A/C unit will not cool a car interior. Among things you can do are:
1. Keep condenser grille clean.

Check for dirt and debris; periodically remove dead insects, leaves, etc., with stiff bristle brush. Straighten any bent fins—carefully.
2. Keep radiator filled to correct level. (See Cooling System section). If fluid needs to be added, add antifreeze rather than water.
3. Keep radiator coolant at a 50/50 water/antifreeze mixture.
4. Flush cooling system and replace with fresh coolant mixture at least every 24 months. (See Cooling System section).
5. Radiator cap should be tight and sealed properly. If sealing gasket is cracked, cut or worn, replace cap with new 15 lb. unit.
6. Check fan belt tension periodically. (See Cooling System section). Replace glazed, frayed or cut fan belts, before they fail entirely.
7. Check periodically for bubbles in A/C sight glass. Sight glass is located in head of receiver/drier vessel. Or on the side of the V.I.R. assembly. Sight glass is no larger than head of large nail. It may be dirty. Wipe clean for best visibility.

PROCEED AS FOLLOWS:
a) With engine and A/C system running, look for passage of refrigerant in sight glass. You'll be looking for a stream of milky white bubbles as they pass through sight glass. It is best to watch sight glass and have someone else start the car and turn on the A/C system. Allow to run for a few minutes.
b) If you observe no bubbles, and air flow from A/C unit in the car is passing cold air, everything is OK.
c) If no bubbles appear in sight glass, and air flow from the A/C unit in the car is not delivering cold air, the system may be low on refrigerant and could need a re-charge.
d) If bubbles appear, system is low on refrigerant.
e) If you suspect refrigerant loss based on tests performed above, have system checked by a professional A/C service shop. They can confirm refrigerant loss, recharge the system and check for system leakage.

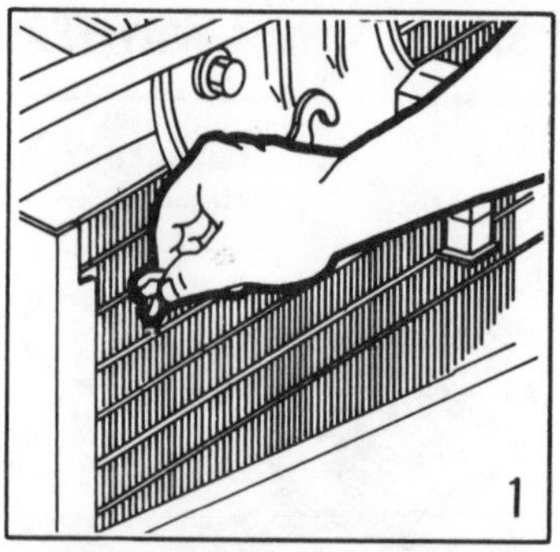

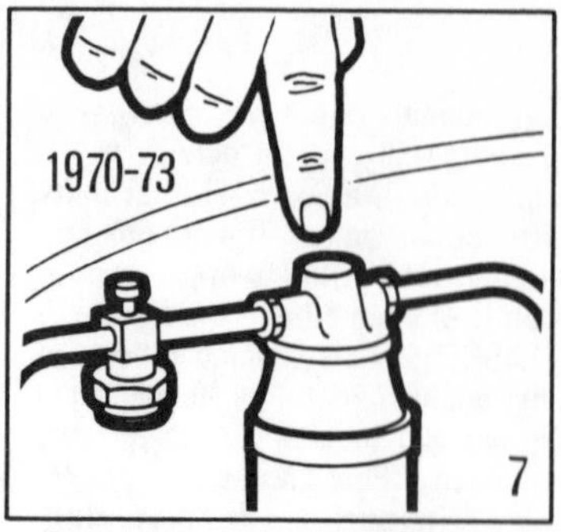

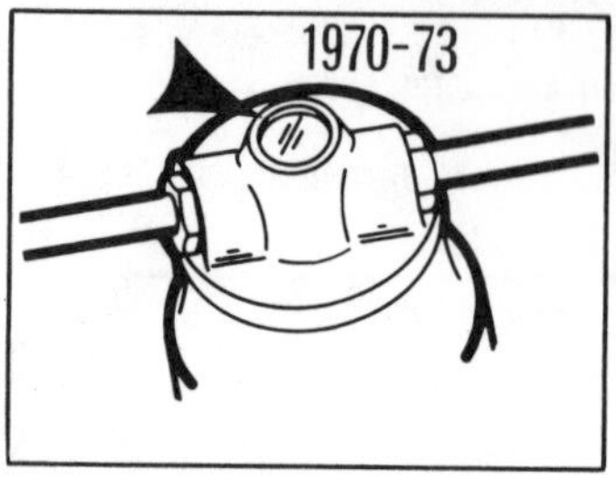

NOTE: Once a week or so, even in winter, run A/C system for about 5 minutes as you drive. This keeps system internally lubricated, prevents hoses hardening.

TUNE-UP SPECIFICATIONS

YEAR	ENGINE No. Cyl. Displacement (cu. in.)	SPARK PLUGS Type	Gap (in.)	DISTRIBUTOR Point Dwell (deg.)	Point Gap (in.)	IGNITION TIMING Man. Trans.● (deg.) ■	Auto Trans.● (deg.) ■	IDLE SPEED Man. Trans.● (rpm) ▲	Auto Trans. (rpm) ▲
1970	6-250 1 bbl	R-46T	.035	31-34°	.019	TDC⑩	4°B	830-750	630-600
	8-350 2 bbl	R-46S	.030	28-32°	.016	10°B⑩	10°B	750	575
	8-350 4 bbl	R-45S	.030	28-32°	.016	10°B⑩	10°B	650	575
	8-350 4 bbl	R-43S	.030	28-32°	.016	14°B⑩	14°B	750	625
	8-455 2 bbl	R-45S	.030	28-32°	.016	—	8°B	—	575
	8-455 4 bbl①	R-44S	.030	28-32°	.016	—	12½°	—	600
	8-455 4 bbl②	R-45S	.030	28-32°	.016	—	8°B	—	575
	8-455 4 bbl③	R-44S	.030	28-32°	.016	12°⑩	12°B	700	650
	8-455 4 bbl③	R-44S	.030	28-32°	.016	8°B⑩	8°B	700	650
1971	6-250 1 bbl	R-46TS	.035	31-34°	.019	4°B⑩	4°B	600⑤	500⑤
	8-350 2 bbl	R-46S	.040	28-32°	.016	10°B⑩	10°B	750	600
	8-350 4 bbl	R-45S④	.040	28-32°	.016	10°B⑩	12°B	750	600
	8-455 2 bbl	R-46S	.040	28-32°	.016	—	8B°	—	600
	8-455 4 bbl	R-46S	.040	28-32°	.016	—	8B°	—	600
	8-455 4 bbl	R-45S	.040	28-32°	.016	10°⑩	10°B	750	600
	8-455 4 bbl	R-45S	.040	28-32°	.016	12°B⑩	10°B	750	600
1972	8-350 2 bbl	R-46S	.040	28-32°	.016	8°B⑩	8°B(6°B)	750	650/550
	8-350 4 bbl	R-46S	.040	28-32°	.016	8°B⑩	12°B	750	600
	8-455 4 bbl	R-46S	.040	28-32°	.016	10°B⑩	8B°	750	600
	8-455 4 bbl	R-46S	.040	28-32°	.016	10°B⑩	8B°	750	600
	8-455 4 bbl	R-45S	.040	28-32°	.016	12°B⑩	10B°	750	650
1973	6-250 1 bbl	R-46T	.035	33°	.019	6°B⑩	6°B	700/450	600/450
	8-350 2 bbl	R-46S	.040	30°	.016	—	14°B	—	650/550
	8-350 4 bbl	R-46S	.040	30°	.016	—	12°B	—	650/550
	8-350 4 bbl	R-45S	.040	30°	.016	12°⑩	—	1000/600	—
	8-455 4 bbl	R-45S	.040	30°	.016	10°B⑩	8°B	1000/750	650/550
1974	6-250 1 bbl	R-46T	.035	33°	.019	8°B⑩	8°B	850/450	600/450
	8-350 4 bbl	R-46S	.040	30°	.016	—	12°B	—	650/550
	8-350 4 bbl	R-46S	.040	30°	.016	—	14°B	—	650/550
	8-455 4 bbl	R-46S	.040	30°	.016	—	8°B	—	650/550
	8-455 4 bbl	R-46SX	.080	⑥	⑥	—	8°B	—	650/550
1975	6-231 2 bbl	R-44SX	.060	⑥	⑥	12°B⑩	12°B	800/600	700/600
	6-250 1 bbl	R-46TX	.060	⑥	⑥	10°B⑩	10°B	800/450	600/450
	8-260 2 bbl	R-46SX	.080	⑥	⑥	16°B⑩	18°B⑦	700/750	650/550
	8-350 4 bbl	R-46SX	.080	⑥	⑥	—	20°B	—	650/550
	8-455 4 bbl	R-46SX	.080	⑥	⑥	—	16°B	—	650/550
1976	V6-231 2 bbl	R-44SX	.060	⑥	—⑥	12°B⑩	12°B	600/800	650
	6-250 1 bbl	R-46TX	.060	—⑥	—⑥	10°B⑩	10°B	425/850⑧	425/550
	8-260 2 bbl	R-46SX	.080	—⑥	—⑥	16°B⑩	⑨	750	550/650
	8-350 4 bbl	R-46SX	.080	—⑥	—⑥	—	20°B	—	550/650
	8-455 4 bbl	R-46SX	.080	—⑥	—⑥	—	16°B	—	550/650
1977	6-231	See Underhood Specifications Sticker							
	8-260								
	8-350								
	8-403								

▲ Adjust automatic transmissions in Drive (AMC/Ford/GM) or Neutral (Chrysler), all manual transmissions are adjusted in Neutral.
● Figure in parentheses indicate California engine.
■ All figures are Before Top Dead Center.
① Cutlass
② Vista Cruiser
③ 442
④ R-46S for automatic transmission
⑤ Without A/C
550—automatic transmission
500—manual transmission
⑥ Electronic ignition
⑦ 16B—California
⑧ 425/600—Cal.
⑨ 18°B—Fed
16°B—Cal.
⑩ Set timing with carburetor adjusted to the following speeds

	All V8	Without A/C	With A/C
	1970-75	1100	850

TDC Top Dead Center
B Before Top Dead Center
— Not applicable

NOTE: The underhood specifications sticker often reflects tune-up specification changes made in production. Sticker figures must be used if they disagree with those in this chart.

CAPACITIES

YEAR	ENGINE No. Cyl. Displacement (cu. in.)	ENGINE OIL Add 1 qt. with New Filter	TRANSMISSION Pts. to Refill after Draining MANUAL 3-speed	MANUAL 4-speed	AUTOMATIC	DRIVE AXLE (pts.)	COOLING SYSTEM with Heater (qts.)	COOLING SYSTEM with Air Cond. (qts.)
1970	6-250	4	3.5	—	6	3.7	12.2	12.2
	8-350	4	3.5	2.25	6	3.7	15.2	15.7
	8-455	4	3.5	2.25	6	3.7	17.5	18
1971	6-250	4	3.5	—	6	4.25	12.2	12.2
	8-350	4	3.5	2.25	6	4.25	15.2	15.7
	8-455	4	3.5	—	6	4.25	17.5	18
1972	8-350	4	3.5	2.25	6	4.25①	15.2	15.7
	8-455	4	—	—	6	4.25①	17	17.5
1973	6-250	4	3.5	—	6	4.25	12.5	—
	8-350	4	3.5	2.25	6	4.25①②	15.9④	③④
	8-455	4	—	2.25	6	4.25①②	17.0⑤	18⑤
1974	6-250	4	3.5	—	6	4.25	15.5	—
	8-350	4	—	—	6	4.25②	20.0	20.0
	8-455	4	—	—	6	5.50	21.0⑥	21.5⑥
1975	6-231	4	—	3.0	6	2.80	13.3	14.2
	6-250	4	3.5	—	6	4.25	17.0	17.0
	8-260	4	3.5	—	6	4.25	17.0	17.0
	8-350	4	—	—	6	4.25②	20.0	20.0
	8-455	4	—	—	6	5.50	21.0⑥	21.5⑥
1976	6-231	4	3.5	3.0	6	2.80	13.3	14.2
	6-250	4	3.5	—	6	4.25	17	17
	8-260	4	3.5	⑦	6	4.25	17	17
	8-350	4	—	—	6	4.25②	20	20
	8-455	4	—	—	6	5.5	21⑥	21.5⑥
1977	6-231	4	3.5	3.0	6	2.80	13.3	14.2
	8-260	4	3.5	⑦	6	4.25	17	17
	8-350	4	—	—	6	4.25②	20	20
	8-403	4	—	—	6	4.25②	20.0	20.0

- ● Specifications do not include converter
- ① Limited slip differential—5.4 pts
- ② Vista Cruiser—5.5 pts
- ③ Cutlass—16 qts
- ④ Heavy duty cooling—21 qts
- ⑤ Heavy duty cooling—22 qts
- ⑥ Heavy duty cooling—22.5 qts
- — Not applicable
- ⑦ 3.5 (Dexron) with 5-speed

Dodge/Plymouth

Lubrication and Oil Change

BRAKE FLUID LEVEL CHECK

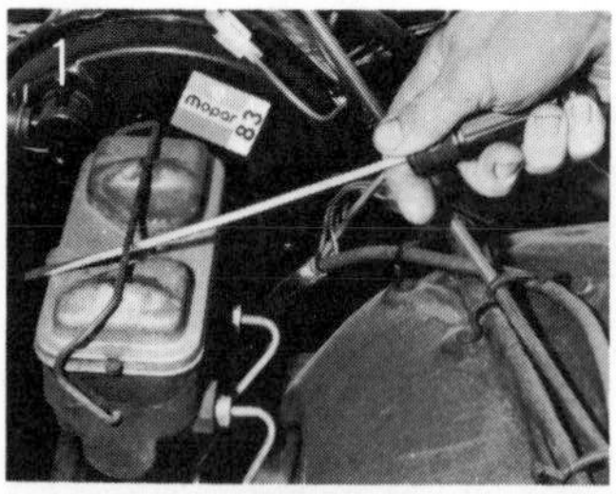

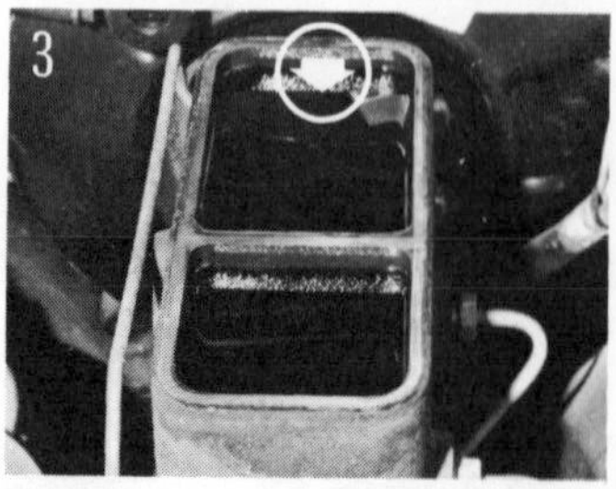

Check brake fulid level in master cylinder every six months . . . sooner if braking feels inadequate. Add when low. Recommended grade: Extra Heavy Duty; Grade 70R3 as printed on can (check owner's handbook) Master cylinder is located under hood on left side. It is oblong container about 6″ long with cap held down by wire clip. Check brake fluid level as follows:

1. Pry wire retaining clip off cap top with screwdriver.
2. Remove cap and gasket by lifting up.
3. Fluid level should be within ¼ inch of top rim. If lower than this, add fresh fluid to appropriate level.

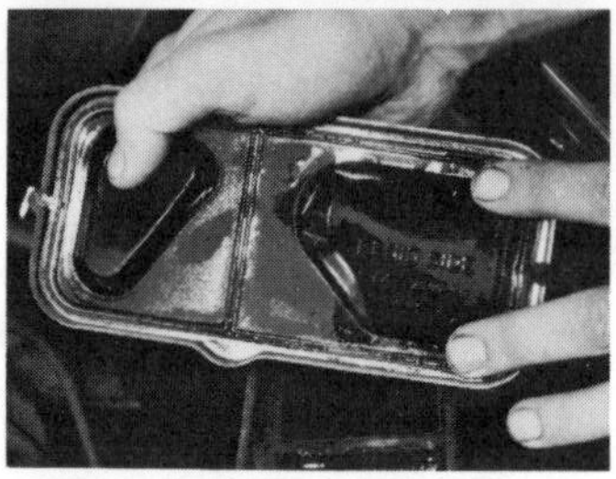

DO NOT OVERFILL

4. Replace cap and gasket; secure retaining clip over cap. If fluid level was low, check again in a few days.
5. If fluid repeatedly checks low, there is a leak somewhere in the system. See SAFETY SYSTEMS—

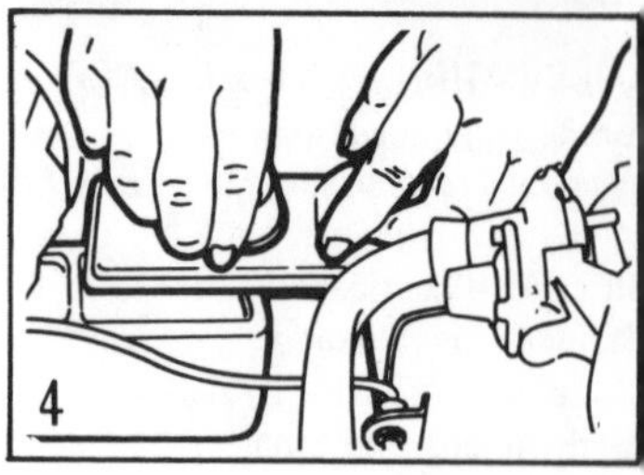

WHEEL CYLINDER CHECK. Have mechanic check further. Neglect can be dangerous.

NOTE: On cars with front disc brakes, it is normal for the fluid level to drop slightly as the brake pads wear down.

MANUAL TRANSMISSION FLUID LEVEL CHECK

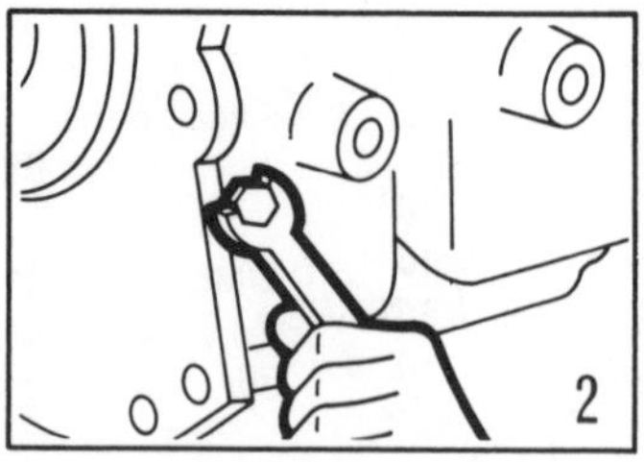

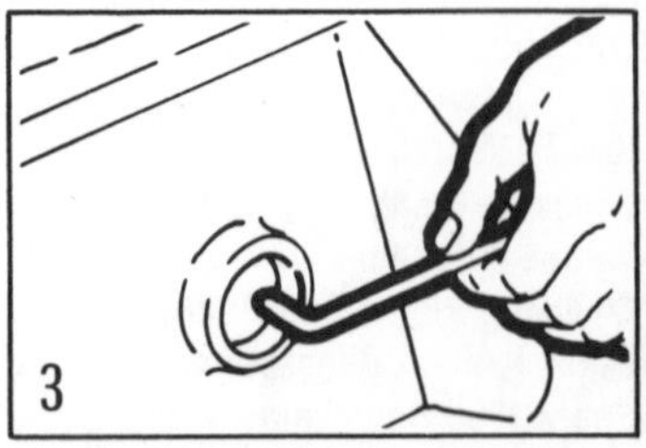

Chrysler Says . . . Check manual transmission fluid level every 6000 miles. Car should be parked level. Recommended grade: DEXRON automatic transmission fluid—SAE 90 gear lubricant may also be used in warm climates or if gear rattle at idle or whine under acceleration becomes objectionable. Do not mix the two lubricants. DEXRON is pink while gear oil is dark brown.

Tools Needed . . . Adjustable wrench and bulb syringe.

1. Locate the transmission filler plug on the side of the transmission from underneath the car. Some transmissions have a drain plug as well. The filler plug is always the upper plug.
2. Clean the area around the plug before loosening. Remove the filler plug with an adjustable wrench.
3. Check that the fluid level is up to the bottom of the filler plug hole.

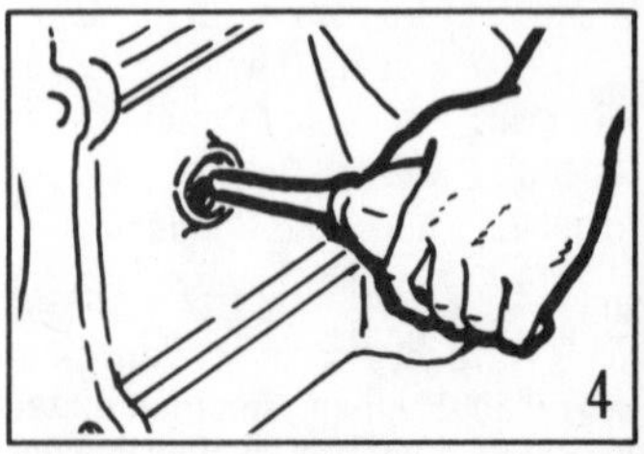

4. Add fluid as necessary with a bulb syringe until fluid begins to run out.
5. Install filler plug and tighten.

AUTOMATIC TRANSMISSION FLUID LEVEL CHECK

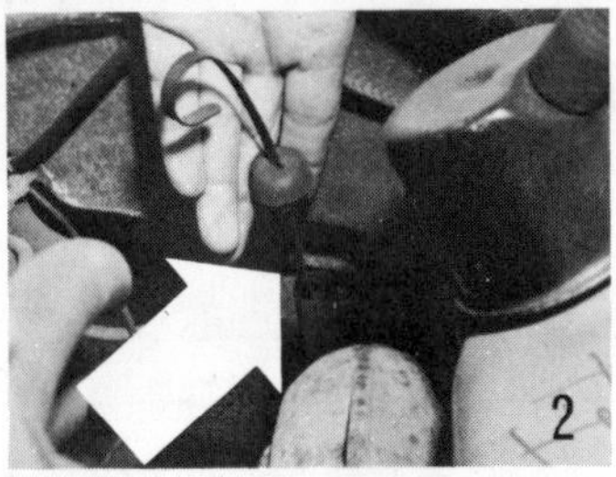

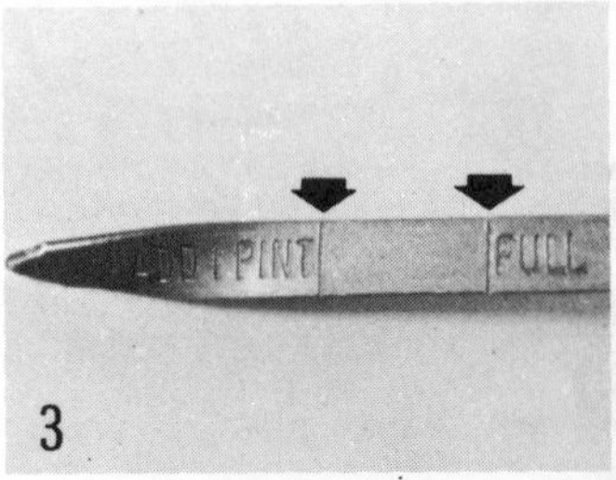

Chrysler Says . . . Check automatic transmission fluid (ATF) level every 6000 miles. Recommended grade: DEXRON ATF

Tools . . . Long neck filler funnel

1. Engine must be warmed up and idling. Park car on level ground. With brake applied, shift selector lever through all gear positions, ending in Neutral.
2. Pull out dipstick, located at rear of engine compartment on right side. Wipe it clean and push it all the way back in. Remove it again and check reading.
3. If fluid is below F (full) mark, add DEXRON slowly to bring level up. Add fluid slowly, frequently checking the level. Do not overfill as the transmission may overheat, and have to be drained at a service station.

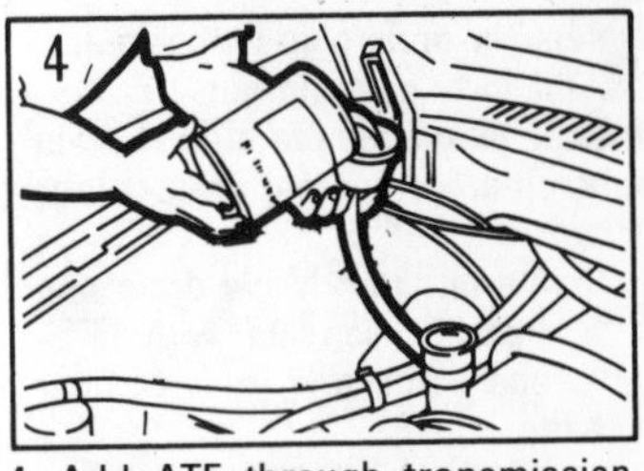

4. Add ATF through transmission dipstick hole using a long-neck filler funnel.

REAR AXLE LUBRICANT

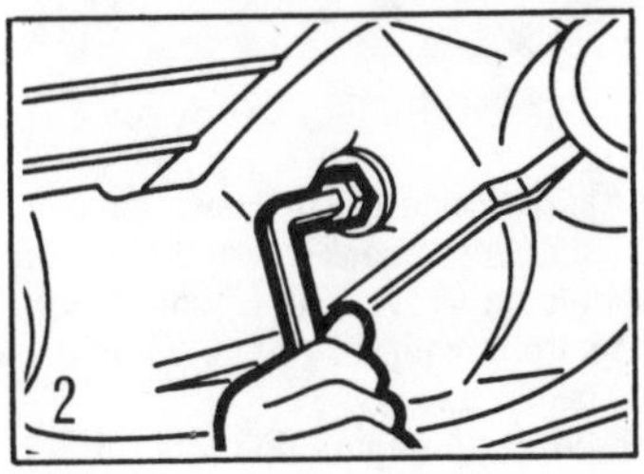

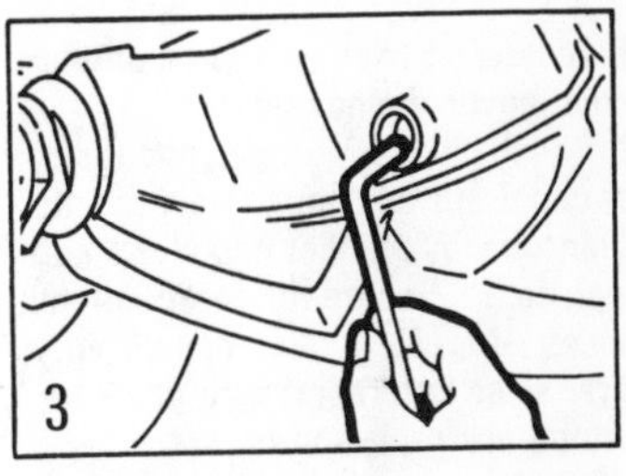

Chrysler Says . . . Check rear axle lube level every 6000 miles. Recommended grade: Hypoid gear lube (SAE 90). Cars with limited slip differential require special fluid.

Tools . . . Adjustable hand wrench; fluid level check device (made from coat hanger wire; bend at 90° angle 2" from end.); bulb syringe.

1. Locate filler plug on forward side of rear axle housing, or on cover plate.
2. Wipe plug area clean; remove plug with wrench.
3. Insert wire level check device; remove. Adequate fluid level should show lubricant to last ⅛-inch of wire, before bend.
4. If fluid level is low, add as needed, with a hand bulb syringe, until level shows to last ⅛-inch of wire, before bend.

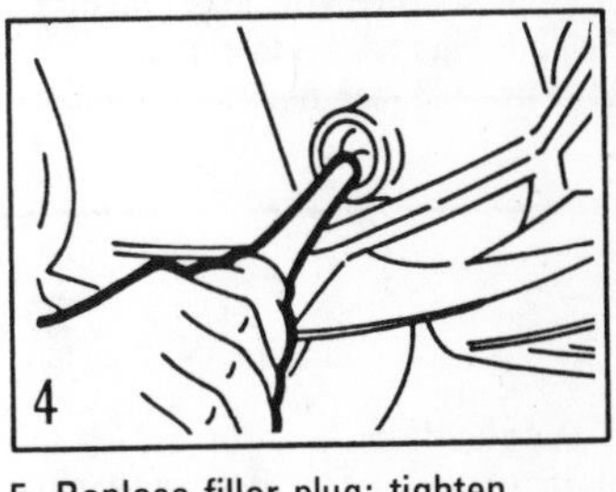

5. Replace filler plug; tighten.

OIL AND FILTER CHANGE

Chrysler Says . . . Change oil every 3000 miles (1970-74 models) or 6000 miles (1975-77 models); change filter every 6000 miles. Recommended grade: SE. Check oil level on dipstick (engine off) at least once a week.

Tools and Materials . . . Adjustable wrench; oil filter strap wrench; drain pan for old oil (at least 5 qt. capacity); oil pour spout; 4 qt. oil (5 qt. if changing filter); new oil filter.

Safety tip . . . use work gloves.

1. If engine is cold, start up and idle for about 5 minutes.
2. Park car on level ground. Turn engine off.
3. Locate oil drain plug on underside

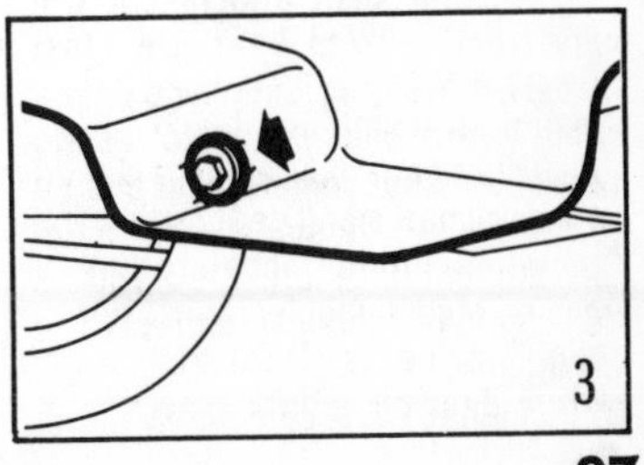

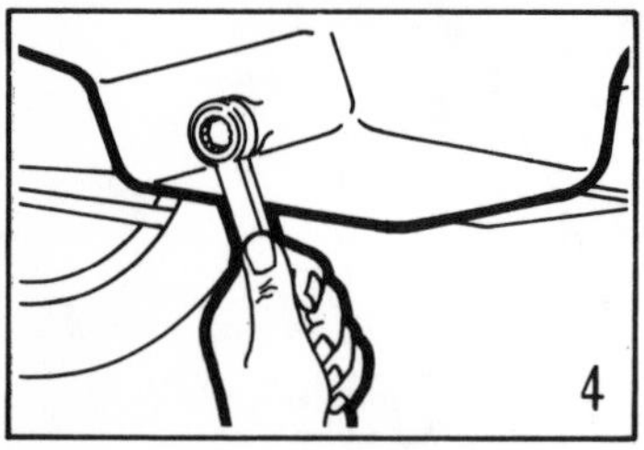

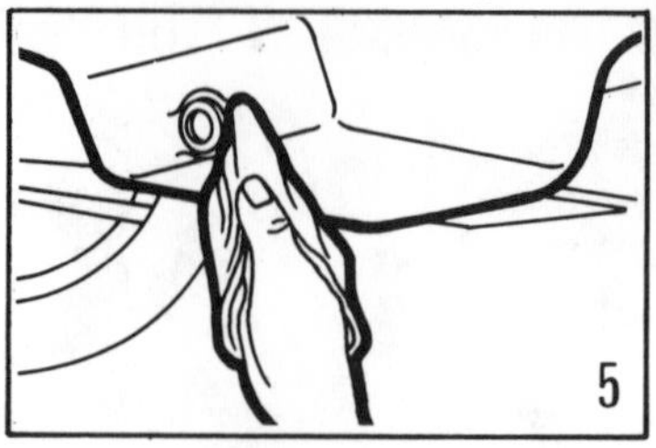

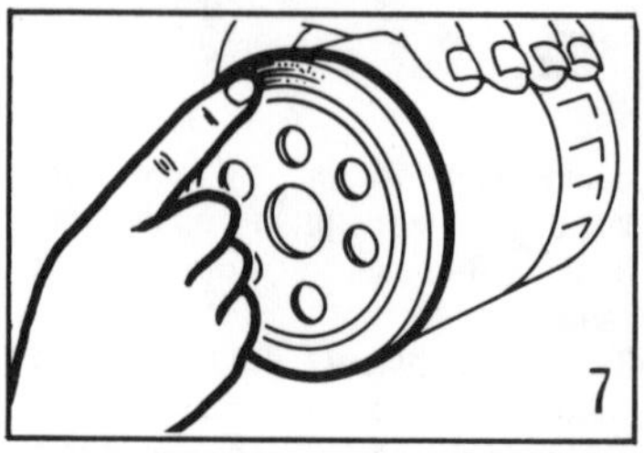

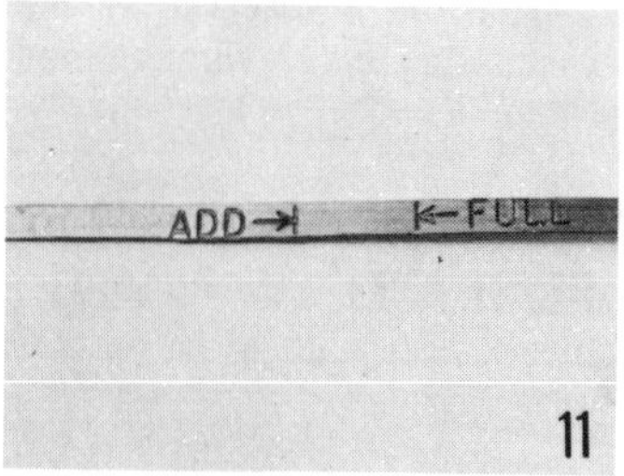

of engine. Place drain pan under plug.
4. Remove drain plug with wrench. Let ALL dirty oil drain out.
5. Wipe plug and area around drain hole clean. Replace drain plug; tighten it.
6. Locate oil filter. Move drain pan under filter. Loosen filter with oil filter wrench. Unscrew; remove filter by hand.
7. Smear fresh oil over surface of rubber gasket (washer) of new filter. Install new filter by hand only. Do NOT use wrench. Turn filter until gasket makes contact. Tighten an additional half turn only . . . NO MORE.
8. Locate oil filler on top of engine valve cover. Remove cap.
9. Punch oil pouring spout into top of oil can. Pour all cans of new oil into filler tube. Wipe filler cap clean and replace it. Besure to re-attach all hoses. (NOTE: If filler cap is very dirty, rinse in turpentine or gasoline. Dry before replacing.)
10. Check new oil level at dipstick. Pull out dipstick, wipe clean.
11. Push dipstick back into engine. Be sure to insert all the way. Remove dipstick and check new oil level. It should be above "SAFE" line. If not, be sure to check if you put in all the oil called for.
12. Start up engine and idle for 3-5 minutes. Oil signal light on instrument panel will glow red when engine is first started. Light should go out in 30 seconds or less.
13. Stop engine and check for oil leaks at drain plug and filter. If you find any, check tightness of plug and/or filter, also for condition of filter gasket to see that it has not become pinched or damaged when installing. Recheck oil level, which should now be at "SAFE".

SPEEDOMETER CABLE LUBRICATION

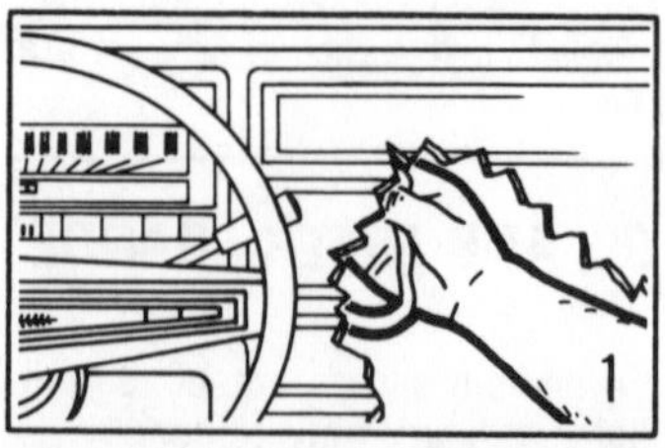

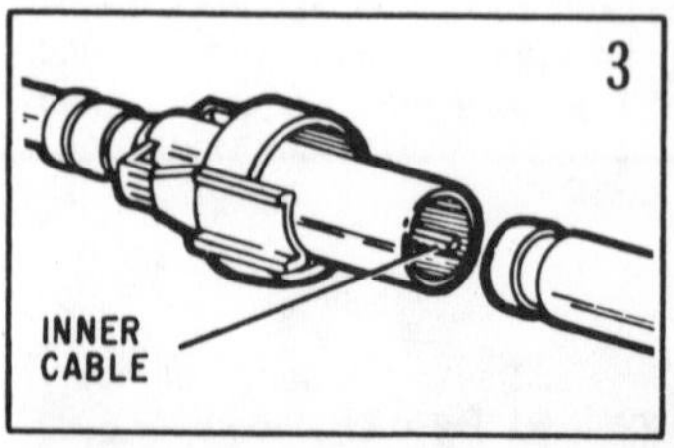

If speedometer pointer tends to quiver or jump, or if unit makes a low, rasping or clicking sound, graphite lubrication may be needed.
1. Locate cable shaft attachment directly behind speedometer dial.
2. The cable shaft attachment will vary from year to year. On most models, there is a plastic tang on the cable which engages a slot at the rear of the speedometer. Lift this up to disengage. On some other models, the cable is attached with a "C"-clip. Slide this clip sideways to disengage.
3. Pull inner cable completely out of inner casing. Note carefully which end is top. Check for wear or frayed ends. If damaged, replace inner cable with new one.
4. Apply generous amount of speedometer cable lubricant into cable casing. Replace inner cable in shaft, noting that bottom end is inserted first. Turn inner cable as it is being reinserted. Twist cable when all the way in, to lock into position at lower end.
5. Reconnect cable to speedometer head under instrument panel.

DOOR HINGES AND STOPS

(lubricate every 6 months)
1. Brush any dirt accumulations from door hinges and stops. Use old tooth brush or rag.
2. Apply dab of white polyethylene grease to door hinges, trunk hinges, hood hinges, door stops.

DOOR LOCKS

(lubricate every 6 months)
1. Insert door key half way into lock.
2. Spray aerosol lock lubricant into lock.
3. Push key rest of way into lock; turn back and forth several times.

Cooling System

It is recommended . . . that radiator coolant (water/antifreeze mixture) level be checked once or twice a month. Do this when engine is cold. Check more often if you do a lot of hard driving.
Keep coolant up to recommended level in radiator. If coolant checks frequently low, look for leaks. Tighten all hose clamps occasionally. For best results, keep a 50/50 water/antifreeze mixture year round. Change complete coolant mixture every 24 months.
CAUTION: If you must check coolant in a hot engine, cover radiator cap

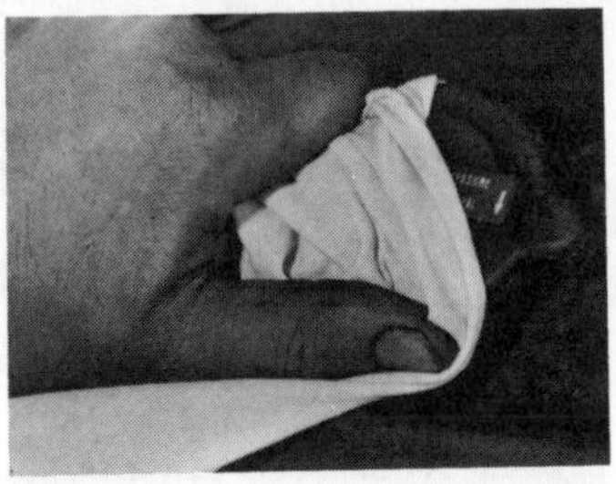

with thick rag before releasing. Remove cap slowly . . . press down and turn.
On cars equipped with a coolant recovery system, simply check the

level visible through the translucent reservoir on the right side of the radiator. If it is necessary to add coolant, add to the reservoir, not the radiator.

RADIATOR CAP CHECK

Check radiator cap occasionally for worn or cracked gasket. If cap doesn't seal properly, fluid will be lost and engine will overheat.
Replace worn cap with new cap rated 13 to 15 lbs. pressure. On cars with coolant recovery system, use 16 lb. cap.

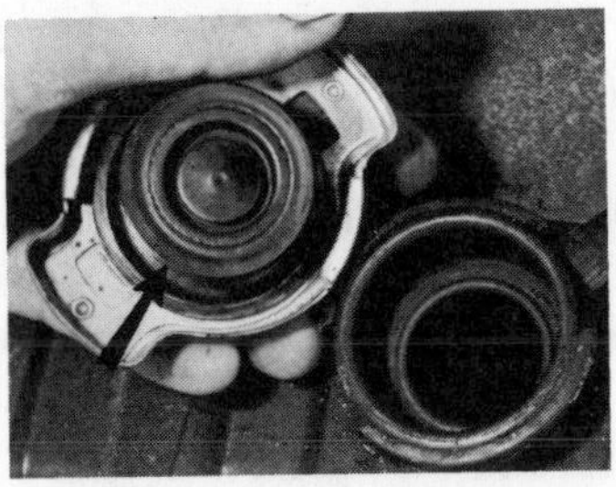

REPLACING THE THERMOSTAT

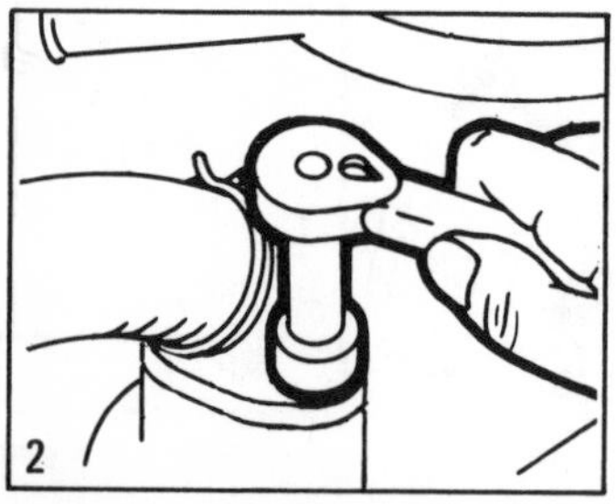

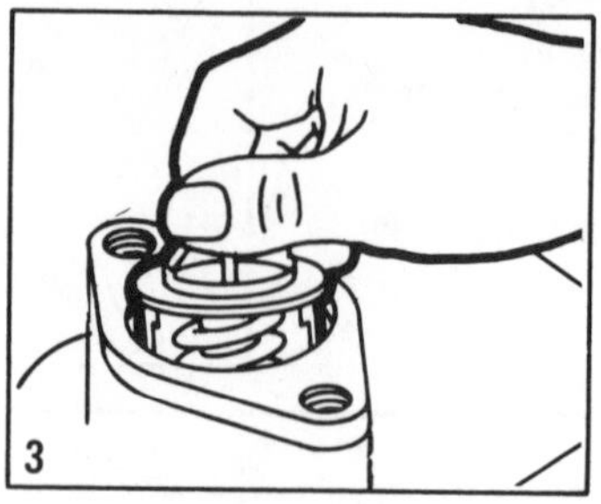

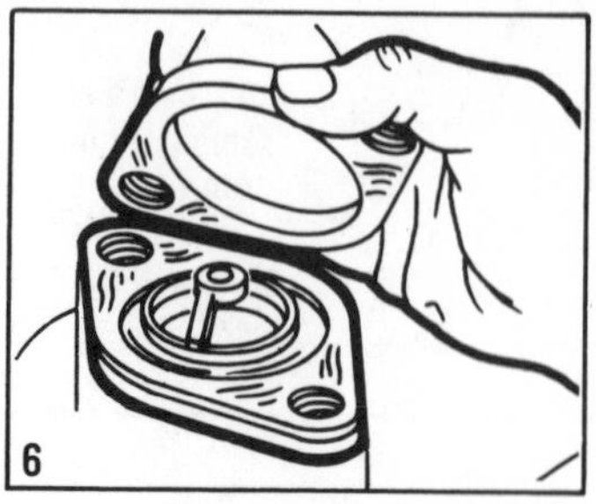

A faulty thermostat will usually cause engine overheating. Replace with new thermostat.

Tools and Materials . . . new thermostat; gasket sealer; adjustable wrench

1. Drain radiator of about half its coolant. (See Hose Replacement section)

2. Loosen and remove both retaining bolts and lift thermostat housing off the engine.

NOTE: If you're careful it won't be necessary to remove radiator hose.

3. Remove old thermostat.

4. Scrape thermostat housing flange and engine block surface to remove old gasket debris.

5. Drop new thermostat into place—spring down (toward engine).

6. Install new gasket with sealer applied to both sides.

7. Replace thermostat housing and tighten both retaining bolts. (Only when engine is cold)

FAN BELT ADJUSTMENT

The fan belt not only drives the radiator fan, it turns the water pump and drives the alternator. Another belt drives the power steering pump. It's easy to see that the condition and proper tension of the belts are vital, since engine cooling, electrical power, and steering depend on them. The belts deserve an occasional look and tension check.

1. Inspect fan belt occasionally. If worn, frayed or cracked on inner driving surface, replace.

CAUTION: An overtightened belt may damage alternator and water pump, or power steering pump bearings.

2. Check tension occasionally. Press thumb at midpoint of belt span be-

tween pulleys. If belt depresses more than ½ inch, tightening is needed. A too-loose belt will not drive alternator and pumps effectively.

3. Adjust to proper tension of ¼ inch deflection. Adjust as follows:

A. Loosen mounting bolts at top and bottom so alternator can pivot on lower bolt and upper bolt can slide in bracket.

B. Pull alternator out slightly to put tension on belt, and hold while tightening upper bolt.

C. Check tension. Repeat adjustment as necessary.

D. When tension is correct, tighten lower bolt.

HOSE REPLACEMENT

Coolant drain and refill work may be done alone; when changing hoses, coolant must also be drained as part of job. Discard all hoses with cracks or soft spots. Check hose clamps for tightness and good condition.

1. Remove radiator cap. Open radiator petcock (See 2). Drain coolant into catch basin. If near 24 months old, discard old coolant.

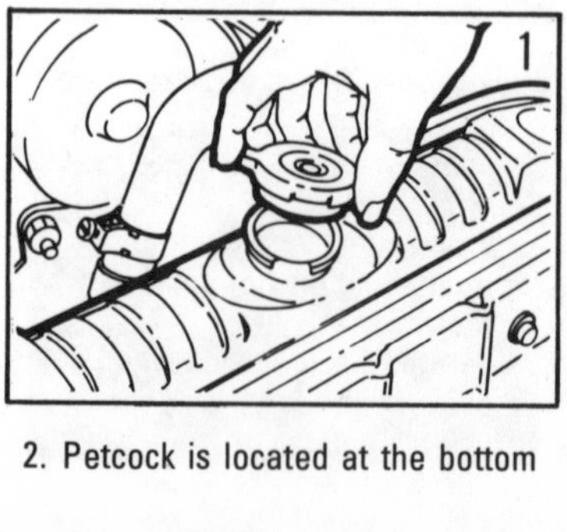

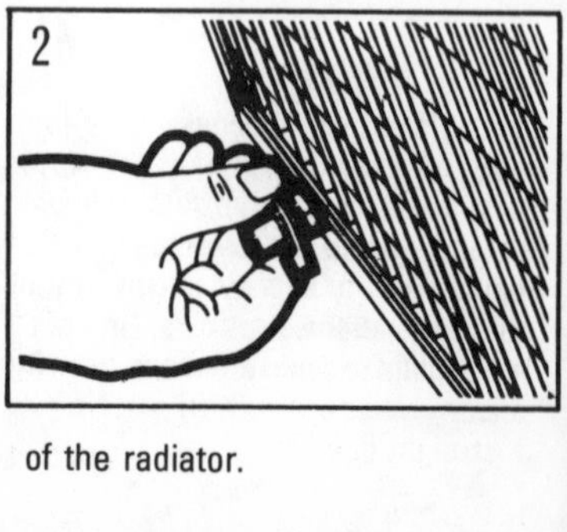

2. Petcock is located at the bottom of the radiator.

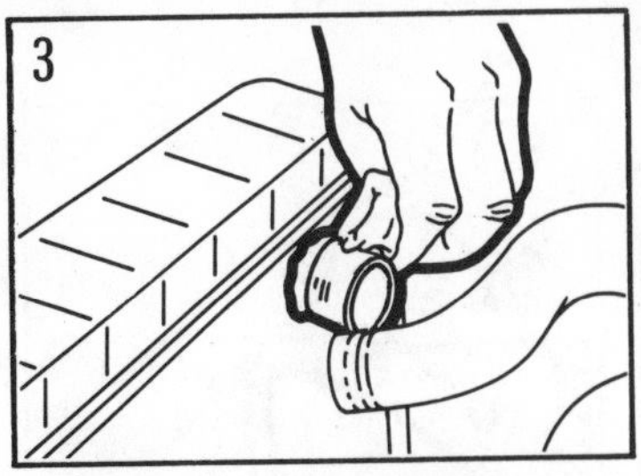

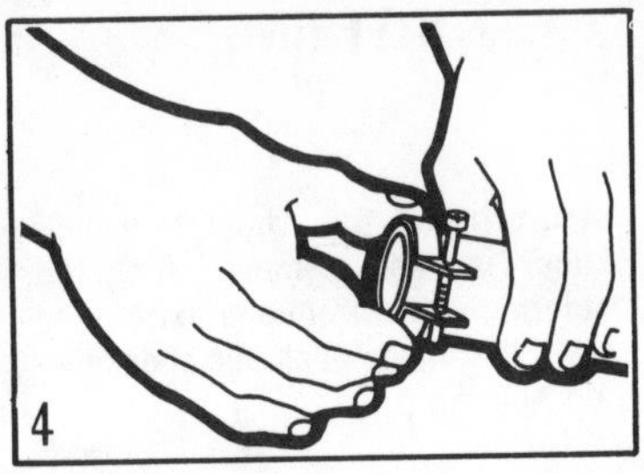

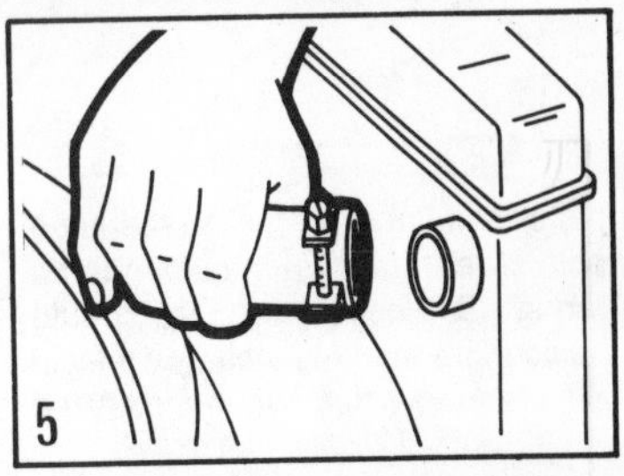

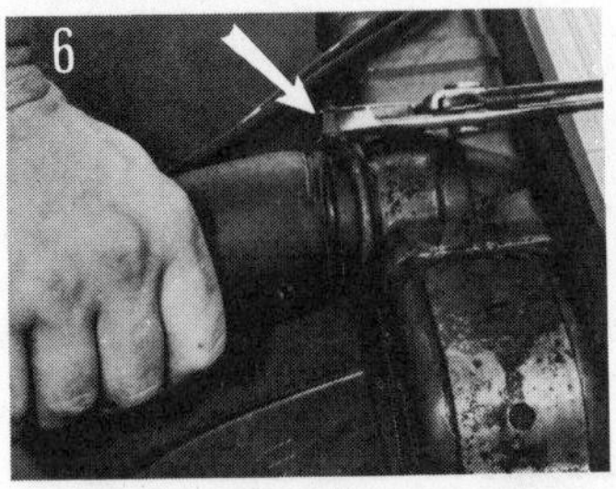

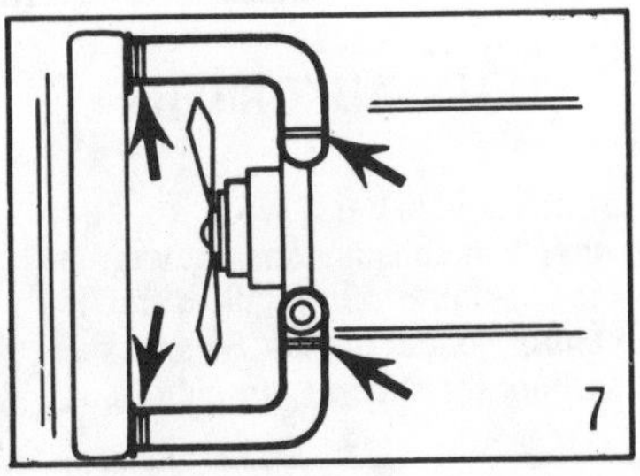

3. Wipe all hose connections clean. Use emery cloth to get rid of residue.
4. If old hose clamps are badly rusted or damaged, replace with new units.
5. Slip clamps over each hose end. Slip hose ends all the way onto cleaned up hose connections.
6. Place hose clamp ¼ inch from hose end. Tighten. Close petcock. Refill with 50/50 coolant/water mix.
7. Start engine; allow to warm up. Check for coolant leaks.
8. Road test car; watch temperature gauge.

Suspension and Tires

The front wheels mount to hubs which rotate on spindles. Each spindle is attached to an upper and lower suspension ball joint, and connects to the steering linkage tie rods. Upper and lower suspension control arms link the spindles to the car's unitized body, permitting it to move up and down in relation to the wheels with a hinge effect. Each front suspension unit is sprung independently utilizing a torsion bar and shock absorber. Dodge and Plymouth models use a pair of longitudinal mounted torsion bars which locate between each lower control arm and the reinforced structural members of the body. The rear suspension consists of multi-leaf springs suspending a solid rear axle, and a pair of telescopic shock absorbers.

HOW TO PINPOINT HANDLING PROBLEMS

Your car's suspension system consists of wheels, tires, springs, shock absorbers, sway (or stabilizer) bars, ball joints, steering linkage. If any of these items is out of adjustment or badly worn, you may notice any of these symptoms:

- car pulls to one side when braking
- car wanders when driving a straight line
- overall ride may be either hard or bouncy
- effect is needed to steer vehicle
- tires show uneven wear
- tires squeal when cornering
- front of car dips or bounces when braking
- car rocks side-to-side when going over rough road
- wheels bounce or make slapping sound on road
- steering wheel vibrates in hands
- front of car vibrates at highway speeds

Any of above symptoms indicates corrective action is needed. Delay can: ruin tires; cause damage/failure to other suspension parts; create safety hazard.

STEERING

If steering linkage, front suspension and steering column components are in good condition, there should be no more than 1½ inch free play in the steering wheel when measured at the rim of the wheel. If a loud knock is heard when turning the steering wheel from one extreme to the other, have mechanic check pinion bearing preload.

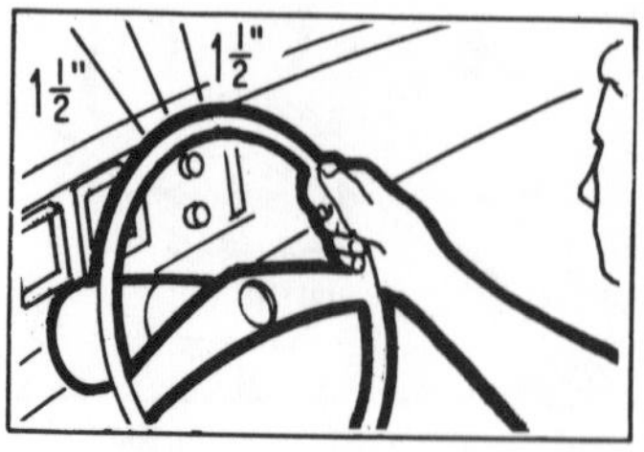

SHOCK ABSORBERS

Shock absorbers work to keep wheels in constant contact with the road. Result is safe handling and ride control; longer tire life. So shock absorbers (or shocks) are important.

HOW TO CHECK FOR BAD SHOCKS

1. Check under car and locate shock absorber near each wheel.
2. Heavy oil streaks on outer shock housing indicate need for replacement.
3. Stand at front of car and apply body weight in a pumping action to front bumper or fender. Release pressure and allow car to stop rocking. Car should not bounce more than one more time after releasing pressure. Repeat at rear. If bouncing continues more than once, replacement is needed. Replace shocks in pairs (front pair or rear pair).

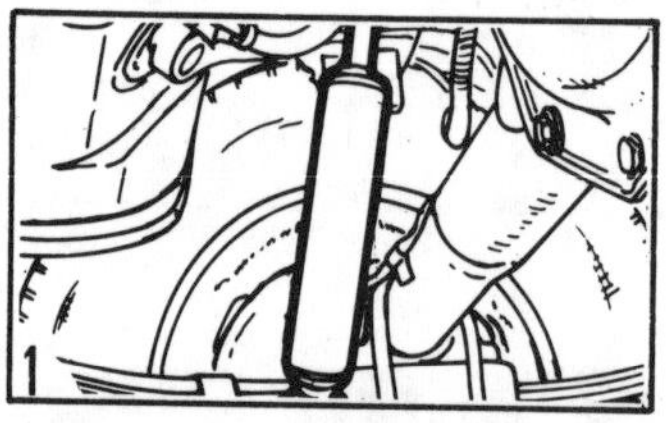

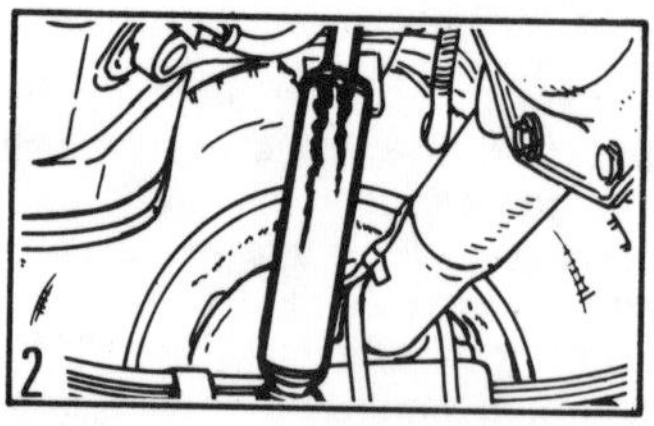

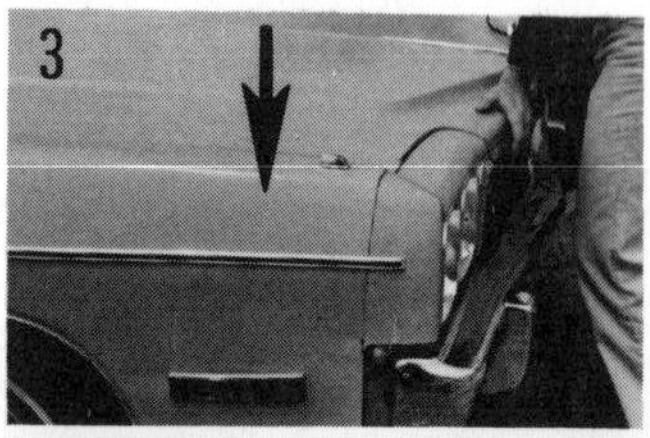

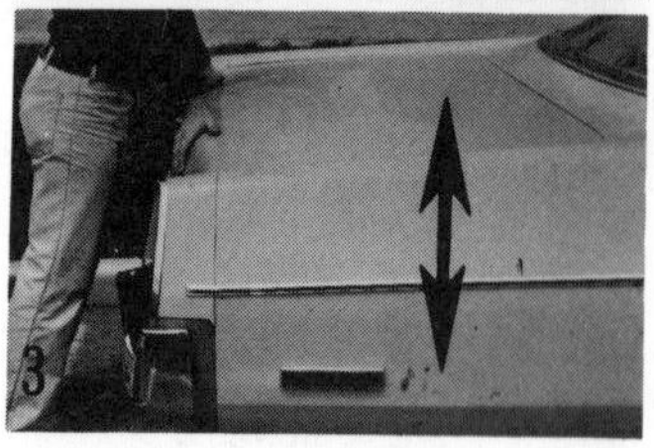

TOW HITCH INFORMATION

If your car is used for trailer towing you should check:
A. Cooling System; be sure radiator is at proper level in radiator. See Cooling System Section for checks to perform.
B. Check Transmission Fluid; keep topped up to proper level.
C. Check Rear Shock Absorbers; you may benefit from installation of new rear shocks.
D. Check Tire Pressures; best traction and handling can be ensured if tire pressures are properly maintained.

For safer and more trouble-free trailer towing, consider:
A. Automatic Transmission Cooler; helps remove excess heat from automatic transmission fluid built up during towing mileage. Also helps avoid radiator overheating. Some units can be self-installed.
B. Radiator Over-Flow Tank Kit; addition of a reservoir to catch radiator coolant overflow preventing coolant loss. Easy to install, these units help a tow car run cooler, avoid overheating due to coolant loss.
C. Heavy-Duty Shock Absorbers or Air Shocks; important to have on rear wheels if you intend to do a lot of towing or load carrying within the car itself. Don't forget to consider replacing factory shocks, when they are worn out, with heavy-duty units at the front as well.
D. Variable Load Flasher; this unit will accommodate the added load of trailer turn signal lamps on trailer when these are hooked into your car's electrical system.

Ignition System

CHECKING IGNITION SYSTEM

NOTE: Beginning in 1972, electronic ignition became available as optional equipment on some models. In 1973 and later models, electronic ignition is standard. Electronic ignition eliminates the breaker points and condenser. However, it is still necessary to check the cap and rotor every 12,000 miles. And the plugs must be replaced at regular intervals too; 12,000 miles (1973-74), 15,000 miles (1975-77 models without catalytic converter), or 30,000 miles (1975-77 models with converter).
The ignition system consists of spark plugs; plug wires; distributor; rotor; points; condenser; coil. These units work to create a good hot spark inside the engine (ignition) at exactly the right moment (timing). If ignition is weak or timing is off, engine may be hard to start, run poorly, waste gas, lose power, backfire or not run at all.

TUNE-UP SERVICES

Chrysler Says . . . Replace plugs and points every 12,000 miles, on 1970-72 cars
Tools and Materials . . . Parts: set of points; condenser; 6 spark plugs. Tools: gap gauge; 13/16 in. spark plug socket ⅝ in. spark plug socket on 1975-77 Sixes), screwdriver; open end, box or combination wrenchs; timing equipment (see Ignition Timing).
Safety Tip . . . Change only one spark plug at a time to avoid cross-wiring and possible engine damage.

CHECKING POINTS, AND ROTOR

1. To open distributor, snap retaining clips off with screwdriver, lift cap off but keep wires connected.

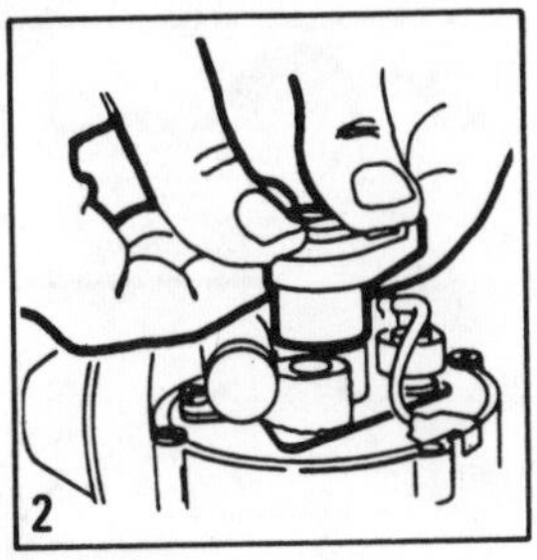

2. Pull rotor off (straight up). Replace if cracked or metallic tip is badly burned.

3. On 1970-72 models, pry points apart with screwdriver. If worn or burned, replace. If OK, check point gap.

OTHER IGNITION CHECK POINTS

Inspect spark plug wires. If cracked or brittle, entire set should be replaced. Also, center high tension wire. Inspect distributor cap. Wipe inside clean occasionally with dry, lint-free rag. If cap is cracked or rotor contacts are excessively burned, replace cap.

SPARK PLUG REPLACEMENT

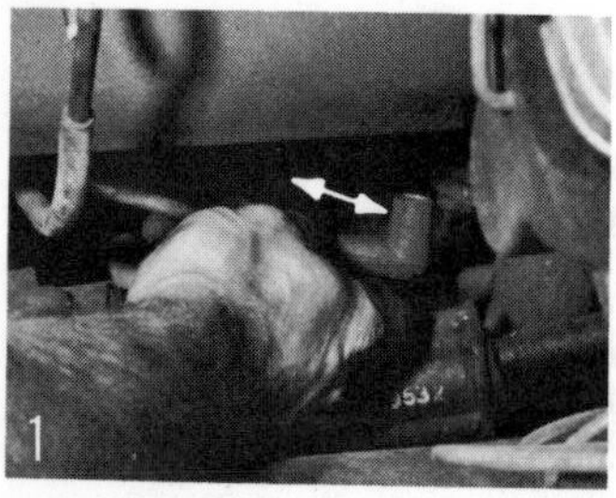

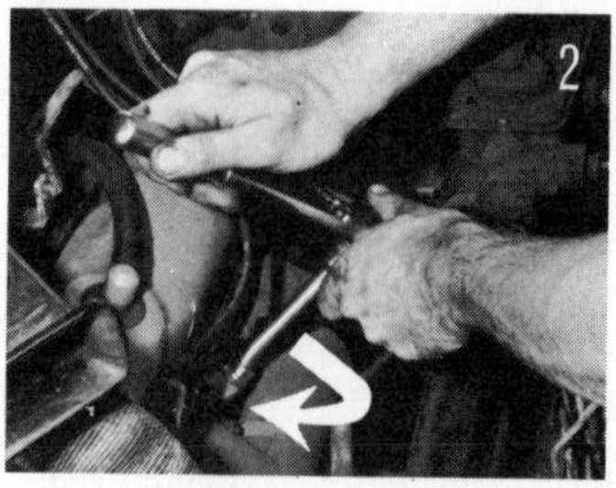

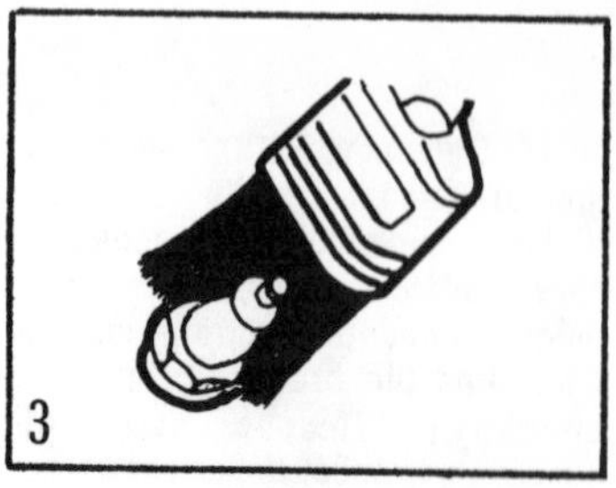

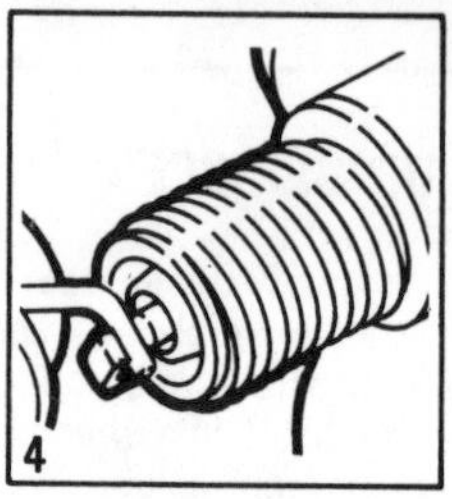

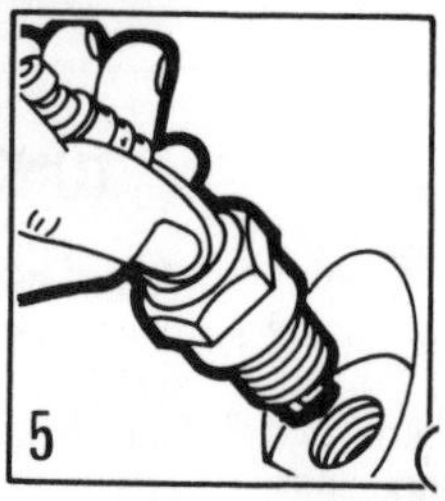

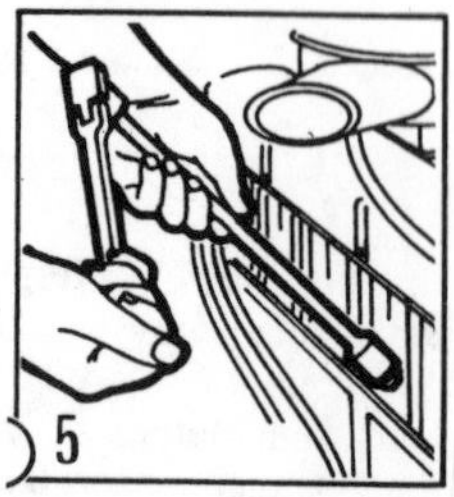

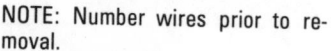

NOTE: Number wires prior to removal.

1. Plug spark plug wire by grasping rubber boot. Do not jerk wire off. If stuck, turn boot, pulling gently.
2. Loosen spark plug using socket wrench.
3. Wipe loose dirt from around plug before removing. Do not let dirt drop into engine through plug hole. Unscrew plug.
4. Check plug electrode gap on new spark plug. Adjust to .035 in.

Plug gap is correct when the gauge drags slightly as it is pulled between plug electrodes.

5. Thread new plug into plug hole by hand. Hand tighten. Do not force or cross thread. Use socket wrench to tighten firmly but do not force. Replace plug wire. Press boot firmly.

LOCATION OF POINTS AND CONDENSER (1970-72 Models Only)

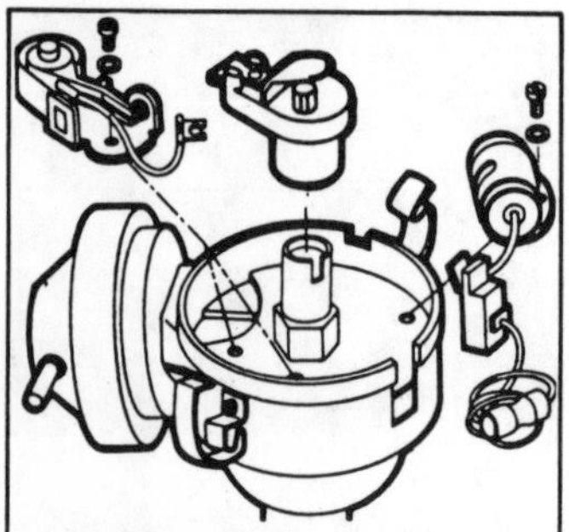

Location inside distributor

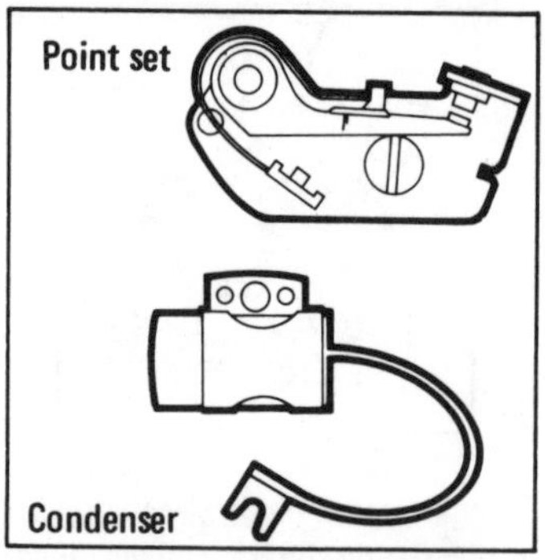

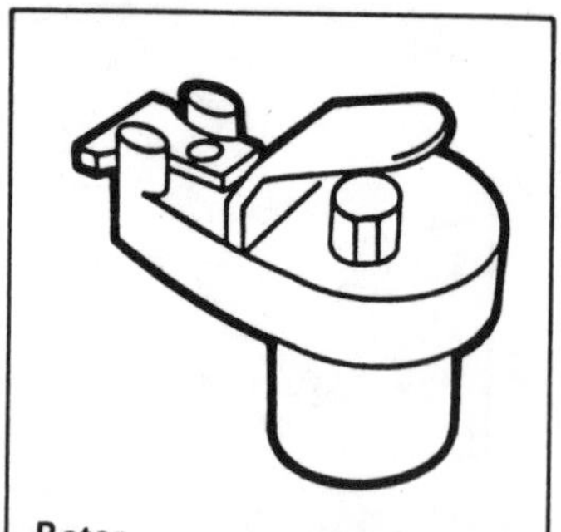

Rotor

The distributor holds the points, rotor and condenser.

Points and condenser work together. Always replace condenser also when installing new points.

If your car has electronic ignition, periodic replacement of distributor parts is not required. If you suspect ignition trouble because of engine misfire, have the distributor checked out by a professional mechanic.

REMOVING POINTS AND CONDENSER (1970-72 Models Only)

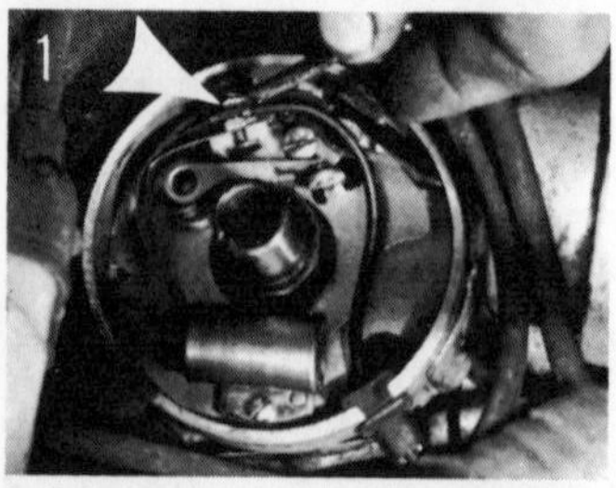

1. Loosen nut, and disconnect primary wire and condenser lead wire.

2. Remove screw which holds condenser; remove condenser.

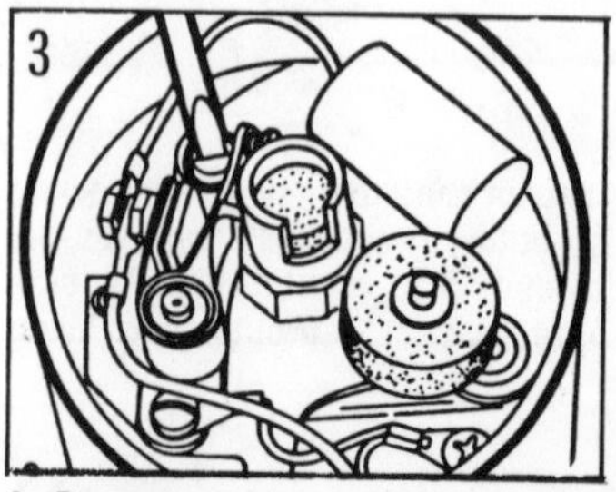

3. Remove screws holding points to distributor, remove points.

4. Wipe all dirt from distributor plate and cam.
5. Inspect primary wire for frayed insulation, dirty connection. Clean connection or have wire repaired as necessary.

CAUTION: When removing screws from distributor in following steps, be sure to avoid any screws accidentally falling through distributor opening into engine. Use magnetic screwdriver.

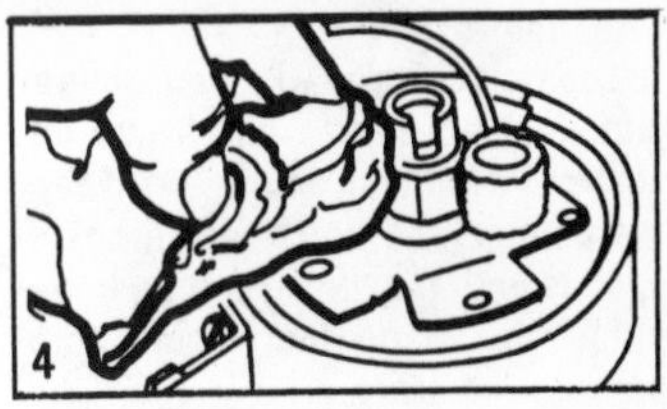

INSTALLING POINTS AND CONDENSER (1970-72 Models Only)

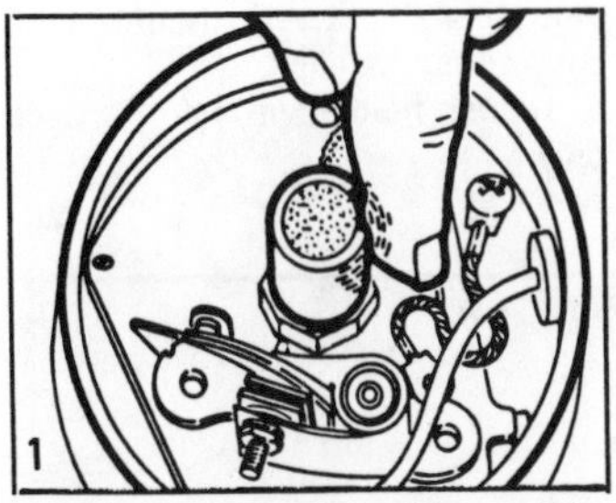

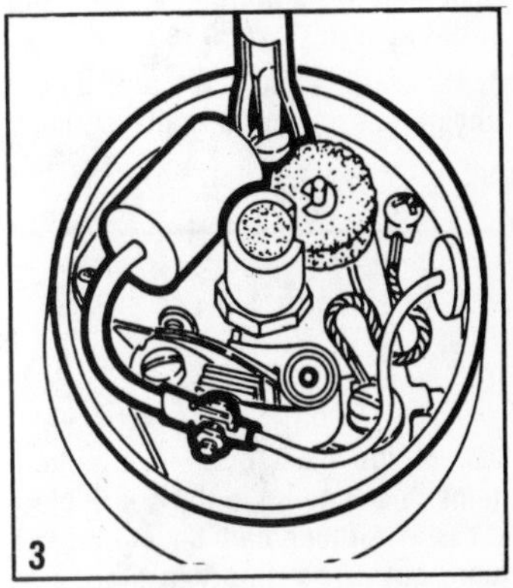

1. Apply small amount of heat resistant lube to distributor cam. (Lube usually supplied with new points. If not, purchase separately.)
2. Position new points in distributor and fasten with attaching screws. CAUTION: use magnetic screwdriver, or screwdriver with clip.
3. Attach new condenser to distributor with attaching screw.
4. Attach primary wire and condenser lead wire to point set. Don't let contacts touch distributor body or breaker plate. (Some models: wire from points attaches to condenser.)

SETTING THE CONTACT GAP (1970-72 Models Only)

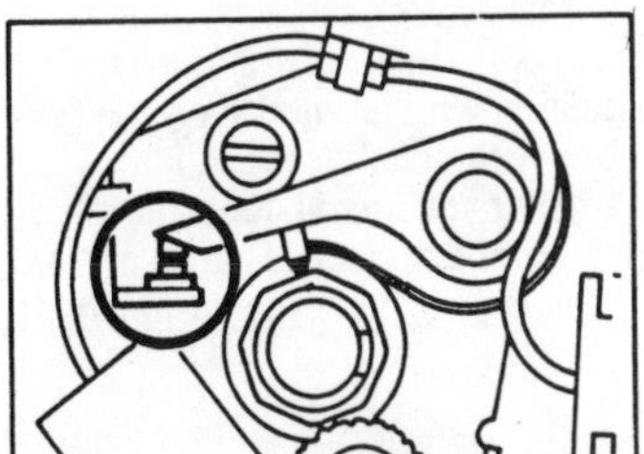

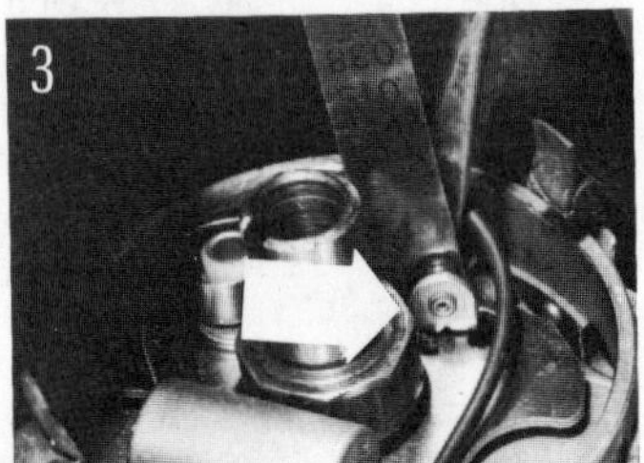

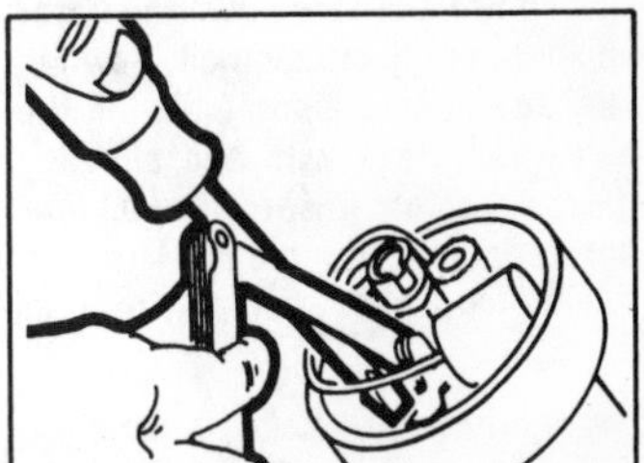

1. Electrical contacts of point set MUST BE PARALLEL. If needed, bend stationary contact with needlenose pliers. Bend fixed bracket only.
2. Turn engine by ignition key (you'll need a helper) until rubbing block on points is one of the high points of the distributor cam. You may use wrench on lower pulley to do this.
3. Look up correct point gap on engine compartment sticker. Insert proper gap gauge between open point contacts. Slightly loosen point attaching screws. Insert screwdriver in breaker plate notch near point contacts. Twist screwdriver to open or close points as needed. Tighten screws when correct gap is obtained.
4. Recheck gap after screws are tightened. Readjust if needed.
5. Align tab inside rotor with notch on distributor shaft and push rotor onto shaft. Rotor must be fully seated on shaft.
6. Install distributor cap by aligning tabs on cap with notch on body. Snap retaining clips in place.

IGNITION TIMING

NOTE: On cars equipped with electronic ignition, regular adjustment of ignition timing is not necessary. Adjusting timing is the important finishing touch to any tune-up. While not difficult, job requires timing light and dwell meter.

1. Locate timing marks and pointer (notches) on engine and lower engine pulley. Clean away dirt. Mark the pointer and notch which corresponds with the timing setting in degrees shown on the engine compartment sticker.
2. Hook up timing light according to instructions supplied with it.
3. Disconnect the one or two vacuum lines from the distributor. Plug with pencil tip or golf tee.
4. Hook up tachometer and adjust engine idle speed to specifications.

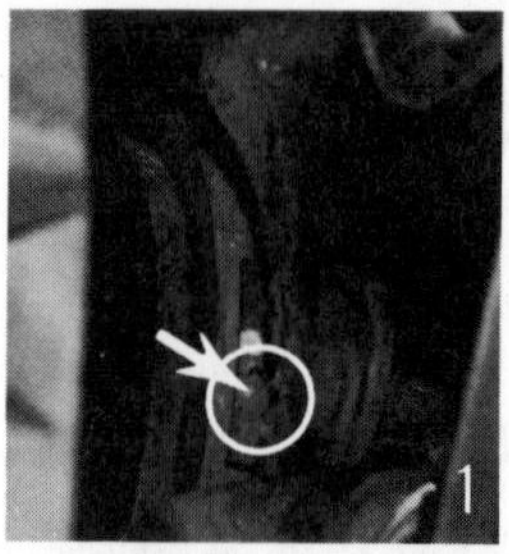

Idle attachment screw is located where gas pedal linkage attaches to carburetor.

5. Aim timing light at pulley mark(s). If the chalked marks do not align,

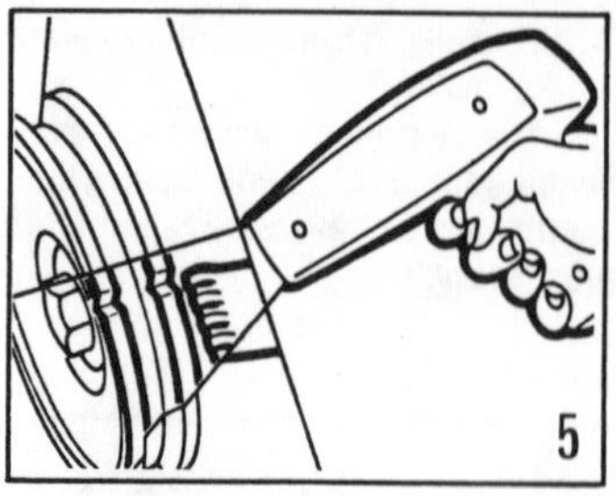

loosen distributor hold-down bolt and slowly rotate distributor until chalked marks align.

6. Tighten hold-down bolt. Recheck timing.

REPLACING SPARK PLUG WIRES

One of the most often overlooked items in a tune-up is the spark plug wires. Your car can be in perfect tune, but if the plug wires are not carrying the spark to the plugs, your engine will run poorly. The original equipment wires that came with your car are usually good for a year or two before needing replacement. On newer cars, the higher underhood temperatures created by emission controls breaks down the wires ability to conduct electricity sooner. The spark plug boot ends of the wires will crack with age allowing the spark to arc towards the engine, not reaching the plugs. The distributor cap ends of the wires will often collect moisture, and corrode right there in your distributor cap. Sometimes a wire will contact a hot part of the engine, such as the exhaust manifold and burn through the insulation. Other times, a wire will become oil soaked and gummy, breaking down the insulation. Often, when carbon core wires get old, they will break off inside, with no visible signs of breakage on the outside. Always use good quality spark plug wire. A carbon core or cut-rate brand may seem attractive at first, but will cost you more in the long run with reduced engine efficiency and more frequent replacement.

1. Replace one wire at a time. This will keep you out of trouble with crossed wires. When removing wires, twist back and forth as you pull up. This will help free up stuck wires.
2. Take the old wire and match it up with the new one for length. If you are cutting your own, make sure there is good metal to metal contact between the end of the wire and the pinch-on connectors.
3. Make sure each wire seats all the way down in the distributor cap. First push down the wire, then the boot. The wire should click in place.
4. After you are all done, make sure all wires are clear of choke or throttle linkage on hot exhaust manifolds.

Use the firing order illustration to guide you when replacing your ignition wires and/or distributor cap.

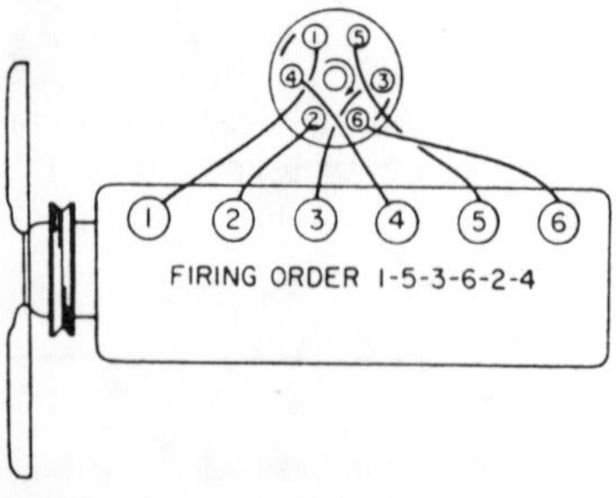

Slant six

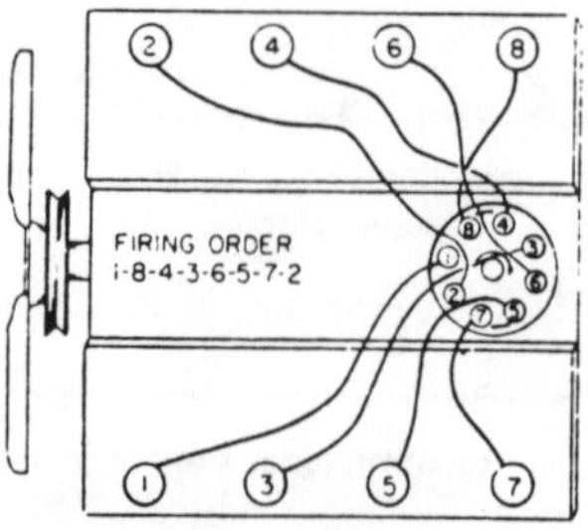

318 and 360 cu in. V8s

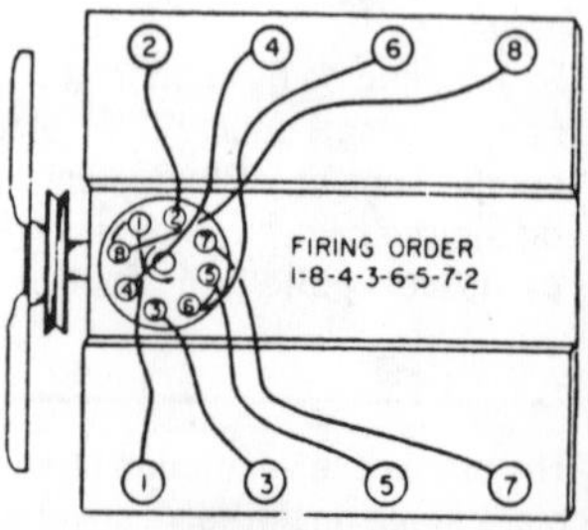

383, 400, and 440 cu in. V8s

Fuel System

When gasoline is brought from the fuel tank, it mixes with air in the carburetor. This gas/air mixture then passes thru a network of small hoses, valves and filters, enters engine thru the intake manifold, passes thru the intake valves and is burned in the combustion chamber. The burned exhaust gas is then passed thru the exhaust valves to the exhaust system and to the outside air. In order to keep your car's engine running cleanly with minimal pollution, and avoid dangerous carbon monoxide fumes inside the vehicle, certain items should be checked from time to time.

REPLACING THE AIR FILTER

The large round canister that sits on top of the engine holds the air filter element. Check it twice a year, or sooner in dusty areas.

1. Remove the wing nut and lift up the air cleaner lid.
2. Lift out the circular air cleaner element. Discard if excessively dirty, or if oil contaminated more than half its circumference. Replace at two year or 24,000 mile intervals regardless of mileage.
3. If reuseable, tap against a hard surface to remove any loose dirt. Wipe out inside of air cleaner canister and lid. Install element and lid and tighten wing nut.

FUEL FILTER REPLACEMENT

All models are equipped with a throwaway filter which is located in the fuel line near the carburetor. On 1970-74 models the filter should be replaced every 2 years/24,000 miles, whichever occurs first. On 1975 models, replace the fuel filter every 15,000 miles. On 1976-77 models, replace the fuel filter every 30,000 miles.

To replace the filter, proceed in the following manner:

CAUTION: Do not smoke while performing this procedure.

1. Squeeze the clips securing the old filter assembly to the fuel line with pliers in order to open them.
2. Work the ends of both old rubber hoses off of the fuel line and lift out the filter with the hoses attached. Be careful not to drop gasoline on the manifolds if they are hot.
3. Using the clips supplied, install the pieces of rubber hose that come with the new filter over the necks on either side of it.
4. Install the filter hose assembly in the fuel line with clips, being sure that the arrow on the filter is pointing in the direction of fuel flow. Cut the hose to the correct length, if necessary.
5. Check to be sure that the fuel lines are not coming into contact with any other engine components.
6. Start the engine and check for leaks.

CRANKCASE VENTILATION FILTER CLEANING

The crankcase ventilation filter is the black dome on the valve cover with a thick hose leading to the air cleaner. Its purpose is to filter the incoming air for the crankcase ventilation system. At six month intervals (1970-71 models) or once a year (1972-77 models), the filter is removed and cleaned.

1. Remove the hose which runs to the carburetor air cleaner from the crankcase inlet air cleaner (breather

cap).
2. Inspect the hose and clean or replace it, as necessary.
3. Remove the crankcase air cleaner assembly from the valve cover.
4. Wash the assembly in kerosene.
5. Invert the assembly and wet the filter element by filling it with SAE 30 engine oil.
6. Allow the excess oil to drain off and install it on the engine. Connect the hose back to the air cleaner.

PCV VALVE REPLACEMENT

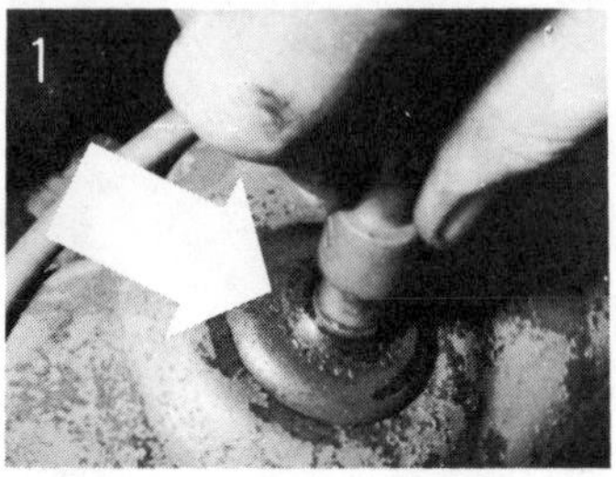

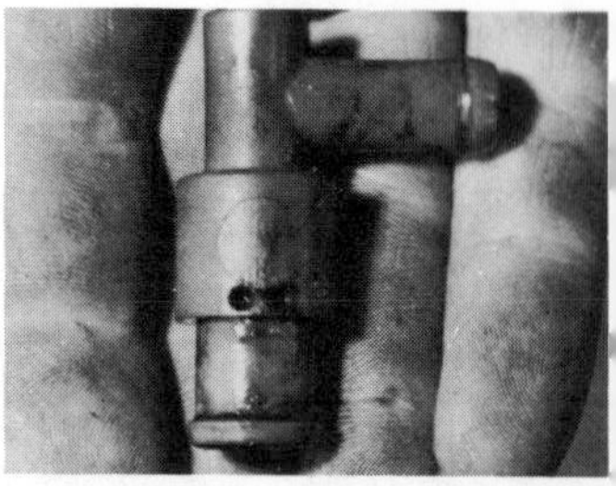

The PCV valve is located in a grommet on the valve cover and has a heavy hose running from it to the rear of the carburetor. It should be checked twice a year (1970-71 models) or once a year (1972-77 models) and replaced every 12 months (1970-71 models) or two years (1972-77 models).

1. Grasp the hose and PCV valve and pull out of the valve cover.
2. Disconnect other end of hose from carburetor. Remove PCV valve from hose.
3. Shake the PCV valve. If it clicks, it is not clogged and is OK. Flush hose out with cleaning solvent and dry. If the PCV valve is clogged, it cannot be cleaned. Replace it.
4. Connect the PCV valve and hose and insert in valve cover. Connect the hose to the carburetor.

Safety Systems

PARKING LIGHTS, TURN SIGNALS, STOP AND BACK-UP LIGHTS

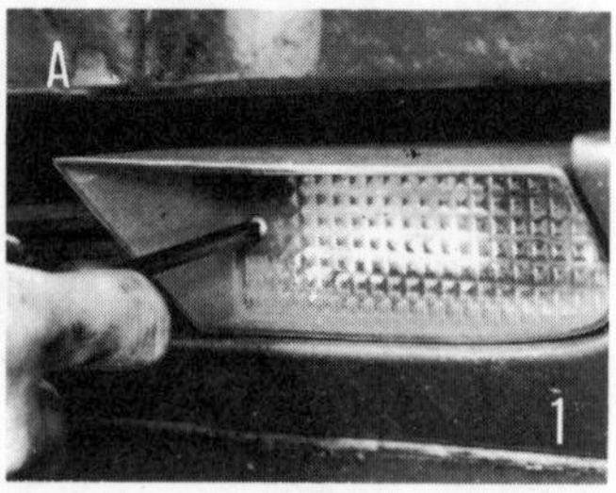

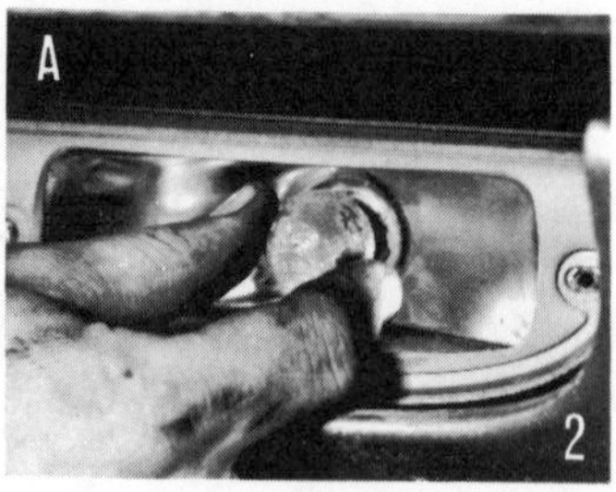

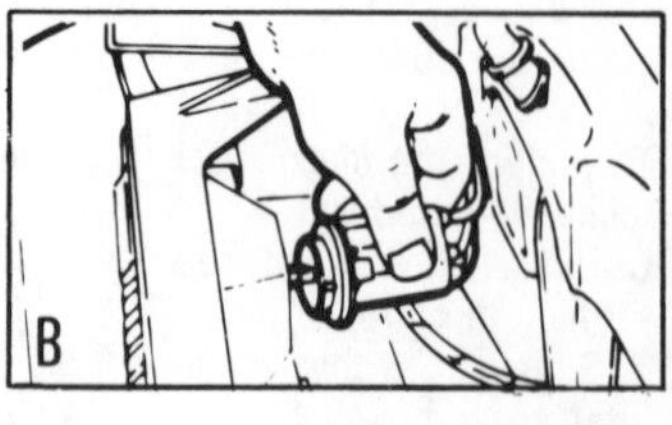

Parking lights, turn signals, and stop lights function with dual-element bulbs. Back-up lights are single element types. To replace:
A. Front parking lights and turn signals on all models and rear lights on station wagons. Remove lens to expose bulb(s). Push in on bulb while turning counterclockwise to release bulb from socket. Remove and replace with new bulb. Replace lens.
B. On sedans and convertibles, rear bulbs are reached from inside rather than outside. Locate bulb housing inside trunk or rear compartment. Twist socket to release from housing. Push in on bulb, turn counterclockwise and remove bulb.
NOTE: When inserting new dual element bulb, note that knobs on side of bulb base are different distances from base tip. Match knobs to socket slots for proper fit.

REPLACING INTERIOR DOME LIGHT

Pry the dome light lens out from the housing. To avoid blowing the fuse, make sure that the doors are closed and domelight switch in the OFF position. Push in on the bulb and turn it clockwise to remove from socket. Insert new bulb and install in reverse order.

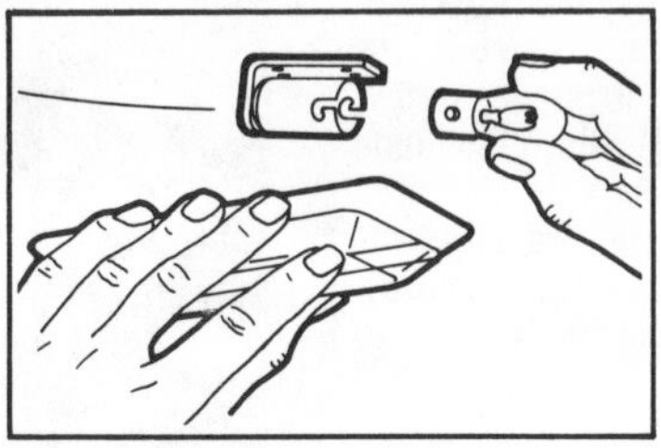

REPLACING HEADLIGHT SEALED BEAMS

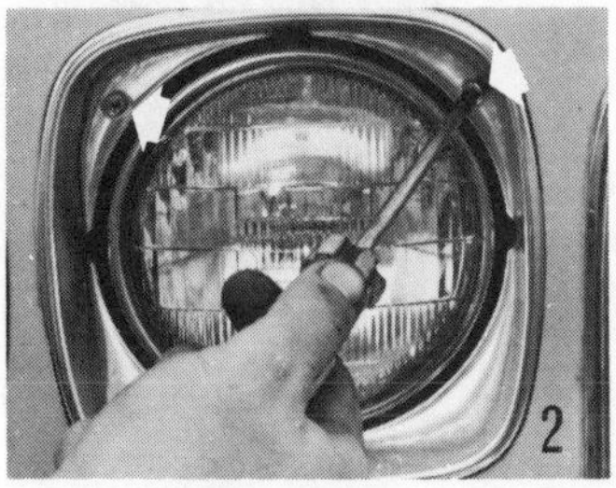

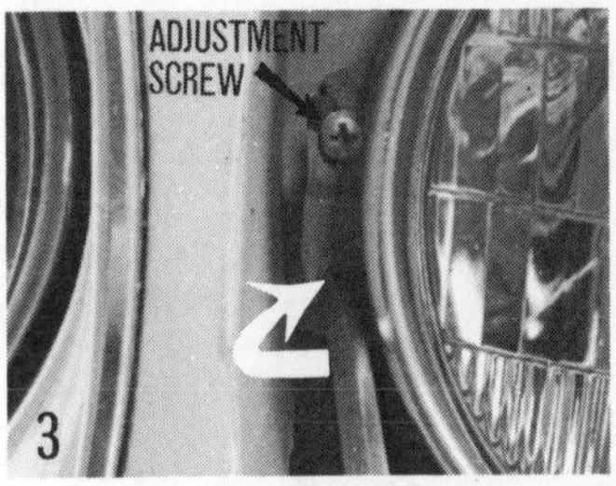

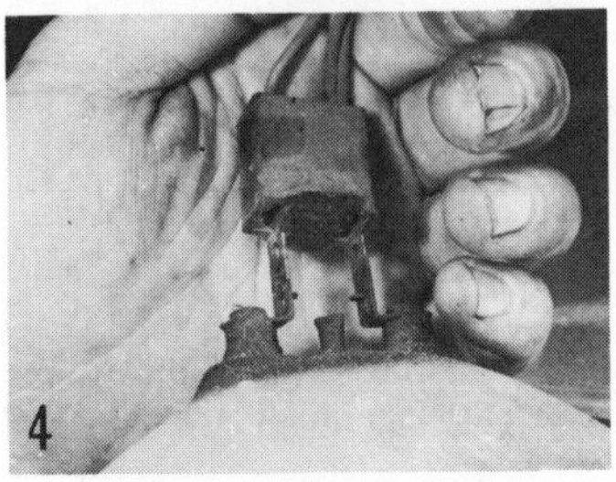

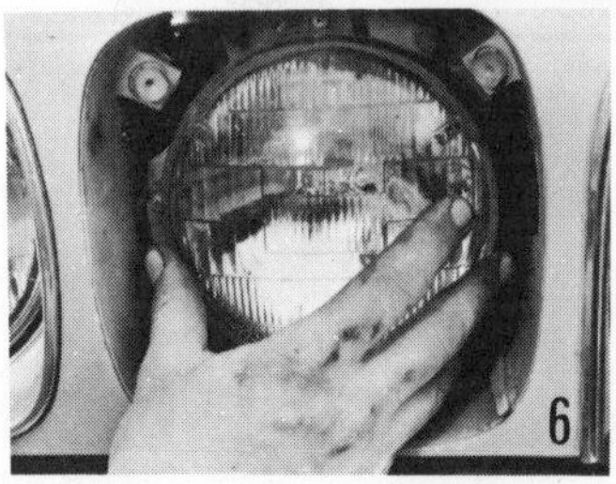

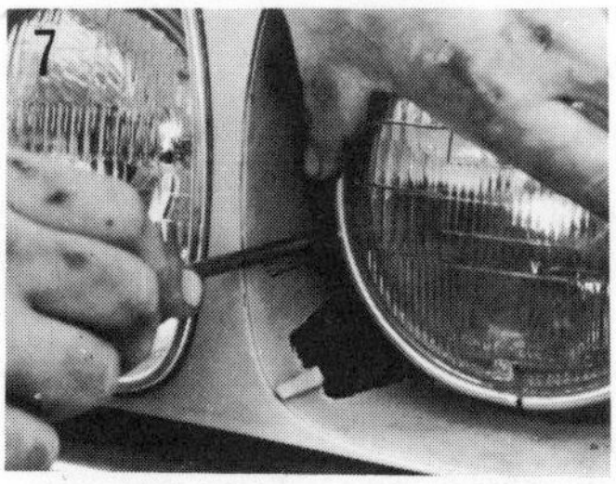

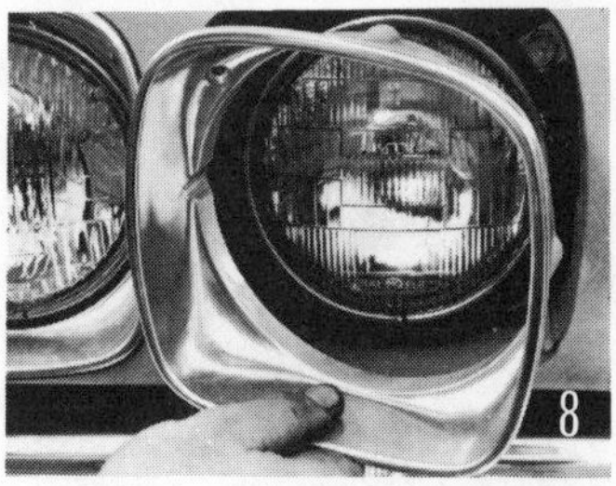

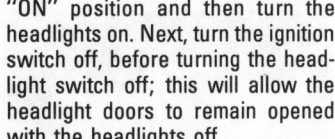

1. On models with concealed headlights, turn the ignition switch to the "ON" position and then turn the headlights on. Next, turn the ignition switch off, before turning the headlight switch off; this will allow the headlight doors to remain opened with the headlights off.
2. Unfasten the screws which secure the headlight bezel and remove the bezel.
3. Remove the three headlight retaining ring screws and remove the ring while supporting the sealed beam unit with your hand.

CAUTION: Do not disturb the two headlight aiming screws.

4. Remove the sealed beam unit from the car and pull the electrical connector straight off the back of it.

CAUTION: Do not interchange the inner and outer headlight sealed beam units on models with dual headlights. The outer bulbs are two element types and marked by the number "2" on the face of the glass. The inner bulbs are single element types and are marked with the number 1.

5. Attach the connector plug to the new headlight.
6. Position the new bulb in housing. Make sure the lugs on the back of the bulb fit into recesses in the housing.
7. Install the retaining ring.
8. Replace the headlight trim bezel.

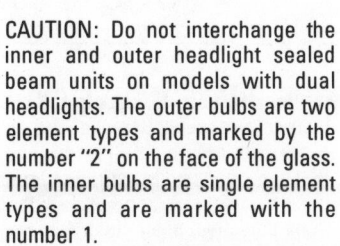

REPLACING WINDSHIELD WIPER BLADES

To replace the wiper blade assembly, lift the wiper arm up and depress the release lever (using a screwdriver if necessary) where the blade assembly is attached to the arm. Separate the assembly from the arm. To install, merely snap the new blade assembly into place.

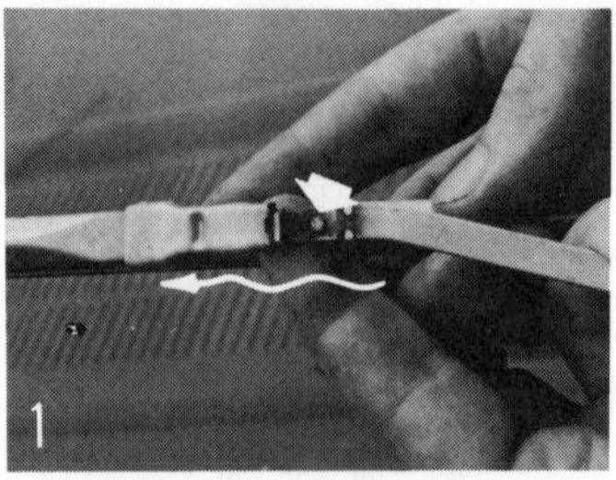

To replace the rubber blade insert only, depress the red (or black) dots on the blade assembly and slide the insert out lengthwise. When installing a new insert, bend the insert slightly upward to engage retaining channels.

HORN PROBLEMS

If horn sounds and does not stop, this is due to short circuit in wiring. Disconnect wiring connector under hood and have professional service shop check horn wiring circuit.

STEERING PROBLEMS

See steering system check in Suspension Section. Check tire pressures. Have a professional service shop check all components in the front end and steering system.

SERVICING WINDSHIELD WASHER SYSTEM

If washer fails to squirt properly, raise hood and check system hose connections. Be sure washer fluid container has fluid. Check spout openings for clogging.
Keep container filled with fluid mixture of washer solvent and water. If road spray buildup on windshield is a chronic problem, add 1 tablespoon dishwasher detergent to solvent/water mixture when re-filling container.

CHECKING BRAKE WHEEL CYLINDERS

All cars employ a dual hydraulic brake system. If a leak develops in one hydraulic system, the other system, which is totally independent of the other, will remain functional. This means you will have braking at two wheels. In addition, a warning light will light up on the dash if there is a pressure drop. However, a small amount of leakage may develop that will not cause a sudden reduction of braking or actuate the light. For this reason, if you suspect anything at all, take a look. On cars with drum brakes, check the inside of the tire and wheel. If it is wet, daub some up with your finger and smell it. Brake fluid is sweet to the smell. On cars with disc front brakes, remove the tire and wheel and check the caliper for leakage. Have a mechanic correct any leaks immediately.

Electrical System

CHECK BATTERY FLUID

1. Remove plastic filler caps on top of battery. Fluid should be up to lower end of filler hole and covering the plates. If fluid is low add clean, cold tap water. If your area has hard water, use only distilled water available at auto supply, food or drug stores.
2. Replace any lost caps immediately.

CAUTION: NEVER LIGHT A MATCH OR SMOKE near the top of a battery. Batteries give off explosive hydrogen gas.

NOTE: Battery that often checks low on fluid could mean:

A. Battery is getting old, due for replacement; have charge capacity checked at service shop.

B. Connections may be corroded or loose; clean/replace as needed (see below).

C. Alternator or voltage regulator not functioning properly; this happens far less often than A or B above.

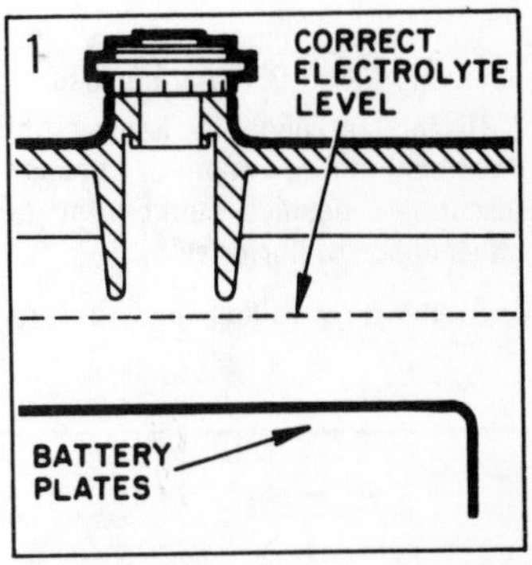

CLEAN THOSE BATTERY TERMINALS

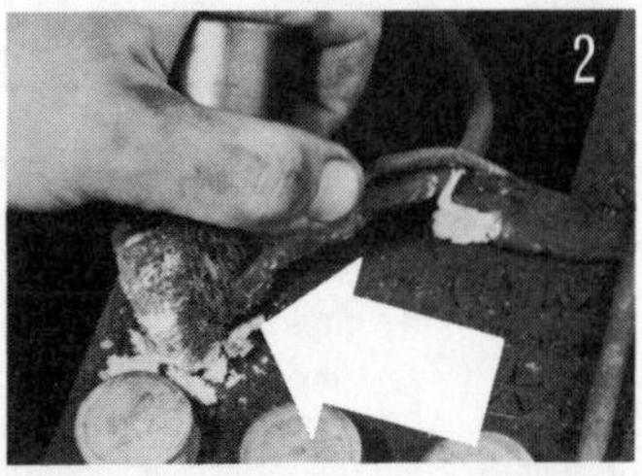

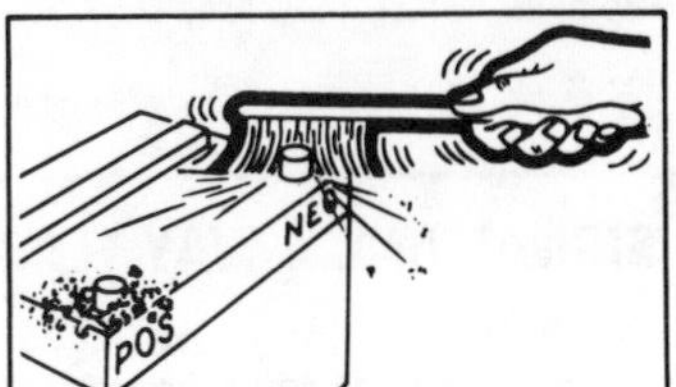

As time goes by, battery terminals build up a dry powdery, whitish material. This material is corrosive and will gradually eat thru battery cables if not cleaned off periodically.

1. Loosen and remove battery connections.
2. Brush off all loose corrosion; use stiff bristle brush. Do not get this material into eyes or on open cuts. Wash off at once.
3. If corrosion build-up is extremely heavy and brushing does not remove all of it, mix 2 tablespoons baking soda to 1 cup water. Pour solution directly onto terminals and connectors. Allow to soak a few minutes and rinse off. Continue brushing to remove all traces of corrosion build-up. Do not allow cleaning solution to enter battery.
4. Replace connectors on battery terminal posts and tighten. Do not hammer connections onto posts, but be sure they will not come loose with vibration.
5. Liberally smear battery terminal posts and cable connectors with petroleum jelly.

REPLACE FAULTY BATTERY CABLES

If battery cable strands become frayed, broken or corroded, replace cable immediately. Delay in correcting this condition could lead to sudden failure to start the engine. Can also weaken battery.

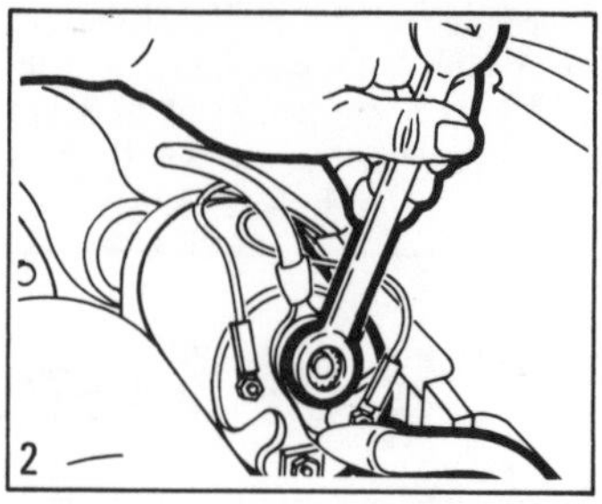

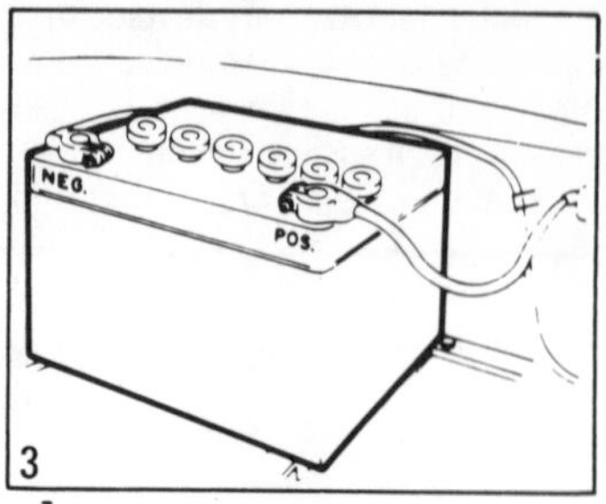

1. Loosen and remove battery connections. Clean OFF any corrosion.

2. Disconnect negative cable from its attachment to engine or chassis. Disconnect positive cable from its attachment to starter relay.

3. Attach new cables making sure positive and negative cables are on proper terminals. They are not identical.

4. Replace connectors on battery terminal posts and tighten.

5. Liberally smear battery terminal posts and cable connectors with petroleum jelly.

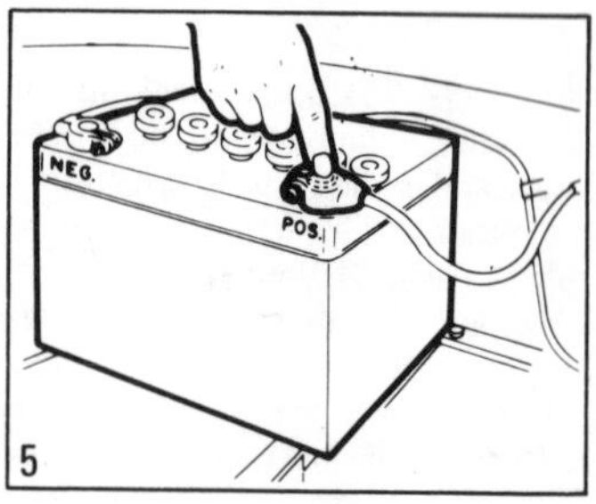

BATTERY HOLDDOWN

The clamp device which holds the battery in place consists of two long bolts which mount in the battery tray, two nuts and a crossbar. 1975-77 models have a plastic heat shield which surrounds the battery. Periodically, check the hold-down bolts for tightness and corrosion buildup. Clean off corrosion with wire brush and baking soda. Severely corroded hold-down components should be replaced before they break.

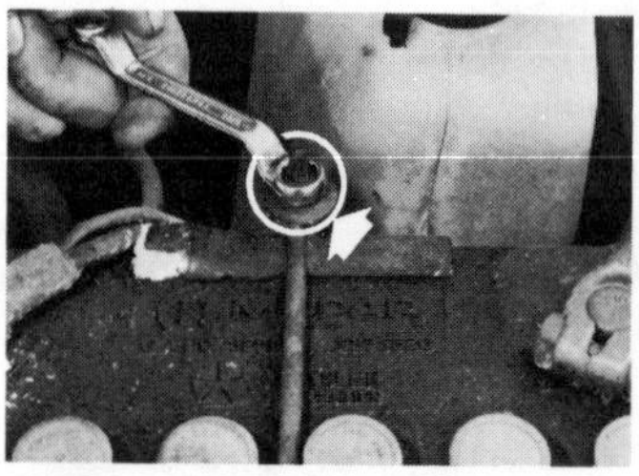

TURN SIGNAL AND 4-WAY FLASHERS

Turn signal and 4-way emergency flashers will operate only if: A. All light bulbs on circuit are OK, and B. Flasher units are not burned out. The car has two flasher units that work independent of each other. On 1970-73 models, the turn signal flasher is located behind the ashtray and the 4-way flasher on the brake pedal bracket. On 1974-77 models, both flashers plug into the fuse block. To replace either type of flasher, simply unplug the unit from its connector. Take the old flasher with you when you purchase the new one. Replace only with same type flasher.

ALTERNATOR CHECKS

Dashboard ammeter gauge should show slight discharge when you first turn ignition key while starting. This proves gauge is OK. When engine starts, gauge should first jump to the charge side, then slowly fall back to the center with engine at idle speed. If ammeter shows discharge at idle speed, alternator isn't charging properly. Common causes are:

A. Fan belts are loose and slipping on alternator pulley. Tighten or replace belts.

B. Battery terminals, cables are loose or corroded. Clean; tighten; replace bad cables.

If A or B do not correct problem, alternator or voltage regulator may be faulty. This happens far less often, and can only be checked by mechanic with proper electrical testing equipment.

Alternator Caution: Alternator can be permanently damaged by shortcircuiting terminal connections. When working around or moving alternator, always keep metal tools or engine parts from terminals.

FUSE LOCATION

On 1970-73 models, the fusebox is located under the dash, to the left of the brake pedal bracket. To gain access to the fuses, unsnap the two retaining clips and disconnect the fusebox from the firewall connector. Each fuse socket has a number indicating which circuit the fuse protects.

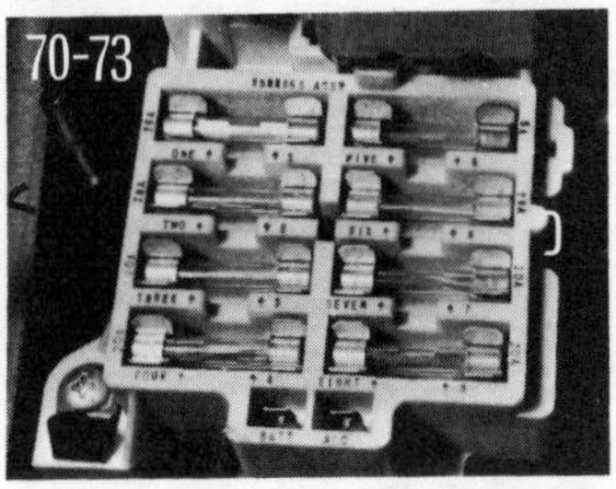

On 1974-77 models, the fusebox is located to the left of the steering column and swings down for easy access. Simply rotate the fusebox retaining key 90 degrees and the fusebox will hinge down. The fuse location breakdown on these models is as follows:

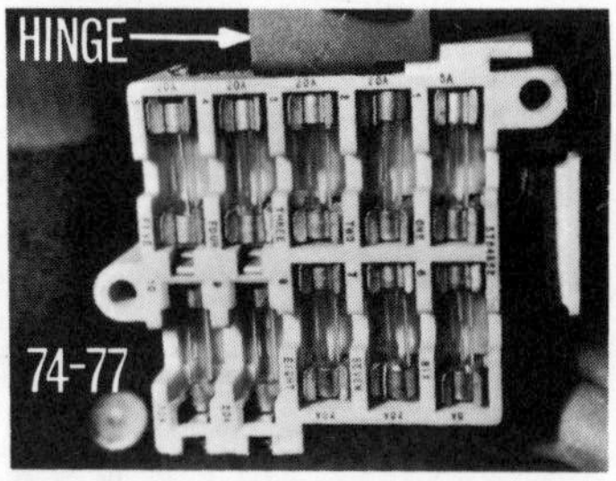

CAVITY	FUSE	ITEMS FUSED
1.	5 AMP	LAMPS: CLUSTER, WINDSHIELD WIPER AND HEADLAMP SWITCH TITLE, ASH TRAY, OIL GAUGE, TEMPERATURE GAUGE, TAILGATE LOCK SWITCH, REAR WINDOW DEFOGGER, HEATED REAR WINDOW, STEREO TAPE, RADIO, CLOCK, HEATER AND AIR CONDITIONER CONTROL LAMPS.
2.	20 AMP	LAMPS: SIDE MARKER, TAIL, LICENSE, PARKING AND INSTRUMENT LAMPS, ATC AMPLIFIER.
3.	20 AMP	LAMPS: STOP, DOME, AFT DOME, TRUNK, GLOVE BOX, MAP, COURTESY, HEADLAMP SWITCH TITLE AND IGNITION SWITCH, vanity, VISOR LAMPS. TIME DELAY RELAY, KEY-IN AND HEADLAMP ON BUZZER, CLOCK, AND CIGARETTE LIGHTER.
4.	20 AMP	HORN (DUAL) AND HORN RELAY.
5.	20 AMP	LAMPS: DUAL BRAKE, OIL PRESSURE, OPEN DOOR AND SEAT BELT. ELECTRIC DECK LID, POWER WINDOW SAFETY RELAY, SEAT BELT WARNING TIME DELAY RELAY AND BUZZER. PO MODELS—HIGH TEMPERATURE AND E.G.R. LAMPS.
6.	5 AMP	RADIO WITH TAPE PLAYER.
7.	5 AMP	VOLTAGE LIMITER, RADIO CAPACITOR, FUEL & TEMP GAUGE. OIL GAUGE (PD-0-00).
8.	20 AMP	BACK-UP AND TURN SIGNAL LAMPS, TURN SIGNAL FLASHER, SPEED CONTROL, REAR WINDOW DEFOGGER, AIR CONDITIONER CLUTCH, ACT VENT RELAY, CORNERING LAMPS DC MODELS. POWER ANTENNA C MODELS.
9.	30 AMP	AIR CONDITIONER BLOWER MOTOR, HEATER BLOWER MOTOR, HEATED REAR WINDOW RELAY AND TAILGATE LOCK.
10.	20 AMP	HAZARD FLASHER

REAR WINDOW DEFOGGER SYSTEM (1975-77 Models)

Do not clean inside of rear window fitted with defogger system with any abrasive material. This could destroy carbon-copper wires. Use only soft rag and mild detergent/water mixture. Dry carefully.

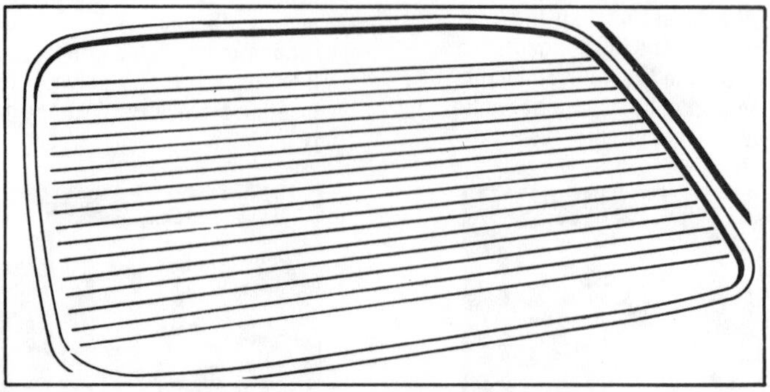

Air Conditioner

CHECKPOINTS AND SERVICES

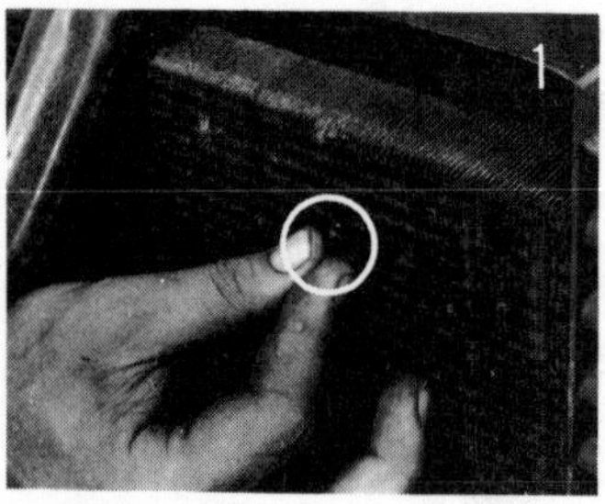

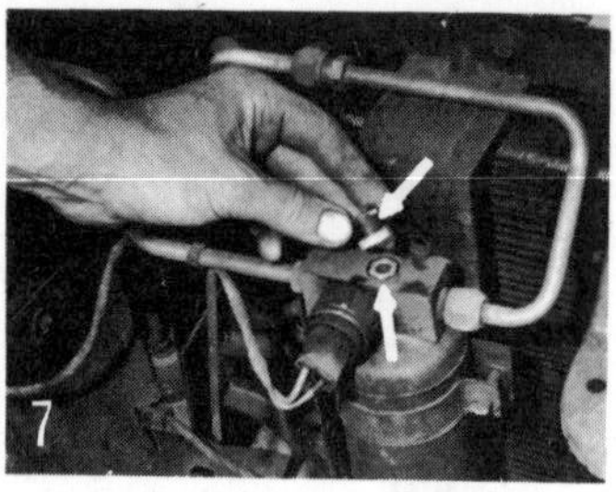

WARNING!—Never attempt to tighten fittings, disassemble or do any work on your car's A/C system. Consult a professional mechanic about A/C system problems and their correction. Your auto air conditioner (A/C) is a delicate, closed system. If air, dirt or water get into it, or if refrigerant escapes, the A/C unit will not cool a car interior. Among things you can do are:

1. Keep condenser grill clean. Check for dirt and debris; periodically remove dead insects, leaves, etc., with stiff bristle brush. Straighten any bent fins—carefully.
2. Keep radiator filled to correct level. (See Cooling System section). If fluid needs to be added, add antifreeze rather than water.
3. Keep radiator coolant at a 50/50 water/antifreeze mixture.
4. Flush cooling system and replace with fresh coolant mixture at least every 24 months. (See Cooling System section).
5. Radiator cap should be tight and sealed properly. If sealing gasket is cracked, cut or worn, replace cap with new 15 lb. unit.
6. Check fan belt tension periodically. (See Cooling System section). Replace glazed, frayed or cut fan belts, before they fail entirely.
7. Check periodically for bubbles in A/C sight glass. Sight glass is located in head of receiver/drier vessel. Or in metal tubing leading from top of receiver/drier. Sight glass is no larger than head of large nail. It may be dirty. Wipe clean for best visibility.

PROCEED AS FOLLOWS:

a) With engine and A/C system running, look for passage of refrigerant in sight glass. You'll be looking for a stream of milky white bubbles as they pass through sight glass. It is best to watch sight glass and have someone else start the car and turn on the A/C system. Allow to run for a few minutes.

b) If you observe no bubbles, and air flow from A/C unit in the car is passing cold air, everything is OK.

c) If no bubbles appear in sight glass, and air flow from the A/C unit in the car is not delivering cold air, the system may be low on refrigerant and could need a re-charge.

d) If bubbles appear, system is low on refrigerant.

e) If you suspect refrigerant loss based on tests performed above, have system checked by a professional A/C service shop. They can confirm refrigerant loss, recharge the system and check for system leakage.

NOTE: Once a week or so, even in winter, run A/C system for about 5 minutes as you drive. This keeps system internally lubricated, prevents hoses hardening.

TUNE-UP SPECIFICATIONS

YEAR	ENGINE No. Cyl. Displacement (cu. in.)	SPARK PLUGS Type	Gap (in.)	DISTRIBUTOR Point Dwell (deg.)	Point Gap (in.)	IGNITION TIMING Man. Trans.● (deg.)■	Auto Trans.● (deg.)■	IDLE SPEED Man. Trans.● (rpm)▲	Auto Trans. (rpm)▲
1970	6-225 (145 hp)	N-14Y	.035	41-46	.020	TDC	TDC	700	650
	8-318 (230 hp)	N-14Y	.035	30-34	.017	TDC	TDC	750	700
	8-383 (290 hp)	J-14Y	.035	28-32	.018	TDC	2½B	750	650
	8-440 (350 hp)	J-11Y	.035	28-32	.018	TDC	2½B	750	750
	8-400 (350 hp)	J-13Y	.035	28-33	.018	—	12½B	—	650
	8-440 (390 hp)	J-11Y	.035	27-32①	.017	5B	5B	900	900
1971	6-225 (145 hp)	N-14Y	.035	41-46	.020	TDC(2½B)	TDC(2½B)	750	750
	8-318 (230 hp)	N-14Y	.035	30-34	.017	TDC	TDC	750	700
	8-360 (255 hp)	N-13Y	.035	30-34	.017	2½B	2½B	750	700
	8-383 (275 hp)	J-14Y	.035	28-32	.018	TDC	2½B	750	700
	8-383 (300 hp)	J-11Y	.035	28-32	.018	TDC	2½B	900	800
	8-440 (335 hp)	J-13Y	.035	28-32	.018	—	5B	—	750
	8-440 (370 hp)	J-11Y	.035	28-32	.018	TDC	2½B	900	800
1972	8-318 (150 hp)	N-13Y	.035	30-34	.017	—	TDC	—	750(700)
	8-360 (175 hp)	N-13Y	.035	30-34	.017	—	TDC	—	750
	8-400 (190 hp)	J-13Y	.035	28-32	.018	—	5B②	—	700
	8-440 (225 hp)	J-11Y	.035	28-32	.018	—	10B	—	750(700)
1973	8-318 (150 hp)	N-13Y	.035	Electronic		—	TDC	—	700
	8-360 (170 hp)	N-13Y	.035	Electronic		—	TDC	—	750
	8-400 (185 hp)	J-13Y	.035	Electronic		—	10B	—	700
	8-440 (220 hp)	J-11Y	.035	Electronic		—	10B	—	700
1974	8-360 (180 hp)	N-12Y	.035	Electronic		—	5B	—	750
	8-400 (185 hp)	J-13Y	.035	Electronic		—	5B	—	750
	8-400 (260 hp)	J-13Y	.035	Electronic		—	5B	—	900(750)
	8-440 (275 hp)	J-11Y	.035	Electronic		—	10B	—	750
1975	8-318 (150 hp)	N-13Y	.035	Electronic		—	2B	—	750
	8-360 (All)	N-12Y	.035	Electronic		—	6B	—	750
	8-400 (185 hp)	J-13Y	.035	Electronic		—	10B	—	750
	8-400 (205 hp)	J-13Y	.035	Electronic		—	8B	—	750
	8-440 (275 hp)	RY-87P	.040	Electronic		—	8B	—	750
1976-77	8-318③ (150 hp)	RN-12Y	.035	Electronic		—	2B	—	750
	8-318④ (150 hp)	RN-12Y	.035	Electronic		—	2A	—	750
	8-360 (170 hp)	RN-12Y	.035	Electronic		—	6B	—	700
	8-360Cal (175 hp)	RN-12Y	.035	Electronic		—	6B	—	750
	8-400 (175 hp)	RJ-13Y	.035	Electronic		—	10B	—	700
	8-400Cal (185 hp)	RJ-13Y	.035	Electronic		—	8B	—	750
	8-400LB (210 hp)	RJ-13Y	.035	Electronic		—	10B	—	720
	8-400HP (240 hp)	RJ-86P	.035	Electronic		—	6B	—	750
	8-440 (205 hp)	RJ-13Y	.035	Electronic		—	8B	—	750
	8-440HP (255 hp)	RJ-11Y	.035	Electronic		—	10B	—	750

▲ Adjust automatic transmissions in Drive (AMC/Ford/GM) or Neutral (Chrysler), all manual transmissions are adjusted in Neutral.
● Figure in parentheses indicate California engine.
■ A After Top Dead Center B Before Top Dead Center TDC Top Dead Center
Cal California
LB Lean Burn
① Both sets 37°—40°
② Non-California cars built after Feb. 2, 7½B
③ With Catalytic Converter
④ With Air Pump only

NOTE: The underhood specifications sticker often reflects tune-up specification changes made in production. Sticker figures must be used if they disagree with those in this chart.

CAPACITIES

YEAR	ENGINE No. Cyl. Displacement (cu. in.)	ENGINE OIL Add 1 qt. with New Filter	TRANSMISSION Pts. to Refill after Draining MANUAL 3-speed	MANUAL 4-speed	AUTOMATIC	DRIVE AXLE (pts.)	COOLING SYSTEM with Heater (qts.)	COOLING SYSTEM with Air Cond. (qts.)
1970	6-225	4	4.75	—	17	2	13	15
	8-318	4	4.75	—	16	4	16	19
	8-383	4	4.75	—	19	4	16	17
	8-383	4	4.75	—	16	4	16	17
	8-440	4	—	—	19	4	17	18
1971	6-225	4	4.75	—	17	4.5	13	13
	8-318	4	4.75	—	17	4.5	16	16.5
	8-360	4	4.75	—	16	4.5	15.5	15
	8-383	4	4.75	—	16①	4.5	14.5	15
	8-440	4	—	—	19	4	15.5	17
1972	8-318	4	—	—	17	4.5	16	17.5
	8-360	4	—	—	16.3	4.5	16	16
	8-400	4	—	—	19	4.5	14.5	15
	8-440	4	—	—	16.3	4.5	14.5	14.5
1973	8-318	4	—	—	17	4.5	16	17.5
	8-360	4	—	—	16.3	4.5	15.5	16
	8-400	4	—	—	19	4.5	16	17
	8-440	4	—	—	19	4.5	15.5	15.5
1974	8-360	4	—	—	16.1	4.5	16.5	16.5
	8-400	4	—	—	18.9②	4.5	16.5	16.5
	8-440	4	—	—	16.1	4.5	16	16
1975-77	8-318	4	—	—	17⑤④	4.5	17.5	17.5
	8-360	4	—	—	16.5④⑤	4.5	16	16
	8-400	4	—	—	19⑤	4.5	16.5	16.5
	8-440	4③	—	—	19⑤	4.5	16	16

① 2-bbl—19 pts
② 16.1 pts with HP 400
③ 5 qts with HP 440
④ 11¾ in. torque converter—19 pts
⑤ With auxiliary cooler—20.5 pts

Fairlane/Torino

Lubrication and Oil Change

BRAKE FLUID LEVEL CHECK

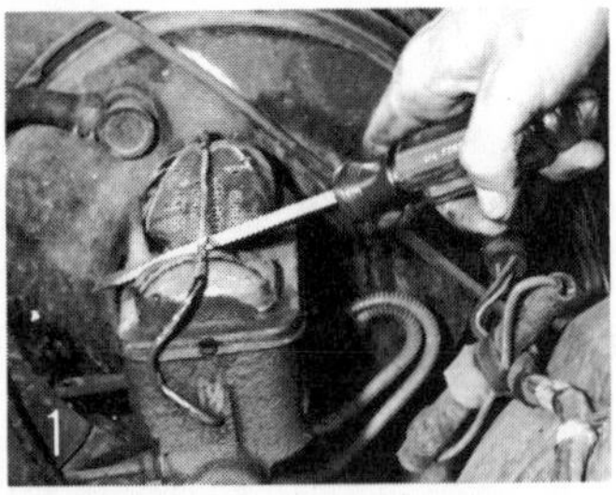
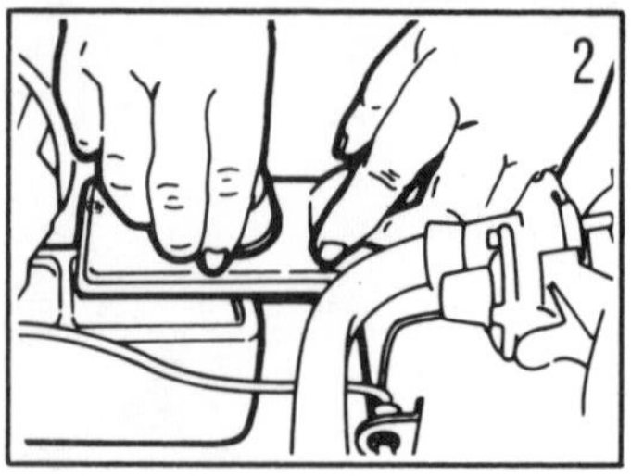
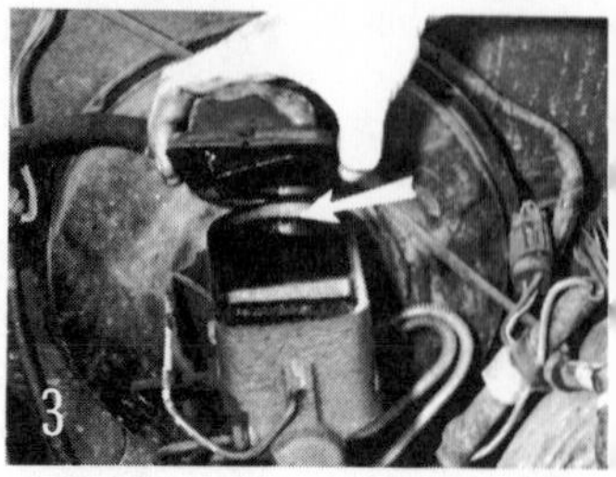

Check brake fluid level in master cylinder every three months . . . sooner if braking feels inadequate. Add when low. Recommended grade: Extra Heavy Duty; Grade 70R3 as printed on can (check owner's handbook).

Master cylinder is located under hood on left side. It is oblong container about 6" long with cap held down by wire clip. Check brake fluid level as follows:

1. Pry wire retaining clip off cap top with screwdriver.
2. Remove cap and gasket by lifting up.
3. Fluid level should be within ¼ inch of top rim. If lower than this, add fresh fluid to appropriate level.

DO NOT OVERFILL

4. Replace cap and gasket; secure retaining clip over cap. If fluid level was low, check again in a few days.
5. If fluid repeatedly checks low, there is a leak somewhere in the system. See SAFETY SYSTEMS—WHEEL CYLINDER CHECK. Have mechanic check further. Neglect can be dangerous.

MANUAL TRANSMISSION FLUID LEVEL CHECK

FORD SAYS . . . check manual transmission fluid every 6000 miles. Car should be parked level. Recommended grade: Standard Transmission Fluid (SAE 90).

TOOLS NEEDED . . . fluid level check device (make from coat hanger wire; bend at 90° angle 2" from end); adjustable wrench; bulb syringe.

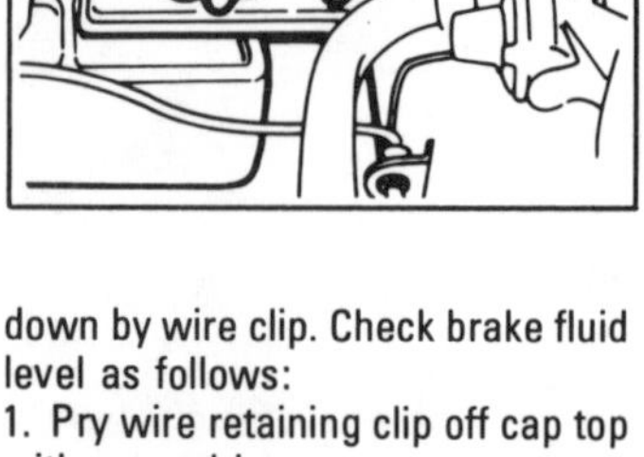
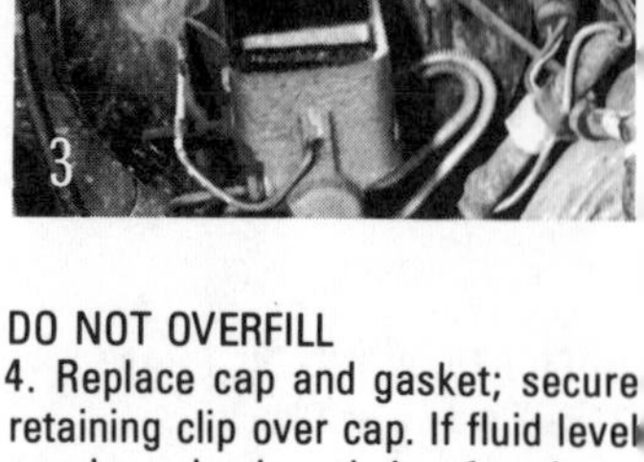
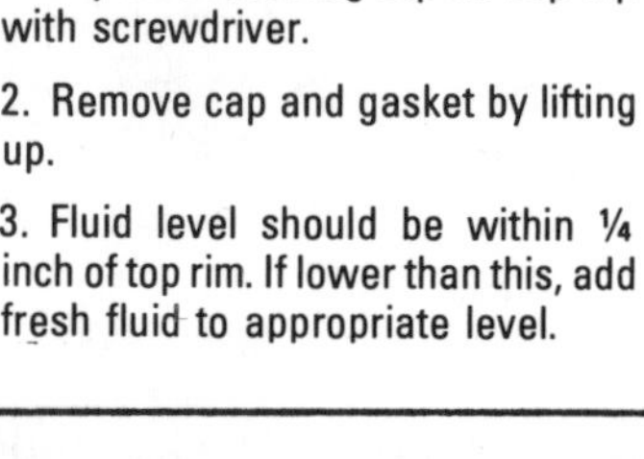
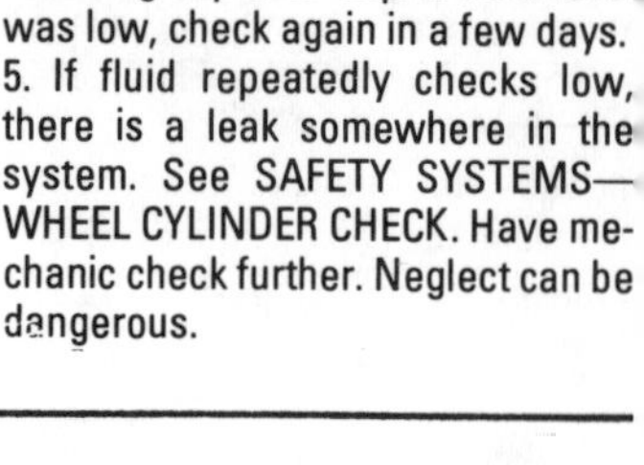

1. Locate transmission fluid filler plug on right side of transmission housing from underneath car.
2. Wipe road dirt from filler plug area before loosening. Remove plug with adjustable wrench.
3. Insert fluid level check device. Fluid level should be right up to bottom edge of filler hole.
4. Add fluid as needed with hand bulb syringe.
5. Replace filler plug; tighten.

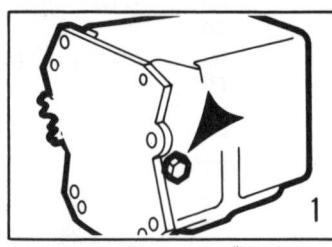

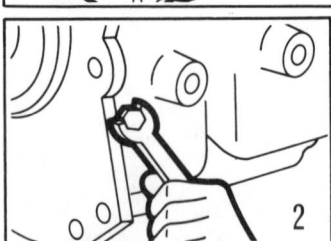

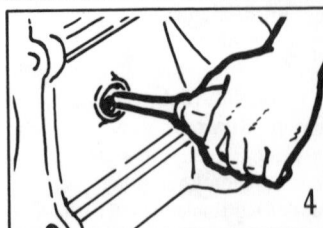

AUTOMATIC TRANSMISSION FLUID LEVEL CHECK

FORD SAYS . . . check automatic transmission fluid (ATF) level every 6000 miles. Recommended grade: ATF Type F.

TOOLS . . . Long neck filler funnel and clean rag.

1. Engine must be warmed up and

running. Place shift lever in PARK position.
2. Pull out dipstick. Wipe clean. Push dipstick all the way back in; remove it again.
3. If fluid is below ADD mark, add ATF to bring level up. DO NOT OVERFILL.
4. Add ATF thru transmission dipstick hole by means of long-neck filler funnel.

REAR AXLE LUBRICANT

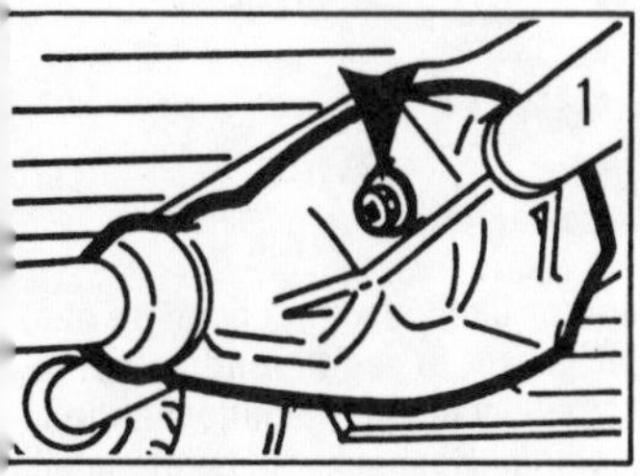

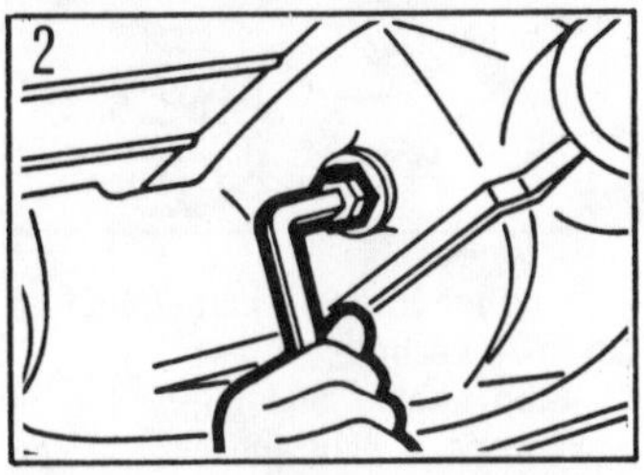

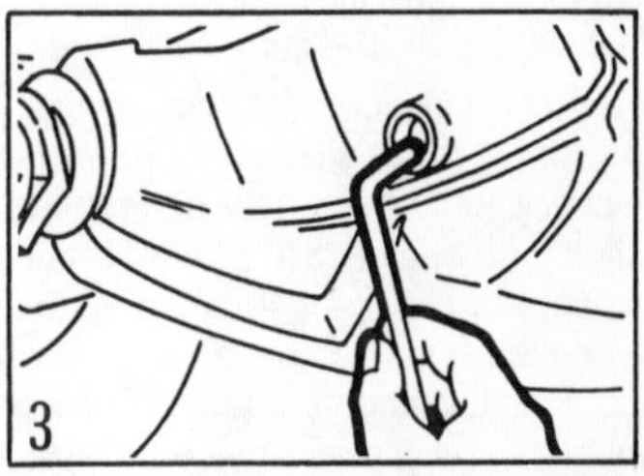

FORD SAYS . . . check rear axle lube level every 6000 miles. Recommended grade: Hypoid gear lube (SAE 90).

TOOLS . . . ⅜ in. ratchet handle and short extension; fluid level check device (made from coat hanger wire; bend at 90° angle 2″ from end); bulb syringe.
1. Locate filler plug on forward side of rear axle housing.
2. Wipe plug area clean; remove plug with ratchet and extension. Insert square end to remove plug.

3. Insert wire level check device; remove. Adequate fluid level should show lubricant on last ¼-inch of wire.
4. If fluid level is low, add as needed, with a hand bulb syringe, until level

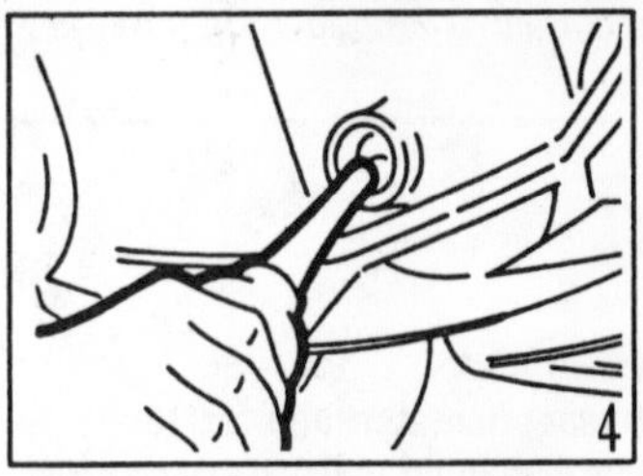

shows on last ¼-inch of wire.
5. Replace filler plug; tighten.

OIL AND FILTER CHANGE

FORD SAYS . . . Change oil every 4000 miles, change filter every 8000 miles. Recommended grade: MS or SE (check owner's handbook). Check oil level at least once a week.
TOOLS & MATERIALS . . . adjustable hand wrench; medium size screwdriver; oil filter removal wrench; drain pan for old oil (at least 5 qt. capacity); oil pouring spout; 5 qt. oil; new oil filter; oil and lubricants as specified below.
SAFETY TIP . . . Always support the car with safety stands when working underneath.

1. If engine is cold, start up and idle for about 5 minutes.
2. Park car on level ground. Turn engine off.
3. Locate oil drain plug on underside of engine. Place drain pan under plug.
4. Remove drain plug with wrench.

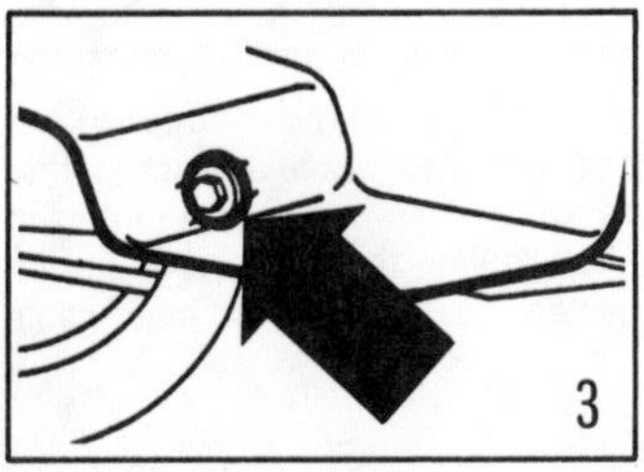

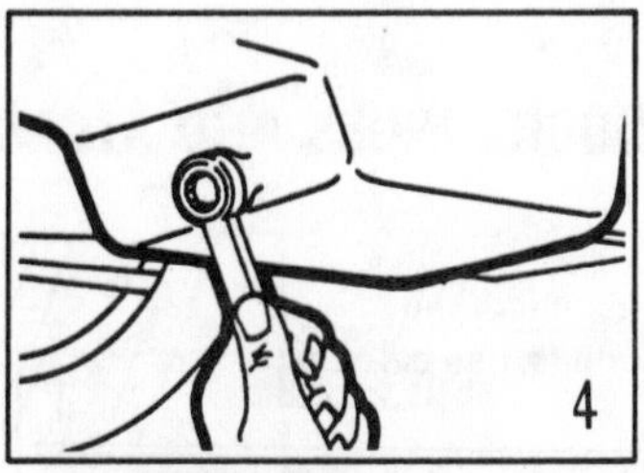

Let ALL dirty oil drain out.
5. Wipe plug and area around drain hole clean. Replace drain plug; tighten it.

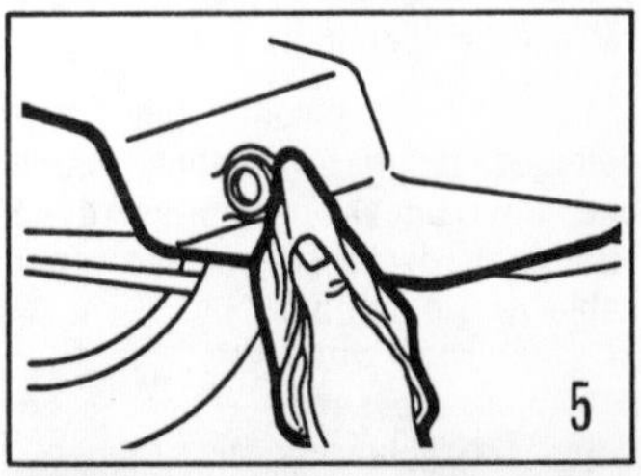

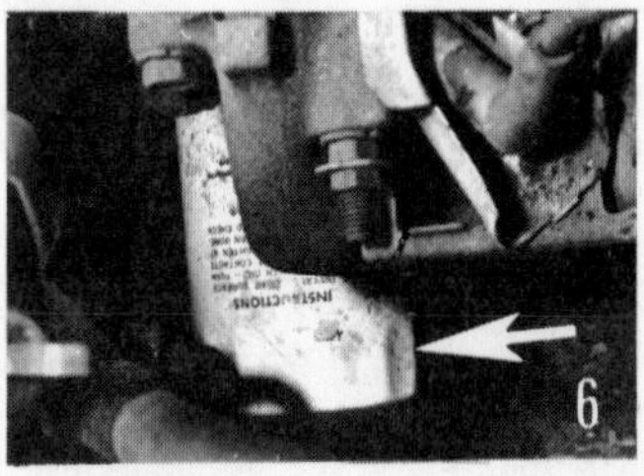

6. Locate oil filter. Move drain pan under filter. Loosen filter with oil filter wrench. Unscrew; remove filter by hand.

7. Smear fresh oil over surface of rubber gasket (washer) of new filter. Install new filter by hand only. Do NOT use wrench. Turn filter until gasket makes contact. Tighten an additional half turn only . . . NO MORE.

8. Locate oil filler hole on top of engine. Remove cap.

9. Punch oil pouring spout into top of oil can. Pour all cans of new oil into filler tube. Wipe filler cap clean and replace it.

10. Check new oil level at dipstick. Pull out dipstick, wipe clean.

11. Push dipstick back into engine. Be sure to insert all the way. Remove dipstick and check new oil level. It should be above "SAFE" line. If not, be sure to check if you put in all the oil called for.

12. Start up engine and idle for 3-5 minutes. Oil signal light on instrument panel will glow red when en-

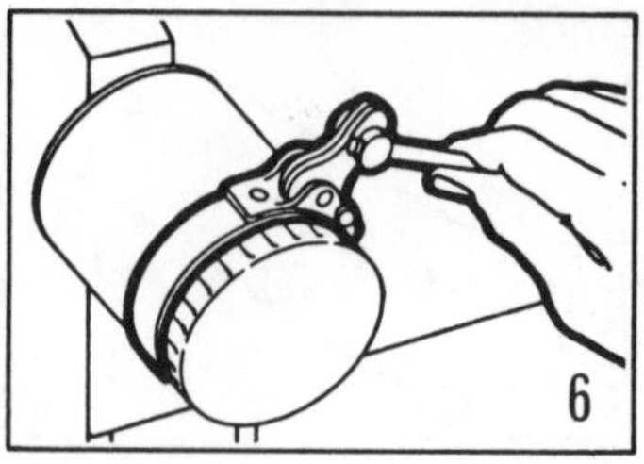

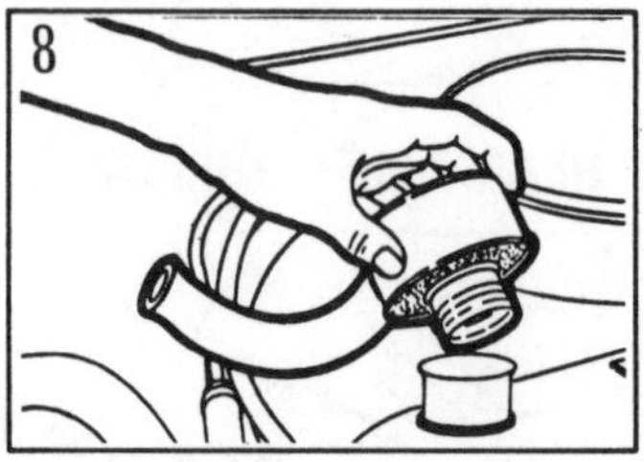

gine is first started. Light should go out in 30 seconds or less.

13. Stop engine and check for oil leaks at drain plug and filter. If you find any, check tightness of plug

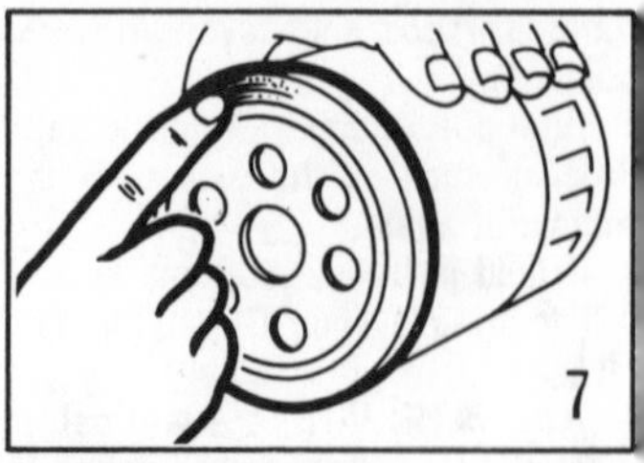

and/or filter, also for condition of filter gasket to see that it has not become pinched or damaged when installing. Recheck oil level, which should now be at "SAFE".

SPEEDOMETER CABLE LUBRICATION

If speedometer pointer tends to quiver or jump, or if unit makes a low, rasping sound, lubrication may be needed.

1. Locate cable shaft attachment directly behind speedometer dial.

2. Remove retaining clip. Unscrew cable from speedometer.

3. Pull inner cable completely out of outer casing. Note carefully which end is top. Check for wear or frayed strands. If damaged, replace inner cable with new one.

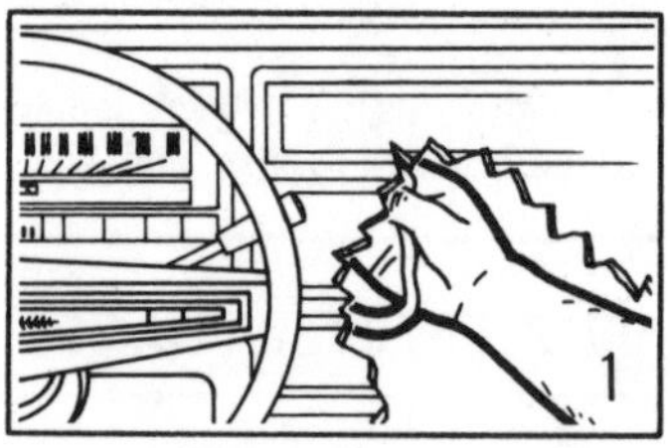

4. Apply generous amount of speedometer cable lubricant into cable casing. Replace inner cable in shaft, noting that top end is not inserted accidentally. Turn inner cable

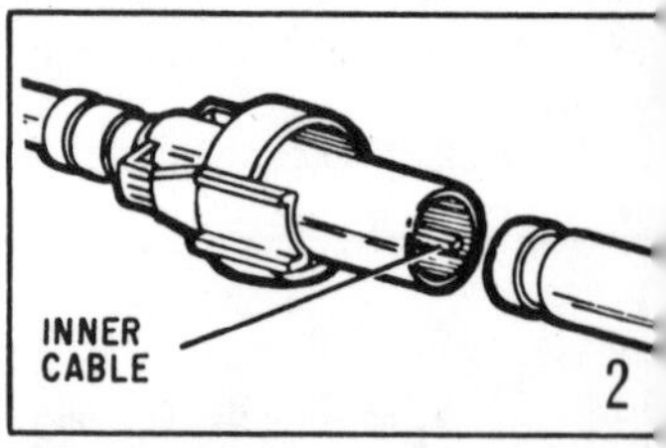

as it is being re-inserted. Twist cable when all the way in, to lock into position at lower end.

5. Reconnect cable to speedometer head under instrument panel.

DOOR HINGES AND STOPS

(lubricate every 6 months)

1. Brush any dirt accumulations from door hinges and stops. Use old tooth brush or rag.

2. Apply dab of white polyethylene grease to door hinges, trunk hinges, hood hinges, door stops.

DOOR LOCKS

(lubricate every 6 months)
1. Insert door key half way into lock.
2. Spray aerosol lock lubricant into lock.
3. Push key rest of way into lock; turn back and forth several times.

Cooling System

IT IS RECOMMENDED . . . that radiator coolant (water/antifreeze mixture) level be checked once or twice a month. Do this when engine is cold. Check more often if you do a lot of hard driving. On models with clear expansion tanks, check coolant level visually when hot.
Keep coolant up to recommended level in radiator. If coolant checks frequently low, look for leaks.

Tighten all hose clamps occasionally. For best results, keep a 50/50 water/antifreeze mixture year round. Change complete coolant mixture every 24 months.

CAUTION: If you must check coolant in a hot engine, cover radiator cap with thick rag before releasing. Remove cap slowly . . . press down and turn.

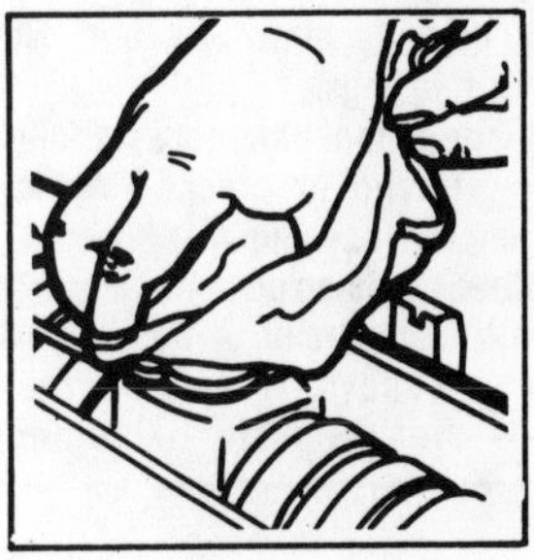

REPLACING THE THERMOSTAT

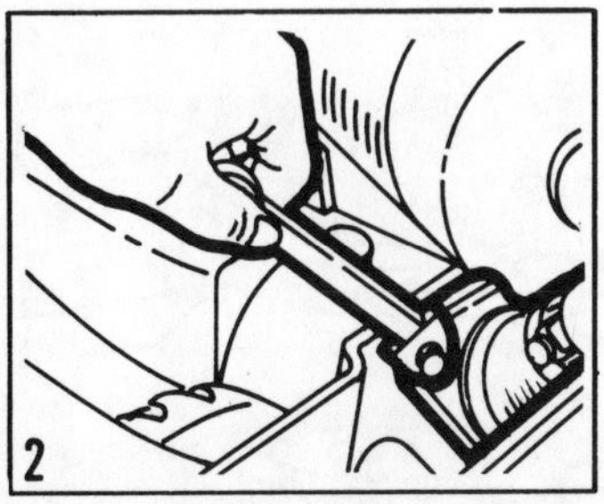

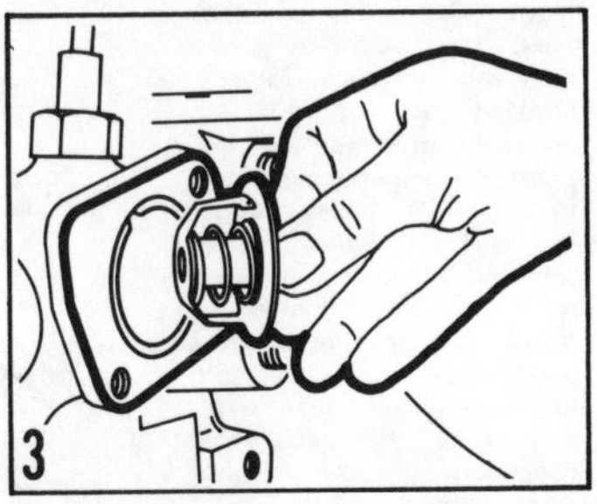

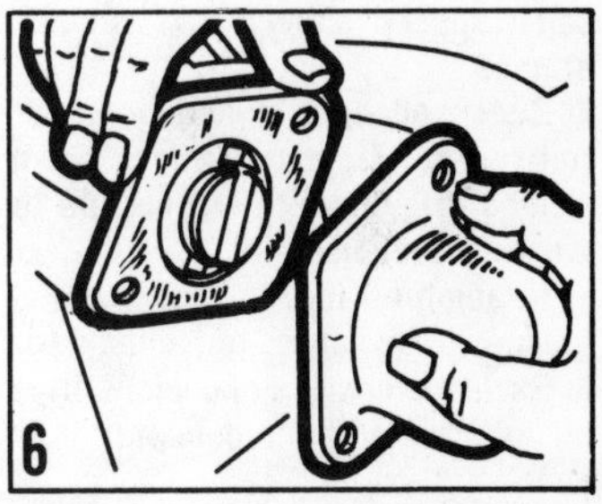

A faulty thermostat will usually cause engine overheating. Replace with new thermostat.

TOOLS AND MATERIALS . . .
New thermostat
Gasket
Adjustable wrench

1. Drain radiator of about half its coolant. (See Hose Replacement section).
2. Loosen and remove both retaining bolts and lift thermostat housing off the engine.

NOTE: If you're careful it won't be necessary to remove radiator hose.

3. Remove old thermostat.
4. Scrape thermostat housing flange and engine block surface to remove old gasket debris.
5. Drop new thermostat into place—spring down.
6. Install new gasket with sealer applied to both sides.
7. Replace thermostat housing and tighten both retaining bolts.

ENGINE OVERHEATING

YOUR CAR
OVERHEATS BECAUSE
radiator coolant is too low
fan belt is too loose
of a broken or leaking hose
thermostat does not function
radiator is plugged with sediment
water pump does not function properly

TO CORRECT IT
fill to correct level;
check for leaks
adjust tension or replace frayed belt

replace hose; tighten clamps replace thermostat	consult professional mechanic (may need radiator removal and servicing, or total replacement)	replace water pump (may make squeaky noise; or leak at pump shaft)

FAN BELT ADJUSTMENT

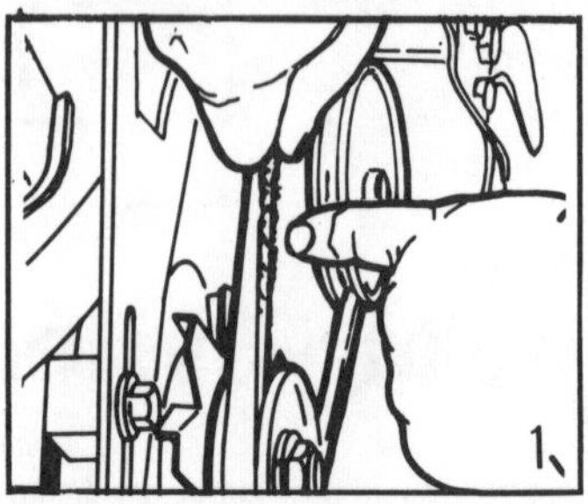

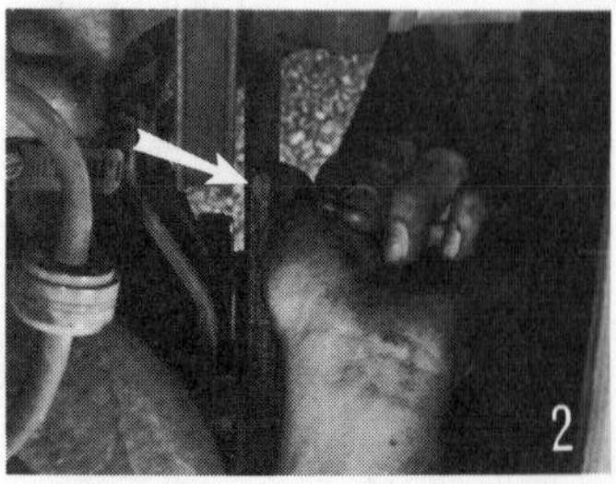

The fan belt not only drives the radiator fan, it turns the water pump and drives the alternator. It's easy to see that the condition and proper tension of the belt are vital, since almost all engine cooling and electrical power is dependent on it. The belt deserves an occasional look and tension check.

CAUTION: An overtightened belt may damage alternator and water pump bearings.

1. Inspect fan belt occasionally. If worn, frayed or cracked on inner driving surface, replace.
2. Check tension occasionally. Press thumb at midpoint of belt span between pulleys. If belt depresses more than ½ inch, tightening is needed. A too-loose belt will not drive alternator and water pump effectively.
3. Adjust to proper tension of ¼ inch deflection. Adjust as follows:

A. Loosen mounting bolts at top and bottom so alternator can pivot on lower bolt and upper bolt can slide in bracket.

B. Pull alternator out slightly to put tension on belt, and hold while tightening upper bolt.

C. Check tension. Repeat adjustment as necessary.

D. When tension is correct, tighten lower bolt.

FIND THOSE COOLING SYSTEM LEAKS

1. Inspect all hoses. If any are weak, soft in spots or show cracks, replace at once.
2. Check all hose connections for tightness. Tighten loose hose clamps; they tend to loosen due to engine vibration.
3. If radiator steams or hisses when engine is switched off, check for leaks. Look for signs of coolant drips on radiator or around heater tank joint.

Leaks are possible at:
Upper or lower radiator hoses
Water pump (gaskets or seal)
Heater core or connecting hoses
Automatic transmission cooler lines (at bottom of radiator)
Faulty radiator pressure cap
Faulty cylinder head gasket
Cracked cylinder head or block

Due to the number of joints, cooling systems have many places to leak from. Check clamp tightness. If leaks persist an anti-leak additive in the coolant may help. Noisy water pumps may benefit from a lubricating additive in the coolant. Use a cooling system cleaner when flushing during a drain and refill job. It will help remove rust and scale. Remember — additives will not cure chronic problems. But they will effect a short-term remedy in many cases.

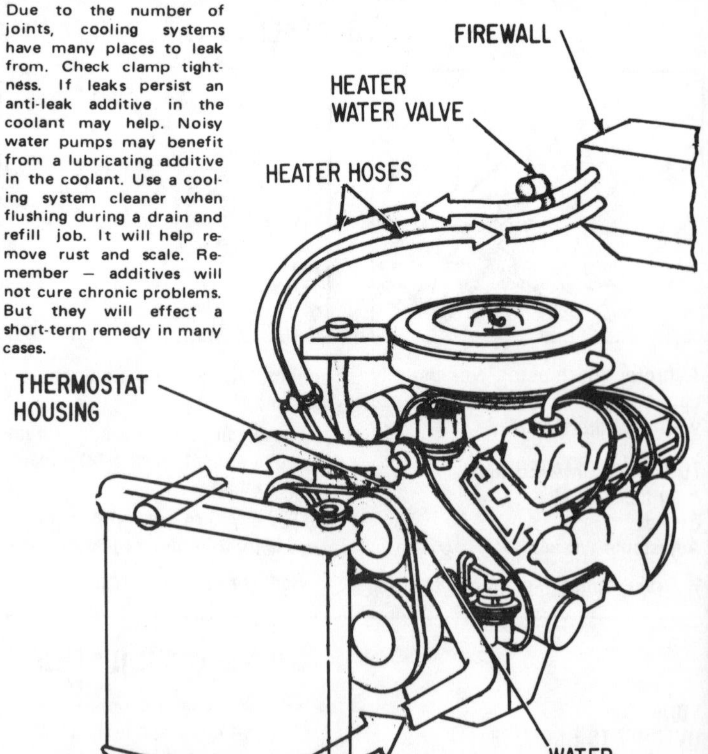

RADIATOR CAP CHECK

Check radiator cap occasionally for worn or cracked gasket. If cap doesn't seal properly, fluid will be lost and engine will overheat. Replace worn cap with new cap rated 13 to 15 lbs. pressure.

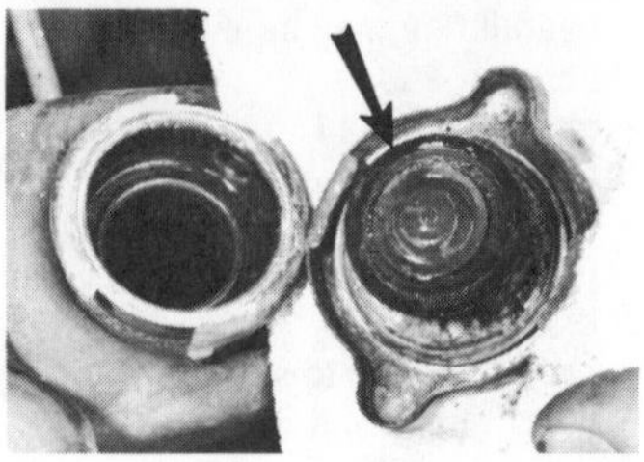

HOSE REPLACEMENT

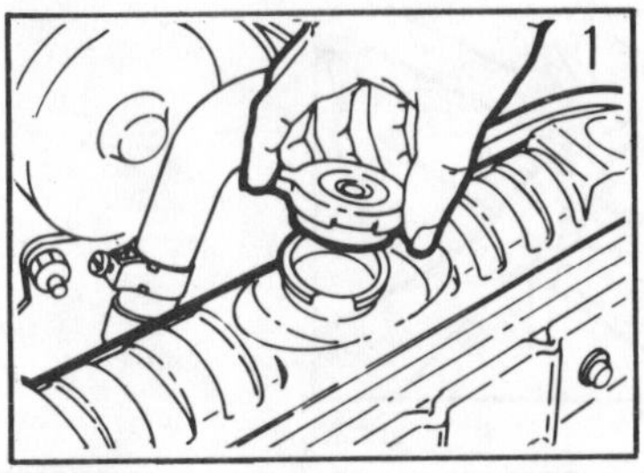

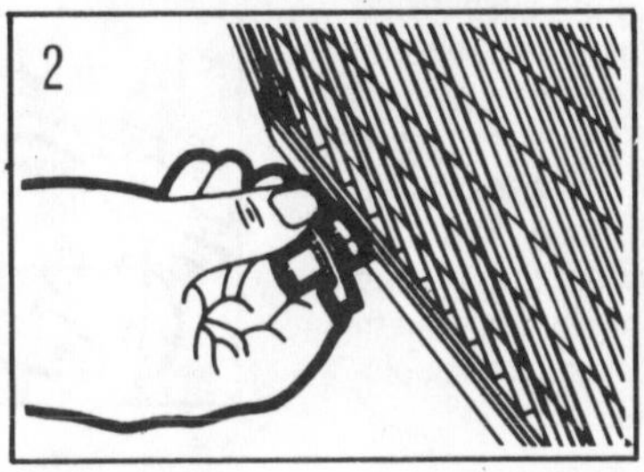

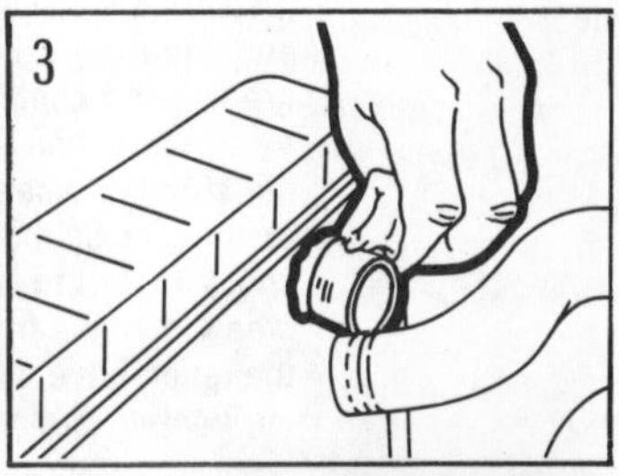

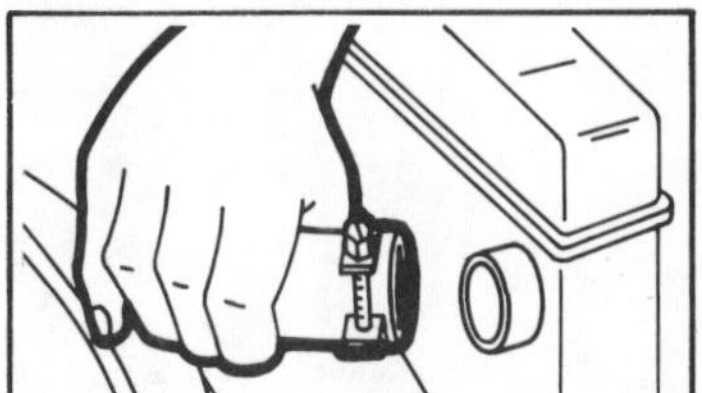

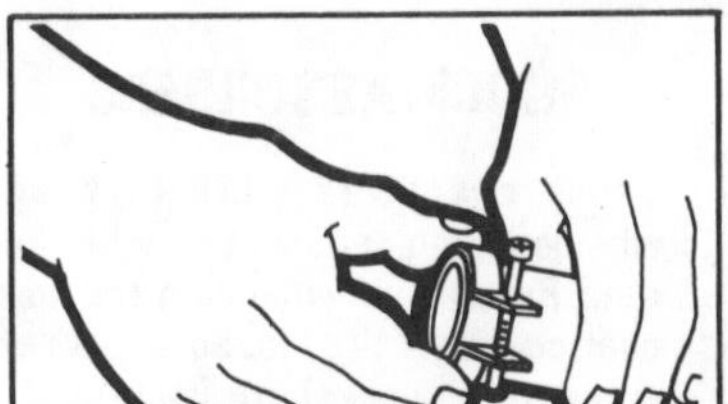

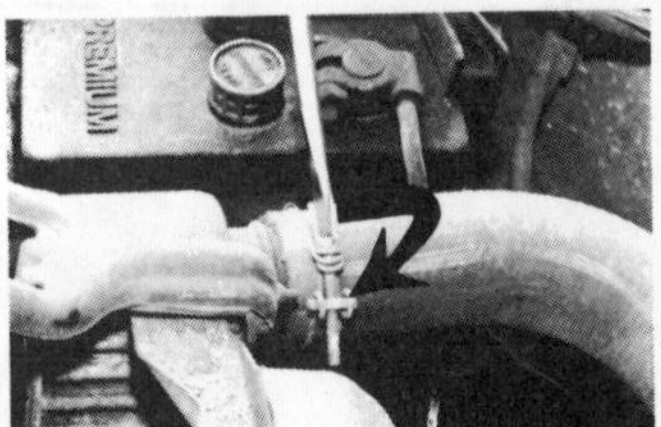

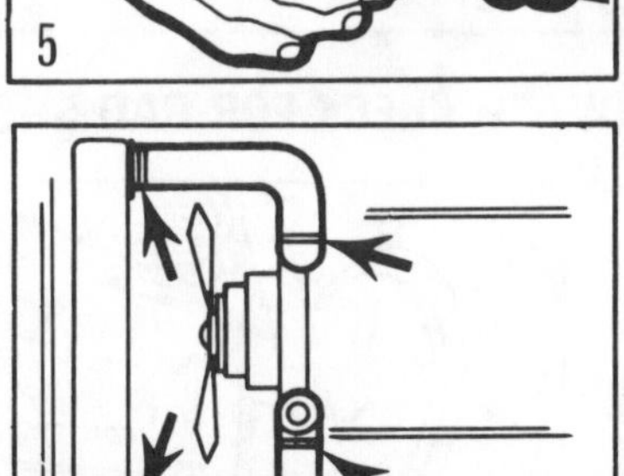

Coolant drain and refill work may be done alone; when changing hoses, coolant must also be drained as part of job. Discard all hoses with cracks or soft spots. Check hose clamps for tightness and good condition.

1. Remove radiator cap. Open radiator petcock (See 2). Drain coolant into catch basin. If near 24 months old, discard old coolant.
2. Petcock is located at the bottom of the radiator.
3. Wipe all hose connections clean. Use emery cloth to get rid of residue.
4. If old hose clamps are badly rusted or damaged, replace with new units.
5. Slip clamps over each hose end. Slip hose ends all the way onto cleaned up hose connections.
6. Place hose clamp ¼ inch from hose end. Tighten. Close petcock. Refill with 50/50 coolant/water mix.
7. Start engine; allow to warm up. Check for coolant leaks.
8. Road test car; watch for temperature warning light.

Suspension and Tires

The front wheels mount and rotate on the spindles, which are attached to upper and lower ball joints. A coil spring is mounted between the control arms on each side. A shock absorber is located in the center of each spring. The rear suspension is a trailing link design. The rear axle is located by one upper and two lower control arms and a lateral bar. A coil spring and shock absorber are located on each side of the axle.

Your car's suspension system consists of wheels, tires, springs, shock absorbers, sway (or stabilizer) bars, ball joints, steering linkage. If any of these items is out of adjustment or badly worn, you may notice any of these symptoms:

- car pulls to one side when braking
- car wanders when driving a straight line
- overall ride may be either hard or bouncy
- effort is needed to steer vehicle
- tires show uneven wear
- tires squeal when cornering
- front of car dips or bounces when braking
- car rocks side-to-side when going over rough road
- wheels bounce to make slapping sound on road
- steering wheel vibrates in hands
- front of car vibrates at highway speeds

Any of above symptoms indicates corrective action is needed. Delay can: ruin tires; cause damage/failure to other suspension parts; create safety hazard.

STEERING

If steering linkage, front suspension and steering column components are in good condition, there should be not more than 1½ inch free play in the steering wheel when measured at the rim of the wheel. If a loud knock is heard when turning the steering wheel from one extreme to the other, have mechanic check pinion bearing preload.

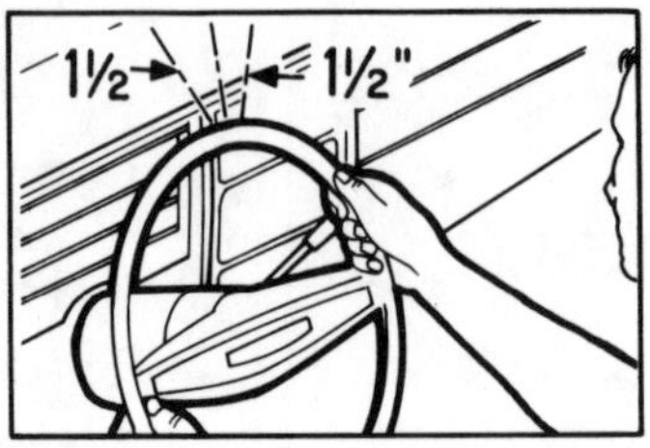

SHOCK ABSORBERS

Shock absorbers work to keep wheels in constant contact with the road. Result is safe handling and ride control; longer tire life. So shock absorbers (or shocks) are important.

HOW TO CHECK FOR BAD SHOCKS

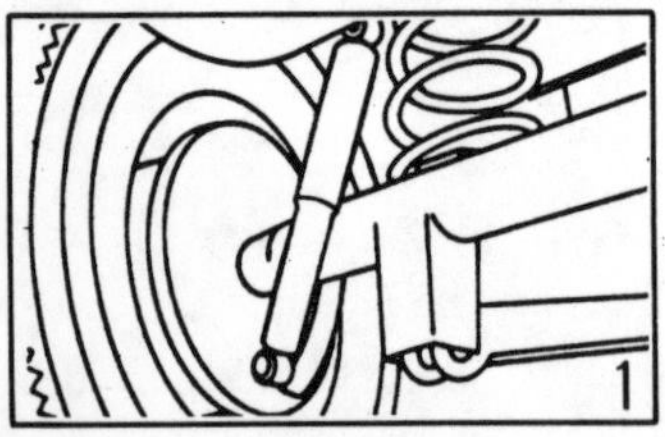

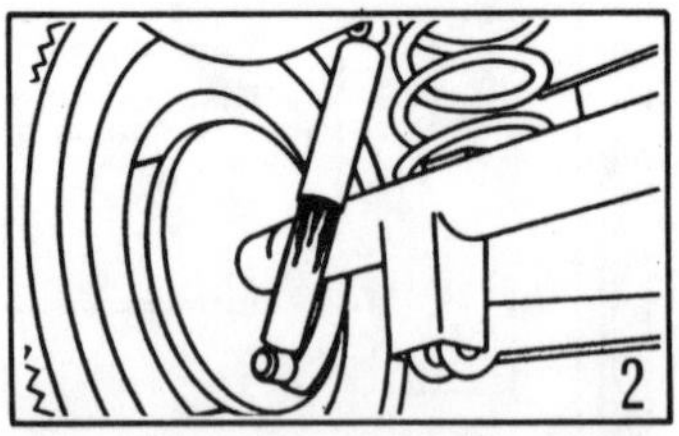

1. Check under car and locate shock absorber near each wheel.

2. Heavy oil streaks on outer shock housing indicate need for replacement.

3. Stand at front of car and apply body weight in pumping action to front bumper or fender. Release pressure and allow car to stop rocking. Car should not bounce more than one more time after releasing pressure. Repeat at rear. If bouncing continues more than once, replacement is needed. Replace shocks in pairs (front pair or rear pair).

TOW HITCH INFORMATION

If your car is used for trailer towing you should check:

A. Cooling System; be sure coolant is at proper level in radiator. See Cooling System Section for checks to perform.

B. Check Transmission Fluid; keep topped up to proper level.
C. Check Rear Shock Absorbers; you may benefit from installation of new rear shocks.
D. Check Tire Pressures; best traction and handling can be ensured if tire pressures are properly maintained.
For safer and more trouble-free trailer towing, consider:
A. Automatic Transmission Cooler; helps remove excess heat from automatic transmission fluid built up during towing mileage. Also helps avoid radiator overheating. Some units can be self-installed.
B. Radiator Over-Flow Tank Kit; addition of a reservoir to catch radiator coolant overflow preventing coolant loss. Easy to install, these units help a tow car run cooler, avoid overheating due to coolant loss.
C. Heavy-Duty Shock Absorbers or Air Shocks; important to have on rear wheels if you intend to do a lot of towing or load carrying within the car itself. Don't forget to consider replacing factory shocks, when they are worn out, with heavy-duty units at the front as well.
D. Variable Load Flasher; this unit will accommodate the added load of trailer turn signal lamps on trailer when these are hooked into your car's electrical system.

FRONT END ALIGNMENT

When steering, handling and/or tire wear indicate front end alignment may be needed, this work can only be done at an automotive service shop. DO NOT PUT OFF NEEDED FRONT END ALIGNMENT. At the same time, have ball joints and steering linkage checked.

Ignition System

TUNE-UP SERVICES

The ignition system consists of spark plugs; plug wires; distributor; rotor; points; condenser; coil. These units work to create a good hot spark inside the engine (ignition) at exactly the right moment (timing). If ignition is weak or timing is off, engine may be hard to start, run poorly, waste gas, lose power, backfire or not run at all. All 1975 and later models, 1974 models sold in California, and most 1974 models sold in 49 states (except some early 250-6 cylinder, 302 V8 and 351 V8 equipped models) use the new breakerless (solid state) ignition system. The breakerless system eliminates the breaker points and condenser completely. The only maintenance necessary is to check the cap, rotor, and ignition wire condition when replacing spark plugs.
FORD SAYS—Replace plugs and points every 12,000 miles (1970-74) and plugs every 15,000 to 20,000 miles (1975-76).
TOOLS & MATERIALS—Parts: set of points, condenser, 6 or 8 spark plugs. Tools: gap gauge, 13/16 in. (BF or BRF plugs) or ⅝ in. (ARF plugs), spark plug socket, screwdriver, open end, box or combination wrenches, timing equipment (see ignition timing).

CHECKING POINTS, AND ROTOR

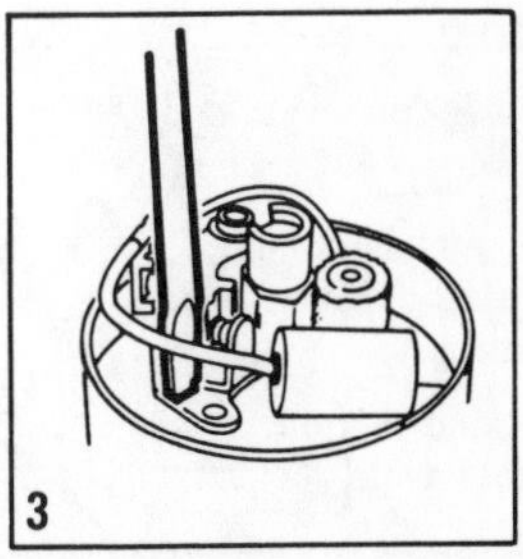

The distributor holds the points, rotor and condenser.
1. To open distributor, snap retaining clips off the screwdriver, lift cap off but keep wires connected.
2. Pull rotor off (straight up). Replace if cracked or metallic tip is badly burned.
3. Pry points apart with screwdriver. If worn or burned, replace. If OK, check point gap.

OTHER IGNITION CHECK POINTS

Inspect spark plug wires. If cracked or brittle, entire set should be replaced. Also center, high tension wire. Inspect distributor cap. Wipe inside clean occasionally with dry, lint-free rag. If cap is cracked or rotor contacts are excessively burned, replace cap.

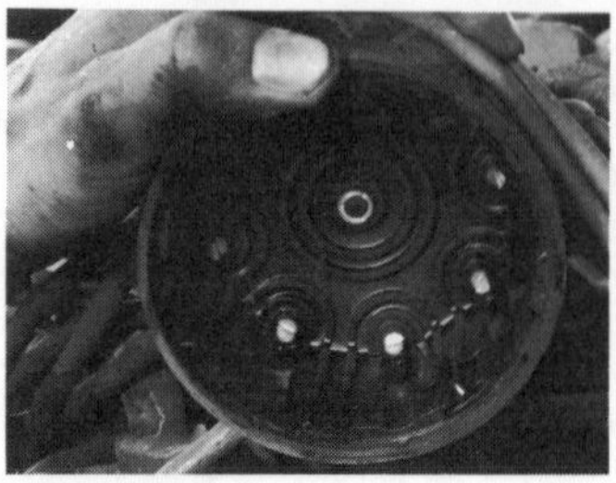

SPARK PLUG REPLACEMENT

1

2

3

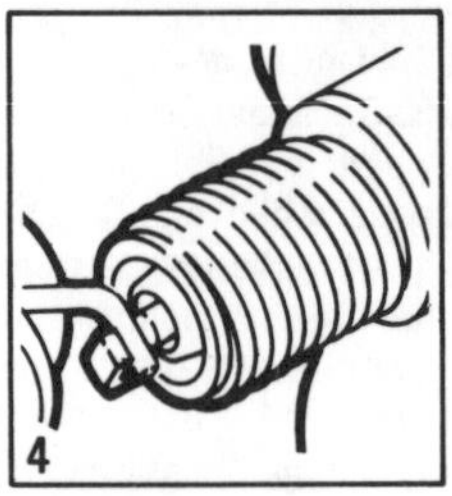
4

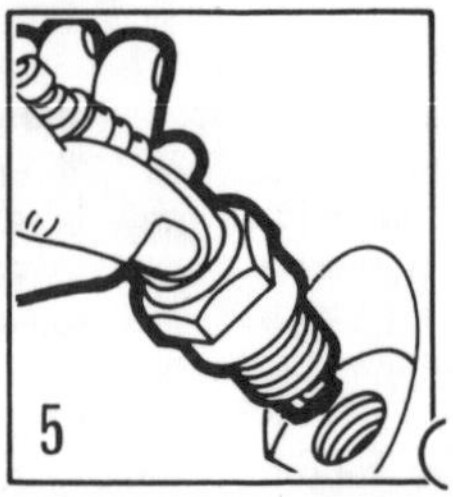
5

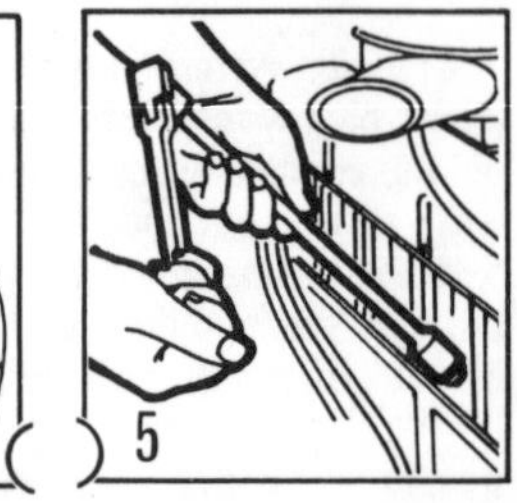
5

1. Remove spark plug wire by grasping rubber boot. Do not jerk wire off. If stuck, turn boot, pulling gently.
2. Loosen spark plug using socket wrench.
3. Wipe or brush loose dirt from around plug before removing. Do not let dirt drop into engine through plug hole. Unscrew plug.
4. Check plug electrode gap on new spark plug. Adjust to specifications in tune-up chart.
Plug gap is correct when the gauge drags slightly as it is pulled between plug electrodes.
5. Thread new plug into plug hole by hand. Hand tighten. Do not force or cross thread. Use socket wrench to tighten firmly but do not force. Replace plug wire. Press boot firmly.

REMOVING POINTS

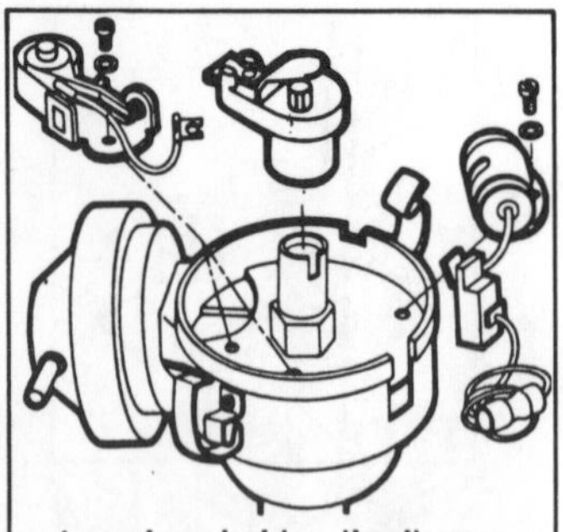
Location inside distributor

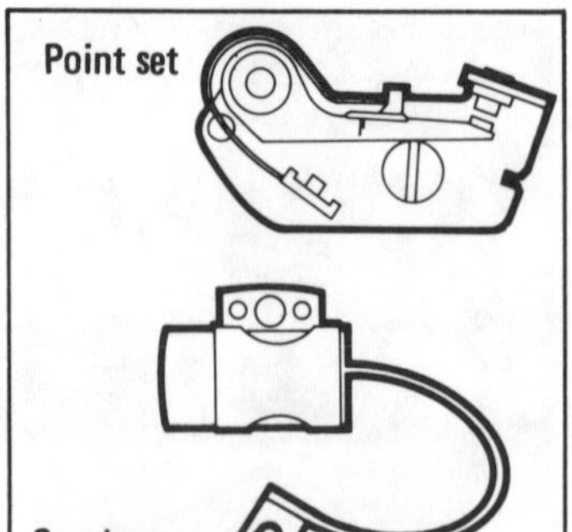

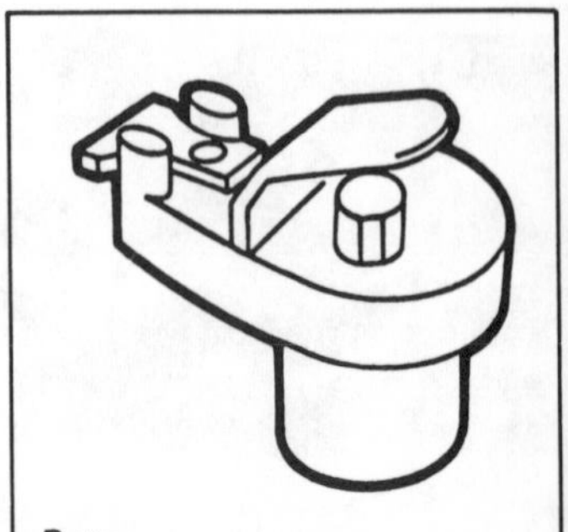
Rotor

Points and condenser work together. Always replace condenser when installing new points.
On models equipped with the breakerless electronic ignition, there is no routine maintenance or parts re-

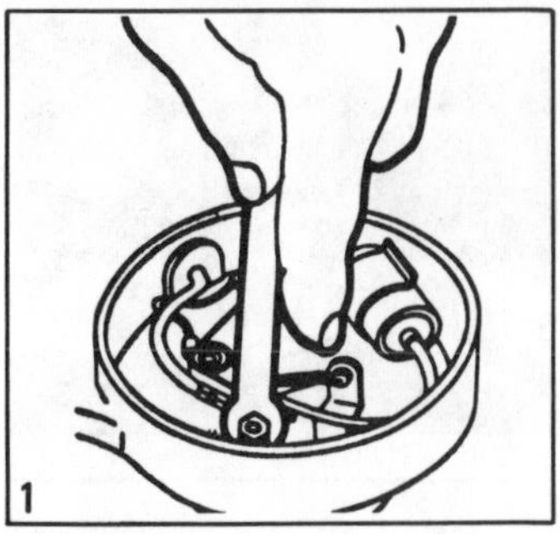

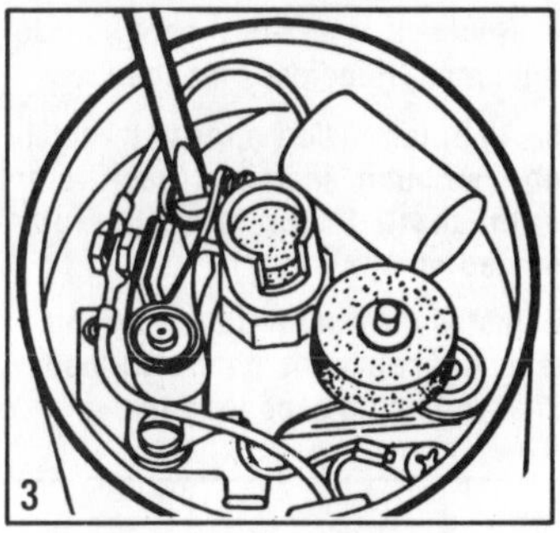

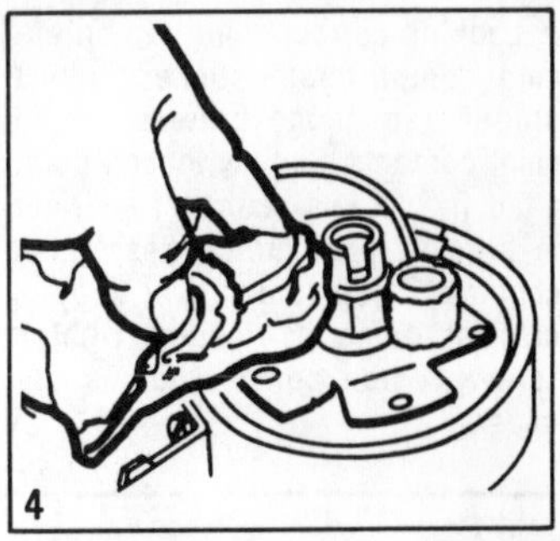

placement. Do check distributor cap condition, rotor, and ignition wires when replacing spark plugs.

1. Loosen nut, and disconnect primary wire and condenser lead wire.
2. Remove screw which holds condenser; remove condenser.
3. Remove screws holding points to distributor; remove points.

4. Wipe all dirt from distributor plate and cam.

5. Inspect primary wire for frayed insulation, dirty connection. Clean connection or have wire repaired as necessary.

CAUTION: When removing screws from distributor, be sure to avoid any screws accidentally falling through distributor opening into engine. Use magnetic screwdriver.

INSTALLING POINTS AND CONDENSER

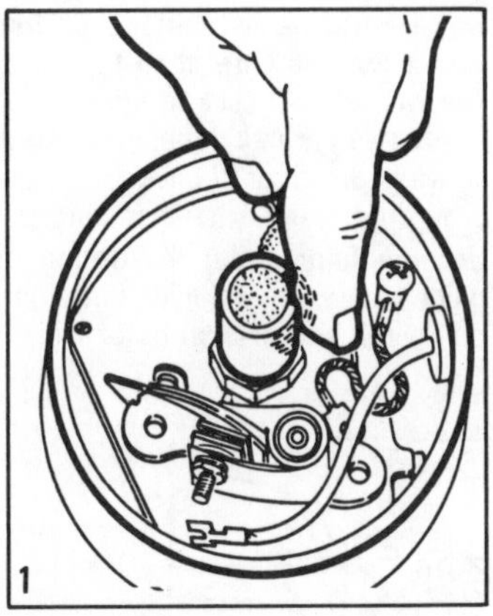

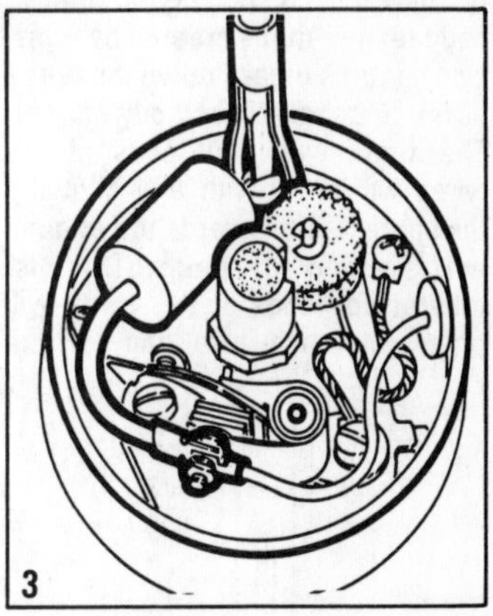

1. Apply small amount of heat resistant lube to distributor cam. (Lube usually supplied with new points. If not, purchase separately.)
2. Position new points in distributor and fasten with attaching screws. CAUTION: use magnetic screwdriver, or screwdriver with clip.
3. Attach new condenser to distributor with attaching screw.
4. Attach primary wire and condenser lead wire to point set. Don't let contacts touch distributor body or breaker plate. (Some models: wire from points attaches to condenser.)

RESETTING THE CONTACT GAP

1. Electrical contacts of point set MUST BE PARALLEL. If needed, bend stationary contact with needle-nose pliers. Bend fixed bracket only.

2. Turn engine by ignition key (you'll need a helper) until rubbing block on points is one of the high points of the distributor cam. You may use wrench on lower pulley to do this.

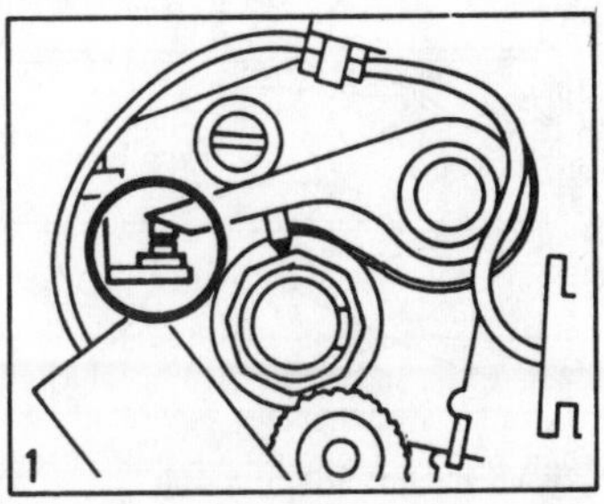

3. Look up correct point gap on engine compartment sticker. Insert proper gap gauge between open point contacts. Slightly loosen point attaching screws. Insert screwdriver in breaker plate notch near point contacts. Twist screwdriver to open or close points as needed. Tighten screws when correct gap is obtained.

4. Recheck gap after screws are tightened. Readjust if needed.

5. Align tab inside rotor with notch on distributor shaft and push rotor onto shaft. Rotor must be fully seated on shaft.

6. Install distributor cap by aligning tabs on cap with notch on body. Snap retaining clips in place.

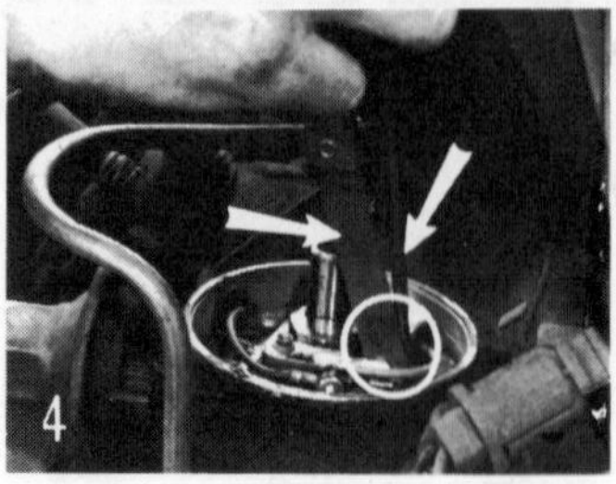

REPLACING SPARK PLUG WIRES

One of the most often overlooked items in a tune-up is the spark plug wires. Your car can be in perfect tune, but if the plug wires are not carrying the spark to the plugs, your engine will run poorly. The original equipment wires that came with your car are usually good for a year or two before needing replacement. On newer cars, the higher under-hood temperatures created by emission controls breaks down the wires ability to conduct electricity sooner. The spark plug boot ends of the wires will crack with age allowing the spark to arc towards the engine, not reaching the plugs. The distributor cap ends of the wires will often collect moisture, and corrode right there in your distributor cap. Sometimes a wire will contact a hot part of the engine, such as the exhaust manifold and burn through the insulation. Other times, a wire will become oil soaked and gummy, breaking down the insulation. Often, when carbon core wires get old, they will break off inside, with no visible signs of breakage on the outside. Always use good quality spark plug wire. A carbon core or cut-rate brand may seem attractive at first, but will cost you more in the long run with reduced engine efficiency and more frequent replacement.

1. Replace one wire at a time. This will keep you out of trouble with crossed wires. When removing wires, twist back and forth as you pull up. This will help free up stuck wires.

2. Take the old wire and match it up with the new one for length. If you are cutting your own, make sure there is good metal to metal contact between the end of the wire and the pinch-on connectors.

3. Make sure each wire seats all the way down in the distributor cap. First push down the wire, then the boot. The wire should click in place.

4. After you are all done, make sure all wires are clear of choke or throttle linkage, or hot exhaust manifolds.

Use the firing order illustration to guide you when replacing your ignition wires and/or distributor cap.

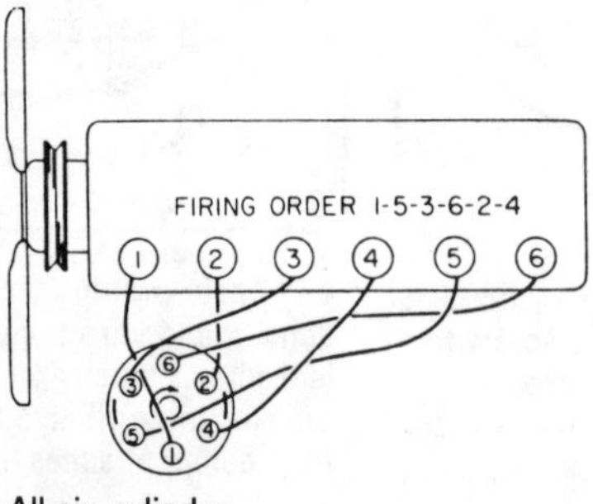

All six cylinder

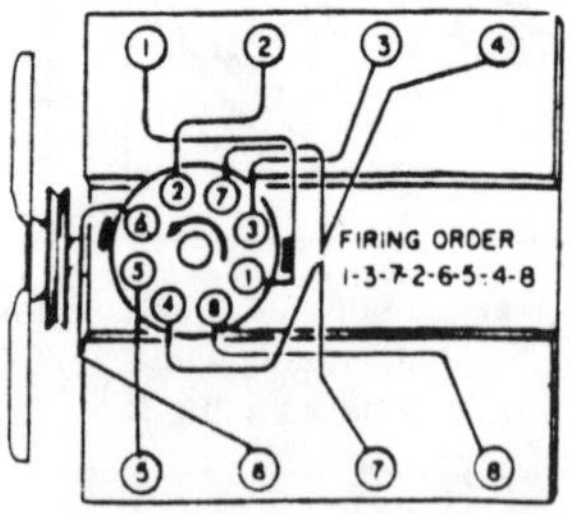

351 and 400 V8

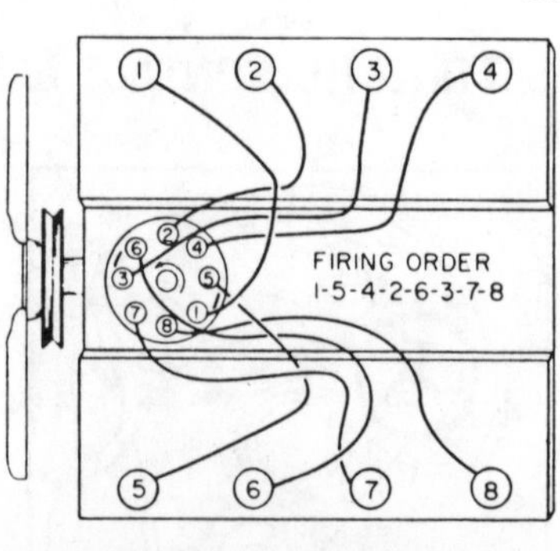

All V8 except 351 and 400

Use the firing order illustration to guide you when replacing your ignition wires and/or distributor cap.

IGNITION TIMING

Adjusting timing is the important finishing touch to any tune-up. While not difficult, job requires timing light and dwell meter.

1. Locate timing marks and pointer (notches) on engine and lower engine pulley. Clean away dirt. Mark the pointer and notch which corresponds with the timing setting in degrees shown on the engine compartment sticker.
2. Hook up timing light according to instructions supplied with it.
3. Disconnect the one or two vacuum lines from the distributor. Plug with pencil tip or golf tee.
4. Hook up tachometer and adjust engine idle speed.
5. Aim timing light at pulley mark(s). If the chalked marks do not align, loosen distributor hold-down bolt and slowly rotate distributor until chalked marks align.
6. Tighten hold-down bolt. Recheck timing.

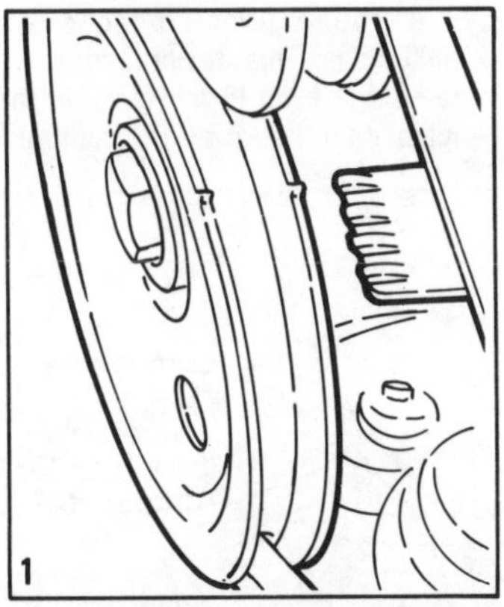

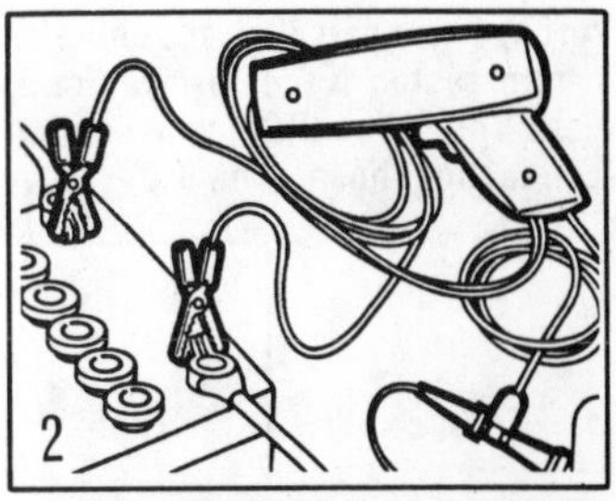

Fuel System

When gasoline is brought from the fuel tank, it mixes with air in the carburetor. This gas/air mixture enters engine thru the intake manifold, passes thru the intake valves and is burned in the combustion chamber. The burned exhaust gas is then passed thru the exhaust valves to the exhaust system and to the outside air. In order to keep your car's engine running cleanly with minimal pollution, and avoid dangerous carbon monoxide fumes inside the vehicle, certain items should be checked from time to time.

AIR AND CRANKCASE FILTER REPLACEMENT

The large round can that sits on top of the engine holds the air cleaner. Twice a year:

1. Remove wing nut, and remove air cleaner lid.
2. Lift out circular air cleaner cartridge. Discard if more than 12 months old or excessively dirty.
3. Pull crankcase filter out of filter can. Wipe inside of can and lid.
4. Install crankcase filter. Install in reverse order.

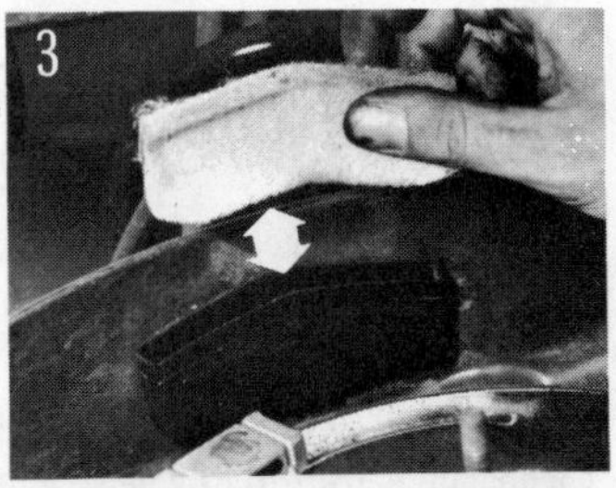

EMISSION CONTROL SYSTEMS

An important part of a car's emission control system is the Positive Crankcase Ventilation (PCV) valve and its connecting hose. The PCV valve should be replaced once every 24,000 miles. This device keeps dirt and sludge from forming inside the engine. Make sure all PCV connections are tight. Check that the connecting hoses are clear and not clogged. Replace any brittle or broken hoses.

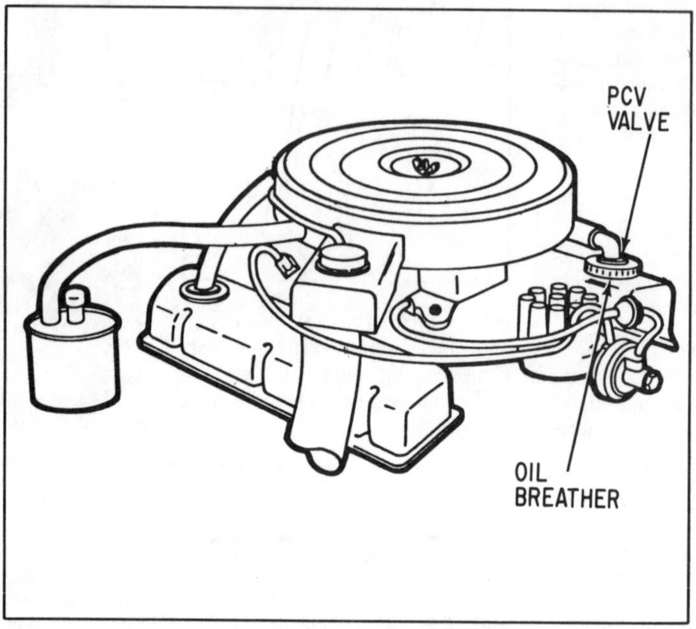

PCV VALVE REPLACEMENT

The PCV valve is located on top of the valve cover, in front of the air cleaner.

1. Grasp hose holding PCV valve. Pull straight out.
2. Note where other end of hose is connected. Pull off.
3. Remove PCV valve from hose. Flush hose out with cleaning solvent. Dry hose. Install new PCV valve in hose.
4. Attach end of hose to its original connection and insert PCV valve into proper opening.

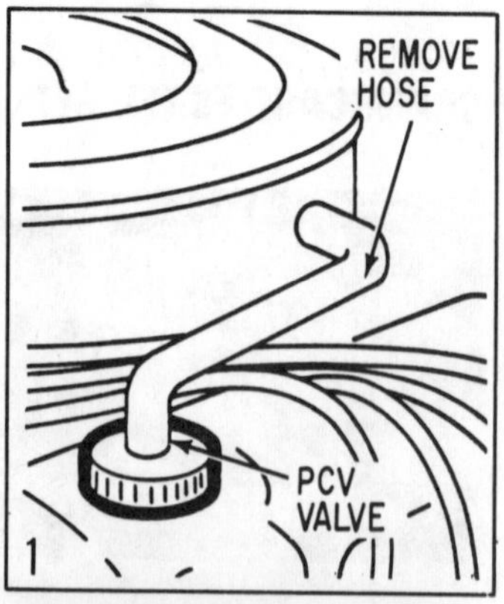

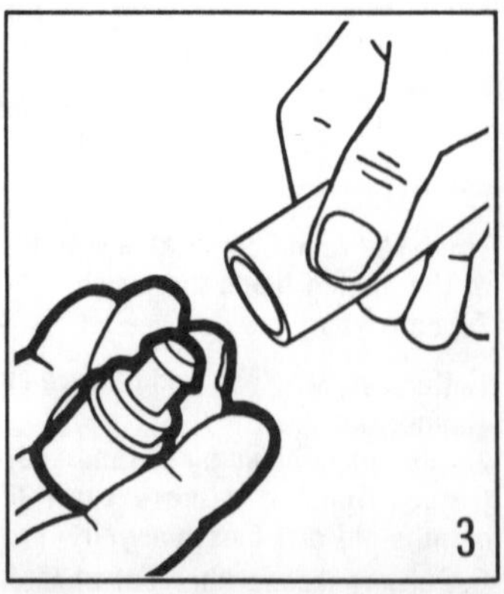

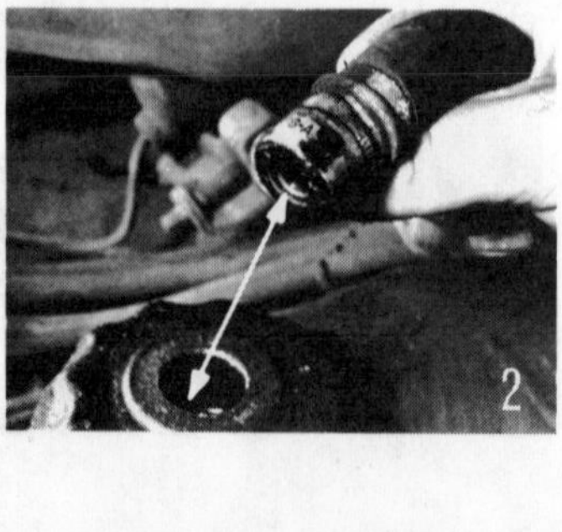

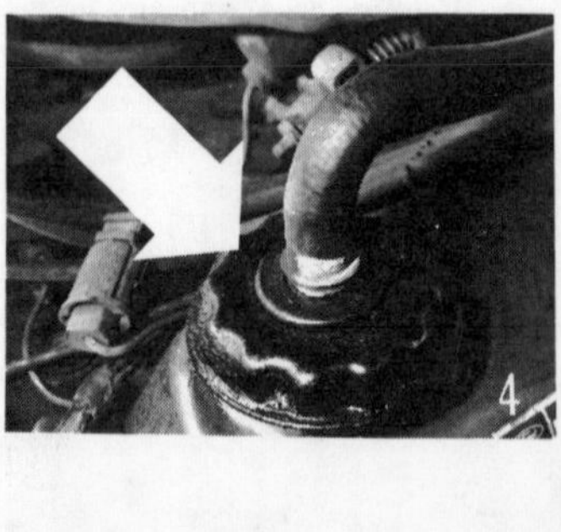

FUEL FILTER REPLACEMENT

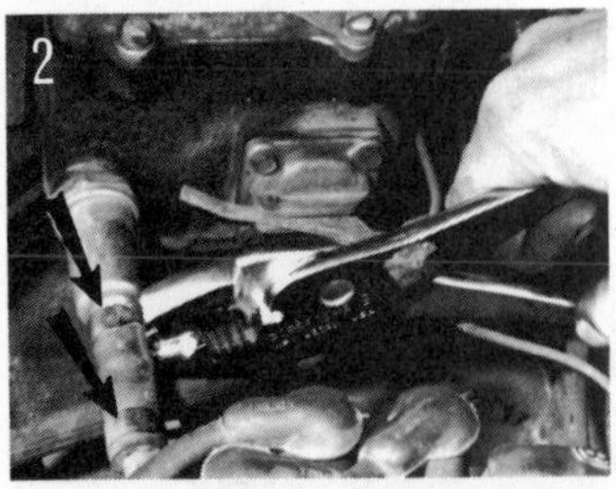

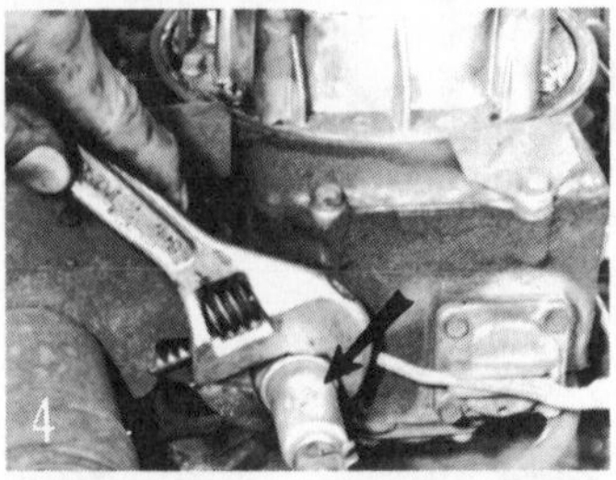

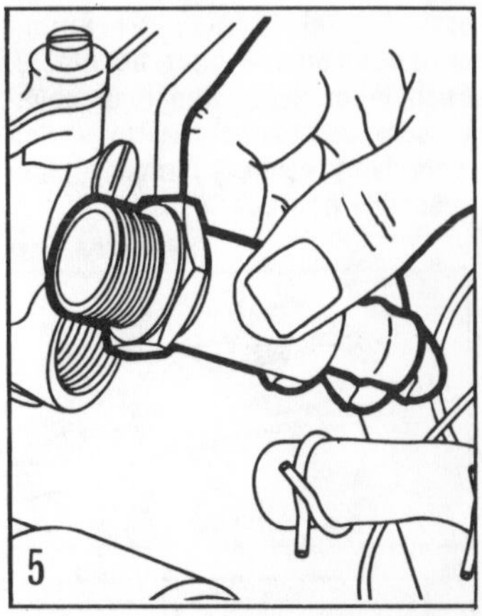

The fuel filter is located behind the large fuel line inlet nut on the carburetor. Replace the filter every year or 12,000 miles. The fuel filter prevents dirt, rust, and scale from both the gas station's tank and your own fuel tank from reaching the carburetor. A dirty filter will starve the engine and cause poor running.

1. Locate the fuel filter in line to carburetor. Place a rag under the filter housing to collect fuel that will drain out when filter is removed.
2. Pinch the ends of clamps together, and move toward center of hose. Use the smallest possible amount of tension, to avoid damaging the clamps. You can get a special tool designed for this job that will make handling the clamps much easier.
3. Pull the hose off filter and fuel line.
4. Fit an adjustable wrench to the six-sided portion of the filter body, and unscrew it from the carburetor. Discard old unit.
5. Position a new gasket onto the new filter, screw housing into carburetor and tighten.
6. Position new clamps in center of a new hose. If the old clamps are to be reused, make sure they have not lost their tension.
7. Install hose on fuel line and filter. Pinch the clamp ends together, and position well onto fuel line and filter.

Note: After replacing filter, remove rag used to catch spilled fuel, and then start engine. Check for leaks. Addition of a can of carburetor cleaner to the fuel tank occasionally will aid in keeping the entire fuel system clean.

Safety Systems

PARKING LIGHTS, TURN SIGNALS AND STOP LIGHTS

All above lighting functions are performed by four dual-element bulbs. Front parking light and turn signal bulbs are mounted in the parking light housing in the grille. To replace, raise hood and reach socket from behind grille. To replace rear taillight, stop light, turn signal bulbs, raise trunk lid or rear door. Reach socket from inside car. Twist socket counterclockwise in housing. When socket is removed, push down on bulb and turn counterclockwise to remove from socket. Insert new dual-element bulb in correct position (see note) and re-install socket in housing.

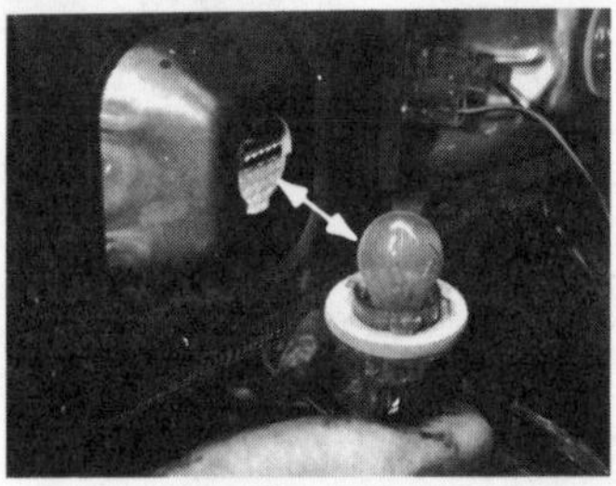

NOTE: When inserting new dual element bulb, note that knobs on side of bulb base are different distances from base tip. Match knobs to socket slots for proper fit.

STATION WAGON REAR LIGHTS

To replace lights on 1970-72 station wagons: left side—remove interior trim panel; right side—remove spare wheel & cover. Remove socket twist bulb counterclockwise to remove outside retaining screws; pull assembly out. Remove socket; twist bulb counterclockwise to remove.

LICENSE PLATE LIGHTS

On sedans, disconnect terminal from inside trunk. Remove retaining screws; remove light assembly. Push in on bulb; turn bulb counterclockwise to remove. On station wagons, disconnect terminal; snap assembly from rear bumper.

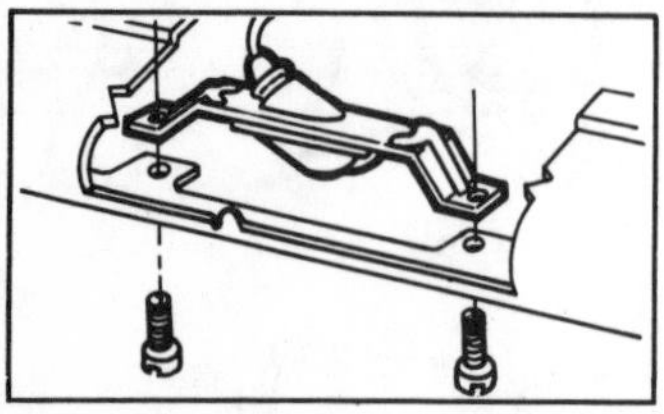

SIDE MARKER LIGHTS

Front: Reach up under fender; turn socket counterclockwise to remove. Pull bulb straight out.
Rear: Open trunk; remove trim panel to expose assembly. Twist socket counterclockwise to remove. Pull bulb straight out.

INTERIOR DOME LIGHT

This is a cartridge type bulb. Pry the dome light lens out from the housing. To avoid blowing the fuse, make sure that the doors are closed and the dome light switch is in the OFF position. Carefully lever the bulb straight out of the housing. Insert new bulb and re-install dome light lens.

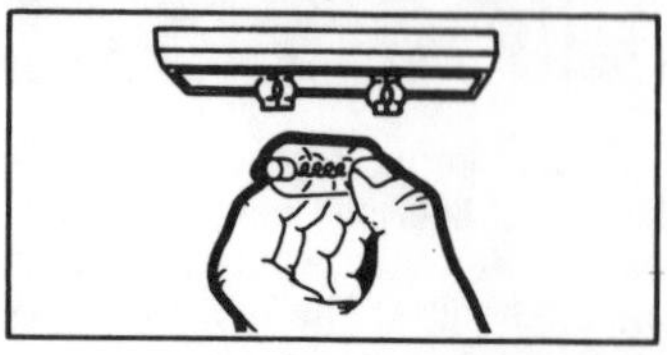

HEADLIGHT REPLACEMENT

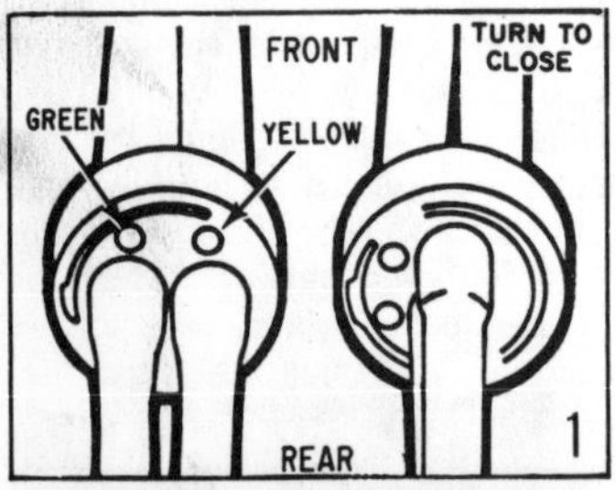

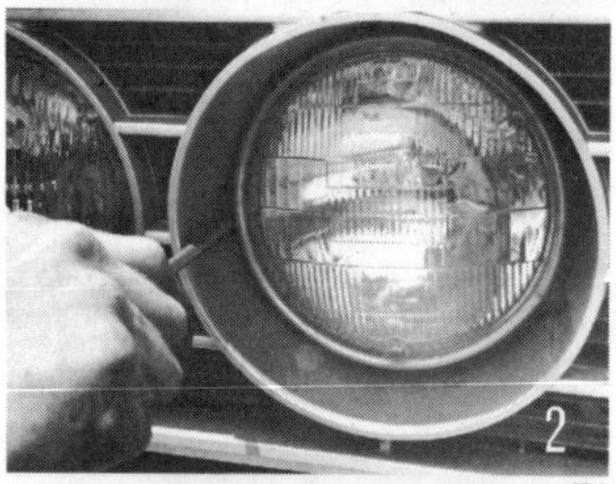

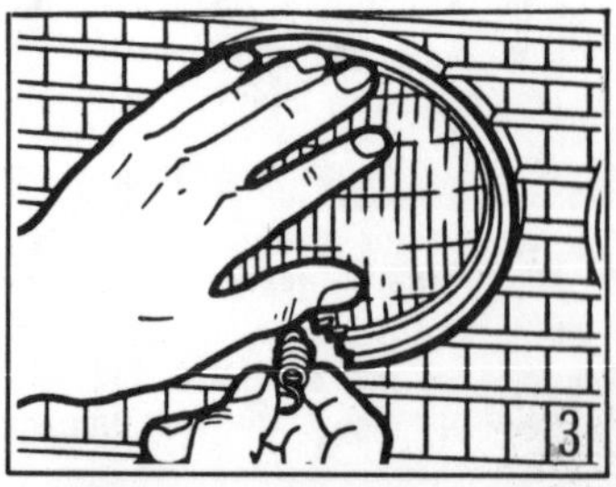

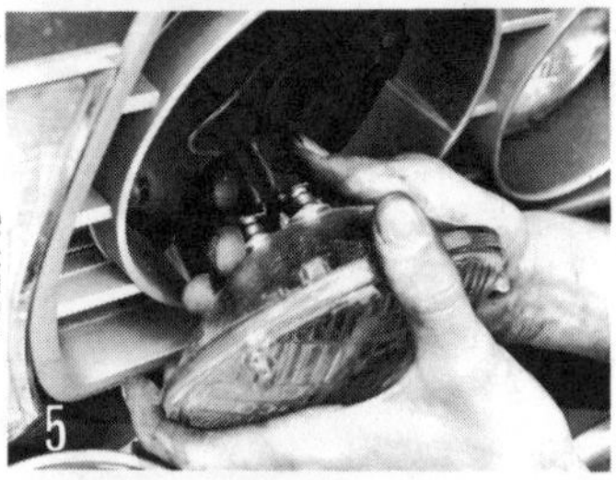

1. If the car is equipped with headlight covers, close the by-pass switch located between the headlight switch and the vacuum motor to open the cover.
2. On some models remove screws and remove headlight door. On others remove trim ring.
3. On 1970-72 models place hand over headlight assembly to steady it. Unhook the spring from the retaining ring.
4. Remove retainer ring screws, and remove retainer ring. Be careful not to confuse retainer ring screws with the headlight aiming screws.
5. Pull bulb forward, disconnect wire terminal.
6. Attach the wire terminal to the new bulb, and place bulb into position, locating the bulb glass tabs in the positioning slots.
7. Attach retainer ring to assembly with the three retainer screws. On earlier models reconnect spring to retaining ring.
8. Replace trim ring assembly and headlight door if so equipped. If equipped with headlight covers, open by-pass valve to lower covers.

HORN PROBLEMS

If horn sounds and does not stop, this is due to short circuit in wiring. Disconnect wiring connector under hood and have professional service shop check horn wiring circuit.

WINDSHIELD WIPER BLADE REPLACEMENT

To replace wiper blade, lift up on spring release tab on wiper arm connector. Pull wiper blade off. Snap new blade into place.

To replace rubber insert only, press down, away from wiper blade to free it. Slide insert from blade. Insert new wiper. Bend insert upward slightly to engage retaining clips.

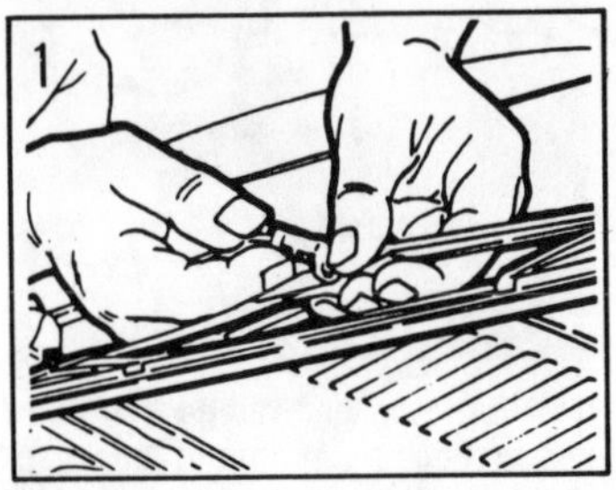

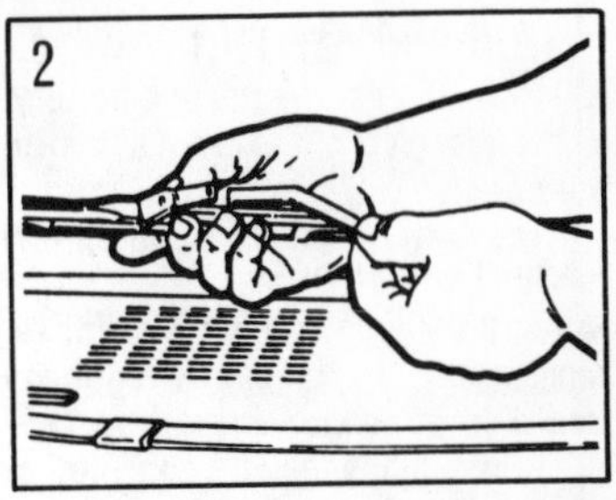

STEERING PROBLEMS

See steering system check in Suspension Section. Check tire pressures. Have a professional service shop check all components in the front end and steering system.

WHEEL CYLINDER CHECK

Drum brakes employ individual wheel cylinders to apply braking pressure to shoes. Check for brake fluid leaks on inside of wheel.
Disc brakes employ calipers on individual wheels. Remove wheel and inspect caliper for signs of fluid leaks. Have mechanic correct leaks.

WASHER SYSTEM

If washer fails to squirt properly, raise hood and check system hose connections. Be sure washer fluid container has fluid. Check spout openings for clogging.
Keep container filled with fluid mixture of washer solvent and water. If road spray buildup on windshield is a chronic problem, add 1 tablespoon dishwasher detergent to solvent/water mixture when re-filling container.

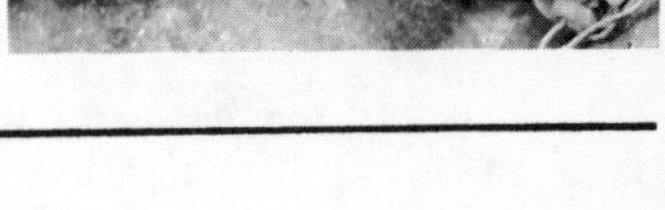

Electrical System

CHECK BATTERY FLUID

To ensure starting ability at all times check your battery condition periodically. You'll need to check battery electrolyte (fluid) level in each of the six cells. Check battery cable connections for tightness and inspect for accumulated corrosion.

SAFETY NOTE: Wear gloves when working on battery.

1. Remove plastic filler caps on top of battery. Fluid should be up to lower end of filler hole and covering the plates. If fluid is low add clean, cold tap water. If your area has hard water, use only distilled water available at auto supply, food or drug stores.

2. Replace any lost caps immediately.
CAUTION: NEVER LIGHT A MATCH OR SMOKE near the top of a battery. Batteries give off explosive hydrogen gas.
NOTE: Battery that often checks low on fluid could mean:
A. Battery is getting old, due for replacement; have charge capacity checked at service shop.
B. Connections may be corroded or loose; clean/replace as needed (see below).

C. Alternator or voltage regulator not functioning properly; this happens far less often than A or B above.

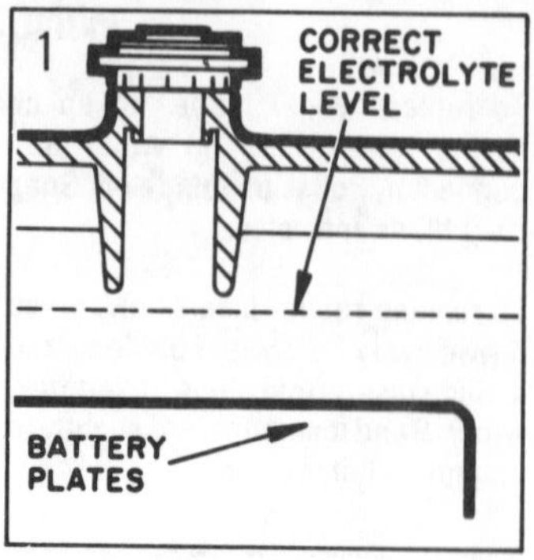

CLEAN THOSE BATTERY TERMINALS

As time goes by, battery terminals build up a dry powdery, whitish material. This material is corrosive and will gradually eat thru battery cables if not cleaned off periodically.

1. Loosen and remove battery connections.
2. Brush off all loose corrosion; use

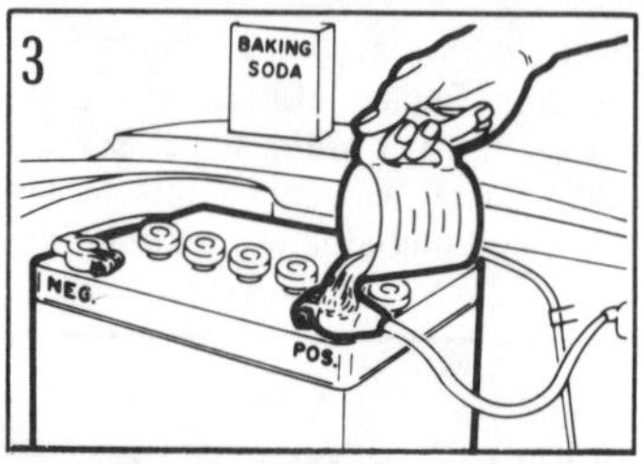

stiff bristle brush. Do not get this material into eyes or on open cuts. Wash off at once.
3. If corrosion build-up is extremely heavy and brushing does not remove all of it, mix 2 tablespoons baking soda to 1 cup water. Pour solution directly onto terminals and connectors. Allow to soak a few minutes

and rinse off. Continue brushing to remove all traces of corrosion build-up. Do not allow cleaning solution to enter battery.
4. Replace connectors on battery terminal posts and tighten.
5. Liberally smear battery terminal posts and cable connectors with petroleum jelly.

REPLACE FAULTY BATTERY CABLES

If battery cable strands become frayed, broken or corroded, replace cable immediately. Delay in correcting this condition could lead to sudden failure to start the engine. Can also weaken battery.

1. Loosen and remove battery. Clean off any corrosion buildup.
2. Disconnect negative cable from its attachment to engine or chassis. Disconnect positive cable from its attachment to starter relay.
3. Attach new cables making sure positive and negative cables are on proper terminals. They are not identical.
4. Replace connectors on battery terminal posts and tighten.
5. Liberally smear battery terminal posts and cable connectors with petroleum jelly.

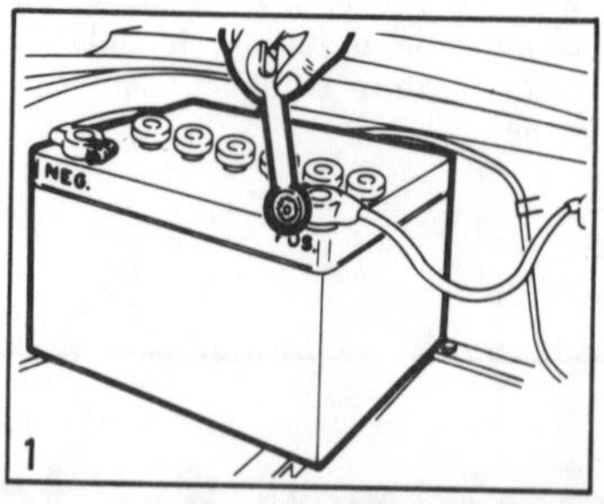

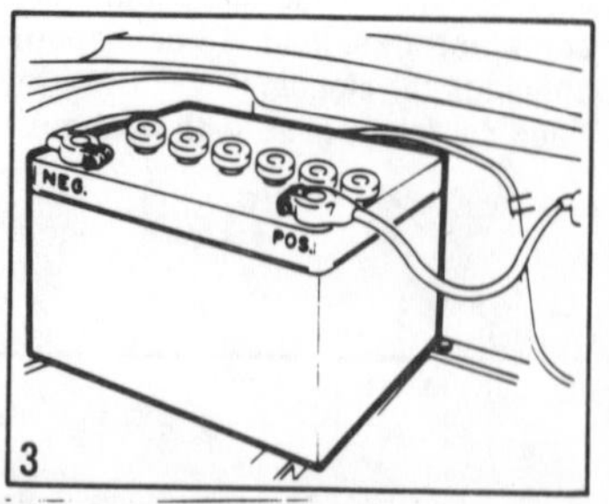

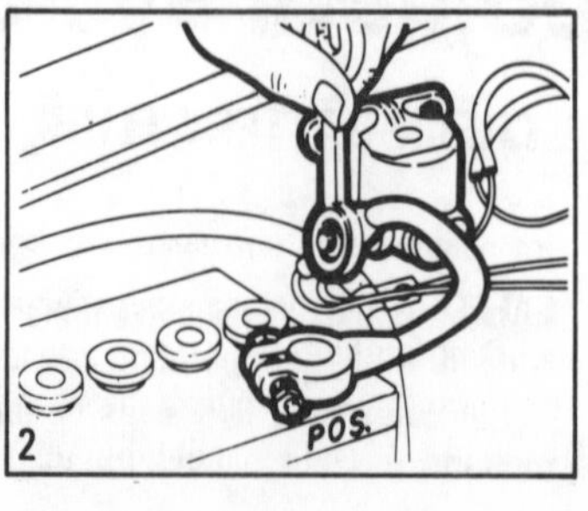

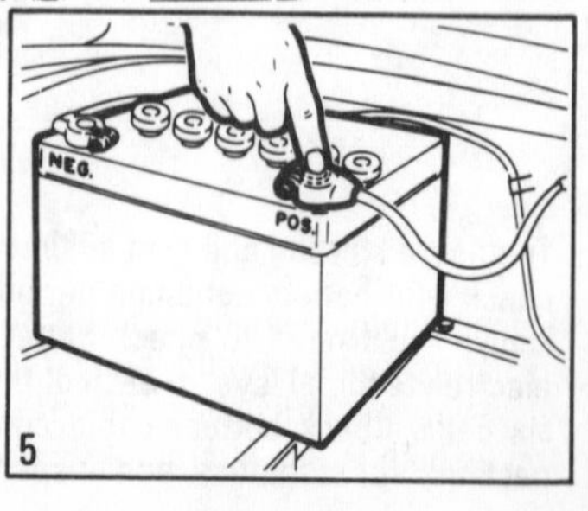

BATTERY HOLDDOWN

The clamp device which holds battery in place should be checked periodically. If loose, tighten. Clean off corrosion buildup. Severely corroded holddown components should be replaced before they break.

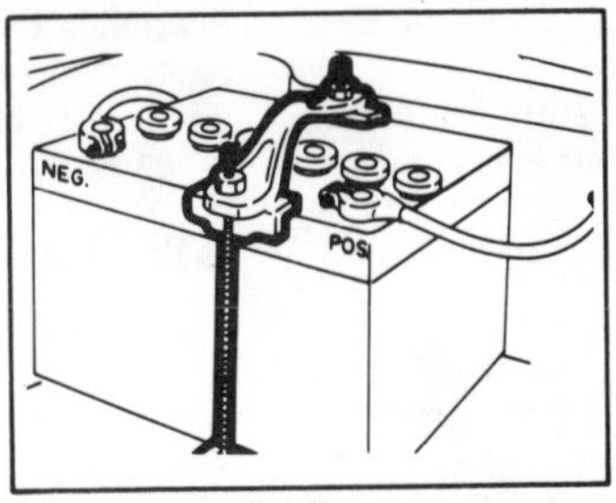

ELECTRICAL FUSES

Fuses are a safeguard for a car's electrical system. If a greater current is developed than that which the wiring harness is equipped to handle, the fuses blow out. This stops the possibility of overlaoding the wires and startingan electrical fire. Spare fuses should always be carried, of the amperage specified by the owners manual. NEVER REPLACE A FUSE WITH ONE OF A HIGHER AMPERAGE. ALWAYS REPLACE WITH FUSE OF THE SAME AMPERAGE.

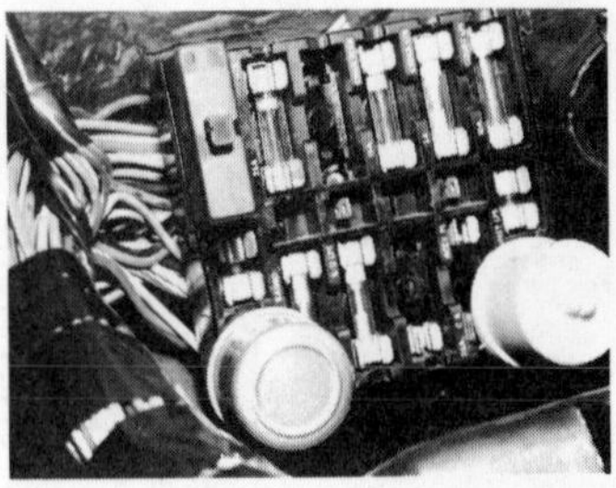

TURN SIGNAL AND 4-WAY FLASHER

Year	1970	1971	1972-1976
Type of Mounting	Clamp Bracket	Clamp Bracket	On Fuse Panel
Turn Signal Flasher	Back of instrument panel to the right of steering column	Back of instrument panel to the left of steering column	On Fuse Panel
Emergency Flasher	Back of instrument panel to the left of steering column	Taped to 1401 harness between instrument panel and fuse panel	On Fuse Panel

Turn signals and 4-way emergency flashers will operate only if: A. All light bulbs are OK. B. Flasher units are not burned out. The car has two flasher units that work independently of each other. Turn signal flasher is located behind instrument panel on extreme left. Emergency flasher is located as illustration shows. To remove either flasher, grasp with fingers, twist and pull flasher toward front of car. Pull connector from flasher. REPLACE ONLY WITH SAME TYPE FLASHER.

ALTERNATOR

Red alternator warning light on instrument panel should glow red when you first turn ignition key. This proves bulb is OK. Alternator warning light should go off when engine is running at normal operating speed. If alternator warning light glows red at operating speed, alternator isn't charging battery properly. Common causes are:

A. Fan belts are loose and slipping on alternator pulley. Tighten or re-

place belts.
B. Battery terminals, cables are loose or corroded. Clean; tighten; replace bad cables.
If A or B do not correct problem, alternator or voltage regulator may be faulty. This happens far less often, and can only be checked by mechanic with proper electrical testing equipment.
Alternator Caution: Alternator can be permanently damaged by short-circuiting terminal connections. When working around or moving alternator, always keep metal tools or engine parts from terminals.

REAR WINDOW DEFOGGER SYSTEM

Do not clean inside of rear window fitted with defogger system with any abrasive material. This could destroy carbon-copper wires. Use only soft rag and mild detergent/water mixture. Dry carefully.

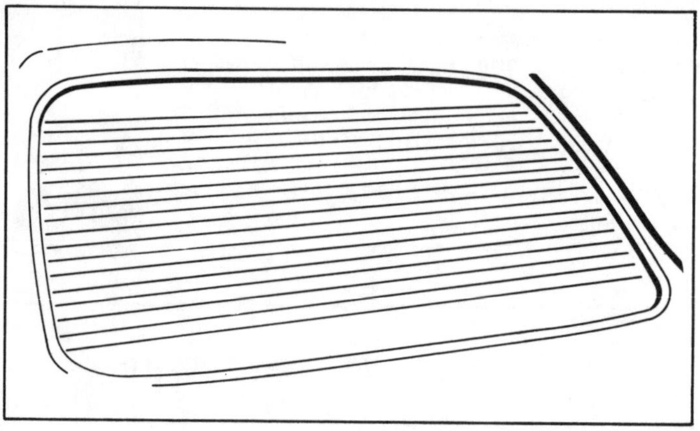

Air Conditioner

CHECK POINTS AND SERVICES

WARNING!—Never attempt to tighten fittings, disassemble or do any work on your car's A/C system. Consult a professional mechanic about A/C system problems and their correction. Your auto air conditioner (A/C) is a delicate, closed system. If air, dirt or water get into it, or if refrigerant escapes, the A/C unit will not cool a car interior. Among things you can do are:
1. Keep condenser grille clean. Check for dirt and debris; periodically remove dead insects, leaves, etc., with stiff bristle brush. Straighten any bent fins—carefully.
2. Keep radiator filled to correct level. (See Cooling System section). If fluid needs to be added, add antifreeze rather than water.
3. Keep radiator coolant at a 50/50 water/antifreeze mixture.
4. Flush cooling system and replace with fresh coolant mixture at least every 24 months. (See Cooling System section).
5. Radiator cap should be tight and sealed properly. If sealing gasket is cracked, cut or worn, replace cap with new 15 lb. unit.
6. Check fan belt tension periodically. (See Cooling System section). Replace glazed, frayed or cut fan belts, before they fail entirely.
7. Check periodically for bubbles in A/C sight glass. Sight glass is located in head of receiver/drier vessel. Or in metal tubing leading from top of receiver/drier. Sight glass is no larger than head of large nail. It may be dirty. Wipe clean for best visibility.

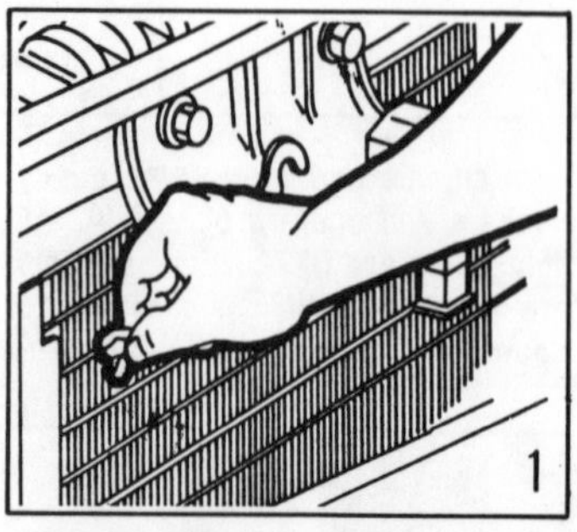
1

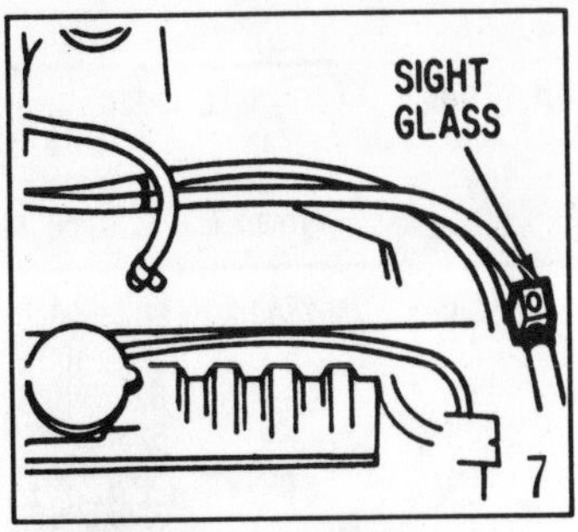

PROCEED AS FOLLOWS:
a) With engine and A/C system running, look for passage of refrigerant in sight glass. You'll be looking for a stream of milky white bubbles as they pass through sight glass. It is best to watch sight glass and have someone else start the car and turn on the A/C system. Allow to run for a few minutes.
b) If you observe no bubbles, and air flow from A/C unit in the car is passing cold air, everything is OK.
c) If no bubbles appear in sight glass, and air flow from the A/C unit in the car is not delivering cold air, the system may be low on refrigerant and could need a re-charge.
d) If bubbles appear, system is low on refrigerant.
e) If you suspect refrigerant loss based on tests performed above, have system checked by a professional A/C service shop. They can

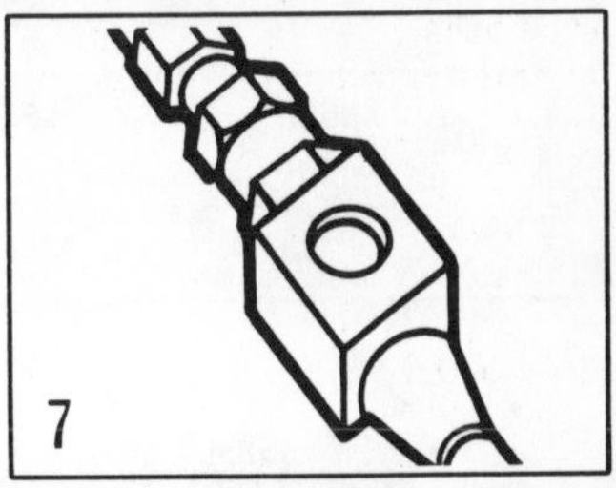

confirm refrigerant loss, recharge the system and check for system leakage.
NOTE: Once a week or so, even in winter, run A/C system for about 5 minutes as you drive. This keeps system internally lubricated, prevents hoses hardening.

TUNE-UP SPECIFICATIONS

YEAR	ENGINE No. Cyl. Displacement (cu. in.)	SPARK PLUGS Type	SPARK PLUGS Gap (in.)	DISTRIBUTOR Point Dwell (deg.)	DISTRIBUTOR Point Gap (in.)	IGNITION TIMING Man. Trans.● (deg.)■	IGNITION TIMING Auto Trans.● (deg.)■	IDLE SPEED Man. Trans.● (rpm)▲	IDLE SPEED Auto Trans. (rpm)▲
1970	6-250	BF-82	0.035	49	0.025	6B	6B	750/500⑧	600/500⑧
	8-302	BF-42	0.035	27	0.021	6B	6B	800/500⑧	600/500⑧
	8-351C (250 hp)	AF-42	0.035	27	0.021	6B	6B	700/500⑧	600
	8-351W (250 hp)	BF-42	0.035	27	0.021	10B	10B	700/500⑧	575 [600/500⑧]
	8-351C (300 hp)	BF-32	0.035	27	0.021	6B	6B	800/500⑧	600 [600/500⑧]
	8-429 (360 hp)	BF-42	0.035	27/29⑦	0.021/⑦ 0.017	6B	6B	700	600
	8-429CJ (370 hp)	AF-32	0.035	27/29⑦	0.021/⑦ 0.017	10B	10B	700 [700/500⑧]	650
1971	6-250	BRF-82	0.034	36	0.027/⑦ 0.025	6B	6B	750	600
	8-302	BRF-42	0.034	27	0.021	6B	6B	800/500⑧	575 [600/500⑧]
	8-351C (240 hp)	ARF-42	0.034	27	0.021	6B	6B	700/500⑧	600
	8-351W (240 hp)	BRF-42	0.034	27	0.021	6B	6B	700/500⑧	575 [600/500⑧]
	8-351CJ (280 hp)	ARF-42	0.034	27	0.021	6B	6B	800/500⑧	600
	8-351C (285 hp)	ARF-32	0.034	27	0.021	6B	6B	800/500⑧	600
	8-429 (360 hp)	BRF-42	0.034	27/29⑦	0.021/⑦ 0.017	4B	4B	700	600 [600/500⑧]
	8-429CJ (370 hp)	ARF-42	0.034	25	0.020	10B	10B	750	600 [650/500⑧]
	8-429SCJ	ARF-42	0.034	28	0.020	10B	10B	650/500⑧	700/500⑧
1972	6-250	BRF-82	0.034	37	0.027	6B	6B	700/500⑧	600/500⑧
	8-302	BRF-42	0.034	28	0.017	6B	6B	800/500⑧	575 [600/500⑧]
	8-351C (165 hp)	ARF-42	0.034	28	0.017	6B	6B	750/500⑧	575/500①⑧
	8-351W (165 hp)	BRF-42	0.034	28	0.017	—	6B	—	575 [600/500⑧]
	8-351CJ (266 hp)	ARF-42	0.034	28④	0.017②	16B	16B	1000/500⑧	700/500③⑧
	8-400	ARF-42	0.034	28	0.017	—	6B	—	625/500⑧
	8-429	ARF-42	0.034	28	0.017	—	10B	—	600/500⑧

FAIRLANE/TORINO

YEAR	ENGINE No. Cyl. Displacement (cu. in.)	SPARK PLUGS Type	Gap (in.)	DISTRIBUTOR Point Dwell (deg.)	Point Gap (in.)	IGNITION TIMING Man. Trans.● (deg.)■	Auto Trans.● (deg.)■	IDLE SPEED Man. Trans.● (rpm) ▲	Auto Trans. (rpm) ▲
1973	6-250	BRF-42	0.034	37	0.027	6B	6B	750/500⑧	600/500⑧
	8-302	BRF-42	0.034	28	0.017	6B	6B	800/500⑧	625/500⑧
	8-351W(156hp)	BRF-42	0.034	28	0.017	——	6B	——	625/500⑧
	8-351C(159hp)	ARF-42	0.034	28	0.017	——	10B	——	625/500⑧
	8-351CJ(246hp)	ARF-42	0.034	28④	0.017②	16B	18B	1000/500⑧	800/500⑧
	8-400	ARF-42	0.034	28	0.017	——	6B	——	625/500⑧
	8-429	ARF-42	0.034	28	0.017	——	10B	——	650/500⑧
	8-460PI	ARF-42	0.034	28	0.017	——	10B	——	600/500⑧
1974	6-250	BRF-82	⑥	37⑤	0.027⑤	6B	6B	800/500⑧	625/500⑧
	8-302	BRF-42	⑥	28⑤	0.017⑤	10B	6B	800/500⑧	625/500⑧
	8-351W(162hp)	BRF-42	⑥	28⑤	0.017⑤	——	6B	——	600/500⑧
	8-351C(163hp)	ARF-42	⑥	28⑤	0.017⑤	——	14B	——	600/500⑧
	8-351CJ(255hp)	ARF-42	0.034	28⑤	0.017②	20B	20B	1000/500⑧	800/500⑧
	8-400	ARF-42	0.044	Breakerless		——	12B	——	625/500⑧
	8-460 (195, 220hp)	ARF-52	0.044	Breakerless		——	14B	——	650/500⑧
	8-460PI(260hp)	ARF-52	0.044	Breakerless		——	10B	——	700/500⑧
1975	8-351W(154hp)	ARF-42	0.044	Breakerless		——	6B	——	600/500⑧
	8-351M(148hp)	ARF-42	0.044	Breakerless		——	6B	——	700/500⑧
	8-400	ARF-42	0.044	Breakerless		——	6B	——	625/500⑧
	8-460(216hp)	ARF-52	0.044	Breakerless		——	14B	——	650/600⑧
	8-460PI(226hp)	ARF-52	0.044	Breakerless		——	14B	——	700/600⑧
1976	8-302 2bbl	ARF-52	.044	Breakerless		See Engine Service Decal		750	650
	8-302 4bbl	ARF-42	.044	Breakerless				750	650
	8-351 2bbl	ARF-52	.044	Breakerless				——	650
	8-351 4bbl	ARF-42	.044	Breakerless				——	650
	8-400 2bbl	ARF-52	.044	Breakerless				——	650
	8-400 4bbl	ARF-52	.044	Breakerless				——	650
	8-460PI 4bbl	ARF-52	.044	Breakerless				——	650
1977	8-302 2bbl 8-351 2bbl 8-400 2bbl	See Underhood Specifications Sticker							

▲ Adjust automatic transmissions in Drive (AMC/Ford/GM) or Neutral (Chrysler), all manual transmissions are adjusted in Neutral.
● Figure in parentheses indicate California engine.
■ All figures are Before Top Dead Center.

NOTE: The underhood specifications sticker often reflects tune-up specification changes made in production. Sticker figures must be used if they disagree with those in this chart.

① Figure is 625/500 for California engines.
② Figure is 0.020 for manual transmission w/dual point distributor.
③ Figure is 800/500 for California engines.
④ 30-33° dwell (both contacts operating) on vehicles with manual transmission and dual point distributor.
⑤ All 1974 California cars use breakerless ignition.
⑥ 40 states—0.034 in.; California—0.044 in. plug gap.
⑦ When two figures are separated by a slash, the first figure is for engines equipped with dual diaphragm distributors and the second figure is for engines equipped with single diaphragm distributors.
⑧ Figures in brackets are for solenoid equipped vehicles only; if not equipped with solenoid, use figure not in brackets. In cases where two figures are separated by a slash, the first is for idle speed with solenoid energized and automatic transmission in Drive, while the second is for idle speed with solenoid disconnected and automatic transmission in Neutral.

B Before Top Dead Center.
C Cleveland.
CJ Cobra Jet.
HO High Output.
NA Not available.
SCJ Super Cobra Jet.
W Windsor.
M Modified Cleveland.
PI Police Interceptor.
—— Not applicable.

CAPACITIES

YEAR	ENGINE No. Cyl. Displacement (cu. in.)	ENGINE OIL Add 1 qt. with New Filter	TRANSMISSION Pts. to Refill after Draining MANUAL 3-speed	4-speed	AUTOMATIC	DRIVE AXLE (pts.)	COOLING SYSTEM with Heater (qts.)	with Air Cond. (qts.)
1970	6-250	3.5	3.5	—	18	4	11.5	11.5
	8-302	4	3.5	4	18	5	15.5	16.5
	8-351	4	3.5	4	22	5	15.5	16.5
	8-429	6①	—	4	26	5	19.5	19.5
1971	6-250	3.5	3.5	—	18	4	11	11
	8-302	4	3.5	—	18	4	15	15.5
	8-351	4	3.5	4	22	5	15.5	16.5
	8-429	6①	—	4	26	5	19.5	19.5
1972-73	6-250	3.5	3.5	—	18	4	11.5	11.5
	8-302	4	3.5	—	18	4	15	15
	8-351	4	—	4	20.5②	4	15.5	16
	8-400	4	—	—	26	4	17.5	17.5
	8-429	4	—	—	26	5	19	18
1974	6-250	4	—	—	③	4	11.5	—
	8-302	4	3.5	—	③	4	15.7	15.7
	8-351	4	—	—	④	4	⑤	⑤
	8-400	4	—	—	25	5	17.7	18.3
	8-460	6	—	—	25	5	18.9	19.5
1975	8-351	3½⑧	—	—	⑥	4	⑦	⑦
	8-400	3½⑧	—	—	⑥	5	17.1	17.5
	8-460	4	—	—	⑥	5	19.2	19.2
1976	8-351W	4	—	—	③	5	15.9	16.2
	8-351M	4	—	—	③	5	17.1	17.5
	8-400	4	—	—	25	5	17.1	17.5
	8-460 4bbl	4	—	—	25	5	19.2	19.2
	8-460PI	6⑨	—	—	25	5	19.7	19.7
1977	8-302	4	—	—	③	4	15.7	15.7
	8-351M	4	—	—	③	5	17.1	17.5
	8-400	4	—	—	25	5	17.1	17.5

① 429-2 bbl—4 qts.
② 26 pts. for 351CJ.
③ C4—18 or 20 pts., FMX—22 pts.
④ 351-2V with C6—25 pts., 351-4V with C6—21 pts.
⑤ 351W-2V—16.4 qts. w/heater; 16.8 w/AC.
⑥ C4—20 pts., FMX—22 pts., C6—25 pts.
⑦ 351 Windsor—15.9 qts. w/heater; 16.2 w/AC.
351 Modified—17.1 qts. w/heater; 17.5 w/AC.
⑧ Add only ½ qt. of oil for new service filter.
⑨ 7.5 with oil cooler.
— Not applicable

Service Record

Date/Mileage	Service	Next Due

Ford

Lubrication and Oil Change

BRAKE FLUID LEVEL CHECK

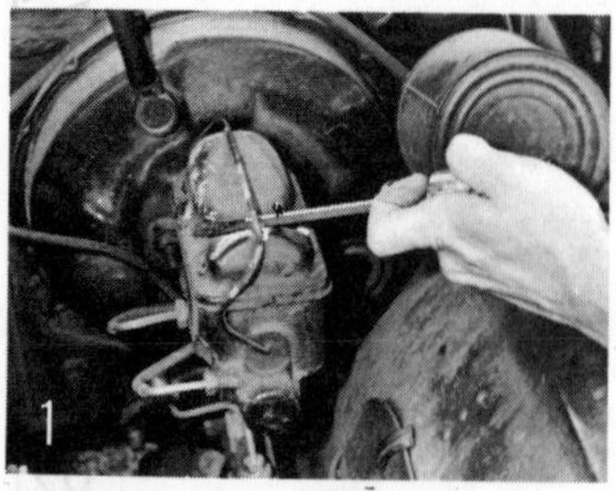

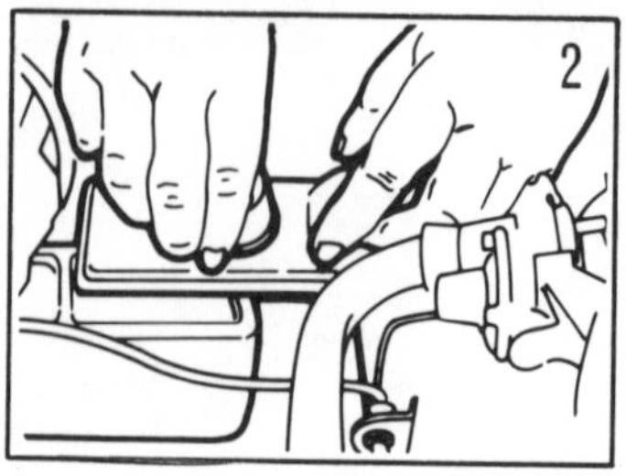

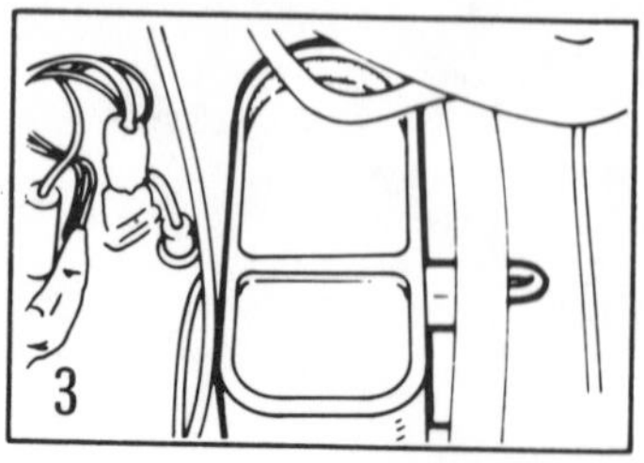

Check brake fluid level in master cylinder every three months . . . sooner if braking feels inadequate. Add when low. Recommended grade: DOT 3.

Master cylinder is located under hood on left side. It is oblong container about 6″ long with cap held down by wire clip. Check brake fluid level as follows:

1. Pry wire retaining clip off cap top with screwdriver.
2. Remove cap and gasket by lifting up.
3. Fluid level should be within ¼ inch of top rim. If lower than this, add fresh fluid to appropriate level.
DO NOT OVERFILL
4. Replace cap and gasket; secure retaining clip over cap. If fluid level was low, check again in a few days.
5. If fluid repeatedly checks low, there is a leak somewhere in the system. Have mechanic check further. Neglect can be dangerous.

MANUAL TRANSMISSION FLUID LEVEL CHECK

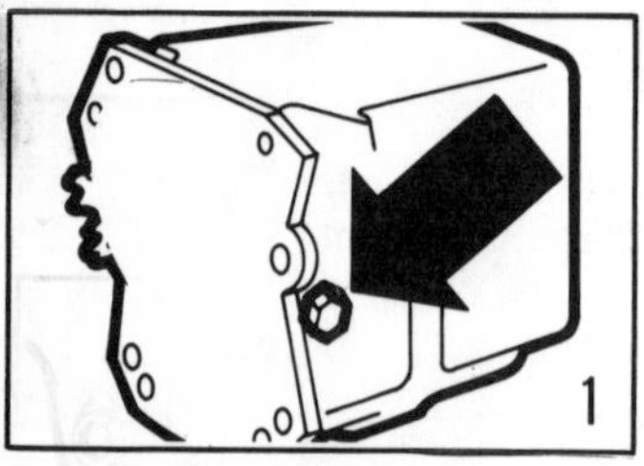

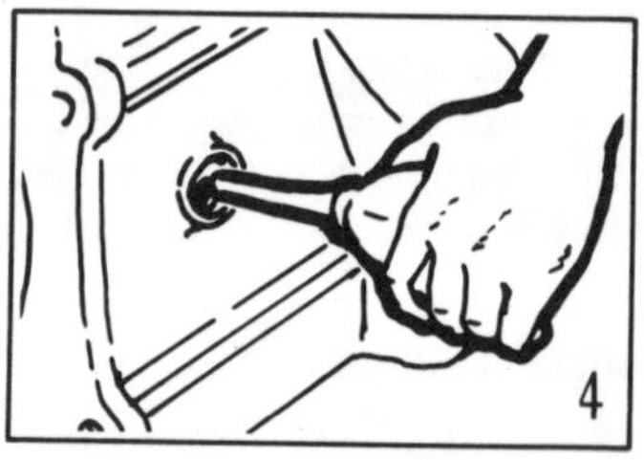

FORD SAYS . . . check manual transmission fluid every 6000 miles. Car should be parked level. Recommended grade: Standard Transmission Fluid (SAE 90).
TOOLS NEEDED . . . adjustable wrench; bulb syringe with flexible nozzle.

1. Locate transmission fluid filler plug on right side of transmission housing from underneath car.
2. Wipe road dirt from filler plug area before loosening. Remove plug with adjustable wrench.
3. Insert your finger. Fluid level should be right up to bottom edge of filler hole.
4. Add fluid as needed with hand bulb syringe.
5. Replace filler plug; tighten.

AUTOMATIC TRANSMISSION FLUID LEVEL CHECK

FORD SAYS . . . check automatic transmission fluid (ATF) level every 6000 miles. Recommended grade: ATF Type F.

TOOLS . . . Long neck filler funnel.

1. Engine must be warmed up and running. Place shift lever in PARK position.
2. Pull out dipstick. Wipe clean.

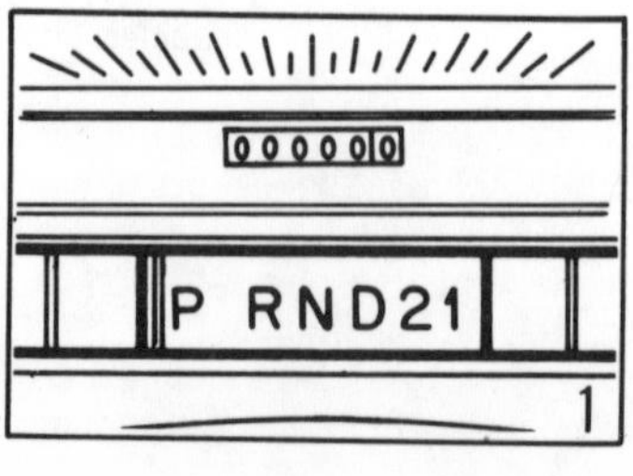

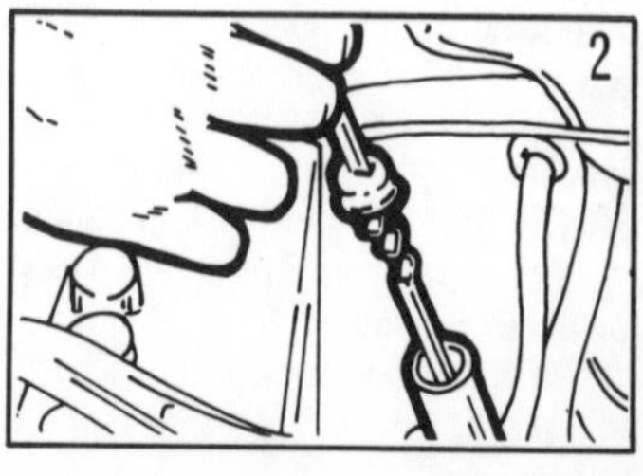

Push dipstick all the way back in; remove it again.

3. If fluid is below ADD mark, add ATF to bring level up. DO NOT OVERFILL.

4. Add ATF thru transmission dipstick hole by means of long-neck filler funnel.

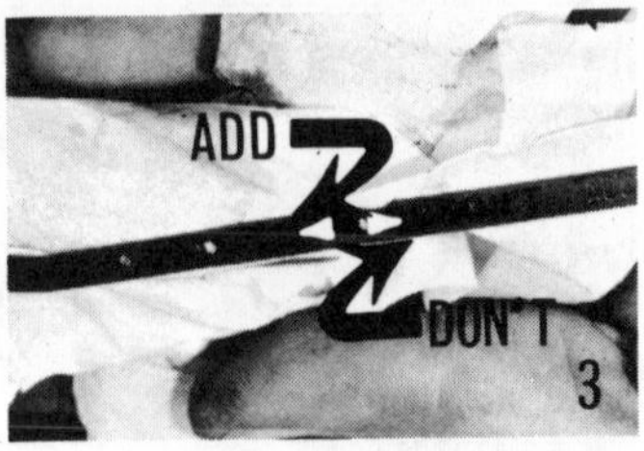

REAR AXLE LUBRICANT

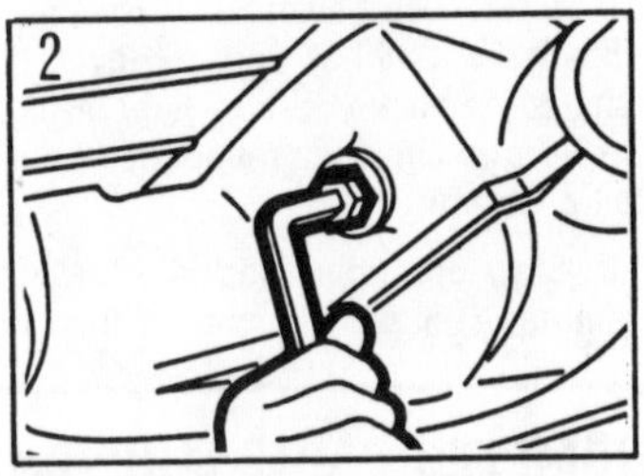

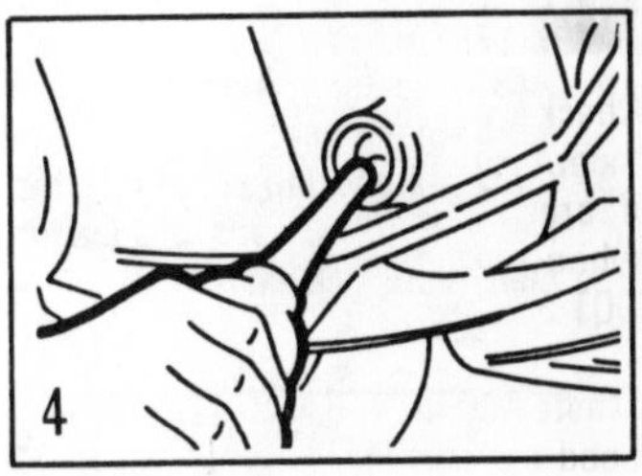

FORD SAYS . . . check rear axle lube level every 6000 miles. Recommended grade: Hypoid gear lube (SAE 90).
TOOLS . . . adjustable hand wrench; bulb syringe.

1. Locate filler plug on forward side of rear axle housing.
2. Wipe plug area clean; remove plug with wrench.
3. Insert your finger, remove. Adequate fluid level should show lubricant right up to the bottom edge of the filler hole.
4. If fluid level is low, add as needed, with a hand bulb syringe, until level shows on last ¼-inch of wire.
5. Replace filler plug; tighten.

OIL AND FILTER CHANGE

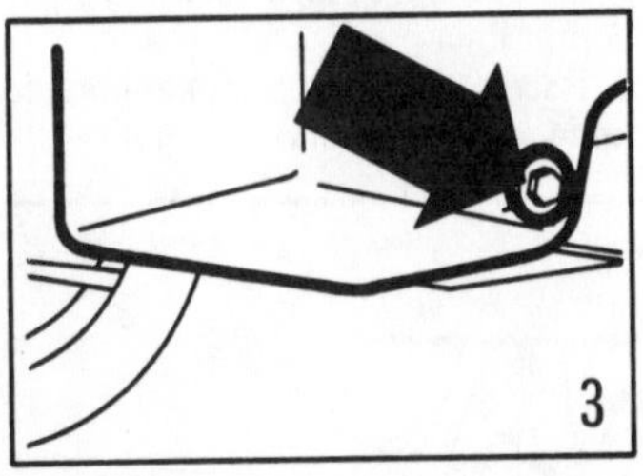

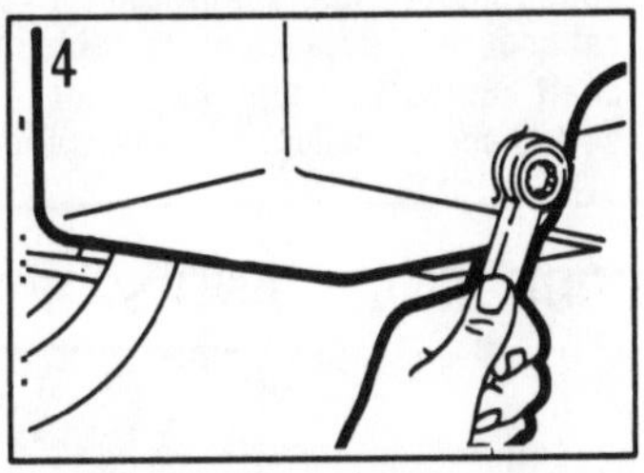

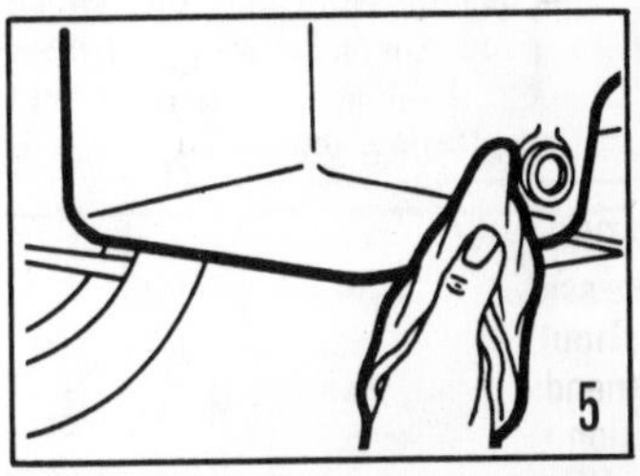

FORD SAYS . . . Change oil every 6,000 miles, change filter every 12,000 miles. Recommended grade: MS or SE (check owner's handbook). Check oil level at least once a week.
TOOLS & MATERIALS . . . adjustable hand wrench; medium size screwdriver; oil filter removal wrench; drain pan for old oil (at least 5 qt. capacity); oil pouring spout; 5 qt. oil; new oil filter; oil and lubricants as specified below.
SAFETY TIP . . . use work gloves.

1. If engine is cold, start up and idle for about 5 minutes.

2. Park car on level ground. Turn engine off.

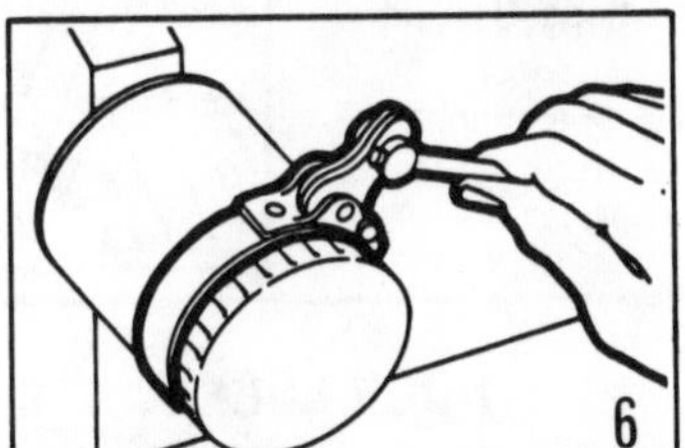

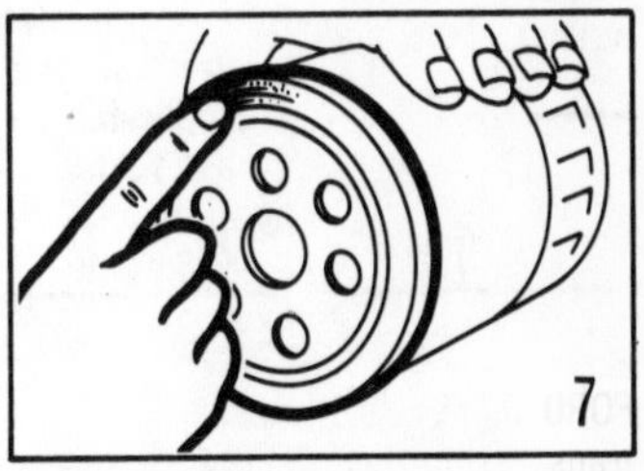

3. Locate oil drain plug on underside of engine. Place drain pan under plug.

4. Remove drain plug with wrench. Let ALL dirty oil drain out.

5. Wipe plug and area around drain hole clean. Replace drain plug; tighten it.

6. Locate oil filter. Move drain pan under filter. Loosen filter with oil filter wrench. Unscrew; remove filter by hand.

7. Smear fresh oil over surface of rubber gasket (washer) of new filter.

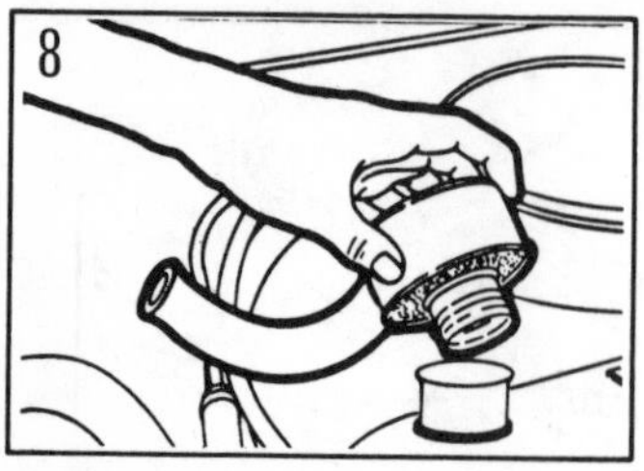

Install new filter by hand only. Do NOT use wrench. Turn filter until gasket makes contact. Tighten an additional half turn only . . . NO MORE.

8. Locate oil filler hole on top of engine. Remove cap.

9. Punch oil pouring spout into top of oil can. Pour all cans of new oil into filler tube. Wipe filler cap clean and replace it.

10. Check new oil level at dipstick. Pull out dipstick, wipe clean.

11. Push dipstick back into engine. Be sure to insert all the way. Remove dipstick and check new oil level. It should be above "SAFE" line. If not, be sure to check if you put in all the oil called for.

12. Start up engine and idle for 3-5 minutes. Oil signal light on instrument panel will glow red when engine is first started. Light should go out in 30 seconds or less.

13. Stop engine and check for oil leaks at drain plug and filter. If you find any, check tightness of plug and/or filter, also for condition of filter gasket to see that it has not become pinched or damaged when installing. Recheck oil level, which should now be at "SAFE".

SPEEDOMETER CABLE LUBRICATION

If speedometer pointer tends to quiver or jump, or if unit makes a low, rasping sound, lubrication may be needed.

1. Locate cable shaft attachment directly behind speedometer dial.
2. Remove retaining clip. Unscrew cable from speedometer.
3. Pull inner cable completely out of outer casing. Note carefully which end is top. Check for wear or frayed strands. If damaged, replace inner cable with new one.

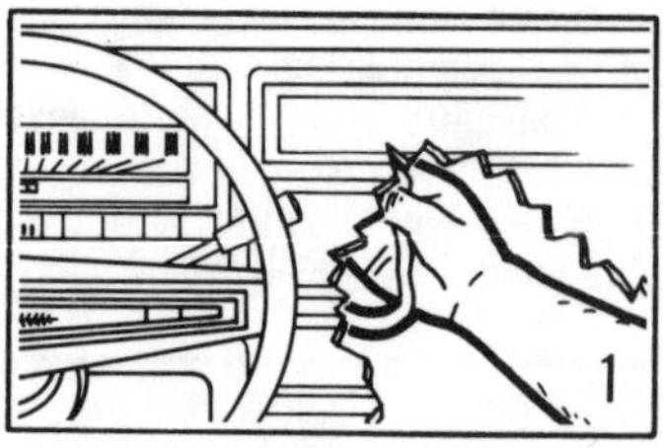

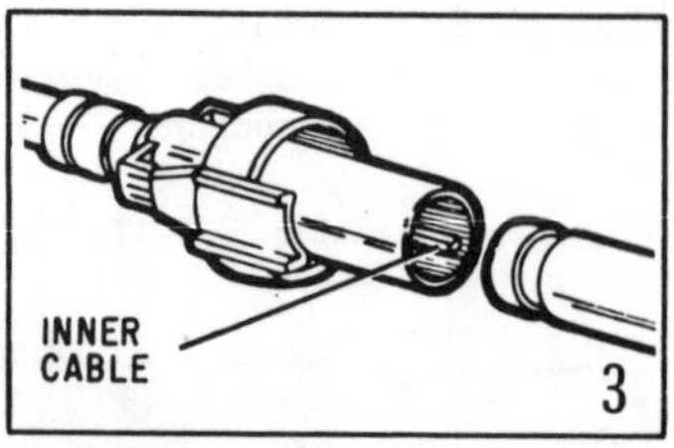

4. Apply generous amount of speedometer cable lubricant into cable casing. Replace inner cable in shaft, noting that top end is not inserted accidentally. Turn inner cable as it is being re-inserted. Twist cable when all the way in, to lock into position at lower end.
5. Reconnect cable to speedometer head under instrument panel.

DOOR HINGES AND STOPS

(lubricate every 6 months)
1. Brush any dirt accumulations from door hinges and stops. Use old tooth brush or rag.
2. Apply dab of white polyethylene grease to door hinges, trunk hinges, hood hinges, door stops.

DOOR LOCKS

(lubricate every 6 months)
1. Insert door key half way into lock.
2. Spray aerosol lock lubricant into lock.
3. Push key rest of way into lock; turn back and forth several times.

Cooling System

IT IS RECOMMENDED . . . that radiator coolant (water/antifreeze mixture) level be checked once or twice a month. Do this when engine is cold. Check more often if you do a lot of hard driving. On models with clear expansion tanks, check coolant level visually when hot.
Keep coolant up to recommended level in radiator. If coolant checks frequently low, look for leaks.

Tighten all hose clamps occasionally. For best results, keep a 50/50 water/antifreeze mixture year round. Change complete coolant mixture every 24 months.

CAUTION: If you must check coolant in a hot engine, cover radiator cap with thick rag before releasing. Remove cap slowly . . . press down and turn.

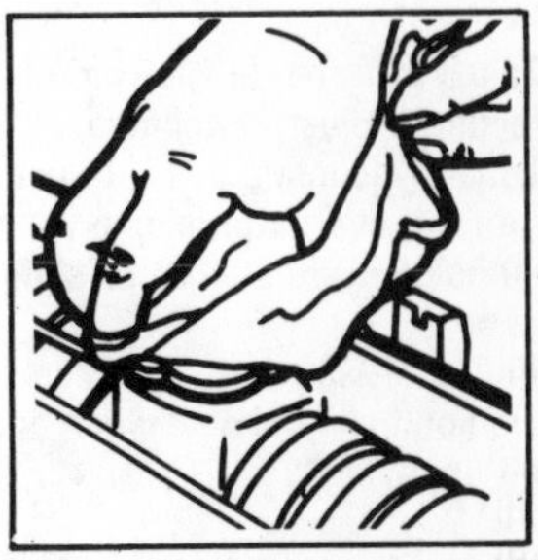

REPLACING THE THERMOSTAT

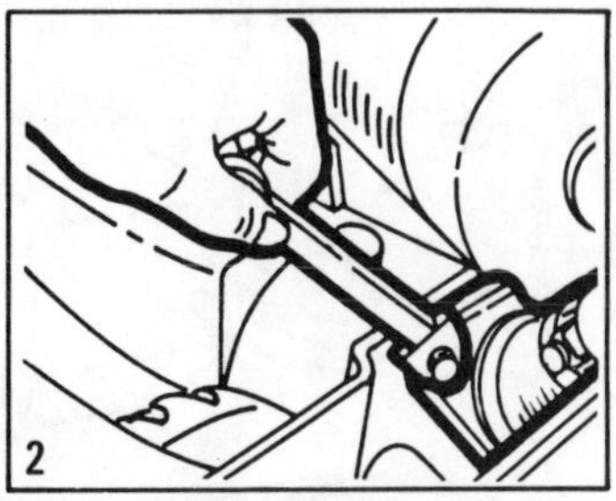

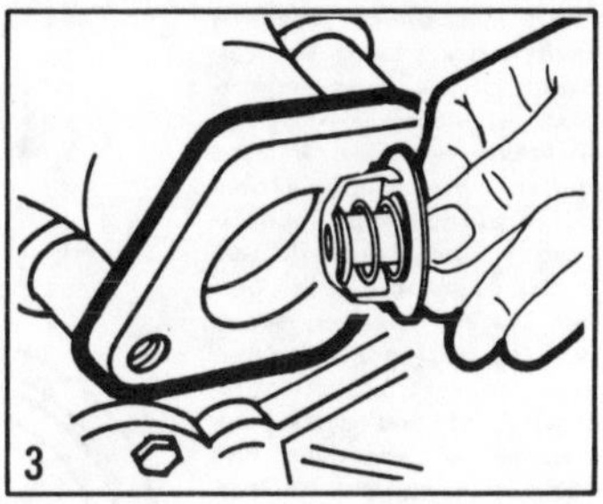

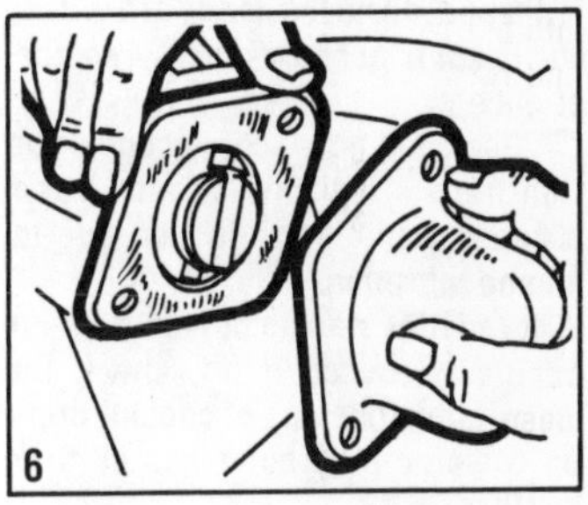

A faulty thermostat will usually cause engine overheating. Replace with new thermostat.

TOOLS AND MATERIALS . . .
New thermostat
Gasket
Adjustable wrench

1. Drain radiator of about half its coolant. (See Hose Replacement section).
2. Loosen and remove both retaining bolts and lift thermostat housing off the engine.

NOTE: If you're careful it won't be necessary to remove radiator hose.

3. Remove old thermostat.
4. Scrape thermostat housing flange and engine block surface to remove old gasket debris.
5. Drop new thermostat into place—spring down.
6. Install new gasket with sealer applied to both sides.
7. Replace thermostat housing and tighten both retaining bolts.

ENGINE OVERHEATING

YOUR CAR OVERHEATS BECAUSE

radiator coolant is too low
fan belt is too loose
of a broken or leaking hose
thermostat does not function
radiator is plugged with sediment
water pump does not function properly

TO CORRECT IT

fill to correct level; check for leaks
adjust tension or replace frayed belt
replace hose; tighten clamps
replace thermostat
consult a professional mechanic (may need radiator removal and servicing, or total replacement)
replace water pump (may make squeaky noise; or leak at pump shaft)

FAN BELT ADJUSTMENT

The fan belt not only drives the radiator fan, it turns the water pump and drives the alternator. It's easy to see that the condition and proper tension of the belt are vital, since almost all engine cooling and electrical power is dependent on it. The belt deserves an occasional look and tension check.

CAUTION: An overtightened belt may damage alternator and water pump bearings.

1. Inspect fan belt occasionally. If worn, frayed or cracked on inner driving surface, replace.
2. Check tension occasionally. Press thumb at midpoint of belt span between pulleys. If belt depresses

more than ½ inch, tightening is needed. A too-loose belt will not drive alternator and water pump effectively.

3. Adjust to proper tension of ¼ inch deflection. Adjust as follows:

A. Loosen mounting bolts at top and bottom so alternator can pivot on lower bolt and upper bolt can slide in bracket.

B. Pull alternator out slightly to put tension on belt, and hold while tightening upper bolt.

C. Check tension. Repeat adjustment as necessary.

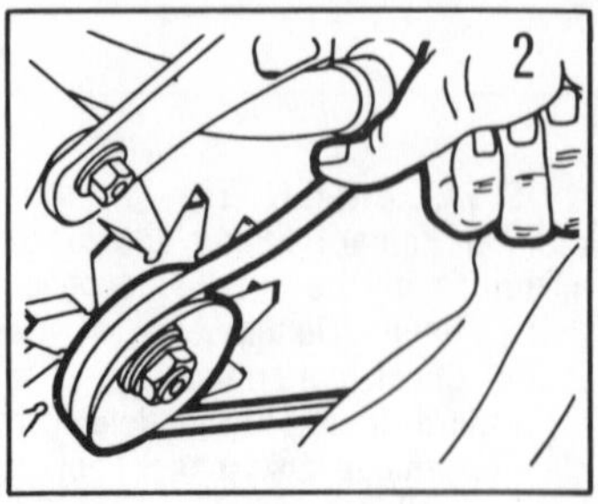

D. When tension is correct, tighten lower bolt.

FIND THOSE COOLING SYSTEM LEAKS

1. Inspect all hoses. If any are weak, soft in spots or show cracks, replace at once.

2. Check all hose connections for tightness. Tighten loose hose clamps; they tend to loosen due to engine vibration.

3. If radiator steams or hisses when engine is switched off, check for leaks. Look for signs of coolant drips on radiator or around heater tank joint.

Leaks are possible at:
Upper or lower radiator hoses
Water pump (gaskets or seal)
Heater core or connecting hoses
Automatic transmission cooler lines (at bottom of radiator)
Faulty radiator pressure cap
Faulty cylinder head gasket
Cracked cylinder head or block

Due to the number of joints, cooling systems have many places to leak from. Check clamp tightness. If leaks persist an anti-leak additive in the coolant may help. Noisy water pumps may benefit from a lubricating additive in the coolant. Use a cooling system cleaner when flushing during a drain and refill job. It will help remove rust and scale. Remember — additives will not cure chronic problems. But they will effect a short-term remedy in many cases.

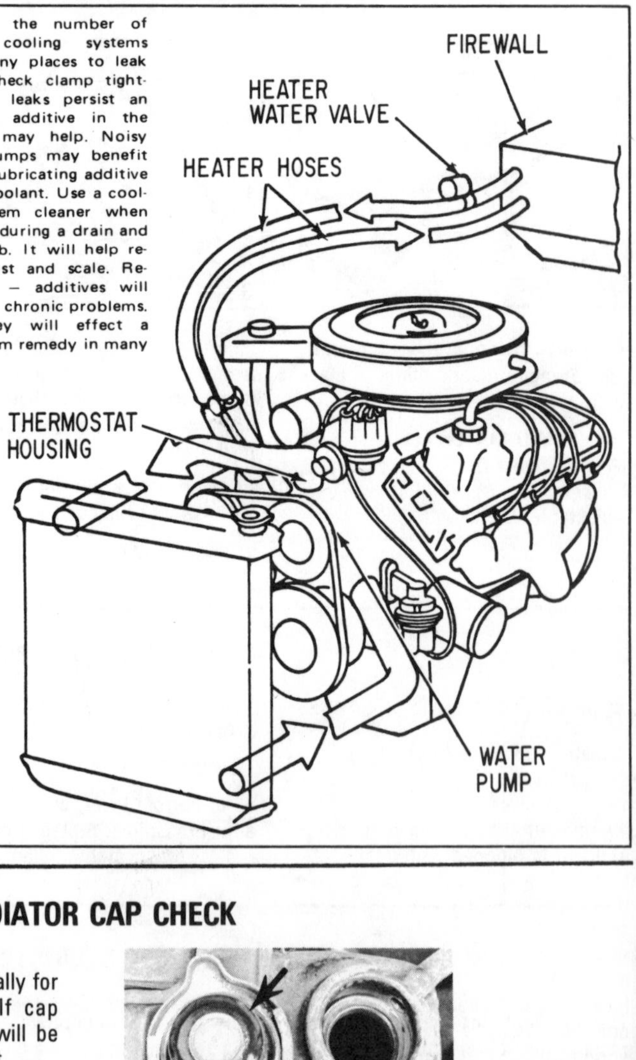

RADIATOR CAP CHECK

Check radiator cap occasionally for worn or cracked gasket. If cap doesn't seal properly, fluid will be lost and engine will overheat. Replace worn cap with new cap rated 13 to 15 lbs. pressure.

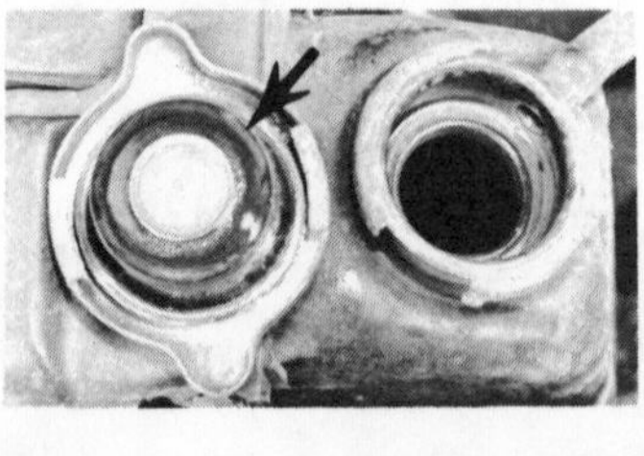

HOSE REPLACEMENT

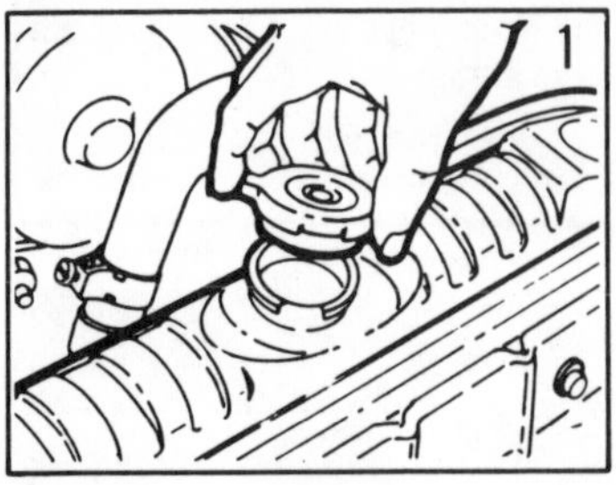

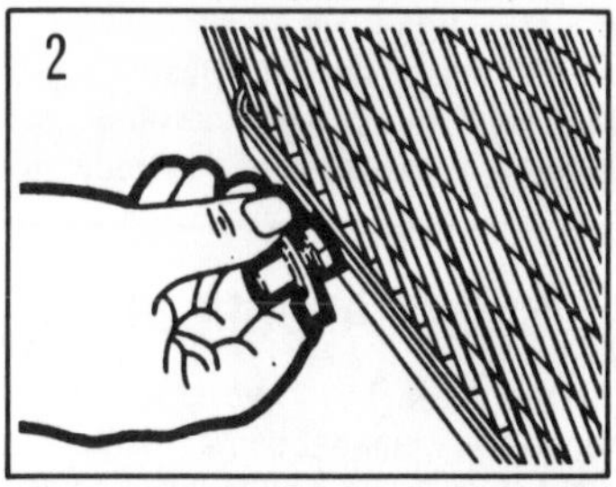

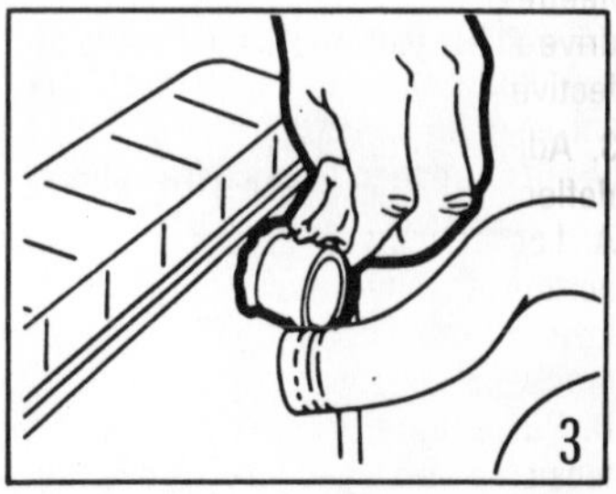

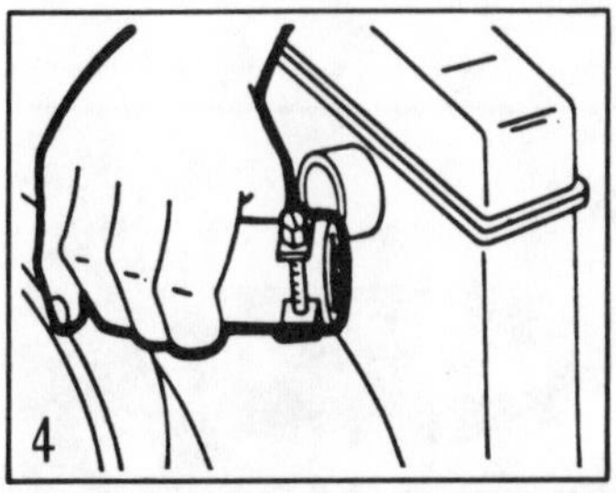

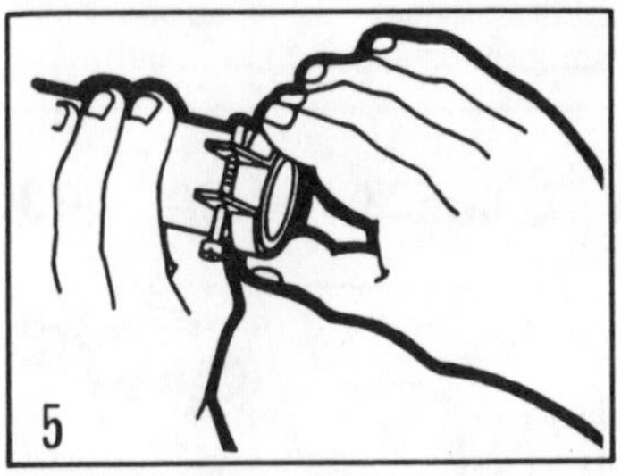

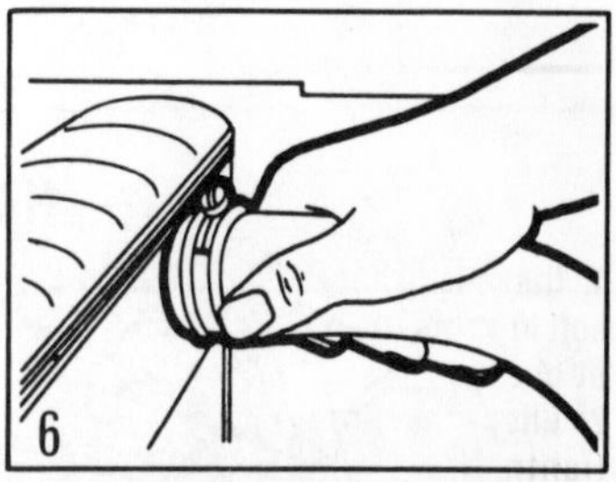

Coolant drain and refill work may be done alone; when changing hoses, coolant must also be drained as part of job. Discard all hoses with cracks or soft spots. Check hose clamps for tightness and good condition.
1. Remove radiator cap. Open radiator petcock (See 2). Drain coolant into catch basin. If near 24 months old, discard old coolant.
2. Petcock is located at the bottom of the radiator.
3. Wipe all hose connections clean. Use emery cloth to get rid of residue.
4. If old hose clamps are badly rusted or damaged, replace with new units.

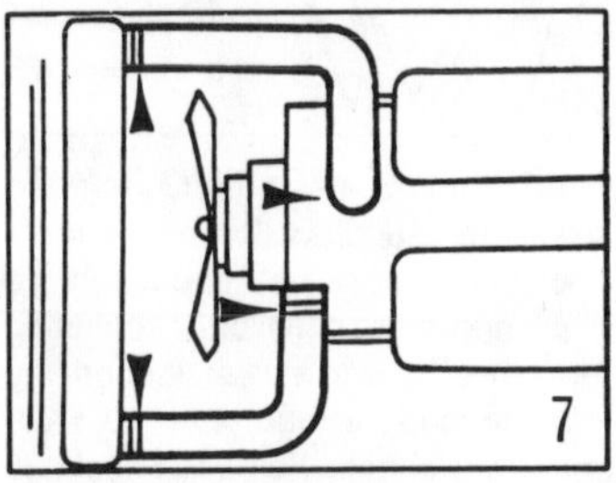

5. Slip clamps over each hose end. Slip hose ends all the way onto cleaned up hose connections.
6. Place hose clamp ¼ inch from hose end. Tighten. Close petcock.

Refill with 50/50 coolant/water mix.
7. Start engine; allow to warm up. Check for coolant leaks.
8. Road test car; watch for temperature warning light.

Suspension and Tires

The front wheels mount and rotate on the spindles, which are attached to upper and lower ball joints. A coil spring is mounted between the control arms on each side. A shock absorber is located in the center of each spring. The rear suspension is a trailing link design. The rear axle is located by one upper and two lower control arms and a lateral bar. A coil spring and shock absorber are located on each side of the axle.

Your car's suspension system consists of wheels, tires, springs, shock absorbers, sway (or stabilizer) bars, ball joints, steering linkage. If any of these items is out of adjustment or badly worn, you may notice any of these symptoms:

- car pulls to one side when braking
- car wanders when driving a straight line
- overall ride may be either hard or bouncy
- effort is needed to steer vehicle
- tires show uneven wear
- tires squeal when cornering
- front of car dips or bounces when braking
- car rocks side-to-side when going over rough road
- wheels bounce to make slapping sound on road
- steering wheel vibrates in hands
- front of car vibrates at highway speeds

Any of above symptoms indicates corrective action is needed. Delay can: ruin tires; cause damage/failure to other suspension parts; create safety hazard.

STEERING

If steering linkage, front suspension and steering column components are in good condition, there should be not more than 1½ inch free play in the steering wheel when measured at the rim of the wheel. If a loud knock is heard when turning the steering wheel from one extreme to the other, have mechanic check pinion bearing preload.

SHOCK ABSORBERS

Shock absorbers work to keep wheels in constant contact with the road. Result is safe handling and ride control; longer tire life. So shock absorbers (or shocks) are important.

HOW TO CHECK FOR BAD SHOCKS

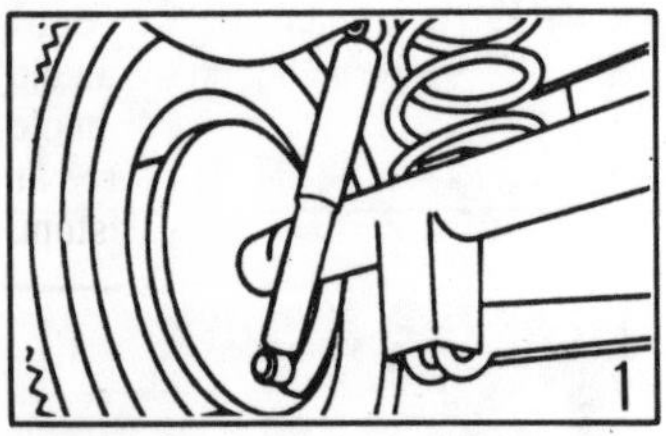

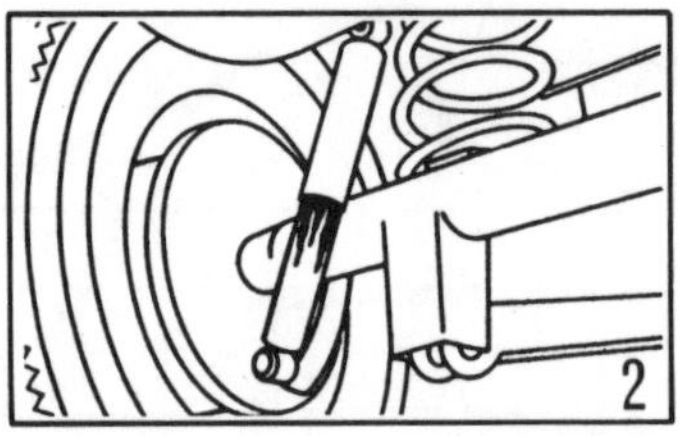

1. Check under car and locate shock absorber near each wheel.

2. Heavy oil streaks on outer shock housing indicate need for replacement.

3. Stand at front of car and apply body weight in pumping action to front bumper or fender. Release pressure and allow car to stop rocking. Car should not bounce more than one more time after releasing pressure. Repeat at rear. If bouncing continues more than once, replacement is needed. Replace shocks in pairs (front pair or rear pair).

TOW HITCH INFORMATION

If your car is used for trailer towing you should check:
A. Cooling System; be sure coolant is at proper level in radiator. See Cooling System Section for checks to perform.
B. Check Transmission Fluid; keep topped up to proper level.
C. Check Rear Shock Absorbers; you may benefit from installation of new rear shocks.
D. Check Tire Pressures; best traction and handling can be ensured if tire pressures are properly maintained.
For safer and more trouble-free trailer towing, consider:
A. Automatic Transmission Cooler; helps remove excess heat from automatic transmission fluid built up during towing mileage. Also helps avoid radiator overheating. Some units can be self-installed.
B. Radiator Over-Flow Tank Kit; addition of a reservoir to catch radiator coolant overflow preventing coolant loss. Easy to install, these units help a tow car run cooler, avoid overheating due to coolant loss.
C. Heavy-Duty Shock Absorbers or Air Shocks; important to have on rear wheels if you intend to do a lot of towing or load carrying within the car itself. Don't forget to consider replacing factory shocks, when they are worn out, with heavy-duty units at the front as well.
D. Variable Load Flasher; this unit will accommodate the added load of trailer turn signal lamps on trailer when these are hooked into your car's electrical system.

FRONT END ALIGNMENT

When steering, handling and/or tire wear indicate front end alignment may be needed, this work can only be done at an automotive service shop. DO NOT PUT OFF NEEDED FRONT END ALIGNMENT. At the same time, have ball joints and steering linkage checked.

Ignition System

The distributor holds the points, rotor and condenser.
Two types of ignition systems are used on the Ford. A conventional system using breaker points and condenser is used on all 1970-73 models and on many early production 1974 models equipped with the 351 V8. A breakerless (solid state) ignition system using an armature and magnetic pickup coil assembly in the distributor and a solid state amplifier module located in-line between the coil and distributor is installed in all 1974 models sold in California, and all Federal 1975 models as standard equipment, and on most 49 states 1974 models except some early production 1974 models equipped with the 351 V8.
Both systems employ a distributor which is driven by the camshaft at one-half crankshaft rpm, a high-voltage rotor, distributor cap and spark plug wiring, and an oil filled conventional type coil.

The two systems differ in the manner in which they convert electrical primary voltage (12 volts) from the battery into secondary voltage (20,000 volts or greater) to fire the spark plugs. In the conventional ignition system, the breaker points open and close as the moveable breaker arm rides the rotating distributor cam eccentric, thereby opening and closing the current to the ignition coil. When the points open, they interrupt the flow of primary current to the coil, causing a collapse of the magnetic field in the coil and creating a high-tension spark which is used to fire the spark plugs. In the breakerless system, a distributor shaft-mounted armature rotates past a magnetic pickup coil assembly causing fluctuations in the magnetic field generated by the pickup coil. These fluctuations in turn, cause the amplifier module to turn the ignition coil current off and on, creating the high-tension spark to fire the spark plugs. The amplifier module electronically controls the dwell, which is controlled mechanically in a conventional system by the duration that the points remain closed.
The solid state ignition system does not use points or a condenser as did the conventional system. You should still check the rotor, cap and wires as you would on a conventional system.

TUNE-UP SERVICES

FORD SAYS . . . Replace plugs and points every 12,000 miles.
TOOLS & MATERIALS . . . Parts: set of points; condenser; 8 spark plugs. Tools: gap gauge; 13/16 in. or ⅝ in. spark plug socket; screwdriver; open end, box or combination wrenches; timing equipment (see Ignition Timing).
SAFETY TIP . . . Change only one spark plug at a time to avoid cross-wiring and possible engine damage.

CHECKING POINTS AND ROTOR

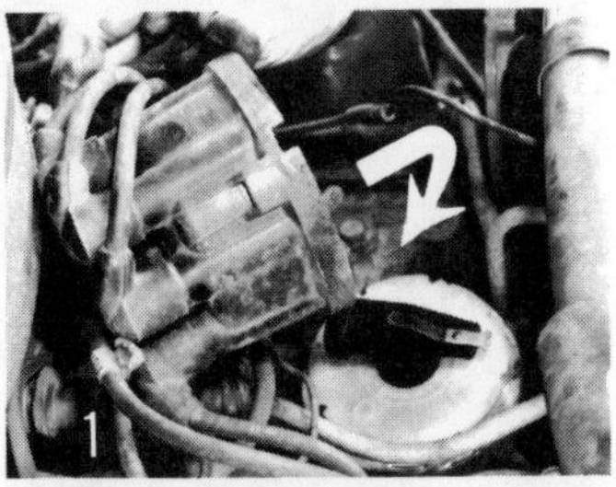

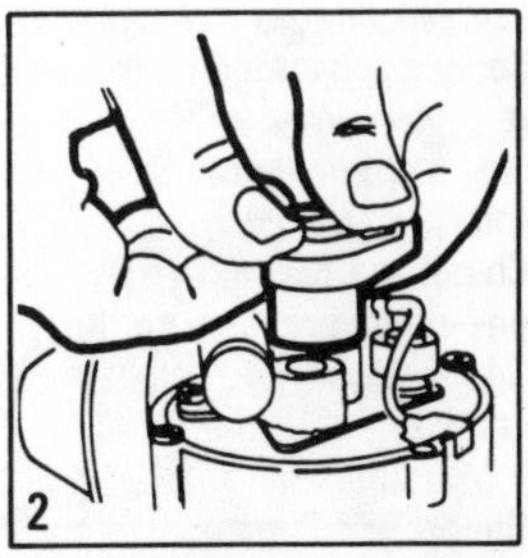

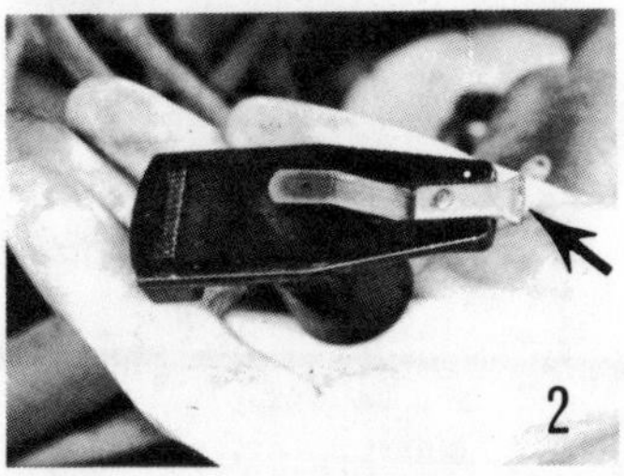

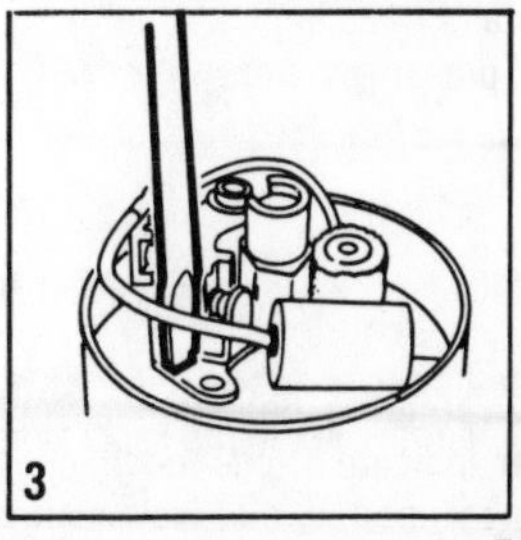

1. To open distributor, snap retaining clips off with screwdriver, lift cap off but keep wires connected.
2. Pull rotor off (straight up). Replace if cracked or metallic tip is badly burned.
3. On conventional systems, pry points apart with screwdriver. If worn or burned, replace. If OK, check point gap.

OTHER IGNITION CHECK POINTS

Inspect spark plug wires. If cracked or brittle, entire set should be replaced. Also center, high tension wire. Inspect distributor cap. Wipe inside clean occasionally with dry, lint-free rag. If cap is cracked or rotor contacts are excessively burned, replace cap.

HOOKING UP A TACHOMETER

On conventional ignition systems, connect the red lead (positive) wire of the meter to the distributor primary wire connection on the positive (+) side of the coil, and the black ground (negative) wire of the meter to a good ground on the engine (e.g., thermostat housing nut).

On the solid state system, there is a terminal on the ignition coil labelled TACH TEST. Connect the tachometer red lead to this terminal, with the black tachometer lead going to a good ground.

Some tachometers may not work with solid state ignition, or may hook up differently than described above. Before you hook yours up, check the instructions that came with your tachometer to be sure it will work with solid state ignition.

SPARK PLUG REPLACEMENT

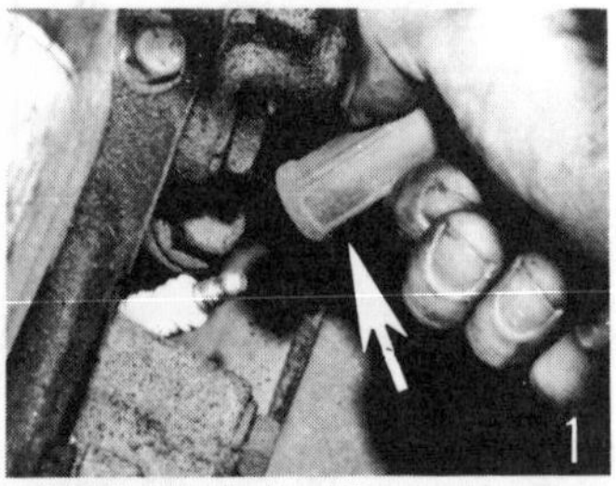

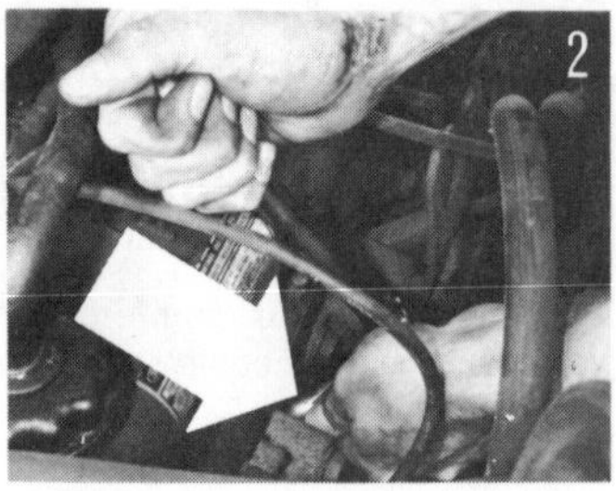

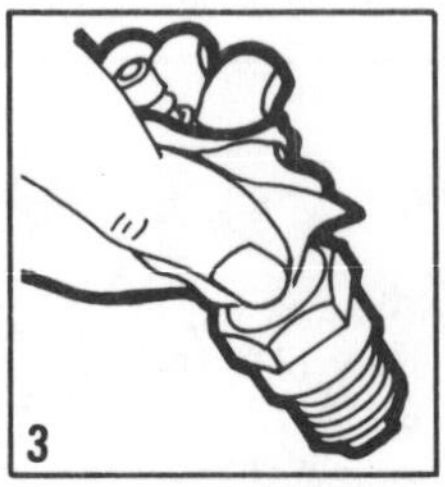

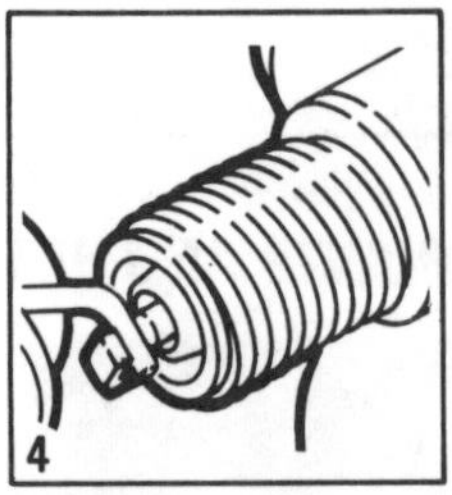

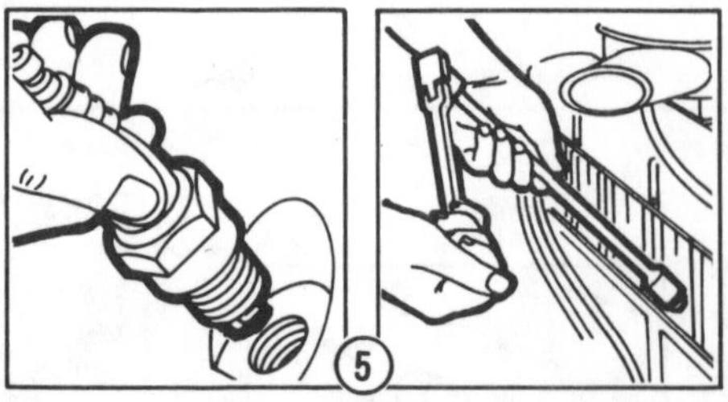

1. Remove spark plug wire by grasping rubber boot. Do not jerk wire off. If stuck, turn boot, pulling gently.
2. Loosen spark plug using socket wrench.
3. Wipe or brush loose dirt from around plug before removing. Do not let dirt drop into engine through plug hole. Unscrew plug.
4. Check plug electrode gap on new spark plug. Adjust to specification shown in the tune-up chart.

Plug gap is correct when the gauge drags slightly as it is pulled between plug electrodes.

5. Thread new plug into plug hole by hand. Hand tighten. Do not force or cross thread. Use socket wrench to tighten firmly but do not force. Replace plug wire. Press boot firmly.

REPLACING SPARK PLUG WIRES

1. Remove only one wire at a time from the engine.
2. Match the wire removed with the same length wire in the replacement set.
3. Route the replacement wire in the same way as the original.
4. After all wires are replaced, check that all wires on 1974 and earlier distributors are seated in the distributor cap. Check that all boots are in place.
5. If you run into difficulty, go to the Firing Order illustrations for help.

Use the firing order illustration to guide you when replacing your ignition wires and/or distributor cap.

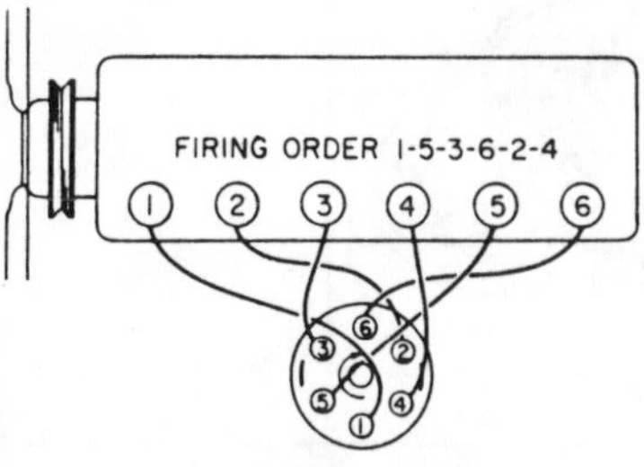

240 cu. in. 6 cyl.

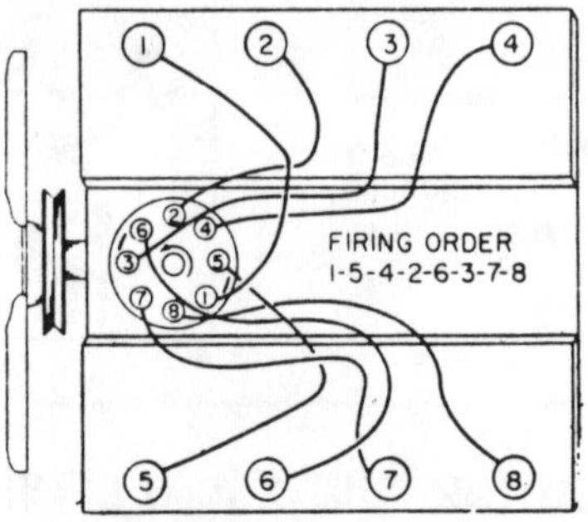

V8 except 351, 400 cu. in.

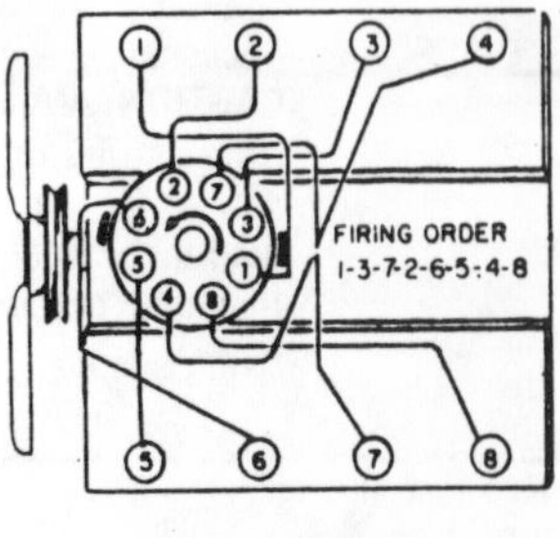

V8 351, 400 cu. in.

IGNITION TIMING

Adjusting timing is the important finishing touch to any tune-up. While not difficult, job requires timing light and dwell meter.

1. Locate timing marks and pointer (notches) on engine and lower engine pulley. Clean away dirt. Mark the pointer and notch which corresponds with the timing setting in degrees shown on the engine compartment sticker.
2. Hook up timing light according to instructions supplied with it.
3. Disconnect the one or two vacuum lines from the distributor. Plug with pencil tip or golf tee.
4. Hook up tachometer and adjust engine idle speed. Idle adjustment screw is located where gas pedal linkage attaches to carburetor.
5. Aim timing light at pulley mark(s).

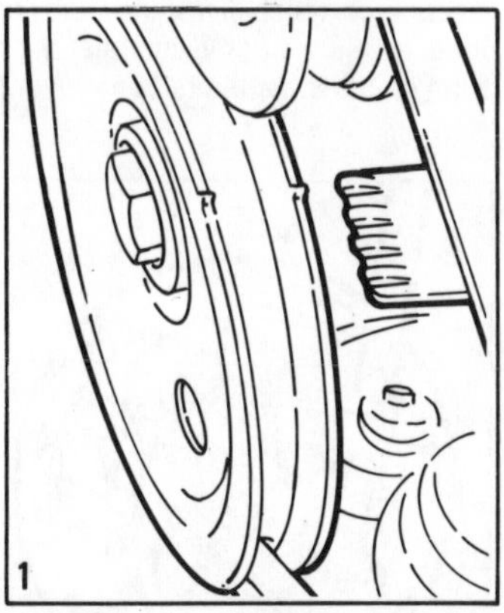

If the chalked marks do not align, loosen distributor hold-down bolt and slowly rotate distributor until chalked marks align.

6. Tighten hold-down bolt. Recheck timing.

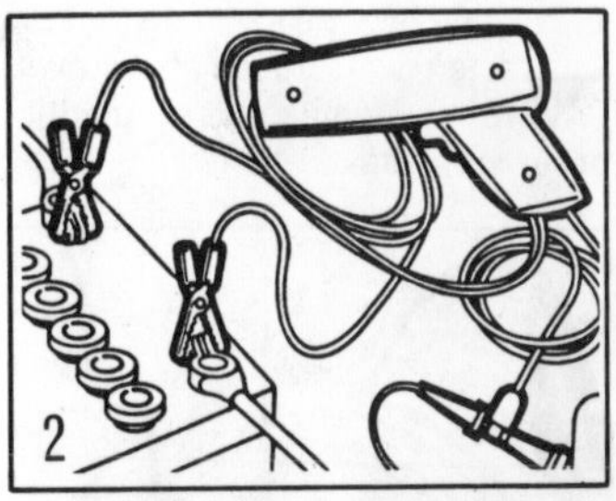

REMOVING POINTS

Conventional Ignition

Points and condenser work together. Always replace condenser when installing new points.

1. Loosen nut, and disconnect primary wire and condenser lead wire.
2. Remove screw which holds condenser; remove condenser.
3. Remove screws holding points to distributor; remove points.

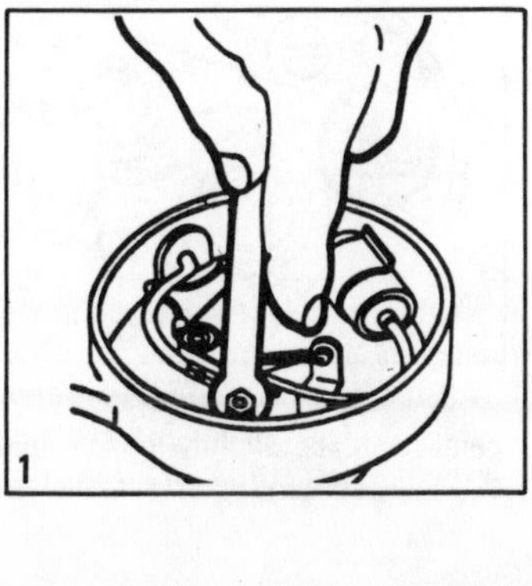

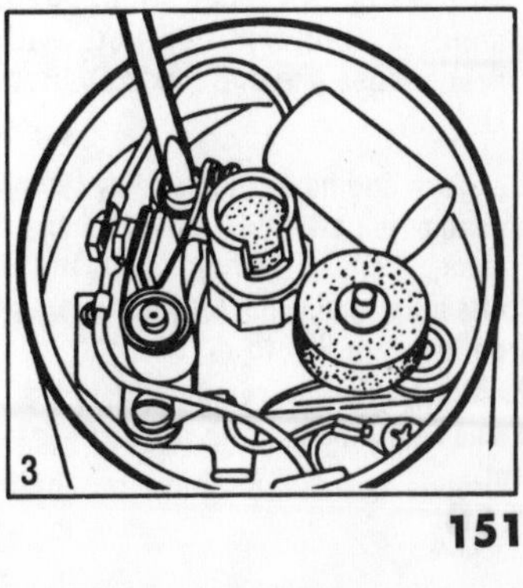

4. Wipe all dirt from distributor plate and cam.
5. Inspect primary wire for frayed insulation, dirty connection. Clean connection or have wire repaired as necessary.
CAUTION: When removing screws from distributor, be sure to avoid any screws accidentally falling through distributor opening into engine. Use magnetic screwdriver.

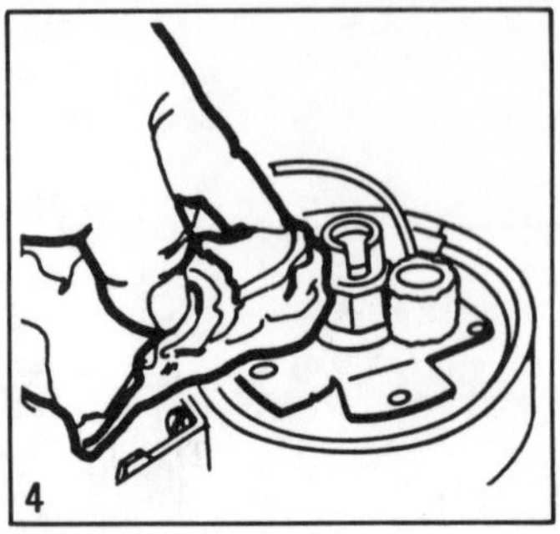

INSTALLING POINTS AND CONDENSER

1. Apply small amount of heat resistant lube to distributor cam. (Lube usually supplied with new points. If not, purchase separately.)
2. Position new points in distributor and fasten with attaching screws. CAUTION: use magnetic screwdriver, or screwdriver with clip.
3. Attach new condenser to distributor with attaching screw.
4. Attach primary wire and condenser lead wire to point set. Don't let contacts touch distributor body or breaker plate. (Some models: wire from points attaches to condenser.)

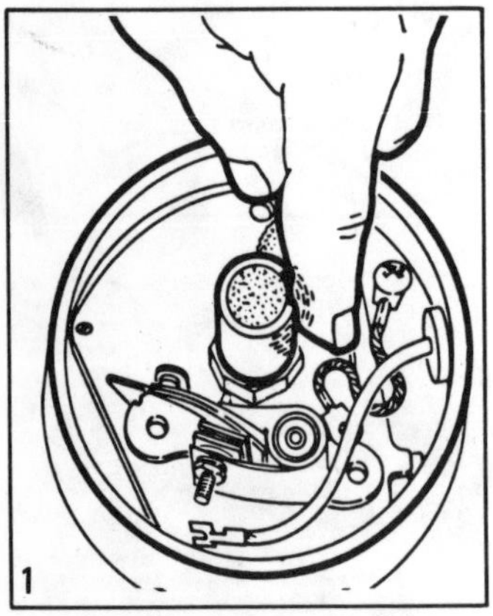

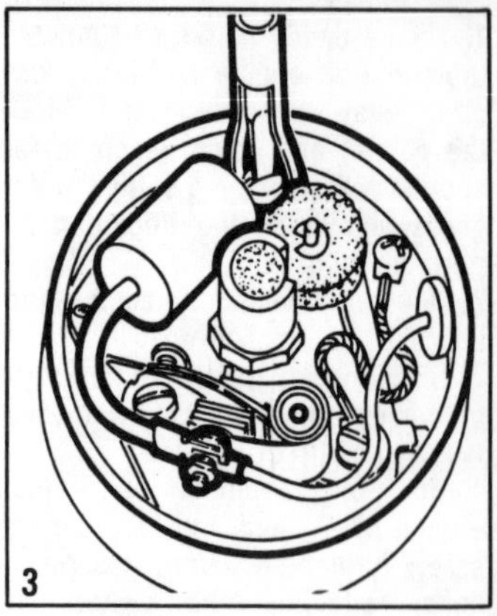

RESETTING THE CONTACT GAP

1. Electrical contacts of point set MUST BE PARALLEL. If needed, bend stationary contact with needle-nose pliers. Bend fixed bracket only.

2. Turn engine by ignition key (you'll need a helper) until rubbing block on points is one of the high points of the distributor cam. You may use wrench on lower pulley to do this.

3. Look up correct point gap on engine compartment sticker. Insert proper gap gauge between open

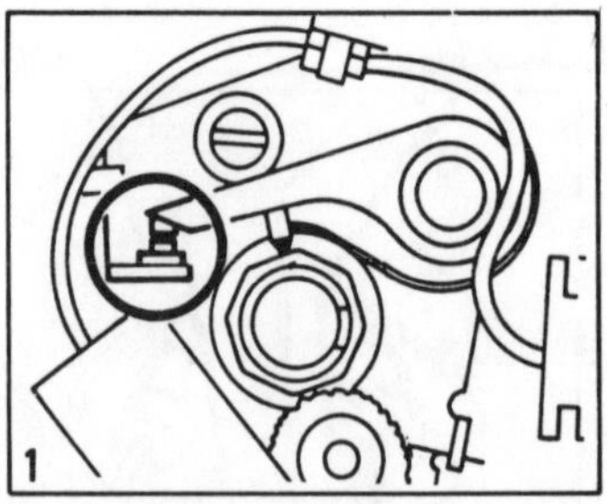

point contacts. Slightly loosen point attaching screws. Insert screwdriver

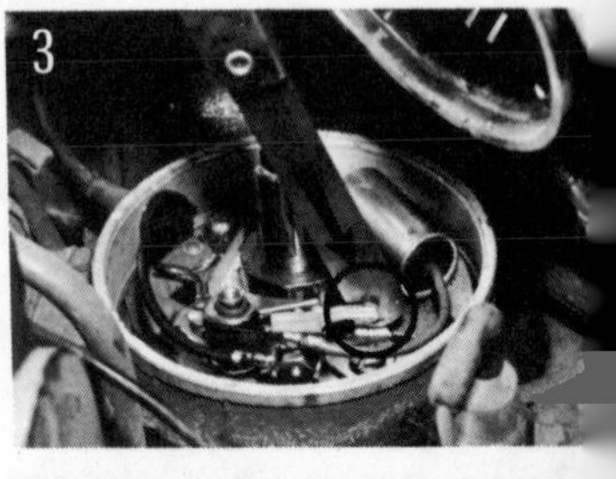

in breaker plate notch near point contacts. Twist screwdriver to open or close points as needed. Tighten screws when correct gap is obtained.

4. Recheck gap after screws are tightened. Readjust if needed.

5. Align tab inside rotor with notch on distributor shaft and push rotor onto shaft. Rotor must be fully seated on shaft.

6. Install distributor cap by aligning tabs on cap with notch on body. Snap retaining clips in place.

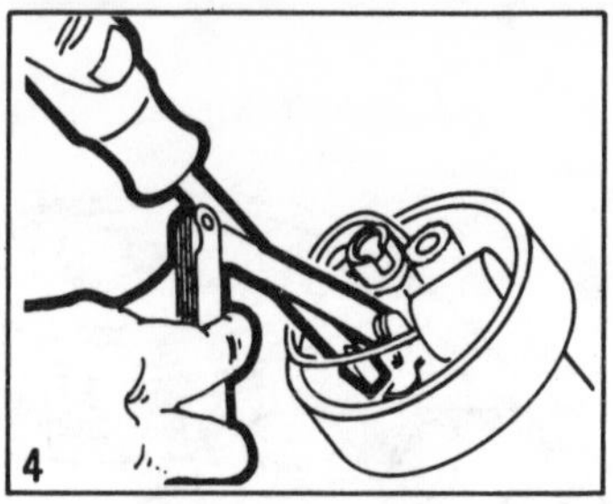

Fuel System

When gasoline is brought from the fuel tank, it mixes with air in the carburetor. This gas/air mixture then enters engine through the intake manifold, passes through the intake valves and is burned in the combustion chamber. The burned exhaust gas is then passed through the exhaust valves to the exhaust system and to the outside air. In order to keep your car's engine running cleanly with minimal pollution, and avoid dangerous carbon monoxide fumes inside the vehicle, certain items should be checked from time to time.

AIR AND CRANKCASE FILTER REPLACEMENT

The large round can that sits on top of the engine holds the air cleaner. Twice a year:

1. Remove wing nut, and remove air cleaner lid.
2. Lift out circular air cleaner cartridge. Discard if more than 12 months old or excessively dirty.
3. Pull crankcase filter out of filter can. Wipe inside of can and lid.
4. Install crankcase filter. Put elbow on filter neck.

EMISSION CONTROL SYSTEMS

An important part of a car's emission control system is the Positive Crankcase Ventilation (PCV) valve and its connecting hose. The PCV valve should be replaced once every 24,000 miles. This device keeps dirt and sludge from forming inside the engine. Make sure all PCV connections are tight. Check that the connecting hoses are clear and not clogged. Replace any brittle or broken hoses.

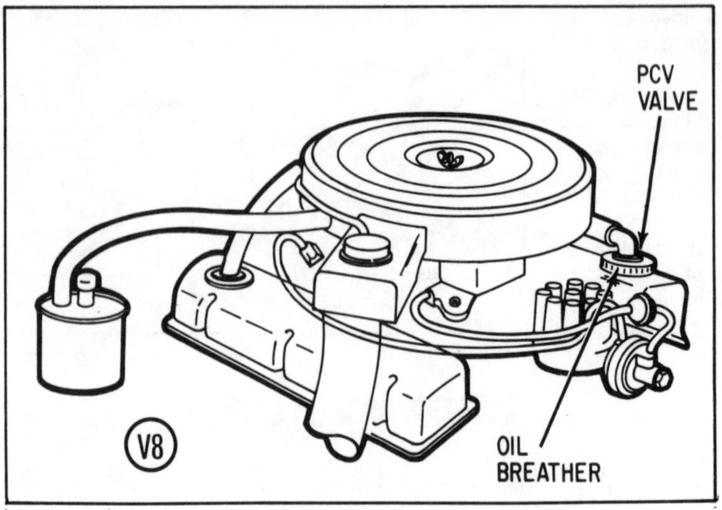

PCV VALVE REPLACEMENT

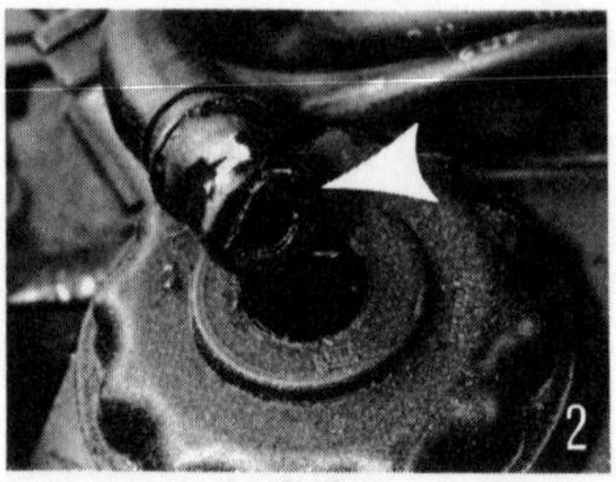

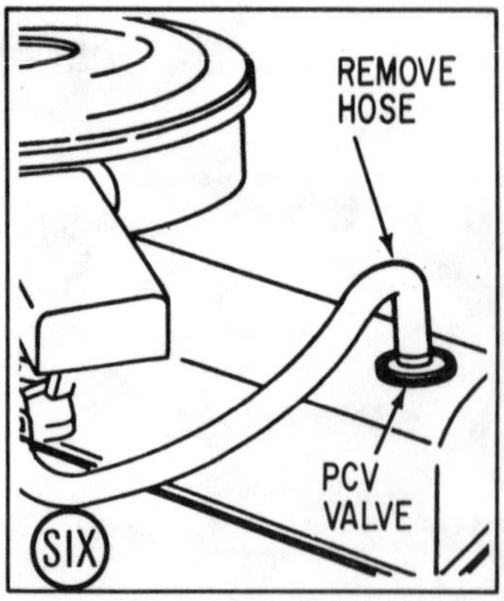

The PCV valve is located on top of the valve cover, in front of the air cleaner.

1. Grasp hose holding PCV valve. Pull straight out.
2. Note where other end of hose is connected. Pull off.
3. Remove PCV valve from hose. Flush hose out with cleaning solvent. Dry hose. Install new PCV valve in hose.
4. Attach end of hose to its original connection and insert PCV valve into proper opening.

FUEL FILTER REPLACEMENT

The fuel filter is located behind the large fuel line inlet nut on the carburetor. Replace the filter every year or 12,000 miles. The fuel filter prevents dirt, rust, and scale from both the gas station's tank and your own fuel tank from reaching the carburetor. A dirty filter will starve the engine and cause poor running.

1. Locate the fuel filter in line to carburetor. Place a rag under the filter housing to collect fuel that will drain out when filter is removed.
2. Pinch the ends of clamps together, and move toward center of hose. Use the smallest possible amount of tension, to avoid damaging the clamps. You can get a special tool designed for this job that will make handling the clamps much easier.
3. Pull the hose off filter and fuel line.
4. Fit an adjustable wrench to the six-sided portion of the filter body, and unscrew it from the carburetor.

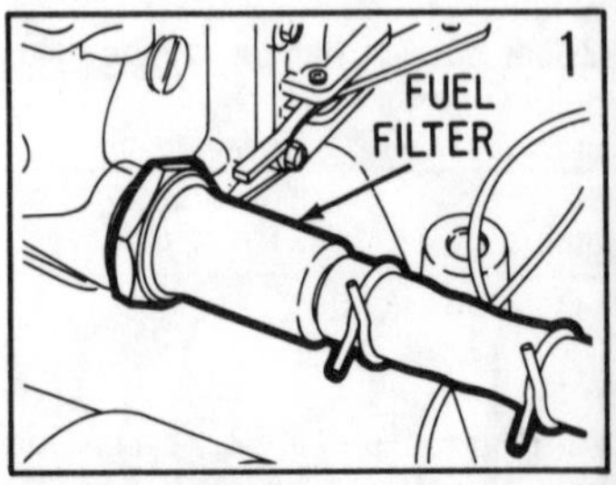

Discard old unit.

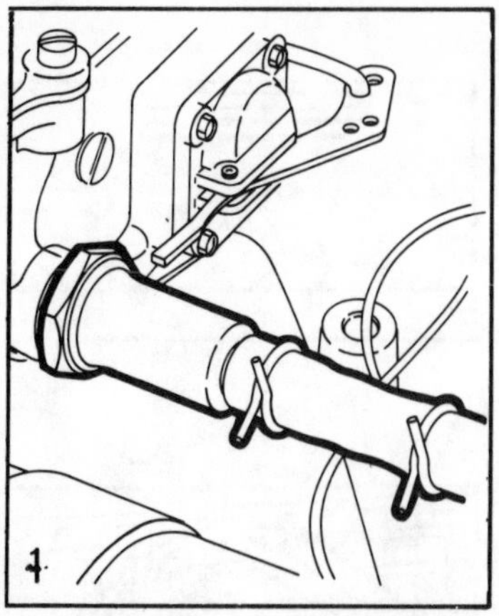

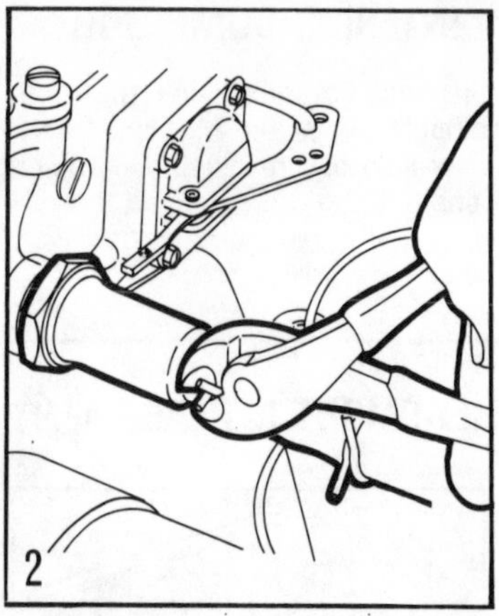

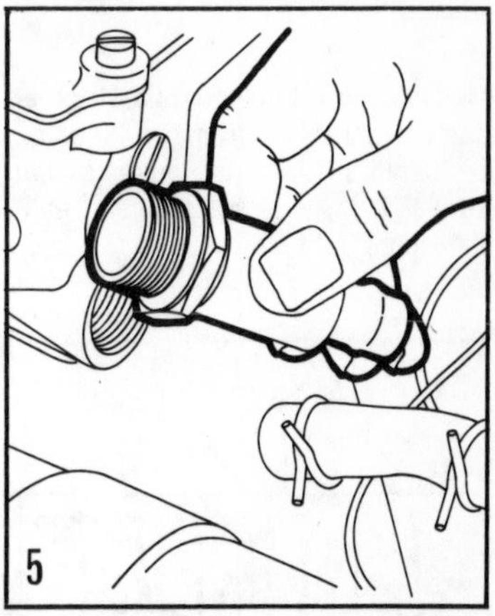

5. Position a new gasket onto the new filter, screw housing into carburetor and tighten.
6. Position new clamps in center of a new hose. If the old clamps are to be reused, make sure they have not lost their tension.
7. Install hose on fuel line and filter. Pinch the clamp ends together, and position well onto fuel line and filter. Note: After replacing filter, remove rag used to catch spilled fuel, and then start engine. Check for leaks.

Addition of a can of carburetor cleaner to the fuel tank occasionally will aid in keeping the entire fuel system clean.

Safety Systems

PARKING LIGHTS, TURN SIGNALS AND STOP LIGHTS

All above lighting functions are performed by dual-element bulbs. Front parking light and turn signal bulbs are mounted in the parking light housing in the grille. To remove the parking light on a Ford, remove the trim ring or lens retaining screws, and remove the ring or lens. Twist the bulb socket counterclockwise to remove the bulb assembly. Push down on the bulb turning counterclockwise to remove the bulb. To replace rear taillight, stop light, turn signal bulbs, raise trunk lid or rear door. Reach socket from inside car. Twist socket counterclockwise in housing. When socket is removed, push down on bulb and turn counterclockwise to remove from socket. Insert new dual-element bulb in correct position (see note) and re-install socket in housing.
NOTE: When inserting new dual element bulb, note that knobs on side of bulb base are different distances from base tip. Match knobs to socket slots for proper fit.

STATION WAGON REAR LIGHTS

To replace lights on station wagons: left side—remove interior trim panel; right side—remove spare wheel & cover. Remove socket twist bulb counterclockwise to remove outside retaining screws; pull assembly out. Remove socket; twist bulb counterclockwise to remove.

SIDE MARKER LIGHTS

Front: Reach up under fender; turn socket counterclockwise to remove. Pull bulb straight out.
Rear: Open trunk; remove trim panel to expose assembly. Twist socket counterclockwise to remove. Pull bulb straight out.

LICENSE PLATE LIGHTS

On sedans, disconnect terminal from inside trunk. Remove retaining screws; remove light assembly. Push in on bulb; turn bulb counterclockwise to remove. On station wagons, disconnect terminal; snap assembly from rear bumper.

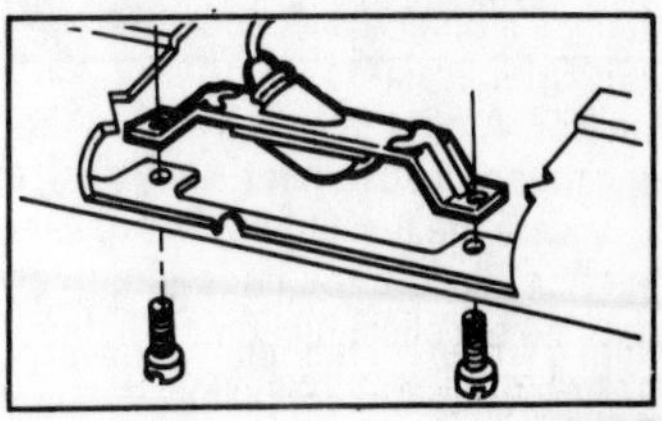

INTERIOR DOME LIGHT

This is a cartridge type bulb. Pry the dome light lens out from the housing. To avoid blowing the fuse, make sure that the doors are closed and the dome light switch is in the OFF position. Carefully lever the bulb straight out of the housing. Insert new bulb and re-install dome light lens.

HEADLIGHT REPLACEMENT

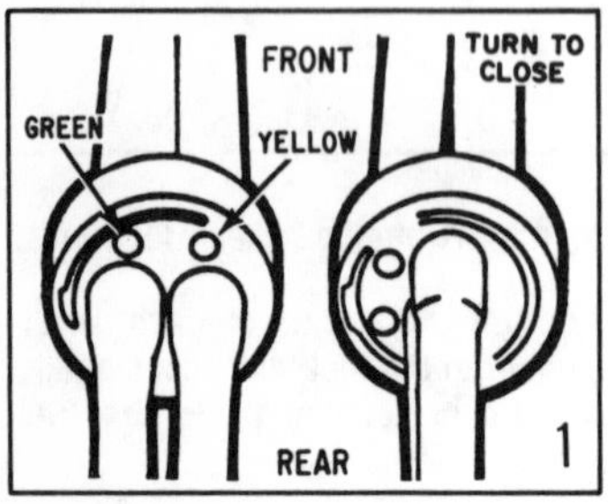

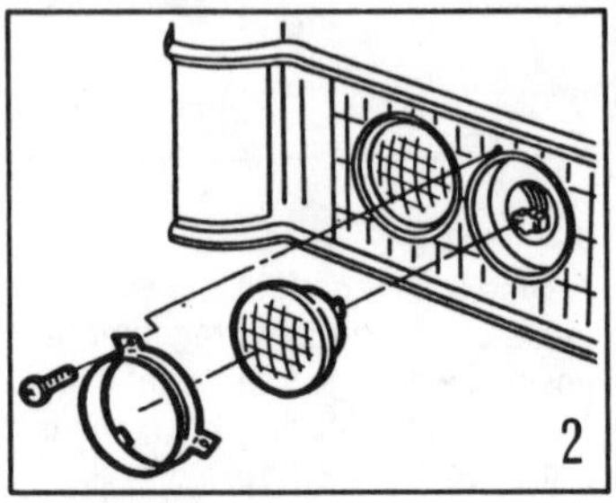

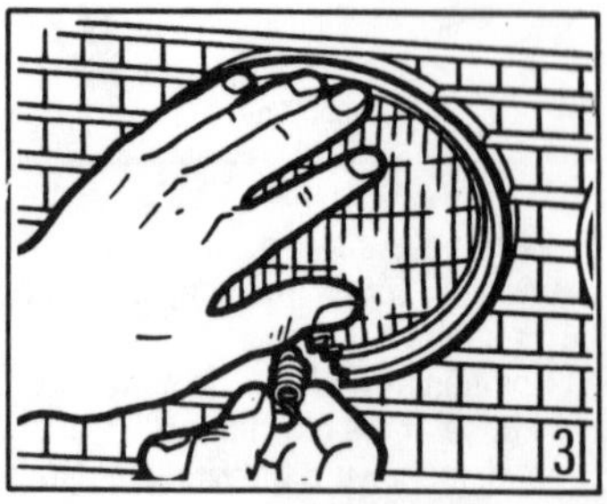

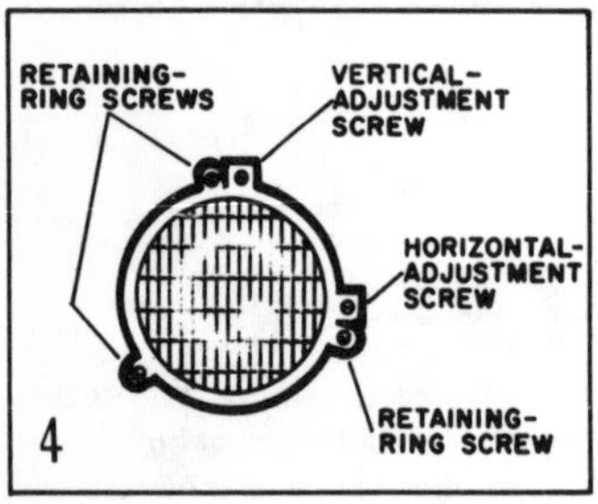

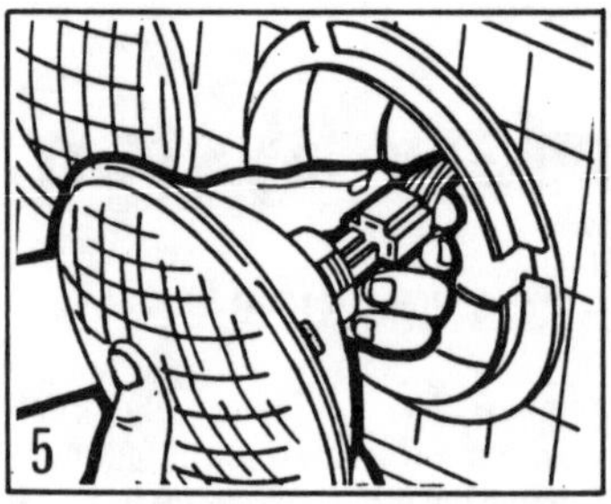

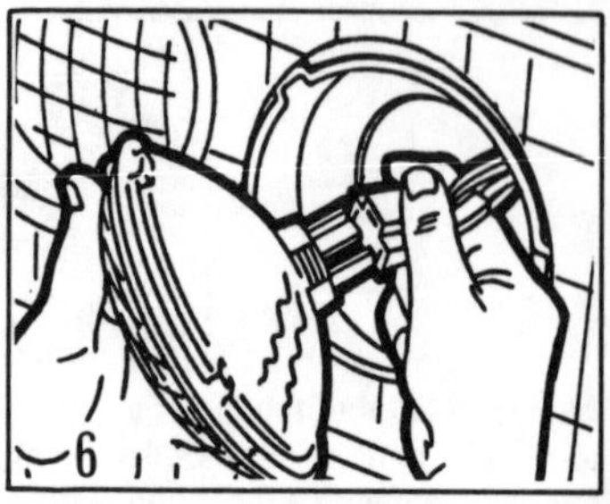

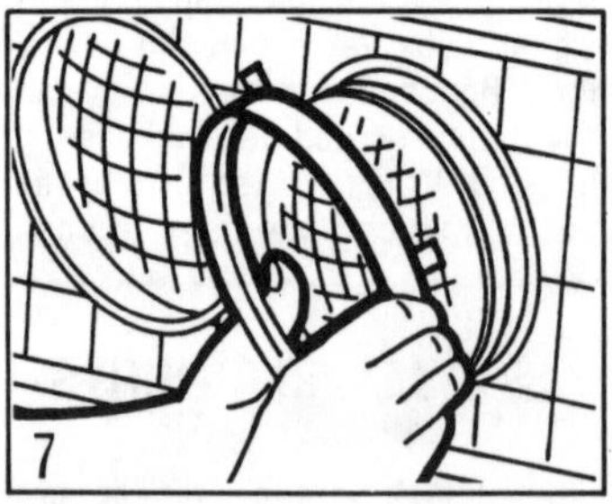

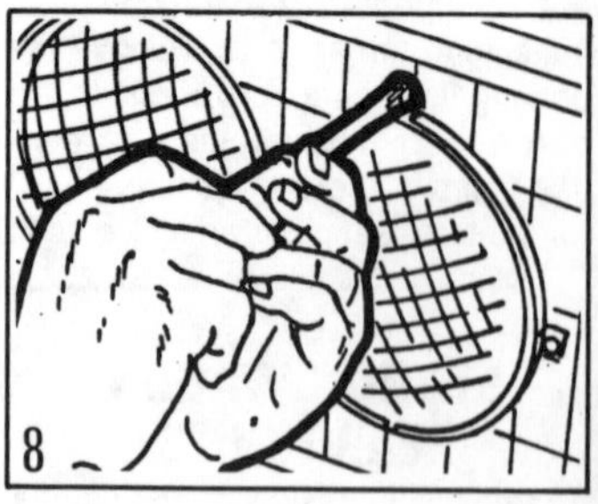

1. If the car is equipped with headlight covers, close the by-pass switch located between the headlight switch and the vacuum motor to open the cover.
2. On some early models remove screws and remove headlight trim ring.
3. On 1970-72 models place hand over headlight assembly to steady it. Unhook the spring from the retaining ring.
4. Remove retainer ring screws, and remove retainer ring. Be careful not to confuse retainer ring screws with the headlight aiming screws.
5. Pull bulb forward, disconnect wire terminal.
6. Attach the wire terminal to the new bulb, and place bulb into position, locating the bulb glass tabs in the positioning slots.
7. Attach retainer ring to assembly with the three retainer screws. On earlier models reconnect spring to retaining ring.
8. Replace trim ring assembly (early model only). If equipped with headlight covers, open by-pass valve to lower covers.

WINDSHIELD WIPER BLADE REPLACEMENT

To replace wiper blade, lift up on spring release tab on wiper arm connector. Pull wiper blade off. Snap new blade into place.
Some Fords are equipped with a pin type wiper blade. To remove this type, insert a screwdriver into the spring opening on the top of the blade and press down while pulling

the wiper blade out. To install this type of blade, simply push the blade onto the arm until it locks.

To replace rubber insert only, press down, away from wiper blade to free it. Slide insert from blade. Insert new wiper. Bend insert upward slightly to engage retaining clips.

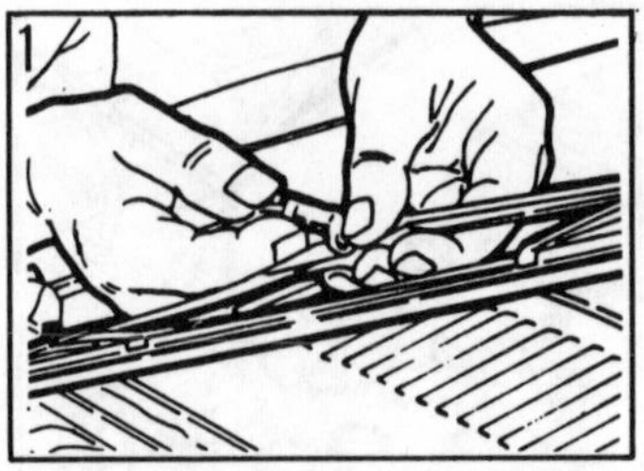

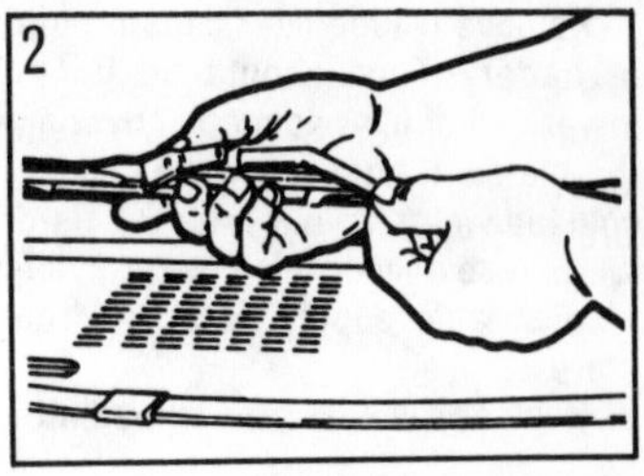

HORN PROBLEMS

If horn sounds and does not stop, this is due to short circuit in wiring. Disconnect wiring connector under hood and have professional service shop check horn wiring circuit.

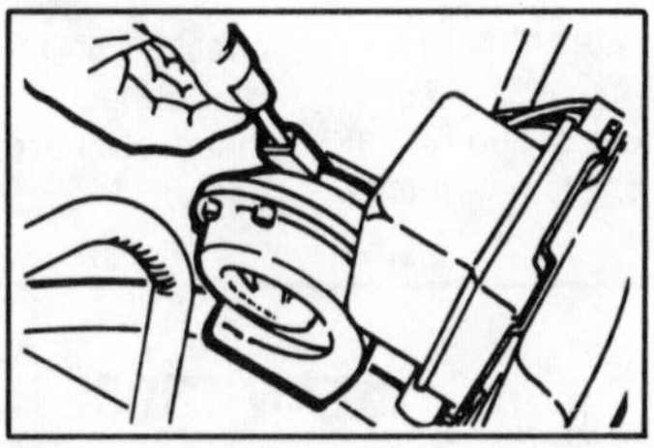

STEERING PROBLEMS

See steering system check in Suspension Section. Check tire pressures. Have a professional service shop check all components in the front end and steering system.

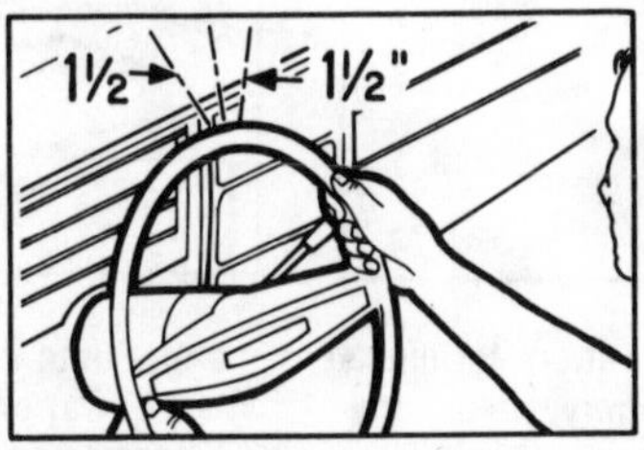

WASHER SYSTEM

If washer fails to squirt properly, raise hood and check system hose connections. Be sure washer fluid container has fluid. Check spout openings for clogging.
Keep container filled with fluid mixture of washer solvent and water. If road spray buildup on windshield is a chronic problem, add 1 tablespoon dishwasher detergent to solvent/water mixture when re-filling container.

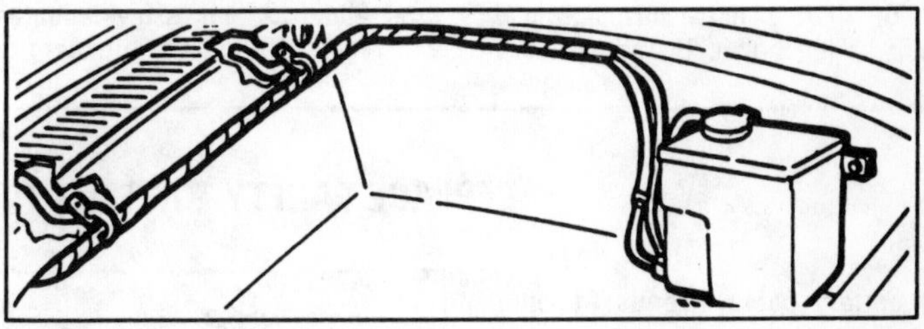

Electrical System

CHECK BATTERY FLUID

To ensure starting ability at all times check your battery condition periodically. You'll need to check battery electrolyte (fluid) level in each of the six cells. Check battery cable connections for tightness and inspect for accumulated corrosion.
SAFETY NOTE: Wear gloves when working on battery.

1. Remove plastic filler caps on top of battery. Fluid should be up to lower end of filler hole and covering the plates. If fluid is low add clean, cold tap water. If your area has hard water, use only distilled water available at auto supply, food or drug stores.
2. Replace any lost caps immediately.
CAUTION: NEVER LIGHT A MATCH OR SMOKE near the top of a battery. Batteries give off explosive hydrogen gas.
NOTE: Battery that often checks low on fluid could mean:
A. Battery is getting old, due for replacement; have charge capacity

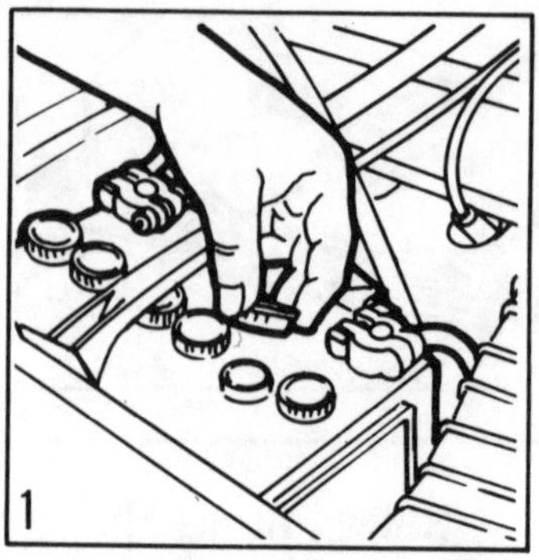

checked at service shop.
B. Connections may be corroded or loose; clean/replace as needed (see below).

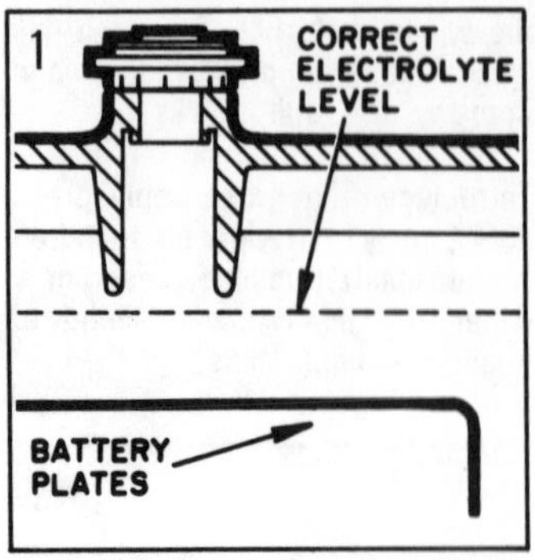

C. Alternator or voltage regulator not functioning properly; this happens far less often than A or B above.

CLEAN THOSE BATTERY TERMINALS

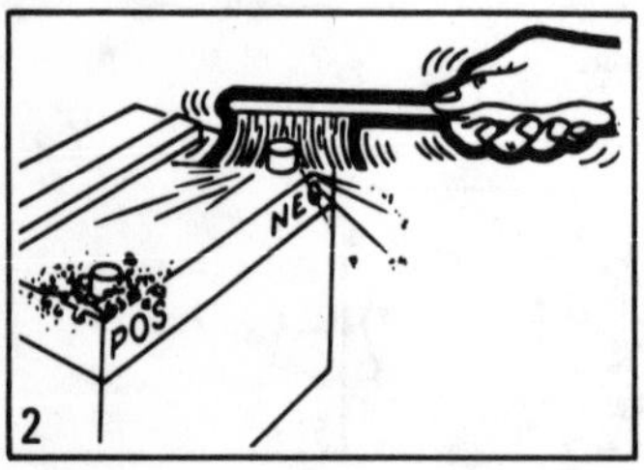

As time goes by, battery terminals build up a dry powdery, whitish material. This material is corrosive and will gradually eat thru battery cables if not cleaned off periodically.
1. Loosen and remove battery connections.
2. Brush off all loose corrosion; use stiff bristle brush. Do not get this material into eyes or on open cuts. Wash off at once.
3. If corrosion build-up is extremely heavy and brushing does not remove all of it, mix 2 tablespoons baking soda to 1 cup water. Pour solution directly onto terminals and connectors. Allow to soak a few minutes and rinse off. Continue brushing to remove all traces of corrosion build-up. Do not allow cleaning solution to enter battery.
4. Replace connectors on battery terminal posts and tighten.
5. Liberally smear battery terminal posts and cable connectors with petroleum jelly.

REPLACE FAULTY BATTERY CABLES

If battery cable strands become frayed, broken or corroded, replace cable immediately. Delay in correcting this condition could lead to sudden failure to start the engine. Can also weaken battery.

1. Loosen and remove battery connections. Clean OFF any corrosion.

2. Disconnect negative cable from its attachment to engine or chassis. Disconnect positive cable from its attachment to starter relay.

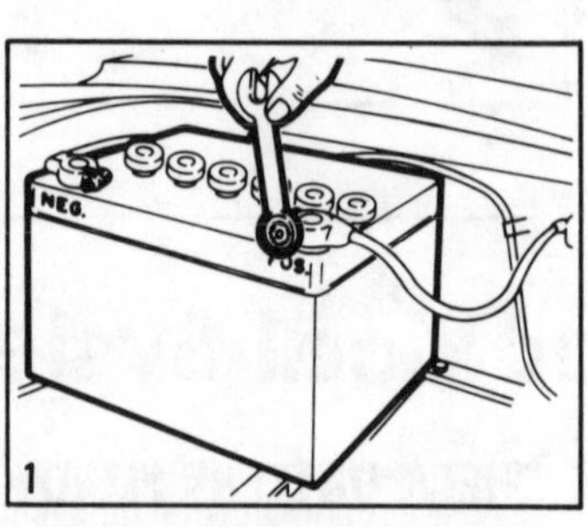

3. Attach new cables making sure positive and negative cables are on

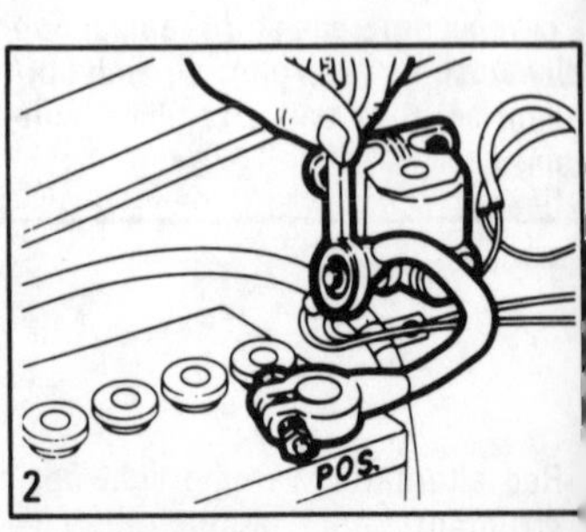

proper terminals. They are not identical.

4. Replace connectors on battery terminal posts and tighten.
5. Liberally smear battery terminal posts and cable connectors with petroleum jelly.

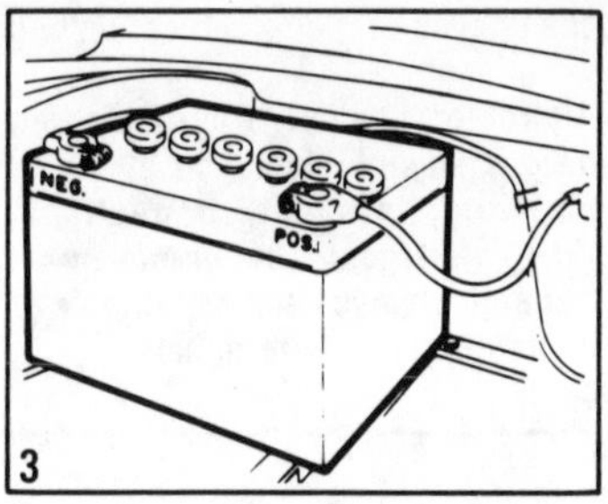

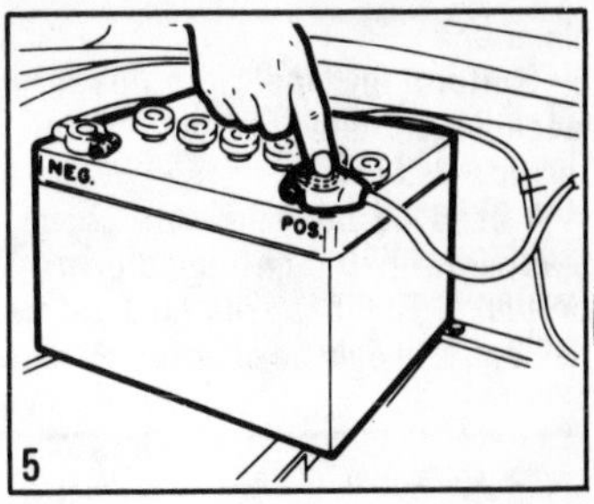

BATTERY HOLDDOWN

The clamp device which holds battery in place should be checked periodically. If loose, tighten. Clean off corrosion buildup. Severely corroded holddown components should be replaced before they break.

ELECTRICAL FUSES

Fuses are a safeguard for a car's electrical system. If a greater current is developed than that which the wiring harness is equipped to handle, the fuses blow out. This stops the possibility of overloading the wires and starting an electrical fire. Spare fuses should always be carried, of the amperage specified by the owner's manual. NEVER REPLACE A FUSE WITH ONE OF A HIGHER AMPERAGE. ALWAYS REPLACE WITH A FUSE OF THE SAME AMPERAGE.

TURN SIGNAL AND 4-WAY FLASHER

Turn signals and 4-way emergency flashers will operate only if: A. All light bulbs are OK. B. Flasher units are not burned out. The car has two flasher units that work independently of each other. Turn signal flasher is located behind instrument panel on extreme left. Emergency flasher is located as illustration shows. To remove either flasher, grasp with fingers, twist and pull flasher toward front of car. Pull connector from flasher. REPLACE ONLY WITH SAME TYPE FLASHER.

ALTERNATOR

Red alternator warning light on instrument panel should glow red when you first turn ignition key. This proves bulb is OK. Alternator warning light should go off when engine is running at normal operating speed. If alternator warning light glows red at operating speed, alternator isn't charging battery properly. Common causes are:
A. Fan belts are loose and slipping on alternator pulley. Tighten or re-

place belts.
B. Battery terminals, cables are loose or corroded. Clean; tighten; replace bad cables.
If A or B do not correct problem, alternator or voltage regulator may be faulty. This happens far less often, and can only be checked by mechanic with proper electrical testing equipment.
Alternator Caution: Alternator can be permanently damaged by short-circuiting terminal connections. When working around or moving alternator, always keep metal tools or engine parts from terminals.

REAR WINDOW DEFOGGER SYSTEM

Do not clean inside of rear window fitted with defogger system with any abrasive material. This could destroy carbon-copper wires. Use only soft rag and mild detergent/water mixture. Dry carefully.

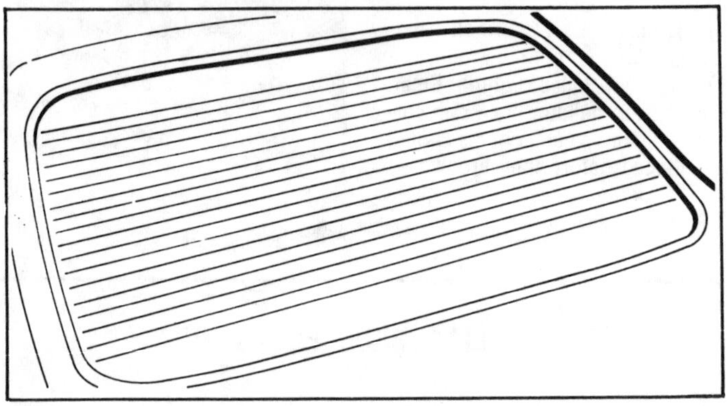

Air Conditioner

CHECK POINTS AND SERVICES

WARNING!—Never attempt to tighten fittings, disassemble or do any work on your car's A/C system. Consult a professional mechanic about A/C system problems and their correction. Your auto air conditioner (A/C) is a delicate, closed system. If air, dirt or water get into it, or if refrigerant escapes, the A/C unit will not cool a car interior. Among things you can do are:
1. Keep condenser grille clean. Check for dirt and debris; periodically remove dead insects, leaves, etc., with stiff bristle brush. Straighten any bent fins—carefully.
2. Keep radiator filled to correct level. (See Cooling System section). If fluid needs to be added, add antifreeze rather than water.
3. Keep radiator coolant at a 50/50 water/antifreeze mixture.

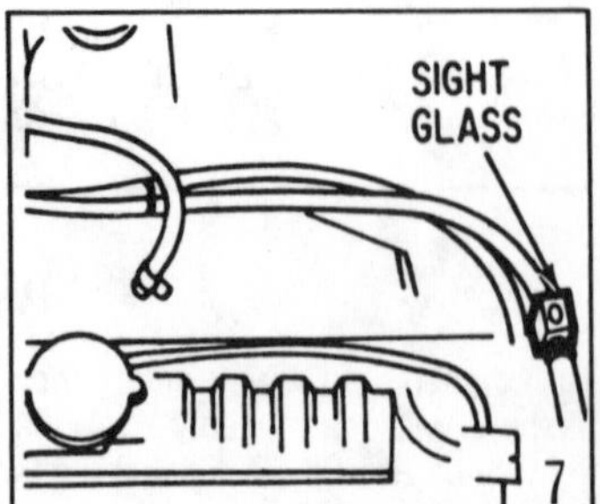

4. Flush cooling system and replace with fresh coolant mixture at least every 24 months. (See Cooling System section).
5. Radiator cap should be tight and sealed properly. If sealing gasket is cracked, cut or worn, replace cap with new 15 lb. unit.
6. Check fan belt tension periodically. (See Cooling System section). Replace glazed, frayed or cut fan belts, before they fail entirely.
7. Check periodically for bubbles in A/C sight glass. The sight glass on Fords was last used in 1974. Sight glass is located in head of receiver/drier vessel. Or in metal tubing leading from top of receiver/drier. Sight

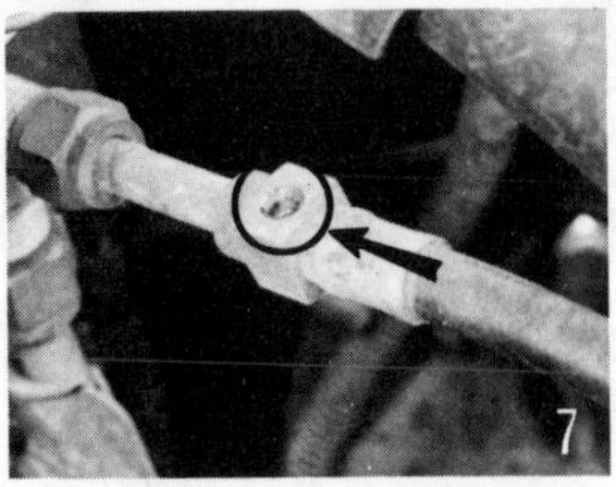

glass is no larger than head of large nail. It may be dirty. Wipe clean for best visibility.

PROCEED AS FOLLOWS:

a) With engine and A/C system running, look for passage of refrigerant in sight glass. You'll be looking for a stream of milky white bubbles as they pass through sight glass. It is best to watch sight glass and have someone else start the car and turn on the A/C system. Allow to run for a few minutes.

b) If you observe no bubbles, and air flow from A/C unit in the car is passing cold air, everything is OK.

c) If no bubbles appear in sight glass, and air flow from the A/C unit in the car is not delivering cold air, the system may be low on refrigerant and could need a re-charge.

d) If bubbles appear, system is low on refrigerant.

e) If you suspect refrigerant loss based on tests performed above, have system checked by a professional A/C service shop. They can confirm refrigerant loss, recharge the system and check for system leakage.

NOTE: Once a week or so, even in winter, run A/C system for about 5 minutes as you drive. This keeps system internally lubricated, prevents hoses hardening.

TUNE-UP SPECIFICATIONS

YEAR	ENGINE No. Cyl. Displacement (cu. in.)	SPARK PLUGS Type	SPARK PLUGS Gap (in.)	DISTRIBUTOR Point Dwell (deg.)	DISTRIBUTOR Point Gap (in.)	IGNITION TIMING Man. Trans.● (deg.)■	IGNITION TIMING Auto Trans.● (deg.)■	IDLE SPEED Man. Trans.● (rpm)▲	IDLE SPEED Auto Trans. (rpm)▲
1970	6-240 (150 hp)	BF-42	.034	35-40	.027	6B	6B	800/500⑩	500
	8-302 (210 hp)	BF-42	.034	24-29	.021	6B	68	575 [800/500⑩]	575 [600/500⑩]
	8-351 (250 hp)	BF-42	.034	24-29	.021	10B	10B	575 [700/500⑩]	575 [600/500⑩]
	8-390 (270 hp)	BF-42	.034	24-29③	.021③	6B	6B	750/500⑩	600/500⑩
	8-428PI (360 hp)	BF-32	.034	24-29	.021	—	6B	—	600/500⑩
	8-429 (320 hp)	BRF-42	.034	24-29③	.021③	—	6B	—	600/500⑩
	8-429 (360 hp)	BRF-42	.034	24-29③	.021③	6B	6B	700/500⑩	600/500⑩
1971	6-240 (140 hp)	BRF-42	.034	33-38	.027	6B	6B	800/500⑩	600/500⑩
	8-302 (210 hp)	BRF-42	.034	24-29	.021	6B	6B	575 [775/500⑩]	575 [600/500⑩]
	8-351W (240 hp)	BRF-42	.034	24-29	.021	6B	6B	575 [775/500⑩]	575 [600/500⑩]
	8-351C (240 hp)	ARF-42	.034	24-29	.021	—	6B	—	625/550⑩
	8-390 (255 hp)	BRF-42	.034	24-29	.021	—	6B	—	600/475⑩
	8-400 (260 hp)	ARF-42	.034	26-31	.017	—	10B(6B)	—	625/500⑩
	8-429PI (370 hp)	ARF-42	.034	27½-29½	.020	—	10B	—	650/500⑩
	8-429 (320 hp)	BRF-42	.034	24-29③	.021③	—	4B	—	600
	8-429 (360 hp)	BRF-42	.034	24-29③	.021③	4B	4B	700	600
1972	6-240 (103 hp)	BRF-42	.034	35-39	.027	—	6B	—	500
	8-302 (140 hp)	BRF-42	.034	26-30	.017	—	6B	—	575 [600/500⑩]
	8-351W (153 hp)	BRF-42	.034	26-30	.017	—	6B		575 [600/500⑩]
	8-351C (163 hp)	ARF-42	.034	26-30	.017	—	6B		600/500⑩
	8-400 (172 hp)	ARF-42	.034	26-30	.017	—	6B	—	625/500⑩
	8-429 (208 hp)	BRF-42	.034	26-30	.017	—	10B	—	600/500⑩
	8-429PI (N.A. hp)	ARF-42	.034	26-30	.017	—	10B	—	650/500⑩
1973	8-351W (153 hp)	BRF-42	.034	26-30	.017	—	6B	—	575 [600/500⑩]
	8-351C (163 hp)	ARF-42	.034	26-30	.017	—	6B	—	600/500⑩
	8-400 (172 hp)	ARF-42	.034	26-30	.017	—	6B	—	625/500⑩
	8-429 (208 hp)	BRF-42	.034	26-30	.017	—	10B	—	600/500⑩
	8-460PI (267, 274 hp)	ARF-42	.034	26-30	.017	—	10B	—	650/500⑩

TUNE-UP SPECIFICATIONS

YEAR	ENGINE No. Cyl. Displacement (cu. in.)	SPARK PLUGS Type	SPARK PLUGS Gap (in.)	DISTRIBUTOR Point Dwell (deg.)	DISTRIBUTOR Point Gap (in.)	IGNITION TIMING Man. Trans.● (deg.)■	IGNITION TIMING Auto Trans.● (deg.)■	IDLE SPEED Man. Trans.● (rpm) ▲	IDLE SPEED Auto Trans. (rpm) ▲
1974	8-351W (162 hp)	BRF-42	.034④	26-30⑥	.014-.020⑥	—	6B		600/500⑩
	8-351C (163 hp)	ARF-42	.044	26-30⑥	.014-0.20⑥	—	14B	—	700/500⑩
	8-400 (170 hp)	ARF-42	.044 (.054)	Electronic		—	12B	—	625/500⑩
	8-460 (195 hp)	ARF-52	.054 (.044)	Electronic		—	14B	—	650(675)/500
	8-460PI (275 hp)	ARF-52	.054	Electronic		—	10B	—	700/500⑩
1975	8-351M (148, 150 hp)	ARF-42	.044	Electronic		—	8B	—	700
	8-400 (144, 158 hp)	ARF-42	.044	Electronic		—	6B⑦	—	625
	8-460 (218 hp)	ARF-52	.044	Electronic		—	14B	—	650
	8-460PI (226 hp)	ARF-52	.044	Electronic		—	14B	—	650
1976	8-351M (All hp)	ARF-42/52⑧	.044	Electronic		—	⑧	—	650(650)/675⑧⑩
	8-400 (All hp)	ARF-42/52⑧	.044	Electronic		—	⑧	—	650(625)
	8-460 (All hp)	ARF-52	.044	Electronic		—	8/14B ⑧ @ 650	—	650
	8-460PI (226 hp)	ARF-52	.044	Electronic		—	14B@ 650	—	650
1977	8-351 8-400 8-460	See Underhood Specifications Sticker							

▲ Adjust automatic transmissions in Drive (AMC/Ford/GM) or Neutral (Chrysler), all manual transmissions are adjusted in Neutral.
● Figure in parentheses indicate California engine.
■ All figures are Before Top Dead Center.

NOTE: The underhood specifications sticker often reflects tune-up specification changes made in production. Sticker figures must be used if they disagree with those in this chart.

① Not used
② A/C off
③ For engines equipped with single diaphragm distributors adjust point dwell to 26-31 degrees and point gap to .017 inch
④ .044 on California models and all cars using Solid State Ignition
⑤ Not used
⑥ Solid State Ignition used on all engines nationwide on cars assembled after May, 1974.
⑦ 8B with 3.25:1 rear axle, Code 9 or R on Certification label
⑧ Depends on emission equipment, check underhood specification sticker
⑨ Not used
⑩ In all cases where two figures are separated by a slash, the first is for idle speed with solenoid energized and the automatic transmission in Drive, while the second is for idle speed with solenoid disconnected and automatic transmission in Neutral. Brackets around figures separated by a slash indicates that some engines were equipped with solenoids, while others were not. If there is no solenoid on the engine, set the idle sped to the figure not in brackets.

TDC Top Dead Center
W Windsor
— Not applicable
B Before Top Dead Center
C Cleveland
M Modified Cleveland
PI Police Interceptor
N.A. Not available

CAPACITIES

YEAR	ENGINE No. Cyl. Displacement (cu. in.)	ENGINE OIL Add 1 qt. with New Filter	TRANSMISSION Pts. to Refill after Draining MANUAL 3-speed	MANUAL 4-speed	AUTOMATIC	DRIVE AXLE (pts.)	COOLING SYSTEM with Heater (qts.)	COOLING SYSTEM with Air Cond. (qts.)
1970	6-240	4	3.5	—	See chart below	5	14.4	14.4
	8-302	4	3.5	—		4.5	15.4	15.6
	8-351	4	3.5	—		4.5	16.5	16.9
	8-390	4	3.5	—		4.5	20.1	20.5
	8-428P	4	—	—		4.5	19.7	19.7
	8-429	4	—	—		4.5	18.6	19.0

CAPACITIES

YEAR	ENGINE No. Cyl. Displacement (cu. in.)	ENGINE OIL Add 1 qt. with New Filter	TRANSMISSION Pts. to Refill after Draining MANUAL 3-speed	MANUAL 4-speed	AUTOMATIC	DRIVE AXLE (pts.)	COOLING SYSTEM with Heater (qts.)	COOLING SYSTEM with Air Cond. (qts.)
1971	6-240	4	3.5	—		5	14.1	14.1
	8-302	4	3.5	—		4.5	15.2	15.6
	8-351	4	3.5	—		4.5	16.3	16.7
	8-390	4	—	—		4.5	20.3	26.3
	8-400	4	—	—		4.5	17.6	17.6
	8-429	4	—	—		4.5	18.8	18.8
1972	6-240	4	—	—		4	14.2	14.2
	8-302	4	—	—		4.5	15.2	15.2
	8-351	4	—	—		4.5	16.3	16.3
	8-400	4	—	—		5	17.7	18.3
	8-429	4	—	—		5	18.8	19.5
1973	8-351	4	—	—		4.5	16.3	16.3
	8-400	4	—	—		5	17.7	18.3
	8-429	4	—	—		5	18.8	19.5
1974	8-351	4	—	—		4.5	16.3	①
	8-400	4	—	—		5	18.0	18.0
	8-460	4	—	—		5	19.4	19.4
1975-76	8-351	4	—	—		4.5	17.1	17.6
	8-400	4	—	—		4.5	17.1	17.6
	8-460	4	—	—		5.0	18.5	18.5
1977	8-351							
	8-400							
	8-460							

AUTOMATIC TRANSMISSION REFILL CAPACITIES (Pts.)

Year	Code ▲	Capacities
'70-'72	XY	22
'70-'72	W	20.5
'70-'77	U, Z	25.5

▲ Transmission code can be found on the serial number plate or the vehicle certification label.

① 351W—17.1 qts; 351C—16.3 qts; 351M—16.3 qts
P Police
—— Not applicable

Service Record

Date/Mileage	Service	Next Due

Gremlin/Hornet

Lubrication and Oil Change

BRAKE FLUID LEVEL CHECK

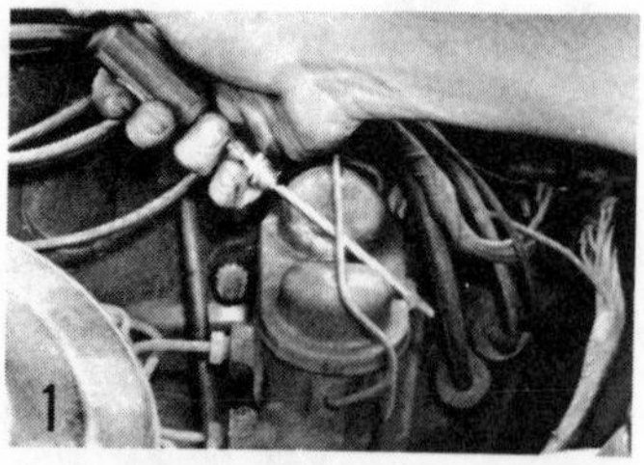

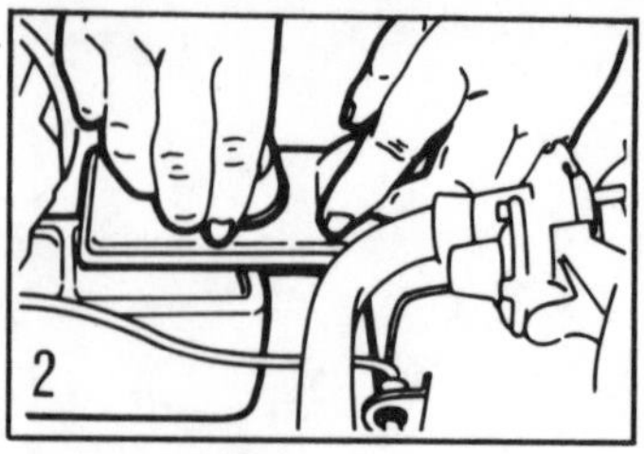

Check brake fluid level in master cylinder every three months . . . sooner if braking feels inadequate. Add when low. Recommended grade: DOT 3.

Master cylinder is located under hood on left side. It is oblong container about 6" long with cap held down by wire clip. Check brake fluid level as follows:

1. Pry wire retaining clip off cap top with screwdriver.
2. Remove cap and gasket by lifting up.
3. Fluid level should be within ¼ inch of top rim. If lower than this, add fresh fluid to appropriate level.

DO NOT OVERFILL

4. Replace cap and gasket; secure retaining clip over cap. If fluid level was low, check again in a few days.
5. If fluid repeatedly checks low, there is a leak somewhere in the system. See SAFETY SYSTEMS—WHEEL CYLINDER CHECK. Have mechanic check further. Neglect can be dangerous.

MANUAL TRANSMISSION FLUID LEVEL CHECK

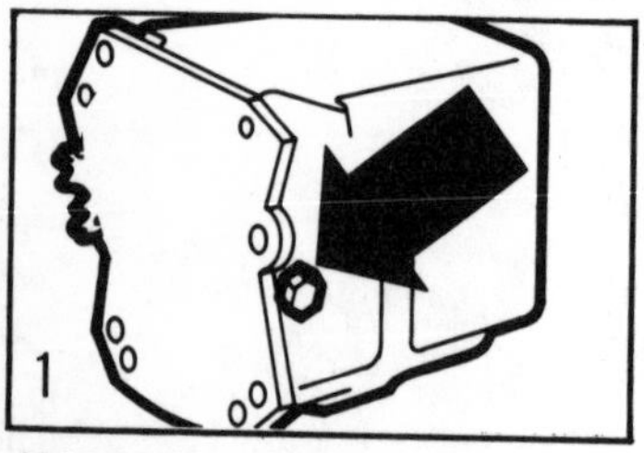

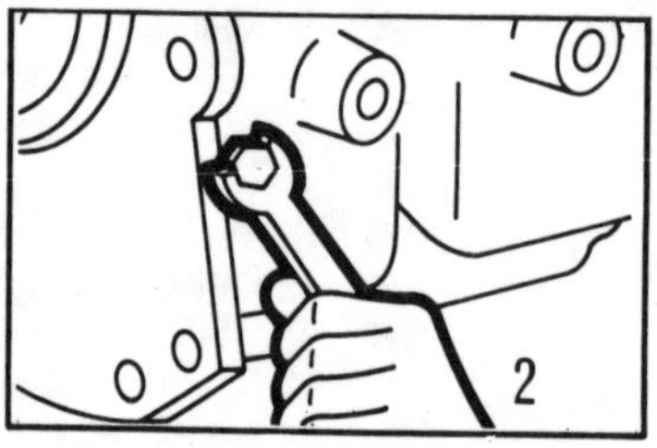

AMC SAYS . . . check manual transmission fluid every 6000 miles. Car should be parked level. Recommended grade: Standard Transmission Fluid (SAE 90).

TOOLS NEEDED . . . fluid level check device (make from coat hanger wire; bend at 90° angle 2" from end); adjustable wrench; bulb syringe.

1. Locate transmission fluid filler plug on right side of transmission housing from underneath car.
2. Wipe road dirt from filler plug area before loosening. Remove plug with adjustable wrench.
3. Insert fluid level check device. Fluid level should be right up to bottom edge of filler hole.
4. Add fluid as needed with hand bulb syringe.

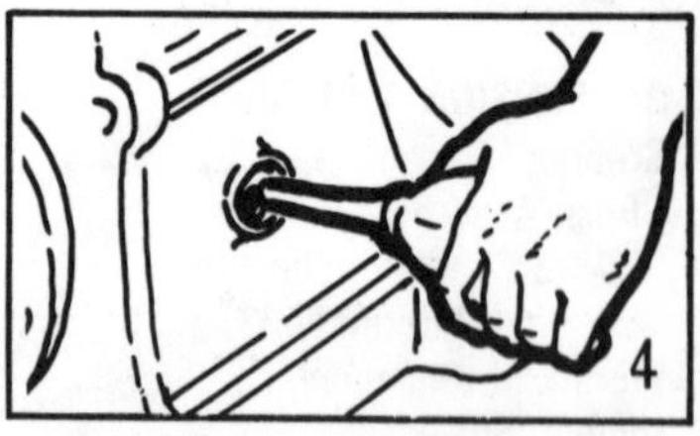

5. Replace filler plug; tighten.

AUTOMATIC TRANSMISSION FLUID LEVEL CHECK

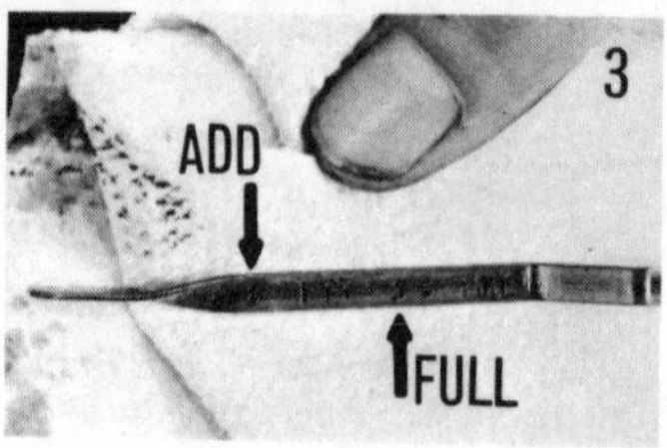

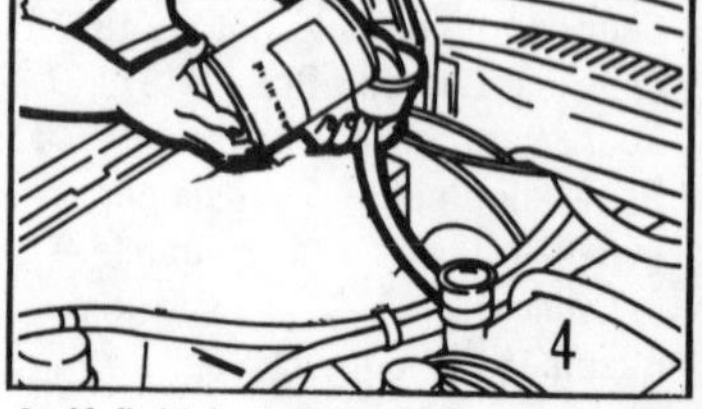

AMC SAYS . . . check automatic transmission fluid DEXRON® level every 6000 miles. Recommended grade: DEXRON® (Type A).

TOOLS . . . Long neck filler funnel.

1. Engine must be warmed up and running. Place shift lever in PARK position.

2. Pull out dipstick. Wipe clean. Push dipstick all the way back in; remove it again.

3. If fluid is below ADD mark, add ATF to bring level up. DO NOT OVERFILL.
4. Add ATF thru transmission dipstick hole by means of long-neck filler funnel.

REAR AXLE LUBRICANT

AMC SAYS . . . check rear axle lube level every 6000 miles. Recommended grade: Hypoid gear lube (SAE 90).

TOOLS . . . adjustable hand wrench; fluid level check device (made from coat hanger wire; bend at 90° angle 2" from end); bulb syringe.

1. Locate filler plug on forward side of rear axle housing.
2. Wipe plug area clean; remove plug with wrench.
3. Insert wire level check device; remove. Adequate fluid level should show lubricant on last ¼-inch of wire.
4. If fluid level is low, add as needed, with a hand bulb syringe, until level shows on last ¼-inch of wire.
5. Replace filler plug; tighten.

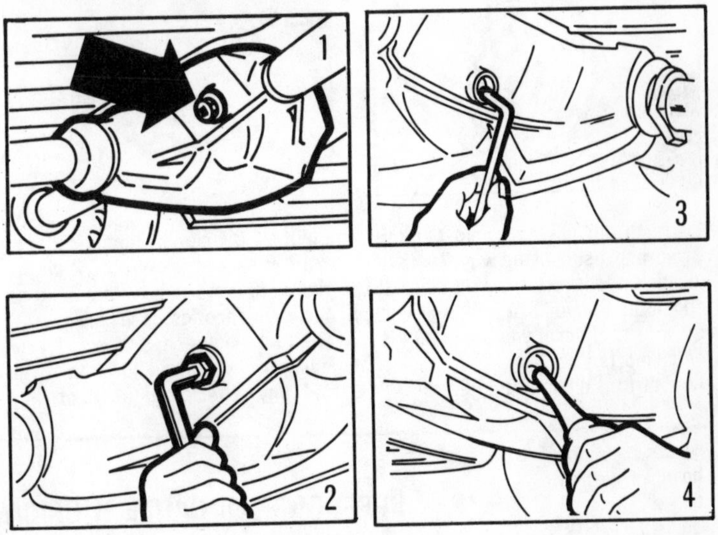

OIL AND FILTER CHANGE

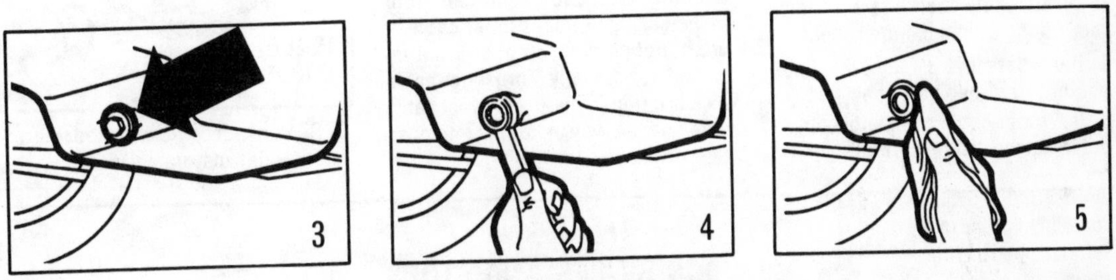

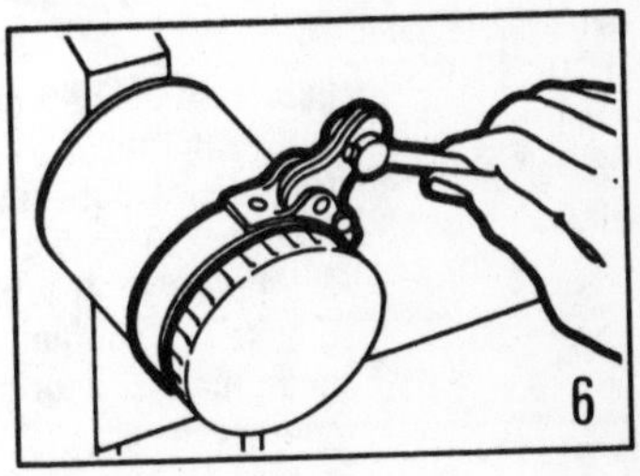

AMC SAYS . . . Change oil and filter every 6000 miles. Recommended grade: MS or SE (check owner's handbook). Check oil level at least once a week.

TOOLS & MATERIALS . . . adjustable hand wrench; medium size screwdriver; oil filter removal wrench; drain pan for old oil (at least 5 qt. capacity); oil pouring spout; 5 qt. oil; new oil filter; oil and lubricants as specified below.

SAFETY TIP . . . use work gloves.

1. If engine is cold, start up and idle for about 5 minutes.
2. Park car on level ground. Turn engine off.
3. Locate oil drain plug on underside of engine. Place drain pan under plug.
4. Remove drain plug with wrench. Let ALL dirty oil drain out.
5. Wipe plug and area around drain hole clean. Replace drain plug; tighten it.
6. Locate oil filter. Move drain pan under filter. Loosen filter with oil filter wrench. Unscrew; remove filter by hand.
7. Smear fresh oil over surface of rubber gasket (washer) of new filter. Install new filter by hand only. Do NOT use wrench. Turn filter until gasket makes contact. Tighten an additional half turn only . . . NO MORE.
8. Locate oil filler tube on top of engine. Remove cap.
9. Punch oil pouring spout into top of oil can. Pour all cans of new oil into filler tube. Wipe filler cap clean and replace it. Be sure to re-attach all hoses. (NOTE: If filler cap is very dirty, rinse in turpentine Dry before replacing.)
10. Check new oil level at dipstick. Pull out dipstick, wipe clean.

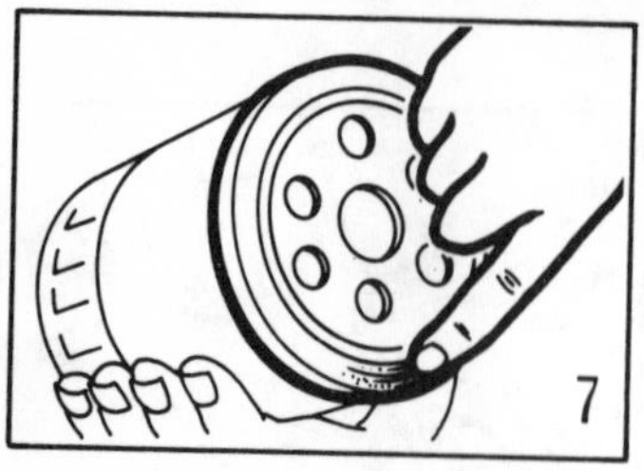

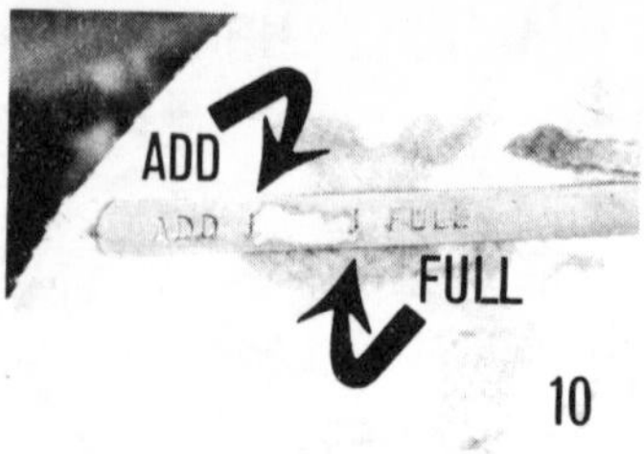

11. Push dipstick back into engine. Be sure to insert all the way. Remove dipstick and check new oil level. It should be above "SAFE" line. If not, be sure to check if you put in all the oil called for.
12. Start up engine and idle for 3-5 minutes. Oil signal light on instrument panel will glow red when engine is first started. Light should go out in 30 seconds or less.
13. Stop engine and check for oil leaks at drain plug and filter. If you find any, check tightness of plug and/or filter, also for condition of filter gasket to see that it has not become pinched or damaged when installing. Recheck oil level, which should now be at "SAFE".

SPEEDOMETER CABLE LUBRICATION

If speedometer pointer tends to quiver or jump, or if unit makes a low, rasping sound, lubrication may be needed.

1. Locate cable shaft attachment directly behind speedometer dial.
2. Press flat surface; pull cable back and out from behind panel.
3. Pull inner cable completely out of outer casing. Note carefully which end is top. Check for wear or frayed strands. If damaged, replace inner cable with new one.
4. Apply generous amount of speedometer cable lubricant into cable casing. Replace inner cable in shaft, noting that top end is not inserted accidentally. Turn inner cable as it is being re-inserted. Twist cable when all the way in, to lock into position at lower end.

5. Re-connect cable to speedometer head under instrument panel.

DOOR HINGES AND STOPS

(lubricate every 6 months)
1. Brush any dirt accumulations from door hinges and stops. Use old tooth brush or rag.
2. Apply dab of white polyethylene grease to door hinges, trunk hinges, hood hinges, door stops.

DOOR LOCKS

(lubricate every 6 months)
1. Insert door key half way into lock.
2. Spray aerosol lock lubricant into lock.
3. Push key rest of way into lock; turn back and forth several times.

Cooling System

IT IS RECOMMENDED . . . that radiator coolant (water/antifreeze mixture) level be checked once or twice a month. Do this when engine is cold. Check more often if you do a lot of hard driving.
Keep coolant up to recommended level in radiator. If coolant checks frequently low, look for leaks. Tighten all hose clamps occasionally. For best results, keep a 50/50 water/antifreeze mixture year round. Change complete coolant mixture every 24 months.

CAUTION: If you must check coolant in a hot engine, cover radiator cap with thick rag before releasing. Remove cap slowly . . . press down and turn.

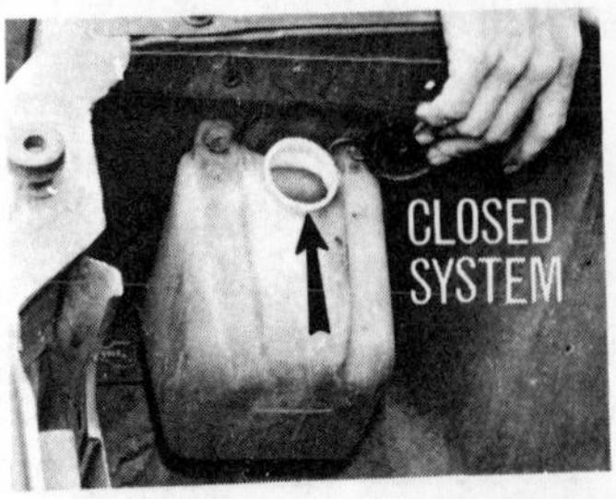

REPLACING THE THERMOSTAT

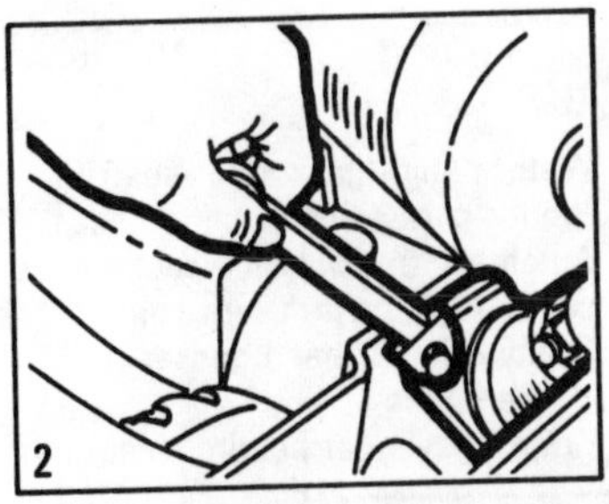

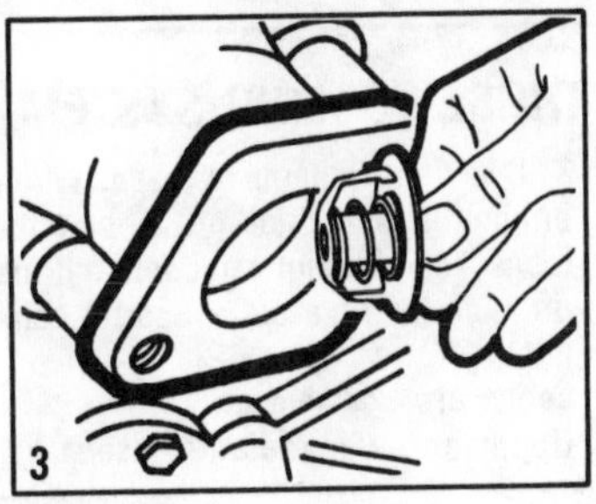

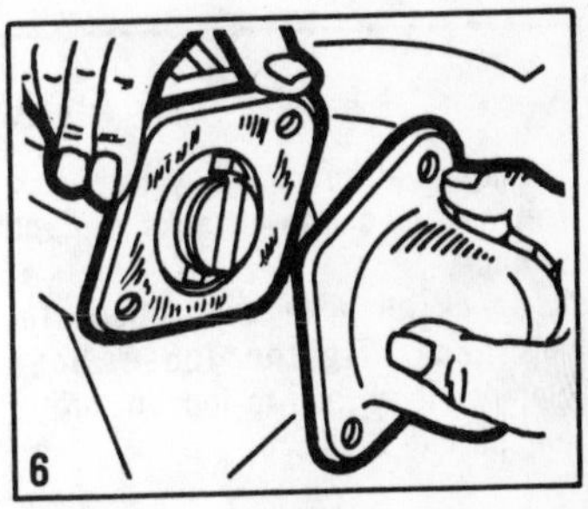

A faulty thermostat will usually cause engine overheating. Replace with new thermostat.

TOOLS AND MATERIALS . . .
New thermostat
Gasket sealer
Adjustable wrench

1. Drain radiator of about half its coolant. (See Hose Replacement section)
2. Loosen and remove the retaining bolts and lift thermostat housing off the engine.

NOTE: If you're careful it won't be necessary to remove radiator hose.

3. Remove old thermostat.
4. Scrape thermostat housing flange and engine block surface to remove old gasket debris.
5. Drop new thermostat into place—spring down.
6. Install new gasket with sealer applied to both sides.
7. Replace thermostat housing and tighten both retaining bolts.

RADIATOR CAP CHECK

Check radiator cap occasionally for worn or cracked gasket. If cap doesn't seal properly, fluid will be lost and engine will overheat. Replace worn cap with new cap rated 13 to 15 lbs. pressure.

FAN BELT ADJUSTMENT

The fan belt not only drives the radiator fan, it turns the water pump and drives the alternator. Another belt drives the power steering pump. It's easy to see that the condition and proper tension of the belts are

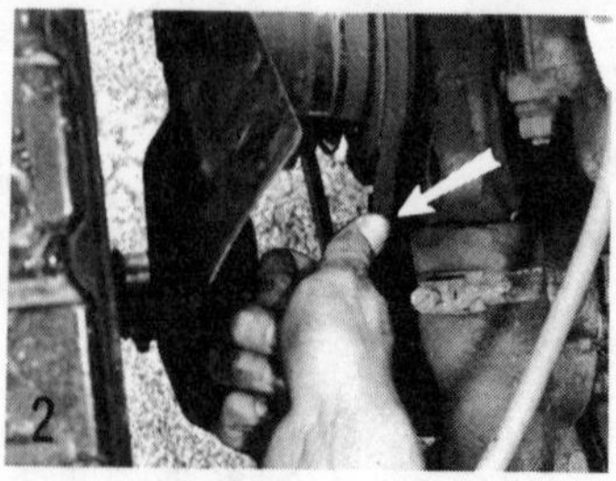

vital, since engine cooling, electrical power, and steering depend on them. The belts deserve an occasional look and tension check.

1. Inspect fan belt occasionally. If worn, frayed or cracked on inner driving surface, replace.

CAUTION: An overtightened belt may damage alternator and water pump, or power steering pump bearings.

2. Check tension occasionally. Press thumb at midpoint of belt span between pulleys. If belt depresses more than ½ inch, tightening is needed. A too-loose belt will not drive alternator and pumps effectively.

3. Adjust to proper tension of ¼ inch deflection. Adjust as follows:

A. Loosen mounting bolts at top and bottom so alternator can pivot on lower bolt and upper bolt can slide in bracket.

B. Pull alternator out slightly to put tension on belt, and hold while tightening upper bolt.

C. Check tension. Repeat adjustment as necessary.

D. When tension is correct, tighten lower bolt.

FIND THOSE COOLING SYSTEM LEAKS

1. Inspect all hoses. If any are weak, soft in spots or show cracks, replace at once.

2. Check all hose connections for tightness. Tighten loose hose clamps; they tend to loosen due to engine vibration.

3. If radiator steams or hisses when engine is switched off, check for leaks. Look for signs of coolant drips on radiator or around header tank joint.

Leaks are possible at:

Upper or lower radiator hoses
Water pump (gaskets or seal)
Heater core or connecting hoses
Automatic transmission cooler lines
Faulty radiator pressure cap
Faulty cylinder head gasket
Choke hoses
Cracked cylinder head or block

Due to the number of joints, cooling systems have many places to leak from. Check clamp tightness. If leaks persist an anti-leak additive in the coolant may help. Noisy water pumps may benefit from a lubricating additive in the coolant. Use a cooling system cleaner when flushing during a drain and refill job. It will help remove rust and scale. Remember – additives will not cure chronic problems. But they will effect a short-term remedy in many cases.

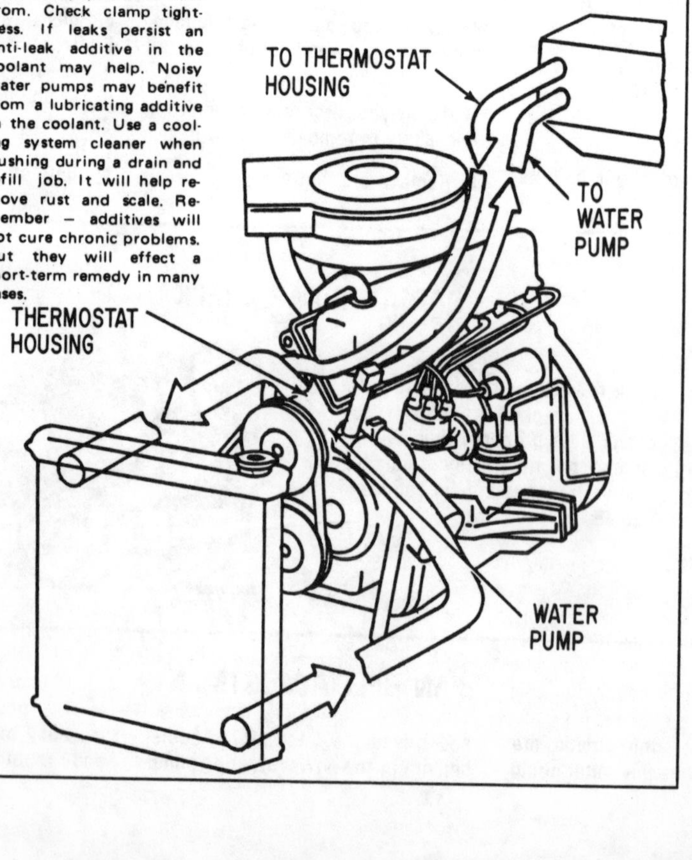

ENGINE OVERHEATING

YOUR CAR OVERHEATS BECAUSE	TO CORRECT IT
radiator coolant is too low	fill to correct level; check for leaks
fan belt is too loose	adjust tension or replace frayed belt
of a broken or leaking hose	replace hose; tighten clamps
thermostat does not function	replace thermostat
radiator is plugged with sediment	consult professional mechanic (may need radiator removal and servicing, or total replacement)
water pump does not function properly	replace water pump (may make squeaky noise; or leak at pump shaft)

HOSE REPLACEMENT

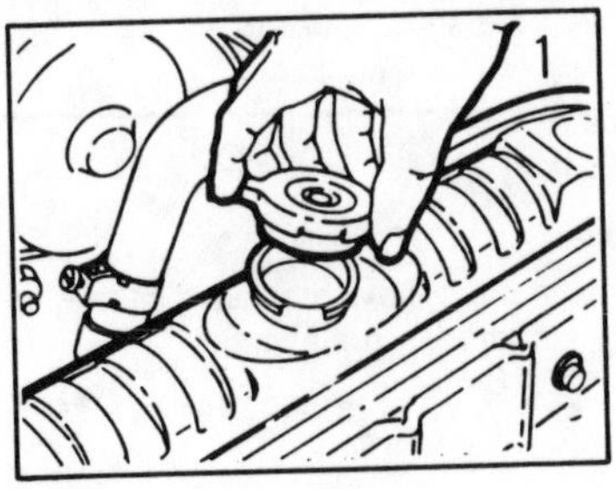

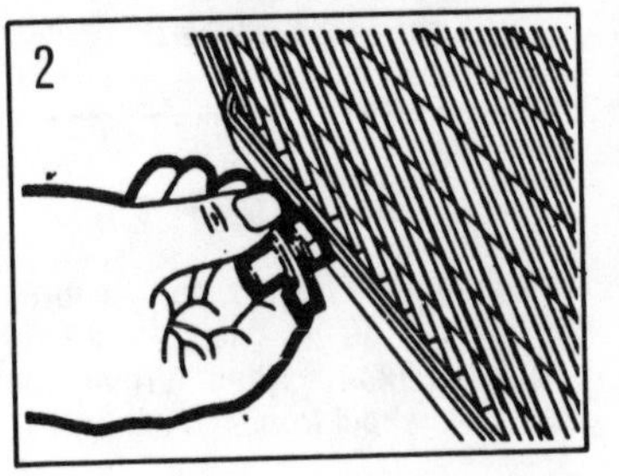

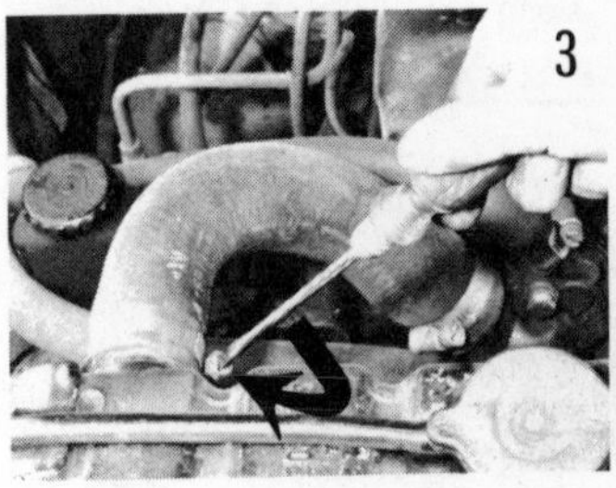

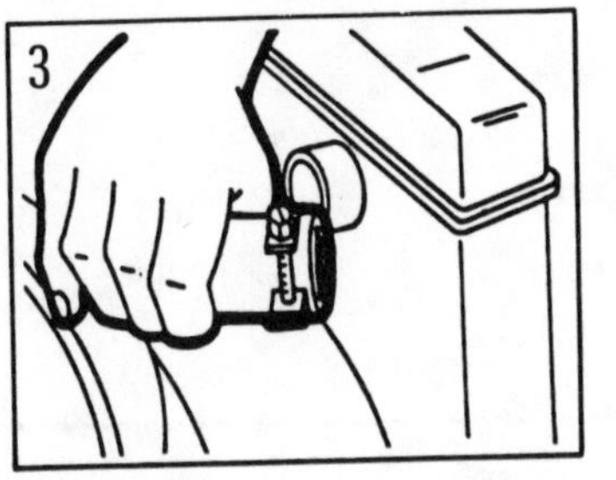

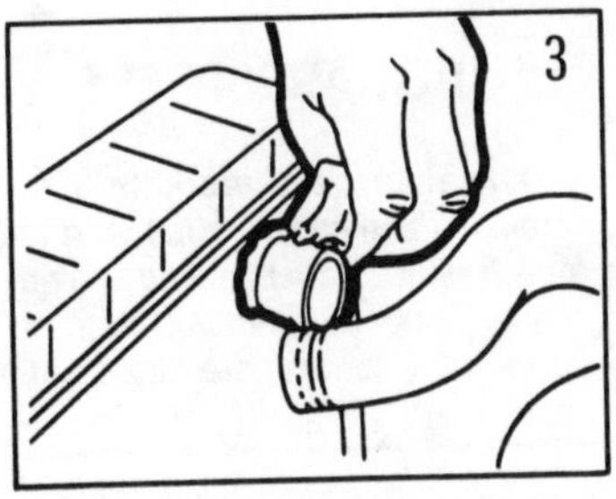

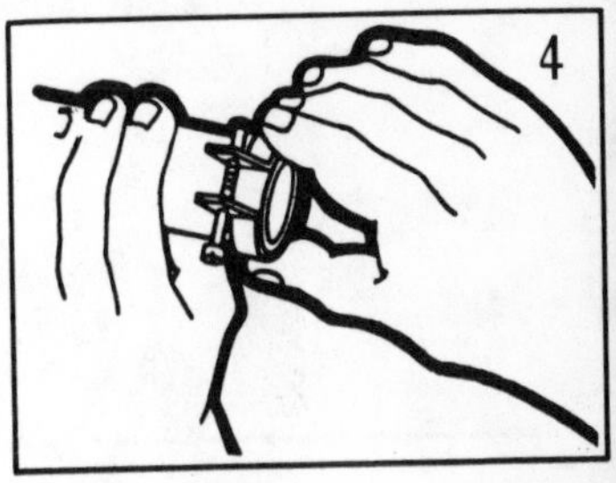

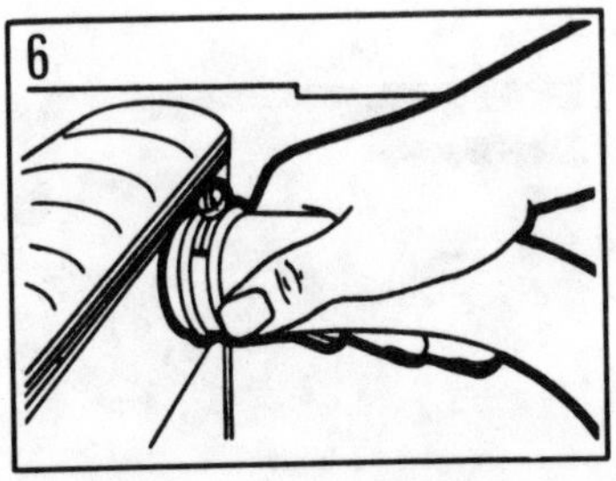

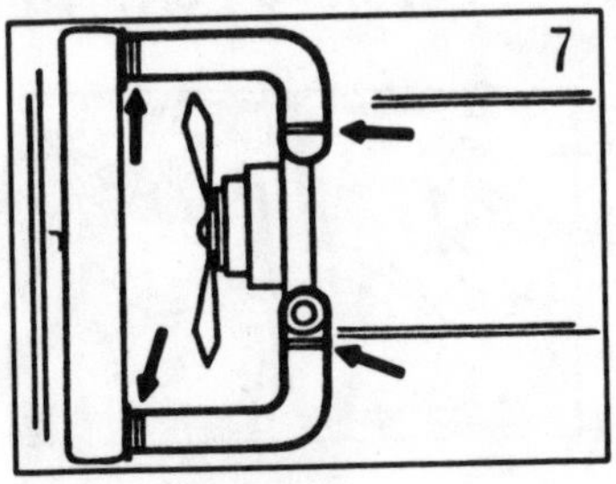

Coolant drain and refill work may be done alone; when changing hoses, coolant must also be drained as part of job. Discard all hoses with cracks or soft spots. Check hose clamps for tightness and good condition.

1. Remove radiator cap. Open radiator petcock. Drain coolant into catch basin. If near 24 months old, discard old coolant.
2. Petcock is located at the bottom of the radiator.
3. Wipe all hose connections clean. Use emery cloth to get rid of residue.
4. If old hose clamps are badly rusted or damaged, replace with new units.
5. Slip clamps over each hose end. Slip hose ends all the way onto cleaned up hose connections.
6. Place hose clamp ¼ inch from hose end. Tighten. Close petcock. Refill with 50/50 coolant/water mix.
7. Start engine; allow to warm up. Check for coolant leaks.
8. Road test car; watch for temperature warning light.

Suspension and Tires

The front wheels mount and rotate on the spindles, which are attached to upper and lower ball joints. Upper and lower control arms link the spindles to the car's frame, and permit the frame and body to move up and down in relation to the position of the wheels with a hinge effect. The spring is mounted to the top of the upper control arm on either side, with the upper end located by the top of a spring housing. A shock absorber is located inside each spring. The rear suspension consists of leaf springs suspending the solid rear axle. The rear shock absorbers are mounted ahead of the rear axle on either side.

Your car's suspension system consists of wheels, tires, springs, shock absorbers, sway (or stabilizer) bars, ball joints, steering linkage. If any of these items is badly worn, you may notice any of these symptoms:

- car pulls to one side when braking
- car wanders when driving a straight line
- overall ride may be either hard or bouncy
- effort is needed to steer vehicle
- tires show uneven wear
- tires squeal when cornering
- front of car dips or bounces when braking
- car rocks side-to-side when going over rough road
- wheels bounce or make slapping sound on road
- steering wheel vibrates in hands
- front of car vibrates at highway speeds

Any of above symptoms indicates corrective action is needed. Delay can: ruin tires; cause damage/failure to other suspension parts; create safety hazard.

STEERING

If steering linkage, front suspension and steering column components are in good condition, there should be no more than 1½ inch free play in the steering wheel when measured at the rim of the wheel. If a loud knock is heard when turning the steering wheel from one extreme to the other, have mechanic check pinion bearing preload.

SHOCK ABSORBERS

Shock absorbers work to keep wheels in constant contact with the road. Result is safe handling and ride control; longer tire life. So shock absorbers (or shocks) are important.

HOW TO CHECK FOR BAD SHOCKS

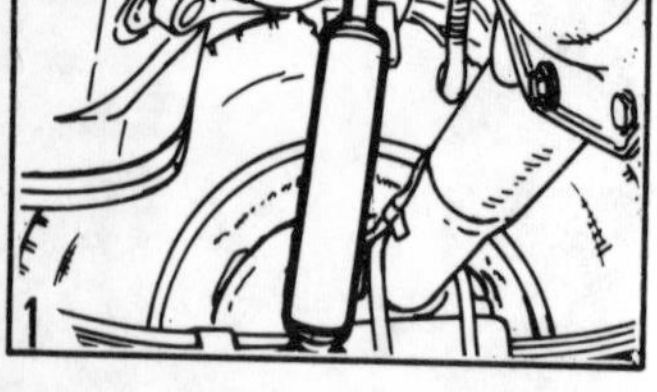

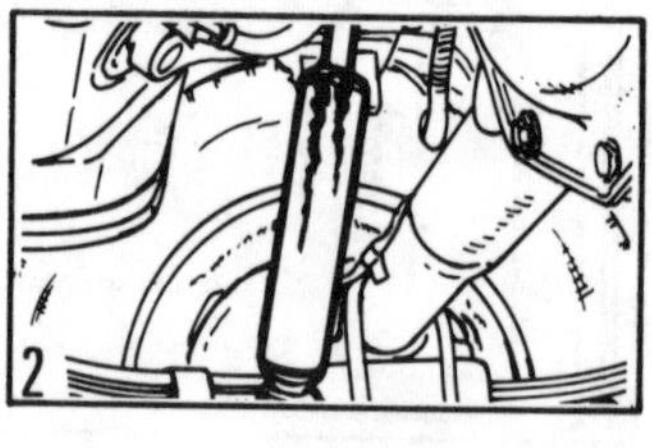

1. Check under car and locate shock absorber near each wheel.

2. Heavy oil streaks on outer shock housing indicate need for replacement.

3. Stand at front of car and apply body weight in a pumping action to front bumper or fender. Release pressure and allow car to stop rocking. Car should not bounce more than one more time after releasing pressure. Repeat at rear. If bouncing continues more than once, replacement is needed. Replace shocks in pairs (front pair or rear pair).

TOW HITCH INFORMATION

If your car is used for trailer towing you should check:

A. Cooling System; be sure coolant is at proper level in radiator. See Cooling Section for checks to perform.

B. Check Transmission Fluid; keep topped up to proper level.

C. Check Rear Shock Absorbers; you may benefit from installation of new rear shocks.

D. Check Tire Pressures; best traction and handling can be ensured if tire pressures are properly maintained.

For safer and more trouble-free trailer towing, consider:

A. Automatic Transmission Cooler; helps remove excess heat from automatic transmission fluid built up during towing mileage. Also helps avoid radiator overheating. Some units can be self-installed.

B. Radiator Over-Flow Tank Kit; addition of a reservoir to catch radiator coolant overflow preventing coolant loss. Easy to install, these units help a tow car run cooler, avoid overheating due to coolant loss.

C. Heavy-Duty Shock Absorbers or Air Shocks; important to have on rear wheels if you intend to do a lot of towing or load carrying within the car itself. Don't forget to consider replacing factory shocks, when they are worn out, with heavy-duty units at the front as well.

D. Variable Load Flasher; this unit will accommodate the added load of trailer turn signal lamps on trailer when these are hooked into your car's electrical system.

FRONT END ALIGNMENT

When steering, handling and/or tire wear indicate front end alignment may be needed, this work can only be done at an automotive service shop. DO NOT PUT OFF NEEDED FRONT END ALIGNMENT. At the same time, have ball joints and steering linkage checked.

Ignition System

TUNE-UP SERVICES—1970-74

The ignition system consists of spark plugs; plug wires; distributor; rotor; points; condenser; coil. These units work to create a good hot spark inside the engine (ignition) at exactly the right moment (timing). If ignition is weak or timing is off, engine may be hard to start, run poorly, waste gas, lose power, backfire or not run at all.

AMC SAYS . . . Replace plugs and points every 12,000 miles.

TOOLS & MATERIALS . . . Parts: set of points; condenser; spark plugs. Tools: gap gauge; 13/16 in. spark plug socket; screwdriver; open end, box or combination wrenches; timing equipment
(see Ignition Timing).

SAFETY TIP . . . Change only one spark plug at a time to avoid crosswiring and possible engine damage.

OTHER IGNITION CHECK POINTS

Inspect spark plug wires. If cracked or brittle, entire set should be replaced. Also, center high tension wire. Inspect distributor cap. Wipe inside clean occasionally with dry, lint-free rag. If cap is cracked or rotor contacts are excessively burned, replace cap.

BREAKERLESS IGNITION AMC BID SYSTEM 1975-77

The ignition system consists of a control unit, coil, breakerless distributor, spark plugs, spark plug cables

AMC SAYS: Replace plugs every 30,000 mi.

TOOLS & MATERIALS . . . Parts: 6 or 8 spark plugs. Tools: spark plug socket, screwdriver, open end, box, or combination wrenches, timing equipment.

SAFETY TIP . . . Change only one spark plug wire at a time to avoid crosswiring and possible engine damage.

If your car has breakerless ignition, periodic replacement of distributor parts is not required. If you suspect ignition trouble because of engine misfire, have the distributor checked out by a professional mechanic.

CHECKING POINTS, AND ROTOR—1970-74

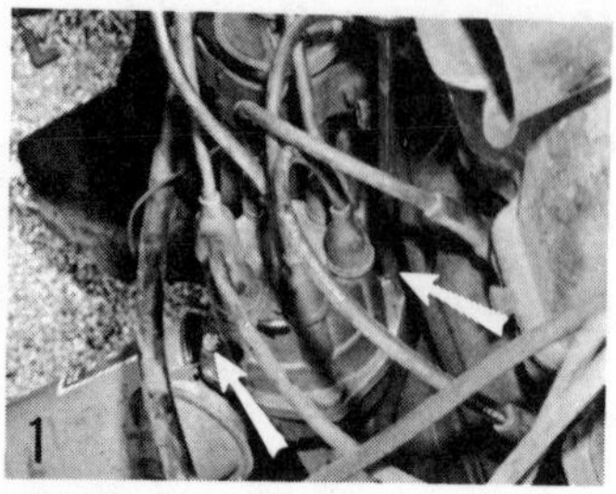

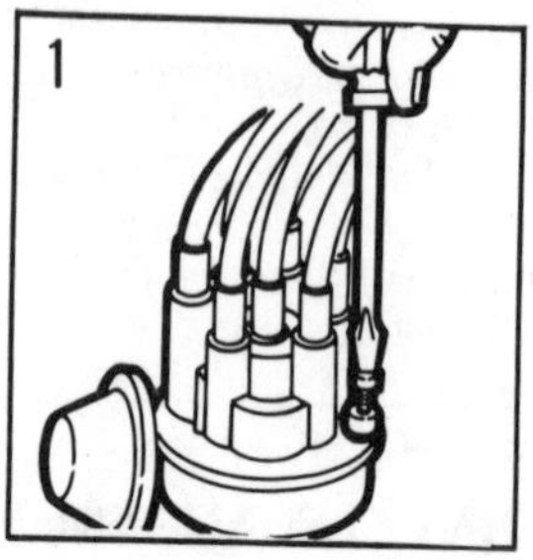

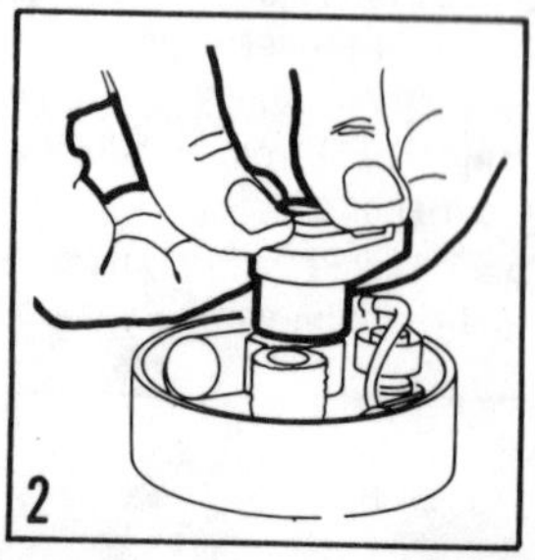

The distributor holds the points, rotor and condenser.

1. To open distributor, turn holddowns with a screwdriver. Lift cap off but keep wires connected.
2. Pull rotor off (straight up). Replace if cracked or metallic tip is badly burned.
3. Pry points apart with screwdriver. If worn or burned, replace. If OK, check point gap.

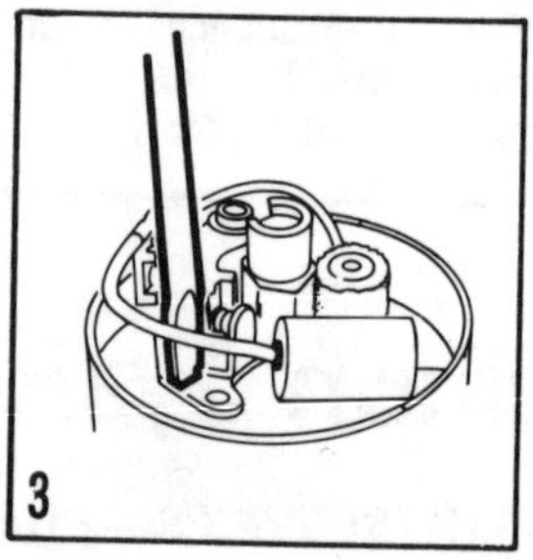

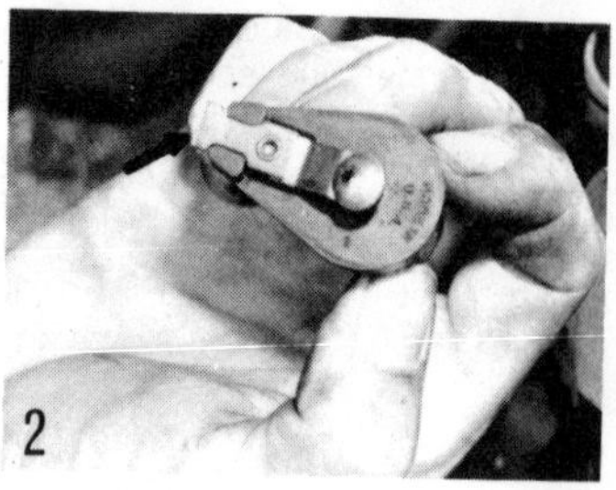

CHECKING CAP AND ROTOR—1975-77

Other ignition check points: inspect spark plug wires. If cracked or brittle, entire set should be replaced. Check center high tension cable, distributor cap and rotor. If either cap or rotor is excessively burned, it should be replaced.

1. To open distributor, turn holddown screws with a screwdriver. Lift off cap.
2. Pull rotor straight up and off of shaft. It tip is excessively burned, replace it.
3. If cap is cracked or rotor contacts are burned, replace cap. When switching wires to new cap, do them one at a time to avoid crosswiring.

SPARK PLUG REPLACEMENT

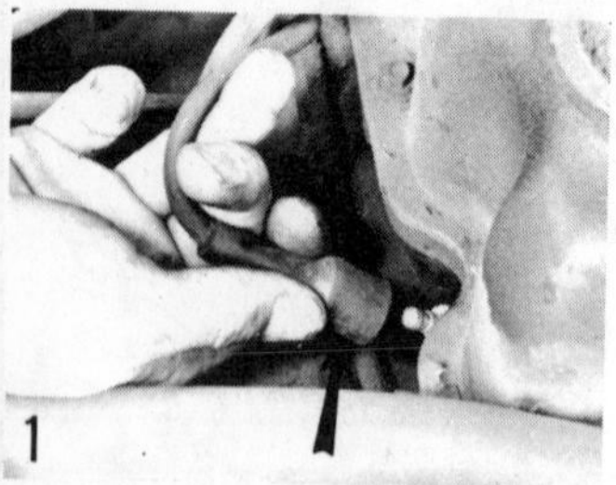

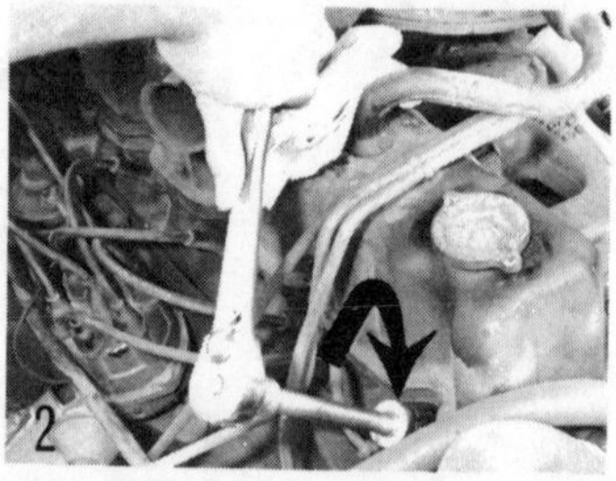

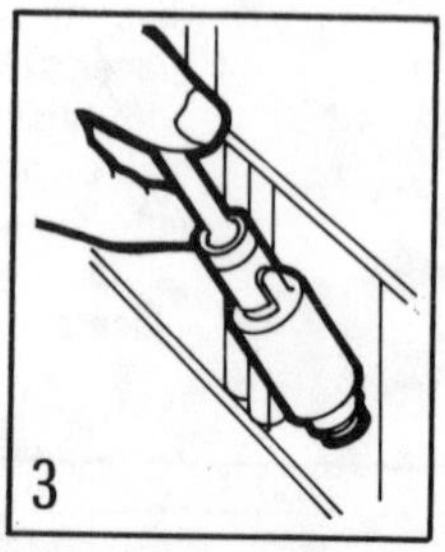

1. Remove spark plug wire by grasping rubber boot. Do not jerk wire off. If stuck, turn boot, pulling gently.
2. Loosen spark plug using socket wrench.
3. Wipe loose dirt from around plug before removing. Do not let dirt drop into engine through plug hole. Unscrew plug.

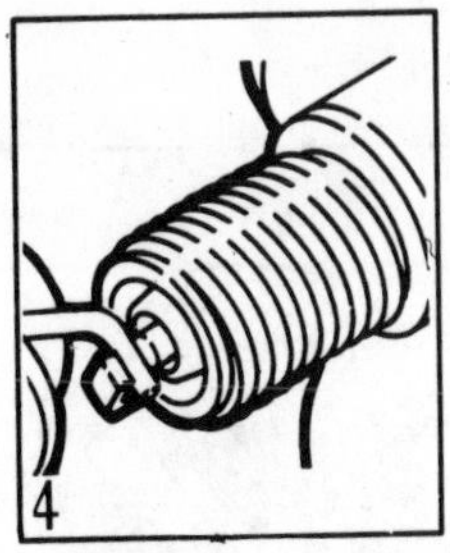

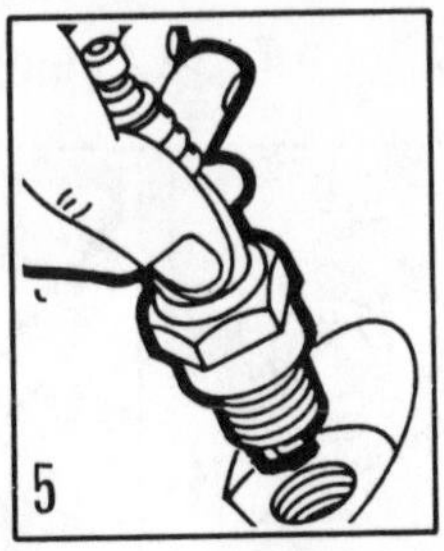

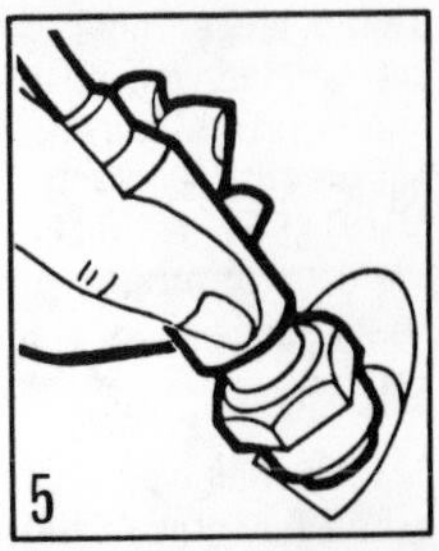

4. Check plug electrode gap on new spark plug. Adjust to gap shown in the Specifications Chart
Plug gap is correct when the gauge drags slightly as it is pulled between plug electrodes.
5. Thread new plug into plug hole by hand. Hand tighten. Do not force or cross thread. Use socket wrench to tighten firmly but do not force. Replace plug wire. Press boot firmly.

REMOVING POINTS—Six Cylinder

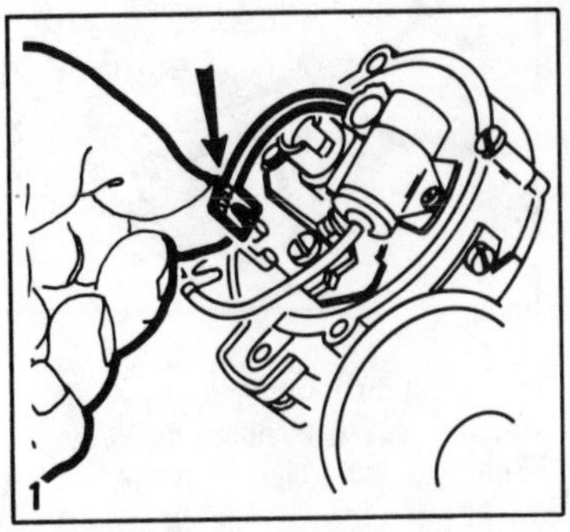

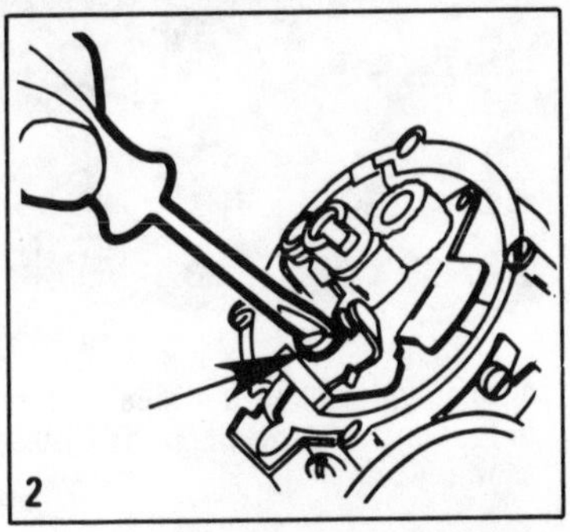

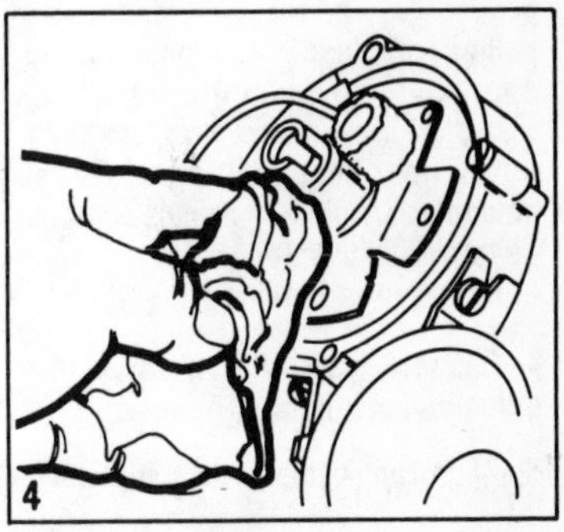

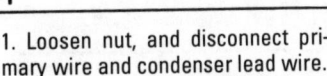

1. Loosen nut, and disconnect primary wire and condenser lead wire.
2. Remove screw which holds condenser; remove condenser.
3. Remove screws holding points to distributor, remove points.
4. Wipe all dirt from distributor plate and cam.
5. Inspect primary wire for frayed insulation, dirty connection. Clean connection or have wire repaired as necessary.

CAUTION: When removing screws from distributor in following steps, be sure to avoid any screws accidentally falling through distributor opening into engine. Use magnetic screwdriver.

INSTALLING POINTS AND CONDENSER—Six Cylinder

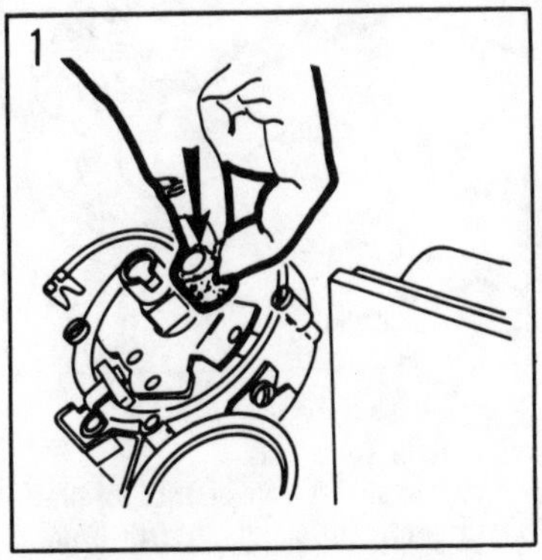

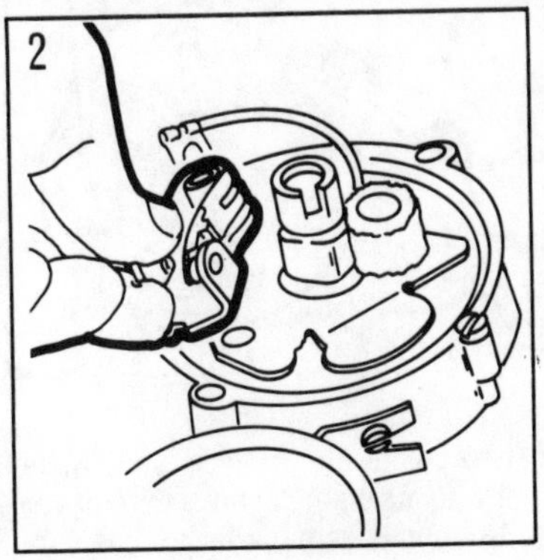

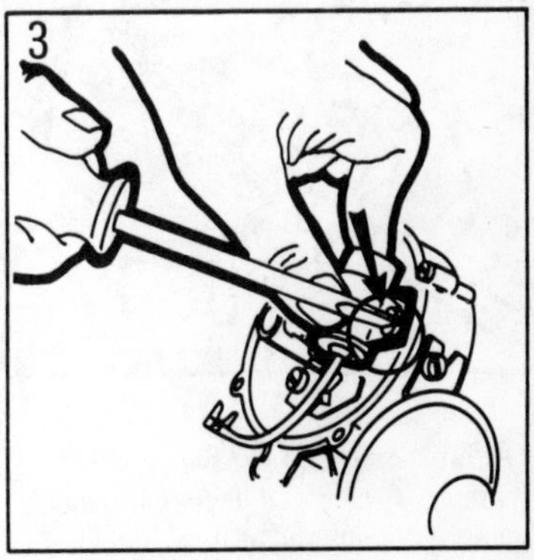

1. Apply small amount of heat resistant lube to distributor cam. (Lube usually supplied with new points. If not, purchase separately.)
2. Position new points in distributor and fasten with attaching screws. CAUTION: use magnetic screwdriver, or screwdriver with clip.
3. Attach new condenser to distributor with attaching screw.
4. Attach primary wire and condenser lead wire to point set. Don't let contacts touch distributor body or breaker plate. (Some models: wire from points attaches to condenser.)

RESETTING THE CONTACT GAP—Six Cylinder

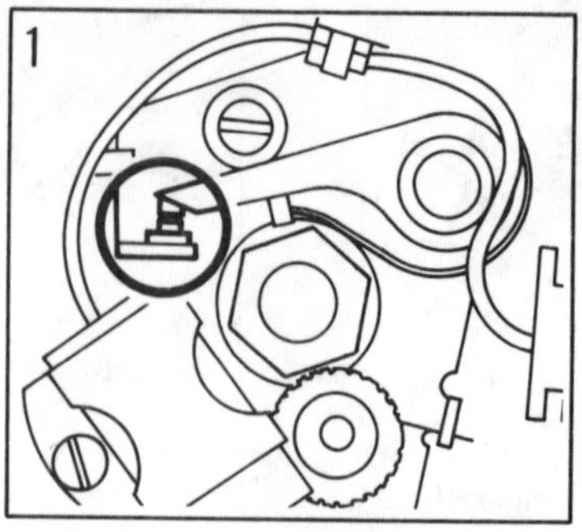

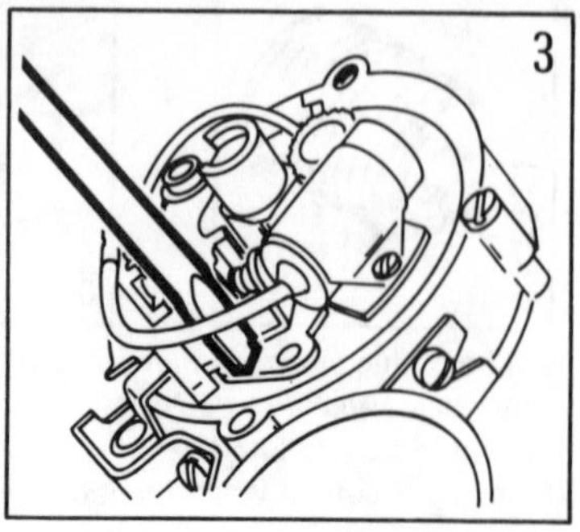

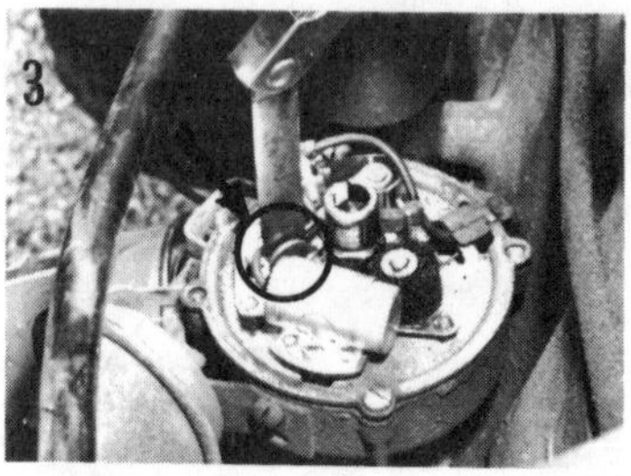

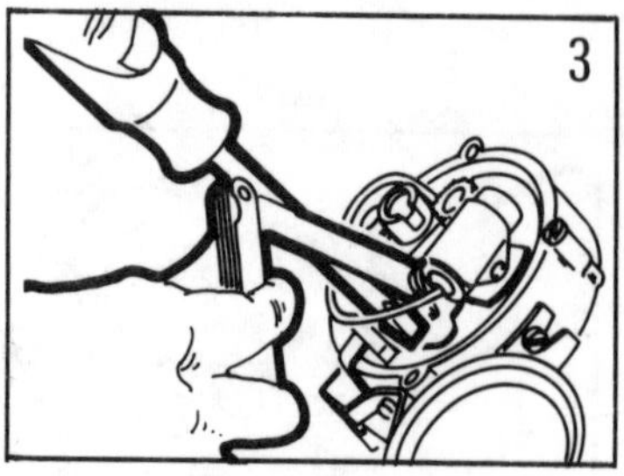

1. Electrical contacts of point set MUST BE PARALLEL. If needed, bend stationary contact with needle-nose pliers. Bend fixed bracket only.

2. Turn engine by ignition key (you'll need a helper) until rubbing block on points is one of the high points of the distributor cam. You may use wrench on lower pulley to do this, but TURN ONLY CLOCKWISE TO THE RIGHT—NEVER COUNTERCLOCKWISE.

3. Look up correct point gap on engine compartment sticker. Insert proper gap gauge between open point contacts. Slightly loosen point attaching screws on 6 cyl engines. Insert screwdriver in breaker plate notch near point contacts. Twist screwdriver to open or close points as needed. Tighten screws when correct gap is obtained.

4. Recheck gap after screws are tightened. Readjust if needed.

5. Align tab inside rotor with notch on distributor shaft and push rotor onto shaft. Rotor must be fully seated on shaft.

6. Install distributor cap by aligning tabs on cap with notch on body. Snap retaining clips in place.

REMOVING POINTS—V8

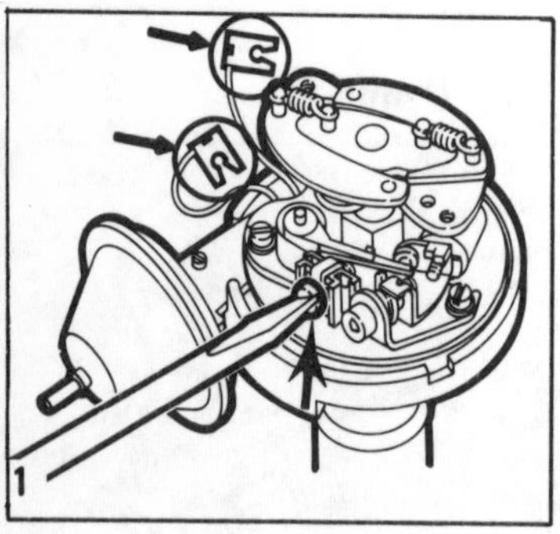

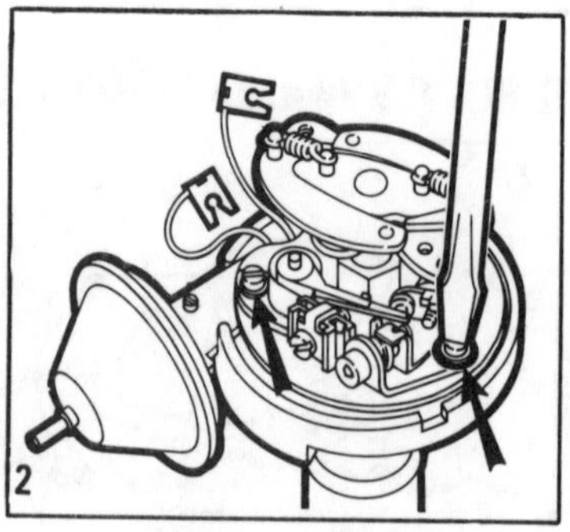

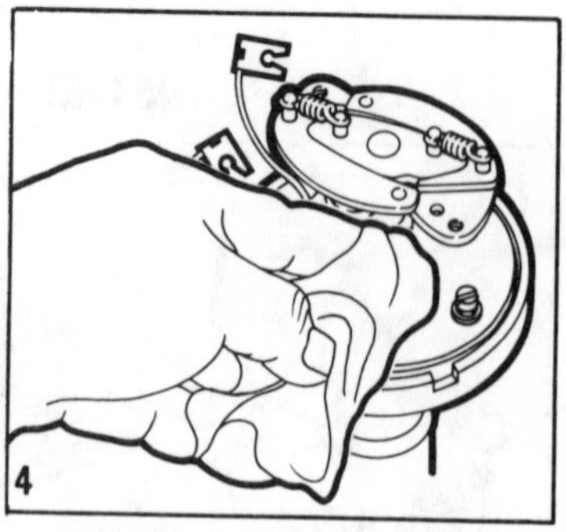

Points and condenser work together. Always replace condenser also when installing new points.

1. Disconnect the two wire terminals connected to the points set. Notice that the condenser connector is on the outside.
2. Loosen, but do not remove the two points attaching screws. Slide the points off the screws to remove.
3. Remove screw which holds condenser. DO NOT DROP SCREW.

NOTE: Later models use a combined points and condenser. When you remove points you also remove condenser. You can also install these points in early cars.
4. Wipe all dirt from distributor plate and cam with clean, lint-free rag.

CAUTION: When removing screws from distributor, be sure to avoid any screws accidentally falling through distributor opening into engine. Use magnetic screwdriver.

INSTALLING POINTS AND CONDENSER—V8

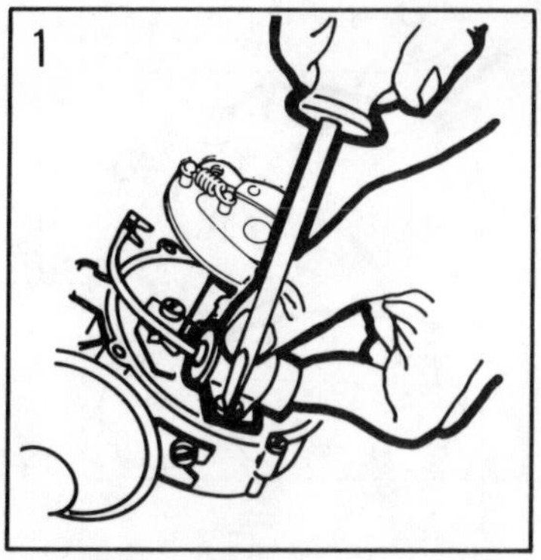

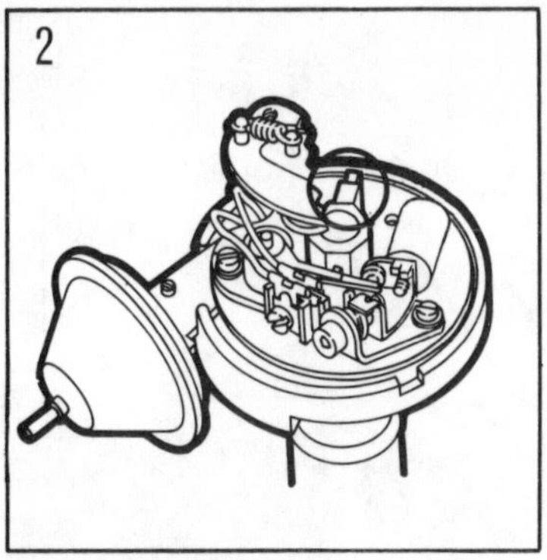

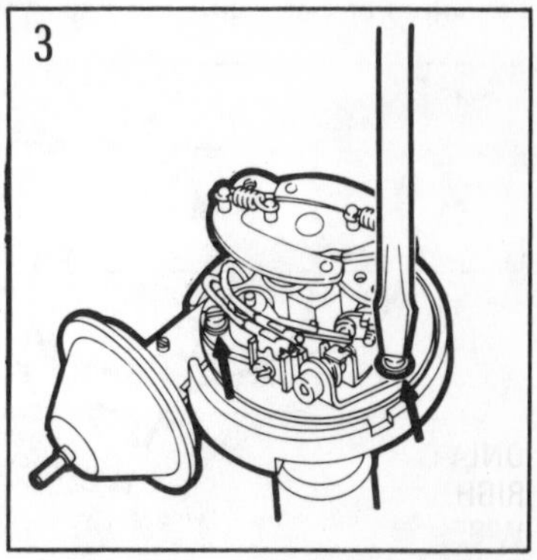

1. Attach new condenser with screw.
2. Rotate or replace cam lubricator. Fiber cam lubricator must be turned 180° every 12,000 mi., replaced every 24,000. When replacing, simply pull it up and off stud; push new lubricator down over stud.
DO NOT attempt to add oil or grease to fiber lubricator.
3. Position new points set in distributor by sliding onto screws. Tighten screws.

RESETTING THE CONTACT GAP—V8

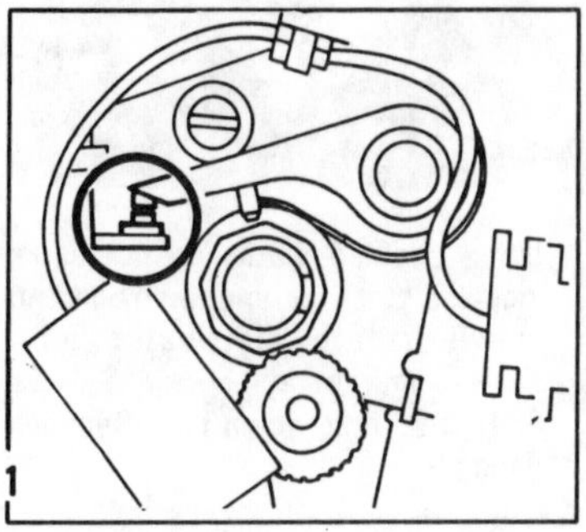

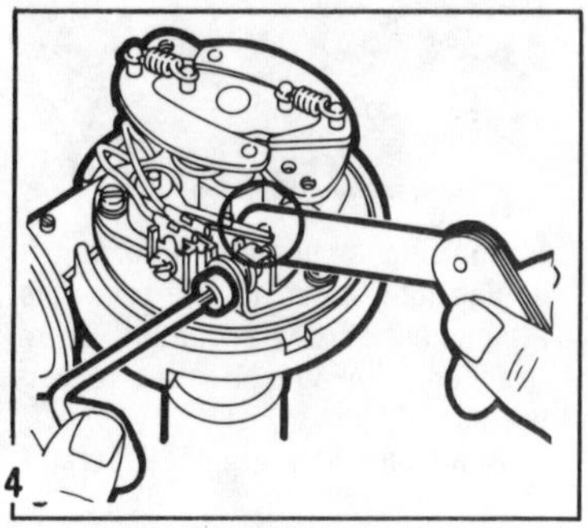

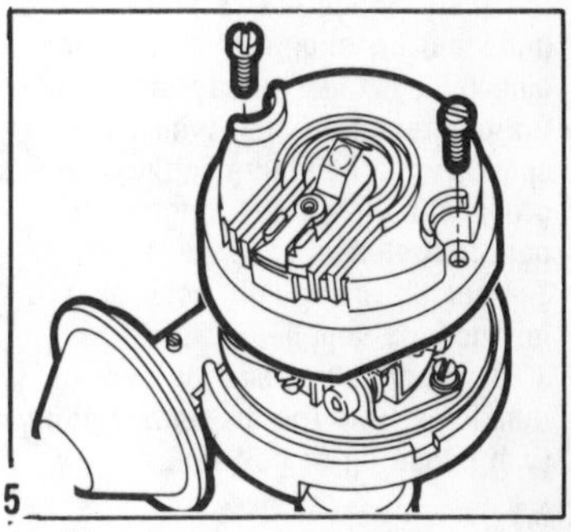

1. Check that point contacts meet squarely. If they do not, bend bracket supporting fixed contact using needle-nosed pliers.
2. Turn engine by ignition key (you'll need a helper) until rubbing block on point set is on one of the high spots of distributor cam. You may use wrench on lower engine pulley to do this.
3. Insert a ⅛ in. allen wrench into points adjusting screw. Correct gap is .016 in. for new points.
4. Insert correct size feeler gauge. Adjust gap with wrench until feeler gauge can be moved in and out between contacts with only slight drag.
5. Install rotor on advance weight assembly. The two lugs on the bottom of the rotor are shaped differently, so it can only be installed one way. Tighten screws.
6. Install cap be depressing screws and turning latches onto body of distributor. Insert the coil wire into the cap.
7. Point gap can be adjusted with the engine running. Insert the allen wrench through the cap window, slowly turn the adjusting screw clockwise until the engine just starts to misfire, and then turn it back ½ turn.

REPLACING SPARK PLUG WIRES

1. Remove only one wire at a time from the engine.
2. Match the wire removed with the same length wire in the replacement set.
3. Route the replacement wire in the same way as the original.
4. After all wires are replaced, check that all wires on 1974 and earlier distributors are seated in the distributor cap. Check that all boots are in place.
5. If you run into difficulty, go to the Firing Order illustrations for help.

GREMLIN/HORNET

Use the firing order illustration to guide you when replacing your ignition wires and/or distributor cap.

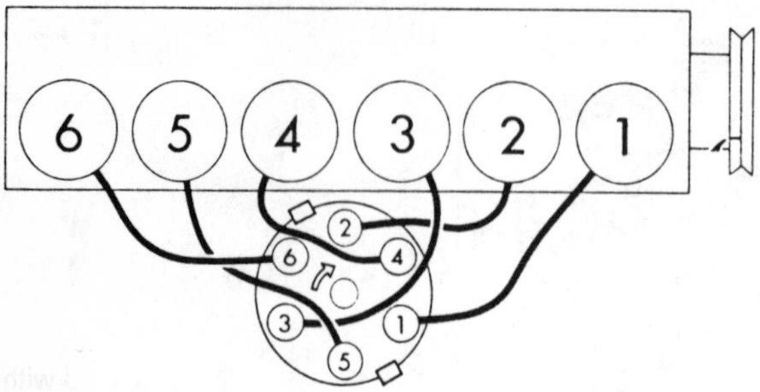

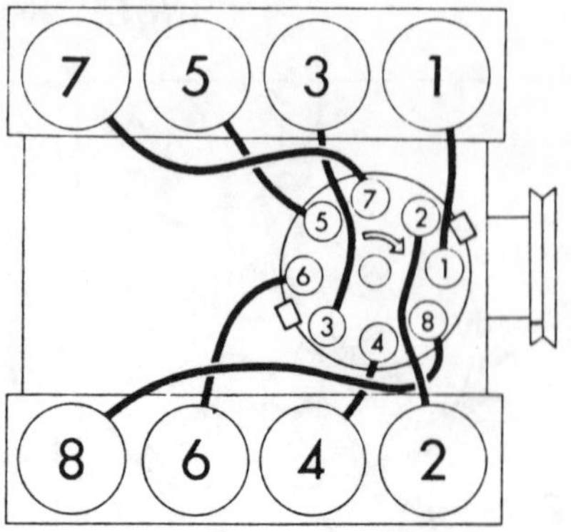

IGNITION TIMING

Adjusting timing is the important finishing touch to any tune-up. While not difficult, job requires timing light and dwell meter.

1. Locate timing marks and pointer (notches) on engine and lower engine pulley. Clean away dirt. Mark the pointer and notch which corresponds with the timing setting in degrees shown on the engine compartment sticker.
2. Hook up timing light according to instructions supplied with it.
3. Disconnect the one or two vacuum lines from the distributor. Plug with pencil tip or golf tee.

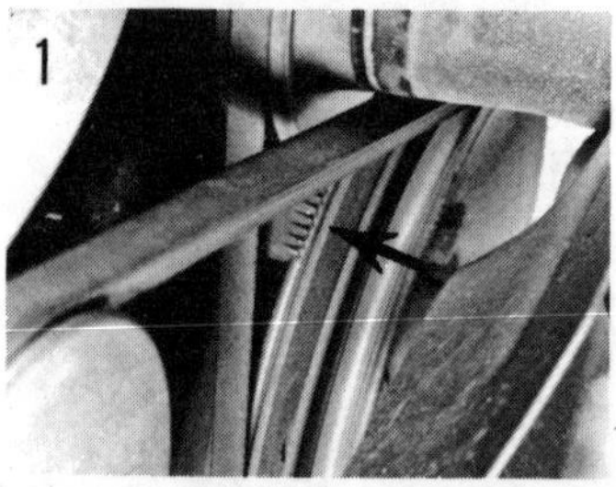

4. Hook up tachometer and adjust engine idle speed to 600 rpm. Idle attachment screw is located where gas pedal linkage attaches to carburetor.
5. Aim timing light at pulley mark(s).

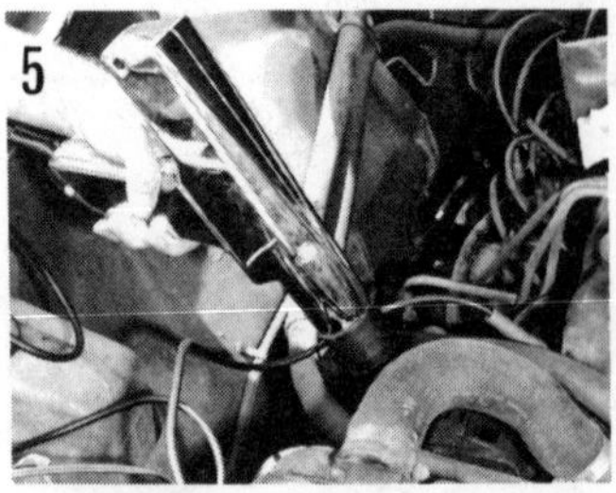

If the chalked marks do not align, loosen distributor holddown bolt and slowly rotate distributor until chalked marks align.

6. Tighten hold-down bolt. Recheck timing.

Fuel System

When gasoline is brought from the fuel tank, it mixes with air in the carburetor. This gas/air mixture enters engine thru the intake manifold, passes thru the intake valves and is burned in the combustion chamber. The burned exhaust gas is then passed thru exhaust valves to the exhaust system and to the outside air. In order to keep your car's engine running clearly with minimal pollution, and avoid dangerous carbon monoxide fumes inside the vehicle, certain items should be checked from time to time.

EMISSION CONTROLS SYSTEM

The most important part of a car's emission control system is the Positive Crankcase Ventilation (PCV) valve and its connecting hose. The PCV valve should be replaced once every 12 months. This device keeps dirt and sludge from forming inside the engine. Make sure all PCV connections are tight. Check that the connecting hoses are clear and not clogged. Replace any brittle or broken hoses.

KEEP THE AIR INTAKE CLEAN

The large round can that sits on top of the engine holds the air cleaner. Twice a year:

1. Remove wing nut, and remove air cleaner lid.

2. Lift out circular air cleaner cartridge. Discard if more than 12 months old or excessively dirty.

3. Remove elbow.

4. Pull crankcase filter out of filter can. Wipe inside of can and lid with clean cloth.

5. Install crankcase filter. Put elbow on filter neck.

6. Install in reverse order.

PCV VALVE REPLACEMENT

The PCV valve is located on top of the valve cover, in front of the air cleaner.

1. Grasp hose holding PCV valve. Pull straight out.

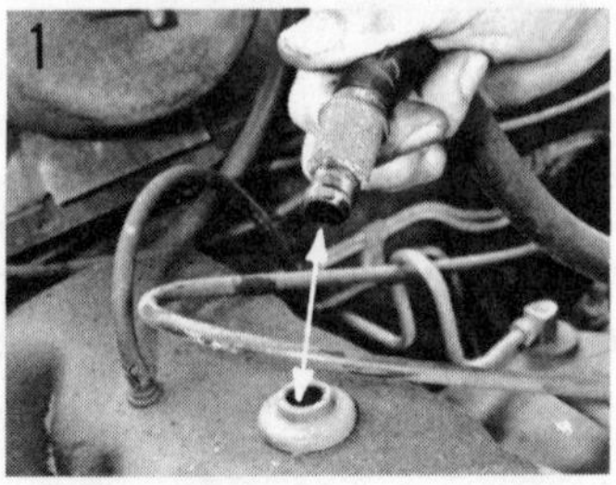

2. Note where other end of hose is connected. Pull off.
3. Remove PCV valve from hose. Flush hose out with cleaning solvent. Dry hose. Install new PCV valve in hose.

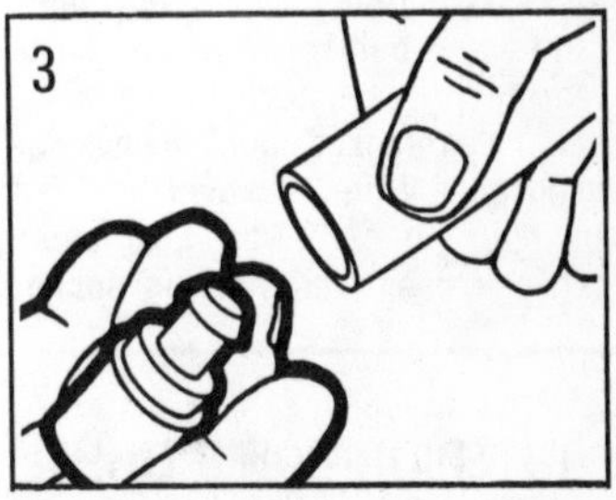

4. Attach end of hose to its original connection and insert PCV valve into proper opening.

FUEL FILTER REPLACEMENT

Replace the filter every year or 12,000 miles. The fuel filter prevents dirt, rust, and scale from both the gas station's tank and your own fuel tank from reaching the carburetor. A dirty filter will starve the engine and cause poor running.

1. Locate the fuel filter in line to carburetor. Place a rag under the filter housing to collect fuel that will drain out when filter is removed.
2. Pinch the ends of clamps together, and move toward center of hose. Use the smallest possible amount of tension, to avoid damaging the clamps. You can get a special tool designed for this job that will make handling the clamps much easier.
3. Pull the hose off filter and fuel line.
4. Position new clamps in center of a new hose. If the old clamps are to be reused, make sure they have not lost their tension.
5. Install hose on fuel line and filter. Pinch the clamp ends together, and position well onto fuel line and filter.

Note: After replacing filter, remove rag used to catch spilled fuel, and then start engine. Check for leaks. Addition of a can of carburetor cleaner to the fuel tank occasionally will aid in keeping the entire fuel system clean.

Safety Systems

PARKING LIGHTS, TURN SIGNALS AND STOP LIGHTS

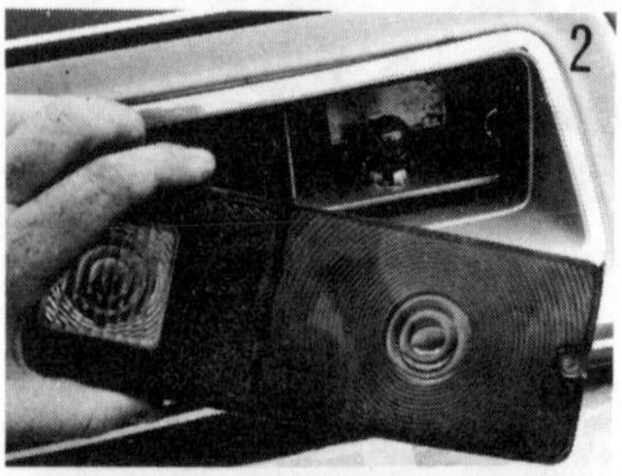

All above lighting functions are performed by four dual-element bulbs. Front parking light and turn signal bulbs are mounted in the parking light housing in the grille. To replace, remove the lens, push down on bulb while turning it counterclockwise to remove it from the socket.
To replace rear taillight, stop light, turn signal bulbs, raise trunk lid or rear door. Reach socket from inside car. Twist socket counterclockwise in housing. When socket is removed, push in on bulb and turn counterclockwise to remove from socket.

Insert new dual-element bulb in correct position (see note) and re-install socket in housing.
NOTE: When inserting new dual

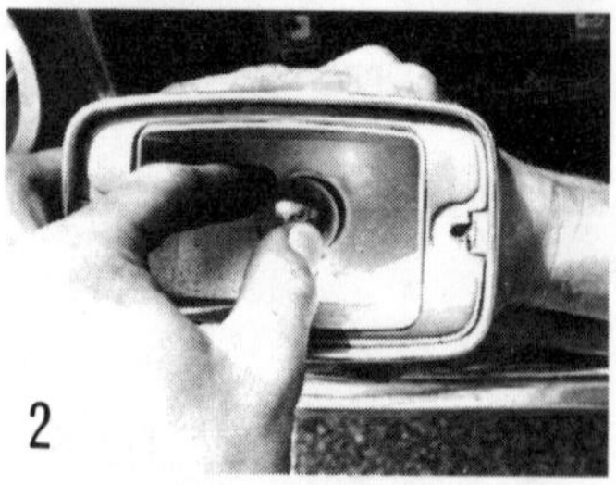

element bulb, note that knobs on side of bulb base are different distances from base tip. Match knobs to socket slots for proper fit.

INTERIOR DOME LIGHT

This is a cartridge type bulb. Pry the dome light lens out from the housing. To avoid blowing the fuse, make sure that the doors are closed and domelight switch in the OFF position. Push in on the bulb and turn it clockwise to remove from socket. Insert new bulb and install in reverse order.

BACK-UP LIGHTS

To replace back-up light bulbs, raise trunk lid. Reach bulb socket from inside car. Turn bulb socket counterclockwise and pull out. Push down on bulb turning counterclockwise to remove from socket. Insert new bulb and reinstall in reverse order.

LICENSE PLATE LIGHTS

Remove screw lens and housing that attaches to bottom of bumper. Push in on bulb turning counterclockwise to remove.

SIDE MARKER LIGHT

1. Remove the retaining screws, and remove the lense.

2. Turn bulb socket counterclockwise to remove from housing. Pull bulb straight out. Do not turn bulb.

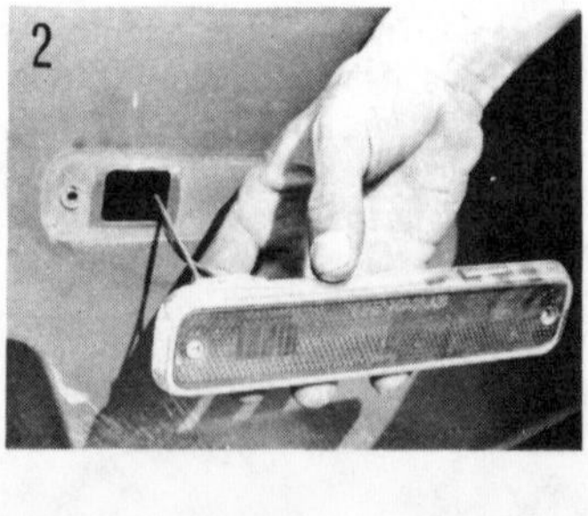

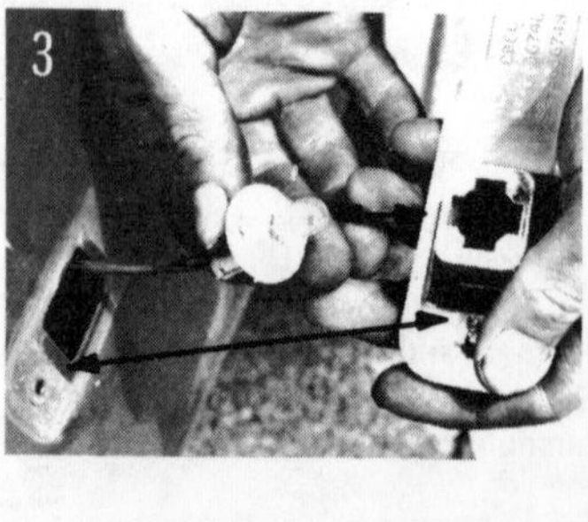

HEADLIGHT REPLACEMENT

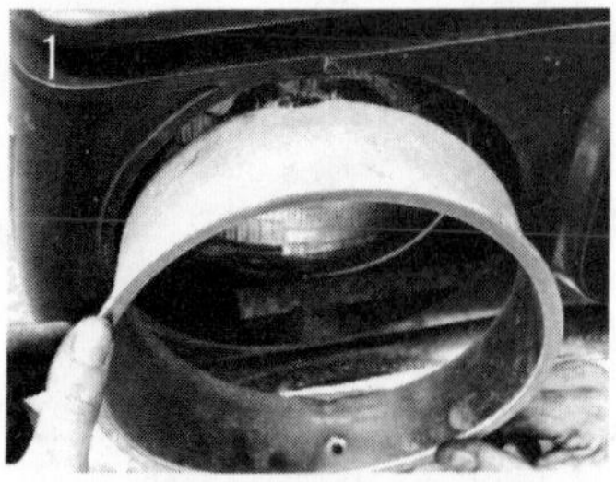

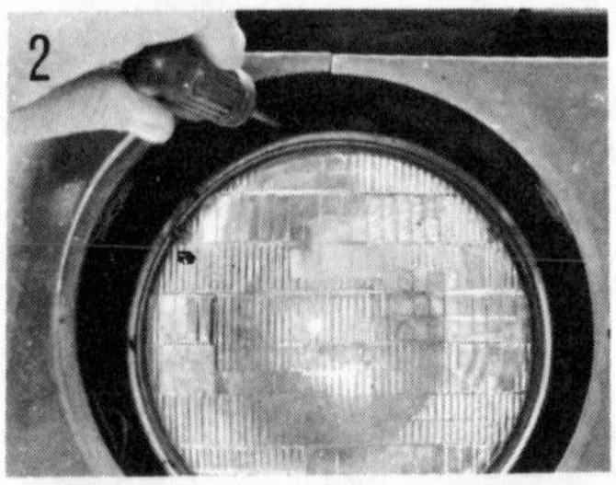

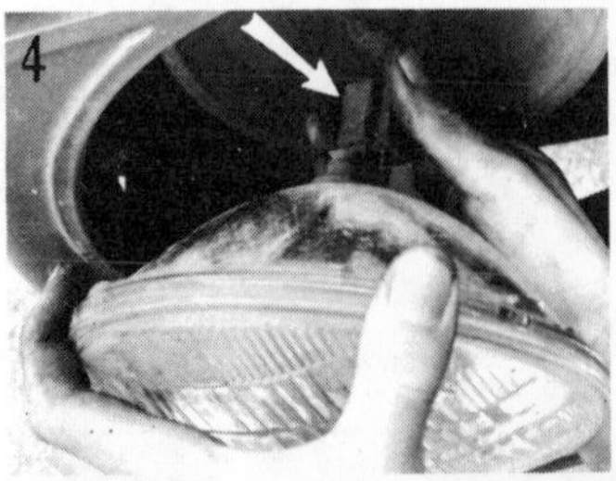

1. Remove both headlight cover retaining screws and cover.

2. Loosen, but do not remove, headlight retaining ring attaching screws. NOTE: Do not mistake headlight adjustment screws for the three retaining ring screws.

3. Rotate retaining ring to left until large openings in attaching screw slots are aligned with screw heads. Remove ring.

4. Pull lamp (sealed beam) out of headlight shell toward front of car; disconnect wiring connector from sealed beam unit.

5. Connect wire connector to new sealed beam unit.

6. Position new sealed beam unit in headlight shell. Be sure knobs on back of bulb (near outer edge) enter slots in shell.

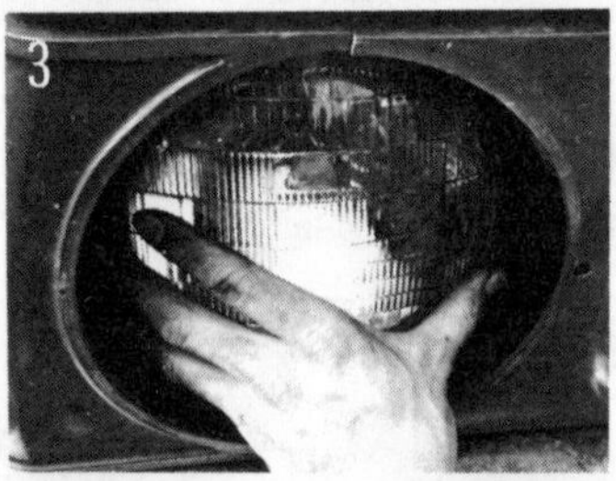

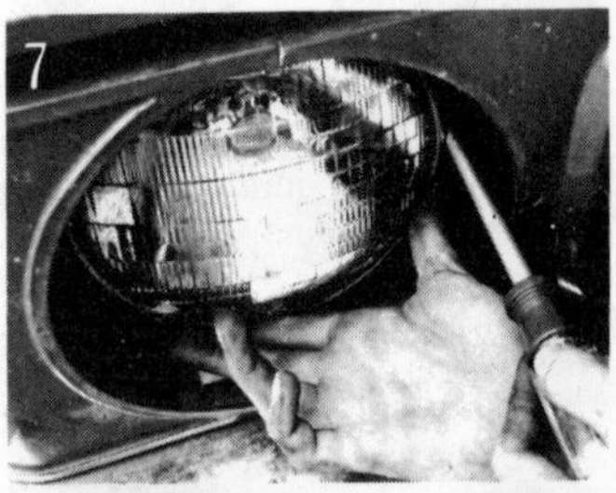

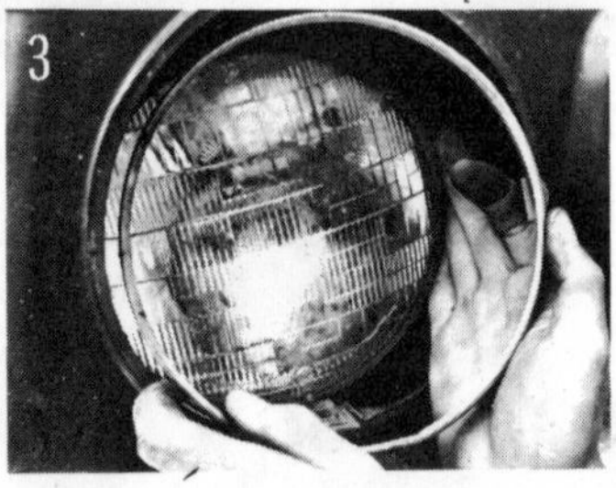

7. Position retaining ring on retainer screws; turn ring to right. Tighten screws.

8. Position headlight cover; install attaching screws.

WINDSHIELD WIPER BLADE REPLACEMENT

To replace wiper blade, lift up on spring release tab on wiper arm connector. Pull wiper blade off. Snap new blade into place.

To replace rubber insert only, press down, away from wiper blade to free it. Slide insert from blade. Insert new wiper. Bend insert upward slightly to engage retaining clips.

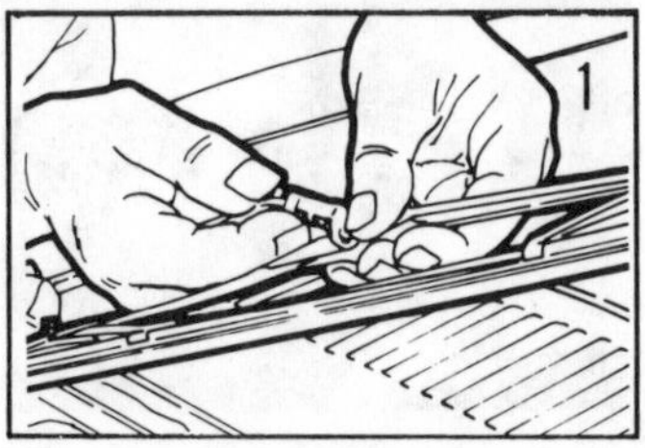

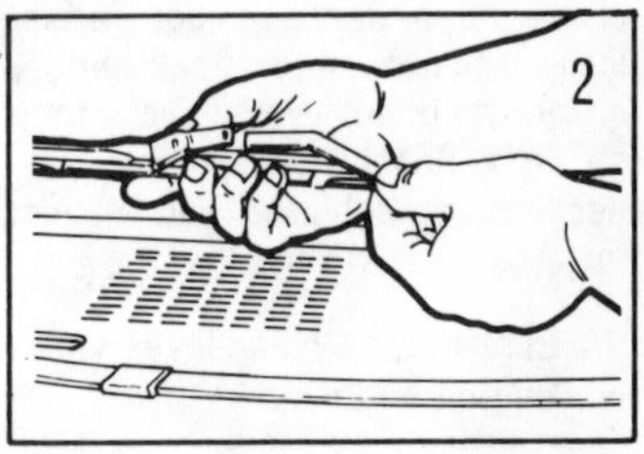

HORN PROBLEMS

If horn sounds and does not stop, this is due to short circuit in wiring. Disconnect wiring connector under hood and have professional service shop check horn wiring circuit.

STEERING PROBLEMS

See steering system check in Suspension Section. Check tire pressures. Have a professional service shop check all components in the front end and steering system.

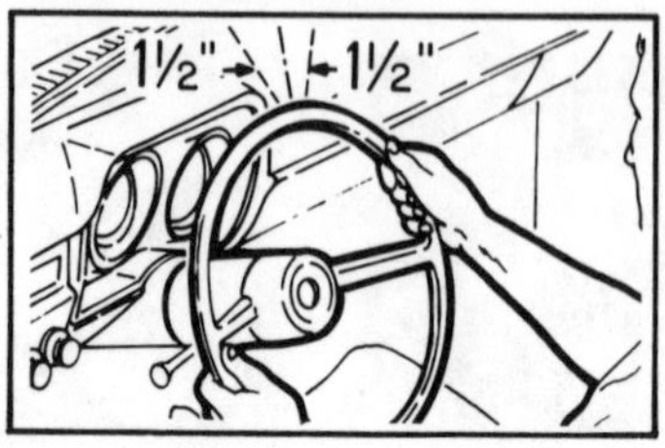

WASHER SYSTEM

If washer fails to squirt properly, raise hood and check system hose connections. Be sure washer fluid container has fluid. Check spout openings for clogging.
Keep container filled with fluid mixture of washer solvent and water. If road spray buildup on windshield is a chronic problem, add 1 tablespoon dishwasher detergent to solvent/water mixture when re-filling container.

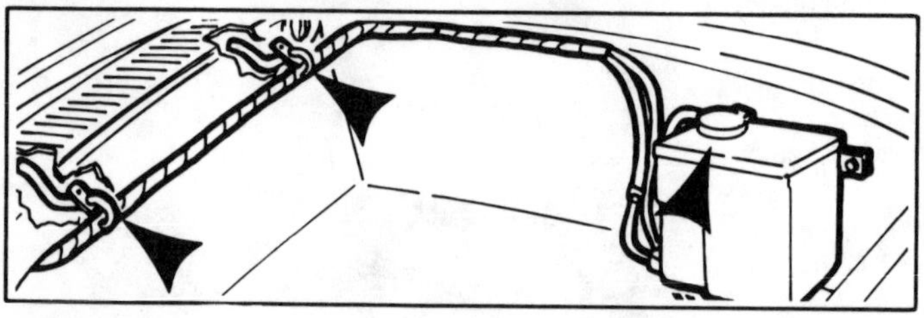

Electrical System

CHECK BATTERY FLUID

To ensure starting ability at all times check your battery condition periodically. You'll need to check battery electrolyte (fluid) level in each of the six cells. Check battery cable connections for tightness and inspect for accumulated corrosion.

SAFETY NOTE: Wear gloves when working on battery.

1. Remove plastic filler caps on top of battery. Fluid should be up to lower end of filler hole and covering the plates. If fluid is low add clean, cold tap water. If your area has hard water, use only distilled water available at auto supply, food or drug stores.

2. Replace any lost caps immediately.

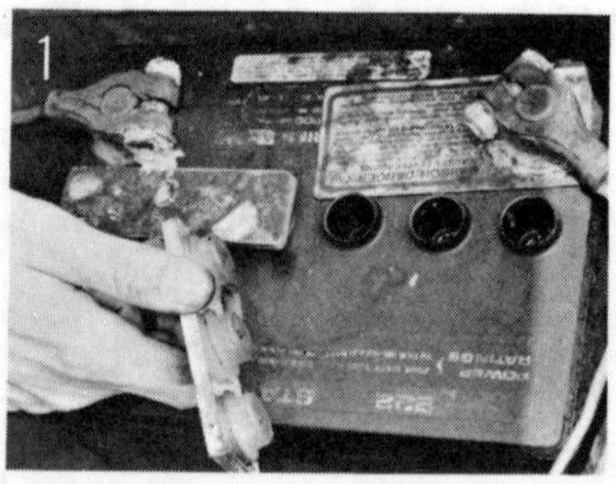

CAUTION: NEVER LIGHT A MATCH OR SMOKE near the top of a battery. Batteries give off explosive hydrogen gas.

NOTE: Battery that often checks low on fluid could mean:

A. Battery is getting old, due for replacement; have charge capacity checked at service shop.

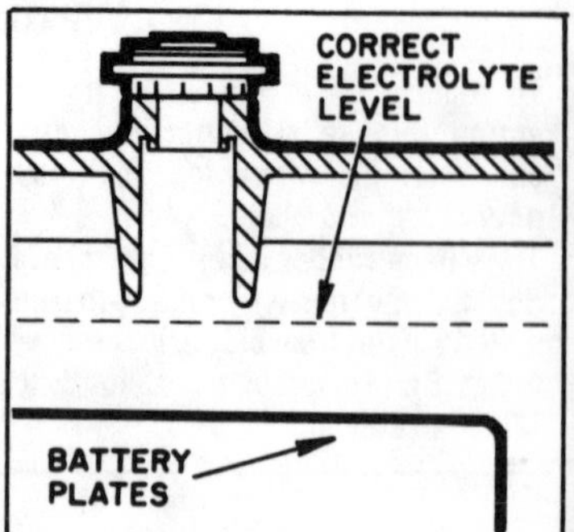

B. Connections may be corroded or loose; clean/replace as needed (see below).

C. Alternator or voltage regulator not functioning properly; this happens far less often than A or B above.

CLEAN THOSE BATTERY TERMINALS

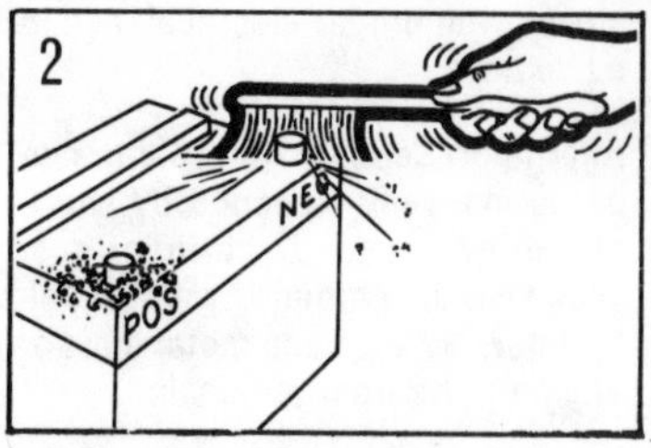

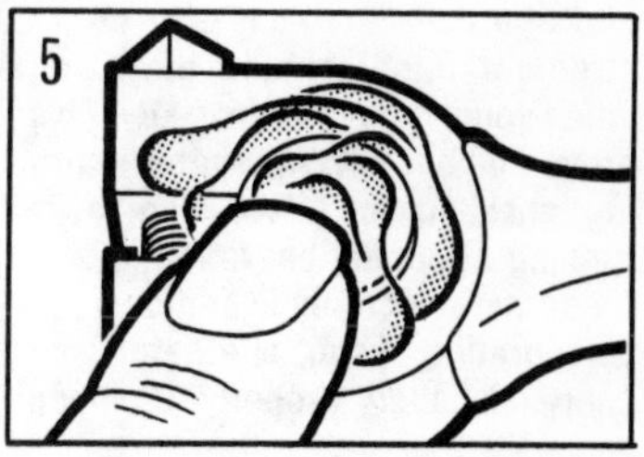

As time goes by, battery terminals build up a dry powdery, whitish material. This material is corrosive and will gradually eat thru battery cables if not cleaned off periodically.

1. Loosen and remove battery connections.
2. Brush off all loose corrosion; use stiff bristle brush. Do not get this material into eyes or on open cuts. Wash off at once.
3. If corrosion build-up is extremely heavy and brushing does not remove all of it, mix 2 tablespoons baking soda to 1 cup water. Pour solution directly onto terminals and connectors. Allow to soak a few minutes and rinse off. Continue brushing to remove all traces of corrosion build-up. Do not allow cleaning solution to enter battery.
4. Replace connectors on battery terminal posts and tighten. Do not hammer connections onto posts, but be sure they will not come loose with vibration.
5. Liberally smear battery terminal posts and cable connectors with petroleum jelly.

REPLACE FAULTY BATTERY CABLES

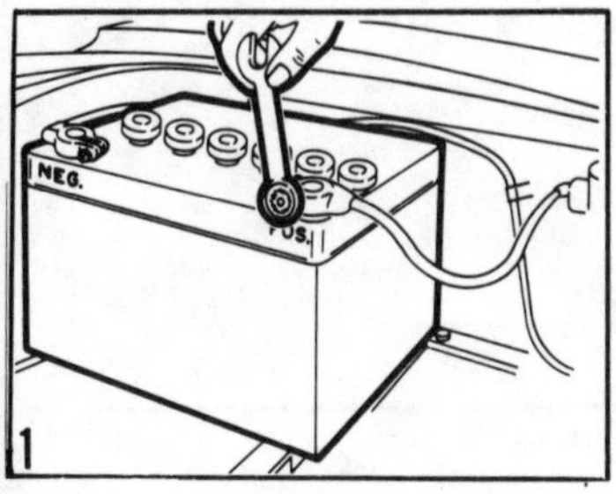

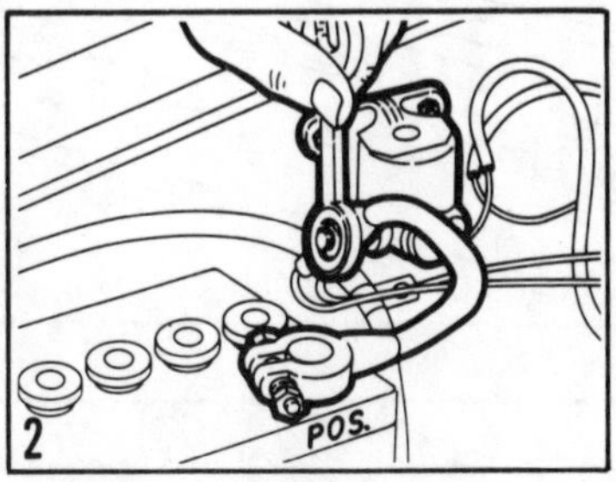

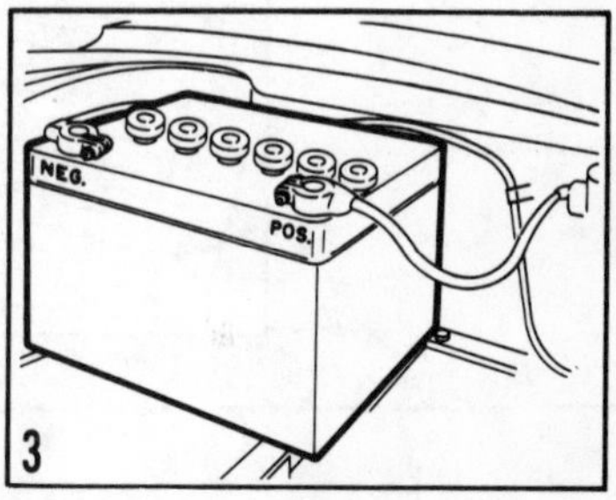

If battery cable strands become frayed, broken or corroded, replace cable immediately. Delay in correcting this condition could lead to sudden failure to start the engine. Can also weaken battery.

1. Loosen and remove battery connections. Clean off any corrosion buildup.
2. Disconnect negative cable from its attachment to engine or chassis. Disconnect positive cable from its attachment to starter relay.
3. Attach new cables making sure positive and negative cables are on proper terminals. They are not identical.
4. Replace connectors on battery terminal posts and tighten.
5. Liberally smear battery terminal posts and cable connectors with petroleum jelly.

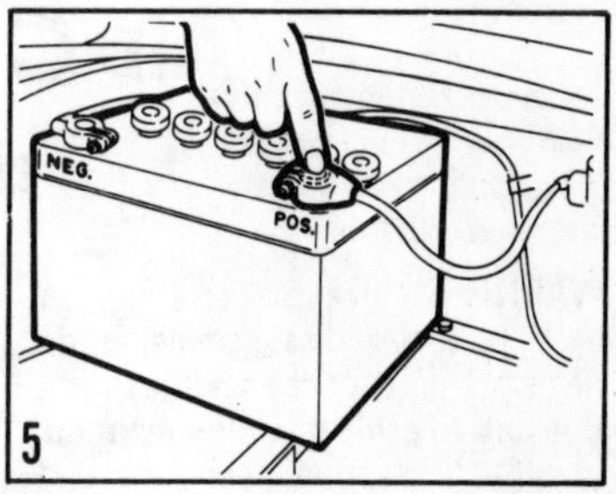

TURN SIGNAL AND 4-WAY FLASHER

Turn signals and 4-way emergency flashers will operate only if: A. All light bulbs are OK. B. Flasher units are not burned out. The car has two flasher units that work independently of each other. Turn signal flasher is located behind instrument panel on extreme left. Emergency flasher is located to the right of the steering column. To remove grasp with fingers, twist and pull flasher toward front of car. Pull connector from flasher. REPLACE ONLY WITH SAME TYPE FLASHER.

ALTERNATOR

Red alternator warning light on instrument panel should glow red when you first turn ignition key. This proves bulb is OK. Alternator warning light should go off when engine is running at normal operating speed. If alternator warning light glows red at operating speed, alternator isn't charging battery properly. Common causes are:

A. Fan belts are loose and slipping on alternator pulley. Tighten or replace belts.

B. Battery terminals, cables are loose or corroded. Clean; tighten; replace bad cables.

If A or B do not correct problem, alternator or voltage regulator may be faulty. This happens far less often, and can only be checked by mechanic with proper electrical testing equipment.

Alternator Caution: Alternator can be permanently damaged by short-circuiting terminal connections. When working around or moving alternator, always keep metal tools or engine parts from terminals.

REAR WINDOW DEFOGGER SYSTEM

Do not clean inside of rear window fitted with defogger system with any abrasive material. This could destroy carbon-copper wires. Use only soft rag and mild detergent/water mixture. Dry carefully.

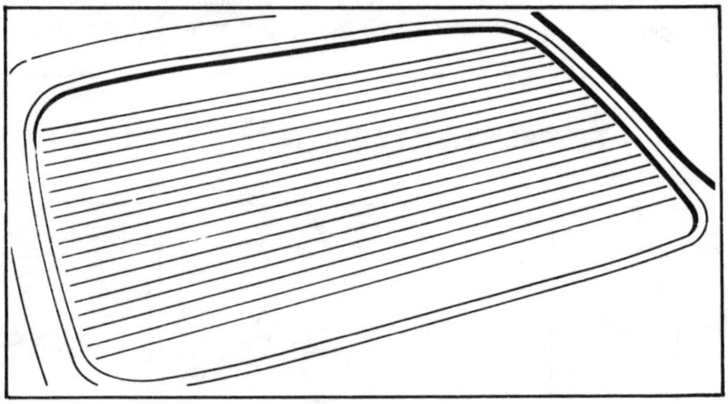

Air Conditioning System

CHECK POINTS AND SERVICES

WARNING!—Never attempt to tighten fittings, disassemble or do any work on your car's A/C system. Consult a professional mechanic about A/C system problems and their correction. Your auto air conditioner (A/C) is a delicate, closed system. If air, dirt or water get into it, or if refrigerant escapes, the A/C unit will not cool a car interior. Among things you can do are:

1. Keep condenser grille clean. Check for dirt and debris; periodically remove dead insects, leaves, etc., with stiff bristle brush. Straighten any bent fins—carefully.
2. Keep radiator filled to correct level. (See Cooling System section). If fluid needs to be added, add antifreeze rather than water.
3. Keep radiator coolant at a 50/50 water/antifreeze mixture.

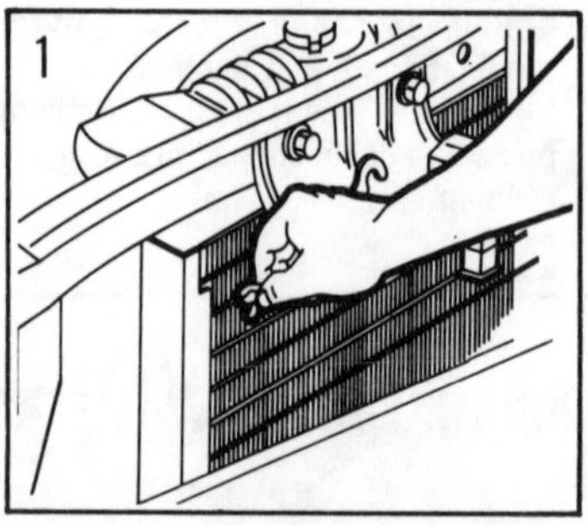

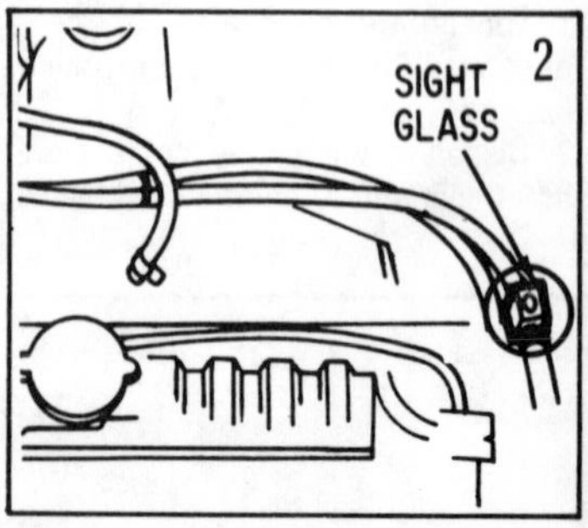

4. Flush cooling system and replace with fresh coolant mixture at least every 24 months. (See Cooling System section).
5. Radiator cap should be tight and

sealed properly. If sealing gasket is cracked, cut or worn, replace cap with new 15 lb. unit.

6. Check fan belt tension periodically. (See Cooling System section). Replace glazed, frayed or cut fan belts, before they fail entirely.

7. Check periodically for bubbles in A/C sight glass. Sight glass is located in head of receiver/drier vessel. Or in metal tubing leading from top of receiver/drier. Sight glass is no larger than head of large nail. It may be dirty. Wipe clean for best visibility.

PROCEED AS FOLLOWS:

a) With engine and A/C system running, look for passage of refrigerant in sight glass. You'll be looking for a

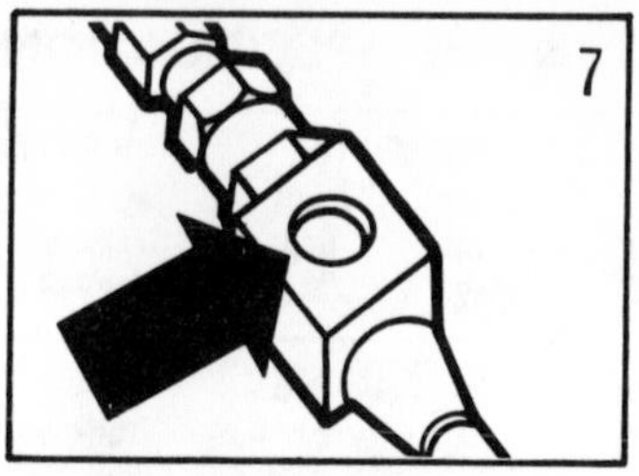

7

stream of milky white bubbles as they pass through sight glass. It is best to watch sight glass and have someone else start the car and turn on the A/C system. Allow to run for a few minutes.

b) If you observe no bubbles, and air flow from A/C unit in the car is passing cold air, everything is OK.

c) If no bubbles appear in sight glass, and air flow from the A/C unit in the car is not delivering cold air, the system may be low on refrigerant and could need a re-charge.

d) If bubbles appear, system is low on refrigerant.

e) If you suspect refrigerant loss based on tests performed above, have system checked by a professional A/C service shop. They can confirm refrigerant loss, recharge the system and check for system leakage.

NOTE: Once a week or so, even in winter, run A/C system for about 5 minutes as you drive. This keeps system internally lubricated, prevents hoses hardening.

CAPACITIES

YEAR	ENGINE No. Cyl. Displacement (cu. in.)	ENGINE OIL Add 1 qt. with New Filter	TRANSMISSION Pts. to Refill after Draining MANUAL 3-speed	MANUAL 4-speed	AUTOMATIC	DRIVE AXLE (pts.)	COOLING SYSTEM with Heater (qts.)	with Air Cond. (qts.)
1970	6-232	4	1.5①	—	18.5	3	10.5	10.5
	8-304	4	3	2.5	18.5	4	14	14
	8-360	4	—	2.5	20	4	13	13
1971	6-232	4	1.5①	—	18.5	3③	10.5	10.5
	6-258	4	2.5	—	18.5	3③	10.5	10.5
	8-304	4	2.5	2.5	18.5	4	14	14
	8-360	4	3	2.5	20	4	13	13
1972	6-232	4	1.5①	—	17	3③	10.5	10.5
	6-258	4	2.5	—	17	3③	10.5	10.5
	8-304	4	2.5	2.5	17	4	14	14
	8-360	4	2.5	2.5	19	4	13	13
1973	6-232	4	2.5	—	17	3③	10.5	10.5
	6-258	4	2.5	—	17	3③	10.5	10.5
	8-304	4	2.5	2.5	17	4	14	14
	8-360	4	2.5	2.5	19	4	13	14
1974	6-232	4	2.5	—	17	3③	11	11.5
	6-258	4	2.5	—	17	3③	11	11.5
	8-304	4	2.5	2.5	17	4	16	16
	8-360	4	2.5	2.5	19	4	15.5	15.5
1975	6-232	4	2.5②	—	17	3③	11	11.5
	6-258	4	2.5②	—	17	3③	11	11.5
	8-304	4	3.5	—	17	4	16	16
	8-360	4	—	—	19	4	15.5	15.5
1976-77	6-232	4	2.5②	—	17	3③	11	11.5
	6-258	4	2.5②	—	17	3③	11	11.5
	8-304	4	3.5	—	17	4	16	16
	8-360	4	—	—	19	4	15.5	15.5

① Fully synchronized: 2.5 pts
② 4 pts with O.D.
③ 8.875" Ring Gear: 4 pts

TUNE-UP SPECIFICATIONS

YEAR	ENGINE No. Cyl. Displacement (cu. in.)	SPARK PLUGS Type	SPARK PLUGS Gap (in.)	DISTRIBUTOR Point Dwell (deg.)	DISTRIBUTOR Point Gap (in.)	IGNITION TIMING Man. Trans.● (deg.)■	IGNITION TIMING Auto Trans.● (deg.)■	IDLE SPEED Man. Trans.● (rpm)▲	IDLE SPEED Auto Trans. (rpm)▲
1970	6-232	N-14Y	.035	33	.016	3B	3B	600	550
	8-304	N-12Y	.035	30	.016	5B	5B	650	600
	8-360	N-12Y	.035	30	.016	5B	5B	650	600
1971	6-232	N-12Y	.035	33	.016	3B	5B	700	600
	6-258	N-12Y	.035	33	.016	5B	5B	700	600
	8-304	N-12Y	.035	30	.016	2½B	2½B	750	650
	8-360	N-12Y	.035	30	.016	5B	5B	750	700
1972	6-232	N-12Y	.035	33	.016	5B(3B)	5B(3B)	600(700)	550(600)
	6-258	N-12Y	.035	33	.016	5B(3B)	5B(3B)	600(700)	550(600)
	8-304	N-12Y	.035	30	.016	5B	5B	750	650(700)
	8-360	N-12Y	.035	30	.016	5B	5B	750	700
1973	6-232	N-12Y	.035	33	.016	5B(3B)	5B(3B)	700	600
	6-258	N-12Y	.035	33	.016	5B(3B)	5B(3B)	700	600
	8-304	N-12Y	.035	30	.016	5B	5B	750	700
	8-360	N-12Y	.035	30	.016	5B	5B	750	700
1974	6-232	N-12Y	.035	33	.016	5B(3B)	5B(3B)	700	600
	6-258	N-12Y	.035	33	.016	5B(3B)	5B(3B)	700	600
	8-304	N-12Y	.035	30	.016	5B	5B(2½B)	750	700
	8-360	N-12Y	.035	30	.016	5B	5B	750	700
1975	6-232	N-12Y	.035	Electronic		5B	5B	600	550(700)
	6-258	N-12Y	.035	Electronic		3B	3B	600	550(700)
	8-304	N-12Y	.035	Electronic		5B	5B	750	700
	8-360	N-12Y	.035	Electronic		5B	5B	750	700
1976	6-232	N-12Y	.035	Electronic		8B	8B	850	550(700)
	6-258	N-12Y	.035	Electronic		6B	8B	850	550(700)
	8-304	N-12Y	.035	Electronic		5B	10B(5B)	750	700
	8-360	N-12Y	.035	Electronic		—	10B(5B)	700	700
1977	6-232	See Underhood Specifications Sticker							
	6-258								
	8-304								

▲ Adjust automatic transmissions in Drive (AMC/Ford/GM) or Neutral (Chrysler), all manual transmissions are adjusted in Neutral.

■ All Figures are Before Top Dead Center.

● Figure in parentheses indicate California engine.

NOTE: The underhood specifications sticker often reflects tune-up specification changes made in production. Sticker figures must be used if they disagree with those in this chart.

Le Mans/Tempest/GTO

Lubrication and Oil Change

CHECKING OIL LEVEL

GM SAYS . . . Check engine oil level at every fuel stop

Tools and Materials . . . Clean rag, oil as needed, oil can spout or funnel
Recommended Grade of Oil . . . SE

1. Wait five minutes if engine has been running. The car must be level.

2. Locate the dipstick in the tube at the side of the engine.

3. Pull the dipstick out and wipe it dry with the clean rag.

4. Replace the dipstick, wait ten seconds, and pull it out again. Check the oil level. Replace the dipstick.

5. Add oil if the level is below FULL. If it is at ADD, you can add a full quart. Add oil at the oil filler cap opening on the engine valve rocker cover or at the front of the engine.
Caution: Overfilling can damage engine seals and cause rapid oil consumption.

BRAKE FLUID LEVEL CHECK

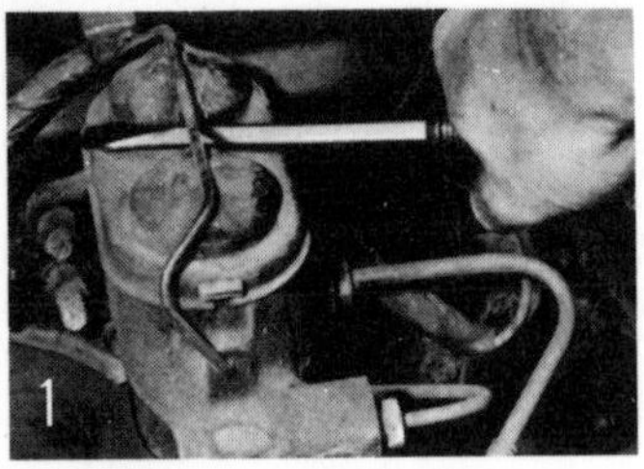

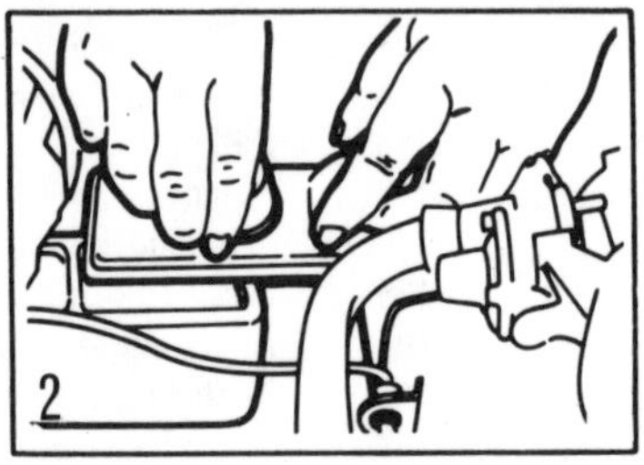

GM SAYS . . . Check brake fluid level every six months

Tools and Materials . . . Clean rag, fluid as needed, screwdriver

Recommended Grade of Brake Fluid . . . Conforming to DOT 3 specifications
1. Locate the master brake cylinder at the left rear of the engine compartment. Clean off all dirt from around cap. The car must be level.

2. Pry the wire retaining clip off the cap top with a screwdriver.

3. Remove the cap and gasket by lifting up.

4. Fluid level should be within $\frac{1}{4}$ in. of lowest edge of each reservoir. Add fluid as necessary.

5. Replace cap and gasket; secure retaining clip. If level was low, check again soon. If fluid is repeatedly low, there is a leak; have a mechanic check the system.
Caution: Don't leave brake fluid containers or master cylinder open any longer than necessary. Brake fluid picks up damaging moisture from the air.

MANUAL TRANSMISSION FLUID LEVEL CHECK

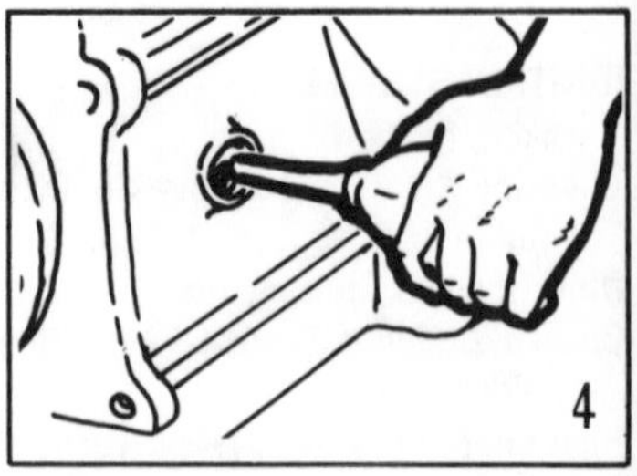

GM SAYS . . . Check transmission fluid level every four months
Tools and Materials . . . Adjustable wrench, screwdriver, suction gun, fluid as needed
Recommended grade of lubricant . . . SAE 80W or 80W-90 GL-5 gear lubricant, five speed transmission requires Dexron® II
1. Locate transmission fluid filler plug on side of transmission housing under car. The car must be level.
2. Wipe off and remove filler plug.
3. Insert screwdriver to check level. Fluid level should be up to bottom edge of filler hole.
4. Add lubricant as needed with suction gun.
5. Replace and tighten filler plug.

AUTOMATIC TRANSMISSION FLUID LEVEL CHECK

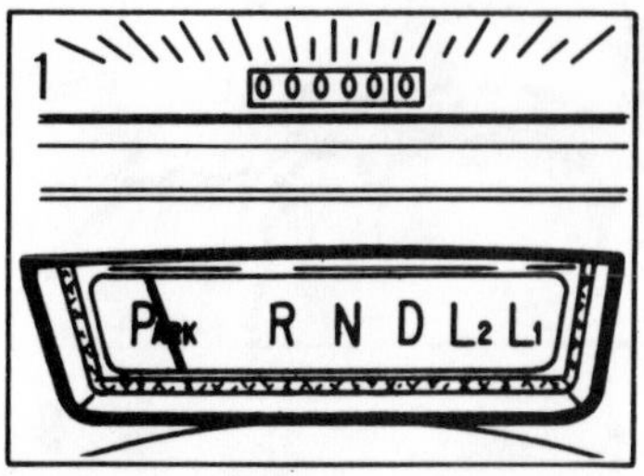

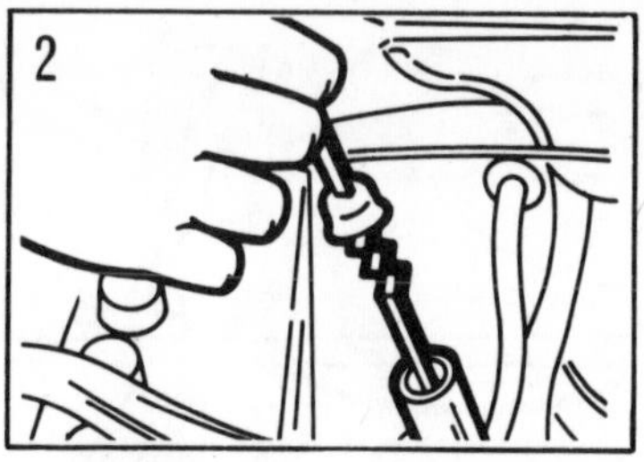

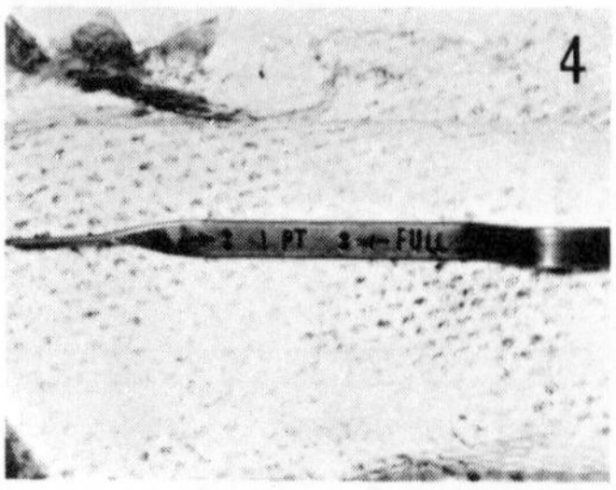

GM SAYS . . . Check transmission fluid level at every oil change (6000 mi. through 1974, 7500 mi. starting 1975)

Tools and Materials . . . Funnel, fluid as needed, clean rag

Recommended grade of lubricant . . . Dexron® II or Type A

1. The engine should be thoroughly warmed up and running. The car must be level. The transmission must be in Park.
2. Locate the dipstick at the rear of the engine. Pull it out, wipe it off, and replace it.
3. Wait ten seconds; pull out the dipstick and check the level.
4. If the fluid on the dipstick is hot, it should be between ADD and FULL. If it is warm, it should be at the ADD mark. The distance between ADD and FULL is one pint.
5. Use the funnel to add fluid through the dipstick tube.

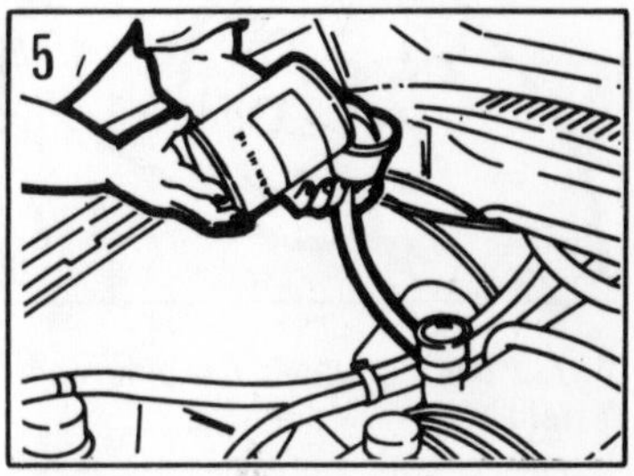

Caution: Overfilling will cause foaming and fluid loss.

CHECKING REAR AXLE LUBRICANT LEVEL

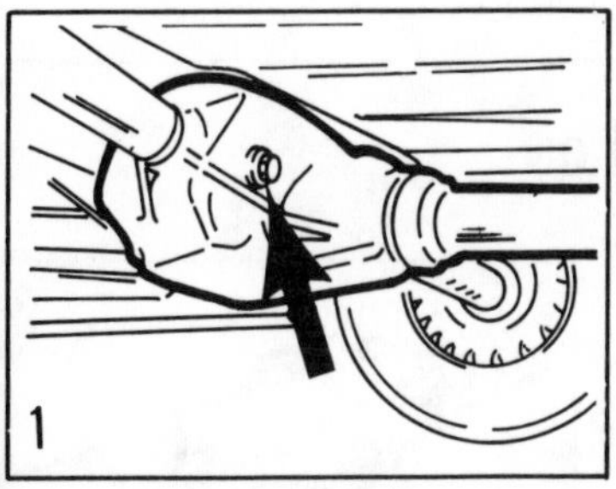

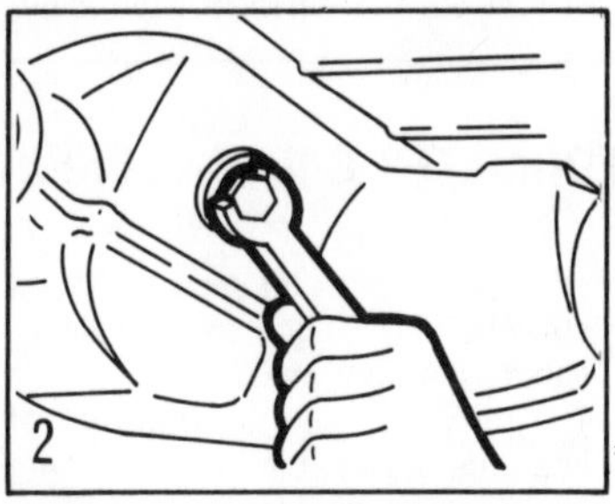

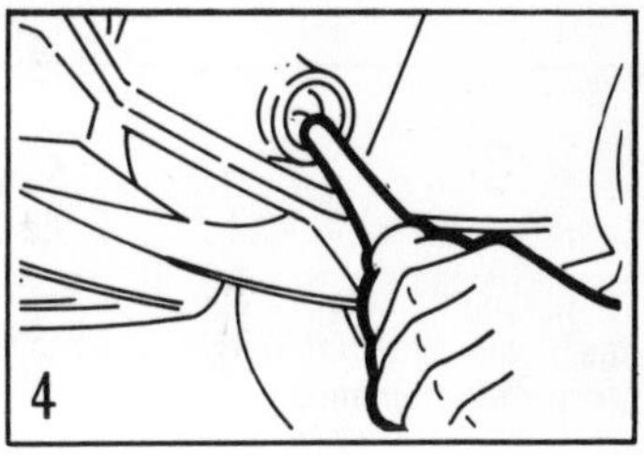

GM SAYS . . . Check rear axle lubricant level at every oil change (6000 mi. through 1974, 7500 mi. thereafter)

Tools and Materials . . . Adjustable wrench, rag, screwdriver, suction gun, lubricant as needed

Recommended grade of lubricant . . . SAE 80W or 80W-90 GL-5 gear lubricant, limited slip, Safe-T-Track, or Positraction axles require a special lubricant

1. The car must be level. Locate the filler plug on the forward side or rear cover of the rear axle center (differential) housing.
2. Wipe the area clean and remove the filler plug.
3. Insert the screwdriver to check the level. The fluid should be right up to the plug opening.
4. Add lubricant as needed with suction gun.
5. Replace and tighten the filler plug.

CHANGING ENGINE OIL AND FILTER

GM SAYS . . . Change engine oil every 6000 mi. through 1974, 7500 mi. thereafter; change filter at every second oil change

Tools and Materials . . . Adjustable wrench, oil pouring spout or funnel, filter wrench, oil drain pan of six or more quarts capacity, amount of oil specified in Capacities Chart, filter

1. Engine must be warm and the car must be parked on the level.
2. Locate the drain plug on the engine oil pan.

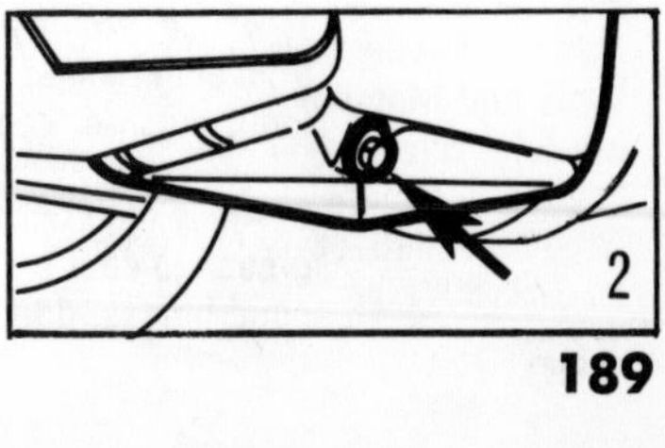

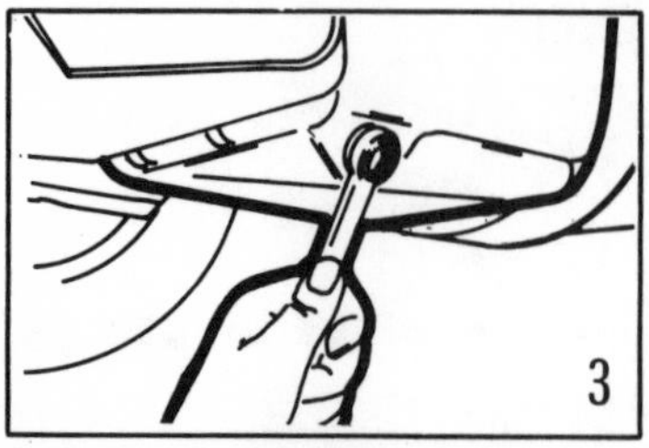

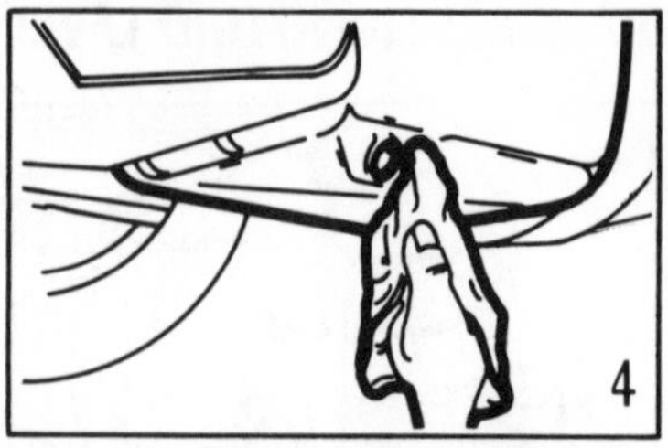

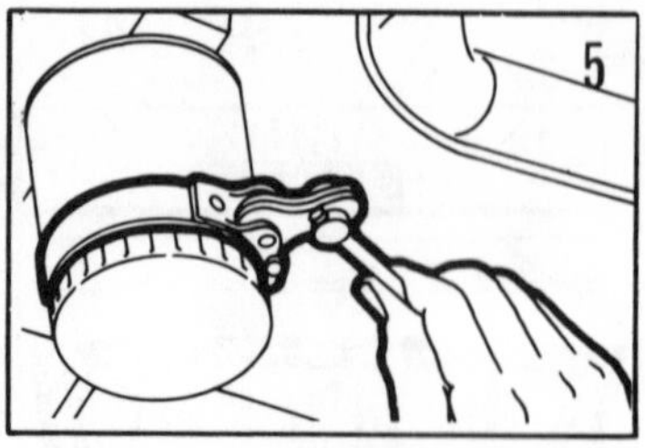

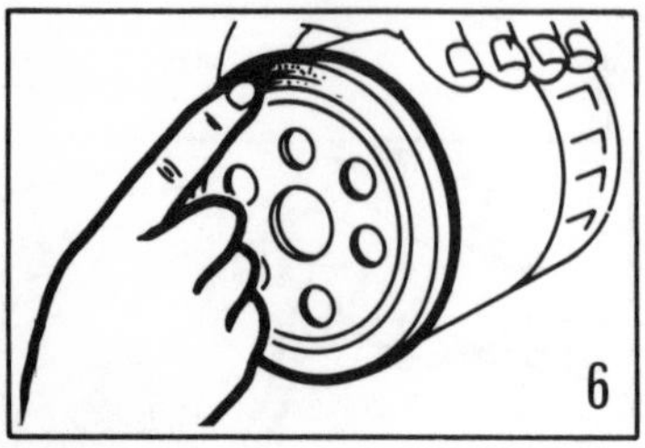

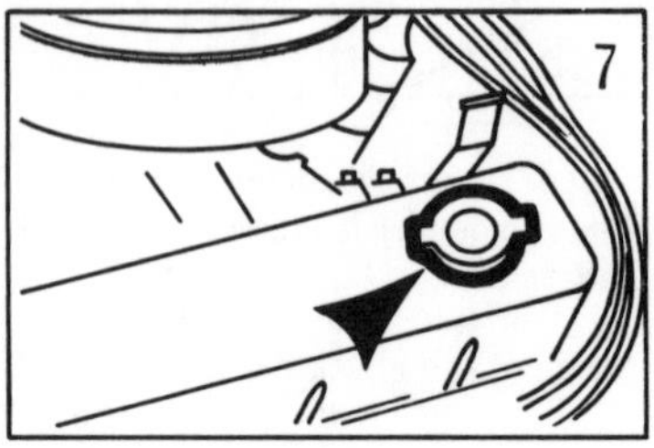

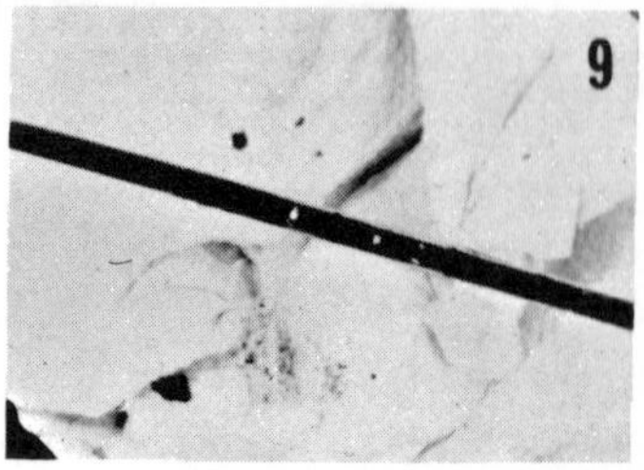

3. Put the pan under the plug and carefully remove the plug.

4. Let all the dirty oil drain out. When it stops, wipe off the area and replace the plug.

5. Locate the filter and place the pan under it. Unscrew the filter with the special wrench and remove it. Dump the contents into the pan.

6. Wipe off the filter mounting area. Rub clean oil on the new filter gasket. Screw the filter on, but tighten only by hand.

7. Remove the oil filler cap from the engine rocker arm cover or the tube at the front of the engine.

8. Pour the required number of quarts of oil into the filler cap opening.

9. Pull out the dipstick, wipe it off, and check the level. It is normal for it to be slightly above FULL.

10. Start the engine. The oil pressure light should go out or pressure should show on the gauge in 30 seconds or less. If it doesn't, stop the engine and correct the problem.

11. Check for leaks around the filter or drain plug with the engine running. Stop the engine and recheck the level.

SPEEDOMETER CABLE LUBRICATION

If the speedometer is jerky or noisy, the cable is either damaged or in need of lubrication.

1. Locate the cable attachment behind the speedometer dial.
2. Unclip or unscrew, as required, the outer cable housing from the speedometer.
3. Pull inner cable completely out of outer casing. Note carefully which end is top. Check for wear or frayed strands. If damaged, replace inner cable with new one.
4. Apply a small amount of speedometer cable lubricant into cable casing. Replace inner cable in shaft, noting that top end is not inserted accidentally. Turn inner cable as it is being re-inserted. Twist cable when all the way in, to lock into position at lower end.

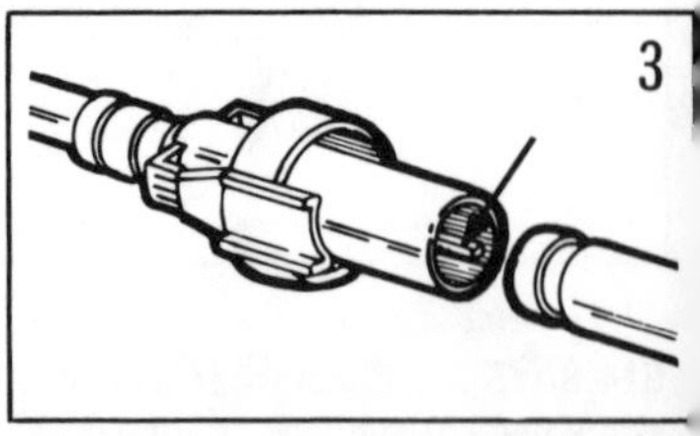

5. Reconnect cable to speedometer head under instrument panel.

DOOR HINGES AND STOPS

(lubricate every 6 months)
1. Brush any dirt accumulations from door hinges and stops. Use old tooth brush or rag.

2. Apply dab of white waterproof grease to door hinges, trunk hinges, hood hinges, door stops.

DOOR LOCKS

(lubricate every 6 months)
1. Insert door key half way into lock.
2. Spray aerosol lock lubricant into lock.
3. Push key rest of way into lock; turn back and forth several times.

Cooling System

IT IS RECOMMENDED . . . that radiator coolant (water/antifreeze mixture) level be checked once or twice a month. Do this when engine is cold. Check more often if you do a lot of hard driving. Coolant is checked visually on models with expansion tanks.
Keep coolant up to recommended level in radiator. If coolant checks frequently low, look for leaks. Tighten all hose clamps ocassionally. For best results, keep a 50/50 water/antifreeze mixture year round. Change complete coolant

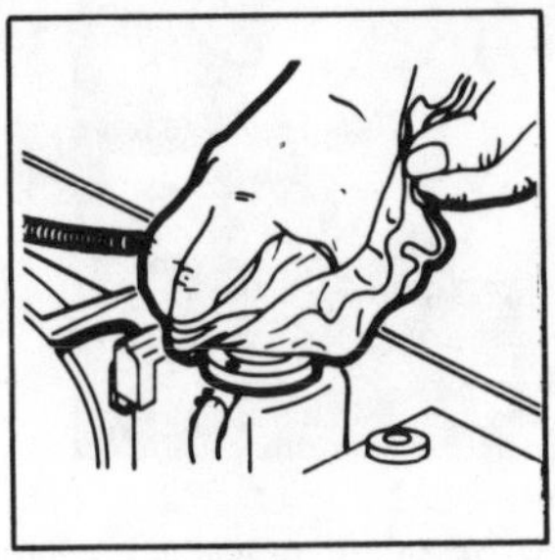

mixture every 24 months.
CAUTION: If you must check coolant in a hot engine, cover radiator cap

with thick rag before releasing. Remove cap slowly . . . press down and turn.

REPLACING THE THERMOSTAT

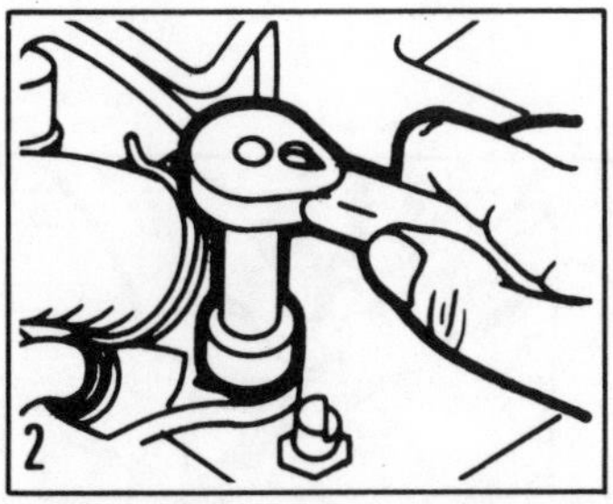

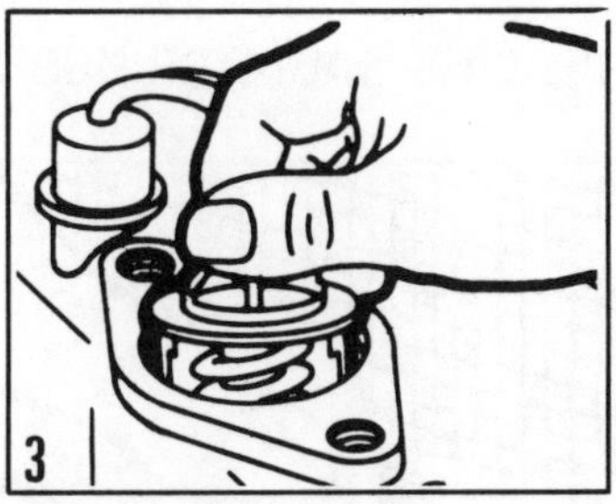

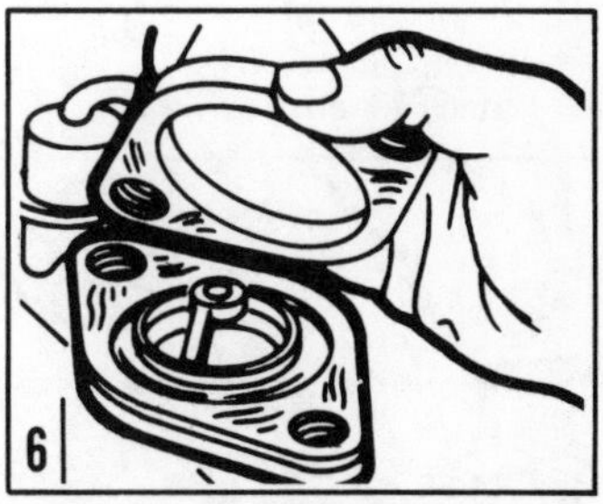

Poor heater output is often caused by a thermostat stuck open; occasionally one sticks shut causing immediate overheating. The thermostat is located inside the housing where the top radiator hose connects to the engine.
Tools and Materials . . . New thermostat, gasket, box or socket wrench, container for coolant

1. Drain radiator of about half its coolant. (See Changing Anti-Freeze)
2. Loosen and remove both retaining bolts and lift thermostat housing off the engine.
NOTE: If you're careful it won't be necessary to remove radiator hose.
3. Remove old thermostat.
4. Scrape thermostat housing flange and engine block surface to remove old gasket debris.
5. Drop new thermostat into place—spring down.
6. Install new gasket with sealer applied to both sides.
7. Replace thermostat housing and tighten both retaining bolts.
8. Refill the system and let the engine warm up with the heater on. Check the level.

CHECKING THE RADIATOR CAP

Check radiator cap occasionally for worn or cracked gasket. If cap doesn't seal properly, fluid will be lost and engine will overheat. Replace worn cap with new cap rated 15 lbs. pressure.

ADJUSTING THE FAN BELT

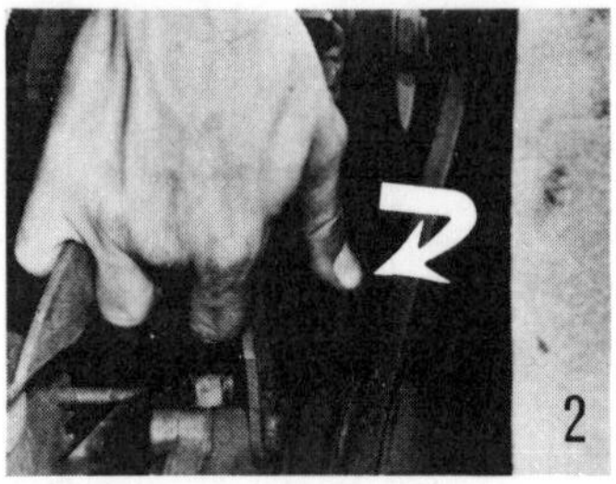

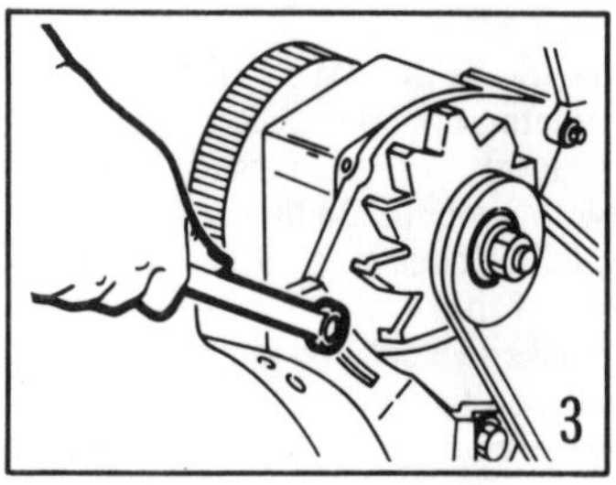

The fan belt not only drives the radiator fan, it turns the water pump and drives the alternator. It's easy to see that the condition and proper tension of the belt are vital, since almost all engine cooling and electrical power is dependent on it. The belt deserves an occasional look and tension check.

1. Inspect fan belt occasionally. If worn, frayed or cracked on inner driving surface, replace.

CAUTION: An overtightened belt may damage alternator and water pump bearing.

2. Check tension occasionally. Press thumb at midpoint of belt span between pulleys. If belt depresses more than ½ inch, tightening is needed. A too-loose belt will not drive alternator and water pump effectively.

3. To adjust loosen alternator pivot and adjustment bolts, pivot the alternator until the belt is properly tensioned (¼ in. deflection) and then tighten bolts. Tighten first the adjustment bolt, then the pivot bolt.

REPLACING RADIATOR HOSES

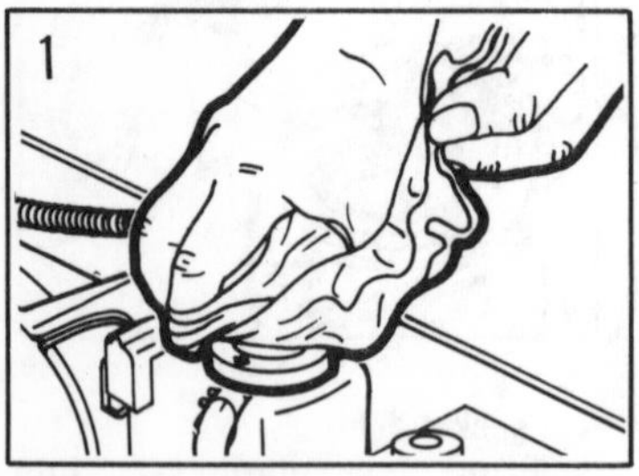

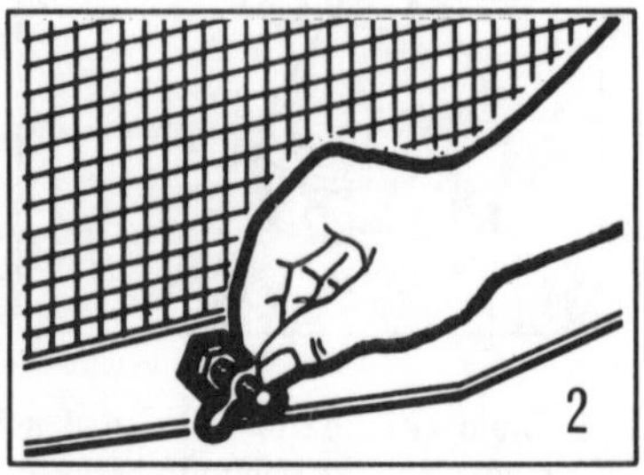

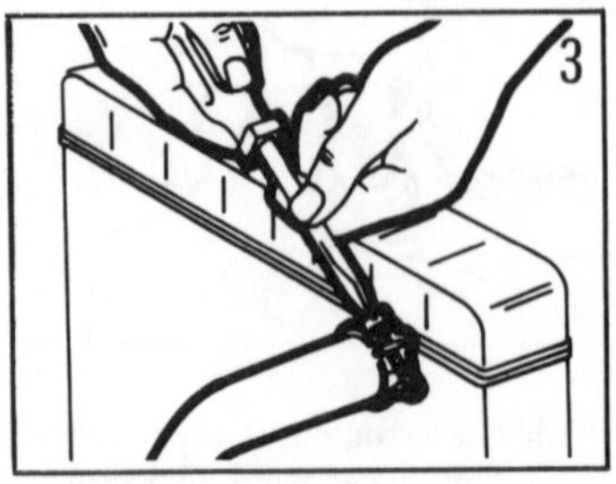

Tools and Materials . . . Screwdriver, knife, sandpaper, coolant container Coolant drain and refill work may be done alone; when changing hoses, coolant must also be drained as part of job. Check hose clamps for tightness and good condition.

Discard all hoses with cracks or soft spots.

1. Remove radiator cap. Open radiator petcock (See 2). Drain coolant into catch basin. If near 24 months old or discolored, discard old coolant.

2. Petcock or drain plug is located at the bottom rear of the radiator. Open petcock or remove plug to drain.

3. Loosen clamps at each end of hose(s). Work loose; pull off. If old hose clamps are rusted or damaged, replace with new units.

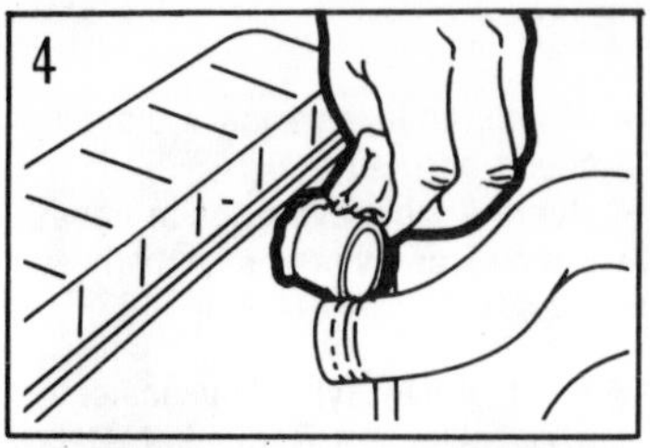

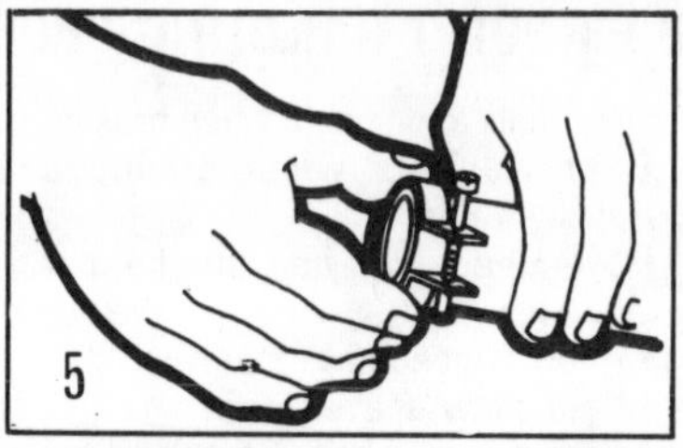

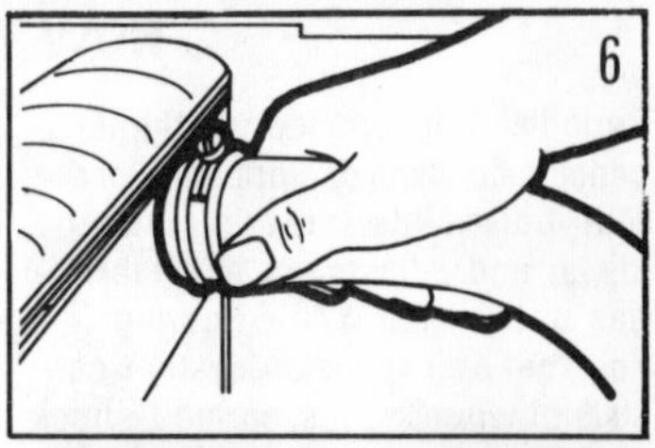

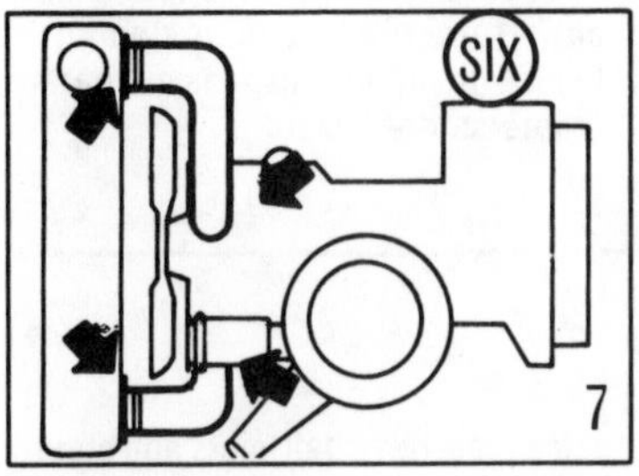

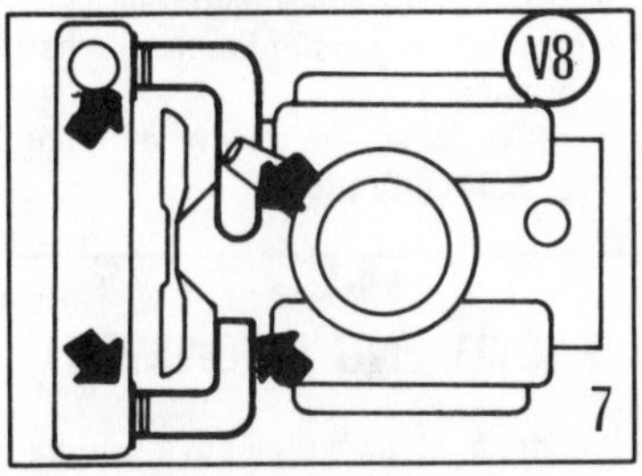

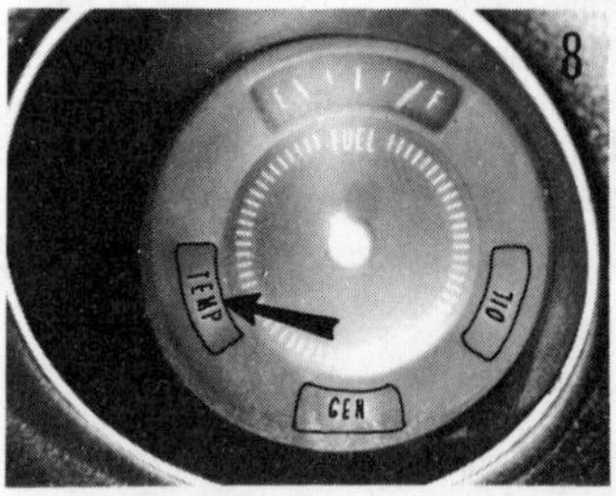

4. Wipe all hose connections clean. Use sandpaper to get rid of residue. Check all hoses for weak spots, as well as cracks inside and out.
5. Slip clamps over each hose end. Slip hose ends all the way onto cleaned up hose connections.
6. Place hose clamp ¼ inch from hose end. Tighten. Close petcock. Refill with 50/50 coolant/water mix.
7. Start engine; allow to warm up with the heater on. Check for coolant leaks. Recheck the level.
8. Road test car; watch for temperature warning light or gauge.

CHANGING ANTI-FREEZE

GM SAYS . . . Change coolant mixture at least every two years, sooner if discoloration is noticed

Tools and Materials . . . Amount of anti-freeze equal to half the coolant capacity, drain container, adjustable wrench, funnel

CAUTION: Anti-freeze can kill grass and is a powerful poison; dispose of it carefully and flush away any spillage. It also stains painted surfaces.

1. Remove the radiator cap.
2. Open the radiator petcock at the lower rear of the radiator. Let the coolant drain.
3. Locate the block drain plug or plugs. There is one on the side of inline engines and one on each side of V-type engines. Remove these plugs. If nothing comes out, poke around inside the hole with a screwdriver to dislodge blockage.
4. DO NOT DO THIS IF YOUR ENGINE IS WARM! Fill the radiator with water from a hose. Let it drain out the engine block and radiator drains. Repeat the operation until only clean water comes out.
5. If you have a coolant catch tank, remove and flush that out.
6. Replace the plugs; close the petcock.
7. Pour in an amount of anti-freeze equal to half the coolant capacity (see the capacity chart). A 50% mixture gives the best possible boiling and freezing points and assures rust protection.
8. Fill the radiator with water. Start the engine and let it warm up with the heater on (the heater is part of the system). Leave the cap off and add water until the radiator stays full.

9. Replace the radiator cap. If you have a coolant catch tank, fill it to the normal level with the 50% anti-freeze/water solution.
10. On systems without the catch tank, some coolant will be lost out the overflow tube during initial operation. This is not a defect, so long as the level doesn't drop more than about two inches below the filler neck. Keep the coolant at this level.

Suspension and Tires

The front wheels turn on the wheel bearings, which are mounted on the steering spindles (knuckles). There is a pivot point at the top and bottom of each knuckle, called a ball joint. The lower ball joint usually wears out before the upper. The ball joints attach the knuckle to the upper and lower control arms at each side. A coil spring is mounted between the control arms at each side and a shock absorber is inside each spring. The rear suspension consists of coil springs, upper and lower control arms on each side, and shock absorbers.

HOW TO PINPOINT HANDLING PROBLEMS

Periodic maintenance of the suspension consists of lubrication of the four ball joints, steering linkage joints, and adjustment and lubrication of the front wheel bearings.

Your car's suspension system consists of wheels, tires, springs, shock absorbers, sway (or stabilizer) bars, ball joints, steering linkage. If any of these items is out of adjustment or badly worn, you may notice any of these symptoms:

- car pulls to one side when braking
- car wanders when driving a straight line
- overall ride may be either hard or bouncy
- effort is needed to steer vehicle
- tires show uneven wear
- tires squeal when cornering
- front of car dips or bounces when braking
- car rocks side-to-side when going over rough road
- wheels bounce to make slapping sound on road
- steering wheel vibrates in hands
- front of car vibrates at highway speeds

Any of above symptoms indicates corrective action is needed. Delay can: ruin tires; cause damage/failure to other suspension parts; create safety hazard.

FRONT END ALIGNMENT

When steering, handling and/or tire wear indicate front end alignment may be needed, this work can only be done at an automotive service shop. DO NOT PUT OFF NEEDED FRONT END ALIGNMENT. At the same time, have ball joints and steering linkage checked.

STEERING

If steering linkage, front suspension and steering column components are in good condition, there should be not more than 1½ inch free play in the steering wheel when measured at the rim of the wheel. If a loud knock is heard when turning the steering wheel from one extreme to the other, have a mechanic check the steering system.

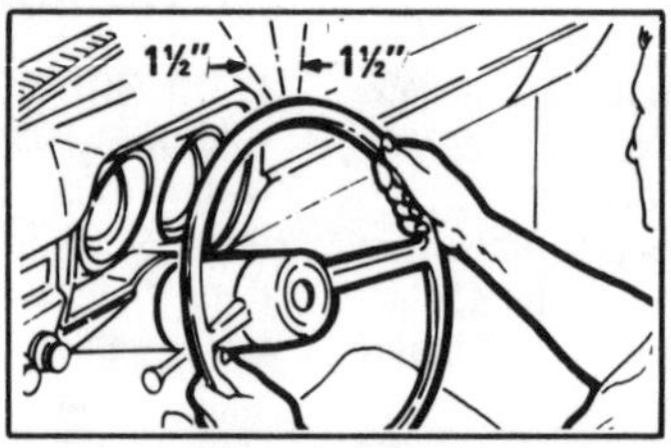

CHECKING YOUR SHOCK ABSORBERS

Shock absorbers work to keep wheels in constant contact with the road. Result in safe handling and ride control; longer tire life. So shock absorbers (or shocks) are important.

1. Check under car and locate shock absorber near each wheel.
2. Heavy oil streaks on outer shock housing indicate need for replacement.
3. Stand at front of car and apply body weight in a pumping action to front bumper or fender. Release pressure and allow car to stop rocking. Car should not bounce more than one more time after releasing pressure. Repeat at rear. If bouncing continues more than once, replacement is needed. Replace shocks in pairs (front pair or rear pair).

TOW HITCH INFORMATION

If your car is used for trailer towing you should check:
A. Cooling System; be sure coolant is at proper level in radiator. See Cooling System Section for checks to perform.
B. Check Transmission Fluid; keep topped up to proper level.
C. Check Rear Shock Absorbers; you may benefit from installation of new rear shocks.
D. Check Tire Pressures; best traction and handling can be ensured if tire pressures are properly maintained.
E. Check maintenance interval recommendations with dealer or owner's manual. These intervals are shorter for trailer towing.
F. Check with dealer or owner's manual to be sure that the car is properly equipped to handle the weight of the trailer being considered.

For safer and more trouble-free trailer towing, consider:
A. Automatic Transmission Cooler; helps remove excess heat from automatic transmission fluid built up during towing mileage. Also helps avoid radiator overheating.
B. Radiator Over-Flow Tank Kit; addition of a reservoir to catch radiator coolant overflow preventing coolant loss. Easy to install, these units help a tow car run cooler, avoid overheating due to coolant loss.
C. Heavy-Duty Shock Absorbers or Air Shocks; important to have on rear wheels if you intend to do a lot of towing or load carrying within the car itself. Don't forget to consider replacing factory shocks, when they are worn out, with heavy-duty units at the front as well.
D. Variable Load Flasher; this unit will accommodate the added load of trailer turn signal lamps on trailer when these are hooked into your car's electrical system.
E. Flex or Clutch-type Fan; these move more cooling air at low speeds and reduce load on the engine at high speeds.

Ignition System

CHECKING IGNITION SYSTEM

The ignition system consists of spark plugs; plug wires; distributor; rotor; points; condenser; coil. These units work to create a good hot spark inside the engine (ignition) at exactly the right moment (timing). If ignition is weak or timing is off, engine may be hard to start, run poorly, waste gas, lose power, backfire or not run at all.

CHECKING POINTS AND ROTOR—Six Cylinder through 1974

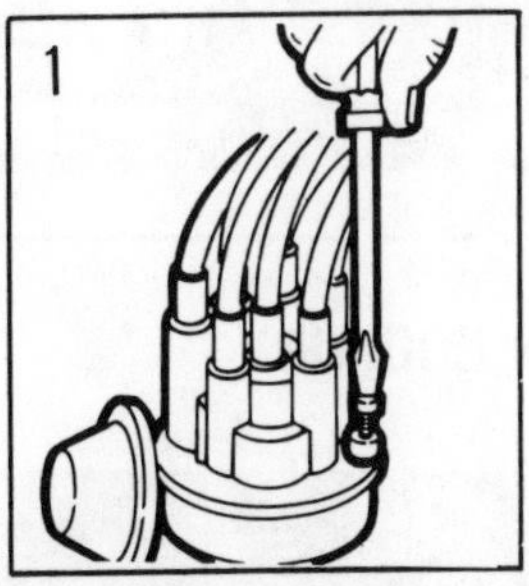

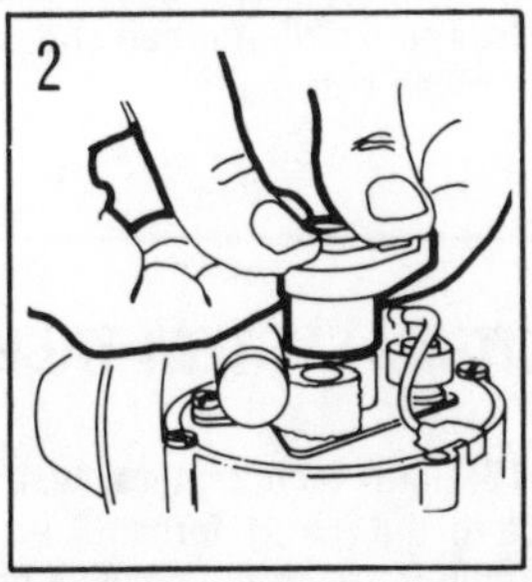

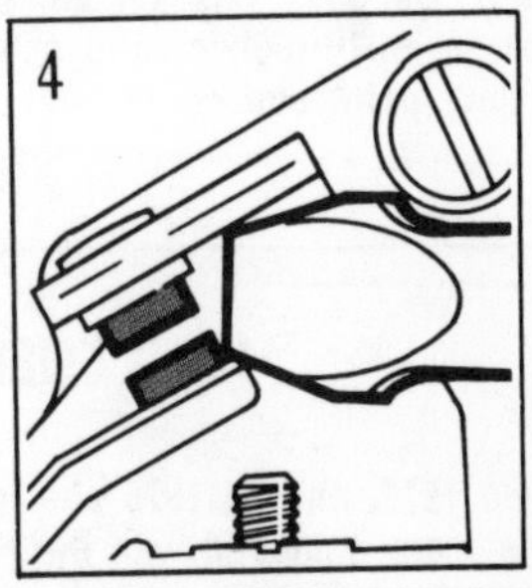

1. To open the distributor, loosen the two screws retaining the cap. Remove the coil (center) wire and lift the cap off, but keep the other wires attached.

2. Pull the rotor off (straight up). If it is cracked or metallic tip is badly burned, replace it.

3. Check the metal contacts inside the cap. Replace the cap if they are corroded or there are any cracks.

4. Pry the points apart with a screwdriver. If worn or burned, replace. If OK, check the gap.

OTHER IGNITION CHECKPOINTS

Inspect spark plug wires. If cracked or brittle, entire set should be replaced. Also, check center coil high tension wire. Inspect distributor cap. Wipe inside clean occasionally with dry, lint-free rag. If cap is cracked or rotor contacts are excessively burned, replace cap.

CHECKING POINTS AND ROTOR—V8 through 1974

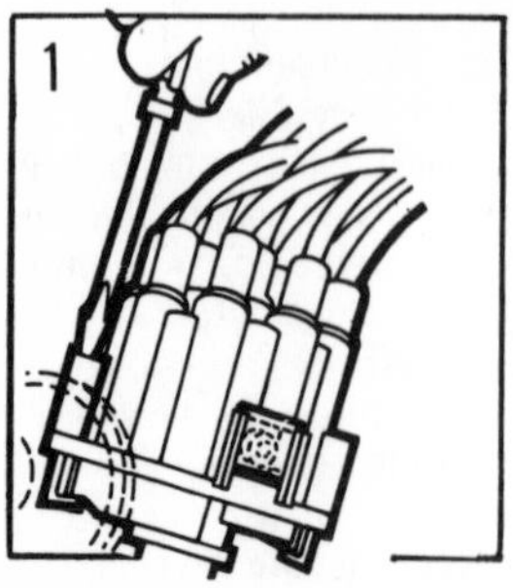

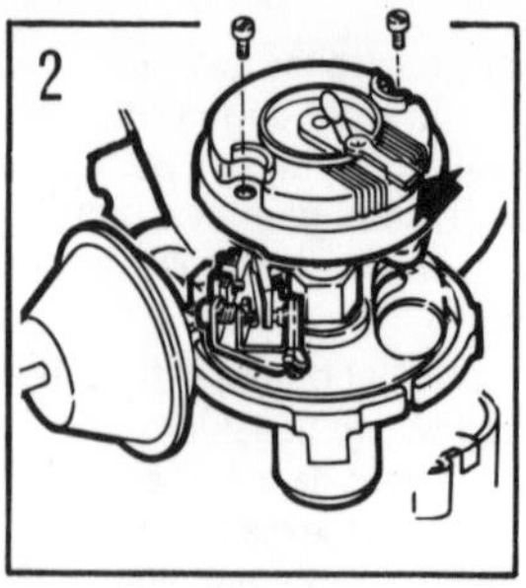

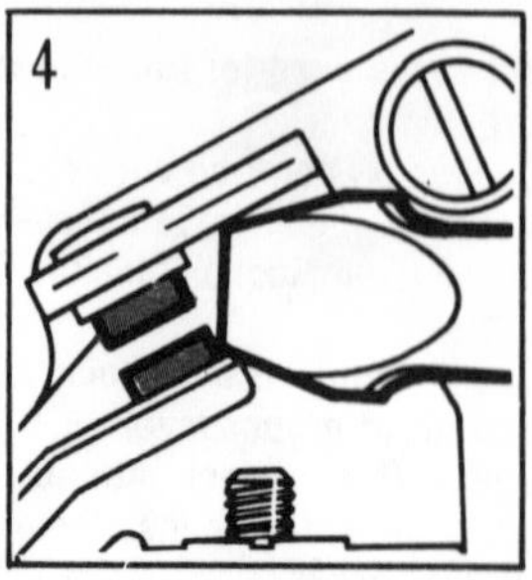

1. To open the distributor, depress the screw in the cap and rotate the latch off the distributor (there are two latches). Remove the coil (center) wire and lift off the cap. Keep the other wires attached.
2. Remove the two screws and lift off the rotor. If it is cracked or metallic tip is badly burned, replace it.
3. Check the metal contacts inside the cap. Replace the cap if they are corroded or there are any cracks.
4. Pry the points apart with a screwdriver. If worn or burned, replace. If OK, check the gap.

OTHER IGNITION CHECKPOINTS

Inspect spark plug wires. If cracked or brittle, entire set should be replaced. Also, check center coil high tension wire. Inspect distributor cap. Wipe inside clean occasionally with dry, lint-free rag. If cap is cracked or rotor contacts are excessively burned, replace cap.

CHECKING IGNITION SYSTEM—All 1975 and Later Engines

These engines all use the General Motors HEI (High Energy Ignition) system. No internal distributor maintenance or adjustments are required. Because this system produces a much higher voltage than ordinary point and condenser systems, the condition of the spark plug or high tension wires should be checked occasionally. There is no need to check timing on a regular basis, since there are no wearing parts. The distributor cap should be kept clean externally.

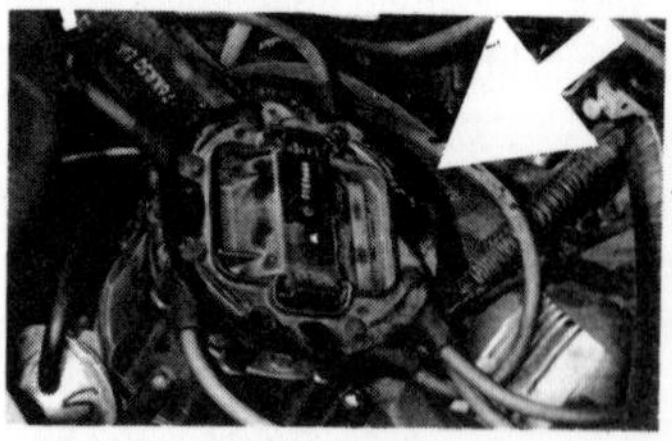

HIGH ENERGY IGNITION SYSTEM TACHOMETER HOOKUP

Some 1974, and all 1975 and later cars are equipped with the High Energy Ignition System which uses a different tachometer hookup than was used in previous years.

1. On the V6 and V8 engines, connect the tachometer to the TACH terminal on the distributor and to a suitable ground.

NOTE: Some tachometers must connect to the TACH terminal on the distributor and to the positive terminal on the battery. If there is any doubt check the tachometer manufacturer's instructions.

2. On the inline six cylinder, connect the tachometer to the TACH terminal on the coil, opposite the BAT terminal, and to a ground.

SPARK PLUG REPLACEMENT

GM SAYS . . . Replace spark plugs every 12-18,000 miles on models through 1974, every 22,500 miles on 1975 and later models, sooner if poor performance or missing is noted
Tools and Materials . . . New plugs

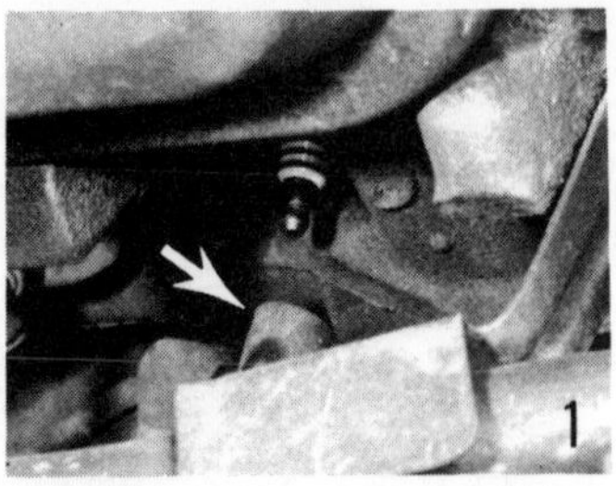

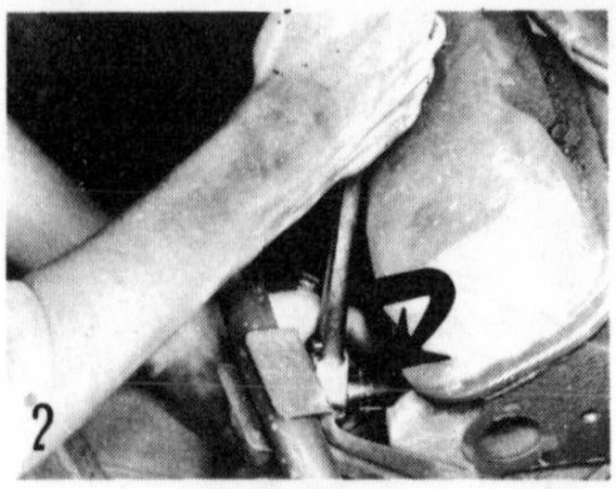

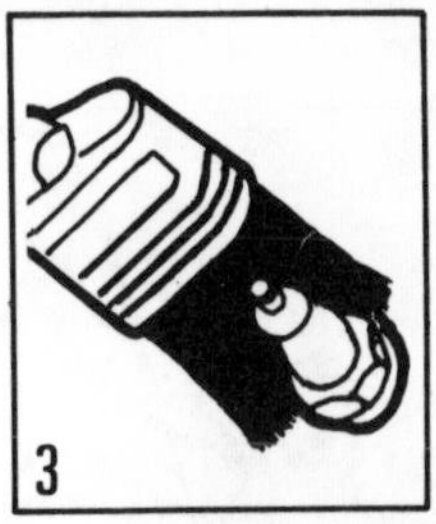

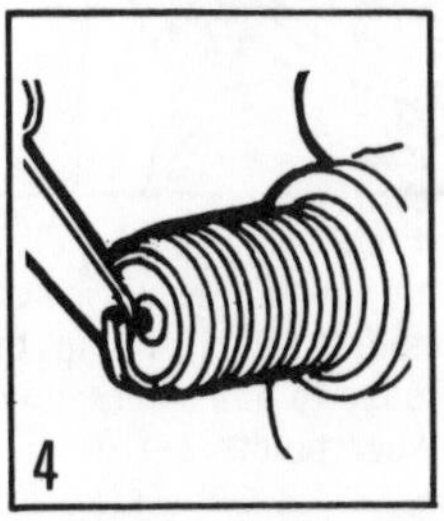

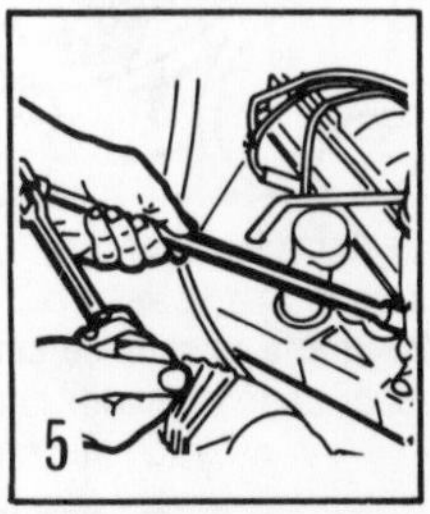

of type listed in Tune-Up Chart, spark plug socket to fit new plugs (either 5/8 or 13/16 in.), spark plug gap gauge

1. Remove spark plug wire by grasping rubber boot. Do not jerk wire off. If stuck, turn boot, pulling gently.

2. Loosen spark plug using socket wrench.

3. Wipe or brush loose dirt from around plug before removing. Do not let dirt drop into engine through plug hole. Unscrew plug.

4. Check plug electrode gap on new spark plug. Adjust to the specified gap, using the bending tool on the gauge. Plug gap is correct when the gauge drags slightly as it is pulled between plug electrodes.

5. Thread new plug into plug hole by hand. Hand tighten. Do not force or cross thread. Use socket wrench to tighten firmly but do not force. Replace plug wire. Press boot firmly.

REPLACING IGNITION POINTS AND CONDENSER

GM SAYS . . . Replace every 12,000 miles
Tools and Materials . . . Magnetic screwdriver, feeler gauges, replacement points and condenser
Points and condenser work together. Always replace condenser also when installing new points.

REPLACING IGNITION POINTS AND CONDENSER—Six Cylinder through 1974

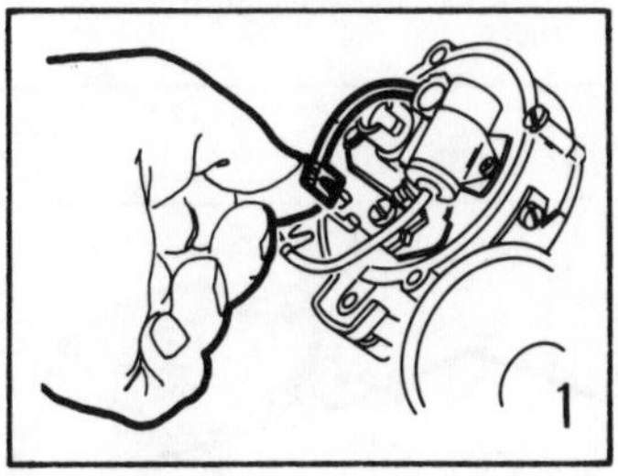

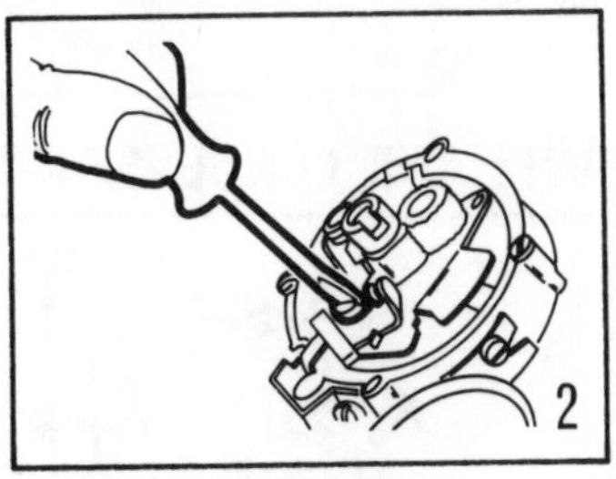

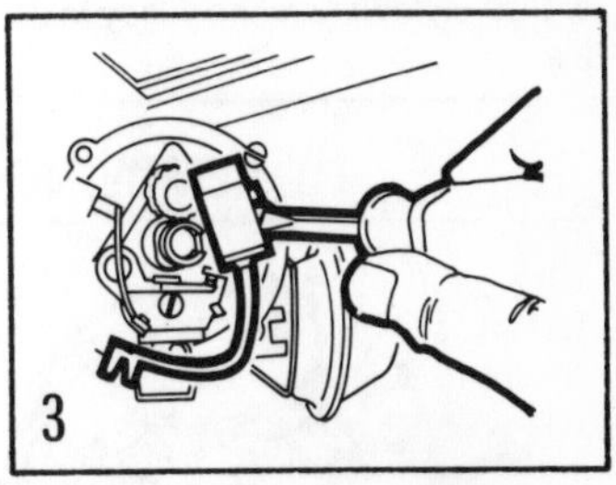

1. Disconnect the two wire terminals connected to the point set. Notice that the condenser connector is on the outside.

2. Remove points attaching screw being very careful not to drop screw inside distributor.

3. Remove screw which holds condenser. DO NOT DROP SCREW.

4. Wipe all dirt from distributor plate and cam with clean, lint-free rag.

INSTALLING POINTS AND CONDENSER

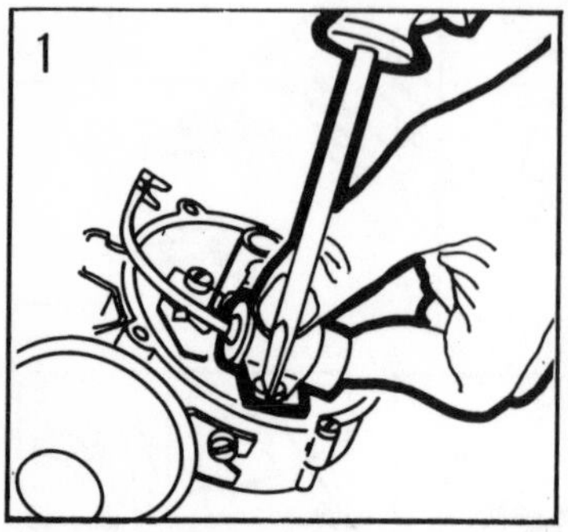

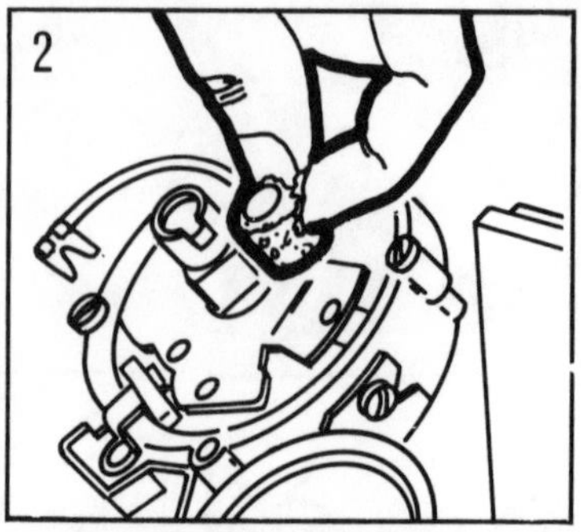

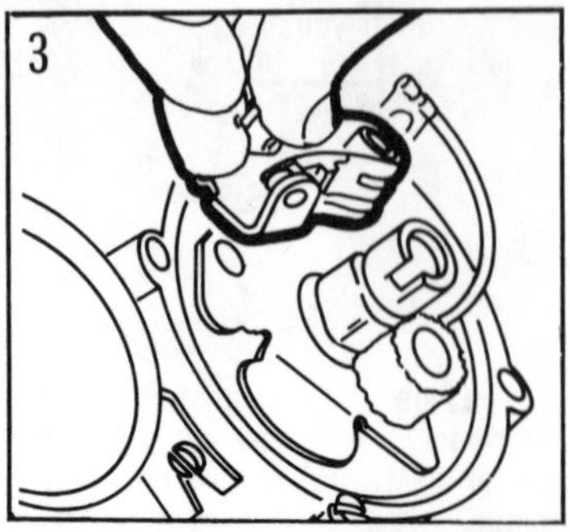

1. Attach new condenser with screw.
2. Rotate or replace cam lubricator. Fiber cam lubricator must be turned 180° every 12,000 mi., replaced every 24,000. When replacing, simply pull it up and off stud; push new lubricator down over stud. DO NOT attempt to add oil or grease to fiber lubricator.
3. Position new points set in distributor. Attach retaining screw lightly. Replace both wire terminals. The condenser wire goes on the outside of the two.

SETTING THE CONTACT GAP

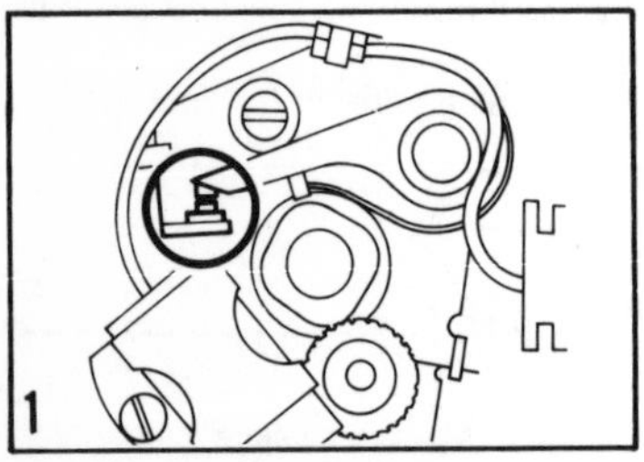

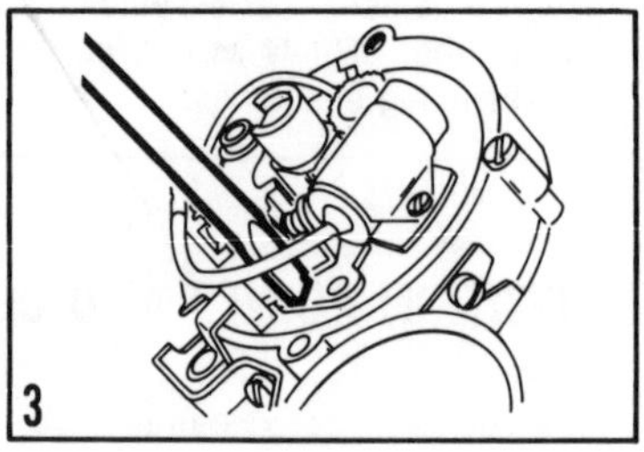

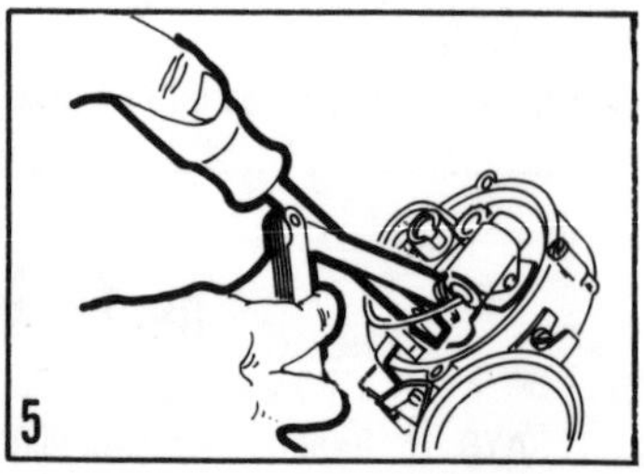

1. Check that point contacts meet squarely. If they do not, bend bracket supporting fixed contact using needle-nosed pliers.
2. Turn engine by ignition key (you'll need a helper) until rubbing block on point set is on one of the high spots of distributor cam. You may use wrench on lower engine pulley to do this.
3. Insert screwdriver in slot near point contacts; twist to open or close gap.
4. Correct gap is in Tune-Up Specifications Chart.
5. Insert correct size feeler gauge. Adjust gap with screwdriver until feeler gauge can be moved in and out between contacts with only slight drag.
6. Tighten point set holddown screw. Recheck gap; it might have changed from tightening holddown screw. Re-adjust if needed.
7. Align tab inside rotor with notch on distributor shaft and push rotor onto shaft. Rotor must be fully seated on shaft.
8. Replace distributor cap; install screws.

REMOVING POINTS AND CONDENSER—V8 through 1974

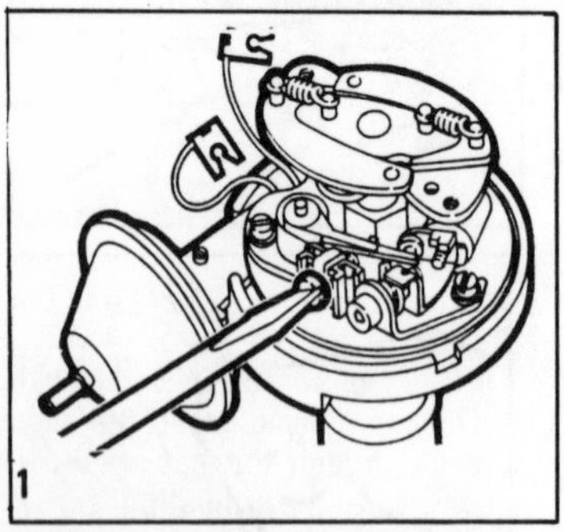

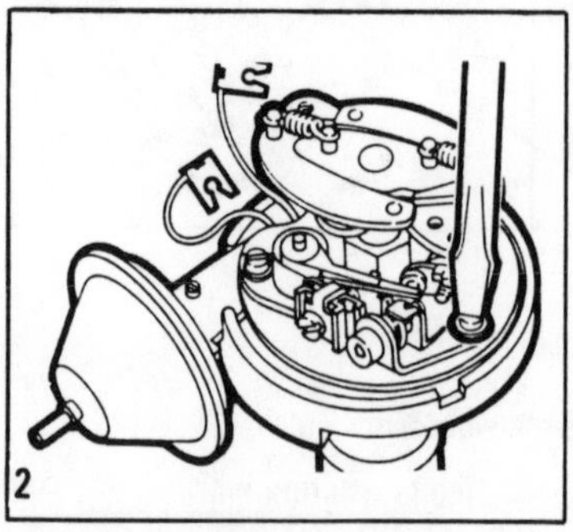

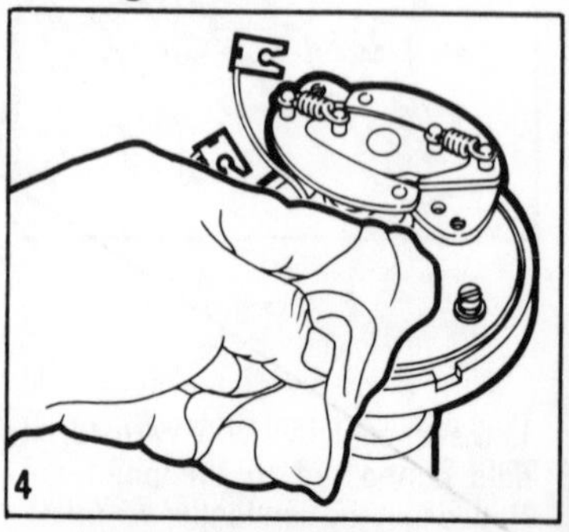

1. Disconnect the two wire terminals connected to the point set. Notice that the condenser connector is on the outside.
2. Loosen, but do not remove the two points attaching screws. Slide the points off the screws to remove.
3. Remove screw which holds condenser. DO NOT DROP SCREW.

NOTE: Later models use a combined points and condenser set. When you remove points you also remove condenser. You can also install these sets in early cars.

4. Wipe all dirt from distributor plate and cam with clean, lint-free rag.

INSTALLING POINTS AND CONDENSER

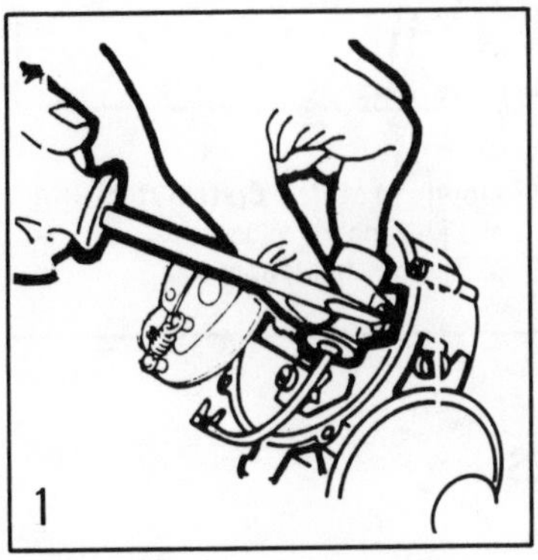

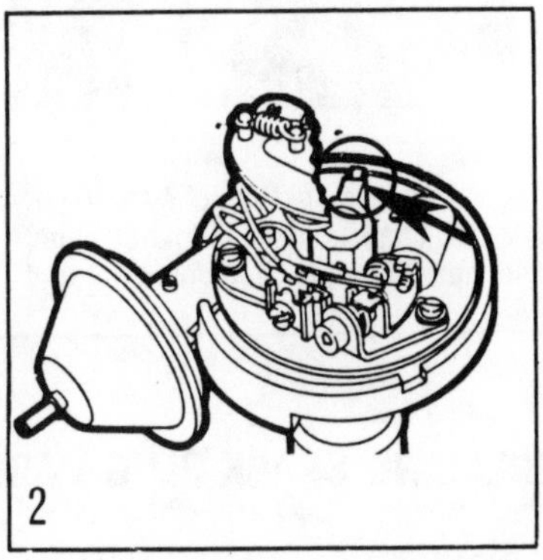

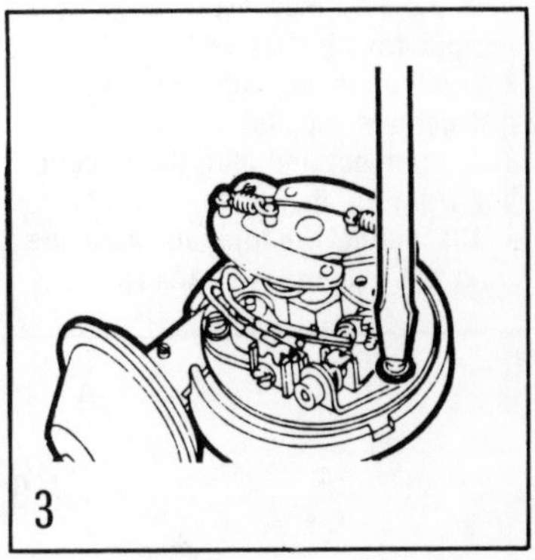

1. Attach new condenser with screw.
2. Rotate or replace cam lubricator. Fiber cam lubricator must be turned 180° every 12,000 mi., replaced every 24,000. When replacing, simply pull it up and off stud; push new lubricator down over stud. DO NOT attempt to add oil or grease to fiber lubricator.
3. Position new points set in distributor by sliding onto screws. Tighten screws.

SETTING THE CONTACT GAP

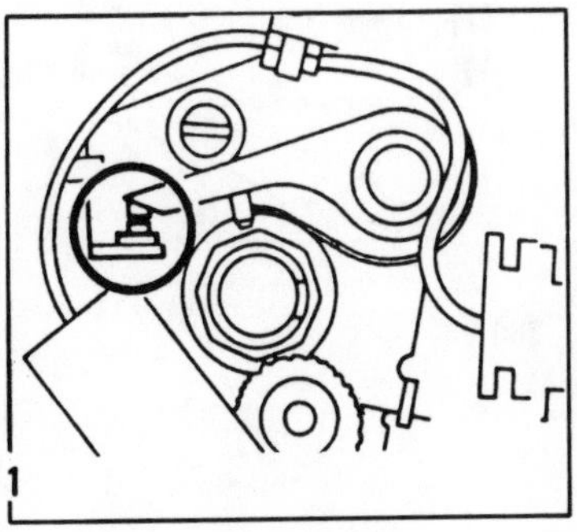

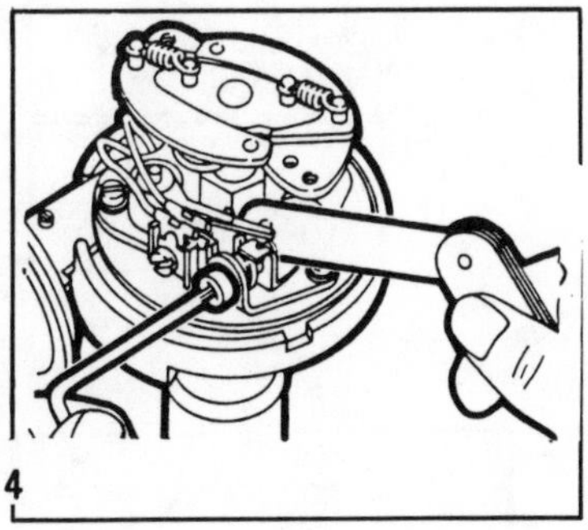

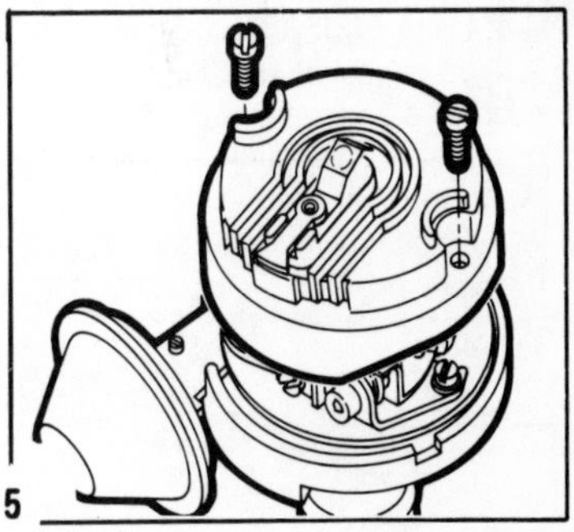

1. Check that point contacts meet squarely. If they do not, bend bracket supporting fixed contact using needle-nosed pliers.
2. Turn engine by ignition key (you'll need a helper) until rubbing block on point set is on one of the high spots of distributor cam. You may use wrench on lower engine pulley to do this.
3. Insert a ⅛ in. allen wrench into points adjusting screw. Correct gap is in the Tune-Up Specification Chart.
4. Insert correct size feeler gauge. Adjust gap with wrench until feeler gauge can be moved in and out between contacts with only slight drag.
5. Install rotor on advance weight assembly. The two lugs on the bottom of the rotor are shaped differently, so it can only be installed one way. Tighten screws.
6. Install cap by depressing screws and turning latches onto body of distributor. Insert the coil wire into the cap.
7. Point gap can be adjusted with the engine running. Insert the allen wrench though the cap window, slowly turn the adjusting screw clockwise until the engine just starts to misfire, and then turn it back ½ turn.

ADJUSTING IGNITION TIMING

Adjusting timing is the important finishing touch to any tune-up. While not difficult, job requires timing light. Timing setting is given in the Tune-Up Specifications Chart.

1. Locate timing marks and pointer (notches) on engine and lower engine pulley. Clean away dirt. Mark the pointer notches with chalk.
2. Hook up timing light according to instructions supplied with it.
3. Disconnect and plug the vacuum line from the distributor.
4. Disconnect the fuel tank vent line from the evaporative canister.

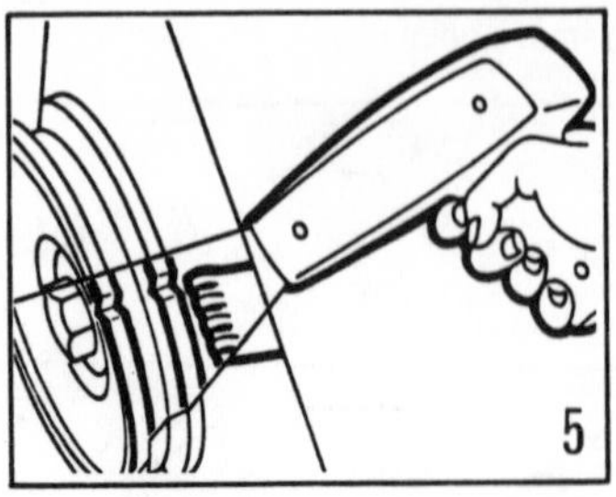

5. Aim timing light at pulley mark(s). If the chalked marks do not align, loosen distributor holddown nut and slowly rotate distributor until chalked marks align.
6. Tighten holddown nut.

REPLACING SPARK PLUG WIRES

Use the firing order illustration to guide you when replacing your ignition wires and/or distributor cap.

1. Remove only one wire at a time from the engine.
2. Match the wire removed with the same length wire in the replacement set.
3. Route the replacement wire in the same way as the original.
4. After all wires are replaced, check that all wires on 1974 and earlier distributors are seated in the distributor cap. Check that all boots are in place.
5. If you run into difficulty, go to the Firing Order illustrations for help.

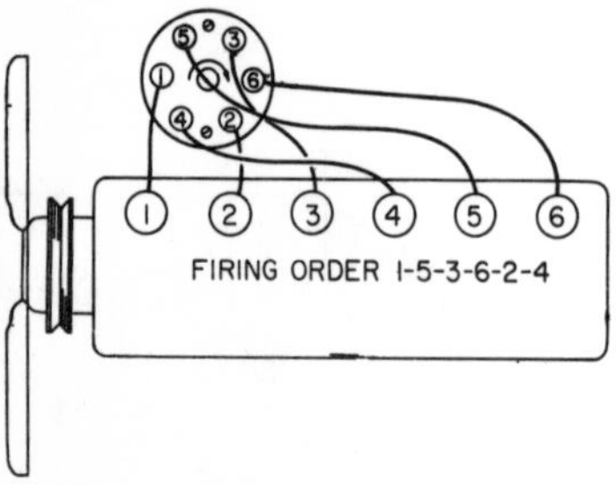

250 Six

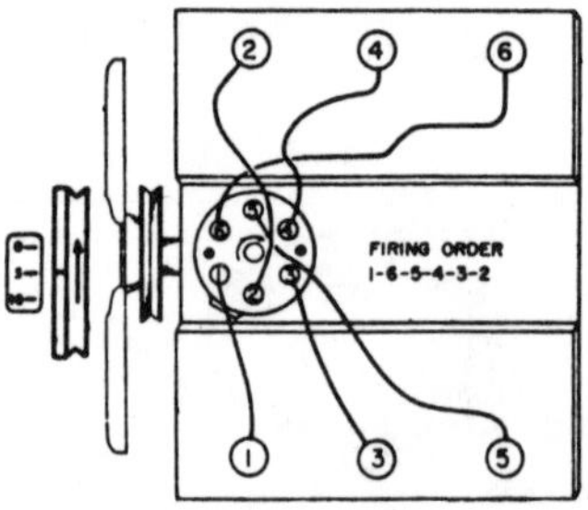

V6

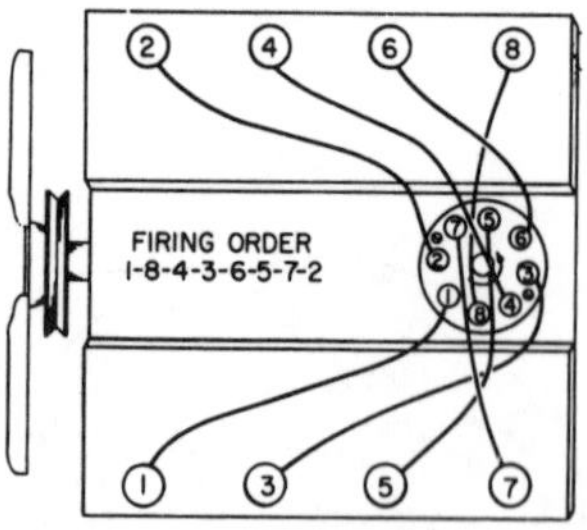

260 V8

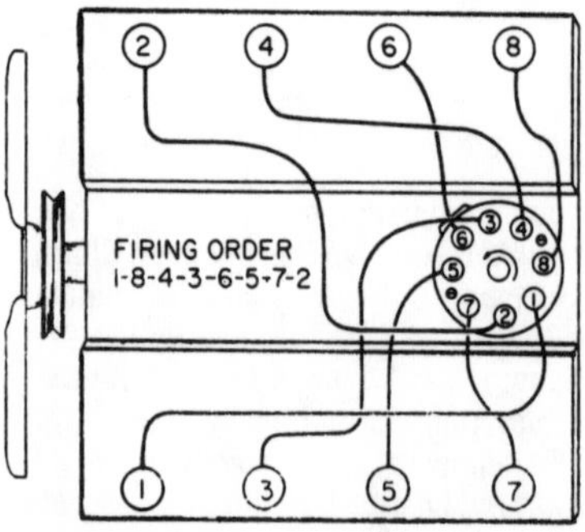

350, 400, 455 V8

Fuel System

When gasoline is brought from the fuel tank, it mixes with air in the carburetor. This gas/air mixture enters engine thru the intake manifold, passes thru the intake valves and is burned in the combustion chamber. The burned exhaust gas is then passed thru the exhaust valves to the exhaust system and to the outside air. In order to keep your car's engine running cleanly with minimal pollution, and avoid dangerous carbon monoxide fumes inside the vehicle, certain items should be checked from time to time.

REPLACING THE AIR FILTER AND CRANKCASE VENTILATION FILTER

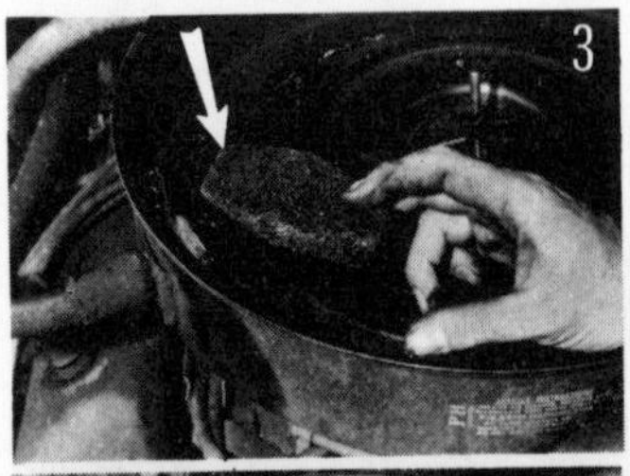

The large round can that sits on top of the engine is the air cleaner. The filter element inside should be replaced every 24,000 miles.

1. Unscrew the wing nut and remove the air cleaner cover.
2. Remove and discard the old dirty filter.
3. Check the small crankcase breather filter. If dirty, lift out and replace it.
4. Using a clean rag, wipe out the inside of air cleaner. Install new filter and replace top cover.

FUEL FILTER REPLACEMENT

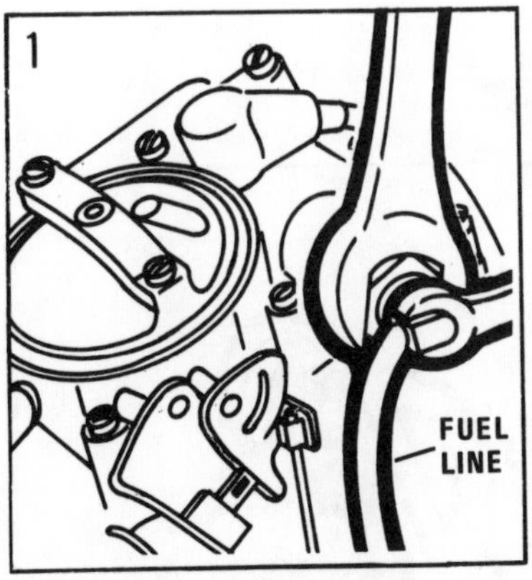

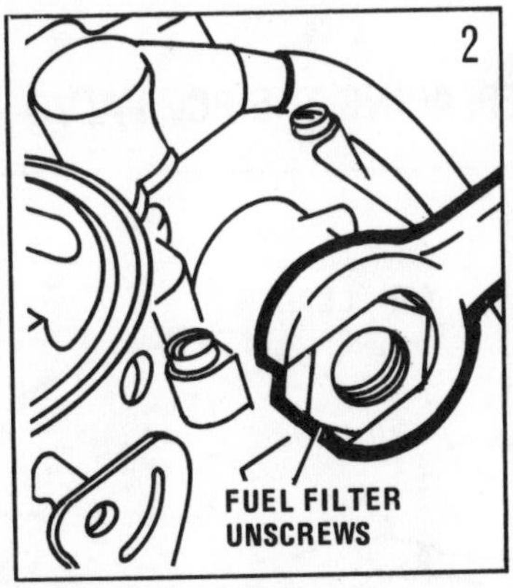

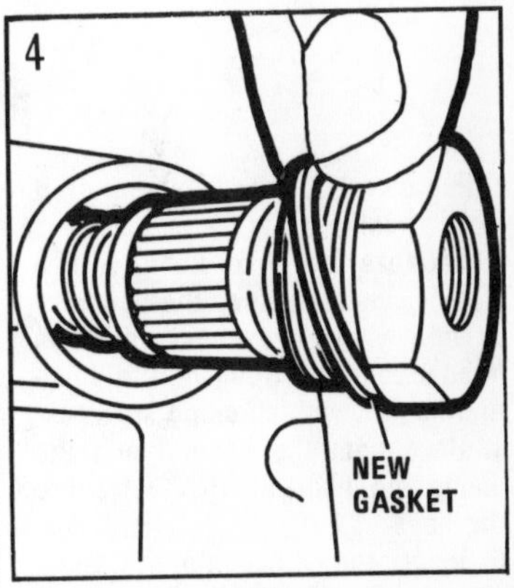

The fuel filter is located behind the large fuel line inlet nut on the carburetor. Replace the filter every year or 12,000 miles. The fuel filter prevents dirt, rust, and scale from both the gas station's tank and your own fuel tank from reaching the carburetor. A dirty filter will starve the engine and cause poor running.

1. Place an absorbent rag under fuel line connection to absorb gas spills. Unscrew fuel line connection with ½ in. wrench while holding the larger nut with a 1 in. wrench. Be careful, fuel line fitting threads are easily stripped.
2. Remove the large filter retaining nut from the carburetor. The spring behind the filter will push it out. Remove the filter and the spring.
3. Install the spring and new filter element. Some carburetors are equipped with a paper element, others with a bronze unit. The bronze filter must have the small cone section facing out and a gasket between the filter and the retaining nut.
4. Install the new gasket on the retaining nut and screw it into place.

CAUTION: DO NOT OVERTIGHTEN

5. Reconnect the fuel line. Discard the gas soaked rag safely.
6. Start the engine and check for leaks. Addition of a can of carburetor cleaner to the fuel tank occasionally will aid in keeping the entire fuel system clean.

REPLACING THE PCV VALVE—Six Cylinder

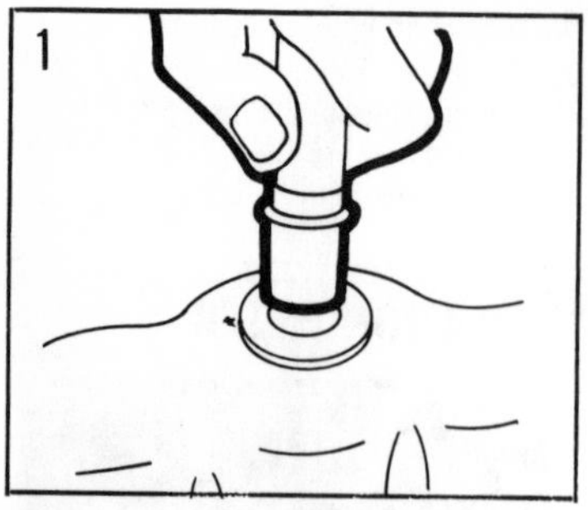

An important part of a car's emission control system is the Positive Crankcase Ventilation (PCV) valve and its connecting hose. The PCV valve should be replaced once every 24,000 miles. This device keeps dirt and sludge from forming inside the engine. Make sure all PCV connections are tight. Check that the connecting hoses are clear and not clogged. Replace any brittle or broken hoses.

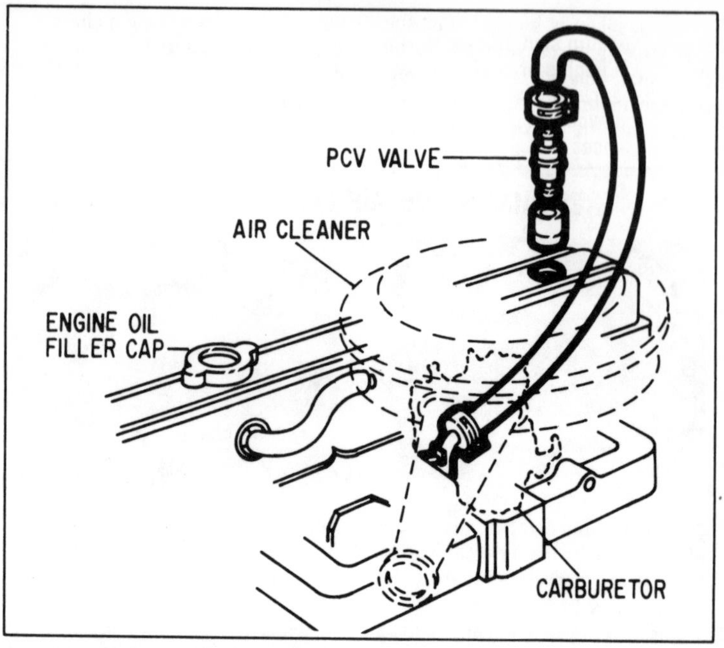

1. Pull valve from its location in rear part of valve cover.
2. Squeeze the hose clamp with a pair of pliers. Remove the valve.
3. Note where the other end of the hose connects. Remove the hose and flush it with cleaning solvent.
4. Reconnect the hose. Pinch the clamp and insert the PCV valve into the hose.
5. Insert the valve into the valve cover.

REPLACING THE PCV VALVE—V8

1. Pull valve from its location in left front of valve cover.
2. Squeeze the hose clamp with a pair of pliers. Remove the valve.
3. Note where the other end of the hose connects. Remove the hose and flush it with cleaning solvent.
4. Reconnect the hose. Pinch the clamp and insert the PCV valve into the hose.
5. Insert the valve into the valve cover.

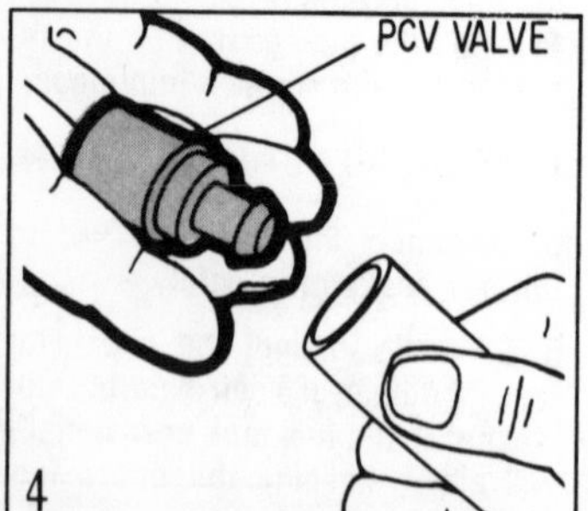

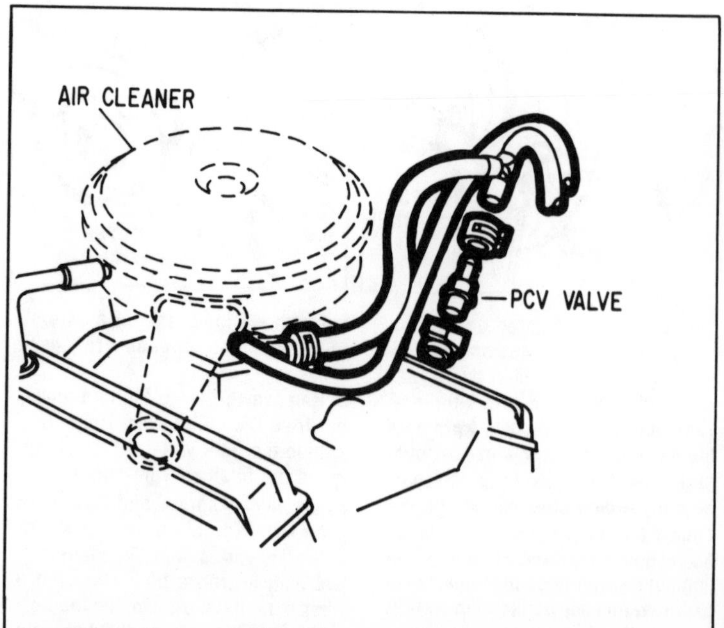

Safety Systems

Headlights, turn signals, stop lights, and parking lights are an important part of your car's safety system. They permit you to see and be seen. Keep all lenses clean and make frequent checks to be sure that all of your lights are functioning properly. Replace any cracked lenses as soon as possible. When replacing a bulb, make a note of the number which is usually printed on the base. If you don't have a number, take the old bulb with you so that you match it for the correct replacement.

REPLACING TURN SIGNAL, STOP, AND BACK-UP LIGHT BULBS

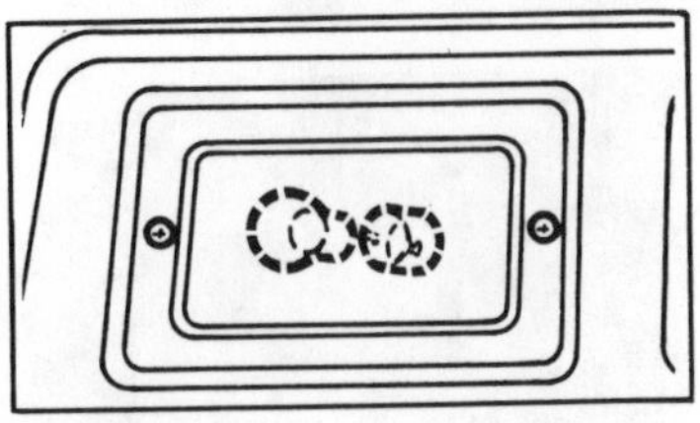

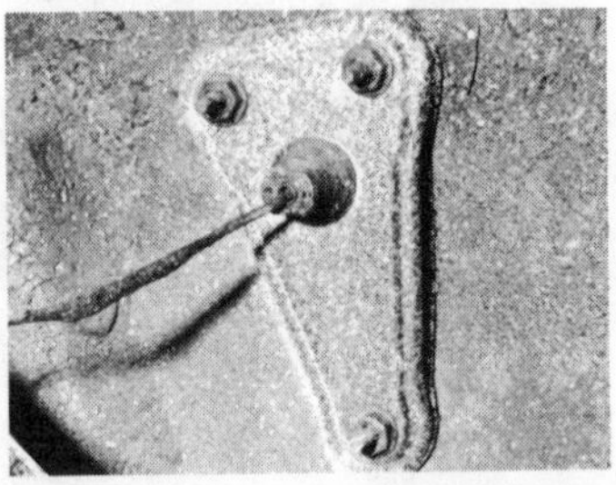

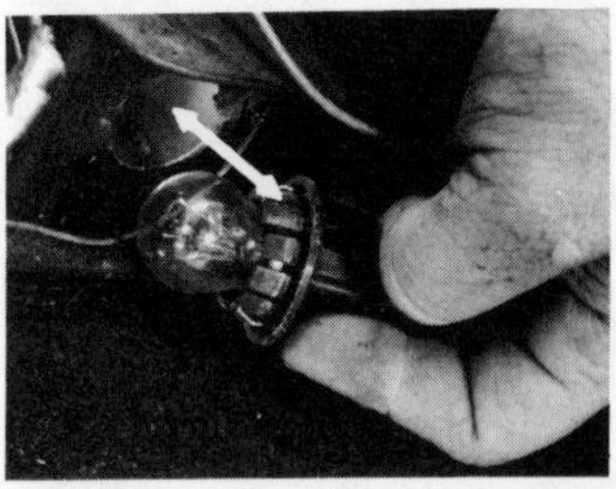

To replace a turn signal, stop light, or back-up light bulb, remove the lens, push down on bulb while turning it counterclockwise to remove it from the socket. Install the new bulb in reverse order. Be sure to match the knobs on the bulb base with the slots in the socket. If there are no screws on the lens, you will have to remove the socket from the back of the light unit. In some cases, you may have to remove the light unit in order to remove the socket.

REPLACING INTERIOR DOME LIGHT

This is a cartridge type bulb; be sure to purchase correct replacement. Pry dome light lens out from housing. To avoid blowing fuse, make sure doors are closed and dome light switch is in OFF position. Carefully lever the bulb straight out of housing. Insert new bulb and re-install dome light lens.

HEADLIGHT REPLACEMENT—Round Lights

1. Remove the headlight trim retaining screws and remove the trim.
2. Unhook the spring from the headlight retaining ring.
3. Remove the two retaining ring screws. Do not disturb the long aiming screws at the top and side.
4. Remove the retaining ring. Disconnect the wiring plug and remove the bulb.
5. Attach the connector plug to the new headlight.
6. Position the new bulb in housing. Make sure that the number molded into the lens is at the top.
7. Install the retaining ring and pull the spring into place.
8. Replace the headlight trim panel.

WINDSHIELD WIPER BLADE REPLACEMENT

To replace wiper blade, lift up on spring release tab on wiper arm connector. Pull wiper blade off. Snap new blade into place.

To replace rubber insert only, press down, away from wiper blade to free it. Slide insert from blade. Insert new wiper. Bend insert upward slightly to engage retaining clips.

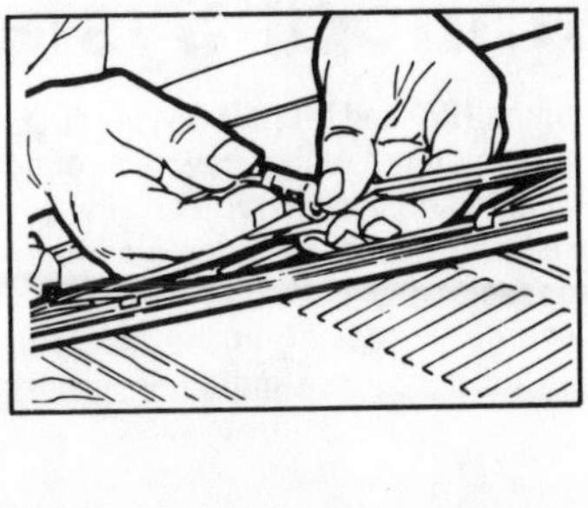

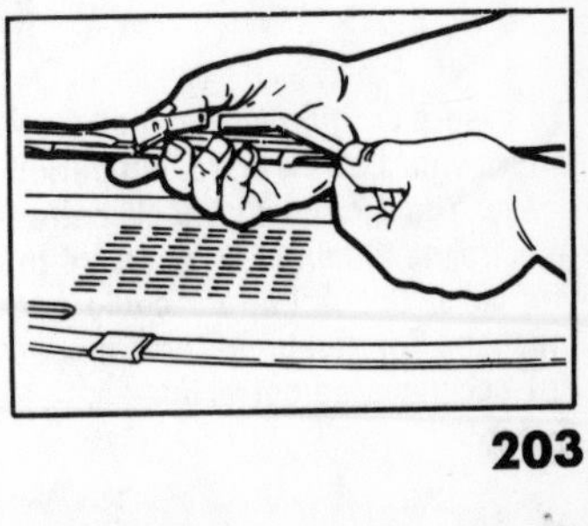

HEADLIGHT REPLACEMENT—Rectangular Lights

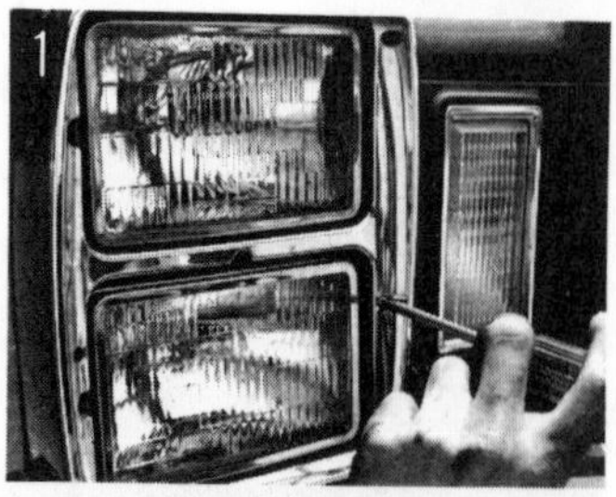

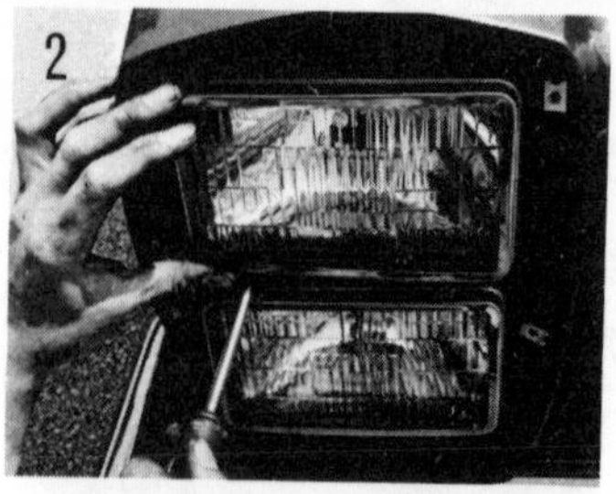

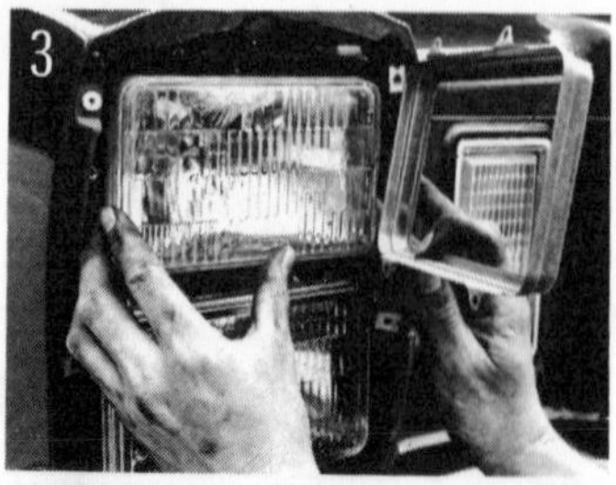

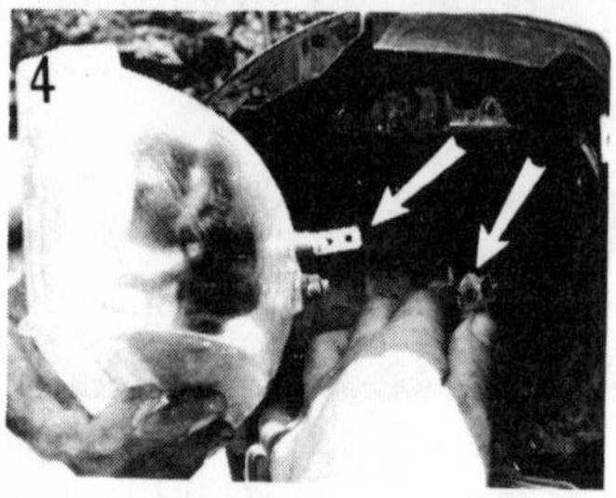

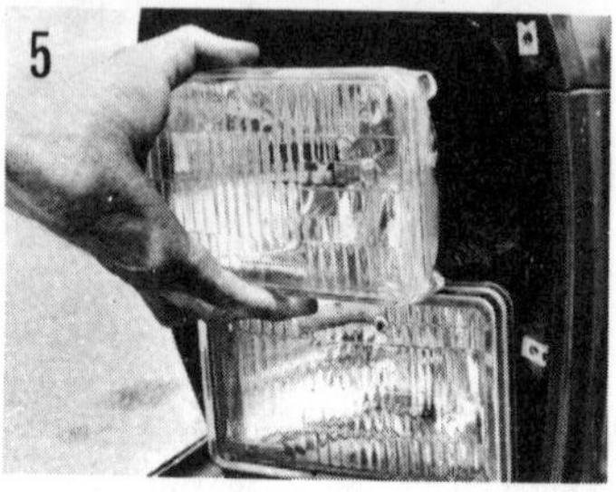

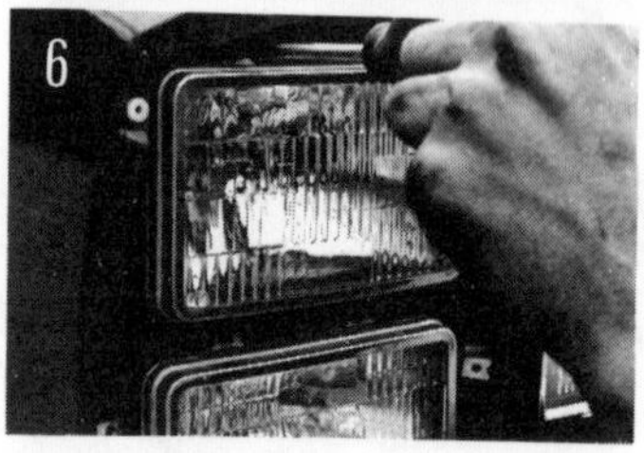

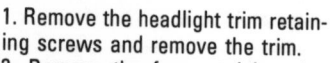

1. Remove the headlight trim retaining screws and remove the trim.
2. Remove the four retaining ring screws. Do not disturb the long aiming screws at the top and side.
3. Remove the retaining ring. Disconnect the wiring plug and remove the bulb.
4. Attach the connector plug to the new headlight.
5. Position the new bulb.
6. Replace the retaining ring with the four screws.
7. Replace the headlight trim panel.

HORN PROBLEMS

If horn sounds and does not stop, this is due to short circuit in wiring. Disconnect wiring connector under hood and have professional service shop check horn wiring circuit.

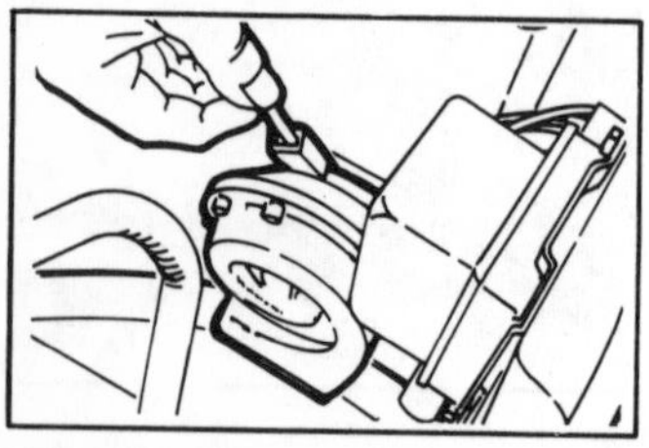

STEERING PROBLEMS

See steering system check in Suspension Section. Check tire pressures. Have a professional service shop check all components in the front end and steering system.

SERVICING WINDSHIELD WASHERS

If washer fails to squirt properly, raise hood and check system hose connections. Be sure washer fluid container has fluid. Check spout openings for clogging.

Keep container filled with fluid mixture of washer solvent and water. If road spray buildup on windshield is a chronic problem, add 1 tablespoon dishwasher detergent to solvent/water mixture when re-filling container.

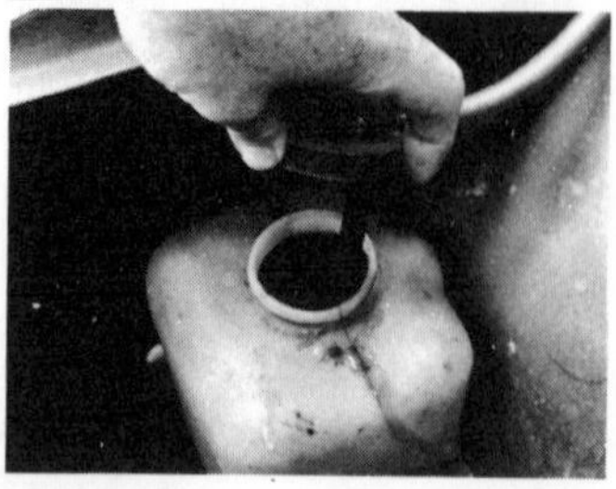

Electrical System

To ensure starting ability at all times check your battery condition periodically. You'll need to check battery electrolyte (fluid) level in each of the six cells. Check battery cable connections for tightness and inspect for accumulated corrosion.

Some 1976 and all 1977 GM products are equipped with a new type of no maintenance battery. This battery requires no maintenance other than occasionally checking its state of charge by looking at the indicator on the top. If the indicator is dark with a green dot showing in the center, the battery is fully charged. If the indicator is dark but there is no green dot showing, the battery should be charged. If the indicator is light, the battery should be replaced.

CHECKING BATTERY LEVEL

1. Remove plastic filler caps on top of battery. Fluid should be up to lower end of filler hole and covering the plates. If fluid is low add clean, cold tap water. If your area has hard water, use only distilled water available at auto supply, food or drug stores.
2. Replace any lost caps immediately.

CAUTION: NEVER LIGHT A MATCH OR SMOKE near the top of a battery. Batteries give off explosive hydrogen gas.

NOTE: Battery that often checks low on fluid could mean:

A. Battery is getting old, due for re-

1

placement; have charge capacity checked at service shop.

B. Connections may be corroded or loose; clean/replace as needed (see below).

C. Alternator or voltage regulator not

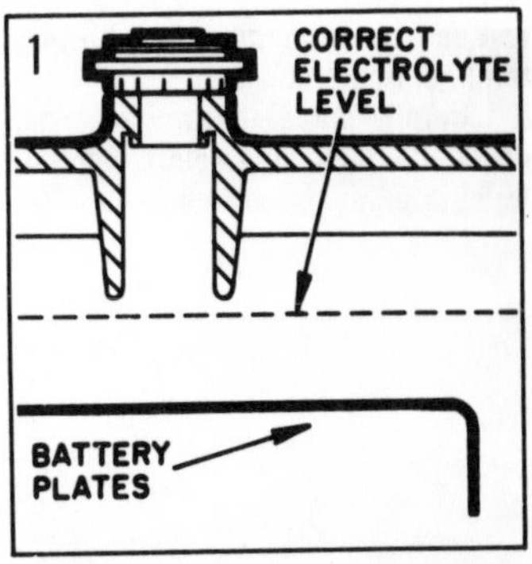

1

functioning properly; this happens far less often than A or B above.

CLEANING BATTERY TERMINALS

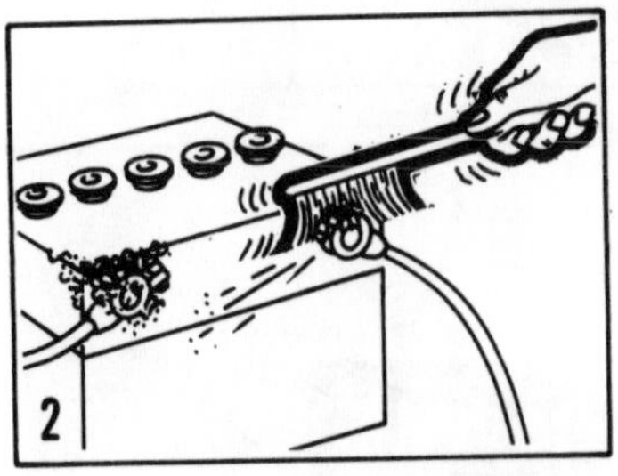

2

As time goes by, battery terminals build up a dry powdery, whitish material. This material is corrosive and will gradually eat thru battery cables if not cleaned off periodically.

1. Loosen and remove battery connections.
2. Brush off all loose corrosion; use stiff bristle brush. Do not get this material into eyes or on open cuts.

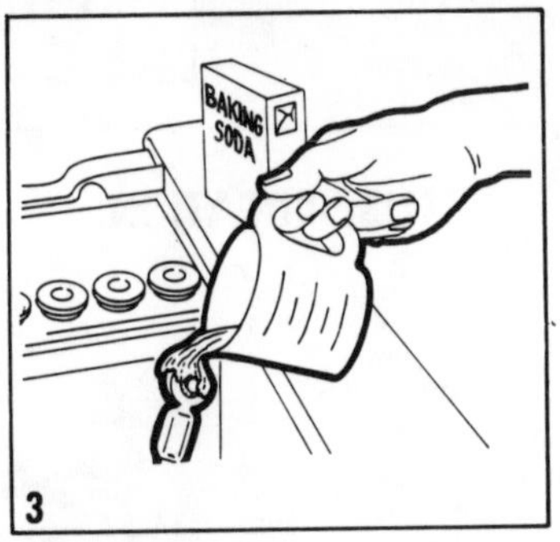

3

Wash off at once.

3. If corrosion build-up is extremely heavy and brushing does not remove all of it, mix 2 tablespoons baking soda to 1 cup water. Pour solution directly onto terminals and connectors. Allow to soak a few minutes and rinse off. Continue brushing to

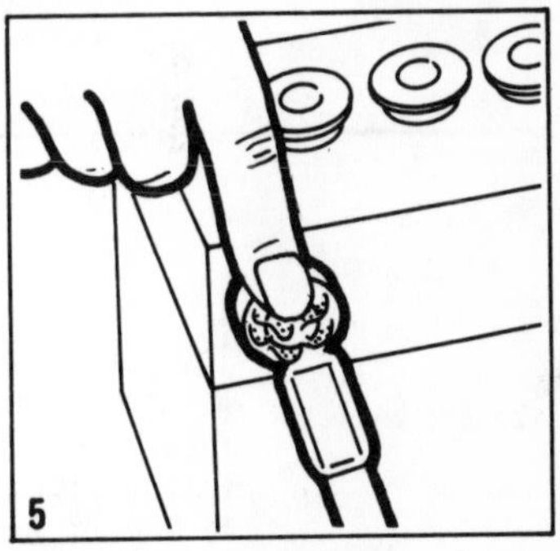

5

remove all traces of corrosion build-up. Do not allow cleaning solution to enter battery.

4. Replace connectors on battery terminal posts and tighten.
5. Liberally smear battery terminal posts and cable connectors with petroleum jelly.

REPLACING BATTERY CABLES

1

If battery cable strands become frayed, broken or corroded, replace cable immediately. Delay in correcting this condition could lead to sudden failure to start the engine. Can

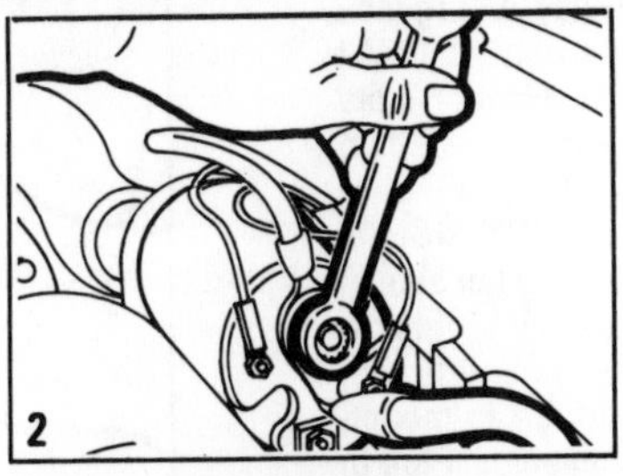

2

also weaken battery.

1. Loosen and remove battery connections. Clean OFF any corrosion.
2. Disconnect negative cable from its attachment to engine or chassis.

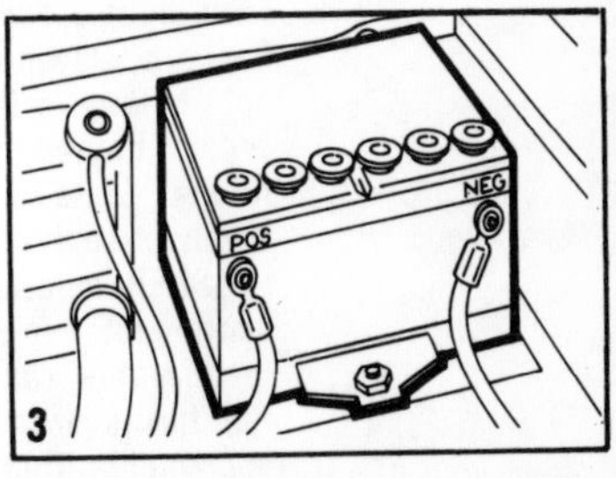

3

Disconnect positive cable from its attachment to starter relay.

3. Attach new cables making sure positive and negative cables are on

proper terminals. They are not identical.
4. Replace connectors on battery terminal posts and tighten.
5. Liberally smear battery terminal posts and cable connectors with petroleum jelly.

The clamp device which holds battery in place should be checked periodically. If loose, tighten. Clean off corrosion buildup. Severely corroded holddown components should be replaced before they break.

BATTERY HOLDDOWN

The clamp device which holds battery in place should be checked periodically. If loose, tighten. Clean off corrosion build-up. Severely corroded holddown components should be replaced before they break.

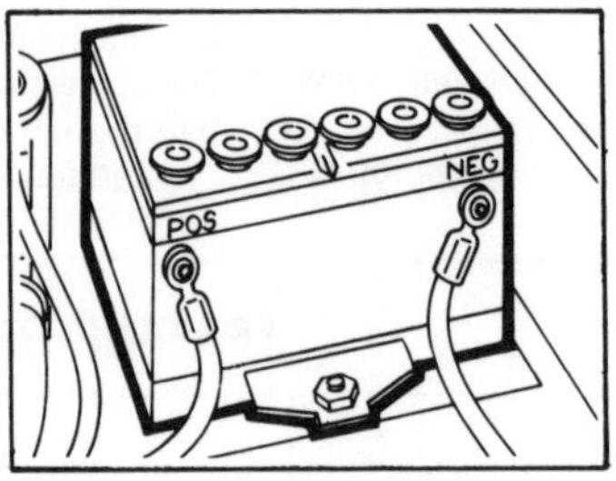

FUSE LOCATION

The fuse box is located to the left of the steering column, directly over the dimmer switch. Each fuse is clearly marked as to function and correct amperage. Always replace fuse with one of same amperage. If fuses are always blowing, have checked by professional mechanic.

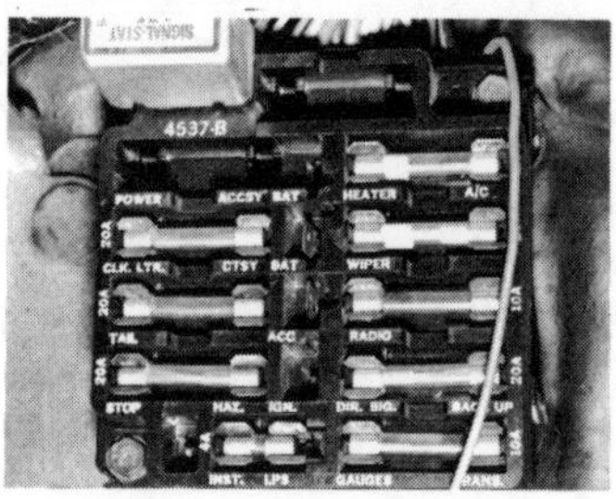

TURN SIGNAL AND 4-WAY FLASHER

Turn signals and 4-way emergency flashers will operate only if: A. All light bulbs are OK. B. Flasher units are not burned out. The car has two flasher units that work independently of each other. TURN SIGNAL FLASHER: located behind left side of instrument panel on lower instrument panel reinforcement brace. Pull flasher from spring clip mounting. Unplug from connector. Plug in new flasher. Replace in spring clip mounting. EMERGENCY FLASHER: located in fuse block. Simply unplug and insert new flasher. REPLACE ONLY WITH SAME TYPE FLASHER.

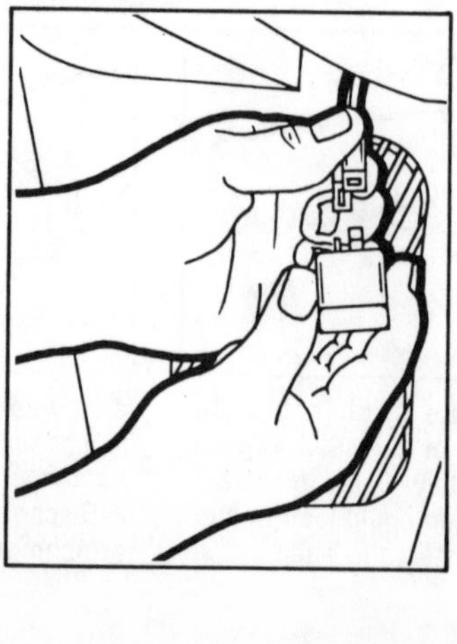

ALTERNATOR CHECKS

If Alt. warning light glows red or ammeter shows discharge at operating speed, alternator isn't charging battery properly. Common causes are:

A. Fan belts are loose and slipping on alternator pulley. Tighten or replace belts.

B. Battery terminals, cables are loose or corroded. Clean; tighten; replace bad cables.

If A or B do not correct problem, alternator or voltage regulator may be faulty. This happens far less often, and can only be checked by mechanic with proper electrical testing equipment.

Alternator Caution: Alternator can be permanently damaged by shortcircuiting terminal connections. When working around or moving alternator, always keep metal tools or engine parts from terminals.

REAR WINDOW DEFOGGER SYSTEM

Do not clean inside of rear window fitted with defogger system with any abrasive material. This could destroy carbon-copper wires. Use only soft rag and mild detergent/water mixture. Dry carefully.

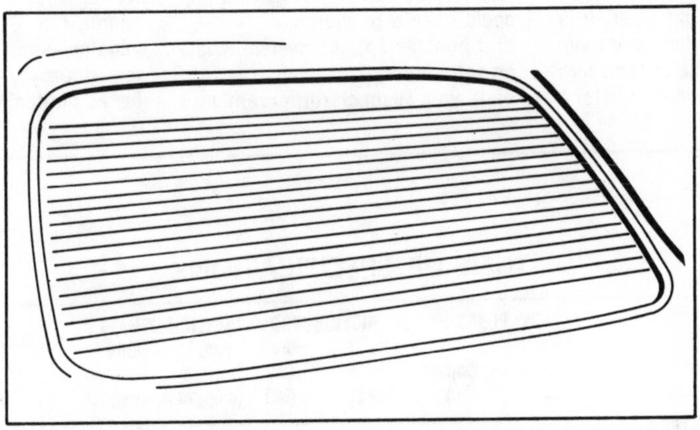

Air Conditioning System

WARNING!—Never attempt to tighten fittings, disassemble or do any work on your car's A/C system. Consult a professional mechanic about A/C system problems and their correction. Your auto air conditioner (A/C) is a delicate, closed system. If air, dirt or water get into it, or if refrigerant escapes, the A/C unit will not cool a car interior. Among things you can do are:

1. Keep condenser grille clean. Check for dirt and debris; periodically remove dead insects, leaves, etc., with stiff bristle brush. Straighten any bent fins—carefully.
2. Keep radiator filled to correct level. (See Cooling System section). If fluid needs to be added, add antifreeze rather than water.
3. Keep radiator coolant at a 50/50 water/antifreeze mixture.

1

4. Flush cooling system and replace with fresh coolant mixture at least every 24 months. (See Cooling System section).
5. Radiator cap should be tight and sealed properly. If sealing gasket is cracked, cut or worn, replace cap with new 15 lb. unit.

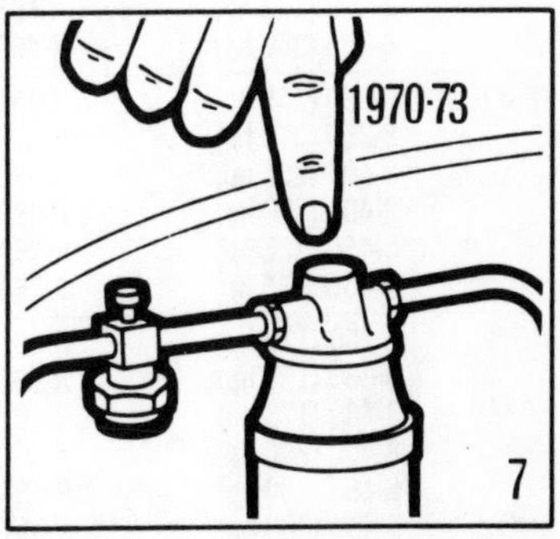

7

6. Check fan belt tension periodically. (See Cooling System section). Replace glazed, frayed or cut fan belts, before they fail entirely.
7. Check periodically for bubbles in A/C sight glass. Sight glass is located in head of receiver/drier vessel. Or on the side of the V.I.R. as-

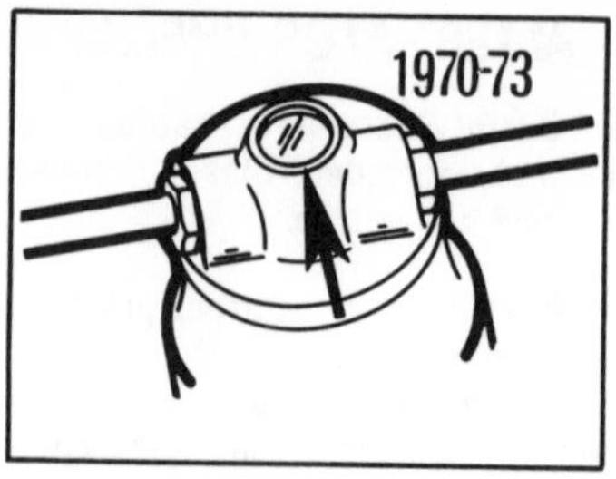

sembly. Sight glass is no larger than head of large nail. It may be dirty. Wipe clean for best visibility.

PROCEED AS FOLLOWS:

a) With engine and A/C system running, look for passage of refrigerant in sight glass. You'll be looking for a stream of milky white bubbles as they pass through sight glass. It is best to watch sight glass and have someone else start the car and turn on the A/C system. Allow to run for a few minutes.

b) If you observe no bubbles, and air flow from A/C unit in the car is passing cold air, everything is OK.

c) If no bubbles appear in sight glass, and air flow from the A/C unit in the car is not delivering cold air, the system may be low on refrigerant and could need a re-charge.

d) If bubbles appear, system is low on refrigerant.

e) If you suspect refrigerant loss based on tests performed above, have system checked by a professional A/C service shop. They can confirm refrigerant loss, recharge the system and check for system leakage.

NOTE: Once a week or so, even in winter, run A/C system for about 5 minutes as you drive. This keeps system internally lubricated, prevents hoses hardening.

TUNE-UP SPECIFICATIONS

YEAR	ENGINE No. Cyl. Displacement (cu. in.)	SPARK PLUGS Type	SPARK PLUGS Gap (in.)	DISTRIBUTOR Point Dwell (deg.)	DISTRIBUTOR Point Gap (in.)	IGNITION TIMING Man. Trans.● (deg.)■	IGNITION TIMING Auto Trans.● (deg.)■	IDLE SPEED Man. Trans.● (rpm)▲	IDLE SPEED Auto Trans. (rpm)▲
1970	6-250 (155 hp)	R-46T	.035	32½	.019	TDC	4B	830/750③	630/600③
	8-350 (255 hp)	R-46S	.035	30	.016	9B	9B	800	650
	8-400 (265 hp)	R-46S	.035	30	.016	9B	9B	800	650
	8-400 (330 hp)	R-45S	.035	30	.016	9B	9B	950	650
	8-400 (350 hp)	R-46S	.035	30	.016	9B	9B	950	650
	8-400 (366 hp)	R-46S	.035	30	.016	9B	9B	950	650
	8-400 (370 hp)	R-46S	.035	30	.016	15B	15B	1000/650③	750/500③
	8-455 (360 hp)	R-46S	.035	30	.016	9B	9B	950	650
1971	6-250 (145 hp)	R-45T	.035	32½	.019	4B	4B	850/550③	650/500③
	8-350 (250 hp)	R-47S	.035	30	.016	12B	12B	800	600
	8-400 (265 hp)	R-47S	.035	30	.016	—	8B	—	600
	8-400 (300 hp)	R-46S	.035	30	.016	12B	12B	1000/600③	700
	8-455 (325 hp)	R-46S	.035	30	.016	—	12B	—	650
	8-455 (335 hp)	R-46S	.035	30	.016	12B	12B	1000/600③	700
1972	6-250 (110 hp)	R-45T	.035	32½	.019	4B	4B	700/450③	600/450③
	8-350 (160 hp)	R-46TS	.035	30	.016	8B	10B	800	625
	8-400 (175 hp)	R-46TS	.035	30	.016	—	10B	—	625
	8-400 (200 hp)	R-46TS	.035	30	.016	8B	10B	1000/600③	700/500③
	8-455 (250 hp)	R-45TS	.035	30	.016	—	10B	—	650/500③
	8-455 (300 hp)	R-45TS	.035	—	—	8B	10B	1000/600③	700/500③
1973	6-250 (100 hp)	R-46T	.035	32½	.019	6B	6B	700/450③	600
	8-350 SE (150 hp)	R-46TS	.040	30	.016	10B	12B	900/600③	650
	8-350 DE (175 hp)	R-46TS	.040	30	.016	10B	12B	900/600③	650
	8-400 SE (170 hp)	R-46TS	.040	30	.016	10B	12B	—	650
	8-400 DE (185 hp)	R-46TS	.040	30	.016	10B	12B	—	650
	8-400 DE (230 hp)	R-45TS	.040	30	.016	10B	12B	1000/600③	650
	8-455 DE (250 hp)	R-45TS	.040	30	.016	10B	12B	—	650
	8-455 S.D. DE (310 hp)	R-44TS	.040	30	.016	10B	12B	1000/600③	750/500③

TUNE-UP SPECIFICATIONS

YEAR	ENGINE No. Cyl. Displacement (cu. in.)	SPARK PLUGS Type	SPARK PLUGS Gap (in.)	DISTRIBUTOR Point Dwell (deg.)	DISTRIBUTOR Point Gap (in.)	IGNITION TIMING Man. Trans.● (deg.)■	IGNITION TIMING Auto Trans.● (deg.)■	IDLE SPEED Man. Trans.● (rpm) ▲	IDLE SPEED Auto Trans. (rpm) ▲
1974	6-250	R-46T	.035	32½	.019	6B	6B	850/450③	600/450③
	8-350 2 bbl	R-46TS	.040	30	.016	10B	12B(10B)	900/600③	650(625)
	8-350 4 bbl	R-46TS	.040	30	.016	10B	12B(10B)	1000/600③	650(625)
	8-400 2 bbl	R-46TS	.040	30	.016	10B	12B(10B)	——	650(625)
	8-400 4 bbl	R-45TS	.040	30	.016	10B	12B(10B)	1000/600③	650(625)
	8-455	R-45TS	.040	30	.016	10B	12B(10B)	——	650(625)
1975	6-250 (100 hp)	R-46TX	.060	Electronic		10B	10B	850	550(600)
	8-350 2 bbl (155 hp)	R-46TSX	.060	Electronic		——	16B	——	600
	8-350 4 bbl (170 hp)	R-46TSX	.060	Electronic		——	16B(12B)	——	650(625)
	8-400 2 bbl (175 hp)	R-46TSX	.060	Electronic		——	16B	——	650
	8-400 4 bbl (210 hp)	R-45TSX	.060	Electronic		——	16B(12B)	——	650(600)
	8-455 4 bbl (215 hp)	R-45TSX	.060	Electronic		——	16B(10B)	——	650(675)
1976	6-250 (100 hp)	R-46TX	.060	Electronic		6B	10B	850	550(600)②
	8-260 (110 hp)	R-46SX	.080	Electronic		16B(14B)	18B(14B)	750	550(600)②
	8-350 2 bbl (155 hp)	R-46TSX	.060	Electronic		——	16B	——	550①
	8-350 4 bbl (175 hp)	R-45TSX	.060	Electronic		——	16B	——	600①
	8-400 2 bbl (170 hp)	R-46TSX	.060	Electronic		——	16B	——	550①
	8-400 4 bbl (185 hp)	R-45TSX	.060	Electronic		——	16B	——	575①
	8-455 (200 hp)	R-45TSX	.060	Electronic		——	16B(12B)	——	550(600)①
1977	6-231	See Underhood Specifications Sticker							
	8-302								
	8-350								
	8-400								
	8-403								

▲ Adjust automatic transmissions in Drive (AMC/Ford/GM) or Neutral (Chrysler), all manual transmissions are adjusted in Neutral.
■ All figures are Before Top Dead Center.
● Figure in parentheses indicate California engine.
① 675 with air conditioning on and compressor clutch wires disconnected.
② 575 for non-California engines with air conditioning.
③ Where two idle speed figures are separated by a slash, the second is with the needle speed solenoid disconnected.
B—Before Top Dead Center
TDC—Top Dead Center

—— Not applicable
SE—Single Exhaust
DE—Dual Exhaust
S.D.—Super Duty
2 bbl, 4 bbl—Carburetor type, 2 barrel, 4 barrel

NOTE: The underhood specifications sticker often reflects tune-up specification changes made in production. Sticker figures must be used if they disagree with those in this chart.

CAPACITIES

YEAR	ENGINE No. Cyl. Displacement (cu. in.)	ENGINE OIL Add 1 qt. with New Filter	TRANSMISSION Pts. to Refill after Draining MANUAL 3-speed	MANUAL 4-speed	AUTOMATIC	DRIVE AXLE (pts.)	COOLING SYSTEM with Heater (qts.)	COOLING SYSTEM with Air Cond. (qts.)
1970	6-250	4	3.5	——	6	3②	13	——
	8-350	5	3.5①	2.5	6	3②	19.9	19.9
	8-400	5	2.5	2.5	7.5	3②	18.3	18.3
	8-455	5	2.5	2.5	7.5	3②	17.5	17.5
1971	6-250	4	3.5	——	6	3②	13	12.4
	8-350	5	3.5①	2.5	6	3②	20	20.5
	8-400	5	2.8	2.5	7.5	3②	18.6	20.8
	8-455	5	2.8	2.5	7.5	3②	17.9	16.8
1972	6-250	4	3.5	——	6	3②	13	12.4
	8-350	5	3.5	2.5	6	3②	20	20.5
	8-400	5	2.8	2.5	7.5	3②	18.6	20.8
	8-455	5	——	2.5	7.5	3②	17.9	19

CAPACITIES

YEAR	ENGINE No. Cyl. Displacement (cu. in.)	ENGINE OIL Add 1 qt. with New Filter	TRANSMISSION Pts. to Refill after Draining MANUAL 3-speed	MANUAL 4-speed	AUTOMATIC	DRIVE AXLE (pts.)	COOLING SYSTEM with Heater (qts.)	COOLING SYSTEM with Air Cond. (qts.)
1973	6-250	4	3.5	—	7.5	4.3	13.3	—
	8-350	5	3.5	2.5	7.5	4.3⑤	22	23.1
	8-400 2 bbl	5	3.5①	2.5	7.5	4.3⑤	22	23.1
	8-400 4 bbl	5	3.5①	2.5	7.5	4.3⑤	23	24
	8-455	5	—	2.5	7.5	4.3⑤	21.1	22.2
1974	6-250	4	3.5	—	7.5	3	13.3	—
	8-350	5	3.5①	2.5	7.5	3⑦	22	23.2
	8-400 2 bbl	5	—	2.5	7.5	3⑦	22	23.2
	8-400 4 bbl	5	—	2.5	7.5	3⑦	23	24
	8-455	5	—	—	7.5	3⑦	21.2	21.3
1975	6-250	4	3.5	—	7.5	3	14.8	14.8
	8-350	5	—	—	7.5	3⑦	21.8	21.8
	8-400	5	—	—	7.5	3⑦	23.8	21.8
	8-455	5	—	—	7.5	3⑦	21.6	21.6
1976-77	6-250	4	3.5	—	7.5	4.3	15	15
	8-260	4	3.5	3.5	7.5	4.3	19.6	20.1
	8-350	5	—	—	7.5	4.3	21.3	23.2
	8-400 2 bbl	5	—	—	7.5	4.3⑧	21.3	23.2
	8-400 4 bbl	5	—	—	7.5	4.3⑧	21.3	23.6
	8-455	5	—	—	7.5	4.3⑧	22.3	21.6

① 2.8 with Muncie heavy-duty transmission
② 5 with 8⅞ in. diameter ring gear axle
③ Not used
④ Not used
⑤ 5.5 with 8⅞ in. diameter ring gear axle in station wagon
⑥ Not used
⑦ 4.9 on station wagons and with optional axle on sedans
⑧ 5.3 with 8⅞ in. diameter ring gear axle in station wagons
2 bbl—2 barrel
4 bbl—4 barrel
—— Not applicable

Maverick/Comet

Lubrication and Oil Change

LUBRICATION CHECK

FORD SAYS . . . Change oil and filter every 6000 miles. Recommended grade: MS or SE (check owner's handbook). Check oil level at least once a week.

TOOLS & MATERIALS . . . adjustable hand wrench; medium size screwdriver; oil filter removal wrench; drain pan for old oil (at least 5 qt. capacity); oil pouring spout; 5 qt. oil; new oil filter; oil and lubricants as specified below.

SAFETY TIP . . . use work gloves.

BRAKE FLUID LEVEL CHECK

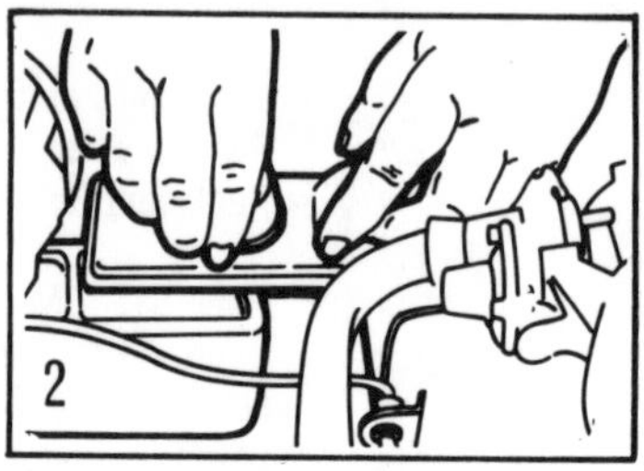

Check brake fluid level in master cylinder every three months . . . sooner if braking feels inadequate. Add when low. Recommended grade: DOT 3.

Master cylinder is located under hood on left side. It is an oblong container about 6" long with cap held down by wire clip. Check brake fluid level as follows:

1. Pry wire retaining clip off cap top with screwdriver.
2. Remove cap and gasket by lifting up.
3. Fluid level should be within ¼ inch of top rim. If lower than this, add fresh fluid to appropriate level. DO NOT OVERFILL
4. Replace cap and gasket; secure retaining clip over cap. If fluid level was low, check again in a few days.
5. If fluid repeatedly checks low, there is a leak somewhere in the system. See SAFETY SYSTEMS—WHEEL CYLINDER CHECK. Have mechanic check further. Neglect can be dangerous.

MANUAL TRANSMISSION FLUID LEVEL CHECK

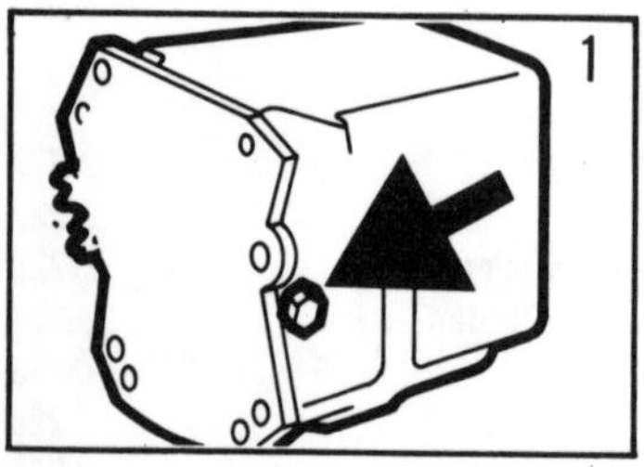

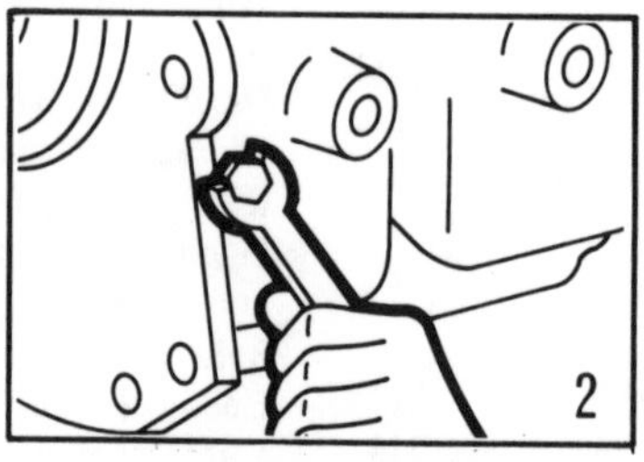

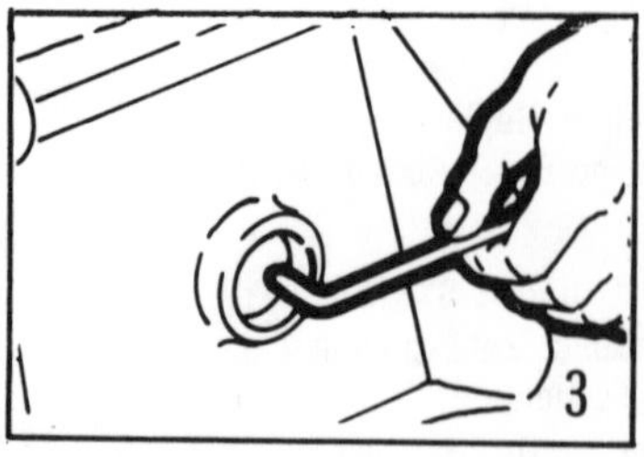

FORD SAYS . . . check manual transmission fluid every 6000 miles (1970-74 models), or 10,000 miles (1975-77). Car should be parked level. Recommended grade: Standard Transmission Fluid (SAE 90)

TOOLS NEEDED . . . fluid level check device (make from coat hanger wire; bend at 90° angle 2" from end; adjustable wrench; bulb syringe.

1. Locate transmission fluid filler plug on right side of transmission housing from underneath car.
2. Wipe road dirt from filler plug area before loosening. Remove plug with adjustable wrench.
3. Insert fluid level check device. Fluid level should be right up to bottom edge of filler hole.
4. Add fluid as needed with hand bulb syringe.

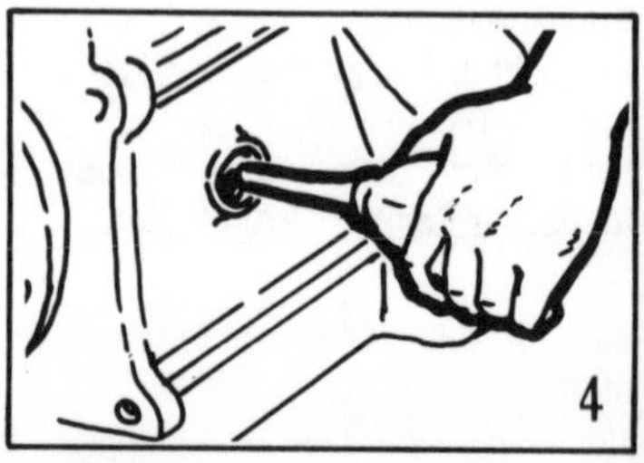

5. Replace filler plug; tighten.

AUTOMATIC TRANSMISSION FLUID LEVEL CHECK

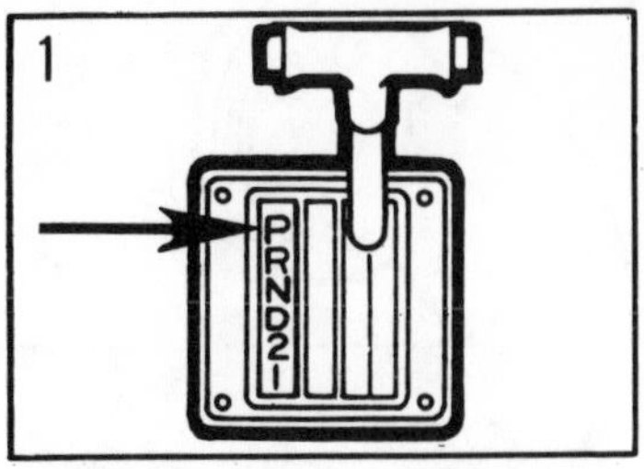

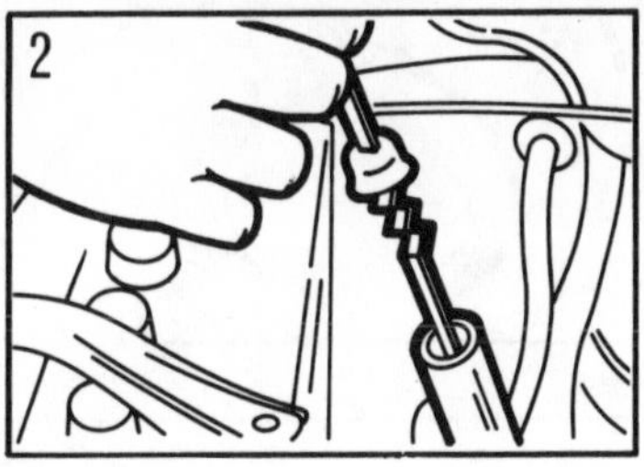

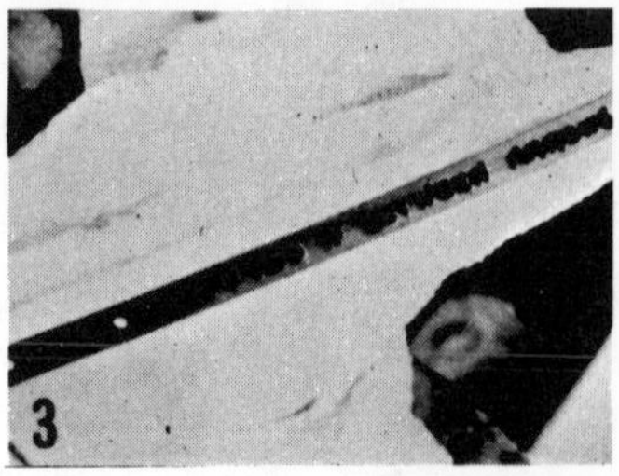

FORD SAYS . . . check automatic transmission fluid (ATF) level every 6000 miles (1970-74 models, or 10,000 miles (1975-77 models). Recommended grade: ATF Type F.
TOOLS . . . Long neck filler funnel.
1. Engine must be warmed up and running. Place shift lever in PARK position.

2. Pull out dipstick. Wipe clean. Push dipstick all the way back in; remove it again.
3. If fluid is below ADD mark, add ATF to bring level up. DO NOT OVERFILL.
4. Add ATF thru transmission dipstick hole by means of long-neck filler funnel.

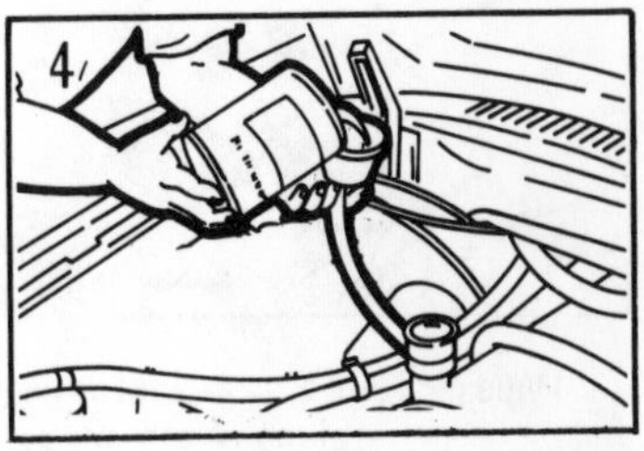

REAR AXLE LUBRICANT

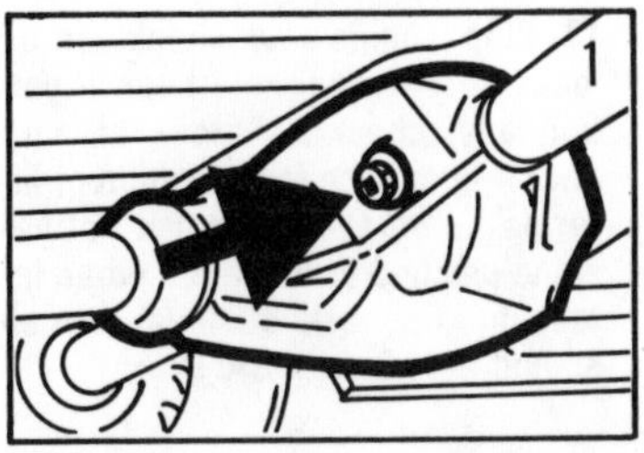

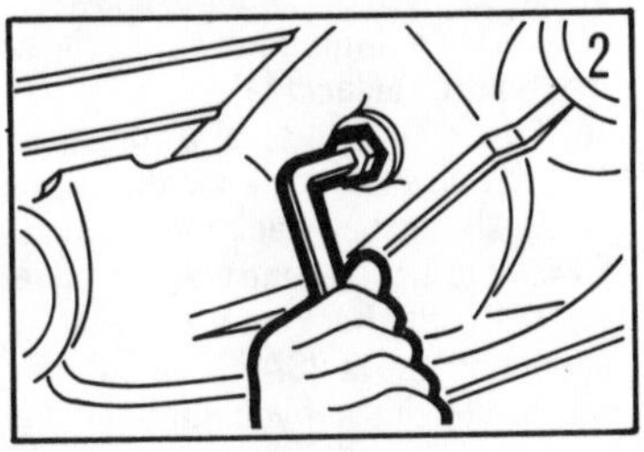

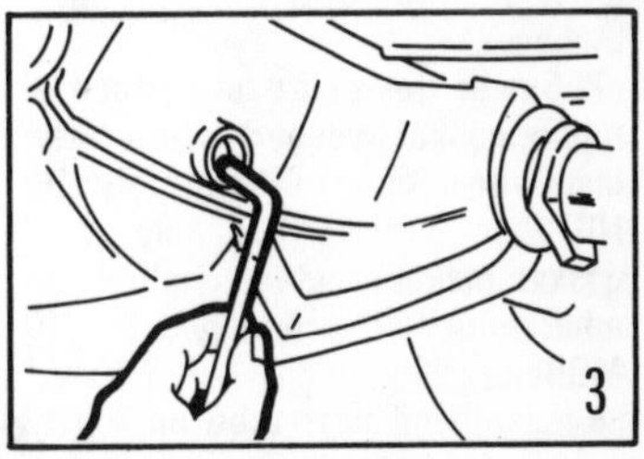

FORD SAYS . . . check rear axle lube level every 6000 miles (1970-74 models), or 10,000 miles (1975-77 models). Recommended grade: Hypoid gear lube (SAE 90)
TOOLS . . . adjustable hand wrench; fluid level check device (made from coat hanger wire; bend at 90° angle 2" from end); bulb syringe.
1. Locate filler plug on forward side of rear axle housing.
2. Wipe plug area clean; remove plug with wrench.
3. Insert wire level check device; remove. Adequate fluid level should show lubricant on last ¼-inch of wire.
4. If fluid level is low, add as needed, with a hand bulb syringe, until level shows on last ¼-inch of wire.

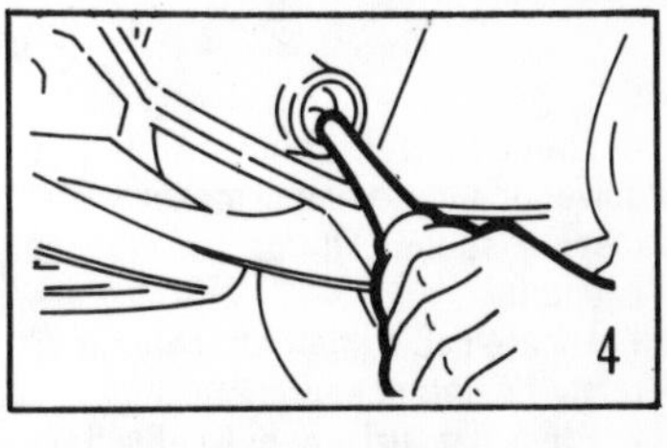

5. Replace filler plug; tighten.

OIL AND FILTER CHANGE

1. If engine is cold, start up and idle for about 5 minutes.
2. Park car on level ground. Turn engine off.
3. Locate oil drain plug on underside of engine. Place drain pan under plug.
4. Remove drain plug with wrench. Let ALL dirty oil drain out.

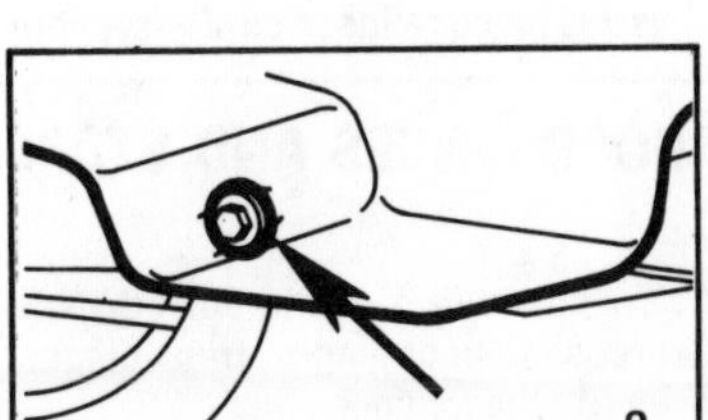

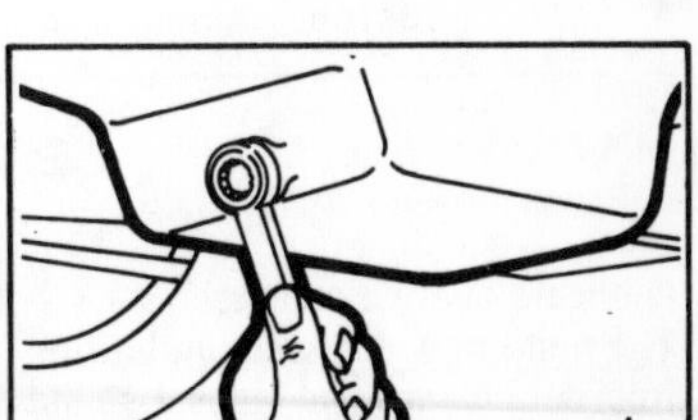

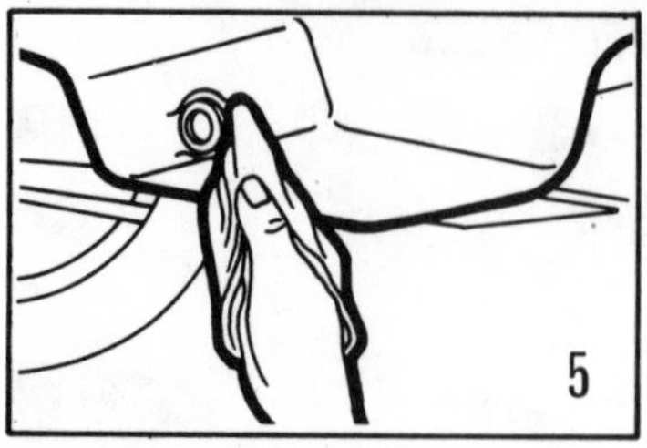

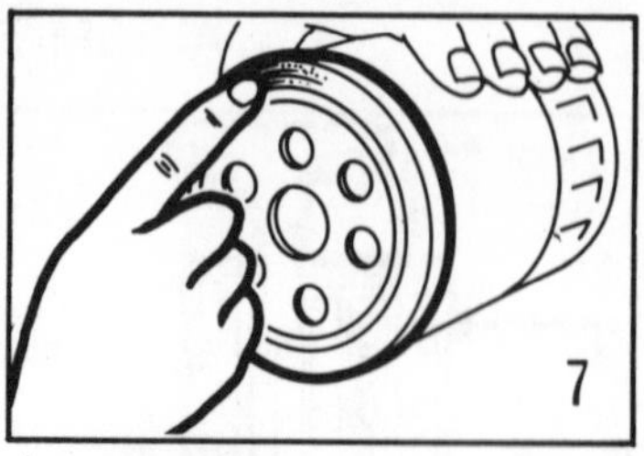

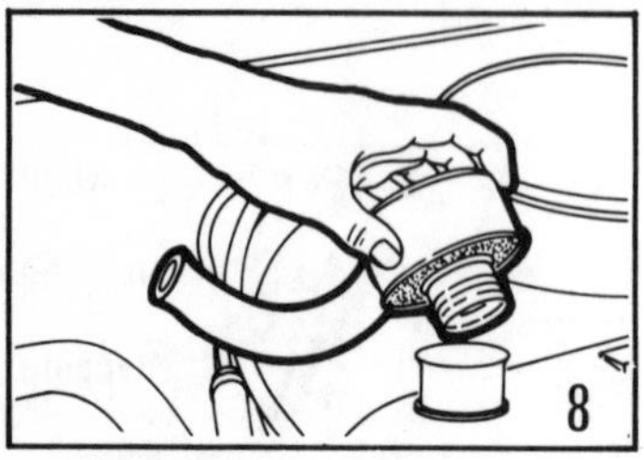

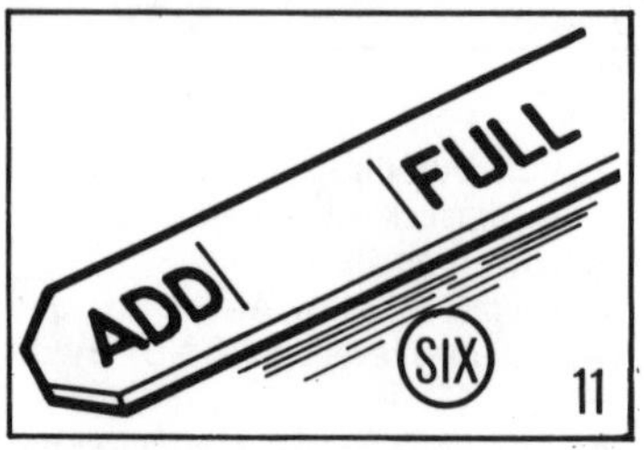

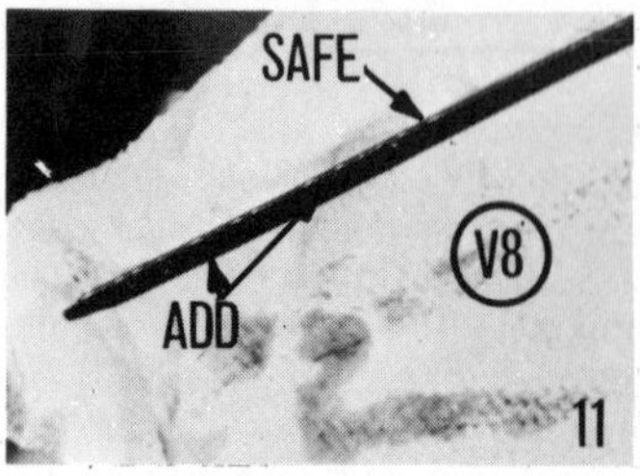

5. Wipe plug and area around drain hole clean. Replace drain plug; tighten it.

6. Locate oil filter. Move drain pan under filter. Loosen filter with oil filter wrench. Unscrew; remove filter by hand.

7. Smear fresh oil over surface of rubber gasket (washer) of new filter. Install new filter by hand only. Do NOT use wrench. Turn filter until gasket makes contact. Tighten an additional half turn only . . . NO MORE.

8. Locate oil filler tube on top of engine. Remove cap.

9. Punch oil pouring spout into top of oil can. Pour all cans of new oil into filler tube. Wipe filler cap clean and replace it. Be sure to re-attach all hoses. (NOTE: If filler cap is very dirty, rinse in turpentine or gasoline. Dry before replacing.)

10. Check new oil level at dipstick. Pull out dipstick, wipe clean.

11. Push dipstick back into engine. Be sure to insert all the way. Remove dipstick and check new oil level. It should be above "SAFE" line. If not, be sure to check if you put in all the oil called for.

12. Start up engine and idle for 3-5 minutes. Oil signal light on instrument panel will glow red when engine is first started. Light should go out in 30 seconds or less.

13. Stop engine and check for oil leaks at drain plug and filter. If you find any, check tightness of plug and/or filter, also for condition of filter gasket to see that it has not become pinched or damaged when installing. Recheck oil level, which should now be at "SAFE".

SPEEDOMETER CABLE LUBRICATION

If speedometer pointer tends to quiver or jump, or if unit makes a low, rasping sound, lubrication may be needed.

1. Locate cable shaft attachment directly behind speedometer dial.
2. Press flat surface; pull cable back and out from behind panel.
3. Pull inner cable completely out of outer casing. Note carefully which end is top. Check for wear or frayed strands. If damaged, replace inner cable with new one.
4. Apply generous amount of speedometer cable lubricant into cable casing. Replace inner cable in shaft, noting that top end is not inserted accidentally. Turn inner cable as it is being re-inserted. Twist cable when all the way in, to lock into position at lower end.
5. Re-connect cable to speedometer head under instrument panel.

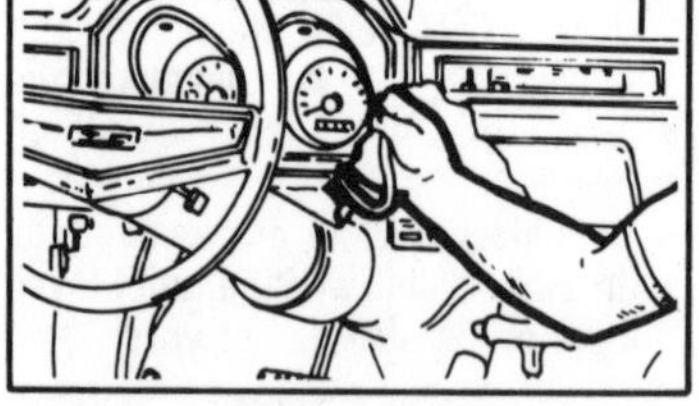

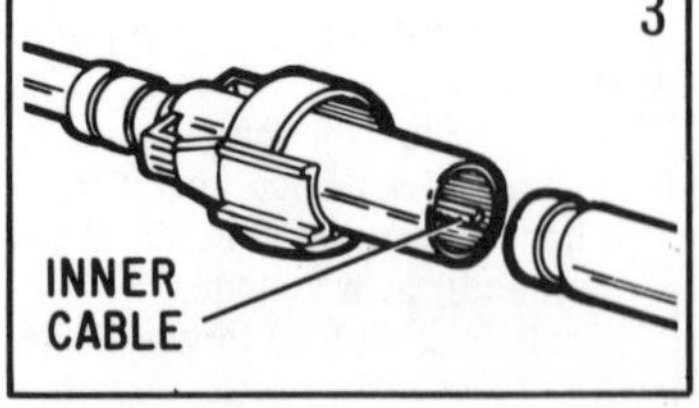

DOOR HINGES AND STOPS

(lubricate every 6 months)

1. Brush any dirt accumulations from door hinges and stops. Use old tooth brush or rag.
2. Apply dab of white polyethylene grease to door hinges, trunk hinges, hood hinges, door stops.

DOOR LOCKS

(lubricate every 6 months)
1. Insert door key half way into lock.
2. Spray aerosol lock lubricant into lock.
3. Push key rest of way into lock; turn back and forth several times.

Suspension and Tires

The front wheels mount and rotate on the spindles, which are attached to upper and lower ball joints. Upper and lower control arms link the spindles to the car's frame, and permit the frame and body to move up and down in relation to the position of the wheels with a hinge effect. The spring is mounted to the top of the upper control arm on either side, with the upper end located by the top of a spring housing. A shock absorber is located inside each spring. The rear suspension consists of leaf springs suspending the solid rear axle. The rear shock absorbers are mounted ahead of the rear axle on either side.

Your car's suspension system consists of wheels, tires, springs, shock absorbers, sway (or stabilizer) bars, ball joints, steering linkage. If any of these items is out of adjustment or badly worn, you may notice any of these symptoms:

- car pulls to one side when braking
- car wanders when driving a straight line
- overall ride may be either hard or bouncy
- effort is needed to steer vehicle
- tires show uneven wear
- tires squeal when cornering
- front of car dips or bounces when braking
- car rocks side-to-side when going over rough road
- wheels bounce or make slapping sound on road
- steering wheel vibrates in hand
- front of car vibrates at highway speeds

Any of above symptoms indicates corrective action is needed. Delay can: ruin tires; cause damage/failure to other suspension parts; create safey hazard.

STEERING

If steering linkage, front suspension and steering column components are in good condition, there should be no more than 1½ inch free play in the steering wheel when measured at the rim of the wheel. If a loud knock is heard when turning the steering wheel from one extreme to the other, have mechanic check pinion bearing preload.

SHOCK ABSORBERS

Shock absorbers work to keep wheels in constant contact with the road. Result is safe handling and ride control; longer tire life. So shock absorbers (or shocks) are important.

HOW TO CHECK FOR BAD SHOCKS

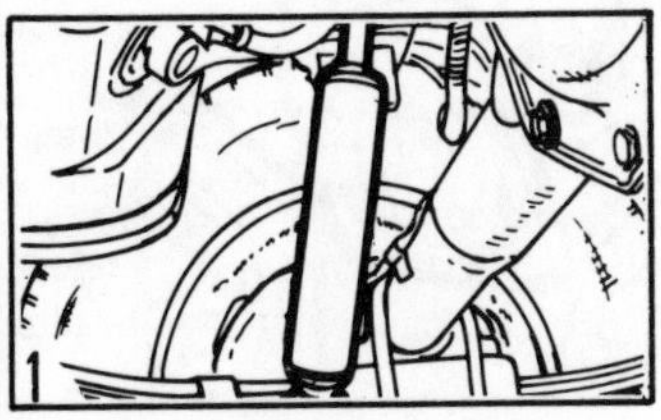

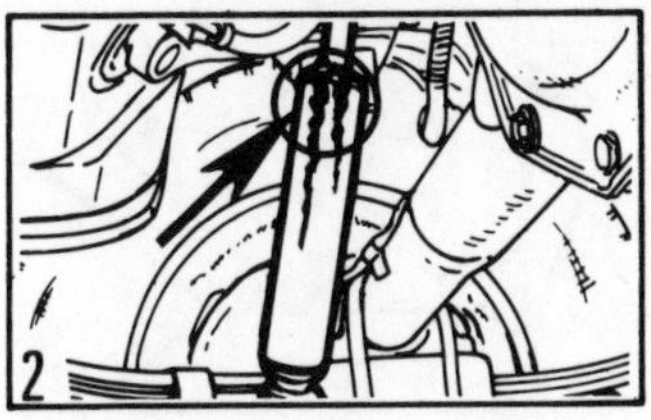

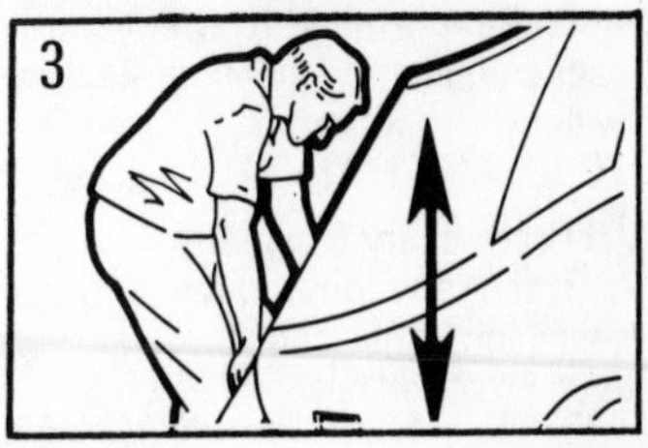

1. Check under car and locate shock absorber near each wheel.
2. Heavy oil streaks on outer shock housing indicate need for replacement.
3. Stand at front of car and apply body weight in a pumping action to front bumper or fender. Release pressure and allow car to stop rocking. Car should not bounce more than one more time after releasing pressure. Repeat at rear. If bouncing continues more than once, replacement is needed. Replace shocks in pairs (front pair or rear pair).

TOW HITCH INFORMATION

If your car is used for trailer towing you should check:
A. Cooling System; be sure radiator is at proper level in radiator. See Cooling System Section for checks to perform.
B. Check Transmission Fluid; keep topped up to proper level.
C. Check Rear Shock Absorbers; you may benefit from installation of new rear shocks.
D. Check Tire Pressures; best traction and handling can be ensured if tire pressures are properly maintained.
For safer and more trouble-free trailer towing, consider:
A. Automatic Transmission Cooler; helps remove excess heat from automatic transmission fluid built up during towing mileage. Also helps avoid radiator overheating. Some units can be self-installed.
B. Radiator Over-Flow Tank Kit; addition of a reservoir to catch radiator coolant overflow preventing coolant loss. Easy to install, these units help a tow car run cooler, avoid overheating due to coolant loss.
C. Heavy-Duty Shock Absorbers or Air Shocks; important to have on rear wheels if you intend to do a lot of towing or load carrying within the car itself. Don't forget to consider replacing factory shocks, when they are worn out, with heavy-duty units at the front as well.
D. Variable Load Flasher; this unit will accommodate the added load of trailer turn signal lamps on trailer when these are hooked into your car's electrical system.

FRONT END ALIGNMENT

When steering, handling and/or tire wear indicate front end alignment may be needed, this work can only be done at an automotive service shop. DO NOT PUT OFF NEEDED FRONT END ALIGNMENT. At the same time, have ball joints and steering linkage checked.

Cooling System

IT IS RECOMMENDED . . . that radiator coolant (water/antifreeze mixture) level be checked once or twice a month. Do this when engine is cold. Check more often if you do a lot of hard driving.
Keep coolant up to recommended level in radiator. If coolant checks frequently low, look for leaks. Tighten all hose clamps occasionally.

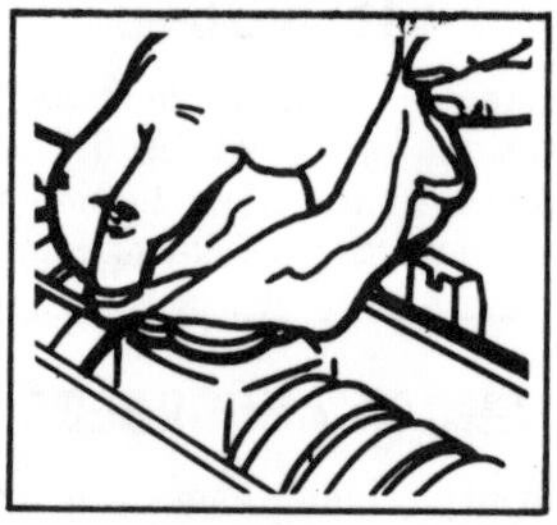

For best results, keep a 50/50 water/antifreeze mixture year round. Change complete coolant mixture every 24 months.
CAUTION: If you must check coolant in a hot engine, cover radiator cap with thick rag before releasing. Remove cap slowly . . . press down and turn.

REPLACING THE THERMOSTAT

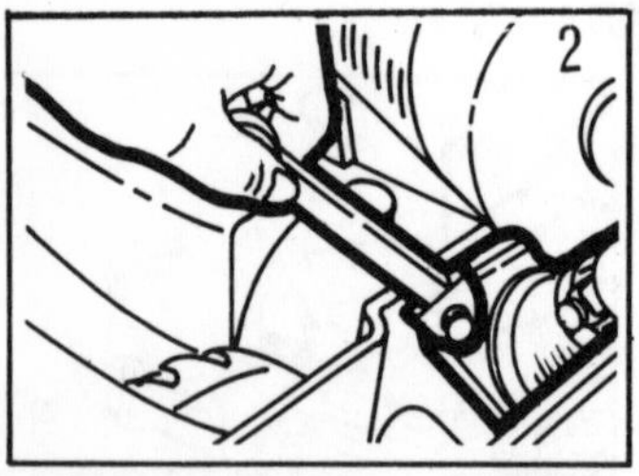

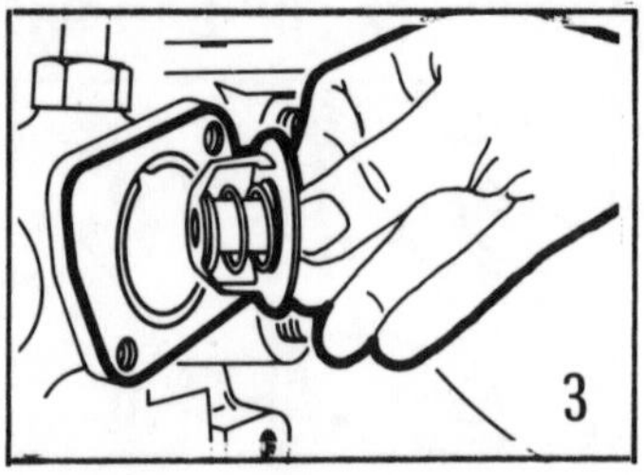

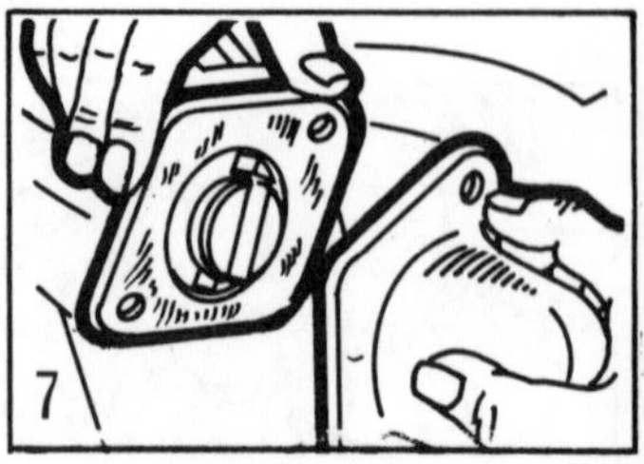

A faulty thermostat will usually cause engine overheating. Replace with new thermostat.
TOOLS AND MATERIALS . . .
New thermostat
Gasket sealer
Adjustable wrench
1. Drain radiator of about half its coolant. (See Hose Replacement section)
2. Loosen and remove both retaining bolts and lift thermostat housing off the engine.
NOTE: If you're careful it won't be necessary to remove radiator hose.
3. Remove old thermostat.
4. Scrape thermostat housing flange and engine block surface to remove old gasket debris.
5. Drop new thermostat into place—spring down.
6. Install new gasket with sealer applied to both sides.
7. Replace thermostat housing and tighten both retaining bolts.

ENGINE OVERHEATING

YOUR CAR OVERHEATS BECAUSE
radiator coolant is too low
fan belt is too loose
of a broken or leaking hose
thermostat does not function
radiator is plugged with sediment
water pump does not function properly

TO CORRECT IT
fill to correct level; check for leaks
adjust tension or replace frayed belt
replace hose; tighten clamps
replace thermostat
consult professional mechanic (may need radiator removal and servicing, or total replacement)
replace water pump (may make squeaky noise; or leak at pump shaft)

FAN BELT ADJUSTMENT

The fan belt not only drives the radiator fan, it turns the water pump and drives the alternator. Another belt drives the power steering pump. It's easy to see that the condition and proper tension of the belts are vital, since engine cooling, electrical cooling, electrical power, and steering depend on them. The belts deserve an occasional look and tension check.

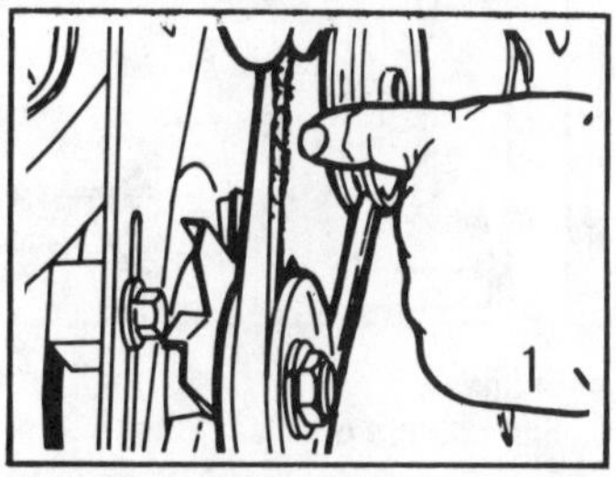

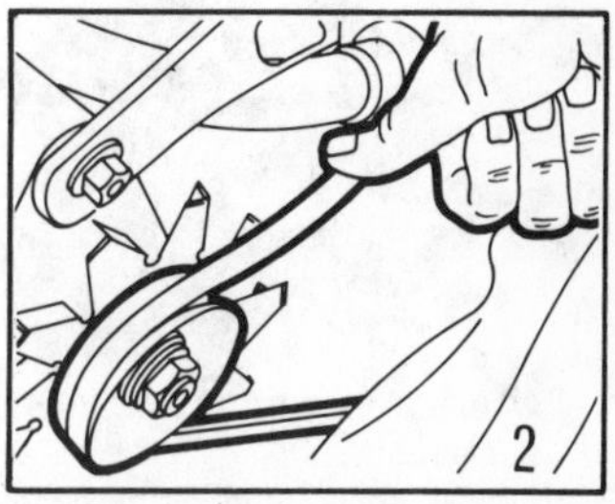

1. Inspect fan belt occasionally. If worn, frayed or cracked on inner driving surface, replace.
CAUTION: An overtightened belt may damage alternator and water pump, or power steering pump bearings.
2. Check tension occasionally. Press thumb at midpoint of belt span between pulleys. If belt depresses more than ½ inch, tightening is needed. A too-loose belt will not drive alternator and pumps effectively.
3. Adjust to proper tension of ¼ inch deflection. Adjust as follows:
A. Loosen mounting bolts at top and bottom so alternator can pivot on lower bolt and upper bolt can slide in bracket.
B. Pull alternator out slightly to put tension on belt, and hold while tightening upper bolt.
C. Check tension. Repeat adjustment as necessary.
D. When tension is correct, tighten lower bolt.

RADIATOR CAP CHECK

Check radiator cap occasionally for worn or cracked gasket. If cap doesn't seal properly, fluid will be lost and engine will overheat. Replace worn cap with new cap rated 13 to 15 lbs. pressure.

HOSE REPLACEMENT

Coolant drain and refill work may be done alone; when changing hoses, coolant must also be drained as part of job. Discard all hoses with cracks or soft spots. Check hose clamps for tightness and good condition.
1. Remove radiator cap. Open radiator petcock (See 2). Drain coolant into catch basin. If near 24 months old, discard old coolant.

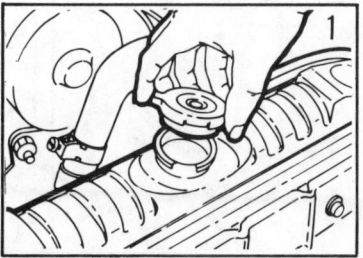

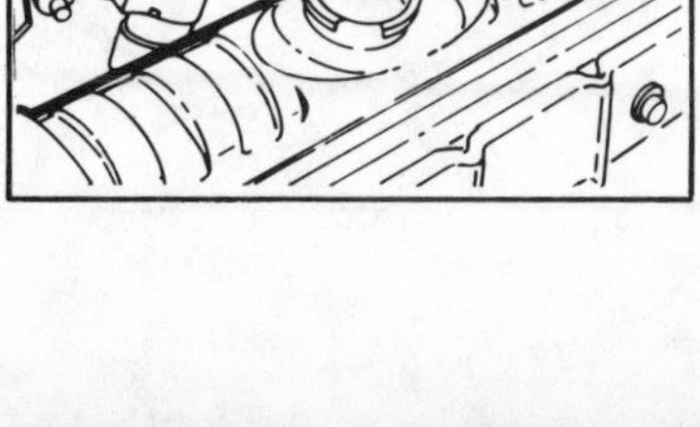

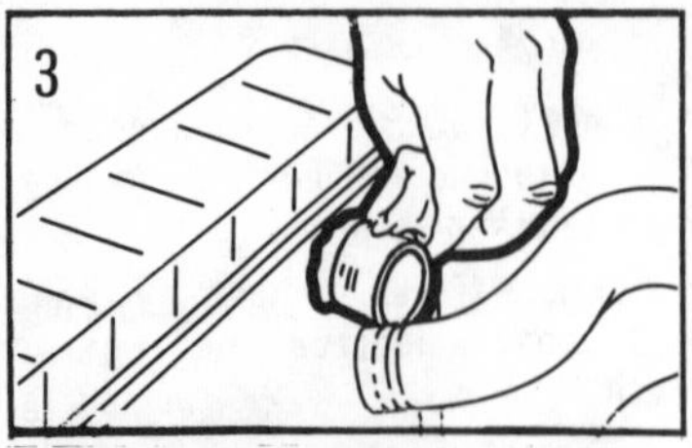

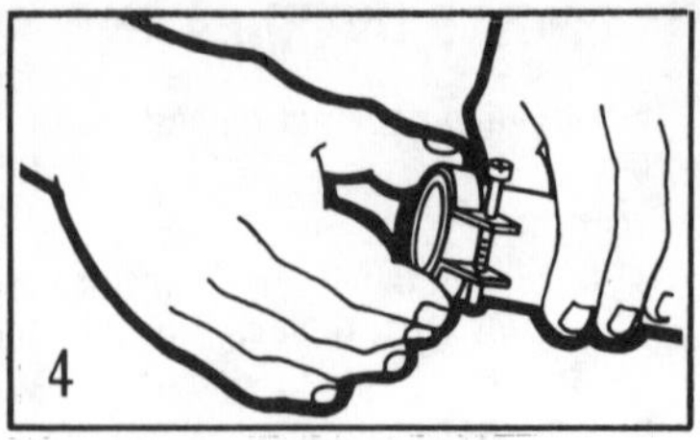

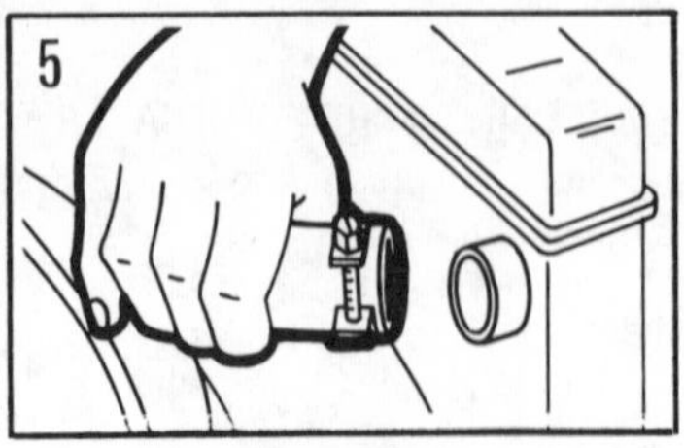

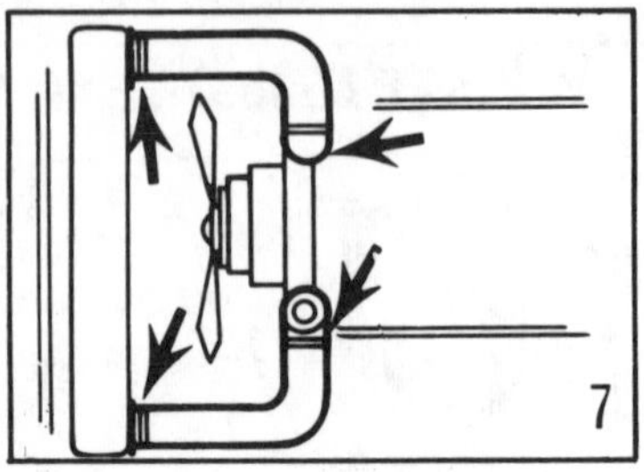

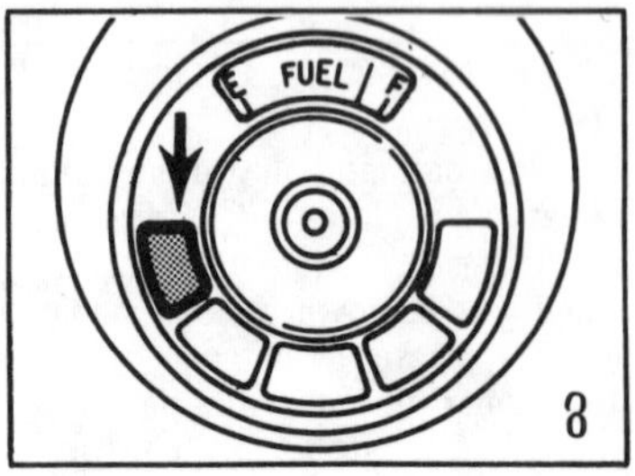

2. Petcock is located at the bottom of the radiator.
3. Wipe all hose connections clean. Use emery cloth to get rid of residue.
4. If old hose clamps are badly rusted or damaged, replace with new units.
5. Slip clamps over each hose end. Slip hose ends all the way onto cleaned up hose connections.
6. Place hose clamp ¼ inch from hose end. Tighten. Close petcock. Refill with 50/50 coolant/water mix.
7. Start engine; allow to warm up. Check for coolant leaks.
8. Road test car; watch for temperature warning light.

FIND THOSE COOLING SYSTEM LEAKS

1. Inspect all hoses. If any are weak, soft in spots or show cracks, replace at once.
2. Check all hose connections for tightness. Tighten loose hose clamps; they tend to loosen due to engine vibration.
3. If radiator steams or hisses when engine is switched off, check for leaks. Look for signs of coolant drips on radiator or around heater tank joint.

Leaks are possible at:
Upper or lower radiator hoses
Water pump (gaskets or seal)
Heater core or connecting hoses
Automatic transmission cooler lines
Faulty radiator pressure cap
Faulty cylinder head gasket
Choke hoses
Cracked cylinder head or block

Due to the number of joints, cooling systems have many places to leak from. Check clamp tightness. If leaks persist an anti-leak additive in the coolant may help. Noisy water pumps may benefit from a lubricating additive in the coolant. Use a cooling system cleaner when flushing during a drain and refill job. It will help remove rust and scale. Remember — additives will not cure chronic problems. But they will effect a short-term remedy in many cases.

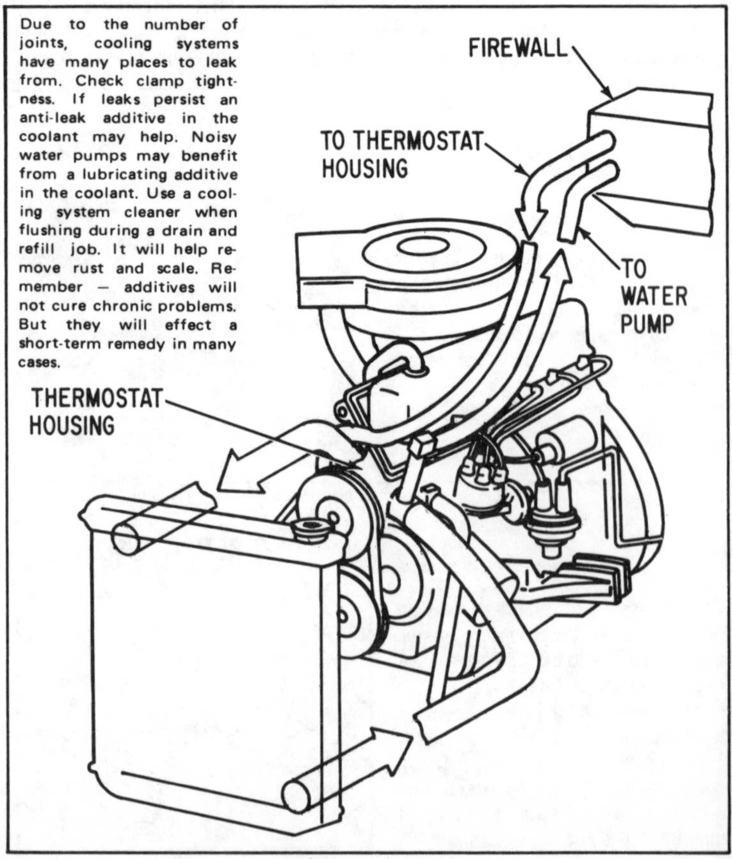

Ignition System

SOLID STATE IGNITION

Beginning 1974, Ford is utilizing a solid state or "breakerless" ignition system on all engines in the state of California. All 1975 and later engines use this maintenance-saving ignition system. This system is unique in that it eliminates the contact breaker points, replacing them with a permanent magnet, low voltage generator.

Briefly, the system works as follows; When the ignition is on and the distributor is rotating, the low voltage generator in the distributor produces alternating current which is then sent to the electronic control module. The module senses the signal from the low voltage generator as the alternating current wave swings from positive to negative each time one of the gear teeth on the armature passes the magnetic field in the coil of the generator. When a gear tooth is directly opposite the magnetic field, the alternating current wave is at crossover (neither negative nor positive). The control module senses this and cuts off electricity (low voltage) to the coil, causing it to fire (high voltage). After the coil fires, the timing circuitry in the module redirects the low tension voltage to the coil.

Other than the low voltage generator and the control module, the rest of the system is conventional in appearance, with a conventional distributor cap and rotor. Spark advance or retard is accomplished by moving the plate for the low voltage generator in the distributor.

TACHOMETER CONNECTION—ELECTRONIC IGNITION

Install a tachometer alligator clip into the "Tach Test" cavity as shown. If the coil connector must be removed, grasp the wires and pull horizontally until it disconnects from the terminals.

An alligator type clip from the tachometer test lead can also be connected to the DEC (Distributor Electronic Control) without removing the connector.

TUNE-UP SERVICES (Conventional and Solid-State)

The conventional ignition system consists of spark plugs; plug wires; distributor; rotor; points; condenser; coil. These units work to create a good hot spark inside the engine (ignition) at exactly the right moment (timing). If ignition is weak or timing is off, engine may be hard to set, run poorly, waste gas, lose power, backfire or not run at all.

FORD SAYS . . . Replace plugs and points every 12,000 miles (1970-74) 15,000 miles (1975-77).

TOOLS & MATERIALS . . . Parts: set of points; condenser; 8 spark plugs. Tools: gap gauge; 13/16 in. or 5/8 in. ('75-77 302V8) spark plug socket; screwdriver; open end, box or combination wrenches; timing equipment (see Ignition Timing).

SAFETY TIP . . . Change only one spark plug at a time to avoid cross-wiring and possible engine damage.

CHECKING POINTS, AND ROTOR

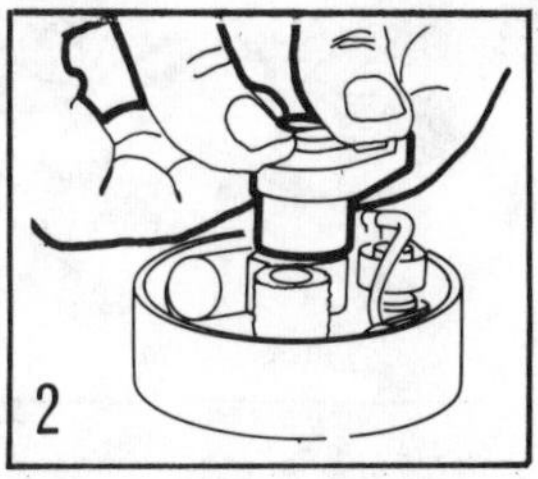

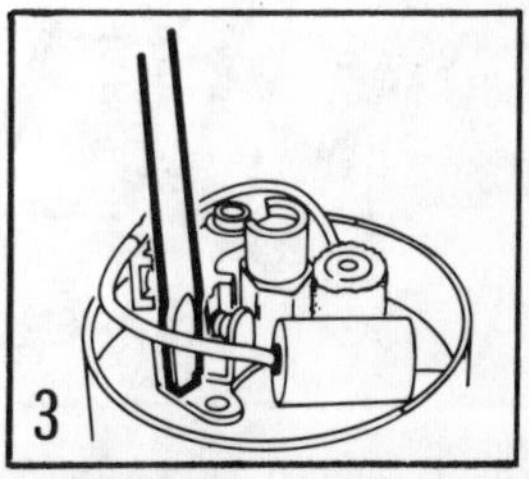

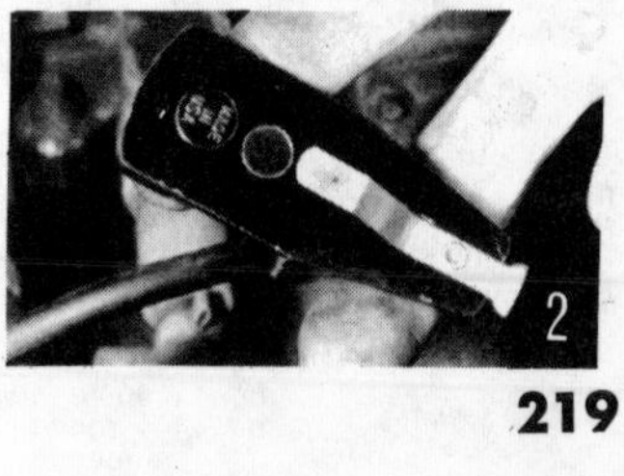

1. To open distributor, snap retaining clips off with screwdriver, lift cap off but keep wires connected.
2. Pull rotor off (straight up). Replace if cracked or metallic tip is badly burned.
3. Pry points (if so equipped) apart with screwdriver. If worn or burned, replace. If OK, check point gap.

OTHER IGNITION CHECK POINTS

Inspect spark plug wires. If cracked or brittle, entire set should be replaced. Also, center high tension wire. Inspect distributor cap. Wipe inside clean occasionally with dry, lint-free rag. If cap is cracked or rotor contacts are excessively burned, replace cap.

SPARK PLUG REPLACEMENT

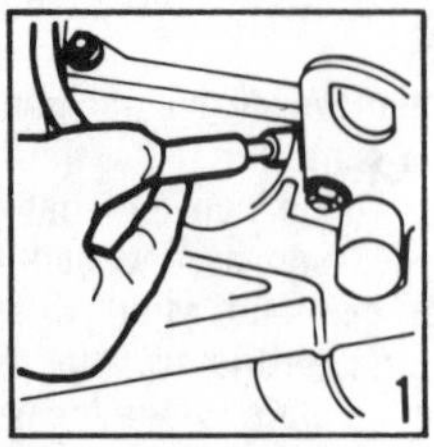

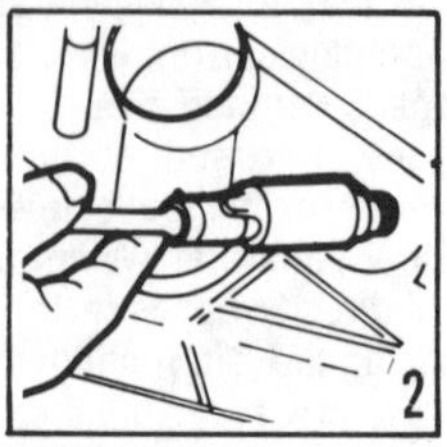

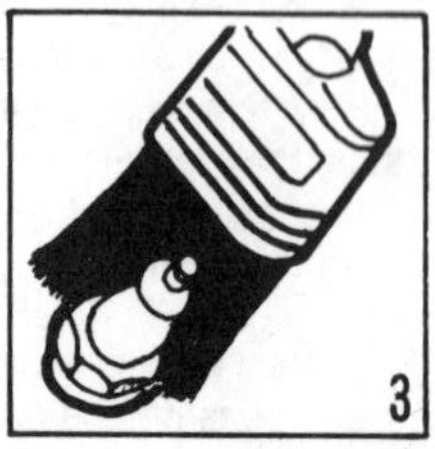

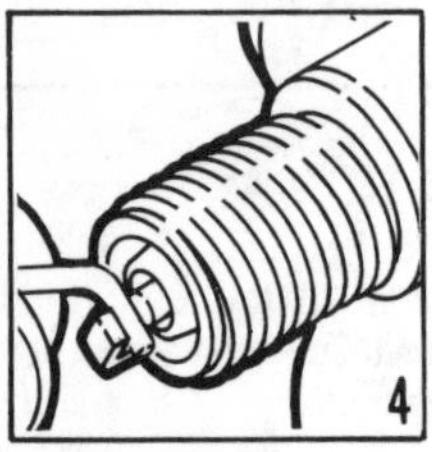

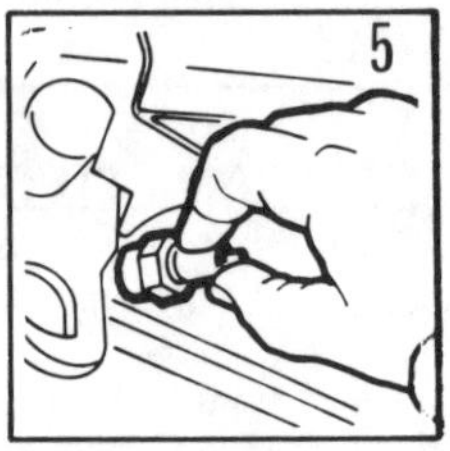

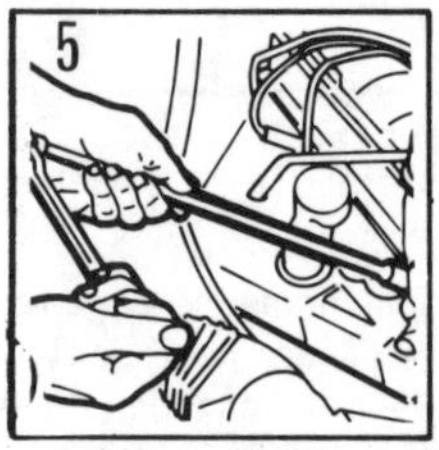

1. Plug spark plug wire by grasping rubber boot. Do not jerk wire off. If stuck, turn boot, pulling gently.
2. Loosen spark plug using socket wrench.
3. Wipe loose dirt from around plug before removing. Do not let dirt drop into engine through plug hole. Unscrew plug.
4. Check plug electrode gap on new spark plug. Adjust to:
gap shown in the Specifications Chart
Plug gap is correct when the gauge drags slightly as it is pulled between plug electrodes.
5. Thread new plug into plug hole by hand. Hand tighten. Do not force or cross thread. Use socket wrench to tighten firmly but do not force. Replace plug wire. Press boot firmly. (Periodic timing adjustment not necessary on cars equipped with solid-state ignition)

IGNITION TIMING

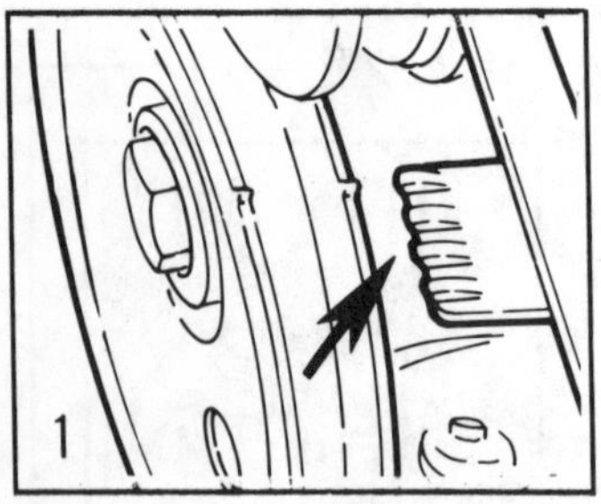

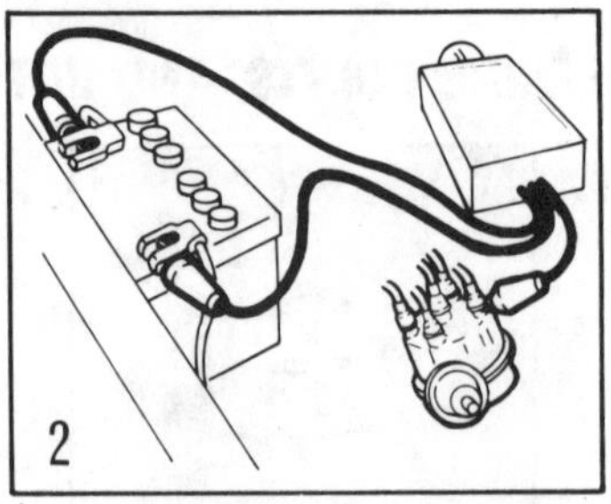

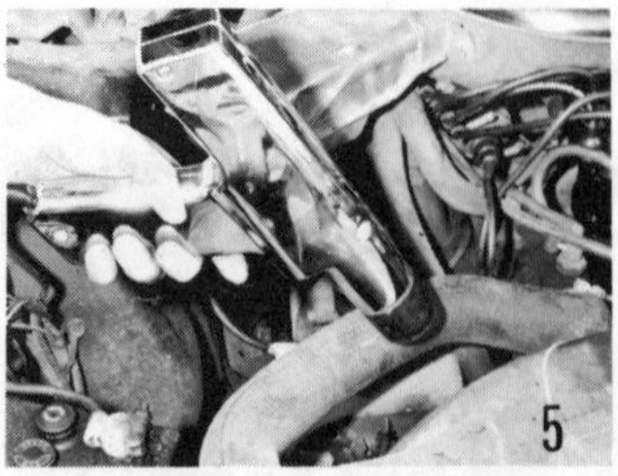

Adjusting timing is the important finishing touch to any tune-up. While not difficult, job requires timing light and dwell meter.

1. Locate timing marks and pointer (notches) on engine and lower engine pulley. Clean away dirt. Mark the pointer and notch which corresponds with the timing setting in degrees shown on the engine compartment sticker.
2. Hook up timing light according to instructions supplied with it.
3. Disconnect the one or two vacuum lines from the distributor. Plug with pencil tip or golf tee.
4. Hook up tachometer and adjust engine idle speed to 600 rpm. Idle attachment screw is located where gas pedal linkage attaches to carburetor.
5. Aim timing light at pulley mark(s). If the chalked marks do not align, loosen distributor holddown bolt and slowly rotate distributor until chalked marks align.
6. Tighten hold-down bolt. Recheck timing.

LOCATION OF POINTS AND CONDENSER—1970-74

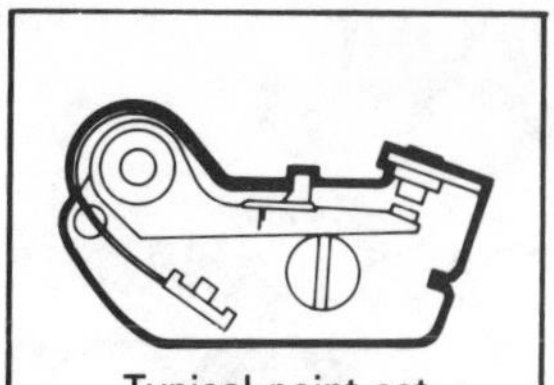
Typical point set.

Points and condenser are located beneath the distributor cap. Always replace condenser when installing new points.
If your car has breakerless ignition, periodic replacement of distributor parts is not required. If you suspect ignition trouble because of engine misfire, have the distributor checked out by a professional mechanic.

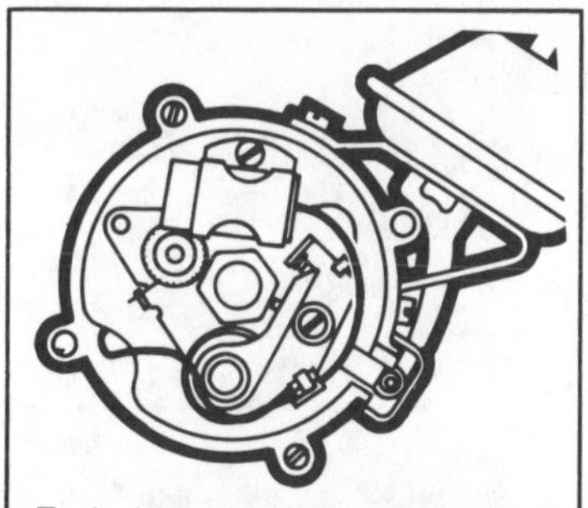
Typical location inside distributor.

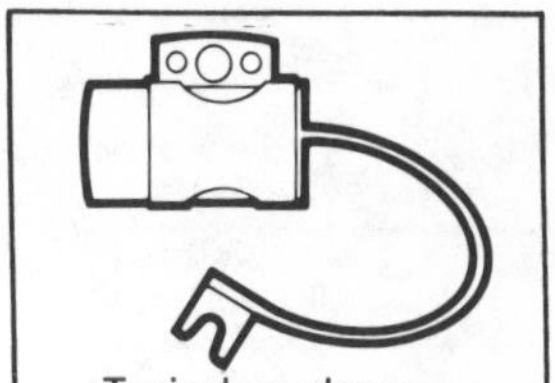
Typical condenser.

REMOVING POINTS—1970-74

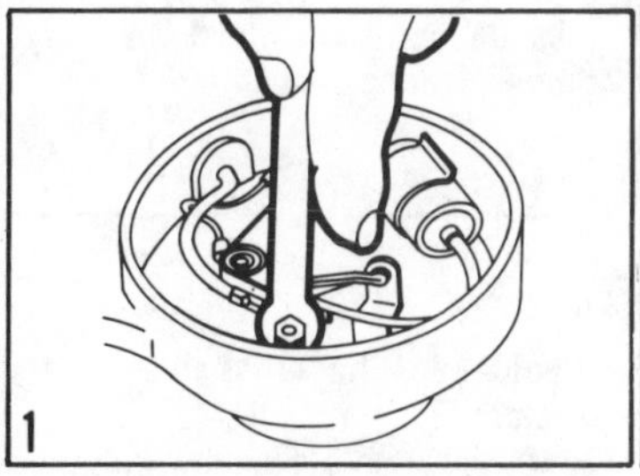

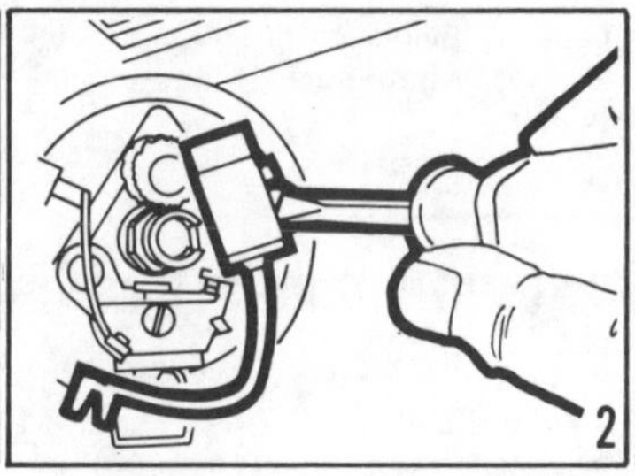

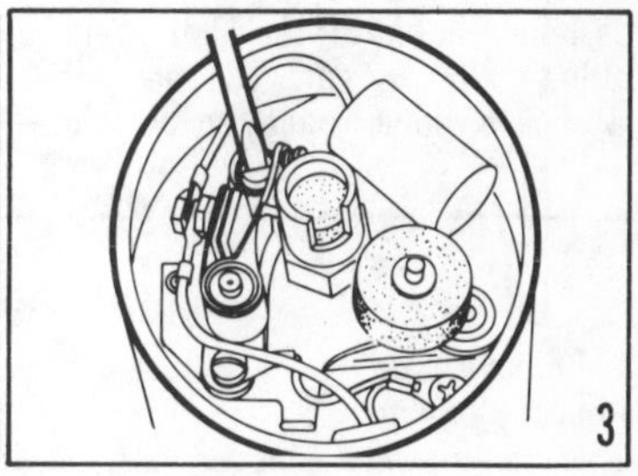

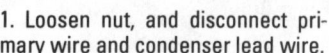

1. Loosen nut, and disconnect primary wire and condenser lead wire.
2. Remove screw which holds condenser; remove condenser.
3. Remove screws holding points to distributor, remove points.
4. Wipe all dirt from distributor plate and cam.
5. Inspect primary wire for frayed insulation, dirty connection. Clean connection or have wire repaired as necessary.

CAUTION: When removing screws from distributor in following steps, be sure to avoid any screws accidentally falling through distributor opening into engine. Use magnetic screwdriver.

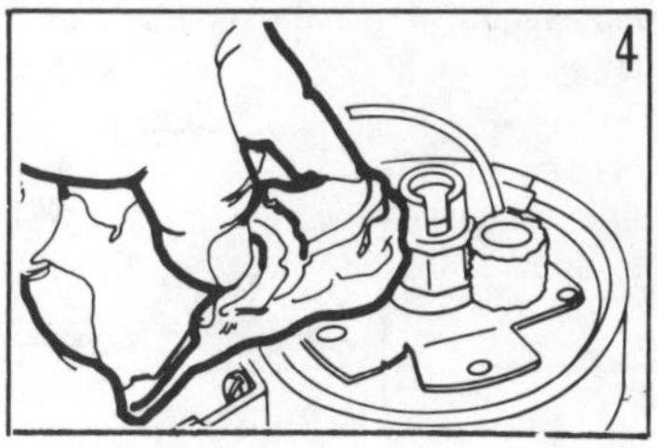

INSTALLING POINTS AND CONDENSER—1970-74

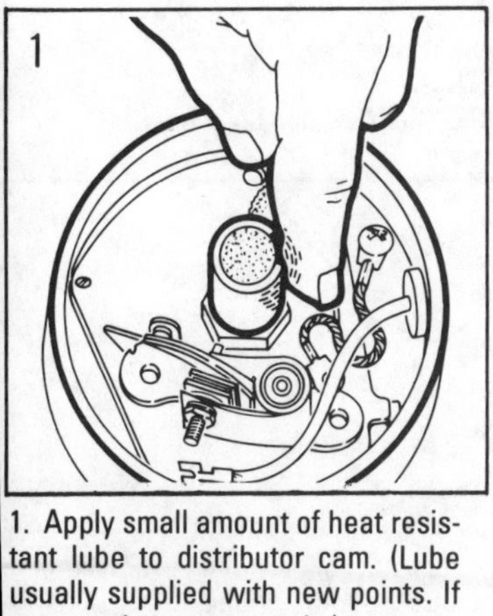

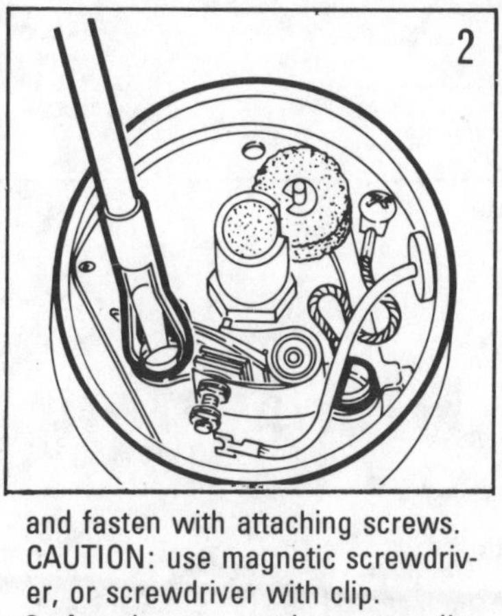

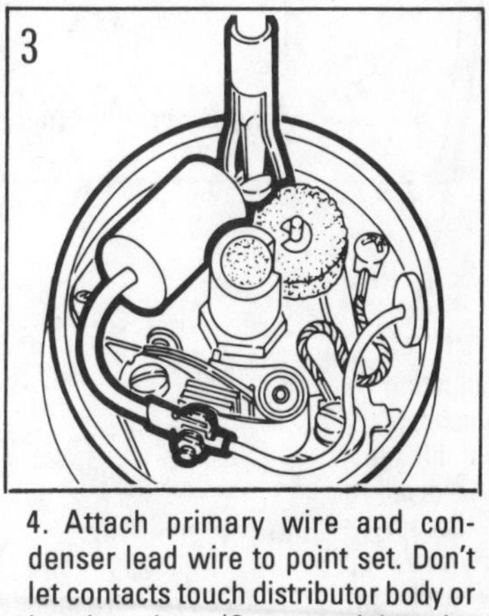

1. Apply small amount of heat resistant lube to distributor cam. (Lube usually supplied with new points. If not, purchase separately.)
2. Position new points in distributor and fasten with attaching screws. CAUTION: use magnetic screwdriver, or screwdriver with clip.
3. Attach new condenser to distributor with attaching screw.
4. Attach primary wire and condenser lead wire to point set. Don't let contacts touch distributor body or breaker plate. (Some models; wire from points attaches to condenser.)

RESETTING THE CONTACT GAP—1970-74

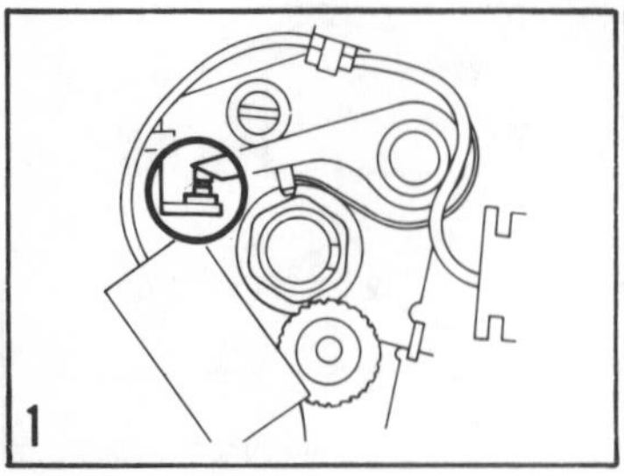

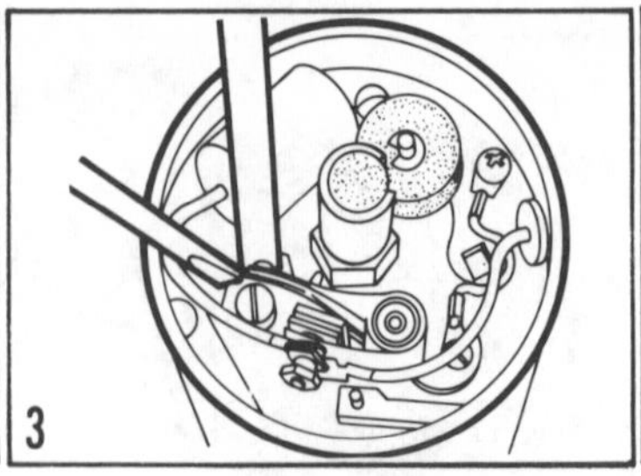

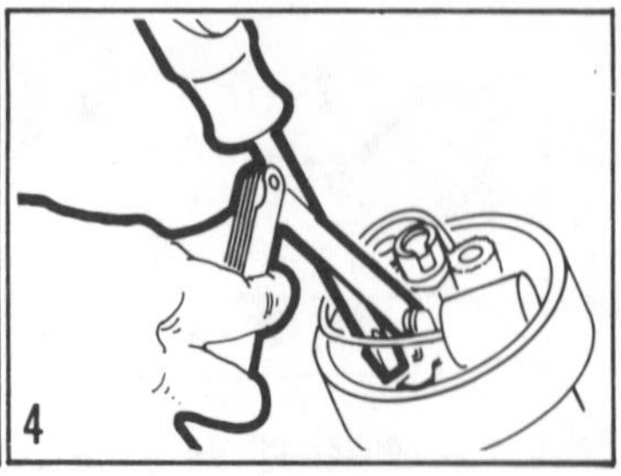

1. Electrical contacts of point set MUST BE PARALLEL. If needed, bend stationary contact with needle-nose pliers. Bend fixed bracket only.
2. Turn engine by ignition key (you'll need a helper) until rubbing block on points is one of the high points of the distributor cam. You may use wrench on lower pulley to do this.
3. Look up correct point gap on engine compartment sticker. Insert proper gap gauge between open point contacts. Slightly loosen point attaching screws. Insert screwdriver in breaker plate notch near point contacts. Twist screwdriver to open or close points as needed. Tighten screws when correct gap is obtained.
4. Recheck gap after screws are tightened. Readjust if needed.
5. Align tab inside rotor with notch on distributor shaft and push rotor onto shaft. Rotor must be fully seated on shaft.
6. Install distributor cap by aligning tabs on cap with notch on body. Snap retaining clips in place.

REPLACING SPARK PLUG WIRES

1. Remove only one wire at a time from the engine.
2. Match the wire removed with the same length wire in the replacement set.
3. Route the replacement wire in the same way as the original.
4. After all wires are replaced, check that all wires on 1974 and earlier distributors are seated in the distributor cap. Check that all boots are in place.
5. If you run into difficulty, go to the Firing Order illustrations for help.

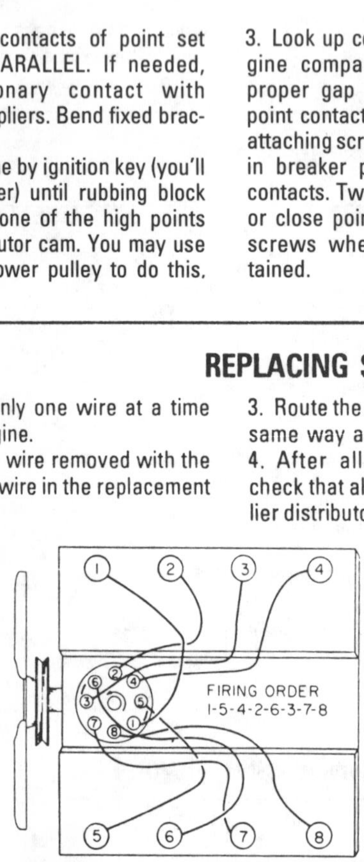

Firing Order—V8 Engine

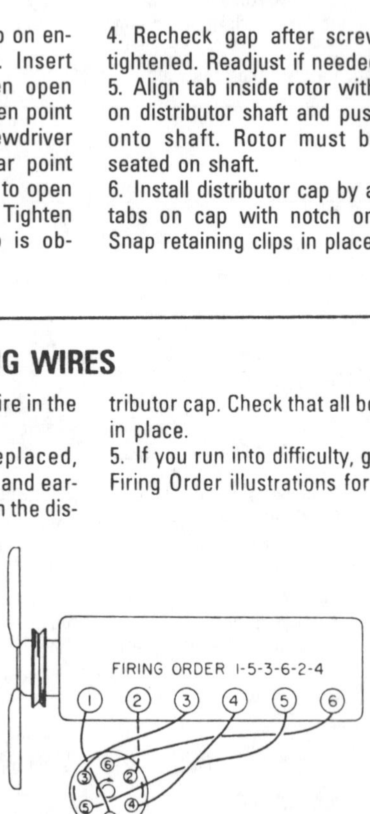

Firing Order—Six Cylinder Engines

Fuel System

When gasoline is brought from the fuel tank, it mixes with air in the carburetor. This gas/air mixture then enters engine thru the intake manifold, passes thru the intake valves and is burned in the combustion chamber. The burned exhaust gas is then passed thru the exhaust valves to the exhaust system and to the outside air. In order to keep your car's engine running cleanly with minimal pollution, and avoid dangerous carbon monoxide fumes inside the vehicle, certain items should be checked from time to time.

KEEP THE AIR INTAKE CLEAN

The large round can that sits on top of the engine holds the air cleaner. Twice a year:

1. Remove wing nut, and remove air cleaner lid.
2. Lift out circular air cleaner cartridge. Discard if more than 12 months old or excessively dirty.
3. Pull off wire clip that retains filter and elbow. Remove elbow.
4. Pull crankcase filter out of filter can. Wipe inside of can and lid with clean cloth.
5. Install crankcase filter. Put elbow on filter neck. Install wire clip onto filter. Install in reverse order.

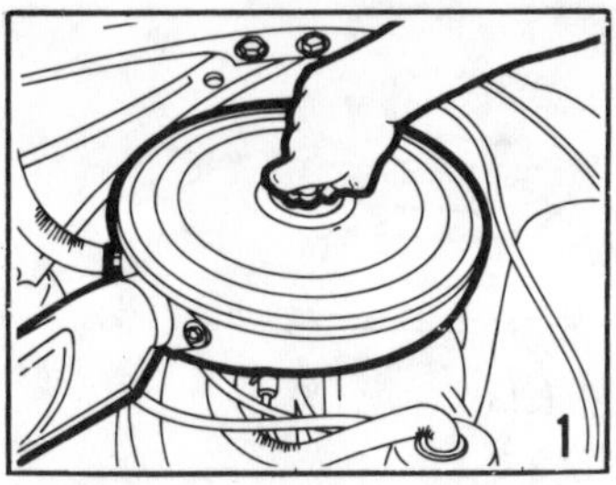

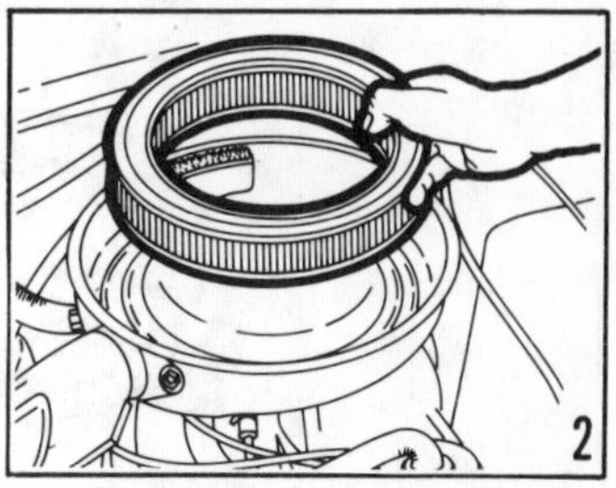

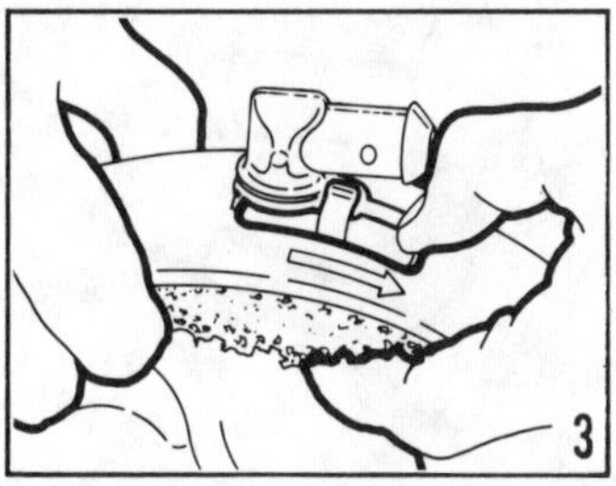

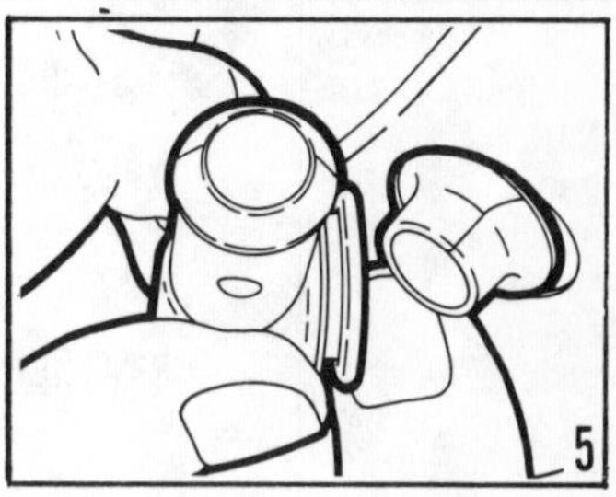

FUEL FILTER REPLACEMENT

Replace the filter every year or 12,000 miles. The fuel filter prevents dirt, rust, and scale from both the gas station's tank and your own fuel tank from reaching the carburetor. A dirty filter will starve the engine and cause poor running.

1. Locate the fuel filter in line to carburetor. Place a rag under the filter housing to collect fuel that will drain out when filter is removed.
2. Pinch the ends of clamps together, and move toward center of hose. Use the smallest possible amount of tension, to avoid damaging the clamps. You can get a special tool designed for this job that will make handling the clamps much

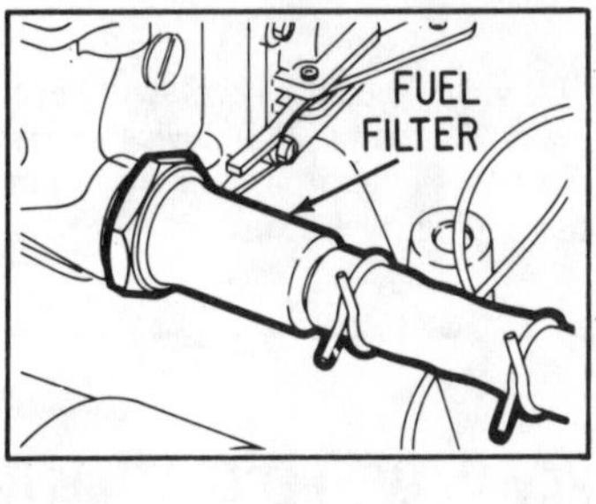

easier.

3. Pull the hose off filter and fuel line.
4. Fit an adjustable wrench to the six-sided portion of the filter body, and unscrew it from the carburetor. Discard old unit.
5. Position a new gasket onto the new filter, screw the housing into the carburetor and tighten.
6. Position new clamps in center of a new hose. If the old clamps are to be reused, make sure they have not lost their tension.
7. Install hose on fuel line and filter. Pinch the clamp ends together, and position well onto fuel line and filter.

Note: After replacing filter, remove rag used to catch spilled fuel, and then start engine. Check for leaks. Addition of a can of carburetor cleaner to the fuel tank occasionally will aid in keeping the entire fuel system clean.

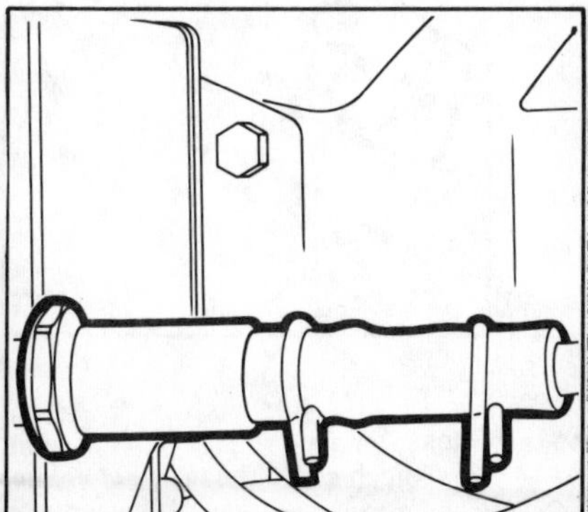

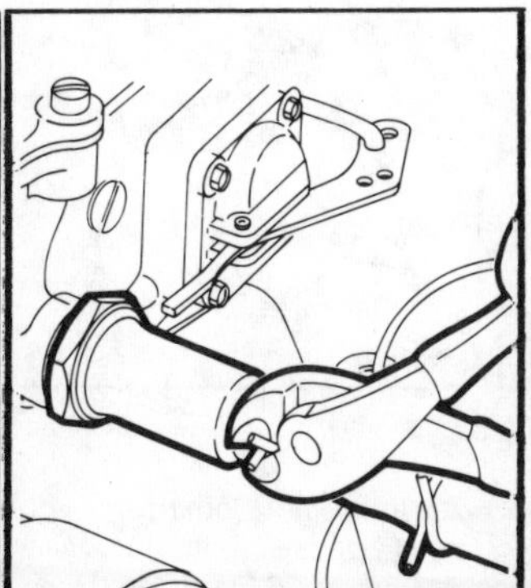

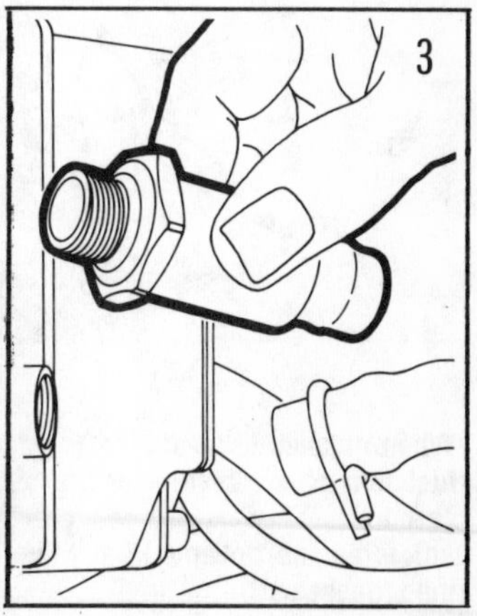

EMISSION CONTROLS SYSTEMS

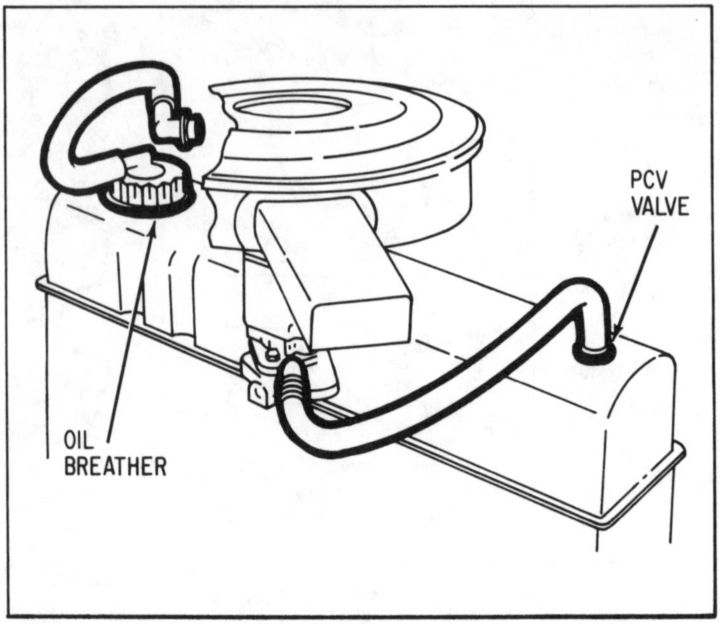

The most important part of a car's emission control system is the Positive Crankcase Ventilation (PCV) valve and its connecting hose. The PCV valve should be replaced once every 12 months. This device keeps dirt and sludge from forming inside the engine. Make sure all PCV connections are tight. Check that the connecting hoses are clear and not clogged. Replace any brittle or broken hoses.

PCV VALVE REPLACEMENT

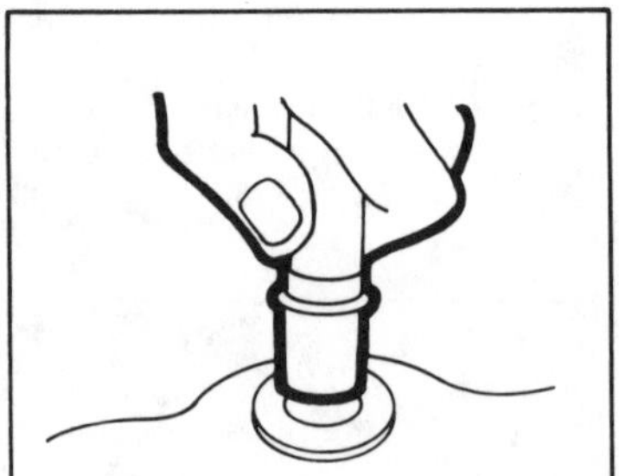

The PCV valve is located on top of the valve cover, in front of the air cleaner.

1. Grasp hose holding PCV valve. Pull straight out.
2. Note where other end of hose is connected. Pull off.
3. Remove PCV valve from hose. Flush hose out with cleaning solvent. Dry hose. Install new PCV valve in hose.
4. Attach end of hose to its original connection and insert PCV valve into proper opening.

Safety Systems

PARKING LIGHTS, TURN SIGNALS AND STOP LIGHTS

All above lighting functions are performed by four dual-element bulbs. Front parking light and turn signal bulbs are mounted in the parking light housing in the grille. To replace, raise hood and reach socket from behind grille. To replace rear taillight, stop light, turn signal bulbs, raise trunk lid or rear door. Reach socket from inside car. Twist socket counterclockwise in housing. When socket is removed, push in on bulb and turn counterclockwise to remove from socket. Insert new dual-element bulb in correct position (see note) and re-install socket in housing.

NOTE: When inserting new dual element bulb, note that knobs on side of bulb base are different distances from base tip. Match knobs to socket slots for proper fit.

BACK-UP LIGHTS

To replace back-up light bulbs, raise trunk lid. Reach bulb socket from inside car. Turn bulb socket counterclockwise and pull out. Push down on bulb turning counterclockwise to remove from socket. Insert new bulb and reinstall in reverse order.

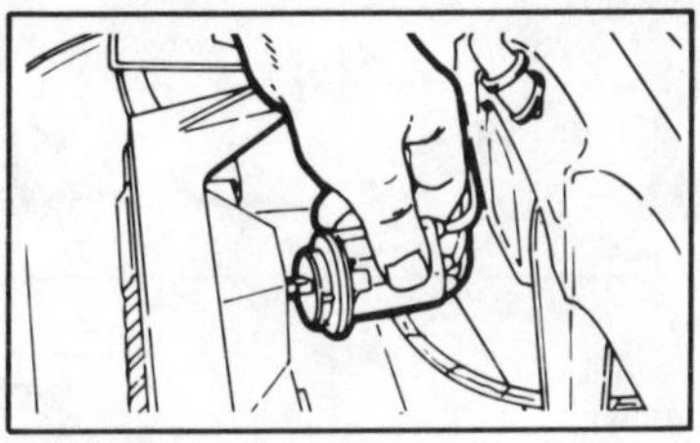

SIDE MARKER LIGHT

Reach up under fender and turn bulb socket counterclockwise to remove from housing. Pull bulb straight out. Do not turn bulb.

LICENSE PLATE LIGHTS

Remove screw lens and housing that attaches to bottom of bumper. Push in on bulb turning counterclockwise to remove.

INTERIOR DOME LIGHT

This is a cartridge type bulb. Pry the dome light lens out from the housing. To avoid blowing the fuse, make sure that the doors are closed and domelight switch in the OFF position. Push in on the bulb and turn it clockwise to remove from socket. Insert new bulb and install in reverse order.

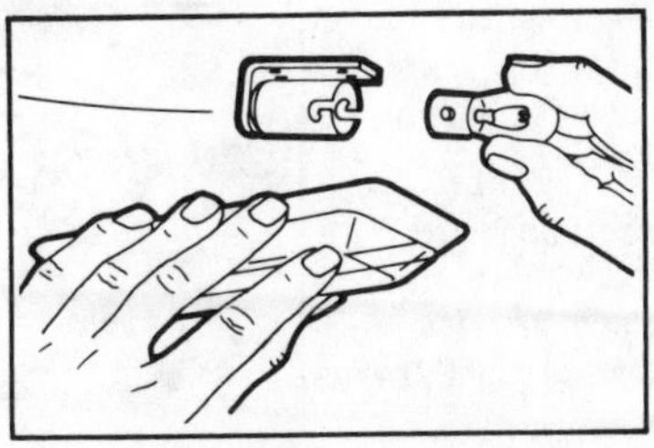

HEADLIGHT REPLACEMENT

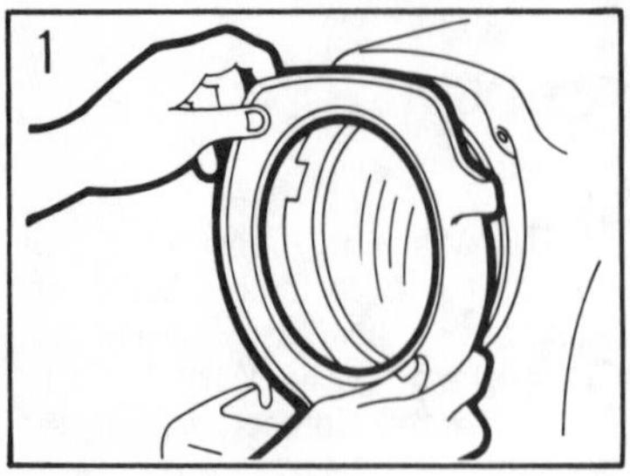

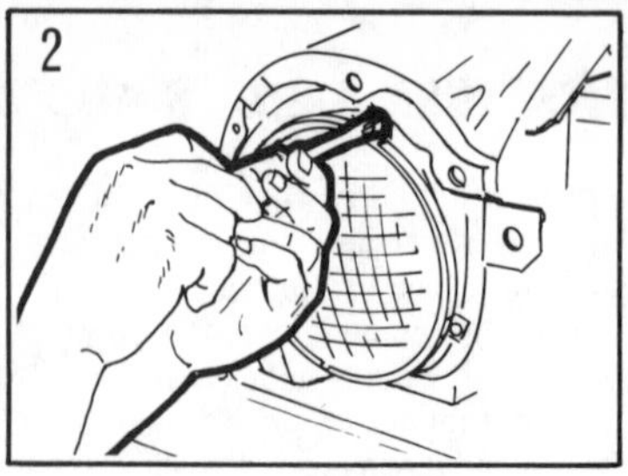

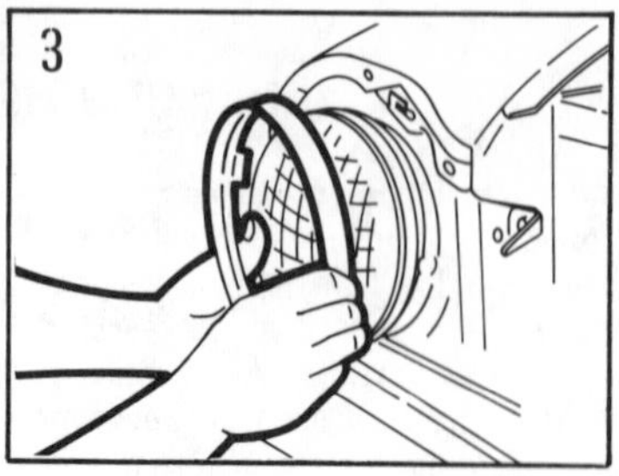

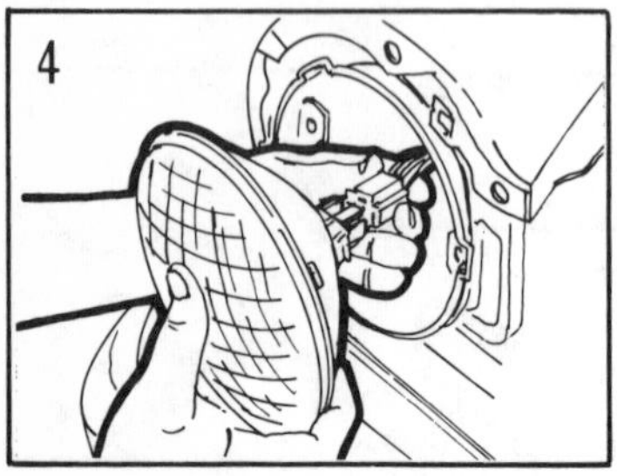

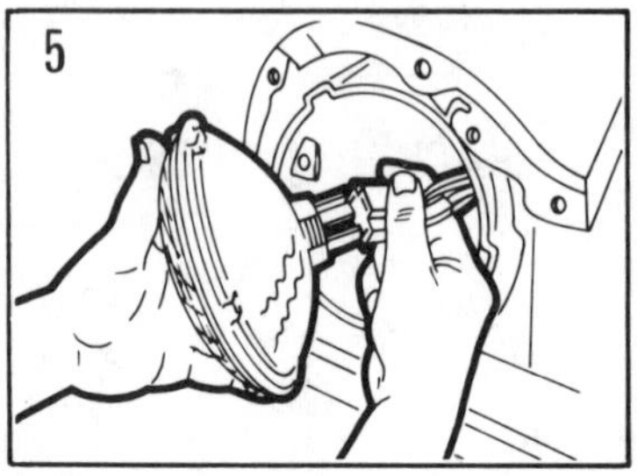

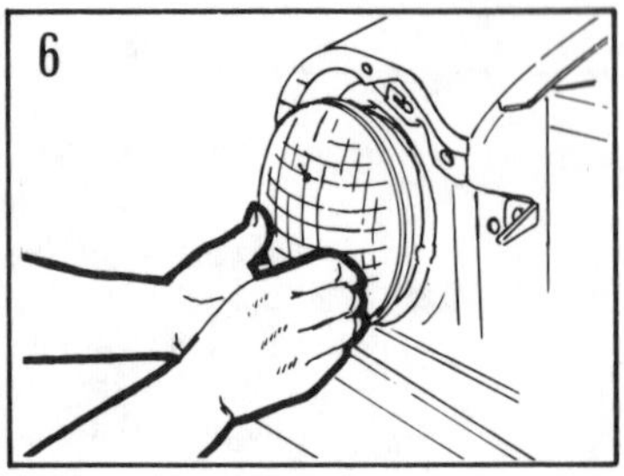

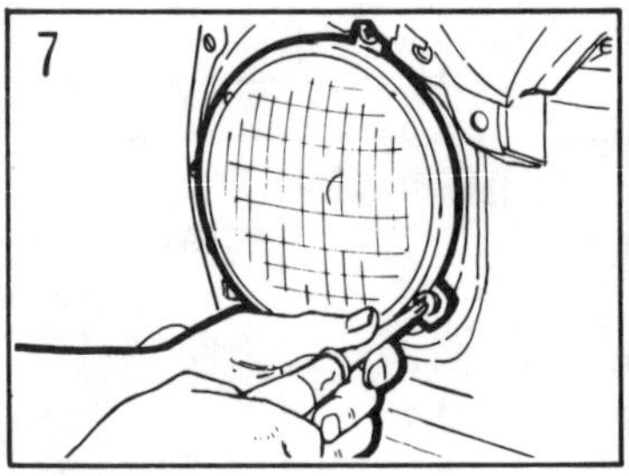

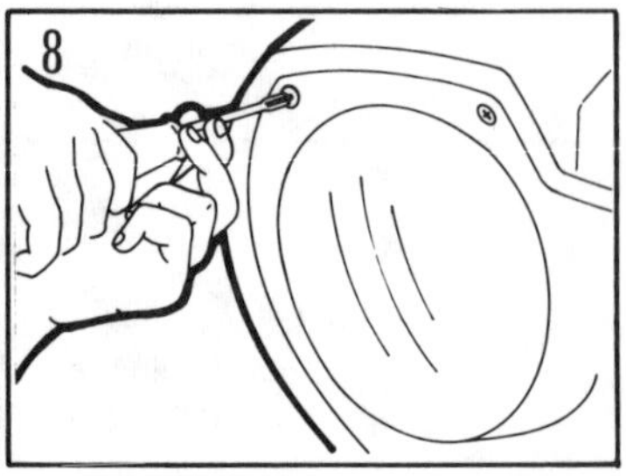

1. Remove both headlight cover retaining screws and cover.
2. Loosen, but do not remove, headlight retaining ring attaching screws. NOTE: Do not mistake headlight adjustment screws for the three retaining ring screws.
3. Rotate retaining ring to left until large openings in attaching screw slots are aligned with screw heads. Remove ring.
4. Pull lamp (sealed beam) out of headlight shell toward front of car; disconnect wiring connector from sealed beam unit.
5. Connect wire connector to new sealed beam unit.
6. Position new sealed beam unit in headlight shell. Be sure knobs on back of bulb (near outer edge) enters slots in shell.
7. Position retaining ring on retainer screws; turn ring to right. Tighten screws.
8. Position headlight cover; install attaching screws.

WHEEL CYLINDER CHECK

Drum brakes employ individual wheel cylinders to apply braking pressure to shoes. Check for brake fluid leaks on inside of wheel. Disc brakes employ calipers on individual wheels. Remove wheel and inspect caliper for signs of fluid leaks. Have mechanic correct leaks.

WINDSHIELD WIPER BLADE REPLACEMENT

To replace wiper blade, lift up on spring release tab on wiper arm connector. Pull wiper blade off. Snap new blade into place.

To replace rubber insert only, press down, away from wiper blade to free it. Slide insert from blade. Insert new wiper. Bend insert upward slightly to engage retaining clips.

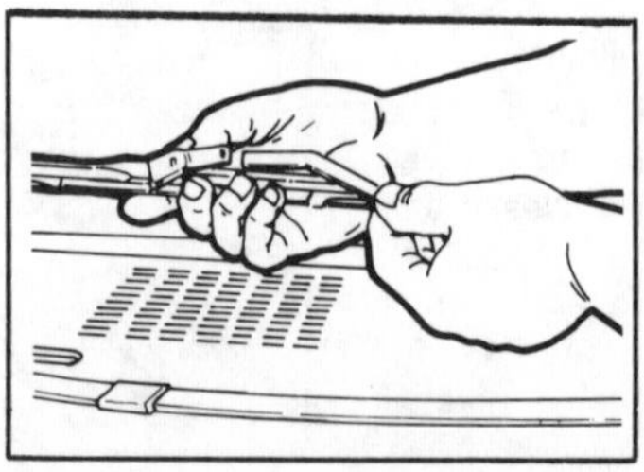

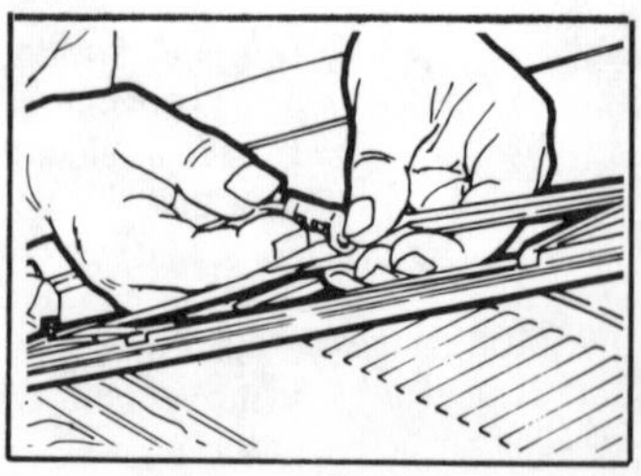

HORN PROBLEMS

If horn sounds and does not stop, this is due to short circuit in wiring. Disconnect wiring connector underhood and have professional service shop check horn wiring circuit.

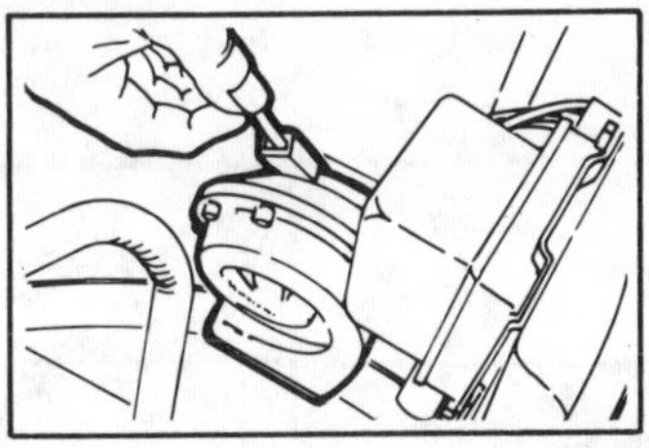

STEERING PROBLEMS

See steering system check in Suspension Section. Check tire pressures. Have a professional service shop check all components in the front end and steering system

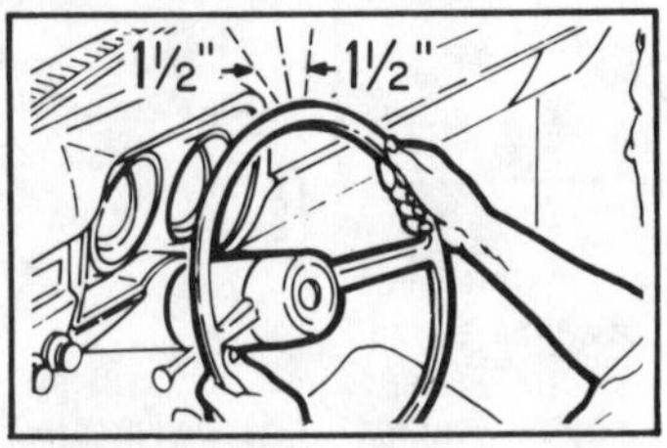

WASHER SYSTEM

If washer fails to squirt properly, raise hood and check system hose connections. Be sure washer fluid container has fluid. Check spout openings for clogging.
Keep container filled with fluid mixture of washer solvent and water. If road spray buildup on windshield is a chronic problem, add 1 tablespoon dishwasher detergent to solvent/water mixture when re-filling container.

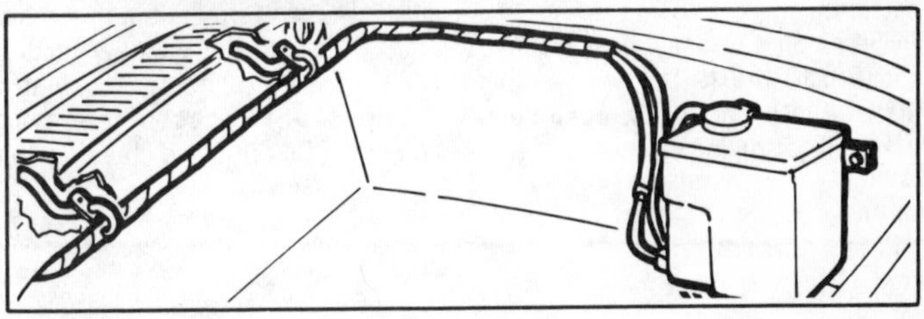

Electrical System

CHECKPOINTS AND SERVICES

To ensure starting ability at all times check your battery condition periodically. You'll need to check battery electrolyte (fluid) level in each of the six cells. Check battery cable connections for tightness and inspect for accumulated corrosion.
SAFETY NOTE: Wear gloves when working on battery.

CHECK BATTERY FLUID

1. Remove plastic filler caps on top of battery. Fluid should be up to lower end of filler hole and covering the plates. If fluid is low add clean, cold tap water. If your area has hard water, use only distilled water available at auto supply, food or drug stores.
2. Replace any lost caps immediately.

CAUTION: NEVER LIGHT A MATCH OR SMOKE near the top of a battery. Batteries give off explosive hydrogen gas.

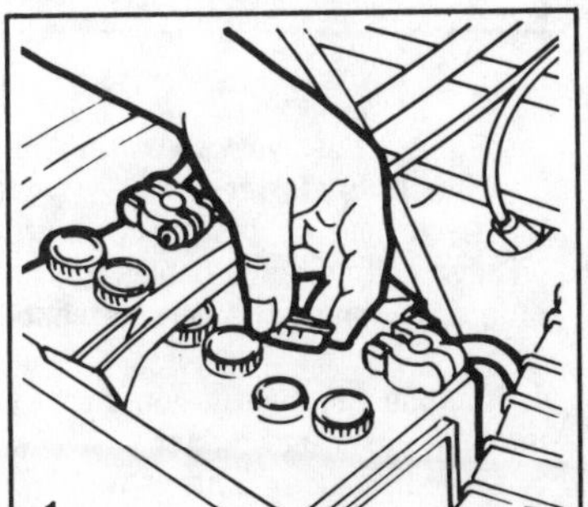

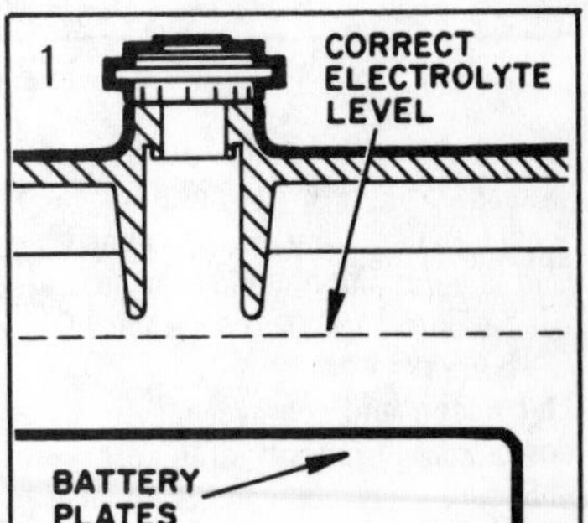

NOTE: Battery that often checks low on fluid could mean:
A. Battery is getting old, due for replacement; have charge capacity checked at service shop.
B. Connections may be corroded or loose; clean/replace as needed (see below).
C. Alternator or voltage regulator not functioning properly; this happens far less often than A or B above.

CLEAN THOSE BATTERY TERMINALS

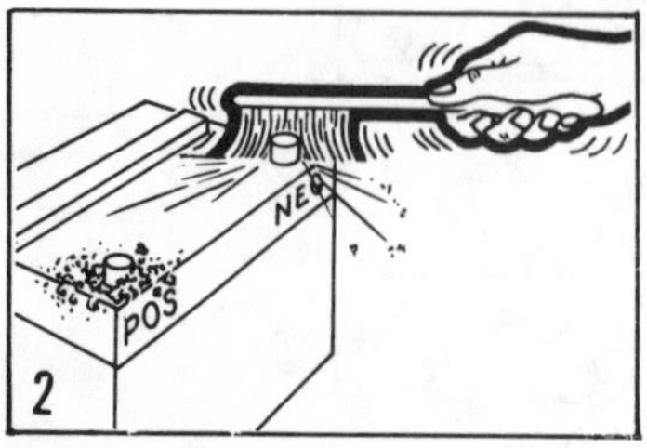

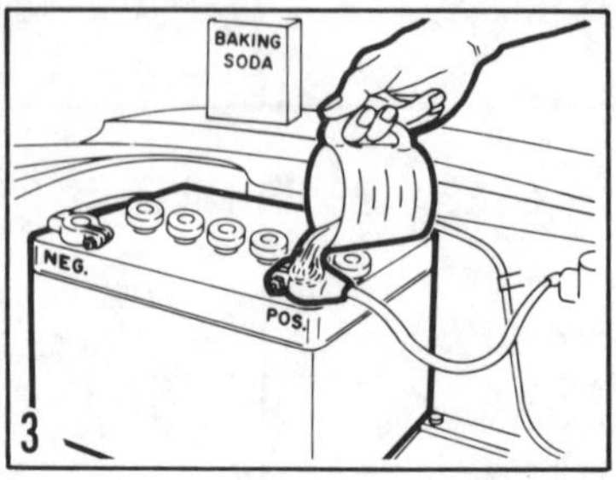

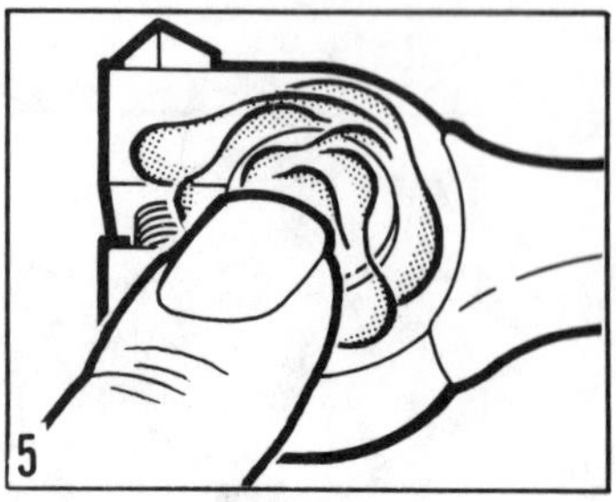

As times goes by, battery terminals build up a dry powdery, whitish material. This material is corrosive and will gradually eat thru battery cables if not cleaned off periodically.
1. Loosen and remove battery connections.
2. Brush off all loose corrosion; use stiff bristle brush. Do not get this material into eyes or on open cuts. Wash off at once.
3. If corrosion build-up is extremely heavy and brushing does not remove all of it, mix 2 tablespoons baking soda to 1 cup water. Pour solution directly onto terminals and connectors. Allow to soak a few minutes and rinse off. Continue brushing to remove all traces of corrosion build-up. Do not allow cleaning solution to enter battery.
4. Replace connectors on battery terminal posts and tighten. Do not hammer connections onto posts, but be sure they will not come loose with vibration.
5. Liberally smear battery terminal posts and cable connectors with petroleum jelly.

REPLACE FAULTY BATTERY CABLES

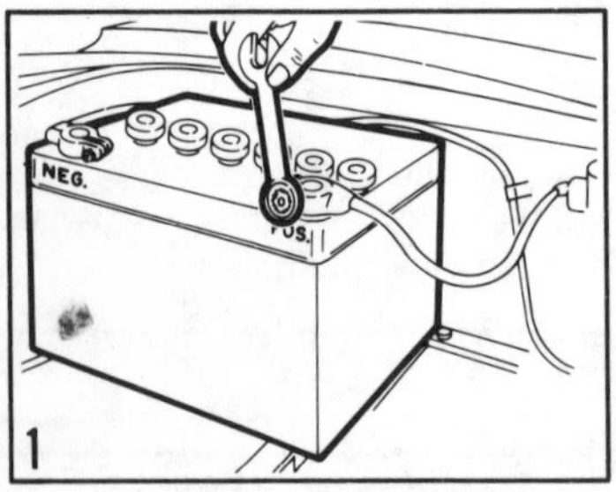

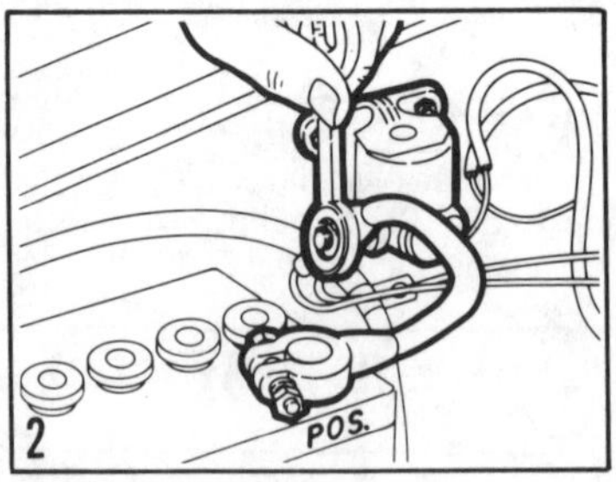

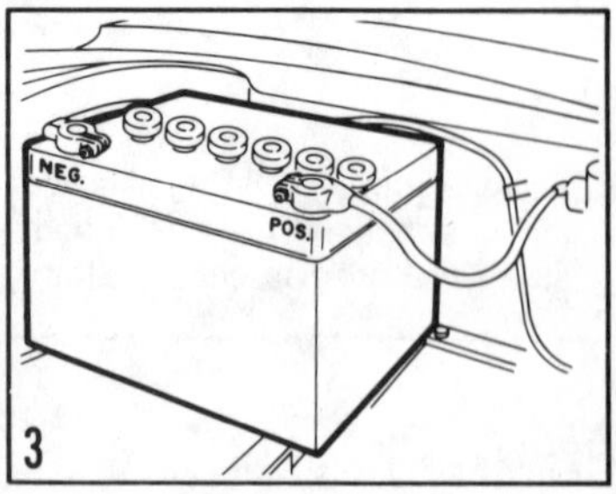

If battery cable strands become frayed, broken or corroded, replace cable immediately. Delay in correcting this condition could lead to sudden failure to start the engine. Can also weaken battery.
1. Loosen and remove battery connections. Clean off any corrosion buildup.
2. Disconnect negative cable from its attachment to engine or chassis. Disconnect positive cable from its attachment to starter relay.
3. Attach new cables making sure positive and negative cables are on proper terminals. They are not identical.
4. Replace connectors on battery terminal posts and tighten.
5. Liberally smear battery terminal posts and cable connectors with petroleum jelly.

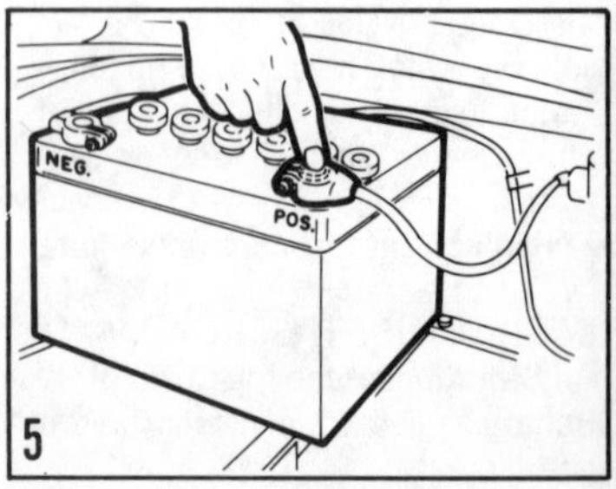

BATTERY HOLDDOWN

The clamp device which holds battery in place should be checked periodically. If loose, tighten. Clean off corrosion buildup. Severely corroded holddown components should be replaced before they break.

ELECTRICAL FUSES—1970-75

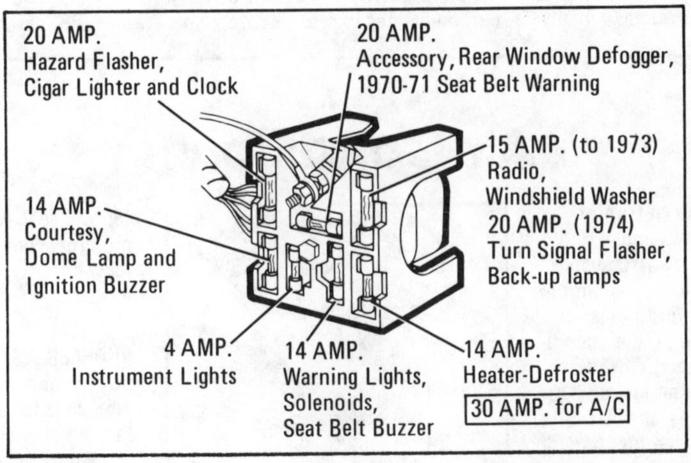

TURN SIGNAL AND 4-WAY FLASHER

Turn signals and 4-way emergency flashers will operate only if: A. All light bulbs are OK. B. Flasher units are not burned out. The car has two flasher units that work independently of each other. Turn signal flasher is located behind instrument panel on extreme left. Emergency flasher is located as illustration shows. To remove either flasher, grasp with fingers, twist and pull flasher toward front of car. Pull connector from flasher. REPLACE ONLY WITH SAME TYPE FLASHER.

ALTERNATOR

Red alternator warning light on instrument panel should glow red when you first turn ignition key. This proves bulb is OK. Alternator warning light should go off when engine is running at normal operating speed. If alternator warning light glows red at operating speed, alternator isn't charging battery properly. Common causes are:

A. Fan belts are loose and slipping on alternator pulley. Tighten or replace belts.

B. Battery terminals, cables are loose or corroded. Clean; tighten; replace bad cables.

If A or B do not correct problem, alternator or voltage regulator may be faulty. This happens far less often, and can only be checked by mechanic with proper electrical testing equipment.

Alternator Caution: Alternator can be permanently damaged by short-circuiting terminal connections. When working around or moving alternator, always keep metal tools or engine parts from terminals.

REAR WINDOW DEFOGGER SYSTEM

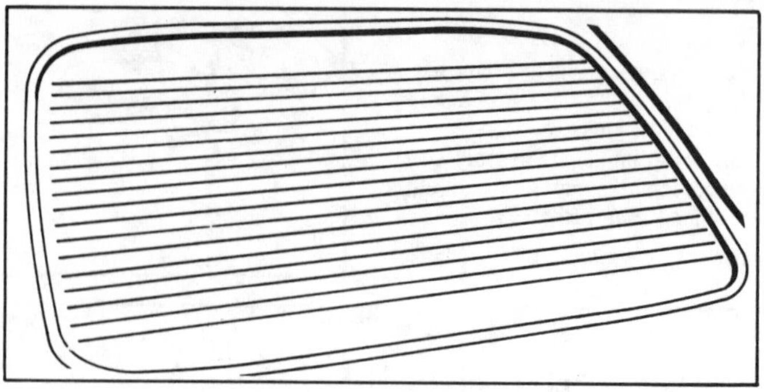

Do not clean inside of rear window fitted with defogger system with any abrasive material. This could destroy carbon-copper wires. Use only soft rag and mild detergent/water mixture. Dry carefully.

Air Conditioner

WARNING!—Never attempt to tighten fittings, disassemble or do any work on your car's A/C system. Consult a professional mechanic about A/C system problems and their correction. Your auto air condition (A/C) is a delicate, closed system. If air, dirt or water get into it, or if refrigerant escapes, the A/C unit will not cool a car interior. Among things you can do are:

1. Keep condenser grill clean. Check for dirt and debris; periodically remove dead insects, leaves, etc., with stiff bristle brush. Straighten any bent fins—carefully.
2. Keep radiator filled to correct level. (See Cooling System section). If fluid needs to be added, add antifreeze rather than water.
3. Keep radiator coolant at a 50/50 water/antifreeze mixture.
4. Flush cooling system and replace with fresh coolant mixture at least every 24 months. (See Cooling System section).
5. Radiator cap should be tight and sealed properly. If sealing gasket is cracked, cut or worn, replace cap with new 15 lb. unit.
6. Check fan belt tension periodically. (See Cooling System section). Replace glazed, frayed or cut fan belts, before they fail entirely.
7. Check periodically for bubbles in A/C sight glass. Sight glass is located in head of receiver/drier vessel. Or in metal tubing leading from top of receiver/drier. Sight glass is no larger than head of large nail. It may be dirty. Wipe clean for best visibility.

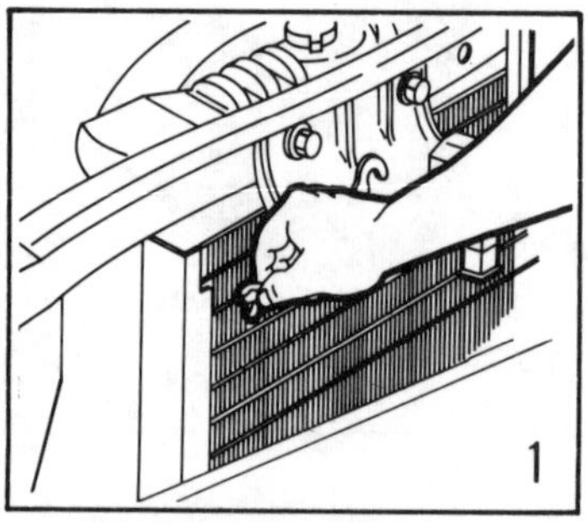

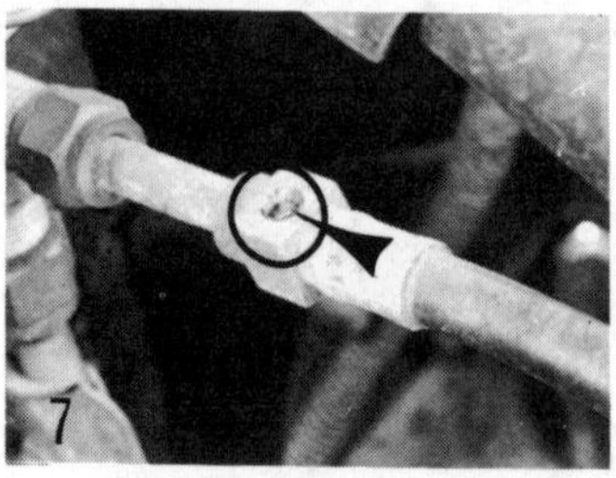

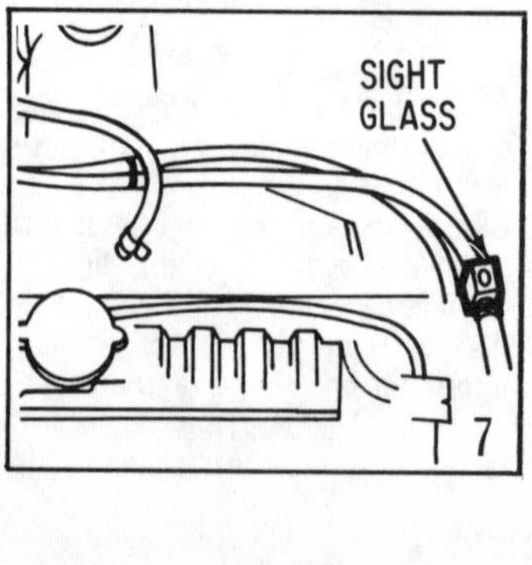

PROCEED AS FOLLOWS:

a) With engine and A/C system running, look for passage of refrigerant in sight glass. You'll be looking for a stream of milky white bubbles as they pass through sight glass. It is best to watch sight glass and have someone else start the car and turn on the A/C system. Allow to run for a few minutes.

b) If you observe no bubbles, and air flow from A/C unit in the car is passing cold air, everything is OK.

c) If no bubbles appear in sight glass, and air flow from the A/C unit in the car is not delivering cold air, the system may be low on refrigerant and could need a re-charge.

d) If bubbles appear, system is low on refrigerant.

e) If you suspect refrigerant loss based on tests performed above, have system checked by a professional A/C service shop. They can confirm refrigerant loss, re-charge the system and check for system leakage.

NOTE: Once a week or so, even in winter, run A/C system for about 5 minutes as you drive. This keeps system internally lubricated, prevents hoses hardening.

TUNE-UP SPECIFICATIONS

YEAR	ENGINE No. Cyl. Displacement (cu. in.)	SPARK PLUGS Type	Gap (in.)	DISTRIBUTOR Point Dwell (deg.)	Point Gap (in.)	IGNITION TIMING Man. Trans.● (deg.)■	Auto Trans.● (deg.)■	IDLE SPEED Man. Trans.● (rpm)▲	Auto Trans. (rpm)▲
1970	6-170	BF-82	0.032-0.036	35-40	0.027	6B	6B	800/500④⑥	600/500⑤⑥
	6-200	BF-82	0.032-0.036	35-40	0.027	6B	6B	800/500④⑥	600/500⑤⑥
	6-250	BF-82	0.032-0.036	37-42	0.025	—	6B	—	600/500⑤⑥
1971	6-170	BRF-82	0.032-0.036	33-38	0.027	6B	—	750	—
	6-200	BRF-82	0.032-0.036	33-38	0.027	6B	6B	800/500④⑥	600/500⑤⑥
	6-250	BRF-82	0.032-0.036	34-39① 33-38②	0.025① 0.027②	6B	6B	750/500⑥	600/500⑤⑥
	8-302	BRF-42	0.032-0.036	24-29	0.021	6B	6B	800/500⑥	600/500⑤⑥
1972	6-170	BRF-82	0.032-0.036	35-39	0.027	6B	—	750	—
	6-200	BRF-82	0.032-0.036	35-39	0.027	6B	6B	800/500④⑥	600/500⑤⑥
	6-250	BRF-82	0.032-0.036	35-39	0.027	6B	6B	750/500⑥	600/500⑤⑥
	8-302	BRF-42	0.032-0.036	26-30	0.017	6B	6B	800/500⑥	600/500⑤⑥
1973	6-200	BRF-82	0.032-0.036	33-39	0.027	6B	6B	800/500⑥	600/500⑥
	6-250	BRF-82	0.032-0.036	33-39	0.027	6B	6B	750/500⑥	600/500⑥
	8-302	BRF-42	0.032-0.036	24-30	0.017	6B	6B	800/500⑥	600/500⑥
1974 49 states	6-200	BRF-82	0.032-0.036	33-39	0.027	6B	6B	800/500⑥	600/500⑥
	6-250	BRF-82	0.032-0.036	33-39	0.027	—	6B	—	650/500⑥
	8-302	BRF-42	0.032-0.036	24-30	0.017	10B	12B	800/500⑥	600/500⑥
1974 California	6-250	BRF-82	0.042-0.046	Breakerless		6B	6B	750/500⑥	600/500⑥
	8-302	BRF-42	0.052-0.056	Breakerless		6B	6B	800/500⑥	650/500⑥
1975	6-200	BRF-82	0.044	Breakerless		6B	6B	750/500⑥	600/500⑥
	6-250	BRF-82	0.044	Breakerless		6B	6B	800/500⑥	600/500⑥
	8-302	ARF-42	0.044	Breakerless		6B	6B	900/500⑥	650/500⑥
1976-77	6-200	BRF-82	0.044	Breakerless		10B	10B	800/500⑥	650/500⑥
	6-250	BRF-82	0.044	Breakerless		6B③	14B③	850/500⑥	600/500⑥
	8-302	ARF-82	0.044	Breakerless		12B	12B	750/500⑥	650/500⑥
1977	6-200 6-250 8-302	See Underhood Specifications Sticker							

▲ Adjust automatic transmissions in Drive (AMC/Ford/GM) or Neutral (Chrysler), all manual transmissions are adjusted in Neutral.

■ All figures are Before Top Dead Center.

● Figure in parentheses indicate California engine.

① Single diaphragm distributor.

② Dual diaphragm distributor.

③ 8B with air conditioning.

④ 750 w/o solenoid.

⑤ 550 w/o solenoid.

⑥ On models equipped with throttle solenoids, the high idle speed figure is adjusted with the solenoid activated, using the solenoid screw adjustment. The lower idle speed figure on solenoid-equipped cars is adjusted (with the solenoid wire disconnected at the inline connector) with the carburetor idle speed screws. On models not equipped with throttle solenoids (1970-72 models only), the idle speed is adjusted with the curb idle adjusting screw on the carburetor.

NOTE: The underhood specifications sticker often reflects tune-up specification changes made in production. Sticker figures must be used if they disagree with those in this chart.

MAVERICK/COMET

CAPACITIES

YEAR	ENGINE No. Cyl. Displacement (cu. in.)	ENGINE OIL Add 1 qt. with New Filter	TRANSMISSION Pts. to Refill after Draining MANUAL 3-speed	MANUAL 4-speed	AUTOMATIC	DRIVE AXLE (pts.)	COOLING SYSTEM with Heater (qts.)	with Air Cond. (qts.)
1970	170, 200	4.5	3.5	3.5	16	2.5	9.0	9.0①
	250	4.5	3.5	—	18	2.5	10.0	10.0
1971	170, 200	4.5	3.5	3.5	16	2.5	9.0	9.0①
	250	4.5	3.5	3.5	18	2.5	9.5	9.5
	302	5.0	4.0	3.5	18	4.0	13.5	14.2
1972	170, 200	4.5	3.5	3.5	16	4.0	9.0	9.0①
	250	4.5	3.5	3.5	18	4.0	9.5	10.5
	302	5.0	4.0	3.5	18	4.0	13.5	14.2
1973	200	4.5	3.5	3.5	16	4.0	9.0	9.0
	250	4.5	3.5	3.5	18	4.0	9.7	9.7
	302	5.0	4.0	3.5	18	4.0	13.5	14.2
1974-77	200	5.0	4.0	3.5	16	4.0	9.0	9.0
	250	5.0	4.0	3.5	18	4.0	9.7	9.7
	302	5.0	4.0	3.5	18	4.0	13.5	14.2

① 170 engines not available with air conditioning.

Mustang

Lubrication and Oil Change

BRAKE FLUID LEVEL CHECK

Check brake fluid level in master cylinder every three months . . . sooner if braking feels inadequate. Add when low. Recommended grade: Extra Heavy Duty; Grade DOT 3 as printed on can (check owner's handbook).

Master cylinder is located under hood on left side. It is oblong container about 6″ long with cap held down by wire clip. Check brake fluid level as follows:

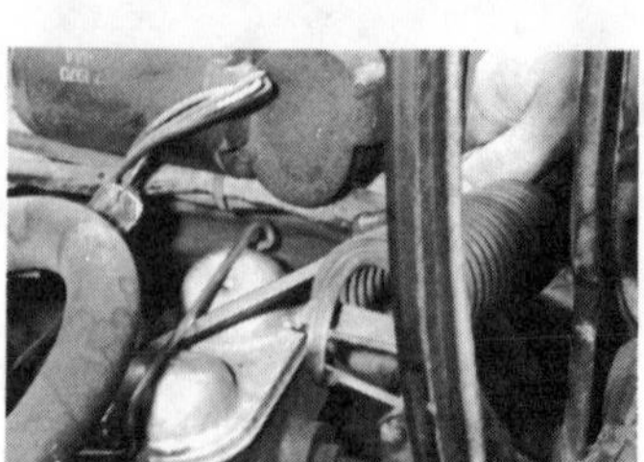

1. Pry wire retaining clip off cap top with screwdriver.
2. Remove cap and gasket by lifting up.
3. Fluid level should be within ¼ inch of top rim. If lower than this, add fresh fluid to appropriate level.
DO NOT OVERFILL
4. Replace cap and gasket; secure retaining clip over cap. If fluid level was low, check again in a few days.
5. If fluid repeatedly checks low, there is a leak somewhere in the system. See SAFETY SYSTEMS—WHEEL CYLINDER CHECK. Have mechanic check further. Neglect can be dangerous.

MANUAL TRANSMISSION FLUID LEVEL CHECK

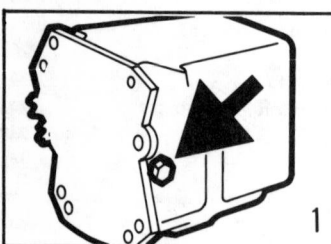

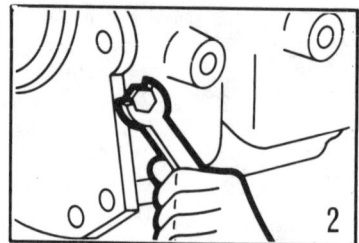

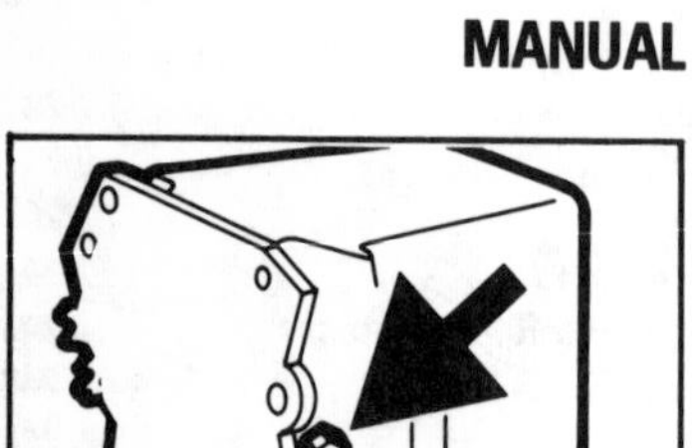

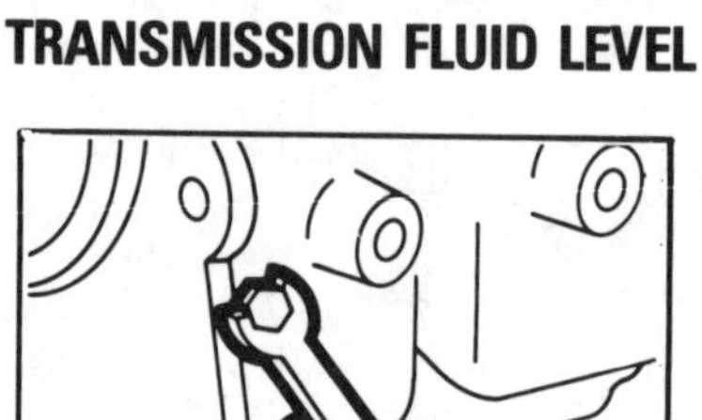

FORD SAYS . . . check manual transmission fluid every 6000 miles (8000 miles-1973). Car should be parked level. Recommended grade: Standard Transmission Fluid (SAE 90).

TOOLS NEEDED . . . fluid level check device (make from coat hanger wire; bend at 90° angle 2″ from end); adjustable wrench; bulb syringe.

1. Locate transmission fluid filler plug on right side of transmission housing from underneath car.
2. Wipe road dirt from filler plug area before loosening. Remove plug with adjustable wrench.
3. Insert fluid level check device. Fluid level should be right up to bottom edge of filler hole.
4. Add fluid as needed with hand bulb syringe.

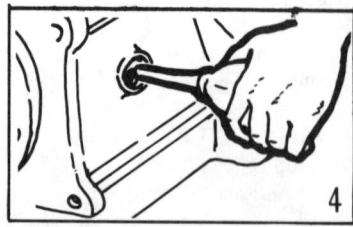

5. Replace filler plug; tighten.

AUTOMATIC TRANSMISSION FLUID LEVEL CHECK

FORD SAYS . . . check automatic transmission fluid (ATF) level every 6000 miles (8000 miles-1973). Recommended grade: ATF Type F.

TOOLS . . . Long neck filler funnel.

1. Engine must be warmed up and running. Place shift lever in PARK position.
2. Pull out dipstick. Wipe clean.

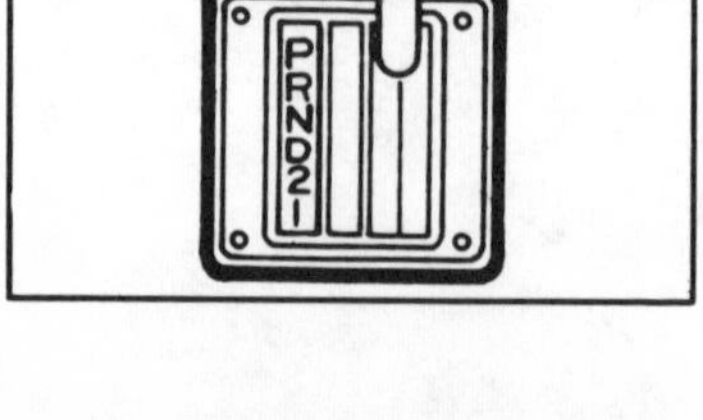

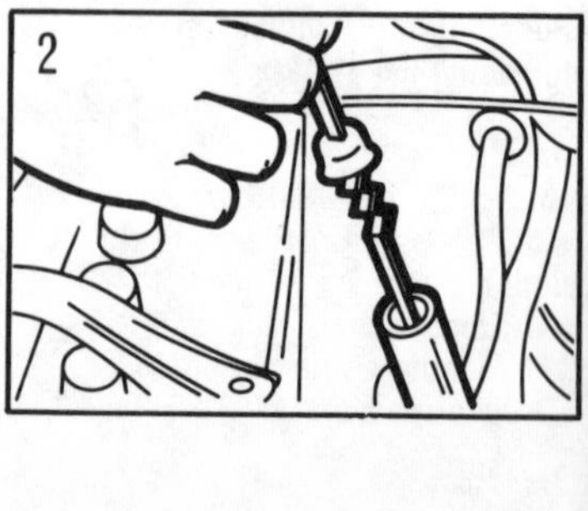

Push dipstick all the way back in; remove it again.

3. If fluid is below ADD mark, add ATF to bring level up. DO NOT OVERFILL.

4. Add ATF thru transmission dipstick hole by means of long-neck filler funnel.

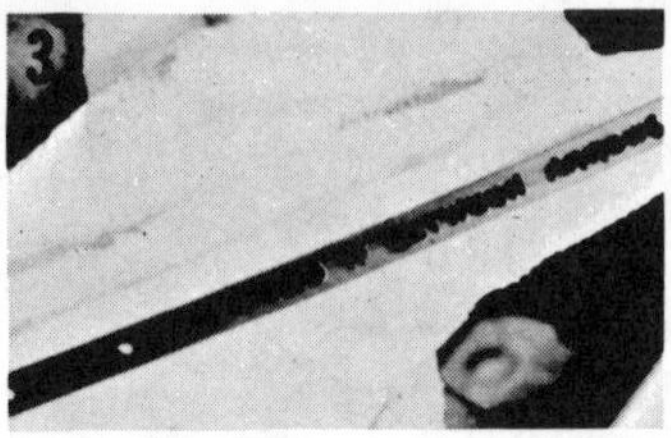

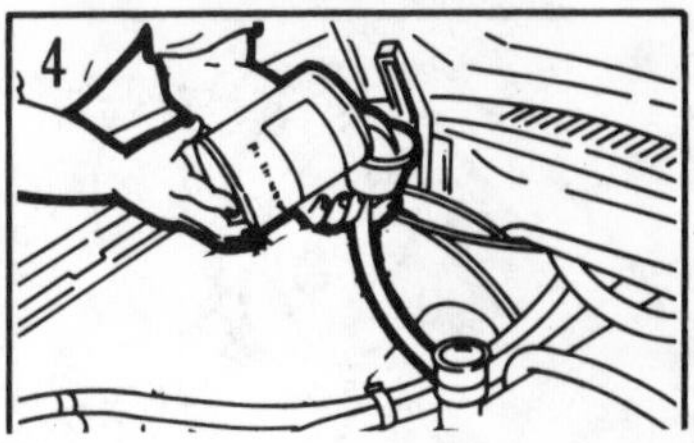

REAR AXLE LUBRICANT

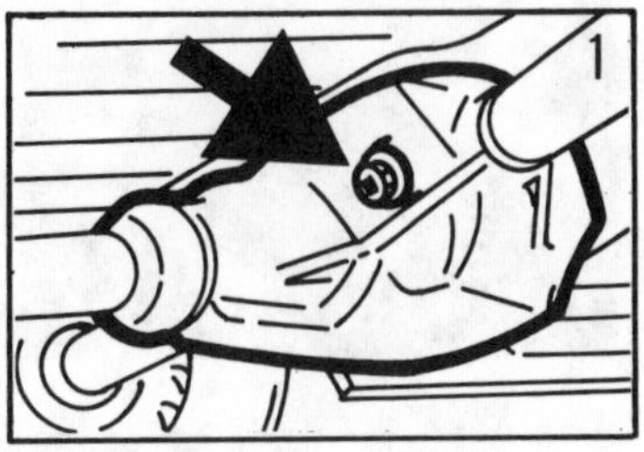

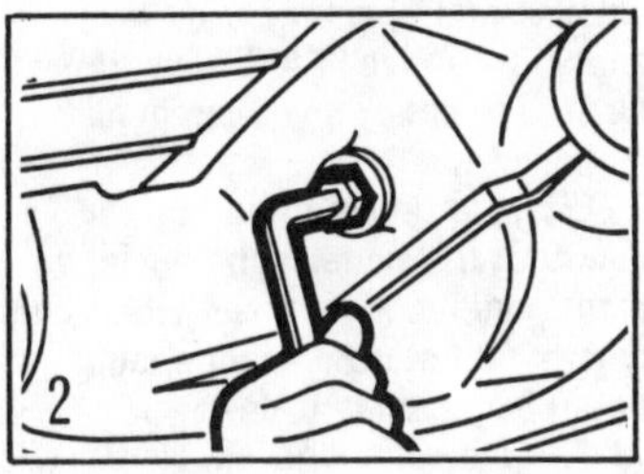

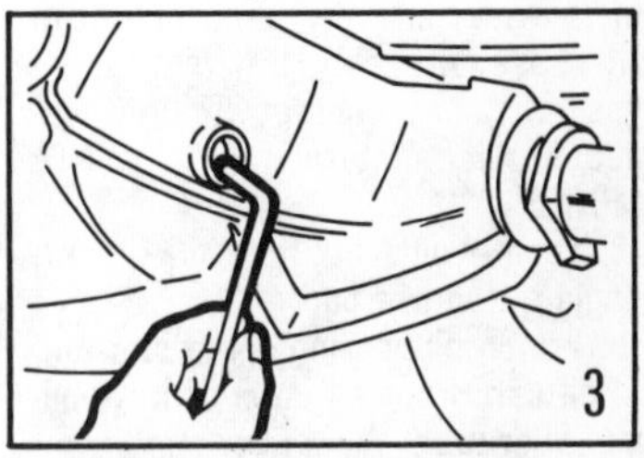

FORD SAYS . . . check rear axle lube level every 6000 miles. Recommended grade: Hypoid gear lube (SAE 90).

TOOLS . . . adjustable hand wrench; fluid level check device (made from coat hanger wire; bend at 90° angle 2" from end); bulb syringe.

1. Locate filler plug on forward side of rear axle housing.

2. Wipe plug area clean; remove plug with wrench.

3. Insert wire level check device; remove. Adequate fluid level should show lubricant on last ¼-inch of wire.

4. If fluid level is low, add as needed, with a hand bulb syringe, until level shows on last ¼-inch of wire.

5. Replace filler plug; tighten.

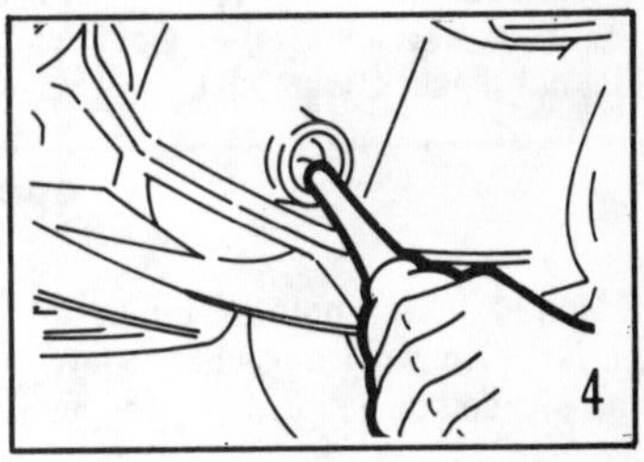

OIL AND FILTER CHANGE

FORD SAYS . . . Change oil every 6000 miles (1970-72), every 4000 miles (1973). Recommended grade: MS or SE (check owner's handbook). Check oil level at least once a week.

TOOLS & MATERIALS . . . adjustable hand wrench; medium size screwdriver; oil filter removal wrench; drain pan for old oil (at least 5 qt. capacity); oil pouring spout; 5 qt. oil; new oil filter; oil and lubricants as specified below.

SAFETY TIP . . . use work gloves.

1. If engine is cold, start up and idle for about 5 minutes.

2. Park car on level ground. Turn engine off.

3. Locate oil drain plug on underside of engine. Place drain pan under plug.

4. Remove drain plug with wrench. Let ALL dirty oil drain out.

5. Wipe plug and area around drain hole clean. Replace drain plug; tighten it.

6. Locate oil filter. Move drain pan under filter. Loosen filter with oil filter wrench. Unscrew; remove filter by hand.

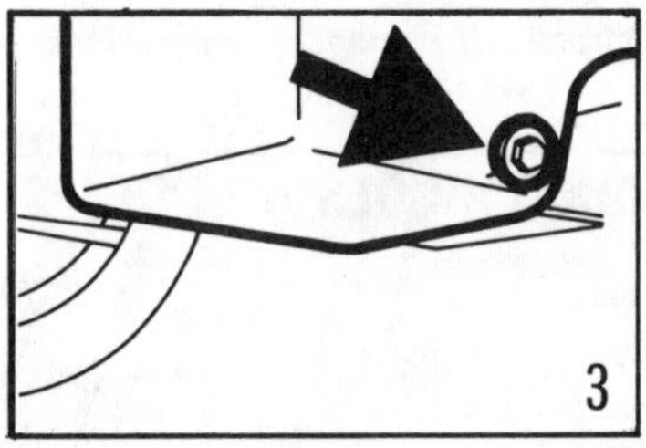

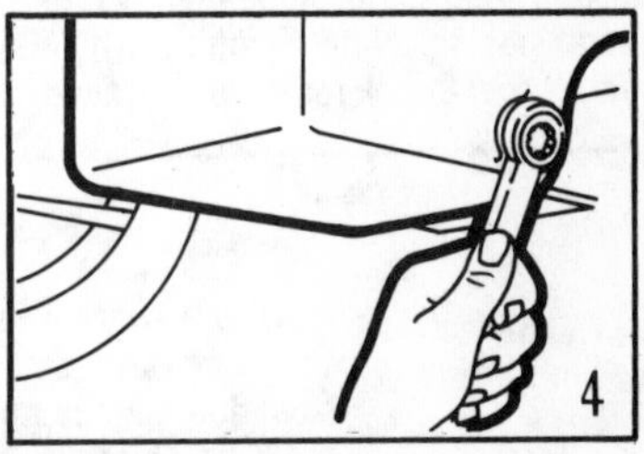

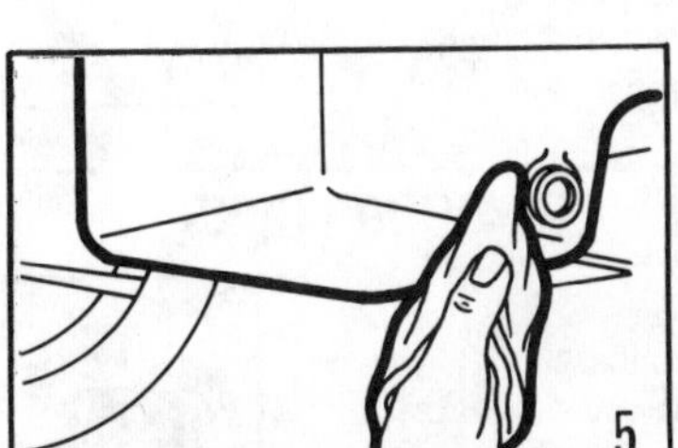

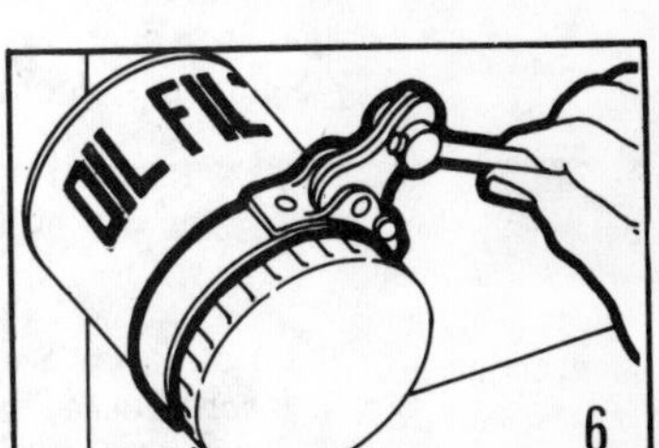

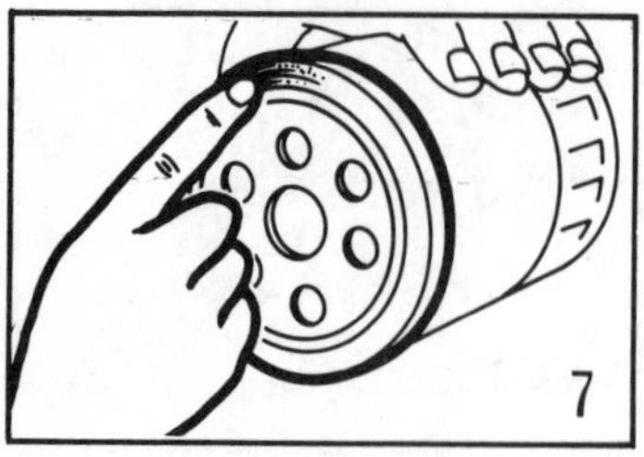

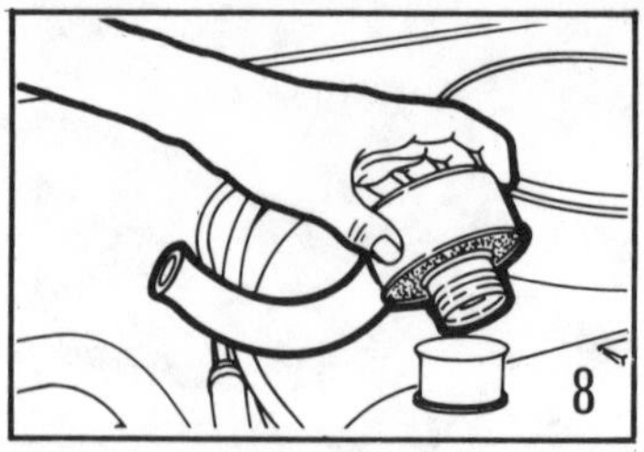

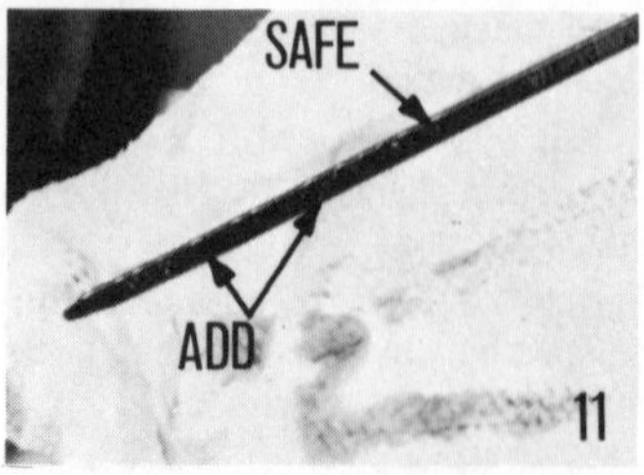

7. Smear fresh oil over surface of rubber gasket (washer) of new filter. Install new filter by hand only. Do NOT use wrench. Turn filter until gasket makes contact. Tighten an additional half turn only . . . NO MORE.

8. Locate oil filler hole on top of engine. Remove cap.

9. Punch oil pouring spout into top of oil can. Pour all cans of new oil into filler tube. Wipe filler cap clean and replace it.

10. Check new oil level at dipstick. Pull out dipstick, wipe clean.

11. Push dipstick back into engine. Be sure to insert all the way. Remove dipstick and check new oil level. It should be above "SAFE" line. If not, be sure to check if you put in all the oil called for.

12. Start up engine and idle for 3-5 minutes. Oil signal light on instrument panel will glow red when engine is first started. Light should go out in 30 seconds or less.

13. Stop engine and check for oil leaks at drain plug and filter. If you find any, check tightness of plug and/or filter, also for condition of filter gasket to see that it has not become pinched or damaged when installing. Recheck oil level, which should now be at "SAFE".

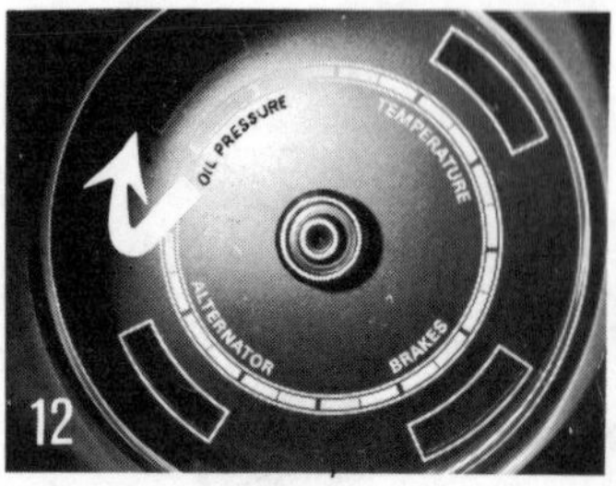

SPEEDOMETER CABLE LUBRICATION

If speedometer pointer tends to quiver or jump, or if unit makes a low, rasping sound, lubrication may be needed.

1. Locate cable shaft attachment directly behind speedometer dial.
2. Remove retaining clip. Unscrew cable from speedometer.
3. Pull inner cable completely out of outer casing. Note carefully which end is top. Check for wear or frayed strands. If damaged, replace inner cable with new one.

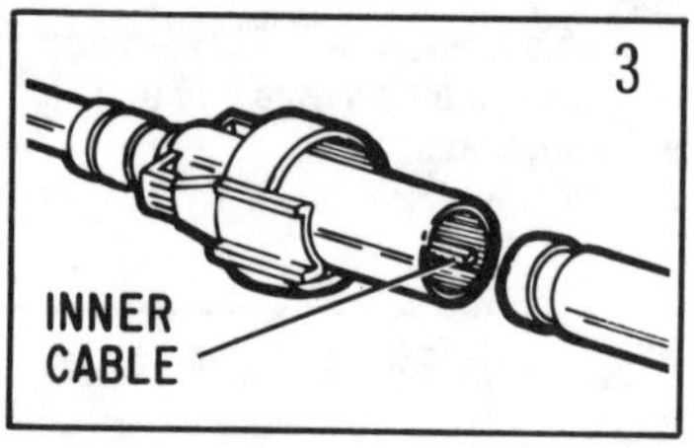

4. Apply generous amount of speedometer cable lubricant into cable casing. Replace inner cable in shaft, noting that top end is not inserted accidentally. Turn inner cable as it is being re-inserted. Twist cable when all the way in, to lock into position at lower end.

5. Reconnect cable to speedometer head under instrument panel.

DOOR HINGES AND STOPS

(lubricate every 6 months)

1. Brush any dirt accumulations from door hinges and stops. Use old tooth brush or rag.
2. Apply dab of white polyethylene grease to door hinges, trunk hinges, hood hinges, door stops.

DOOR LOCKS

(lubricate every 6 months)

1. Insert door key half way into lock.
2. Spray aerosol lock lubricant into lock.
3. Push key rest of way into lock; turn back and forth several times.

Cooling System

IT IS RECOMMENDED . . . that radiator coolant (water/antifreeze mixture) level be checked once or twice a month. Do this when engine is cold. Check more often if you do a lot of hard driving. On models with clear expansion tanks, check coolant level visually when hot.
Keep coolant up to recommended level in radiator. If coolant checks frequently low, look for leaks.

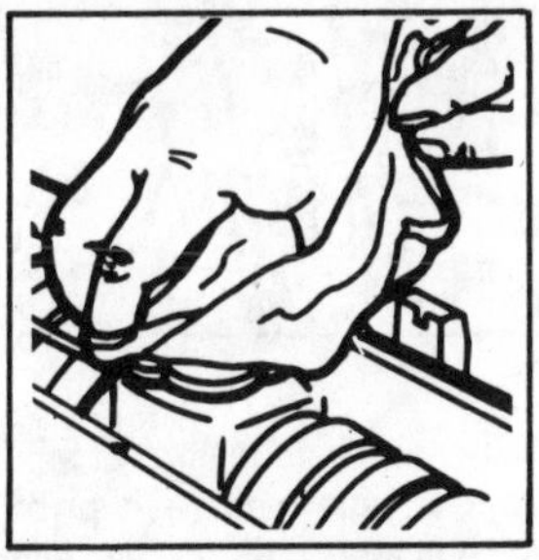

Tighten all hose clamps occasionally. For best results, keep a 50/50 water/antifreeze mixture year round. Change complete coolant mixture every 24 months.

CAUTION: If you must check coolant in a hot engine, cover radiator cap with thick rag before releasing. Remove cap slowly . . . press down and turn.

REPLACING THE THERMOSTAT

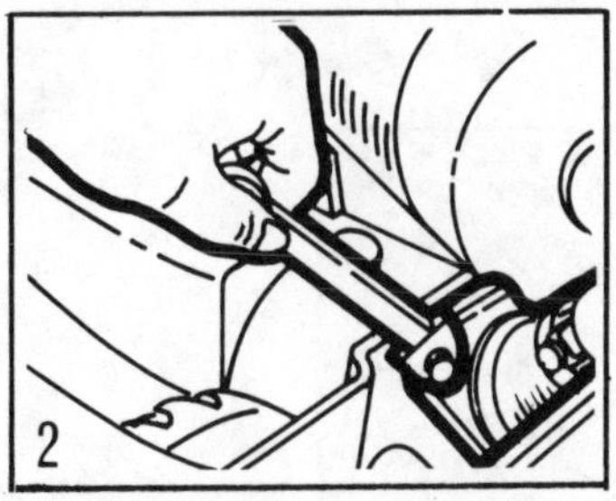

2

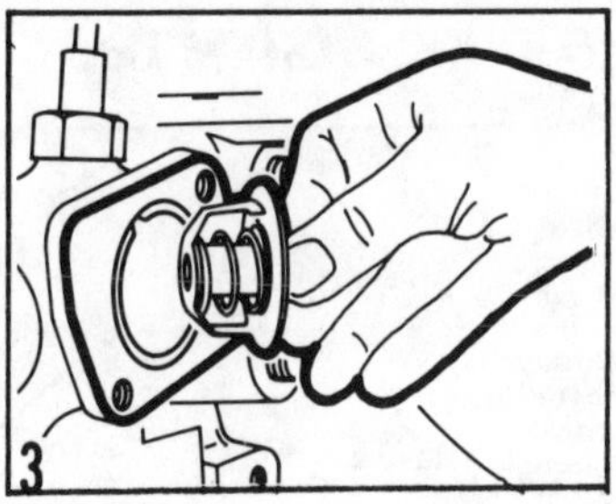

3

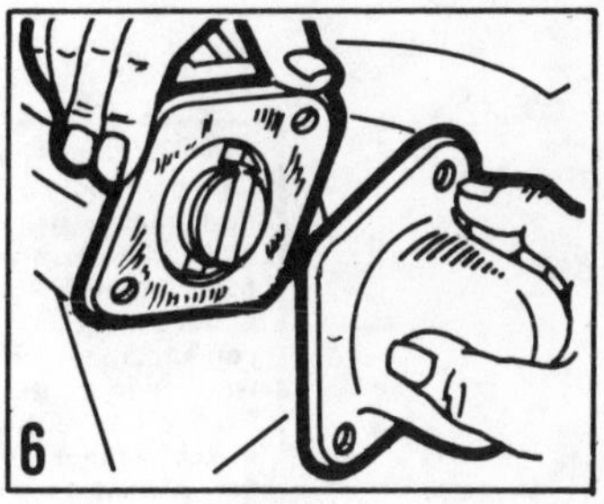

6

A faulty thermostat will usually cause engine overheating. Replace with new thermostat.
TOOLS AND MATERIALS . . .
New thermostat
Gasket
Adjustable wrench
1. Drain radiator of about half its coolant. (See Hose Replacement section).
2. Loosen and remove both retaining bolts and lift thermostat housing off the engine.
NOTE: If you're careful it won't be necessary to remove radiator hose.
3. Remove old thermostat.
4. Scrape thermostat housing flange and engine block surface to remove old gasket debris.
5. Drop new thermostat into place—spring down.
6. Install new gasket with sealer applied to both sides.
7. Replace thermostat housing and tighten both retaining bolts.

ENGINE OVERHEATING

YOUR CAR OVERHEATS BECAUSE	TO CORRECT IT
radiator coolant is too low	fill to correct level; check for leaks
fan belt is too loose	adjust tension or replace frayed belt
of a broken or leaking hose	replace hose; tighten clamps
thermostat does not function	replace thermostat
radiator is plugged with sediment	consult professional mechanic (may need radiator removal and servicing, or total replacement)
water pump does not function properly	replace water pump (may make squeaky noise; or leak at pump shaft)

FAN BELT ADJUSTMENT

The fan belt not only drives the radiator fan, it turns the water pump and drives the alternator. It's easy to see that the condition and proper tension of the belt are vital, since almost all engine cooling and electrical power is dependent on it. The belt deserves an occasional look and tension check.

CAUTION: An overtightened belt may damage alternator and water pump bearings.

1. Inspect fan belt occasionally. If worn, frayed or cracked on inner driving surface, replace.
2. Check tension occasionally. Press thumb at midpoint of belt span between pulleys. If belt depresses more than ½ inch, tightening is needed. A too-loose belt will not drive alternator and water pump effectively.
3. Adjust to proper tension of ¼ inch deflection. Adjust as follows:

A. Loosen mounting bolts at top and bottom so alternator can pivot on lower bolt and upper bolt can slide in bracket.

B. Pull alternator out slightly to put tension on belt, and hold while tightening upper bolt.

C. Check tension. Repeat adjustment as necessary.

D. When tension is correct, tighten lower bolt.

COOLING SYSTEM LEAKS

Due to the number of joints, cooling systems have many places to leak from. Check clamp tightness. If leaks persist an anti-leak additive in the coolant may help. Noisy water pumps may benefit from a lubricating additive in the coolant. Use a cooling system cleaner when flushing during a drain and refill job. It will help remove rust and scale. Remember — additives will not cure chronic problems. But they will effect a short-term remedy in many cases.

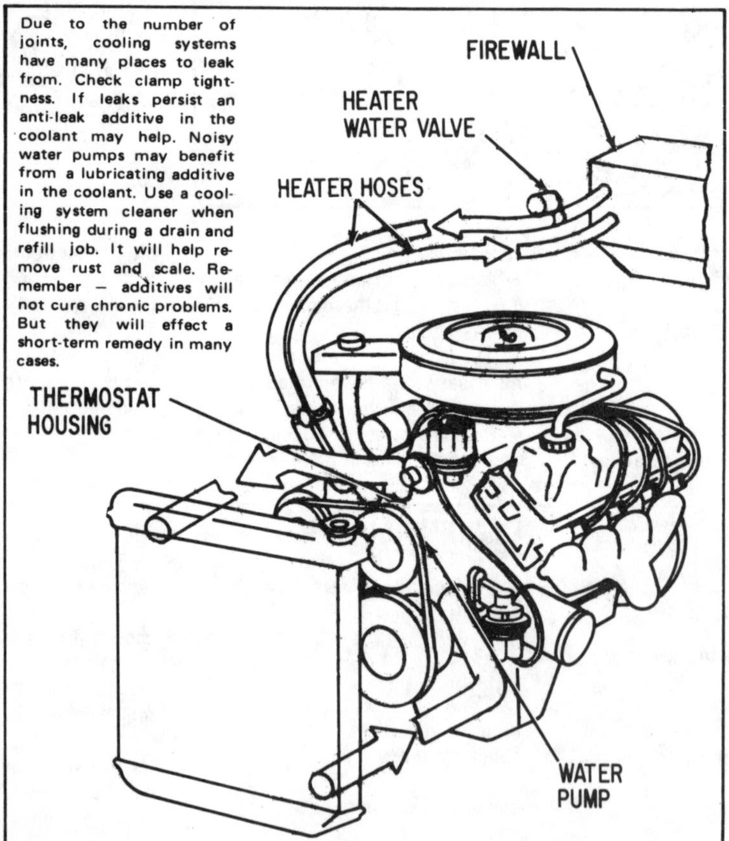

1. Inspect all hoses. If any are weak, soft in spots or show cracks, replace at once.
2. Check all hose connections for tightness. Tighten loose hose clamps; they tend to loosen due to engine vibration.
3. If radiator steams or hisses when engine is switched off, check for leaks. Look for signs of coolant drips on radiator or around heater tank joint.

Leaks are possible at:

Upper or lower radiator hoses
Water pump (gaskets or seal)
Heater core or connecting hoses
Automatic transmission cooler lines (at bottom of radiator)
Faulty radiator pressure cap
Faulty cylinder head gasket
Cracked cylinder head or block

RADIATOR CAP CHECK

Check radiator cap occasionally for worn or cracked gasket. If cap doesn't seal properly, fluid will be lost and engine will overheat. Replace worn cap with new cap rated 13 to 15 lbs. pressure.

HOSE REPLACEMENT

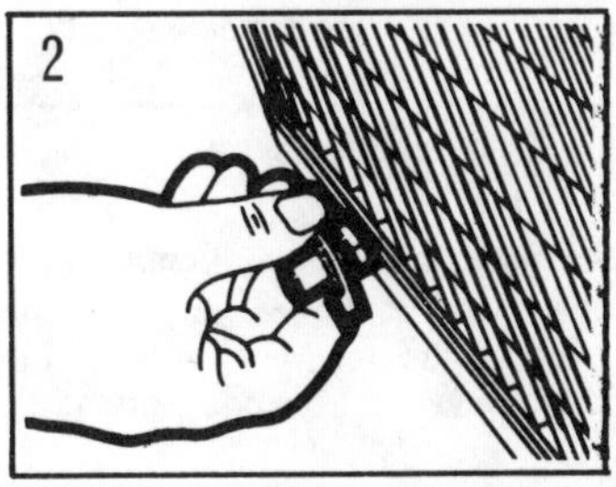

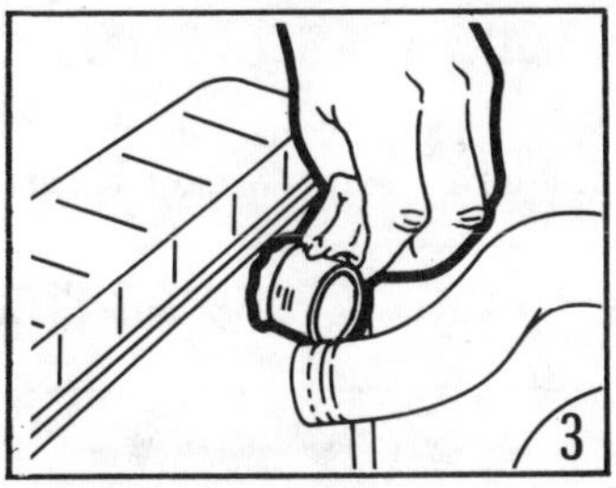

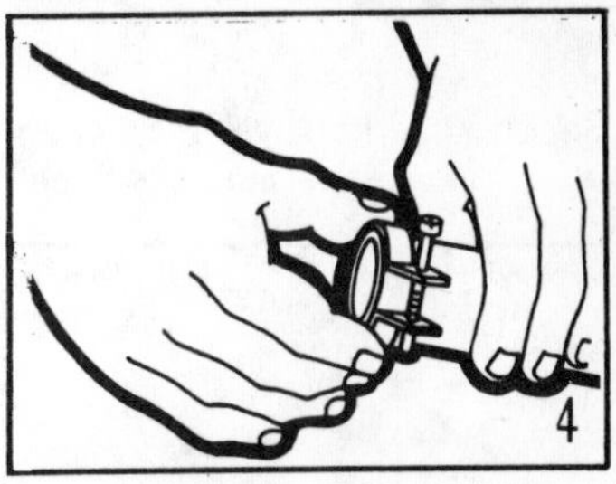

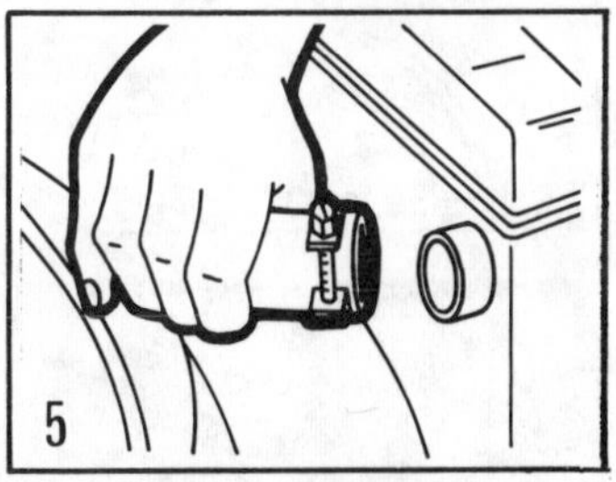

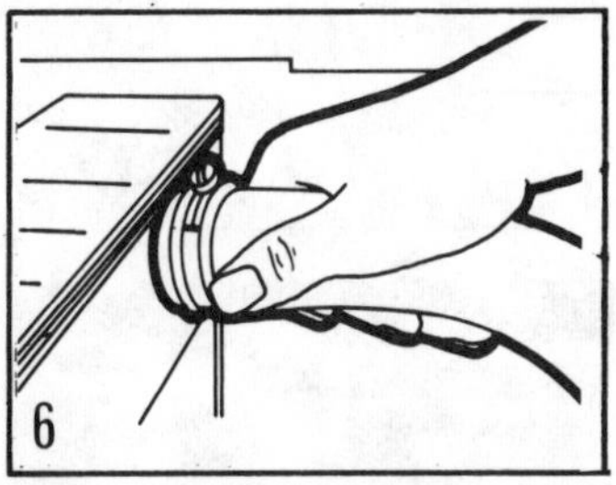

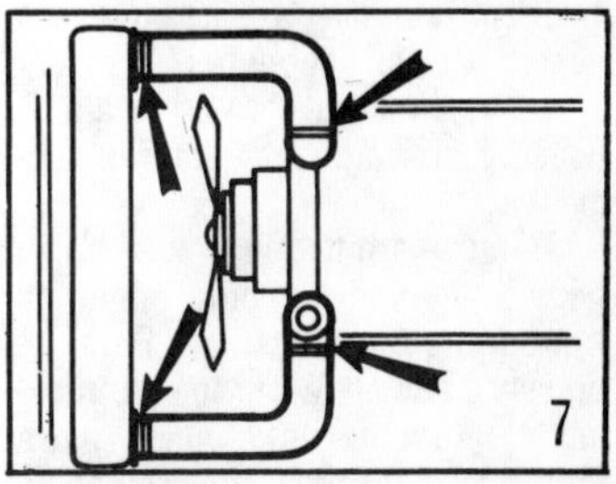

Coolant drain and refill work may be done alone; when changing hoses, coolant must also be drained as part of job. Discard all hoses with cracks or soft spots. Check hose clamps for tightness and good condition.

1. Remove radiator cap. Open radiator petcock (See 2). Drain coolant into catch basin. If near 24 months old, discard old coolant.
2. Petcock is located at the bottom of the radiator.
3. Loosen clamp at each end of hose(s). Work hose loose; pull it off. Wipe all hose connections clean. Use emery cloth to get rid of residue.
4. If old hose clamps are badly rusted or damaged, replace with new units.
5. Slip clamps over each hose end. Slip hose ends all the way onto cleaned up hose connections.
6. Place hose clamp ¼ inch from hose end. Tighten. Close petcock. Refill with 50/50 coolant/water mix.
7. Start engine; allow to warm up. Check for coolant leaks.
8. Road test car; watch for temperature warning light.

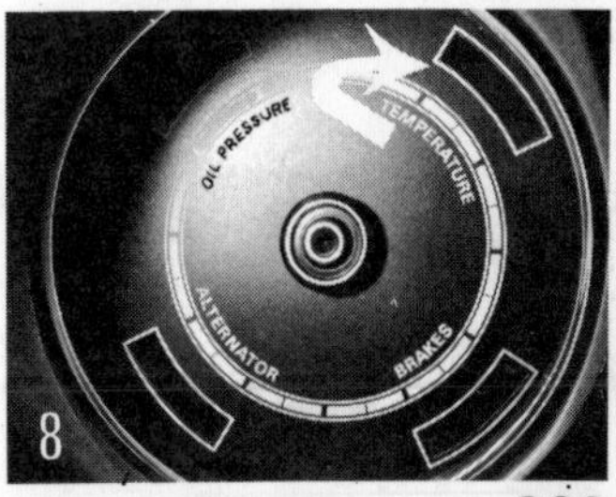

Suspension and Tires

The front wheels mount and rotate on the spindles, which are attached to upper and lower ball joints. A coil spring is mounted between the control arms on each side. A shock absorber is located in the center of each spring. The rear suspension is a trailing link design. The rear axle is located by one upper and two lower control arms and a lateral bar. A coil spring and shock absorber are located on each side of the axle.

Your car's suspension system consists of wheels, tires, springs, shock absorbers, sway (or stabilizer) bars, ball joints, steering linkage. If any of these items is out of adjustment or badly worn, you may notice any of these symptoms:

- car pulls to one side when braking
- car wanders when driving a straight line
- overall ride may be either hard or bouncy
- effort is needed to steer vehicle
- tires show uneven wear
- tires squeal when cornering
- front of car dips or bounces when braking
- car rocks side-to-side when going over rough road
- wheels bounce to make slapping sound on road
- steering wheel vibrates in hands
- front of car vibrates at highway speeds

Any of above symptoms indicates corrective action is needed. Delay can: ruin tires; cause damage/failure to other suspension parts; create safety hazard.

STEERING

If steering linkage, front suspension and steering column components are in good condition, there should be not more than 1½ inch free play in the steering wheel when measured at the rim of the wheel. If a loud knock is heard when turning the steering wheel from one extreme to the other, have mechanic check pinion bearing preload.

SHOCK ABSORBERS

Shock absorbers work to keep wheels in constant contact with the road. Result is safe handling and ride control; longer tire life. So shock absorbers (or shocks) are important.

HOW TO CHECK FOR BAD SHOCKS

1. Check under car and locate shock absorber near each wheel.
2. Heavy oil streaks on outer shock housing indicate need for replacement.
3. Stand at front of car and apply body weight in pumping action to front bumper or fender. Release pressure and allow car to stop rocking. Car should not bounce more than one more time after releasing pressure. Repeat at rear. If bouncing continues more than once, replacement is needed. Replace shocks in pairs (front pair or rear pair).

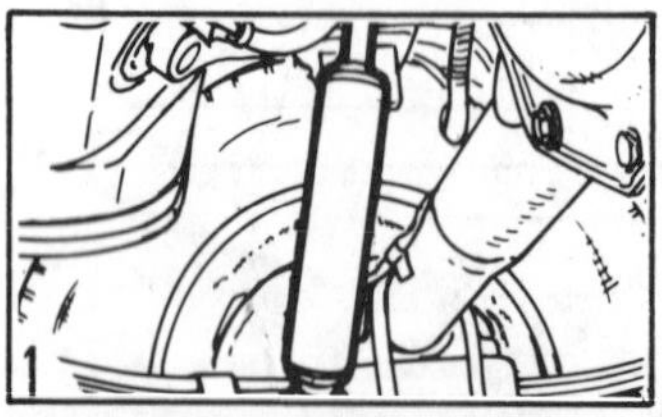

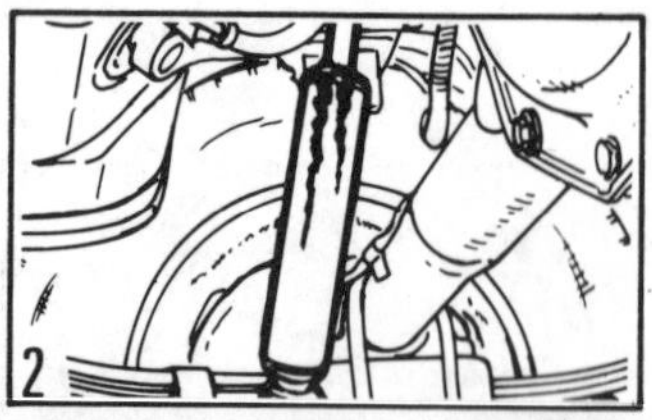

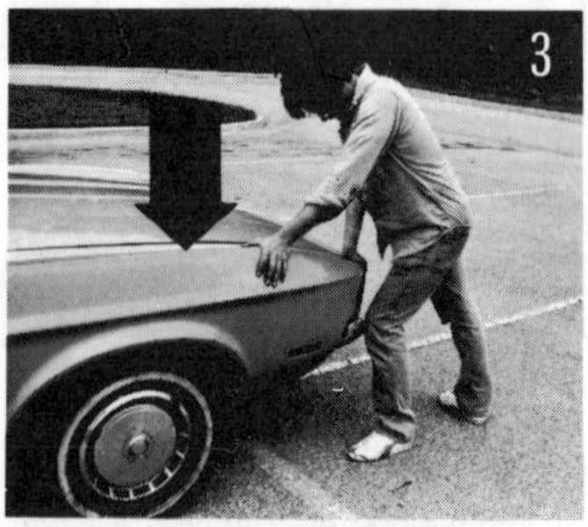

TOW HITCH INFORMATION

If your car is used for trailer towing you should check:

A. Cooling System; be sure coolant is at proper level in radiator. See Cooling System Section for checks to perform.

B. Check Transmission Fluid; keep topped up to proper level.

C. Check Rear Shock Absorbers;

you may benefit from installation of new rear shocks.
D. Check Tire Pressures; best traction and handling can be ensured if tire pressures are properly maintained.

For safer and more trouble-free trailer towing, consider:
A. Automatic Transmission Cooler; helps remove excess heat from automatic transmission fluid built up during towing mileage. Also helps avoid radiator overheating. Some units can be self-installed.

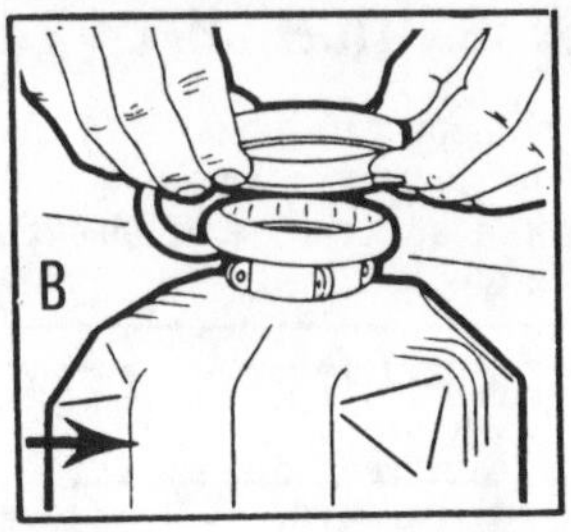

B. Radiator Over-Flow Tank Kit; addition of a reservoir to catch radiator coolant overflow preventing coolant loss. Easy to install, these units help a tow car run cooler, avoid overheating due to coolant loss.
C. Heavy-Duty Shock Absorbers or Air Shocks; important to have on rear wheels if you intend to do a lot of towing or load carrying within the car itself. Don't forget to consider replacing factory shocks, when they are worn out, with heavy-duty units at the front as well.
D. Variable Load Flasher; this unit will accommodate the added load of trailer turn signal lamps on trailer when these are hooked into your car's electrical system.

FRONT END ALIGNMENT

When steering, handling and/or tire wear indicate front end alignment may be needed, this work can only be done at an automotive service shop. DO NOT PUT OFF NEEDED FRONT END ALIGNMENT. At the same time, have ball joints and steering linkage checked.

Ignition System

TUNE-UP SERVICES

The ignition system consists of spark plugs; plug wires; distributor; rotor; points; condenser; coil. These units work to create a good hot spark inside the engine (ignition) at exactly the right moment (timing). If ignition is weak or timing is off, engine may be hard to start, run poorly, waste gas, lose power, backfire or not run at all.
FORD SAYS . . . Replace plugs and points every 12,000 miles.
TOOLS & MATERIALS . . . Parts: set of points; condenser; 8 spark plugs. Tools: gap gauge; 13/16 in. spark plug socket; screwdriver; open end, box or combination wrenches; timing equipment (see Ignition Timing).
SAFETY TIP . . . Change only one spark plug at a time to avoid cross-wiring and possible engine damage.

CHECKING POINTS, AND ROTOR

The distributor holds the points, rotor and condenser.

Use the firing order illustration to guide you when replacing your ignition wires and)or distributor cap.
1. To open distributor, snap retaining clips off with screwdriver, lift cap off but keep wires connected.

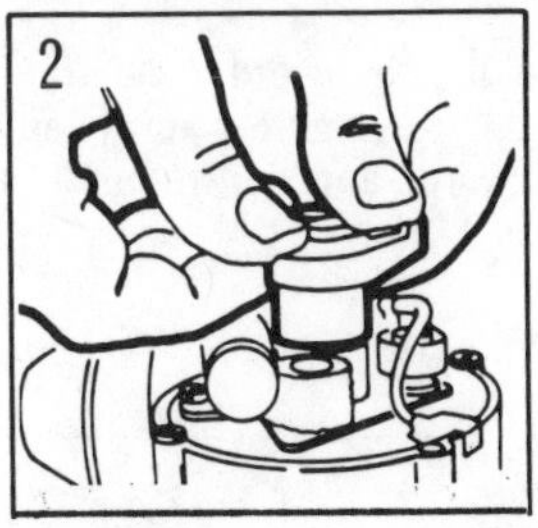

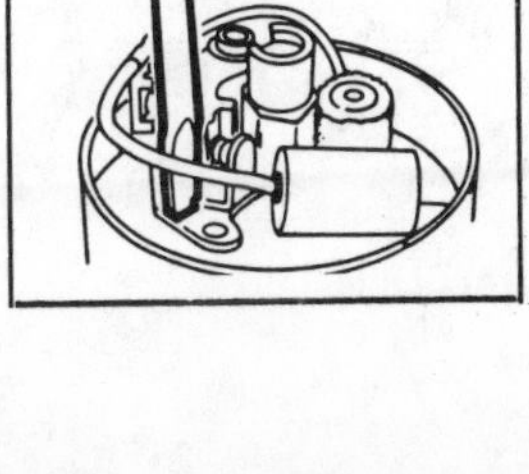

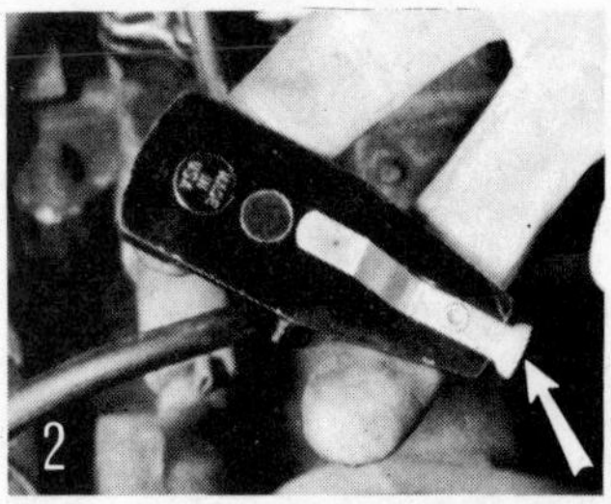

2. Pull rotor off (straight up). Replace if cracked or metallic tip is badly burned.
3. Pry points apart with screwdriver. If worn or burned, replace. If OK, check point gap.

OTHER IGNITION CHECK POINTS

Inspect spark plug wires. If cracked or brittle, entire set should be replaced. Also center, high tension wire. Inspect distributor cap. Wipe inside clean occasionally with dry, lint-free rag. If cap is cracked or rotor contacts are excessively burned, replace cap.

SPARK PLUG REPLACEMENT

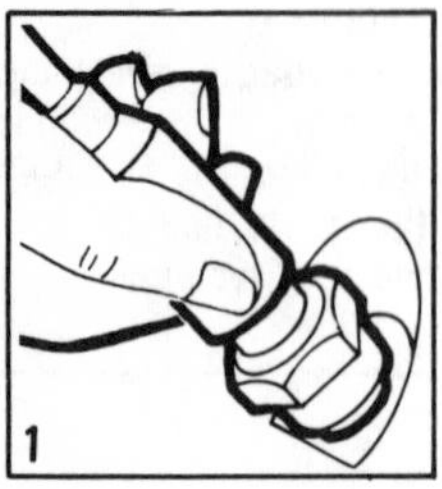

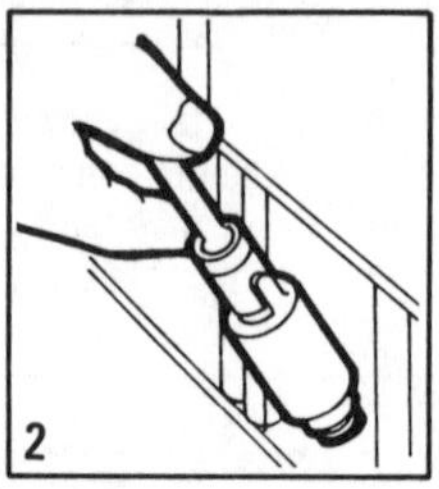

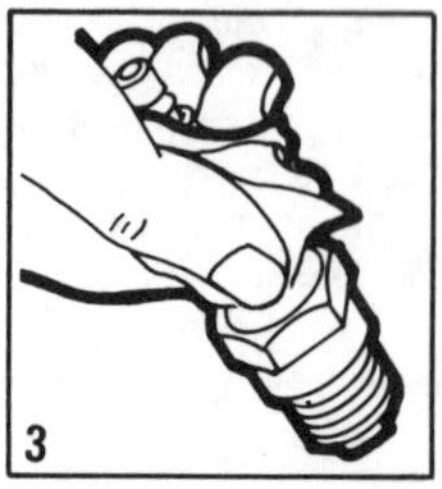

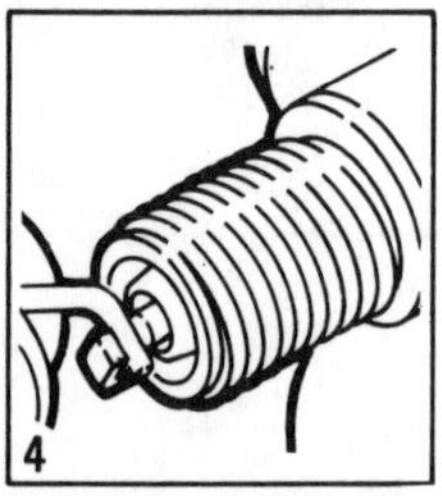

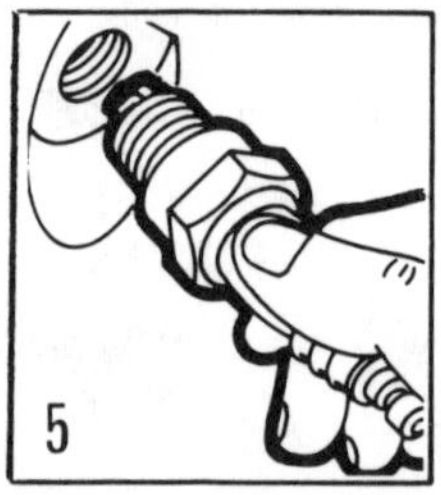

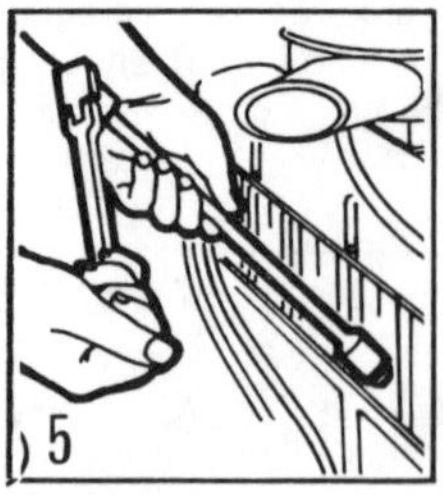

1. Remove spark plug wire by grasping rubber boot. Do not jerk wire. If stuck, turn boot, pulling gently.
2. Loosen spark plug using socket wrench.
3. Wipe or brush loose dirt from around plug before removing. Do not let dirt drop into engine through plug hole. Unscrew plug.
4. Check plug electrode gap on new spark plug. Adjust to: .035 (1970) in. .034 (1971-73) in.
Plug gap is correct when the gauge drags slightly as it is pulled between plug electrodes.
5. Thread new plug into plug hole by hand. Hand tighten. Do not force or cross thread. Use socket wrench to tighten firmly but do not force. Replace plug wire. Press boot firmly.

REPLACING SPARK PLUG WIRES

Use the firing order illustration to guide you when replacing your ignition wires and/or distributor cap.

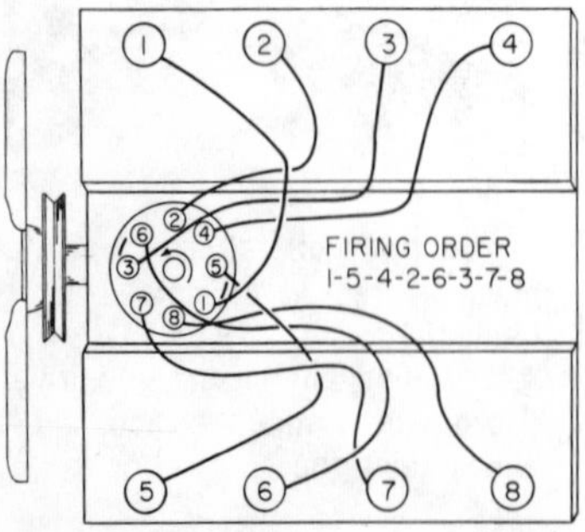

All V8 except 351

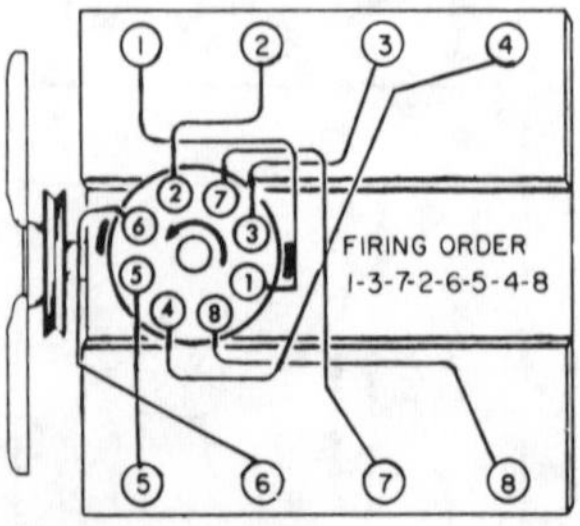

351 and 400 V8

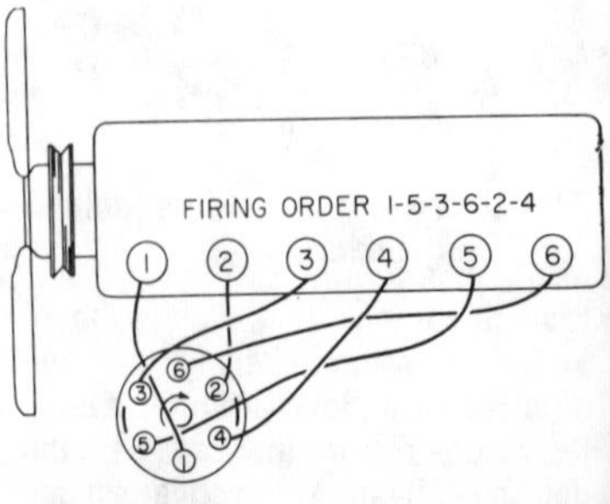

All six cylinder

REMOVING POINTS AND CONDENSER

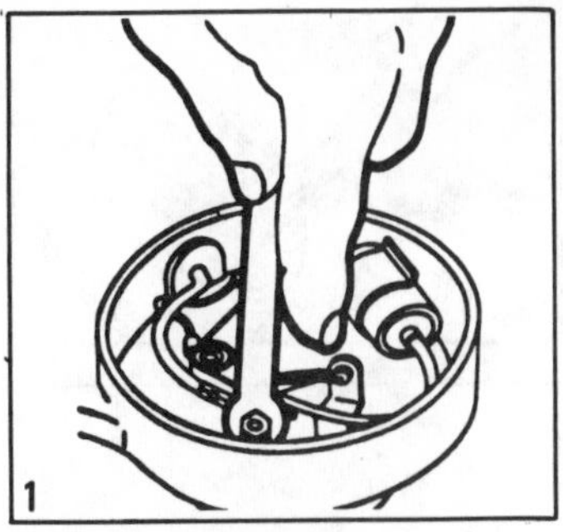

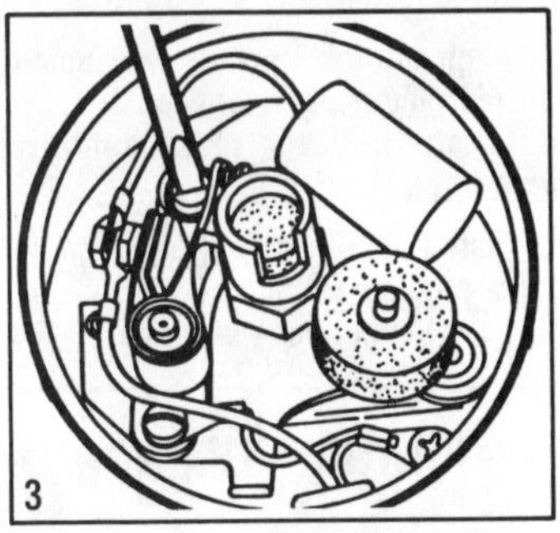

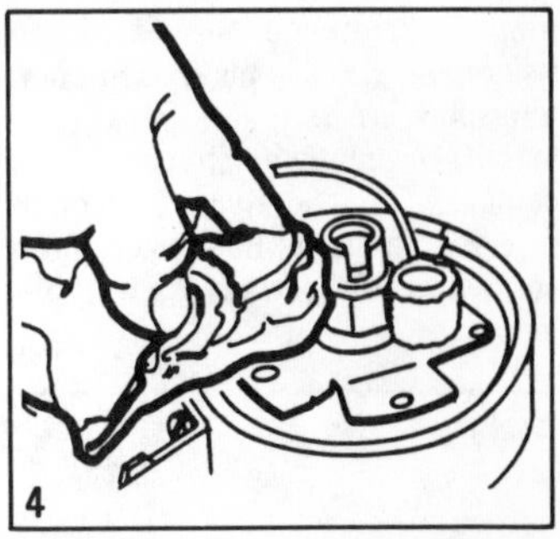

Points and condenser work together. Always replace condenser when installing new points.

1. Loosen nut, and disconnect primary wire and condenser lead wire.
2. Remove screw which holds condenser; remove condenser.
3. Remove screws holding points to distributor; remove points.
4. Wipe all dirt from distributor plate and cam.
5. Inspect primary wire for frayed insulation, dirty connection. Clean connection or have wire repaired as necessary.

CAUTION: When removing screws from distributor, be sure to avoid any screws accidentally falling through distributor opening into engine. Use magnetic screwdriver.

INSTALLING POINTS AND CONDENSER

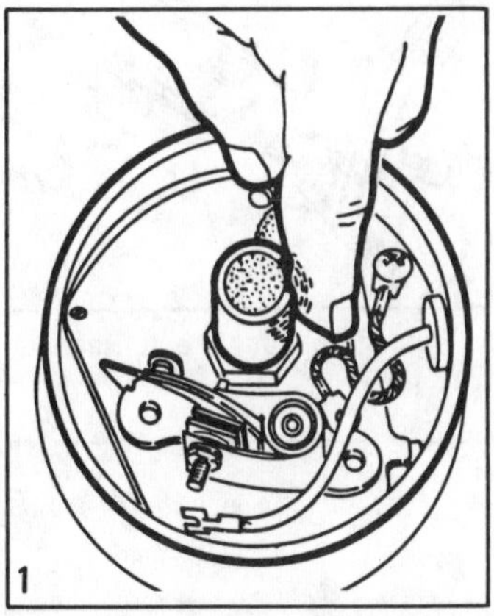

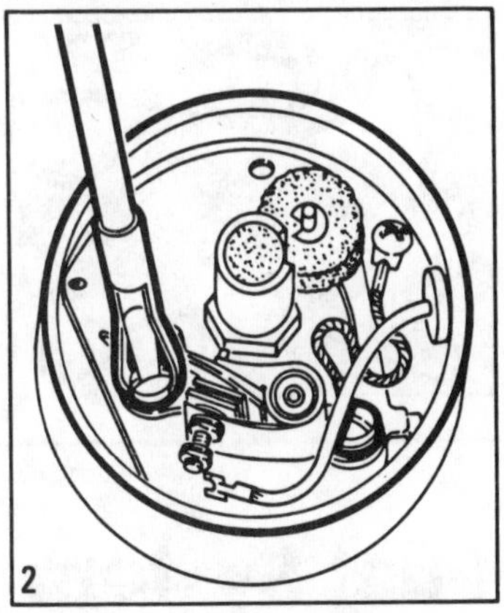

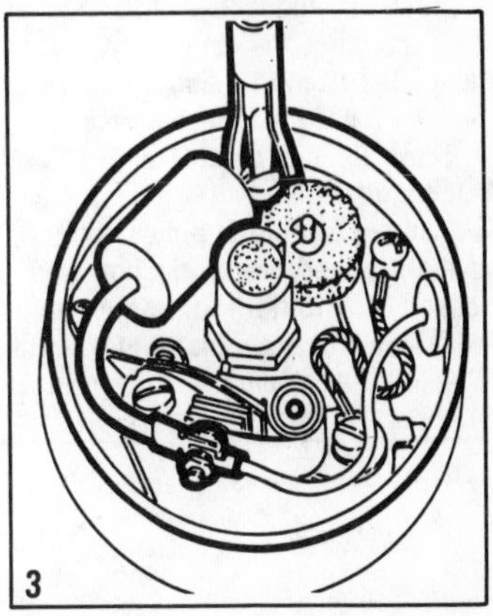

1. Apply small amount of heat resistant lube to distributor cam. (Lube usually supplied with new points. If not, purchase separately.)
2. Position new points in distributor and fasten with attaching screws. CAUTION: use magnetic screwdriver, or screwdriver with clip.
3. Attach new condenser to distributor with attaching screw.
4. Attach primary wire and condenser lead wire to point set. Don't let contacts touch distributor body or breaker plate. (Some models: wire from points attaches to condenser.)

RESETTING THE CONTACT GAP

1. Electrical contacts of point set MUST BE PARALLEL. If needed, bend stationary contact with needle-nose pliers. Bend fixed bracket only.
2. Turn engine by ignition key (you'll need a helper) until rubbing block on points is one of the high points of the distributor cam. You may use wrench on lower pulley to do this.

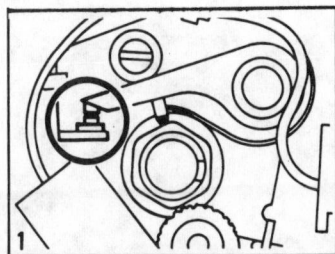

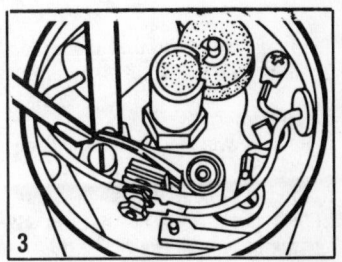

3. Look up correct point gap on engine compartment sticker. Insert proper gap gauge between open point contacts. Slightly loosen point attaching screws. Insert screwdriver in breaker plate notch near point contacts. Twist screwdriver to open or close points as needed. Tighten screws when correct gap is obtained.

4. Recheck gap after screws are tightened. Readjust if needed.

5. Align tab inside rotor with notch on distributor shaft and push rotor onto shaft. Rotor must be fully seated on shaft.

6. Install distributor cap by aligning tabs on cap with notch on body. Snap retaining clips in place.

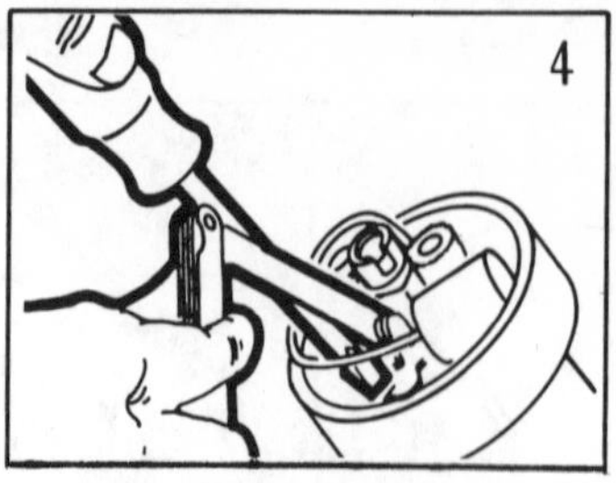

IGNITION TIMING

Adjusting timing is the important finishing touch to any tune-up. While not difficult, job requires timing light and dwell meter.

1. Locate timing marks and pointer (notches) on engine and lower engine pulley. Clean away dirt. Mark the pointer and notch which corresponds with the timing setting in degrees shown on the engine compartment sticker.
2. Hook up timing light according to instructions supplied with it.
3. Disconnect the one or two vacuum lines from the distributor. Plug with pencil tip or golf tee.
4. Hook up tachometer and adjust engine idle speed.
5. Aim timing light at pulley mark(s). If the chalked marks do not align, loosen distributor hold-down bolt and slowly rotate distributor until chalked marks align.

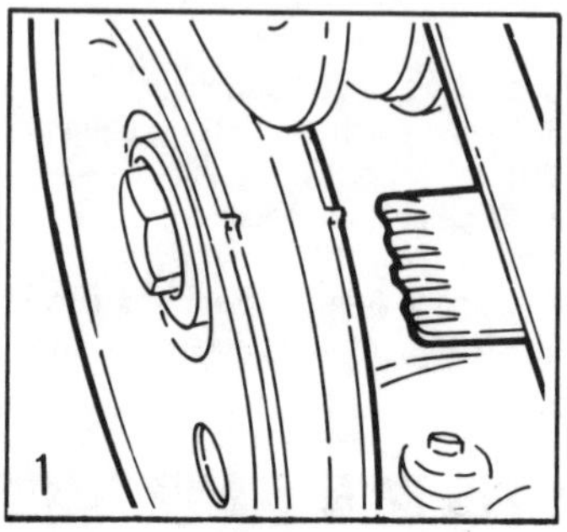

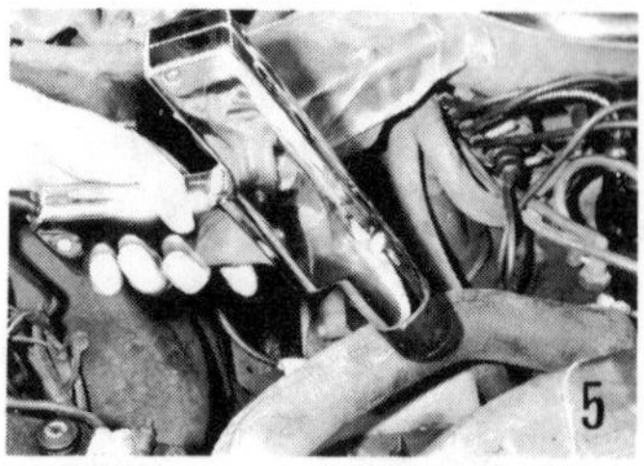

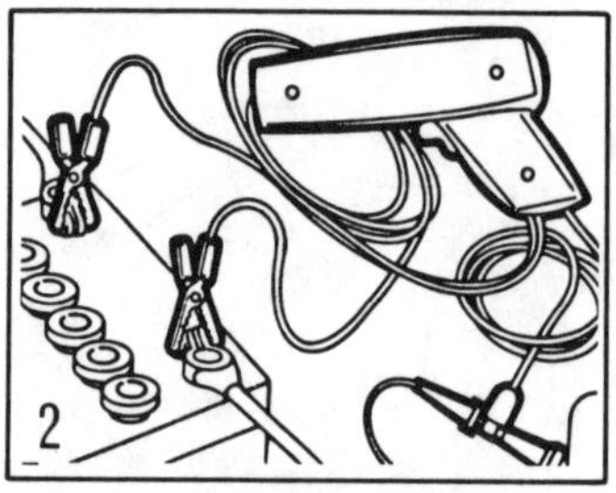

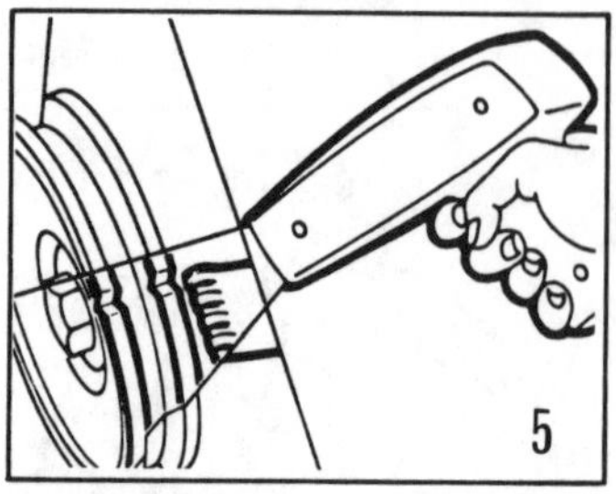

6. Tighten hold-down bolt. Recheck timing.

Fuel System

When gasoline is brought from the fuel tank, it mixes with air in the carburetor. This gas/air mixture then enters engine through the intake manifold, passes through the intake valves and is burned in the combustion chamber. The burned exhaust gas is then passed through the exhaust valves to the exhaust system and to the outside air. In order to keep your car's engine running cleanly with minimal pollution, and avoid dangerous carbon monoxide fumes inside the vehicle, certain items should be checked from time to time.

AIR AND CRANKCASE FILTER REPLACEMENT

The large round can that sits on top of the engine holds the air cleaner.

Twice a year:
1. Remove wing nut, and remove air cleaner lid.
2. Lift out circular air cleaner cartridge. Discard if more than 12 months old or excessively dirty.

3. Pull crankcase filter out of filter can. Wipe inside of can and lid.
4. Install crankcase filter. Install in reverse order.

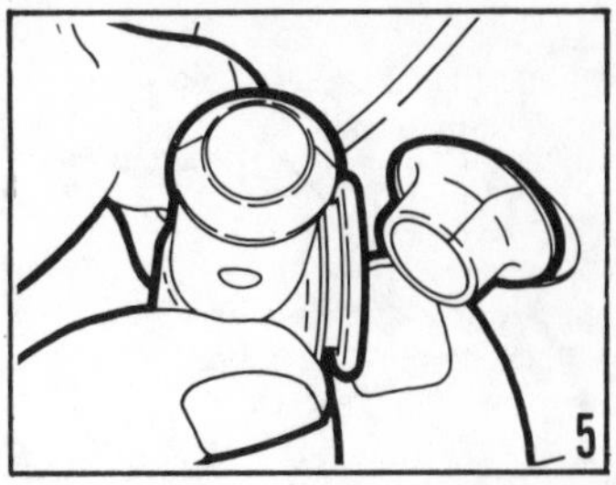

EMISSION CONTROL SYSTEMS

An important part of a car's emission control system is the Positive Crankcase Ventilation (PCV) valve and its connecting hose. The PCV valve should be replaced once every 12,000 miles. This device keeps dirt and sludge from forming inside the engine. Make sure all PCV connections are tight. Check that the connecting hoses are clear and not clogged. Replace any brittle or broken hoses.

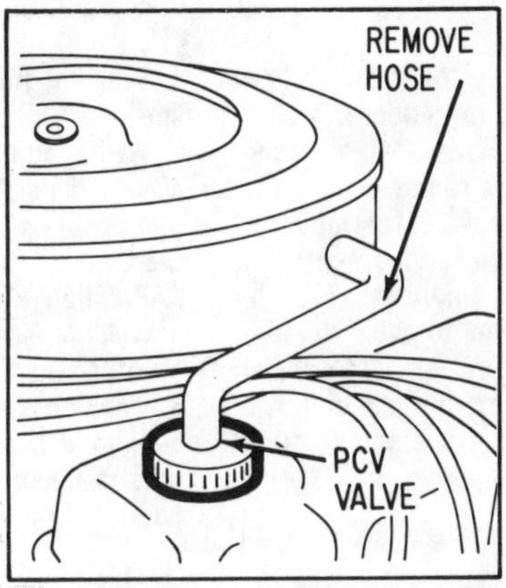

PCV VALVE REPLACEMENT

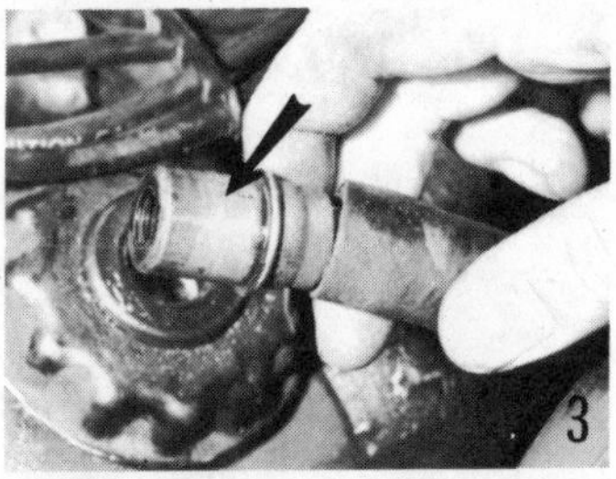

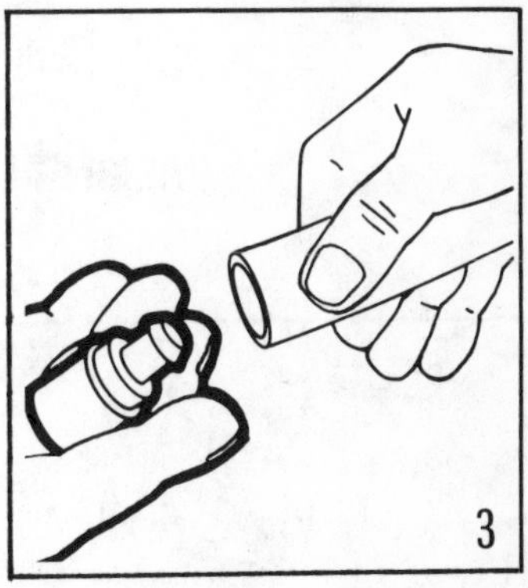

The PCV valve is located on top of the valve cover, in front of the air cleaner.
1. Grasp hose holding PCV valve. Pull straight out.
2. Note where other end of hose is connected. Pull off.
3. Remove PCV valve from hose. Flush hose out with cleaning solvent. Dry hose. Install new PCV valve in hose.
4. Attach end of hose to its original connection and insert PCV valve into proper opening.

FUEL FILTER REPLACEMENT

The fuel filter is located behind the large fuel line inlet nut on the carburetor. Replace the filter every year or 12,000 miles. The fuel filter prevents dirt, rust, and scale from both the gas station's tank and your own fuel tank from reaching the carburetor. A dirty filter will starve the engine and cause poor running.

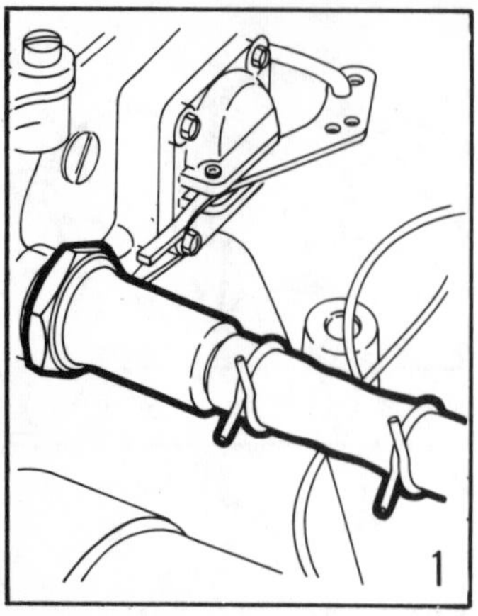

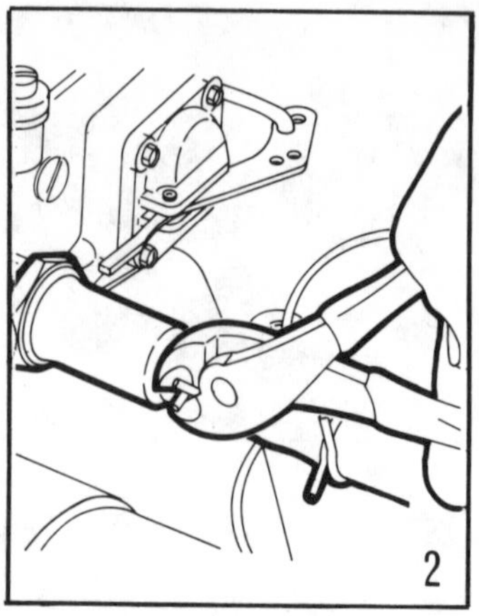

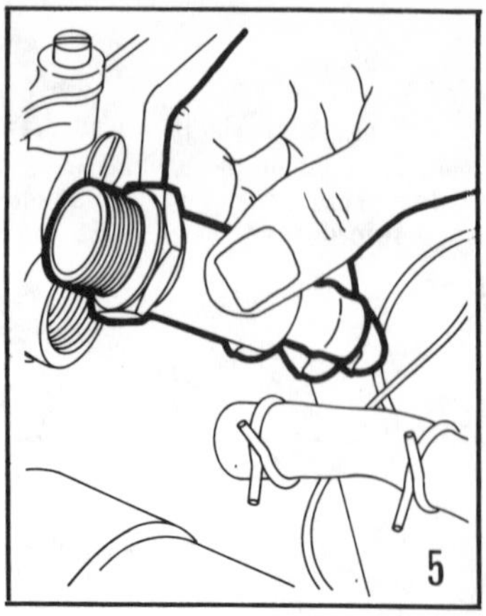

1. Locate the fuel filter in line to carburetor. Place a rag under the filter housing to collect fuel that will drain out when filter is removed.
2. Pinch the ends of clamps together, and move toward center of hose. Use the smallest possible amount of tension, to avoid damaging the clamps. You can get a special tool designed for this job that will make handling the clamps much easier.
3. Pull the hose off filter and fuel line.
4. Fit an adjustable wrench to the six-sided portion of the filter body, and unscrew it from the carburetor. Discard old unit.
5. Position a new gasket onto the new filter, screw housing into carburetor and tighten.
6. Position new clamps in center of a new hose. If the old clamps are to be reused, make sure they have not lost their tension.
7. Install hose on fuel line and filter. Pinch the clamp ends together, and position well onto fuel line and filter.
Note: After replacing filter, remove rag used to catch spilled fuel, and then start engine. Check for leaks. Addition of a can of carburetor cleaner to the fuel tank occasionally will aid in keeping the entire fuel system clean.

Safety Systems

LIGHTING SYSTEM

PARKING LIGHTS, TURN SIGNALS AND STOP LIGHTS

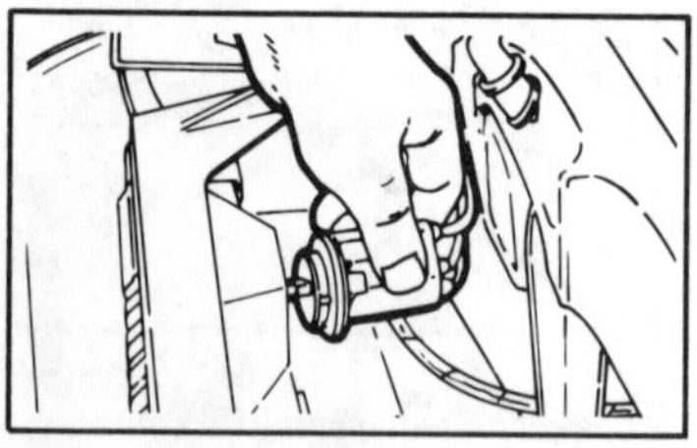

All above lighting functions are performed by four dual-element bulbs. Front parking light and turn signal bulbs are mounted in the parking light housing in the bumper. To replace, remove the lens. To replace rear taillight, stop light, turn signal bulbs, raise trunk lid. Reach socket from inside car. Twist socket counterclockwise in housing. When socket is removed, push down on bulb and turn counterclockwise to remove from socket. Insert new dual-element bulb in correct position (see note) and re-install socket in housing.
NOTE: When inserting new dual element bulb, note that knobs on side of bulb base are different distances from base tip. Match knobs to socket slots for proper fit.

SIDE MARKER LIGHTS

Front: Reach up under fender; turn socket counterclockwise to remove. Pull bulb straight out.
Rear: Open trunk; remove trim panel to expose assembly. Twist socket counterclockwise to remove. Pull bulb straight out.

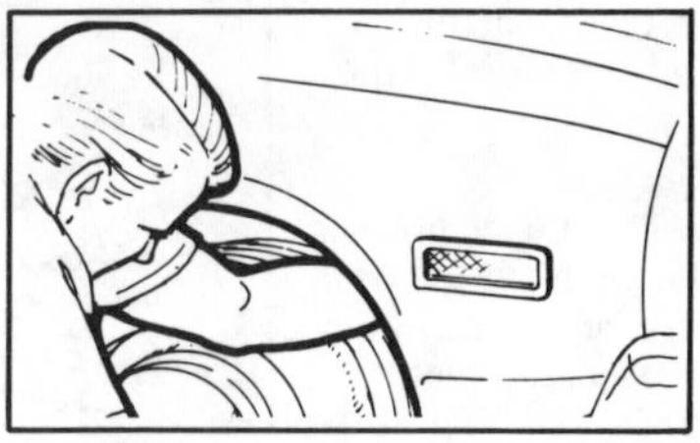

LICENSE PLATE LIGHTS

Disconnect terminal from inside trunk. Remove retaining screws; remove light assembly. Push in on bulb; turn bulb counterclockwise to remove.

INTERIOR DOME LIGHT

This is a cartridge type bulb. Pry the dome light lens out from the housing. To avoid blowing the fuse, make sure that the doors are closed and the dome light switch is in the OFF position. Carefully lever the bulb straight out of the housing. Insert new bulb and re-install dome light lens.

HEADLIGHT REPLACEMENT

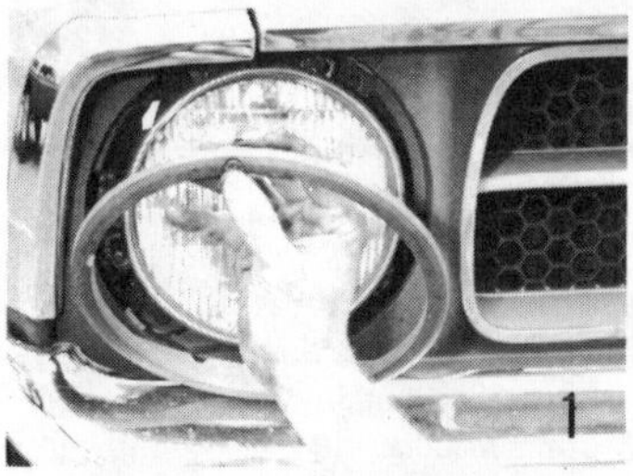

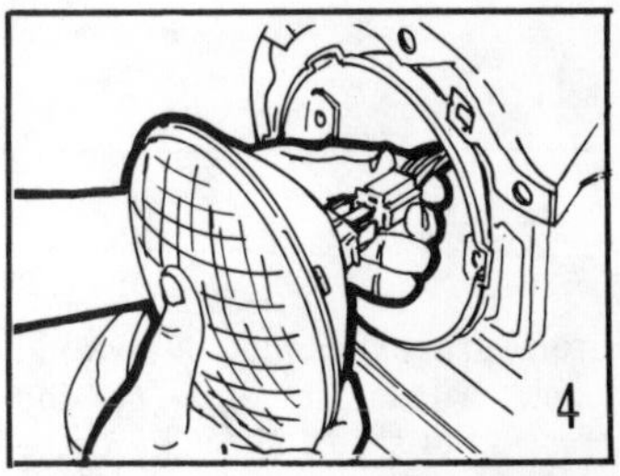

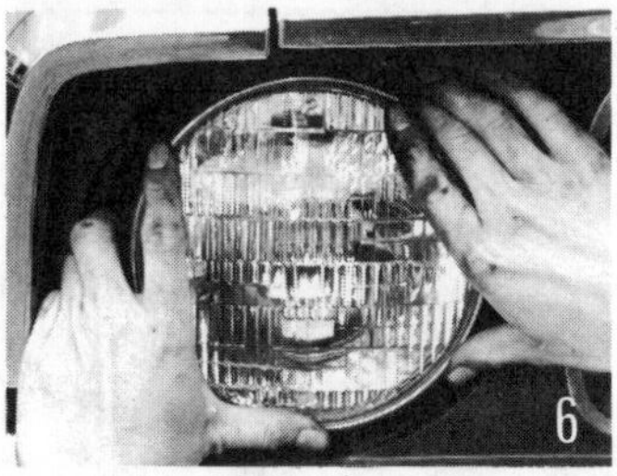

1. On some models remove screws and remove headlight trim ring.
2. On 1970 models place hand over headlight assembly to steady it. Unhook the spring from the retaining ring.
3. Remove retainer ring screws, and remove retainer ring. Be careful not to confuse retainer ring screws with the headlight aiming screws.
4. Pull bulb forward, disconnect wire terminal.
5. Attach the wire terminal to the new bulb, and place bulb into position, locating the bulb glass tabs in the positioning slots.
6. Attach retainer ring to assembly with the three retainer screws. On earlier models reconnect spring to retaining ring.
7. Replace trim ring assembly (early model only) or headlight door.

WINDSHIELD WIPER BLADE REPLACEMENT

To replace wiper blade, lift up on spring release tab on wiper arm connector. Pull wiper blade off. Snap new blade into place.
To replace rubber insert only, press down, away from wiper blade to free it. Slide insert from blade. Insert new wiper. Bend insert upward slightly to engage retaining clips.

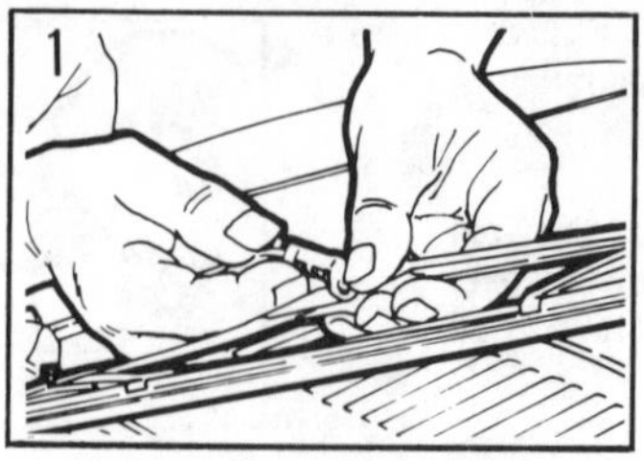

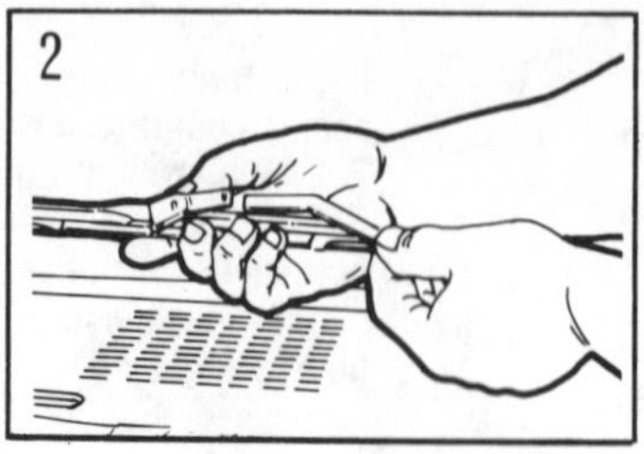

HORN PROBLEMS

If horn sounds and does not stop, this is due to short circuit in wiring. Disconnect wiring connector under hood and have professional service shop check horn wiring circuit.

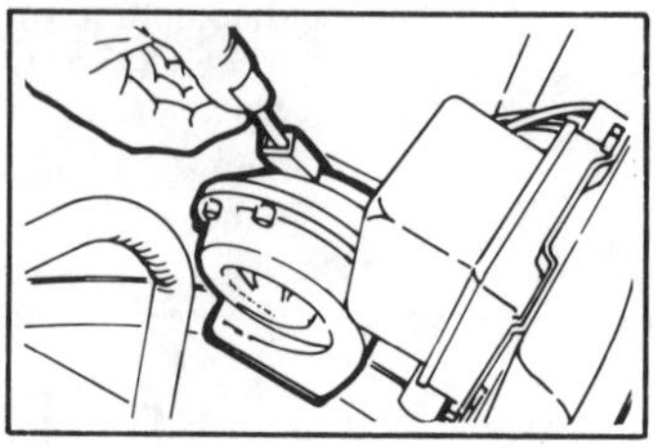

STEERING PROBLEMS

See steering system check in Suspension Section. Check tire pressures. Have a professional service shop check all components in the front end and steering system.

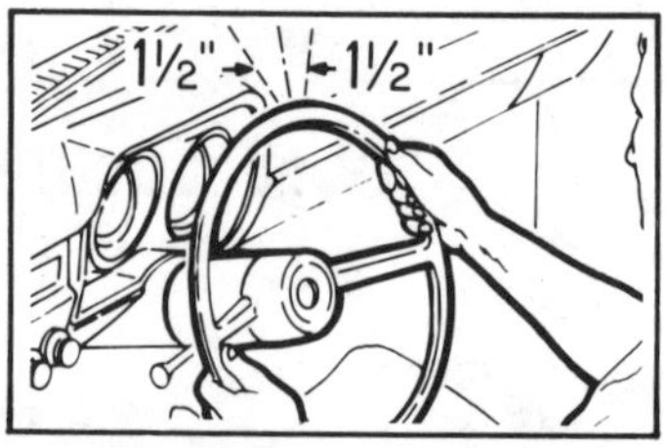

WHEEL CYLINDER CHECK

Drum brakes employ individual wheel cylinders to apply braking pressure to shoes. Check for brake fluid leaks on inside of wheel.
Disc brakes employ calipers on individual wheels. Remove wheel and inspect caliper for signs of fluid leaks. Have mechanic correct leaks.

WASHER SYSTEM

If washer fails to squirt properly, raise hood and check system hose connections. Be sure washer fluid container has fluid. Check spout openings for clogging.
Keep container filled with fluid mixture of washer solvent and water. If road spray buildup on windshield is a chronic problem, add 1 tablespoon dishwasher detergent to solvent/water mixture when re-filling container.

Electrical System

CHECK BATTERY FLUID

To ensure starting ability at all times check your battery condition periodically. You'll need to check battery electrolyte (fluid) level in each of the six cells. Check battery cable connections for tightness and inspect for accumulated corrosion.
SAFETY NOTE: Wear gloves when working on battery.

1. Remove plastic filler caps on top of battery. Fluid should be up to lower end of filler hole and covering the plates. If fluid is low add clean, cold tap water. If your area has hard water, use only distilled water available at auto supply, food or drug stores.
2. Replace any lost caps immediately.

CAUTION: NEVER LIGHT A MATCH OR SMOKE near the top of a battery.

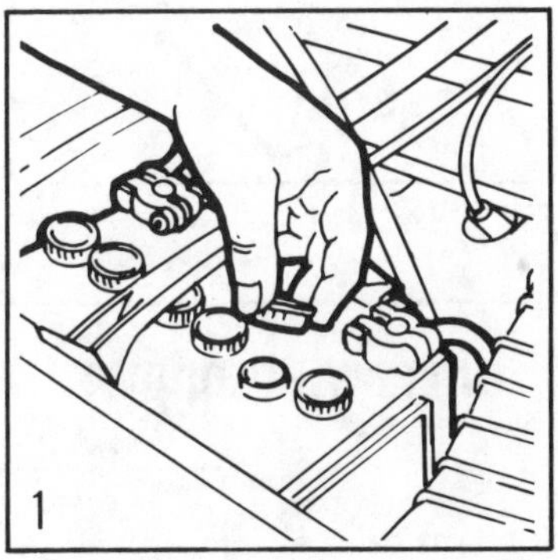

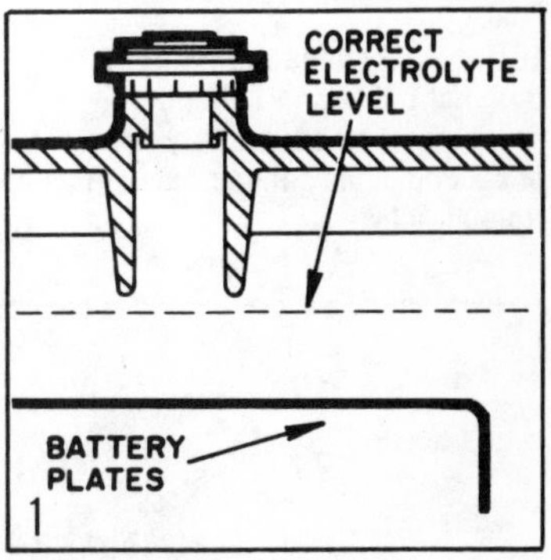

Batteries give off explosive hydrogen gas.
NOTE: Battery that often checks low on fluid could mean:
A. Battery is getting old, due for replacement; have charge capacity checked at service shop.
B. Connections may be corroded or loose; clean/replace as needed (see below).
C. Alternator or voltage regulator not functioning properly; this happens far less often than A or B above.

CLEAN THOSE BATTERY TERMINALS

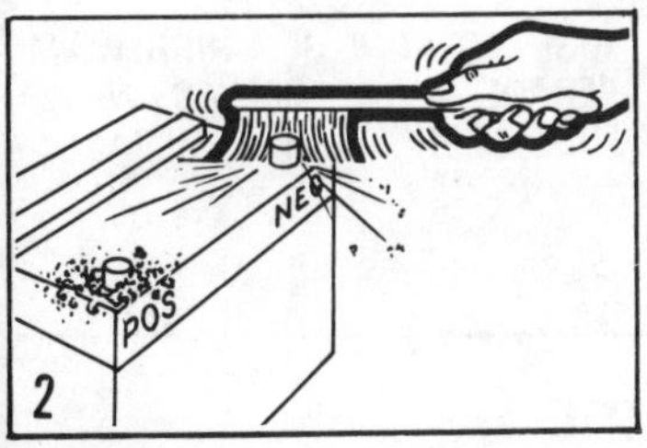

As time goes by, battery terminals build up a dry powdery, whitish material. This material is corrosive and will gradually eat thru battery cables if not cleaned off periodically.
1. Loosen and remove battery connections.
2. Brush off all loose corrosion; use stiff bristle brush. Do not get this material into eyes or on open cuts. Wash off at once.
3. If corrosion build-up is extremely heavy and brushing does not remove all of it, mix 2 tablespoons baking soda to 1 cup water. Pour solution directly onto terminals and connectors. Allow to soak a few minutes and rinse off. Continue brushing to remove all traces of corrosion build-up. Do not allow cleaning solution to enter battery.
4. Replace connectors on battery terminal posts and tighten.
5. Liberally smear battery terminal posts and cable connectors with petroleum jelly.

REPLACE FAULTY BATTERY CABLES

If battery cable strands become frayed, broken or corroded, replace cable immediately. Delay in correcting this condition could lead to sudden failure to start the engine. Can also weaken battery.
1. Loosen and remove battery connections. Clean OFF any corrosion.
2. Disconnect negative cable from

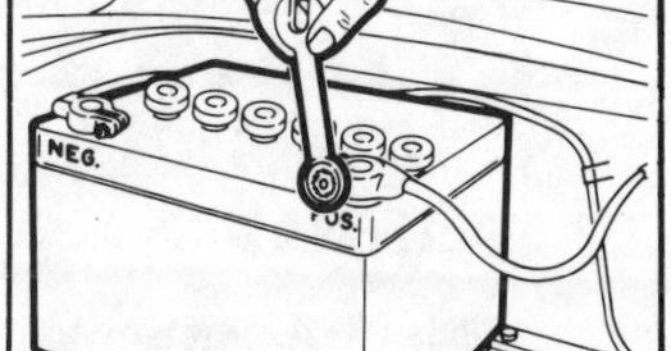

its attachment to engine or chassis. Disconnect positive cable from its attachment to starter relay.

3. Attach new cables making sure positive and negative cables are on proper terminals. They are not identical.

4. Replace connectors on battery terminal posts and tighten.

5. Liberally smear battery terminal posts and cable connectors with petroleum jelly.

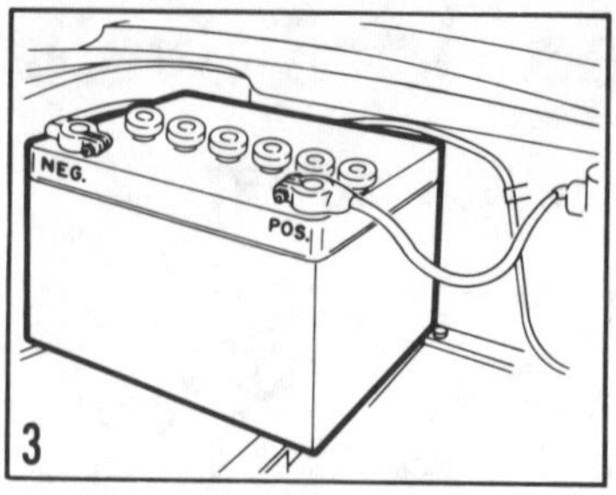

3

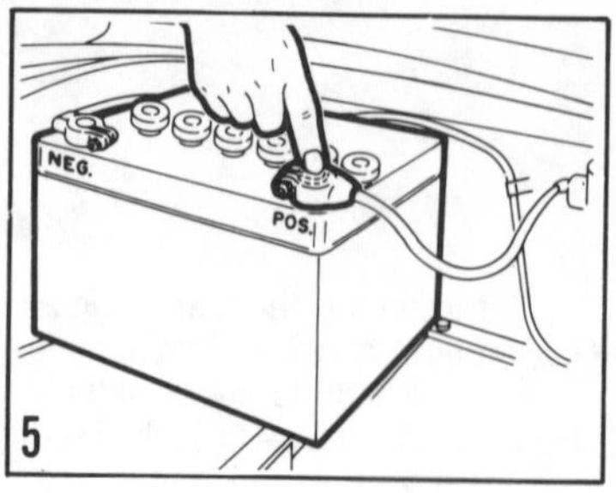

5

BATTERY HOLDDOWN

The clamp device which holds battery in place should be checked periodically. If loose, tighten. Clean off corrosion buildup. Severely corroded holddown components should be replaced before they break.

ELECTRICAL FUSES

Fuses are a safeguard for a car's electrical system. If a greater current is developed than that which the wiring harness is equipped to handle, the fuses blow out. This stops the possibility of overloading the wires and starting an electrical fire. Spare fuses should always be carried, of the amperage specified by the owner's manual. NEVER REPLACE A FUSE WITH ONE OF A HIGHER AMPERAGE. ALWAYS REPLACE WITH A FUSE OF THE SAME AMPERAGE.

TURN SIGNAL AND 4-WAY FLASHER

Turn signals and 4-way emergency flashers will operate only if: A. All light bulbs are OK. B. Flasher units are not burned out. The car has two flasher units that work independently of each other. To remove either flasher, grasp with fingers, twist and pull flasher toward front of car. Pull connector from flasher. REPLACE ONLY WITH SAME TYPE FLASHER.

Year	Type of Mounting	Turn Signal Flasher Location	Hazard Flasher Location
1970	Clamp Bracket	Back of instrument panel to the right of ash tray	Back of instrument panel above and to left of ash tray
1971-73	Tab and Slot	Bracket above glove box	Taped to harness above fuse panel

ALTERNATOR

Red alternator warning light on instrument panel should glow red when you first turn ignition key. This proves bulb is OK. Alternator warning light should go off when engine is running at normal operating speed. If alternator warning light glows red at operating speed, alternator isn't charging battery properly. Commor

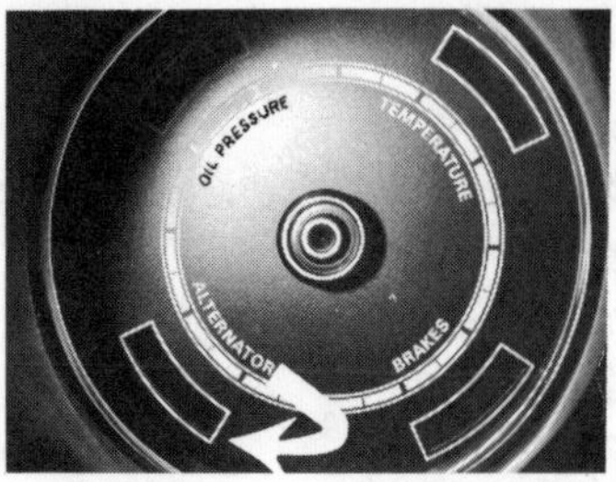

causes are:
A. Fan belts are loose and slipping on alternator pulley. Tighten or replace belts.
B. Battery terminals, cables are loose or corroded. Clean; tighten; replace bad cables.
If A or B do not correct problem, alternator or voltage regulator may be faulty. This happens far less often, and can only be checked by mechanic with proper electrical testing equipment.
Alternator Caution: Alternator can be permanently damaged by short-circuiting terminal connections. When working around or moving alternator, always keep metal tools or engine parts from terminals.

REAR WINDOW DEFOGGER SYSTEM

Do not clean inside of rear window fitted with defogger system with any abrasive material. This could destroy carbon-copper wires. Use only soft rag and mild detergent/water mixture. Dry carefully.

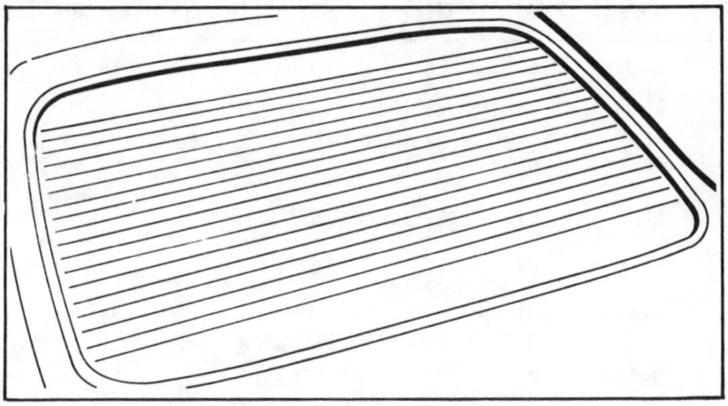

Air Conditioner

CHECKPOINTS AND SERVICES

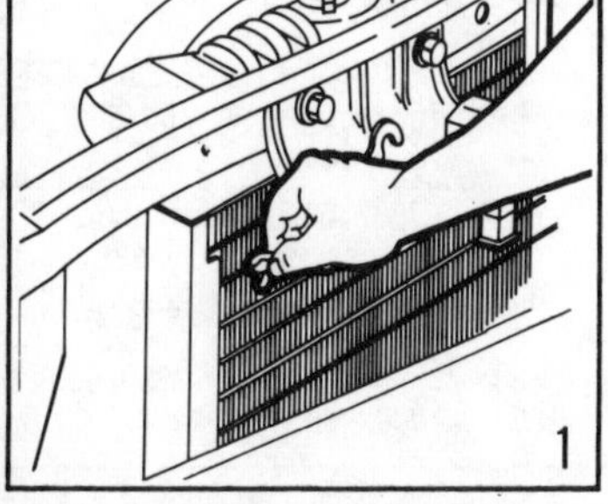

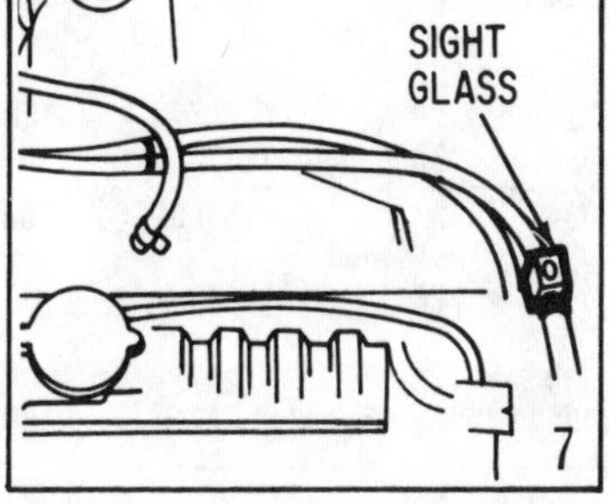

WARNING!—Never attempt to tighten fittings, disassemble or do any work on your car's A/C system. Consult a professional mechanic about A/C system problems and their correction. Your auto air conditioner (A/C) is a delicate, closed system. If air, dirt or water get into it, or if refrigerant escapes, the A/C unit will not cool a car interior. Among things you can do are:
1. Keep condenser grille clean. Check for dirt and debris; periodically remove dead insects, leaves, etc., with stiff bristle brush. Straighten any bent fins—carefully.
2. Keep radiator filled to correct level. (See Cooling System section). If fluid needs to be added, add antifreeze rather than water.
3. Keep radiator coolant at a 50/50 water/antifreeze mixture.
4. Flush cooling system and replace with fresh coolant mixture at least every 24 months. (See Cooling System section).
5. Radiator cap should be tight and sealed properly. If sealing gasket is cracked, cut or worn, replace cap with new 15 lb. unit.
6. Check fan belt tension periodically. (See Cooling System section). Replace glazed, frayed or cut fan belts, before they fail entirely.

7. Check periodically for bubbles in A/C sight glass. Sight glass is located in head of receiver/drier vessel. Or in metal tubing leading from top of receiver/drier. Sight glass is no larger than head of large nail. It may be dirty. Wipe clean for best visibility.

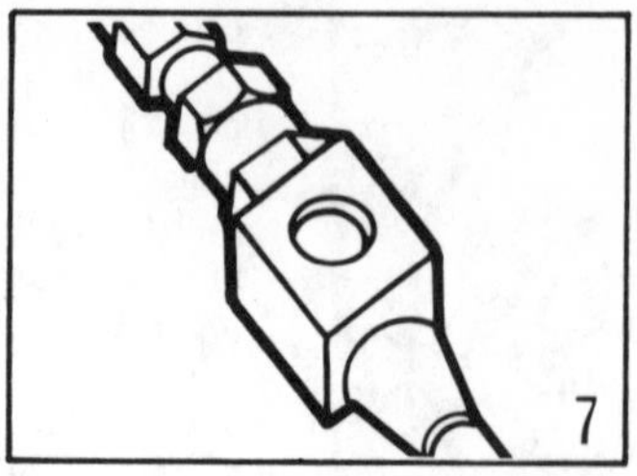

TUNE-UP SPECIFICATIONS

YEAR	ENGINE No. Cyl. Displacement (cu. in.)	SPARK PLUGS Type	SPARK PLUGS Gap (in.)	DISTRIBUTOR Point Dwell (deg.)	DISTRIBUTOR Point Gap (in.)	IGNITION TIMING Man. Trans.● (deg.)■	IGNITION TIMING Auto Trans.● (deg.)■	IDLE SPEED Man. Trans.● (rpm) ▲	IDLE SPEED Auto Trans. (rpm) ▲
1970	6-200	BF-82	0.035	38	0.027	6B	6B	750①	550②
	6-250	BF-82	0.035	38	0.025	6B	6B	750/500⑦	600/500⑦
	8-302 (210 hp)	BF-42	0.035	27	0.021	6B	6B	800/500⑦	600/500⑦
	8-302 (290 hp)	AF-32	0.035	32	0.020	16B	—	800/500⑦	—
	8-351C (250 hp)	AF-42	0.035	27	0.021	6B	6B	700/500⑦	600
	8-351W	BF-42	0.035	27	0.021	10B	10B	700/500⑦	575 (600/500)⑦
	8-351C (300 hp)	AF-42	0.035	27	0.021	6B	6B	800/500⑦	600 (600/500)⑦
	8-428	BF-32	0.035	32	0.020	6B	6B	725	675 (675/500)⑦
	8-429	AF-32	0.035	27/29⑧	0.017/0.021⑧	10B	10B	650/500⑦	700/500⑦
1971	6-250	BRF-82	0.034	36	0.027/0.025⑧	6B	68	750	600
	8-302	BRF-42	0.034	27	0.021	6B	6B	800/500⑦	575 (600/500)⑦
	8-351C	ARF-42	0.034	27	0.021	6B	6B	700/500⑦	575 (600/500)⑦
	8-351W	BRF-42	0.034	27	0.021	6B	6B	700/500⑦	575 (600/500)⑦
	8-351CJ	ARF-42	0.034	27	0.021	6B	6B	800/500⑦	600
	8-351 Boss	ARF-32	0.034	27/29⑧	0.021/0.017⑧	6B	68	800	590
	8-429	ARF-42	0.034	28	0.020	10B	10B	650/500⑦	600/500⑦
1972	6-250	ARF-42	0.034	37	0.027	6B	6B	750/500⑦	600/500⑦
	8-302	BRF-42	0.034	28	0.017	6B	6B	800/500⑦	575 (600/500)⑦
	8-351C	ARF-42	0.034	28	0.017	6B	10B	750/500⑦	575/500③⑦
	8-351W	.BRF-42	0.034	28	0.017	—	6B	—	575 (600/500)⑦
	8-351CJ	ARF-42	0.034	28	0.017④	16B	6B	1000/500⑦	700/500⑤⑦
	8-351HO	ARF-42	0.034	28	0.020	10B	—	1000/500⑦	—
1973	6-250	BRF-82	0.034	37	0.027/0.025⑧	6B	68	750/500⑦	600/500⑦
	8-302	BRF-42	0.034	28	0.017	6B	6B	800/500⑦	575 (600/500)⑦
	8-351	BRF-42	0.034	28	0.017	—	6B	—	575 (600/500)⑦
	8-351CJ	ARF-42	0.034	28	0.017⑥	16B	16B	1000/500⑦	800/500⑦

▲ Adjust automatic transmissions in Drive (AMC/Ford/GM) or Neutral (Chrysler), all manual transmissions are adjusted in Neutral.
■ All figures are Before Top Dead Center.
● Figure in parentheses indicates solenoid equipped vehicle.
① W/A.C.—800
② W/A.C.—600
③ 625/500—Calif. Engines
④ Man. Trans.—0.020
⑤ 800/500—Calif. Engines
⑥ 0.020—Man. Trans. w/Dual point distributor
⑦ Lowest figure is with Solenoid disconnected
⑧ Top figure for dual diaphragm distributors; Lower figure for single diaphragm distributors
C—Cleveland, high performance
W—Windsor
CJ—Cobra Jet
HO—High Output

CAPACITIES

YEAR	ENGINE No. Cyl. Displacement (cu. in.)	ENGINE OIL Add 1 qt. with New Filter	TRANSMISSION Pts. to Refill after Draining MANUAL 3-speed	MANUAL 4-speed	AUTOMATIC	DRIVE AXLE (pts.)	COOLING SYSTEM with Heater (qts.)	with Air Cond. (qts.)
1970	6-200	3.5	3.5	—	16	2.25	9	9
	6-250	3.5	3.5	—	18	4	10	10
	8-302	4	3.5	4	18	4	13.5	15
	8-351	4	3.5	4	22	5	14.5	16
	8-428	4	—	4	26	5	19.5	19.5
	8-429 Boss	8	—	4	25½	5	19.6	—
1971	6-250	3.5	3.5	—	18	4	11	11
	8-302	4	3.5	—	18	4	15	15.5
	8-351	4	3.5	4	22	5	15.5	16
	8-429	6	—	4	26	5	19.5	19.5
1972-73	6-250	3.5	—	—	18	4	11	11
	8-302	4	—	—	18	4	15	15.5
	8-351	4	4	4	22	5	16	16

— Not applicable

Service Record

Date/Mileage	Service	Next Due

Mustang II

Lubrication and Oil Change

It is important to choose an oil of the proper viscosity for climatic and operational conditions. Viscosity is an index of the oil's thickness at different temperatures. A thicker oil (higher numerical rating) is needed for high temperature operation, whereas thinner oil (lower numerical rating) is required for cold weather operation. Due to the need for an oil that embodies both these characteristics in parts of the country where there is wide temperature variation within a small period of time, multigrade oils have been developed. Basically, a multigrade oil is thinner at low temperatures and thicker at high temperatures. For example, a 20W-40 oil exhibits the characteristics of a 20 weight oil when the car is first started and the oil is cold. Its lighter weight allows it to travel to the lubricating surfaces quicker and offer less resistance to starter motor cranking than, let's say, a straight 30 weight oil. But after the engine reaches operating temperature, the 20W-40 oil begins acting like a straight 40 weight oil, its heavier weight providing greater lubricating protection and less susceptibility to foaming than a straight 30 weight oil.

CHECKING THE BRAKE FLUID LEVEL

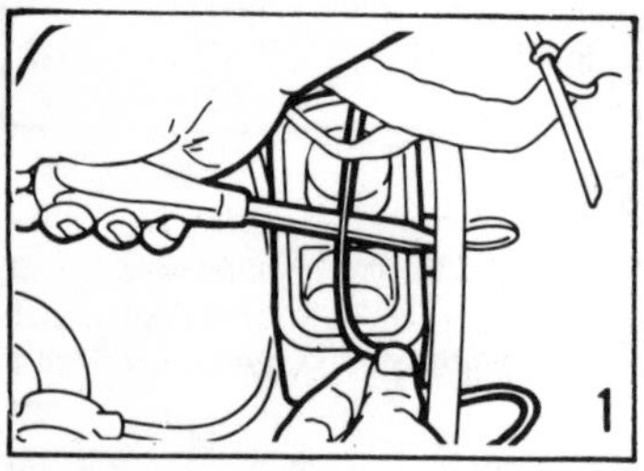

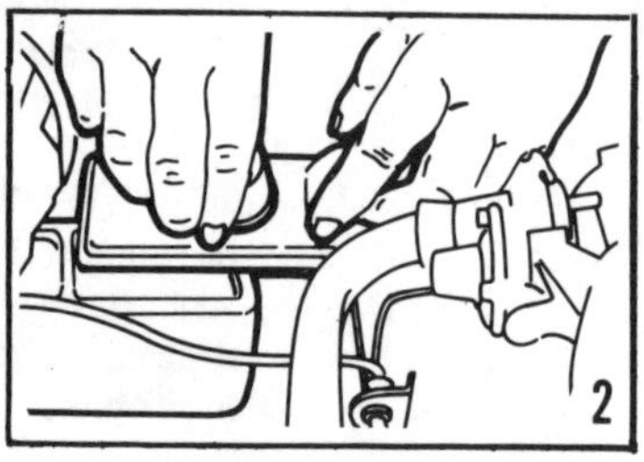

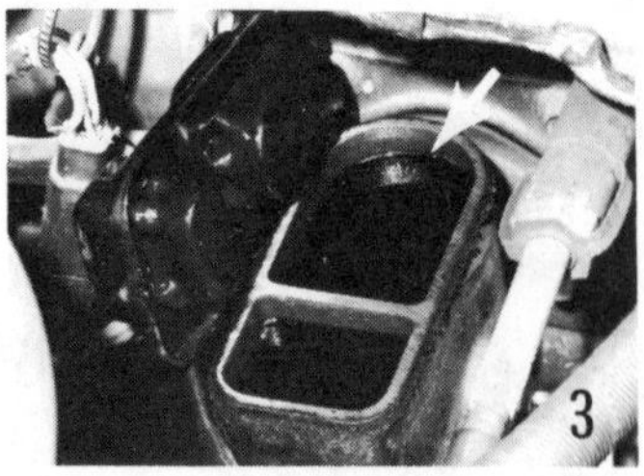

You should check the brake fluid level every three months, sooner if the brake pedal feels spongy or you notice fluid leaking from any brake line. The master cylinder is located under the hood on the left hand side of the firewall. You should top it up as necessary with brake fluid meeting SAE 70 R3 specifications which is usually stamped on the top of the can.

1. Pry wire retaining clip off cap top with screwdriver.
2. Remove cap and gasket by lifting up.
3. Fluid level should be within ¼ inch of top rim. If lower than this, add fresh fluid to appropriate level.

DO NOT OVERFILL

4. Replace cap and gasket; secure retaining clip over cap. If fluid level was low, check again in a few days.
5. If fluid repeatedly checks low, there is a leak somewhere in the system. Have mechanic check further. Neglect can be dangerous.

CHECKING THE MANUAL TRANSMISSION FLUID

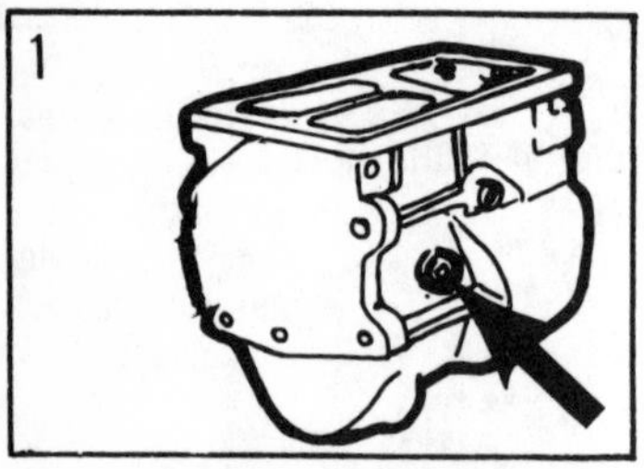

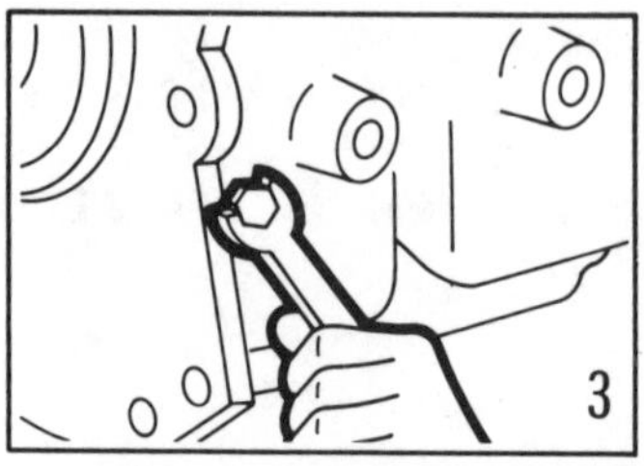

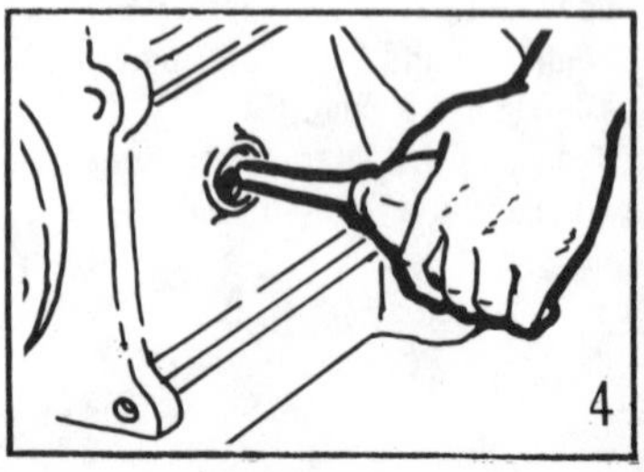

The fluid level in the manual transmission should be checked every 6 months or 6,000 miles.

1. With the car standing perfectly level, apply the parking brake, set the transmission in Neutral, stop the engine and block all four wheels.
2. Wipe all dirt and grease from the filler plug on the side of the transmission.
3. Using a sliding T-bar handle or an adjustable wrench, remove the filler plug.
4. Insert your finger in the opening; the lubricant should be level with the bottom of the filler hole. If required, add SAE 90 manual transmission fluid to the proper level using a syringe with a flexible extension. Install the filler plug.

CHECKING THE AUTOMATIC TRANSMISSION FLUID

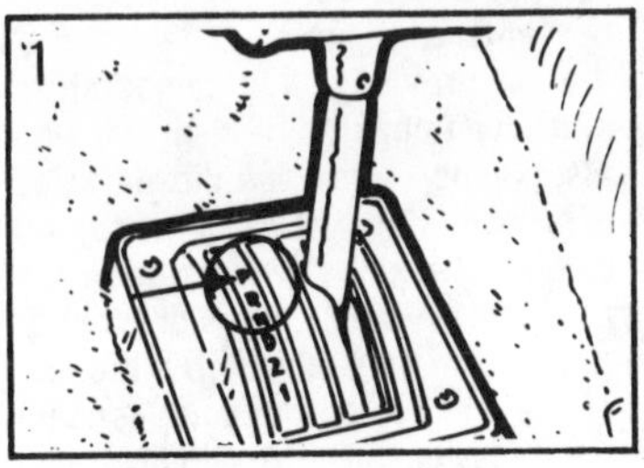

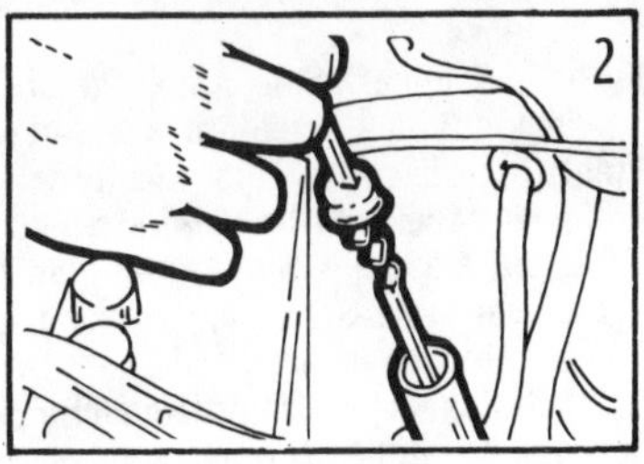

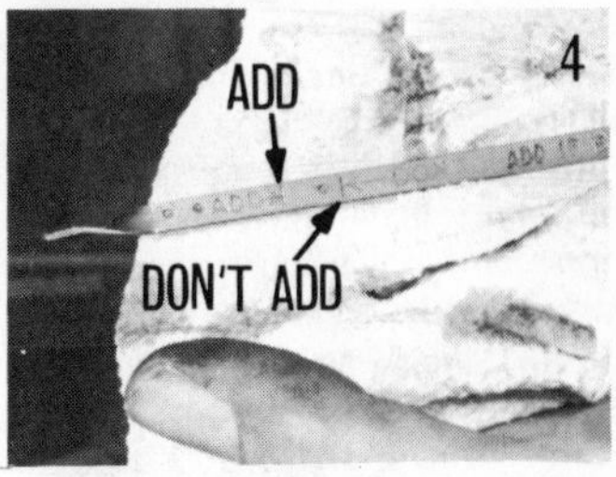

The automatic transmission fluid level should be checked every 12 months or 12,000 miles. The level should also be checked if abnormal shifting behavior is noticed.

1. With the car standing on a level surface, firmly apply the parking brake. Run the engine at idle until normal operating temperature is reached. Then, with the right foot firmly planted on the brake pedal, shift the transmission selector through all of the positions, allowing sufficient time in each range to engage the transmission. Shift the selector into Park (P).
2. With the engine still running, pull out the transmission dipstick, located at the right rear of the engine compartment.
3. Wipe it clean and reinsert it, pushing it down until it seats in the tube.
4. Pull it out and check the level. The level should be between the "ADD" and "FULL" marks. Add ATF Type F as required through the dipstick tube.

CAUTION: Do not overfill the transmission, as foaming and loss of fluid through the vent may cause the transmission to malfunction.

5. If you have to add fluid, obtain a long neck flexible filler funnel and a clear bottle that will hold a pint of fluid. Transfer about a pint of fluid to the bottle and add it using the long

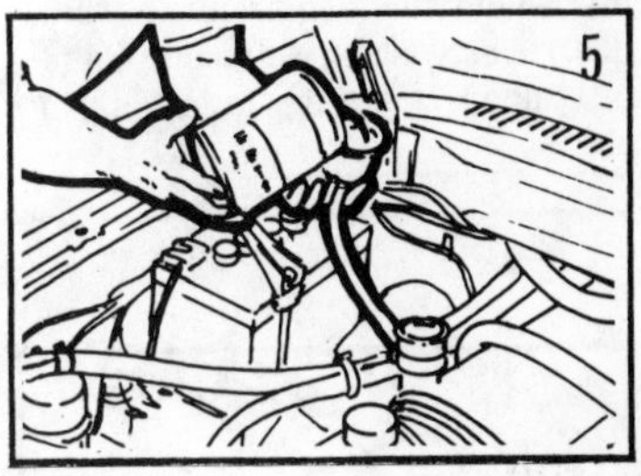

neck funnel. Remember that only about a pint of fluid is needed to raise the level from ADD to FULL, so add it slowly and check the level if you are unsure how much you added.

CHECKING THE REAR AXLE FLUID

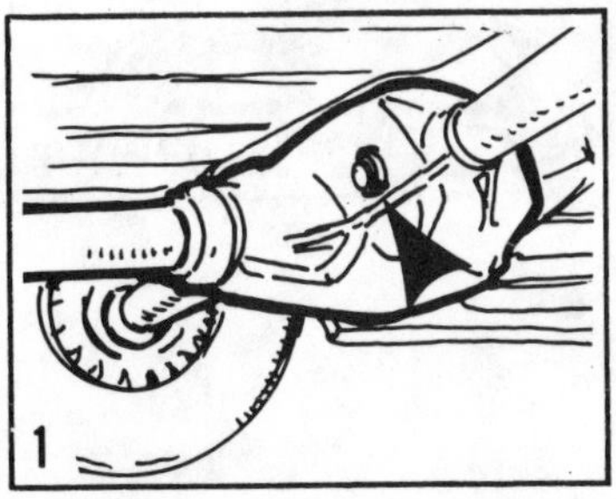

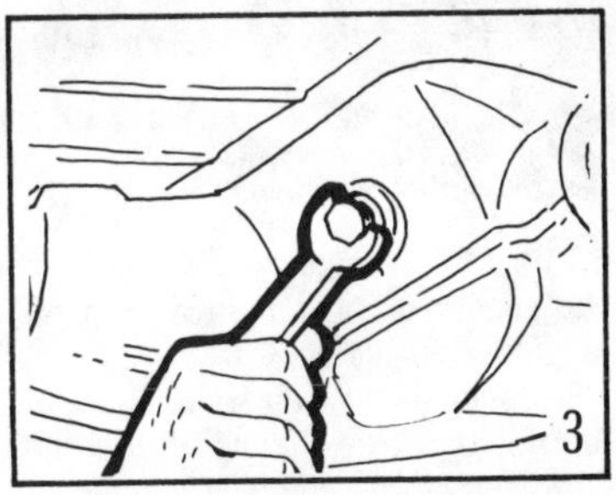

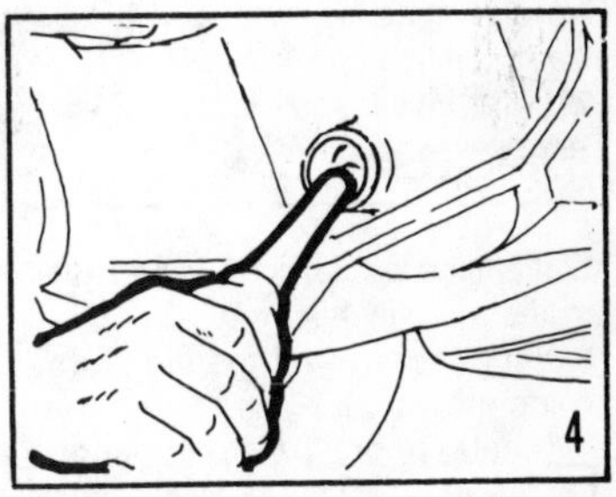

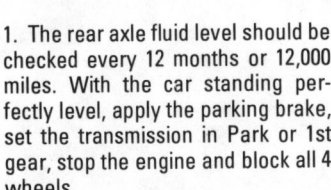

1. The rear axle fluid level should be checked every 12 months or 12,000 miles. With the car standing perfectly level, apply the parking brake, set the transmission in Park or 1st gear, stop the engine and block all 4 wheels.
2. Wipe all dirt and grease from the filler plug area.
3. Using a sliding T-bar handle (3/8 in.) or an adjustable wrench, remove the filler plug. The fluid level must be maintained at 1/4 in. from the bottom of the filler plug hole.
4. To check the fluid level in the axle insert your finger in the opening; if you can feel fluid, then the level is alright. If you can not feel the fluid, add some SAE 80 or 90 hypoid gear lube using a syringe with a flexible extension.
5. If as you are removing the filler plug, the fluid begins to drip out, simply retighten the plug as the fluid level is alright.

CHECKING THE OIL LEVEL

The oil level in the engine should be checked at fuel stops. The check should be made with the engine warm and switched off for a period of about one minute so that the oil has time to drain down into the

crankcase.
1. Pull out the dipstick, wipe it clean and reinsert it.
2. The level of the oil must be kept within the "SAFE" area, above the "ADD 1" mark on the dipstick. If the oil level is kept above the "SAFE" area, heavy oil consumption will result. If the level remains below the "ADD 1" mark, severe engine damage may result.
3. The "ADD 1" and "ADD 2" refer to US measure quarts. Remember that in Canada, the Imperial measure quart is used and it is equal to 5/4 of a US quart. When topping up, make sure that the oil is the same type and viscosity rating as the oil already in the crankcase.

When adding oil to the crankcase or changing the oil or filter, it is important that oil of an equal quality to original equipment be used in your car. The use of inferior oils may void your warranty. Generally speaking, oil that has been rated "SE, heavy-duty detergent" by the American Petroleum Institute will prove satisfactory.

Oil of the SE variety performs a multitude of functions in addition to its basic job of reducing friction of the engine's moving parts. Through a balanced formula of polymeric dispersants and metallic detergents, the oil prevents high temperature and low temperature deposits and also keeps sludge and dirt particles in suspension. Acids, particularly sulphuric acid, as well as other by-products of combustion of sulphur fuels, are neutralized by the oil. These acids, if permitted to concentrate, may cause corrosion and rapid wear of the internal parts of the engine.

OIL AND FILTER CHANGE

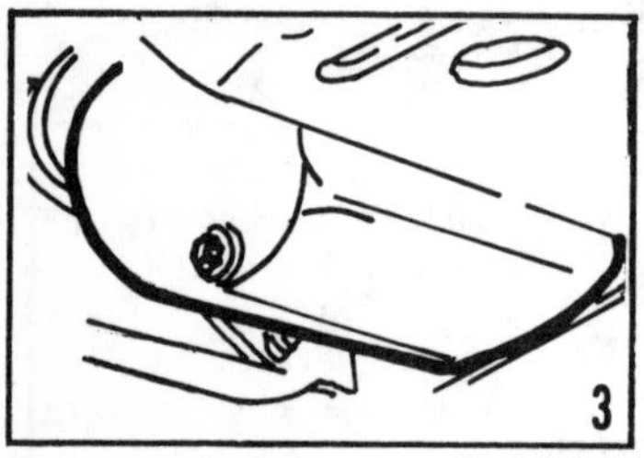
3

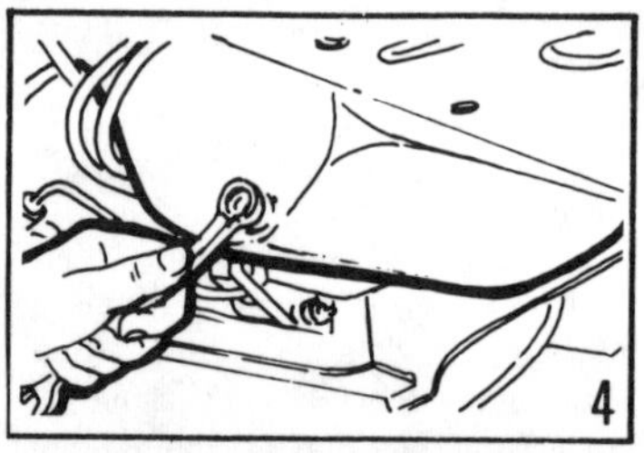
4

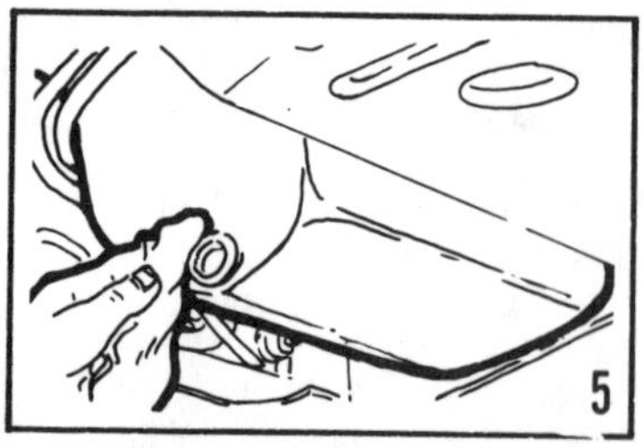
5

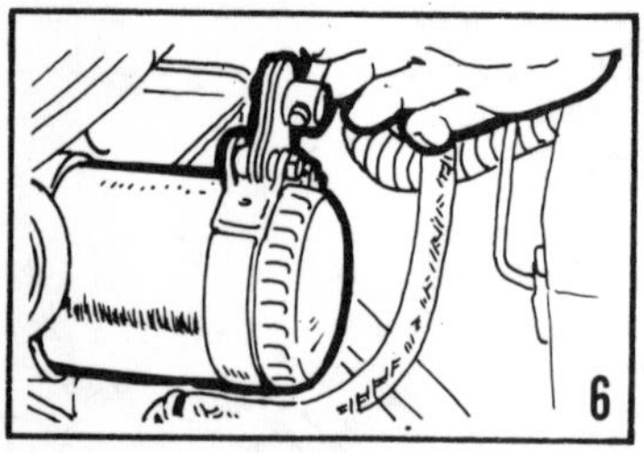
6

7

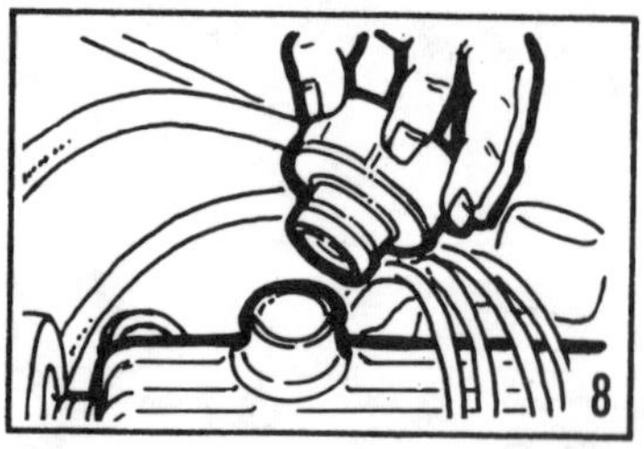
8

1. If engine is cold, start up and idle for about 5 minutes.
2. Park car on level ground. Turn engine off.
3. Locate oil drain plug on underside of engine. Place drain pan under plug.
4. Remove drain plug with wrench. Let ALL dirty oil drain out.
5. Wipe plug and area around drain hole clean. Replace drain plug; tighten it.
6. Locate oil filter. Move drain pan under filter. Loosen filter with oil filter wrench. Unscrew; remove filter by hand.
7. Smear fresh oil over surface of rubber gasket (washer) of new filter. Install new filter by hand only. Do NOT use wrench. Turn filter until gasket makes contact. Tighten an additional half turn only . . . NO MORE.
8. Locate oil filler tube on top of engine. Remove cap.
9. Punch oil pouring spout into top of oil can. Pour all cans of new oil into filler tube. Wipe filler cap clean and replace it. Be sure to re-attach all hoses. (NOTE: If filler cap is very dirty, rinse in solvent. Dry before replacing.)
10. Check new oil level at dipstick. Pull out dipstick, wipe clean.
11. Push dipstick back into engine. Be sure to insert all the way. Remove dipstick and check new oil level. It should be above "SAFE" line. If not, be sure to check if you put in all the oil called for.
12. Start up engine and idle for 3-5 minutes. Oil signal light on instrument panel will glow red when engine is first started. Light should go

11

out in 30 seconds or less.
13. Stop engine and check for oil leaks at drain plug and filter. If you find any, check tightness of plug and/or filter, also for condition of filter gasket to see that it has not become pinched or damaged when installing. Recheck oil level, which should now be at "SAFE".

SPEEDOMETER CABLE LUBRICATION

What you will be lubricating is the speedometer inner cable which runs from the speedometer to the transmission. There are a few bends in the cable routing, so do not try and force the cable out, just pull it out smoothly and slowly. If it gets stuck check the cable outer casing for kinks or bends which could be stopping its movement.

1. Locate cable shaft attachment directly behind speedometer dial.

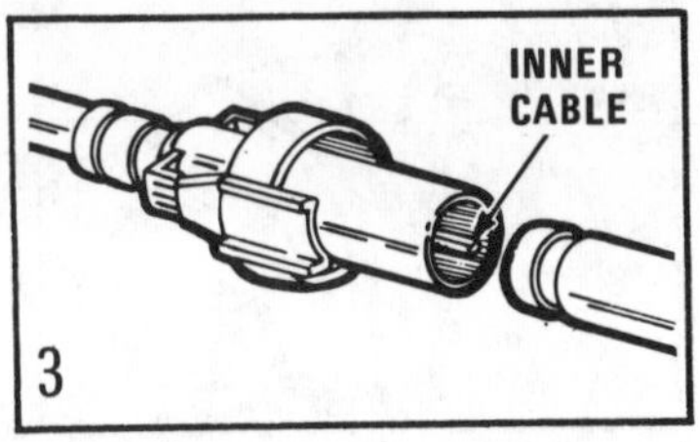

2. Press the quick disconnect clip and pull the cable assembly back and out from behind the dash panel.
3. Pull inner cable completely out of outer casing. Note carefully which end is top. Check for wear or frayed strands. If damaged, replace inner cable with new one.
4. Apply generous amount of speedometer cable lubricant into cable casing. Replace inner cable in shaft, noting that top end is not inserted accidentally. Turn inner cable as it is being re-inserted. Twist cable when all the way in, to lock into position at lower end.
5. Re-connect cable to speedometer head under instrument panel.

DOOR HINGE AND LOCK LUBRICATION

If you have ever had a door lock freeze on you, you will appreciate the value of lubricating your door locks. Lubricating them also helps fight against rust forming inside and ruining the lock. If your door makes noise when you are opening it, it is time to lubricate it. Both jobs are very simple, but when you are lubricating the door lock, it will be easier if the lubricant comes with a long thin tube which you can insert inside the lock. This will do a better job without much spilling. Each of these jobs should be done every six months.

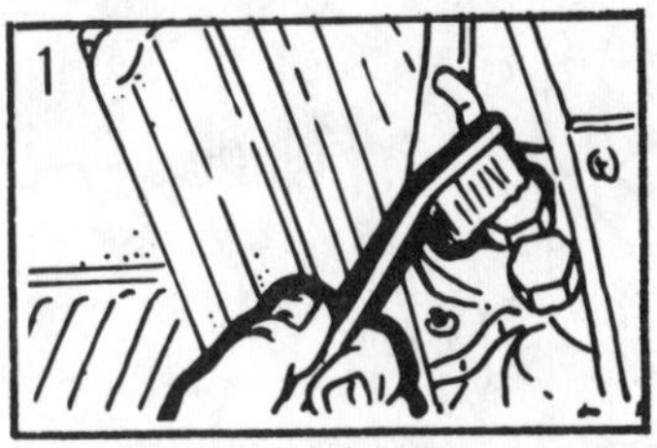

(lubricate every 6 months)
1. Brush any dirt accumulations from door hinges and stops. Use old tooth brush or rag.
2. Apply dab of white polyethylene grease to door hinges, trunk hinges, hood hinges, door stops.

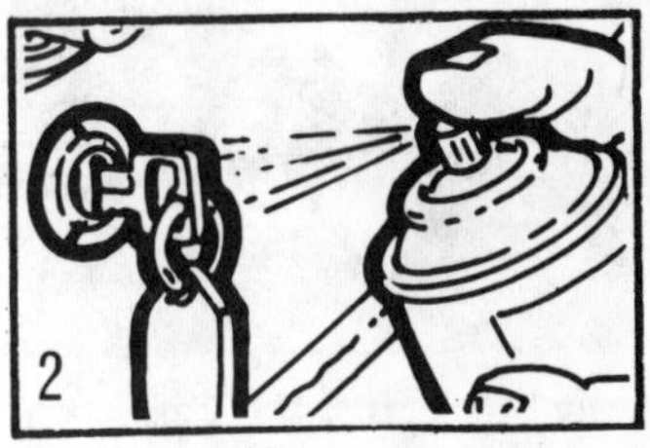

(lubricate every 6 months)
1. Insert door key half way into lock.
2. Spray aerosol lock lubricant into lock.
3. Push key rest of way into lock; turn back and forth several times.

DRAIN HOLE CLEANING

The doors and rocker panels of your car are equipped with drain holes to allow water to drain out of the inside of the body panels. If the drain holes become clogged with dirt, leaves, pine needles, etc., the water will remain inside the panels, causing rust. To prevent this, open the drain holes with a screwdriver. If your car is equipped with rubber dust valves instead, simply open the dust valve with your finger.

Cooling System

REPLACING THE THERMOSTAT

1. Drain the cooling system so that the level of coolant in the engine is below the thermostat housing.

2. Remove the thermostat housing attaching bolts. On the 2300 cc Four, the housing is located at the upper front part of the cylinder head. On the 2800 cc V6, the housing is located at the bottom of the water pump, connected to the lower radiator hose. On the 4900 cc (302) V8, the housing is located at the front of the intake manifold.

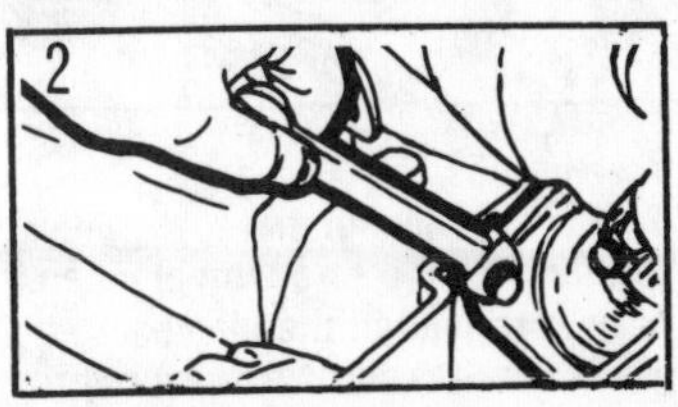

3. Remove the housing, thermostat, and discard the old gasket. On 302 V8 engines, twist the thermostat to remove it.
4. Clean the gasket mating surfaces and the thermostat housing. Test the operation of the thermostat as outlined under "Cooling System Troubleshooting."
5. Using a good thermostat and new gasket, and O-ring (V6), install the thermostat in the housing. On 302 V8 engines, twist the thermostat so that it fits into the recess in the housing.

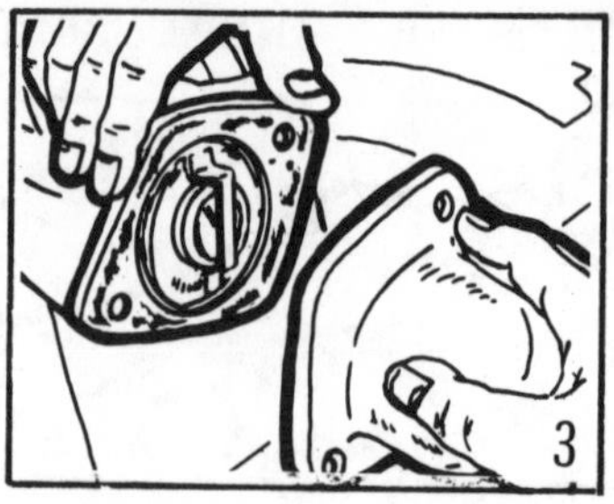

Coat the gasket with water-resistant sealer.
6. Install the housing and tighten the

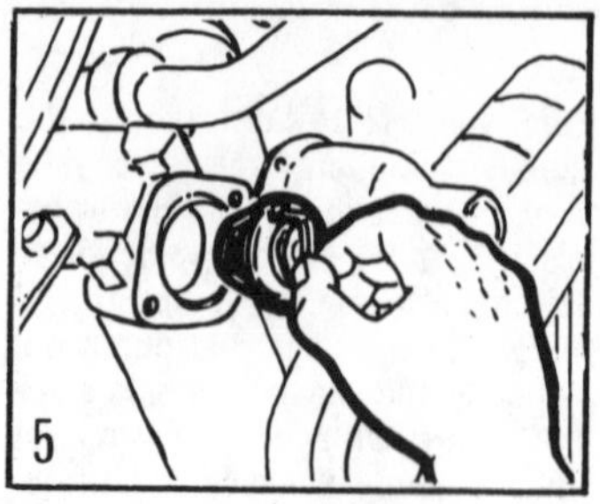

attaching bolts to 12-15 ft. lbs.
7. Refill the cooling system.

FAN BELT ADJUSTMENT

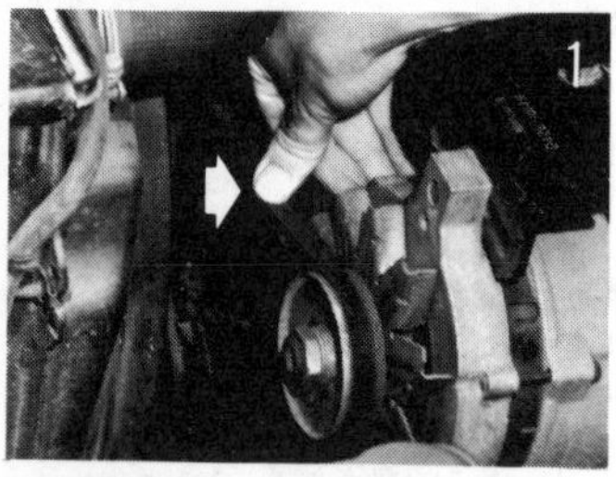

Every 12 months or 12,000 miles, you should check the condition of the fan belt. You should replace any belt that is worn, glazed, or stretched too much to be tightened.
The fan belt not only drives the radiator fan, it turns the water pump and drives the alternator. It's easy to see that the condition and proper tension of the belt are vital, since almost all engine cooling and electrical power are dependent on it.
1. Position a ruler perpendicular to the drive belt at its longest run. Test

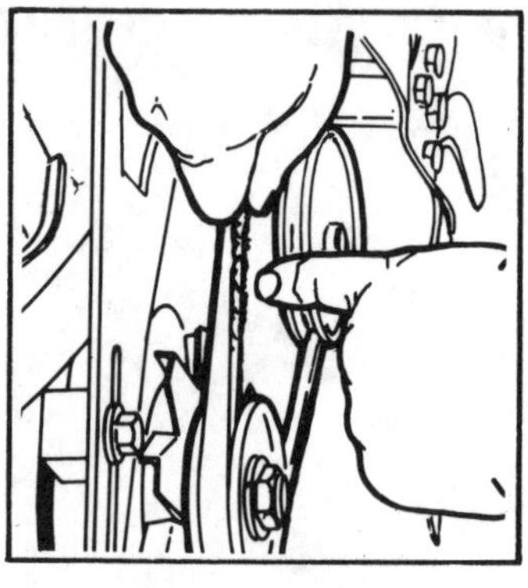

the tightness of the belt by pressing it firmly with your thumb. The deflection should not exceed ¼ in.
2. If the deflection exceeds ¼ in., loosen the alternator mounting and adjusting arm bolts.
3. On 4, 6 and V8 cylinder models, use a pry bar, such as a pipe or broom handle, to move the alter-

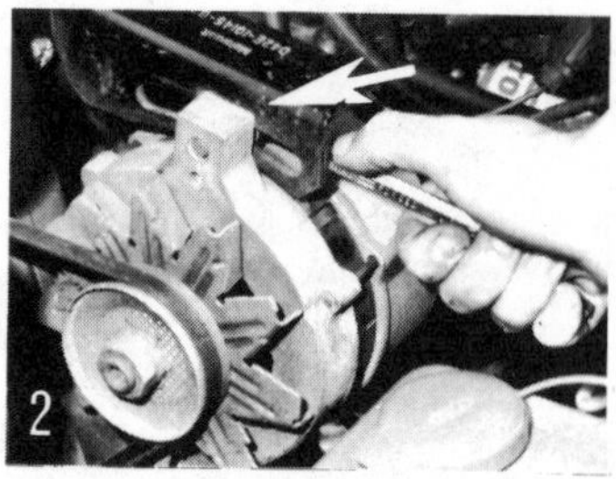

nator toward or away from the engine until the proper tension is reached.
CAUTION: Apply tension to the front of the alternator only. Positioning the pry bar against the rear end housing will damage the alternator.
4. Holding the alternator in place to maintain tension, tighten the adjusting arm bolt. Recheck the belt tension. When the belt is properly tensioned, tighten the alternator mounting bolt.

REPLACING THE RADIATOR HOSES

To replace the radiator hoses, you must first drain the radiator. Hoses should be replaced when they begin to feel soft and surface cracks begin to appear in them. It is usually good practice to check them twice a year and replace them every two years. When you replace the radiator hoses, you will need a screwdriver, something to drain the coolant into, and some emery paper or sandpaper. In order to save time and aggravation, when you are replacing the hose clamps on the new hoses, position the hose clamp so that the screw on it is readily accessible. This

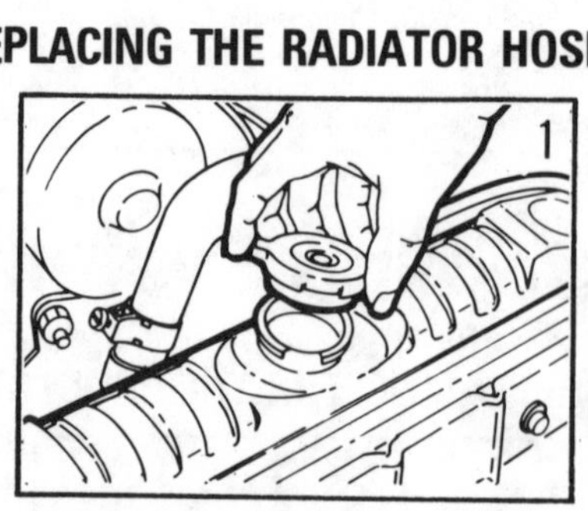

way, you will not have to "hunt" around with the screwdriver when it is time to tighten the clamp.
1. Remove radiator cap. Open

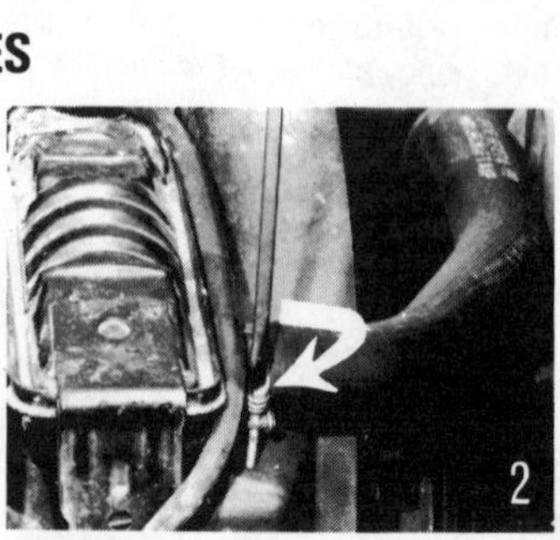

radiator petcock at bottom of radiator. Drain radiator.
2. Loosen clamp at each end of hose(s). Work hose loose; pull it off.

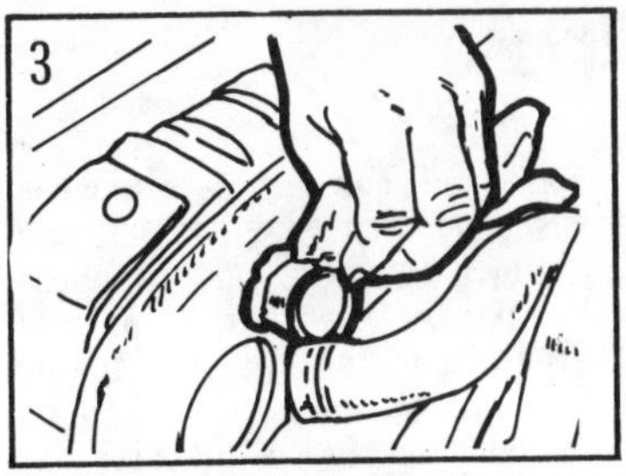

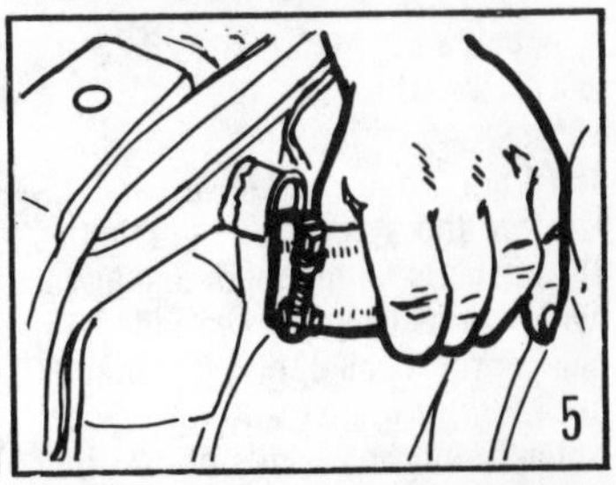

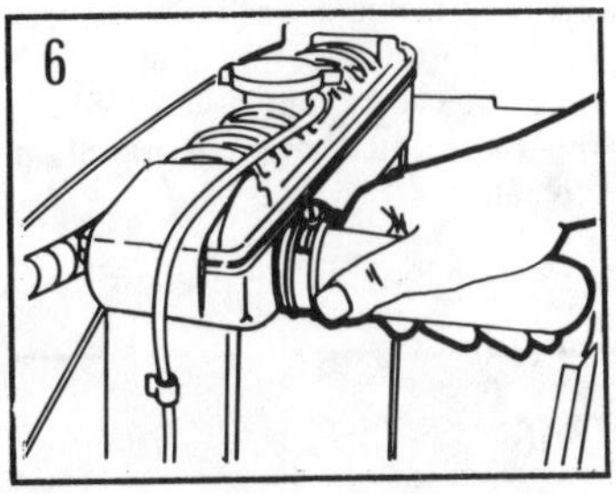

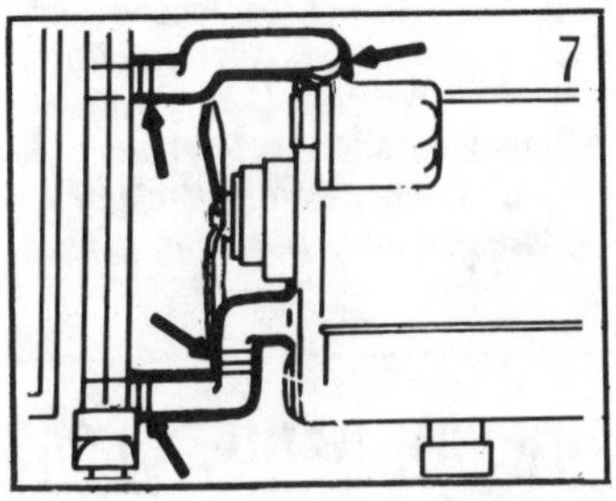

3. Wipe all hose connections clean. Use emery cloth to get rid of residue.
4. If old hose clamps are badly rusted or damaged, replace with new units.
5. Slip clamps over each hose end. Slip hose ends all the way onto cleaned up hose connections.
6. Place hose clamp about ¼ inch from hose end. If you find the hose is a very tight fit, spray a little silicone lubricant in the end; this will make it slide on more easily. Tighten. Close radiator petcock. Refill radiator.
7. Start engine; allow to warm up. Check for coolant leaks.
8. Road test car; watch for temperature warning light.

CHECKING THE RADIATOR CAP

Check radiator cap occasionally for worn or cracked gasket. If cap doesn't seal properly, fluid will be lost and engine will overheat.
Replace worn cap with new cap rated 13 to 15 lbs. pressure.
The radiator cap is found on the top of the radiator in the 4 and V6 engines. On the V8, it is in the top of the upper radiator hose. Some radiator caps, those used with a sealed system do not have the cap 'ears' found on most radiator caps. Removing these is a little bit harder, so use a cloth wrapped around it to prevent you from skinning your knuckles.

CHANGING THE ANTI-FREEZE

If the coolant is extremely dirty, add a good flushing additive to the radiator and run the engine the amount of time recommended on the can.
1. Turn off the engine and remove the radiator cap. Be careful when removing the cap if the engine is hot.
2. Open the petcock in the bottom of the radiator by turning its ears in a counterclockwise direction.
3. When all the coolant has drained out of the system, insert a garden hose into the radiator cap opening. Turn the water on in the hose and start the engine.
4. Allow the engine and the hose to run until the water coming out of the radiator is clean.
5. Turn off the engine and remove the hose. Allow the water to drain out of the system, then close the radiator petcock.
6. Pour the required amount of anti-freeze into the radiator and fill the rest of the system with water.
7. You can determine the required amount of antifreeze by checking the Capacities Chart, and checking this against the protection chart usually found on the anti-freeze container. Run the engine for at least five minutes to allow air to escape. Fill the radiator to 1 in. below the filler neck and turn off the engine. Recheck the level in the radiator after the car has been driven a short distance.

Suspension and Tires

The front wheels mount to, and rotate on, the spindles. The spindles are attached to the upper and lower control arms by the upper and lower ball joints. A coil spring is mounted between the upper and lower control arms on both sides of the front suspension. A pair of shock absorbers provide suspension dampening. The shocks are attached to the lower control arms and the tops of the spring housings.

A rod-type stabilizing strut mounts between two rubber pads at the front crossmember and each lower control arm. The strut aids the lower end of the spindle through its cycle of vertical movement and serves to cushion the fore and aft thrust of the suspension. A stabilizer bar is used to control suspension roll.

The Mustang II employs a semi-elliptic leaf spring rear suspension. The axle housing is supported by a pair of conventional, longitudinally mounted leaf springs. The housing is secured to the center of the springs by two U-bolts, retaining plates, spring pads and nuts. Each spring is suspended from the underbody side rail by a hanger at the front and a shackle at the rear. A pair of staggered mounted, telescopic shock absorbers are mounted (one in front of and one to the rear of the axle housing) between the leaf spring retaining plates and brackets welded to the crossmember.

Listed below are some items which will help you diagnose handling problems.

HOW TO PINPOINT HANDLING PROBLEMS

Manual Steering

HARD STEERING
1. Improper (low) tire pressure
2. Inadequate lubricant
3. Inadequately lubricated front-end parts
4. Bind in steering column
5. Excessive caster
6. Cross-shaft adjustment too tight

CAR VEERS TO ONE SIDE
1. Tire pressures or tread wear unequal
2. Improper front-end alignment
3. Improperly adjusted brakes
4. Faulty shock absorbers or springs

CAR WANDERS
1. Tire pressures improper
2. Improper front-end alignment
3. Play in pitman arm
4. Loose wheel bearings
5. Binding in steering linkage
6. Steering box loose on frame
7. Worn ball joints

POOR RETURN OF STEERING
1. Tires overinflated
2. Improper caster adjustment
3. Bind in steering column
4. Improper front-end lubrication. Steering gear adjustments too tight HARD STEERING

Power Steering

1. Improper (low) tire pressure
2. Loose or glazed pump drive belt
3. Low fluid level
4. Poorly lubricated front-end parts
5. Bind in steering column
6. Inadequate pump output pressure, due to worn pump parts or malfunctioning pressure regulator valve
7. Obstructions in pump lines
8. Excessive caster
9. Cross-shaft adjustment too tight

CAR VEERS TO ONE SIDE
1. Tire pressures or tread wear unequal
2. Improper front-end alignment
3. Improperly adjusted brakes
4. Faulty shock absorbers or springs

CAR WANDERS
1. Tire pressures improper
2. Improper front-end alignment
3. Play in pitman arm
4. Loose wheel bearings
5. Binding in steering linkage
6. Steering unit valve (rotary valve, spool valve, or pivot lever) malfunctioning
7. Worn ball joints

POWER STEERING NOISY
1. Belts loose or glazed
2. Fluid level low
3. Air in system
4. Kinked hydraulic lines
5. Foreign matter clogging hydraulic lines
6. Flow control valve sticking
7. Steering unit valve (rotary valve, spool valve, or pivot lever) worn
8. Worn pump parts
9. Steering gear mountings loose
10. Interference in front end

POOR RETURN OF STEERING
1. Tires overinflated
2. Improper caster adjustment
3. Bind in steering column
4. Improper front-end lubrication
5. Steering gear adjustments too tight

CHECKING YOUR SHOCK ABSORBERS

A shock absorber operates on the principle of forcing fluid through restricted openings in its internal valves. The opening in the valves helps control the motion of the car's springs as they react to the bumps in the road. The shocks aid in ride control, handling, tire life and steering, so their proper functioning is important.

1. Check under car and locate shock absorber near each wheel.

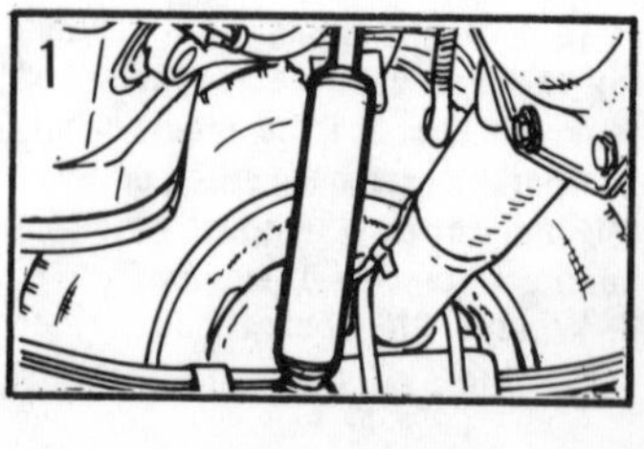

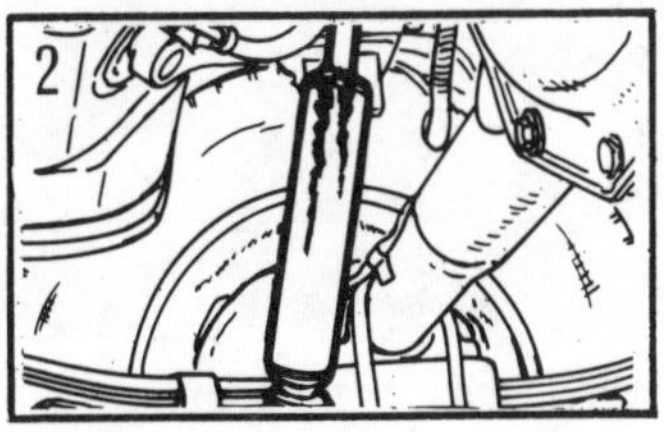

2. Heavy oil streaks on outer shock housing indicate need for replacement.

3. Stand at front of car and apply body weight in a pumping action to front bumper or fender. Release pressure and allow car to stop rocking. Car should not bounce more than one more time after releasing pressure. Repeat at rear. If bouncing continues more than once, replacement is needed. Replace shocks in pairs (front pair or rear pair).

4. If your car is equipped with air shocks, in addition to the above, check all the air lines for proper connections and general integrity. You can check for leaks by filling the shock with air and listening underneath for air leaks around the shocks. If you suspect an air leak but are unsure where it is, try applying a soapy water solution to the lines and connections; bubbles will appear at the point of the leak.

TOW HITCH INFORMATION

You should not tow any more than 1,000 lbs. with your Mustang II; towing any more than this amount for any prolonged period of time will seriously affect engine lifespan. When you are towing you should remember that your car is not going to react as it usually does; acceleration and braking will take longer, crosswinds will have more of an effect, and handling will be trickier than normal. When you are towing, remember to keep the items in your trailer lashed down securely and to keep a closer eye on the operating systems of your car which will be subjected to harder usage.

If your car is used for trailer towing you should check:

A. Cooling System; be sure coolant is at proper level in radiator. See Cooling System Section for checks to perform.

B. Check Transmission Fluid; keep topped up to proper level.

C. Check Rear Shock Absorbers; you may benefit from installation of new rear shocks.

D. Check Tire Pressures; best traction and handling can be ensured if tire pressures are properly maintained.

For safer and more trouble-free

trailer towing, consider:

A. Automatic Transmission Cooler; helps remove excess heat from automatic transmission fluid built up during towing mileage. Also helps avoid radiator overheating. Some units can be self-installed.

B. Radiator Over-Flow Tank Kit; addition of a reservoir to catch radiator coolant overflow preventing coolant loss. Easy to install, these units help a tow car run cooler, avoid overheating due to coolant loss.

C. Heavy-Duty Shock Absorbers or Air Shocks; important to have on rear wheels if you intend to do a lot of towing or load carrying within the car itself. Don't forget to consider replacing factory shocks, when they are worn out, with heavy-duty units at the front as well.

D. Variable Load Flasher; this unit will accommodate the added load of trailer turn signal lamps on trailer when these are hooked into your car's electrical system.

Ford recommends a non-equalizing hitch for the load your Mustang II is capable of carrying. You should not tow trailer over this weight. Before towing your trailer anywhere, it's a good idea to practice turning, stopping and backing up so that you will know how the car will handle before you hit the road.

When you are backing up your trailer, turn the steering wheel in the direction that you want the trailer to go, and remember, do not cut the wheel hard. A little bit of correction at the wheel turns into a lot of correction at the trailer. You should also check the trailer lights before you tow. When you start checking them, you will need a current tester to see if electricity is being supplied to the bulbs. If you are towing a boat trailer, don't forget to check all the connections for corrosion, especially near salt water. A coat of grease around the lens may keep some of the water from seeping in and corroding the bulb fittings.

When you're towing, don't forget to increase your tire pressure 3-5 lbs. and make doubly sure the lug nuts are on tight. It is also a good idea to check them again after you have towed the trailer 50-75 miles.

Ignition System

CHECKING YOUR IGNITION SYSTEM

The primary components of your ignition system are: the coil, primary and spark plug wires, the distributor and its internal components, and the spark plugs. Mustang IIs use two different types of ignition systems, the conventional and the breakerless. The conventional system was used on all 1974 models; the breakerless system on all models starting in 1975.

The two systems differ in the manner in which they convert electrical primary voltage (12 volt) from the battery into secondary voltage (20,000 volts or greater) to fire the spark plugs. In the conventional ignition system, the breaker points open and close as the movable breaker arm rides the rotating distributor cam eccentric, thereby opening and closing the current to the ignition coil. When the points open, they interrupt the flow of primary current to the coil, causing a collapse of the magnetic field in the coil and creating a high tension spark which is used to fire the spark plugs. In the breakerless system, a distributor shaft-mounted armature rotates past a magnetic pickup coil assembly causing fluctuations in the magnetic field generated by the pickup coil. These fluctuations in turn, cause the amplifier module to turn the ignition coil current off and on, creating the high tension spark to fire the spark plugs. The amplifier module electronically controls the dwell, which is controlled mechanically in a conventional system by the duration which the points remain closed.

On the conventional system, the points and condenser should be replaced every 12 months or 12,000 miles. On both systems, you should check the spark plug and coil wires, the condition of the distributor cap and rotor, and the coil condition. To check the points:

1. To ease access to the distributor, remove the air cleaner and position it to one side.

2. Disconnect the secondary cable from the coil at the center of the

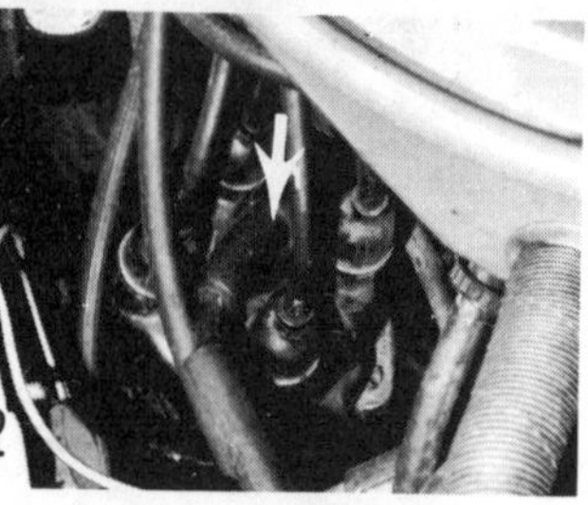
2

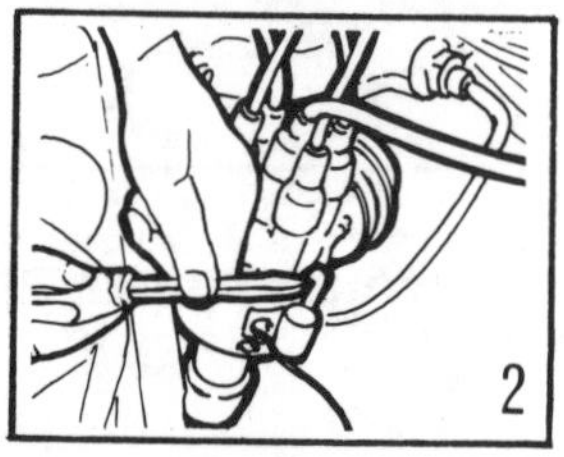
2

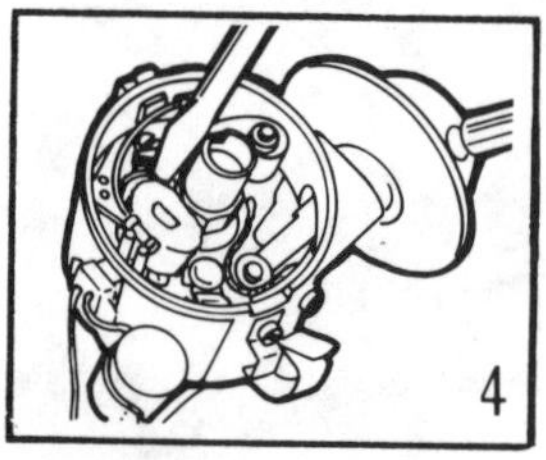
4

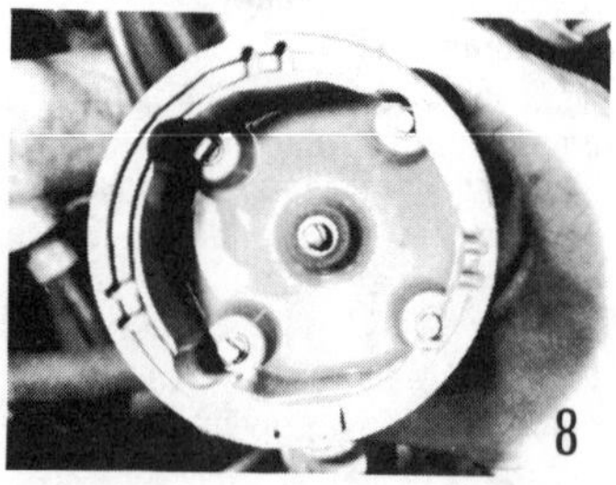
8

distributor cap. On distributors using clasps to secure the cap, pry the retaining clasps from either side of the cap using a flat blade screwdriver. On distributors using cross-head screws with "L-shaped" levers to secure the cap, press down on the screw head with a flat blade screwdriver and while maintaining pressure, rotate the screw head and retaining lever in either direction to free it from the distributor body. Then, lift off the cap (wires installed) and position it to one side.

3. Mark the position of the rotor by scribing a mark on the distributor body. Pull the rotor straight up and off. Discard it if it is cracked, burned or excessively worn at the tip.

4. Insert a screwdriver between the stationary and breaker arms of the points and examine the condition of the contacts. Replace the points if the contacts are blackened, pitted, or if the metal transfer exceeds that of the specified point gap (see "Tune-Up Specifications"). Also replace the points if the breaker arm has lost its tension (nonadjustable types) or if the rubbing block has become worn or loose. Contact points which have become slightly burned (light gray) may be cleaned with a point file.

5. In order for the points to function properly, the contact faces must be aligned. The alignment must be checked with the points closed. To close the points, install an open-end wrench on the crankshaft pulley/damper bolt and turn the engine over in its normal direction of rotation until the points can be seen to close. This may be more easily accomplished with the spark plugs removed.

6. If the contact faces are not centered, bend the stationary arm to suit. Never bend the breaker arm. Discard the points if they cannot be centered correctly.

7. If your Mustang II has the breakerless ignition system, there are no points to check. Instead, when you remove the distributor cap, check the area underneath the rotor for cleanliness. If there is any dirt in there, first try to clean it with compressed air, if this is not available, wipe it out very carefully with a clean lint free cloth.

8. Check the inside of the distributor cap for surface cracks, pitting and burned contacts. If any of these are present, discard the cap. Check the plug and coil wire for cracks in the insulation; if they are in poor condition, replace them.

SPARK PLUG REPLACEMENT

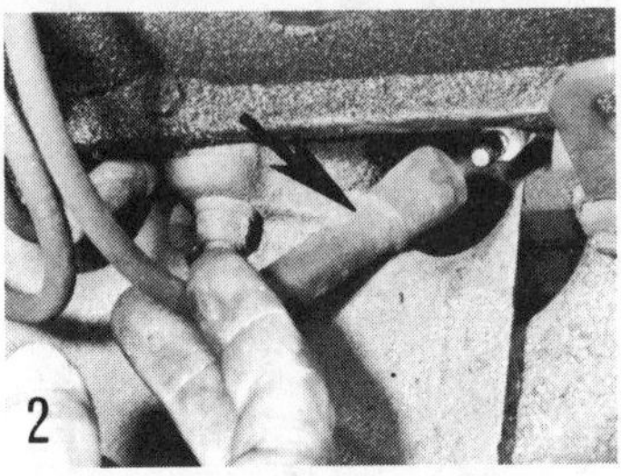

2

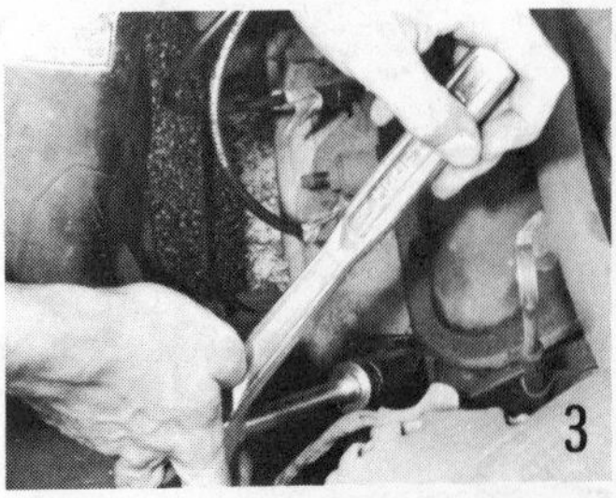

3

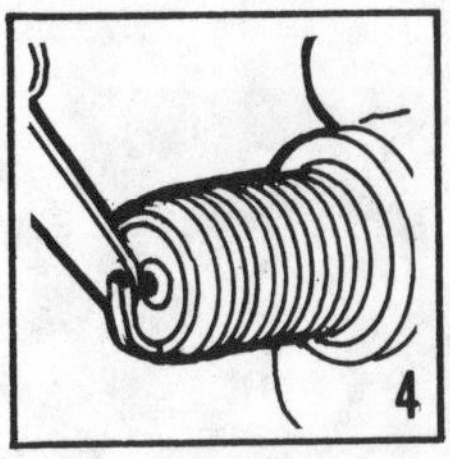

4

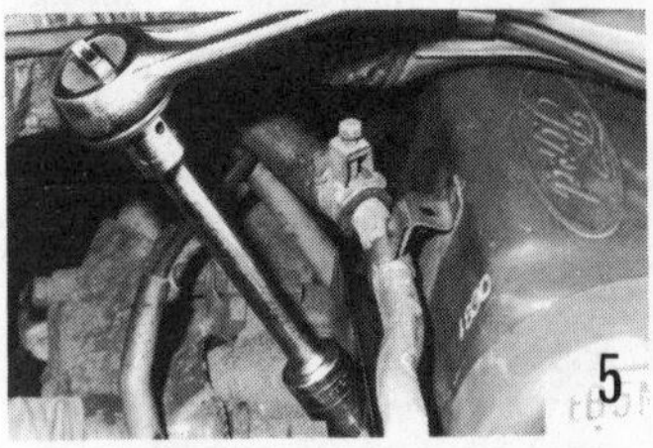

5

Every six months or 6,000 miles, the spark plugs should be removed for inspection. At this time they should be cleaned and regapped. At 12-month or 12,000-mile intervals, the plugs should be replaced.

1. Prior to removal, number each spark plug wire with a piece of masking tape bearing the cylinder number.
2. Remove each spark plug wire by grasping its rubber boot on the end and twisting slightly to free the wire from the plug.
3. Using a 13/16 or ⅝ in. spark plug socket, turn the plugs counterclockwise to remove them.
4. The gap must be checked with a feeler gauge before installing the plug in the engine. With the ground electrode positioned parallel to the center electrode, a wire gauge of the proper diameter must pass through the opening with a slight drag. If the air gap between the two electrodes is not correct, the ground electrode must be bent to bring it to specifications.
5. After the plugs are gapped correctly, they may be inserted into their holes and hand-tightened. Be careful not to cross-thread the plugs. Torque the plugs to the proper specification with a 13/16 or ⅝ in. (302 V8) socket and a torque wrench.
6. Install each spark plug wire on its respective plug, making sure that each spark plug end is making good metal-to-metal contact in its wire socket. Do not allow any foreign matter to enter the cylinders through the spark plug holes.
7. On Mustang IIs with the V6 engine, to gain access to the first spark plug on the right-side, you must reposition the alternator. This can be done by loosening the mounting and adjustment bolts and sliding the alternator upward.
8. On the V8, to gain access to the last two plugs on the right-side, you must remove the battery and battery holder. Also, the Thermactor by-pass valve should be repositioned for easy access to the first two plugs on the right-side.
9. If the spark plugs are to be reused check the porcelain insulator for cracks and the electrodes for excessive wear. Replace the entire set if one plug is damaged. Clean the reusable plugs with a stiff wire brush, or have them cleaned in a plug sandblasting machine (found in many service stations). Uneven wear of the center or ground electrode may be corrected by leveling off the unevenly worn section with a file.

REMOVING AND INSTALLING POINTS AND CONDENSER

1. To replace the points and condenser, loosen the nut at the center of the point assembly and slide the distributor primary lead and the condenser lead away from the terminal.
2. Remove the condenser retaining screw and the point assembly retaining screw(s) and remove the points and condenser.
3. While the points are out, clean the

2

3

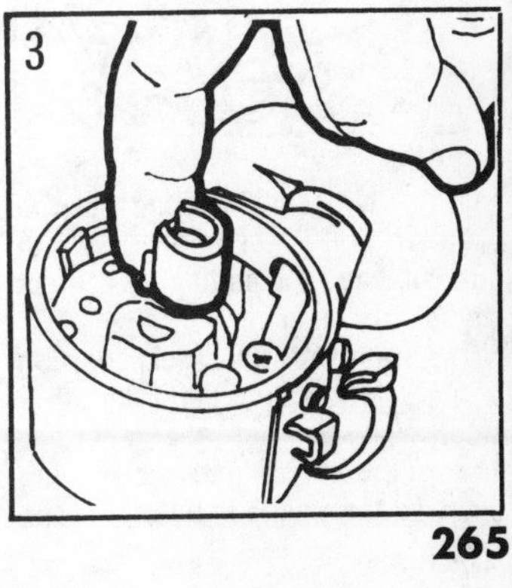

3

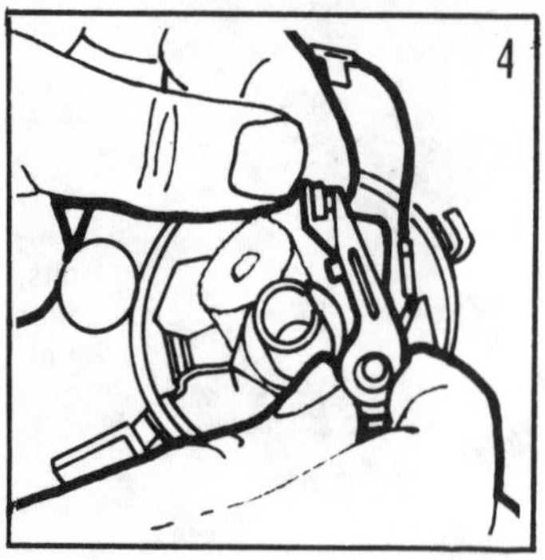

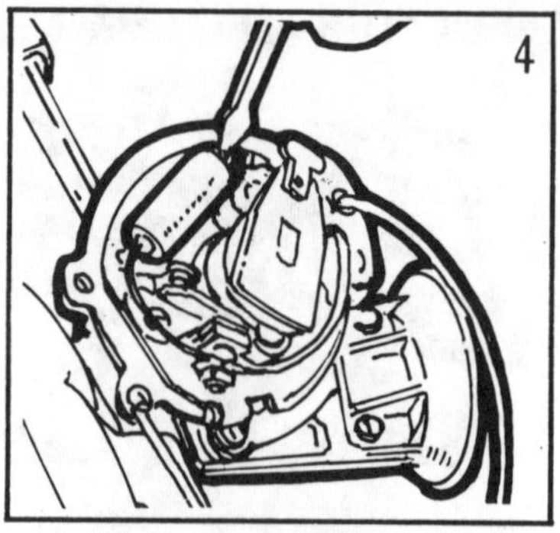

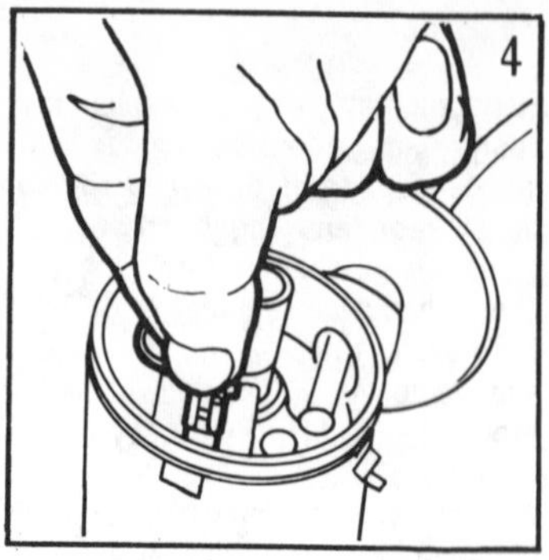

distributor base plate with an alcohol soaked rag to remove any oil film which might impede completion of the ground circuit. Also, lubricate the breaker cam lobes with a very light coating of silicone base grease.

4. Install the new points and condenser and tighten their retaining screws. Connect the electrical leads for both at the primary terminal. Make sure that the contacts are aligned horizontally and vertically as previously described.

The breaker points must be correctly gapped before proceeding any further.

5. Install an open-end wrench on the crankshaft pulley/damper bolt and turn the engine over by hand in the normal direction of rotation until the rubbing block on the point assembly is resting on the high point of a breaker cam lobe.

6. Loosen the point attaching screws slightly. Insert a feeler gauge of the proper thickness between the

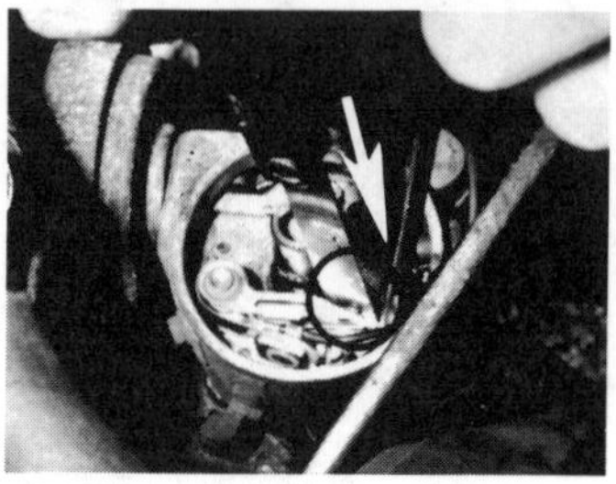

point contacts (see "Tune-Up Specifications").

NOTE: Wipe the feeler gauge clean of any grease or oil which will contaminate the point contacts.

7. The gap is correct when the loosely held feeler gauge passes through the contacts with a slight drag. If the gap needs adjusting, insert the tip of a screwdriver in the notch beside the points and twist to open or close the gap as necessary. Then, without disturbing the setting, tighten the breaker point attaching screw(s). Recheck the gap after tightening.

8. Replace the rotor on top of the distributor shaft, making sure that the tab inside the rotor aligns with the slot on the distributor shaft. Position the distributor cap on top of the distributor.

9. On distributors using clasps to secure the cap, snap the clasps into the slots in the cap. On distributors using cross-head screws with "L-shaped" levers to secure the cap, press down on the screw head and rotate the retaining lever until it is beneath the retaining boss on the distributor body, and then release the screw. Check that the cap is fully seated, and that the spark plug wires fit snugly into the cap. Connect the secondary cable from the coil at the distributor cap.

Use the firing order illustration to guide you when replacing your ignition wires and/or distributor cap.

ADJUSTING THE POINT GAP

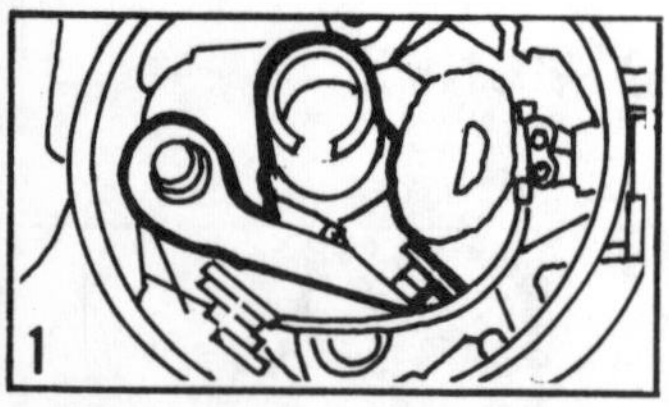

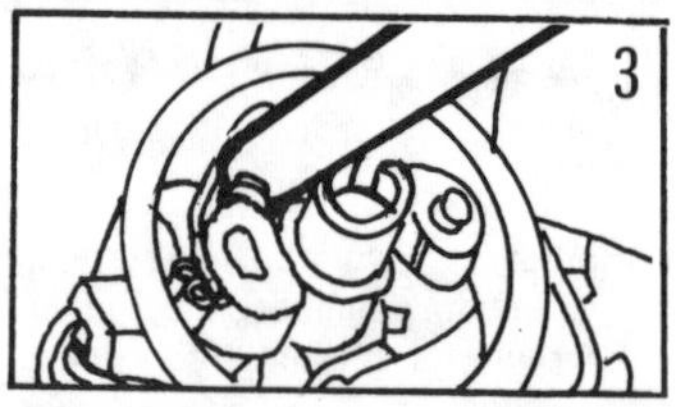

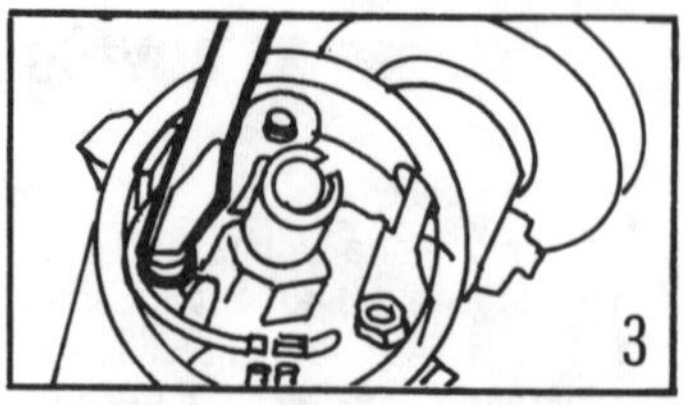

1. If the two contact points of the breaker point assembly are not parallel, bend the stationary contact slightly to correct.

NOTE: Bend only the bracket portion of the points, do not bend the other side.

2. Turn the engine until the rubbing block on the points is on one of the high points of the distributor cam. This can be accomplished either by having an assistant quickly turn the ignition switch to the "start" position and release it, or by placing the proper size wrench on the bolt in the center of the lower pulley on the front of the engine.

3. Insert the correct size feeler gauge between the open contacts of the points. To determine the correct feeler gauge size, see the point gap column on the "Tune-Up Specifications" chart in the front of this chapter. The gauge should fit between the contacts with a slight amount of drag. Always insert the gauge so that it is parallel with the

contacts on the points.
4. If the point gap is too large or too small, adjust as follows:
Slightly loosen the point attaching screws and insert a screwdriver in the notch in the breaker plate at the top of the points. Twist the screwdriver to open or close the points as required. Tighten the breaker point attaching screws when the correct gap is obtained.
5. Recheck the point gap to make sure it did not change when the breaker point attaching screws were tightened.
6. Push the distributor rotor onto the distributor shaft after aligning the tab inside the rotor with the notch on the shaft. Make sure the rotor is fully seated on the shaft.
7. Align the tab inside the base of the distributor cap with the notch in the lip of the distributor body opening. Install the cap on the distributor and make sure it is fully seated. Snap the distributor cap retaining clips into place on the side of the cap.
8. Install the coil high-tension wire. On models with air conditioning, after adjusting the ignition timing, install the alternator attaching bolts, install and adjust the air conditioner compressor belt, and tighten the attaching bolts on the alternator.

REPLACING THE SPARK PLUG WIRES

All you will need for this job will be the new set of spark plug wires. These are sold in kits of two basic types, the types where the wires are already formed, and the kind where you have to put the spark plug wire together yourself. The preformed kits are by far the easiest to install, but with the other kit you can tailor the wire to fit your need exactly with as little surplus wire as possible. Either way, when working on spark plug wires, you only work on one at a time.

1. Lay the new wires out before you so you can match up an old wire with its replacement to ensure a correct fit.
2. Starting from the rear, twist the boot on the last plug and remove it, then remove the wire from the harness.
3. Twist off the boot on the top of the distributor cap and remove the spark plug wire.
4. Compare it with the new wires and choose the one which most nearly matches it in length. If you are using the kit where you make the wire, do not forget to add about an inch on each end for the amount of wire inside the boot.
5. Insert the wire boot on the plug and make sure it is on snug. Push the wire on the harness and insert the other boot on the distributor cap, twisting it down if necessary to make sure it is snug.
6. All you have to do is follow these steps for the other plugs and your wiring job will be complete.

Use the firing order illustration to guide you when replacing your ignition wires and/or distributor cap.

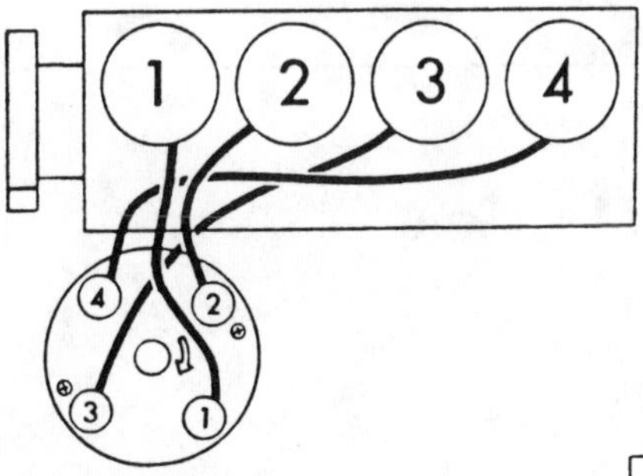

2300 cc Four

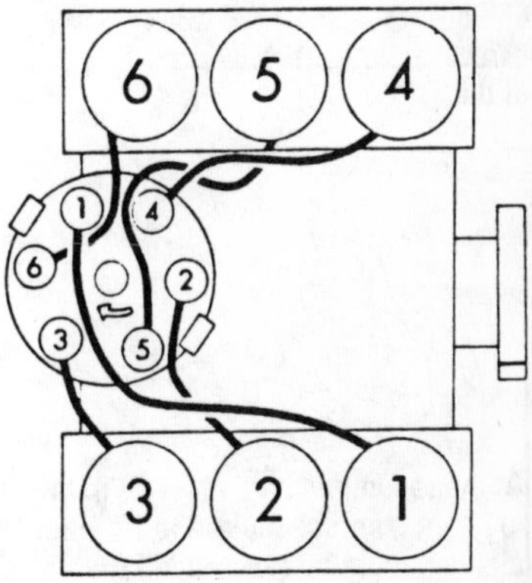

2800 cc V6

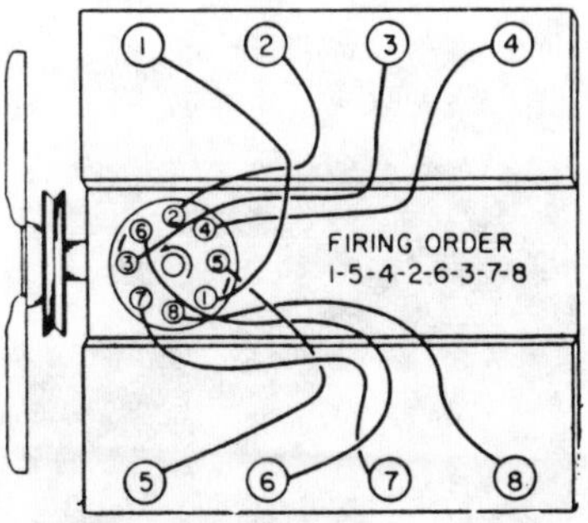

302 CID V8

ADJUSTING THE IGNITION TIMING

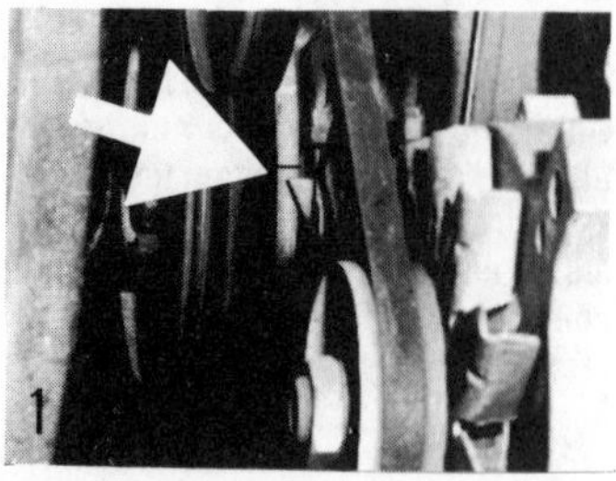

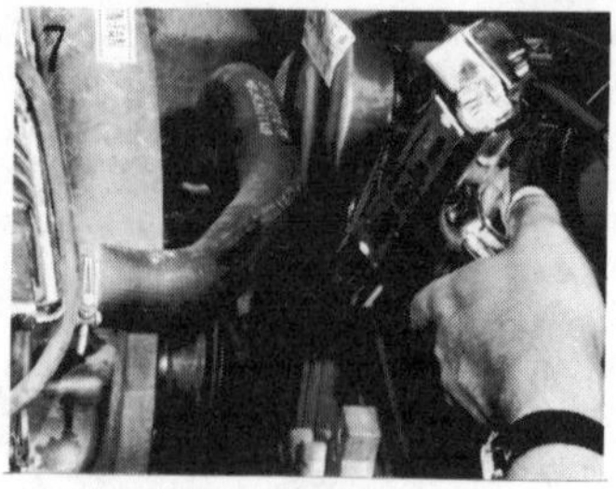

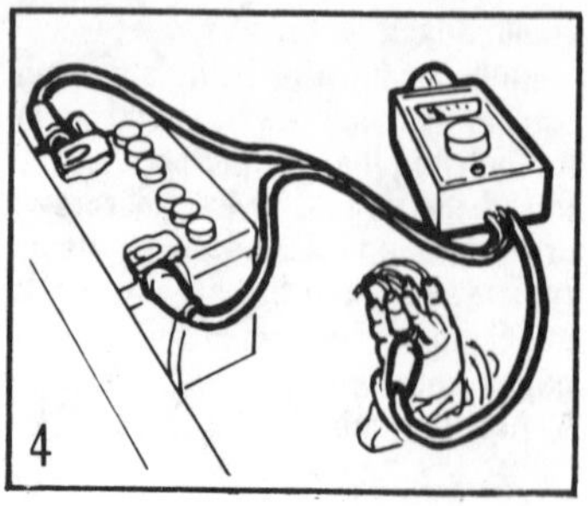

Ford recommends that the ignition timing be checked every 12 months or 12,000 miles. The timing adjustment should always follow a breaker point gap adjustment and be performed with the engine at normal operating temperature.

1. Locate the crankshaft damper/pulley and timing pointer at the front of the engine, and clean them with a solvent soaked rag or wire brush so that the marks can be seen.
2. Scribe a mark on the crankshaft damper/pulley and pointer with chalk or luminescent (day glo) paint to highlight the correct timing setting.
3. Disconnect the vacuum hose(s) at the distributor vacuum capsule and plug it (them) with a pencil, golf tee, or some other small tapered object.
4. Connect a stroboscopic timing light to the No. 1 cylinder spark plug (see firing order illustrations) and to the battery terminals according to the manufacturer's instructions.
5. Connect a tachometer to the engine. On 1974 models equipped with conventional ignition, attach one lead to the distributor primary wire connection at the coil and the other lead to a good ground. On 1975 and later models equipped with solid state (breakerless) ignition, connect one lead to the "TACH TEST" connection atop the ignition coil, and the other wire to a good ground.
6. Make sure that all of the timing light wires and tachometer wires are well clear of the engine. Start the engine and set the idle speed (if necessary) to the speed specified in the "Tune-Up Specifications" chart, using the idle speed adjusting screw(s).
7. Then, with the engine running, aim the timing light at the pointer and at the marks on the damper/pulley. If the marks made with the chalk or paint coincide when the timing light flashes (at the specified rpm), the engine is timed correctly. If the marks do not coincide, stop the engine. Loosen the distributor locknut and start the engine again. While observing the timing light flashes on the markers, grasp the distributor vacuum capsule—not the distributor cap—and rotate the distributor until the marks do coincide. Then, stop the engine and tighten the distributor locknut, taking care not to disturb the setting. As a final check, start the engine once more to make sure that the timing marks still align. NOTE: If necessary, readjust the idle speed to that listed in the tune-up specs. Timing is only correct at the specified rpm.
8. Once the engine is timed, reconnect the vacuum hose(s) to the distributor.

Fuel System

REPLACING THE AIR FILTER

At the recommended intervals in the maintenance schedule, the air filter element must be replaced. If the vehicle is operated under dusty conditions, the element should be changed sooner. On all V8 models, the air filter cover is retained with a single wing nut atop the cover. On 4 cylinder and V6 models, the cover is retained by either two wing nuts or by four metal clips.

1. To replace the element, unscrew the wing nut(s) or unsnap the metal clips, lift off the cover and discard the old element.

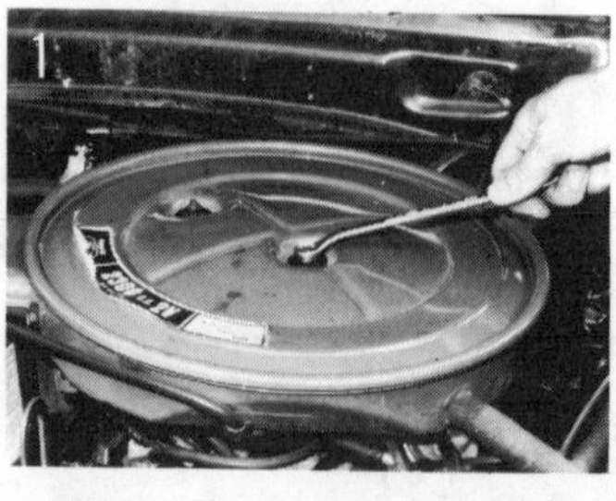

2. While the cover is removed, check the choke plate and external

linkage for freedom of movement.
3. Brush away all dirt and spray the plate corners and linkage with a small amount of penetrating cleaner/lubricant.
4. Wipe the air filter housing clean with a solvent-moistened rag and install the new element with the word "FRONT" facing front.
5. Then install the cover and fasten the clips or wing nut(s).
6. Make sure that all of the emission

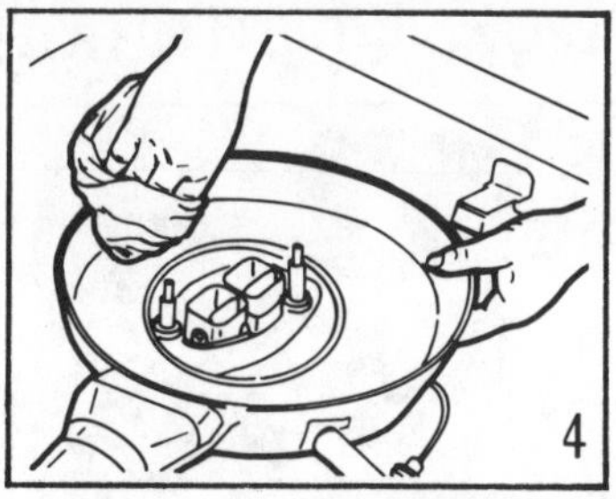

control hoses and ducts fit tightly to

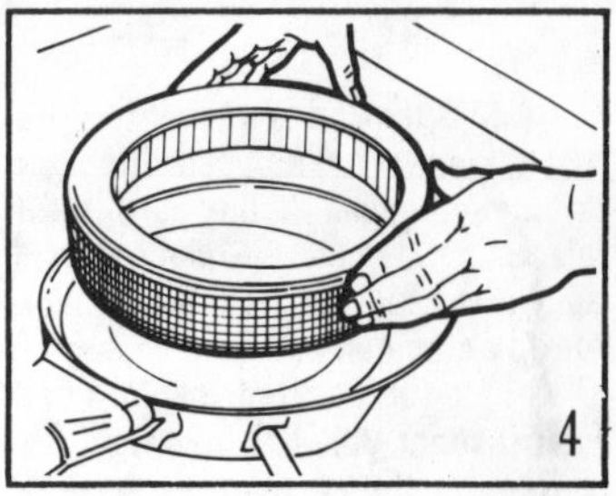

their connections at the air cleaner.

REPLACING THE CRANKCASE VENTILATION FILTER

1. Remove the lid of the air cleaner by unscrewing the wing nut(s) for the V6 and V8 or by unsnapping the clips on the 2300 cc.
2. Lift out and discard the small crankcase ventilation filter pad located in the bottom of the air cleaner.
3. Place a new filter in the pocket and replace the air cleaner lid.

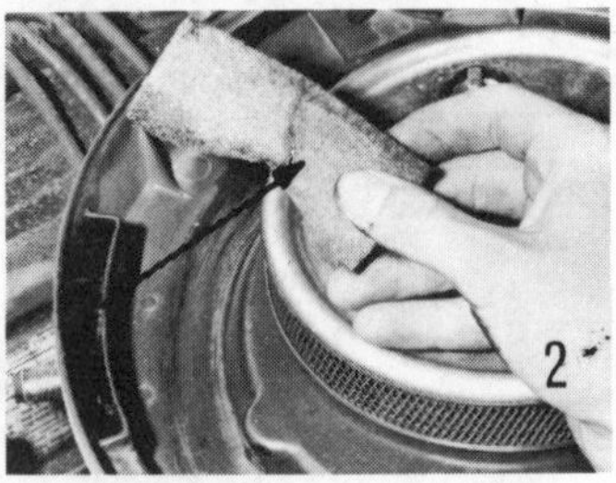

PCV VALVE REPLACEMENT

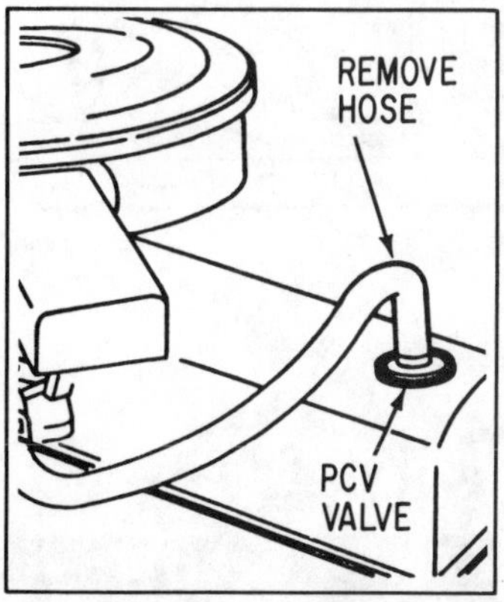

To replace the PCV valve, you must first know where it is, and on present models this can be a problem. On the 2300 cc engine, the valve is in the line between the intake manifold and the oil separator. On the 2800 cc V6, it is in the carburetor spacer. On the 302 V8, it is in the oil filler cap. Removal is simply a matter of pulling the hose off and pulling out the valve except on the V6. On this engine you first have to remove the hose clamp, and then, with a 9/16 in. open end wrench, you can unscrew the PCV valve.

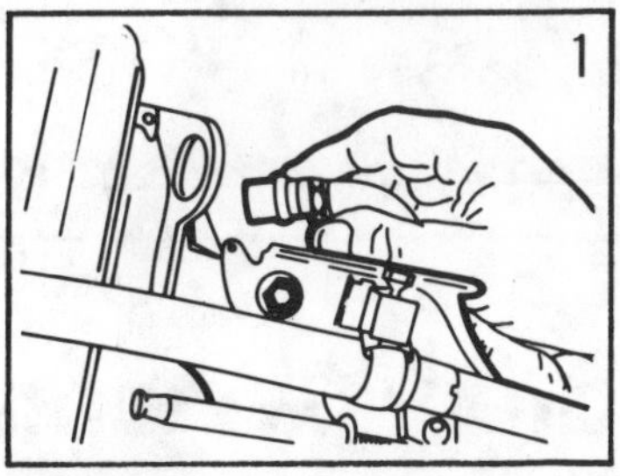

1. Remove the PCV system components, filler cap, PCV valve, hoses, tubes, fittings, etc. from the engine.
2. Soak the rubber ventilation hose(s) in a low volatility petroleum base solvent.
3. Clean the rubber ventilation hose(s) by passing a suitable cleaning brush through them.
4. Thoroughly wash the rubber hoses in a low volatility petroleum base solvent and dry with compressed air.
5. Thoroughly wash the crankcase breather cap, if so equipped, in a low volatility petroleum base solvent and shake dry. Do not dry with compressed air; damage to the filtering media may result.
6. Thoroughly clean tubes, fittings,

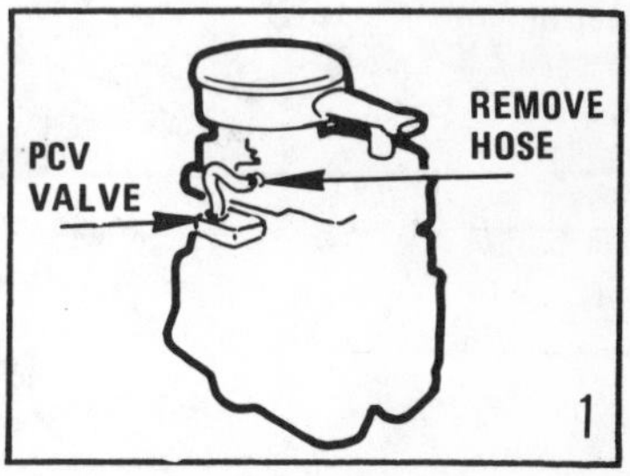

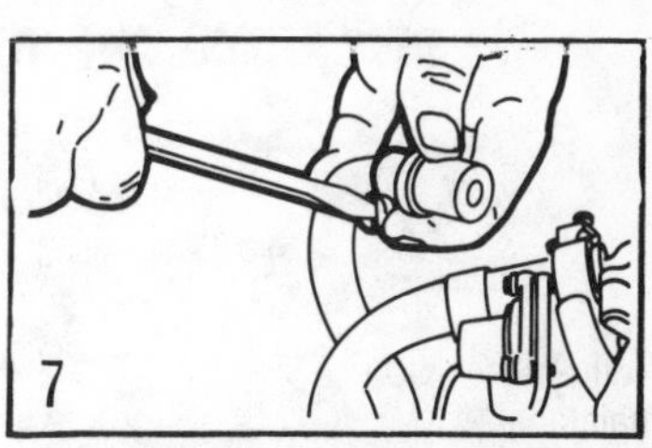

connections to assure unobstructed flow of emission gases.
7. Install new PCV valve and reinstall previously removed hoses, tubes, fittings, etc. to their proper location.
8. Replace any system component that shows signs of damage, wear or deterioration as required.
9. Replace any hose or tube that cannot be cleaned satisfactorily.

REPLACING THE FUEL FILTER

Every 12,000 miles or 12 months, the fuel filter must be replaced. The filter is located inline at the carburetor inlet on most models. Some early V6 equipped Mustang IIs use an inline fuel filter located near the fuel pump. The procedure for replacing the fuel filter (except V6) is as follows:

1. Remove the air filter.
2. Loosen the retaining clamp(s) securing the fuel inlet hose to the fuel filter. If the hose has crimped retaining clamps, these must be cut off and replaced.
3. Pull the hose off the fuel filter.
4. Unscrew the fuel filter from the

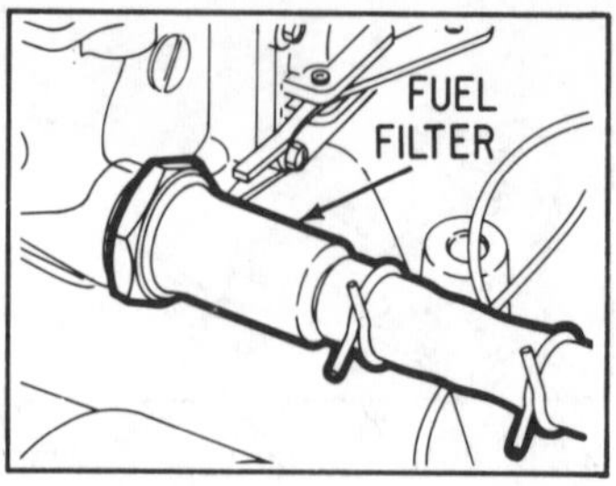

carburetor and discard the gasket, if so equipped.

5. Install a new gasket, if so equipped, and screw the filter into the carburetor.
6. Install a new retaining clamp onto the fuel hose. Push the hose onto the fuel filter and tighten the clamp.
7. Start the engine and check for leaks.
8. Install the air filter.

On V6 equipped Mustang IIs, replacement is a simple procedure of loosening the hose clamps, removing the old filter and installing a new one. Always make sure that the clamps have enough tension to prevent fuel leakage at the filter connections.

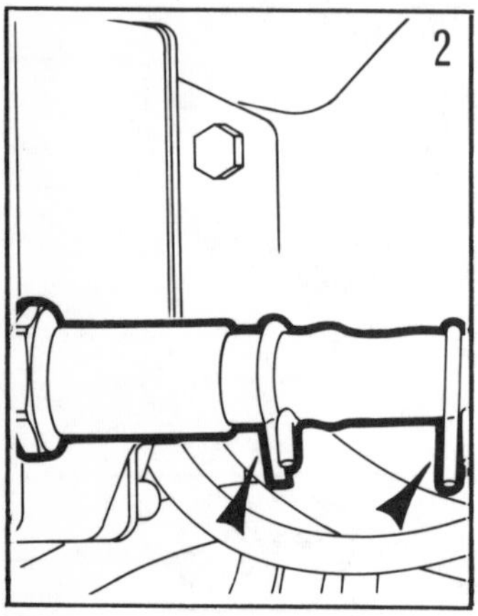

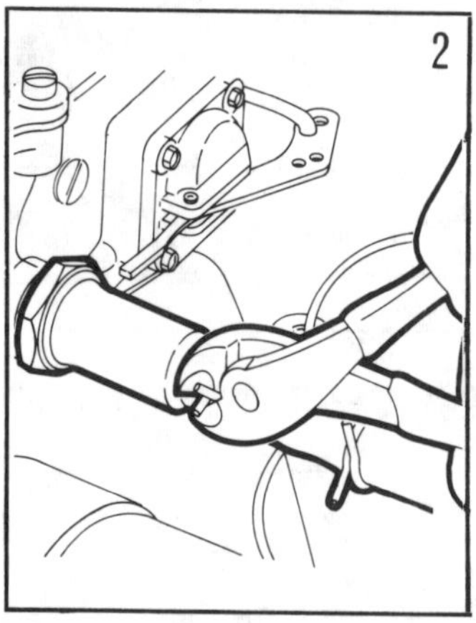

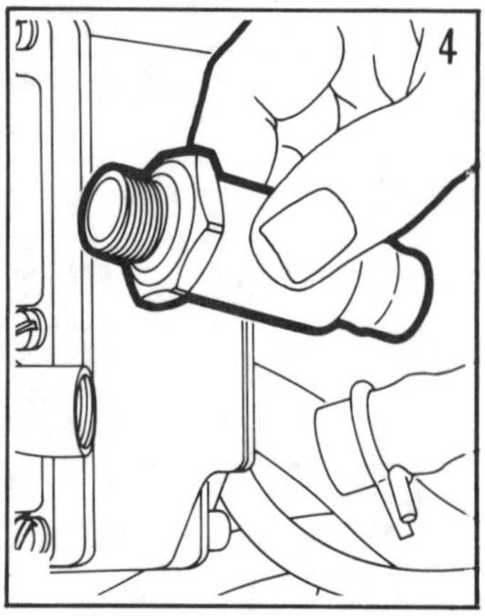

Safety Systems

REPLACING THE TURN SIGNAL, STOP AND BACK-UP LIGHT BULBS

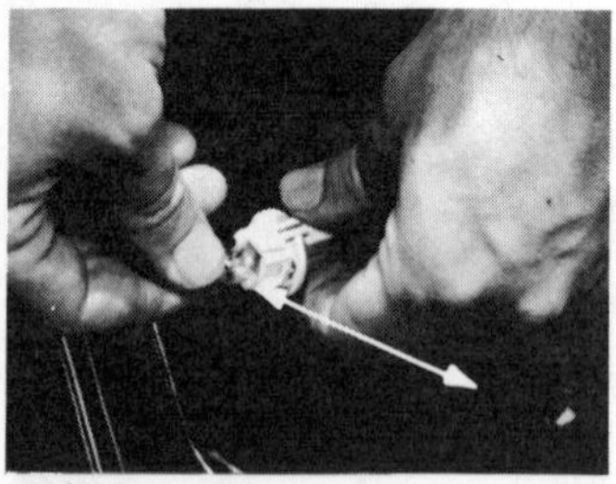

All of these lighting functions are performed by four bulbs. The front parking lights and front turn signal bulbs are mounted in the parking light housing in the grille. Each of these dual-element bulbs performs two functions for their respective

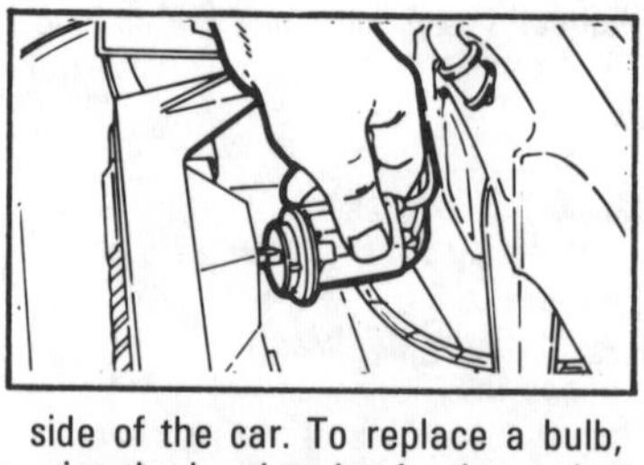

side of the car. To replace a bulb, raise the hood and twist the socket counterclockwise in its housing. When the socket has been removed, push down on the bulb and turn it counterclockwise to remove it from the socket.

The rear taillight, stop light, and turn signal functions are performed by

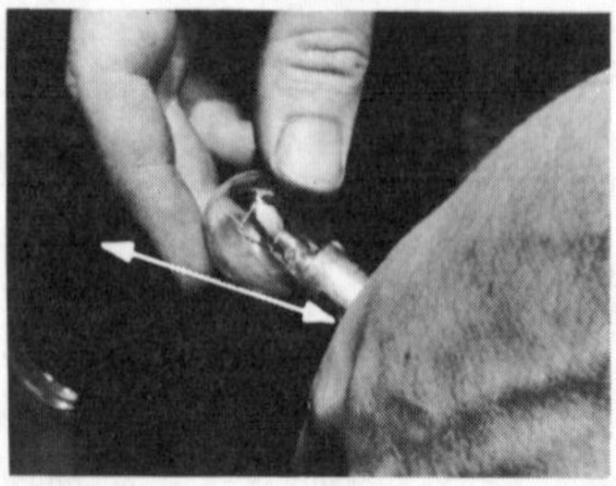

dual-element bulbs on each side of the car.

1. To replace a bulb, raise the trunk lid or rear door and turn the bulb socket counterclockwise.
2. When the socket has been removed, push down on the bulb and

turn it counterclockwise to remove it from the socket.
1. To replace a back-up light bulb, raise the trunk lid or rear door and turn the bulb socket counterclockwise.
2. To remove the bulb from the socket, push down on it and turn it counterclockwise.
3. To reach the light bulb socket on hatchback models, you must first remove the plastic trim panel covering them. It is held on with phillips head screws.

REPLACING THE INTERIOR DOME LIGHT

To gain access to the dome light bulb, pry the dome light lens out from the housing. After making sure the doors are closed and the headlight switch is not turned to the dome light "on" position, pry the bulb straight out of the housing.

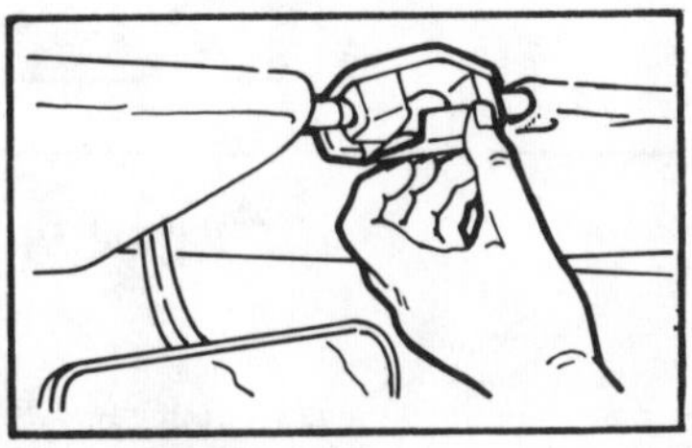

REPLACING THE HEADLIGHTS

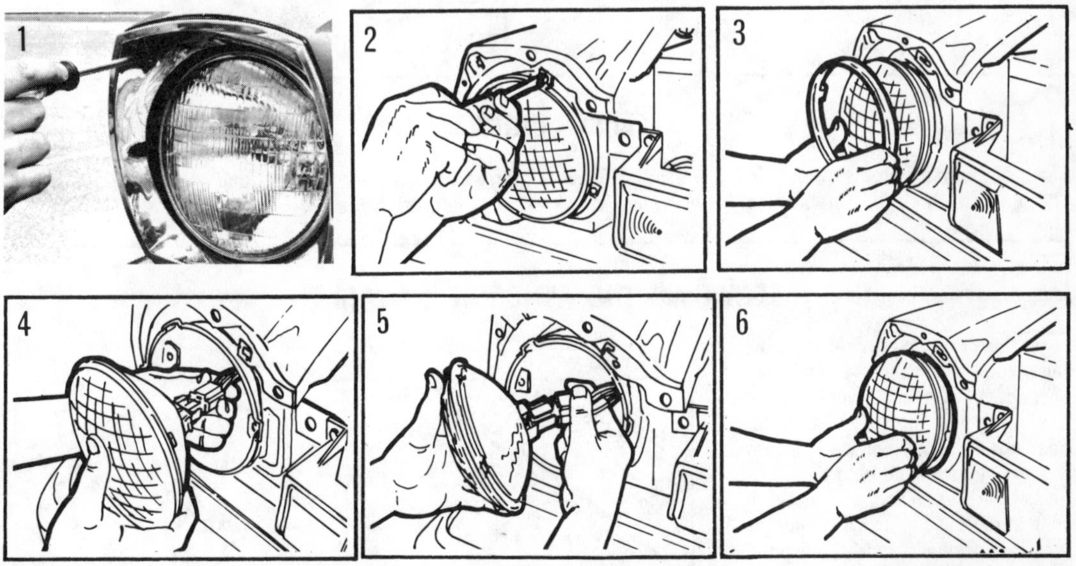

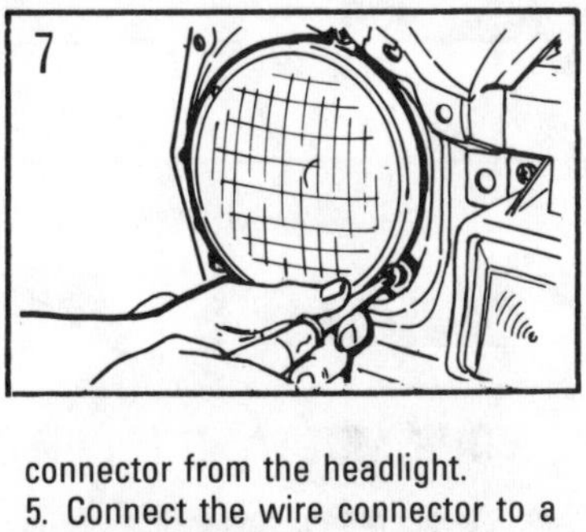

1. Remove the two headlight cover retaining screws and the cover.
2. Loosen, but do not remove, the three headlight retaining ring attaching screws.
NOTE: Do not mistake the headlight adjustment screws for the three retaining ring screws.
3. Rotate the headlight retaining ring to the left until the large openings in the attaching screw slots are aligned with the heads of the screws. Remove the ring.
4. Pull the headlight toward the front of the car and disconnect the wiring connector from the headlight.
5. Connect the wire connector to a new headlight.
6. Position the headlight in the headlight pot making sure the tabs on the back of the headlight enter the slots in the pot.
7. Position the retaining ring on the retaining screws and turn the ring to the right. Tighten the screws.
8. Position the headlight cover and install the attaching screws.

WINDSHIELD WIPER BLADE REPLACEMENT

To replace wiper blade, lift up on spring release tab on wiper arm connector. Pull wiper blade off. Snap new blade into place.
To replace rubber insert only, press down, away from wiper blade to free it. Slide insert from blade. Insert new wiper. Bend insert upward slightly to engage retaining clips.

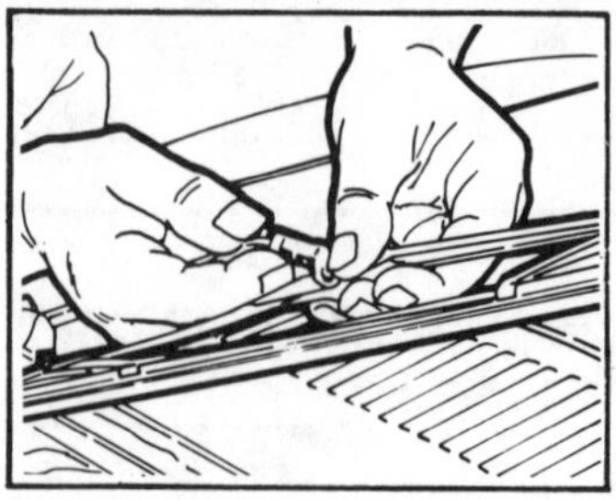

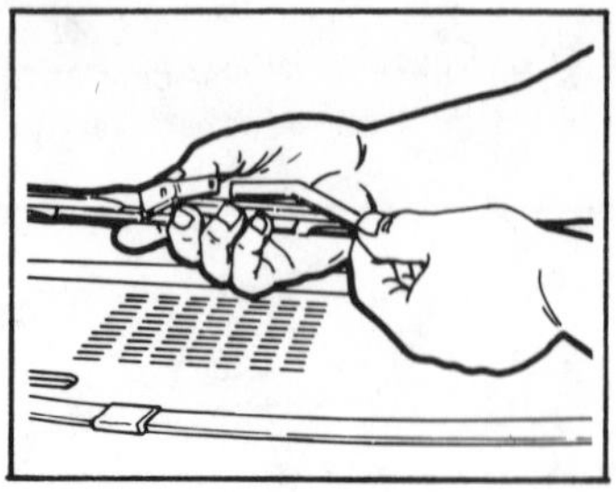

HORN PROBLEMS

If horn sounds and does not stop, this is due to short circuit in wiring. Disconnect wiring connector under hood and have professional service shop check horn wiring circuit.

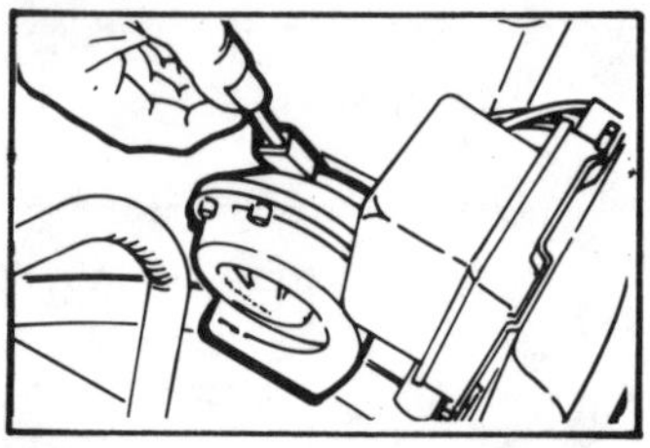

STEERING PROBLEMS

See handling problems check in Suspension Section. Check tire pressures. Have a professional service shop check all components in the front end and steering system.

SERVICING THE WINDSHIELD WASHER

If washer fails to squirt properly, raise hood and check system hose connections. Be sure washer fluid container has fluid. Check spout openings for clogging.
Keep container filled with fluid mixture of washer solvent and water. If road spray buildup on windshield is a chronic problem, add 1 tablespoon dishwasher detergent to solvent/water mixture when re-filling container.

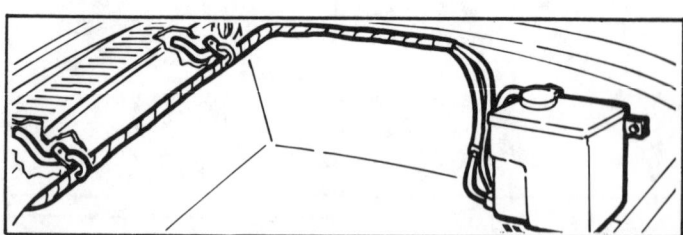

Electrical System

UNDERSTANDING YOUR MUSTANG II's ELECTRICAL SYSTEM

For any electrical system to operate there must be a complete circuit. This means that the power flow from the battery must make a complete circle. When an electrical component is operating, power flows from the battery to the component, passes through the component causing the component to perform its function, then returns to the battery through the ground of the circuit. This ground is usually (but not always) the metal part of the car upon which the electrical component is mounted.

Perhaps the easiest way to visualize this is to think of connecting a light bulb, with two wires attached to it, to your car battery. The battery in your car has two posts, negative and positive. If one of the two wires attached to the light bulb was attached to the negative post and the other wire was attached to the positive post, you would have a complete circuit. Current from the battery would flow out one post, through the wire attached to it, and then to the light bulb, causing it to light. It would then leave the light bulb, travel through the other wire and return to the other post of the battery. The normal automotive circuit differs from this simple circuit in two ways. First, instead of having a return wire from the bulb to the battery, the light bulb returns the current to the battery through the chassis of the vehicle. Since the negative battery cable is attached to the chassis and the chassis is made of electrically conductive metal, the chassis of the vehicle can serve as a ground wire to complete the circuit. Secondly, most automotive circuits contain switches to turn components on and off as required.

There are many types of switches, but the most common simply serves to prevent the passage of current when it is turned off. Since the switch is a part of the complete circuit, when the switch is turned off it breaks the circuit.

Some electrical components which require a large amount of current also have a relay in their circuit. A relay is simply an electrically operated switch, operated remotely by a control switch. The purpose of the relay is to avoid the current loss induced by routing the heavy current carrier circuit to the remote switch location. The horn circuit uses a relay.

Did you ever notice how your instrument panel lights get brighter the faster your car goes? That happens because your alternator (which supplies the battery) puts out more current at speeds above idle. This is a very normal thing, however, it is possible for larger surges of current to pass through the electrical system of your car. If such a surge were to reach an electrical component it would be burnt out. To prevent this, fuses are connected into the current supply wires of most of the major electrical systems of your car. When an electrical current of more power than a component is designed to operate on tries to pass through that component's fuse, the fuse blows (melts) and breaks the circuit to the component, saving it from destruction.

The fuse also protects the component from damage if the power supply wire to the component is grounded before the current reaches the component. Every complete circuit from a power source must include a component which is using the power. Let's go back to the earlier example of the light bulb with two attached wires being hooked to a battery. If you were to disconnect the light bulb from the wires and touch the two wires together (don't try it), the result would be a display of sparks. A similar thing happens (on a smaller scale) when the power supply wire to a component or the electrical component itself becomes grounded before the normal ground connection for the circuit. To prevent damage to the system, the fuse for the circuit blows to interrupt the circuit and protect the components from damage. Because grounding a wire from a power source makes a complete circuit (less the required component to use the power), this phenomenon is called a short circuit. The most common causes of a short circuit are the insulation on a wire breaking or rubbing through to expose the current carrying core of the wire to the metal parts of the car, or a shorted switch.

Some electrical systems on the car are protected by a circuit breaker. A circuit breaker is basically a self-repairing fuse. When either of the above described events takes place in a system which is protected by a circuit breaker, the circuit breaker opens the circuit in the same way that a fuse does. However, when the short is removed from the circuit or the surge subsides, the circuit breaker resets itself and does not have to be replaced as a fuse does.

All Mustang II models use a fuse link in the charging system. The fuse link is a short length of insulated wire, several gauge sizes smaller than the system it protects. The fuse link melts if a booster battery is wired into the system incorrectly, or if a component of the electrical system is shorted to ground. When the fuse link melts, it leaves an open circuit in the charging system and, consequently, the alternator will not charge the battery. A melted fuse link can be identified by bare wire ends or bubbled insulation. It is located in the engine wire harness on or near the starter solenoid.

CHECKING THE BATTERY LEVEL

The electrolyte level in the battery should be checked every few weeks. Remove the battery caps and check to see if the fluid level in the battery is up to the split rings in the bottom of the filler wells. If it is not, you can top it off with plain water unless you live in an area known to have hard water. If you do live in one of these areas, you should use distilled water. Fill the battery only to the split rings in the bottom of the filler wells. If you overfill the battery, the electrolyte will run out onto the pavement and you will be left with a battery full of plain water. Never light a match or use an open flame near the top of the battery, as the battery gives off highly explosive hydrogen gas.

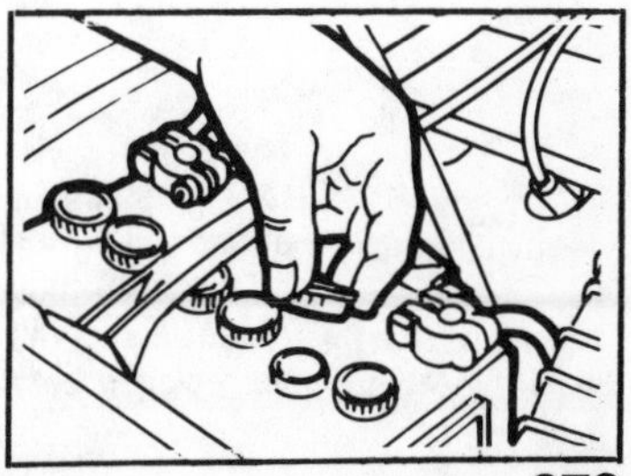

CLEANING THE BATTERY TERMINALS

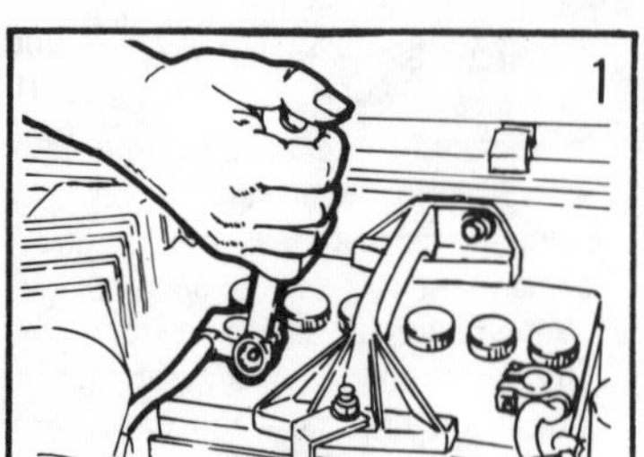

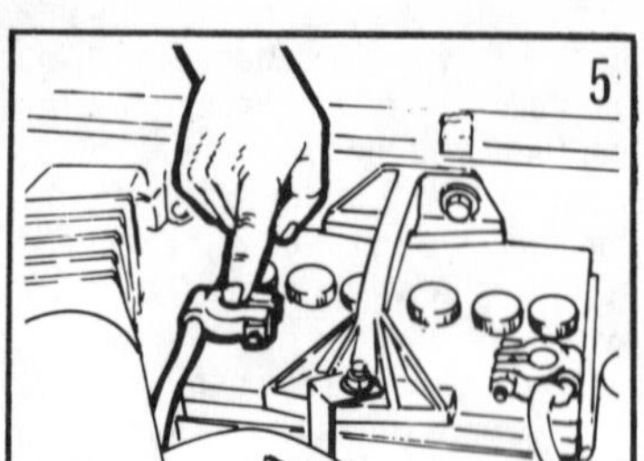

As time goes by, battery terminals build up a dry powdery, whitish material. This material is corrosive and will gradually eat thru battery cables if not cleaned off periodically.

1. Loosen and remove battery connections.
2. Brush off all loose corrosion; use stiff bristle brush. Do not get this material into eyes or on open cuts. Wash off at once.
3. If corrosion build-up is extremely heavy and brushing does not remove all of it, mix 2 tablespoons baking soda to 1 cup water. Pour solution directly onto terminals and connectors. Allow to soak a few minutes and rinse off. Continue brushing to remove all traces of corrosion build-up. Do not allow cleaning solution to enter battery.
4. Replace connectors on battery terminal posts and tighten. Do not hammer connection onto posts, but be sure they will not come loose with vibration.
5. Liberally smear battery terminal posts and cable connectors with petroleum jelly.

REPLACING THE BATTERY CABLES

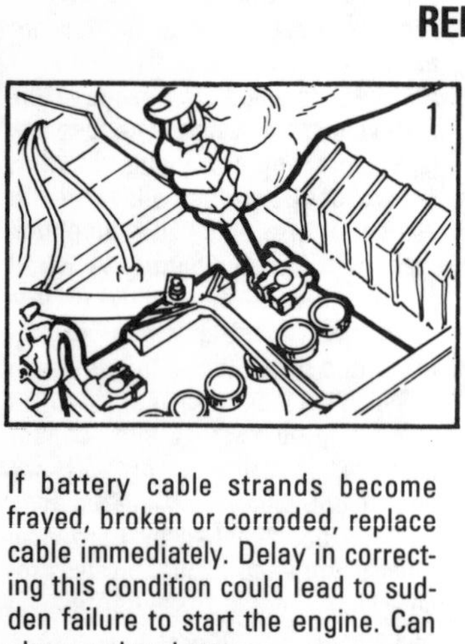

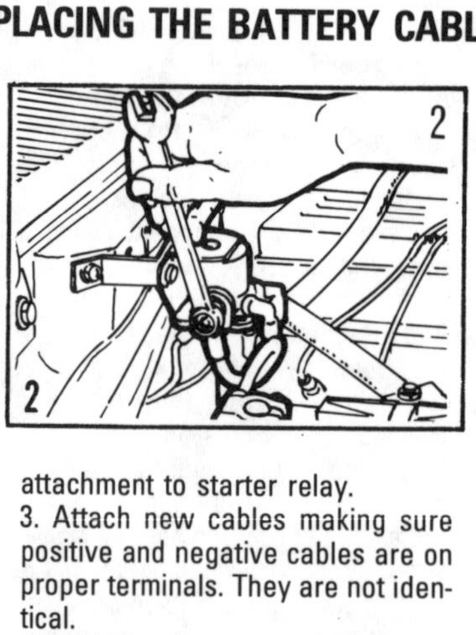

If battery cable strands become frayed, broken or corroded, replace cable immediately. Delay in correcting this condition could lead to sudden failure to start the engine. Can also weaken battery.

1. Loosen and remove battery connections. Clean OFF any corrosion.
2. Disconnect negative cable from its attachment to engine or chassis. Disconnect positive cable from its attachment to starter relay.
3. Attach new cables making sure positive and negative cables are on proper terminals. They are not identical.
4. Liberally smear battery terminal posts and cable connectors with petroleum jelly.
5. Replace connectors on battery terminal posts and tighten.

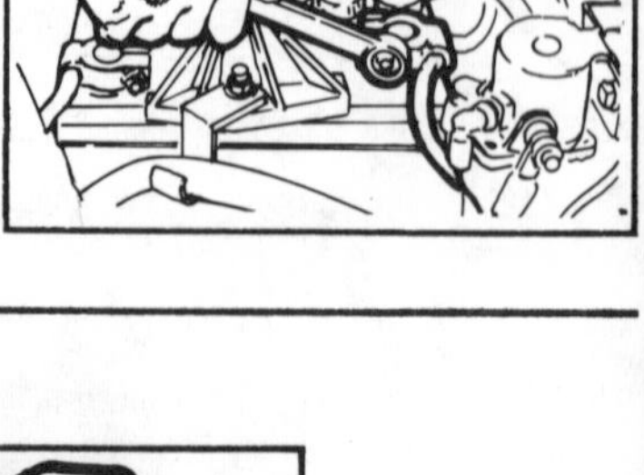

BATTERY HOLDDOWN

The clamp device which holds battery in place should be checked periodically. If loose, tighten. Clean off corrosion buildup. Severely corroded holddown components should be replaced before they break.

FUSE LOCATION

The fuse box is located to the right of the steering column, above the accelerator pedal. If you are going to replace fuses, one of the handiest devices available is a small fuse puller available at most auto parts stores. This will help you avoid breaking the old fuses as you remove them, and makes the job a lot easier than attempting it with a screwdriver. The Mustang II uses 4, 6, 7½, 15, 20, and 30 amp fuses. It is a good idea to buy some of these and leave them in your glove compartment so that when one blows, you will have one to replace it.

TURN SIGNAL AND FOUR WAY FLASHER

These flashers are both located on the fuse box. They are removed by simply unplugging them from their quick disconnect terminals. If your turn signal bulbs are alright, but will not flash on and off, the problem lies in the flasher unit.

ALTERNATOR CHECKS

Red alternator warning light on instrument panel should glow red when you first turn ignition key. This proves bulb is OK. Alt. warning light should go off when engine is running at normal operating speed.
If Alt. warning light glows red at operating speed, alternator isn't charging battery properly. Common causes are:
A. Fan belts are loose and slipping on alternator pulley. Tighten or replace belts.
B. Battery terminals, cables are loose or corroded. Clean; tighten; replace bad cables.

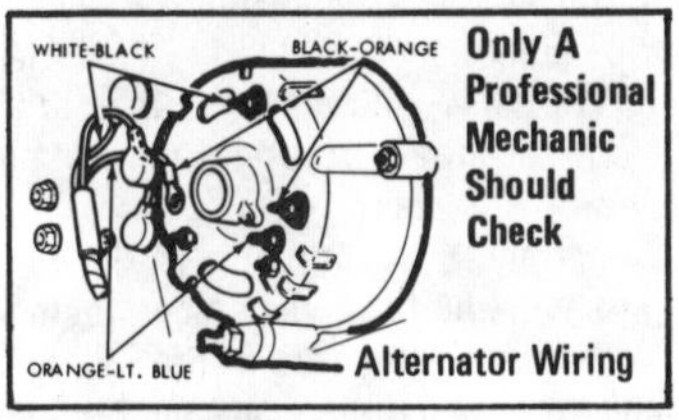

Alternator Wiring

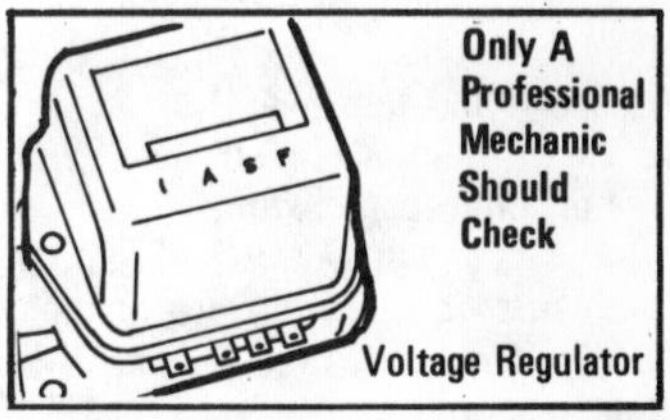

Voltage Regulator

If A or B do not correct problem, alternator or voltage regulator may be faulty. This happens far less often, and can only be checked by mechanic with proper electrical testing equipment.
Alternator Caution: Alternator can be permanently damaged by shortcircuiting terminal connections. When working around or moving alternator, always keep metal tools or engine parts from terminals.

REAR WINDOW DEFOGGER

Do not clean inside of rear window fitted with defogger system with any abrasive material. This could destroy carbon-copper wires. Use only soft rag and mild detergent/water mixture. Dry carefully.
When you clean the inside of the rear window, always clean with a side to side motion. An up and down motion might tear the defroster wires which would make the defroster stop operating.

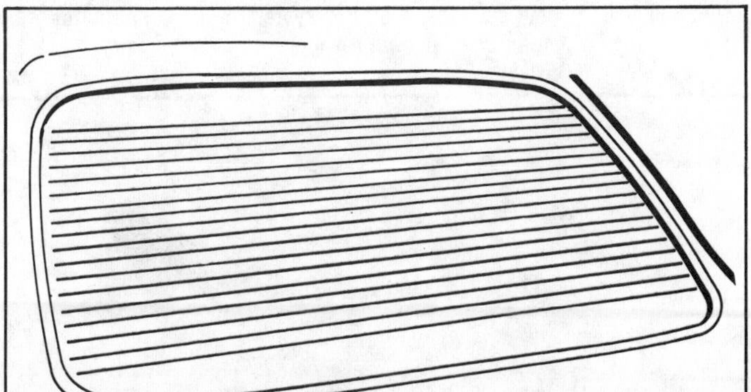

Air Conditioner

WARNING!—Never attempt to tighten fittings, disassemble or do any work on your Mustang II A/C system. Consult a professional mechanic about A/C system problems and their correction. Your auto air conditioner (A/C) is a delicate, closed system. If air, dirt or water get into it, or if refrigerant escapes, the A/C unit will not cool a car interior. Among things you can do are:

1. Keep condenser grill clean. Check for dirt and debris; periodically remove dead insects, leaves, etc., with stiff bristle brush. Straighten any bent fins—carefully.
2. Keep radiator filled to correct level. (See Cooling System section). If fluid needs to be added, add antifreeze rather than water.
3. Keep radiator coolant at a 50/50 water/antifreeze mixture.
4. Flush cooling system and replace with fresh coolant mixture at least every 24 months. (See Cooling System section).
5. Radiator cap should be tight and sealed properly. If sealing gasket is cracked, cut or worn, replace cap with new 12-15 lb. unit.
6. Check fan belt tension periodically. (See Cooling System section). Replace glazed, frayed or cut fan belts, before they fail entirely.
7. Check periodically for bubbles in A/C sight glass. The sight glass was last used in 1974. On 1975 and later models, pressure testing equipment is needed to check the condition of the refrigerant. Sight glass is located in head of receiver/drier vessel. Or in metal tubing leading from top of receiver/drier. Sight glass is no larger than head of large nail. It may be dirty. Wipe clean for best visibility.

Once a year, before hot weather sets in, it is advisable to check the refrigerant charge in the air conditioner system. This may be accomplished by looking at the sight glass located in the engine compartment, next to the radiator.

1. Wipe the sight glass clean with a cloth wrapped around the eraser end of a pencil.
2. Connect a tachometer to the engine with the positive line connected to the distributor side of the ignition coil and the negative line connected to a good ground, such as the steering box.
3. Have a friend operate the air conditioner controls while you look at the sight glass. Have your friend set the dash panel control to maximum cooling. Start the engine and idle at 1,500 rpm.
4. While looking at the sight glass, signal your friend to turn the blower switch to the High position.
5. If a few bubbles appear immediately after the blower is turned on and then disappear, the system is sufficiently charged with refrigerant. If, on the other hand, a large amount of bubbles, foam or froth continue after the blower has operated for a few seconds, then the system is in need of additional refrigerant. If no bubbles appear at all, then there is either sufficient refrigerant in the system, or it is bone dry.
6. The way to clear this question up is to have your friend turn the blower switch off and on (engine running at 1,500 rpm) about every 10 seconds or so while you look at the sight glass. This will cycle the magnetic clutch. If the system is properly charged, bubbles will appear in the sight glass a few seconds after the blower is turned off and disappear when the blower is turned on although they may linger awhile in extremely hot weather.
7. If no bubbles appear when the blower is in the "OFF" position, then the system should be serviced by an authorized dealer and checked for leaks.

AIR CONDITIONING COMPRESSOR DRIVE BELT

1. Position a ruler perpendicular to the drive belt at its longest run. Test the tightness of the belt by pressing it firmly with your thumb. The deflection should not exceed ¼ in.
2. If the engine is equipped with an idler pulley, loosen the idler pulley adjusting bolt, insert a pry bar between the pulley and the engine (or in the idler pulley adjusting slot), and adjust the tension accordingly. If the engine is not equipped with an idler pulley, the alternator must be moved to accomplish this adjustment, as outlined under "Adjusting the Fan Belt."
3. When the proper tension is reached, tighten the idler pulley adjusting bolt (if so equipped) or the alternator adjusting and mounting bolts.

TUNE-UP SPECIFICATIONS

YEAR	ENGINE No. Cyl. Displacement (cu. in.)	SPARK PLUGS Type	SPARK PLUGS Gap (in.)	DISTRIBUTOR Point Dwell (deg.)	DISTRIBUTOR Point Gap (in.)	IGNITION TIMING Man. Trans.● (deg.)■	IGNITION TIMING Auto Trans.● (deg.)■	IDLE SPEED Man. Trans.● (rpm)▲	IDLE SPEED Auto Trans. (rpm)▲
1974	4-140 (2300 cc)	AGRF-52	.034	35-41	.027	6B @ 750	6B @ 750	750N	750D
	6-170.8 (2800 cc)	AGR-42	.044	35-41	.024	12B @ 750	12B @ 650	750N	750D
1975	4-140 (2300 cc)	AGRF-52	.034	Electronic		6B @ 550	6B @ 550 (10B @ 550)	750N	650D
	6-170.8 (2800 cc)	AGR-42	.034	Electronic		6B @ 850	10B @ 700 (8B @ 700)	850N	700D
	8-302 (4900 cc)	ARF-42	.044	Electronic		——	20B	——	700D
1976	4-140 (2300 cc)	AGRF-52	.034	Electronic		6B @ 550	20B @ 550	850N	750D
	6-170.8 (2800 cc)	AGR-42	.034	Electronic		10B @ 850 (8B @ 650)	12B @ 700① (6B @ 650)	850N	700D (800D)
	8-302 (4900 cc)	ARF-42	.044	Electronic		——	6B @ 650 (8B @ 500)	——	700D
1977	4-140 (2300 cc) 6-170.8 (2800 cc) 8-302 (4900 cc)	See Underhood Specifications Sticker							

▲ Adjust automatic transmissions in Drive (AMC/Ford/GM) or Neutral (Chrysler), all manual transmissions are adjusted in Neutral.
■ All figures are Before Top Dead Center.
● Figure in parentheses indicate California engine.
—— Not applicable

NOTE: The underhood specifications sticker often reflects tune-up specification changes made in production. Sticker figures must be used if they disagree with those in this chart.

CAPACITIES

YEAR	ENGINE No. Cyl. Displacement (cu. in.)	ENGINE OIL Add 1 qt. with New Filter	TRANSMISSION Pts. to Refill after Draining MANUAL 3-speed	MANUAL 4-speed	AUTOMATIC	DRIVE AXLE (pts.)	COOLING SYSTEM with Heater (qts.)	COOLING SYSTEM with Air Cond. (qts.)
1974	4-140 (2300 cc)	4	——	4.0	16.0	4.0	8.8	9.2
	6-170.8 (2800 cc)	4.5①	——	4.0	15.0	4.0	12.5	12.8
1975-76	4-140 (2300 cc)	4.0	——	3.5	16.0	4.0	8.5	9.1
	6-170.8 (2800 cc)	4.5①	——	3.5	15.0	4.0	12.3	13.2
	8-302 (4900 cc)	4.0	——	3.5	15.0	4.0	16.3	16.3
1977	4-140 (2300 cc)	4.0	——	3.5	16.0	4.5	2.5	9.1
	6-170.8 (2800 cc)	4.5①	——	3.5	15.0	4.5	12.3	13.2
	8-302 (4900 cc)	4.0	——	3.5	15.0	4.5	16.3	16.3

① Add only ½ qt. for new filter
—— Not applicable

Service Record

DATE/MILEAGE	SERVICE	NEXT DUE

Nova/Ventura/Apollo/Omega/Skylark

Lubrication and Oil Change

CHECKING OIL LEVEL

GM SAYS . . . Check engine oil level at every fuel stop
Tools and Materials . . . Clean rag, oil as needed, oil can spout or funnel
Recommended Grade of Oil . . . SE
1. Wait five minutes if engine has been running. The car must be level.
2. Locate the dipstick in the tube at the side of the engine.
3. Pull the dipstick out and wipe it dry with the clean rag.
4. Replace the dipstick, wait ten seconds, and pull it out again. Check the oil level. Replace the dipstick.
5. Add oil if the level is below FULL. If it is at ADD, you can add a full quart. Add oil at the oil filler cap opening on the engine valve rocker cover or at the front of the engine.
Caution: Overfilling can damage engine seals and cause rapid oil consumption.

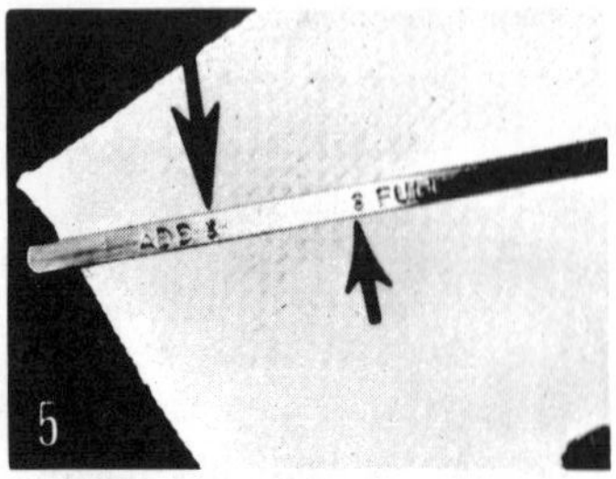

BRAKE FLUID LEVEL CHECK

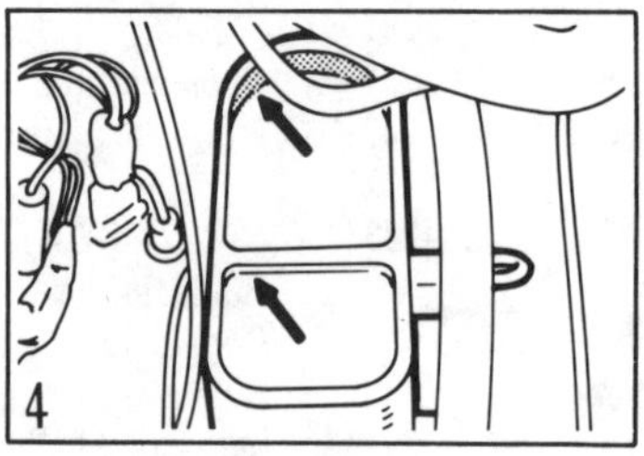

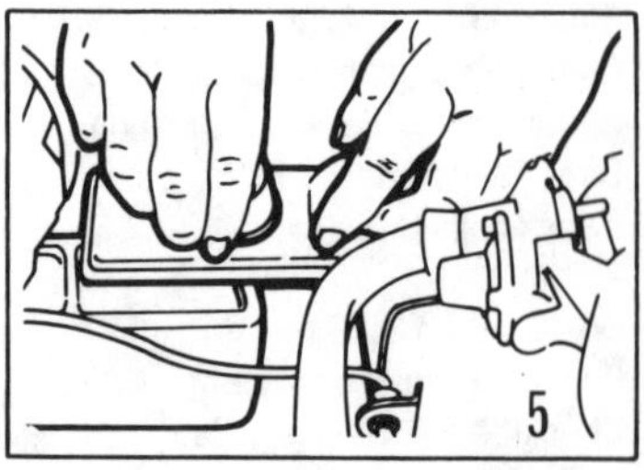

GM SAYS . . . Check brake fluid level every six months
Tools and Materials . . . Clean rag, fluid as needed, screwdriver
Recommended Grade of Brake Fluid . . . Conforming to DOT 3 specifications

1. Locate the master brake cylinder at the left rear of the engine compartment. Clean off all dirt from around cap. The car must be level.
2. Pry the wire retaining clip off the cap top with a screwdriver.
3. Remove the cap and gasket by lifting up.
4. Fluid level should be within ¼ in. of lowest edge of each reservoir. Add fluid as necessary.
5. Replace cap and gasket; secure retaining clip. If level was low, check again soon. If fluid is repeatedly low, there is a leak; have a mechanic check the system.

Caution: Don't leave brake fluid containers or master cylinder open any longer than necessary. Brake fluid picks up damaging moisture from the air.

CHECKING MANUAL TRANSMISSION FLUID LEVEL

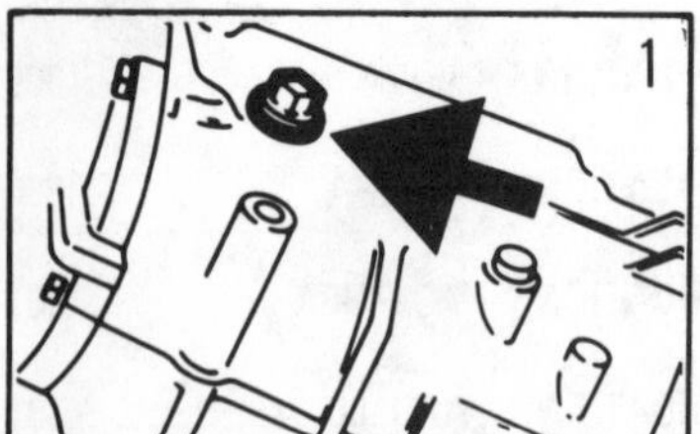

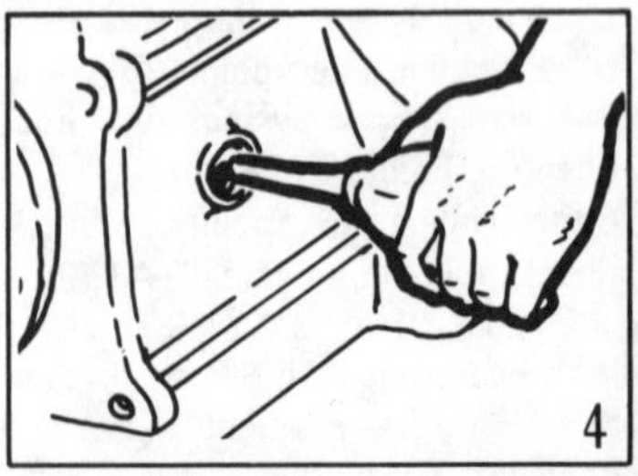

GM SAYS . . . Check transmission fluid level every four months

Tools and Materials . . . Adjustable wrench, screwdriver, suction gun, fluid as needed
Recommended grade of lubricant . . . SAE 80W or 80W-90 GL-5 gear lubricant, five speed transmission requires DEXRON® II

1. Locate transmission fluid filler plug on side of transmission housing under car. The car must be level.
2. Wipe off and remove filler plug.
3. Insert screwdriver to check level. Fluid level should be up to bottom edge of filler hole.
4. Add lubricant as needed with suction gun.
5. Replace and tighten filler plug.

CHECKING AUTOMATIC TRANSMISSION FLUID LEVEL

GM SAYS . . . Check transmission fluid level at every oil change (6000 mi. through 1974, 7500 mi. starting 1975)

Tools and Materials . . . Funnel, fluid as needed, clean rag
Recommended grade of lubricant . . . Dexron® II or Type A

1. The engine should be thoroughly warmed up and running. The car must be level. The transmission must be in Park.
2. Locate the dipstick at the rear of the engine. Pull it out, wipe it off, and replace it.
3. Wait ten seconds; pull out the dipstick and check the level.
4. If the fluid on the dipstick is hot, it should be between ADD and FULL. If it is warm, it should be at the ADD mark. The distance between ADD and FULL is one pint.

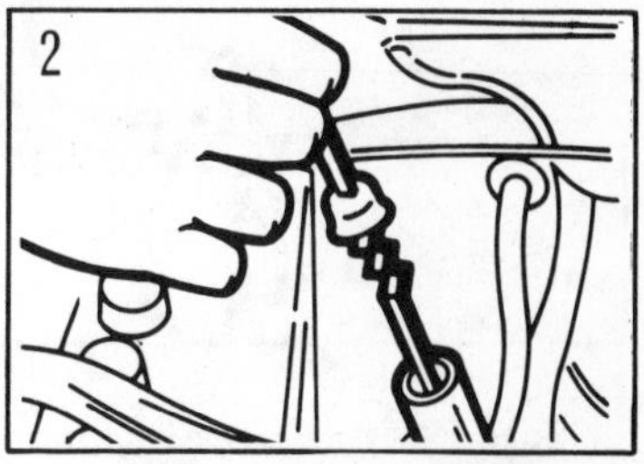

5. Use the funnel to add fluid through the dipstick tube.

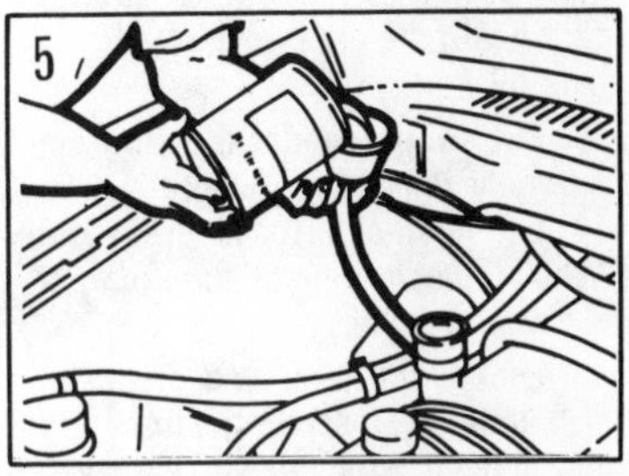

Caution: Overfilling will cause foaming and fluid loss.

CHECKING REAR AXLE LUBRICANT LEVEL

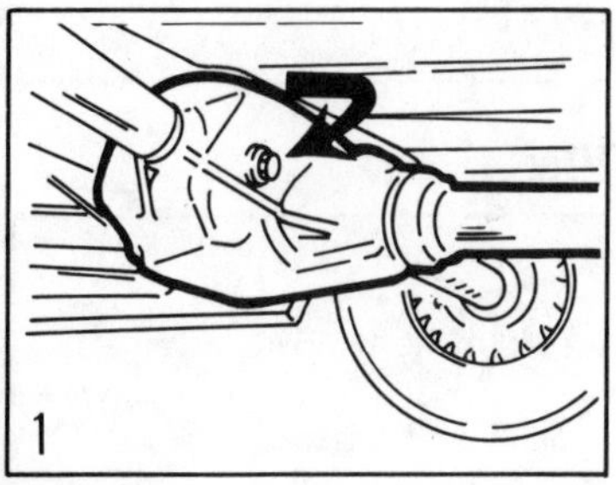

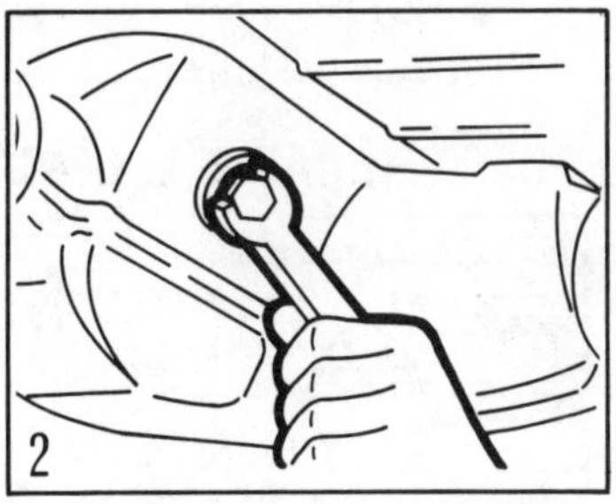

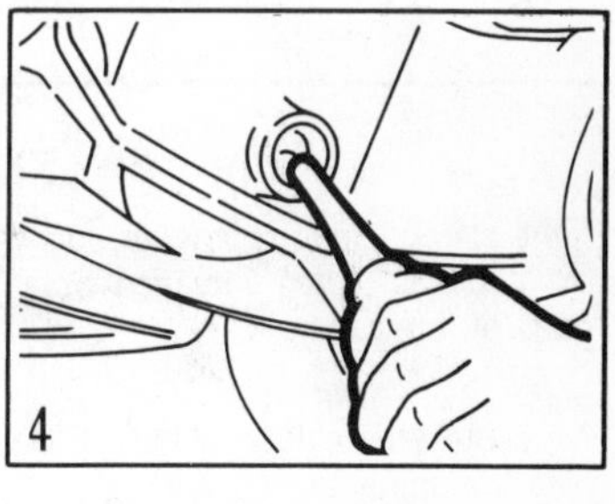

GM SAYS . . . Check rear axle lubricant level at every oil change (6000 mi. through 1974, 7500 mi. thereafter)

Tools and Materials . . . Adjustable wrench, rag, screwdriver, suction gun, lubricant as needed
Recommended grade of lubricant . . . SAE 80W or 80W-90 GL-5 gear lubricant, limited slip or Positraction axles require a special lubricant

1. The car must be level. Locate the filler plug on the forward side or rear cover of the rear axle center (differential) housing.
2. Wipe the area clean and remove the filler plug.
3. Insert the screwdriver to check the level. The fluid should be right up to the plug opening.
4. Add lubricant as needed with suction gun.
5. Replace and tighten the filler plug.

CHANGING ENGINE OIL AND FILTER

GM SAYS . . . Change engine oil every 6000 mi. through 1974, 7500 mi. thereafter; change filter at every second oil change
Tools and Materials . . . Adjustable wrench, oil pouring spout or funnel, filter wrench, oil drain pan of six or more quarts capacity, amount of oil specified in Capacities Chart, filter

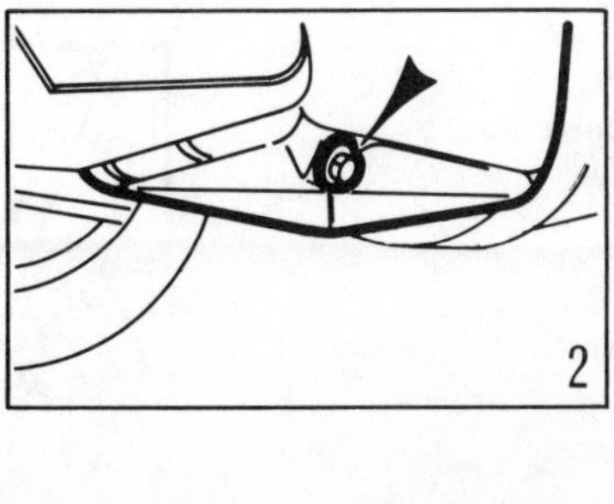

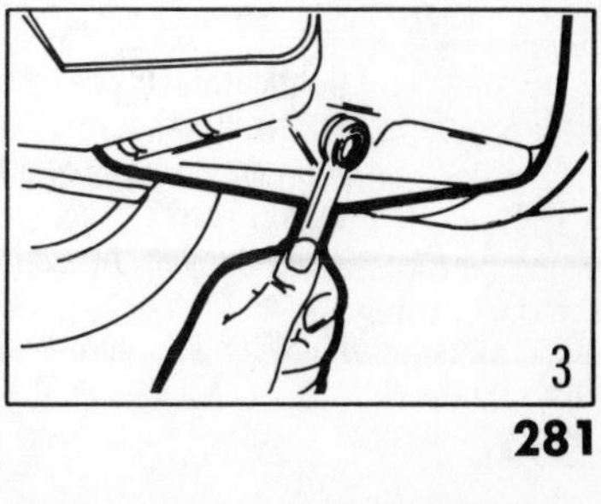

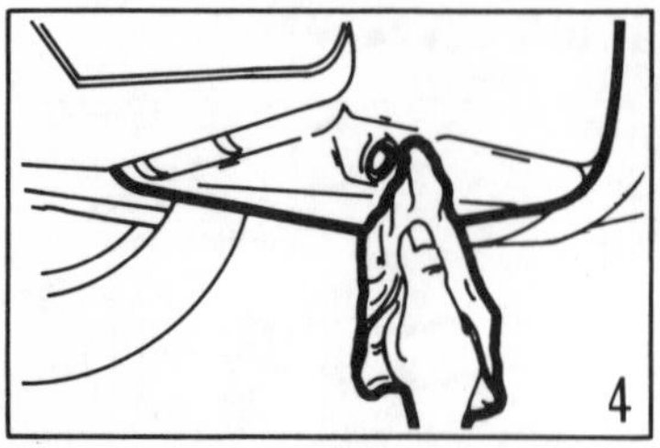

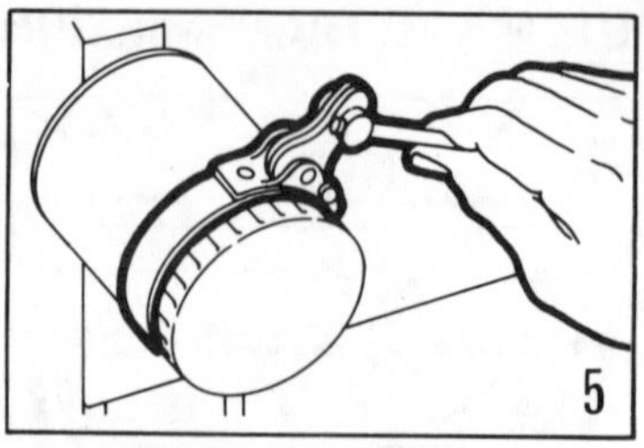

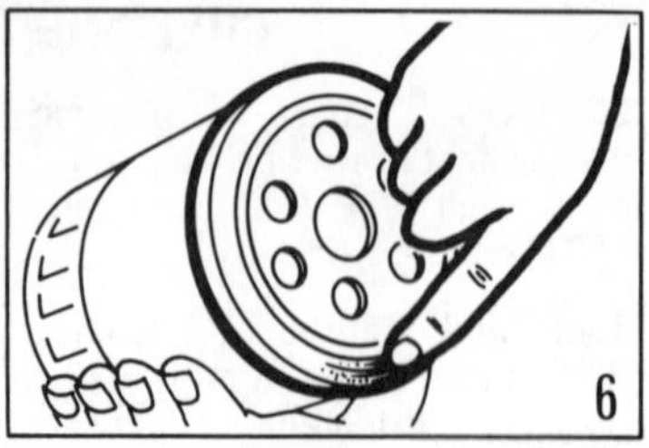

1. Engine must be warm and the car must be parked on the level.

2. Locate the drain plug on the engine oil pan.

3. Put the pan under the plug and carefully remove the plug.

4. Let all the dirty oil drain out. When it stops, wipe off the area and replace the plug.

5. Locate the filter and place the pan under it. Unscrew the filter with the special wrench and remove it. Dump the contents into the pan.

6. Wipe off the filter mounting area. Rub clean oil on the new filter gasket. Screw the filter on, but tighten only by hand.

7. Remove the oil filler cap from the

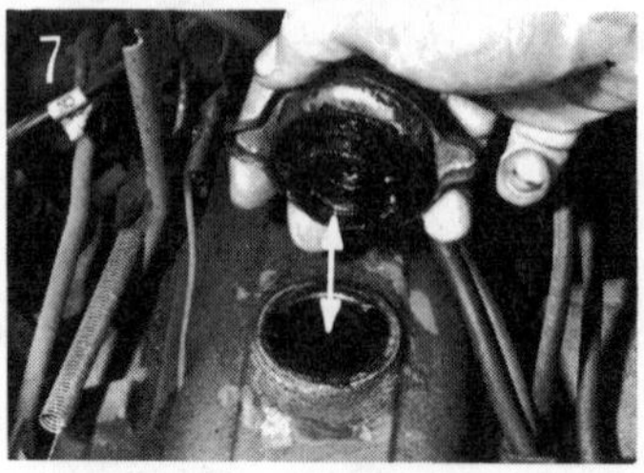

engine rocker arm cover or the tube at the front of the engine.

8. Pour the required number of quarts of oil into the filler cap opening.

9. Pull out the dipstick, wipe it off, and check the level. It is normal for it to be slightly above FULL.

10. Start the engine. The oil pressure light should go out or pressure should show on the gauge in 30 seconds or less. If it doesn't, stop the engine and correct the problem.

11. Check for leaks around the filter or drain plug with the engine running. Stop the engine and recheck the level.

SPEEDOMETER CABLE LUBRICATION

If the speedometer is jerky or noisy, the cable is either damaged or in need of lubrication.

1. Locate the cable attachment behind the speedometer dial.

2. Unclip or unscrew, as required, the outer cable housing from the speedometer.

3. Pull inner cable completely out of outer casing. Note carefully which end is top. Check for wear or frayed strands. If damaged, replace inner cable with new one.

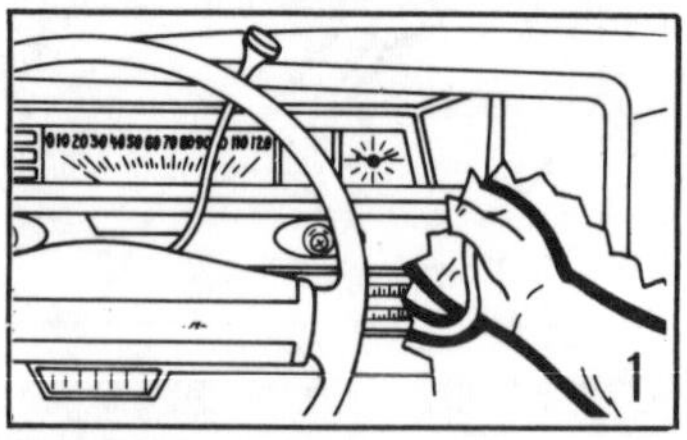

4. Apply a small amount of speedometer cable lubricant into cable casing. Replace inner cable in shaft, noting that top end is not inserted accidentally. Turn inner cable

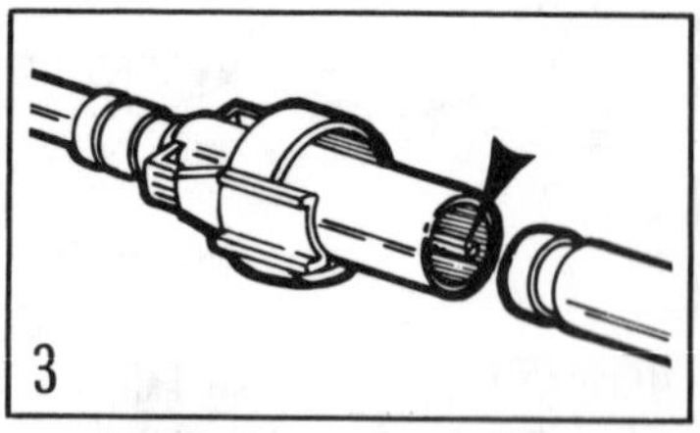

as it is being re-inserted. Twist cable when all the way in, to lock into position at lower end.

5. Reconnect cable to speedometer head under instrument panel.

DOOR HINGES AND STOPS

(lubricate every 6 months)

1. Brush any dirt accumulations from door hinges and stops. Use old tooth brush or rag.

2. Apply dab of white waterproof grease to door hinges, trunk hinges, hood hinges, door stops.

DOOR LOCKS

(lubricate every 6 months)
1. Insert door key half way into lock.
2. Spray aerosol lock lubricant into lock.
3. Push key rest of way into lock; turn back and forth several times.

Cooling System

IT IS RECOMMENDED . . . that radiator coolant (water/antifreeze mixture) level be checked once or twice a month. Do this when engine is cold. Check more often if you do a lot of hard driving. Coolant is checked visually on models with expansion tanks.
Keep coolant up to recommended level in radiator. If coolant checks frequently low, look for leaks. Tighten all hose clamps occasionally. For best results, keep a 50/50 water/antifreeze mixture year round. Change complete coolant mixture every 24 months.
CAUTION: If you must check coolant in a hot engine, cover radiator cap with thick rag before releasing. Remove cap slowly . . . press down and turn.

REPLACING THE THERMOSTAT

Poor heater output is often caused by a thermostat stuck open; occasionally one sticks shut causing immediate overheating. The thermostat is located inside the housing where the top radiator hose connects to the engine.

TOOLS AND MATERIALS . . .
New thermostat
Gasket
Box or socket wrench
Container for coolant

1. Drain radiator of about half its coolant. (See Changing Anti-Freeze).
2. Loosen and remove both retaining bolts and lift thermostat housing off the engine.

NOTE: If you're careful it won't be necessary to remove radiator hose.

3. Remove old thermostat.
4. Scrape thermostat housing flange and engine block surface to remove old gasket debris.
5. Drop new thermostat into place—spring down.

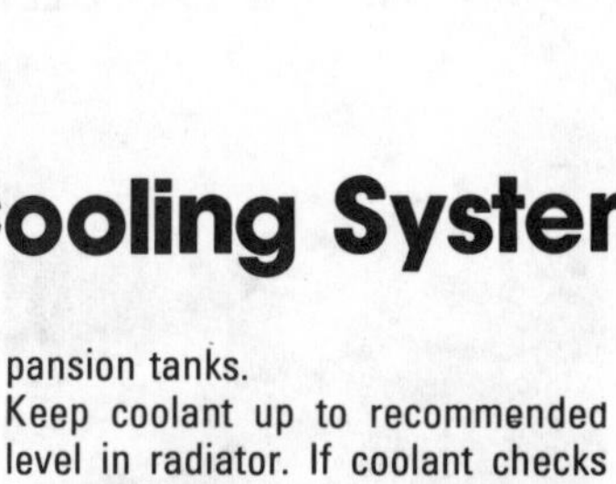

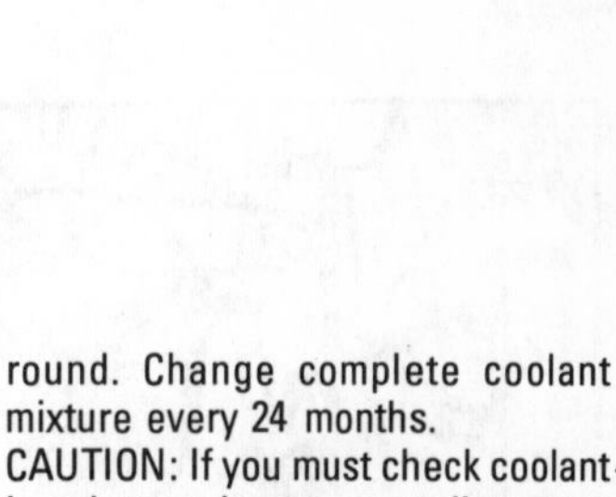

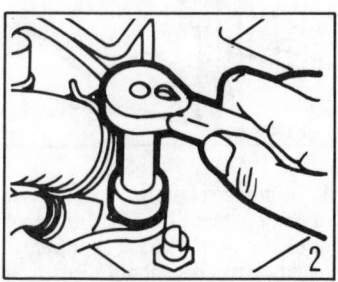

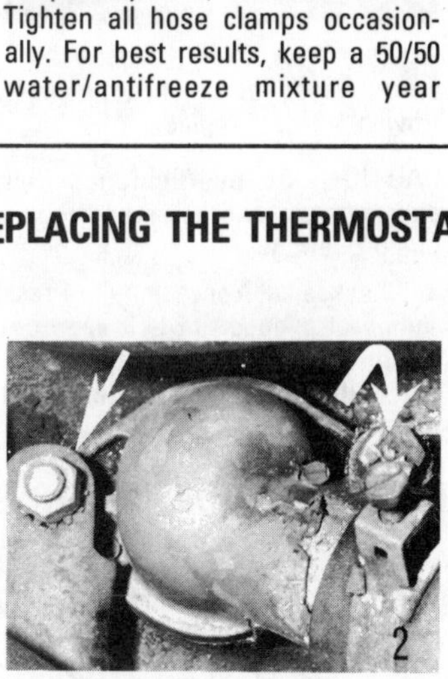

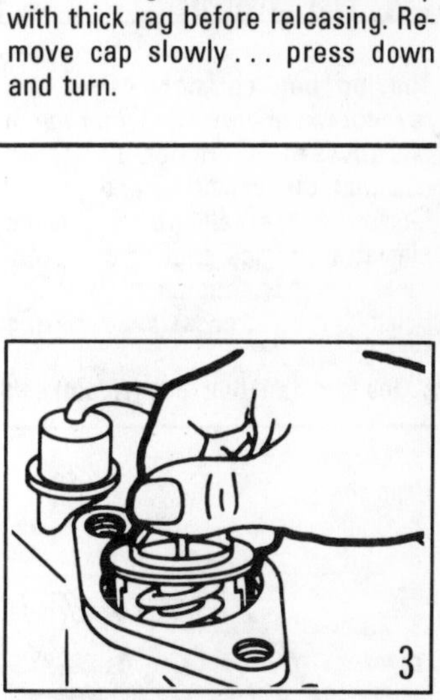

6. Install new gasket with sealer applied to both sides.
7. Replace thermostat housing and tighten both retaining bolts.

8. Refill the system and let the engine warm up with the heater on. Check the level.

CHECKING THE RADIATOR CAP

Check radiator cap occasionally for worn or cracked gasket. If cap doesn't seal properly, fluid will be lost and engine will overheat. Replace worn cap with new cap rated 15 lbs. pressure.

ADJUSTING THE FAN BELT

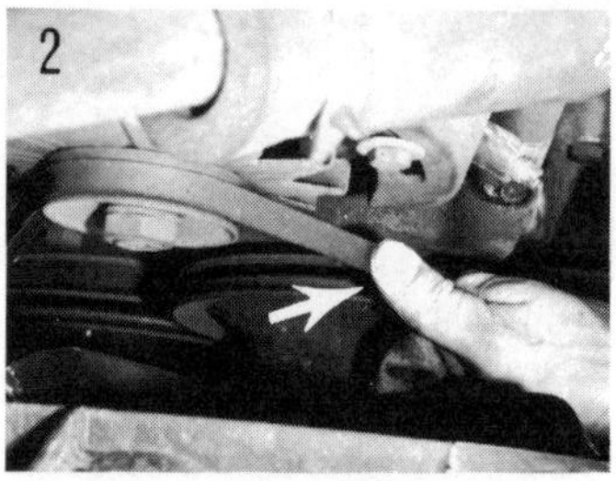

The fan belt not only drives the radiator fan, it turns the water pump and drives the alternator. It's easy to see that the condition and proper tension of the belt are vital, since almost all engine cooling and electrical power is dependent on it. The belt deserves an occasional look and tension check.

1. Inspect fan belt occasionally. If worn, frayed or cracked on inner driving surface, replace.

CAUTION: An overtightened belt may damage alternator and water pump bearings.

2. Check tension occasionally. Press thumb at midpoint of belt span between pulleys. If belt depresses more than ½ inch, tightening is needed. A too-loose belt will not drive alternator and water pump effectively.

3. To adjust loosen alternator pivot and adjustment bolts, pivot the alternator until the belt is properly tensioned (¼ in. deflection) and then tighten bolts. Tighten first the adjustment bolt, then the pivot bolt.

REPLACING RADIATOR HOSES

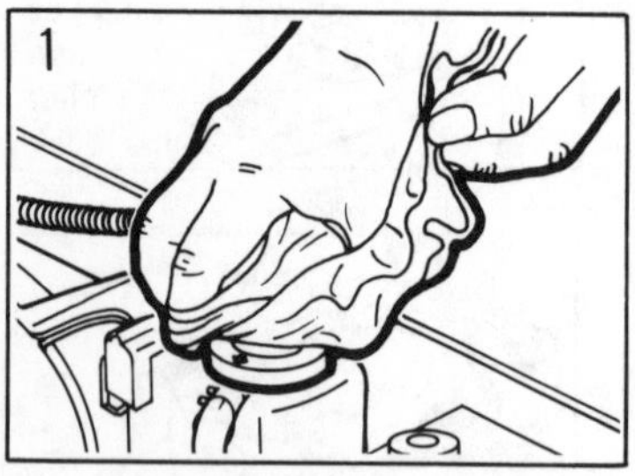

Tools and Materials . . . Screwdriver, knife, sandpaper, coolant container Coolant drain and refill work may be done alone; when changing hoses, coolant must also be drained as part of job. Check hose clamps for tightness and good condition.

Discard all hoses with cracks or soft spots.

1. Remove radiator cap. Open radiator petcock (See 2). Drain coolant into catch basin. If near 24 months old or discolored, discard old coolant.

2. Petcock or drain plug is located at the bottom rear of the radiator. Open petcock or remove plug to drain.

3. Loosen clamps at each end of hose(s). Work loose; pull off. If old hose clamps are rusted or damaged, replace with new units.

4. Wipe all hose connections clean. Use sandpaper to get rid of residue. Check all hoses for weak spots, as well as cracks inside and out.

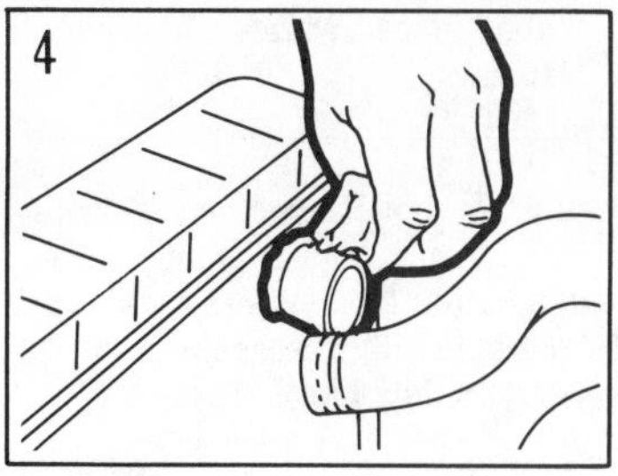

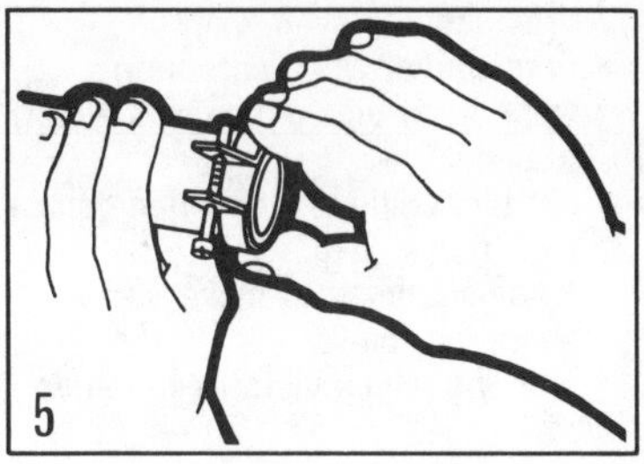

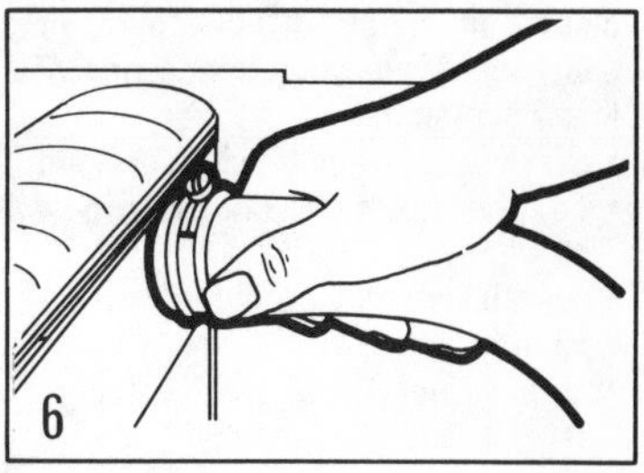

5. Slip clamps over each hose end. Slip hose ends all the way onto cleaned up hose connections.
6. Place hose clamp ¼ inch from hose end. Tighten. Close petcock. Refill with 50/50 coolant/water mix.
7. Start engine; allow to warm up with the heater on. Check for coolant leaks. Recheck the level.
8. Road test car; watch for temperature warning light or gauge.

CHANGING ANTI-FREEZE

GM SAYS . . . Change coolant mixture at least every two years, sooner if discoloration is noticed

Tools and Materials . . . Amount of anti-freeze equal to half the coolant capacity, drain container, adjustable wrench, funnel

Caution: Anti-freeze can kill grass and is a powerful poison; dispose of it carefully and flush away any spillage. It also stains painted surfaces.

1. Remove the radiator cap.
2. Open the radiator petcock at the lower rear of the radiator. Let the coolant drain.
3. Locate the block drain plug or plugs. There is one on the side of inline engines and one on each side of V-type engines. Remove these plugs. If nothing comes out, poke around inside the hole with a screwdriver to dislodge the blockage.
4. DO NOT DO THIS IF YOUR ENGINE IS WARM! Fill the radiator with water from a hose. Let it drain out the engine block and radiator drains. Repeat the operation until only clean water comes out.
5. If you have a coolant catch tank, remove and flush that out.
6. Replace the plugs; close the petcock.
7. Pour in an amount of anti-freeze equal to half the coolant capacity (see the capacity chart). A 50% mixture gives the best possible boiling and freezing points and assures rust protection.
8. Fill the radiator with water. Start the engine and let it warm up with the heater on (the heater is part of the system). Leave the cap off and add water until the radiator stays full.
9. Replace the radiator cap. If you have a coolant catch tank, fill it to the normal level with the 50% anti-freeze/water solution.
10. On systems without the catch tank, some coolant will be lost out the overflow tube during initial operation. This is not a defect, so long as the level doesn't drop more than about two inches below the filler neck. Keep the coolant at this level.

Suspension and Tires

How To Pinpoint Handling Problems
The front wheels turn on the wheel bearings, which are mounted on the steering spindles (knuckles). There is a pivot point at the top and bottom of each knuckle, called a ball joint. The lower ball joint usually wears out before the upper. The ball joints attach the knuckle to the upper and lower control arms at each side. A coil spring is mounted between the control arms at each side and a shock absorber is inside each spring. The rear suspension consists of leaf springs and staggered shock absorbers. The staggered arrangement controls wheel hop under hard acceleration or braking.

Periodic maintenance of the suspension consists of lubrication of the four ball joints, steering linkage joints, and adjustment and lubrication of the front wheel bearings.

Your car's suspension system consists of wheels, tires, springs, shock absorbers, sway (or stabilizer) bars, ball joints, steering linkage. If any of these items is out of adjustment or badly worn, you may notice any of these symptoms:

- car pulls to one side when braking
- car wanders when driving a straight line
- overall ride may be either hard or bouncy
- effort is needed to steer vehicle
- tires show uneven wear
- tires squeal when cornering
- front of car dips or bounces when braking
- car rocks side-to-side when going over rough road
- wheels bounce to make slapping sound on road
- steering wheel vibrates in hands
- front of car vibrates at highway speeds

Any of above symptoms indicates corrective action is needed. Delay can: ruin tires; cause damage/failure to other suspension parts; create safety hazard.

STEERING

If steering linkage, front suspension and steering column components are in good condition, there should be not more than 1½ inch free play in the steering wheel when measured at the rim of the wheel. If a loud knock is heard when turning the steering wheel from one extreme to the other, have a mechanic check the steering system.

FRONT END ALIGNMENT

When steering, handling and/or tire wear indicate front end alignment may be needed, this work can only be done at an automotive service shop. DO NOT PUT OFF NEEDED FRONT END ALIGNMENT. At the same time, have ball joints and steering linkage checked.

CHECKING YOUR SHOCK ABSORBERS

Shock absorbers work to keep wheels in constant contact with the road. Result is safe handling and ride control; longer tire life. So shock absorbers (or shocks) are important.

1. Check under car and locate shock absorber near each wheel.
2. Heavy oil streaks on outer shock housing indicate need for replacement.
3. Stand at front of car and apply body weight in a pumping action to front bumper or fender. Release pressure and allow car to stop rocking. Car should not bounce more than one more time after releasing pressure. Repeat at rear. If bouncing continues more than once, replacement is needed. Replace shocks in pairs (front pair or rear pair).

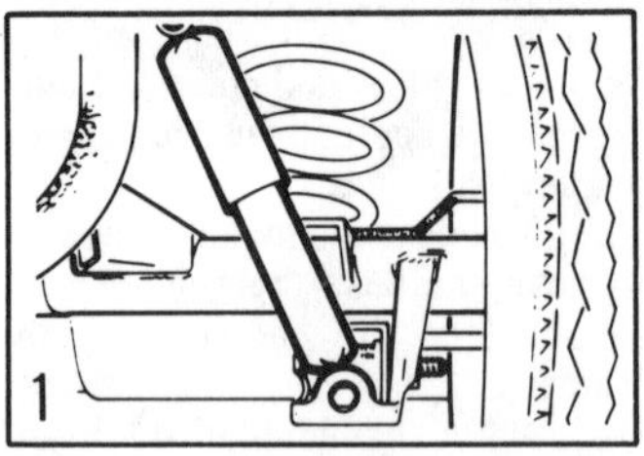

TOW HITCH INFORMATION

If your car is used for trailer towing you should check:

A. Cooling System; be sure coolant is at proper level in radiator. See Cooling System Section for checks to perform.

B. Check Transmission Fluid; keep topped up to proper level.

C. Check Rear Shock Absorbers; you may benefit from installation of new rear shocks.

D. Check Tire Pressures; best traction and handling can be ensured if tire pressures are properly maintained.

E. Check maintenance interval recommendations with dealer or owner's manual. These intervals are shorter for trailer towing.

F. Check with dealer or owner's manual to be sure that the car is properly equipped to handle the weight of the trailer being considered.

For safer and more trouble-free trailer towing, consider:
A. Automatic Transmission Cooler; helps remove excess heat from automatic transmission fluid built up during towing mileage. Also helps avoid radiator overheating.
B. Radiator Over-Flow Tank Kit; addition of a reservoir to catch radiator coolant overflow preventing coolant loss. Easy to install, these units help a tow car run cooler, avoid overheating due to coolant loss.
C. Heavy-Duty Shock Absorbers or Air Shocks; important to have on rear wheels if you intend to do a lot of towing or load carrying within the car itself. Don't forget to consider replacing factory shocks, when they are worn out, with heavy-duty units at the front as well.
D. Variable Load Flasher; this unit will accommodate the added load of trailer turn signal lamps on trailer when these are hooked into your car's electrical system.
E. Flex or Clutch-Type Fan; these move more cooling air at low speeds and reduce load on the engine at high speeds.

Ignition System

The ignition system consists of spark plugs; plug wires; distributor; rotor; points; condenser; coil. These units work to create a good hot spark inside the engine (ignition) at exactly the right moment (timing). If ignition is weak or timing is off, engine may be hard to start, run poorly, waste gas, lose power, backfire or not run at all.

CHECKING IGNITION SYSTEM— Six and Four Cylinder through 1974

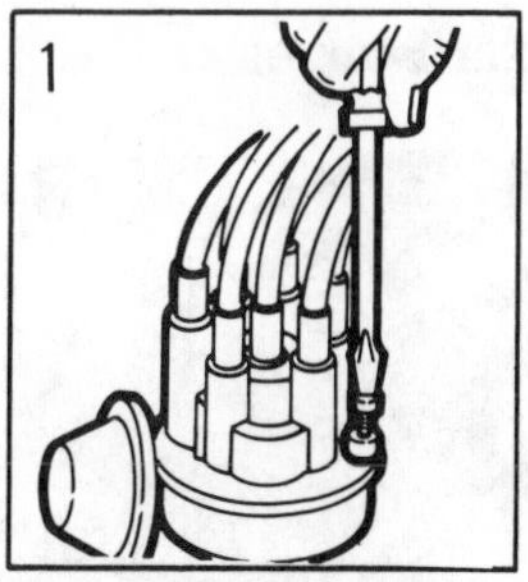

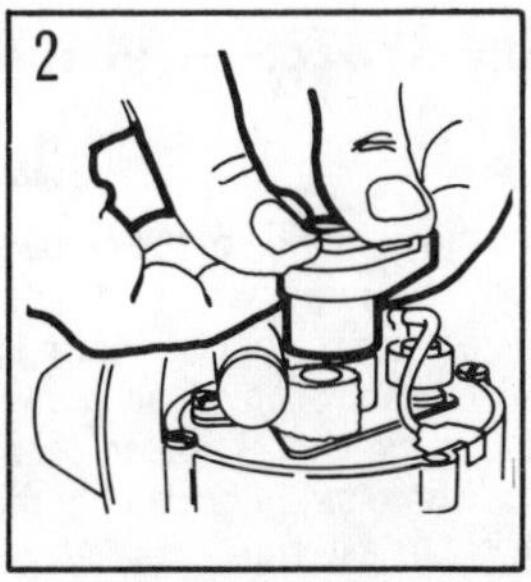

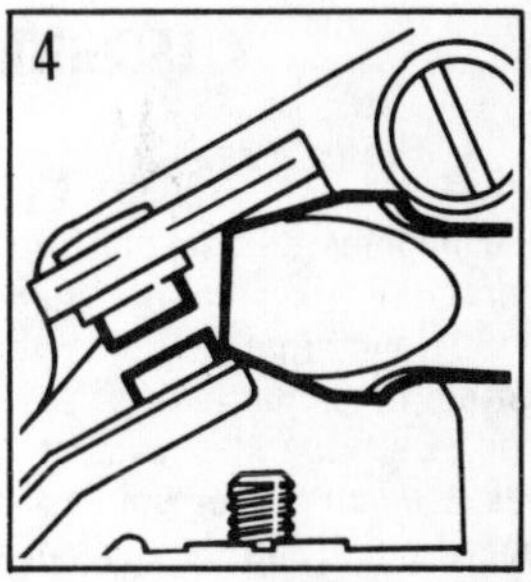

CHECKING POINTS AND ROTOR

1. To open the distributor, loosen the two screws retaining the cap. Remove the coil (center) wire and lift the cap off, but keep the other wires attached.
2. Pull the rotor off (straight up). If it is cracked or metallic tip is badly burned, replace it.
3. Check the metal contacts inside the cap. Replace the cap if they are corroded or there are any cracks.
4. Pry the points apart with a screwdriver. If worn or burned, replace. If OK, check the gap.

OTHER IGNITION CHECK POINTS

Inspect spark plug wires. If cracked or brittle, entire set should be replaced. Also, check center coil high tension wire. Inspect distributor cap. Wipe inside clean occasionally with dry, lint-free rag. If cap is cracked or rotor contacts are excessively burned, replace cap.

CHECKING IGNITION SYSTEM—V8 through 1974

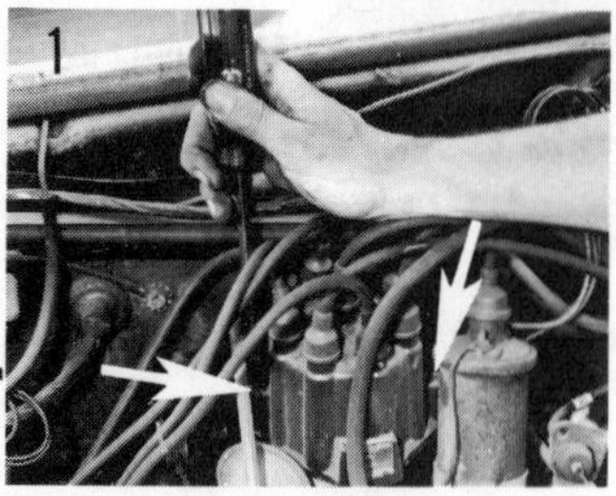

CHECKING POINTS AND ROTOR

1. To open the distributor, depress the screw in the cap and rotate the latch off the distributor (there are two latches). Remove the coil (center) wire and lift off the cap. Keep the other wires attached.

2. Remove the two screws and lift off the rotor. If it is cracked or metallic tip is badly burned, replace it.

3. Check the metal contacts inside the cap. Replace the cap if they are corroded or there are any cracks.

4. Pry the points apart with a screwdriver. If worn or burned, replace. If OK, check the gap.

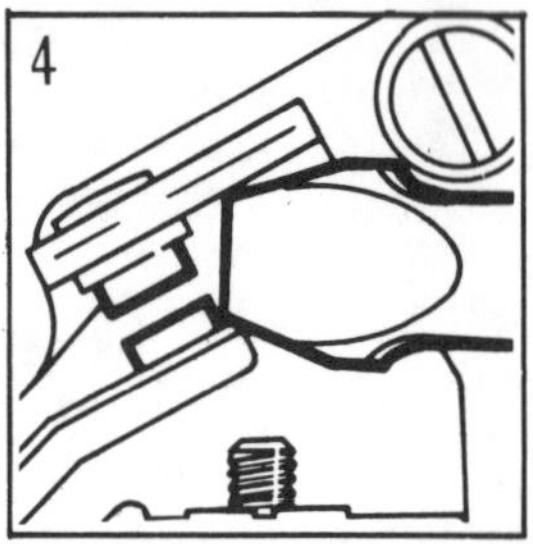

OTHER IGNITION CHECK POINTS

Inspect spark plug wires. If cracked or brittle, entire set should be replaced. Also, check center coil high tension wire. Inspect distributor cap. Wipe inside clean occasionally with dry, lint-free rag. If cap is cracked or rotor contacts are excessively burned, replace cap.

CHECKING IGNITION SYSTEM—All 1975 and Later Engines

These engines all use the General Motors HEI (High Energy Ignition) system. No internal distributor maintenance or adjustments are required. Because this system produces a much higher voltage than ordinary point and condenser systems, the condition of the spark plug or high tension wires should be checked occasionally. There is no need to check timing on a regular basis, since there are no wearing parts. The distributor cap should be kept clean externally.

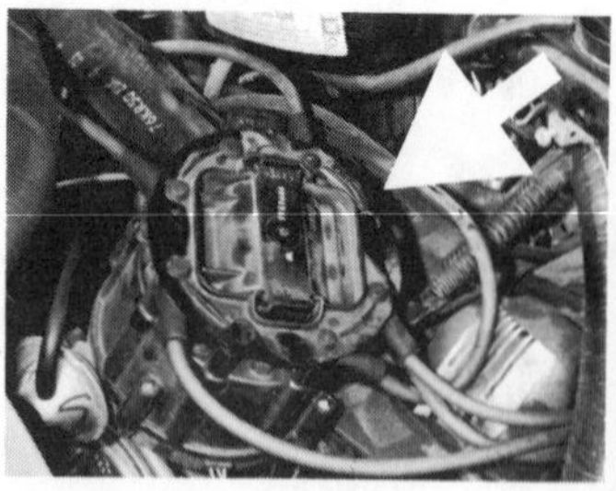

High Energy Ignition System Tachometer Hookup

Some 1974, and all 1975 and later Buicks are equipped with the High Energy Ignition System which uses a different tachometer hookup than was used in previous years.

1. On the V6 and V8 engines, connect the tachometer to the TACH terminal on the distributor and to a suitable ground.

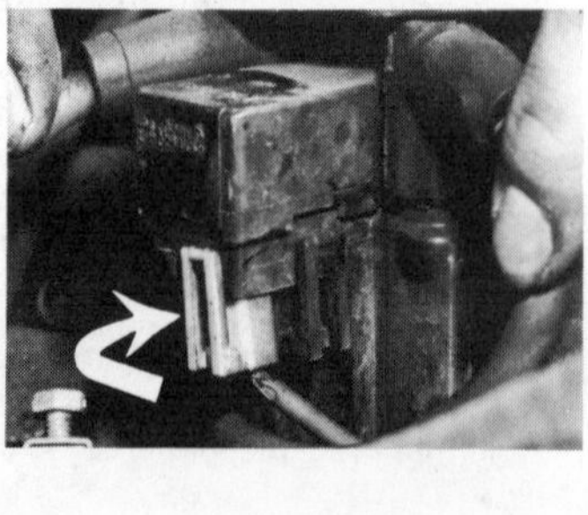

NOTE: Some tachometers must connect to the TACH terminal on the distributor and to the positive terminal on the battery. If there is any doubt check the tachometer manufacturer's instructions.

2. On the inline six cylinder, connect the tachometer to the TACH terminal on the coil, opposite the BAT terminal, and to a ground.

SPARK PLUG REPLACEMENT

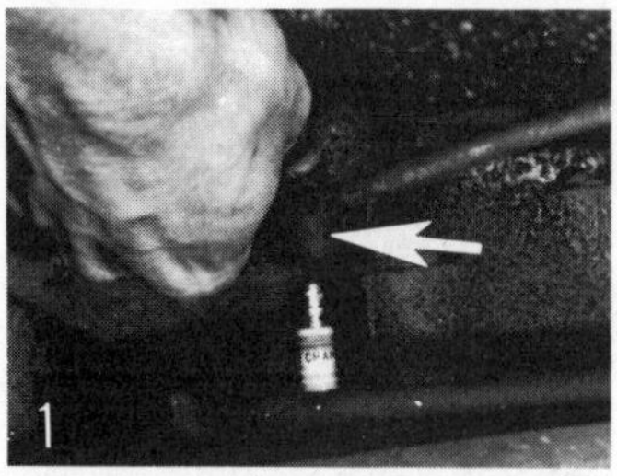

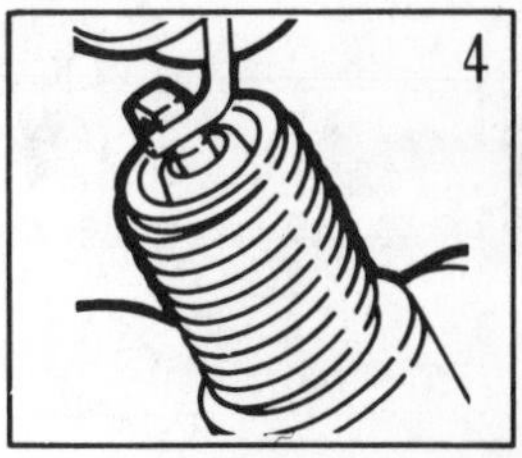

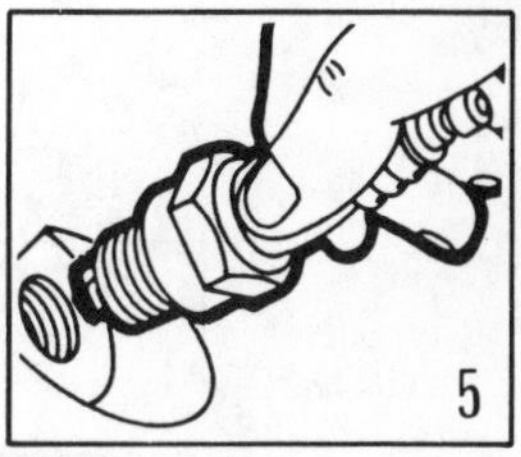

GM SAYS . . . Replace spark plugs every 12-18,000 miles on models through 1974, every 22,500 miles on 1975 and later models, sooner if poor performance or missing is noted

Tools and Materials . . . New plugs of type listed in Tune-Up Chart, spark plug socket to fit new plugs (either 5/8 or 13/16 in.), spark plug gap gauge

1. Remove spark plug wire by grasping rubber boot. Do not jerk wire off. If stuck, turn boot, pulling gently.

2. Loosen spark plug using socket wrench.

3. Wipe or brush loose dirt from around plug before removing. Do not let dirt drop into engine through plug hole. Unscrew plug.

4. Check plug electrode gap on new spark plug. Adjust to the specified gap, using the bending tool on the gauge.

Plug gap is correct when the gauge drags slightly as it is pulled between plug electrodes.

5. Thread new plug into plug hole by hand. Hand tighten. Do not force or cross thread. Use socket wrench to tighten firmly but do not force. Replace plug wire. Press boot firmly.

REPLACING SPARK PLUG WIRES

1. Remove only one wire at a time from the engine.

2. Match the wire removed with the same length wire in the replacement set.

3. Route the replacement wire in the same way as the original.

4. After all wires are replaced, check that all wires on 1974 and earlier distributors are seated in the distributor cap. Check that all boots are in place.

5. If you run into difficulty, go to the Firing Order illustrations for help.

Use the firing order to guide you when replacing your ignition wires and/or distributor cap.

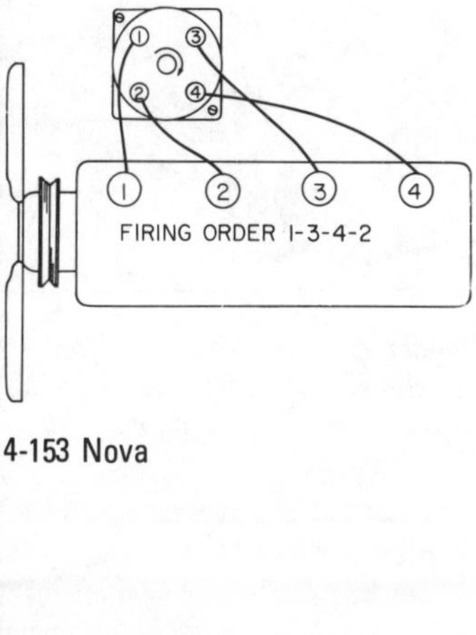

4-153 Nova

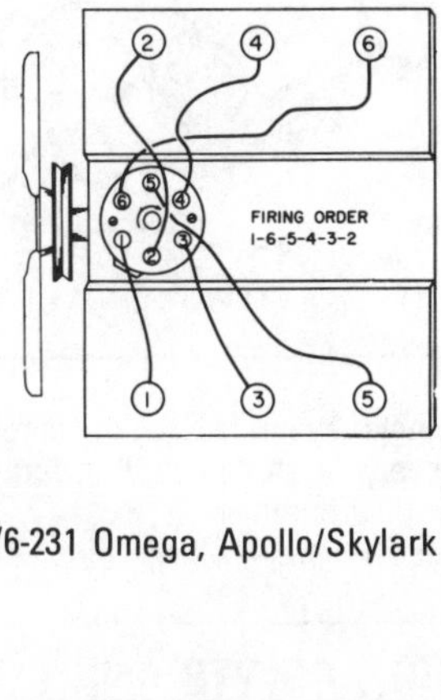

V6-231 Omega, Apollo/Skylark

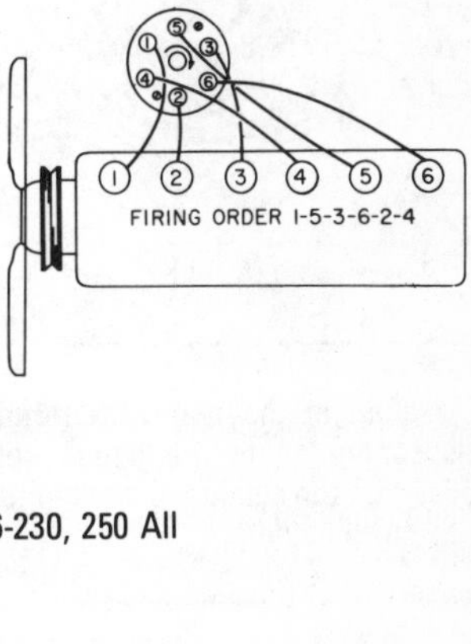

6-230, 250 All

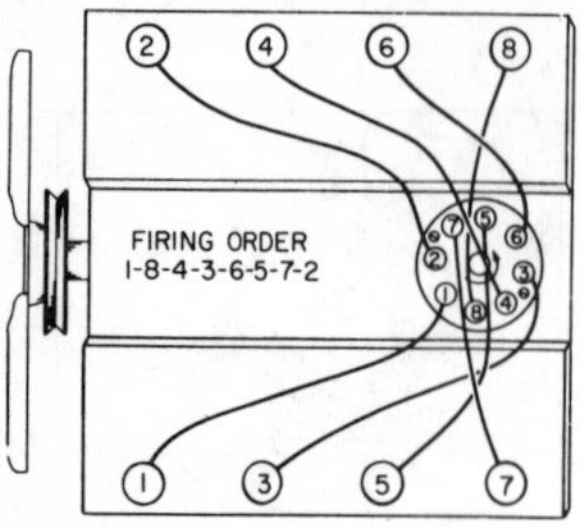

V8-260 Omega, Ventura, Apollo/ Skylark

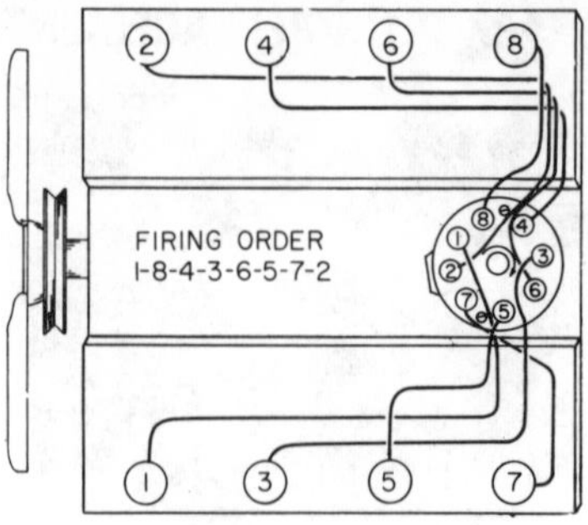

V8-262, 305, 307, 350, 396 Nova; V8-307 Ventura

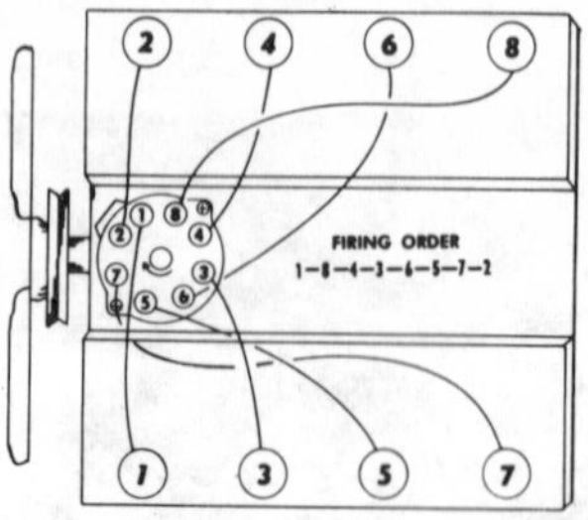

V8-350 Apollo/Skylark; 1975-76 Omega, Ventura

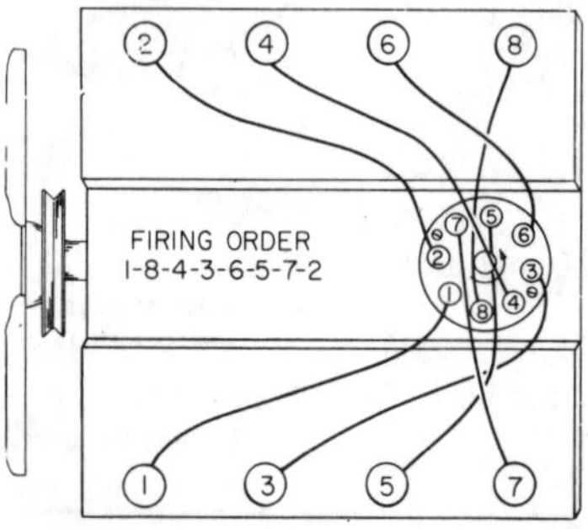

V8-350 1973-74 Omega; All 1977 V8-350 except Nova

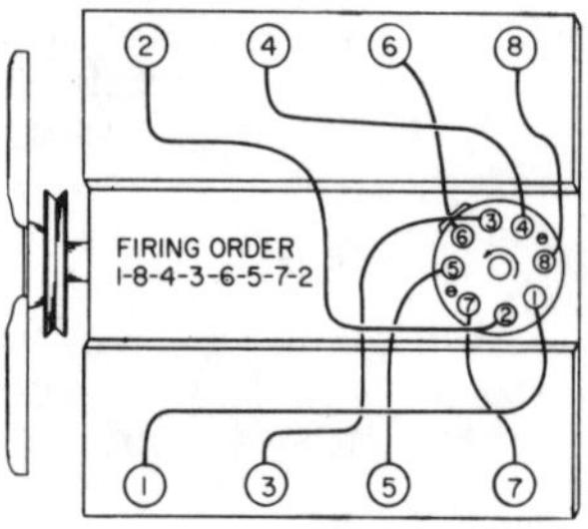

V8-350 1971-74 Ventura; 1977 V8-302

REMOVING POINTS AND CONDENSER—Six and Four Cylinder through 1974

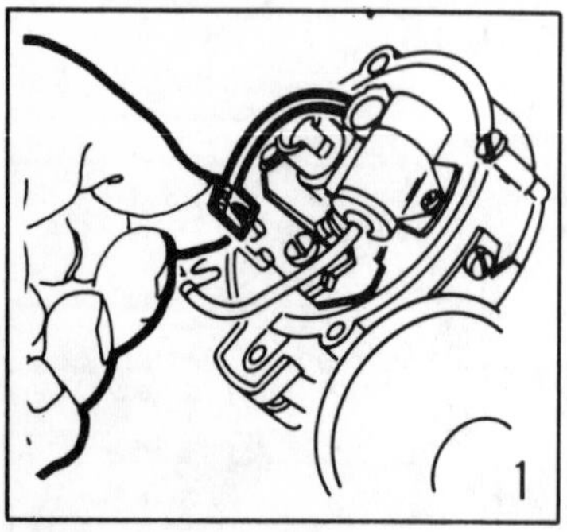

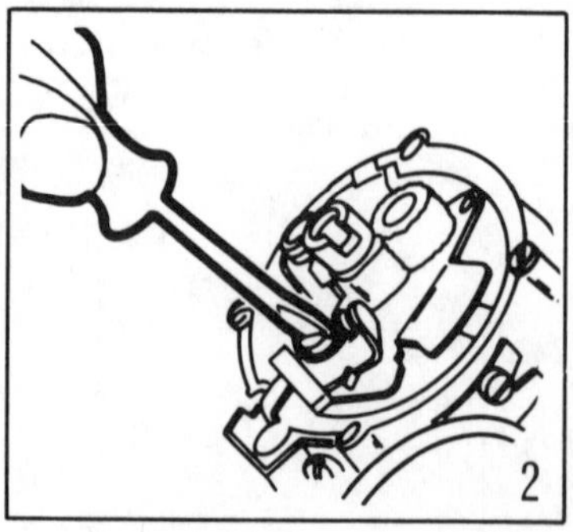

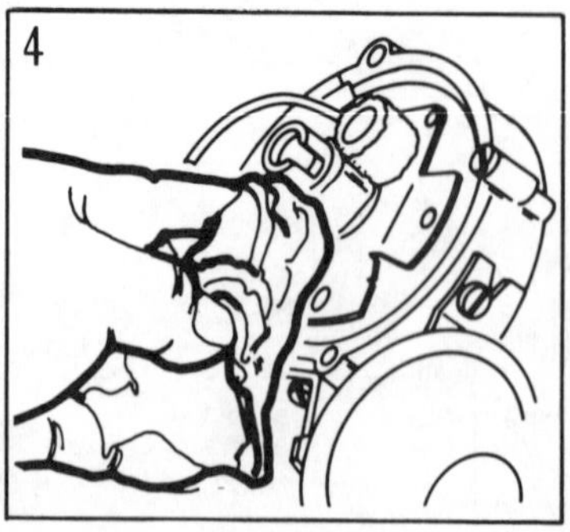

1. Disconnect the two wire terminals connected to the points set. Notice that the condenser connector is on the outside.
2. Remove points attaching screw being very careful not to drop screw inside distributor.
3. Remove screw which holds condenser. DO NOT DROP SCREW.
4. Wipe all dirt from distributor plate and cam with clean, lint-free rag.

INSTALLING IGNITION POINTS AND CONDENSER

GM SAYS . . . Replace every 12,000 miles
Tools and Materials . . . Magnetic screwdriver, feeler gauges, replacement points and condenser
Points and condenser work together. Always replace condenser also when installing new points.

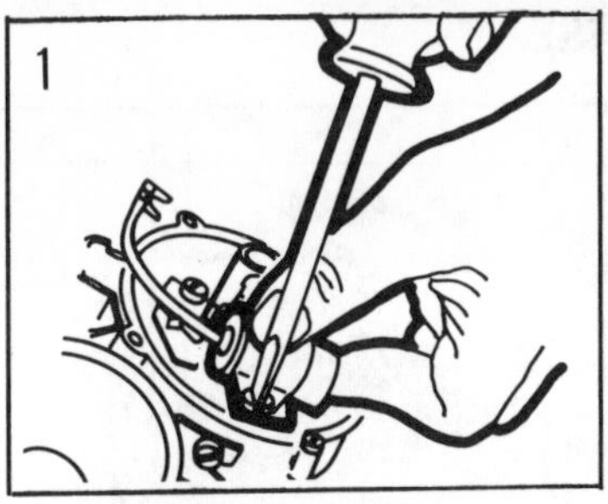

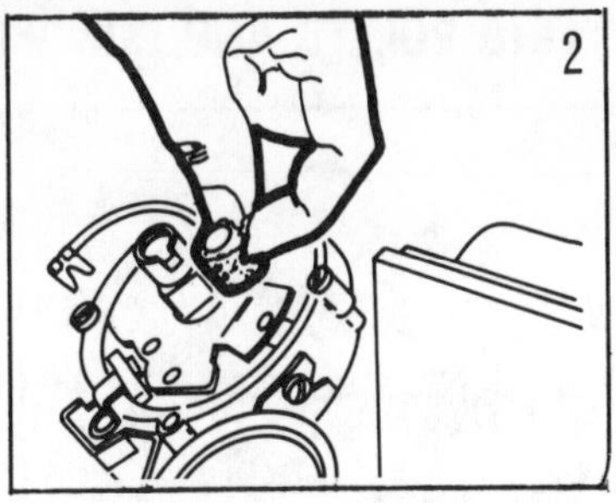

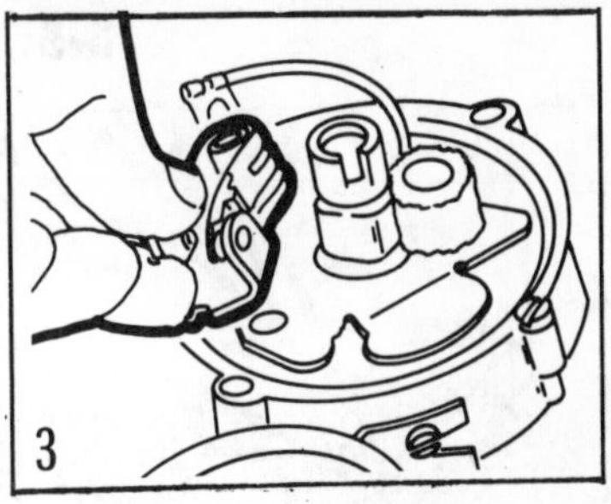

1. Attach new condenser with screw.
2. Rotate or replace cam lubricator. Fiber cam lubricator must be turned 180° every 12,000 mi., replaced every 24,000. When replacing, simply pull it up and off stud; push new lubricator down over stud. DO NOT attempt to add oil or grease to fiber lubricator.
3. Position new points set in distributor. Attach retaining screw lightly. Replace both wire terminals. The condenser wire goes on the outside of the two.

CAUTION: When removing screws from distributor, be sure to avoid any screws accidentally falling through distributor opening into engine. Use magnetic screwdriver.

RESETTING THE CONTACT GAP

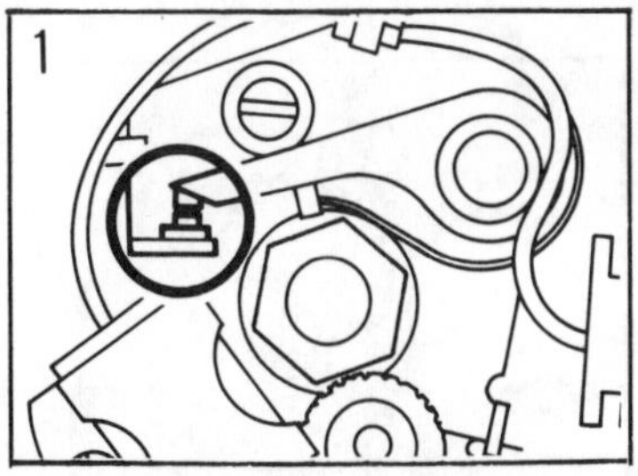

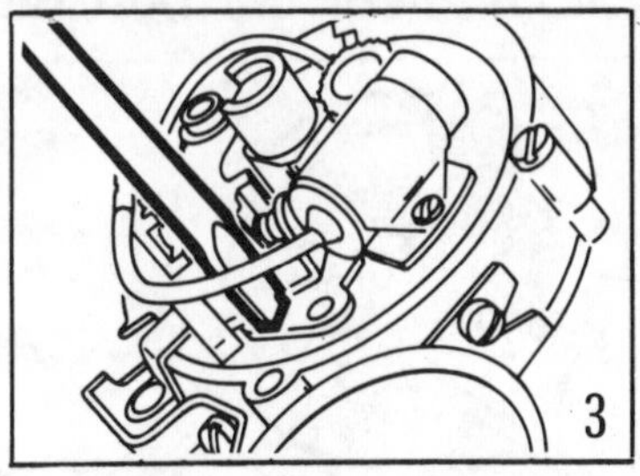

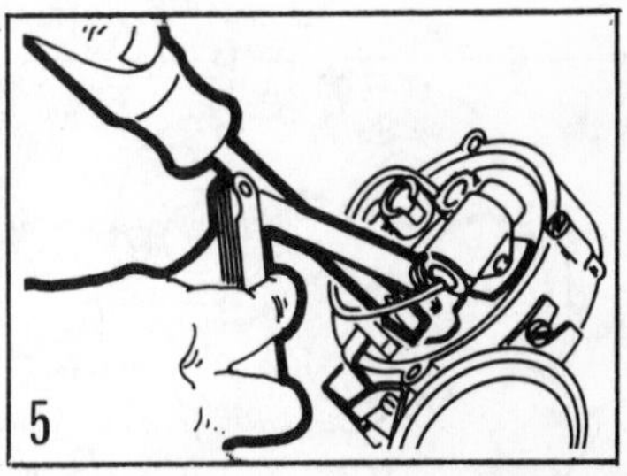

1. Check that point contacts meet squarely. If they do not, bend bracket supporting fixed contact using needle-nosed pliers.
2. Turn engine by ignition key (you'll need a helper) until rubbing block on point set is on one of the high spots of distributor cam. You may use wrench on lower engine pulley to do this.
3. Insert screwdriver in slot near point contacts; twist to open or close gap.
4. Correct gap is in Tune-Up Specifications Chart.
5. Insert correct size feeler gauge. Adjust gap with screwdriver until feeler gauge can be moved in and out between contacts with only slight drag.
6. Tighten point set holddown screw. Recheck gap; it might have changed from tightening holddown screw. Re-adjust if needed.
7. Align tab inside rotor with notch on distributor shaft and push rotor onto shaft. Rotor must be fully seated on shaft.
8. Replace distributor cap; install screws.

REMOVING POINTS AND CONDENSER—V8 through 1974

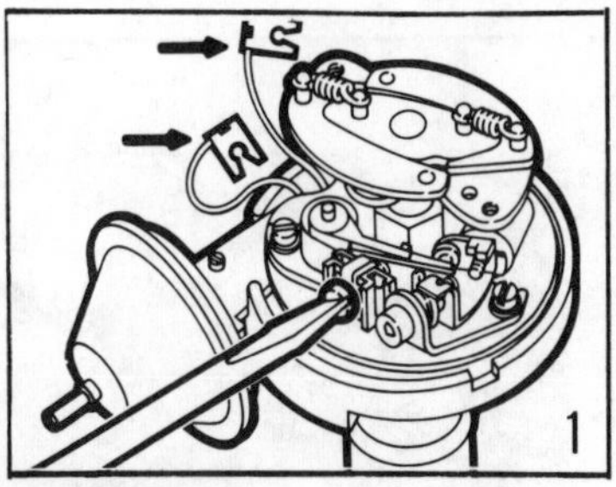

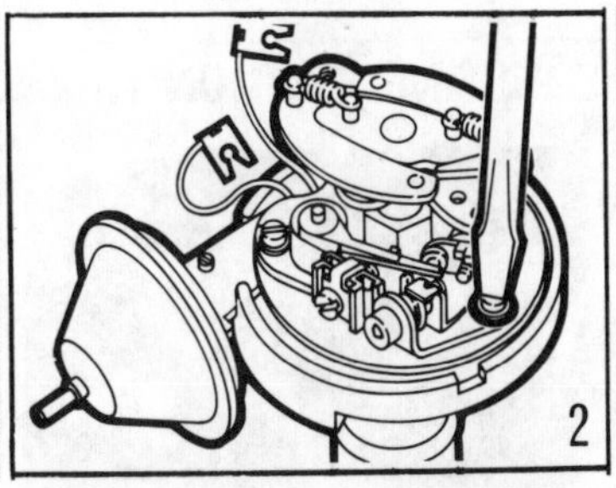

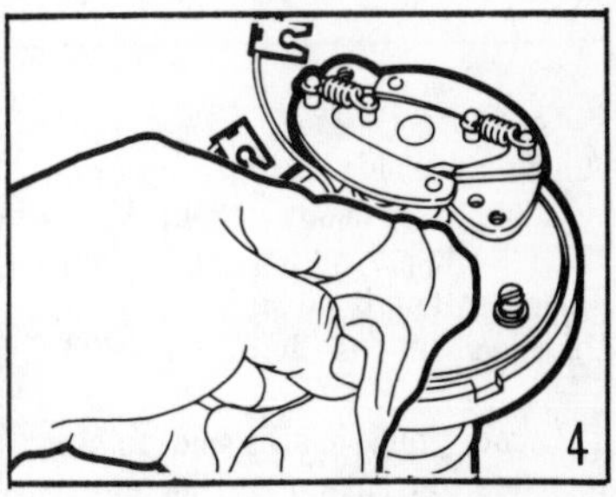

1. Disconnect the two wire terminals connected to the point set. Notice that the condenser connector is on the outside.
2. Loosen, but do not remove the two points attaching screws. Slide the points off the screws to remove.
3. Remove screw which holds condenser. DO NOT DROP SCREW.
NOTE: Later models use a combined points and condenser set. When you remove points you also remove condenser. You can also install these sets in early cars.
4. Wipe all dirt from distributor plate and cam with clean, lint-free rag.

INSTALLING POINTS AND CONDENSER

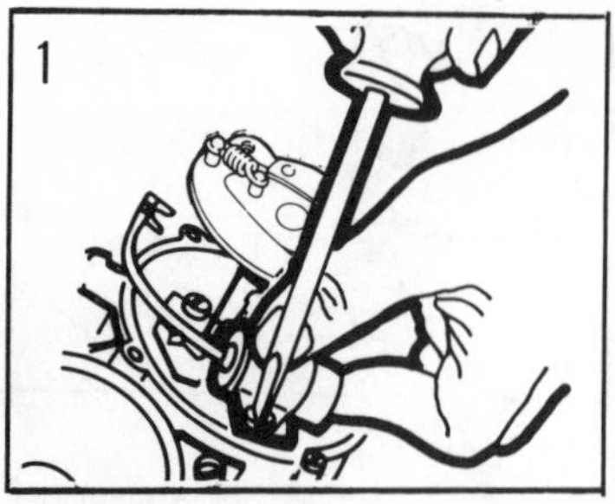

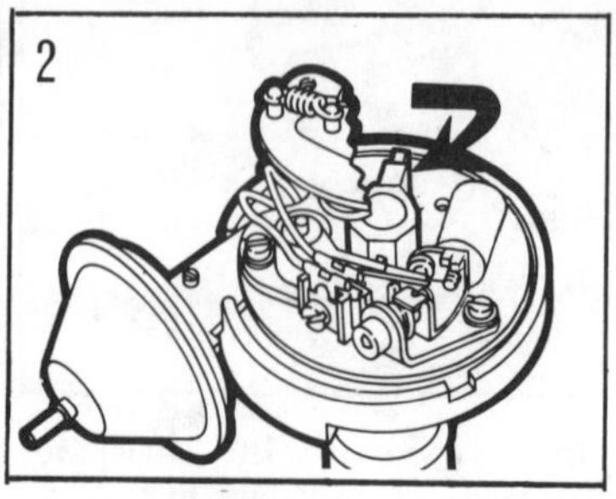

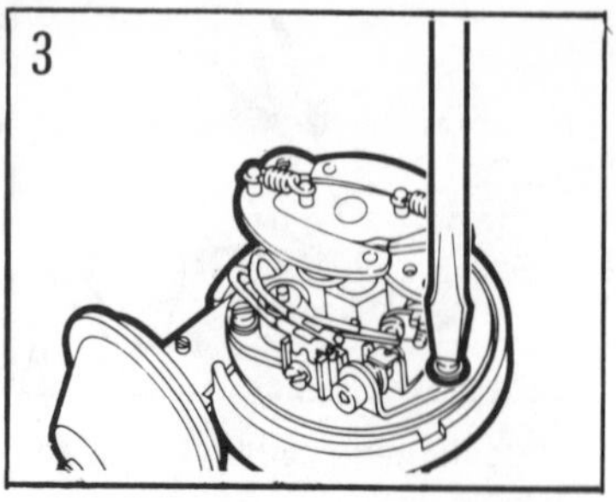

1. Attach new condenser with screw.
2. Rotate or replace cam lubricator. Fiber cam lubricator must be turned 180° every 12,000 mi., replaced every 24,000. When replacing, simply pull it up and off stud; push new lubricator down over stud. DO NOT attempt to add oil or grease to fiber lubricator.
3. Position new points set in distributor by sliding onto screws. Tighten screws.

CAUTION: When removing screws from distributor, be sure to avoid any screws accidentally falling through distributor opening into engine. Use magnetic screwdriver.

RESETTING THE CONTACT GAP

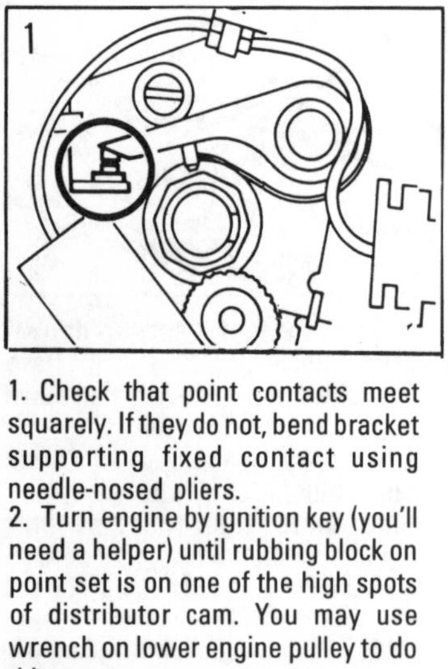

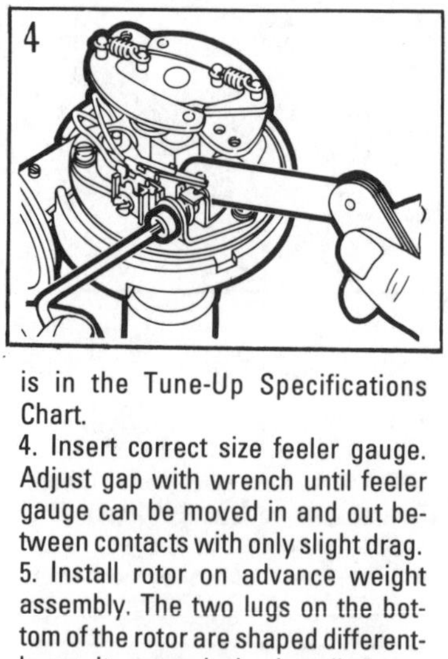

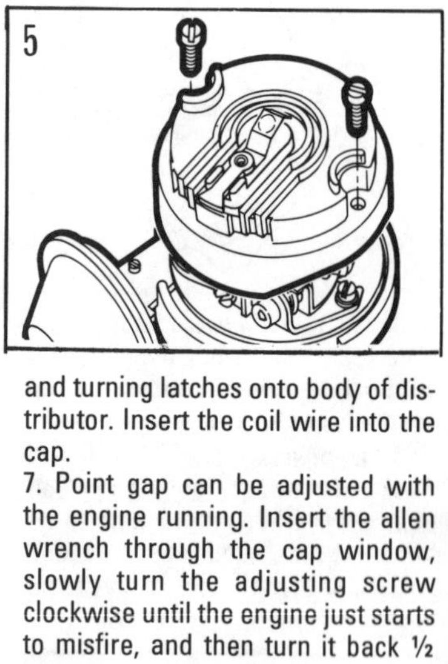

1. Check that point contacts meet squarely. If they do not, bend bracket supporting fixed contact using needle-nosed pliers.
2. Turn engine by ignition key (you'll need a helper) until rubbing block on point set is on one of the high spots of distributor cam. You may use wrench on lower engine pulley to do this.
3. Insert a ⅛ in. allen wrench into points adjusting screw. Correct gap is in the Tune-Up Specifications Chart.
4. Insert correct size feeler gauge. Adjust gap with wrench until feeler gauge can be moved in and out between contacts with only slight drag.
5. Install rotor on advance weight assembly. The two lugs on the bottom of the rotor are shaped differently, so it can only be installed one way. Tighten screws.
6. Install cap by depressing screws and turning latches onto body of distributor. Insert the coil wire into the cap.
7. Point gap can be adjusted with the engine running. Insert the allen wrench through the cap window, slowly turn the adjusting screw clockwise until the engine just starts to misfire, and then turn it back ½ turn.

ADJUSTING IGNITION TIMING

Adjusting timing is the important finishing touch to any tune-up. While not difficult, job requires timing light. Timing setting is given in the Tune-Up Specifications Chart.

1. Locate timing marks and pointer (notches) on engine and lower engine pulley. Clean away dirt. Mark the pointer notches with chalk.
2. Hook up timing light according to instructions supplied with it.
3. Disconnect and plug the vacuum line from the distributor.

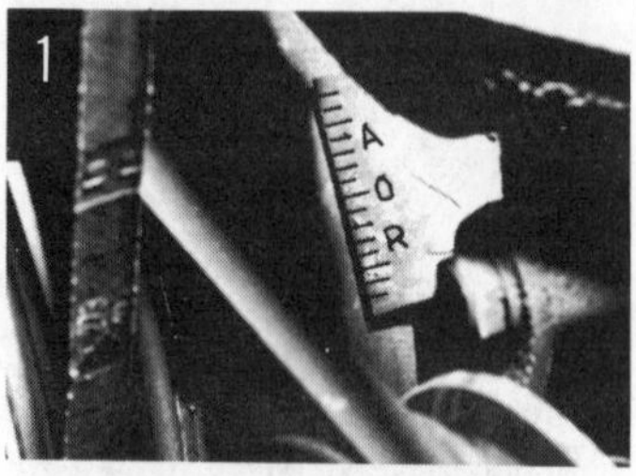

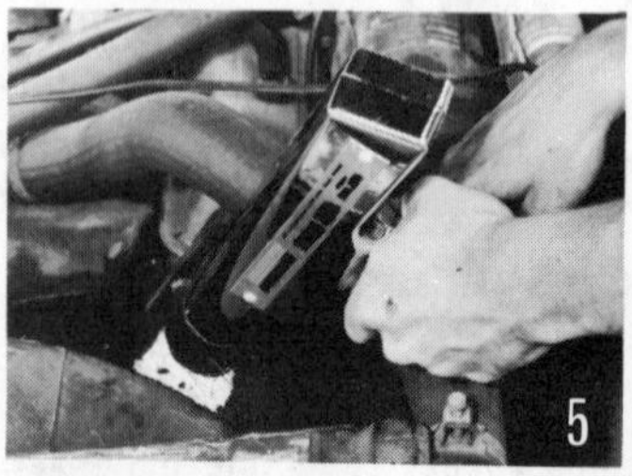

4. Disconnect the fuel tank vent line from the evaporative canister.
5. Aim timing light at pulley mark(s). If the chalked marks do not align, loosen distributor hold-down nut and slowly rotate distributor until chalked marks align.
6. Tighten hold-down nut.

Fuel System

When gasoline is brought from the fuel tank, it mixes with air in the carburetor. This gas/air mixture enters engine thru the intake manifold, passes thru the intake valves and is burned in the combustion chamber. The burned exhaust gas is then passed thru the exhaust valves to the exhaust system and to the outside air. In order to keep your car's engine running cleanly with minimal pollution, and avoid dangerous carbon monoxide fumes inside the vehicle, certain items should be checked from time to time.

An important part of a car's emission control system is the Positive Crankcase Ventilation (PCV) valve and its connecting hose. The PCV valve should be replaced once every 24,000 miles. This device keeps dirt and sludge from forming inside the engine. Make sure all PCV connections are tight. Check that the connecting hoses are clear and not

clogged. Replace any brittle or broken hoses.

REPLACING THE AIR FILTER AND CRANKCASE VENTILATION FILTER

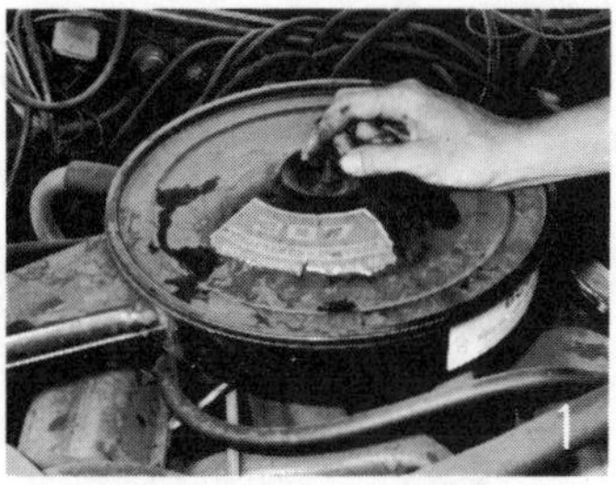

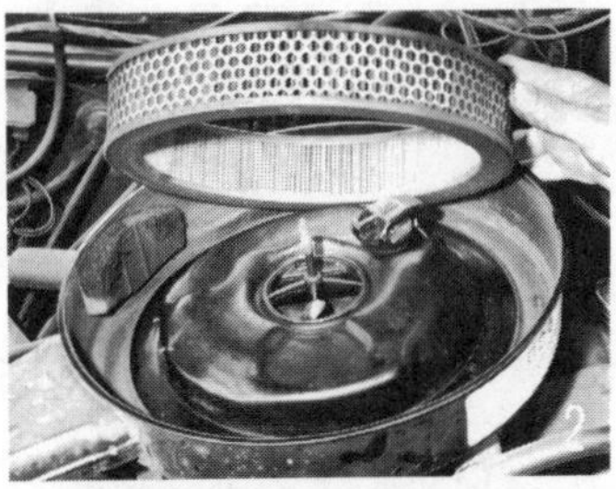

The large round can that sits on top of the engine is the air cleaner. The filter element inside should be replaced every 12,000 miles.

1. Unscrew the wing nut and remove the air cleaner cover.

2. Remove and discard the old dirty filter.

3. Check the small crankcase breather filter. If dirty, lift out and replace it.

4. Using a clean rag, wipe out the inside of air cleaner. Install new filter and replace top cover.

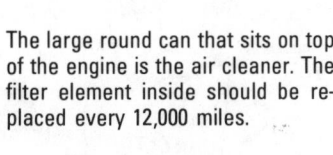

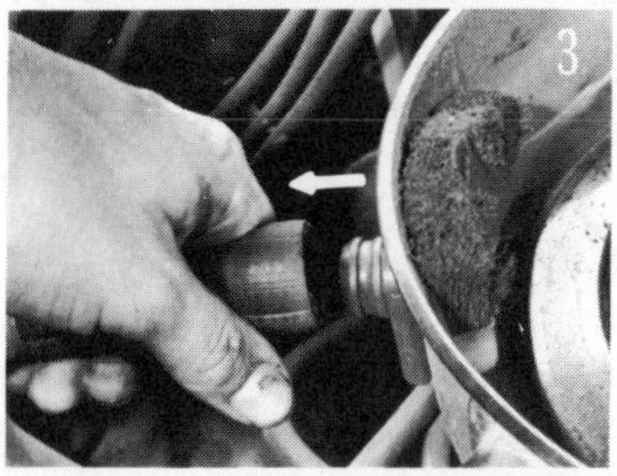

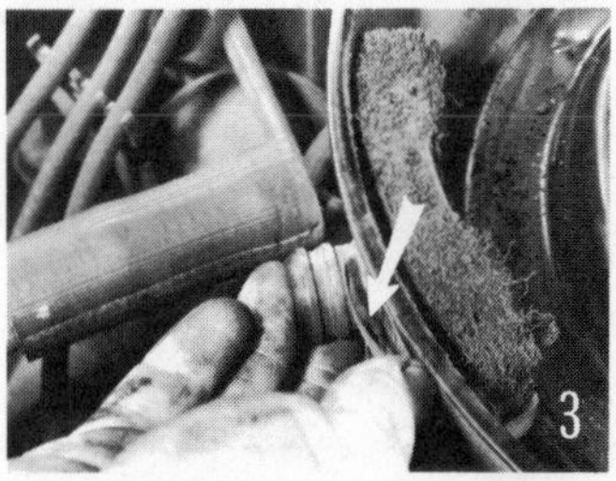

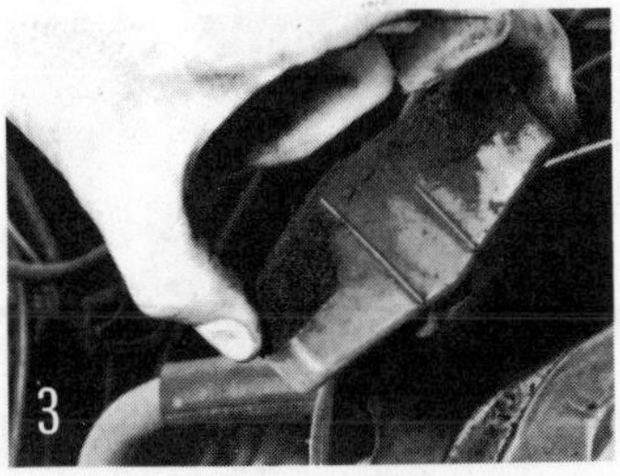

REPLACING THE PCV VALVE

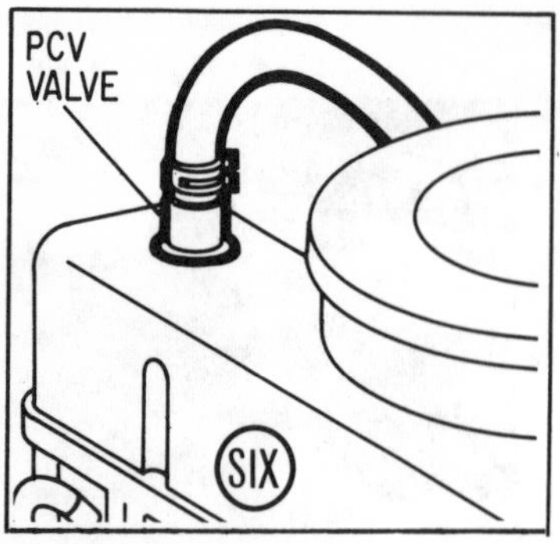

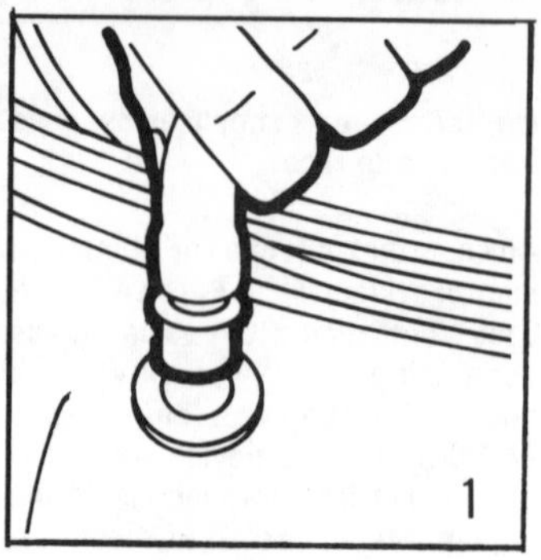

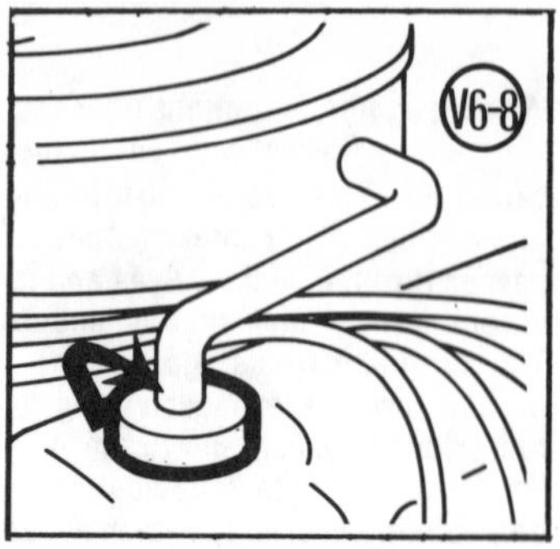

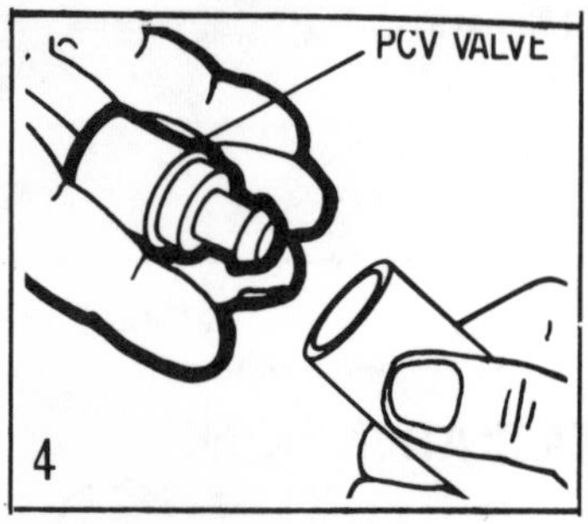

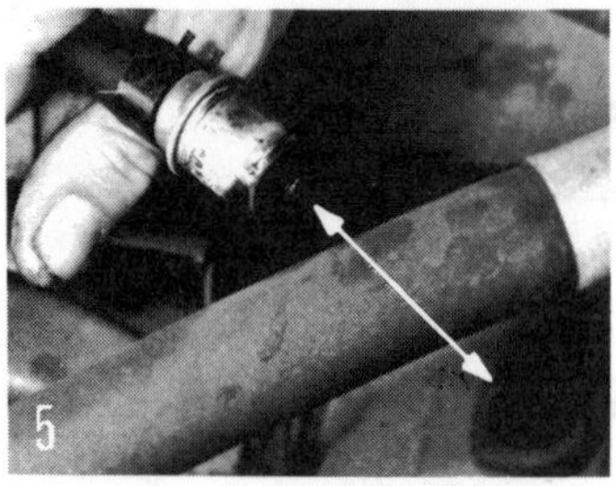

1. Pull valve from its location in rear part of valve cover.
2. Squeeze the hose clamp with a pair of pliers. Remove the valve.
3. Note where the other end of the hose connects. Remove the hose and flush it with cleaning solvent.
4. Reconnect the hose. Pinch the clamp and insert the PCV valve into the hose.
5. Insert the valve into the valve cover.

FUEL FILTER REPLACEMENT

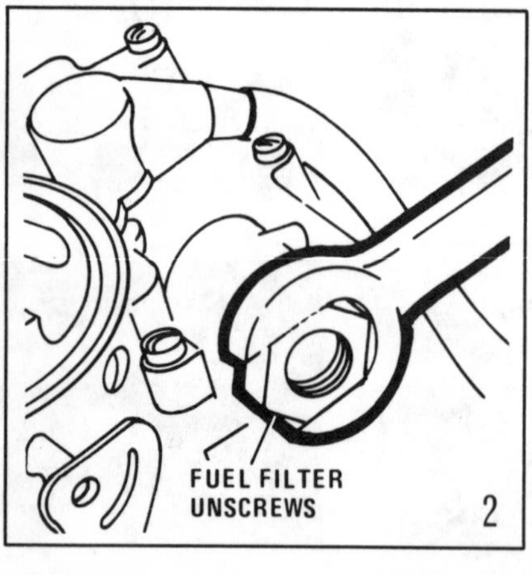

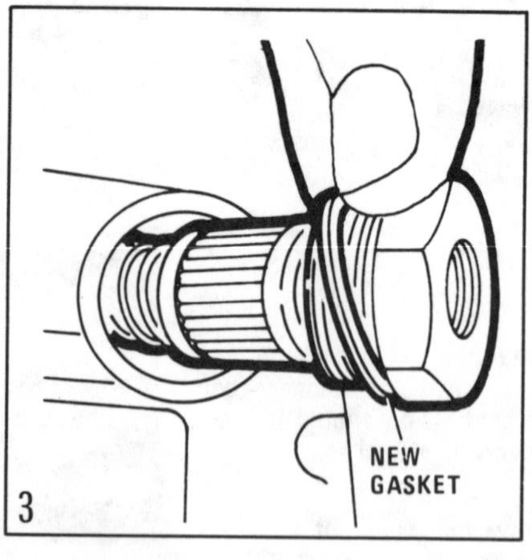

The fuel filter is located behind the large fuel line inlet nut on the carburetor. Replace the filter every year or 12,000 miles. The fuel filter prevents dirt, rust, and scale from both the gas station's tank and your own fuel tank from reaching the carburetor. A dirty filter will starve the engine and cause poor running.

1. Place an absorbent rag under fuel line connection to absorb gas spills.

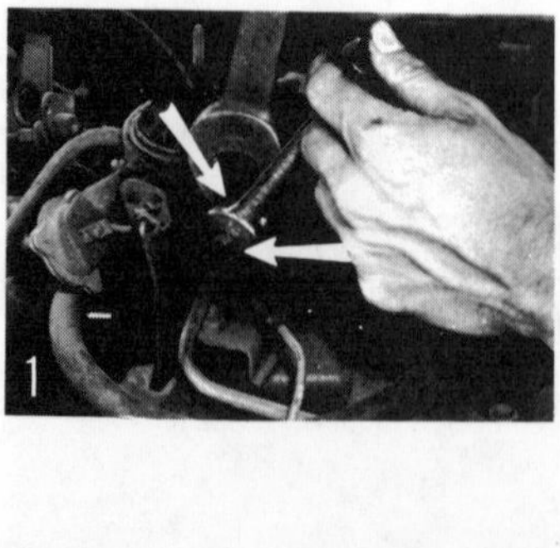

Unscrew fuel line connection with ½ in. wrench while holding the larger nut with a 1 in. wrench. Be careful, fuel line fitting threads are easily stripped.

2. Remove the large filter retaining nut from the carburetor. The spring behind the filter will push it out. Remove the filter and the spring.
3. Install the spring and new filter element. Some carburetors are

equipped with a paper element, others with a bronze unit. The bronze filter must have the small cone section facing out and a gasket between the filter and the retaining nut.

4. Install the new gasket on the retaining nut and screw it into place. CAUTION: DO NOT OVERTIGHTEN
5. Reconnect the fuel line. Discard the gas soaked rag safely.
6. Start the engine and check for leaks. Addition of a can of carburetor cleaner to the fuel tank occasionally will aid in keeping the entire fuel system clean.

Safety Systems

Headlights, turn signals, stop lights, and parking lights are an important part of your car's safety system. They permit you to see and be seen. Keep all lenses clean and make frequent checks to be sure that all of your lights are functioning properly. Replace any cracked lenses as soon as possible. When replacing a bulb, make a note of the number which is usually printed on the base. If you don't have a number, take the old bulb with you so that you match it for the correct replacement.

REPLACING TURN SIGNAL, STOP, AND BACK-UP LIGHT BULBS

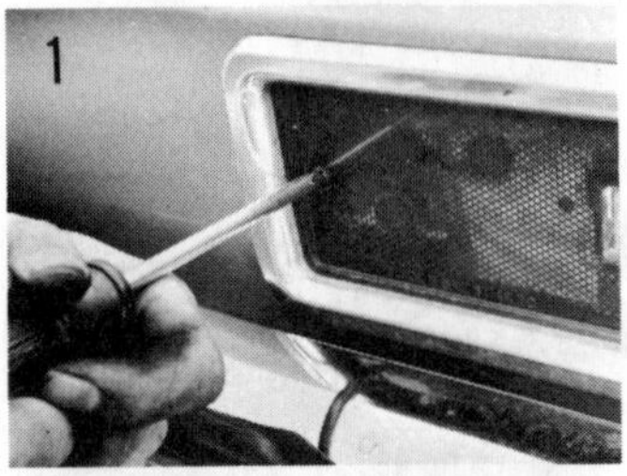

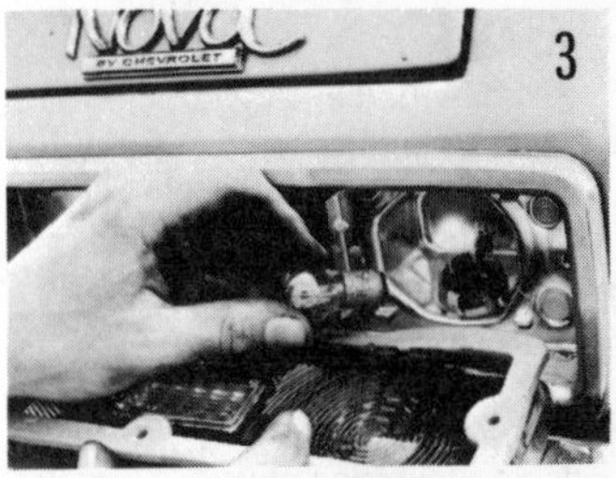

To replace a turn signal, stop light, or back-up light bulb, remove the lens, push down on bulb while turning it counterclockwise to remove it from the socket. Install the new bulb in reverse order. Be sure to match the knobs on the bulb base with the slots in the socket. If there are no screws on the lens, you will have to remove the socket from the back of the light unit. In some cases, you may have to remove the light unit in order to remove the socket.

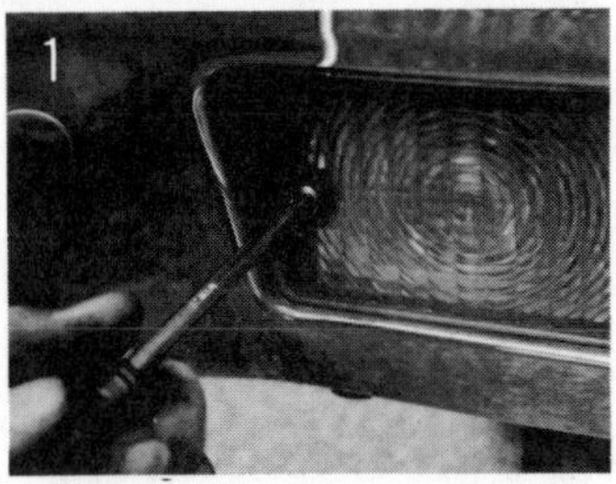

REPLACING INTERIOR DOME LIGHT

This is a cartridge type bulb; be sure to purchase correct replacement. Pry dome light lens out from housing. To avoid blowing fuse, make sure doors are closed and dome light switch is in OFF position. Carefully lever the bulb straight out of housing. Insert new bulb and re-install dome light lens.

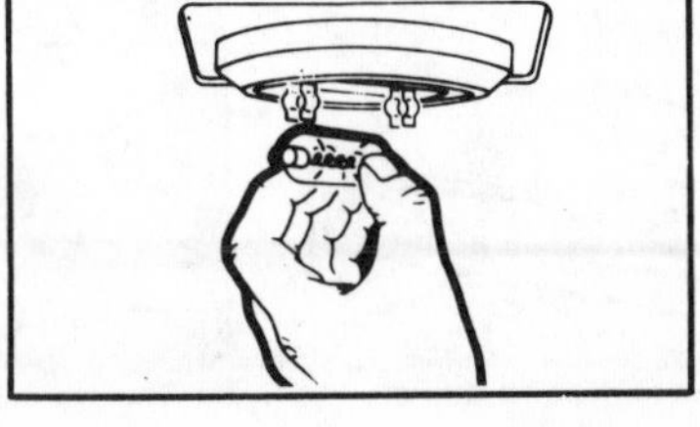

REPLACING HEADLIGHT SEALED BEAMS

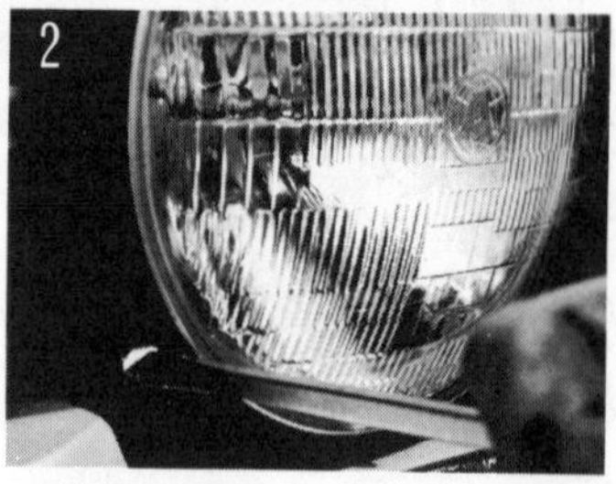

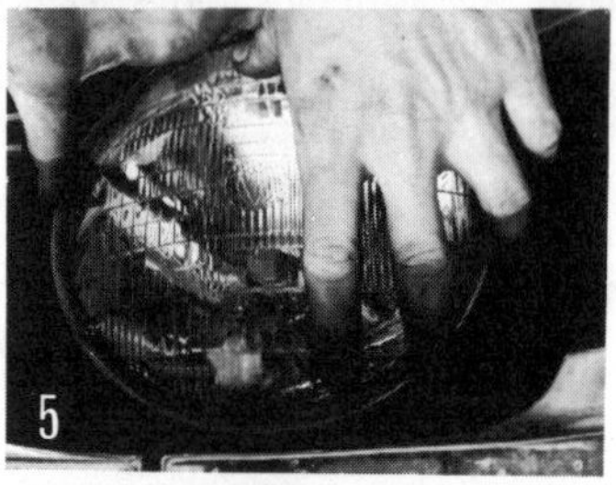

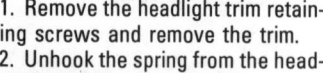

1. Remove the headlight trim retaining screws and remove the trim.
2. Unhook the spring from the headlight retaining ring.
3. Remove the two retaining ring screws. Do not disturb the long aiming screws at the top and side.
4. Remove the retaining ring. Disconnect the wiring plug and remove the bulb.
5. Attach the connector plug to the new headlight.
6. Position the new bulb in housing. Make sure that the number molded into the lens is at the top.
7. Install the retaining ring and pull the spring into place.
8. Replace the headlight trim panel.

WINDSHIELD WIPER BLADE REPLACEMENT

To replace wiper blade, lift up on spring release tab on wiper arm connector. Pull wiper blade off. Snap new blade into place.

To replace rubber insert only, press down, away from wiper blade to free it. Slide insert from blade. Insert new wiper. Bend insert upward slightly to engage retaining clips.

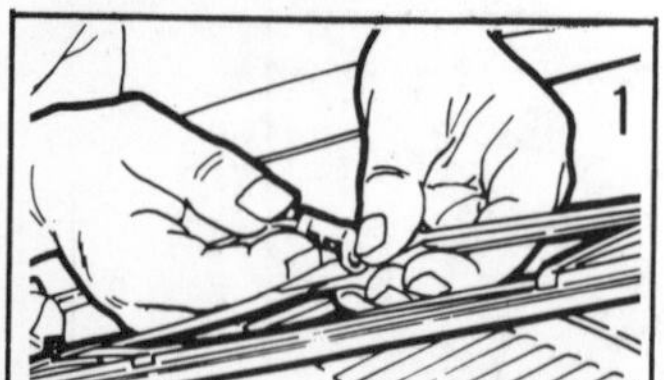

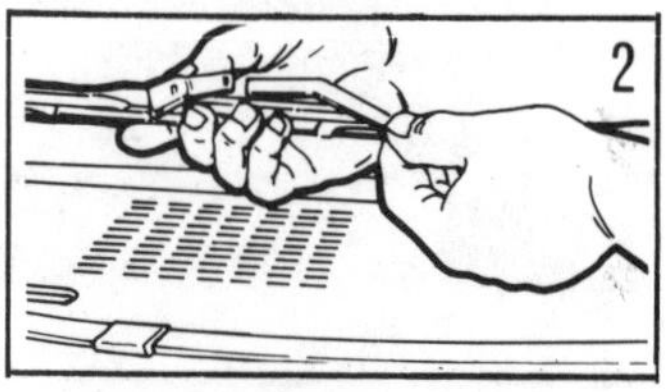

HORN PROBLEMS

If horn sounds and does not stop, this is due to short circuit in wiring. Disconnect wiring connector under hood and have professional service shop check horn wiring circuit.

STEERING PROBLEMS

See steering system check in Suspension Section. Check tire pressures. Have a professional service shop check all components in the front end and steering system.

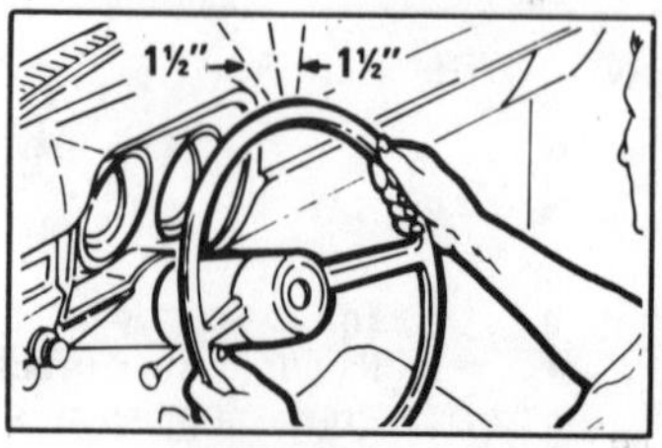

SERVICING WINDSHIELD WASHERS

If washer fails to squirt properly, raise hood and check system hose

connections. Be sure washer fluid container has fluid. Check spout openings for clogging.
Keep container filled with fluid mixture of washer solvent and water. If road spray buildup on windshield is a chronic problem, add 1 tablespoon dishwasher detergent to solvent/water mixture when re-filling container.

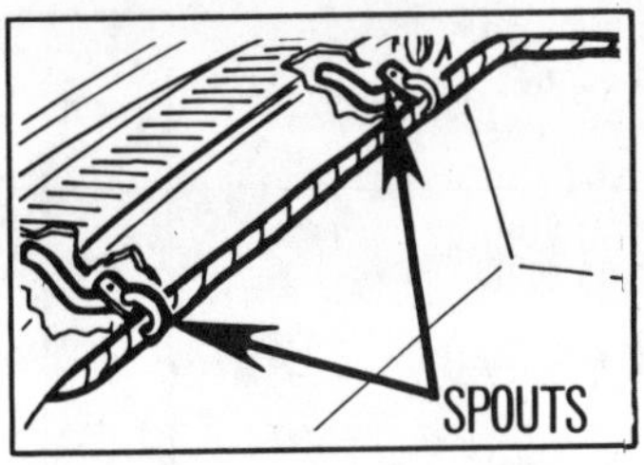

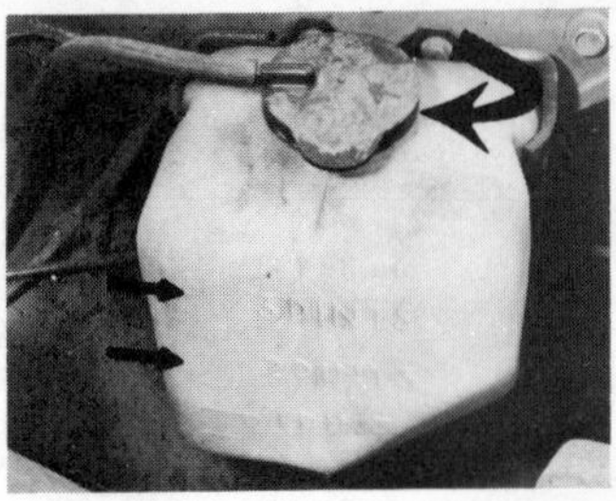

Electrical System

To ensure starting ability at all times check your battery condition periodically. You'll need to check battery electrolyte (fluid) level in each of the six cells. Check battery cable connections for tightness and inspect for accumulated corrosion.

Some 1976 and all 1977 GM products are equipped with a new type of no maintenance battery. This battery requires no maintenance other than occasionally checking its state of charge by looking at the indicator on the top. If the indicator is dark with a green dot showing in the center, the battery is fully charged. If the indicator is dark but there is no green dot showing, the battery should be charged. If the indicator is light, the battery should be replaced.

CHECKING BATTERY LEVEL

1. Remove plastic filler caps on top of battery. Fluid should be up to lower end of filler hole and covering the plates. If fluid is low add clean, cold tap water. If your area has hard water, use only distilled water available at auto supply, food or drug stores.
2. Replace any lost caps immediately.

CAUTION: NEVER LIGHT A MATCH OR SMOKE near the top of a battery. Batteries give off explosive hydrogen gas.

NOTE: Battery that often checks low on fluid could mean:

A. Battery is getting old, due for replacement; have charge capacity checked at service shop.

B. Connections may be corroded or loose; clean/replace as needed (see below).

C. Alternator or voltage regulator not functioning properly; this happens far less often than A or B above.

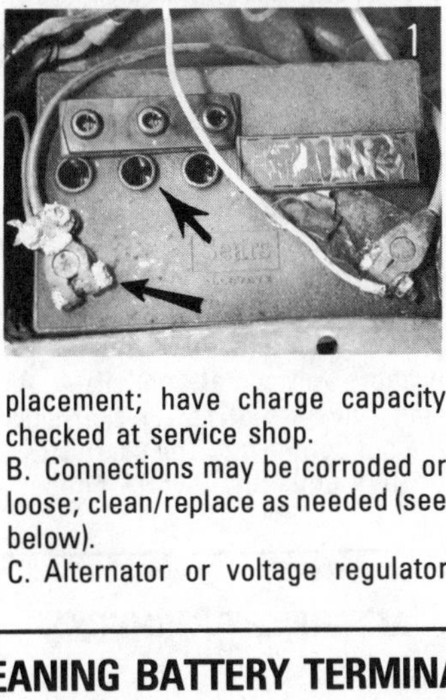

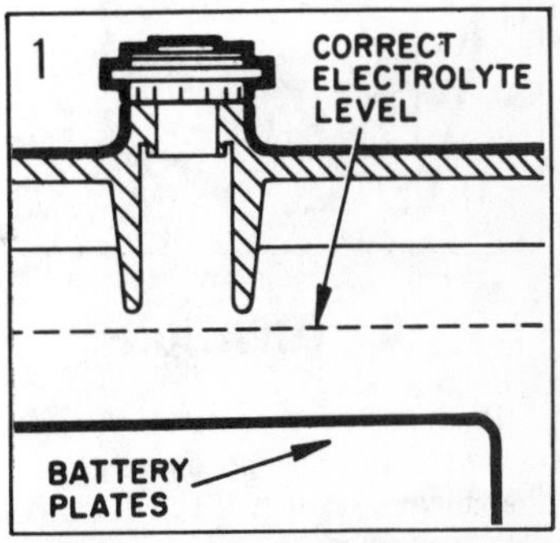

CLEANING BATTERY TERMINALS

As time goes by, battery terminals build up a dry powdery, whitish material. This material is corrosive and will gradually eat thru battery cables if not cleaned off periodically.

1. Loosen and remove battery connections.
2. Brush off all loose corrosion; use stiff bristle brush. Do not get this material into eyes or on open cuts. Wash off at once.
3. If corrosion build-up is extremely heavy and brushing does not remove all of it, mix 2 tablespoons baking

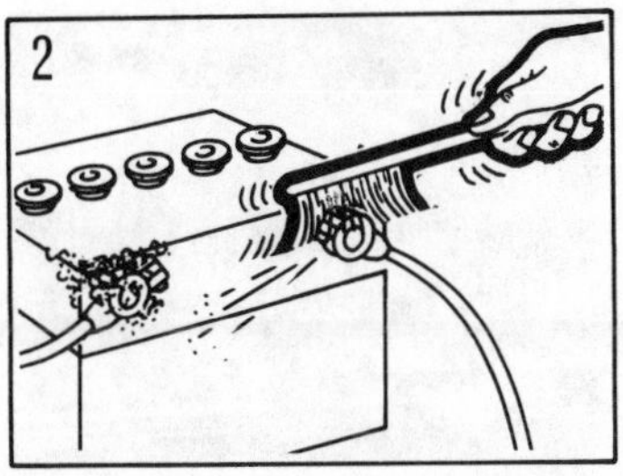

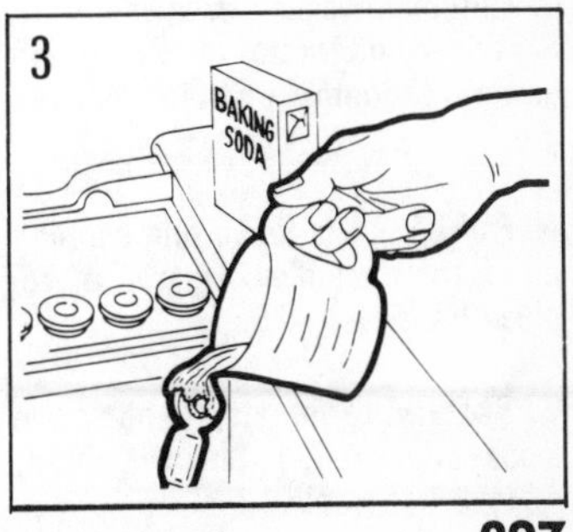

soda to 1 cup water. Pour solution directly onto terminals and connectors. Allow to soak a few minutes and rinse off. Continue brushing to remove all traces of corrosion build-up. Do not allow cleaning solution to enter battery.
4. Replace connectors on battery terminal posts and tighten.
5. Liberally smear battery terminal posts and cable connectors with petroleum jelly.

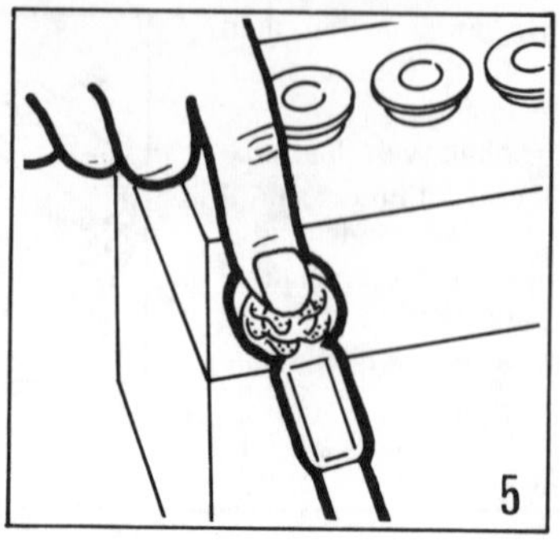
5

BATTERY HOLDDOWN

The clamp device which holds battery in place should be checked periodically. If loose, tighten. Clean off corrosion buildup. Severely corroded holddown components should be replaced before they break.

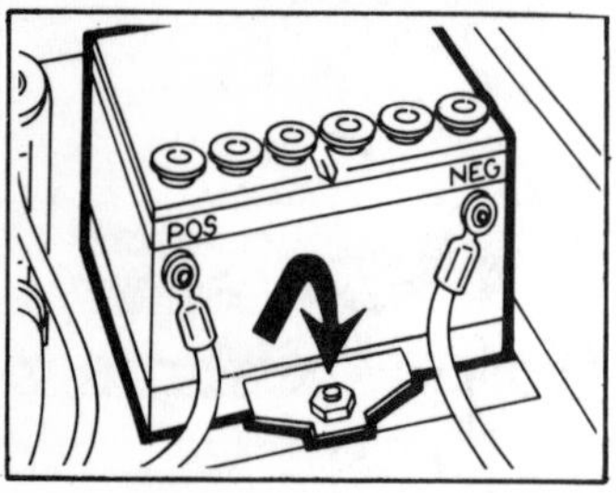

FUSE LOCATION

The fuse box is located to the left of the steering column, directly over the dimmer switch. Each fuse is clearly marked as to function and correct amperage. Always replace fuse with one of same amperage. If fuses are always blowing, have checked by professional mechanic.

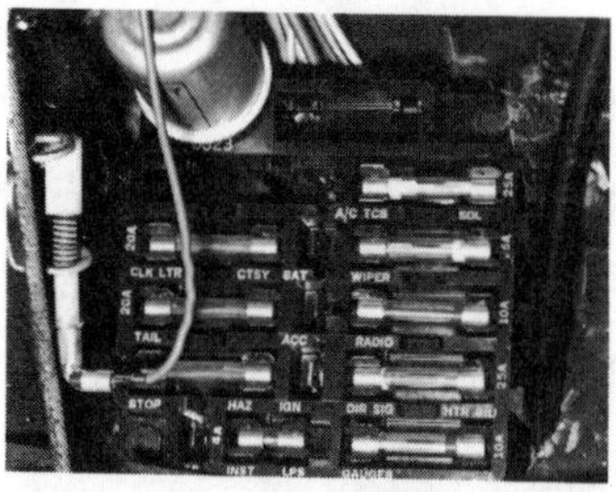

TURN SIGNAL AND 4-WAY FLASHER

Turn signals and 4-way emergency flashers will operate only if: A. All light bulbs are OK. B. Flasher units are not burned out. The car has two flasher units that work independently of each other. TURN SIGNAL FLASHER: located behind left side of instrument panel or near steering column. Pull flasher from spring clip mounting. Unplug from connector. Plug in new flasher. Replace in spring clip mounting. EMERGENCY FLASHER: located in fuse block. Simply unplug and insert new flasher. REPLACE ONLY WITH SAME TYPE FLASHER.

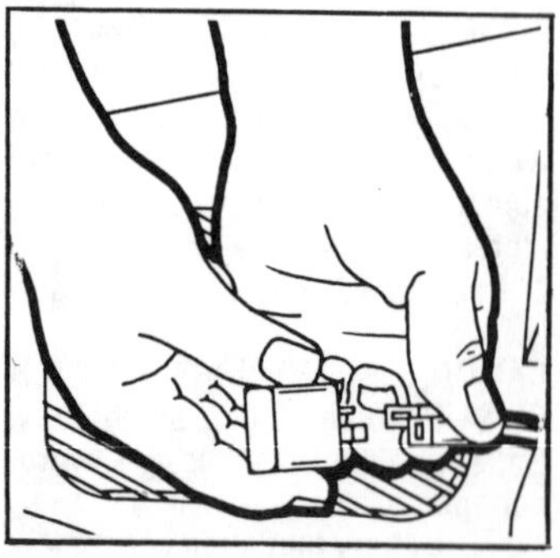

ALTERNATOR CHECKS

If Alt. warning light glows red or ammeter shows discharge at operating speed, alternator isn't charging battery properly. Common causes are:

A. Fan belts are loose and slipping on alternator pulley. Tighten or replace belts.

B. Battery terminals, cables are loose or corroded. Clean; tighten; replace bad cables.

If A or B do not correct problem, alternator or voltage regulator may be faulty. This happens far less often, and can only be checked by mechanic with proper electrical testing equipment.

Alternator Caution: Alternator can be permanently damaged by short-circuiting terminal connections. When working around or moving alternator, always keep metal tools or engine parts from terminals.

REPLACING BATTERY CABLES

If battery cable strands become frayed, broken or corroded, replace cable immediately. Delay in correcting this condition could lead to sudden failure to start the engine. Can also weaken battery.

1. Loosen and remove battery connections. Clean OFF any corrosion.
2. Disconnect negative cable from its attachment to engine or chassis. Disconnect positive cable from its attachment to starter relay.
3. Attach new cables making sure positive and negative cables are on proper terminals. They are not identical.
4. Replace connectors on battery terminal posts and tighten.
5. Liberally smear battery terminal posts and cable connectors with petroleum jelly.

Air Conditioning System

WARNING!—Never attempt to tighten fittings, disassemble or do any work on your car's A/C system. Consult a professional mechanic about A/C system problems and their correction. Your auto air conditioner (A/C) is a delicate, closed system. If air, dirt or water get into it, or if refrigerant escapes, the A/C unit will not cool a car interior. Among things you can do are:

1. Keep condenser grille clean. Check for dirt and debris; periodically remove dead insects, leaves, etc., with stiff bristle brush. Straighten any bent fins—carefully.
2. Keep radiator filled to correct level. (See Cooling System section). If fluid needs to be added, add antifreeze rather than water.
3. Keep radiator coolant at a 50/50 water/antifreeze mixture.
4. Flush cooling system and replace with fresh coolant mixture at least every 24 months. (See Cooling System section).
5. Radiator cap should be tight and sealed properly. If sealing gasket is cracked, cut or worn, replace cap with new 15 lb. unit.
6. Check fan belt tension periodically. (See Cooling System section). Replace glazed, frayed or cut fan belts, before they fail entirely.
7. Check periodically for bubbles in A/C sight glass. Sight glass is located in head of receiver/drier vessel. Or on the side of the V.I.R. assembly. Sight glass is no larger than head of large nail. It may be dirty. Wipe clean for best visibility.

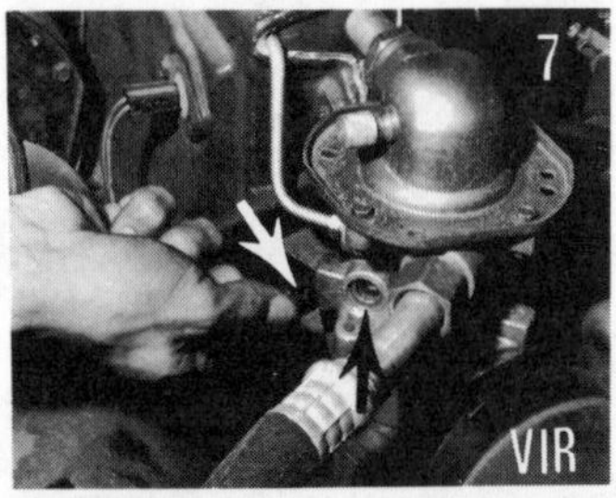

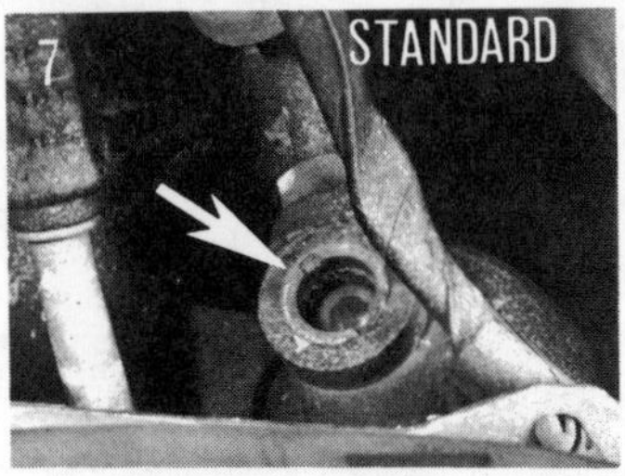

PROCEED AS FOLLOWS:

a) With engine and A/C system running, look for passage of refrigerant in sight glass. You'll be looking for a stream of milky white bubbles as they pass through sight glass. It is best to watch sight glass and have someone else start the car and turn on the A/C system. Allow to run for a few minutes.

b) If you observe no bubbles, and air flow from A/C unit in the car is passing cold air, everything is OK.

c) If no bubbles appear in sight glass, and air flow from the A/C unit in the car is not delivering cold air, the system may be low on refrigerant and could need a re-charge.

d) If bubbles appear, system is low on refrigerant.

e) If you suspect refrigerant loss based on tests performed above, have system checked by a professional A/C service shop. They can confirm refrigerant loss, recharge the system and check for system leakage.

NOTE: Once a week or so, even in winter, run A/C system for about 5 minutes as you drive. This keeps system internally lubricated, prevents hoses hardening.

TUNE-UP SPECIFICATIONS

YEAR	ENGINE No. Cyl. Displacement (cu. in.)	SPARK PLUGS Type	SPARK PLUGS Gap (in.)	DISTRIBUTOR Point Dwell (deg.)	DISTRIBUTOR Point Gap (in.)	IGNITION TIMING Man. Trans.● (deg.)■	IGNITION TIMING Auto Trans.● (deg.)■	IDLE SPEED Man. Trans.● (rpm)▲	IDLE SPEED Auto Trans. (rpm)▲
	Nova								
1970	4-153	R-46N	.035	31-34	.019	TDC	4B	750	650
	6-230, 250	R-46N	.035	31-34	.019	TDC	4B	700	550/400⑤
	8-307	R-45	.035	29-31	.019	2B	8B	700	600/450⑤
	8-350 2 bbl	R-44	.035	29-31	.019	TDC	4B	750	600/450⑤
	8-350 4 bbl	R-44	.035	29-31	.019	TDC	4B	700	600
1971	6-250	R-46TS	.035	31-34	.019	4B	4B	550	500
	8-307	R-45TS	.035	29-31	.019	4B	8B	600	550①
	8-350 2 bbl	R-45TS	.035	29-31	.019	2B	6B	600	550①
	8-350 4 bbl	R-44TS	.035	29-31	.019	4B	8B	600	550①
1972	6-250	R-46T	.035	31-34	.019	4B	4B	700	600
	8-307	R-44T	.035	29-31	.019	4B	8B	900	600
	8-350 2 bbl	R-44T	.035	29-31	.019	6B	6B	900	600
	8-350 4 bbl	R-44T	.035	29-31	.019	4B	8B	800	600
1973	6-250	R-46T	.035	31-34	.019	6B	6B	700/450⑤	600/450⑤
	8-307	R-44T	.035	29-31	.019	4B	8B	900/450⑤	600/450⑤
	8-350 2 bbl	R-44T	.035	29-31	.019	8B	8B	900/450⑤	600/450⑤
	8-350 4 bbl	R-44T	.035	29-31	.019	8B	12B	900/450⑤	600/450⑤
1974	6-250	R-46T	.035	31-34	.019	6B	6B	800/450⑤	600/450⑤
	8-350 2 bbl	R-44T	.035	29-31	.019	4B	8B	900/450⑤	600/450⑤
	8-350 4 bbl	R-44T	.035	29-31	.019	4B	8B	900/450⑤	600/450⑤
1975	6-250	R-46TX	.060	Electronic		10B	10B	800/425⑤	550/425⑤ (600/425)⑤
	8-262	R-44TX	.060	Electronic		8B	8B	800	600
	8-350 2 bbl	R-44TX	.060	Electronic		6B	6B	800	600
	8-350 4 bbl	R-44TX	.060	Electronic		6B	8B(6B)	800	600
1976	6-250	R-46TS	.035	Electronic		8B	6B	850	550①(600)
	8-305	R-45TS	.045	Electronic		6B	8B(TDC)	800	600
	8-350	R-45TS	.045	Electronic		8B(6B)	8B(6B)	800	600
1977	6-250	See Underhood Specification Sticker							
	8-305								
	8-350								
	Omega								
1973	6-250	R-46T	.035	33	.019	6B	6B	700/450⑤	600/450⑤
	8-350 2 bbl	R-46S	.040	30	.016	——	14B	——	650/500⑤
	8-350 4 bbl	R-46S	.040	30	.016	——	12B	——	650/500⑤
1974	6-250	R-46T	.035	33	.019	8B	8B	850/450⑤	600/450⑤
	8-350	R-46S	.040	30	.016	——	12B	——	650/500⑤
1975	6-250	R-46TX	.060	Electronic		10B	10B	800/425⑤	600/425⑤
	8-260	R-46SX	.080	Electronic		16B	18B(14B)	750	650/550⑤
	8-350	R-45TSX	.060	Electronic		——	12B	——	600
1976	6-250	R-46TX	.060	Electronic		10B	10B	850/425⑤	550/425⑤ (600/425)⑤
	8-260	R-46SX	.080	Electronic		16B	18B(14B)	750	550(600)②
	8-350	R-45TSX	.060	Electronic		——	12B	——	600
1977	6-231	See Underhood Specification Sticker							
	6-250								
	8-260								
	8-350								

TUNE-UP SPECIFICATIONS

YEAR	ENGINE No. Cyl. Displacement (cu. in.)	SPARK PLUGS Type	SPARK PLUGS Gap (in.)	DISTRIBUTOR Point Dwell (deg.)	DISTRIBUTOR Point Gap (in.)	IGNITION TIMING Man. Trans.● (deg.)■	IGNITION TIMING Auto Trans.● (deg.)■	IDLE SPEED Man. Trans.● (rpm)▲	IDLE SPEED Auto Trans. (rpm)▲
				Ventura					
1971	6-250	R-45T	.035	31-24	.019	4B	4B	500	500
	8-307	R-45TS	.035	29-31	.019	4B	8B	600	550
1972	6-250	R-45T	.035	31-34	.019	4B	4B	700/450⑤	600/450⑤
	8-307	R-45TS	.035	29-31	.019	4B	8B	900/450⑤	600/450⑤
	8-350	R-46TS	.035	29-31	.019	10B	10B	800	625
1973	6-250	R-46T	.035	31-34	.019	6B	6B	700/450⑤	600
	8-350	R-46TS	.040	29-31	.019	10B	12B	900/600⑤	650
	8-350 dual exh.	R-46TS	.040	29-31	.019	10B	12B	900/600⑤	650
1974	6-250	R-46T	.035	32½	.019	6B	6B	850/450⑤	600/450⑤
	8-350 2 bbl	R-46TS	.040	30	.019	10B	12B(10B)	900/600⑤	650(625)
	8-350 4 bbl	R-46TS	.040	30	.019	10B	12B(10B)	1000/600⑤	650(625)
1975	6-250	R-46TX	.060	Electronic		10B	10B	850	550(600)
	8-260	R-46SX	.080	Electronic		16B	18B(16B)	——	600
	8-350 2 bbl	R-45TSX	.060	Electronic		——	12B	——	650(625)
	8-350 4 bbl	R-45TSX	.060	Electronic		——	12B	——	650(625)
1976	6-250	R-46TX	.060	Electronic		10B	10B	850	550(600)③
	8-260	R-46SX	.080	Electronic		16B(14B)	18B(14B)	750	550(600)
	8-350 2 bbl	R-45TSX	.060	Electronic		——	12B	——	600
	8-350 4 bbl	R-45TSX	.060	Electronic		——	12B	——	600
1977	4-151 6-231 8-260 8-350			See Underhood Specifications Sticker					
				Apollo/Skylark					
1974	6-250	R-46T	.035	32	.019	8B	6B	950/450⑤	600/450⑤
	8-350	R-45TS	.040	30	.016	——	4B	——	650/500⑤
1975	V6-231	R-44SX	.060	Electronic		12B	12B	800/600⑤	700
	6-250	R-46TX	.060	Electronic		10B	10B	850	550
	8-260	R-46SX	.080	Electronic		——	18B(14B)	——	650
	8-350	R-45TSX	.060	Electronic		12B	12B	——	600
1976	V6-231	R-44SX	.060	Electronic		12B	12B	800/600⑤	600
	8-260	R-46SX	.080	Electronic		——	18B(14B)	——	550/650⑤ (600/650)⑤④
	8-350	R-45TSX	.060	Electronic		——	12B	——	600
1977	6-231 8-260 8-350			See Underhood Specification Sticker					

▲ Adjust automatic transmissions in Drive (AMC/Ford/GM) or Neutral (Chrysler), all manual transmissions are adjusted in Neutral.
■ All figures are Before Top Dead Center.
● Figure in parentheses indicate California engine.
2 bbl. 4 bbl—Carburetor type, 2 barrel, 4 barrel
TDC—Top Dead Center
① With the air conditioner on
② 650 with air conditioning
③ 575 with air conditioning, except in California
④ Lower figure with air conditioning on
⑤ Where two figures are separated by a slash, lower figure is with solenoid disconnected, unless specified otherwise

NOTE: The underhood specifications sticker often reflects tune-up specification changes made in production. Sticker figures must be used if they disagree with those in this chart.

CAPACITIES

YEAR	ENGINE No. Cyl. Displacement (cu. in.)	ENGINE OIL Add 1 qt. with New Filter	TRANSMISSION Pts. to Refill after Draining MANUAL 3-speed	MANUAL 4-speed	AUTOMATIC	DRIVE AXLE (pts.)	COOLING SYSTEM with Heater (qts.)	COOLING SYSTEM with Air Cond. (qts.)
Nova								
1970	4-153	3.5①	3	—	6	3.8④	9	9
	6-230, 250	4	3	—	6②	3.8④	12	13
	8-307	4	3	—	6②	3.8④	15	16
	8-350	4	3	3	6.5②③	3.8④	16	16
	8-396	4	3	3	8	4.3	23	24
1971	6-250	4	3	—	6②	3.8	12	—
	8-307	4	3	—	6②	3.8	15	16
	8-350	4	3	3	6.5②	3.8	16	16
1972	6-250	4	3	—	6②	4.3	12	—
	8-307	4	3	—	6②	4.3	15	16
	8-350	4	3	3	6.5②	4.3	16	16
1973	6-250	4	3	—	6②	4.3	12.5	—
	8-307	4	3	—	5	4.3	15.5	16.5
	8-350	4	3	3	5	4.3	15.5	16.5
1974	6-250	4	3	—	8	4.3	12.5	—
	8-350	4	3	3	8	4.3	15.5	16.5
1975	6-250	4	3	—	8	4.3	15	15
	8-262	4	3	—	8	4.3	17	18
	8-350	4	3	3	8	4.3	17	17
1976	6-250	4	3	—	8	4.3	15	15
	8-305	4	3	—	8	4.3	17	18
	8-350	4	3	3	8	4.3	17	17
1977	6-250	4	3	—	8	4.3	15	15
	8-305	4	3	—	8	4.3	17	18
	8-350	4	3	3	8	4.3	17	17
Omega								
1973	6-250	4	3.5	—	6	4.3	12.5	—
	8-350	4	3.5	—	6	4.3⑤	15.9	16.5
1974	6-250	4	3.5	—	6	4.3	15.5	—
	8-350	4	—	—	6	4.3	18.5	19.5
1975	6-250	4	3.5	—	6	4.3	15.5	19.5
	8-260	4	3.5	—	6	4.3	18.5	19.5
	8-350	4	—	—	6	4.3	18.5	19.5
1976	6-250	4	3.5	—	6	3.5⑥	15.5	16.5
	8-260	4	3.5	3.5 ⑦	6	3.5⑥	23	23.5
	8-350	4	—	—	6	3.5⑥	21.5	22
1977	6-231	4	3.5	—	6	3.5⑥	16.6	16.7
	6-250	4	3.5	—	6	3.5⑥	15.5	16.5
	8-260	4	3.5	3.5 ⑦	6	3.5⑥	23	23.5
	8-350	4	—	—	6	3.5⑥	21.5	22

CAPACITIES

YEAR	ENGINE No. Cyl. Displacement (cu. in.)	ENGINE OIL Add 1 qt. with New Filter	TRANSMISSION Pts. to Refill after Draining MANUAL 3-speed	MANUAL 4-speed	AUTOMATIC	DRIVE AXLE (pts.)	COOLING SYSTEM with Heater (qts.)	COOLING SYSTEM with Air Cond. (qts.)
				Ventura				
1971	6-250	4	3	—	6	3.8	12	—
	8-307	4	3	—	6②	3.8	15	16
1972	6-250	4	3	—	6	3.8	12	16
	8-307	4	3	—	6②	3.8	15	16
	8-350	5	—	—	5	3.8	19.4	20.3
1973	6-250	4	3.5	—	6	4.3	12.1	—
	8-350	5	3.5	2.5	5	4.3	19.2	19.3
1974	6-250	4	3.5	—	6	4.3	12.1	—
	8-350	5	3.5	2.5	7.5	4.3	19.2	19.3
1975	6-250	4	3.5	—	5	3.8	13.5	13.5
	8-260	4	3.5	—	5	3.8	18.5	19.5
	8-350	5	—	—	5	3.8	18.5	19.5
1976	6-250	4	3.5	—	5	3.8	13.5	13.5
	8-260	4	3.5	3.5	5	3.8	18.5	19.5
	8-350	5	—	—	5	3.8	18.5	19.5
1977	4-151	—	—	—	—	—	—	—
	6-231	4	3.5	—	6	4.3	16.6	16.7
	8-260	4	—	3.5	5	3.8	18.5	19.5
	8-350	5	3.5	—	5	3.8	18.5	19.5
				Apollo/Skylark				
1974-75	V6-231	4	3.5	—	6	4.3	16.6	16.7
	6-250	4	3.5	—	6	4.3	16.9	17
	8-260	4	—	—	6	4.3	22.4	22.9
	8-350	4	—	—	6	4.3	18.9	19.3
1976	V6-231	4	3.5	—	6	4.3	16.6	16.7
	8-260	4	—	—	6	4.3	22.4	22.9
	8-350	4	—	—	6	4.3	18.9	19.3
1977	6-231	4	3.5	—	6	4.3	16.6	16.7
	8-260	4	—	—	6	4.3	22.4	22.9
	8-350	4	—	—	6	4.3	18.9	19.3

① Add ½ quart for new filter on four-cylinder engine
② 5 pts. with three-speed Turbo Hydra-Matic 350
③ 8 pts. with 360 hp. engine
④ 4.3 pts. with 8⅞ in. diameter ring gear rear axle
⑤ 5.4 pts. with limited slip differential
⑥ 4.3 pts. with 8½ in. diameter ring gear rear axle
— Not available
⑦ 3.5 (Dexron) with 5-speed

NOTE: Automatic transmission figures do not include torque converter

Service Record

DATE/MILEAGE	SERVICE	NEXT DUE

Pacer

Lubrication and Oil Change

BRAKE FLUID LEVEL CHECK

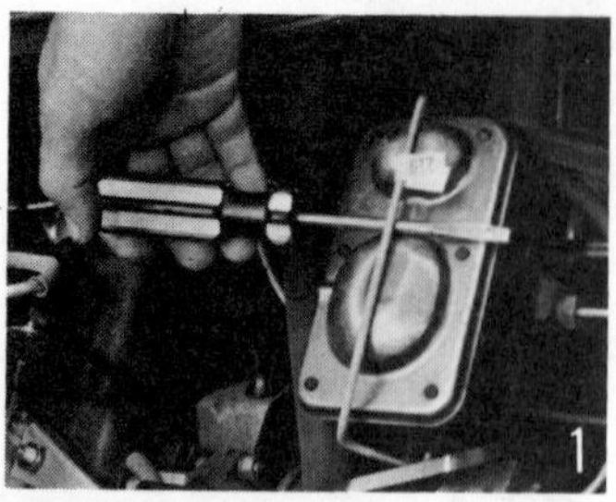

Check brake fluid level in master cylinder every three months . . . sooner if braking feels inadequate. Add when low. Recommended grade: DOT 3

Master cylinder is located under hood on left side. It is oblong container about 6″ long with cap held down by wire clip. Check brake fluid level as follows:

1. Pry wire retaining clip off cap top with screwdriver.
2. Remove cap and gasket by lifting up.
3. Fluid level should be within ¼ inch of top rim. If lower than this, add fresh fluid to appropriate level. DO NOT OVERFILL
4. Replace cap and gasket; secure retaining clip over cap. If fluid level was low, check again in a few days.
5. If fluid repeatedly checks low, there is a leak somewhere in the system. See SAFETY SYSTEMS—WHEEL CYLINDER CHECK. Have mechanic check further. Neglect can be dangerous.

MANUAL TRANSMISSION FLUID LEVEL CHECK

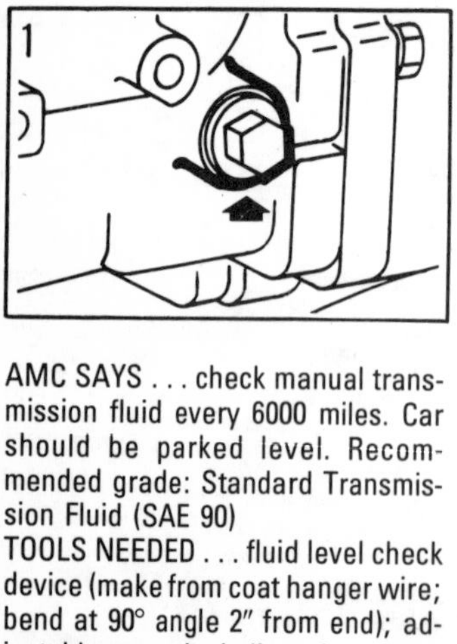

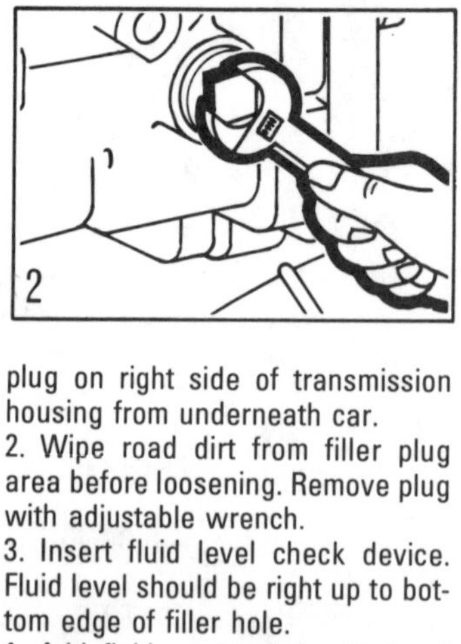

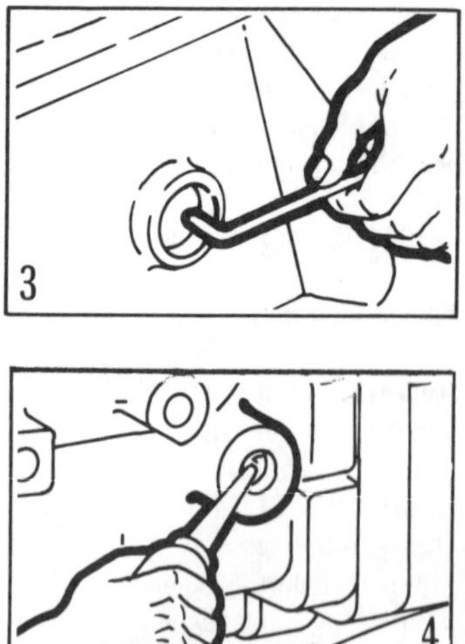

AMC SAYS . . . check manual transmission fluid every 6000 miles. Car should be parked level. Recommended grade: Standard Transmission Fluid (SAE 90)

TOOLS NEEDED . . . fluid level check device (make from coat hanger wire; bend at 90° angle 2″ from end); adjustable wrench; bulb syringe.

1. Locate transmission fluid filler plug on right side of transmission housing from underneath car.
2. Wipe road dirt from filler plug area before loosening. Remove plug with adjustable wrench.
3. Insert fluid level check device. Fluid level should be right up to bottom edge of filler hole.
4. Add fluid as needed with hand bulb syringe.

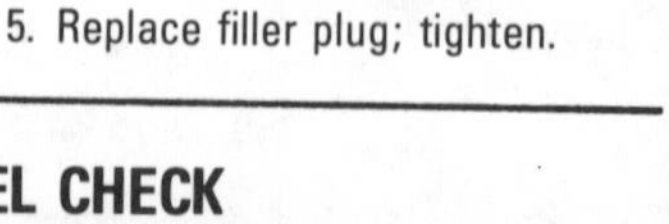

5. Replace filler plug; tighten.

AUTOMATIC TRANSMISSION FLUID LEVEL CHECK

AMC SAYS . . . check automatic transmission fluid DEXRON® level every 6000 miles. Recommended grade: DEXRON® (Type A)

TOOLS . . . Long neck filler funnel

1. Engine must be warmed up and running. Place shift lever in Neutral position.
2. Pull out dipstick. Wipe clean.

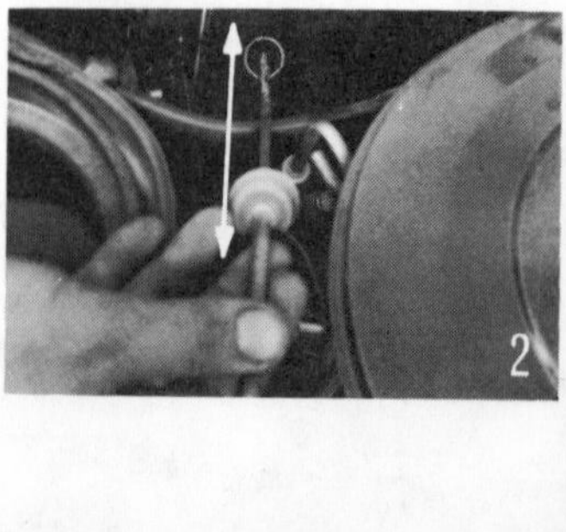

Push dipstick all the way back in; remove it again.
3. If fluid is below ADD mark, add ATF to bring level up. DO NOT OVERFILL.
4. Add ATF thru transmission dipstick hole by means of long-neck filler funnel.

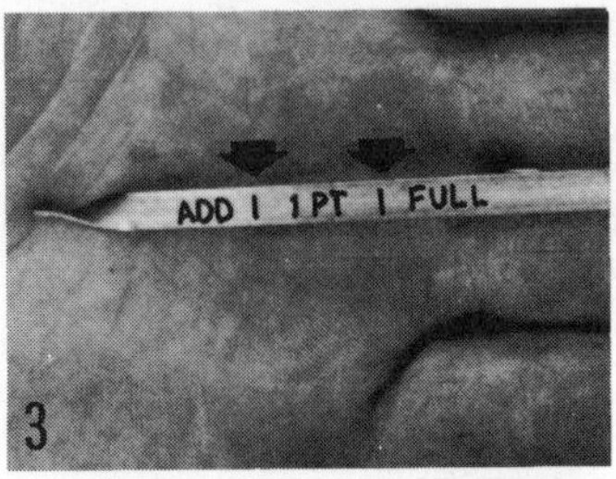

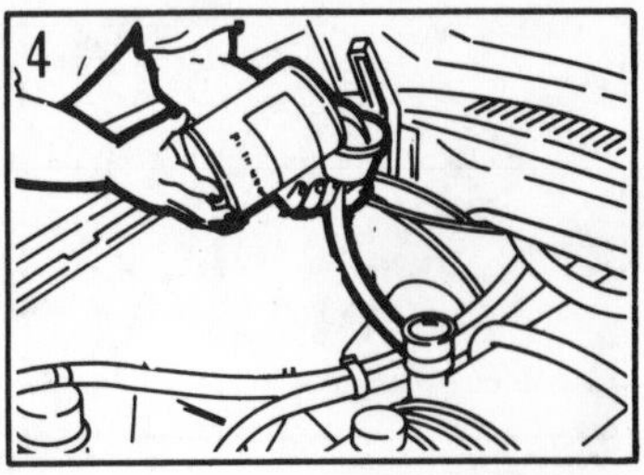

REAR AXLE LUBRICANT

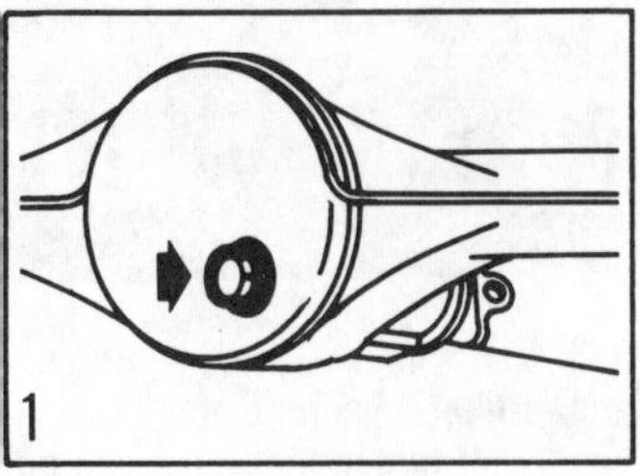

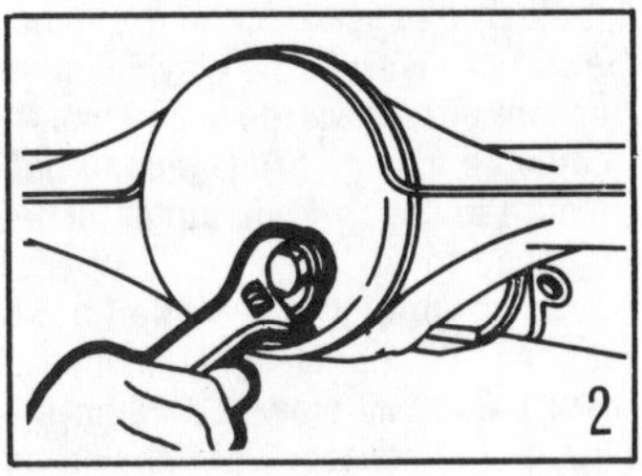

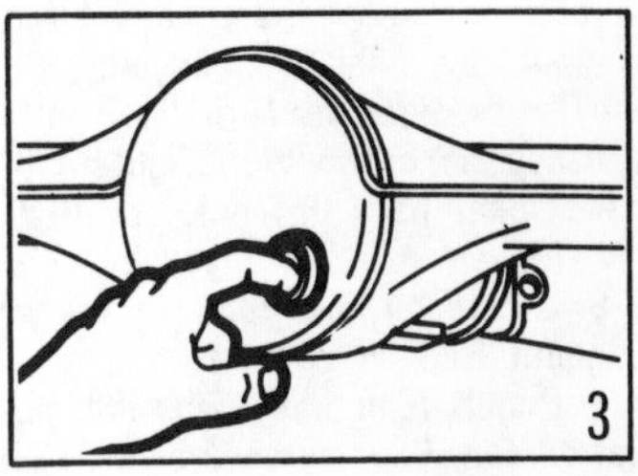

AMC SAYS . . . check rear axle lube level every 6000 miles. Recommended grade: Hypoid gear lube (SAE 90)
TOOLS . . . adjustable hand wrench; fluid level check device (made from coat hanger wire; bend at 90° angle 2″ from end); bulb syringe.
1. Locate filler plug on rear of rear axle housing.

2. Wipe plug area clean; remove plug with wrench.
3. Insert wire level check device; remove. Adequate fluid level should show lubricant on last ¼-inch of wire.
4. If fluid level is low, add as needed, with a hand bulb syringe, until level shows on last ¼-inch of wire.
5. Replace filler plug; tighten.

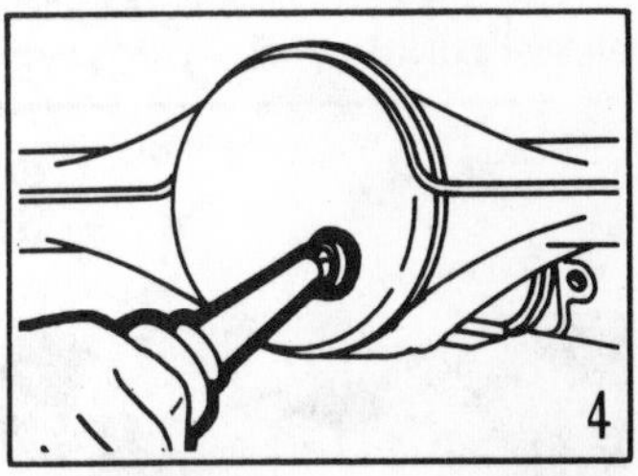

OIL AND FILTER CHANGE

AMC SAYS . . . Change oil and filter every 6000 miles. Recommended grade: MS or SE (check owner's handbook). Check oil level at least once a week.
TOOLS & MATERIALS . . . adjustable hand wrench; medium size screwdriver; oil filter removal wrench; drain pan for old oil (at least 5 qt. capacity); oil pouring spout; 5 qt. oil; new oil filter; oil and lubricants as specified below.
SAFETY TIP . . . use work gloves.
1. If engine is cold, start up and idle for about 5 minutes.
2. Park car on level ground. Turn engine off.
3. Locate oil drain plug on underside of engine. Place drain pan under plug.
4. Remove drain plug with wrench. Let ALL dirty oil drain out.

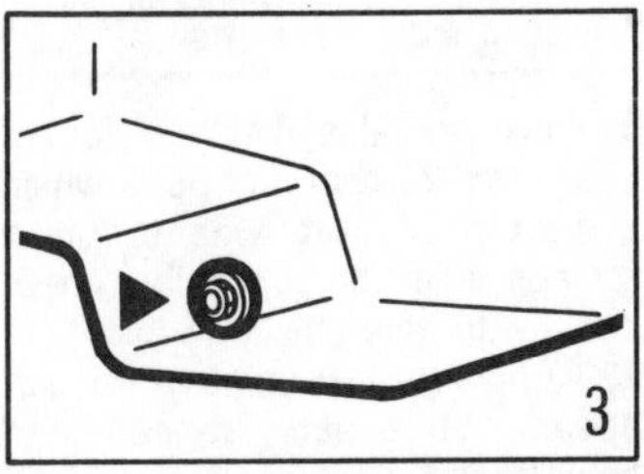

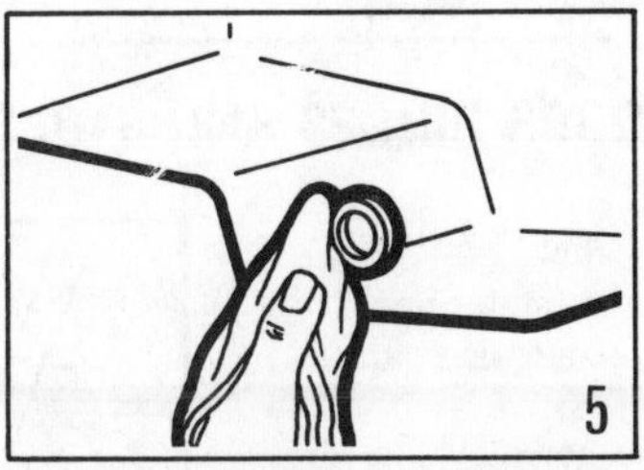

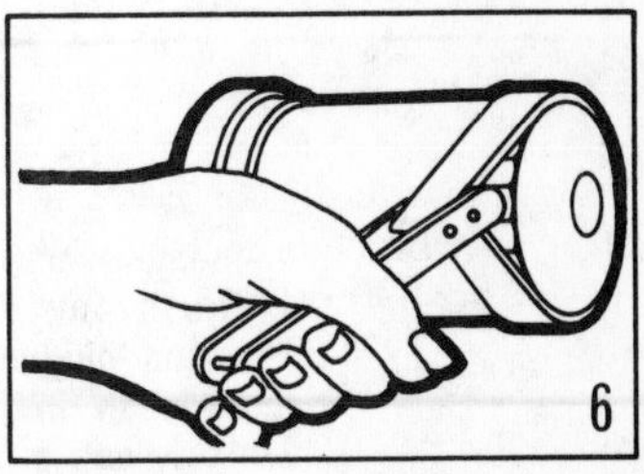

5. Wipe plug and area around drain hole clean. Replace drain plug; tighten it.
6. Locate oil filter. Move drain pan

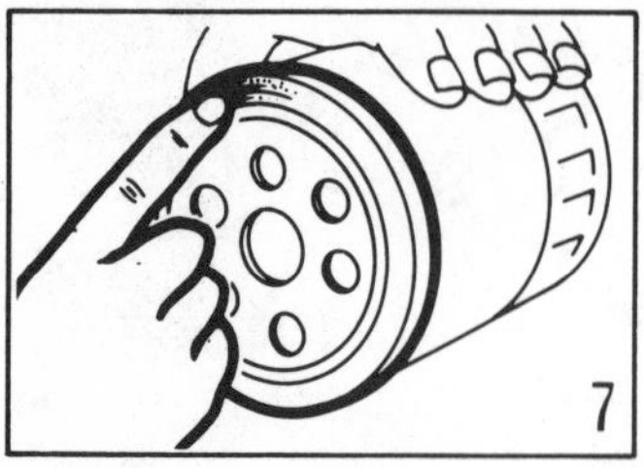

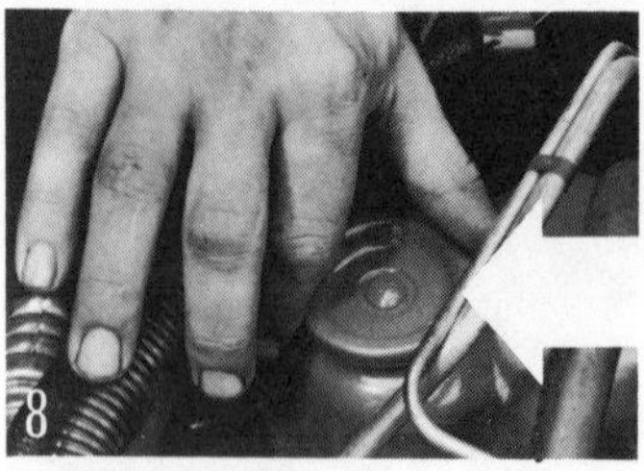

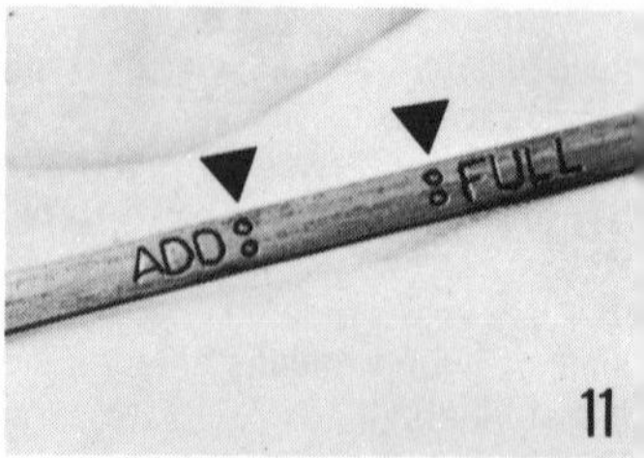

under filter. Loosen filter with oil filter wrench. Unscrew; remove filter by hand.

7. Smear fresh oil over surface of rubber gasket (washer) of new filter. Install new filter by hand only. Do NOT use wrench. Turn filter until gasket makes contact. Tighten an additional half turn only . . . NO MORE.

8. Locate oil filler tube on top of engine. Remove cap.

9. Punch oil pouring spout into top of oil can. Pour all cans of new oil into filler tube. Wipe filler cap clean and replace it. Be sure to re-attach all hoses. (NOTE: If filler cap is very dirty, rinse in turpentine or gasoline. Dry before replacing.)

10. Check new oil level at dipstick. Pull out dipstick, wipe clean.

11. Push dipstick back into engine. Be sure to insert all the way. Remove dipstick and check new oil level. It should be above "SAFE" line. If not, be sure to check if you put in all the oil called for.

12. Start up engine and idle for 3-5 minutes. Oil signal light on instrument panel will glow red when engine is first started. Light should go out in 30 seconds or less.

13. Stop engine and check for oil leaks at drain plug and filter. If you find any, check tightness of plug and/or filter, also for condition of filter gasket to see that it has not become pinched or damaged when installing. Recheck oil level, which should now be at "SAFE".

SPEEDOMETER CABLE LUBRICATION

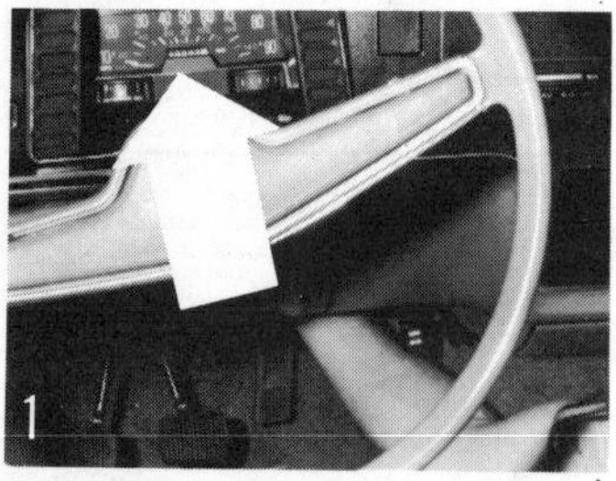

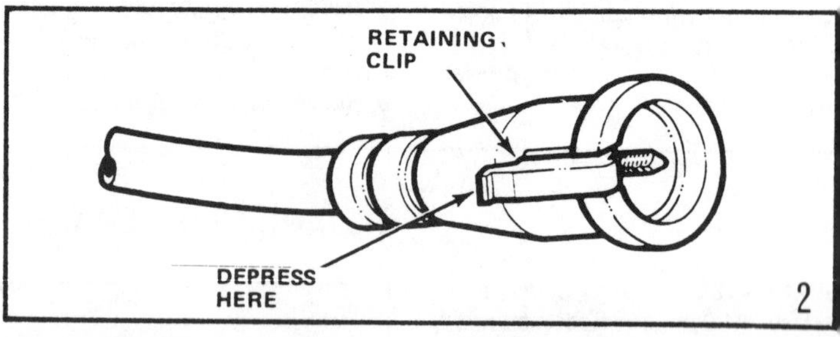

If speedometer pointer tends to quiver or jump, or if unit makes a low, rasping sound, lubrication may be needed.

1. Locate cable shaft attachment directly behind speedometer dial.
2. Press flat surface; pull cable back and out from behind panel.
3. Pull inner cable completely out of outer casing. Note carefully which end is top. Check for wear or frayed strands. If damaged, replace inner cable with new one.
4. Apply generous amount of speedometer cable lubricant into cable casing. Replace inner cable in shaft, noting that top end is not inserted accidentally. Turn inner cable as it is being re-inserted. Twist cable when all the way in, to lock into position at lower end.
5. Re-connect cable to speedometer head under instrument panel.

DOOR HINGES AND STOPS

(lubricate every 6 months)

1. Brush any dirt accumulations from door hinges and stops. Use old tooth brush or rag.
2. Apply dab of white polyethylene grease to door hinges, trunk hinges, hood hinges, door stops.

DOOR LOCKS

(lubricate every 6 months)
1. Insert door key half way into lock.
2. Spray aerosol lock lubricant into lock.
3. Push key rest of way into lock; turn back and forth several times.

Cooling System

IT IS RECOMMENDED . . . that radiator coolant (water/antifreeze mixture) level be checked once or twice a month. Do this when engine is cold. Check more often if you do a lot of hard driving.
Keep coolant up to recommended level in radiator. If coolant checks frequently low, look for leaks. Tighten all hose clamps occasionally. For best results, keep a 50/50 water/antifreeze mixture year

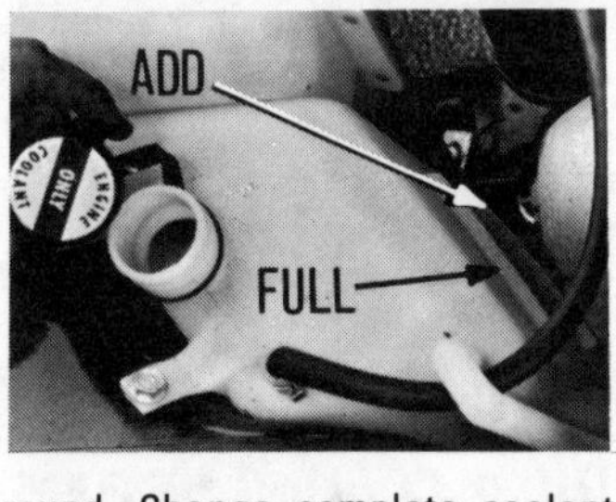

round. Change complete coolant mixture every 24 months.

CAUTION: If you must check coolant in a hot engine, cover radiator cap with thick rag before releasing. Remove cap slowly . . . press down and turn.
On cars equipped with a coolant recovery system, simply check the level visible through the translucent reservoir on the right side of the radiator. If it is necessary to add coolant, add to the reservoir, not the radiator.

REPLACING THE THERMOSTAT

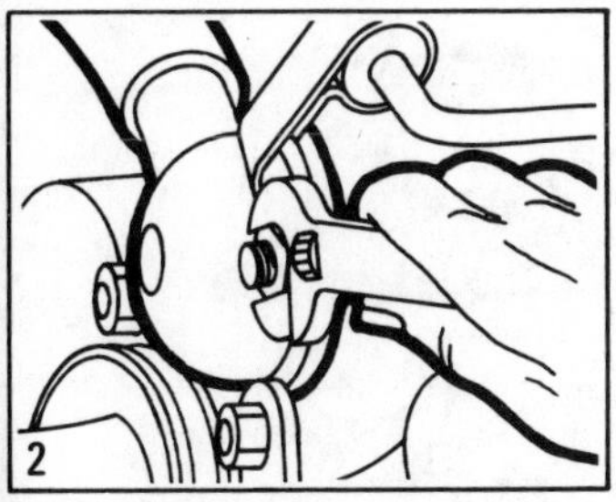

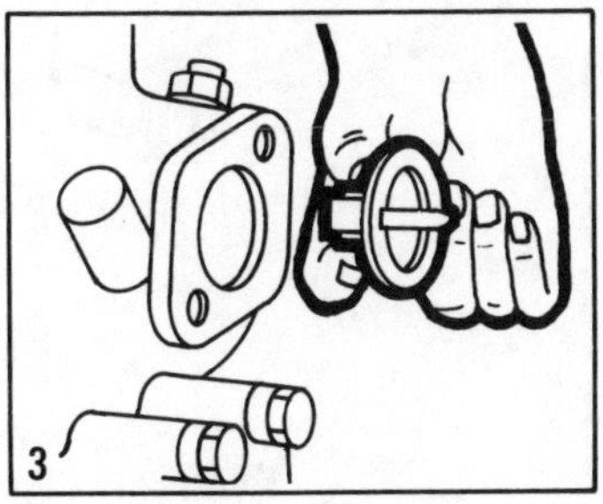

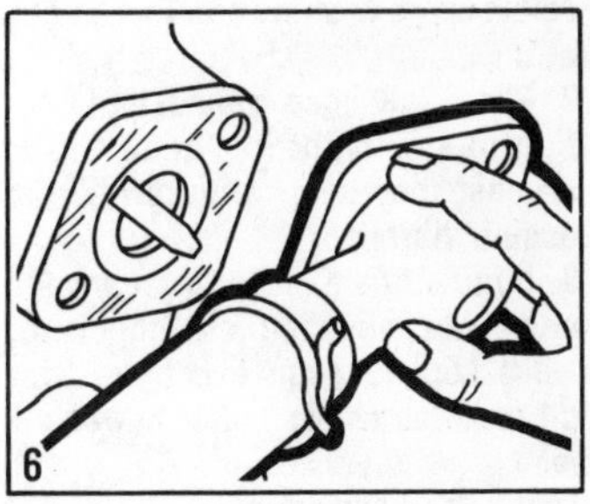

A faulty thermostat will usually cause engine overheating. Replace with new thermostat.
TOOLS AND MATERIALS . . .
New thermostat
Gasket sealer
Adjustable wrench
1. Drain radiator of about half its coolant. (See Hose Replacement section)
2. Loosen and remove both retaining bolts and lift thermostat housing off the engine.
NOTE: If you're careful it won't be necessary to remove radiator hose.
3. Remove old thermostat.
4. Scrape thermostat housing flange and engine block surface to remove old gasket debris.
5. Drop new thermostat into place—spring down.
6. Install new gasket with sealer applied to both sides.
7. Replace thermostat housing and tighten both retaining bolts.

FAN BELT ADJUSTMENT

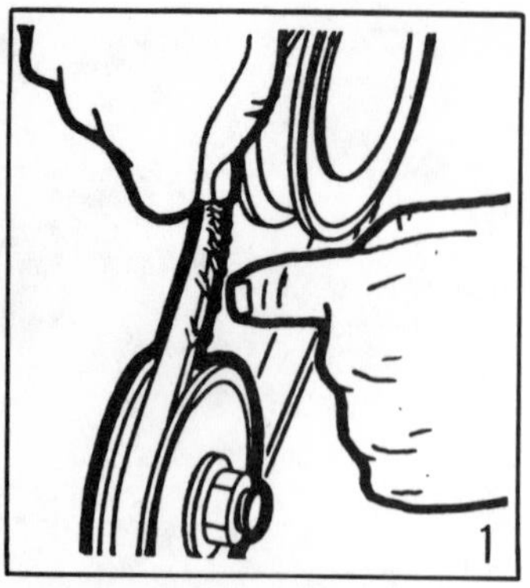

The fan belt not only drives the radiator fan, it turns the water pump and drives the alternator. Another belt drives the power steering pump. It's easy to see that the condition and proper tension of the belts are vital, since engine cooling, electrical power, and steering depend on them. The belts deserve an occasional look and tension check.

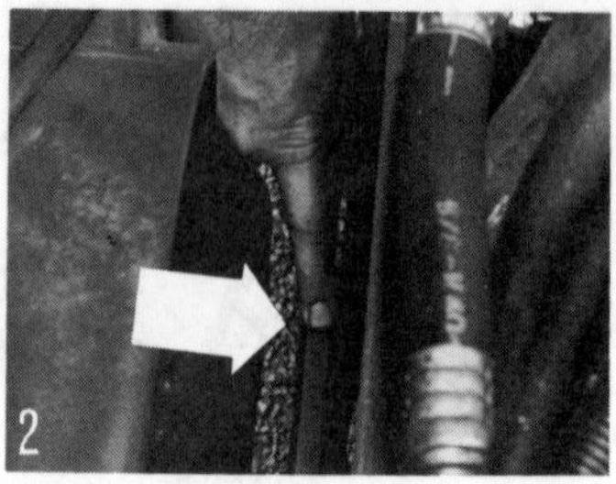

1. Inspect fan belt occasionally. If worn, frayed or cracked on inner driving surface, replace.

CAUTION: An overtightened belt may damage alternator and water pump, or power steering pump bearings.

2. Check tension occasionally. Press thumb at midpoint of belt span between pulleys. If belt depresses more than ½ inch, tightening is needed. A too-loose belt will not drive alternator and pumps effectively.

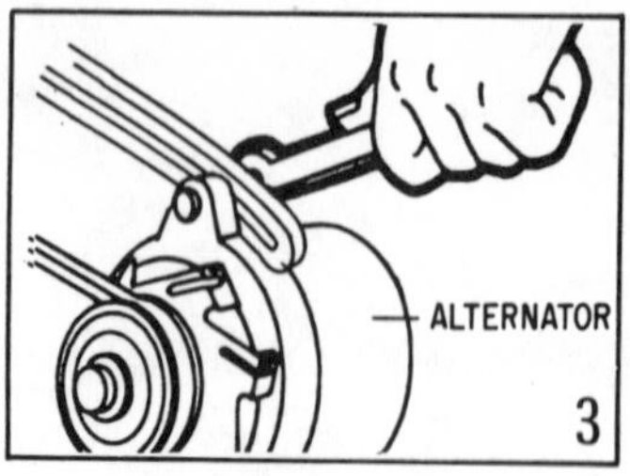

3. Adjust to proper tension of ¼ inch deflection. Adjust as follows:

A. Loosen mounting bolts at top and bottom so alternator can pivot on lower bolt and upper bolt can slide in bracket.

B. Pull alternator out slightly to put tension on belt, and hold while tightening upper bolt.

C. Check tension. Repeat adjustment as necessary.

D. When tension is correct, tighten lower bolt.

FIND THOSE COOLING SYSTEM LEAKS

1. Inspect all hoses. If any are weak, soft in spots or show cracks, replace at once.
2. Check all hose connections for tightness. Tighten loose hose clamps; they tend to loosen due to engine vibration.
3. If radiator steams or hisses when engine is switched off, check for leaks. Look for signs of coolant drips on radiator or around header tank joint.

Leaks are possible at:
Upper or lower radiator hoses
Water pump (gaskets or seal)
Heater core or connecting hoses
Automatic transmission cooler lines
Faulty radiator pressure cap
Faulty cylinder head gasket
Cracked cylinder head or block

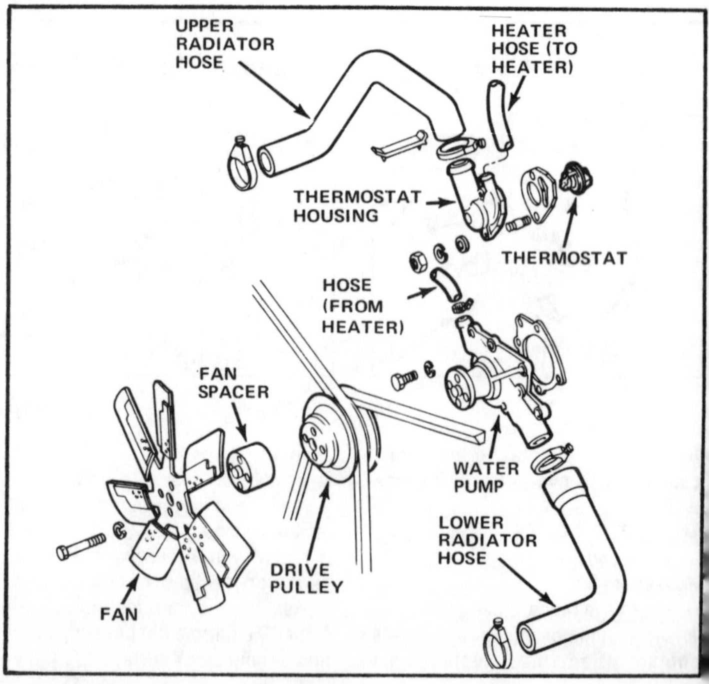

RADIATOR CAP CHECK

Check radiator cap occasionally for worn or cracked gasket. If cap doesn't seal properly, fluid will be lost and engine will overheat. Replace worn cap with new cap rated 13 to 15 lbs. pressure.

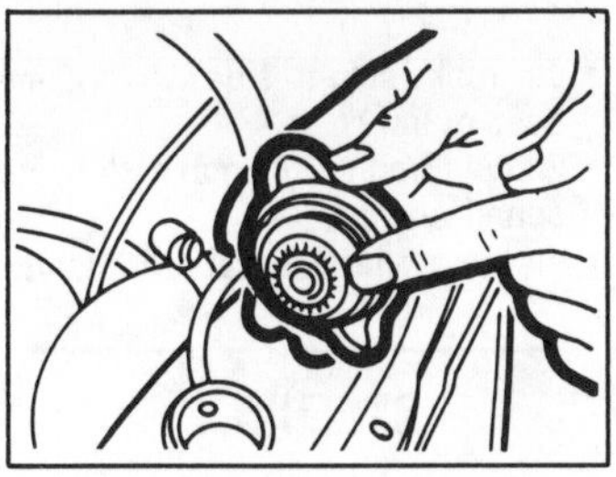

HOSE REPLACEMENT

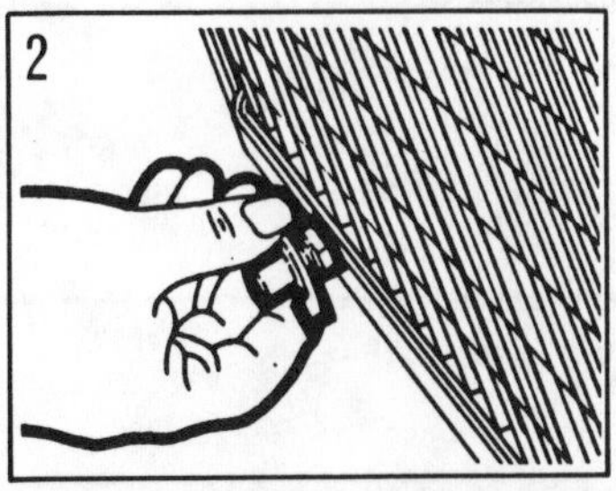

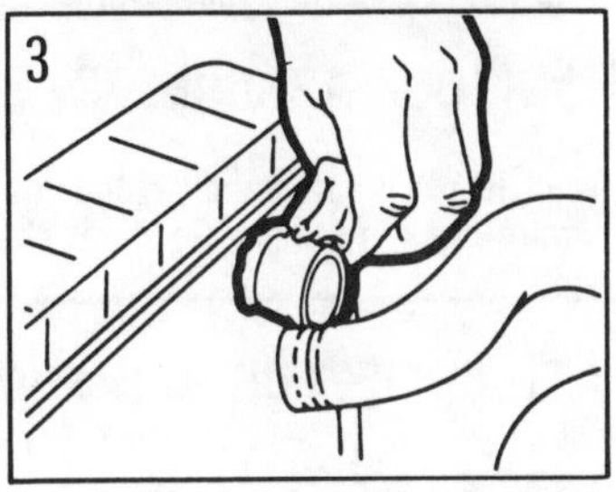

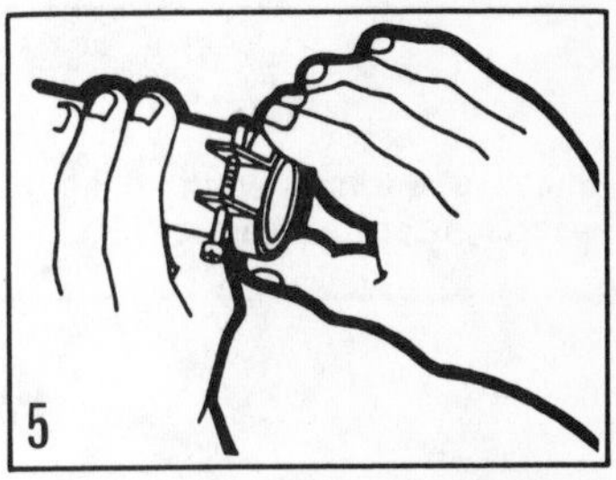

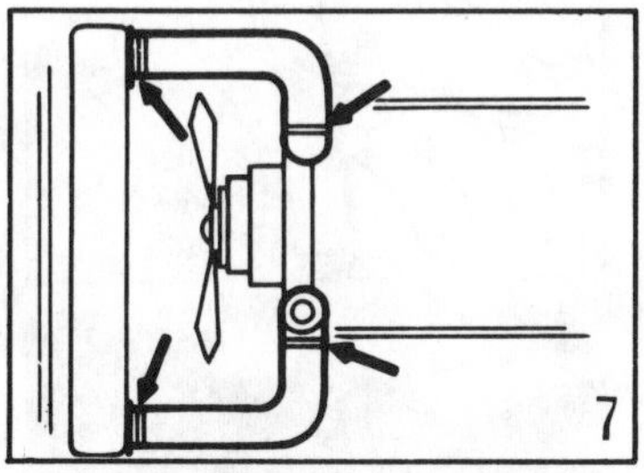

Coolant drain and refill work may be done alone; when changing hoses, coolant must also be drained as part of job. Discard all hoses with cracks or soft spots. Check hose clamps for tightness and good condition.
1. Remove radiator cap. Open radiator petcock (See 2). Drain coolant into catch basin. If near 24 months old, discard old coolant.
2. Petcock is located at the bottom of the radiator.
3. Wipe all hose connections clean. Use emery cloth to get rid of residue.
4. If old hose clamps are badly rusted or damaged, replace with new units.
5. Slip clamps over each hose end. Slip hose ends all the way onto cleaned up hose connections.
6. Place hose clamp ¼ inch from hose end. Tighten. Close petcock. Refill with 50/50 coolant/water mix.
7. Start engine; allow to warm up. Check for coolant leaks.
8. Road test car; watch for temperature warning light.

Suspension and Tires

The front wheels mount and rotate on the spindles, which are attached to upper and lower ball joints. Upper and lower control arms link the spindles to the car's frame, and permit the frame and body to move up and down in relation to the position of the wheels with a hinge effect. The spring is mounted to the top of the upper control arm on either side, with the upper end located by the top of a spring housing. A shock absorber is located inside each spring. The rear suspension consists of leaf springs suspending the solid rear axle. The rear shock absorbers are mounted ahead of the rear axle on either side.

Your car's suspension system consists of wheels, tires, springs, shock absorbers, sway (or stabilizer) bars, ball joints, steering linkage. If any of these items is out of adjustment or badly warn, you may notice any of

these symptoms:
- car pulls to one side when braking
- car wanders when driving a straight line
- overall ride may be either hard or bouncy
- effort is needed to steer vehicle
- tires show uneven wear
- tires squeal when cornering
- front of car dips or bounces when braking
- car rocks side-to-side when going over rough road
- wheels bounce or make slapping sound on road
- steering wheel vibrates in hands
- front of car vibrates at highway speeds

Any of above symptoms indicates corrective action is needed. Delay can: ruin tires; cause damage/failure to other suspension parts; create safety hazard.

STEERING

If steering linkage, front suspension and steering column components are in good condition, there should be no more than 1½ inch free play in the steering wheel when measured at the rim of the wheel. If a loud knock is heard when turning the steering wheel from one extreme to the other, have mechanic check pinion bearing preload.

SHOCK ABSORBERS

Shock absorbers work to keep wheels in constant contact with the road. Result is safe handling and ride control; longer tire life. So shock absorbers (or shocks) are important.

HOW TO CHECK FOR BAD SHOCKS

1. Check under car and locate shock absorber near each wheel.

2. Heavy oil streaks on outer shock housing indicate need for replacement.

3. Stand at front of car and apply body weight in a pumping action to front bumper or fender. Release pressure and allow car to stop rocking. Car should not bounce more than one more time after releasing pressure. Repeat at rear. If bouncing continues more than once, replacement is needed. Replace shocks in pairs (front pair or rear pair).

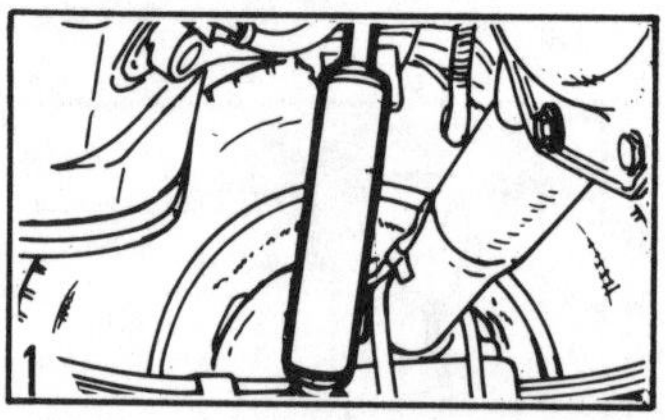

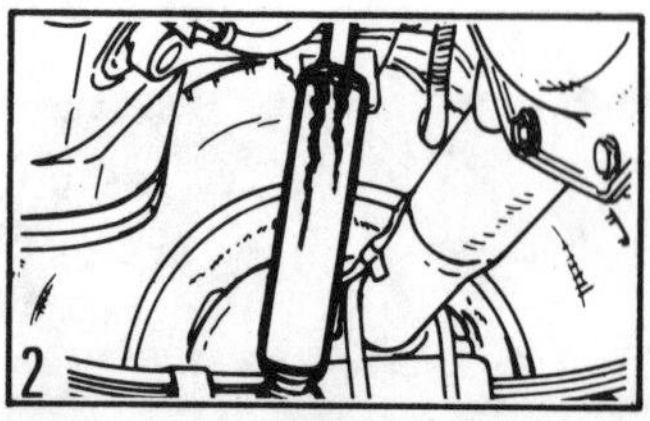

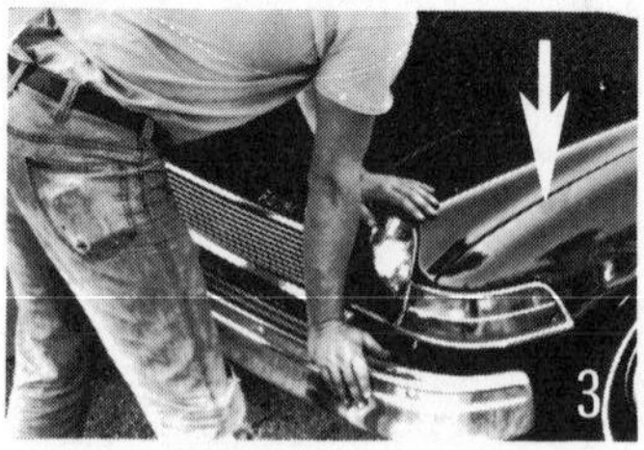

TOW HITCH INFORMATION

If your car is used for trailer towing you should check:
A. Cooling System; be sure radiator is at proper level in radiator. See Cooling System Section for checks to perform.
B. Check Transmission Fluid; keep topped up to proper level.
C. Check Rear Shock Absorbers; you may benefit from installation of new rear shocks.
D. Check Tire Pressures; best traction and handling can be ensured if tire pressures are properly maintained.

For safer and more trouble-free trailer towing, consider:
A. Automatic Transmission Cooler; helps remove excess heat from automatic transmission fluid built up during towing mileage. Also helps avoid radiator overheating. Some units can be self-installed.
B. Radiator Over-Flow Tank Kit; addition of a reservoir to catch radiator coolant overflow preventing coolant loss. Easy to install, these units help a tow car run cooler, avoid overheating due to coolant loss.
C. Heavy-Duty Shock Absorbers or Air Shocks; important to have on rear wheels if you intend to do a lot of towing or load carrying within the car itself. Don't forget to consider replacing factory shocks, when they are worn out, with heavy-duty units at the front as well.
D. Variable Load Flasher; this unit will accommodate the added load of trailer turn signal lamps on trailer when these are hooked into your car's electrical system.

FRONT END ALIGNMENT

When steering, handling and/or tire wear indicate front end alignment may be needed, this work can only be done at an automotive service shop. DO NOT PUT OFF NEEDED FRONT END ALIGNMENT. At the same time, have ball joints and steering linkage checked.

Ignition System

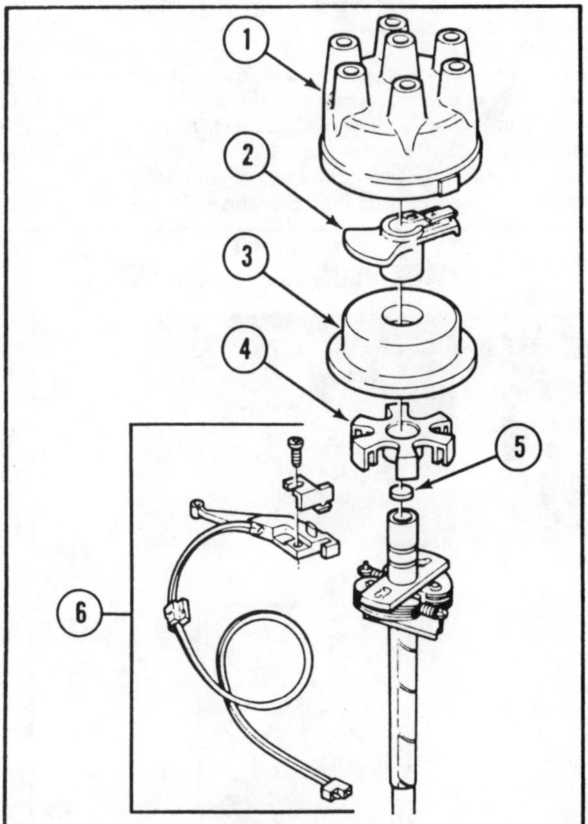

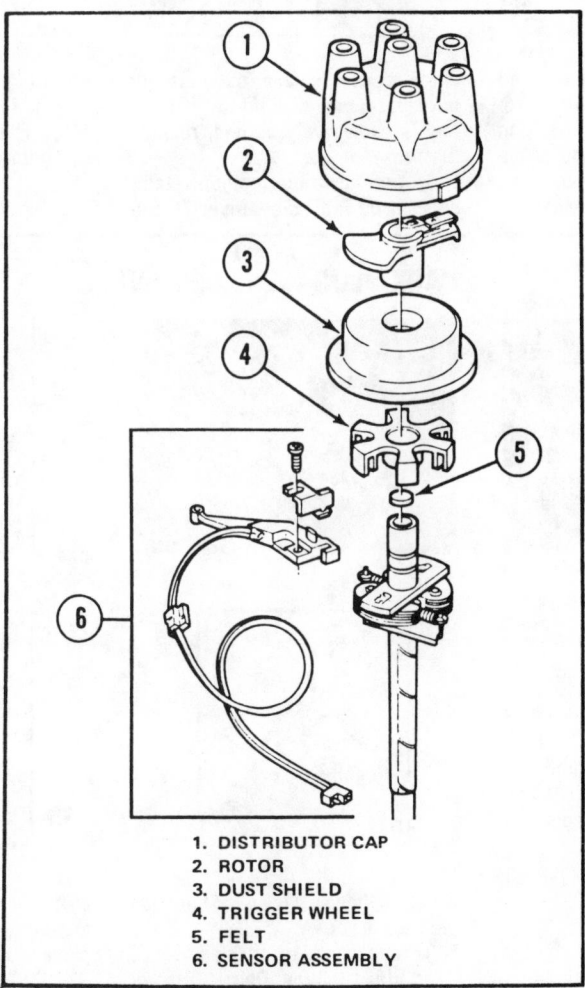

1. DISTRIBUTOR CAP
2. ROTOR
3. DUST SHIELD
4. TRIGGER WHEEL
5. FELT
6. SENSOR ASSEMBLY

The ignition system consists of spark plugs, plug wires, distributor, control unit, rotor, sensor, trigger wheel and coil. These units work to create a good hot spark inside the engine (ignition) at exactly the right moment (timing). If ignition is weak or timing is off, engine may be hard to start, run poorly, waste gas, lose power, backfire or not run at all.

TUNE-UP SERVICES

AMC SAYS . . . Replace plugs every 30,000 miles.
TOOLS & MATERIALS . . . Parts: 6 spark plugs. TOOLS; gap gauge, 13/16 in. spark plug socket, timing equipment, box or combination wrenches.

SAFETY TIP . . . Change only one spark plug at a time to avoid crosswiring and possible engine damage.

OTHER IGNITION CHECKPOINTS

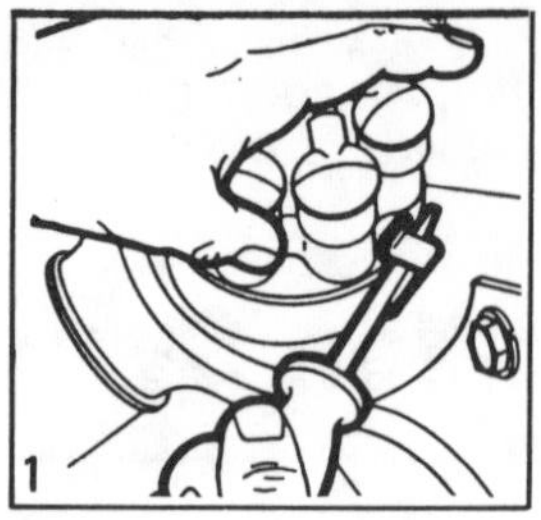

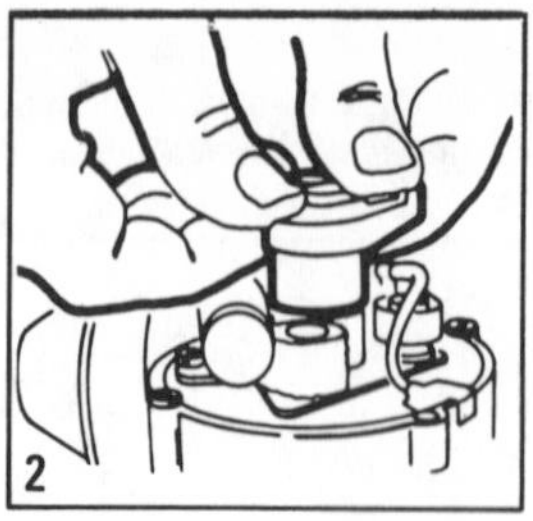

Inspect spark plug wiries. If cracked or brittle, entire set should be replaced. Also, center high tension wire. Inspect distributor cap. Wipe inside clean occasionally with a dry, lint free cloth. If cap is cracked, or rotor contacts are excessively burned, replace cap. If rotor contact end is excessively burned, replace the rotor.

1. To open distributor, snap retaining clips off with screwdriver, lift cap off but keep wires connected.
2. Pull rotor off (straight up). Replace if cracked or metallic tip is badly burned.

SPARK PLUG REPLACEMENT

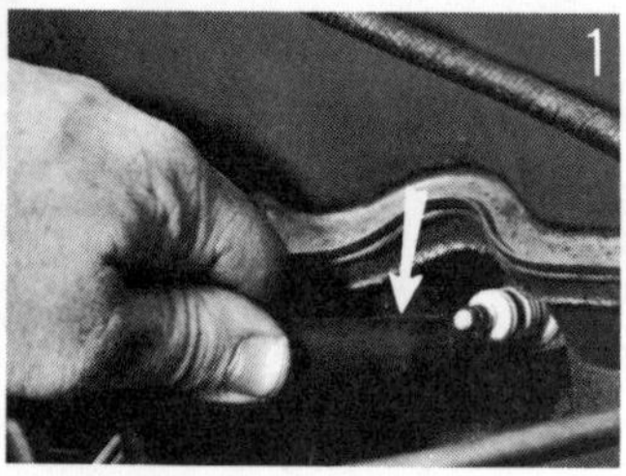

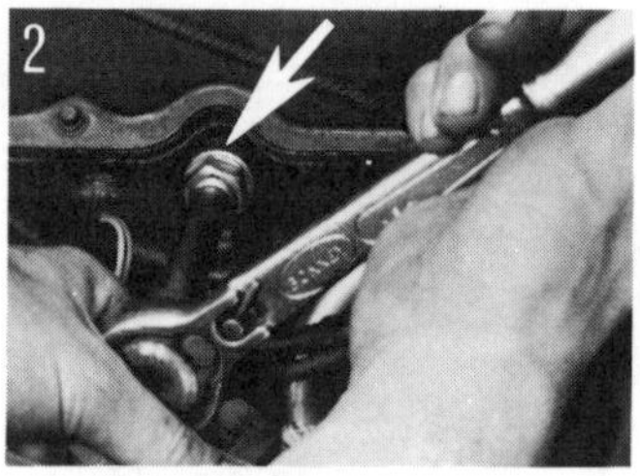

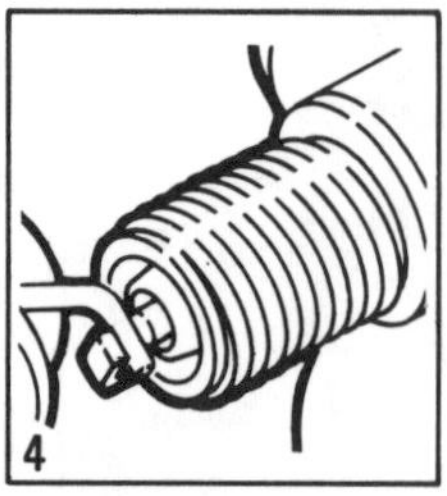

1. Plug spark plug wire by grasping rubber boot. Do not jerk wire off. If stuck, turn boot, pulling gently.

2. Loosen spark plug using socket wrench.

3. Wipe loose dirt from around plug before removing. Do not let dirt drop into engine through plug hole. Unscrew plug.

4. Check plug electrode gap on new spark plug. Adjust to:
   All plugs: .035″

Plug gap is correct when the gauge drags slightly as it is pulled between plug electrodes.

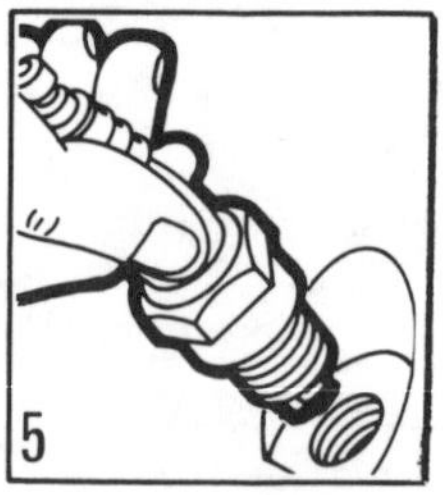

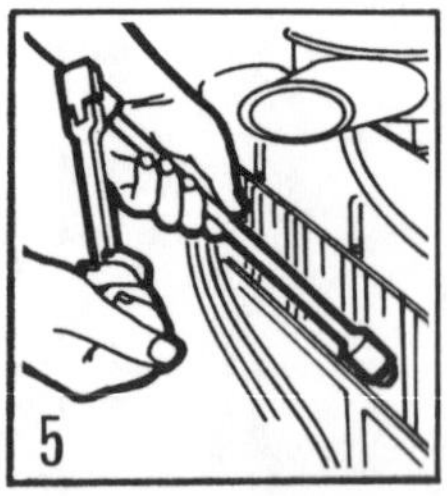

5. Thread new plug into plug hole by hand. Hand tighten. Do not force or cross thread. Use socket wrench to tighten firmly but do not force. Replace plug wire. Press boot firmly.

REPLACING SPARK PLUG WIRES

One of the most often overlooked items in a tune-up is the spark plug wires. Your car can be in perfect tune, but if the plug wires are not carrying the spark to the plugs, your engine will run poorly. The original equipment wires that came with your car are usually good for a year or two before needing replacement.

On newer cars, the higher underhood temperatures created by emission controls breaks down the wires ability to conduct electricity sooner. The spark plug boot ends of the wires will crack with age allowing the spark to arc towards the engine, not reaching the plugs. The distributor cap ends of the wires will often collect moisture, and corrode right there in your distributor cap. Sometimes a wire will contact a hot part of the engine, such as the exhaust manifold and burn through the insulation. Other times, a wire will become oil soaked and gummy, breaking down the insulation. Often, when carbon core wires get old, they will break off inside, with no visible signs of breakage on the outside. Always use good quality spark plug wire. A carbon core or cut-rate brand may seem attractive at first, but will cost you more in the long run with reduced engine efficiency and more frequent replacement.

1. Replace one wire at a time. This will keep you out of trouble with crossed wires. When removing wires, twist back and forth as you pull up. This will help free up stuck wires.

2. Take the old wire and match it up with the new one for length. If you are cutting your own, make sure there is good metal to metal contact between the end of the wire and the pinch-on connectors.

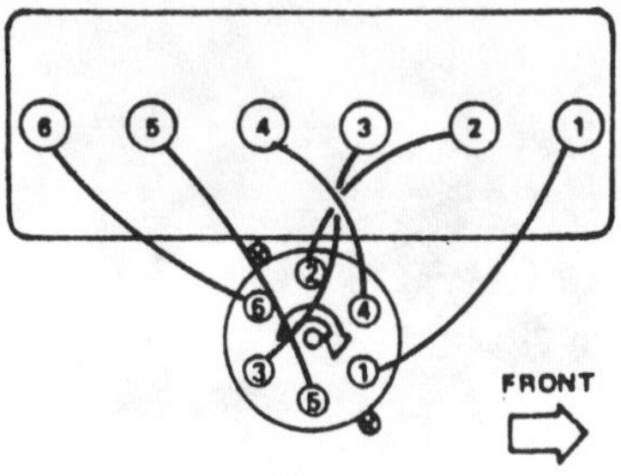

CLOCKWISE ROTATION
1-5-3-6-2-4

3. Make sure each wire seats all the way down in the distributor cap. First push down the wire, then the boot. The wire should click in place.

4. After you are all done, make sure all wires are clear of choke or throttle linkage, or hot exhaust manifolds.

Use the firing order illustration to guide you when replacing your ignition wires and/or distributor cap.

IGNITION TIMING

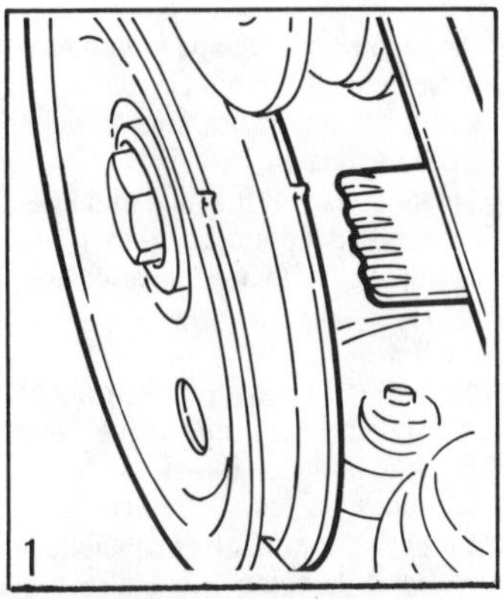

Adjusting timing is the important finishing touch to any tune-up. While not difficult, job requires timing light and dwell meter.

1. Locate timing marks and pointer (notches) on engine and lower engine pulley. Clean away dirt. Mark the pointer and notch which corresponds with the timing setting in degrees shown on the engine compartment sticker.

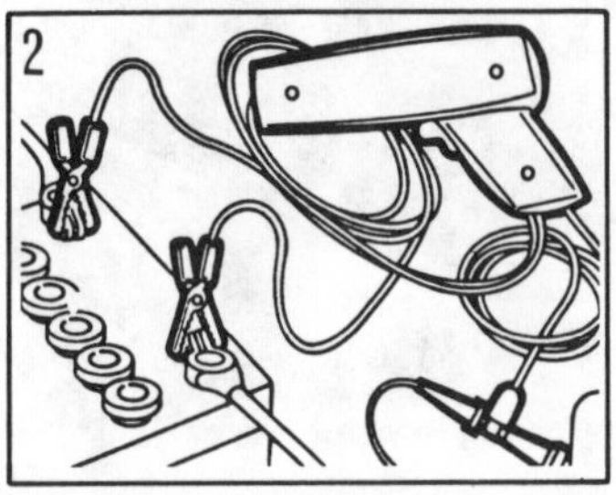

2. Hook up timing light according to instructions supplied with it.

3. Disconnect the one or two vacuum lines from the distributor. Plug with pencil tip or golf tee.

4. Hook up tachometer and adjust engine idle speed to RPM specified on underhood sticker. Idle attachment screw is located where gas pedal linkage attaches to carburetor.

5. Aim timing light at pulley mark(s). If the chalked marks do not align, loosen distributor hold-down bolt and slowly rotate distributor until chalked marks align.

6. Tighten hold-down bolt. Recheck timing.

Fuel System

When gasoline is brought from the fuel tank, it mixes with air in the carburetor. This gas/air mixture then enters engine through the intake manifold, passes through the intake valves and is burned in the combustion chamber. The burned exhaust gas is then passed through the exhaust valves to the exhaust system and to the outside air. In order to keep your car's engine running cleanly with minimal pollution, and avoid dangerous carbon monoxide fumes inside the vehicle, certain items should be checked from time to time.

KEEP THE AIR INTAKE CLEAN

The large round can that sits on top of the engine holds the air cleaner. Twice a year:

1. Remove wing nut, and remove air cleaner lid.

2. Lift out circular air cleaner cartridge. Discard if more than 12

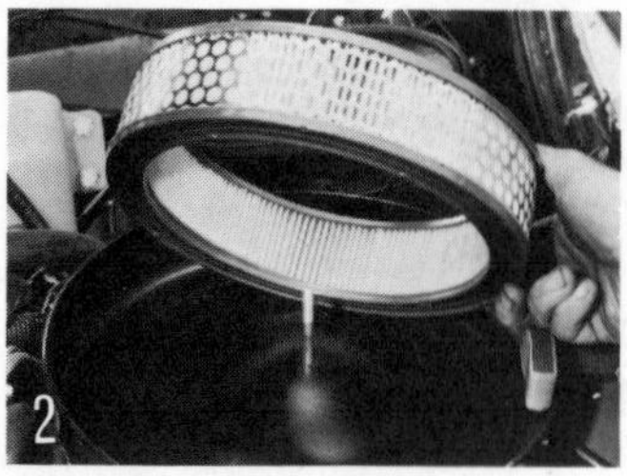

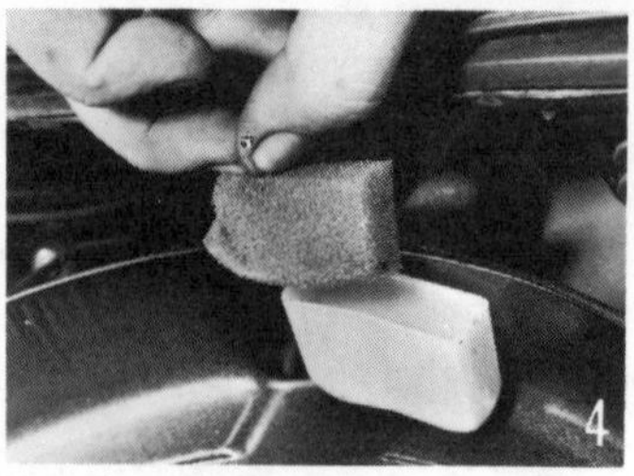

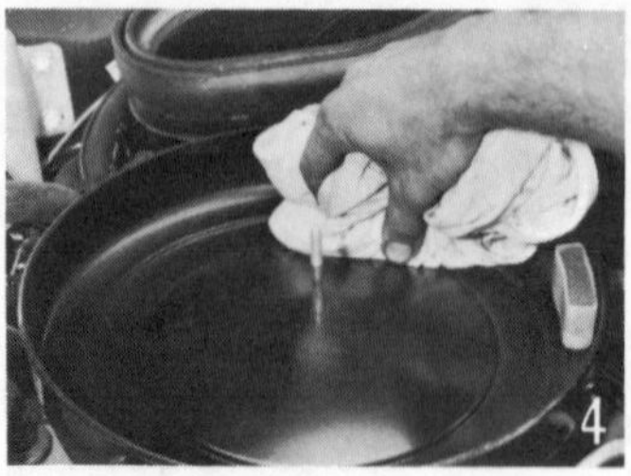

months old or excessively dirty.
3. Pull crankcase filter out of filter can. Wipe inside of can and lid with clean cloth.
4. Install crankcase filter. Install in reverse order.

FUEL FILTER REPLACEMENT

Replace the filter every year or 12,000 miles. The fuel filter prevents dirt, rust, and scale from both the gas station's tank and your own fuel tank from reaching the carburetor. A dirty filter will starve the engine and cause poor running.

1. Locate the fuel filter in line to carburetor. Place a rag under the filter housing to collect fuel that will drain out when filter is removed.
2. Pinch the ends of clamps together, and move toward center of hose. Use the smallest possible amount of tension, to avoid damaging the clamps. You can get a special tool designed for this job that will make handling the clamps much easier.

3. Pull the hose off filter and fuel line.
4. Position new clamps in center of a new hose. If the old clamps are to be reused, make sure they have not lost their tension.
5. Install hose on fuel line and filter. Pinch the clamp ends together, and position well onto fuel line and filter.

Note: After replacing filter, remove rag used to catch spilled fuel, and then start engine. Check for leaks. Addition of a can of carburetor cleaner to the fuel tank occasionally will aid in keeping the entire fuel system clean.

PCV VALVE REPLACEMENT

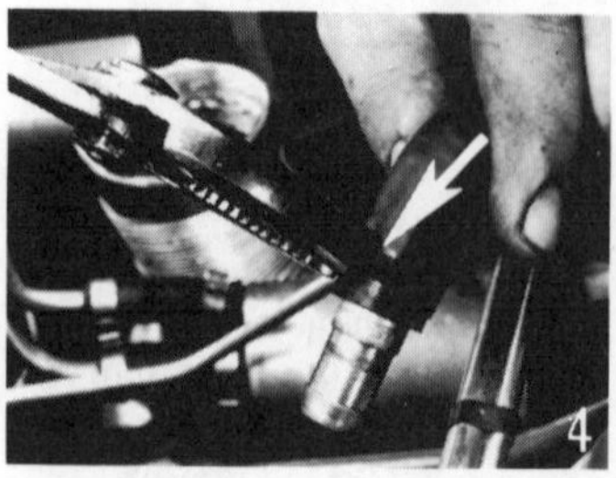

The most important part of a car's emission control system is the Positive Crankcase Ventilation (PCV) valve and its connecting hose. The PCV valve should be replaced once every 12 months. This device keeps dirt and sludge from forming inside the engine. Make sure all PCV connections are tight. Check that the connecting hoses are clear and not clogged. Replace any brittle or broken hoses.

The PCV valve is located on top of the valve cover, in front of the air cleaner.
1. Grasp hose holding PCV valve. Pull straight out.
2. Note where other end of hose is connected. Pull off.
3. Remove PCV valve from hose. Flush hose out with cleaning solvent. Dry hose. Install new PCV valve in hose.
4. Attach end of hose to its original connection and insert PCV valve into proper opening.

Safety Systems

PARKING LIGHTS, TURN SIGNALS AND STOP LIGHTS

All above lighting functions are performed by four dual-element bulbs. Front parking light and turn signal bulbs are mounted in the parking light housing in the grille. To replace, remove lens to expose bulb(s). Push in on bulb while turning counterclockwise to release bulb from socket. Remove and replace with new bulb. Replace lens.

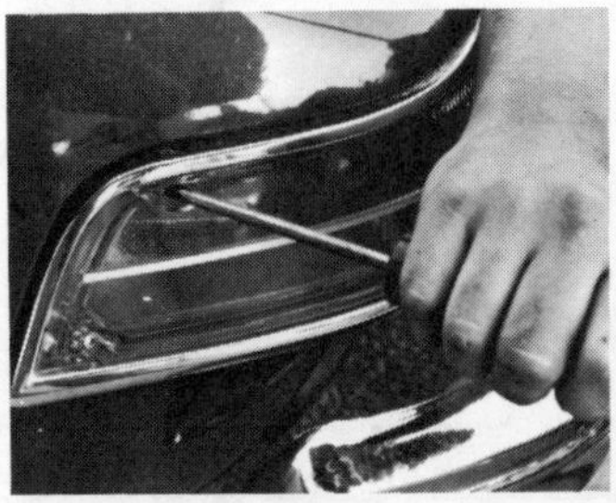

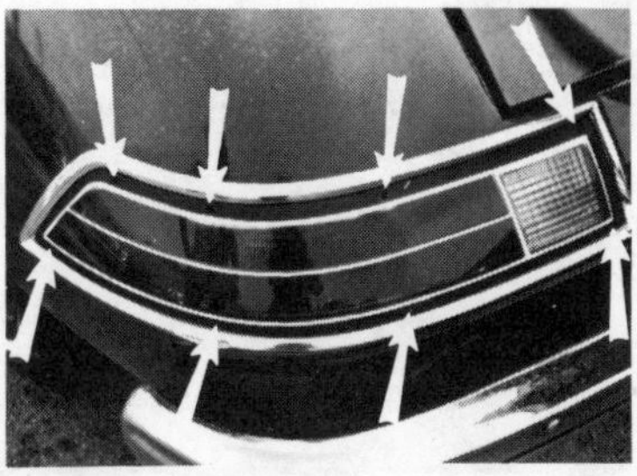

NOTE: When inserting new dual element bulb, note that knobs on side of bulb base are different distances from base tip. Match knobs to socket slots for proper fit.

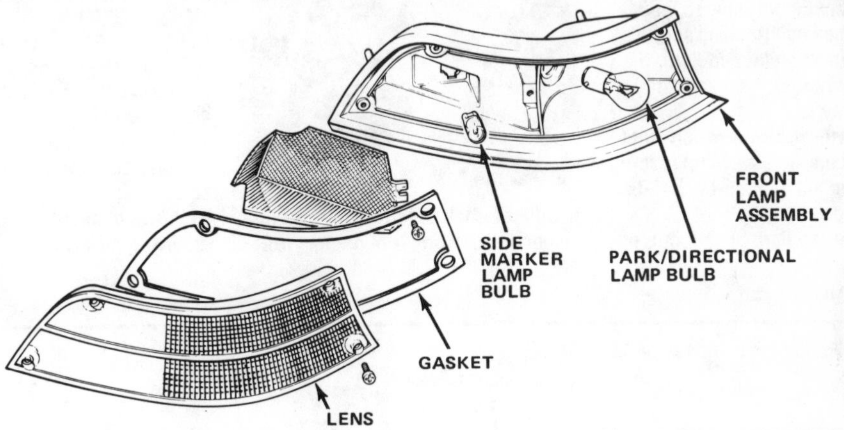

BACK-UP LIGHTS

Remove the screws that retain the lens. Push in on bulb, turning counterclockwise to remove.

LICENSE PLATE LIGHTS

Remove screws lens and housing that attaches to bottom of bumper. Push in on bulb turning counterclockwise to remove.

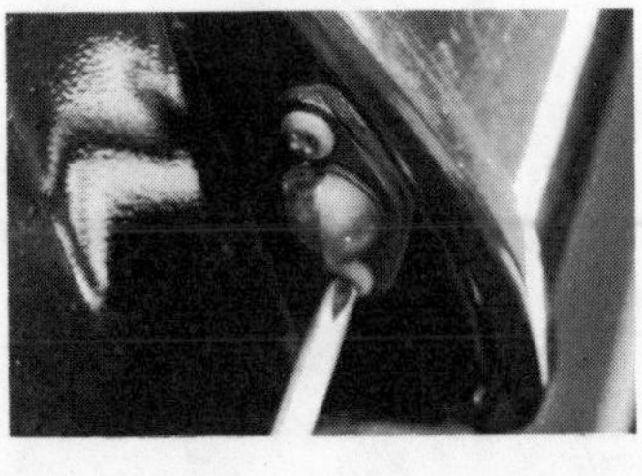

INTERIOR DOME LIGHT

This is a cartridge type bulb. Pry the dome light lens out from the housing. To avoid blowing the fuse, make sure that the doors are closed and dome light switch in the OFF position. Push in on the bulb and turn it clockwise to remove from socket. Insert new bulb and install in reverse order.

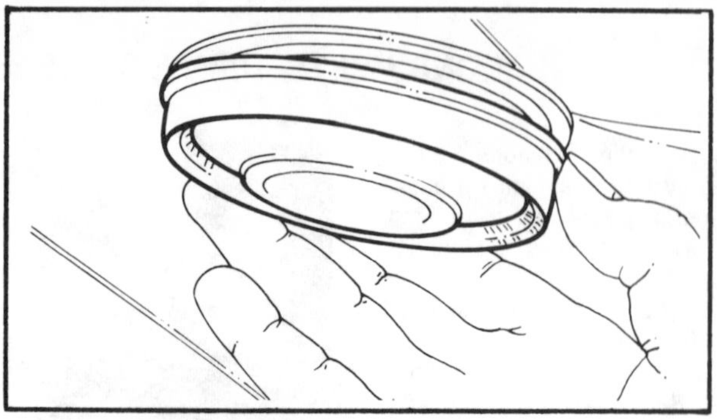

SEALED BEAM HEADLIGHT REPLACEMENT

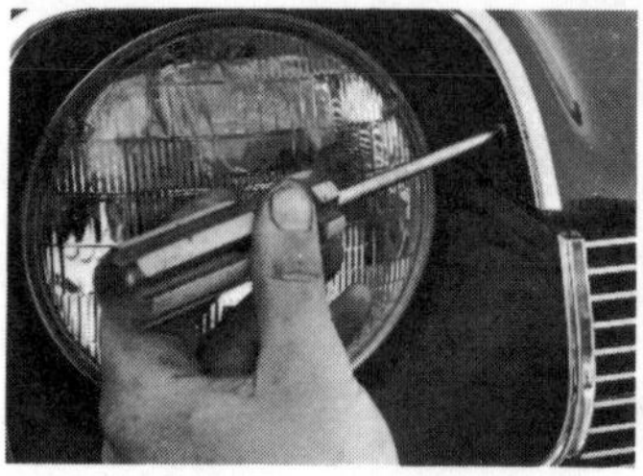

1. Remove both headlight cover retaining screws and cover.
2. Loosen, but do not remove, headlight retaining ring attaching screws. NOTE: Do not mistake headlight adjustment screws for the three retaining ring screws.
3. Rotate retaining ring to left until large openings in attaching screw slots are aligned with screw heads. Remove ring.
4. Pull lamp (sealed beam) out of headlight shell toward front of car; disconnect wiring connector from sealed beam unit.
5. Connect wire connector to new sealed beam unit.
6. Position new sealed beam unit in headlight shell. Be sure nobs on back of bulb (near outer edge) enter slots in shell.
7. Position retaining ring on retainer screws; turn ring to right. Tighten screws.
8. Position headlight cover; install attaching screws.

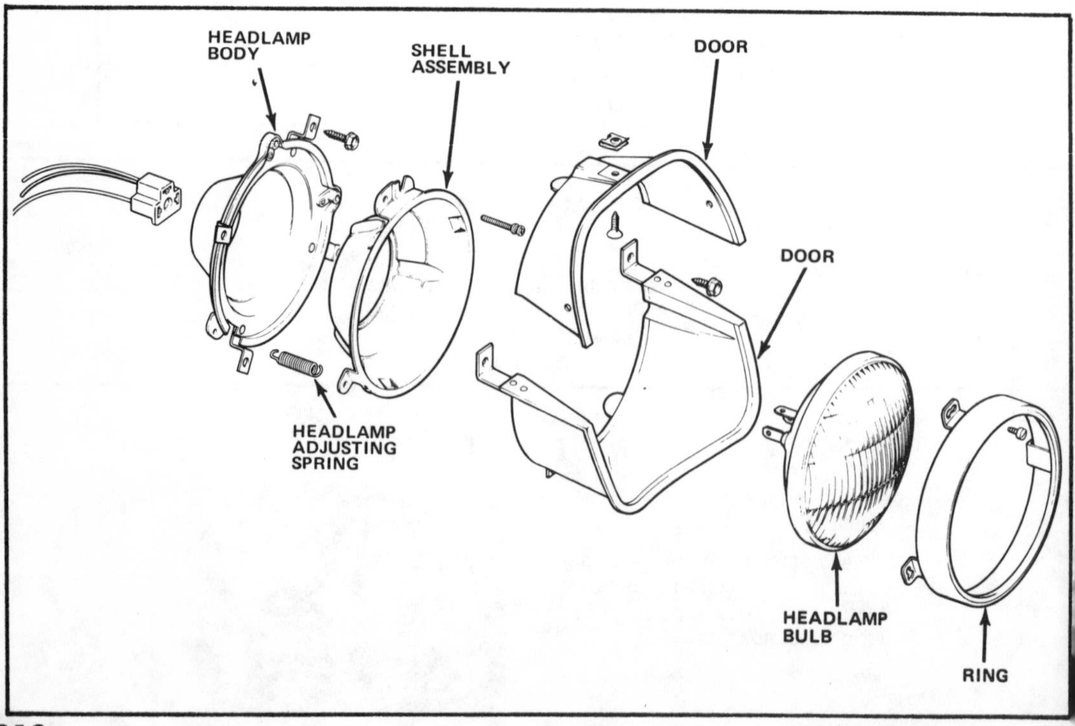

WINDSHIELD WIPER BLADE REPLACEMENT

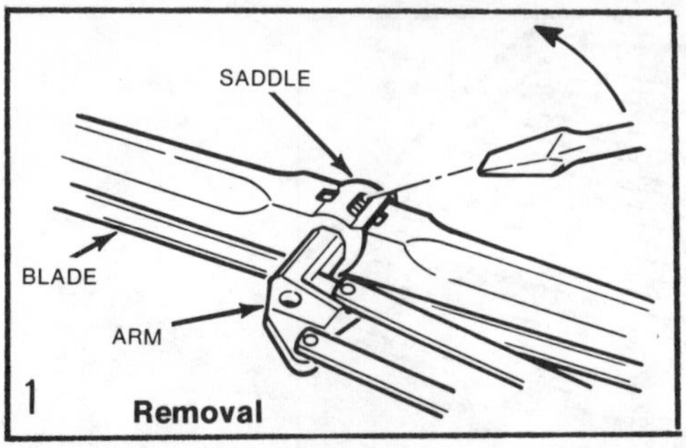

1 **Removal**

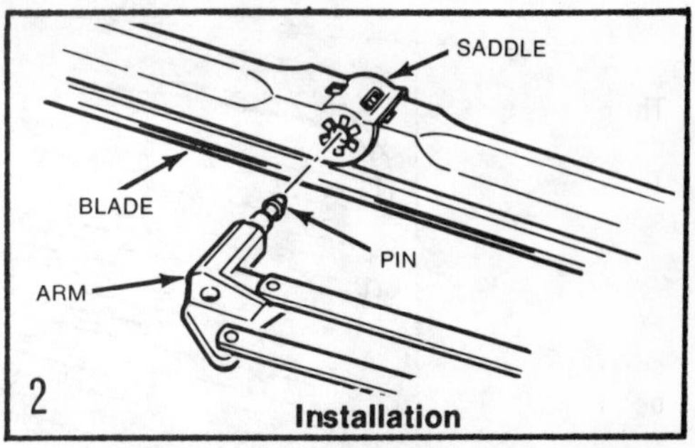

2 **Installation**

To replace wiper blade, lift up on spring release tab on wiper arm connector. Pull wiper blade off. Snap new blade into place.
To replace rubber insert only, press down, away from wiper blade to free it. Slide insert from blade. Insert new wiper. Bend insert upward slightly to engage retaining clips.

HORN PROBLEMS

If horn sounds and does not stop, this is due to short circuit in wiring. Disconnect wiring connector under hood and have professional service shop check horn wiring circuit.

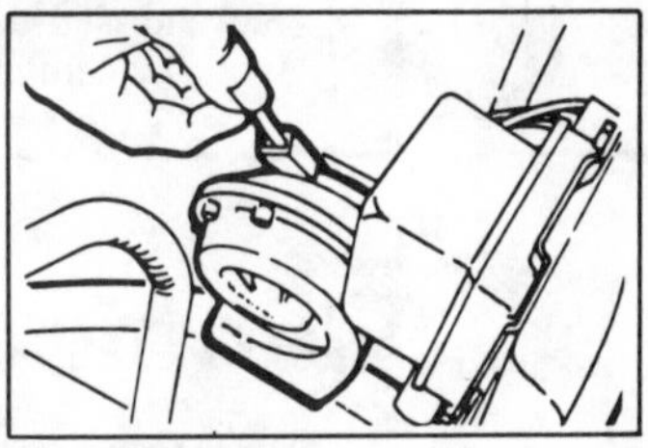

STEERING PROBLEMS

See steering system check in Suspension Section. Check tire pressures. Have a professional service shop check all components in the front end and steering system.

WHEEL CYLINDER CHECK

Drum brakes employ individual wheel cylinders to apply braking pressure to shoes. Check for brake fluid leaks on inside of wheel. Disc brakes employ calipers on individual wheels. Remove wheel and inspect caliper for signs of fluid leaks. Have mechanic correct leaks.

WASHER SYSTEM

If washer fails to squirt properly, raise hood and check system hose connections. Be sure washer fluid container has fluid. Check spout openings for clogging.
Keep container filled with fluid mixture of washer solvent and water. If road spray buildup on windshield is a chronic problem, add 1 tablespoon dishwasher detergent to solvent/water mixture when re-filling container.

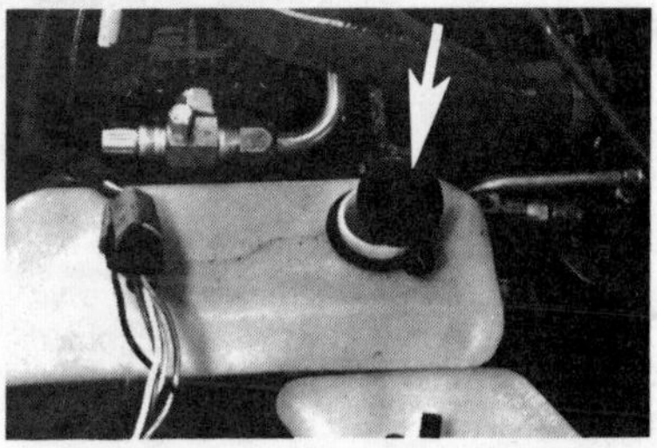

REAR WINDOW DEFOGGER SYSTEM

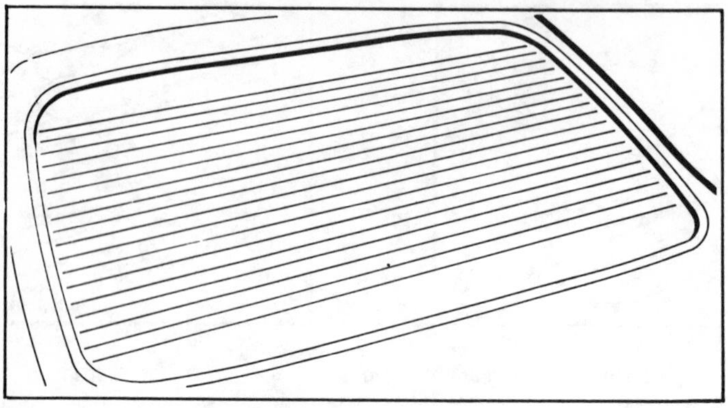

Do not clean inside of rear window fitted with defogger system with any abrasive material. This could destroy carbon-copper wires. Use only soft rag and mild detergent/water mixture. Dry carefully.

Electrical System

CHECKPOINTS AND SERVICES

To ensure starting ability at all times check your battery condition periodically. You'll need to check battery electrolyte (fluid) level in each of the six cells. Check battery cable connections for tightness and inspect for accumulated corrosion.
SAFETY NOTE: Wear gloves when working on battery.

CHECK BATTERY FLUID

1. Remove plastic filler caps on top of battery. Fluid should be up to lower end of filler hole and covering the plates. If fluid is low add clean, cold tap water. If your area has hard water, use only distilled water available at auto supply, food or drug stores.
2. Replace any lost caps immediately.

CAUTION: NEVER LIGHT A MATCH OR SMOKE near the top of a battery. Batteries give off explosive hydrogen gas.

NOTE: Battery that often checks low on fluid could mean:

A. Battery is getting old, due for replacement; have charge capacity checked at service shop.

B. Connections may be corroded or loose; clean/replace as needed (see below).

C. Alternator or voltage regulator not functioning properly; this happens far less often than A or B above.

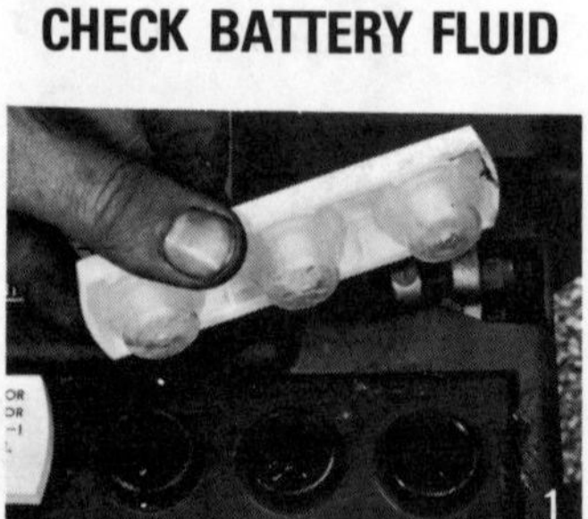

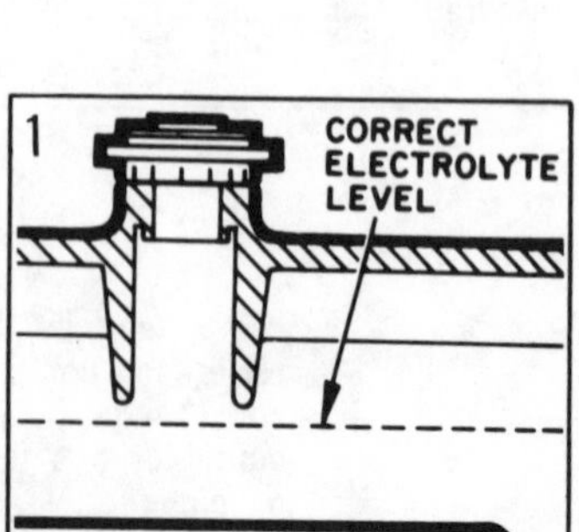

CLEAN THOSE BATTERY TERMINALS

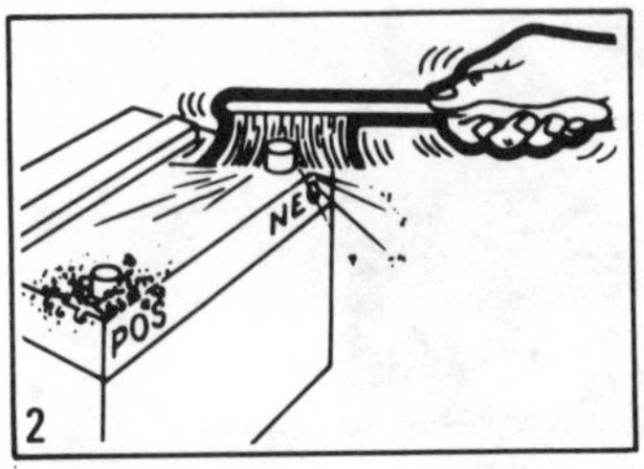

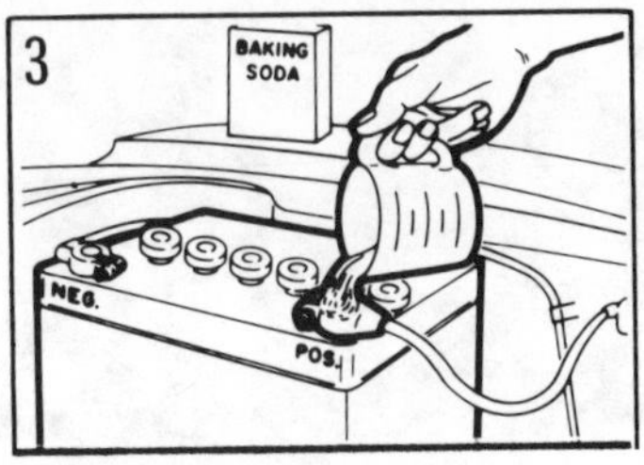

As time goes by, battery terminals build up a dry powdery, whitish material. This material is corrosive and will gradually eat thru battery cables if not cleaned off periodically.

1. Loosen and remove battery connections.
2. Brush off all loose corrosion; use stiff bristle brush. Do not get this material into eyes or on open cuts. Wash off at once.
3. If corrosion build-up is extremely heavy and brushing does not remove all of it, mix 2 tablespoons baking soda to 1 cup water. Pour solution directly onto terminals and connectors. Allow to soak a few minutes and rinse off. Continue brushing to remove all traces of corrosion build-up. Do not allow cleaning solution to enter battery.
4. Replace connectors on battery terminal posts and tighten. Do not hammer connections onto posts, but be sure they will not come loose with vibration.
5. Liberally smear battery terminal posts and cable connectors with petroleum jelly.

REPLACE FAULTY BATTERY CABLES

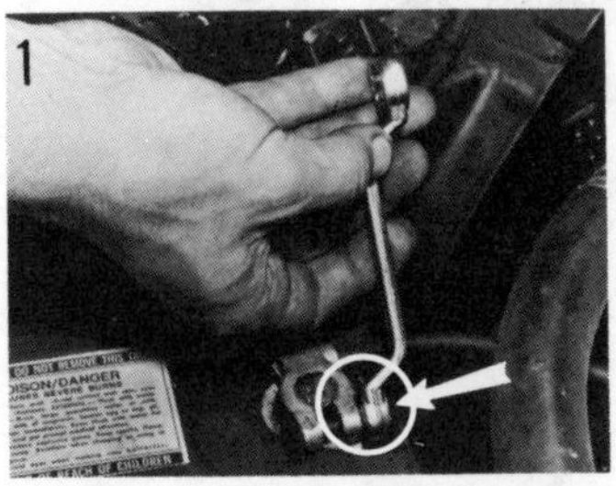

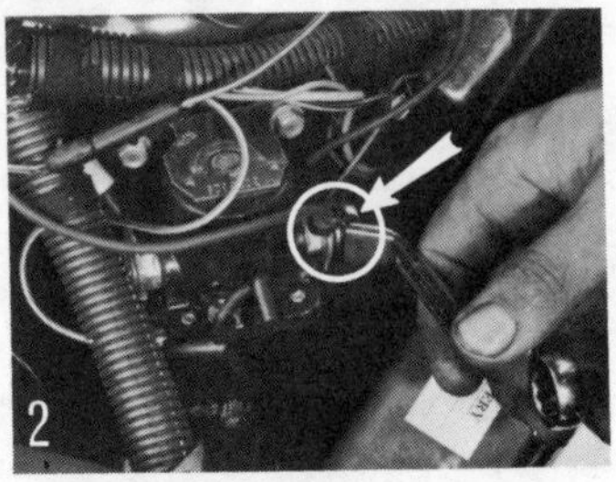

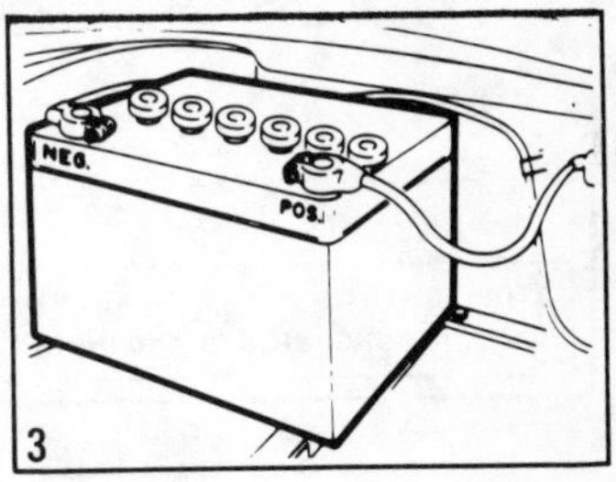

If battery cable strands become frayed, broken or corroded, replace cable immediately. Delay in correcting this condition could lead to sudden failure to start the engine. Can also weaken battery.

1. Loosen and remove battery connections. Clean off any corrosion buildup.
2. Disconnect negative cable from its attachment to engine or chassis. Disconnect positive cable from its attachment to starter relay.
3. Attach new cables making sure positive and negative cables are on proper terminals. They are not identical.
4. Replace connectors on battery terminal posts and tighten.
5. Liberally smear battery terminal posts and cable connectors with petroleum jelly.

ALTERNATOR

Red alternator warning light on instrument panel should glow red when you first turn ignition key. This proves bulb is OK. Alternator warning light should go off when engine is running at normal operating speed. If alternator warning light glows red at operating speed, alternator isn't charging battery properly. Common causes are:

A. Fan belts are loose and slipping on alternator pulley. Tighten or replace belts.

B. Battery terminals, cables are loose or corroded. Clean; tighten; replace bad cables.

If A or B do not correct problem, alternator or voltage regulator may be faulty. This happens far less often, and can only be checked by mechanic with proper electrical testing equipment.

Alternator Caution: Alternator can be permanently damaged by short-circuiting terminal connections. When working around or moving alternator, always keep metal tools on engine parts from terminals.

ELECTRICAL FUSES

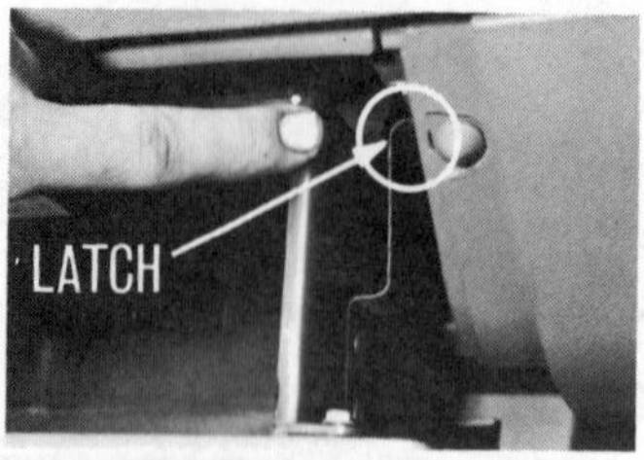

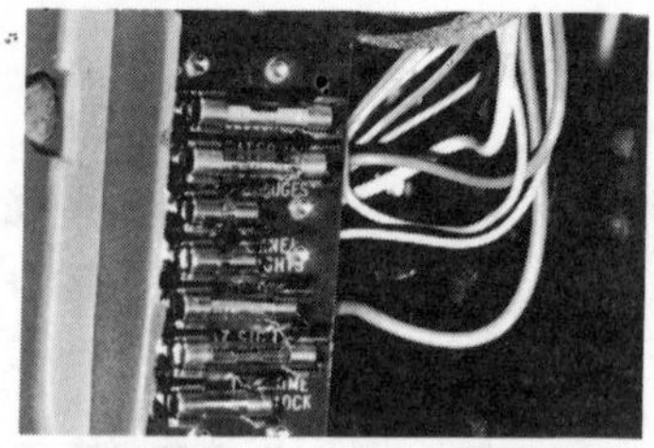

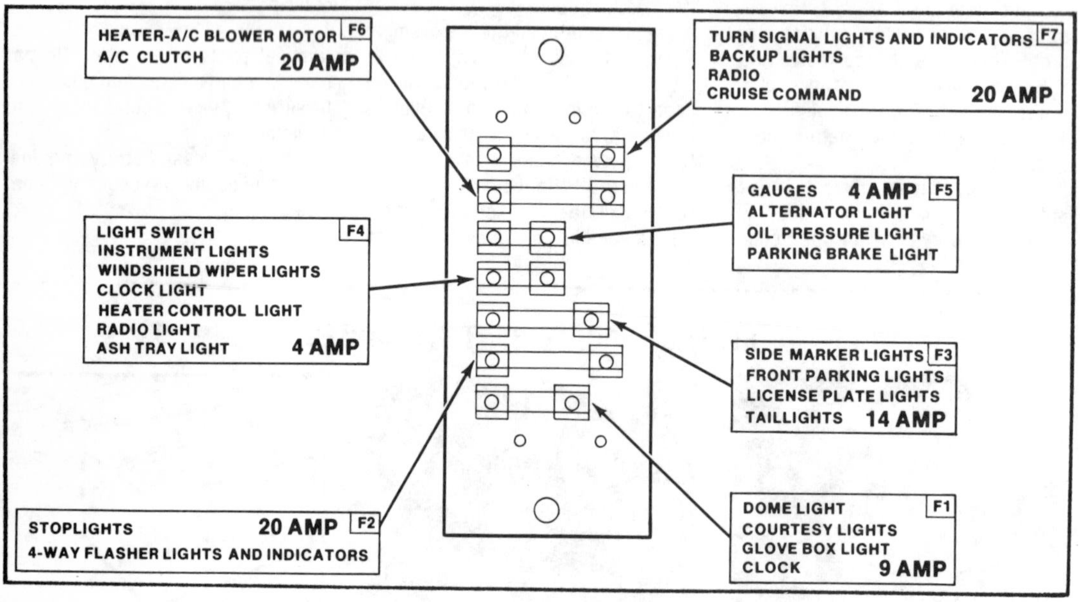

Air Conditioning

WARNING!—Never attempt to tighten fittings, disassemble or do any work on your car's A/C system. Consult a professional mechanic about A/C system problems and their correction. Your auto air conditioner (A/C) is a delicate, closed system. If air, dirt or water get into it, or if refrigerant escapes, the A/C unit will not cool a car interior. Among things you can do are:

1. Keep condenser grill clean. Check for dirt and debris; periodically remove dead insects, leaves, etc., with stiff bristle brush. Straighten any bent fins—carefully.
2. Keep radiator filled to correct level. (See Cooling System section). If fluid needs to be added, add antifreeze rather than water.
3. Keep radiator coolant at a 50/50 water/antifreeze mixture.
4. Flush cooling system and replace with fresh coolant mixture at least every 24 months. (See Cooling System section).
5. Radiator cap should be tight and sealed properly. If sealing gasket is cracked, cut or worn, replace cap with new 15 lb. unit.
6. Check fan belt tension periodically. (See Cooling System section). Replace glazed, frayed or cut fan belts, before they fail entirely.
7. Check periodically for bubbles in A/C sight glass. Sight glass is located in head of receiver/drier vessel. Or in metal tubing leading from top of receiver/drier. Sight glass is no larger than head of large nail. It may be dirty. Wipe clean for best visibility.

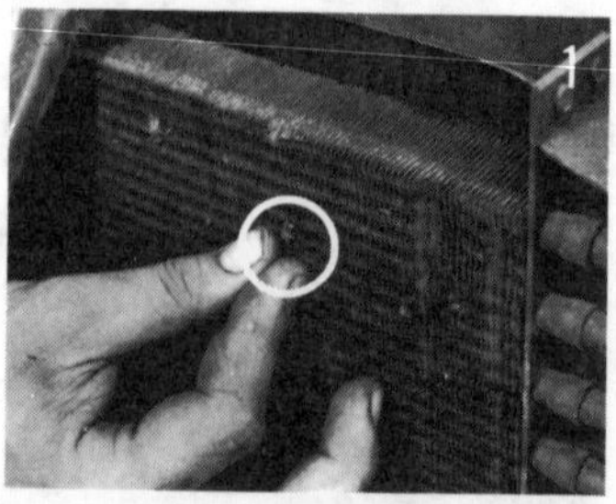

7

PROCEED AS FOLLOWS:

a) With engine and A/C system running, look for passage of refrigerant in sight glass. You'll be looking for a stream of milky white bubbles as they pass through sight glass. It is best to watch sight glass and have someone else start the car and turn on the A/C system. Allow to run for a few minutes.

b)If you observe no bubbles, and air flow from A/C unit in the car is passing cold air, everything is OK.

c) If no bubbles appear in sight glass, and air flow from the A/C unit in the car is not delivering cold air, the system may be low on refrigerant and could need a re-charge.

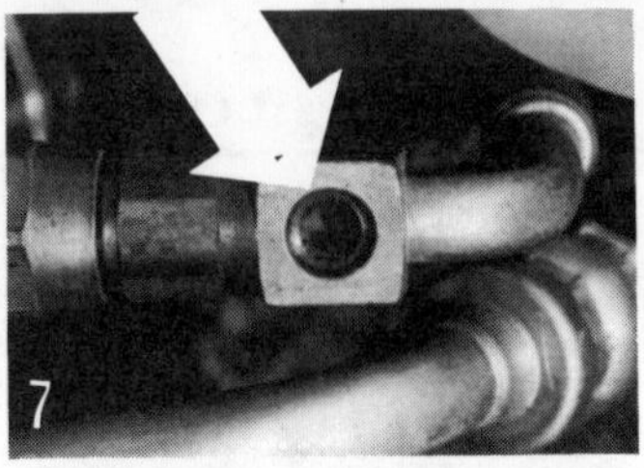

d) If bubbles appear, system is low on refrigerant.

e) If you suspect refrigerant loss based on test performed above, have system checked by a professional A/C service shop. They can confirm refrigerant loss, recharge the system and check for system leakage.

NOTE: Once a week or so, even in winter, run A/C system for about 5 minutes as you drive. This keeps system internally lubricated, prevents hoses hardening.

TUNE-UP SPECIFICATIONS

YEAR	ENGINE No. Cyl. Displacement (cu. in.)	SPARK PLUGS Type	SPARK PLUGS Gap (in.)	DISTRIBUTOR Point Dwell (deg.)	DISTRIBUTOR Point Gap (in.)	IGNITION TIMING Man. Trans.● (deg.)■	IGNITION TIMING Auto Trans.● (deg.)■	IDLE SPEED Man. Trans.● (rpm)▲	IDLE SPEED Auto Trans. (rpm)▲
1975	6-232	N-12Y	0.35	Electronic		5B	5B	600	550(700)
	6-258	N-12Y	0.35	Electronic		3B	3B	600	550(700)
1976	6-232	N-12Y	0.35	Electronic		8B	8B	850	550(700)
	6-258 1 bbl	N-12Y	0.35	Electronic		6B	8B	850	550(700)
	6-258 2 bbl	N-12Y	0.35	Electronic		6B	8B	600	700
1977	6-232								
	6-258 1 bbl			See Underhood Specifications Sticker					
	6-258 2 bbl								

▲ Adjust automatic transmissions in Drive (AMC/Ford/GM) or Neutral (Chrysler), all manual transmissions are adjusted in Neutral.
■ All figures are Before Top Dead Center.
● Figure in parentheses indicate California engine.
NOTE: The underhood specifications sticker often reflects tune-up specification changes made in production. Sticker figures must be used if they disagree with those in this chart.

CAPACITIES

YEAR	ENGINE No. Cyl. Displacement (cu. in.)	ENGINE OIL Add 1 qt. with New Filter	TRANSMISSION Pts. to Refill after Draining MANUAL 3-speed	MANUAL 4-speed	AUTOMATIC	DRIVE AXLE (pts.)	COOLING SYSTEM with Heater (qts.)	COOLING SYSTEM with Air Cond. (qts.)
1975	6-232	4	3.5①	—	17②	3	14	14.5
	6-258	4	3.5①	—	17②	3	14	14.5
1976	6-232	4	3.5①	—	17②	3	14	14.5
	6-258	4	3.5①	—	17②	3	14	14.5
1977	6-232	4	3.5①	3.5	17②	3	14	14.5
	6-258	4	3.5①	3.5	17②	3	14	14.5

① 4 pts. with overdrive
② Figures include torque converter

Service Record

Date/Mileage	Service	Next Due

Pinto/Bobcat

Lubrication and Oil Change

LUBRICATION CHECK

Oil is the single most important item in keeping the engine in your Pinto running. Without it, the internal components would quickly overheat and seize. Either too much, or too little is not good for the engine and will increase engine wear, so it is very important to keep a constant check on the oil level. For Pintos, you should check the oil at least once a week, when you stop for gas is a good time, since the car will be stopped on a level surface, but remember to let the oil have a minute or two to drain back into the oil pan or you will not get a correct reading. The dipstick, a long thin rod with a curved handle, is located on the

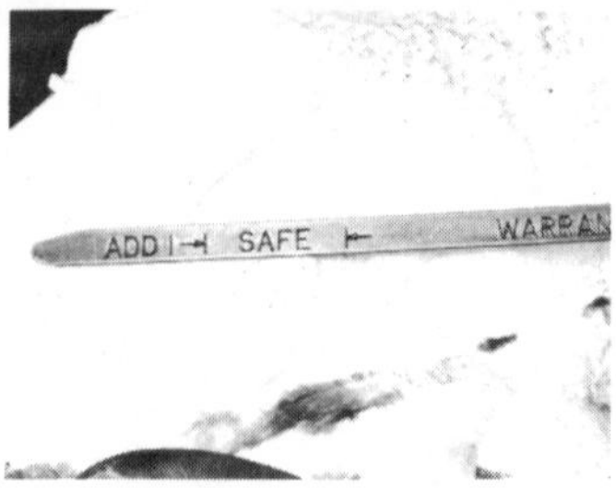

driver's side of the engine, and has either Add-Safe (for the 2000 and 2300 cc engines), or Min-Max (for the 1600 and 2800 cc engines) markings on the dipstick. The oil level must be kept between these two marks at all times. To check the oil, open the hood and position it securely on the hood support rod. Reach in and remove the dipstick and wipe it clean on a lint-free rag. Reinsert it, then pull it out and check the level showing on the lower part of the dipstick. If you are unsure of the first reading, wipe the dipstick off again and try it again until you receive an accurate reading. Remember, if you are in Canada, that an Imperial quart is more than the standard quart used in the US; make sure that you do not overfill the engine. One other thing to remember when you are adding oil, is to make sure that you add oil of the same viscosity.

BRAKE FLUID LEVEL CHECK

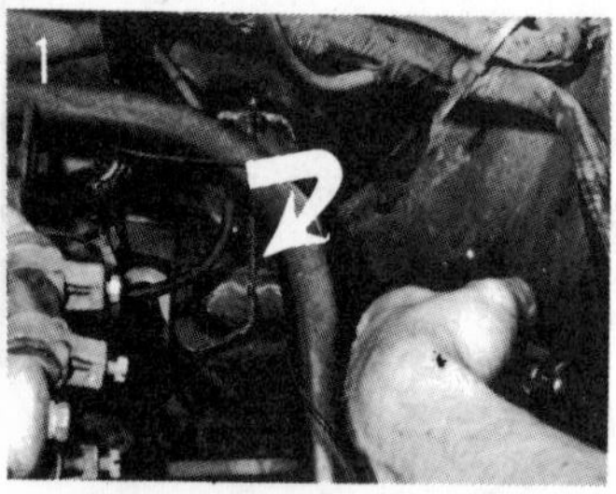

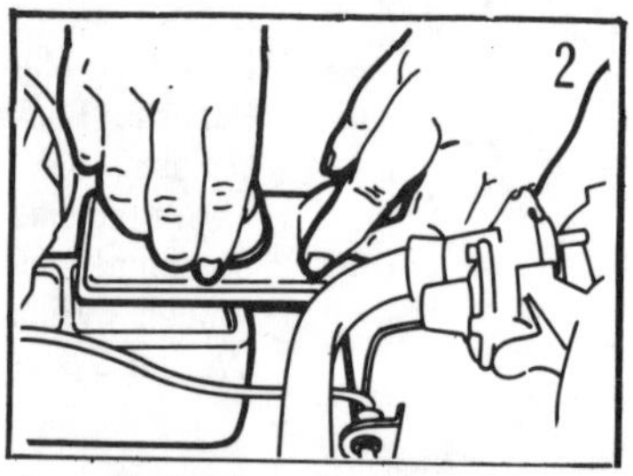

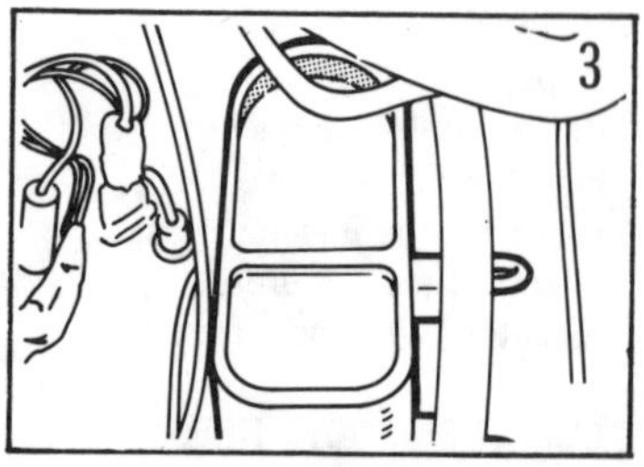

You should check the fluid level in the master cylinder at least every six months. The master cylinder is located on the firewall to the left of the engine. If the brake pedal begins to feel spongy, check the fluid level in the master cylinder, as this is often a sign of low brake fluid. If, after you fill the master cylinder, it checks low again after a short period of time, check all the brake lines for leaks, and have the brake system checked by a qualified mechanic.

When adding brake fluid, you should check the can to make sure that it meets the specifications for your car. Fluid that has the letters SAE 70 R3 and DOT 3 should be used in your Pinto.

1. Pry wire retaining clip off cap top with screwdriver.

2. Remove cap and gasket by lifting up.

3. Fluid level should be within ¼ inch of top rim. If lower than this, add fresh fluid to appropriate level. DO NOT OVERFILL

4. Replace cap and gasket; secure retaining clip over cap. If fluid level was low, check again in a few days.

5. If fluid repeatedly checks low, there is a leak somewhere in the system. Have mechanic check further. Neglect can be dangerous.

MANUAL TRANSMISSION FLUID LEVEL CHECK

You should check the manual transmission fluid every six months. To do it, you will need SAE 80 manual transmission fluid, an adjustable wrench or ⅜ in. drive ratchet and an extension, and a hand bulb syringe. To check the fluid:

1. Locate transmission fluid filler plug on right side of transmission housing from underneath car.

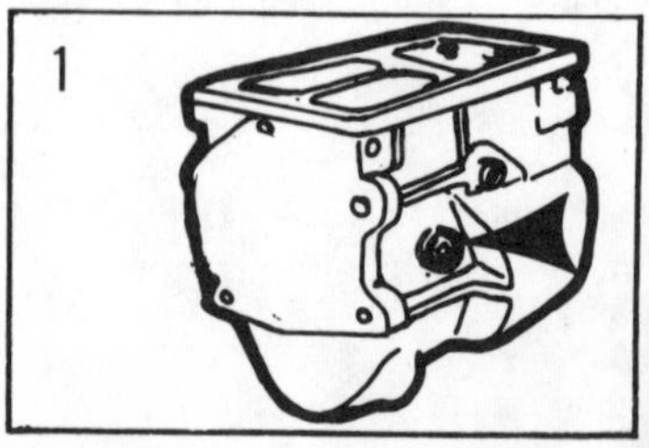

2. Wipe road dirt from filler plug area before loosening. Remove plug with wrench.

3. If the fluid begins to leak out before you have completely removed the plug, retighten the plug as the level is alright. If no fluid has leaked out and you have completely removed the plug, insert your finger in the opening; the fluid level should be

up to the edge of the filler hole.

4. Add fluid as needed with hand

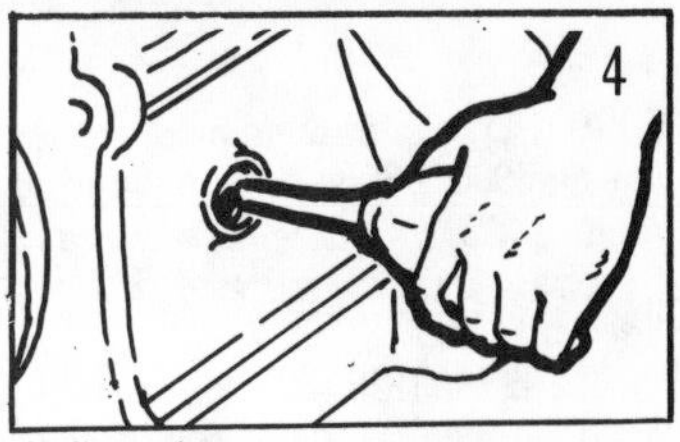

bulb syringe.

5. Replace filler plug; tighten.

AUTOMATIC TRANSMISSION FLUID LEVEL CHECK

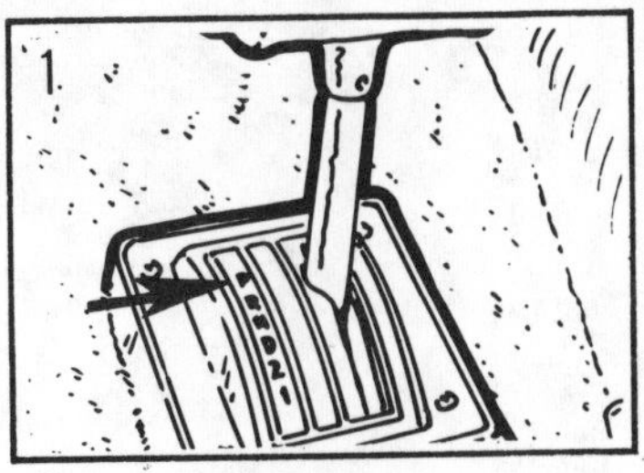

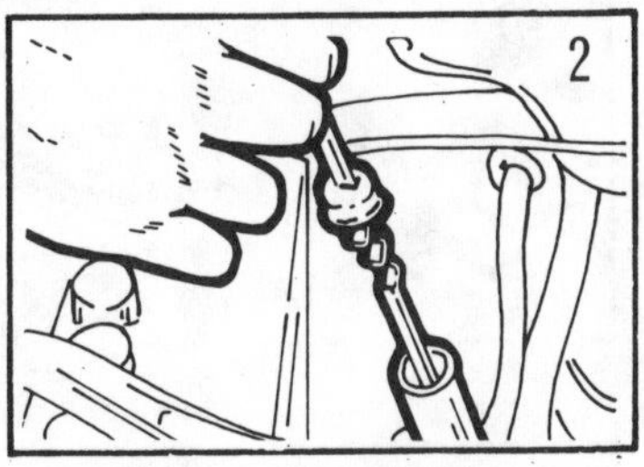

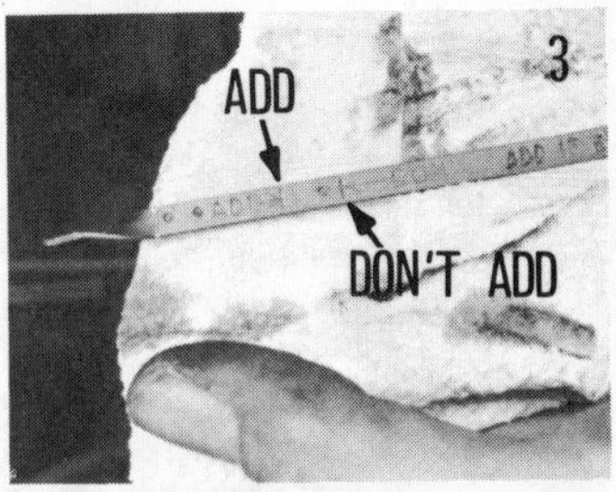

You should check the automatic transmission fluid level about once a month, sooner if the transmission sounds noisier than normal. The transmission uses automatic transmission fluid (ATF) Type F. This is the only type of transmission fluid to be used in your transmission. Aside from the ATF, you will need a long neck filler funnel to make adding the fluid easier. Remember not to add too much fluid as this will affect the performance of the transmission.

1. Engine must be warmed up and running. Place shift lever in PARK position.

2. Pull out dipstick. Wipe clean. Push dipstick all the way back in; remove it again.

3. If fluid is below ADD mark, add ATF to bring level up. DO NOT OVERFILL.

4. Add ATF thru transmission

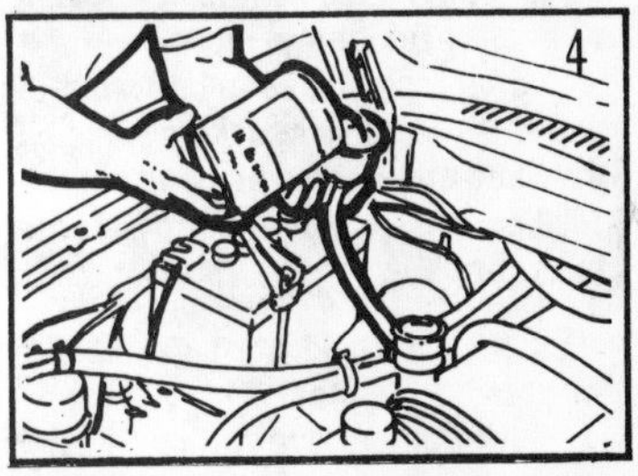

dipstick hole by means of long-neck filler funnel.

REAR AXLE LUBRICANT

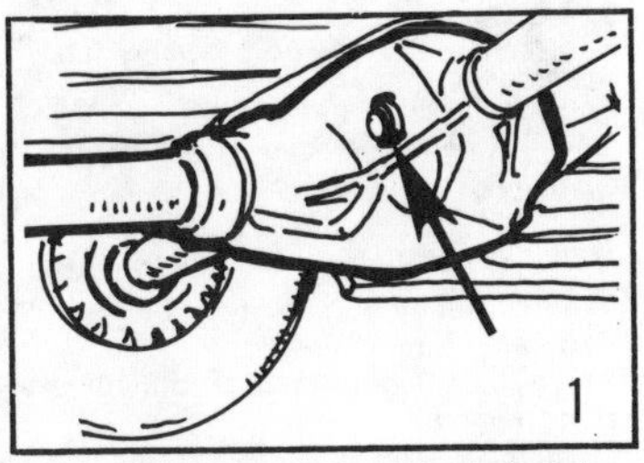

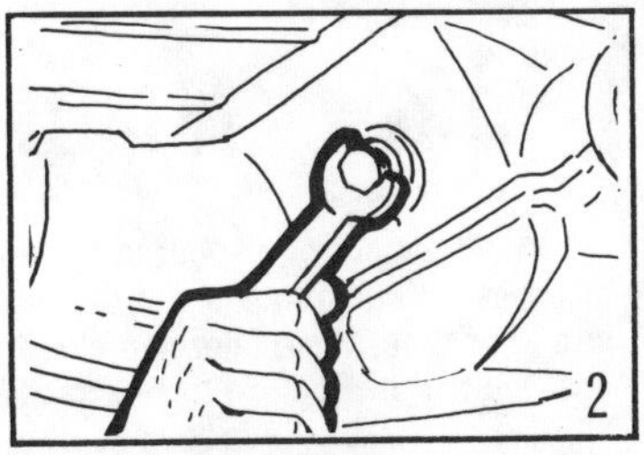

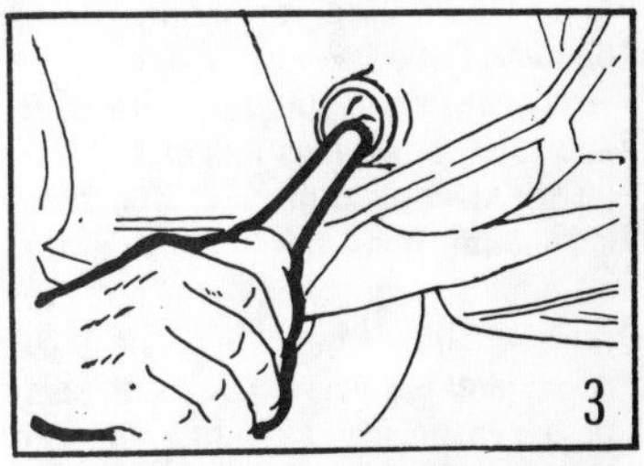

You should check the rear axle lubricant level every six months or six thousand miles, whichever comes first. The filler plug is on the driver's side of the differential housing, and you will need a ratchet (3/8 in. drive) and an extension to remove the plug, along with a syringe and SAE 80 or 90 hypoid gear oil. Before you even think about going underneath the car, first make sure the parking brake is set with the transmission in Neutral or Park, and the rear wheels blocked. After you do this, then you can begin the operation.

1. Locate filler plug on forward side of rear axle housing.

2. Wipe plug area clean; remove plug with wrench.

3. If the fluid begins to leak out as you are removing the plug, tighten the plug as the oil level is adequate. If you get the plug out and no fluid spills out, insert your finger in the opening and check for the level of fluid. It should be up to the bottom edge of the hole, if not add some with the syringe.

4. When the fluid level is adequate, replace and tighten the filler plug.

OIL AND FILTER CHANGE

FORD SAYS . . . Change oil and filter every 6000 miles. Recommended grade: MS or SE (check owner's handbook). Check oil level at least once a week.
TOOLS & MATERIALS . . . adjustable hand wrench; medium size screwdriver; oil filter removal wrench; drain pan for old oil (at least 5 qt. capacity); oil pouring spout; 4 qt. oil for 1600 cc Pinto; 5 qt. oil for 2000, 2300 cc Pinto; new oil filter; oil and lubricants as specified below.
SAFETY TIP . . . use work gloves.

To change your oil and filter, first check the Capacities Chart and see how much oil you are going to need. After this, you will need a container of sufficient quantity to hold the oil (make sure you get one that will fit underneath the engine), an adjustable wrench, an oil filter wrench and an oil filter. Instead of the adjustable wrench previously mentioned, it would be a good idea to buy a set of metric wrenches or sockets since all the Pinto and Bobcat engines but the 1600 cc. are held together by metric fasteners.

1. If engine is cold, start up and idle for about 5 minutes.
2. Park car on level ground. Turn engine off.
3. Locate oil drain plug on underside of engine. Place drain pan under plug.
4. Remove drain plug with wrench. Let ALL dirty oil drain out.
5. Wipe plug and area around drain hole clean. Replace drain plug; tighten it.
6. Locate the oil filter; on the 2000 and 2300 cc. engines it is on the left (driver's) side, on the 1600 and 2800 cc. engines it is on the right side. On all engines you should be able to reach the filter from above. The 1600 cc. oil filter is smaller than most, so a rubber insert may have to be added to your filter wrench.
7. Smear fresh oil over surface of rubber gasket (washer) of new filter. Install new filter by hand only. Do NOT use wrench. Turn filter until gasket makes contact. Tighten an additional half turn only . . . NO MORE.
8. Locate oil filler tube on top of engine. Remove cap.

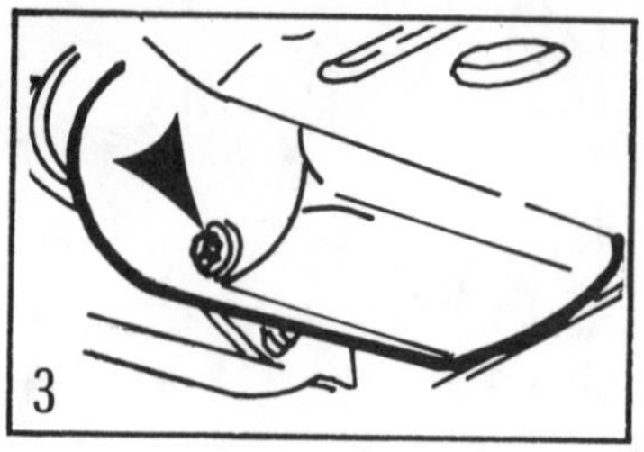
3

7

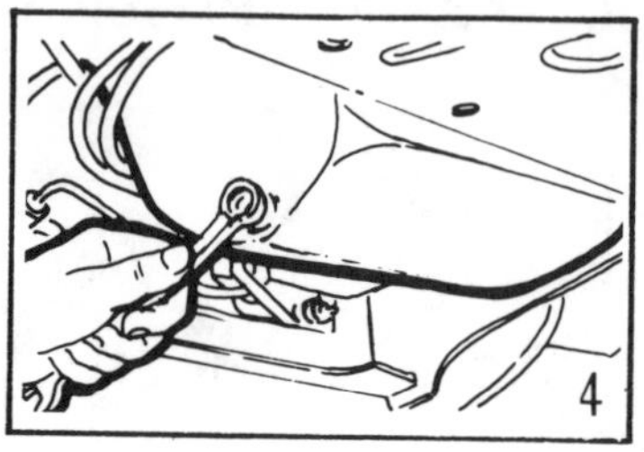
4

8

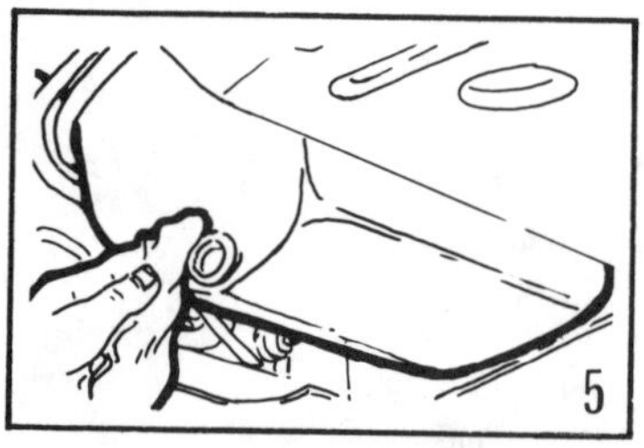
5

11

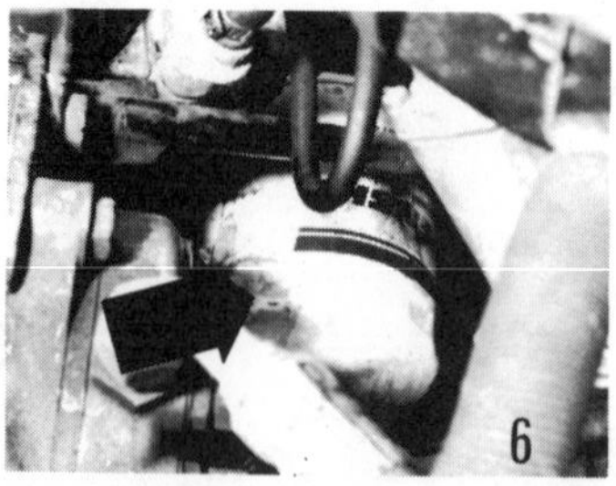
6

12

9. Punch oil pouring spout into top of oil can. Pour all cans of new oil into filler tube. Wipe filler cap clean and replace it. Be sure to re-attach all hoses. (NOTE: If filler cap is very dirty, rinse in solvent. Dry before replacing.)
10. Check new oil level at dipstick. Pull out dipstick, wipe clean.
11. Push dipstick back into engine. Be sure to insert all the way. Remove dipstick and check new oil level. It should be above the MAX line on the 1600 and 2800 cc. engines and above the SAFE line on the others. If not, make sure you put in all the oil which was required.

12. Start up engine and idle for 3-5 minutes. Oil signal light on instrument panel will glow red when engine is first started. Light should go out in 30 seconds or less.

13. Stop engine and check for oil leaks at drain plug and filter. If you find any, check tightness of plug and/or filter, also for condition of filter gasket to see that it has not become pinched or damaged when installing. Recheck oil level.

SPEEDOMETER CABLE LUBRICATION

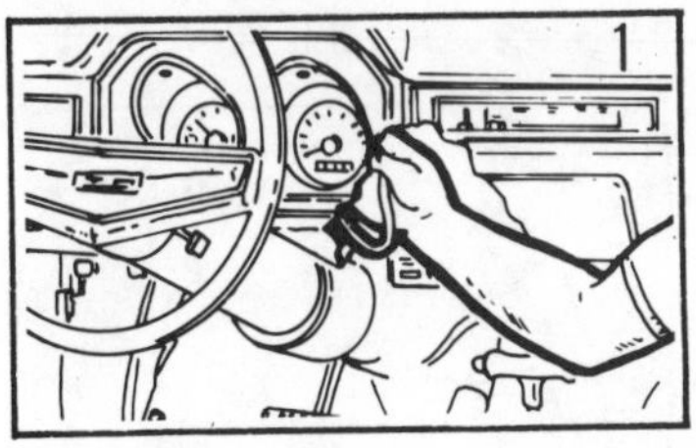

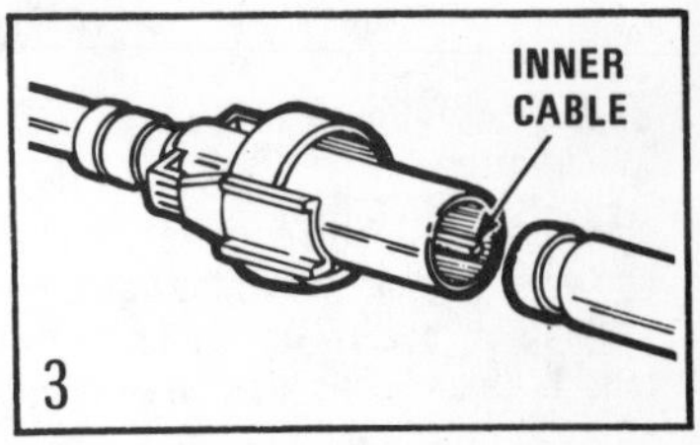

If speedometer pointer tends to quiver or jump, or if unit makes a low, rasping sound, lubrication may be needed.

1. Locate cable shaft attachment directly behind speedometer dial.
2. Press flat surface; pull cable back and out from behind panel.
3. Pull inner cable completely out of outer casing. Note carefully which end is top. Check for wear or frayed strands. If damaged, replace inner cable with new one.
4. Apply generous amount of speedometer cable lubricant into cable casing. Replace inner cable in shaft, noting that top end is not inserted accidentally. Turn inner cable as it is being re-inserted. Twist cable when all the way in, to lock into position at lower end.
5. Re-connect cable to speedometer head under instrument panel.

DOOR HINGE AND LOCK LUBRICATION

If you have ever had a door lock freeze on you, you will appreciate the value of lubricating your door locks. Lubricating them also helps fight against rust forming inside and ruining the lock. If your door makes noise when you are opening it, it is time to lubricate it. Both jobs are very simple, but when you are lubricating the door lock, it will be easier if the lubricant comes with a long thin tube which you can insert inside the lock. This will do a better job without much spilling. Each of these jobs should be done every six months.

1. Brush any dirt accumulations from door hinges and stops. Use old tooth brush or rag.
2. Apply dab of white polyethylene grease to door hinges, trunk hinges, hood hinges, door stops.

DOOR LOCKS

(lubricate every 6 months)

1. Insert door key half way into lock.
2. Spray aerosol lock lubricant into lock.
3. Push key rest of way into lock; turn back and forth several times.

DRAIN HOLE CLEANING

The doors and rocker panels of your car are equipped with drain holes to allow water to drain out of the inside of the body panels. If the drain holes become clogged with dirt, leaves, pine needles, etc., the water will remain inside the panels, causing rust. To prevent this, open the drain holes with a screwdriver. If your car is equipped with rubber dust valves instead, simply open the dust valve with your finger.

Cooling System

FIND THOSE COOLING SYSTEM LEAKS

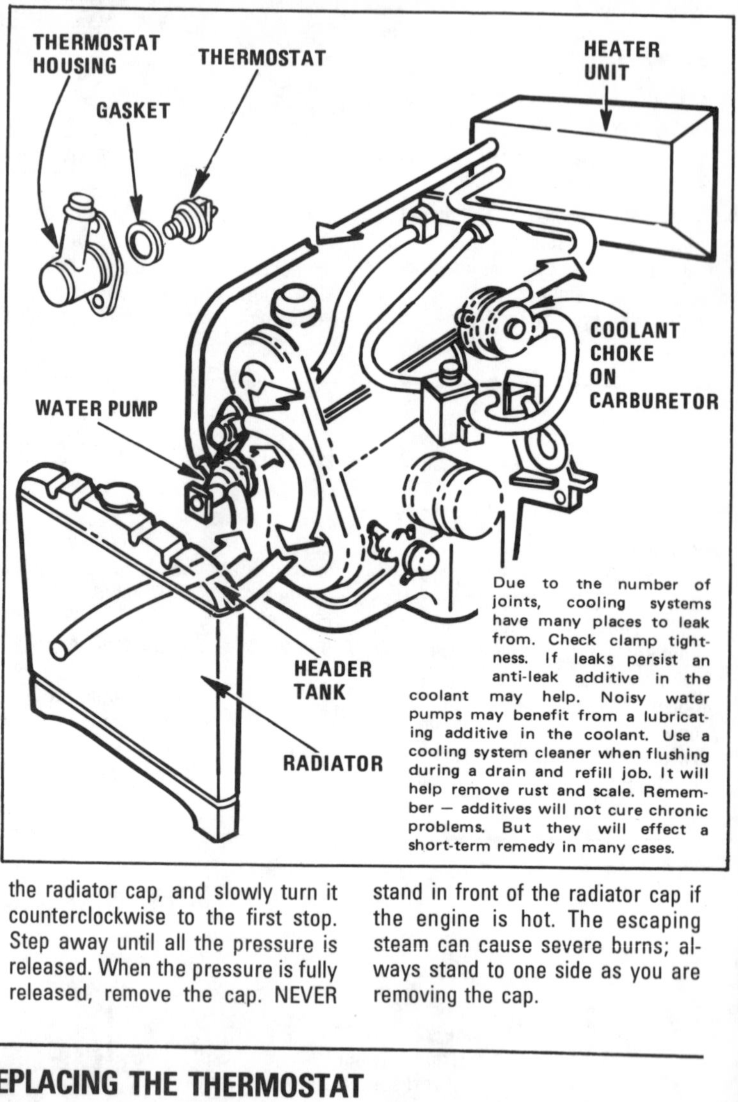

Due to the number of joints, cooling systems have many places to leak from. Check clamp tightness. If leaks persist an anti-leak additive in the coolant may help. Noisy water pumps may benefit from a lubricating additive in the coolant. Use a cooling system cleaner when flushing during a drain and refill job. It will help remove rust and scale. Remember — additives will not cure chronic problems. But they will effect a short-term remedy in many cases.

Anyone who has ever had an engine overheat and boil over on them knows (or should know) the value of keeping an eye on the cooling system. It really does not take much effort to go out once a week when the engine is cool and check the coolant level. Most newer cars come equipped with coolant recovery kits which makes the checking job even easier. If your car does not have one, it is a good idea to look into them as antifreeze which is boiled away down the overflow tube is money lost. If your car has a coolant recovery system, check the level of fluid in the reservoir and add a 50/50 mix of antifreeze and water to bring the level up to the proper mark on the reservoir. On all cars, whether they have a coolant recovery system or not, when the engine is cold, the water level in the radiator should be checked. The coolant level in the engine should be kept about 1½ in. below the filler neck. If you have to check the coolant level on a hot engine, first wrap a thick cloth around the radiator cap, and slowly turn it counterclockwise to the first stop. Step away until all the pressure is released. When the pressure is fully released, remove the cap. NEVER stand in front of the radiator cap if the engine is hot. The escaping steam can cause severe burns; always stand to one side as you are removing the cap.

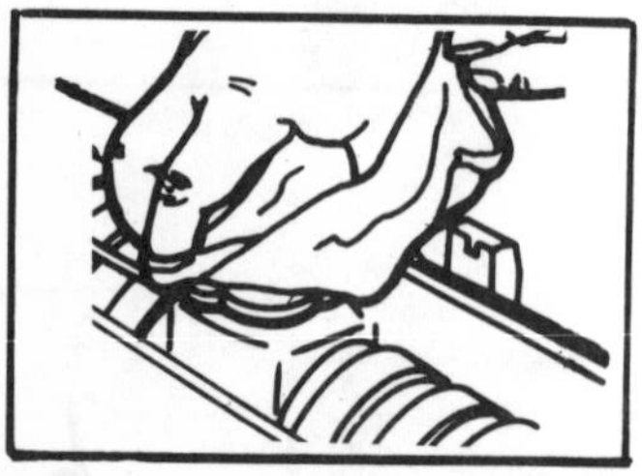

REPLACING THE THERMOSTAT

A faulty thermostat will usually cause engine overheating. Replace with new thermostat.

To replace the thermostat, you first have to know where it is:

1600 cc engine: on the top front of the cylinder head

2000 cc engine: on the top front of the cylinder head

2300 cc engine: on the top front of the cylinder head to the right of the water pump

2800 cc engine: on the bottom of the water pump cover.

If you still are not sure where it is, follow the top radiator hose (or the bottom radiator hose if you have a V6) on the four cylinder models to the point where it enters the engine. Under the metal connector is the thermostat.

A faulty thermostat will cause the engine to overheat and stop the coolant from circulating in the radiator.

1. Drain radiator of about half its coolant. (See How To Replace Hoses).
2. Loosen and remove both retaining bolts and lift thermostat housing off the engine.

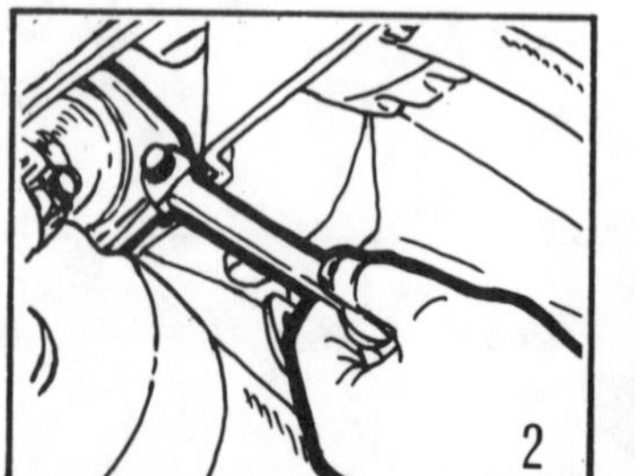

2

NOTE: If you're careful it won't be necessary to remove radiator hose.

3. Remove the old thermostat; also the retaining ring if you are working on a 2000 cc engine.
4. Scrape thermostat housing flange and engine block surface to remove old gasket debris.
5. Drop new thermostat into place—spring down.
6. Install new gasket with sealer applied to both sides.
7. Replace thermostat housing and tighten both retaining bolts.

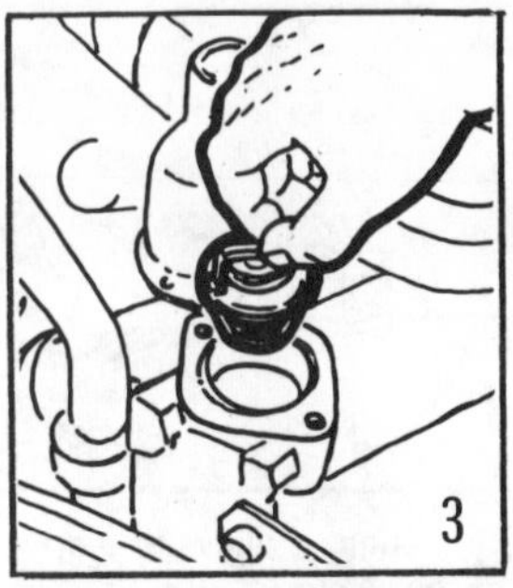

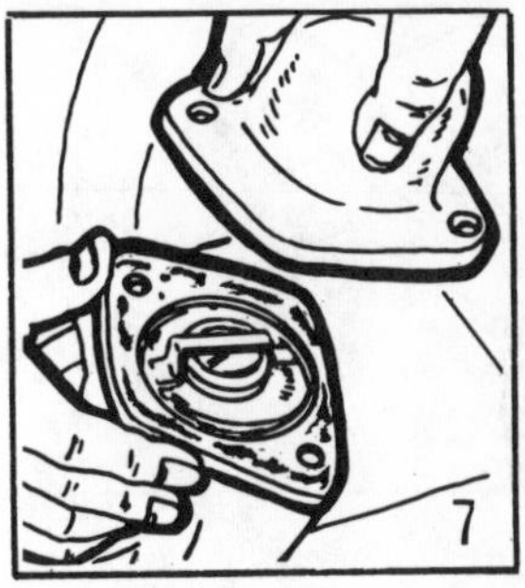

FAN BELT ADJUSTMENT

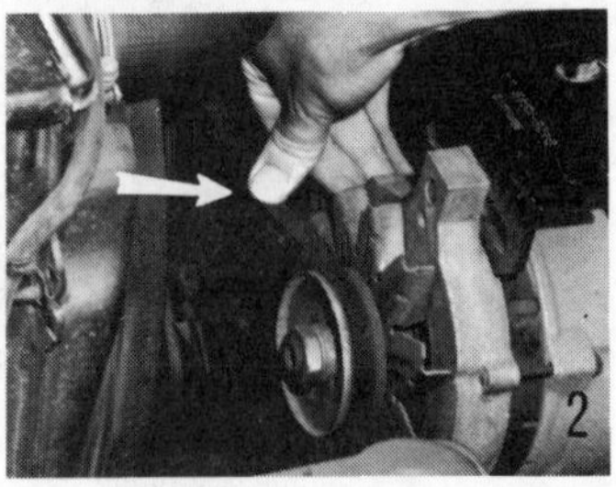

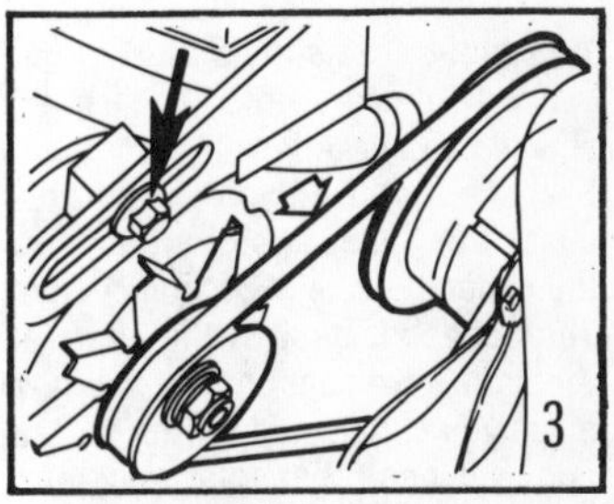

The fan belt not only drives the radiator fan, it turns the water pump and drives the alternator. It's easy to see that the condition and proper tension of the belt are vital, since almost all engine cooling and electrical power are dependent on it. The belt deserves an occasional look and tension check.
1. Inspect fan belt occasionally. If worn, frayed or cracked on inner driving surface, replace.
CAUTION: An overtightened belt may damage alternator and water pump bearings.
2. Check tension occasionally. Press thumb at midpoint of belt span between pulleys. If belt depresses more than ½ inch, tightening is needed. A too-loose belt will not drive alternator and water pump effectively.
3. Adjust to proper tension of ¼ inch deflection.

REPLACING THE RADIATOR HOSES

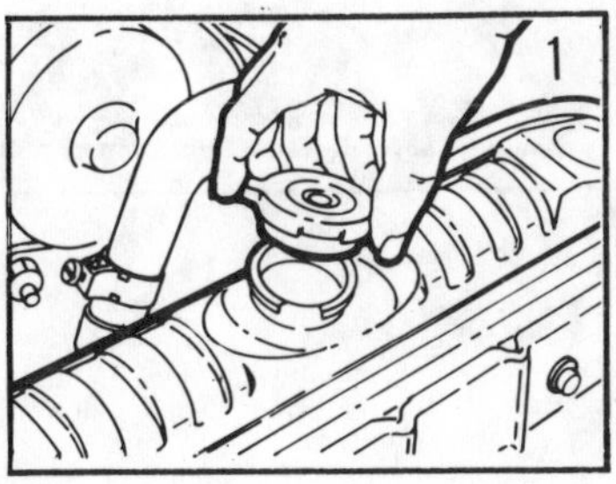

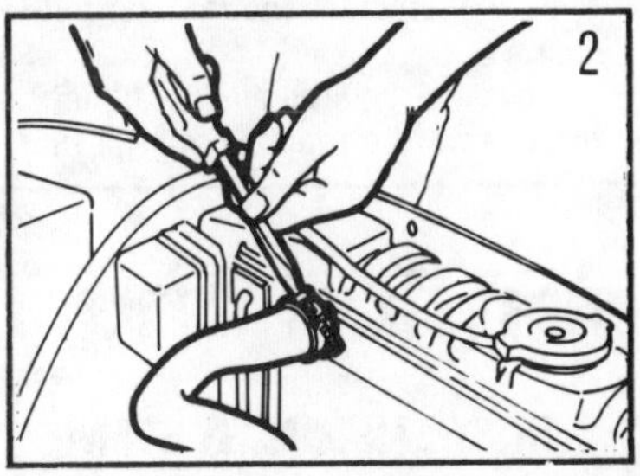

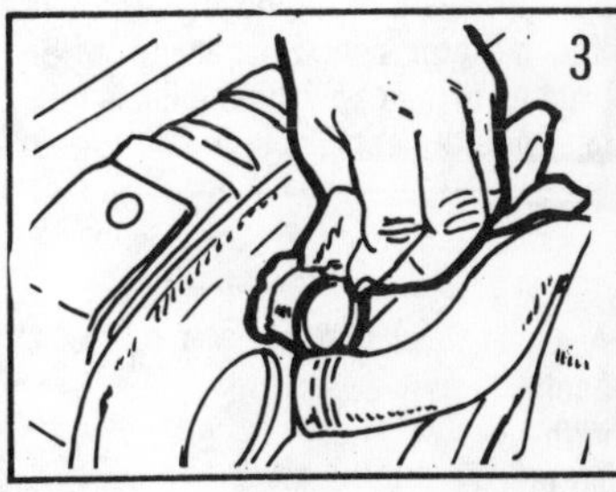

Coolant drain and refill work may be done alone; when changing hoses, coolant must also be drained as part of job. Discard all hoses with cracks or soft spots. Check hose clamps for tightness and good condition.

1. Remove radiator cap. Open radiator petcock at bottom of radiator. Drain radiator.
2. Loosen clamp at each end of hose(s). Work hose loose; pull it off.
3. Wipe all hose connections clean. Use emery cloth to get rid of residue.
4. If old hose clamps are badly rusted or damaged, replace with new units.
5. Slip clamps over each hose end. Slip hose ends all the way onto cleaned up hose connections.

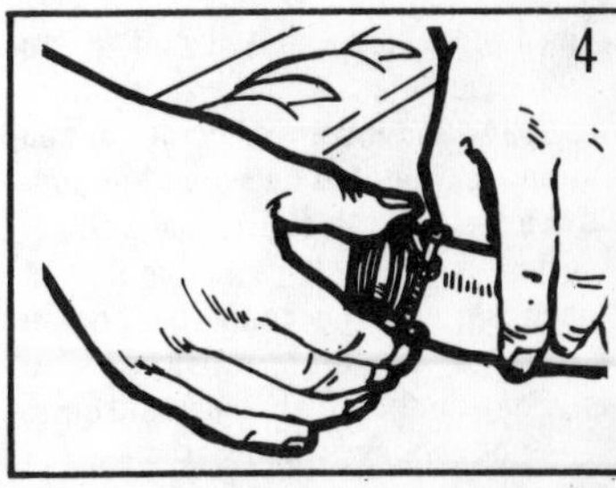

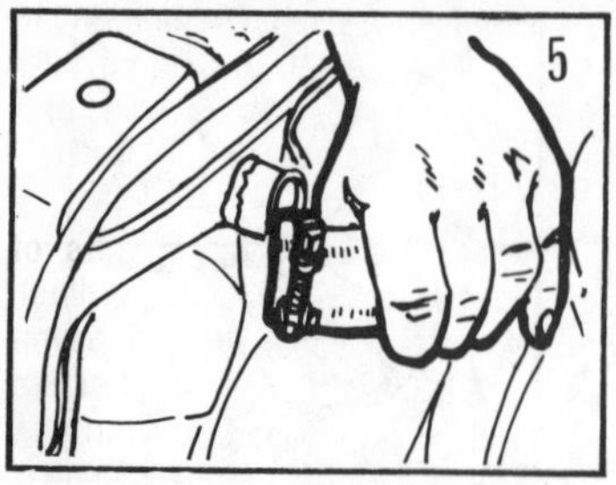

6. Place hose clamp about ¼ inch from hose end. Tighten. Close radiator petcock. Refill radiator.

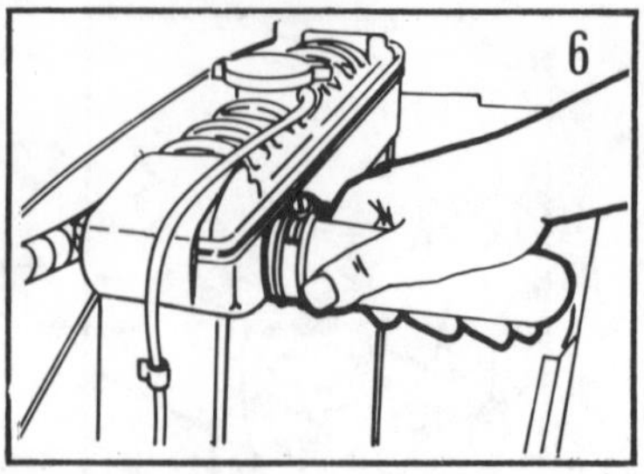

7. Start engine; allow to warm up. Check for coolant leaks.

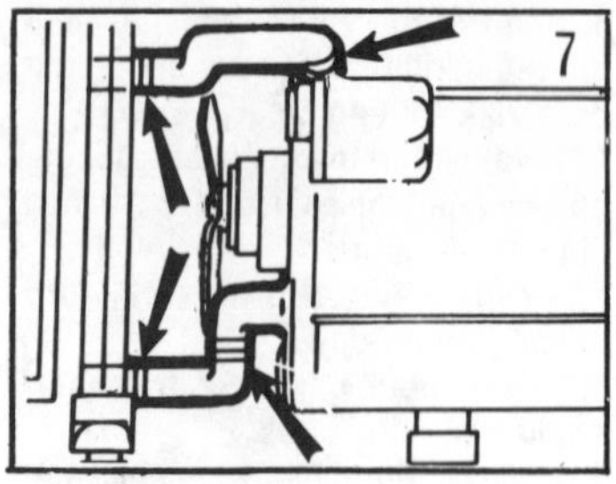

8. Road test car; watch for temperature warning light.

CHANGING THE ANTI-FREEZE

Your anti-freeze should be changed every two years, and its strength should be checked every Spring and Fall. The first thing you should do is check the Capacities Chart and see the capacity of your cooling system. Then check it against the chart on the antifreeze container to see how much you should add for the protection you need. For this procedure, you will need a place to drain the radiator, preferably some place with a drain so the coolant will not just flow out and pollute the environment; a hose to flush the system with, a can of flushing additive, and a pair of pliers or vise grips to open the petcock with.

1. If the coolant is extremely dirty, add a good flushing additive to the radiator and run the engine the amount of time recommended on the can.
2. Turn off the engine and remove the radiator cap. Be careful when removing the cap if the engine is hot.
3. Open the petcock in the bottom of

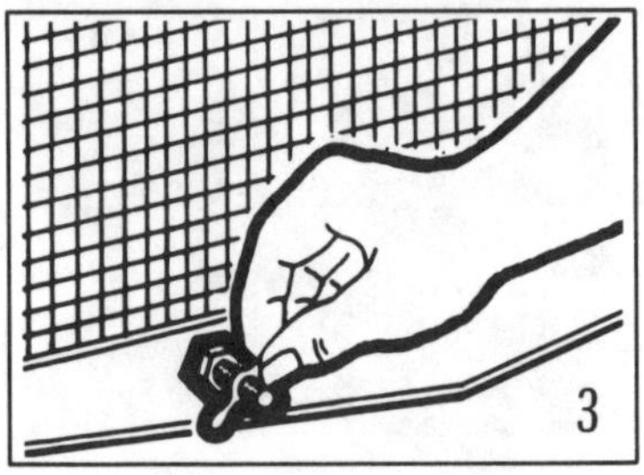

the radiator by turning its ears in a counterclockwise direction.
4. When all the coolant has drained out of the system, insert a garden hose into the radiator cap opening. Turn the water on in the hose and start the engine.
5. Allow the engine and the hose to run until the water coming out of the radiator is clean. Turn off the engine and remove the hose.
6. Allow the water to drain out of the system, then close the radiator petcock.
7. Pour the required amount of antifreeze into the radiator and fill the rest of the system with water. Run the engine for at least five minutes to allow air to escape.
8. Fill the radiator to 1 in. below the filler neck and turn off the engine. Recheck the level in the radiator after the car has been driven a short distance.

RADIATOR CAP CHECK

Check radiator cap occasionally for worn or cracked gasket. If cap doesn't seal properly, fluid will be lost and engine will overheat. Replace worn cap with new cap rated 12 to 15 lbs. pressure.

Suspension and Tires

SUSPENSION SYSTEM

The front wheels mount and rotate on the spindles, which are attached to upper and lower ball joints. A coil spring is mounted between the control arms on both sides. A shock absorber is located in the center of each spring. The rear suspension consists of leaf springs and stagger-mounted shock absorbers. The right shock is mounted ahead of the rear axle; the left shock behind the rear axle.

Your car's suspension system consists of wheels, tires, springs, shock absorbers, sway (or stabilizer) bars, ball joints, steering linkage. If any of these items is out of adjustment or badly worn, you may notice any of these symptoms:

- car pulls to one side when braking
- car wanders when driving a straight line
- overall ride may be either hard or bouncy
- effort is needed to steer vehicle
- tires show uneven wear
- tires squeal when cornering
- front of car dips or bounces when braking

- car rocks side-to-side when going over rough road
- wheels bounce or make slapping sound on road
- steering wheel vibrates in hands
- front of car vibrates at highway speeds

Any of above symptoms indicates corrective action is needed. Delay can: ruin tires; cause damage/failure to other suspension parts; create safety hazard.

Pinto and Bobcats front wheels mount to, and rotate on, the spindles. The spindles are attached to the upper and lower control arms by the upper and lower ball joints. A coil spring is mounted between the upper and lower control arms on both sides of the front suspension. A pair of shock absorbers provide suspension dampening. The shocks are attached to the lower control arms and the tops of the spring housings.

Additional suspension dampening is provided by a pair of strut bars which attach to the lower control arms and the body of the vehicle.

The rear suspension consists of conventional three-leaf, longitudinal, semielliptic springs, located asymmetrically to the rear axle carrier and fastened by U-bolt clamps. Standard telescopic shock absorbers control vertical rebound.

HANDLING TROUBLESHOOTING

Manual Steering

HARD STEERING

1. Improper (low) tire pressure
2. Inadequate lubricant
3. Inadequately lubricated front-end parts
4. Bind in steering column
5. Excessive caster
6. Cross-shaft adjustment too tight

CAR VEERS TO ONE SIDE

1. Tire pressures or tread wear unequal
2. Improper front-end alignment
3. Improperly adjusted brakes
4. Faulty shock absorbers or springs

CAR WANDERS

1. Tire pressures improper
2. Improper front-end alignment
3. Play in pitman arm
4. Loose wheel bearings
5. Binding in steering linkage
6. Steering box loose on frame
7. Worn ball joints

POOR RETURN OF STEERING

1. Tires overinflated
2. Improper caster adjustment
3. Bind in steering column
4. Improper front-end lubrication. Steering gear adjustments too tight

Power Steering

HARD STEERING

1. Improper (low) tire pressure
2. Loose or glazed pump drive belt
3. Low fluid level
4. Poorly lubricated front-end parts
5. Bind in steering column
6. Inadequate pump output pressure, due to worn pump parts or malfunctioning pressure regulator valve
7. Obstructions in pump lines
8. Excessive caster
9. Cross-shaft adjustment too tight

CAR VEERS TO ONE SIDE

1. Tire pressures or tread wear unequal
2. Improper front-end alignment
3. Improperly adjusted brakes
4. Faulty shock absorbers or springs

CAR WANDERS

1. Tire pressures improper
2. Improper front-end alignment
3. Play in pitman arm
4. Loose wheel bearings
5. Binding in steering linkage
6. Steering unit valve (rotary valve, spool valve, or pivot lever) malfunctioning
7. Worn ball joints

POWER STEERING NOISY

1. Belts loose or glazed
2. Fluid level low
3. Air in system
4. Kinked hydraulic lines
5. Foreign matter clogging hydraulic lines
6. Flow control valve sticking
7. Steering unit valve (rotary valve, spool valve, or pivot lever) worn
8. Worn pump parts
9. Steering gear mountings loose
10. Interference in front end

POOR RETURN OF STEERING

1. Tires overinflated
2. Improper caster adjustment
3. Bind in steering column
4. Improper front-end lubrication
5. Steering gear adjustments too tight

STEERING

If steering linkage, front suspension and steering column components are in good condition, there should be no more than 3/8 inch free play in the steering wheel when measured at the rim of the wheel. If a loud knock is heard when turning the steering wheel from one extreme to the other, have mechanic check pinion bearing preload.

SHOCK ABSORBERS

Shock absorbers work to keep wheels in constant contact with the road. Result is safe handling and ride control; longer tire life. So shock absorbers (or shocks) are important.

HOW TO CHECK FOR BAD SHOCKS

1. Check under car and locate shock absorber near each wheel.

2. Heavy oil streaks on outer shock housing indicate need for replacement.

3. Stand at front of car and apply body weight in a pumping action to front bumper or fender. Release pressure and allow car to stop rocking. Car should not bounce more than once more time after releasing pressure. Repeat at rear. If bouncing continues more than one, replacement is needed. Replace shocks in pairs (front pair or rear pair).

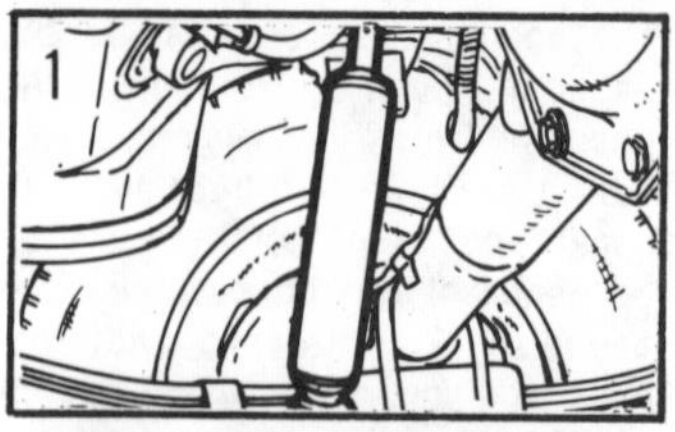

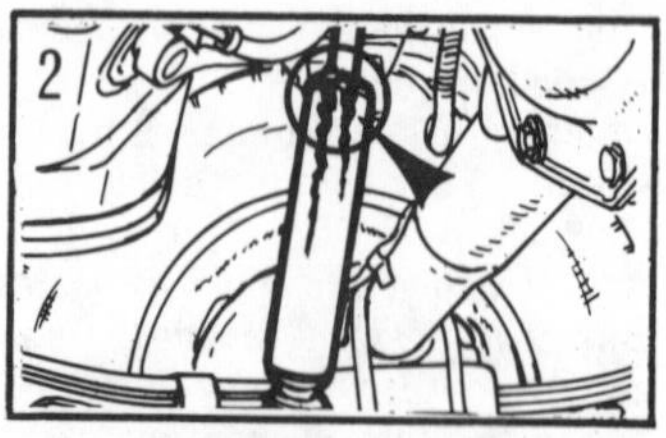

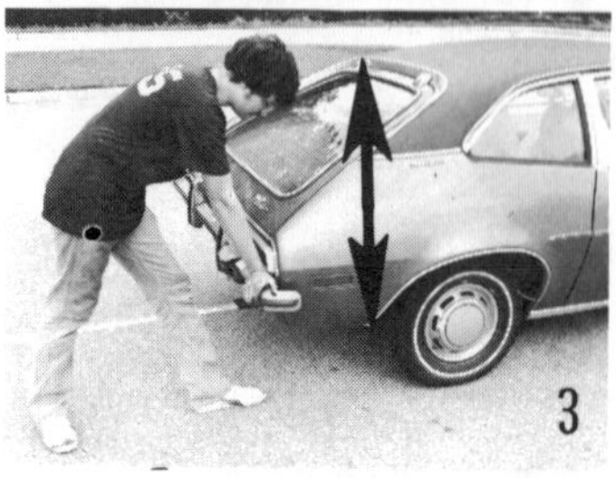

TOW HITCH INFORMATION

If your Pinto is used for trailer towing you should check:
A. Cooling System; be sure radiator is at proper level in radiator. See Cooling System Section for checks to perform.
B. Check Transmission Fluid; keep topped up to proper level.
C. Check Rear Shock Absorbers; you may benefit from installation of new rear shocks.
D. Check Tire Pressures; best traction and handling can be ensured if tire pressures are properly maintained.
For safer and more trouble-free trailer towing, consider:
A. Automatic Transmission Cooler; helps remove excess heat from automatic transmission fluid built up during towing mileage. Also helps avoid radiator overheating. Some units can be self-installed.

B. Radiator Over-Flow Tank Kit; addition of a reservoir to catch radiator coolant overflow preventing coolant loss. Easy to install, these units help a tow car run cooler, avoid overheating due to coolant loss.

C. Heavy-Duty Shock Absorbers or Air Shocks; important to have on rear wheels if you intend to do a lot of towing or load carrying within the car itself. Don't forget to consider replacing factory shocks, when they are worn out, with heavy-duty units at the front as well.

D. Variable Load Flasher; this unit will accommodate the added load of trailer turn signal lamps on trailer when these are hooked into your car's electrical system.
Ford recommends that you tow no more than 1,000 lbs. with your car. The most important thing to remember when you are towing is that you are towing. Your car is not going to react the way it normally does. Acceleration times are going to be longer and stopping is going to take more distance. Crosswinds will also affect your car more with a trailer attached. Before you drive off, make sure all the lights on the trailer are working, if not, a test light will aid in tracking down the trouble spots.

FRONT END ALIGNMENT

When steering, handling and/or tire wear indicate front end alignment may be needed, this work can only be done at an automotive service shop. DO NOT PUT OFF NEEDED FRONT END ALIGNMENT. At the same time, have ball joints and steering linkage checked.

Ignition System

CHECKING YOUR IGNITION SYSTEM

The primary components of your ignition system are: the coil, primary and spark plug wires, the distributor and its internal components, and the spark plugs. Pintos use two different types of ignition systems, the conventional and the breakerless. The conventional system was used on all models through 1974, the breaker-

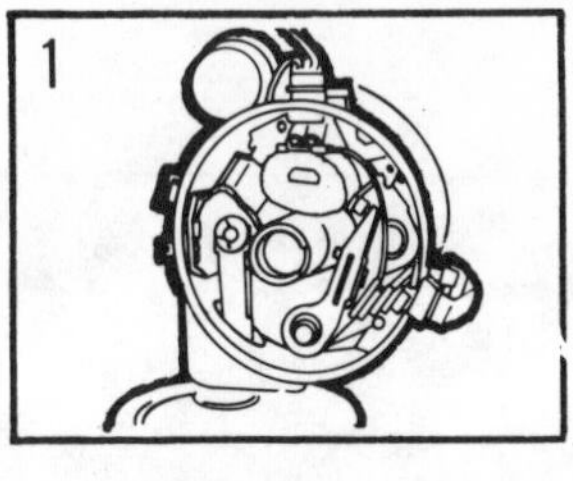

less on all models starting in 1975. All Bobcats use the breakerless system.

The two systems differ in the manner in which they convert electrical primary voltage (12 volt) from the battery into secondary voltage (20,000 volts or greater) to fire the spark plugs. In the conventional ignition system, the breaker points open and close as the movable breaker arm rides the rotating distributor cam eccentric, thereby opening and closing the current to the ignition coil. When the points open, they interrupt the flow of primary current to the coil, causing a collapse of the magnetic field in the coil and creating a high tension spark which is used to fire the spark plugs. In the breakerless system, a distributor shaft-mounted armature rotates past a magnetic pickup coil assembly causing fluctuations in the magnetic field generated by the pickup coil. These fluctuations in turn, cause the amplifier module to turn the ignition coil current off and on, creating the high tension spark to fire the spark plugs.

The amplifier module electronically controls the dwell, which is controlled mechanically in a conventional system by the duration which the points remain closed.

On the conventional system, the points and condenser should be replaced every 12 months or 12,000 miles. On both systems, you should check the spark plug and coil wires, the condition of the distributor cap and rotor, and the coil condition. To check the points, remove the air cleaner and position it to one side.

1. Disconnect the secondary cable from the coil at the center of the distributor cap. On distributors using clasps to secure the cap, pry the retaining clasps from either side of the cap using a flat blade screwdriver. On distributors using cross-head screws with "L-shaped" levers to

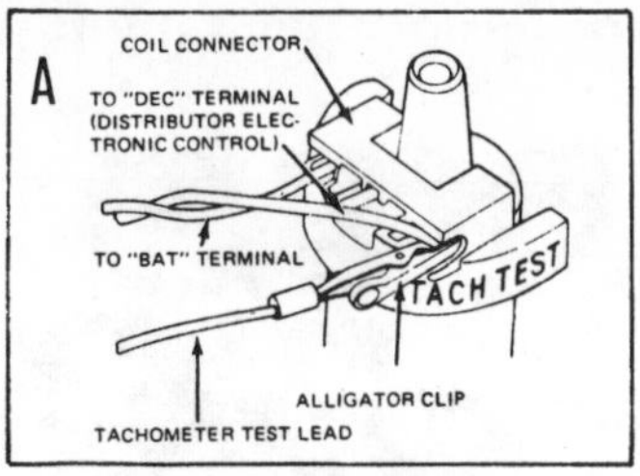

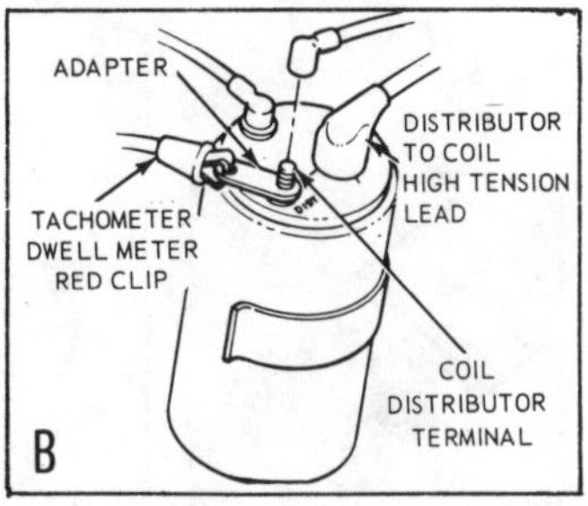

secure the cap, press down on the screw head with a flat blade screwdriver and while maintaining pressure, rotate the screw head and retaining lever in either direction to free it from the distributor body. Then, lift off the cap (wires installed) and position it to one side.

2. Mark the position of the rotor by scribing a mark on the distributor body. Pull the rotor straight up and off. Discard it if it is cracked, burned or excessively worn at the tip.

3, Insert a screwdriver between the stationary and breaker arms of the points and examine the condition of the contacts. Replace the points if the contacts are blackened, pitted, or if the metal transfer exceeds that of the specified point gap (see "Tune-Up Specifications"). Also replace the points if the breaker arm has lost its tension (nonadjustable types) or if the rubbing block has become worn or loose. Contact points which have become slightly burned (light gray) may be cleaned with a point file.

4. In order for the points to function properly, the contact faces must be aligned. The alignment must be checked with the points closed. To close the points, install an open-end wrench on the crankshaft pulley/damper bolt and turn the engine over in its normal direction of rotation until the points can be seen to close. This may be more easily accomplished with the spark plugs removed.

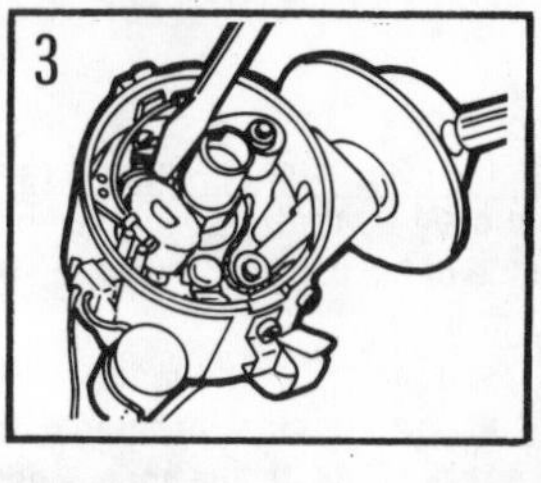

5. If the contact faces are not centered, bend the stationary arm to suit. Never bend the breaker arm. Discard the points if they cannot be centered correctly.

6. Check the inside of the distributor cap for surface cracks, pitting and burned contacts. If any of these are present, discard the cap. Check the plug and coil wire for cracks in the insulation; if they are in poor condition, replace them.

7. If your Pinto-Bobcat has the breakerless ignition system, there are no points to check. Instead, when you remove the distributor cap, check the area underneath the rotor for cleanliness. If there is any dirt in there, first try to clean it with compressed air, if this is not available, wipe it out very carefully with a clean lint free cloth.

The new solid state ignition coil connector allows a tachometer test lead with an alligator-type clip to be connected to the DEC (Distributor Electronic Control) terminal without removing the connector.

When engine rpm must be checked, install the tachometer alligator clip into the "TACH TEST" cavity as shown. If the coil connector must be removed, grasp the wires and pull horizontally until it disconnects from the terminals.

See the two figures illustrating how to hook up a tach to both conventional and breakerless ignition systems.

REPLACING THE SPARK PLUGS

1. If the spark plug wires are not numbered as to their cylinder, place a piece of masking tape on each wire and number it.
2. Grasp each wire by the rubber boot at the end. Pull the wires from the spark plugs. If the boots stick to the plugs, remove them with a twisting motion. Do not attempt to remove the spark plug wires from the plugs by pulling on the wire itself as this will damage the spark plug wires.
3. Using a 13/16 in. spark plug socket, loosen each plug several turns. Be careful not to contact the positive battery terminal with the spark plug wrench.
4. If compressed air is available, blow off the area around each spark plug hole. Otherwise, use a rag or other suitable material and remove any loose particles from around each plug hole. In either case, make sure that foreign matter is not allowed to enter the cylinders.
5. Unscrew the plugs the rest of the way and remove them from the engine.

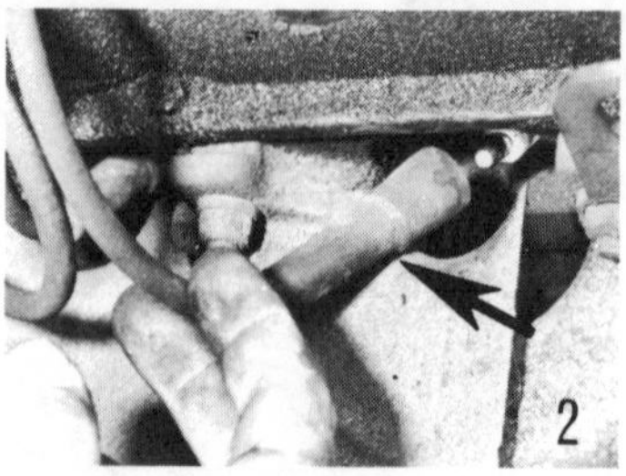

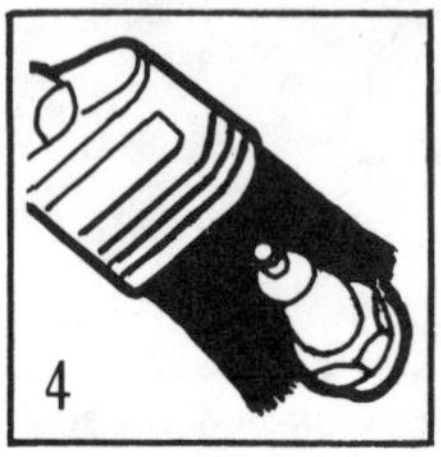

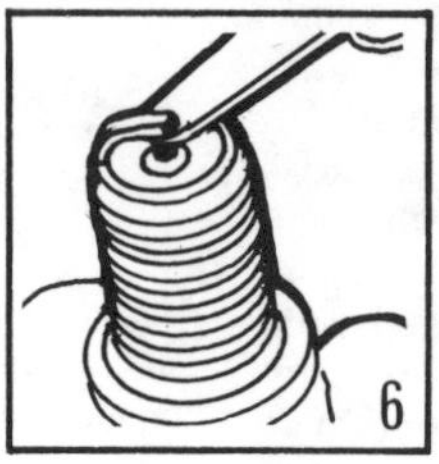

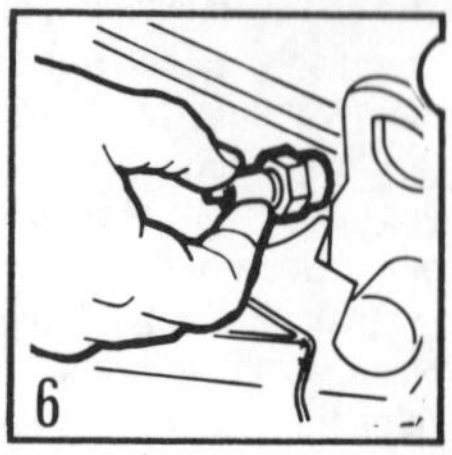

6. Check plug electrode gap on new spark plug. Plug gap is correct when the gauge drags slightly as it is pulled between plug electrodes.

Insert the plugs into the engine and tighten them hand tight. Do not crossthread the plugs.

7. Tighten the plugs to 10-15 ft lbs. on 14 MM plugs; 15-25 ft lbs on 18MM plugs, and 15-20 ft lbs. on the V6.
8. Install the spark plug wires on their respective plugs, making sure each wire is firmly connected.

REPLACING SPARK PLUG WIRES

All you will need for this job will be the new set of spark plug wires. These are sold in kits of two basic types, the types where the wires are already formed, and the kind where you have to put the spark plug wire together yourself. The preformed kits are by far the easiest to install, but with the other kit you can tailor the wire to fit your need exactly with as little surplus wire as possible. Either way, when working on spark plug wires, you only work on one at a time.

1. Lay the new wires out before you so you can match up an old wire with its replacement to ensure a correct fit.

2. Starting from the rear, twist the boot on the last plug and remove it, then remove the wire from the harness.

3. Twist off the boot on the top of the distributor cap and remove the spark plug wire.

4. Compare it with the new wires and choose the one which most nearly matches it in length. If you are using the kit where you make the wire, do not forget to add about an inch on each end for the amount of wire inside the boot.

5. Insert the wire boot on the plug and make sure it is on snug. Push the wire on the harness and insert the other boot on the distributor cap, twisting it down if necessary to make sure it is snug.

6. All you have to do is follow these steps for the other plugs and your wiring job will be complete.

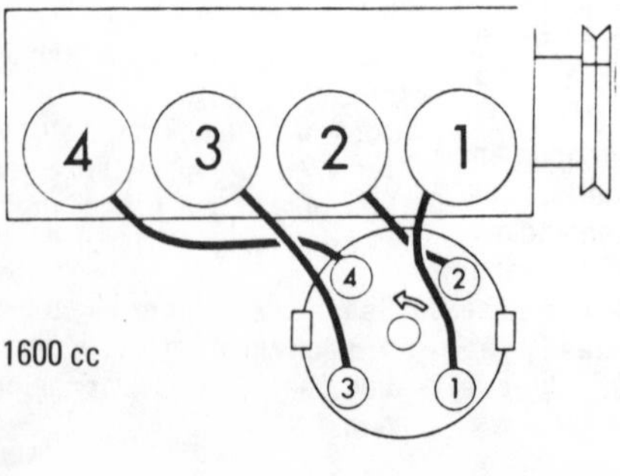

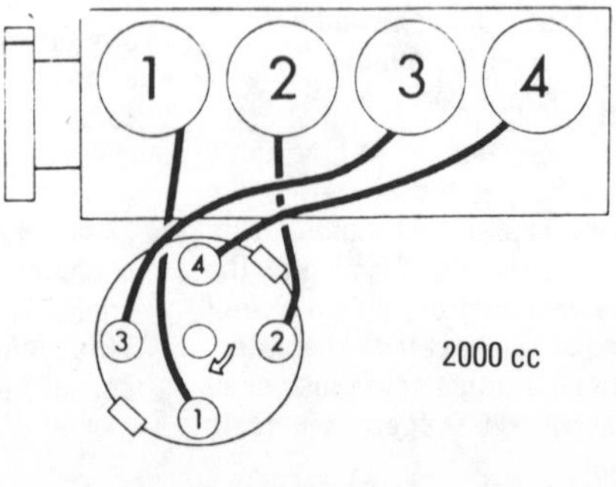

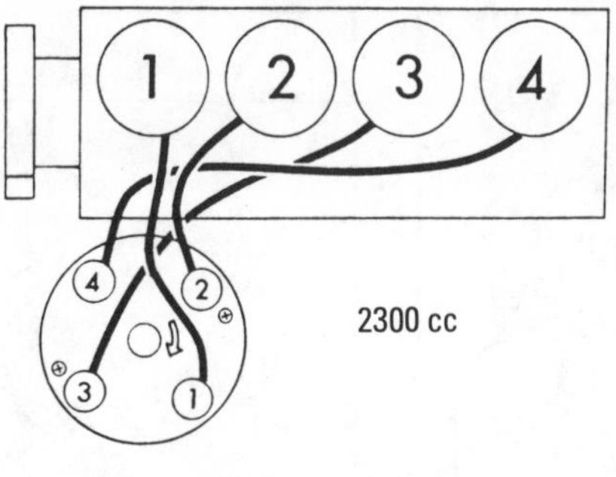

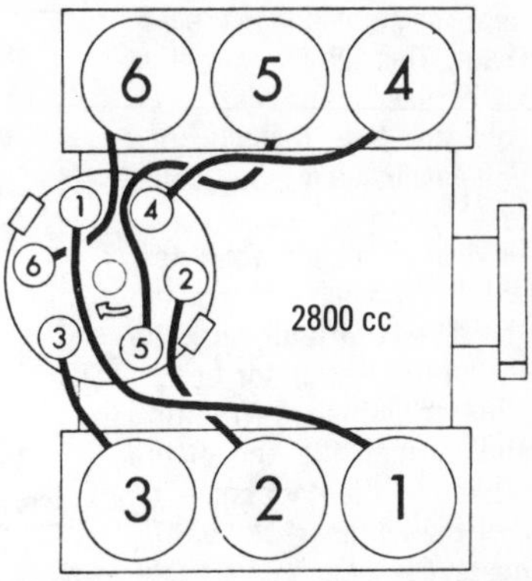

INSTALLING THE IGNITION POINTS AND CONDENSER

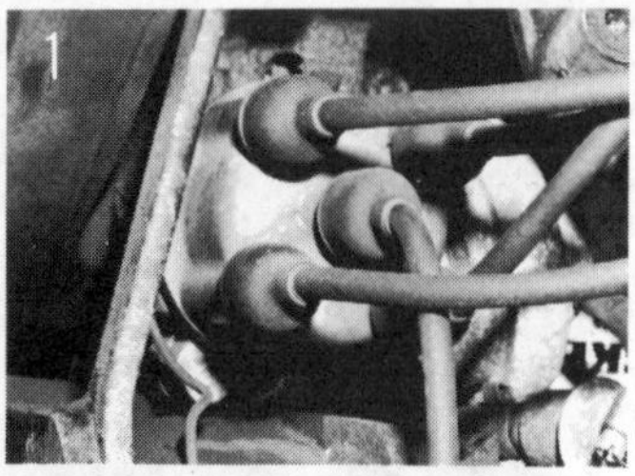

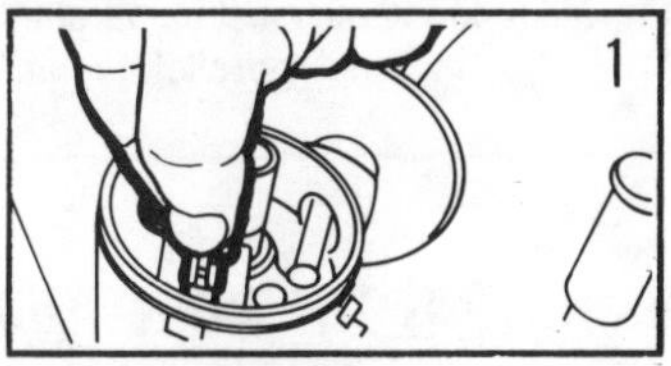

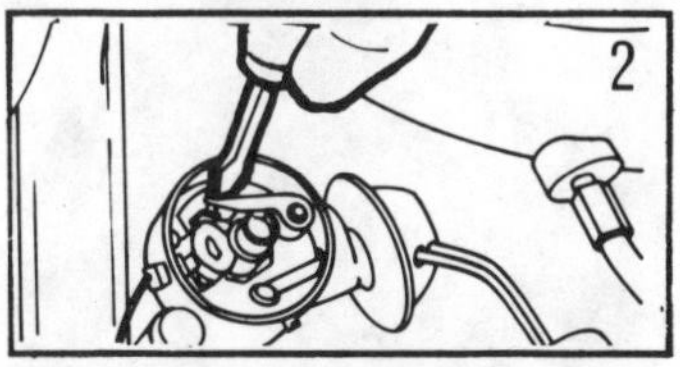

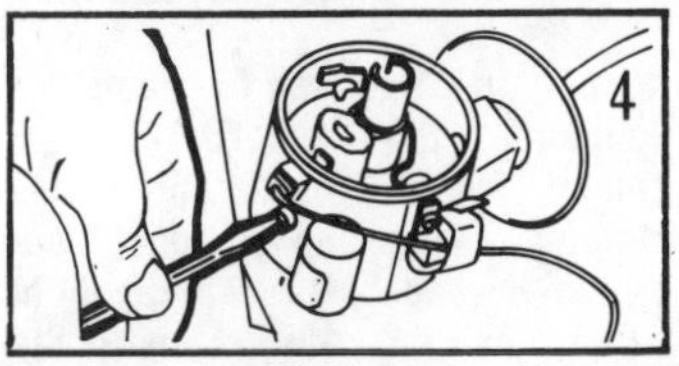

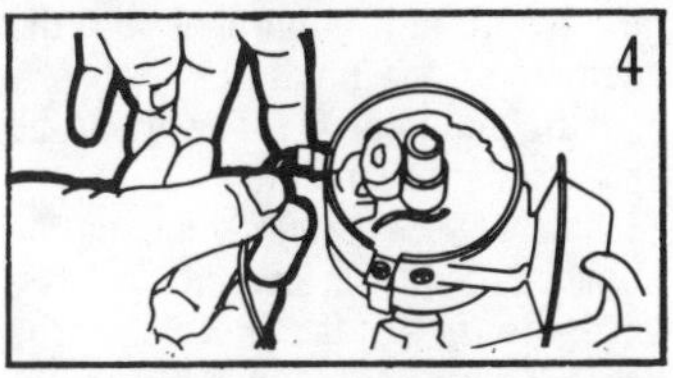

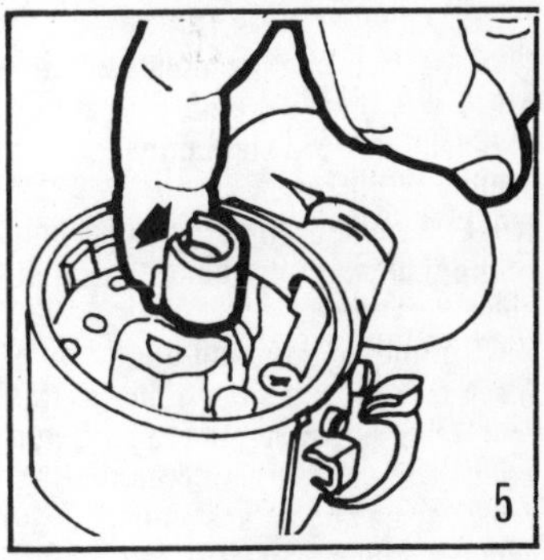

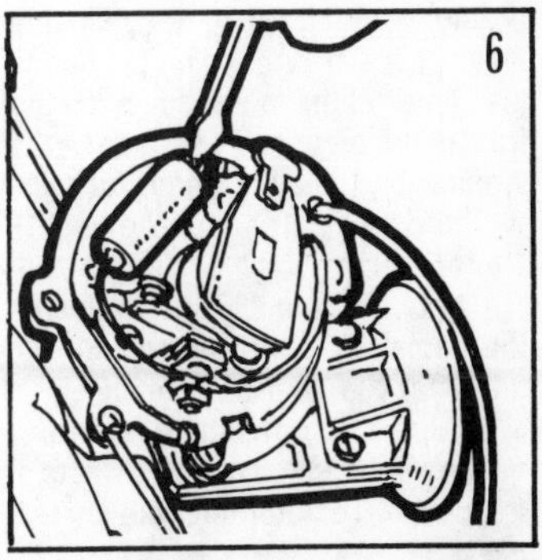

CAUTION: When removing screws from distributor in following steps be sure to avoid any screws accidentally falling through distributor opening into engine. Use magnetic screwdriver.

1. Remove the distributor cap; on the 1600 cc and 2300 cc., loosen the screw that attaches the distributor primary wire and the condenser lead wire to the center of the breaker points. On the 2000 cc., disconnect the condenser from the breaker points by pulling the breaker point wire from the condenser connector near the circumference of the distributor body.

2. On the 1600 cc and 2300 cc., using a magnetic or locking screwdriver, remove the screw that attaches the condenser to the distributor breaker plate and remove the condenser and screw from the distributor.

3. Remove the one or two breaker point attaching screw(s) with a magnetic screwdriver and remove the points and their attaching screw(s) from the distributor. You should use a magnetic screwdriver for this so that you do not lose the tiny point attaching screws while you are removing them.

4. On the 2000 cc., remove the screw that attaches the condenser to the distributor body. Grasp the condenser and wire and work the rubber grommet out of the distributor body. Disconnect the ignition switch wire connector from the coil and disconnect the wire attached to the condenser from the coil.

5. Wipe all dirt and grease from the distributor plate and cam with a lint-free rag. Apply a small amount of

special heat-resistant lube to the distributor cam. This lube is supplied with most breaker point kits. If you did not get this lube (usually in a small pull-apart capsule), buy some from a local auto parts store.

6. On the 2000 cc., position the new condenser and wire assembly on the side of the distributor and work the grommet into the distributor body. Install the condenser attaching screw and position the end of the wire attached to the condenser on the post of the coil marked "dist." Install the ignition switch wire on the coil post over the condenser wire.

7. Position your new points on the breaker plate of the distributor, making sure the tab (2300 cc only), on the bottom of the points engages the indentation on the breaker plates. Install and tighten the breaker point attaching screws.

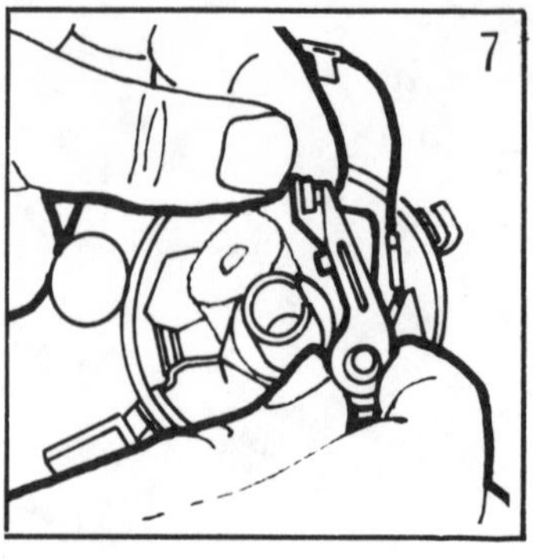

On the 2300 cc, position the distributor primary wire and the condenser lead wire on their attaching screw on the points and tighten the attaching screw. The connectors on the end of the wires must be parallel to each other and parallel to the ground when they are tightened. If this is not done, one of the connectors might contact the breaker plate and short out the primary side of the ignition. In most cases this will prevent the engine from starting.

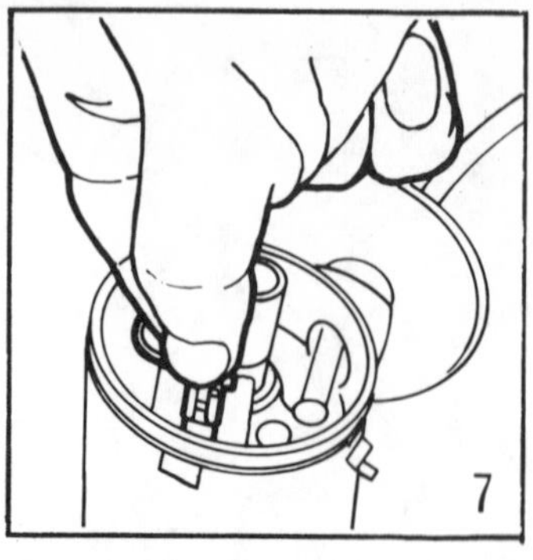

8. Adjust the breaker points as shown.

ADJUSTING THE POINT GAP

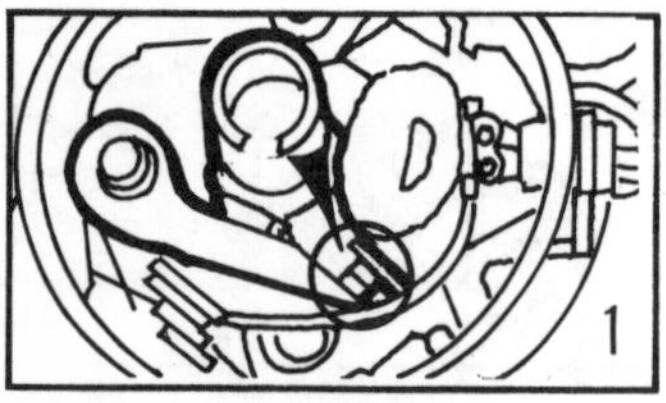

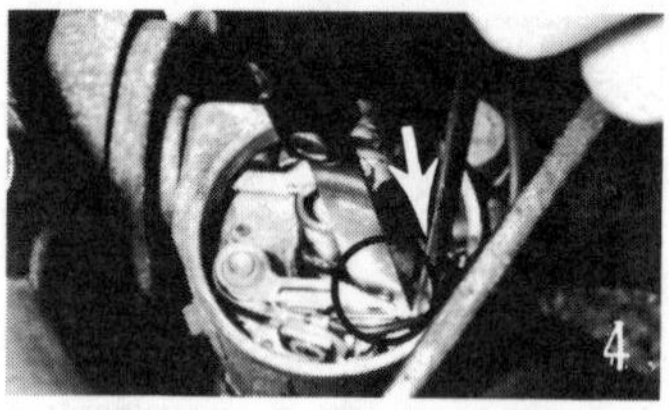

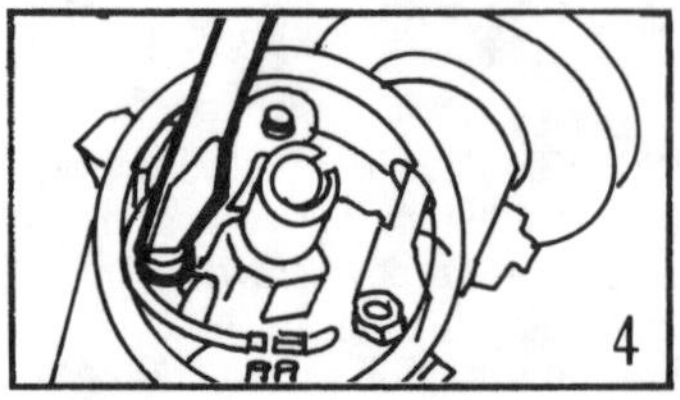

1. If the two contact points of the breaker point assembly are not parallel, bend the stationary contact slightly to correct.

NOTE: Bend only the bracket portion of the points, do not bend the other side.

2. Turn the engine until the rubbing block on the points is on one of the four high points of the distributor cam. This can be accomplished either by having an assistant quickly turn the ignition switch to the "start" position and release it, or by placing the proper size wrench on the bolt in the center of the lower pulley on the front of the engine. If you choose the wrench on pulley method, turn the wrench clockwise (to the right). Never turn the pulley counterclockwise on a 2000 cc engine as the camshaft drive belt could slip and alter the camshaft timing.

3. Insert the correct size feeler gauge between the open contacts of the points. To determine the correct feeler gauge size, see the point gap column on the "Tune-Up Specifications" chart in the front of this chapter. The gauge should fit between the contacts with a slight amount of drag. Always insert the gauge so that it is parallel with the contacts on the points.

4. If the point gap is too large or too small, adjust as follows:

1600 cc, 2300cc—Slightly loosen the point attaching screws and insert a screwdriver in the notch in the breaker plate at the top of the points. Twist the screwdriver to open or close the points as required. Tighten the breaker point attaching screws when the correct gap is obtained.

2000 cc—Slightly loosen the point attaching screw and insert a screwdriver blade between the boss on the breaker plate and the notch on the points. Twist the screwdriver to open or close the points as required. Tighten the breaker point attaching screw when the correct gap is obtained.

5. Recheck the point gap to make sure it did not change when the breaker point attaching screws were tightened.

6. Push the distributor rotor onto the distributor shaft after aligning the tab inside the rotor with the notch on the shaft. Make sure the rotor is fully seated on the shaft.

7. Align the tab inside the base of the distributor cap with the notch in the lip of the distributor body opening. Install the cap on the distributor and make sure it is fully seated. Snap the distributor cap retaining clips into place on the side of the cap.

8. Install the coil high-tension wire. On models with air conditioning, after adjusting the ignition timing, install the alternator attaching bolts, install and adjust the air conditioner compressor belt, and tighten the attaching bolts on the alternator.

ADJUSTING THE IGNITION TIMING

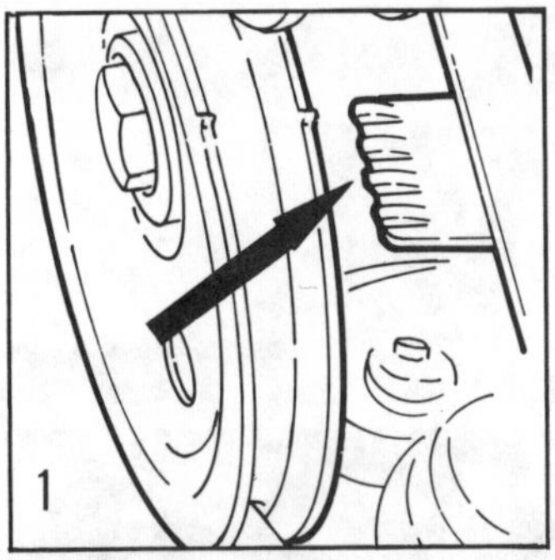

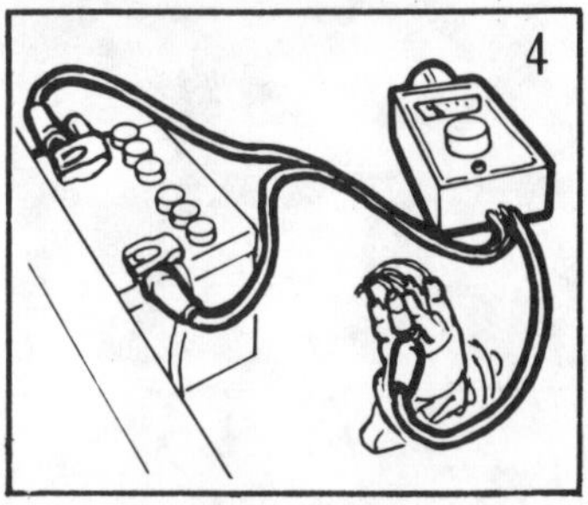

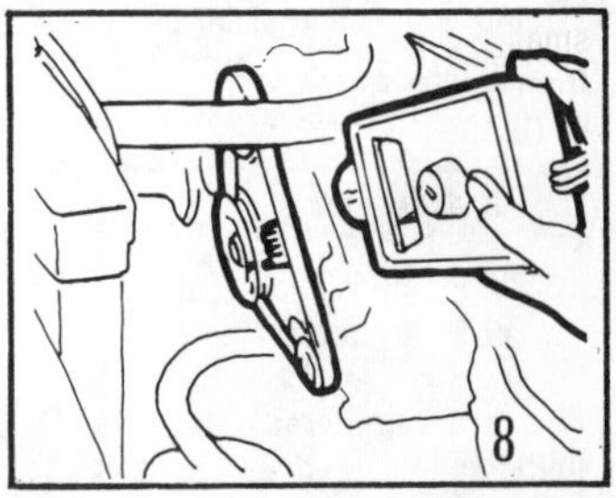

1. Locate the timing marks and pointer on the lower engine pulley and engine front cover.

2. Clean the timing marks and pointer.

3. Mark the proper timing mark (see "Tune-Up Specifications") and the pointer with white chalk or day-glo paint. Attach a tachometer to the engine.

4. Attach a timing light according to the manufacturer's instructions. If the timing light has three wires, one (usually blue or green) must be installed, with an adapter, between the end of the no. 1 spark plug wire and spark plug. The other leads are connected to the positive (usually red lead) battery terminal and the negative (usually black lead) battery terminal.

5. Disconnect the one or two vacuum lines from the distributor. After removing the lines, plug the open end with the tip of a pencil or a golf tee.

6. Check to be sure the timing light wires are clear of the engine fan and start the engine.

CAUTION: When working on a vehicle with the engine running, the following precautions must be observed: Work only in a well-ventilated area. Be certain the transmission is in Neutral and the parking brake firmly applied. Always keep your hands, clothing, and tools clear of the moving radiator fan.

7. Adjust the carburetor to reduce the engine idle speed to the specification shown in the tune-up chart.

8. Aim the timing light at the timing mark and pointer on the front of the engine. If the marks you put on the timing mark and pointer are not aligned when the timing light flashes, turn off the engine and proceed to step nine. If the two marks do align, adjust the engine to normal idle speed, turn off the engine, and remove the test equipment.

9. On those models with a 1600 cc, 2300 cc, or 2800 cc engine, loosen the distributor lockscrew just enough that the distributor can be turned. On those models with a 2000 cc engine, loosen the distributor lock bolt just enough so the distributor can be turned.

NOTE: The distributor lock bolt on the 2000 cc engine has a 13 mm metric head.

The distributor lock bolt or screw is located at the base of the distributor where the distributor shaft enters the engine. Turn the distributor slightly in the direction of distributor rotor rotation to retard the spark. Turn the distributor slightly in the opposite direction of rotation to advance the spark. Tighten the lockscrew or bolt.

10. Start the engine and recheck the timing. If the timing mark and the pointer still do not align, repeat step nine.

11. Adjust the engine to normal idle speed, turn off the engine, and remove the test equipment.

Fuel Systems

When gasoline is brought from the fuel tank, it mixes with air in the carburetor. This gas/air mixture enters engine thru the intake manifold, passes thru the intake valves and is burned in the combustion chamber. The burned exhaust gas is then passed thru the exhaust valves to the exhaust system and to the outside air. In order to keep your car's engine running cleanly with minimal pollution, and avoid dangerous carbon monoxide fumes inside the vehicle, certain items should be checked from time to time.

Among these are the air filter, the fuel filter, the crankcase ventilation filter, the oil filler cap (1600 cc. only), and the PCV valve.

1600 CC ENGINE ONLY

Remove the oil filler cap from the front of the valve cover and disconnect the hose from the cap. Immerse the cap in a pan filled with mineral spirits or other suitable solvent. Agitate the cap in the pan, then remove and shake it dry. Connect the hose to the cap and install it on the valve cover.

REPLACING THE AIR FILTER AND CRANKCASE VENTILATION FILTER

1. Remove air cleaner lid by removing retaining clips. Lift out circular air cleaner cartridge. Remove loose dust. Discard if more than 12 months old or if excessively dirty.

2. Wipe inside of can and lid clean with lint-free cloth.

3. Discard small crankcase filter located in pocket on inside bottom half of can. Insert new crankcase filter.

4. Insert air cleaner cartridge. Replace lid, secure retaining clips.

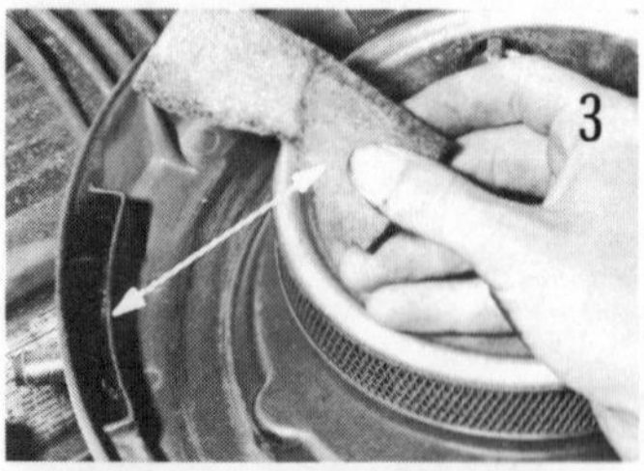

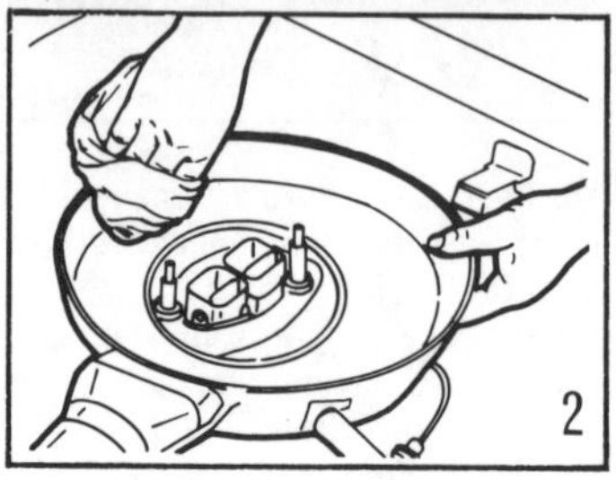

PCV VALVE SERVICE

On the 1600 and 2000 cc engines, the PCV valve is located in the top of the oil separator. The 2300 cc engine PCV valve is located midway between the carburetor and the oil separator. On the V6, it is located in the carburetor spacer.

1. Remove the PCV system components, filler cap, PCV valve, hoses, tubes, fittings, etc. from the engine.
2. Soak the rubber ventilation hose(s) in a low volatility petroleum base solvent.
3. Clean the rubber ventilation hose(s) by passing a suitable cleaning brush through them.
4. Thoroughly wash the rubber hoses in a low volatility petroleum base solvent and dry with compressed air.
5. Thoroughly wash the crankcase breather cap, if so equipped, in a low volatility petroleum base solvent and shake dry. Do not dry with compressed air; damage to the filtering media may result.
6. Thoroughly clean tubes, fittings, connections to assure unobstructed flow of emission gases.
7. Install new PCV valve and reinstall previously removed hoses, tubes, fittings, etc. to their proper location.
8. Replace any system component that shows signs of damage, wear or deterioration as required.

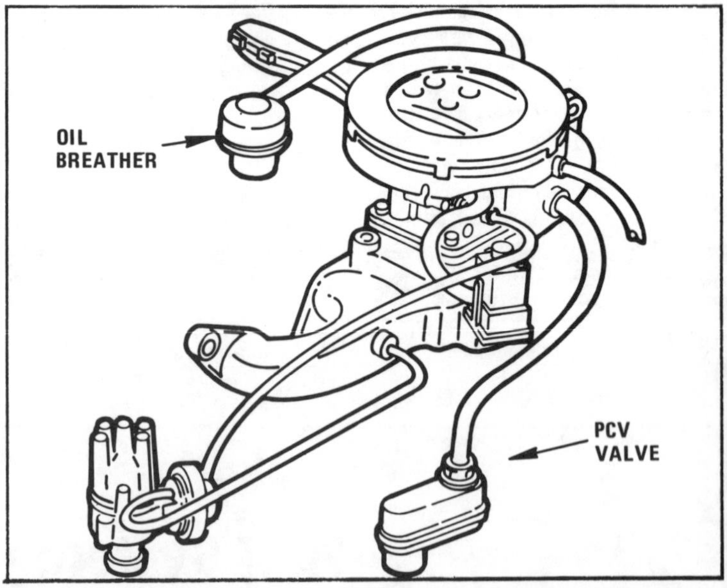

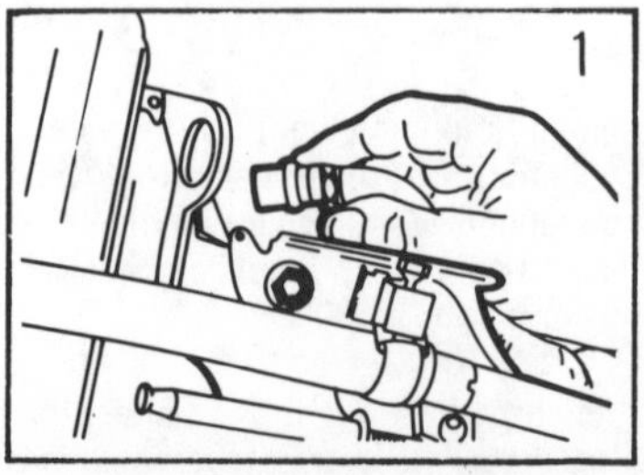

9. Replace any hose or tube that cannot be cleaned satisfactorily.

V6 PCV VALVE REMOVAL

1. Remove the air cleaner; loosen the screw on the clamp and remove the hose from the PCV valve.

2. With a 9/16 in. open end wrench, unscrew the PCV valve from the carburetor spacer.

3. Install a new valve and replace the hose and air cleaner.

REPLACING THE FUEL FILTER

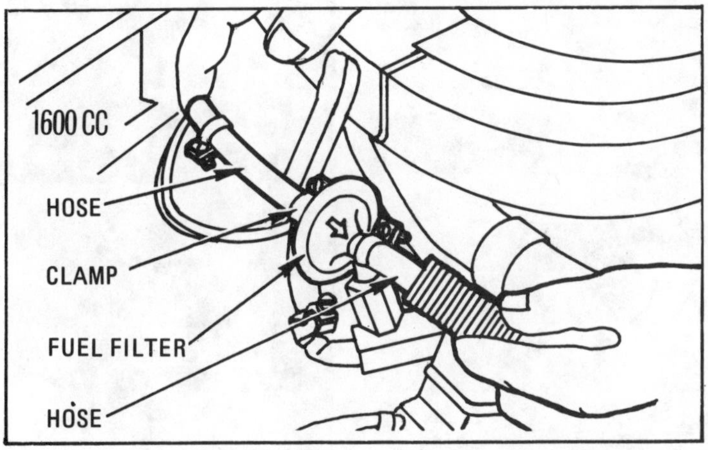

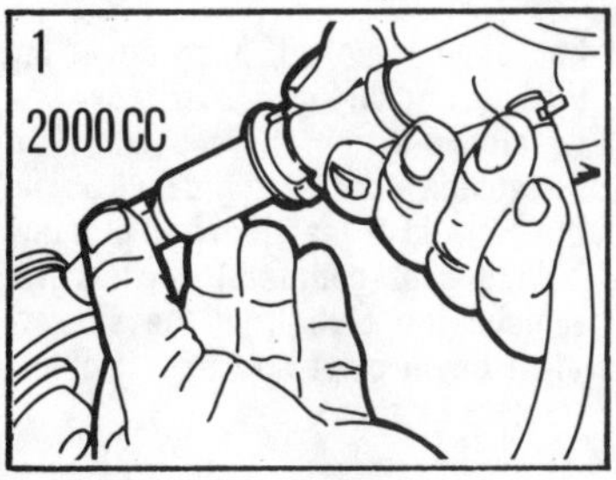

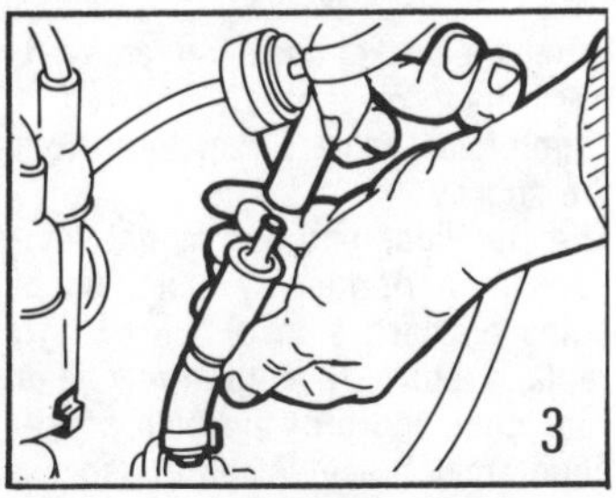

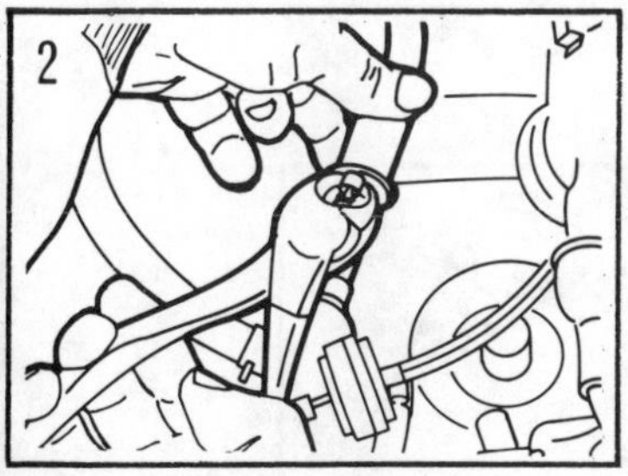

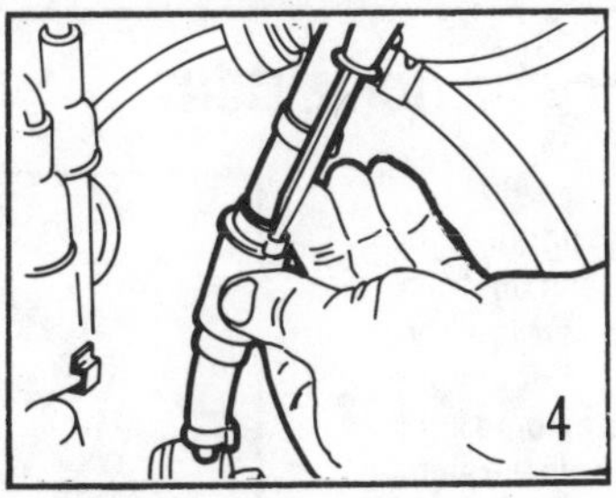

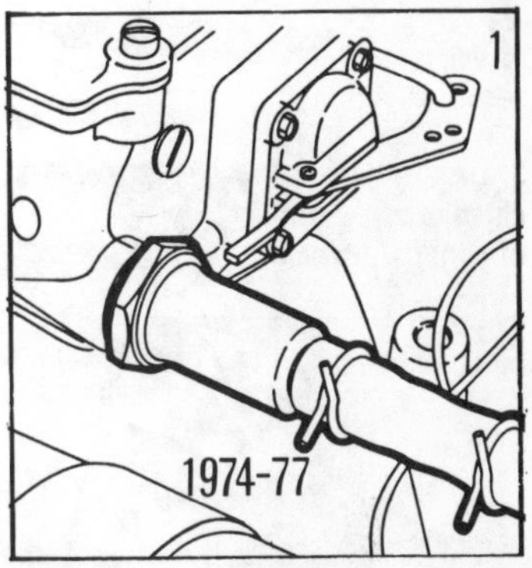

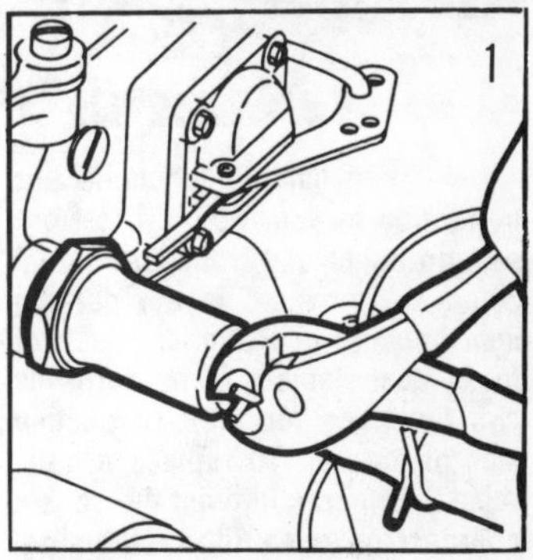

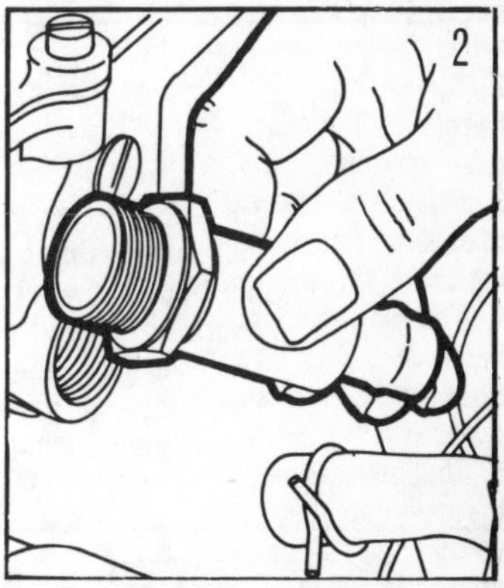

1600 CC ENGINES

On the 1600 cc engines, the fuel filter is in the fuel line located below the battery. Access to the filter can be made easier by removing the battery, however it is not necessary.

1. Locate the fuel filter in the fuel line and loosen the screws in the filter clamps.
2. Remove the fuel lines from the old filter and install the new filter in the lines. Make sure the arrow on the filter points toward the line to the carburetor.
3. Tighten the filter clamps and install the battery.

2000 CC ENGINES—1971-73

1. Locate the fuel filter in the fuel line from the fuel pump to the carburetor.
2. Squeeze the tabs on the fuel filter clamps together and move the clamps away from the filter.
3. Remove the old filter from the fuel line and install a new one.
4. Compress the tabs on the fuel filter clamps and position the clamps on the fuel lines near the filter.

1974-77 ALL ENGINES

1. Remove the air cleaner. Loosen the clamp securing the inlet hose to the fuel filter and unscrew the filter from the carburetor.
2. Install a new filter and connect the fuel inlet hose and clamp.
3. Tighten the filter and crimp the clamp securely. Start the engine and check for fuel leaks.

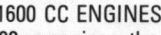

Safety Systems

REPLACING THE TURN SIGNAL, STOP AND BACK-UP LIGHT BULBS

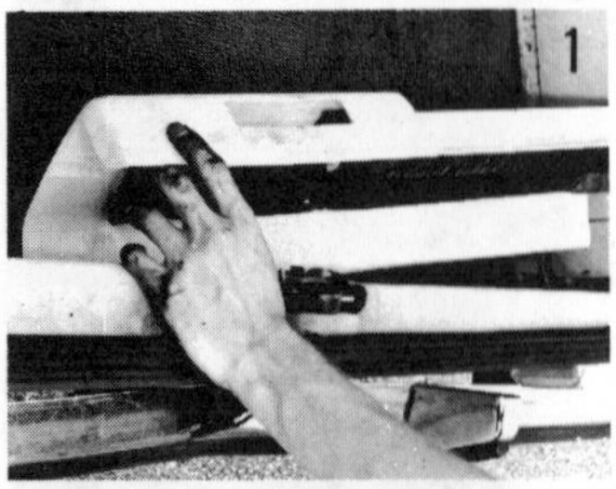

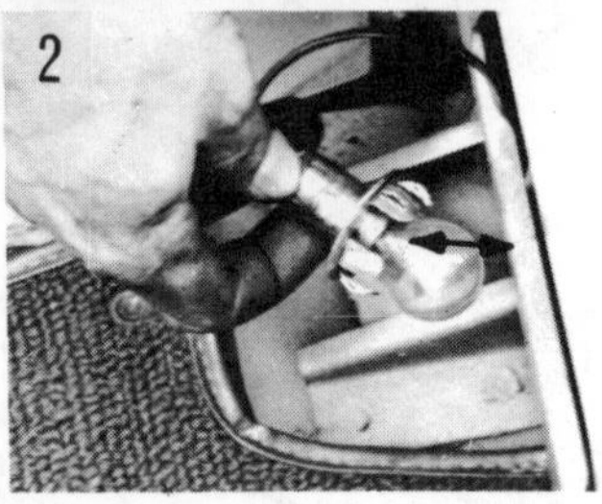

All of these lighting functions are performed by four bulbs. The front parking lights and front turn signal bulbs are mounted in the parking light housing in the grille. Each of these dual-element bulbs performs two functions for their respective side of the car. To replace a bulb, raise the hood and twist the socket counterclockwise in its housing.

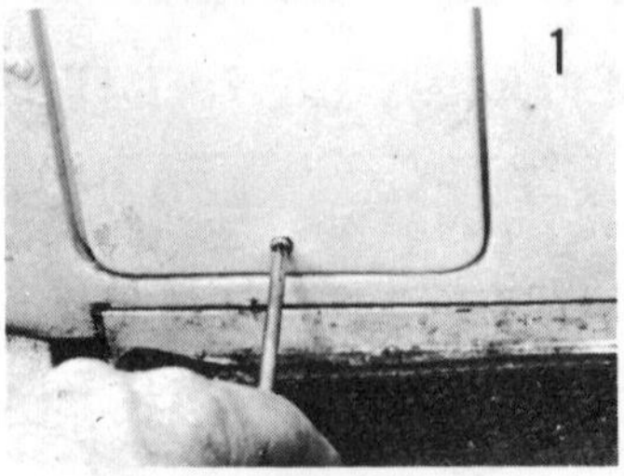

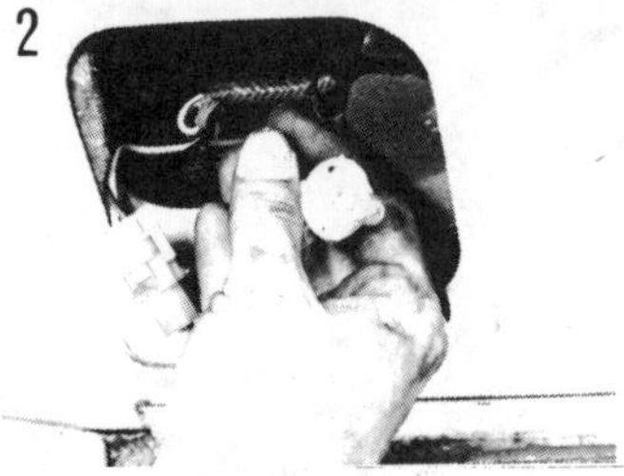

When the socket has been removed, push down on the bulb and turn it counterclockwise to remove it from the socket.
The stop light, and turn signal functions are performed by dual-element bulbs on each side of the car. To replace a bulb, raise the trunk lid or rear door and turn the bulb socket counterclockwise. When the socket

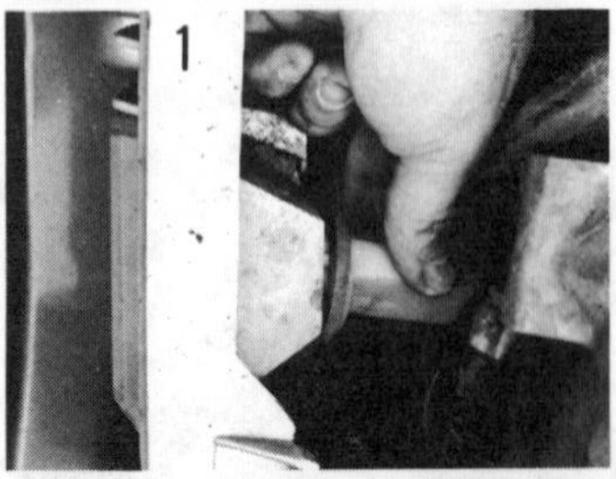

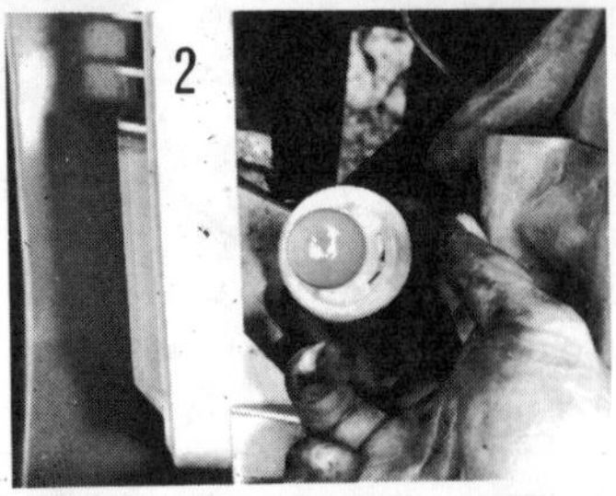

has been removed, push down on the bulb and turn it counterclockwise to remove it from the socket.
To replace a back-up light bulb, raise the trunk lid or rear door and turn the bulb socket counterclockwise. To remove the bulb from the socket, push down on it and turn it counterclockwise.

DOME LIGHT

To gain access to the dome light bulb, pry the dome light lens out from the housing. After making sure the doors are closed and the headlight switch is not turned to the dome light "on" position, pry the bulb straight out of the housing.

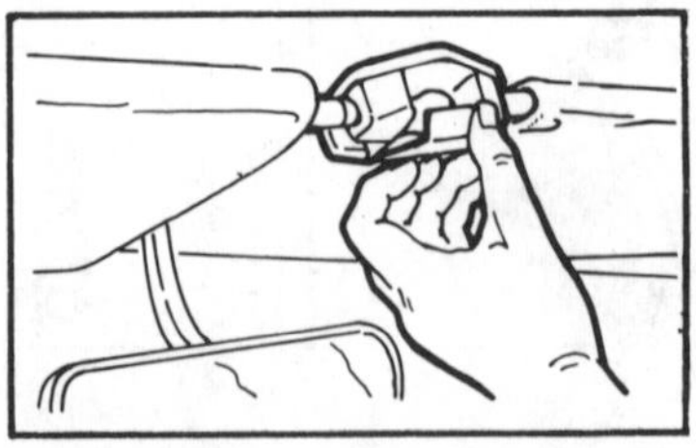

FRONT SIDE MARKER LIGHT

Reach up under fender and turn bulb socket counterclockwise to remove from housing. Pull bulb straight out. Do not turn bulb.

HEADLIGHT REPLACEMENT

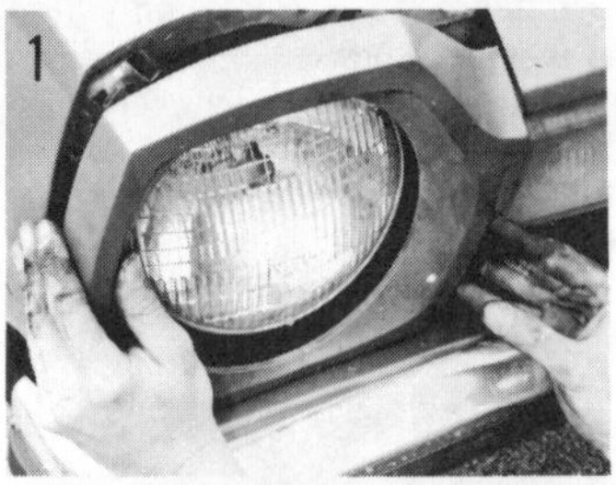

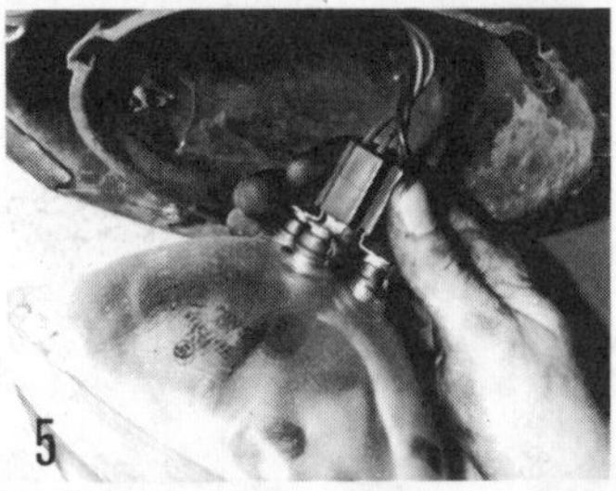

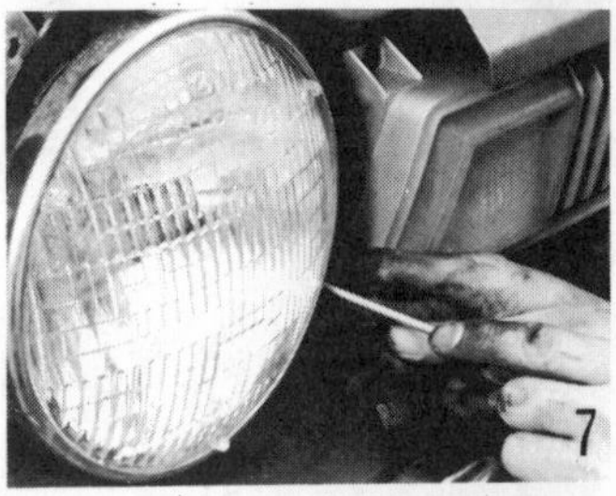

1. Remove both headlight cover retaining screws and cover.
2. Loosen, but do not remove, headlight retaining ring attaching screws. NOTE: Do not mistake headlight adjustment screws for the three retaining ring screws.
3. Rotate retaining ring to left until large openings in attaching screw slots are aligned with screw heads. Remove ring.
4. Pull lamp (sealed beam) out of headlight shell toward front of car; disconnect wiring connector from sealed beam unit.
5. Connect wire connector to new sealed beam unit.
6. Position new sealed beam unit in headlight shell. Be sure nobs on back of bulb (near outer edge) enter slots in shell.
7. Position retaining ring on retainer screws; turn ring to right. Tighten screws.
8. Position headlight cover; install attaching screws.

WINDSHIELD WIPER BLADE REPLACEMENT

To remove the wiper blades, lift up on the spring release tab on the wiper blade-to-wiper arm connector and pull the wiper blade off the wiper arm.

There are two types of replacement rubbers for the windshield wipers; one requires replacement of the entire wiper blade, but the other type allows replacement of only the rubber wiper blade insert.

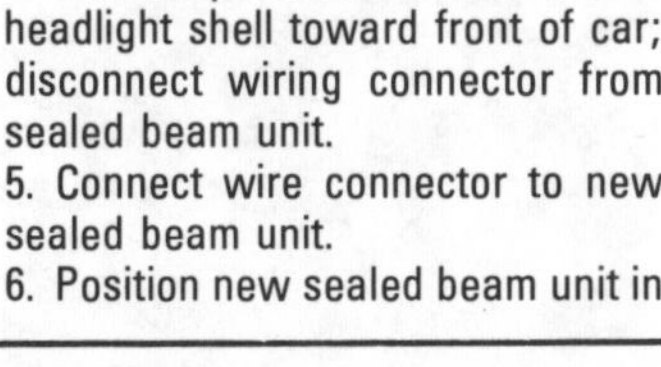

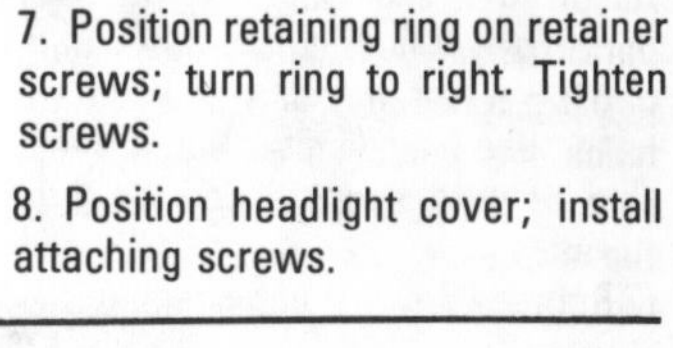

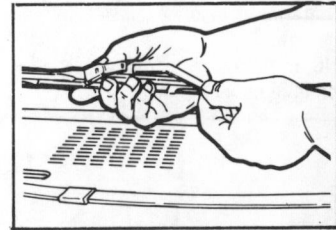

If you have bought an entire replacement blade, simply snap it back into place on the wiper arm. If you have bought a rubber insert only, press the old rubber insert down, away from the wiper blade, to free it from the retaining clips on the ends of the wiper blades. Slide the insert from the blade. Position the new insert in the wiper blade, then bend it upward slightly to engage the retaining clips.

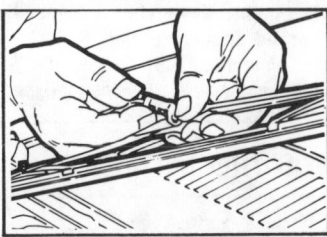

HORN PROBLEMS

If horn sounds and does not stop, this is due to short circuit in wiring. Disconnect wiring connector under hood and have professional service shop check horn wiring circuit.

STEERING PROBLEMS

See steering system check in Suspension Section. Check tire pressures. Have a professional service shop check all components in the front end and steering system.

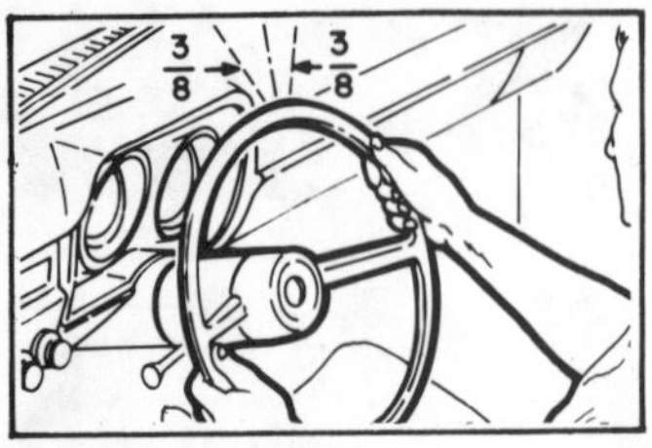

WHEEL CYLINDER CHECK

Drum brakes employ individual wheel cylinders to apply braking pressure to shoes. Check for brake fluid leaks on inside of wheel. Disc brakes employ calipers on individual wheels. Remove wheel and inspect caliper for signs of fluid leaks. Have mechanic correct leaks.

WASHER SYSTEM

If washer fails to squirt properly, raise hood and check system hose connections. Be sure washer fluid container has fluid. Check spout openings for clogging.

Keep container filled with fluid mixture of washer solvent and water. If road spray buildup on windshield is a chronic problem, add 1 tablespoon dishwasher detergent to solvent/water mixture when re-filling container.

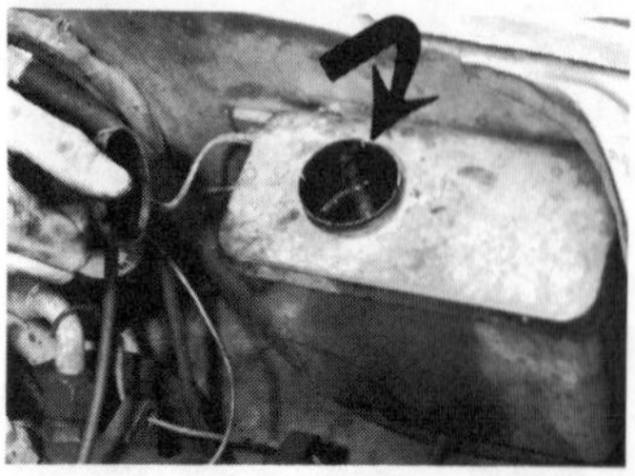

Electrical System

CHECKING THE BATTERY LEVEL

1. Remove plastic filler caps on top of battery. Fluid level should be up to the split ring in the filler opening. If fluid is low add clean, cold tap water. If your area has hard water, use only distilled water available at auto supply, food or drug stores.
2. Replace any lost caps immediately.

CAUTION: NEVER LIGHT A MATCH OR SMOKE near the top of a battery. Batteries give off explosive hydrogen gas.

NOTE: Battery that often checks low on fluid could mean:

A. Battery is getting old, due for replacement; have charge capacity checked at service shop.

B. Connections may be corroded or loose; clean/replace as needed (see below).

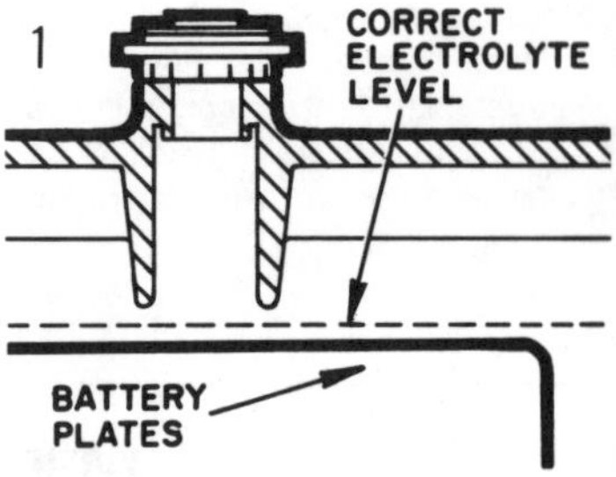

C. Alternator or voltage regulator not functioning properly; this happens far less often than A or B above.

CLEANING THE BATTERY TERMINALS

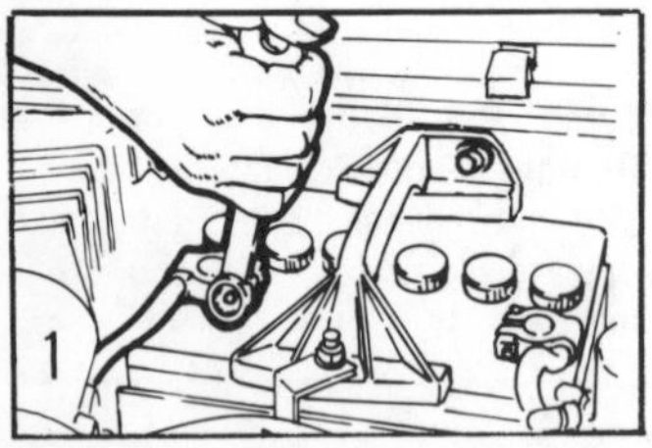

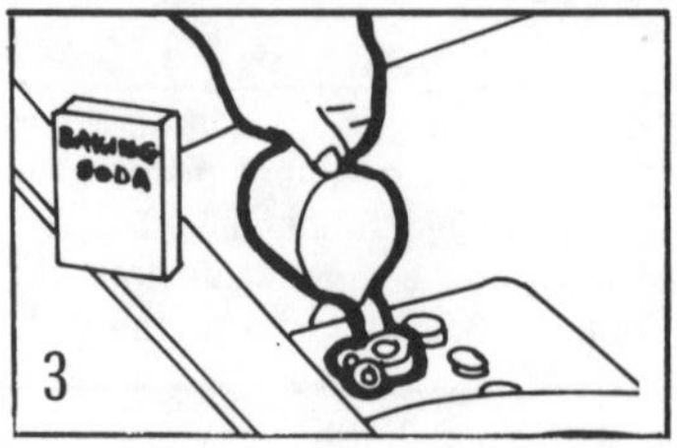

As time goes by, battery terminals build up a dry powdery, whitish material. This material is corrosive and will gradually eat thru battery cables if not cleaned off periodically.

1. Loosen and remove battery connections.
2. Brush off all loose corrosion; use stiff bristle brush. Do not get this material into eyes or on open cuts. Wash off at once.
3. If corrosion build-up is extremely heavy and brushing does not remove all of it, mix 2 tablespoons baking soda to 1 cup water. Pour solution directly onto terminals and connectors. Allow to soak a few minutes and rinse off. Continue brushing to remove all traces of corrosion build-up. Do not allow cleaning solution to enter battery.
4. Replace connectors on battery terminal posts and tighten.
5. Liberally smear battery terminal posts and cable connectors with petroleum jelly.

REPLACING THE BATTERY CABLES

If battery cable strands become frayed, broken or corroded, replace cable immediately. Delay in correcting this condition could lead to sudden failure to start the engine. It can also weaken your battery.

1. Disconnect and remove the battery negative cable; then disconnect and remove the positive cable.
2. Loosen and remove battery connections. Clean OFF any corrosion.
3. Disconnect negative cable from its attachment to engine or chassis. Disconnect positive cable from its attachment to starter relay.
4. Attach new cables making sure positive and negative cables are on proper terminals. They are not identical.
5. Replace connectors on battery terminal posts and tighten.
6. Liberally smear battery terminal posts and cable connectors with petroleum jelly.

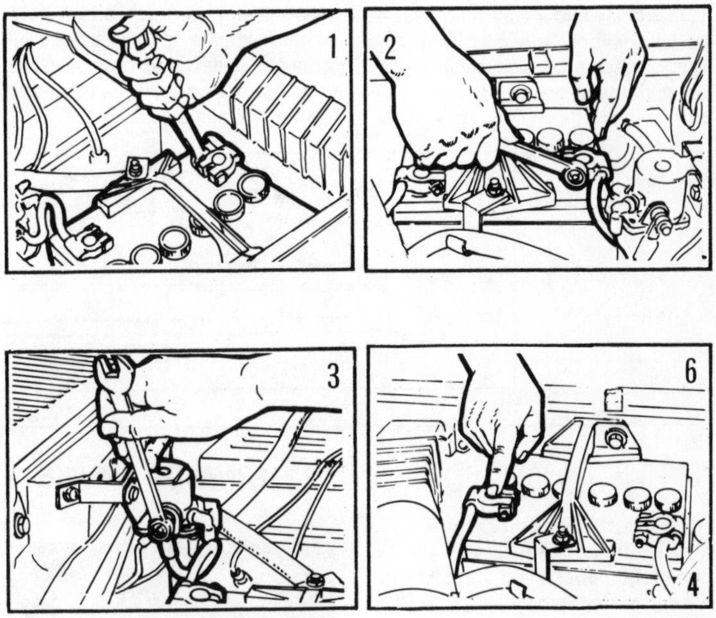

BATTERY HOLDDOWN

The clamp device which holds battery in place should be checked periodically. If loose, tighten. Clean off corrosion buildup. Severely corroded holddown components should be replaced before they break.

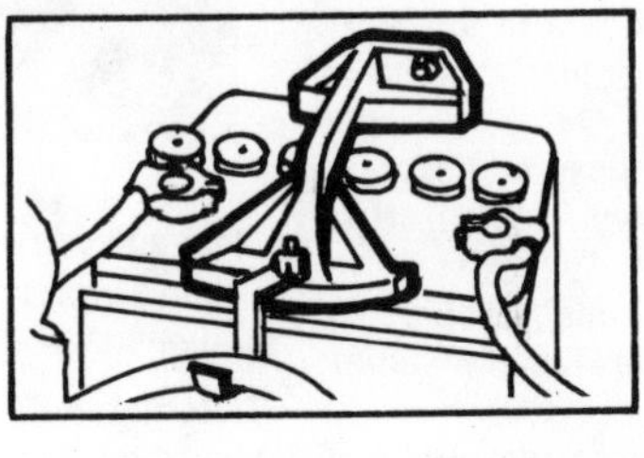

FUSE BOX LOCATION

The fuse box on your Pinto or Bobcat is located to the right of the steering column, below the instrument cluster.

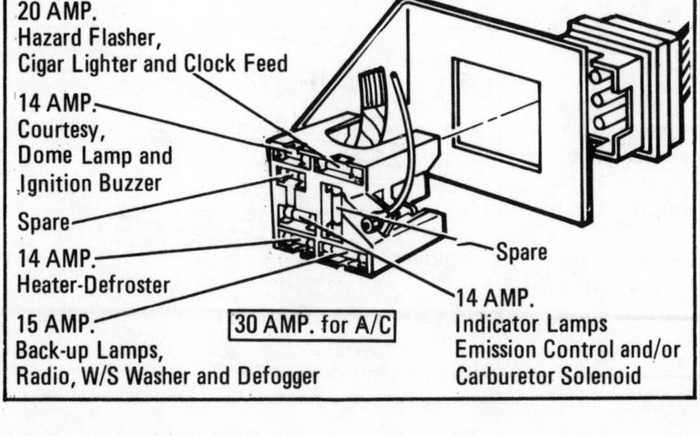

TURN SIGNAL AND 4-WAY FLASHER

Turn signals and 4-way emergency flashers will operate only if: A. All light bulbs are OK. B. Flasher units are not burned out. Pintos and Bobcats have two flasher units that work independently of each other. Turn signal flasher is located behind instrument panel directly over glove box door opening. Emergency flasher is in same position slightly to left. To remove either flasher grasp with fingers, twist and pull flasher toward front of car. Pull connector from flasher. REPLACE ONLY WITH SAME TYPE FLASHER.

ALTERNATOR CHECKS

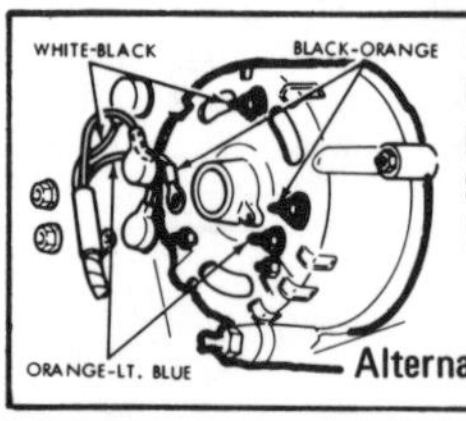

Only A Professional Mechanic Should Check

Alternator Wiring

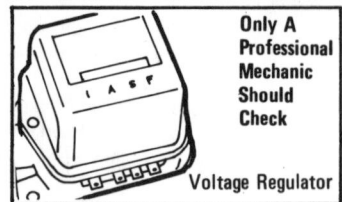

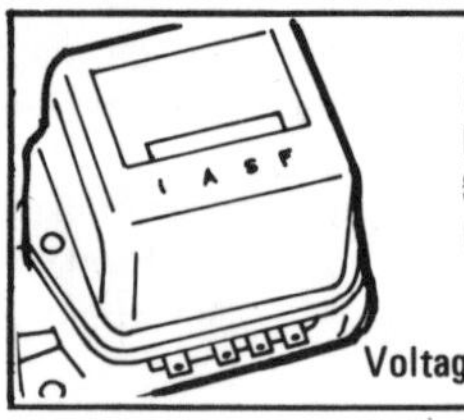

Only A Professional Mechanic Should Check

Voltage Regulator

Red alternator warning light on instrument panel should glow red when you first turn ignition key. This proves bulb is OK. Alt. warning light should go off when engine is running at normal operating speed.

If Alt. warning light glows red at operating speed, alternator isn't charging battery properly. Common causes are:

A. Fan belts are loose and slipping on alternator pulley. Tighten or replace belts.

B. Battery terminals, cables are loose or corroded. Clean; tighten; replace bad cables.

If A or B do not correct problem, alternator or voltage regulator may be faulty. This happens far less often, and can only be checked by mechanic with proper electrical testing equipment.

Alternator Caution: Alternator can be permanently damaged by short-circuiting terminal connections. When working around or moving alternator, always keep metal tools or engine parts from terminals.

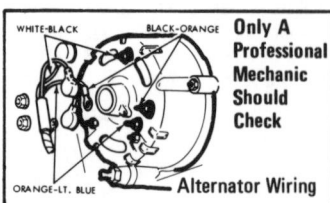

REAR WINDOW DEFOGGER

Do not clean inside of the rear window fitted with defogger system with any abrasive material. This could destroy carbon-copper wires; use only soft rag and mild detergent/water mixture. Dry carefully.

When you clean the inside of the rear window, always clean with a side to side motion. An up and down motion might tear the defroster wires which would make the defroster stop operating.

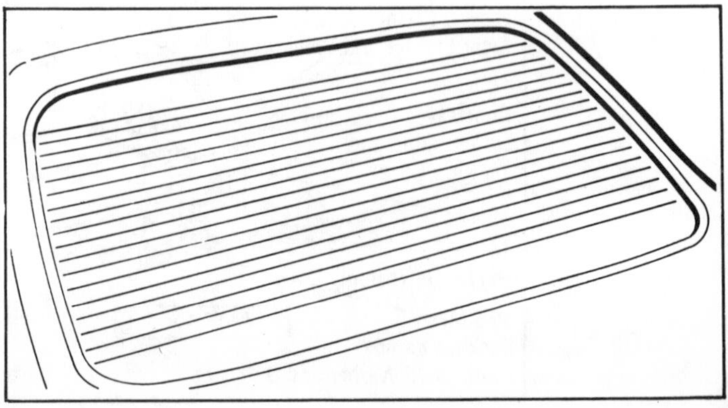

Air Conditioning Systems

CHECKPOINTS AND SERVICES

WARNING!—Never attempt to tighten fittings, disassemble or do any work on your Pinto or Bobcats A/C system. Consult a professional mechanic about A/C system problems and their correction. Your auto air conditioner (A/C) is a delicate, closed system. If air, dirt or water get into it, or if refrigerant escapes, the A/C unit will not cool a car interior. Among things you can do are:

1. Keep condenser grill clean. Check for dirt and debris; periodically remove dead insects, leaves, etc., with stiff bristle brush. Straighten any bent fins—carefully.
2. Keep radiator filled to correct level. (See Cooling System section). If fluid needs to be added, add antifreeze rather than water.
3. Keep radiator coolant at a 50/50 water/antifreeze mixture.
4. Flush cooling system and replace with fresh coolant mixture at least every 24 months. (See Cooling System section).
5. Radiator cap should be tight and sealed properly. If sealing gasket is cracked, cut or worn, replace cap with new 12-15 lb. unit.
6. Check fan belt tension periodically. (See Cooling System section).

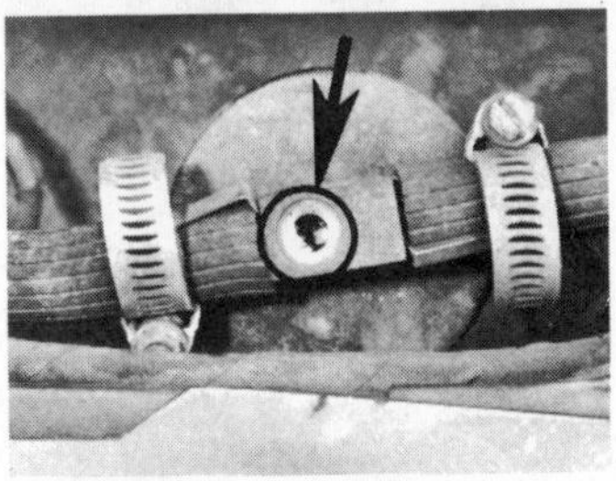

Replace glazed, frayed or cut fan belts, before they fail entirely.

7. Check periodically for bubbles in A/C sight glass. The sight glass was last used in 1973. Sight glass is located in head of receiver/drier vessel. Or in metal tubing leading from top of receiver/drier. Sight glass is no larger than head of large nail. It may be dirty. Wipe clean for best visibility.

PROCEED AS FOLLOWS:

a) With engine and A/C system running, look for passage of refrigerant in sight glass. You'll be looking for a stream of milky white bubbles as they pass through sight glass. It is best to watch sight glass and have someone else start the car and turn on the A/C system. Allow to run for a few minutes.

b) If you observe no bubbles, and air flow from A/C unit in the car is passing cold air, everything is OK.

c) If no bubbles appear in sight glass, and air flow from the A/C unit in the car is not delivering cold air, the system may be low on refrigerant and could need a re-charge.

d) If bubbles appear, system is low on refrigerant.

e) If you suspect refrigerant loss based on tests performed above, have system checked by a professional A/C service shop. They can confirm refrigerant loss, recharge the system and check for system leakage.

Since there is no sight glass on 1974 and later models, if you suspect the air conditioning is not working, first see if the belt is slipping, or if any of the compressor electrical connections have come off. You should also check the fuse box for a blown fuse. If everything checks out, take the car to a qualified air conditioning service facility for a thorough inspection.

NOTE: Once a week or so, even in winter, run A/C system for about 5 minutes as you drive. This keeps system internally lubricated, prevents hoses hardening.

CAPACITIES

YEAR	ENGINE No. Cyl. Displacement (cu. in.)	ENGINE OIL Add 1 qt. with New Filter	TRANSMISSION Pts. to Refill after Draining MANUAL 3-speed	MANUAL 4-speed	AUTOMATIC	DRIVE AXLE (pts.)	COOLING SYSTEM with Heater (qts.)	COOLING SYSTEM with Air Cond. (qts.)
1971-72	4-97.6 (1600 cc)	3	—	2.5	—	2.2	7¾	—
	4-122 (2000 cc)	4	—	2.5	16	2.2	8½	—
1973	4-97.6 (1600 cc)	3	—	2.8	—	2.2	7⅘	—
	4-122 (2000 cc)	4	—	2.8	16	2.2	8½	8½
1974	4-122 (2000 cc)	4	—	2.8	16	3.0	8½	8½
	4-140 (2300 cc)	4	—	2.8	16	3.0	8⅘	9⅓
1975-76	4-140 (2300 cc)	4	—	2.8	16①	2.2②	8.7	9.0
	6-170.8(2800 cc)	4.5③	—	2.8	16①	2.2②	12½	13.2
1977	4-140 (2300 cc)	4	—	2.8	16①	2.2②	8.7	9.0
	6-170.8(2800 cc)	4.5③	—	2.8	16①	2.2②	12½	13.2

① 14 with optional C4 transmission.
② 4-4½ when equipped with optional 8 in. axle.
③ Add only ½ qt. for new filter.

TUNE-UP SPECIFICATIONS

YEAR	ENGINE No. Cyl. Displacement (cu. in.)	SPARK PLUGS Type	SPARK PLUGS Gap (in.)	DISTRIBUTOR Point Dwell (deg.)	DISTRIBUTOR Point Gap (in.)	IGNITION TIMING Man. Trans.● (deg.)■	IGNITION TIMING Auto Trans. (deg.)■	IDLE SPEED Man. Trans.● (rpm)▲	IDLE SPEED Auto Trans. (rpm)▲
1971	4-97.6 (1600 cc)	AGR-22	.030	40	.025	12B	—	800/500①	—
	4-122 (2000 cc)	BRF-42	.034	40	.025	6B	12B	750/500①	650/500①
1972	4-97.6 (1600 cc)	AGR-22	.030	40	.025	12B	—	800/500①	—
	4-122 (2000 cc)	BRF-42	.034	40	.025	6B	12B	750/500①	650/500①
1973	4-97.6 (1600 cc)	AGR-32	.034	40	.025	12B	—	800/500①	—
	4-122 (2000 cc)	BRF-42	.034	40	.025	6B-10B	6B-10B	750/500①	650/500①
1974	4-122 (2000 cc)	BRF-42	.034	39	.025	6B (3B @ 650)	6B (3B @ 650)	750	650
	4-140 (2300 cc)	AGRF-52	.034	39	.025	6B	6B	750	650
1975	4-140 (2300 cc)	AGRF-52	.034	Electronic		6B	6B (10B)	550	550
	6-170.8(2800 cc)	AGR-42	.034	Electronic		6B	10B (8B)	850	700
1976	4-140 (2300 cc)	AGRF-52	.034	Electronic		6B @ 550	20B @ 550	850	750
	6-170.8(2800 cc)	AGR-42	.034	Electronic		10B @ 700 (8B @ 650)	12B @ 700 (8B @ 700)	850	700
1977	4-140 (2300 cc) 6-170.8(2800 cc)	See Underhood Specifications Sticker							

▲ Adjust automatic transmissions in Drive (AMC/Ford/GM) or Neutral (Chrysler), all manual transmissions are adjusted in Neutral.
■ All figures are Before Top Dead Center.
● Figure in parentheses indicate California engine.
① First figure is for idle speed with solenoid energized and automatic transmission in Drive, while the second figure is for idle speed with solenoid disconnected and automatic transmission in Neutral. Cars without a solenoid use lower figure.

NOTE: The underhood specifications sticker often reflects tune-up specification changes made in production. Sticker figures must be used if they disagree with those in this chart.

Regal/Skylark/Century

Lubrication and Oil Change

LUBRICATION CHECK

GM SAYS . . . Change oil every 6000 miles; change filter every 12,000 miles. Recommended grade: SE. Check oil level at least once a week.

TOOLS & MATERIALS . . . adjustable wrench; medium size screwdriver; oil filter removal wrench; drain pan for old oil (at least 5 qt. capacity); oil pouring spout; 4 qt. oil (5 qt. if changing filter; new oil filter; oil and lubricants as specified below.

SAFETY TIP . . . use work gloves.

BRAKE FLUID LEVEL CHECK

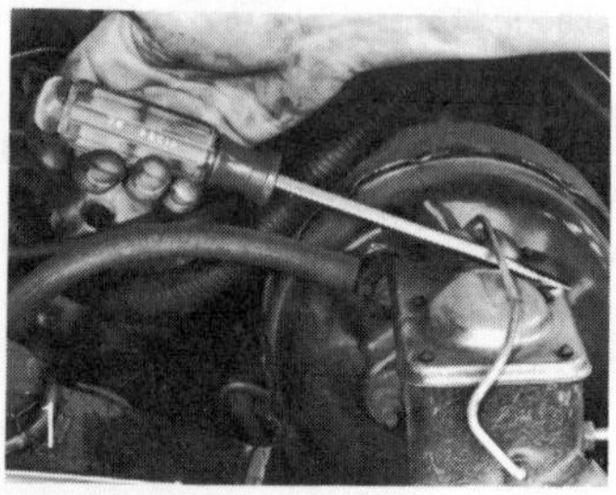

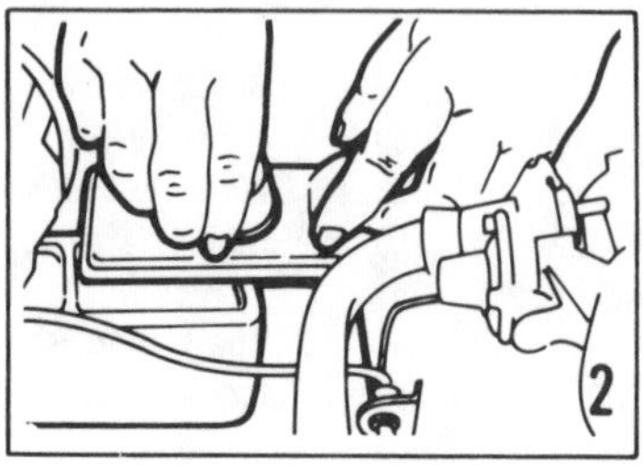

Check brake fluid level in master cylinder every three months . . . sooner if braking feels inadequate. Add when low.

Recommended grade: DOT 3

1. Pry wire retaining clip off cap top with screwdriver.
2. Remove cap and gasket by lifting up.
3. Fluid level should be within ¼ inch of top rim. If lower than this, add fresh fluid to appropriate level.

DO NOT OVERFILL

4. Replace cap and gasket; secure retaining clip over cap. If fluid level was low, check again in a few days.
5. If fluid repeatedly checks low, there is a leak somewhere in the system.

MANUAL TRANSMISSION FLUID LEVEL CHECK

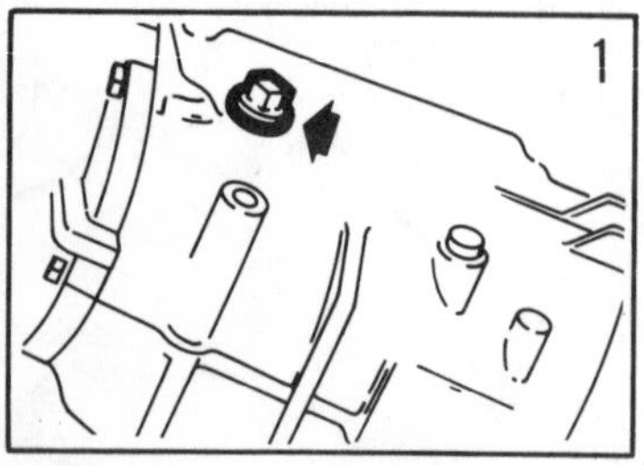

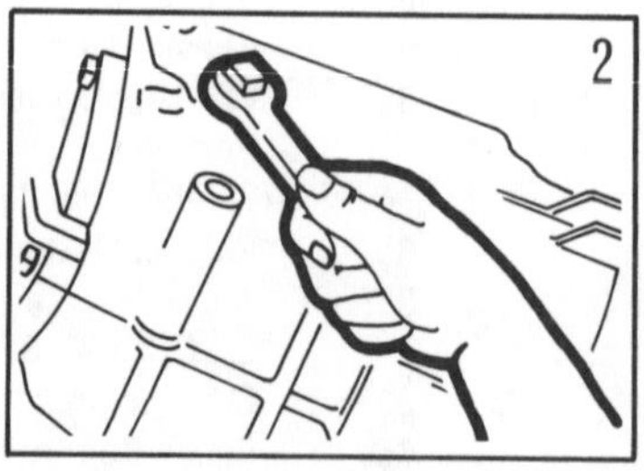

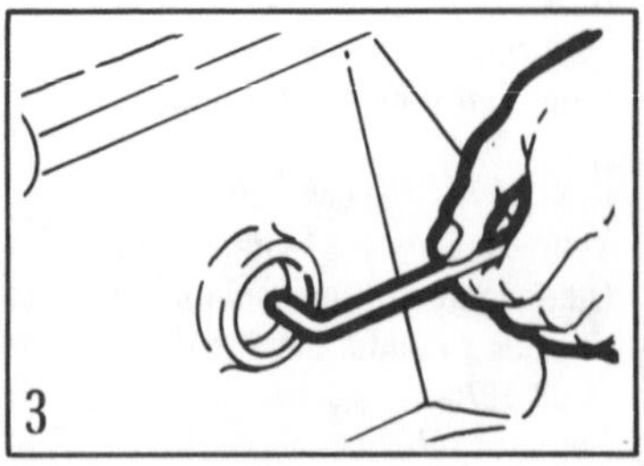

GM SAYS . . . Check the manual transmission lubricant level every 6 months or 7,500 miles. Recommended grade; SAE 80W-90 GL-5 gear lube.

TOOLS . . . adjustable hand wrench; fluid level check device (made from coat hanger wire; bend at 90° angle 2″ from end.); bulb syringe.

1. Locate transmission fluid filler plug on right side of transmission housing from underneath car.
2. Wipe road dirt from filler plug area before loosening. Remove plug with adjustable wrench.
3. Insert fluid level check device. Fluid level should be right up to bottom edge of filler hole.
4. Add fluid as needed with hand bulb syringe.
5. Replace filler plug; tighten.

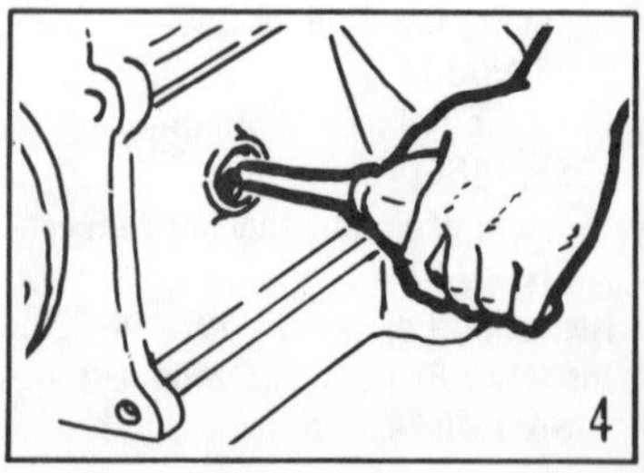

AUTOMATIC TRANSMISSION FLUID LEVEL CHECK

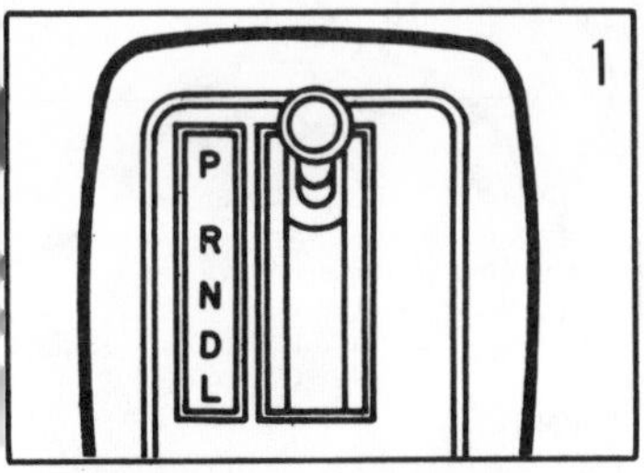

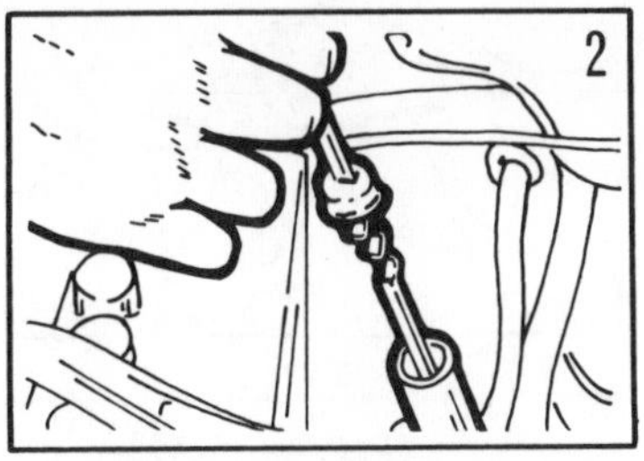

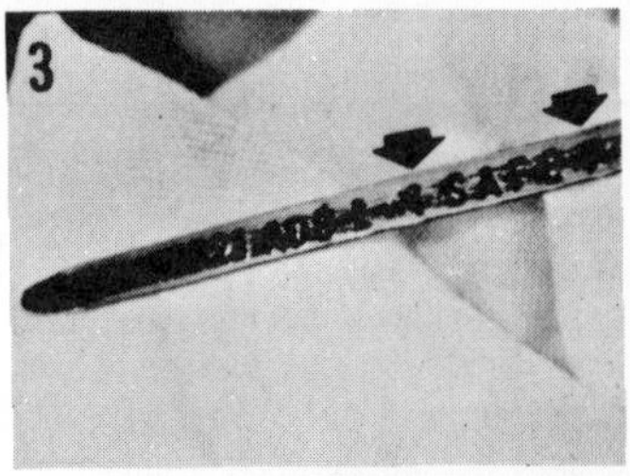

GM SAYS . . . check automatic transmission fluid (ATF) level every 6000 miles. Recommended grade: DEXRON® or Type A
TOOLS . . . Long neck filler funnel

1. Engine must be warmed up and running. Place shift lever in PARK position.

2. Pull out dipstick. Wipe clean. Push dipstick all the way back in; remove it again.

3. If fluid is below ADD mark, add ATF to bring level up. DO NOT OVERFILL.

4. Add ATF thru transmission dipstick hole by means of long-neck filler funnel.

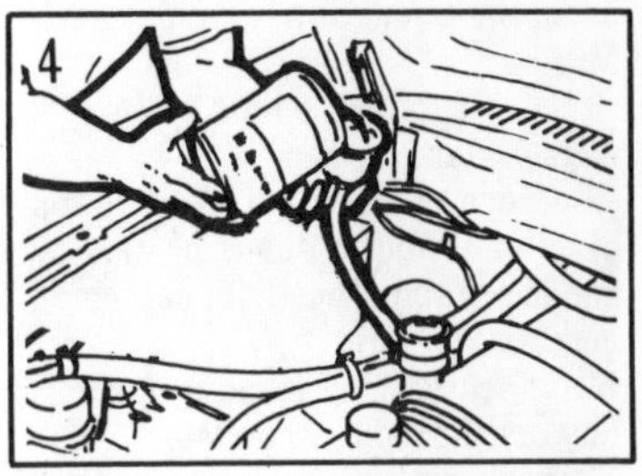

REAR AXLE LUBRICANT

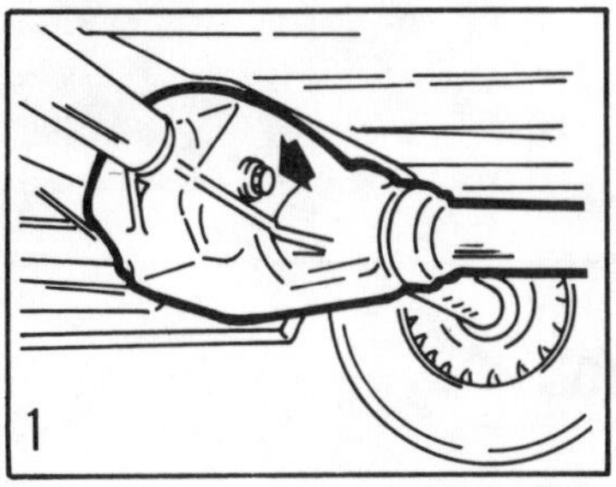

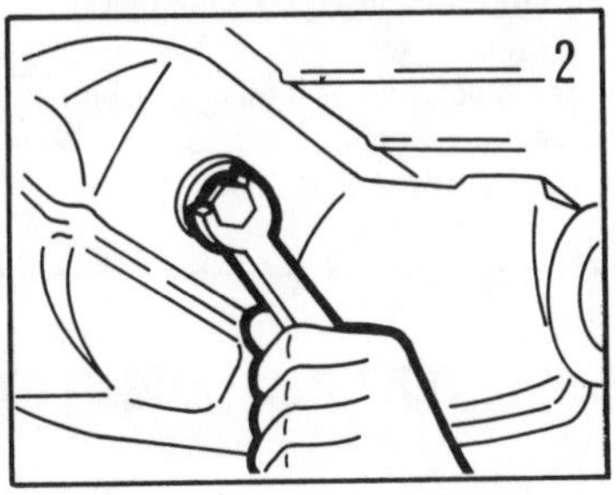

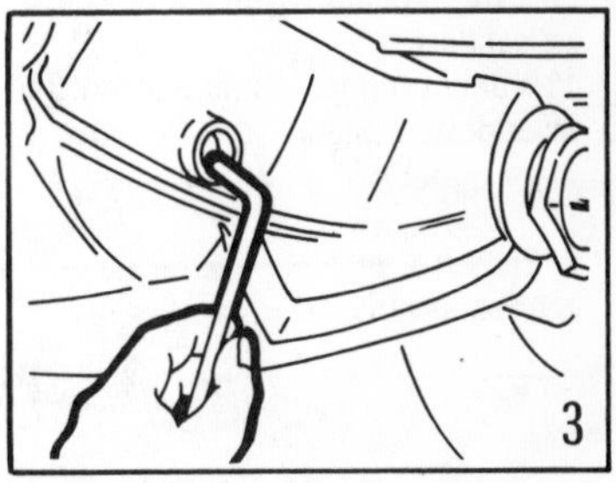

GM SAYS . . . check rear axle lube level every 6000 miles. Recommended grade: Hypoid gear lube (SAE 90). Positraction axles require special positraction lubricant.

TOOLS . . . adjustable hand wrench; fluid level check device (made from coat hanger wire; bend at 90° angle 2″ from end.); bulb syringe.

1. Locate filler plug on forward side of rear axle housing.

2. Wipe plug area clean; remove plug with wrench.
3. Insert wire level check device; remove. Adequate fluid level should show lubricant on last ¼-inch of wire.
4. If fluid level is low, add as needed, with a hand bulb syringe, until level shows on last ¼-inch of wire.
5. Replace filler plug; tighten.
If speedometer pointer tends to quiver or jump, or if unit makes a low, rasping sound, lubrication may be needed.

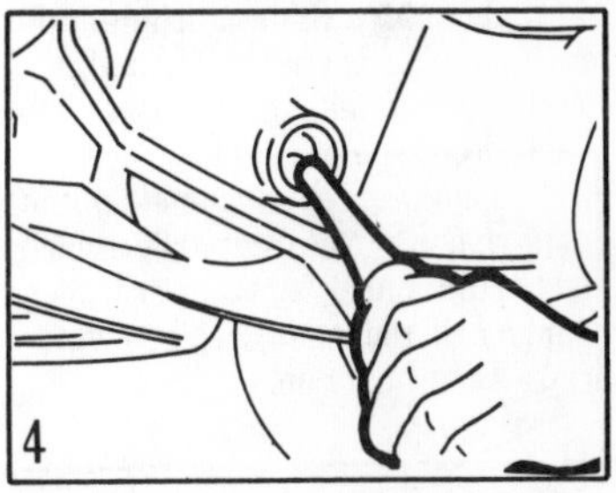

OIL AND FILTER CHANGE

1. If engine is cold, start up and idle for about 5 minutes.
2. Park car on level ground. Turn engine off.
3. Locate oil drain plug on underside of engine. Place drain pan under plug.
4. Remove drain plug with wrench. Let ALL dirty oil drain out.

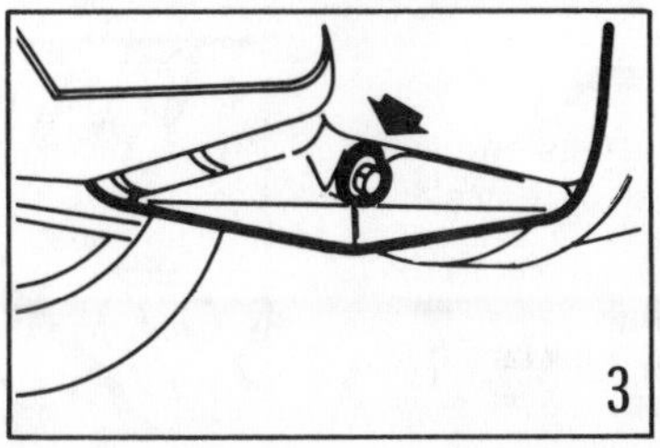

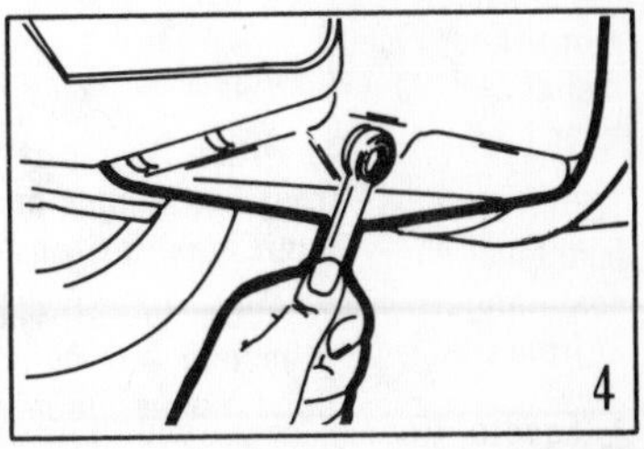

5. Wipe plug and area around drain hole clean. Replace drain plug; tighten it.
6. Locate oil filter. Move drain pan under filter. Loosen filter with oil filter wrench. Unscrew; remove filter by hand.
7. Smear fresh oil over surface of rubber gasket (washer) of new filter. Install new filter by hand only. Do NOT use wrench. Turn filter until gasket makes contact. Tighten an additional half turn only . . . NO MORE.
8. Locate oil filler tube on top of engine. Remove cap.
9. Punch oil pouring spout into top of oil can. Pour all cans of new oil into filler tube. Wipe filler cap clean and replace it.
10. Check new oil level at dipstick. Pull out dipstick, wipe clean.
11. Push dipstick back into engine. Be sure to insert all the way. Remove dipstick and check new oil level. It should be above "FULL" line. If not, be sure to check if you put in all the oil called for.
12. Start up engine and idle for 3-5 minutes. Oil signal light on instrument panel will glow red when engine is first started. Light should go out in 30 seconds or less.
13. Stop engine and check for oil leaks at drain plug and filter. If you find any, check tightness of plug and/or filter, also for condition of filter gasket to see that it has not become pinched or damaged when installing. Recheck oil level, which should now be at "FULL".

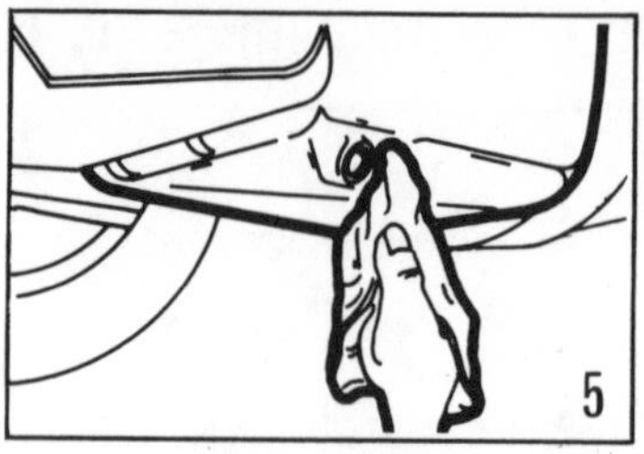
5

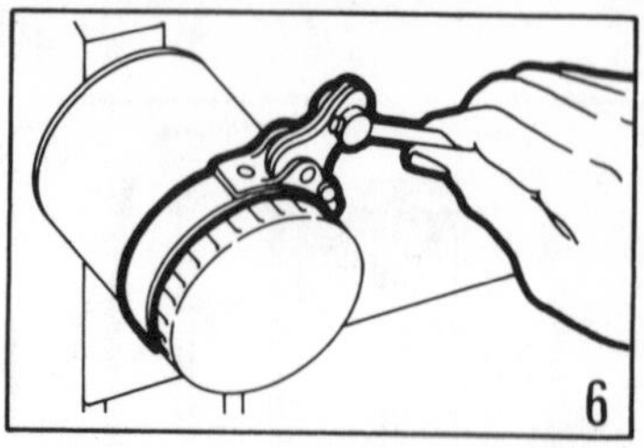
6

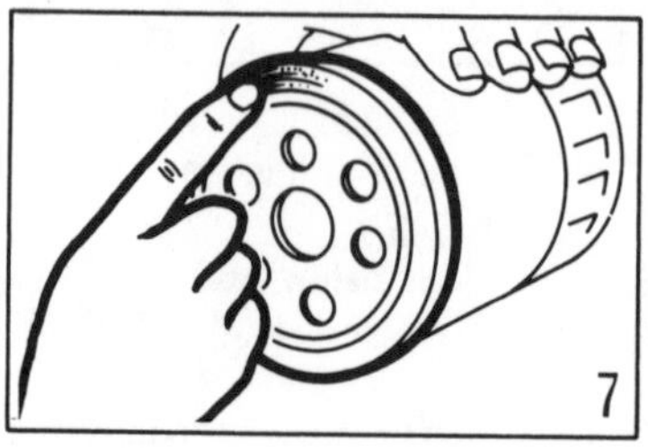
7

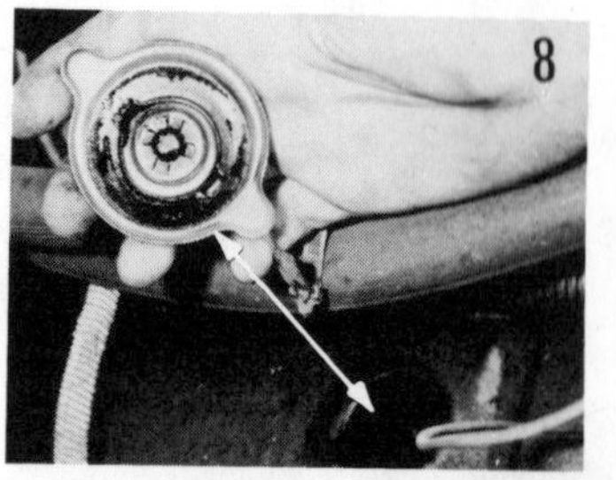
8

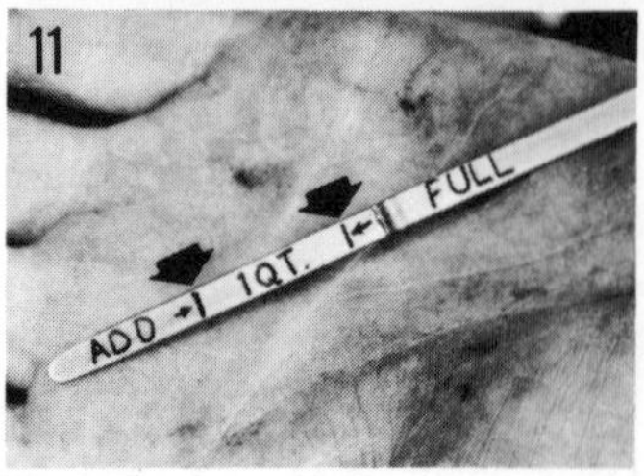

11

SPEEDOMETER CABLE LUBRICATION

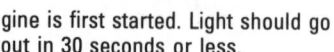

1. Locate cable shaft attachment directly behind speedometer dial.
2. Remove retaining clip. Unscrew cable from speedometer.
3. Pull inner cable completely out of outer casing. Note carefully which end is top. Check for wear or frayed strands. If damaged, replace inner cable with new one.
4. Apply generous amount of speedometer cable lubricant into cable casing. Replace inner cable in shaft, noting that top end is not inserted accidentally. Turn inner cable as it is being re-inserted. Twist cable when all the way in, to lock into position at lower end.
5. Reconnect cable to speedometer head under instrument panel.

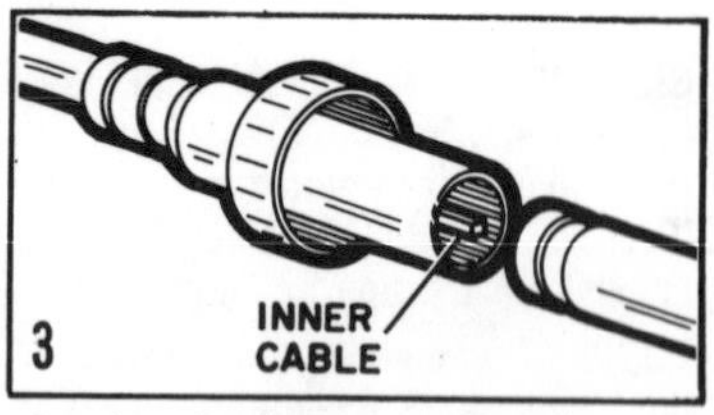

3

DOOR HINGES AND STOPS

(lubricate every 6 months)

1. Brush any dirt accumulations from door hinges and stops. Use old tooth brush or rag.

2. Apply dab of white polyethylene grease to door hinges, trunk hinges, hood hinges, door stops.

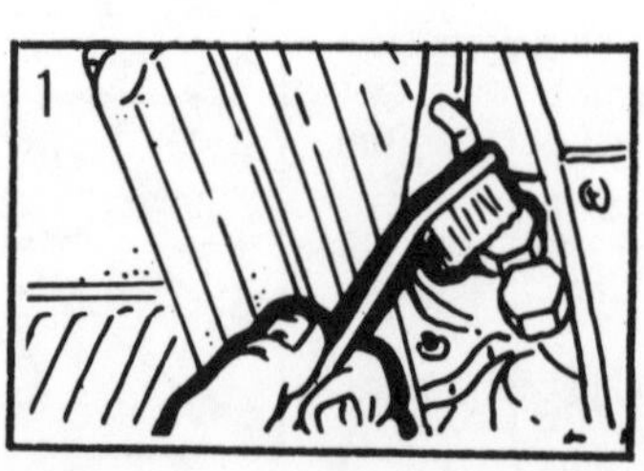
1

DOQR LOCKS

(lubricate every 6 months)
1. Insert door key half way into lock.
2. Spray aerosol lock lubricant into lock.
3. Push key rest of way into lock; turn back and forth several times.

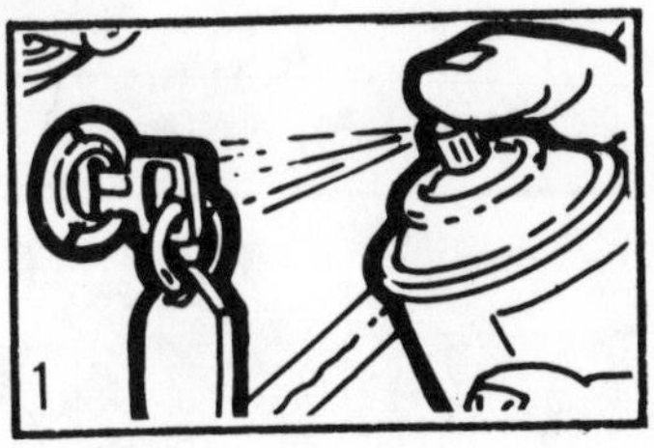

Cooling System

IT IS RECOMMENDED . . . that radiator coolant (water/antifreeze mixture) level be checked once or twice a month. Do this when engine is cold. Check more often if you do a lot of hard driving. Coolant is checked visually on models with expansion tanks.
Keep coolant up to recommended level in radiator. If coolant checks frequently low, look for leaks.

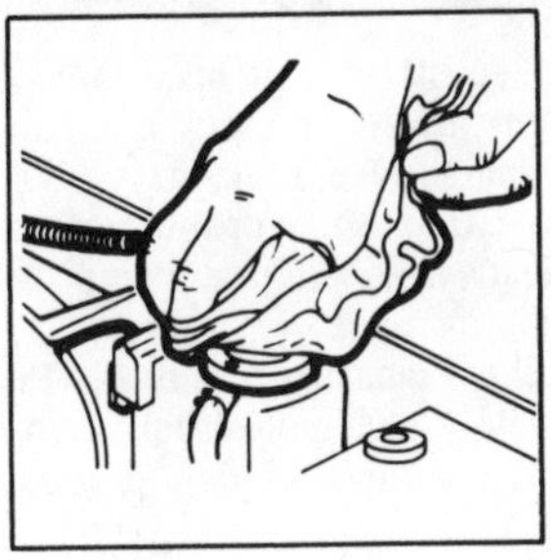

Tighten all hose clamps occasionally. For best results, keep a 50/50 water/antifreeze mixture year round. Change complete coolant mixture every 24 months.

CAUTION: If you must check coolant in a hot engine, cover radiator cap with thick rag before releasing. Remove cap slowly . . . press down and turn.

REPLACING THE THERMOSTAT

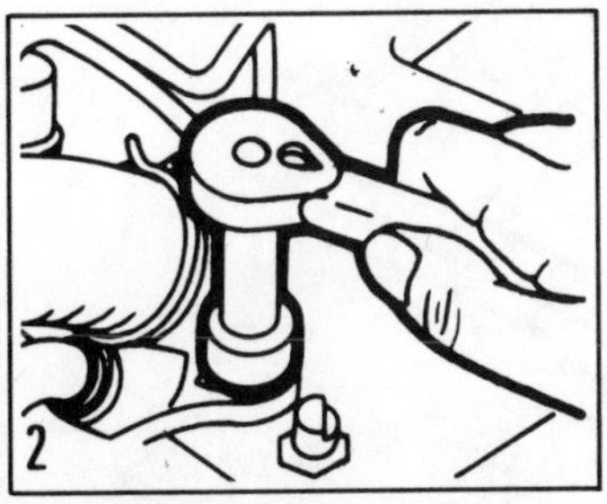

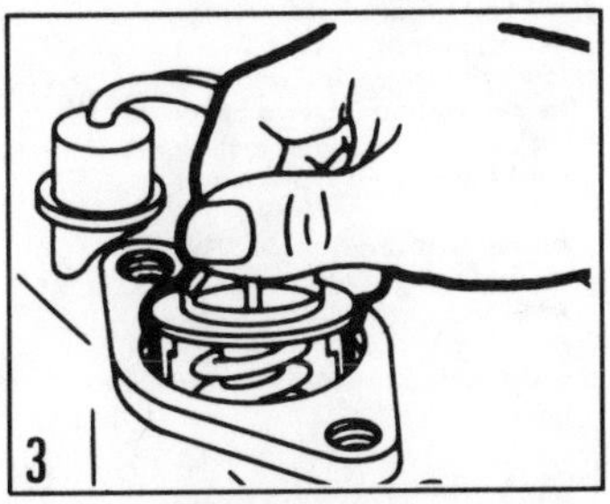

A faulty thermostat will usually cause engine overheating. The thermostat is located inside the housing where the top radiator hose connects to the engine.
TOOLS AND MATERIALS . . .
New thermostat
Gasket
Adjustable wrench

1. Drain radiator of about half its coolant. (See How To Replace Hoses)
2. Loosen and remove both retaining bolts and lift thermostat housing off the engine.
NOTE: If you're careful it won't be necessary to remove radiator hose.
3. Remove old thermostat.

4. Scrape thermostat housing flange and engine block surface to remove old gasket debris.
5. Drop new thermostat into place—spring down.
6. Install new gasket with sealer applied to both sides.
7. Replace thermostat housing and tighten both retaining bolts.

TOUBLESHOOT ENGINE OVERHEATING

YOUR CAR OVERHEATS BECAUSE
radiator coolant is too low
fan belt is too loose
of a broken or leaking hose
thermostat does not function
radiator is plugged with sediment

water pump does not function properly

TO CORRECT IT

fill to correct level; check for leaks

adjust tension or replace frayed belt

replace hose; tighten clamps

replace thermostat

consult professional mechanic (may need radiator removal and servicing, or total replacement)

replace water pump (may make squeaky noise; or leak at pump shaft)

FAN BELT ADJUSTMENT

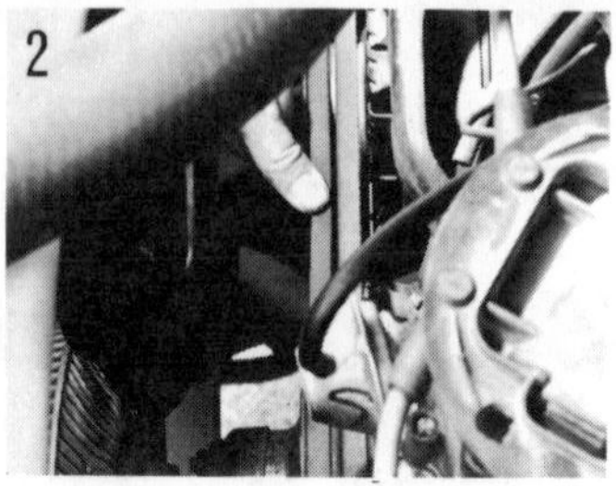

The fan belt not only drives the radiator fan, it turns the water pump and drives the alternator. It's easy to see that the condition and proper tension of the belt are vital, since almost all engine cooling and electrical power is dependent on it. The belt deserves an occasional look and tension check.

1. Inspect fan belt occasionally. If worn, frayed or cracked on inner driving surface, replace.
CAUTION: an overtightened belt may damage alternator and water pump bearings.
2. Check tension occasionally. Press thumb at midpoint of belt span between pulleys. If belt depresses more than ½ inch, tightening is needed. A too-loose belt will not drive alternator and water pump effectively.
3. To adjust loosen alternator mounting bolts, pivot the alternator over until the belt is properly tensioned (¼ in. deflection) and then tighten bolts.

FIND THOSE COOLING SYSTEM LEAKS

1. Inspect all hoses. If any are weak, soft in spots or show cracks, replace at once.
2. Check all hose connections for tightness. Tighten loose hose clamps; they tend to loosen due to engine vibration.
3. If radiator steams or hisses when engine is switched off, check for leaks. Look for signs of coolant drips on radiator or around header tank joint.

Leaks are possible at:
Upper or lower radiator hoses
Water pump (gaskets or seal)
Heater core or connecting hoses
Automatic transmission cooler lines (at bottom of radiator)
Faulty radiator pressure cap
Faulty cylinder head gasket
Cracked cylinder head or block

Due to the number of joints, cooling systems have many places to leak from. Check clamp tightness. If leaks persist an anti-leak additive in the coolant may help. Noisy water pumps may benefit from a lubricating additive in the coolant. Use a cooling system cleaner when flushing during a drain and refill job. It will help remove rust and scale. Remember — additives will not cure chronic problems. But they will effect a short-term remedy in many cases.

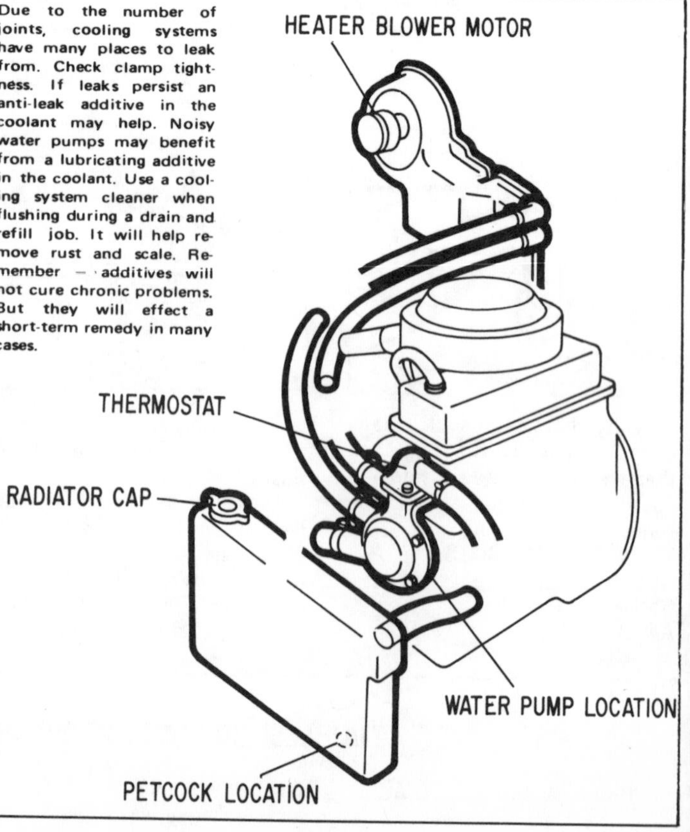

RADIATOR CAP CHECK

Check radiator cap occasionally for worn or cracked gasket. If cap doesn't seal properly, fluid will be lost and engine will overheat. Replace worn cap with new cap rated 15 lbs. pressure.

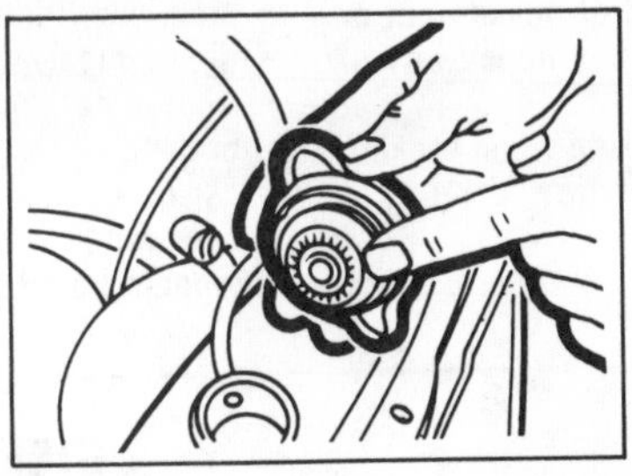

HOSE REPLACEMENT

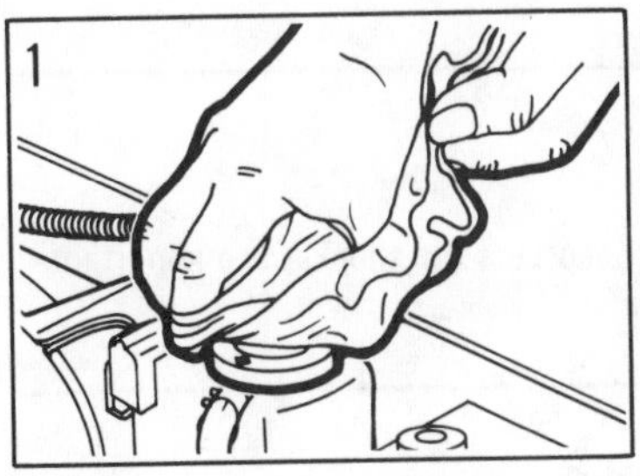

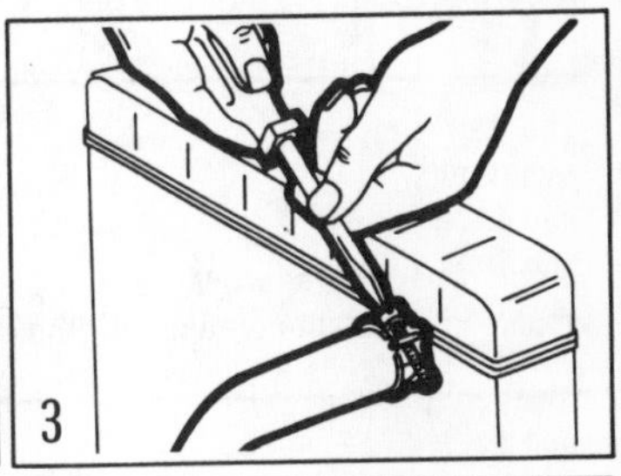

Coolant drain and refill work may be done alone; when changing hoses, coolant must also be drained a part of job. Discard all hoses with cracks or soft spots. Check hose clamps for tightness and good condition.

1. Remove radiator cap. Open radiator petcock. Drain coolant into catch basin. If near 24 months old, discard old coolant.
2. Petcock or drain plug is located at the bottom left of the radiator. Open petcock or remove plug to drain.
3. Loosen clamps at each end of hose(s). Work loose; pull off. If old hose clamps are rusted or damaged, replace with new units.
4. Wipe all hose connections clean. Use emery cloth to get rid of residue. Check all hoses for weak spots, as well as cracks inside and out.
5. Slip clamps over each hose end. Slip hose ends all the way onto cleaned up hose connections.

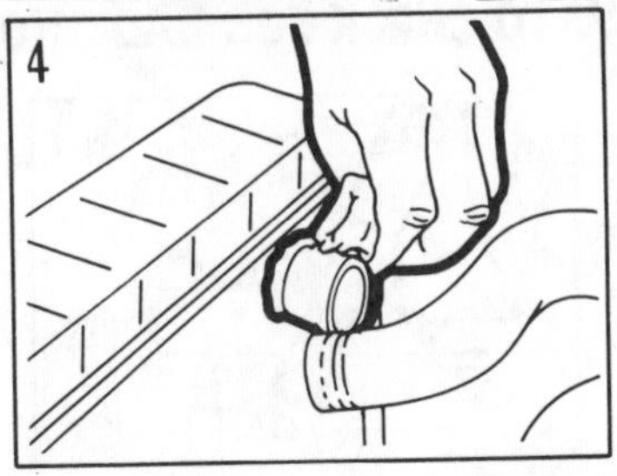

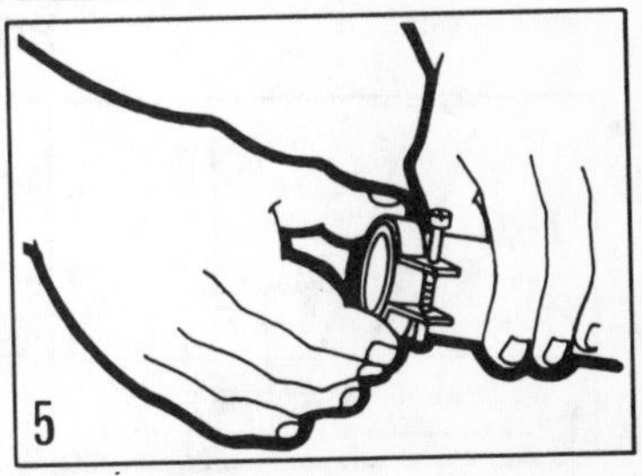

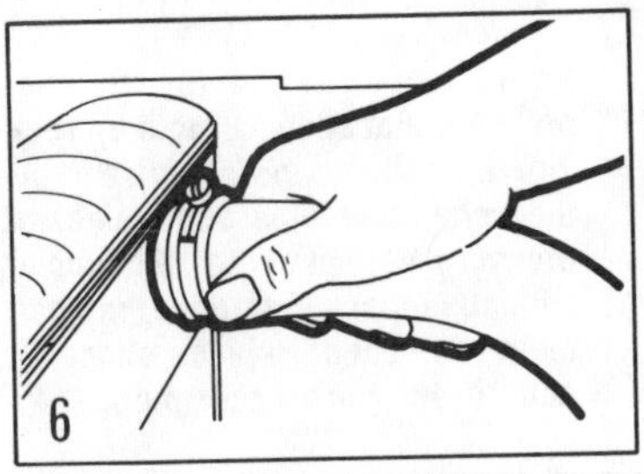

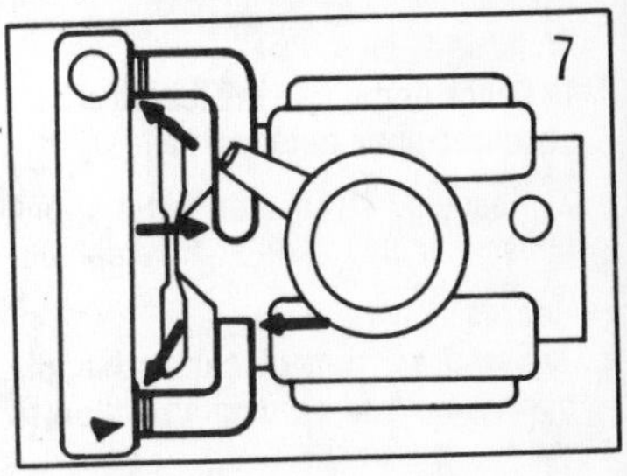

6. Place hose clamp ¼ inch from hose end. Tighten. Close petcock. Refill with 50/50 coolant/water mix.
7. Start engine; allow to warm up. Check for coolant leaks.
8. Road test car; watch for temperature warning light.

Suspension and Tires

The front wheels mount and rotate on the spindles, which are attached to upper and lower ball joints. A coil spring is mounted between the control arms on both sides. A shock absorber is located in the center of each spring. The rear suspension consists of coil springs, upper and lower control arms, and shock absorbers.

Your car's suspension system consists of wheels, tires, springs, shock absorbers, sway (or stabilizer) bars, ball joints, steering linkage. If any of these items is out of adjustment or badly worn, you may notice any of these symptoms:

- car pulls to one side when braking
- car wanders when driving a straight line
- overall ride may be either hard or bouncy
- effort is needed to steer vehicle
- tires show uneven wear
- tires squeal when cornering
- front of car dips or bounces when braking
- car rocks side-to-side when going over rough road
- wheels bounce to make slapping sound on road
- steering wheel vibrates in hands
- front of car vibrates at highway speeds

Any of above symptoms indicates corrective action is needed. Delay can: ruin tires; cause damage/failure to other suspension parts; create safety hazard.

STEERING

If steering linkage, front suspension and steering column components are in good condition, there should be not more than 1½ inch free play in the steering wheel when measured at the rim of the wheel. If a loud knock is heard when turning the steering wheel from one extreme to the other, have mechanic check pinion bearing preload.

SHOCK ABSORBERS

Shock absorbers work to keep wheels in constant contact with the road. Result is safe handling and ride control; longer tire life. So shock absorbers (or shocks) are important.

HOW TO CHECK FOR BAD SHOCKS

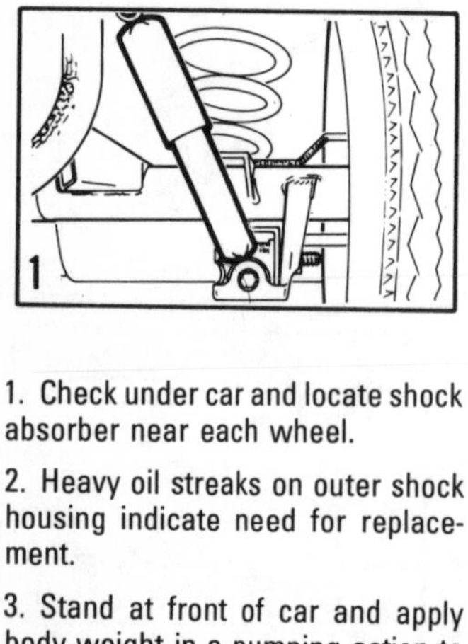

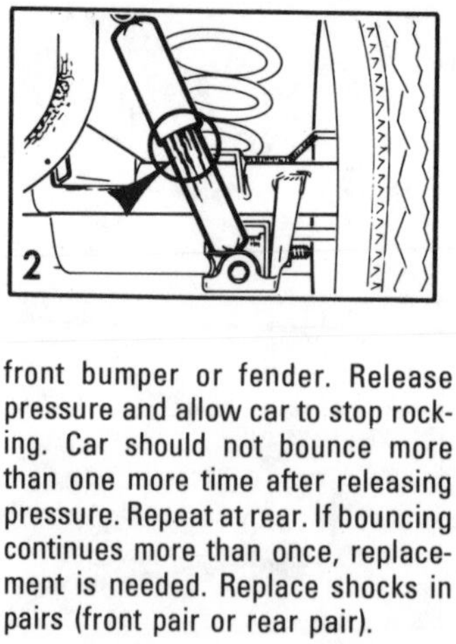

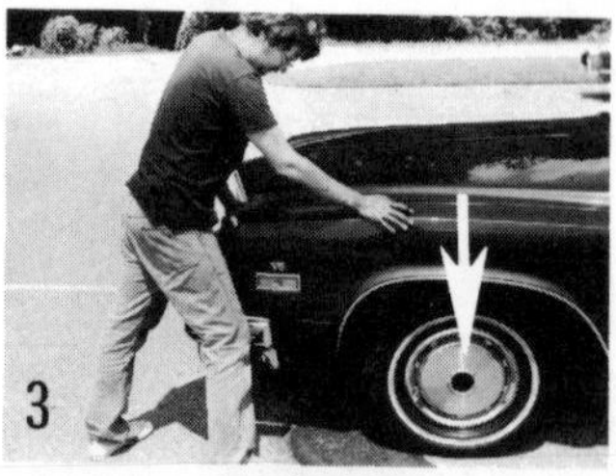

1. Check under car and locate shock absorber near each wheel.

2. Heavy oil streaks on outer shock housing indicate need for replacement.

3. Stand at front of car and apply body weight in a pumping action to front bumper or fender. Release pressure and allow car to stop rocking. Car should not bounce more than one more time after releasing pressure. Repeat at rear. If bouncing continues more than once, replacement is needed. Replace shocks in pairs (front pair or rear pair).

TOW HITCH INFORMATION

If your car is used for trailer towing you should check:

A. Cooling System; be sure coolant is at proper level in radiator. See Cooling System Section for checks to perform.

B. Check Transmission Fluid; keep topped up to proper level.

C. Check Rear Shock Absorbers; you may benefit from installation of new rear shocks.

D. Check Tire Pressures; best traction and handling can be ensured if tire pressures are properly maintained.

For safer and more trouble-free trailer towing, consider:

A. Automatic Transmission Cooler; helps remove excess heat from automatic transmission fluid built up

during towing mileage. Also helps avoid radiator overheating. Some units can be self-installed.
B. Radiator Over-Flow Tank Kit; addition of a reservoir to catch radiator coolant overflow preventing coolant loss. Easy to install, these units help a tow car run cooler, avoid overheating due to coolant loss.
C. Heavy-Duty Shock Absorbers or Air Shocks; important to have on rear wheels if you intend to do a lot of towing or load carrying within the car itself. Don't forget to consider replacing factory shocks, when they are worn out, with heavy-duty units at the front as well.
D. Variable Load Flasher; this unit will accommodate the added load of trailer turn signal lamps on trailer when these are hooked into your car's electrical system.

FRONT END ALIGNMENT

When steering, handling and/or tire wear indicate front end alignment may be needed, this work can only be done at an automotive service shop. DO NOT PUT OFF NEEDED FRONT END ALIGNMENT. At the same time, have ball joints and steering linkage checked.

Ignition System

TUNE-UP SERVICES—1970-74 Standard Ignition

The ignition system consists of spark plugs; plug wires; distributor; rotor; points; condenser; coil. These units work to create a good hot spark inside the engine (ignition) at exactly the right moment (timing). If ignition is weak or timing is off, engine may be hard to start, run poorly, waste gas, lose power, backfire or not run at all.
TOOLS & MATERIALS . . . Parts: set of points; condenser, 8 spark plugs. Tools: feeler gauge; 13/16 in. (1970) or ⅝ in. spark plug socket; open end box or combination wrenches; timing equipment.

SAFETY TIP . . . Change only one spark plug at a time to avoid cross-wiring and possible engine damage.

OTHER IGNITION CHECK POINTS

Inspect spark plug wires. If cracked or brittle, entire set should be replaced. Also, center high tension wire. Inspect distributor cap. Wipe inside clean occasionally with dry, lint-free rag. If cap is cracked or rotor contacts are excessively burned, replace cap.

CHECKING POINTS AND ROTOR—V8 (1970-74)

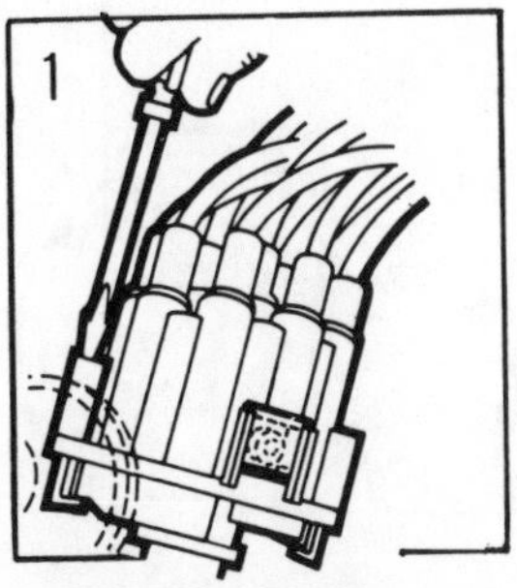

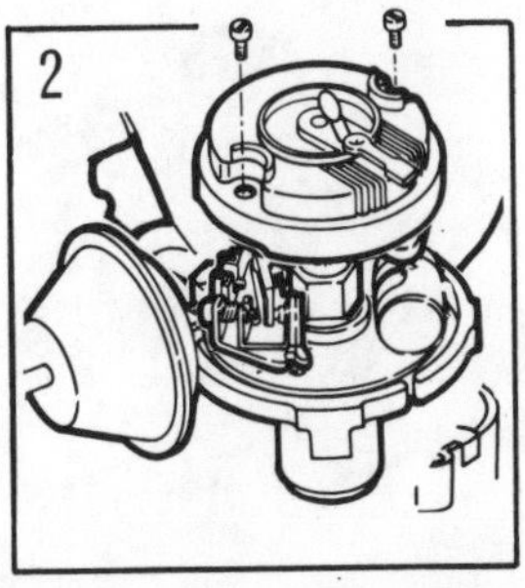

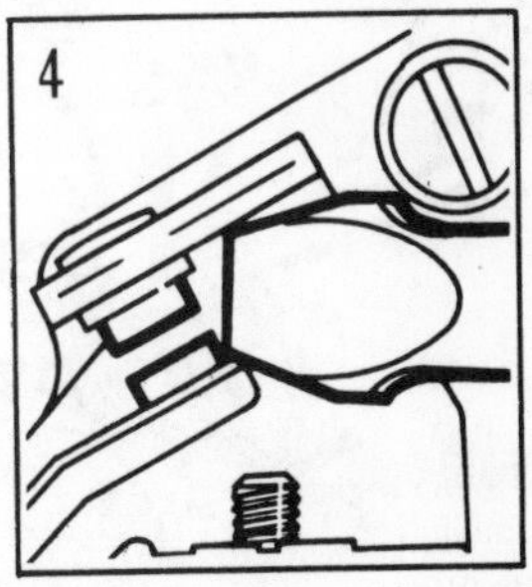

The distributor holds the points, rotor and condenser.
1. To open the distributor, depress the screw in the cap and rotate the latch off the distributor (there are two latches). Remove the coil wire and lift off the cap. Keep the other wires attached.
2. Remove the two screws and lift off the rotor. If it is cracked or metallic tip is badly burned, replace it.
3. Check the metal contacts inside the cap. Replace the cap if they are corroded or there are any cracks.
4. Pry the points apart with a screwdriver. If worn or burned, replace. If OK, check the gap.

REMOVING POINTS V8 (1970-74)

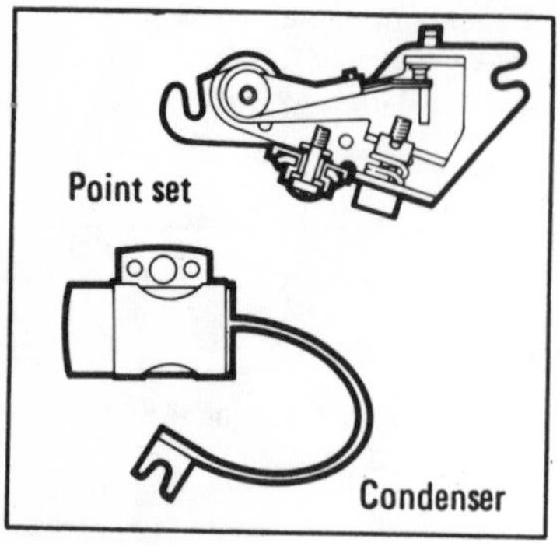

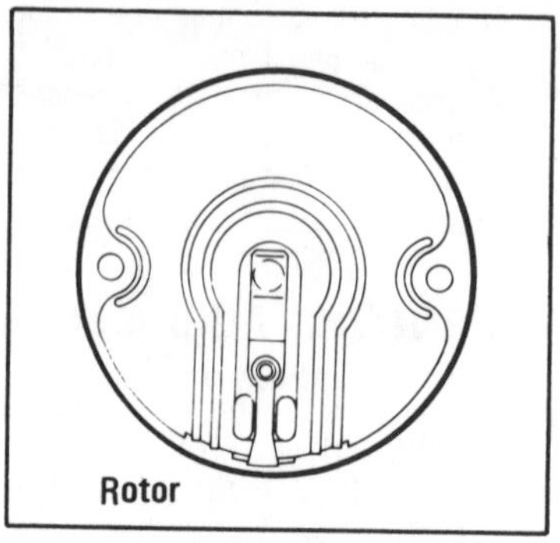

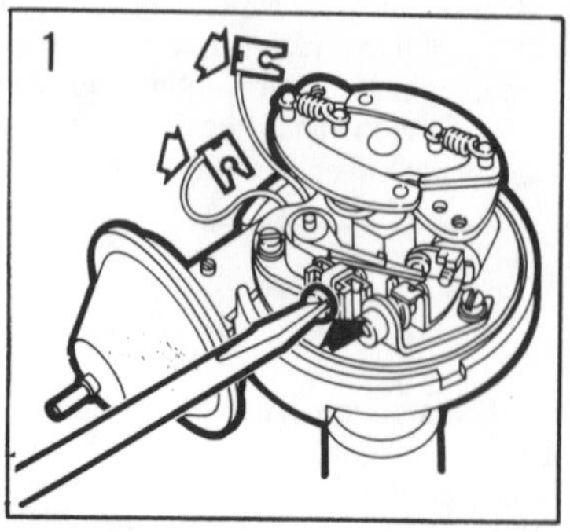

1. Disconnect the two wire terminals connected to the points set. Notice that the condenser connector is on the outside.
2. Loosen, but do not remove the two points attaching screws. Slide the points off the screws to remove.
3. Remove screw which holds condenser. DO NOT DROP SCREW.

NOTE: Later models use a combined points and condenser. When you remove points you also remove condenser. You can also install these points in early cars.

4. Wipe all dirt from distributor plate and cam with clean, lint-free rag.

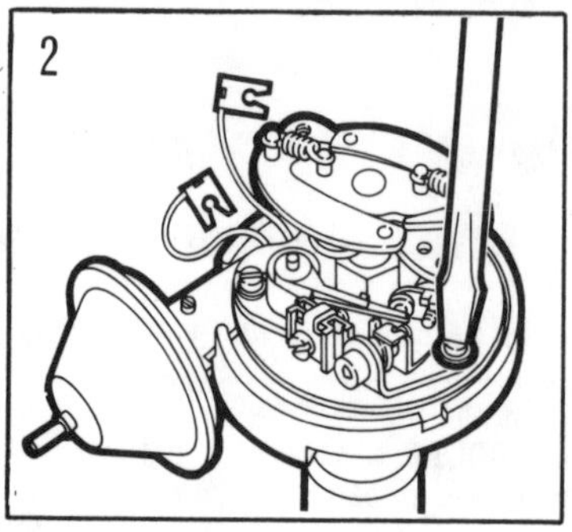

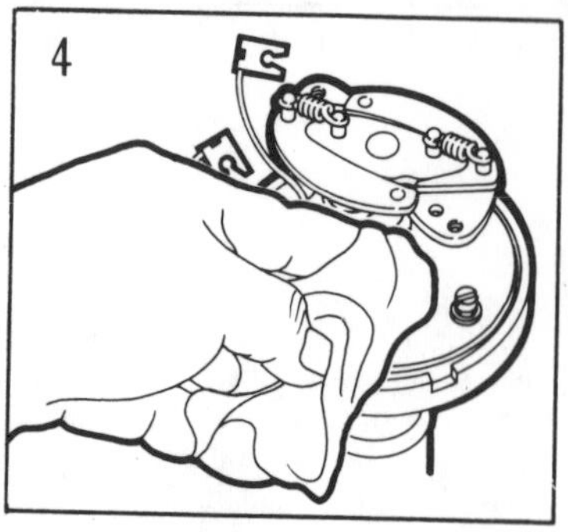

CAUTION: When removing screws from distributor, be sure to avoid any screws accidentally falling through distributor opening into engine. Use magnetic screwdriver.

INSTALLING POINTS AND CONDENSER—V8 (1970-74)

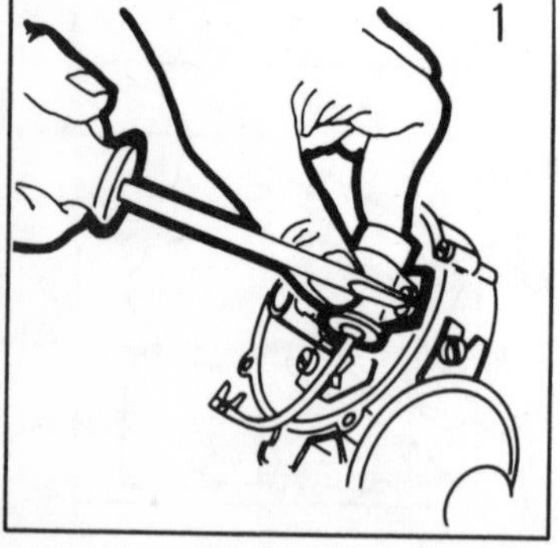

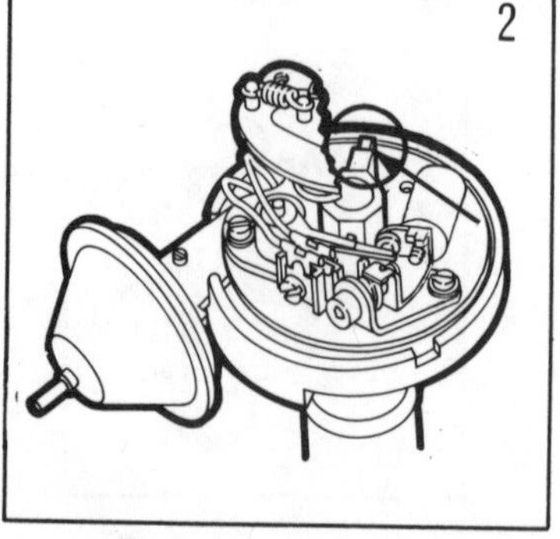

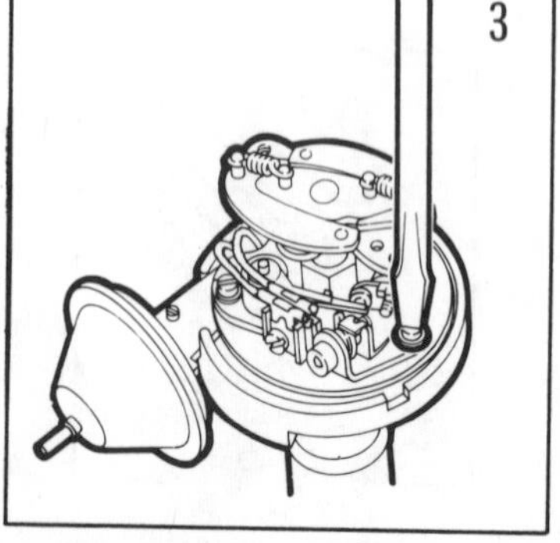

1. Attach new condenser with screw.
2. Rotate or replace cam lubricator. Fiber cam lubricator must be turned 180° every 12,000 mi., replaced every 24,000. When replacing, simply pull it up and off stud; push new lubricator down over stud. DO NOT attempt to add oil or grease to fiber lubricator.
3. Position new points set in distributor by sliding onto screws. Tighten screws.

RESETTING THE CONTACT GAP—V8 (1970-74)

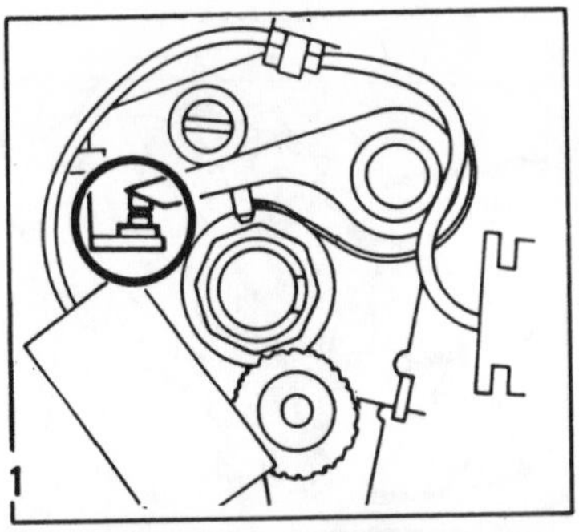

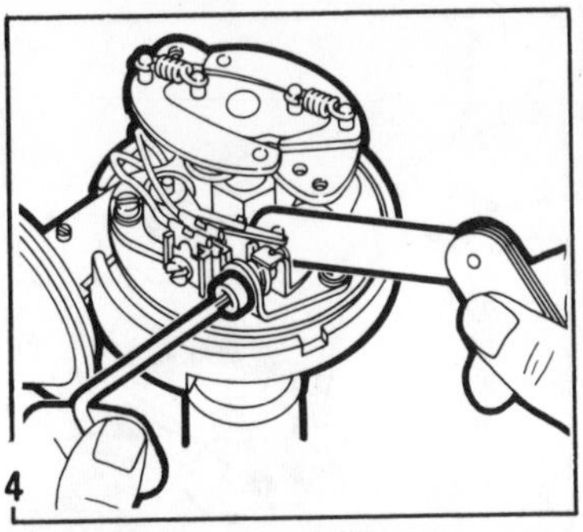

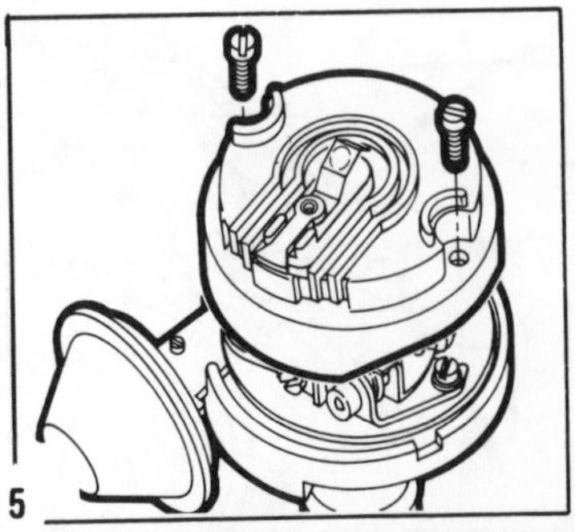

1. Check that point contacts meet squarely. If they do not, bend bracket supporting fixed contact using needle-nosed pliers.
2. Turn engine by ignition key (you'll need a helper) until rubbing block on point set is on one of the high spots of distributor cam. You may use wrench on lower engine pulley to do this.
3. Insert a ⅛ in. allen wrench into points adjusting screw. Correct gap is shown in the Specifications Chart.
4. Insert correct size feeler gauge. Adjust gap with wrench until feeler gauge can be moved in and out between contacts with only slight drag.
5. Install rotor on advance weight assembly. The two lugs on the bottom of the rotor are shaped differently, so it can only be installed one way. Tighten screws.
6. Install cap by depressing screws and turning latches onto body of distributor. Insert the coil wire into the cap.
7. Point gap can be adjusted with the engine running. Insert the allen wrench through the cap window, slowly turn the adjusting screw clockwise until the engine just starts to misfire, and then turn it back ½ turn.

CHECKING POINTS AND ROTOR—Six (1970-74)

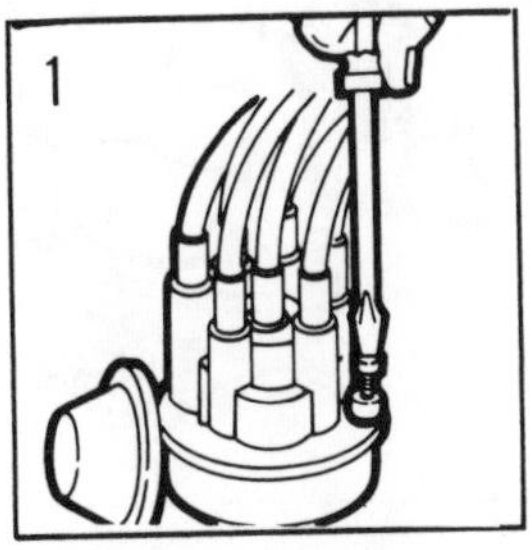

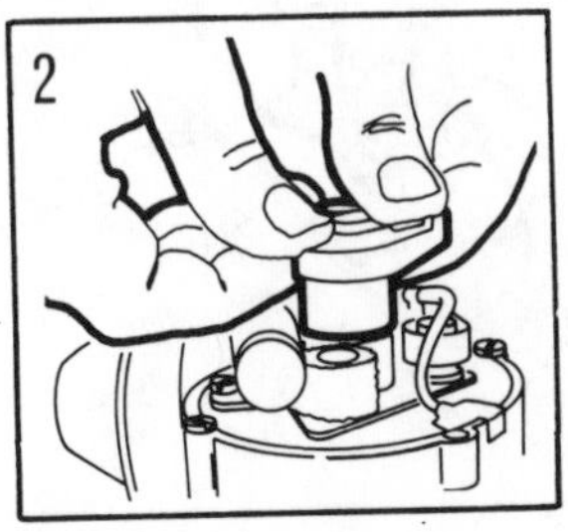

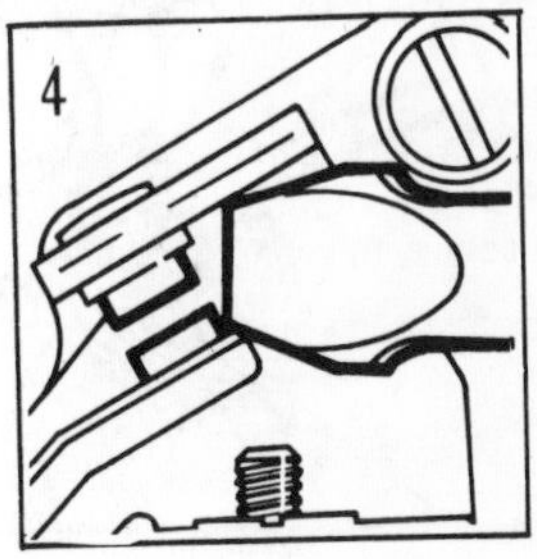

1. To open the distributor, remove the two screws retaining the cap. Remove the coil wire and lift the cap off, but keep the other wires attached.
2. Pull the rotor off (straight up). If it is cracked or metallic tip is badly burned, replace it.
3. Check the metal contacts inside the cap. Replace the cap if they are corroded or there are any cracks.
4. Pry the points apart with a screwdriver. If worn or burned, replace. If OK, check the gap.

LOCATION OF POINTS AND CONDENSER—Six (1970-74)

Points and condenser work together. Always replace condenser also when installing new points.

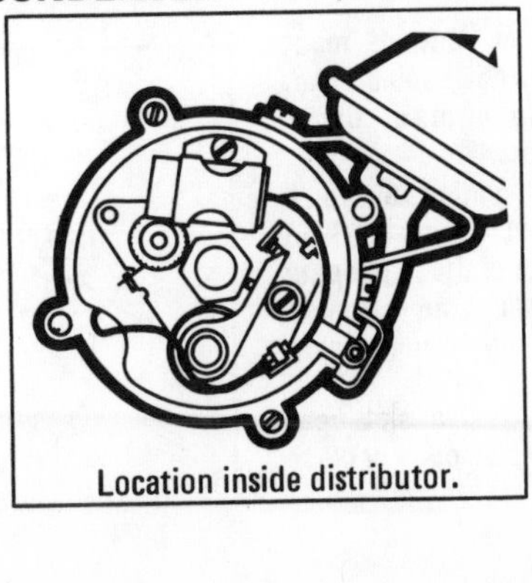

Location inside distributor.

REMOVING POINTS—Six (1970-74)

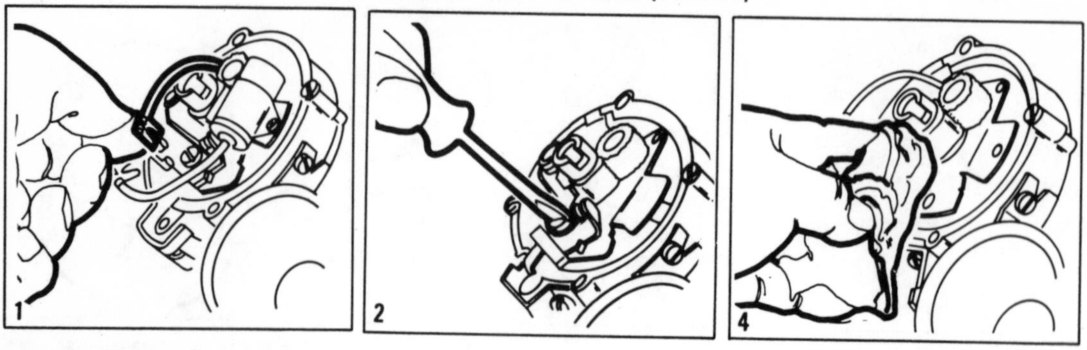

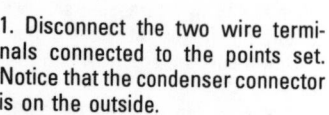

1. Disconnect the two wire terminals connected to the points set. Notice that the condenser connector is on the outside.
2. Remove points attaching screw being very careful not to drop screw inside distributor.
3. Remove screw which holds condenser. DO NOT DROP SCREW.
4. Wipe all dirt from distributor plate and cam with clean, lint-free rag.

CAUTION: When removing screws from distributor, be sure to avoid any screws accidentally falling through distributor opening into engine. Use magnetic screwdriver.

INSTALLING POINTS AND CONDENSER—Six (1970-74)

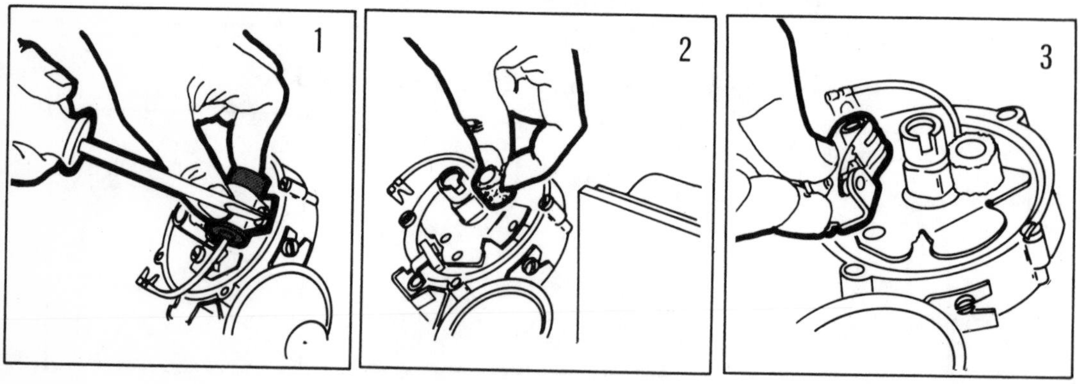

1. Attach new condenser with screw.
2. Rotate or replace cam lubricator. Fiber cam lubricator must be turned 180° every 12,000 mi., replaced every 24,000. When replacing, simply pull it up and off stud; push new lubricator down over stud. DO NOT attempt to add oil or grease to fiber lubricator.
3. Position new points set in distributor. Attach retaining screw lightly. Replace both wire terminals. The condenser wire goes on the outside of the two.

RESETTING THE CONTACT GAP—Six (1970-74)

1. Check that point contacts meet squarely. If they do not, bend bracket supporting fixed contact using needle-nosed pliers.
2. Turn engine by ignition key (you'll need a helper) until rubbing block on point set is on one of the high spots of distributor cam. You may use wrench on lower engine pulley to do this.
3. Insert screwdriver in slot near point contacts; twist to open or close gap.

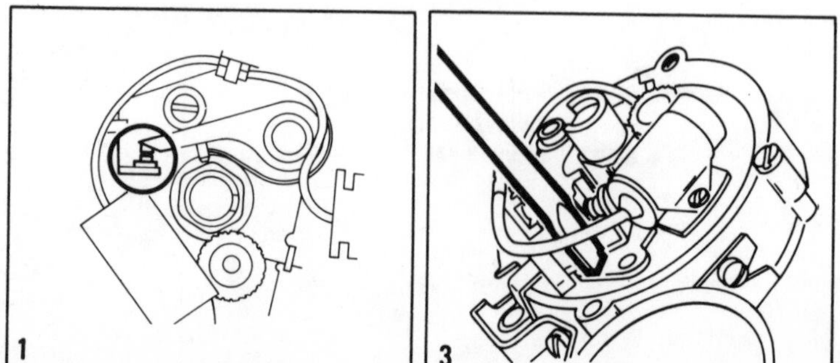

4. Correct gap is shown in the Specifications Chart.

5. Insert correct size feeler gauge. Adjust gap with screwdriver until feeler gauge can be moved in and out between contacts with only slight drag.

6. Tighten point set holddown screw. Recheck gap; it might have changed from tightening holddown screw. Re-adjust if needed.

7. Align tab inside rotor with notch on distributor shaft and push rotor onto shaft. Rotor must be fully seated on shaft.

8. Replace distributor cap; install screws.

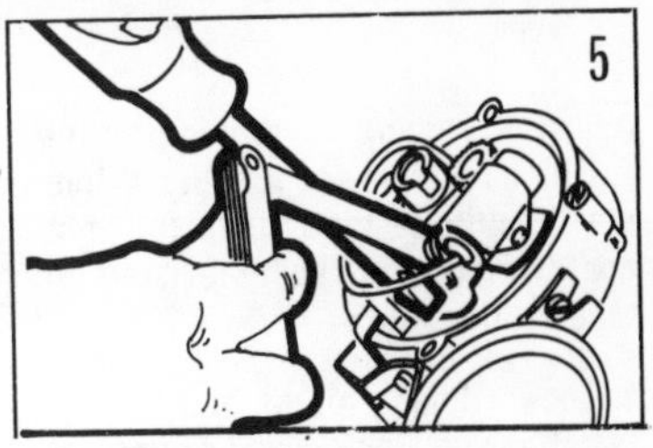

TUNE-UP SERVICES ELECTRONIC IGNITION (1974-77)

Cars equipped with electronic ignition systems require very little care. Spark plugs, ignition wires and timing can be checked periodically as outlined above. Major service to the electronic ignition system should be handled by your mechanic.

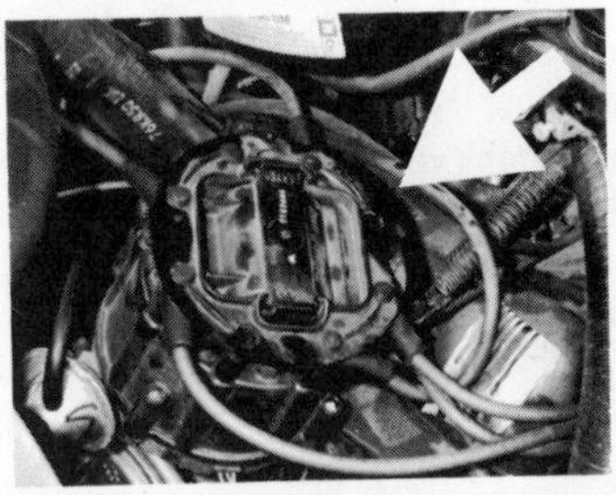

HIGH ENERGY IGNITION SYSTEM TACHOMETER HOOKUP

Some 1974, and all 1975 and later Buicks are equipped with the High Energy Ignition System which uses a different tachometer hookup than was used in previous years.

1. On the V6 and V8 engines, connect the tachometer to the TACH terminal on the distributor and to a suitable ground.

NOTE: Some tachometers must connect to the TACH terminal on the distributor and to the positive terminal on the battery. If there is any doubt check the tachometer manufacturer's instructions.

2. On the inline six cylinder, connect the tachometer to the TACH terminal on the coil, opposite the BAT terminal, and to a ground.

SPARK PLUG REPLACEMENT

1. Remove spark plug wire by grasping rubber boot. Do not jerk wire. If stuck, turn boot, pulling gently.

2. Loosen spark plug using socket wrench.

3. Wipe or brush loose dirt from around plug before removing. Do not let dirt drop into engine through plug hole. Unscrew plug.

4. Check plug electrode gap on new spark plug. Adjust to specification. Plug gap is correct when the gauge drags slightly as it is pulled between plug electrodes.

5. Thread new plug into plug hole by hand. Hand tighten. Do not force or cross thread. Use socket wrench to tighten firmly but do not force. Replace plug wire. Press boot firmly.

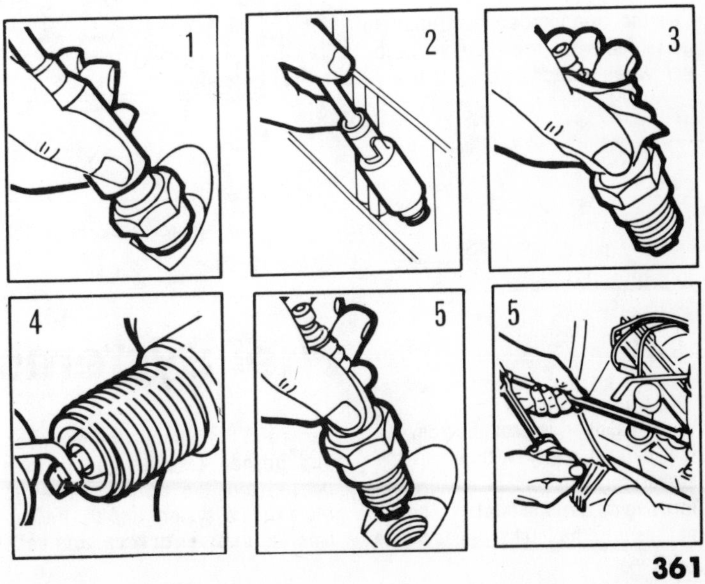

IGNITION TIMING

Adjusting timing is the important finishing touch to any tune-up. While not difficult, job requires timing light and dwell meter. Timing is listed on tune-up decal.

1. Locate timing marks and pointer (notches) on engine and lower engine pulley. Clean away dirt. Mark the pointer notches with chalk.
2. Hook up timing light according to instructions supplied with it.
3. Disconnect and plug the vacuum line from the distributor.
4. Disconnect the fuel tank vent line from the vaporative canister.
5. Aim timing light at pulley mark(s). If the chalked marks do not align, loosen distributor hold-down nut and slowly rotate distributor until chalked marks align.
6. Tighten hold-down nut.

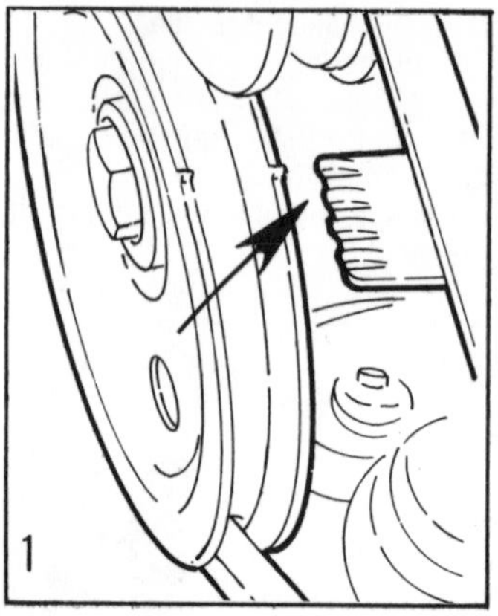

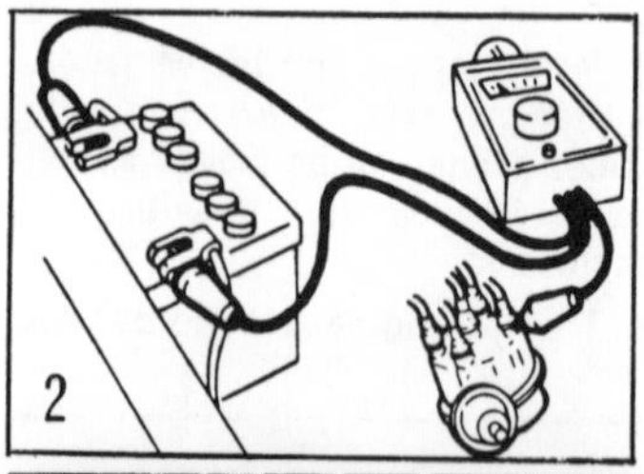

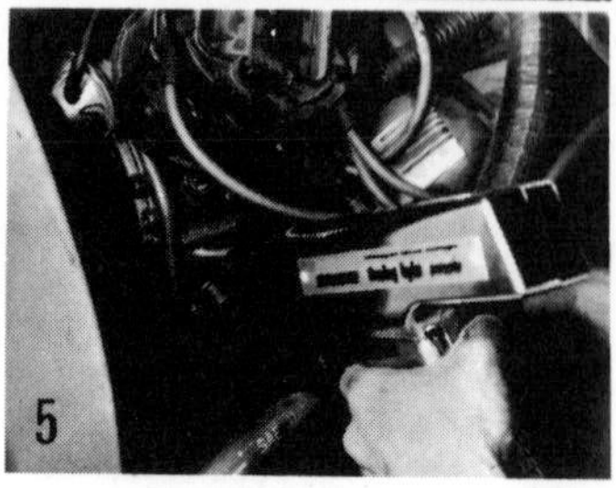

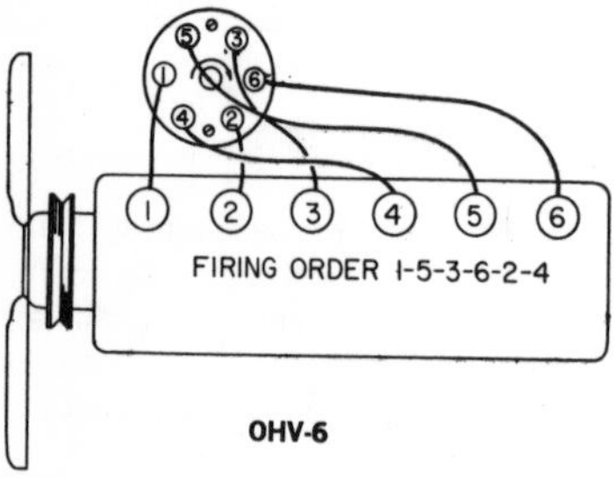

OHV-6

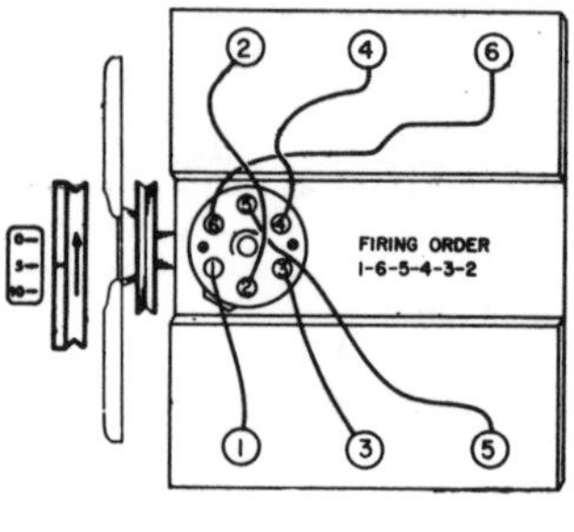

V6 engine

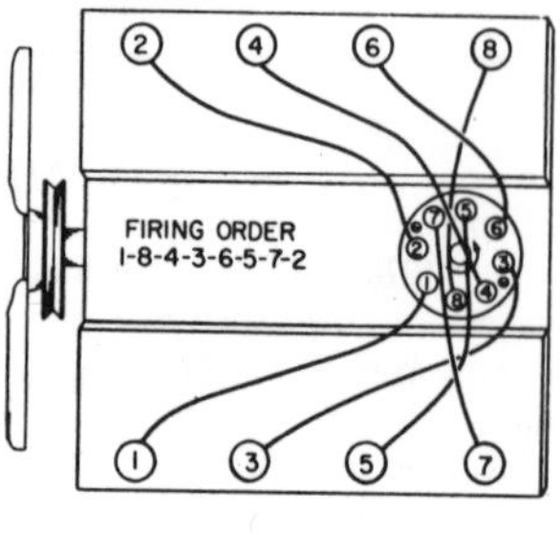

260 V8

Use the firing order illustration to guide you when replacing your ignition wires and/or distributor cap.

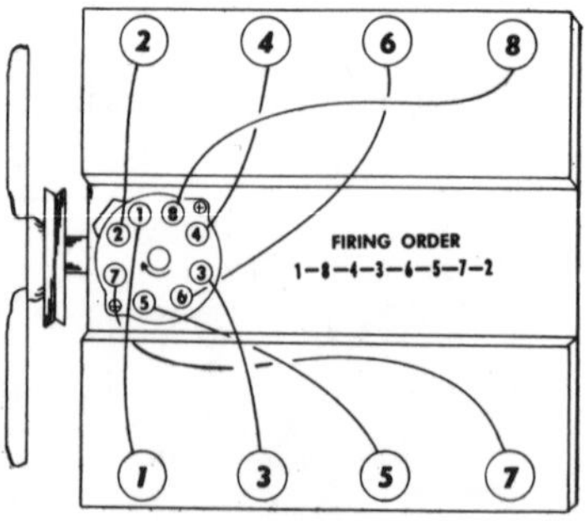

350, 400, 455 cu in.

Fuel Systems

When gasoline is brought from the fuel tank, it mixes with air in the carburetor. This gas/air mixture enters engine thru the intake manifold, passes thru the intake valves and is burned in the combustion chamber. The burned exhaust gas is then passed thru the exhaust valves to the exhaust system and to the outside air. In order to keep your car's engine running cleanly with minimal pollution, and avoid dangerous carbon monoxide fumes inside the vehicle, certain items should be checked from time to time.

KEEP THE AIR INTAKE CLEAN

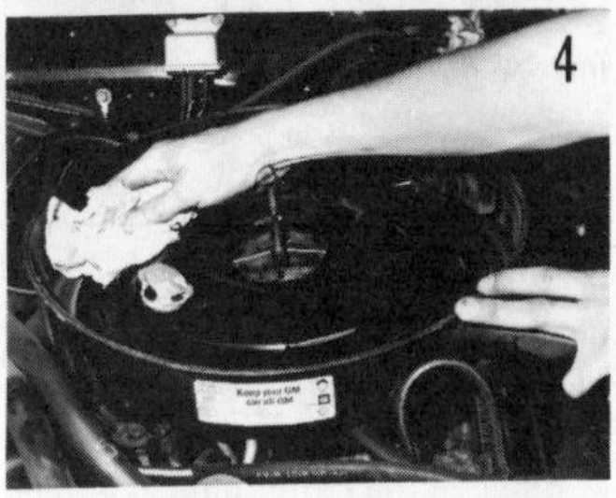

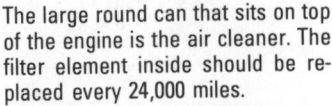

The large round can that sits on top of the engine is the air cleaner. The filter element inside should be replaced every 24,000 miles.

1. Unscrew the wing nut and remove the air cleaner cover.

2. Remove and discard the old dirty filter.

3. Check the small crankcase breather filter. If dirty, lift out and replace it.

4. Using a clean rag, wipe out of the inside of air cleaner. Install new filter and replace top cover.

EMISSION CONTROL SYSTEM

An important part of a car's emission control system is the Positive Crankcase Ventilation (PCV) valve and its connecting hose. The PCV valve should be replaced once every 24,000 miles. This device keeps dirt and sludge from forming inside the engine. Make sure all PCV connections are tight. Check that the connecting hoses are clear and not clogged. Replace any brittle or broken hoses.

PCV VALVE REPLACEMENT

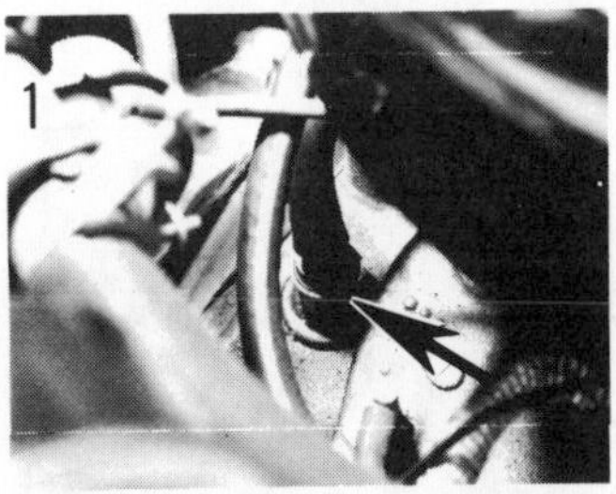

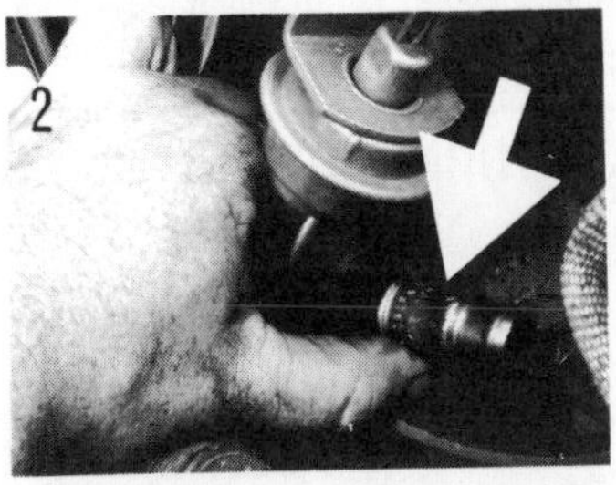

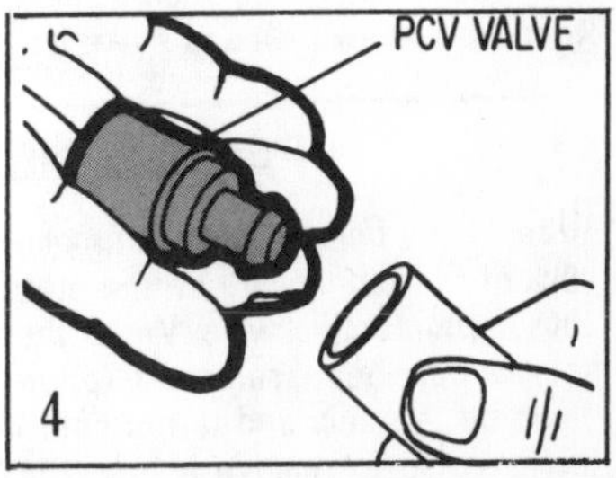

1. Pull valve from its location in the intake manifold.
2. Squeeze the hose clamp with a pair of pliers. Remove the valve.
3. Note where the other end of the hose connects. Remove the hose and flush it with cleaning solvent.
4. Reconnect the hose. Pinch the clamp and insert the PCV valve into the hose.
5. Insert the valve into the valve cover.

FUEL FILTER REPLACEMENT

The fuel filter is located behind the large fuel line inlet nut on the carburetor. Replace the filter every year or 12,000 miles. The fuel filter prevents dirt, rust, and scale from both the gas station's tank and your own fuel tank from reaching the carburetor. A dirty filter will starve the engine and cause poor running.

1. Place an absorbent rag under fuel line connection to absorb gas spills. Unscrew fuel line connection with ½

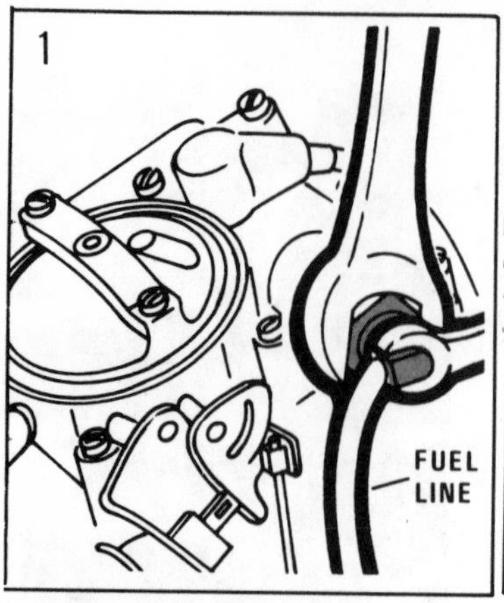

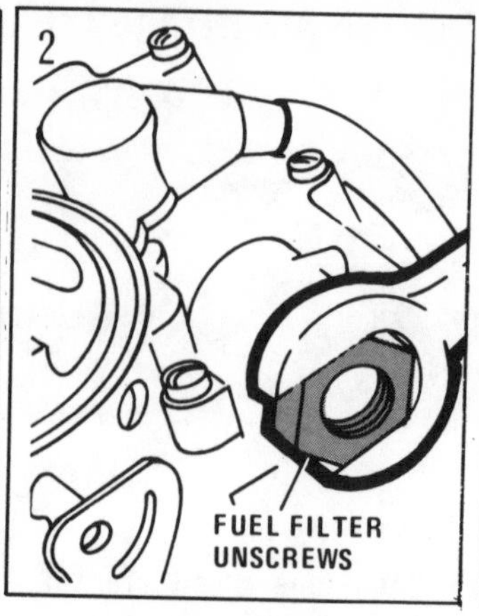

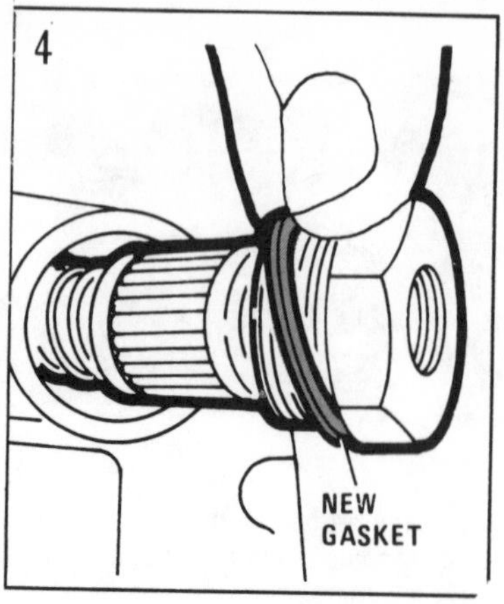

in. wrench while holding the larger nut with a 1 in. wrench. Be careful, fuel line fitting threads are easily stripped.

2. Remove the larger filter retaining nut from the carburetor. The spring behind the filter will push it out. Remove the filter and the spring.

3. Install the spring and new filter element. Some carburetors are equipped with a paper element, others with a bronze unit. The bronze filter must have the small cone section facing out and a gasket between the filter and the retaining nut.

4. Install the new gasket on the retaining nut and screw it into place. CAUTION: DO NOT OVERTIGHTEN

5. Reconnect the fuel line. Discard the gas soaked rag safely.

6. Start the engine and check for leaks. Addition of a can of carburetor cleaner to the fuel tank occasionally will aid in keeping the entire fuel system clean.

Safety Systems

LIGHTING SYSTEM

Headlights, turn signals, stop lights, and parking lights are an important part of your car's safety system. They permit you to see and be seen. Keep all lenses clean and make frequent checks to be sure that all of your lights are functioning properly. Replace any cracked lenses as soon as possible. When replacing a bulb, make a note of the number which is usually printed on the base. If you don't have a number, take the old bulb with you so that you match it for the correct replacement.

PARKING LIGHTS, TURN SIGNALS AND STOP LIGHTS

To replace a bulb, raise the trunk lid back of rear door and turn the bulb socket counterclockwise. When the socket has been removed, push down on the bulb and turn it counterclockwise to remove it from the socket. Install the new bulb in reverse order. Be sure to match the knobs on the bulb base with the slots in socket.

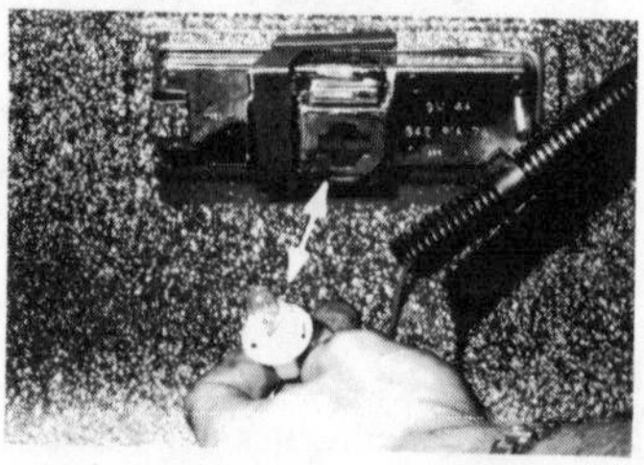

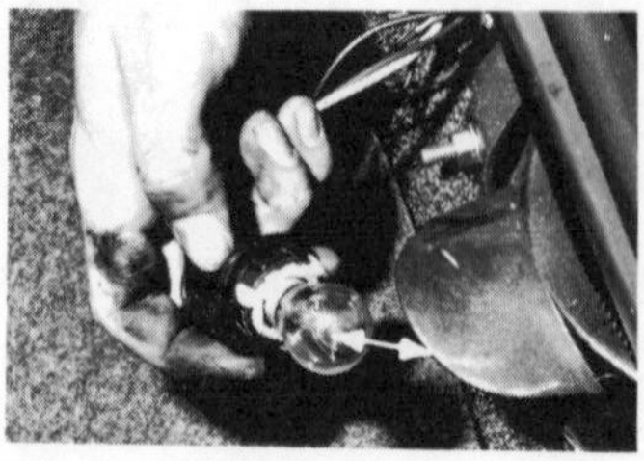

SIDE MARKER LIGHT

Reach up inside fender and turn bulb socket counterclockwise to remove from housing. Pull bulb straight out.

LICENSE PLATE LIGHTS

Remove the screws that retain the lens to the bumpers. Push in on bulb, turning counterclockwise to remove.

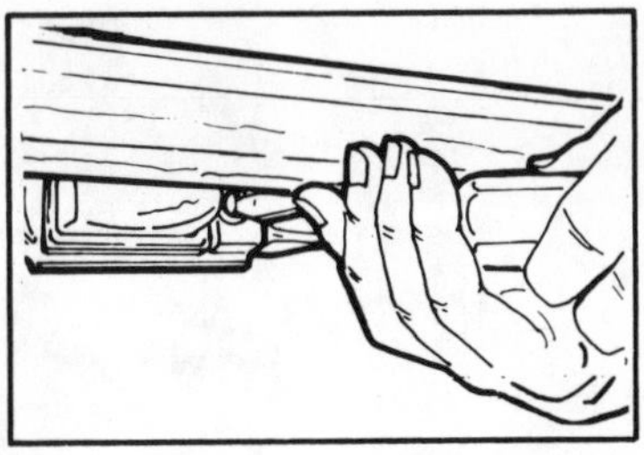

INTERIOR DOME LIGHT

This is cartridge type bulb; be sure to purchase correct replacement. Pry dome light lens out from housing. To avoid blowing fuse, make sure doors are closed and dome light switch is in OFF position. Carefully lever the bulb straight out of housing. Insert new bulb and re-install dome light lens.

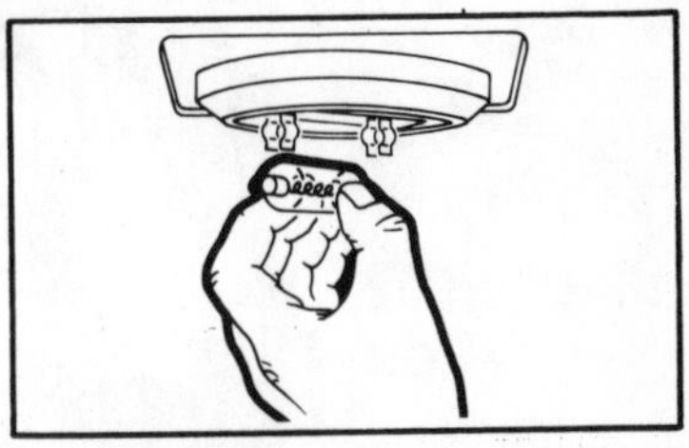

HEADLIGHT REPLACEMENT—Four Headlight System

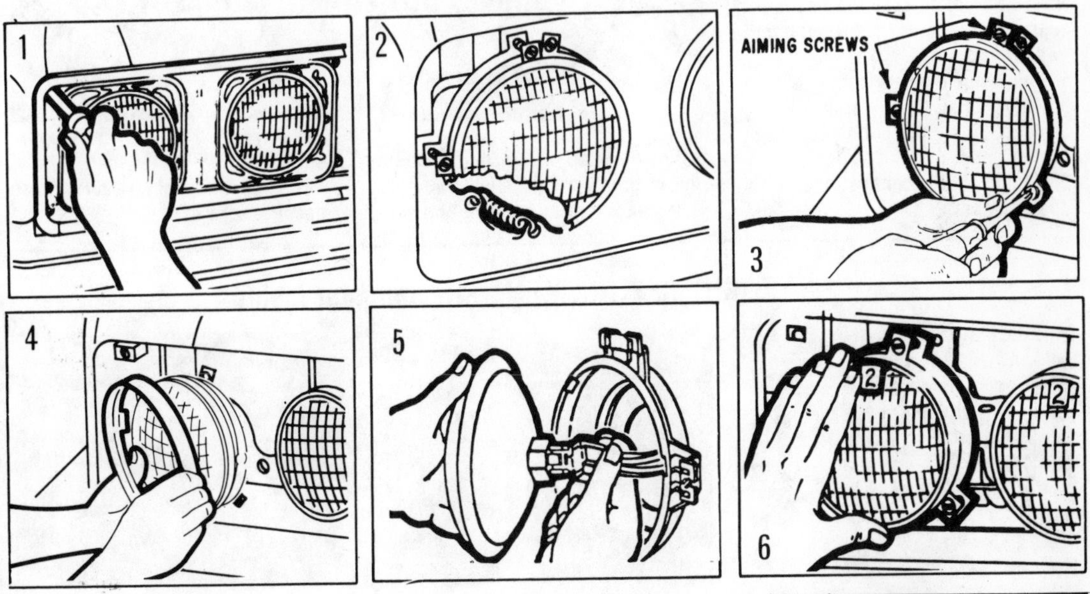

1. Remove the headlight trim retaining screws and remove the trim.

2. Unhook the spring from the headlight ring.

3. Remove the two retaining ring screws. Do not disturb the long aiming screws located at 9 and 12 o'clock.

4. Remove the retaining ring. Disconnect the wiring plug and remove the bulb.

5. Attach the connector plug to the new headlight.

6. Position the new bulb in housing. Make sure that the number molded into the lens is at the top.

7. Install the retaining ring and pull the spring into place.

8. Replace the headlight trim panel.

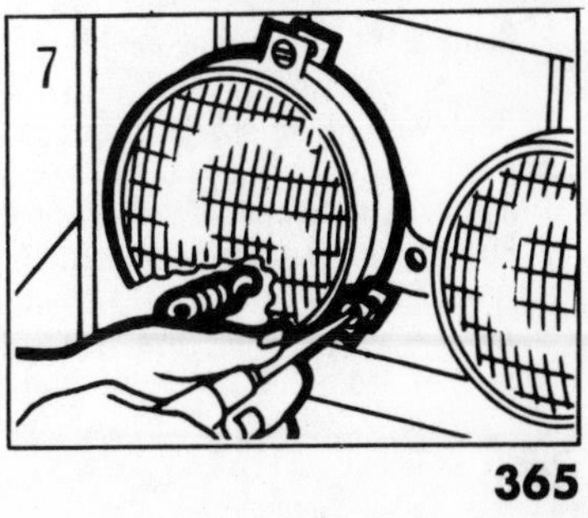

HEADLIGHT REPLACEMENT—Two Headlight System

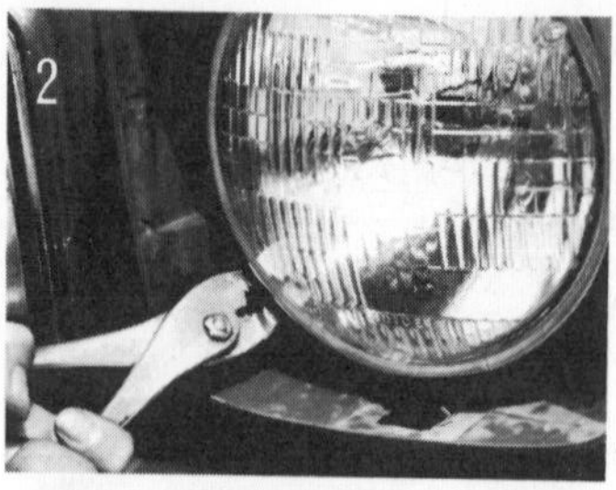

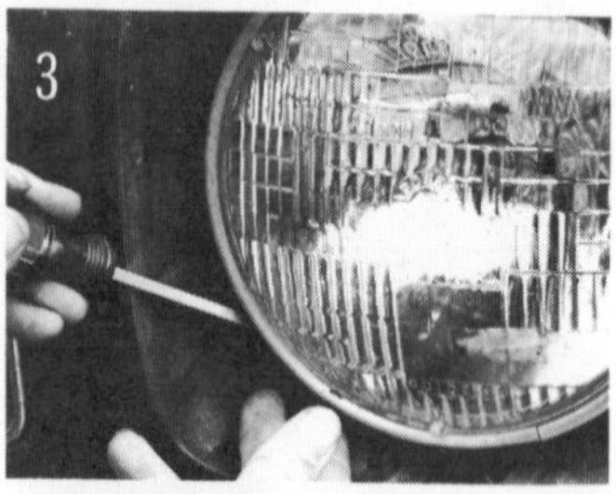

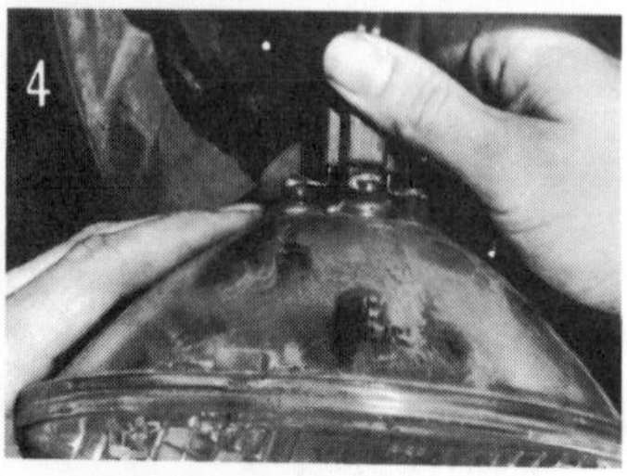

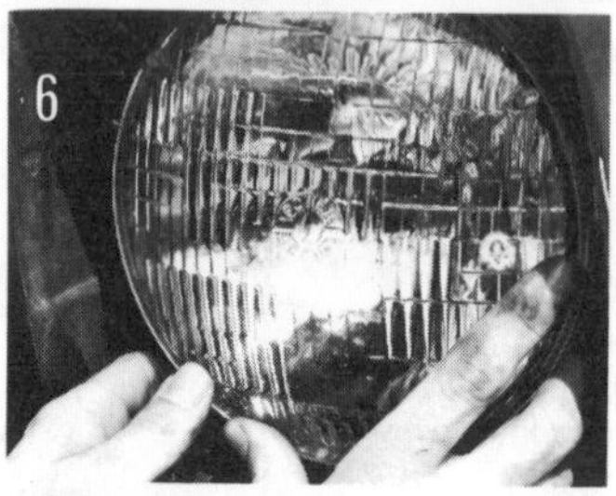

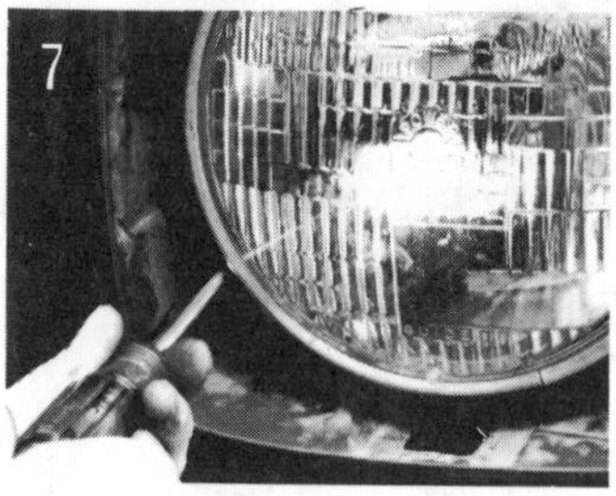

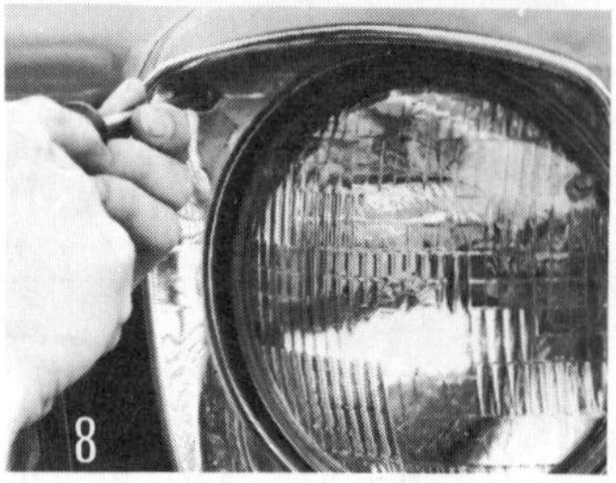

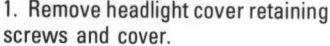

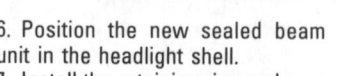

1. Remove headlight cover retaining screws and cover.
2. Unhook the spring from the headlight retaining ring.
3. Unscrew the retaining ring and remove it.

NOTE: Do not mistake the headlight adjustment screws for the retaining ring screws.

4. Pull lamp (sealed beam) out of headlight shell toward front of car; disconnect wiring connector from sealed beam unit.
5. Connect wire connector to new sealed beam unit.
6. Position the new sealed beam unit in the headlight shell.
7. Install the retaining ring and connect the spring.
8. Position headlight cover; install attaching screws.

HEADLIGHT REPLACEMENT—Rectangular Lights

1. Remove the headlight cover retaining screws and cover.
2. Remove the headlight retainer screws.
3. Remove the headlight retainer.
4. Pull the lamp (sealed beam) out of the headlight shell toward the front of the car. Disconnect the wiring connector from the sealed beam unit.

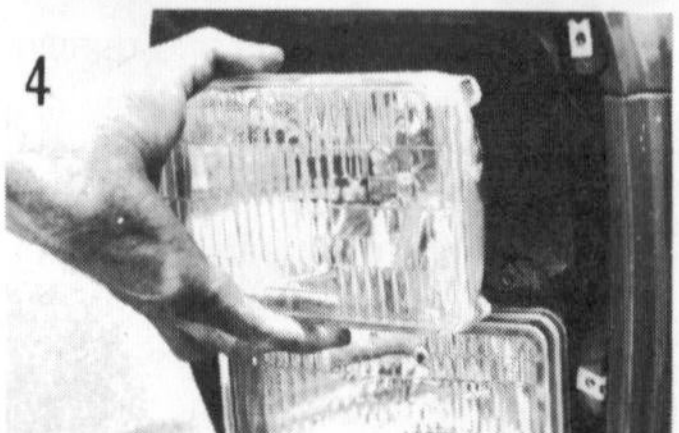

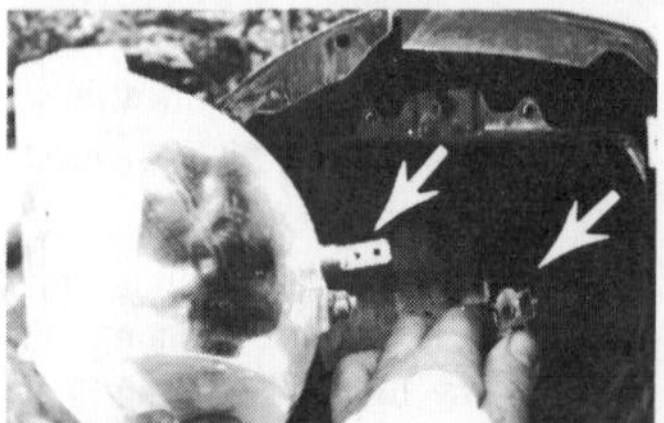

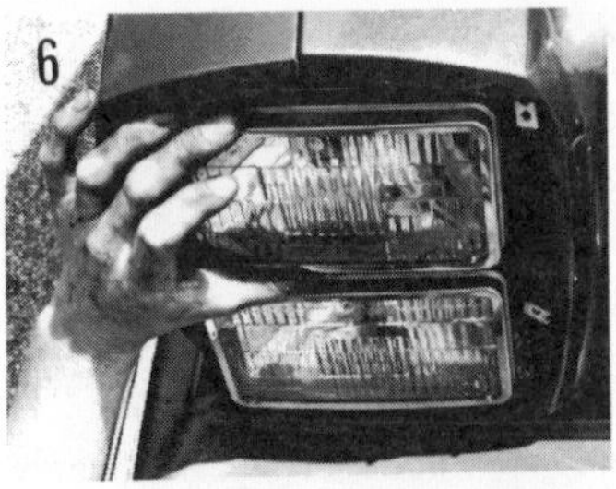

5. Attach the wiring connector to the rear of the sealed beam unit.

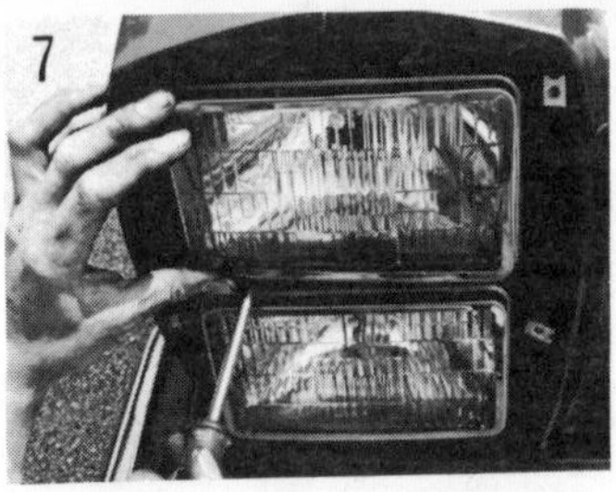

6. Position the new sealed beam unit in the headlight shell.

7. Install the headlight retainer.
8. Position the headlight cover and install the attaching screws.

WINDSHIELD WIPER BLADE REPLACEMENT

To replace wiper blade, lift up on spring release tab on wiper arm connector. Pull wiper blade off. Snap new blade into place.

To replace rubber insert only, press down, away from wiper blade to free it. Slide insert from blade. Insert new wiper. Bend insert upward slightly to engage retaining clips.

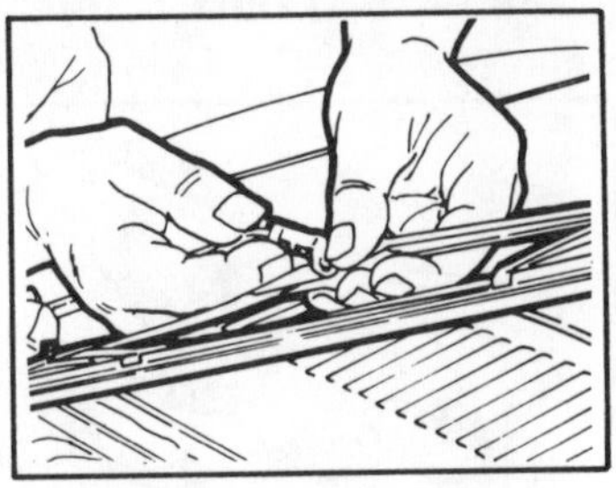

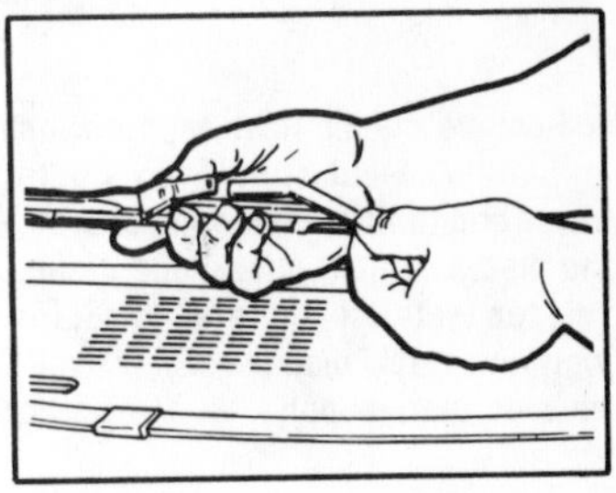

HORN PROBLEMS

If horn sounds and does not stop, this is due to short circuit in wiring. Disconnect wiring connector under hood and have professional service shop check horn wiring circuit.

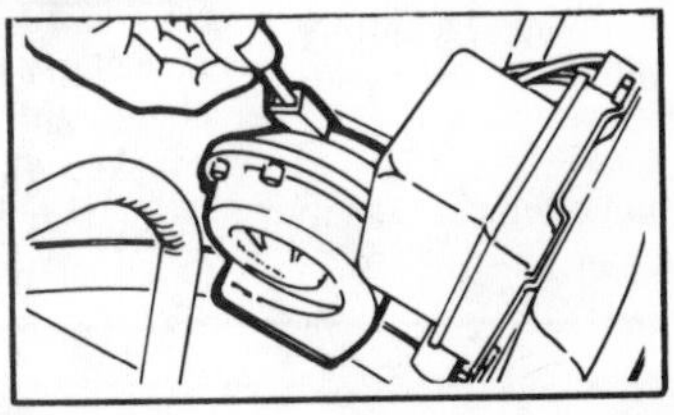

STEERING PROBLEMS

See steering system check in Suspension Section. Check tire pressures. Have a professional service shop check all components in the front end and steering system.

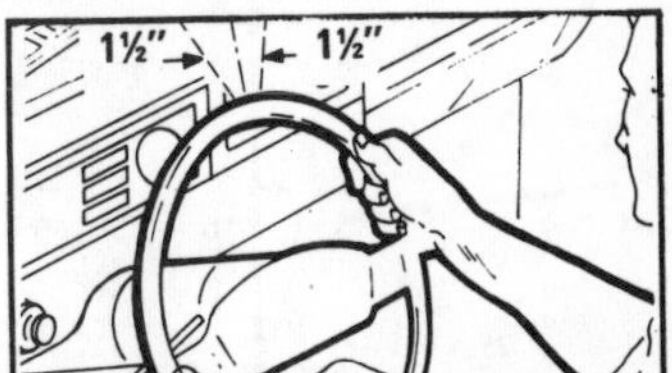

WASHER SYSTEM

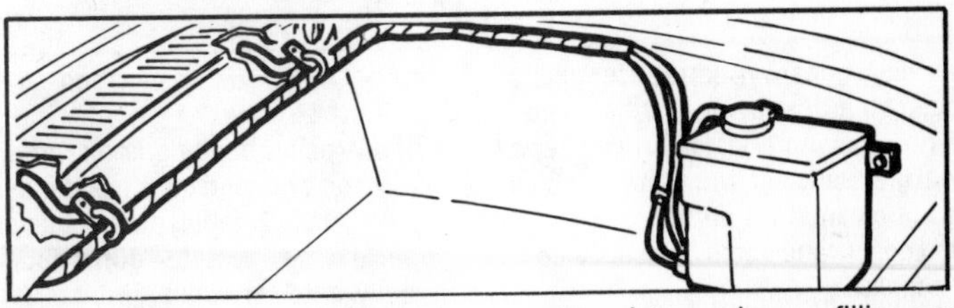

If washer fails to squirt properly raise hood and check system hose connections. Be sure washer fluid container has fluid. Check spout openings for clogging.

Keep container filled with fluid mixture of washer solvent and water. If road spray buildup on windshield is a chronic problem, add 1 tablespoon dishwasher detergent to solvent/water mixture when re-filling container.

Electrical System

CHECKPOINTS AND SERVICES

To ensure starting ability at all times check your battery condition periodically. You'll need to check battery electrolyte (fluid) level in each of the six cells. Check battery cable connections for tightness and inspect for accumulated corrosion.
SAFETY NOTE: Wear gloves when working on battery.
Some 1976 and all 1977 GM products are equipped with a new type of no maintenance battery. This battery requires no maintenance other than occasionally checking its state of charge by looking at the indicator on the top. If the indicator is dark with a green dot showing in the center, the battery is fully charged. If the indicator is dark but there is no green dot showing, the battery should be charged. If the indicator is light, the battery should be replaced.

CHECK BATTERY FLUID

1. Remove plastic filler caps on top of battery. Fluid should be up to lower end of filler hole and covering the plates. If fluid is low add clean, cold tap water. If your area has hard water, use only distilled water available at auto supply, food or drug stores.
2. Replace any lost caps immediately.

CAUTION: NEVER LIGHT A MATCH OR SMOKE near the top of a battery. Batteries give off explosive hydrogen gas.

NOTE: Battery that often checks low on fluid could mean:

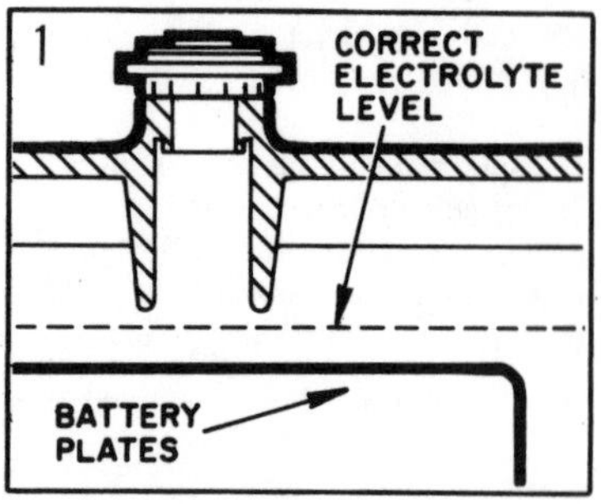

A. Battery is getting old, due for replacement; have charge capacity checked at service shop.
B. Connections may be corroded or loose; clean/replace as needed (see below).
C. Alternator or voltage regulator not functioning properly; this happens far less often than A or B, above.

CLEAN THOSE BATTERY TERMINALS

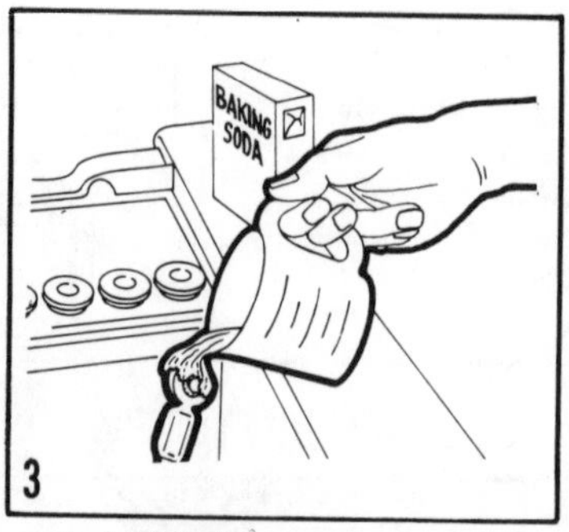

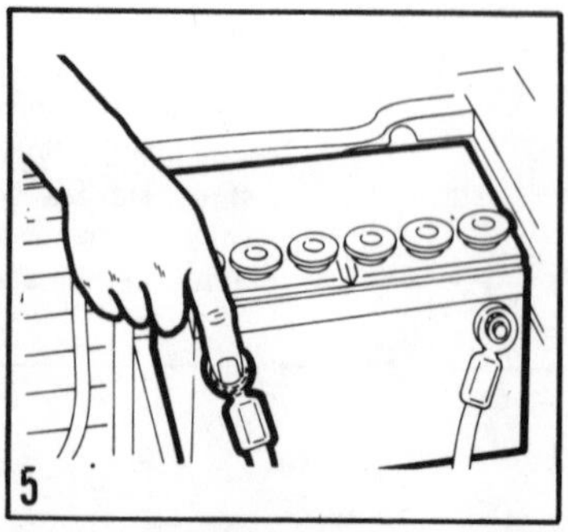

As time goes by, battery terminals build up a dry powdery, whitish material. This material is corrosive and will gradually eat thru battery cables if not cleaned off periodically.
1. Loosen and remove battery connections.
2. Brush off all loose corrosion; use stiff bristle brush. Do not get this material into eyes or on open cuts. Wash off at once.
3. If corrosion build-up is extremely heavy and brushing does not remove all of it, mix 2 tablespoons baking soda to 1 cup water. Pour solution directly onto terminals and connectors. Allow to soak a few minutes and rinse off. Continue brushing to remove all traces of corrosion build-up. Do not allow cleaning solution to enter battery.

4. Replace connectors on battery terminal posts and tighten.
5. Liberally smear battery terminal posts and cable connectors with petroleum jelly.

REPLACE FAULTY BATTERY CABLES

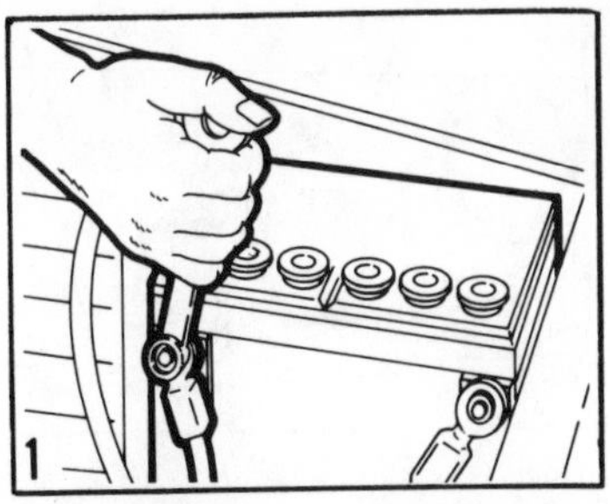

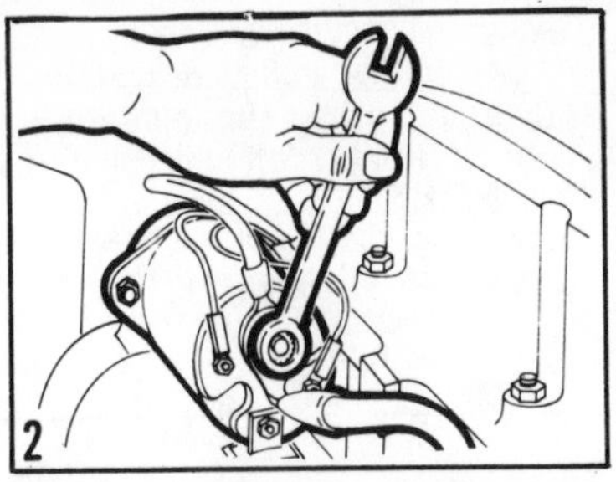

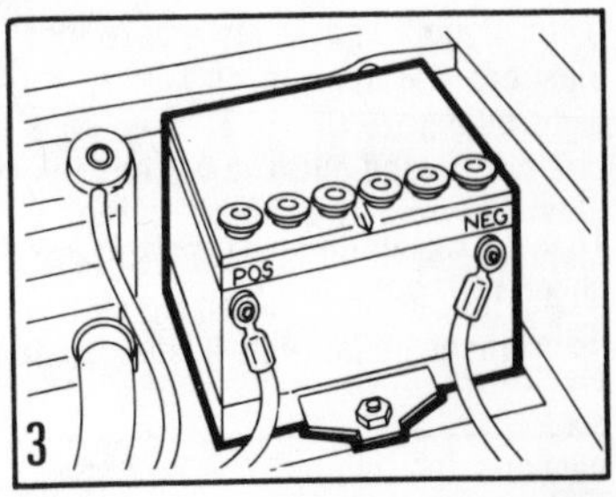

If battery cable strands become frayed, broken or corroded, replace cable immediately. Delay in correcting this condition could lead to sudden failure to start the engine. Can also weaken battery.

1. Loosen and remove battery connections. Clean OFF any corrosion.
2. Disconnect negative cable from its attachment to engine or chassis. Disconnect positive cable from its attachment to starter relay.
3. Attach new cables making sure positive and negative cables are on proper terminals. They are not identical.
4. Replace connectors on battery terminal posts and tighten.
5. Liberally smear battery terminal posts and cable connectors with petroleum jelly.

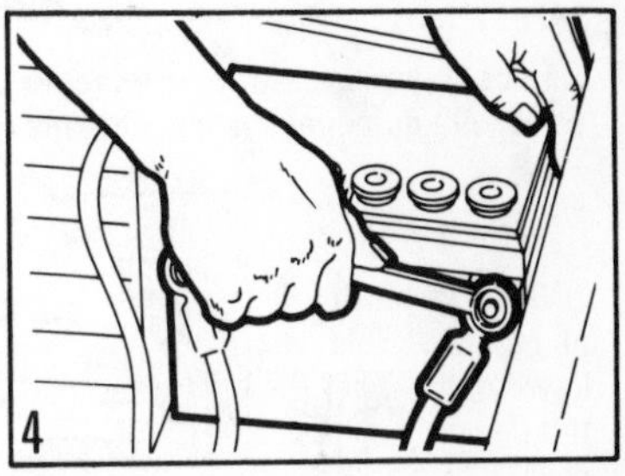

BATTERY HOLDDOWN

The clamp device which holds battery in place should be checked periodically. If loose, tighten. Clean off corrosion buildup. Severely corroded holddown components should be replaced before they break.

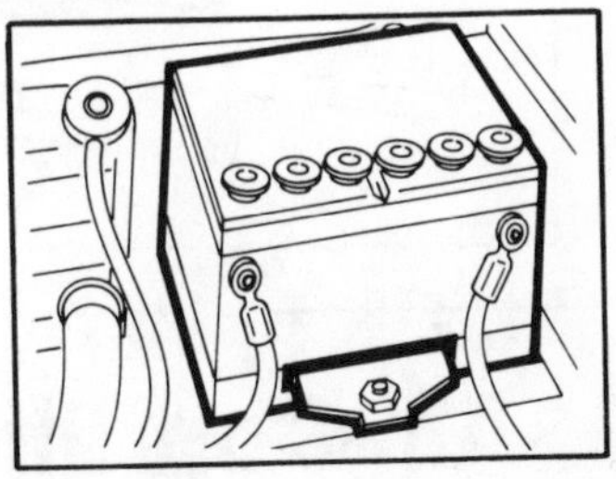

ELECTRICAL FUSES

The fuse box is located to the left of the steering column, directly over the dimmer switch. Each fuse is clearly marked as to function and correct amperage. Always replace fuse with one of same amperage. If fuses are always blowing, have checked by professional mechanic.

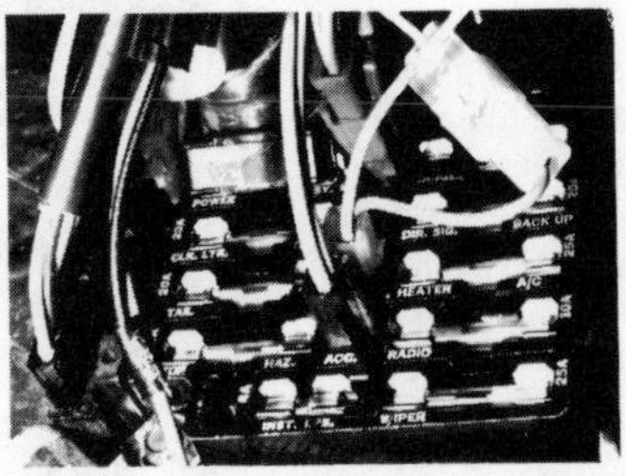

ALTERNATOR

If Alt. warning light glows red at operating speed, alternator isn't charging battery properly. Common causes are:

A. Fan belts are loose and slipping on alternator pulley. Tighten or replace belts.

B. Battery terminals, cables are loose or corroded. Clean; tighten; replace bad cables.

If A or B do not correct problem, alternator or voltage regulator may be faulty. This happens far less often, and can only be checked by mechanic with proper electrical testing equipment.

Alternator Caution: Alternator can be permanently damaged by short-circuiting terminal connections. When working around or moving alternator, always keep metal tools or engine parts from terminals.

TURN SIGNAL AND 4-WAY FLASHER

Turn signals and 4-way emergency flashers will operate only if: A. All light bulbs are OK. B. Flasher units are not burned out. The car has two flasher units that work independently of each other. TURN SIGNAL FLASHER: located behind left side of instrument panel. Pull flasher from spring clip mounting. Unplug from connector. Plug in new flasher. Replace in spring clip mounting. EMERGENCY FLASHER: located in fuse block. Simply unplug and insert new flasher. REPLACE ONLY WITH SAME TYPE FLASHER.

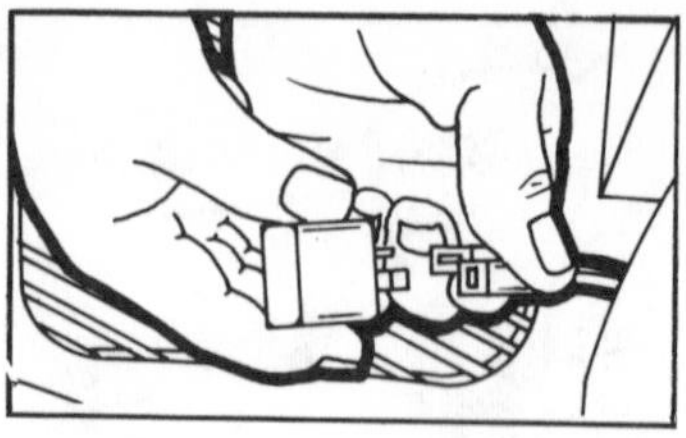

REAR WINDOW DEFOGGER SYSTEM

Do not clean inside of rear window fitted with defogger system with any abrasive material. This could destroy carbon-copper wires. Use only soft rag and mild detergent/water mixture. Dry carefully.

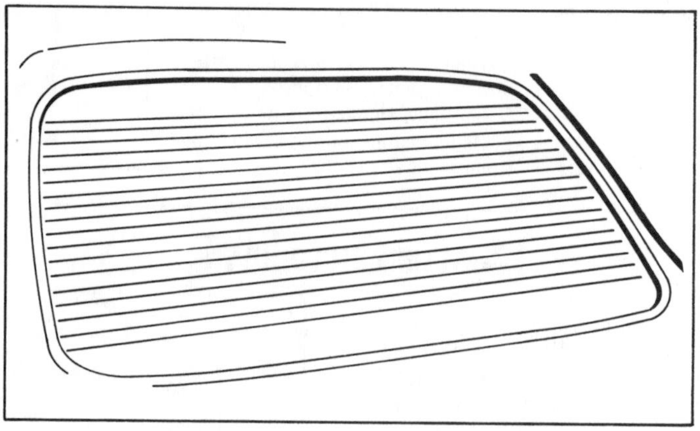

Air Conditioning System

WARNING!—Never attempt to tighten fittings, disassemble or do any work on your car's A/C system. Consult a professional mechanic about A/C system problems and their correction. Your auto air conditioner (A/C) is a delicate, closed system. If air, dirt or water get into it, or if refrigerant escapes, the A/C unit will not cool a car interior. Among things you can do are:

1. Keep condenser grille clean. Check for dirt and debris; periodically remove dead insects, leaves, etc., with stiff bristle brush. Straighten any bent fins—carefully.
2. Keep radiator filled to correct level. (See Cooling System section). If fluid needs to be added, add antifreeze rather than water.
3. Keep radiator coolant at a 50/50 water/antifreeze mixture.
4. Flush cooling system and replace with fresh coolant mixture at least every 24 months. (See Cooling System section).

5. Radiator cap should be tight and sealed properly. If sealing gasket is cracked, cut or worn, replace cap with new 15 lb. unit.
6. Check fan belt tension periodically. (See Cooling System section). Replace glazed, frayed or cut fan belts, before they fail entirely.
7. Check periodically for bubbles in A/C sight glass. Sight glass is located in head of receiver/drier vessel. Or on the side of the V.I.R. assembly. Sight glass is no larger than head of large nail. It may be dirty. Wipe clean for best visibility.

PROCEED AS FOLLOWS:

a) With engine and A/C system running, look for passage of refrigerant in sight glass. You'll be looking for a stream of milky white bubbles as they pass through sight glass. It is

best to watch sight glass and have someone else start the car and turn on the A/C system. Allow to run for a few minutes.
b) If you observe no bubbles, and air flow from A/C unit in the car is passing cold air, everything is OK.
c) If no bubbles appear in sight glass, and air flow from the A/C unit in the car is not delivering cold air, the system may be low on refrigerant and could need a re-charge.
d) If bubbles appear, system is low on refrigerant.
e) If you suspect refrigerant loss based on tests performed above, have system checked by a professional A/C service shop. They can confirm refrigerant loss, recharge the system and check for system leakage.

NOTE: Once a week or so, even in winter, run A/C system for about 5 minutes as you drive. This keeps system internally lubricated, prevents hoses hardening.

TUNE-UP SPECIFICATIONS

YEAR	ENGINE No. Cyl. Displacement (cu. in.)	SPARK PLUGS Type	SPARK PLUGS Gap (in.)	DISTRIBUTOR Point Dwell (deg.)	DISTRIBUTOR Point Gap (in.)	IGNITION TIMING Man. Trans.● (deg.)■	IGNITION TIMING Auto Trans.● (deg.)■	IDLE SPEED Man. Trans.● (rpm)▲	IDLE SPEED Auto Trans. (rpm)▲
1970	6-250	R46T	.035	32	.019	TDC	4B	750①	600①
	8-350	R45TS	.030	30	.016	6B	6B	700	600
	8-455	R-44TS	.030	30	.016	6B②	6B②	700	600
1971	6-250	R46T	.035	32	.019	4B	4B	550	600
	8-350	R45TS	.030	30	.016	6B	10B③	800	600
	8-455	R45TS	.030	30	.016	6B②	6B②	700	600
1972	8-350	R45TS	.040	30	.016	4B	4B	800④	650④
	8-455	R45TS	.040	30	.016	4B⑤	4B⑤	900④	650④
1973	8-350	R45TS	.040	30	.016	4B	4B	800④	650④
	8-455	R45TS	.040	30	.016	4B⑤	4B⑤	900④	650④
1974	6-250	R46T	.035	32	.019	8B	6B	950⑥	600
	8-350	R45TS	.040	30	.016	—	4B	—	650④
	8-455	R45TS	.040	30	.016	—	4B	—	650④
1975	V6-231	R44SX	.060	Electronic		12B	12B	800	600
	6-250	R46TX	.060	Electronic		10B	10B	800	600
	8-260	R46SX	.060	Electronic		—	⑦	—	600
	8-350	R45SX	.060	Electronic		—	12B	—	600
1976	V6-231	R44SX	.060	Electronic		12B	12B	600⑧	600
	8-260	R46SX	.060	Electronic		—	18B⑩	—	550⑨
	8-350	R45SX	.060	Electronic		—	12B	—	600
1977	6-231								
	8-350 2 bbl			See Underhood Specifications Sticker					
	8-350 4 bbl								

▲ Adjust automatic transmissions in Drive (AMC/Ford/GM) or Neutral (Chrysler), all manual transmissions are adjusted in Neutral.
■ All figures are Before Top Dead Center.
● Figure in parentheses indicate California engine.

NOTE: The underhood specifications sticker often reflects tune-up specification changes made in production. Sticker figures must be used if they disagree with those in the chart.

① 400—Solenoid disconnected
② 10°B—Stage 1 engine
③ 6° B—4 bbl engine
④ 600—M.T.; 500—A.T. with the solenoid disconnected
⑤ 8°B—M.T.; 10° B—A.T. Stage 1 engine
⑥ 450—Solenoid disconnected
⑦ See engine service decal
⑧ 800—Solenoid connected
⑨ 650—Solenoid connected
⑩ 14°—California engines

CAPACITIES

YEAR	ENGINE No. Cyl. Displacement (cu. in.)	ENGINE OIL Add 1 qt. with New Filter	TRANSMISSION Pts. to Refill after Draining MANUAL 3-speed	4-speed	AUTOMATIC	DRIVE AXLE (pts.)	COOLING SYSTEM with Heater (qts.)	with Air Cond. (qts.)
1970	6-250	4	3.4	—	6 ②	3	16	16
	8-350	4	3.4	—	6 ②	3	16.5	16.5
	8-350GS	4	3.5	3	7 ②	3	16.5	16.5
	8-455	4	3.5	3	7②	4.25	19.2	19.7
1971	6-250	4	3.4	—	6②	4.25	16	16
	8-350	4	3.4	—	6②	4.25	16.5	16.5
	8-350GS	4	3.4	3	6②	4.25	16.5	16.5
	6-455	4	—	3	7②	5.5	19.2	19.7
1972	8-350	4	3.4	—	6②	4.25	16.5	16.9
	8-350GS	4	3.4	3	6②	4.25	16.2	16.6
	8-455	4	—	3	7②	5.5	19.2	19.7
1973	8-350	4	3.4	—	6②	4.25	16.5	16.9
	8-350GS	4	3.4	3.4	6②	4.25	16.5	16.9
	8-455	4	3.4	3.4	6②	4.25	16.2	16.6
1974	6-250	4	3.5	—	6②	4.25	14.0	16.0
	8-350	4	—	—	6②	4.25	16.5	16.9
	8-455	4	—	—	6②	4.25	16.2	16.6
1975	V6-231	4	3.5	—	6②	4.25	15.35	15.32
	6-250	4	3.5	—	6②	4.25	16.92	17.0
	8-260	4	—	—	6②	4.25	18.9	19.3
	8-350	4	—	—	6②	4.25	16.88	17.16
1976-77	V6-231	4	3.12	—	6②	4.25	15.35	16.32
	8-260	4	—	①	6②	4.25	18.9	19.3
	8-350	4	3.12	—	6②	4.25	16.88	17.16

GS Gran Sport
— Not applicable
① 5 spd—3.5 pts. of Dexron® II
② Specs. do not include torque converter

Valiant/Dart/Aspen/Volare

Lubrication and Oil Change

BRAKE FLUID LEVEL CHECK

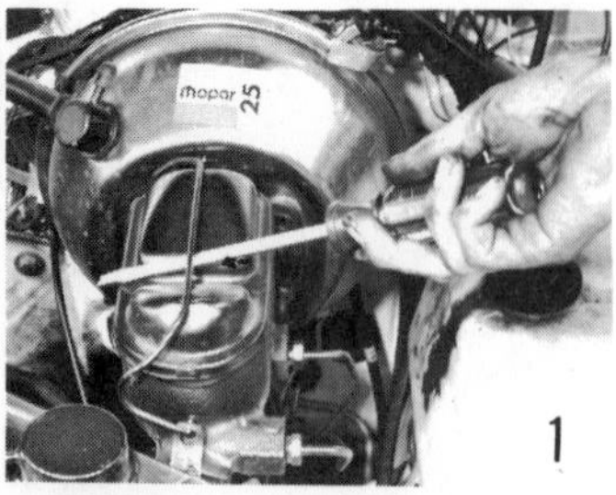

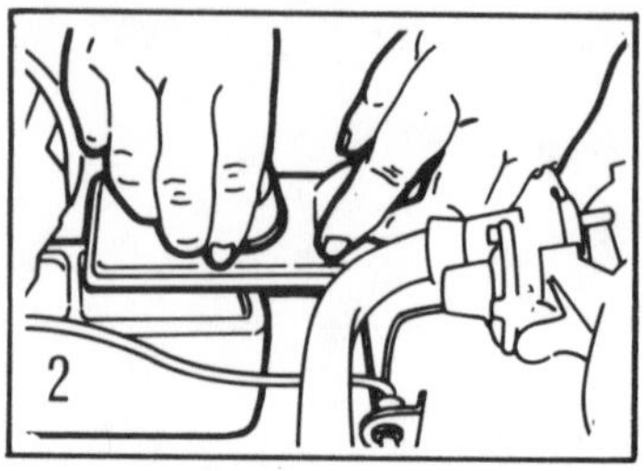

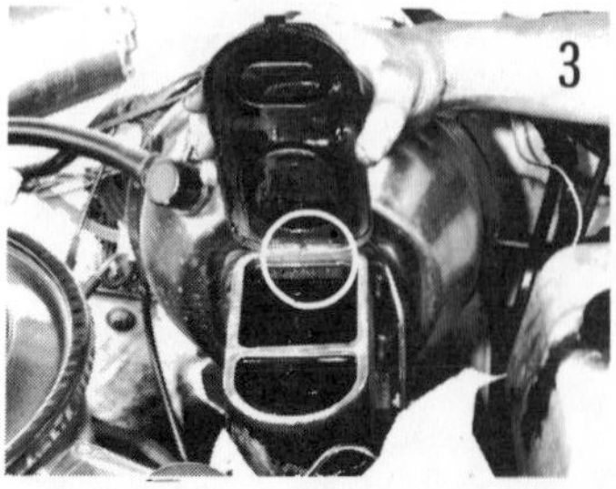

Check brake fluid level in master cylinder every six months . . . sooner if braking feels inadequate. Add when low. Recommended grade: Extra Heavy Duty; Grade 70R3 as printed on can (check owner's handbook). Master cylinder is located under hood on left side. It is oblong container about 6" long with cap held down by wire clip. Check brake fluid level as follows:

1. Pry wire retaining clip off cap top with screwdriver.

2. Remove cap and gasket by lifting up.

3. Fluid level should be within ¼ inch of top rim. If lower than this, add fresh fluid to appropriate level. DO NOT OVERFILL

4. Replace cap and gasket; secure retaining clip over cap. If fluid level was low, check again in a few days.

5. If fluid repeatedly checks low, there is a leak somewhere in the system. See SAFETY SYSTEMS—WHEEL CYLINDER CHECK. Have mechanic check further. Neglect can be dangerous.

NOTE: On cars with front disc brakes, it is normal for the fluid level to drop slightly as the brake pads wear down.

MANUAL TRANSMISSION FLUID LEVEL CHECK

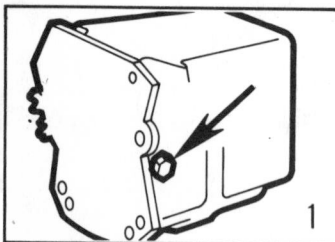

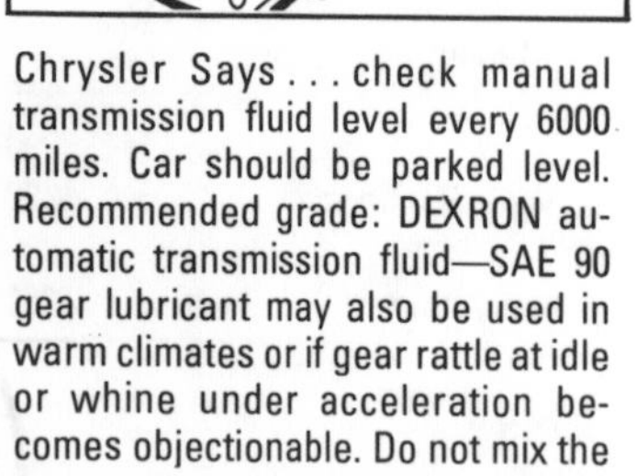

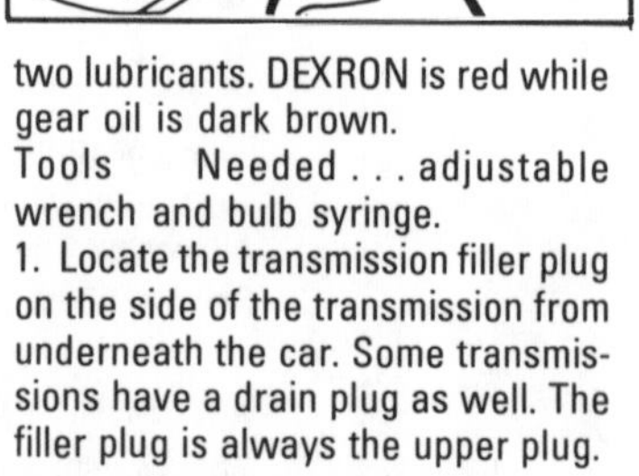

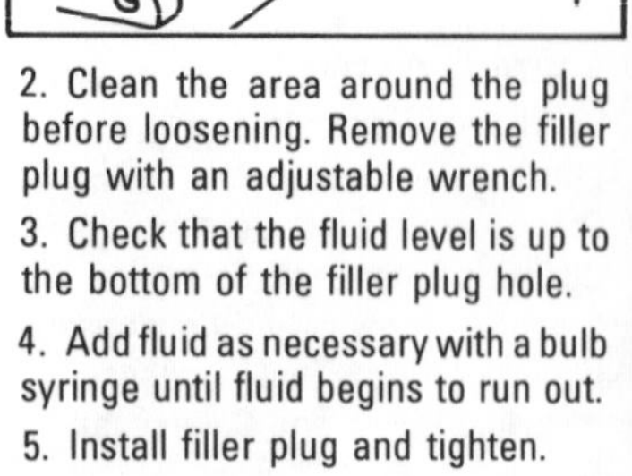

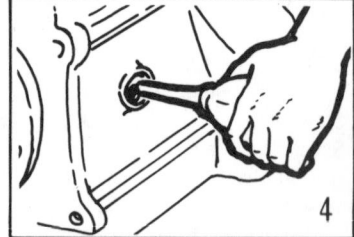

Chrysler Says . . . check manual transmission fluid level every 6000 miles. Car should be parked level. Recommended grade: DEXRON automatic transmission fluid—SAE 90 gear lubricant may also be used in warm climates or if gear rattle at idle or whine under acceleration becomes objectionable. Do not mix the two lubricants. DEXRON is red while gear oil is dark brown.

Tools Needed . . . adjustable wrench and bulb syringe.

1. Locate the transmission filler plug on the side of the transmission from underneath the car. Some transmissions have a drain plug as well. The filler plug is always the upper plug.

2. Clean the area around the plug before loosening. Remove the filler plug with an adjustable wrench.

3. Check that the fluid level is up to the bottom of the filler plug hole.

4. Add fluid as necessary with a bulb syringe until fluid begins to run out.

5. Install filler plug and tighten.

AUTOMATIC TRANSMISSION FLUID LEVEL CHECK

Chrysler Says . . . check automatic transmission fluid (ATF) level every 6000 miles. Recommended grade: DEXRON ATF

Tools . . . Long neck filler funnel

1. Engine must be warmed up and idling. Park car on level ground. With brake applied, shift selector lever through all gear positions, ending in Neutral.

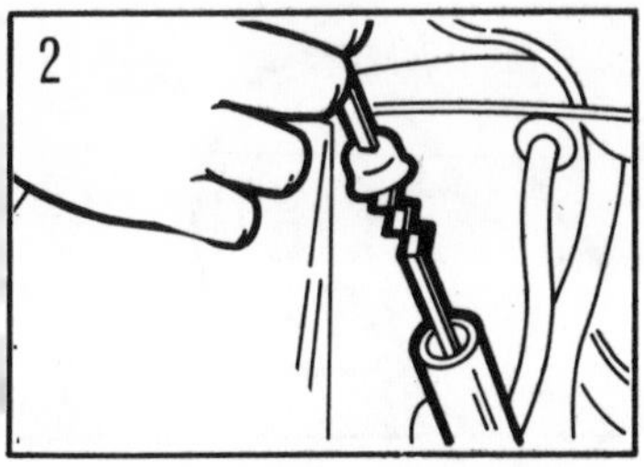

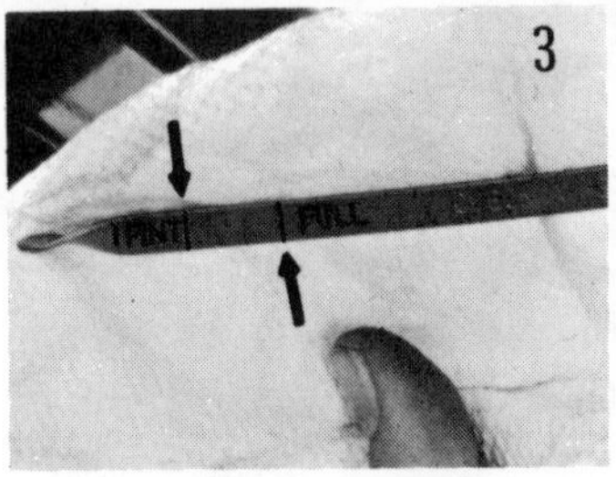

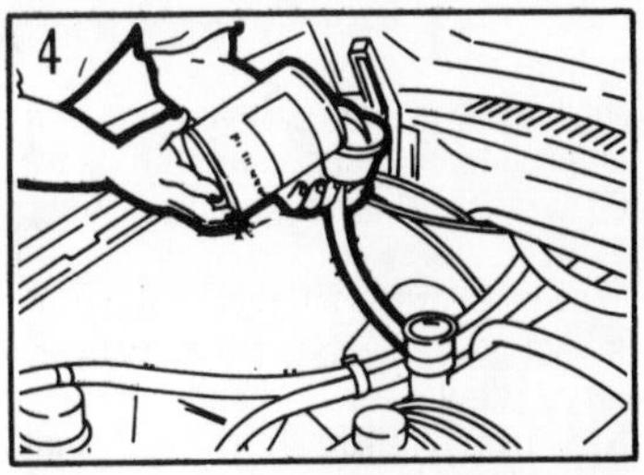

2. Pull out dipstick, located at rear of engine compartment on right side. Wipe it clean and push it all the way back in. Remove it again and check reading.

3. If fluid is below F (full) mark, add DEXRON slowly to bring level up. Add fluid slowly, frequently checking the level. Do not overfill as the transmission may overheat, and have to be drained at a service station.

4. Add ATF through transmission dipstick hole using a long-neck filler funnel.

REAR AXLE LUBRICANT

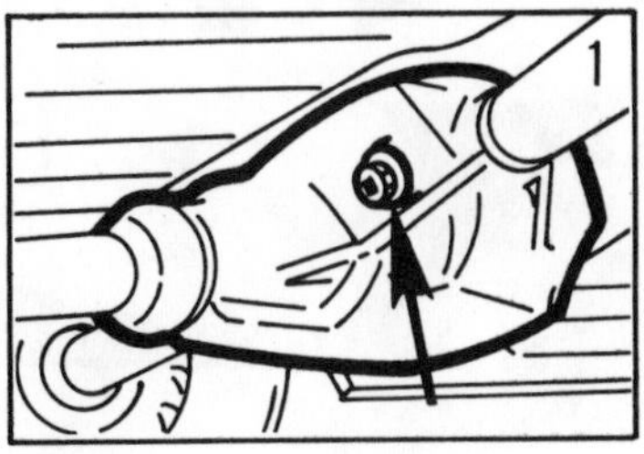

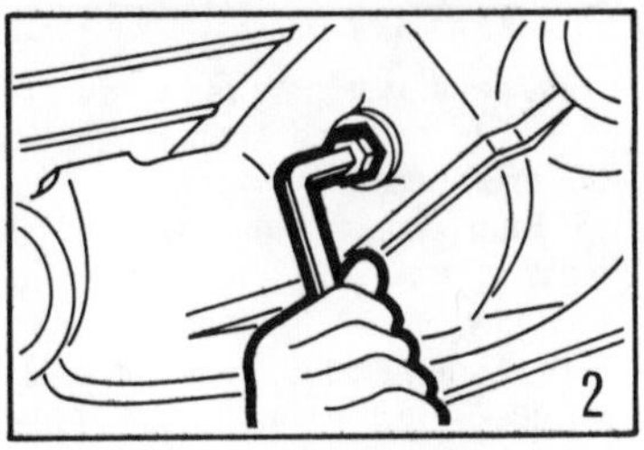

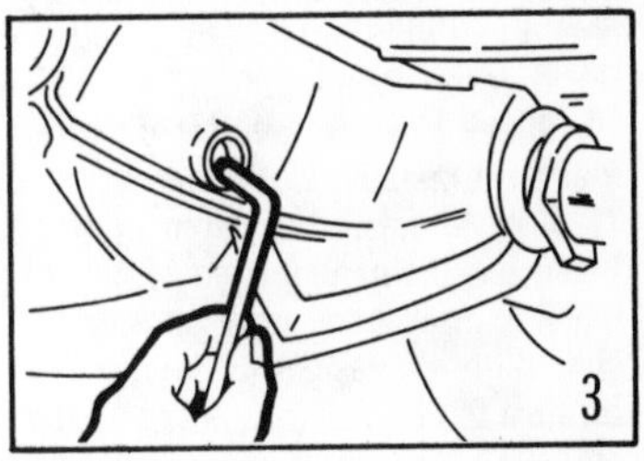

CHRYSLER SAYS . . . check rear axle lube level every 6000 miles. Recommended grade: Hypoid gear lube (SAE 90). Cars with limited slip differential require special fluid.

TOOLS . . . adjustable hand wrench; fluid level check device (made from coat hanger wire; bend at 90° angle 2" from end); bulb syringe.

1. Locate filler plug on forward side of rear axle housing, or on cover plate.

2. Wipe plug area clean; remove plug with wrench.

3. Insert wire level check device; remove. Adequate fluid level should show lubricant to last ⅛-inch of wire, before bend.

4. If fluid level is low, add as needed, with a hand bulb syringe, until level shows to last ⅛-inch of wire, before bend.

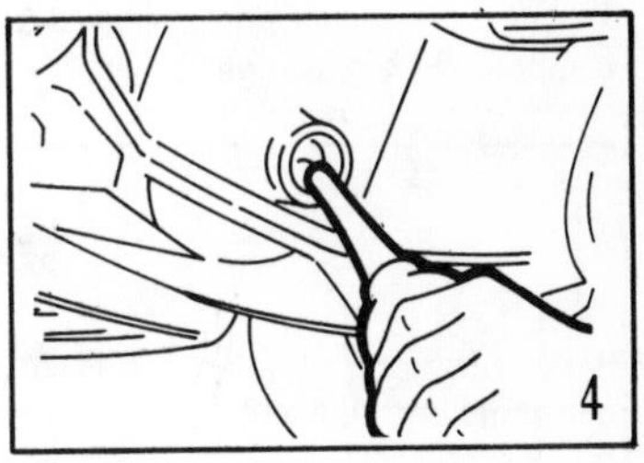

5. Replace filler plug; tighten.

OIL AND FILTER CHANGE

Chrysler Says . . . change oil every 3000 miles (1970-74 models) or 6000 miles (1975-77 models); change filter every 6000 miles. Recommended grade: SE. Check oil level on dipstick (engine off) at least once a week.

Tools and Materials . . . adjustable wrench; oil filter strap wrench; drain pan for old oil (at least 5 qt. capacity); oil pour spout; 4 qt. oil (5 qt. if changing filter); new oil filter.

Safety tip . . . use work gloves.

1. If engine is cold, start up and idle for about 5 minutes.

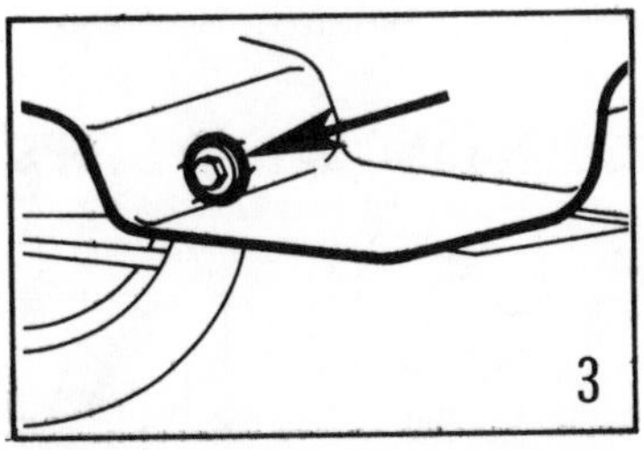

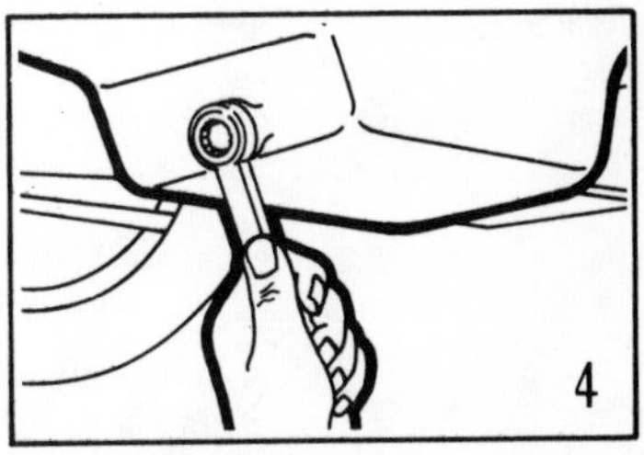

2. Park car on level ground. Turn engine off.

3. Locate oil drain plug on underside of engine. Place drain pan under plug.

4. Remove drain plug with wrench. Let ALL dirty oil drain out.

5. Wipe plug and area around drain

hole clean. Replace drain plug; tighten it.

6. Locate oil filter. Move drain pan under filter. Loosen filter with oil filter wrench. Unscrew; remove filter by hand.

7. Smear fresh oil over surface of rubber gasket (washer) of new filter. Install new filter by hand only. Do NOT use wrench. Turn filter until gasket makes contact. Tighten an additional half turn only . . . NO MORE.

8. Locate oil filler on top of engine valve cover. Remove cap.

9. Punch oil pouring spout into top of oil can. Pour all cans of new oil into filler tube. Wipe filler cap clean and replace it. Be sure to re-attach all hoses. (NOTE: If filler cap is very dirty, rinse in turpentine or gasoline. Dry before replacing.)

10. Check new oil level at dipstick. Pull out dipstick, wipe clean.

11. Push dipstick back into engine. Be sure to insert all the way. Remove dipstick and check new oil level. It should be above "SAFE" line. If not, be sure to check if you put in all the oil called for.

12. Start up engine and idle for 3-5 minutes. Oil signal light on instrument panel will glow red when engine is first started. Light should go out in 30 seconds or less.

13. Stop engine and check for oil leaks at drain plug and filter. If you find any, check tightness of plug and/or filter, also for condition of filter gasket to see that it has not become pinched or damaged when installing. Recheck oil level, which should now be at "SAFE".

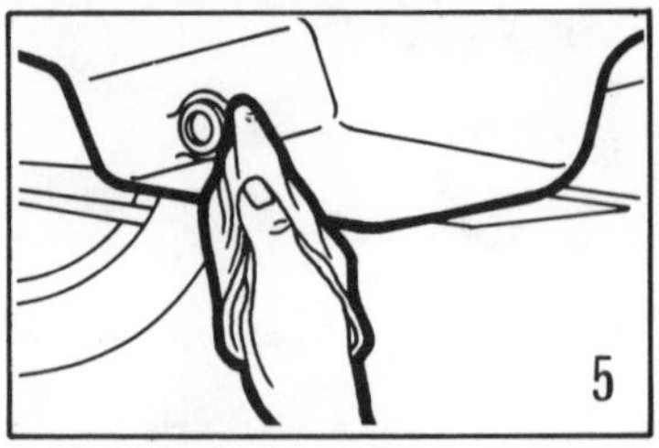

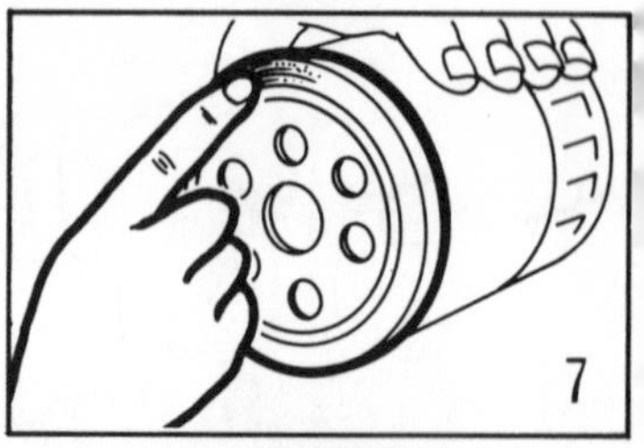

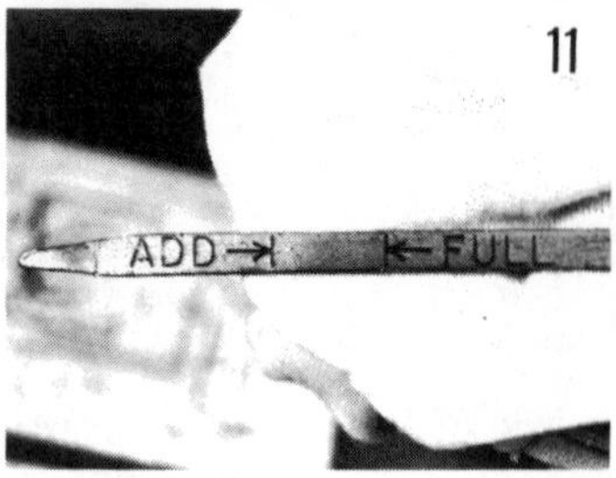

SPEEDOMETER CABLE LUBRICATION

If speedometer pointer tends to quiver or jump, or if unit makes a low, rasping or clicking sound, graphite lubrication may be needed.

1. Locate cable shaft attachment directly behind speedometer dial.

2. The cable shaft attachment will vary from year to year. On most models, there is a plastic tang on the cable which engages a slot at the rear of the speedometer. Lift this up to disengage. On some other models, the cable is attached with a "C"-clip. Slide this clip sideways to disengage.

3. Pull inner cable completely out of inner casing. Note carefully which end is top. Check for wear or frayed ends. If damaged, replace inner cable with new one.

4. Apply generous amount of speedometer cable lubricant into cable casing. Replace inner cable in shaft, noting that bottom end is inserted first. Turn inner cable as it is being reinserted. Twist cable when all the way in, to lock into position at lower end.

5. Reconnect cable to speedometer head under instrument panel.

DOOR HINGES AND STOPS

(lubricate every 6 months)

1. Brush any dirt accumulations from door hinges and stops. Use old tooth brush or rag.

2. Apply dab of white polyethylene grease to door hinges, trunk hinges, hood hinges, door stops.

DOOR LOCKS

(lubricate every 6 months)
1. Insert door key half way into lock.
2. Spray aerosol lock lubricant into lock.
3. Push key rest of way into lock; turn back and forth several times.

Cooling System

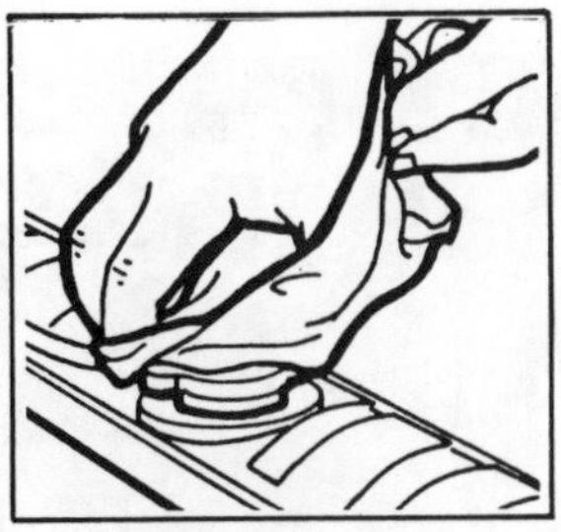

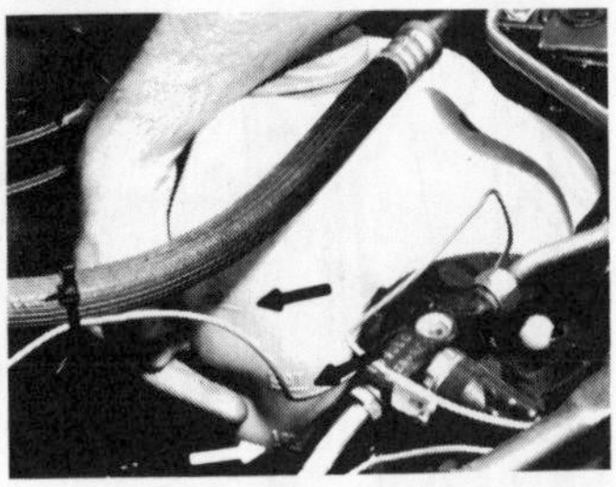

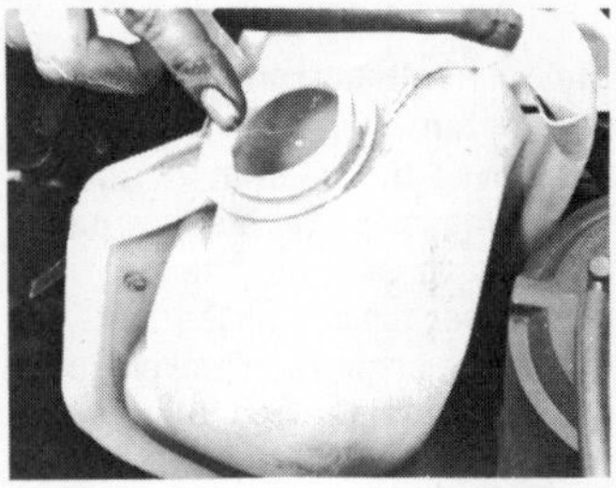

IT IS RECOMMENDED . . . that radiator coolant (water/antifreeze mixture) level be checked once or twice a month. Do this when engine is cold. Check more often if you do a lot of hard driving.
Keep coolant up to recommended level in radiator. If coolant checks frequently low, look for leaks.

Tighten all hose clamps occasionally. For best results, keep a 50/50 water/antifreeze mixture year round. Change complete coolant mixture every 24 months.

CAUTION: If you must check coolant in a hot engine, cover radiator cap with thick rag before releasing. Remove cap slowly . . . press down and turn.
On cars equipped with a coolant recovery system, simply check the level visible through the translucent reservoir on the right side of the radiator. If it is necessary to add coolant, add to the reservoir, not the radiator.

REPLACING THE THERMOSTAT

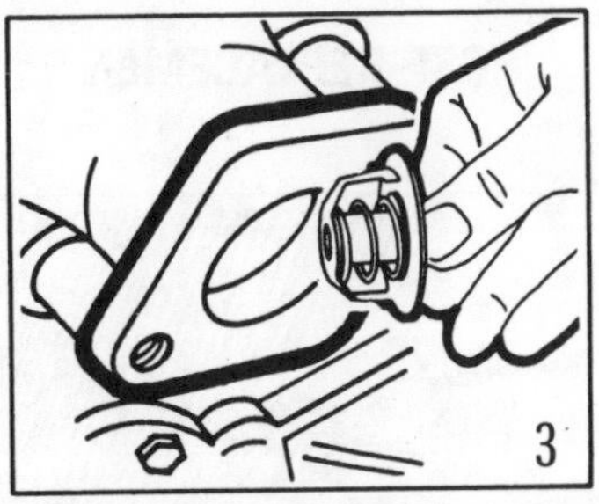

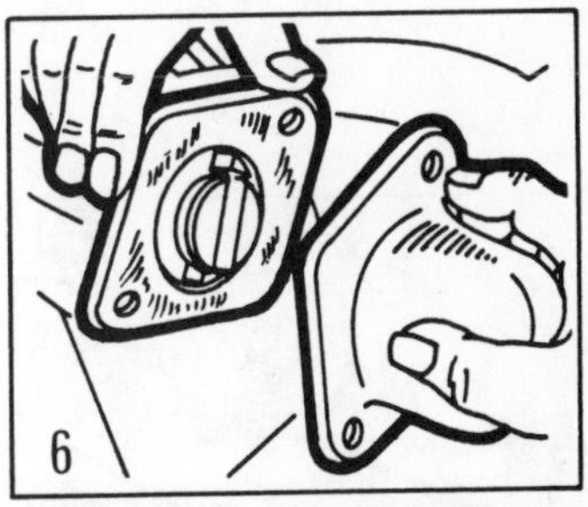

A faulty thermostat will usually cause engine overheating. Replace with new thermostat.

TOOLS AND MATERIALS . . .
New thermostat
Gasket sealer
Adjustable wrench

1. Drain radiator of about half its coolant. (See Hose Replacement section)
2. Loosen and remove both retaining bolts and lift thermostat housing off the engine.
NOTE: If you're careful it won't be necessary to remove radiator hose.
3. Remove old thermostat.
4. Scrape thermostat housing flange and engine block surface to remove old gasket debris.
5. Drop new thermostat into place—spring down (toward engine).
6. Install new gasket with sealer applied to both sides.
7. Replace thermostat housing and tighten both retaining bolts.

RADIATOR CAP CHECK (Only when engine is cold)

Check radiator cap occasionally for worn or cracked gasket. If cap doesn't seal properly, fluid will be lost and engine will overheat.
Replace worn cap with new cap rated 13 to 15 lbs. pressure. On cars with coolant recovery system, use 16 lb. cap.

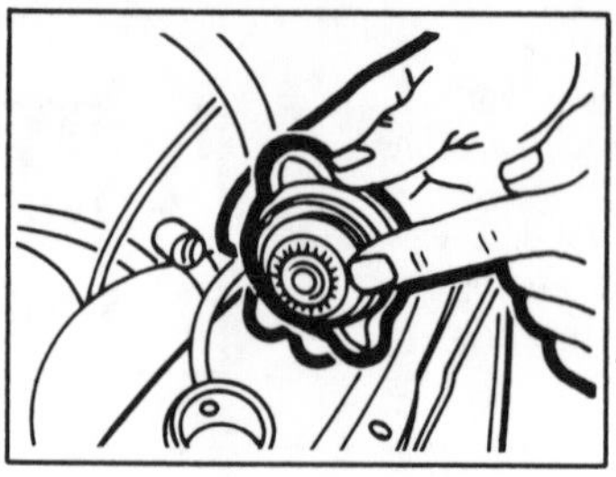

FAN BELT ADJUSTMENT

The fan belt not only drives the radiator fan, it turns the water pump and drives the alternator. Another belt drives the power steering pump. It's easy to see that the condition and proper tension of the belts are vital, since engine cooling, electrical power, and steering depend on them. The belts deserve an occasional look and tension check.

1. Inspect fan belt occasionally. If worn, frayed or cracked on inner driving surface, replace.

CAUTION: An overtightened belt may damage alternator and water pump, or power steering pump bearings.

2. Check tension occasionally. Press thumb at midpoint of belt span between pulleys. If belt depresses more than ½ inch, tightening is needed. A too-loose belt will not drive alternator and pumps effectively.

3. Adjust to proper tension of ¼ inch deflection. Adjust as follows:

A. Loosen mounting bolts at top and bottom so alternator can pivot on lower bolt and upper bolt can slide in bracket.

B. Pull alternator out slightly to put tension on belt, and hold while tightening upper bolt.

C. Check tension. Repeat adjustment as necessary.

D. When tension is correct, tighten lower bolt.

HOSE REPLACEMENT

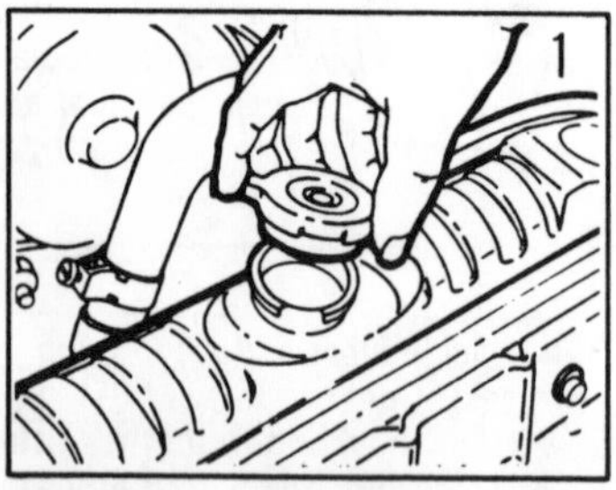

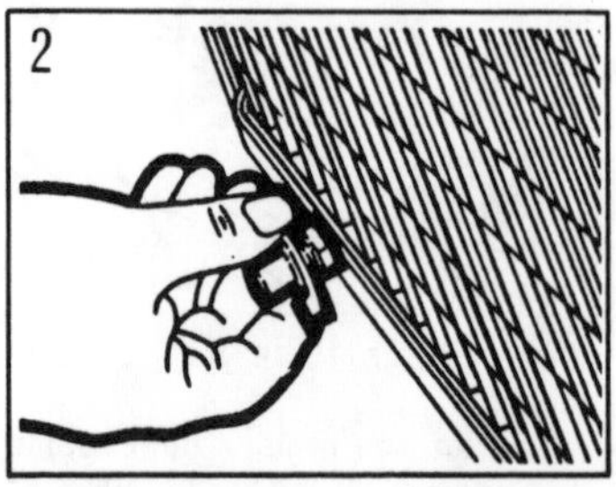

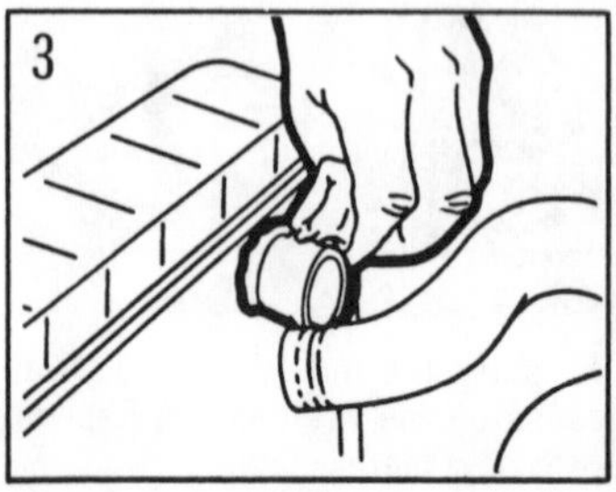

Coolant drain and refill work may be done alone; when changing hoses, coolant must also be drained as part of job. Discard all hoses with cracks or soft spots. Check hose clamps for tightness and good condition.

1. Remove radiator cap. Open radiator petcock (See 2). Drain coolant into catch basin. If near 24 months old, discard old coolant.

2. Petcock is located at the bottom of the radiator.

3. Wipe all hose connections clean. Use emery cloth to get rid of residue.

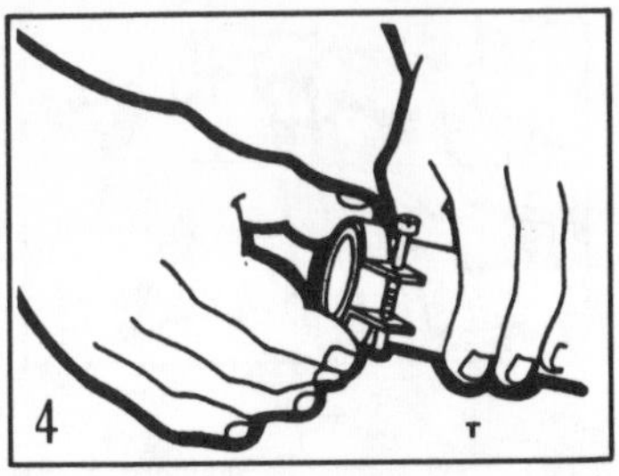

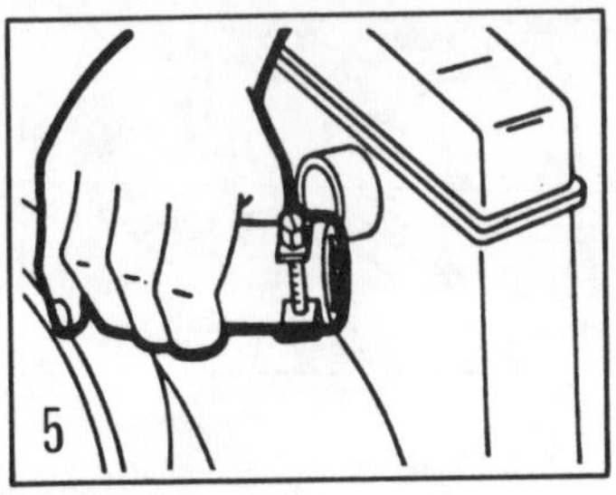

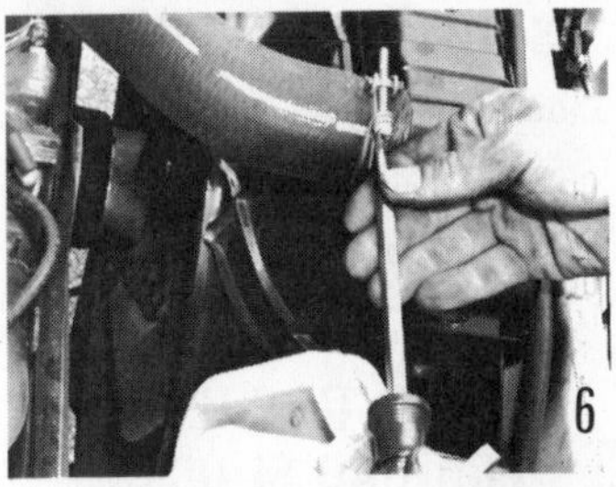

4. If old hose clamps are badly rusted or damaged, replace with new units.
5. Slip clamps over each hose end. Slip hose ends all the way onto cleaned up hose connections.
6. Place hose clamp ¼ inch from hose end. Tighten. Close petcock. Refill with 50/50 coolant/water mix.
7. Start engine; allow to warm up. Check for coolant leaks.
8. Road test car; watch temperature gauge.

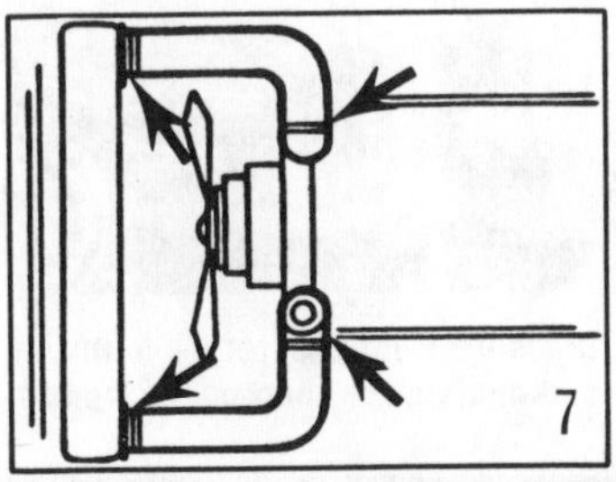

Suspension and Tires

The front wheels mount to hubs which rotate on spindles. Each spindle is attached to an upper and lower suspension ball joint, and connects to the steering linkage tie rods. Upper and lower suspension control arms link the spindles to the car's unitized body, permitting it to move up and down in relation to the wheels with a hinge effect. Each front suspension unit is sprung independently utilizing a torsion bar and shock absorber. Dart and Valiant models use a pair of longitudinal torsion bars while the Aspen and Volare use a pair of transverse torsion bars.

The rear suspension consists of multi-leaf springs suspending a solid rear axle, and a pair of telescopic shock absorbers.

HOW TO PINPOINT HANDLING PROBLEMS

Your car's suspension system consists of wheels, tires, springs, shock absorbers, sway (or stabilizer) bars, ball joints, steering linkage. If any of these items is out of adjustment or badly worn, you may notice any of these symptoms:

- car pulls to one side when braking
- car wanders when driving a straight line
- overall ride may be either hard or bouncy
- effort is needed to steer vehicle
- tires show uneven wear
- tires squeal when cornering
- front of car dips or bounces when braking
- car rocks side-to-side when going over rough road
- wheels bounce or make slapping sound on road
- steering wheel vibrates in hands
- front of car vibrates at highway speeds

Any of above symptoms indicates corrective action is needed. Delay can: ruin tires; cause damage/failure to other suspension parts; create safety hazard.

STEERING

If steering linkage, front suspension and steering column components are in good condition, there should be no more than 1½ inch free play in the steering wheel when measured at the rim of the wheel. If a loud knock is heard when turning the steering wheel from one extreme to the other, have mechanic check pinion bearing preload.

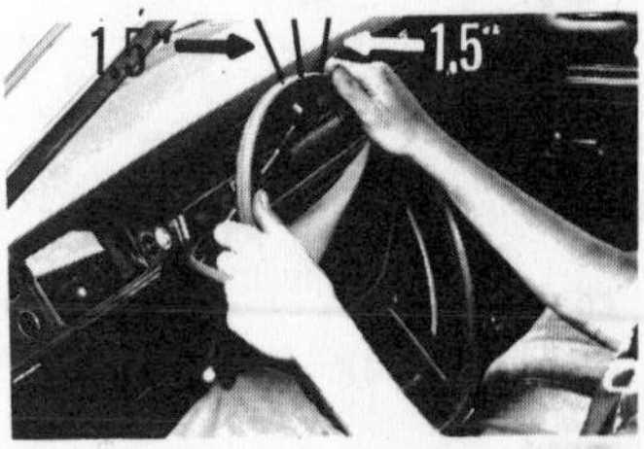

SHOCK ABSORBERS

Shock absorbers work to keep wheels in constant contact with the road. Result is safe handling and ride control; longer tire life. So shock absorbers (or shocks) are important.

HOW TO CHECK FOR BAD SHOCKS

1. Check under car and locate shock absorber near each wheel.
2. Heavy oil streaks on outer shock housing indicate need for replacement.
3. Stand at front of car and apply body weight in a pumping action to front bumper or fender. Release pressure and allow car to stop rocking. Car should not bounce more than one more time after releasing

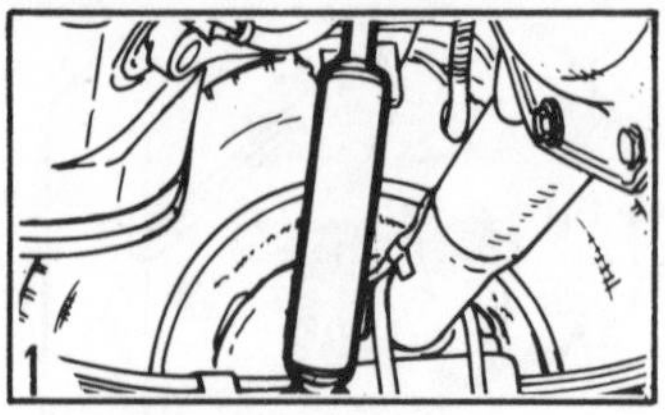

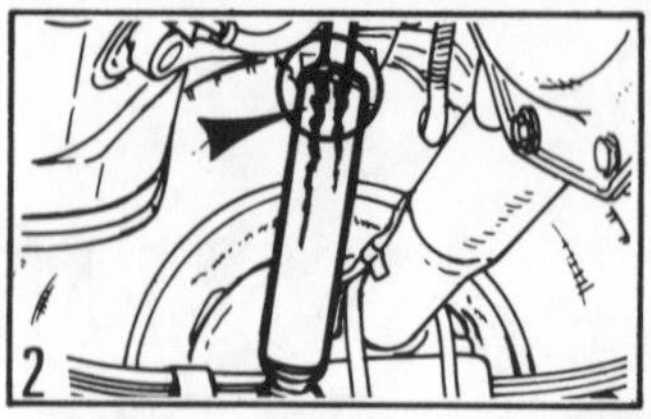

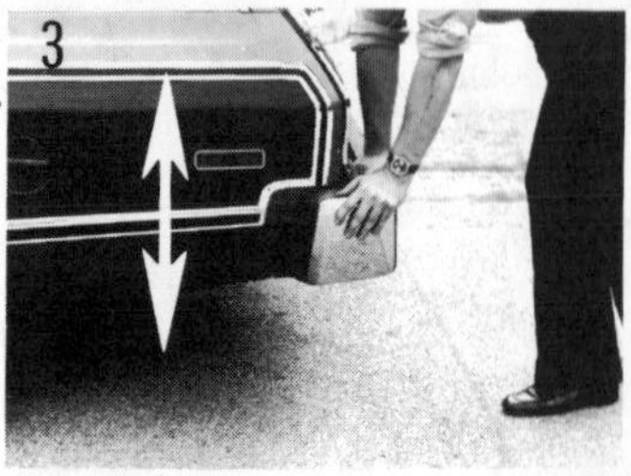

pressure. Repeat at rear. If bouncing continues more than once, replacement is needed. Replace shocks in pairs (front pair or rear pair).

TOW HITCH INFORMATION

If your car is used for trailer towing you should check:

A. Cooling System; be sure radiator is at proper level in radiator. See Cooling System Section for checks to perform.

B. Check Transmission Fluid; keep topped up to proper level.

C. Check Rear Shock Absorbers; you may benefit from installation of new rear shocks.

D. Check Tire Pressures; best traction and handling can be ensured if tire pressures are properly maintained.

For safer and more trouble-free trailer towing, consider:

A. Automatic Transmission Cooler; helps remove excess heat from automatic transmission fluid built up during towing mileage. Also helps avoid radiator overheating. Some units can be self-installed.

B. Radiator Over-Flow Tank Kit; addition of a reservoir to catch radiator coolant overflow preventing coolant loss. Easy to install, these units help a tow car run cooler, avoid overheating due to coolant loss.

C. Heavy-Duty Shock Absorbers or Air Shocks; important to have on rear wheels if you intend to do a lot of towing or load carrying within the car itself. Don't forget to consider replacing factory shocks, when they are worn out, with heavy-duty units at the front as well.

D. Variable Load Flasher; this unit will accommodate the added load of trailer turn signal lamps on trailer when these are hooked into your car's electrical system.

Ignition System

SPARK PLUG REPLACEMENT

NOTE: Number wires prior to removal

1. Plug spark plug wire by grasping rubber boot. Do not jerk wire off. If stuck, turn boot, pulling gently.

2. Loosen spark plug using socket wrench.

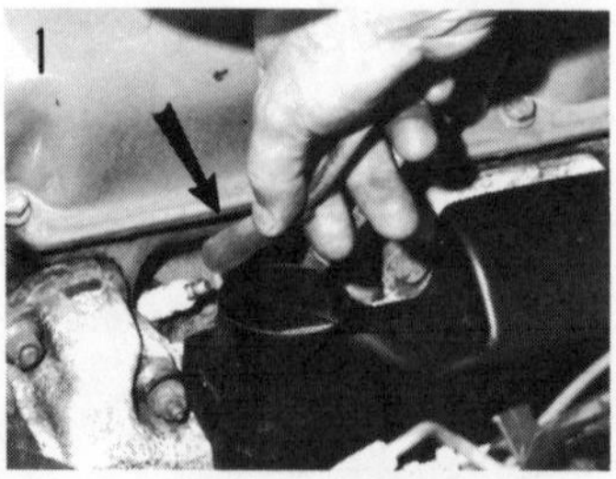

3. Wipe loose dirt from around plug before removing. Do not let dirt drop into engine through plug hole. Unscrew plug.
4. Check plug electrode gap on new spark plug. Adjust to: .035 in.
On all but the 1975-77 Slant Six, make sure that the metal gasket is installed at the top of the plug threads. This gasket is important for a good compression seal.
Plug gap is correct when the gauge drags slightly as it is pulled between plug electrodes.
5. Thread new plug into plug hole by hand. Hand tighten. Do not force or cross thread. Use socket wrench to tighten firmly but do not force. Replace plug wire. Press boot firmly.

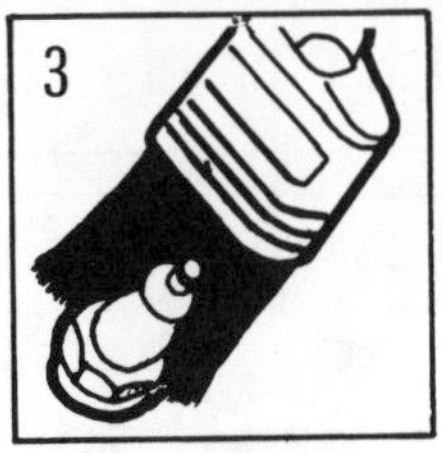

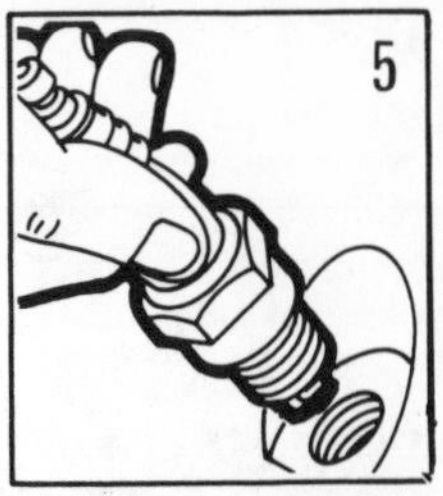

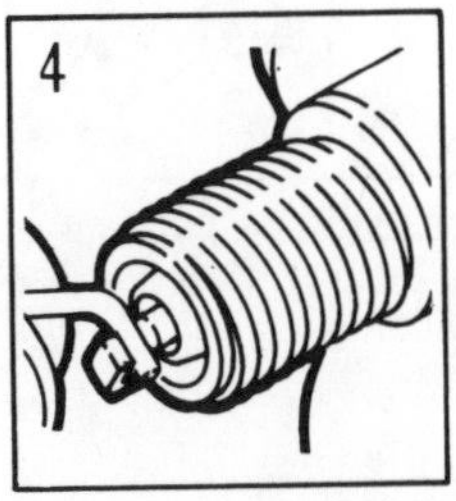

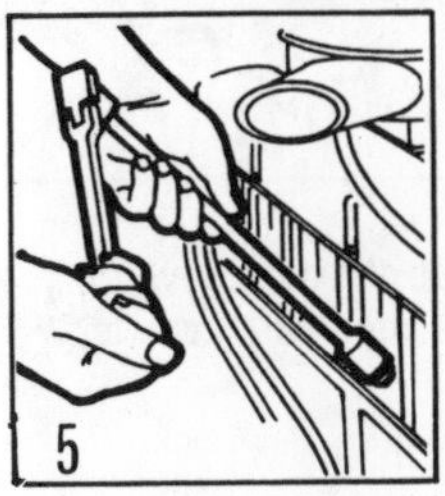

CHECKING IGNITION SYSTEM

NOTE: Beginning in 1972, electronic ignition became available as optional equipment on some models. In 1973 and later models, electronic ignition is standard. Electronic ignition eliminates the breaker points and condenser. However, it is still necessary to check the cap and rotor every 12,000 miles. And the plugs must be replaced at regular intervals too; 12,000 miles (1973-74), 15,000 miles (1975-77 models without catalytic converter), or 30,000 miles (1975-77 models with converter).

The ignition system consists of spark plugs; plug wires; distributor; rotor; points; condenser; coil. These units work to create a good hot spark inside the engine (ignition) at exactly the right moment (timing). If ignition is weak or timing is off, engine may be hard to start, run poorly, waste gas, lose power, backfire or not run at all.
CHRYSLER SAYS . . . Replace plugs

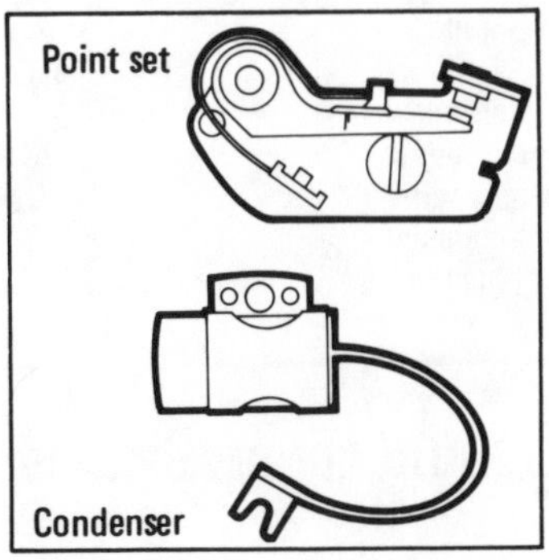

and points every 12,000 miles on 1970-72 cars.
TOOLS AND MATERIALS . . . Parts: set of points; condenser; spark plugs. Tools: gap gauge; 13/16 in. spark plug socket, (5/8 in. spark plug socket on 1975-77 sixes); screwdriver; open end, box or combination wrenches; timing equipment (see Ignition Timing).
SAFETY TIP . . . Change only one spark plug at a time to avoid

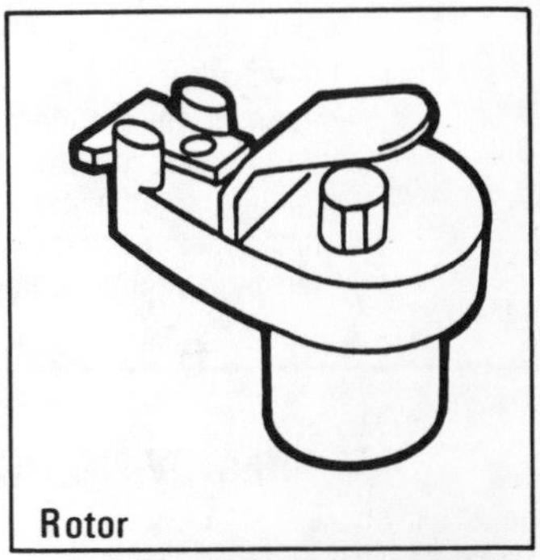

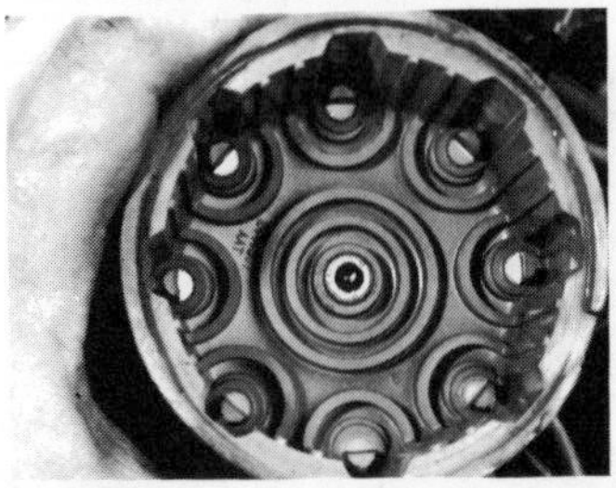

crosswiring and possible engine damage.

OTHER IGNITION CHECK POINTS

Inspect spark plug wires. If cracked or brittle, entire set should be replaced. Also, center high tension wire. Inspect distributor cap. Wipe inside clean occasionally with dry, lint-free rag. If cap is cracked or rotor contacts are excessively burned, replace cap.

CHECKING POINTS AND ROTOR

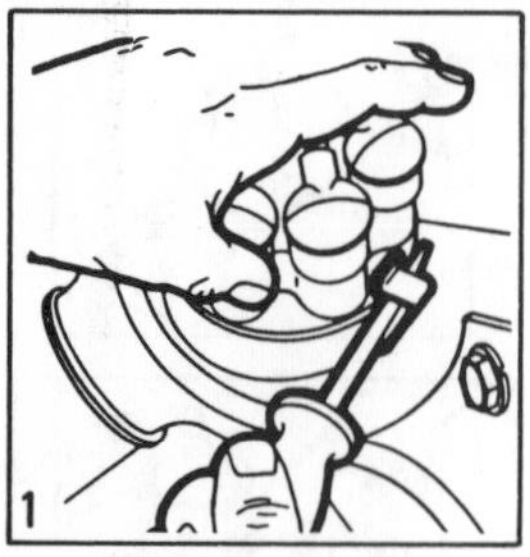

1. To open distributor, snap retaining clips off with screwdriver, lift cap off but keep wires connected.

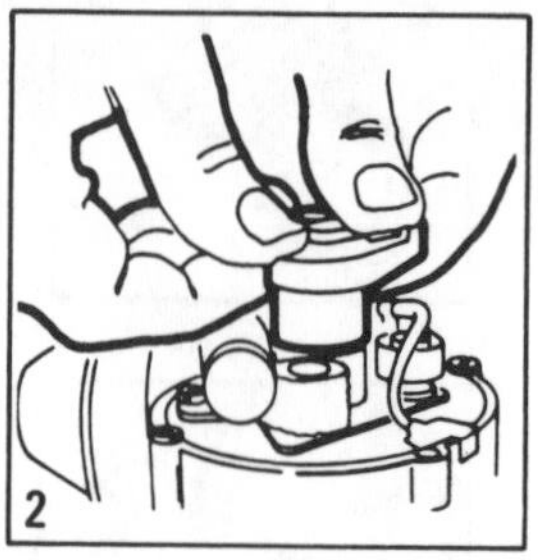

2. Pull rotor off (straight up). Replace if cracked or metallic tip is badly burned.

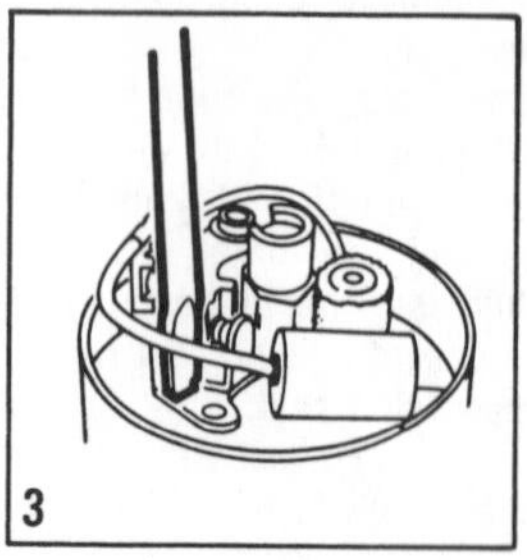

3. On 1970-72 models, pry points apart with screwdriver. If worn or burned, replace. If OK, check point gap.

LOCATION OF POINTS AND CONDENSER—1970-72 Models Only

Points and condenser work together. Always replace condenser also when installing new points.
If your car has electronic ignition, periodic replacement of distributor parts is not required. If you suspect ignition trouble because of engine misfire, have the distributor checked out by a professional mechanic.

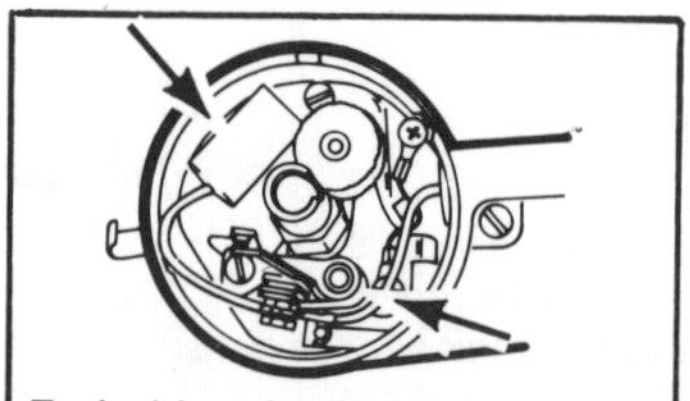

Typical location inside distributor.

REMOVING POINTS AND CONDENSER—1970-72 Models Only

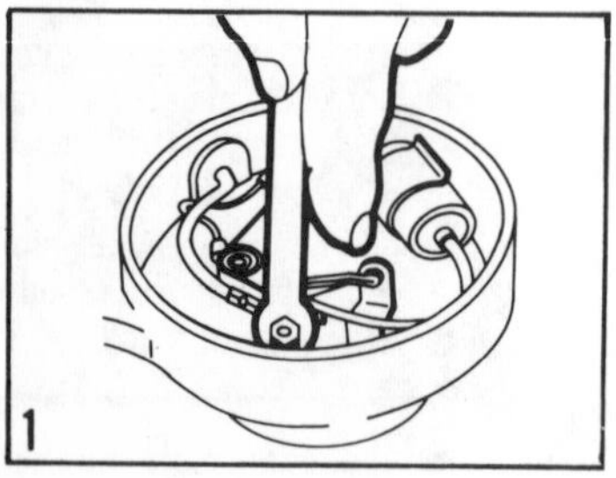

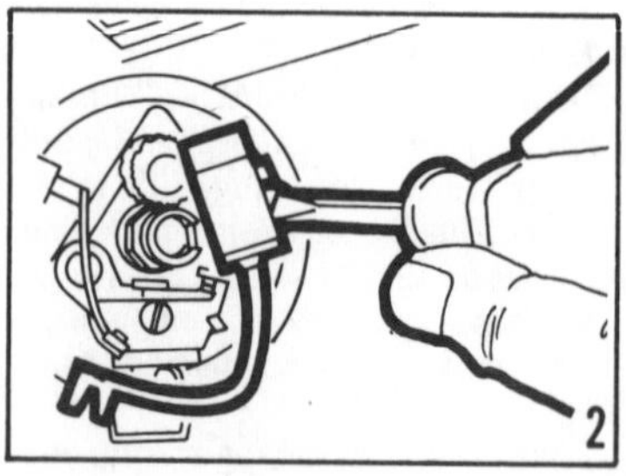

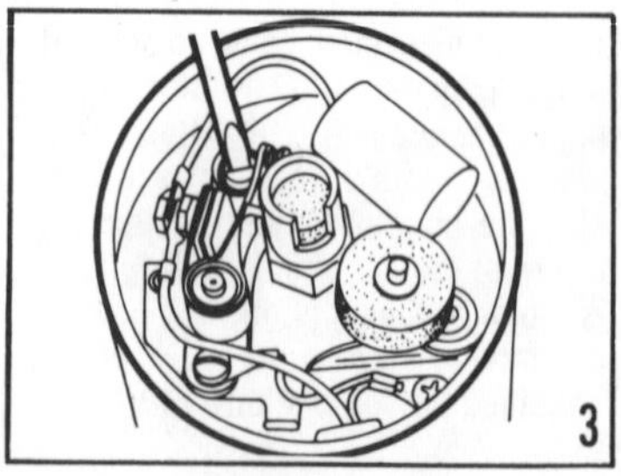

1. Loosen nut, and disconnect primary wire and condenser lead wire.
2. Remove screw which holds condenser; remove condenser.
3. Remove screws holding points to distributor, remove points.
4. Wipe all dirt from distributor plate and cam.
5. Inspect primary wire for frayed insulation, dirty connection. Clean connection or have wire repaired as necessary.

CAUTION: When removing screws from distributor in following steps, be sure to avoid any screws accidentally falling through distributor opening into engine. Use magnetic screwdriver.

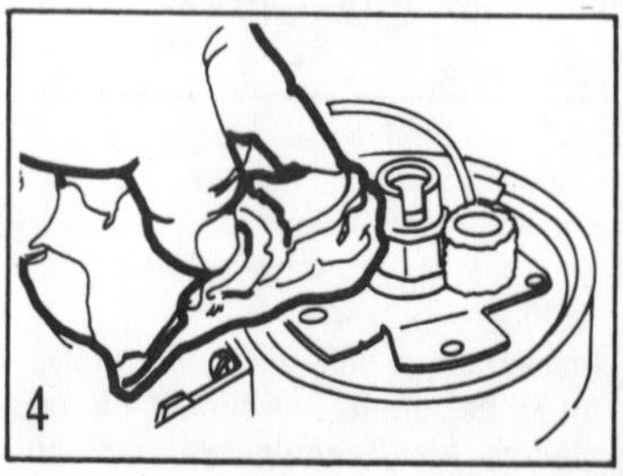

INSTALLING POINTS AND CONDENSER—1970-72 Models Only

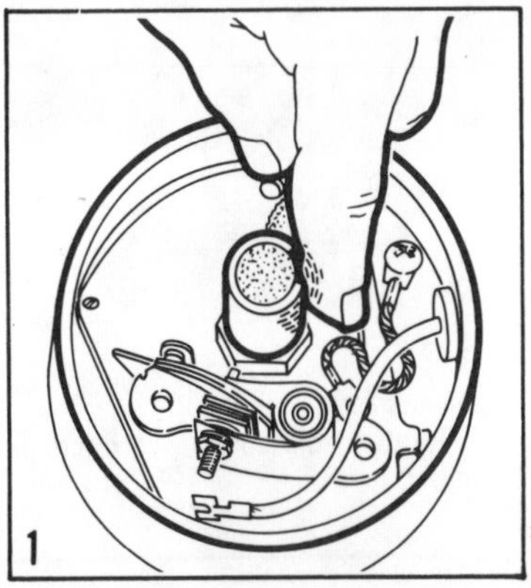
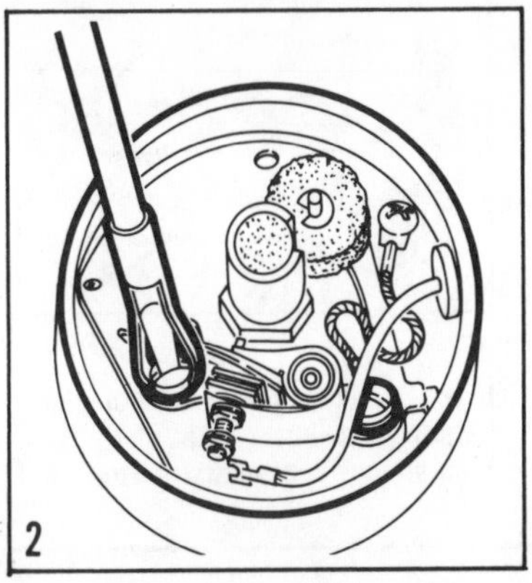
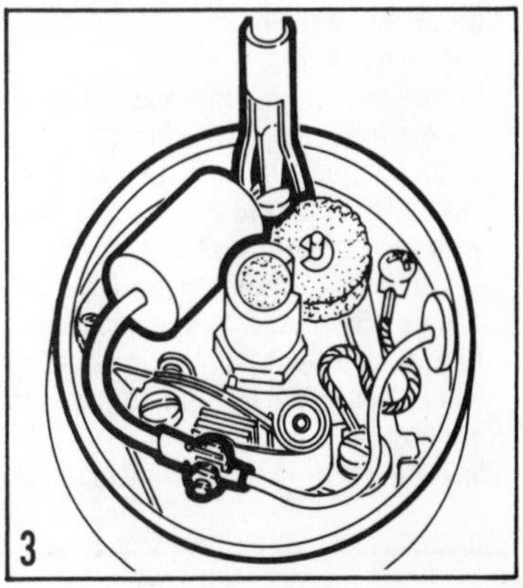

1. Apply small amount of heat resistant lube to distributor cam. (Lube usually supplied with new points. If not, purchase separately.)
2. Position new points in distributor and fasten with attaching screws. CAUTION: Use magnetic screwdriver, or screwdriver with clip.
3. Attach new condenser to distributor with attaching screw.
4. Attach primary wire and condenser lead wire to point set. Don't let contacts touch distributor body or breaker plate. (Some models: wire from points attaches to condenser.)

SETTING THE CONTACT GAP—1970-72 Models Only

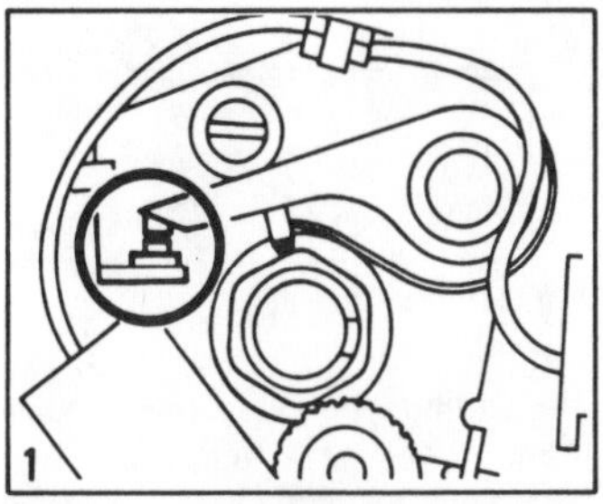

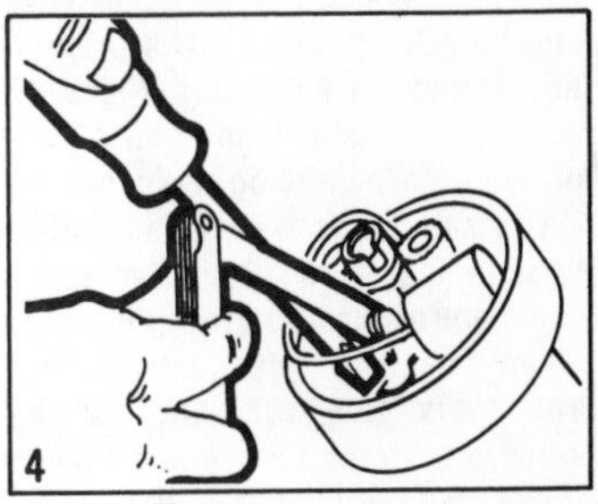

1. Electrical contacts of point set MUST BE PARALLEL. If needed, bend stationary contact with needle-nose pliers. Bend fixed bracket only.
2. Turn engine by ignition key (you'll need a helper) until rubbing block on points is one of the high points of the distributor cam. You may use wrench on lower pulley to do this, but TURN ONLY CLOCKWISE TO THE RIGHT —NEVER COUNTERCLOCKWISE.

3. Look up correct point gap on engine compartment sticker. Insert proper gap gauge between open point contacts. Slightly loosen point attaching screws. Insert screwdriver in breaker plate notch near point contacts. Twist screwdriver to open or close points as needed. Tighten screws when correct gap is obtained.

4. Recheck gap after screws are tightened. Readjust if needed.

5. Align tab inside rotor with notch on distributor shaft and push rotor onto shaft. Rotor must be fully seated on shaft.

6. Install distributor cap by aligning tabs on cap with notch on body. Snap retaining clips in place.

IGNITION TIMING

NOTE: On cars equipped with electronic ignition, regular adjustment of ignition timing is not necessary.
Adjusting timing is the important finishing touch to any tune-up. While not difficult, job requires timing light and dwell meter.
1. Locate timing marks and pointer (notches) on engine and lower gine pulley. Clean away dirt. Mark the

1

pointer and notch which corresponds with the timing setting in degrees shown on the engine compartment sticker.
2. Hook up timing light according to instructions supplied with it.
3. Disconnect the one or two vacuum lines from the distributor. Plug with pencil tip or golf tee.
4. Hook up tachometer and adjust engine idle speed to specifications. Idle attachment screw is located where gas pedal linkage attaches to carburetor.
5. Aim timing light at pulley mark(s).

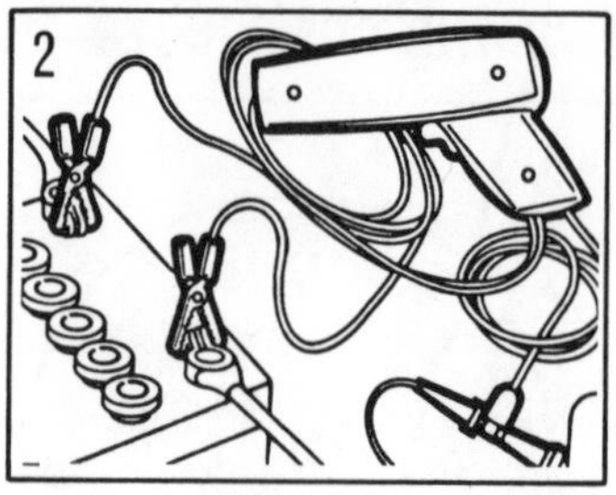

If the chalked marks do not align, loosen distributor hold-down bolt and slowly rotate distributor until

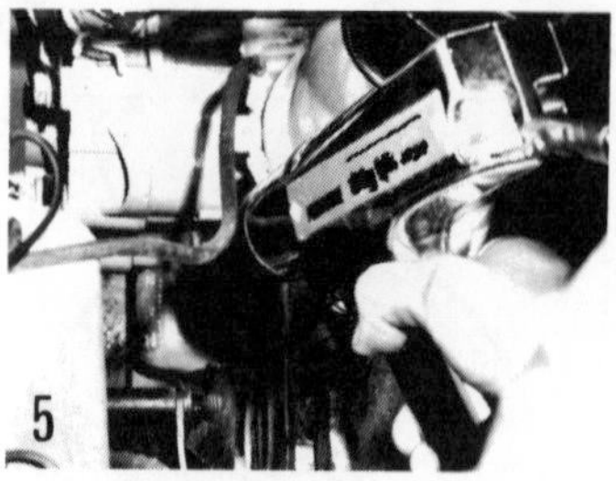

chalked marks align.
6. Tighten hold-down bolt. Recheck timing.

REPLACING SPARK PLUG WIRES

One of the most often overlooked items in a tune-up is the spark plug wires. Your car can be in perfect tune, but if the plug wires are not carrying the spark to the plugs, your engine will run poorly. The original equipment wires that came with your car are usually good for a year or two before needing replacement. On newer cars, the higher underhood temperatures created by emission controls breaks down the wires ability to conduct electricity sooner. The spark plug boot ends of the wires will crack with age allowing the spark to arc towards the engine, not reaching the plugs. The distributor cap ends of the wires will often collect moisture, and corrode right there in your distributor cap. Sometimes a wire will contact a hot part of the engine, such as the exhaust manifold and burn through the insulation. Other times, a wire will become oil soaked and gummy, breaking down the insulation. Often, when carbon core wires get old, they

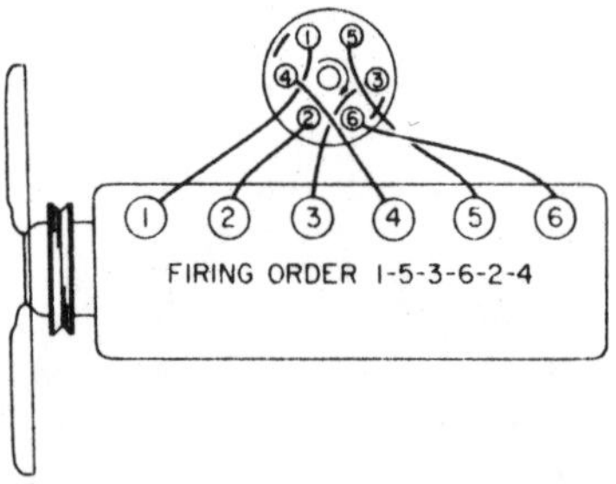

Slant Six

will break off inside, with no visible signs of breakage on the outside. Always use good quality spark plug wire. A carbon core or cut-rate brand may seem attractive at first, but will cost you more in the long run with reduced engine efficiency and more frequent replacement.
1. Replace one wire at a time. This will keep you out of trouble with crossed wires. When removing wires, twist back and forth as you pull up. This will help free up stuck wires.
2. Take the old wire and match it up

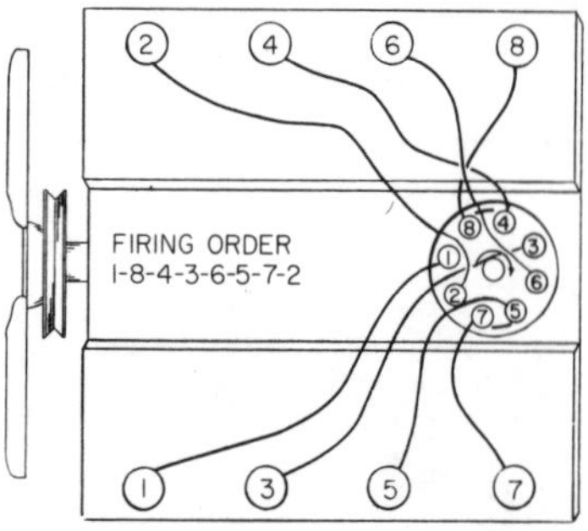

318, 340 and 360 V8s

with the new one for length. If you are cutting your own, make sure there is good metal to metal contact between the end of the wire and the pinch-on connectors.
3. Make sure each wire seats all the way down in the distributor cap. First push down the wire, then the boot. The wire should click in place.
4. After you are all done, make sure all wires are clear of choke or throttle linkage, or hot exhaust manifolds. Use the firing order illustration to guide you when replacing your ignition wires and/or distributor cap.

Fuel System

When gasoline is brought from the fuel tank, it mixes with air in the carburetor. This gas/air mixture enters engine thru the intake manifold, passes thru the intake valves and is burned in the combustion chamber. The burned exhaust gas is then passed thru the exhaust valves to the exhaust system and to the outside air. In order to keep your car's engine running cleanly with minimal pollution, and avoid dangerous carbon monoxide fumes inside the vehicle, certain items should be checked from time to time.

REPLACING THE AIR FILTER

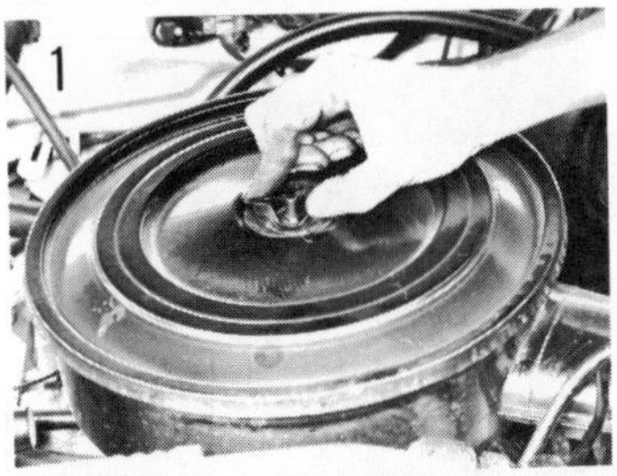

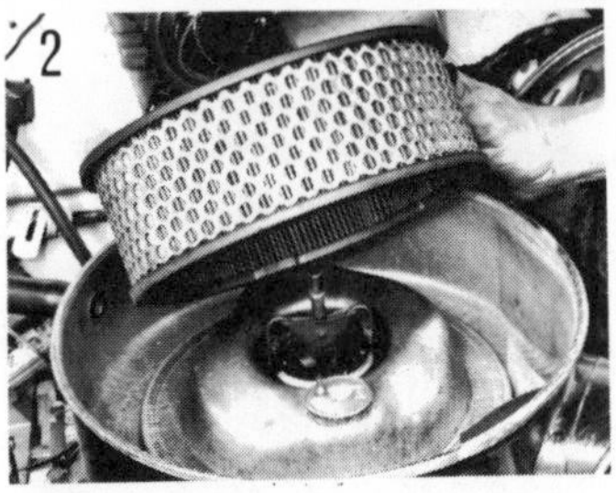

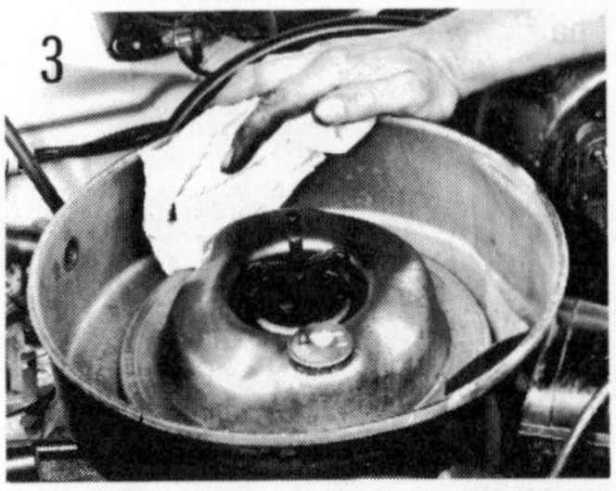

The large round canister that sits on top of the engine holds the air filter element. Check it twice a year, or sooner in dusty areas.

1. Remove the wing nut and lift up the air cleaner lid.

2. Lift out the circular air cleaner element. Discard if excessively dirty, or if oil contaminated more than half its circumference. Replace at two year or 24,000 mile intervals regardless of mileage.

3. If reuseable, tap against a hard surface to remove any loose dirt. Wipe out inside of air cleaner canister and lid. Install element and lid and tighten wing nut.

FUEL FILTER REPLACEMENT

All models are equipped with a throw-away filter which is located in the fuel line near the carburetor. On 1970-74 models the filter should be replaced every 2 years/24,000 miles, whichever occurs first. On 1975 models, replace the fuel filter every 15,000 miles. On 1976-77 models, replace the fuel filter every 30,000 miles.

To replace the filter, proceed in the following manner:

CAUTION: Do not smoke while performing this procedure.

1. Squeeze the clips securing the old filter assembly to the fuel line with pliers in order to open them.
2. Work the ends of both old rubber hoses off of the fuel line and lift out the filter with the hoses attached. Be careful not to drop gasoline on the manifolds if they are hot.
3. Using the clips supplied, install the pieces of rubber hose that come with the new filter over the necks on either side of it.
4. Install the filter hose assembly in the fuel line with clips, being sure that the arrow on the filter is pointing in the direction of fuel flow. Cut the hose to the correct length, if necessary.

5. Check to be sure that the fuel lines are not coming into contact with any other engine components.
6. Start the engine and check for leaks.

CRANKCASE VENTILATION FILTER CLEANING

The crankcase ventilation filter is the black dome on the valve cover with a thick hose leading to the air cleaner. Its purpose is to filter the incoming air for the crankcase ventilation system. At six month intervals (1970-71 models) or once a year (1972-77 models), the filter is removed and cleaned.

1. Remove the hose which runs to the carburetor air cleaner from the crankcase inlet air cleaner (breather cap).
2. Inspect the hose and clean or replace it, as necessary.
3. Remove the crankcase air cleaner assembly from the valve cover.
4. Wash the assembly in kerosene.
5. Invert the assembly and wet the filter element by filling it with SAE 30 engine oil.
6. Allow the excess oil to drain off

and install it on the engine. Connect the hose back to the air cleaner.

PCV VALVE REPLACEMENT

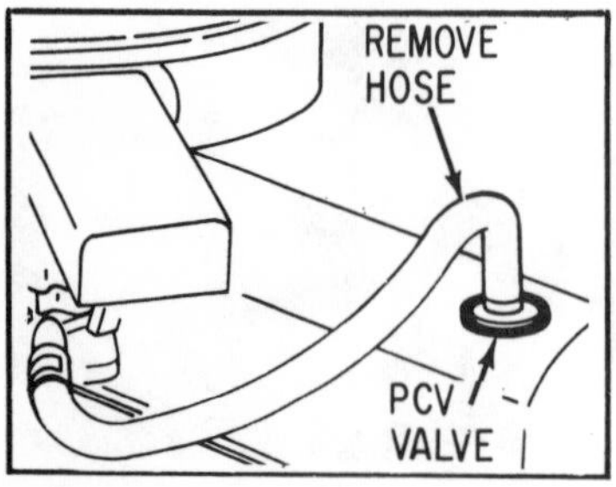

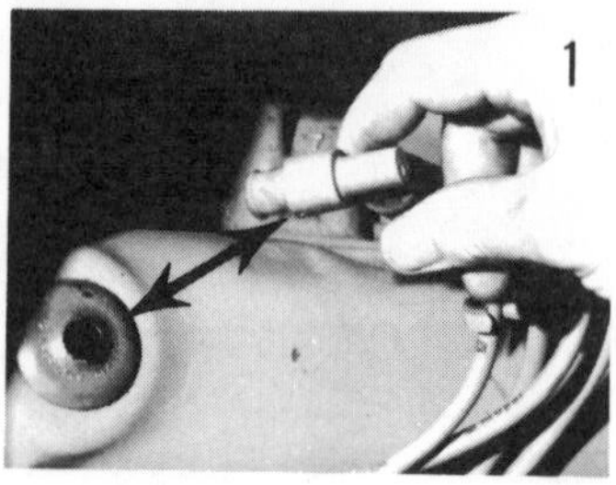

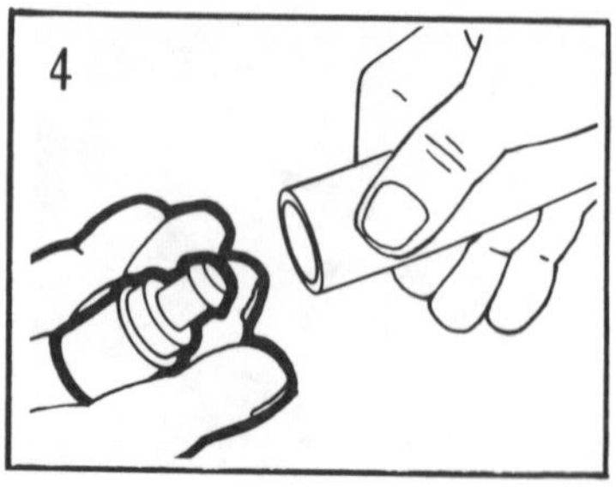

The PCV valve is located in a grommet on the valve cover and has a heavy hose running from it to the rear of the carburetor. It should be checked twice a year (1970-71 models) or once a year (1972-77 models) and replaced every 12 months (1970-71 models) or two years (1972-77 models).

1. Grasp the hose and PCV valve and pull out of the valve cover.

2. Disconnect other end of hose from carburetor. Remove PCV valve from hose.

3. Shake the PCV valve. If it clicks, it is not clogged and is OK. Flush hose out with cleaning solvent and dry. If the PCV valve is clogged, it cannot be cleaned. Replace it.

4. Connect the PCV valve and hose and insert in valve cover. Connect the hose to the carburetor.

Safety Systems

PARKING LIGHTS, TURN SIGNALS, STOP AND BACK-UP LIGHTS

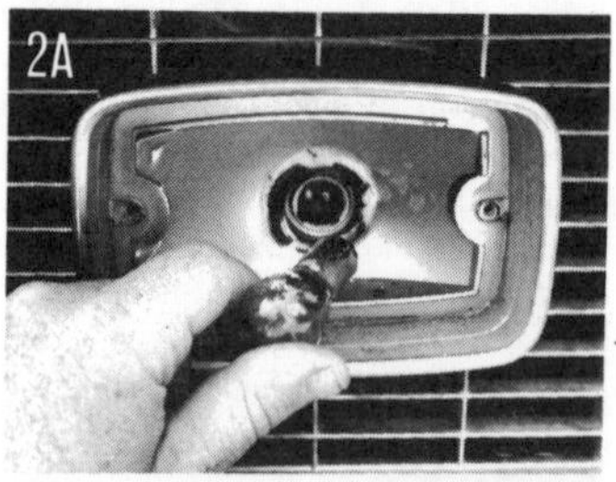

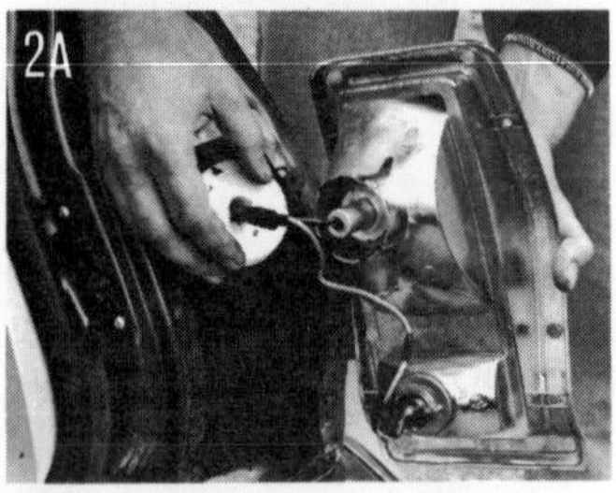

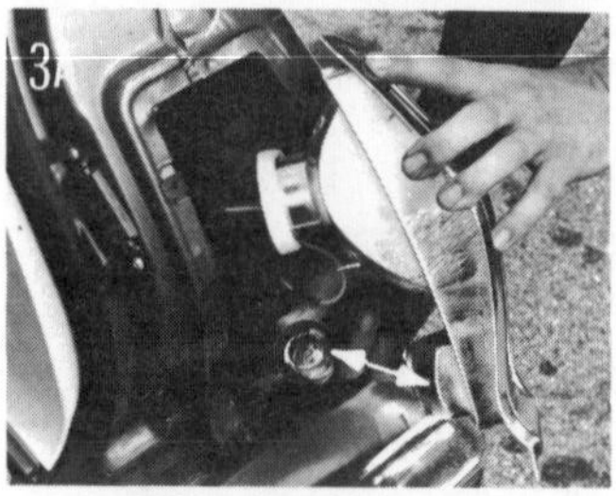

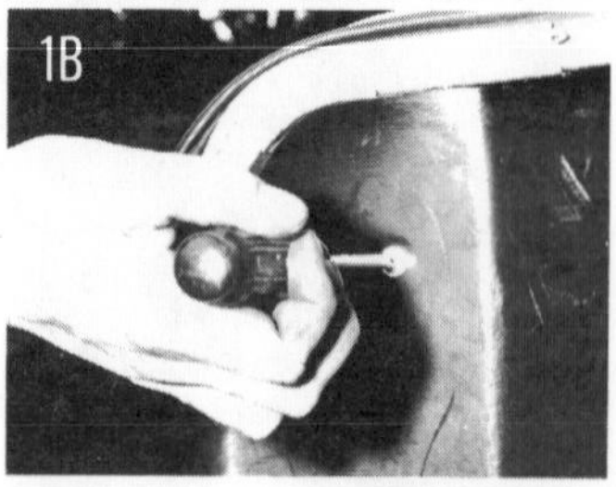

Parking lights, turn signals, and stop lights function with dual-element bulbs. Back-up lights are single element types. To replace:

A. Front parking lights and turn signals on all models and rear lights on station wagons. Remove lens to expose bulb(s). Push it on bulb while turning counterclockwise to release bulb from socket. Remove and replace with new bulb. Replace lens.

B. On sedans and hatchbacks, rear bulbs are reached from inside rather than outside. Locate bulb housing inside trunk or rear compartment. Twist socket to release from housing. Push in on bulb, turn counterclockwise and remove bulb.

NOTE: When inserting new dual element bulb, note that knobs on side of bulb base are different distances from base tip. Match knobs to socket slots for proper fit.

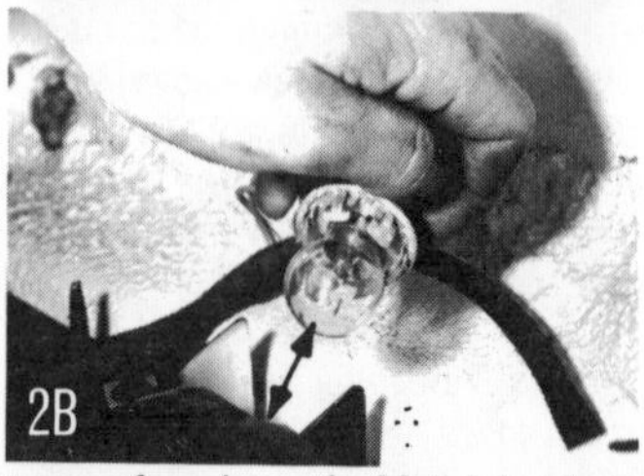

LICENSE PLATE LIGHT

Remove the screws that retain the lens to the bumpers. Push in on bulb, turning counterclockwise to remove.

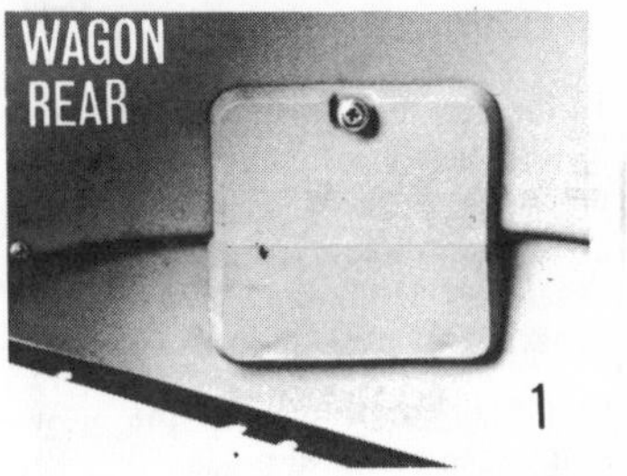

REPLACING INTERIOR DOME LIGHT

Pry the dome light lens out from the housing. To avoid blowing the fuse, make sure that the doors are closed and dome light switch is in the OFF position. Push in on the bulb and turn it clockwise to remove from socket. Insert new bulb and install in reverse order.

SIDE MARKER LIGHT

Reach up inside fender and turn bulb socket counterclockwise to remove from housing. Pull bulb straight out.

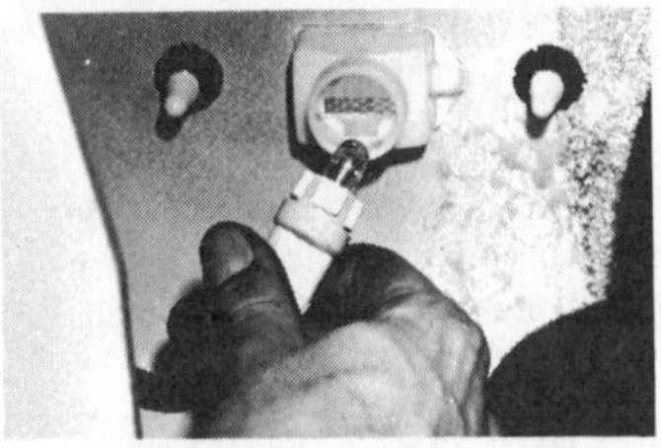

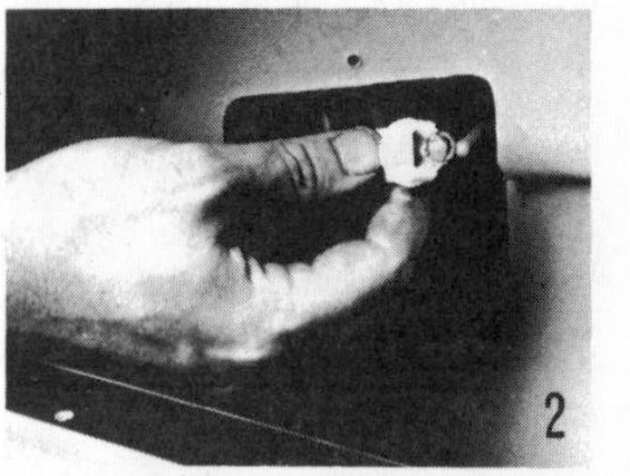

HEADLIGHT REPLACEMENT

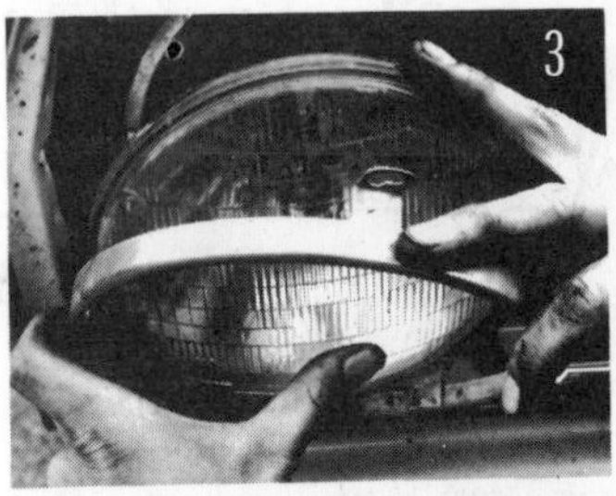

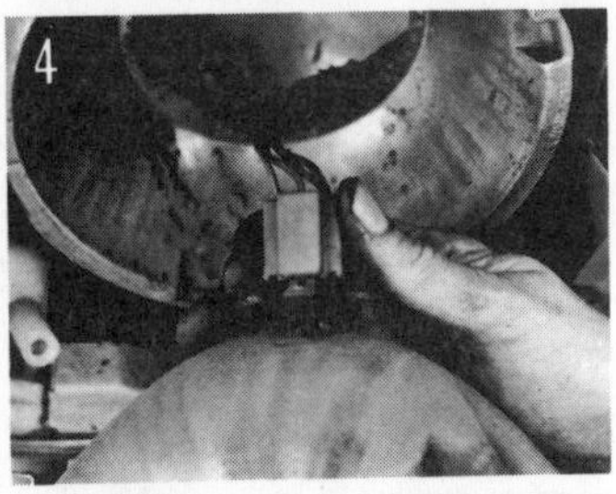

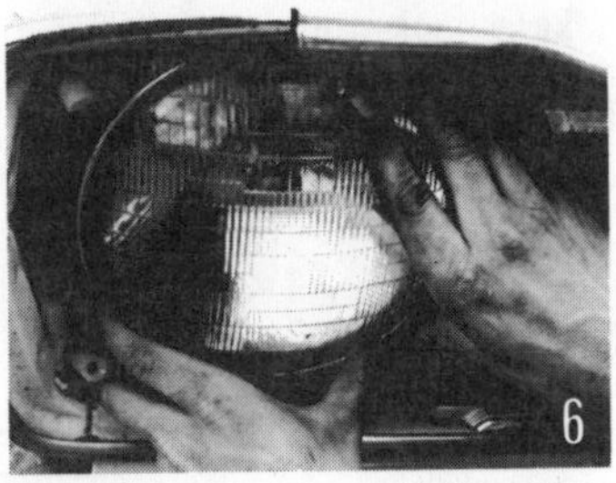

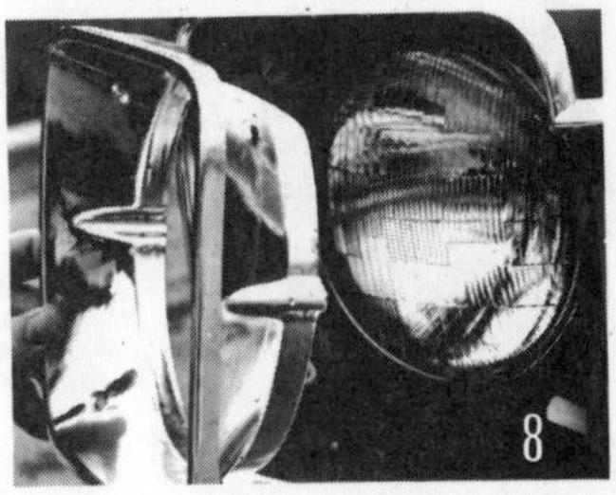

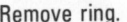

1. Remove both headlight cover retaining screws and cover.
2. Loosen, but do not remove, headlight retaining ring attaching screws. NOTE: Do not mistake headlight adjustment screws for the three retaining ring screws.
3. Rotate retaining ring to left until large openings in attaching screw slots are aligned with screw heads. Remove ring.
4. Pull lamp (sealed beam) out of headlight shell toward front of car; disconnect wiring connector from sealed beam unit.
5. Connect wire connector to new sealed beam unit. NOTE: If possible, use a #6014 headlight. It's brighter than the #6012 which is being phased out.
6. Position new sealed beam unit in headlight shell. Be sure knobs on back of bulb (near outer edge) enter slots in shell.
7. Position retaining ring on retainer screws; turn ring to right. Tighten screws.
8. Position headlight cover; install attaching screws.

REPLACING WINDSHIELD WIPER BLADES

To replace the wiper blade assembly, lift the wiper arm up and depress the release lever (using a screwdriver if necessary) where the blade assembly is attached to the arm. Separate the assembly from the arm.

To install, merely snap the new blade assembly into place.

To replace the rubber blade insert only, depress the red (or black) dots on the blade assembly and slide the insert out lengthwise. When installing a new insert, bend the insert slightly upward to engage retaining channels.

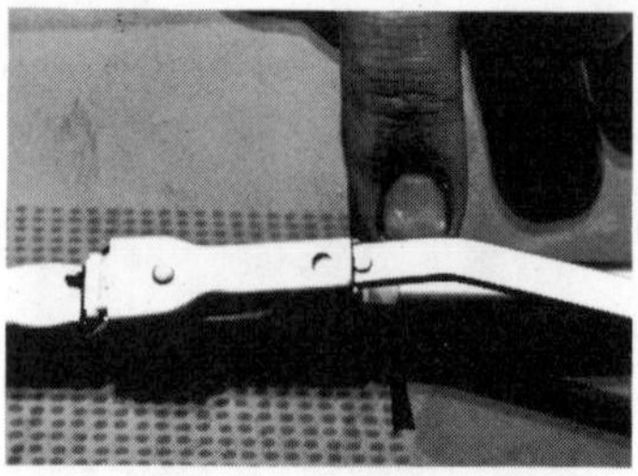

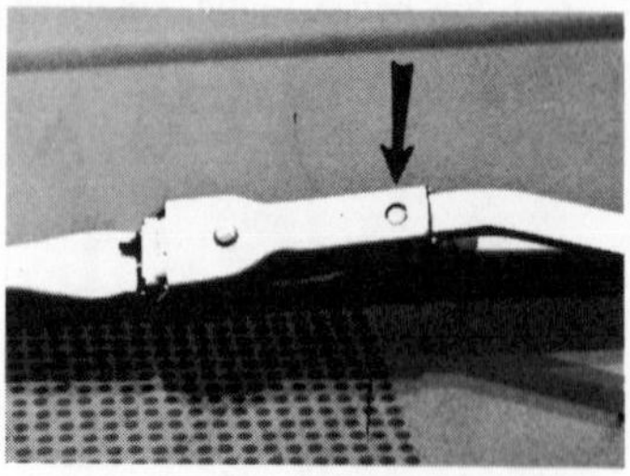

HORN PROBLEMS

If horn sounds and does not stop, this is due to short circuit in wiring. Disconnect wiring connector under hood and have professional service shop check horn wiring circuit.

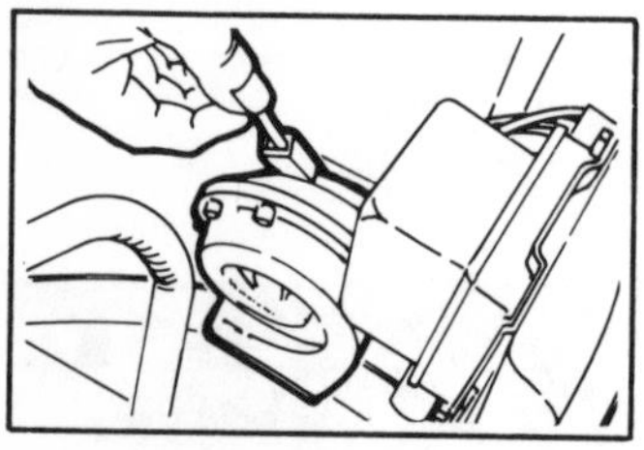

STEERING PROBLEMS

See steering system check in Suspension Section. Check tire pressures. Have a professional service shop check all components in the front end and steering system.

SERVICING WINDSHIELD WASHER SYSTEM

If washer fails to squirt properly, raise hood and check system hose connections. Be sure washer fluid container has fluid. Check spout openings for clogging.

Keep container filled with fluid mixture of washer solvent and water. If road spray buildup on windshield is a chronic problem, add 1 tablespoon dishwasher detergent to solvent/water mixture when re-filling container.

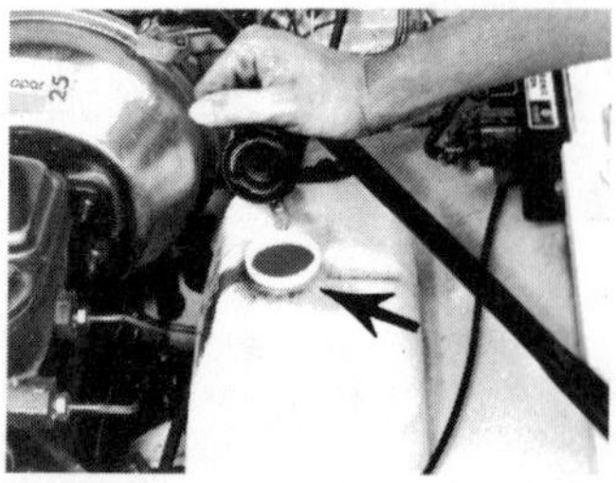

CHECKING BRAKE WHEEL CYLINDERS

All cars employ a dual hydraulic brake system. If a leak develops in one hydraulic system, the other system, which is totally independent of the other, will remain functional. This means you will have braking at two wheels. In addition, a warning light will light up on the dash if there is a pressure drop. However, a small amount of leakage may develop that will not cause a sudden reduction of braking or actuate the light. For this reason, if you suspect anything at all, take a look. On cars with drum brakes, check the inside of the tire and wheel. If it is wet, daub some up with your finger and smell it. Brake fluid is sweet to the smell. On cars with disc front brakes, remove the tire and wheel and check the caliper for leakage. Have a mechanic correct any leaks immediately.

Electrical System

CHECK BATTERY FLUID

1. Remove plastic filler caps on top of battery. Fluid should be up to lower end of filler hole and covering the plates. If fluid is low add clean, cold tap water. If your area has hard water, use only distilled water available at auto supply, food or drug stores.
2. Replace any lost caps immediately.

CAUTION: NEVER LIGHT A MATCH

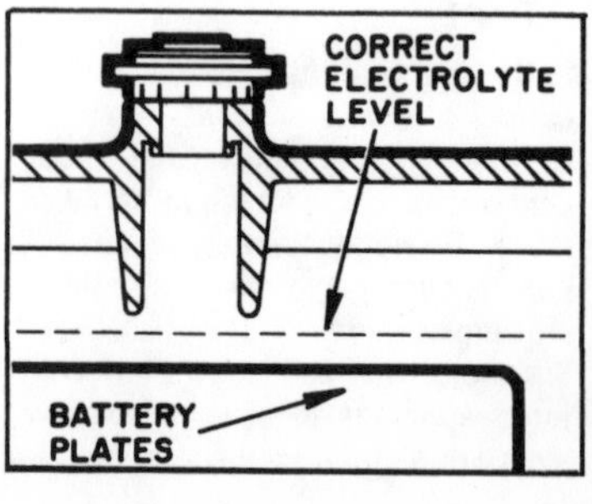

OR SMOKE near the top of a battery. Batteries give off explosive hydrogen gas.
NOTE: Battery that often checks low on fluid could mean:
A. Battery is getting old, due for replacement; have charge capacity checked at service shop.
B. Connections may be corroded or loose; clean/replace as needed (see below).
C. Alternator or voltage regulator not functioning properly; this happens far less often than A or B above.

CLEAN THOSE BATTERY TERMINALS

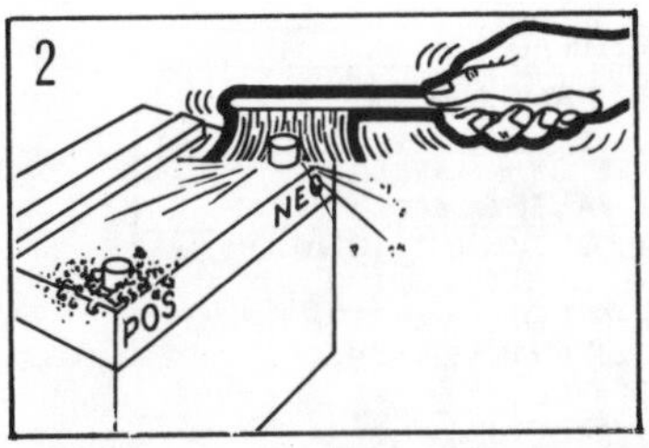

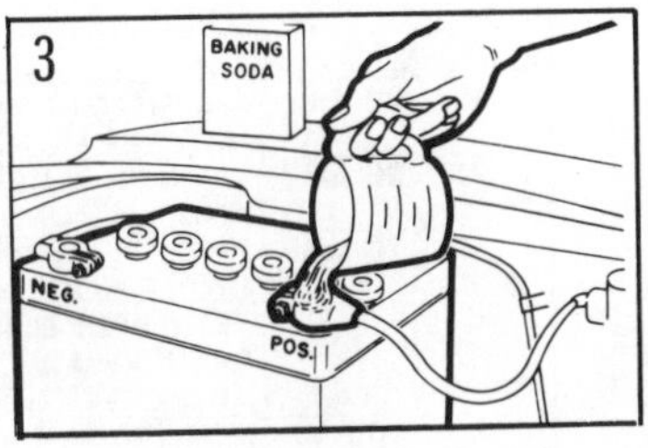

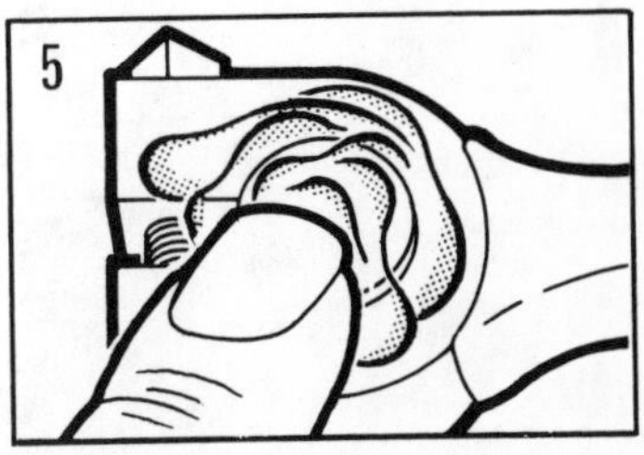

As time goes by, battery terminals build up a dry powdery, whitish material. This material is corrosive and will gradually eat thru battery cables if not cleaned off periodically.
1. Loosen and remove battery connections.
2. Brush off all loose corrosion; use stiff bristle brush. Do not get this material into eyes or on open cuts. Wash off at once.
3. If corrosion build-up is extremely heavy and brushing does not remove all of it, mix 2 tablespoons baking soda to 1 cup water. Pour solution directly onto terminals and connectors. Allow to soak a few minutes and rinse off. Continue brushing to remove all traces of corrosion build-up. Do not allow cleaning solution to enter battery.
4. Replace connectors on battery terminal posts and tighten. Do not hammer connections onto posts, but be sure they will not come loose with vibration.
5. Liberally smear battery terminal posts and cable connectors with petroleum jelly.

REPLACE FAULTY BATTERY CABLES

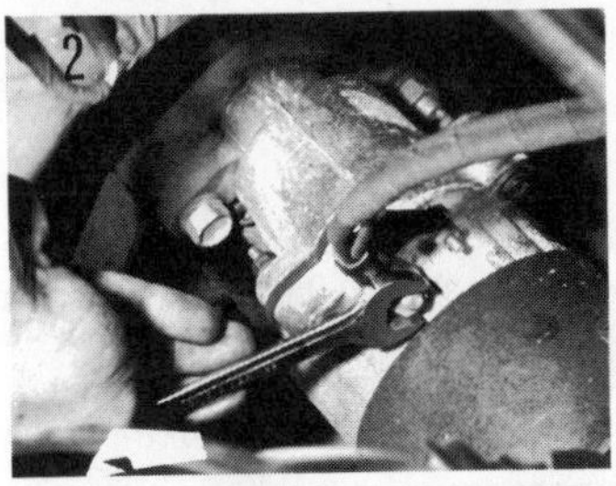

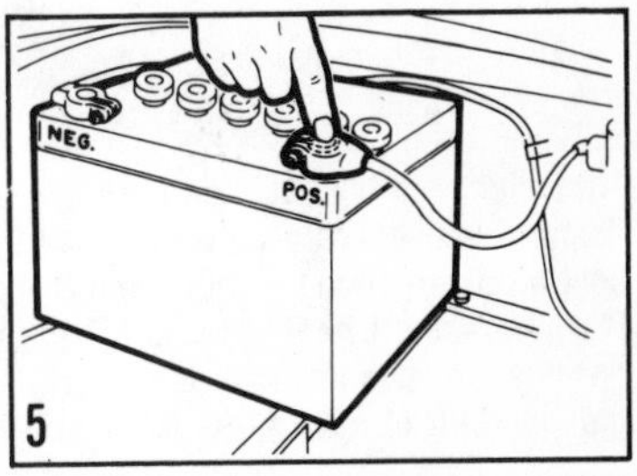

If battery cable strands become frayed, broken or corroded, replace cable immediately. Delay in correcting this condition could lead to sudden failure to start the engine. Can also weaken battery.
1. Loosen and remove battery cables. Clean off any corrosion buildup.
2. Disconnect negative cable from its attachment to engine or chassis. Disconnect positive cable from its attachment to starter relay.
3. Attach new cables making sure positive and negative cables are on proper terminals. They are not identical.
4. Replace connectors on battery terminal posts and tighten.
5. Liberally smear battery terminal posts and cable connectors with petroleum jelly.

BATTERY HOLDDOWN

The clamp device which holds the battery in place consists of two long bolts which mount in the battery tray, two nuts and a crossbar. 1975-77 models have a plastic heat shield which surrounds the battery. Periodically, check the hold down bolts for tightness and corrosion buildup. Clean off corrosion with wire brush and baking soda. Severely corroded holddown components should be replaced before they break.

FUSE LOCATION

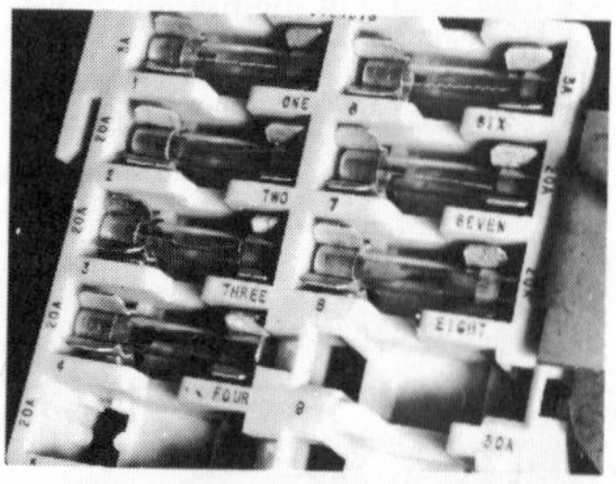

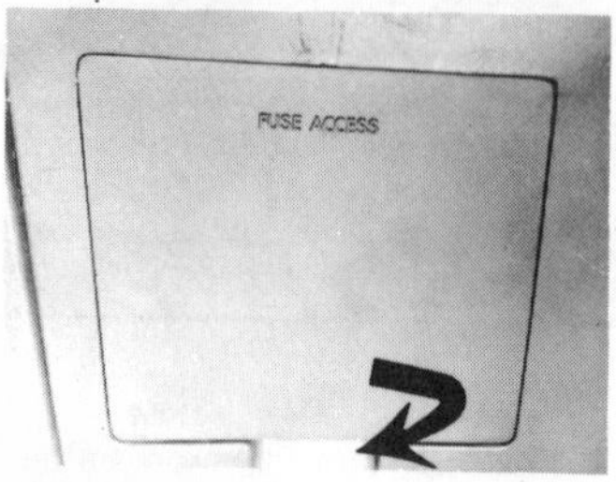

On Valiant and Dart models, the fusebox is located under the dash, to the left of the steering column. To gain access to the fuses, remove the fusebox retaining screw and lower the fusebox. The circuit each fuse protects is indicated by a number on the block.

On Volare and Aspen models, the fusebox is located behind a special access door at the lower left side of the dash. The fuse location breakdown is as follows:

CAVITY	FUSE	ITEMS FUSED
1.	30 AMP	A/C BLOWER MOTOR AND HEATER BLOWER MOTOR
2.	20 AMP	PARK, TAIL, LICENSE, SIDE MARKER AND INSTRUMENT PANEL LAMPS
3.	20 AMP	STOP, DOME, MAP, GLOVE BOX, IGNITION, UNDER HOOD AND TRUNK LAMPS; KEY-IN BUZZER, IGNITION LAMP TIME DELAY RELAY, CLOCK (CONVENTIONAL) AND CIGAR LIGHTER
4.	20 AMP	HORN (DUAL) AND HORN RELAY
5.	30 AMP C/BRKR.	POWER WINDOW MOTORS, POWER DOOR LOCK SOLENOID AND POWER SEATS
6.	20 AMP	POWER DOOR LOCK RELAY
7.	5 AMP	ASH TRAY, GEAR SELECTOR, CONSOLE, A/C AND HEATER CONTROL, INSTRUMENT, CLOCK, RADIO (AM-FM-MPX) AND SWITCH TITLE LAMPS
8.	5 AMP	SEAT BELT, BRAKE WARNING AND OIL PRESSURE LAMPS; WINDOW LIFT SAFETY AND HEATED BACKLITE RELAYS; VOLTAGE LIMITER, FUEL AND TEMP GAUGE. SEAT BELT BUZZER AND TIME DELAY RELAY
9.	20 AMP	A/C CLUTCH, SPEED CONTROL AND REAR WINDOW DEFOGGER
10.	20 AMP	TURN SIGNAL, BACK-UP AND REVERSE GEAR LAMPS
11.	5 AMP	RADIO
12.	20 AMP	HAZARD FLASHER

TURN SIGNAL AND 4-WAY FLASHERS

Turn signal and 4-way emergency flashers will operate only if: A. All light bulbs on circuit are OK, and B. Flasher units are not burned out. The car has two flasher units that work independent of each other. On Dart and Valiant models, the turn signal flasher is located behind the ashtray and the 4-way flasher behind the dash to the left of the steering column. On Volare and Aspen models, both flashers plug into the fuse block. To replace either type of flasher, simply unplug the unit from its connector. Take the old flasher with you when you purchase the new one. Replace only with same type flasher.

ALTERNATOR CHECKS

Dashboard ammeter gauge should show slight discharge when you first turn ignition key while starting. This proves gauge is OK. When engine starts, gauge should first jump to the charge side, then slowly fall back to the center with engine at idle speed. If ammeter shows discharge at idle speed, alternator isn't charging properly. Common causes are:

A. Fan belts are loose and slipping on alternator pulley. Tighten or replace belts.

B. Battery terminals, cables are loose or corroded. Clean; tighten; replace bad cables.

If A or B do not correct problem, alternator or voltage regulator may be faulty. This happens far less often, and can only be checked by mechanic with proper electrical testing equipment.

Alternator Caution: Alternator can be permanently damaged by short-circuiting terminal connections. When working around or moving alternator, always keep metal tools or engine parts from terminals.

REAR WINDOW DEFOGGER SYSTEM—1973-77 Models

Do not clean inside of rear window fitted with defogger system with any abrasive material. This could destroy carbon-copper wires. Use only soft rag and mild detergent/water mixture. Dry carefully.

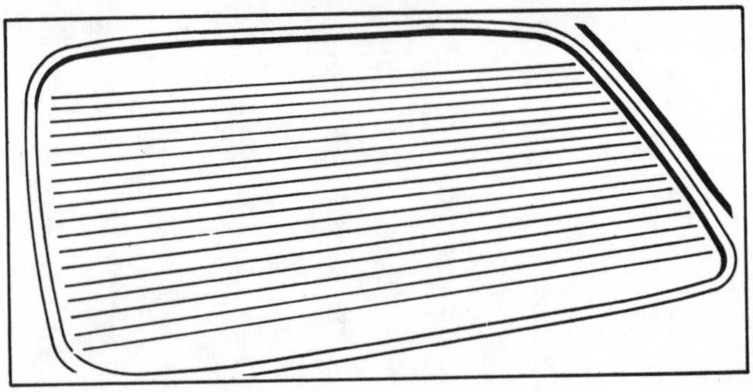

Air Conditioner

CHECKPOINTS AND SERVICES

WARNING!—Never attempt to tighten fittings, disassemble or do any work on your car's A/C system. Consult a professional mechanic about A/C system problems and their correction. Your auto air conditioner (A/C) is a delicate, closed system. If air, dirt or water get into it, or if refrigerant escapes, the A/C unit will not cool a car interior. Among things you can do are:

1. Keep condenser grill clean. Check for dirt and debris; periodically remove dead insects, leaves, etc., with stiff bristle brush. Straighten any bent fins—carefully.
2. Keep radiator filled to correct level. (See Cooling System section). If fluid needs to be added, add anti-freeze rather than water.
3. Keep radiator coolant at a 50/50 water/antifreeze mixture.
4. Flush cooling system and replace with fresh coolant mixture at least every 24 months. (See Cooling System section).
5. Radiator cap should be tight and sealed properly. If sealing gasket is cracked, cut or worn, replace cap with new 15 lb. unit.
6. Check fan belt tension periodically. (See Cooling System section). Replace glazed, frayed or cut fan belts, before they fail entirely.

1

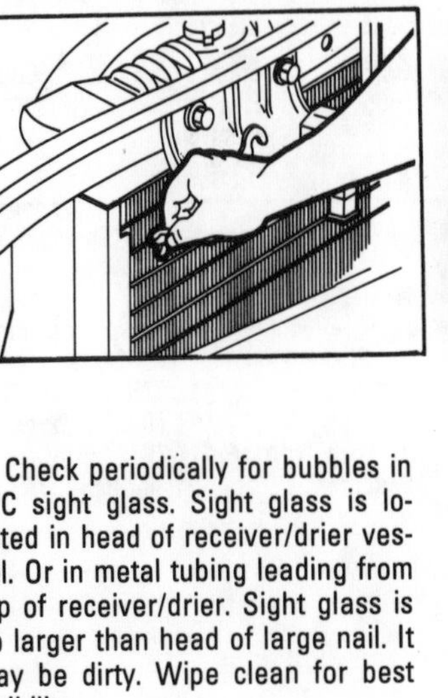

7

7. Check periodically for bubbles in A/C sight glass. Sight glass is located in head of receiver/drier vessel. Or in metal tubing leading from top of receiver/drier. Sight glass is no larger than head of large nail. It may be dirty. Wipe clean for best visibility.

PROCEED AS FOLLOWS:

a) With engine and A/C system running, look for passage of refrigerant in sight glass. You'll be looking for a stream of milky white bubbles as they pass through sight glass. It is best to watch sight glass and have someone else start the car and turn on the A/C system. Allow to run for a few minutes.

b) If you observe no bubbles, and air flow from A/C unit in the car is passing cold air, everything is OK.

c) If no bubbles appear in sight glass, and air flow from the A/C unit in the car is not delivering cold air, the system may be low on refrigerant and could need a re-charge.

d) If bubbles appear, system is low on refrigerant.

e) If you suspect refrigerant loss based on tests performed above, have system checked by a professional A/C service shop. They can confirm refrigerant loss, recharge the system and check for system leakage.

NOTE: Once a week or so, even in winter, run A/C system for about 5 minutes as you drive. This keeps system internally lubricated, prevents hoses hardening.

VALIANT/DART/ASPEN/VOLARE

TUNE-UP SPECIFICATIONS

YEAR	ENGINE No. Cyl. Displacement (cu. in.)	SPARK PLUGS Type	SPARK PLUGS Gap (in.)	DISTRIBUTOR Point Dwell (deg.)	DISTRIBUTOR Point Gap (in.)	IGNITION TIMING Man. Trans. ● (deg.) ■	IGNITION TIMING Auto Trans. ● (deg.) ■	IDLE SPEED Man. Trans. ● (rpm) ▲	IDLE SPEED Auto Trans. (rpm) ▲
1970	6-198	N-14Y	.035	41-46	.020	2½B	TDC	750	750①
	6-225	N-14Y	.035	41-56	.020	TDC	TDC	700	650①
	8-318	N-14Y	.035	30-34	.017	TDC	TDC	750	700
	8-340	N-9Y	.035	27-32②	.017	5B	5B	900	900
1971	6-198	N-14Y	.035	41-46	.020	2½B	2½B	800	800
	6-225	N-14Y	.035	41-46	.020	TDC(2½B)	TDC(2½B)	750	750
	8-318	N-14Y	.035	30-34	.017	TDC	TDC	750	700
	8-340	N-9Y	.035	27-32②	.017	5B	5B	900	900
1972	6-198	N-14Y	.035	41-46	.020	2½B	2½B	800(700)	800(700)
	6-225	N-14Y	.035	41-46	.020	TDC(2½B)	TDC(2½B)	750(700)	750(700)
	8-318	N-13Y	.035	30-34	.017	TDC	TDC	750	750(700)
	8-340	N-9Y	.035	30-34	.017	TDC(2½B)	2½B	900(850)	750
1973	6-198	N-14Y	.035	Electronic		2½B	2½B	800	750
	6-225	N-14Y	.035	Electronic		TDC	TDC	750	750
	8-318	N-13Y	.035	Electronic		2½B	TDC	750	700
	8-360	N-9Y	.035	Electronic		5B	2½B	850	850
1974	6-198	N-14Y	.035	Electronic		2½B	2½B	800	750
	6-225	N-14Y	.035	Electronic		TDC	TDC	800	750
	8-318	N-13Y	.035	Electronic		TDC	TDC	750	750
	8-360	N-12Y	.035	Electronic		5B(2½B)	5B	850	850
1975	6-225	BL-13Y	.035	Electronic		TDC	TDC	800	750
	8-318	N-13Y	.035	Electronic		2B	2B	750	750
	8-360	N-13Y	.035	Electronic		—	2B	—	750
1976-77	6-225	RBL-13Y	.035	Electronic		6B(2B)	2B	750(800)	750
	8-318	RN-12Y	.035	Electronic		2B	2B③	750	750
	8-360 2V	RN-12Y	.035	Electronic		—	6B	—	700
	8-360 HP	RN-12Y	.035	Electronic		—	2B	—	850

▲ Adjust automatic transmissions in Drive (AMC/Ford/GM) or Neutral (Chrysler), all manual transmissions are adjusted in Neutral.
■ All figures are Before Top Dead Center.
● Figure in parentheses indicate California engine.

NOTE: The underhood specifications sticker often reflects tune-up specification changes made in production. Sticker figures must be used if they disagree with those in this chart.

① A/C on
② Adjust both sets of points to this figure. With both sets connected, total reading should be 37-42 degrees
③ With air pump and no catalyst, figure is 2° After Top Dead Center

B Before Top Dead Center
TDC Top Dead Center
2V 2 barrel
HP High Performance

CAPACITIES

YEAR	ENGINE No. Cyl. Displacement (cu. in.)	ENGINE OIL Add 1 qt. with New Filter	TRANSMISSION Pts. to Refill after Draining MANUAL 3-speed	MANUAL 4-speed	AUTOMATIC	DRIVE AXLE (pts.)	COOLING SYSTEM with Heater (qts.)	with Air Cond. (qts.)
1970	6-198	4	6.5	—	17	2	13	14
	6-225	4	6.5	—	17	2	13	14
	8-318	4	4.75	7.5	16	4	16	17
	8-340	4	4.75	7	16	4	15.5	15.5
1971	6-198	4	6.5	—	17	2	13	14
	6-225	4	6.5	—	17	2	13	14
	6-318	4	4.75	—	17	4.5	16	17.5
	8-340	4	4.75	7	16.3	4.5	15.5	15.5
1972	6-198	4	6.5	—	17	2	13	14
	6-225	4	6.5	—	17	2	13	14
	8-318	4	4.75	—	17	4.5	16	15
	8-340	4	4.75	7	16.3	4.5	15	15
1973	6-198	4	6.5	—	17	2	13	13
	6-225	4	6.5	—	17	2	13	14
	8-318	4	4.75	—	17	4.5	16	17.5
	8-340	4	4.75	7	16.3	4.5	15.5	15.5
1974	6-198	4	6.5	—	13.5	2	13	—
	6-225	4	4.75	—	13.5	2	13	14.0
	8-318	4	4.75	7.0	13.5	4.5	16	17.5
	8-360	4	4.75	7.0	14.0	4.5	16	16.0
1975-77	6-225	4	3.5	7.0	13.5	2	13	14
	8-318	4	4.75	7.0	13.5	4.5	16	17.5
	8-360	4	—	—	14.0	4.5	16	16

NOTE: All automatic transmission figures include torque converter
— Not applicable

Service Record

Date/Mileage	Service	Next Due

Vega/Astre

Lubrication and Oil Change

LUBRICATION CHECK

Checking the oil is one of the most important, and easy, maintenance tasks you can perform. Use a name brand oil that is certified grade SE. Check your owner's manual for the proper viscosity to use. This can vary according to the weather conditions expected during the oil change interval.

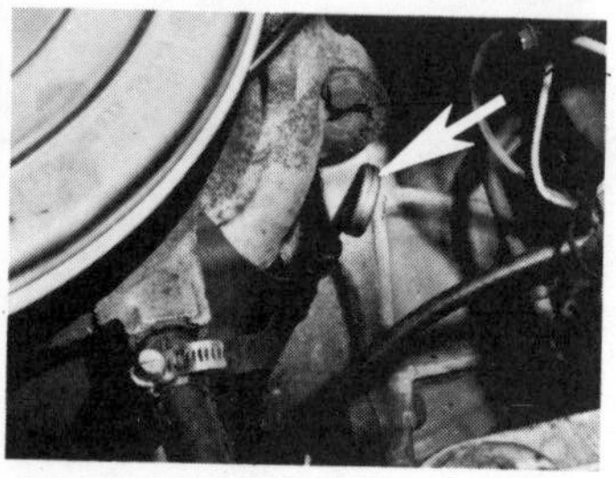

The engine oil level should be checked on a regular basis, at least every time you stop for gas. Always wait a few minutes, to allow the oil to return to the pan or you'll get a false reading. The proper level is between the FULL and ADD marks on the dipstick.

Pull out the dipstick on the left side of the engine. Do not take a reading at this time. Wipe the dipstick off with a clean rag. Replace the dipstick and then remove it again. Check the oil level on the dipstick. If the level is at the ADD mark, adding one full quart at the filler will bring it to the full FULL mark. Never add a full quart if the level is not down to the ADD mark, because this will result in overfilling. Replace the dipstick, making sure it's fully seated.

GM SAYS . . . Change oil every 6000 miles; on 1971-74 models or 7500 miles; on 1975 and later models. Chevrolet recommends that oil filter only be changed every other oil change, but it's a good idea to change it every time you change the oil. Recommended grade: SE. Check oil level at least once a week.

TOOLS & MATERIALS . . . 9/16 box wrench or adjustable wrench; medium size screwdriver; oil filter removal wrench; drain pan for old oil (at least 5 qt. capacity); oil pouring spout; 3 qt. oil (4 qt. if changing filter); new oil filter; oil and lubricants as specified below.

SAFETY TIP . . . use work gloves.

BRAKE FLUID LEVEL CHECK

Check brake fluid level in master cylinder every three months . . . sooner if braking feels inadequate. Add when low.

Recommended grade: Extra Heavy Duty

1. Pry wire retaining clip off cap top with screwdriver.
2. Remove cap and gasket by lifting up.
3. Fluid level should be within ¼ inch of top rim. If lower than this, add fresh fluid to appropriate level.

DO NOT OVERFILL

4. Replace cap and gasket; secure retaining clip over cap. If fluid level was low, check again in a few days.
5. If fluid repeatedly checks low, there is a leak somewhere in the system. See SAFETY SYSTEMS—WHEEL CYLINDER CHECK. Have mechanic check further. Neglect can be dangerous.

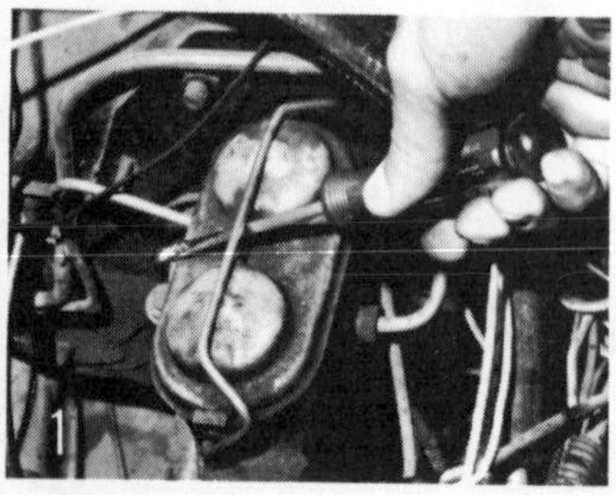

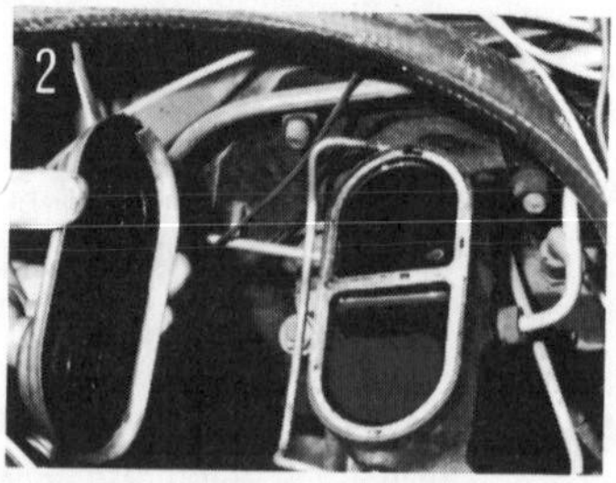

MANUAL TRANSMISSION FLUID LEVEL CHECK

GM SAYS . . . check manual transmission fluid every 6000 miles. Car should be parked level. Recommended grade: Standard Transmission Fluid (SAE 90).

TOOLS NEEDED . . . fluid level check device and adjustable wrench; bulb syringe.

1. Locate transmission fluid filler plug on right side of transmission housing from underneath car.

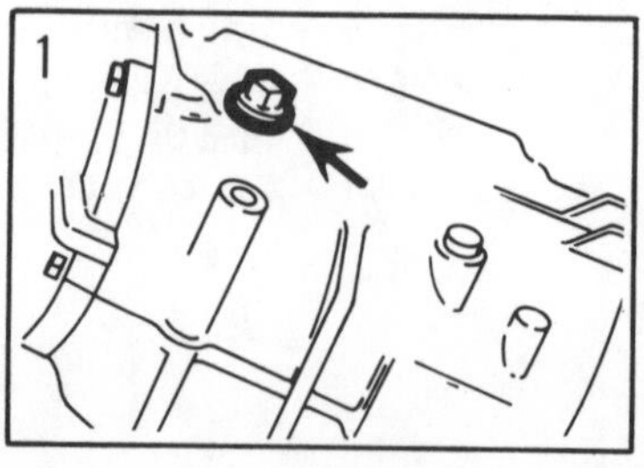

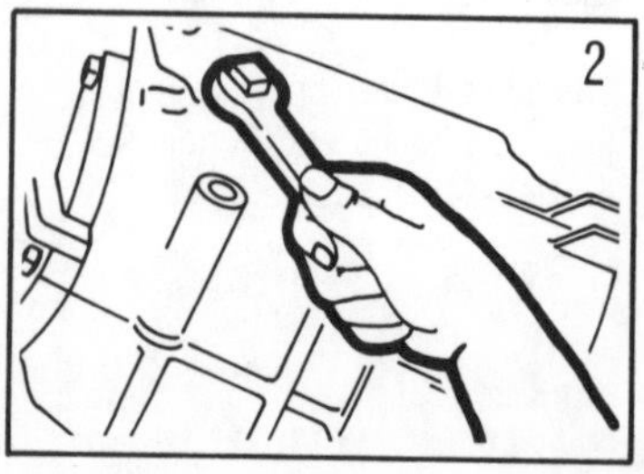

2. Wipe road dirt from filler plug area before loosening. Remove plug with adjustable wrench.
3. Insert your finger in the hole, the fluid should be at or near the bottom of the hole.
4. Add fluid as needed with hand bulb syringe.
5. Replace filler plug; tighten.

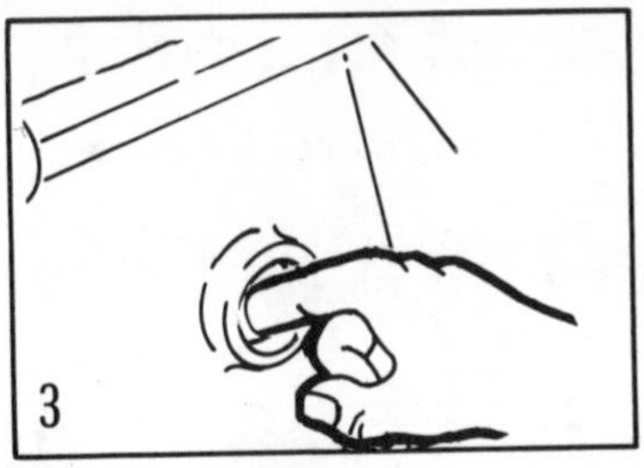

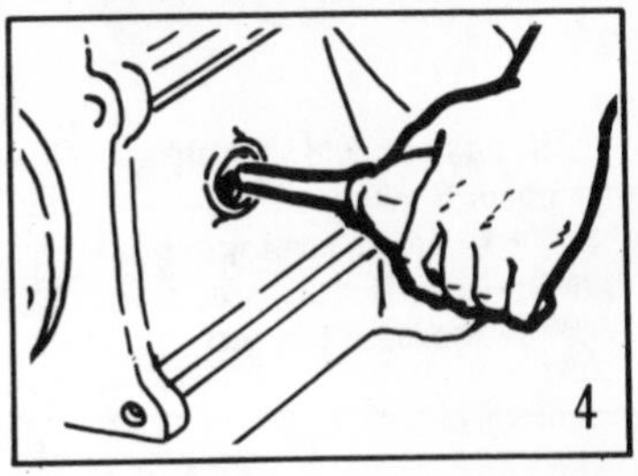

AUTOMATIC TRANSMISSION FLUID LEVEL CHECK

GM SAYS . . . check automatic transmission fluid (ATF) level every 6000 miles. Recommended grade: DEXRON® or Type A.
TOOLS . . . Long neck filler funnel

1. Engine must be warmed up and running. Place shift lever in PARK position.
2. Pull out dipstick. Wipe clean. Push dipstick all the way back in; remove it again.
3. If fluid is below ADD mark, add ATF to bring level up. DO NOT OVERFILL.
4. Add ATF thru transmission dipstick hole by means of long-neck filler funnel.

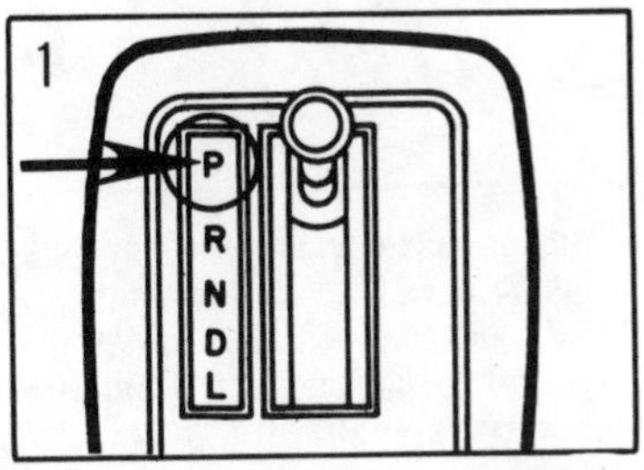

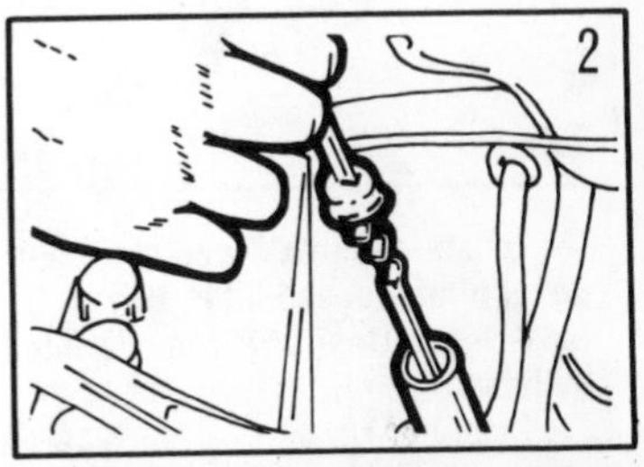

REAR AXLE LUBRICANT

GM SAYS . . . check rear axle lube level every 6000 miles. Recommended grade: Hypoid gear lube (SAE 90). Positraction axles require special positraction lubricant.

TOOLS . . . 9/16 box wrench (1971-73 models) or 3/8 drive ratchet with small extension (1974 and later models) and squeeze bulb filler to add lubricant.

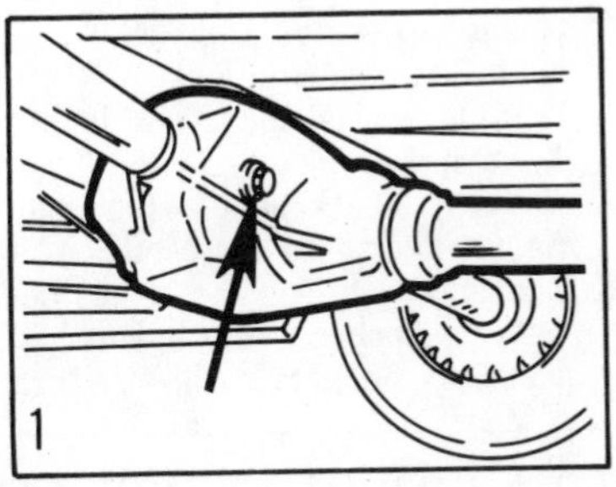

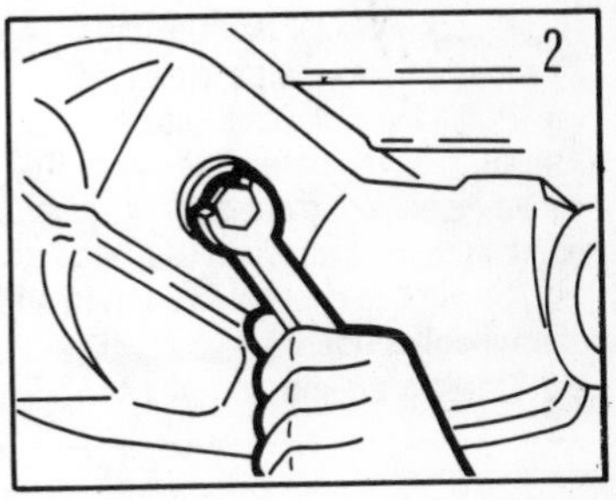

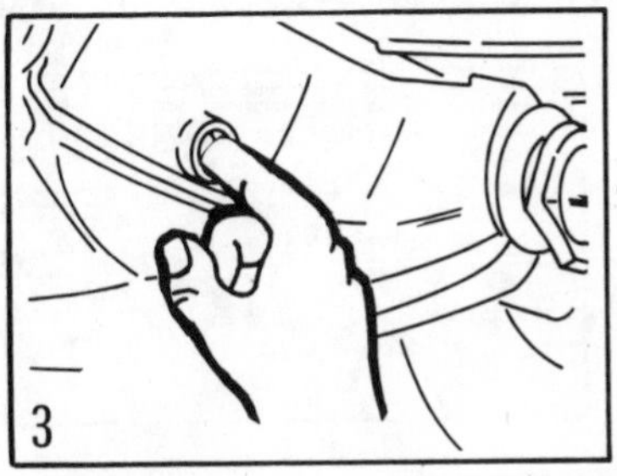

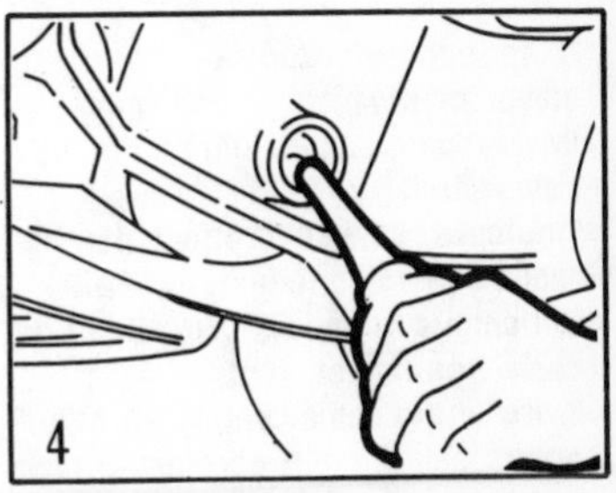

1. Locate filler plug on side of rear axle housing.
2. Wipe plug area clean; remove plug with wrench.
3. Insert your finger in the hole, the fluid should be at or near the bottom of the hole.
4. If fluid level is low, add as needed, with a hand bulb syringe.
5. Replace filler plug; tighten.

OIL AND FILTER CHANGE

1. If engine is cold, start up and idle for about 5 minutes.
2. Park car on level ground. Turn engine off. If you are going to change the oil filter, turn the front wheels hard right to gain clearance for filter removal.
3. Locate oil drain plug on underside of engine. Place drain pan under plug.
4. Remove drain plug with wrench. Let ALL dirty oil drain out.
5. Wipe plug and area around drain hole clean. Replace drain plug; tighten it.

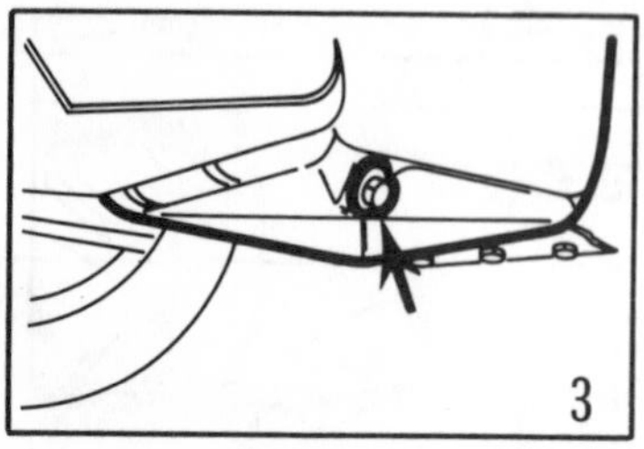

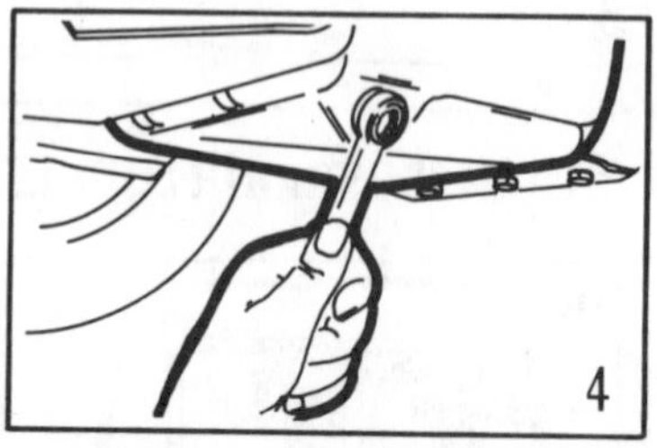

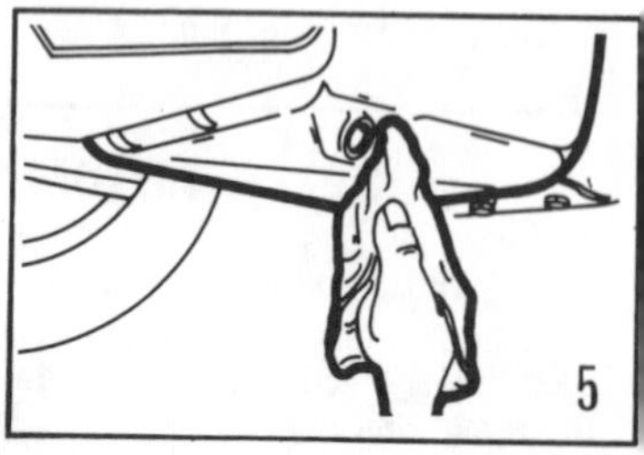

6. Locate oil filter. Move drain pan under filter. Loosen filter with oil filter wrench. Unscrew; remove filter by hand.
7. Smear fresh oil over surface of rubber gasket (washer) of new filter. Install new filter by hand only. Do NOT use wrench. Turn filter until gasket makes contact. Tighten an additional half turn only . . . NO MORE.
8. Locate oil filler hole on top of engine. Remove cap.
9. Punch oil pouring spout into top of oil can. Pour all cans of new oil into filler tube. Wipe filler cap clean and replace it.

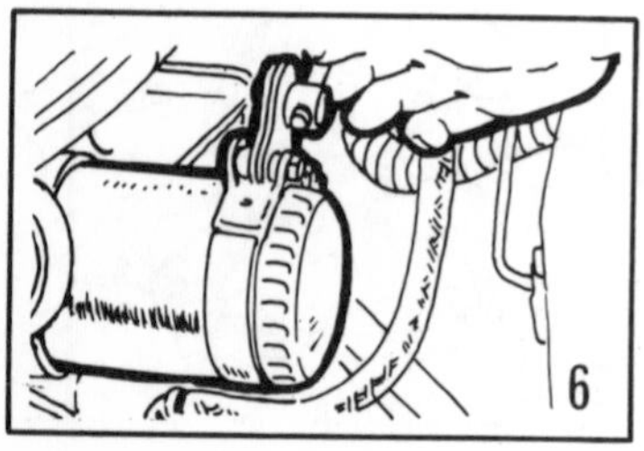

10. Check new oil level at dipstick. Pull out dipstick, wipe clean.
11. Push dipstick back into engine. Be sure to insert all the way. Remove dipstick and check new oil level. It should be above "FULL" line. If not, be sure to check if you put in all the oil called for.
12. Start up engine and idle for 3-5 minutes. Oil signal light on instrument panel will glow red when engine is first started. Light should go out in 30 seconds or less.
13. Stop engine and check for oil leaks at drain plug and filter. If you find any, check tightness of plug and/or filter, also for condition of filter gasket to see that it has not become pinched or damaged when installing. Recheck oil level, which should now be at "FULL".

SPEEDOMETER CABLE LUBRICATION

If speedometer pointer tends to quiver or jump, or if unit makes a low, rasping sound, lubrication may be needed.
1. Locate cable shaft attachment directly behind speedometer dial.
2. Remove retaining clip. Unscrew cable from speedometer.
3. Pull inner cable completely out of outer casing. Note carefully which end is top. Check for wear or frayed strands. If damaged, replace inner cable with new one.

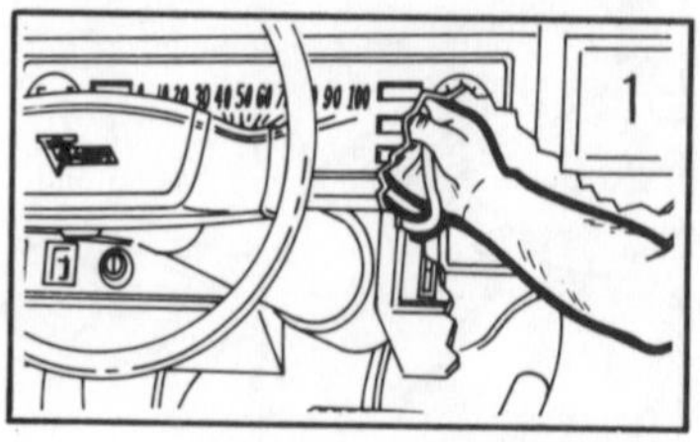

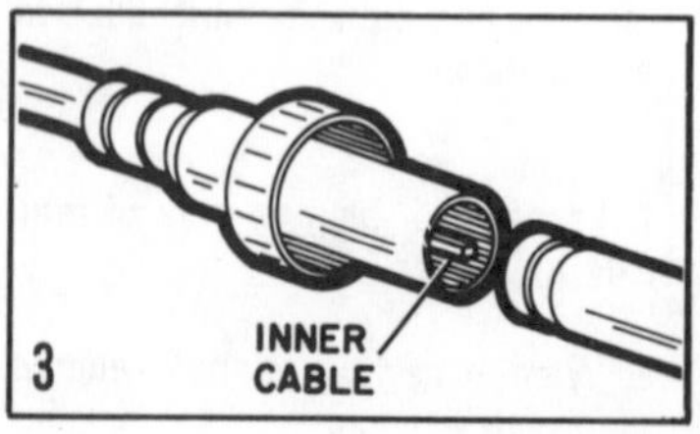

4. Apply generous amount of speedometer cable lubricant into cable casing. Replace inner cable in shaft, noting that top end is not in-

serted accidentally. Turn inner cable as it is being re-inserted. Twist cable when all the way in, to lock into position at lower end.

5. Re-connect cable to speedometer head under instrument panel.

DOOR HINGES AND STOPS

(lubricate every 6 months)

1. Brush any dirt accumulations from door hinges and stops. Use old tooth brush or rag.

2. Apply dab of white polyethylene grease to door hinges, trunk hinges, hood hinges, door stops.

DOOR LOCKS

(lubricate every 6 months)

1. Insert door key half way into lock.

2. Spray aerosol lock lubricant into lock.

3. Push key rest of way into lock; turn back and forth several times.

Cooling System

IT IS RECOMMENDED . . . that radiator coolant (water/antifreeze mixture) level be checked once or twice a month. Do this when engine is cold. Check more often if you do a lot of hard driving. Coolant is checked visually on models with expansion tanks.

Keep coolant up to recommended level in radiator. If coolant checks frequently low, look for leaks.

Tighten all hose clamps occasionally. For best results, keep a 50/50 water/antifreeze mixture year round. Change complete coolant mixture every 24 months.

CAUTION: If you must check coolant in a hot engine, cover radiator cap with thick rag before releasing. Remove cap slowly . . . press down and turn.

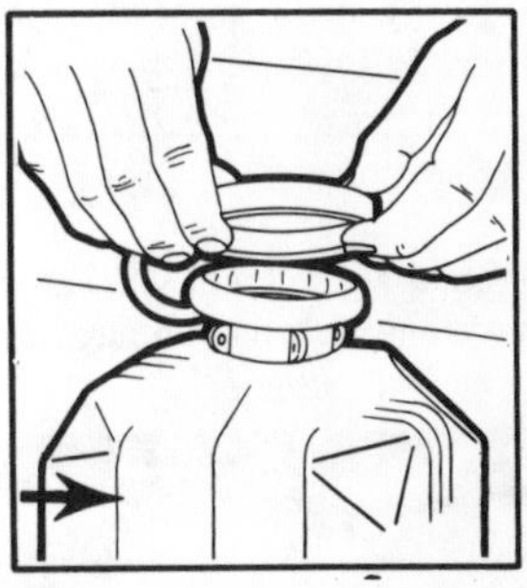

REPLACING THE THERMOSTAT

A faulty thermostat will usually cause engine overheating. The thermostat is located inside the housing where the top radiator hose connects to the engine.

TOOLS AND MATERIALS . . .
New thermostat
Gasket sealer
Socket set or adjustable wrench

1. Drain radiator of about half its coolant. (See How To Replace Hoses)

2. Loosen and remove both retaining bolts and lift thermostat housing off the engine.

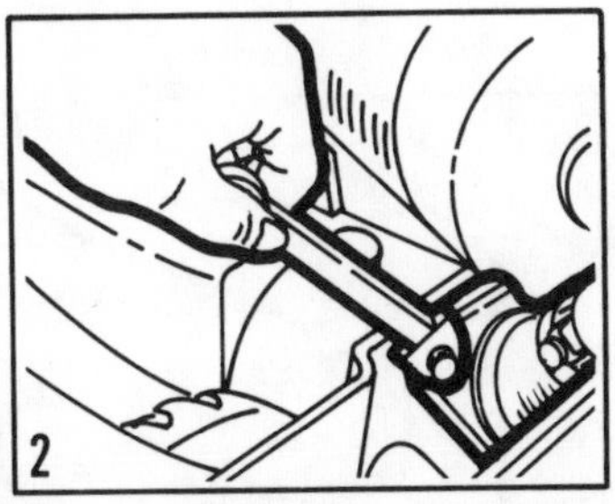

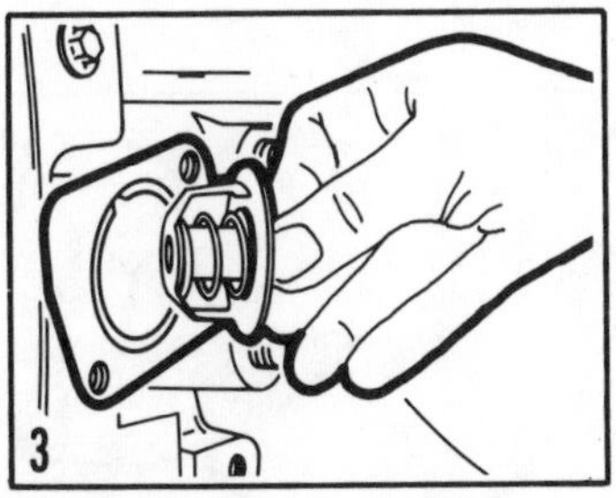

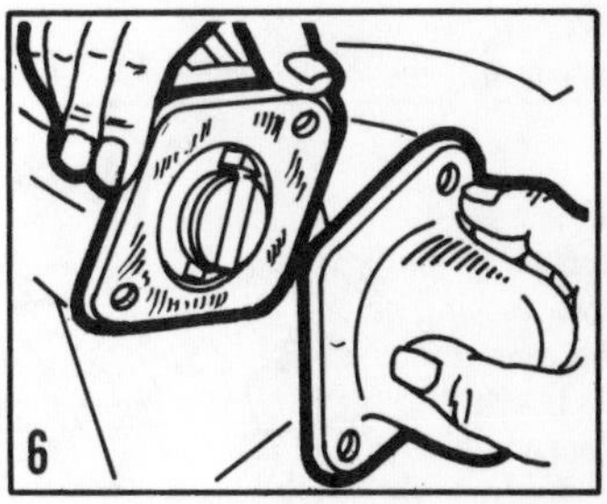

NOTE: If you're careful it won't be necessary to remove radiator hose.

3. Remove old thermostat.

4. Scrape thermostat housing flange and engine block surface to remove old gasket debris.

5. Drop new thermostat into place—spring down.

6. Install new gasket with sealer applied to both sides.

7. Replace thermostat housing and tighten both retaining bolts.

FAN BELT ADJUSTMENT

The fan belt not only drives the radiator fan, it turns the water pump and drives the alternator. It's easy to see that the condition and proper tension of the belt are vital, since almost all engine cooling and electrical power is dependent on it. The belt deserves an occasional look and tension check.

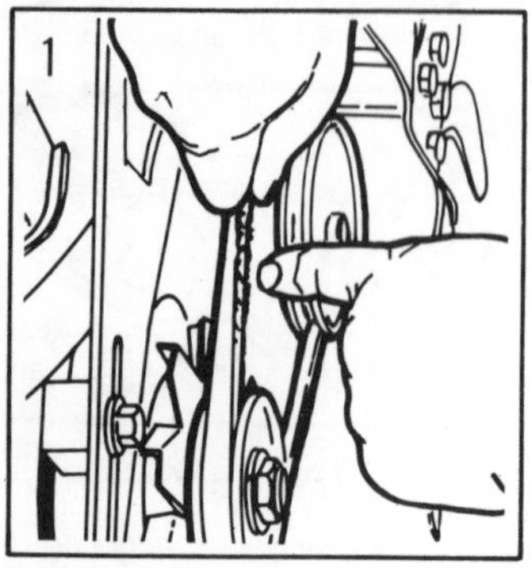

1. Inspect fan belt occasionally. If worn, frayed or cracked on inner driving surface, replace.

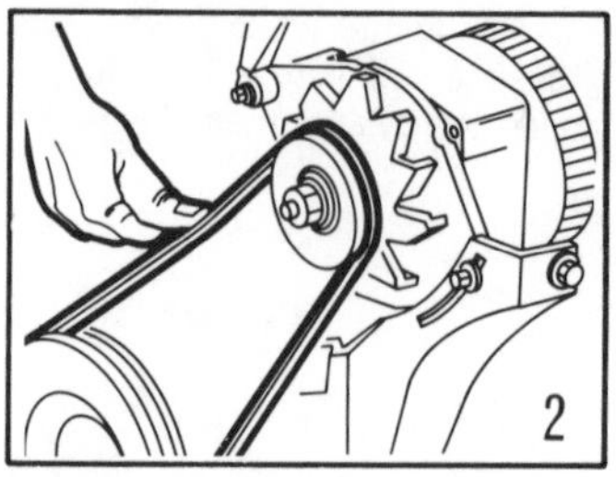

CAUTION: An overtightened belt may damage alternator and water pump bearings.

2. Check tension occasionally. Press thumb at midpoint of belt span between pulleys. If belt depresses more than ½ inch, tightening is needed. A too-loose belt will not drive alternator and water pump effectively.

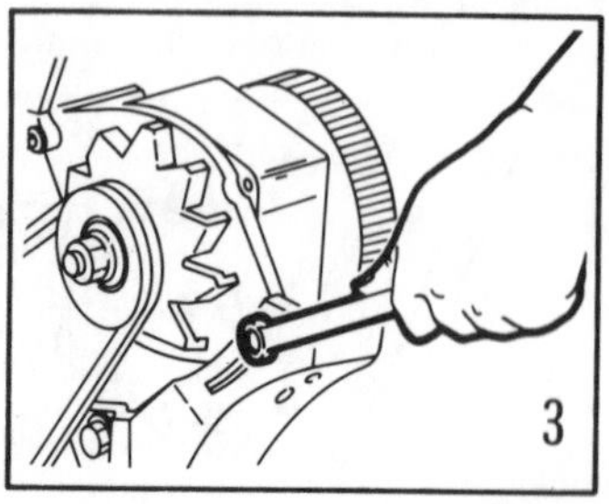

3. Adjust to proper tension of ¼ inch deflection.

HOSE REPLACEMENT

Coolant drain and refill work may be done alone; when changing hoses, coolant must also be drained as part of job. Discard all hoses with cracks or soft spots. Check hose clamps for tightness and good condition.

1. Remove radiator cap. Open radiator petcock (See 2). Drain coolant into catch basin. If near 24 months old, discard old coolant.

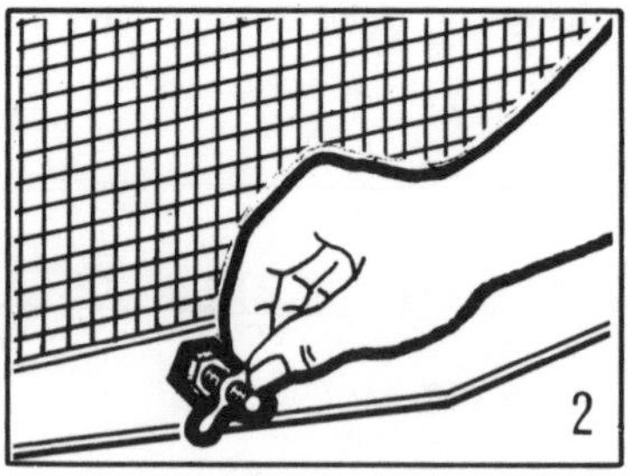

2. Petcock is located on the bottom left of radiator on '71 and '73 and later Vegas and all Astres. To drain a '72 Vega radiator, you must disconnect the lower radiator hose.

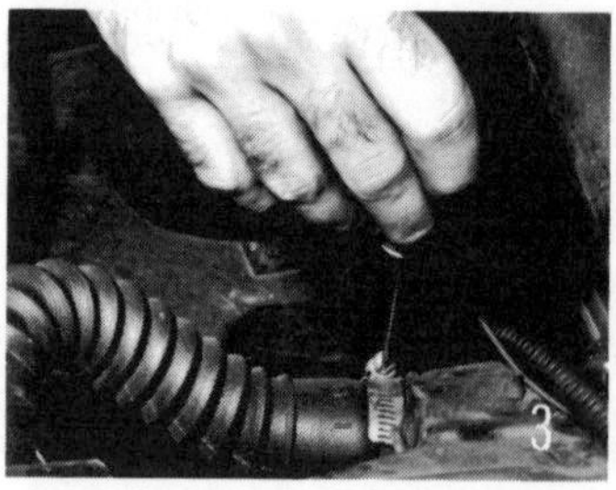

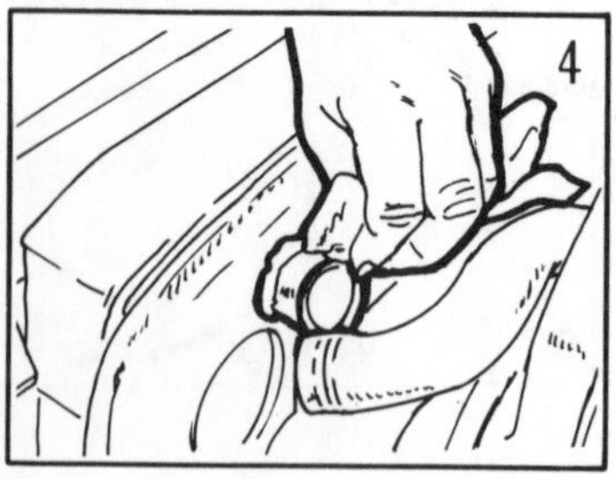

3. Loosen clamps at each end of hose(s). Work loose; pull off. If old hose clamps are rusted or damaged, replace with new units.

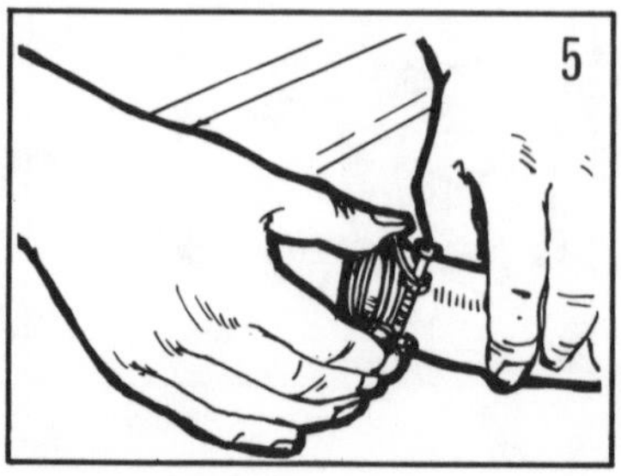

4. Wipe all hose connections clean. Use emery cloth to get rid of residue. Check all hoses for weak spots, as well as cracks inside and out.

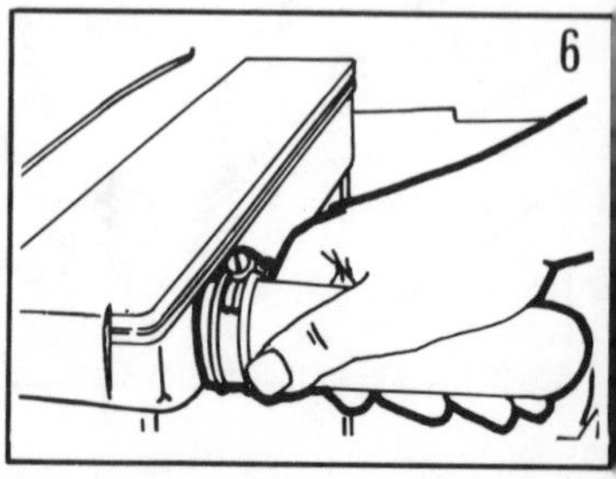

5. Slip clamps over each hose end.

Slip hose ends all the way onto cleaned up hose connections.
6. Place hose clamp ¼ inch from hose end. Tighten. Close petcock. Refill with 50/50 coolant/water mix.
7. Start engine; allow to warm up. Check for coolant leaks.
8. Road test car; watch for temperature warning light. (Vega GT instruments may differ from above).

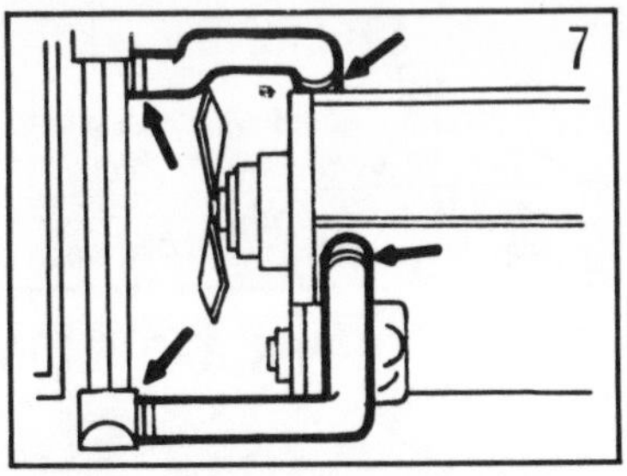

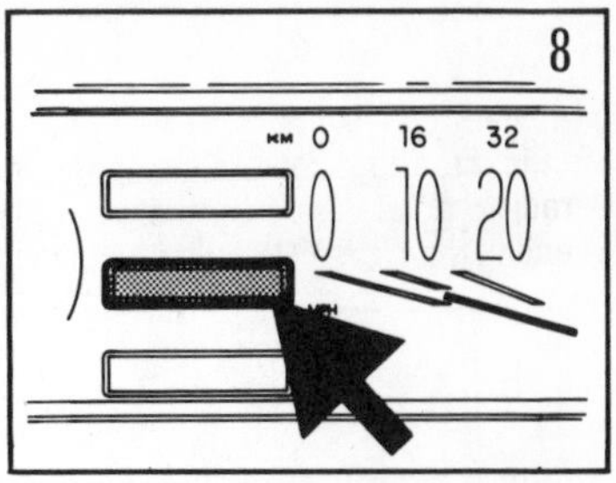

CHANGING THE ANTI-FREEZE

If the coolant is extremely dirty, add a good flushing additive to the radiator and run the engine the amount of time recommended on the can. Turn off the engine and remove the radiator cap. Be careful when removing the cap if the engine is hot. Open the petcock in the bottom of the radiator by turning its ears in a counterclockwise direction. On the 1972 Vega, remove the bottom radiator hose to drain. When all the coolant has drained out of the system, insert a garden hose into the radiator cap opening. Turn the water on in the hose and start the engine. Allow the engine and the hose to run until the water coming out of the radiator is clean. Turn off the engine and remove the hose. Allow the water to drain out of the system, then close the radiator petcock or replace radiator hose. Pour the required amount of antifreeze into the radiator and fill the rest of the system with water. You can determine the required amount of antifreeze by checking the Capacities Chart, and checking this against the protection chart usually found on the antifreeze container. Run the engine for at least five minutes to allow air to escape. Fill the radiator to 1 in. below the filler neck and turn off the engine. Recheck the level in the radiator after the car has been driven a short distance.

Suspension and Tires

The independent front suspension is very similar to that used on larger Chevrolet and Pontiac vehicles. Each wheel is suspended by unequal length control arms. The steering knuckle, which supports the wheel, is attached to the upper and lower control arms by ball joints. The coil spring is located between the lower control arm and the frame. The tubular shock absorber is mounted inside the spring. Vehicles equipped with the optional ride and handling package (standard on GT) have a stabilizer bar mounted in rubber bushings to the body and connecting the lower control arms. The rear suspension is also very similar to that used on larger GM vehicles. A coil spring suspended live rear axle is located by two lower and two upper control arms. The tubular shock absorbers are mounted behind the axle. Vehicles equipped with the optional ride and handling package have a stabilizer bar connecting the lower control arms.

1976 and later models use a new type of suspension similar to that used on the Monza and Sunbird. It uses lower control arms and a tie-rod to control lateral movement. A torque arm running parallel to the driveshaft is used to control axle wind-up. A stabilizer bar is also used and the upper control arms are no longer used.

The front wheels mount and rotate on the spindles, which are attached to upper and lower ball joints. A coil spring is mounted between the control arms on both sides. A shock absorber is located in the center of each spring. The rear suspension consists of coil springs, upper and lower control arms, and shock absorbers.

HANDLING TROUBLESHOOTING

Your car's suspension system consists of wheels, tires, springs, shock absorbers, sway (or stabilizer) bars, ball joints, steering linkage. If any of these items is out of adjustment or badly worn, you may notice any of these symptoms:

- car pulls to one side when braking
- car wanders when driving a straight line
- overall ride may be either hard or bouncy
- effort is needed to steer vehicle
- tires show uneven wear
- tires squeal when cornering
- front of car dips or bounces when braking
- car rocks side-to-side when going over rough road
- wheels bounce or make slapping sound on road
- steering wheel vibrates in hands
- front of car vibrates at highway speeds

Any of above symptoms indicates corrective action is needed. Delay can: ruin tires; cause damage/failure to other suspension parts; create safety hazard.

STEERING

If steering linkage, front suspension and steering column components are in good condition, there should be no more than 1½ inch free play in the steering wheel when measured at the rim of the wheel. If a loud knock is heard when turning the steering wheel from one extreme to the other, have mechanic check pinion bearing preload.

HOW TO CHECK FOR BAD SHOCKS

Shock absorbers work to keep wheels in constant contact with the road. Result is safe handling and ride control; longer tire life. So shock absorbers (or shocks) are important.

1. Check under car and locate shock absorber near each wheel.
2. Heavy oil streaks on outer shock housing indicate need for replacement.

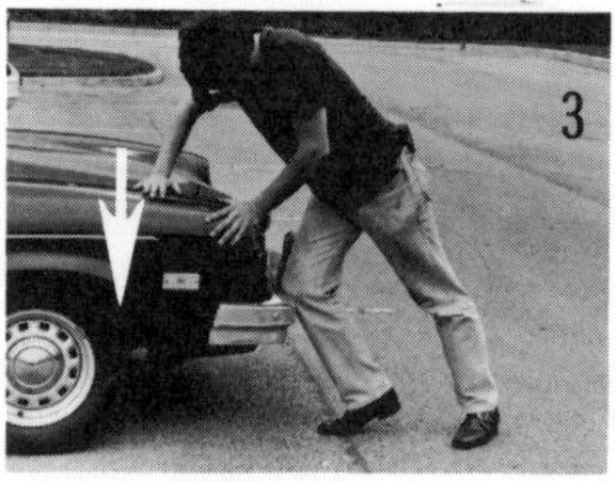

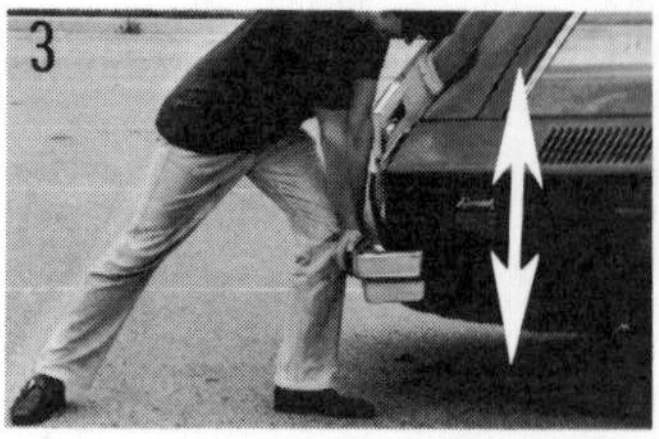

3. Stand at front of car and apply body weight in a pumping action to front bumper or fender. Release pressure and allow car to stop rocking. Car should not bounce more than one more time after releasing pressure. Repeat at rear. If bouncing continues more than once, replacement is needed. Replace shocks in pairs (front pair or rear pair).

TOW HITCH INFORMATION

If your car is used for trailer towing you should check:
A. Cooling System; be sure coolant is at proper level in radiator. See Cooling System Section for checks to perform.
B. Check Transmission Fluid; keep topped up to proper level.
C. Check Rear Shock Absorbers; you may benefit from installation of new rear shocks.
D. Check Tire Pressures; best traction and handling can be ensured if tire pressures are properly maintained.

For safer and more trouble-free trailer towing, consider:
A. Automatic Transmission Cooler; helps remove excess heat from automatic transmission fluid built up during towing mileage. Also helps avoid radiator overheating. Some units can be self-installed.
B. Radiator Over-Flow Tank Kit; addition of a reservoir to catch radiator coolant overflow preventing coolant loss. Easy to install, these units help a tow car run cooler, avoid overheating due to coolant loss.
C. Heavy-Duty Shock Absorbers or Air Shocks; important to have on rear wheels if you intend to do a lot of towing or load carrying within the car itself. Don't forget to consider replacing factory shocks, when they are worn out, with heavy-duty units at the front as well.
D. Variable Load Flasher; this unit will accommodate the added load of trailer turn signal lamps on trailer when these are hooked into your car's electrical system.

FRONT END ALIGNMENT

When steering, handling and/or tire wear indicate front end alignment may be needed, this work can only be done at an automotive service shop. DO NOT PUT OFF NEEDED FRONT END ALIGNMENT. At the same time, have ball joints and steering linkage checked.

Ignition System

TUNE-UP SERVICES

The ignition system consists of spark plugs; plug wires; distributor; rotor; points; condenser; coil. These units work to create a good hot spark inside the engine (ignition) at exactly the right moment (timing). If ignition is weak or timing is off, engine may be hard to start, run poorly, waste gas, lose power, backfire or not run at all.

1975 and later Vegas and Astres are equipped with the High Energy Ignition (HEI) system. This system is a transistorized ignition that eliminates the conventional system's points and condenser, thus eliminating a major part of a tune-up. The voltage delivered by this system is also far greater than the conventional system, enabling longer spark plug life as the hotter plug won't be as susceptible to fouling. There is no regular servicing of the distributor as with previous units, but cap and wire condition should be checked periodically. Spark plugs are still replaced as a part of normal maintenance.

GM SAYS . . . Replace plugs and points every 12,000 miles.

TOOLS & MATERIALS . . . Parts: set of points; condenser; 4 spark plugs. Tools: gap gauge; 5/8 in. spark plug socket; screwdriver; open end, box or combination wrenches; timing equipment.
(see Ignition Timing).

SAFETY TIP . . . Change only one spark plug at a time to avoid cross-wiring and possible engine damage.

CHECKING POINTS AND ROTOR

The distributor holds the points, rotor and condenser.

1. To open the distributor, remove the two screws retaining the cap. Remove the coil wire and lift the cap off, but keep the other wires attached.
2. Pull the rotor off (straight up). If it is cracked or metallic tip is badly burned, replace it.
3. Check the metal contacts inside the cap. Replace the cap if they are corroded or there are any cracks.
4. Pry the points apart with a screwdriver. If worn or burned, replace. If OK, check the gap.

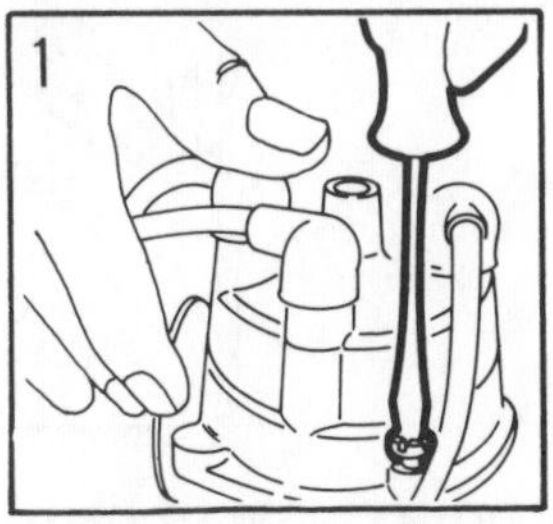

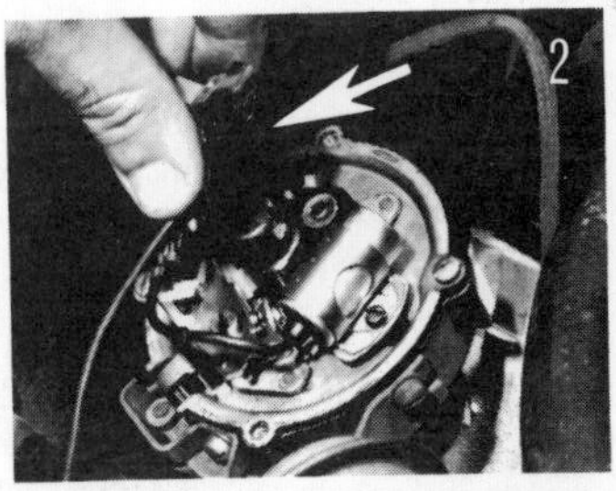

OTHER IGNITION CHECK POINTS

Inspect spark plug wires. If cracked or brittle, entire set should be replaced. Also, center high tension wire. Inspect distributor cap. Wipe inside clean occasionally with dry, lint-free rag. If cap is cracked or rotor contacts are excessively burned, replace cap.

SPARK PLUG REPLACEMENT

1. Remove spark plug wire by grasping rubber boot. Do not yank wire off. If stuck, turn boot, pulling gently.
2. Loosen spark plug using socket wrench.
3. Wipe or brush loose dirt from around plug before removing. Do not let dirt drop into engine through plug hole. Unscrew plug.

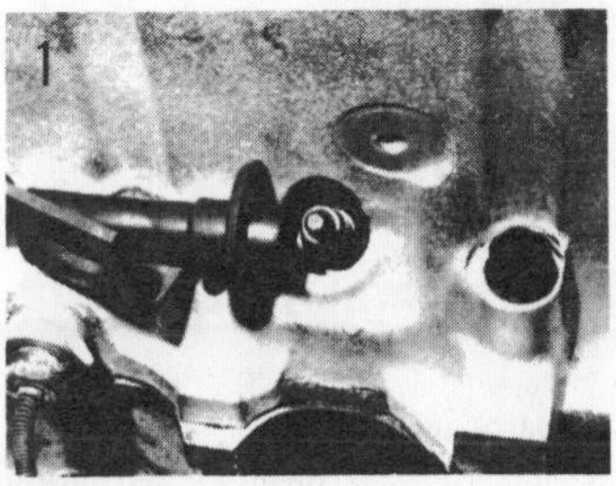

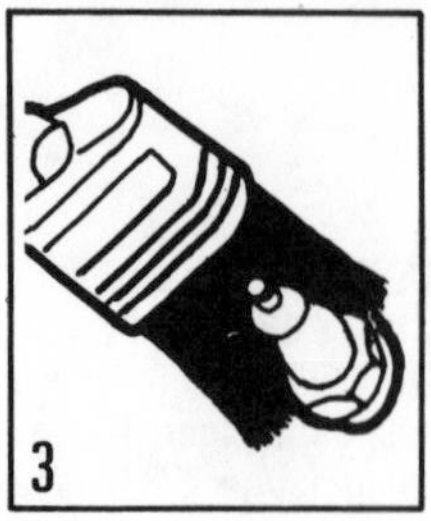

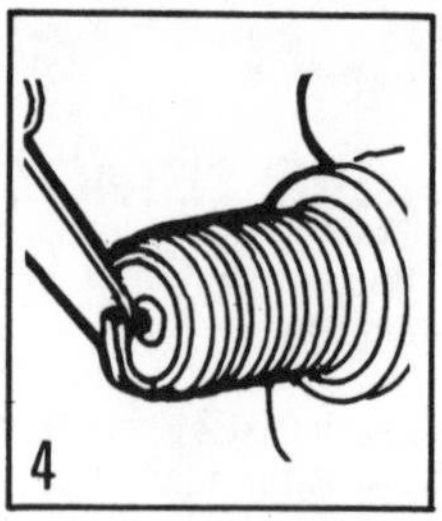

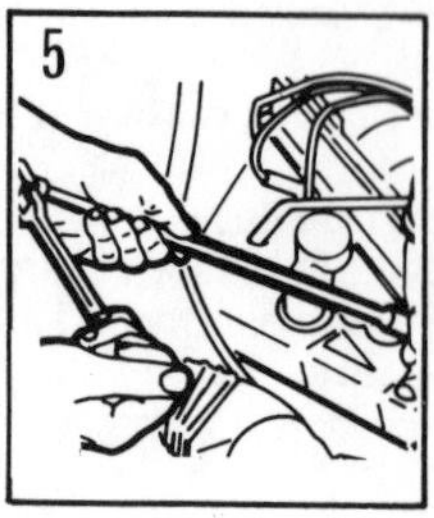

4. Check plug electrode gap on new spark plug. Adjust to 0.035 in. Plug gap is correct when the gauge drags slightly as it is pulled between plug electrodes.

5. Thread new plug into plug hole by hand. Hand tighten. Do not force or cross thread. Use socket wrench to tighten firmly but do not force. Replace plug wire. Press boot firmly.

REPLACING SPARK PLUG WIRES

Use the firing order illustration to guide you when replacing your ignition wires and/or distributor cap.

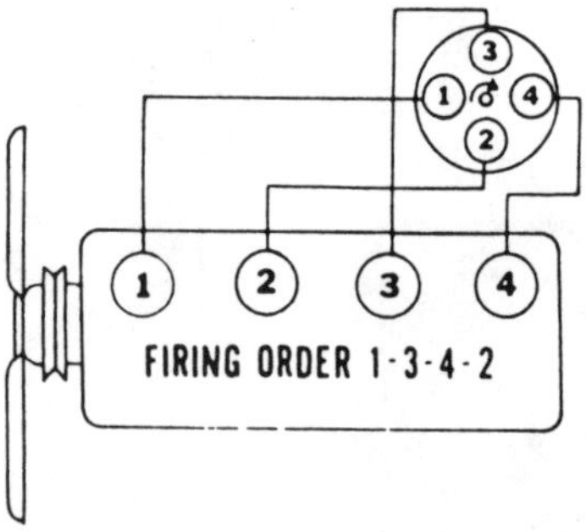

LOCATION OF POINTS AND CONDENSER—1971-74

Points and condenser work together. Always replace condenser also when installing new points.

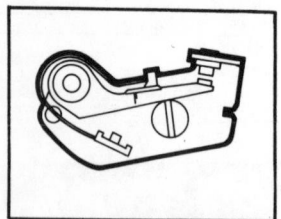

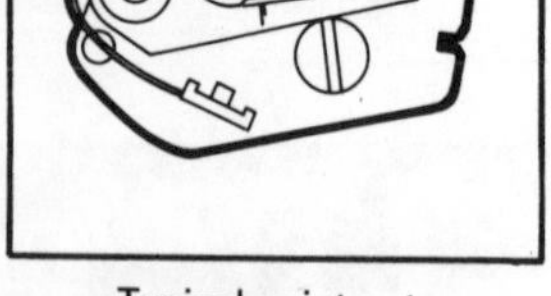
Typical point set.

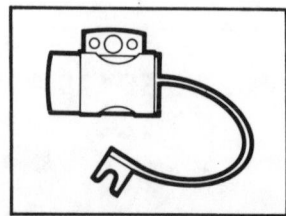

Typical condenser.

Typical location inside distributor.

REMOVING POINTS AND CONDENSER

CAUTION: When removing screws from distributor in following steps, be sure to avoid any screws accidentally falling through distributor opening into engine. Use magnetic screwdriver.

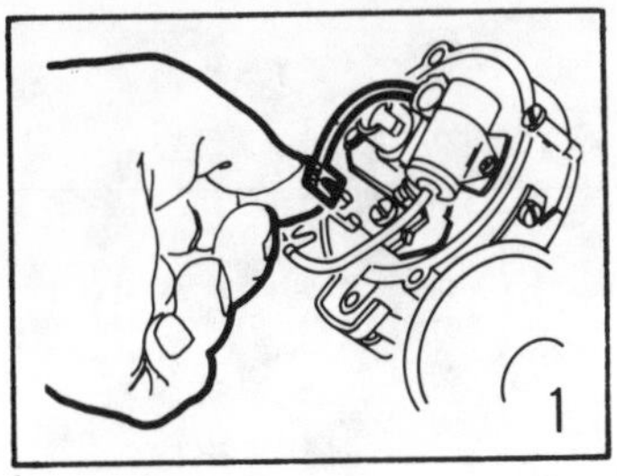

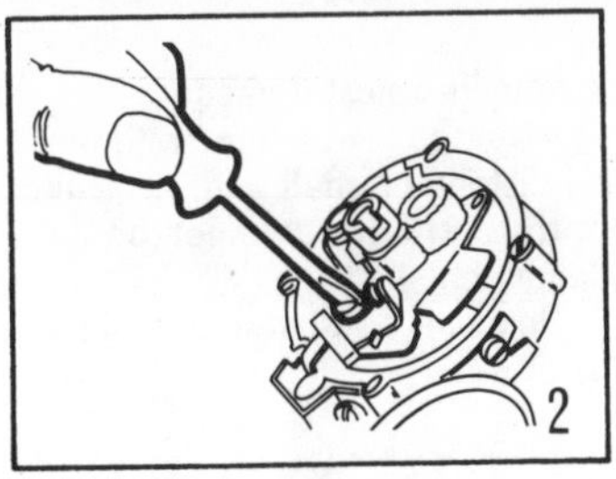

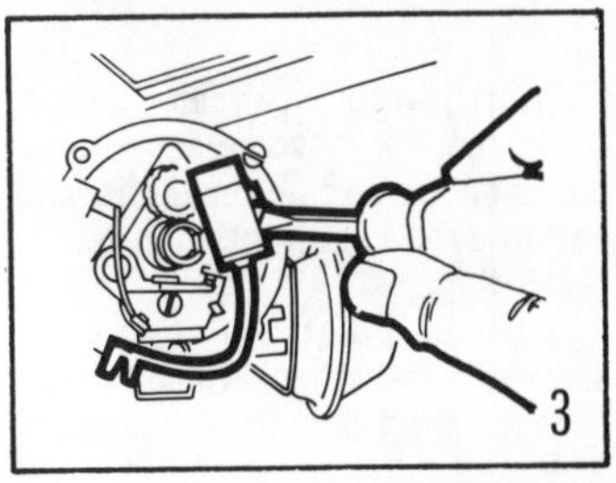

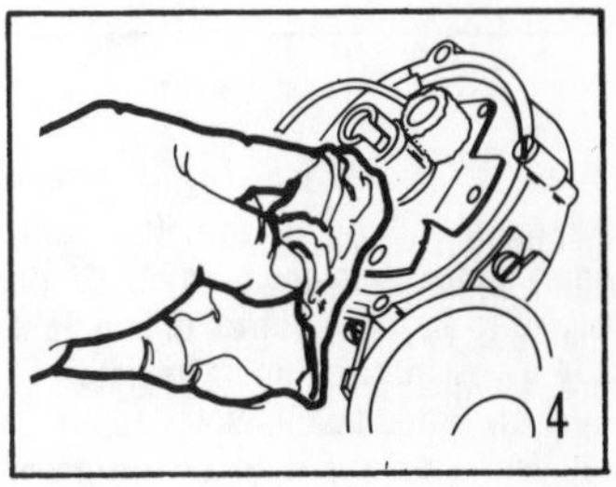

1. Disconnect the two wire terminals connected to the points set. Notice that the condenser connector is on the outside.

2. Remove points attaching screw being very careful not to drop screw inside distributor.

3. Remove screw which holds condenser. DO NOT DROP SCREW.

4. Wipe all dirt from distributor plate and cam with clean, lint-free rag.

INSTALLING POINTS AND CONDENSER—1971-74

1. Attach new condenser with screw.

2. Rotate or replace cam lubricator. Fiber cam lubricator must be turned 180° every 12,000 mi., replaced every 24,000. When replacing, simply pull it up and off stud; push new lubricator down over stud. DO NOT attempt to add oil or grease to fiber lubricator.

3. Position new points set in distributor. Attach retaining screw lightly. Replace both wire terminals. The condenser wire goes on the outside of the two.

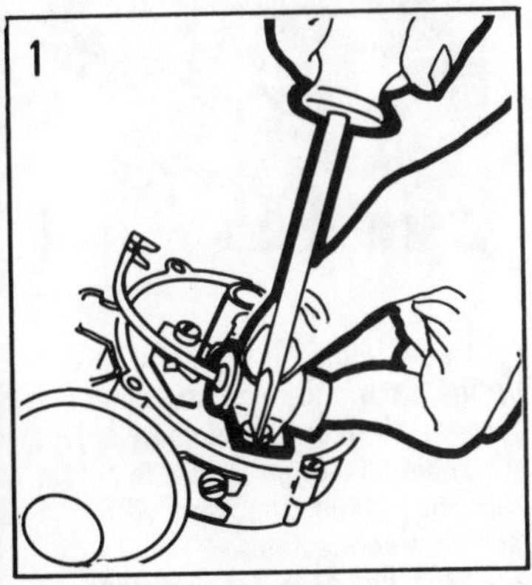

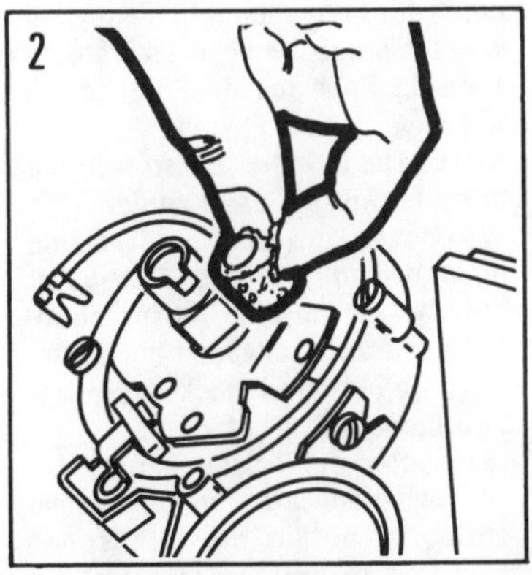

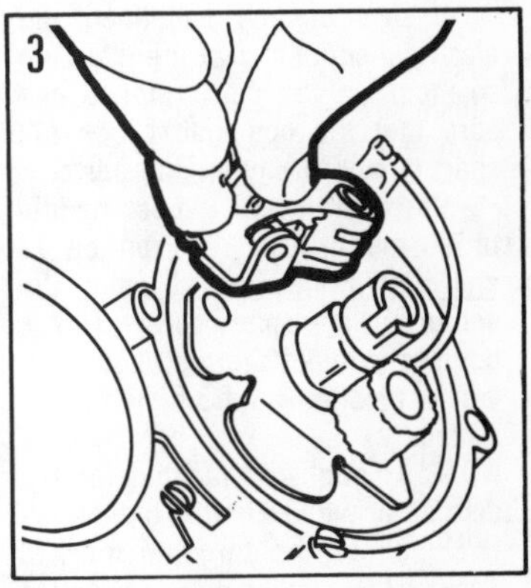

RESETTING THE CONTACT GAP

1. Check that point contacts meet squarely. If they do not, bend bracket supporting fixed contact using needle-nosed pliers.

2. Turn engine by ignition key (you'll need a helper) until rubbing block on point set is on one of the four high spots of distributor cam. You may use ¾ in. wrench on lower engine pulley to do this.

3. Insert screwdriver in slot near point contacts; twist to open or close gap.

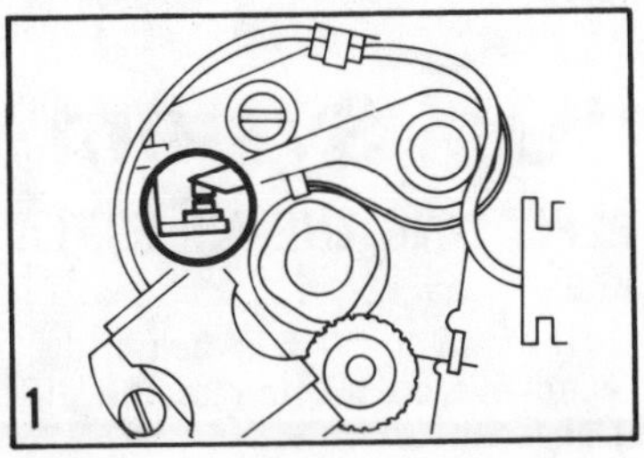

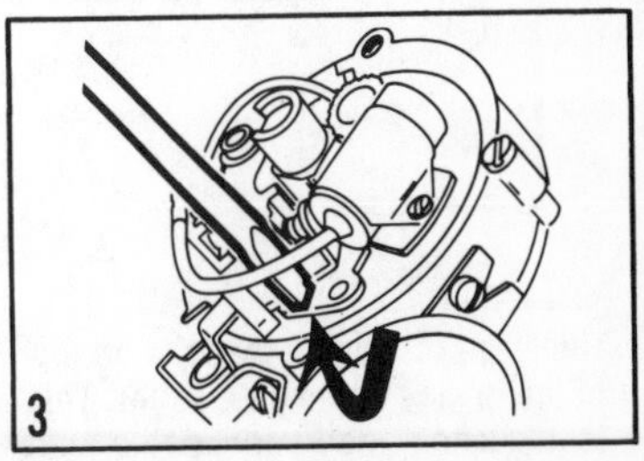

4. Correct gap is .019 in. for new points; .016 in. for used points.

5. Insert correct size feeler gauge. Adjust gap with screwdriver until feeler gauge can be moved in and out between contacts with only slight drag.
6. Tighten point set holddown screw. Recheck gap; it might have changed from tightening holddown screw. Re-adjust if needed.
7. Align tab inside rotor with notch on distributor shaft and push rotor onto shaft. Rotor must be fully seated on shaft.
8. Replace distributor cap; install screws.

5

IGNITION TIMING

Adjusting timing is the important finishing touch to any tune-up. While not difficult, job requires timing light and dwell meter. Timing is listed in Tune-Up Specifications.

1. Warm up the engine to normal operating temperature. Stop the engine and connect the timing light to the No. 1 (front) spark plug wire. Clean off the timing marks and mark the pulley notch with chalk.
2. Disconnect and plug the vacuum line at the distributor.
3. Disconnect the fuel tank line from the top of the evaporative emission carbon canister.
4. If so equipped, disconnect the electrical connector at the idle stop solenoid on the carburetor. Make sure that the connector does not short circuit to any engine parts.
5. Start the engine and set the idle to 700 rpm or less (1000 rpm on '73 and later models) by adjusting the carburetor idle speed screw. This is done to prevent the distributor advance mechanism from being actuated.

NOTE: To hook up a tachometer to a distributor with HEI, attach the positive lead to the terminal marked Tach on the coil; the negative lead to a ground. All tachometers may not connect this way. Check with manufacturer for compatibility with HEI.

1

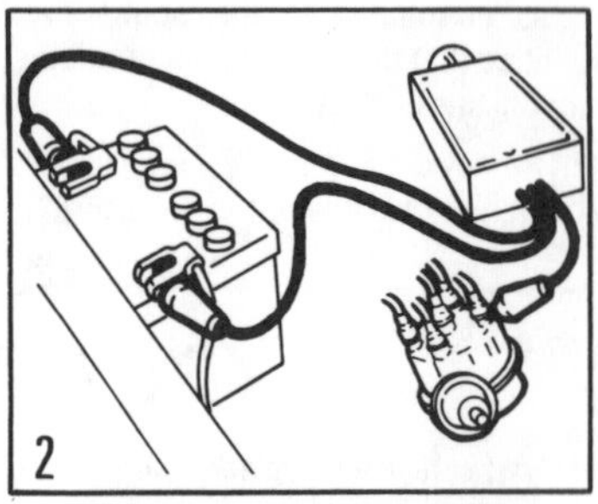
2

6. Aim the timing light at the pointer marks. Be careful not to touch the fan, because it may appear to be standing still. If the pulley notch does not appear to be aligned with the proper timing mark (refer to Tune-Up Specifications) the timing will have to be adjusted.

NOTE: The 0° mark is also referred to as TDC or top dead center.

7. Loosen the distributor clamp locknut and turn the distributor slowly to adjust. Turn counterclockwise to advance timing (toward before), and clockwise to retard (toward 0° or after).
8. Tighten the locknut.
9. Adjust the carburetor idle speed screw to obtain the idle speed specified in the Tune-Up Specifications with the solenoid disconnected.
10. Reconnect the electrical connector to the idle stop solenoid. Speed up the engine to allow the solenoid plunger to extend and then adjust the solenoid plunger screw to obtain the idle speed specified with the solenoid connected.
11. Stop the engine and reconnect the vacuum line and the evaporative canister line. Disconnect the timing light.

6

Fuel System

REPLACING THE AIR FILTER

The large round can that sits on top of the engine is the air cleaner. This is a closed, non-serviceable unit which is discarded and replaced with a new unit every 50,000 miles.

1. Unscrew the 7/16 in. bolt or the wing nut on the top of the air cleaner.

2. Lift the front of the cleaner up and pull the crankcase vent pipe from the valve cover.

3. Remove the air cleaner by lifting it straight off.

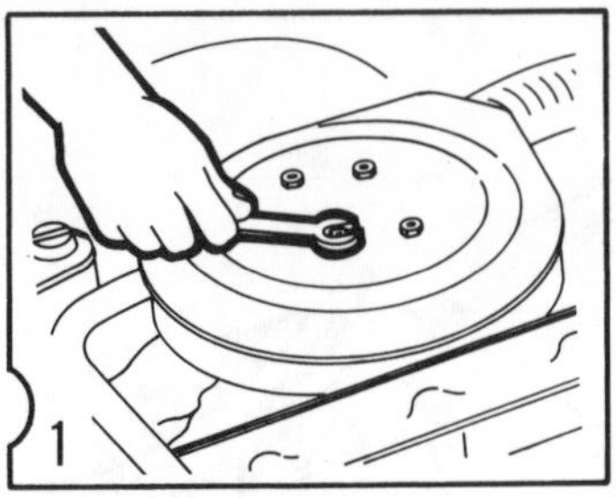

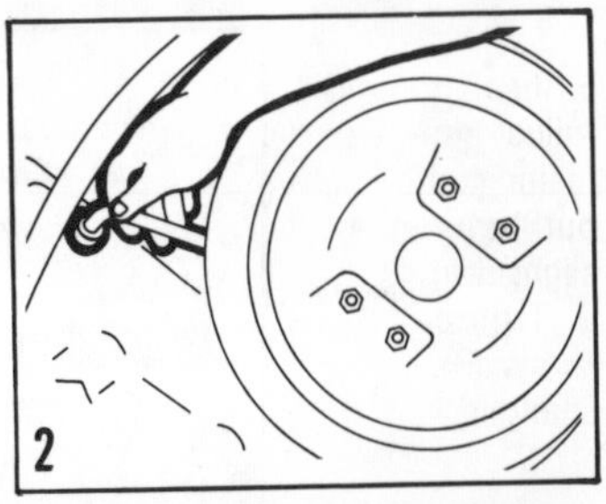

4. Remove the rubber grommet from the old air cleaner before discarding it. Install the grommet on the new unit.

5. Install the new air cleaner on the engine making sure that the vent pipe is in place. Replace the bolt or wing nut.

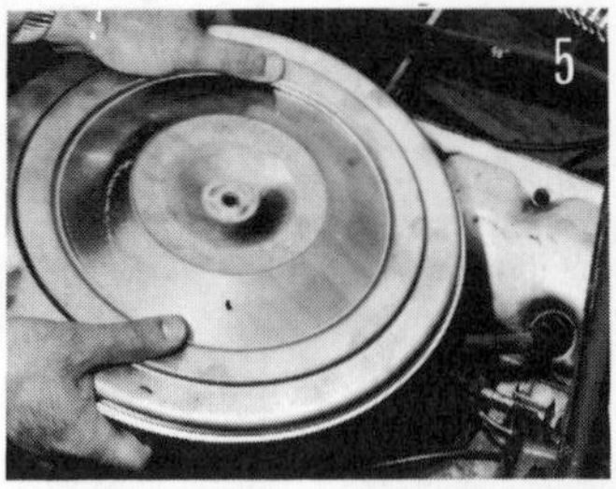

FUEL FILTER REPLACEMENT

The fuel filter is located behind the large fuel line inlet nut on the carburetor. Replace the filter every year or 12,000 miles. The fuel filter prevents dirt, rust, and scale from both the gas station's tank and your own fuel tank from reaching the carburetor. A dirty filter will starve the engine and cause poor running.

1. Place an absorbent rag under fuel line connection to absorb gas spills. Unscrew fuel line connection with ½ in. wrench while holding the larger nut with a 1 in. wrench. Be careful, fuel line fitting threads are easily stripped.
2. Remove the large filter retaining nut from the carburetor. The spring

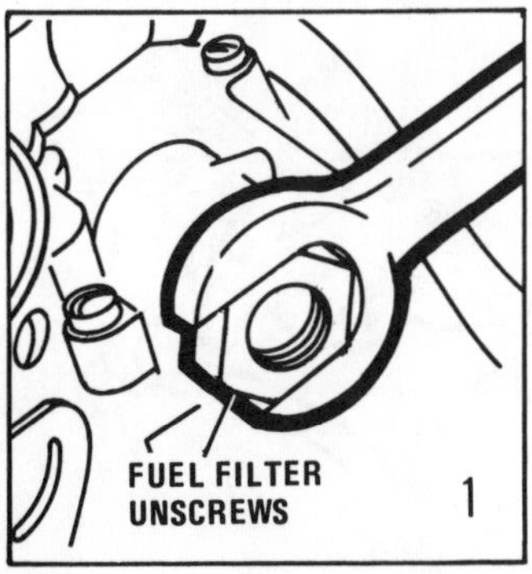

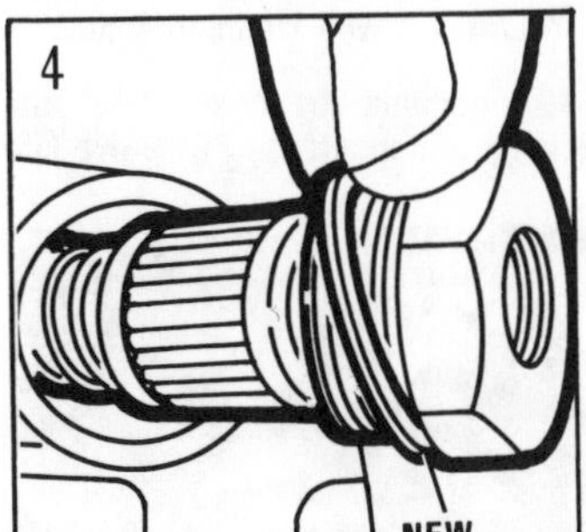

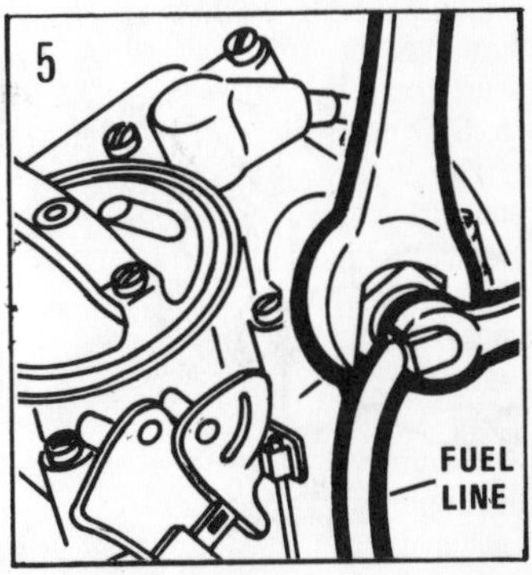

behind the filter will push it out. Remove the filter and the spring.
3. Install the spring and new filter element. Some carburetors are equipped with a paper element, others with a bronze unit. The bronze filter must have the small cone section facing out and a gasket between the filter and the retaining nut.
4. Install the new gasket on the retaining nut and screw it into place. CAUTION: DO NOT OVERTIGHTEN
5. Reconnect the fuel line. Discard the gas soaked rag safely.
6. Start the engine and check for leaks. Addition of a can of carburetor cleaner to the fuel tank occasionally will aid in keeping the entire fuel system clean.

EMISSION CONTROL SYSTEMS

An important part of a car's emission control system is the Positive Crankcase Ventilation (PCV) valve and its connecting hose. The PCV valve should be replaced once every 24,000 miles. This device keeps dirt and sludge from forming inside the engine. Make sure all PCV connections are tight. Check that the connecting hoses are clear and not clogged. Replace any brittle or broken hoses.

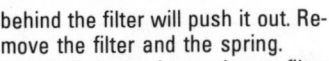

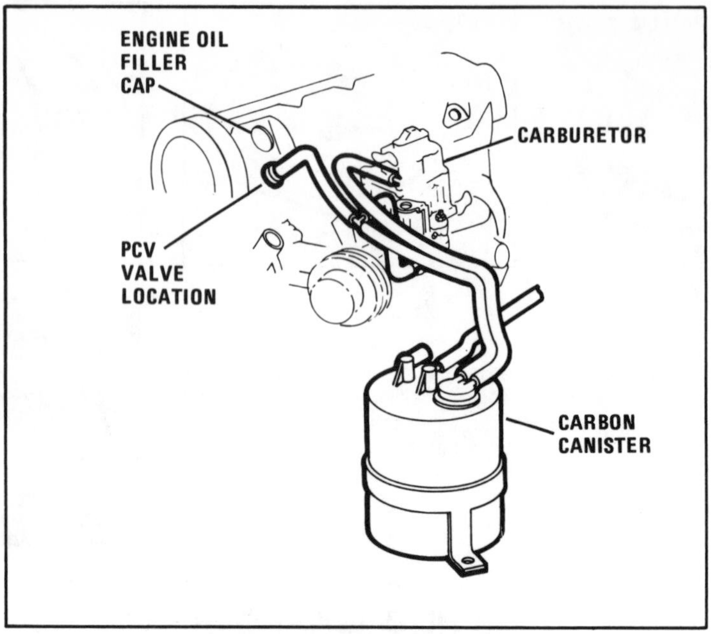

PCV VALVE REPLACEMENT

1. Pull valve from its location in front part of valve cover just below the oil filler cap.

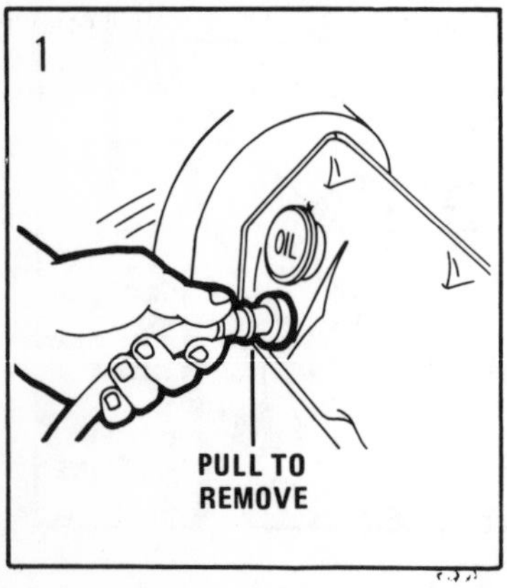

2. Squeeze the hose clamp with a pair of pliers. Remove the valve.

3. Note where the other end of the hose connects. Remove the hose and flush it with cleaning solvent.

4. Reconnect the hose. Pinch the clamp and insert the PCV valve into the hose.

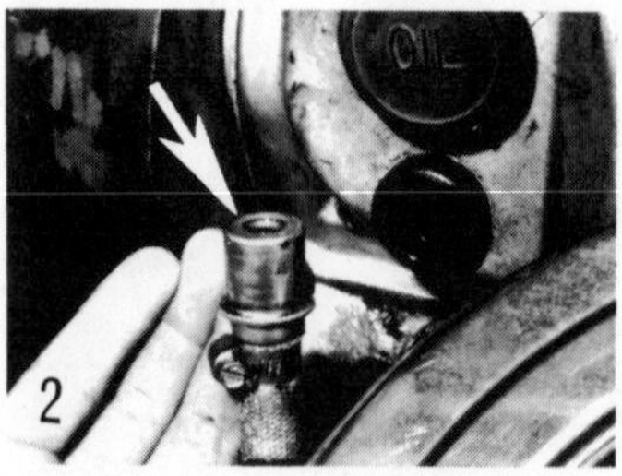

5. Insert the valve into the valve cover.

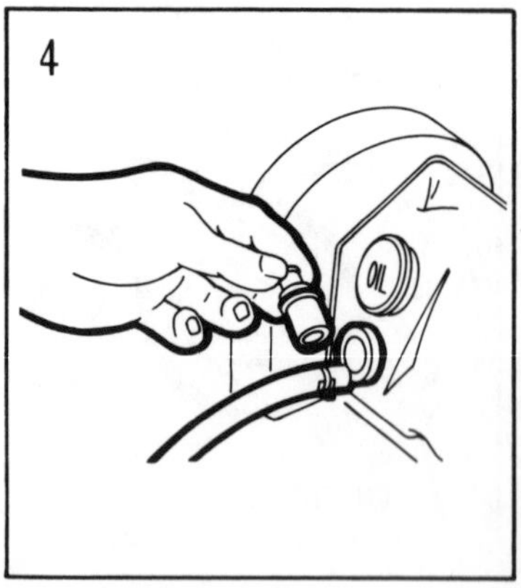

Safety Systems

FRONT TURN SIGNAL, PARKING LIGHT, SIDE MARKER

Parking lights, turn signals, and stop lights function with dual-element bulbs. To replace bulbs:

A. Front parking lights and turn signals on all models and rear lights on station wagons. Remove lens to expose bulb(s). Push in on bulb while turning counterclockwise to release bulb from socket. Remove and replace with new bulb. Replace lens.

B. On sedans and hatchbacks, rear bulbs are reached from inside rather than outside. Locate bulb housing inside trunk or rear compartment. Twist socket to release from housing. Push in on bulb, turn counterclockwise and remove bulb.

NOTE: When inserting new dual element bulb, note that knobs on side of bulb base are different distances from base tip. Match knobs to socket slots for proper fit.

BACK-UP LIGHTS

To replace back-up light bulbs, raise trunk lid or rear door. Reach bulb socket from inside car. Turn bulb socket counterclockwise and pull out. Push down on bulb turning counterclockwise to remove from socket. Remove lens on station wagons.

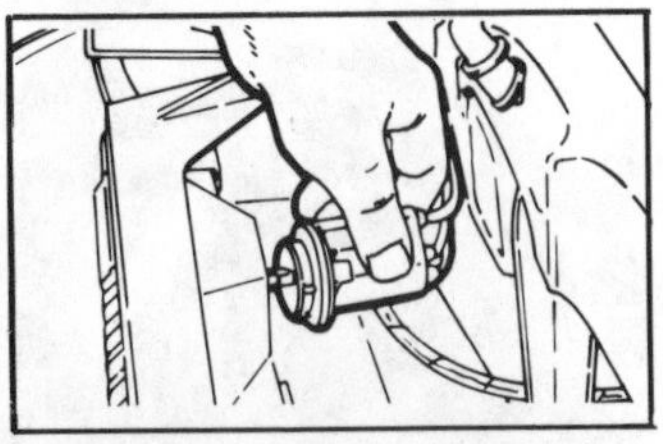

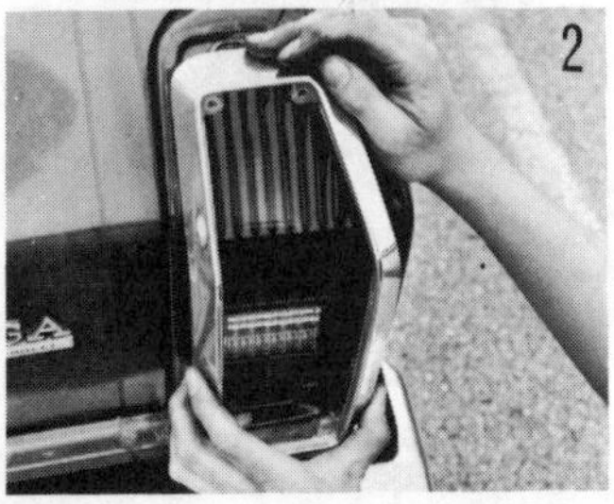

FRONT SIDE MARKER LIGHT

Reach up under fender and turn bulb socket counterclockwise to remove from housing. Pull bulb straight out. Remove lens on 1974 and later models.

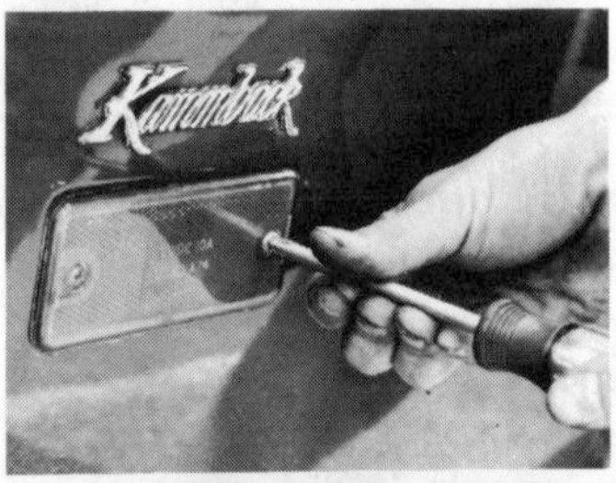

LICENSE PLATE LIGHT

Remove screw lens and housing that attaches to bottom of bumper. Push in on bulb turning counterclockwise to remove. On 1974 and later models, reach bulb socket from inside car. Turn bulb socket counterclockwise and pull out. Push down on bulb turning counterclockwise to remove from socket.

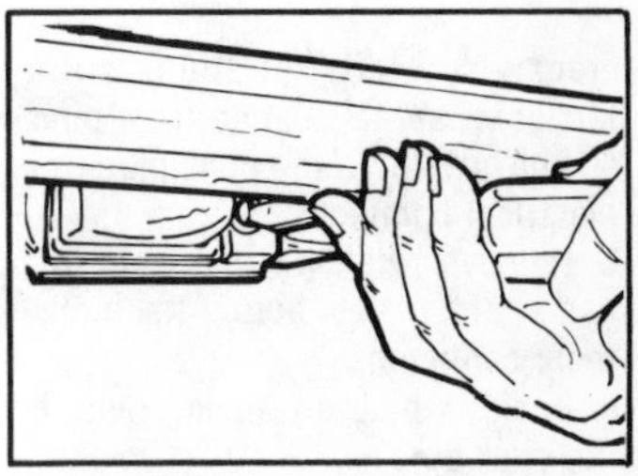

INTERIOR DOME LIGHT

This is cartridge type bulb; be sure to purchase correct replacement. Pry dome light lens out from housing. To avoid blowing fuse, make sure doors are closed and dome light switch is in OFF position. Carefully lever the bulb straight out of housing. Insert new bulb and reinstall dome light lens.

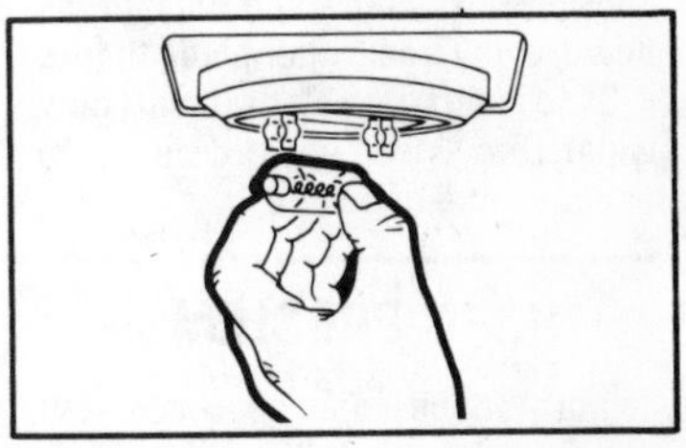

HEADLIGHT REPLACEMENT

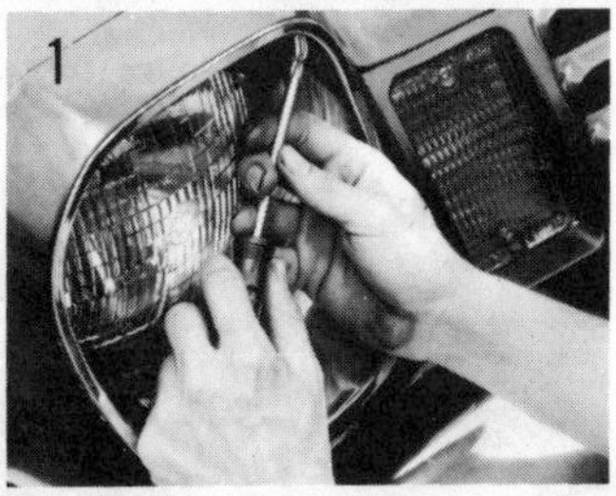

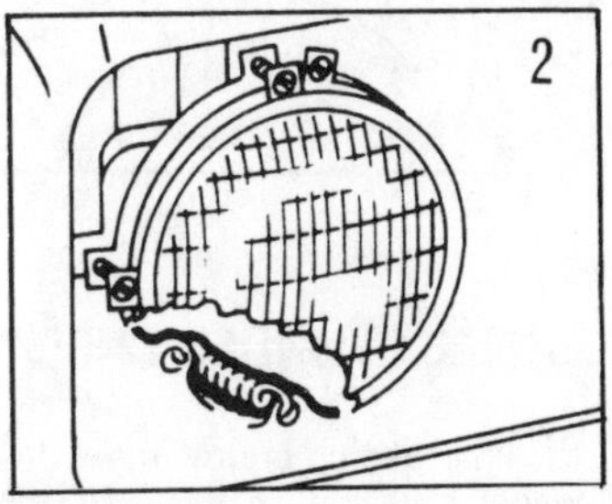

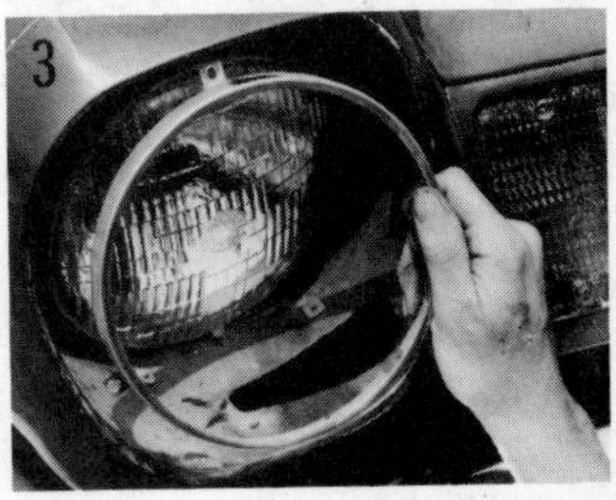

1. Remove the headlight trim ring retaining screws located near the outer edge. Do not confuse these with the two headlight aiming screws.
2. Use a hook to pull the retaining spring off to release the rim. Remove the rim.
3. Rotate the right headlight

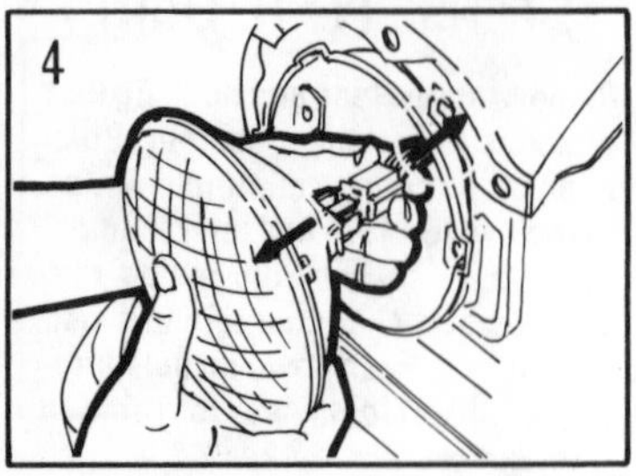

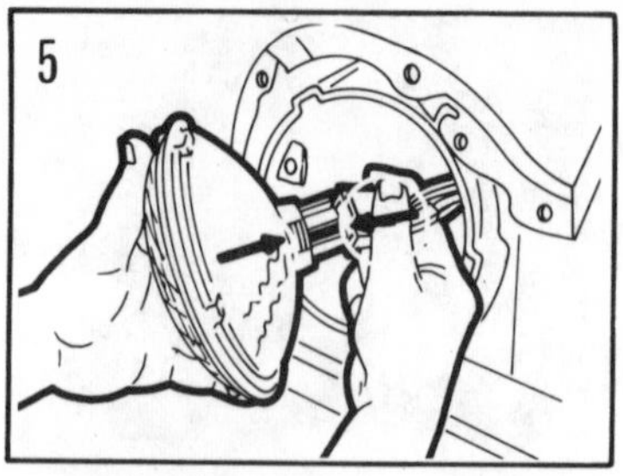

clockwise, left headlight counterclockwise, to release from pins.
4. Pull bulb forward and unplug from electrical connector.
5. Remove retaining ring from bulb and attach to new bulb. Attach electrical connector.
6. Position bulb on aiming pins. Fit rim over bulb.
7. Pull retaining spring into position to hold rim.

8. Insert and tighten headlight rim retaining screws.

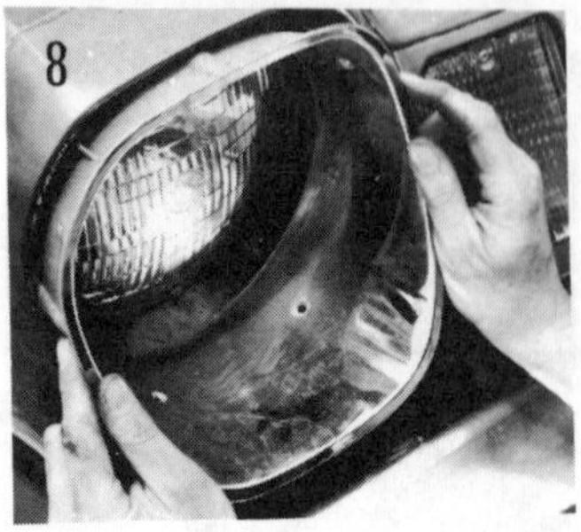

WINDSHIELD WIPER BLADE REPLACEMENT

To replace wiper blade, lift up on spring release tab on wiper arm connector. Pull wiper blade off. Snap new blade into place.
To replace rubber insert only, press down, away from wiper blade to free it. Slide insert from blade. Insert new wiper. Bend insert upward slightly to engage retaining clips.

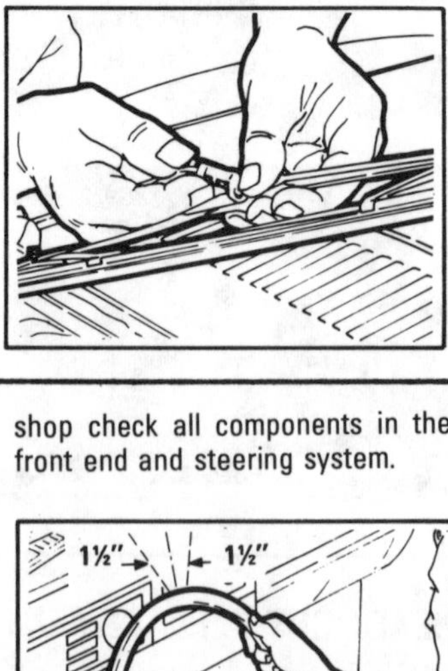

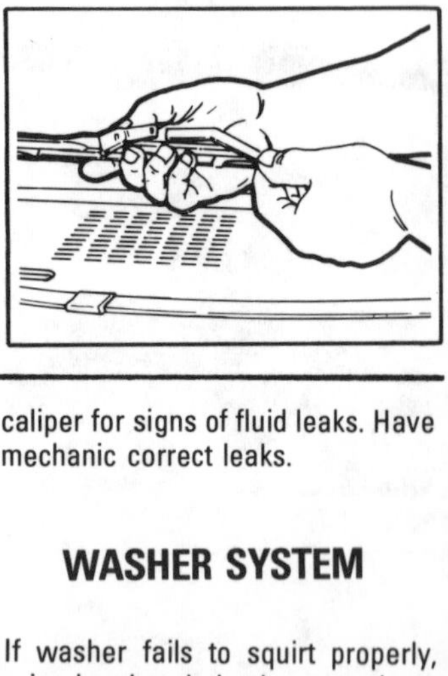

HORN PROBLEMS

If horn sounds and does not stop, this is due to short circuit in wiring. Disconnect wiring connector under hood and have professional service shop check horn wiring circuit.

STEERING PROBLEMS

See steering system check in Suspension Section. Check tire pressures. Have a professional service shop check all components in the front end and steering system.

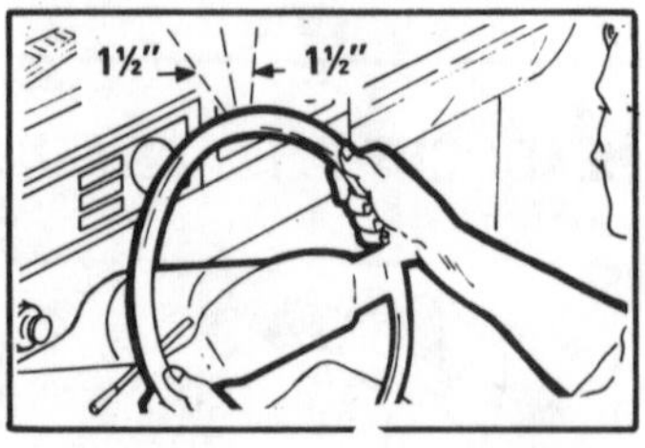

WHEEL CYLINDER CHECK

Drum brakes employ individual wheel cylinders to apply braking pressure to shoes. Check for brake fluid leaks on inside of wheel. Disc brakes employ calipers on individual wheels. Remove wheel and inspect caliper for signs of fluid leaks. Have mechanic correct leaks.

WASHER SYSTEM

If washer fails to squirt properly, raise hood and check system hose connections. Be sure washer fluid container has fluid. Check spout openings for clogging.

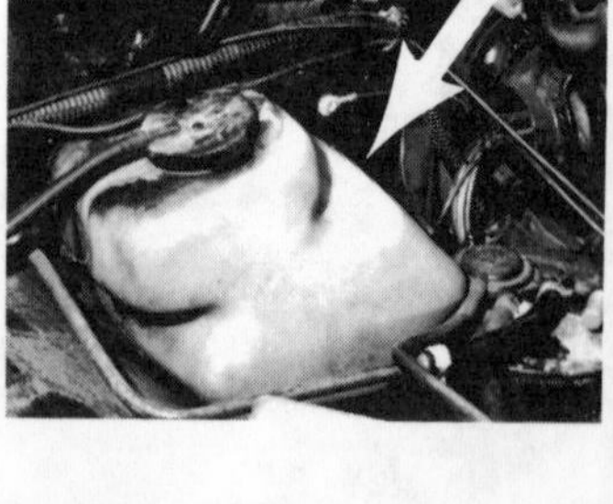

Keep container filled with fluid mixture of washer solvent and water. If road spray buildup on windshield is a chronic problem, add 1 tablespoon dishwasher detergent to solvent/water mixture when re-filling container.

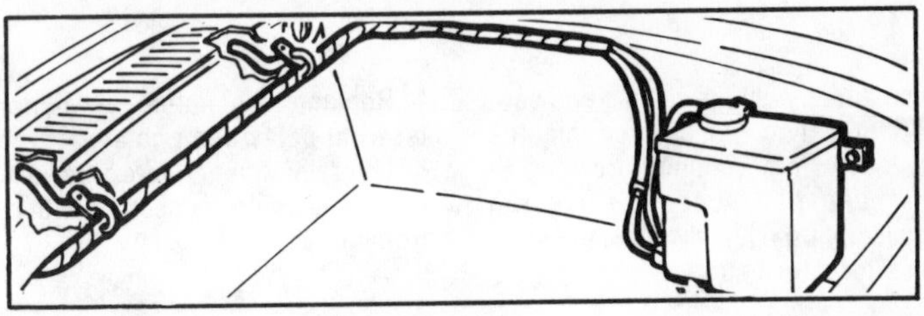

Electrical System

CHECKPOINTS AND SERVICES

To ensure starting ability at all times check your battery condition periodically. You'll need to check battery electrolyte (fluid) level in each of the six cells. Check battery cable connections for tightness and inspect for accumulated corrosion. Jumpstarting information and troubleshooting charts in the General Information section will show you how to get your car going again when it won't start.

SAFETY NOTE: Wear gloves when working on battery.

All 1976 and later Vegas and Astres are equipped with a new type of no maintenance battery. This battery requires no maintenance other than occasionally checking its state of charge by looking at the indicator on the top. If the indicator is dark with a green dot showing in the center, the battery is fully charged. If the indicator is dark but there is no green dot showing, the battery should be charged. If the indicator is light, the battery should be replaced.

CHECK BATTERY FLUID

1. Remove plastic filler caps on top of battery. Fluid should be up to lower end of filler hole and covering the plates. If fluid is low add clean, cold tap water. If your area has hard water, use only distilled water available at auto supply, food or drug stores.
2. Replace any lost caps immediately.

CAUTION: NEVER LIGHT A MATCH OR SMOKE near the top of a battery. Batteries give off explosive hydrogen gas.

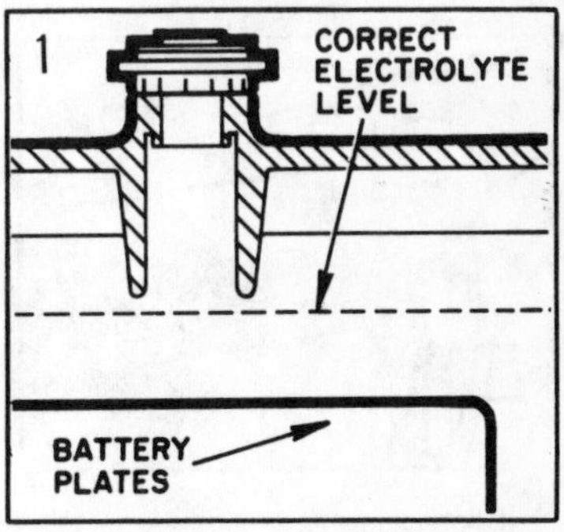

NOTE: Battery that often checks low on fluid could mean:

A. Battery is getting old, due for replacement; have charge capacity checked at service shop.

B. Connections may be corroded or loose; clean/replace as needed (see below).

C. Alternator or voltage regulator not functioning properly; this happens far less often than A or B above.

CLEANING BATTERY TERMINALS

As time goes by, battery terminals build up a dry powdery, whitish material. This material is corrosive and will gradually eat thru battery cables if not cleaned off periodically.

1. Loosen and remove battery connections.
2. Brush off all loose corrosion; use stiff bristle brush. Do not get this material into eyes or on open cuts. Wash off at once.
3. If corrosion build-up is extremely heavy and brushing does not remove all of it, mix 2 tablespoons baking soda to 1 cup water. Pour solu-

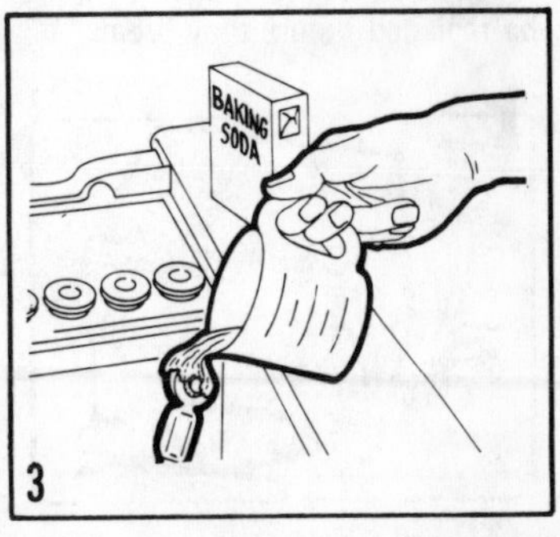

tion directly onto terminals and connectors. Allow to soak a few minutes and rinse off. Continue brushing to remove all traces of corrosion build-up. Do not allow cleaning solution to enter battery.

4. Replace connectors on battery terminal posts and tighten.
5. Liberally smear battery terminal posts and cable connectors with petroleum jelly.

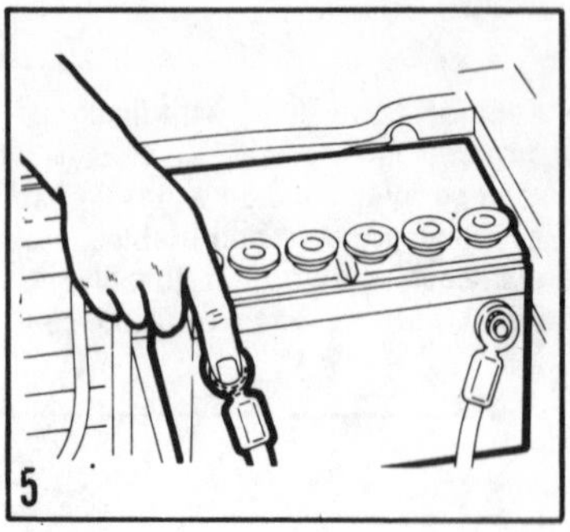
5

REPLACING BATTERY CABLES

If battery cable strands become frayed, broken or corroded, replace cable immediately. Delay in correcting this condition could lead to sudden failure to start the engine. Can also weaken battery.

1. Loosen and remove battery cables. Clean any corrosion build-up.
2. Disconnect negative cable from its attachment to engine or chassis. Disconnect positive cable from its attachment to starter relay.
3. Attach new cables making sure positive and negative cables are on proper terminals. They are not identical.

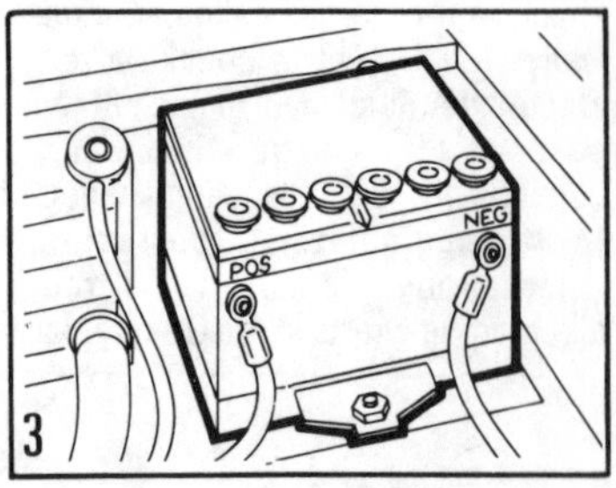

3

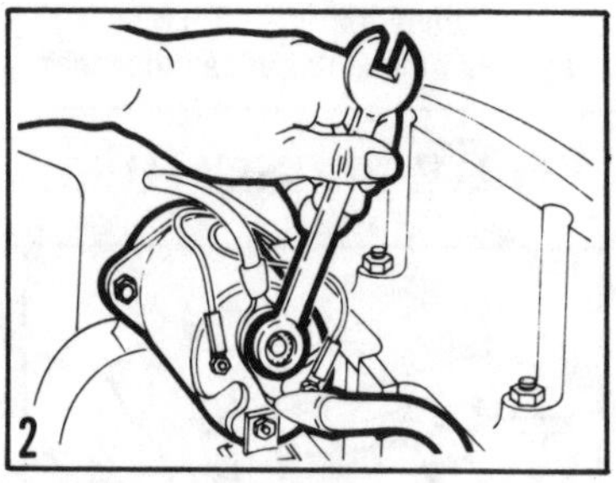
2

1

4. Replace connectors on battery terminal posts and tighten.
5. Liberally smear battery terminal posts and cable connectors with petroleum jelly.

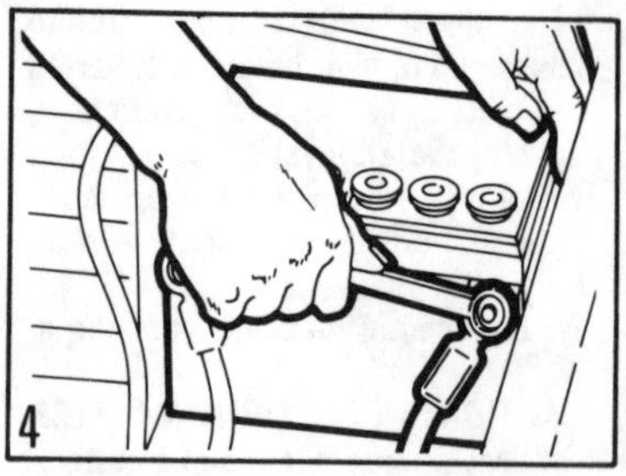
4

BATTERY HOLDDOWN

The clamp device which holds battery in place should be checked periodically. If loose, tighten. Clean off corrosion build-up. Severely corroded holddown components should be replaced before they break.

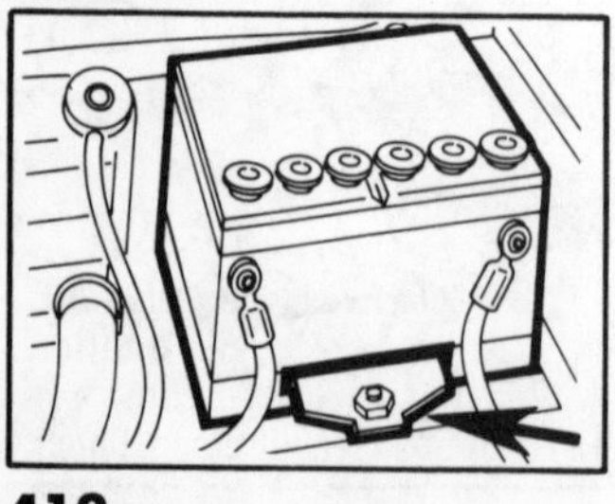

FUSE LOCATION

The fuse box is located to the left of the steering column, directly over the dimmer switch. Each fuse is clearly marked as to function and correct amperage. Always replace fuse with one of same amperage. If fuses are always blowing, have checked by professional mechanic.

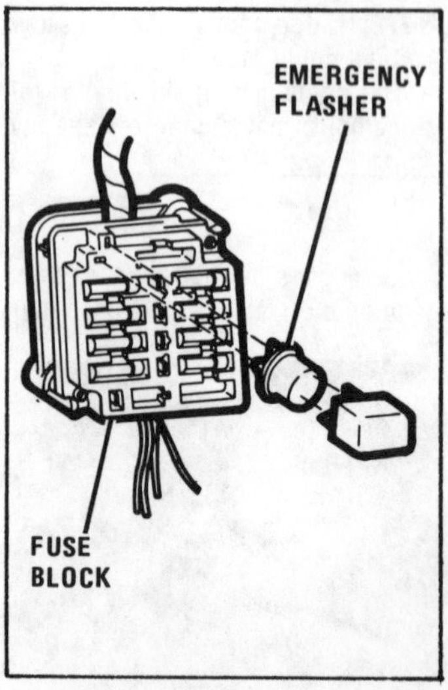

TURN SIGNAL AND 4-WAY FLASHER

Turn signals and 4-way emergency flashers will operate only if: A. All light bulbs are OK. B. Flasher units are not burned out. Vega and Astre have two flasher units that independently of each other. TURN SIGNAL FLASHER: located behind left side of instrument panel. Pull flasher from spring clip mounting. Unplug from connector. Plug in new flasher. Replace in spring clip mounting.

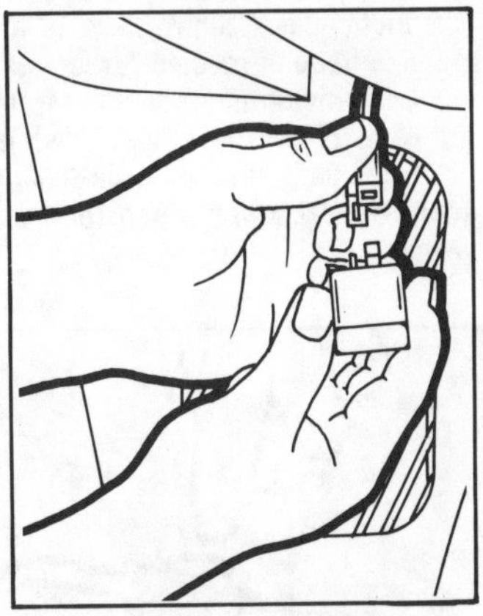

EMERGENCY FLASHER: located in fuse block. Simply unplug and insert new flasher. REPLACE ONLY WITH SAME TYPE FLASHER.

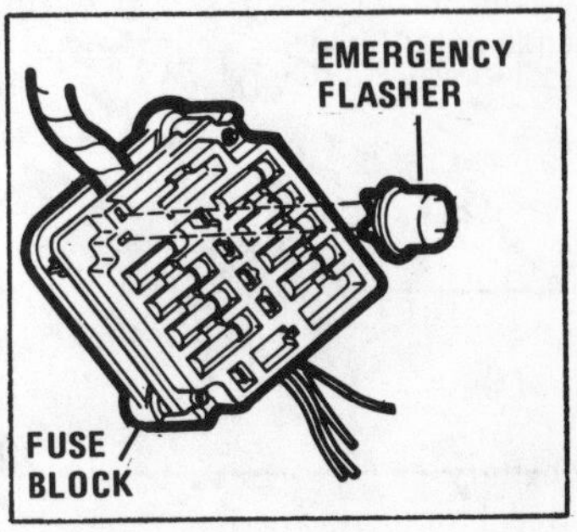

ALTERNATOR CHECKS

If Alt. warning light glows red at operating speed, alternator isn't charging battery properly. Common causes are:
A. Fan belts are loose and slipping on alternator pulley. Tighten or replace belts.
B. Battery terminals, cables are loose or corroded. Clean; tighten; replace bad cables.
If A or B do not correct problem, alternator or voltage regulator may be faulty. This happens far less often, and can only be checked by mechanic with proper electrical testing equipment.

Alternator Caution: Alternator can be permanently damaged by short-circuiting terminal connections. When working around or moving alternator, always keep metal tools or engine parts from terminals.

REAR WINDOW DEFOGGER SYSTEM

Do not clean inside of rear window fitted with defogger system with any abrasive material. This could destroy carbon-copper wires. Use only soft rag and mild detergent/water mixture. Dry carefully.

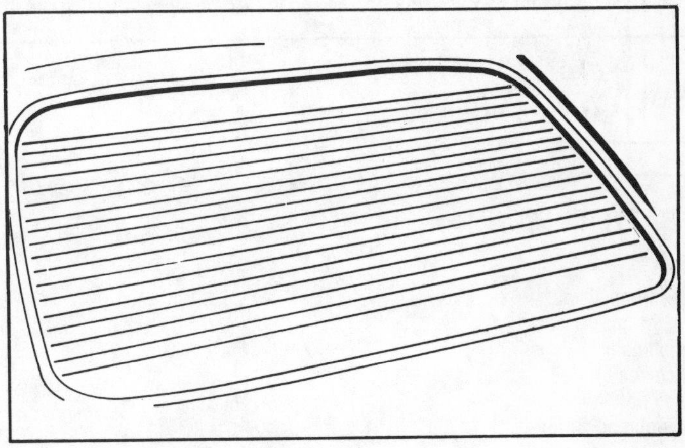

Air Conditioner

CHECK POINTS AND SERVICES

WARNING!—Never attempt to tighten fittings, disassemble or do any work on your car's A/C system. Consult a professional mechanic about A/C system problems and their correction. Your auto air conditioner (A/C) is a delicate, closed system. If air, dirt or water get into it, or if refrigerant escapes, the A/C unit will not cool a car interior. Among things you can do are:
1. Keep condenser grill clean. Check

for dirt and debris; periodically remove dead insects, leaves, etc., with stiff bristle brush. Straighten any bent fins—carefully.

2. Keep radiator filled to correct level. (See Cooling System section). If fluid needs to be added, add antifreeze rather than water.
3. Keep radiator coolant at a 50/50 water/antifreeze mixture.
4. Flush cooling system and replace with fresh coolant mixture at least every 24 months. (See Cooling System section).
5. Radiator cap should be tight and sealed properly. If sealing gasket is cracked, cut or worn, replace cap with new 15 lb. unit.
6. Check fan belt tension periodically. (See Cooling System section). Replace glazed, frayed or cut fan belts, before they fail entirely.
7. Check periodically for bubbles in A/C sight glass. Sight glass is located in head of receiver/dryer vessel. Or in metal tubing leading from top of receiver/drier. Sight glass is no larger than head of large nail. It may be dirty. Wipe clean for best visibility.

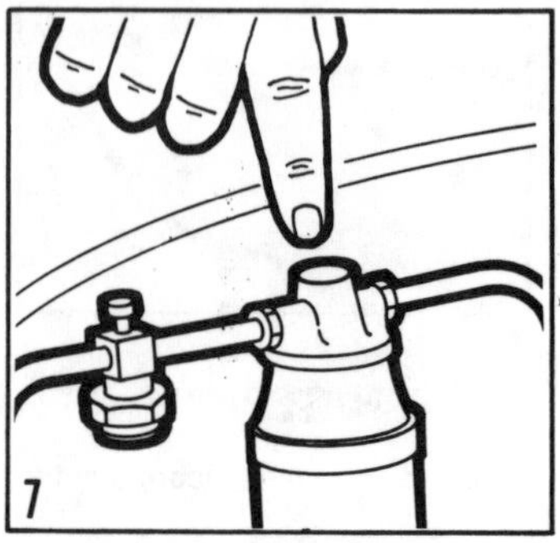

PROCEED AS FOLLOWS:
a) With engine and A/C system running, look for passage of refrigerant in sight glass. You'll be looking for a stream of milky white bubbles as they pass through sight glass. It is best to watch sight glass and have someone else start the car and turn on the A/C system. Allow to run for a

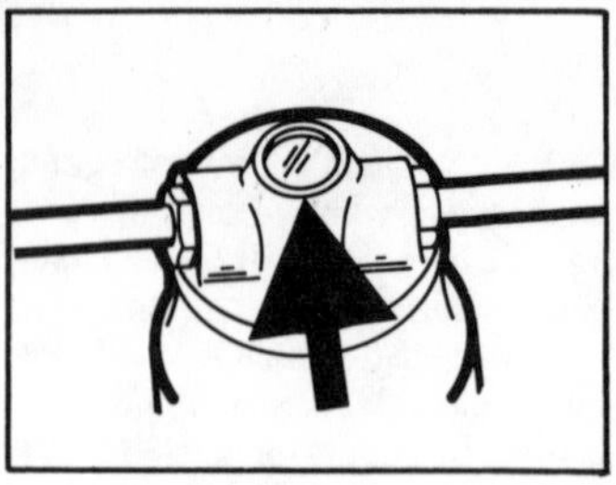

few minutes.
b) If you observe no bubbles, and air flow from A/C unit in the car is passing cold air, everything is OK.
c) If no bubbles appear in sight glass, and air flow from the A/C unit in the car is not delivering cold air, the system may be low on refrigerant and could need a re-charge.
d) If bubbles appear, system is low on refrigerant.
e) If you suspect refrigerant loss based on tests performed above, have system checked by a professional A/C service shop. They can confirm refrigerant loss, recharge the system and check for system leakage.
NOTE: Once a week or so, even in winter, run A/C system for about 5 minutes as you drive. This keeps system internally lubricated, prevents hoses hardening.

TUNE-UP SPECIFICATIONS

YEAR	ENGINE No. Cyl. Displacement (cu. in.)	SPARK PLUGS Type	SPARK PLUGS Gap (in.)	DISTRIBUTOR Point Dwell (deg.)	DISTRIBUTOR Point Gap (in.)	IGNITION TIMING Man. Trans.● (deg.)■	IGNITION TIMING Auto Trans.● (deg.)■	IDLE SPEED Man. Trans.● (rpm)▲	IDLE SPEED Auto Trans. (rpm)▲
1971	4-140	R42TS	0.035	31-34	0.019	6B	6B	850/700②	650/550②
	4-140	R42TS	0.035	31-34	0.019	6B	10B	1200/700②	650/550②
1972	4-140	R42TS	0.035	31-34	0.019	6B	6B(4B)	850(1200) 700①	700①/550②
	4-140	R42TS	0.035	31-34	0.019	8B	8B	1200/700①	700①/550②
1973	4-140	R42TS	0.035	31-34	0.019	8B	8B	1000/700②	750①
	4-140	R42TS	0.035	31-34	0.019	10B	12B	1200/700①②	750①
1974	4-140	R42TS	0.035	31-34	0.019	10B	12B	1000/700②	750/550②
	4-140	R42TS	0.035	31-34	0.019	10B	12B	1200/700②	750/500②
1975	4-140	R43TSX	0.060③	Electronic		8B	10B	1200/700②	750/500②
	4-140	R43TSX	0.060③	Electronic		10B	12B	700④	750/550②
1976	4-140	R43TS	0.035	Electronic		10B	12B	1200/750②	750/550②
	4-140	R43TS	0.035	Electronic		8B	10B	700④ (1000/700②)	750/550② (750/600②)
1977	4-140 4-140	See Underhood Specification Sticker							

▲ Adjust automatic transmissions in Drive (AMC/Ford/GM) or Neutral (Chrysler), all manual transmissions are adjusted in Neutral.
■ All figures are Before Top Dead Center.
● Figure in parentheses indicate California engine.

NOTE: The underhood specifications sticker often reflects tune-up specification changes made in production. Sticker figures must be used if they disagree with those in this chart.

① For air-conditioned vehicles, adjust idle speed to 800 rpm with A/C on.
② Where two figures are separated by a slash, the first figure is for idle speed with solenoid connected, while the second is for idle speed with solenoid disconnected.
③ If fouling occurs, reset gap to .035
④ Solenoid adjustment screw dropped.
B Before Top Dead Center.
—— Not applicable.

CAPACITIES

YEAR	ENGINE No. Cyl. Displacement (cu. in.)	ENGINE OIL Add 1 qt. with New Filter	TRANSMISSION Pts. to Refill after Draining MANUAL 3-speed	MANUAL 4-speed	AUTOMATIC	DRIVE AXLE (pts.)	COOLING SYSTEM with Heater (qts.)	COOLING SYSTEM with Air Cond. (qts.)
1971	4-140	3	2.4	3	6	2.3	6.5	6.5
1972	4-140	3	2.4	3	6①	2.8	6.5	6.5
1973	4.140	3	2.4	3	6①	2.8	8.6	9.0
1974	4-140	3	3.0	3	6①	2.8	8.6	9.0
1975-76	4.140	3	3.0	3②	6①	2.8	8.0	9.0
1977	4-140	3	3.0	3②	6①	2.8	8.0	9.0

① 8 pts. with 3-speed Turbo Hydra-Matic transmission. All figures do not include torque converter.
② 3.5 Dexron® with 5-speed.

Service Record

Date/Mileage	Service	Next Due

Datsun 510/610/710

Lubrication and Oil Change

BRAKE FLUID LEVEL CHECK

Check brake and clutch fluid levels in the master cylinder every time the oil level is checked . . . sooner if braking feels inadequate or if clutch is not operating properly. Add fluid when low.
Recommended grade: SAE 70R-3 (DOT 3).
Master cylinders are located under the hood on the left side. They are clear plastic containers. Fluid level will appear through the plastic.
1. Compare level with mark or ridge, or if unmarked, keep at least ¾ full. Snap off cap and add fluid, if necessary.
2. Replace cap securely. DO NOT

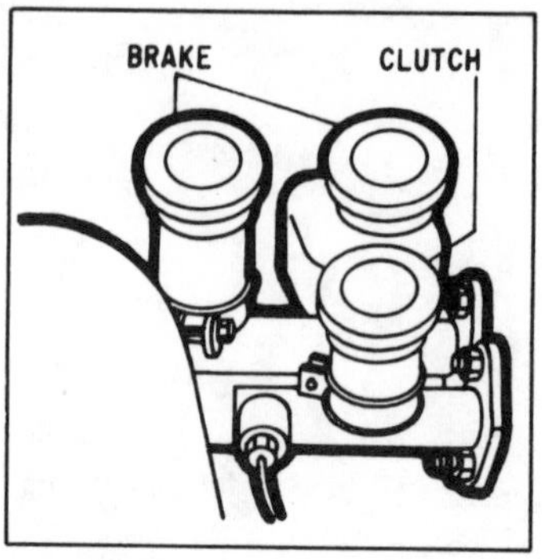

OVERFILL.
3. If fluid level was low, check again in a few days.

4. If fluid repeatedly checks low, there is a leak somewhere in the system.
Have mechanic check further. Neglect can be dangerous.

MANUAL TRANSMISSION FLUID LEVEL CHECK

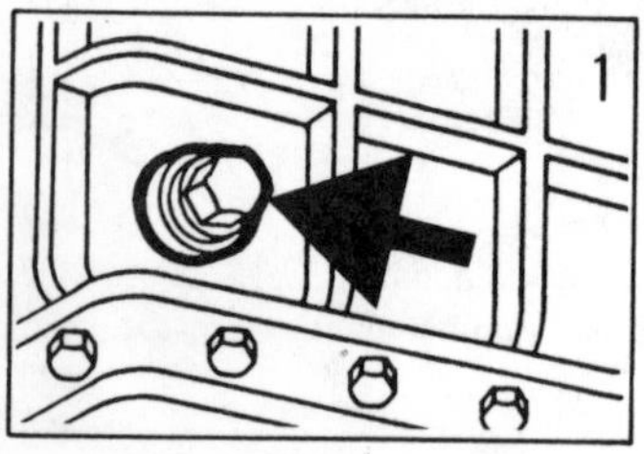

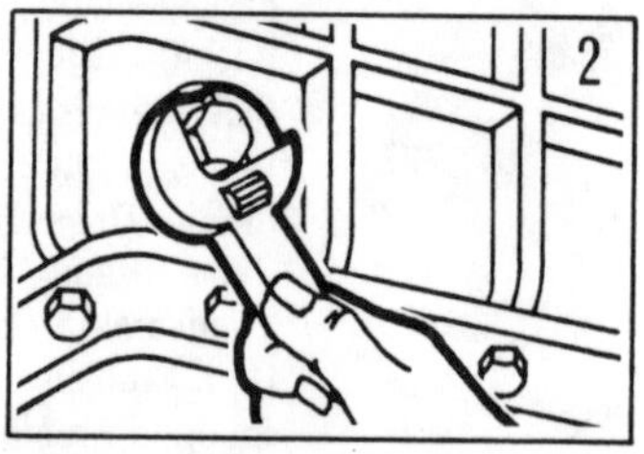

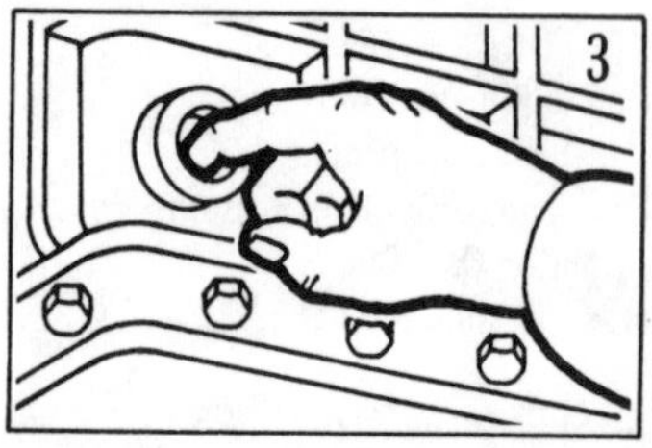

DATSUN SAYS . . . Check manual transmission fluid every 3 months (6 months on 610/710). Car should be parked level. Recommended grade: Standard Transmission Fluid (SAE 90).
TOOLS NEEDED: adjustable wrench, bulb syringe.
1. Locate transmission fluid plug on back of transmission, left side, from underneath car.

2. Wipe road dirt from filler plug area before loosening. Remove plug with adjustable wrench.
3. If fluid leaks out while removing drain plug, level is adequate and plug removal is unnecessary. If no leakage occurs, insert finger in hole; fluid level should be up to tip of finger.
4. Add fluid as needed with hand bulb syringe.

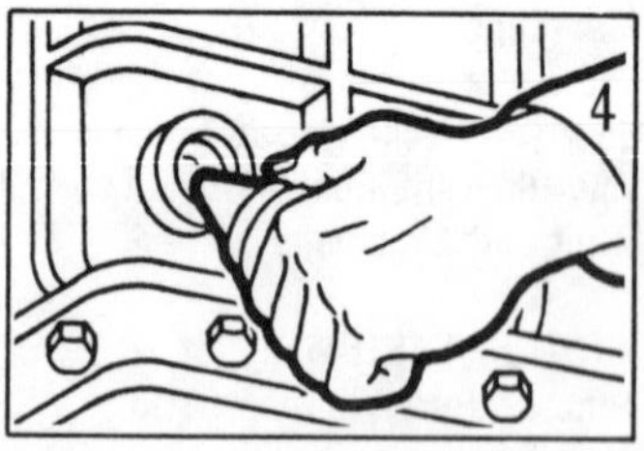

5. Replace filler plug; tighten.

AUTOMATIC TRANSMISSION FLUID LEVEL CHECK

DATSUN SAYS . . . Check automatic transmission fluid (ATF) every three months or 3,000 miles (6 months on 610/710). Recommended Grade: DEXRON Type A.
TOOLS . . . Long neck filler funnel.
1. Engine must be warmed up and running. Place shift lever in PARK position.

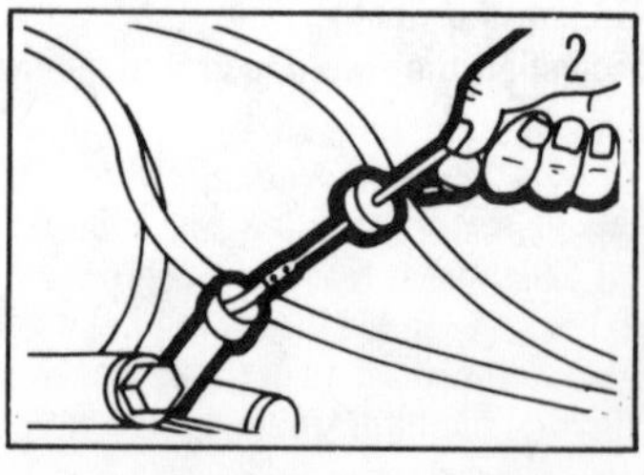

2. Pull out dipstick. Wipe clean. Push dipstick all the way back in; remove it again.
3. If fluid is below "H" mark, add ATF to bring level up. DO NOT OVERFILL.
4. Add ATF thru transmission dipstick hole by means of long-neck filler funnel.

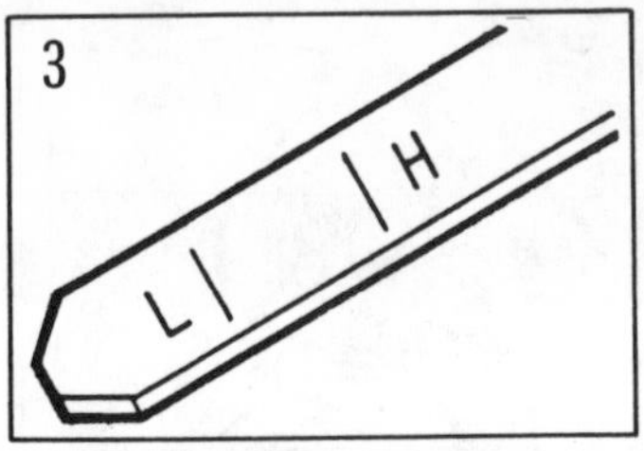

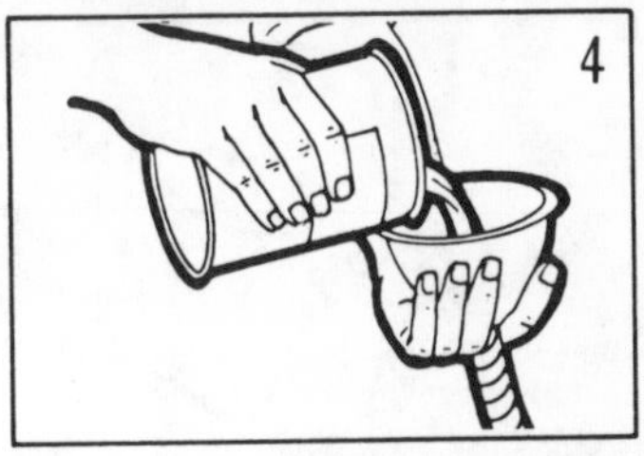

REAR AXLE LUBRICANT CHECK

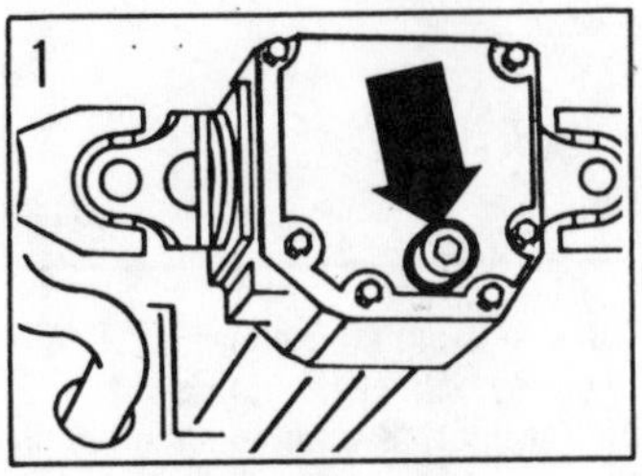

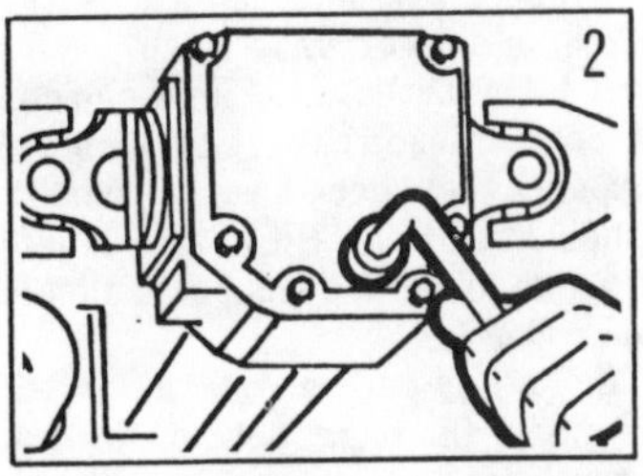

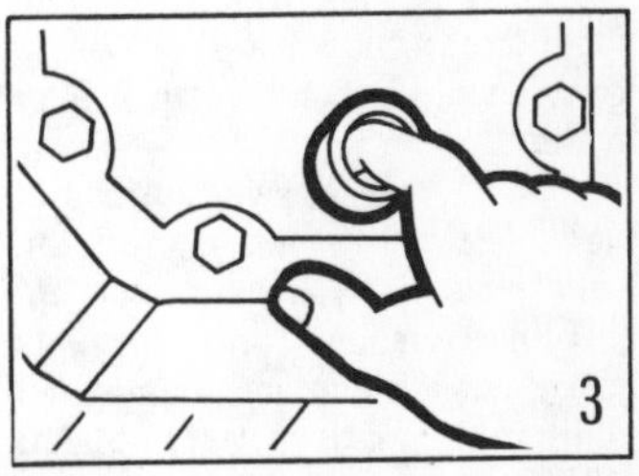

DATSUN SAYS . . . check rear axle lube level every 3,000 miles, 6,000 miles on 610/710. Recommended gear lube (SAE 90).
TOOLS . . . drain plug wrench; bulb syringe.
1. Locate filler plug on rear of rear axle housing.
2. Wipe plug area clean; remove plug with drain plug wrench.
3. If fluid leaks out while removing drain plug, level is adequate and plug removal is unnecessary. If no leakage occurs, insert finger in hole; fluid level should be up to tip of finger.
4. If fluid level is low, add as needed, with a hand bulb syringe until level reaches the edge of filler plug hole.
5. Replace filler plug; tighten.

OIL AND FILTER CHANGE

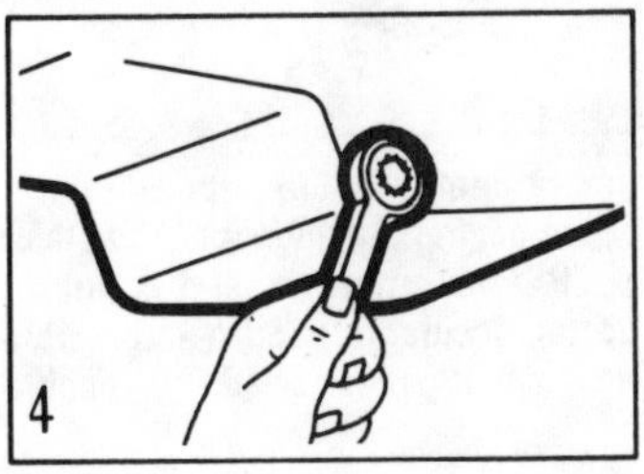

DATSUN SAYS . . . On the 510, change the oil every 3,000, miles the filter every 6,000 miles; for the 610, change the oil every 4,000 miles and the filter every 8,000 miles; the 710 requires an oil and filter change every 6,250 miles. You should check the oil at least once a week, and add oil which is at least an SE grade.
TOOLS & MATERIALS . . . adjustable wrench; medium size screwdriver; oil filter removal wrench; drain pan for old oil; oil pouring spout; new oil filter (if required); other lubricants as specified.
SAFETY TIP . . . use work gloves.
1. If engine is cold, start up and idle for about 5 minutes.
2. Park car on level ground. Turn engine off.
3. Locate oil drain plug on underside of engine. Place drain pan under plug.
4. Remove drain plug with wrench.

Let ALL dirty oil drain out.

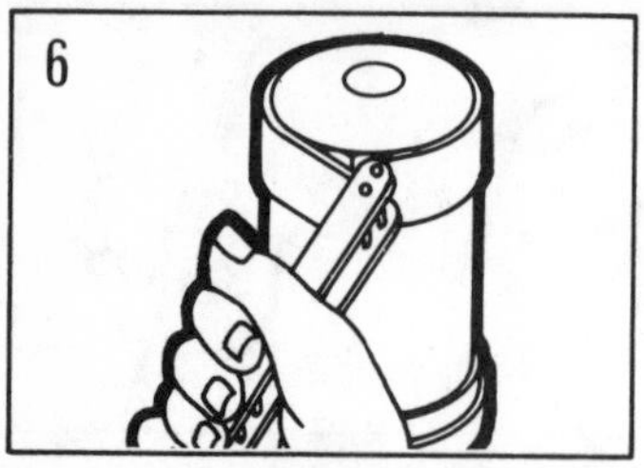

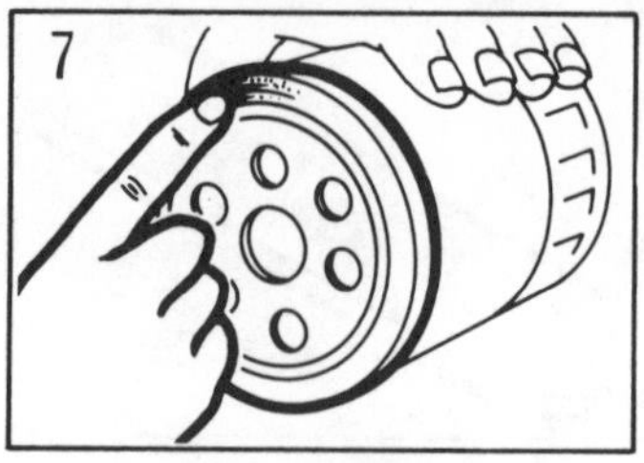

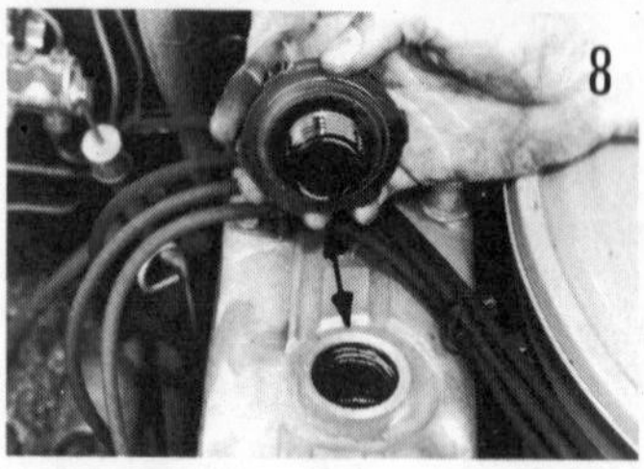

5. Wipe plug and area around drain hole clean. Replace drain plug; tighten it.
6. Locate oil filter. Move drain pan under filter. Loosen filter with oil filter wrench. Unscrew; remove filter by hand.
7. Smear fresh oil over surface of rubber gasket (washer) of new filter. Install new filter by hand only. Do NOT use wrench. Turn filter until gasket makes contact. Tighten an additional half turn only . . . NO MORE.
8. Locate oil filler hole on top of engine. Remove cap.
9. Punch oil pouring spout into top of oil can. Pour all cans of new oil into filler tube. Wipe filler cap clean and replace it.
10. Check new oil level at dipstick. Pull out dipstick, wipe clean.
11. Push dipstick back into engine. Be sure to insert all the way. Remove dipstick and check new oil level. It should be above "HIGH" line. If not, be sure to check if you put in all the oil called for.
12. Start up engine and idle for 3-5 minutes. Oil signal light on instrument panel will glow red when engine is first started. Light should go out in 30 seconds or less.
13. Stop engine and check for oil

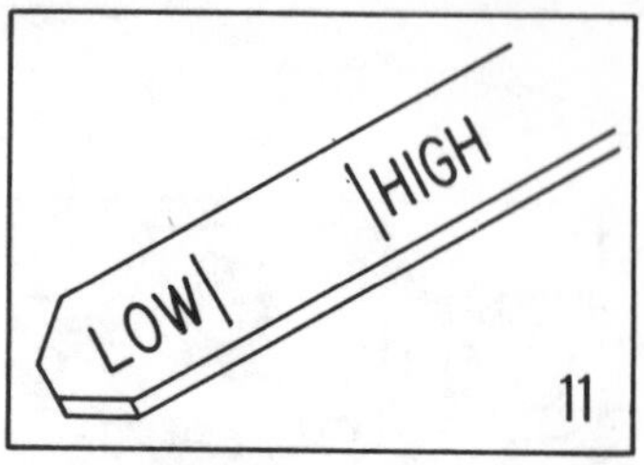

leaks at drain plug and filter. If you find any, check tightness of plug and/or filter, also for condition of filter gasket to see that it has not become pinched or damaged when installing. Recheck oil level, which should now be at "HIGH."

SPEEDOMETER CABLE LUBRICATION

If speedometer pointer tends to quiver or jump, or if unit makes a low, rasping sound, lubrication may be needed.
1. Locate cable shaft attachment directly behind speedometer dial.
2. Unscrew cable from speedometer.
3. Pull inner cable completely out of outer casing. Note carefully which end is top. Check for wear or frayed strands. If damaged, replace inner cable with new one.
4. Apply generous amount of

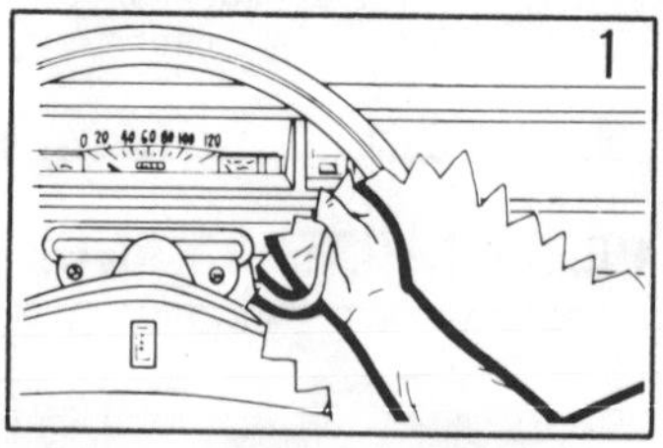

speedometer cable lubricant into cable casing. Replace inner cable in shaft, noting that top end is not inserted accidentally. Turn inner cable as it is being re-inserted. Twist cable

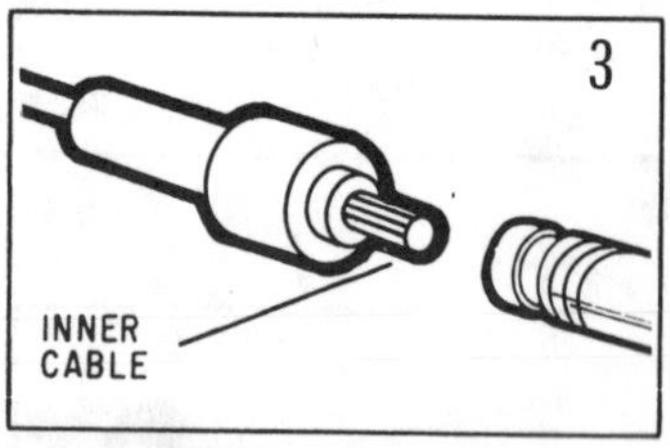

when all the way in, to lock into position at lower end.
5. Reconnect cable to speedometer head under instrument panel.

DOOR HINGES AND STOPS

(lubricate every 6 months)
1. Brush any dirt accumulations from door hinges and stops. Use old tooth brush or rag.
2. Apply dab of white polyethylene grease to door hinges, trunk hinges, hood hinges, door stops.

DOOR LOCKS

(lubricate every 6 months)
1. Insert door key half way into lock.
2. Spray aerosol lock lubricant into lock.
3. Push key rest of way into lock; turn back and forth several times.

Cooling System

IT IS RECOMMENDED . . . that radiator coolant (water/antifreeze mixture) level be checked once or twice a month. Do this when engine is cold. Check more often if you do a lot of hard driving. On models with clear expansion tanks, check coolant level visually when hot.
Keep coolant up to recommended level in radiator. If coolant checks frequently low, look for leaks.

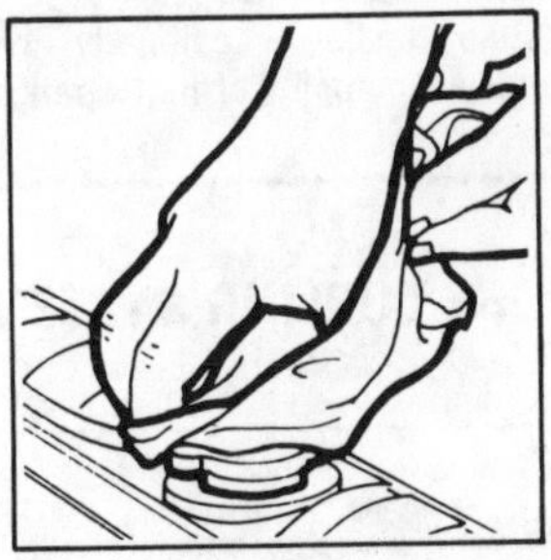

Tighten all hose clamps occasionally. For best results, keep a 50/50 water/antifreeze mixture year round. Change complete coolant mixture every 24 months.
CAUTION: If you must check coolant in a hot engine, cover radiator cap with thick rag before releasing. Remove cap slowly . . . press down and turn.

REPLACING THE THERMOSTAT

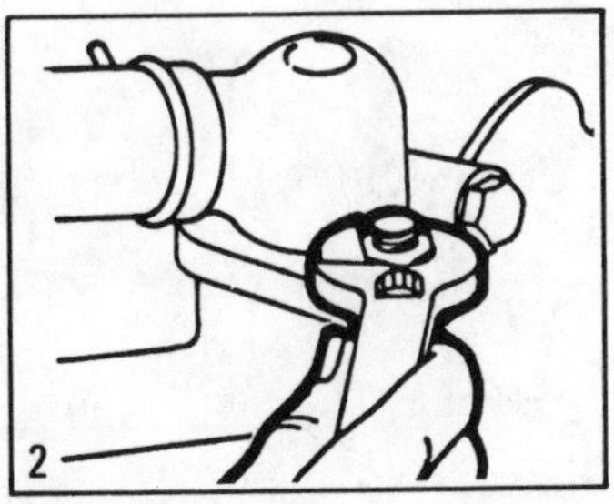

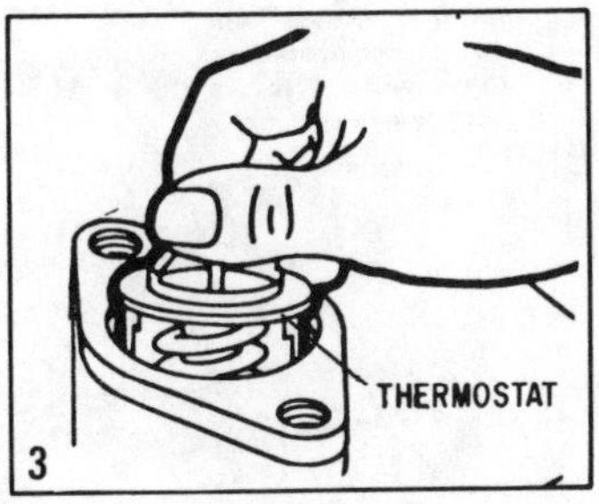

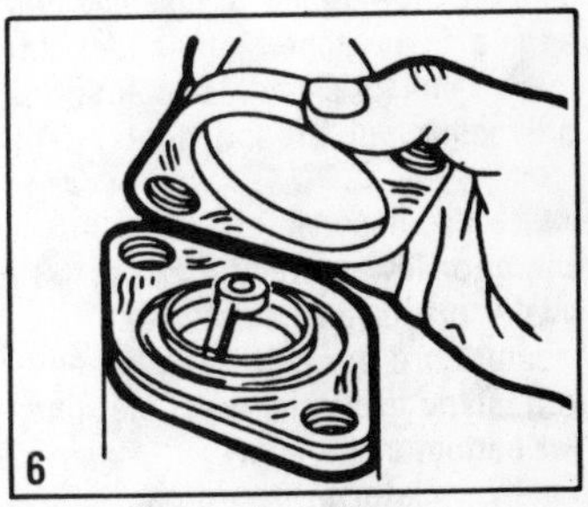

A faulty thermostat will usually cause engine overheating. Replace with new thermostat.
TOOLS AND MATERIALS . . .
New thermostat
Gasket
Adjustable wrench
1. Drain radiator of about half its coolant. (See How To Replace Hoses).
2. Loosen and remove both retaining bolts and lift thermostat housing off the engine.
NOTE: If you're careful it won't be necessary to remove radiator hose.
3. Remove old thermostat.
4. Scrape thermostat housing flange and engine block surface to remove old gasket debris.
5. Drop new thermostat into place—spring down.
6. Install new gasket with sealer applied to both sides.
7. Replace thermostat housing and tighten both retaining bolts.

FAN BELT ADJUSTMENT

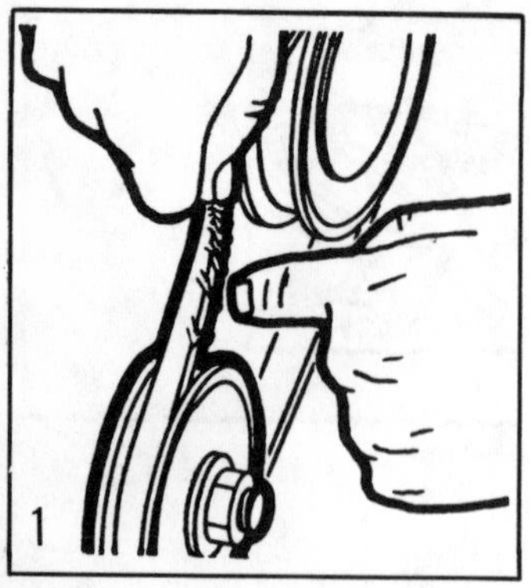

1

2

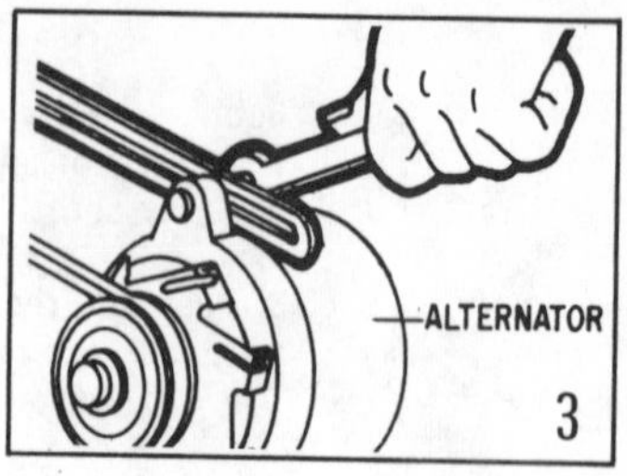

3

The fan belt not only drives the radiator fan, it turns the water pump and drives the alternator. It's easy to see that the condition and proper tension of the belt are vital, since almost all engine cooling and electrical power is dependent on it. The belt deserves an occasional look and tension check.

CAUTION: An overtightened belt may damage alternator and water pump bearings.

1. Inspect fan belt occasionally. If worn, frayed or cracked on inner driving surface, replace.
2. Check tension occasionally. Press thumb at midpoint of belt span between pulleys. If belt depresses more than ½ inch, tightening is needed. A too-loose belt will not drive alternator and water pump effectively.
3. Adjust to proper tension of ¼-½ inch deflection. To adjust, loosen alternator adjustment and attaching bolts. Pull on alternator until proper deflection is attained and tighten bolts.

FIND THOSE COOLING SYSTEM LEAKS

1. Inspect all hoses. If any are weak, soft in spots or show cracks, replace at once.
2. Check all hose connections for tightness. Tighten loose hose clamps; they tend to loosen due to engine vibration.
3. If radiator steams or hisses when engine is switched off, check for leaks. Look for signs of coolant drips on radiator or around heater tank joint.

Leaks are possible at:
Upper or lower radiator hoses
Water pump (gaskets or seal)
Heater core or connecting hoses
Automatic transmission cooler lines (at bottom of radiator)
Faulty radiator pressure cap
Faulty cylinder head gasket
Cracked cylinder head or block

Due to the number of joints, cooling systems have many places to leak from. Check clamp tightness. If leaks persist an anti-leak additive in the coolant may help. Noisy water pumps may benefit from a lubricating additive in the coolant. Use a cooling system cleaner when flushing during a drain and refill job. It will help remove rust and scale. Remember — additives will not cure chronic problems. But they will effect a short-term remedy in many cases.

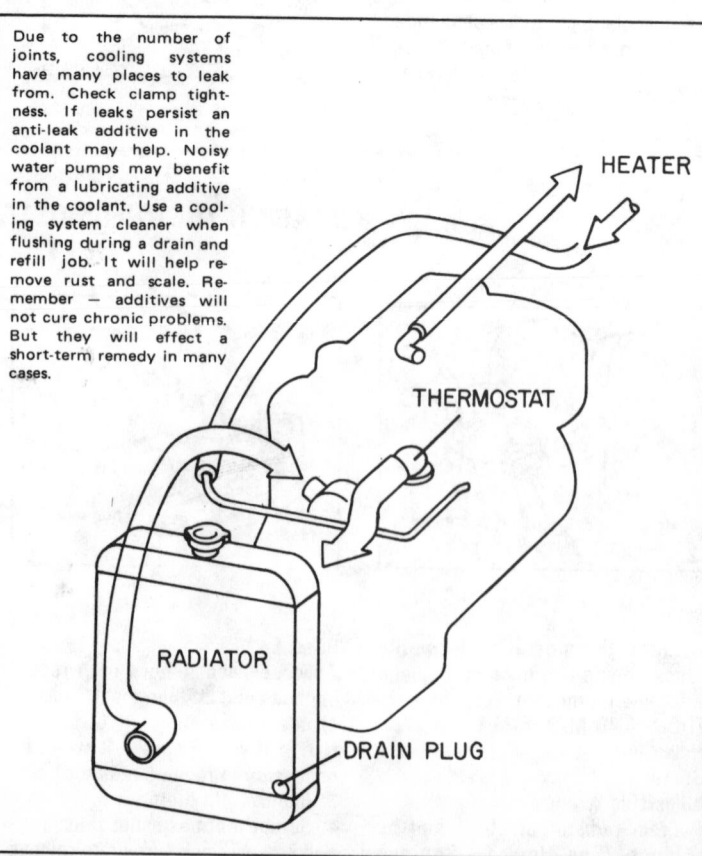

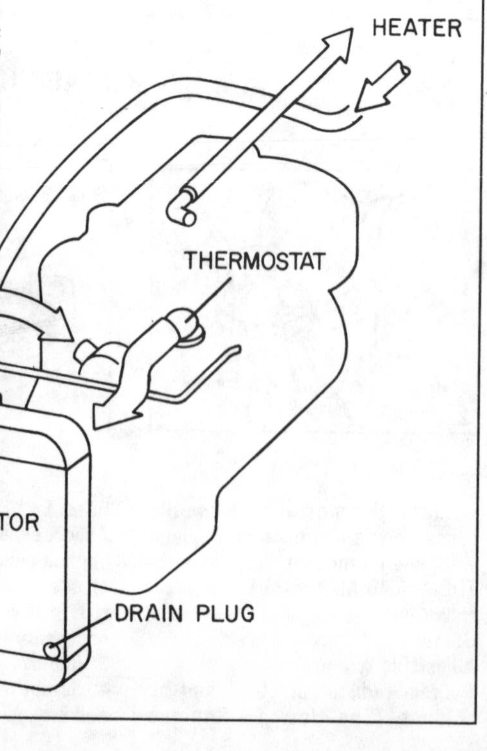

RADIATOR CAP CHECK

Check radiator cap occasionally for worn or cracked gasket. If cap doesn't seal properly, fluid will be lost and engine will overheat. Replace worn cap with new cap rated 13 lbs. pressure.

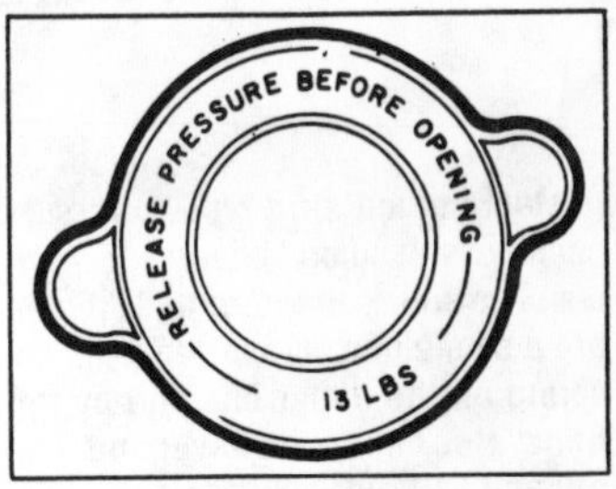

HOSE REPLACEMENT

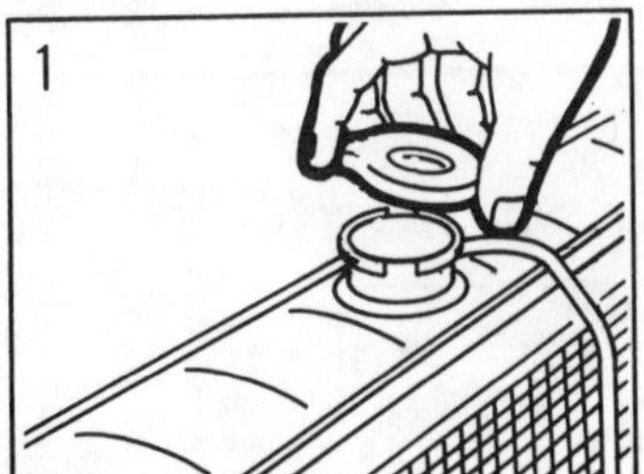

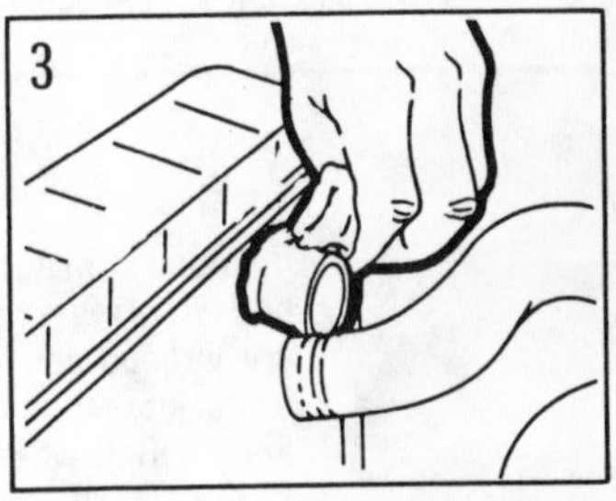

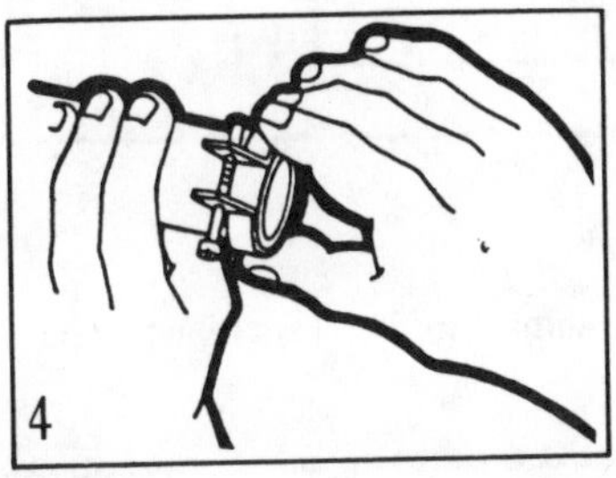

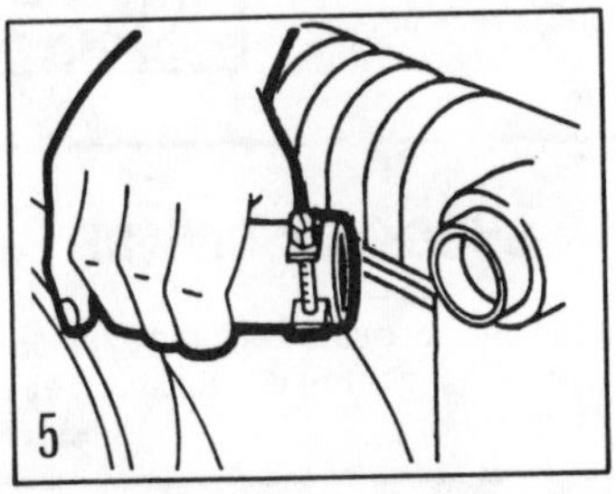

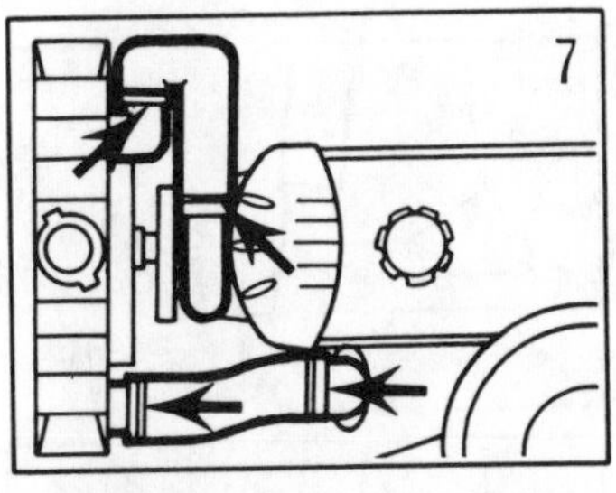

Coolant drain and refill work may be done alone; when changing hoses, coolant must also be drained as part of job. Discard all hoses with cracks or soft spots. Check hose clamps for tightness and good condition.

1. Remove radiator cap. Open radiator petcock (See 2). Drain coolant into catch basin. If near 24 months old, discard old coolant.
2. Petcock is located on the bottom of the radiator.
3. Remove hose clamp and remove hose. Wipe all hose connections clean. Use emery cloth to get rid of residue.
4. If old hose clamps are badly rusted or damaged, replace with new units.
5. Slip clamps over each hose end. Slip hose ends all the way onto cleaned up hose connections.
6. Place hose clamp ¼ inch from hose end. Tighten. Close petcock. Refill with 50/50 coolant/water mix.
7. Start engine; allow to warm up. Check for coolant leaks.
8. Road test car; watch temperature warning gauge to avoid overheating.

Suspension and Tires

SUSPENSION SYSTEM

A MacPherson strut-type front suspension is used on sedans and wagons. The shock absorber and spindle are a single unit, supported by a coil spring on the upper end and by the transverse link on the lower end. The 510 and 610 rear suspension is fully independent and is a semi-trailing arm design with a suspension member, suspension arms, coil springs and hydraulic shock absorbers. All 710s and wagons have leaf springs and solid rear axle.

Your car's suspension system consists of wheels, tires, springs, shock absorbers, sway (or stabilizer) bars, ball joints, steering linkage. If any of these items is out of adjustment or badly worn, you may notice any of these symptoms:

- car pulls to one side when braking
- car wanders when driving a straight line
- overall ride may be either hard or bouncy
- effort is needed to steer vehicle
- tires show uneven wear
- tires squeal when cornering
- front of car dips or bounces when braking
- car rocks side-to-side when going over rough road
- wheels bounce to make slapping sound on road
- steering wheel vibrates in hands
- front of car vibrates at highway speeds

Any of above symptoms indicates corrective action is needed. Delay can: ruin tires; cause damage/failure to other suspension parts; create safety hazard.

STEERING

If steering linkage, front suspension and steering column components are in good condition, there should be not more than 1½ inch free play in the steering wheel when measured at the rim of the wheel. If a loud knock is heard when turning the steering wheel from one extreme to the other, have mechanic check pinion bearing preload.

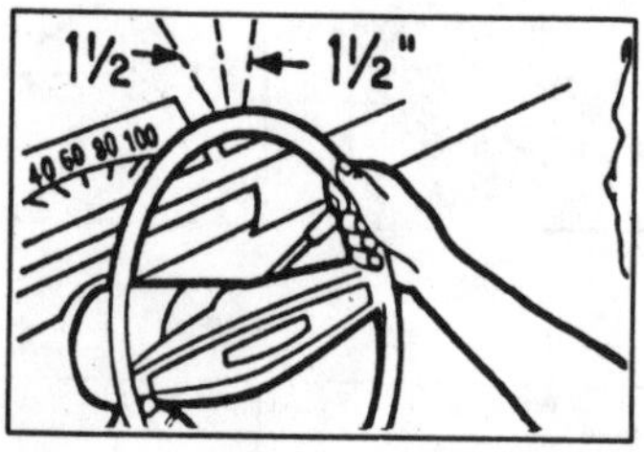

SHOCK ABSORBERS

Shock absorbers work to keep wheels in constant contact with the road. Result is safe handling and ride control; longer tire life. So shock absorbers (or shocks) are important.

HOW TO CHECK FOR BAD SHOCKS

1. Check under car and locate shock absorber near each wheel.
2. Heavy oil streaks on outer shock housing indicate need for replacement.
3. Stand at front of car and apply body weight in pumping action to front bumper or fender. Release pressure and allow car to stop rocking. Car should not bounce more than one more time after releasing pressure. Repeat at rear. If bouncing continues more than once, replacement is needed. Replace shocks in pairs (front pair or rear pair).

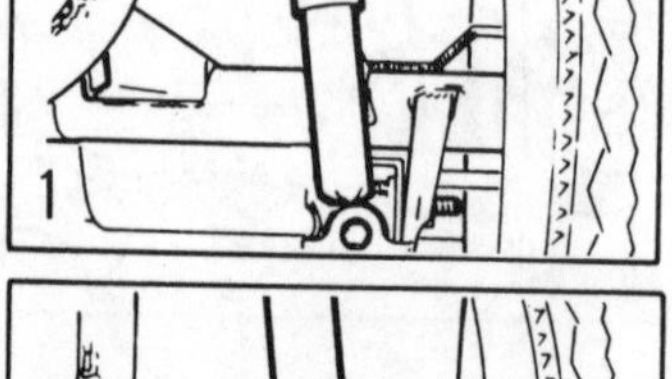

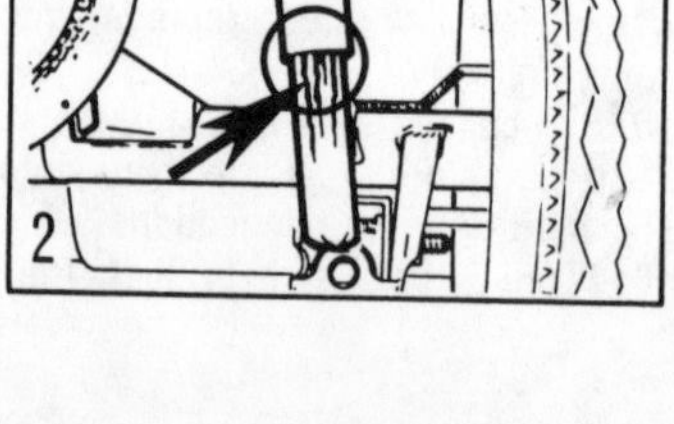

TOW HITCH INFORMATION

If your car is used for trailer towing you should check:
A. Cooling System; be sure coolant is at proper level in radiator. See Cooling System Section for checks to perform.
B. Check Transmission Fluid; keep topped up to proper level.
C. Check Rear Shock Absorbers; you may benefit from installation of new rear shocks.
D. Check Tire Pressures; best traction and handling can be ensured if tire pressures are properly maintained.
For safer and more trouble-free trailer towing, consider:
A. Automatic Transmission Cooler; helps remove excess heat from automatic transmission fluid built up during towing mileage. Also helps avoid radiator overheating. Some units can be self-installed.
B. Radiator Over-Flow Tank Kit; addition of a reservoir to catch radiator coolant overflow preventing coolant loss. Easy to install, these units help a tow car run cooler, avoid overheating due to coolant loss.
C. Heavy-Duty Shock Absorbers or Air Shocks; important to have on rear wheels if you intend to do a lot of towing or load carrying within the car itself. Don't forget to consider replacing factory shocks, when they are worn out, with heavy-duty units at the front as well.
D. Variable Load Flasher; this unit will accommodate the added load of trailer turn signal lamps on trailer when these are hooked into your car's electrical system.

FRONT END ALIGNMENT

When steering, handling and/or tire wear indicate front end alignment may be needed, this work can only be done at an automotive service shop. DO NOT PUT OFF NEEDED FRONT END ALIGNMENT. At the same time, have ball joints and steering linkage checked.

Ignition System

TUNE-UP SERVICES

The ignition system consists of spark plugs; plug wires; distributor; rotor; points; condenser; coil. These units work to create a good hot spark inside the engine (ignition) at exactly the right moment (timing). If ignition is weak or timing is off, engine may be hard to start, run poorly, waste gas, lose power, backfire or not run at all.
1975-76 610s and 710s sold in California are equipped with electronic ignition which replaces the points with a pick-up coil. This pick-up coil does not require replacement, however the gap should be checked and adjusted when performing a tune-up.
1971-73 510s and 1973 610s are equipped with dual point distributors which require different timing and point gap adjustment procedures. For specific instructions, see the sections on dual point distributors.
Datsun recommends that points, plugs and condenser be replaced every 12 months or 12,000 miles unless you have electronic ignition. With electronic ignition, points and condenser should not have to be replaced, but you should check the gap of the points once a year or if you suspect a problem in the ignition.
TOOLS & MATERIALS . . . Parts: set of points; condenser; 4 spark plugs. Tools: gap gauge; 13/16 in. spark plug socket; screwdriver; open end, box or combination metric wrenches; timing equipment.
SAFETY TIP . . . Change only one spark plug at a time to avoid crosswiring and possible engine damage.

CHECKING POINTS AND ROTOR

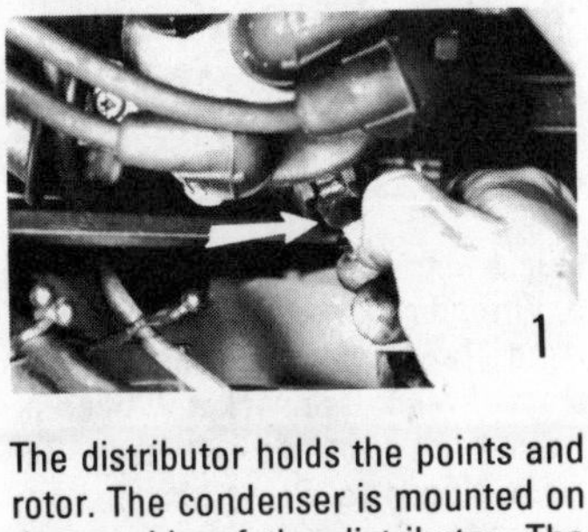

The distributor holds the points and rotor. The condenser is mounted on the outside of the distributor. The cap forms the top of the distributor.
1. To open distributor, snap retaining clips off with screwdriver, lift cap off but keep wires connected.
2. Pull rotor off (straight up). Replace if badly burned.

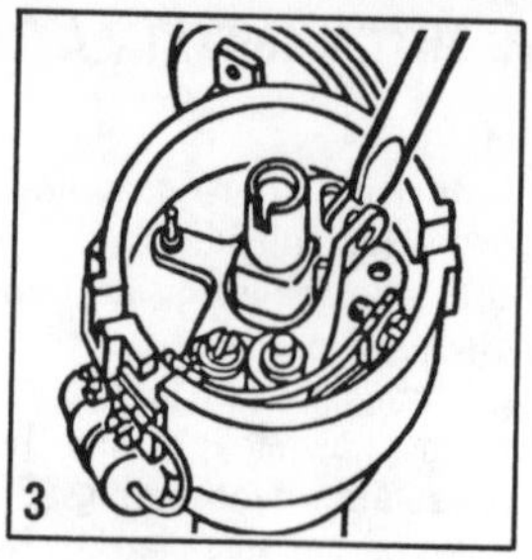

3. Pry points apart with screwdriver. If worn or burned, replace. If OK, check point gap.

OTHER IGNITION CHECK POINTS

Inspect spark plug wires. If cracked or brittle, entire set should be replaced. Also center, high tension wire. Inspect distributor cap. Wipe inside clean occasionally with dry, lint-free rag. If cap is cracked or rotor contacts are excessively burned, replace cap.

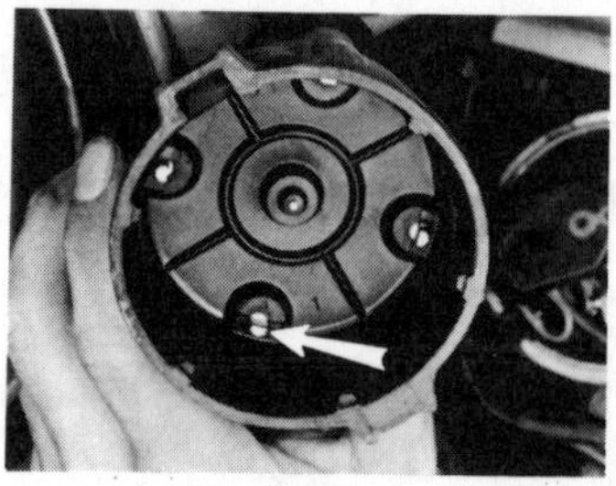

SPARK PLUG REPLACEMENT

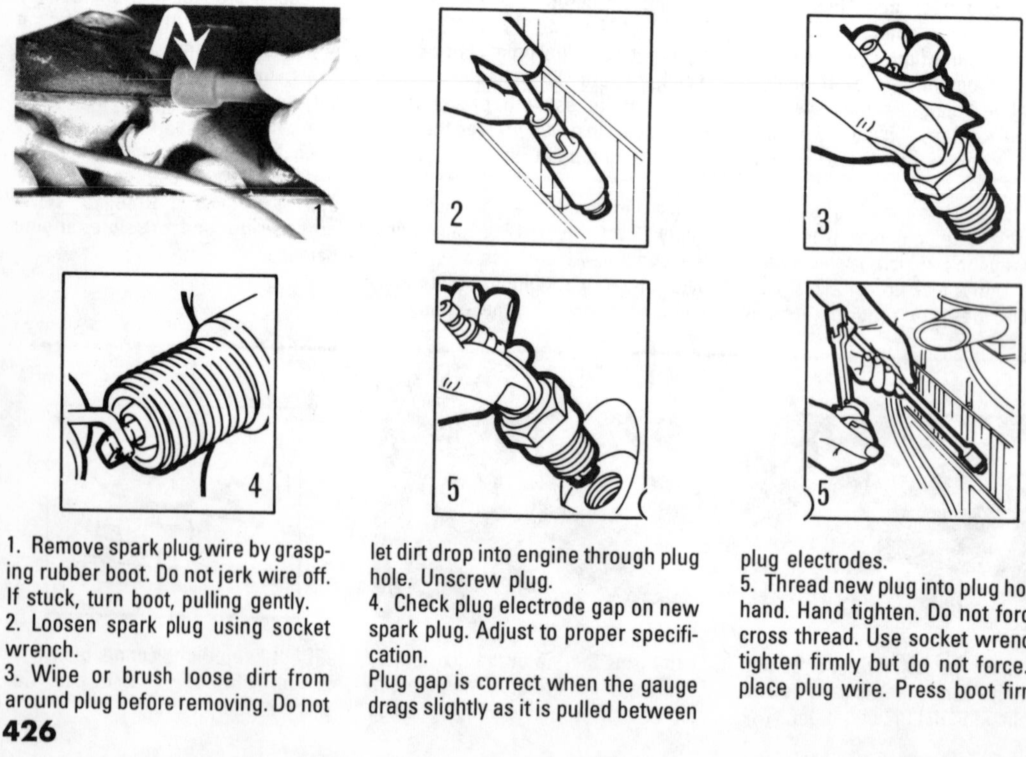

1. Remove spark plug wire by grasping rubber boot. Do not jerk wire off. If stuck, turn boot, pulling gently.
2. Loosen spark plug using socket wrench.
3. Wipe or brush loose dirt from around plug before removing. Do not let dirt drop into engine through plug hole. Unscrew plug.
4. Check plug electrode gap on new spark plug. Adjust to proper specification.
Plug gap is correct when the gauge drags slightly as it is pulled between plug electrodes.
5. Thread new plug into plug hole by hand. Hand tighten. Do not force or cross thread. Use socket wrench to tighten firmly but do not force. Replace plug wire. Press boot firmly.

LOCATION OF POINTS AND CONDENSER

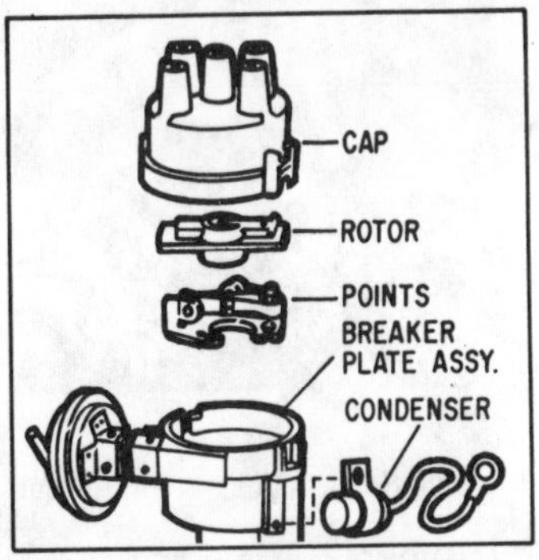

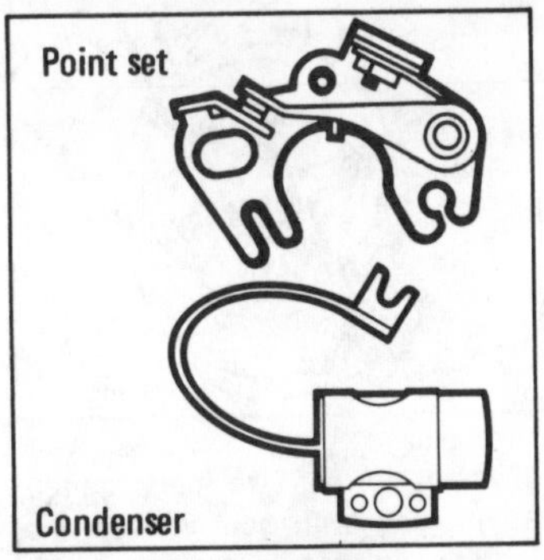

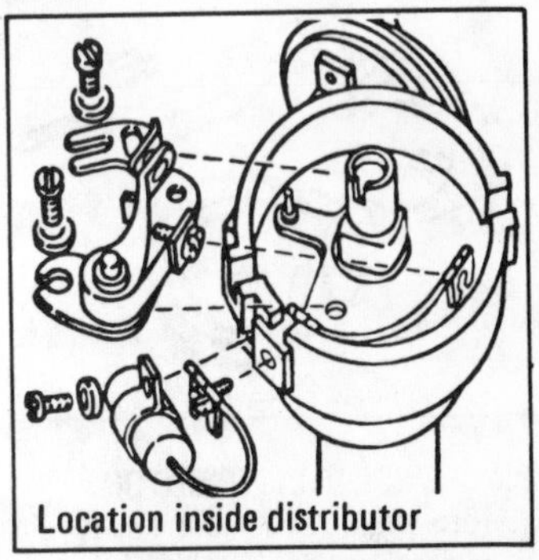

Points and condenser work together. Always replace condenser when installing new points. While you may find slight differences in location or attachments of these parts from one car to another they're all basically the same. The condenser is attached to the outside rather than inside.

REMOVING POINTS AND CONDENSER

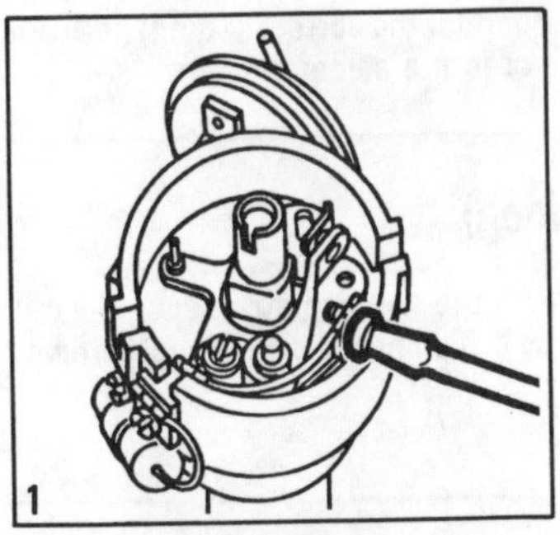

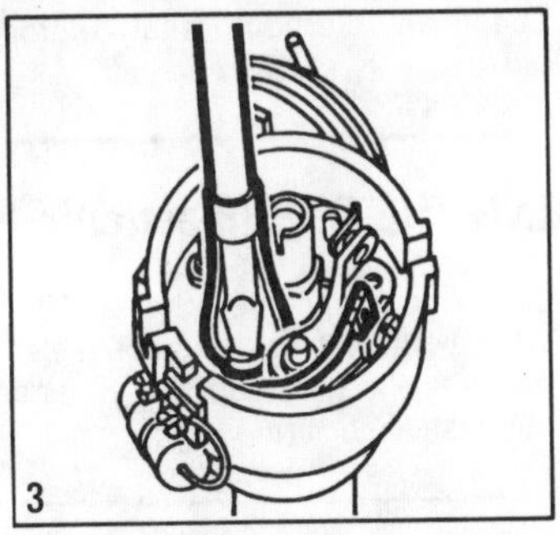

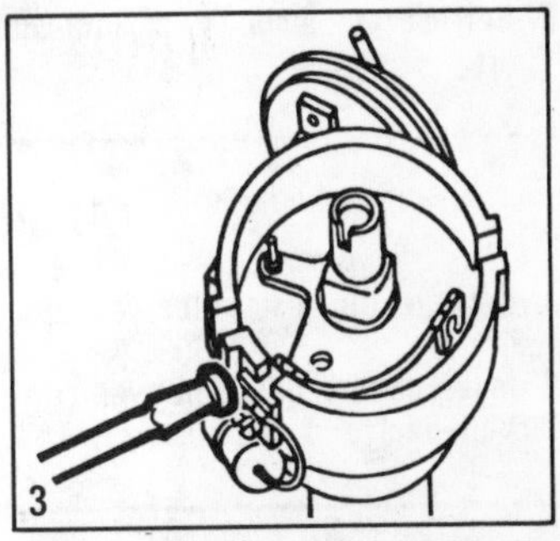

1. Disconnect the wire terminal connected to the points set.
2. Remove points attaching screws being very careful not to drop screws inside distributor.
3. Remove screw holding condenser to side of distributor and condenser wire terminal screw. DO NOT DROP SCREW.
4. Wipe all dirt from distributor plate and cam.

CAUTION: When removing screws from distributor, be sure to avoid any screws accidentally falling through distributor opening into engine. Use magnetic screwdriver.

INSTALLING POINTS AND CONDENSER

1. Lubricate cam head assembly with grease.
2. Position new points set in distributor. Attach retaining screws lightly. Replace wire terminal.
3. Attach new condenser to side of distributor with screw. Attach wire terminal and tighten screw.

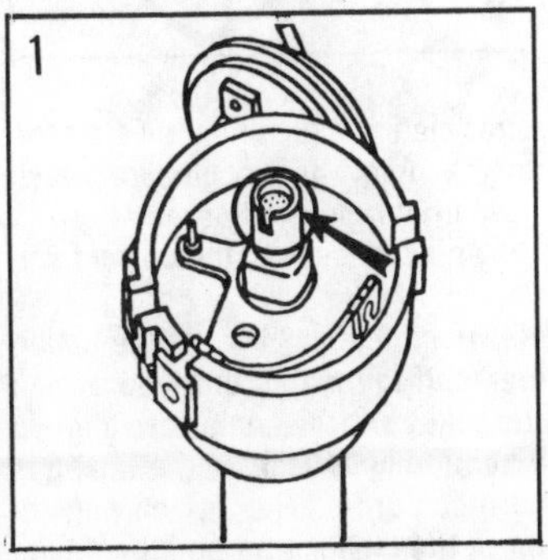

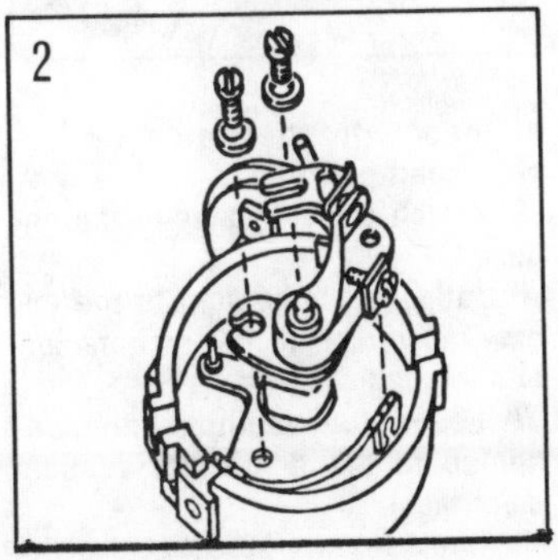

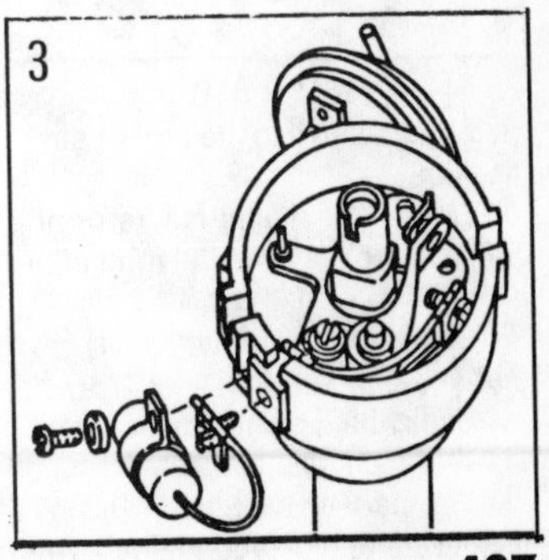

SETTING THE CONTACT GAP

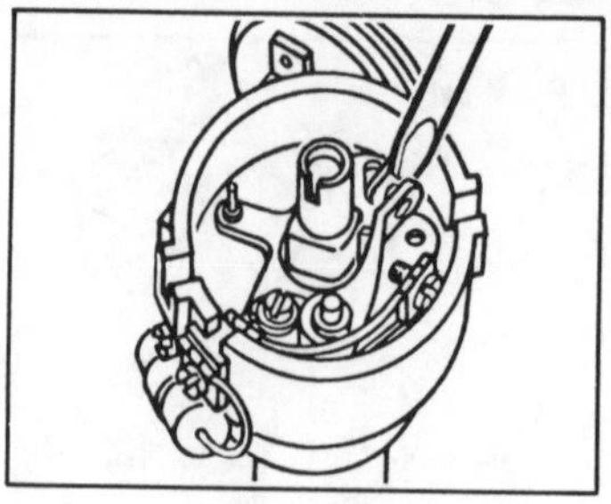

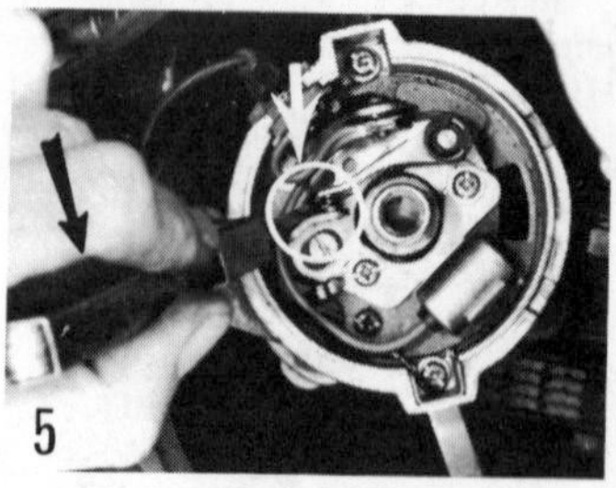

SINGLE POINT DISTRIBUTOR

1. Turn engine by ignition key (you'll need a helper) until rubbing block or point set is on one of the four high spots of distributor cam. You may use a wrench on lower engine pulley to do this.
2. Insert screwdriver in adjusting screw near point contacts; turn to open or close gap.
3. Correct gap is shown in Tune-Up Chart.
4. Insert correct size feeler gauge; adjust gap with screwdriver until feeler gauge can be moved between contacts with only slight drag.
5. Tighten point set holddown screws. Recheck gap; it might have changed from tightening the holddown screws. Readjust if needed.
6. Align rotor with distributor shaft and push rotor onto shaft. Rotor must be fully seated on shaft.
7. Replace distributor cap; install clips.

DUAL POINT DISTRIBUTOR

The two sets of breaker points are adjusted with a feeler gauge in the same manner as those in a single point distributor, except that you do the actual adjusting by twisting a screwdriver in the point set notch. Check the "Tune-Up Specifications" chart for the correct setting; both are set to the same opening.

ADJUSTING THE GAP (Electronic Ignition)

1. Remove the distributor cap and rotor.
2. Insert a feeler gauge between the pick-up coil and the reluctor. The proper gap should be between .008-.016 in. Do not use a steel feeler gauge to check the gap. Use either a non-metallic or brass one.
3. If the gap is not correct, adjust it by loosening the pick-up coil screws.

IGNITION TIMING

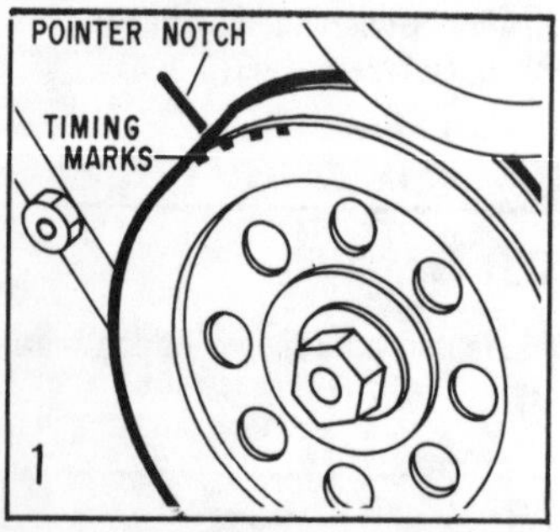

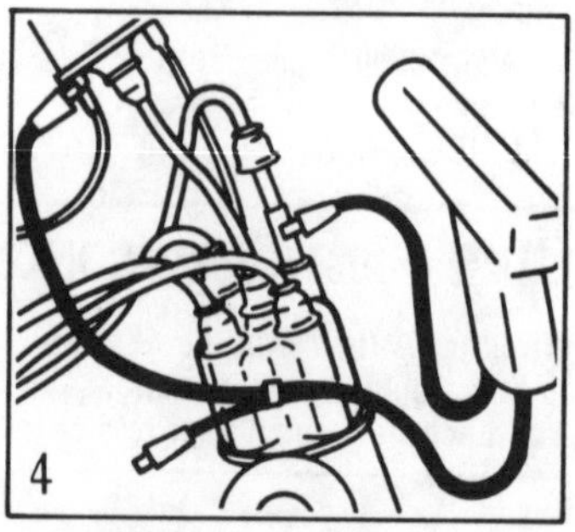

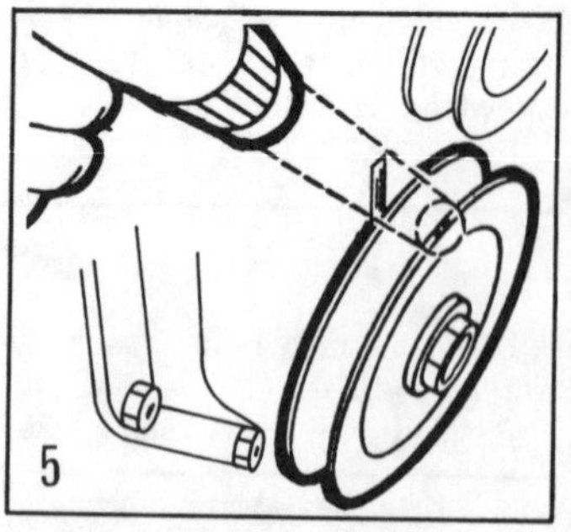

1. Set the dwell to the proper specification.
2. Locate the timing marks on the crankshaft pulley and the front of the engine.
3. Clean off the timing marks so that you can see them.
4. Use chalk or white paint to color the mark on the crankshaft pulley and the mark on the scale which will indicate the correct timing when aligned with the notch on the crankshaft pulley.
5. Attach a tachometer to the engine.
6. Attach a timing light to the engine, according to the manufacturer's instructions.
7. Leave the vacuum line connected to the distributor vacuum diaphragm.
8. Check to make sure that all of the wires clear the fan and then start the engine. Allow the engine to reach nomal operating temperature.
9. Adjust the idle to the correct setting.
10. Aim the timing light at the timing marks. If the marks that you put on the pulley and the engine are aligned when the light flashes, the timing is correct. Turn off the engine and remove the tachometer and the timing

light. If the marks are not in alignment, proceed with the following steps.
11. Turn off the engine.
12. Loosen the distributor lockbolt just enough so that the distributor can be turned with a little effort.
13. Start the engine. Keep the wires of the timing light clear of the fan.
14. With the timing light aimed at the pulley and the marks on the engine, turn the distributor in the direction of rotor rotation to retard the spark, and in the opposite direction of rotor rotation to advance the spark. Align the marks on the pulley and the engine with the flashes of the timing light. Tighten the holddown bolt.

REPLACING SPARK PLUG WIRES

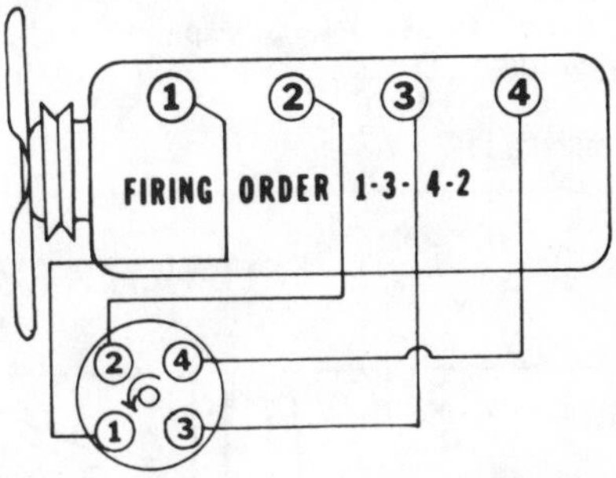

One of the most often overlooked items in a tune-up is the spark plug wires. Your car can be in perfect tune, but if the plug wires are not carrying the spark to the plugs, your engine will run poorly. The original equipment wires that came with your car are usually good for a year or two before needing replacement. On newer cars, the higher underhood temperatures created by emission controls breaks down the wires ability to conduct electricity sooner. The spark plug boot ends of the wires will crack with age allowing the spark to arc towards the engine, not reaching the plugs. The distributor cap ends of the wires will often collect moisture, and corrode right there in your distributor cap. Sometimes a wire will contact a hot part of the engine, such as the exhaust manifold and burn through the insulation. Other times, a wire will become oil soaked and gummy, breaking down the insulation. Often, when carbon core wires get old, they will break off inside, with no visible signs of breakage on the outside. Always use good quality spark plug wire. A carbon core or cut-rate brand may seem attractive at first, but will cost you more in the long run with reduced engine efficiency and more frequent replacement.

1. Replace one wire at a time. This will keep you out of trouble with crossed wires. When removing wires, twist back and forth as you pull up. This will help free up stuck wires.
2. Take the old wire and match it up with the new one for length. If you are cutting your own, make sure there is good metal contact between the end of the wire and the pinch-on connectors.
3. Make sure each wire seats all the way down in the distributor cap. First push down the wire, then the boot. The wire should click in place.
4. After you are all done, make sure all wires are clear of choke or throttle linkage, or hot exhaust manifolds. Use the firing order illustration to guide you when replacing your ignition wires and/or distributor cap.

Fuel System

When gasoline is brought from the fuel tank, it mixes with air in the carburetor. This gas/air mixture then passes thru a network of small hoses, valves and filters, enters engine thru the intake manifold, passes thru the intake valves and is burned in the combustion chamber. The burned exhaust gas is then passed thru the exhaust valves to the exhaust system and to the outside air. In order to keep your car's engine running cleanly with minimal pollution, and avoid dangerous carbon monoxide fumes inside the vehicle, certain items should be checked from time to time.

KEEP THE AIR INTAKE CLEAN

The large round can that sits on top of the engine contains the air filter. The air filter is a paper type which does not require servicing until replacement, which is every 24,000 miles.

1. Unscrew the wing nut at the top of the air cleaner.

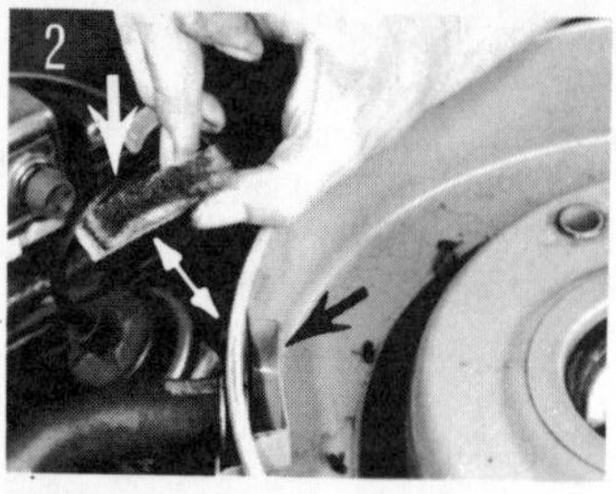

2. Remove the top cover. Lift out circular air cleaner cartridge. Check the small crankcase breather filter. If dirty, lift out and replace it.

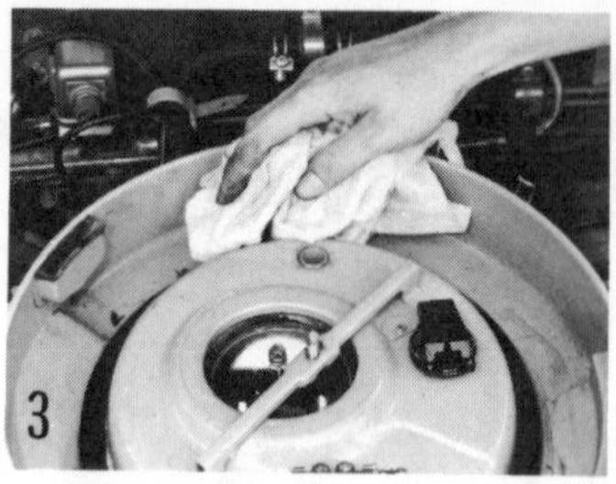

3. Wipe inside of can and lid clean with lint-free cloth.

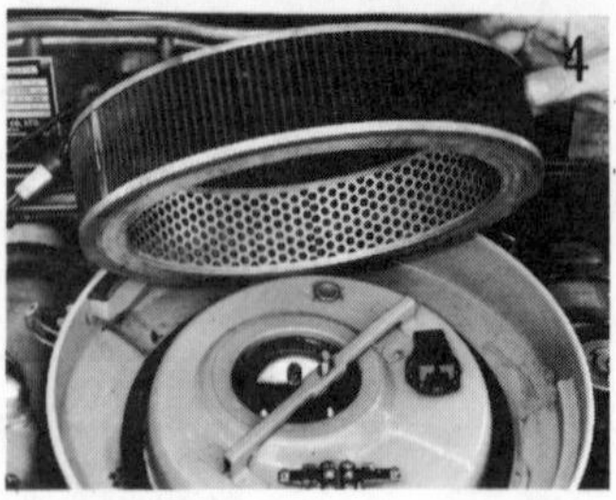

4. Insert new air cleaner cartridge, replace lid and secure wing nut.

FUEL FILTER REPLACEMENT

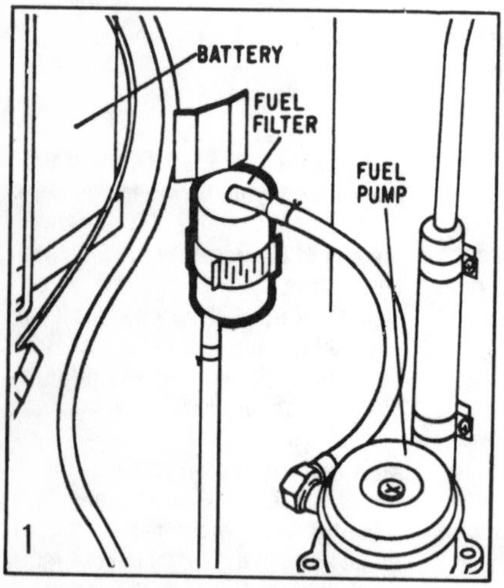

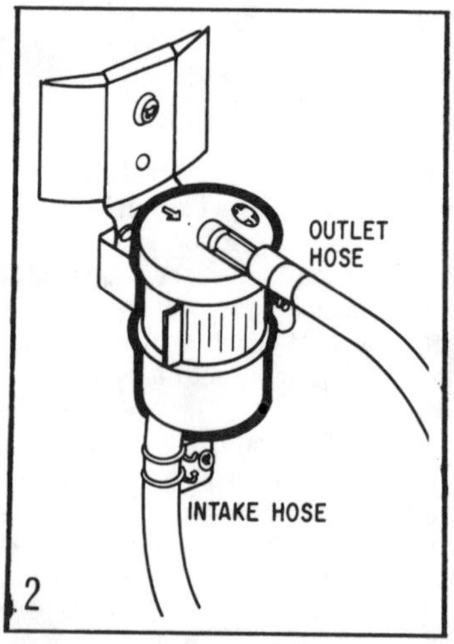

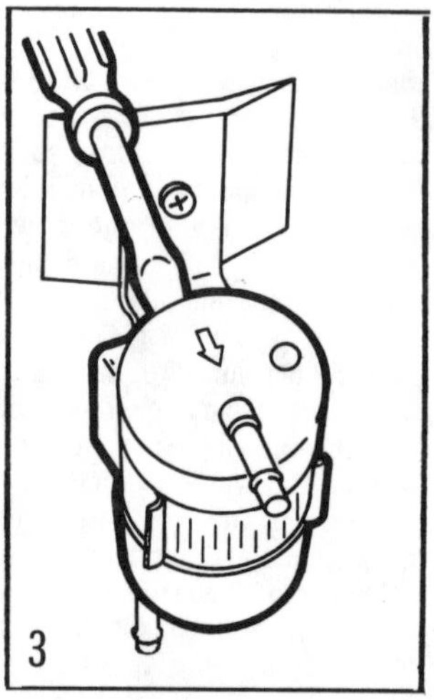

The fuel filter is located in the right inner fender in the engine compartment. It is a cartridge type filter. Replace the filter every year or 12,000 (24,000 on 610/710s) miles. The fuel filter prevents dirt, rust, and scale from both the gas station's tank and your own fuel tank from reaching the carburetor. A dirty filter will starve the engine and cause poor running.

1. Locate fuel filter on right side fender wall.
2. Disconnect the inlet and outlet hoses from fuel filter. Make certain that the inlet hose (bottom) doesn't fall below the fuel tank level or the gasoline will drain out.
3. Pry the fuel filter from its clip and replace the assembly.
4. Replace the intake and outlet lines; secure hose clamps tightly to avoid leaks.
5. Start the engine and check for leaks. Addition of a can of carburetor cleaner to the fuel tank occasionally will aid in keeping the entire fuel system clean.

PCV VALVE REPLACEMENT

An important part of a car's emission control system is the Positive Crankcase Ventilation (PCV) valve and its connecting hose. The PCV valve should be replaced once every 24,000 miles. This device keeps dirt and sludge from forming inside the engine. Make sure all PCV connections are tight. Check that the connecting hoses are clear and not

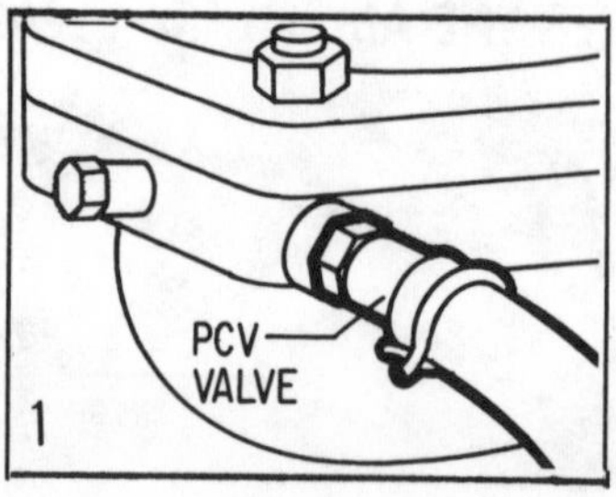

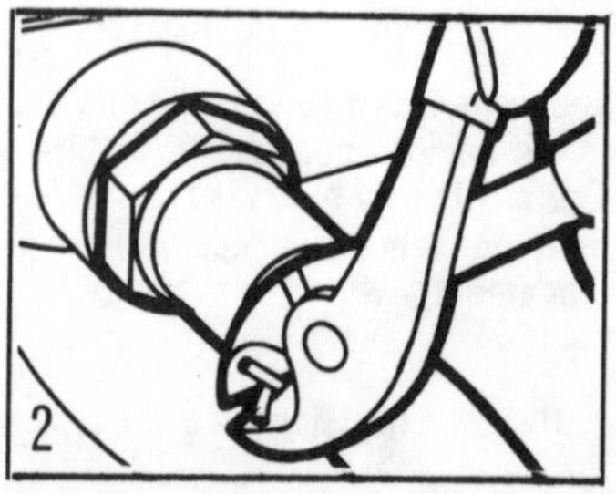

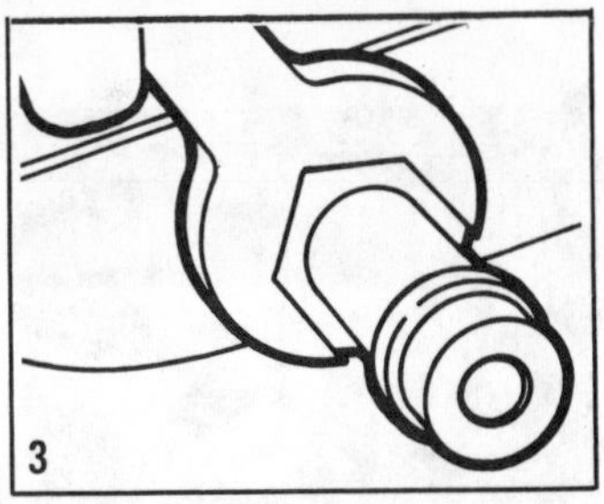

clogged. Replace any brittle or broken hoses.

1. PCV valve is located in the manifold below the carburetor.
2. Squeeze hose clamp with pliers. Remove hose.
3. Unscrew PCV valve and remove from its location in manifold.
4. Note where other end of hose connects. Remove hose and flush with cleaning solvent.
5. Replace PCV in manifold and reconnect hose and clamps.

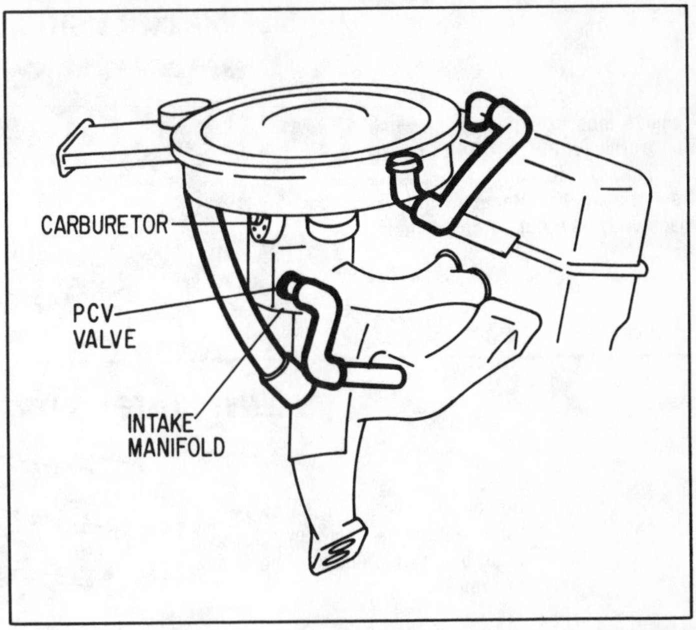

Safety Systems

PARKING LIGHTS, TURN SIGNALS AND STOP LIGHTS

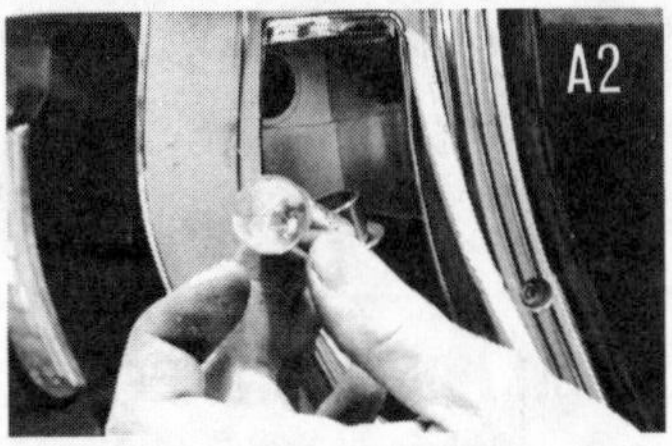

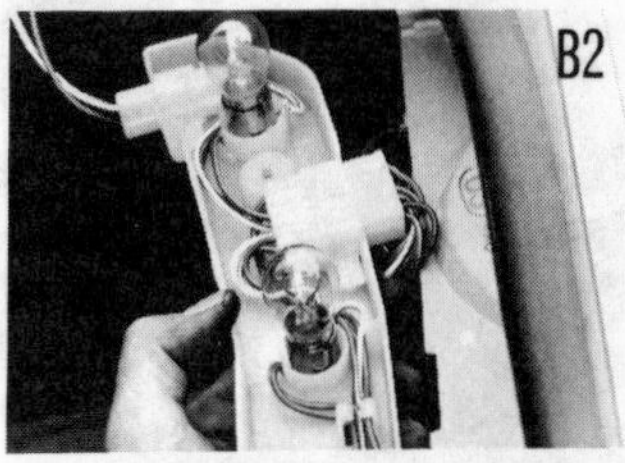

Parking lights, turn signals, and stop lights function with dual-element bulbs.

A. Front parking lights, turn signals, side marker lights: remove lens to expose bulb(s). Push in on bulb while turning counterclockwise to release the bulb from the socket. Remove and replace with a new bulb. Replace lens.
B. Rear Light Comb. on sedans, to replace rear light bulbs (except license plate), raise trunk lid. Reach bulb socket from inside car. Turn bulb socket counterclockwise to remove from socket. On station wagon, remove lens to reach rear bulbs.

BACK-UP LIGHTS

To replace back-up light bulbs, raise trunk lid. Reach bulb socket from inside car. Turn bulb socket counterclockwise and pull out. Push down on bulb turning counterclockwise to remove from socket. Remove lens on station wagons.

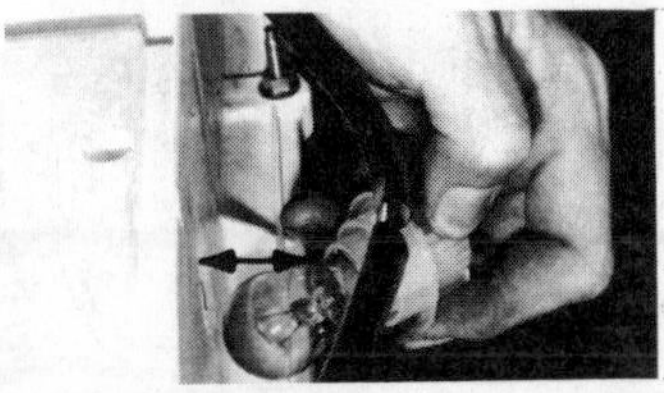

SIDE MARKER LIGHT

Remove lens to expose bulb. Push on bulb while turning counterclockwise to release the bulb from the socket. Remove and replace with new bulb. Replace lens.

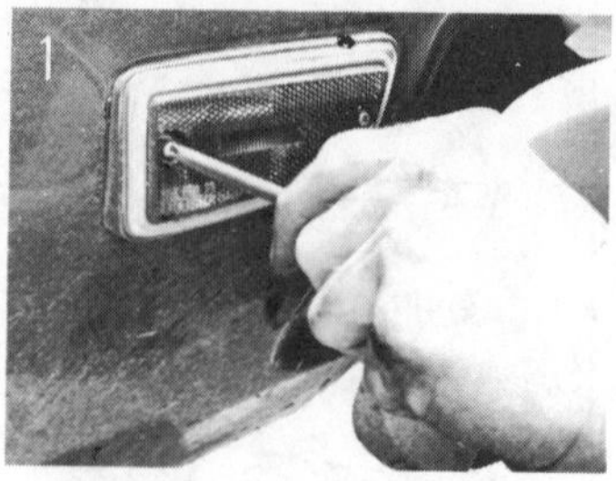

LICENSE PLATE LIGHTS

Remove the retaining screws, and remove the lens from bumper. Push in on bulb turning counterclockwise to remove.

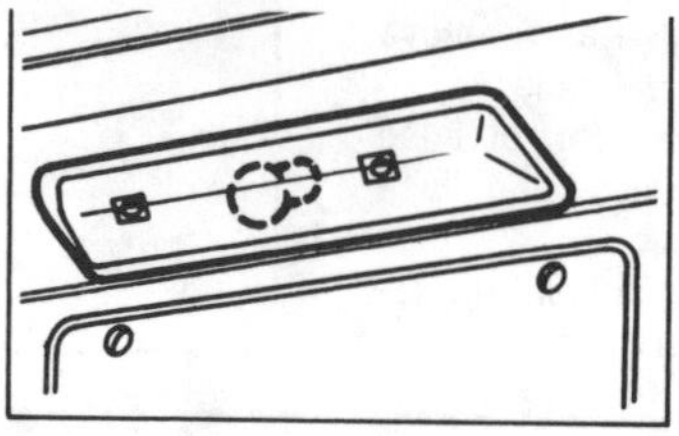

INTERIOR DOME LIGHT

This is cartridge type bulb; be sure to purchase correct replacement. Pry dome light lens out from housing. To avoid blowing fuse, make sure doors are closed and dome light switch is in OFF position. Carefully lever the bulb straight out of housing. Insert new bulb and reinstall dome light lens.

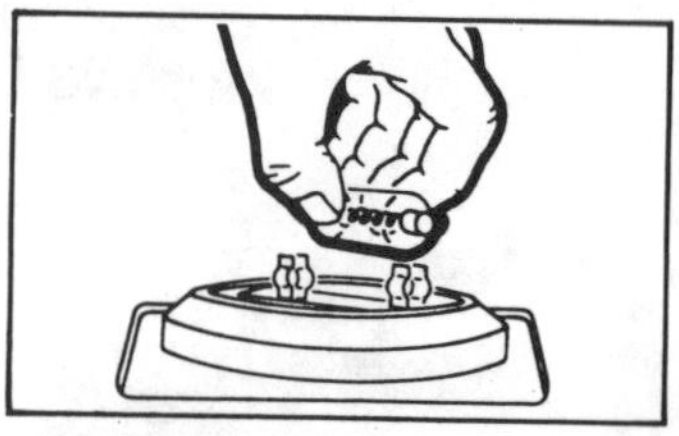

SEALED BEAM HEADLIGHT REPLACEMENT

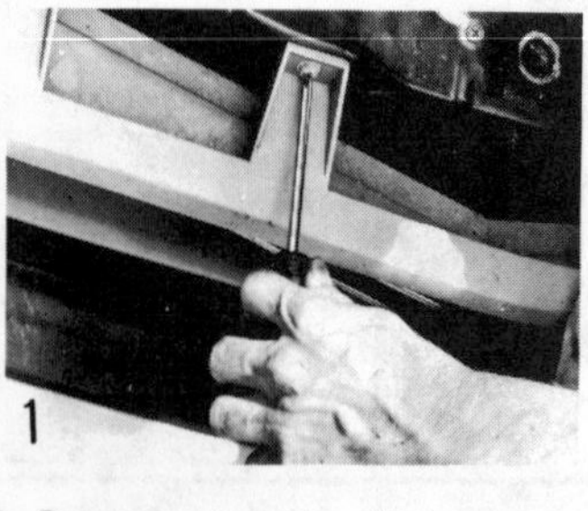

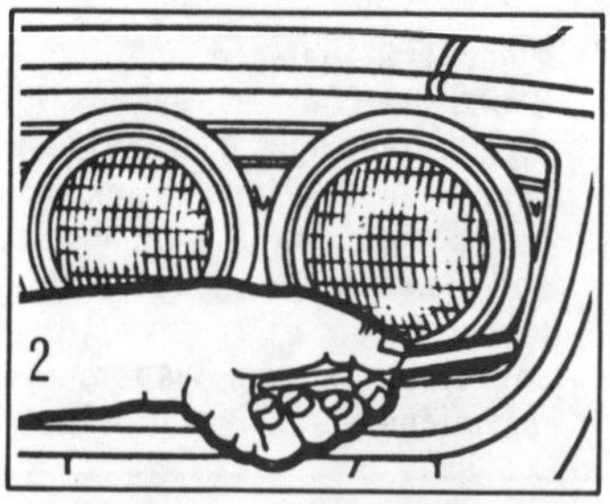

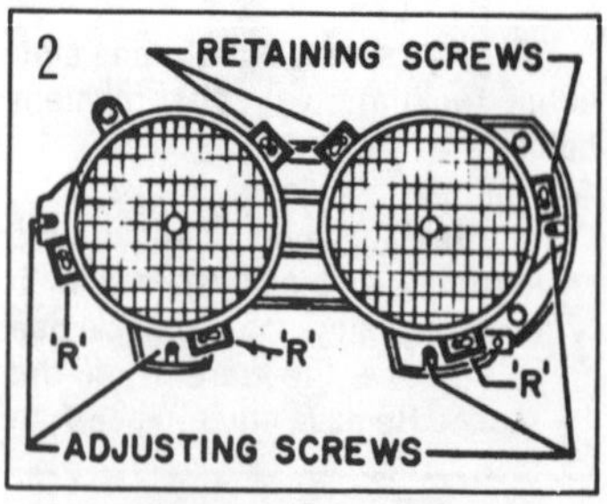

1. Remove either headlight rim or grille retaining screws, and remove the rim or grille.
2. Remove trim ring retaining screws located near the outside, being careful not to confuse these with headlight aiming screws. (Coupe only)
3. Remove the inner ring and pull the headlight out. Disconnect and remove the bulb.

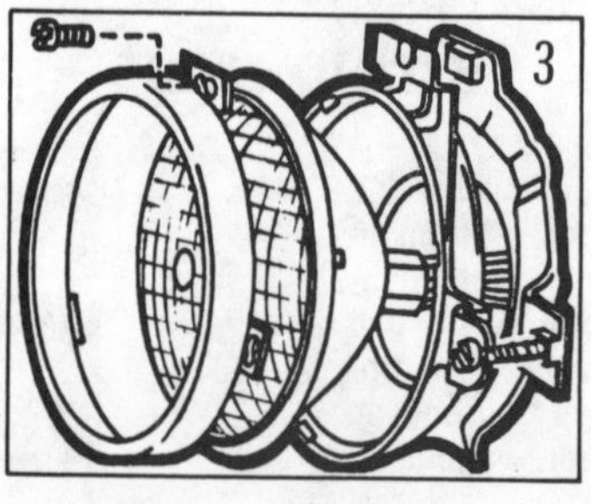

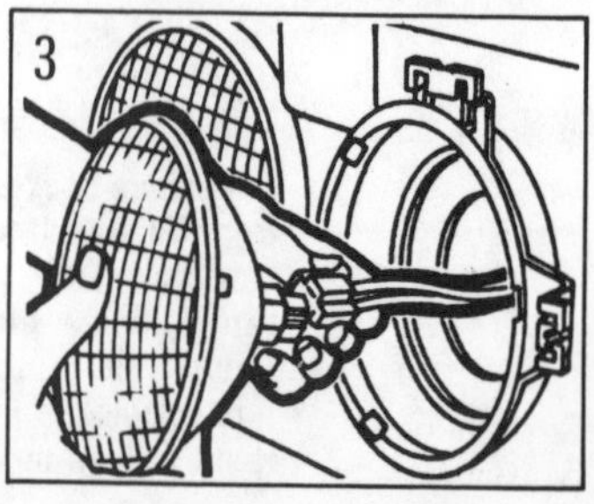

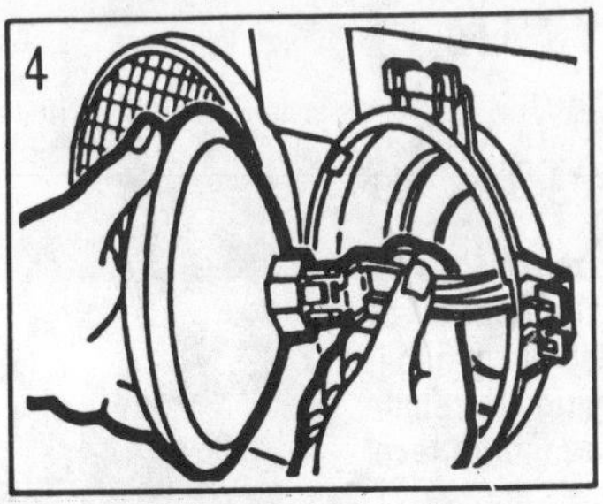

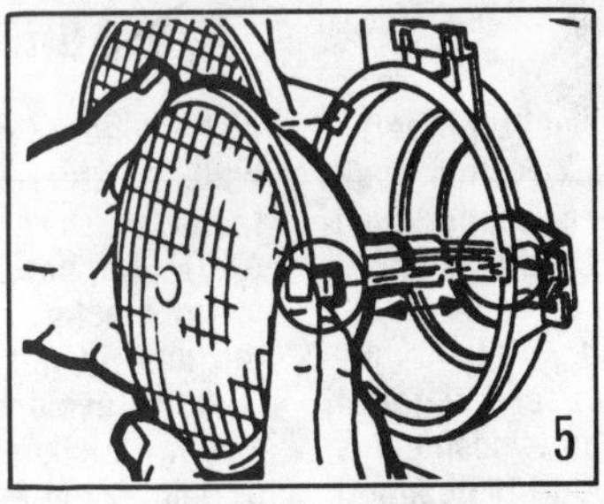

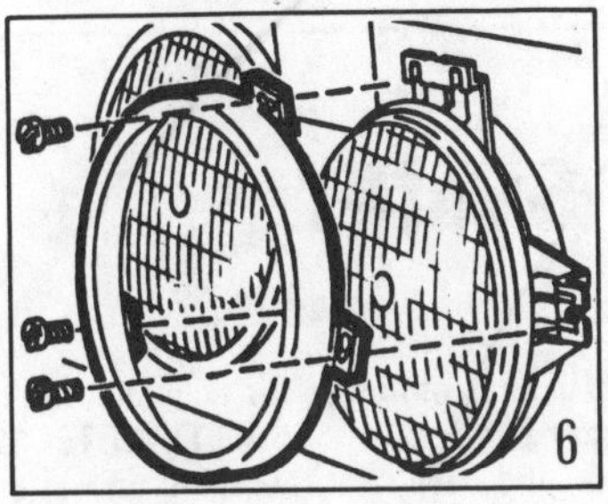

4. Connect the plug to the rear of the new bulb unit.
5. Position new sealed beam in headlight shell. Be sure that knobs on back of light (near outer edge) enter slots in shell.
6. Place retaining ring over sealed beam and fasten with three screws.
7. Install trim ring and tighten screws.

WINDSHIELD WIPER BLADE REPLACEMENT

To replace wiper blade, lift up on spring release tab on wiper arm connector. Pull wiper blade off. Snap new blade into place.
To replace rubber insert only, press down, away from wiper blade to free it. Slide insert from blade. Insert new wiper. Bend insert upward slightly to engage retaining clips.

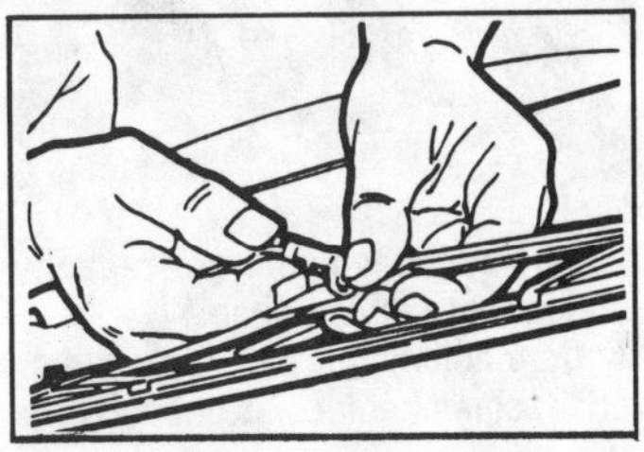

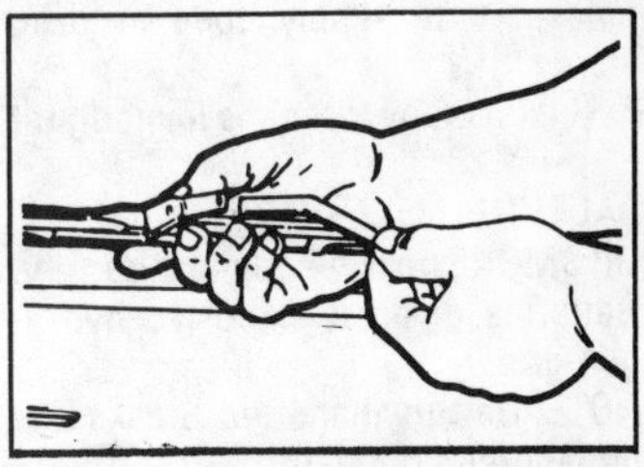

HORN PROBLEMS

If horn sounds and does not stop, this is due to short circuit in wiring. Disconnect wiring connector under hood and have professional service shop check horn wiring circuit.

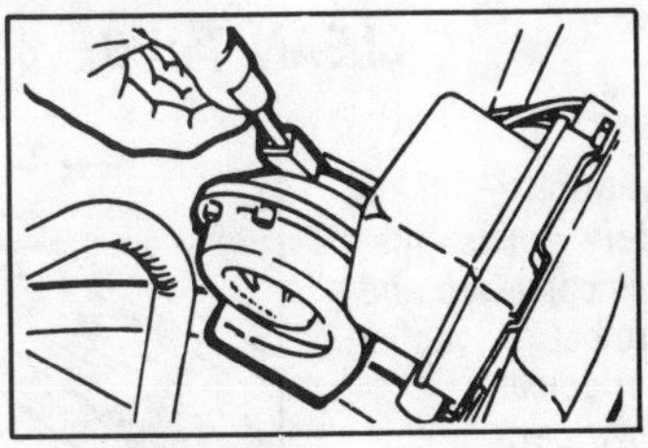

STEERING PROBLEMS

See steering system check in Suspension Section. Check tire pressures. Have a professional service shop check all components in the front end and steering system.

WASHER SYSTEM

If washer fails to squirt properly, raise hood and check system hose connections. Be sure washer fluid container has fluid. Check spout openings for clogging.
Keep container filled with fluid mixture of washer solvent and water. If road spray buildup on windshield is a chronic problem, add 1 tablespoon dishwasher detergent to solvent/water mixture when re-filling container.
NOTE: The car's windshield washer pump mechanism is lubricated by the fluid in the windshield washer tank. To avoid damaging the pump mechanism, keep an adequate level of fluid in the tank at all times.

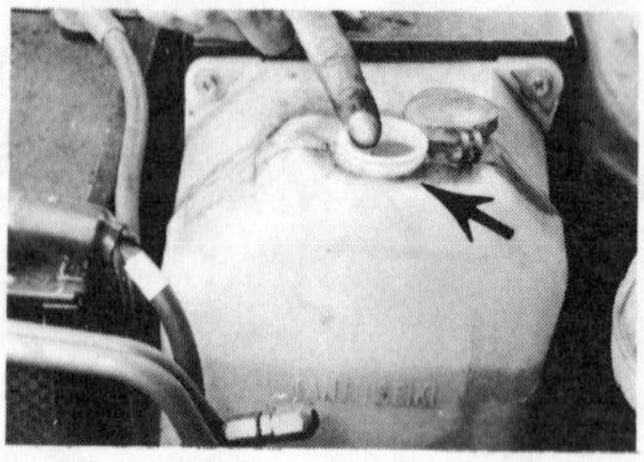

Electrical System

To ensure starting ability at all times check your battery condition periodically. You'll need to check battery electrolyte (fluid) level in each of the six cells. Check battery cable connections for tightness and inspect for accumulated corrosion.
SAFETY NOTE: Wear gloves when working on battery.

CHECK BATTERY FLUID

1. Remove plastic filler caps on top of battery. Fluid should be up to lower end of filler hole and covering the plates. If fluid is low add clean, cold tap water. If your area has hard water, use only distilled water available at auto supply, food or drug stores.
2. Replace any lost caps immediately.
CAUTION: NEVER LIGHT A MATCH OR SMOKE near the top of a battery. Batteries give off explosive hydrogen gas.
NOTE: Battery that often checks low on fluid could mean:
A. Battery is getting old, due for re-

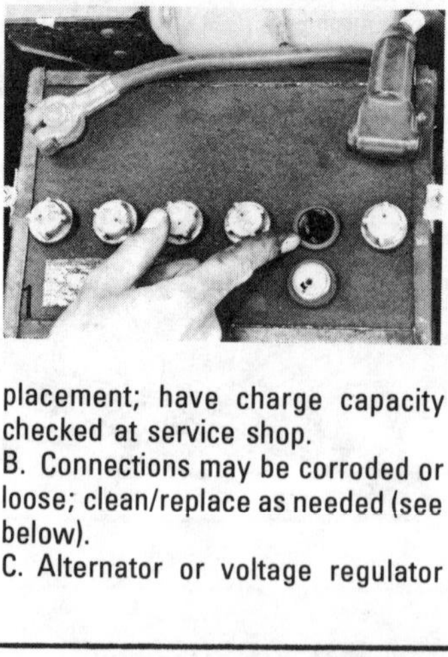

placement; have charge capacity checked at service shop.
B. Connections may be corroded or loose; clean/replace as needed (see below).
C. Alternator or voltage regulator

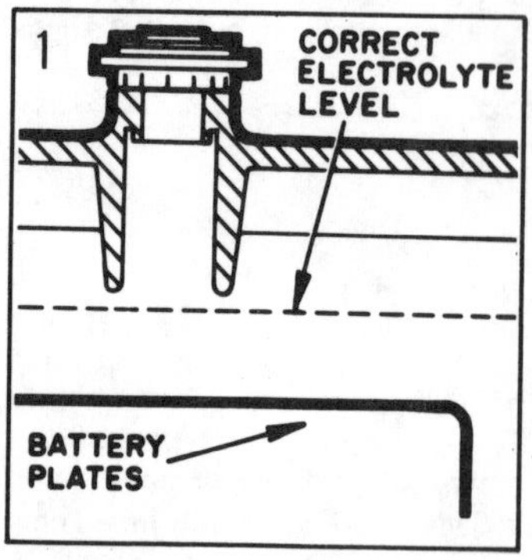

not functioning properly; this happens far less often than A or B above.

CLEAN THOSE BATTERY TERMINALS

As time goes by, battery terminals build up a dry powdery, whitish material. This material is corrosive and will gradually eat thru battery cables if not cleaned off periodically.
1. Loosen and remove battery connections.
2. Brush off all loose corrosion; use stiff bristle brush. Do not get this material into eyes or on open cuts. Wash off at once.
3. If corrosion build-up is extremely heavy and brushing does not remove

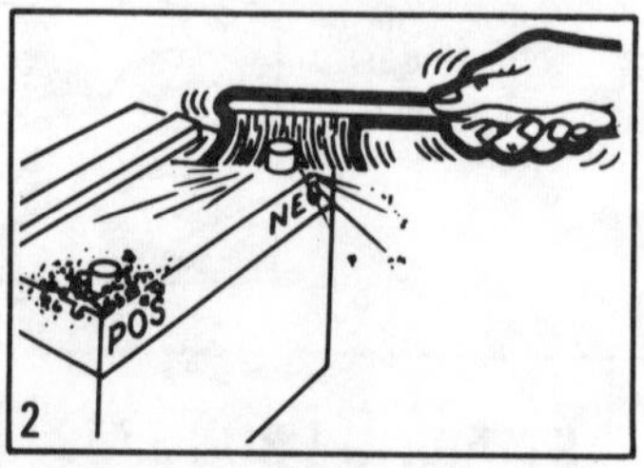

all of it, mix 2 tablespoons baking soda to 1 cup water. Pour solution directly onto terminals and connec-

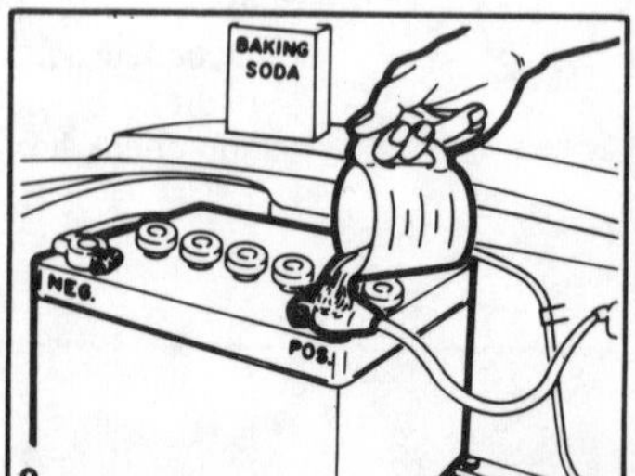

tors. Allow to soak a few minutes and rinse off. Continue brushing to

remove all traces of corrosion build-up. Do not allow cleaning solution to enter battery.
4. Replace connectors on battery terminal posts and tighten.
5. Liberally smear battery terminal posts and cable connectors with petroleum jelly.

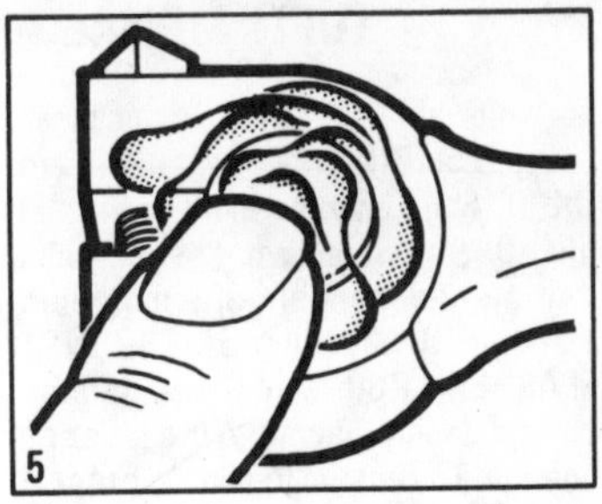

REPLACE FAULTY BATTERY CABLES

If battery cable strands become frayed, broken or corroded, replace cable immediately. Delay in correcting this condition could lead to sudden failure to start the engine. Can also weaken battery.
1. Loosen and remove battery connections. Clean OFF any corrosion.
2. Disconnect negative cable from its attachment to engine or chassis. Disconnect positive cable from its attachment to starter relay.
3. Attach new cables making sure positive and negative cables are on proper terminals. They are not identical.
4. Replace connectors on battery terminal posts and tighten.
5. Liberally smear battery terminal posts and cable connectors with petroleum jelly.

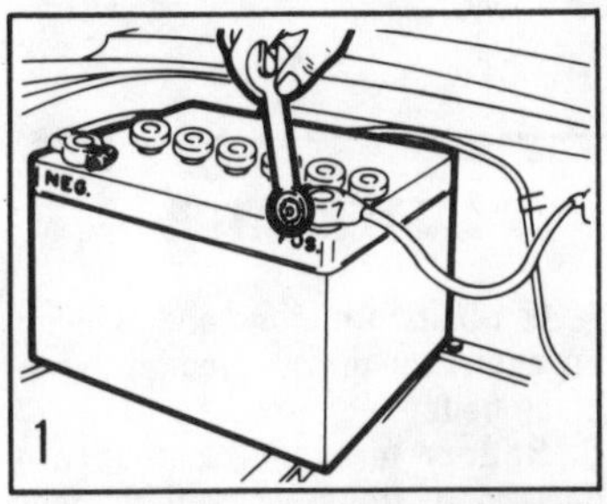

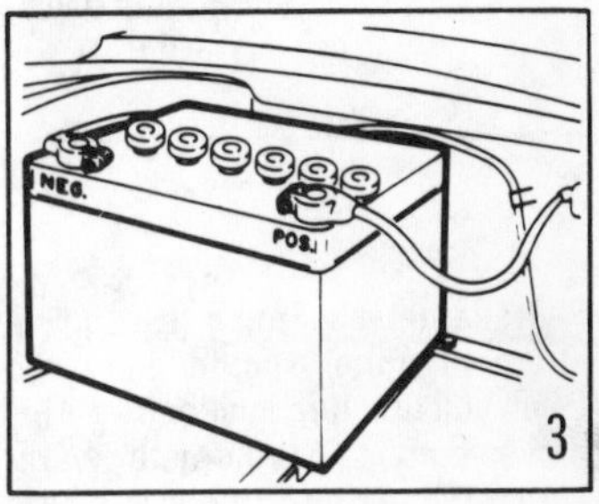

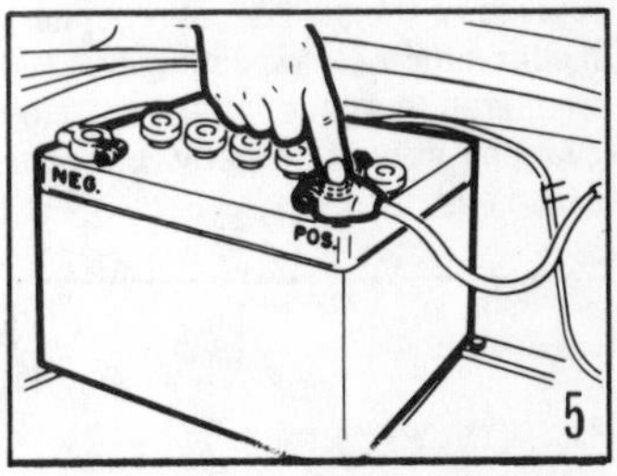

BATTERY HOLDDOWN

The clamp device which holds battery in place should be checked periodically. If loose, tighten. Clean off corrosion buildup. Severely corroded holddown components should be replaced before they break.

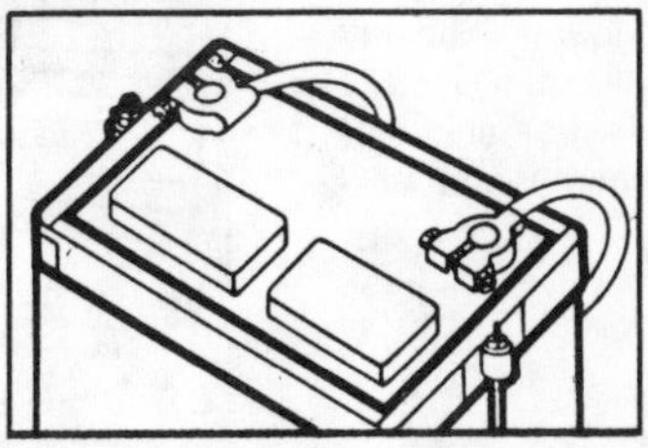

ELECTRICAL FUSES

The fuse box is located on the right side of the steering column on the engine firewall. The fuse box cover is clearly marked as to function and correct amperage of each fuse. Always replace fuse with one of the same amperage. If fuses are continually blowing, have system checked by professional mechanic.

TURN SIGNAL AND 4-WAY FLASHER

Turn signals and 4-way flashers will operate only if: A. All light bulbs are OK. B. Flasher units are not burned out. Datsun has two flasher units that are independent of each other. TURN SIGNAL and EMERGENCY FLASHER: Both units are located behind dash adjacent to the steering column. To remove, unscrew bracket retaining screw and disconnect the wiring connection.
To install, connect wire terminal to new assembly, and attach to side of steering column with screws.
REPLACE ONLY WITH SAME TYPE FLASHER.

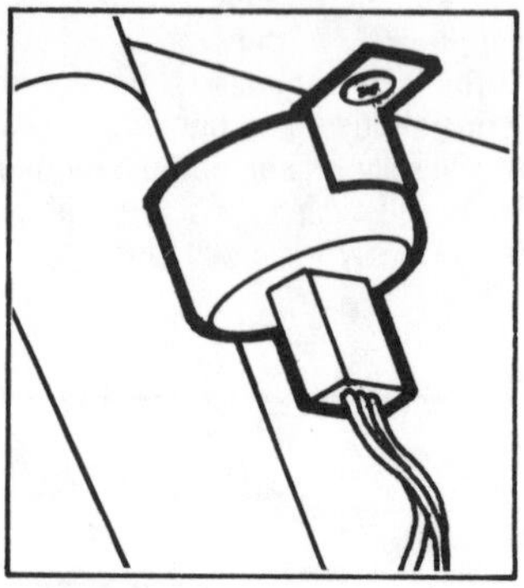

ALTERNATOR

Red alternator warning light on instrument panel should glow red when you first turn ignition key. This proves bulb is OK. Alternator warning light should go off when engine is running at normal operating speed. If alternator warning light glows red at operating speed, alternator isn't charging battery properly. Common causes are:
A. Fan belts are loose and slipping on alternator pulley. Tighten or replace belts.
B. Battery terminals, cables are loose or corroded. Clean; tighten; replace bad cables.
If A or B do not correct problem, alternator or voltage regulator may be faulty. This happens far less often, and can only be checked by mechanic with proper electrical testing equipment.
Alternator Caution: Alternator can be permanently damaged by shortcircuiting terminal connections. When working around or moving alternator, always keep metal tools or engine parts from terminals.

REAR WINDOW DEFOGGER SYSTEM

Do not clean inside of rear window fitted with defogger system with any abrasive material. This could destroy carbon-copper wires. Use only soft rag and mild detergent/water mixture. Dry carefully.

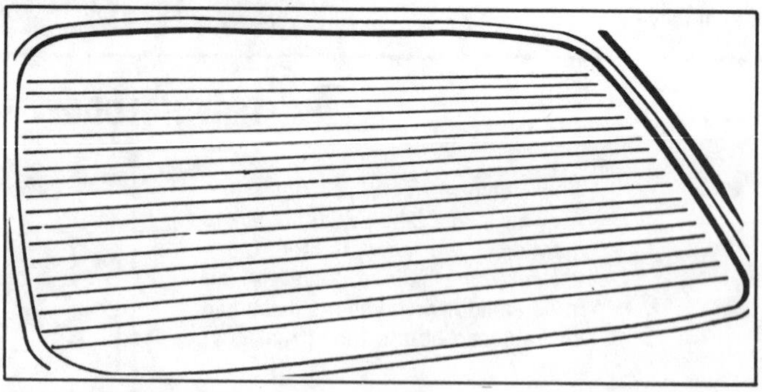

Air Conditioner

CHECK POINTS AND SERVICES

WARNING!—Never attempt to tighten fittings, disassemble or do any work on your car's A/C system. Consult a professional mechanic about A/C system problems and their correction. Your auto air conditioner (A/C) is a delicate, closed system. If air, dirt or water get into it, or if refrigerant escapes, the A/C unit will not cool a car interior. Among things you can do are:

1. Keep condenser grille clean. Check for dirt and debris; periodically remove dead insects, leaves, etc., with stiff bristle brush. Straighten any bent fins—carefully.
2. Keep radiator filled to correct level. (See Cooling System section). If fluid needs to be added, add antifreeze rather than water.
3. Keep radiator coolant at a 50/50 water/antifreeze mixture.
4. Flush cooling system and replace with fresh coolant mixture at least every 24 months. (See Cooling System section).
5. Radiator cap should be tight and sealed properly. If sealing gasket is cracked, cut or worn, replace cap with new 13 lb. unit.
6. Check fan belt tension periodically. (See Cooling System section). Replace glazed, frayed or cut fan belts, before they fail entirely.
7. Check periodically for bubbles in A/C sight glass. Sight glass is located in head of receiver/drier vessel. Sight glass is no larger than the head of a large nail. It may be dirty. Wipe clean for best visibility.

PROCEED AS FOLLOWS:

a) With engine and A/C system running, look for passage of refrigerant

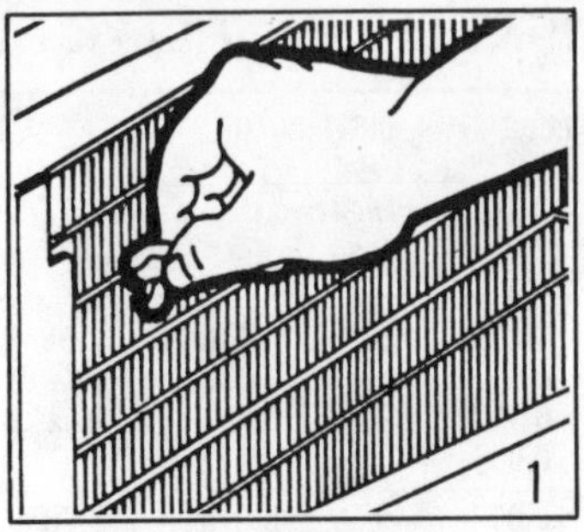

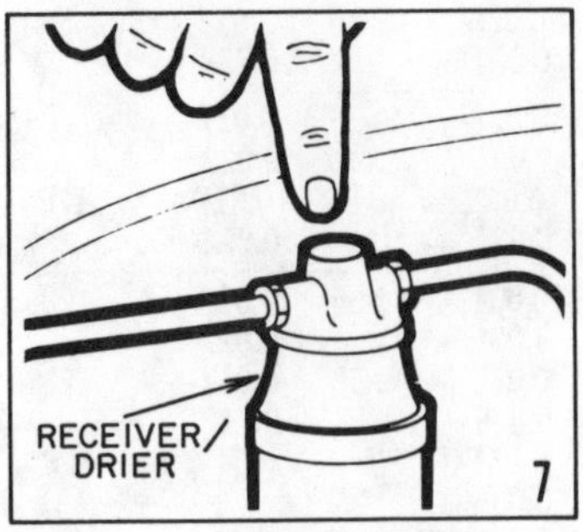

in sight glass. You'll be looking for a stream of milky white bubbles as they pass through sight glass. It is best to watch sight glass and have someone else start the car and turn on the A/C system. Allow to run for a few minutes.

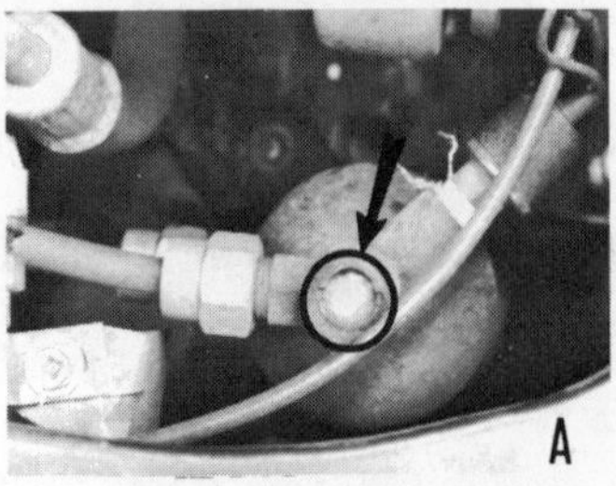

b) If you observe no bubbles, and air flow from A/C unit in the car is passing cold air, everything is OK.

c) If no bubbles appear in sight glass, and air flow from the A/C unit in the car is not delivering cold air, the system may be low on refrigerant and could need a re-charge.

d) If bubbles appear, system is low on refrigerant.

e) If you suspect refrigerant loss based on tests performed above, have system checked by a professional A/C service shop. They can confirm refrigerant loss, recharge the system and check for system leakage.

NOTE: Once a week or so, even in winter, run A/C system for about 5 minutes as you drive. This keeps system internally lubricated, prevents hoses hardening.

TUNE-UP SPECIFICATIONS

YEAR	MODEL	SPARK PLUGS Type	SPARK PLUGS Gap (in.)	DISTRIBUTOR Point Dwell (deg.)	DISTRIBUTOR Point Gap (in.)	IGNITION TIMING Man. Trans. (deg.) ■	IGNITION TIMING Auto Trans. (deg.) ■	IDLE SPEED Man. Trans. (rpm) ■	IDLE SPEED Auto Trans. (rpm) ■
1970-71	510	BP-6E	0.028-0.032	49-55	0.018-0.022	10B @ 600-700	10B @ 575-650	600-700	575-650
	510 with emiss. control	BP-6E	0.032-0.036	49-55	0.018-0.022	5A @ 700	5A @ 600	700	600
1972	510	BP-5ES	0.032-0.036	49-55	0.018-0.022	7B @ 700	7B @ 600	700	600
1973	510, 610	BP-6ES	0.028-0.031	49-55	0.018-0.022	5B @ 800	5B @ 650	800	650
1974	610	B6ES	0.028-0.031	49-55	0.017-0.022	12B @ 750	12B @ 650	750	650
	710	B6ES	0.028-0.031	49-55	0.017-0.022	12B @ 800		800	650
1975-76	610	BP-6ES	0.031-0.035	49-55	0.017-0.022	12B	12B	750	650
	710	BP-6ES	0.031-0.035	49-55	0.017-0.022	12B	12B	750	650
	710, 610 (California)	BP-6ES	0.031-① 0.035	②	②	12B	12B	750	650
1977	610, 710	See Underhood Specification Sticker							

■ Manual transmission is in Neutral; Automatic transmission is in Drive
① 1976: .039-.043
② Gap 0.008-0.016 in.—electronic ignition

NOTE: The underhood specifications sticker often reflects tune-up specification changes made in production. Sticker figures must be used if they disagree with those in this chart.

CAPACITIES

YEAR	MODEL	ENGINE OIL With Filter	ENGINE OIL Without Filter	TRANSMISSION (Pts. to Refill after Draining) MANUAL	TRANSMISSION (Pts. to Refill after Draining) AUTOMATIC	DRIVE AXLE (pts.)	COOLING SYSTEM (qts.)
1970-73	510	5.2	4.4	6.4	11.4①⑤	1.7	6.8, 7.2②
1973	610	5.0	4.5	4.0	11.8⑤	1.8	9.0
	610 station wagon	5.0	4.5	4.0	11.8⑤	2.8	9.0
1974	610	4.5	—	4.0	10.9⑤	1.75③	6.88
	710	4.45	—	4.5	10.9⑤	2.75	6.88
1975-77	610	4.5	4.0	4.25	11.8⑤	1.4④	7.25
	710	4.5	4.0	4.25	11.8⑤	2.75	7.25

① 1.5 pts. w/cooler
② w/heater
③ w/manual trans.—2.12
w/auto. trans.—2.75
④ Wagon—1.75
⑤ Total capacity

Datsun 1200/B210

Lubrication and Oil Change

LUBRICATION CHECK

DATSUN SAYS: Change engine oil every 3,000 (6,000 on B210) miles; change oil filter every 6,000 miles. Recommended grade: S.E. Check oil level at least once a week.

TOOLS & MATERIALS . . . adjustable wrench; medium size screwdriver; oil filter removal wrench; drain pan for old oil (4 quart capacity); oil pouring spout; 3 qts. oil for engine (4 qts. with filter); new oil filter (if required); other lubricants as specified.

SAFETY TIP . . . use work gloves.

BRAKE FLUID LEVEL CHECK

Check brake and clutch fluid levels in the master cylinder every time the oil level is checked . . . sooner if braking feels inadequate or if clutch is not operating properly. Add fluid when low.

Recommended grade: DOT 3

Master cylinders are located under the hood on the left side. They are clear plastic containers. Fluid level will appear through the plastic.

1. Compare level with mark or ridge, or if unmarked, keep at least ¾ full. Snap off cap and add fluid, if necessary.

2. Replace cap securely. DO NOT OVERFILL.

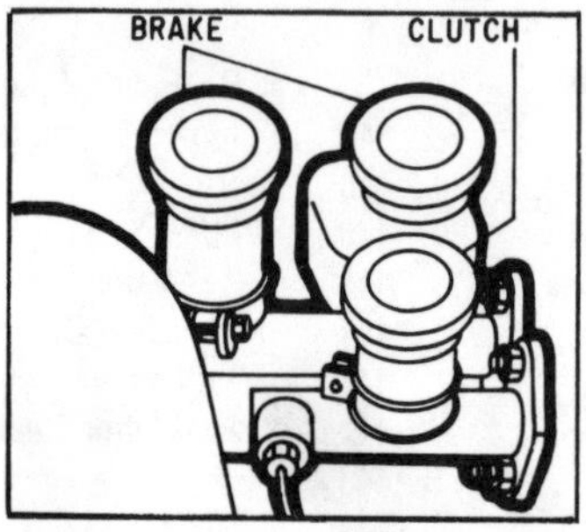

3. If fluid level was low, check again in a few days.

4. If fluid repeatedly checks low, there is a leak somewhere in the system.

Have mechanic check further. Neglect can be dangerous.

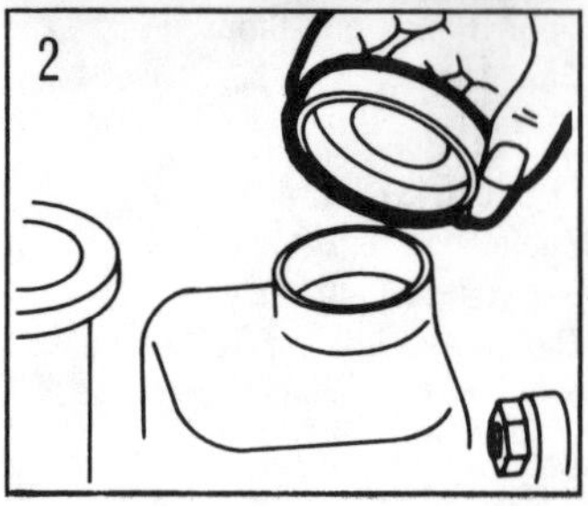

MANUAL TRANSMISSION FLUID LEVEL CHECK

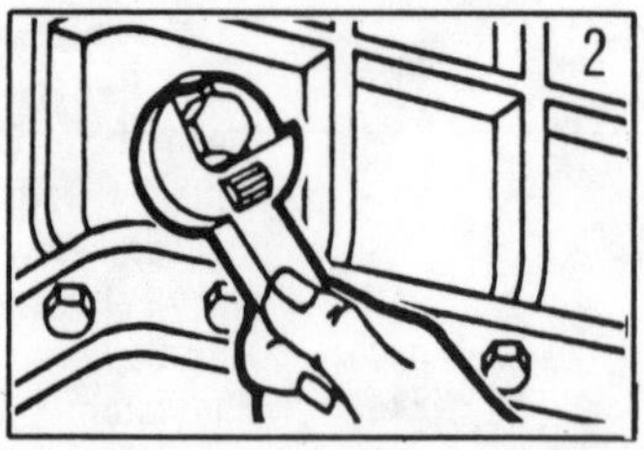

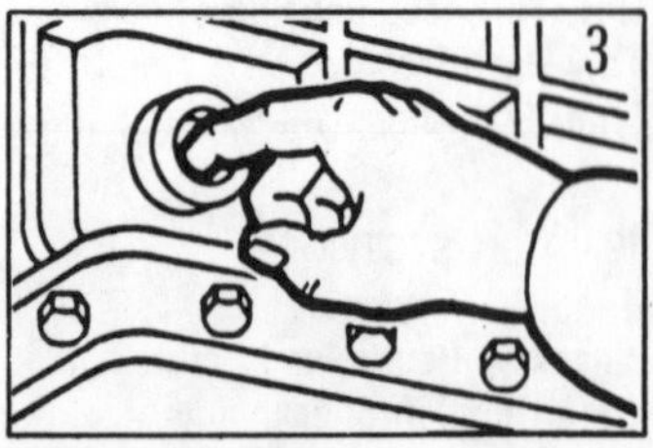

DATSUN SAYS . . . Check manual transmission fluid every 3 months (6 months on B210). Car should be parked level. Recommended grade: Standard Transmission Fluid (SAE 90).

TOOLS NEEDED: adjustable wrench; bulb syringe.

1. Locate transmission fluid plug on back of transmission, left side, from underneath car.

2. Wipe road dirt from filler plug area before loosening. Remove plug with adjustable wrench.

3. If fluid leaks out while removing drain plug, level is adequate and plug removal is unnecessary. If no leakage occurs, insert finger in hole; fluid level should be up to tip of finger.

4. Add fluid as needed with hand bulb syringe.

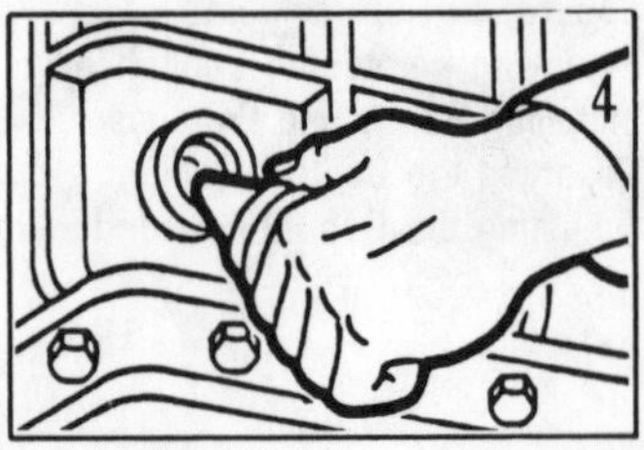

5. Replace filler plug; tighten.

AUTOMATIC TRANSMISSION FLUID LEVEL CHECK

DATSUN SAYS . . . check automatic transmission fluid (ATF) every three months or 3,000 miles (6 months/ 6,000 miles on B210).

TOOLS NEEDED . . . Long neck filler funnel.

1. Engine must be warmed up and running. Place shift lever in PARK position.
2. Pull out dipstick. Wipe clean. Push dipstick all the way back in; remove it again.
3. If fluid is below "H" mark, add ATF to bring level up. DO NOT OVERFILL.
4. Add ATF thru transmission dipstick hole by means of long-neck filler funnel.

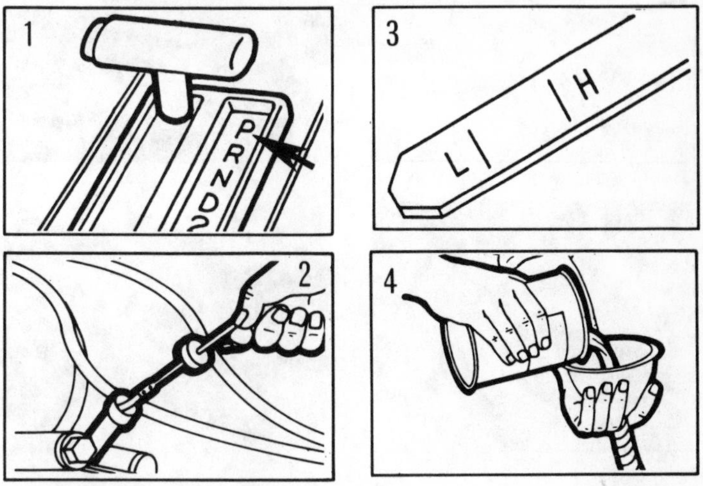

REAR AXLE LUBRICANT

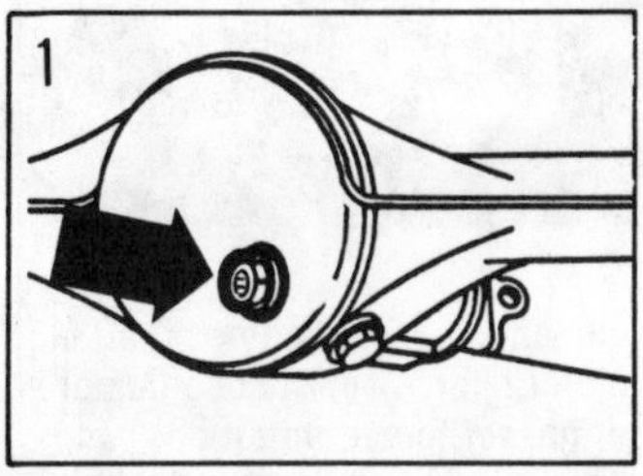

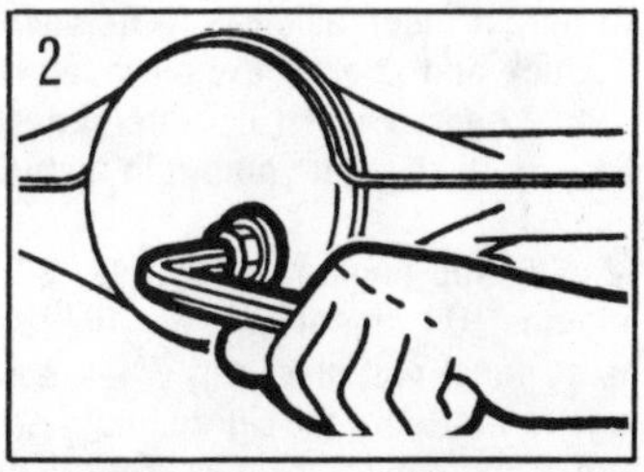

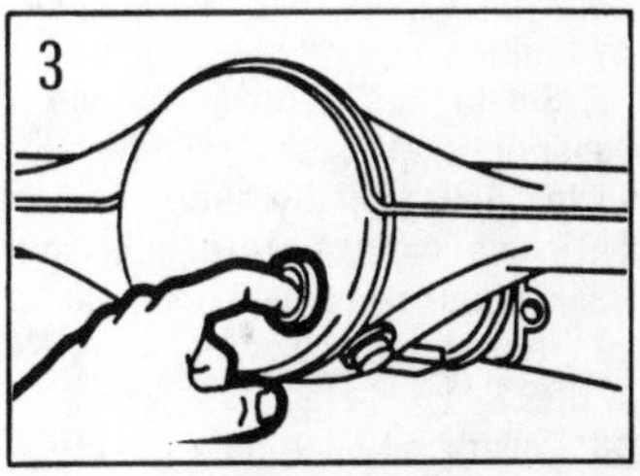

DATSUN SAYS . . . check rear axle lube level every 3,000 miles (6,000 miles on B210). Recommended gear lube (SAE 90).

TOOLS . . . drain plug wrench; bulb syringe.

1. Locate filler plug on rear of rear axle housing.
2. Wipe plug area clean; remove plug with drain plug wrench.
3. If fluid leaks out while removing drain plug, level is adequate and plug removal is unnecessary. If no leakage occurs, insert finger in hole; fluid level should be up to tip of finger.
4. If fluid level is low, add as needed, with a hand bulb syringe until level reaches the edge of filler plug hole.
5. Replace filler plug; tighten.

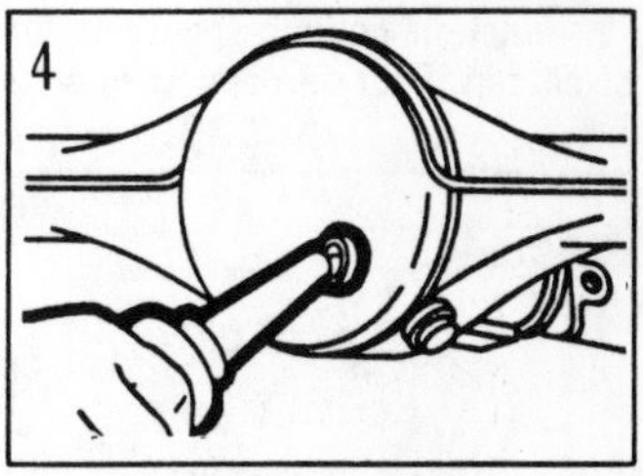

OIL AND FILTER CHANGE

1. If engine is cold, start up and idle for about 5 minutes.
2. Park car on level ground. Turn engine off.
3. Locate oil drain plug on underside of engine. Place drain pan under plug.
4. Remove drain plug with wrench. Let ALL dirty oil drain out.

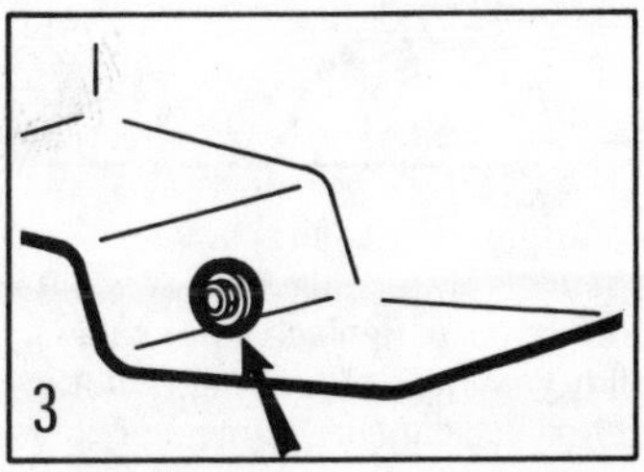

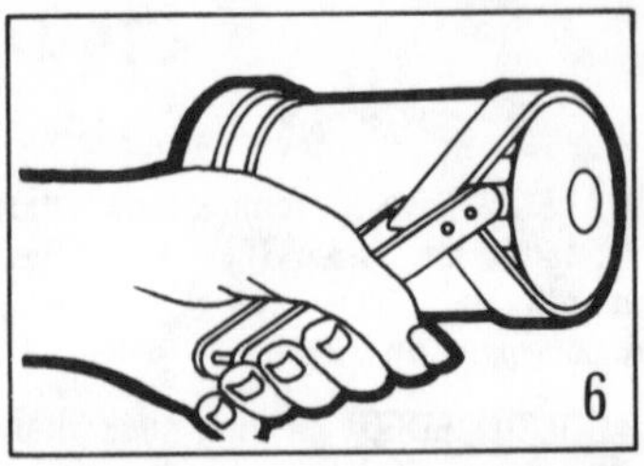

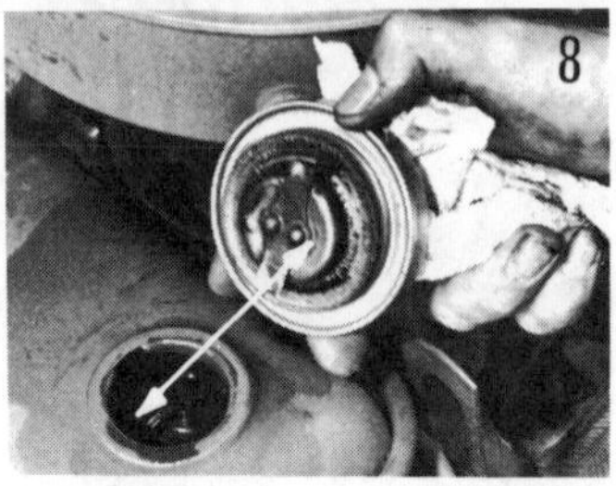

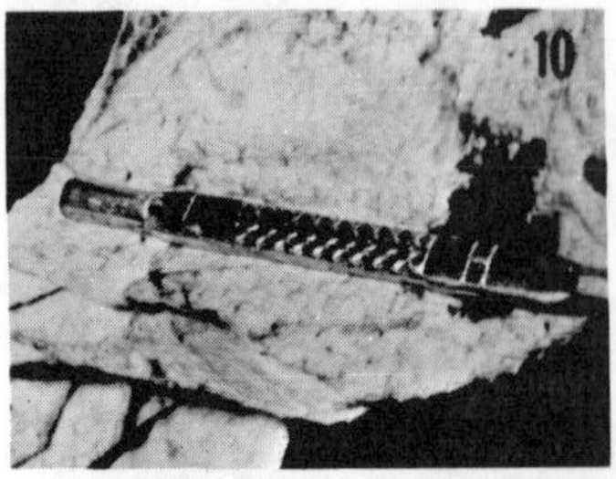

5. Wipe plug and area around drain hole clean. Replace drain plug; tighten it.

6. Locate oil filter. Move drain pan under filter. Loosen filter with oil filter wrench. Unscrew; remove filter by hand.

7. Smear fresh oil over surface of rubber gasket (washer) of new filter. Install new filter by hand only. Do NOT use wrench. Turn filter until gasket makes contact. Tighten an additional half turn only . . . NO MORE.

8. Locate oil filler hole on top of engine. Remove cap.

9. Punch oil pouring spout into top of oil can. Pour all cans of new oil into filler tube. Wipe filler cap clean and replace it.

10. Check new oil level at dipstick. Pull out dipstick, wipe clean.

11. Push dipstick back into engine. Be sure to insert all the way. Remove dipstick and check new oil level. It should be above "HIGH" line. If not, be sure to check if you put in all the oil called for.

12. Start up engine and idle for 3-5 minutes. Oil signal light on instrument panel will glow red when engine is first started. Light should go out in 30 seconds or less.

13. Stop engine and check for oil leaks at drain plug and filter. If you

find any, check tightness of plug and/or filter, also for condition of filter gasket to see that it has not become pinched or damaged when installing. Recheck oil level, which should now be at "HIGH."

SPEEDOMETER CABLE LUBRICATION

If speedometer pointer tends to quiver or jump, or if unit makes a low, rasping sound, lubrication may be needed.

1. Locate cable shaft attachment directly behind speedometer dial.

2. Unscrew cable from speedometer.

3. Pull inner cable completely out of outer casing. Note carefully which end is top. Check for wear or frayed strands. If damaged, replace inner cable with new one.

4. Apply generous amount of speedometer cable lubricant into cable casing. Replace inner cable in shaft, noting that top end is not inserted accidentally. Turn inner cable

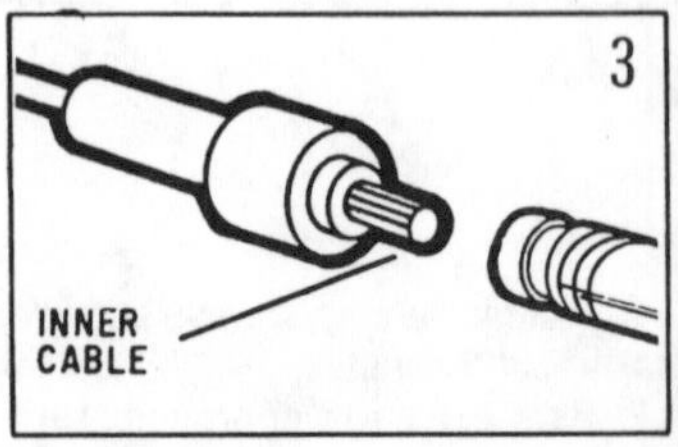

as it is being re-inserted. Twist cable when all the way in, to lock into position at lower end.

5. Reconnect cable to speedometer head under instrument panel.

DOOR HINGES AND STOPS

(lubricate every 6 months)

1. Brush any dirt accumulations from door hinges and stops. Use old tooth brush or rag.

2. Apply dab of white polyethylene grease to door hinges, trunk hinges, hood hinges, door stops.

DOOR LOCKS

(lubricate every 6 months)

1. Insert door key half way into lock.

2. Spray aerosol lock lubricant into lock.

3. Push key rest of way into lock; turn back and forth several times.

Cooling System

IT IS RECOMMENDED . . . that radiator coolant (water/antifreeze mixture) level be checked once or twice a month. Do this when engine is cold. Check more often if you do a lot of hard driving. On models with clear expansion tanks, check coolant level visually when hot.
Keep coolant up to recommended level in radiator. If coolant checks frequently low, look for leaks.

Tighten all hose clamps occasionally. For best results, keep a 50/50 water/antifreeze mixture year round. Change complete coolant mixture every 24 months.

CAUTION: If you must check coolant in a hot engine, cover radiator cap with thick rag before releasing. Remove cap slowly . . . press down and turn.

REPLACING THE THERMOSTAT

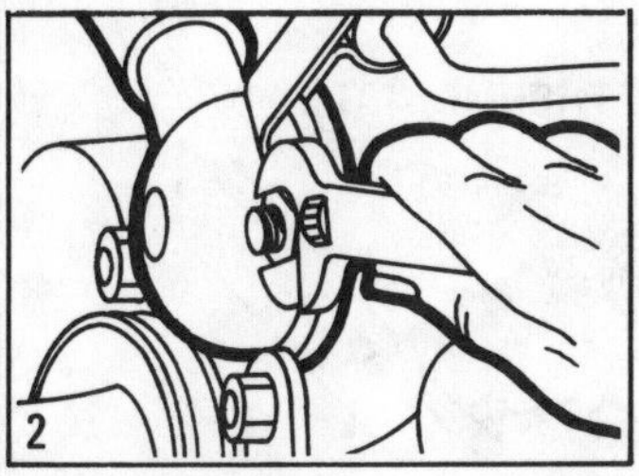

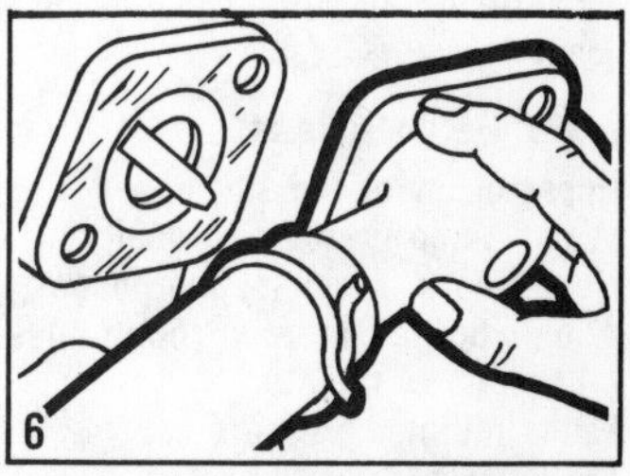

A faulty thermostat will usually cause engine overheating. Replace with new thermostat.

TOOLS AND MATERIALS . . .

New thermostat
Gasket
Adjustable wrench

1. Drain radiator of about half its coolant. (See How To Replace Hoses).
2. Loosen and remove both retaining bolts and lift thermostat housing off the engine.
NOTE: If you're careful it won't be necessary to remove radiator hose.
3. Remove old thermostat.
4. Scrape thermostat housing flange and engine block surface to remove old gasket debris.
5. Drop new thermostat into place—spring down.
6. Install new gasket with sealer applied to both sides.
7. Replace thermostat housing and tighten both retaining bolts.

FAN BELT ADJUSTMENT

The fan belt not only drives the radiator fan, it turns the water pump and drives the alternator. It's easy to see that the condition and proper tension of the belt are vital, since almost all engine cooling and electrical power is dependent on it. The belt deserves an occasional look and tension check.

CAUTION: An overtightened belt may damage alternator and water pump bearings.

1. Inspect fan belt occasionally. If worn, frayed or cracked on inner driving surface, replace.
2. Check tension occasionally. Press thumb at midpoint of belt span between pulleys. If belt depresses more than ½ inch, tightening is needed. A too-loose belt will not drive alternator and water pump effectively.

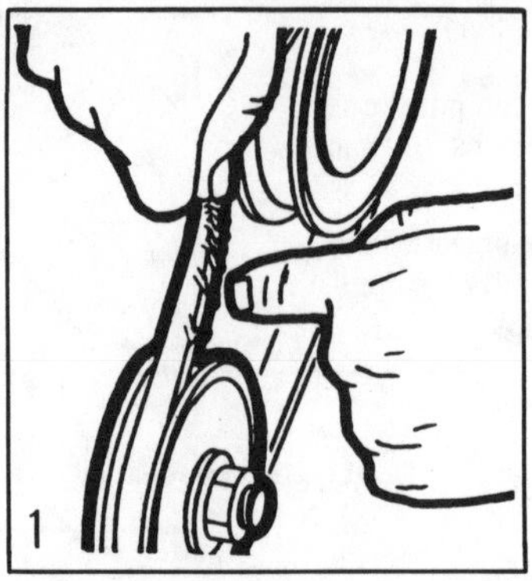

3. Adjust to proper tension of ¼-½ inch deflection. To adjust, loosen alternator adjustment and attaching bolts. Pull on alternator until proper deflection is attained and tighten bolts.

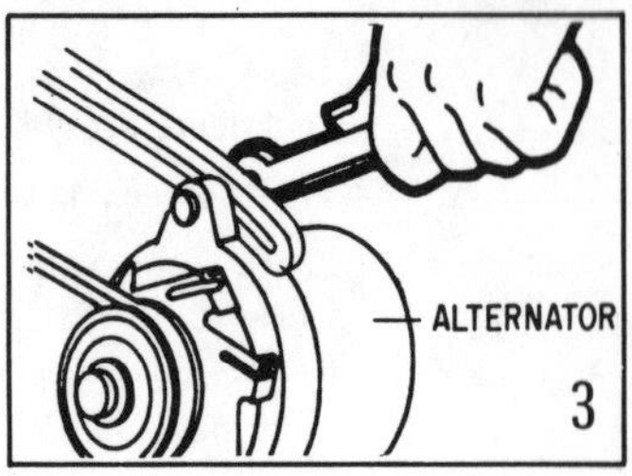

FIND THOSE COOLING SYSTEM LEAKS

1. Inspect all hoses. If any are weak, soft in spots or show cracks, replace at once.

2. Check all hose connections for tightness. Tighten loose hose clamps; they tend to loosen due to engine vibration.

3. If radiator steams or hisses when engine is switched off, check for leaks. Look for signs of coolant drips on radiator or around heater tank joint.

Leaks are possible at:

Upper or lower radiator hoses
Water pump (gaskets or seal)
Heater core or connecting hoses
Automatic transmission cooler lines (at bottom of radiator)
Faulty radiator pressure cap
Faulty cylinder head gasket
Cracked cylinder head or block

Due to the number of joints, cooling systems have many places to leak from. Check clamp tightness. If leaks persist an anti-leak additive in the coolant may help. Noisy water pumps may benefit from a lubricating additive in the coolant. Use a cooling system cleaner when flushing during a drain and refill job. It will help remove rust and scale. Remember – additives will not cure chronic problems. But they will effect a short-term remedy in many cases.

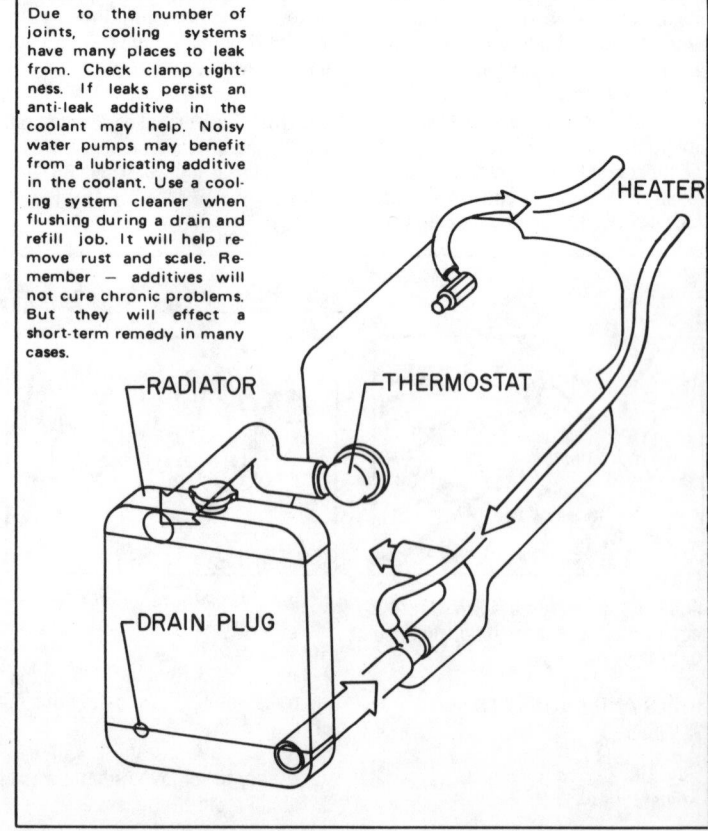

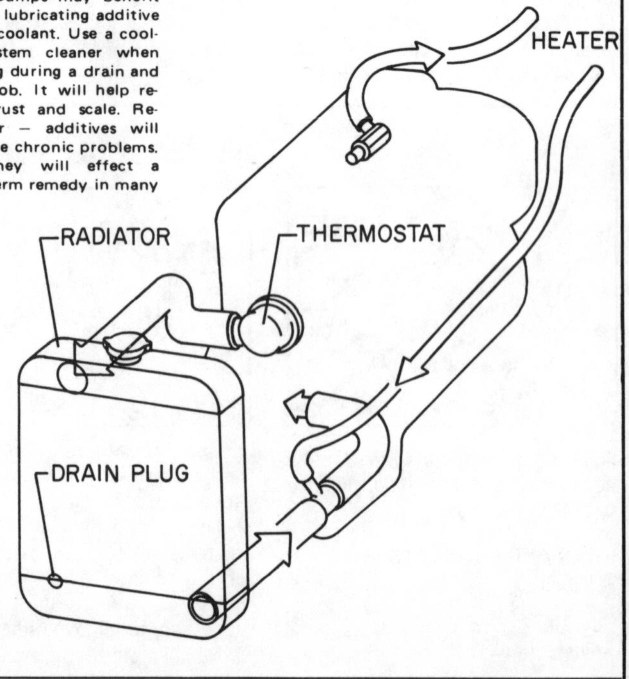

RADIATOR CAP CHECK

Check radiator cap occasionally for worn or cracked gasket. If cap doesn't seal properly, fluid will be lost and engine will overheat. Replace worn cap with new cap rated 13 lbs. pressure.

HOSE REPLACEMENT

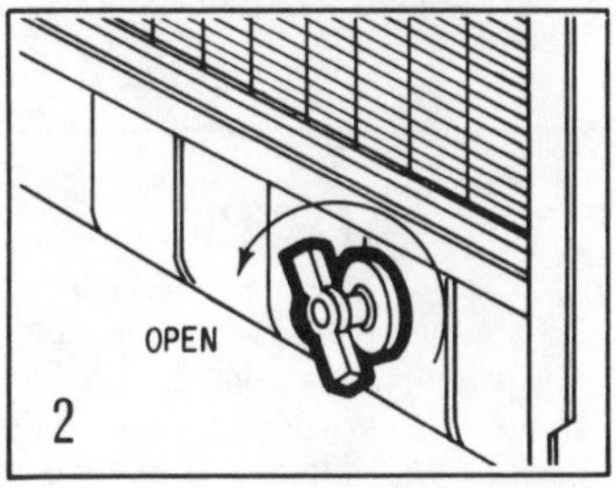

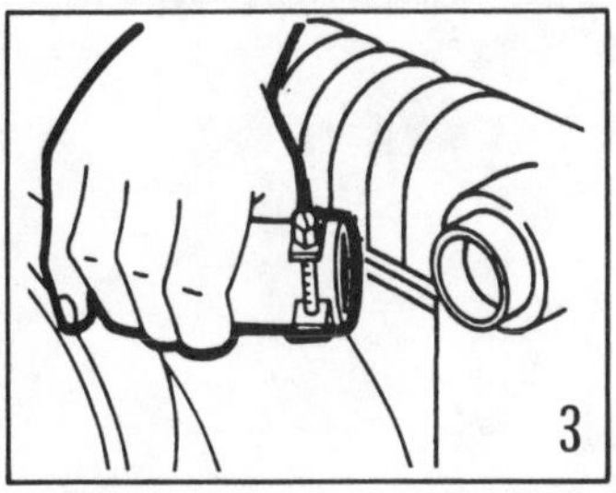

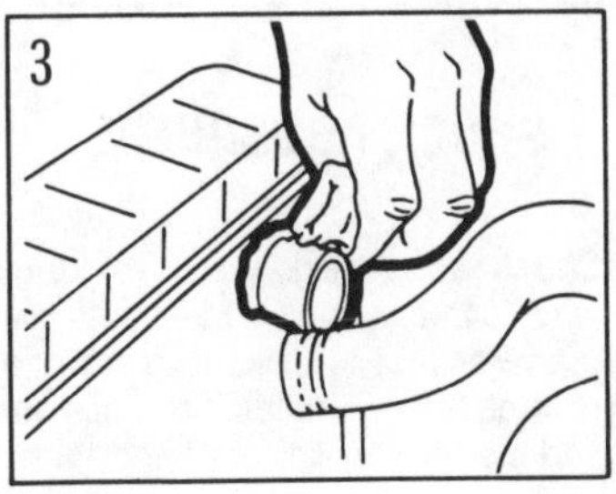

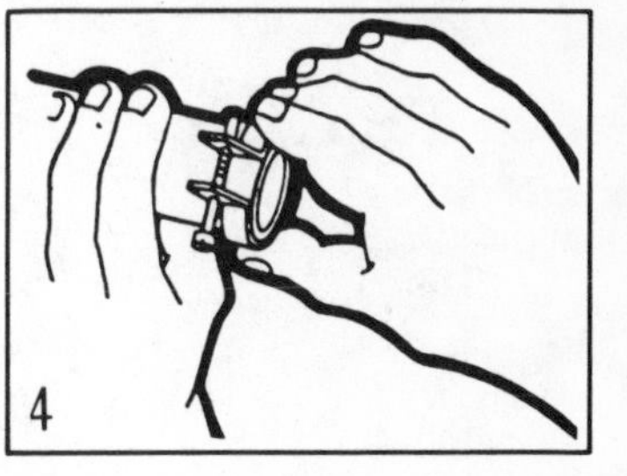

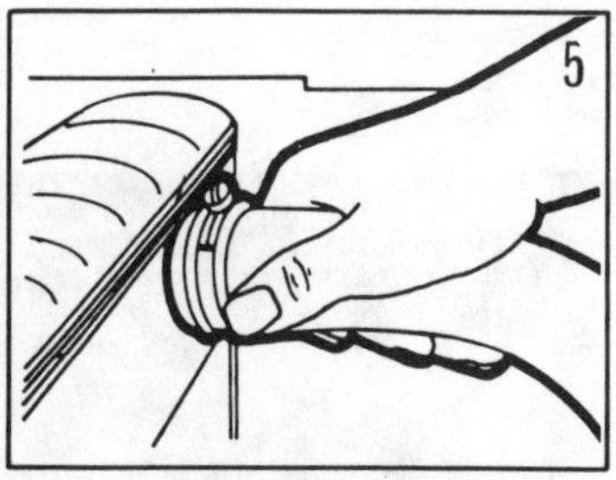

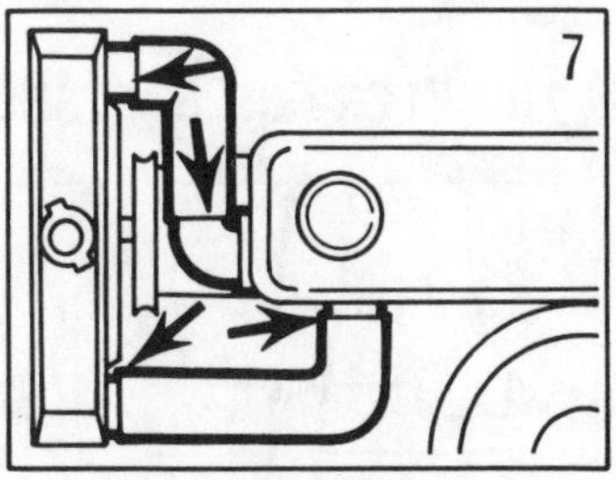

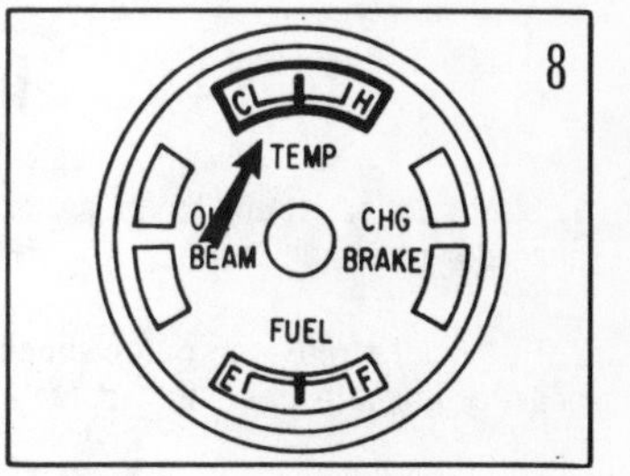

Coolant drain and refill work may be done alone; when changing hoses, coolant must also be drained as part of job. Discard all hoses with cracks or soft spots. Check hose clamps for tightness and good condition.

1. Remove radiator cap. Open radiator petcock (See 2). Drain coolant into catch basin. If near 24 months old, discard old coolant.

2. Petcock is located on the bottom of the radiator on the Datsun.

3. Remove hose clamp and remove hose. Wipe all hose connections clean. Use emery cloth to get rid of residue.

4. If old hose clamps are badly rusted or damaged, replace with new units.

5. Slip clamps over each hose end. Slip hose ends all the way onto cleaned up hose connections.

6. Place hose clamp ¼ inch from hose end. Tighten. Close petcock. Refill with 50/50 coolant/water mix.

7. Start engine; allow to warm up. Check for coolant leaks.

8. Road test car; watch temperature warning gauge to avoid overheating.

Suspension and Tires

SUSPENSION SYSTEM

The front suspension is a Mac Pherson strut type. The shock absorber and spindle are combined to a single unit which is supported by the coil spring at the upper end, and by the transverse link at the lower end. The rear suspension consists of semielliptic leaf springs, hydraulic shock absorbers, and rubber bumpers.

Your car's suspension system consists of wheels, tires, springs, shock absorbers, sway (or stabilizer) bars, ball joints, steering linkage. If any of these items is out of adjustment or badly worn, you may notice any of these symptoms:

- car pulls to one side when braking
- car wanders when driving a straight line
- overall ride may be either hard or bouncy
- effort is needed to steer vehicle
- tires show uneven wear
- tires squeal when cornering
- front of car dips or bounces when braking
- car rocks side-to-side when going over rough road
- wheels bounce to make slapping sound on road
- steering wheel vibrates in hands
- front of car vibrates at highway speeds

Any of above symptoms indicates corrective action is needed. Delay can: ruin tires; cause damage/failure to other suspension parts; create safety hazard.

STEERING

If steering linkage, front suspension and steering column components are in good condition, there should be not more than 1½ inch free play in the steering wheel when measured at the rim of the wheel. If a loud knock is heard when turning the steering wheel from one extreme to the other, have mechanic check pinion bearing preload.

SHOCK ABSORBERS

Shock absorbers work to keep wheels in constant contact with the road. Result is safe handling and ride control; longer tire life. So shock absorbers (or shocks) are important.

HOW TO CHECK FOR BAD SHOCKS

1. Check under car and locate shock absorber near each wheel.

2. Heavy oil streaks on outer shock housing indicate need for replacement.

3. Stand at front of car and apply body weight in pumping action to front bumper or fender. Release pressure and allow car to stop rocking. Car should not bounce more than one more time after releasing pressure. Repeat at rear. If bouncing continues more than once, replacement is needed. Replace shocks in pairs (front pair or rear pair).

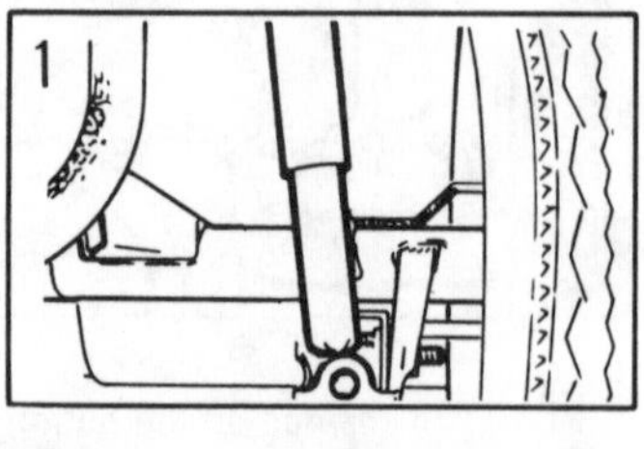

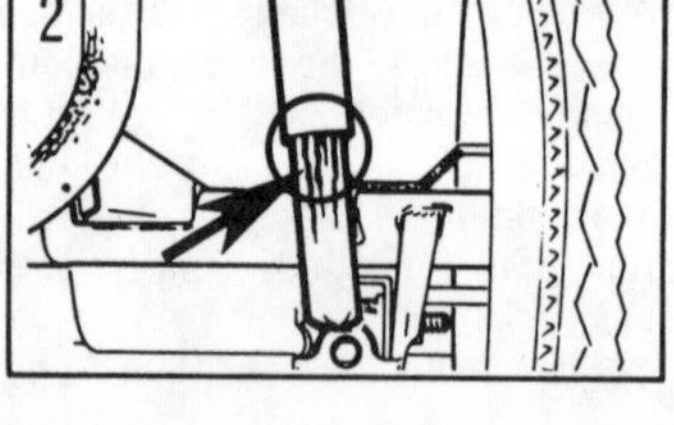

TOW HITCH INFORMATION

If your car is used for trailer towing you should check:
A. Cooling System; be sure coolant is at proper level in radiator. See Cooling System Section for checks to perform.
B. Check Transmission Fluid; keep topped up to proper level.
C. Check Rear Shock Absorbers; you may benefit from installation of new rear shocks.
D. Check Tire Pressures; best traction and handling can be ensured if tire pressures are properly maintained.
For safer and more trouble-free trailer towing, consider:
A. Automatic Transmission Cooler; helps remove excess heat from automatic transmission fluid built up during towing mileage. Also helps avoid radiator overheating. Some units can be self-installed.
B. Radiator Over-Flow Tank Kit; addition of a reservoir to catch radiator coolant overflow preventing coolant loss. Easy to install, these units help a tow car run cooler, avoid overheating due to coolant loss.
C. Heavy-Duty Shock Absorbers or Air Shocks; important to have on rear wheels if you intend to do a lot of towing or load carrying within the car itself. Don't forget to consider replacing factory shocks, when they are worn out, with heavy-duty units at the front as well.
D. Variable Load Flasher; this unit will accommodate the added load of trailer turn signal lamps on trailer when these are hooked into your car's electrical system.

FRONT END ALIGNMENT

When steering, handling and/or tire wear indicate front end alignment may be needed, this work can only be done at an automotive service shop. DO NOT PUT OFF NEEDED FRONT END ALIGNMENT. At the same time, have ball joints and steering linkage checked.

Ignition System

TUNE-UP SERVICES

The ignition system consists of spark plugs; plug wires; distributor; rotor; points; condenser; coil. These units work to create a good hot spark inside the engine (ignition) at exactly the right moment (timing). If ignition is weak or timing is off, engine may be hard to start, run poorly, waste gas, lose power, backfire or not run at all.
1975-76 B210s sold in California are equipped with electronic ignition which replaces the points with a pick-up coil. This pick-up coil does not require replacement, however the gap should be checked and adjusted if necessary when you suspect a problem in the ignition system.
DATSUN SAYS . . . Replace points, plugs and condenser every 12 months or 12,000 miles (12 months or 20,000 miles on B210).
TOOLS & MATERIALS . . . Parts: set of points; condenser; 4 spark plugs. Tools: gap gauge; 13/16 in. spark plug socket; screwdriver; open end, box or combination metric wrenches; timing equipment.
SAFETY TIP . . . Change only one spark plug at a time to avoid crosswiring and possible engine damage.

CHECKING POINTS AND ROTOR

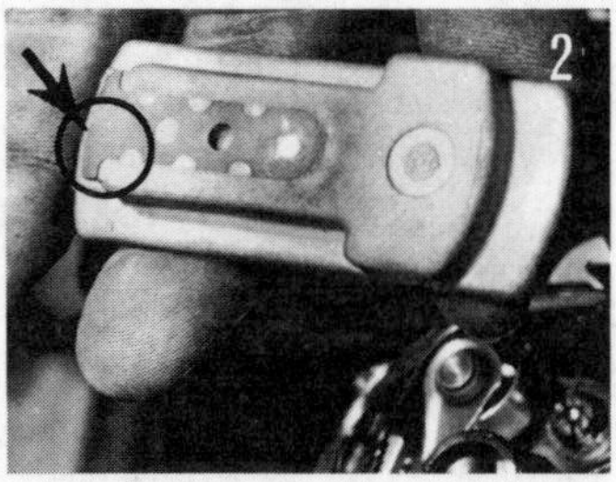

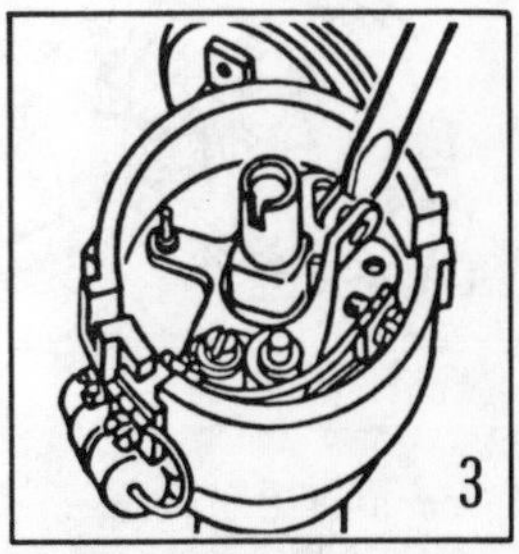

The distributor holds the points and rotor. The condenser is mounted on the outside of the distributor. The cap forms the top of the distributor.
1. To open distributor, snap retaining clips off with screwdriver, lift cap off but keep wires connected.
2. Pull rotor off (straight up). Replace if badly burned.
3. Pry points apart with screwdriver. If worn or burned, replace. If OK, check point gap.

OTHER IGNITION CHECK POINTS

Inspect spark plug wires. If cracked or brittle, entire set should be replaced. Also center, high tension wire. Inspect distributor cap. Wipe inside clean occasionally with dry, lint-free rag. If cap is cracked or rotor contacts are excessively burned, replace cap.

SPARK PLUG REPLACEMENT

1. Remove spark plug wire by grasping rubber boot. Do not jerk wire If stuck, turn boot, pulling gently.
2. Loosen spark plug using socket wrench.
3. Wipe or brush loose dirt from around plug before removing. Do not let dirt drop into engine through plug hole. Unscrew plug.
4. Check plug electrode gap on new spark plug. Adjust to specifications. Plug gap is correct when the gauge drags slightly as it is pulled between plug electrodes.
5. Thread new plug into plug hole by hand. Hand tighten. Do not force or cross thread. Use socket wrench to tighten firmly but do not force. Replace plug wire. Press boot firmly.

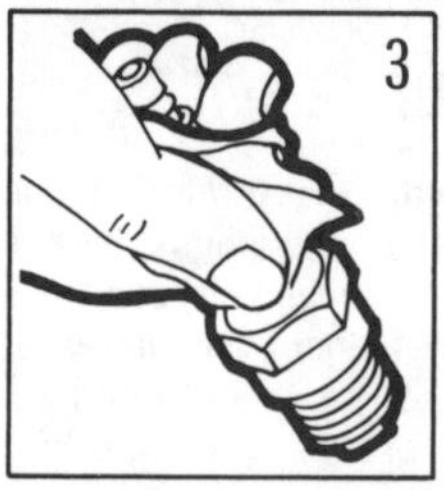

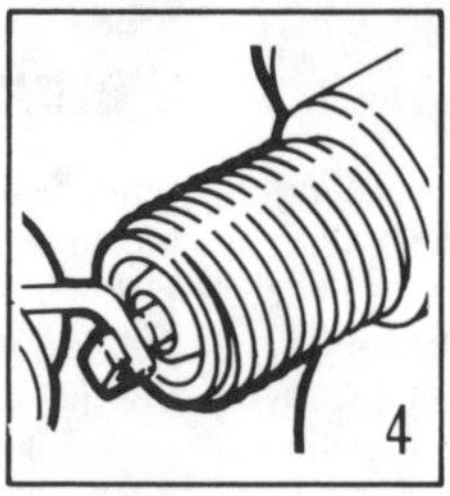

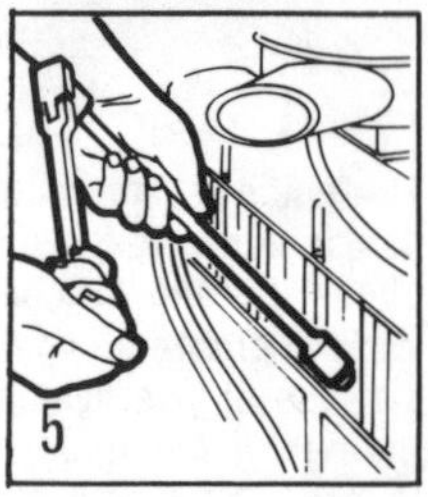

REMOVING POINTS AND CONDENSER

1. Disconnect the wire terminal connected to the points set.

2. Remove points attaching screws being very careful not to drop screws inside distributor.

3. Remove screw holding condenser to side of distributor and condenser wire terminal screw. DO NOT DROP SCREW.

4. Wipe all dirt from distributor plate and cam.

CAUTION: When removing screws from distributor, be sure to avoid any screws accidentally falling through distributor opening into engine. Use magnetic screwdriver.

INSTALLING POINTS AND CONDENSER

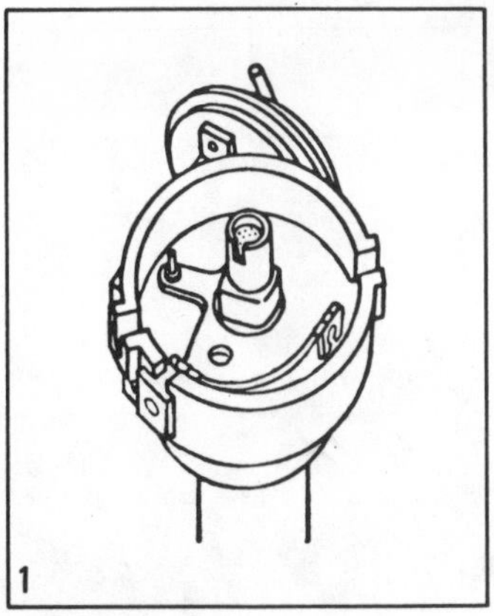

1. Lubricate cam head assembly with grease.

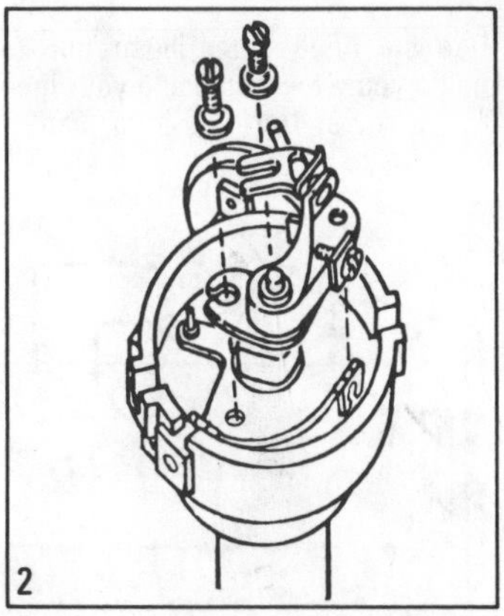

2. Position new points set in distributor. Attach retaining screws lightly. Replace wire terminal.

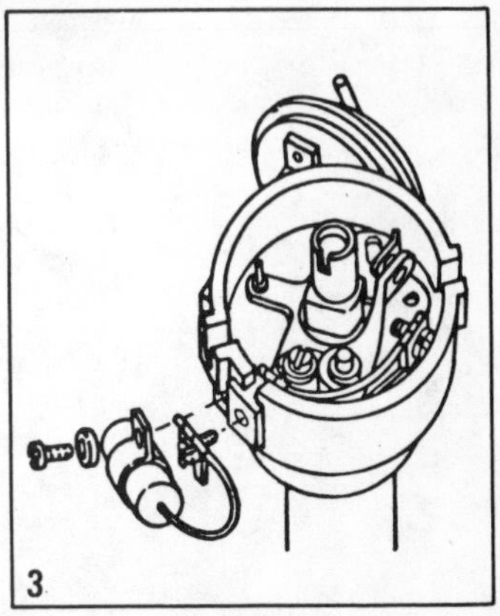

3. Attach new condenser to side of distributor with screw. Attach wire terminal and tighten screw.

RESETTING THE CONTACT GAP

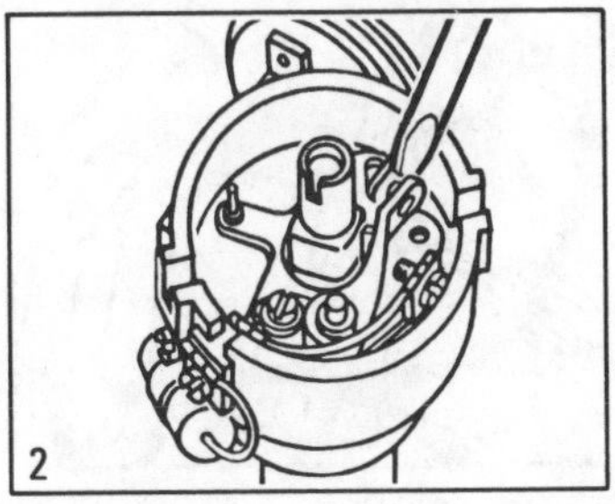

1. Turn engine by ignition key (you'll need a helper) until rubbing block or point set is on one of the four high spots of distributor cam. You may use a wrench on lower engine pulley to do this.
2. Insert screwdriver in adjusting screw near point contacts; turn to open or close gap.

3. Correct gap is shown in the specifications chart.

4. Insert correct size feeler gauge; adjust gap with screwdriver until feeler gauge can be moved between contacts with only slight drag.

5. Tighten point set holddown screw. Recheck gap; it might have changed from tightening the holddown screws. Readjust if needed.

6. Align rotor with distributor shaft and push rotor onto shaft. Rotor must be fully seated on shaft.

7. Replace distributor cap; install clips.

ADJUSTING THE GAP (Electronic Ignition)

1. Remove the distributor cap and rotor.
2. Insert a feeler gauge between the pick-up coil and the reluctor. The proper gap should be between .008-.016 in. Do not use a steel feeler gauge to check the gap. Use either a plastic or brass feeler gauge.
3. If the gap is not correct, adjust it by loosening the pick-up coil screws.

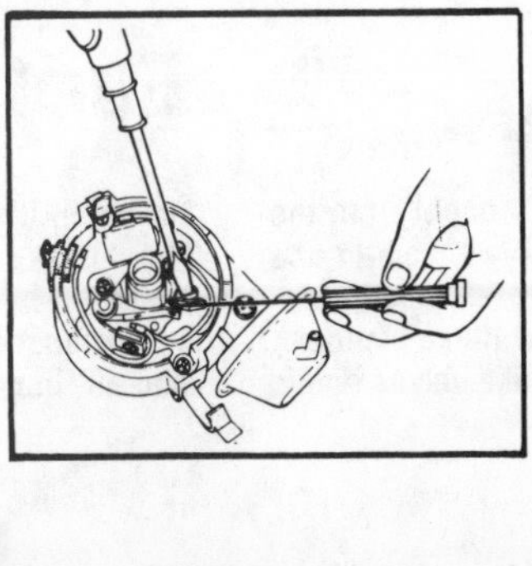

REPLACING SPARK PLUG WIRES

Use the firing order illustration to guide you when replacing your ignition wires and/or distributor cap.

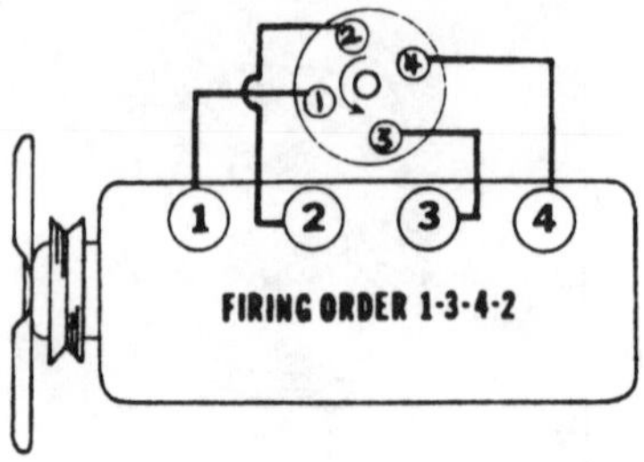

1200 and B210

IGNITION TIMING

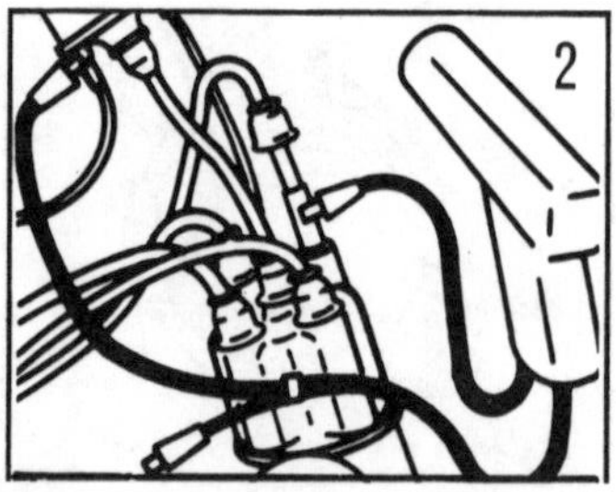

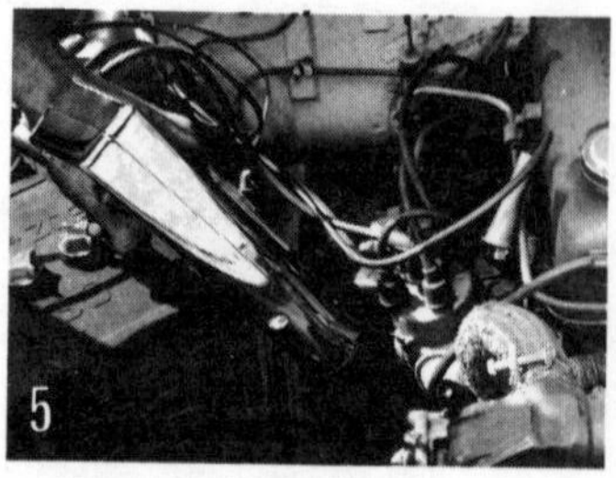

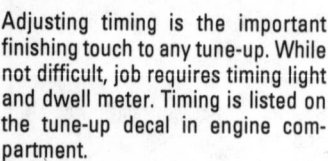

Adjusting timing is the important finishing touch to any tune-up. While not difficult, job requires timing light and dwell meter. Timing is listed on the tune-up decal in engine compartment.

1. Locate pointer notch on engine and timing marks on lower engine pulley. Clean away dirt. Mark the pointer notch with chalk.
2. Hook up the timing light according to instructions supplied with it.
3. Disconnect and plug the vacuum line from the distributor.
4. Hook up tachometer and adjust engine idle speed to 800 RPM. Idle adjustment screw is located where gas pedal linkage attaches to carburetor.
5. Aim timing light at pulley marks. If the chalked marks do not align, loosen distributor holddown clamp and slowly rotate distributor until chalked marks align.
6. Tighten holddown clamp and recheck timing.

Fuel System

When gasoline is brought from the fuel tank, it mixes with air in the carburetor. This gas/air mixture enters engine thru the intake manifold, passes thru the intake valves and is burned in the combustion chamber. The burned exhaust gas is then passed thru the exhaust valves to the exhaust system and to the outside air. In order to keep your car's engine running cleanly with minimal pollution, and avoid dangerous carbon monoxide fumes inside the vehicle, certain items should be checked from time to time.

KEEP THE AIR INTAKE CLEAN

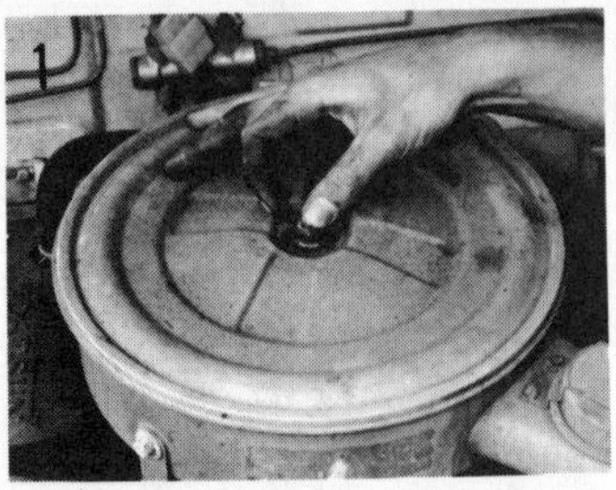

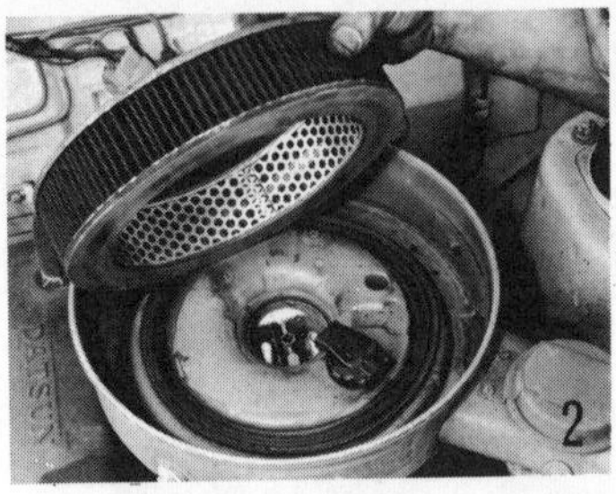

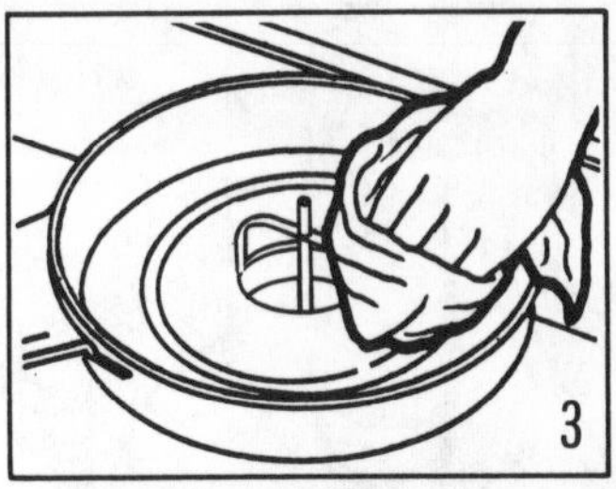

The large round can that sits on top of the engine contains the air filter. The air filter is a paper type which does not require servicing until replacement, which is every 24,000 miles.

1. Unscrew the wing nut at the top of the air cleaner.

2. Remove the top cover. Lift out circular air cleaner cartridge.

3. Wipe inside of can and lid clean with lint-free cloth.

4. Insert new air cleaner cartridge, replace lid and secure wing nut.

EMISSION CONTROL SYSTEMS

An important part of a car's emission control system is the Positive Crankcase Ventilation (PCV) valve and its connecting hose. The PCV valve should be replaced once every 24,000 miles. This device keeps dirt and sludge from forming inside the engine. Make sure all PCV connections are tight. Check that the connecting hoses are clear and not clogged. Replace any brittle or broken hoses.

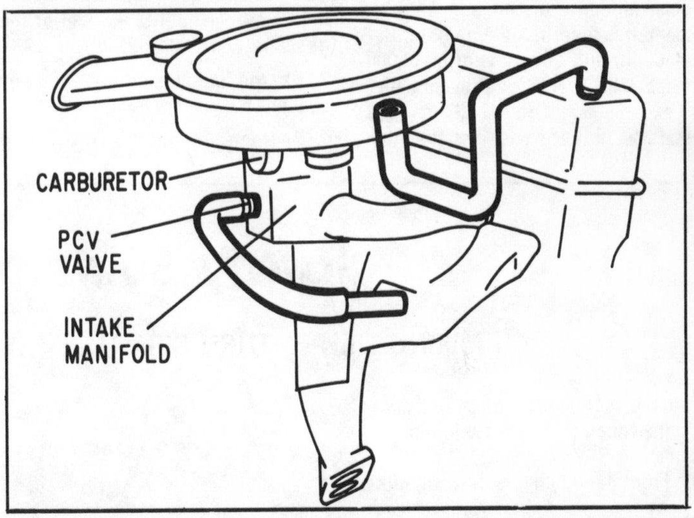

PCV VALVE REPLACEMENT

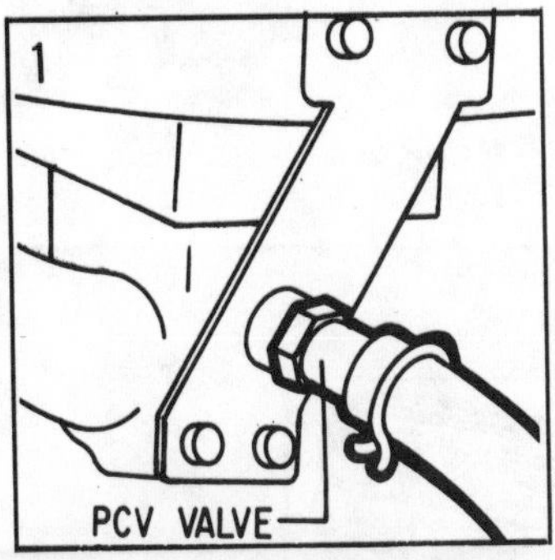

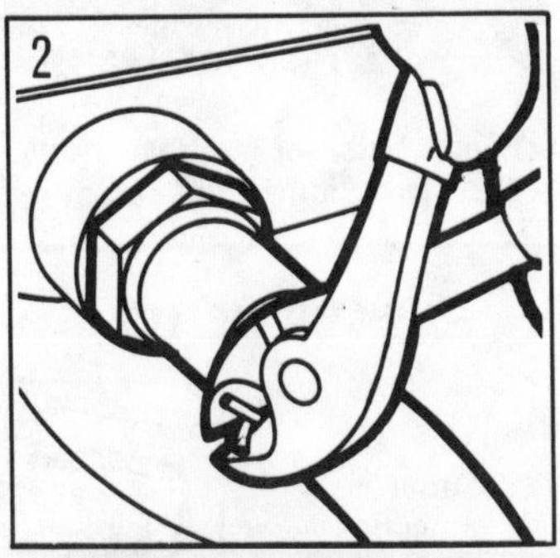

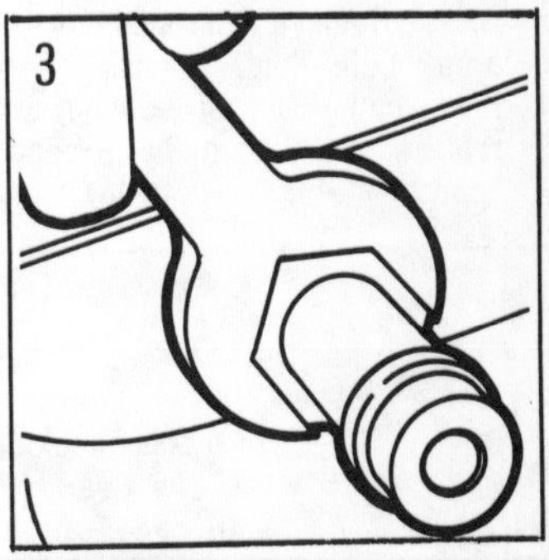

1. PCV valve is located in the manifold below the carburetor.
2. Squeeze hose clamp with pliers. Remove hose.
3. Unscrew PCV valve and remove from its location in manifold.
4. Note where other end of hose connects. Remove hose and flush with cleaning solvent.
5. Replace PCV in manifold and reconnect hose and clamps.

FUEL FILTER REPLACEMENT

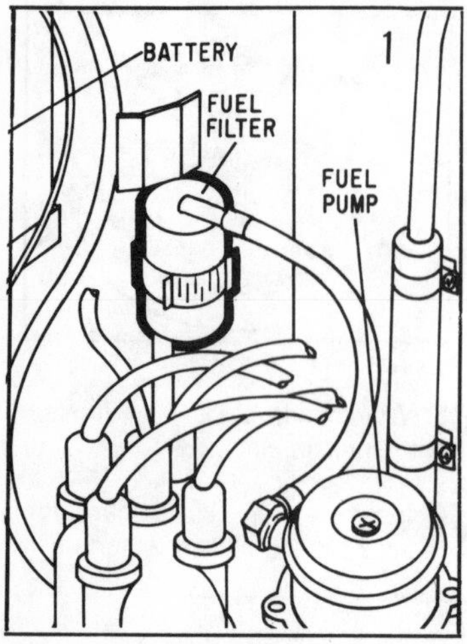

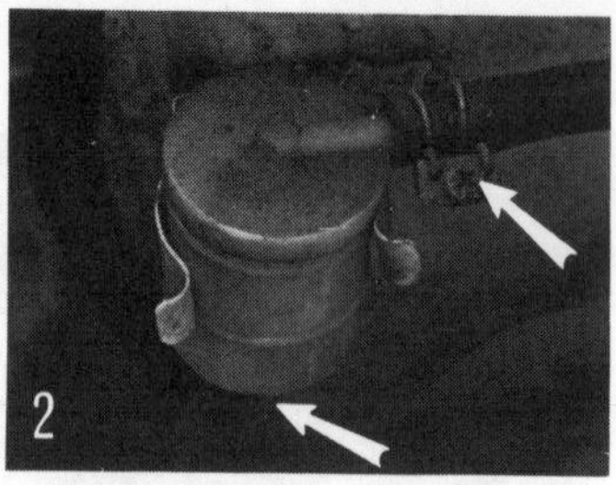

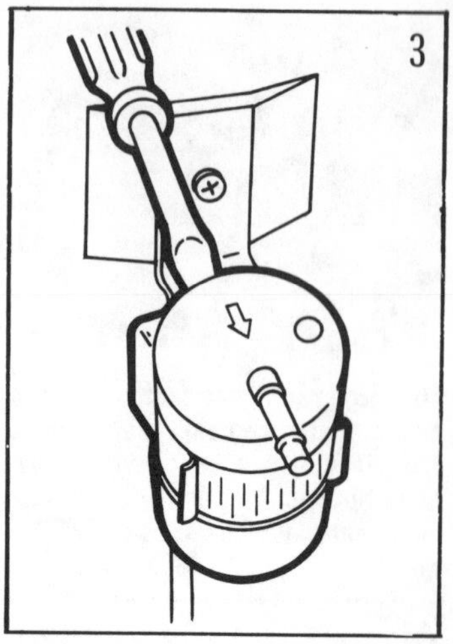

The fuel filter is located in the right inner fender in the engine compartment. It is a cartridge type filter. Replace the filter every year or 12,000 miles. The fuel filter prevents dirt, rust, and scale from both the gas station's tank and your own fuel tank from reaching the carburetor. A dirty filter will starve the engine and cause poor running.

1. Locate fuel filter on right side fender wall.
2. Disconnect the inlet and outlet hoses from fuel filter. Make certain that the inlet hose (bottom) doesn't fall below the fuel tank level or the gasoline will drain out.
3. Pry the fuel filter from its clip and replace the assembly.
4. Replace the intake and outlet lines; secure hose clamps tightly to avoid leaks.
5. Start the engine and check for leaks. Addition of a can of carburetor cleaner to the fuel tank occasionally will aid in keeping the entire fuel system clean.

Safety Systems

PARKING LIGHTS, TURN SIGNALS AND STOP LIGHTS

Parking lights, turn signals, and stop lights function with dual-element bulbs.

A. Front parking lights, turn signals, side marker lights: remove lens to expose bulb(s). Push in on bulb while turning counterclockwise to release the bulb from the socket. Remove and replace with a new bulb. Replace lens.
B. Rear Light Comb. on sedans, to replace rear light bulbs (except license plate), raise trunk lid.

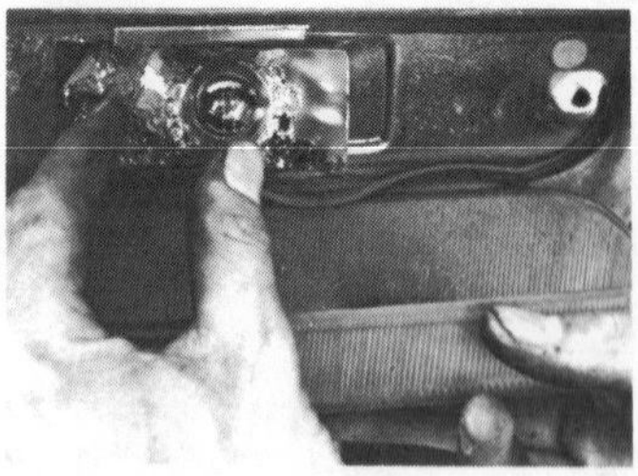

Reach bulb socket from inside car. Turn bulb socket counterclockwise to remove from socket.

BACK-UP LIGHTS

To replace back-up light bulbs, raise trunk lid. Reach bulb socket from inside car. Turn bulb socket counterclockwise and pull out. Push down on bulb turning counterclockwise to remove from socket.

WINDSHIELD WIPER BLADE REPLACEMENT

To replace wiper blade, lift up on spring release tab on wiper arm connector. Pull wiper blade off. Snap new blade into place.

To replace rubber insert only, press down, away from wiper blade to free it. Slide insert from blade. Insert new wiper. Bend insert upward slightly to engage retaining clips.

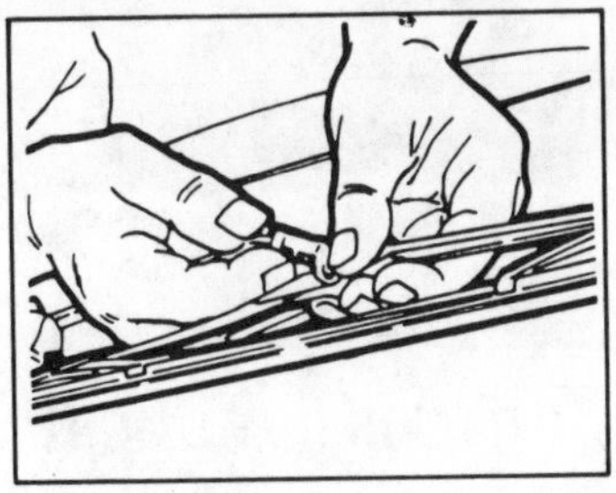

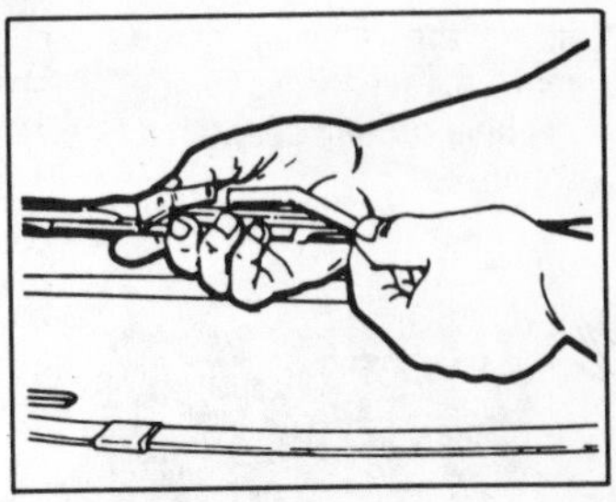

HORN PROBLEMS

If horn sounds and does not stop, this is due to short circuit in wiring. Disconnect wiring connector under hood and have professional service shop check horn wiring circuit.

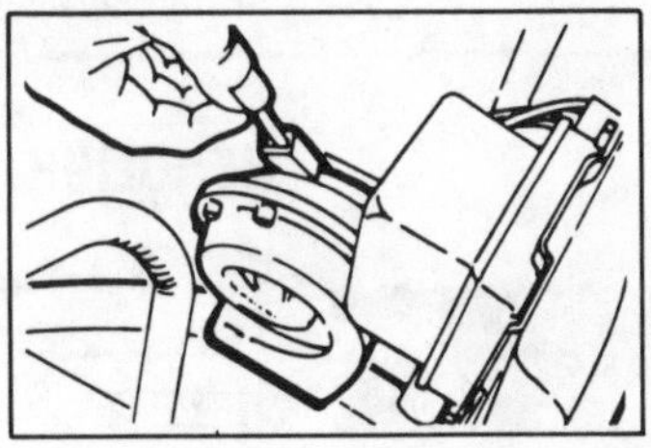

STEERING PROBLEMS

See steering system check in Suspension Section. Check tire pressures. Have a professional service shop check all components in the front end and steering system.

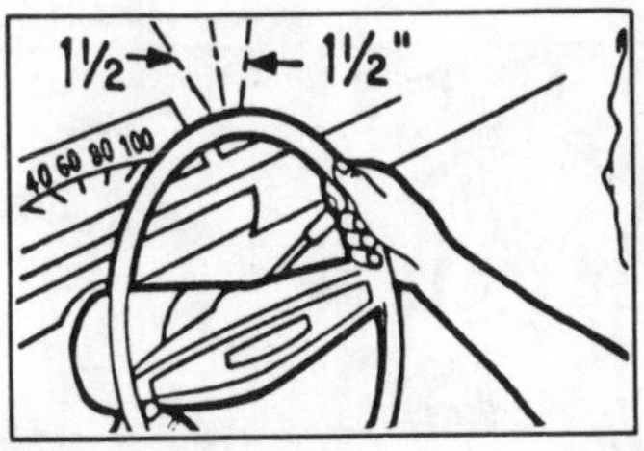

WASHER SYSTEM

If washer fails to squirt properly, raise hood and check system hose connections. Be sure washer fluid container has fluid. Check spout openings for clogging.
Keep container filled with fluid mixture of washer solvent and water. If road spray buildup on windshield is a chronic problem, add 1 tablespoon dishwasher detergent to solvent/water mixture when re-filling container.
NOTE: The car's windshield washer pump mechanism is lubricated by the fluid in the windshield washer tank. To avoid damaging the pump mechanism, keep an adequate level of fluid in the tank at all times.

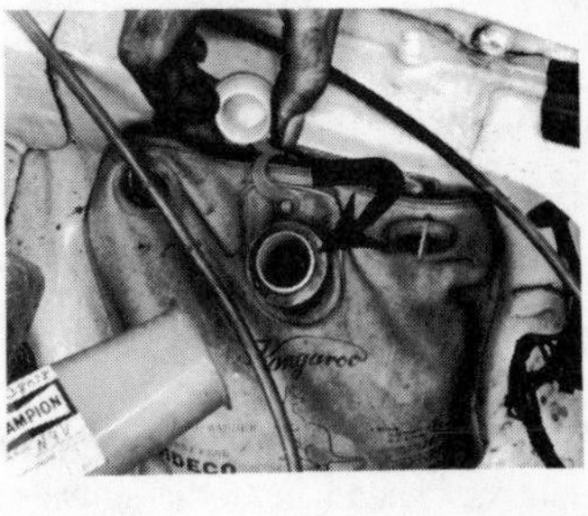

SIDE MARKER LIGHT

Remove the retaining screws, and remove the lens from bumper. Push in on bulb turning counterclockwise to remove.

INTERIOR DOME LIGHT

This is cartridge type bulb; be sure to purchase correct replacement. Pry dome light lens out from housing. To avoid blowing fuse, make sure doors are closed and dome light switch is in OFF position. Carefully lever the bulb straight out of housing. Insert new bulb and reinstall dome light lens.

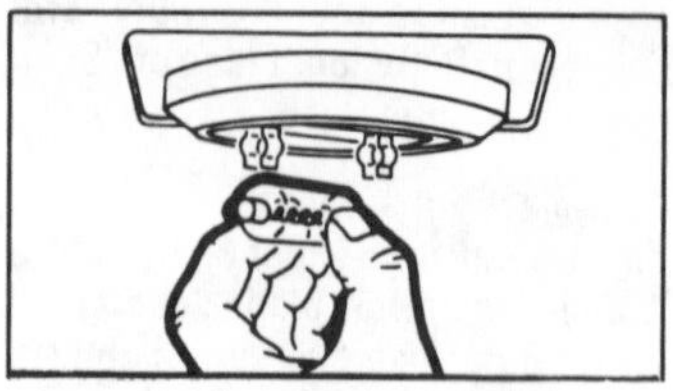

LICENSE PLATE LIGHTS

Remove lens to expose bulb. Push on bulb while turning counterclockwise to release the bulb from the socket. Remove and replace with new bulb. Replace lens.

HEADLIGHT REPLACEMENT

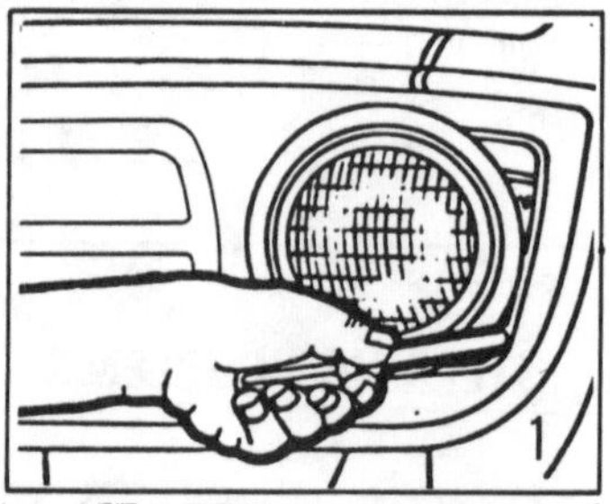

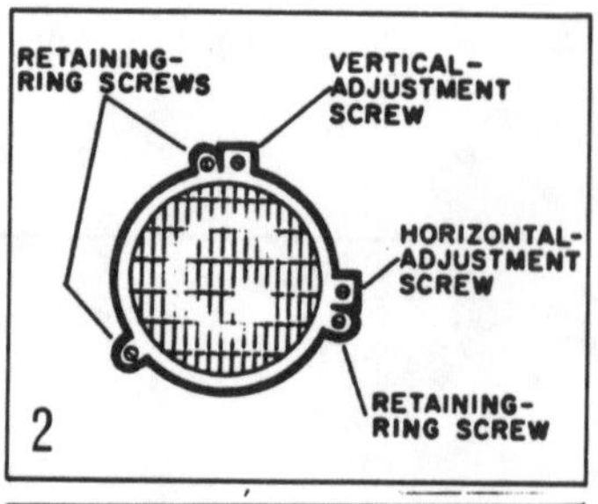

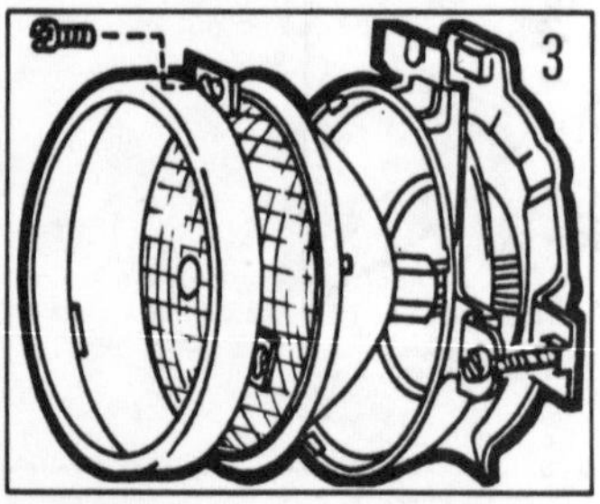

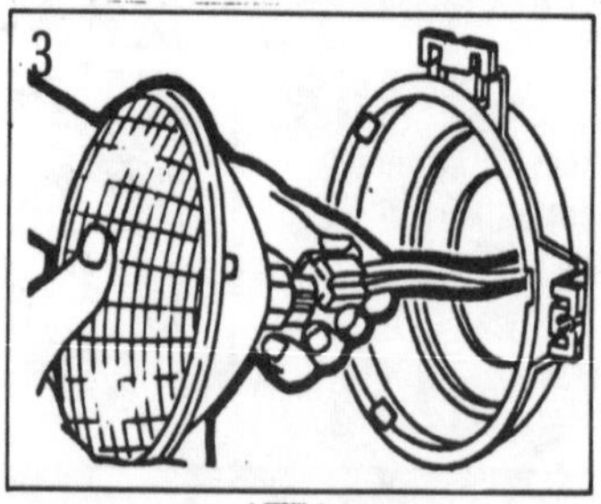

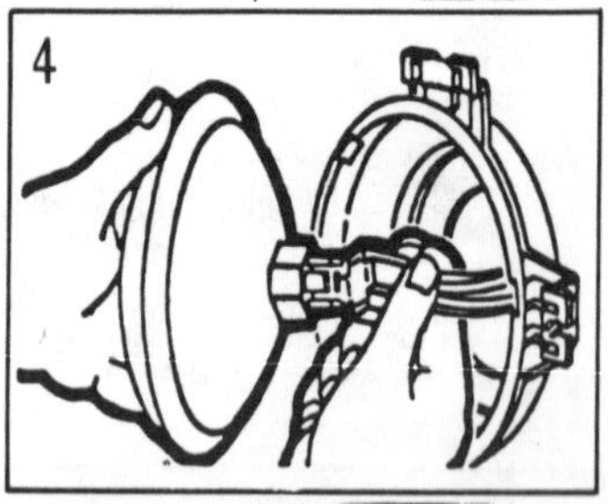

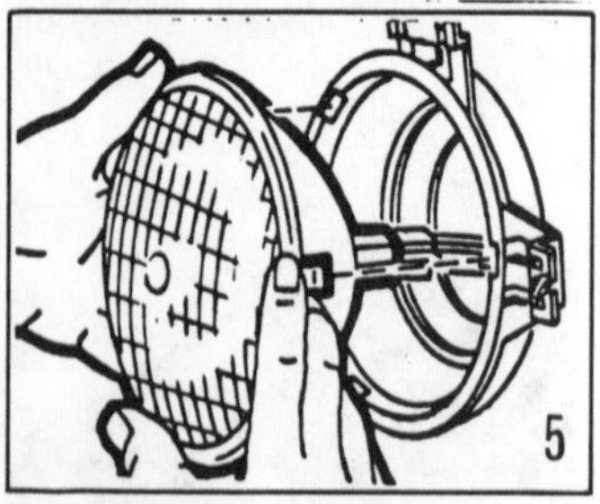

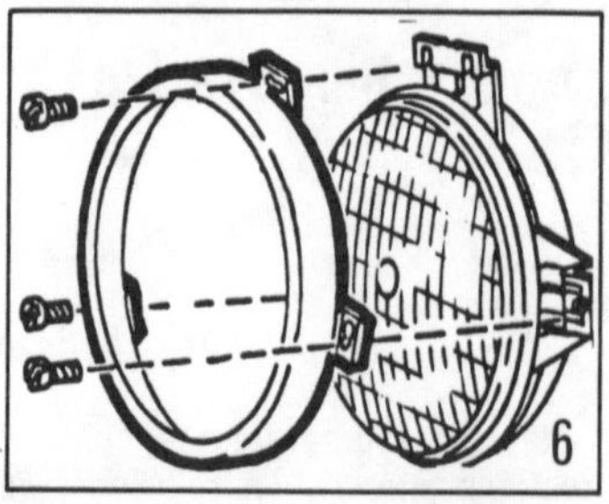

1. Remove either headlight rim or grille retaining screws, and remove the rim or grille.
2. Remove trim ring retaining screws located near the outside, being careful not to confuse these with headlight aiming screws. (Coupe only)
3. Remove the inner ring and pull the headlight out. Disconnect and remove the bulb.
4. Connect the plug to the rear of the new bulb unit.
5. Position new sealed beam in headlight shell. Be sure that knobs on back of light (near outer edge) enter slots in shell.
6. Place retaining ring over sealed beam and fasten with three screws.
7. Install trim ring and tighten screws.

Electrical System

CHECK POINTS AND SERVICES

To ensure starting ability at all times check your battery condition periodically. You'll need to check battery electrolyte (fluid) level in each of the six cells. Check battery cable connections for tightness and inspect for accumulated corrosion.

SAFETY NOTE: Wear gloves when working on battery.

CHECK BATTERY FLUID

1. Remove plastic filler caps on top of battery. Fluid should be up to lower end of filler hole and covering the plates. If fluid is low add clean, cold tap water. If your area has hard water, use only distilled water available at auto supply, food or drug stores.

2. Replace any lost caps immediately.

CAUTION: NEVER LIGHT A MATCH OR SMOKE near the top of a battery. Batteries give off explosive hydrogen gas.

NOTE: Battery that often checks low on fluid could mean:

A. Battery is getting old, due for replacement; have charge capacity checked at service shop.

B. Connections may be corroded or loose; clean/replace as needed (see below).

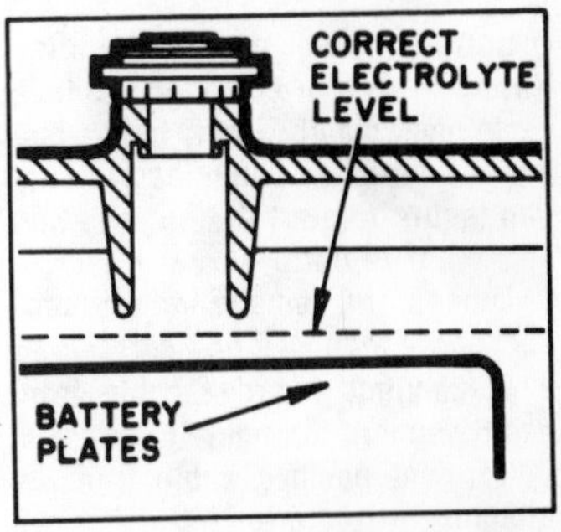

C. Alternator or voltage regulator not functioning properly; this happens far less often than A or B above.

CLEAN THOSE BATTERY TERMINALS

As time goes by, battery terminals build up a dry powdery, whitish material. This material is corrosive and will gradually eat thru battery cables if not cleaned off periodically.

1. Loosen and remove battery connections.

2. Brush off all loose corrosion; use stiff bristle brush. Do not get this material into eyes or on open cuts. Wash off at once.

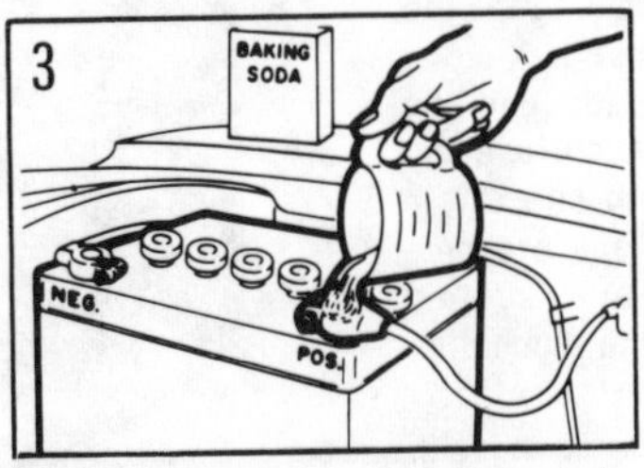

3. If corrosion build-up is extremely heavy and brushing does not remove all of it, mix 2 tablespoons baking soda to 1 cup water. Pour solution directly onto terminals and connectors. Allow to soak a few minutes and rinse off. Continue brushing to remove all traces of corrosion build-up. Do not allow cleaning solution to enter battery.

4. Replace connectors on battery terminal posts and tighten.

5. Liberally smear battery terminal posts and cable connectors with petroleum jelly.

BATTERY HOLDDOWN

The clamp device which holds battery in place should be checked periodically. If loose, tighten. Clean off corrosion buildup. Severely corroded holddown components should be replaced before they break.

REPLACE FAULTY BATTERY CABLES

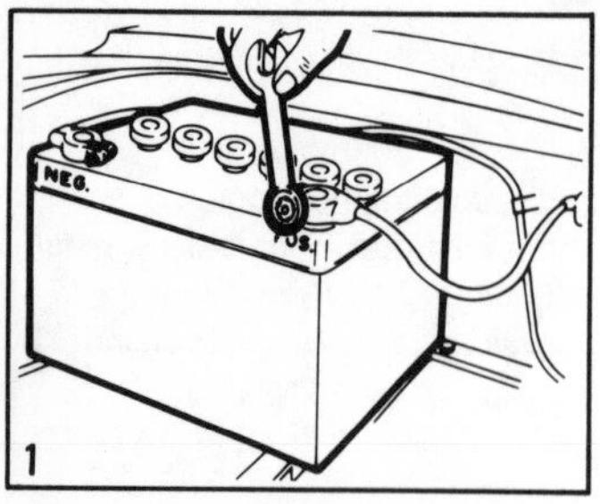

1

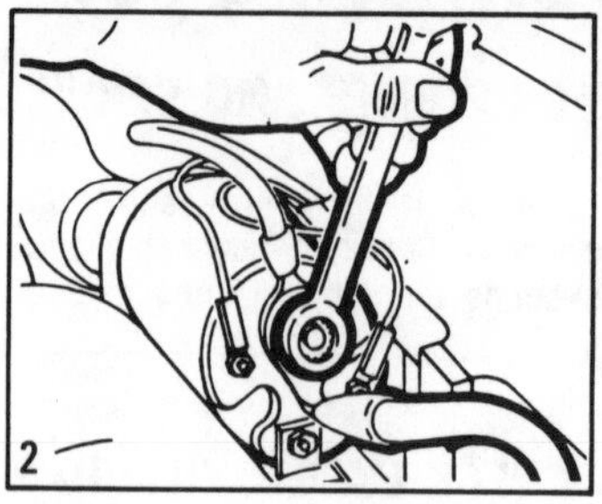
2

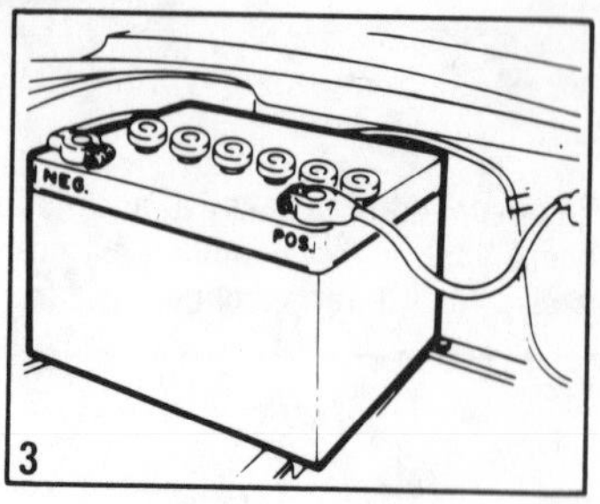

3

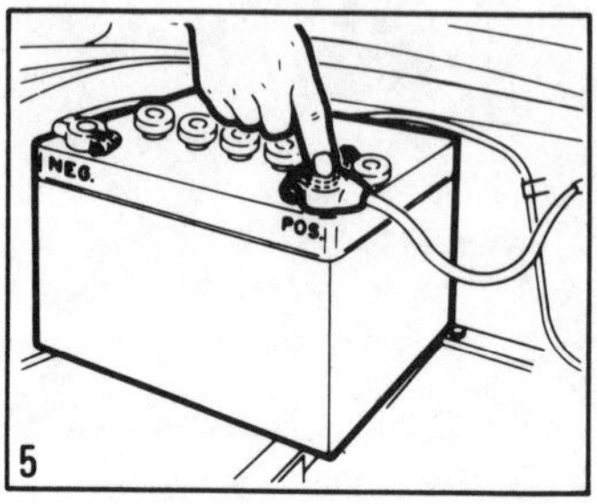

5

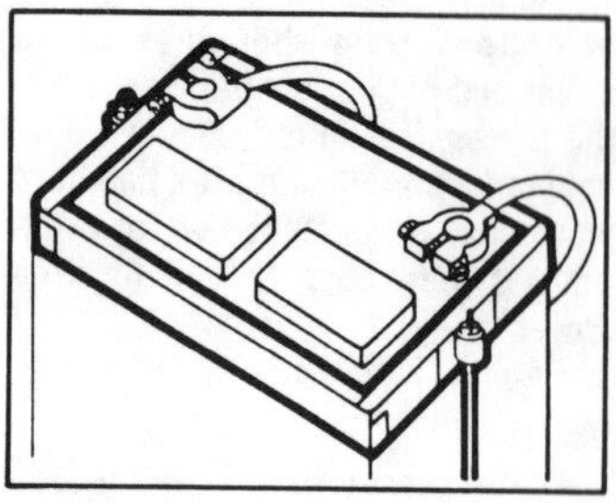

If battery cable strands become frayed, broken or corroded, replace cable immediately. Delay in correcting this condition could lead to sudden failure to start the engine. Can also weaken battery.

1. Loosen and remove battery connections. Clean OFF any corrosion.
2. Disconnect negative cable from its attachment to engine or chassis. Disconnect positive cable from its attachment to starter relay.
3. Attach new cables making sure positive and negative cables are on proper terminals. They are not identical.
4. Replace connectors on battery terminal posts and tighten.
5. Liberally smear battery terminal posts and cable connectors with petroleum jelly.

ELECTRICAL FUSES

The fuse box is located on the right side of the steering column on the engine firewall. The fuse box cover is clearly marked as to function and correct amperage of each fuse. Always replace fuse with one of the same amperage. If fuses are continually blowing, have system checked by professional mechanic.

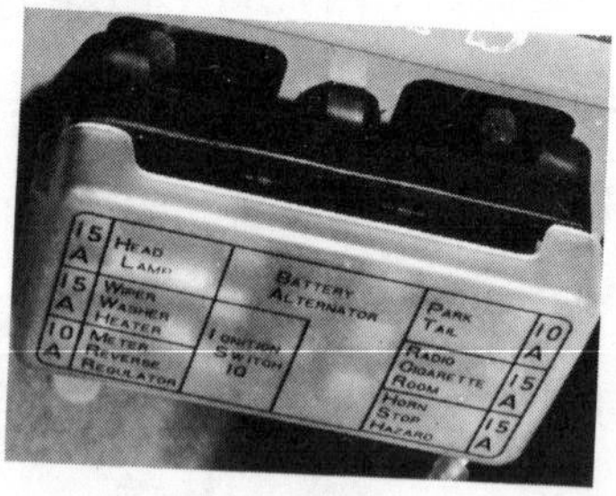

TURN SIGNAL AND 4-WAY FLASHER

Turn signals and 4-way flashers will operate only if: A. All light bulbs are OK. B. Flasher units are not burned out. Datsun has two flasher units that are independent of each other. TURN SIGNAL and EMERGENCY FLASHER: Both units are located behind dash adjacent to the steering column. To remove, unscrew bracket retaining screw and disconnect the wiring connection.

To install, connect wire terminal to new assembly, and attach to side of steering column with screws.

REPLACE ONLY WITH SAME TYPE FLASHER.

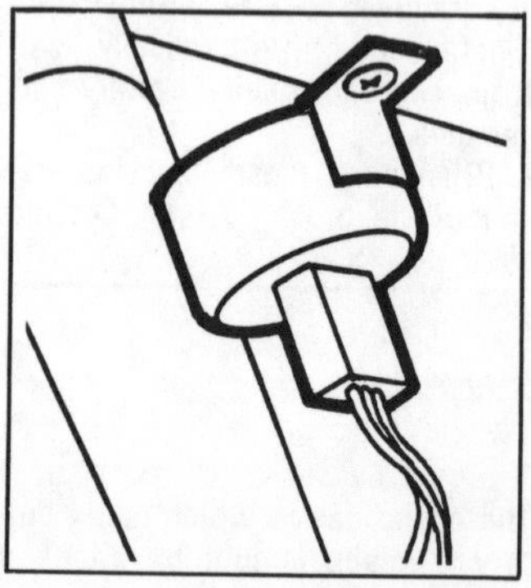

ALTERNATOR

Red alternator warning light on instrument panel should glow red when you first turn ignition key. This proves bulb is OK. Alternator warning light should go off when engine is running at normal operating speed. If alternator warning light glows red at operating speed, alternator isn't charging battery properly. Common causes are:

A. Fan belts are loose and slipping on alternator pulley. Tighten or replace belts.

B. Battery terminals, cables are loose or corroded. Clean; tighten; replace bad cables.

If A or B do not correct problem, alternator or voltage regulator may be faulty. This happens far less often, and can only be checked by mechanic with proper electrical testing equipment.

Alternator Caution: Alternator can be permanently damaged by shortcircuiting terminal connections. When working around or moving alternator, always keep metal tools or engine parts from terminals.

REAR WINDOW DEFOGGER SYSTEM

Do not clean inside of rear window fitted with defogger system with any abrasive material. This could destroy carbon-copper wires. Use only soft rag and mild detergent/water mixture. Dry carefully.

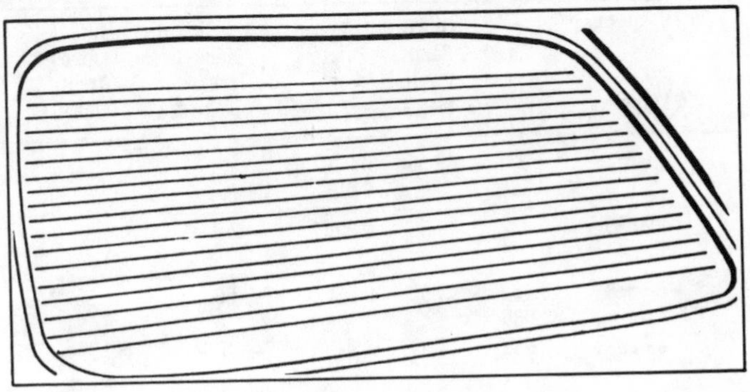

Air Conditioning System

WARNING!—Never attempt to tighten fittings, disassemble or do any work on your car's A/C system. Consult a professional mechanic about A/C system problems and their correction. Your auto air conditioner (A/C) is a delicate, closed system. If air, dirt or water get into it, or if refrigerant escapes, the A/C unit will not cool a car interior. Among things you can do are:

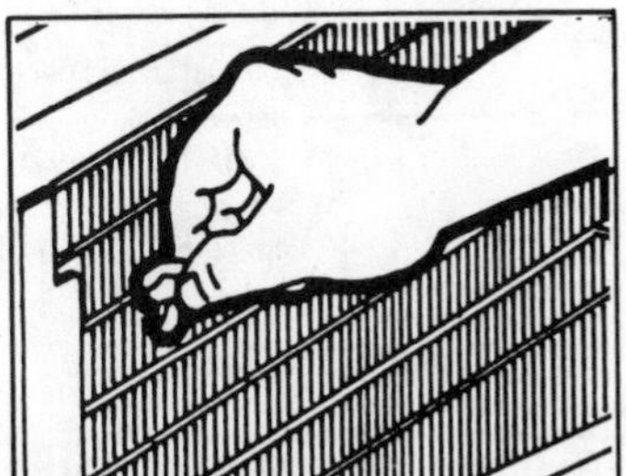

1

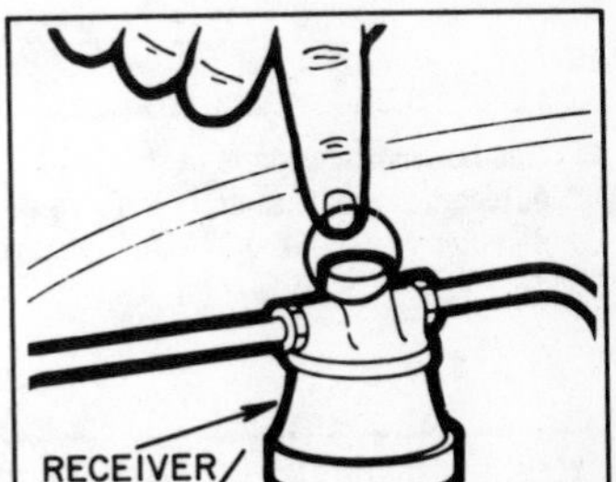

7

1. Keep condenser grille clean. Check for dirt and debris; periodically remove dead insects, leaves, etc., with stiff bristle brush. Straighten any bent fins—carefully.
2. Keep radiator filled to correct level. (See Cooling System section). If fluid needs to be added, add antifreeze rather than water.
3. Keep radiator coolant at a 50/50 water/antifreeze mixture.
4. Flush cooling system and replace with fresh coolant mixture at least every 24 months. (See Cooling System section).
5. Radiator cap should be tight and sealed properly. If sealing gasket is cracked, cut or worn, replace cap with new 13 lb. unit.
6. Check fan belt tension periodically. (See Cooling System section). Replace glazed, frayed or cut fan belts, before they fail entirely.
7. Check periodically for bubbles in A/C sight glass. Sight glass is lo-

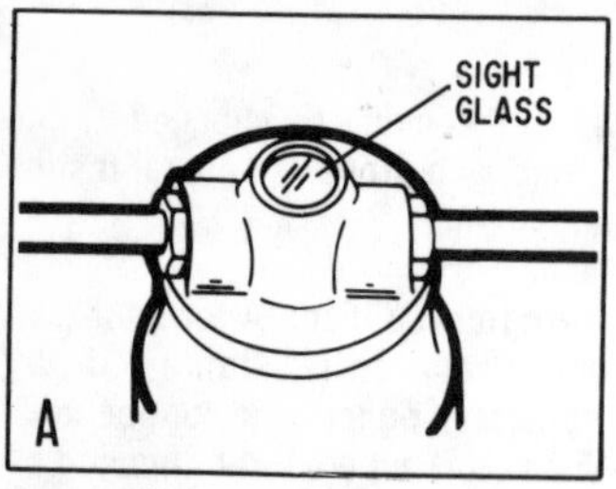

cated in head of receiver/drier vessel. Sight glass is no larger than the head of a large nail. It may be dirty. Wipe clean for best visibility.

PROCEED AS FOLLOWS:

a) With engine and A/C system running, look for passage of refrigerant in sight glass. You'll be looking for a stream of milky white bubbles as they pass through sight glass. It is best to watch sight glass and have someone else start the car and turn on the A/C system. Allow to run for a few minutes.

b) If you observe no bubbles, and air flow from A/C unit in the car is passing cold air, everything is OK.

c) If no bubbles appear in sight glass, and air flow from the A/C unit in the car is not delivering cold air, the system may be low on refrigerant and could need a re-charge.

d) If bubbles appear, system is low on refrigerant.

e) If you suspect refrigerant loss based on tests performed above, have system checked by a professional A/C service shop. They can confirm refrigerant loss, recharge the system and check for system leakage.

NOTE: Once a week or so, even in winter, run A/C system for about 5 minutes as you drive. This keeps system internally lubricated, prevents hoses hardening.

TUNE-UP SPECIFICATIONS

YEAR	MODEL	SPARK PLUGS		DISTRIBUTOR		IGNITION TIMING		IDLE SPEED	
		Type	Gap (in.)	Point Dwell (deg.)	Point Gap (in.)	Man. Trans. (deg.) ■	Auto Trans. (deg.) ■	Man. Trans. (rpm) ■	Auto Trans. (rpm) ■
1971	1200	BP-6E	0.031-0.035	49-55	0.018-0.022	5B	—	700	—
1972	1200	BP-5ES	0.032-0.036	49-55	0.020	5B	5B	700	600
1973	1200	BP-5ES	0.032-0.036	49-55	0.020	5B	5B	700	600
1974	B210	BP-5ES	0.031-0.035	49-55	0.017-0.022	5B	5B	800	650
1975	B210 (Federal)	BP-5ES	0.031-0.035	49-55	0.017-0.022	10B	10B	700	650
	B210 (California)	BP-6ES	0.031-0.035	①	①	10B	10B	750	650
1976	B210 (Federal)	BP-5ES	0.031-0.035	49-55	0.017-0.022	10B	10B	700	650
	B210 (California)	BP-5ES	0.031-0.035	①	①	10B	8B	700	650
1977	B210	See Underhood Specifications Sticker							

■ Manual transmission is in Neutral; Automatic transmission is in Drive

① Reluctor gap 0.008-0.016 in.—electronic ignition

NOTE: The underhood specifications sticker often reflects tune-up specification changes made in production. Sticker figures must be used if they disagree with those in this chart.

CAPACITIES

YEAR	MODEL	ENGINE OIL With Filter	ENGINE OIL Without Filter	TRANSMISSION Pts. to Refill after Draining MANUAL	TRANSMISSION Pts. to Refill after Draining AUTOMATIC	DRIVE AXLE (pts.)	COOLING SYSTEM (qts.)
1971-73	1200		2.9	4.3	11.8②	1.8	5.7
1974	B210	3.45	—	2.5	10.9②	1.88	5.45
1975-77	B210	4.2	3.7	2.7	12.0②	2.0	①

① 6¼ manual transmission
6 automatic transmission

② Total capacity

Toyota Corolla

Lubrication and Oil Change

BRAKE FLUID LEVEL CHECK

Check brake and clutch fluid levels in the master cylinders every time the oil level is checked . . . sooner if the braking feels inadequate, or the clutch will not disengage properly. Add fluid when low. Master cylinders are located under the hood on the left side, and are made of translucent plastic, making removal of the cap unnecessary except when adding fluid. Recommended Grade: (Both) Extra heavy duty. **DOT 3**

1. If fluid level does not reach top ridge, remove cap and gasket by lifting up.
2. Add recommended fluid to reach level. DO NOT OVERFILL.
3. Replace cap and gasket. If fluid level was low, check again in a few days.
4. If fluid level repeatedly checks low, there is a leak somewhere in the system.

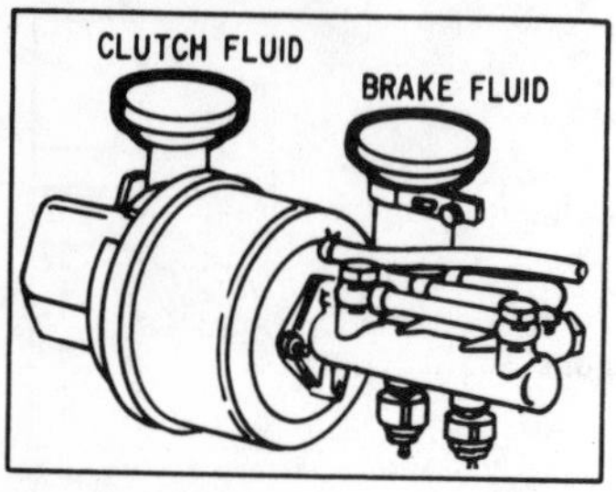

MANUAL TRANSMISSION FLUID LEVEL CHECK

TOYOTA SAYS . . . check manual transmission fluid level every 6000 miles. Car should be parked level. Recommended grade: API grade GL-4, SAE 80.

TOOLS NEEDED . . . adjustable wrench, bulb syringe.

1. Locate the transmission filler plug on the side of the transmission from underneath the car.
2. Wipe road dirt from filler plug area before loosening. Remove plug with adjustable wrench.
3. Insert your finger to check fluid level. The fluid should be right up to the bottom edge of the hole.
4. Add fluid as needed with hand bulb syringe.
5. Replace filler plug; tighten.

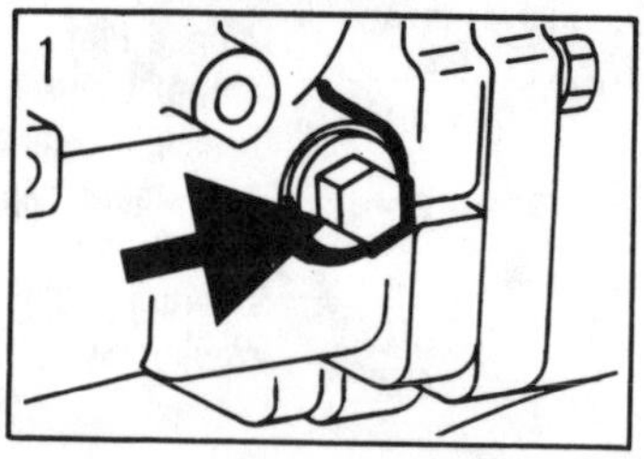

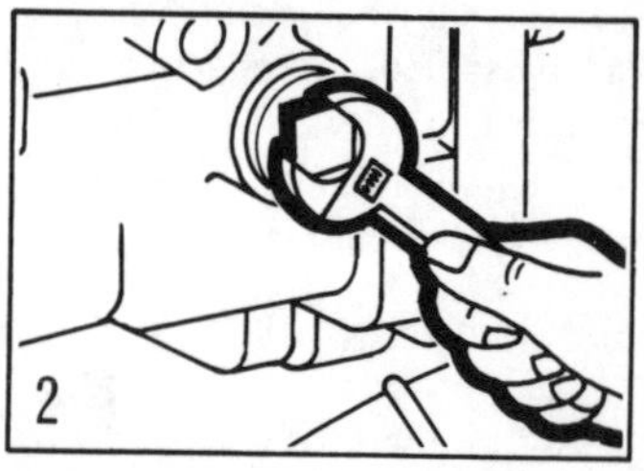

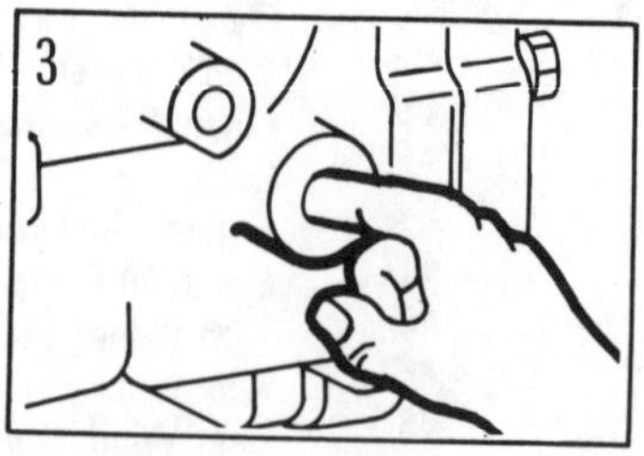

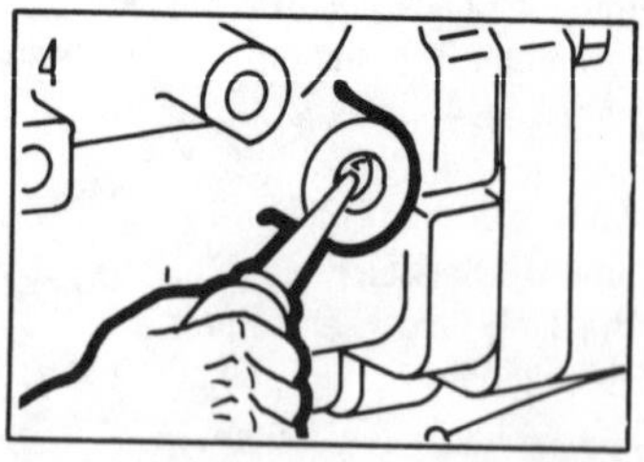

AUTOMATIC TRANSMISSION FLUID LEVEL CHECK

TOYOTA SAYS . . . check automatic transmission fluid (ATF) level every 3000 miles. Recommended grade: ATF Type F.

TOOLS NEEDED . . . Long neck filler funnel.

1. Start the engine and idle it for a few minutes. Apply the parking brake. Shift the transmission

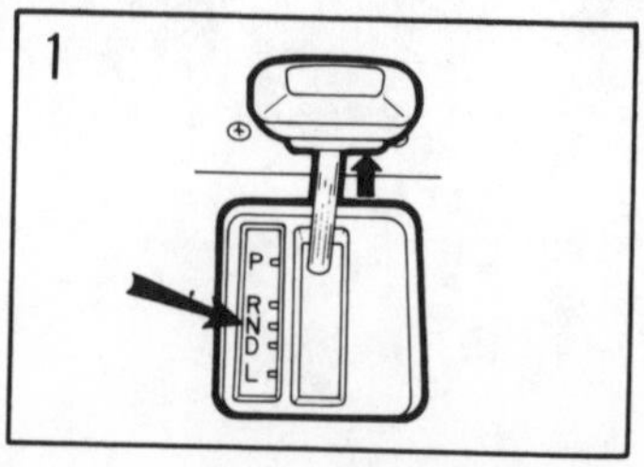

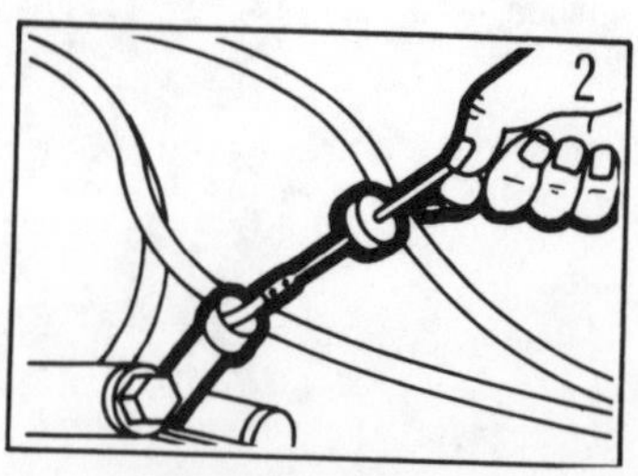

through every range, and return it to Neutral.
2. Pull out dipstick. Wipe clean. Push dipstick all the way back in; remove it again.
3. Choose the "hot" or "cold" range on the stick according to the transmission temperature. If fluid is between notches, do not add. If fluid is below lower mark, add enough ATF to bring level up as necessary. DO NOT OVERFILL.
4. Add ATF thru transmission dipstick hole by means of long-neck filler funnel.

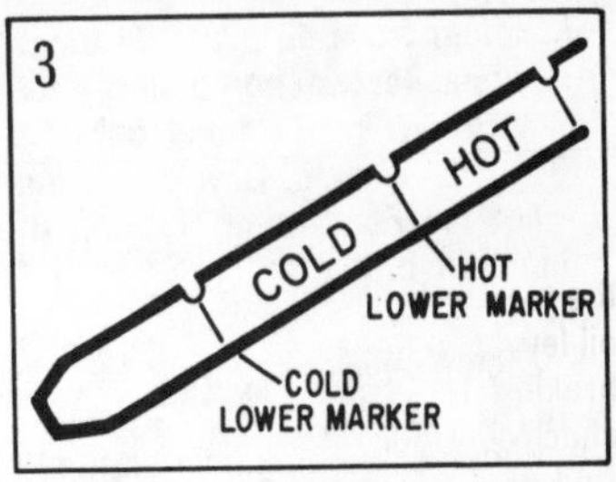

REAR AXLE LUBRICANT

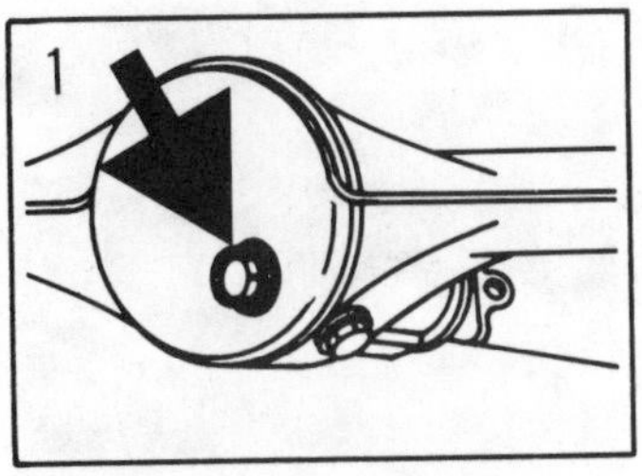

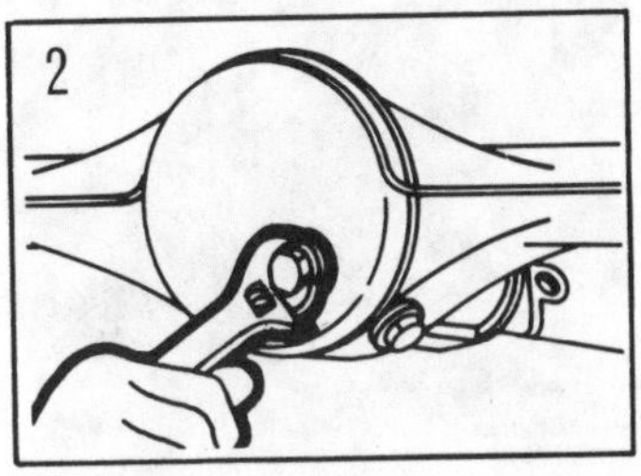

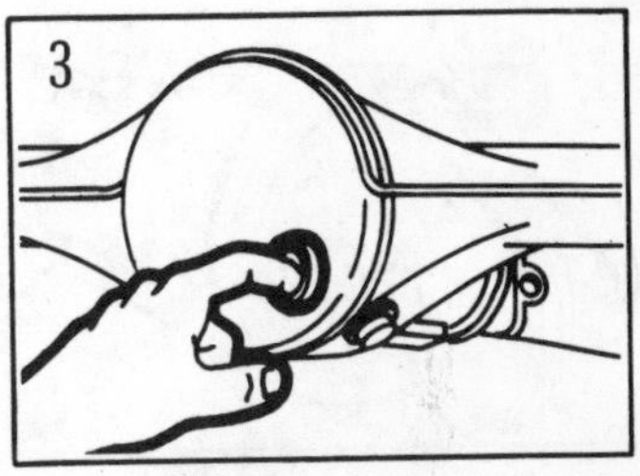

TOYOTA SAYS . . . check rear axle lube level every 6000 miles. Recommended grade: APIGL-5 (SAE 90).
TOOLS . . . adjustable hand wrench; bulb syringe.
1. Locate filler plug on forward side of rear axle housing.
2. Wipe plug area clean; remove plug with wrench.
3. Adequate fluid level should show lubricant at level of filler plug.
4. If fluid level is low, add as needed, with a hand bulb syringe.
5. Replace filler plug; tighten.

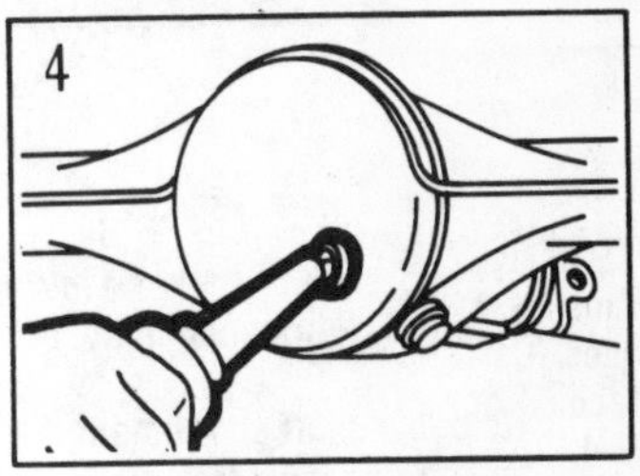

OIL AND FILTER CHANGE

TOYOTA SAYS . . . Check oil and filter initially at 1,000 miles; then change oil every 3,000 miles or three months; and change the filter every 6,000 miles or six months. Recommended grade: SE. Check oil level at least once a week.
TOOLS & MATERIALS . . . adjustable wrench; medium size screwdriver; oil filter removal wrench; drain pan for old oil (5 quart cap.); oil pouring spout; new oil filter (if required); other lubricants as specified below.

1. If engine is cold, start up and idle for about 5 minutes.
2. Park car on level ground. Turn engine off.
3. Locate oil drain plug on underside of engine. Place drain pan under plug.
4. Remove drain plug with wrench. Let ALL dirty oil drain out.
5. Wipe plug and area around drain hole clean. Replace drain plug; tighten it.
6. Locate oil filter. Move drain pan under filter. Loosen filter with oil filter wrench. Unscrew; remove filter by hand.

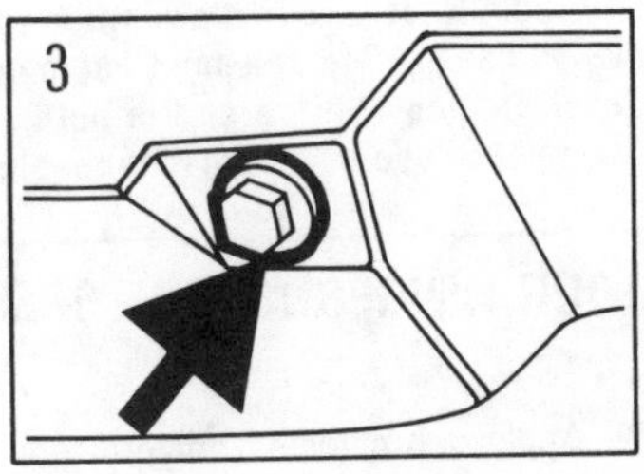

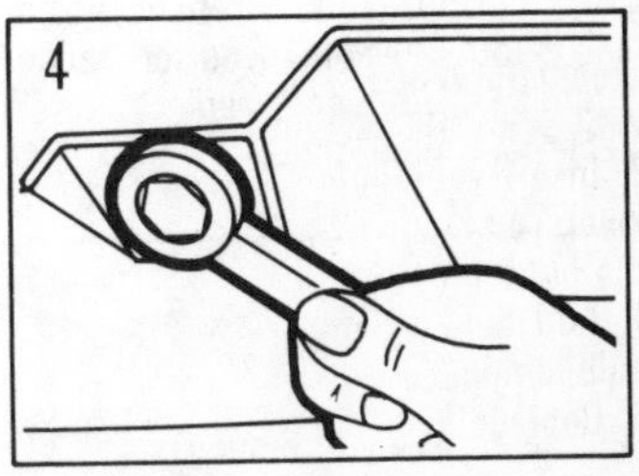

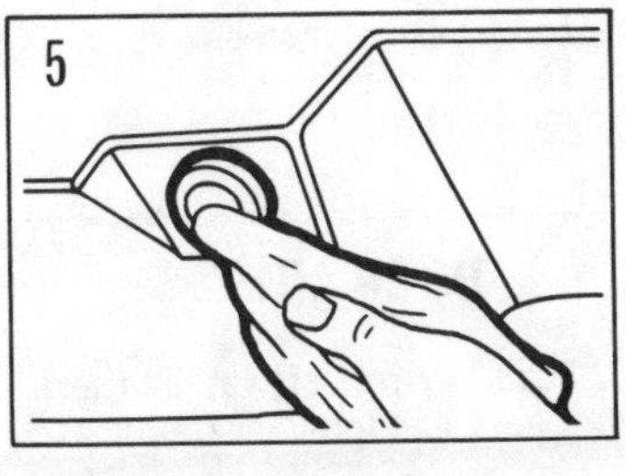

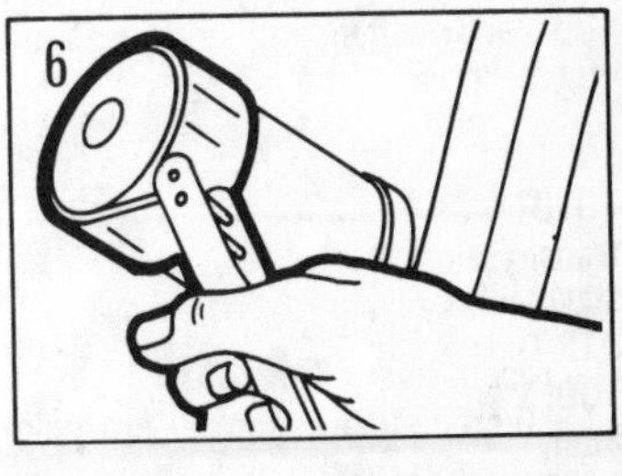

7. Smear fresh oil over surface of rubber gasket (washer) of new filter. Install new filter by hand only. Do NOT use wrench. Turn filter until gasket makes contact. Tighten an additional half turn only . . . NO MORE.

8. Locate oil filler cap on top of engine. Remove cap.

9. Punch oil pouring spout into top of oil can. Pour all cans of new oil into filler hole. Wipe filler cap clean and replace it. Be sure to reattach all hoses.

NOTE: If filler cap is very dirty, rinse in turpentine or gasoline. Dry before replacing.

10. Check new oil level at dipstick. Pull out dipstick, wipe clean.

11. Push dipstick back into engine. Be sure to insert all the way. Remove dipstick and check new oil level. It should be above "F" line. If not, be sure to check if you put in all the oil called for.

12. Start up engine and idle for 3-5 minutes. Oil signal light on instrument panel will glow red when engine is first started. Light should go out in 30 seconds or less.

13. Stop engine and check for oil leaks at drain plug and filter. If you find any, check tightness of plug and/or filter, also for condition of filter gasket to see that it has not become pinched or damaged when installing. Recheck oil level, which should now be at "F".

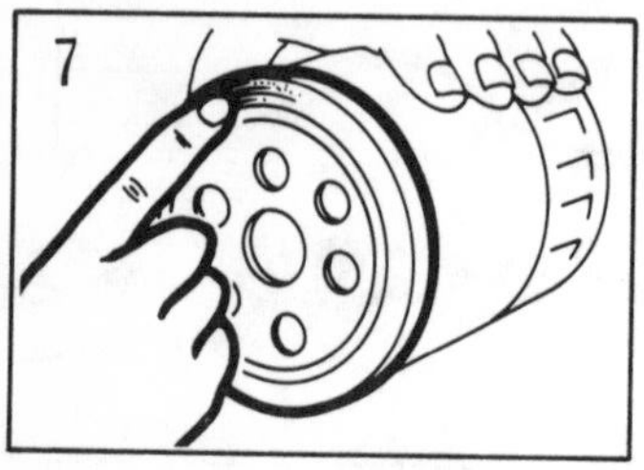
7

8

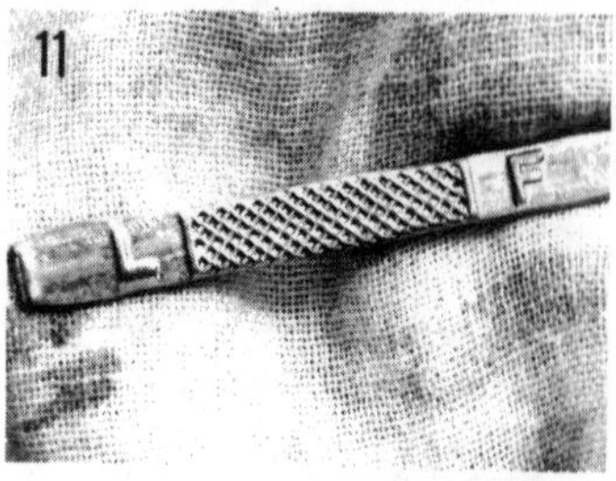
11

SPEEDOMETER CABLE LUBRICATION

If speedometer pointer tends to quiver or jump, or if unit makes a low, rasping sound, lubrication may be needed.

1. Locate cable shaft attachment directly behind speedometer dial.
2. Reach around behind dash and unscrew cable; press flat surface and pull out from behind panel.
3. Pull inner cable completely out of outer casing. Note carefully which end is top. Check for wear or frayed strands. If damaged, replace inner cable with new one.

1

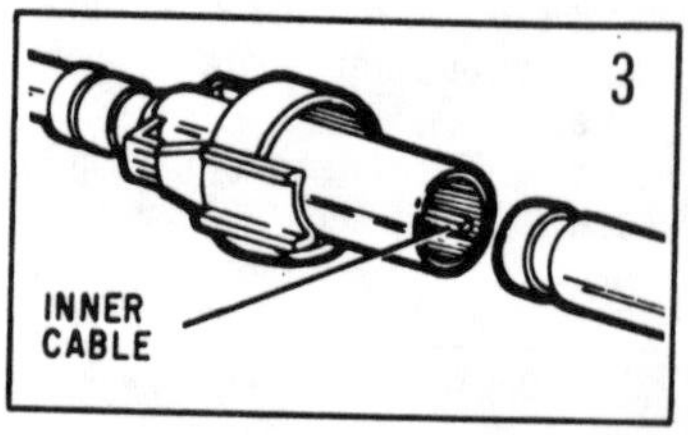

3

4. Apply generous amount of speedometer cable lubricant into cable casing. Replace inner cable in shaft, noting that top end is not inserted accidentally. Turn inner cable as it is being re-inserted. Twist cable when all the way in, to lock into position at lower end.
5. Reconnect cable to speedometer head under instrument panel.

DOOR HINGES AND STOPS

(lubricate every 6 months)

1. Brush any dirt accumulations from door hinges and stops. Use old tooth brush or rag.
2. Apply dab of white polyethylene grease to door hinges, trunk hinges, hood hinges, door stops.

DOOR LOCKS

(lubricate every 6 months)

1. Insert door key half way into lock.
2. Spray aerosol lock lubricant into lock.
3. Push key rest of way into lock; turn back and forth several times.

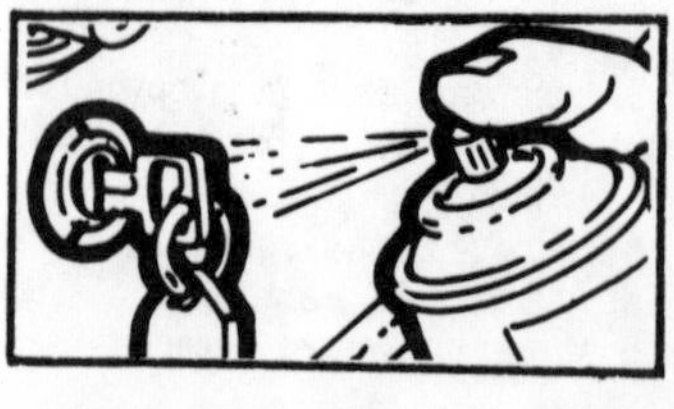

Cooling System

IT IS RECOMMENDED . . . that radiator coolant (water/antifreeze mixture) level be checked once or twice a month. Do this when engine is cold. Check more often if you do a lot of hard driving. On models with clear expansion tanks, check coolant level visually when hot.
Keep coolant up to recommended level in radiator. If coolant checks frequently low, look for leaks. Tighten all hose clamps occasionally. For best results, keep a 50/50 water/antifreeze mixture year round. Change complete coolant mixture every 12,000 miles.
CAUTION: If you must check coolant in a hot engine, cover radiator cap with thick rag before releasing. Remove cap slowly . . . press down and turn.

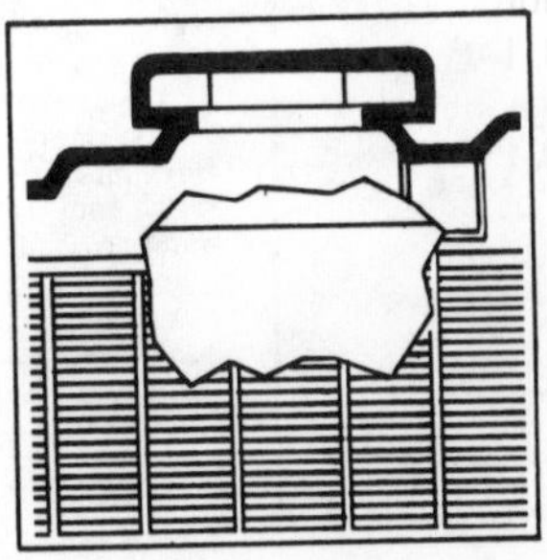

REPLACING THE THERMOSTAT

A faulty thermostat will usually cause engine overheating. Replace with new thermostat.

TOOLS AND MATERIALS . . .
New thermostat
Gasket
Adjustable wrench

1. Drain radiator of about half its coolant. (See How To Replace Hoses).
2. Loosen and remove both retaining bolts and lift thermostat housing off the engine.
NOTE: If you're careful it won't be necessary to remove radiator hose.
3. Remove old thermostat.
4. Scrape thermostat housing flange and engine block surface to remove old gasket debris.
5. Drop new thermostat into place—spring down.
6. Install new gasket with sealer applied to both sides.
7. Replace thermostat housing and tighten both retaining bolts.

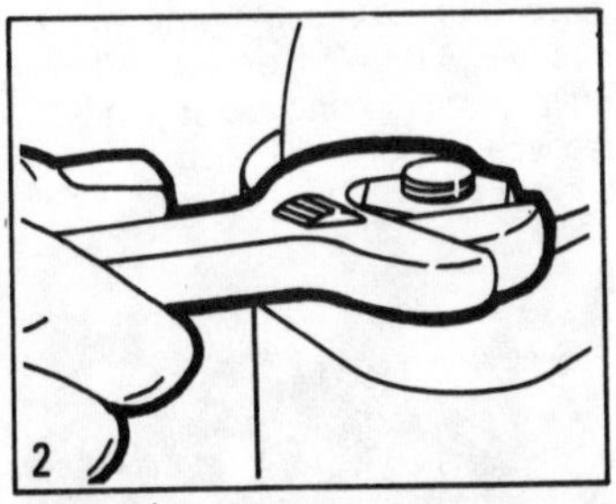
2

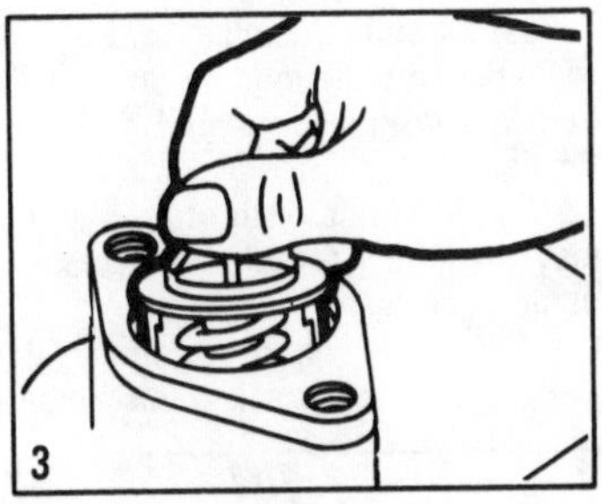
3

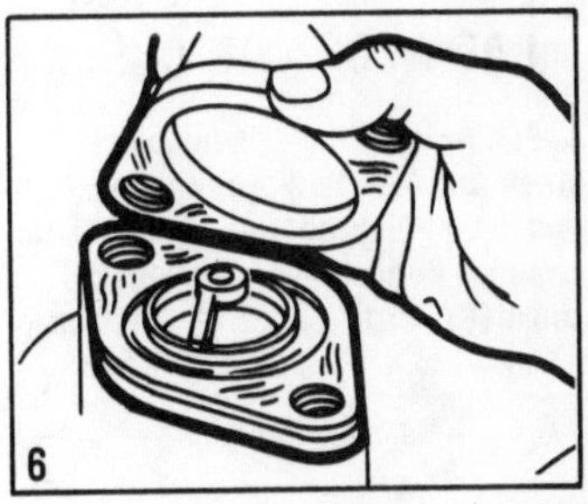
6

FIND THOSE COOLING SYSTEM LEAKS

1. Inspect all hoses. If any are weak, soft in spots or show cracks, replace at once.
2. Check all hose connections for tightness. Tighten loose hose clamps; they tend to loosen due to engine vibration.
3. If radiator steams or hisses when engine is switched off, check for leaks. Look for signs of coolant drips on radiator or around heater tank joint.

Leaks are possible at:
Upper or lower radiator hoses
Water pump (gaskets or seal)
Heater core or connecting hoses
Automatic transmission cooler lines (at bottom of radiator)
Faulty radiator pressure cap
Faulty cylinder head gasket
Cracked cylinder head or block

Due to the number of joints, cooling systems have many places to leak from. Check clamp tightness. If leaks persist an anti-leak additive in the coolant may help. Noisy water pumps may benefit from a lubricating additive in the coolant. Use a cooling system cleaner when flushing during a drain and refill job. It will help remove rust and scale. Remember — additives will not cure chronic problems. But they will effect a short-term remedy in many cases.

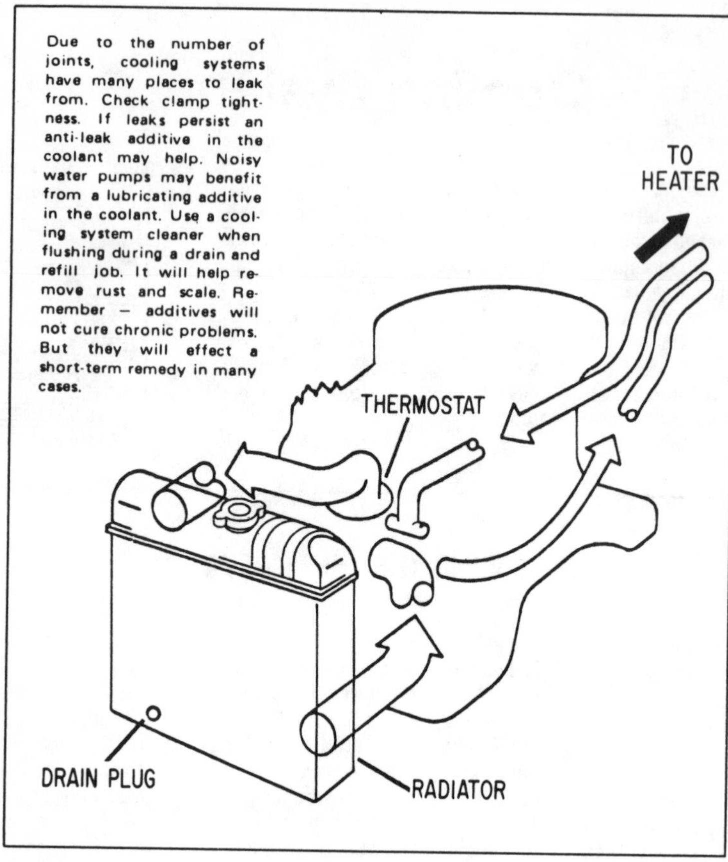

RADIATOR CAP CHECK

Check radiator cap occasionally for worn or cracked gasket. If cap doesn't seal properly, fluid will be lost and engine will overheat.
Replace worn cap with new cap rated 13 to 15 lbs. pressure.

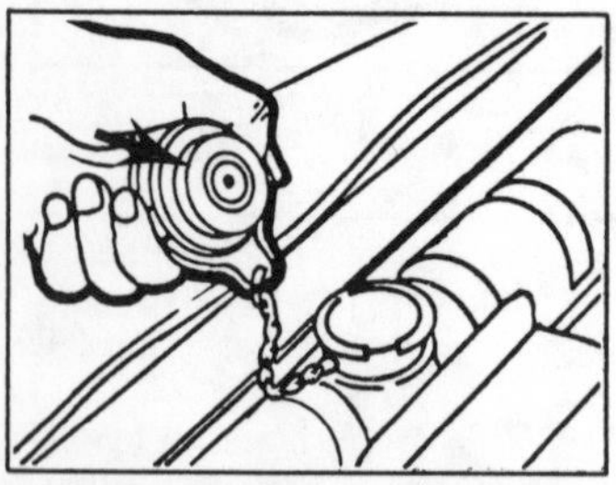

FAN BELT ADJUSTMENT

The fan belt not only drives the radiator fan, it turns the water pump and drives the alternator. It's easy to see that the condition and proper tension of the belt are vital, since almost all engine cooling and electrical power is dependent on it. The belt deserves an occasional look and tension check.

CAUTION: An overtightened belt may damage alternator and water pump bearings.

1. Inspect fan belt occasionally. If worn, frayed or cracked on inner

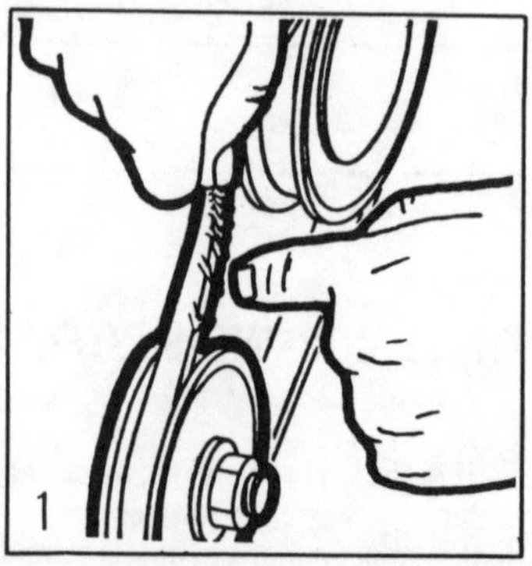

driving surface, replace.

2. Check tension occasionally. Press thumb at midpoint of belt span between pulleys. If belt depresses more than ½ inch, tightening is needed. A too-loose belt will not drive alternator and water pump effectively.

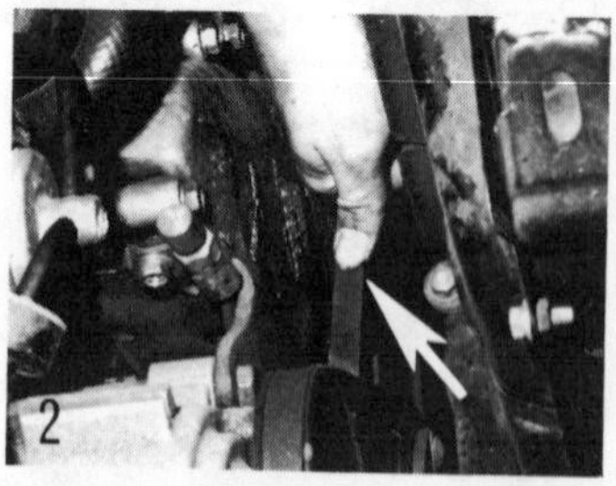

3. Adjust to proper tension of ¼ inch deflection.

HOSE REPLACEMENT

Coolant drain and refill work may be done alone; when changing hoses, coolant must also be drained as part of job. Discard all hoses with cracks or soft spots. Check hose clamps for tightness and good condition.

1. Remove radiator cap. Open radiator petcock (See 2). Drain coolant into catch basin. If near 24 months old, discard old coolant.
2. Petcock is located at the bottom of the radiator.
3. Wipe all hose connections clean. Use emery cloth to get rid of residue.
4. If old hose clamps are badly rusted or damaged, replace with new units.
5. Slip clamps over each hose end. Slip hose ends all the way onto cleaned up hose connections.
6. Place hose clamp ¼ inch from hose end. Tighten. Close petcock. Refill with 50/50 coolant/water mix. NOTE: On the 1600 engine, after filling the radiator, loosen the temperature gauge sending unit releasing all air trapped in the system and then add more coolant.
7. Start engine; allow to warm up. Check for coolant leaks.

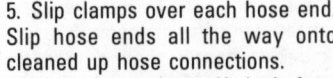

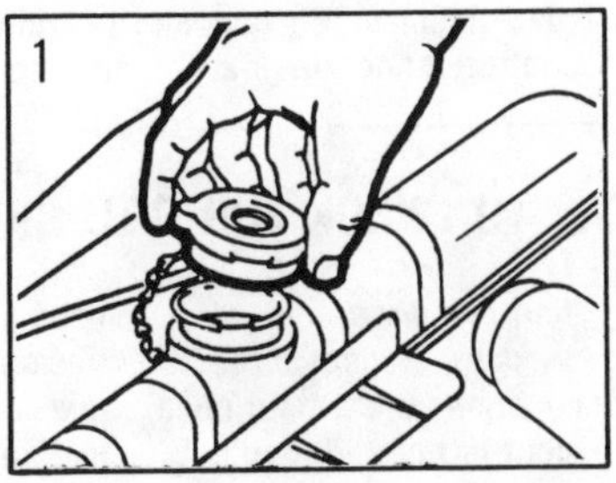

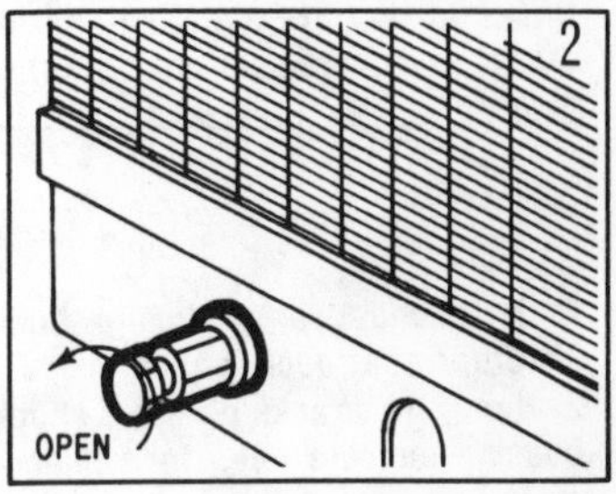

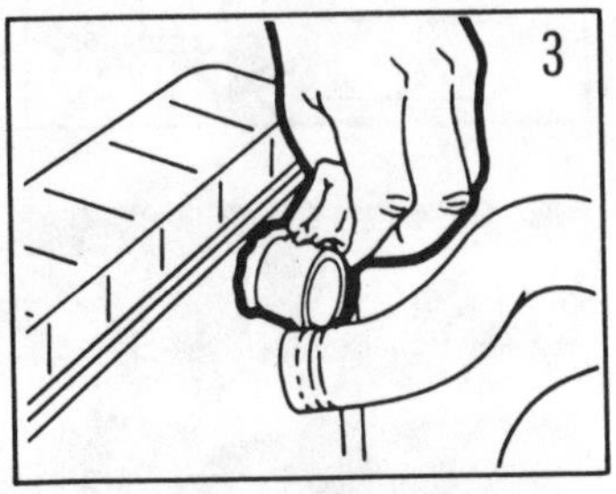

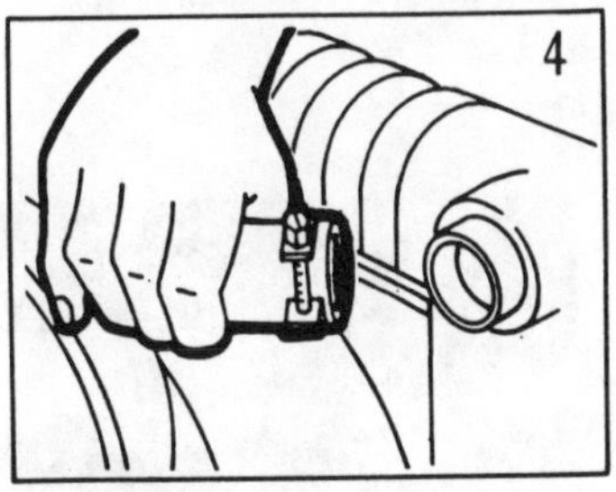

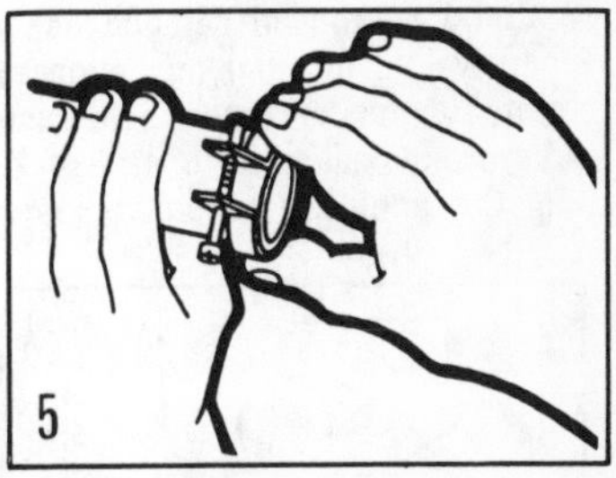

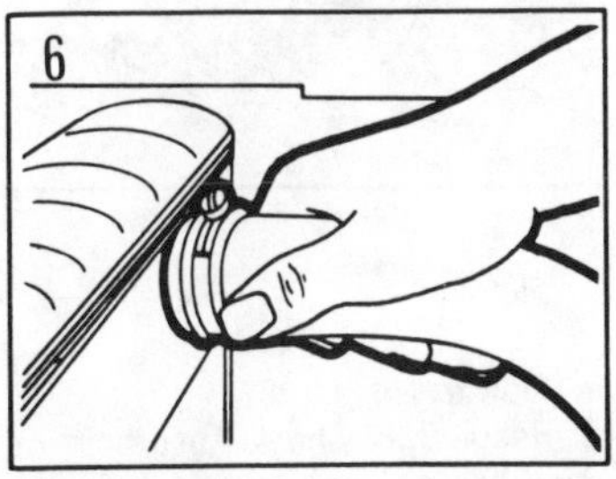

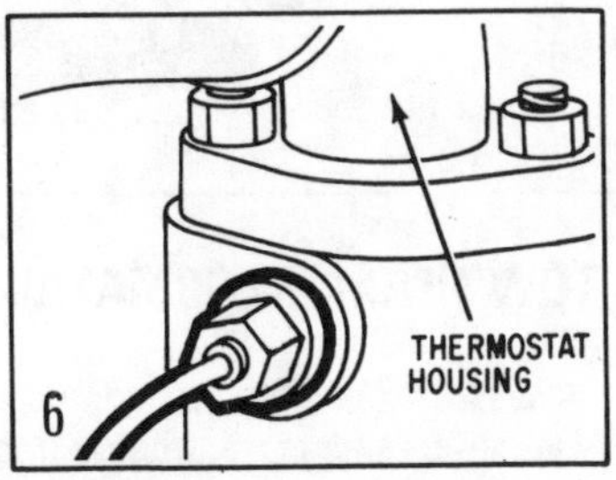

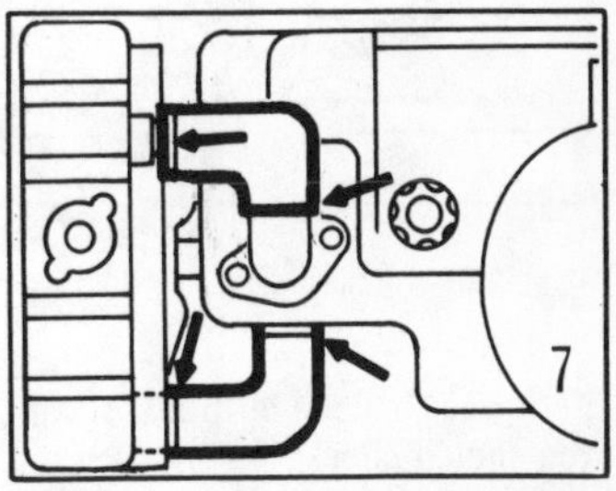

Suspension and Tires

The Corolla front suspension is a MacPherson strut type. The shock absorber and spindle are combined to a single unit which is supported by the coil spring at the upper end, and by the control arm at the lower end. The rear suspension consists of semi-elliptic leaf springs, and telescopic shock absorbers.

Your car's suspension system consists of wheels, tires, springs, shock absorbers, sway (or stabilizer) bars, ball joints, steering linkage. If any of these items is out of adjustment or badly worn, you may notice any of these symptoms:

- car pulls to one side when braking
- car wanders when driving a straight line
- overall ride may be either hard or bouncy
- effort is needed to steer vehicle
- tires show uneven wear
- tires squeal when cornering
- front of car dips or bounces when braking
- car rocks side-to-side when going over rough road
- wheels bounce to make slapping sound on road
- steering wheel vibrates in hands
- front of car vibrates at highway speeds

Any of above symptoms indicates corrective action is needed. Delay can: ruin tires; cause damage/failure to other suspension parts; create safety hazard.

STEERING

If steering linkage, front suspension and steering column components are in good condition, there should be not more than 1½ inch free play in the steering wheel when measured at the rim of the wheel. If a loud knock is heard when turning the steering wheel from one extreme to the other, have mechanic check pinion bearing preload.

SHOCK ABSORBERS

Shock absorbers work to keep wheels in constant contact with the road. Result is safe handling and ride control; longer tire life. So shock absorbers (or shocks) are important.

HOW TO CHECK FOR BAD SHOCKS

1. Check under car and locate shock absorber near each wheel.
2. Heavy oil streaks on outer shock housing indicate need for replacement.
3. Stand at front of car and apply body weight in pumping action to front bumper or fender. Release pressure and allow car to stop rocking. Car should not bounce more than one more time after releasing pressure. Repeat at rear. If bouncing continues more than once, replacement is needed. Replace shocks in pairs (front pair or rear pair).

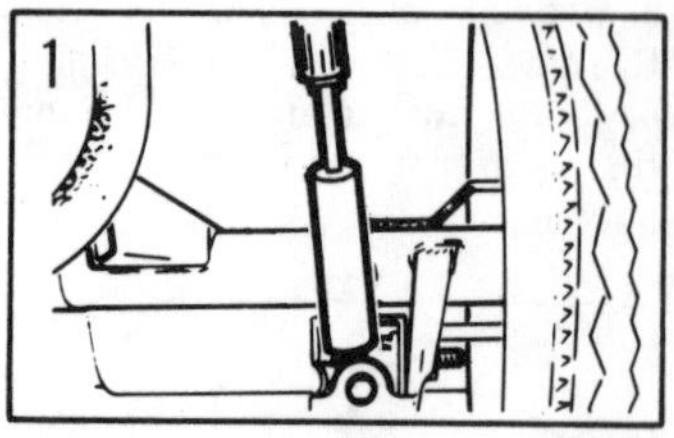

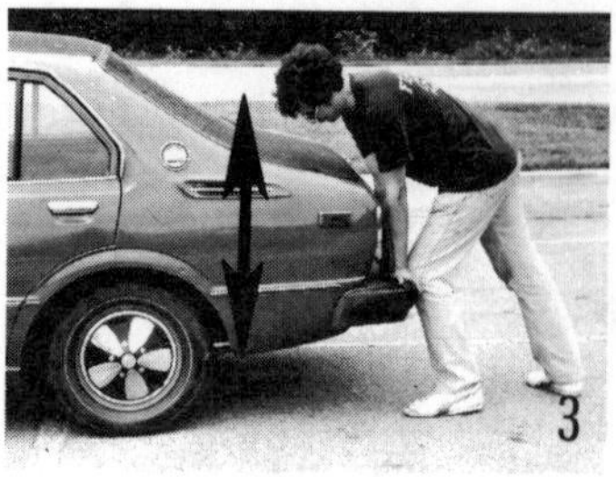

TOW HITCH INFORMATION

If your car is used for trailer towing you should check:
A. Cooling System; be sure coolant is at proper level in radiator. See Cooling System Section for checks to perform.
B. Check Transmission Fluid; keep topped up to proper level.
C. Check Rear Shock Absorbers; you may benefit from installation of new rear shocks.
D. Check Tire Pressures; best traction and handling can be ensured if tire pressures are properly maintained.

For safer and more trouble-free trailer towing, consider:
A. Automatic Transmission Cooler; helps remove excess heat from automatic transmission fluid built up during towing mileage. Also helps avoid radiator overheating. Some units can be self-installed.
B. Radiator Over-Flow Tank Kit; addition of a reservoir to catch radiator coolant overflow preventing coolant loss. Easy to install, these units help a tow car run cooler, avoid overheating due to coolant loss.
C. Heavy-Duty Shock Absorbers or Air Shocks; important to have on rear wheels if you intend to do a lot of towing or load carrying within the car itself. Don't forget to consider replacing factory shocks, when they are worn out, with heavy-duty units at the front as well.
D. Variable Load Flasher; this unit will accommodate the added load of trailer turn signal lamps on trailer when these are hooked into your car's electrical system.

FRONT END ALIGNMENT

When steering, handling and/or tire wear indicate front end alignment may be needed, this work can only be done at an automotive service shop. DO NOT PUT OFF NEEDED FRONT END ALIGNMENT. At the same time, have ball joints and steering linkage checked.

Ignition System

TUNE-UP SERVICES

The ignition system consists of spark plugs; plug wires; distributor; rotor; points; condenser; coil. These units work to create a good hot spark inside the engine (ignition) at exactly the right moment (timing). If ignition is weak or timing is off, engine may be hard to start, run poorly, waste gas, lose power, backfire or not run at all.

Starting in 1975, transistorized ignition is standard on all Corollas.

The transistorized ignition system employed by Toyota works very much like the conventional system previously described. Regular breaker points are used, but instead of switching primary current to the coil off-and-on, they are used to trigger a switching transistor. The transistor, in turn, switches the coil primary current on and off.

Since only a very small amount of current is needed to operate the transistor, the points will not become burned or pitted, as they would if they had full primary current to be higher than usual because the use of a higher current would normally cause the points to fail much more rapidly. For more information, see the Corona/Mark II section.

Also available on 1975 Corollas sold outside of California, is a dual point distributor.

With both these types of ignition system, the recommended replacement interval for points is 24,000 miles.

TOYOTA SAYS: On conventional ignition replace plugs and points every 12,000 miles.

Plugs, points (transistorized ignition) replace every 24,000 miles

TOOLS AND MATERIALS . . . Parts: set of points; condenser; 4 spark plugs. Tools: wire gap gauge (plugs); feeler gauge (points); 13/16 in., spark plug socket; screwdriver; open end, box or combination metric wrenches; timing equipment (see Ignition Timing).

CHECKING POINTS AND ROTOR

The distributor holds the points and rotor. The condenser is attached to the outside of the distributor. The cap forms the top of the distributor.

1. To open distributor, snap retaining clips off with screwdriver, lift cap off but keep wires connected.
2. Pull rotor off (straight up). Replace if cracked or metallic tip is badly burned. Lift off flat radio static shield.
3. Pry points apart with screwdriver. If worn or burned, replace. If OK, check point gap.

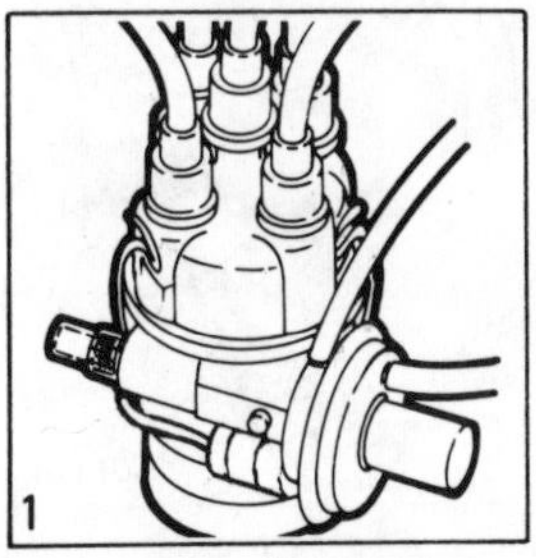

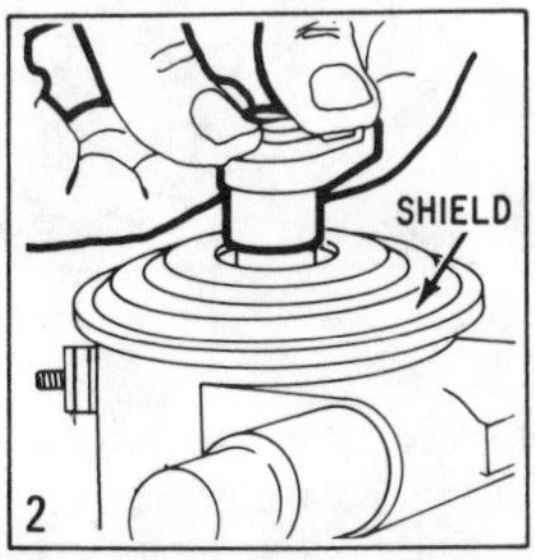

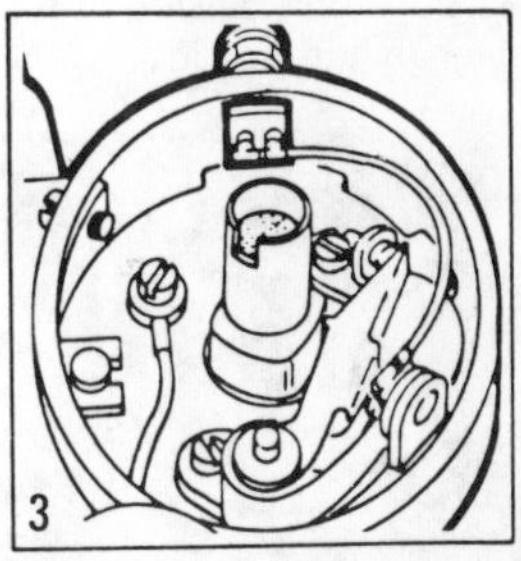

OTHER IGNITION CHECK POINTS

Inspect spark plug wires. If cracked or brittle, entire set should be replaced. Also center, high tension wire. Inspect distributor cap. Wipe inside clean occasionally with dry, lint-free rag. If cap is cracked or rotor contacts are excessively burned, replace cap.

SPARK PLUG REPLACEMENT

1. Remove spark plug wire by grasping rubber boot. Do not jerk wire off. If stuck, turn boot, pulling gently. Remove metal insert from around plugs (1200 cc engine only).
2. Loosen spark plug using socket wrench.
3. Wipe or brush loose dirt from around plug before removing. Do not

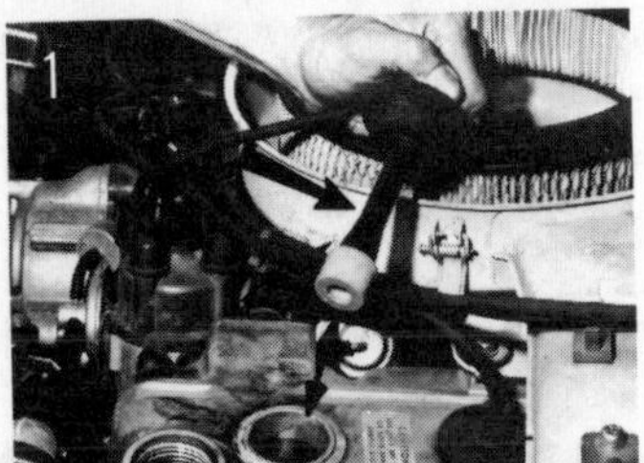

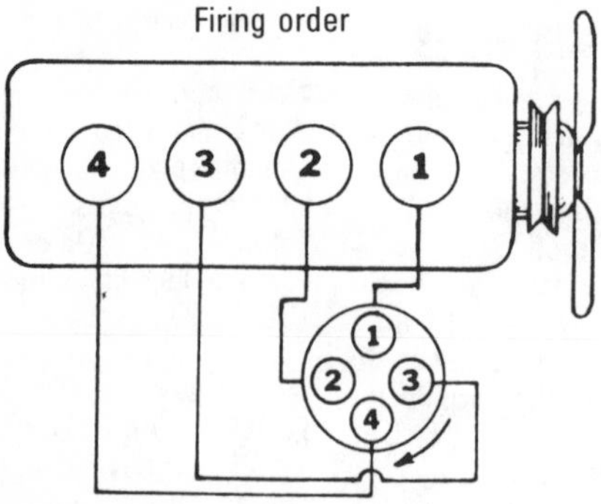

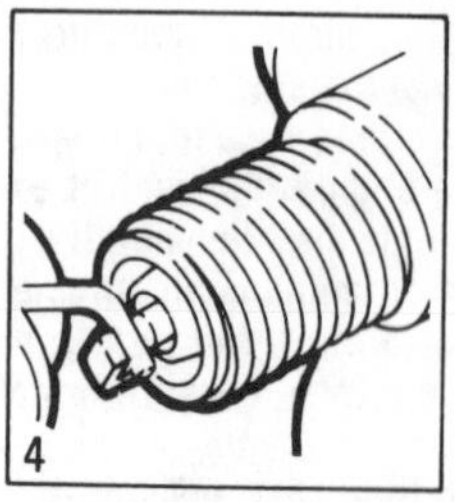

let dirt drop into engine through plug hole. Unscrew plug.

4. Check plug electrode gap on new spark plug. Adjust to 0.031 in. Plug gap is correct when the gauge drags slightly as it is pulled between plug electrodes.

5. Thread new plug into plug hole by hand. Hand tighten. Do not force or cross thread. Use socket wrench to tighten firmly but do not force. Replace plug wire. Press boot firmly.

REMOVING POINTS

Points and condenser work together. Always replace condenser when installing new points. While you may find slight differences in location or attachment of these parts from one car to another, they're all basically the same. The condenser is attached to the outside of the distributor rather than inside.

1. Disconnect the wire terminal connected to the points set. Remove condenser wire terminal from side of distributor.

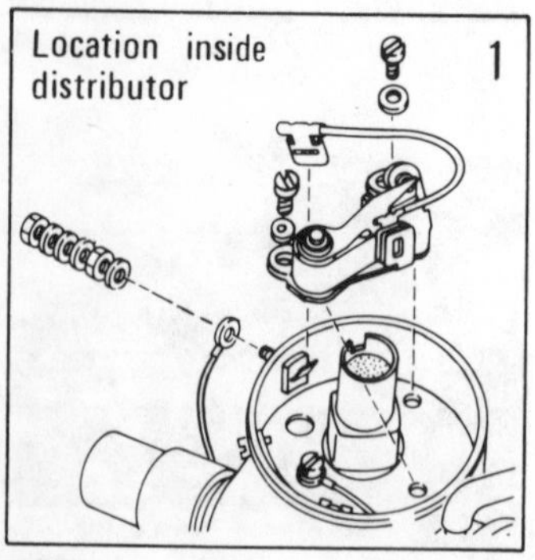

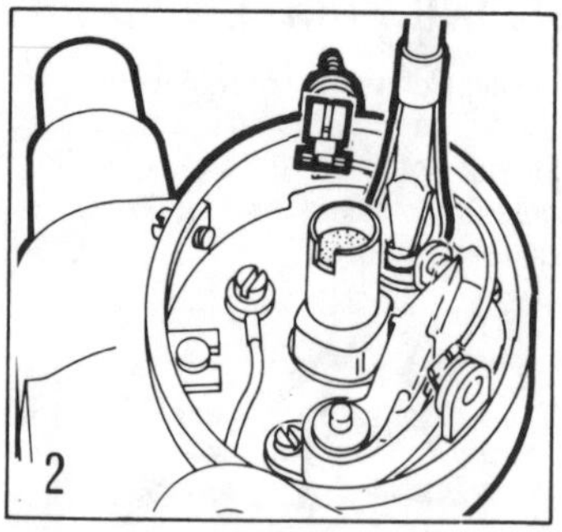

2. Remove points attaching screws being very careful not to drop screws inside distributor.
Remove the second set of points the same way, if equipped.

3. Remove screw attaching condenser to side of distributor if used. DO NOT DROP SCREW.

4. Wipe all dirt from distributor plate and cam.

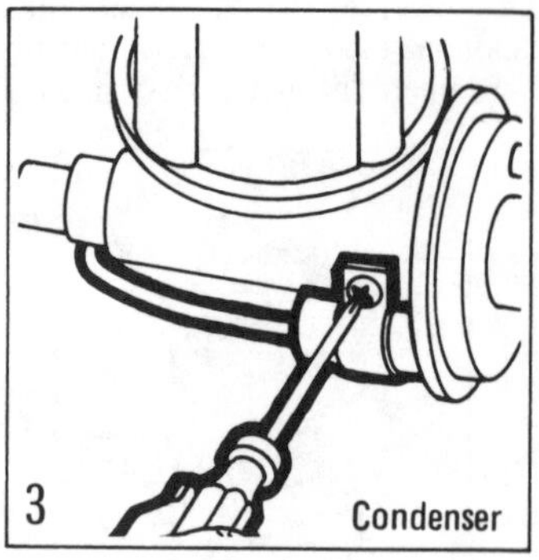

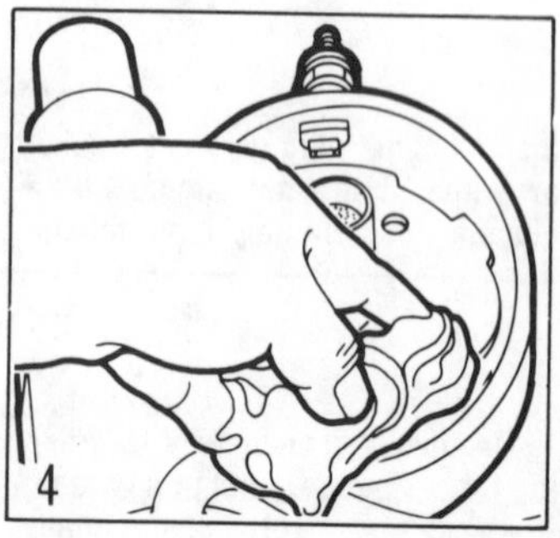

CAUTION: When removing screws from distributor, be sure to avoid any screws accidentally falling through distributor opening into engine. Use magnetic screwdriver.

INSTALLING POINTS AND CONDENSER

1. Apply small amount of heat resistant lube to distributor cam (lube sometimes supplied with new point sets, if not, purchase separately). Attach new condenser with screw if used.
2. Position new points sets in distributor. Attach retaining screws lightly.
3. Attach primary wire; attach condenser lead wire to condenser lead terminal. Do not allow either wire to touch distributor body or breaker plate.

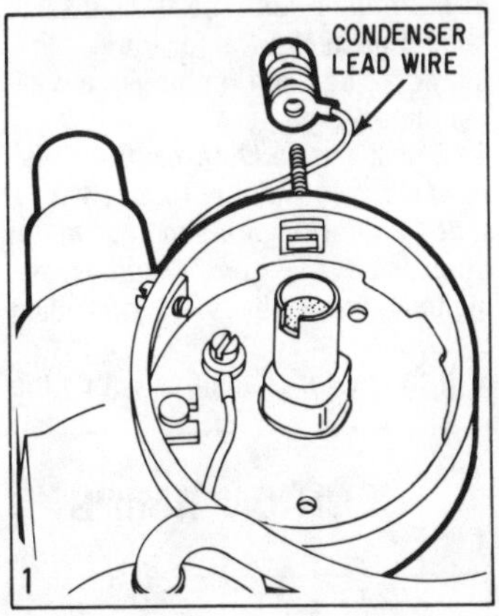

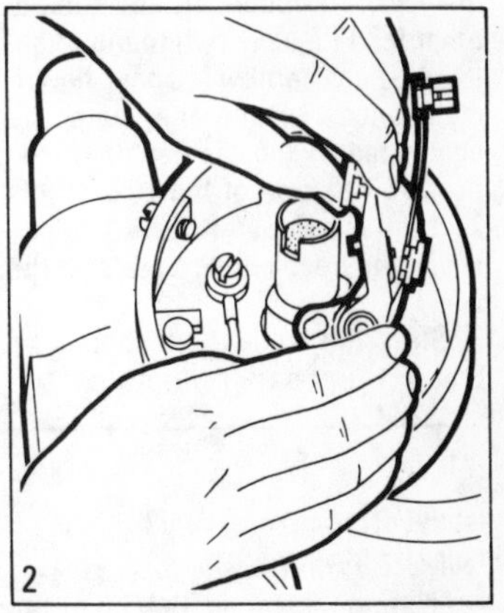

RESETTING THE CONTACT GAP

1. Check that point contacts meet squarely. If they do not, bend bracket supporting fixed contact using needle-nosed pliers.
2. Turn engine by ignition key (you'll need a helper) until rubbing block on point set is on one of the four high spots of distributor cam. You may use wrench on lower engine pulley to do this.
3. Insert screwdriver in slot near point contacts; twist to open or close gap.
4. Correct point gap is .018 in.
5. Insert correct size feeler gauge between open point contacts. If adjustment is needed, twist screwdriver to open or close points as needed.
6. Tighten screws when correct gap is obtained. Recheck gap; it might have changed from tightening holddown screws. Readjust if needed.

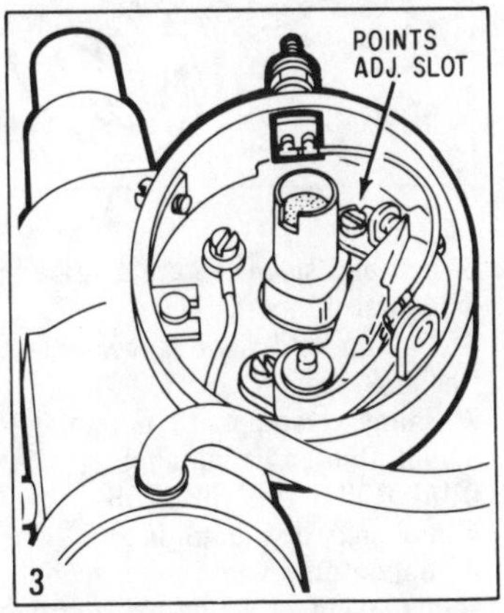

If your Corolla has dual ignition points, adjust them as you would on a single point system.

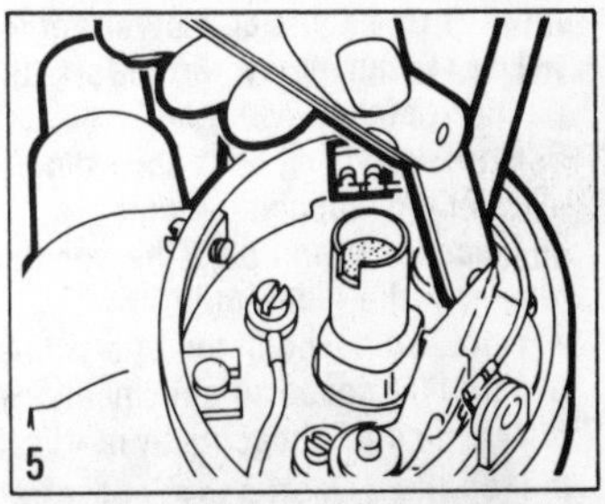

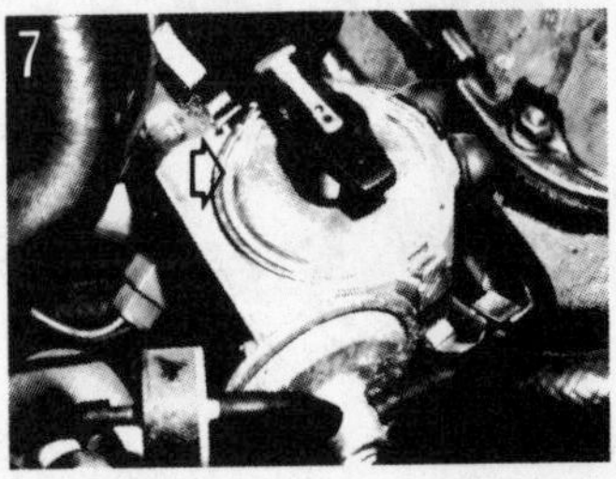

7. Replace radio static shield; align tab inside rotor with notch on distributor shaft; push rotor onto shaft. Rotor must be fully seated.
8. Replace distributor cap; install clips.

DWELL ANGLE

1. Connect a dwell meter to the ignition system, according to the manufacturer's instructions.
a. When checking the dwell on a conventional ignition system, connect one meter lead (usually black) to a metallic part of the car to ground the meter; the other lead (usually red) is connected to the coil primary post (the one with the small lead which runs to the distributor body);

b. When checking dwell on a model with transistorized ignition, ground one meter lead (usually black) to a metallic part of the car; hook up the other lead (usually red) to the negative (−) coil terminal. Under no circumstances should the meter be connected to the distributor or the positive (+) side of the coil.
2. If the dwell meter has a set line, adjust the needle until it rests on the line.
3. Start the engine. It should be warmed-up and running at the specified idle speed.
CAUTION: Be sure to keep fingers, tools, clothes, hair, and wires clear of the engine fan. The transmission should be in Neutral (or Park), parking brake set, and running in a well-ventilated area.
4. Check the reading on the dwell meter. If you have a Toyota with a four-cylinder engine and your meter doesn't have a four-cylinder scale, multiply the eight-cylinder reading by two.
5. If the meter reading is within the range specified in the "Tune-Up Specifications" chart, shut the engine off and disconnect the dwell meter.
6. If the dwell is not within specifications, shut the engine off and adjust the point gap as previously outlined. Increasing the point gap decreases the dwell angle and vice versa.
7. Adjust the points until dwell is within specifications, then disconnect the dwell meter. Adjust the timing.

IGNITION TIMING

SINGLE POINT
Adjusting timing is the important finishing touch to any tune-up. While not difficult, job requires timing light and dwell meter. Timing is listed on tune-up decal, in engine compartment of car.
1. Locate timing marks and pointer notches on engine and lower engine pulley. Clean away dirt. Mark the pointer notches with chalk.
2. Hook up timing light according to instructions supplied with it.
3. Disconnect and plug the vacuum line from the distributor.
4. Hook up tachometer and adjust engine idle speed to specifications.
5. Aim timing light at pulley marks. If the chalked marks do not align loosen distributor hold down screw or bolt and slowly rotate distributor until chalked marks align.

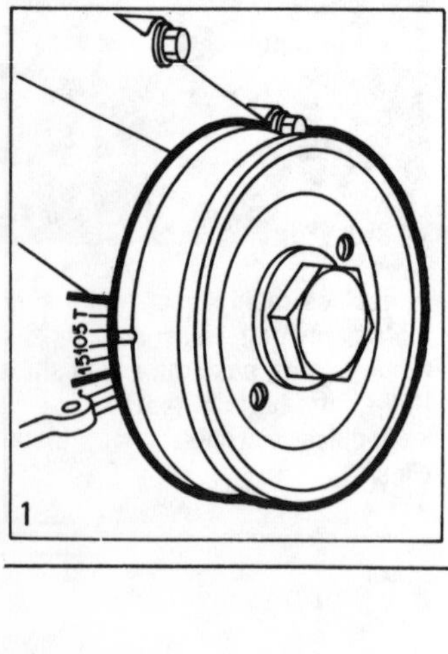

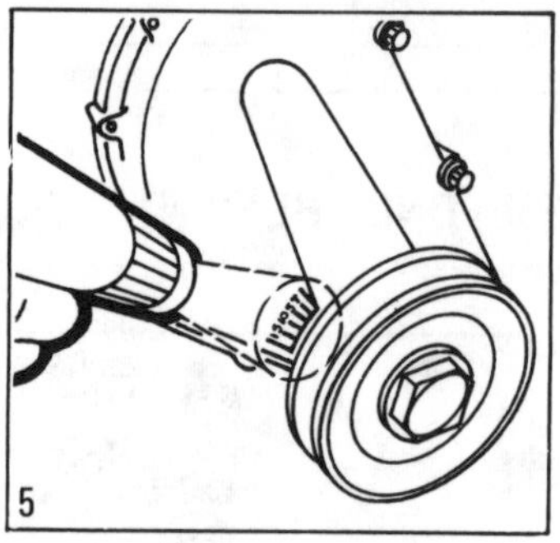

6. Tighten hold down screw or bolt. Recheck timing.
7. Readjust engine to normal idle speed. Detach timing light.
DUAL POINT DISTRIBUTOR
A dual point distributor is offered as an option on some Corolla models, sold outside of California, starting 1975.
To adjust the dual point system, proceed as follows:
1. Adjust the timing for the main set of points as previously outlined in the "Single Point" section.
2. Use a jumper wire to ground the terminal on the thermoswitch connector after removing the connector from the thermoswitch. The thermoswitch is threaded into the intake manifold and is connected to the dual point system relay. Be careful not to confuse it with any of the emission control system switches which are connected to the computer.

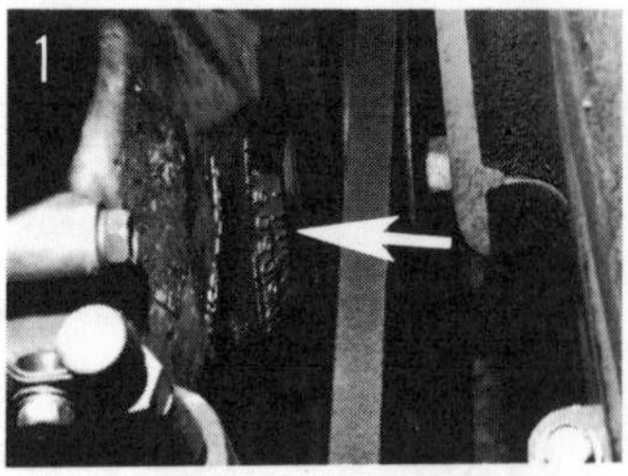

3. Check the timing with a light as described above, the timing should be 22° before top dead center (BTDC).
4. If the timing is off, connect a dwell meter to the negative side of the coil, and adjust the sub-points so that the dwell angle is 52°. The sub-points are adjusted in the same manner as the main points.
5. Remove the test equipment and reconnect the thermoswitch.

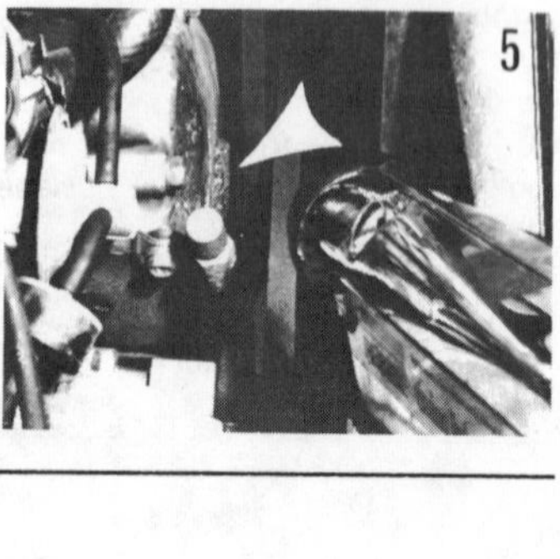

Fuel System

When gasoline is brought from the fuel tank, it mixes with air in the carburetor. This gas/air mixture enters engine thru the intake manifold, passes thru the intake valves and is burned in the combustion chamber.

The burned exhaust gas is then passed thru the exhaust valves to the exhaust system and to the outside air. In order to keep your car's engine running cleanly with minimal pollution, and avoid dangerous carbon monoxide fumes inside the vehicle, certain items should be checked from time to time.

KEEP THE AIR INTAKE CLEAN

The large round can that sits on top of the engine holds the air cleaner. Twice a year:

1. Remove air cleaner lid by removing wing nut, and, if so equipped, retaining clips.
2. Lift out air cleaner cartridge. Discard cartridge if used more than 18,000 miles, or if excessively dirty.
3. Wipe out air cleaner with a clean cloth.
4. Replace cartridge, install lid, and wing nut. Snap retaining clips.

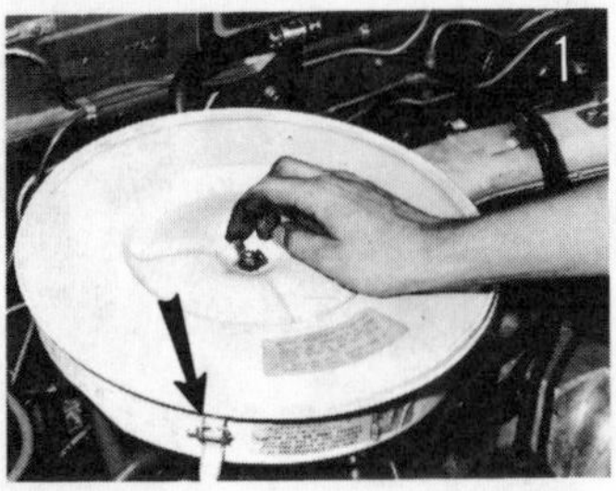

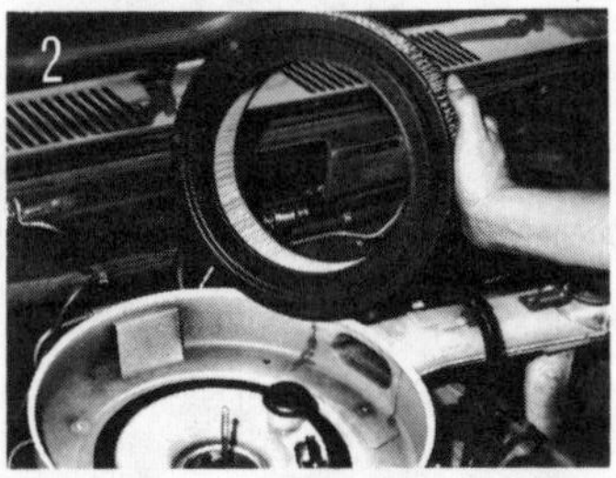

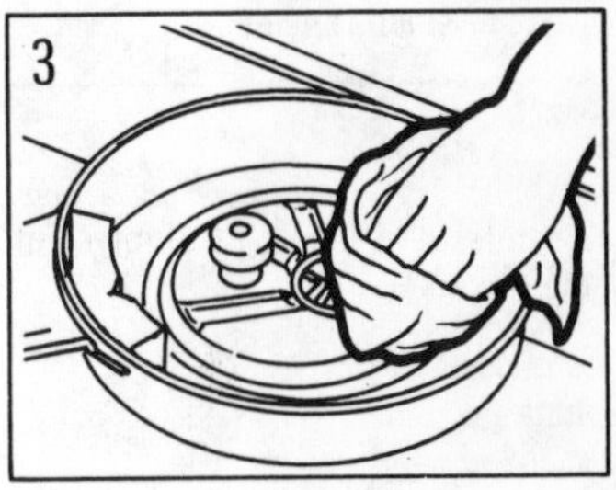

EMISSION CONTROL SYSTEMS

The most important part of a car's emission control system is the Positive Crankcase Ventilation (PCV) valve and its connecting hose. The PCV valve should be replaced every 12,000 miles (24,000 after 1972). This device keeps dirt and sludge from forming inside the engine. Make sure all PCV connections are tight. Check that the connecting hoses are clear and not clogged. Replace any brittle or broken hoses.

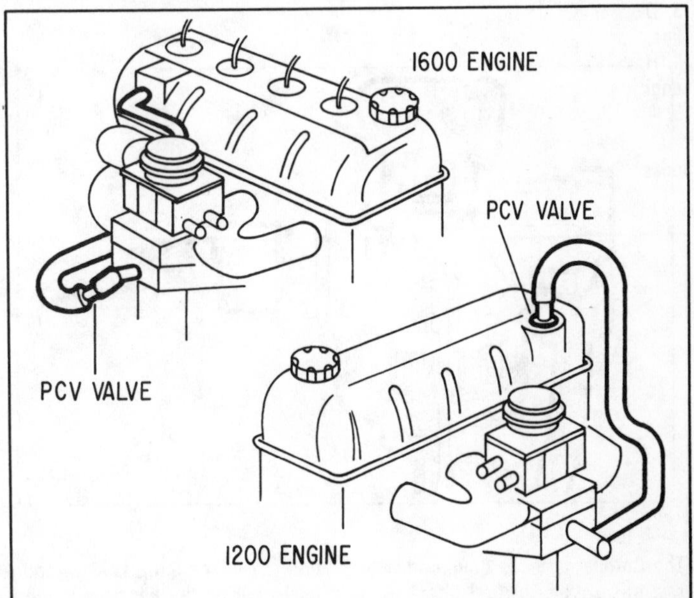

PCV VALVE REPLACEMENT

1. Pull valve from its location in rear part of valve cover (1200 cc engine). On 1600 cc engine valve is located in the hose line leading to intake manifold.
2. Squeeze the hose clamp(s) with a pair of pliers, remove the hose(s). Pull out valve.
3. Note where other end of the long hose connects. Remove the hose and flush it with solvent.
4. Reconnect the hose. Pinch the

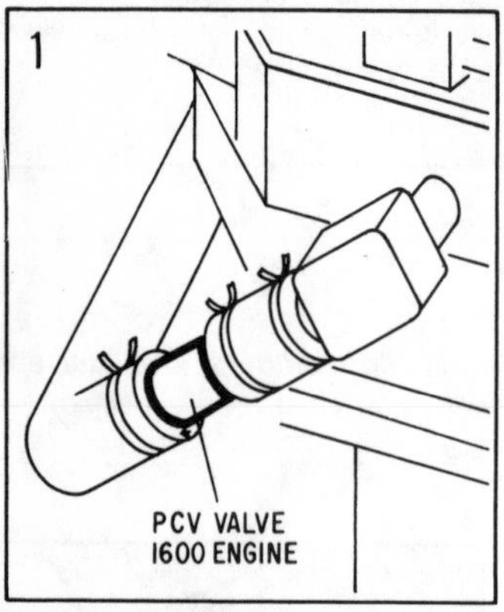

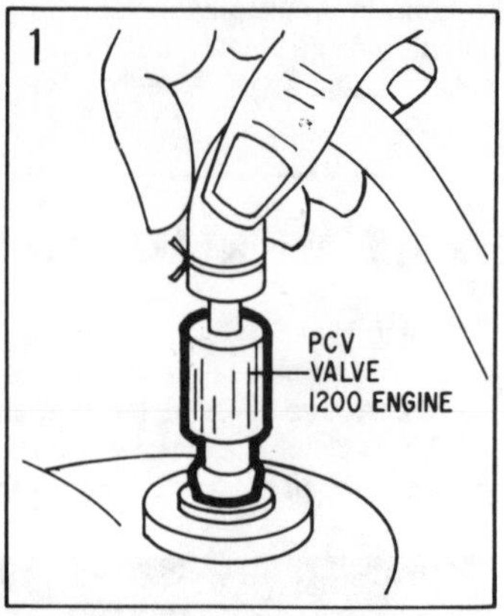

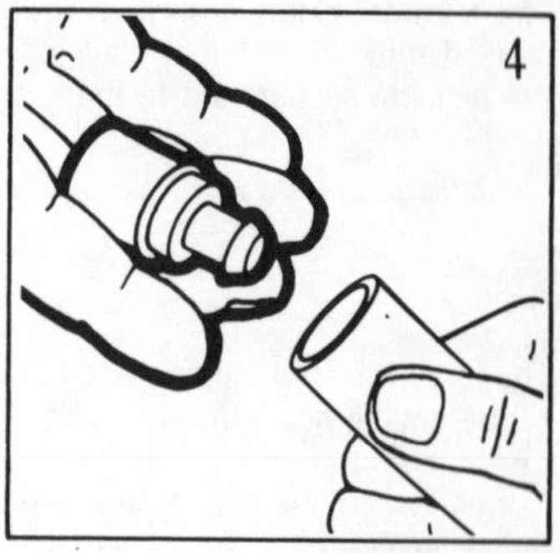

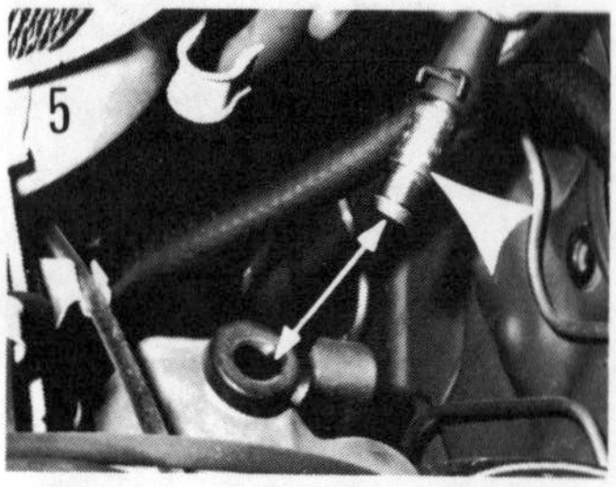

clamp(s) and insert PCV valve into the hose(s).

5. Insert the valve into the valve cover. (1600 only.)

FUEL FILTER REPLACEMENT

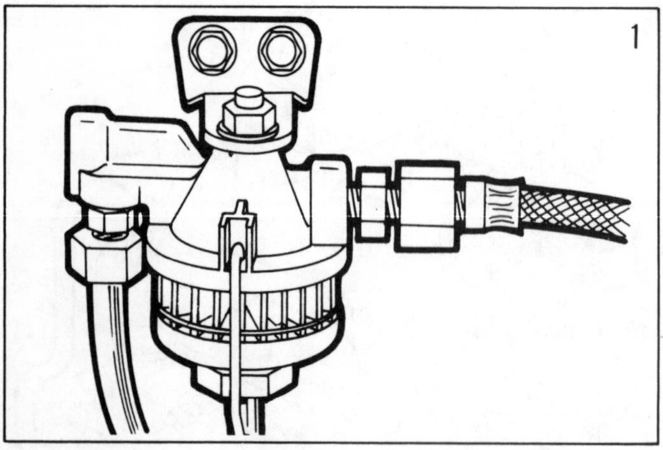

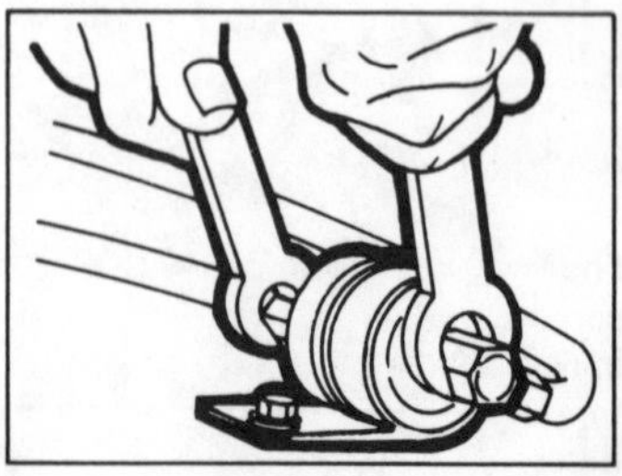

The Corolla series is equipped with two basic types of fuel filters. The 1200 series uses a cartridge type with a disposable element, while the 1600 series uses a throwaway type. Both types should be replaced every 30,000 (24,000 after 1972) miles as a dirty filter will starve the engine and cause poor running.

1. This type is located in the fuel line; it is not necessary to remove unit to replace filter. Loosen and remove nut on the filter bowl bail.
2. Withdraw the bowl, element spring, element and the bowl gasket.
3. Wash all of the parts in solvent and examine them for damage. Install a new filter element and bowl gasket.
4. Install components in the reverse order of their removal. Do not fully tighten the bail nut.

5. Seat the bowl by turning it slightly; tighten the bail nut full and check for leaks.

1. Unfasten the fuel intake hose. Use a wrench to loosen the attachment nut and another wrench on the opposite side to keep the filter from turning.
2. Remove the flexible fuel line from the other side of the filter. Unfasten the attaching screws from the filter bracket.
3. Install the new filter and reconnect the fuel lines. Start the engine and check for leaks.

1
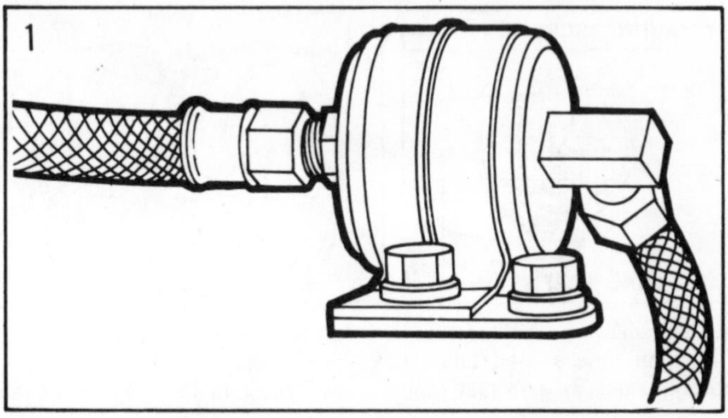

Safety Systems

PARKING LIGHTS, TURN SIGNALS AND STOP LIGHTS

Front combination parking light and turn signal bulbs are mounted in the parking light housing in the bumper. To replace, remove the retaining screws and remove the lens. To replace rear tail light, stop light, turn signal bulbs, on sedan, raise trunk lid and reach socket from inside trunk. On wagon, remove retaining screws and remove lens. Push down on bulb turning counterclockwise to remove. Insert new dual-element bulb in correct position (see note) and re-install socket in housing.

NOTE: When inserting new dual element bulb, note that knobs on side of bulb base are different distances from base tip. Match knobs to socket slots for proper fit.

BACK-UP LIGHTS

Sedans, to replace back-up light bulbs, raise trunk lid, and remove socket. On wagons, remove retaining screws and remove lens. Push down on bulb and turn counterclockwise to remove. Install new dual element bulb (see note) and replace socket or lens.

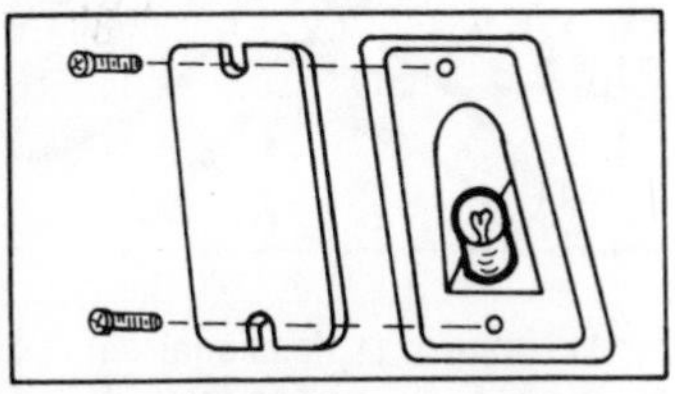

SIDE MARKER LIGHT

Front . . . Remove the retaining screws, and remove the lens. Push in on bulb, turning counterclockwise to remove.
Rear . . . On sedans, raise trunk lid. Reach bulb socket from inside car. Turn socket counterclockwise to remove. On wagon, remove three retaining screws and remove lens cover. Push down on bulb and turn counterclockwise to remove.

LICENSE PLATE LIGHTS

Remove screws and remove housing from bumper of sedan. On wagon, remove screws, lens cover and gasket. Push in on bulb turning counterclockwise.

INTERIOR DOME LIGHT

Unscrew dome light lens and remove from housing. To avoid blowing fuse, make sure doors are closed and dome light switch is in OFF position. Carefully lever the bulb straight out of the housing. Insert new bulb and re-install dome light lens.

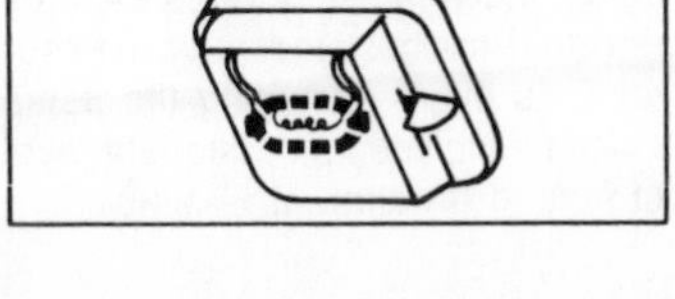

HEADLIGHT REPLACEMENT

1. Remove headlight trim ring retaining screws and remove the trim ring.

1

2. Remove the three short inner ring screws. Do not remove or tamper with the two longer screws, these are the headlight adjustment screws.

3. Remove the inner ring and pull the headlight out. Disconnect and remove the bulb.

4. Connect the plug to the rear of the

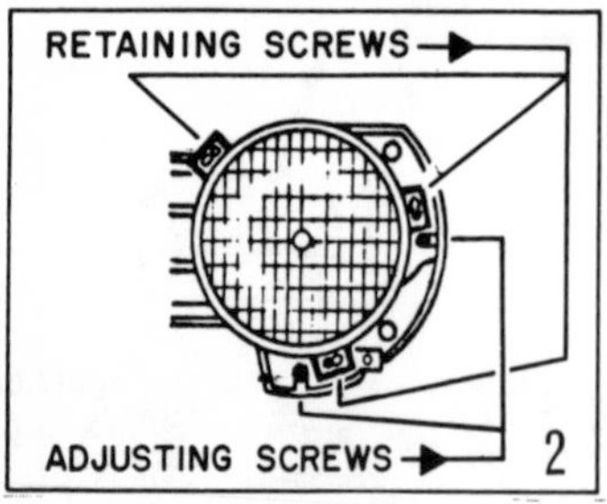

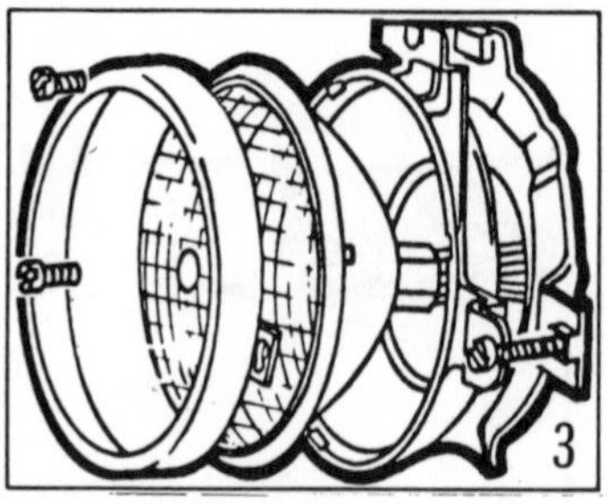

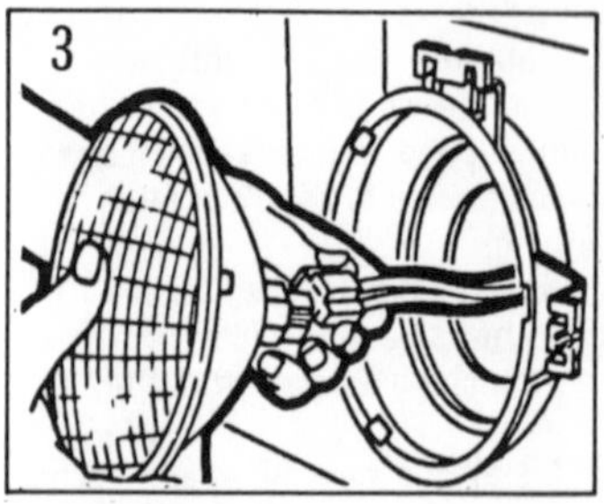

new bulb unit.
5. Position new sealed beam in headlight shell. Be sure that knobs on back of light (near outer edge) enter slots in shell.
6. Place retaining ring over sealed beam and fasten with three screws.
7. Install trim ring and tighten screws.

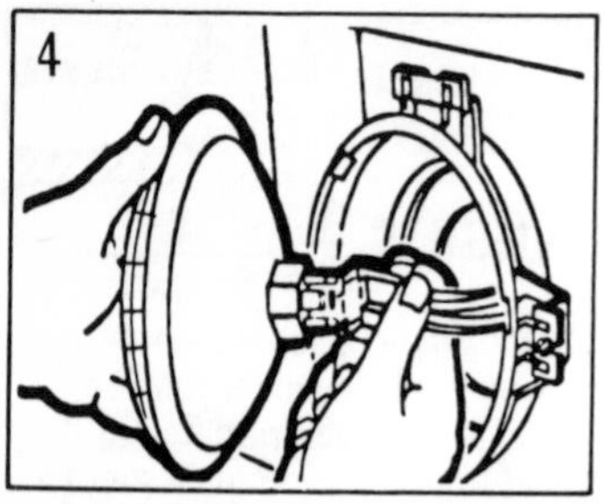

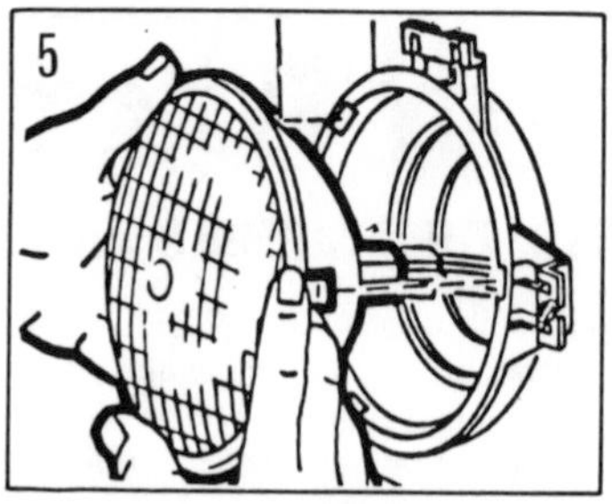

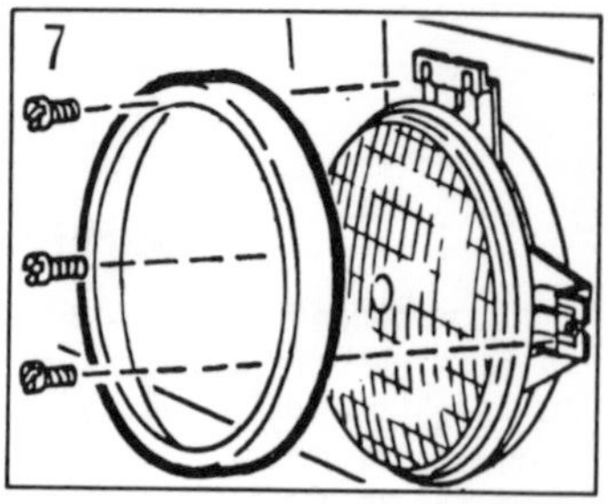

WINDSHIELD WIPER BLADE REPLACEMENT

To remove wiper blades lift up on spring release tab on wiper blade to wiper arm connector. Pull wiper blade off wiper arm. Snap replacement blade assembly into place. On later models, you can replace the wiper blade insert. Press the old

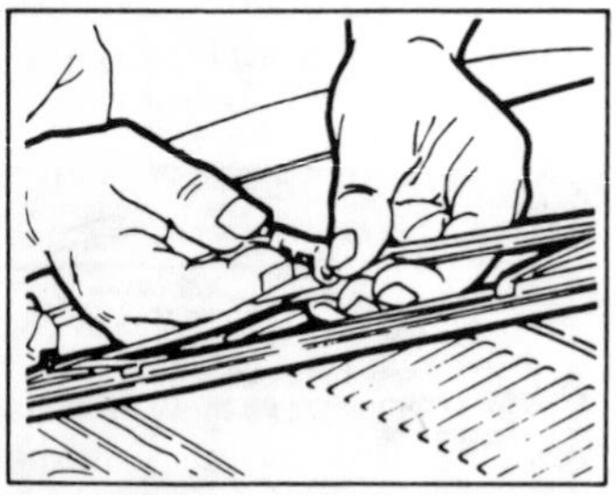

rubber insert down, away from wiper blade to free it from its retaining clips on blade ends. Slide insert from blade. Position new insert on wiper blade. Bend insert upward slightly to engage retaining clips.

HORN PROBLEMS

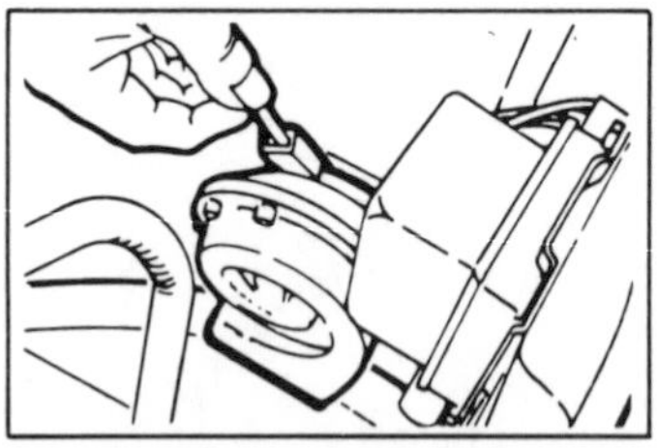

If horn sounds and does not stop, this is due to short circuit in wiring. Disconnect wiring connector under hood and have professional service shop check horn wiring circuit.

STEERING PROBLEMS

See steering system check in Suspension Section. Check tire pres-

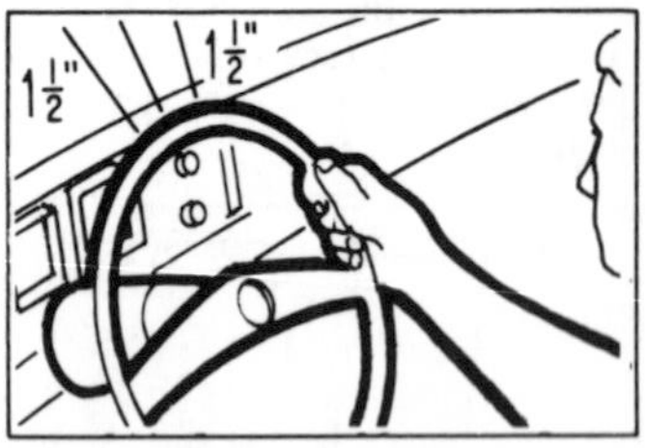

sures. Have a professional service shop check all components in the front end and steering system.

WASHER SYSTEM

If washer fails to squirt properly, raise hood and check system hose connections. Be sure washer fluid container has fluid. Check spout openings for clogging.

Keep container filled with fluid mixture of washer solvent and water. If road spray buildup on windshield is a chronic problem, add 1 tablespoon dishwasher detergent to solvent/water mixture when re-filling container.

NOTE: The car's windshield washer pump mechanism is lubricated by the fluid in the windshield washer tank. To avoid damaging the pump mechanism, keep an adequate level of fluid in the tank at all times.

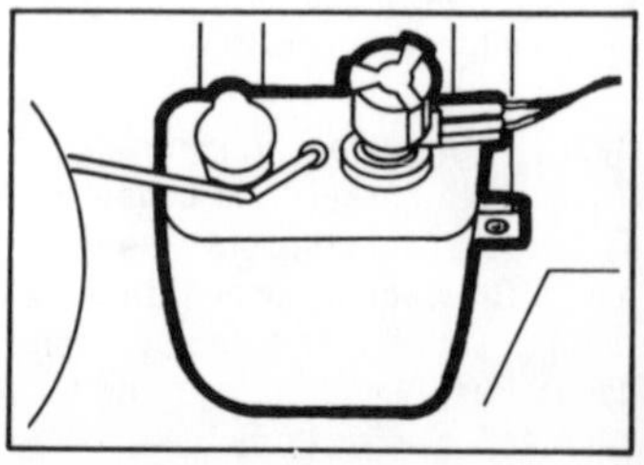

Electrical System

CHECK BATTERY FLUID

To ensure starting ability at all times check your battery condition periodically. You'll need to check battery electrolyte (fluid) level in each of the six cells. Check battery cable connections for tightness and inspect for accumulated corrosion.
SAFETY NOTE: Wear gloves when working on battery.

1. Remove plastic filler caps on top of battery. Fluid should be up to lower end of filler hole and covering the plates. If fluid is low add clean, cold tap water. If your area has hard water, use only distilled water available at auto supply, food or drug stores.
2. Replace any lost caps immediately.

CAUTION: NEVER LIGHT A MATCH OR SMOKE near the top of a battery. Batteries give off explosive hydrogen gas.

NOTE: Battery that often checks low on fluid could mean:
A. Battery is getting old, due for replacement; have charge capacity checked at service shop.
B. Connections may be corroded or loose; clean/replace as needed (see below).
C. Alternator or voltage regulator not functioning properly; this happens far less often than A or B above.

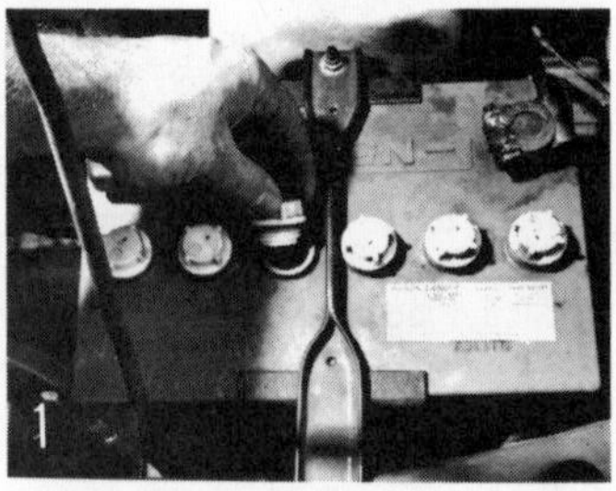
1

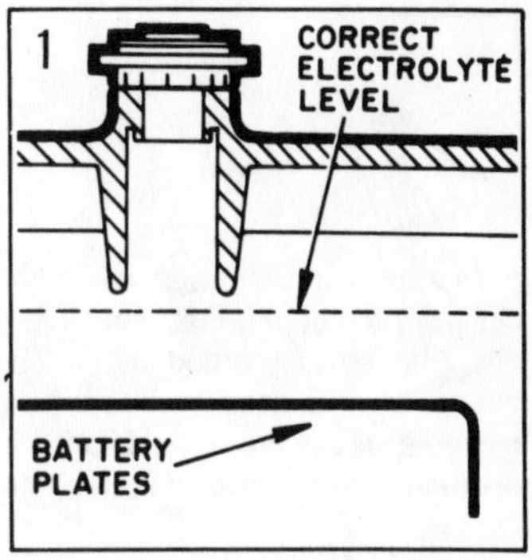

1

CLEAN THOSE BATTERY TERMINALS

As time goes by, battery terminals build up a dry powdery, whitish material. This material is corrosive and will gradually eat thru battery cables if not cleaned off periodically.
1. Loosen and remove battery connections.
2. Brush off all loose corrosion; use stiff bristle brush. Do not get this material into eyes or on open cuts. Wash off at once.
3. If corrosion build-up is extremely heavy and brushing does not remove all of it, mix 2 tablespoons baking soda to 1 cup water. Pour solution directly onto terminals and connectors. Allow to soak a few minutes and rinse off. Continue brushing to remove all traces of corrosion build-up. Do not allow cleaning solution to enter battery.
4. Replace connectors on battery terminal posts and tighten.
5. Liberally smear battery terminal posts and cable connectors with petroleum jelly.

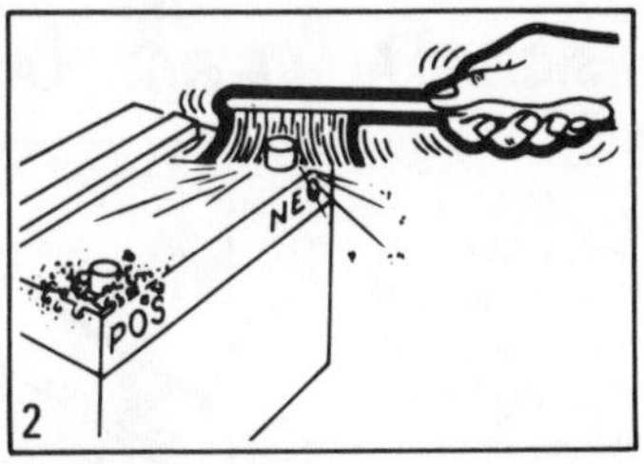

2

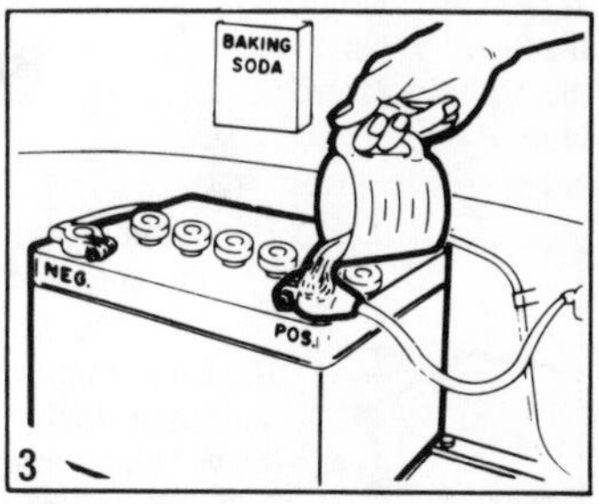

3

REPLACE FAULTY BATTERY CABLES

If battery cable strands become frayed, broken or corroded, replace cable immediately. Delay in correcting this condition could lead to sudden failure to start the engine. Can also weaken battery.
1. Loosen and remove battery connections. Clean OFF any corrosion.
2. Disconnect negative cable from its attachment to engine or chassis. Disconnect positive cable from its attachment to starter relay.
3. Attach new cables making sure positive and negative cables are on proper terminals. They are not identical.
4. Replace connectors on battery terminal posts and tighten.
5. Liberally smear battery terminal posts and cable connectors with petroleum jelly.

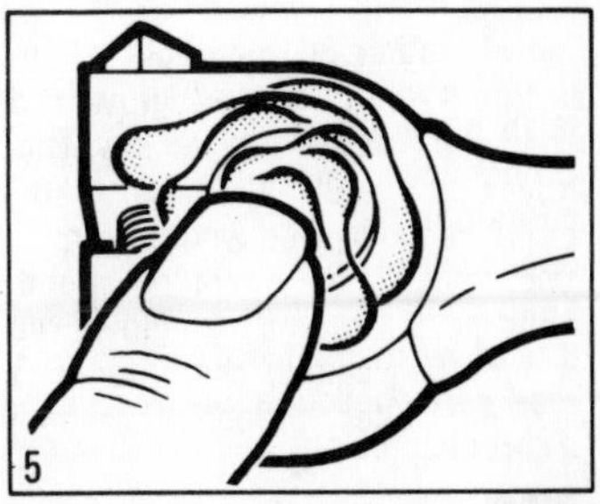
5

BATTERY HOLDDOWN

The clamp device which holds battery in place should be checked periodically. If loose, tighten. Clean off corrosion buildup. Severely corroded holddown components should be replaced before they break.

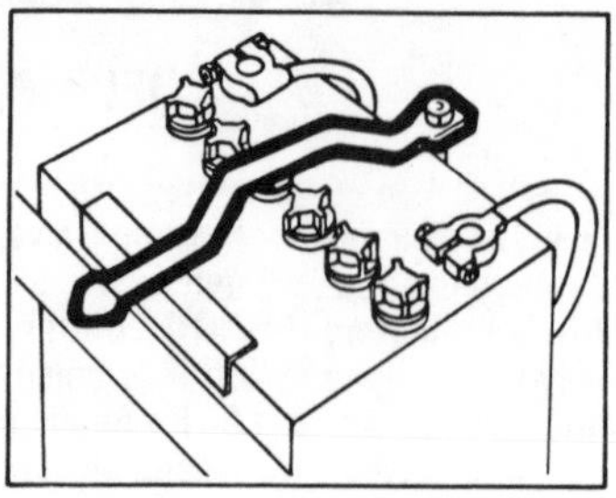

ELECTRICAL FUSES

If any lights, switches or electrical circuits do not operate, check for possible blown (burned out) fuse. Fuses are located in fuse box mounted under the left side of the instrument panel inside car. Replace blown fuse with same amperage new fuse. If fuses blow regularly, have car checked by professional service shop for possible short circuit.

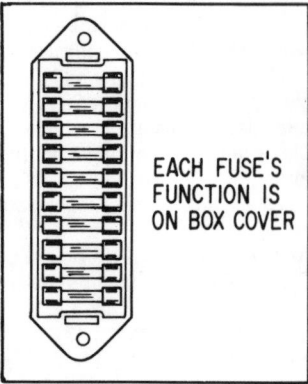

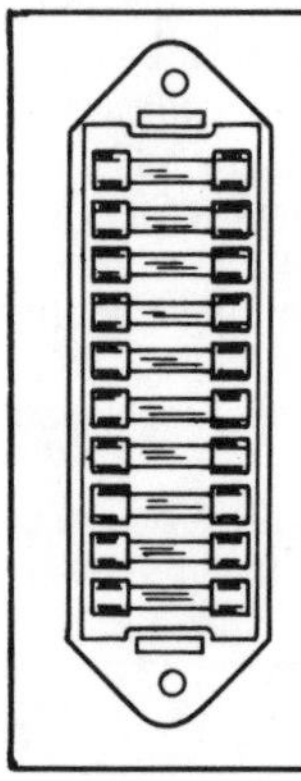
EACH FUSE'S
FUNCTION IS
ON BOX COVER

TURN SIGNAL AND 4-WAY FLASHER

Turn signals and 4-way flashers will operate only if: A. All light bulbs are OK. B. Flasher unit is not burned out. The flasher unit is located on the left, under the dash. To replace, remove the wiring connector, grasp with fingers and pull connector out. To remove flasher, remove screw from bracket. REPLACE ONLY WITH SAME TYPE FLASHER.

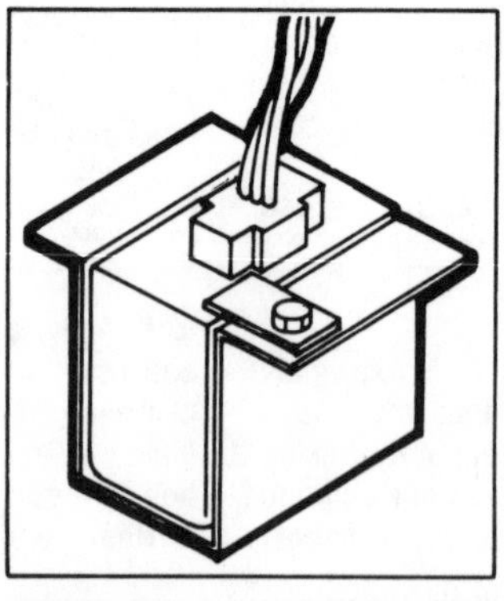

ALTERNATOR

Red alternator warning light on instrument panel should glow red when you first turn ignition key. This proves bulb is OK. Alternator warning light should go off when engine is running at normal operating speed. If alternator warning light glows red at operating speed, alternator isn't charging battery properly. Common causes are:

A. Fan belts are loose and slipping on alternator pulley. Tighten or replace belts.

B. Battery terminals, cables are loose or corroded. Clean; tighten; replace bad cables.

If A or B do not correct problem, alternator or voltage regulator may be faulty. This happens far less often, and can only be checked by mechanic with proper electrical testing equipment.

Alternator Caution: Alternator can be permanently damaged by short-circuiting terminal connections. When working around or moving alternator, always keep metal tools or engine parts from terminals.

REAR WINDOW DEFOGGER SYSTEM

Do not clean inside of rear window fitted with defogger system with any abrasive material. This could destroy carbon-copper wires. Use only soft rag and mild detergent/water mixture. Dry carefully.

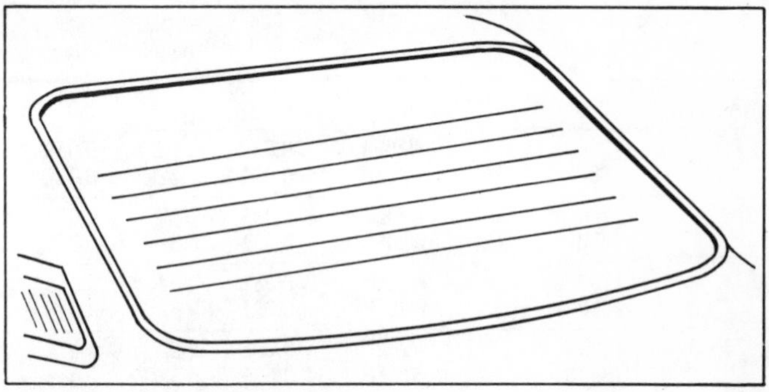

Air Conditioner

WARNING!—Never attempt to tighten fittings, disassemble or do any work on your car's A/C system. Consult a professional mechanic about A/C system problems and their correction. Your auto air conditioner (A/C) is a delicate, closed system. If air, dirt or water get into it, or if refrigerant escapes, the A/C unit will not cool a car interior. Among things you can do are:

1. Keep condenser grille clean. Check for dirt and debris; periodically remove dead insects, leaves, etc., with stiff bristle brush. Straighten any bent fins—carefully.
2. Keep radiator filled to correct level. (See Cooling System section). If fluid needs to be added, add antifreeze rather than water.
3. Keep radiator coolant at a 50/50 water/antifreeze mixture.
4. Flush cooling system and replace with fresh coolant mixture at least every 12,000 miles. (See Cooling System section).
5. Radiator cap should be tight and sealed properly. If sealing gasket is cracked, cut or worn, replace cap with new 15 lb. unit.
6. Check fan belt tension periodically. (See Cooling System section). Replace glazed, frayed or cut fan belts, before they fail entirely.
7. Check periodically for bubbles in the A/C sight glass. Sight glass is located in the head of the receiver/drier vessel. Sight glass is no larger than the head of a large nail. It may be dirty. Wipe clean for best visibility.

PROCEED AS FOLLOWS:

a) With engine and A/C system running, look for passage of refrigerant in sight glass. You'll be looking for a stream of milky white bubbles as they pass through sight glass. It is best to watch sight glass and have someone else start the car and turn on the A/C system. Allow to run for a few minutes.

b) If you observe no bubbles, and air flow from A/C unit in the car is passing cold air, everything is OK.

c) If no bubbles appear in sight glass, and air flow from the A/C unit in the car is not delivering cold air, the system may be low on refrigerant and could need a re-charge. Shut off the system and do not operate it.

d) If bubbles appear, system is low on refrigerant.

e) If you suspect refrigerant loss based on tests performed above, have system checked by a professional A/C service shop. They can confirm refrigerant loss, recharge the system and check for system leakage.

NOTE: Once a week or so, even in winter, run A/C system for about 5 minutes as you drive. This keeps system internally lubricated, prevents hoses hardening.

TOYOTA COROLLA

TUNE-UP SPECIFICATIONS

YEAR	MODEL	SPARK PLUG Type	SPARK PLUG Gap (in.)	DISTRIBUTOR Point Dwell (deg.)	DISTRIBUTOR Point Gap (in.)	IGNITION TIMING Man. Trans. (deg.) ■	IGNITION TIMING Auto Trans. (deg.) ■	IDLE SPEED Man. Trans. (rpm) ■	IDLE SPEED Auto Trans. (rpm) ■
1970	1200	W20EP	0.031	52	0.018	5A	5A	650	650
1971	1200	W20EP	0.031	52	0.018	5A	5A	650	650
	1600	W20EP	0.031	52	0.018	5B	5B	750	650
1972	1200	W20EP	0.031	52	0.018	5B	—	650	—
	1600	W20EP	0.031	52	0.018	5B	5B	750	650
1973	1200	W20EP	0.031	52	0.018	5B	—	600	—
	1600	W20EP	0.031	52	0.018	5B	5B	750	650
1974	1200	W20EP	0.031	52	0.018	5B	—	750	—
	1600①	W20EP	0.031	52	0.018	5B	5B	750	800
	1600②	W20EP	0.031	52	0.018	10B	10B	850	850
1975-76	1600	W16EP	0.030	52③	0.018	10B④	10B④	850	850
1977	1600	See Underhood Specification Sticker							

■ Manual transmission is in Neutral; Automatic transmission is in Drive
① USA—except California
② California only
③ Dual-point—main 57°; sub 52°
④ Dual-point—main 12B; sub 19-22B

NOTE: The underhood specifications sticker often reflects tune-up specification changes made in production. Sticker figures must be used if they disagree with those in this chart.

CAPACITIES

YEAR	MODEL	ENGINE OIL With Filter	ENGINE OIL Without Filter	TRANSMISSION Pts. to Refill after Draining MANUAL	TRANSMISSION Pts. to Refill after Draining AUTOMATIC	DRIVE AXLE (pts.)	COOLING SYSTEM (qts.)
1970-74	Corolla 1200	3.7	2.9	1.8	5.0	2.0	5.6
1971-74	Corolla 1600	3.9	3.0	1.6	5.0①	2.0	6.8
1975-77	Corolla 1600	4.6	3.7	1.6	6.1	2.2	8.2

① 3-speed: 6.1

Toyota Corona/Mark II

Lubrication and Oil Change

BRAKE FLUID LEVEL CHECK

Check brake and clutch fluid levels in the master cylinder every time the oil level is checked . . . sooner if braking feels inadequate, or clutch will not disengage properly. Add fluid when low.

Recommended grade: SAE 70R-3 (DOT 3).

Master cylinders are located under the hood on the left side. They are clear plastic containers. Fluid level will appear through the plastic.

1. Compare level with mark or ridge, or if unmarked, keep at least 3/4 full. Snap off cap and add fluid, if necessary.

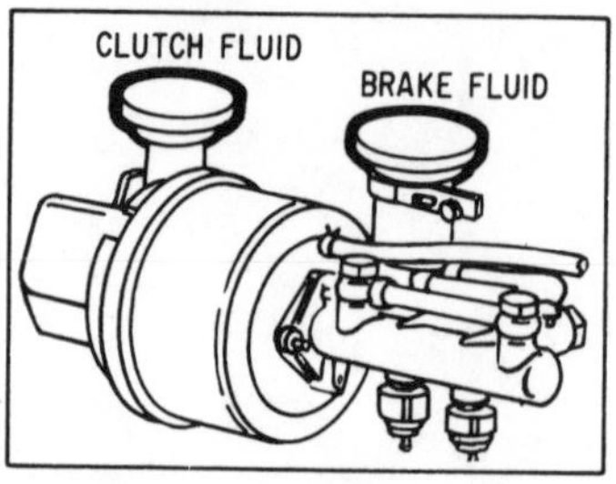

2. Replace cap securely. DO NOT OVERFILL.
3. If fluid level was low, check again in a few days.
4. If fluid repeatedly checks low, there is a leak somewhere in the system.

MANUAL TRANSMISSION FLUID LEVEL CHECK

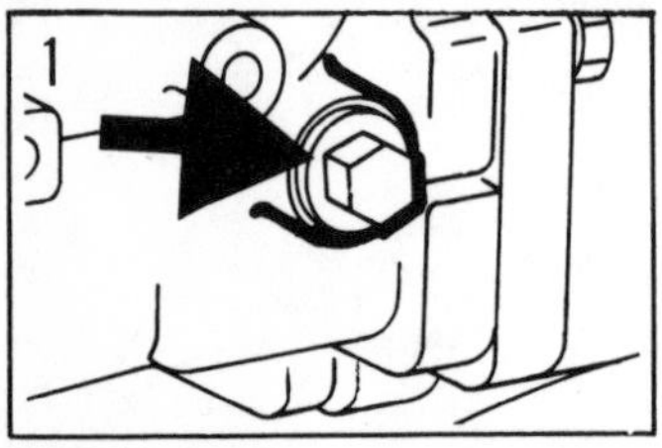

TOYOTA SAYS . . . check manual transmission fluid level every 6000 miles. Car should be parked level. Recommended grade: API grade GL-4, SAE80.

TOOLS NEEDED . . . adjustable wrench, bulb syringe.

1. Locate the transmission filler plug on the side of the transmission from underneath the car.

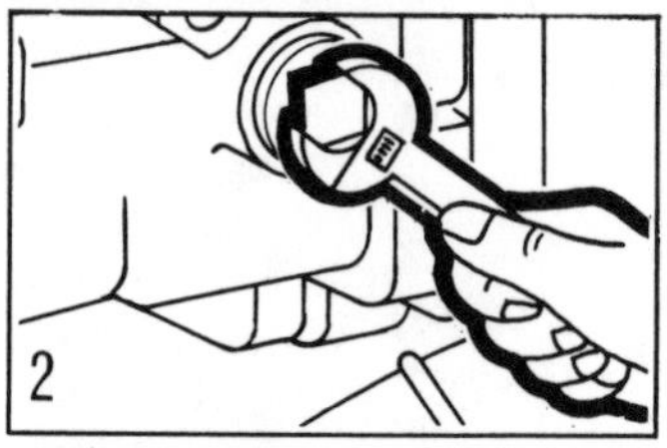

2. Wipe road dirt from filler plug area before loosening. Remove plug with adjustable wrench.
3. Insert your finger to check fluid level. The fluid should be right up to the bottom edge of the hole.
4. Add fluid as needed with hand bulb syringe.
5. Replace filler plug; tighten.

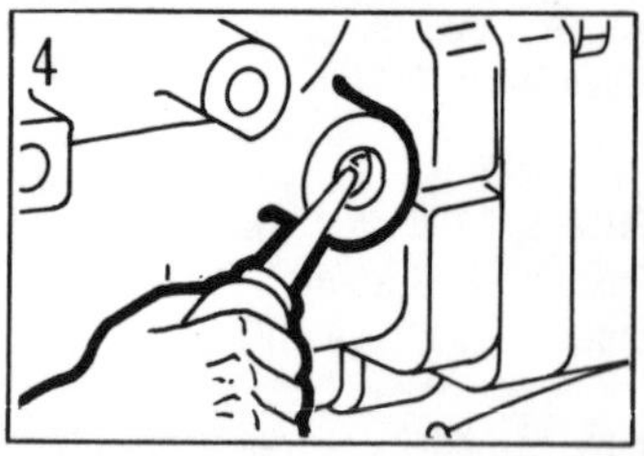

AUTOMATIC TRANSMISSION FLUID LEVEL CHECK

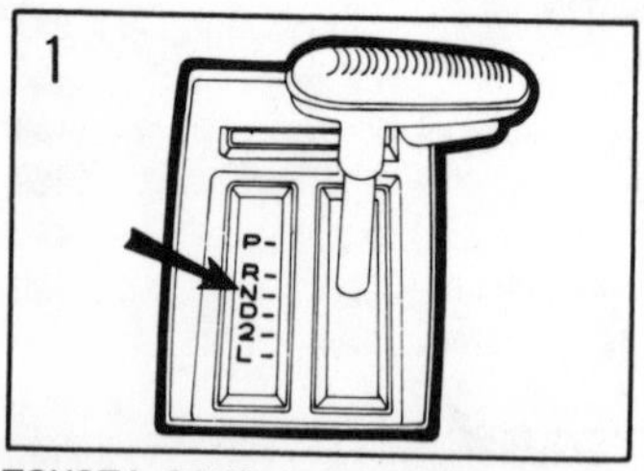

TOYOTA SAYS . . . check automatic transmission fluid (ATF) every 3000 miles. Recommended grade: Type F.

TOOLS NEEDED . . . Long neck filler funnel.

1. Start the engine and idle it for a few minutes. Apply the parking brake. Shift the transmission through every range, and return it to Neutral.

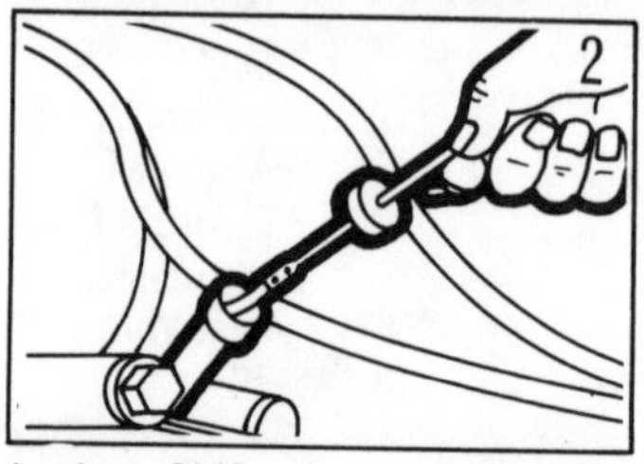

2. Pull out dipstick. Wipe clean. Push dipstick all the way back in; remove it again.
3. Choose the "hot" or "cold" range on the stick according to the transmission temperature. If fluid is between notches, do not add. If fluid is below lower mark, add enough ATF to bring level up as necessary. DO NOT OVERFILL.
4. Add ATF thru transmission dipstick hole by means of long-neck filler funnel.

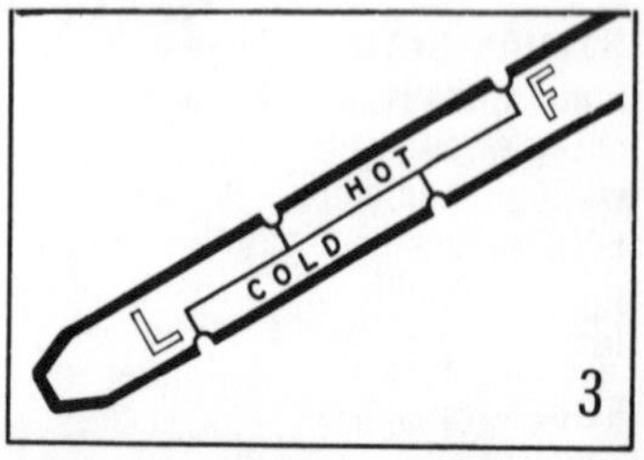

REAR AXLE LUBRICANT

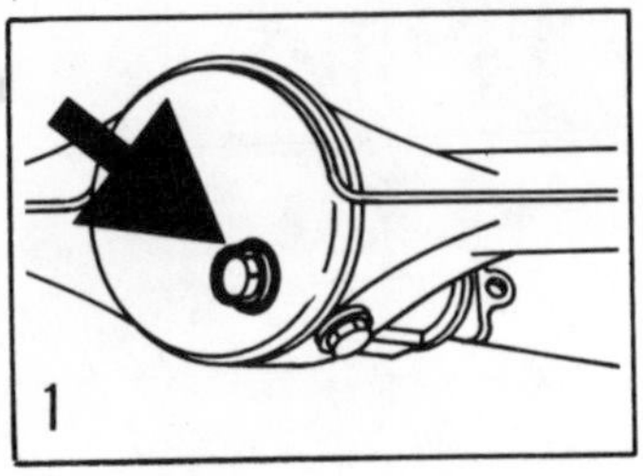

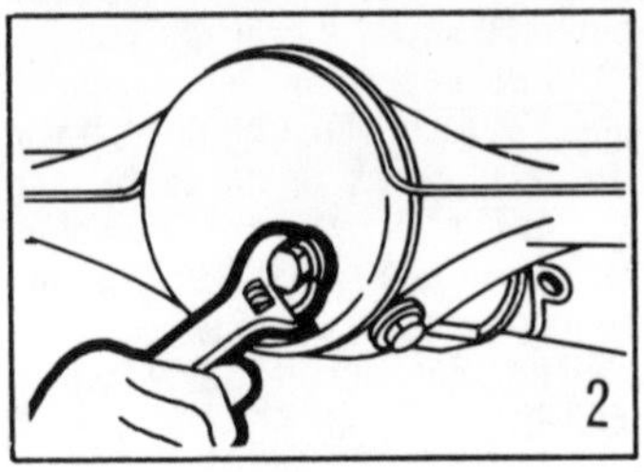

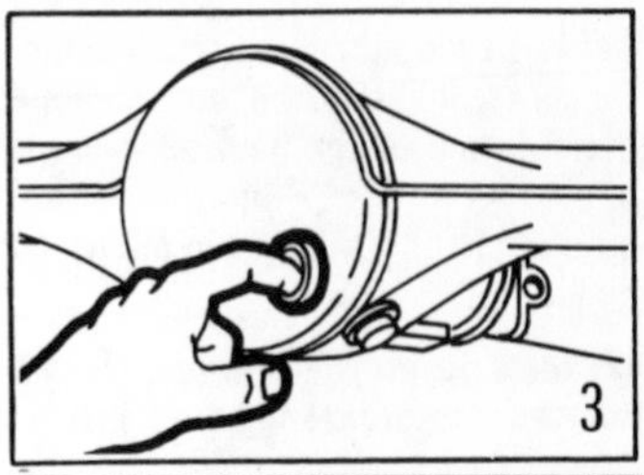

TOYOTA SAYS . . . check rear axle lube level every 6000 miles. Recommended grade: APIGL-5 (SAE 90).
TOOLS . . . adjustable hand wrench; bulb syringe.
1. Locate filler plug on forward side of rear axle housing.
2. Wipe plug area clean; remove plug with wrench.
3. Adequate fluid level should show lubricant at level of filler plug.
4. If fluid level is low, add as needed, with a hand bulb syringe.
5. Replace filler plug; tighten.

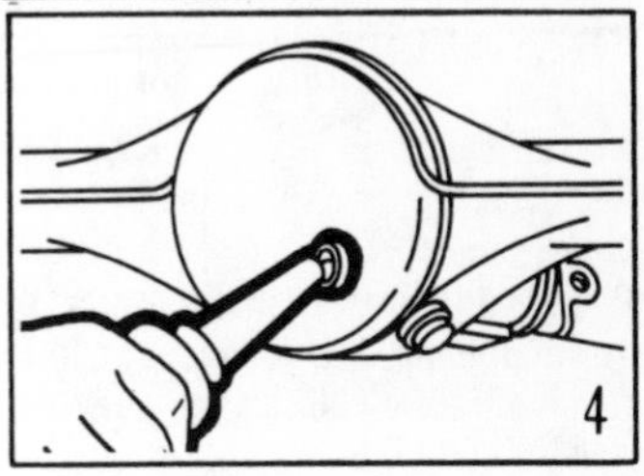

OIL AND FILTER CHANGE

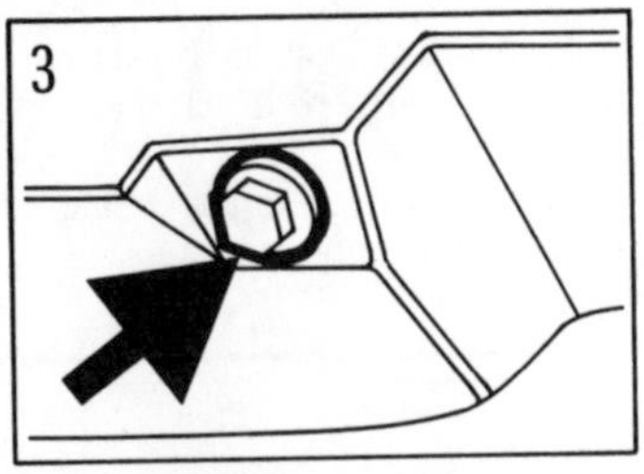

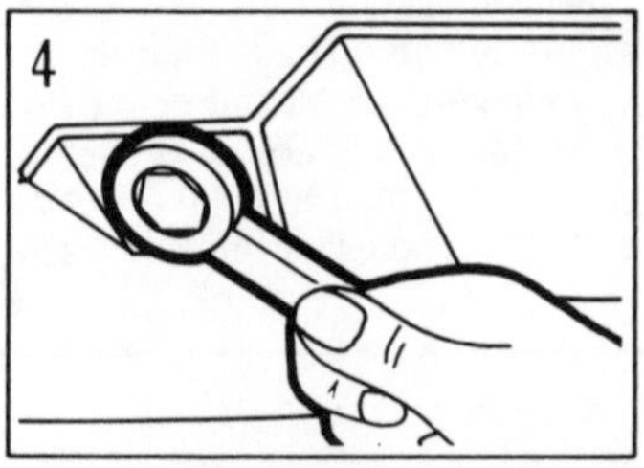

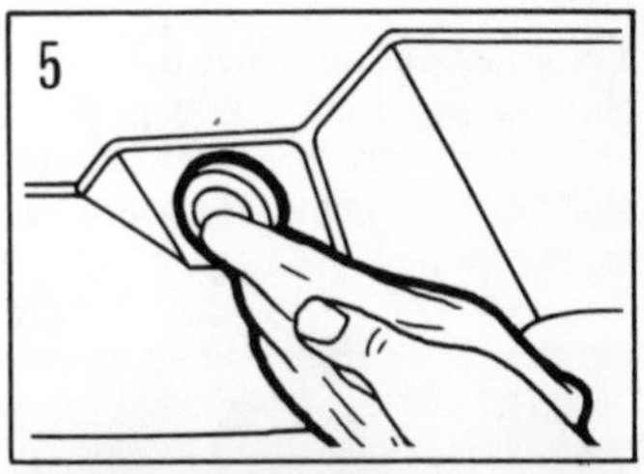

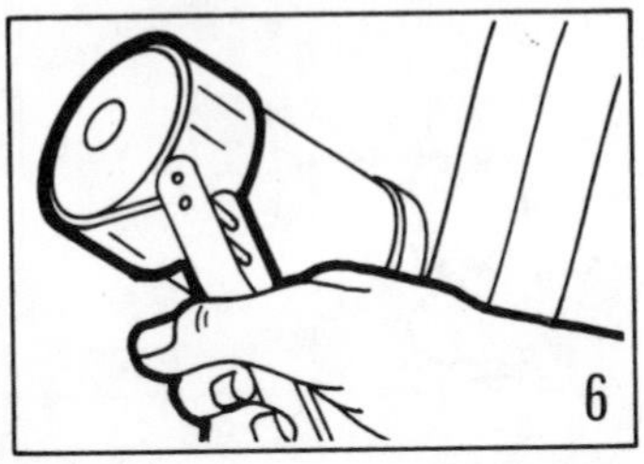

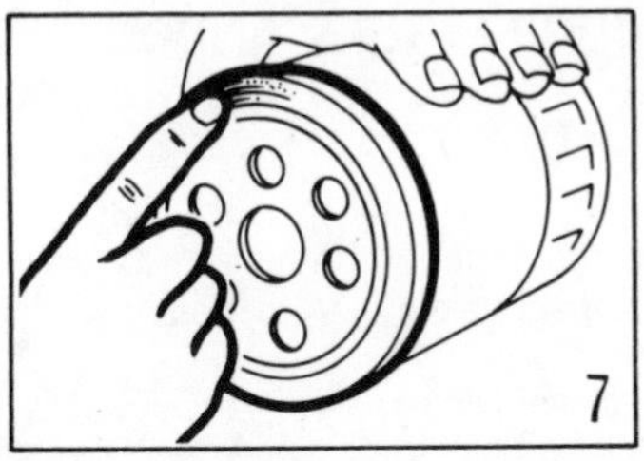

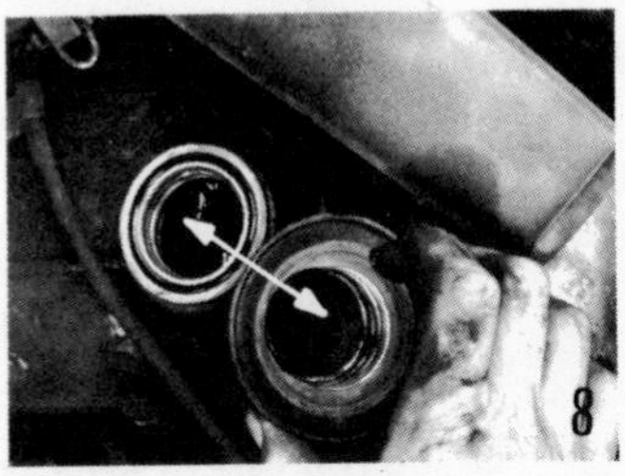

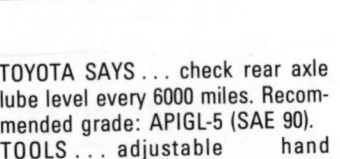

TOYOTA SAYS . . . Change oil and filter initially at 1000 miles; then change oil every 3000 miles or 3 months; and change the filter every 6000 miles or 6 months. Recommended grade: SE. Check oil level at least once a week.

TOOLS & MATERIALS . . . adjustable wrench; medium size screwdriver; oil filter removal wrench; drain pan for old oil; oil pouring spout; new oil filter (if required); other lubricants as specified.

1. If engine is cold, start up and idle for about 5 minutes.
2. Park car on level ground. Turn engine off.
3. Locate oil drain plug on underside of engine. Place drain pan under plug.
4. Remove drain plug with wrench. Let ALL dirty oil drain out.
5. Wipe plug and area around drain hole clean. Replace drain plug; tighten it.
6. Locate oil filter. Move drain pan under filter. Loosen filter with oil filter wrench. Unscrew; remove filter by hand.
7. Smear fresh oil over surface of rubber gasket (washer) of new filter. Install new filter by hand only. Do NOT use wrench. Turn filter until gasket makes contact. Tighten an additional half turn only . . . NO MORE.
8. Locate oil filler cap on top of engine. Remove cap.
9. Punch oil pouring spout into top of oil can. Pour all cans of new oil into filler hole. Wipe filler cap clean and replace it. Be sure to reattach all hoses.

NOTE: If filler cap is very dirty, rinse in turpentine or gasoline. Dry before replacing.

10. Check new oil level at dipstick. Pull out dipstick, wipe clean.

11. Push dipstick back into engine. Be sure to insert all the way. Remove dipstick and check new oil level. It should be above "F" line. If not, be sure to check if you put in all the oil called for.

12. Start up engine and idle for 3-5 minutes. Oil signal light on instrument panel will glow red when engine is first started. Light should go out in 30 seconds or less.

13. Stop engine and check for oil leaks at drain plug and filter. If you find any, check tightness of plug and/or filter, also for condition of filter gasket to see that it has not become pinched or damaged when installing. Recheck oil level, which should now be at "F".

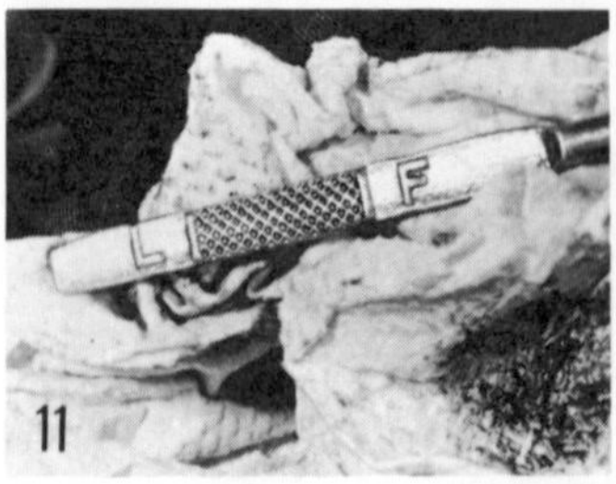

SPEEDOMETER CABLE LUBRICATION

If speedometer pointer tends to quiver or jump, or if unit makes a low, rasping sound, lubrication may be needed.

1. Locate cable shaft attachment directly behind speedometer dial.

2. Remove retaining clip. Unscrew cable from speedometer.

3. Pull inner cable completely out of outer casing. Note carefully which end is top. Check for wear or frayed strands. If damaged, replace inner cable with new one.

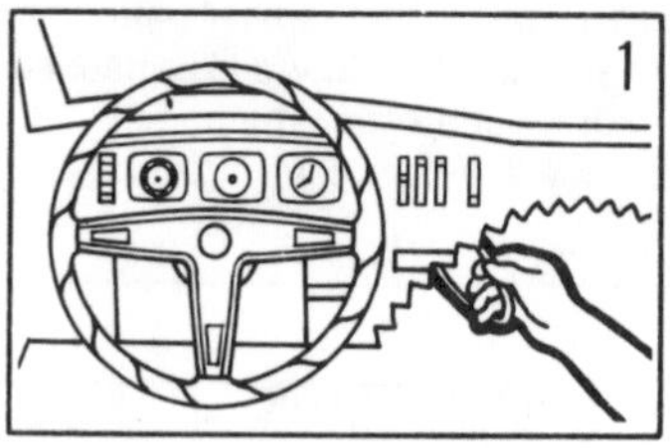

4. Apply generous amount of speedometer cable lubricant into cable casing. Replace inner cable in shaft, noting that top end is not inserted accidentally. Turn inner cable as it is being re-inserted. Twist cable when all the way in, to lock into position at lower end.

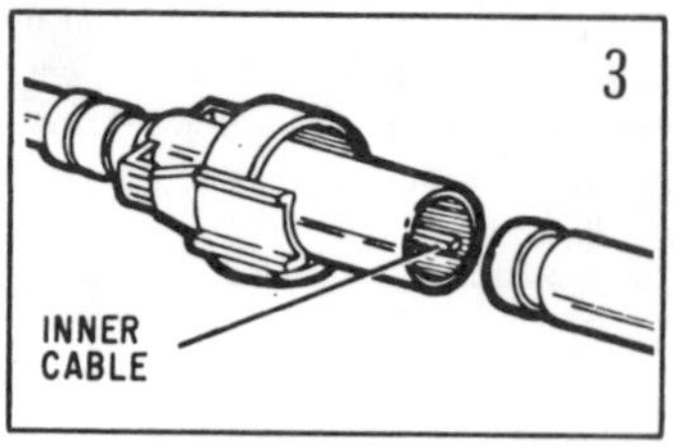

5. Reconnect cable to speedometer head under instrument panel.

DOOR HINGES AND STOPS

(lubricate every 6 months)

1. Brush any dirt accumulations from door hinges and stops. Use old tooth brush or rag.
2. Apply dab of white polyethylene grease to door hinges, trunk hinges, hood hinges, door stops.

DOOR LOCKS

(lubricate every 6 months)

1. Insert door key half way into lock.
2. Spray aerosol lock lubricant into lock.
3. Push key rest of way into lock; turn back and forth several times.

Cooling System

IT IS RECOMMENDED . . . that radiator coolant (water/antifreeze mixture) level be checked once or twice a month. Do this when engine is cold. Check more often if you do a lot of hard driving. On models with clear expansion tanks, check coolant level visually when hot.
Keep coolant up to recommended level in radiator. If coolant checks frequently low, look for leaks. Tighten all hose clamps occasionally. For best results, keep a 50/50 water/antifreeze mixture year round. Change complete coolant mixture every 12,000 miles.

CAUTION: If you must check coolant in a hot engine, cover radiator cap with thick rag before releasing. Remove cap slowly . . . press down and turn.

REPLACING THE THERMOSTAT

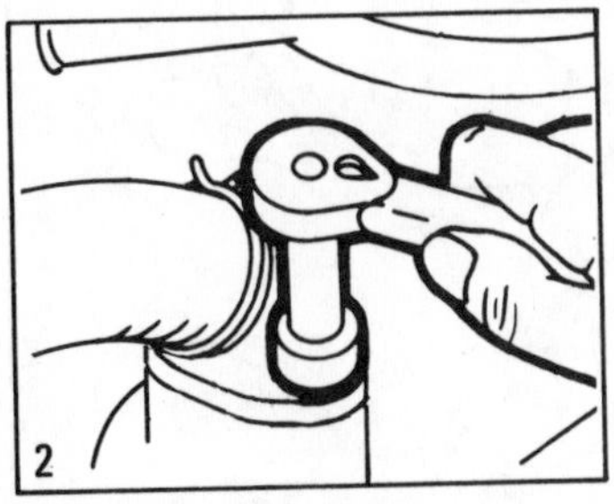

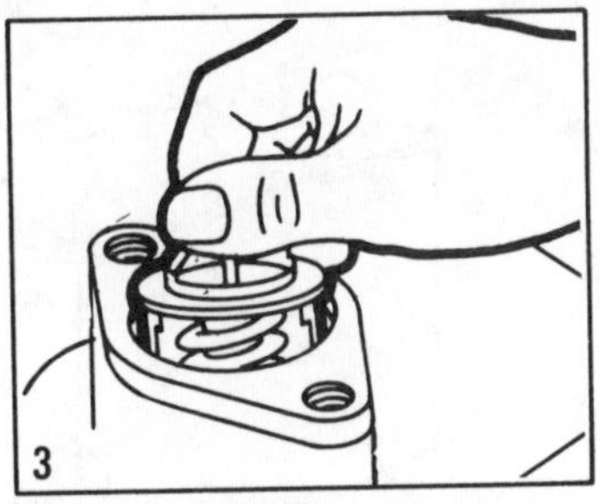

A faulty thermostat will usually cause engine overheating. Replace with new thermostat.

TOOLS AND MATERIALS . . .
New thermostat
Gasket
Adjustable wrench
1. Drain radiator of about half its coolant. (See How To Replace Hoses)
2. Loosen and remove both retaining bolts and lift thermostat housing off the engine.

NOTE: If you're careful it won't be necessary to remove radiator hose.

3. Remove old thermostat.
4. Scrape thermostat housing flange and engine block surface to remove old gasket debris.
5. Drop new thermostat into place—spring down.
6. Install new gasket with sealer applied to both sides.
7. Replace thermostat housing and tighten both retaining bolts.

FAN BELT ADJUSTMENT

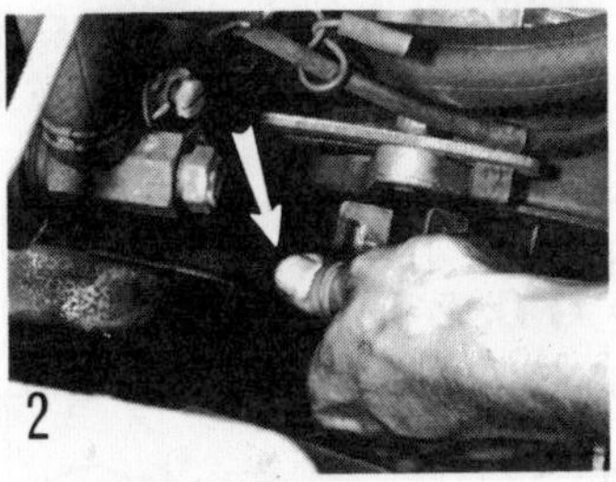

The fan belt not only drives the radiator fan, it turns the water pump and drives the alternator. It's easy to see that the condition and proper tension of the belt are vital, since almost all engine cooling and electrical power is dependent on it. The belt deserves an occasional look and tension check.
CAUTION: An overtightened belt may damage alternator and water pump bearings.
1. Inspect fan belt occasionally. If worn, frayed or cracked on inner driving surface, replace.
2. Check tension occasionally. Press thumb at midpoint of belt span between pulleys. If belt depresses more than ½ inch, tightening is needed. A too-loose belt will not drive alternator and water pump effectively.
3. Adjust to proper tension of ¼ inch deflection.

FIND THOSE COOLING SYSTEM LEAKS

1. Inspect all hoses. If any are weak, soft in spots or show cracks, replace at once.
2. Check all hose connections for tightness. Tighten loose hose clamps; they tend to loosen due to engine vibration.
3. If radiator steams or hisses when engine is switched off, check for leaks. Look for signs of coolant drips on radiator or around heater tank joint.

Leaks are possible at:
Upper or lower radiator hoses
Water pump (gaskets or seal)
Heater core or connecting hoses
Automatic transmission cooler lines (at bottom of radiator)
Faulty radiator pressure cap
Faulty cylinder head gasket
Cracked cylinder head or block

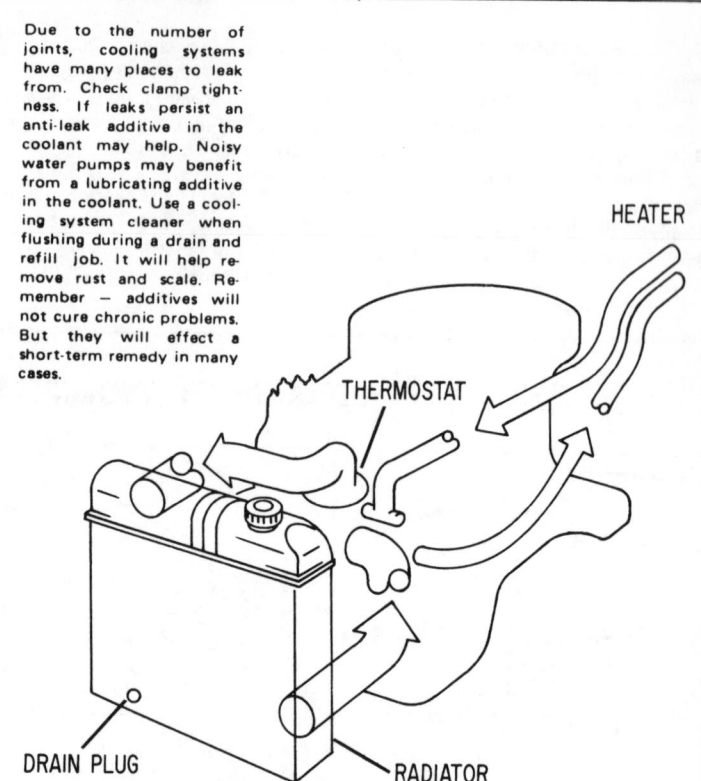

Due to the number of joints, cooling systems have many places to leak from. Check clamp tightness. If leaks persist an anti-leak additive in the coolant may help. Noisy water pumps may benefit from a lubricating additive in the coolant. Use a cooling system cleaner when flushing during a drain and refill job. It will help remove rust and scale. Remember — additives will not cure chronic problems. But they will effect a short-term remedy in many cases.

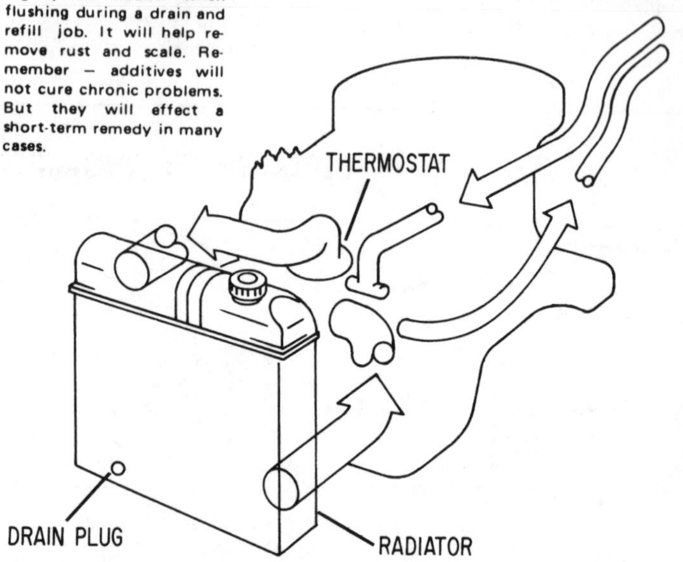

RADIATOR CAP CHECK

Check radiator cap occasionally for worn or cracked gasket. If cap doesn't seal properly, fluid will be lost and engine will overheat. Replace worn cap with new cap rated 13 to 15 lbs. pressure.

HOSE REPLACEMENT

Coolant drain and refill work may be done alone; when changing hoses, coolant must also be drained as part of job. Discard all hoses with cracks or soft spots. Check hose clamps for tightness and good condition.

1. Remove radiator cap. Open radiator petcock. Drain coolant into catch basin. If near 24 months old, discard old coolant.
2. Petcock is located at the bottom

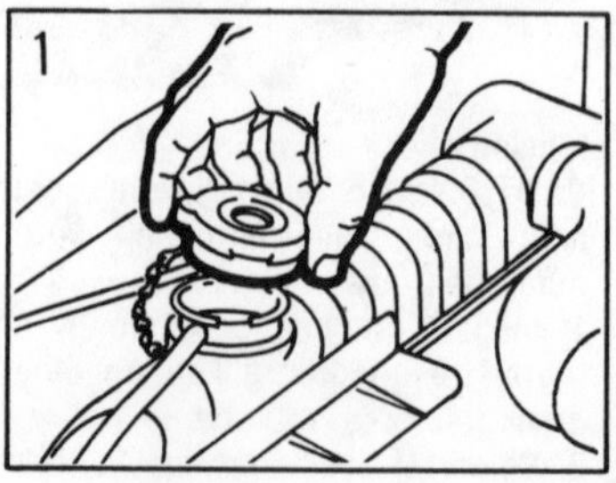

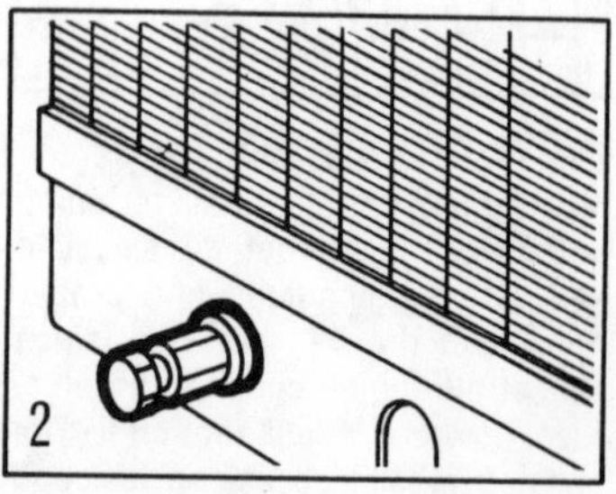

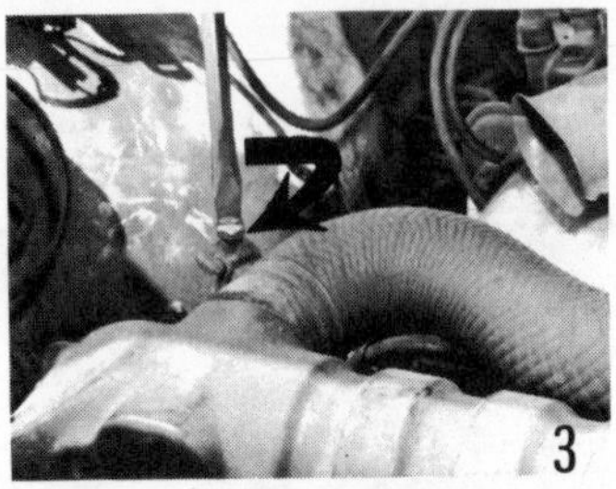

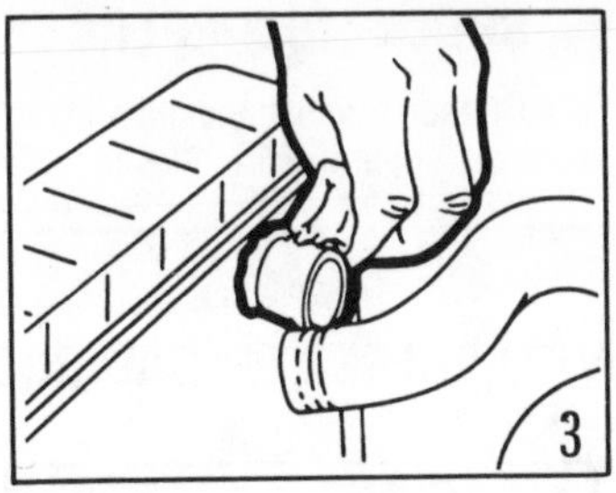

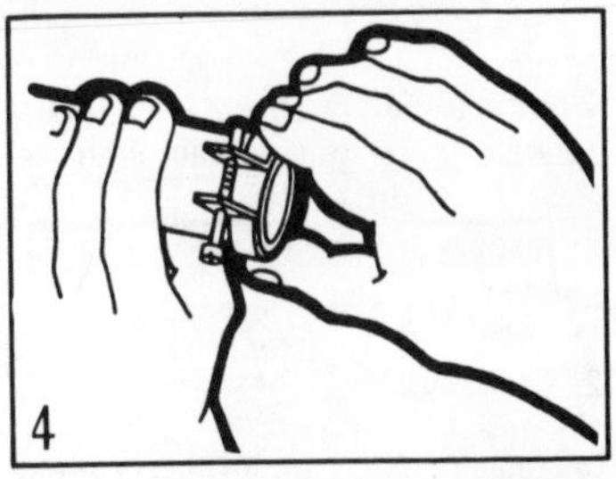

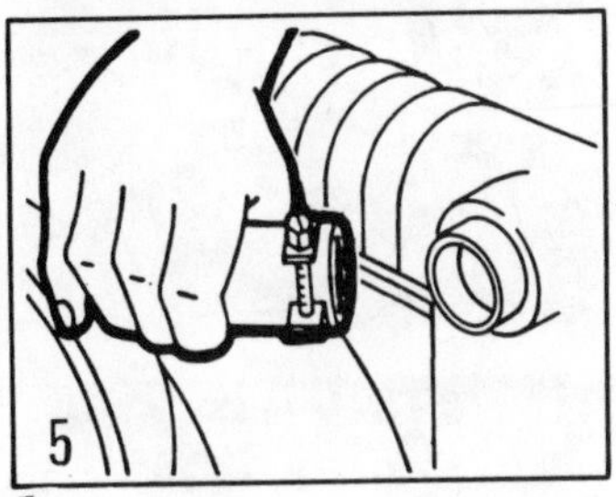

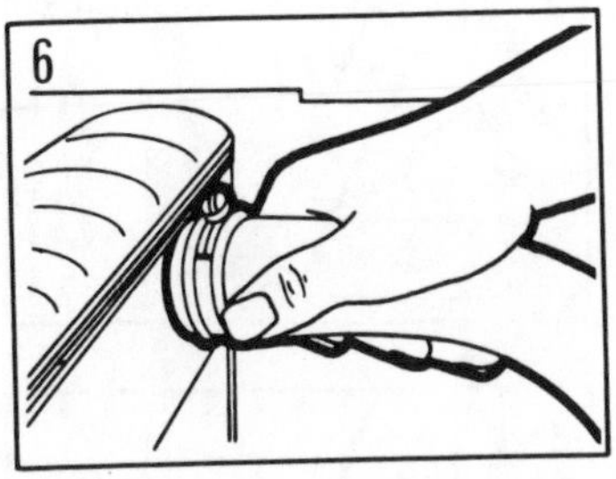

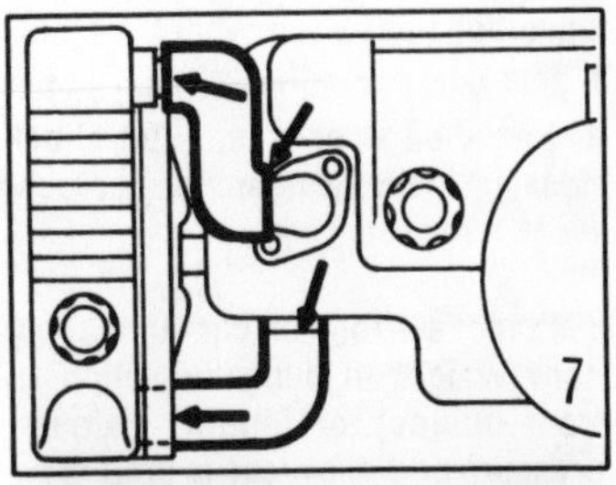

of the radiator.
3. Wipe all hose connections clean. Use emery cloth to get rid of residue.
4. If old hose clamps are badly rusted or damaged, replace with new units.
5. Slip clamps over each hose end. Slip hose ends all the way onto cleaned up hose connections.
6. Place hose clamp ¼ inch from hose end. Tighten. Close petcock. Refill with 50/50 coolant/water mix.
7. Start engine; allow to warm up. Check for coolant leaks.
8. Road test car; watch temperature gauge to avoid overheating.

Suspension and Tires

SUSPENSION SYSTEM

The front suspension is independent, with control arms and coil springs, and uses rubber bushings and a strut bar to absorb vibrations and shock. The shock absorbers are mounted inside the coil springs, together with the springs, act to reduce up and down vibration. The rear suspension is composed of asymmetrical semi-elliptic leaf springs with double acting telescopic shock absorbers.

Your car's suspension system consists of wheels, tires, springs, shock absorbers, sway (or stabilizer) bars, ball joints, steering linkage. If any of these items is out of adjustment or badly worn, you may notice any of these symptoms:

- car pulls to one side when braking
- car wanders when driving a straight line
- overall ride may be either hard or bouncy
- effort is needed to steer vehicle
- tires show uneven wear
- tires squeal when cornering
- front of car dips or bounces when braking
- car rocks side-to-side when going over rough road
- wheels bounce to make slapping sound on road
- steering wheel vibrates in hands
- front of car vibrates at highway speeds

Any of above symptoms indicates corrective action is needed. Delay can: ruin tires; cause damage/failure to other suspension parts; create safety hazard.

STEERING

If steering linkage, front suspension and steering column components are in good condition, there should be not more than 1½ inch free play in the steering wheel when measured at the rim of the wheel. If a loud knock is heard when turning the steering wheel from one extreme to the other, have mechanic check pinion bearing preload.

SHOCK ABSORBERS

Shock absorbers work to keep wheels in constant contact with the road. Result is safe handling and ride control; longer tire life. So shock absorbers (or shocks) are important.

HOW TO CHECK FOR BAD SHOCKS

1. Check under car and locate shock absorber near each wheel.

2. Heavy oil streaks on outer shock housing indicate need for replacement.

3. Stand at front of car and apply body weight in pumping action to front bumper or fender. Release pressure and allow car to stop rocking. Car should not bounce more than one more time after releasing pressure. Repeat at rear. If bouncing continues more than once, replacement is needed. Replace shocks in pairs (front pair or rear pair).

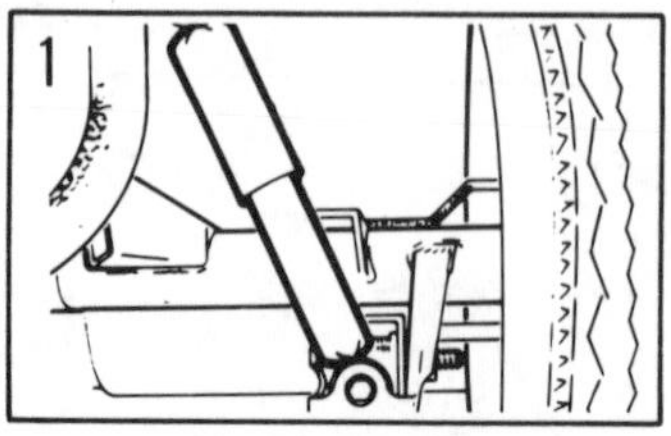

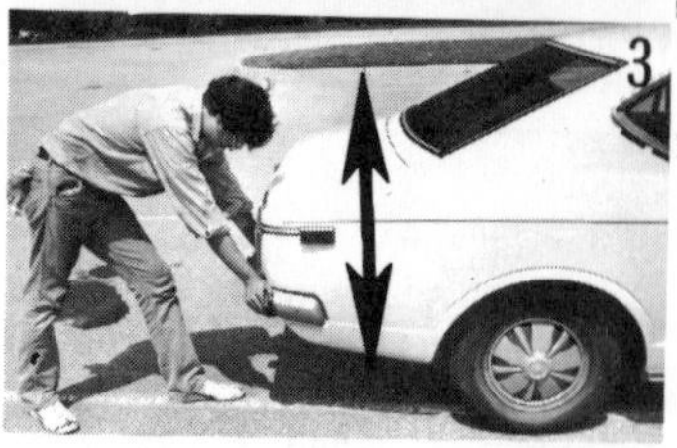

TOW HITCH INFORMATION

If your car is used for trailer towing you should check:

A. Cooling System; be sure coolant is at proper level in radiator. See Cooling System Section for checks to perform.

B. Check Transmission Fluid; keep topped up to proper level.

C. Check Rear Shock Absorbers; you may benefit from installation of new rear shocks.

D. Check Tire Pressures; best traction and handling can be ensured if tire pressures are properly maintained.

For safer and more trouble-free trailer towing, consider:

A. Automatic Transmission Cooler; helps remove excess heat from automatic transmission fluid built up during towing mileage. Also helps avoid radiator overheating. Some units can be self-installed.

B. Radiator Over-Flow Tank Kit; addition of a reservoir to catch radiator coolant overflow preventing coolant loss. Easy to install, these units help a tow car run cooler, avoid overheating due to coolant loss.

C. Heavy-Duty Shock Absorbers or Air Shocks; important to have on rear wheels if you intend to do a lot of towing or load carrying within the car itself. Don't forget to consider replacing factory shocks, when they are worn out, with heavy-duty units at the front as well.

D. Variable Load Flasher; this unit will accommodate the added load of trailer turn signal lamps on trailer when these are hooked into your car's electrical system.

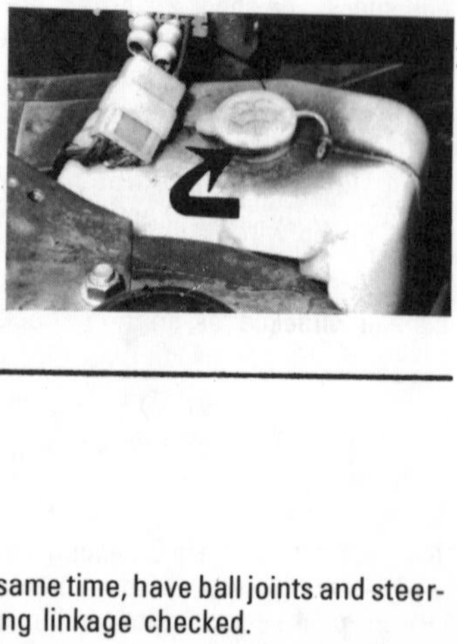

FRONT END ALIGNMENT

When steering, handling and/or tire wear indicate front end alignment may be needed, this work can only be done at an automotive service shop. DO NOT PUT OFF NEEDED FRONT END ALIGNMENT. At the same time, have ball joints and steering linkage checked.

Ignition System

As already stated, the condenser is used to absorb any extra high-voltage passing through the points. Since, in the transistorized system, there is no high current, no condenser is needed or used.

As a result of the lower stress placed on them, the points only have to be replaced every 24,000 miles instead of the usual 12,000 miles.

The Toyota transistorized ignition system may be quickly identified by the lack of a condenser on the outside of the distributor and by the addition of a control box, which is connected between the distributor and the primary side of the coil.

The engines used in the Corona are: 8R-C, 1858 cc, used in 1970-71; the 18R-C, 1980 cc, used in 1972-74; and the 20-R, 2189 cc, used in 1975 and later models. Tbe Corona Mark II has used the 8R-C and 18R-C through 1972. 1972 and later models use the six cylinder 2M and 4M series.

The conventional ignition system consists of spark plugs; plug wires; distributor; rotor; points; condenser; coil. These units work to create a good hot spark inside the engine (ignition) at exactly the right moment (timing). If ignition is weak or timing is off, engine may be hard to start, run poorly, waste gas, lose power, backfire or not run at all.

Transistorized ignition was first used on 1974 6 cylinder engines sold in California. With the introduction of 1975 models, usage has been extended to all Toyota vehicles sold in the United States.

The transistorized ignition system employed by Toyota works very much like the conventional system previously described. Regular breaker points are used, but instead of switching primary current to the coil off-and-on, they are used to trigger a switching transistor. The transistor, in turn, switches the coil primary current on and off.

Since only a very small amount of current is needed to operate the transistor, the points will not become burned or pitted, as they would if they had full primary current passing through them. This also allows the primary current to be higher than usual because the use of a higher current would normally cause the points to fail much more rapidly.

TUNE-UP SERVICES

TOYOTA SAYS: Replace plugs and points every 12,000 (24,000 with transistorized ignition) miles.

TOOLS & MATERIALS . . . Parts: set of points; condenser; 4 spark plugs; Tools: wire gap gauge (plugs); feeler gauge (points); spark plug socket, 13/16 in.; screwdriver; open end, box or combination metric wrenches; timing equipment (see Ignition Timing).

CHECKING POINTS AND ROTOR

The distributor holds the points and rotor. The condenser is attached to the outside of the distributor. The cap forms the top of the distributor.

1. To open distributor, snap retaining clips off with screwdriver, lift cap off but keep wires connected.

2. Pull rotor off (straight up). Replace if cracked or metallic tip is badly burned. Lift off flat radio static shield.

3. Pry points apart with screwdriver. If worn or burned, replace. If OK, check point gap.

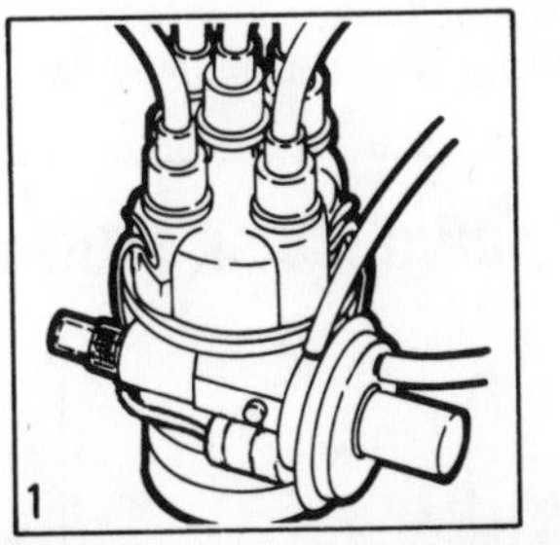

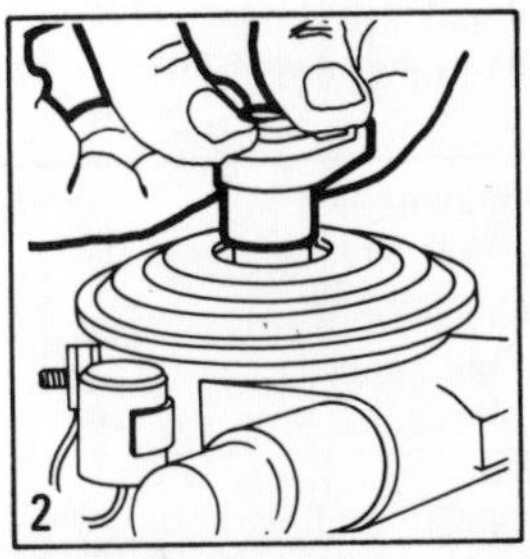

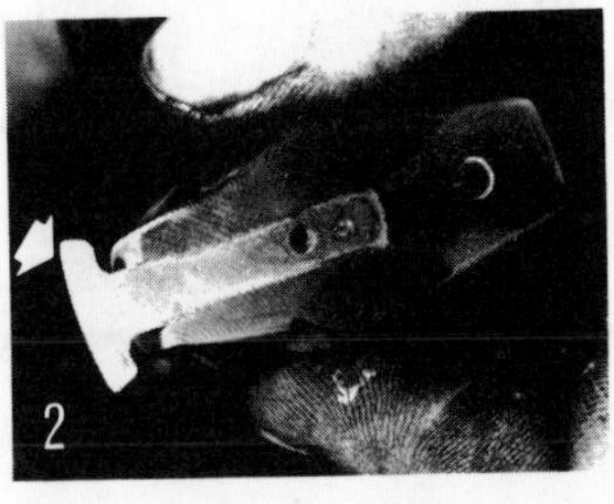

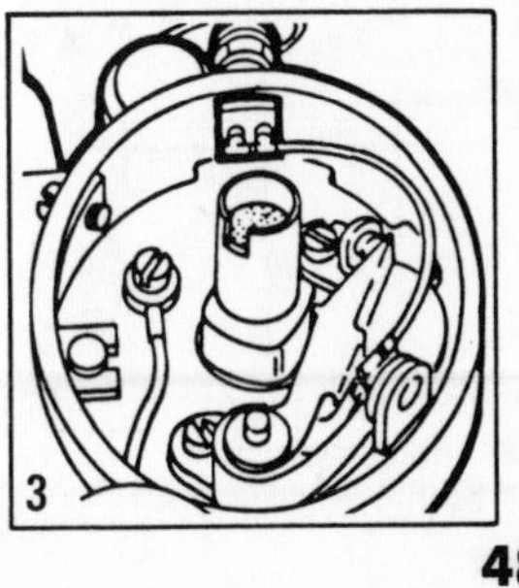

OTHER IGNITION CHECK POINTS

Inspect spark plug wires. If cracked or brittle, entire set should be replaced. Also center, high tension wire. Inspect distributor cap. Wipe inside clean occasionally with dry, lint-free rag. If cap is cracked or rotor contacts are excessively burned, replace cap.

SPARK PLUG REPLACEMENT

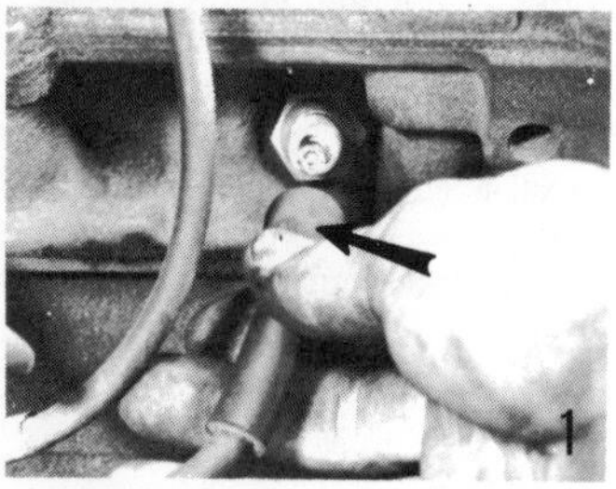

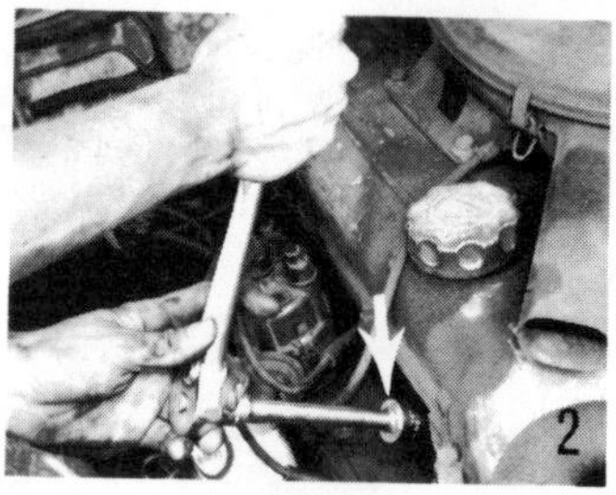

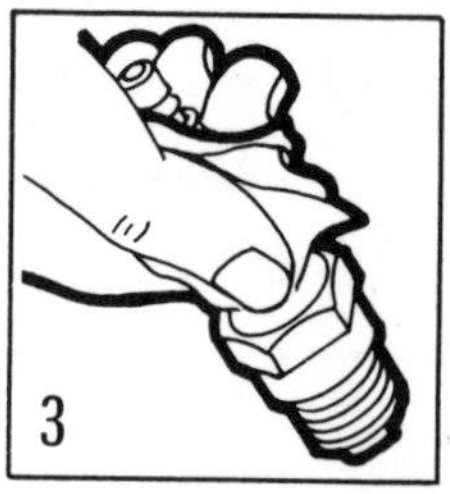

1. Remove spark plug wire by grasping rubber boot. Do not jerk wire. If stuck, turn boot, pulling gently.
2. Loosen spark plug using socket wrench.
3. Wipe or brush loose dirt from around plug before removing. Do not let dirt drop into engine through plug hole. Unscrew plug.
4. Check plug electrode gap on new spark plug. Adjust to 0.030-0.031. Plug gap is correct when the gauge drags slightly as it is pulled between plug electrodes.
5. Thread new plug into plug hole by hand. Hand tighten. Do not force or cross thread. Use socket wrench to tighten firmly but do not force. Replace plug wire. Press boot firmly.

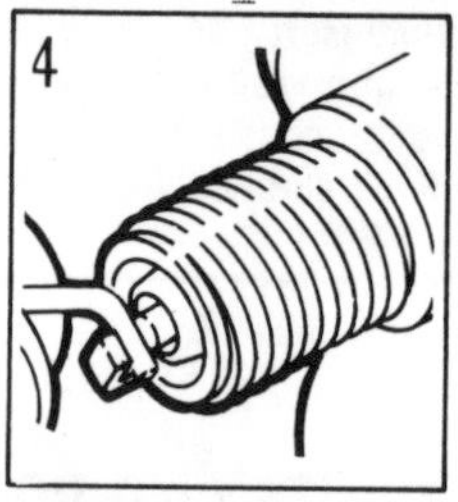

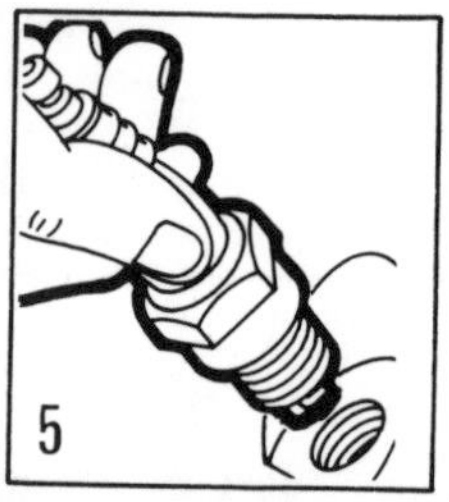

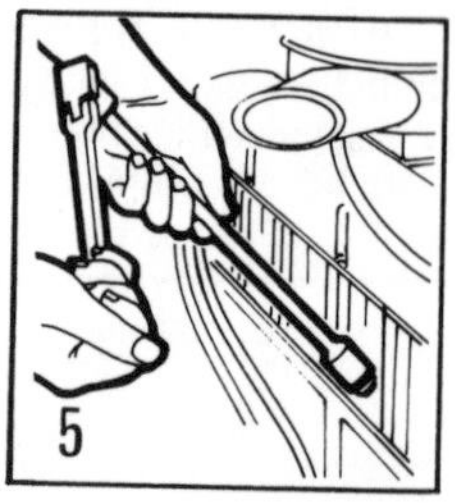

REPLACING SPARK PLUG WIRES

Use the firing order illustration to guide you when replacing your ignition wires and/or distributor cap.

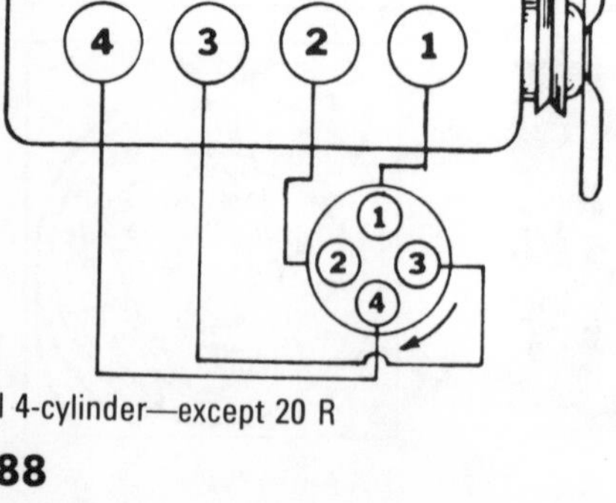

All 4-cylinder—except 20 R

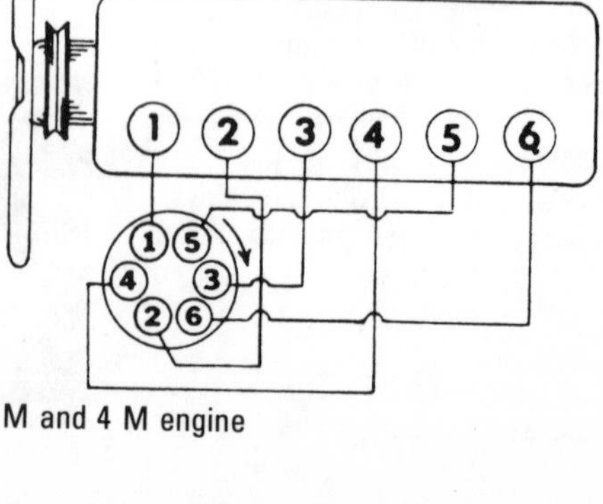

2 M and 4 M engine

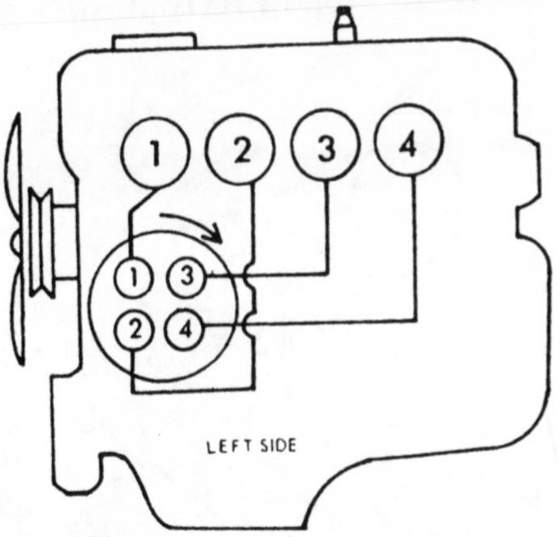

20 R ENGINE

LOCATION OF POINTS AND CONDENSER

Points and condenser on conventional ignition work together. Always replace condenser when installing new points. While you may find slight differences in location or attachment of these parts from one car to another, they're all basically the same. The condenser is attached to the outside of the distributor rather than inside.

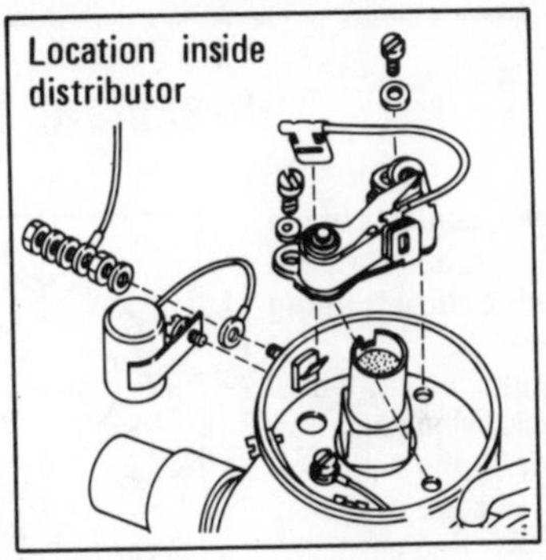

REMOVING POINTS

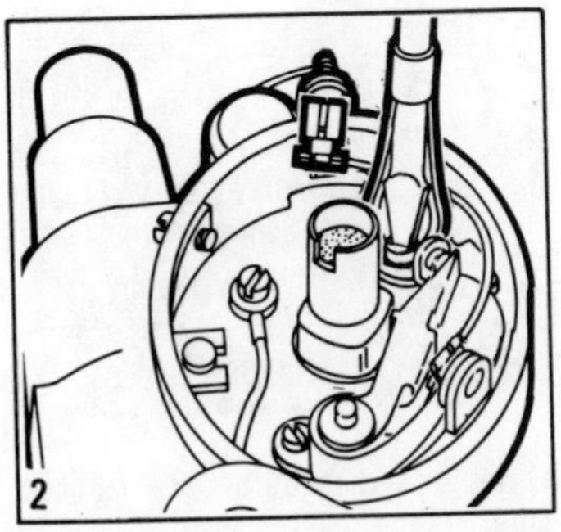

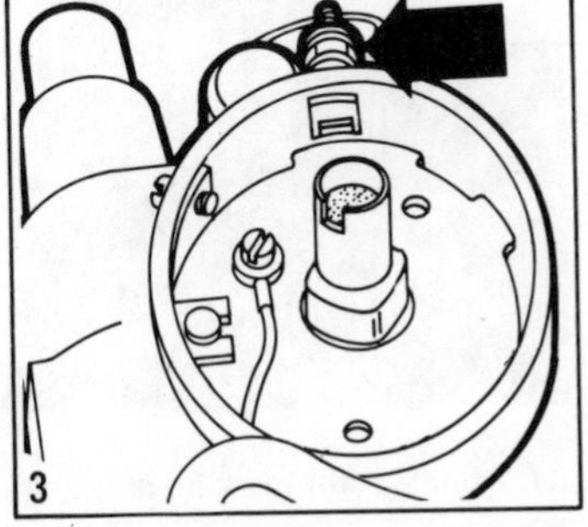

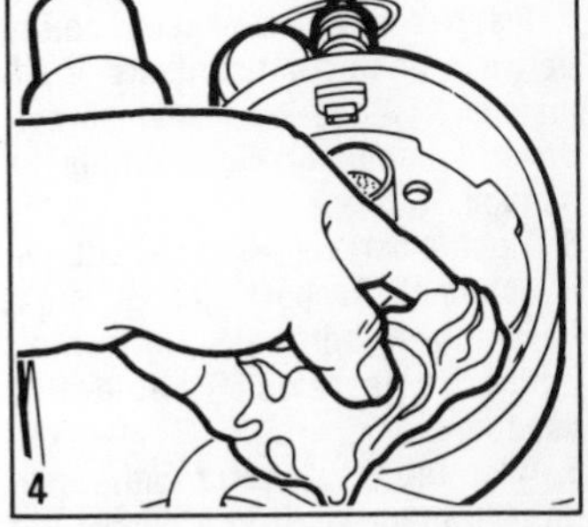

1. Disconnect the wire terminal connected to the points set. On conventional ignition remove condenser wire terminal from side of distributor.
2. On conventional ignition remove points attaching screws being very careful not to drop screws inside distributor.
3. Remove screw attaching condenser to side of distributor. DO NOT DROP SCREW.
4. Wipe all dirt from distributor plate and cam.

CAUTION: When removing screws from distributor, be sure to avoid any screws accidentally falling through distributor opening into engine. Use magnetic screwdriver.

INSTALLING POINTS AND CONDENSER

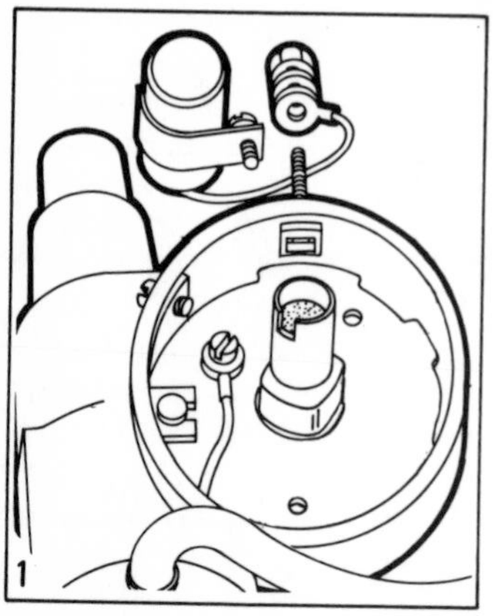

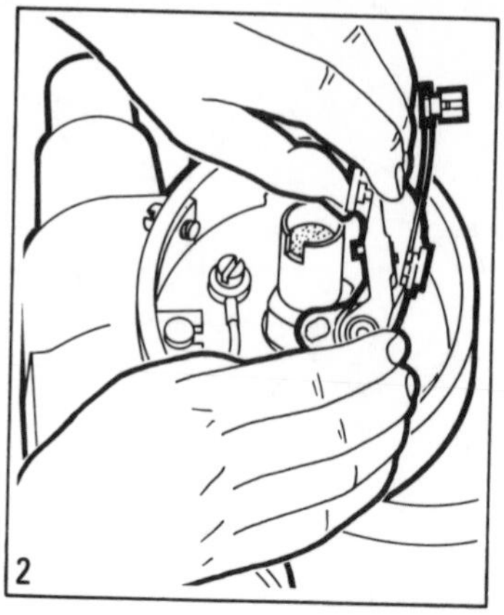

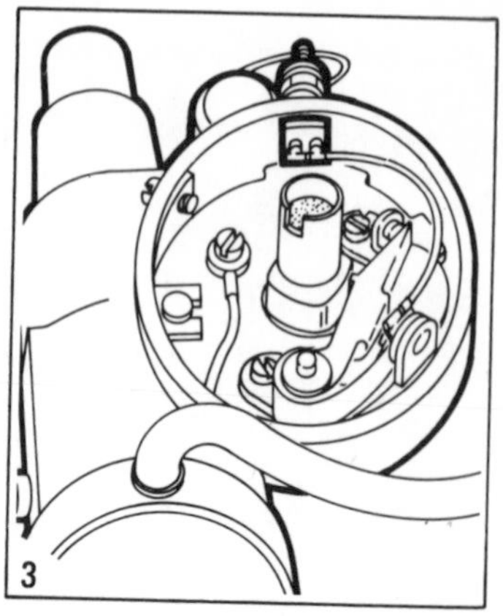

1. Apply small amount of heat resistant lube to distributor cam (lube sometimes supplied with new point sets, if not, purchase separately). On conventional ignition attach new condenser with screw.
2. Position new points set in distributor. Attach retaining screws lightly.
3. Attach primary wire; on conventional ignition attach condenser lead wire to condenser lead terminal. Do not allow either wire to touch distributor body or breaker plate.

RESETTING THE CONTACT GAP

1. Check that point contacts meet squarely. If they do not, bend bracket supporting fixed contact using needle-nosed pliers.
2. Turn engine by ignition key (you'll need a helper) until rubbing block on point set is on one of the high spots of distributor cam. You may use wrench on lower engine pulley to do this.
3. Insert screwdriver in slot near point contacts; twist to open or close gap.
4. Correct point gap is .018 in.
5. Insert correct size feeler gauge between open point contacts. If adjustment is needed, twist screwdriver to open or close points as needed.
6. Tighten screws when correct gap is obtained. Recheck gap; it might have changed from tightening holddown screws. Readjust if needed.
7. Align tab inside rotor with notch on distributor shaft and push rotor onto shaft. Rotor must be fully seated.
8. Replace distributor cap; install clips.

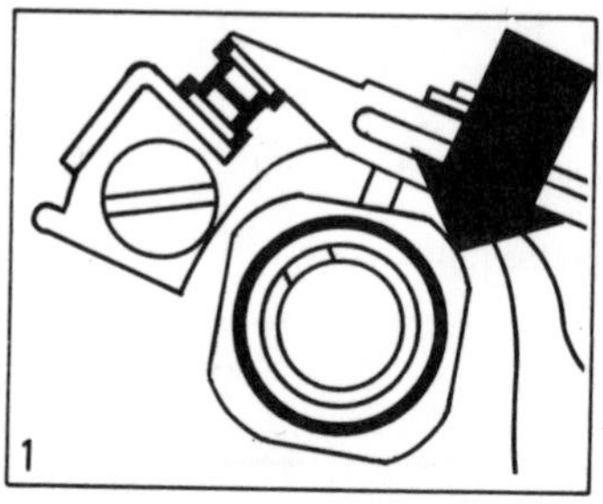

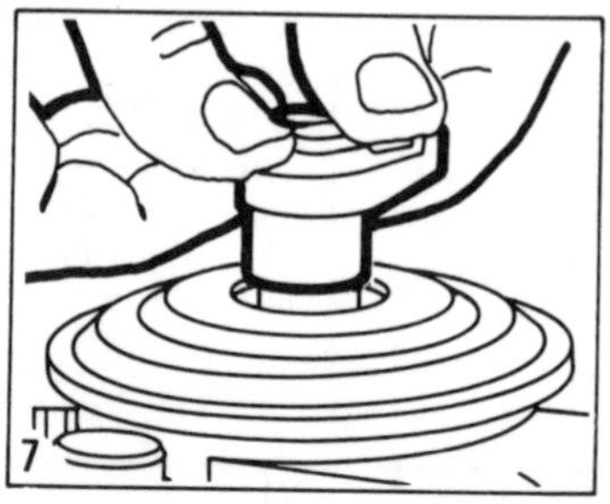

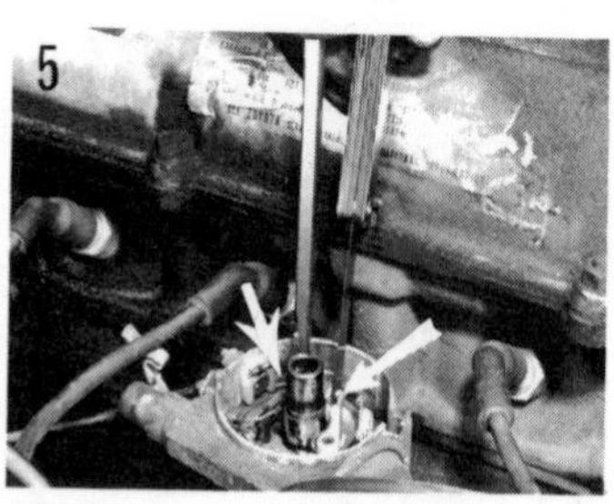

DWELL ANGLE

1. Connect a dwell meter or tach to the ignition system, according to the manufacturer's instructions.

a. When checking the dwell on a conventional ignition system, connect one meter lead (usually black) to a metallic part of the car to ground the meter; the other lead (usually red) is connected to the coil primary

post (the one with the small lead which runs to the distributor body).
b. When checking dwell on a model with transistorized ignition, ground one meter lead (usually black) to a metallic part of the car; hook up the other lead (usually red) to the negative (−) coil terminal. Under no circumstances should the meter be connected to the distributor or the positive (+) side of the coil.
2. If the dwell meter has a set line, adjust the needle until it rests on the line.
3. Start the engine. It should be warmed-up and running at the specified idle speed.
CAUTION: Be sure to keep fingers, tools, clothes, hair, and wires clear of the engine fan. The transmission should be in Neutral (or Park), parking brake set, and running in a well-ventilated area.
4. Check the reading on the dwell meter. If you have a Toyota with a four-cylinder engine and your meter doesn't have a four-cylinder scale, multiply the eight-cylinder reading by two.
5. If the meter reading is within the range specified in the "Tune-Up Specifications" chart, shut the engine off and disconnect the dwell meter.

6. If the dwell is not within specifications, shut the engine off and adjust the point gap as previously outlined. Increasing the point gap decreases the dwell angle and vice versa.

7. Adjust the points until dwell is within specifications, then disconnect the dwell meter. Adjust the timing.

IGNITION TIMING

1. Warm-up the engine. Connect a tachometer and check the engine idle speed to be sure that is is within the specification given in the "Tune-Up Specifications" chart. See Dwell Angle for information on how to hook up a tach.

2. If the timing marks are difficult to see, use a dab of paint or chalk to make them more visible.

3. Connect a timing light according to the manufacturer's instructions. If the light has three wires, one (usually blue or green) must be installed with an adapter between the No. 1 spark plug lead and the spark plug. The other leads are connected to the positive (+) battery terminal (usually a red lead) and the other to the negative (−) battery terminal (usually a black lead).

4. Disconnect the vacuum line(s) from the distributor vacuum unit. Plug it (them) with a pencil or golf tee(s).

5. Be sure that the timing light wires are clear of the fan and start the engine.

CAUTION: Keep fingers, clothes, tools, hair, and leads clear of the

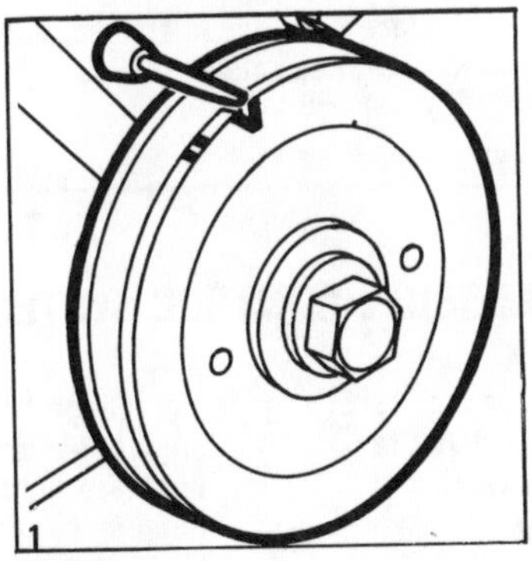

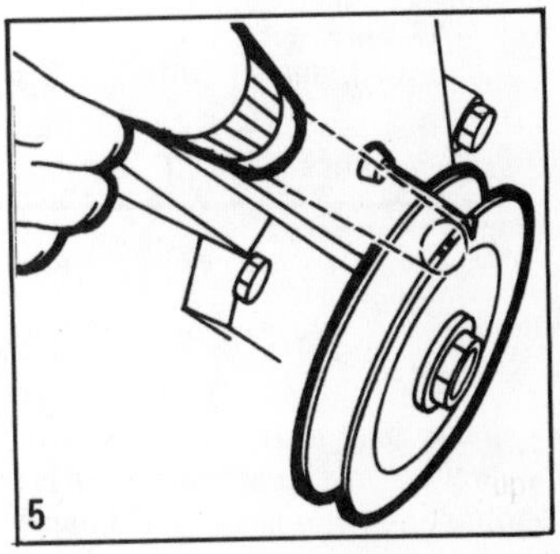

spinning engine fan. Be sure that you are running the engine in a well-ventilated area.
6. Allow the engine to run at the specified idle speed with the gearshift in Neutral with manual transmission and Drive (D) with automatic transmission.
CAUTION: Be sure that the parking brake is set and that the front wheels are blocked to prevent the car from rolling forward, especially when Drive is selected with an automatic.
7. Point the timing marks at the marks indicated in the chart and illustrations below. With the engine at idle, timing should be at the specification given on the "Tune-Up Specifications" chart.
8. If the timing is not at the specification, loosen the pinch-bolt at the base of the distributor just enough so that the distributor can be turned. Turn the distributor to advance or retard the timing as required. Once the proper marks are seen to align with the timing light, timing is correct.
9. Stop the engine and tighten the pinch-bolt. Start the engine and recheck timing. Stop the engine; disconnect the tachometer and timing light. Connect the vacuum line(s) to the distributor vacuum unit.

Fuel Systems

When gasoline is brought from the fuel tank, it mixes with air in the carburetor. This gas/air mixture enters engine thru the intake manifold, passes thru the intake valves and is burned in the combustion chamber. The burned exhaust gas is then passed thru the exhaust valves to the exhaust system and to the outside air. In order to keep your car's engine running cleanly with minimal pollution, and avoid dangerous carbon monoxide fumes inside the vehicle, certain items should be checked from time to time.

REPLACING THE AIR FILTER

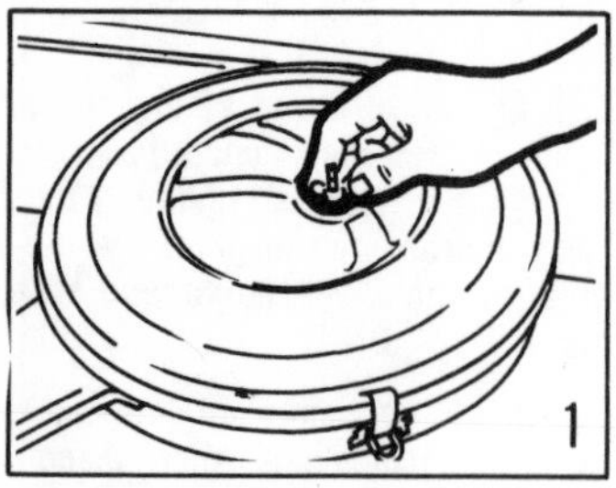

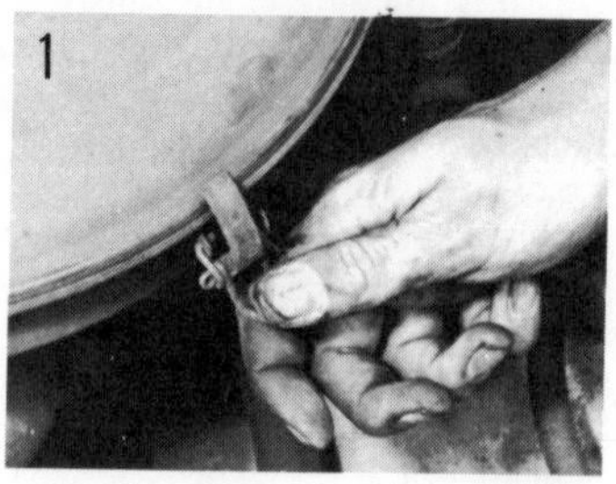

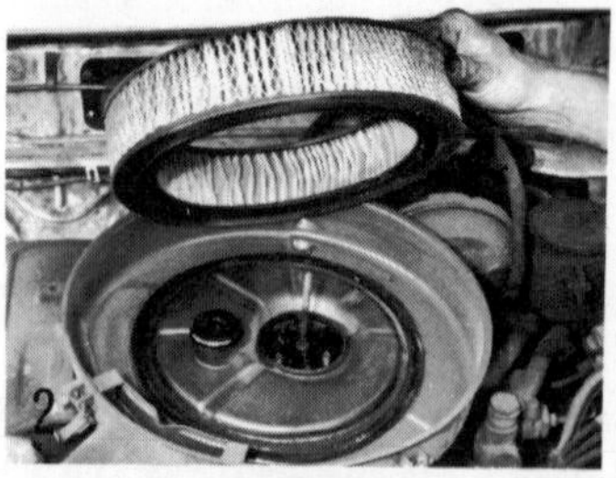

The large round can that sits on top of the engine holds the air cleaner. Twice a year:

1. Remove air cleaner lid by removing wing nut, and, if so equipped, retaining clips.
2. Lift out air cleaner cartridge. Discard cartridge if used more than 18,000 miles (24,000 miles on Corona's after 1972).
3. Wipe out air cleaner with a clean cloth.
4. Replace cartridge, install lid, and wing nut. Snap retaining clips.

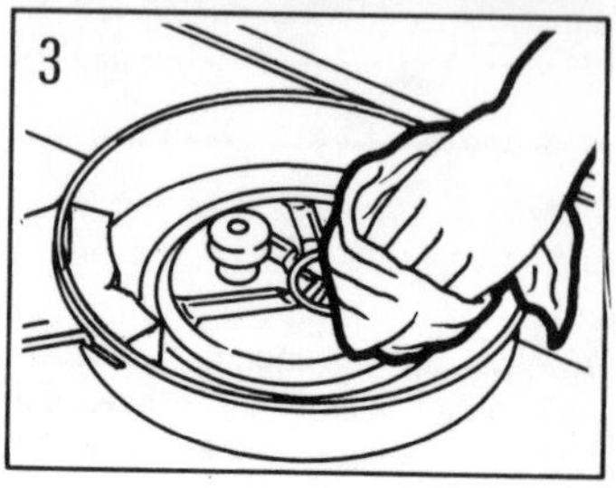

EMISSION CONTROL SYSTEMS

An important part of a car's emission control system is the Positive Crankcase Ventilation (PCV) valve and its connecting hose. The PCV valve should be replaced once every 24,000 miles. This device keeps dirt and sludge from forming inside the engine. Make sure all PCV connections are tight. Check that the connecting hoses are clear and not clogged. Replace any brittle or broken hoses.

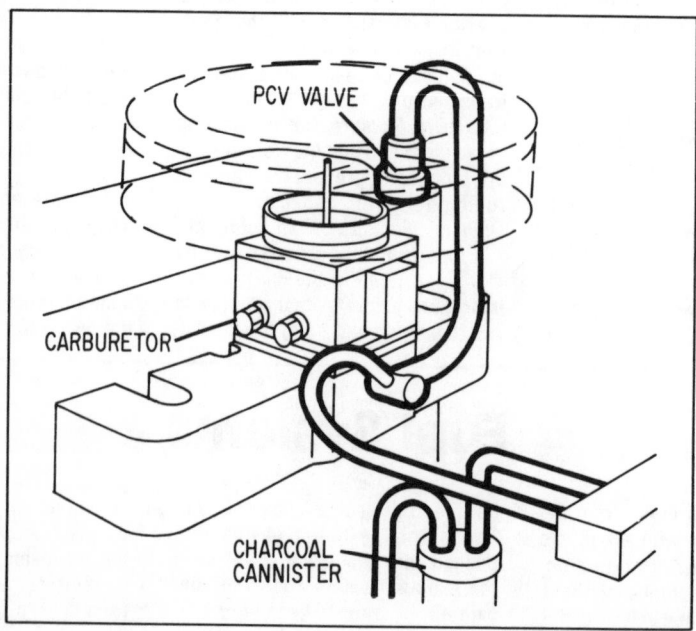

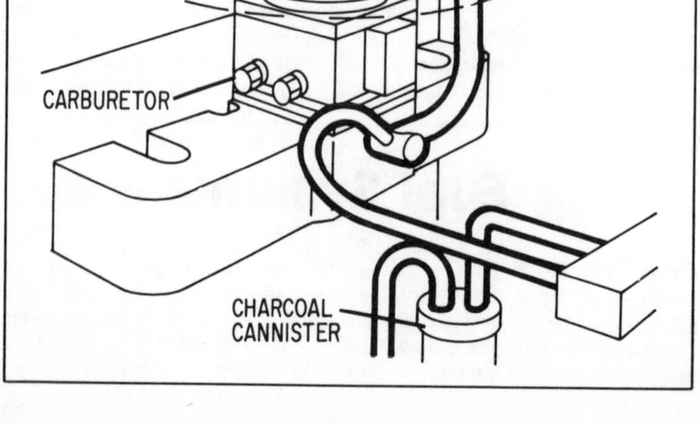

PCV VALVE REPLACEMENT

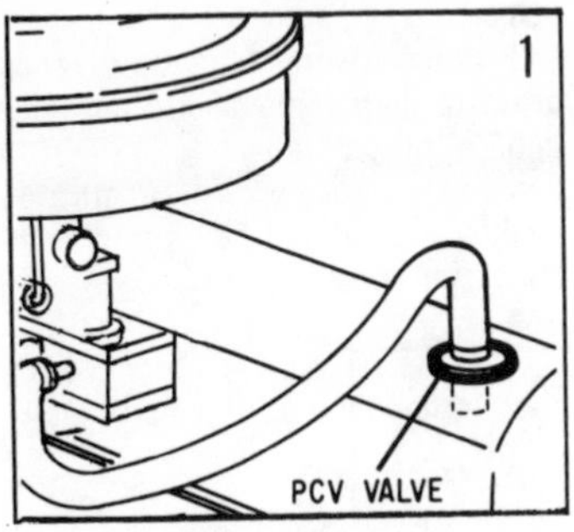

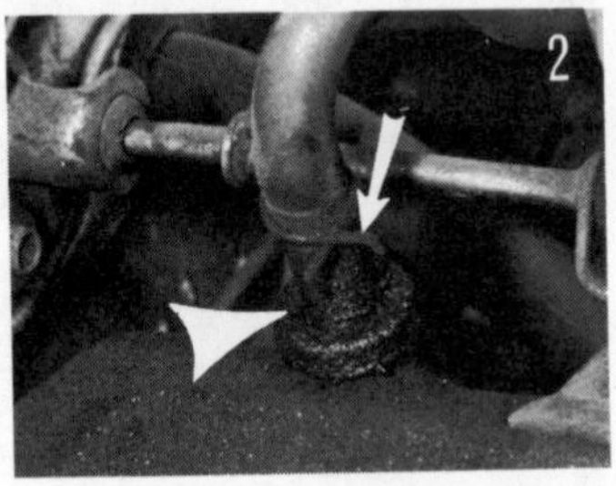

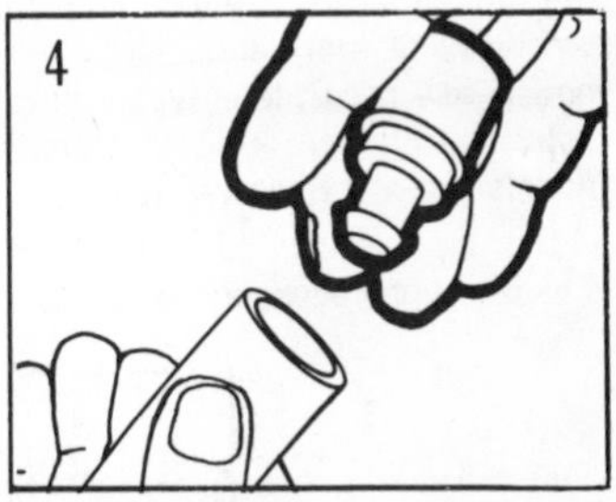

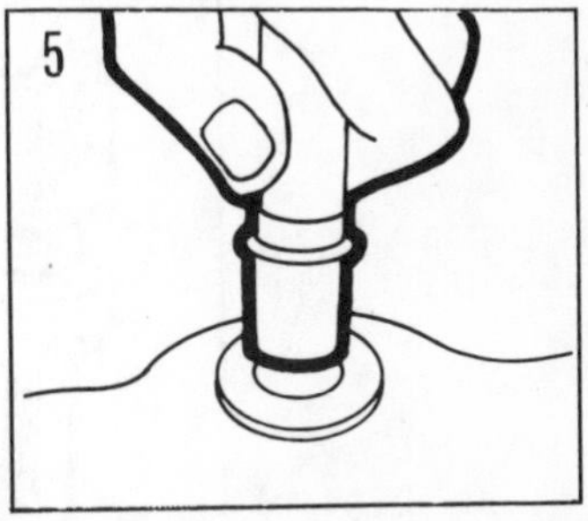

1. Pull valve from its location in rear part of valve cover.
2. Squeeze the hose clamp with a pair of pliers, remove hose. Pull out valve.
3. Note where the other end of the hose connects. Remove the hose and flush it with cleaning solvent.
4. Reconnect the hose. Pinch the clamp and insert the PCV valve into the hose.
5. Insert the valve into the valve cover.

FUEL FILTER REPLACEMENT—Throwaway Type

1. Unfasten the fuel intake hose. Use a wrench to loosen the attachment nut and another wrench on the opposite side to keep the filter from turning.
2. Remove the flexible fuel line from the other side of the filter. Unfasten the attaching screws from the filter bracket.
3. Install the new filter and reconnect the fuel lines. Start the engine and check for leaks.

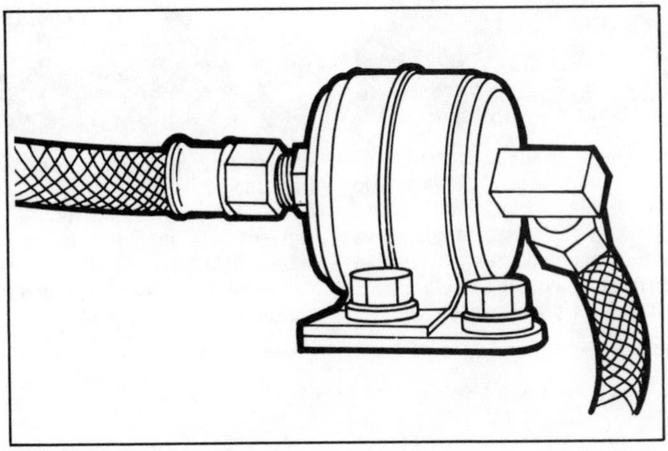

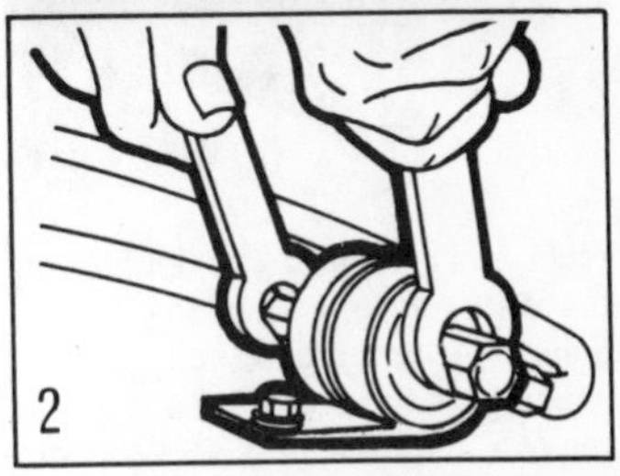

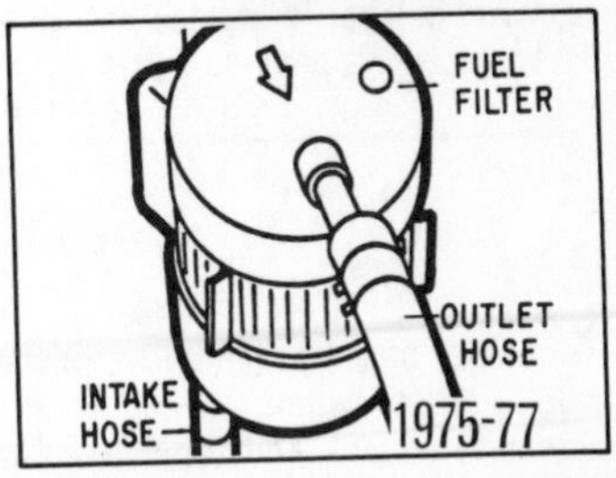

FUEL FILTER RELACEMENT—Cartridge Type

The Corona series is equipped with two types of fuel filters. The older models use a cartridge type with a disposable element, while the newer models use a throwaway type.

1. This type is located in the fuel line; it is not necessary to remove unit to replace filter. Loosen and remove nut on the filter bowl bail.
2. Withdraw the bowl, element spring, element and the bowl gasket.
3. Wash all of the parts in solvent and examine them for damage. Install a new filter element and bowl gasket.
4. Install components in the reverse order of their removal. Do not fully tighten the bail nut.
5. Seat the bowl by turning it slightly; tighten the bail nut full and check for leaks.

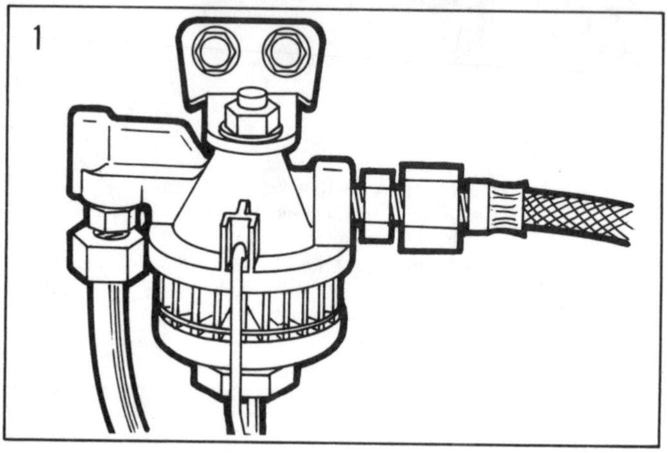

Safety Systems

PARKING LIGHTS, TURN SIGNALS AND STOP LIGHTS

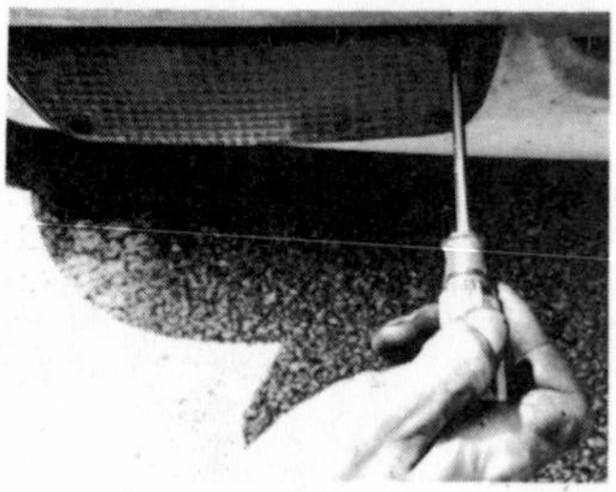

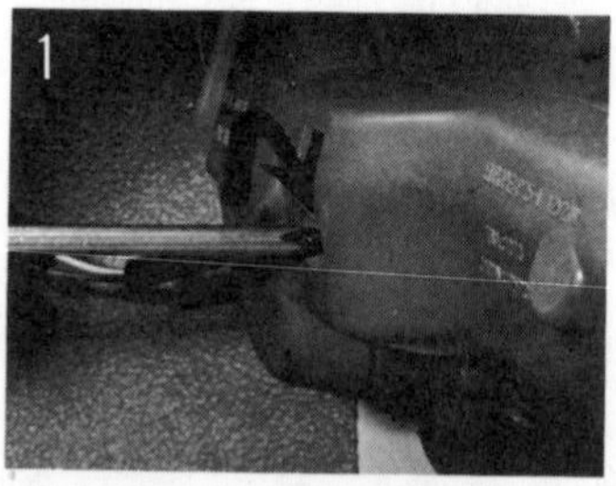

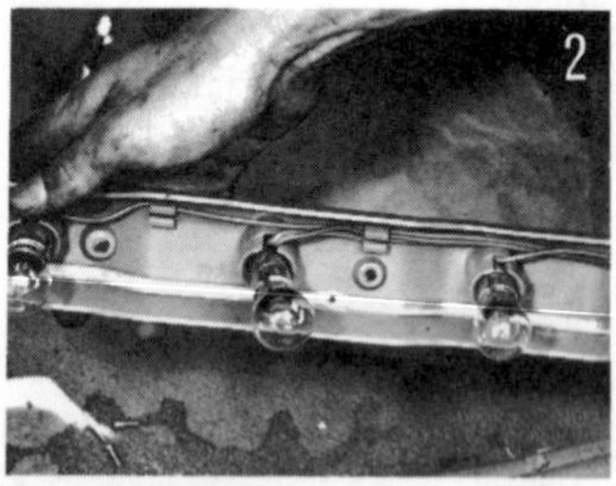

Front parking lights are mounted in the parking light housings in the grille. The turn signal bulbs are in housings in the bumper. To replace, remove the retaining screws and remove the lens. To replace rear tail light, stop light, back-up lights, turn signal bulbs on sedan, raise trunk lid and pull off back of housing. On wagon, remove retaining screws and remove light assembly, and then twist socket counterclockwise in housing to remove it. On both sedans and wagons, push down on bulb and turn counterclockwise to remove from socket.

NOTE: When inserting new dual element bulb, note that knobs on side of bulb base are different distances from base tip. Match knobs to socket slots for proper fit.

BACK-UP LIGHTS

To replace back-up light bulbs, raise trunk lid. On wagon, remove three retaining screws and remove light assembly. Reach bulb socket from inside car. Turn bulb socket counterclockwise and pull out. Push down element bulb in correct position (see note) and reinstall socket in housing.

SIDE MARKER LIGHT

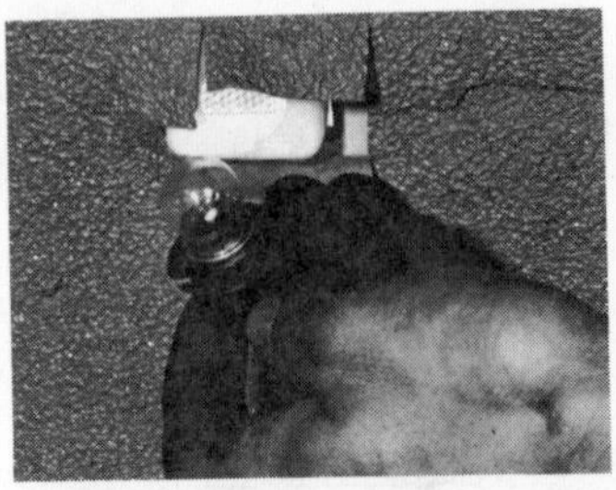

Front . . . Remove the retaining screws, and remove the lens. Push in on bulb, turning counterclockwise to remove.

Rear . . . On sedans, raise trunk lid. Reach bulb socket from inside car. Turn socket counterclockwise to remove. On wagon, remove three retaining screws and remove lens cover. Push down on bulb and turn counterclockwise to remove.

LICENSE PLATE LIGHTS

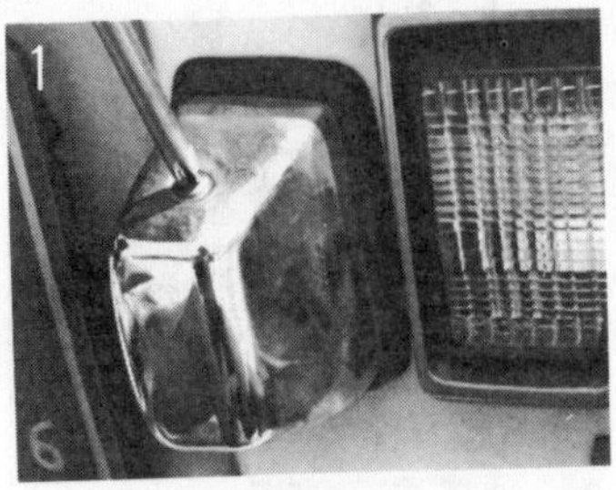

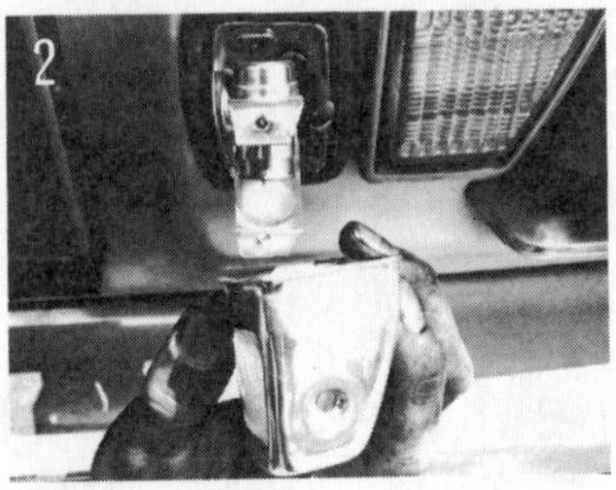

Remove screws and remove from housing on bumper of sedan. On wagon, remove screws, lens cover and gasket. Push in on bulb turning counterclockwise to remove.

INTERIOR DOME LIGHT

Unscrew dome light lens and remove from housing. To avoid blowing fuse, make sure doors are closed and dome light switch is in OFF position. Carefully lever the bulb straight out of the housing. Insert new bulb and re-install dome light lens.

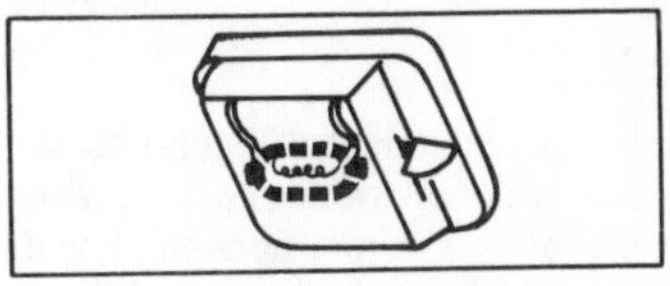

WINDSHIELD WIPER BLADE REPLACEMENT

To remove wiper blades lift up on spring release tab on wiper blade-to-wiper arm connector. Pull wiper blade off wiper arm. There are two types of replacement wipers for Corona windshield wipers. One requires replacement of entire wiper blade. Simply snap replacement blade assembly into place. The other allows replacement of only the rubber wiper blade insert. Press the old rubber insert down away from wiper blade to free it from its retaining clips on blade ends; slide in insert from blade. Position new insert in wiper blade. Bend insert upward slightly to engage retaining clips.

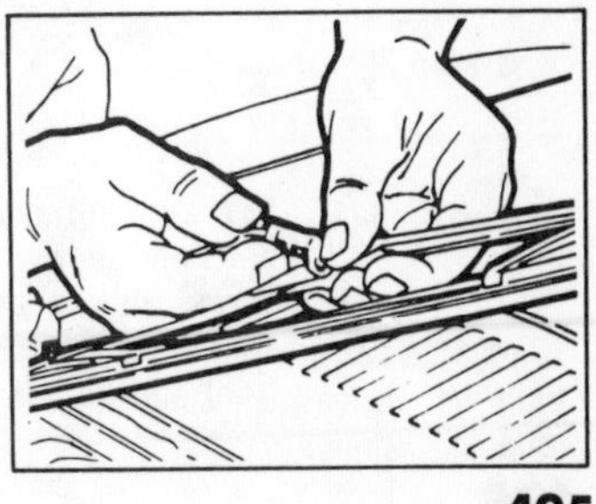

HEADLIGHT REPLACEMENT

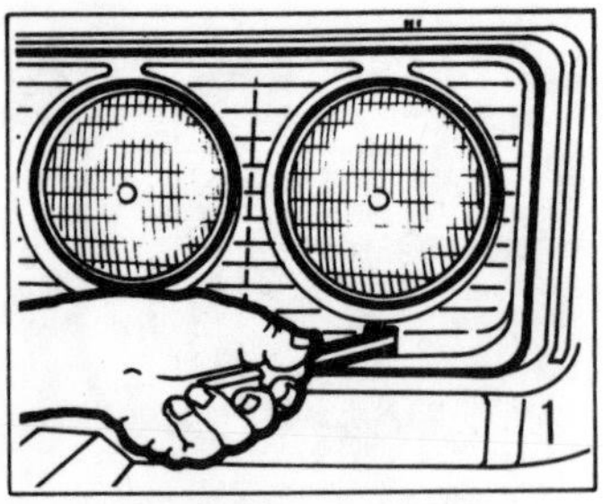

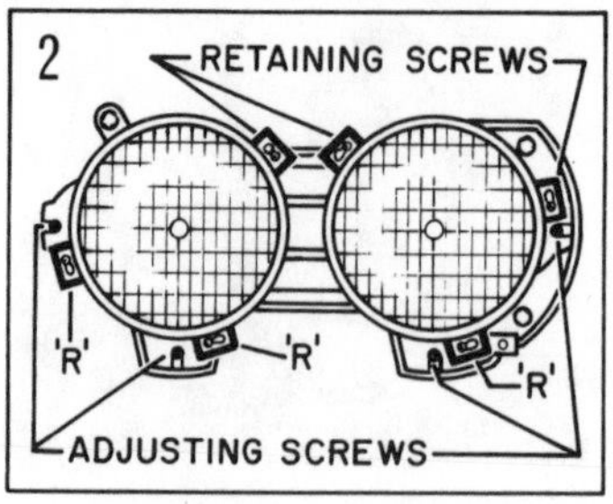

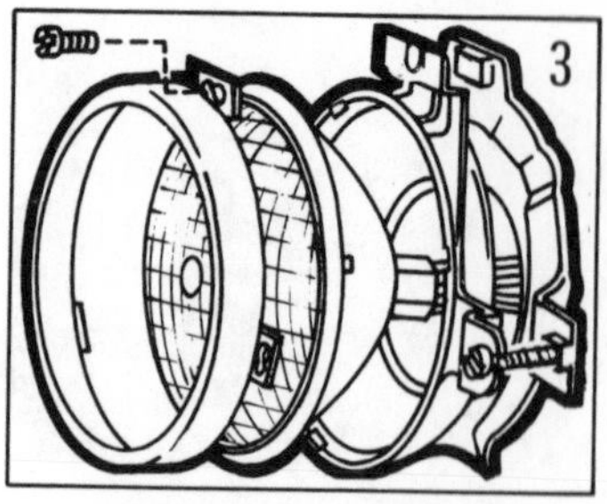

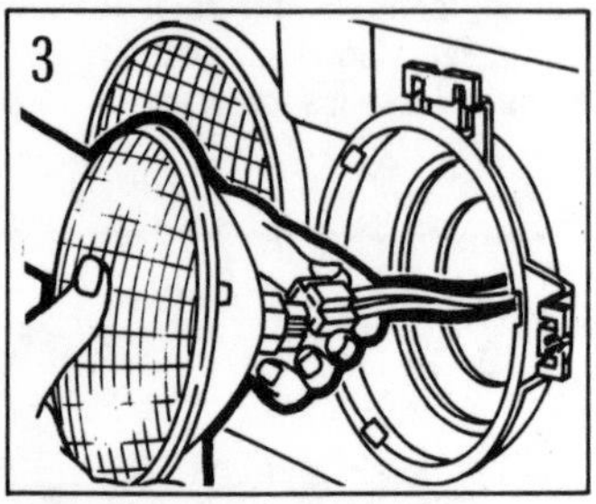

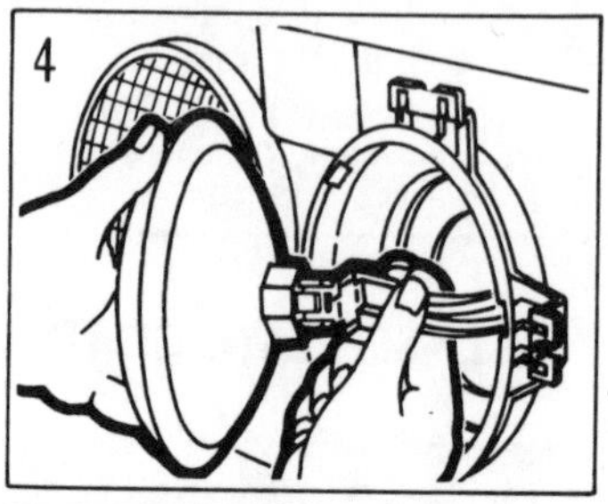

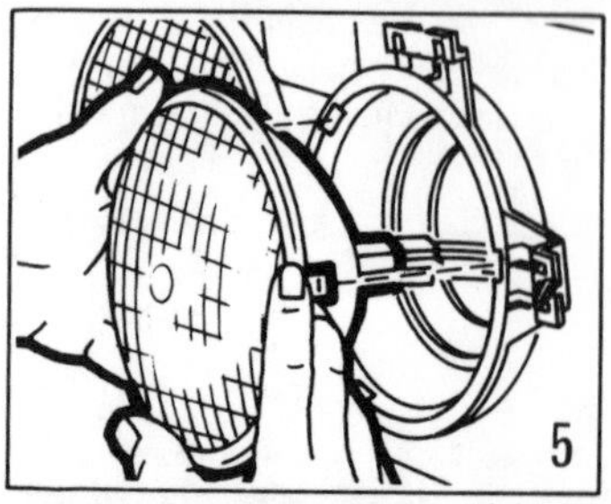

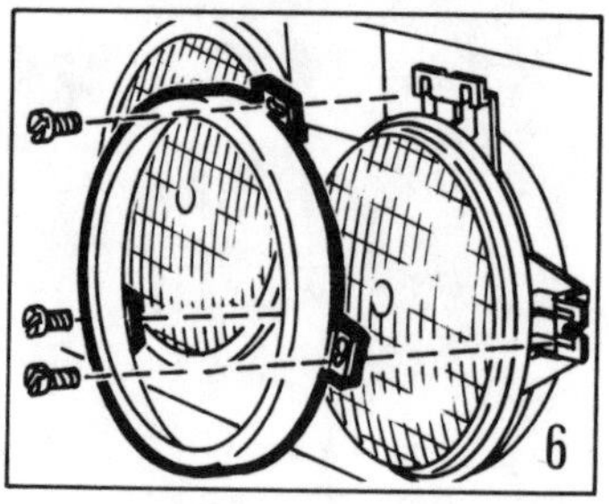

1. Remove either headlight rim or grille retaining screws, and remove the rim or grille.
2. Remove the three short inner ring screws. Do not remove or tamper with the two longer screws, these are the headlight adjustment screws.
3. Remove the inner ring and pull the headlight out. Disconnect and remove the bulb.
4. Connect the plug to the rear of the new bulb unit.
5. Position new sealed beam in headlight shell. Be sure that knobs on back of light (near outer edge) enter slots in shell.
6. Place retaining ring over sealed beam and fasten with three screws.
7. Install trim ring and tighten screws.

HORN PROBLEMS

If horn sounds and does not stop, this is due to short circuit in wiring. Disconnect wiring connector under hood and have professional service shop check horn wiring circuit.

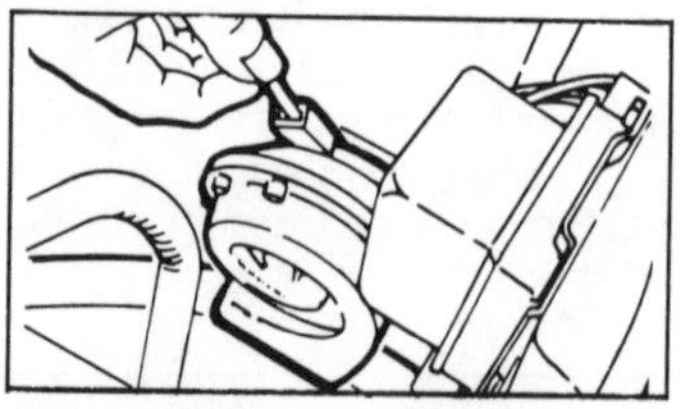

STEERING PROBLEMS

See steering system check in Suspension Section. Check tire pressures. Have a professional service shop check all components in the front end and steering system.

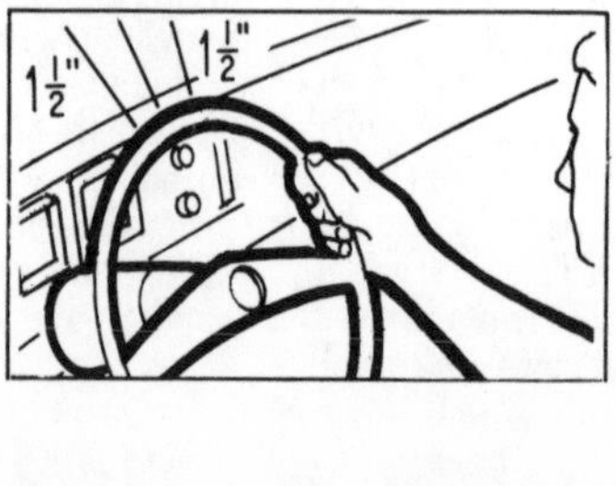

WASHER SYSTEM

If washer fails to squirt properly, raise hood and check system hose connections. Be sure washer fluid container has fluid. Check spout openings for clogging.

Keep container filled with fluid mixture of washer solvent and water. If road spray buildup on windshield is a chronic problem, add 1 tablespoon dishwasher detergent to solvent/water mixture when re-filling container.

NOTE: The cars windshield washer pump mechanism is lubricated by the fluid in the windshield washer tank. To avoid damaging the pump mechanism, keep an adequate level of fluid in the tank at all times.

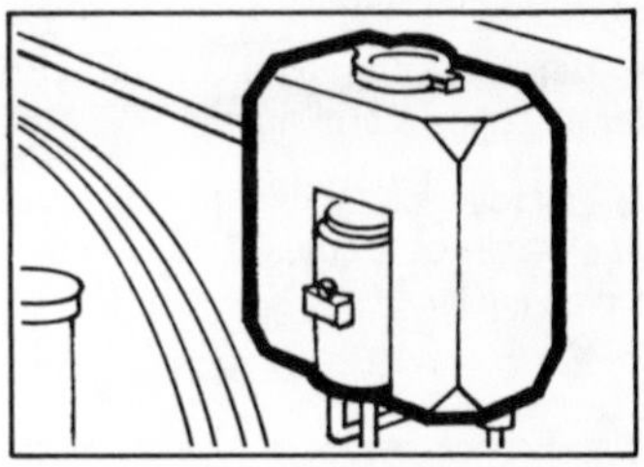

Electrical System

CHECK BATTERY FLUID LEVEL

To ensure starting ability at all times check your battery condition periodically. You'll need to check battery electrolyte (fluid) level in each of the six cells. Check battery cable connections for tightness and inspect for accumulated corrosion.

SAFETY NOTE: Wear gloves when working on battery.

1. Remove plastic filler caps on top of battery. Fluid should be up to lower end of filler hole and covering the plates. If fluid is low add clean, cold tap water. If your area has hard water, use only distilled water available at auto supply, food or drug stores.

2. Replace any lost caps immediately.

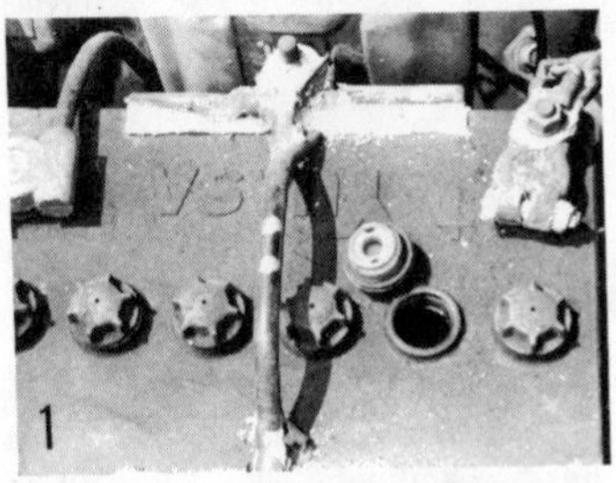

CAUTION: NEVER LIGHT A MATCH OR SMOKE near the top of a battery. Batteries give off explosive hydrogen gas.

NOTE: Battery that often checks low on fluid could mean:

A. Battery is getting old, due for replacement; have charge capacity checked at service shop.

B. Connections may be corroded or loose; clean/replace as needed (see below).

C. Alternator or voltage regulator not functioning properly; this happens far less often than A or B above.

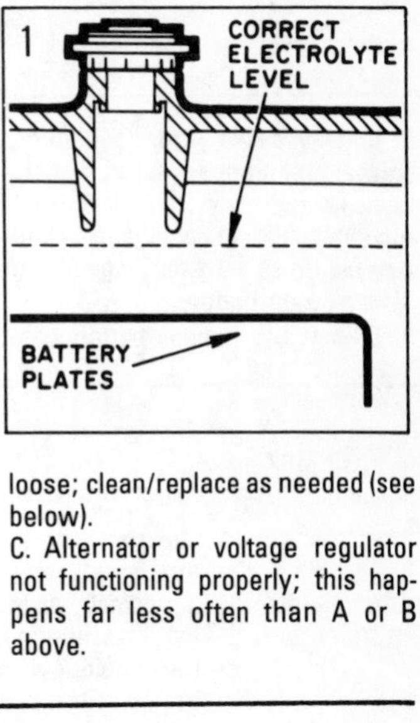

CLEAN THOSE BATTERY TERMINALS

As time goes by, battery terminals build up a dry powdery, whitish material. This material is corrosive and will gradually eat thru battery cables if not cleaned off periodically.

1. Loosen and remove battery connections.

2. Brush off all loose corrosion; use stiff bristle brush. Do not get this material into eyes or on open cuts. Wash off at once.

3. If corrosion build-up is extremely heavy and brushing does not remove all of it, mix 2 tablespoons baking soda to 1 cup water. Pour solution directly onto terminals and connectors. Allow to soak a few minutes and rinse off. Continue brushing to remove all traces of corrosion

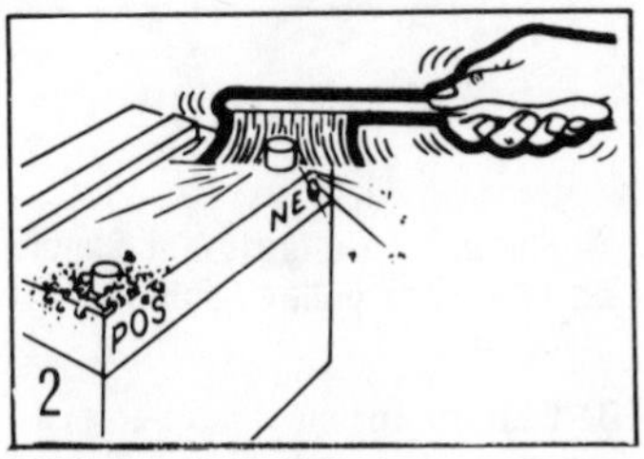

build-up. Do not allow cleaning solution to enter battery.

4. Replace connectors on battery terminal posts and tighten.

5. Liberally smear battery terminal posts and cable connectors with petroleum jelly.

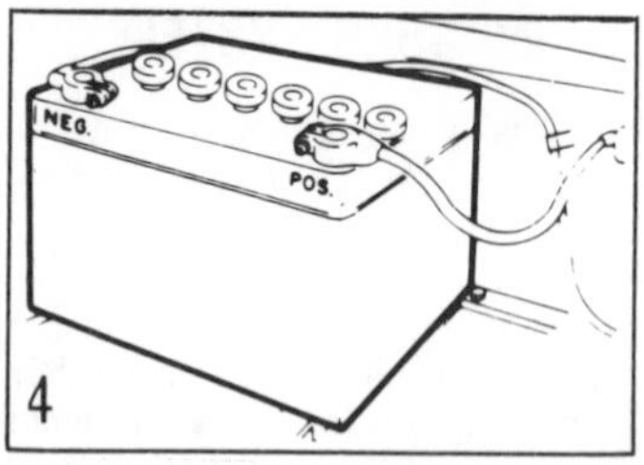

REPLACE FAULTY BATTERY CABLES

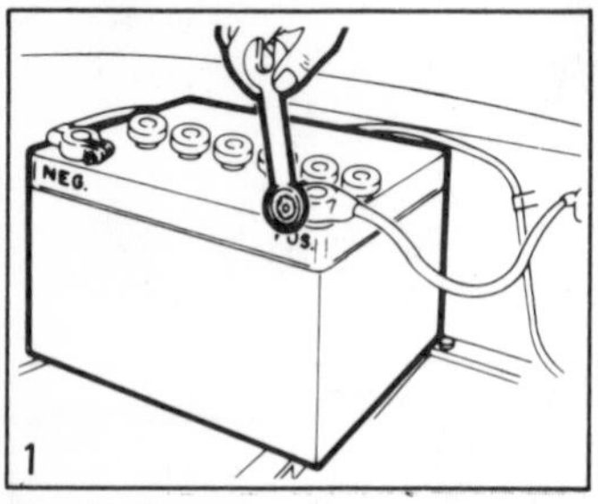

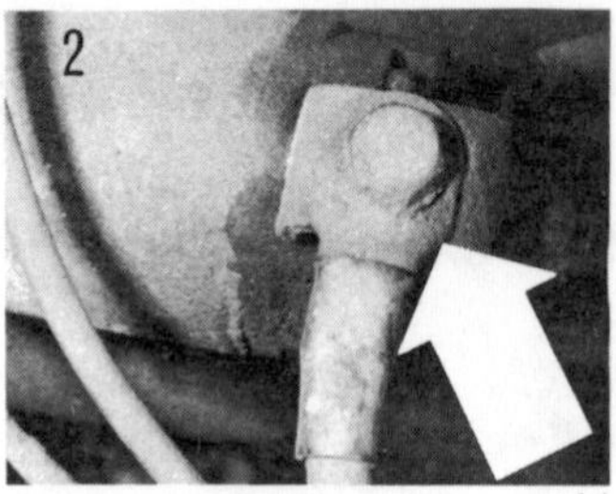

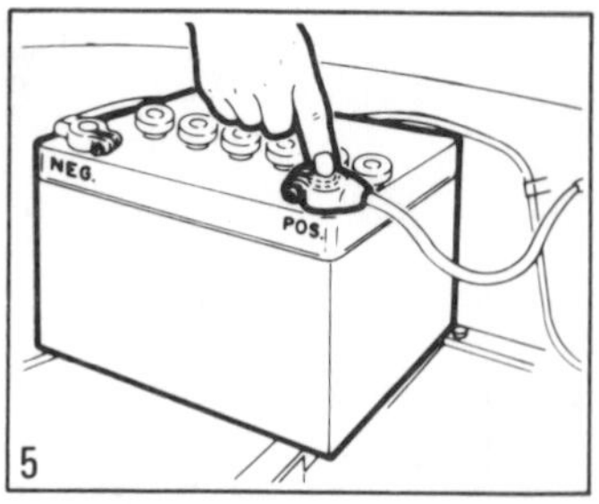

If battery cable strands become frayed, broken or corroded, replace cable immediately. Delay in correcting this condition could lead to sudden failure to start the engine. Can also weaken battery.

1. Loosen and remove battery connections. Clean OFF any corrosion.
2. Disconnect negative cable from its attachment to engine or chassis. Disconnect positive cable from its attachment to starter relay.
3. Attach new cables making sure positive and negative cables are on proper terminals. They are not identical.
4. Replace connectors on battery terminal posts and tighten.
5. Liberally smear battery terminal posts and cable connectors with petroleum jelly.

BATTERY HOLDDOWN

The clamp device which holds battery in place should be checked periodically. If loose, tighten. Clean off corrosion buildup. Severely corroded holddown components should be replaced before they break.

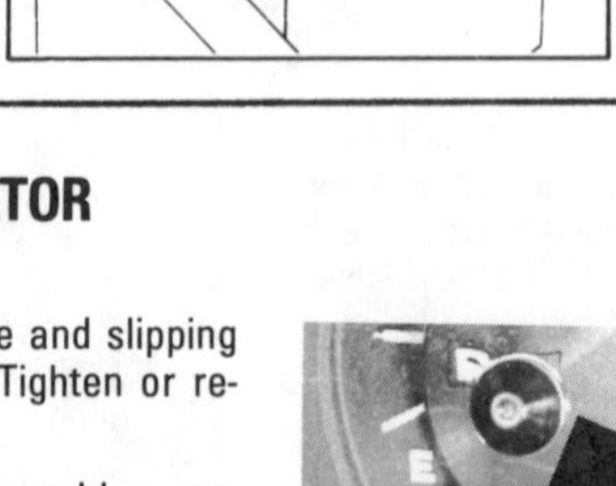

ALTERNATOR

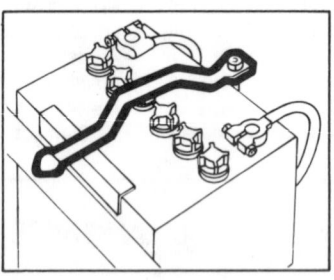

Red alternator warning light on instrument panel should glow red when you first turn ignition key. This proves bulb is OK. Alternator warning light should go off when engine is running at normal operating speed. If alternator warning light glows red at operating speed, alternator isn't charging battery properly. Common causes are:

A. Fan belts are loose and slipping on alternator pulley. Tighten or replace belts.

B. Battery terminals, cables are loose or corroded. Clean; tighten; replace bad cables.

If A or B do not correct problem, alternator or voltage regulator may be faulty. This happens far less of-

ten, and can only be checked by mechanic with proper electrical testing equipment.

Alternator Caution: Alternator can be permanently damaged by short-circuiting terminal connections.

When working around or moving alternator, always keep metal tools or engine parts from terminals.

ELECTRICAL FUSES

If any lights, switches or electrical circuits do not operate, check for possible blown (burned out) fuse. Fuses are located in fuse box mounted under the left side of the instrument panel inside car. Replace blown fuse with same amperage new fuse. If fuses blow regularly, have car checked by professional service shop for possible short circuit.

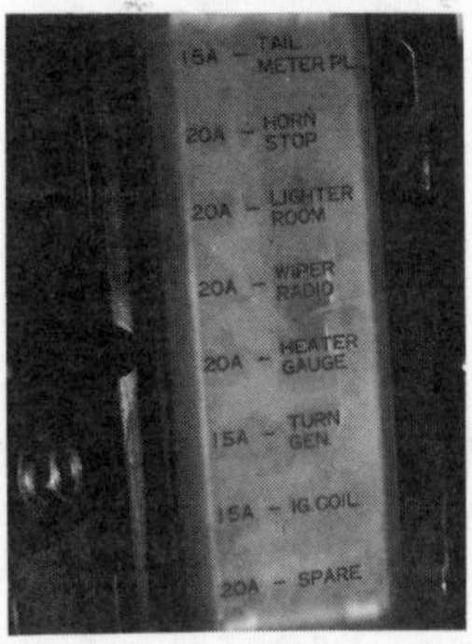

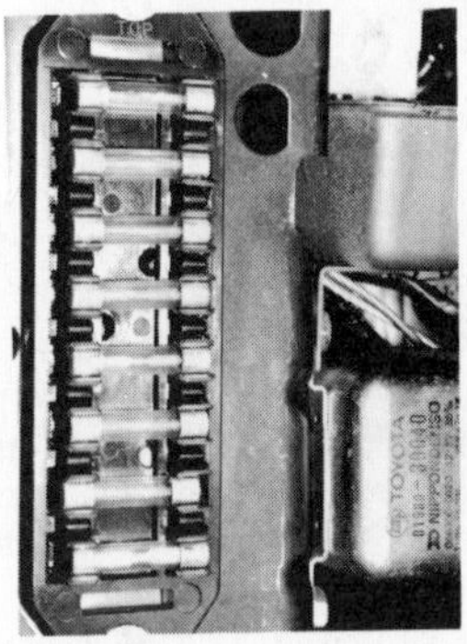

TURN SIGNAL AND 4-WAY FLASHER

Turn signals and 4-Way flashers will operate only if: A. All light bulbs are OK. B. Flasher unit is not burned out. The flasher unit is located on the left, under the dash. To replace, remove the wiring connector, grasp with fingers and pull connector out. To remove flasher, remove screw from bracket. REPLACE ONLY WITH SAME TYPE FLASHER.

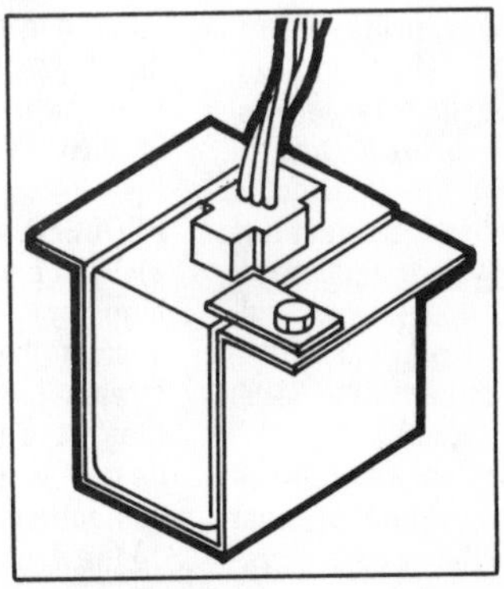

REAR WINDOW DEFOGGER SYSTEM

Do not clean inside of rear window fitted with defogger system with any abrasive material. This could destroy carbon-copper wires. Use only soft rag and mild detergent/water mixture. Dry carefully.

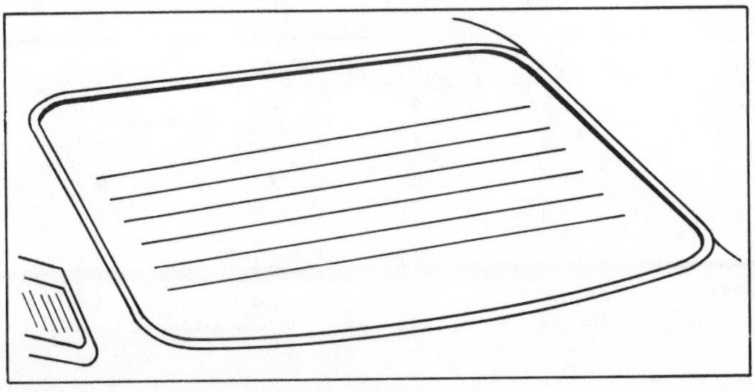

Air Conditioning System

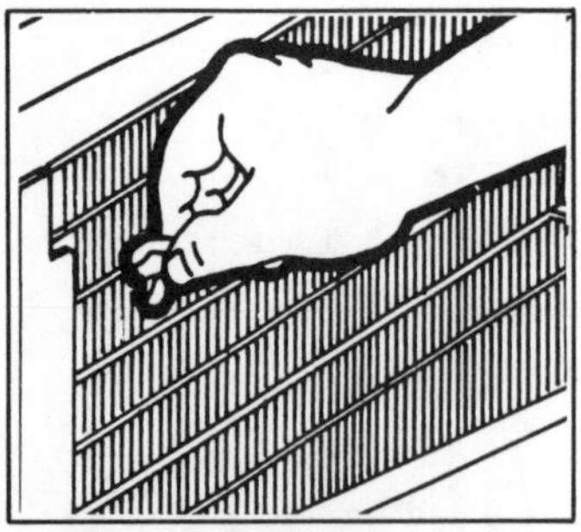

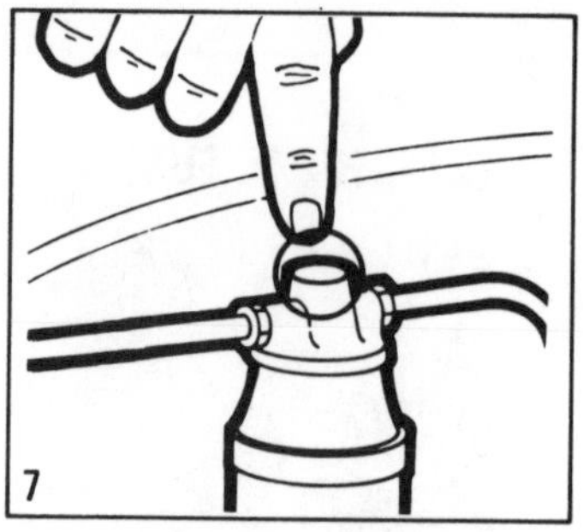
7

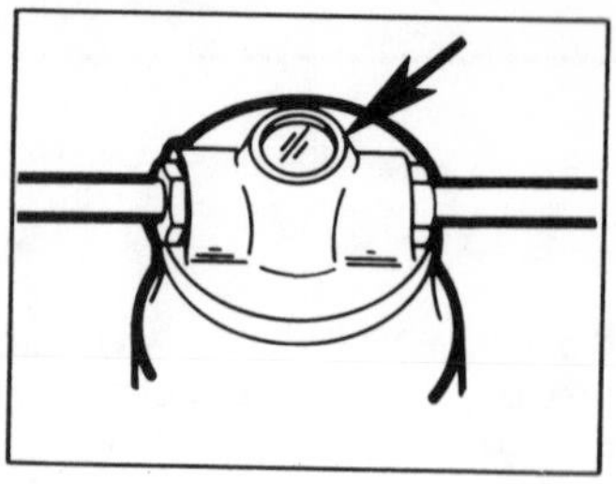

WARNING!—Never attempt to tighten fittings, disassemble or do any work on your car's A/C system. Consult a professional mechanic about A/C system problems and their correction. Your auto air conditioner (A/C) is a delicate, closed system. If air, dirt or water get into it, or if refrigerant escapes, the A/C unit will not cool a car interior. Among things you can do are:

1. Keep condenser grille clean. Check for dirt and debris; periodically remove dead insects, leaves, etc., with stiff bristle brush. Straighten any bent fins—carefully.
2. Keep radiator filled to correct level. (See Cooling System section). If fluid needs to be added, add antifreeze rather than water.
3. Keep radiator coolant at a 50/50 water/antifreeze mixture.
4. Flush cooling system and replace with fresh coolant mixture at least every 12,000 miles. (See Cooling System section).
5. Radiator cap should be tight and sealed properly. If sealing gasket is cracked, cut or worn, replace cap with new 15 lb. unit.
6. Check fan belt tension periodically. (See Cooling System section). Replace glazed, frayed or cut fan belts, before they fail entirely.
7. Check periodically for bubbles in the A/C sight glass. Sight glass is located in the head of the receiver/drier vessel. Sight glass is no larger than the head of a large nail. It may be dirty. Wipe clean for best visibility.

PROCEED AS FOLLOWS:

a) With engine and A/C system running, look for passage of refrigerant in sight glass. You'll be looking for a stream of milky white bubbles as they pass through sight glass. It is best to watch sight glass and have someone else start the car and turn on the A/C system. Allow to run for a few minutes.

b) If you observe no bubbles, and air flow from A/C unit in the car is passing cold air, everything is OK.

c) If no bubbles appear in the sight glass, and air flow from the A/C unit in the car is not delivering cold air, the system may be low on refrigerant and could need a recharge. Shut off the system and do not operate it.

d) If bubbles appear, system is low on refrigerant.

e) If you suspect refrigerant loss based on tests performed above, have system checked by a professional A/C service shop. They can confirm refrigerant loss, recharge the system and check for system leakage.

NOTE: Once a week or so, even in winter, run A/C system for about 5 minutes as you drive. This keeps system internally lubricated, prevents hoses hardening.

CAPACITIES

YEAR	MODEL	ENGINE OIL With Filter	ENGINE OIL Without Filter	TRANSMISSION MANUAL	TRANSMISSION AUTOMATIC	DRIVE AXLE (pts.)	COOLING SYSTEM (qts.)
1970-71	Corona 1900	5.6	4.6	2.1	7.4	2.2	8.4
1972-73	Corona 2000	5.2	4.2	4.1	7.4	2.2	8.4
1974	Corona 2000	5.3	4.0	2.9①	6.1	2.6	8.4
1975-77	Corona 2200	5.3	4.4	2.9①	6.1	2.6	8.5
1970-71	Mark II 1900	5.3	4.3	2.1	7.4	2.2	7.8
1972 (early)	Mark II 2000	5.2	4.2	2.1	7.4	2.2	7.8
1972 (late)-77	Mark II 6 cyl	5.6	4.6	1.8	7.4	2.6	11.4

① 2.7 with 5-speed

TUNE-UP SPECIFICATIONS

YEAR	MODEL	SPARK PLUGS Type	SPARK PLUGS Gap (in.)	DISTRIBUTOR Point Dwell (deg.)	DISTRIBUTOR Point Gap (in.)	IGNITION TIMING Man. Trans. (deg.) ■	IGNITION TIMING Auto Trans. (deg.) ■	IDLE SPEED Man. Trans. (rpm) ■	IDLE SPEED Auto Trans. (rpm) ■
1970	8R-C	W20EP	0.031	52	0.018	TDC	TDC	650	650
	2M	W20EP	0.031	41	0.018	TDC	TDC	650	650
1971	8-RC	W20EP	0.031	52	0.018	10B	10B	650	650
	2M	W20EP	0.031	41	0.018	TDC	TDC	650	650
1972	18R-C	W20EP	0.031	52	0.018	7B	7B	650	650
	2M	W16EP	0.030	41	0.018	7B	7B	700	600
	4M	W14EP	0.031	41	0.018	7B	5B	700	650
1973	18R-C	W20EP	0.031	52	0.018	7B	7B	650	650
	4M	W14EP	0.031	41	0.018	7B	5B	700	650
1974	18R-C	W20EP③	0.031	52	0.018	7B	7B	650	850
	4M	W16EP	0.031	41	0.018	5B	5B	700	750
1975-76	20R	W16EP	0.030	52	0.018	8B	8B	850	850
	4M①	W16EP	0.030	41	0.018	10B	10B	800	750
	4M②	W16EP	0.030	41	0.018	5B	5B	800	750
1977	See Underhood Specifications Sticker								

■ Manual transmission is in Neutral; Automatic transmission is in Drive
① Except Calif.
② Calif.
③ Calif. w/EGR: W 16EP

NOTE: The underhood specifications sticker often reflects tune-up specification changes made in production. Sticker figures must be used if they disagree with those in this chart.

Service Record

DATE/MILEAGE	SERVICE	NEXT DUE

Volkswagen Type 1

Lubrication and Oil Change

LUBRICATION CHECK

A key part of keeping your VW running at peak performance is regular oil changes and lubrication. The required tools are few and the lubricants widely available, so there's no excuse for neglect.

VW SAYS... Change oil and clean oil strainer every 3000 miles.
On 1975-76 cars, the oil change interval is lengthened to 5000 mile intervals. If your car is used under adverse conditions, however, change the oil more frequently. Recommended grade: MS or SE
Check the oil level at least once a week

TOOLS & MATERIALS
10mm box wrench or socket and ratchet handle set
medium sized screwdriver
drain pan for old oil (at least 4 qt. capacity)
oil pouring spout
oil strainer gaskets and copper gaskets for nuts
oil and lubricants as specified below
SAFETY TIPS . . . Use jackstands to support the car,
never get under a car held only by a jack. Or, use a
pair of sturdy drive-on ramps.
Wear work gloves when changing oil to avoid
burns.

BRAKE FLUID LEVEL CHECK

Check brake fluid level in master cylinder reservoir every three months . . . sooner if braking feels inadequate. Add when low. Recommended grade: DOT 3 or 4 as printed on can.
The brake reservoir is located in the luggage compartment on the driver's side. It is a translucent plastic container with a screw-on cap. Brake fluid is easily checked by making sure that level is above the seam of the "see through" reservoir. Add fluid if level is below the seam. Secure cap firmly.
DO NOT OVERFILL
If fluid repeatedly checks low, there is a leak somewhere in the system. See SAFETY SYSTEMS—WHEEL CYLINDER.

Have mechanic check further. Neglect can be dangerous because leaks can either soak brake linings with fluid, making them ineffective, or completely disable either front or rear brakes.

OIL CHANGE AND OIL STRAINER CLEANING

1. If engine is cold, start up and idle for about 5 minutes.
2. Park car on level ground. Turn engine off.
3. Place drain pan under oil strainer cover, located in center of engine.
4. Using 10mm wrench, remove all but one nut, pry cover down with screwdriver, and allow oil to drain.
5. Remove the last nut and remove the oil strainer and gaskets.

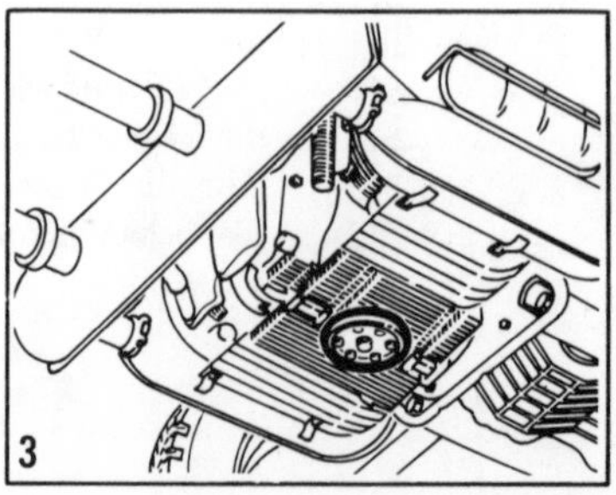
3

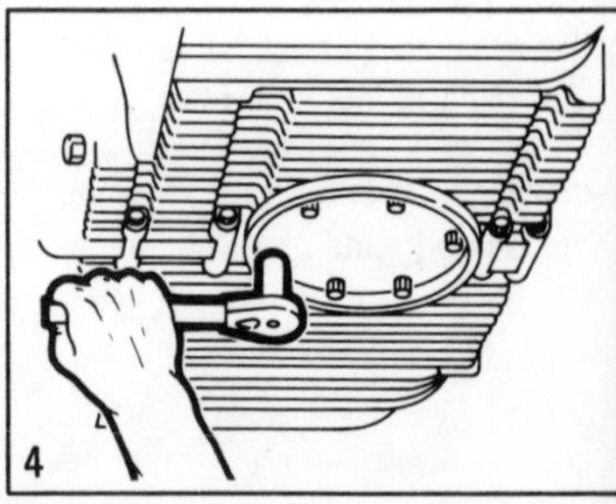
4

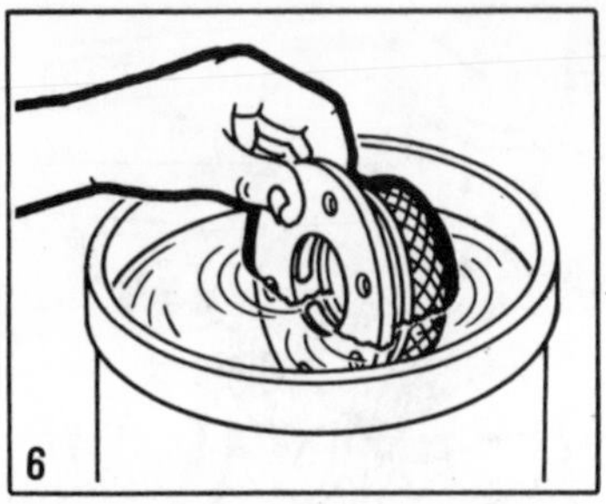

6

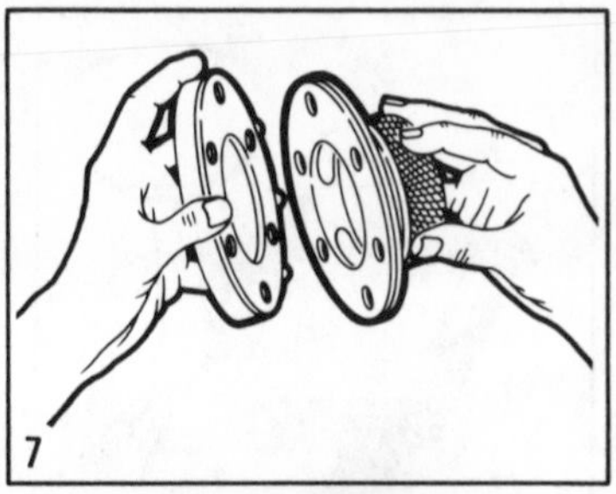

7

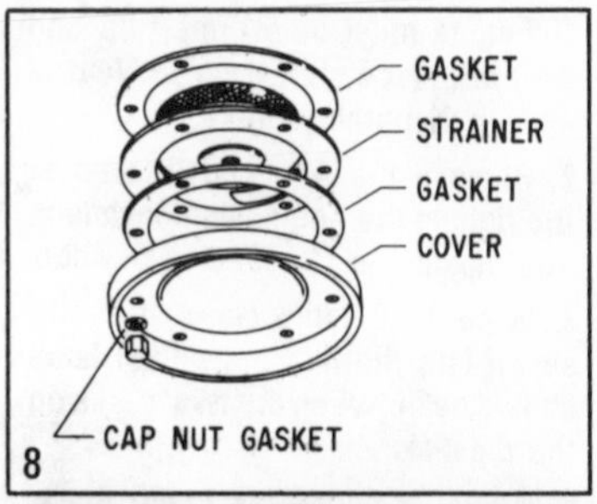

8

6. Clean the strainer and cover in solvent.
7. Install a new gasket on the cover studs. Position the strainer over the studs.
8. Install a second gasket and then the cover. Use new copper gaskets on the cover nuts. DO NOT OVER-TIGHTEN THE CAP NUTS.
9. Locate the oil filler tube on top of the engine. Remove cap.
10. Punch oil pouring spout into top of oil can. Pour two cans and about half of the third can of oil into the filler tube. Wipe filler cap clean and replace it.
11. Check new oil level at dipstick.

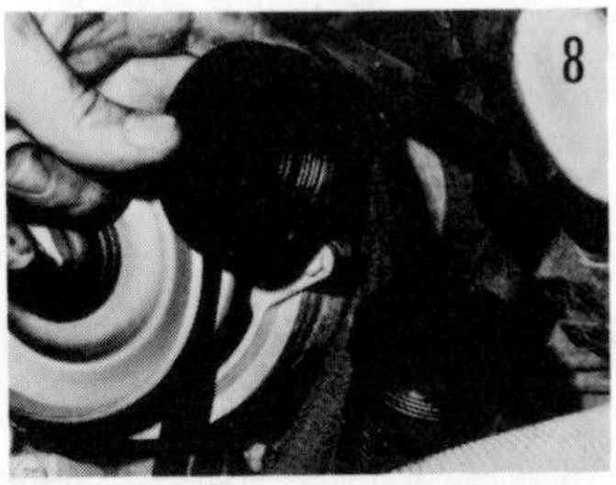

8

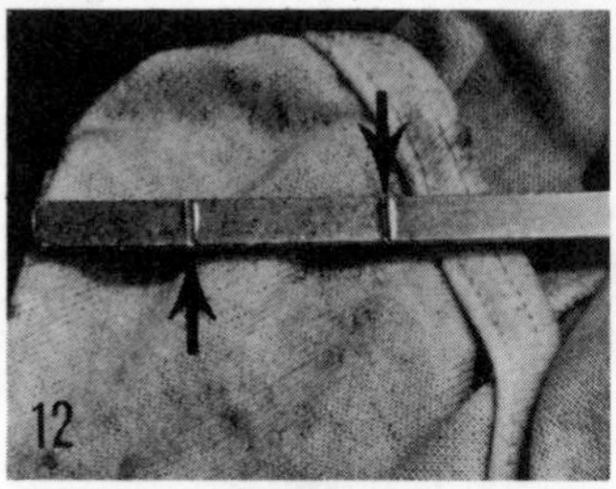

12

Pull out dipstick, wipe clean.
12. Push dipstick all the way back in. Remove and check oil level. It should be between the marks. If not, add just enough oil to bring the level to the top line.
13. Start engine and idle 3-5 minutes. The oil light on instrument panel will glow when engine is first started. Light should go out in 30 seconds or less.
14. Stop engine and check strainer cover for leaks. Recheck oil level, which should now be at the top line.

MANUAL TRANSAXLE FLUID LEVEL CHECK

VW SAYS . . . check manual transaxle fluid every 6000 miles. Car should be level. Recommended grade: Standard transmission gear oil (SAE 90-80 in very cold climates).
TOOLS NEEDED . . . drain plug wrench suction gun or squeeze bulb syringe
1. Locate transmission filler plug on side of transaxle housing from underneath the car.
2. Wipe road dirt from filler plug area before loosening. Remove plug with wrench.
3. Insert your finger into the hole. Oil should be level with the bottom edge of the filler hole.
4. Add gear oil as needed with suction gun or squeeze bulb syringe.
5. Replace filler plug; tighten.

1

2

3

4

AUTOMATIC STICKSHIFT FLUID LEVEL CHECK

VW SAYS . . . check automatic transmission fluid (ATF) level every 6000 miles. Recommended grade: ATF Type A or Dexron®.
TOOLS NEEDED . . . long-neck filler funnel

1. Engine must be warmed up and shut off. Place shift lever in Neutral and apply parking brake.
2. Remove the ATF cap located at the right in the engine compartment. The dipstick is attached to the cap.
3. Wipe the dipstick clean and reinsert it into the filler. The fluid level should be between the two marks on the dipstick.
4. If fluid is below the lower mark, add enough ATF to bring level up as necessary. DO NOT OVERFILL.
5. Add ATF through tube by means of long-neck filler funnel.

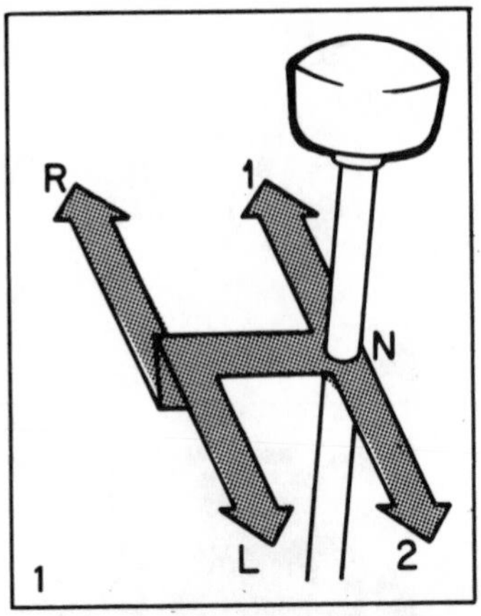

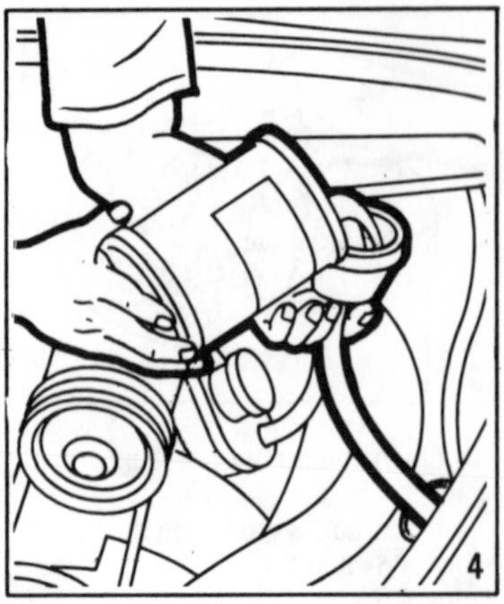

FRONT END LUBRICATION

VW SAYS . . . every 6000 miles, lubricate the four grease fittings on the front axle of regular Beetles. This must be done with the front wheels off the ground. Grease until excess appears at the sides.

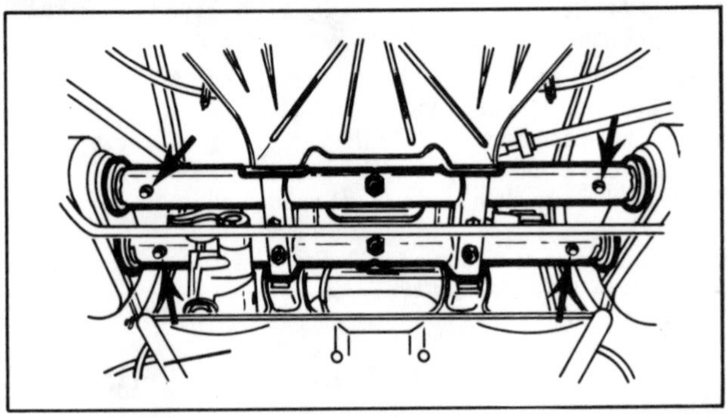

OTHER LUBRICATION CHECKS

Keep the windshield washer container full of water and enough solvent to prevent freezing in winter. Keep the spare tire at 42 psi. Occasionally remove the plug and lubricate the door locks with a light oil. On older models, remove the door hinge caps, and oil. On newer models, lube with a pressure grease gun until new grease appears.

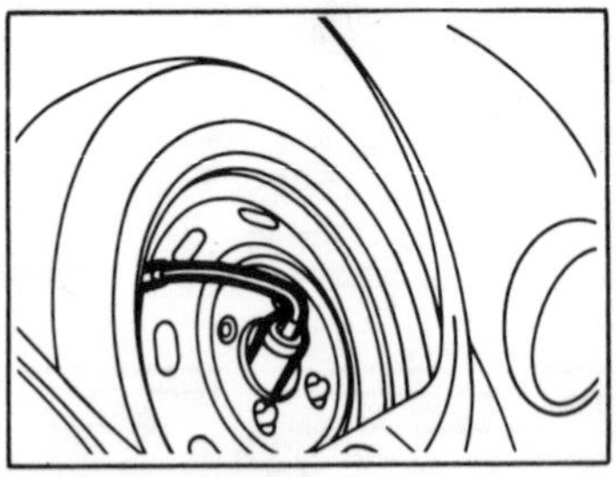

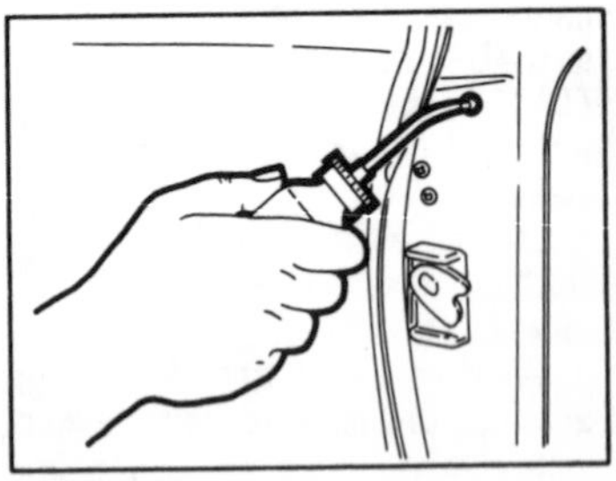

SPEEDOMETER CABLE LUBRICATION

If speedometer pointer tends to quiver or jump, or if unit makes a low, rasping sound, lubrication may be needed.
1. Open the luggage compartment. Remove the instrument panel cover. On '73 and later Super Beetles, go up behind the dash.
2. Remove the cable from the speedometer by unscrewing it.

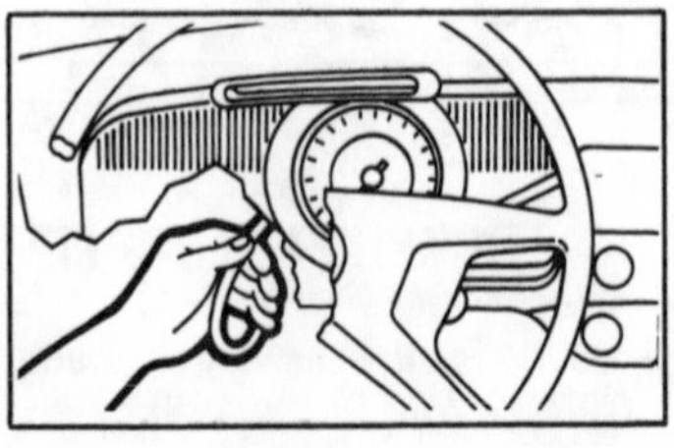

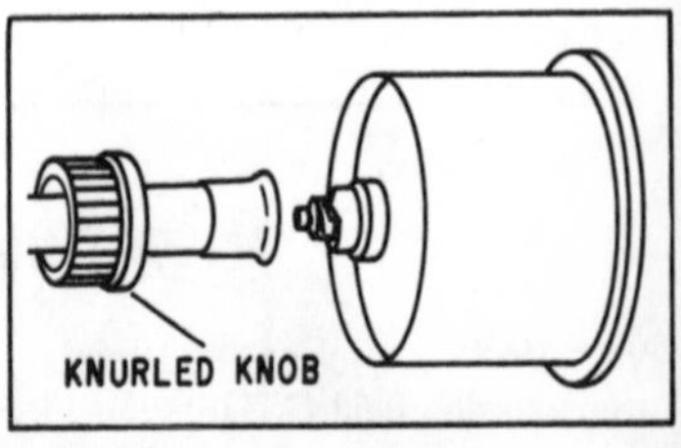

3. Pry off the left front hub cap.
4. Knock the cable retaining pin out of the dust cover.
5. Pull the cable out through the axle. Carefully note which end is top. Check for wear or frayed strands. If damaged, replace inner cable.
6. Apply generous amount of speedometer cable lubricant into cable casing. From the top, push the cable down into the guide channel and into the sheath. Be careful you're inserting the correct end first.
7. Fasten the cable at the dust cover with a cotter pin.
8. Reconnect cable to speedometer head and replace cover.

DISTRIBUTOR LUBRICATION

Every 6000 miles, put a few drops of a light oil on the felt pad under the distributor rotor. This will lubricate the ignition advance mechanism. On some older distributors, this is not required.

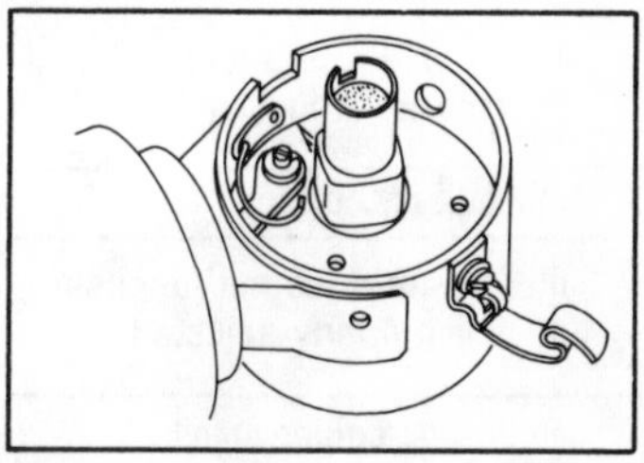

WHEEL BEARING LUBRICATION

On all but '74 models, front and rear wheel bearings should be disassembled and repacked in grease every 30,000 miles. This is a job requiring professional knowledge and tools.

Cooling System

The VW depends on the cooling system and the engine lubricating system to maintain the correct engine temperature. The cooling system consists of a belt driven fan which forces air over the cylinders and cylinder heads. Sheet metal shrouds surround the engine so that the cooling air is contained and directed. Engine oil also provides cooling and this is why oil quality and level are even more critical on a VW than a conventional car. All VWs have an oil cooler, a small oil radiator, located inside the cooling shroud. Accessory oil coolers are available, which you can have installed or install yourself, that provide additional engine cooling for heavy duty operation such as trailer towing. For almost all heater/cooling system work or inspection it may be necessary to get under the car. Do not attempt to do any work under the vehicle while it is supported only by the jack. Use safety stands or ramps. Block the wheels. It's a good idea to carry a spare fan belt. Belts have a way of going in the most remote places and at the most inopportune times. The original VW tool kit comes with a wrench to fit the pulley bolt. If you don't have one, purchase a wrench that fits and you'll be able to adjust or replace the belt yourself.

REPLACING THE THERMOSTAT

A faulty thermostat can cause either overheating or slow warmup. Check that the thermostat is fully closed when the engine is cold, and wide open when the engine is idling hot. Replace if defective. Located under car.

TOOLS AND MATERIALS
Adjustable wrench or socket and ratchet handle
New thermostat

1. Remove screws, and remove air duct plate from lower right of engine.
2. Remove mounting bolt from underside of thermostat bracket.
3. Loosen bracket mounting nut.

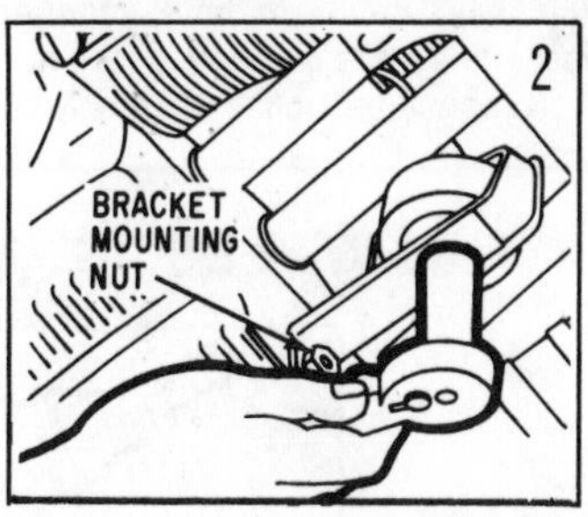

4. Push upper portion of bracket away from you so that bracket will rotate away from thermostat.
5. Unscrew thermostat (counterclockwise).

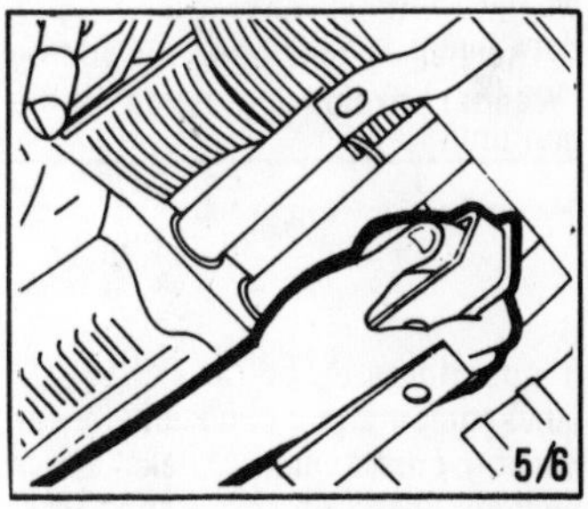

6. Screw new thermostat onto actuating rod. When fully screwed on, move up and down to ensure cooling flaps are free. Leave in full up position.

7. Turn the bracket back to its original position so that rod is in slot in upper portion.
8. Slide the bracket up and down on its mount until top of bracket just touches top of thermostat. Be careful not to pull thermostat down in doing this.
9. Tighten thermostat bracket mounting nut.
10. Pull thermostat downward, and install thermostat mounting bolt through lower bracket.
11. Install air duct plate.

ENGINE OVERHEATING

OVERHEATS BECAUSE	TO CORRECT IT
engine oil level is too low, or viscosity is incorrect	fill to correct level or replace with proper grade of oil; check for leaks
fan belt is too loose	adjust tension or replace worn belt
thermostat does not function or is improperly adjusted	have checked and, if necessary, have replaced or adjusted by professional mechanic
engine oil cooler or oil pressure relief valve is clogged or not working	have checked and, if necessary, have replaced by professional mechanic
of heavy duty operation, such as trailer towing or extra loads	allow engine to cool, proceed more slowly, and use lower gear
engine is out of tune (ignition timing may be incorrect)	adjust ignition timing

FAN BELT ADJUSTMENT

The fan belt drives the cooling fan and generator. Since there is no natural air flow through the engine, and since the oil cooler is dependent upon the fan, it should be easy to see that any slippage of the belt will result in overheating. The belt deserves an occasional look and tension check.

1. Inspect fan belt occasionally. Press thumb at midpoint of belt span between pulleys. If belt depresses more than ½ inch, tightening is needed. A too loose belt will not drive the cooling fan or generator/alternator effectively.
2. The belt is tensioned by adding (loosens) or removing (tightens) the spacer shims between the pulley halves. Place extra shims on the outside of the pulley, under the nut.
3. Use a screwdriver in the slot in the inner pulley to hold it during loosening and tightening of the nut. Correct belt tension is extremely important for proper engine cooling and electrical charging.

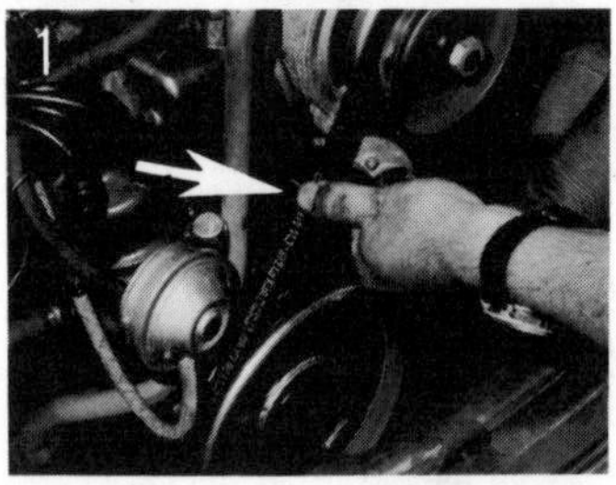

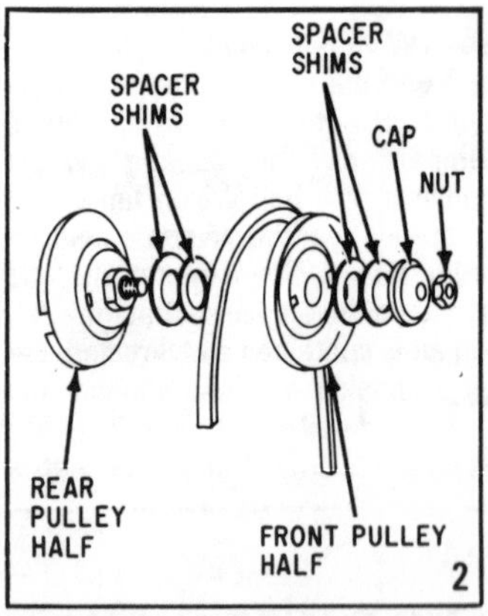

PLUG WIRE BOOTS

Check these seals occasionally for cracks or brittleness. Leaks allow needed cooling air to escape. They are replaced by simply pulling spark plug leads off, and pulling the old boot off the end of the connector. Slide the new boot on carefully in exactly the same position. Then, install the lead and make sure it seals properly. If necessary, slide it to a position on the connector which will ensure a tight seal against the shrouding.

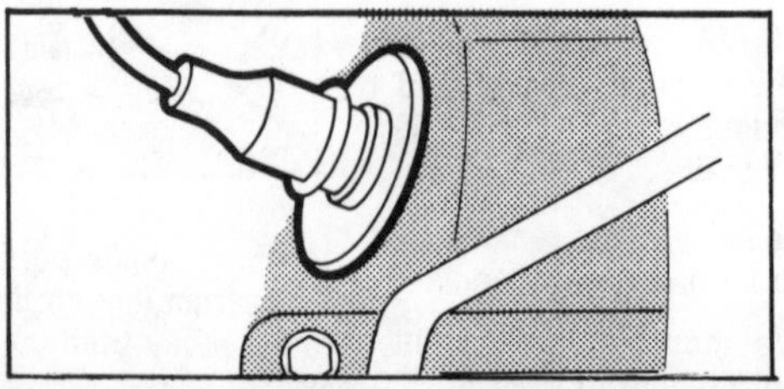

FIND THOSE COOLING SYSTEM LEAKS

1. Inspect both heater hoses. If either is cracked or broken, replace it. Leaky heater hoses deprive the engine of cooling air, make the heater ineffective.
2. Inspect heater hose clamps. Make sure they hold hoses securely onto fittings, and have not loosened due to vibration.
3. With engine off, check cooling fan air intake behind fan housing for foreign material.
4. Inspect spark plug rubber boots for cracks, brittleness, and replace if necessary.
5. Make sure all screws in shrouding are in place and tight.
6. Make sure rubber seal around rear of engine compartment is not cracked. Have replaced if necessary.

Leaks are possible at:
Heater hoses • Shrouding assembly points • Spark plug rubber boots

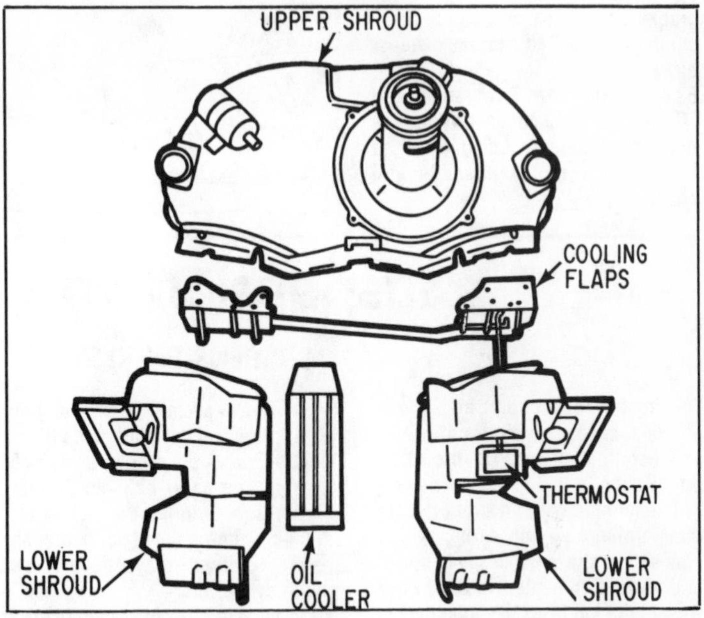

HOSE REPLACEMENT

Inspect all hoses. If any are dented or cracked, replace at once. Check all hose connections for tightness. Tighten loose hose clamps; they tend to loosen due to engine vibration.
1. Loosen both hose clamps with a Phillips screwdriver.
2. Carefully pull hose off fan housing connection. Then, pull lower portion of hose off heater box sleeve.
3. Press down on top of heater box sleeve to make sure it is fully seated.
4. Transfer hose clamps to new hose.
5. Connect hose at top and bottom. Make sure it slides on as far as it will go, and that heater box sleeve stays in position.
6. Position and tighten hose clamps.

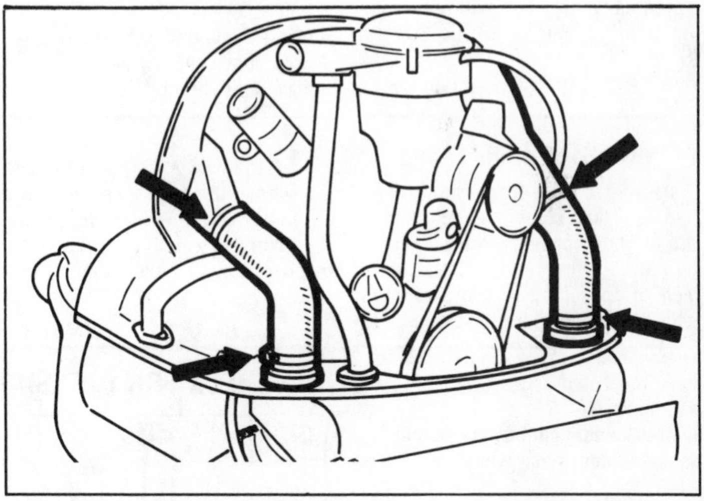

POINTS TO CHECK

Check fins on bottom of oil pan and cylinders and heads for heavy deposits of grease and dirt. If fins are clogged, have engine steam cleaned.

Check hoses for leaks at arrowed points. Leaks will deprive the engine of required cooling air. See Hose Replacement section at right.

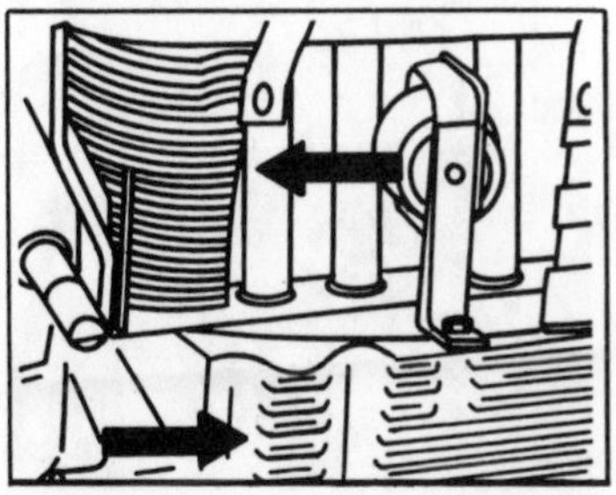

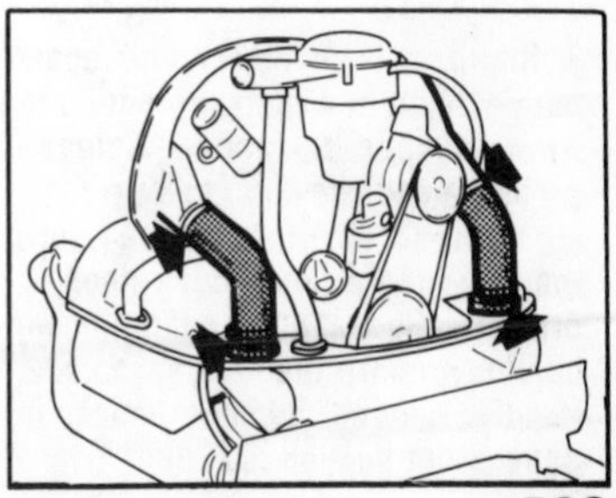

Check the rubber gasket at the rear of the engine compartment for cracks. Leaks here may cause recirculation of cooling system exhaust air.
Remember that if the red "Generator" light comes on it means there is no engine cooling. Stop the engine as soon as possible and check cause.

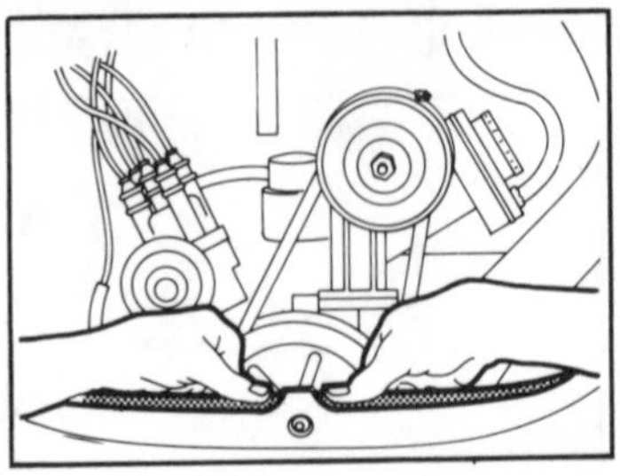

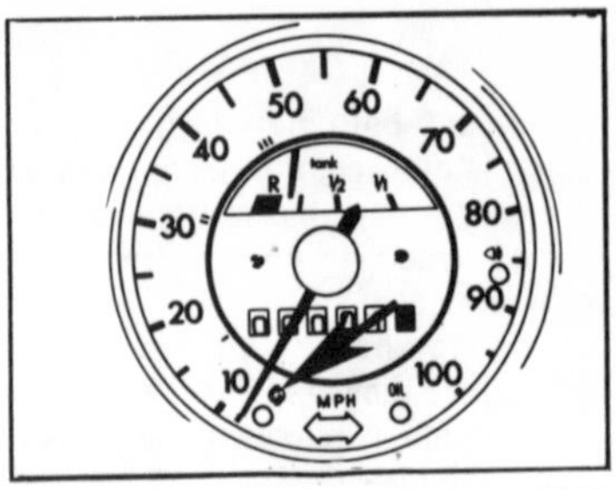

Suspension and Tires

SUSPENSION SYSTEM

The front wheels mount and rotate on the spindles, which are attached to steering knuckles. On the standard Beetle, torsion bars run across the front of the car and support it via dual, trailing torsion arms, which connect to the knuckles via upper and lower ball joints. On the Super Beetle, the knuckles are mounted to the lower end of a suspension strut which supports the body via a coil spring at the top. A ball joint is required only on the lower end of the steering knuckle on the Super Beetle.
Your car's suspension system consists of wheels, tires, torsion bars (coil springs on the front of the Super Beetle), shock absorbers, sway bars (or stabilizer bars), ball joints, steering linkage, steering damper. If any of these items is out of adjustment or badly worn, you may notice any of these symptoms:

- car pulls to one side when braking
- car wanders when driving a straight line
- overall ride may be either hard or bouncy
- effort is needed to steer vehicle
- tires show uneven wear
- tires squeal when cornering
- front of car dips or bounces when braking
- car rocks side-to-side when going over rough road
- wheels bounce or make slapping sound on road
- steering wheel vibrates in hands
- front of car vibrates at highway speeds

Any of above symptoms indicates corrective action is needed. Delay can: ruin tires; cause damage/failure to other suspension parts; create safety hazard.

STEERING

If steering linkage, front suspension and steering column components are in good condition, there should be no more than one and one half inch of free play in the steering wheel when measured at the rim of the wheel. If a loud knock is heard when turning the steering wheel from one extreme to the other, have mechanic check pinion bearing preload.

SHOCK ABSORBERS

Shock absorbers work to keep wheels in constant contact with the road. Result in safe handling and ride control; longer tire life. So shock absorbers (or shocks) are important.

HOW TO CHECK FOR BAD SHOCKS

1. Check under car and locate shock absorber near each wheel.

2. Heavy oil streaks on outer shock housing indicate need for replacement.

3. Stand at front of car and apply body weight in a pumping action to front bumper or fender. Release pressure and allow car to stop rocking. Car should not bounce more than one more time after releasing pressure. Repeat at rear. If bouncing continues more than once, replacement is needed. Replace shocks in pairs (front pair or rear pair).

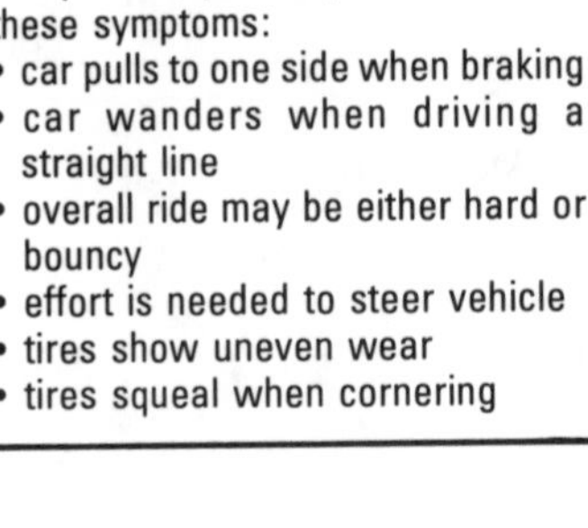

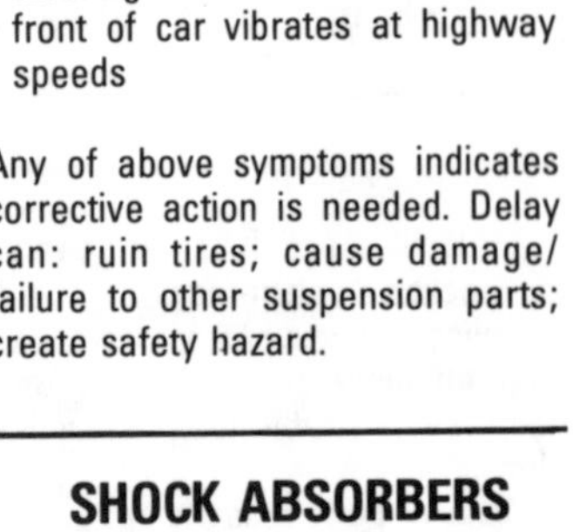

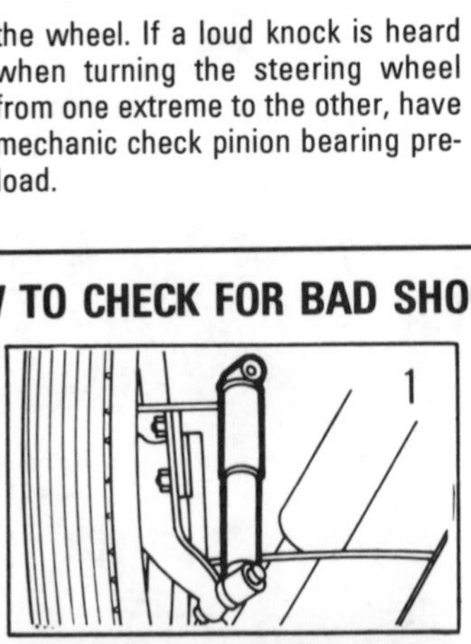

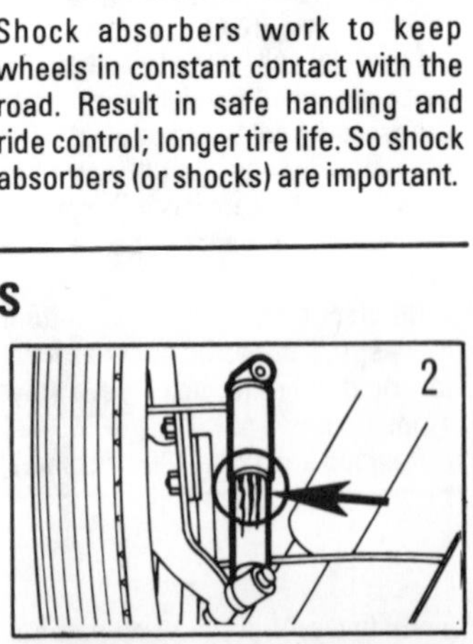

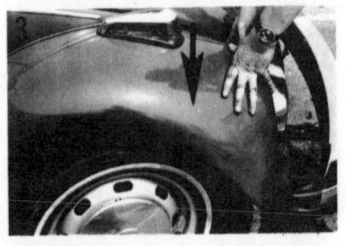

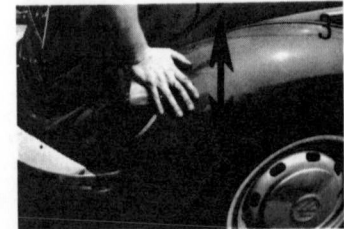

TOW HITCH INFORMATION

If your VW is used for trailer towing you should check:

A. Cooling System; make sure that fan belt is in good condition and properly tensioned. See Cooling System for checks to perform.

B. Check ATF level on automatic stickshift models. Maintain at proper level.

C. Check rear shock absorbers; you may benefit from installation of new rear shocks.

D. Check Tire Pressures; best traction and handling will be ensured if tire pressures are properly maintained. Never exceed 882 lbs. trailer weight when towing with your VW.

For safer and more trouble-free trailer towing, consider:
A. Engine oil cooler; helps maintain lower engine temperature during towing. Helps avoid engine overheating. Some units can be self-installed.

B. Heavy Duty Shock Absorbers; important to have on rear wheels if you intend to do a lot of towing or load carrying within the car itself. Don't forget to consider replacing factory shocks, when they are worn out, with heavy duty units at the front as well.
C. Variable Load Flasher; this unit will accommodate the added load of trailer turn signal lamps on trailer when these are hooked into your car's electrical system.

FRONT END ALIGNMENT

When steering, handing and/or tire wear indicate front end alignment may be needed, this work can only be done at an automotive service shop. DO NOT PUT OFF NEEDED FRONT END ALIGNMENT. At the same time, have ball joints and steering linkage checked.

Ignition System

TUNE-UP SERVICES

The ignition system consists of spark plugs; plug wires; distributor; rotor; points; condenser; coil. These units work to create a good hot spark inside the engine (ignition) at exactly the right moment (timing). If ignition is weak or timing is off, engine may be hard to start, run poorly, waste gas, lose power, backfire or not run at all. VW SAYS . . . Replace plugs and points every 12,000 miles (15,000 miles on 1975-76 models).

TOOLS & MATERIALS . . . Parts: set of points; condenser; 4 spark plugs. Tools: gap gauge; 13/16 in. spark plug socket and handle; screwdriver; open end, box or combination metric wrenches; timing equipment (see Ignition Timing).

SAFETY TIP . . . Change only one spark plug at a time to avoid cross-wiring and possible engine damage.

OTHER IGNITION CHECK POINTS

Inspect spark plug wires. If cracked or brittle, entire set should be replaced. Also, center high tension wire. Inspect distributor cap. Wipe inside clean occasionally with dry, lint-free rag. If cap is cracked or rotor contacts are excessively burned, replace cap.

CHECKING POINTS, AND ROTOR

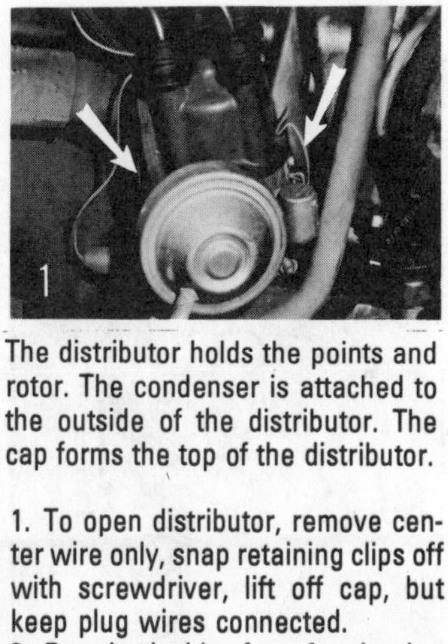

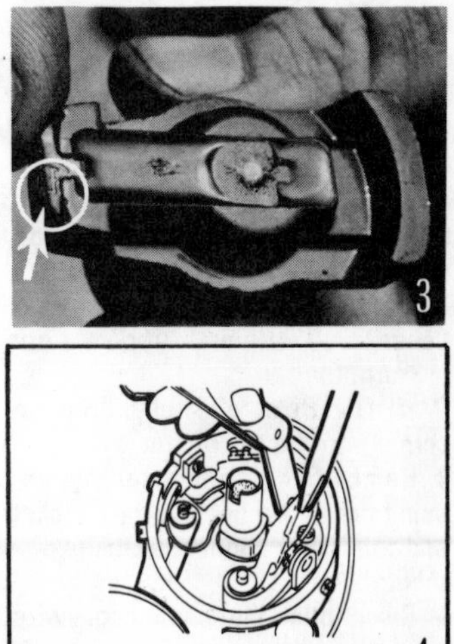

The distributor holds the points and rotor. The condenser is attached to the outside of the distributor. The cap forms the top of the distributor.

1. To open distributor, remove center wire only, snap retaining clips off with screwdriver, lift off cap, but keep plug wires connected.
2. Examine inside of cap for pitted or burned metal contacts, hairline cracks, excessive wear of button at center, or carbon tracks.
3. Pull rotor off straight up. If it is cracked, or tip or center contact is burned, replace it.
4. Pry points apart with screwdriver. If pitted or burned, replace. If OK, check gap with feeler gauge, for proper setting of .016.

SPARK PLUG REPLACEMENT

1. Pull spark plug wire by grasping rubber boot. Do not jerk wire off. If stuck, turn boot, pulling gently.

2. Loosen spark plug using socket wrench.

3. Wipe loose dirt from around plug before removing. Do not let dirt drop into engine through plug hole. Unscrew plug.

4. Check plug electrode gap on new plug. Adjust to .024 in. on all Beetles. Plug gap is correct when the gauge drags slightly as it is pulled between plug electrodes.

5. Thread new plug into plug hole by hand. Hand tighten. Do not force or cross thread. Use socket wrench to tighten firmly but do not force. Replace plug wire. Press boot firmly.

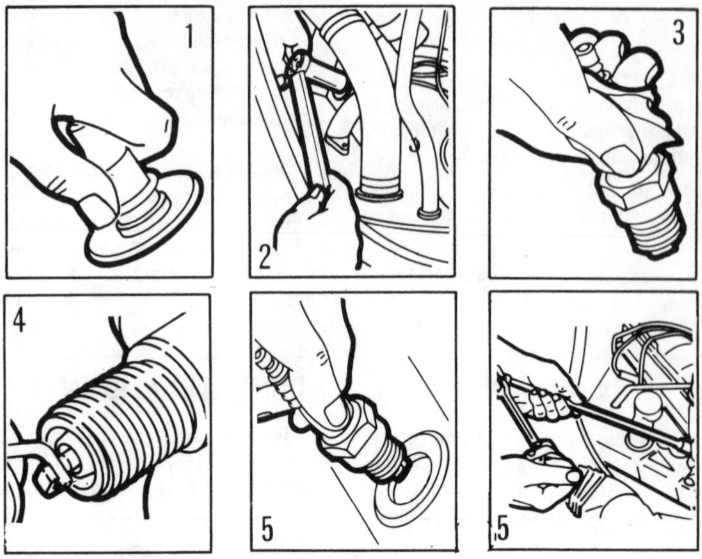

POINTS AND CONDENSER

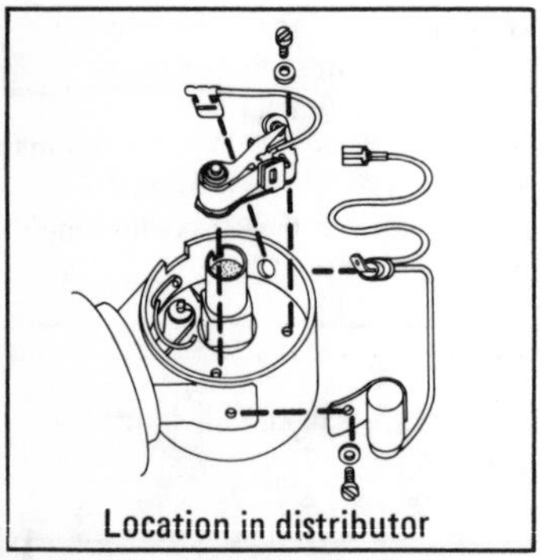

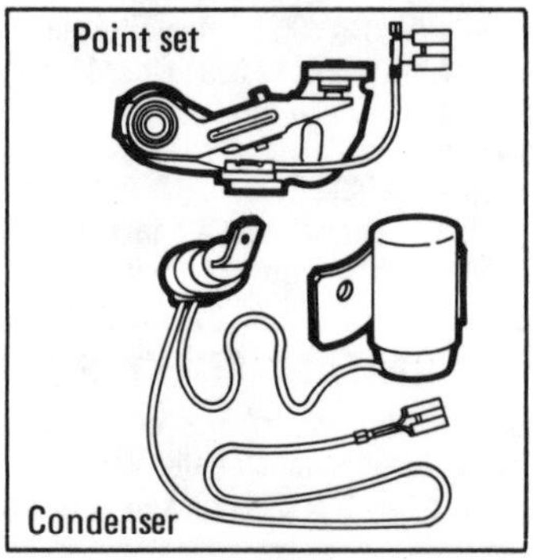

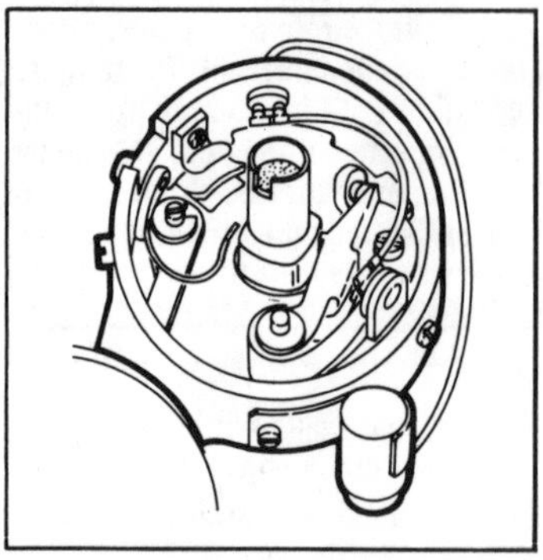

Points and Condenser work together. Always replace condenser when installing new points. The condenser is attached to the outside of the distributor.

REMOVING POINTS AND CONDENSER

1. Disconnect the points wire from the condenser connection at the side of the distributor.
2. Remove the screw from the stationary breaker point. Lift points out of distributor.
CAUTION: Be careful not to drop the screw into the distributor.
3. Remove the condenser by undoing the screw holding the bracket and condenser connection to the distributor.
4. Disconnect the condenser wire from the coil.

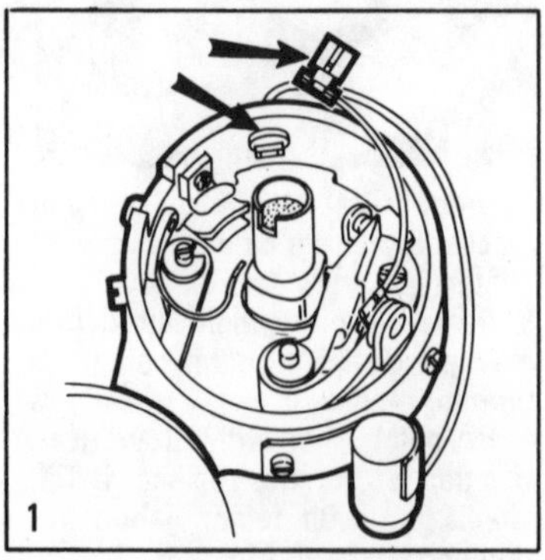

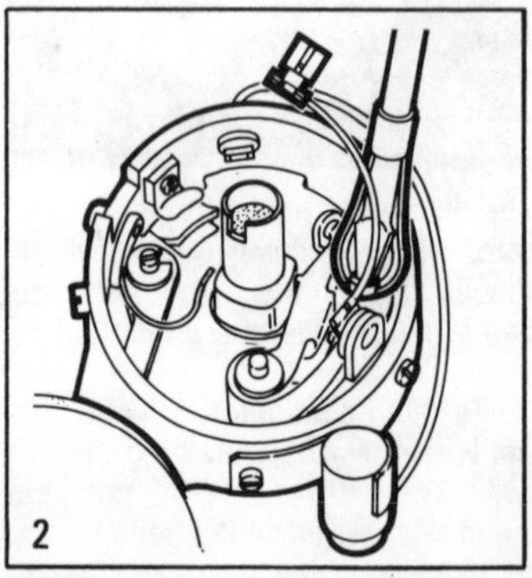

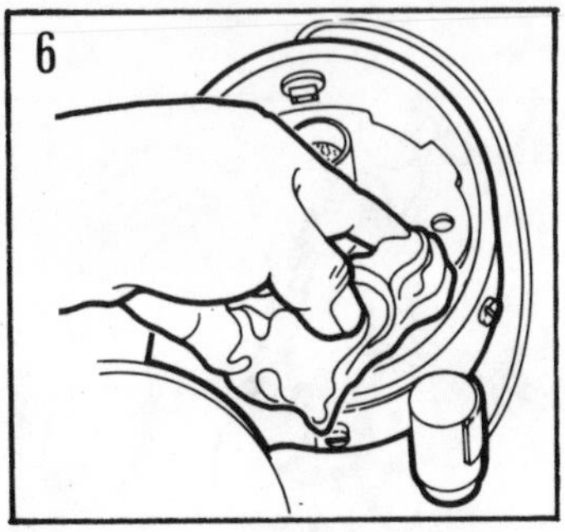

5. If necessary, remove connector grommet. Pull connector grommet out of distributor.
6. Wipe all dirt and grease from the distributor plate and cam with clean, lint-free rag.

CAUTION: When removing screws from distributor, be sure to avoid any screws accidentally falling through distributor opening into engine. Use magnetic screwdriver, or safety clip screwdriver.

INSTALLING POINTS AND CONDENSER

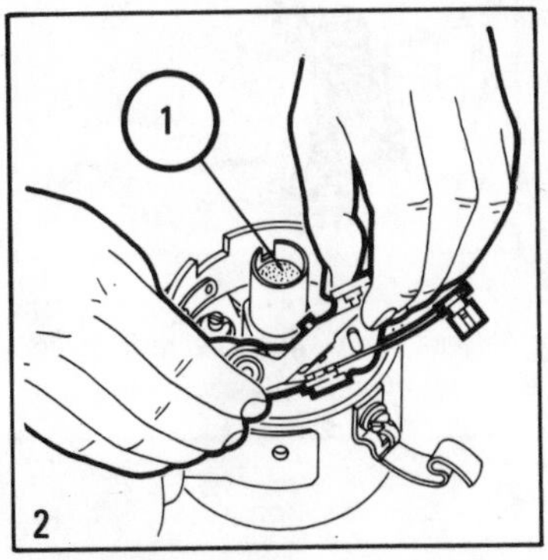

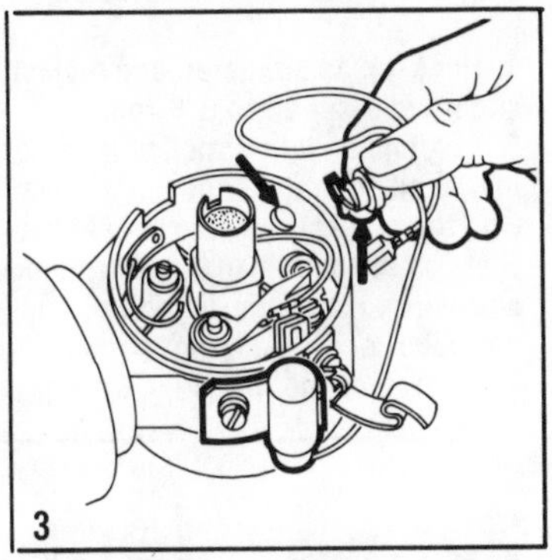

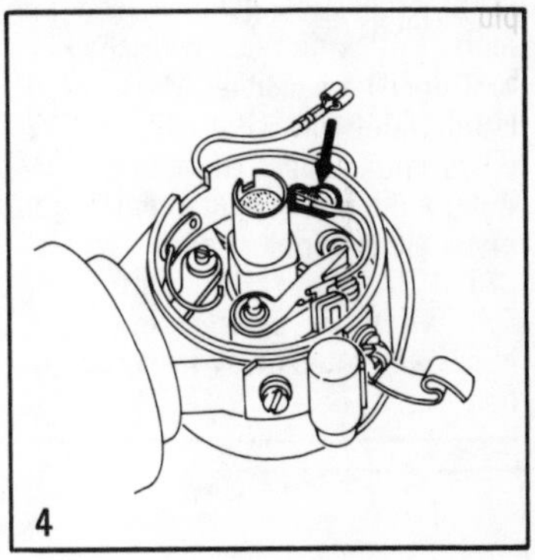

1. Apply small amount of heat resistant lube to distributor cam (lube sometimes supplied with new point sets, if not, purchase separately).
2. Position new points in distributor and fasten with the attaching screw.
3. Insert connector grommet through side of distributor, and attach new condenser to distributor with attaching screw. On some distributors, install connector grommet bracket. Connect wire to coil.
4. Connect points wire to condenser connection.

RESETTING THE CONTACT GAP

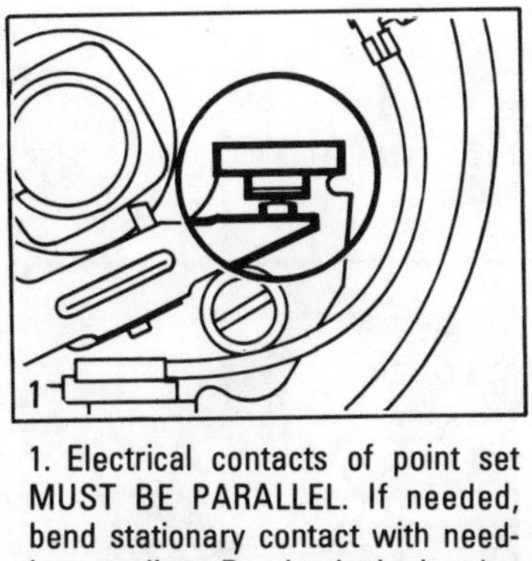

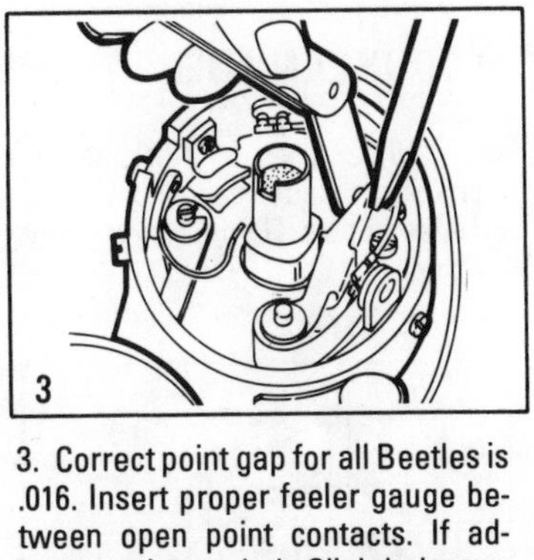

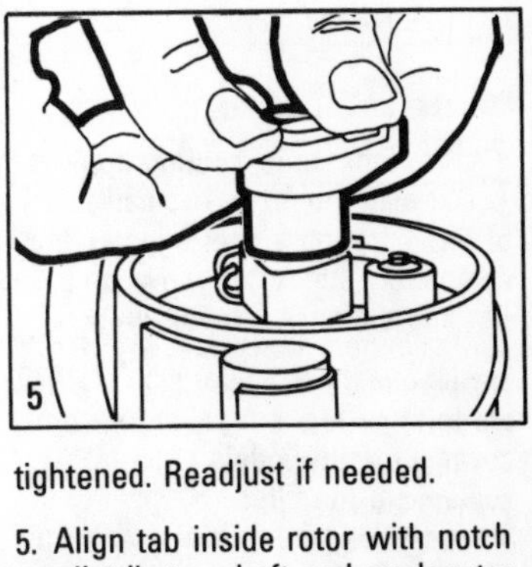

1. Electrical contacts of point set MUST BE PARALLEL. If needed, bend stationary contact with needlenose pliers. Bend only the bracket portion of points—not the other side.
2. Turn engine by ignition key (you'll need a helper) until rubbing block on points is on one of the four high points of distributor cam. You may use wrench on lower pulley to do this.
3. Correct point gap for all Beetles is .016. Insert proper feeler gauge between open point contacts. If adjustment is needed: Slightly loosen point attaching screw. Insert screwdriver between boss on breaker plate and notch on points. Twist screwdriver to open or close points as needed. Tighten screws when correct gap is obtained.
4. Recheck point gap after screw is tightened. Readjust if needed.

5. Align tab inside rotor with notch on distributor shaft and push rotor onto shaft. Rotor must be fully seated on shaft.

6. Install distributor cap by aligning tabs on cap with notch on body. Snap retaining clips in place.

7. Install center distributor wire.

IGNITION TIMING

Adjusting timing is the important finishing touch to any tune-up. This is not a difficult job but it does require a timing light, dwell meter or combination dwell/tach and a piece of chalk. This equipment will cost about $20 and up depending on type and quality. Since timing is a minor service adjustment not requiring any parts installation, you may wish to have this done at a service garage. If you have equipment, proceed as follows:

1. Locate the timing marks on the lower crankshaft pulley. Clean the marks and wipe them with chalk so that they'll be visible. Mark the 0° (1970), 5° ATDC (1971-76), or 7½° BTDC (1974 California models).
2. Hook up timing light according to instructions supplied with it.

CAUTION: Make sure that timing light wires are clear of fan. Keep hands and tools away from fan and belt.

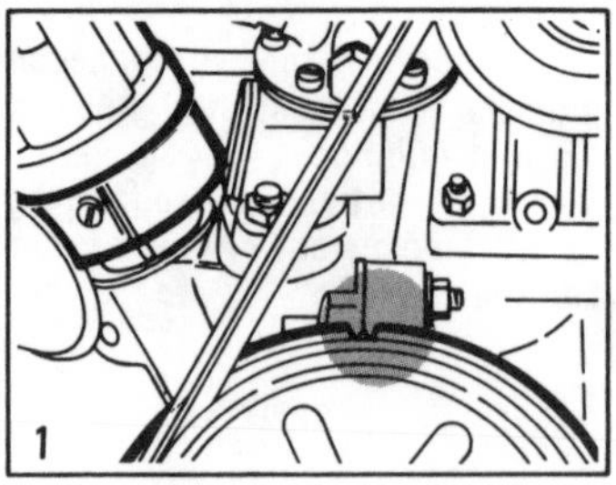

3. Disconnect the vacuum line on 1970 and 1974 California models only. Leave the line connected on all other models.
4. Hook up tachometer and adjust engine idle speed to 900 rpm.
5. Aim timing light at pulley mark. If the chalked notch does not align with the crankcase seam, loosen the clamp at the bottom of the distributor and slowly rotate the distributor until the notch and seam align.
6. Tighten clamp. Recheck timing.

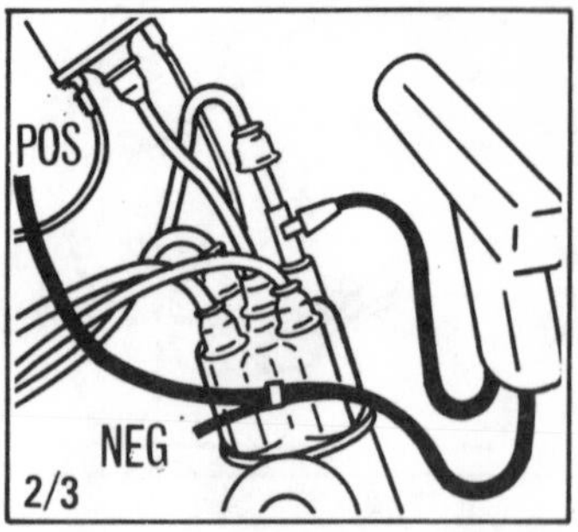

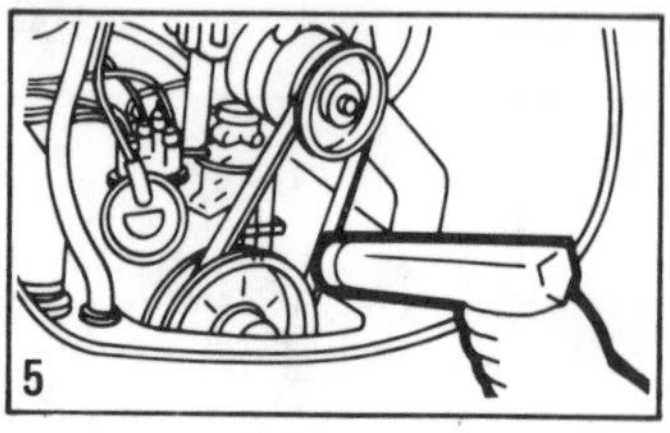

7. Readjust engine idle to 850 rpm. Detach timing light.

Fuel System

When gasoline is brought from the fuel tank, it mixes with air in the carburetor, or on 1975-76 models the fuel injector. This fuel/air mixture then enters the engine through the intake manifold, passes through the intake valves and is burned in the combustion chamber. On fuel injection models, the fuel is injected upstream from the intake manifold. The burned exhaust gas is then passed through the exhaust valves to the exhaust system and into the outside air. In order to keep your VW engine running cleanly with minimal pollution, certain items should checked from time to time.

HOW TO CLEAN FUEL STRAINER

VW recommends replacement at 12,000 mile intervals. A small speck of dirt entering a fuel injector may completely block the flow of fuel, causing expensive repair work.

1. Remove the fuel filter plug on 1970 models, pump cover screw and cover on later models.
2. Remove the filter screen.
3. Clean the screen in solvent, and air dry.
4. Carefully wipe any sediment from the pump.
5. Replace screen with larger end going in first on 1970 models, screen downward on later models.
6. Position plug in side of pump or top cover on pump. Make sure gasket is under plug on 1970 models, gaskets are under cover and screw on later models. Tighten cover screw or plug.

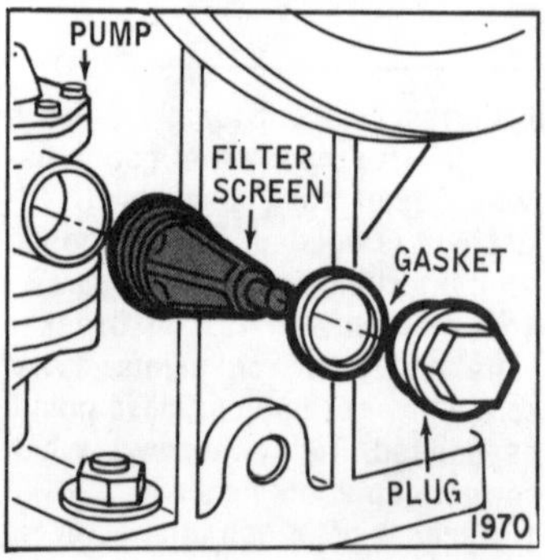

7. Operate the engine, and check for leaks.

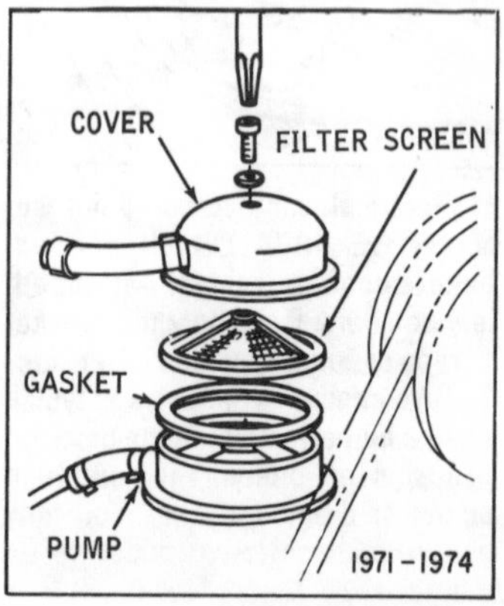

FUEL FILTER REPLACEMENT

On 1975-76 Beetles, the fuel filter should be replaced every 15,000 miles or every year. It is located at the front of the car near the fuel tank. Be sure the car is supported firmly by jack stands before getting underneath.

1. The fuel filter is located near the fuel pump in the pump's suction line. The suction line is the line running from the gas tank to the "S" connection at the fuel pump.
2. Clamp the lines shut, so that no gas dribbles out. You can use wooden clothespins for this.
3. Release the retaining pin and bracket.
4. Disconnect the lines from both ends of the filter.
5. Install the new filter in the same manner.

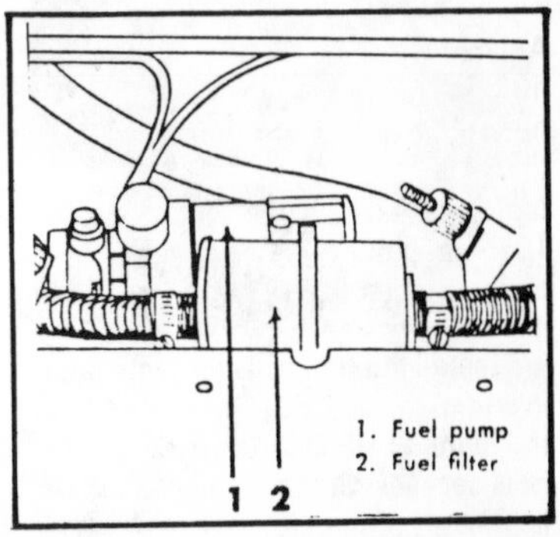

KEEP THE AIR INTAKE CLEAN

The large can or box that sits on top of the engine is the air cleaner. 1970-72 Beetles have an oil bath air cleaner. 1973 models may have either an oil bath or a paper element air cleaner. All 1974-76 models have a paper element air cleaner. The servicing requirements for both these types of air cleaners are shown below. Servicing is required twice a year.

OIL BATH TYPE

1. Detach all hoses, making a note of where they go.
2. Loosen the clamp screw on the large heated air hose and pull it off.
3. Remove the screw on the air cleaner bracket and loosen the screw on the air cleaner clamp.
4. Carefully lift the air cleaner off. Do not tilt, or you will spill oil.
5. Unclip the top, and separate the two halves.
6. Drain the old oil out of the bottom.
7. Clean the top and bottom with a clean rag.
8. Refill the line with clean engine oil (.9 pint).
9. Install air cleaner in original position. Make sure to reconnect all hoses in original position.

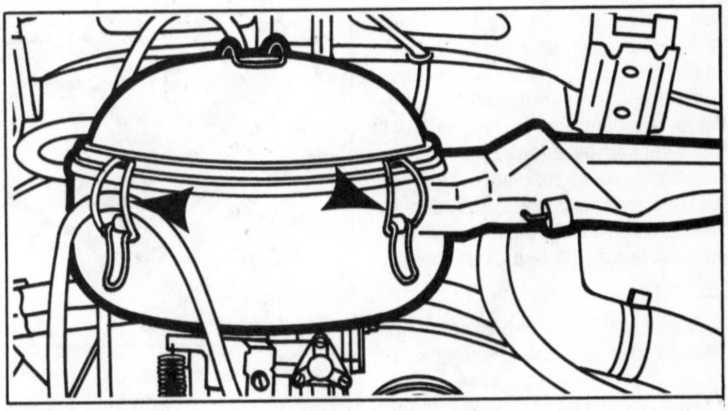

PAPER ELEMENT TYPE

1. Detach all small hoses, noting where they go.
2. Loosen the clamp screw, and pull the large heated air hose off.
3. Loosen the air cleaner clamp screw, and pull the air cleaner off.
4. Release the four clips, and pull the top off.
5. Shake dirt off the filter, and inspect it. If it is dirty, replace, do not attempt to clean it.
6. Install filter element, making sure it is properly seated.

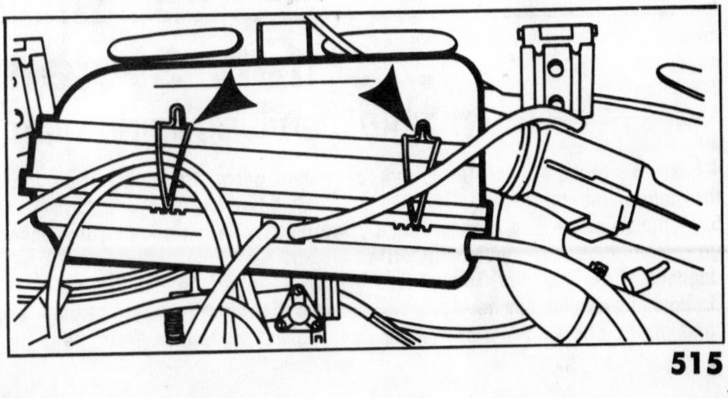

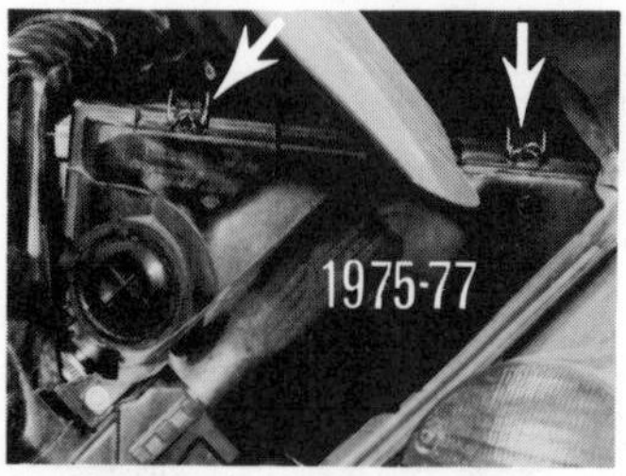

7. Install the top, and clip it into position.
8. Reinstall air cleaner, making sure it is parallel with the fan housing. Do not overtighten clamp screw.
9. Reconnect all hoses in proper position.

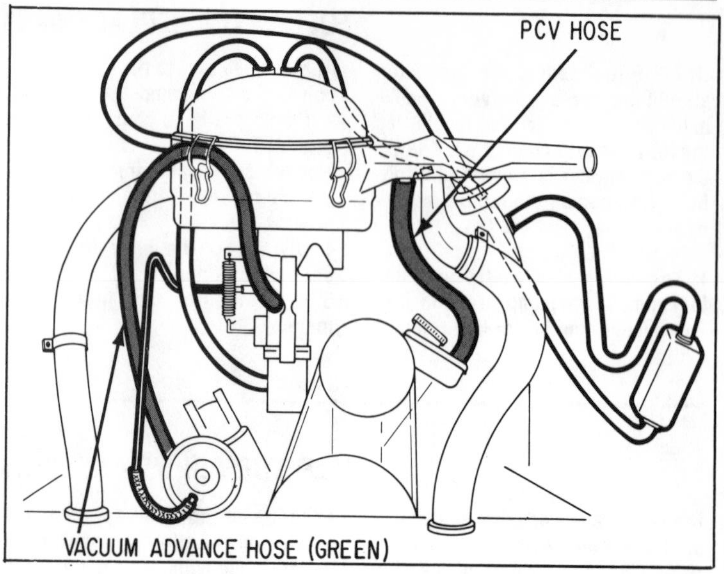

EMISSION CONTROLS SYSTEMS

An important part of a car's emission controls is the Positive Crankcase Ventilation system. The connecting hoses should be inspected every 6 months for clogging or deterioration. This system helps prevent the formation of sludge and dirt in the engine.

EMISSION SYSTEM CHECKS

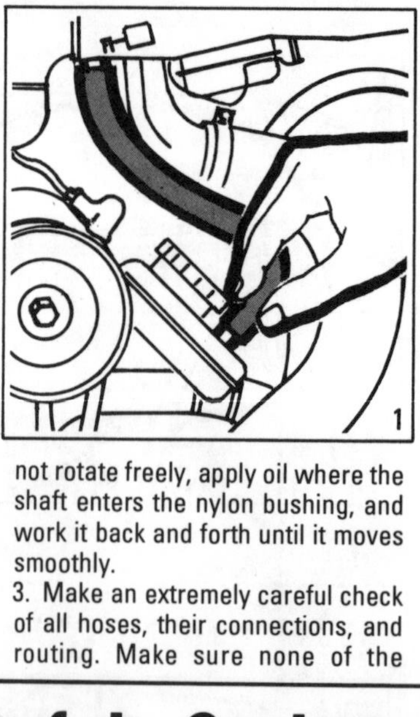

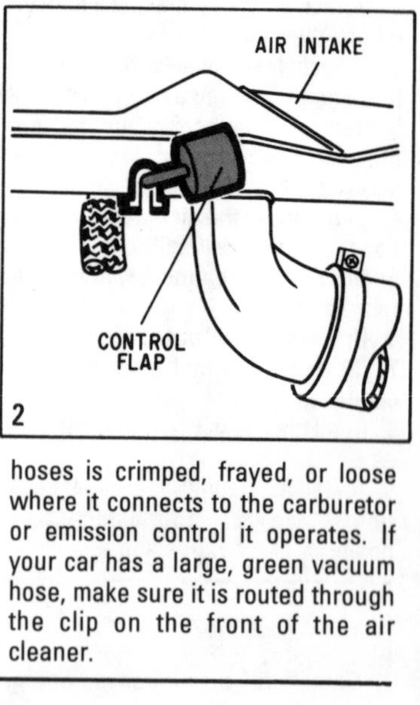

Emission controlled engines clean combustion through use of various precise controls on things like ignition timing and carburetor air temperature. Improper operation of any of these controls, or any vacuum leak caused by a loose connection can cause rough running, hesitation, or increased emissions. Periodically make all the checks described below to ensure smooth and clean engine operation:

1. Remove the hose which connects the air cleaner intake with the oil filler. make sure the hose is not frayed or cracked, and blow through it to ensure it is not clogged. If dirty, clean or replace.

2. Check the counterweighted control flap on the air intake. If it does not rotate freely, apply oil where the shaft enters the nylon bushing, and work it back and forth until it moves smoothly.
3. Make an extremely careful check of all hoses, their connections, and routing. Make sure none of the hoses is crimped, frayed, or loose where it connects to the carburetor or emission control it operates. If your car has a large, green vacuum hose, make sure it is routed through the clip on the front of the air cleaner.

Safety Systems

FRONT TURN SIGNAL, PARKING LIGHT, SIDE MARKER

These two bulbs are located within the fender mounted lens. A No. 57 bulb handles the side marker function. A No. 1034 bulb handles the turn signal and parking light. To replace, remove the two Phillips head screws and lift the lens off. Wipe any dirt or moisture from the inside of the lens. Push down on bulb and turn counterclockwise to remove from socket. Insert new bulb.
NOTE: When inserting new bulb, note that knobs on side of base are different distances from base tip. Match knobs to socket slots for proper fit. Check that the lens gasket is correctly positioned and not cracked or rotten. Replace, if necessary. Reinstall the lens. DO NOT overtighten the screws or you will break the lens.

REAR TURN SIGNAL, STOP-TAIL, BACK-UP LIGHTS

These three (1970-72) or four (1973-76) bulbs are located under the single rear lens on the fender. To replace, unscrew the four Phillips head screws and take off the lens. Wipe any dirt or moisture from the inside of the lens. Push down on bulb and turn counterclockwise to remove from socket. Insert new bulb and install in reverse order.

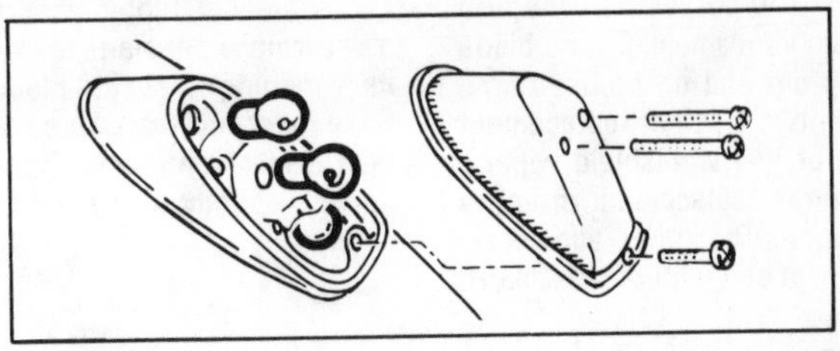

INTERIOR DOME LIGHT

Depress the tab on right side of light with screwdriver, and lift assembly out to stops. Press on right side stop and lift light all the way out. Hold spring at one end of bulb, and lift bulb out to one side, and remove it. Install new bulb at one end, and then push into spring at other end. Install assembly, seating it properly.

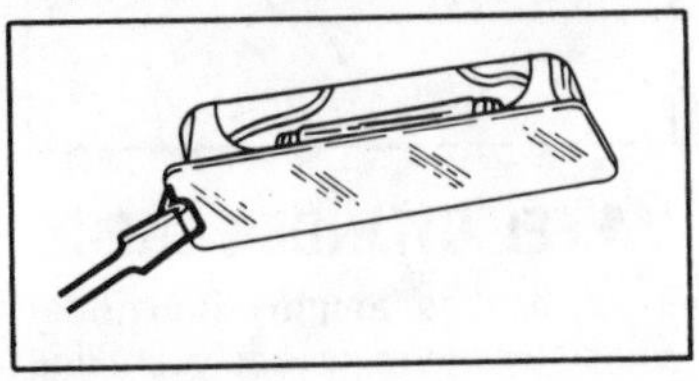

LICENSE PLATE LIGHTS

Open engine compartment lid. Remove two screws and remove lens assembly. Push bulb in, turn, and remove it. Install replacement bulb by pushing in and turning in opposite direction. Clean lens and check that the release cable grommet is correctly positioned.

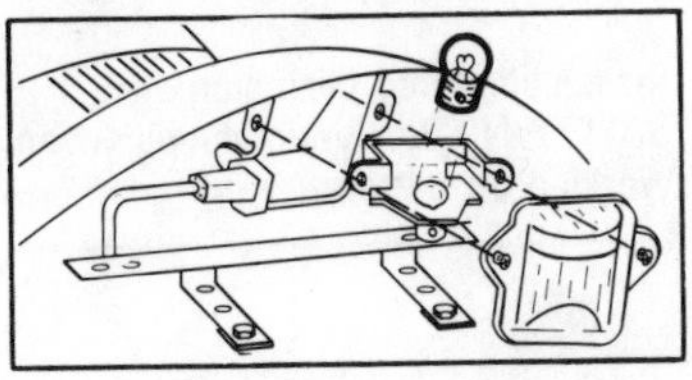

HEADLIGHT REPLACEMENT

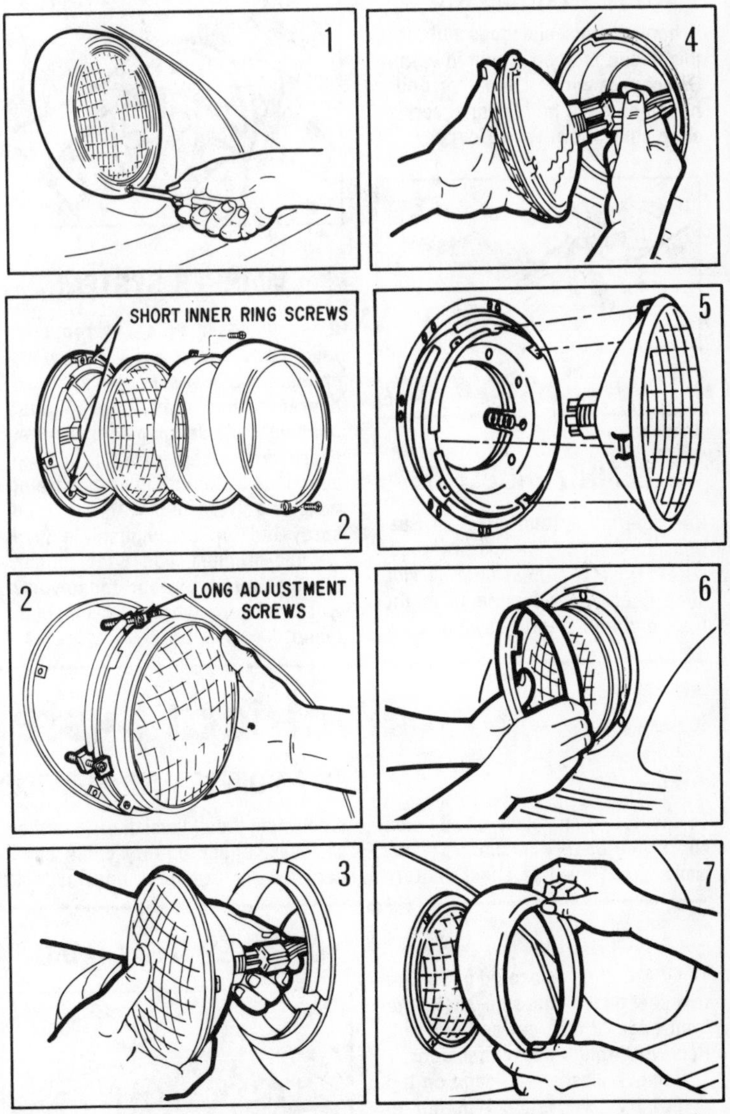

1. Loosen the screw at the bottom of the trim ring. Use the loose screw to pull off the trim ring.
2. Remove the three short inner ring screws. Do not remove or tamper with the two longer screws, these are the headlight adjustment screws.
3. Remove the inner ring and pull the headlight out. Disconnect and remove the bulb.
4. Connect the plug to the rear of the new bulb unit.
5. Position new sealed beam in headlight shell. Be sure that knobs on back of light (near outer edge) enter slots in shell.
6. Place retaining ring over sealed beam and fasten with three screws.
7. Install ring and tighten screw.

WINDSHIELD WIPER BLADE REPLACEMENT

To remove wiper blades lift arm away from windshield. Rotate blade and snap out and off crooked arm. There are two types of replacement rubbers for VW windshield wipers. One requires replacement of entire wiper blade. The other allows replacement of only wiper blade insert.

Press the old rubber insert down, away from wiper blade to free it from its retaining clips on blade ends. Slide insert in wiper blade. Position new insert from blade. Bend insert upward slightly to engage retaining clips.

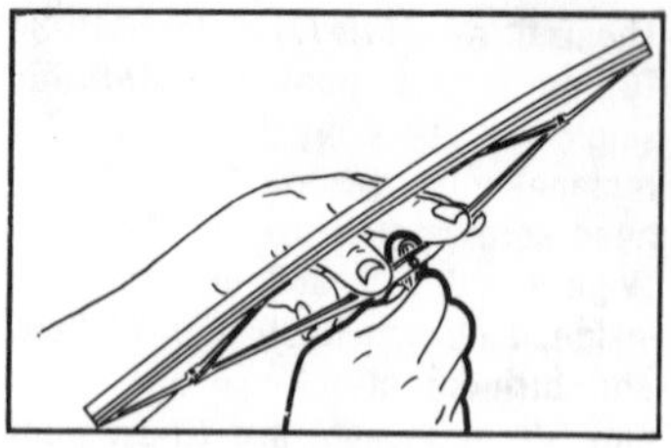

HORN PROBLEMS

If horn sounds and does not stop, this is due to short circuit in wiring. Disconnect wiring connector under hood and have professional service shop check horn wiring circuit.

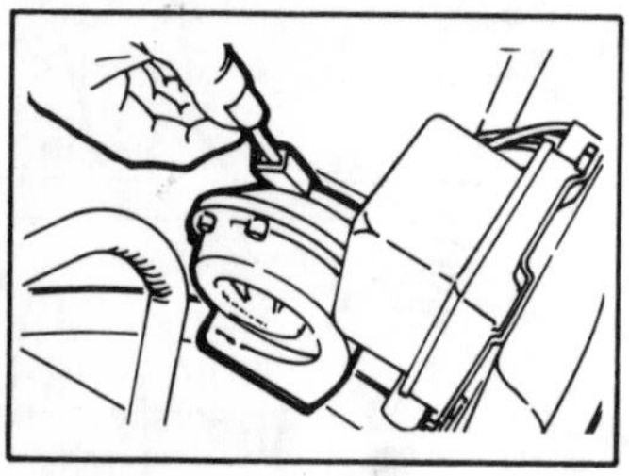

STEERING PROBLEMS

See steering system check in Suspension Section. Check tire pressures. Have a professional service shop check all components in the front end and steering system.

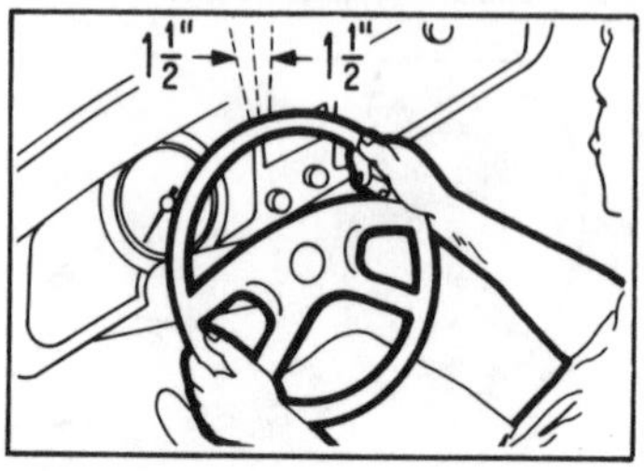

WASHER SYSTEM

If washer fails to squirt properly, raise hood and check system hose connections. Be sure washer fluid container has fluid. Check spout openings for clogging. Ensure that spare tire is kept at 42 psi. Keep container filled with fluid mixture of washer solvent and water. If road spray buildup on windshield is a chronic problem, add 1 tablespoon dishwasher detergent to solvent/water mixture when re-filling container.

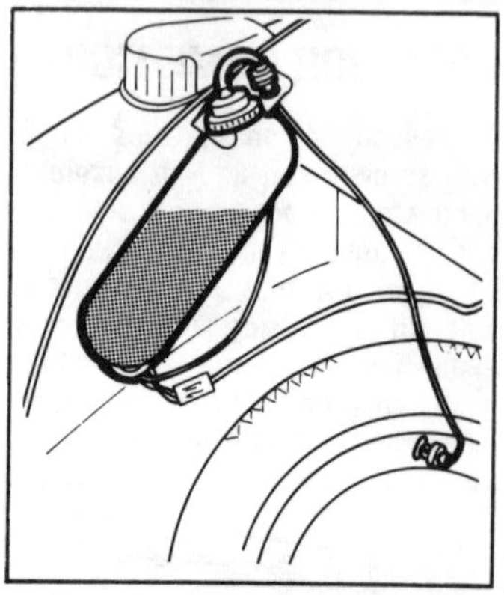

WHEEL CYLINDER CHECK

Drum brakes employ individual wheel cylinders to apply braking pressure to shoes. Check for brake fluid leaks on inside of wheel. If leaks are apparent, have mechanic service at once. Failure to do so could mean partial failure of brake system, damage to linings.

Electrical Systems

CHECKPOINTS AND SERVICES

To ensure starting ability at all times check your battery condition periodically. You'll need to check battery electrolyte (fluid) level in each of the six cells. Check battery cable connections for tightness and inspect for accumulated corrosion.
SAFETY NOTE: Wear gloves when working on battery.

CHECK BATTERY FLUID

The VW battery is located under the rear seat on the right side. Lift up the front edge of the seat and pull out. Remove through passenger door.

1. Remove plastic filler caps on top of battery. Fluid should be up to lower end of filler hole and covering the plates. If fluid is low add clean, cold tap water. If your area has hard water, use only distilled water available at auto supply, food or drug stores.

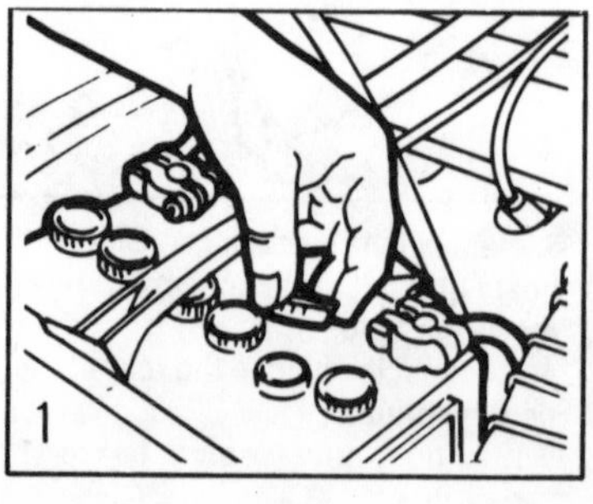

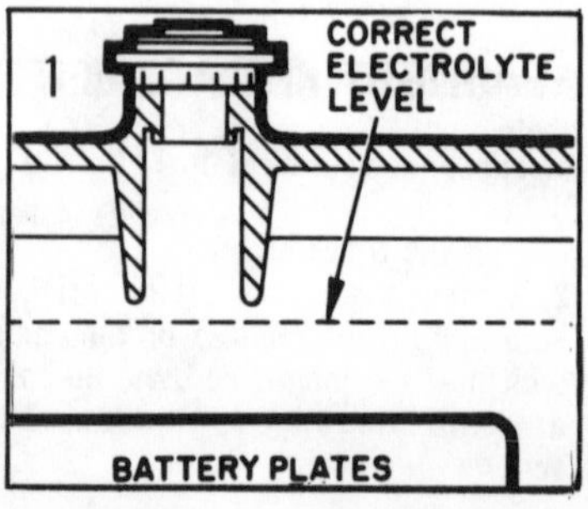

2. Replace any lost caps immediately.

CAUTION: NEVER LIGHT A MATCH OR SMOKE near the top of a battery. Batteries give off explosive hydrogen gas.

NOTE: Battery that often checks low on fluid could mean:

A. Battery is getting old, due for replacement; have charge capacity checked at service shop.

B. Connections may be corroded or loose; clean/replace as needed (see below).

C. Alternator or voltage regulator not functioning properly; this happens far less often than A or B above.

CLEAN THOSE BATTERY TERMINALS

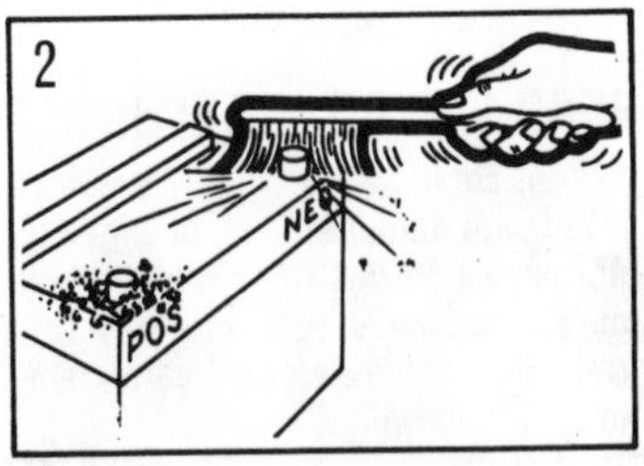

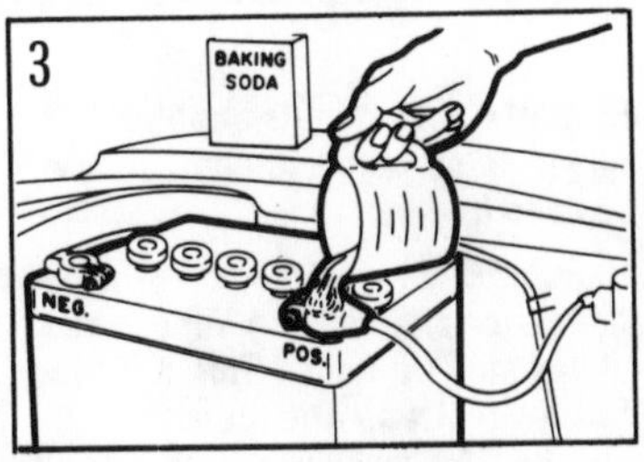

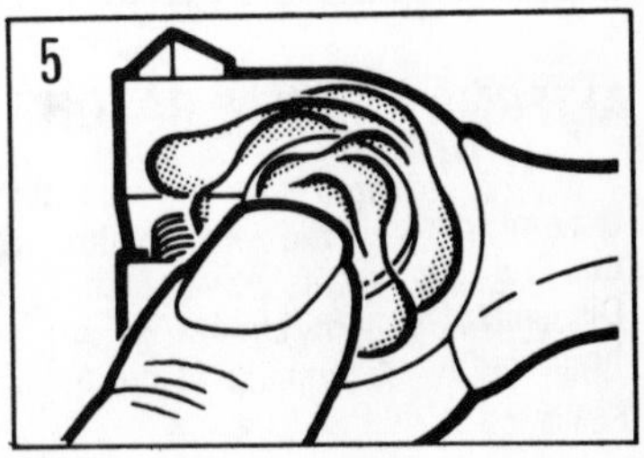

As time goes by, battery terminals build up a dry powdery, whitish material. This material is corrosive and will gradually eat thru battery cables if not cleaned off periodically.

1. Loosen and remove battery connections.
2. Brush off all loose corrosion; use stiff bristle brush. Do not get this material into eyes or on open cuts. Wash off at once.
3. If corrosion build-up is extremely heavy and brushing does not remove all of it, mix 2 tablespoons baking soda to 1 cup water. Pour solution directly onto terminals and connectors. Allow to soak a few minutes and rinse off. Continue brushing to remove all traces of corrosion build-up. Do not allow cleaning solution to enter battery.
4. Replace connectors on battery terminal posts and tighten. Do not hammer connections onto posts, but be sure they will not come loose with vibration.
5. Liberally smear battery terminal posts and cable connectors with petroleum jelly.

REPLACE FAULTY BATTERY CABLES

If battery cable strands become frayed, broken or corroded, replace cable immediately. Delay in correcting this condition could lead to sudden failure to start the engine. Can also weaken battery.

1. Loosen and remove battery connections. Clean off any corrosion.
2. Disconnect negative cable from its attachment to engine or chassis. Disconnect positive cable from its attachment to starter relay.
3. Attach new cables making sure positive and negative cables are on proper terminals. They are not identical.
4. Replace connectors on battery terminal posts and tighten.
5. Liberally smear battery terminal posts and cable connectors with petroleum jelly.

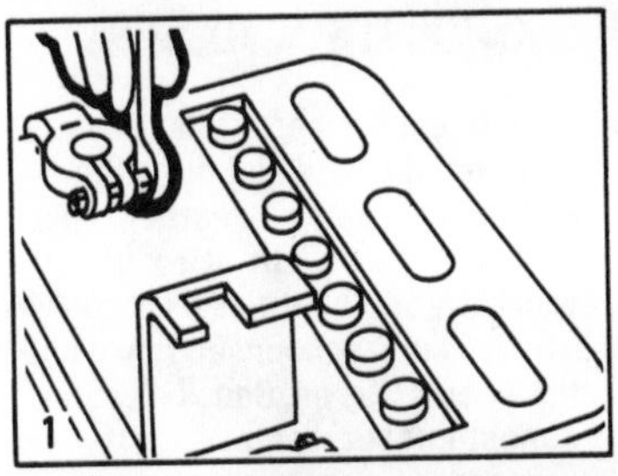

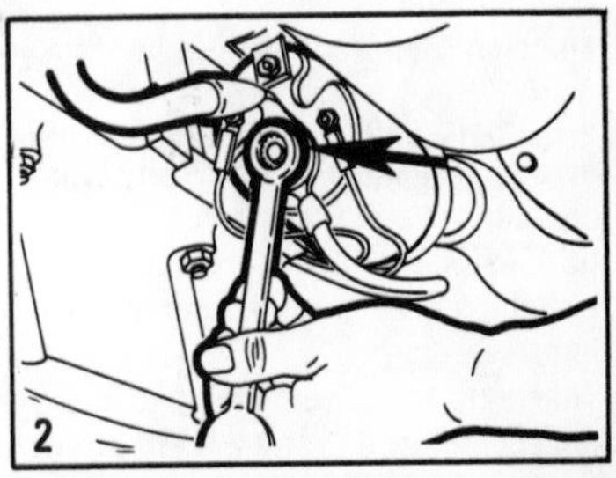

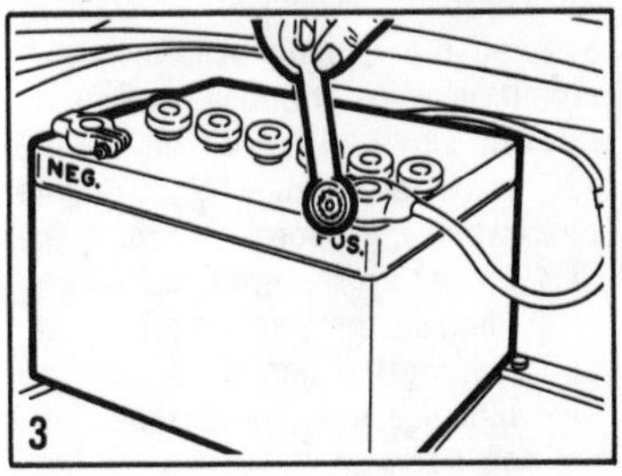

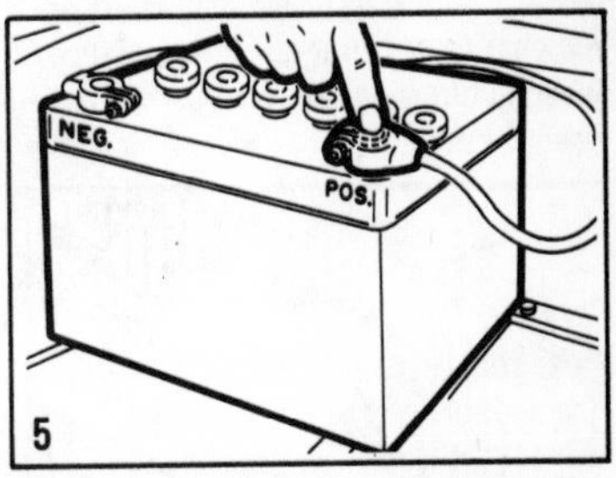

TURN SIGNAL AND 4-WAY FLASHER

Turn signals and 4-way flashers will operate only if:

A. All light bulbs are OK. B. Flasher unit is not burned out. Beetles and Super Beetles have one flasher relay which operates turn signals and emergency flasher. On the Super Beetle the flasher is located behind the fuse box under the dash. The flasher relay is square, the round unit is the headlight dimmer relay. On the Beetle, open the luggage compartment and remove the dash cover.

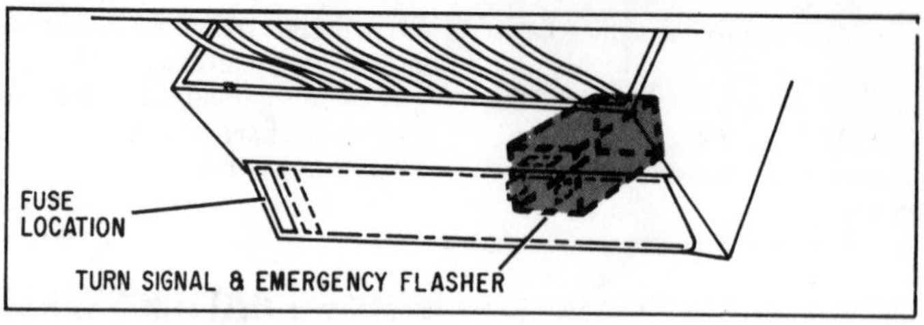

ALTERNATOR/GENERATOR

Red warning light on instrument panel should glow red when you first turn ignition key. This proves bulb is OK. Warning light should go off when engine is running at normal operating speed.

If warning light glows red at operating speed generator/alternator isn't charging battery properly. Common causes are:

A. Fan belts are loose and slipping on generator/alternator pulley. Tighten or replace belts.

B. Battery terminals, cables are loose or corroded. Clean; tighten; replace bad cables.

If A or B do not correct problem generator/alternator or voltage regulator may be faulty. This happens far less often, and can only be checked by mechanic with proper electrical testing equipment.

Alternator Caution: Alternator can be permanently damaged by short-circuiting terminal connections. When working around or moving alternator, always keep metal tools or engine parts from terminal.

REAR WINDOW DEFOGGER

Do not clean inside of rear window fitted with defogger system with any abrasive material. This could destroy carbon-copper wires. Use only soft rag and mild detergent/water mixture. Dry carefully.

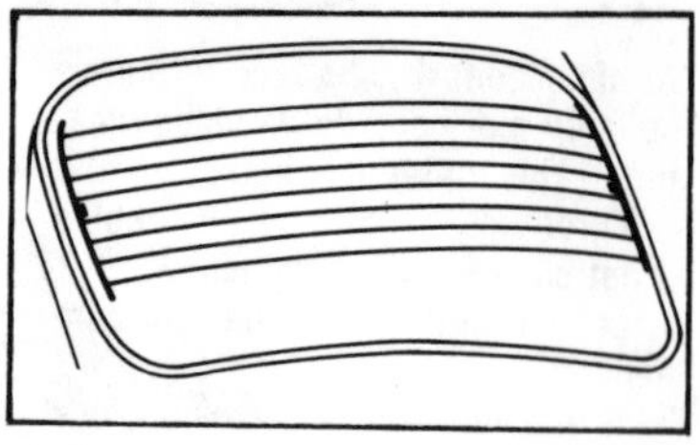

Air Conditioner

CHECK POINTS AND SERVICES

WARNING! Never attempt to tighten fittings, disassemble or do any work on your VWs A/C system. Consult a professional mechanic about A/C system problems and their correction.

Your auto air conditioner (A/C) is a delicate, closed system. If air, dirt or water get into it, or if refrigerant escapes, the A/C unit will not cool a car interior. Among things you can do are:

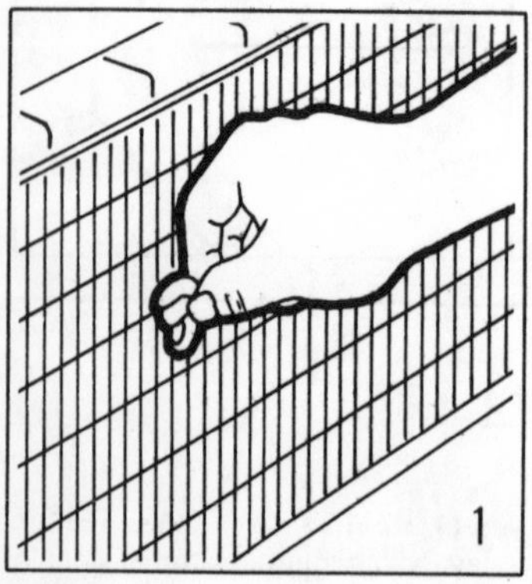
1

1. Keep condenser grilles clean. Check for dirt and debris; periodically remove dead insects, leaves, etc., with stiff bristle brush. Straighten any bent fins—carefully.
2. Make sure condenser fan operates when A/C is on. Check electrical connections or replace parts as necessary.
3. Keep the cooling system in top condition as described in the Cooling System section. While the Beetle A/C does not directly affect engine temperature, it does increase the load placed on the engine. Keeping all cooling system parts in top shape, and keeping the engine in top tune will minimize the chances of overheating damage.
4. Check fan and compressor belt tension periodically. (See Cooling System section). Replace glazed, frayed or cut belts, before they fail entirely.
5. Check periodically for bubbles in A/C sight glass. Sight glass is located in head of receiver/drier vessel, which is located in the right front fenderwell. Sight glass is no larger than head of large nail. It may be dirty. Wipe clean for best visibility.

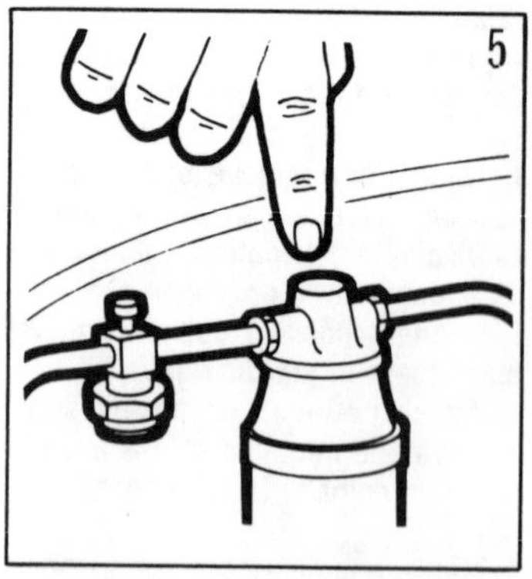
5

PROCEED AS FOLLOWS:

a) With engine and A/C system running, look for passage of refrigerant in sight glass. You'll be looking for a stream of milky white bubbles as they pass through sight glass. It is best to watch sight glass and have someone else start the car and turn

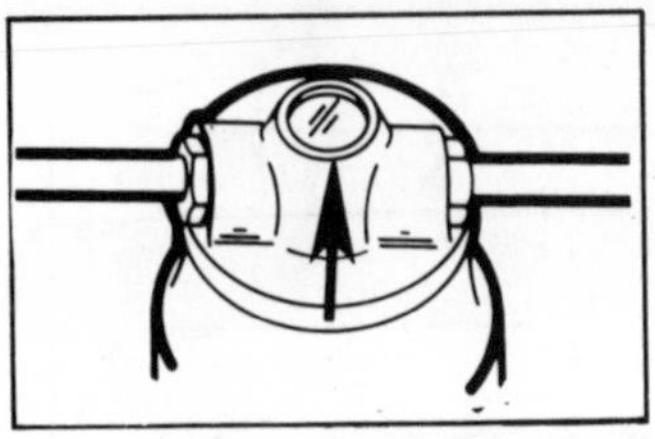

on the A/C system. Allow to run for a few minutes.

b) If you observe no bubbles, and air flow from A/C unit in the car is passing cold air, everything is OK.
c) If no bubbles appear in sight glass, and air flow from the A/C unit in the car is not delivering cold air, the system may be low on refrigerant and could need a re-charge.
d) If bubbles appear, system is low on refrigerant.
e) If you suspect refrigerant loss based on tests performed above, have system checked by a professional A/C service shop. They can confirm refrigerant loss, recharge the system and check for system leakage.

NOTE: Once a week or so, even in winter, run A/C system for about 5 minutes as you drive. This keeps system internally lubricated, prevents hoses hardening.

TUNE-UP SPECIFICATIONS

YEAR	ENGINE No. Cyl. Displacement (c.c.)	SPARK PLUGS Type	SPARK PLUGS Gap (in.)	DISTRIBUTOR Point Dwell (deg.)	DISTRIBUTOR Point Gap (in.)	IGNITION TIMING Man. Trans. (deg.)	IGNITION TIMING Auto Trans. (deg.)	IDLE SPEED Man. Trans. (rpm)	IDLE SPEED Auto Trans. (rpm)
1970	4-1600	Bosch W145T1	.024	44-50	.016	TDC	TDC	800-900	900-1000
1971	4-1600	Bosch W145T1	.024	44-50	.016	5ATDC	5ATDC	800-900	900-1000
1972	4-1600	Bosch W145T1	.024	44-50	.016	5ATDC	5ATDC	800-900	900-1000
1973	4-1600	Bosch W145T1	.024	44-50	.016	5ATDC	5ATDC	800-900	900-1000
1974	4-1600	Bosch W145T1	.024	44-50	.016	7½BTDC	7½BTDC	800-900	900-1000
1974 California	4-1600	Bosch W145T1	.024	44-50	.016	5ATDC	5ATDC	800-900	900-1000
1975	4-1600	Bosch W145T1	.024	44-50	.016	5ATDC	TDC	875	875
1976	4-1600	Bosch W145T1	.024	44-50	.016	5ATDC	TDC	875	925
1977	See Underhood Specifications Sticker								

NOTE: The underhood specifications sticker often reflects tune-up specification changes made in production. Sticker figures must be used if they disagree with those in this chart.
BTDC Before Top Dead Center
TDC Top Dead Center
ATDC After Top Dead Center

CAPACITIES

YEAR	ENGINE No. Cyl. Displacement (c.c.)	ENGINE OIL	TRANSMISSION Pts. to Refill after Draining MANUAL	TRANSMISSION Pts. to Refill after Draining AUTOMATIC	DRIVE AXLE (pts.)
1970-77	4-1600	2.5	6.3	7.6	6.3①

① 5.4 when changed

Service Record

DATE/MILEAGE	SERVICE	NEXT DUE

Volkswagen Type 2

Lubrication and Oil Change

LUBRICATION CHECK

VW SAYS . . . Change oil and clean oil strainer every 3000 miles on 1970-71 models, change oil every 3000 miles and filter every 6000 miles on 1972-76 models. Recommended grade: MS or SE.
Check the oil level at least once a week.
TOOLS AND MATERIALS . . . 10 mm box wrench or socket and ratchet handle set (1970-71), 21 mm box wrench or socket and ratchet handle set (1972-76), medium size screwdriver, drain pan for old oil (at least 4 qt. capacity), oil pouring spout, special VW oil filter wrench (1972-76), oil strainer gaskets and copper washers (1970-71), oil and lubricants as specified below.
SAFETY TIP . . . use work gloves.

BRAKE FLUID LEVEL CHECK

On 1970 buses, the brake fluid reservoir is located ahead of the steering column under the instrument panel. Look for the brake fluid reservoir on 1971-72 models behind the driver's seat. Move the seat forward to see the reservoir. The reservoir is located under the driver's seat on 1973-76 models, level can be seen through the cut-out in the cover.

Keep the fluid level above the seam on the reservoir (½—¾″ below cap) on 1970-72 models, between the upper and lower edges of the reservoir on 1973-76 models.

DO NOT OVERFILL

Check brake fluid level in master cylinder reservoir every three months . . . sooner if braking feels inadequate.

Add when low. Recommended grade: DOT 3 or 4 as printed on can. If fluid repeatedly checks low, there is a leak somewhere in the system. See SAFETY SYSTEMS—WHEEL CYLINDER.

Have mechanic check further. Neglect can be dangerous because leaks can either soak brake linings with fluid, making them ineffective,

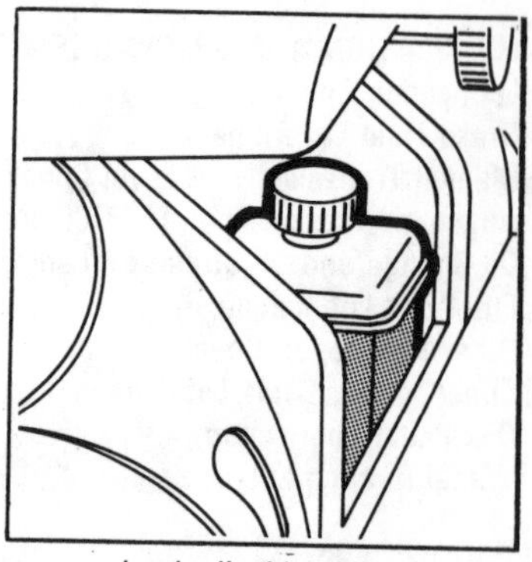

or completely disable either front or rear brakes.

MANUAL TRANSAXLE FLUID LEVEL CHECK

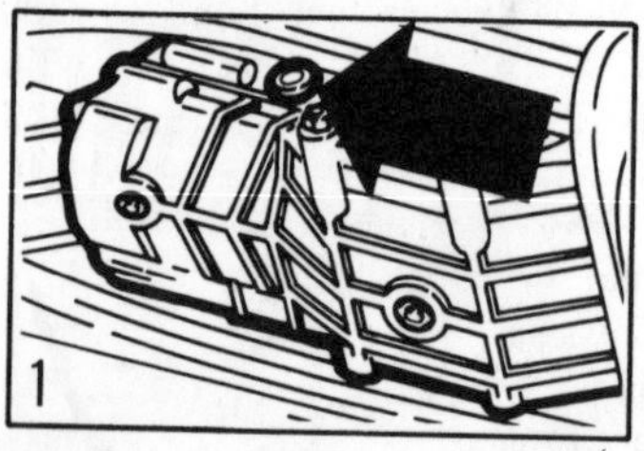

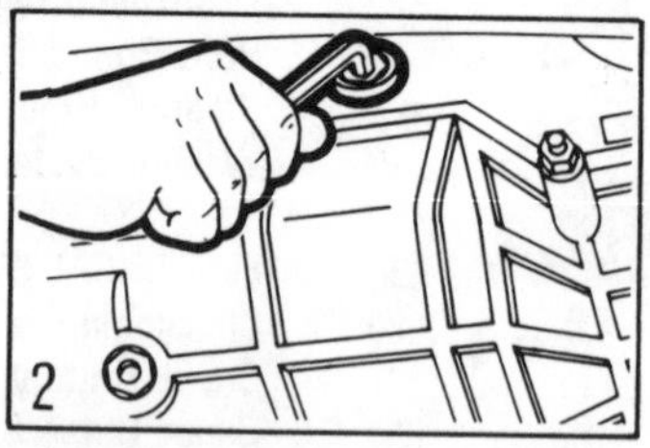

VW SAYS . . . Check manual transaxle fluid every 6000 miles. Car should be level. Recommended grade: Standard transmission gear oil (SAE 90—use 80 in very cold climates).
TOOLS NEEDED . . . Drain plug wrench. Suction gun or squeeze bulb syringe.
1. Locate transmission filler plug on side of transaxle housing from underneath the car.
2. Wipe road dirt from filler plug area before loosening. Remove plug with wrench.
3. Insert your finger into the hole. Oil should be level with the bottom edge of the filler hole.
4. Add gear oil as needed with suction gun or squeeze bulb syringe.

5. Replace filler plug; tighten.

AUTOMATIC TRANSMISSION FLUID CHANGE

VW SAYS . . . change automatic transmission fluid (ATF) every 30,000 miles or 18,000 under heavy duty conditions such as trailer towing or frequent full load carrying.
TOOLS . . . long neck filler funnel,

adjustable wrench or socket set, drain pan (at least 3 qts. capacity). SUPPLIES . . . oil pan gasket, 3 qts. ATF.

1. Run engine until normal operating temperature is reached.
2. Park the bus on level ground and turn the engine off.
3. Place drain pan under transmission drain plug.
4. Remove the drain plug and allow the fluid to drain.
5. Unscrew the oil pan bolts and drop the pan.
6. Remove the circular oil strainer from the transmission.

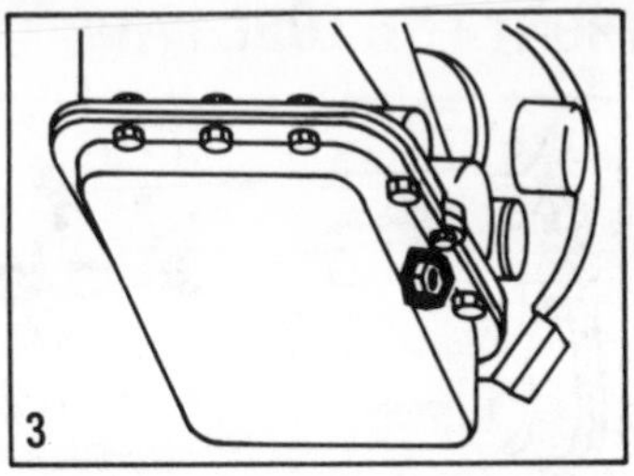

7. Clean both the pan and the strainer in solvent.
8. Install the strainer and the pan. Use a new gasket on the pan. DON'T OVERTIGHTEN THE OIL PAN BOLTS

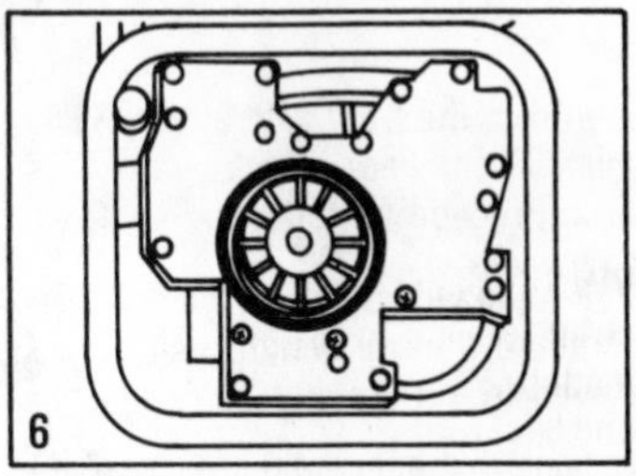

9. Fill the transmission with 2.6 qts. of ATF. Do not add the full three quarts.

10. Run the engine and recheck the fluid level.

OIL CHANGE AND OIL STRAINER CLEANING

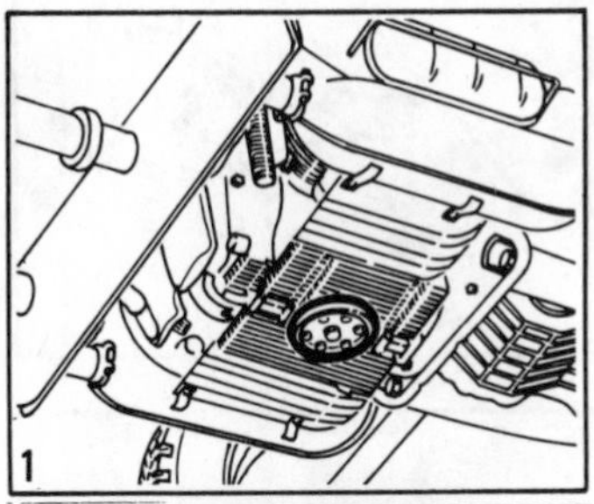

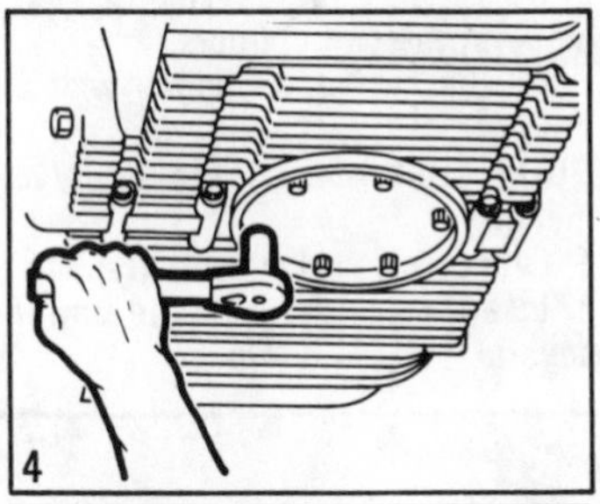

1. If engine is cold, start up and idle for about 5 minutes.
2. Park car on level ground. Turn engine off.
3. Place drain pan under oil strainer cover, located in center of engine.
4. On a 1970-71 bus, use a 10 mm wrench to remove all but one nut, pry cover down with screwdriver, and allow oil to drain.
5. Remove the last nut and remove the oil strainer and gaskets.
6. On 1972-76 models, remove the 21 mm drain plug to the side of the oil strainer and allow the oil to drain.
7. Remove center nut and remove the strainer.
8. Clean the strainer in solvent.
9. Install a new gasket on the cover

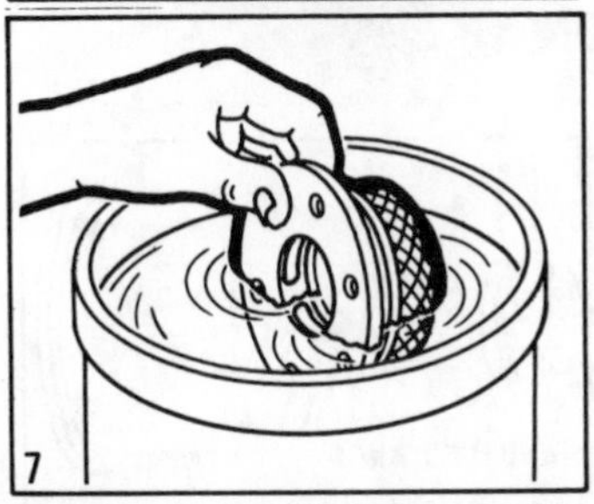

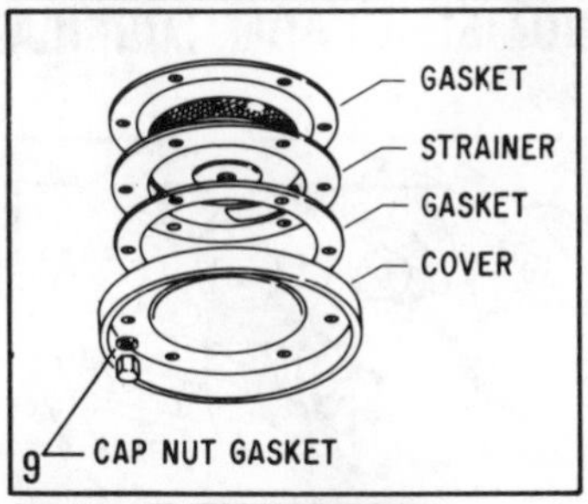

stud(s). Position the strainer over the stud(s).

10. Install a second gasket and then the cover. Use new copper gaskets on the cover nuts or bolt.
11. On '72 and later engines, remove oil filter with special VW oil filter wrench. Lube filter gasket with clean oil, and install, tightening gently the amount specified on the filter.
12. Locate the oil filler tube on top of the engine. Remove cap.
13. Punch oil pouring spout into top of oil can. Pour two cans (three cans with filters) and about ¾ of another can of oil into the filler tube. Wipe filler cap clean and replace it.
14. Check new oil level at dipstick. Pull out dipstick, wipe clean.
15. Push dipstick all the way back in.

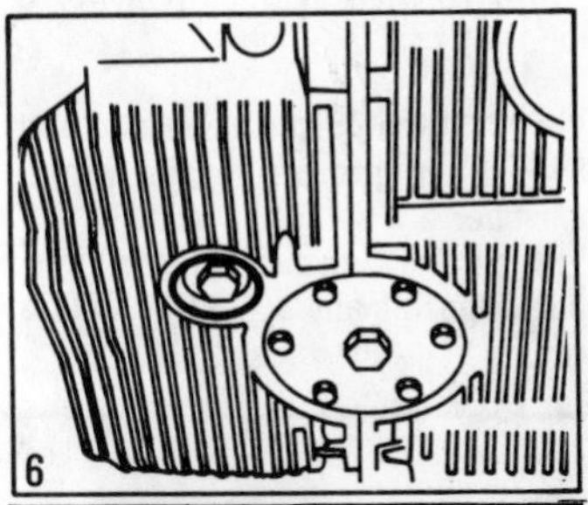

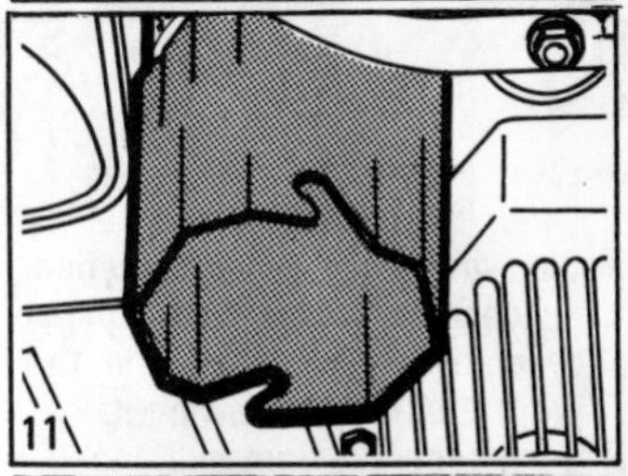

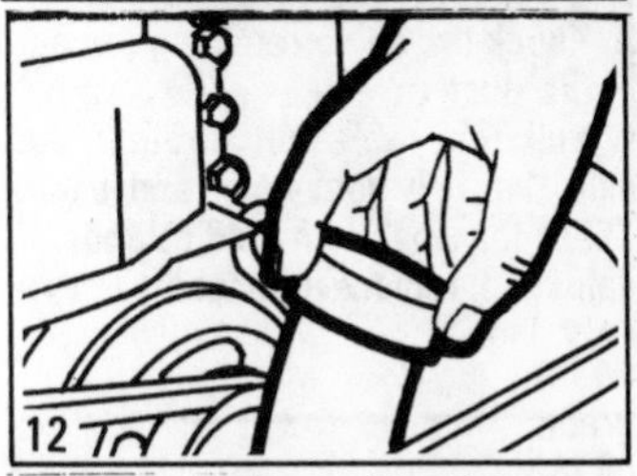

Remove and check oil level. It should be between the marks. If not, add just enough oil to bring the level to the top line.

16. Start engine and idle 3-5 minutes. The oil light on instrument panel will glow when engine is first started. Light should go out in 30 seconds or less.
17. Stop engine and check strainer cover for leaks. Recheck oil level, which should now be at the top line.

FRONT END LUBRICATION

Lubricate the front axle every 18,000 miles or one year, whichever occurs first. Proceed as follows:

1. Put the vehicle up on a lift or axle stand so that all weight will be removed from the wheels.

2. Locate the five fittings (two on each side, one at center), and clean thoroughly with a clean rag.

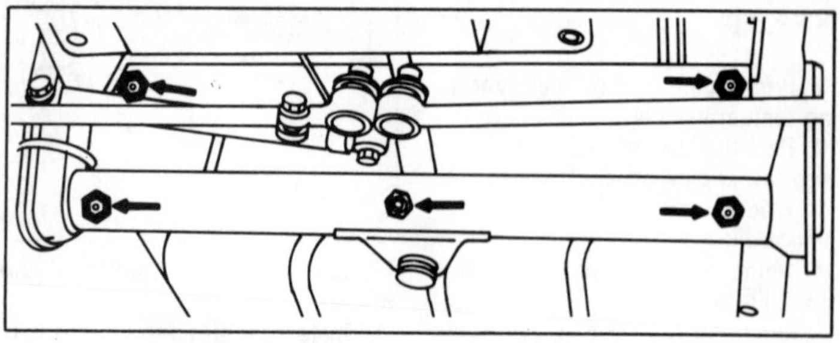

3. Lube each fitting with lithium based grease until fresh grease emerges at the sealing rings.

4. Carefully remove all excess grease that gets onto hoses or tires, as rubber is decomposed by grease.

OTHER LUBRICATION CHECKS

DOOR HINGES (lubricate every 6 months)

1. Pry off the plastic cover and add SAE 30 motor oil to the hinge chamber if it's not full.
2. Press the plug back into the hinge and wipe off any spilled oil with a rag.
3. Squirt oil into the sliding door hinge at the two cut-outs.
4. Oil the rear door hinges with a drop of oil.

DOOR LOCKS (lubricate every 6 months)

1. Lubricate your key with graphite.
2. Insert it into the lock and turn it several times in the lock.

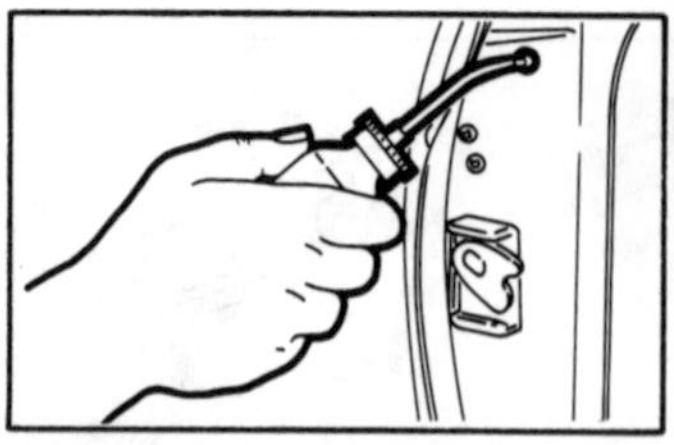

SPEEDOMETER CABLE LUBRICATION

If speedometer pointer tends to quiver or jump, or if unit makes a low rasping sound, lubrication is needed.
1. Reach under the instrument panel and remove the cable from the speedometer by unscrewing it.
2. Pry off the left front hub cap.
3. Knock the cable retaining pin out of the dust cover.
4. Pull the cable out through the axle. Carefully note which end is top. Check for wear or frayed strands. If damaged, replace inner cable with a new one.

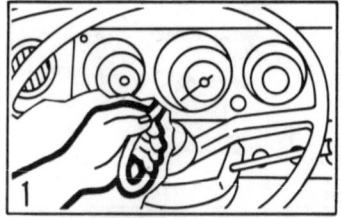

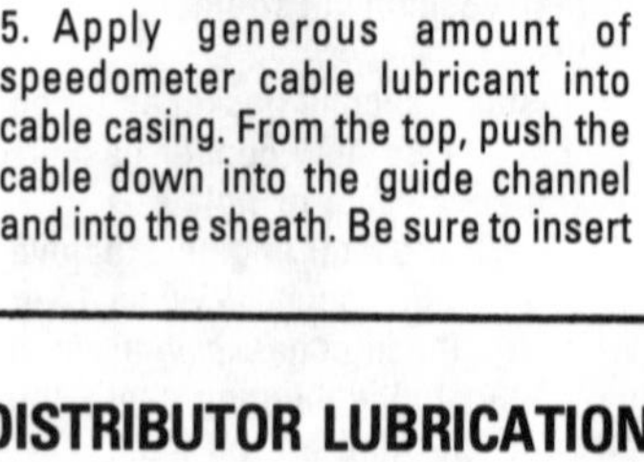

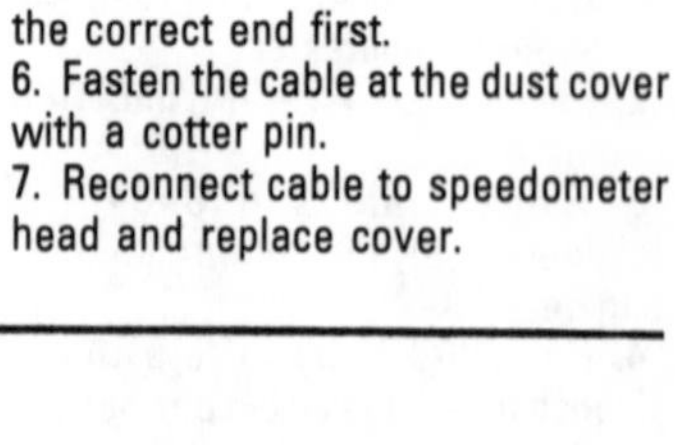

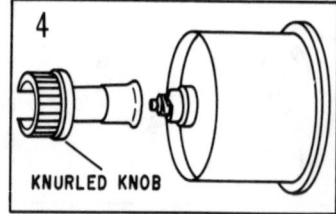

5. Apply generous amount of speedometer cable lubricant into cable casing. From the top, push the cable down into the guide channel and into the sheath. Be sure to insert the correct end first.
6. Fasten the cable at the dust cover with a cotter pin.
7. Reconnect cable to speedometer head and replace cover.

DISTRIBUTOR LUBRICATION

Every 6000 miles, put a few drops of a light oil on the felt pad under the distributor rotor. This will lubricate the ignition advance mechanism. On some older distributors, this is not required.

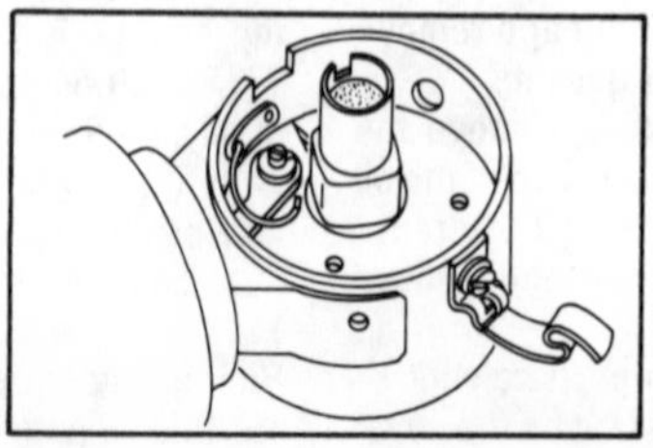

WHEEL BEARING LUBRICATION

Front and rear wheel bearings should be disassembled and repacked in grease every 30,000 miles. This is a job requiring professional knowledge and tools.

Cooling System

The VW depends on the cooling system and the engine lubricating system to maintain the correct engine temperature. The cooling system consists of a belt driven fan which forces air over the cylinders and cylinder heads. Sheet metal shrouds surround the engine so that the cooling air is contained and directed. Engine oil also provides cooling and this is why oil quality and level are even more critical on a VW than a conventional car. All VWs have an oil cooler, a small oil radiator, located inside the cooling shroud. Accessory oil coolers are available, which you can have installed or install yourself, that provide additional engine cooling for heavy duty operation such as trailer towing. A faulty thermostat can cause either overheating or slow warm-up. Check that the thermostat is fully closed when the engine is cold, and wide open when the engine is idling hot. Replace if defective. Located under car. For almost all heater/cooling system work or inspection it may be necessary to get under the car. Do not attempt to do any work under the vehicle while it is supported only by the jack. Use safety stands or ramps. Block the wheels.

REPLACING THE THERMOSTAT

A faulty thermostat can cause either overheating or slow warm-up. Check that the thermostat is fully closed when the engine is cold, and wide open when the engine is idling hot. Replace if defective. Located under car.

1. Remove screws, remove air duct place from lower right of engine.
2. Remove mounting bolt from underside of thermostat bracket.
3. Loosen bracket mounting nut.
4. Push upper portion of bracket

away from you. Rotate bracket away from thermostat.

5. Unscrew thermostat (counterclockwise).
6. Screw new thermostat onto actuating rod. When fully screwed on, move up and down to ensure cooling flaps are free. Leave in full up position.
7. Turn the bracket back to its original position so that rod is in slot in upper portion.
8. Slide the bracket up and down on its mount until top of bracket just touches top of thermostat. Do not pull thermostat down in doing this.
9. Tighten thermostat bracket mounting nut.
10. Pull thermostat downward, and install thermostat mounting bolt through lower bracket.
11. Install air duct plate.

1. Remove the mounting bolts, and remove the lower right side cooling duct from underneath the engine.
2. Unscrew the cable connection from the front of the thermostat.
3. Unscrew and remove the bolt from the rear of the thermostat.
4. In replacing, first position the thermostat and install the mounting

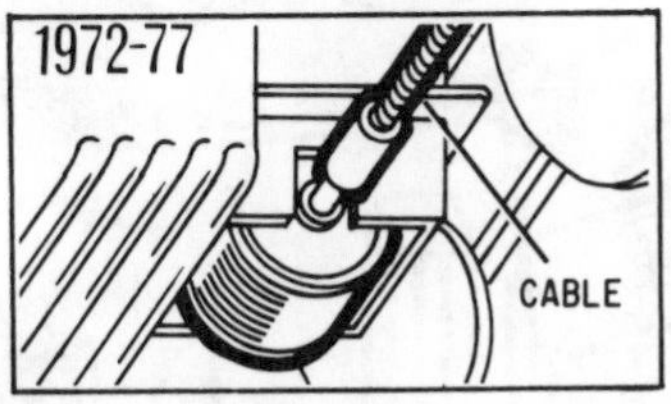

bolt, after engine cools.

5. Screw on the cable connection. Make sure the cable runs in the groove of the wheel provided for it.
6. Loosen the screw and square nut that holds the cable to the control flap shaft. Hold the flaps in the fully closed position, and tighten the nut and screw so the cable will hold the flaps fully closed.

FAN BELT ADJUSTMENT

The fan belt drives the cooling fan and generator. Since there is no natural air flow through the engine, and since the oil cooler is dependent upon the fan, it should be easy to see that the slippage of the belt will re-

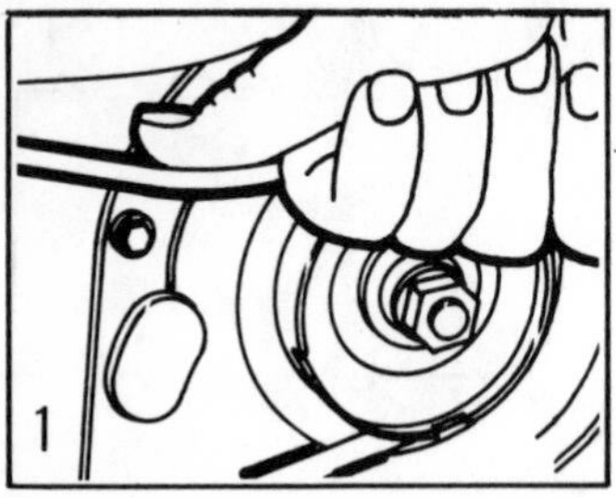

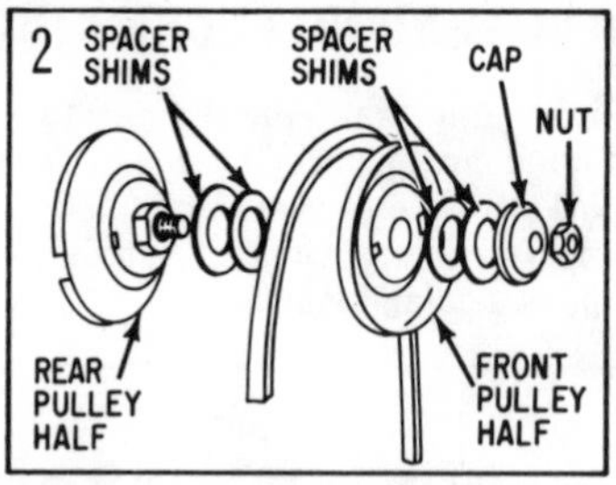

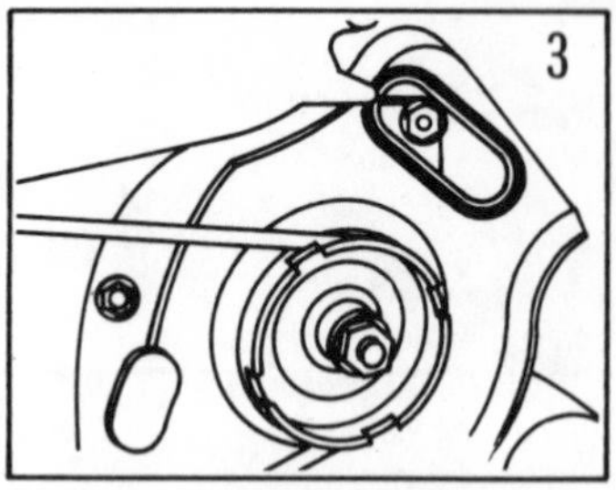

sult in overheating. The belt deserves an occasional look and tension check.

1. Inspect fan belt occasionally. Press thumb at midpoint of belt span between pulleys. If belt depresses more than ½ inch, tightening is needed. A too loose belt will not drive the cooling fan or generator/alternator effectively.

2. The 1970-71 belt is tensioned by adding (loosens) or removing (tightens) the spacer shims under the outer pulley half. Place extra shims on the outside of the pulley, under the nut.

3. Use a screwdriver in the slot in the inner pulley to hold it during loosening and tightening of the nut.

4. The 1972-76 belt is tensioned by moving the alternator in or out as necessary. Remove the plastic cover from the alternator.

5. Loosen the alternator bolts (one is an allen head—use proper tool) and push the alternator to the right until the belt tension is correct. Tighten the bolts.

FIND THOSE COOLING SYSTEM LEAKS

1. Inspect both heater hoses. If either is cracked or broken, replace it. Leaky heater hoses deprive the engine of cooling air, make the heater ineffective.

2. Inspect heater hose clamps. Make sure they hold hoses securely onto fittings, and have not loosened due to vibration.

3. With engine off, check cooling fan air intake behind fan housing for foreign material.

4. Inspect spark plug rubber boots for cracks, brittleness, and replace if necessary.

5. Make sure all screws in shrouding are in place and tight.

6. Make sure rubber seal around rear of engine compartment is not cracked. Have replaced if necessary.

Leaks are possible at:
Heater hoses
Shrouding assembly points
Spark plug rubber boots

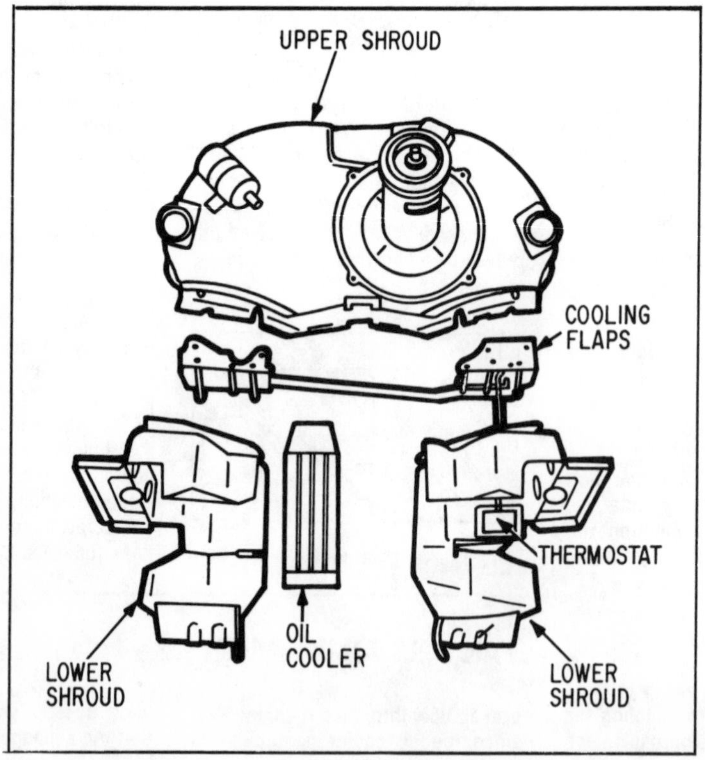

HOSE REPLACEMENT

Inspect all hoses. If any are dented or cracked, replace at once.

Check all hose connections for tightness. Tighten loose hose clamps; they tend to loosen due to engine vibration.

1. Loosen both hose clamps with a Phillips screwdriver.
2. Carefully pull hose off fan housing connection. Then, pull lower portion of hose off heater box sleeve.
3. Press down on top of heater box sleeve to make sure it is fully seated.
4. Transfer hose clamps to new hose.
5. Connect hose at top and bottom. Make sure it slides on as far as it will go, and that heater box sleeve stays in position.
6. Position and tighten hose clamps.

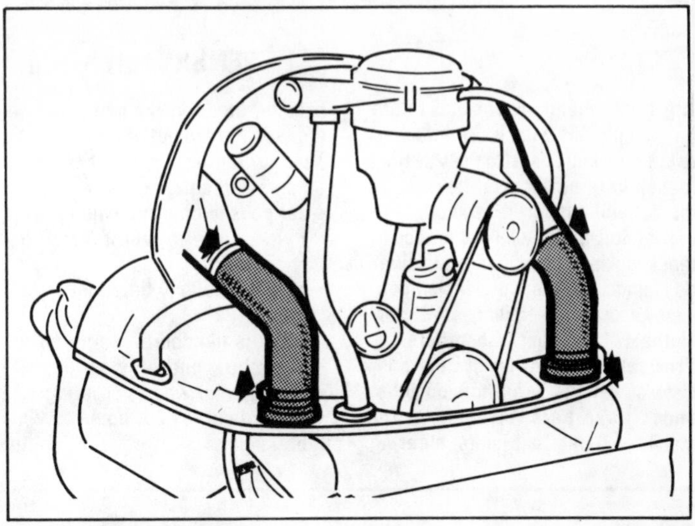

PLUG WIRE BOOTS

Check these seals occasionally for cracks or brittleness. Leaks allow needed cooling air to escape. They are replaced by simply pulling spark plug leads off, and pulling the old boot off the end of the connector. Slide the new boot on carefully in exactly the same position. Then, install the lead and make sure it seals properly. If necessary, slide it to a position on the connector which will ensure a tight seal against the shrouding.

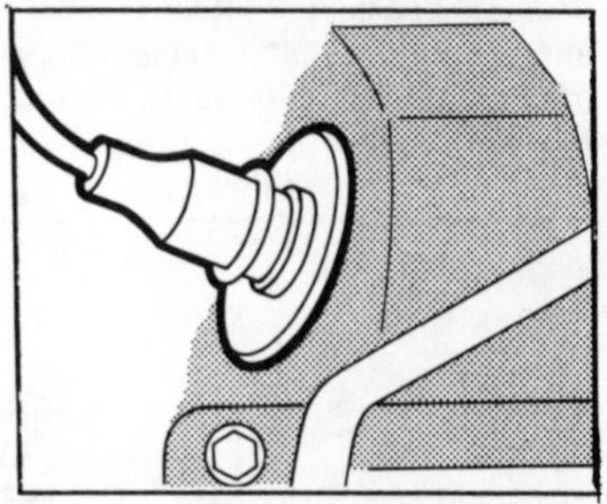

POINTS TO CHECK

Check fins on bottom of oil pan, cylinders and heads for heavy deposits of grease and dirt. If fins are clogged, have engine steam cleaned.

Check the rubber gasket at the rear of the engine compartment for cracks. Leaks here may cause recirculation of hot air.

Check hoses for leaks at arrowed points. Leaks will deprive the engine of required cooling air. See Hose Replacement section at left.

Remember that if the red "Generator" light comes on it means there is no engine cooling. Stop the engine as soon as possible and check cause.

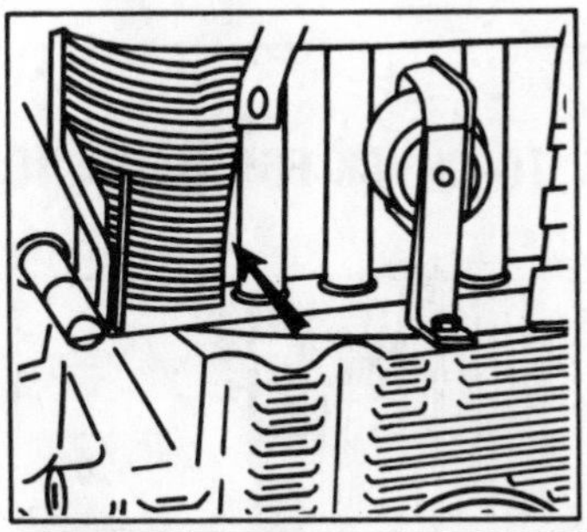

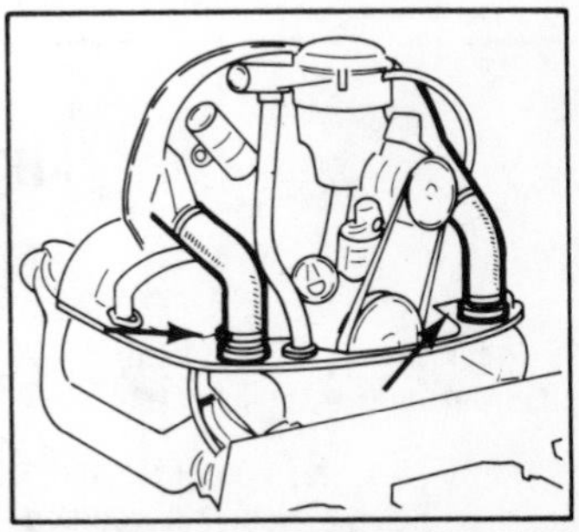

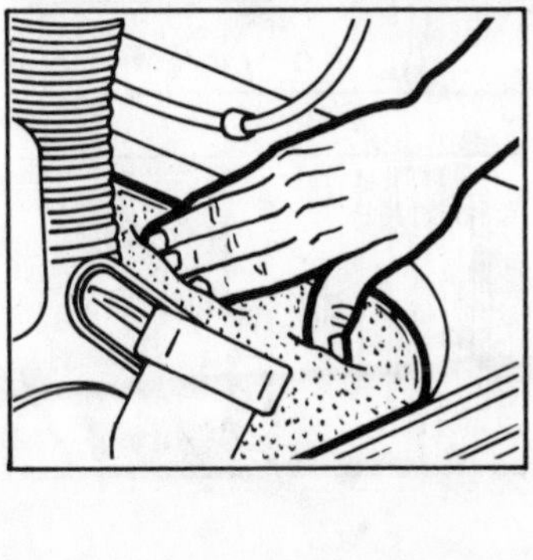

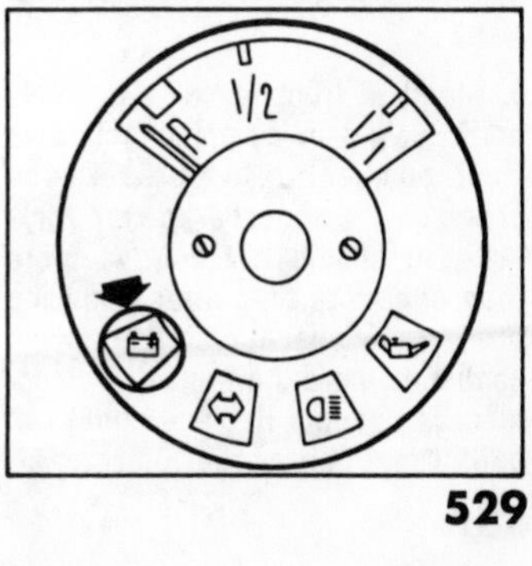

Suspension and Tires

SUSPENSION SYSTEM

The front wheels mount and rotate on the spindles, which are attached to steering knuckles. On the VW Bus, torsion bars run across the front of the car and support it via dual, trailing torsion arms, which connect to the knuckles via upper and lower ball joints. The rear suspension consists of diagonal trailing arms, torsion bars, and shock absorbers.

Your car's suspension system consists of wheels, tires, torsion bars, shock absorbers, sway bars (or stabilizer bars), ball joints, steering linkage, steering damper. If any of these items are out of adjustment or badly worn, you may notice any of these symptoms:

- car pulls to one side when braking
- car wanders when driving a straight line
- overall ride may be either hard or bouncy
- effort is needed to steer vehicle
- tires show uneven wear
- tires squeal when cornering
- front of car dips or bounces when braking
- car rocks side-to-side when going over rough road
- wheels bounce to make slapping sound on road
- steering wheel vibrates in hands
- front of car vibrates at highway speeds

Any of the above symptoms indicates corrective action is needed. Delay can: ruin tires; cause damage/failure to other suspension parts; create safety hazard.

STEERING

If steering linkage, front suspension and steering column components are in good condition, there should be no more than one and one half inch of free play in the steering wheel when measured at the rim of the wheel. If a loud knock is heard when turning the steering wheel from one extreme to the other, have mechanic check pinion bearing preload.

SHOCK ABSORBERS

Shock absorbers work to keep wheels in constant contact with the road. Result is safe handling and ride control; longer tire life. So shock absorbers (or shocks) are important.

HOW TO CHECK FOR BAD SHOCKS

1. Check under car and locate shock absorber near each wheel.

2. Heavy oil streaks on outer shock housing indicate need for replacement.

3. Stand at front of car and apply body weight in pumping action to front bumper or fender. Release pressure and allow car to stop rocking. Car should not bounce more than one more time after releasing pressure. Repeat at rear. If bouncing continues more than once, replacement is needed. Replace shocks in pairs (front pair or rear pair).

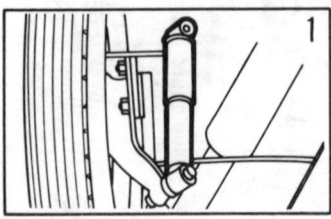

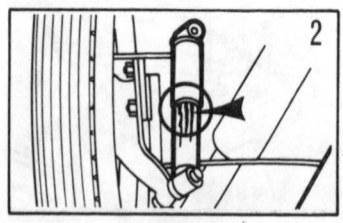

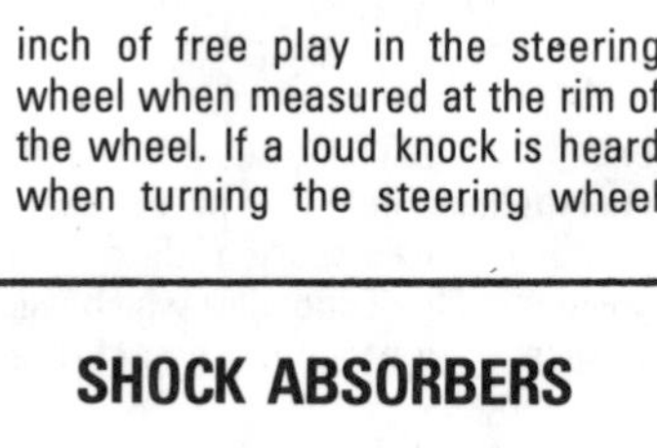

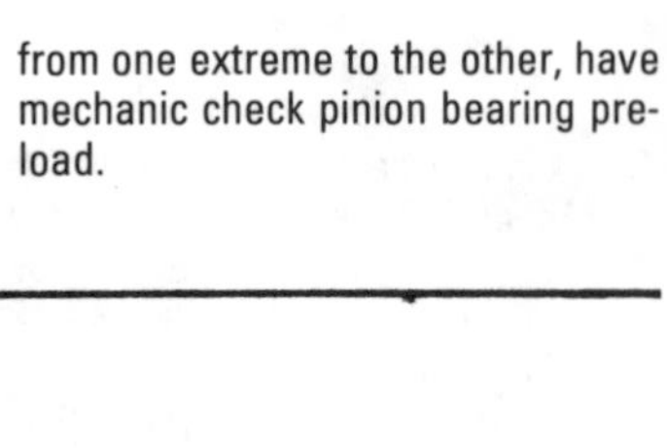

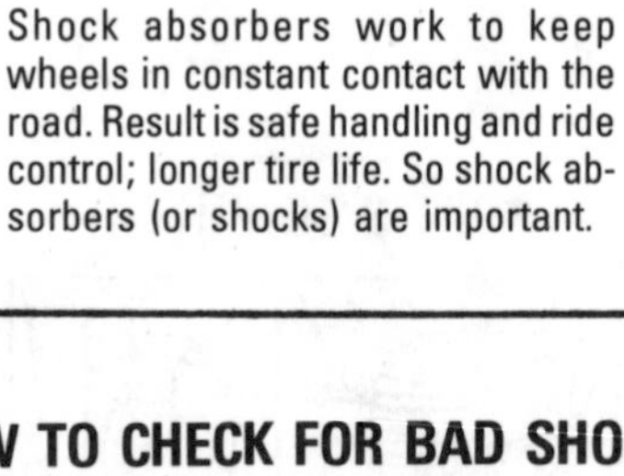

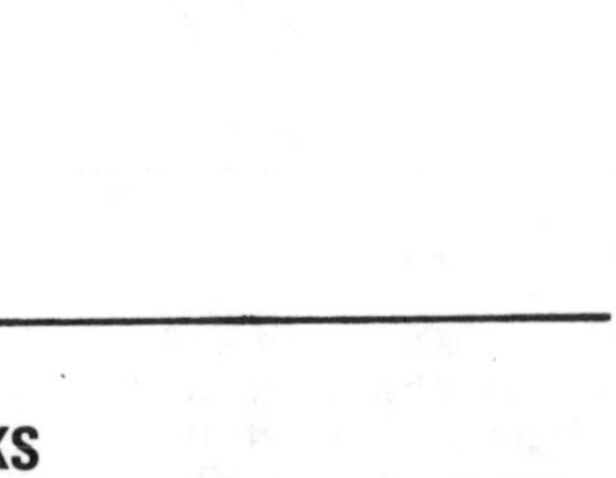

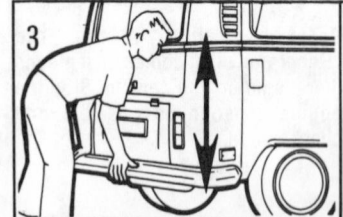

TOW HITCH INFORMATION

If your VW is used for trailer towing you should check:

A. Cooling system; make sure that fan belt is in good condition and properly tensioned. See Cooling system for checks to perform.

B. Check rear shock absorbers; you may benefit from installation of new rear shocks.

C. Check tire pressures; best traction and handling will be ensured if tire pressures are properly maintained. Never exceed a load of 1340 lbs. (trailer without brakes) or 2240 lbs. (trailer with brakes).

For safer and more trouble-free trailer towing, consider:

A. Engine oil cooler; helps maintain lower engine temperature during towing. Helps avoid engine overheating. Some units can be self-installed.

B. Heavy Duty Shock Absorbers; important to have on rear wheels if you intend to do a lot of towing or load carrying within the car itself. Don't forget to consider replacing factory shocks, when they are worn out, with heavy duty units at the front as well.

C. Variable Load Flasher; this unit will accommodate the added load of trailer turn signal lamps on trailer when these are hooked into your car's electrical system.

FRONT END ALIGNMENT

When steering, handling and/or tire wear indicate front end alignment may be needed, this work can only be done at an automotive service shop. DO NOT PUT OFF NEEDED FRONT END ALIGNMENT. At the same time, have ball joints and steering linkage checked.

Ignition System

TUNE-UP SERVICES

The ignition system consists of spark plugs; plug wires; distributor; rotor; points; condenser; coil. These units work to create a good hot spark inside the engine (ignition) at exactly the right moment (timing). If ignition is weak or timing is off, engine may be hard to start, run poorly, waste gas, lose power, backfire or not run at all.

VW SAYS . . . Replace plugs and points every 12,000 miles (1970-74 models) or 15,000 miles (1975-76 models).

TOOLS & MATERIALS . . . Parts: set of points; condenser; 4 spark plugs. Tools: gap gauge; 13/16 in. spark plug socket; screwdriver; open end, box or combination metric wrenches; timing equipment (see Ignition Timing).

SAFETY TIP . . . Change only one spark plug at a time to avoid crosswiring and possible engine damage.

CHECKING POINTS AND ROTOR

1

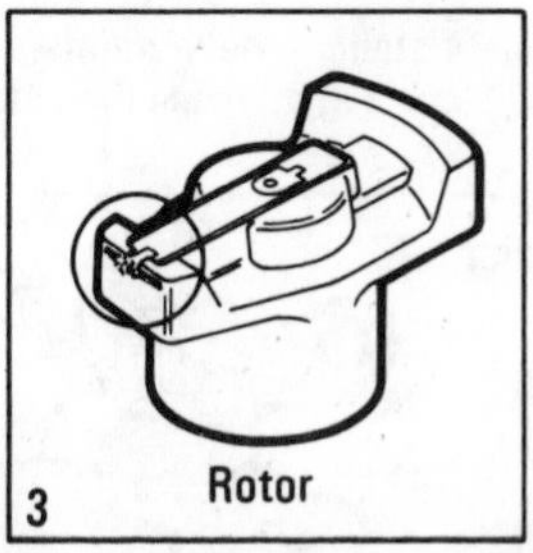

3

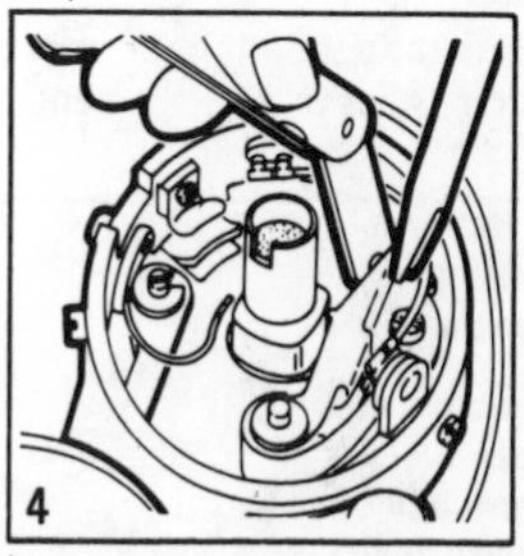
4

The distributor holds the points and rotor. The condenser is attached to the outside of the distributor.

1. To open distributor, remove center wire only, snap retaining clips off with screwdriver, lift cap off but keep wires connected.
2. Examine inside of cap for pitted or burned metal contacts and hairline cracks.
3. Pull rotor off (straight up). If it is cracked or metallic tip is badly burned, replace it.
4. Pry points apart with screwdriver. If pitted or burned, replace. If OK, check point gap with feeler gauge, for proper setting of .016.

OTHER IGNITION CHECK POINTS

Inspect spark plug wires. If cracked or brittle, entire set should be replaced. Also center, high tension wire. Inspect distributor cap. Wipe inside clean occasionally with dry, lint-free rag. If cap is cracked or rotor contacts are excessively burned, replace cap. Inspect coil. It seldom needs replacing, but if it is cracked or damaged, replace it.

SPARK PLUG REPLACEMENT

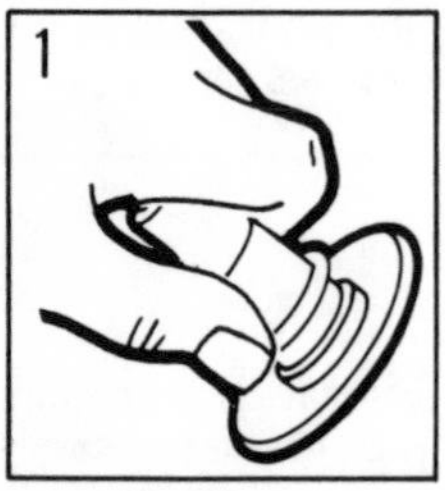

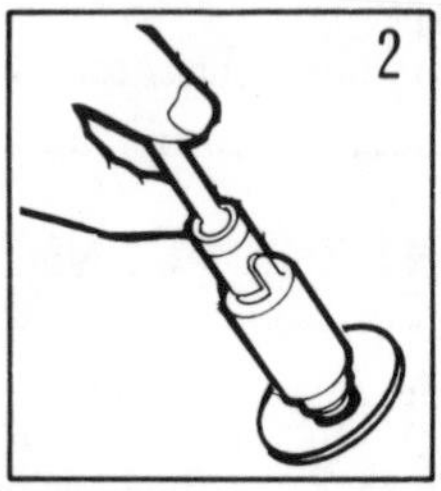

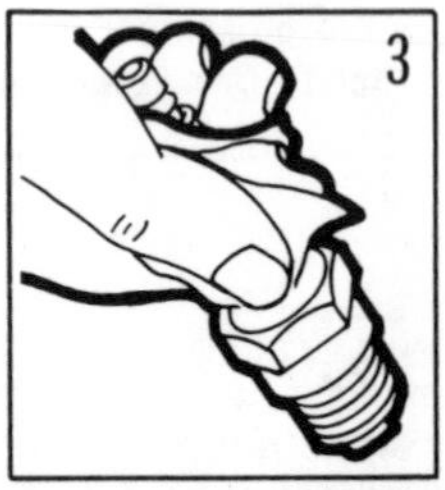

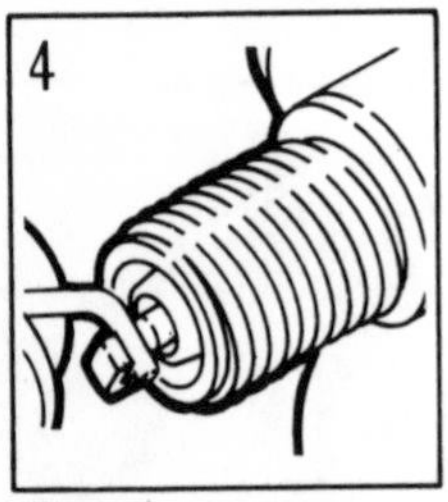

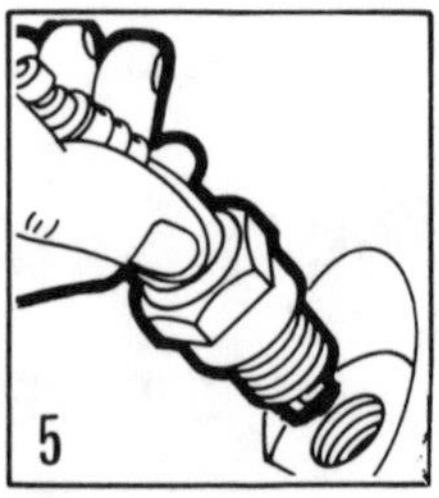

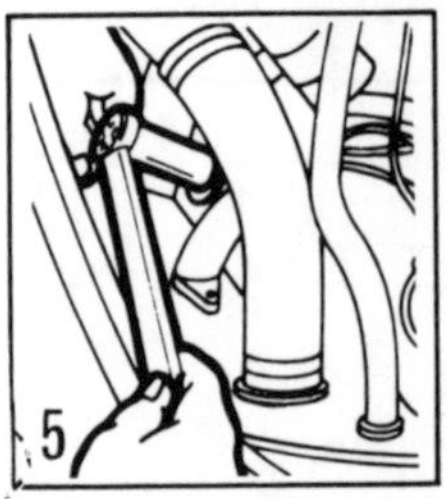

1. Remove spark plug wire by grasping rubber boot. Do not jerk wire off. If stuck, turn boot, pulling gently.

2. Loosen spark plug using socket wrench.

3. Wipe or brush loose dirt from around plug before removing. Do not let dirt drop into engine through plug hole. Unscrew plug.

4. Check plug electrode gap on new spark plug. Adjust to specifications. Plug gap is correct when the gauge drags slightly as it is pulled between plug electrodes.

5. Thread new plug into plug hole by hand. Hand tighten. Do not force or cross thread. Use socket wrench to tighten firmly but do not force. Replace plug wire. Press boot firmly.

LOCATION OF POINTS AND CONDENSER

Points and condenser work together. Always replace condenser when installing new points. The condenser is attached to the outside of the distributor.

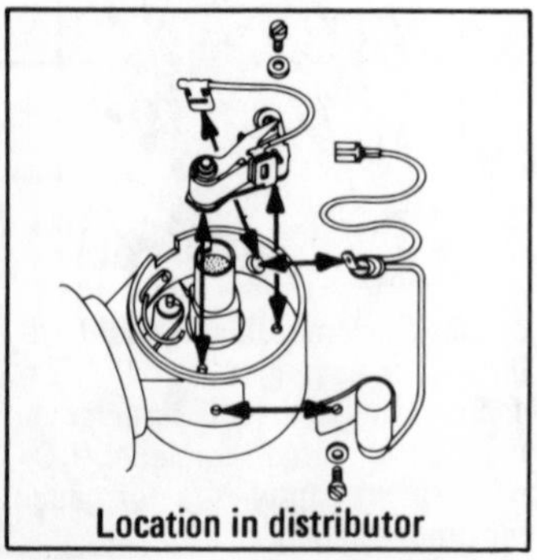

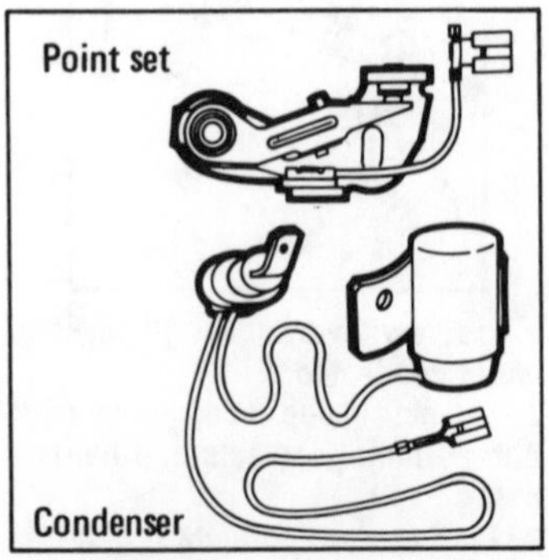

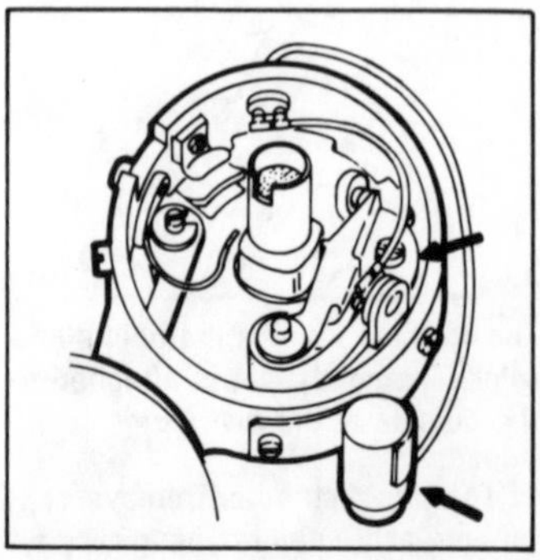

REMOVING POINTS AND CONDENSER

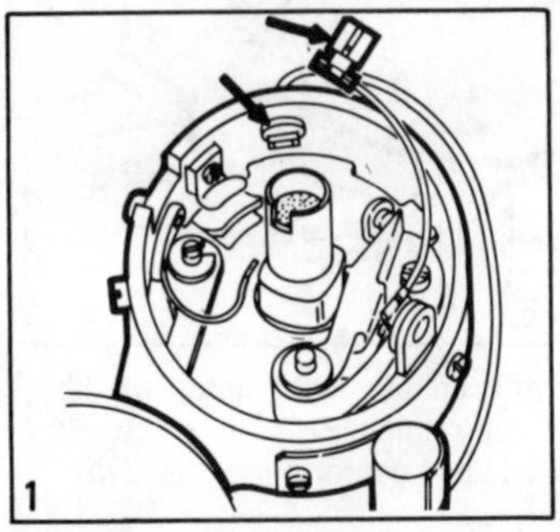

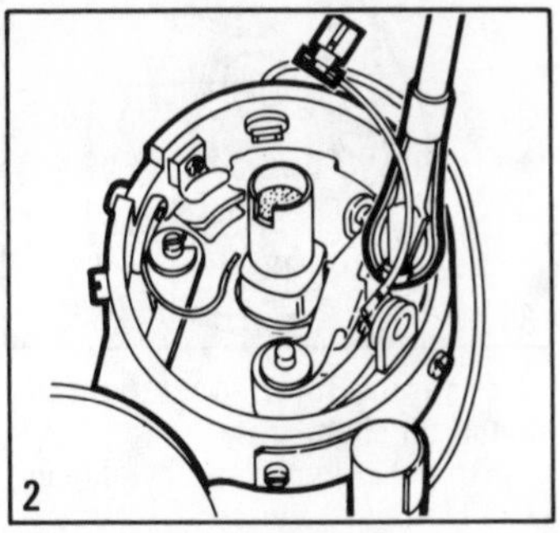

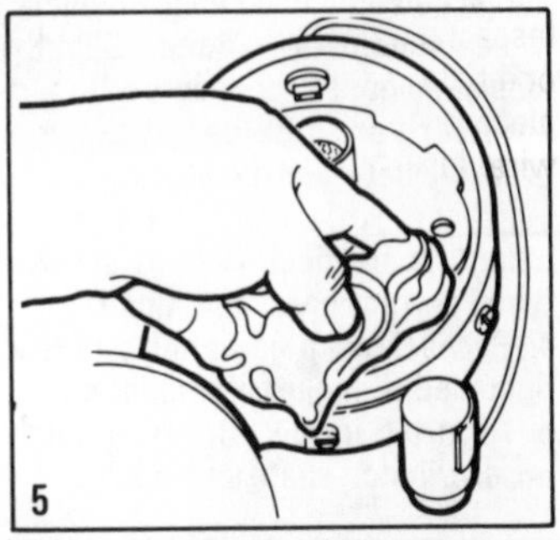

1. Disconnect the points wire from the condenser connection at the side of the distributor.

2. Remove the screw from the stationary breaker point. Lift points out of distributor.

CAUTION: Be careful not to drop the screw into the distributor.

3. Remove the condenser by undoing the screw holding the bracket and condenser connection to the distributor.

4. Disconnect the condenser wire from the coil.

5. Wipe all dirt and grease from the distributor plate and cam with clean, lint-free rag.

CAUTION: When removing screws from distributor, be sure to avoid any screws accidentally falling through distributor opening into engine. Use magnetic screwdriver.

INSTALLING POINTS AND CONDENSER

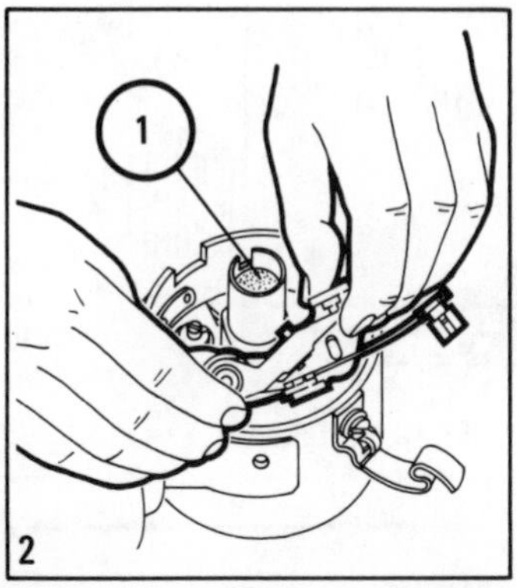

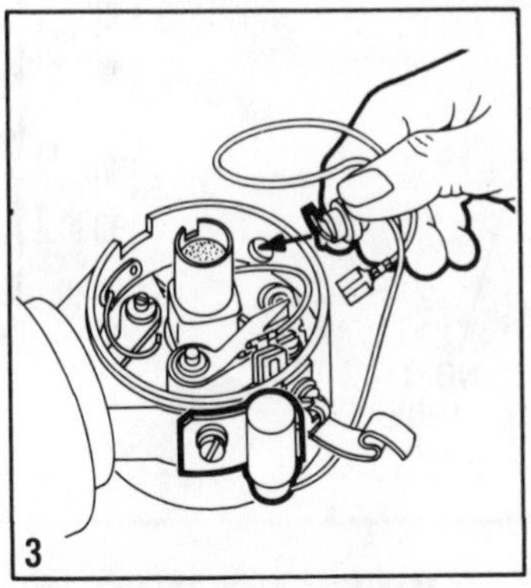

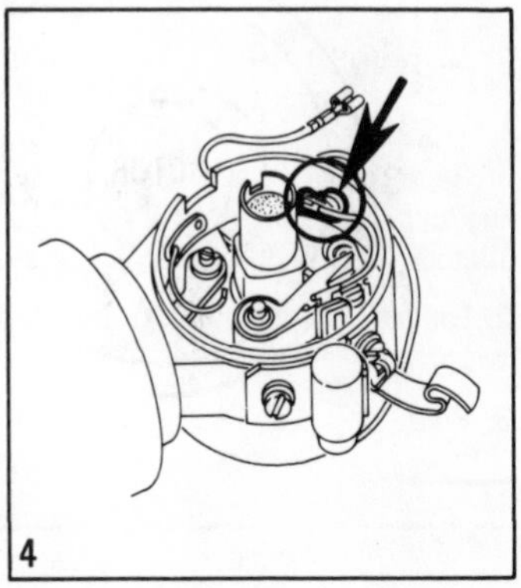

1. Apply small amount of heat resistant lube to distributor cam (lube sometimes supplied with new point sets, if not, purchase separately).

2. Position new points in distributor and fasten with the attaching screw. Connect points wire to terminal on inside of distributor.

3. Attach new condenser to distributor with attaching screw. Connect wire to coil.

4. Connect points wire to condenser terminal.

RESETTING THE CONTACT GAP

1. Electrical contacts of point set MUST BE PARALLEL. If needed, bend stationary contact with needle-nosed pliers. Bend only the bracket portion of points—not the other side.

2. Turn engine by ignition key (you'll need a helper) until rubbing block on points is on one of the four high points of distributor cam. You may use wrench on lower pulley to do this.

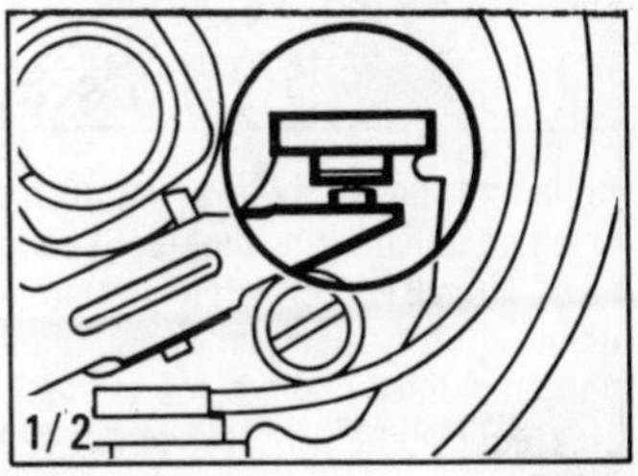

3. Correct point gap for all Type 2 models is .016. Insert proper feeler gauge between open point contacts. If adjustment is needed: Slightly loosen point attaching screw. Insert screwdriver between boss on breaker plate and notch on points. Twist screwdriver to open or close points as needed. Tighten screws when correct gap is obtained.
4. Recheck point gap after screw is tightened. Readjust if needed.
5. Align tab inside rotor with notch on distributor shaft and push rotor

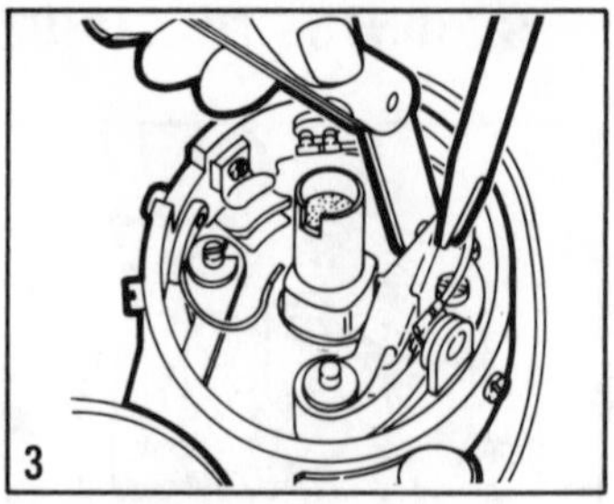

onto shaft. Rotor must be fully seated on shaft.
6. Install distributor cap by aligning

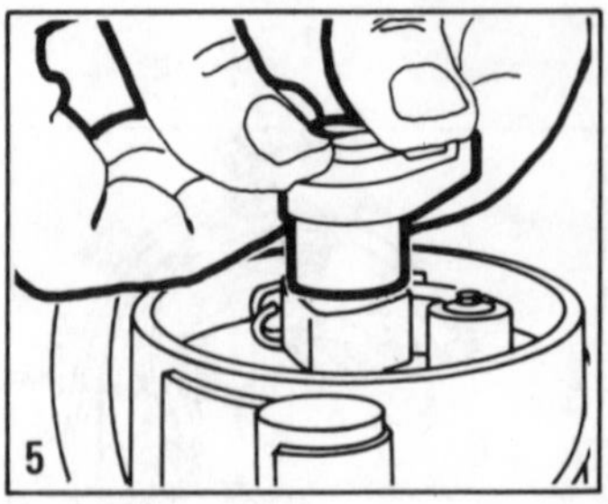

tabs on cap with notch on body. Snap retaining clips in place.
7. Install center distributor wire.

REPLACING SPARK PLUG WIRES

Use the firing order illustration to guide you when replacing your ignition wires and/or distributor cap.

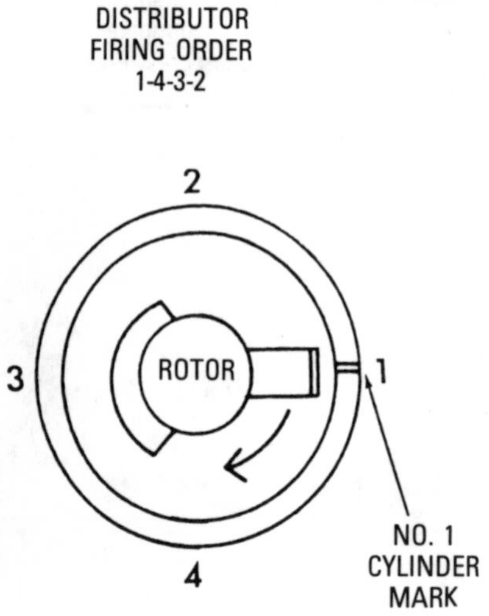

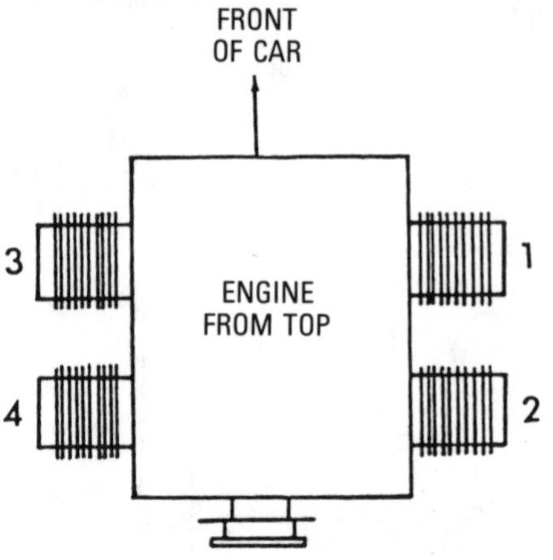

CYLINDER NUMBERING

IGNITION TIMING

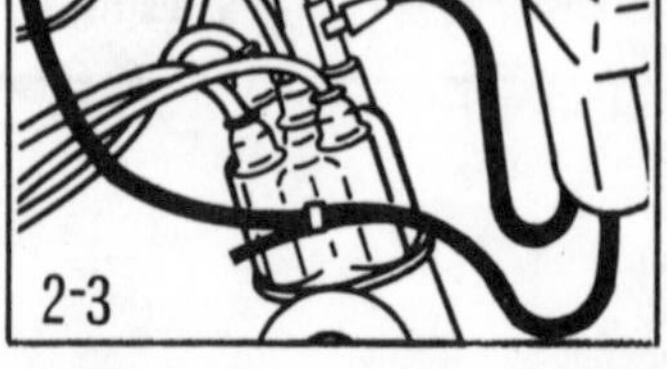

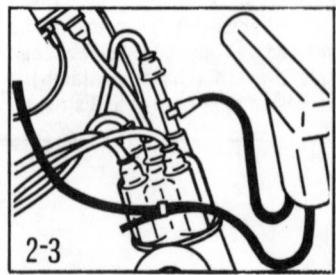

Adjusting timing is the important finishing touch to any tune-up. This is not a difficult job but it does require a timing light, dwell meter or combination dwell/tach and a piece of chalk. This equipment will cost about $20 and up depending on type and quality. Since timing is a minor service adjustment not requiring any parts installation, you may wish to have this done at a service garage. If you have equipment proceed as follows:

1. Locate timing marks on crankshaft pulley (lower). Clean away dirt. Mark the timing notch with the chalk.
2. Hook up timing light according to instructions supplied with it.
CAUTION: Make sure that timing

light wires are clear of drive belt. Keep hands and tools away from belt.
3. Disconnect the vacuum line on 1970 models only. Leave the line connected on all other models.
4. Hook up tachometer and adjust engine idle speed to specifications, if necessary.
5. Aim timing light at pulley mark. If the chalked notch does not align with the crankcase seam, loosen the clamp at the bottom of the distributor and slowly rotate the distributor until the notch and seam align.
6. Tighten clamp. Recheck timing.
7. Detach timing light.

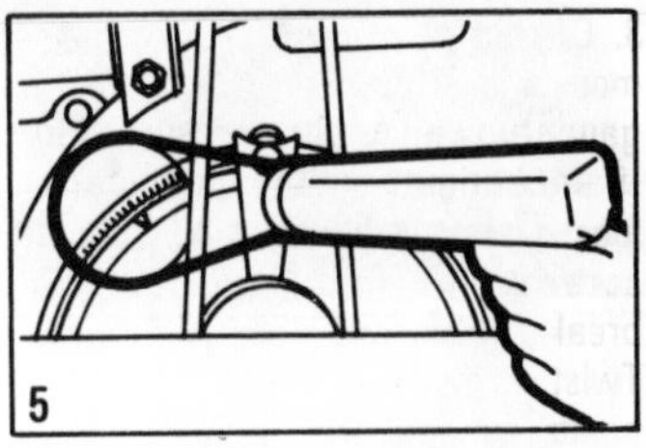

Fuel System

When gasoline is brought from the fuel tank, it mixes with air in the carburetor. This gas/air mixture enters engine thru the intake manifold, passes thru the intake valves and is burned in the combustion chamber. The burned exhaust gas is then passed thru the exhaust valves to the exhaust system and to the outside air. In order to keep your car's engine running cleanly with minimal pollution, and avoid dangerous carbon monoxide fumes inside the vehicle, certain items should be checked from time to time.

FUEL FILTER CLEANING/REPLACEMENT

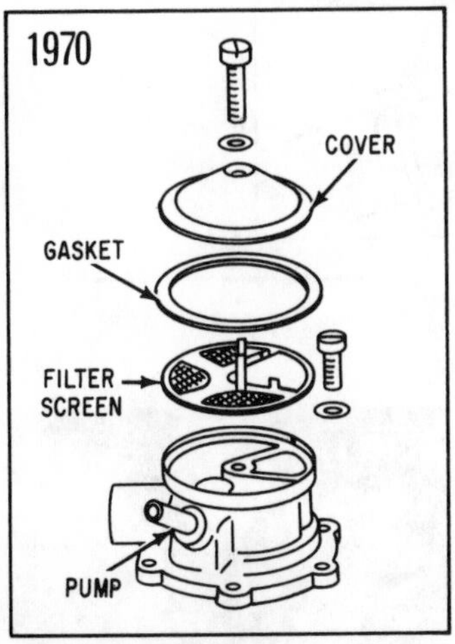

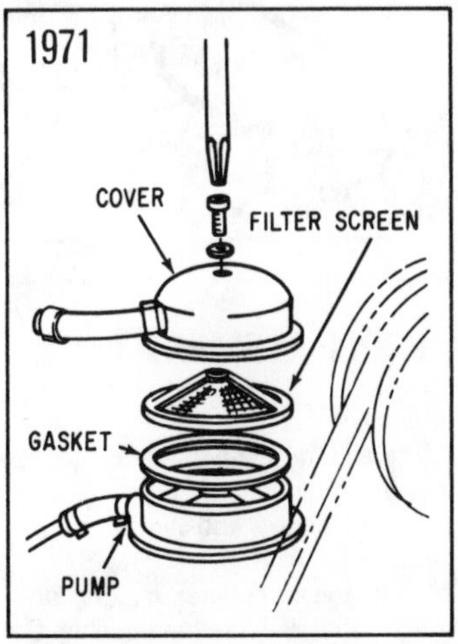

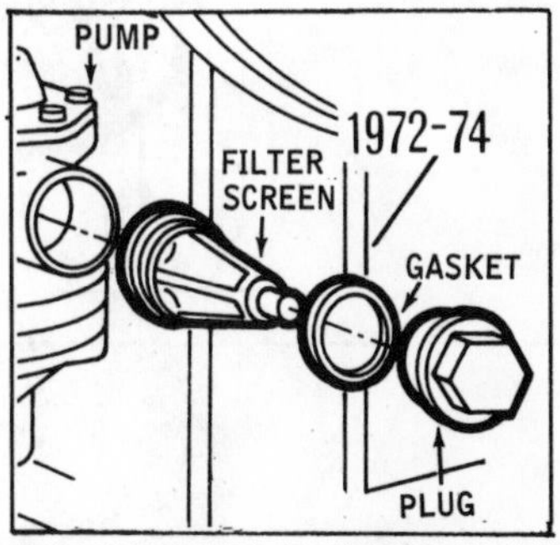

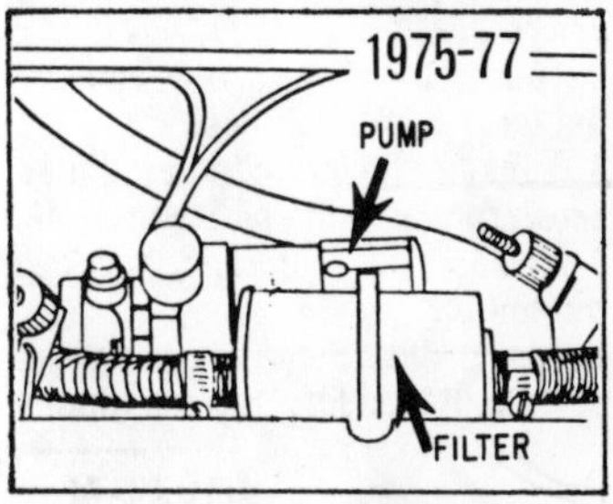

On 1970-71 models:
1. Remove the fuel pump top cover bolt and lift off the cover.
2. Remove the filter screen.
3. Clean the filter in solvent and air dry.
4. Carefully wipe any sediment from the pump.
5. Replace screen with studs facing up.
6. Position top cover on pump and install bolt.
NOTE: After cleaning filter screen, re-check for fuel leaks with engine running and fuel passing through the system.

On 1972-74 models:
1. Locate the fuel pump up under the engine, between #1 cylinder and the flywheel. The filter screen is located behind a hexagonal plug on the side of the fuel pump housing.
2. Remove the cover plug and take out the thimble-like filter screen.
3. Clean the filter in solvent and air dry.
4. Install the filter and cover plug with a new gasket, if possible.
5. After installation, run the engine and check for leaks.

On 1975-77 models with fuel injection:
1. Open the fuel tank filler cap to relieve any excess pressure in the system.
2. Locate the disposable in-line filter between the fuel tank and electric fuel pump near the front axle.
3. Clamp off the inlet and outlet fuel lines to the filter with clothes pins.
4. Loosen the hose clamps and remove the filter. Discard it.
5. Install the new filter with the arrow pointing in the direction of fuel flow. Tighten the hose clamps. Remove the clothes pins.
6. After installation, run the engine and check for leaks.

KEEP THE AIR INTAKE CLEAN

The large can or box that sits on top of the engine is the air cleaner. 1970-72 buses have an oil bath air cleaner. 1973-76 models have a paper element air cleaner. Access to the air cleaner is through the lid in the rear floor.

OIL BATH TYPE

1. Detach all hoses, making a note of where they go.
2. Loosen the clamp screw on the large heated air hose and pull it off.
3. Remove the screw on the air cleaner bracket and loosen the screw on the air cleaner clamp.
4. Carefully lift the air cleaner off. Do not tilt, or you will spill oil.
5. Unclip the top, and separate the two halves.
6. Drain the old oil out of the bottom.
7. Clean the top and bottom with a clean rag.
8. Refill the line with clean engine oil (.9 pint).
9. Install air cleaner in original position. Make sure to reconnect all hoses in original position.

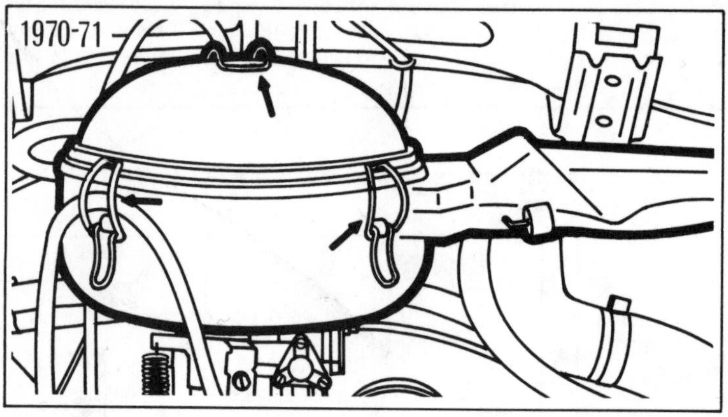

PAPER ELEMENT TYPE

1. Detach all small hoses, noting where they go.
2. Loosen the clamp screw, and pull the large heated air hose off.
3. Loosen the air cleaner clamp screw, and pull the air cleaner off.
4. Release the four clips, and pull the top off.
5. Shake dirt off the filter, and inspect it. If it is dirty, replace, do not attempt to clean it.
6. Install filter element, making sure it is properly seated.
7. Install the top, and clip it into position.
8. Reinstall air cleaner, making sure it is parallel with the fan housing. Do not overtighten clamp screw.
9. Reconnect all hoses in proper position.

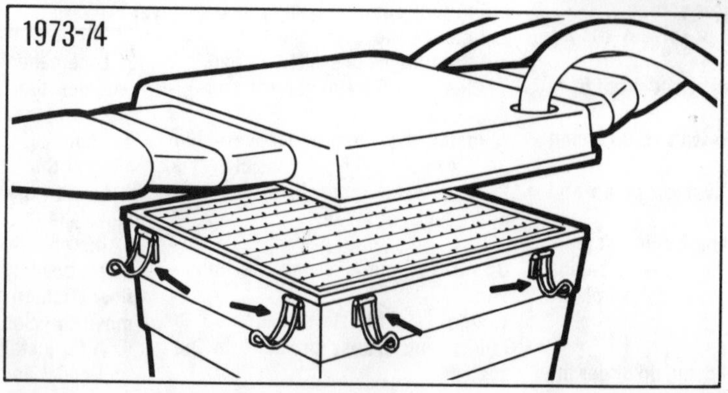

EMISSION CONTROL SYSTEMS

An important part of a car's emission controls is the Positive Crankcase Ventilation system. The connecting hoses should be inspected every 6 months for clogging or deterioration. This system helps prevent the formation of sludge and dirt in the engine.

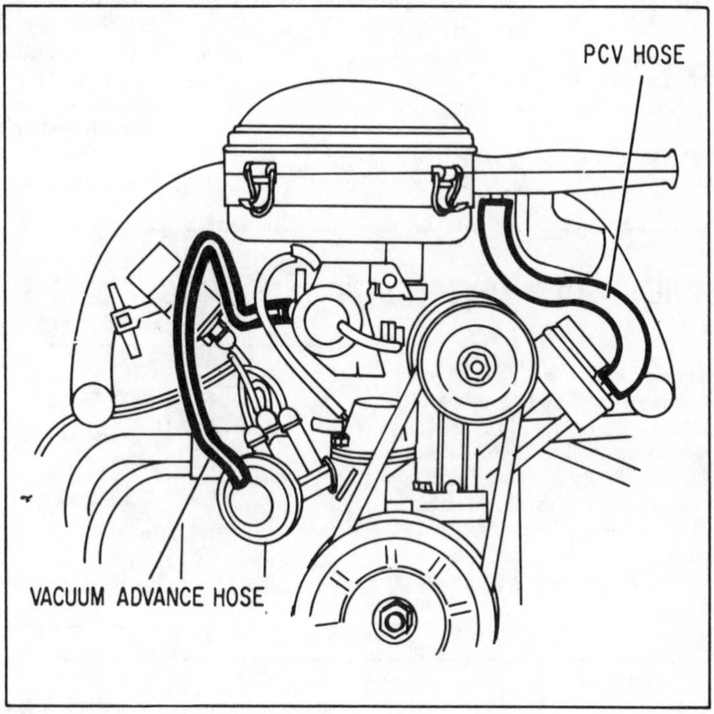

EMISSION SYSTEM CHECKS

Emission controlled engines achieve clean combustion through use of various precise controls on things like ignition timing and carburetor air temperature. Improper operation of any of these controls, or any vacuum leak caused by a loose connection can cause rough running, hesitation, or increased emissions. Periodically make all the checks described below to ensure smooth and clean engine operation:

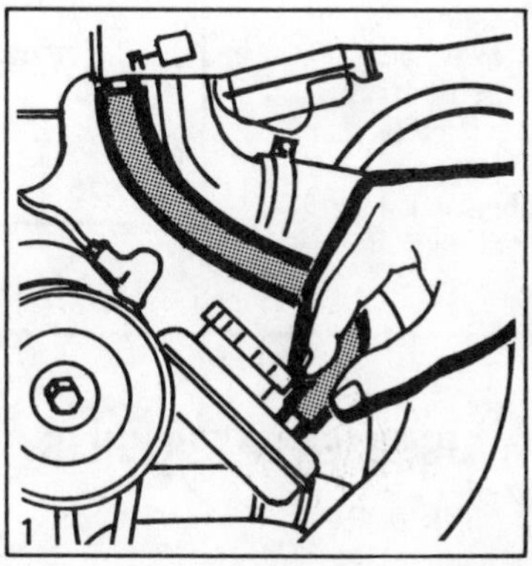

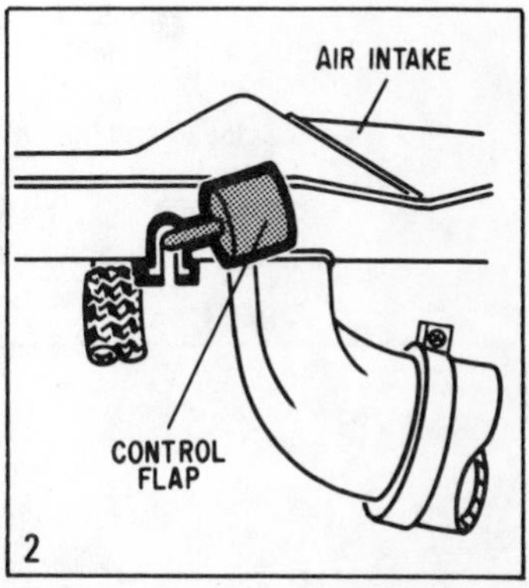

1. Remove the hose which connects the air cleaner intake with the oil filler. Make sure the hose is not frayed or cracked, and blow through it to ensure it is not clogged. If dirty, clean or replace.

2. Check the counterweighted control flap on the air intake on 70-71 buses. If it does not rotate freely, apply oil where the shaft enters the nylon bushing, and work it back and forth until it moves smoothly.

3. Make an extremely careful check of all hoses, their connections, and routing. Make sure none of the hoses is crimped, frayed, or loose where it connects to the carburetor or emission control it operates. If your 1970-71 has a large, green vacuum hose, make sure it is routed through the clip on the front of the air cleaner.

Safety Systems

PARKING LIGHTS AND TURN SIGNALS

A No. 1034 bulb functions as the turn signal and parking light. To replace, remove the two Phillips head screws and lift the lens off. Wipe any dirt or moisture from the inside of the lens.

Push down on bulb and turn counterclockwise to remove from socket.

Insert new bulb. Small side marker bulbs are replaced in the same manner as those; use a No. 57 bulb. On 1974-76 models, both of these bulbs are under a single lens.

NOTE: When inserting new bulb, note that knobs on side of base are different distances from base tip. Match knobs to socket slots for proper fit. Check that the lens gasket is correctly positioned and not cracked or rotted. Replace, if necessary. Reinstall the lens. DO NOT overtighten the screws or you will break the lens.

REAR TURN SIGNAL, STOP-TAIL, BACK-UP LIGHTS

These three bulbs are located under the single rear lens on the fender. To replace, unscrew the three Phillips head screws and take off the lens. Wipe any dirt or moisture from the inside of the lens. Push down on bulb and turn counterclockwise to remove from the socket. Insert the new bulb and install in reverse order.

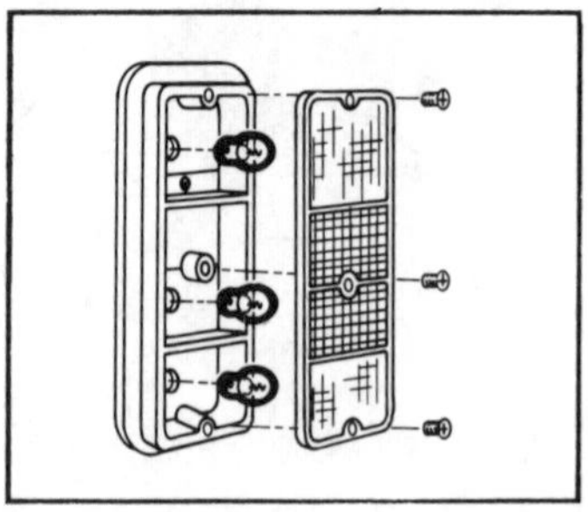

INTERIOR DOME LIGHT

This is a cartridge type bulb; be sure to purchase correct replacement. Carefully pry the light housing out of the headliner using a screwdriver in the housing slot. To avoid blowing fuse, make sure that doors are closed and light switch is off (center position). Carefully lift the bulb straight out of the housing. Insert new bulb and re-install housing.

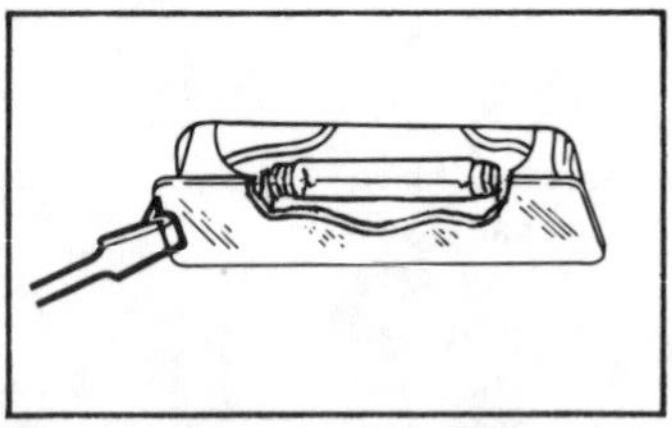

LICENSE PLATE LIGHTS

Open engine compartment lid. Remove two screws and remove lens assembly. Push bulb in, turn, and remove it. Install replacement bulb by pushing in and turning in opposite direction. Clean lens and check that the release cable grommet is correctly positioned.

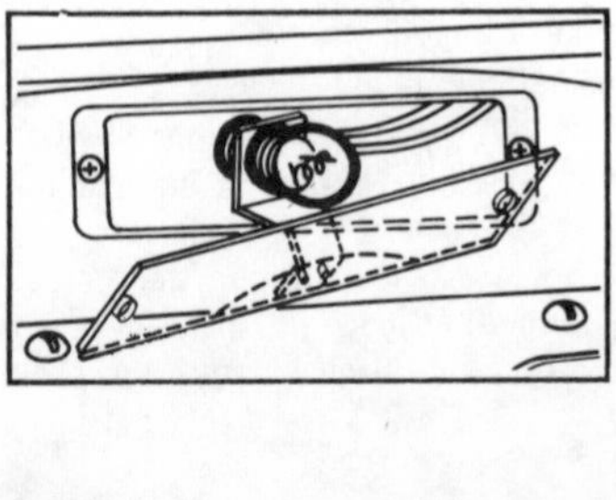

HEADLIGHT REPLACEMENT

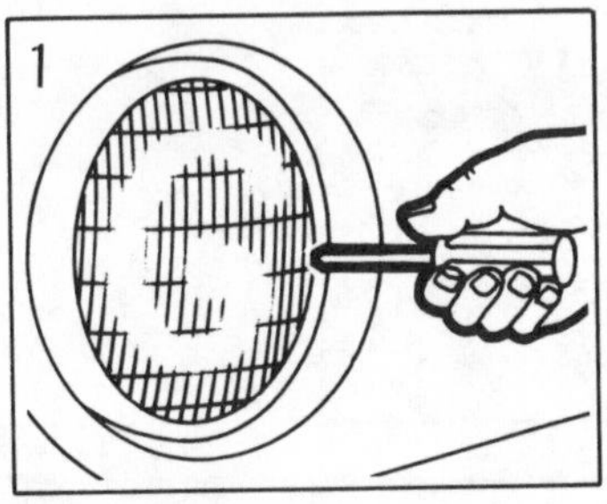

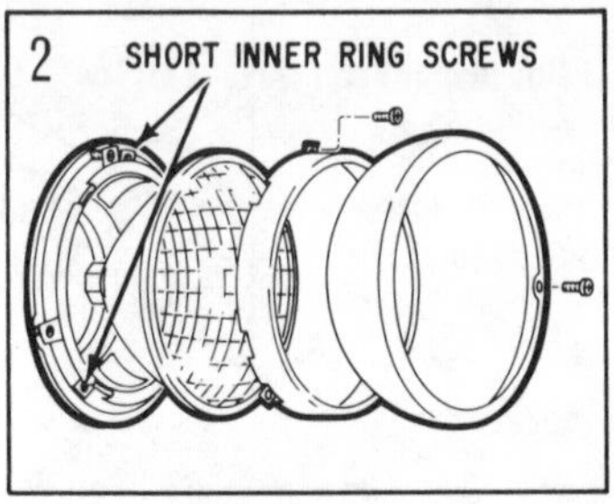

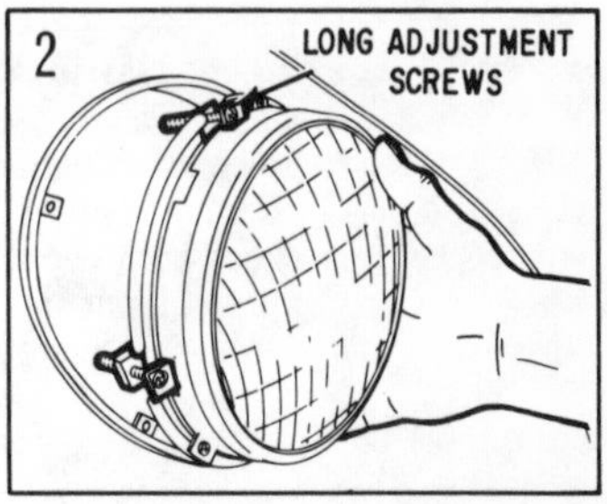

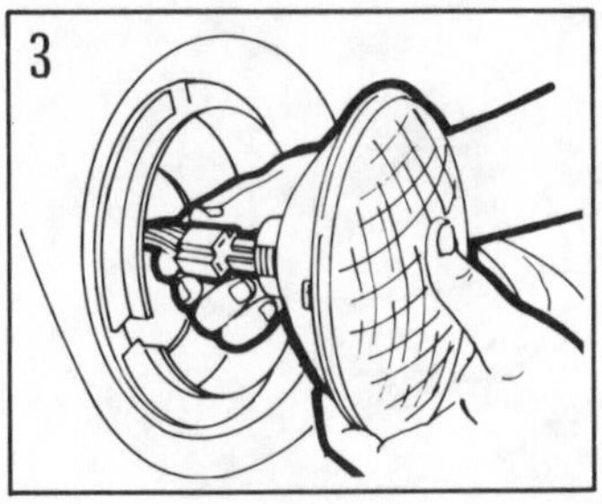

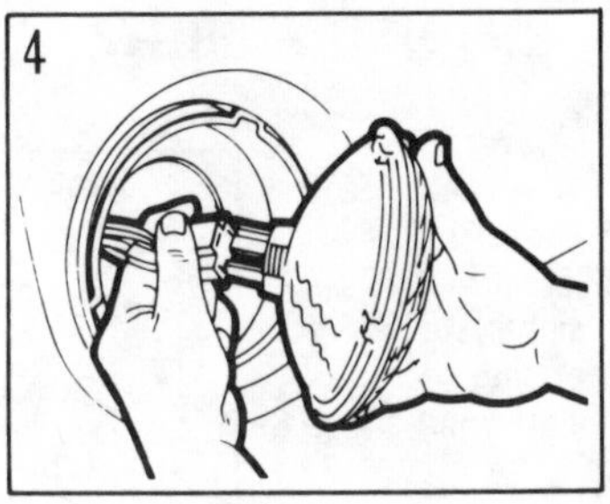

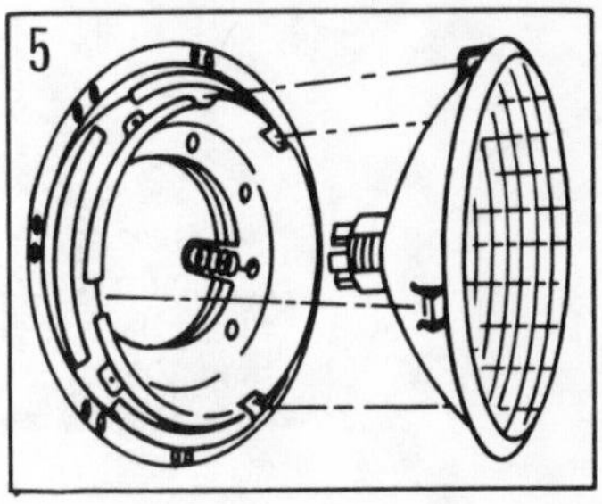

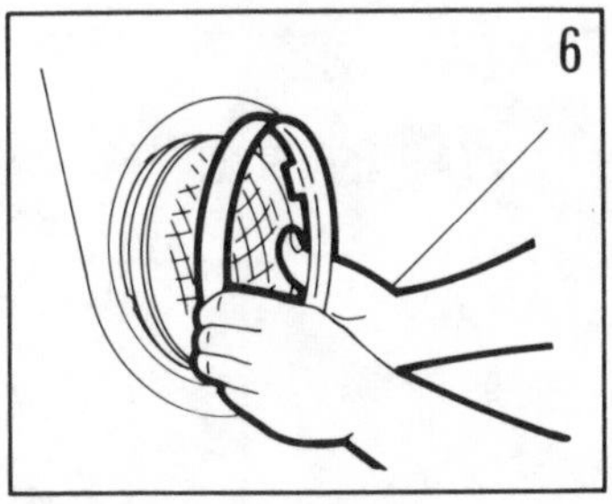

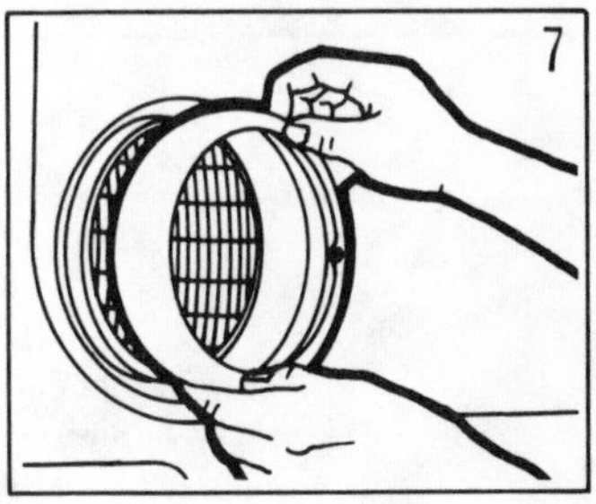

1. Loosen the single screw in the edge of trim ring. Use the loose screw to pull off the trim ring.
2. Remove the three short inner ring screws. Do not remove or tamper with the two longer screws, these are the headlight adjustment screws.
3. Remove the inner ring and pull the headlight out. Disconnect and remove the bulb.
4. Connect the plug to the rear of the new bulb unit.
5. Position new sealed beam in headlight shell. Be sure that knobs on back of light (near outer edge) enter slots in shell.
6. Place retaining ring over sealed beam and fasten with three screws.
7. Install trim ring and tighten screws.

WINDSHIELD WIPER BLADE REPLACEMENT

To remove wiper blades, lift arm away from windshield. Rotate blade and snap out and off crooked arm. There are two types of replacement rubbers for VW windshield wipers. One requires replacement of entire wiper blade. Simply snap it into place. The other allows replacement of only rubber wiper blade insert. Press the old rubber insert down, away from wiper blade to free it from its retaining clips on blade ends. Slide insert from blade. Position new insert in wiper blade. Bend insert upward slightly to engage retaining clips.

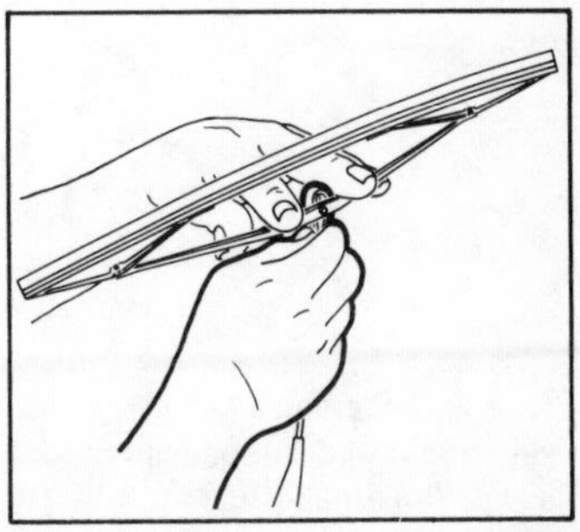

HORN PROBLEMS

If horn fails to sound, this usually means failure of horn contacts to touch each other within steering column. Have mechanic check. Also check horn wiring connector under the front fenders.

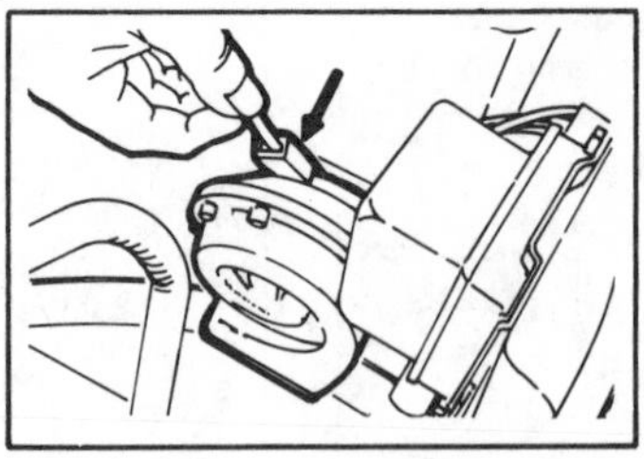

STEERING PROBLEMS

See steering system check in Suspension Section. Check tire pressures. Have a professional service shop check all components in the front end and steering system.

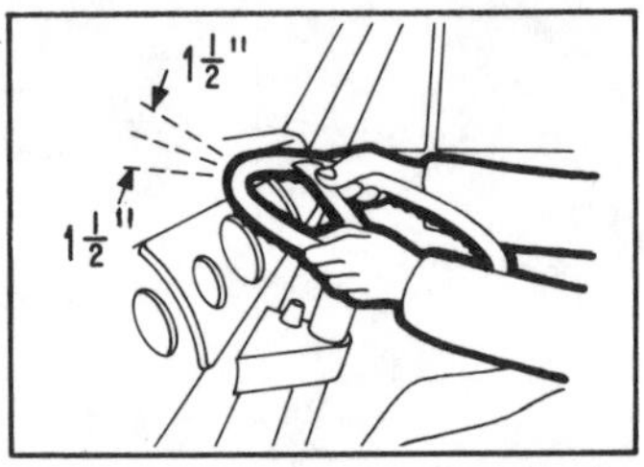

WASHER SYSTEM

If the washer doesn't squirt properly, check all the system hose connections. Be sure the washer reservoir is full and pressurized. The reservoir is located on the passenger's side below the dash. Remove the plastic cover to check it. Use an air pump to pressurize the washer container. Add a windshield washer solvent to cut road film and prevent winter freezing. Keep air pressure at 42 psi.

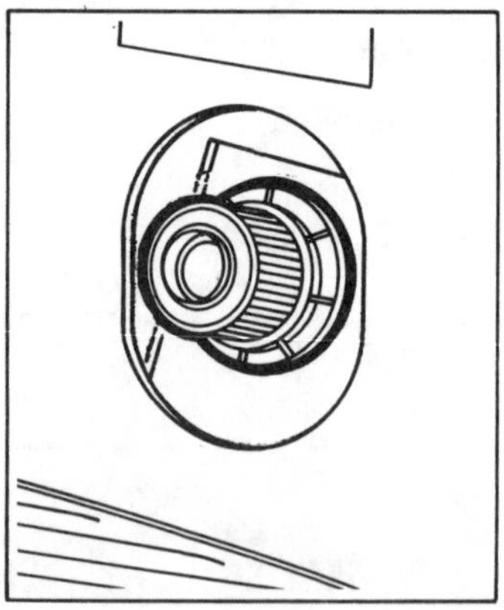

Electrical System

CHECK POINTS AND SERVICES

To ensure starting ability at all times check your battery condition periodically. You'll need to check battery electrolyte (fluid) level in each of the six cells. Check battery cable connections for tightness and inspect for accumulated corrosion.

SAFETY NOTE: Wear gloves when working on battery.

CHECK BATTERY FLUID

The bus battery is located in the right hand corner of the engine compartment. Remove the plastic top cover from the battery. Use a mirror to look into each cell, otherwise you'll have to remove the battery to perform this service.

1. Remove the plastic filler caps on top of battery. Fluid should be up to lower end of filler hole and covering the plates. If fluid is low add clean, cold tap water. If your area has hard water, use only distilled water available at auto supply, food or drug stores.
2. Replace any lost caps immediately.

CAUTION: NEVER LIGHT A MATCH OR SMOKE near the top of a battery.

Batteries give off explosive hydrogen gas.

NOTE: Battery that often checks low on fluid could mean:

A. Battery is getting old, due for replacement; have charge capacity

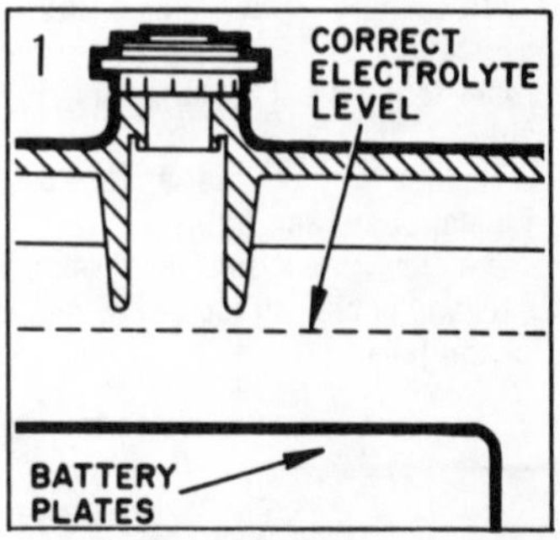

checked at service shop.

B. Connections may be corroded or loose; clean/replace as needed (see below).

C. Alternator or voltage regulator not functioning properly; this happens far less often than A or B above.

CLEAN THOSE BATTERY TERMINALS

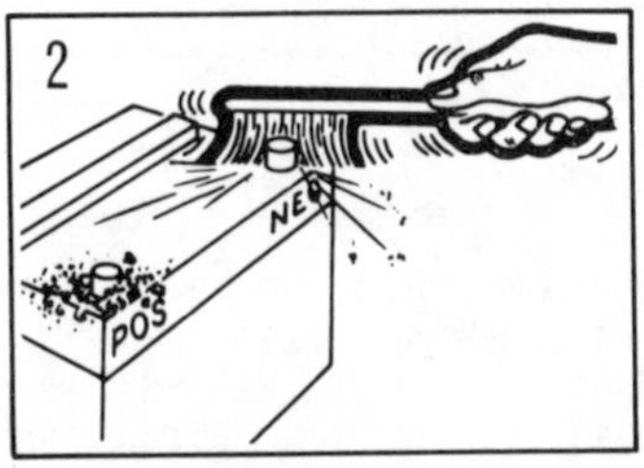

As time goes by, battery terminals build up a dry powdery, whitish material. This material is corrosive and will gradually eat thru battery cables if not cleaned off periodically.

1. Loosen and remove battery connections.
2. Brush off all loose corrosion; use

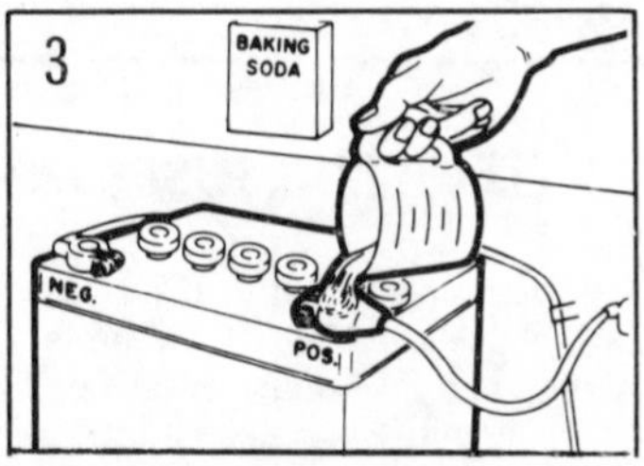

stiff bristle brush. Do not get this material into eyes or on open cuts. Wash off at once.

3. If corrosion build-up is extremely heavy and brushing does not remove all of it, mix 2 tablespoons of baking soda to 1 cup water. Pour solution directly onto terminals and connectors. Allow to soak a few minutes

and rinse off. Continue brushing to remove all traces of corrosion build-up. Do not allow cleaning solution to enter battery.

4. Replace connectors on battery terminal posts and tighten.
5. Liberally smear battery terminal posts and cable connectors with petroleum jelly.

REPLACE FAULTY BATTERY CABLES

If battery cable strands become frayed, broken or corroded, replace cable immediately. Delay in correcting this condition could lead to sudden failure to start the engine. Can also weaken battery.

1. Loosen and remove battery connections. Clean OFF any corrosion.
2. Disconnect negative cable from its attachment to engine or chassis.

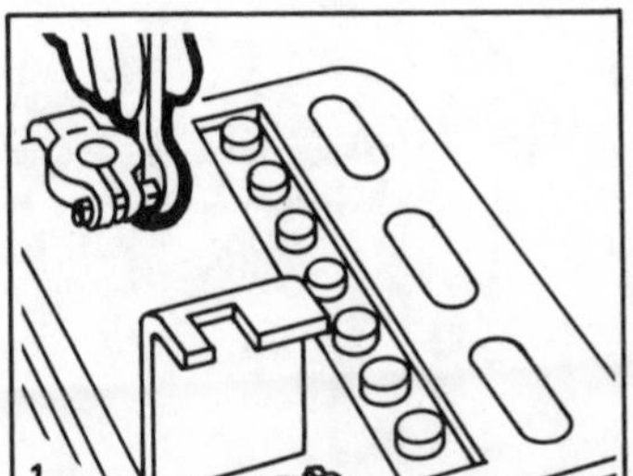

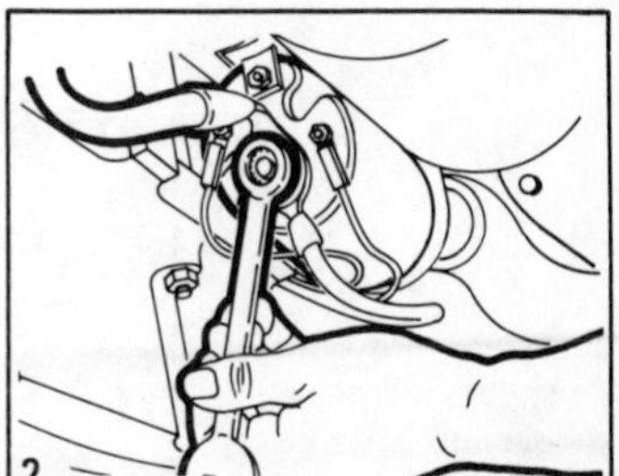

Disconnect positive cable from its attachment to starter relay.
3. Attach new cables making sure positive and negative cables are on proper terminals. They are not identical.
4. Replace connectors on battery terminal posts and tighten.
5. Liberally smear battery terminal posts and cable connectors with petroleum jelly.

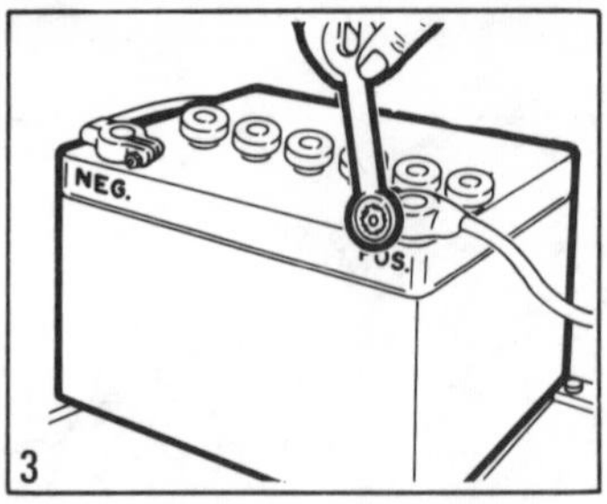

3

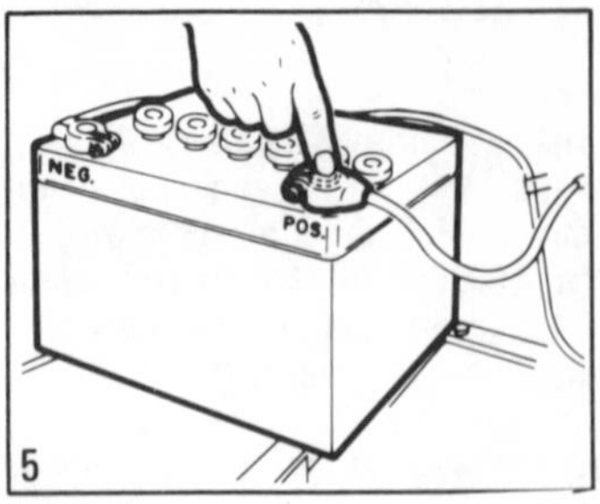

5

BATTERY HOLDDOWN

The clamp device which holds battery in place should be checked periodically. If loose, tighten. Clean off corrosion buildup. Severely corroded holddown components should be replaced before they break.

ELECTRICAL FUSES

If any lights, switches or electrical circuits do not operate, check for possible blown (burned out) fuse. Fuses are located in fuse box mounted under instrument panel to the left of the steering column. Replace blown fuse with same amperage new fuse. If fuses blow regularly, have car checked by professional service shop for possible short circuit. Fuses usually fail so that there is a visible separation in the bright metallic conductor. The fuse box is marked to indicate what items each fuse serves, so you can easily tell which fuse is faulty by finding out what electrical accessories do not operate. The amperage is marked on the fuse itself.

TURN SIGNAL AND 4-WAY FLASHER

Turn signals and 4-way flashers will operate only if:
A. All light bulbs are OK. B. Flasher unit is not burned out. Type 2 vehicles have one flasher relay which operates turn signals and emergency flashers. On the bus, the flasher is located in the center socket of the bracket behind the fuse box.

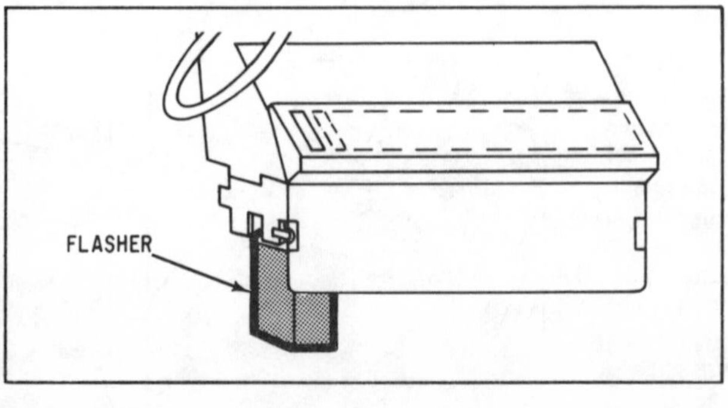

ALTERNATOR/GENERATOR

Red alternator/generator warning light on instrument panel should glow red when you first turn ignition key. This proves bulb is OK. Alternator/generator warning light should go off when engine is running at normal operating speed.
If alternator/generator warning light glows red at operating speed, alternator/generator isn't charging battery properly. Common causes are:
A. Fan belts are loose and slipping on alternator pulley. Tighten or replace belts.
B. Battery terminals, cables are loose or corroded. Clean; tighten; replace bad cables.
If A or B do not correct problem, alternator/generator or voltage regulator may be faulty. This happens far less often, and can only be checked by mechanic with proper electrical testing equipment.
Alternator Caution: Alternator can be permanently damaged by short-circuiting terminal connections. When working around or moving alternator, always keep metal tools or engine parts from terminals.

REAR WINDOW DEFOGGER SYSTEM

Do not clean inside of rear window fitted with defogger system with any abrasive material. This could destroy carbon-copper wires. Use only soft rag and mild detergent/water mixture. Dry carefully.

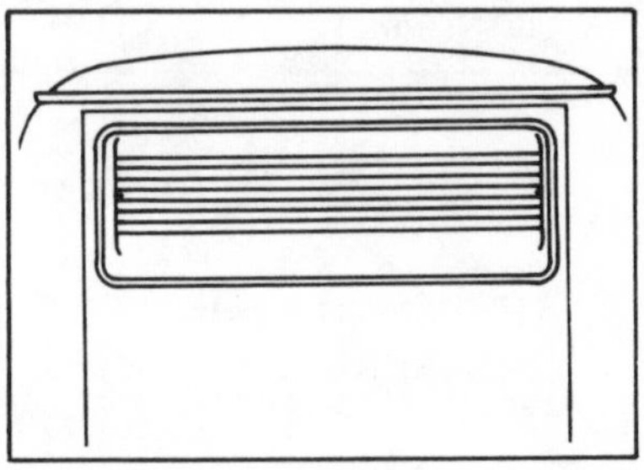

Air Conditioner

WARNING!—Never attempt to tighten fittings, disassemble or do any work on your VW's A/C system. Consult a professional mechanic about A/C system problems and their correction.
Your auto air conditioner (A/C) is a delicate, closed system. If air, dirt or water get into it, or if refrigerant escapes, the A/C unit will not cool a car interior. Among things you can do are:

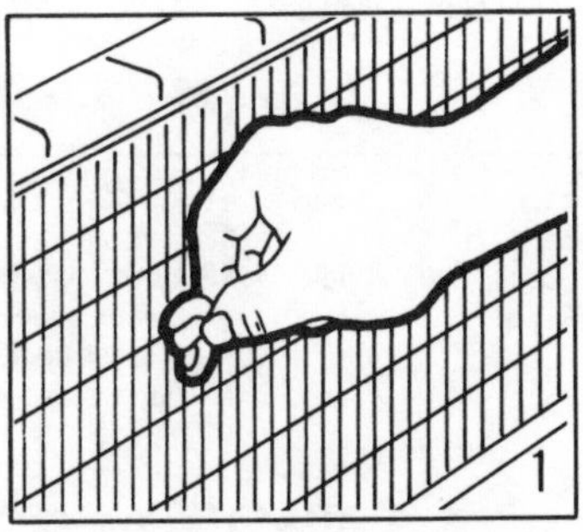

1

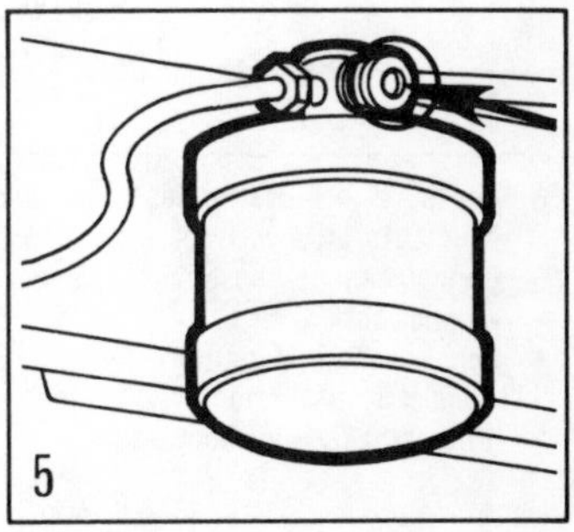

5

1. Keep condenser grilles clean. Check for dirt and debris; periodically remove dead insects, leaves, etc., with stiff bristle brush. Straighten any bent fins—carefully.
2. Make sure condenser fan operates when A/C is on. Check electrical connections or replace parts as necessary.
3. Keep the cooling system in top condition as described in the Cooling System section. While the VWs A/C does not directly affect engine temperature, it does increase the load placed on the engine. Keeping all cooling system parts in top shape, and keeping the engine in top tune will minimize the chances of overheating damage.
4. Check fan and compressor belt tension periodically. (See Cooling System section). Replace glazed, frayed or cut belts, before they fail entirely.
5. Check periodically for bubbles in A/C sight glass. Sight glass is located in head of receiver/drier vessel, which is in line inside A/C unit or under bus on left side. Sight glass is no larger than head of large nail. It may be dirty. Wipe clean for best

visibility.

PROCEED AS FOLLOWS:

a) With engine and A/C system running, look for passage of refrigerant in sight glass. You'll be looking for a stream of milky white bubbles as they pass through sight glass. It is best to watch sight glass and have someone else start the car and turn on the A/C system. Allow to run for a few minutes.

b) If you observe no bubbles, and air flow from A/C unit in the car is passing cold air, everything is OK.

c) If no bubbles appear in sight glass, and air flow from the A/C unit in the car is not delivering cold air, the system may be low on refrigerant and could need a re-charge.

d) If bubbles appear, system is low on refrigerant.

e) If you suspect refrigerant loss based on tests performed above, have system checked by a professional A/C service shop. They can confirm refrigerant loss, recharge the system and check for system leakage.

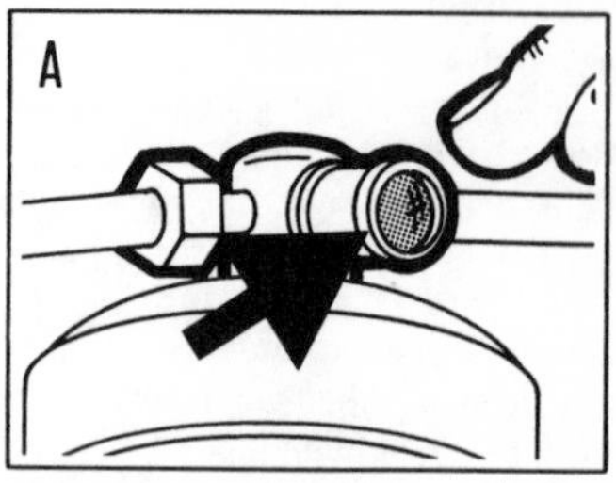

NOTE: Once a week or so, even in winter, run A/C system for about 5 minutes as you drive. This keeps system internally lubricated, prevents hoses hardening.

TUNE-UP SPECIFICATIONS

YEAR	ENGINE No. Cyl. Displacement (c.c.) ●	SPARK PLUGS Type	SPARK PLUGS Gap (in.)	DISTRIBUTOR Point Dwell (deg.)	DISTRIBUTOR Point Gap (deg.)	IGNITION TIMING Man. Trans. (deg.)	IGNITION TIMING Auto Trans. (deg.)	IDLE SPEED Man. Trans. (rpm)	IDLE SPEED Auto Trans. (rpm)
1970	4-1600 (B)	Bosch W145T1 Champion L88A	.024	44-50	.016	TDC②	—	800-900	—
1971	4-1600 (AE)	Bosch W145T1 Champion L88A	.024	44-50	.016	5ATDC①	—	800-900	—
1972	4-1700 (CB)	Bosch W145T2 Champion N88	.024	44-50	.016	5ATDC①	—	800-900	—
1973	4-1700 (CB)	Bosch W145T2 Champion N88	.024	44-50	.016	10ATDC①	—	800-900	—
	4-1700 (CD)	Bosch W145T2 Champion N88	.024	44-50	.016	—	5ATDC①	—	900-1000
1974	4-1800 (AW)	Bosch W145T2 Champion N88	.024	44-50	.016	10ATDC①	5ATDC①	800-900	900-1000
1975	4-1800 (ED)	Bosch W145M2 Champion N288	.024	44-50	.016	5ATDC③	5ATDC③	900	900
1976	4-2000 (GD)	Bosch W145M2 Champion N288	.028	44-50	.016	7½BTDC③	7½BTDC③	900	950
1977	See Underhood Specification Sticker								

① At idle, throttle valve closed, vacuum hose(s) on
② At idle, throttle valve closed, vacuum hose(s) off
③ Carbon canister hose at air cleaner disconnected; at idle; vacuum hose(s) on
● Engine code in parentheses
MT Manual Transmission
AT Automatic Transmission
BTDC Before Top Dead Center
ATDC After Top Dead Center
NOTE: The underhood specifications sticker often reflects tune-up specification changes made in production. Sticker figures must be used if they disagree with those in this chart.
— Not applicable

CAPACITIES

YEAR	ENGINE No. Cyl. Displacement (c.c.)	ENGINE OIL	TRANSMISSION Pts. to Refill after Draining MANUAL	TRANSMISSION Pts. to Refill after Draining AUTOMATIC	DRIVE AXLE (pts.)
1970-71	4-1600	2.5	7.4	12.6①	3.0
1972-76	4-1700, 1800, 2000	3.7②	7.4	12.6①	3.0

① Figure given is with torque converter; when changed, figure is 6.3 ② 4.4 w/filter — Not applicable

Volkswagen Rabbit/Dasher/Scirocco

Lubrication and Oil Change

LUBRICATION CHECK

VW SAYS . . . Change oil and oil filter strainer every 7500 miles
Recommended grade: MS or SE
Check the oil level at least once a week

TOOLS & MATERIALS
15mm box wrench or metric socket and ratchet handle set
medium sized screwdriver
drain pan for old oil (at least 5 qt. capacity)
oil pouring spout
oil and lubricants as specified below

SAFETY TIP . . . wear gloves

BRAKE FLUID LEVEL CHECK

Check brake fluid level in master cylinder reservoir every three months . . . sooner if braking feels inadequate. Add when low. Recommended grade: DOT 3 or 4 as printed on can.

The brake reservoir is located in the engine compartment on the driver's side. It is a translucent plastic container with a screw-on cap. Brake fluid is easily checked by making sure that level is above the seam of the "see through" reservoir. Add fluid if level is below the seam. Secure cap firmly.
DO NOT OVERFILL
If fluid repeatedly checks low, there is a leak somewhere in the system.
See SAFETY SYSTEMS—WHEEL CYLINDER.
Have mechanic check further. Neglect can be dangerous because leaks can either soak brake linings with fluid, making them ineffective,

or completely disable either front or rear brakes.

MANUAL TRANSAXLE FLUID LEVEL CHECK

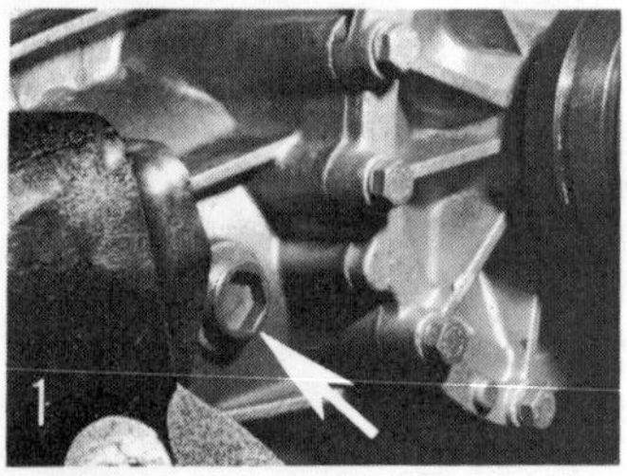

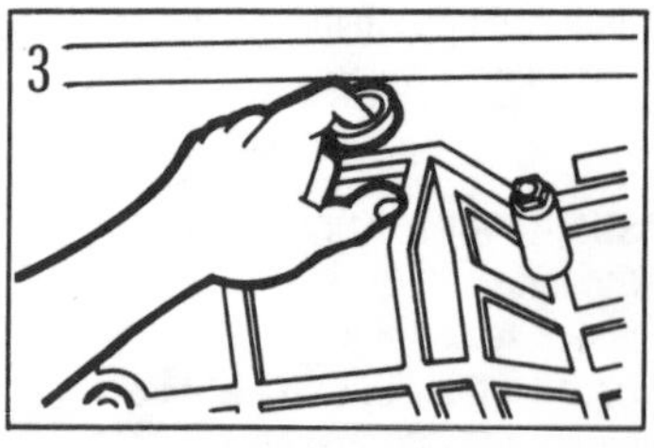

VW SAYS . . . check manual transaxle fluid every 15,000 miles. Car should be safely supported. Recommended grade: Standard transmission gear oil (SAE 90—80 in very cold climates).
TOOLS NEEDED . . . drain plug wrench
suction gun or squeeze bulb syringe
1. Locate transmission filler plug on side of transaxle housing from underneath the car.
2. Wipe road dirt from filler plug area before loosening. Remove plug with wrench.
3. Insert your finger into the hole. Oil should be level with the bottom edge of the filler hole.
4. Add gear oil as needed with suction gun or squeeze bulb syringe.

5. Replace filler plug; tighten.

AUTOMATIC TRANSMISSION FLUID LEVEL CHECK

VW SAYS . . . check automatic transmission fluid (ATF) level every 6000 miles. Recommended grade: ATF Type A or Dexron®.

TOOLS NEEDED . . . long-neck filler funnel

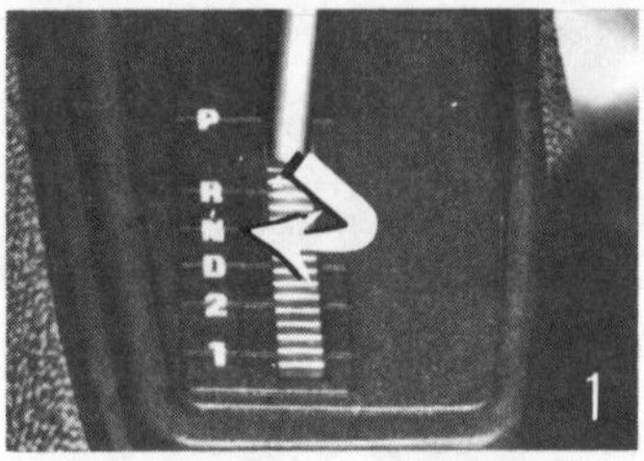

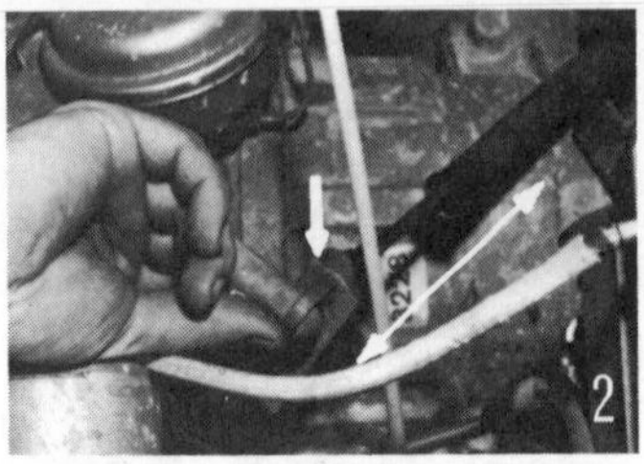

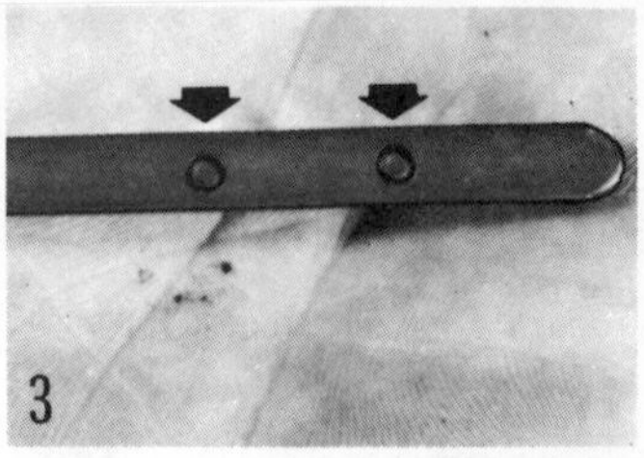

The Dasher automatic transmission dipstick is located at the left rear of the engine. On Rabbits and Sciroccos, it is located at the right side of the engine compartment near the battery.

1. Idle the engine for a few minutes with the selector in Neutral. Apply the parking brake.
2. Remove the dipstick, wipe it clean, reinsert it, and withdraw it again.
3. The fluid level should be within the two marks. Top up with Dexron® or Type A automatic transmission fluid. Bear in mind that the difference between the two marks is less than one pint. Use a long-necked funnel to add the fluid. Every 30,000 miles (20,000 when towing or other heavy-duty use) the fluid should be drained and replaced.

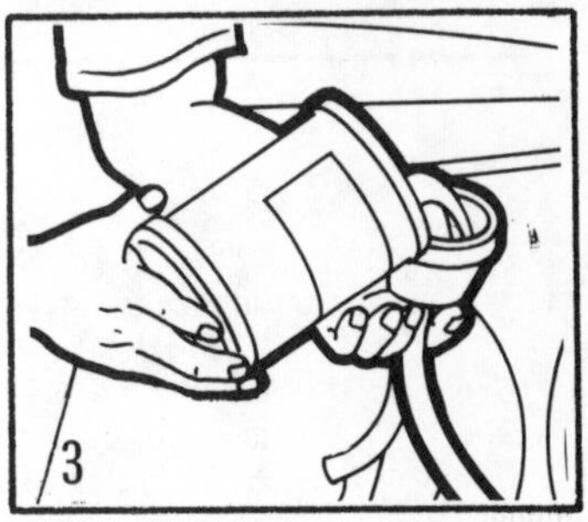

OIL AND FILTER CHANGE

1. If engine is cold, start up and idle for about 5 minutes.
2. Park car on level ground. Turn engine off.
3. Locate oil drain plug on underside of engine. Place drain pan under plug.
4. Remove drain plug with wrench. Let ALL dirty oil drain out.
5. Wipe plug and area around drain hole clean. Replace drain plug; tighten it.
6. Locate oil filter. Move drain pan under filter. Loosen filter with oil filter wrench. Unscrew; remove filter by hand.
7. Smear fresh oil over surface of rubber gasket (washer) of new filter. Install new filter by hand only. Do NOT use wrench. Turn filter until gasket makes contact. Tighten an additional half turn only . . . NO MORE.
8. Locate oil filler hole on top of engine. Remove cap.
9. Punch oil pouring spout into top of oil can. Pour all cans of new oil into filler tube. Wipe filler cap clean and replace it.
10. Check new oil level at dipstick. Pull out dipstick, wipe clean.
11. Push dipstick back into engine. Be sure to insert all the way. Remove dipstick and check new oil level. It should be above "MAX" line. If not, be sure to check if you put in all the oil called for.
12. Start up engine and idle for 3-5 minutes. Oil signal light on instrument panel will glow red when engine is first started. Light should go out in 30 seconds or less.
13. Stop engine and check for oil leaks at drain plug and filter. If you find any, check tightness of plug and/or filter, also for condition of filter gasket to see that it has not become pinched or damaged when installing. Recheck oil level, which should now be at "MAX."

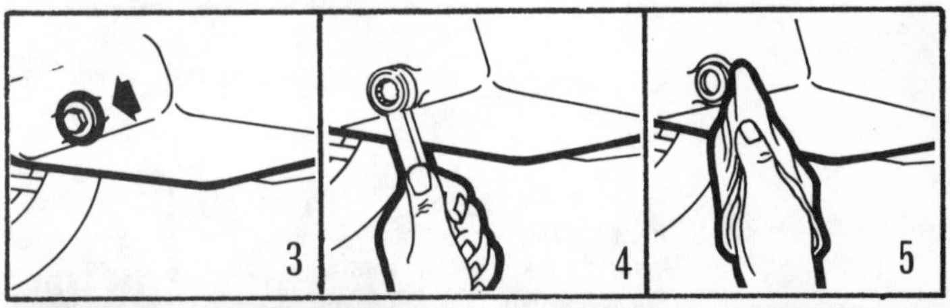

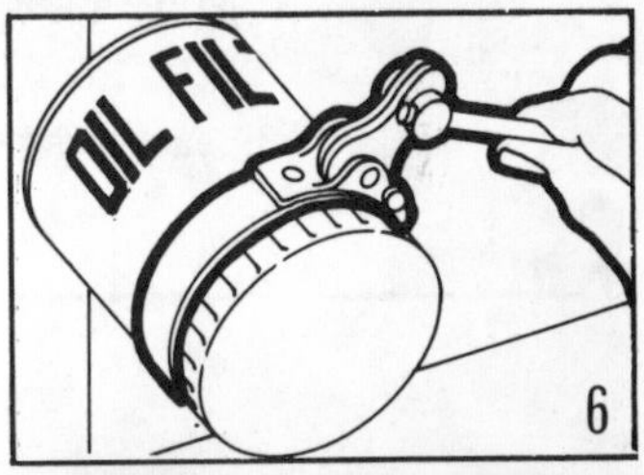

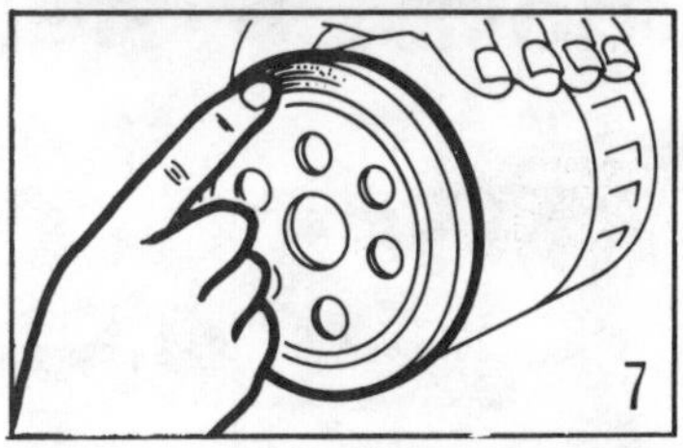

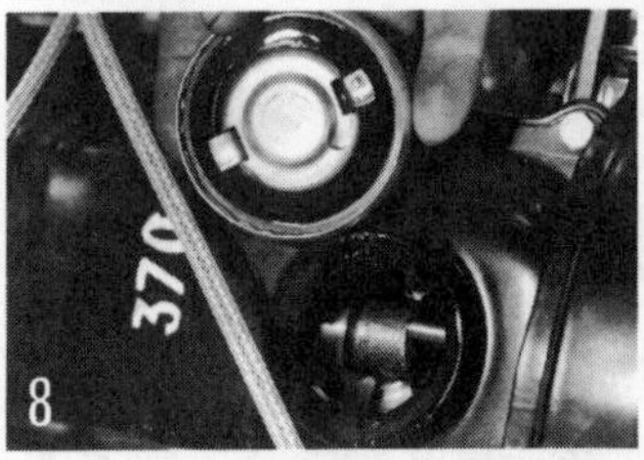

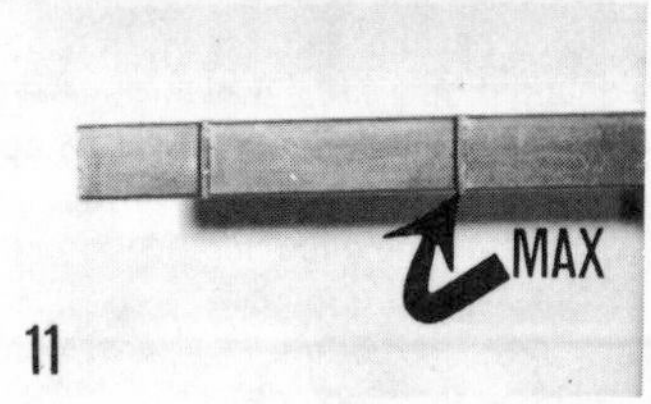

SPEEDOMETER CABLE LUBRICATION

If speedometer pointer tends to quiver or jump, or if unit makes a low, rasping sound, lubrication may be needed.

1. Locate cable shaft attachment directly behind speedometer dial.
2. Unscrew cable from speedometer.
3. Pull inner cable completely out of outer casing. Note carefully which end is top. Check for wear or frayed strands. If damaged, replace inner cable with new one.
4. Apply generous amount of speedometer cable lubricant into cable casing. Replace inner cable in shaft, noting that top end is not inserted accidentally. Turn inner cable as it is being re-inserted. Twist cable when all the way in, to lock into position at lower end.
5. Re-connect cable to speedometer head under instrument panel.

DOOR HINGES AND STOPS

(lubricate every 6 months)

1. Brush any dirt accumulations from door hinges and stops. Use old tooth brush or rag.
2. Apply dab of white polyethylene grease to door hinges, trunk hinges, hood hinges, door stops.

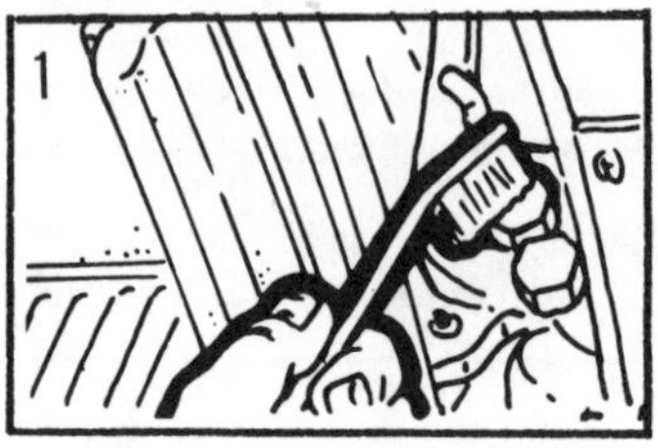

DOOR LOCKS

(lubricate every 6 months)

1. Insert door key half way into lock.
2. Spray aerosol lock lubricant into lock.
3. Push key rest of way into lock; turn back and forth several times.

Cooling System

The cooling system consists of a belt-driven, external water pump, thermostat, radiator, and thermo-switch controlled electric cooling fan. When the engine is cold the thermostat is closed and blocks the water from the radiator so that the coolant is only circulated through the engine. When the engine warms up, the thermostat opens and the radiator is included in the coolant circuit. The thermo-switch is positioned in the bottom of the radiator and turns the electrical fan on at 199° F, off at 186° F. This reduces power loss and engine noise.

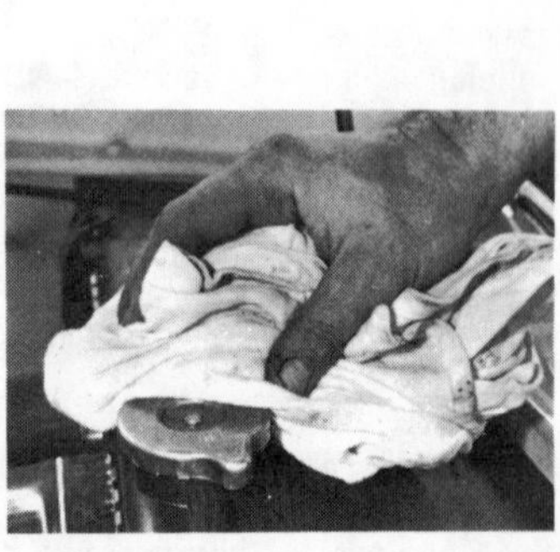

IT IS RECOMMENDED . . . that radiator coolant (water/antifreeze mixture) level be checked once or twice a month. Do this when engine is cold. Check more often if you do a lot of hard driving. Coolant is checked visually on models with expansion tanks. On models without expansion tanks, the coolant level should be kept at the embossed mark or Max mark in the radiator neck. Keep coolant up to recommended level in radiator. If coolant checks frequently low, look for leaks. Tighten all hose clamps occasionally. For best results, keep a 50/50 water/antifreeze mixture year round. Change complete coolant mixture every 24 months.

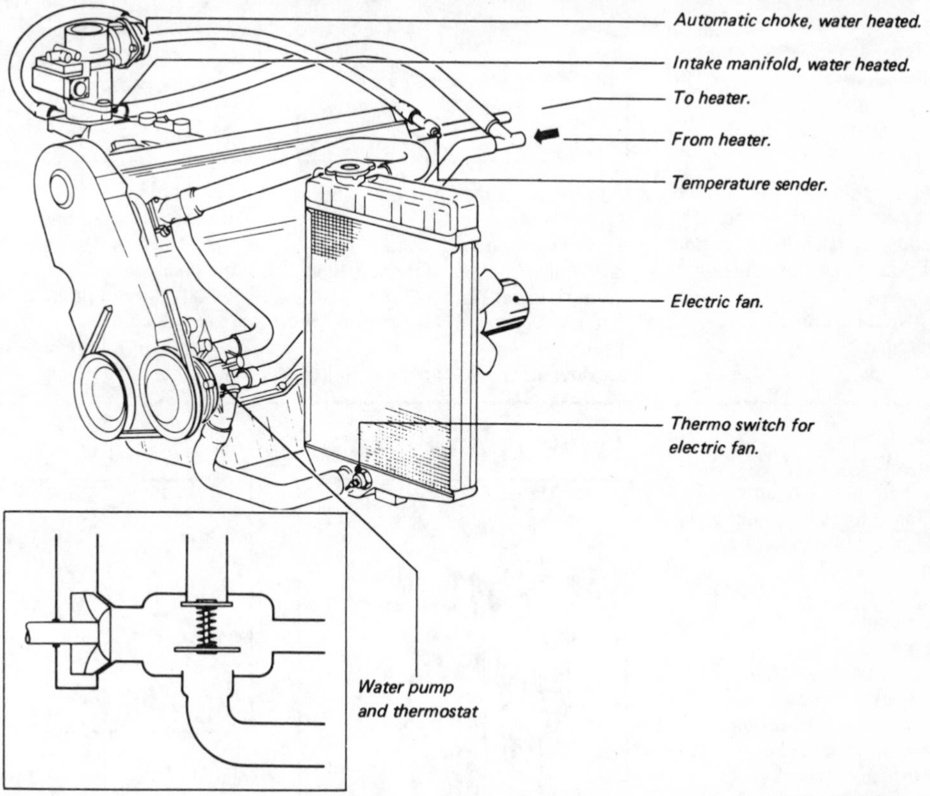

REPLACING THE THERMOSTAT

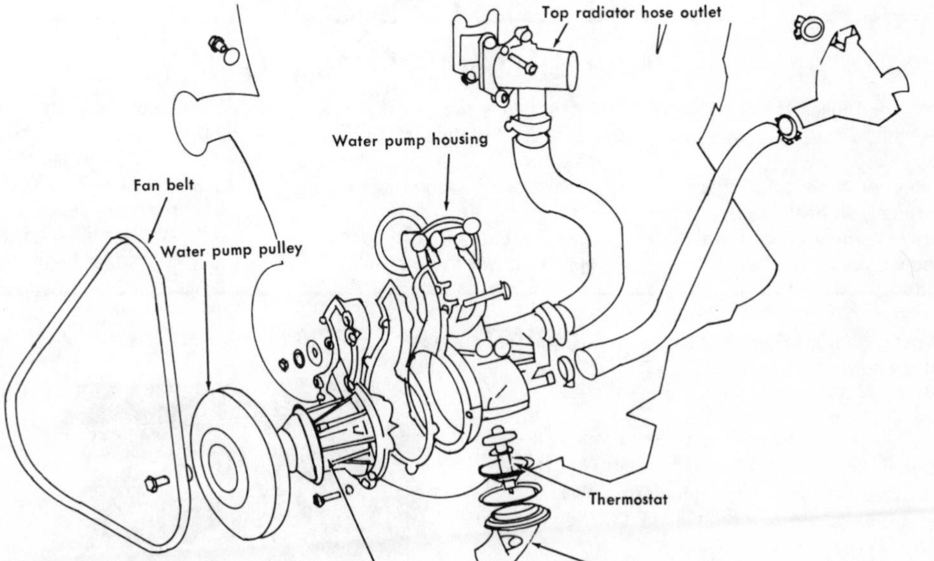

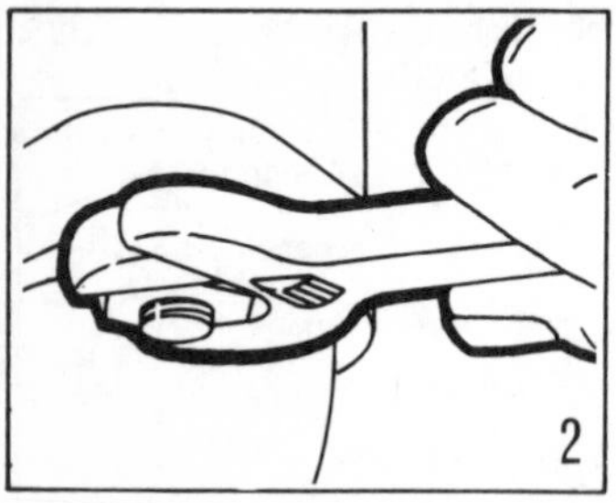

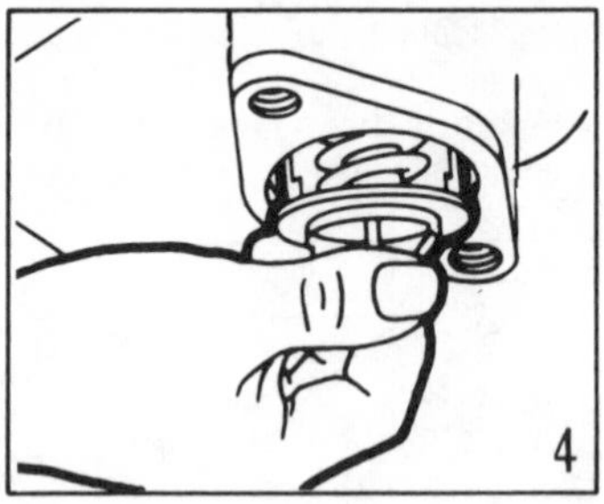

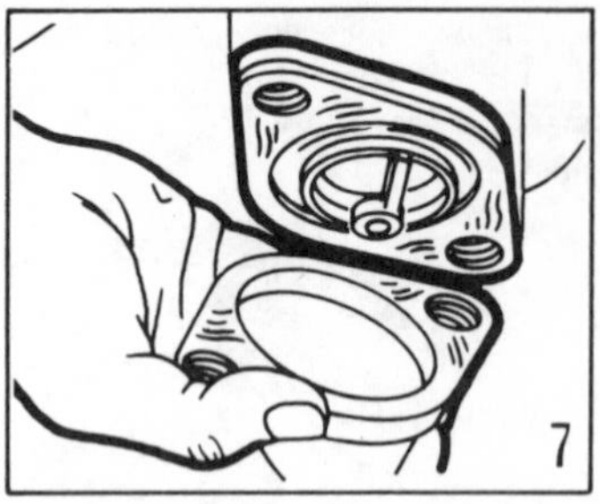

A faulty thermostat will usually cause engine overheating. The thermostat is located in the bottom radiator hose neck on the water pump.

TOOLS AND MATERIALS . . .
New thermostat
Gasket sealer
Adjustable wrench or metric socket set

1. Drain the cooling system.
2. Remove the two retaining bolts from the lower water pump neck. It's not necessary to disconnect the hose.
3. Move neck, with hoses attached, out of the way.
4. Remove the thermostat.
5. Install a new seal on the water pump neck.
6. Install the thermostat with the spring end up.
7. Replace the water pump neck and tighten the two retaining bolts.

FAN BELT ADJUSTMENT

The fan belt not only drives the radiator fan, it turns the water pump and drives the alternator. It's easy to see that the condition and proper tension of the belt are vital, since almost all engine cooling and electrical power is dependent on it. The belt deserves an occasional look and tension check.

1. Inspect fan belt occasionally. If worn, frayed or cracked on inner driving surface, replace.

CAUTION: An overtightened belt may damage alternator and water pump bearings.

2. Check tension occasionally. Press

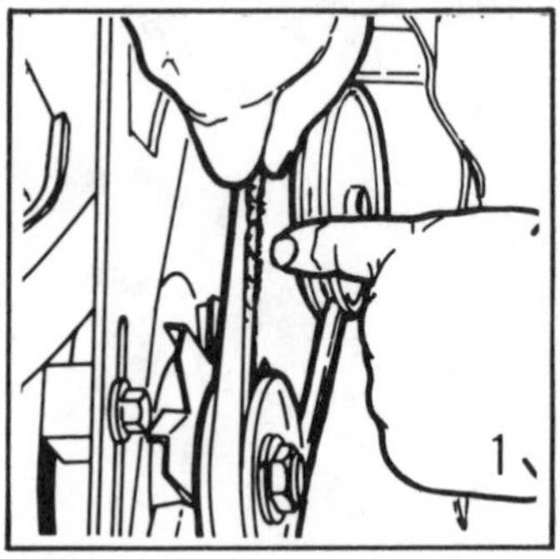

thumb at midpoint of belt span between pulleys. If belt depresses more than ½ inch, tightening is

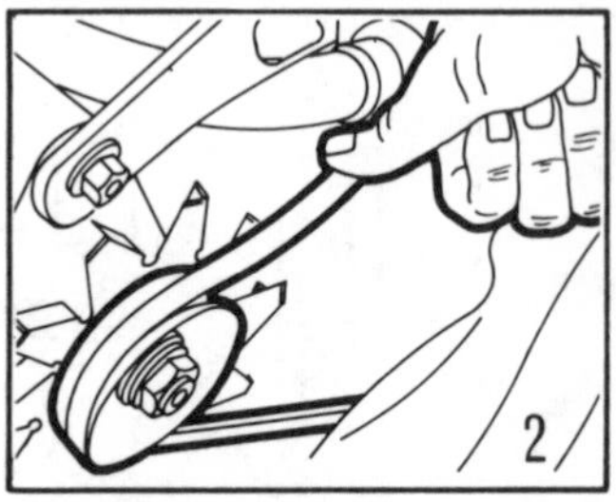

needed. A too-loose belt will not drive alternator and water pump effectively.

3. Adjust to proper tension of ¼ inch deflection.

FIND THOSE COOLING SYSTEM LEAKS

1. Inspect all hoses. If any are weak, soft in spots or show cracks, replace at once.
2. Check all hose connections for tightness. Tighten loose hose clamps; they tend to loosen due to engine vibration.
3. If radiator steams or hisses when engine is switched off, check for leaks. Look for signs of coolant drips on radiator or around header tank joint.

Leaks are possible at:
Upper or lower radiator hoses
Water pump (gaskets or seal)
Heater core or connecting hoses
Automatic transmission cooler lines (at bottom of radiator)
Faulty radiator pressure cap
Faulty cylinder head gasket
Cracked cylinder head or block

RADIATOR CAP CHECK

Check radiator cap occasionally for worn or cracked gasket. If cap doesn't seal properly, fluid will be lost and engine will overheat.

HOSE REPLACEMENT

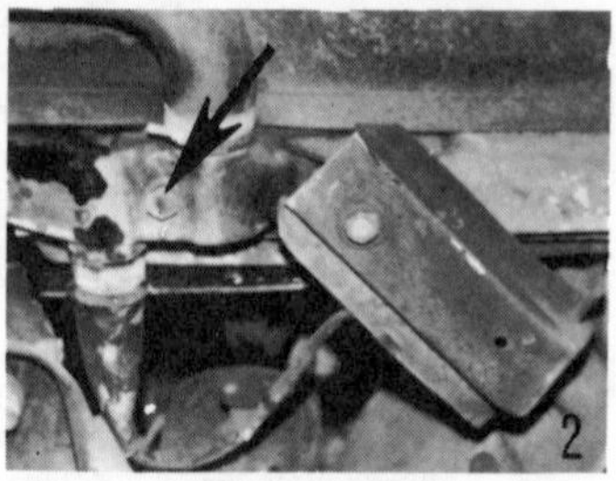
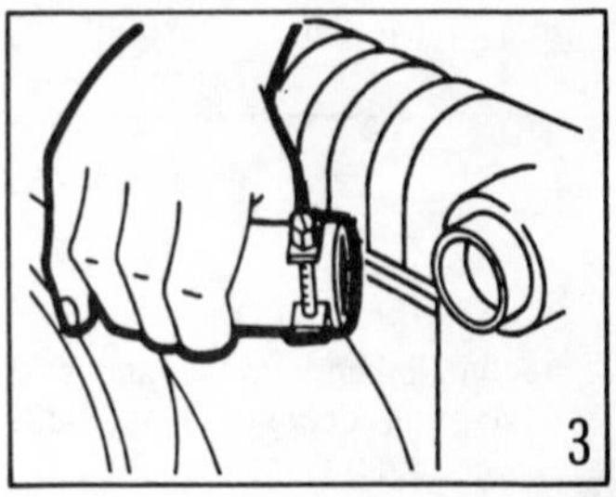
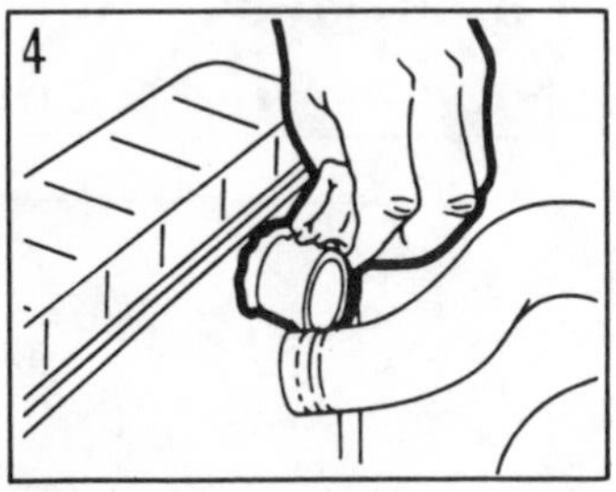
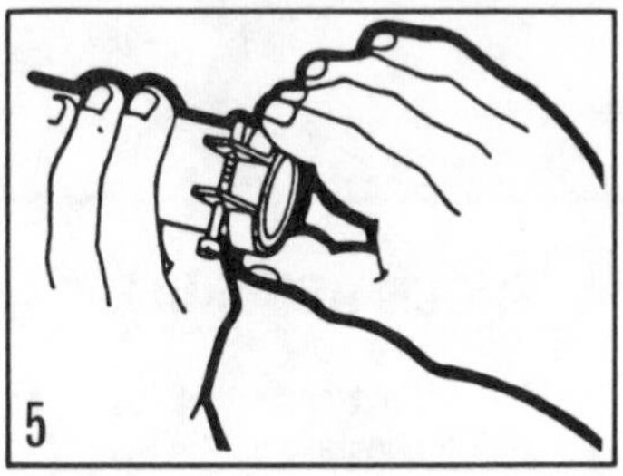
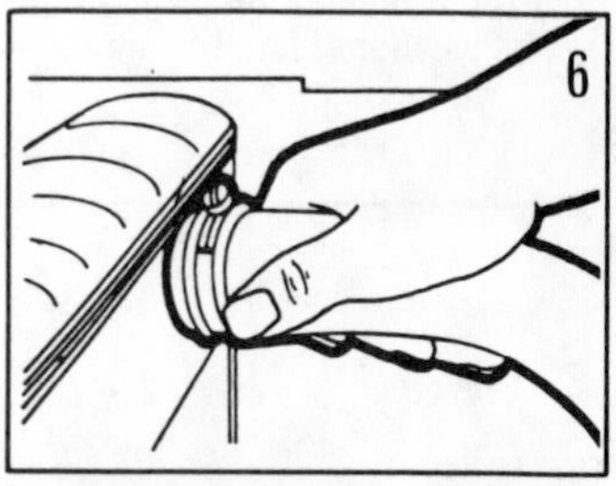

Coolant drain and refill work may be done alone; when changing hoses, coolant must also be drained as part of job. Discard all hoses with cracks or soft spots. Check hose clamps for tightness and good condition.

1. Remove radiator cap. Open radiator petcock (See 2). Drain coolant into catch basin. If near 24 months old, discard old coolant.
2. The petcock is located at the bottom of the radiator.
3. Loosen clamps at each end of hose(s). Work loose; pull off. If old hose clamps are rusted or damaged, replace with new units.
4. Wipe all hose connections clean. Use emery cloth to get rid of residue. Check all hoses for weak spots, as well as cracks inside and out.
5. Slip clamps over each hose end. Slip hose ends all the way onto cleaned up hose connections.
6. Place hose clamp ¼ inch from hose end. Tighten. Close petcock. Refill with 50/50 coolant/water mix.
7. Start engine; allow to warm up. Check for coolant leaks.

8. Road test car; watch for temperature warning light.

Suspension and Tires

The front suspension is a simple strut design. It consists of a lower control arm, ball joint, and suspension strut. In a MacPherson strut design, such as this, the shock absorbers strut serves as a locating member of the suspension as well as a damper. A shock absorber insert is located inside the body of the strut. A concentric coil spring is the springing medium. A stabilizer bar is used to reduce front body roll.

The Dasher rear suspension consists of a rear axle beam containing a full length torsion bar. A trailing arm is welded to the axle beam tube on each side. The trailing arms mount to the unit body in rubber bushings. A coil spring provides the additional suspension at each wheel. A Panhard rod locates the axle against lateral forces.

The Rabbit/Scirocco rear suspension consists of individual trailing arms connected by a cross-chassis torsion beam. Each wheel is suspended by a coil spring mounted over a shock absorber strut unit. The torsion beam acts as a rear stabilizer bar, twisting to resist body roll.

Your car's suspension system consists of wheels, tires, coil springs, shock absorbers, sway bars (or stabilizer bars), ball joints, steering linkage, steering damper. If any of these items is out of adjustment or badly worn, you may notice any of these symptoms:

- car pulls to one side when braking
- car wanders when driving a straight line
- overall ride may be either hard or bouncy
- effort is needed to steer vehicle
- tires show uneven wear
- tires squeal when cornering
- front of car dips or bounces when braking
- car rocks side-to-side when going over rough road
- wheels bounce or make slapping

sound on road
- steering wheel vibrates in hands
- front of car vibrates at highway speeds

Any of above symptoms indicates corrective action is needed. Delay can: ruin tires; cause damage/failure to other suspension parts; create safety hazard.

STEERING

If steering linkage, front suspension and steering column components are in good condition, there should be no more than one and one half inch of free play in the steering wheel when measured at the rim of the wheel. If a loud knock is heard when turning the steering wheel from one extreme to the other, have mechanic check pinion bearing preload.

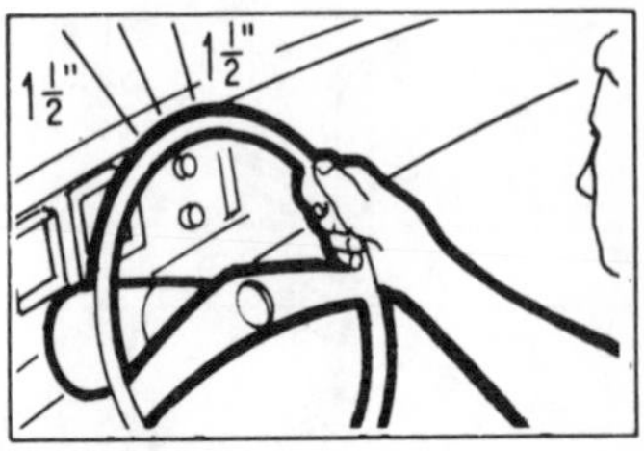

SHOCK ABSORBERS

Shock absorbers work to keep wheels in constant contact with the road. Result is safe handling and ride control; longer tire life. So shock absorbers (or shocks) are important.

HOW TO CHECK FOR BAD SHOCKS

1. Check under car and locate shock absorber near each wheel.
2. Heavy oil streaks on outer shock housing indicate need for replacement.
3. Stand at front of car and apply body weight in a pumping action to front bumper or fender. Release pressure and allow car to stop rocking. Car should not bounce more than one more time after releasing pressure. Repeat at rear. If bouncing continues more than once, replacement is needed. Replace shocks in pairs (front pair or rear pair).

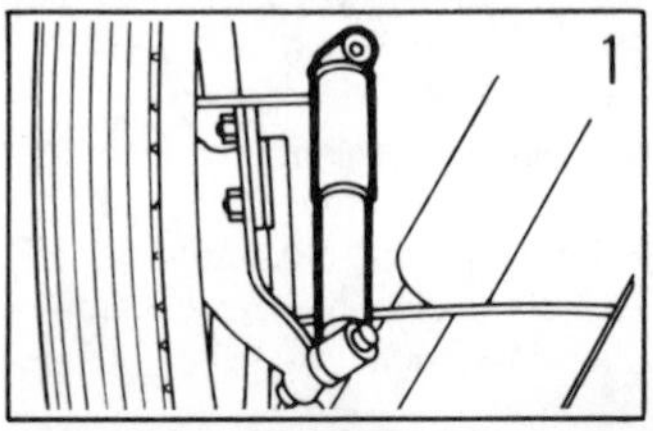

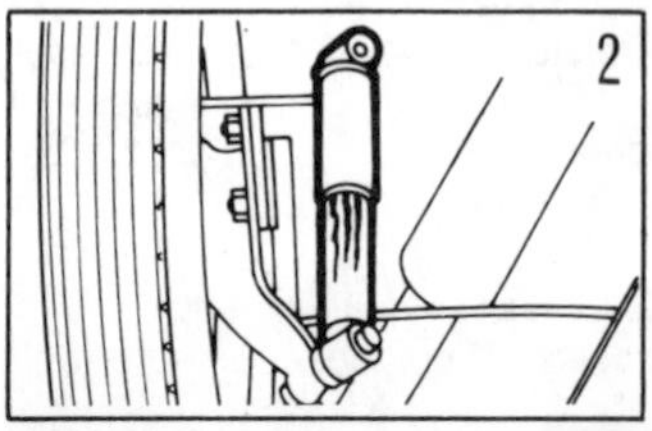

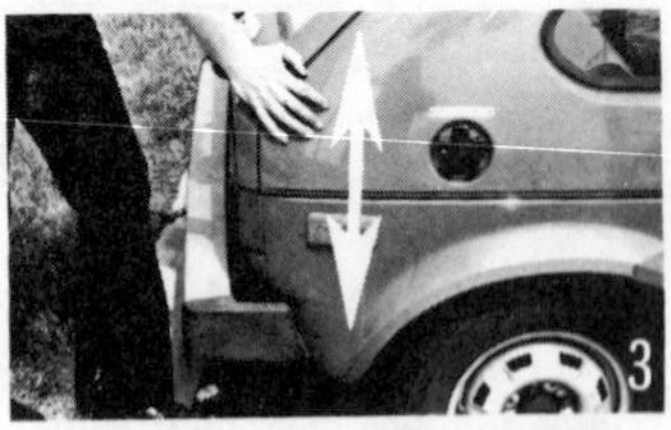

TOW HITCH INFORMATION

If your car is used for trailer towing you should check:
A. Cooling System; be sure coolant is at proper level in radiator. See Cooling System Section for checks to perform.
B. Check Transmission Fluid; keep topped up to proper level.
C. Check Rear Shock Absorbers; you may benefit from installation of new rear shocks.
D. Check Tire Pressures; best traction and handling can be ensured if tire pressures are properly maintained.

For safer and more trouble-free trailer towing, consider:
A. Automatic Transmission Cooler; helps remove excess heat from automatic transmission fluid built up during towing mileage. Also helps avoid radiator overheating. Some units can be self-installed.
B. Heavy-Duty Shock Absorbers or Air Shocks; important to have on rear wheels if you intend to do a lot of towing or load carrying within the

car itself. Don't forget to consider replacing factory shocks, when they are worn out, with heavy-duty units at the front as well.
C. Variable Load Flasher; this unit will accommodate the added load of trailer turn signal lamps on trailer when these are hooked into your car's electrical system.

FRONT END ALIGNMENT

When steering, handling and/or tire wear indicate front end alignment may be needed, this work can only be done at an automotive service shop. DO NOT PUT OFF NEEDED FRONT END ALIGNMENT. At the same time, have ball joints and steering linkage checked.

Ignition System

TUNE-UP SERVICES

The ignition system consists of spark plugs; plug wires; distributor; rotor; points; condenser; coil. These units work to create a good hot spark inside the engine (ignition) at exactly the right moment (timing). If ignition is weak or timing is off, engine may be hard to start, run poorly, waste gas, lose power, backfire or not run at all. VW SAYS . . . Replace plugs and points every 15,000 miles.
TOOLS & MATERIALS . . . Parts: set of points; condenser; 4 spark plugs. Tools: gap gauge; 13/16 in. spark plug socket; screwdriver; open end, box or combination metric wrenches; timing equipment (see Ignition Timing).
SAFETY TIP . . . Change only one spark plug at a time to avoid cross-wiring and possible engine damage.

CHECKING POINTS AND ROTOR

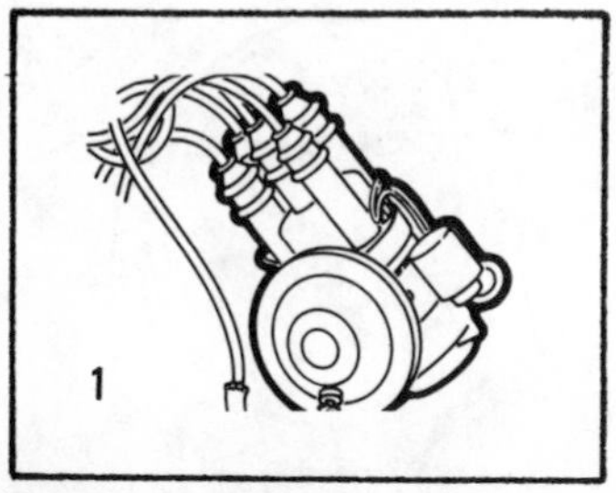

The distributor holds the points and rotor. The condenser is attached to the outside of the distributor. The cap forms the top of the distributor.
1. To open distributor, remove center wire only, snap retaining clips off with screwdriver, lift off cap, but keep plug wires connected.
2. Examine inside of cap for pitted or burned metal contacts, hairline cracks, excessive wear of button at center, or carbon tracks.

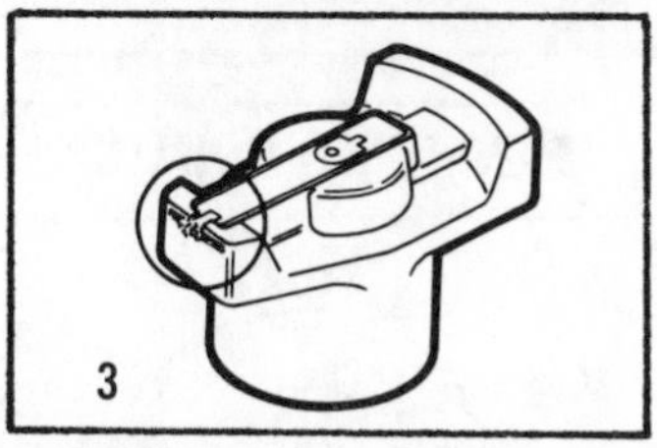

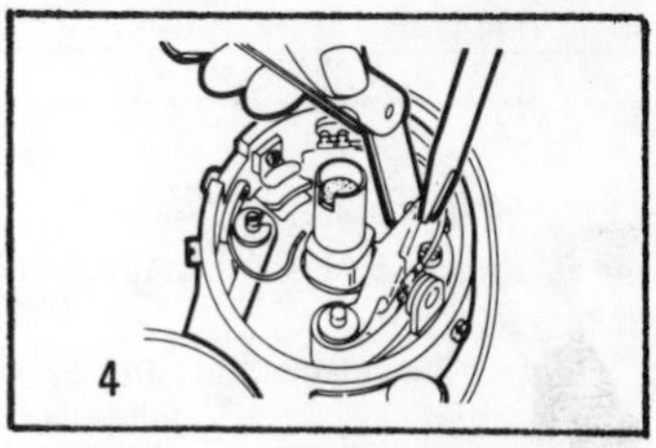

3. Pull rotor off straight up. If it is cracked, or tip or center contact is burned, replace it.
4. Pry points apart with screwdriver. If pitted or burned, replace. If OK, check gap with feeler gauge, for proper setting of .016.

OTHER IGNITION CHECK POINTS

Inspect spark plug wires. If cracked or brittle, entire set should be replaced. Also, center high tension wire. Inspect distributor cap. Wipe inside clean occasionally with dry, lint-free rag. If cap is cracked or rotor contacts are excessively burned, replace cap.

SPARK PLUG REPLACEMENT

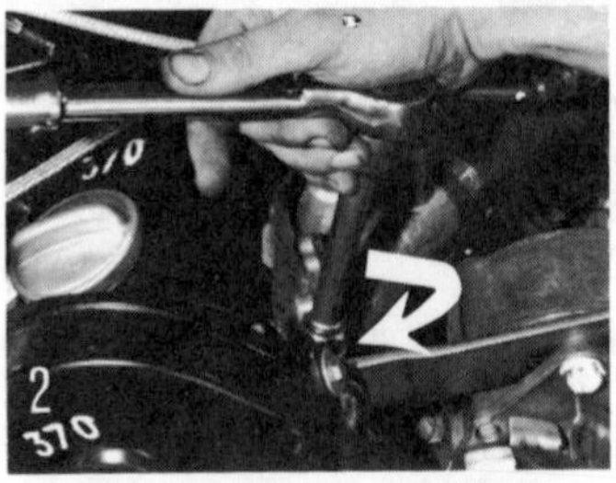

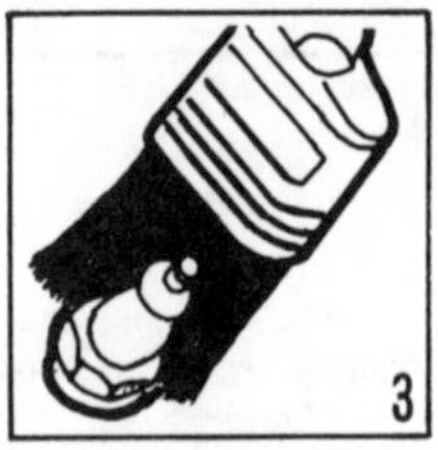

1. Pull spark plug wire by grasping rubber boot. Do not yank wire off. If stuck, turn boot, pulling gently.
2. Loosen spark plug using socket wrench.
3. Wipe loose dirt from around plug before removing. Do not let dirt drop into engine through plug hole. Unscrew plug.
4. Check plug electrode gap on new plug. Adjust to .028 in. on all cars. Plug gap is correct when the gauge drags slightly as it is pulled between plug electrodes. Lightly oil threads before installing plug.

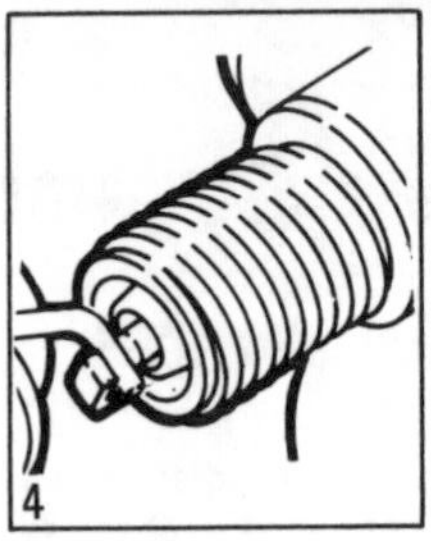

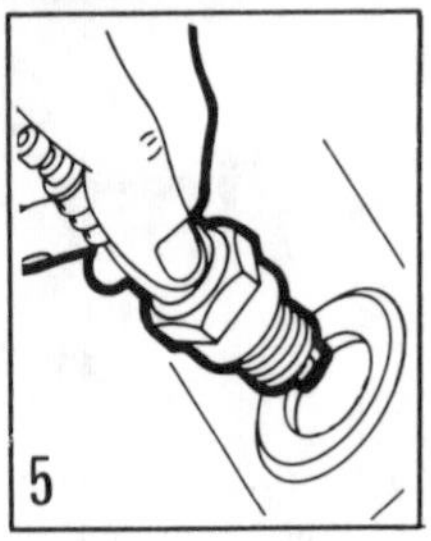

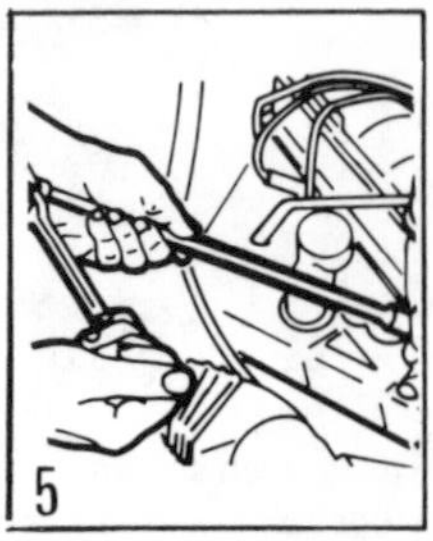

5. Thread new plug into plug hole by hand. Hand tighten. Do not force or cross thread. Use socket wrench to tighten firmly but do not force. Replace plug wire. Press boot firmly into place.

LOCATION OF POINTS AND CONDENSER

Points and condenser work together. Always replace condenser when installing new points. The condenser is attached to the outside of the distributor.

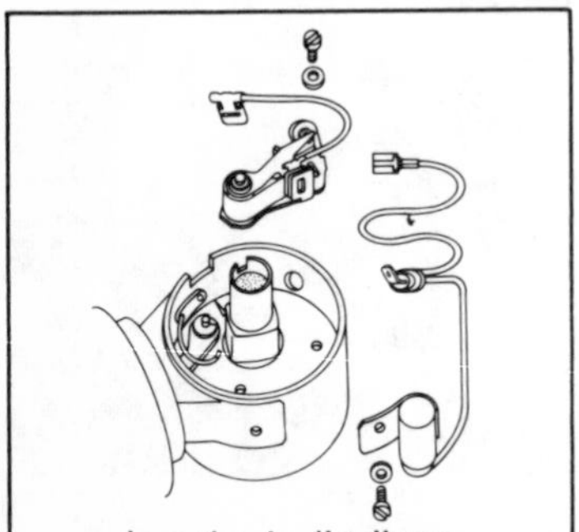
Location in distributor

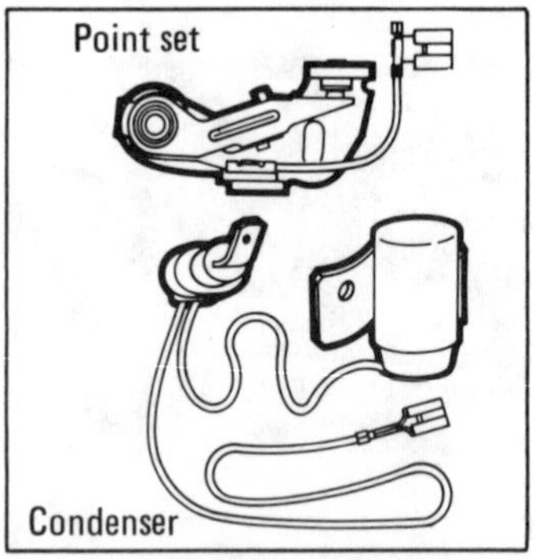

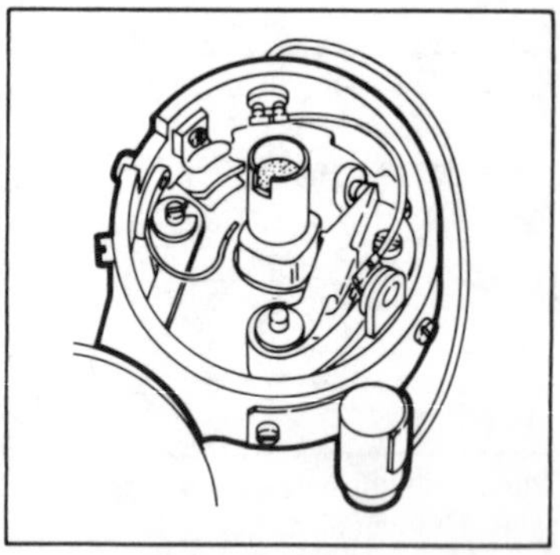

REMOVING POINTS

1. Disconnect the points wire from the condenser connection at the side of the distributor.
2. Remove the screw from the stationary breaker point. Lift points out of distributor.
CAUTION: Be careful not to drop the screw into the distributor.
3. Remove the condenser by undoing the screw holding the bracket and condenser connection to the distributor.
4. Disconnect the condenser wire from the coil.

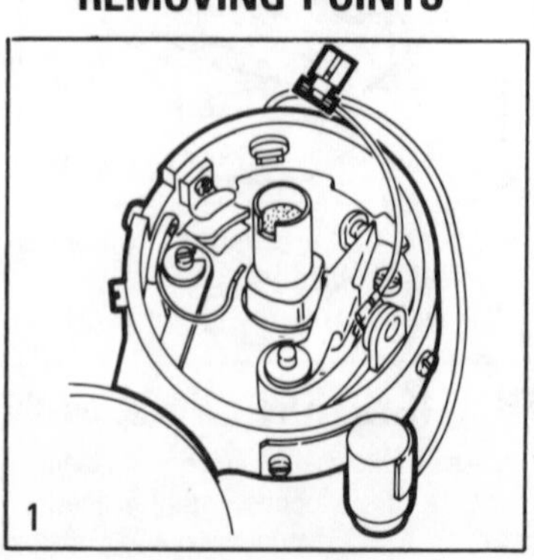

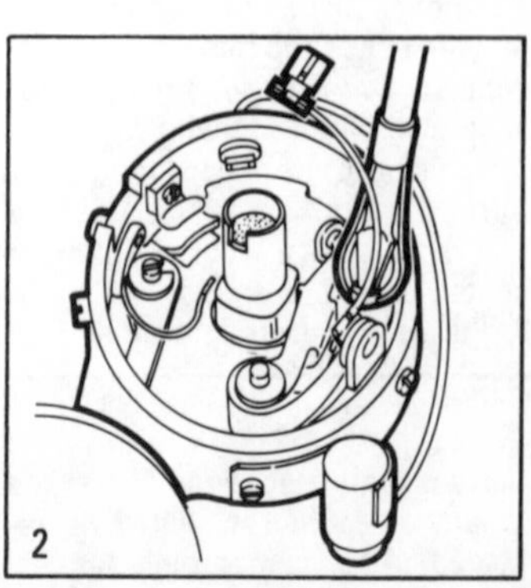

5. If necessary, remove connector grommet. Pull connector grommet out of distributor.
6. Wipe all dirt and grease from the distributor plate and cam with clean, lint-free rag.

CAUTION: When removing screws from distributor, be sure to avoid any screws accidentally falling through distributor opening into engine. Use magnetic screwdriver, or safety clip screwdriver.

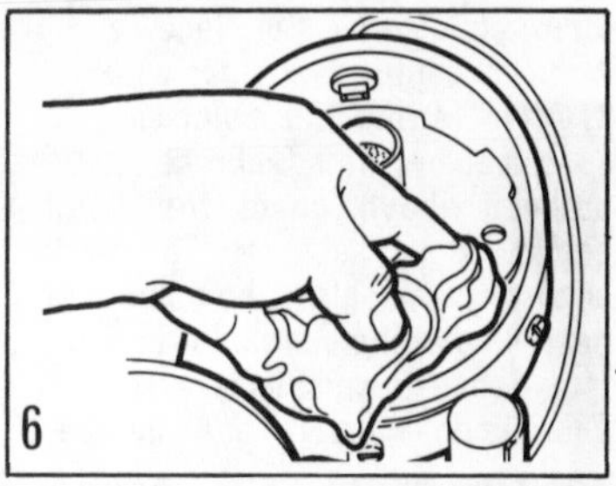

INSTALLING POINTS AND CONDENSER

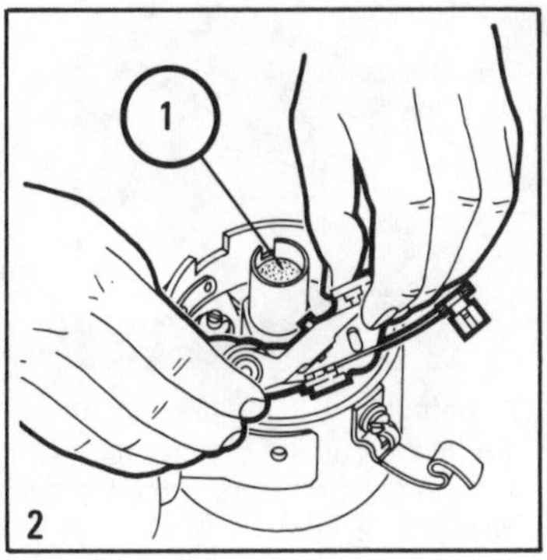

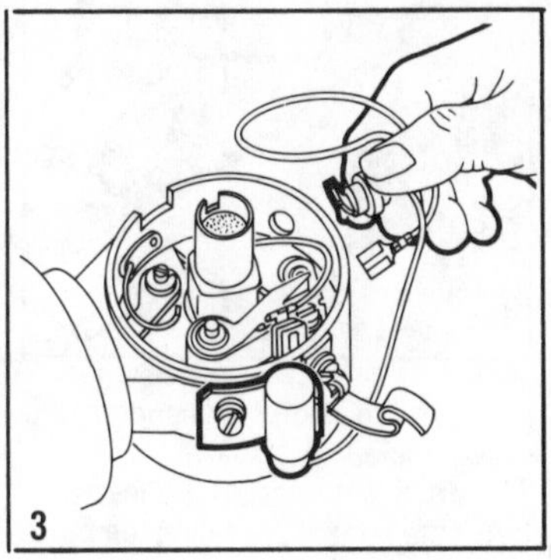

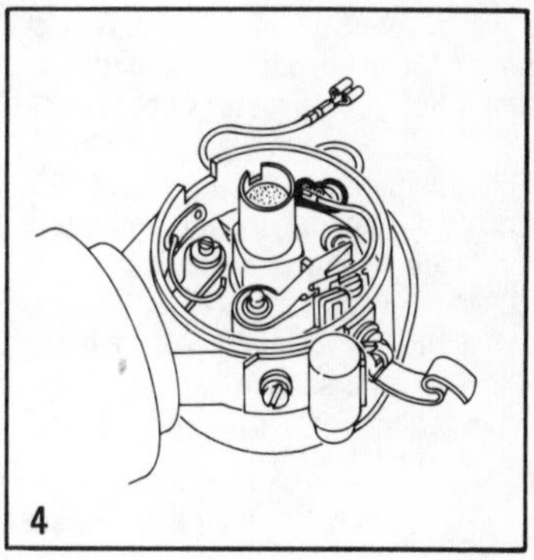

1. Apply small amount of heat resistant lube to distributor cam (lube sometimes supplied with new point sets, if not, purchase separately).
2. Position new points in distributor and fasten with the attaching screw.
3. Insert connector grommet through side of distributor, and attach new condenser to distributor with attaching screw. On some distributors, install connector grommet bracket. Connect wire to coil.

4. Connect points wire to condenser connection.

SETTING THE CONTACT GAP

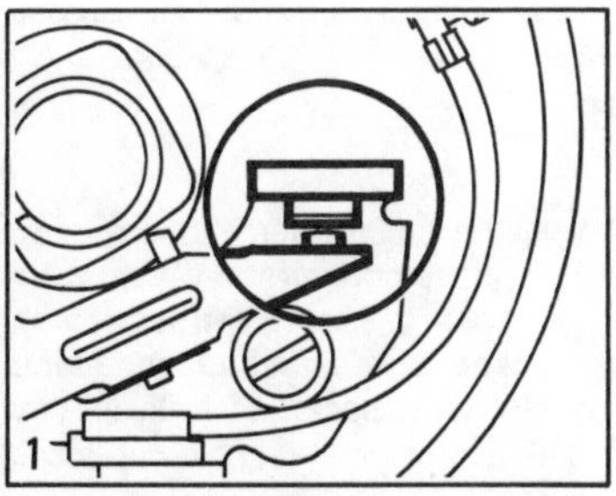

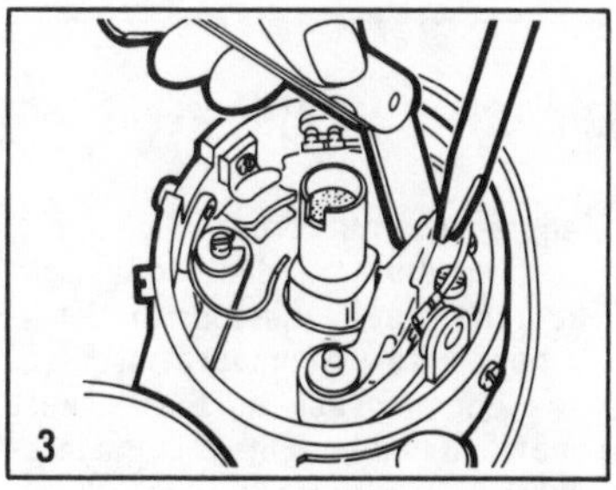

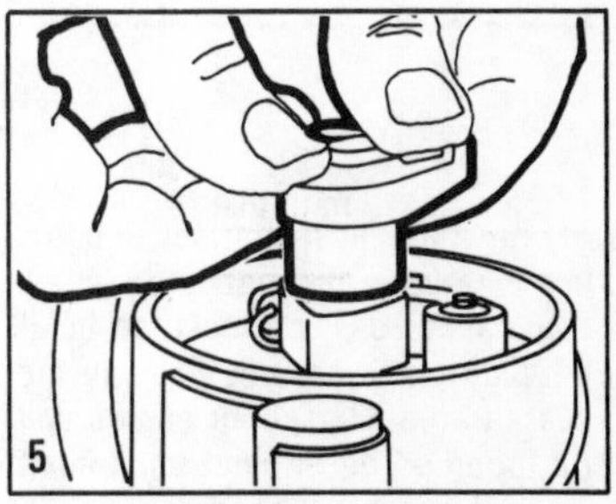

1. Electrical contacts of point set MUST BE PARALLEL. If needed, bend stationary contact with needle-nosed pliers. Bend only the bracket portion of points—not the other side.
2. Turn engine by ignition key (you'll need a helper) until rubbing block on points is on one of the four high points of distributor cam. You may use wrench on lower pulley to do this.
3. Correct point gap for all cars is .016. Insert proper feeler gauge between open point contacts. If adjustment is needed: Slightly loosen point attaching screw. Insert screwdriver between boss on breaker plate and notch on points. Twist screwdriver to open or close points as needed. Tighten screws when correct gap is obtained.
4. Recheck point gap after screw is tightened. Readjust if needed.
5. Align tab inside rotor with notch on distributor shaft and push rotor onto shaft. Rotor must be fully seated on shaft.
6. Install distributor cap by aligning tabs on cap with notch on body.

Snap retaining clips in place.
7. Install center distributor wire.
8. After setting the point gap to specification with a feeler gauge as outlined above, check the dwell angle with a dwell meter. The dwell angle or cam angle is the number of degrees that the distributor cam rotates while the points are closed. There is an inverse relationship between dwell angle and point gap. Increasing the point gap will decrease the dwell angle and vice versa. Checking the dwell angle with a meter is a far more accurate method of measuring point opening than the feeler gauge method.
9. Attach the dwell meter according to the manufacturer's instruction sheet. The negative lead is grounded and the positive lead is connected to the No. 1 primary wire terminal that runs from the coil to the distributor. Start the engine, let it idle and reach operating temperature, and observe the dwell angle on the meter. The reading should fall within the allowable range given in the Tune-Up Specifications chart. If it does not, the gap will have to be reset.

IGNITION TIMING

Adjusting timing is the important finishing touch to any tune-up. This is not a difficult job but it does require a timing light, dwell meter or combination dwell/tach and a piece of chalk. This equipment will cost about $20 and up depending on type and quality. Since timing is a minor service adjustment not requiring any parts installation, you may wish to have this done at a service garage. If you have equipment, proceed as follows:

1. Attach the timing light as outlined above or according to the manufacturer's instructions. Hook up a dwell/tachometer since you'll need an rpm indication for correct timing.
2. Locate the timing mark opening in the clutch or torque converter housing at the rear of the engine directly behind the distributor. The OT mark stands for TDC or 0° advance. The 3 mark designates 3° ATDC. Mark them with chalk so that they will be

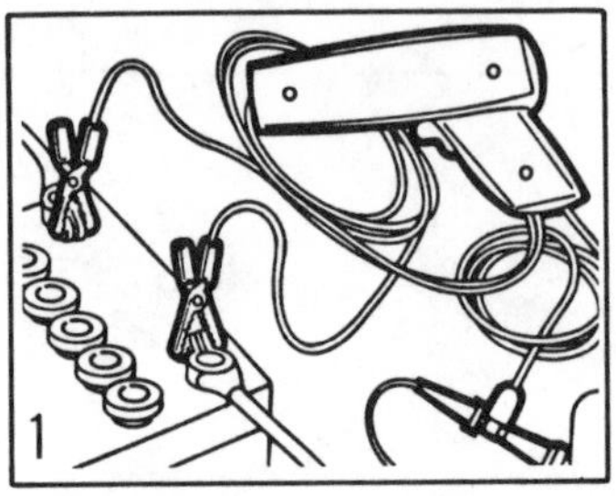

more visible. Don't disconnect the vacuum line.
3. Start the engine and allow it to reach the normal operating temperature. The engine should be running at normal idle speed.
4. Shine the timing light at the marks.
5. The light should now be flashing when the 3° line and the V-shaped pointer are aligned.
6. If not, loosen the distributor holddown bolt and rotate the distributor very slowly to align the marks.

7. Tighten the mounting nut when the ignition timing is correct.
8. Recheck the timing when the distributor is secured.

With ignition timing correctly adjusted, the spark plugs will fire at the exact instant in which the piston is nearing the top of the compression stroke.

With ignition timing correctly adjusted, the spark plugs will fire at the exact instant in which the piston is nearing the top of the compression stroke, thus providing maximum power and economy.

REPLACING SPARK PLUG WIRES

One of the most overlooked items in a tune-up is the spark plug wires. Your car can be in perfect tune, but if the plug wires are not carrying the spark to the plugs, your engine will run poorly. The original equipment wires that came with your care are usually good for a year or two before needing replacement. On newer cars, the higher underhood temperatures created by emission controls breaks down the wires' ability to conduct electricity sooner. The spark plug boot ends of the wires will crack with age allowing the spark to arc towards the engine, not reaching the plugs. The distributor cap ends of the wires will often collect moisture, and corrode right there in your distributor cap. Sometimes a wire will contact a hot part of the engine, such as the exhaust manifold and burn through the insulation. Other times, a wire will become oil soaked and gummy, breaking down the insulation. Often, when carbon core wires get old, they will break off inside, with no visible signs of breakage on the outside. Always use good quality spark plug wire. A carbon core or cut-rate brand may seem attractive at first, but will cost you more in the long run with reduced engine efficiency and more frequent replacement.

1. Replace one wire at a time. This will keep you out of trouble with crossed wires. When removing wires, twist back and forth as you pull up. This will help free up stuck wires.
2. Take the old wire and match it up with the new one for length. If you are cutting your own, make sure there is good metal to metal contact between the end of the wire and the pinch-on connectors.
3. Make sure each wire seats all the way down in the distributor cap. First push down the wire, then the boot. The wire should click in place.

4. After you are all done, make sure all wires are clear of choke or throttle linkage, or hot exhaust manifolds. Use the firing order illustration to guide you when replacing your ignition wires and/or distributor cap.

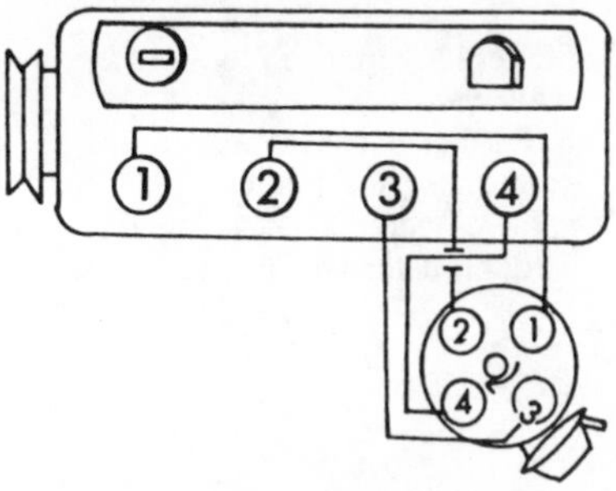

FIRING ORDER—1-3-4-2

Fuel System

When gasoline is brought from the fuel tank, it mixes with air in the carburetor or fuel injector. This gas/air mixture then enters the engine thru the intake manifold, passes thru the intake valves and is burned in the combustion chamber. The burned exhaust gas is then passed thru the exhaust valves to the exhaust system and to the outside air. In order to keep your engine running cleanly with minimal pollution, and avoid dangerous carbon monoxide fumes inside the vehicle, certain items should be checked from time to time.

FUEL FILTER

The fuel filter is a strainer screen located under the top cover of the fuel pump. On 1974 models it should be replaced every 12,000 miles; on later models, it should be replaced every 15,000 miles or each year.

In addition to the fuel pump strainer screen, all fuel injected models are equipped with an in-line filter. 1976-77 Dashers and 1976-77 Sciroccos with the high performance engine are equipped with fuel injection.

On some models this fuel filter is located in the engine compartment. It can easily be found by tracing the fuel line back from the fuel injector. Other models use a similar type of filter, but this is located on the underside of the car, on the right side by the fuel tank. This filter is a fairly large silver container attached in the fuel line near the tank.

To remove either type, the clips, nuts, or hose clamps must be removed and the fuel lines taken off the filter. The engine compartment filter can be reached by opening the hood and removing the connections from the top of the engine. The fuel tank located filter must be removed

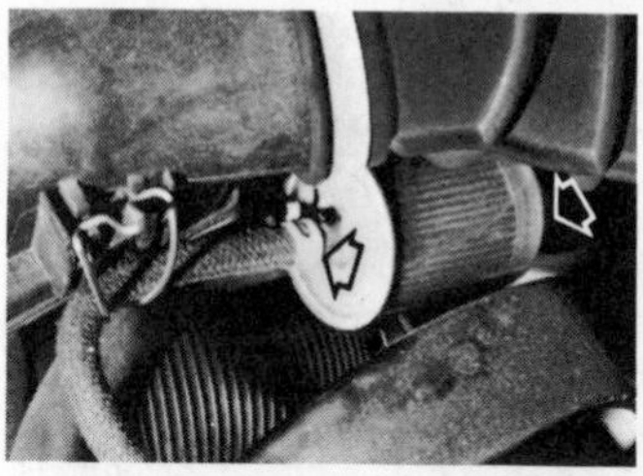

from under the car; make sure that you plug the line from the tank so that fuel doesn't spill out. Remember to support the car safely on jack stands when working underneath.

EMISSION CONTROL SYSTEMS

Crankcase ventilation is the only emission control system that the average owner should concern himself with. All other maintenance and service should be referred to the dealer or service garage. The purpose of the crankcase ventilation system is twofold. It keeps harmful vapor by-products of combustion from escaping into the atmosphere and prevents the buildup of crankcase pressure which can lead to oil leaks. Crankcase vapors are recirculated from the camshaft cover through a hose to the air cleaner. Here they are mixed with the air/fuel mixture and burned in the combustion chamber.

HOW TO CLEAN FUEL STRAINER

1. Remove the pump cover screw and cover.
2. Remove the filter screen.
3. Clean the screen in solvent, and air dry.
4. Carefully wipe any sediment from the pump.
5. Replace screen with screen downward.
6. Position top cover on pump. Make sure gaskets are under cover and screw. Tighten cover screw.
7. Operate the engine, and check for leaks.

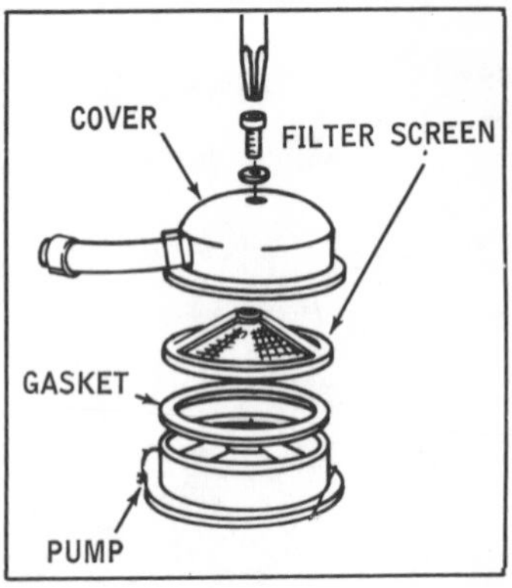

KEEP THE AIR INTAKE CLEAN

Volkswagen recommends that the air cleaner element be removed and cleaned every 15,000 miles and replaced every 30,000 miles or two years. The air filter is a key part of the engine. A restrictive, dirty element will cause a reduction in fuel economy and performance and an increase in exhaust emissions.

The air filter is inside the plastic intake box which is connected to the carburetor or fuel injection system by a large round hose (1974-75 Dashers have a round air cleaner). To gain access to the filter, unsnap the clip type retainers and separate the housing. The air filter lifts right out.

If you are cleaning the filter, shake or vacuum the dirt accumulation from the filter. Before putting the filter back in, check it for any rips and make sure the outer rubber edge is intact. If not, replace the filter, it's cheap insurance. Take a clean rag and wipe out the inside of the air cleaner. Install the filter back in the housing. Fit the housing halves together and resnap the clips.

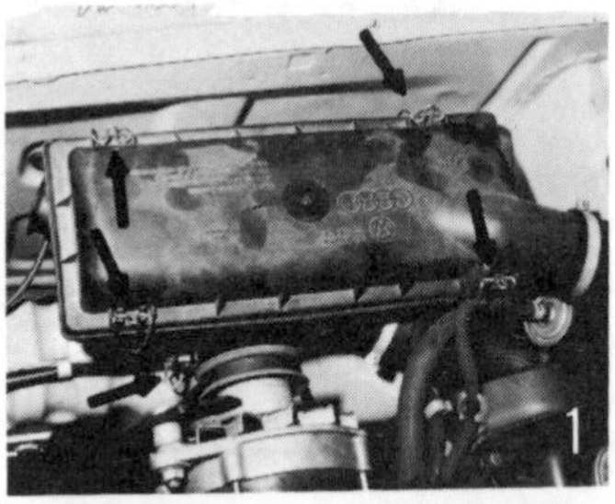

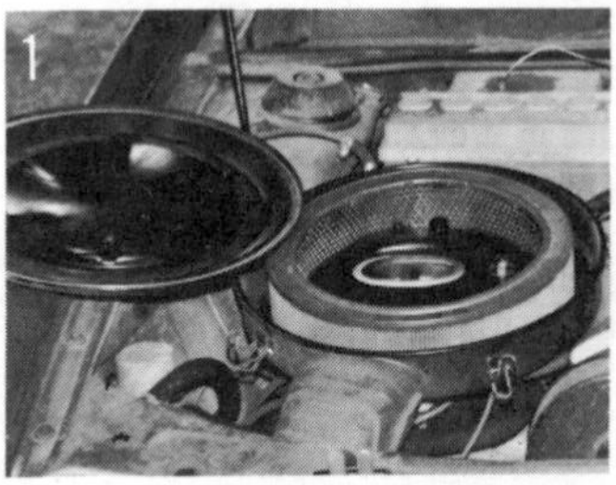

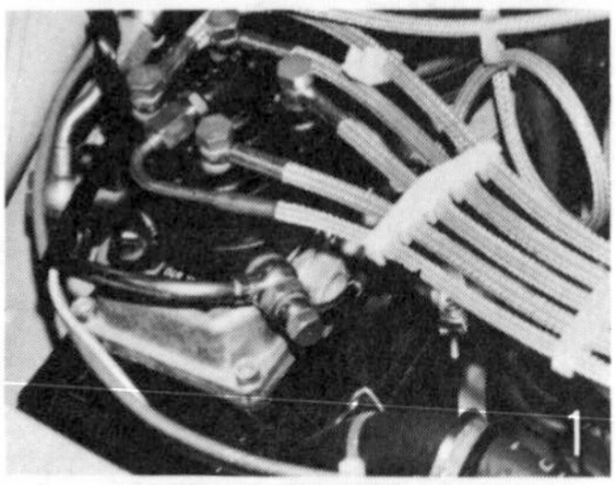

FUEL INJECTED CARS

CRANKCASE VENTILATION SYSTEM SERVICE

Every 15,000 miles or each year, remove the vent hoses in the system and check their condition. Note where each hose goes before removing them. If the hoses are clogged or cracked and falling apart, replace them. The Dasher has a crankcase ventilation valve, the other models do not. This valve is not normally replaced, as is common on American cars, but removed and cleaned at 15,000 mile or one year intervals.

The valve is located in the line to the camshaft cover. Remove it. Immerse the valve in carburetor cleaning solvent. Shake it dry and replace it.

Safety Systems

FRONT TURN SIGNAL, PARKING LIGHT, SIDE MARKER

To replace a Rabbit or Dasher side marker bulb, unscrew the Phillips head screws, remove the lens, gently press the bulb into its socket, turn it and remove it. Install the new bulb and replace the lens. Don't overtighten the screws or you'll crack the lens. On the Scirocco, remove the lens and pull the rubber cap off. Remove the bulb holder by pressing the lugs outward. Remove the old bulb and replace it. Install the holder and the lens.

Dasher and Rabbit turn/park lights are replaced by removing the lens. Gently press the bulb down into its housing and turn it to remove. Install the new bulb. Replace the lens, but be sure to properly position the gasket. To replace a Scirocco turn/park bulb, open the hood, pull off the rubber cap on the rear of the light housing, squeeze the lugs on the housing together and remove it from the light. Press the bulb into its socket and turn it to the left to remove. Insert the new bulb and insert the housing into the light. Make sure that the lugs are engaged. Replace the rubber cap.

NOTE: When inserting new bulb, note that knobs on side of base are different distances from base tip. Match knobs to socket slots for proper fit. Check that the lens gasket is correctly positioned and not cracked or rotted. Replace, if necessary. Reinstall the lens. DO NOT overtighten the screws or you will break the lens.

REAR TURN SIGNAL, STOP-TAIL, BACK-UP LIGHTS

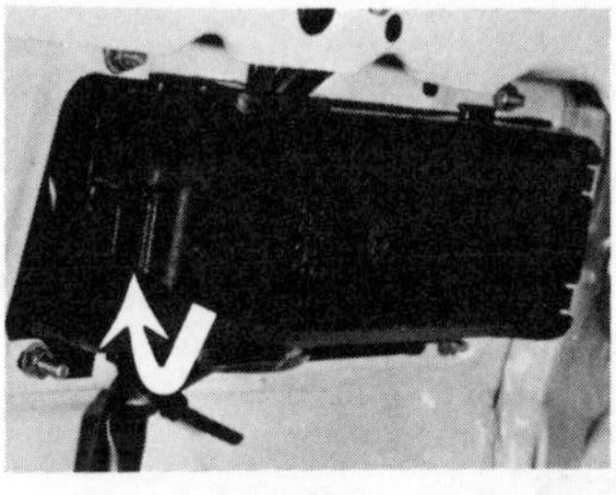

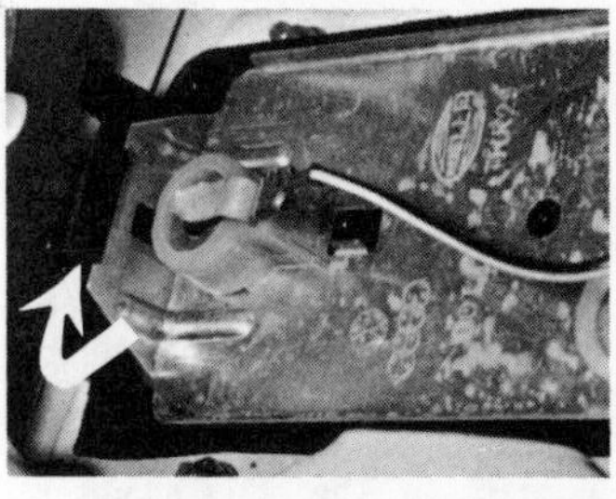

All rear lights are serviced from within the luggage compartment. On the Rabbit and Scirocco, unscrew the knurled screw and remove the tail light cover. Depress the spring clip on the inboard side and pull the bulb housing. Press the bulb into its housing and turn it to remove. Install the new bulb and replace the cover. Don't overtighten the knurled screw. On the Dasher, pry the clip on the tail light cover and remove the cover. Squeeze the bulb housing and center and pull it out. Bulbs are replaced in the same way as the Rabbit/Scirocco. Snap the bulb housing and cover back into place.

LICENSE PLATE LIGHTS

To replace the license light bulb(s), unscrew the two Phillips head screws and remove the lens. Push in on the bulb to remove. Both bulbs must be functioning for the light to work. Replace the lens, but don't overtighten the screws.

INTERIOR DOME LIGHT

To replace the interior light on the Rabbit or Scirocco, press against the spring clip and lift out the bulb housing. This is a cartridge bulb. Pull it from the holder and insert the replacement bulb. Reinstall the housing into the headliner. The Dasher bulb is replaced in the same manner except that the housing is removed by inserting a screwdriver in the housing cut out on the switch side and carefully prying it out.

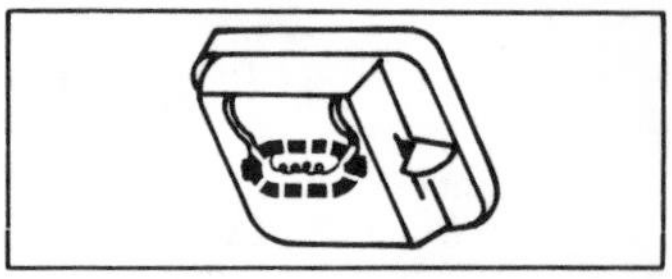

HEADLIGHT REPLACEMENT

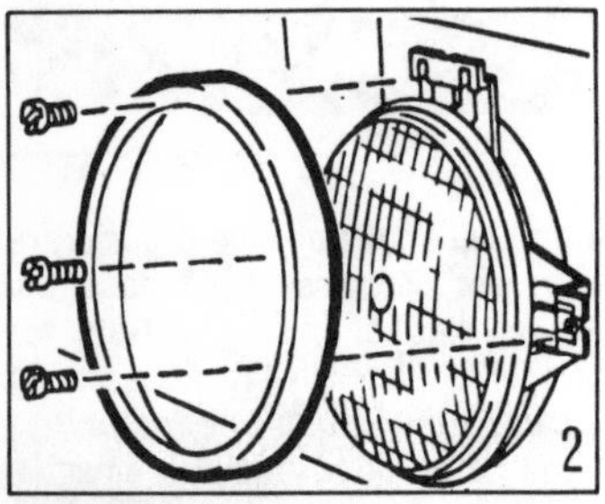

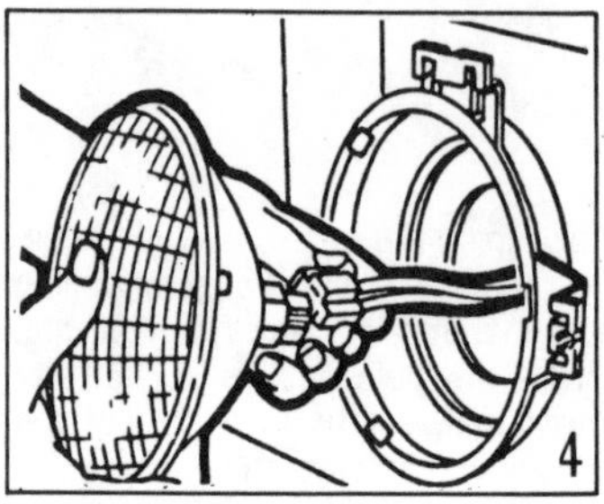

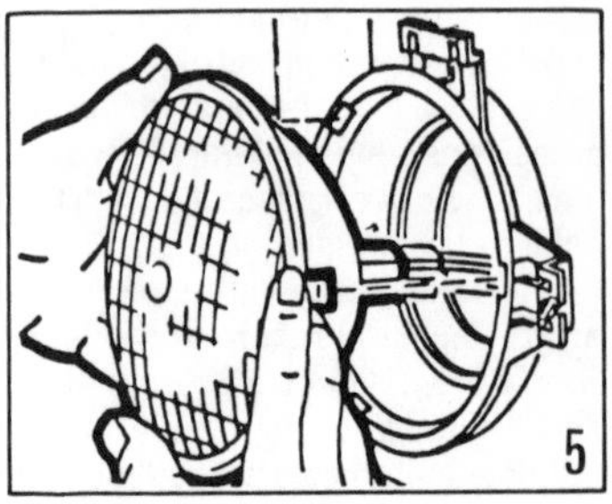

1. Remove the grille.
2. Remove the three headlight retaining ring screws. Do not disturb the two headlight aiming screws or it will be necessary to reaim the headlights.
3. Remove headlight retaining ring.
4. Pull the headlight out of the housing and unplug the multi-connector.
5. Replace the new bulb in the reverse order of removal. Make sure that the three lugs on the bulb engage the slots in the housing.

WINDSHIELD WIPER BLADE REPLACEMENT

To remove wiper blades lift arm away from windshield. Rotate blade and snap out and off crooked arm. There are two types of replacement rubbers for VW windshield wipers. One requires replacement of entire wiper blade. The other allows replacement of only wiper blade insert. Press the old rubber insert down, away from wiper blade to free it from its retaining clips on blade ends. Slide insert in wiper blade. Position new insert from blade. Bend insert upward slightly to engage retaining clips.

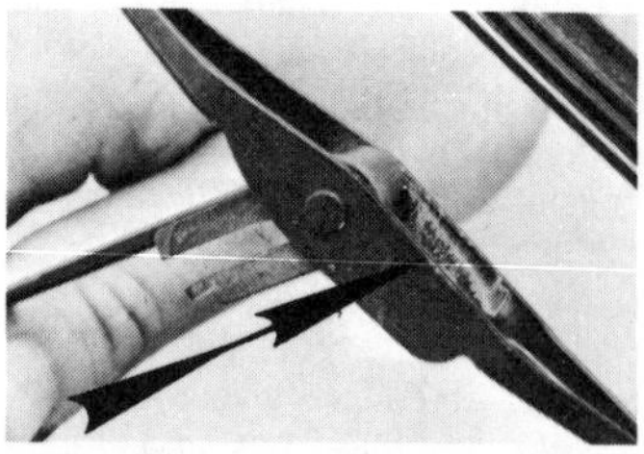

HORN PROBLEMS

If horn sounds and does not stop, this is due to short circuit in wiring. Disconnect wiring connector under hood and have professional service shop check horn wiring circuit.

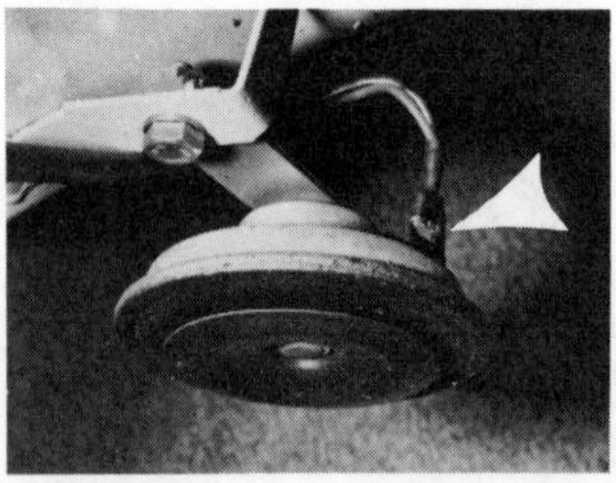

STEERING PROBLEMS

See steering system check in Suspension Section. Check tire pressures. Have a professional service shop check all components in the front end and steering system.

WHEEL CYLINDER CHECK

Disc brakes employ calipers on individual wheels. Remove wheel and inspect caliper for signs of fluid leaks. Have mechanic correct leaks. Drum brakes employ individual wheel cylinders to apply braking pressure to shoes. Check for brake fluid leaks on inside of wheel.

WASHER SYSTEM

If washer fails to squirt properly, raise hood and check system hose connections. Be sure washer fluid container has fluid. Check spout openings for clogging.

Keep container filled with fluid mixture of washer solvent and water. If road spray buildup on windshield is a chronic problem, add 1 tablespoon dishwasher detergent to solvent/water mixture when re-filling container.

NOTE: The car's windshield washer pump mechanism is lubricated by the fluid in the windshield washer tank. To avoid damaging the pump mechanism, keep an adequate level of fluid in the tank at all times.

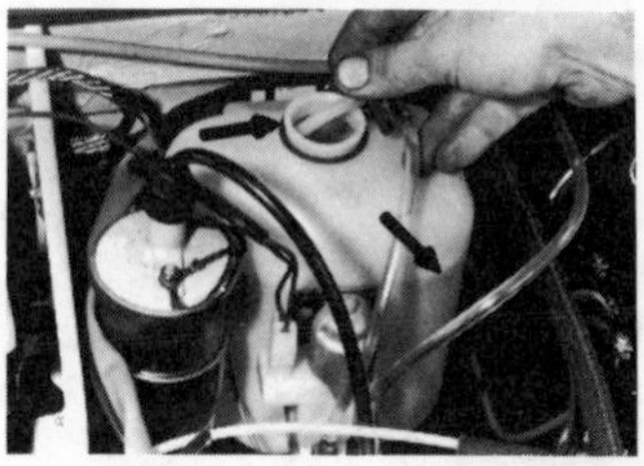

Electrical System

To ensure starting ability at all times check your battery condition periodically. You'll need to check battery electrolyte (fluid) level in each of the six cells. Check battery cable connections for tightness and inspect for accumulated corrosion.

SAFETY NOTE: Wear gloves when working on battery.

CHECK BATTERY FLUID

1. Remove plastic filler caps on top of battery. Fluid should be up to lower end of filler hole and covering the plates. If fluid is low add clean, cold tap water. If your area has hard water, use only distilled water available at auto supply, food or drug stores.
2. Replace any lost caps immediately.

CAUTION: NEVER LIGHT A MATCH OR SMOKE near the top of a battery. Batteries give off explosive hydrogen gas.

NOTE: Battery that often checks low on fluid could mean:

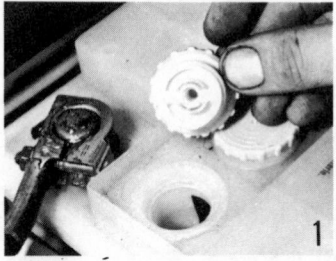

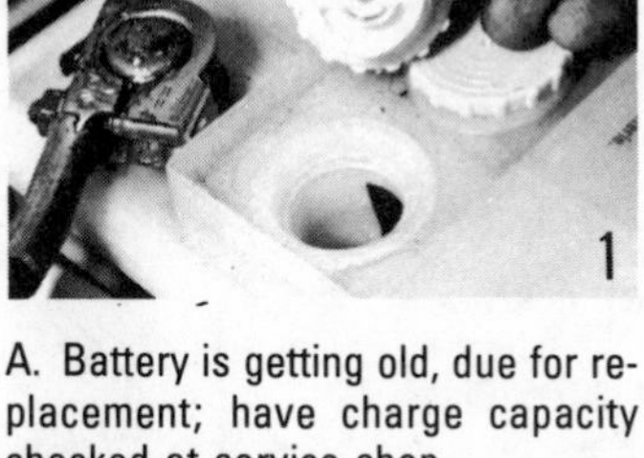

A. Battery is getting old, due for replacement; have charge capacity checked at service shop.

B. Connections may be corroded or loose; clean/replace as needed (see below).

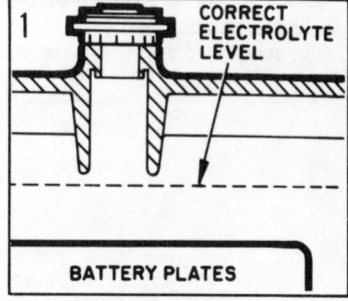

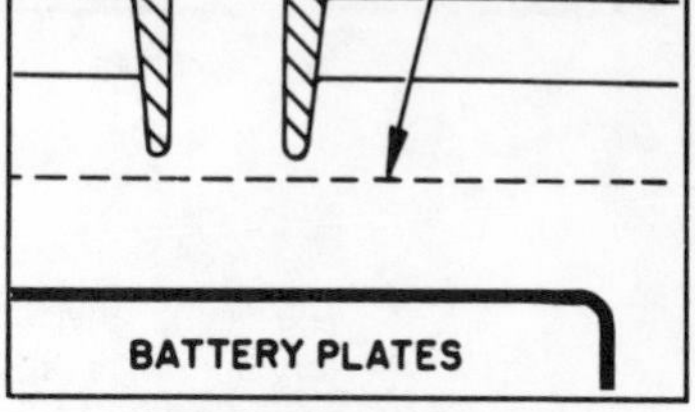

C. Alternator or voltage regulator not functioning properly; this happens far less often than A or B above.

CLEAN THOSE BATTERY TERMINALS

As time goes by, battery terminals build up a dry powdery, whitish material. This material is corrosive and will gradually eat thru battery cables if not cleaned off periodically.

1. Loosen and remove battery connections.
2. Brush off all loose corrosion; use stiff bristle brush. Do not get this material into eyes or on open cuts. Wash off at once.
3. If corrosion build-up is extremely heavy and brushing does not remove all of it, mix 2 tablespoons baking soda to 1 cup water. Pour solution directly onto terminals and connectors. Allow to soak a few minutes and rinse off. Continue brushing to remove all traces of corrosion build-up. Do not allow cleaning solution to enter battery.
4. Replace connectors on battery terminal posts and tighten. Do not hammer connections onto posts, but be sure they will not come loose with vibration.
5. Liberally smear battery terminal posts and cable connectors with petroleum jelly.

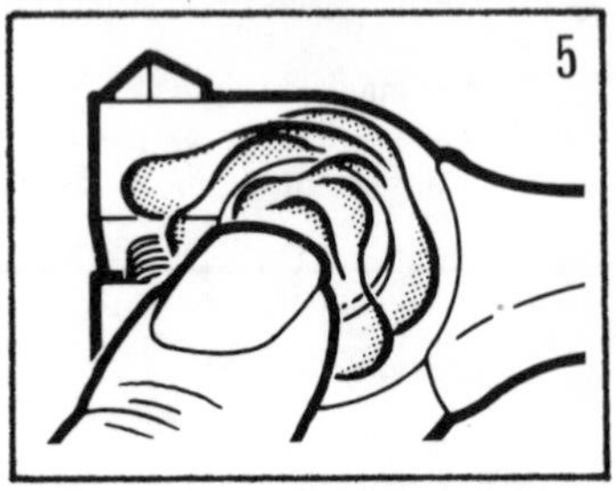

REPLACE FAULTY BATTERY CABLES

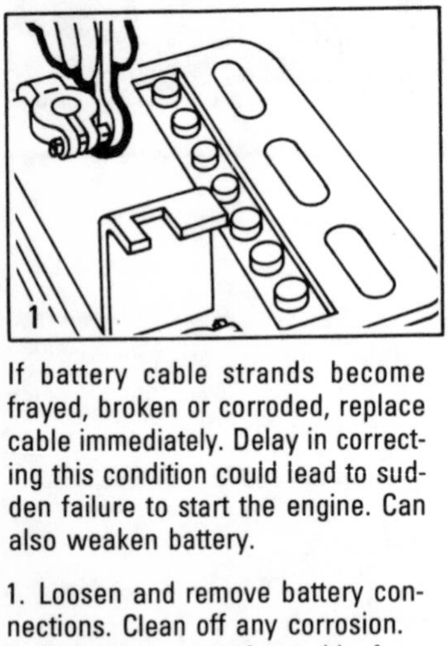

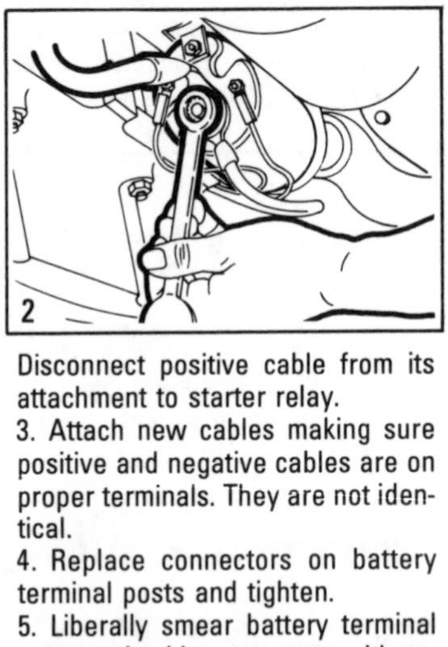

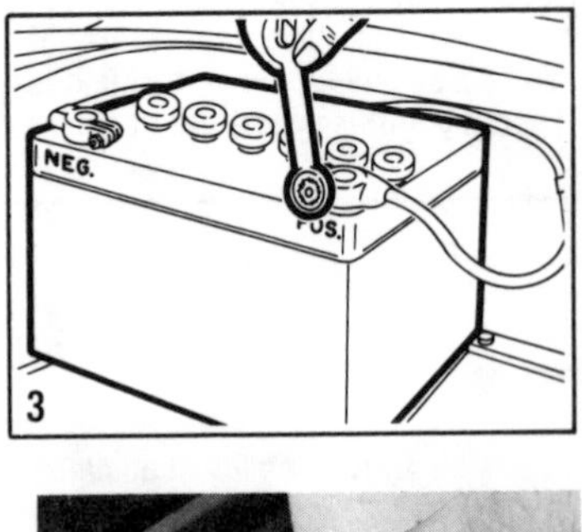

If battery cable strands become frayed, broken or corroded, replace cable immediately. Delay in correcting this condition could lead to sudden failure to start the engine. Can also weaken battery.

1. Loosen and remove battery connections. Clean off any corrosion.
2. Disconnect negative cable from its attachment to engine or chassis. Disconnect positive cable from its attachment to starter relay.
3. Attach new cables making sure positive and negative cables are on proper terminals. They are not identical.
4. Replace connectors on battery terminal posts and tighten.
5. Liberally smear battery terminal posts and cable connectors with petroleum jelly.

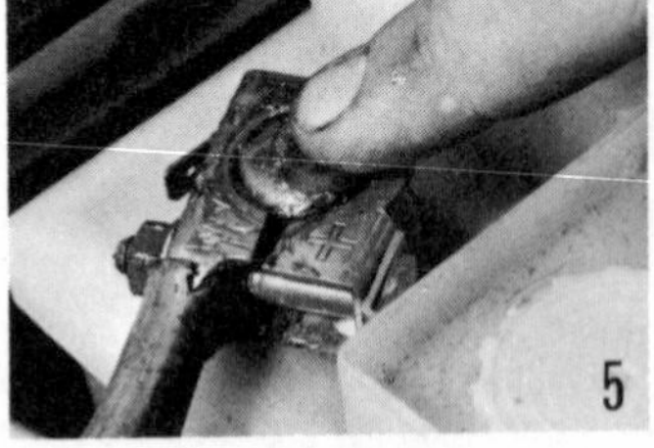

BATTERY HOLDDOWN

The clamp device which holds battery in place should be checked periodically. If loose, tighten. Clean off corrosion buildup. Severely corroded holddown components should be replaced before they break.

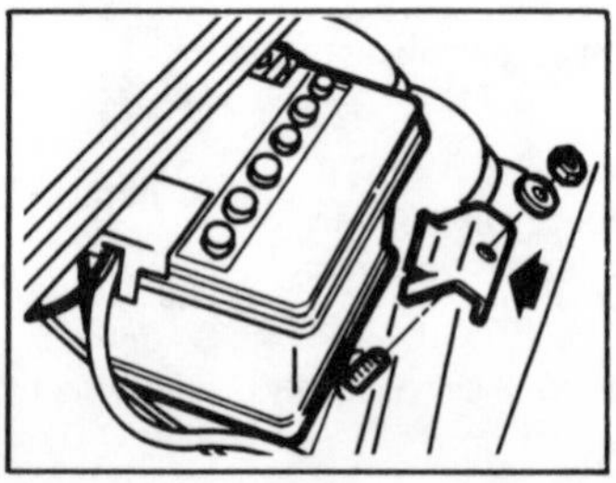

FUSES, RELAYS AND FLASHERS

The fuses, relays, and flashers are all located in one central compartment on all models. The compartment is located on the left side of the engine compartment on 1974-75 Dashers and under the left hand side of the dash on all other models. Fuses are the ceramic type with a metal strip through the center. A blown fuse will have a broken metal strip. To replace a blown fuse, merely twist it out of the connectors and insert the new one the same way. Relays and flashers pull out of their socket. Insert the replacement relay firmly into the relay box.

ALTERNATOR

Red warning light on instrument panel should glow red when you first turn ignition key. This proves bulb is OK. Warning light should go off when engine is running at normal operating speed.

If warning light glows red at operating speed alternator isn't charging battery properly. Common causes are:

A. Fan belts are loose and slipping on alternator pulley. Tighten or replace belts.

B. Battery terminals, cables are loose or corroded. Clean; tighten; replace bad cables.

If A or B do not correct problem alternator or voltage regulator may be faulty. This happens far less often, and can only be checked by mechanic with proper electrical testing equipment.

Alternator Caution: Alternator can be permanently damaged by short-circuiting terminal connections. When working around or moving alternator, always keep metal tools or engine parts from terminal. Disconnect the battery when working on alternator.

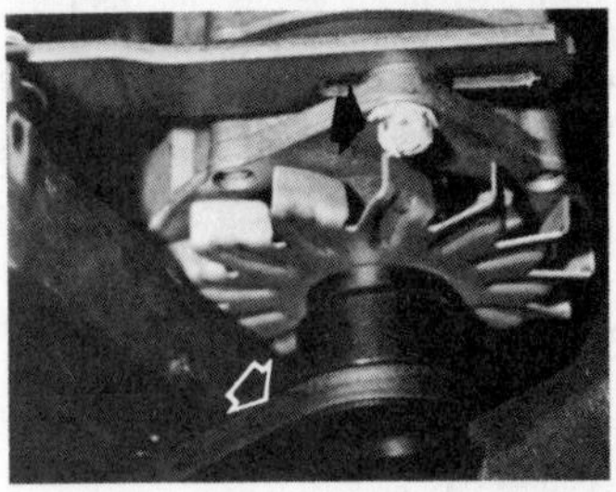

REAR WINDOW DEFOGGER SYSTEM

Do not clean inside of rear window fitted with defogger system with any abrasive material. This could destroy carbon-copper wires. Use only soft rag and mild detergent/water mixture. Dry carefully.

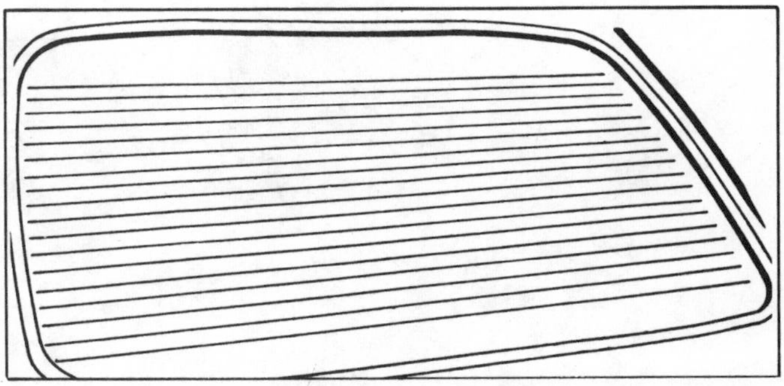

Air Conditioner

WARNING!—Never attempt to tighten fittings, disassemble or do any work on your VWs A/C system. Consult a professional mechanic about A/C system problems and their correction.

Your auto air conditioner (A/C) is a delicate, closed system. If air, dirt or water get into it, or if refrigerant es-

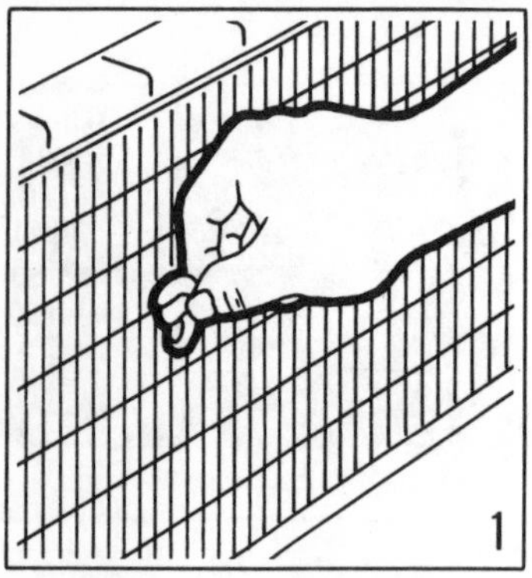
1

capes, the A/C unit will not cool a car interior. Among things you can do are:

1. Keep condenser grilles clean. Check for dirt and debris; periodically remove dead insects, leaves, etc., with stiff bristle brush. Straighten any bent fins—carefully.
2. Make sure condenser fan operates when A/C is on. Check electrical connections or replace parts as necessary.
3. Keep the cooling system in top condition as described in the Cooling System section. While the A/C does not directly affect engine temperature, it does increase the load placed on the engine. Keeping all cooling system parts in top shape, and keeping the engine in top tune will minimize the chances of overheating.
4. Check fan and compressor belt tension periodically. (See Cooling System section). Replace glazed, frayed or cut belts, before they fail entirely.
5. Check periodically for bubbles in A/C sight glass. Sight glass is located in head of receiver/drier vessel, which is located in the engine compartment. Sight glass is no larger than head of large nail. It may be dirty. Wipe clean for best visibility.

PROCEED AS FOLLOWS:

a) With engine and A/C system running, look for passage of refrigerant in sight glass. You'll be looking for a stream of milky white bubbles as they pass through sight glass. It is best to watch sight glass and have someone else start the car and turn on the A/C system. Allow to run for a few minutes.

b) If you observe no bubbles, and air flow from A/C unit in the car is passing cold air, everything is OK.

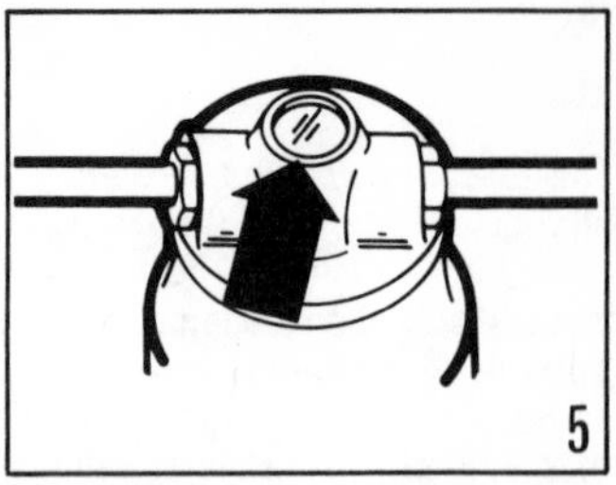
5

c) If no bubbles appear in sight glass, and air flow from the A/C unit in the car is not delivering cold air, the system may be low on refrigerant and could need a re-charge.

d) If bubbles appear, system is low on refrigerant.

e) If you suspect refrigerant loss based on tests performed above, have system checked by a professional A/C service shop. They can confirm refrigerant loss, recharge the system and check for system leakage.

NOTE: Once a week or so, even in winter, run A/C system for about 5 minutes as you drive. This keeps system internally lubricated, prevents hoses hardening.

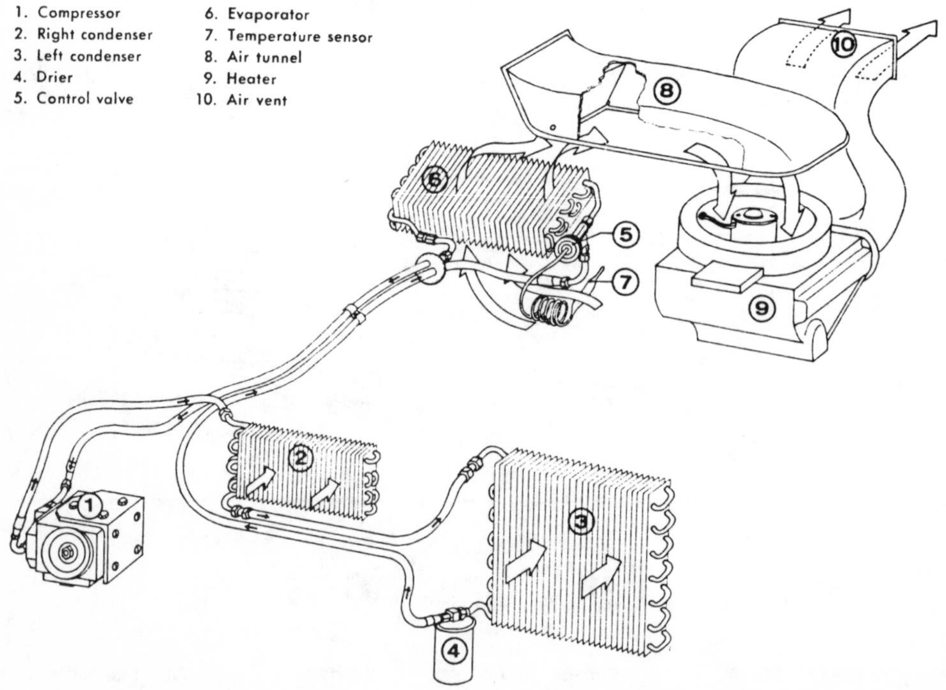

TUNE-UP SPECIFICATIONS

YEAR	MODEL	SPARK PLUGS Type	SPARK PLUGS Gap (in.)	DISTRIBUTOR Point Dwell (deg.)	DISTRIBUTOR Point Gap (in.)	IGNITION TIMING Man. Trans. (deg.)	IGNITION TIMING Auto Trans. (deg.)	IDLE SPEED Man. Trans. (rpm)	IDLE SPEED Auto Trans. (rpm)
1974	Dasher	Bosch W175T30	0.024-0.028	44-50①	0.016	3 ATDC @ idle	3 ATDC @ idle	850-1000	850-1000
1975	Dasher	Bosch W200T30	0.024-0.028	44-50	0.016	3 ATDC @ idle	3 ATDC @ idle	850-1000	850-1000
1976-77	Dasher	Bosch W215T30	0.024-0.028	44-50	0.016	3 ATDC @ idle	3 ATDC @ idle	900-1000	900-1000
1975-77	Rabbit/Scirocco	Bosch W200T30	0.024-0.028	44-50	0.016	3 ATDC @ idle	3 ATDC @ idle	900-1000	900-1000

① 47°-53° for California models
② Vacuum hose on

NOTE: The underhood specifications sticker often reflects tune-up specification changes made in production. Sticker figures must be used if they disagree with those in this chart.

CAPACITIES

YEAR	MODEL	ENGINE OIL With Filter	ENGINE OIL Without Filter	TRANSMISSION Pts. to Refill after Draining MANUAL	TRANSMISSION Pts. to Refill after Draining AUTOMATIC	DRIVE AXLE (pts.)	COOLING SYSTEM (qts.)
1974-75	Dasher	3.7	3.2	3.4	3.2	3①	6.4
1976-77	Dasher	3.2	2.6	2.6	3.2	3①	6.4②
1975-77	Rabbit/Scirocco	3.7	3.2	3.4	3.2	1.6①	6.8

① Automatic transmission only, manual transmission figure includes drive axle
② 6.9 qts. on models with coolant expansion tank

Service Record

DATE/MILEAGE	SERVICE	NEXT DUE

General Information

JUMP STARTING FROM ANOTHER CAR

It is important that jumper cable connections between both batteries be made from NEGATIVE to NEGATIVE and from POSITIVE to POSITIVE. Incorrect hookup could damage both vehicles. Identify positive terminal by + mark on battery base or terminal post, or by checking to find (positive) battery cable that connects to starter relay. Negative terminal is marked (−) and connects to engine block, or chassis.

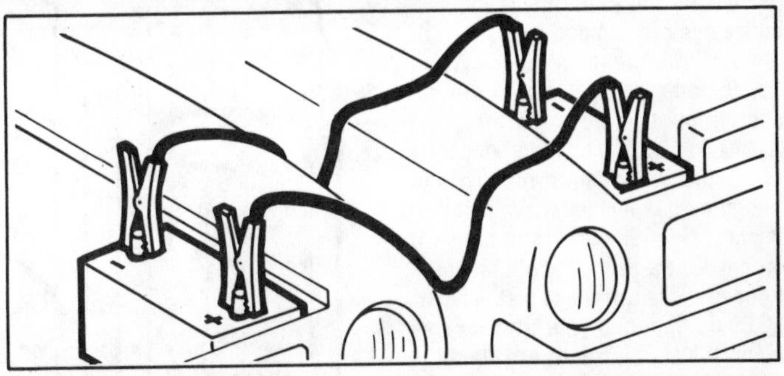

KEEP THE FUEL SYSTEM CLEAR

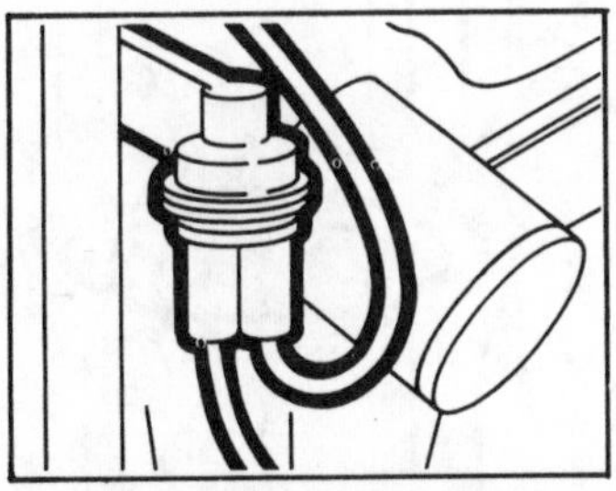

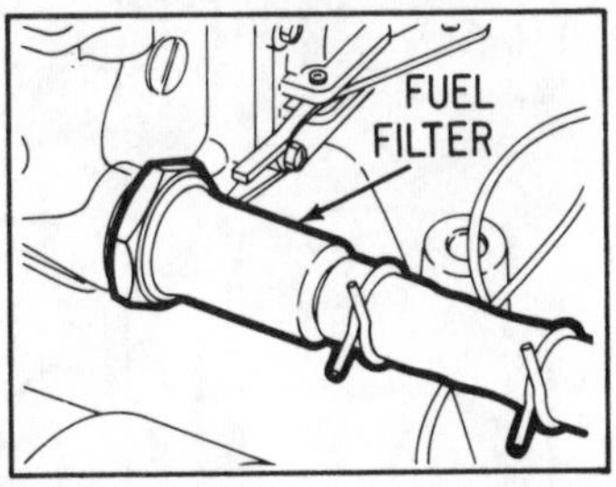

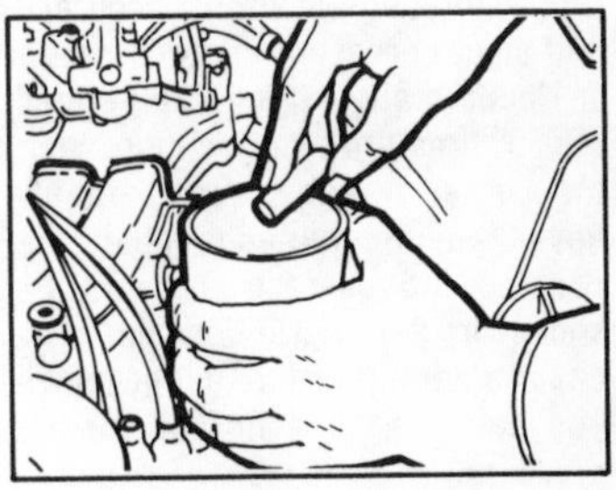

1. Locate fuel pump attached to engine block on left side. Tubing from fuel pump carries gasoline to carburetor. Check for leaks at all connections in this line.
2. Fuel passes thru a filter before entering carburetor. Engine may run poorly or stop due to clogged filter. Replace fuel filter at recommended intervals.
3. To check fuel flow to carburetor: detach fuel line at fuel filter inlet; hold end of line into a cup (not styrofoam); have someone turn starter key. If a good supply of fuel comes out of the line, the filter is probably clogged. If no fuel comes thru or flow is restricted, fuel pump may be faulty.

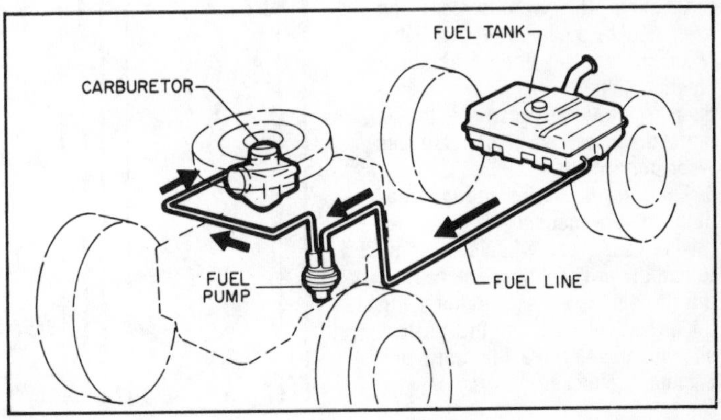

CAUTION: Before cranking engine, be sure hands and clothing are clear of fan blades.

FUEL CAP INSPECTION

Water and/or dirt in the gas tank can cause many problems. Rough running, a blocked carburetor, and possible frozen fuel lines in winter can all result from water or dirt in the fuel tank. Make sure that the fuel cap fits tightly on the filler neck. If the sealing gasket is worn, cut, or cracked, replace the cap. The addition of a fuel line antifreeze additive to the gas tank during the winter will help prevent frozen fuel lines.

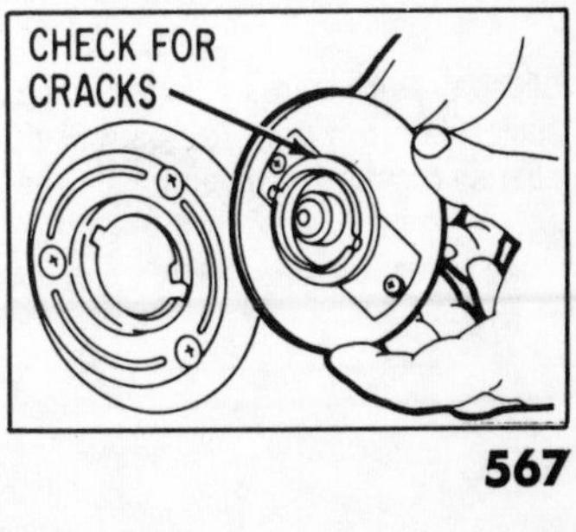

TIRE WEAR PATTERNS

1. Tread Wear Bars. These appear when your tires are ready for replacement due to normal wear. The indicators are molded into the bottoms of the tread grooves. When bands appear in two or more adjacent grooves, replace the tire.
2. Incorrect Camber. When one side of the tire wears more rapidly than the other, suspect incorrect camber. If that side is worn smoothly, it means that a front end alignment is needed. Take the car to a specialist.
3. Overinflation. If your tires look as if only the center treads are wearing, you have been overinflating them. Find the proper inflation pressure in your owner's manual. Check the tires with gauge of known accuracy and adjust pressure as necessary.
4. Underinflation. If the outer edges of your tires are wearing more than the center threads, you probably have them underinflated. Inflate the tires to the correct pressure as shown in the chart. Consider purchasing a tire pressure gauge which you can use to maintain correct pressure.
5. Cupping. This wear pattern can be caused by a number of problems. Misalignment resulting from bent steering linkage can cause this condition. A wheel/tire assembly that is out of balance can also cause this wear pattern.
6. Feathering. Saw-toothed wear patterns are caused by incorrect toe-in. Your front wheels must be turned inward slightly at the front. If this "toe-in" is excessive, however, the tires will wear in the pattern shown above. Have the front end alignment checked.

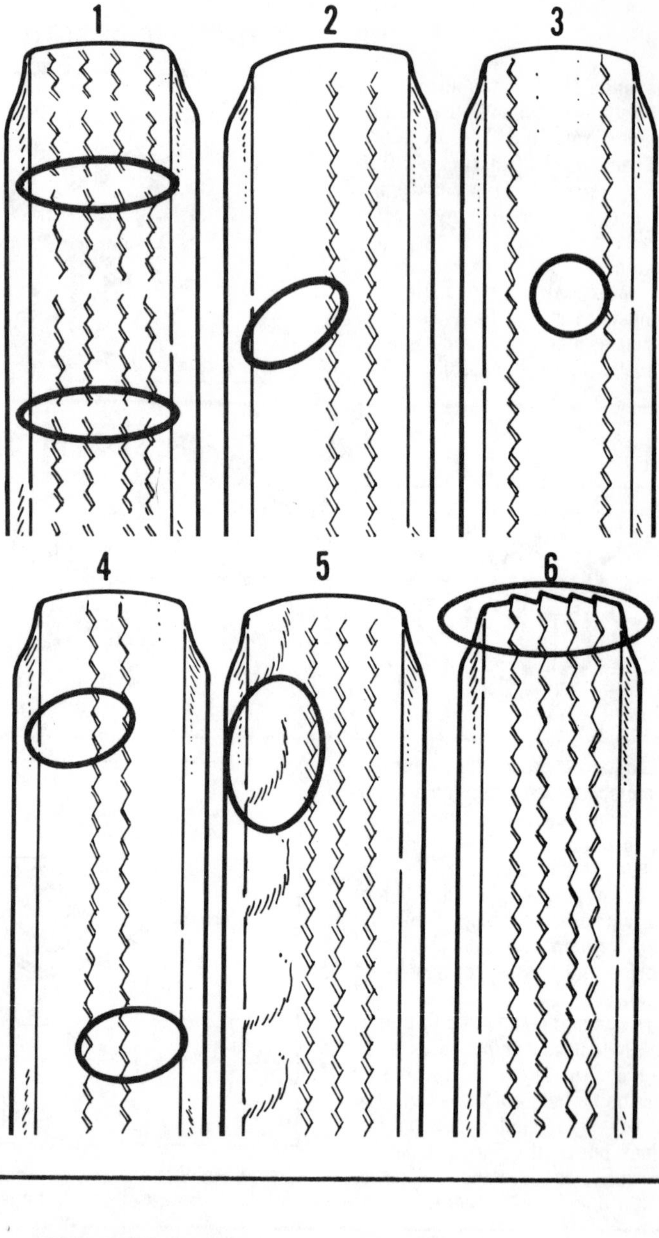

TIRE PRESSURES

Check tire pressures when tires are cool. Use a tire pressure gauge; do not rely on gas station air hose pressure indicators. A once-a-week check should ensure maximum life from your tires, plus better handling and performance on the highway.

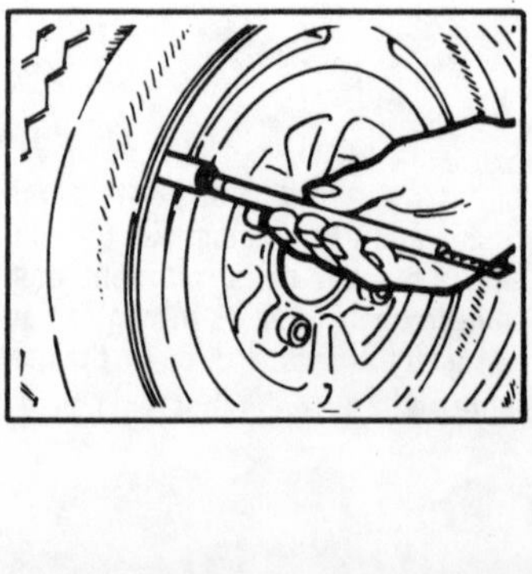

TIRE CHECKS

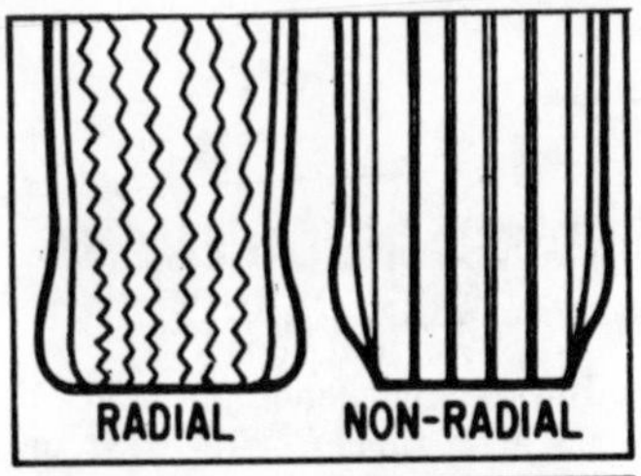

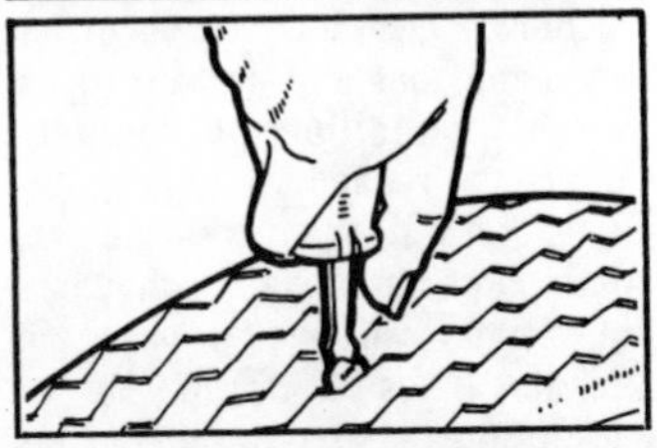

Radial tires will appear underinflated compared to standard tires. Check pressure with gauge. Safe tread depth is at least 1/16 inch.

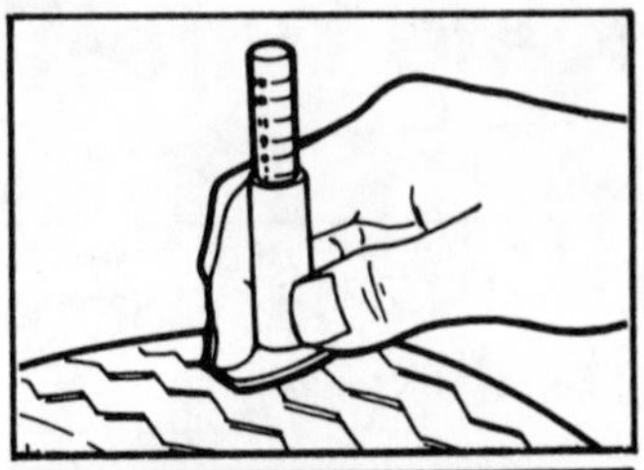

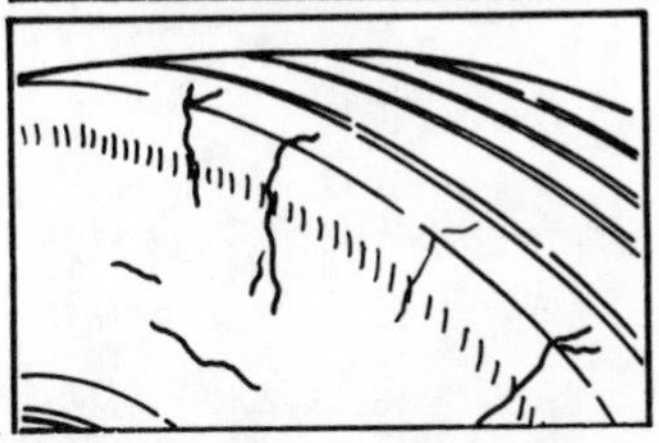

Remove stones or glass chips embedded in tread. Check for sidewall cracks or abrasion.

TIRE ROTATION

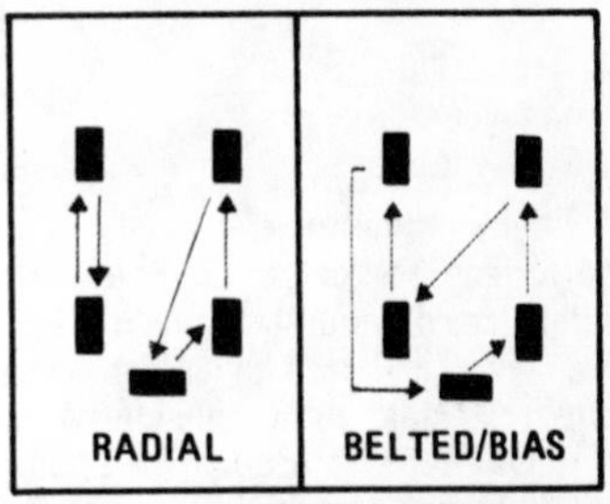

Rotate tires every 5,000 miles. Do not rotate snow tires with standard tires.

NOTE: Radial tires are rotated differently than standard tires. And with either type, you can employ 4-tire or 5-tire rotation pattern depending on whether spare is used. For 4-tire rotation, simply by-pass spare.

STUDDED TIRES

Studded tires should be removed from the car as soon as threat of snow and ice has ended. Many states require studded tires be removed by a certain date. Studded tires should always be remounted in the same wheel position when put back in service each winter. Mark tires LR (left rear), etc; mark which sidewall faces out.

EXHAUST SYSTEM CHECKPOINTS

Besides annoying noise, a leaky or defective exhaust system is potentially very dangerous to vehicle occupants when engine is running. Twice a year—or whenever exhaust/muffler noises seem to be louder than usual—an inspection of the exhaust system should be performed.

Check for muffler holes or broken seams.

Look for black sooty streaks that indicate exhaust gas leakage from cracks. Also check for thin areas of exhaust system metal components. Check hangers that attach exhaust system to vehicle. All connections should be solid, movement relatively limited. Weak or broken hangers must be replaced as soon as possible.

Check for loose pipe connections. For total safety, all defective exhaust/muffler system units should be replaced immediately.

Engine Tune-Up

Engine tune-up is a procedure performed to restore engine performance, deteriorated due to normal wear and loss of adjustment. The three major areas considered in a routine tune-up are compression, ignition, and carburetion, although valve adjustment may be included.

A tune-up is performed in three steps: analysis, in which it is determined whether normal wear is responsible for performance loss, and which parts require replacement or service; parts replacement or service; and adjustment, in which engine adjustments are returned to original specifications. Since the advent of emission control equipment, precision adjustment has become increasingly critical, in order to maintain pollutant emission levels.

ANALYSIS

The procedures below are used to indicate where adjustments, parts service or replacement are necessary within the realm of a normal tune-up. If, following these tests, all systems appear to be functioning properly, proceed to the Troubleshooting Section for further diagnosis.

—Remove all spark plugs, noting the cylinder in which they were installed. Remove the air cleaner, and position the throttle and choke in the full open position. Disconnect the coil high tension lead from the coil and the distributor cap. Insert a compression gauge into the spark plug port of each cylinder, in succession, and crank the engine with the starter to obtain the highest possible reading. Record the readings, and compare the highest to the lowest on the compression pressure limit chart. If the difference exceeds the limits on the chart, or if all readings are excessively low, proceed to a wet compression check (see Troubleshooting Section).

—Evaluate the spark plugs according to the spark plug chart in the Troubleshooting Section, and proceed as indicated in the chart.

Maxi. Press. Lbs. Sq. In.	*Min. Press. Lbs. Sq. In.*	*Max. Press. Lbs. Sq. In.*	*Min. Press. Lbs. Sq. In.*
134	101	188	141
136	102	190	142
138	104	192	144
140	105	194	145
142	107	196	147
146	110	198	148
148	111	200	150
150	113	202	151
152	114	204	153
154	115	206	154
156	117	208	156
158	118	210	157
160	120	212	158
162	121	214	160
164	123	216	162
166	124	218	163
168	126	220	165
170	127	222	166
172	129	224	168
174	131	226	169
176	132	228	171
178	133	230	172
180	135	232	174
182	136	234	175
184	138	236	177
186	140	238	178

—Remove the distributor cap, and inspect it inside and out for cracks and/or carbon tracks, and inside for excessive wear or burning of the rotor contacts. If any of these faults are evident, the cap must be replaced.

—Check the breaker points for burning, pitting or wear, and the contact heel resting on the distributor cam for excessive wear. If defects are noted, replace the entire breaker point set.

—Remove and inspect the rotor. If the contacts are burned or worn, or if the rotor is excessively loose on the distributor shaft (where applicable), the rotor must be replaced.

—Inspect the spark plug leads and the coil high tension lead for cracks or brittleness. If any of the wires appear defective, the entire set should be replaced.

—Check the air filter to ensure that it is functioning properly.

PARTS REPLACEMENT AND SERVICE

The determination of whether to replace or service parts is at the mechanic's discretion; however, it is suggested that any parts in questionable condition be replaced rather than reused.

—Clean and regap, or replace, the spark plugs as needed. Lightly coat the threads with engine oil and install the plugs. CAUTION: Do not over-torque taperseat spark plugs, or plugs being installed in aluminum cylinder heads.

—If the distributor cap is to be reused, clean the inside with a dry rag, and remove corrosion from the rotor contact points with fine emery cloth. Remove the spark plug wires one by one, and clean the wire ends and the inside of the towers. If the boots are loose, they should be replaced.

If the cap is to be replaced, transfer the wires one by one, cleaning the wire ends and replacing the boots if necessary.

—If the original points are to remain in service, clean them lightly with emery cloth, lubricate the contact heel with grease specifically designed for this purpose. Rotate the crankshaft until the heel rests on a high point of the distributor cam, and adjust the point gap to specifications.

When replacing the points, remove the original points and condenser, and wipe out the inside of the distributor housing with a clean, dry rag. Lightly lubricate the contact heel and pivot point, and install the points and condenser. Rotate the crankshaft until the heel rests on a high point of the distributor cam, and adjust the point gap to specifications. NOTE: Always replace the condenser when changing the points.

—If the rotor is to be reused, clean the contacts with solvent. Do not alter the spring tension of the rotor center contact. Install the rotor and the distributor cap.

—Replace the coil high tension lead and/or the spark plug leads as necessary.

—Clean the carburetor using a spray solvent (e.g., Gumout® Spray). Remove the varnish from the throttle bores, and clean the linkage. Disconnect and plug the fuel line, and run the engine until it runs out of fuel. Partially fill the float chamber with solvent, and reconnect the fuel line. In extreme cases, the jets can be pressure flushed by inserting a rubber plug into the float vent, running the spray nozzle through it, and spraying the solvent until it squirts out of the venturi fuel dump.

—Clean and tighten all wiring connections in the primary electrical circuit.

Additional Services

The following services should be performed in conjunction with a routine tune-up to ensure efficient performance.

—Inspect the battery and fill to the proper level with distilled water. Remove the cable clamps, clean clamps and posts thoroughly, coat the posts lightly with petroleum jelly, reinstall and tighten.

—Inspect all belts, replace and/or adjust as necessary.

—Test the PCV valve (if so equipped), and clean or replace as indicated. Clean all crankcase ventilation hoses, or replace if cracked or hardened.

—Adjust the valves (if necessary) to manufacturer's specifications.

ADJUSTMENTS

—Connect a dwell-tachometer between the distributor primary lead and ground. Remove the distributor cap and rotor (unless equipped with Delco externally adjustable distributor). With the ignition off, crank the engine with a remote starter switch and measure the point dwell angle. Adjust the dwell angle to specifications. NOTE: Increasing the gap decreases the dwell angle and vice-versa. Install the rotor and distributor cap.

—Synchronize the throttles and mixture of multiple carburetors (if so equipped) according to procedures given in the individual car sections.

—Adjust the idle speed, mixture, and idle quality, as specified in the car sections. Final idle adjustments should be made the with air cleaner installed. CAUTION: Due to strict emission control requirements on

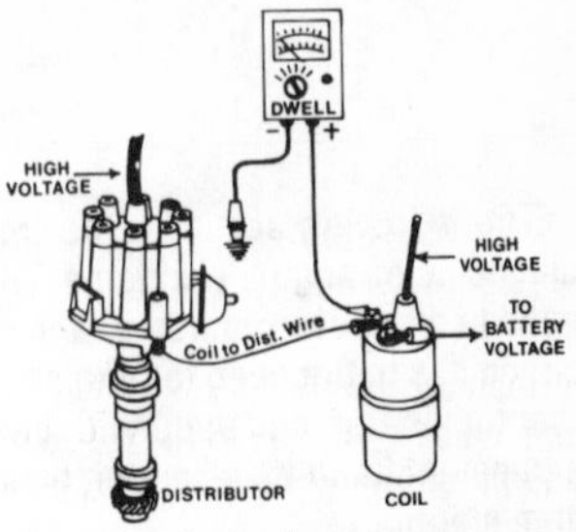

Dwell meter hook-up

1969 and later models, special test equipment (CO meter, SUN Tester) may be necessary to properly adjust idle mixture to specifications.

—Connect a timing light according to the manufacturer's specifications. Identify the proper timing marks with chalk or paint. NOTE: Luminescent (day-glo) paint is excellent for this purpose. Start the engine, and run it until it reaches operating temperature. Disconnect and plug any distributor vacuum lines, and adjust idle to the speed required to adjust timing, according to specifications. Loosen the distributor clamp and adjust timing to specifications by rotating the distributor in the engine. NOTE: To advance timing, rotate distributor opposite normal direction of rotor rotation, and vice-versa.

Troubleshooting

The following section is designed to aid in the rapid diagnosis of engine problems. The systematic format is used to diagnose problems ranging from engine starting difficulties to the need for engine overhaul. It is assumed that the user is equipped with basic hand tools and test equipment (tach-dwell meter, timing light, voltmeter, and ohm-meter).

Troubleshooting is divided into two sections. The first, General Diagnosis, is used to locate the problem area. In the second, Specific Diagnosis, the problem is systematically evaluated.

①—It is extremely difficult to evaluate vehicle noises. While the above are general definitions of engine noises, those starred (*) should be considered as possibly originating elsewhere in the car. To aid diagnosis, the following list considers other potential sources of these sounds.

Metallic grind:
Throwout bearing; transmission gears, bearings, or synchronizers; differential bearings, gears; something metallic in contact with brake drum or disc.
Metallic tap:
U-joints; fan-to-radiator (or shroud) contact.
Scrape:
Brake shoe or pad dragging; tire to body contact; suspension contacting undercarriage or exhaust; something non-metallic contacting brake shoe or drum.
Tick:
Transmission gears; differential gears; lack of radio suppression; resonant vibration of body panels; windshield wiper motor or transmission; heater motor and blower.
Squeal:
Brake shoe or pad not fully releasing; tires (excessive wear, uneven wear, improper inflation); front or rear wheel alignment (most commonly due to improper toe-in).
Hiss or whistle:
Wind leaks (body or window); heater motor and blower fan.
Roar:
Wheel bearings; wind leaks (body and window).

GENERAL DIAGNOSIS

PROBLEM: *Symptom*	*SPECIFIC DIAGNOSIS*: *See number listed*
Engine won't start:	
Starter doesn't turn	1.1, 2.1
Starter turns, engine doesn't	2.1
Starter turns engine very slowly	1.1, 2.4
Starter turns engine normally	3.1, 4.1
Starter turns engine very quickly	6.1
Engine fires intermittently	4.1
Engine fires consistently	5.1, 6.1
Engine runs poorly:	
Hard starting	3.1, 4.1, 5.1, 8.1
Rough idle	4.1, 5.1, 8.1
Stalling	3.1, 4.1, 5.1, 8.1
Engine dies at high speeds	4.1, 5.1
Hesitation (on acceleration from standing stop)	5.1, 8.1
Poor pickup	4.1, 5.1, 8.1
Lack of power	3.1, 4.1, 5.1, 8.1
Backfire through the carburetor	4.1, 8.1, 9.1
Backfire through the exhaust	4.1, 8.1, 9.1
Blue exhaust gases	6.1, 7.1
Black exhaust gases	5.1
Running on (after the ignition is shut off)	3.1, 8.1
Susceptible to moisture	4.1
Engine misfires under load	4.1, 7.1, 8.4, 9.1
Engine misfires at speed	4.1, 8.4
Engine misfires at idle	3.1, 4.1, 5.1, 7.1, 8.4

PROBLEM: *Symptoms*	*Probable Cause*
Engine noises: ①	
Metallic grind while starting	Starter drive not engaging completely
Constant grind or rumble	*Starter drive not releasing, worn main bearings
Constant knock	Worn connecting rod bearings
Knock under load	Fuel octane too low, worn connecting rod bearings
Double knock	Loosen piston pin
Metallic tip	*Collapsed or sticky valve lifter, excessive valve clearance, excessive end play in a rotating shaft
Scrape	*Fan belt contacting a stationary surface
Tick while starting	S.U. electric fuel pump (normal), starter brushes
Constant tick	*Generator brushes, shreaded fan belt
Squeal	*Improperly tensioned fan belt
Hiss or roar	*Steam escaping through a leak in the cooling system or the radiator overflow vent
Whistle	*Vacuum leak
Wheeze	Loose or cracked spark plug

SPECIFIC DIAGNOSIS

This section is arranged so that following each test, instructions are given to proceed to another, until a problem is diagnosed.

INDEX

Group		*Topic*
1	*	Battery
2	*	Cranking system
3	*	Primary electrical system
4	*	Secondary electrical system
5	*	Fuel system
6	*	Engine compression
7	**	Engine vacuum
8	**	Secondary electrical system
9	**	Valve train
10	**	Exhaust system
11	**	Cooling system
12	**	Engine lubrication

*—The engine need not be running.
**—The engine must be running.

SAMPLE SECTION

Test and Procedure	*Results and Indications*	*Proceed to*
4.1—Check for spark: Hold each spark plug wire approximately 1/4" from ground with gloves or a heavy, dry rag. Crank the engine and observe the spark.	→ If no spark is evident: →	4.2
	→ If spark is good in some cases: →	4.3
	→ If spark is good in all cases: →	4.6

DIAGNOSIS

1.1—Inspect the battery visually for case condition (corrosion, cracks) and water level.	If case is cracked, replace battery:	1.4
	If the case is intact, remove corrosion with a solution of baking soda and water (CAUTION: *do not get the solution into the battery*), and fill with water:	1.2
1.2—Check the battery cable connections: Insert a screwdriver between the battery post and the cable clamp. Turn the headlights on high beam, and observe them as the screwdriver is gently twisted to ensure good metal to metal contact.	If the lights brighten, remove and clean the clamp and post; coat the post with petroleum jelly, install and tighten the clamp:	1.4
	If no improvement is noted:	1.3

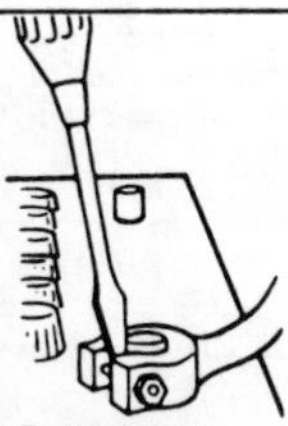

Testing battery cable connections using a screwdriver

1.3—Test the state of charge of the battery using an individual cell tester or hydrometer.

Spec. Grav. Reading	*Charged Condition*
1.260-1.280	Fully Charged
1.230-1.250	Three Quarter Charged
1.200-1.220	One Half Charged
1.170-1.190	One Quarter Charged
1.140-1.160	Just About Flat
1.110-1.130	All The Way Down

State of battery charge

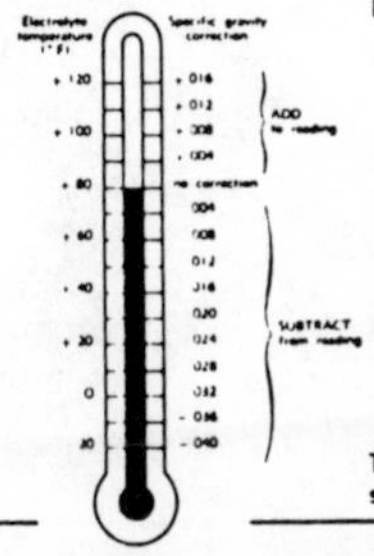

The effect of temperature on the specific gravity of battery electrolyte

If indicated, charge the battery. NOTE: *If no obvious reason exists for the low state of charge (i.e., battery age, prolonged storage), the charging system should be tested:* 1.4

Test and Procedure	*Results and Indications*	*Proceed to*
1.4—Visually inspect battery cables for cracking, bad connection to ground, or bad connection to starter.	If necessary, tighten connections or replace the cables:	2.1

Tests in Group 2 are performed with coil high tension lead disconnected to prevent accidental starting.

Test and Procedure	*Results and Indications*	*Proceed to*
2.1—Test the starter motor and solenoid: Connect a jumper from the battery post of the solenoid (or relay) to the starter post of the solenoid (or relay).	If starter turns the engine normally:	2.2
	If the starter buzzes, or turns the engine very slowly:	2.4
	If no response, replace the solenoid (or relay).	3.1
	If the starter turns, but the engine doesn't, ensure that the flywheel ring gear is intact. If the gear is undamaged, replace the starter drive.	3.1
2.2—Determine whether ignition override switches are functioning properly (clutch start switch, neutral safety switch), by connecting a jumper across the switch(es), and turning the ignition switch to "start".	If starter operates, adjust or replace switch:	3.1
	If the starter doesn't operate:	2.3
2.3—Check the ignition switch "start" position: Connect a 12V test lamp between the starter post of the solenoid (or relay) and ground. Turn the ignition switch to the "start" position, and jiggle the key. 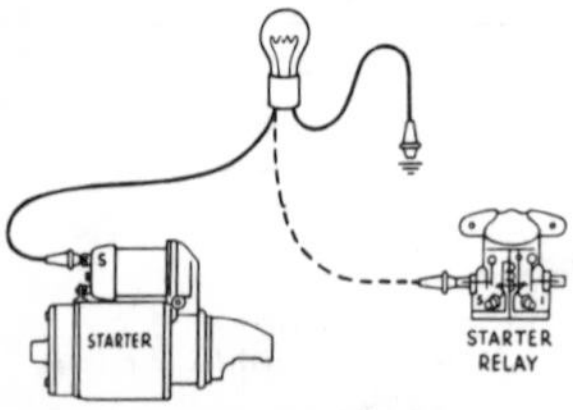 Checking the ignition switch "start" position	If the lamp doesn't light when the switch is turned, check the ignition switch for loose connections, cracked insulation, or broken wires. Repair or replace as necessary:	3.1
	If the lamp flickers when the key is jiggled, replace the ignition switch.	3.3
2.4—Remove and bench test the starter, according to specifications.	If the starter does not meet specifications, repair or replace as needed:	3.1
	If the starter is operating properly:	2.5
2.5—Determine whether the engine can turn freely: Remove the spark plugs, and check for water in the cylinders. Check for water on the dipstick, or oil in the radiator. Attempt to turn the engine using an 18″ flex drive and socket on the crankshaft pulley nut or bolt.	If the engine will turn freely only with the spark plugs out, and hydrostatic lock (water in the cylinders) is ruled out, check valve timing:	9.2
	If engine will not turn freely, and it is known that the clutch and transmission are free, the engine must be disassembled for further evaluation:	
3.1—Check the ignition switch "on" position: Connect a jumper wire between the distributor side of the coil and ground, and a 12V test lamp between the switch side of the coil and ground. Remove the high tension lead from the coil. Turn the ignition switch on and jiggle the key.	If the lamp lights:	3.2
	If the lamp flickers when the key is jiggled, replace the ignition switch:	3.3
	If the lamp doesn't light, check for loose or open connections. If none are found, remove the ignition switch and check for continuity. If the switch is faulty, replace it:	3.3

Tests and Procedures	*Results and Indications*	*Proceed to*
3.2—Check the ballast resistor or resistance wire for an open circuit, using an ohmmeter.	Replace the resistor or the resistance wire if the resistance is zero.	3.3
3.3—Visually inspect the breaker points for burning, pitting, or excessive wear. Gray coloring of the point contact surfaces is normal. Rotate the crankshaft until the contact heel rests on a high point of the distributor cam, and adjust the point gap to specifications.	If the breaker points are intact, clean the contact surfaces with fine emery cloth, and adjust the point gap to specifications. If pitted or worn, replace the points and condenser, and adjust the gap to specifications: NOTE: *Always lubricate the distributor cam according to manufacturer's recommendations when servicing the breaker points.*	3.4
3.4—Connect a dwell meter between the distributor primary lead and ground. Crank the engine and observe the point dwell angle.	If necessary, adjust the point dwell angle: NOTE: *Increasing the point gap decreases the dwell angle, and vice-versa.*	3.6
	If dwell meter shows little or no reading:	3.5

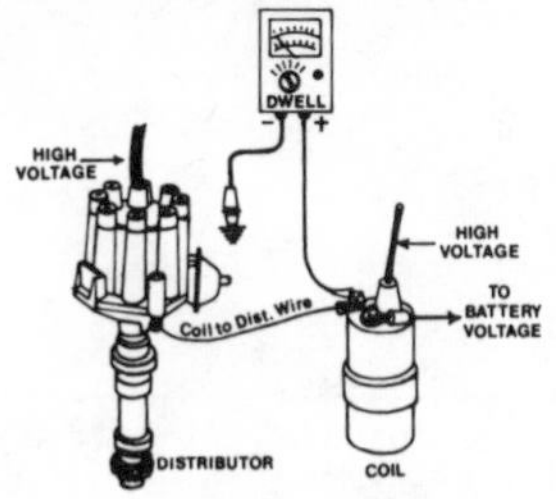

Dwell meter hook-up

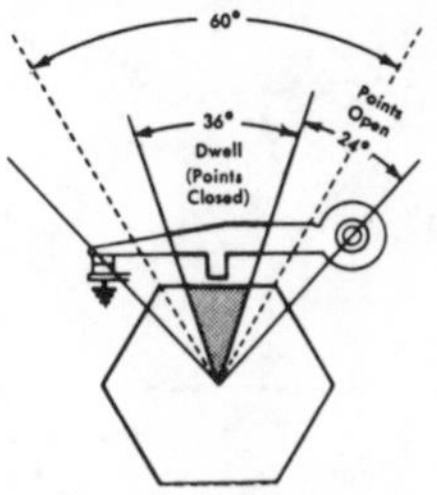

Dwell angle

Tests and Procedures	*Results and Indications*	*Proceed to*
3.5—Check the condenser for short: Connect an ohmmeter across the condenser body and the pigtail lead.	If any reading other than infinite resistance is noted, replace the condenser:	3.6

Checking the condenser for short
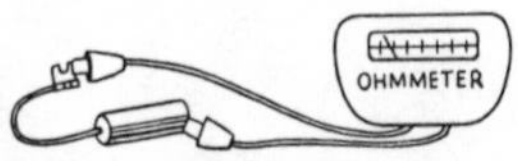

Tests and Procedures	*Results and Indications*	*Proceed to*
3.6—Test the coil primary resistance: Connect an ohmmeter across the coil primary terminals, and read the resistance on the low scale. Note whether an external ballast resistor or resistance wire is utilized.	Coils utilizing ballast resistors or resistance wires should have approximately 1.0Ω resistance; coils with internal resistors should have approximately 4.0Ω resistance. If values far from the above are noted, replace the coil:	4.1

Testing the coil primary resistance
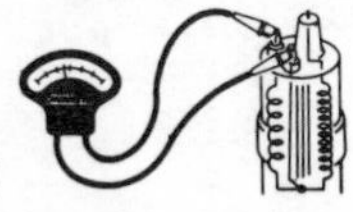

Tests and Procedures	*Results and Indications*	*Proceed to*
4.1—Check for spark: Hold each spark plug wire approximately ¼″ from ground with gloves or a heavy, dry rag. Crank the engine, and observe the spark.	If no spark is evident:	4.2
	If spark is good in some cylinders:	4.3
	If spark is good in all cylinders:	4.6
4.2—Check for spark at the coil high tension lead: Remove the coil high tension lead from the distributor and position it approximately ¼″ from ground. Crank the engine and observe spark. CAUTION: *This test should not be performed on cars equipped with transistorized ignition.*	If the spark is good and consistent:	4.3
	If the spark is good but intermittent, test the primary electrical system starting at 3.3:	3.3
	If the spark is weak or non-existent, replace the coil high tension lead, clean and tighten all connections and retest. If no improvement is noted:	4.4

Test and Procedure	Results and Indications	Proceed to
4.3—Visually inspect the distributor cap and rotor for burned or corroded contacts, cracks, carbon tracks, or moisture. Also check the fit of the rotor on the distributor shaft (where applicable).	If moisture is present, dry thoroughly, and retest per 4.1:	4.1
	If burned or excessively corroded contacts, cracks, or carbon tracks are noted, replace the defective part(s) and retest per 4.1:	4.1
	If the rotor and cap appear intact, or are only slightly corroded, clean the contacts thoroughly (including the cap towers and spark plug wire ends) and retest per 4.1:	
	If the spark is good in all cases:	4.6
	If the spark is poor in all cases:	4.5
4.4—Check the coil secondary resistance: Connect an ohmmeter across the distributor side of the coil and the coil tower. Read the resistance on the high scale of the ohmmeter. 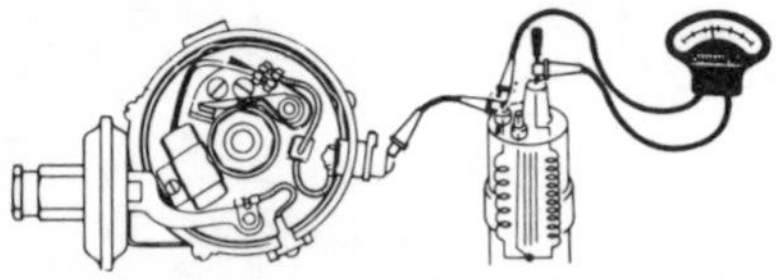 Testing the coil secondary resistance	The resistance of a satisfactory coil should be between 4KΩ and 10KΩ. If the resistance is considerably higher (i.e., 40KΩ) replace the coil, and retest per 4.1: NOTE: *This does not apply to high performance coils.*	4.1
4.5—Visually inspect the spark plug wires for cracking or brittleness. Ensure that no two wires are positioned so as to cause induction firing (adjacent and parallel). Remove each wire, one by one, and check resistance with an ohmmeter.	Replace any cracked or brittle wires. If any of the wires are defective, replace the entire set. Replace any wires with excessive resistance (over 8000Ω per foot for suppression wire), and separate any wires that might cause induction firing.	4.6
4.6—Remove the spark plugs, noting the cylinders from which they were removed, and evaluate according to the chart below.	See below.	See below.

	Condition	Cause	Remedy	Proceed to
	Electrodes eroded, light brown deposits.	Normal wear. Normal wear is indicated by approximately .001″ wear per 1000 miles.	Clean and regap the spark plug if wear is not excessive: Replace the spark plug if excessively worn:	4.7
	Carbon fouling (black, dry, fluffy deposits).	If present on one or two plugs:		
		Faulty high tension lead(s).	Test the high tension leads:	4.5
		Burnt or sticking valve(s).	Check the valve train: (Clean and regap the plugs in either case.)	9.1
		If present on most or all plugs: Overly rich fuel mixture, due to restricted air filter, improper carburetor adjustment, improper choke or heat riser adjustment or operation.	Check the fuel system:	5.1

	Condition	Cause	Remedy	Proceed to
	Oil fouling (wet black deposits)	Worn engine components. NOTE: *Oil fouling may occur in new or recently rebuilt engines until broken in.*	Check engine vacuum and compression:	6.1
			Replace with new spark plug	
	Lead fouling (gray, black, tan, or yellow deposits, which appear glazed or cinder-like).	Combustion by-products.	Clean and regap the plugs: (Use plugs of a different heat range if the problem recurs.)	4.7
	Gap bridging (deposits lodged between the electrodes).	Incomplete combustion, or transfer of deposits from the combustion chamber.	Replace the spark plugs:	4.7
	Overheating (burnt electrodes, and extremely white insulator with small black spots).	Ignition timing advanced too far.	Adjust timing to specifications:	8.2
		Overly lean fuel mixture.	Check the fuel system:	5.1
		Spark plugs not seated properly.	Clean spark plug seat and install a new gasket washer: (Replace the spark plugs in all cases.)	4.7
	Fused spot deposits on the insulator.	Combustion chamber blow-by.	Clean and regap the spark plugs:	4.7
	Pre-ignition (melted or severely burned electrodes, blistered or cracked insulators, or metallic deposits on the insulator).	Incorrect spark plug heat range.	Replace with plugs of the proper heat range:	4.7
		Ignition timing advanced too far.	Adjust timing to specifications:	8.2
		Spark plugs not being cooled efficiently.	Clean the spark plug seat, and check the cooling system:	11.1
		Fuel mixture too lean.	Check the fuel system:	5.1
		Poor compression.	Check compression:	6.1
		Fuel grade too low.	Use higher octane fuel:	4.7

Test and Procedure	Results and Indications	Proceed to
4.7—Determine the static ignition timing: Using the flywheel or crankshaft pulley timing marks as a guide, locate top dead center on the *compression* stroke of the No. 1 cylinder. Remove the distributor cap.	Adjust the distributor so that the rotor points toward the No. 1 tower in the distributor cap, and the points are just opening:	4.8

Test and Procedure	*Results and Indications*	*Proceed to*
4.8—Check coil polarity: Connect a voltmeter negative lead to the coil high tension lead, and the positive lead to ground (NOTE: *reverse the hook-up for positive ground cars*). Crank the engine momentarily.  Checking coil polarity	If the voltmeter reads up-scale, the polarity is correct:	5.1
	If the voltmeter reads down-scale, reverse the coil polarity (switch the primary leads):	5.1
5.1—Determine that the air filter is functioning efficiently: Hold paper elements up to a strong light, and attempt to see light through the filter.	Clean permanent air filters in gasoline (or manufacturer's recommendation), and allow to dry. Replace paper elements through which light cannot be seen:	5.2
5.2—Determine whether a flooding condition exists: Flooding is identified by a strong gasoline odor, and excessive gasoline present in the throttle bore(s) of the carburetor.	If flooding is not evident:	5.3
	If flooding is evident, permit the gasoline to dry for a few moments and restart.	
	If flooding doesn't recur:	5.6
	If flooding is persistant:	5.5
5.3—Check that fuel is reaching the carburetor: Detach the fuel line at the carburetor inlet. Hold the end of the line in a cup (not styrofoam), and crank the engine.	If fuel flows smoothly:	5.6
	If fuel doesn't flow (NOTE: *Make sure that there is fuel in the tank*), or flows erratically:	5.4
5.4—Test the fuel pump: Disconnect all fuel lines from the fuel pump. Hold a finger over the input fitting, crank the engine (with electric pump, turn the ignition or pump on); and feel for suction.	If suction is evident, blow out the fuel line to the tank with low pressure compressed air until bubbling is heard from the fuel filler neck. Also blow out the carburetor fuel line (both ends disconnected):	5.6
	If no suction is evident, replace or repair the fuel pump:	5.6
	NOTE: *Repeated oil fouling of the spark plugs, or a no-start condition, could be the result of a ruptured vacuum booster pump diaphragm, through which oil or gasoline is being drawn into the intake manifold (where applicable).*	
5.5—Check the needle and seat: Tap the carburetor in the area of the needle and seat.	If flooding stops, a gasoline additive (e.g., Gumout) will often cure the problem:	5.6
	If flooding continues, check the fuel pump for excessive pressure at the carburetor (according to specifications). If the pressure is normal, the needle and seat must be removed and checked, and/or the float level adjusted:	5.6
5.6—Test the accelerator pump by looking into the throttle bores while operating the throttle.	If the accelerator pump appears to be operating normally:	5.7
	If the accelerator pump is not operating, the pump must be reconditioned. Where possible, service the pump with the carburetor(s) installed on the engine. If necessary, remove the carburetor. Prior to removal:	5.7
5.7—Determine whether the carburetor main fuel system is functioning: Spray a commercial starting fluid into the carburetor while attempting to start the engine.	If the engine starts, runs for a few seconds, and dies:	5.8
	If the engine doesn't start:	6.1

Test and Procedures	*Results and Indications*	*Proceed to*
5.8—Uncommon fuel system malfunctions: See below:	If the problem is solved:	6.1
	If the problem remains, remove and recondition the carburetor.	

Condition	*Indication*	*Test*	*Usual Weather Conditions*	*Remedy*
Vapor lock	Car will not restart shortly after running.	Cool the components of the fuel system until the engine starts.	Hot to very hot	Ensure that the exhaust manifold heat control valve is operating. Check with the vehicle manufacturer for the recommended solution to vapor lock on the model in question.
Carburetor icing	Car will not idle, stalls at low speeds.	Visually inspect the throttle plate area of the throttle bores for frost.	High humidity, 32-40° F.	Ensure that the exhaust manifold heat control valve is operating, and that the intake manifold heat riser is not blocked.
Water in the fuel	Engine sputters and stalls; may not start.	Pump a small amount of fuel into a glass jar. Allow to stand, and inspect for droplets or a layer of water.	High humidity, extreme temperature changes.	For droplets, use one or two cans of commercial gas dryer (Dry Gas) For a layer of water, the tank must be drained, and the fuel lines blown out with compressed air.

Test and Procedure	*Results and Indications*	*Proceed to*
6.1—Test engine compression: Remove all spark plugs. Insert a compression gauge into a spark plug port, crank the engine to obtain the maximum reading, and record.	If compression is within limits on all cylinders:	7.1
	If gauge reading is extremely low on all cylinders:	6.2
	If gauge reading is low on one or two cylinders:	6.2
	(If gauge readings are identical and low on two or more adjacent cylinders, the head gasket must be replaced.)	

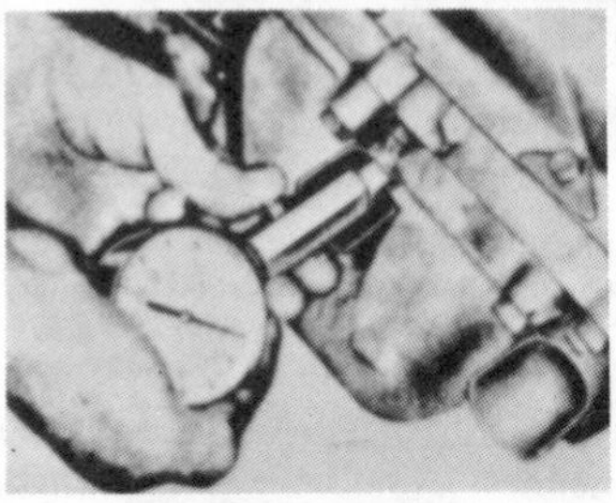

Testing compression
(© Chevrolet Div. G.M. Corp.)

Maxi. Press. Lbs. Sq. In.	*Min. Press. Lbs. Sq. In.*	*Maxi. Press. Lbs. Sq. In.*	*Min. Press. Lbs. Sq. In.*	*Max. Press. Lbs. Sq. In.*	*Min. Press. Lbs. Sq. In.*	*Max. Press. Lbs. Sq. In.*	*Min. Press. Lbs. Sq. In.*
134	101	162	121	188	141	214	160
136	102	164	123	190	142	216	162
138	104	166	124	192	144	218	163
140	105	168	126	194	145	220	165
142	107	170	127	196	147	222	166
146	110	172	129	198	148	224	168
148	111	174	131	200	150	226	169
150	113	176	132	202	151	228	171
152	114	178	133	204	153	230	172
154	115	180	135	206	154	232	174
156	117	182	136	208	156	234	175
158	118	184	138	210	157	236	177
160	120	186	140	212	158	238	178

Compression pressure limits
(© Buick Div. G.M. Corp.)

Test and Procedure	*Results and Indications*	*Proceed to*
6.2—Test engine compression (wet): Squirt approximately 30 cc. of engine oil into each cylinder, and retest per 6.1.	If the readings improve, worn or cracked rings or broken pistons are indicated:	Next Chapter
	If the readings do not improve, burned or excessively carboned valves or a jumped timing chain are indicated:	7.1
	NOTE: *A jumped timing chain is often indicated by difficult cranking.*	

Test and Procedure	*Results and Indications*	*Proceed to*
7.1—Perform a vacuum check of the engine: Attach a vacuum gauge to the intake manifold beyond the throttle plate. Start the engine, and observe the action of the needle over the range of engine speeds.	See below.	See below

	Reading	*Indications*	*Proceed to*
	Steady, from 17-22 in. Hg.	Normal.	8.1
	Low and steady.	Late ignition or valve timing, or low compression:	6.1
	Very low	Vacuum leak:	7.2
	Needle fluctuates as engine speed increases.	Ignition miss, blown cylinder head gasket, leaking valve or weak valve spring:	6.1, 8.3
	Gradual drop in reading at idle.	Excessive back pressure in the exhaust system:	10.1
	Intermittent fluctuation at idle.	Ignition miss, sticking valve:	8.3, 9.1
	Drifting needle.	Improper idle mixture adjustment, carburetors not synchronized (where applicable), or minor intake leak. Synchronize the carburetors, adjust the idle, and retest. If the condition persists:	7.2
	High and steady.	Early ignition timing:	8.2

7.2—Attach a vacuum gauge per 7.1, and test for an intake manifold leak. Squirt a small amount of oil around the intake manifold gaskets, carburetor gaskets, plugs and fittings. Observe the action of the vacuum gauge.	If the reading improves, replace the indicated gasket, or seal the indicated fitting or plug:	8.1
	If the reading remains low:	7.3
7.3—Test all vacuum hoses and accessories for leaks as described in 7.2. Also check the carburetor body (dashpots, automatic choke mechanism, throttle shafts) for leaks in the same manner.	If the reading improves, service or replace the offending part(s):	8.1
	If the reading remains low:	6.1

Test and Procedure	Results and Indications	Proceed to
8.1—Check the point dwell angle: Connect a dwell meter between the distributor primary wire and ground. Start the engine, and observe the dwell angle from idle to 3000 rpm.	If necessary, adjust the dwell angle. NOTE: *Increasing the point gap reduces the dwell angle and vice-versa.* If the dwell angle moves outside specifications as engine speed increases, the distributor should be removed and checked for cam accuracy, shaft endplay and concentricity, bushing wear, and adequate point arm tension (NOTE: *Most of these items may be checked with the distributor installed in the engine, using an oscilloscope*):	8.2
8.2—Connect a timing light (per manufacturer's recommendation) and check the dynamic ignition timing. Disconnect and plug the vacuum hose(s) to the distributor if specified, start the engine, and observe the timing marks at the specified engine speed.	If the timing is not correct, adjust to specifications by rotating the distributor in the engine: (Advance timing by rotating distributor opposite normal direction of rotor rotation, retard timing by rotating distributor in same direction as rotor rotation.)	8.3
8.3—Check the operation of the distributor advance mechanism(s): To test the mechanical advance, disconnect all but the mechanical advance, and observe the timing marks with a timing light as the engine speed is increased from idle. If the mark moves smoothly, without hesitation, it may be assumed that the mechanical advance is functioning properly. To test vacuum advance and/or retard systems, alternately crimp and release the vacuum line, and observe the timing mark for movement. If movement is noted, the system is operating.	If the systems are functioning:	8.4
	If the systems are not functioning, remove the distributor, and test on a distributor tester:	8.4
8.4—Locate an ignition miss: With the engine running, remove each spark plug wire, one by one, until one is found that doesn't cause the engine to roughen and slow down.	When the missing cylinder is identified:	4.1
9.1—Evaluate the valve train: Remove the valve cover, and ensure that the valves are adjusted to specifications. A mechanic's stethoscope may be used to aid in the diagnosis of the valve train. By pushing the probe on or near push rods or rockers, valve noise often can be isolated. A timing light also may be used to diagnose valve problems. Connect the light according to manufacturer's recommendations, and start the engine. Vary the firing moment of the light by increasing the engine speed (and therefore the ignition advance), and moving the trigger from cylinder to cylinder. Observe the movement of each valve.	See below	See below

Observation	*Probable Cause*	*Remedy*	*Proceed to*
Metallic tap heard through the stethoscope.	Sticking hydraulic lifter or excessive valve clearance.	Adjust valve. If tap persists, remove and replace the lifter:	10.1
Metallic tap through the stethoscope, able to push the rocker arm (lifter side) down by hand.	Collapsed valve lifter.	Remove and replace the lifter:	10.1
Erratic, irregular motion of the valve stem.*	Sticking valve, burned valve.	Recondition the valve and/or valve guide:	Next Chapter
Eccentric motion of the pushrod at the rocker arm.*	Bent pushrod.	Replace the pushrod:	10.1
Valve retainer bounces as the valve closes.*	Weak valve spring or damper.	Remove and test the spring and damper. Replace if necessary:	10.1

*—When observed with a timing light.

Test and Procedure	*Results and Indications*	*Proceed to*
9.2—Check the valve timing: Locate top dead center of the No. 1 piston, and install a degree wheel or tape on the crankshaft pulley or damper with zero corresponding to an index mark on the engine. Rotate the crankshaft in its direction of rotation, and observe the opening of the No. 1 cylinder intake valve. The opening should correspond with the correct mark on the degree wheel according to specifications.	If the timing is not correct, the timing cover must be removed for further investigation:	
10.1—Determine whether the exhaust manifold heat control valve is operating: Operate the valve by hand to determine whether it is free to move. If the valve is free, run the engine to operating temperature and observe the action of the valve, to ensure that it is opening.	If the valve sticks, spray it with a suitable solvent, open and close the valve to free it, and retest. If the valve functions properly:	 10.2
	If the valve does not free, or does not operate, replace the valve:	10.2
10.2—Ensure that there are no exhaust restrictions: Visually inspect the exhaust system for kinks, dents, or crushing. Also note that gasses are flowing freely from the tailpipe at all engine speeds, indicating no restriction in the muffler or resonator.	Replace any damaged portion of the system:	11.1
11.1—Visually inspect the fan belt for glazing, cracks, and fraying, and replace if necessary. Tighten the belt so that the longest span has approximately ½″ play at its midpoint under thumb pressure.	Replace or tighten the fan belt as necessary:	11.2

Checking the fan belt tension
(© Nissan Motor Co. Ltd.)

Test and Procedure	*Results and Indications*	*Proceed to*
11.2—Check the fluid level of the cooling system.	If full or slightly low, fill as necessary:	11.5
	If extremely low:	11.3
11.3—Visually inspect the external portions of the cooling system (radiator, radiator hoses, thermostat elbow, water pump seals, heater hoses, etc.) for leaks. If none are found, pressurize the cooling system to 14-15 psi.	If cooling system holds the pressure:	11.5
	If cooling system loses pressure rapidly, reinspect external parts of the system for leaks under pressure. If none are found, check dipstick for coolant in crankcase. If no coolant is present, but pressure loss continues:	11.4
	If coolant is evident in crankcase, remove cylinder head(s), and check gasket(s). If gaskets are intact, block and cylinder head(s) should be checked for cracks or holes. If the gasket(s) is blown, replace, and purge the crankcase of coolant:	12.6
	NOTE: *Occasionally, due to atmospheric and driving conditions, condensation of water can occur in the crankcase. This causes the oil to appear milky white. To remedy, run the engine until hot, and change the oil and oil filter.*	
11.4—Check for combustion leaks into the cooling system: Pressurize the cooling system as above. Start the engine, and observe the pressure gauge. If the needle fluctuates, remove each spark plug wire, one by one, noting which cylinder(s) reduce or eliminate the fluctuation.  Radiator pressure tester (© American Motors Corp.)	Cylinders which reduce or eliminate the fluctuation, when the spark plug wire is removed, are leaking into the cooling system. Replace the head gasket on the affected cylinder bank(s).	
11.5—Check the radiator pressure cap: Attach a radiator pressure tester to the radiator cap (wet the seal prior to installation). Quickly pump up the pressure, noting the point at which the cap releases.  Testing the radiator pressure cap (© American Motors Corp.)	If the cap releases within ± 1 psi of the specified rating, it is operating properly:	11.6
	If the cap releases at more than ± 1 psi of the specified rating, it should be replaced:	11.6
11.6—Test the thermostat: Start the engine cold, remove the radiator cap, and insert a thermometer into the radiator. Allow the engine to idle. After a short while, there will be a sudden, rapid increase in coolant temperature. The temperature at which this sharp rise stops is the thermostat opening temperature.	If the thermostat opens at or about the specified temperature:	11.7
	If the temperature doesn't increase: (If the temperature increases slowly and gradually, replace the thermostat.)	11.7

Test and Procedure	*Results and Indication*	*Proceed to*
11.7—Check the water pump: Remove the thermostat elbow and the thermostat, disconnect the coil high tension lead (to prevent starting), and crank the engine momentarily.	If coolant flows, replace the thermostat and retest per 11.6:	11.6
	If coolant doesn't flow, reverse flush the cooling system to alleviate any blockage that might exist. If system is not blocked, and coolant will not flow, recondition the water pump.	—
12.1—Check the oil pressure gauge or warning light: If the gauge shows low pressure, or the light is on, for no obvious reason, remove the oil pressure sender. Install an accurate oil pressure gauge and run the engine momentarily.	If oil pressure builds normally, run engine for a few moments to determine that it is functioning normally, and replace the sender.	—
	If the pressure remains low:	12.2
	If the pressure surges:	12.3
	If the oil pressure is zero:	12.3
12.2—Visually inspect the oil: If the oil is watery or very thin, milky, or foamy, replace the oil and oil filter.	If the oil is normal:	12.3
	If after replacing oil the pressure remains low:	12.3
	If after replacing oil the pressure becomes normal:	—
12.3—Inspect the oil pressure relief valve and spring, to ensure that it is not sticking or stuck. Remove and thoroughly clean the valve, spring, and the valve body.  Oil pressure relief valve (© British Leyland Motors)	If the oil pressure improves:	—
	If no improvement is noted:	12.4
12.4—Check to ensure that the oil pump is not cavitating (sucking air instead of oil): See that the crankcase is neither over nor underfull, and that the pickup in the sump is in the proper position and free from sludge.	Fill or drain the crankcase to the proper capacity, and clean the pickup screen in solvent if necessary. If no improvement is noted:	12.5
12.5—Inspect the oil pump drive and the oil pump:	If the pump drive or the oil pump appear to be defective, service as necessary and retest per 12.1:	12.1
	If the pump drive and pump appear to be operating normally, the engine should be disassembled to determine where blockage exists:	Next Chapter
12.6—Purge the engine of ethylene glycol coolant: Completely drain the crankcase and the oil filter. Obtain a commercial butyl cellosolve base solvent, designated for this purpose, and follow the instructions precisely. Following this, install a new oil filter and refill the crankcase with the proper weight oil. The next oil and filter change should follow shortly thereafter (1000 miles).		

Carburetor Troubleshooting

TROUBLESHOOTING

NOTE: Carburetor problems cannot be isolated effectively unless all other engine systems are functioning correctly and the engine is properly tuned.

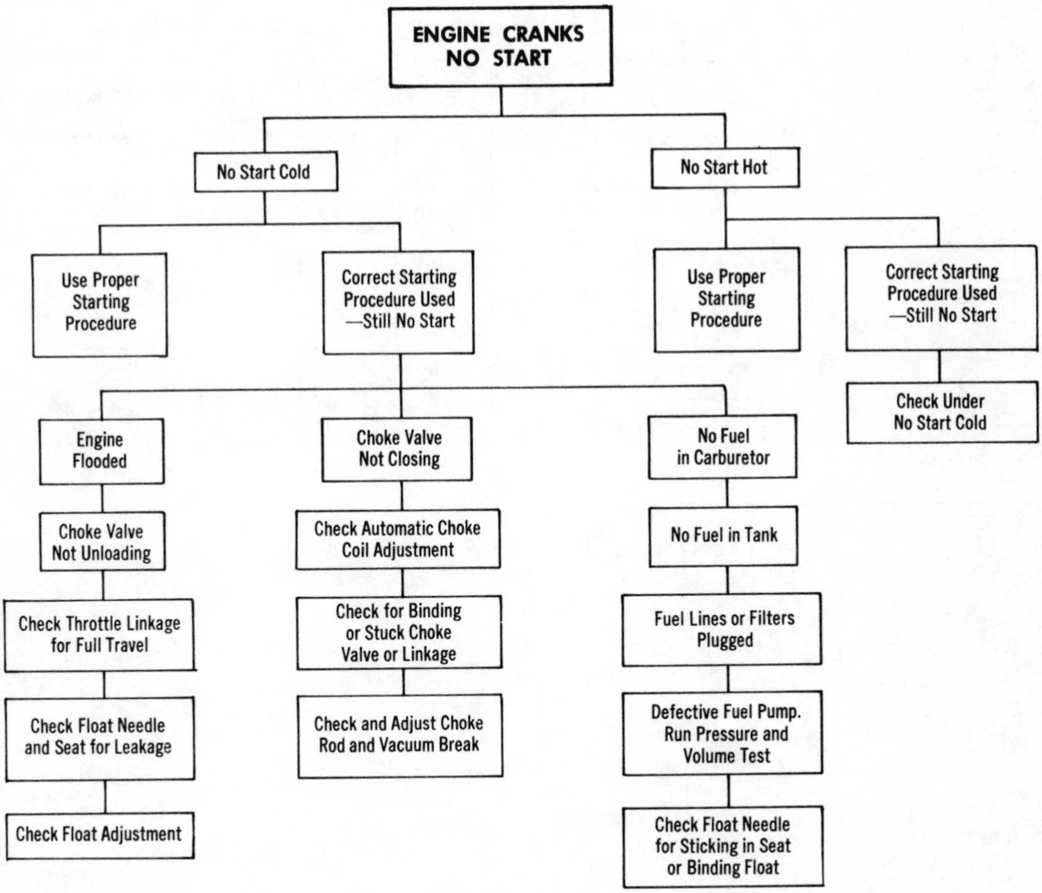

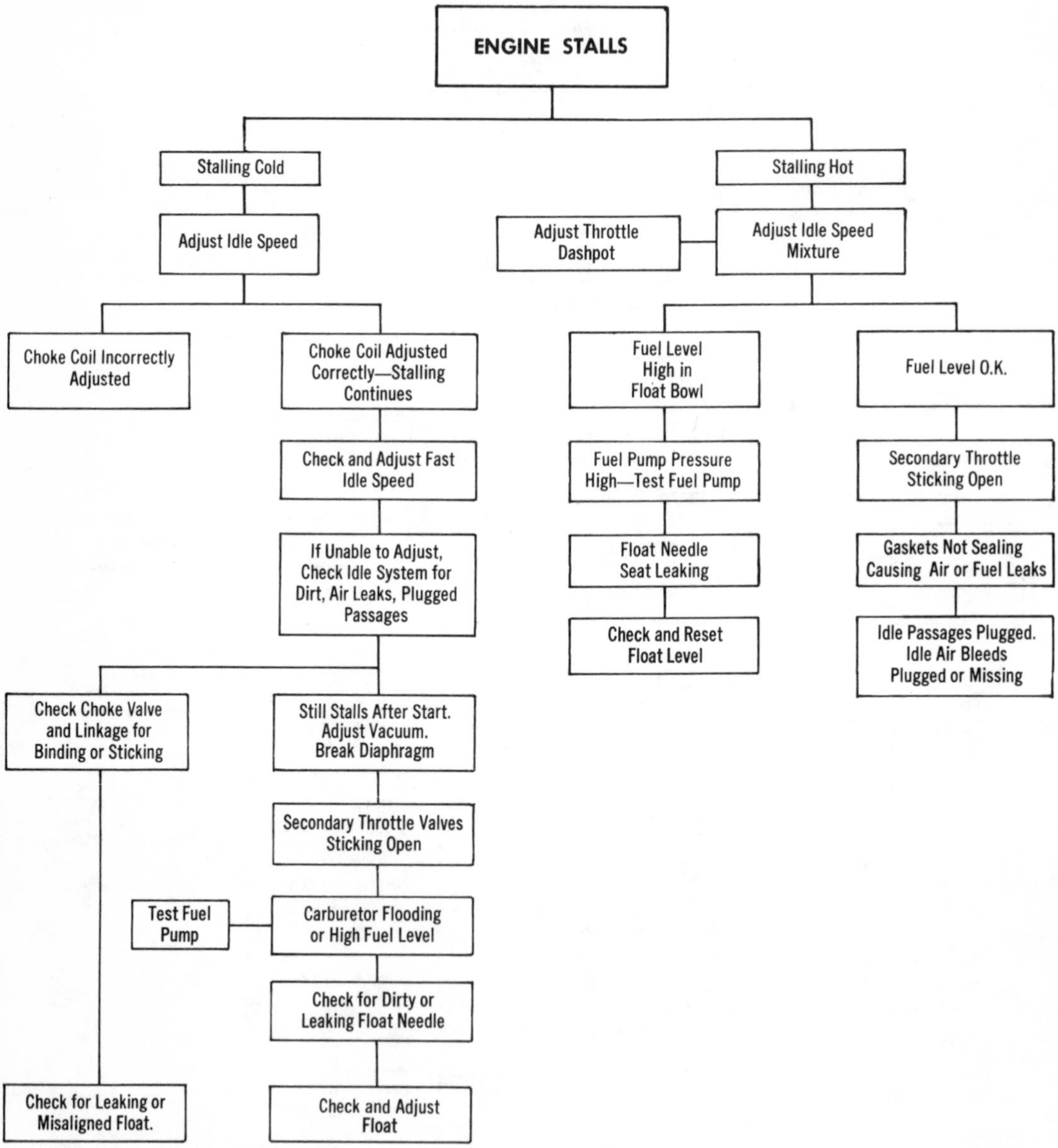
ENGINE STALLS
Stalling Cold
Adjust Idle Speed
Choke Coil Incorrectly Adjusted
Choke Coil Adjusted Correctly—Stalling Continues
Check and Adjust Fast Idle Speed
If Unable to Adjust, Check Idle System for Dirt, Air Leaks, Plugged Passages
Check Choke Valve and Linkage for Binding or Sticking
Check for Leaking or Misaligned Float.
Still Stalls After Start. Adjust Vacuum. Break Diaphragm
Secondary Throttle Valves Sticking Open
Test Fuel Pump
Carburetor Flooding or High Fuel Level
Check for Dirty or Leaking Float Needle
Check and Adjust Float
Stalling Hot
Adjust Throttle Dashpot
Adjust Idle Speed Mixture
Fuel Level High in Float Bowl
Fuel Pump Pressure High—Test Fuel Pump
Float Needle Seat Leaking
Check and Reset Float Level
Fuel Level O.K.
Secondary Throttle Sticking Open
Gaskets Not Sealing Causing Air or Fuel Leaks
Idle Passages Plugged. Idle Air Bleeds Plugged or Missing

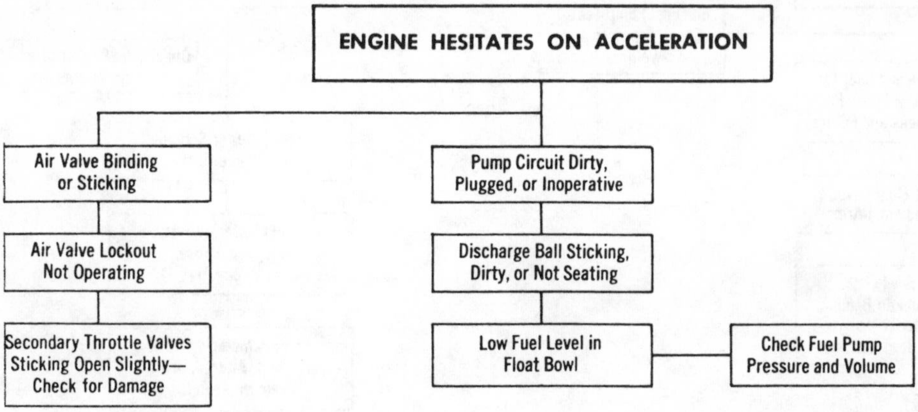
ENGINE HESITATES ON ACCELERATION
Air Valve Binding or Sticking
Air Valve Lockout Not Operating
Secondary Throttle Valves Sticking Open Slightly—Check for Damage
Pump Circuit Dirty, Plugged, or Inoperative
Discharge Ball Sticking, Dirty, or Not Seating
Low Fuel Level in Float Bowl
Check Fuel Pump Pressure and Volume

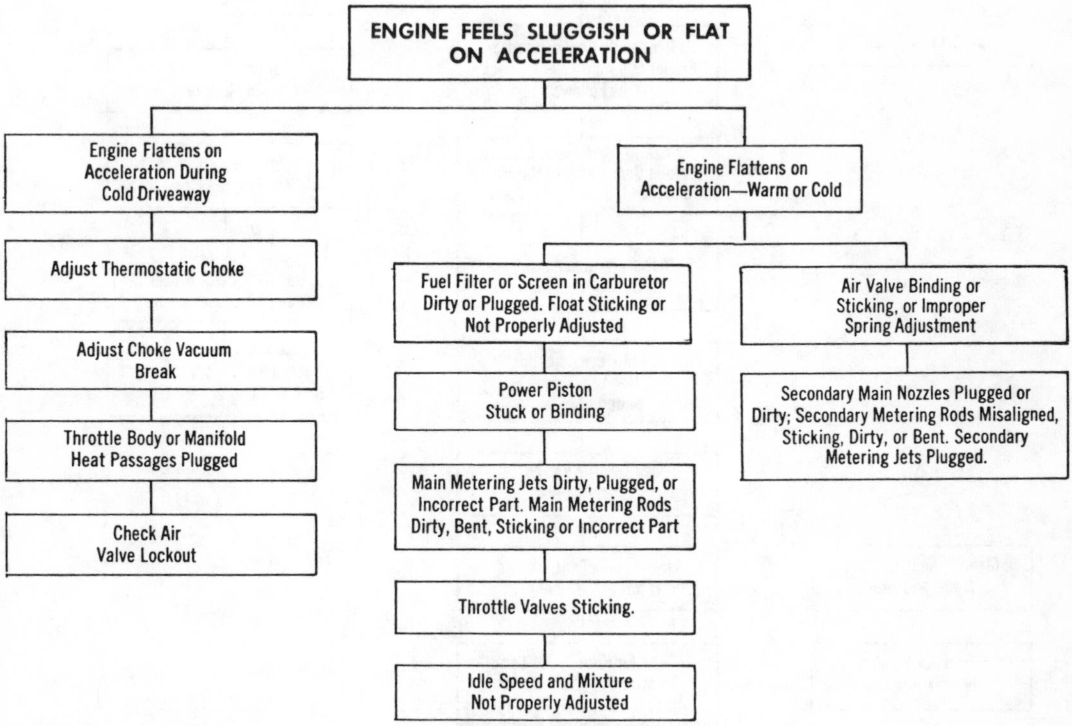
ENGINE FEELS SLUGGISH OR FLAT ON ACCELERATION
Engine Flattens on Acceleration During Cold Driveaway
Adjust Thermostatic Choke
Adjust Choke Vacuum Break
Throttle Body or Manifold Heat Passages Plugged
Check Air Valve Lockout
Engine Flattens on Acceleration—Warm or Cold
Fuel Filter or Screen in Carburetor Dirty or Plugged. Float Sticking or Not Properly Adjusted
Power Piston Stuck or Binding
Main Metering Jets Dirty, Plugged, or Incorrect Part. Main Metering Rods Dirty, Bent, Sticking or Incorrect Part
Throttle Valves Sticking.
Idle Speed and Mixture Not Properly Adjusted
Air Valve Binding or Sticking, or Improper Spring Adjustment
Secondary Main Nozzles Plugged or Dirty; Secondary Metering Rods Misaligned, Sticking, Dirty, or Bent. Secondary Metering Jets Plugged.

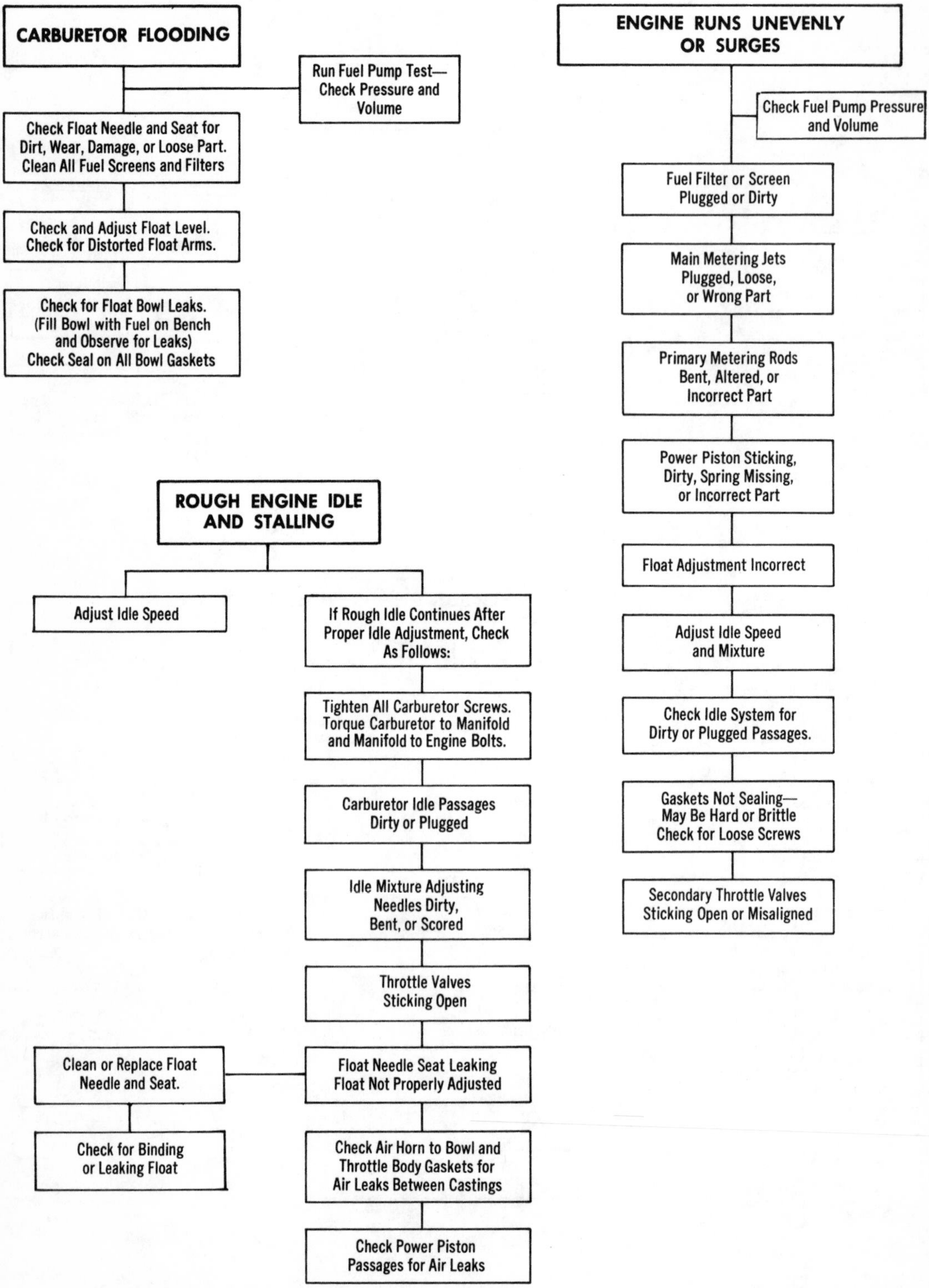
CARBURETOR FLOODING
Run Fuel Pump Test—Check Pressure and Volume
Check Float Needle and Seat for Dirt, Wear, Damage, or Loose Part. Clean All Fuel Screens and Filters
Check and Adjust Float Level. Check for Distorted Float Arms.
Check for Float Bowl Leaks. (Fill Bowl with Fuel on Bench and Observe for Leaks) Check Seal on All Bowl Gaskets
ENGINE RUNS UNEVENLY OR SURGES
Check Fuel Pump Pressure and Volume
Fuel Filter or Screen Plugged or Dirty
Main Metering Jets Plugged, Loose, or Wrong Part
Primary Metering Rods Bent, Altered, or Incorrect Part
Power Piston Sticking, Dirty, Spring Missing, or Incorrect Part
Float Adjustment Incorrect
Adjust Idle Speed and Mixture
Check Idle System for Dirty or Plugged Passages.
Gaskets Not Sealing—May Be Hard or Brittle Check for Loose Screws
Secondary Throttle Valves Sticking Open or Misaligned
ROUGH ENGINE IDLE AND STALLING
Adjust Idle Speed
If Rough Idle Continues After Proper Idle Adjustment, Check As Follows:
Tighten All Carburetor Screws. Torque Carburetor to Manifold and Manifold to Engine Bolts.
Carburetor Idle Passages Dirty or Plugged
Idle Mixture Adjusting Needles Dirty, Bent, or Scored
Throttle Valves Sticking Open
Float Needle Seat Leaking Float Not Properly Adjusted
Clean or Replace Float Needle and Seat.
Check for Binding or Leaking Float
Check Air Horn to Bowl and Throttle Body Gaskets for Air Leaks Between Castings
Check Power Piston Passages for Air Leaks

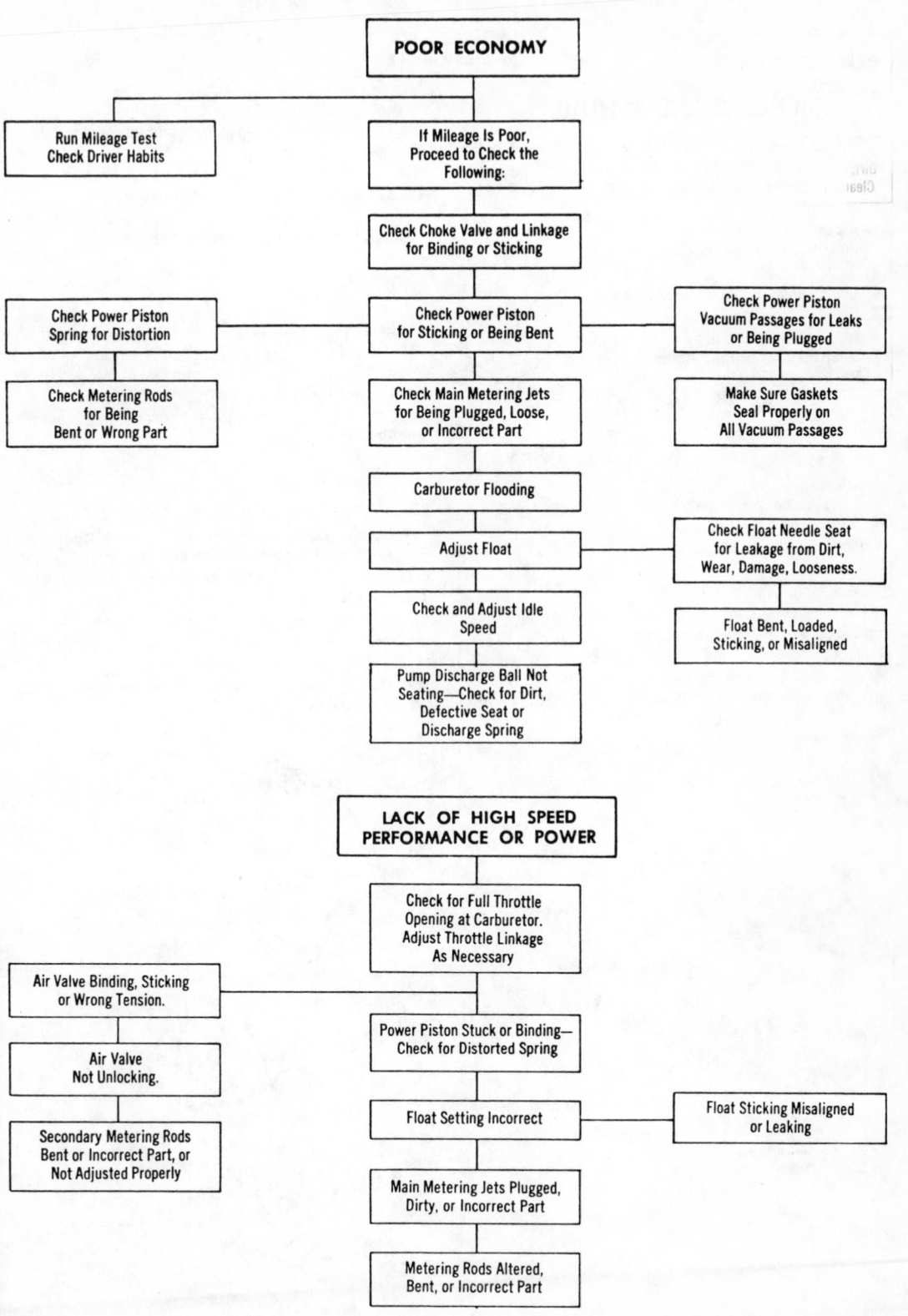

POOR ECONOMY

- Run Mileage Test Check Driver Habits
- If Mileage Is Poor, Proceed to Check the Following:
  - Check Choke Valve and Linkage for Binding or Sticking
  - Check Power Piston for Sticking or Being Bent
    - Check Power Piston Spring for Distortion
      - Check Metering Rods for Being Bent or Wrong Part
    - Check Power Piston Vacuum Passages for Leaks or Being Plugged
      - Make Sure Gaskets Seal Properly on All Vacuum Passages
  - Check Main Metering Jets for Being Plugged, Loose, or Incorrect Part
  - Carburetor Flooding
  - Adjust Float
    - Check Float Needle Seat for Leakage from Dirt, Wear, Damage, Looseness.
      - Float Bent, Loaded, Sticking, or Misaligned
  - Check and Adjust Idle Speed
  - Pump Discharge Ball Not Seating—Check for Dirt, Defective Seat or Discharge Spring

LACK OF HIGH SPEED PERFORMANCE OR POWER

- Check for Full Throttle Opening at Carburetor. Adjust Throttle Linkage As Necessary
  - Air Valve Binding, Sticking or Wrong Tension.
    - Air Valve Not Unlocking.
      - Secondary Metering Rods Bent or Incorrect Part, or Not Adjusted Properly
- Power Piston Stuck or Binding—Check for Distorted Spring
- Float Setting Incorrect
  - Float Sticking Misaligned or Leaking
- Main Metering Jets Plugged, Dirty, or Incorrect Part
- Metering Rods Altered, Bent, or Incorrect Part

Clutch

PROBLEMS AND SOLUTIONS

When diagnosing problems in any area, there is no substitute for careful examination and experience. The following are some symptoms that may accompany clutch troubles.

1. Excessive noise.
2. Clutch chatter or grab.
3. Clutch slip.
4. Clutch drag or failure to release.
5. Pedal pulsation.
6. Low clutch facing life.
7. Gear lock up or hard shifting.
8. Hard pedal.

EXCESSIVE NOISE

There are five common sources of clutch noise:

1. Release bearing.
2. Clutch shaft pilot bearing.
3. Transmission pinion shaft bearing.
4. Transmitted engine noises.
5. Clutch linkage noises.

RELEASE BEARING

Release bearing noises vary with the degree of bearing failure. A dry or damaged bearing usually makes a shrill or scraping sound when depressing the clutch pedal to the point of release finger-to-bearing contact. This means that the noise should be audible at the lower end of clutch pedal free-play. Continued use of a car, with the release bearing in this condition, is damaging to the clutch release fingers.

Usual cause of release bearing failure is overwork—caused by riding the clutch. Other causes are not enough pedal free-play, lack of lubricant in the bearing, clutch release fingers worn or out of true.

PILOT BEARING

Clutch shaft pilot bearing noises can be heard only when the bearing is in operation. This is at any time crankshaft speed is different from that of the clutch shaft (clutch disengaged with transmission in gear).

This is a high pitched squeal, caused by a dry bearing. Requires replacement.

TRANSMISSION PINION SHAFT BEARING

A rough, or otherwise damaged, transmission pinion (input) shaft bearing noise can be heard only when the clutch is engaged, with transmission in any shift position. The noise is usually quite noticeable with the gears in neutral. This noise should diminish and completely disappear as the transmission pinion gear slows down and stops after clutch release. This noise is easily distinguished from release bearing noise because of the opposite conditions of encounter.

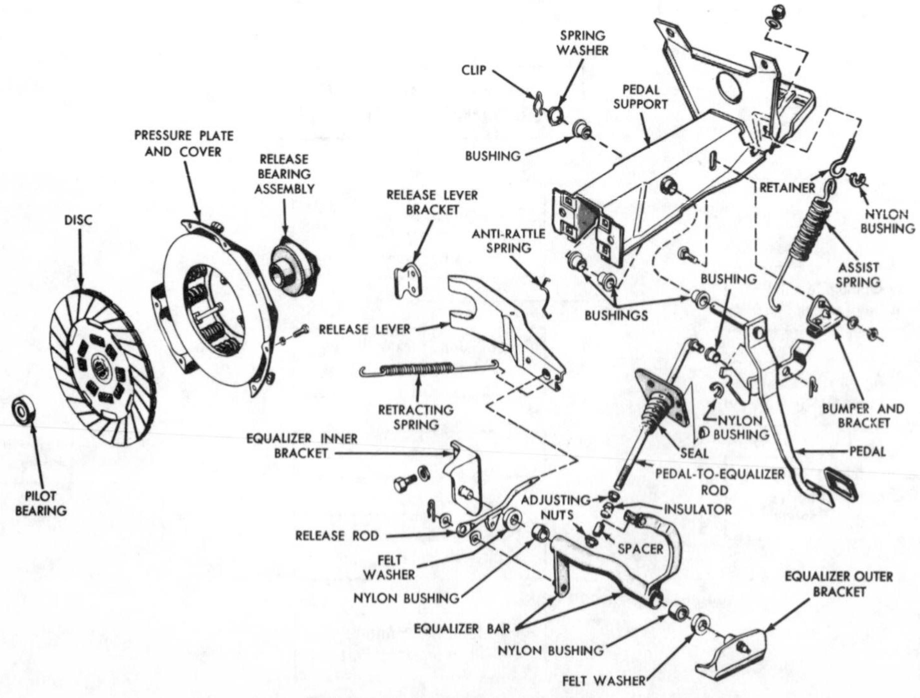

Typical clutch linkage (© Ford Motor Co)

TRANSMITTED ENGINE NOISES

Assuming that the clutch pedal has the required amount of free-play, there should be no objectionable amount of engine noise transmitted to the passenger area via the clutch. Some engine noises are transmitted through the positive pressure of the clutch release bearing and fingers to the clutch housing. Here they are amplified by the shape of the clutch housing and heard in the passenger compartment in the guise of clutch or transmission trouble. Engine noise transmission can usually be modified through clutch pedal manipulation.

CLUTCH LINKAGE NOISE

Clutch linkage noise is usually a clicking or snapping sound that can be heard or felt in the pedal itself when moving it completely up or down. Locating the cause of trouble and correcting it is a matter of repositioning and lubrication. The trouble may be in the clutch assist spring, the retract spring, the release bearing lever, or even at the release bearing.

CLUTCH CHATTER OR GRAB

Usually the cause of clutch chatter or grab can be located within the clutch assembly. To correct the trouble will require the removal of the clutch. However, symptoms resembling clutch trouble may be misleading and originate in other areas.

In order to isolate the cause of the problem, we suggest that the following items be checked in this order.

1. Be sure that the clutch linkage is in adjustment and not binding. If necessary, lubricate, align and adjust linkage.
2. Check for worn or loose engine or transmission mounts. If necessary, tighten or replace mounts.
3. Check for wear, looseness or misalignment of universal joints. Check attaching bolts on clutch pressure plate, transmission and clutch housing. Tighten, align or replace as necessary.
4. Check freedom of movement of the clutch release bearing on its sleeve. Free up or replace as necessary.
5. Check for oil or grease on the flywheel, friction disc or pressure plate.
6. Check for trueness of the friction disc, and that the disc hub is not binding on the splines of the transmission input shaft (clutch shaft).
7. Be sure that the disc or the pressure plate is not broken.
8. Examine clutch pressure plate and cover plate assembly for cracks or heat discoloration.
9. Check pressure plate and flywheel for warpage.

CLUTCH SLIP

Clutch slippage is usually most noticeable when pulling away, and during acceleration from a standing start. A severe, but positive, test for slippage is to start the engine, set the parking brake and apply the service brakes; shift the transmission into high gear and release the clutch pedal while accelerating the engine. A clutch in good condition should hold and stall the engine. If the clutch slips, the cause may be one or more of the following:

1. Improper linkage adjustment (not enough free-play).
2. Broken or disconnected parts.
3. Clutch linkage or lever mechanism binding or broken, not allowing full pressure plate application.
4. Friction disc oil-saturated or excessively worn.
5. Pressure plate worn, springs weak from temper loss or failure (damaging heat will usually cause parts to appear blue).
6. Clutch plate not seated (after installation of a new plate).

CLUTCH DRAG OR FAILURE TO RELEASE

There are many reasons for clutch drag (spin) or failure to release. The following conditions, therefore, apply to unmodified versions of standard vehicles. Changing the driven plate mass (replacing the standard driven plate with a heavy duty unit), changing transmission oil viscosity, etc. may influence clutch spin-time. Three seconds is a good, typical, spin-time for the standard transmission and clutch, driven under normal conditions, in average temperate zone climates.

The friction disc and some of the transmission gears spin briefly after clutch disengagement, so normal clutch action should not be confused with a dragging clutch.

Clutch drag, failure to release or abnormal spin-time may be caused by one or more of the following:

1. Improper clutch linkage adjustment or release fork off pivot.
2. Clutch plate hub binding on the transmission input (pinion) shaft.
3. A warped or bent friction disc or pressure plate; or loose friction material on the driven disc.
4. The transmission input shaft may be binding or sticking in the pilot bearing.
5. Misalignment of transmission to the engine.
6. Transmission lubricant low or not heavy enough.

PEDAL PULSATION

This condition can be felt by applying light foot pressure to the clutch pedal with the engine idling. It may be caused by any of the following:

1. Bent or uneven clutch release finger adjustment.
2. Excessive flywheel runout due to bent wheel or crankshaft flange; or the flywheel may not be properly seated on the crankshaft flange.
3. Release bearing cocked on transmission bearing retainer.
4. Poor alignment of transmission with the engine.

LOW CLUTCH FACING LIFE

This sort of complaint warrants a close study of the operator's driving habits. Poor clutch facing wear may be caused by any of the following:

1. Riding the clutch.
2. Drag strip type operation.
3. Continuous overloading, or the hauling of heavy trailers or other equipment.
4. Holding the car from drifting backward on a grade; by slipping the clutch instead of using the brakes.

5. Improper pedal linkage adjustment (free-play and pedal height).
6. Rough surface on flywheel or pressure plate.
7. Presence of oil or water on clutch facing.
8. Weak pressure plate springs, causing clutch creep or slip.

GEAR LOCK UP OR HARD SHIFTING

This trouble is so closely related to Clutch Drag Or Failure To Release that diagnosis should be conducted in the same way as given under that heading. If, after checking the items listed and finding that the transmission still locks up or is hard to shift, the trouble probably lies in the transmission cover or shifter assembly, or in the transmission proper. In that case, transmission work is needed.

HARD PEDAL

A stiff clutch pedal or a clutch release that requires abnormal pedal pressure may result from one or more of the following:

1. Dry and binding clutch linkage and levers.
2. Linkage out of alignment.
3. Improper (heavy) retracting spring.
4. Dry or binding release bearing sleeve or transmission bearing retainer.
5. Assist spring missing or improperly adjusted.
6. Wrong type clutch assembly (heavy duty) being used.

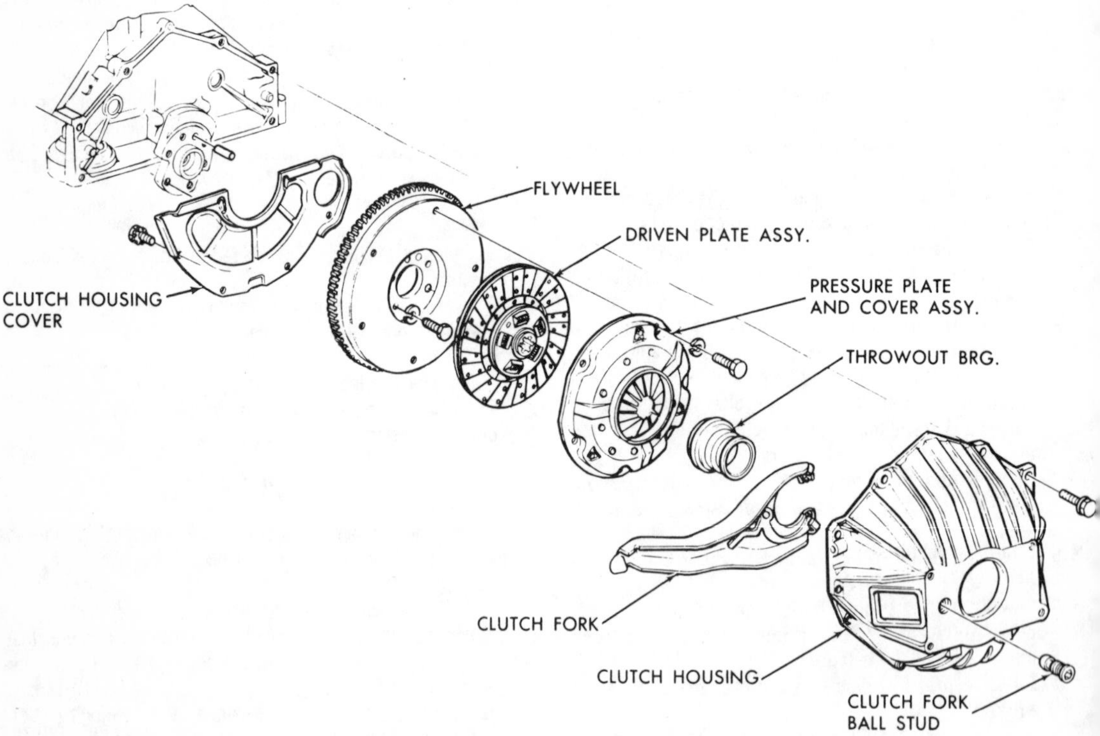

Manual Transmissions

DIAGNOSIS

JUMPING OUT OF HIGH GEAR

1. Misalignment of transmission case or clutch housing.
2. Worn pilot bearing in crankshaft.
3. Bent transmission shaft.
4. Worn high speed sliding gear.
5. Worn teeth in clutch shaft.
6. Insufficient spring tension on shifter rail plunger.
7. Bent or loose shifter fork.
8. End-play in clutch shaft.
9. Gears not engaging completely.
10. Loose or worn bearings on clutch shaft or mainshaft.

STICKING IN HIGH GEAR

1. Clutch not releasing fully.
2. Burred or battered teeth on clutch shaft.
3. Burred or battered transmission main-shaft.
4. Frozen synchronizing clutch.
5. Stuck shifter rail plunger.
6. Gearshift lever twisting and binding shifter rail.
7. Battered teeth on high speed sliding gear or on sleeve.
8. Lack of lubrication.
9. Improper lubrication.
10. Corroded transmission parts.
11. Defective mainshaft pilot bearing.

JUMPING OUT OF SECOND GEAR

1. Insufficient spring tension on shifter rail plunger.
2. Bent or loose shifter fork.
3. Gears not engaging completely.
4. End-play in transmission mainshaft.
5. Loose transmission gear bearing.
6. Defective mainshaft pilot bearing.
7. Bent transmission shaft.
8. Worn teeth on second speed sliding gear or sleeve.
9. Loose or worn bearings on transmission mainshaft.
10. End-play in countershaft.

STICKING IN SECOND GEAR

1. Clutch not releasing fully.
2. Burred or battered teeth on sliding sleeve.
3. Burred or battered transmission main-shaft.
4. Frozen synchronizing clutch.
5. Stuck shifter rail plunger.
6. Gearshift lever twisting and binding shifter rail.
7. Lack of lubrication.
8. Second speed transmission gear bearings locked will give same effect as gears stuck in second.
9. Improper lubrication.
10. Corroded transmission parts.

JUMPING OUT OF LOW GEAR

1. Gears not engaging completely.
2. Bent or loose shifter fork.
3. End-play in transmission mainshaft.
4. End-play in countershaft.
5. Loose or worn bearings on transmission mainshaft.
6. Loose or worn bearings in countershaft.
7. Defective mainshaft pilot bearing.

STICKING IN LOW GEAR

1. Clutch not releasing fully.
2. Burred or battered transmission main-shaft.
3. Stuck shifter rail plunger.
4. Gearshift lever twisting and binding shifter rail.
5. Lack of lubrication.
6. Improper lubrication.
7. Corroded transmission parts.

JUMPING OUT OF REVERSE GEAR

1. Insufficient spring tension on shifter rail plunger.
2. Bent or loose shifter fork.
3. Badly worn gear teeth.
4. Gears not engaging completely.
5. End-play in transmission mainshaft.
6. Idler gear bushings loose or worn.
7. Loose or worn bearings on transmission mainshaft.
8. Defective mainshaft pilot bearing.

STICKING IN REVERSE GEAR

1. Clutch not releasing fully.
2. Burred or battered transmission main-shaft.
3. Stuck shifter rail plunger.
4. Gearshift lever twisting and binding shifter rail.
5. Lack of lubrication.
6. Improper lubrication.
7. Corroded transmission parts.

FAILURE OF GEARS TO SYNCHRONIZE

1. Binding pilot bearing on main-shaft, will synchronize in high gear only.
2. Clutch not releasing fully.
3. Detent springs weak or broken.
4. Weak or broken springs under balls in sliding gear sleeve.
5. Binding bearing on clutch shaft.
6. Binding countershaft.
7. Binding pilot bearing in crankshaft.
8. Badly worn gear teeth.
9. Scored or worn cones.
10. Improper lubrication.
11. Constant mesh gear not turning freely on transmission mainshaft. Will synchronize in that gear only.

Diagnostic Charts

STARTING SYSTEM DIAGNOSIS

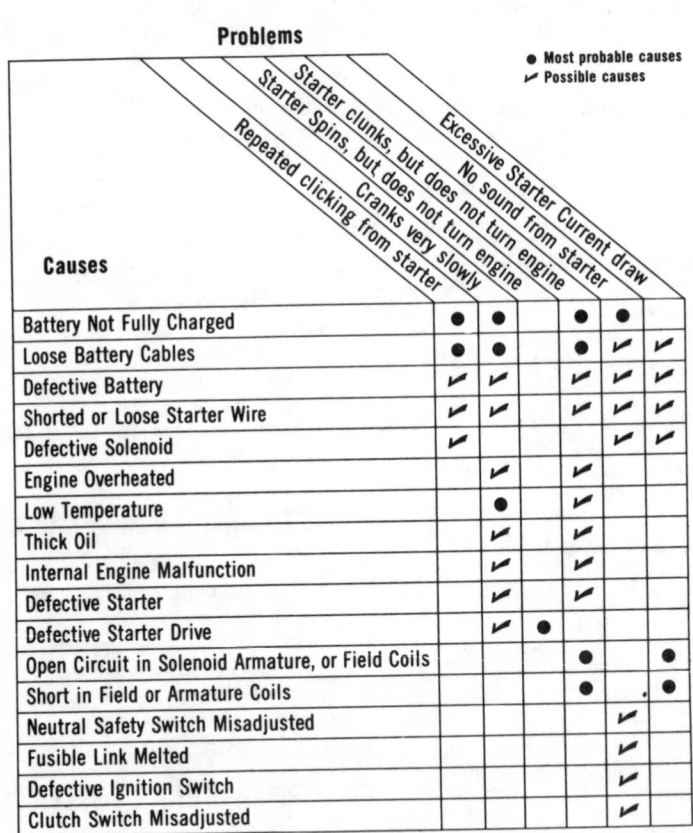

● Most probable causes
✓ Possible causes

Causes \ Problems	Repeated clicking from starter	Cranks very slowly	Starter Spins, but does not turn engine	Starter clunks, but does not turn engine	No sound from starter	Excessive Starter Current draw
Battery Not Fully Charged	●	●		●	●	
Loose Battery Cables	●	●		●	✓	✓
Defective Battery	✓	✓		✓	✓	✓
Shorted or Loose Starter Wire	✓	✓		✓	✓	✓
Defective Solenoid	✓				✓	✓
Engine Overheated		✓		✓		
Low Temperature		●		✓		
Thick Oil		✓		✓		
Internal Engine Malfunction		✓		✓		
Defective Starter		✓		✓		
Defective Starter Drive		✓	●			
Open Circuit in Solenoid Armature, or Field Coils				●		●
Short in Field or Armature Coils				●		●
Neutral Safety Switch Misadjusted					✓	
Fusible Link Melted					✓	
Defective Ignition Switch					✓	
Clutch Switch Misadjusted					✓	

CLUTCH AND MANUAL TRANSMISSION DIAGNOSIS

● Most probable causes
✓ Possible causes

Causes \ Problems	Noisy in Forward Speeds	Noisy in Reverse	Noisy in Neutral	Hard Shifting	Jumping Out of Gear	Sticking in Gear	Gears Clash	Locks in Two Gears	Leaks
Low or Wrong Lubricant	✓	✓	✓	✓		✓	✓		✓
Transmission Misaligned or Loose	✓	✓	✓		✓				
Maindrive Gear or Bearing Damaged	●	✓	✓			✓	✓		
Speedometer Drive Noise	✓	✓							
Mainshaft Gears or Bearing Damaged	●	✓	✓		●				
Incorrect End Play on Shafts	✓	✓	✓		✓				
Reverse Idler Gear or Shaft Damaged		●	✓						
Incorrect Clutch Adjustment			●	✓		●	●		
Shift Linkage Misadjusted				●	✓	✓		●	
Bent Shifter Forks or Shafts				✓	✓	✓		✓	
Damaged Synchronizers				✓	✓	✓	●		
Speed Too High on Downshift				●			✓		
Front Main Bearing Damaged	✓	✓	✓		✓				
Bent Output Shaft					✓				
High Idle Speed							✓		
Wait 3-4 Sec. Before Shifting Into a Non-synchronized Gear							●		
Bent Shift Rods								✓	
Overfilled									●
Seals at Covers or Extension Housing Bad									✓
Loose Main Drive Gear Bearing Retainer									✓
Operating Shaft Seals Bad									✓
Worn Extension Housing Bushing									✓

CHRYSLER TORQUEFLITE AUTOMATIC TRANSMISSION DIAGNOSIS

Causes

✓ Possible causes

Problems	Oil level	Control linkage	Oil pressure check	Kickdown band	Low-reverse band	Improper engine idle	Servo linkage	Accumulator	Valve body assembly	Manual valve lever	Air pressure check	Servo link	Governor	Gear shift cable	Regulator valve	Strainer	Converter control valve	Breather clogged	Cooler or lines
Harsh N to D or N to R shift			✓	✓	✓	✓	✓		✓	✓									
Delayed Shift—N to D	✓		✓						✓										
Runaway on upshift—2-3 kickdown	✓	✓	✓	✓				✓	✓			✓							
Harsh upshift and 3-2 kickdown		✓	✓	✓				✓	✓			✓							
No upshift	✓	✓	✓	✓				✓	✓	✓	✓	✓	✓						
No kickdown on normal downshift	✓	✓	✓	✓				✓	✓		✓		✓	✓					
Erratic shifts	✓	✓	✓			✓								✓	✓	✓			
Slips in forward drive positions	✓		✓					✓	✓		✓								
Slips in Reverse only			✓		✓		✓		✓		✓								
Slips in all positions	✓		✓						✓		✓				✓				
No drive in any positions	✓		✓						✓	✓	✓					✓			
No drive in forward positions			✓	✓				✓	✓		✓	✓			✓				
No drive in Reverse			✓		✓		✓		✓		✓		✓						
Drives in Neutral									✓	✓				✓					
Drags or locks				✓	✓		✓					✓							
Noises	✓								✓	✓			✓		✓		✓		
Hard to fill or blows out	✓								✓							✓	✓	✓	✓
Transmission overheats	✓			✓	✓				✓				✓		✓		✓		✓

This transmission is used on all Chrysler Corporation cars since 1967 and on American Motors products since 1972.

FORD C-6 AUTOMATIC TRANSMISSION DIAGNOSIS

Causes

● Most probable causes
✓ Possible causes

Problems	Fluid level	Vacuum diaphragm	Manual linkage	Governor	Valve body	Pressure regulator	Intermediate band	Low-reverse clutch	Intermediate servo	Engine idle speed	Downshift linkage	Perform air pressure check	Extension tear oil seal	Perform pressure check	Engine performance
No drive in D, 2, and 1			✓		✓							✓		✓	
1-2 or 2-3 shift points erratic	✓	✓	✓	✓	✓						✓	✓		✓	
Rough 1-2 upshifts		✓			✓	✓	✓		✓			✓		✓	
Rough 2-3 upshifts		✓			✓	✓	✓		✓			✓		✓	
Dragged out 1-2 shift	✓	✓			✓	✓	✓		✓			✓		✓	
No 1-2 or 2-3 shift		✓	✓	✓	✓		✓		✓		✓	✓		✓	
No 3-1 shift in D				✓	✓										
No forced downshifts		✓			✓						✓				
Runaway engine on 3-2 downshift		✓			✓	✓	✓		✓			✓		✓	
Rough 3-2 or 3-1 shift at closed throttle		✓			✓	✓			✓	✓					
Shifts 1-3 in D		✓		✓	✓		✓		✓						
Creeps excessively										●					
Slips in first gear, D	✓	✓			✓	✓						✓		✓	
Slips in second gear	✓	✓			✓	✓	✓		✓			✓		✓	
Slips or chatters in R	✓	✓			✓	✓		✓				✓		✓	
No drive in D only			✓		✓							✓		✓	
No drive in 2 only	✓		✓		✓				✓			✓		✓	
No drive in 1 only	✓		✓		✓							✓		✓	
No drive in R only	✓		✓		✓			✓				✓		✓	
No drive in any lever position	✓		✓		✓	✓						✓		✓	
Lockup in 2 only								●							
Parking lock broken			✓												
Transmission overheats		✓				✓						✓		✓	
Maximum speed too low															✓
Transmission noisy in N and P	✓					✓									
Transmission noisy in all gears	✓					✓									
Fluid leak	✓	✓							✓				✓		
Car moves forward in N			✓												

This transmission is available on many Ford Motor Company cars from 1967.

GENERAL MOTORS TURBO HYDRA-MATIC 350 AUTOMATIC TRANSMISSION DIAGNOSIS

Causes

● Most probable causes
✓ Possible causes

Problems	Low oil level/water in oil	Vacuum leak	Modulator and/or valve	Strainer and/or gasket	Governor valve/screen	Valve body gasket/plate	Pressure regulator valve	1-2 shift valve	2-3 shift valve	Manual low-control valve	Detent valve and linkage	2-3 accumulator	Manual valve linkage	Pump gears	Gasket screen-pressure
Slips in all ranges	✓		✓	✓		✓	✓						✓		✓
Drive slips—no First gear	✓		✓	✓		✓	✓						✓		✓
No 1-2 upshift		✓			✓	✓	✓	✓							
Slips, 1-2 upshift	✓		✓			✓	✓	✓				✓			
Harsh 1-2 upshift		✓	✓				✓								
No 2-3 upshift						✓			✓						
2-3 upshift early or late		✓			✓	✓	✓		✓		✓				
Slips, 2-3 upshift	✓		✓			✓	✓		✓						
No full throttle downshift		✓	✓				✓		✓			✓			
2-3 upshift, full throttle only		✓									✓				
Car drives in Neutral											●				
Slips in Reverse	✓		✓	✓		✓	✓	✓					✓	✓	✓
1-2 or 2-3 shifts noisy	●														
Noisy in all ranges	✓			✓		✓									✓
Spews oil out of the breather	✓			✓											

This transmission is available on many General Motors cars since 1969.

BRAKE DIAGNOSIS

Problems

● Most probable causes
✓ Possible causes

Causes	Brake Tell-Tale Glows During Stop	Brakes Chatter (Roughness)	Brakes Squeak During Application	Scraping Noise from Brakes	Uneven Braking Action (Front to Rear)	Uneven Braking Action (Pulls to Side)	Brakes Drag	Brakes Slow to Release	Brakes Slow to Respond	Excessive Braking Action	Excessive Brake Pedal Effort	Pedal Travel Gradually Increases	Excessive Brake Pedal Travel
Leaking Brake Line or Connection	●				✓							●	✓
Leaking Wheel Cylinder or Piston Seal	✓					✓				✓		●	✓
Leaking Master Cylinder	✓											●	✓
Restricted Brake Fluid Passage					✓	✓	✓	✓	✓		✓	✓	
Air In Brake System	●				✓								●
Contaminated or Improper Brake Fluid	✓						✓	✓	✓				
Faulty Metering Valve (Disc Only)	✓				✓		✓	✓	✓	✓	✓		✓
Sticking Wheel Cylinder or Caliper Pistons					✓	✓	✓	✓			✓		
Improperly Adjusted Master Cylinder Push Rod	✓						●	✓					✓
Leaking Vacuum System									✓		●		
Restricted Air Passage In Power Unit								✓	●		✓		
Improperly Assembled Power Unit							●	✓	✓	✓	✓		
Damaged Power Unit							✓	✓	✓	✓	✓		
Brake Assembly Attachments—Missing or Loose		✓		✓	✓	✓	✓						✓
Brake Pedal Linkage Interference or Binding							●	●	✓		✓		
Worn Out Brake Lining—Replace			✓	✓	✓	✓					✓		
Uneven Brake Lining Wear—Replace	✓		✓	✓	✓	✓							✓
Glazed Brake Lining—Sand Lightly			✓		✓	✓			✓		●		
Incorrect Lining Material—Replace		✓	●		✓	✓			✓	✓	✓		
Contaminated Brake Lining—Replace		✓	✓	✓	●	●			✓	●			
Linings Damaged By Abusive Use—Replace			✓	✓	✓	✓				●	✓		
Excessive Brake Lining Dust—Remove with Air			✓		●	●				●	✓		
Brake Drums or Rotors Heat Spotted or Scored		●	✓		✓	✓				✓			
Out-of-Round or Vibrating Brake Drums		●											
Out-of-Parallel Brake Rotors		●											
Excessive Rotor Run-Out		✓											
Faulty Automatic Adjusters	✓				✓	✓	✓					●	✓
Weak or Incorrect Brake Shoe Return Springs			✓	●	✓	✓	●	✓		✓			
Drums Tapered or Threaded				●									
Incorrect Wheel Cylinder Sizes					✓	✓				✓	✓		
Improperly Adjusted Parking Brake							✓						
Incorrect Front End Alignment						●							
Incorrect Tire Pressure					✓	✓							
Incorrect Wheel Bearing Adjustment		✓		✓									✓
Loose Front Suspension Attachments		✓		●		✓							
Out-of-Balance Wheel Assemblies		●											
Driver Riding Brake Pedal					✓		✓				✓	✓	✓
Faulty Proportioning Valve							✓	✓	✓		✓		
Insufficient Brake Shoe Pad Lubricant			●	●	✓		✓	✓					

DISC BRAKE DIAGNOSIS

Problems

● Most probable causes
✓ Possible causes

Causes	Excessive Pedal Travel	Hard Pedal	Grabbing or Pulling	Fading Pedal	Noise and Chatter	Dragging Brakes
Master Cylinder Fluid Low	●		✓	✓		
Air in Hydraulic System	●		✓			
Hoses Soft or Weak	●			✓		
Caliper Seals Soft or Broken	●		●		✓	●
Power Brake Malfunctioning		●				
Lining Soiled With Brake Fluid		●	●			
Lines or Hoses Kinked or Collapsed		●	●			●
Caliper Pistons Frozen or Seized		●	●		✓	●
Master Cylinder Cups Swollen		●				●
Master Cylinder Bore Rough		●	●	●		
Caliper Cylinder Bore Rough or Worn		●	●	●	✓	●
Pedal Push Rod and Linkage Binding		●	✓			
Metering Valve Not Working		●	●			
Hydraulic Connections Loose or Ruptured	✓		✓	●		
Caliper Cylinder Seals Worn or Damaged	✓			●	✓	●
Bleed Screw Open	✓			●		
Lines or Hoses Ruptured	✓			●		
Disc Has Excessive Internal Runout					●	✓
Disc Out of Parallel			✓		●	✓
Disc Has Casting Imperfections					●	✓
Restricted Port in Master Cylinder		✓				●
Residual Pressure Check Valve		✓				●
Push Rod on Master Cylinder Out of Adjustment		✓				●
Caliper Loose			●		✓	
Poor Quality Brake Fluid				●		
Poor Quality Brake Lining				●	●	

AIR CONDITIONING DIAGNOSIS

● Most probable causes
✓ Possible causes

Causes \ Problems	Compressor Discharge Pressure Too High	Compressor Discharge Pressure Too Low	P.O.A. Valve Inlet Pressure Too High	P.O.A. Valve Inlet Pressure Too Low	Nozzle Outlet Temperature Too Warm	Nozzle Outlet Temperature Too Cold	Blown Thermal Limiter	Compressor Clutch Slips	Evaporator Pressure Too High	Water Blowing Out Discharge Nozzle	Compressor Not Operating	Water Drains Onto Floor
Engine Overheated	●				✓			✓	✓			
Overcharge of Refrigerant or Air in System	●				✓			✓	✓			
Restriction in Condenser	●				✓		✓	✓				
Restriction in Receiver-Dehydrator		●		✓	✓		✓					
Restriction in Any High Pressure Line	●	✓		✓	✓		✓	✓	✓			
Condenser Air Flow Blocked	●				✓		✓	✓	✓			
P.O.A. Valve Inlet Pressure Too High	●											
Insufficient Refrigerant		●		✓	●		●				✓	
Defective Compressor		●	✓		✓			✓	✓		●	
Plug in Refrigerant System	✓	●	✓	✓	✓		✓	✓	✓		✓	
P.O.A. Valve Inlet Pressure Too Low		●				✓	✓				✓	
P.O.A. Valve Stuck Open					✓	✓	✓				✓	
Capillary Tube to Evaporator Tube Contact	✓		●		✓	✓		●	✓			
Expansion Valve Inoperative	✓	✓	●	✓	●		●	✓	●		✓	
Inlet Screen Plugged or Valve Fails		✓		●	✓		✓				✓	
Restriction in System Hoses or Tubes	✓	✓		●	✓	✓	✓	✓	✓		✓	
Poor Seal Evaporator to Evaporator Inlet Case		✓		✓	●							
Poor Seal Evaporator to Heater Case		✓		✓	●							
Defective or Missing Evaporator Drain Hose										●		●
Air Ducts Not Properly Connected		✓		✓	●	✓						
Vacuum Hoses Not Connected Properly					●	✓						
P.O.A. Valve Faulty			●		●	●						
Low Charge or Discharged System		✓	✓	✓	✓		●		✓		✓	
Thermal Limiter Improperly Installed							●				✓	
Thermal Limiter Blown											●	
Faulty Superheat Shut Off Switch							●				✓	
Head Pressure Too High								●				
Pulley Wobbles								●				
Loose Compressor Drive Belt		✓	✓		✓				●		●	
Defective Clutch or Coil		✓	✓		✓				●		●	
Restriction in Suction Line		✓	✓		✓				●		✓	
Defective Suction Throttling Valve		✓	✓	●					✓			
Defective Expansion Valve	✓		●	✓	✓		✓		✓			
Plugged or Kinked Evaporator Drain Hose										●		
Broken Compressor Drive Belt											●	
No Power to Clutch							✓				●	
Faulty Switch or Wiring								✓			●	

COOLING SYSTEM DIAGNOSIS

● Most probable causes
✓ Possible causes

Causes \ Problems	External Leakage	Internal Leakage	Poor Circulation	Overheating	Overflow Loss	Corrosion	Temp Too Low (Slow Engine Warm Up)	Water Pump Noisy
Hose Leaking	●			●				
Water Pump Leaking	●			●				
Damaged Gasket	●	●		●				
Leaking Heater Core	●			✓				
Cracked Cylinder Block	●	●		✓				
Faulty Pressure Cap	●	●		●	●			
Oil Cooler Fittings Loose	●	●		✓				
Faulty Head Gasket	●	●		✓				
Loose Cylinder Head Bolts	●	●		✓				
Cracked Valve Port		●		✓				
Cracked Cylinder Wall		●		✓				
Leaking Oil Cooler		●						
Low Coolant Level			●	●				
Collapsed Radiator Hose			●	●				
Fan Belt Loose			●	✓				✓
Air Leak Through Bottom Hose	✓		●					
Faulty Thermostat			●	●			●	
Water Pump Impeller Broken			●					●
Restricted Radiator Core			●	●				
Restricted Engine Water Jacket			●					
Incorrect Ignition Timing				●				
Inaccurate Temperature Gauge				●			●	
Excessive Engine Idling				●				
Frozen Coolant				●				
Faulty Vacuum By Pass Valve			✓	●				
Overfilling					●			
Blown Head Gasket	✓				●			
Coolant Foaming					●			
Insufficient Corrosion Inhibitor			✓	✓		●		
Extended Use of Anti-Freeze			✓	✓		●		
High Mineral and Lime Content of Coolant			✓	✓		●		
Faulty Temperature Sending Unit							●	
Faulty Heater Controls			✓				●	
Defective Seal								●
Bearing Corroded								●

FRONT SUSPENSION DIAGNOSIS

● Most probable causes
✓ Possible causes

Causes \ Problems	Front Wheel Shimmy	Pull to One Side	Excessive Play in Steering	Wheel Tramp	Excessive Tire Wear	Hard Steering	Wandering	Front End Noise
Out of Balance Tires	●			●	✓			
Worn or Out of Adjustment Wheel Bearings	✓					✓		
Worn Tie Rod Ends	✓							
Worn Ball Joints	✓							
Incorrect Wheel Alignment	●	✓			✓	✓	●	
Incorrect Ride Height	✓							
Low or Uneven Tire Pressures		●			●	●	✓	
Front or Rear Brake Dragging		✓						
Grease or Brake Fluid on Brake Linings		✓						
Broken or Sagging Front Spring		✓				✓	✓	
Incorrect Steering Gear Adjustment			✓					
Worn Front End Parts			●					●
Shock Absorber Inoperative or Loose				✓		✓	✓	✓
Ball Joint Needs Lubrication						✓		✓
Loose Stabilizer Bar								✓
Loose Lugnuts								✓
Loose Brake Parts								✓
Improper Tire Size					✓			
Bent or Worn Steering Linkage						✓	✓	

TIRE WEAR DIAGNOSIS

● Most probable causes
✓ Possible causes

Problems	Underinflation	Overinflation	Excessive speed	Excessive camber	Incorrect toe-in	Wheel unbalanced	Corrections
Bald spots						●	Dynamic or static balance the wheels
Feathered Edge					●		Adjust toe-in
Wear on one side				●			Adjust camber to specifications
Cracked Treads	✓		●				Adjust pressure to specifications with tire cool or replace tire
Rapid wear at center		●					Adjust pressure to specifications with tire cool
Rapid wear at shoulders	●						Adjust pressure to specifications with tire cool

Driving for Economy

Whether you drive a Cadillac, a Volkswagen, a moving van, or a milk truck, you can improve your miles per gallon by remembering a few basic rules and applying them to the driving situations you encounter. While short formulas never tell the whole story, here is one to keep in mind the next time you fill up:

Travel at low, steady speeds
+Maintain your car's momentum
+Anticipate conditions ahead
+Accelerate gently
+Be patient

=MORE MILES PER GALLON

The forces you're up against don't know or care how much money you spend for gasoline.

Air resistance
+Rolling resistance
+Acceleration resistance
+Gravity resistance
+Engine resistance

=FEWER MILES
PER GALLON

Besides knowing the facts and opposing forces, inspiration will also be important. Like pole-vaulting, in which one's opponent is the crossbar, or sprinting, where the runner fights a stopwatch, driving for economy is an individual event in which you're competing both with yourself and with the miles per gallon figure calculated from the speedometer and gas pump. By approaching driving for economy as a challenge, and not as drudgery, your gas mileage may even exceed that of less-inspired friends who happen to own smaller cars. Economy-run reporters who confide that "you won't approach the gas mileage of Mr. XYZ, but here are some little tips for you" imply that Mr. XYZ has some magical abilities which you lack. Don't believe it—give that little extra effort and you'll see.

SMOOTH AND STEADY WINS THE MILES PER GALLON RACE

LOW SPEED SAVES GAS

The expense of driving at higher speeds is evident in figure 4-1. When traveling at a constant speed, each model was most economical at about 30 to 40 miles per hour. At speeds over 40 mph, higher air resistance attacks a car's frontal area and causes economy to drop sharply. When you double your speed, you need eight times as much horsepower to fight air resistance. At speeds below 40, tire rolling resistance is the major factor causing low gas mileage. Another study revealed that a car getting 19.7 miles per gallon at 40 mph delivered only 18.3 at 50 mph, 16.2 at 60 mph, and just 14.2 at a speed of 70.

Your car will deliver its best gas mileage at moderate speeds in the neighborhood of 35-40 miles per hour. When it's not possible to maintain this most economical speed, do the next best thing and travel as slowly, as possible without becoming a safety hazard. A 10% increase in your speed (e.g., from 50 to 55 mph) will require a 33% increase in the horsepower you need to overcome

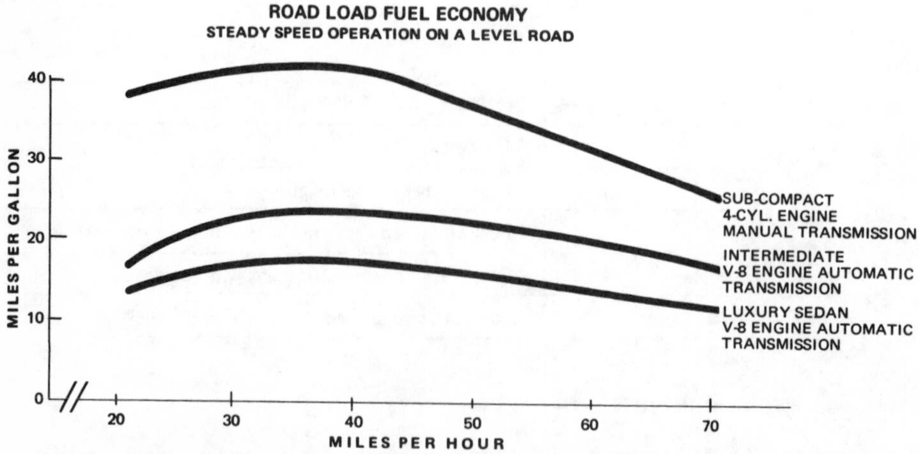

Fig. 4–1. Speeds of 35–40 mph are best for maximum economy. *Source:* G. J. Huebner, Jr., and D. J. Gasser, "General Factors Affecting Vehicle Fuel Consumption" (paper presented at National Automobile Engineering Meeting, Society of Automotive Engineers, Detroit, Michigan, May 15, 1973.)

air resistance. Greater increases are even more costly and are shown in the following table:

Increase in Speed	Increase in Horsepower Required to Overcome Air Resistance
10%	33%
20%	73%
30%	120%
40%	175%
50%	240%
60%	310%

Regardless of the vehicle, higher speeds mean less economy. However, don't feel too sorry for the driver of a diesel-engined car. For example, the fuel mileage of the diesel-powered Mercedes-Benz 220D drops from 50 miles per gallon at 30 mph down to 25 mpg at a speed of 70.

MAINTAIN A CONSTANT SPEED

By keeping your speed as steady as possible, you'll conserve your car's momentum and reduce its fuel consumption. Unnecessary changes in speed can be quite wasteful. For example, by letting your speed fluctuate between 55 and 65 mph, instead of maintaining a constant 60, you can lose between 1 and 1.5 miles per gallon. When you're traveling at a steady speed, acceleration resistance isn't present and it doesn't matter as much how heavy your car happens to be. If your car doesn't have a cruise control device, you can practice until you can do almost as well as the machine. When driving on an open highway, glance at your speedometer every 10 seconds or so. If your spot-checks show, for example, readings of 57, 60, 65, 59, 56, you're not doing very well. Keep practicing until the readings are very neatly constant, for example: 60, 60, 61, 59, 60. This type of practice is an excellent application of the little extra effort we talked about earlier.

ACCELERATE GRADUALLY

A "jackrabbit" start may be good for bunnies, but it's very expensive for your car. A rapid getaway can use twice as much gasoline as a more moderate, gradual start. In moving off from a stop, try to get into a high gear as soon as the engine will accept the load. With an automatic transmission, this means a very light foot on the throttle so that high gear will be chosen as early as possible. With a manual transmission, don't over-speed the engine in the lower gears—learn to shift up at the minimum speed that the engine will accept in the next higher gear.

If you drive an emission-controlled car equipped with a transmission-controlled ignition spark retard mechanism (see Chapter Five), it's even more important for you to get into high gear as soon as possible. In these cars, unnecessary use of the spark-retarding lower gears will keep your engine running inefficiently for a longer time.

BRAKE SPARINGLY

The world's most expensive magic trick is the one you perform when you change gasoline into brake lining dust. Every time you step on the brake, you're dissipating momentum that the engine worked hard to build up. Don't use the brake more often than is really necessary. Just as a polite cowboy might tip his hat to ladies on the street, some drivers touch their brake at practically every turn in the road.

Frequent panic stops are a sign that you aren't driving as economically as you could. While panic stops are necessary at the time they're made, most of them reflect that the car was traveling too fast in the first place. Although you don't hear much about "jackrabbit stops," they aren't economical either. Some of the worst braking offenses include charging a stop sign only to screeech to a halt; braking unnecessarily while traveling uphill; rushing into a turn, then applying the brake; not releasing the handbrake completely; and "riding" the brake. As an indication of how little the brakes can be used, consider that two men once drove from Detroit to Los Angeles without once touching their specially-sealed brake pedal. While you needn't go to this extreme, remember that hitting the brake isn't free—it's paid for by your gasoline dollar.

PASS SMOOTHLY

If you're driving for maximum miles per gallon, you probably won't be passing anything except gas stations. However, when you must pass, accelerate as gradually as possible and increase speed only to the level that safety requires. This may be difficult to do, as we all have a bit of race-driver within us that tempts us to whip right out there and show the other guy what a real car can do. Making an impression on the person you're passing will also make an impression on your fuel bill.

MERGE SMOOTHLY

We've all been in the sidewalk or doorway situation where we meet another person and play the guessing game of who goes first. Its baseball counterpart is the "I've-got-it-you-take-it" outfield catch. When merging onto an interstate or other major highway, the same thing happens. Interaction with other cars tends to upset the smoothness of your economical driving. If you simply blast onto the highway with eyes straight ahead, you've wasted gasoline as well as risked your neck. If you timidly creep up to the highway itself, you'll be forced to accelerate for all you're worth just to keep your car at its present length. Either strategy will reduce your miles per gallon. By trying to "fit in" with the traffic with which you're merging, and by making use of the full acceleration distance provided by the highway engineers, you can maintain your momentum, speed up more slowly, and save gas.

SOME LITTLE THINGS THAT MEAN A LOT

STEADY AT THE WHEEL

By keeping the steering wheel as motionless as possible, you'll minimize the side-to-side movement that increases both the distance you must travel and your tires' rolling resistance along the way. Each little change in direction interrupts your car's considerable momentum and causes the front tires to be paid just a little more horsepower for their work.

A DRAG ERASER

If your car is equipped with disc brakes, and if you sometimes drive for long distances on a very straight road, here's a tip that can make a slight reduction in your rolling resistance. Disc brake pads, instead of retracting away from the rotor, will drag lightly against it after you've released the brake pedal. Your front wheel bearings, if adjusted properly, will have a very small amount of looseness, or "play." If you were to keep your foot off the brake, then make a left turn followed by a right turn, play in the wheel bearings would move the rotor just enough to push the brake pads very slightly back into their housings and reduce their drag on the rotor. Once you're on that straight piece of road, the normal act of passing and returning to your lane can provide enough sideward force to retract the pads ever so slightly.

DON'T PUMP THE GAS PEDAL

It wouldn't help your gas mileage if the neighborhood kids decided to refill their squirt guns from your gas tank. However, every time you press down on the gas pedal, you activate a squirt-gun-like device called the accelerator pump. Thinking that you want to accelerate, the faithful gadget shoots some raw gasoline into the engine. The purpose of the accelerator pump is to smooth the transition from steady speed to acceleration. Some economy run drivers have been known to disconnect the accelerator pump in order to avoid the squirt-gun effect—however, this is nether necessary nor safe for everyday driving purposes. By moving the gas pedal very slowly when you decide to accelerate, you can fool the accelerator pump and save the gas it would otherwise squirt into the engine. After turning the engine off, removing the air cleaner, and holding the choke valve open, you can manipulate the throttle and see for yourself how much gasoline is being wasted. With the help of someone observing the carburetor throat, you can even practice pressing on the gas pedal until you have a better feel for how fast it can move before the accelerator pump goes into action. For safety, make sure you have the engine turned off and are not smoking when either observing or practicing. Because raw gasoline squirted into a stopped engine will thin the oil, it's also advisable to do your accelerator-pump practicing just before you change oil.

RULE OUT THAT BARREL

On most foreign cars equipped with a two-barrel carburetor, one will do the work under normal conditions, while the second will operate only at high speeds or when extra power is needed. When in the same gear, pressing to a certain point of the accelerator pedal movement will cause a slight surge in the engine's power and a change in the sound it's making. By becoming familiar with the point at which your second barrel is activated, you can avoid the drop in economy that accompanies its use. (Note: THE PRECEDING ADVICE GOES DOUBLE FOR READERS DRIVING FOUR-BARREL CARBURETORS.)

However, most American cars with two barrel carburetors (except Pintos and late model Vegas) do not have this progressive opening sequence. Therefore, both barrels are always operating, which requires the driver to have a very light foot.

OPEN WINDOWS WASTE GAS

At highway speeds, an open window will increase your car's air resistance and lower your miles per gallon. On a warm day, it's better to crack the vent windows slightly and use the flow-through ventilation with which your car may be equipped. If you don't have flow-through ventilation, crack open as many windows as necessary and use cool air from the conventional heater-defroster air system. If it's too hot, don't turn on the fan—open more windows. Economy run drivers have been known to swelter inside their cars in order to avoid opening a window and suffering the penalty of increased air resistance. At very low speeds, air resistance is less important and it's not as expensive to lower the windows. However, you can leave them up and your friends will think you have air conditioning.

TURN OFF THE HEATER FAN

When traveling at speeds over 40 miles per hour, you're wasting gasoline by turning on the heater-defroster fan. At these speeds, normal air resistance will force plenty of air through the intake of your heating-ventilation system. Unnecessary use of the fan places an extra load on the alternator, which in turn places an extra load on the engine. The electric fan, depending on its size, design, and running speed, may consume between 4 and 24 amperes of electrical current. An alternator forced to supply 40 to 50 amperes will lower gas mileage by .5 to .9 miles per gallon. As with so many other consumers of your gasoline dollar, the electric fan should be used only when you need it.

SPARE THE AIR

If your car has air conditioning, use it sparingly. The fan in an air-conditioned car will tend to draw electrical currents in the higher parts of the 4-24 ampere range just mentioned. Use of the air conditioner will also require engine horsepower to operate the compressor unit and to activate the magnetic clutch which keeps the compressor engaged. Figure 4-2 compares the average miles per gallon of test cars with and without their air conditioning units in operation. Depending on the speed traveled, drivers lost between 1.0 and 2.2 miles per gallon by turning on the air conditioner.

AVOID UNNECESSARY IDLING

That breakfast-table warm-up might make your car warm and toasty by the time you've finished your pancakes, but you've been getting zero miles per gallon in the process. It's much more economical to start out from cold and warm up the entire car at the same time—at least you'll be getting miles from gasoline otherwise wasted in a standing car. The same advice applies to drive-in banks, movies, ice-cream stands, churches, hamburger stands and gas stations. If you know that you're going to be stationary for more than a minute, you'll save gas by shutting off and restarting instead of allowing the engine to idle.

WHILE YOU CAR WARMS UP

Any professional athlete knows that it takes a gradual warm-up before going full tilt. Arm-conscious baseball pitchers don't take all those warm-up tosses just so the management can sell more popcorn. Your car also needs to warm up before it can run most efficiently—in cold-weather driving, this may take over five miles.

After sitting in the driveway during a wintry night, your car is as stiff as an arthritic statue—engine oil is like molasses, wheel bearing grease has the consistency of window caulking, and other lubricants are also too thick to properly flow between the moving parts to which they're assigned. After you've started the engine, wait until the oil pressure warning light goes off, then move off and drive more slowly than usual for the first few miles. Rolling resistance during this period will be very high, and you'll save gas by going slower against the extra drag.

When starting a cold engine, don't speed it up to the point where it sounds like pistons are about to come bursting through the hood. Besides wasting gasoline, this can damage moving parts that are not yet fully lubricated. Instead of racing a balky engine, let it idle for a minute or so until it is smooth enough to move the car.

WHEN YOU'RE GOING THE WRONG WAY

When you're traveling down a busy two-way road and discover that you're headed in the wrong direction, there's an economical answer to your problem. Figure 4-3 shows two ways of handling this dilemma. You can turn right, as driver B did, then attempt to turn left in order to get going in the desired direction. However, driver B has a problem: before he can turn back onto the

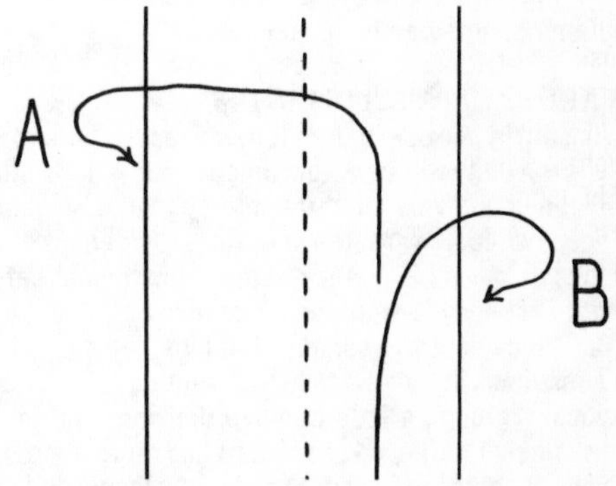

Fig. 4–3. Two possible ways to turn around when you discover you're headed in the wrong direction. Text tells why driver A saves gas.

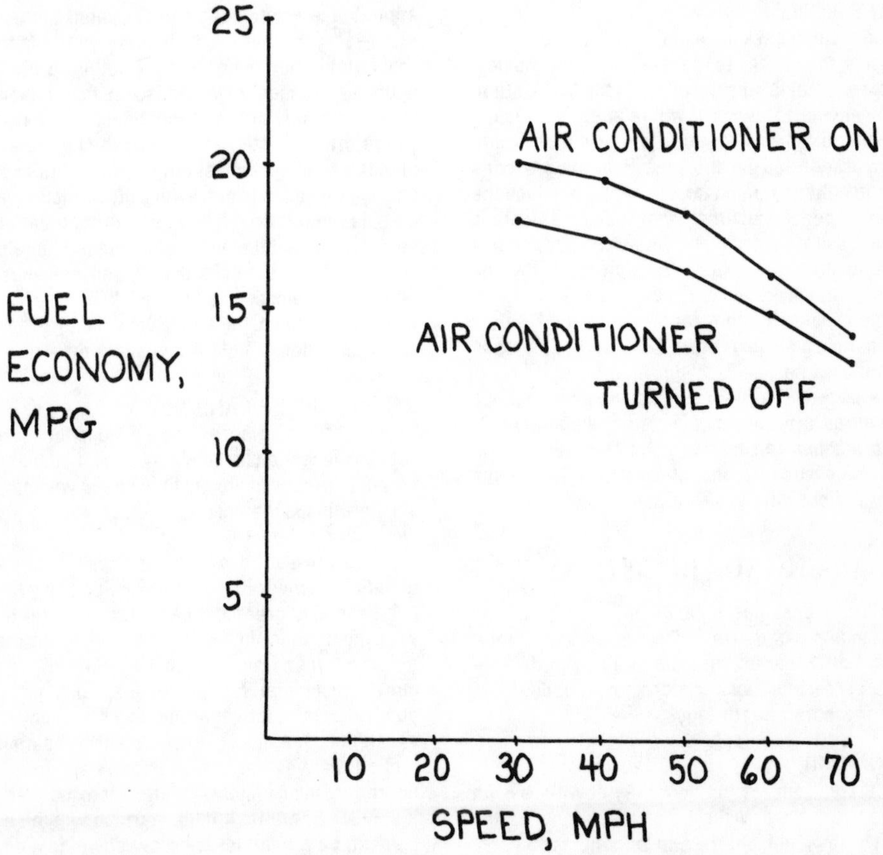

Fig. 4–2. While air conditioner use hurts economy at moderate speeds, at 70 mph there isn't much difference.

highway, he must wait until two lanes of traffic are clear—a long wait on many busy roads. Driver A, on the other hand, drove a little further in the wrong direction until he could make a convenient turn into a parking lot or street on the left side of the road. Once there, he only needed to wait until one lane of traffic was clear, which is more probable than two lanes being clear at the same time. If the road is very crowded, driver A will be headed in the proper direction while driver B is still back there playing the "It's-OK-to-the-left-what-about-the-right?" game and idling away his gasoline.

MAKING THAT DIFFICULT LEFT TURN

It's all but impossible to turn left onto a four-lane road that is crowded with cars, but uncontrolled by a stop light. Yet many drivers sit at the intersection and waste their gas while they're praying for an opening that stretches across all four lanes at the same time. A safer and more economical approach is to turn right and go a short distance until you can turn left into a street or lot, then come back in the direction you wanted to go in the first place. Through a little creative thinking and going with the flow of traffic, you can often find more economical ways of getting to your destination. As in this and the preceding section, it can be more economical to "use" the traffic flow instead of fighting it.

WHEN YOU REVERSE

When you want to back up, use the brakes to stop the car completely, then shift into reverse and apply the gas. It's more economical to stop the car with the brakes than it is with the engine. Likewise, if you're already traveling backward, use the brake to stop before you shift into First or Drive and step on the gas. Reversing a car's momentum in either direction takes energy, of which the engine is an expensive source. With today's automatic and synchromesh transmissions, it's all too easy to use the engine to do a job more efficiently done by the brakes.

If you have enough room, and if laws and safety conditions permit, making a U-turn will help you maintain your momentum and use less gas than would be required by a back-and-forth reversing maneuver. Since highway U-turns are almost universally illegal, U-turn reverses of direction can save you gas primarily in parking lots, service stations and other areas where the reverse gear might otherwise be used.

TAKING TO THE HILLS

In getting the best gas mileage that your car and driving conditions can deliver, hills can be very important. Like the stock market, they either go up or down—and, as the successful stock trader knows, each direction calls for a different strategy.

THE DOWN START

When starting from rest on your way down a hill, let gravity give you a hand. With a manual shift, allow the car to drift a few feet before you engage the clutch. Depending on your car and the steepness of the hill, you may even be able to start off in Second instead of First. Allowing gravity to change your momentum from stopped to moving will mean less wear on your clutch and more miles to your gallon. If you drive an automatic, you can also make use of gravity's pull on your car. Just keep a soft touch on the gas pedal and gravity will help you get into your economical high gear in a very short time.

The greater ease of accelerating downhill is one reason why it's a good idea to stop on the right side of a downhill road whenever you need to read the map or stop for gasoline, food, or whatever. Your engine is at its thirstiest when you ask it to accelerate up a hill.

SKIPPING A GEAR

Though something more likely to be done by a novice driver, skipping a gear when accelerating downhill can reduce wasteful throttle manipulations (remember the accelerator pump) involved in the ritual of shifting through all the gears when they're not really necessary. Going from 1st to 3rd or from 2nd to 4th can save gas when you're accelerating downhill—but be careful not to lug the engine.

THE UP START

Starting from rest on an uphill road calls for your foot on the brake until the very instant that you begin to accelerate. Otherwise the engine will have to reverse the car's momentum from downhill drift to uphill acceleration. For an automatic transmission. this is relatively easy—all you have to do is keep your left foot on the brake until your right foot has begun to press the gas pedal. With a manual transmission, the problem can be a little harder on both your clutch and your gas mileage. If you're driving a stick shift, keep the handbrake applied until the clutch is almost engaged and the engine is just starting to move the car. With a little practice, you should be able to start on a hill without drifting back at all. The secret is correct timing in releasing the handbrake—too soon and you'll drift, too late and you may stall the engine. Needless to say, the stick driver is going to waste both gasoline and clutch lining if he rides the clutch in order to hold his position on a hill.

DRIVING THE UPS AND DOWNS

Except for the most extreme circumstances, don't ever accelerate while climbing a hill. You'll be using gasoline far out of proportion to the little speed you may pick up. If acceleration is inefficient on a level road, it's downright wasteful on the way up a hill.

If you drive a heavy car, especially one with an automatic transmission, don't poke along on your way up a hill. Gradually press the gas pedal in order to maintain your momentum, but remember not to accelerate. Automatic transmissions tend to "lock up" and become more efficient at higher speeds, so it pays to climb quickly. Learn not to approach a hill with any more initial speed than you need in order to easily maintain momentum on the way up. Likewise, don't put your foot to the floorboard in an impossible attempt to maintain speed on a very steep grade. If a hill starts to win the momentum contest, be a good loser—slow down as it dictates and continue climbing at a rate that feels comfortable.

In a small car, allow your speed to drop slightly as you

climb. Keep the gas pedal steady if you're not slowing down too quickly, press down gradually if you are. If you're driving a manual transmission, don't be afraid to downshift if necessary—you'll get better gas mileage by allowing the engine to run at a more efficient speed. Don't worry about traveling slowly as you reach the peak. This speed is easily picked up as you gradually accelerate on the way back down.

Regardless of the car you're driving, let gravity help you gain speed on the downhill side. Any extra gas you use here may well be wasted by a sharp curve on the way down or by a stop sign at the bottom. Follow the stock trader's example and don't invest good gasoline into a hill that's on its way down.

For some readers, placing the transmission in Neutral and coasting downhill may be a strong temptation. However, don't do it—for a number of good reasons:

1. It's illegal in many places.
2. In today's steering-lock-equipped cars, a driver coasting with the engine off might remove the ignition key by force of habit, thus locking the steering wheel when the car is moving at high speed.
3. It can damage the internal parts of an automatic transmission.
4. It increases the load on the brakes and makes them more likely to overheat and fail on a steep hill.

YOUR DRIVING ENVIRONMENT

Knowing what's going to happen before it does is an asset in any business and likewise with driving for economy. The sooner you know what's ahead, the quicker you can prepare for it in order to use less gasoline along the way. Don't just think about where your car is right now. Consider the conditions you'll be facing in a few feet, in fifty yards, or maybe even a couple of miles. By anticipating upcoming conditions, you can immediately react with gas-saving actions that will enable you to maintain your momentum, accelerate more slowly, drive more steadily, or avoid a wasteful sudden stop. While your "messengers" of advance warning can take many forms, the following are among the most important:

READ THE SIGNS

"Stop sign ahead" should automatically tell you to get off the gas pedal and gradually slow down. Ignore this advance notice and you'll be just another magician who turns gasoline into brake lining dust. Other such warnings are "Traffic signals ahead" and "Toll booth ahead." Whenever a sign tells you that anything is ahead, it's bound to have some effect on what you should do if you're driving for economy.

"Hill next two miles, trucks gear down" practically screams that any gas you use between here and the steep hill is going to be wasted on the way down. Another hint that you should lighten up on the gas is the presence of a mountain elevation or summit marker.

"Curves ahead" isn't advertising a girlie show, but describing a driving condition where you can save gas by flowing slowly and smoothly, instead of rushing from one curve to the next. If you happen to be following someone you'd like to pass, back off and forget about it as soon as you see this sign.

"Merge ahead" tells you that you're going to have to interact with cars going in the same direction, and that you'd better check your speed, traffic spacing, and length of acceleration lane if you're going to get through the experience while using the least possible amount of gasoline.

"No passing zone," "School zone," "Narrow bridge ahead" are all signs which can increase your miles per gallon. By anticipating stops, slow-downs, and other special conditions, you can take your foot off the gas pedal earlier and slow down more gradually. Whether a sign warns of a rough road, a troll under the bridge, or a nudist colony crosswalk, chances are it's something for

Illus. 4–1. When you see a sign like this one, your car has valuable potential energy—don't use any more gas than necessary in getting from here to the down-hill slope.

Illus. 4–2. If you were thinking about passing that driver up ahead, relax for a few curves and enjoy the scenery.

Illus. 4–3. Sign at right tips off the fact that this hill is going to start down very abruptly once you get to the top.

which you'll have to slow up. After all, there aren't many signs urging that you drive faster.

USE YOUR SHARE OF THE ROAD

By anticipating successive curves and how you can stay in your lane in order to get through them in the shortest distance, you can shorten the length of a trip, better maintain your car's momentum, reduce your tires' rolling resistance, and get better gas mileage. Not much better, but remember that all these little things add up. In general, by keeping to the inside of curves, you'll minimize the length of any trip. But be sure to stay in your own lane while you're doing it.

READING THE RED LIGHTS

On frequently-traveled roads, learn to "read" the red lights ahead. If the lights are synchronized to encourage a certain speed, try to maintain that speed. If you see that a light is going to turn red before you reach it, ease up on the gas and approach the light as slowly as you can. If the light turns green, you've maintained your momentum and can accelerate more economically. If it's still red when you arrive, you've saved some gasoline during your gradual approach. Hurry-up-and-wait isn't good for your gas mileage. If you know that a certain stop light stays red for a long time, don't ruin your gas mileage by rushing to it when it's green, but you're still far away. Even if you do have to stop for a seemingly perpetual red light, you can save gas by turning off the motor while you're waiting.

CHANGING LANES

Just as an airplane pilot likes to travel at the altitude where the winds happen to be most favorable, you should try to "read" the flow of the various lanes available to you in congested driving situations. Observation of the lane patterns in your everyday driving can help you pinpoint exactly where lane 1 begins to slow down and lane 2 begins to speed up. It's not economical to zig-zag down the road, jumping into every open spot that arises, but you should likewise not limit yourself to one lane and ignore the others. Race drivers practice courses until they know the precise location where they must hit the gas when coming out of each turn. While driving to work in the morning is a little less thrilling, you can still profit from the race driver's example and practice different strategies until you find the one that works best for you in the lane patterns you're up against.

When travelling in traffic, always watch the red lights and traffic flow ahead so that you can maintain your car's momentum by moving into the lane with the least congestion. Through awareness of the cars around you and allowing acceleration room between you and the car ahead, you can make a south changeover without the need kto stand on the gas pedal. Temporarily switching to a slower lane can sometimes be advantageous. For example, if a heavy truck is stopped at the red light near the bottom of a hill, the natural tendency is to choose the passing lane so that you won't have to creep up the hill behind him. However, since other drivers will share this tendency, they may have the passing lane backed up a long way. Under these circumstances, you're better off behind the truck—at least he and you will be through the intersection by the time the light turns red again, while the backed-up drivers may end up waiting for the same red light twice. Don't ignore a possible strategy just because it seems unconventional.

DON'T TAILGATE

Whether driving in traffic or on the freeway, tailgating wastes gas. In addition to its safety hazards, tailgating ruins the tempo of your driving and leads to jerky, momentum-wasting changes which become necessary in order to avoid rear-ending the car ahead. When driving for economy, you can't afford to change speeds every time the brake-tapper in front decides to accelerate, decelerate or swerve, depending on how he's doing in the card game he and his passengers might be playing. If possible, pass the slower driver; if not, drop back and try to find a relaxing song on the radio. Don't let the driving behavior of others anger you into losing sight of your miles-per-gallon goal.

USE THE REAR VIEW MIRRORS

Proper use of the mirrors will enhance the smoothness of your driving by keeping you aware of the changing conditions around you. When driving for speed, you're passing everything on the road and most of the action is taking place up front—in this case, the mirrors are slightly less important. However, when you're driving for economy and the people around you aren't, there will be more activity behind you than if you were driving faster.

Many a middle-distance runner has been "boxed-in" while running on the inside lane of a tiny indoor track. With a runner in front of him, a runner beside him, and a runner directly behind, there's no way he can improve his position. He's forced to follow the pace of the man in front, which may be the exact opposite of the pace that is best for him. The same situation can come up in driving on any multiple-lane highway. If you're approaching a slower driver at the same time that a faster driver is approaching you, be sure to pace your pass so that you aren't boxed-in behind the driver ahead and forced to slow down. Anticipation of who-is-going-to-be-where-and-when is a key to economical driving, and frequent glances at your rear-view mirrors can help immeasurably.

YOU'RE WATCHING THE WRONG CAR

Everybody knows that, in the most important car is the one directly in front of you. After all, if you make a mistake, he's the one you're going to hit. That's a fine rule of thumb for safe driving, but when driving for economy we should take this for granted and try to go one step further. In this case, it's really one car (or more) farther ahead. Instead of concentrating entirely on the car directly ahead, look also at the car that's ahead of him.

If you were to watch commuter or other heavy traffic from the air, it would look like a giant screen-door spring expanding and contracting as it wiggles down the highway. Cars spread out as each takes its turn to accelerate, then bunch together as they take turns slowing down. The normal reaction is to accelerate as soon as the person in front of you begins to accelerate and to slow down as soon as he begins to slow down. This alternate hurry-up-and-wait and wait-and-hurry-up activity detracts from the smoothness which driving for economy demands. However, unless you're driving a bulldozer, it will be impossible for you to maintain a steady speed.

The next best thing is to reduce the amount of speeding-up and slowing-down you have to do, and the secret is to watch cars that are further ahead than the one in front. Whenever the second car ahead begins to accelerate, anticipate your own movement by taking your foot off the brake and starting to accelerate very slightly—by the time your turn comes, you'll already be moving and won't have to accelerate as quickly to keep up with the flow. Likewise, as the cars ahead start slowing down, begin to reduce your own speed before you really have to. By looking further ahead and beginning your speed changes earlier, you'll be able to enjoy the economy of smoother driving and smaller momentum changes. As you practice this strategy, you'll continue to get a better feel for the acceleration and deceleration "countdowns" which can give you gas-saving advance notice of necessary changes in your speed.

Even better advance notice is possible when driving in traffic through a tunnel, on a wet road, or at night. The shiny walls and roof of the tunnel will reflect the brake lights of cars further ahead, giving you a slow-down cue even when you can't see the cars themselves. Likewise, the successive switching off of brake lights gives you advance notice that you need in order to accelerate sooner and more slowly. Like the tunnel walls, a shiny or wet road surface will reflect the brake lights of the second car in front, except from underneath the car ahead. Likewise for night driving, in which anticipation is naturally more difficult because of lower visibility.

If you happen to be directly behind a truck or other large vehicle, your looking-ahead strategy will not be possible. In this case, it's appropriate to do a courteous turn for your fellow drivers—back off and let a few of them in front of you.

BEND WITH THE WIND

With today's engines, wind doesn't have much effect on how fast you can go. However, it can be a factor in deciding how fast you should go. By watching flags, factory smoke, bushes, trees and skinny telephone poles, you can determine if the wind is for you or against you. Drive a little more slowly when the wind is against you—air resistance depends on the relative speed between you and the air, not just on your speedometer reading. With the wind at your back, higher speeds will be much less expensive. Recall once again that the increase in air resistance is far out of proportion to the increase in your speed, and that a 10% increase in speed means a 33% increase in the horsepower your car needs to overcome air resistance.

In one gas mileage study, a standard size car was driven at high speed with and against a stiff wind. Going 70 mph into the 18 mph wind, the car was able to achieve only 11.6 miles per gallon. However, when driven 70 mph with the wind at its back, the car's mileage increased to 16.6 miles per gallon.

DRIVING AN AUTOMATIC

If you're driving a car with an automatic transmission, don't despair. Look at the bright side—by increasing your miles per gallon by 15%, you'll save more money than the stick driver who makes the same improvement. If that's not bright enough, consider the following:

Most cars with an automatic transmission are provided with a lower, more economical rear axle ratio to help compensate for economy lost through torque converter slippage. In addition, since the torque converter dampens uneven running which often occurs with lean air-fuel mixtures, an engine used with an automatic transmission can use a slightly leaner carburetor mixture than the same engine hooked up to a manual transmission. Another compensating factor is that high speeds tend to lessen the disadvantage of an automatic transmission. This is because greater air resistance lowers the economy of any car, regardless of transmission type, and because the torque converter becomes more efficient at higher speeds.

Besides applying the general techniques discussed so far, you can get more miles per gallon from your automatic by doing the following: Keep the car in high gear whenever possible. This may sometimes require a very light foot in order to avoid the selection of a lower gear. In some situations, it may be advantageous to use your left foot for braking. When you're trying to maintain your momentum by avoiding the brake, yet feel that a sudden stop or slow-down may become necessary, having your left foot in position near the brake will reduce your reaction time. Any time you are traveling downhill or decelerating, it's a good idea to keep your braking foot poised near the pedal—however, be sure not to "ride" the brake. Since your automatic transmission "locks up"

Illus. 4-4. If your windshield view looks like this, you're in the "pipeline" and shouldn't yield to the temptations of uneconomical driving.

and is more efficient at higher speeds, make a strong charge at the hills which lie ahead. Maintain or gradually build up speed as you approach the hill, then gradually press the gas pedal to maintain it on the way up.

ATTITUDE IS IMPORTANT

Driving for economy requires a certain state of mind. You should be relaxed enough that you aren't in a hurry and are free of the temptations of tail-gating, lane-jumping, and race-driver passing techniques. On the other hand, you must be alert to your driving environment and possible changes in it which may affect your speed, acceleration, and braking decisions. In short, driving for economy requires that you think economy. Every time you move the gas pedal, brake pedal, steering wheel or shift lever, one of the main thoughts in your mind should be—how is this going to affect my gas mileage?

RELAX IN THE "PIPELINE"

You'll encounter some situations where your speed is sharply reduced and in which you may become totally frustrated. It's morning rush hour and there are 5000 cars in front of yours; or you're following a cement mixer on a one-lane road; or you're stuck in the crowd that's taking a 14-mile detour. In these circumstances, it's sometimes hard to think sanity, let alone economy. But try. Whether you curse the mayor, sing Christmas carols, or play tic-tac-toe on the windshield, it isn't going to make one minute of difference in the time at which you'll arrive at your destination. When in these "pipeline" situations where you're trapped and can't do anything about it, try to relax and let the pipeline carry you at its own rate. However, along the way, get the best gas mileage you can by anticipating the movement of the cars in front of you and by applying various other tips presented here. This situation is one in which the AM-FM radio, stereo-tape outfit or shortwave unit can be a handy gas saver. If listening to the radio or tape deck calms you down, you're going to drive more economically. However, don't pump the gas pedal in tune with the music.

ENJOYING THE TRIP

Though sometimes more boring than frustrating, long trips can benefit from the same philosophy that is useful in the "pipeline." Radio equipment and gauges can help fight fatigue and impatience, as can keeping track of your average speed or competing with yourself to improve your gas mileage from one fill-up to the next.

HOW FAST ARE YOU REALLY GOING?

When you're driving for economy, it helps to know how fast you're going. Your speedometer may not be as accurate as you think, especially if you have oversize or

Two-Mile Time *min.*	*sec.*	*Actual Speed* *mph*	*One-Mile Time* *sec.*
1	40	72	50
1	44	69	52
1	48	66.5	54
1	52	64	56
1	56	62	58
2	0	60	60
2	4	58	62
2	8	56	64
2	12	54.5	66
2	16	53	68
2	20	51.5	70
2	24	50	72
2	28	48.5	74
2	32	47.5	76
2	36	46	78
2	40	45	80

snow tires on your car. Snow tires, which are larger in diameter than their summer counterparts, can fool your speedometer into reporting that you're going as much as five miles per hour slower than you really are. Thinking that you're going 55 when you're really going 60 may not seem like much, but it can be important to air resistance as well as to the radar cop down the road. At 60 mph, you'll require almost 30% more horsepower to overcome air resistance than you would at 55.

You can easily give your speedometer a lie detector test while driving on any highway equipped with mile markers. In addition, some roads have special mile-marked sections for the specific purpose of testing your speed. Drive at a constant speed which is comfortable, and which you can easily maintain over a distance of either one or two miles. Have a passenger time how long it takes to complete the course, then refer to the following table to determine your actual speed:

For example, if you maintain a constant speed over the one-mile course, a time of 68 seconds would indicate that your average speed was a very economical 53 mph. Be sure to check your speedometer accuracy from time to time, especially after you have switched to a new set of tires.

The Basics of Engine Operation

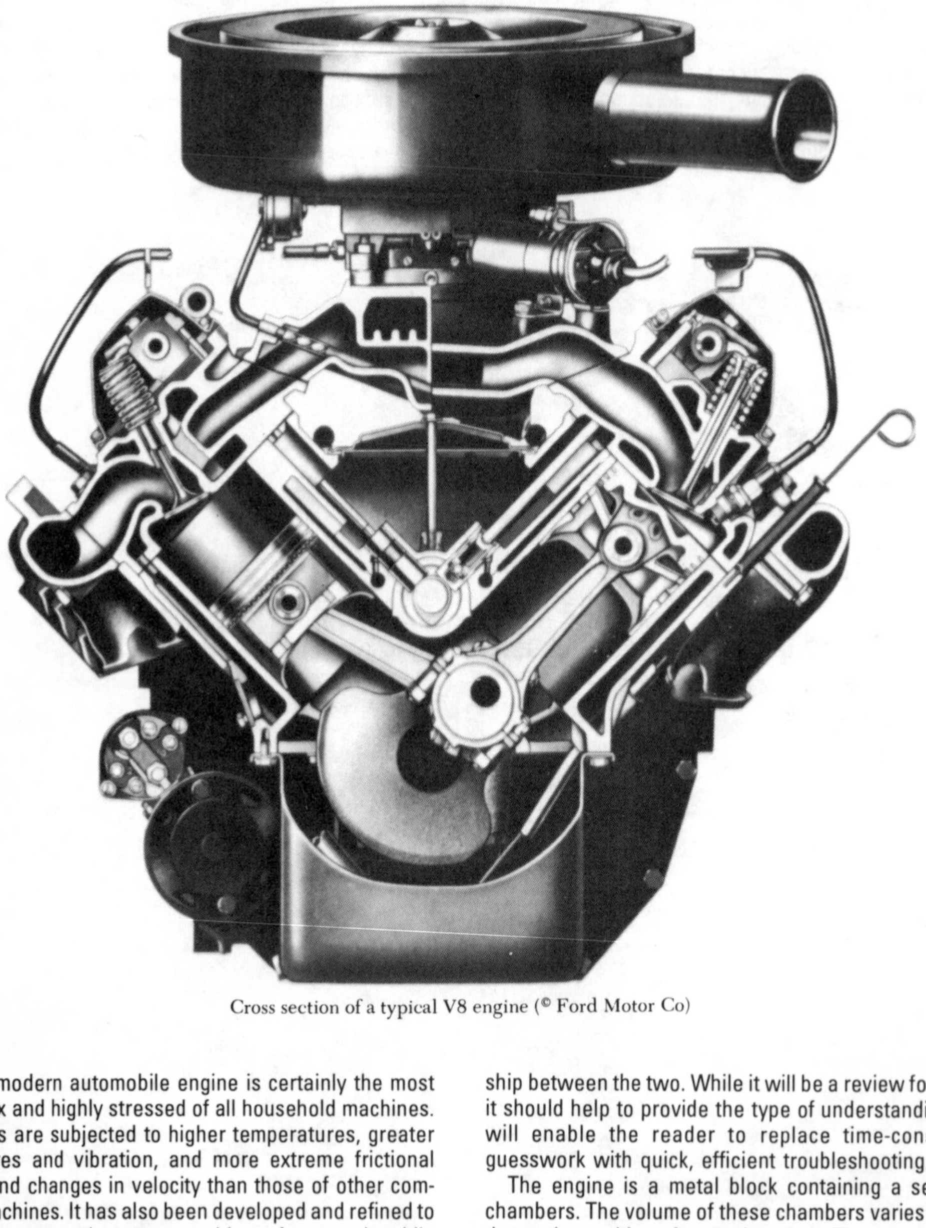

Cross section of a typical V8 engine (© Ford Motor Co)

The modern automobile engine is certainly the most complex and highly stressed of all household machines. Its parts are subjected to higher temperatures, greater pressures and vibration, and more extreme frictional loads and changes in velocity than those of other common machines. It has also been developed and refined to a greater extent than most machines. As a result, while the basic operating principles are fairly simple, the specifics are quite complex, and even the smallest deviation from the norm in the dimensions or the condition of a part, or in the setting of an individual adjustment can result in an obvious operating defect.

This first section is designed to relate engine operating principles to the most common malfunctions so that the troubleshooter may visualize the physical relationship between the two. While it will be a review for many, it should help to provide the type of understanding that will enable the reader to replace time-consuming guesswork with quick, efficient troubleshooting.

The engine is a metal block containing a series of chambers. The volume of these chambers varies in relation to the position of a rotating shaft. There is a port for each chamber which provides for the admission of combustible material and another port for the expulsion of burned gases. The combustion chambers' volumes must be variable in order for the engine to be able to make use of the expansion of the burning gases. This ability also enables the chamber to compress the gases before combustion, and to purge itself of burned material and refill itself with a combustible charge after combustion

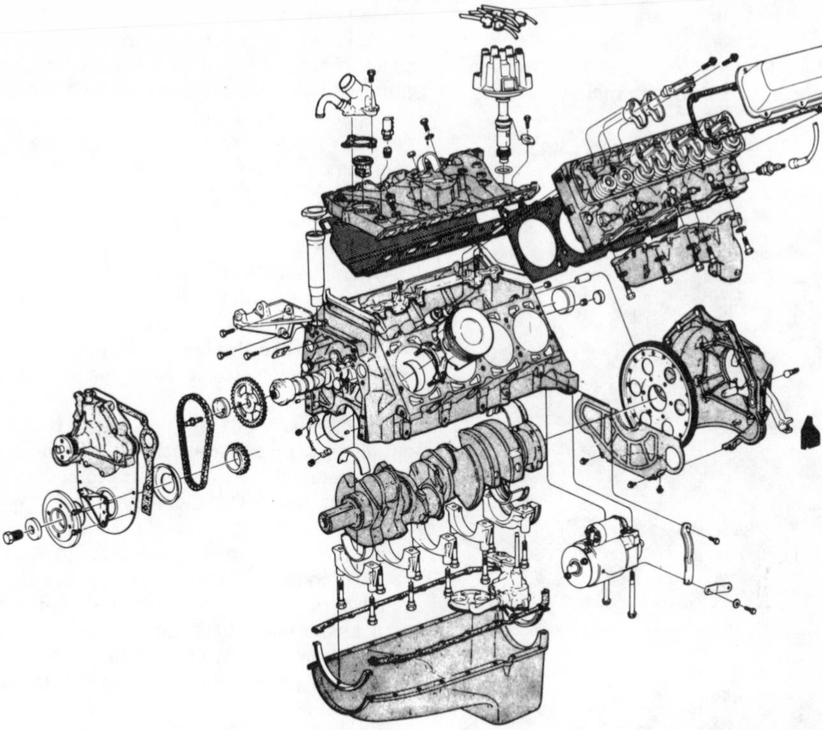

An exploded view of a typical water-cooled V8 engine (© G.M. Corp)

has taken place. (A description of how these four functions are accomplished follows the material on basic engine construction.)

The upper engine block is usually an iron or aluminum alloy casting, consisting of outer walls which form hollow water jackets around the four, six, or eight cylinder walls. The lower block provides an appropriate number of rigid mounting points for the bearings which hold the crankshaft in place, and is known as the crankcase. The hollow jackets of the upper block add to the rigidity of the structure and contain the liquid coolant which carries the heat away from the cylinders and other parts of the block. The block of an air-cooled engine consists of a crankcase which provides for the rigid mounting of the crankshaft and for the studs which hold the cylinders rigidly in place. The cylinders are usually individual, single-wall castings, and are finned for cooling.

The block (both air-cooled and water-cooled) also provides rigid mounts for the engine's camshaft and its drive gears or drive chain. In water-cooled engines, studs are installed in the top of the block to provide for the rigid mounting of the cylinder heads on the top of the

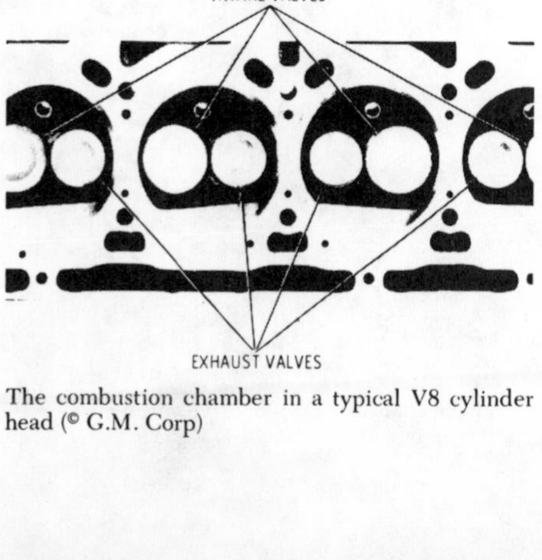

The combustion chamber in a typical V8 cylinder head (© G.M. Corp)

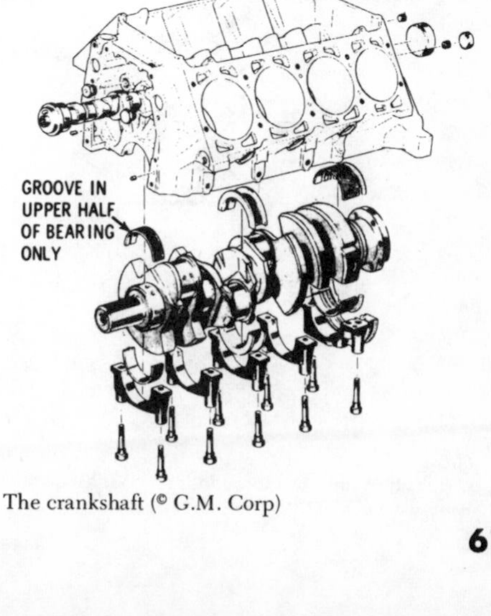

The crankshaft (© G.M. Corp)

block. The water and oil pumps are usually mounted directly to the block.

The crankshaft is a long iron alloy or steel fabrication which consists of bearing points or journals, which turn

A typical V8 cylinder block, bottom view (© G.M. Corp)

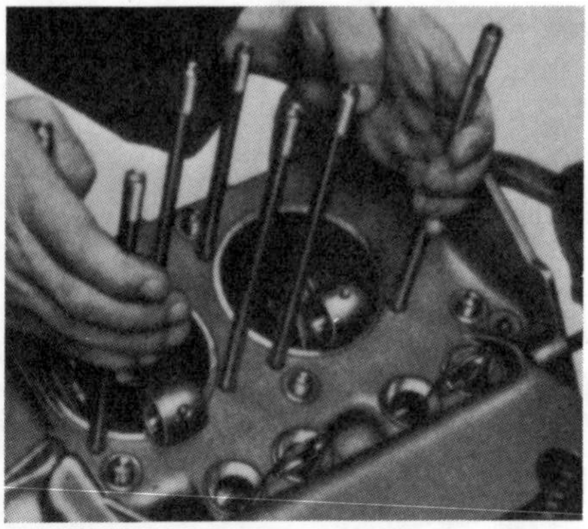

The crankcase of an air cooled engine (© Volkswagon of America, Inc)

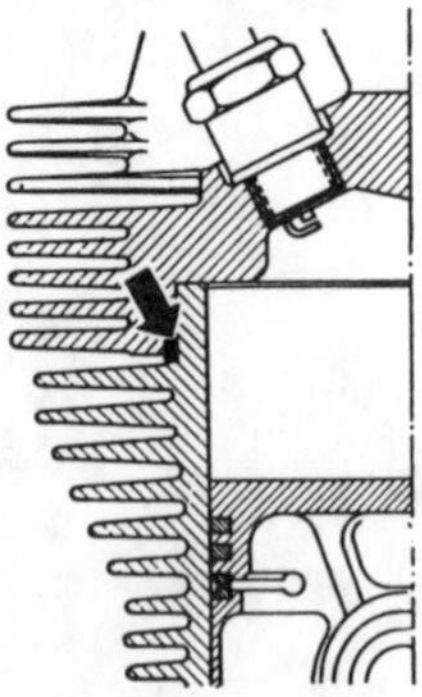

Cross-section of an air-cooled cylinder showing the cooling fins on the cylinder (© Volkswagon of America, Inc)

on their own axes, and counterweighted crank throws or crankpins which are located several inches from the center of the shaft and turn in a circle. The crankpins are centered under the cylinders which are machined into the upper block. Aluminum pistons with iron sealing rings are located in the cylinders and are linked to the crankpins via steel connecting rods. The rods connect with the pistons at their upper ends via piston pins and bushings, and at their lower ends fasten to the crankpins around the bearings.

When the crankshaft turns, the pistons move up and down within the cylinders, and the connecting rods convert their reciprocating motion into the rotary motion of the crankshaft. A flywheel at the rear of the crankshaft provides a large, stable mass for smoothing out the rotation.

The cylinder heads form tight covers for the tops of the cylinders, and contain machined chambers into which the contents of the cylinders are forced as the pistons reach the upper limit of their travel. Two poppet valves in each cylinder are opened and closed by the action of the camshaft and valve train. The camshaft is driven at one-half crankshaft speed and operates the valves remotely through pushrods and rocker levers via its eccentric lobes or cams. Each combustion chamber contains one intake valve and one exhaust valve. The cylinder heads also provide mounting threads for spark plugs which screw right through the heads so their lower tips protrude into the combustion chambers.

Lubricating oil, which is stored in a pan at the bottom of the engine and force-fed to almost all the parts of the engine by a gear type pump, lubricates the entire engine and also seals the piston rings.

The engine operates on a four-stroke cycle which is described below.

1. Intake Stroke: The intake stroke begins with the piston near the top of its travel, the exhaust valve nearly closed, and the intake valve opening rapidly. As the piston nears the top of its travel and begins its descent, the exhaust valve closes fully, the intake valve reaches a fully open position, and the volume of the combustion

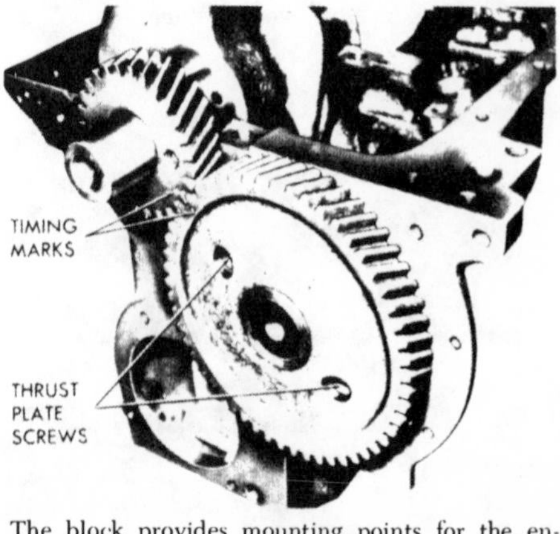

The block provides mounting points for the engine's camshaft and its drive mechanism (© G.M. Corp)

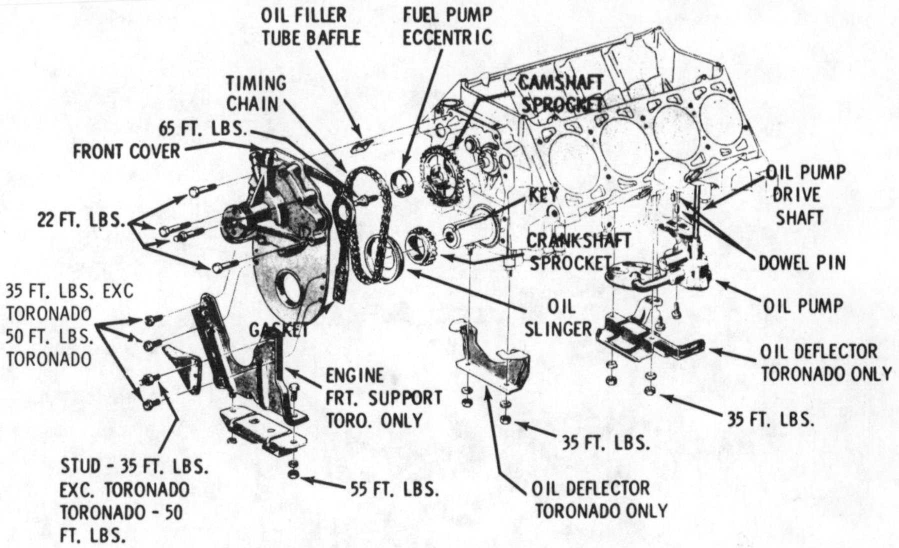

The water and oil pumps are usually mounted directly to the block (© G.M. Corp)

chamber begins to increase, creating a vacuum. As the piston descends, an air/fuel mixture is drawn from the carburetor into the cylinder through the intake manifold. (The intake manifold is simply a series of tubes which links each cylinder with the carburetor and the carburetor is a device for using the motion of air moving into the engine to mix just the right amount of fuel into the air stream.) The intake stroke ends with the piston having passed the bottom of its travel. The intake valve reaches a closed position just after the piston has begun its upstroke. The cylinder is now filled with the fuel/air mixture.

2. Compression Stroke: As the piston ascends, the fuel/air mixture is forced into the small chamber machined into the cylinder head. This compresses the mixture until it occupies ⅛th to 1/11th of the volume that it

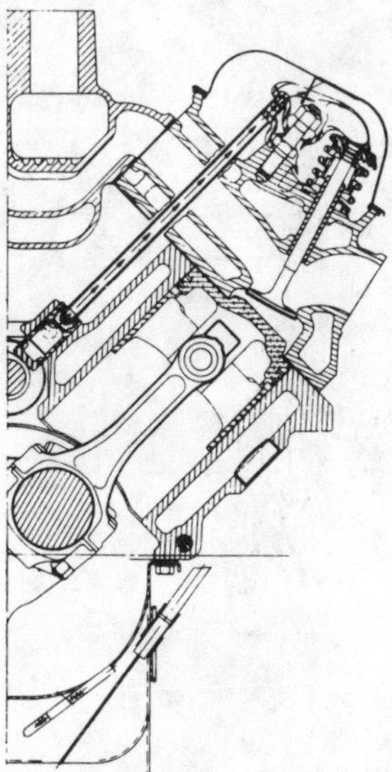

The camshaft operates the valves through push-rods and rocker levers (© G.M. Corp)

A typical piston and rod assembly (© G.M. Corp)

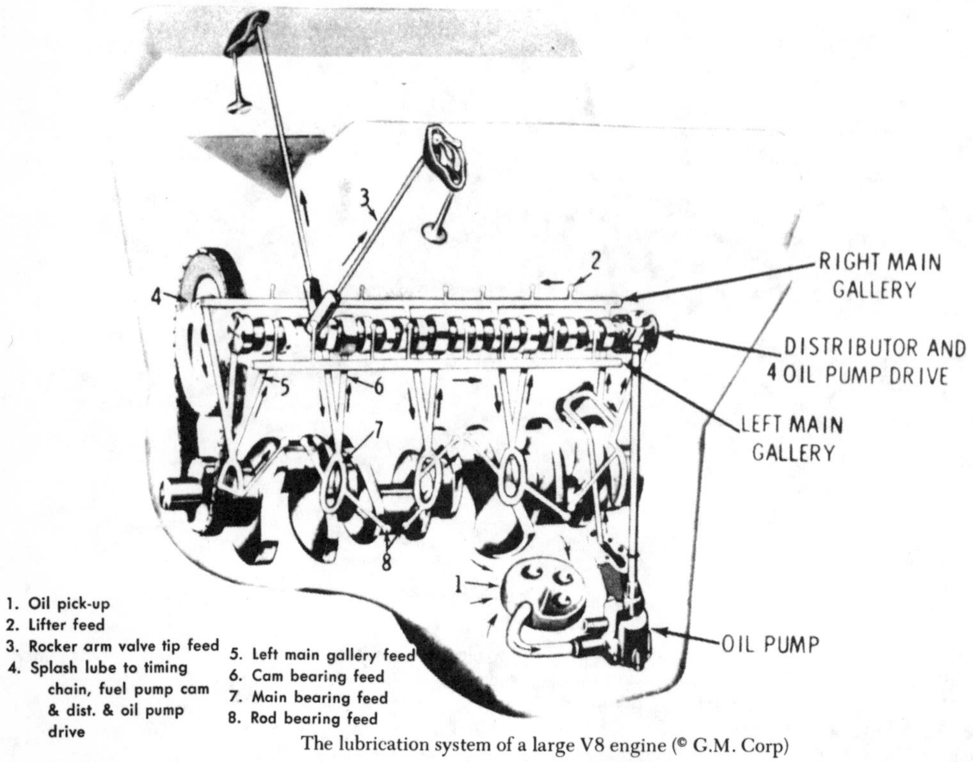

The lubrication system of a large V8 engine (© G.M. Corp)

did at the time the piston began its ascent. This compression raises the temperature of the mixture and increases its pressure, vastly increasing the force generated by the expansion of gases during the power stroke.

3. Power Stroke: The fuel/air mixture is ignited by the spark plug just before the piston reaches the top of its stroke so that a very large portion of the fuel will have burned by the time the piston begins descending again. The heat produced by combustion increases the pressure in the cylinder, forcing the piston down with great force.

4. Exhaust Stroke: As the piston approaches the bottom of its stroke, the exhaust valve begins opening and the pressure in the cylinder begins to force the gases out around the valve. The ascent of the piston then forces nearly all the rest of the unburned gases from the cylinder. The cycle begins again as the exhaust valve closes, the intake valve opens and the piston begins descending and bringing a fresh charge of fuel and air into the combustion chamber.

Several cars that have been imported into the United States use two-stroke cycle engines. These operate with only a compression stroke and a power stroke. Intake of fuel and air mixture and purging of exhaust gases takes place between the power and compression strokes while the piston is near the bottom of its travel. Ports in the cylinder walls replace poppet valves located in the cylinder heads on four-stroke cycle engines. The crankcase is kept dry of oil, and the entire engine is lubricated by mixing the oil with the fuel so that a fine mist of oil covers all moving parts. The ports are designed so the fuel and air are trapped in the engine's crankcase during

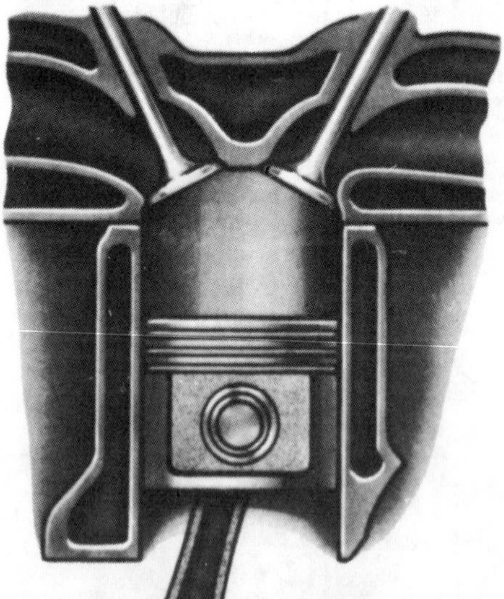

The appearance of the combustion chamber at the beginning of the compression stroke (© G.M. Corp)

most of the downstroke of the piston, thus making the crankcase a compression chamber that force-feeds the combustion chambers after the ports are uncovered. The pistons serve as the valves, covering the ports whenever they should be closed.

This should provide a basic understanding of what is going on inside the engine. The ignition, fuel, and engine auxiliary systems will be described later, each in its own troubleshooting section.

Troubleshooting When the Engine Won't Start

Check:

1. The Starting System
2. The Ignition System
3. The Fuel System
4. Compression

The Starting System

HOW IT WORKS

The battery is the first link in the chain of mechanisms which work together to provide cranking of the automobile engine. In most modern cars, the battery is a lead-acid electrochemical device consisting of six two-volt (2 V) subsections connected in series so the unit is capable of producing approximately 12 V of electrical pressure. Each subsection, or cell, consists of a series of positive and negative plates held a short distance apart in a solution of sulfuric acid and water. The two types of plates are of dissimilar metals. This causes a chemical reaction to be set up, and it is this reaction which produces current flow from the battery when its positive and negative terminals are connected to an electrical appliance such as a lamp or motor. The continued transfer of electrons would eventually convert the sulfuric acid in the electrolyte to water, and make the two plates identical in chemical composition. As electrical energy is removed from the battery, its voltage output tends to drop. Thus, measuring battery voltage and battery electrolyte composition are two ways of checking the ability of the unit to supply power. During the starting of the engine, electrical energy is removed from the battery. However, if the charging circuit is in good condition and the operating conditions are normal, the power removed from the battery will be replaced by the generator (or alternator) which will force electrons back through the battery, reversing the normal flow, and restoring the battery to its original chemical state.

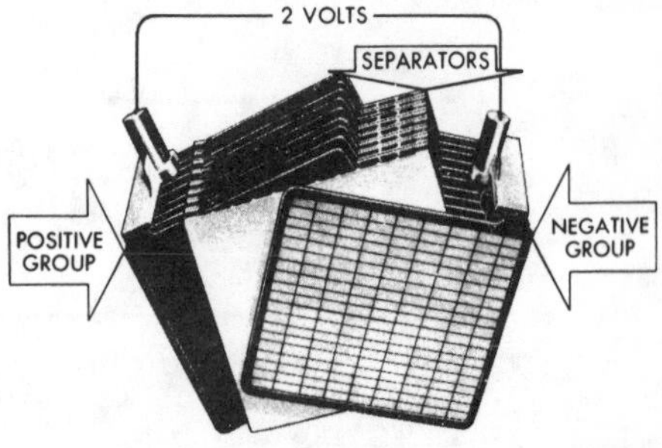

The battery plates which make up one of the six cells (© G.M. Corp)

The battery and starting motor are linked by very heavy electrical cables designed to minimize resistance to the flow of current. Generally, the major power supply cable that leaves the battery goes directly to the starter, while other electrical system needs are supplied by a smaller cable. During starter operation, power flows from the battery to the starter and is grounded through the car's frame and the battery's negative ground strap.

The starting motor is a specially designed, direct current electric motor capable of producing a very great amount of power for its size. One thing that allows the motor to produce a great deal of power is its tremendous rotating speed. It drives the engine through a tiny pinion gear (attached to the starter's armature), which drives the very large flywheel ring gear at a greatly reduced speed. Another factor allowing it to produce so much power is that only intermittent operation is required of it. Thus, little allowance for air circulation is required, and the windings can be built into a very small space.

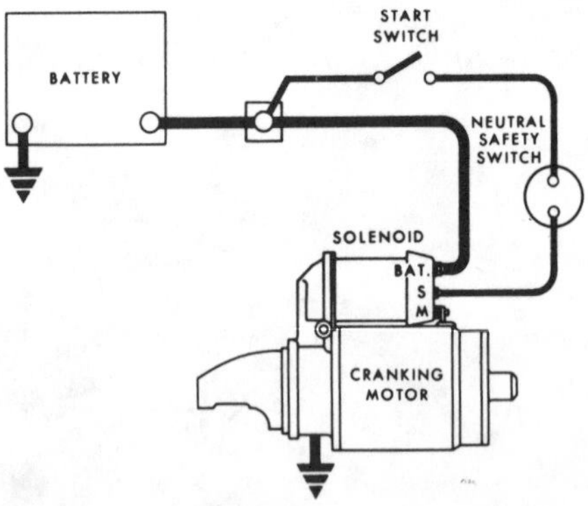

The starting circuit (© G.M. Corp)

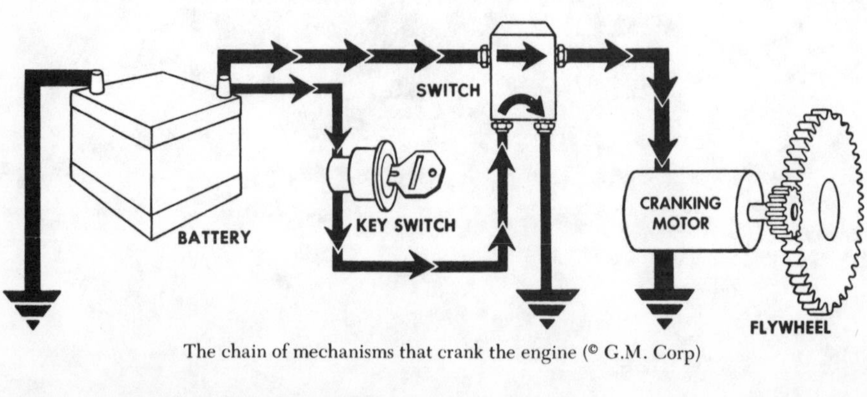

The chain of mechanisms that crank the engine (© G.M. Corp)

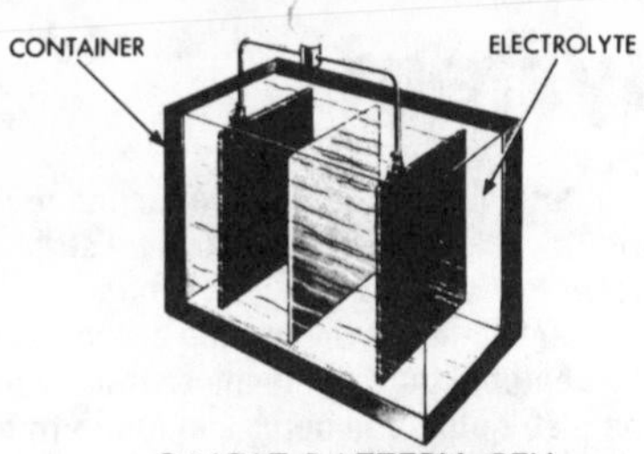

Simplified drawing of a battery cell (Courtesy, Delco-Remy) (© G.M. Corp)

The starter solenoid is a magnetic device which employs the small current supplied by the starting switch circuit of the ignition switch. This magnetic action moves a plunger which mechanically engages the starter and electrically closes the heavy switch which connects it to the battery. The starting switch circuit consists of the starting switch contained within the ignition switch, a transmission neutral safety switch or clutch pedal switch, and the wiring necessary to connect these in series with the starter solenoid or relay.

A pinion, which is a small gear, is mounted to a one-way drive clutch. This clutch is splined to the starter armature shaft. When the ignition switch is moved to the "start" position, the solenoid plunger slides the pinion toward the flywheel ring gear via a collar and spring. If the teeth on the pinion and flywheel match properly, the pinion will engage the flywheel immediately. If the gear teeth butt one another, the spring will be compressed and will force the gears to mesh as soon as the starter turns far enough to allow them to do so. As the solenoid plunger reaches the end of its travel, it closes the contacts that connect the battery and starter and then the engine is cranked.

As soon as the engine starts, the flywheel ring gear begins turning fast enough to drive the pinion at an extremely high rate of speed. At this point, the one-way clutch begins allowing the pinion to spin faster than the starter shaft so that the starter will not operate at excessive speed. When the ignition switch is released from the starter position, the solenoid is de-energized, and a spring contained within the solenoid assembly pulls the gear out of mesh and interrupts the current flow to the starter.

Some starters employ a separate relay, mounted away from the starter, to switch the motor and solenoid current on and off. The relay thus replaces the solenoid electrical switch, but does not eliminate the need for a solenoid mounted on the starter used to mechanically engage the starter drive gears. The relay is used to reduce the amount of current the starting switch must carry.

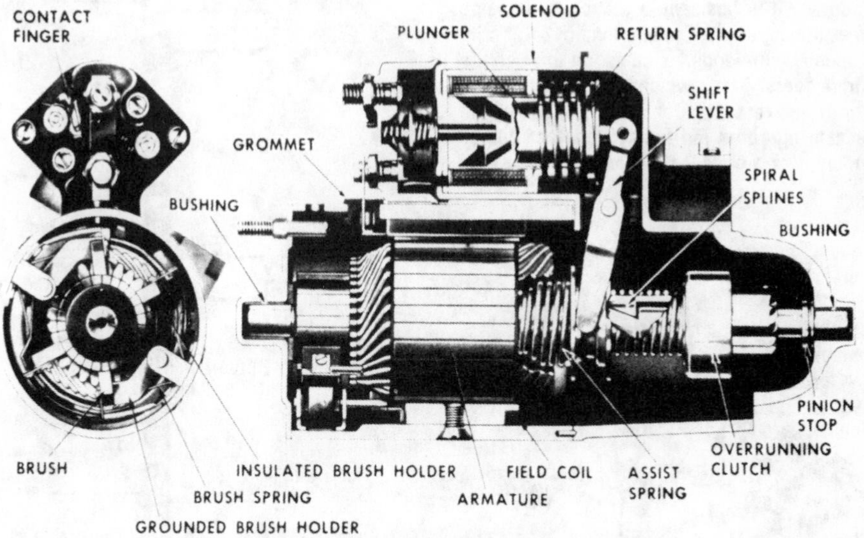

A typical starting motor (© G.M. Corp)

The Ignition System

HOW IT WORKS

The coil is the heart of the ignition system. It consists of two coils of wire wound about an iron core. These coils are insulated from each other and the whole assembly is enclosed in an oil-filled case. The primary coil is connected to the two primary terminals located on top of the coil and consists of relatively few turns of a heavier wire. The secondary circuit consists of many turns of fine wire and is connected to the high-tension connection on top of the coil. Energizing the coil primary with battery voltage produces current flow through the primary winding; this in turn produces a very large, intense magnetic field. Interrupting the flow of primary current causes the field to collapse. Just as current moving through a wire produces a magnetic field, moving a field across a wire will produce a current. As the magnetic field collapses, its lines of force cross the secondary winding, inducing a current in that winding. The force of the induced current is concentrated because of the relative shortness of the secondary coil of wire.

The distributor is the controlling element of the system, switching the primary current on and off and distributing the current to the proper spark plug each time a spark is produced. It is basically a stationary housing surrounding a rotating shaft. The shaft is driven at one-half engine speed by the engine's camshaft through the distributor drive gears. A cam which is situated near the top of the shaft has one lobe for each cylinder of the engine. The cam operates the ignition contact points, which are mounted on a plate located on bearings within the distributor housing. A rotor is attached to the top of the distributor shaft. When the bakelite distributor cap is in place, on top of the unit's metal housing, a spring-loaded contact connects the portion of the rotor directly above the center of the shaft to the center connection on top of the distributor. The outer end of the rotor passes very close to the contacts connected to the four, six, or eight high-tension connections around the outside of the distributor cap.

Under normal operating conditions, power from the battery is fed through a resistor or resistance wire to the primary circuit of the coil and is then grounded through the ignition points in the distributor. During cranking, the full voltage of the battery is supplied through an auxiliary circuit routed through the solenoid switch. In an eight-cylinder engine, the distributor cam will allow the points to close about 60 crankshaft degrees before the firing of the spark plug. Current will begin flowing through the

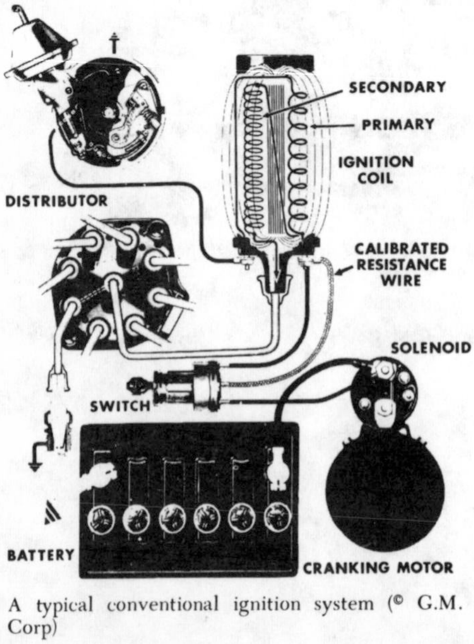

A typical conventional ignition system (© G.M. Corp)

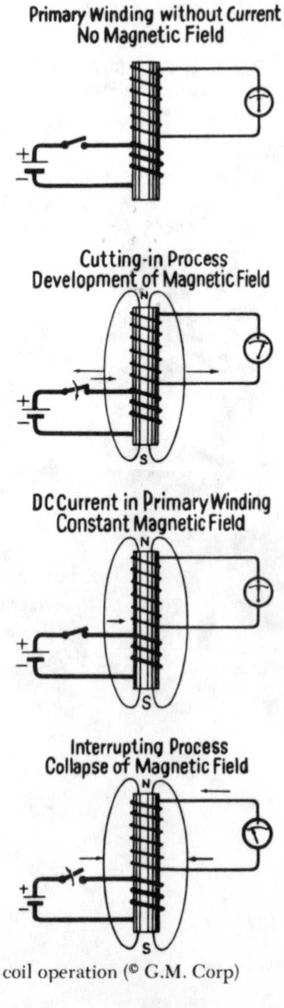

Ignition coil operation (© G.M. Corp)

primary wiring to the positive connection on the coil, through the primary winding of the coil, through the ground wire between the negative connection on the coil and the distributor, and to ground through the contact points. Shortly after the engine is ready to fire, the current flow through the coil primary will have reached a near maximum value, and an intense magnetic field will have formed around the primary windings. The distributor cam will separate the contact points at the proper time for ignition and the primary field will collapse, causing current to flow in the secondary circuit. A capacitor, known as the "condenser," is installed in the circuit in parallel with the contact points in order to absorb some of the force of the electrical surge that occurs during collapse of the magnetic field. The condenser consists of several layers of aluminum foil separated by insulation. These layers of foil, upon an increase in voltage, are capable of storing electricity, making the condenser a sort of electrical surge tank. Voltages just after the points open may reach 250 V because of the vast amount of energy stored in the primary windings and their magnetic field. A condenser which is defective or improperly grounded will not absorb the shock from the fast-moving stream of electrons when the points open and these electrons will force their way across the point gap, causing burning and pitting.

The very high voltage induced in the secondary windings will cause a surge of current to flow from the coil tower to the center of the distributor, where it will travel along the connecting strip along the top of the rotor. The surge will arc its way across the short gap between the contact on the outer end of the rotor and the connection in the cap for the high-tension lead of the cylinder to be fired. After passing along the high-tension lead, it will travel down the center electrode of the spark plug, which is surrounded by ceramic insulation, and arc its way over to the side electrode, which is grounded through threads which hold the plug in the cylinder head. The heat generated by the passage of the spark will ignite the contents of the cylinder.

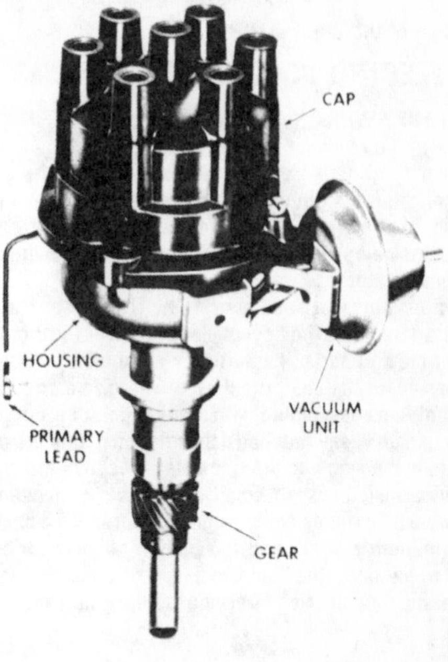

The location of the vacuum advance unit (© G.M. Corp)

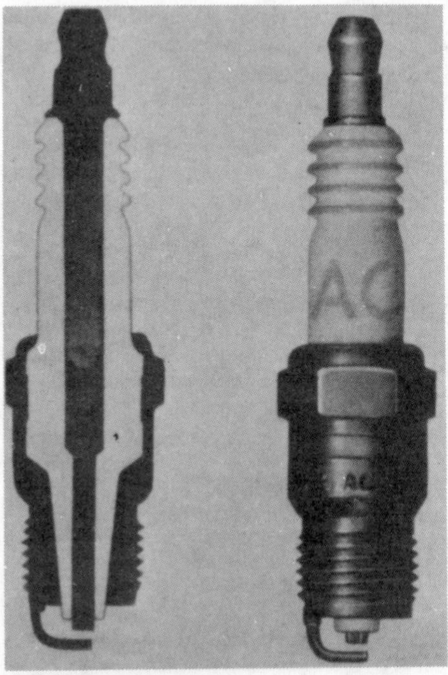

Cross-section of a spark plug. The white portion is the insulator. (© G.M. Corp)

Most distributors employ both centrifugal and vacuum advance mechanisms to advance the point at which ignition occurs for optimum performance and economy. Spark generally occurs a few degrees before the piston reaches top dead center (TDC) in order that very high pressures will exist in the cylinder as soon as the piston is capable of using the energy—just a few degrees after TDC. Centrifugal advance mechanisms employ hinged flyweights working in opposition to springs to turn the top portion of the distributor shaft, including the cam and rotor, ahead of the lower shaft. This advances the point at which the cam causes the points to open. A more advanced spark is required at higher engine speeds because the speed of combustion does not increase in direct proportion to increases in engine speed, but tends to lag behind at high revolutions. If peak cylinder pressures are to exist at the same point, advance must be used to start combustion earlier.

Vacuum advance is used to accomplish the same thing when part-throttle operation reduces the speed of combustion because of less turbulence and compression, and poorer scavenging of exhaust gases. Carburetor vacuum below the throttle plate is channeled to a vacuum diaphragm mounted on the distributor. The higher the manifold vacuum, the greater the motion of the diaphragm against spring pressure. A rod between the diaphragm and the plate on which the contact points are mounted rotates the plate on its bearings causing the cam to open the points earlier in relation to the position of the crankshaft.

ELECTRONIC IGNITION SYSTEMS

HOW THEY WORK

Electronic ignition systems use the same type of ignition coil to generate a hot spark, and employ the same type of rotor, distributor cap, wiring, and spark plugs to provide that spark to the cylinders. The main difference is that they employ a transistor to start and stop the flow of primary current.

A transistor is a solid-state relay. This means that it can start and stop the flow of electric current without the use of moving parts. It is turned on and off by a current much smaller than that required to energize a coil. Thus, the problems associated with ignition point burning and wear can be vastly reduced if the ignition points are used to supply the signal to the transistor. Because the signal to the transistor is so small, the points can even be replaced by a simple type of signal generator which uses a permanent magnet and the motion of the distributor shaft to generate the signal in a pick-up coil without any mechanical contact or direct passage of current.

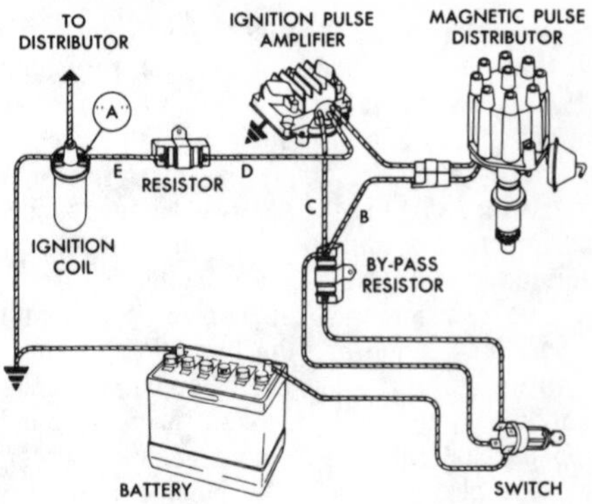

Diagram of a General Motors electronic ignition system (© G.M. Corp)

The switching transistor is part of an amplifier unit, which, in several stages, amplifies the original signal supplied by the pick-up coil, in some units. In others, a capacitor is first charged, and then is discharged across the primary circuit of the coil when ignition is required.

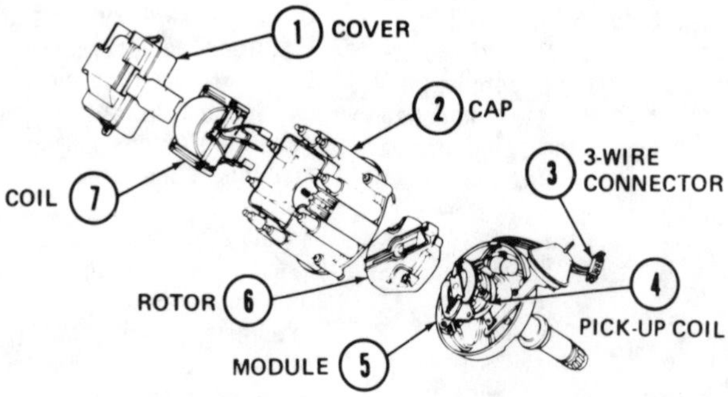

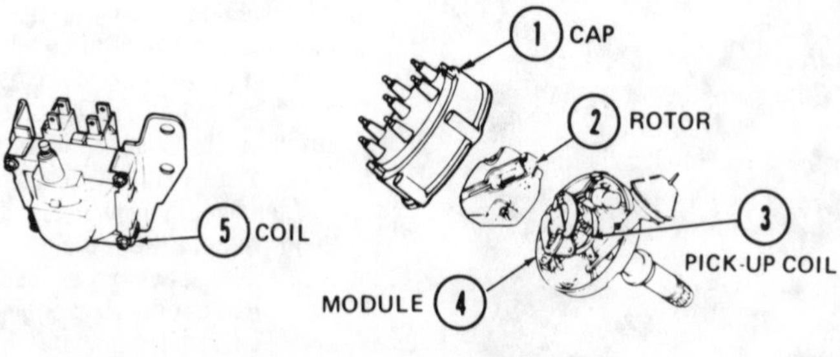

The Fuel System

HOW IT WORKS

The fuel burned in a gasoline engine is a mixture of hydrocarbon liquids—all with different boiling points. The purpose of the fuel system is to mix the proper amount of fuel with the air that the engine demands, effectively evaporate most of the fuel, and conduct the air/fuel mixture to the engine cylinders. The fuel system also regulates the flow of mixture to the engine for control of power output.

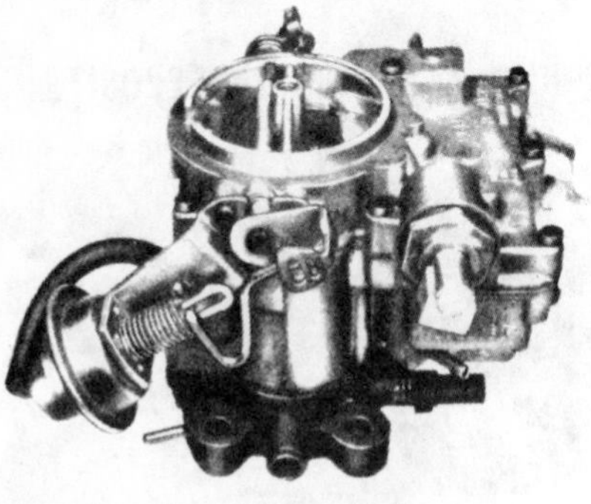

A typical carburetor (© G.M. Corp)

The fuel is stored in a tank which generally serves to allow for settling of water and other foreign material by picking up the fuel several inches off the bottom of the tank. A strainer is frequently used in the pick-up inside the tank.

Most engines employ a mechanical fuel pump which is driven by an eccentric on the camshaft. The pump is a flexible diaphragm mounted inside a housing. The eccentric on the camshaft forces the diaphragm down for intake of fuel and a spring forces the diaphragm back up. When fuel is not required by the carburetor, the spring remains compressed and the diaphragm remains motionless during what would normally be a discharge stroke for the pump. A line connects the fuel pick-up in the tank with the pump so the suction created by the pump can pull fuel from the tank to the pump inlet. A similar line connects the pump outlet to the carburetor. Some vehicles use electrically driven pumps that operate much as the engine-driven pump, but use solenoids to move the pump diaphragm up and down. A few vehicles employ in-tank centrifugal, electrical pumps.

The carburetor stores the fuel in a vented tank known as the "float bowl." A float-operated valve maintains the level of fuel in the bowl within a narrow range. As the fuel level rises, the float will rise and close off the valve, thus causing the movement of the fuel pump diaphragm to be reduced because of reduced discharge of fuel.

The carburetor handles all the air which the engine receives and regulates its flow through the action of a throttle. The air passes through a slight restriction in the carburetor, known as a "venturi." The venturi causes some of the atmospheric pressure that is pushing the air to be lost as the air speeds up in passing through the restriction. The pressure in the venturi drops as the air flow increases. In order to improve the accuracy of the metering at low speeds, a booster venturi is frequently used. It is a much smaller venturi, mounted above the regular one, in the center of the carburetor bore.

A main metering system, consisting of a nozzle and a discharge tube which carries the fuel to a spot inside the venturi in the throttle bore, conducts the fuel to the airstream during most driving conditions. Since vacuum in the venturi is proportional to the amount of air passing through it, the air/fuel ratio is fairly accurately governed by the amount of vacuum available to lift fuel from the bowl to the discharge. If the carburetor uses a booster venturi, fuel is discharged at the center of the booster to provide the best possible metering at low speeds. The arm which carries fuel to the booster venturi and supports it is usually integral with several other carburetor

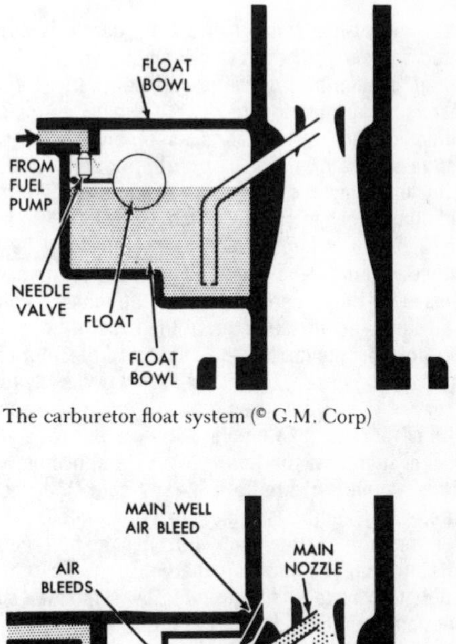

The carburetor float system (© G.M. Corp)

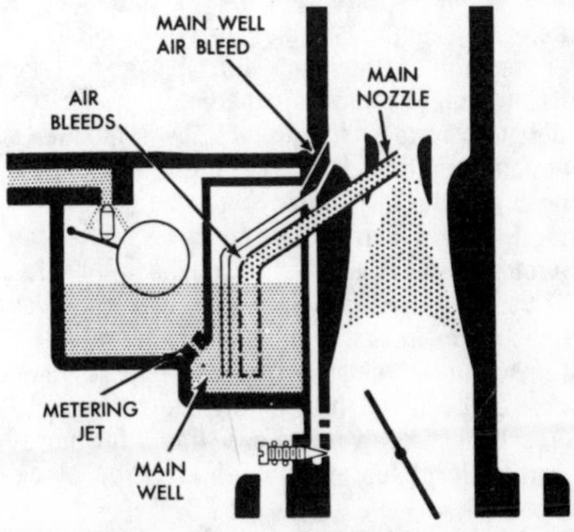

The carburetor main circuit (© G.M. Corp)

parts, such as idle or accelerator pump passages. The assembly is known as the "venturi cluster" and can be separated from the main body of the carburetor during disassembly. In some carburetors, a metering rod, which is positioned by the throttle linkage, throttles the flow of fuel through the main discharge nozzle for increased metering accuracy.

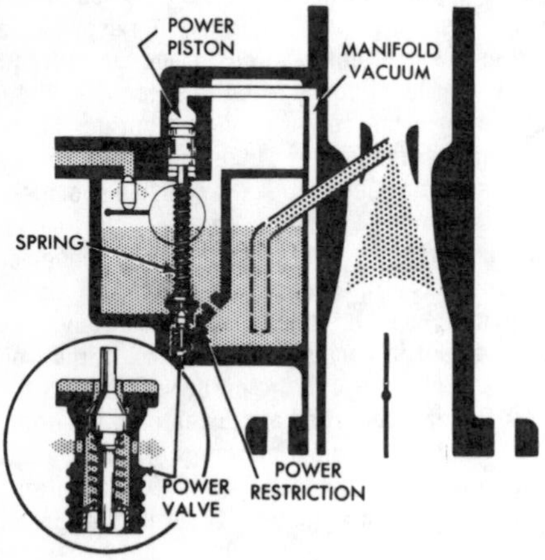

The carburetor power system (© G.M. Corp)

The flow of fuel through the main nozzle is supplemented at very high throttle openings by a power enrichment system that provides sufficient fuel to ensure fullest use of the air inducted by the engine at full power conditions. This system consists of an auxiliary fuel passage and metering valve on carburetors which do not employ metering rods, and an auxiliary metering rod positioning mechanism on those which do. In either case, a piston is kept in an inactive position by high manifold vacuum. When manifold vacuum becomes very low, as at full throttle, the piston either opens the valve in the auxiliary fuel passage, or, in the case of units using metering rods, moves the rod slightly further out of the main metering nozzle, or "jet." A spring generally forces the system to operate when manifold vacuum drops off.

The carburetor also employs an idle passage which conducts fuel from the float bowl to a spot below the throttle. When the throttle is nearly shut, the vacuum created in the venturi is negligible, but manifold vacuum under the throttle is very high, and pulls the fuel required at idle through this small auxiliary system. Flow of fuel through this system is adjustable by a mixture screw accessible from outside the carburetor.

The carburetor also employs a pump that is operated by the throttle linkage to discharge a spray of fuel into the airstream during sudden increases in throttle opening. This pump provides instant response to sudden changes in conditions.

Many carburetors use two or four venturis to provide better distribution of fuel to the engine or to permit progressive use of two sets of venturis for more accurate metering of fuel over a wider range of air flow conditions.

The fuel is conducted by a series of tubes from the carburetor to the intake ports of the engine block. These tubes are known as the "intake manifold" and branch away from the carburetor base. Small tubes are used all the way from the carburetor to each cylinder to avoid the restriction to mixture flow that would result if large ducts were suddenly narrowed down to the size of the intake valves. The high velocity in the intake manifold also helps the fuel to be more completely evaporated by the time it reaches the combustion chambers.

Evaporation is also aided by designing the carburetor to thoroughly atomize the fuel and by heating the manifold slightly with exhaust manifold heat. Some exhaust manifold heating systems employ a thermostatic valve to channel the flow of hot gases either toward or away from the intake manifold walls depending on temperature conditions.

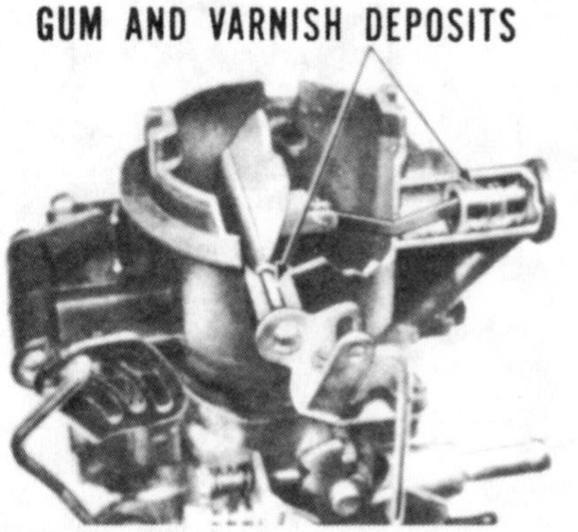

Spots where gum and varnish form on carburetors using choke pistons (Courtesy, Chrysler Corp)

During cold-engine operating conditions, evaporation of fuel is very poor. The carburetor uses a choke to permit smooth cold-engine operation. The choke is constructed much like the throttle, but is located above the venturi so that closing it will produce a vacuum that will increase the amount of fuel flowing from the carburetor jets into the air stream. This very rich mixture will contain sufficient fuel to provide a combustible mixture, even though the cold temperatures will retard the evaporation process.

The choke is operated by a thermostatic spring, the tension of which is relaxed by heat from the exhaust manifold as the engine warms up. Intake manifold vacuum also affects the position of the choke, which is mounted off center in the carburetor bore. Increased flow of air will thus tend to open the choke and maintain a fairly even vacuum at the fuel metering jets. A vacuum-operated diaphragm may also be used to prevent cold operation from being excessively rich. The diaphragm is linked to the choke through a lever arm and opens the choke slightly as soon as there is a vacuum in the manifold.

An air cleaner is mounted on top of the carburetor to remove dust and dirt from the air and to avoid excessive wear of engine parts. Most recent air filters are made of

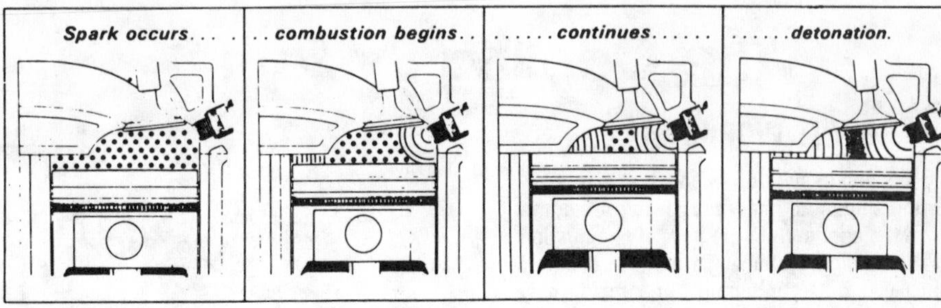

Detonation

a sufficiently porous paper to permit a relatively unrestricted flow of air while catching dust particles.

DETONATION

Detonation, or "knock" or "ping," is a severely damaging form of explosive combustion. During normal engine operation, combustion is only partly complete as the piston passes TDC at the beginning of the power stroke. The full energy of the fuel is released gradually as the piston descends and is converted to mechanical energy almost as fast as heat is created by combustion. Detonation occurs as a result of extreme temperatures and pressures in the cylinders. Cylinder temperatures become so high that the pressure increase caused by combustion near the spark plug raises a great portion of the total charge to a temperature above its ignition point, causing simultaneous combustion at many points in the chamber rather than the normal gradual spreading of the flame. The result is a violent shock to the piston and cylinder walls and searing heat.

Gasoline octane rating refers to the ability of the fuel to resist rapid combustion of the type that damages the engine. Detonation may be caused by use of the wrong spark plug, an incorrect fuel mixture, improper ignition timing, or overheating. However, by far the most common cause, assuming the engine is reasonably well maintained, is use of a fuel of too low an octane rating. Use a reputable brand of gasoline of regular or premium grade, depending on the manufacturer's recommendations for the particular engine. In some cases, this will still result in slight detonation because of variations in individual engines. A fuel with sufficient anti-knock quality should be used to avoid audible detonation.

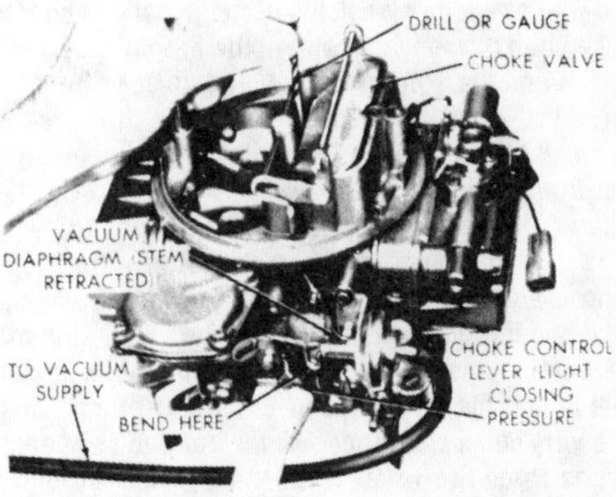

A typical factory manual illustration giving instructions on choke vacuum break adjustment (Courtesy, Chrysler Corp)

VAPOR LOCK AND PERCOLATION

Vapor lock is the evaporation of fuel into vapor due to heat conducted to the fuel pump. This vapor paralyzes the pump. The pump has only limited ability to handle gaseous material. The vapor simply expands and contracts as the diaphragm operates, rather than flowing in and out. Some air-conditioned cars have a return line designed to allow fuel vapor to be shunted back to the fuel tank.

Percolation is a related phenomenon, but occurs in the carburetor. Fuel vapor formed by heat increases the pressure in the float bowl, causing it to overflow into the throttle bores. Flooding problems result when the engine is hot.

The Cooling System

HOW IT WORKS

The cooling system, in spite of its compact size, handles a staggering amount of heat in order to protect the internal parts of the engine from the heat of combustion and friction. The cooling system of a modern car may remove about 6,000 BTU per minute, or considerably more heat than is required to comfortably warm a large home in extreme weather.

The coolant employed now is generally a mixture of water and ethylene glycol. Ethylene glycol is a chemical which, when mixed with water in the proper proportions, both lowers the freezing point and raises the boiling point of the solution. Most commercial antifreezes also contain additives designed to inhibit corrosion and foaming in the system.

The water pump is the heart of the cooling system. This is usually driven off the pulley on the front of the engine crankshaft by V belts. Its bearings are usually sealed ball bearing units located in the long snout of the front pump housing. The pump's impeller is a vaned wheel which fits the inside of the water pump housing with a very close clearance. Water trapped between the vanes is forced to rotate with the impeller around the inside of the water pump housing. The resultant centrifugal force raises the pressure in the pump discharge, causing water to flow through the pump.

The coolant is discharged into the front of the engine block and circulates in the water jackets around the cylinders. It then makes its way upward through ports in the block, head gasket, and head to the water passages around the combustion chambers. It leaves the engine through the front of the block, passing into the thermostat housing which, in V8 engines, is a part of the intake manifold. Here, the water flow splits; part of it returning directly to the water pump inlet through an external bypass hose or internal bypass passage, and part of it passing through the upper radiator hose.

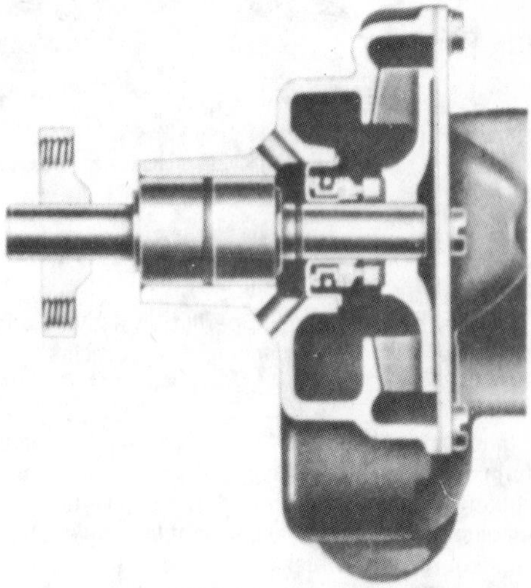

Cross-section of a typical water pump (© G.M. Corp)

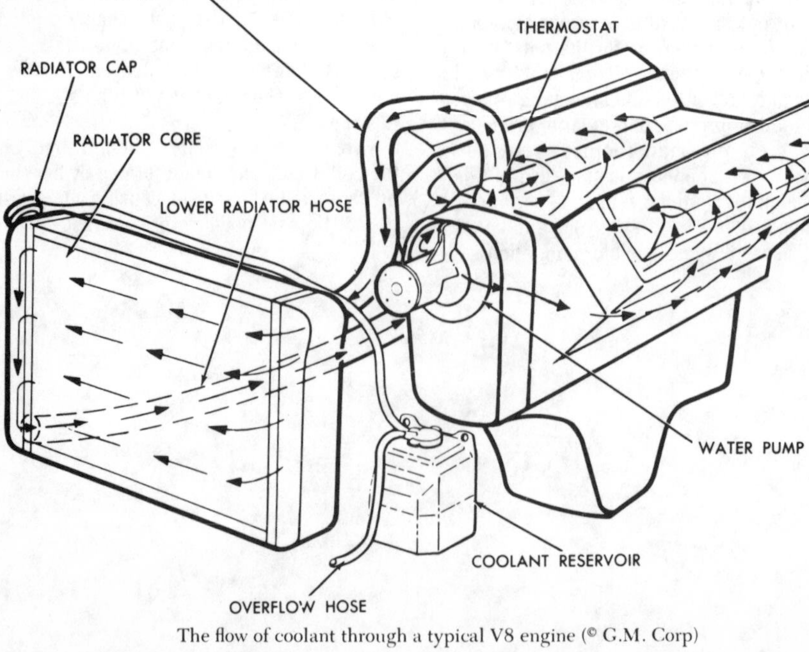

The flow of coolant through a typical V8 engine (© G.M. Corp)

The radiator is a heat exchanger consisting of a large number of thin water tubes fed through upper and lower or right and left side header tanks. Thin metal fins are soldered to the outside surfaces of the water tubes to increase the area of the hot metal surfaces available for transmission of heat to the air. A fan, usually driven off the water pump shaft, aids circulation of air through the radiator, especially at low speeds. Some fans have a thermostatically operated fluid drive clutch to adjust the fan speed to temperature conditions and engine speed.

A heater core, similar in construction to the radiator, receives coolant flow from the lower portion of the thermostat housing where coolant flows at all times. The heater hoses conduct the water to the core and return it to the inlet side of the water pump. The heater core is usually in a heater air duct located in the dash panel.

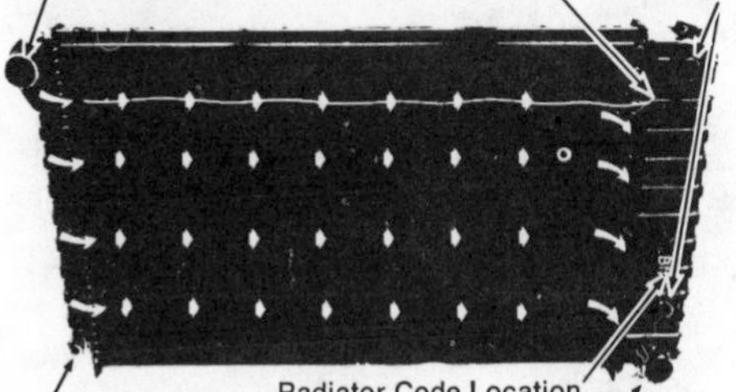

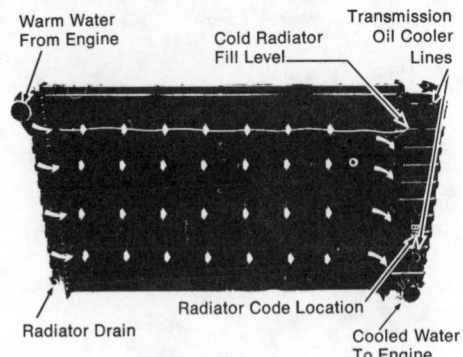

A typical cross-flow radiator (© G.M. Corp)

A pressure cap seals the radiator against coolant leakage through the action of a sprung poppet valve whose rubber sealing ring bears against a surface inside the filler neck. The cap allows the escape of coolant when the system pressure reaches a predetermined level, usually about 15 psi, thus protecting the radiator, hoses, and other system components from excessive pressure. The cap also incorporates a vacuum relief valve which opens only during cooling of the system (when the engine is off) to prevent the formation of vacuum within the system.

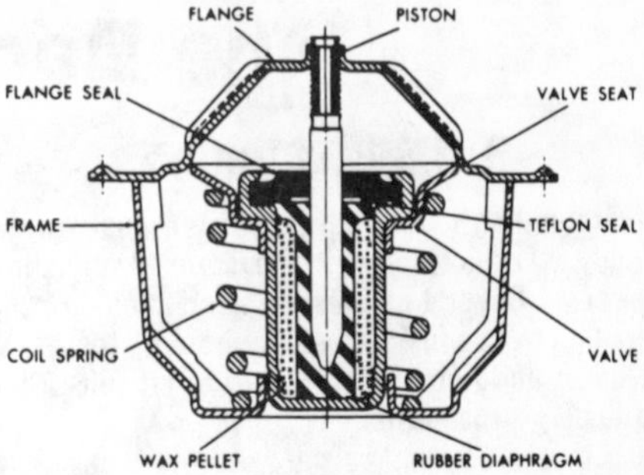

Cross-section of a thermostat (© G.M. Corp)

The system adjusts its cooling capacity to the weather conditions, vehicle speed, and engine load through the action of a thermostat. The thermostat consists of a poppet or hinged flap type of valve actuated by pressure from a fluid-filled bellows or wax pellet. The valve remains tightly closed below the rated opening temperature, forcing all the coolant discharged from the water pump to return directly to the water pump inlet. This practically eliminates loss of heat from the engine during warm-up, while protecting the system from the formation of steam at hot spots. The bypass inlet is situated near the heat-sensing portion of the thermostat so the thermostat will receive a continuous indication of the water temperature, sven when none of the fluid is passing through it.

When coolant temperature reaches the specified level (usually 180-195°), the thermostat will begin opening. The valve will be opened gradually as coolant temperatures rise, and will reach a wide-open position about 25° above the opening temperature. The radiator is slightly larger than required during most operating conditions. Thus, the thermostat is usually at least part-way closed, providing a precise control of engine temperature. One exception is when the engine is idled or turned off immediately after a hard run. The cooling system's capacity to throw off heat is vastly decreased under these conditions but the great amount of heat stored up in the heavy metal of the engine block continues to warm the coolant. It is normal for the engine temperature to rise substantially under these conditions. As long as water is not discharged from the pressure cap, there is nothing wrong with the system.

The Electrical System

BASIC ELECTRICITY

Understanding just a little about the basic theory of electricity will make electrical system troubleshooting much easier. Several gauges are used in electrical troubleshooting to see inside the circuit being tested. Without a basic understanding, it will be difficult to understand testing procedures.

Electricity is defined as the flow of electrons. Electrons are hypothetical particles thought to constitute the basic "stuff" of electricity. In a comparison with water flowing in a pipe, the electrons would be the water. As the flow of water can be measured, the flow of electricity can be measured. The unit of measurement is amperes, frequently abbreviated "amps". An ammeter will measure the actual amount of current flowing in the circuit.

Electricity can be compared to water flowing in a pipe (© G.M. Corp)

Just as water pressure is measured in units such as pounds per square inch, electrical pressure is measured in volts. When a voltmeter's two probes are placed on two "live" portions of an electrical circuit with different electrical pressures, current will flow through the voltmeter and produce a reading which indicates the difference in electrical pressure between the two parts of the circuit.

While increasing the voltage in a circuit will increase the flow of current, the actual flow depends not only on voltage, but on the resistance of the circuit. The standard unit for measuring circuit resistance is an ohm, measured by an ohmmeter. The ohmmeter is somewhat similar to an ammeter, but incorporates its own source of power so that a standard voltage is always present.

An actual electric circuit consists of four basic parts. These are: the power source, such as a generator or battery; a hot wire, which conducts the electricity under a relatively high voltage or pressure to the electrical appliance supplied by the circuit; the load, such as a lamp, motor, resistor, or relay coil; and the ground wire, which carries the current back to the source under very low electrical pressure. In such a circuit, the bulk of the resistance exists between the point where the hot wire is connected to the load, and the point where the load is grounded. In an automobile, the vehicle's frame, which is made of steel, is used as a part of the ground circuit for many of the electrical devices.

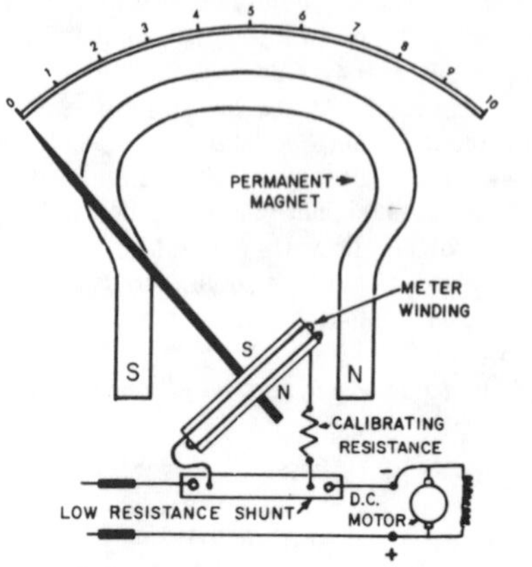

Ammeter circuit

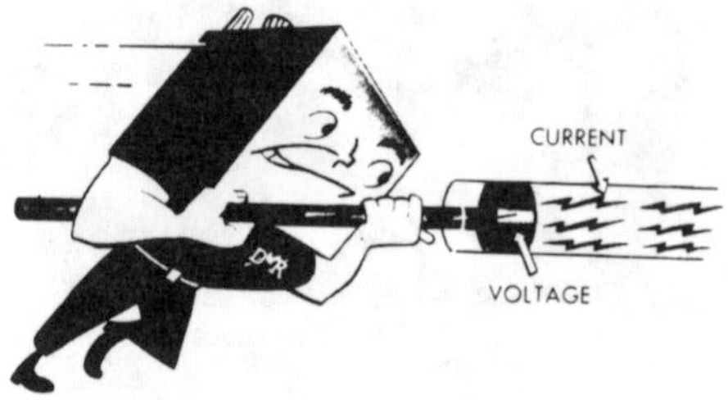

Voltage is the pressure that causes current to flow (© G.M. Corp)

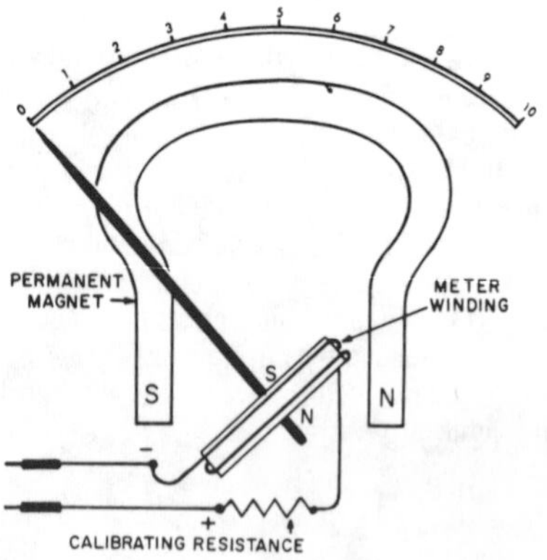

Voltmeter circuit

Remember that, in electrical testing, the voltmeter is connected in parallel with the circuit being tested (without disconnecting any wires) and measures the difference in voltage between the locations of the two probes; that the ammeter is connected in series with the load (the circuit is separated at one point and the ammeter inserted so it becomes a part of the circuit); and that the ohmmeter is self-powered, so that all the power in the circuit should be off and the portion of the circuit to be measured contacted at either end by one of the probes of the meter.

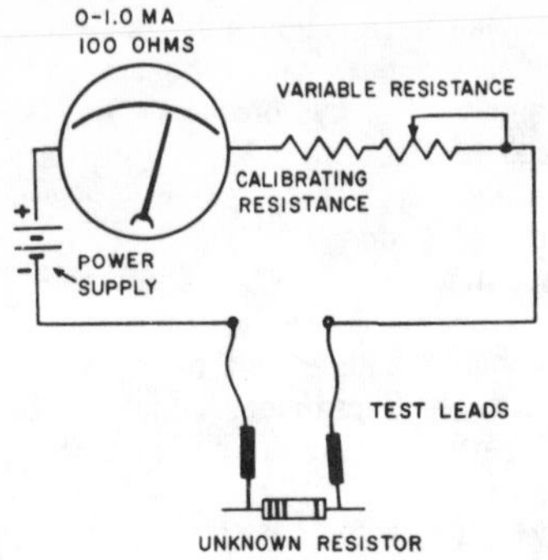

Ohmmeter circuit

THE CHARGING SYSTEM

HOW IT WORKS

The automobile charging system provides electrical power for operation of the vehicle's ignition and starting systems and all the electrical accessories. The battery serves as an electrical surge or storage tank, storing (in chemical form) the energy originally produced by the engine-driven generator. The system also provides a means of regulating generator output to protect the battery from being overcharged and to avoid excessive voltage to the accessories.

The storage battery is a chemical device incorporating parallel lead plates in a tank containing a sulfuric acid-water solution. Adjacent plates are slightly dissimilar, and the chemical reaction of the two dissimilar plates produces electrical energy when the battery is connected to a load such as the starter motor. The chemical reaction is reversible, so that when the generator is producing a voltage (electrical pressure) greater than that produced by the battery, electricity is forced into the battery, and the battery is returned to its fully charged state.

An alternator rotor. Initial current flow comes from the battery (Courtesy of Delco-Remy)

The vehicle's generator is driven mechanically, through V belts, by the engine crankshaft. It consists of two coils of fine wire, one stationary (the "stator"), and one movable (the "rotor"). The rotor may also be known as the "armature", and consists of fine wire wrapped around an iron core which is mounted on a shaft. The electricity which flows through the two coils of wire (provided initially by the battery in some cases) creates an intense magnetic field around both rotor and stator, and the interaction between the two fields creates voltage, allowing the generator to power the accessories and charge the battery.

There are two types of generators; the earlier is the direct current (DC) type. The current produced by the DC generator is generated in the armature and carried off the spinning armature by stationary brushes contacting the commutator. The commutator is a series of smooth metal contact plates on the end of the armature. The commutator plates, which are separated from one another by a very short gap, are connected to the armature circuits so that current will flow in one direction only in the wires carrying the generator output. The generator stator consists of two stationary coils of wire which draw some of the output current of the generator to form a powerful magnetic field and create the interaction of fields which generates the voltage. The generator field is wired in series with the regulator.

Newer automobiles use alternating current generators or "alternators", because they are more efficient, can be rotated at higher speeds, and have fewer brush problems. In an alternator, the field rotates while all the current produced passes only through the stator windings. The brushes bear against continuous slip rings rather than a commutator. This causes the current produced to periodically reverse the direction of its flow. Diodes (electrical one-way switches) block the flow of current from traveling in the wrong direction. A series of diodes is wired together to permit the alternating flow of the stator to be converted to a pulsating, but unidirectional flow at the alternator output. The alternator's field is wired in series with the voltage regulator.

The regulator consists of several circuits. Each circuit has a core, or magnetic coil of wire, which operates a switch. Each switch is connected to ground through one or more resistors. The coil of wire responds directly to system voltage. When the voltage reaches the required level, the magnetic field created by the winding of wire closes the switch and inserts a resistance into the generator field circuit, thus reducing the output. The contacts of the switch cycle open and close many times each second to precisely control voltage.

While alternators are self-limiting as far as maximum current is concerned, DC generators employ a current regulating circuit which responds directly to the total

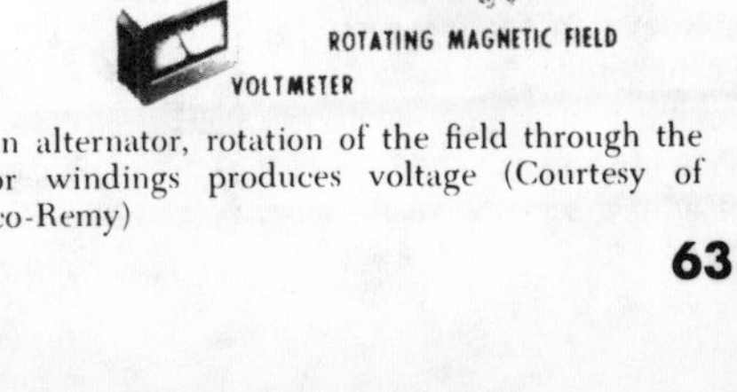

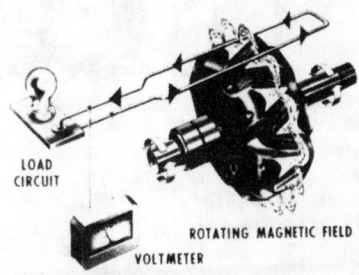

In an alternator, rotation of the field through the stator windings produces voltage (Courtesy of Delco-Remy)

A typical alternator (© G.M. Corp)

amount of current flowing through the generator circuit rather than to the output voltage. The current regulator is similar to the voltage regulator except that all system current must flow through the energizing coil on its way to the various accessories.

SAFETY PRECAUTIONS

Observing these precautions will ensure safe handling of the electrical system components, and will avoid damage to the vehicle's electrical system:

A. Be absolutely sure of the polarity of a booster battery before making connections. Connect the cables positive to positive, and negative to negative. Connect positive cables first and then make the last connection to a ground on the body of the booster vehicle so that arcing cannot ignite hydrogen gas that may have accumulated near the battery. Even momentary connection of a booster battery with the polarity reversed will damage alternator diodes.

B. Disconnect both vehicle battery cables before attempting to charge a battery.

C. Never ground the alternator or generator output or battery terminal. Be cautious when using metal tools around a battery to avoid creating a short circuit between the terminals.

D. Never ground the field circuit between the alternator and regulator.

E. Never run an alternator or generator without load unless the field circuit is disconnected.

F. Never attempt to polarize an alternator.

G. Keep the regulator cover in place when taking voltage and current limiter readings.

H. Use insulated tools when adjusting the regulator.

I. Whenever DC generator-to-regulator wires have been disconnected, the generator must be repolarized. To do this with an externally grounded, light duty generator, momentarily place a jumper wire between the battery terminal and the generator terminal of the regulator. With an internally grounded heavy duty unit, disconnect the wire to the regulator field terminal and touch the regulator battery terminal with it.

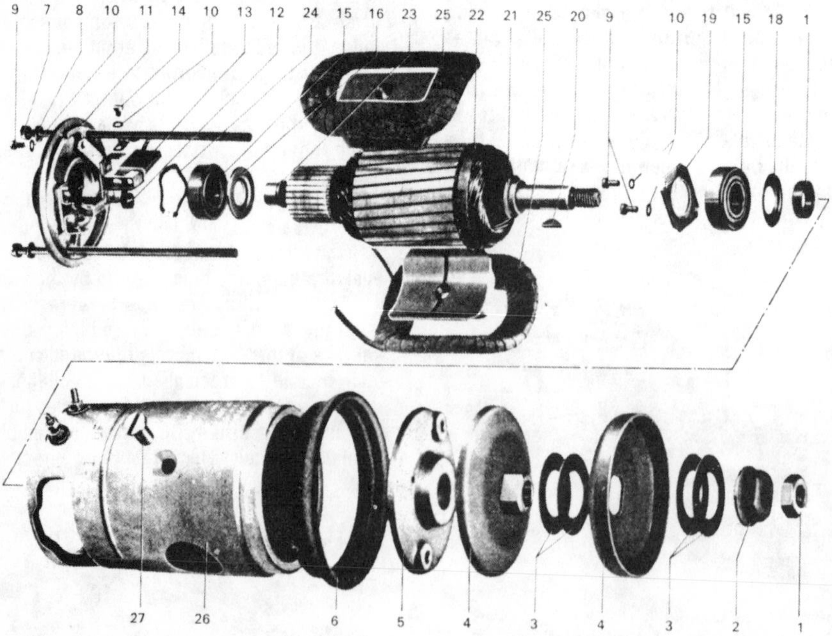

Exploded view of generator

1. Nut for pulley
2. Special washer
3. Shim
4. Pulley
5. End plate
6. End ring
7. Through-bolt
8. Washer
9. Screw
10. Washer
11. End plate with carbon brushes
12. Spring
13. Carbon brushes
14. Screw
15. Ball bearing
16. Splash shield
18. Splash shield
19. Retaining plate
20. Woodruff key
21. Splash shield
22. Armature
23. Armature flange
24. Gasket
25. Field coil
26. Housing
27. Field screw

The Air Conditioning System

HOW IT WORKS

The automotive air conditioning system's basic purpose is to reverse the normal flow of heat. Heat normally flows from an area at a certain temperature to any cooler area. The car's air conditioning system must keep the passenger compartment below the outsife temperature by continuously removing heat.

This is accomplished by a mechanical compressor which is driven off the engine's crankshaft to compress a material which can be readily changed from a liquid to a gas state. The refrigerant in automotive applications is R-12 which has a $-327°$ F boiling point at atmospheric pressure.

The R-12 is metered into a cooling coil (very similar in construction to a car radiator) at about 30 psi. The refrigerant is in liquid form at this point in the cycle. Its boiling point at 30 psi is just above the normal freezing temperature of water. The refrigerant therefore tends to boil, absorbing heat from the coil.

The cooling coil is known as the evaporator. It is normally located inside the car or on the firewall. A blower forces either outside or inside air, depending on the type of system and the control settings, through the evaporator. The air then passes into the passenger compartment through dash-mounted registers. As the air passes through the evaporator coil, heat and moisture are removed.

The refrigerant boils completely inside the evaporator and then passes into the compressor where its pressure is vastly increased. The pressure on the refrigerant as it leaves the compressor is usually 200 psi or more.

The refrigerant then enters the condenser, a heat exchanging coil usually located in front of the car's

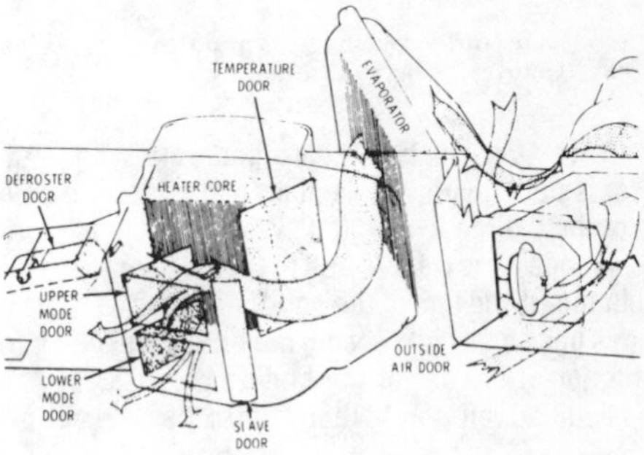

Air flow through the evaporator (Courtesy, G.M. Corp)

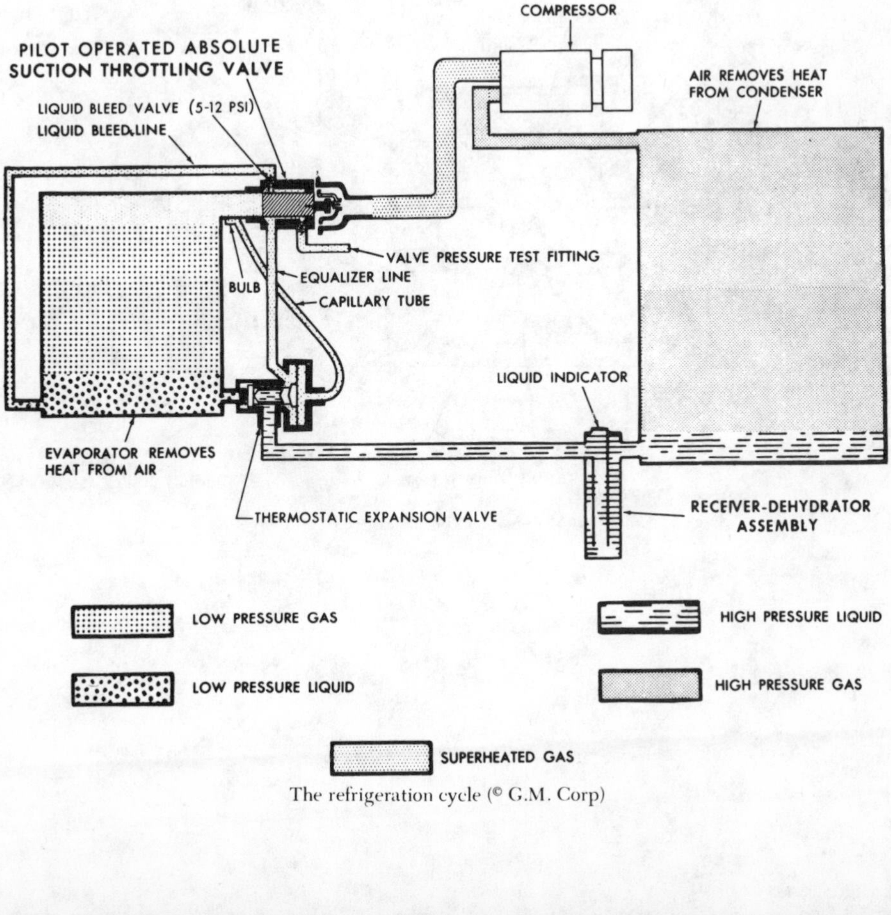

The refrigeration cycle (© G.M. Corp)

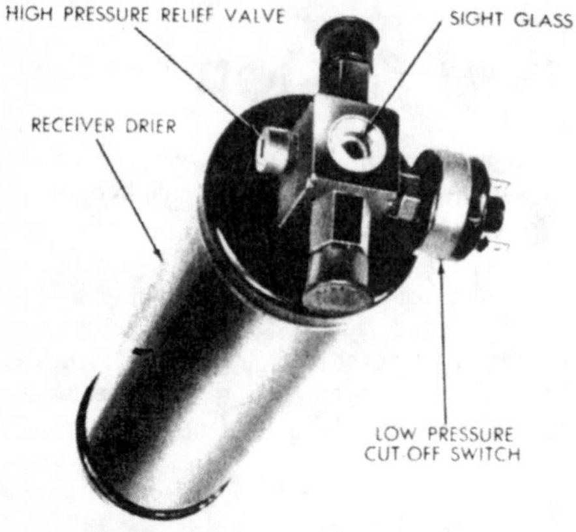

A receiver-drier showing location of the sight glass (Courtesy, Chrysler Corporation)

radiator. The very high pressure generated in the compressor is put to work at this point and raises the boiling point of the R-12 to over 150° F. When the cooling effect of the outside air is transmitted to the refrigerant through the thin tubes and fins of the condenser coil, it cools and changes back to a liquid, losing the heat it picked up from the interior of the car in the boiling process.

The liquified refrigerant then enters the receiver-drier, a small black tank located next to the condenser or on one of the fender wells. This unit has the job of separating liquid refrigerant from any gas that might have left the condenser, and also filters the refrigerant and absorbs any moisture it may contain. It incorporates a sight glass, in most systems, that allows the refrigerant returning to the evaporator to be checked for the presence of gas bubbles.

The refrigerant then flows through a liquid line to the expansion valve. This valve is located near the evaporator, usually (on most factory systems) on or near the firewall. On aftermarket systems, it is located under the dash. It is shaped like a mushroom, and in some systems incorporates the sight glass. This is the valve which controls the flow of refrigerant to the evaporator. The flow is controlled to supply only that amount the evaporator can handle.

The compressor incorporates a magnetic clutch to permit it to be turned off when it is not required. The clutch is operating whenever the flat portion on the front is turning with the belt-driven pulley located on the front of the compressor.

WARNING: Because of the dangerous pressures and temperatures associated with the escape of refrigerant, repairs involving a line or fitting that contains refrigerant should always be left to trained servicemen.

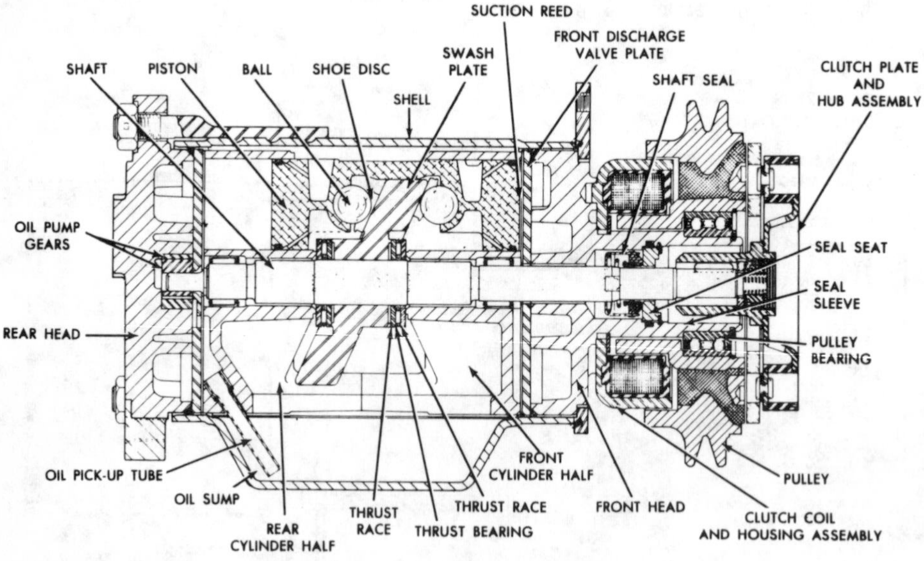

A General Motors type compressor (© G.M. Corp)

Manual Transmission and Clutch

HOW THEY WORK

Because of the way the gasoline engine breathes, it can produce torque, or twisting force, only within a narrow speed range. Most modern engines must turn at about 2,500 rpm to produce their peak torque. By 4,500 rpm they are producing so little torque that continued increases in engine speed produce no power increases.

The transmission and clutch are employed to vary the relationship between engine speed and the speed of the wheels so that adequate engine power can be produced under all circumstances. The clutch allows engine torque to be applied to the transmission input shaft gradually, due to mechanical slippage. The car can, consequently, be started smoothly from a full stop.

The transmission changes the ratio between the rotating speeds of the engine and the wheels by the use of gears. Three-speed or four-speed transmissions are most common. The lower gears allow full engine power to be applied to the rear wheels during acceleration at low speeds.

The clutch driven plate is a thin disc, the center of which is splined to the transmission input shaft. Both sides of the disc are covered with a layer of material which is similar to brake lining and which is capable of allowing slippage without roughness or excessive noise.

The clutch cover is bolted to the engine flywheel and incorporates a diaphragm spring which provides the pressure to engage the clutch. The cover also houses the pressure plate. The driven disc is sandwiched between the pressure plate and the smooth surface of the flywheel when the clutch pedal is released, thus forcing it to turn at the same speed as the engine crankshaft.

The transmission contains a mainshaft which passes all the way through the transmission, from the clutch to the driveshaft. This shaft is separated at one point, so that front and rear portions can turn at different speeds.

Power is transmitted by a countershaft in the lower gears and reverse. The gears of the countershaft mesh with gears on the mainshaft, allowing power to be carried from one to the other. All the countershaft gears are integral with that shaft, while several of the mainshaft gears can either rotate independently of the shaft or be locked to it. Shifting from one gear to the next causes one of the gears to be freed from rotating with the shaft, and locks another to it. Gears are locked and unlocked by internal dog clutches which slide between the center of the gear and the shaft. The forward gears usually employ synchronizers: friction members which smoothly bring gear and shaft to the same speed before the toothed dog clutches are engaged.

The clutch is operating properly if:

1. It will stall the engine when released with the vehicle held stationary.

2. The shift lever can be moved freely between first and reverse gears when the vehicle is stationary and the clutch disengaged.

A clutch pedal free-play adjustment is incorporated in

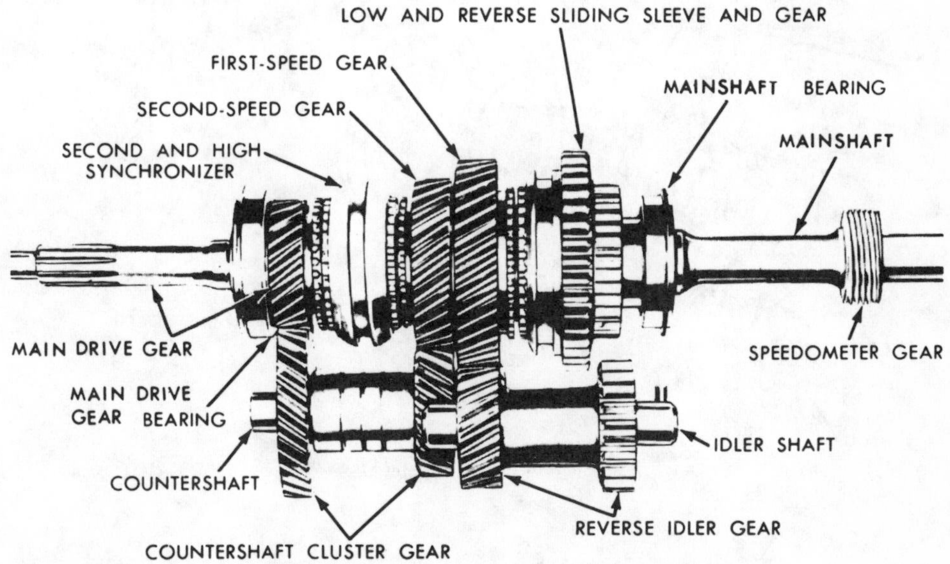

The inner workings of a transmission (© G.M. Corp)

the linkage. If there is about 1-2 in. of motion before the pedal begins to release the clutch, it is adjusted properly. Inadequate free-play wears all parts of the clutch releasing mechanisms and may cause slippage. Excessive free-play may cause inadequate release and hard shifting of gears.

Some clutches use a hydraulic system in place of mechanical linkage. If the clutch fails to release, fill the clutch master cylinder with fluid to the proper level and pump the clutch pedal to fill the system with fluid. Bleed the system in the same way as a brake system. If leaks are located, tighten loose connections or overhaul the master or slave cylinder as necessary.

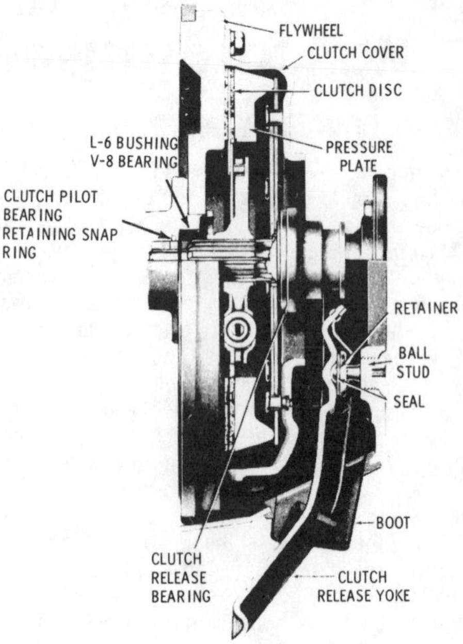

A typical clutch assembly (© G.M. Corp)

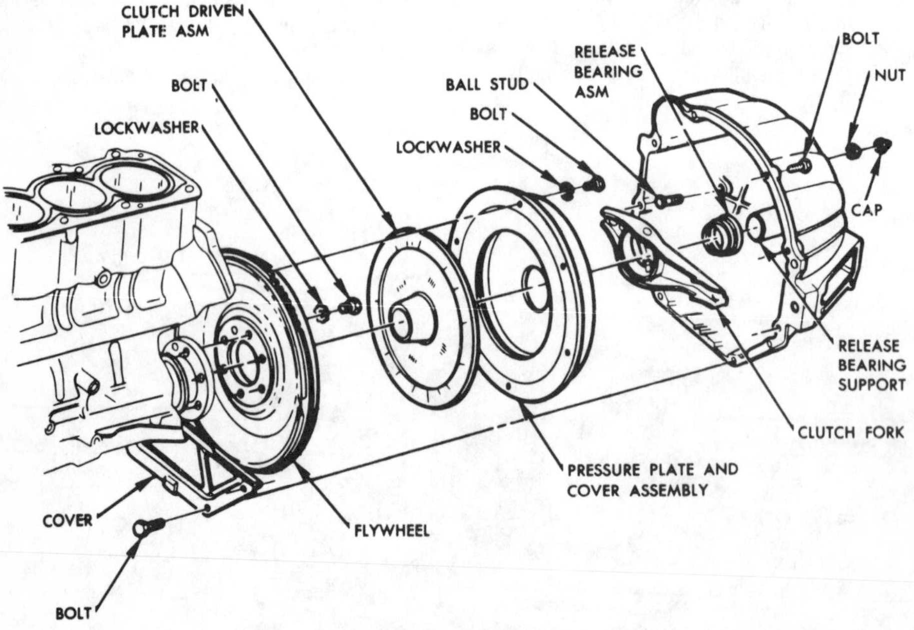

Clutch assembly (Courtesy Chevrolet Motor Division)

Automatic Transmission

HOW IT WORKS

The automatic transmission allows engine torque and power to be transmitted to the rear wheels within a narrow range of engine operating speeds. The transmission will allow the engine to turn fast enough to produce plenty of power and torque at very low speeds, while keeping it at a sensible rpm at high vehicle speeds. The transmission performs this job entirely without driver assistance.

The transmission uses a light fluid as the medium for the transmission of power. This fluid also works in the operation of various hydraulic control circuits and as a lubricant. Because the transmission fluid performs all of these three functions, trouble within the unit can easily travel from one part to another. For this reason, and because of the complexity and unusual operating principles of the transmission, a very sound understanding of the basic principles of operation will simplify troubleshooting.

THE TORQUE CONVERTER

The torque converter replaces the conventional clutch. It has three functions:

1. It allows the engine to idle with the vehicle at a standstill—even with the transmission in gear.
2. It allows the transmission to shift from range to range smoothly, without requiring that the driver close the throttle during the shift.
3. It multiplies engine torque to an increasing extent as vehicle speed drops and throttle opening is increased. This has the effect of making the transmission more responsive and reduces the amount of shifting required.

The torque converter is a metal case which is shaped like a sphere that has been flattened on opposite sides. It is bolted to the rear end of the engine's crankshaft. Generally, the entire metal case rotates at engine speed and serves as the engine's flywheel.

The case contains three sets of blades. One set is attached directly to the case. This set forms the torus or pump. Another set is directly connected to the output shaft, and forms the turbine. The third set is mounted on a hub which, in turn, is mounted on a stationary shaft through a one-way clutch. This third set is known as the stator.

A pump, which is driven off the transmission input shaft, keeps the torque converter full of transmission fluid at all times. Fluid flows continuously through the unit to provide cooling.

Under low-speed acceleration, the torque converter functions as follows:

The torus is turning faster than the turbine. It picks up fluid at the center of the converter and, through centrifugal force, slings it outward. Since the outer edge of the converter moves faster than the portions at the center, the fluid picks up speed.

The fluid then enters the outer edge of the turbine blades. It then travels back toward the center of the converter case along the turbine blades. In impinging upon the turbine blades, the fluid loses the energy picked up in the torus.

If the fluid were now to immediately be returned directly into the torus, both halves of the converter would have to turn at approximately the same speed at all times, and torque input and output would both be the same.

In flowing through the torus and turbine, the fluid

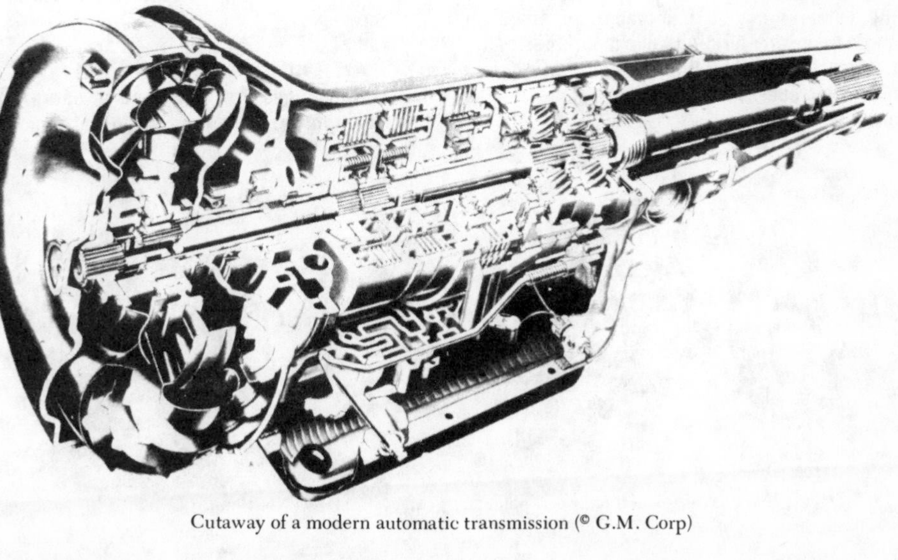

Cutaway of a modern automatic transmission (© G.M. Corp)

picks up two types of flow, or flow in two separate directions. It flows through the turbine blades, and it spins with the engine. The stator, whose blades are stationary when the vehicle is being accelerated at low speeds, converts one type of flow into another. Instead of allowing the fluid to flow straight back into the torus, the stator's curved blades turn the fluid almost 90° toward the direction of rotation of the engine. Thus the fluid does not flow as fast toward the torus, but is already spinning when the torus picks it up. This has the effect of allowing the torus to turns much faster than the turbine. This difference in speed may be compared to the difference in speed between the smaller and larger gears in any gear train. The result is that engine power output is higher, and engine torque is multiplied.

As the speed of the turbine increases, the fluid spins faster and faster in the direction of engine rotation. As a result, the ability of the stator to redirect the fluid flow is reduced. Under cruising conditions, the stator is eventually forced to rotate on its one-way clutch in the direction of engine rotation. Under these conditions, the torque converter begins to behave almost like a solid shaft, with the torus and turbine speeds being almost equal.

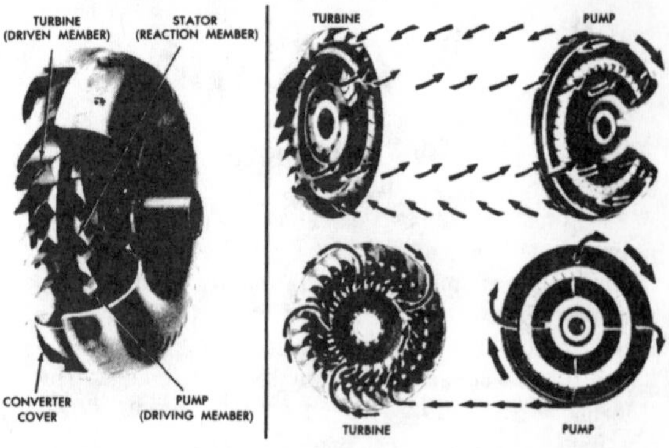

Cutaway view of a torque converter (© G.M. Corp)

THE PLANETARY GEARBOX

The ability of the torque converter to multiply engine torque is limited. Also, the unit tends to be more efficient when the turbine is rotating at relatively high speeds. Therefore, a planetary gearbox is used to carry the power output of the turbine to the driveshaft to make the most efficient use of the converter.

Planetary gears function very similarly to conventional transmission gears. However, their construction is different in that three elements make up one gear system, and in that all three elements are different from one another. The three elements are: an outer gear that is shaped like a hoop, with teeth cut into the inner surface; a sun gear, mounted on a shaft and located at the very center of the outer gear; and a set of three planet gears, held by pins in a ring-like planet carrier and meshing with both the sun gear and the outer gear. Either the outer gear or the sun gear may be held stationary, providing more than one possible torque multiplication factor for each set of gears. Also, if all three gears are forced to rotate at the same speed, the gearset forms, in effect, a solid shaft.

Most modern automatics use the planetary gears to provide either a single reduction ratio of about 1.8:1, or two reduction gears: a low of about 2.5:1, and an intermediate of about 1.5:1. Bands and clutches are used to hold various portions of the gearsets to the transmission case or to the shaft on which they are mounted. Shifting is accomplished, then, by changing the portion of each planetary gearset which is held to the transmission case or to the shaft.

THE SERVOS AND ACCUMULATORS

The servos are hydraulic pistons and cylinders. They resemble the hydraulic actuators used on many familiar machines, such as bulldozers. Hydraulic fluid enters the cylinfer, under pressure, und forces the piston to move to engage the band or clutches.

The accumulators are used to cushion the engagement of the servos. The transmission fluid must pass through the accumulator on the way to the servo. The accumulator housing contains a thin piston which is sprung away from the discharge passage of the accumulator. When fluid passes through the accumulator on the way to the servo, it must move the piston against spring pressure, and this action smoothes out the action of the servo.

THE HYDRAULIC CONTROL SYSTEM

The hydraulic pressure used to operate the servos comes from the main transmission oil pump. This fluid is

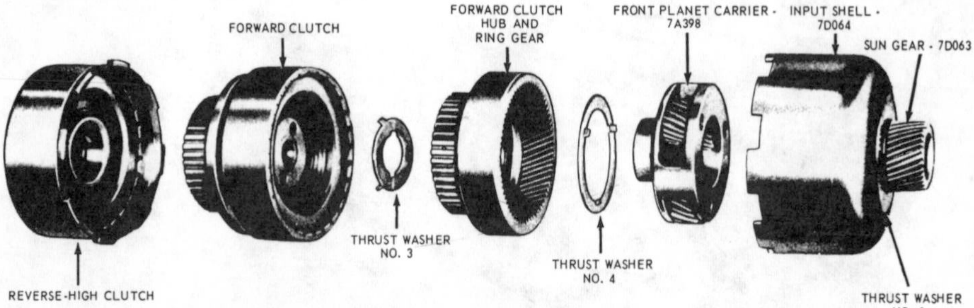

Exploded view of a planetary gearset (Courtesy, Ford Motor Co)

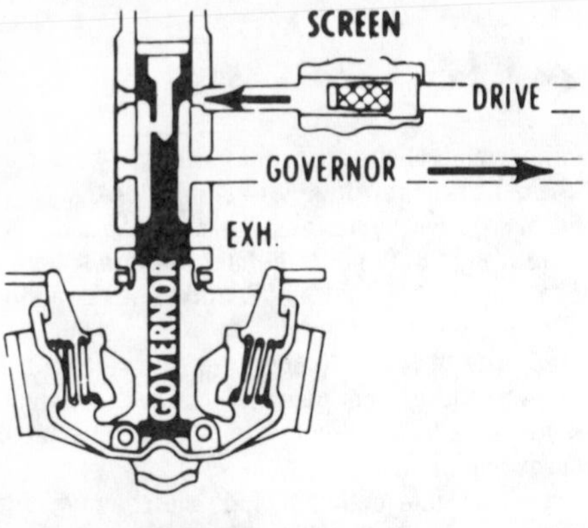

Schematic of a governor (© G.M. Corp)

channeled to the various servos through the shift valves. There is generally a manual shift valve which is operated by the transmission selector lever and an automatic shift valve for each automatic upshift the transmission provides: i.e., two-speed automatics have a low-high shift valve, while three-speeds will have a 1-2 valve, and a 2-3 valve.

There are two pressures which affect the operation of these valves. One is the governor pressure which is affected by vehicle speed. The other is the modulator pressure which is affected by intake manifold vacuum or throttle position. Governor pressure rises with an increase in vehicle speed, and modulator pressure rises as the throttle is opened wider. By responding to these two pressures, the shift valves cause the upshift points to be delayed with increased throttle opening to make the best use of the engine's power output.

Most transmissions also make use of an auxiliary circuit for downshifting. This circuit may be actuated by the throttle linkage or the vacuum line which actuates the modulator, or by a cable or solenoid. It applies pressure to a special downshift surface on the shift valve or valves.

The transmission modulator also governs the line pressure, used to actuate the servos. In this way, the clutches and bands will be actuated with a force matching the torque output of the engine.

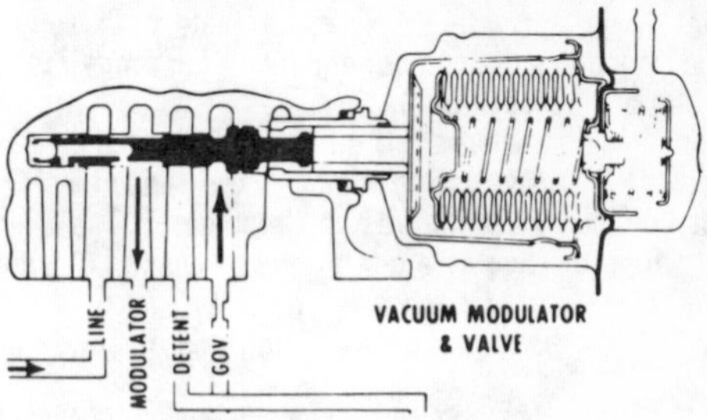

Schematic of a vacuum modulator (© G.M. Corp)

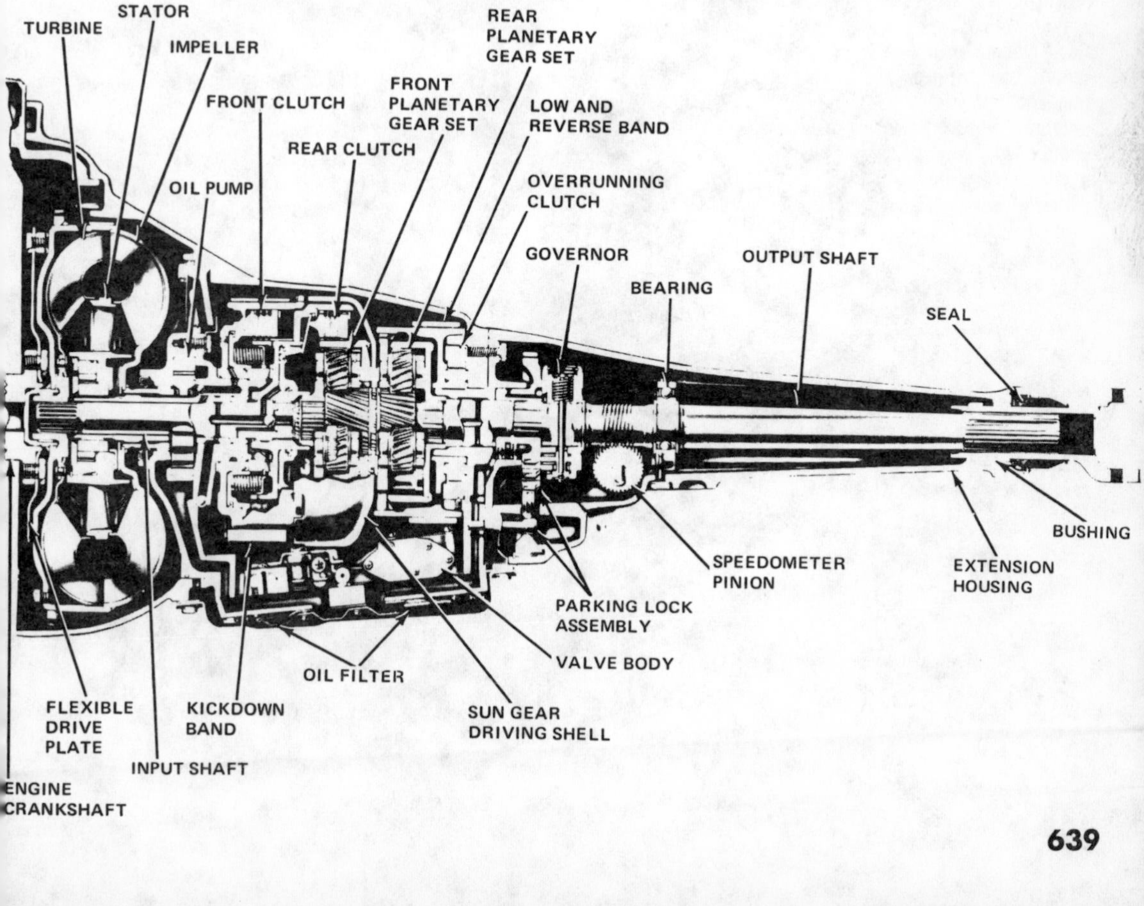

The Rear Axle

HOW IT WORKS

The rear axle is a special type of transmission that reduces the speed of the drive from the engine and transmission and divides the power to the rear wheels. Power enters the rear axle from the driveshaft via the companion flange. The flange is mounted on the drive pinion shaft. The drive pinion shaft and gear which carry the power into the differential turn at engine speed. The gear on the end of the pinion shaft drives a large ring gear the axis of rotation of which is 90° away from that of the pinion. The pinion and gear reduce the speed and multiply the power by the gear ratio of the axle, and change the direction of rotation to turn the axle shafts which drive both wheels. The rear axle gear ratio is found by dividing the number of pinion gear teeth into the number of ring gear teeth.

The ring gear drives the differential case. The case provides the two mounting points for the ends of a pinion shaft on which are mounted two pinion gears. The pinion gears drive the two side gears, one of which is located on the inner end of each axle shaft.

By driving the axle shafts through this arrangement, the differential allows the outer drive wheel to turn faster than the inner drive wheel in a turn.

The main drive pinion and the side bearings, which bear the weight of the differential case, are shimmed to provide proper bearing preload, and to position the pinion and ring gears properly.

NOTE: The proper adjustment of the relationship of the ring and pinion gears is critical. It should be attempted only by those with extensive equipment and/or experience.

Limited-slip differentials include clutches which tend to link each axle shaft to the differential case. Clutches may be engaged either by spring action or by pressure produced by the torque on the axles during a turn. During turning on a dry pavement, the effects of the clutches are overcome, and each wheel turns at the required speed. When slippage occurs at either wheel, however, the clutches will transmit some of the power to the wheel which has the greater amount of traction. Because of the presence of clutches, limited-slip units require a special lubricant. Consult a Chilton Manual or factory information for unit identification and lubricant recommendations.

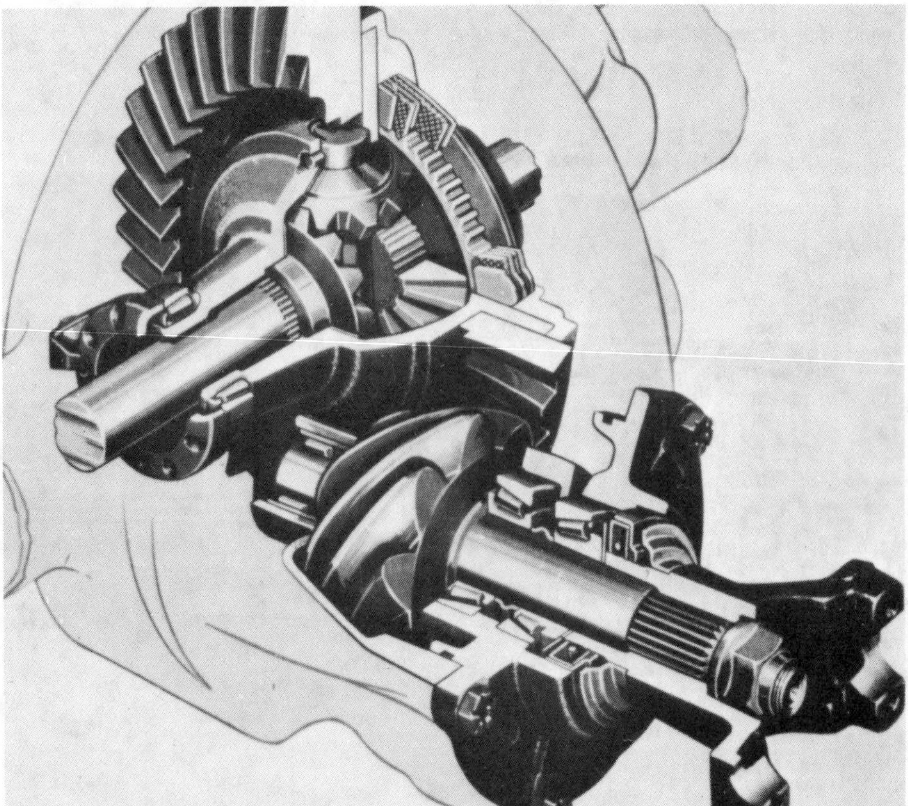

Cutaway of a typical rear axle (© Ford Motor Co)

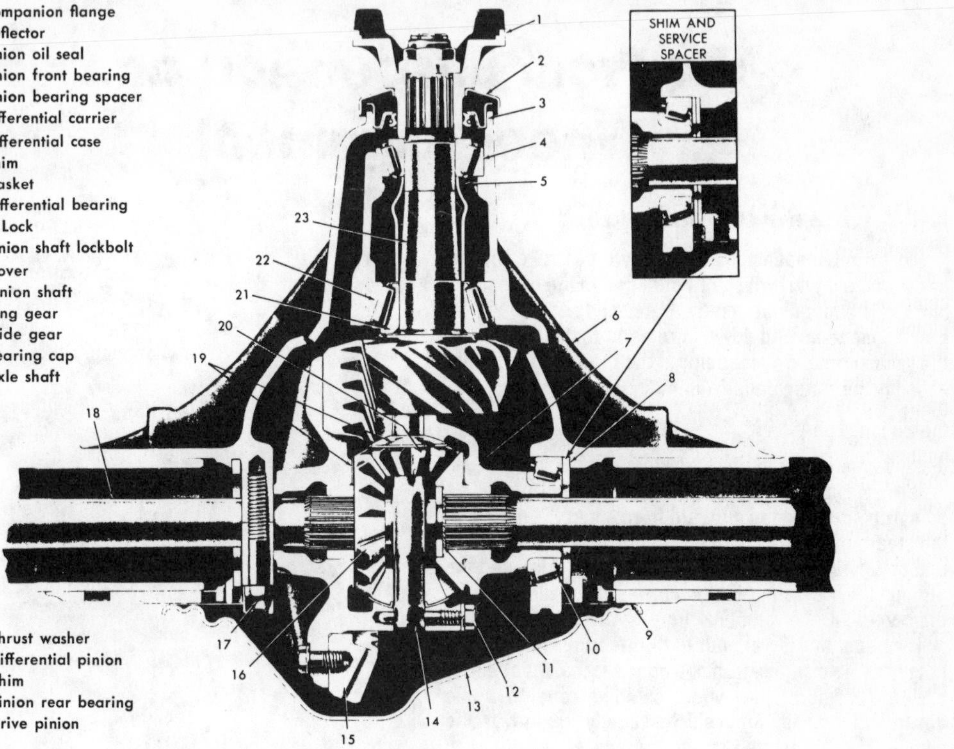

Typical General Motors rear axle—C type (Courtesy of Chevrolet Div. of G.M. Corp)

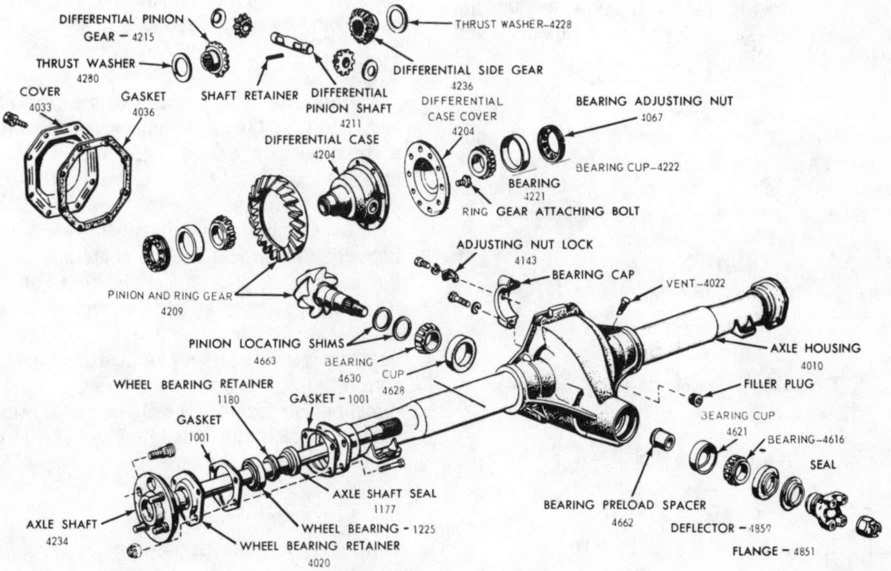

Exploded view of rear axle components.

The Front Suspension and Wheel Alignment

HOW THE FRONT SUSPENSION WORKS

Most front suspensions include two control arms (an upper and a lower) which are attached to the chassis by hinges. The hinges permit the outer ends of the control arms to move up and down in relation to the chassis as the vehicle travels over bumps in the road surface, while keeping the outer ends from moving forward or backward.

The outer ends of the control arms are kept an equal distance apart by steerinv knuckles. The steering knuckles are held in place, at top and bottom, by ball joints. The wheel spindles extend outward from about the middle of the steering knuckles. The ball joints permit the upward and downward motion of the steering knuckles and the turning motion required for cornering, while keeping them vertical. Tie rods link them to the steering gear.

The upper and lower ends of the steering knuckles are not the same distance from the chassis; the upper end is closer. Therefore, the wheel spindles tend to angle downward and lift the vehicle slightly whenever the wheels are not pointed straight ahead.

A list of various terms used in wheel alignment, with their definitions, follows.

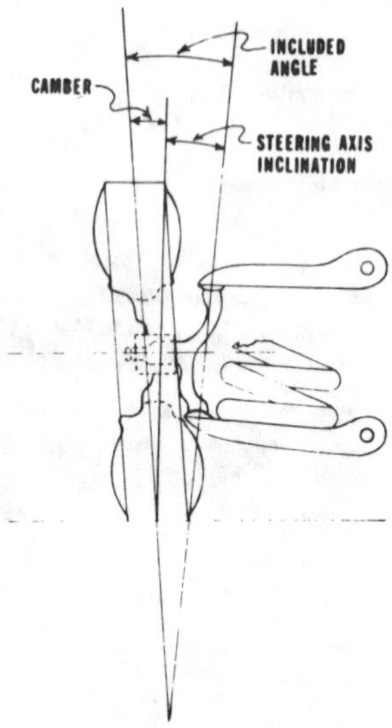

Camber, steering axis and included angle

CAMBER

The wheel is not positioned vertically on most vehicles, but is angled so that the upper edge is further away from the chassis than is the lower edge. Angling the wheel in this manner makes better use of the tire tread during cornering.

CASTER

The vehicle has caster if the upper end of the steering knuckle is positioned slightly behind the lower end. Caster helps the vehicle's steering return to the straight-ahead position, and improves directional stability.

STEERING AXIS INCLINATION

Steering axis inclination results from the fact that the upper end of the steering knuckle is closer to the chassis than the lower end. This angular mounting is what causes the vehicle to lift slightly during cornering. The car's weight thus tends to help the steering return to the center and to aid directional stability.

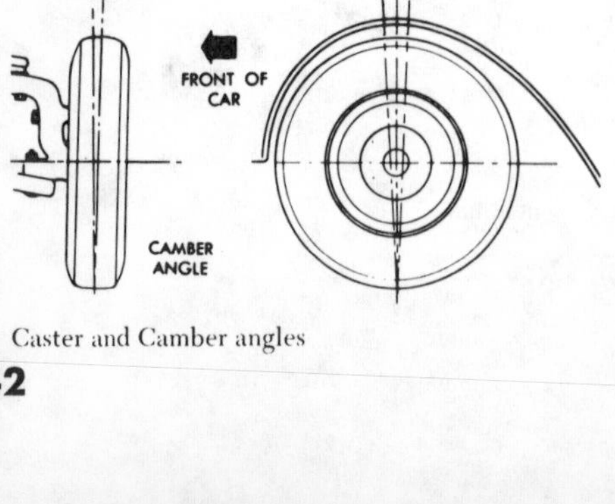

Caster and Camber angles

INCLUDED ANGLE

The included angle is the sum of the steering axis inclination and the caster angles. It is the angle between a line drawn between the two mounting points of the steering knuckle and a line drawn vertically through the center of the wheel.

In each of the above definitions, an imaginary angle between the vertical and the centerline of the wheel or the steering knuckle is described. On an alignment chart, these angles are referred to in degrees of positive caster, camber, etc. If the angle is listed as zero, the unit in question is to be perfectly vertical. If a figure of less than zero is listed, the unit should be angled in the opposite direction. For example, negative caster refers to an adjustment which positions the upper end of the steering knuckle ahead of the lower end, rather than behind.

TOE-IN

On most vehicles, when the front wheels are stationary, they are closer together at the front than at the rear. Aligning the wheels in this manner compensates for various frictional forces that alter the angles between the wheels when the vehicle is moving. Thus, the wheels are brought into a parallel position, relative to each

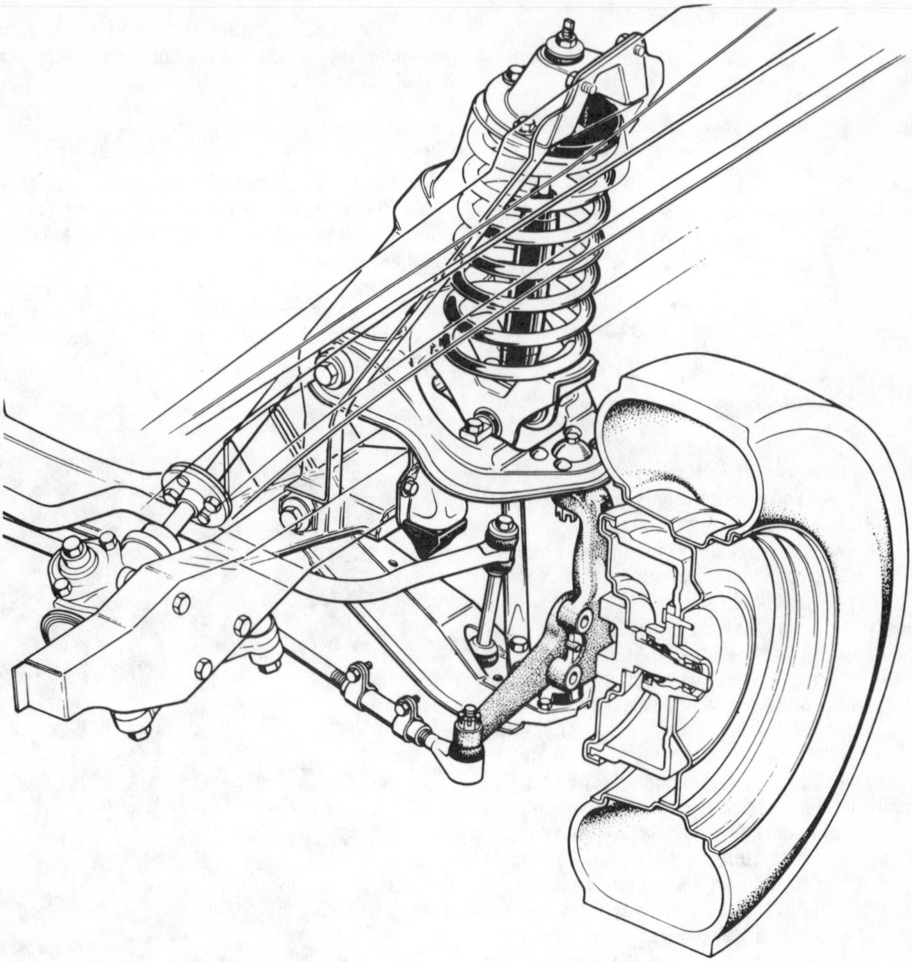

A typical front suspension system (© Ford Motor Co)

other, as the vehicle gains speed. Toe-in is measured in inches; the difference between the distance separating the front and rear centerlines of the wheels.

TOE-OUT

The steering is designed so that the inner wheel turns more sharply toward the center of the turn than the outer wheel turns. This compensates for the fact that the inner wheel actually travels a shorter distance during the turn. Designing the steering in this manner avoids having the front wheels fight each other, thus improving tire life and aiding stability. Where toe-out is to be checked, angles are given for the inner and outer wheel relative to travel in a straight line. Thus, in a left-hand turn, the left (inner) wheel might be 24° from straight ahead, and the right (outer) wheel 20° from straight ahead. For a right turn, the figures would be reversed.

TRACKING

During straight-line operation, the vehicle's rear wheels must duplicate, or run parallel to, the paths of the front wheels. To measure the accuracy of a vehicle's tracking, measure the distance from the right-side lower ball joint to a point on the left side of the rear axle, and repeat the measurement for the left-side lower ball joint and a similar point on the right side of the rear axle. You

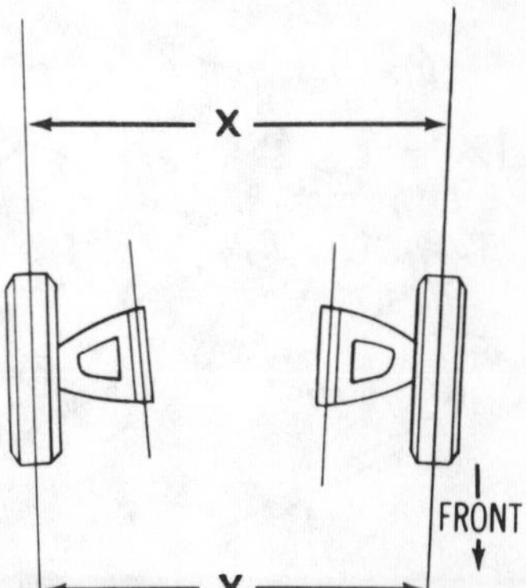

X − Y = Toe-in

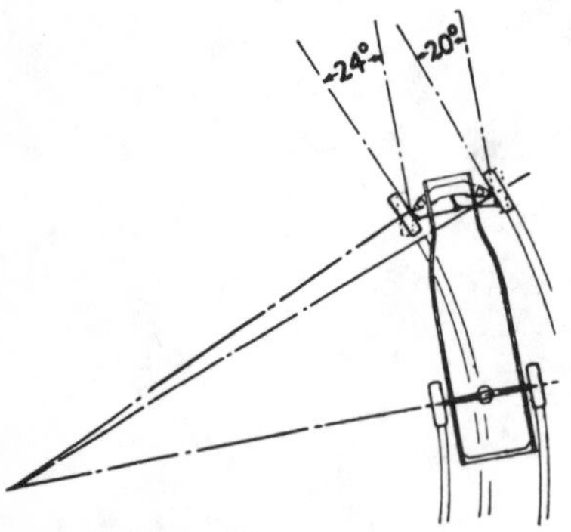

Toe-out. Inside wheel turns a greater number of degrees

may wish to drop a plumb line from each of these four points to the ground and mark the spots in order to avoid interference from various parts of the vehicle's undercarriage. The two diagonal lines should be equal in length to within ¼ in. Otherwise, the frame of the vehicle is bent or the rear axle is off center.

The rear wheels may also be checked for toe-in or toe-out by measuring between the inner surfaces of the tires at front and rear. Toe-in or toe-out in excess of manufacturer's specifications indicates a bent rear axle.

There is a special machine designed to check the alignment of the front wheels. Caster is first adjusted to specifications by moving the upper control arm. This may be accomplished by repositioning shims, changing the length of a strut with adjusting nuts, or by repositioning the mounting point of a strut on the frame. Camber is then accomplished by pulling the entire control arm toward the frame or forcing it further away. This involves repositioning shims equally at the front and rear of the control arm, turning adjusting nuts an equal amount, or repositioning a strut.

There are exceptions to these general rules. For example, on 1965-66 Thunderbirds, these adjustments affect the lower control arm, and on Vegas, camber is adjusted before caster. Consult a manual for the precise method to be used for the vehicle in question.

On all vehicles, toe-in is adjusted after caster and camber are correct by turning the adjusting sleeves on the tie rods. These sleeves should be turned in equal amounts in opposite directions in order to keep the steering wheel centered. If the wheel is off center, it may be centered without affecting toe-in by turning both adjusting sleeves in the same direction.

When caster, camber, and toe-in have been adjusted, steering axis inclination and toe-out figures should be correct. If not, a worn ball joint or bent suspension or steering part is at fault.

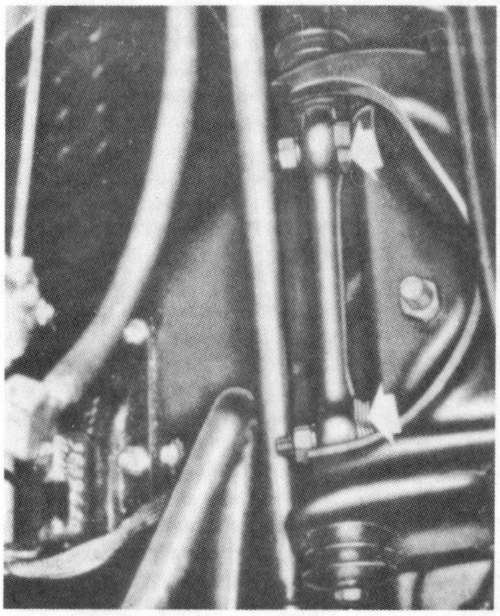

Caster and camber adjusting shim installation (Courtesy of Chevrolet Div. of G.M. Corp)

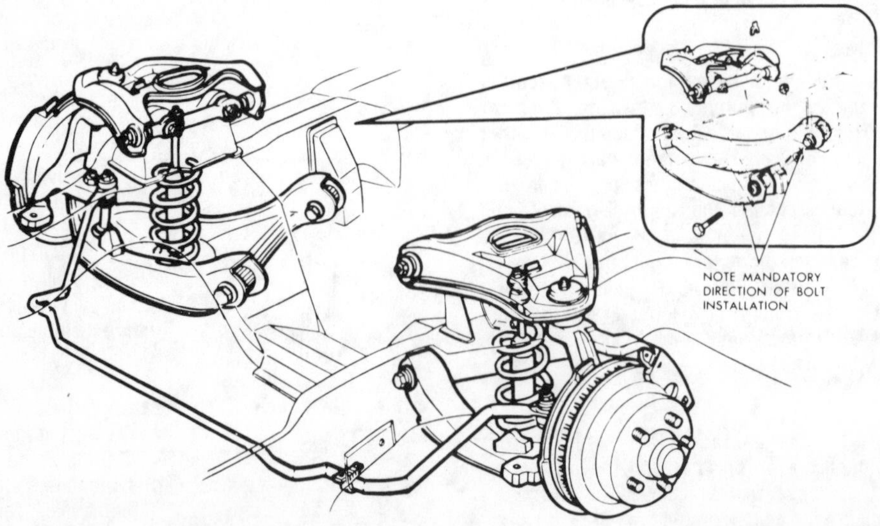

Brakes

HYDRAULIC SYSTEMS

Hydraulic systems are used to actuate the brakes of all modern automobiles. The system transports the power required to force the frictional surfaces of the braking system together from the pedal to the individual brake units at each wheel. A hydraulic system is used for two reasons. First, fluid under pressure can be carried to all parts of an automobile by small hoses—some of which are flexible—without taking up a significant amount of room or posing routing problems. Second, a great mechanical advantage can be given to the brake pedal end of the system, and the foot pressure required to actuate the brakes can be reduced by making the surface area of the master cylinder pistons smaller than that of any of the pistons in the wheel cylinders or calipers.

The master cylinder consists of a fluid reservoir and either a single or double cylinder and piston assembly. Double type master cylinders are designed to separate the front and rear braking systems hydraulically in case of a leak.

Steel lines carry the brake fluid to a point on the vehicle's frame near each of the vehicle's wheels. The fluid is then carried to the slave cylinders by flexible tubes in order to allow for suspension and steering movements.

In drum brake systems, the slave cylinders are called wheel cylinders. Each wheel cylinder contains two pistons, one at either end, which push outward in opposite directions. In disc brake systems, the slave cylinders are part of the calipers. One or four cylinders are used to force the brake pads against the disc, but all cylinders

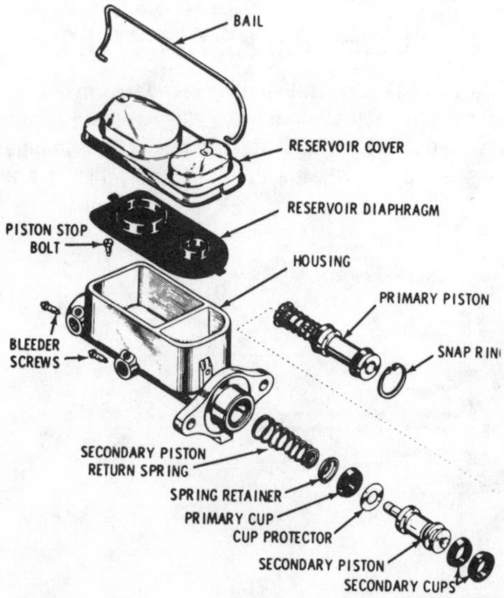

Bendix dual master cylinder (Courtesy of Oldsmobile Div. of G.M. Corp)

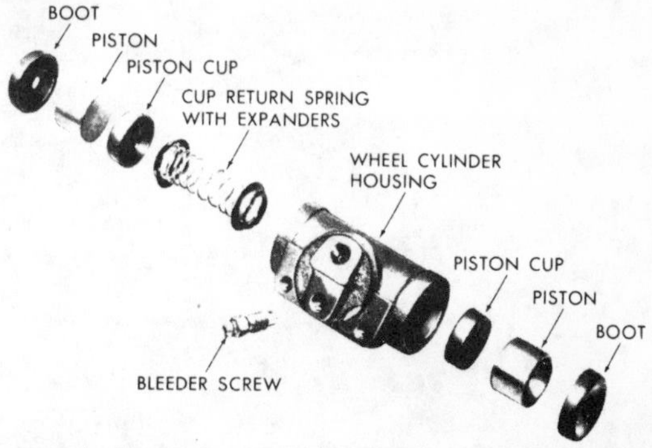

Wheel cylinder (Courtesy of Chevrolet Div. of G.M. Corp)

contain one piston only. All slave cylinder pistons employ some type of seal, usually made of rubber, to minimize the leakage of fluid around the piston. A rubber dust boot seals the outer end of the cylinder against dust and dirt. The boot fits around the outer end of the piston on disc brake calipers, and around the brake actuating rod on wheel cylinders.

The hydraulic system operates as follows: When at rest, the entire system, from the piston(s) in the master cylinder to those in the wheel cylinders or calipers, is full of brake fluid. Upon application of the brake pedal, fluid trapped in front of the master cylinder piston(s) is forced through the lines to the slave cylinders. Here, it forces the pistons outward, in the case of drum brakes, and inward toward the disc, in the case of disc brakes. The motion of the pistons is opposed by return springs mounted outside the cylinders in drum brakes, and by internal springs or spring seals, in disc brakes.

Upon release of the brake pedal, a spring located inside the master cylinder immediately returns the master cylinder piston(s) to the normal position. The pistons contain check valves and the master cylinder has compensating ports drilled in it. These are uncovered as the pistons reach their normal position. The piston check valves allow fluid to flow toward the wheel cylinders or calipers as the pistons withdraw. Then, as the return springs force the brake pads or shoes into the released position, the excess fluid returns to the master cylinder fluid reservoir through the compensating ports. It is during the time the pedal is in the released position that any fluid that has leaked out of the system will be replaced through the compensating ports.

Dual circuit master cylinders employ two pistons, located one behind the other, in the same cylinder. The primary piston is actuated directly by mechanical linkage from the brake pedal. The secondary piston is actuated by fluid trapped between the two pistons. If a leak develops in front of the secondary piston, it moves forward until it bottoms against the front of the master cylinder, and the fluid trapped between the pistons will operate the rear brakes. If the rear brakes develop a

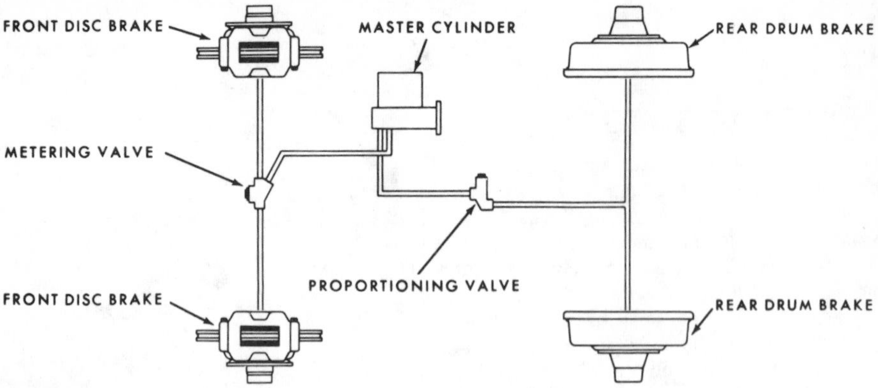

Disc brake hydraulic system

leak, the primary piston will move forward until direct contact with the secondary piston takes place, and it will force the secondary piston to actuate the front brakes. In either case, the brake pedal moves farther when the brakes are applied, and less braking power is available.

All dual-circuit systems use a distributor switch to warn the driver when only half of the brake system is operational. This switch is located in a valve body which is mounted on the firewall or the frame below the master cylinder. A hydraulic piston receives pressure from both circuits, each circuit's pressure being applied to one end of the piston. When the pressures are in balance, the piston remains stationary. When one circuit has a leak, however, the greater pressure in that circuit during application of the brakes will push the piston to one side, closing the distributor switch and activating the brake warning light.

In disc brake systems, this valve body also contains a metering valve and, in some cases, a proportioning valve. The metering valve keeps pressure from traveling to the disc brakes on the front wheels until the brake shoes on the rear wheels have contacted the drums, ensuring that the front brakes will never be used alone. The proportioning valve throttles the pressure to the rear brakes so as to avoid rear wheel lock-up during very hard braking.

These valves may be tested by removing the lines to the front and rear brake systems and installing special brake pressure testing gauges. Front and rear system pressures are then compared as the pedal is gradually depressed. Specifications vary with the manufacturer and design of the brake system.

Brake system warning lights may be tested by depressing the brake pedal and holding it while opening one of the wheel cylinder bleeder screws. If this does not cause the light to go on, substitute a new lamp, make continuity checks, and, finally, replace the switch as necessary.

The hydraulic system may be checked for leaks by applying pressure to the pedal gradually and steadily. If the pedal sinks very slowly to the floor, the system has a leak. This is not to be confused with a springy or spongy feel due to the compression of air within the lines. If the system leaks, there will be a gradual change in the position of the pedal with a constant pressure.

Check for leaks along all lines and at wheel cylinders. If no external leaks are apparent, the problem is inside the master cylinder.

POWER BRAKE BOOSTERS

Power brakes operate just as standard brake systems except in the actuation of the master cylinder pistons. A vacuum diaphragm is located on the front of the master cylinder and assists the driver in applying the brakes,

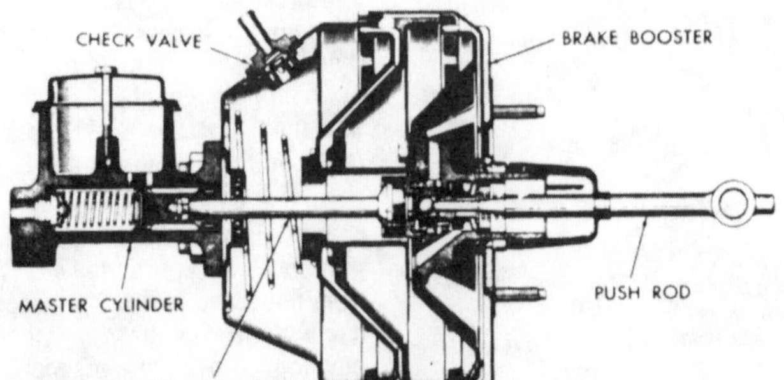

Cutaway view of brake booster and master cylinder (© G.M. Corp)

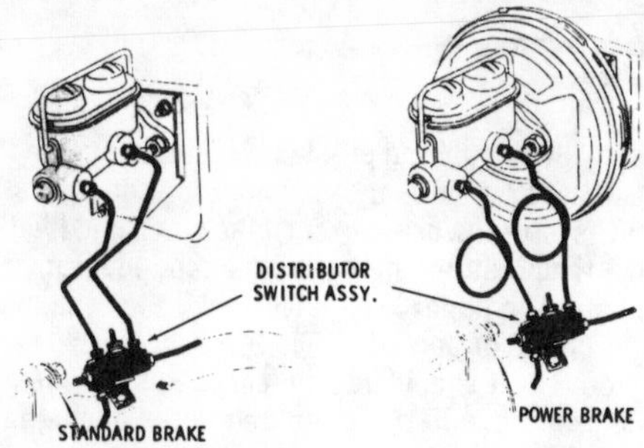

A typical distributor switch assembly (Courtesy, G.M. Corp)

reducing both the effort and travel he must put into moving the brake pedal.

The vacuum diaphragm housing is connected to the intake manifold by a vacuum hose. A check valve is placed at the point where the hose enters the diaphragm housing, so that during periods of low manifold vacuum brake assist vacuum will not be lost.

Depressing the brake pedal closes off the vacuum source and allows atmospheric pressure to enter on one side of the diaphragm. This causes the master cylinder pistons to move and apply the brakes. When the brake pedal is released, vacuum is applied to both sides of the diaphragm, and return springs return the diaphragm and master cylinder pistons to the released position. If the vacuum fails, the brake pedal rod will butt against the end of the master cylinder actuating rod, and direct mechanical application will occur as the pedal is depressed.

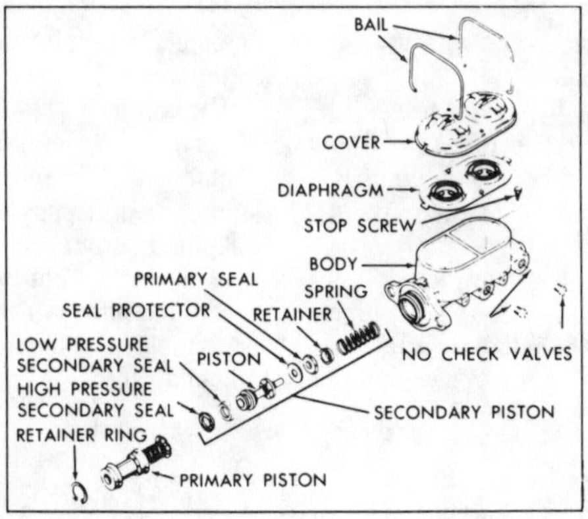

Exploded view of master cylinder

Steering Systems

POWER STEERING

Power steering units are mechanical steering gear units incorporating a power assist. A worm shaft, which is rotated by the shaft coming down from the steering wheel via a flexible coupling, causes a rack piston nut to slide up and down inside the housing. This motion is changed into rotating force by the action of an output shaft sector gear. The rack piston nut is forced up and down inside the housing by the rotation of the worm gear, which forces the nut to move through the action of recirculating balls. The nut fits tightly inside the housing, and is sealed against the sides of the housing by a ring type seal. Power assist is provided by forcing hydraulic fluid into the housing on one side or the other of the rack piston nut.

The hydraulic pressure is supplied by a rotary vane pump, driven by the engine via V belts. The pump incorporates a flow control valve that bypasses the right amount of fluid for the proper operating pressure. The pump contains a fluid reservoir, located above the main body of the pump. The same fluid lubricates all parts of the power steering unit.

A rotary valve, spool valve, or pivot lever, located in the steering box, senses the rotation of the steering wheel and channels fluid to the upper or lower surface of the rack piston nut.

When power steering problems occur, the pump fluid level should first be checked. Note that two levels are given. The lower level is correct if the pump and fluid are at room temperature, after having been inoperative for some time. The upper level is correct if the system has been in operation (about 175°).

The drive belt should also be checked for looseness, cracks, or glazing. Replace the belt if it is damaged, or tighten it if necessary.

MANUAL STEERING

Manual steering units convert the rotating force of the steering wheel into a slower, higher torque rotation of the pitman arm. The force of the arm is then transmitted to the wheels by tie rods. Generally, a flexible coupling connects the shaft coming down from the steering wheel to the worm shaft of the steering box.

The worm shaft rotates the cross-shaft or pitman shaft by having the worm gear on the worm shaft rotate the sector gear, mounted on the cross-shaft. In many designs, the efficiency of the unit is increased by using a ball nut incorporating recirculating balls to transmit the rotating force from the worm to the sector gear.

The bearings which carry the worm shaft are usually adjustable, to compensate for wear. In some designs, an adjusting screw is employed, while in others shims may

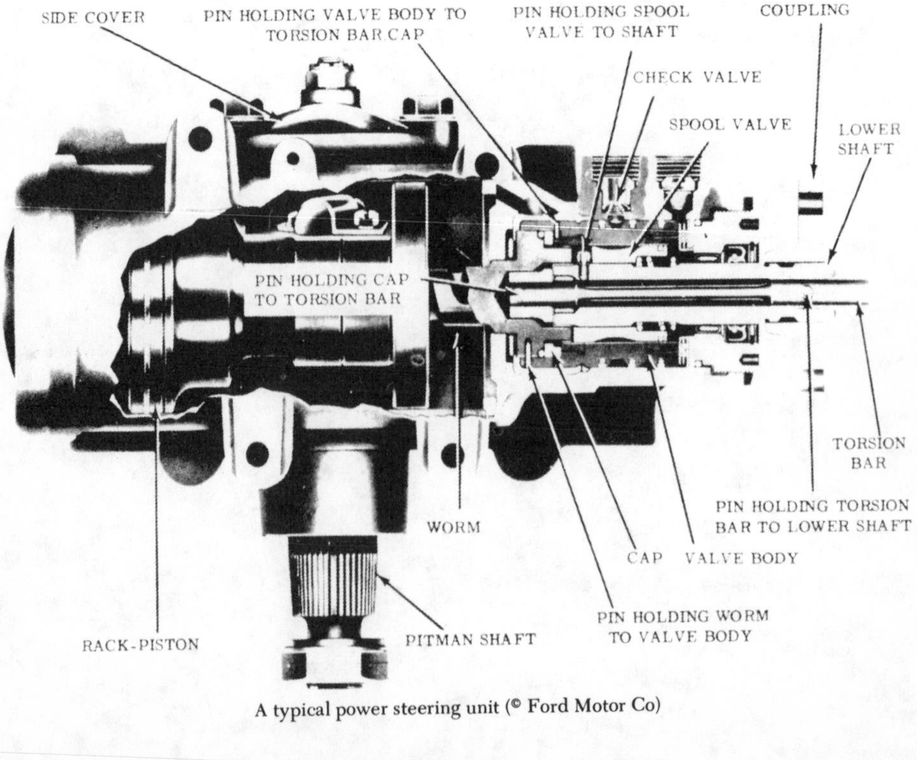

A typical power steering unit (© Ford Motor Co)

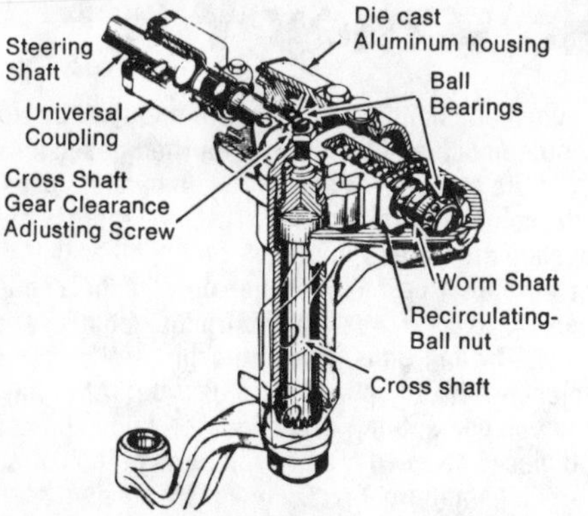

Chrysler steering gear, recirculating ball type (Courtesy of Chrysler Corp)

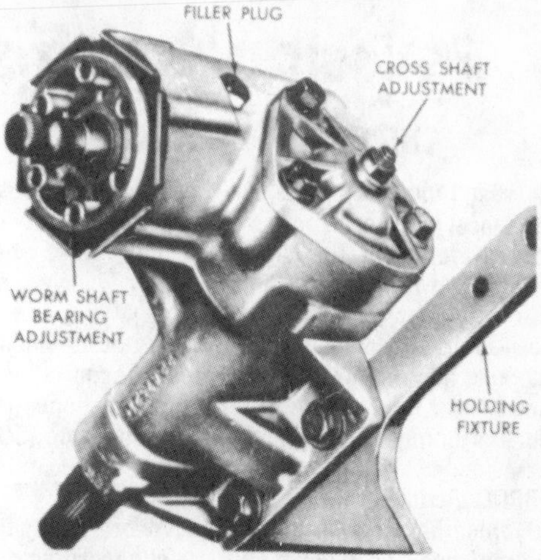

Steering gear adjustment locations (Courtesy of Chrysler Corp)

be used to provide the proper bearing preload. Generally, preload is measured by rotating the steering wheel with a spring scale with the pitman arm disconnected from the lower portions of the steering gear.

An adjusting screw is also provided for positioning the cross-shaft for proper meshing of the worm or ball nut and sector gear. After worm bearing preload is adjusted, play is removed from the unit with the cross-shaft adjusting screw, and a recheck of turning effort is made. The adjusting screw must then be backed off slightly if too great a steering wheel turning torque is required. Consult the manufacturer's instructions to make these adjustments because of variations in actual procedures and torque specifications.

Before beginning to troubleshoot manual steering problems, check the condition and pressure of the tires, and the lubrication of the steering gear. Consult the manufacturer's specifications for proper lubricant. It is usually a heavy oil like that used in rear axles. If there is uneven tire wear, it might be wise to align the front end before trying to track down steering malfunctions.

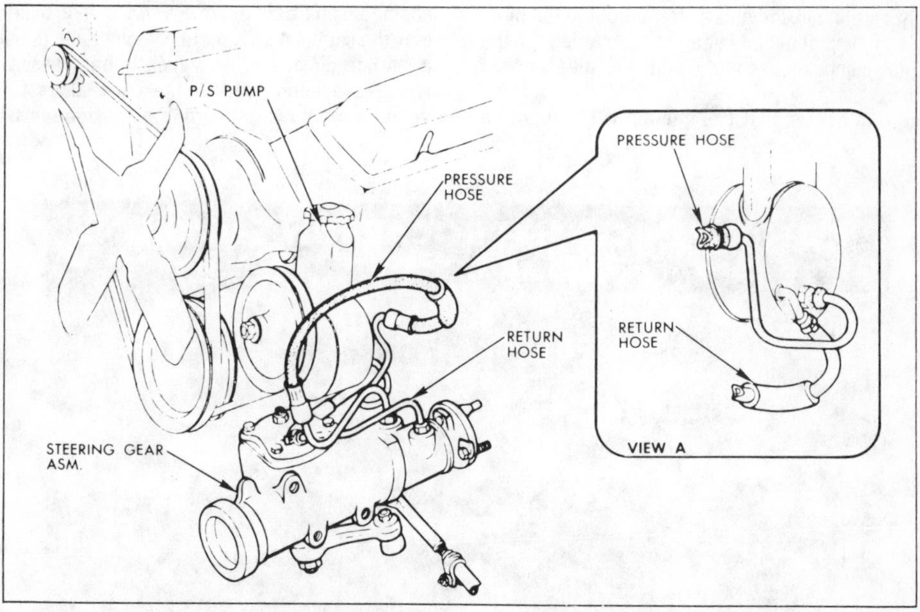

Typical power steering pump mounting

Emission Controls, How They Work

THE ORIGIN OF SMOG

It wasn't too many years ago that smog was considered a local problem in the Los Angeles area. Now we all know differently. There is smog almost any place where there is a large concentration of motor vehicles, and industry.

The internal combustion engine puts three kinds of pollutants into the air, two of them are responsible for smog. The three pollutants are hydrocarbons (HC), oxides of nitrogen (NOx), and carbon monoxide (CO).

HYDROCARBONS

Hydrocarbons is really just a fancy word that means unburned gasoline. If you take a can of gasoline, pour it out on the ground, and let it evaporate, the vapors that go off into the atmosphere are hydrocarbons. Because hydrocarbons are created by the simple evaporation of gasoline, a motor vehicle can pollute the air even when it's not running. This is the reason for the evaporative vapor controls which trap the vapors so they cannot escape into the atmosphere.

If hydrocarbons can be burned they don't cause any problem. Light a match to that gasoline that you poured out on the ground and allow it to burn up completely. The result will be nothing but carbon dioxide and water, which is harmless. The hydrocarbons have been eliminated by burning.

If the internal combustion engine would burn gasoline completely, all the hydrocarbons would be gone and we would get carbon dioxide and water out of the tail pipe. The sad story is that nobody has yet been able to make an internal combustion engine that will give perfect combustion.

It is hard to believe that you can put gasoline into a combustion chamber, burn it with enough heat to drive an automobile and still have unburned gasoline coming out of the tail pipe. Actually the combustion takes place in the combustion chamber so fast, that there is a layer of gasoline around the edges of the chamber that doesn't get burned. This happens not only in the combustion chamber of a car, but in any burning within an enclosed space. The big guns of a battleship are loaded with a projectile backed up by bags of powder. After the gun is fired you can actually crawl into the firing chamber and find pieces of powder and even parts of the cotton bags that did not burn up. On a much smaller scale this happens even in a gun cartridge although you may not see the unburned powder because most of it goes out the barrel with the bullet.

CARBON MONOXIDE

Hydrocarbons that burn up in the combustion chamber are eliminated as far as pollution is concerned, but the way in which they burn determines how much we get of another pollutant, carbon monoxide. A rich mixture burns with two much gasoline, or if you want to look at it the other way around, you could say there is not enough air. When burning takes place the hydrocarbons unite with oxygen. If we have a rich mixture, there is not enough oxygen and so we get carbon monoxide (CO). Carbon monoxide is a deadly poison, the stuff that kills you if you run your car in a closed garage.

The formation of carbon monoxide in the combustion chamber can be cut down by running lean mixtures. This way the combustion is more complete and the end result is carbon dioxide (CO_2), which is harmless. Lean mixtures have been used by the car makers for several years to cut down on carbon monoxide emissions.

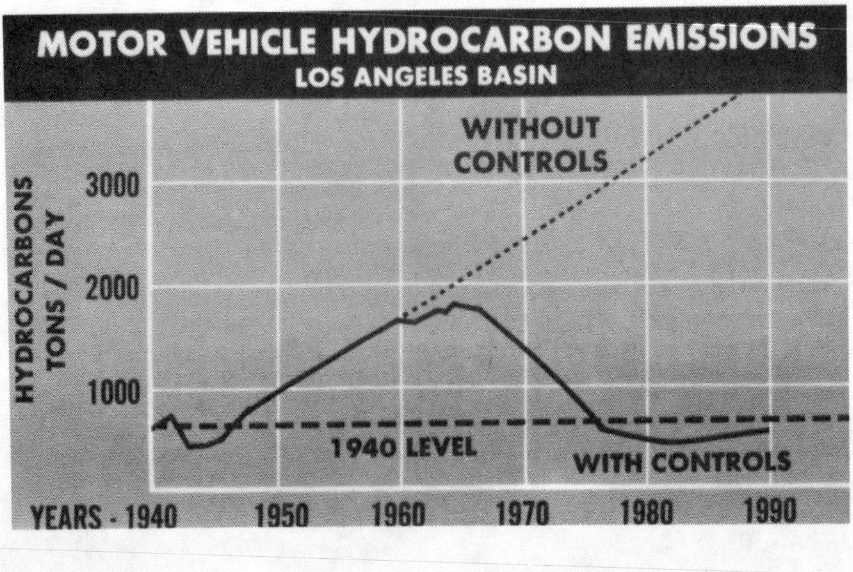

OXIDES OF NITROGEN

The third emission, oxides of nitrogen is created when the peak temperature in the combustion chamber rises over 2,500 degrees Fahrenheit.

We ordinarily think of the air we breathe as being mostly oxygen, because that is the gas we need to stay alive, but actually the air around us is 80% nitrogen. With that much nitrogen in the air that the engine breathes, naturally there is plenty of it in the combustion chamber when the spark plug lights the fire. If the peak temperature in the combustion chamber is 2,500 degrees or hotter, the nitrogen and oxygen in the air combine to form oxides of nitrogen. NOx also forms at lower combustion temperatures but in smaller amounts.

PHOTOCHEMICAL SMOG

It is important to remember that each of the three pollutants is emitted for separate reasons. Hydrocarbons come from unburned fuel, carbon monoxide comes from rich mixtures, and oxides of nitrogen come from too much heat in the combustion chamber.

These three pollutants are not smog. Smog is formed in the atmosphere in a photochemical process by only two of the pollutants after they leave the tail pipe. When hydrocarbons and oxides of nitrogen are exposed to sunlight, chemical reaction creates photochemical smog, which is a whole series of chemicals, called oxidants. It is these oxidants that create all the discomfort and even death when people or plants breathe them.

Carbon monoxide does not enter into the production of smog. It is a deadly gas all by itself, but it is completely odorless so you don't even know it is around until it's too late.

THE SMOG IN LOS ANGELES

Los Angeles is blessed with probably the most livable climate in the world, with sunshine possible any day of the year, and temperatures that hardly ever get below freezing.

Unfortunately, nature created a few flaws in the paradise, mainly a range of mountains to the north that create a sheltered area known as the Los Angeles basin. The lid on the basin is the temperature inversion which is present in the Southern California area over three hundred days out of every year.

TEMPERATURE INVERSION

In most parts of the world, the air near the ground is warm and it gets cooler the greater the altitude. The warm air rises, meets cooler air and cools itself off but the air higher up is still cooler, so the air keeps rising until pollution is carried away. A temperature inversion is a warm air blanket extending from street level up to a few hundred, or even a few thousand feet. Because there is no cooler air at higher levels within the inversion, the air in the inversion becomes a stagnant mass that does not rise. When the top of the warm air blanket is several thousand feet high, there is enough movement within the inversion that the smog rises above the city streets and you have a clear day. When the inversion level is down to where it can be measured in hundreds of feet, the smog builds up and can't go anywhere. This is when you get the eye irritation, headaches and difficult breathing that is characteristic of a smog attack.

Now that the scientists have done all the work and positively identified where the smog comes from, it is very easy to explain it, but you should remember that it took many years of laboratory experiments to pin down the internal combustion engine as being responsible for the production of photochemical smog. Even today, laboratory scientists do not know exactly how photochemical smog is formed or what it consists of. They can put the proper ingredients into a chamber, expose it to sunlight and create smog, but nobody has yet discovered the

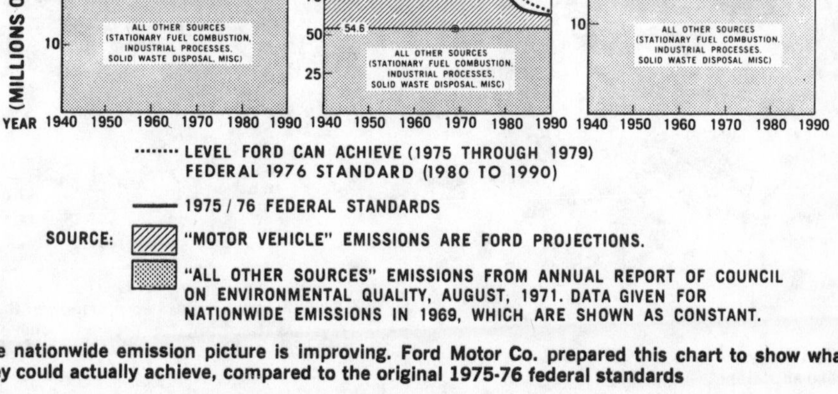

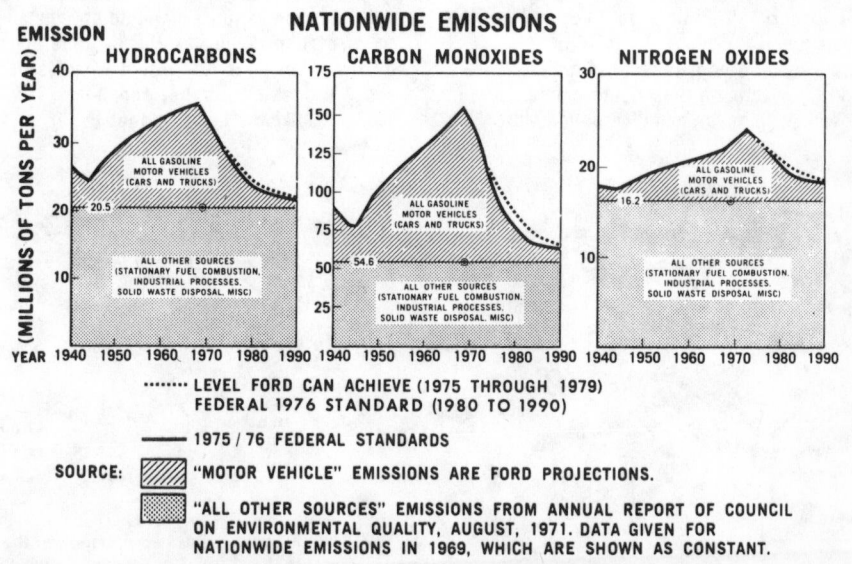

The nationwide emission picture is improving. Ford Motor Co. prepared this chart to show what they could actually achieve, compared to the original 1975-76 federal standards

precise chemical reaction that actually goes on. Experiments are continuing and some day we may be able to get rid of smog simply by spraying something in the air. Until that time comes, the only way to stop it is to keep the automobile from emitting the pollutants that create it.

THE DEVELOPMENT OF CRANKCASE, EXHAUST, AND VAPOR CONTROLS

When work first started in smog research, most people naturally assumed that all the pollutants came out of the tail pipe. The car makers themselves did some experimenting and pointed out that the crankcase road draft tube was responsible for 20% of the hydrocarbon emissions.

CRANKCASE CONTROLS

In an engine, some of the hydrocarbons that cling to the combustion chamber walls and do not burn, are forced out through the exhaust valve when it opens. But there is also a layer of hydrocarbons around the top ring in the space between the top of the piston and the cylinder wall. There never has been a top ring that made a perfect seal, so there is always some leakage or blowby past the ring and down into the crankcase. Because the space above the ring is full of unburned hydrocarbons, these are what go down through the crankcase and out through the road draft tube. There is some NOx and CO mixed in, but crankcase emissions are mostly HC.

Starting on 1961 California cars, and in 1963 nationwide, the manufacturers removed the road draft tube from the crankcase and connected the crankcase opening to the intake manifold through an orifice or a movable valve to control the flow. This positive crankcase ventilation system, or PCV, completely eliminated the emission of hydrocarbons from the crankcase, except at wide open throttle where there is no intake manifold vacuum to pull the pollutants into the engine. At wide open throttle the engine breathed through an open filler cap on the oil filler tube.

In 1966, as a result of legislation, the manufacturers put a closed PCV system on their California cars and in 1968 this closed system was installed nationwide. With the closed system there is absolutely no escape of hydrocarbons into the atmosphere. At wide open throttle the crankcase emissions are drawn into the engine by the suction in the air cleaner.

EXHAUST CONTROLS

Starting in 1966, on California cars, the car makers attacked the problem of exhaust emissions, concentrating mainly on hydrocarbons and carbon monoxide. The easiest way to control carbon monoxide is to run lean mixtures. Most carburetors since 1966 in California or 1968 nationwide have been set on the lean side. Hydrocarbons were controlled partly by changing the shape of the combustion chamber so there were fewer pockets where the gasoline could escape burning.

Unfortunately, those engine modifications did not do a complete job for most of the car makers, and many of them, in the early days of emission controls, had to use an air pump, which takes care of both hydrocarbons and carbon monoxide. The pump, driven by a belt off the front pulley, pumps air through a series of hoses and lines into each exhaust port. Any hydrocarbons or carbon monoxide that come out of the port are oxidized (burned) when they mix with the blast of air under the heat of the exhaust. Actually, the system creates combustion in the exhaust manifold and if you don't believe it, just get under a car equipped with an air-pump after a hard run at night and watch how everything glows.

Chrysler Corporation avoided the use of an air pump for many years, by using an engine modification system. Later on, other car makers also adopted the engine modification system. They were able to do this by very carefully tailoring the spark timing and the mixture so that fewer hydrocarbons and carbon monoxide were produced. What did come out the exhaust port was burned up in the exhaust manifold because of retarded timing which heated up the exhaust.

Heat in the exhaust manifold or exhaust system gets rid of carbon monoxide and hydrocarbons by burning them up, but does not produce oxides of nitrogen because it does not get hot enough.

The crankcase controls that began in 1961 and the

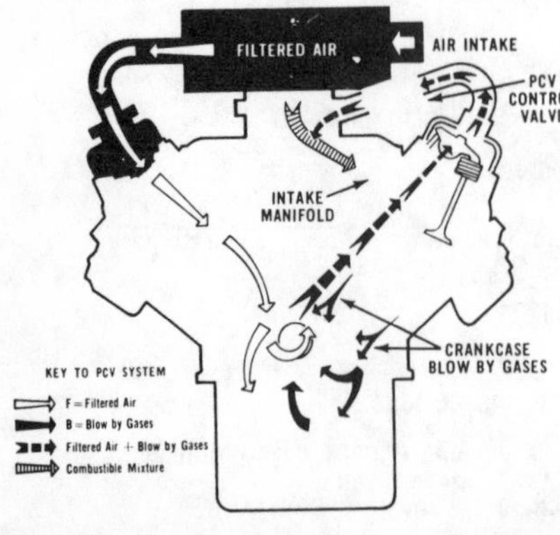

The closed system results in 100% control of crankcase emissions

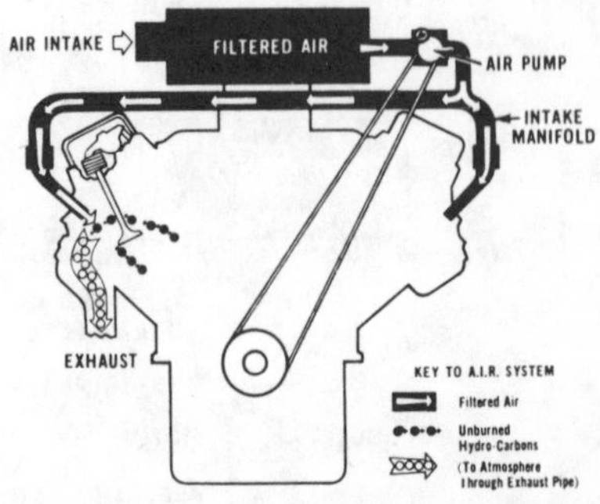

The air pump causes combustion in the exhaust system that burns up the emissions, making them harmless. Every air pump system also includes some engine modifications

exhaust controls that started in 1966 were mainly concerned with hydrocarbons and carbon monoxide. Oxides of nitrogen were recognized as a pollutant that created smog, but hydrocarbons and carbon monoxide were much more easily controlled with the knowledge that was available back then. Public health officials legislated against the emission of hydrocarbons and carbon monoxide, completely ignoring the oxides of nitrogen. This blunder was compounded when the hydrocarbon and carbon monoxide controls came in because the lean mixtures raised peak combustion temperatures to above 2,500 degrees causing emissions of more oxides of nitrogen. Los Angeles residents found out about this the hard way when oxides of nitrogen suddenly became a much greater problem than they ever had been and the familiar brown haze that came with some smog attacks started appearing everywhere. Finally, in 1971, legislation forced the car makers to put NOx controls on new cars. That was the beginning of the transmission controlled spark and speed controlled spark systems, which lowered peak combustion temperatures by retarding the spark. General Motors put the systems on most of their cars in 1970, one year before the law actually required them. Lately, exhaust gas recirculation (EGR) has taken the place of transmission controlled spark. EGR lowers the peak combustion temperature because the exhaust gas will not burn, and it makes the fuel air mixture less powerful.

In the meantime, Californians were being smothered by the exhaust from those 1966 through 1970 vehicles which put out much more oxides of nitrogen than any of the older uncontrolled cars did.

California now requires that devices be fitted to those 1966 through 1970 used cars that do not have oxides of nitrogen controls. California also requires that some type of used car emission control be installed on vehicles as far back as 1955. So far, California is the only State to require this but undoubtedly other States will, if their smog problem gets bad enough.

VAPOR CONTROLS

Starting on 1970 California cars, the manufacturers installed vapor controls to stop the evaporation of gasoline from the fuel tank and the carburetor. The first two years, some systems used the engine crankcase to store the vapors that came out of the fuel tank. When the engine was running, the vapors were purged from the crankcase by the positive crankcase ventilation system. This crankcase storage could cause trouble on cars that were driven on short trips because they never got warm enough to evaporate the gasoline in the crankcase. The PCV system was constantly sucking in fuel vapors that made the engine run rich.

In later years, most car makers, except some imports, went to a canister storage system. A canister in the engine compartment collected the vapors and was purged when the engine was running. The vapors from the canister didn't cause trouble in the operation of the engine because they were drawn off very slowly.

CONTROLS VERSUS DRIVEABILITY

The emission controls on the 1971 through current vehicles are doing a good job of controlling emissions, but the car doesn't run as well as it used to. Driveability has suffered. Surging and hesitation are expected. In fact, if you drive a late model car that does not surge or hesitate at any speed, then someone has probably doctored the car to make it run better.

Gas mileage has not been affected as much by emission controls as you might think. Other factors such as the increased weight of vehicles and the number of power accessories, such as air conditioning, take much more out of gas mileage than the emission controls do.

SYSTEMS OF THE FUTURE

The cars that we have seen since 1971 are just about what we will continue to see as long as the manufacturers keep using standard carburetion and ignition. Some manufacturers have already taken a step in the right

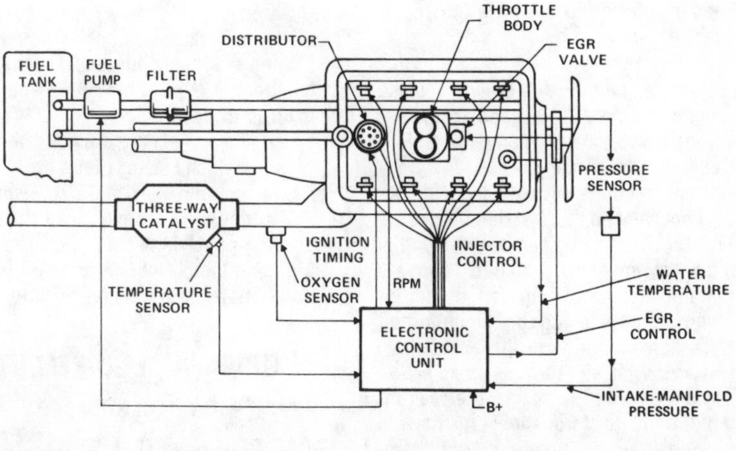

A closed-loop EFI system for 1976 emission standards. In order for the catalytic converter to operate effectively, the exhaust chemistry must be strictly controlled. This requires an exact metering of the air/fuel intake ratio through all phases of engine operation, which in turn requires a constant sensing of various engine conditions and exhaust characteristics. This is all fed to the Electronic Control Unit which computes the engine's exact fuel requirements.

The "muffler full of beads" may be the solution the car makers have been looking for. Its appearance on 1975 cars may mean better driveability

direction by going to electronic ignition. But there will have to be better ways developed of feeding the fuel into the engine so that it only gets enough for perfect combustion and not enough to pollute. Until that happens, perhaps with some type of fuel injection, or a different type of carburetor, we will not have a car that drives well and is clean, at the same time.

CATALYTIC CONVERTERS

The catalytic converter looks like a muffler full of beads. The beads are the catalyst, a substance that causes a chemical reaction, but does not enter into it.

Usually, the catalytic converter is hooked up to an air pump, similar to the pump on air injection systems. When the hot exhaust gases mix with the air in the presence of the catalyst, the HC, CO and NOx are reduced to harmless gases.

The catalyst eventually gets dirty or contaminated by foreign substances from the fuel tank. The fuel has to be absolutely lead free, or the catalyst will be ruined. If it is necessary to change the catalyst, the plan is to have a trapdoor in the converter, and a special vacuum cleaner. Connect the vacuum cleaner to the converter and it sucks out the old catalyst. The new catalyst is inside the vacuum cleaner. By switching the connections, the new catalyst is injected into position inside the converter. It only takes a few seconds with the car on a hoist.

THERMAL REACTOR

The thermal reactor goes on the car's engine in place of the regular exhaust manifold. It is used to oxidize unburned hydrocarbons and carbon monoxide before they can be released into the atmosphere.

Basically, the thermal reactor is an extension of the air injection system concept. What a thermal reactor does is supply a better place for the exhaust combustion to take place. (Remember the glowing exhaust manifold above?) Combustion is aided because there is more time, turbulence, and higher temperatures to burn up the unburned hydrocarbons and carbon monoxide in the exhaust.

Exhaust gases, mixed with air from an air injection pump, are fed from the exhaust ports into the reactor. Baffles at the end of the reactor force the gases back to the center, thus giving them more time in the high temperature area and added turbulence to provide for their more complete combustion. The reactor is insulated, both to keep its internal temperature high and to keep things from getting too hot under the hood.

STRATIFIED CHARGE ENGINES

A stratified charge gasoline engine works something like a diesel engine. Two types of mixture are provided in the combustion chamber: a small, very rich cloud of mixture to promote ignition and a larger, very clean cloud of mixture which contains an excess of oxygen, to aid in more complete combustion.

There are at least two different ways of providing the two different kinds of mixture. Either a fuel injection system having two nozzles, one for rich mixture and one for lean, per cylinder or a separate, small combustion is used for each cylinder, in which the rich mixture is ignited to help more completely burn the leaner mixture in the main combustion chamber by providing sufficient heat to raise all portions of the chamber to above ignition temperature. In this way, a mixture too lean to burn in an ordinary engine may be burned, resulting in lower exhaust emissions.

FUEL INJECTION

Fuel injection may also be used to help decrease the amount of emissions, by providing a more precise control over the fuel/air ratio for each cylinder. In a normally carbureted engine, the mixture varies between cylinders because of their varying distances from the carburetor. As a result, some cylinders get a very rich mixture, while others may get a very lean mixture. So, at best, the carburetor mixture setting is a compromise.

When the fuel is injected directly into the combustion chambers, it is possible to provide identical (and ideal) mixtures to each cylinder.

Also, fuel injection provides a higher fuel delivery pressure which causes better atomization (smaller droplets) of fuel and thus more complete combustion.

With the more complex electronic fuel injection systems, it is possible to tailor the mixture for such variables as engine load, ambient temperature, etc., allowing an even better control of the mixture.

ORIGINAL EQUIPMENT SYSTEMS

CRANKCASE VENTILATION CONTROLS

ROAD DRAFT SYSTEM

Because piston rings don't seal perfectly there is always a little bit of leakage or "blow-by" into the crankcase. This blow-by consists of unburned gasoline and water vapor, which must be removed or the oil pan ends

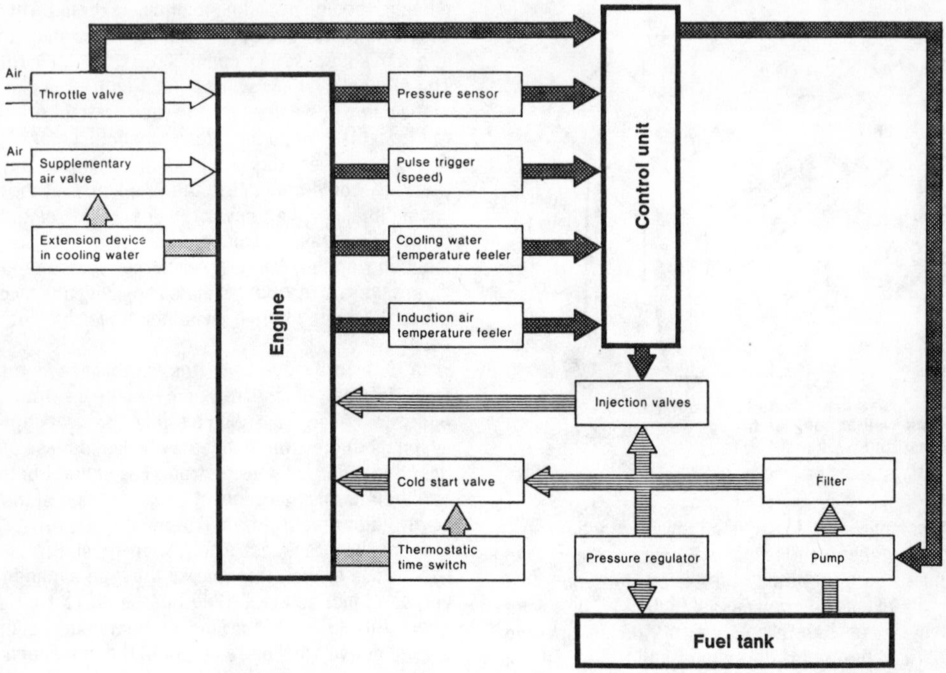

Mercedes-Benz electrically controlled injection system (Courtesy Mercedes-Benz of North America Inc. and Daimler-Benz AG. Stuttgart, Germany)

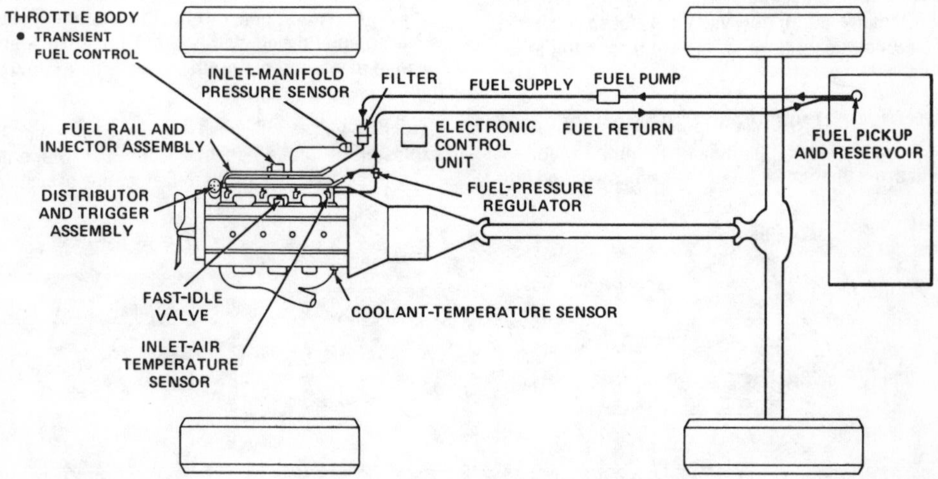

A typical Electronic Fuel Injection (EFI) system installation. The various sensors relay information on applicable engine operating conditions to the Electronic Control Unit. The control unit in turn activates the fuel pump, insuring that the necessary amount of fuel is delivered to the fuel injectors. Any excess fuel is returned to the gas tank via an overflow valve and fuel return line.

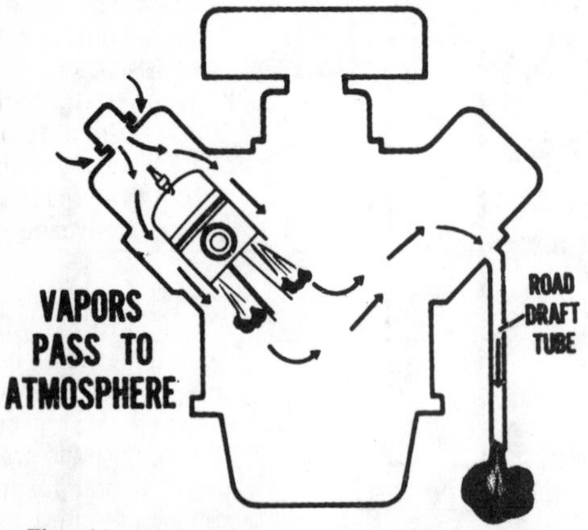

The old road draft system of crankcase ventilation worked well as long as the car was moving, but at idle it didn't work at all

up with corrosive acids from chemical reactions between the water and the gasoline. Engineers recognized a long time ago that the oil and the engine would last longer if they kept the crankcase ventilated. The way it was always done before smog was with an opening somewhere at the top of the engine and a tube off the side of the crankcase that hung down into the airflow under the car. The airflow, or road draft, passed over the tube when the car was moving, drew the undesirable fumes out of the crankcase and pulled in fresh air through the opening on the top. Road draft tubes worked well, while the vehicle was moving, but on a stationary engine or one that didn't move very fast, the engineers had to devise other ways such as fans or vacuum systems to keep the crankcase ventilated. In the days before smog, it didn't matter how you did it just so you had a blast of clean air going through the crankcase to get rid of the fumes.

OPEN POSITIVE CRANKCASE VENTILATION (PCV)

Positive crankcase ventilation uses intake manifold vacuum to draw the fumes out of the crankcase and into the manifold. They are burned in the combustion chamber and go out with the engine exhaust. The crankcase connection can be any place on the engine that has internal air passages connecting with the crankcase. The original systems were an add-on device connected at the same position as the old road draft tube. The hose ran from there up to the intake manifold. Later on, when the systems were designed into the engines, they found that they could connect to the crankcase at the rocker cover, at the valley cover, at either end of the block below the intake manifold or even at the fuel pump mounting flange. The crankcase connection should be where there is the least chance of picking up any oil, so it is usually made at the highest point, which is the rocker cover.

In 1971, Ford moved all of their crankcase connections from the rear of one rocker cover to the front of the opposite cover. This didn't affect the working of the system, but they found that they picked up less oil when the connection was at the front. For years, Pontiac has had their crankcase connection at the front of the valley cover, underneath the intake manifold.

From the crankcase connection most PCV systems use a hose or tube that runs to the intake manifold. But you can't just connect a big hose and let it go at that. There has to be some kind of restriction so that the engine doesn't pull more air out of the crankcase than it does through the carburetor. This restriction can be a plan orifice or a variable orifice, which is called the PCV valve. During the high vacuum at idle or deceleration, the plunger in the valve is pulled against a spring and seats against the end of the valve. In this position the amount of airflow through the valve is limited. At cruising speed, when intake manifold vacuum is a little bit less than it would be at idle, the spring pushes the valve off its seat, making the opening slightly bigger and allowing more airflow. At wide-open throttle, the spring pushes the valve completely off its seat, but because there is no vacuum at wide-open throttle there is no airflow through the valve at that time.

All PCV valves will close if there is an intake manifold explosion or intake backfire. When the intake manifold pops back through the carburetor, the pressure in the

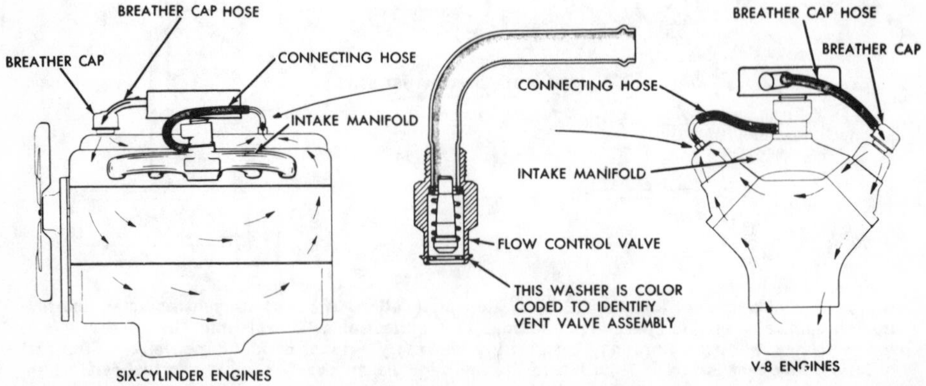

The first positive crankcase ventilation systems took in fresh air through an open breather cap

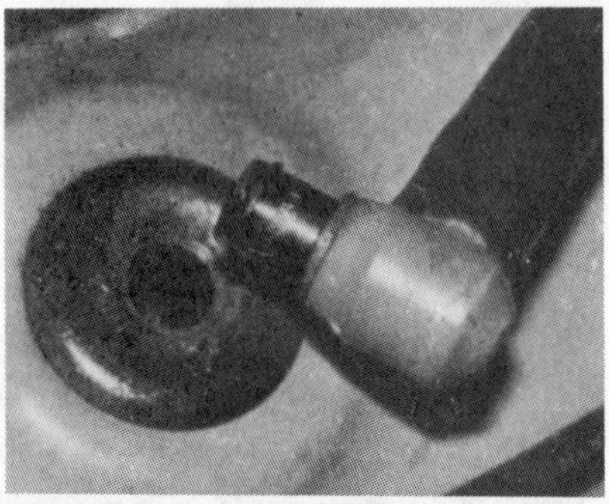

The PCV valve is usually plugged into a grommet on top of the engine. This is a late model Chrysler valve, which looks much different from the earlier hooded models

manifold increases and pushes the PCV valve plunger to the end, preventing this pressure from going down into the crankcase. The fixed orifice provides a similar amount of protection because the intake manifold explosion cannot get through the orifice fast enough to build up pressure in the crankcase. What is feared is that flame might travel along the hose and cause a crankcase explosion. This is impossible as long as the orifice or the PCV valve is in place.

Part of the positive crankcase ventilation system is the fresh air entry. There usually is an opening somewhere on the engine to allow fresh air to enter. Some car makers, particularly those who make import cars with small engines, have PCV systems without a fresh air entry. In that type of system the crankcase runs under vacuum at all times and there is very little flow through the PCV connection. They can get away with this because small engines do not have much blow-by. At wide-open throttle when there is no intake manifold vacuum to apply to the crankcase, the vapors are pushed into the intake manifold by crankcase pressure. This system obviously does not keep the crankcase purged of fumes as well as the type that has the fresh air entry.

In the open system the fresh air entry is usually the oil filler cap, although it can be a separate breather on the rocker cover. In that case, the oil filler cap is the solid type. Inside the fresh air breather cap or separate breather is a mesh type filter that keeps dirt from entering the crankcase.

During wide-open throttle on the open system, there is no vacuum and the crankcase breathes from its own buildup of pressure, through the oil filler cap or breather. This system is not 100% perfect because at wide-open throttle it does allow crankcase vapors to escape into the atmosphere.

CLOSED POSITIVE CRANKCASE VENTILATION (CPCV)

If you want a completely closed system with no leakage of crankcase fumes to the atmosphere, then you have to use what is known as closed positive crankcase ventilation. The PCV valve and the hose from the crankcase to the intake manifold are the same on both open and closed systems. The only difference in the closed system is the way that the fresh air entry is hooked up. Fresh air must enter from the air cleaner into a hose or other connection to the crankcase. Usually the system is set up so that fresh air enters a PCV filter inside the air cleaner, then goes through a hose to the rocker cover.

The advantage of a closed system is that it does not pass fumes from the crankcase into the atmosphere at wide-open throttle or if the PCV valve gets clogged. When the engine is running with intake manifold vacuum, the airflow through the fresh air hose is from the air cleaner to the rocker cover. When the engine is running without manifold vacuum such as at wide-open throttle or if the PCV valve should be plugged, then airflow is by crankcase pressure through the fresh air hose from the rocker cover back to the air cleaner. Once the fumes get inside the air cleaner they are sucked down into the engine, so that there is no way that the crankcase fumes can get outside the engine and into the atmosphere.

California requires that some older cars have their open type PCV systems converted to a closed type. It is not necessary to buy a complete PCV system to do this because the manufacturers make a kit consisting of a fresh air hose and connections between the air cleaner and the rocker cover.

Some imported cars use a closed PCV system that does not have a valve. There is simply a hose connecting the crankcase to the air cleaner. A slight amount of

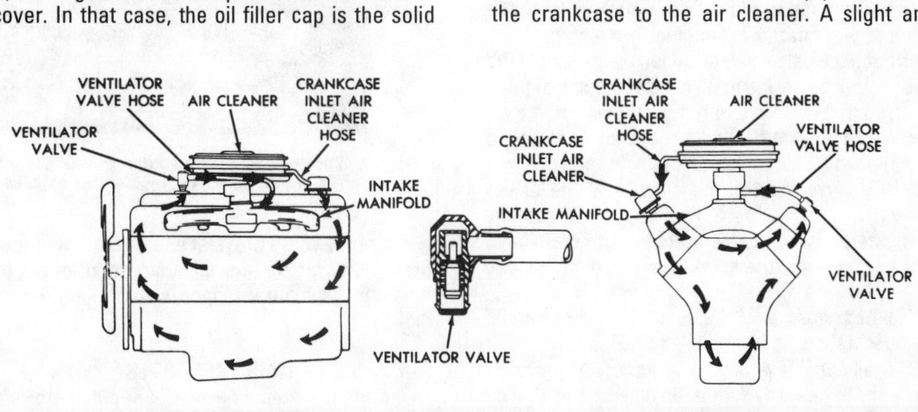

Later systems were closed, with fresh air coming from a tube that connected to the air cleaner

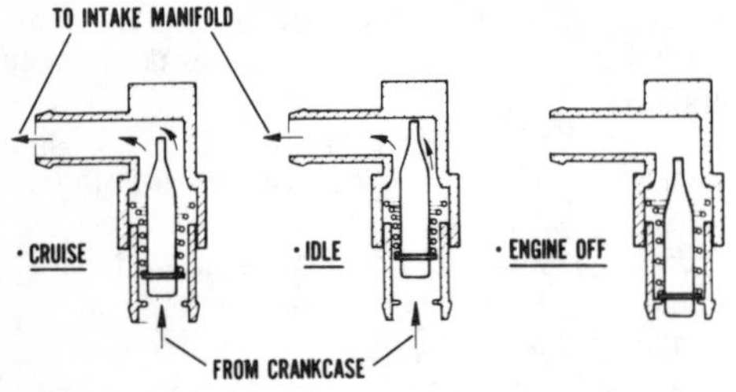

PCV VALVE

The jiggler pin inside the valve takes a position according to manifold vacuum. During an intake manifold explosion (popping back through the carburetor) the valve goes to the "engine off" position and prevents the burning mixture in the manifold from traveling down the hose into the crankcase

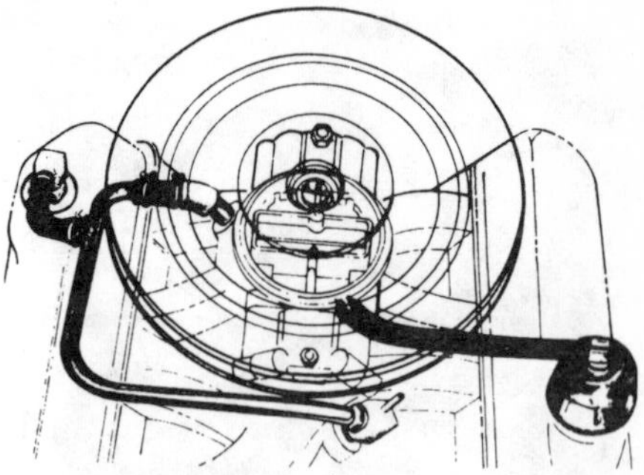

Earlier PCV systems used tubing to take vacuum from each side of the manifold to eliminate pulsing at the valve. Later systems made the connection underneath the carburetor, which accomplished the same purpose without all the tubing

suction in the air cleaner pulls the vapors out of the crankcase, but most of the flow is from crankcase pressure pushing out through the hose. In this system, as in all closed systems, the oil filler cap is the solid type.

SERVICING CRANKCASE VENTILATION SYSTEMS

Service on crankcase ventilation systems amounts mainly to cleaning the hoses, replacing the valve, and either cleaning or replacing the PCV filter. The car makers do not recommend that you attempt to clean the PCV valve because you cannot get it apart to find out if your cleaning was successful. Some of the older cars had valves that could be taken apart and it is alright to clean those types because you can see whether you've gotten them clean.

PCV systems give very little trouble, but there is one thing you must watch if you are replacing a PCV valve with a valve that is not original equipment. Some of the valves on the market are universal, made to fit just about any engine and can easily be installed backwards. A valve that is installed backwards will be closed all the time because intake manifold vacuum will suck the plunger against the end of the valve away from the spring.

If you use a non-standard PCV valve, make sure that it is specified for your particular engine. The amount of air flowing through the valve is determined by the size of the plunger and the holes inside. You can't get inside to measure it, so that you have to rely on the part number.

If you have an older car with so much blow-by that the original equipment PCV valve can't handle the smoke, a universal PCV valve may be the answer. Some of the universal valves pass so much air that you can actually run the engine on what comes up out of the crankcase with the carburetor mixture screws screwed all the way shut.

On an open system, a PCV valve that cannot handle the blow-by will show up in smoke and fumes coming out through the oil cap. On a closed system, you probably won't be able to see any fumes coming out of the air cleaner, but the air filter element will get dirty in a very short time because it is being forced to gulp oil fumes from the crankcase.

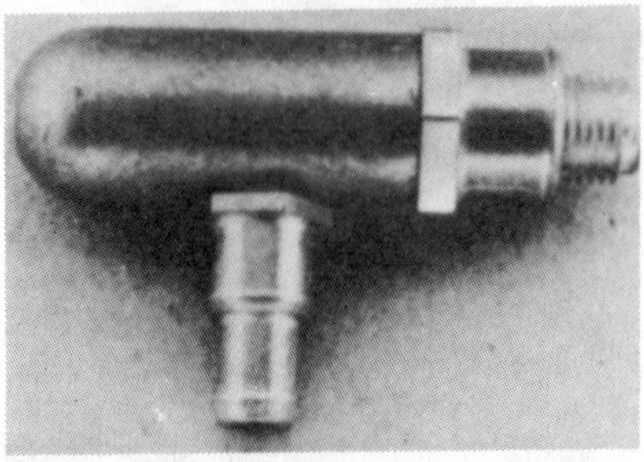

This accessory PCV valve is not original equipment, but it has a high flow which can solve the problem of excessive smoke from the crankcase

The PCV filter is usually at the end of the fresh air hose, inside the air cleaner

For many years Chrysler used a foam wrapper around their paper air cleaner elements to keep the oil off the element. A similar wrapper is now being used on other makes.

AIR PUMP EXHAUST CONTROLS

Air pump systems have a lot of plumbing, with hoses and lines running all over the engine which make them look very complicated, but actually, they are one of the simplest systems for emission control. The pump, driven

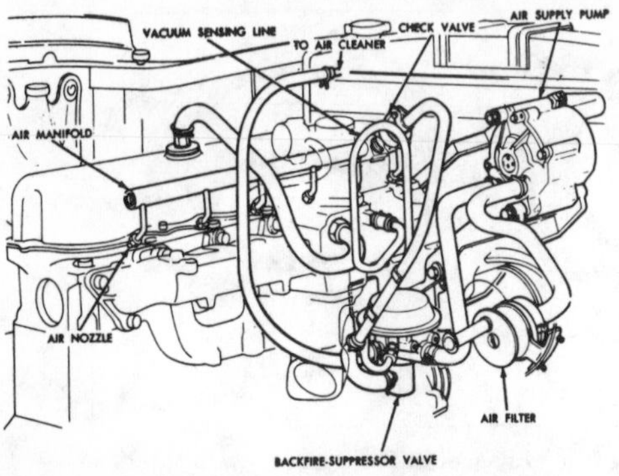

Early air pump systems had complex hose routings. Even so, they gave very little trouble in service

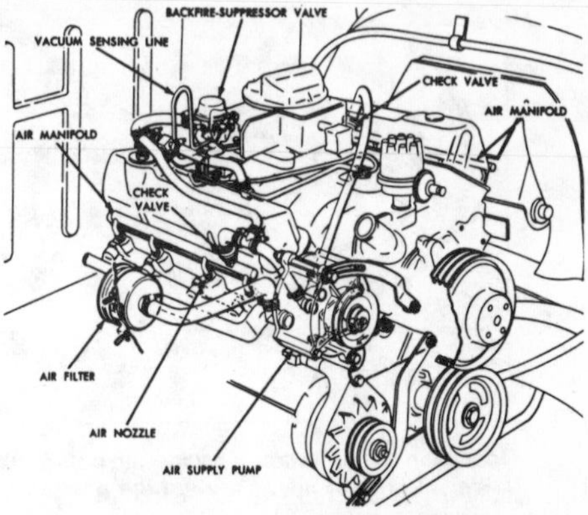

The backfire supressor valve and separate pump air filter have both been done away with on the later systems, except on some imported cars

by a belt at the front of the engine, pumps air under a pressure of only a few pounds into each exhaust port. The hydrocarbons and carbon monoxide that come out the port are very hot. The extra air mixed with them causes a fire in the exhaust manifold that oxidizes the carbon monoxide into harmless carbon dioxide and burns up the hydrocarbons into carbon dioxide and water. Stainless steel nozzles are used to direct the air into the port as close to the exhaust valve as possible. The stainless steel is necessary so that the nozzles will not burn away.

Between the nozzles and the pump is a check valve. The system can be set up so that there is one check valve per bank on a V8 engine or a single check valve for the whole system. The check valve keeps the hot exhaust gases from flowing back into the pump and hoses, and destroying them. The pump parts are made out of a special hard plastic. If you have ever smelled a pump that burned up because of a bad check valve, you'll never forget it.

During closed throttle deceleration, high intake manifold vacuum pulls a lot of extra fuel into the engine and out the exhaust system. If the pump continues pumping during deceleration you can get a lot of popping in the exhaust or even an exhaust explosion that can blow the mufflers apart. To prevent this, some way had to be found to shut off the pump during deceleration. The early systems used on most cars in 1966 and 1967 (and on some imported cars even later), used what was known as an anti-backfire valve or gulp valve. The gulp valve was connected between the pump and the intake manifold. A small sensing line or hose led from the valve diaphragm to the intake manifold. During the high vacuum of deceleration, the vacuum through the sensing line acted on the diaphragm, which pulled the valve open, allowing all of the air from the pump to flow directly into the intake manifold. The anti-backfire valve did not shut off the flow of air to the nozzles, but because it opened the system to the high intake manifold vacuum, almost all of the air from the pump flowed into the intake manifold with very little left to come out of the nozzles. Limiting the air going into the exhaust manifold prevented exhaust system explosions and the extra air entering the intake manifold leaned down the mixtures so that emissions were not so bad during deceleration. The disadvantage of the anti-backfire valve was that the engine kept on running during deceleration. In some cases backing off the throttle at 70 miles per hour would have no effect at all for a few seconds. It felt as if the throttle was stuck wide-open. This was quite a shock if you weren't expecting it, but even after you got used to it, it was still annoying to have a car feel like it was running away with you. Another disadvantage of the gulp valve was its tendency to open when the car first started. The gulp valves operate on a change in vacuum applied to the diaphragm. The change from no vacuum when the engine is not running to immediate vacuum when the engine starts was enough to open the valve for a few seconds. Many engines would shake because of the air entering the intake manifold immediately after they were started. Oldsmobile recognized the problem on V8 engines and provided an air bleed control valve that blocked off the air from the pump to the gulp valve until it built up to a high value. The gulp valve still opened when the engine started, but no air could enter the intake manifold because the control valve was closed.

The gulp valve was obviously not the way to go, so the next development became known as the dump valve, by-pass valve, or diverter valve. It used a diaphragm operated from intake manifold vacuum, the same as the older gulp valve. However, air from the pump ran through the diverter valve at all times. During the high vacuum of deceleration, the diverter valve shut off the air to the nozzles and sent it to the air cleaner. The air entering the air cleaner has no effect on the operation of the car. It was sent to the air cleaner just to cut down on the noise. Later diverter valves, and the ones that are still used today, exhaust the air directly into the atmosphere through either a bronze or a cotton filter.

In both the gulp and the dump type of backfire suppressor valves, the diaphragm has a calibrated hole in it. This means that if you apply a sudden amount of vacuum to the sensing nozzle on the valve, the diaphragm will move against the spring to operate the valve. The hole in the diaphragm bleeds off the vacuum very quickly and the spring pushes the diaphragm back to the off position.

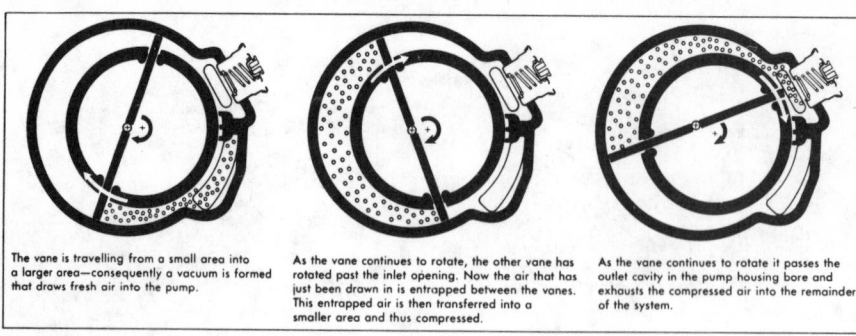

The vane is travelling from a small area into a larger area—consequently a vacuum is formed that draws fresh air into the pump.

As the vane continues to rotate, the other vane has rotated past the inlet opening. Now the air that has just been drawn in is entrapped between the vanes. This entrapped air is then transferred into a smaller area and thus compressed.

As the vane continues to rotate it passes the outlet cavity in the pump housing bore and exhausts the compressed air into the remainder of the system.

Operation of the eccentric vane air pump. The spring-loaded gadget at the upper right is the relief valve, which only opens under high pressure

Because of this bleed feature in the diaphragm, you can check the operation of the valve by disconnecting and reconnecting the hose or by simply pinching the hose and then letting it go. When you pinch the hose, you have to wait a few seconds for the vacuum to stabilize on each side of the diaphragm. When you reconnect the hose, the sudden surge of vacuum will make the valve operate. Of course, you can also check the valve by opening the throttle and allowing the engine to decelerate. In most cases, if you can reach the valve, or listen to the valve and work the throttle at the same time, making the engine decelerate is the easiest way to check the valve because you don't have any hoses or lines to disconnect.

When the pumps first came out, a relief valve was pressed into the side of the pump. The relief valve would open under high rpm to prevent the buildup of excess pressure that might damage the hoses or the pump itself. On some later models, the relief valve is built into the diverter valve, so that the diverter valve actually has a dual function. It diverts and also relieves pressure. If anything goes wrong with the relief valve part of the diverter valve, the entire diverter valve has to be replaced.

All domestic cars use a pump that is manufactured by the Saginaw Division of General Motors. The only variation in the pumps is the location of the mounting ears and the air hose connections. The early pumps used in 1966 and 1967, and on some cars for a few years after that, were made with 3 vanes and rebuilding of them was encouraged. Saginaw furnished parts for the 3-vane pumps until 1970 and then the parts were discontinued. Many mechanics had a lot of trouble reassembling the pumps because of the eccentric arrangement of the vane. In most cases the pumps were being replaced anyway, so that the loss of the supply of parts affected very few shops.

The 3-vane pump was discontinued on most new cars in 1968 when Saginaw came out with a new 2-vane design. The 2-vane pump has never had any parts supply and it is factory-recommended procedure to replace the pump rather than attempt to repair it.

The 3-vane pumps took their fresh air supply from a separate air filter or from the clean side of the engine air cleaner. The most noticeable feature of the 2-vane pump was the elimination of any external air cleaner. The filter

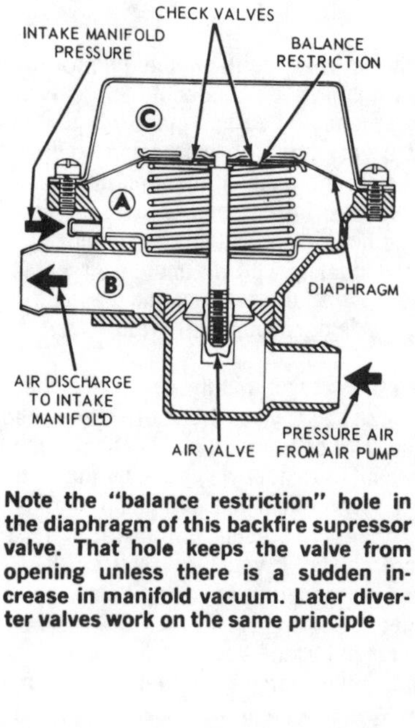

Note the "balance restriction" hole in the diaphragm of this backfire supressor valve. That hole keeps the valve from opening unless there is a sudden increase in manifold vacuum. Later diverter valves work on the same principle

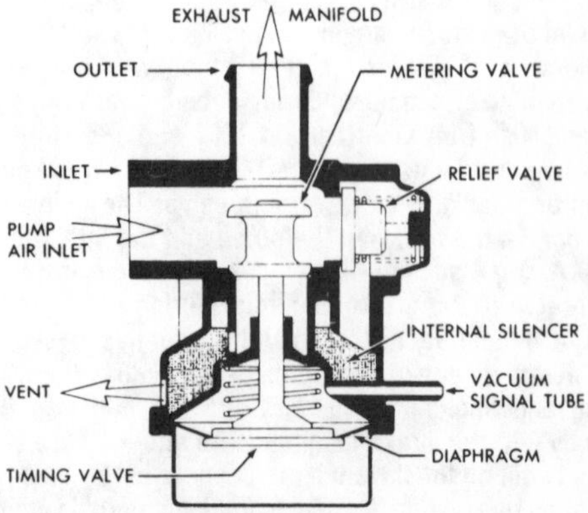

INTERNAL MUFFLER TYPE

Rochester Products latest diverter valve has an internal silencer. The bleed hole in the diaphragm does not show here, but it is definitely there

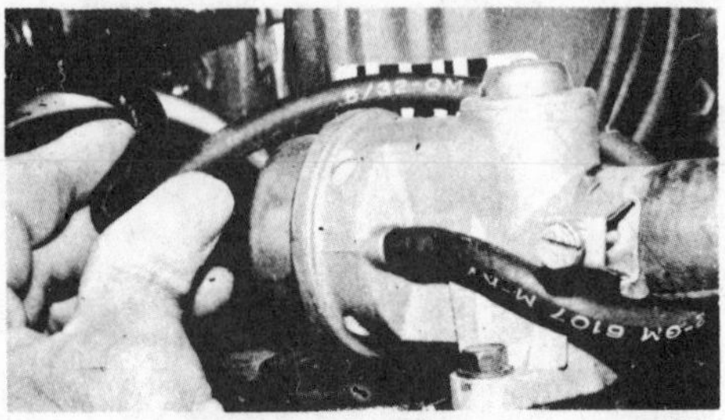

Diverter valves can be checked with the engine idling by pinching the hose, waiting a few seconds, and then releasing it. The valve should exhaust air for a few seconds

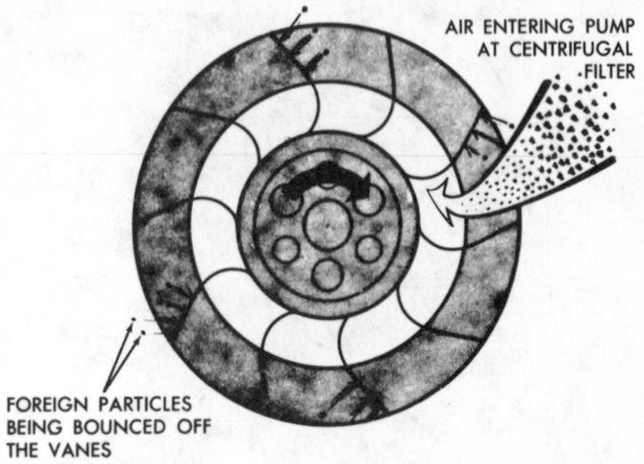

Operation of the filter fan on late model air pumps

fan behind the front pulley of the pump acted as a centrifugal filter and kept dirt from getting into the inside of the pump. Cleaning of the filter fan is not recommended because it is too easy to get the dirt particles down inside of the pump. If the fan is so dirty that the air flow is restricted, then the pulley and filter fan should be removed and a new filter fan pressed on the hub.

It is a difficult job to get the filter fan off the hub without breaking it. Actually, it is designed so that you do have to break the fan to remove it. Anything that attaches to the outside of the 2-vane pump, such as a relief valve, a diverter valve, mounting brackets, the filter fan, the front pulley or any air nozzle connections, can be replaced if necessary and they are available if you order them from a dealer parts department. The internal parts of the 2-vane pump are not available and it should not be taken apart.

The early pump systems used a lot of hoses and tubing, so many that in some cases that you couldn't even see the engine. Some car makers have stuck with the external lines and hoses, but others have built the air passages into the exhaust manifold, the intake manifold, or the cylinder head.

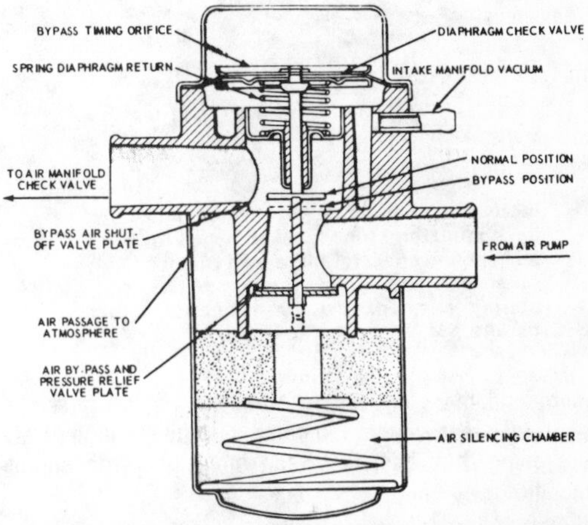

Carter Carburetor Co. makes this diverter valve, which is used on Ford products. A little known feature of this valve is that it not only diverts, but will relieve high pressure as well

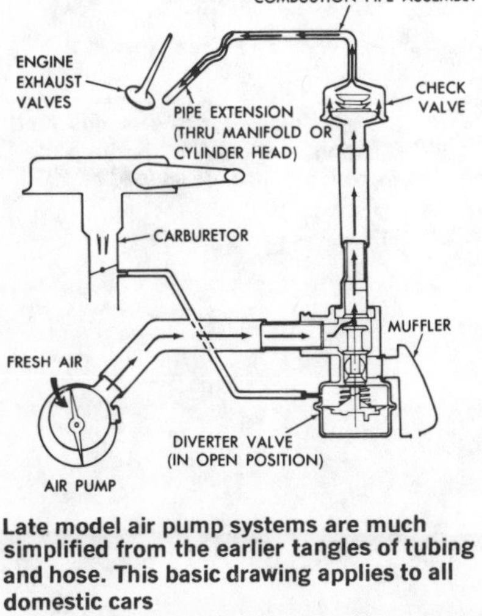

Late model air pump systems are much simplified from the earlier tangles of tubing and hose. This basic drawing applies to all domestic cars

ENGINE MODIFICATION SYSTEMS

When exhaust emission controls were in the planning stage, every car maker except Chrysler Corporation felt that the only way to control exhaust emissions was with the air pump system. Chrysler was doing a lot of experimenting and running test fleets with engine modification systems. By running leaner fuel mixtures, retarded spark, higher idle speed and different combustion chambers, Chrysler thought that they could pass the emission tests without an air pump. When the 1966 California cars rolled off the end of the assembly line, every American manufacturer had an air pump on his engine except Chrysler. Their faith in the engine modification system paid off. One year later, other manufacturers also started to use the engine modification system and the air pump was on the way out.

Air pumps were used less and less by all manufacturers as they relied on the engine modification system until 1972. In that year, to meet the stricter requirements, Chrysler finally had to put its first air pump on California engines. As the requirements get stricter, it becomes

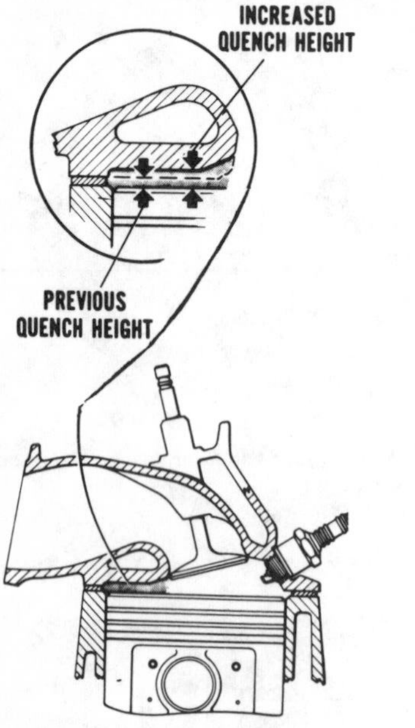

Increased quench height helps emissions by eliminating the "pocket" where unburn ed gasoline collects. Increased quench height has some side effects, such as re quiring lower compression ratios, or higher octane gas

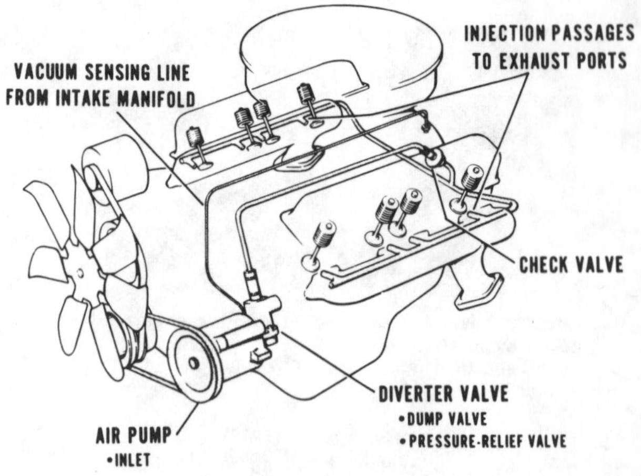

Chrysler 1973 air pump location

more and more difficult to make an engine pass the emissions test without the pump, but the manufacturers are doing their best to lessen emissions with engine modifications only.

CHRYSLER'S CLEAN AIR PACKAGE (CAP) AND CLEAN AIR SYSTEM (CAS)

Chrysler's system was originally called the Clean Air Package and later the name was changed to Clean Air System. The engine modifications in the system are really very simple. A normal, uncontrolled engine pollutes very badly at idle because the mixture is so rich. The rich mixture is what causes unburned hydrocarbons and carbon monoxide to come out the tailpipe. If you run a very lean mixture the engine won't idle unless you open the throttle more to keep it running. With the throttle open further the engine idles too fast. The easiest way to slow it down without affecting the throttle opening or the mixture is to retard the spark. This is the combination that is used at curb idle on all Chrysler engines with the Clean Air System. The idle mixture is lean, the throttle is opened further than it would be normally and the spark is retarded. The retarded spark not only helps slow the engine down, but it also increases the temperature in the exhaust manifold which oxidizes the carbon monoxide and also burns up the hydrocarbons.

To ensure that the mixture will stay lean and not be affected by somebody fiddling with the idle mixture

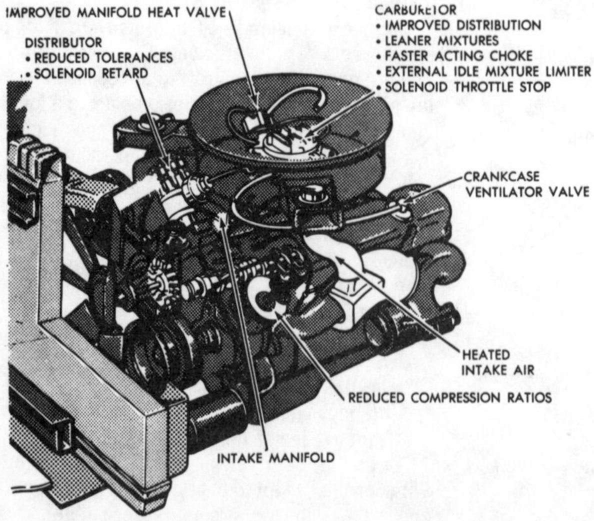

Chrysler pioneered the engine mod ification system. This is the state to which it had developed by 1970

screws, Chrysler has used several different systems to limit the amount of fuel that you can get at idle. The cleverest one of these is an idle mixture limiter built into the carburetor. No matter how far out you unscrew the idle needle, the limiter prevents rich mixtures beyond a certain point. Some carburetors have a pinned needle. If you try to unscrew the mixture needle too far, the pin breaks the needle off and then you have the problem of either drilling it out and fixing the throttle body or replacing the carburetor.

The fuel mixture is also set very lean at acceleration and cruising so that the emissions will be as low as possible. It wasn't necessary to lean it out too much in the cruising range because engines normally do not pollute very much when they are cruising at part-throttle.

The lean mixtures and other changes mentioned so far resulted in, originally, over 50% reduction in hydrocarbon and carbon monoxide emissions during idle and acceleration, but further controls were necessary to control emissions during deceleration on manual transmission cars.

When an engine without emission controls decelerates, it pollutes very badly. The rich idle mixture is sucked into the engine under high vacuum. Very little air comes into the engine because the throttle is closed. Also, the high vacuum pulls the exhaust back through the open exhaust valves and makes a very bad mixture that doesn't burn up. The wider throttle setting used with the Clean Air Package helps to lower emissions on deceleration because it lets more air into the combustion chamber. This reduces the deceleration vacuum and there is less tendency for the exhaust to be pulled back through the open exhaust valves.

Cars with manual transmissions maintain the high vacuum of deceleration much longer than a car with an automatic. The automatic gets an initial high vacuum when the driver takes his foot off the throttle, but this goes away pretty fast because of the slippage in the transmission. The automatic transmission CAP cars did not require any additional controls in most cases, but the manual transmission cars were still polluting heavily during deceleration. Chrysler engineers discovered that the best way to burn up those hydrocarbons on manual transmission cars during deceleration was to advance the spark. Normally the distributor vacuum diaphragm goes to the neutral or no advance position when the throttle is closed. If the engineers hooked up the vacuum diaphragm to the intake manifold, then they would get spark advance during deceleration but they would also have spark advance at idle when they definitely didn't want it. The solution to this problem was the Distributor Vacuum Control Valve or "Spark Valve". The ported vacuum line from the carburetor to the distributor ran through the spark valve. Another line was connected from the valve to intake manifold vacuum. During deceleration, the high intake manifold vacuum moved the valve so that the source of vacuum for the distributor was switched from the carburetor port to the intake manifold. The spark valve would stay in this position as long as the engine was decelerating with about 21½ in. Hg of vacuum or more. When the deceleration vacuum dropped off, the spark valve went back to its normal position and the distributor operated on ported carburetor vacuum the same as any other distributor.

Because you can't maintain deceleration vacuum on an engine that is sitting on the shop floor, the test for the spark valve is to see how many seconds it takes for it to switch back when you decelerate the engine without a load. Because the test is only for a few seconds, many people assume that the valve works that way on the

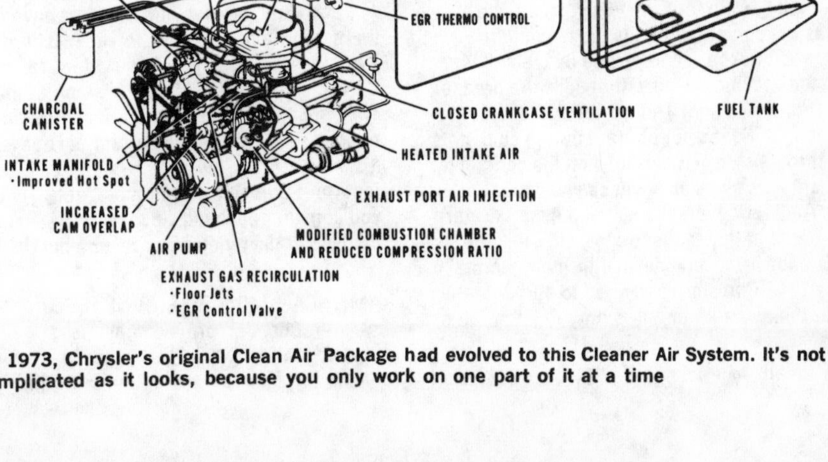

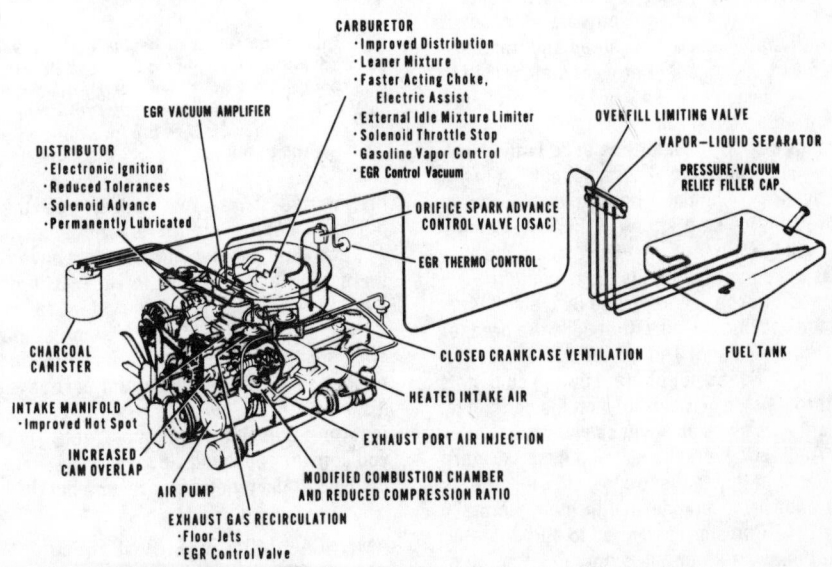

By 1973, Chrysler's original Clean Air Package had evolved to this Cleaner Air System. It's not as complicated as it looks, because you only work on one part of it at a time

engine, only opening for a few seconds when the driver takes his foot off the throttle. Actually, the valve goes to the intake manifold position as long as the engine is decelerating with more than about 21½ in. Hg of vacuum.

Other cars have also used the Chrysler spark valve. All of the spark valves, when used on Chrysler products or other cars, are adjustable by removing the end cap and turning the screw to increase or decrease the spring pressure. However, some car makers do not recommend adjustment.

One of the internal changes in the Clean Air Package was an increased quench height in the combustion chamber. On an overhead valve engine, the quench height is the distance from the top of the piston to the underside of the cylinder head where the smooth part of the head laps over the cylinder. If this space is made very small, the mixture squirts out of the space as the piston rises. This gives a swirling to the mixture which allows a much greater compression ratio without getting any detonation or ping. Without the ping you get the power of the higher compression ratio while using lower octane gas. The quench area is bad for emissions because sometimes the fuel in that little pocket does not burn. Also, it has a tendency to collect carbon, which makes the pocket even smaller, increasing the problem. Opening up the quench area has a definite beneficial effect on emissions, but it forces the car maker to lower compression ratios.

A lot of other refinements have been made in carburetion to try to get better fuel distribution. Some of the CAP carburetors have a single idle mixture screw. This screw adjusts the mixture in both barrels of a two-barrel carburetor at the same time. Other carburetors have an adjustable idle air bleed which is adjusted at the factory.

Chrysler was one of the first to use a throttle dashpot which gave a slower closing throttle, on manual transmission cars. We normally think of the dashpot as being used to stop the engine from stalling when the driver takes his foot off the throttle on an automatic transmission car. This dashpot was not to prevent stalling, but to stop the heavy emissions caused by the rich mixture from a closed throttle during deceleration.

Another clever design Chrysler has used is their solenoid retard vacuum advance. This solenoid is part of the vacuum advance unit and it is hooked up to a ground contact on the throttle stop screw. When the engine throttle is brought back to the curb idle position, the stop screw touches the contact, grounds the circuit, turns on the solenoid, and the spark is retarded by a small electromagnet in the vacuum advance that pulls the breaker plate to the retard position. The advantage of the solenoid retard is that it does not operate during cold start because the throttle stop screw is held off the contact by the fast idle cam. This gives an advanced spark for better cold starting. Another advantage is that the spark retard goes away immediately as soon as the throttle is opened. This allows the engine to run more normally above idle. In 1970, Chrysler finally had to add a heated air cleaner to their system and it is now used on all of their engines.

When the Clean Air Package and Clean Air System first started, it was easy to lean over the engine compartment and point out the various components of the system. Now, so many other items have been added to the engine that it is hard to know where the Clean Air System ends and another system takes up. In 1972, Chrysler added air pumps to some California engines. They also added an NOx spark control and exhaust gas recirculation. The old Clean Air Package is still there, but it's covered up by all the additional controls. When repairing Chrysler Corporation cars, it is much easier if you consider each individual system on its own, without thinking of the whole thing as one big Clean Air System.

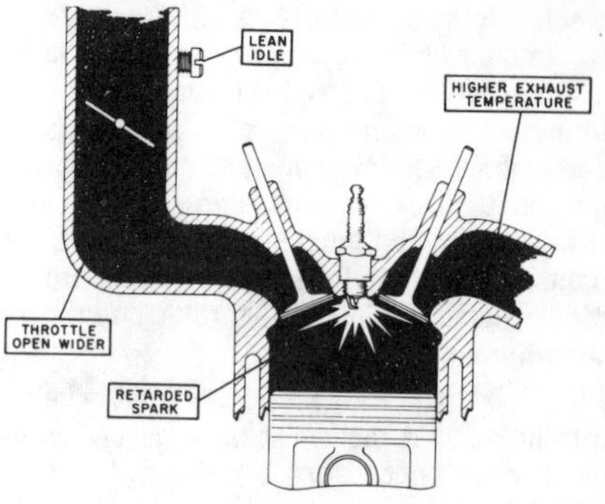

HOW CLEANER AIR SYSTEM LIMITS EMISSIONS AT IDLE

Spark timing and throttle opening work hand in hand. A retarded spark requires a wider throttle opening to maintain the same idle rpm. Or you could say that a wider throttle opening requires a retarded spark, for the same reason. The result is lowered emissions because of a denser mixture and a hotter exhaust

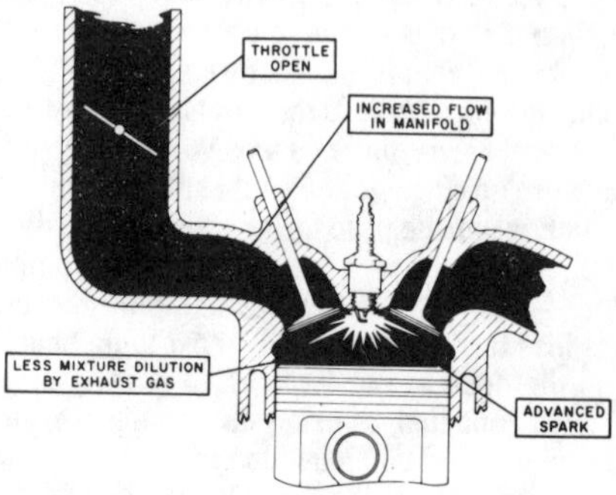

HOW CLEANER AIR SYSTEM LIMITS EMISSIONS ON DECELERATION

This is the result of having a spark valve that advances the spark during deceleration. When combined with the wider throttle opening that was made possible by retarding the spark at idle, there is less mixture dilution and more complete burning

AMERICAN MOTORS ENGINE MOD

After Chrysler proved that the engine modification system would work, the other manufacturers didn't waste any time in coming out with their own versions.

American Motors brought out their Engine Mod system on the 232 6 cylinder engine in 1967. They used a composition cylinder head gasket which was thicker than the usual steel gasket and increased the quench height. The carburetor was set lean and the initial spark setting was retarded from 5 to 8 degrees.

In 1968, the Engine Mod system graduated to the American Motors V8s with automatic transmission. The heated air cleaner also appeared that year as the beginning of more and more units that had to be added to keep the emission levels down. In 1970, they reached the ultimate in gadgetry with a dual diaphragm vacuum advance and a deceleration valve similar to the one Chrysler was using. In 1971, transmission controlled spark took over from the dual diaphragm distributor and deceleration valve. American Motors has kept their system simple since then, sticking with transmission controlled spark on many of their cars. The reason that American Motors has not had to go to some of the complicated spark controls that other manufacturers have used, is that they were not afraid to drop an air pump on an engine when it looked as if the engine modification controls were getting out of hand. The air pump has always been the easiest solution to lowering emissions, although it is a costly one because there is so much hardware.

Late model American Motors cars seem to have just as many emission controls as most of the other cars do. Exhaust gas recirculation, transmission controlled spark, and even the air pump are still very much in the picture. Since American Motors uses the Ford carburetor they also have the Ford electric choke, which heats up the choke coil and gives a quicker choke opening. The term "Engine Mod," in reference to the American Motors engine modification system, has fallen by the wayside somewhat with the introduction of exhaust gas recirculation, transmission controlled spark, and the other systems. When working on an American Motors vehicle, it is better to consider each system individually than to try to consider the engine being controlled by one big Engine Mod system.

FORD'S IMPROVED COMBUSTION (IMCO) SYSTEM

Ford's IMCO system first appeared in the middle of 1967 on the 170 and 200 cubic inch 6 cylinder engines and on the 410 V8 in Mercury cars. None of the modifications that make up the IMCO system are visible when you lift the hood. Part of the system is the heated air cleaner, but the heated air cleaner is also used on other engines. The rest of the system consists of modifications to the carburetor, intake manifold, cylinder heads, combustion chamber, exhaust manifold, camshaft and distributor.

Modifications to the carburetor are mainly changes in the fuel flow to get leaner mixtures. Getting these leaner mixtures was not just a simple case of changing jet sizes, but involved relocating some of the components inside the carburetor such as the idle jet tube. The bowl vent designs were also changed to get better internal venting at all engine speeds.

Some Ford carburetors used an internal idle limiter needle. It was similar to the idle mixture screw, but was covered by a lead seal so that it couldn't be changed. The idle limiter needle was set to a maximum richness value so that no matter how far the idle mixture screw was unscrewed, the mixture would not richen beyond that point. Later models of Ford carburetors used idle limiter caps which are also used by most other manufacturers. Intake manifold changes were made to get better heat on the fuel passages and several of the passages were reshaped to give better distribution. Combustion chambers were changed so that they had the same volume, but less surface for unburned fuel to cling to. The exhaust manifolds were given a more free flowing design and the camshaft was changed so that both intake and exhaust valves had less open time. Both the exhaust manifold and camshaft changes reduced back flow of the exhaust into the combustion chamber at idle, thereby, giving a better mixture that would burn more completely. Initial spark timing was retarded several degrees to get more complete burning of the fuel at idle and both vacuum and centrifugal spark advance curves were tailored to reduce emissions.

As soon as it was proved that the first IMCO system would work, Ford concentrated its efforts on eliminating air pumps from as many engines as possible. To eliminate the pump, they had to go to some of the most complicated systems in the industry. Many Ford engines use a dual diaphragm distributor which retards the spark at idle. Some six-cylinder engines also use a vacuum deceleration valve so that the spark will be advanced during deceleration.

In 1970, Ford started using electronic control of vacuum spark advance. This was their Electronic Distributor Modulator System, sometimes called the "Dist-O-Vac." Vacuum advance was shut off at low speeds and allowed at high speeds. In 1972, the Electronic Distributor Modulator system was changed slightly and given the new name of Electronic Spark Control. In 1973, exhaust gas recirculation, plus a change in the Federal test procedure resulted in the elimination of the electronic spark control from passenger car engines.

Ford has had more trouble with their six-cylinder engines than their V8s. Some of the six-cylinder engines have very complicated emission control systems. Many of these systems, such as Transmission Regulated Spark, Temperature Activated Vacuum, Delay Vacuum By-pass and the Spark Delay Valve, all are used to control distributor vacuum advance. A fair question is, why didn't Ford just eliminate the vacuum advance completely? The answer is that they had to keep it for better driveability, better gas mileage, and to help prevent engine overheating.

One important part of Ford's engine modification system is the fresh air tube, which they call a "zip tube." This tube connects from the grille at the front of the car to the air cleaner and supplies the engine with cool air from outside the engine compartment. The zip tube is used to cool the mixture down and help prevent detonation. The zip tube only affects engine operation on a very hot day when the outside air temperature is around 100°F. On that kind of a day, the temperature of the air inside the engine compartment can easily go to 200°F and that is much too hot to enable the engine to breathe without detonating, under a heavy load.

Ford still uses the term IMCO to describe their engine modification system, but IMCO itself is really not a specific system on the engine. All the term means is that the engine does not have an air pump. As with the other car makers, you should consider each emission control system individually and not try to think of IMCO as being one system, covering the whole engine.

GENERAL MOTORS CONTROLLED COMBUSTION SYSTEM (CCS)

Because the only visual difference in an engine with the controlled combustion system is the heated air cleaner, it looks as if that is all there is to the system.

Actually, the heated air cleaner is only one of many modifications General Motors has made to their engines when they didn't use an air pump. The original CCS system, used in 1968 and 1969, consisted of only 4 modifications. The carburetor was specially calibrated for lean mixtures and the engine idle speed was increased. The distributor was calibrated for emissions and set with initial timing that was retarded. A high temperature thermostat was used to raise the engine operating temperature and a thermostatically controlled air cleaner heated the carburetor air intake. Most of these original modifications were designed to lower hydrocarbons and carbon monoxide, but they did not do much for NOx.

In 1970, transmission controlled spark came in on some engines. In 1973, exhaust gas recirculation (EGR) was added to many engines. General Motors still uses the term CCS as applying to all their emission controlled engines, but CCS in itself is not a specific system.

The most confusing system on General Motors cars, especially Chevrolet, is their Transmission Controlled Spark. Each year changes were made to the TCS system, in some cases making it work exactly opposite to the year before. When you work on a General Motors car with Transmission Controlled Spark, you must use only the specifications and repair procedures for that particular year. A good example of the changes in the Chevrolet Transmission Controlled Spark system are the different vacuum solenoids used. In some years the vacuum solenoid shuts off vacuum spark advance when it is energized. In other years, the solenoid is normally closed so that it shuts off the vacuum when it is not energized. You must be very careful to correctly identify the year of car you are working on, and determine that somebody has not substituted the wrong parts so that the system works backwards from the way it should.

SPARK CONTROLS

TRANSMISSION CONTROLLED SPARK (TCS)

Transmission Controlled Spark first came out in 1970 on General Motors cars, one year earlier than the law required. Transmission Controlled Spark is a system of shutting off the vacuum spark advance in the lower gears or at lower speeds. If the system is speed controlled, it is usually called speed controlled spark. However, American Motors calls their system Transmission Control Spark, although on cars equipped with automatic transmission, it is sensitive to car speed rather than gear position.

In all TCS systems, vacuum to the distributor is turned on and off by a vacuum solenoid. This solenoid receives current when the ignition switch is on and usually is fused in the car fuse block. The solenoid is grounded at the transmission in certain gears and ungrounded in others. The difficulty in checking out the system comes from the fact that there are two kinds of solenoids, normally open to vacuum or normally closed. The normally open solenoid allows vacuum to pass through it and act on the distributor when it is not energized. The normally closed solenoid allows vacuum to pass through the distributor only when it is energized. The early sys-

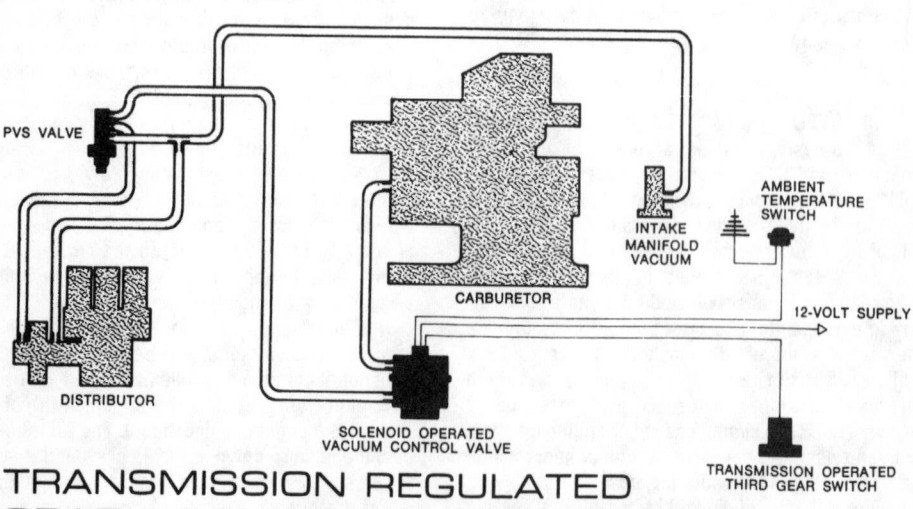

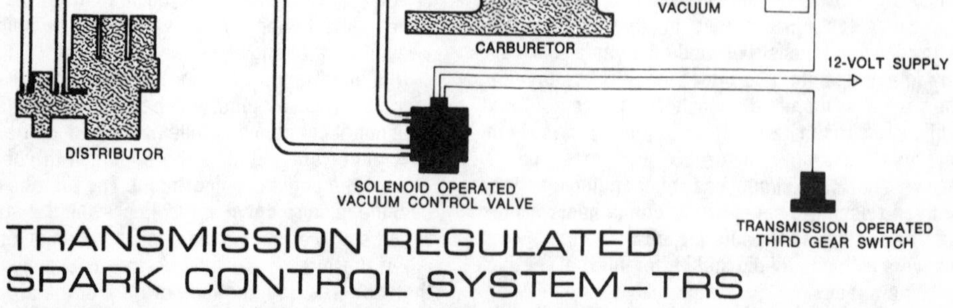

All transmission controlled spark or speed controlled spark systems work in the same basic way, although the hardware varies considerably. Their purpose is to cancel vacuum advance at low speeds or in lower gears

Spark control vacuum solenoids come in many different shapes. This is an AMC solenoid

The Pontiac vacuum solenoid used in early 1973 has a plug-in delay relay

tems all used normally open solenoids. When the solenoid was energized, by the transmission being in the proper gear, it closed the vacuum passage and cut off the vacuum advance. This was a fail-safe system. If the fuse blew or anything happened to break the electrical circuit, then the solenoid would de-energize and you would have vacuum advance at all times.

Some manufacturers stayed with the normally open solenoid through all the years that they used transmission controlled spark. When using a normally open solenoid without a relay, the transmission switch in the solenoid ground circuit must be normally closed. In other words, if you turn the switch on with the engine not running, the transmission switch completes the circuit and the solenoid is energized. When the transmission goes into High gear, which is usually the gear in which vacuum advance is permitted, the transmission switch is opened. This de-energizes the vacuum solenoid and allows the vacuum to pass through it and act on the distributor vacuum advance.

The CEC or Combined Emission Control solenoid used on Chevrolet and also on the General Motors 6 cylinder engine, is a normally closed solenoid used with a normally open transmission switch. This means that when you turn on the ignition switch with the engine not running, nothing happens because the transmission switch is open, breaking the ground circuit. The CEC valve just sits there and does nothing until the transmission goes into High gear. At that time, the transmission switch closes, which energizes the CEC valve and turns on the vacuum to the distributor. The CEC valve has a dual function, which is why it is called a combined emission control. The same plunger in the valve that turns on the vacuum to the distributor also extends and pushes the throttle linkage open for a wider closed-throttle opening when the transmission is in High gear. When the throttle is held open, during deceleration, you don't get the high intake manifold vacuum that pulls so much fuel over from the idle circuit and makes such rich mixtures. This helps emission control.

The stem of the CEC valve is adjustable, but it is never used to set curb idle because at idle it doesn't even touch the throttle linkage. There is an rpm setting for the CEC valve, but it is only necessary to adjust it if the carburetor has been overhauled or somebody has been tampering with the adjustment. The CEC valve can always be recognized because there are vacuum hoses connected to it. The normal anti-dieseling solenoid that you find in the same position on many carburetors does not have vacuum hoses. It has only a single wire. Curb idle is always set with the anti-dieseling solenoid adjustment. Curb idle is never set with the stem of the CEC valve.

An additional control on many transmission controlled spark systems is an ambient temperature switch or a coolant temperature switch. Temperature switches usually provide a ground at low temperatures to turn the solenoid on, and open at high temperatures so that the system is not affected.

With a normally open vacuum solenoid, the solenoid is energized at all times, except in High gear. The temperature switch provides a ground at cold temperatures, but there isn't any way that this ground can be directly hooked up to turn the vacuum solenoid off and allow vacuum advance. To do this, a relay is inserted into the hot wire between the ignition switch and the vacuum solenoid. The temperature control switch provides a ground for the relay at low temperatures. This energizes the relay which then breaks the circuit between the battery and the vacuum solenoid, de-energizes the solenoid, and allows vacuum advance. The relay in this type of a system would be a normally closed relay. In other words, it is closed and allows current to flow to the vacuum solenoid, except when the temperature switch provides a ground to energize the relay.

Some temperature switches also provide a hot override. When the engine temperature gets up to the danger point, the hot override operates the solenoid, sometimes through a relay, to allow vacuum advance.

Additional controls are a time relay and a delay relay. The terminology on these two relays is confusing because they have both been called delay relays. In this book, the time relay is the one that allows vacuum advance for approximately 20 seconds after the ignition key is turned on and the engine started. The delay relay

The basic test of any vacuum spark control is to disconnect the hose at the distributor and connect a vacuum gauge. If the spark control requires rotating the rear wheels, you can use a long hose and position the gauge in the driver's seat while you go around the block

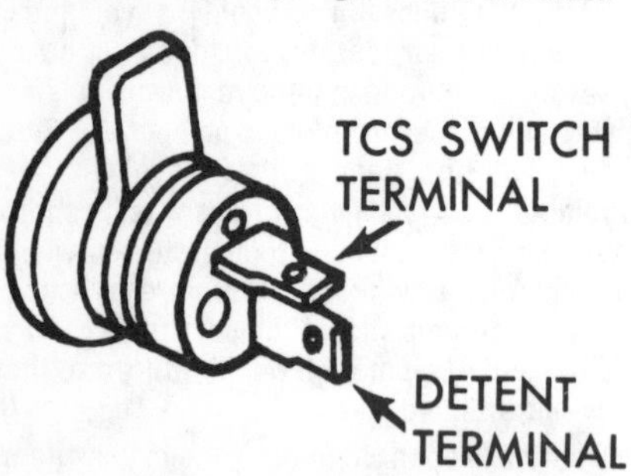

The big General Motors hydramatic has the transmission switch inside, with these two terminals outside

is the one that delays the application of vacuum to the distributor for 20 seconds after the transmission goes into High gear.

The time relay used on Chevrolet vehicles is always mounted on the firewall or somewhere in the engine compartment. The delay relay on Chevrolets is always mounted behind the instrument panel, so there is no chance of getting the two mixed up.

The Pontiac Transmission Controlled Spark used on 1973 models built before March 15th, is a completely different system from the Chevrolet and other General Motors systems. Some of the Pontiac spark controls also operate the exhaust gas recirculation valve. Mounted next to the Pontiac vacuum solenoid is a black delay relay, that delays the application of vacuum advance after the transmission goes into High gear. This delay relay is an innocent looking piece of equipment, but its cost is in the $20.00 range.

After March 15, 1973, Pontiac did away with the delay relay and used a start-up relay which is the same unit as the time relay used by Chevrolet.

SPEED CONTROLLED SPARK (SCS)

This system uses a vacuum solenoid similar to Transmission Controlled Spark. The difference is that speed controlled spark turns the solenoid off to allow vacuum advance at about 35 miles per hour instead of when the transmission goes into a certain gear. The solenoid receives current from the ignition switch and is grounded at the speed switch in the speedometer cable. Below 35 mph, the solenoid is grounded, which energizes it, shutting off the vacuum to the distributor. The small governor inside the speed switch senses the car speed and breaks the contact with ground at approximately 35 mph. This turns the solenoid off and allows vacuum advance. American Motors uses the term "Transmission Controlled Spark" even though, on their automatic transmissions, the spark is controlled by the speed of the car rather than the gear position. Before March 15, 1973, American Motors used an ambient temperature switch at the front of the car. This switch turned off the current to the solenoid below 63°F and allowed vacuum advance at all speeds. After March 15, 1973, American Motors dropped the temperature switch and used a speed controlled spark system that works by governor pressure from the automatic transmission. Since governor pressure is directly related to speed, it amounts to the same thing as using a speed switch. Spark advance is allowed above a governor pressure corresponding to approximately 35 mph.

TEMPERATURE SPARK CONTROLS

Temperature switches are used in several of the spark control systems to cancel the system under cold conditions and allow full vacuum advance so that the engine has better driveability. Some of the temperature switches sense outside air temperature. They are located either at the front of the car at the air intake, in the cowl, or in one of the front door posts. The switches that are sensitive to outside air temperature were eliminated after March 15, 1973 or moved to locations on the engine, so that they are sensitive to engine temperature instead of outside air temperature. To make the switches more sensitive to engine temperature, some of them were enclosed in plastic or metal housings that bolted to the engine. Others were relocated in the air cleaner. In some, the design of the switch was completely changed so that it became a coolant temperature switch that screwed into the block.

Coolant temperature switches have been used for several years to control vacuum spark advance. A coolant temperature switch is usually mechanical. A heat sensitive element inside the switch expands and changes the routing of the vacuum from one nozzle on the switch to another.

Air temperature switches can be either mechanical or electric. The electric ones usually control the flow of electricity to a vacuum solenoid or are in control of the ground circuit from the solenoid.

Another type of temperature switch, used by Pontiac, is screwed into an intake manifold passageway and senses the temperature of the air fuel mixture. The switch is the mechanical type and works much the same way as a coolant temperature switch would. Pontiac

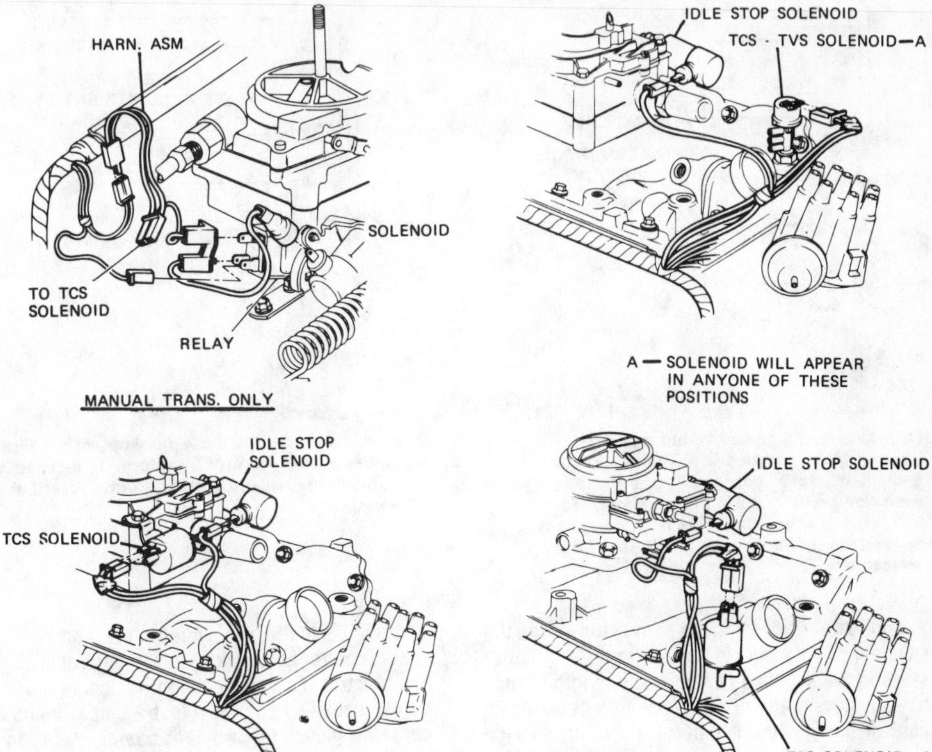

Vacuum solenoids are usually on top of the engine somewhere, but can be in almost any position, even combined with a thermo-vaccum switch, as on Buick.

also uses a switch that screws into the cylinder head and senses the temperature of the metal.

Another coolant temperature switch, that has 3 nozzles and has been used for many years on many different makes of cars, is called the Thermo-Vacuum Switch, Distributor Vacuum Control Switch, or the Ported Vacuum Switch. This switch is connected to intake manifold vacuum, to ported vacuum, and to the distributor vacuum advance. When used on all cars except American Motors, the switch only works when the engine is overheated. At that time, the ported vacuum from the carburetor is shut off and full manifold vacuum is sent to the distributor.

American Motors uses a similar 3-nozzle switch, but the way it works is entirely different. This switch sends intake manifold vacuum to the distributor when the engine is cold and ported vacuum when the engine is at normal operating temperatures. American Motors also has a 3-nozzle switch used with their exhaust gas recirculation system. One of the nozzles is not used and the switch is colored black for identification.

On Ford Motor Company vehicles, the 3-nozzle switch can be hooked up two different ways. The normal way is with 3 different hoses to it, so that it sends either manifold vacuum or ported vacuum to the distributor vacuum advance. The other way is to use the switch with a dual diaphragm distributor and connect it so that manifold vacuum to the retard side of the diaphragm runs through the switch. When the engine overheats, the switch cuts off the manifold vacuum to the retard side and vents the diaphragm to atmosphere through the third nozzle which is covered with a little foam filter. Many of the air temperature and coolant temperature switches look the same, but inside they are entirely different and they operate differently. Always go by part number and not appearance when installing a new switch.

DECELERATION SPARK VALVES

The spark valve was pioneered by Chrysler Corporation, and is used mainly on its manual transmission vehicles. With a ported spark setup, the distributor vacuum advance goes to the neutral or no advance position at idle and also during deceleration. Manual transmission vehicles have a higher vacuum during deceleration because there is no slippage in the transmission. This higher vacuum draws in a lot more fuel and creates a rich mixture that has to be burned up in order to lower emissions. This mixture will burn better if the spark can be advanced during deceleration. The problem is that you do not want the spark advanced at idle. The spark valve does this job very neatly by allowing normal ported vacuum advance at all times except during deceleration. Then it switches over so that full manifold vacuum is sent to the distributor vacuum advance. The switching point for the spark valve is approximately 21 in. Hg of vacuum.

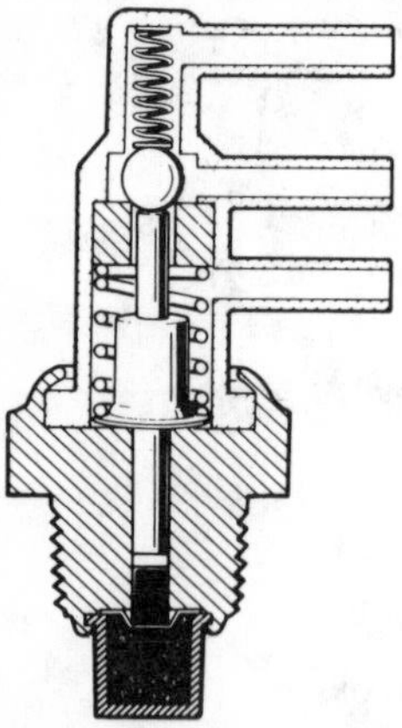

Ford calls this a ported vacuum switch. General Motors names it a Thermo Vacuum Switch. Whatever you call it, it is not an emission control, but simply a device to help cure overheating. This is the way it is hooked up on Fords when the 3-hose hookup is used

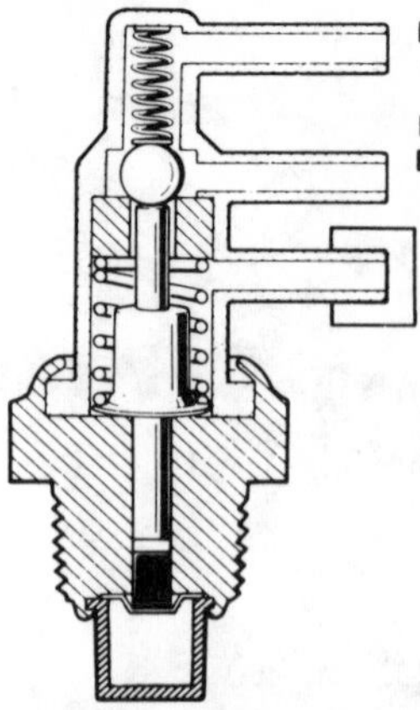

Ford also uses a 2 hose hookup with a filter, called a "Retard-Vent" system. It is used to cancel dual diaphragm distributor retard at idle

As long as manifold vacuum stays above that value, the spark valve sends full manifold vacuum to the distributor which stays in the advance position. The length of time that the valve stays in the advance position depends on the weight of the car, the incline of the road, and the speed.

Spark valves usually are tested on the shop floor by revving the engine and allowing it to decelerate with the transmission in Neutral. With a vacuum gauge at the distributor, you can see the change in vacuum and the number of seconds elapsed before the change—this is the measure of whether the valve is adjusted correctly. Some manufacturers use a different system of adjusting the valve and others do not allow any adjustment at all. They adjust the valve at the factory and if there is anything wrong with it, you are supposed to replace it.

ELECTRONIC SPARK CONTROL (ESC)

Electronic spark control is used only by Ford Motor Company. They have used two systems and both of them are similar. In 1970 and 1971, they used the Electronic Distributor Modulator or "Dist-O-Vac." In 1972, this system was improved and called the "Electronic Spark Control." Actually, the systems are nothing more than speed controlled spark with an electronic control box. The electronic control is mounted behind the instrument panel, usually near the glove compartment. In some cars, the glove compartment has an open top and you can reach in and remove the electronic control from its mounting bracket, without having to crawl underneath the instrument panel.

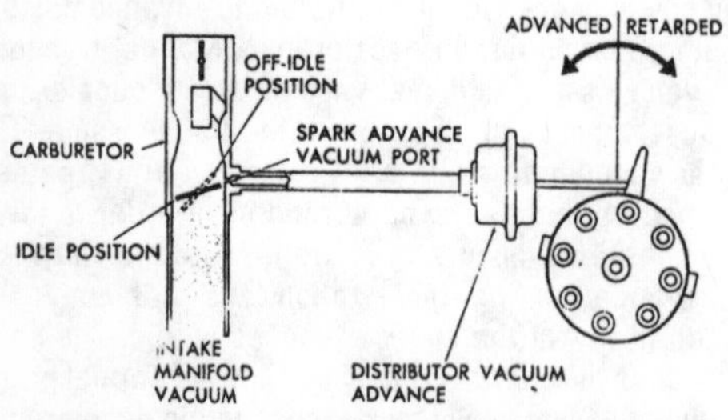

When the vacuum spark advance is "ported" it means the port is above the throttle plate so there is no advance at idle

A speed sensor in the speedometer cable is also behind the instrument panel, only a few inches in front of the speedometer head, or in the engine compartment. This speed control is actually a little AC generator. It sends signals to the electronic control which then turns a vacuum solenoid on or off to control vacuum to the distributor.

In the 1970-71 Dist-O-Vac system, the vacuum solenoid and the electronic control were in a single large box behind the instrument panel. In 1972, the two units were split up and the solenoid was mounted on the intake manifold, but the electronic control remained in the passenger compartment, behind the instrument panel. Relocating the solenoid on the engine eliminated the long vacuum hoses that had to take vacuum all the way through the firewall to the control box.

The electronic spark control systems are nothing to worry about because you are not required to repair any of the electronics. If the other units of the system check okay, but it still won't work, then the trouble has to be in the electronic control box and all you do is replace it.

A temperature switch located in the door post was used with all the electronic systems. The 1970-71 Dist-O-Vac switch is in the ground circuit and is closed when it is cold. The 1972 electronic spark control switch is in the hot circuit and is closed when the temperature is warm. If you replace the switch, warm it up before you go to the trouble of installing it, to see if it is open or closed when it is supposed to be.

In spite of the complexity of the electronic systems, all

they do is control distributor vacuum according to speed. It's an easy thing to hook up a vacuum gauge and drive a car to find out if they are working.

DELAY VACUUM BY-PASS (DVB)

On many engines, Ford uses a spark delay valve between the carburetor port and distributor. The valve is nothing more than a calibrated restriction that delays the application of ported vacuum to the distributor for a few seconds. When the engine is cold, this spark delay can cause problems with driveability. So, Ford set up a system with a vacuum solenoid, a check valve, and a door post temperature switch to by-pass the spark delay valve when the weather was cold. The door post temperature switch is in the hot circuit so that it turns the current to the solenoid on and off. The solenoid has one terminal receiving current from the temperature switch and the other grounded at the solenoid. The delay vacuum by-pass system was one of those defeat devices that the EPA said had to be removed. And so after March 15, 1973, all delay vacuum by-pass systems were deleted. When the engine calibration number on the sticker is followed by an "X", it means that the delay vacuum by-pass has been left off the engine.

PORTED VACUUM ADVANCE

The term "Ported Vacuum Advance" means that the distributor vacuum advance unit is connected to a small port in the carburetor throat, above the throttle valve, when the throttle is in the curb idle position. There is no vacuum above the throttle valve to act on the port, so at curb idle the distributor vacuum advance goes to the neutral or no advance position. When the throttle is opened, the throttle blade passes over the spark port exposing it to vacuum and then the distributor advances. This system has been in use for many years on most makes of cars. However, some cars use full manifold vacuum to the distributor vacuum advance. When the full vacuum system is used, the distributor is fully advanced at idle. Full vacuum advance at idle helps to control overheating.

If a car that was set up at the factory for ported vacuum advance has its hoses switched around by mistake so that it is connected to full manifold vacuum, the engine idle speed would be considerably higher. If you did not know that the switch in hoses had been made, you might try to slow the engine down to a normal idle speed by adjusting the speed screw on the carburetor. Then the engine probably would not pass an idle emission test. This mistake is not discovered very often, but it is something that you should be aware of.

MIXTURE CONTROLS

HEATED AIR CLEANERS

All heated air cleaners use air from a stove surrounding the exhaust manifold. The hot air comes up through a tube to a flapper valve in the air cleaner snorkle. The valve is moveable so that the air to the carburetor can be regulated to give full hot air, full underhood air, or any mixture of the two. The valve is moved either by a temperature bulb that acts on it directly or by a vacuum motor that is controlled by a separate temperature sensor switch in the air cleaner. Vacuum to the vacuum motor runs through the sensor switch which is closed at cold temperatures. As the engine intake air starts to warm up the sensor, the bimetal blade moves to uncover a bleed hole which bleeds off vacuum to the vacuum motor. The spring in the motor then pushes the flapper valve to the underhood air position and the hot air is completely shut off.

Many cars now have a cold air tube or "zip tube" from the underhood opening on the air cleaner snorkle to a fresh air entry in the grille of the car. This way the air cleaner takes in cool outside air instead of hot underhood air. The reason for going after the cool outside air is

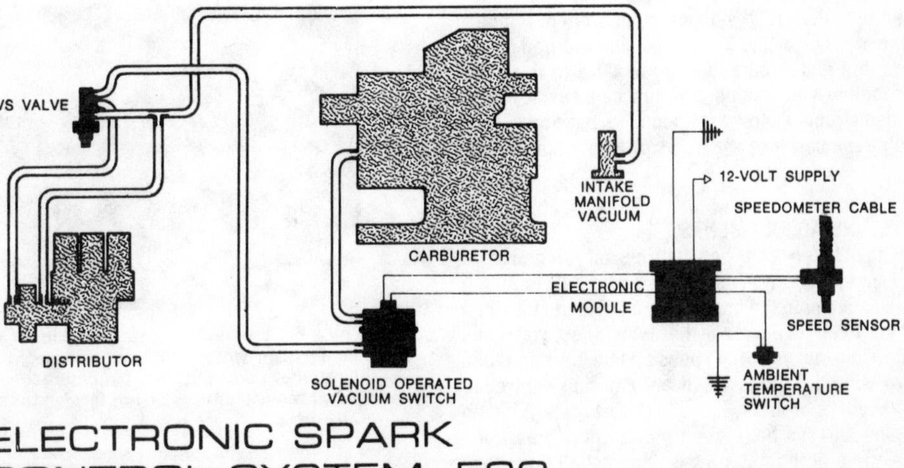

ELECTRONIC SPARK CONTROL SYSTEM-ESC

Ford's Electronic Spark Control is really nothing more than a speed controlled spark system with an electronic box to turn the vacuum solenoid on and off

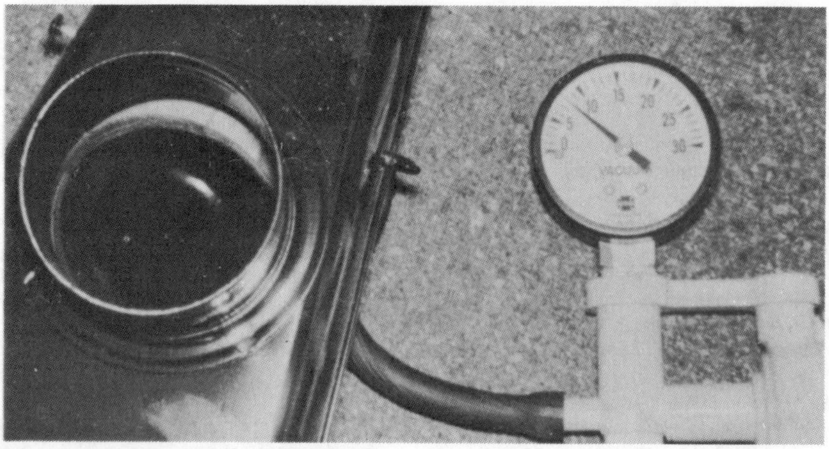

Vacuum motors on heated air cleaners can be checked with a hand operated vacuum pump

Heated air cleaner temperature sensors can be checked with a thermometer, but usually it isn't necessary to be this particular. If the sensor is defective, it probably won't work at all

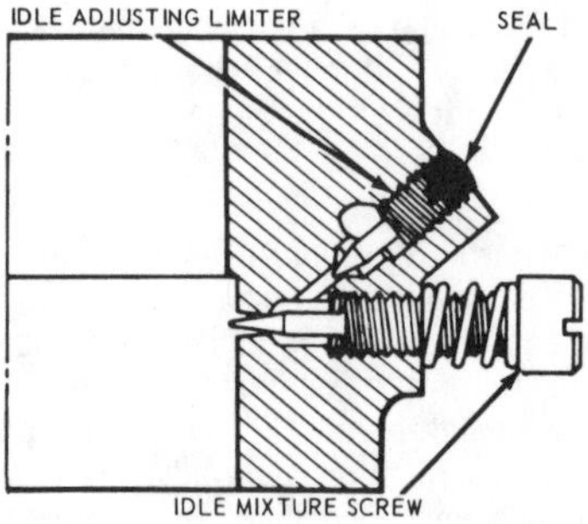

Various means have been used to limit the amount that you can richen the idle mixture. This sealed limiter screw on a Carter YF limits the maximum amount of mixture, no matter how far you back off the mixture adjustment screw

that the air entering the carburetor must be warm, but not too hot. On a hot summer day when the outside air temperature is over 100°F, engine compartment temperature can easily go to 200°F. This superheated air is much too thin and it leans out the mixture to the point that detonation and engine damage can easily occur. The cold air tube keeps the incoming air down to a reasonable temperature and helps prevent engine damage.

IDLE MIXTURE ADJUSTMENTS

In the days before emission controls, all you had to do with idle mixture screws was adjust the carburetor to the highest vacuum or to the best idle you could get and let it go at that. If you adjust a car that way today, you'll still get a good idle, but you won't pass an idle emission test. We have all heard the joke: "If an emission controlled car idles well it's probably illegal". Unfortunately, it's no joke. Many surveys have been made and it has been found in some of them that emissions usually increase after a tune-up because the mechanic adjusts the mixture screws to give the car owner the best idle he can. This is not the way to adjust emission controlled cars.

The most common idle mixture limiter is the limiter cap. When you buy new caps from Ford, they come in this jar, submerged in fluid. Other manufacturers do not furnish the caps any more.

Drivers are going to have to learn, if they haven't already, that they cannot expect the glass smooth idle that they got in the old days.

EMISSIONS INCREASE WITH IMPROPER SERVICE

Malfunction Item	Emission Increase	
	H.C. - PPM*	C.O. - %*
1 cylinder missing	358	-
Rich idle mixture (1-1/2 A.F. mixture)	-	.66
Low idle speed (100 rpm lower than specification)	35	-
Advance timing (6° from specification)	63	-
Plugged P.C.V. valve	43	.34
Choke set rich (2 diameters of choke rod)	40	.18
Heat riser valve stuck open	35	.18
*PPM - Parts per million % - Percentage		

The most scientific way to adjust idle is with a CO meter. If the manufacturer gives specifications for CO outputs at idle, this is the best way to make the adjustment.

LEAN DROP METHOD

An alternate method, and one that some manufacturers feel is the best, is the "Lean Drop" method. In the lean drop procedure, you set the idle to the smoothest you can get and then turn the mixture screws in leaner until engine speed drops off by a certain amount. If the manufacturers specify the lean drop method, do not be afraid to use it because in many cases it is more accurate than using a CO tester that might be out of calibration. Many CO testers, even good ones, are out of calibration simply because they haven't been checked in months or even years.

LEAN BEST IDLE

Another method of idle adjustment is called "Lean Best Idle". This is not a case of adjusting for the best idle you can get and forgetting it, it involves adjusting for the best idle, but making sure that the screws are in to the lean position as far as possible without losing any rpm. The best way to do this is to adjust for the best idle, then turn the screws in until there is a definite drop in rpm. Finally, turn the screws back out until the lost rpm is just regained. This way you have not sacrificed engine speed, but you know you are positively at the leanest setting you can get.

¼ TURN RICH

Another setting specified for idle mixture needles, usually on cars with an air pump, is one quarter turn rich from lean roll. Lean roll is not a very precise point so that it can be hard to find on some engines. But what it means is that you turn the mixture screws in until you get a definite fall off and roll in engine rpm. Then you back out one quarter turn from that point. This gives you a richer mixture than you would normally have. But a rich mixture

Curb idle speed is always adjusted at the anti-dieseling solenoid (lower arrow). The throttle screw (upper arrow) is only for adjusting idle with the solenoid disconnected

Sometimes, as on this Ford, the anti-dieseling solenoid has a separate adjuster, which makes it easier

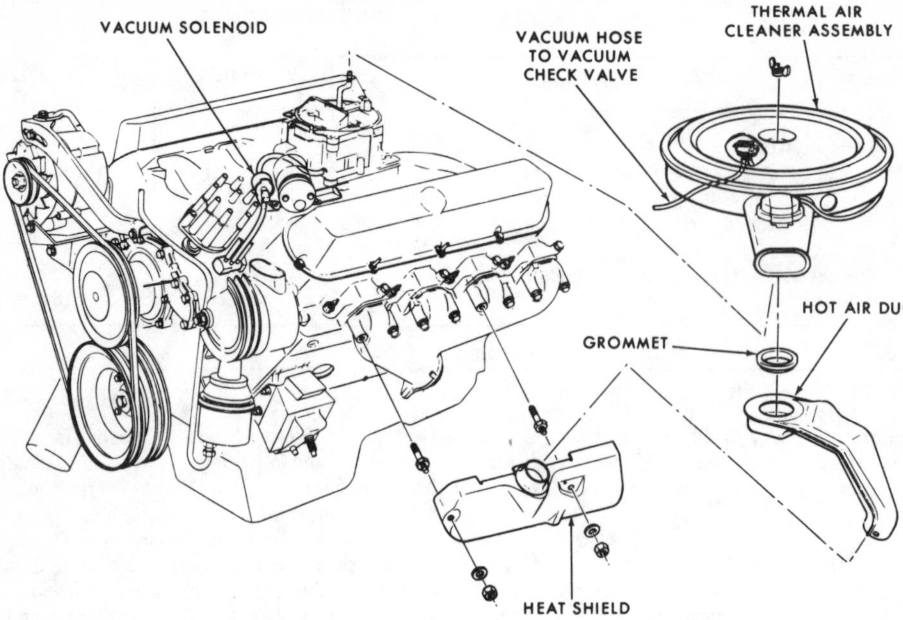

The air cleaner itself is not all there is to the heated air system. The "stove" on the exhaust mani fold is part of it

is what cars with an air pump need because they have to have enough fuel passing through to the engine to keep the fire going in the exhaust manifold and burn up the hydrocarbons and CO. On all cars you must follow the car manufacturers' specifications for setting idle and you must not take it for granted that because it was set one way last year, it is set the same way this year.

THROTTLE POSITIONING DEVICES

Chevrolet's CEC valve, besides being a vacuum solenoid that controls spark advance, also opens the throttle during deceleration in High gear. This helps prevent the rich mixtures that would be pulled through the idle circuit if the throttle were allowed to close to the normal curb idle position. Many imported cars also use throttle positioning devices that are usually vacuum controlled, but may have an electrical back-up. Toyota uses a throttle positioner that operates

DECELERATION ENRICHING VALVES

Some 4 cylinder engines go very lean during deceleration. This causes incomplete combustion and emission levels become very high. If a little extra fuel and air is fed into the intake manifold during deceleration, better combustion results and emission levels are lowered. Actually, the term "Enriching Valve" is a misnomer. It really doesn't make the mixture any richer, it just puts more mixture into the engine. Some of the valves on imported cars are built into the carburetor so that they feed more fuel, but not any air. However, they are used in conjunction with a throttle positioner which gives the engine extra air to mix with the extra fuel.

The separate deceleration enriching valves such as the type used on the Pinto, can sometimes develop a

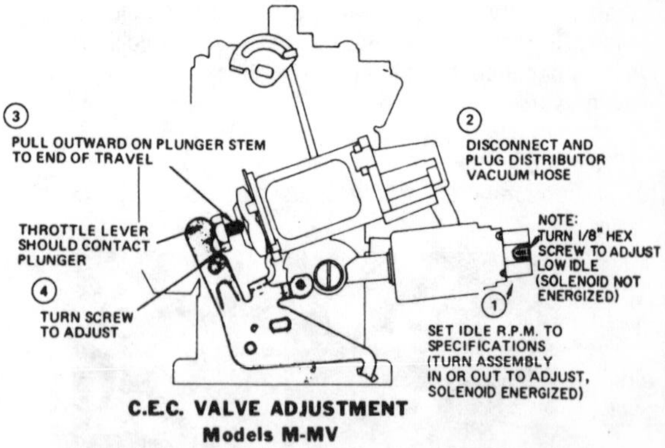

The General Motors CEC valve is not an anti-dieseling solenoid, and must never be used to set curb idle. There is a special rpm specification for adjustment of the CEC valve

vacuum leak in the diaphragm. When this happens, air enters the engine at all times causing rough idle and a lean condition. If the type of valve that is built into the carburetor were to be stuck open, then, of course, there would be of an extremely rich mixture at all times. This is something to be on the lookout for if you have a small imported car with a high CO level.

EVAPORATIVE CONTROLS

Vapor controls are the most simple and trouble-free emission control on the whole car. They are known by various names such as American Motors Evaporative Emission Control, (EEC), General Motors Evaporative

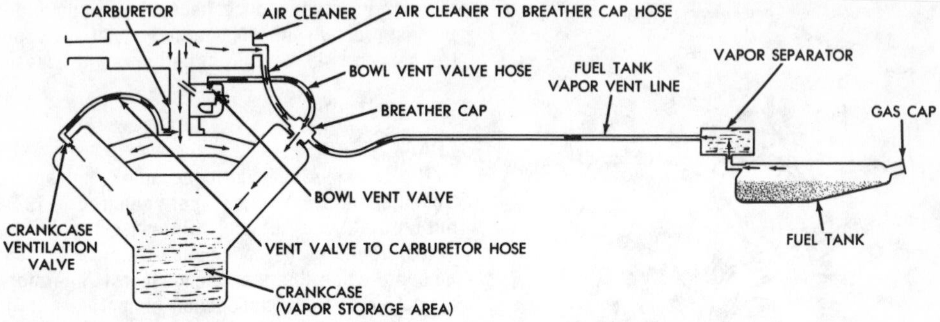

Chrysler's original vapor control system used crankcase storage. The vapor line tied in with the PCV system

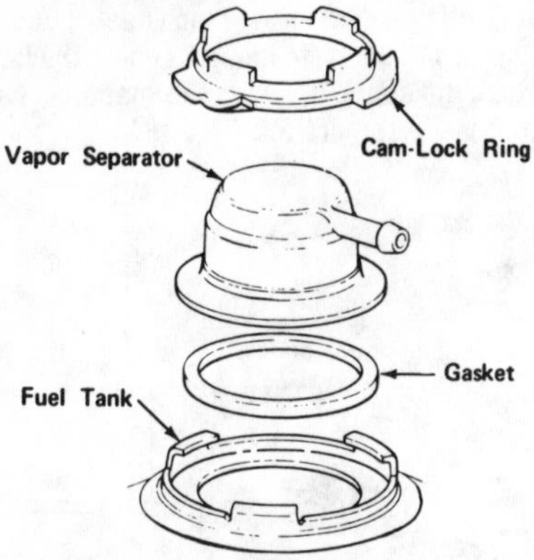

This Ford dome-type separator is held in place by a locking ring, similar to a tank gauge sending unit.

Emission Control, (EEC), or Evaporative Loss Control, (ELC), or Evaporation Control Systems, (ECS), and Evaporative Emission System, (EES). Chrysler calls theirs the Evaporation Control System, (ECS), and Vapor Saver; while Ford sticks by the term Evaporative Emission Control System, (EECS). We call all of the systems vapor control for simplification.

When vapor controls first came out in 1970, there were two ways of storing the vapors from the tank, in the engine crankcase or in a canister full of carbon (charcoal) particles. In later years all of the manufacturers went to the canister system.

Most of the vapor control system is in the tank and in the means of separating the vapors from liquid fuel. All of the tanks have some kind of fill control that keeps an air space at the top of the tank so that liquid fuel will not travel along the vent line to the vapor storage. The early systems had extremely complicated vapor liquid separators that were mounted near the tank. Several vent lines, usually one from each corner of the tank, led to the separator and then a single line went up to the front of the car to either the crankcase or the carbon canister. In later years, the manufacturers discovered that all that complicated plumbing was completely unnecessary. The vapor separator now is simply a small dome on top of the tank usually filled with foam or other substance. The vapors will go through the foam, but any liquid fuel drains back into the tank. The tanks are all completely closed and use a filler cap that will open automatically if either pressure or vacuum builds up in the tank.

Vapor movement through the vapor line to the storage in the engine compartment depends upon many things. If the engine is running, fuel is being pulled out of the tank by the fuel pump and air has to enter to keep from collapsing it. This air enters through the vapor line. In effect then, the carbon canister is not only for vapor storage, but it is the point where air enters the tank

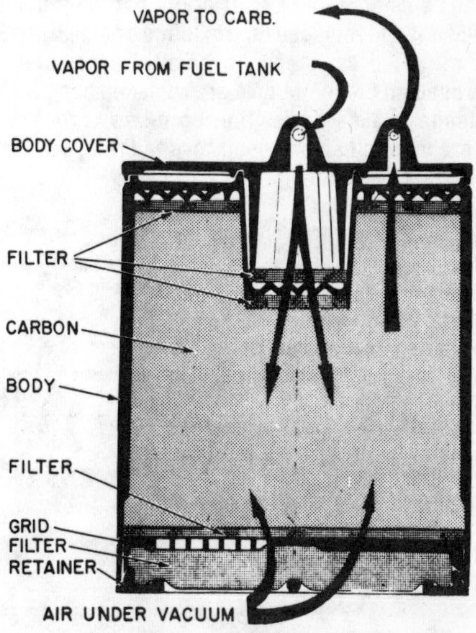

The 2 hose canister is the simplest in operation. Canisters also come in three and four hose models

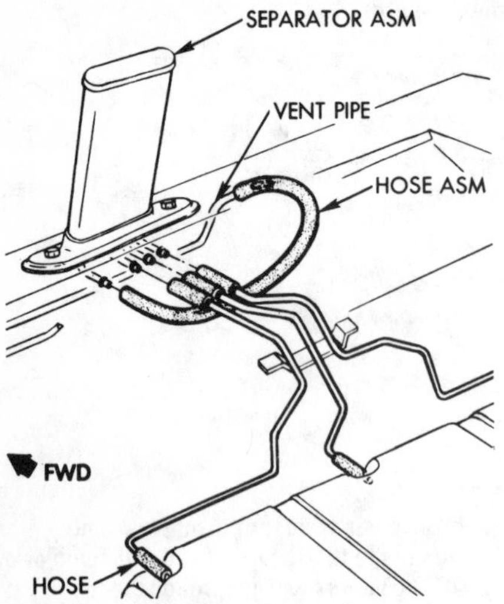

Most of the improvements in vapor control design have been in the vapor separators. The early designs used the stand pipe style separator, which is usually mounted behind the rear seat

anytime gasoline is being withdrawn. Air also enters through the carbon canister if the tank cools off in the evening from the heat of the day. If the carbon canister or vent line should become plugged, the safety feature is the fuel tank cap which will open either under pressure or vacuum to keep from collapsing the tank. Many of the carbon canisters have a filter at the bottom that can be slipped out and replaced on a mileage or time basis. Ford uses a sealed canister. The small-size canisters that were used on earlier models are replaced completely on a mileage or time basis. The large-size Ford canisters that are now in use are good for the life of the car and there is no maintenance necessary. Undoubtedly the biggest problem you will ever have with any vapor control system is leakage from deteriorating hoses.

NOx CONTROLS

SPARK RETARD

The transmission controlled spark and speed controlled spark systems that first appeared in 1971 were put on the cars to control NOx emissions.

NOx forms in the combustion chamber in excessive amounts when the peak combustion temperature gets over 2,500°F. Peak combustion temperature is directly related to spark timing. If the spark occurs at exactly the right instant, you get a maximum amount of pressure and heat in the combustion chamber and the car puts out maximum power. If the spark is retarded slightly, the power falls off because not as much heat is being generated in the combustion chamber. Keeping the heat down by retarding the spark lowers the formation of Nox to the levels that were required in 1970-1972.

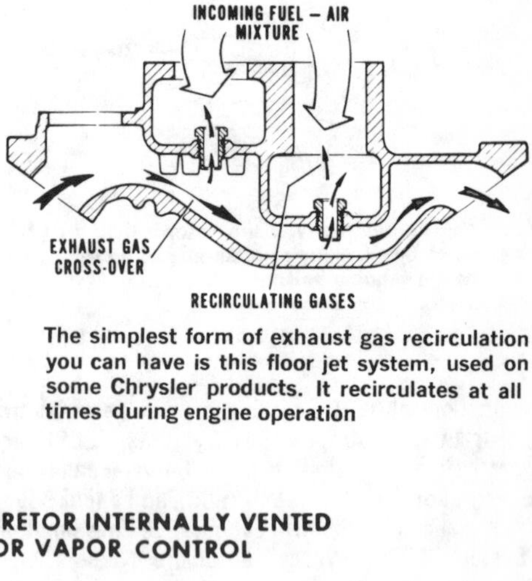

The simplest form of exhaust gas recirculation you can have is this floor jet system, used on some Chrysler products. It recirculates at all times during engine operation

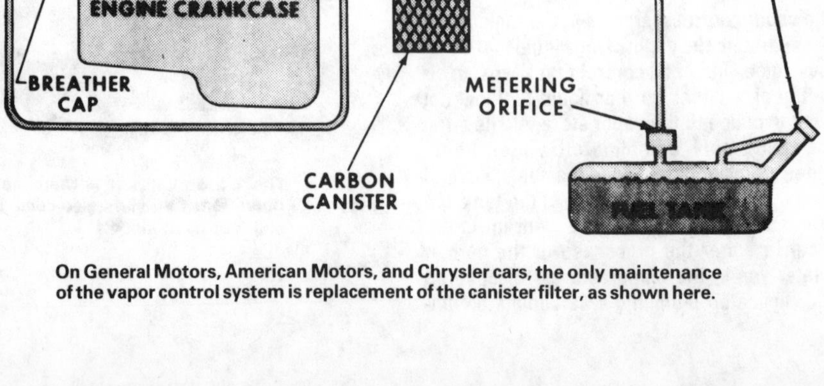

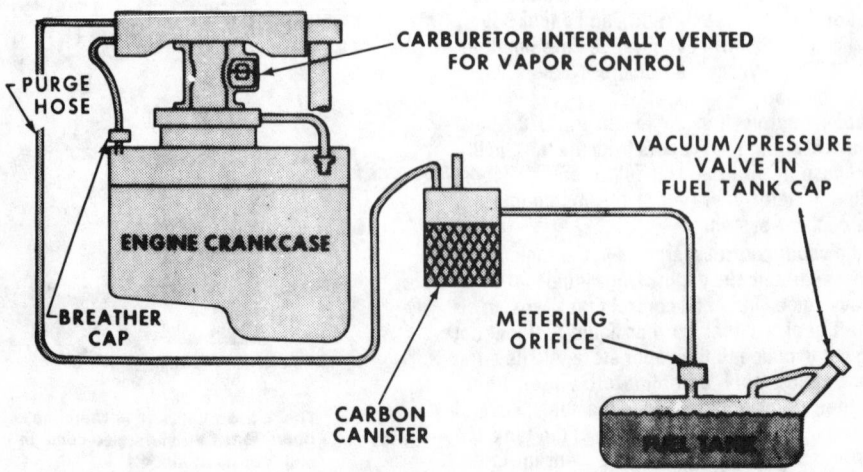

On General Motors, American Motors, and Chrysler cars, the only maintenance of the vapor control system is replacement of the canister filter, as shown here.

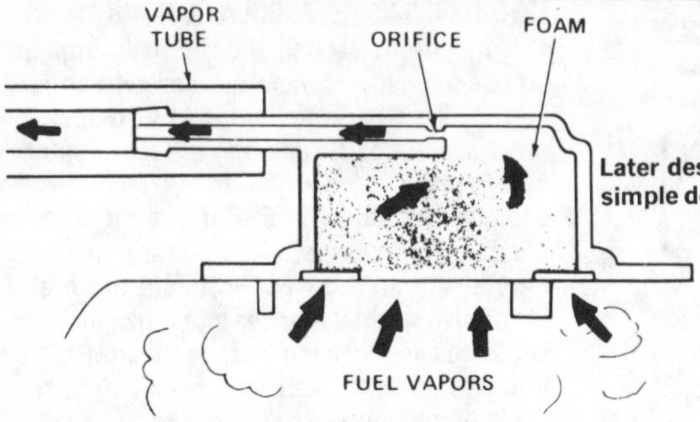

Later designs have a vapor separator that is only a simple dome on the top of the tank

The transmission controlled spark and speed controlled spark systems are covered elsewhere under those headings. Chrysler Corporation did not refer to their system in those terms, but simply called it the NOx control system. The system was only used two years, 1971 and 1972. Manual transmissions were set up fairly simply, allowing vacuum spark advance in High gear only. A solenoid was energized in the lower gears to shut off the vacuum to the distributor. In High gear, a transmission switch opened the ground circuit from the solenoid, de-energizing it and allowing vacuum to advance the spark. The solenoid was mounted at the back of the engine, near the distributor. A temperature switch, mounted on the firewall, sensed the temperature in the plenum chamber at the cowl air intake. The temperature switch was also in the ground circuit from the solenoid. When air temperatures were cold, the temperature switch broke the circuit to ground so that the solenoid was de-energized, allowing vacuum advance. The temperature switch was left off the 1972 manual transmission cars, so that the system consisted simply of a vacuum solenoid and a transmission switch.

The system on the automatic transmission was much more complicated. In 1971, there was a vacuum control, an electronic control box, a thermo switch, a speed switch and a vacuum solenoid. The vacuum switch, the speed switch, and the temperature switch all provided separate grounds for the electronic control. These grounds were reversed in their effects on the vacuum solenoid by the electronic control box. When any one of the 3 units were grounded, the electronic control turned the solenoid off, allowing vacuum advance. To cut off vacuum advance, all 3 of the switches had to be opened. The temperature switch was opened above 70°F. The vacuum switch was opened below 15 in. Hg of intake manifold vacuum, and the speed switch was opened below 30 mph. The only time all 3 switches were opened was in warm weather, below 30 mph, when the engine was accelerated fast enough to drop the intake manifold vacuum below 15 in. Hg. This was quite an ingenious method of controlling vacuum spark advance because this gave advance at all times except when a cutoff of the advance was needed to control emissions.

The temperature switch, vacuum switch, and elec-

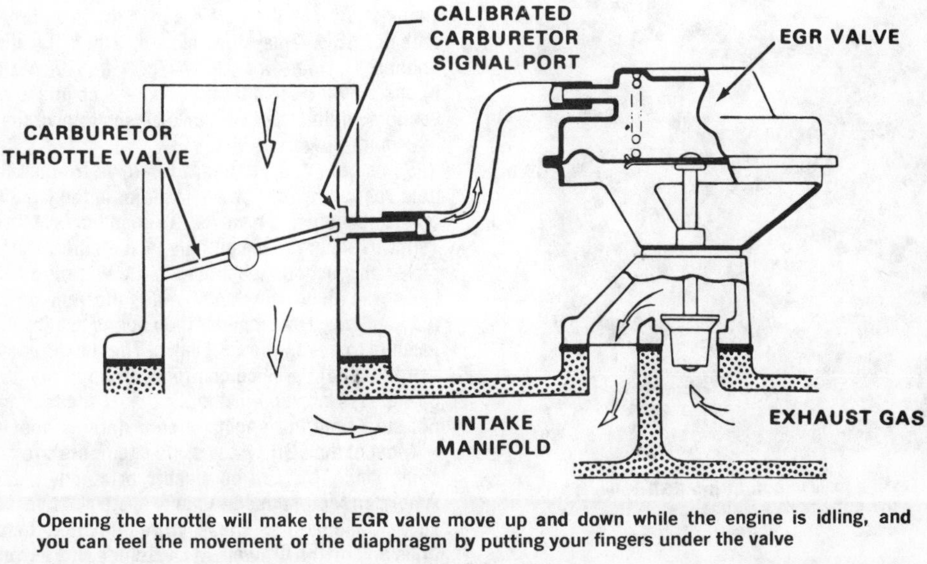

Opening the throttle will make the EGR valve move up and down while the engine is idling, and you can feel the movement of the diaphragm by putting your fingers under the valve

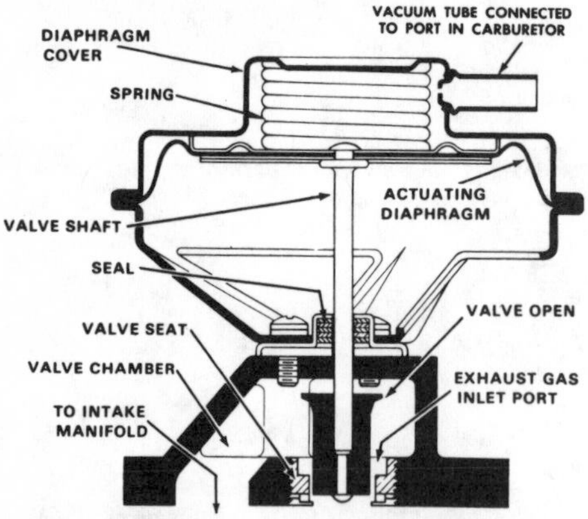

Cutaway of a typical General Motors EGR valve. The Chrysler and Ford valves are similar

tronic control were mounted on the firewall and called the control unit. The temperature part of the control unit stuck through the firewall into the front of the cowl chamber to allow ambient temperatures to act on it.

In 1972, the vacuum part of the control unit was discontinued. This simplified the system greatly and meant that there was vacuum advance above 30 mph in warm weather, but never below 30 mph. One thing you must remember about the electric circuitry in the NOx system is that grounding the electronic control ground circuit turns the solenoid off.

Fewer cars used the transmission control spark system after 1972 because the Federal test procedures were changed and exhaust gas recirculation came in which did a much better job of controlling emissions of NOx.

Testing for vacuum at the EGR valve is easily done with a gauge, as on this Ford

EXHAUST GAS RECIRCULATION (EGR)

Exhaust gas recirculation is used primarily to lower peak combustion temperatures and control the formation of NOx. NOx emission at low combustion temperatures are not bad, but when the temperature goes over 2,500°F, the production of NOx in the combustion chamber shoots way up. You can cut down on the peak combustion temperatures by retarding the spark or by introducing an inert gas to dilute the fuel air mixture. Introducing exhaust gases into the combustion chamber is a little like throwing water-soaked wood on a roaring fire. The water-soaked wood won't burn, so that the fire cools down and doesn't roar nearly as much as it used to. Put a little exhaust gas in the combustion chamber and it takes the place of a certain amount of air fuel mixture. When the spark ignites the mixture, there isn't as much to burn so that the fire is not as hot. Also, the engine doesn't put out as much power.

Exhaust gas recirculation is kept to very low limits. The hole in the EGR valve is very small even when it is wide-open. It's surprising how little exhaust gas it takes to cool down the peak combustion temperatures.

Chrysler had one of the simplest exhaust recirculation systems with their floor jet under the carburetor. Holes were drilled in the bottom of the intake manifold and calibrated jets were screwed into the holes. The holes penetrated into the exhaust crossover passage and allowed the exhaust to come into the intake manifold at all times. The trouble with that system is that it allowed exhaust gas recirculation at idle, which wasn't necessary and didn't make for the smoothest idling engines. Floor jet EGR is still used on some Chrysler engines, but most of them now use a separate EGR valve the same as all the other manufacturers.

The EGR valve is mounted on the intake manifold so that when it opens, exhaust gases are allowed to go from the crossover passage into the throat under the carburetor. The EGR valve is vacuum-operated, sometimes by intake manifold vacuum and on some engines by ported vacuum. The ported vacuum systems are the simplest. At idle, the port is above the throttle blade, so that the EGR valve stays closed. When the throttle is opened, vacuum acts on the port and the EGR valve opens. At wide-open throttle, there is no intake manifold vacuum so that the EGR valve closes to give the engine maximum power.

Some cars operate their EGR valve from intake manifold vacuum. They use an amplifier in the circuit to turn on the vacuum to the valve. The amplifier is controlled by venturi vacuum. A small hole in the carburetor venturi picks up vacuum when the airflow through the carburetor is high enough and sends the vacuum signal to the amplifier. The amplifier then opens to allow manifold vacuum to act on the EGR valve. The amplifier system is used to obtain precise control over when the EGR valve operates. Also, it means that exhaust recirculation does not start until the engine is considerably above idle.

Most of the EGR systems use a temperature control of some kind. This can be electric or strictly mechanical. American Motors used a unique system of two air bleeds called modulators. These were mounted behind the grille and on the firewall. At low temperatures, one of the

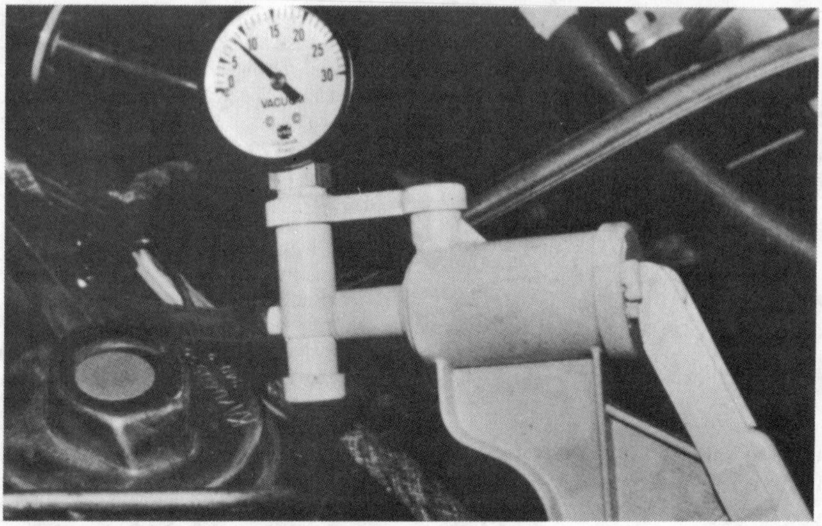

Checking the EGR valve for a leaking diaphragm is best done with a hand vacuum pump

modulators would open and t high temperatures the other opened, allowing air to bleed into the vacuum system to the EGR valve so that the vacuum was weakened and the valve did not open as much. Chrysler used a similar system with an air bleed that sensed temperature inside the cowl plenum chamber. These systems that were sensitive to outside ai temperatures were discontinued after March 15, 1973 as a result of the EPA order.

Ford uses a temperature control that looks like a PVS valve, but only has two nozzles. It shuts off the vacuum to the EGR valve at low temperatures. When Chrysler dropped their air temperature sensor in the plenum chamber, they went to a valve similar to Ford's, but mounted in the radiator. The valve has two nozzles with a hose connected to one and a foam filter on the other. At low temperatures, the valve opens which allows air to enter and weakens the vacuum so that the EGR valve stays closed.

Buick has changed their EGR temperature regulation considerably. In 1972, they didn't use any temperature control at all. In 1973, they had a temperature switch in the hose that shut off the vacuum to the EGR valve at low temperatures. This switch was sensitive to engine compartment temperature and was judged a defeat device by EPA, so that on March 15, 1973, Buick changed the switch to a coolant temperature switch working with a vacuum solenoid. At low temperatures, the coolant switch operated the solenoid to shut off the vacuum to the EGR valve. In 1974, Buick got rid of the electrics in the system and went to a straight coolant-vacuum switch that closed off the vacuum to the EGR valve at low temperatures.

Oldsmobile and Cadillac used a switch in the hose similar to Buick's first switch. After March 15, 1973, they enclosed the switch in a housing so that it was more sensitive to engine temperature rather than underhood temperature.

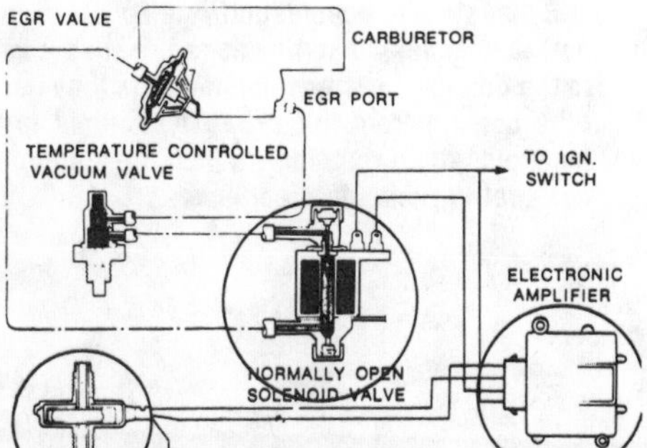

Ford had the ultimate in EGR valve control, an electronic "black box" that turned the exhaust gas recirculation off above 64 mph

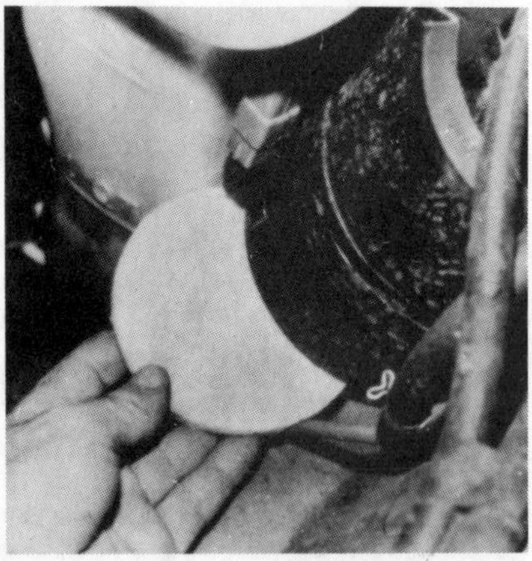

All domestic cars now use the canister for storing vapors

Pontiac probably has the most complicated system of all. Before March 15, 1973, the EGR system was tied in with the transmission control spark system. The two systems were hooked together so that when vacuum spark advance was allowed, there was no EGR. When EGR was allowed, there was no vacuum spark advance. This complicated system was eliminated on March 15, 1973 and from then on the EGR and the transmission control spark systems were separate.

IMPORTED CAR EMISSION CONTROL SYSTEMS

Imported car emission control systems accomplish the same ends as the domestic systems, but usually they do it in a different way. In their crankcase ventilation systems, they sometimes use a valve the same as the domestic systems, but in other instances there is nothing but a hose connecting the crankcase to the air cleaner. This accomplishes the same thing as the valve type systems because the slight suction in the air cleaner draws the fumes out of the crankcase to keep them from going into the atmosphere.

Most imported cars use a heated air cleaner, sometimes with vacuum control to the air valve and sometimes with a simple thermostatic bulb to open and close the valve. Some imported cars use a simple door on their air cleaners which is operated by a lever on the air cleaner snorkle. The lever has two positions, "summer" and "winter," which must be changed manually, depending upon the season.

The imported car air pump systems pump air into the exhaust manifold near the exhaust valve, the same as on domestic systems. There are still quite a few imported cars that use an antibackfire valve which allows pumped air to go into the intake manifold during deceleration. Other imported cars use the more modern diverter valve which vents all of the air from the pump into the atmosphere through a silencer.

Imported cars have made many modifications to their carburetors. They may use fuel cutoff valves that cut out the idle circuit during deceleration to eliminate the rich mixtures. There are also fuel cutoff valves that shut off the idle circuit when the ignition switch is turned off to prevent dieseling.

Throttle positioners and deceleration enrichers are common on imported engines. The throttle positioners open the throttle during deceleration, but sometimes have additional controls that put the positioner into operation in certain gears or above certain speeds.

Deceleration enrichers are built into many Japanese carburetors. During the high vacuum of deceleration, an extra passage opens and allows more fuel to enter underneath the throttle blade. These systems are called the "coasting richer" by many Japanese makers, probably because that was the closest translation they could get to deceleration enricher.

Spark control systems include both transmission controlled spark and a dual point retard system used by Datsun. The dual point system is a clever way of getting a few degrees of retard whenever it is needed to control emissions. The retard breaker points are placed 7 crankshaft degrees away from the normal breaker points in the distributor. A relay is used that can switch the coil primary from the normal to the retarded set of points. Anytime the retard is needed, all that is necessary is to close the switch to activate the relay and the engine is automatically 7 crankshaft degrees retarded. Depending on the year of the car and whether it has an automatic or manual transmission, several different kinds of switches have been used to control the relay. You may find a temperature switch, a throttle position switch, a transmission gear position switch and a second throttle position switch. One of the throttle position switches works when the throttle is closed and the other when the throttle goes to the wide-open position. When used with the transmission gear switch, you might call the system transmission controlled spark, but the difference is that it is not controlling distributor vacuum advance, but a simple mechanical retard of 7 degrees.

Exhaust gas recirculation is also used on many imported vehicles. In some cases they use a valve similar to the domestic system and in others they have a simple tube coming from the exhaust manifold to the intake manifold with a restrictor to limit the amount of exhaust gas that is recirculated.

Towing a Trailer

With the epidemic growth of trailers—especially the less expensive travel trailers—car manufacturers have recently offered an option known known as the "Trailer Package." This group of options, which the manufacturers believe to be advantageous, includes such components as a larger engine, oversized alternator and radiator, heavy-duty shock absorbers and springs, heavy-duty transmission and transmission oil cooler, larger radiator fan, and a radiator shroud. Instead of adding all of the aftermarket trailer components to the car, the vehicle can now be ordered with these items as factory equipment.

The total weight-to-horsepower ratio is very important when buying a car that is not fitted with a trailer package. The most practical upper limit for the ratio is approximately 60 pounds per horsepower while the average is 30–40 lbs/hp. This ratio is calculated by adding the trailer and the tow vehicle weight and then dividing this weight by the rated engine horsepower. One must remember that the weight of the provisions must be considered.

EFFECTS OF PULLING ON THE TOW VEHICLE

As you can imagine, the increased weight of the trailer being pulled will have effects on the tow vehicle. One can only estimate the exact relationship between driving with the trailer and without it, but certain points are certain; the acceleration time of the car is lengthened along with a reduction in gas mileage. The grade climbing ability and the top speed of the vehicle are also reduced.

It is important to remember that you need more time to accelerate when you wish to pass another car if you are towing a trailer. You must also remember to allow for the increased length of the trailer when returning to the right-hand lane.

FACTORS AFFECTING TOWING

It is important to keep in mind the approximate vicinity in which the trailer will be used before buying a tow vehicle since both climate and temperature greatly affect the performance of the average tow vehicle. For example, a unit which was set to run on the eastern coast of the United States would have to be modified to run correctly in the mountainous areas of the West where the air is thinner. Furthermore, the advantages of oversized radiators and transmission coolers are apparent if the unit is to be used in a warm climate as opposed to a colder climate.

No one is expected to stay at home with his trailering rig so the best plan is to equip the vehicle with warm-weather as well as cold-weather components and to deal with thin-air problems as they arise. Any qualified service mechanic can make the proper adjustments when the rig is to be driven through mountainous thin-air regions.

VEHICLE SAFETY

SAFETY ROUTES AND SPEEDS

The key words are "plan ahead." There are some individuals who like surprises but most of us don't. When planning a camping trip, sit down with up-to-date maps and plan the safest and most convenient route. It is no fun getting lost. Also calculate the distance to be covered each day so that the approximate location of each night's campsite can be found. This will enable you to make reservations ahead of time. It will also save time and trouble searching for campsites after a full day of driving.

When it comes to speed recommendations, the figures are always relative. They are dependent on the size and weight of the trailer and the tow vehicle, and the braking and acceleration ability of the entire unit. Actually common sense comes into play a great deal. Remember that you are towing a trailer, the stability of which decreases as speed increases. This in turn causes increased control problems. The trailers manufactured today advertise cruising speeds equal to most driving needs but there are so many variables (e.g., wind and terrain) that maintaining a reasonable speed is important. Also, the faster you go, the more power is needed just to overcome the greater wind resistance created by the trailer. Thus, the fewer miles per gallon you recieve from the tow vehicle. Your most economical cruising speed can be determined only through trial and error.

TRAILER SAFETY CHAINS

The safety chain is a type of link between the trailer frame and the bumper or frame of the car. The reason for these chains is to keep the trailer from separating from the car if the hitch or the hitch connection breaks. These chains are required equipment in some states.

Safety chains (© Airstream Corp.)

The safety chain should be attached to the trailer frame and to the car bumper or frame with a tight connection. Make sure the connection is tight; if the hitch connection breaks, the chain will keep the hitch tongue from striking the ground. The safety chain is a good precaution against a breakaway trailer and the damage that could be caused.

PERIODIC INSPECTION OF THE TOW VEHICLE

It is a good practice to examine the tow vehicle before it is used for towing the trailer any great distance. Follow the paragraphs below in checking the car components.

Make an inspection of the hitch assembly. Check for any stress cracks in the hitch supports or any loose welds or broken bolts. In short, make certain that the hitch is still securely attached to the tow vehicle.

A common—and troublesome—mistake made by trailer owners is the attempt to use the same old hitch on a new, larger trailer. The result can be permanent damage to the car, as well as the trailer, and the possibility of an accident. See that the new trailer and its hitch are compatible (within the same weight classification).

Check the car's shock absorbers by pushing on that part of the body of the vehicle over the shock. Continue pushing until the car is moving briskly in the vertical direction, then stop the pressure. If the vehicle keeps moving up and down, the shock is bad. The car should return to the rest position within one bounce. Also check the shocks to see if any leakage is present. If so, replace them.

The tow vehicle's shock absorbers should be replaced every 10,000 miles, at a maximum. Faulty shocks can greatly increase the twisting motion of the car body causing harder handling and magnifying the possibility of an accident.

Make an inspection of the tow vehicle's tires before any trip. They all should be in good condition and have equal pressure. Using recapped tires or snow tires in the summer is only asking for trouble. Alternating an old tire and a new one on the rear of the car may also cause trouble in stopping and may even cause jackknifing.

These checks, as simple as they might seem, are of great importance. This is, however, not the end of the inspection. Inspect all the mechanical components of the car yourself or have this done by a qualified mechanic. Such things as lubricant in the crankcase and transmission should be checked along with the level of the cooling system and the front-end alignment. Have these things attended to so that a breakdown will not hamper your free time.

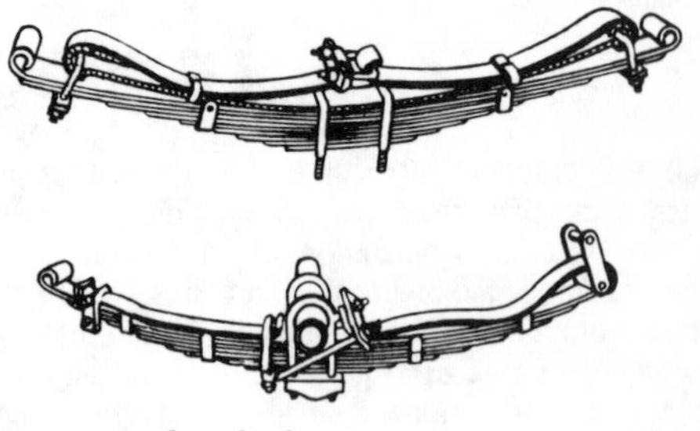

Two types of overload springs

Air bag spring insert

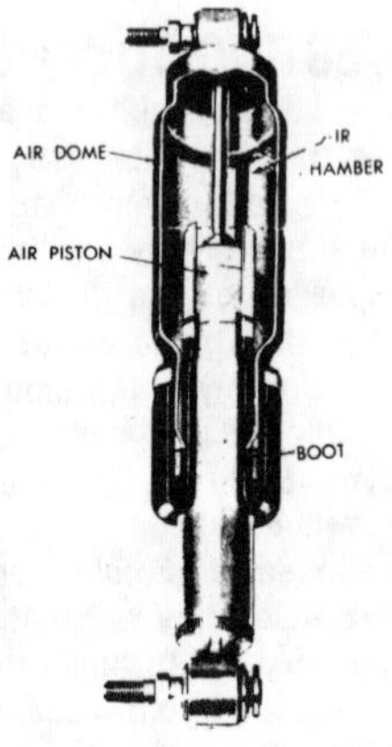

A superlift shock absorber

TOW VEHICLE COMPONENTS

SPRINGS

Overload springs are added to the stock equipment of the tow vehicle to raise the rear of the vehicle to the normal, level, driving position of the car after the

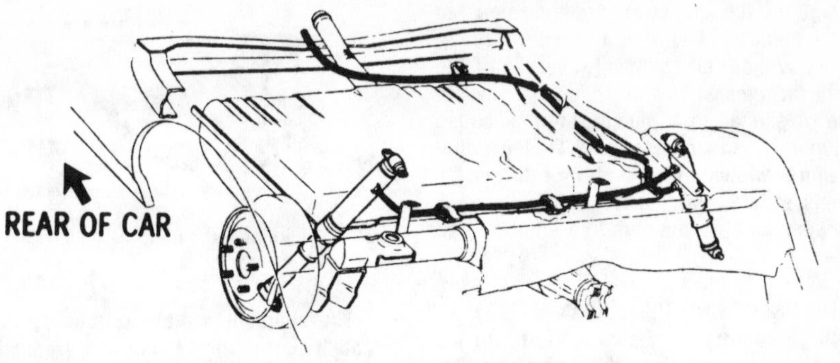

Airshock and pressure line location on the tow vehicle

trailer is attached. Overload springs come in a variety of models ranging from the coil type to leaf spring sets which are added to the factory equipment.

With the advent of air-lift shock absorbers and air bag spring inserts, overload springs are rarely used except on older vehicles. They do, however, give the correct position to the car which otherwise, because of the weight, would be sitting with its nose high in the air. This nose-up angle leads to hazardous driving since all the weight is transferred to the rear axle, leaving none on the front suspension for steering. Such a condition will result in unpredictable handling and extreme tire wear at the rear wheels. Driving at night with the car in a nose-up position is especially dangerous because your headlights are, in effect, improperly aimed. They are pointed too high and will shine into the eyes of oncoming drivers, making it difficult for them to see properly. You also won't be able to see the road surface the way you should.

LIMITED-SLIP DIFFERENTIAL

Since the traction of the tow vehicle plays an important part in the car-trailer package, anything to help traction is an asset. The limited-slip or positive-traction rear axle falls into this category.

The conventional "open" differentials have a tendency to transfer the torque of the engine to the rear wheel with the least resistance. When a vehicle is positioned with its left rear wheel on ice and the right rear wheel on a dry surface, the force of the engine is applied to the left rear wheel causing it to spin freely, never gaining traction. The limited-slip differential has an internal clutching system which transfers the torque from the spinning wheel to the wheel which has the best traction, thus enabling the vehicle to move forward.

This type of differential is a definite advantage in foul weather situations such as snow or rain where traction is a problem. One must remember that the traction of the tow vehicle is of utmost importance for safety. Limited-slip or positive-traction rear axles were available for many years as an option on standard cars. Today they are standard equipment on most cars or trucks fitted with a trailer package. To check for this locking type of differential, just jack the rear of the car until both rear wheels clear the ground. Spin either tire in the direction of forward movement and watch the rotation of the other tire. If the other tire turns in the same direction as the one you are turning, the differential is a clutch type differential; if the other tire turns in the reverse direction, the axle is an open type.

TRANSMISSIONS

Manual

The manual, or "stick," transmission was for years the "most reliable" type of transmission for towing. The positive contact of the clutch disc to the flywheel makes a sure engagement. A closer examination of the clutch mechanism for towing has come about in recent years. When you think about the situation and about how the clutch works, you can see its disadvantages.

The idea of a clutch type transmission is positive engagement with a limited amount of slip. However, when towing a reasonably large trailer with a medium-sized engine, the driver must slip the clutch greatly to start the car moving. Once moving, positive engagement is allowable but one can see this problem magnified by a slippery surface. In order to set the vehicle and trailer in motion, the clutch must be slipped drastically; if not, the wheel will turn freely because of the sudden application of torque on the slippery surface.

Automatic

With the advent of the new type Turbo-Hydromatic® transmission, and other modern three-speed transmissions, old wives' tales about automatics for towing have fallen by the wayside. In fact, the large manufacturers offering the current trailer towing packages recommend the automatic transmission.

Older automatics lived up to the fears of trailer towers mainly because the car itself was not "set up" for towing. Either the differential was of the incorrect ratio or the car wasn't driven correctly. To function correctly, the vehicle must be geared for towing. This point will be discussed in the "Rear Axle Ratio" section.

The advantage of the automatic transmission, as opposed to the manual, is that the torque may be applied gradually without any slipping. The slip of the torque converter accomplishes this action. This is not the same type of slip as in a clutch set-up because there is no wear to any component. This gradual starting procedure allows the transfer of torque to the rear wheels slowly and, consequently, lessens the chance of the wheels braking free of the road surface.

AUTOMATIC TRANSMISSION OIL COOLING

Transmission oil coolers are usually offered in the new trailer towing packages since the extra load of a trailer forces the transmission to work harder than under normal conditions. The extra load causes the transmission to create more heat due to increased friction. This extra heat is transferred to the transmission oil and, if the oil is allowed to become too hot, it will change its chemical composition or become burnt. When this occurs, valve bodies become clogged and the transmission doesn't operate as efficiently as it should. Serious damage to the transmission can result. Thus the need for the extra transmission oil cooling capacity.

You can tell if the transmission fluid is burnt by inspecting it for a burnt smell and discoloration. Burnt transmission fluid is dark brown or black as opposed to its normal bright clear red color. If the transmission fluid is burnt it will also have a distinct burnt odor. Since transmission fluid "cooks" in stages, it may develop forms of sludge or varnish. It is also possible for a leak to develop inside the radiator oil cooler and contaminate the transmission fluid. Pull the transmission dipstick out and place the end on a tissue or paper towl. Particles of sludge can be seen more easily this way. If any of the above conditions do exist, the transmission fluid should be completely drained, the filtering screens cleaned, the transmission inspected for possible damage, and new fluid installed.

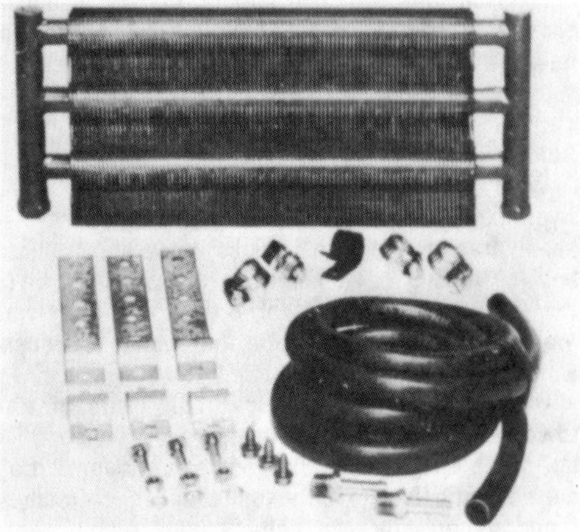

Oil cooler components

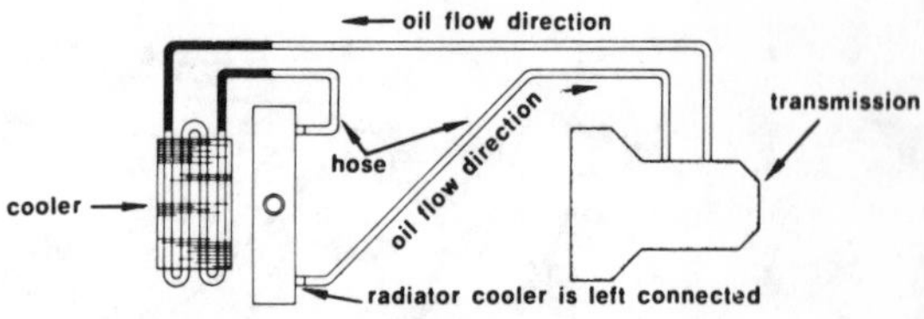

Diagram of the transmission cooling system

The solution to these problems, as mentioned previously, is the installation of a transmission oil cooler. If your tow vehicle is not equipped with an oil cooler and it becomes evident that you need one, you can purchase one at any well-supplied auto parts store or trailer service center. Do not install the oil cooling radiator in front of the water cooling radiator since it will restrict the flow of air through the water cooling radiator. Install it off to the side. An additional benefit of installing a transmission oil cooler is that the engine block will also run cooler since some of the cooling load is removed from the water cooling radiator.

Proper driving techniques can also help keep the transmission oil cool while towing a trailer. Never lug the engine in high gear at low speeds (e.g., climbing a hill). Instead, downshift into the next lower gear. This reduces the heat produced in the transmission by increasing the mechanical efficiency of the torque convertor. Also the engine cooling capacity is increased due to higher fan and water pump speed.

REAR AXLE RATIO VARIATIONS

The rear axle ratio, as pointed out above, is very important to a vehicle which is used to tow a trailer. The average car, as it comes equipped from the factory, has a rear axle ratio suited to normal load conditions. Such vehicles are equipped with differential ratios in the high twos, such as a 2.73 ratio.

The axle ratio is the relationship between the number of turns the driveshaft makes as compared to the number of turns of the drive axles. For example, if the car is equipped with a 2.73 differential, the driveshaft will turn 2.73 times for each time the drive axles turn once. It would be then said that this car has a 2.73 differential. The drive axle ratio, combined with the size of the engine, determines the pulling power of the car.

There is no set differential ratio recommended for all trailers. A 3.63 ratio can be used with a six-cylinder engine effectively while a 3.23 can be used with a V8 with the same amount of success. The trailer packages offered by the vehicle manufacturers recommend specific axle ratios for each engine. These can be checked at your local dealer.

A small class in axle ratios is in order at this point. The axle ratio is based on the direct relationship between the turning of the driveshaft and the turning of the drive axles. The higher the numerical ratio of the differential, the lower the gearing of the axle. For example, a differential with a ratio of 4.11 will cause the engine to turn faster to maintain a 50 mph speed than will an axle with a ratio of 3.23.

The object in choosing a rear axle ratio is to properly combine the torque curve of the engine with the appropriate ratio—keeping in mind the type of pulling which is to be done and formulating the correct ratio. As you can see this is a complicated task. Thankfully, the large car and truck manufacturers calculate the ratios and publish them in the trailer towing packages available for new vehicles.

Concentrate on the correct ratio for towing; the harmful side effects are many at both extremes. If the ratio is too low (numerically), it will require a greater slipping of the clutch mechanism to get the unit moving initially, thus causing wear to the clutch mechanism. On the other hand, if the ratio is too high (numerically), the top speed of the rig is greatly lowered. The tendency with a very high differential ratio is to run the engine above the acceptable rpm range which will cause great damage to the engine. The importance of the correct ratio is evident.

WHEELS AND TIRES

There are so many variables and possibilities in today's tire market that outfitting a rig can become quite confusing.

Selecting tires for your tow vehicle is perhaps the more confusing. Consider exactly what type of driving you will be doing and over what kind of terrain. Will you be traveling at high speeds for long periods of time? Will you be traveling off the road very much? Will there be snow or mud where you will be going? Will your tires be subjected to extremely high road temperatures? There are many factors to be taken into consideration. First, let's discuss the different types of tires.

There is a growing trend away from the conventional bias tires and toward the bias-belted and radial ply tires.

The conventional bias tires are constructed so that the cords run from one wire bead to the other at an angle. Alternate plies run at an opposite angle. This type of construction gives rigidity to both the sidewall and the tread surface.

The construction of the radial tire differs from that of a conventional bias tire in that the cords run from bead to bead at an approximate angle of 90 degrees. This type of construction gives the tread a great amount of rigidity and the side walls a great amount of flexibility. The belts restrict the amount of "squirm" when the tread comes in contact with the pavement, thus improving the tread life.

The bias-belted tire is constructed in much the same manner as the conventional bias tire. There are belts running at an angle and also at a 90° angle to the bead as in the radial ply tire. This type of construction gives rigidity to the tread and the sidewalls of the tire. Tread life is improved over the conventional bias tire but the objectional feeling of instability sometimes found in the flexible sidewalls of the radial is eliminated.

It is true that there is greater safety and longer tread life with tires of a higher load rating. But to achieve this, one must sacrifice the soft ride that original equipment tires provide.

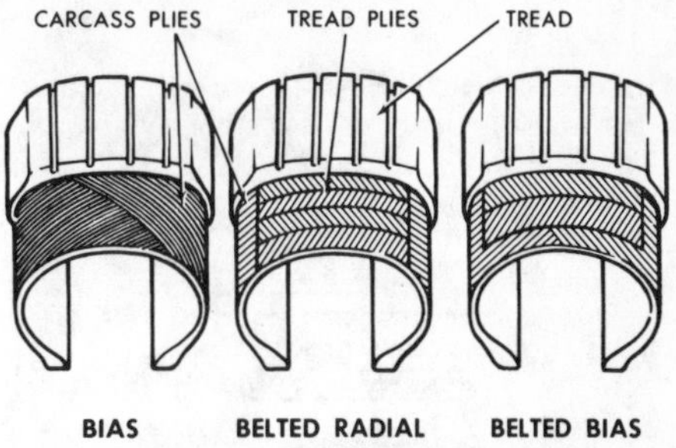

Construction of the bias, belted bias and the radial tire (© Chevrolet Div. G.M. Corp.)

WARNING: Heavy-duty suspensions are a must for the application of radial ply tires. Coupled with a standard, "mushy" suspension, radial tires will "cup" and wear unevenly. Never mix radial ply tires with any other type of tire on the same axle. If you decide to put wide, flotation type tires on your tow vehicle, remember that they must not be installed on narrow rims. Extra-wide rims or wheels must be used.

Tread design should be taken into consideration when selecting the tires for your tow vehicle. Decide what kind of driving you will be doing most often. Will you be driving off the road frequently? Will you be doing a lot of high-speed driving for long periods of time? A combination of both maybe or strictly one or the other? For strictly off-the-road traveling, you will want a heavy-duty tread design that will give you lots of traction and protect the tire against severe road conditions. For strictly highway use, you want a tread that will run quietly, give good mileage, and stay cool while running at high speeds. There are tires available that are designed for both off-road and on-road use. They have a traction type dread design that stays relatively cool and runs quietly. Radials are not recommended for strictly off-the-road use because the stiff tread will cause the sidewall to bulge out when the tire travels over an obstacle such as a rock. The sidewalls will bulge so much that they become susceptible to cuts or punctures.

Tire Pressure

Even pressure in the tow vehicle's tires plays an important part in the stability of the car-trailer unit. Low or uneven tire pressure can result in hard handling, erratic braking, and possible swerving which may result in an accident. Overinflated tires have the tendency to wear in the center and suffer a reduction in overall traction. Do not trust a gas station tire pressure gauge. Surveys have shown such gauges to be as much as 10 psi incorrect. Carry your own tire pressure gauge so each tire can be set at the correct amount.

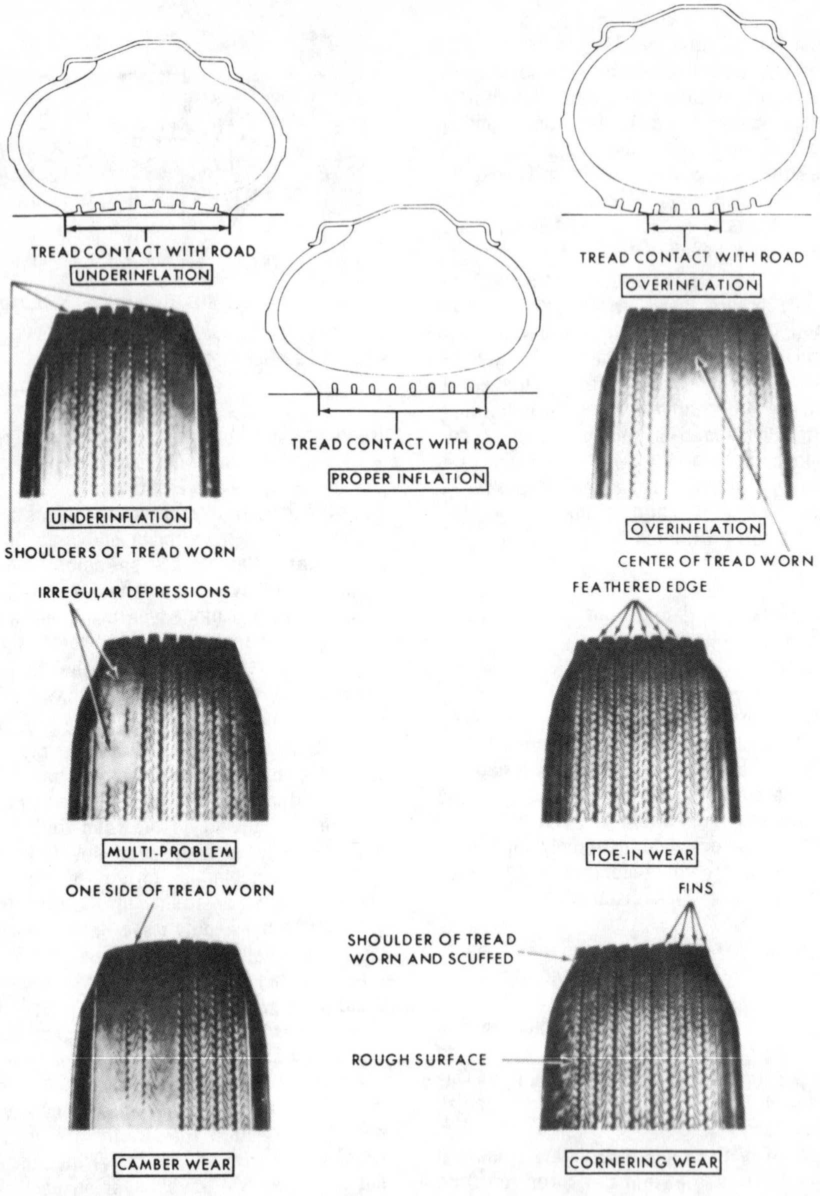

Illustration showing abnormal tire wear patterns caused by improper inflation, misalignment, improper balance or suspension neglect.

Wheels

The tire rim forms the direct union between the car and the tire. It absorbs the direct stress which the tire encounters and transfers it to the steering mechanism. Rims are usually maintenance-free and require little or no service. If a high-speed blowout or any other accident where rim damage is possible occurs, the rims should be checked and replaced if found defective.

It is advisable to have your tires mounted on wheels by a qualified mechanic. Damage to the wheel and the tire might otherwise result.

If it is necessary to install larger tires onto the tow vehicle, do not attempt to install these tires on the narrow rims. Oversized or wider rims should be used for these tires.

AIR SHOCK ABSORBERS

Air shocks are a relatively new addition to the camping field. These are conventional shock absorbers with internal power pistons which expand and contract when air pressure is applied to them. They were first used in racing autos, the suspensions of which had to be raised or lowered to compensate for varying track conditions.

These can be a welcome solution to the rear-end sag problem of tow vehicles. Since the travel trailer has a relatively low hitch height, the installation of the air shock assembly, with no other suspension changes, can regain the normal riding height of the car.

Installation is relatively simple; merely replace the conventional shock absorbers using the same mounting brackets. The only addition is the placement of the air line (which is used to fill the shocks). This line is usually mounted in the trunk of the auto. When the hitch is in place, the shocks can be filled to the proper level so that the car is horizontal; when the trailer is removed they can be deflated to give the car a smoother, more even ride.

Check with your trailer dealer when purchasing the shocks regarding the correct models for your trailering needs and the correct procedures for installing and using the air shock package.

DEALER TRAILER PACKAGES

Since more and more towing is being done with the conventional automobile, the auto manufacturers have offered cars directly from the factory with the heavy-duty equipment necessary for trailer towing. In the past these components had to be added once the conventional auto was purchased.

Mechanical engineers have investigated and calculated which drive train components are necessary to produce a car capable of towing the different classes of trailers with no particular problem. Such components as heavy-duty battery, transmission, cooling system, electrical system, suspension, and engine are already included.

When a new vehicle is to be purchased to tow a trailer, consult the dealer and he will have you look at a special brochure which will present an orderly arrangement of the packages available with each model of car. The charts in this book will provide most of the same information.

4 WHEEL DRIVE

Four-wheel-drive (4wd) vehicles have recently gained popularity in the recreation field. The idea started with those who bought surplus Jeeps and found a new area of fun in off-road driving. Manufacturers gradually entered the 4wd market; today there is a wide variety of four-wheel-drive models on the market.

A 4wd vehicle is basically the conventional two-wheel rear-drive model which has been combined with a front-drive axle. The front axle has a power drive to pull the vehicle while the rear axle pushes it. One can easily see the tremendous increase in traction with the addition of a front-drive axle. Driving a 4wd vehicle in the early days was hazardous and anything but comfortable since the front axle was always engaged and the front suspension was rigid and hard. Today, however, this is all changed. The front differential can be disengaged while the vehicle is on a paved highway and then engaged when off-road traction is necessary. The suspension has also been modified so that comfort will not suffer to any great extent.

Just looking at the added traction of two drive axles, and knowing that traction is the key word when pulling a trailer, shows a 4wd unit to be an excellent tow vehicle. This is not to say, "run out and buy" on the merits shown here. It should be considered however, if you plan to do a great deal of off-road camping. Your local dealer can tell you which vehicles are equipped with the 4wd option and will give you the information regarding the different components.

TOW HITCHES

Before beginning to classify tow hitches into groups, let's break down the hitch into two basic components: the tow bar and the coupler. The tow bar is the unit which is fastened to the car whether it be to the frame or bumper. The coupler is the portion containing the hitch ball which connects to the tongue of the trailer.

There are basically three types of hitches: the frame-mounted; the axle-mounted; and the equalizing type hitch. These will be discussed further under their own headings.

It is important to any tow hitch to be strong but this becomes doubly important when a heavy trailer is to be towed. A custom hitch is rarely necessary with light travel trailers but, as the tongue weight of the trailer increases, the need for such a hitch also increases.

All well-mounted hitches should be fastened at three points on the tow vehicle body. This three-point attachment achieves both stability and strength which is necessary in towing. When buying or installing any type of tow hitch, consult a qualified hitch dealer if you are a novice. This is an important piece of equipment, with an expensive car in front of it and an expensive trailer behind it, so consult a reputable dealer for his advice with regard to the hitch.

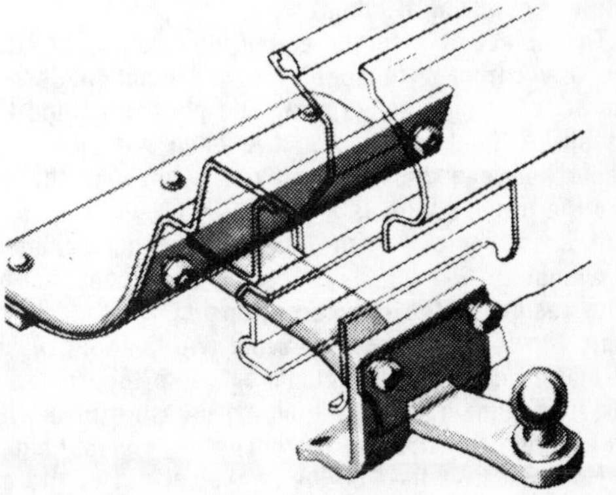

Non-equalizing hitch

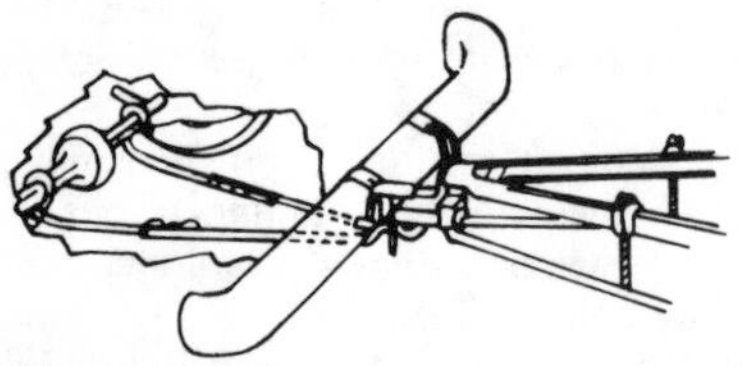

Axle type hitch

Frame and Axle Tow Hitches

Frame hitches are the least expensive to buy. They are usually straight or slightly offset beams which are attached to the frame and the rear bumper of the tow vehicle. The trailer hitch ball is on the other end of the support beam and engages the coupler of the trailer. This type of hitch is not generally used with any type of trailer above 2000 lbs gross vehicle weight and a tongue weight over 200 lbs.

The axle hitch is fastened on either side of the axle housing with two support rods which intersect at the rear bumper and are fastened there. The axle support hitch centers the pulling power of the car on the stable rear axle housing.

This type of hitch is not recommended for towing modern heavier trailers such as travel trailers. Even though the hitch is fastened to the tow vehicle's bumper or frame at the very rear of the car, there is a certain amount of forward-backward flexing and strain put on the axle housing where the other end of the hitch is fastened. A certain amount of forward-backward flexing movement is present with all types of trailer hitches, even if they are properly installed. With types other than the axle hitch, the flexing occurs at points where the least amount of harm is done, such as the frame and the bumper. With the axle hitch, however, the flexing is present on the rear axle housing of the tow vehicle. This can cause bent or cracked axle housings, bent or broken U-bolts that attach the axles to the leaf springs, and (on cars with rear coil springs) damage to the upper and lower control arms.

Trailer Equalizing Hitches

The object of a trailer equalizing hitch is to keep the tow car in a reasonably level condition despite the added weight at the rear. The physics behind the equalizing hitch distributes the hitch weight of the trailer between the front and rear wheels of the car and the trailer's wheels.

It is easy to see in the following example. Placing a weight of 200 lbs in the trunk of a conventional auto results in the downard slope of the vehicle toward the rear. Suppose we weld two five-foot pieces of metal beam a foot' equidistant from the center of the rear bumper. A man applying pressure in the upward direction can raise the car to its original height.

Now we take the 200 lbs of weight out of the car trunk and place a travel trailer with a hitch weight of 200 lbs onto the trailer hitch. The rear of the car will once again slope to the rear but, again, a man can restore the car to level by exerting the same upward pressure on the two beams.

Suppose we fasten the beam supports to the trailer tongue with chains while the man is exerting pressure. With this done, the manual pressure can be released and neither the car nor the trailer will move downward. What has happened? The weight has distributed itself: one-third has been placed on the front wheels of the car; one-third has been placed on the rear wheels. The remaining third has been positioned on the trailer wheels. This is how a weight distribution hitch works.

The solid beams extending from the tow vehicle are usually made of spring steel to flex when severe vertical pressure is applied—as might happen if the tow vehicle happens to hit a deep hole. When the equalizing hitch is properly hooked up, both the trailer and the car are level.

Installation of a Trailer Hitch

Installing a trailer hitch is no job for a novice, if the trailer to be towed is a fairly large one (class II, III). Class I hitches can be installed by almost anyone with common hand tools. Hitch installation should be done by an experienced, competent trailer service center with mechanics who are trained for this operation. This is also no place for penny pinching. The difference in cost between a corner-cutting installation and one done correctly should not be more then a few dollars. This is not to say that you shouldn't shop around to get the best price on a hitch installation, however. You must simply put the emphasis on the quality of the work and not on the price.

There are a lot of companies that design and make prefab trailer hitches to fit each make of car. These can be trusted to be strong enough if the hitch is installed correctly and you do not tow anything heavier than is recommended by the hitch manufacturer.

If by chance you have to have a hitch custom made to fit your car properly, inspect the material that the hitch is to be made of. Check to be sure that the steel is made of a sufficiently heavy gauge, strong enough to carry the load of your trailer. Remember to look for quality and not price. Check around among your trailering friends to find shops that install trailer hitches and have a reputation for good work. Maybe you would like to visit a few of the shops you had in mind and look them over. A certain amount of equipment is essential to installing and fabricating hitches. Metal-bending and cutting tools, welders, hoists, power-impact wrenches, and jackstands to hold parts into place for cutting and fitting should be readily visible. Check over some of the installer's work. You don't have to be an expert to be able to see poor workmanship which indicates indifference, as opposed to pride of a job well done. Examine the welds carefully to see if the beads are of even width; they should look like a line of evenly spaced crescent shapes. Pockmarks, large lumps of burnt material, or otherwise interrupted beads are a sign of poor welding.

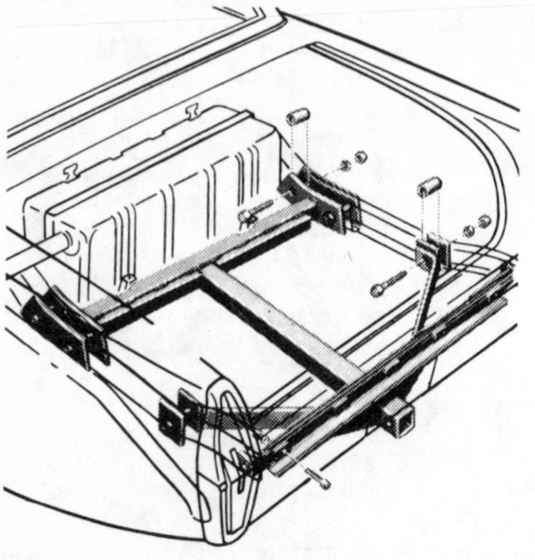

Load equalizing hitch

The tow vehicle might require reinforcement of the frame before the hitch is installed. This is partically true of cars with the unit body frame construction. An experienced hitch installer should be able to tell if the frame on your car needed extra reinforcement.

There seems to be a bit of discrepancy about how a trailer hitch should be attached to a tow vehicle. Some say to bolt it on and others say to weld it. All that can be done here is to give the drawbacks and advantages of both.

The advantages of having the hitch welded on are:

1. Gives a better bond to the frame of the tow vehicle.
2. Spreads the load over a wider area.
3. Will not work loose as bolts might do.

Disadvantages:

1. Welded job is only as good as the person who does the welding.
2. Welds can break without warning.
3. Heat created by welding could warp or distort the frame of the tow vehicle and could even change the properties of the metal, making it softer or more brittle.

The advantages of having the hitch bolted on are:

1. Squeaks and rattles will let you know if the bolts do work loose.
2. Bolted-on hitches are easier to remove for switching over to another vehicle or to just store for the winter.
3. Easier to install.

Disadvantages:

1. The bolts can work loose.
2. Some car manufacturers recommend that holes not be drilled in the frame of the car.
3. Should a bolt fall out, it cannot be replaced with an average bolt; they must be made of a harder grade of steel.
4. The stress is placed on one small area, right where the bolt is placed through the frame.

When installing a trailer hitch, check to make sure that the height of the hitch ball is the same as the height of the coupler on your trailer when it is level. Also allow at least ¼ in. gap between the gas tank and the floor of the car, and all bars and brackets of the installed hitch. The reason for this is that friction from vibration could wear a hole.

Hitch Maintenance

Most people think that installation is all the attention a hitch requires. Not so. To give long years of dependable service, the hitch should be properly maintained. Here are a few pointers on hitch maintenance:

1. Keep the hitch ball tight. Never install a hitch ball without the correct lockwasher and shank nut.
2. Keep all of the nuts and bolts tight that attach the hitch to the car.
3. Lubricate the ball occasionally. Use a light lubricant; a heavy grease will attract and hold harmful abrasives that could do more damage than the grease could help.
4. Check all levers, pins, and working joints for signs of wear. Lubricate them with a light lubricant. Replace them if they show signs of extreme wear and the possiblity of breakage.
5. Spray the hitch and tongue of the trailer with a rust-inhibiting paint from time to time. This should help retard corrosion and extend useful hitch life.
6. Examine the safety chains regularly. Sometimes chains drag on the ground and wear to a point of possible failure if the trailer ever becomes disconnected from the tow vehicle. Replace the chains if they are worn to a point that you think is unsafe.

BRAKES

The tow vehicle serves as the major portion of the braking system of the car-trailer unit. With the new, optional trailer package equipment, manufacturers have kept this fact in mind. Either heavy-duty shoe brakes or disc brakes are offered.

Although heavy-duty shoe brakes offer maximum stopping power, disc brakes are worth the extra

A disc brake

Clutch fan

A flex-type fan

money. Their resistance to fade and the excess buildup of heat which causes brake failure is an asset which cannot be overlooked.

If the vehicle is not equipped with a towing package, the stock, factory equipment brake linings can be replaced with center metallic bonded linings. These are harder than the factory linings and will increase the braking power of the car greatly—especially when the brakes are warm.

FLEXIBLE AUTO FANS

A frequent hazard of towing a trailer is the tendency for the cooling system to overload and overheat. This generally happens with cars which are not equipped with trailer towing packages. To alleviate this problem, either a larger fan or fan shrouding, or a combination of both, are in order. Today, however, a few companies (the best known being Flex-a-lite®) are producing light-weight fiberglass fans for recreational vehicles. The idea was first initiated in racing cars where maximum cooling was needed at low engine speed with a limited amount of component weight.

The fan is composed of a fiberglass-reinforced material which is relatively pliable. This construction provides a unit which is light (approximately one-fourth of the weight of the stock unit) and produces twice the cooling capacity at low engine speed.

The fan works in the following manner: At the idle speed or low engine rpm, the blades of the fan extend at a severe angle, cutting the air at a greater degree and causing a greater amount of air to be sucked through the radiator. As the engine speed increases, the centrifugal force of the fan, which is turning at greater speed, causes the blades to bend, thus decreasing the angle of the blades and also decreasing the amount of air being moved. This lowering of the fan's function is desirable because, as the forward speed of the tow vehicle is increased, more air is channeled through the radiator without the help of the fan. Another advantage of the flex type fan is that at higher engine rpm, there is a limited amount of fan noise which is a characteristic of the large-bladed, stock fans.

CLUTCHING FANS

Newer models, equipped with either trailer packages or air conditioning, are fitted with clutch type fans for engine cooling. This sort of unit has a heat-sensing mechanism built into the center shaft of the fan itself. If the engine is relatively cold, the mechanism will allow the fan to "free-wheel" until the sensor's heat mechanism reacts to the engine approaching running temperature. At this temperature the clutch engages inside the fan and the fan turns again at a one-to-one ratio with the fan shaft.

PASSENGER CAR AND STATION WAGON TIRE LOAD LIMITS

Load Range B (4-ply rating) → 20–32
Load Range C (6-ply rating) → 34–36
Load Range D (8-ply rating) → 38–40

TIRE SIZE OR DESIGNATION								Cold Inflation Pressures—Pounds Per Square Inch										
Bias		Bias and Belted Bias				Radial												
1965 On	Pre 1965	78 Series	70 Series	60 Series	Metric	78 Series	70 Series	20	22	24	26	28	30	32	34	36	38	40
6.00-13					165 R 13			770	820	860	900	930	970	1010	1040	1080	1110	1140
		A78-13	A70-13			AR 78-13	AR 70-13	810	860	900	940	980	1020	1060	1090	1130	1160	1200
6.50-13		B78-13	B70-13		175 R 13	BR 78-13	BR 70-13	890	930	980	1030	1070	1110	1150	1190	1230	1270	1300
		C78-13	C70-13			CR 78-13	CR 70-13	950	1000	1050	1100	1140	1190	1230	1270	1320	1360	1390
7.00-13					185 R 13			980	1030	1080	1130	1180	1230	1270	1310	1360	1400	1440
			D70-13			DR 78-13	DR 70-13	1010	1070	1120	1170	1220	1270	1320	1360	1410	1450	1490
					195 R 13			1060	1110	1170	1220	1280	1320	1370				
			E70-13			ER 78-13	ER 70-13	1070	1130	1190	1240	1300	1350	1400	1440	1490	1540	1580
					155 R 14			780	820	860	900	940	970	1010				
			A70-14				AR 70-14	810	860	900	940	980	1020	1060	1090	1130	1160	1200
6.45-14					165 R 14			860	910	960	1000	1040	1080	1120	1160	1200	1240	1270
	6.00-14							840	900	930	980	1020	1060	1100	1130	1170	1210	1240
		B78-14	B70-14			BR 78-14	BR 70-14	890	930	980	1030	1070	1110	1150	1190	1230	1270	1300
6.95-14					175 R 14			950	1000	1050	1100	1140	1190	1230	1270	1310	1350	1390
		C78-14	C70-14			CR 78-14	CR 70-14	950	1000	1050	1100	1140	1190	1230	1270	1320	1360	1400
	6.50-14							930	990	1030	1080	1130	1170	1210	1250	1300	1330	1370
		D78-14	D70-14			DR 78-14	DR 70-14	1010	1070	1120	1170	1220	1270	1320	1360	1410	1450	1490
7.35-14					185 R 14			1040	1100	1160	1210	1260	1310	1360	1400	1450	1490	1540
	7.00-14							1030	1100	1140	1190	1240	1290	1340	1380	1430	1470	1520
		E78-14	E70-14			ER 78-14	ER 70-14	1070	1130	1190	1240	1300	1350	1400	1440	1490	1540	1580
7.75-14					195 R 14			1150	1210	1270	1330	1390	1440	1500	1550	1600	1650	1690
	7.50-14							1150	1230	1280	1340	1390	1450	1500	1550	1600	1650	1700
		F78-14	F70-14			FR 78-14	FR 70-14	1160	1220	1280	1340	1400	1450	1500	1550	1610	1650	1700
8.25-14					205 R 14			1250	1310	1380	1440	1500	1560	1620	1670	1730	1780	1830
	8.00-14							1240	1320	1380	1440	1500	1560	1620	1670	1730	1780	1830
		G78-14	G70-14			GR 78-14	GR 70-14	1250	1310	1380	1440	1500	1560	1620	1680	1730	1780	1830

PASSENGER CAR AND STATION WAGON TIRE LOAD LIMITS

Load Range B (4-ply rating) → columns 20–32
Load Range C (6-ply rating) → columns 20–36
Load Range D (8-ply rating) → columns 20–40

TIRE SIZE OR DESIGNATION: Bias 1965 On	Bias Pre 1965	Bias and Belted Bias 78 Series	Bias and Belted Bias 70 Series	Bias and Belted Bias 60 Series	Metric	Radial 78 Series	Radial 70 Series	Cold Inflation Pressures—Pounds Per Square Inch: 20	22	24	26	28	30	32	34	36	38	40
8.55-14					215 R 14			1360	1430	1510	1580	1640	1710	1770	1830	1890	1950	2000
	8.50-14							1330	1420	1480	1550	1610	1670	1740	1790	1850	1910	1960
		H78-14	H70-14			HR 78-14	HR 70-14	1360	1430	1510	1580	1650	1710	1770	1830	1890	1950	2010
8.85-14	9.00-14				225 R 14			1430	1510	1580	1660	1730	1790	1860	1920	1990	2050	2100
		J78-14	J70-14			JR 78-14	JR 70-14	1430	1500	1580	1650	1720	1790	1860	1920	1980	2040	2100
			K70-14				KR 70-14	1460	1540	1620	1690	1770	1830	1900	1970	2030	2090	2150
								1540	1640	1700	1780	1850	1930	2000	2060	2130	2200	2260
	9.50-14		L70-14				LR 70-14	1520	1600	1680	1750	1830	1900	1970	2040	2100	2170	2230
					165 R 15	BR 78-15		870	910	960	1000	1050	1090	1130				
								890	930	980	1030	1070	1110	1150				
	6.00-15							890	940	980	1030	1070	1110	1150	1190	1230	1270	1300
6.85-15			C70-15		175 R 15	CR 78-15	CR 70-15	950	1000	1050	1100	1140	1190	1230	1270	1320	1360	1390
		C78-15						950	1000	1050	1100	1140	1190	1230	1270	1320	1360	1400
	6.50-15							980	1040	1080	1130	1180	1230	1270	1320	1360	1400	1440
		D78-15	D70-15			DR 78-15	DR 70-15	1010	1070	1120	1170	1220	1270	1320	1360	1410	1450	1490
7.35-15					185 R 15			1070	1130	1180	1240	1290	1340	1390	1440	1480	1530	1570
		E78-15	E70-15	E60-15		ER 78-15	ER 70-15	1070	1130	1190	1240	1300	1350	1400	1440	1490	1540	1580
7.75-15					195 R 15			1150	1210	1270	1330	1380	1440	1490	1540	1590	1640	1690
	6.70-15							1110	1190	1230	1290	1340	1400	1450	1500	1550	1590	1640
		F78-15	F70-15	F60-15		FR 78-15	FR 70-15	1160	1220	1280	1340	1400	1450	1500	1550	1610	1650	1700
					205 R 15			1240	1300	1370	1430	1490	1550	1610	1660	1720	1770	1820
	7.10-15							1190	1270	1320	1380	1440	1500	1550	1600	1660	1710	1760
		G78-15	G70-15	G60-15		GR 78-15	GR 70-15	1250	1310	1380	1440	1500	1560	1620	1680	1730	1780	1830
8.25-15								1250	1310	1380	1440	1500	1560	1620	1670	1730	1780	1830
					215 R 15			1340	1410	1480	1550	1620	1680	1740	1800	1860	1920	1970
	7.60-15							1310	1400	1450	1520	1580	1640	1710	1760	1820	1880	1930
		H78-15	H70-15			HR 78-15	HR 70-15	1360	1440	1510	1580	1650	1710	1770	1830	1890	1950	2010
8.55-15								1360	1430	1510	1580	1640	1710	1770	1830	1890	1950	2000

PASSENGER CAR AND STATION WAGON TIRE LOAD LIMITS

Load Range B (4-ply rating) → up to 32
Load Range C (6-ply rating) → up to 36
Load Range D (8-ply rating) → up to 40

TIRE SIZE OR DESIGNATION: Bias 1965 On	Bias Pre 1965	Bias and Belted Bias 78 Series	Bias and Belted Bias 70 Series	Bias and Belted Bias 60 Series	Metric	Radial 78 Series	Radial 70 Series	Cold Inflation Pressures—Pounds Per Square Inch: 20	22	24	26	28	30	32	34	36	38	40
8.85-15					225 R 15			1430	1510	1580	1650	1720	1790	1860	1920	1980	2040	2100
	8.00-15							1380	1470	1530	1600	1670	1730	1800	1860	1920	1980	2040
		J78-15	J70-15			JR 78-15	JR 70-15	1430	1500	1580	1650	1720	1790	1860	1920	1980	2040	2100
9.00-15								1460	1540	1620	1690	1760	1830	1900	1970	2030	2090	2150
	8.20-15							1470	1570	1630	1710	1780	1850	1920	1980	2050	2110	2170
			K70-15				KR 70-15	1460	1540	1620	1690	1770	1830	1900	1970	2030	2090	2150
9.15-15		L78-15	L70-15		235 R 15			1510	1600	1680	1750	1830	1900	1970	2030	2100	2160	2230
						LR 78-15	LR 70-15	1520	1600	1680	1750	1830	1900	1970	2040	2100	2170	2230
		M78-15						1610	1700	1780	1860	1940	2020	2090	2160	2230	2300	2370
		N78-15						1700	1790	1880	1970	2050	2130	2210	2280	2360	2430	2500
8.90-15								1700	1810	1880	1970	2050	2130	2210	2290	2360	2430	2500
6.00-16								1075	1135	1195	1250	1300	1350	1400	1450	1500		
6.50-16								1215	1280	1345	1405	1465	1525	1580	1635	1690		
7.00-15								1310	1380	1450	1515	1580	1640	1700	1760	1820		
7.00-16								1365	1440	1515	1585	1650	1715	1780	1840	1900		

NOTES:

1. Ply Rating While there is no industry-wide definition of ply rating, passenger car tires marked "4-ply rating/2-ply" have the same load carrying capacity as a current or most recent 4-ply tire of the same size at the same inflation. Passenger car tires marked "8-ply rating/4-ply" have the same load carrying capacity as 8-ply rating tires of the same size at the same inflation, regardless of the actual number of plies.
2. Load Range The "load range" system is now being used in tire marketing with letters (e.g., Load Range B, C, D, etc.) to identify tires with their particular load and inflation limits and service requirements. While the ply rating system is being gradually phased out, both designations may be used on tire sidewalls and are shown in the tables above. During their interim period Load Range B tires may be marked 4-ply rating/2-ply or 4-ply; Load Range C tires, 6-ply rating/4-ply or 6-ply and Load Range D tires, 8-ply rating/4-ply, 8-ply rating/6-ply or 8-ply.

HIGH FLOTATION TRUCK TIRE LOAD RATINGS

Size	Load Range	Ply Rating	Maximum Tire Loads (pounds) at Various Cold Inflation Pressures (psi)												
			30	35	40	45	50	55	60	65	70	75	80	85	90
8.00-16.5	B	4	1360												
8.00-16.5	C	6	1360	1490	1610	1730									
8.00-16.5	D	8	1360	1490	1610	1730	1840	1945	2045						
8.00-16.5	E	10	1360	1490	1610	1730	1840	1945	2045	2145	2240	2330			
8.00-16.5	F	12	1360	1490	1610	1730	1840	1945	2045	2145	2240	2330	2420	2500	2590
8.75-16.5	B	4	1570												
8.75-16.5	C	6	1570	1720	1850	1990									
8.75-16.5	D	8	1570	1720	1850	1990	2110	2240	2350						
8.75-16.5	E	10	1570	1720	1850	1990	2110	2240	2350	2470	2570	2680			
9.50-16.5	B	4	1860												
9.50-16.5	C	6	1860	2030	2190	2350									
9.50-16.5	D	8	1860	2030	2190	2350	2500	2650	2780						
9.50-16.5	E	10	1860	2030	2190	2350	2500	2650	2780	2920	3050	3170			
10-16.5	B	4	1840												
10-16.5	C	6	1840	2010	2170	2330									
10-16.5	D	8	1840	2010	2170	2330	2480	2620	2750						
10-17.5	C	6	1910	2095	2265	2425									
10-17.5	D	8	1910	2095	2265	2425	2580	2730	2870						
10-17.5	E	10	1910	2095	2265	2425	2580	2730	2870	3010	3140	3270			
10-17.5	F	12	1910	2095	2265	2425	2580	2730	2870	3010	3140	3270	3395	3520	3640
12-16.5	D	8	2370	2590	2800	3000									
12-16.5	E	10	2370	2590	2800	3000	3190	3370	3550						
14-17.5	C	6	3210												
14-17.5	D	8	3210	3500	3790	4060									
14-17.5	E	10	3210	3500	3790	4060	4320	4570	4800						
14-17.5	F	12	3210	3500	3790	4060	4320	4570	4800	5030	5260	5470			
14-17.5	G	14	3210	3500	3790	4060	4320	4570	4800	5030	5260	5470	5680	5890	6090
10-15	B	4	1760												
10-15	C	6	1760	1930	280	2230									
10-15	D	8	1760	1930	280	2230	2370	2510	2640						
10-16	B	4	1840												
10-16	C	6	1840	2010	2170	2330									
10-16	D	8	1840	2010	2170	2330	2480	2620	2750						
11-14	B	4	1820												
11-14	C	6	1820	1990	2150	2300									
11-14	D	8	1820	1990	2150	2300	2450	2590	2730						
11-15	B	4	1900												
11-15	C	6	1900	2080	2250	2410									
11-15	D	8	1900	2080	2250	2410	2560	2710	2850						
11-16	B	4	1980												
11-16	C	6	1980	2160	2330	2500									
11-16	D	8	1980	2160	2330	2500	2650	2810	2950						

NOTE For the tire sizes not listed, consult your tire supplier, or write Rubber Manufacturer's Assoc. for load and inflation information.

CONVENTIONAL TRUCK TIRE LOAD RATINGS

Size	Load Range	Ply Rating	Load Limits (lbs per tire) at Various Cold Inflation Pressures 20	25	30	35	40	45	50	55	60	65	70	75	80	85	90	95	100
4.10-6	B	4	185	210	235	260	280	300	320	335	350	370							
4.80-8	A	2	305	345	385														
4.80-8	B	4	305	345	385	425	455	490	520	550	580	610							
4.80-8	C	6	305	345	385	425	455	490	520	550	580	610	635	660	685	710	735		
4.80-9	A	2	330	375	415														
4.80-9	B	4	330	375	415	455	495	530	560	595	625	655							
4.80-12	B	4	405	465	515	565	610	655	695	735	775	810							
4.80-12	C	6	405	465	515	565	610	655	695	735	775	810	845	880	915	950	980		
5.30-6	A	2	310	355															
5.30-6	B	4	310	355	395	430	465	500	530	560									
5.30-12	B	4	485	550	615	670	725	780	825	875									
5.70-8	B	4	420	480	535	585	630	675	720										
5.70-8	C	6	420	480	535	585	630	675	720	760	800	835	875	910					
5.70-8	D	8	420	480	535	585	630	675	720	760	800	835	875	910	945	930	1015	1045	
6.50-10	C	6	685	775	865	945	1020	1100	1170	1230	1300								
6.50-10	E	10	685	775	865	945	1020	1100	1170	1230	1300	1360	1420	1480	1540	1590	1650	1700	1759
6.90-9	B	4	580	655	730	800	865												
6.90-9	C	6	580	655	730	800	865	925	985	1045	1095								
6.90-9	E	10	580	655	730	800	865	925	985	1045	1095	1150	1200	1250	1300	1345	1400	1435	1480
6.90-12	B	4	690	785	875	955	1035												
6.90-12	C	6	690	785	875	955	1035	1105	1175	1245	1310								
7.00-10	D	8	765	870	970	1060	1140	1230	1300	1380	1450	1520	1590						
7.00-10	E	10	765	870	970	1060	1140	1230	1300	1390	1450	1520	1590	1650	1720	1780			
7.50-10	E	10	825	935	1040	1140	1230	1320	1400	1490	1560	1640	1710	1780					
9.00-10	E	10	1110	1260	1400	1530	1650	1770	1890	2000	2100	2200							

CONVENTIONAL TRUCK TIRE LOAD RATINGS (cont.)

Size	Load Range	Ply Rating	Load Limits (lbs per tire) at Various Cold Inflation Pressures														
			30	35	40	45	50	55	60	65	70	75	80	85	90	95	100
6.50-13 ST	B	4	705	800	895	980											
6.50-13 ST	C	6	705	800	895	980	1060	1130	1200	1275							
7.75-14 ST	B	4	895	1020	1140	1240											
7.75-14 ST	C	6	895	1020	1140	1240	1340	1440	1530								
7.75-15 ST	B	4	895	1020	1140	1240											
7.75-15 ST	C	6	895	1020	1140	1240	1340	1440	1530								
16.5 x 6.5-8	A	2	415														
16.5 x 6.5-8	B	4	415	475	525	570	615										
16.5 x 6.5-8	C	6	415	475	525	570	615	655	695	735	770						
20.5 x 8.0-10	B	4	655	745	820	895											
20.5 x 8.0-10	C	6	655	745	820	895	965	1030	1090								
20.5 x 8.0-10	D	8	655	745	820	895	965	1030	1090	1150	1210	1270	1320				
20.5 x 8.0-10	E	10	655	745	820	895	965	1030	1090	1150	1210	1270	1320	1370	1420	1470	
18.5 x 8.5-8	B	4	560	630	700	760											
18.5 x 8.5-8	C	6	560	630	700	760	820	875	930								
23.5 x 8.5-12	B	4	805	910	1010	1100											
23.5 x 8.5-12	C	6	805	910	1010	1100	1180	1260	1340								

TRAILER TIRE LOAD RATINGS

Size	Load Range	Ply Rating	Load Limits (lbs per tire) at Various Cold Inflation Pressures														
			30	35	40	45	50	55	60	65	70	75	80	85	90	95	100
6.00-16 LT	C	6	1130	1230	1330	1430											
6.50-16 LT	C	6	1270	1390	1500	1610											
6.70-15 LT	C	6	1210	1320	1430	1530											
7.00-13 LT	C	6	1000	1090	1170	1260											
7.00-13 LT	D	8	1000	1090	1170	1260	1340	1420	1490								
7.00-14 LT	C	6	1030	1130	1220	1310											
7.00-14 LT	D	8	1030	1130	1220	1310	1390	1470	1550								
7.00-14 LT	E	10	1030	1130	1220	1310	1390	1470	1550	1620	1700	1770					
7.00-15 LT	C	6	1350	1480	1610	1720											
7.00-15 LT	D	8	1350	1480	1610	1720	1830	1940	2040								
7.00-16 LT	C	6	1430	1560	1680	1800											
7.00-16 LT	D	8	1430	1560	1680	1800	1910	2030	2130								
7.10-15 LT	C	6	1320	1440	1560	1670											
7.50-15 LT	D	8	1560	1710	1840	1980	2100	2220	2330								
7.50-15 LT	E	10	1560	1710	1840	1980	2100	2220	2330	2450	2560	2660					
7.50-16 LT	C	6	1620	1770	1930	2060											
7.50-16 LT	D	8	1620	1770	1930	2060	2190	2310	2440								
7.50-16 LT	E	10	1620	1770	1930	2060	2190	2310	2440	2560	2670	2780					
8.25-16 LT	D	8	1980	2160	2330	2500	2660										
8.25-16 LT	E	10	1980	2160	2330	2500	2660	2820	2960								
9.00-16 LT	D	8	2250	2460	2660	2850	3030										
9.00-16 LT	E	10	2250	2460	2660	2850	3030	3210	3370								
7-14.5	D	8	1140	1240	1350	1440	1530	1620	1710	1790	1870						
7-14.5	E	10	1140	1240	1350	1440	1530	1620	1710	1790	1870	1940	2020	2090			
7-14.5	F	12	1140	1240	1350	1440	1530	1620	1710	1790	1870	1940	2020	2090	2160	2230	2300
8-14.5	E	10	1380	1510	1630	1750	1860	1970	2070	2170	2270	2360	2450	2540			
8-14.5	F	12	1380	1510	1630	1750	1860	1970	2070	2170	2270	2360	2450	2540	2620	2710	2790

SI Metric Tables

The following tables are given in SI (International System) metric units. SI units replace both customary (English) and the older gavimetric units. The use of SI units as a new worldwide standard was set by the International Committee of Weights and Measures in 1960. SI has since been adopted by most countries as their national standard.

These tables are general conversion tables which will allow you to convert customary units, which appear in the text, into SI units.

The following are a list of SI units and the customary units, used in this book, which they replace:

To measure:	Use SI units:	Which replace (customary units):
mass	kilograms (kg)	pounds (lbs)
temperature	Celsius (°C)	Fahrenheit (°F)
length	millimeters (mm)	inches (in.)
force	newtons (N)	pounds force (lbs)
capacities	liters (l)	pints/quarts/gallons (pts/qts/gals)
torque	newton-meters (N·m)	foot pounds (ft lbs)
pressure	kilopascals (kPa)	pounds per square inch (psi)
volume	cubic centimeters (cm^3)	cubic inches (cu in.)
power	kilowatts (kW)	horsepower (hp)

If you have had any prior experience with the metric system, you may have noticed units in this chart which are not familiar to you. This is because, in some cases, SI units differ from the older gravimetric units which they replace. For example, newtons (N) replace kilograms (kg) as a force unit, kilopascals (kPa) replace atmospheres or bars as a unit of pressure, and, although the units are the same, the name Celsius replaces centigrade for temperature measurement.

If you are not using the SI tables, have a look at them anyway; you will be seeing a lot more of them in the future.

ENGLISH TO METRIC CONVERSION: MASS (WEIGHT)

Current mass measurement is expressed in pounds and ounces (lbs. & ozs.). The metric unit of mass (or weight) is the kilogram (kg). Even although this table does not show conversion of masses (weights) larger than 15 lbs, it is easy to calculate larger units by following the data immediately below.

To convert ounces (oz.) to grams (g): multiply th number of ozs. by 28
To convert grams (g) to ounces (oz.): multiply the number of grams by .035

To convert pounds (lbs.) to kilograms (kg): multiply the number of lbs. by .45
To convert kilograms (kg) to pounds (lbs.): multiply the number of kilograms by 2.2

lbs	kg	lbs	kg	oz	kg	oz	kg
0.1	0.04	0.9	0.41	0.1	0.003	0.9	0.024
0.2	0.09	1	0.4	0.2	0.005	1	0.03
0.3	0.14	2	0.9	0.3	0.008	2	0.06
0.4	0.18	3	1.4	0.4	0.011	3	0.08
0.5	0.23	4	1.8	0.5	0.014	4	0.11
0.6	0.27	5	2.3	0.6	0.017	5	0.14
0.7	0.32	10	4.5	0.7	0.020	10	0.28
0.8	0.36	15	6.8	0.8	0.023	15	0.42

ENGLISH TO METRIC CONVERSION: TEMPERATURE

To convert Fahrenheit (°F) to Celsius (°C): take number of °F and subtract 32; multiply result by 5; divide result by 9

To convert Celsius (°C) to Fahrenheit (°F): take number of °C and multiply by 9; divide result by 5; add 32 to total

Fahrenheit (F)		Celsius (C)		Fahrenheit (F)		Celsius (C)		Fahrenheit (F)		Celsius (C)	
°F	°C	°C	°F	°F	°C	°C	°F	°F	°C	°C	°F
−40	−40	−38	−36.4	80	26.7	18	64.4	215	101.7	80	176
−35	−37.2	−36	−32.8	85	29.4	20	68	220	104.4	85	185
−30	−34.4	−34	−29.2	90	32.2	22	71.6	225	107.2	90	194
−25	−31.7	−32	−25.6	95	35.0	24	75.2	230	110.0	95	202
−20	−28.9	−30	−22	100	37.8	26	78.8	235	112.8	100	212
−15	−26.1	−28	−18.4	105	40.6	28	82.4	240	115.6	105	221
−10	−23.3	−26	−14.8	110	43.3	30	86	245	118.3	110	230
−5	−20.6	−24	−11.2	115	46.1	32	89.6	250	121.1	115	239
0	−17.8	−22	−7.6	120	48.9	34	93.2	255	123.9	120	248
1	−17.2	−20	−4	125	51.7	36	96.8	260	126.6	125	257
2	−16.7	−18	−0.4	130	54.4	38	100.4	265	129.4	130	266
3	−16.1	−16	3.2	135	57.2	40	104	270	132.2	135	275
4	−15.6	−14	6.8	140	60.0	42	107.6	275	135.0	140	284
5	−15.0	−12	10.4	145	62.8	44	112.2	280	137.8	145	293
10	−12.2	−10	14	150	65.6	46	114.8	285	140.6	150	302
15	−9.4	−8	17.6	155	68.3	48	118.4	290	143.3	155	311
20	−6.7	−6	21.2	160	71.1	50	122	295	146.1	160	320
25	−3.9	−4	24.8	165	73.9	52	125.6	300	148.9	165	329
30	−1.1	−2	28.4	170	76.7	54	129.2	305	151.7	170	338
35	1.7	0	32	175	79.4	56	132.8	310	154.4	175	347
40	4.4	2	35.6	180	82.2	58	136.4	315	157.2	180	356
45	7.2	4	39.2	185	85.0	60	140	320	160.0	185	365
50	10.0	6	42.8	190	87.8	62	143.6	325	162.8	190	374
55	12.8	8	46.4	195	90.6	64	147.2	330	165.6	195	383
60	15.6	10	50	200	93.3	66	150.8	335	168.3	200	392
65	18.3	12	53.6	205	96.1	68	154.4	340	171.1	205	401
70	21.1	14	57.2	210	98.9	70	158	345	173.9	210	410
75	23.9	16	60.8	212	100.0	75	167	350	176.7	215	414

ENGLISH TO METRIC CONVERSION: LENGTH

To convert inches (ins.) to millimeters (mm): multiply number of inches by 25.4

To convert millimeters (mm) to inches (ins.): multiply number of millimeters by .04

Inches	Decimals	Milli-meters	Inches to millimeters inches	mm
1/64	0.051625	0.3969	0.0001	0.00254
1/32	0.03125	0.7937	0.0002	0.00508
3/64	0.046875	1.1906	0.0003	0.00762
1/16	0.0625	1.5875	0.0004	0.01016
5/64	0.078125	1.9844	0.0005	0.01270
3/32	0.09375	2.3812	0.0006	0.01524
7/64	0.109375	2.7781	0.0007	0.01778
1/8	0.125	3.1750	0.0008	0.02032
9/64	0.140625	3.5719	0.0009	0.02286
5/32	0.15625	3.9687	0.001	0.0254
11/64	0.171875	4.3656	0.002	0.0508
3/16	0.1875	4.7625	0.003	0.0762
13/64	0.203125	5.1594	0.004	0.1016
7/32	0.21875	5.5562	0.005	0.1270
15/64	0.234375	5.9531	0.006	0.1524
1/4	0.25	6.3500	0.007	0.1778
17/64	0.265625	6.7469	0.008	0.2032
9/32	0.28125	7.1437	0.009	0.2286
19/64	0.296875	7.5406	0.01	0.254
5/16	0.3125	7.9375	0.02	0.508
21/64	0.328125	8.3344	0.03	0.762
11/32	0.34375	8.7312	0.04	1.016
23/64	0.359375	9.1281	0.05	1.270
3/8	0.375	9.5250	0.06	1.524
25/64	0.390625	9.9219	0.07	1.778
13/32	0.40625	10.3187	0.08	2.032
27/64	0.421875	10.7156	0.09	2.286
7/16	0.4375	11.1125	0.1	2.54
29/64	0.453125	11.5094	0.2	5.08
15/32	0.46875	11.9062	0.3	7.62
31/64	0.484375	12.3031	0.4	10.16
1/2	0.5	12.7000	0.5	12.70

Inches	Decimals	Milli-meters	Inches to millimeters inches	mm
33/64	0.515625	13.0969	0.6	15.
17/32	0.53125	13.4937	0.7	17.
35/64	0.546875	13.8906	0.8	20.
9/16	0.5625	14.2875	0.9	22.8
37/64	0.578125	14.6844	1	25.4
19/32	0.59375	15.0812	2	50.8
39/64	0.609375	15.4781	3	76.2
5/8	0.625	15.8750	4	101.6
41/64	0.640625	16.2719	5	127.0
21/32	0.65625	16.6687	6	152.4
43/64	0.671875	17.0656	7	177.8
11/16	0.6875	17.4625	8	203.2
45/64	0.703125	17.8594	9	228.6
23/32	0.71875	18.2562	10	254.0
47/64	0.734375	18.6531	11	279.4
3/4	0.75	19.0500	12	304.8
49/64	0.765625	19.4469	13	330.2
25/32	0.78125	19.8437	14	355.6
51/64	0.796875	20.2406	15	381.0
13/16	0.8125	20.6375	16	406.4
53/64	0.828125	21.0344	17	431.8
27/32	0.84375	21.4312	18	457.2
55/64	0.859375	21.8281	19	482.6
7/8	0.875	22.2250	20	508.0
57/64	0.890625	22.6219	21	533.4
29/32	0.90625	23.0187	22	558.8
59/64	0.921875	23.4156	23	584.2
15/16	0.9375	23.8125	24	609.6
61/64	0.953125	24.2094	25	635.0
31/32	0.96875	24.6062	26	660.4
63/64	0.984375	25.0031	27	690.6

ENGLISH TO METRIC CONVERSION: TORQUE

To convert foot-pounds (ft./lbs.) to Newton-meters: multiply the number of ft./lbs. by 1.3

To convert inch-pounds (in./lbs.) to Newton-meters: multiply the number of in./lbs. by .11

in lbs	N-m	in lbs	N-m	in lbs	N-m	in lbs	N-m	in lbs	N-m
0.1	0.01	1	0.11	10	1.13	19	2.15	28	3.16
0.2	0.02	2	0.23	11	1.24	20	2.26	29	3.28
0.3	0.03	3	0.34	12	1.36	21	2.37	30	3.39
0.4	0.04	4	0.45	13	1.47	22	2.49	31	3.50
0.5	0.06	5	0.56	14	1.58	23	2.60	32	3.62
0.6	0.07	6	0.68	15	1.70	24	2.71	33	3.73
0.7	0.08	7	0.78	16	1.81	25	2.82	34	3.84
0.8	0.09	8	0.90	17	1.92	26	2.94	35	3.95
0.9	0.10	9	1.02	18	2.03	27	3.05	36	4.07

ENGLISH TO METRIC CONVERSION: TORQUE

Torque is now expressed as either foot-pounds (ft./lbs.) or inch-pounds (in./lbs.). The metric measurement unit for torque is the Newton-meter (Nm). This unit—the Nm—will be used for all SI metric torque references, both the present ft./lbs. and in./lbs.

ft lbs	N-m	ft lbs	N-m	ft lbs	N-m	ft lbs	N-m
0.1	0.1	33	44.7	74	100.3	115	155.9
0.2	0.3	34	46.1	75	101.7	116	157.3
0.3	0.4	35	47.4	76	103.0	117	158.6
0.4	0.5	36	48.8	77	104.4	118	160.0
0.5	0.7	37	50.7	78	105.8	119	161.3
0.6	0.8	38	51.5	79	107.1	120	162.7
0.7	1.0	39	52.9	80	108.5	121	164.0
0.8	1.1	40	54.2	81	109.8	122	165.4
0.9	1.2	41	55.6	82	111.2	123	166.8
1	1.3	42	56.9	83	112.5	124	168.1
2	2.7	43	58.3	84	113.9	125	169.5
3	4.1	44	59.7	85	115.2	126	170.8
4	5.4	45	61.0	86	116.6	127	172.2
5	6.8	46	62.4	87	118.0	128	173.5
6	8.1	47	63.7	88	119.3	129	174.9
7	9.5	48	65.1	89	120.7	130	176.2
8	10.8	49	66.4	90	122.0	131	177.6
9	12.2	50	67.8	91	123.4	132	179.0
10	13.6	51	69.2	92	124.7	133	180.3
11	14.9	52	70.5	93	126.1	134	181.7
12	16.3	53	71.9	94	127.4	135	183.0
13	17.6	54	73.2	95	128.8	136	184.4
14	18.9	55	74.6	96	130.2	137	185.7
15	20.3	56	75.9	97	131.5	138	187.1
16	21.7	57	77.3	98	132.9	139	188.5
17	23.0	58	78.6	99	134.2	140	189.8
18	24.4	59	80.0	100	135.6	141	191.2
19	25.8	60	81.4	101	136.9	142	192.5
20	27.1	61	82.7	102	138.3	143	193.9
21	28.5	62	84.1	103	139.6	144	195.2
22	29.8	63	85.4	104	141.0	145	196.6
23	31.2	64	86.8	105	142.4	146	198.0
24	32.5	65	88.1	106	143.7	147	199.3
25	33.9	66	89.5	107	145.1	148	200.7
26	35.2	67	90.8	108	146.4	149	202.0
27	36.6	68	92.2	109	147.8	150	203.4
28	38.0	69	93.6	110	149.1	151	204.7
29	39.3	70	94.9	111	150.5	152	206.1
30	40.7	71	96.3	112	151.8	153	207.4
31	42.0	72	97.6	113	153.2	154	208.8
32	43.4	73	99.0	114	154.6	155	210.2

ENGLISH TO METRIC CONVERSION: FORCE

Force is presently measured in pounds (lbs.). This type of measurement is used to measure spring pressure, specifically how many pounds it takes to compress a spring. Our present force unit (the pound) will be replaced in SI metric measurements by the Newton (N). This term will eventually see use in specifications for electric motor brush spring pressures, valve spring pressures, etc.

To convert pounds (lbs.) to Newton (N): multiply the number of lbs. by 4.45

lbs	N	lbs	N	lbs	N	oz	N
0.01	0.04	21	93.4	59	262.4	1	0.3
0.02	0.09	22	97.9	60	266.9	2	0.6
0.03	0.13	23	102.3	61	271.3	3	0.8
0.04	0.18	24	106.8	62	275.8	4	1.1
0.05	0.22	25	111.2	63	280.2	5	1.4
0.06	0.27	26	115.6	64	284.6	6	1.7
0.07	0.31	27	120.1	65	289.1	7	2.0
0.08	0.36	28	124.6	66	293.6	8	2.2
0.09	0.40	29	129.0	67	298.0	9	2.5
0.1	0.4	30	133.4	68	302.5	10	2.8
0.2	0.9	31	137.9	69	306.9	11	3.1
0.3	1.3	32	142.3	70	311.4	12	3.3
0.4	1.8	33	146.8	71	315.8	13	3.6
0.5	2.2	34	151.2	72	320.3	14	3.9
0.6	2.7	35	155.7	73	324.7	15	4.2
0.7	3.1	36	160.1	74	329.2	16	4.4
0.8	3.6	37	164.6	75	333.6	17	4.7
0.9	4.0	38	169.0	76	338.1	18	5.0
1	4.4	39	173.5	77	342.5	19	5.3
2	8.9	40	177.9	78	347.0	20	5.6
3	13.4	41	182.4	79	351.4	21	5.8
4	17.8	42	186.8	80	355.9	22	6.1
5	22.2	43	191.3	81	360.3	23	6.4
6	26.7	44	195.7	82	364.8	24	6.7
7	31.1	45	200.2	83	369.2	25	7.0
8	35.6	46	204.6	84	373.6	26	7.2
9	40.0	47	209.1	85	378.1	27	7.5
10	44.5	48	213.5	86	382.6	28	7.8
11	48.9	49	218.0	87	387.0	29	8.1
12	53.4	50	224.4	88	391.4	30	8.3
13	57.8	51	226.9	89	395.9	31	8.6
14	62.3	52	231.3	90	400.3	32	8.9
15	66.7	53	235.8	91	404.8	33	9.2
16	71.2	54	240.2	92	409.2	34	9.4
17	75.6	55	244.6	93	413.7	35	9.7
18	80.1	56	249.1	94	418.1	36	10.0
19	84.5	57	253.6	95	422.6	37	10.3
20	89.0	58	258.0	96	427.0	38	10.6

ENGLISH TO METRIC CONVERSION: LIQUID CAPACITY

Liquid or fluid capacity is presently expressed as pints, quarts or gallons, or a combination of all of these. In the metric system the liter (l) will become the basic unit. Fractions of a liter would be expressed as deciliters, centiliters, or most frequently (and commonly) as milliliters.

To convert pints (pts.) to liters (l): multiply the number of pints by .47
To convert liters (l) to pints (pts.): multiply the number of liters by 2.1
To convert quarts (qts.) to liters (l): multiply the number of quarts by .95

To convert liters (l) to quarts (qts.): multiply the number of liters by 1.06
To convert gallons (gals.) to liters (l): multiply the number of gallons by 3.8
To convert liters (l) to gallons (gals.): multiply the number of liters by .26

gals	liters	qts	liters	pts	liters
0.1	0.38	0.1	0.10	0.1	0.05
0.2	0.76	0.2	0.19	0.2	0.10
0.3	1.1	0.3	0.28	0.3	0.14
0.4	1.5	0.4	0.38	0.4	0.19
0.5	1.9	0.5	0.47	0.5	0.24
0.6	2.3	0.6	0.57	0.6	0.28
0.7	2.6	0.7	0.66	0.7	0.33
0.8	3.0	0.8	0.76	0.8	0.38
0.9	3.4	0.9	0.85	0.9	0.43
1	3.8	1	1.0	1	0.5
2	7.6	2	1.9	2	1.0
3	11.4	3	2.8	3	1.4
4	15.1	4	3.8	4	1.9
5	18.9	5	4.7	5	2.4
6	22.7	6	5.7	6	2.8
7	26.5	7	6.6	7	3.3
8	30.3	8	7.6	8	3.8
9	34.1	9	8.5	9	4.3
10	37.8	10	9.5	10	4.7
11	41.6	11	10.4	11	5.2
12	45.4	12	11.4	12	5.7
13	49.2	13	12.3	13	6.2
14	53.0	14	13.2	14	6.6
15	56.8	15	14.2	15	7.1
16	60.6	16	15.1	16	7.6
17	64.3	17	16.1	17	8.0
18	68.1	18	17.0	18	8.5
19	71.9	19	18.0	19	9.0
20	75.7	20	18.9	20	9.5
21	79.5	21	19.9	21	9.9
22	83.2	22	20.8	22	10.4
23	87.0	23	21.8	23	10.9
24	90.8	24	22.7	24	11.4
25	94.6	25	23.6	25	11.8
26	98.4	26	24.6	26	12.3
27	102.2	27	25.5	27	12.8
28	106.0	28	26.5	28	13.2
29	110.0	29	27.4	29	13.7
30	113.5	30	28.4	30	14.2

ENGLISH TO METRIC CONVERSION: PRESSURE

The basic unit of pressure measurement used today is expressed as pounds per square inch (psi). The metric unit for p will be the kilopascal (kPa). This will apply to either fluid pressure or air pressure, and will be frequently seen in tire pressure readings, oil pressure specifications, fuel pump pressure, etc.

To convert pounds per square inch (psi) to kilopascals (kPa): multiply the number of psi by 6.89

Psi	kPa	Psi	kPa	Psi	kPa	Psi	kPa
0.1	0.7	37	255.1	82	565.4	127	875.
0.2	1.4	38	262.0	83	572.3	128	882.
0.3	2.1	39	268.9	84	579.2	129	889.
0.4	2.8	40	275.8	85	586.0	130	896.
0.5	3.4	41	282.7	86	592.9	131	903.
0.6	4.1	42	289.6	87	599.8	132	910.
0.7	4.8	43	296.5	88	606.7	133	917.
0.8	5.5	44	303.4	89	613.6	134	923.
0.9	6.2	45	310.3	90	620.5	135	930
1	6.9	46	317.2	91	627.4	136	937.
2	13.8	47	324.0	92	634.3	137	944
3	20.7	48	331.0	93	641.2	138	951.
4	27.6	49	337.8	94	648.1	139	958.
5	34.5	50	344.7	95	655.0	140	965.
6	41.4	51	351.6	96	661.9	141	972
7	48.3	52	358.5	97	668.8	142	979
8	55.2	53	365.4	98	675.7	143	985
9	62.1	54	372.3	99	682.6	144	992
10	69.0	55	379.2	100	689.5	145	999
11	75.8	56	386.1	101	696.4	146	1006
12	82.7	57	393.0	102	703.3	147	1013.
13	89.6	58	399.9	103	710.2	148	1020
14	96.5	59	406.8	104	717.0	149	1027
15	103.4	60	413.7	105	723.9	150	1034
16	110.3	61	420.6	106	730.8	151	1041
17	117.2	62	427.5	107	737.7	152	1048
18	124.1	63	434.4	108	744.6	153	1054
19	131.0	64	441.3	109	751.5	154	1061
20	137.9	65	448.2	110	758.4	155	1068
21	144.8	66	455.0	111	765.3	156	1075
22	151.7	67	461.9	112	772.2	157	1082
23	158.6	68	468.8	113	779.1	158	1089
24	165.5	69	475.7	114	786.0	159	1096
25	172.4	70	482.6	115	792.9	160	1103
26	179.3	71	489.5	116	799.8	161	1110
27	186.2	72	496.4	117	806.7	162	1116
28	193.0	73	503.3	118	813.6	163	1123
29	200.0	74	510.2	119	820.5	164	1130
30	206.8	75	517.1	120	827.4	165	1137
31	213.7	76	524.0	121	834.3	166	1144
32	220.6	77	530.9	122	841.2	167	1151
33	227.5	78	537.8	123	848.0	168	1158
34	234.4	79	544.7	124	854.9	169	116
35	241.3	80	551.6	125	861.8	170	117
36	248.2	81	558.5	126	868.7	171	117

ENGLISH TO METRIC CONVERSION: PRESSURE

The basic unit of pressure measurement used today is expressed as pounds per square inch (psi). The metric unit for psi will be the kilopascal (kPa). This will apply to either fluid pressure or air pressure, and will be frequently seen in tire pressure readings, oil pressure specifications, fuel pump pressure, etc.

To convert pounds per square inch (psi) to kilopascals (kPa): multiply the number of psi by 6.89

Psi	kPa	Psi	kPa	Psi	kPa	Psi	kPa
172	1185.9	216	1489.3	260	1792.6	304	2096.0
173	1192.8	217	1496.2	261	1799.5	305	2102.9
174	1199.7	218	1503.1	262	1806.4	306	2109.8
175	1206.6	219	1510.0	263	1813.3	307	2116.7
176	1213.5	220	1516.8	264	1820.2	308	2123.6
177	1220.4	221	1523.7	265	1827.1	309	2130.5
178	1227.3	222	1530.6	266	1834.0	310	2137.4
179	1234.2	223	1537.5	267	1840.9	311	2144.3
180	1241.0	224	1544.4	268	1847.8	312	2151.2
181	1247.9	225	1551.3	269	1854.7	313	2158.1
182	1254.8	226	1558.2	270	1861.6	314	2164.9
183	1261.7	227	1565.1	271	1868.5	315	2171.8
184	1268.6	228	1572.0	272	1875.4	316	2178.7
185	1275.5	229	1578.9	273	1882.3	317	2185.6
186	1282.4	230	1585.8	274	1889.2	318	2192.5
187	1289.3	231	1592.7	275	1896.1	319	2199.4
188	1296.2	232	1599.6	276	1903.0	320	2206.3
189	1303.1	233	1606.5	277	1909.8	321	2213.2
190	1310.0	234	1613.4	278	1916.7	322	2220.1
191	1316.9	235	1620.3	279	1923.6	323	2227.0
192	1323.8	236	1627.2	280	1930.5	324	2233.9
193	1330.7	237	1634.1	281	1937.4	325	2240.8
194	1337.6	238	1641.0	282	1944.3	326	2247.7
195	1344.5	239	1647.8	283	1951.2	327	2254.6
196	1351.4	240	1654.7	284	1958.1	328	2261.5
197	1358.3	241	1661.6	285	1965.0	329	2268.4
198	1365.2	242	1668.5	286	1971.9	330	2275.3
199	1372.0	243	1675.4	287	1978.8	331	2282.2
200	1378.9	244	1682.3	288	1985.7	332	2289.1
201	1385.8	245	1689.2	289	1992.6	333	2295.9
202	1392.7	246	1696.1	290	1999.5	334	2302.8
203	1399.6	247	1703.0	291	2006.4	335	2309.7
204	1406.5	248	1709.9	292	2013.3	336	2316.6
205	1413.4	249	1716.8	293	2020.2	337	2323.5
206	1420.3	250	1723.7	294	2027.1	338	2330.4
207	1427.2	251	1730.6	295	2034.0	339	2337.3
208	1434.1	252	1737.5	296	2040.8	240	2344.2
209	1441.0	253	1744.4	297	2047.7	341	2351.1
210	1447.9	254	1751.3	298	2054.6	342	2358.0
211	1454.8	255	1758.2	299	2061.5	343	2364.9
212	1461.7	256	1765.1	300	2068.4	344	2371.8
213	1468.7	257	1772.0	301	2075.3	345	2378.7
214	1475.5	258	1778.8	302	2082.2	346	2385.6
215	1482.4	259	1785.7	303	2089.1	347	2392.5

Mechanic's Data

TAP DRILL SIZES

National Coarse or U.S.S.

Screw & Tap Size	Threads Per Inch	Use Drill Number
No. 5	40	39
No. 6	32	36
No. 8	32	29
No. 10	24	25
No. 12	24	17
1/4	20	8
5/16	18	F
3/8	16	5/16
7/16	14	U
1/2	13	27/64
9/16	12	31/64
5/8	11	17/32
3/4	10	21/32
7/8	9	49/64
1	8	7/8
1-1/8	7	63/64
1-1/4	7	1-7/64
1-1/2	6	1-11/32

National Fine or S.A.E.

Screw & Tap Size	Threads Per Inch	Use Drill Number
No. 5	44	37
No. 6	40	33
No. 8	36	29
No. 10	32	21
No. 12	28	15
1/4	28	3
5/16	24	1
3/8	24	Q
7/16	20	W
1/2	20	29/64
9/16	18	33/64
5/8	18	37/64
3/4	16	11/16
7/8	14	13/16
1-1/8	12	1-3/64
1-1/4	12	1-11/64
1-1/2	12	1-27/64

DECIMAL EQUIVALENT SIZE OF THE NUMBER DRILLS

Drill No.	Decimal Equivalent	Drill No.	Decimal Equivalent	Drill No.	Decimal Equivalent
80	.0135	53	.0595	26	.1470
79	.0145	52	.0635	25	.1495
78	.0160	51	.0670	24	.1520
77	.0180	50	.0700	23	.1540
76	.0200	49	.0730	22	.1570
75	.0210	48	.0760	21	.1590
74	.0225	47	.0785	20	.1610
73	.0240	46	.0810	19	.1660
72	.0250	45	.0820	18	.1695
71	.0260	44	.0860	17	.1730
70	.0280	43	.0890	16	.1770
69	.0292	42	.0935	15	.1800
68	.0310	41	.0960	14	.1820
67	.0320	40	.0980	13	.1850
66	.0330	39	.0995	12	.1890
65	.0350	38	.1015	11	.1910
64	.0360	37	.1040	10	.1935
63	.0370	36	.1065	9	.1960
62	.0380	35	.1100	8	.1990
61	.0390	34	.1110	7	.2010
60	.0400	33	.1130	6	.2040
59	.0410	32	.1160	5	.2055
58	.0420	31	.1200	4	.2090
57	.0430	30	.1285	3	.2130
56	.0465	29	.1360	2	.2210
55	.0520	28	.1405	1	.2280
54	.0550	27	.1440		

DECIMAL EQUIVALENT SIZE OF THE LETTER DRILLS

Letter Drill	Decimal Equivalent	Letter Drill	Decimal Equivalent	Letter Drill	Decimal Equivalent
A	.234	J	.277	S	.348
B	.238	K	.281	T	.358
C	.242	L	.290	U	.368
D	.246	M	.295	V	.377
E	.250	N	.302	W	.386
F	.257	O	.316	X	.397
G	.261	P	.323	Y	.404
H	.266	Q	.332	Z	.413
I	.272	R	.339		

DECIMAL EQUIVALENTS OF THE COMMON FRACTIONS

1/64	= .0156
1/32	= .0313
3/64	= .0469
1/16	= .0625
5/64	= .0781
3/32	= .0938
7/64	= .1094
1/8	= .1250
9/64	= .1406
5/32	= .1563
11/64	= .1719
3/16	= .1875
13/64	= .2031
7/32	= .2188
15/64	= .2344
1/4	= .2500
17/64	= .2656
9/32	= .2813
19/64	= .2969
5/16	= .3125
21/64	= .3281
11/32	= .3438
23/64	= .3594
3/8	= .3750
25/64	= .3906
13/32	= .4063
27/64	= .4219
7/16	= .4375
29/64	= .4531
15/32	= .4688
31/64	= .4844
1/2	= .5000
33/64	= .5156
17/32	= .5313
35/64	= .5469
9/16	= .5625
37/64	= .5781
19/32	= .5938
39/64	= .6094
5/8	= .6250
41/64	= .6406
21/32	= .6563
43/64	= .6719
11/16	= .6875
45/64	= .7031
23/32	= .7188
47/64	= .7344
3/4	= .7500
49/64	= .7656
25/32	= .7813
51/64	= .7969
13/16	= .8125
53/64	= .8281
27/32	= .8438
55/64	= .8594
7/8	= .8750
57/64	= .8906
29/32	= .9063
59/64	= .9219
15/16	= .9375
61/64	= .9531
31/32	= .9688
63/64	= .9844

Anti-Freeze Information

FREEZING AND BOILING POINTS OF SOLUTIONS ACCORDING TO PERCENTAGE OF ALCOHOL OR ETHYLENE GLYCOL

Freezing Point of Solution	Alcohol Volume %	Alcohol Solution Boils at	Ethylene Glycol Volume %	Ethylene Glycol Solution Boils at
20°F.	12	196°F.	16	216°F.
10°F.	20	189°F.	25	218°F.
0°F.	27	184°F.	33	220°F.
−10°F.	32	181°F.	39	222°F.
−20°F.	38	178°F.	44	224°F.
−30°F.	42	176°F.	48	225°F.

Note: above boiling points are at sea level. For every 1,000 feet of altitude, boiling points are approximately 2°F. lower than those shown. For every pound of pressure exerted by the pressure cap, the boiling points are approximately 3°F. higher than those shown.

TO INCREASE THE FREEZING PROTECTION OF ANTI-FREEZE SOLUTIONS ALREADY INSTALLED

Cooling System Capacity Quarts	Number of Quarts of ETHYLENE GLYCOL Anti-Freeze Required to Increase Protection													
	From +20°F. to					From +10°F. to					From +0°F. to			
	0°	−10°	−20°	−30°	−40°	0°	−10°	−20°	−30°	−40°	−10°	−20°	−30°	−40°
10	1¾	2¼	3	3½	3¾	¾	1½	2¼	2¾	3¼	¾	1½	2	2½
12	2	2¾	3½	4	4½	1	1¾	2½	3¼	3¾	1	1¾	2½	3¼
14	2¼	3¼	4	4¾	5½	1¼	2	3	3¾	4½	1	2	3	3½
16	2½	3½	4½	5¼	6	1¼	2½	3½	4¼	5¼	1¼	2¼	3¼	4
18	3	4	5	6	7	1½	2¾	4	5	5¾	1½	2½	3¾	4¾
20	3¼	4½	5¾	6¾	7½	1¾	3	4¼	5½	6½	1½	2¾	4¼	5¼
22	3½	5	6¼	7¼	8¼	1¾	3¼	4¾	6	7¼	1¾	3¼	4½	5½
24	4	5½	7	8	9	2	3½	5	6½	7½	1¾	3½	5	6
26	4¼	6	7½	8¾	10	2	4	5½	7	8¼	2	3¾	5½	6¾
28	4½	6¼	8	9½	10½	2¼	4¼	6	7½	9	2	4	5¾	7¼
30	5	6¾	8½	10	11½	2½	4½	6½	8	9½	2¼	4¼	6¼	7¾

Test radiator solution with proper hydrometer. Determine from the table the number of quarts of solution to be drawn off from a full cooling system and replace with undiluted anti-freeze, to give the desired increased protection. For example, to increase protection of a 22-quart cooling system containing Ethylene Glycol (permanent type) anti-freeze, from +20°F. to −20°F. will require the replacement of 6¼ quarts of solution with undiluted anti-freeze.

ANTI-FREEZE CHART
TEMPERATURES SHOWN IN DEGREES FAHRENHEIT +32 IS FREEZING

Cooling System Capacity Quarts	Quarts of ETHYLENE GLYCOL Needed for Protection to Temperatures Shown Below													
	1	2	3	4	5	6	7	8	9	10	11	12	13	14
10	+24°	+16°	+ 4°	−12°	−34°	−62°								
11	+25	+18	+ 8	− 6	−23	−47								
12	+26	+19	+10	0	−15	−34	−57°							
13	+27	+21	+13	+ 3	− 9	−25	−45							
14			+15	+ 6	− 5	−18	−34							
15			+16	+ 8	0	−12	−26							
16			+17	+10	+ 2	− 8	−19	−34	−52°					
17			+18	+12	+ 5	− 4	−14	−27	−42					
18			+19	+14	+ 7	0	−10	−21	−34	−50°				
19			+20	+15	+ 9	+ 2	− 7	−16	−28	−42				
20				+16	+10	+ 4	− 3	−12	−22	−34	−48°			
21				+17	+12	+ 6	0	− 9	−17	−28	−41			
22				+18	+13	+ 8	+ 2	− 6	−14	−23	−34	−47°		
23				+19	+14	+ 9	+ 4	− 3	−10	−19	−29	−40		
24				+19	+15	+10	+ 5	0	− 8	−15	−23	−34	−46°	
25				+20	+16	+12	+ 7	+ 1	− 5	−12	−20	−29	−40	−50°
26					+17	+13	+ 8	+ 3	− 3	− 9	−16	−25	−34	−44
27					+18	+14	+ 9	+ 5	− 1	− 7	−13	−21	−29	−39
28					+18	+15	+10	+ 6	+ 1	− 5	−11	−18	−25	−34
29					+19	+16	+12	+ 7	+ 2	− 3	− 8	−15	−22	−29
30					+20	+17	+13	+ 8	+ 4	− 1	− 6	−12	−18	−25

For capacities over 30 quarts divide true capacity by 3. Find quarts Anti-Freeze for the ⅓ and multiply by 3 for quarts to add.

For capacities under 10 quarts multiply true capacity by 3. Find quarts Anti-Freeze for the tripled volume and divide by 3 for quarts to add.

Towing

TOWING CARS WITH AUTOMATIC TRANSMISSIONS

When towing a disabled car, care must be used to avoid damage to the automatic transmission. None of the automatic transmission cars covered in this book can be push started. If it becomes necessary to tow one of these cars, the following chart should be used for reference.

Transmission	Towing: Maximum Speed	Towing: Maximum Distance (Miles)
AMC Shift Command	35	50
Torque-Command	30	①
Torqueflite	30	①
Ford FMX/CW	30	15
Ford C3, C4	30	15
Ford C6	30	15
Ford C4S	30	15
Powerglide	35	50
Torque Drive	35	50
G.M. Type 300	35	50
G.M. Type 250, 350, 375B	35	50
G.M. Type 375, 400, 425	35	50

①—Do not tow extended distances without disconnecting driveshaft or raising rear wheels.

CHILTON'S BASIC AUTO MAINTENANCE has just shown you how to handle simple maintenance chores, and save money in the process. If you think you'd like to learn more about keeping your car running properly, and even making a few of your own repairs, look into a Chilton Repair and Tune-Up Guide. Chilton publishes a comprehensive line of repair, tune-up and maintenance manuals designed for the do-it-yourselfer to do just that. Check the following list and see if you can be guided to further savings in the care and maintenance of your car, truck, van, recreational vehicle, or motorcycle.

American Cars

AMX & JAVELIN 1968-71 .... (#5605) $8.95

BARRACUDA & CHALLENGER 1965-72 .. (#5807) $6.95

CAMARO 1967-76 .... (#6471) $6.95

CHARGER/CORONET 1971-75 .... (#6316) $6.95

CHEVELLE & MONTE CARLO 1964-75
Including El Camino .... (#6263) $6.95

CHEVETTE 1976-77 .... (#6511) $6.95

CHEVROLET 1968-76
Full size models .... (#6544) $6.95

CHEVY II & NOVA 1962-75 .... (#6267) $6.95

CORVAIR 1960-69 .... (#5607) $8.95

CORVETTE 1953-62 .... (#6576) $6.95

CORVETTE STINGRAY 1963-76 .... (#6322) $7.95

DART & DEMON 1965-72 .... (#5720) $8.95

DART & DEMON 1968-76 .... (#6324) $6.95

DODGE 1968-76
Full size models .... (#6554) $6.95

DODGE CHARGER 1967-70 .... (#6486) $6.95

FAIRLANE & TORINO 1962-75
Including Ranchero and Elite .... (#6320) $6.95

FIREBIRD 1967-74 .... (#5996) $6.95

FORD 1968-76
Full size models .... (#6546) $6.95

GREMLIN & HORNET 1970-74 .... (#5994) $6.95

MAVERICK & COMET 1970-76 .... (#6550) $6.95

MUSTANG 1965-73 .... (#6542) $6.95

MUSTANG II 1974-76 .... (#6538) $6.95

PACER 1975-76 .... (#6473) $6.95

PINTO 1971-76 .... (#6536) $6.95

PLYMOUTH 1968-76
Full size models .... (#6552) $6.95

REBEL/MATADOR 1967-74 .... (#5986) $6.95

ROAD RUNNER & SATELLITE 1968-73
Including Belvedere and GTX .... (#5821) $6.95

TEMPEST, GTO & LE MANS 1968-73 .. (#5905) $6.95

VALIANT & DUSTER 1963-72 .... (#5788) $6.95

VALIANT & DUSTER 1968-76 .... (#6326) $6.95

VEGA 1971-76 .... (#6534) $6.95

Imported Cars

AUDI 1970-73
Super 90, 100 .... (#5092) $7.95

AUDI FOX 1973-75 .... (#6337) $7.95

AUSTIN-HEALEY 1957-69
100-6, 3000, Sprite, Austin America .... (#5496) $8.95

BMW 1959-70
4 cylinder models .... (#5576) $8.95

BMW 1969-74
4 cylinder models .... (#5980) $7.95

CAPRI 1970-76 .... (#6404) $7.95

COLT 1971-76 .... (#6475) $7.95

DASHER 1974-75 .... (#6213) $7.95

DATSUN 1961-72
1500, 1600, 2000, 510, 1200,
410, 411, Patrol, Pick-up .... (#5790) $7.95

DATSUN 1973-75
510, 1200, B210, 610, 710 .... (#6311) $7.95

DATSUN 240Z, 260Z 1970-74 .... (#6215) $7.95

FIAT 1964-70
1100, 1500, 1600, 600, 850, 124 .... (#6485) $7.95

FIAT 1970-73
850, 124, 128 .... (#6018) $7.95

HONDA 1970-74
600, Civic .... (#6020) $7.95

HONDA CIVIC 1973-76
Including CVCC .... (#6508) $7.95

JAGUAR 1960-69
Mk II, 340, 420, XKE ....(#5464) $8.95

JAGUAR 1969-74
XKE 6 and V-12, XJ6, XJ12 ....(#5998) $7.95

MAZDA 1971-73
RX2, RX3 ....(#5906) $7.95

MERCEDES-BENZ 1959-70
190, 200, 220, 230, 250, 280, 300, & diesels(#6065) $7.95

MERCEDES-BENZ 1968-73
220, 230, 250, 280, 300, 350, 450, & diesels(#5907) $8.95

MG 1961-75
1100, Midget, MGB, MGC ....(#6318) $7.95

OPEL 1964-70
Kadett, GT ....(#5792) $7.95

OPEL 1971-75
Kadett. 1900 Manta, GT ....(#6575) $7.95

PEUGEOT 1960-68
403, 404 ....(#5465) $8.95

PEUGEOT 1970-74
304,504, & diesel ....(#5982) $7.95

PORSCHE 1950-68
356, 911, 912 ....(#6572) $7.95

PORSCHE 1969-73
911, 912, 914, 914/6 ....(#5822) $7.95

RABBIT/SCIROCCO 1975 ....(#6341) $7.95

RENAULT 1964-72
Dauphine, Caravelle, R8, R10, R12, R16 (#5794) $7.95

SAAB 1960-70
750, 850, 95, 96, Sonett ....(#6570) $7.95

SAAB 99 1969-75 ....(#5988) $7.95

SIMCA 1963-69
Aronde, 1000, 1182, 1204 ....(#5535) $8.95

SUBARU 1970-74
FF-1, 1200, 1300, 1400 ....(#5978) $7.95

SUNBEAM/HILLMAN
Imp, Arrow, Rapier, Alpine, Tiger,
Minx, Husky ....(#5467) $8.95

TOYOTA 1966-70
Corona, Mk II, Corolla, Crown, Land Cruiser, Pick-up ....(#5795) $7.95

TOYOTA 1970-76
Corolla, Carina, Celica, Corona,
Mk II, Crown ....(#6540) $7.95

TRIUMPH 1963-70
Spitfire, TR-4, TR-250, GT6 ....(#5557) $7.95

TRIUMPH 1969-73
Spitfire, GT6, TR-6 ....(#5910) $7.95

VOLKSWAGEN 1949-71
Type 1 Beetle, Karmann Ghia, Type 2 Bus,
Type 3 ....(#5796) $7.95

VOLKSWAGEN 1970-76
Type 1 Beetle, Super Beetle, Karmann Ghia, Type 2 Bus,
Type 3 Fastback and Squareback, 411, 412 (#6548) $7.95

VOLVO 1956-69
444, 544, P1800, 122S, 140 series, 164 . . .(#6529) $7.95

VOLVO 1970-73
140 series, 164, 1800E, 1800ES ....(#5850) $7.95

Vans, Pick-Ups, and Recreational Vehicles

BLAZER/JIMMY 1969-77
2 and 4 wheel drive ....(#6558) $7.95

BRONCO 1966-73 ....(#5921) $7.95

CAMPER TRAILERS ....(#5851) $6.95

CHEVROLET/GMC PICK-UPS 1970-75
2 and 4 wheel drive ....(#6343) $7.95

CHEVROLET/GMC VANS 1967-74 ......(#6012) $7.95

CHEVROLET LUV PICK-UP 1972-75 .....(#6201) $7.95

DATSUN PICK-UPS 1970-75 ....(#6333) $7.95

DODGE/PLYMOUTH VANS 1967-74 .....(#6006) $7.95

FORD PICK-UPS 1970-75
2 and 4 wheel drive ....(#6335) $7.95

FORD VANS 1966-74 ....(#6010) $7.95

FORD COURIER PICK-UP ....(#6203) $7.95

INBOARD/OUTDRIVES 1968-72
Kiekhaefer Mercury, Evinrude, Johnson, Volvo
Penta ....(#5804) $6.95

INTERNATIONAL SCOUT 1967-73 ......(#5912) $7.95

JEEP UNIVERSAL 1953-76
CJ-3B, CJ-5, CJ-6 ....(#6556) $6.95

JEEP WAGONEER, COMMANDO & CHEROKEE 1966-74
Includes Jeepster ....(#6004) $7.95

MAZDA PICK-UPS 1972-75
B-1600 piston, Rotary pick-up ....(#6274) $7.95

OUTBOARD MOTORS 30 HORSEPOWER AND OVER 1966-72
Chrysler, Kiekhaefer Mercury, Evinrude, Johnson ....(#5803) $6.95

OUTBOARD MOTORS UNDER 30 HORSEPOWER 1966-72
Chrysler, Kiekhaefer Mercury, Evinrude, Johnson ....(#5802) $6.95

RAMCHARGER/TRAILDUSTER 1974-75 ..(#6331) $7.95

SMALL ENGINES
One cylinder 2 and 4 cycle air-cooled types up to 20 cu. in. ....(#5909) $6.95

SNOWMOBILES 1965-72
Arctic Cat, Mercury, Polaris, Evinrude, RUPP, Yamaha ....(#5805) $7.95

SNOWMOBILES 1969-76
Arctic Cat, OMC, Polaris, RUPP, Ski-Doo, Yamaha ....(#6008) $7.95

TOYOTA HI-LUX PICK-UPS 1970-74 .....(#6205) $7.95

TOYOTA LAND CRUISER 1966-74 ......(#6276) $7.95

TRAVEL TRAILERS
single or tandem axle types ....(#5853) $6.95

TRUCK CAMPERS
slide-in and chassie-mount types ......(#5852) $6.95

WINNEBAGO MOTOR HOMES 1968-74
all built on Dodge chassis ....(#6014) $7.95

Motorcycles

BMW MOTORCYCLE
R50, R60, R75 through 1972 ....(#6049) $6.95

BSA
unit construction 250, 441, 500, 650, 750 thru 1972 ....(#6048) $6.95

BULTACO, MONTESA & OSSA 1963-72 (#5888) $7.95

HARLEY-DAVIDSON V-TWINS 1959-72 ..(#5797) $6.95

HARLEY-DAVIDSON V-TWINS 1965-74 ..(#6219) $6.95

HODAKA 1964-73
Ace 90, 100, Wombat, Combat Wombat .(#6027) $7.95

HONDA ELSINORES 1973-75 ....(#6284) $6.95

HONDA FOURS 1969-74
350, 500, 550, 750 ....(#6030) $6.95

HONDA SINGLES 1968-75
50 to 125 ....(#6034) $6.95

HONDA TWINS 1966-72 ....(#5799) $6.95

HONDA XL SERIES 1972-75
XL70, 100, 125, 175, 250, 350 ....(#6217) $6.95

HONDA 125-200 TWINS 1969-76
125, 175, 200 ....(#6469) $6.95

HONDA 350/360 TWINS 1968-75 ....(#6038) $6.95

HONDA 450/500 TWINS 1966-76 ....(#6451) $6.95

KAWASAKI 1966-72
all 2 strokes ....(#6044) $6.95

KAWASAKI SINGLES 1969-75
90 to 350cc singles ....(#6339) $6.95

KAWASAKI TRIPLES 1969-75 ....(#6265) $6.95

KAWASAKI 900 Z1 1973-74 ....(#6025) $7.95

MOTO GUZZI 1966-72
V700, V750, V850 ....(#5908) $7.95
NORTON 750 & 850 1966-73 ....(#5913) $7.95

SUZUKI 1963-72
singles and twins ....(#5800) $6.95

SUZUKI SINGLES & TWINS 1970-74 ...(#6036) $6.95

SUZUKI TRIPLES 1972-74
GT380, GT550, GT750 ....(#6032) $6.95

TRIUMPH MOTORCYCLE 1965-72
unit construction 250, 500, 650, 750 .....(#6046) $6.95

YAMAHA 1964-72
2 stroke and 4 stroke models ....(#5801) $6.95

YAMAHA ENDUROS 1968-74 ....(#6806) $6.95

YAMAHA STREET TWO-STROKES 1967-75
all single and twin cylinder models ....(#6040) $6.95

YAMAHA 4-STROKES 1970-74
500, 650, 750 ....(#6088) $6.95

PRICE POLICY: All prices shown are suggested list prices and are subject to change without notice. Chilton automotive books may be found in most bookstores, department stores, automotive supply outlets and other locations where books are sold. If you have trouble finding the Chilton title you are interested in, send your check or money order, along with the name and code number of the book(s) desired, to:

Chilton Book Company
Sales Service Department
Radnor, Pennsylvania 19089
Make check payable to Chilton Book Company
(Pa. residents add 6% sales tax)